FOUNDATIONS AND FRONTIERS

Psychology

Douglas A. Bernstein

University of South Florida

CENGAGE
Learning·

Australia · Brazil · Mexico · Singapore · United Kingdom · United States

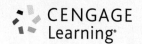

Psychology: Foundations and Frontiers
Douglas A. Bernstein

Product Director: Jon-David Hague

Product Manager: Clayton Austin

Content Developer: Shannon LeMay-Finn

Product Assistant: Kimiya Hojjat

Media Developer: Jasmin Tokatlian

Marketing Manager: Jennifer Levanduski

Content Project Manager: Michelle Clark

Art Director: Jennifer Wahi

Manufacturing Planner: Karen Hunt

Production Service: Lynn Lustberg, MPS Limited

Text and Photo Researcher: Lumina Datamatics

Copy Editor: Christine Sabooni

Text and Cover Designer: Jeff Bane

Cover Image: Main image: Yury Maselov/
Hemera/360/Getty Images; students: Ljupco/
iStock/360/Getty Images.

Compositor: MPS Limited

Library of Congress Control Number: 2014944466

Student Edition:
ISBN: 978-1-305-11430-2

Loose-leaf Edition:
ISBN: 978-1-305-62987-5

Cengage Learning
20 Channel Center Street
Boston, MA 02210
USA

Cengage Learning is a leading provider of customized learning solutions with office locations around the globe, including Singapore, the United Kingdom, Australia, Mexico, Brazil, and Japan. Locate your local office at **www.cengage.com/global**.

Cengage Learning products are represented in Canada by Nelson Education, Ltd.

To learn more about Cengage Learning Solutions, visit **www.cengage.com**.

Purchase any of our products at your local college store or at our preferred online store **www.cengagebrain.com**.

Printed in the Canada
Print Number: 01   Print Year: 2014

BRIEF CONTENTS

For Doris

To the memory of our beloved friend and co-author,
Alison Clarke-Stewart

CONTENTS

4   Sensation and Perception 86

5   Learning 140

6 Memory ... 178

7 Thought and Language ... 218

8 Intelligence 258

9 Consciousness 292

12 Health, Stress, and Coping 426

13 Personality 456

18 Neuropsychology — 664

FEATURES

PREFACE

Psychology is a rich and varied science, covering the breadth and depth of human behavior—everything from fleeting reflexes to enduring memories, from falling asleep to falling in love. In my experience, most students enter the introductory course thinking that psychology concerns itself mainly with personality, psychological testing, mental disorders, psychotherapy, and other aspects of clinical psychology. Many of these students are surprised, then, when they find themselves reading about such topics as the structure of the brain, optical illusions, the effect of jet lag on athletic performance, AIDS and the immune system, and prenatal risk factors, to name just a few. Yet these are all topics under the umbrella that is psychology.

For all its diversity, psychology is also a remarkably integrated discipline whose subfields are linked through common interests and related research questions. As a psychologist and scholar, I created this new version of my introductory psychology textbook to portray the wide range of topics that make up the science of psychology. As a teacher, I focused on the essentials of the discipline—the core concepts of psychology that I hope will be especially accessible and interesting to students. And as the new title suggests, I have tried to describe the research foundations that have made psychological science what it is today, as well as the research frontiers that will be expanding the psychological science of tomorrow. I also tried to present all of this material through an integrated, active pedagogical system designed to help students get the most out of the text.

In the process, I remained dedicated to presenting a textbook that not only is clear and enjoyable to read but that also provides features to support the learning process in all students, regardless of their academic background. Specifically, I set these goals:

- To focus on topics that represent the full range of psychology, from cell to society, without overwhelming the reader with details.

- To provide many active learning exercises that invite students to work with the book's material in ways that can help them understand and remember it.

- To help students develop their ability to think critically and scientifically by examining the ways that psychologists have solved (or are trying to solve) fascinating puzzles of behavior and mental processes.

- To explain the content of psychology with an emphasis on the doing of psychology, grounding all discussions in current and classic research studies. (I help students appreciate the importance of research by exploring one study in detail in a special feature in each chapter.)

My discussion of research in psychology is also designed to remind students that although in some ways "people are people wherever you go," sociocultural factors—including gender, ethnicity, cultural background, and geography—often shape human behavior and mental processes. I repeatedly point out, therefore, that psychological research on the thinking styles, perceptual habits, psychological disorders, social pressures, and other phenomena seen in North America or Europe, for example, may or may not apply to other cultures, or even to subcultures within Western countries.

Rather than isolating discussion of sociocultural material in boxed features, I have woven it into every chapter so that students will encounter it repeatedly as they read. I introduce the importance of sociocultural factors in Chapter 1 and continue to reinforce it through coverage of such topics as the impact of culture and experience on perception (Chapter 4), classrooms across cultures (Chapter 5), ethnic differences in IQ (Chapter 8), social and cultural factors in sexuality (Chapter 10), gender differences in stress responses (Chapter 12), personality, culture, and human development (Chapter 11), gender and cultural differences in depression and suicide (Chapter 14), and cultural factors in aggression (Chapter 16), to cite just a few examples.

What's New in *Foundations and Frontiers?*

In creating *Psychology: Foundations and Frontiers*, I have sought to update, upgrade, and combine all the best features of my two previous introductory psychology textbooks. I hope that the result of my effort is a book that offers even more of what psychology faculty and their students want and need.

Organization

Designed for presentation in a single academic term, the book's chapter organization is similar but not identical to that found in both the brief and full-length versions that it replaces. There are eighteen chapters, including two formerly optional ones on industrial/organizational psychology and neuropsychology. The order of the chapters reflects the way I have always taught my introductory course, but I know that your preference for chapter sequencing may not match mine. Accordingly, you will find that each of the chapters works as a freestanding unit so that you may assign them in whatever order you wish. For example, many instructors prefer to teach the material on human development relatively late in the course, which is why it appears as Chapter 11. However, that chapter can be just as comfortably assigned earlier in the course.

An Emphasis on Active Learning

The emphasis on active learning in my earlier textbooks proved popular with faculty and students, so I have continued to emphasize it in the new book. You will find two kinds of "Try This" features throughout the book.

TRY THIS

- First, dozens of figure and photo captions help students understand and remember a psychological principle or phenomenon by suggesting ways they can demonstrate it for themselves. In the memory chapter, for example, a photo caption suggests that students show the photo to a friend and then ask questions about it to illustrate the operation of constructive memory. These captions are all identified with a Try This symbol.

- Second, I have placed Try This symbols in page margins at even more places where active learning opportunities occur in the narrative. At these points, I ask students to stop reading and try doing something to illustrate or highlight the psychological principle or phenomenon under discussion. For example, in the sensation and perception chapter, I ask the student to focus attention on various targets as a way of appreciating the difference between overt and covert attention shifts.

Active Review

My efforts to promote active learning can also be seen in two other elements of the book:

- A Linkages diagram at the end of each chapter is designed to help students understand and appreciate the ways that the chapter they have just read relates to other subfields of psychology.

- Twenty-item multiple-choice self-tests at the end of each chapter are focused on the applications as well as the definitions of principles, concepts, and phenomena.

Updated Content

As always, I have tried to present the latest as well as the most established results of basic and applied research on topics that are both important in psychological science and of high interest to students. Here is a chapter-by-chapter summary of just some the new or updated material you will find in this new book:

Chapter 1 (Introduction):

- Latest figures on employment settings for psychologists

- Latest figures on graduate degrees in psychology earned by men, women, and members of ethnic minority groups

Chapter 2 (Research Methods in Psychology):

- Latest research methods used to evaluate claims for the effectiveness of eye movement desensitization and reprocessing (EMDR) therapy

Chapter 3 (Biological Aspects of Psychology):

- New information on epigenetic influences in understanding the interacting roles of heredity and environment

- Updated research on stem cells and nerve growth factors and their uses in repairing brain damage

- Latest information on techniques for studying the brain, including commercial and forensic uses

- Latest information on electrical synapses

- Latest information on the use of electrical stimulation as therapy for brain damage

- Information about how experience can change the structure of the brain

- Latest information about adolescent brain development and behavior

- Latest information on optogenetics

Chapter 4 (Sensation and Perception):

- New information about age-related decreases in visual acuity

- New Try This exercise to help illustrate the trichromatic theory of color vision

- New information about loss of olfaction as an early indicator of neurological disorder

- Latest information about research on pheromones in humans

- Latest information about research on acupuncture

- New information about benign paroxysmal positional vertigo

- New information about the sense of equilibrium and astronautics

- Expanded information about the effects of motivation on top-down processing

- Updated and expanded information about the effects of cell phones, texting, personal music players, and laptop computer use on attention—especially drivers and pedestrians

- New Try This exercise on touch sensations

Chapter 5 (Learning):

- Latest information about the mechanisms of classical conditioning

- Latest information about the effects of reinforcers in the brain

- Updated information on applications of operant conditioning

- Updated information on the biological basis of observational learning

- Latest research on the impact of violent television and video games
- Updated information on active learning methods in the classroom
- Latest research about e-media for delivery of college class materials
- Updated information on classrooms across cultures

Chapter 6 (Memory):

- Updated information about scents as memory cues
- Updated information about false memories and eyewitness testimony
- Latest research on the biological basis of memory

Chapter 7 (Thought and Language):

- Updated information on judge and jury decision making
- New section on building effective problem solving skills
- Latest information on advances in artificial intelligence
- Latest information about creativity and its biological roots
- New information about effects of physical environment on creative thinking
- Latest information on decision making in risky situations
- Updated information on group problem solving and decision making
- Latest information about bilingualism and long-term effects on cognition

Chapter 8 (Intelligence):

- Updated information on extraneous influences on intelligence test results
- New research on stereotype threat
- Updated information on the interaction of environmental and genetic factors in intelligence, and on group differences in IQ

Chapter 9 (Consciousness):

- Revised information on the number and labels for stages of sleep
- Updated information about nonconscious and unconscious mental processes
- Updated information about sleep disorders and treating sleep disorders
- New information about the functions of REM sleep and its effect on creativity
- New information about effects of sleep deprivation to reduce impact of trauma

- Latest information about chronotypes, and the "clock genes" that seem to drive them
- Updated information about applications of hypnosis and effects of meditation
- Updated information about neural effects of drugs, including epigenetic effects
- Latest information about the long-term effects of caffeine, nicotine, and opiates
- Latest information on the debate over medical uses of marijuana

Chapter 10 (Motivation and Emotion):

- New information about how eating habits have changed over centuries
- New Try This exercise to illustrate the facial feedback hypothesis
- Latest information on lie detection
- New section on intrinsic and extrinsic sources of motivation
- Updated information about hormonal influences on eating behavior
- Updated information about neurotransmitters and eating behavior
- Latest figures on obesity and new material on its causes and on prevention efforts
- Updated material on anorexia nervosa and bulimia
- Updated information about gender differences in sexuality
- Latest information about well-being and its relation to achievement
- New coverage of the conceptual act model of emotion
- New research on situational factors in reading facial expressions

Chapter 11 (Human Development):

- Updated information about behavioral genetics, genetic influences on development, and the influence of environmental factors on genetic expression
- Updated information on the effects of electronic and social media on infant, child, and adolescent development
- Updated information about midlife transition and the "sandwich generation"
- New and updated information about intellectual abilities in late adulthood, including risk factors and protective or mediating influences
- Updated information about the impact of alcohol, nicotine, and other toxins on infant development

- Latest information about infant thinking and behavior during the sensorimotor stage

- Latest information about influences of nature and the environment on children's brain development

- Updated information about culture and cognitive development

- Updated information about poverty as a developmental danger

- Updated information on long-term effects of early attachment styles

- Updated information about parenting styles and their effects on child development

- Updated information on the development of infants' theory of mind

- Updated statistics on adolescent sexuality and teenage pregnancy

- Updated information about emotional development during emerging adulthood

- New and updated information about longevity

Chapter 12 (Health, Stress, and Coping):

- New information about the long-term effects of stressors early in life

- New statistics on worldwide deaths due to health-damaging behaviors

- Updated information about the cognitive effects of stressors on decision making and problem solving

- Updated information about posttraumatic stress disorder (PTSD)

- New information about the relationship among socioeconomic status, lack of control, and premature death in lower socioeconomic groups

- Updated information about associations between social networks and happiness

- Updated information about personality and resistance to stress

- Updated information about identifying people at elevated risk for health problems

- Updated information about health beliefs and efforts to change them

Chapter 13 (Personality):

- New information about empirical research on psychodynamic theory

- Updated information about applications and biological basis of Five Factor Theory of personality

- New research on Gray's reinforcement sensitivity theory

- Updated information on personality research in nonhumans

- Updated information about the influence of genetics and epigenetics on personality traits

- Updated information about situational factors and the expression of personality traits

- Updated information about the possible impact of early attachment style in childhood and adulthood

- Updated information about the behavioral correlates of internal versus external locus of control

- Updated information about the effects of self-efficacy on achievement and well-being

- New information about the impact of positive psychology in personality

- Updated information about culture and personality

- Updated information about the latest edition of the Minnesota Multiphasic Personality Inventory (MMPI-2 RF)

Chapter 14 (Psychological Disorders):

- Updated information on the incidence of psychological disorders

- Presentation of the new DSM-5 and the forthcoming ICD-11, and information about debates surrounding the changes made in DSM-5

- Updated information on diagnostic reliability and validity

- Updated information about bias in psychological diagnosis

- Updated coverage of causes of psychological disorders, including epigenetics

- New information about the effects of the media-driven attitudes on people's understanding and response to psychological disorders

- Updated information about culture-specific disorders

- Inclusion of *cyberchondria,* a term similar to "medical students' syndrome"

- Updated information about somatic symptom disorders and dissociative disorders

- Updated statistics about the incidence of, and risk factors for, suicide

- Updated information about hallucinations in schizophrenia

- Updated statistics about the incidence of autistic spectrum disorders

- Updated information about mental illness and the law

Chapter 15 (Treatment of Psychological Disorders):

- Updated information about the prevalence of psychological treatments in adults and children in the United States
- Updated information about research on the effectiveness of psychotherapy
- New and updated information about the evolution of evidence-based practice and empirically supported therapies
- Updated information about cultural diversity training for therapists
- Updated information about therapeutic effects of repetitive transcranial magnetic stimulation (rTMS) therapy, deep brain stimulation, and optogenic stimulation
- Updated information about effectiveness, side effects, and costs and benefits of antidepressant drugs
- Updated information about human diversity and drug treatments
- Updated information about the effectiveness of psychoactive medications for mental disorders and their value in combination with psychotherapy
- Updated information about community psychology
- New and updated information about self-help and Internet-based therapy efforts

Chapter 16 (Social Psychology):

- New Try This exercises on attitude similarity and helping behavior
- New information about factors contributing to, or mediating, feelings of empathy
- New information about how social media affect feelings of attraction
- Updated information about terror management theory
- Updated information about the speed, strength, and accuracy of first impressions and factors that influence them
- Updated information about prejudice and its possible causes
- Updated information on the contact hypothesis and the mere-exposure effect in reducing prejudice
- Updated information on factors that contribute to attraction
- Updated information on gender and conformity
- Updated statistics about aggressive behavior in the United States
- Updated information about the possible biological and social factors in aggression

- New information on neuroimaging studies in social psychology

Chapter 17 (Industrial and Organizational Psychology):

- Expanded history of industrial and organizational psychology
- Updated employment statistics for industrial and organizational psychologists
- Updated information about factors that influence job satisfaction
- Updated statistics about workplace violence
- Updated information about leader and follower behaviors
- Updated information about leader-member exchange (LMX) theory

Chapter 18 (Neuropsychology):

- Updated information about how the interconnections of modules in the brain contribute to specific abilities and behaviors
- Updated information about the effects of strokes and the latest rehabilitation approaches
- Updated information about traumatic brain injuries and memory loss
- New information about traumatic brain injuries in sports
- Updated information about consciousness disturbances
- Updated information about brain activity and prosopagnosia
- Updated information about language disorders and frontotemporal degeneration
- Updated statistics about dementia
- New and updated information about the causes and symptoms of Alzheimer's disease
- Latest information about treatments for Alzheimer's disease

Special Features

Several special features of *Foundations and Frontiers* are designed to promote efficient learning and mastery of the material. These include, in each chapter, an integrated pedagogical system as well as sections on Thinking Critically, Focus on Research Methods, and Linkages.

An Integrated Pedagogical System

An integrated pedagogical system is designed to help students get the most out of their reading. Based on the PQ4R study system (discussed in Chapter 6, Memory), learning aids in each chapter include the following elements.

Preview Section To help students survey and question the material, each chapter opens with an outline and a brief preview statement. A question related to the key topic of each main section of the chapter appears at the beginning of each of those main sections, and these questions appear again at the end of the chapter, where they help to organize the chapter summary.

Margin Glossary Key terms are defined in the margin of the page where they appear, reinforcing core concepts without interrupting the flow of reading. All key terms match those in the American Psychological Association's *Thesaurus of Psychological Index Terms* (11th ed.) and in the *APA Dictionary of Psychology*. I believe that using key terms from these sources will help students do their own research by making it easier for them to use key-term searches in the field's most popular databases (PsycINFO & PsycARTICLES). Using these key terms will also improve students' abilities to transfer terms learned in introductory courses to their work in advanced courses. (I have also revised many of the phonetic guides to make it even easier for students to correctly pronounce unfamiliar key terms as well as other terms whose pronunciation is not immediately obvious.)

Instructional Captions Captions for all figures, tables, photographs, and cartoons reiterate core concepts and help students learn to interpret visual information. And, as mentioned earlier, many of these captions prompt students to engage in various kinds of active learning experiences.

In Review Charts In Review study charts summarize information in a convenient tabular format. I have placed two or three In Review charts strategically in each chapter to help students synthesize and assimilate large chunks of information—for example, on drug effects, key elements in personality theories, and stress responses and mediators. Fill-in-the-blank self-testing items at the bottom of each In Review chart further aid student learning and review of the chapter material. The answer key for these items can be found at the back of the book.

Active Review As mentioned earlier, the Active Review section at the end of each chapter includes

- A Linkages diagram containing questions that illustrate three of the ways that material in each chapter is connected to other chapters in the book.

- A chapter summary organized around major topic headings and the related preview questions. The summary is presented in short, easy-to-read paragraphs that focus on the topics introduced by chapter subheadings.

- A twenty-item multiple-choice test designed to help students assess their understanding of the chapter's key points prior to taking quizzes and exams.

Thinking Critically

A special Thinking Critically section in each chapter helps students hone their skills in this vital area. My approach centers on describing research on psychological phenomena in a way that reveals the logic of the scientific method, identifies possible flaws in design or interpretation, and leaves room for more questions and further research. In other words, as an author-teacher, I try to model critical thinking processes for my readers. The Thinking Critically sections are designed to make these processes more explicit and accessible by providing readers with a framework for analyzing evidence before drawing conclusions. The framework is built around five questions that the reader should find useful in analyzing not only published psychological research, but other forms of communication as well, including political speeches, advertising claims, and appeals for contributions. These five questions first appear in Chapter 1, where I introduce the importance of critical thinking, and they are repeated in every chapter's Thinking Critically section.

1. What am I being asked to believe or accept?

2. What evidence is available to support the assertion?

3. Are there alternative ways of interpreting the evidence?

4. What additional evidence would help evaluate the alternatives?

5. What conclusions are most reasonable?

Using this simple yet powerful framework, I explore issues such as subliminal persuasion, recovered memories, and the origins of sexual orientation, to name just a few. Page xv includes a complete list of the Thinking Critically features.

Focus on Research Methods

Psychological scientists have helped us better understand behavior and mental processes through their commitment to empirical research. They have posed vital questions about psychological phenomena and have designed research that can answer (or at least illuminate) those questions. In Chapter 2, I introduce readers to the methods of scientific research and to basic research designs in psychology. Every subsequent chapter features a Focus on Research Methods section that highlights a particular research study to help students appreciate the value of research and the creativity with which psychologists have conducted it. Like the Thinking Critically sections, the Focus on Research Methods features are organized around five questions designed to help readers organize their thinking about research questions and research results.

1. What was the researcher's question?

2. How did the researcher answer the question?

3. What did the researcher find?

4. What do the results mean?

5. What do we still need to know?

These Focus on Research Methods sections help students see how psychologists have used experiments, correlational studies, surveys, observations, and other designs to explore phenomena such as learned helplessness, infant cognition, evolutionary theories of helping, and human sexual behavior. A full list of the Focus on Research features appears on page xv.

Linkages

In my experience, introductory psychology students are better able to appreciate the scope of our discipline when they look at it not as a laundry list of separate topics but as an interrelated set of subfields, each of which contributes to—and benefits from—the work being done in all the others. To help students see these relationships, I have built into the book an integrating tool called Linkages. There are two elements in the Linkages program.

- *Linkages diagrams* At the end of each chapter is a Linkages diagram, which presents a set of questions that illustrate three of the ways that material in the chapter is related to other chapters in the book. For example, the Linkages diagram in Chapter 3, "Biological Aspects of Psychology," contains questions that show how biological psychology is related to consciousness ("Does the brain shut down when I sleep?"), human development ("How do our brains change over a lifetime?"), and treatment of psychological disorders ("How do drugs help people diagnosed with schizophrenia?"). These diagrams are designed to help students keep in mind how the content of each chapter fits into psychology as a whole. To introduce the concept of Linkages, the diagram in Chapter 1 appears within the body of the chapter.

- *Linkages sections* One of the questions in each chapter's Linkages diagram reminds the student of the chapter's discussion of that question in a special section entitled, appropriately enough, Linkages (see page xv for a complete list of Linkages sections).

These elements combine with the text narrative to highlight the network of relationships among psychology's subfields. This Linkages program is designed to help students see the "big picture" of psychology, no matter how many chapters their instructor assigns or in what sequence.

Teaching and Learning Support Package

Many useful instructional and pedagogical materials have been developed to support this textbook and the introductory course. These are designed to enhance and maximize the teaching and learning experience.

MindTap for *Psychology: Foundations and Frontiers*

MindTap for *Psychology: Foundations and Frontiers* engages and empowers students to produce their best work—consistently. By seamlessly integrating course material with videos, activities, apps, and much more, MindTap creates a unique learning path that fosters increased comprehension and efficiency.

For students:

- MindTap delivers real-world relevance with activities and assignments that help students build critical thinking and analytic skills that will transfer to other courses and their professional lives.

- MindTap helps students stay organized and efficient with a single destination that reflects what's important to the instructor, along with the tools students need to master the content.

- MindTap empowers and motivates students with information that shows where they stand at all times—both individually and compared to the highest performers in class.

Additionally, for instructors, MindTap allows you to:

- Control what content students see and when they see it with a learning path that can be used as-is or matched to your syllabus exactly.

- Create a unique learning path of relevant readings and multimedia and activities that move students up the learning taxonomy from basic knowledge and comprehension to analysis, application, and critical thinking.

- Integrate your own content into the MindTap Reader using your own documents or pulling from sources like RSS feeds, YouTube videos, websites, Googledocs, and more.

- Use powerful analytics and reports that provide a snapshot of class progress, time in course, engagement, and completion.

Available Supplements

Cengage Learning Testing, powered by Cognero

Cengage Learning Testing Powered by Cognero® is a flexible, online system that allows you to: import, edit, and manipulate content from the text's test bank or elsewhere, including your own favorite test questions; create multiple test versions in an instant; and deliver tests from your LMS, your classroom, or wherever you want.

Online Instructor's Manual

The instructor's manual (IM) contains a variety of resources to aid instructors in preparing and presenting text material in a manner that meets their personal preferences and course needs. It presents suggestions and resources to enhance and facilitate learning.

Online PowerPoints

These vibrant, Microsoft PowerPoint lecture slides provide concept coverage to assist you with your lecture.

Acknowledgments

Many people provided me with the help, criticism, and encouragement I needed to create *Foundations and Frontiers*. I am of course indebted to my colleagues Louis Penner, Ed Roy, and the late Alison Clarke-Stewart, who, as co-authors of the Bernstein, Penner, Clarke-Stewart, and Roy textbooks *Psychology* and *Essentials of Psychology,* provided invaluable assistance in reviewing this book's manuscript as it developed. I also offer sincere thanks to Professor Paul Spector of the University of South Florida, who took the lead in creating the original version of the chapter on industrial and organizational psychology, and to Joel Shenker, M.D., Ph.D., who took the lead in creating the original chapter on neuropsychology. I am indebted, too, to a number of other colleagues for their expert help and advice on the revision of various chapters that appeared in *Foundations and Frontiers*. These colleagues include, for Chapter 3 and part of Chapter 4, Joel Shenker, M.D., Ph.D.; for part of Chapter 4, Angela Hayden, University of Kentucky; for Chapter 5, Doug Williams, University of Winnipeg; for Chapter 5, Lisa Geraci, Texas A&M University; for Chapter 7, Paul Whitney, Washington State University, for Chapter 8, Rose Mary Webb, Appalachian State University; for Chapter 10, Nancy Dess, Occidental College; for Chapter 12, Catherine Stoney, National Center for Complementary and Alternative Medicine; for Chapters 14 and 15, Vicki Phares, University of South Florida; and for Chapter 17, Nathan Carter, University of Georgia.

I also want to offer heartfelt thanks to my friends and colleagues who did such a wonderful job in creating the supplementary materials for *Foundations and Frontiers*. Most of these people have worked with me for years, and many of them had been graduate student instructors in the University of Illinois introductory psychology program out of which my earlier books emerged. They include Dale Doty, Jessica Hill, Darrell Rudmann, Shelby Kaura, Bob Jacobs, Leslie Sandusky, Robert Flint, Jon Weimer, Peter Vernig, and Mar Novarro.

The process of creating *Foundations and Frontiers* was greatly facilitated by the work of many dedicated people at Cengage Learning. From the sales representatives and sales managers who originally conveyed my colleagues' requests for the text to the marketing staff who worked to tell my colleagues what *Foundations and Frontiers* has to offer, it seems everyone at Cengage had a hand in shaping this book. Several people in the editorial and production areas at Cengage deserve special mention, however, because they did an outstanding job in helping me develop and revise the draft manuscript and turn that manuscript into the beautiful book you are now holding. I wish to thank Clayton Austin and Joann Kozyrev, Product Managers at Cengage, for their efforts in bringing this book to fruition. Development Editor Shannon LeMay-Finn was instrumental in the shaping and development of the manuscript; her editorial expertise and disciplined approach was invaluable to me, as was her unfailing good humor. The work of our copyeditor, Christine Sabooni, revealed and corrected all my little errors and some big ones, too. Thanks to both of you for all your help. And many thanks to Lynn Lustberg for coordinating the myriad production tasks associated with this project and for keeping them, and me, on schedule. I also want to thank Michelle Clark for her work as Production Coordinator and Jasmin Tokatlian for her assistance in managing the print supplements. To Jon-David Hague, product director at Cengage, I offer my sincere thanks. Without these people, and those who worked with them, *Foundations and Frontiers* would not have happened.

Finally, I want to thank my wife, Doris, for the loving support that sustains me in my work and in my life. *Je vous aime beaucoup, ma chérie.*

Doug Bernstein

Introducing Psychology

© agsandrew/Shutterstock.com

Preview

All of the following people hold truly interesting jobs. What do you think they studied to qualify for those jobs? See if you can correctly match each person in the left column with their field of study from the right column.

People	Fields of Study
Anne Marie Apanovitch works for a major drug company and determines which of their marketing strategies are most effective in promoting sales.	Engineering
Rebecca Snyder studies the giant pandas at Zoo Atlanta in an effort to promote captive breeding and ultimately increase the wild population of this endangered species.	Criminal Justice
Michael Moon's job at a software company is to find new ways to make websites easier for consumers to use.	Advertising
Sharon Lundgren, founder of Lundgren Trial Consulting, Inc., prepares witnesses to testify in court and teaches attorneys how to present evidence in the most convincing ways.	Psychology
Evan Byrne investigates the role of memory lapses, fatigue, errors, and other human factors in causing airplane crashes for the U.S. National Transportation Safety Board.	Computer Science
Captain Karen Orts, chief of mental health services at a U.S. Air Force base, provides psychotherapy to military personnel suffering combat-related stress disorders, and teaches leadership courses to commissioned and noncommissioned officers.	Zoology

Because Captain Orts offers psychotherapy, you probably guessed that she is a psychologist, but what academic field did you associate with Rebecca Snyder, who studies giant pandas? It would have been perfectly reasonable to assume that she is a zoologist, but she, too, is a psychologist. So is Evan Byrne, whose work on website design might suggest that he was a computer science major. And although Sharon Lundgren spends her time working with witnesses and conducting mock trials, she is a psychologist, not a lawyer. The fact is that *all* these people are psychologists! They may not all fit your ideas of what psychologists do, but as you will see in this chapter and throughout this book, psychology is much broader and more diverse than you may have expected. Reading this book will give you a fuller understanding of psychology, and we hope that you will find our field as fascinating as we do!

This chapter begins our exploration of psychology with a brief look at some of its interrelated specialty areas, or *subfields*. We then tell the story of how psychology came to be and review several theories and approaches that guide psychologists in their work. We also point out how the activities of psychologists in virtually every subfield are affected by human diversity, especially by age, gender, ethnicity, and other individual characteristics encountered in today's multicultural societies.

THE WORLD OF PSYCHOLOGY: AN OVERVIEW

What is psychology and how did it grow?

Psychology is the science that studies behavior and mental processes and seeks to apply that study in the service of human welfare. It is a science that covers a lot of territory, as illustrated by the vastly different jobs that occupy the six psychologists we described. They are all psychologists because they are all involved in studying, predicting, improving, or explaining some aspect of behavior and mental processes. Some of the world's half-million

Psychology The science of behavior and mental processes.

psychologists focus on what can go wrong in behavior and mental processes—psychological disorders, problems in childhood development, stress-related illnesses, and the like—while others study what goes right. They explore, for example, the factors that lead people to be happy and satisfied with their lives, to achieve at a high level, to be creative, to help others, and to develop their full potential as human beings. This focus on what goes right, on the things that make life most worth living, has become known as **positive psychology** (e.g., Wood & Tarrier, 2010; Waterman, 2013), and you will see many examples of it in the research described throughout this book.

To appreciate how many things come under the umbrella of *behavior and mental processes*, think for a moment about how you would answer the question, Who are you? Would you answer by describing your personality, the sharpness of your vision or hearing, your interests and goals, your job skills and accomplishments, your IQ, your cultural background, or your social skills? Perhaps you would describe a physical or psychological problem that bothers you. You could list these and dozens of other things about yourself, and every one of them would reflect some aspect of what psychologists mean by behavior and mental processes. When psychologists focus their work on particular aspects of behavior and mental processes, they enter one of psychology's many subfields. Let's take a quick look at the typical interests and activities of psychologists in these subfields now; we will focus on many of them in more detail in later chapters.

Subfields of Psychology

When psychologists choose to focus their attention on certain aspects of behavior and mental processes, they enter one of psychology's subfields. Let's take a quick look at the typical interests and activities of psychologists in each subfield. We will describe their work in more detail in later chapters.

Biological Psychology

Biological psychologists, also called *physiological psychologists*, study how the brain and the body's biological processes affect, and are affected by, behavior and mental processes. Have you ever had the odd feeling that a new experience, such as entering a new house, has actually happened to you before? Biological psychologists studying this illusion of *déjà vu* (French for "already seen") suggest that it may be due to a temporary malfunction in the brain's ability to combine incoming information from the senses, creating the impression of two "copies" of a single event (Brown, 2004). In the chapter on biological aspects of psychology, we describe biological psychologists' research on many other topics, such as how your brain controls your movements and speech and what organs help you cope with stress and fight disease.

Cognitive Psychology

TRY THIS Stop reading for a moment and look left and right. Your ability to follow this suggestion, to recognize whatever you saw, and to understand the words you are reading right now are the result of mental, or *cognitive*, abilities. Those abilities allow you to receive information from the outside world, understand it, and act on it. **Cognitive psychologists** (some of whom prefer to be called *experimental psychologists*) study mental abilities such as sensation and perception, learning and memory, thinking, consciousness, intelligence, and creativity. Cognitive psychologists have found, for example, that we don't just receive incoming information—we mentally change it. Notice that the drawing in Figure 1.1 stays physically the same, but two different versions emerge, depending on which of its features *you* emphasize.

Applications of cognitive psychologists' research are all around you. The work of those whose special interest is **engineering psychology**—also known as *human factors*—has helped designers create computer keyboards, mobile phones, MP3 players, websites, aircraft instrument panels, automobile navigation systems, nuclear power plant controls,

positive psychology A field of research that focuses on people's positive experiences and characteristics, such as happiness, optimism, and resilience.

biological psychologists Psychologists who analyze the biological factors influencing behavior and mental processes. Also called *physiological psychologists*.

cognitive psychologists Psychologists who study the mental processes underlying judgment, decision making, problem solving, imagining, and other aspects of human thought or cognition. Also called *experimental psychologists*.

engineering psychology A field in which psychologists study human factors in the use of equipment and help designers create better versions of that equipment.

and even TV remotes that are more logical, easier to use, and less likely to cause errors. You will read more about human factors research and many other aspects of cognitive psychology in several chapters of this book.

Developmental Psychology

Developmental psychologists describe how behavior and mental processes change from birth through old age and try to understand the causes and effects of those changes (see Figure 1.2). Their research on the development of memory and other mental abilities, for example, is used by judges and attorneys in deciding how old a child has to be in order to serve as a reliable witness in court or to be able to choose in a responsible way which divorcing parent to live with. The chapter on human development describes other research by developmental psychologists and how it is being applied in areas such as parenting, evaluating day care, and preserving mental capacity in elderly people.

Personality Psychology

Personality psychologists study individuality—the unique features that characterize each of us. Using personality tests, some of these psychologists seek to describe how your own combination of personality traits, like your fingerprints, differs from everyone else's in terms of traits such as openness to experience, emotionality, reliability, agreeableness, and sociability. Others study the combinations of personality traits that are associated with the appearance of ethnic prejudice, depression, bullying, or vulnerability to stress-related health problems. And personality psychologists interested in positive psychology are trying to identify and understand the human strengths that help people to remain optimistic, even in the face of stress or tragedy, and to find happiness in their lives (Snyder & Lopez, 2009).

FIGURE 1.1
Husband and Father-in-Law

This figure is called "Husband and Father-in-Law" (Botwinick, 1961) because you can see an old man or a young man, depending on how you mentally organize its features. The elderly father-in-law faces to your right and is turned slightly toward you. He has a large nose, and the dark areas represent his coat pulled up to his protruding chin. However, the tip of his nose can also be seen as the tip of a younger man's chin; the younger man is in profile, also looking to your right, but away from you. The old man's mouth is the young man's neckband. Both men are wearing a broad-brimmed hat.

From American Journal of Psychology. *Copyright 1961 by the Board of Trustees of the University of Illinois. Used with permission of the University of Illinois Press.*

Drawing by a nine-year-old   Drawing by an eleven-year-old

(A)   **(B)**

FIGURE 1.2
Where Would You Put a Third Eye?

In a study of how thinking develops, children were asked to show where they would place a third eye if they could have one. Nine-year-old children, who were still in an early stage of mental development, drew the extra eye between their existing eyes, "as a spare." Having developed more advanced thinking abilities, eleven-year-olds drew the third eye in more creative places, such as the palm of their hand "so I can see around corners."

From Shaffer, Developmental psychology: Theory, research and applications. *Copyright © 1985 Wadsworth, a part of Cengage Learning Inc. Reproduced by permission. www.cengage.com/permissions*

developmental psychologists Psychologists who seek to understand, describe, and explore how behavior and mental processes change over a lifetime.

personality psychologists Psychologists who study the characteristics that make individuals similar to or different from one another.

Getting Ready for Surgery

Health psychologists have learned that when patients are mentally prepared for a surgical procedure, they are less stressed by it and recover more rapidly. Their research is now routinely applied in hospitals through programs in which children and adults are given more information about what to expect before, during, and after their operations.

Dorothy Littell Greco/The Image Works

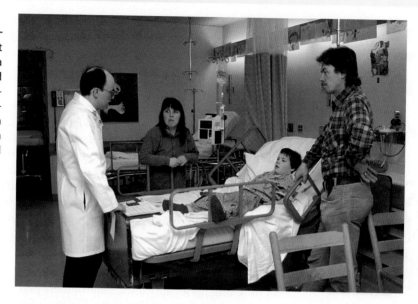

Clinical, Counseling, Community, and Health Psychology

Clinical psychologists and **counseling psychologists** conduct research on the causes and treatment of mental disorders and offer services to help troubled people overcome those disorders. Their research is improving our understanding of the genetic and environmental forces that shape disorders ranging from anxiety and depression to schizophrenia and autism, and it is providing guidance to therapists about which treatment methods are likely to be most effective with each category of disorder.

Community psychologists work to ensure that psychological services reach the homeless and others who need help but tend not to seek it. They also try to prevent psychological disorders by promoting people's resilience and other personal strengths and by working with community leaders and neighborhood organizations to improve local schools and reduce the crime, poverty, and other stressful conditions that often lead to psychological disorders.

Health psychologists study the relationship between behaviors such as smoking or lack of exercise and the likelihood of suffering heart disease, stroke, cancer, or other health problems. They also explore the impact that illnesses such as diabetes, cancer, or multiple sclerosis can have on people's behavior, thinking, emotions, and family relationships. Their research is applied in programs that help people to cope effectively with illness, as well as to reduce the risk of cancer, heart disease, and stroke by changing the behaviors that put them at risk.

Generally, clinical psychologists have Ph.D. degrees in psychology; counseling, community, and health psychologists have either a Ph.D. or a master's degree in psychology. All of these psychologists differ from *psychiatrists*, who are medical doctors specializing in abnormal behavior (psychiatry). You can read more about the work of clinical, counseling, community, and health psychologists in the chapters on health, stress, and coping; psychological disorders; and treatment of psychological disorders.

Educational and School Psychology

Educational psychologists conduct research and develop theories about teaching and learning. The results of their work are applied in programs designed to improve teacher training, refine school curricula, reduce dropout rates, and help students learn more efficiently and remember what they learn. For example, they have supported

clinical and counseling psychologists Psychologists who seek to assess, understand, and change abnormal behavior.

community psychologists Psychologists who work to obtain psychological services for people in need of help and to prevent psychological disorders by working for changes in social systems.

health psychologists Psychologists who study the effects of behavior and mental processes on health and illness and vice versa.

educational psychologists Psychologists who study methods by which instructors teach and students learn and who apply their results to improving those methods.

Got a Match?

Some commercial matchmaking services apply social psychologists' research on interpersonal attraction in an effort to pair up people whose characteristics are most likely to be compatible.

Jeff Morgan 03 / Alamy

the use of the "jigsaw" technique, a type of classroom activity (described in the social psychology chapter) in which children from various ethnic groups must work together to complete a task or solve a problem. These cooperative experiences appear to promote learning, generate mutual respect, and reduce intergroup prejudice (Aronson, 2004).

School psychologists once specialized in IQ testing, diagnosing learning disabilities and other academic problems, and setting up programs to improve students' achievement and satisfaction in school. Today, however, they are also involved in activities such as preventing bullying, early detection of students' mental health problems, and crisis intervention following school violence.

Social Psychology

Social psychologists study the ways that people think about others and how people influence one another. Their research on persuasion has been applied to the creation of safe-sex advertising campaigns designed to stop the spread of AIDS. Social psychologists also explore how peer pressure affects us, what determines whom we like (or even love), and why and how prejudice forms. They have found, for example, that although we may pride ourselves on not being prejudiced, we may actually hold unconscious negative beliefs about certain groups that affect the way we relate to people in those groups. The chapter on social psychology describes these and many other examples of this area of research.

Industrial and Organizational Psychology

Industrial and organizational psychologists conduct research on leadership, stress, competition, pay scales, and other factors that affect the efficiency, productivity, and satisfaction of people in the workplace. They also explore topics such as worker motivation, work team cooperation, conflict resolution procedures, and employee selection methods. Learning more about how businesses and industrial organizations work—or fail to work—allows industrial and organizational psychologists to make evidence-based recommendations for helping them work better. Today, companies all over the world are applying research from industrial and organizational psychology to

school psychologists Psychologists who test IQs, diagnose students' academic problems, and set up programs to improve students' achievement.

social psychologists Psychologists who study how people influence one another's behavior and mental processes, individually and in groups.

industrial and organizational psychologists Psychologists who study ways to improve efficiency, productivity, and satisfaction among workers and the organizations that employ them.

Forensic Psychology

Forensic psychologists may assist police and other agencies in profiling criminals, evaluating the mental competence of defendants, participating in jury selection, and performing many other tasks related to psychology and the law. Actor B. D. Wong's performance as forensic psychiatrist Dr. George Huang on *Law and Order: SVU* was so accurate that the Media Psychology division of the American Psychological Association gave the show its 2004 Golden Psi award for excellence in the fictional portrayal of mental health professionals.

Will Hart/NBC/Photofest

promote the development of *positive organizational behavior*. The results include more effective employee training programs, ambitious but realistic goal-setting procedures, fair and reasonable evaluation tools, and incentive systems that motivate and reward outstanding performance.

Quantitative Psychology

Quantitative psychologists develop and use statistical tools to analyze vast amounts of data collected by their colleagues in all of psychology's subfields. These tools help evaluate the quality of psychological tests, tracing the relationships between childhood experiences and adult behaviors, and even estimating the relative contributions of heredity and environment in shaping intelligence. To what extent are people born smart—or not so smart—and to what extent are their mental abilities created by their environments? This is one of the hottest topics in psychology today, and quantitative psychologists are right in the middle of it.

Other Subfields

Our list of psychology's subfields is still not complete. There are **sport psychologists**, who use visualization and relaxation training programs, for example, to help athletes reduce excessive anxiety, focus attention, and make other changes that let them perform at their best. **Forensic psychologists** assist in jury selection, evaluate defendants' mental competence to stand trial, and deal with other issues involving psychology and the law. And **environmental psychologists** study the effects of the environment on people's behavior and mental processes. The results of their research are applied by architects and interior designers as they plan or remodel residence halls, shopping malls, auditoriums, hospitals, prisons, offices, and other spaces to make them more comfortable and functional for the people who will occupy them. There are also neuropsychologists, military psychologists, consumer psychologists, rehabilitation psychologists, and more.

Further information about the subfields we have mentioned—and some that we haven't—is available on the websites of the American Psychological Association and the Association for Psychological Science.

Where do the psychologists in all these subfields work? Table 1.1 contains a summary of where the approximately 172,000 psychologists in the United States find employment, as well as the kinds of things they typically do in each setting.

quantitative psychologists Psychologists who develop and use statistical tools to analyze research data.

sport psychologists Psychologists who explore the relationships between athletic performance and such psychological variables as motivation and emotion.

forensic psychologists Psychologists who assist in jury selection, evaluate defendants' mental competence to stand trial, and deal with other issues involving psychology and the law.

environmental psychologists Psychologists who study the effects of the physical environment on behavior and mental processes.

TABLE 1.1   TYPICAL ACTIVITIES AND WORK SETTINGS FOR PSYCHOLOGISTS

The fact that psychologists can work in such a wide variety of settings and do so many interesting—and often well-paying—jobs helps account for the popularity of psychology as an undergraduate major (Goldstein, 2010; Dillow & Hoffman, 2008; National Center for Education Statistics, 2014). Psychology courses also provide excellent background for students planning to enter medicine, law, business, and many other fields.

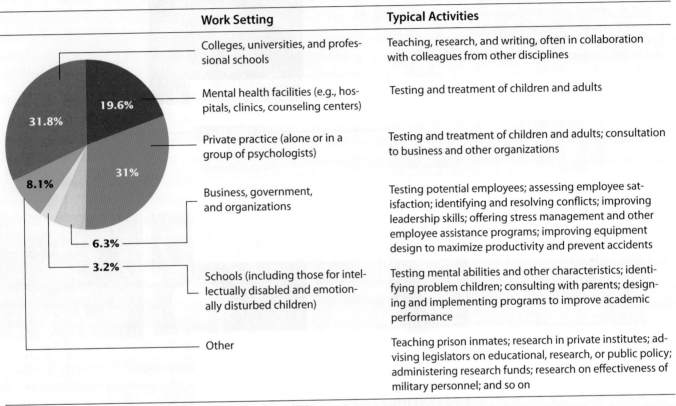

	Work Setting	Typical Activities
	Colleges, universities, and professional schools	Teaching, research, and writing, often in collaboration with colleagues from other disciplines
	Mental health facilities (e.g., hospitals, clinics, counseling centers)	Testing and treatment of children and adults
	Private practice (alone or in a group of psychologists)	Testing and treatment of children and adults; consultation to business and other organizations
	Business, government, and organizations	Testing potential employees; assessing employee satisfaction; identifying and resolving conflicts; improving leadership skills; offering stress management and other employee assistance programs; improving equipment design to maximize productivity and prevent accidents
	Schools (including those for intellectually disabled and emotionally disturbed children)	Testing mental abilities and other characteristics; identifying problem children; consulting with parents; designing and implementing programs to improve academic performance
	Other	Teaching prison inmates; research in private institutes; advising legislators on educational, research, or public policy; administering research funds; research on effectiveness of military personnel; and so on

Source: Employment characteristics of APA members by Membership status, 2012.

Linkages Within Psychology and Beyond

We have listed psychology's subfields as though they were separate, but they often overlap, and so do the activities of the psychologists working in them. When developmental psychologists study the changes that take place in children's thinking skills, for example, their research is linked to the research of cognitive psychologists. Similarly, biological psychologists have one foot in clinical psychology when they look at how chemicals in the brain affect the symptoms of depression. And when social psychologists apply their research on cooperation to promote group learning activities in the classroom, they are linking up with educational psychology. Even when psychologists work mainly in one subfield, they are still likely to draw on, and contribute to, knowledge in other subfields.

So to understand psychology as a whole, you must understand the linkages between its subfields. In this book, to help you recognize these linkages, we highlight three of them in a Linkages diagram at the end of each chapter—similar to the one shown here. Each linkage is represented by a question that connects two subfields, and the chapter given is where you can read more about each question (look for "Linkages" symbols in those chapters). We pay particular attention to one of the questions in each diagram by discussing it in a special Linkages section. If you follow the linkages in these diagrams, you will see more clearly how psychology's many subfields are interconnected. You find this kind of detective work to be interesting, and it will lead you to see many other linkages that we did not mention. Tracing linkages might even improve your grade in the course, because it is often easier to remember material in one topic by relating it to linked material in other topics.

LINKAGES

If you follow the many linkages among psychology's subfields as you read this book, you will come away not only with threads of knowledge about each subfield but also with an appreciation of the fabric of psychology as a whole. We discuss one linkage in detail in each chapter in a special Linkages section.

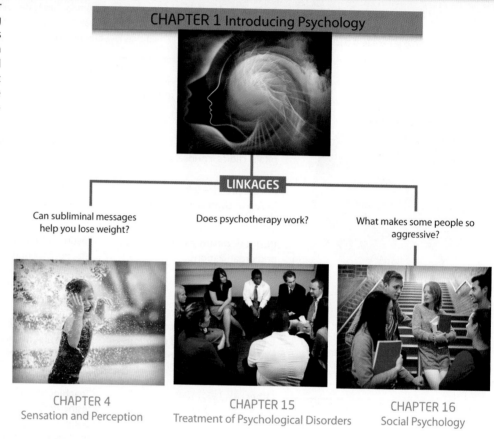

CHAPTER 1 Introducing Psychology

LINKAGES

Can subliminal messages help you lose weight?

Does psychotherapy work?

What makes some people so aggressive?

CHAPTER 4
Sensation and Perception

CHAPTER 15
Treatment of Psychological Disorders

CHAPTER 16
Social Psychology

Links to Other Fields

Just as psychology's subfields are linked to one another, psychology itself is linked to many other fields. Some of these linkages are based on interests that psychologists share with researchers from other disciplines. For example, psychologists work with computer scientists to create artificial intelligence systems that can recognize voices, solve problems, and make decisions in ways that will equal or exceed human capabilities (Haynes, Cohen, & Ritter, 2009; Wang, 2007). Psychologists collaborate with specialists in neuroanatomy, neurophysiology, neurochemistry, genetics, and other disciplines in the field known as **neuroscience**. The goal of this multidisciplinary research enterprise is to examine the structure and function of the nervous system in animals and humans at levels ranging from the individual cell to overt behavior.

Many of the links between psychology and other disciplines appear when research conducted in one field is applied in the other. For example, biological psychologists are learning about the brain with scanning devices developed by computer scientists, physicists, and engineers. Physicians and economists are using research by psychologists to better understand the thought processes that influence (good and bad) decisions about caring for patients and choosing investments. In fact, psychologist Daniel Kahneman won a Nobel Prize in economics for his work in this area. Other psychologists' research on memory has influenced how lineups and "mug shot" photos are displayed to eyewitnesses attempting to identify criminals, how attorneys question eyewitnesses in court, and how lawyers and judges question witnesses and instruct juries. And psychologists' studies of the effect of aging and brain disorders on people's vision, hearing, and mental abilities shape doctors' recommendations about whether and when elderly patients should stop driving cars. This book is filled with more examples of how psychological theories and research have been applied to health care, law, business, engineering, architecture, aviation, and sports, to name just a few.

neuroscience The scientific study of all levels of the nervous system, including neuroanatomy, neurochemistry, neurology, neurophysiology, and neuropharmacology.

Linking Psychology and Law

Cognitive psychologists' research on the quirks of human memory has led to revised guidelines for police and prosecutors when dealing with crime witnesses (U.S. Department of Justice, 1999). These guidelines warn that asking witnesses leading questions (e.g., "Do you remember seeing a gun?") can distort their memories and that false accusations are less likely if witnesses are told that the real criminal might not be in a lineup or in a group of photos (Doyle, 2005).

Masterfile

Research: The Foundation of Psychology

The knowledge that psychologists share across subfields and with other disciplines stems from the research they conduct on many aspects of behavior and mental processes. For example, rather than just speculating about why some people eat too much or too little, psychologists look for answers by using the methods of science. This means that they perform experiments and other scientific procedures to systematically gather and analyze information about behavior and mental processes and then base their conclusions—and their next questions—on the results of those procedures.

The rules and methods of science that guide psychologists in their research are summarized in the chapter on research in psychology. We have placed that chapter early in the book to highlight the fact that without scientific research methods and the foundation of evidence they provide, psychologists' statements and recommendations about behavior and mental processes would carry no more weight than those of astrologers, psychics, or tabloid journalists. Accordingly, we will be relying on the results of scientific research when we tell you what psychology has discovered so far about behavior and mental processes and also when we evaluate their efforts to apply that knowledge to improve the quality of human life.

A Brief History of Psychology

How did scientific research in psychology get started? Psychology is a relatively new discipline, but its roots can be traced through centuries, especially in the history of philosophy. Since at least the time of Socrates, Plato, and Aristotle in ancient Greece, philosophers had been debating psychological topics, such as "What is the nature of the mind and the soul?," "What is the relationship between the mind and the body?," and "Are we born with a certain amount of knowledge, or do we have to learn everything for ourselves?" They even debated whether it is possible to study such things scientifically.

The philosophical view known as *empiricism* was very important to the development of scientific psychology. Beginning in the 1600s, proponents of empiricism—especially

Wilhelm Wundt (1832–1920)

In an early experiment on the speed of mental processes, Wundt (seated) first measured how quickly people could respond to a light by releasing a button they had been holding down. He then measured how much longer the response took when they held down one button with each hand and had to decide, based on the color of the light, which one to release. Wundt reasoned that the additional response time reflected how long it took to perceive the color and decide which hand to move. As noted in the chapter on cognition and language, the logic behind this experiment remains a part of research on cognitive processes today.

INTERFOTO/Personalities/Alamy

consciousness The awareness of external stimuli and our own mental activity.

the British philosophers John Locke, George Berkeley, and David Hume—challenged the long-accepted claim that we are born with knowledge about our world. Instead, empiricists argued that what we know about the world comes to us through experience and observation, not through imagination or intuition. This view suggests that at birth, our minds are like a blank slate (*tabula rasa* in Latin) on which our experiences write a lifelong story. For well over a century now, empiricism has guided psychologists in seeking knowledge about behavior and mental processes through observations governed by the rules of science.

Wundt and the Structuralism of Titchener

The "official" birth date of modern psychology is usually said to be 1879, the year that a physiologist named Wilhelm Wundt (pronounced "voont") established the first formal psychology research laboratory at the University of Leipzig in Germany (Benjamin, 2000). At around this time, German physiologists, including Hermann von Helmholtz and Gustav Fechner (pronounced "FECK-ner"), had been studying vision and other sensory and perceptual processes that empiricism identified as the channels through which human knowledge flows. Fechner's work was especially valuable because he realized that one could study these mental processes by observing people's reactions to changes in sensory stimuli. By exploring, for example, how much brighter a light must become before we see it as twice as bright, Fechner discovered complex but predictable ways that changes in the *physical* characteristics of stimuli produced changes in our *psychological experience* of them. Fechner's approach, which he called *psychophysics*, paved the way for much of the research described in the chapter on sensation and perception.

Wundt, too, used the methods of laboratory science to study sensory-perceptual systems, but the focus of his work was **consciousness**, the mental experiences created by these systems. Wundt wanted to identify the basic elements of consciousness and describe how they are organized and how they relate to one another (Schultz & Schultz, 2004). He developed ingenious laboratory methods to study the speed of decision making and other mental events, and in an attempt to observe conscious experience, Wundt used the technique of *introspection*, which means "looking inward." After training research participants in this method, he repeatedly showed a light or made a sound and asked participants to describe the sensations and feelings these stimuli created. Wundt concluded that "quality" (e.g., cold or blue) and "intensity" (e.g., brightness or loudness) are the two essential elements of sensation, and that feelings can be described in terms of pleasure or displeasure, tension or relaxation, and excitement or depression (Schultz & Schultz, 2004). In conducting this kind of research, Wundt began psychology's transformation from the *philosophy* of mental processes to the *science* of mental processes.

Edward Titchener, an Englishman who had been a student of Wundt's, used introspection in his own laboratory at Cornell University. He studied Wundt's basic elements of consciousness, as well as images and other aspects of conscious experience that are harder to quantify (see Figure 1.3). One result was that Titchener added "clearness" as an element of sensation (Schultz & Schultz, 2004). Titchener called his approach *structuralism* because he was trying to define the structure of consciousness.

Wundt was not alone in the scientific study of mental processes, nor was his work universally accepted. Some of his fellow German scientists, including Hermann Ebbinghaus, believed that analyzing consciousness through introspection was not as important as exploring the capacities and limitations of mental processes such as learning and memory. Ebbinghaus's own laboratory experiments—in which he served as the only participant—formed the basis for some of what we know about memory today.

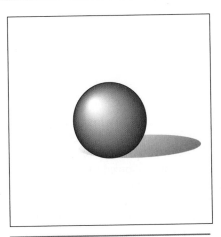

FIGURE 1.3
A Stimulus for Introspection

TRY THIS Look at this object, and try to ignore what it is. Instead, try to describe only your conscious experience, such as redness, brightness, and roundness, and how intense and clear the sensations and images are. If you can do this, you would have been an excellent research assistant in Titchener's laboratory.

Gestalt Psychologists

Around 1912, other German colleagues, including Max Wertheimer, Kurt Koffka, and Wolfgang Köhler, argued against Wundt's efforts to break down human experience or consciousness into its component parts. They were called *Gestalt psychologists* because they pointed out that the whole shape (*Gestalt* in German) of conscious experience is not the same as the sum of its parts. Wertheimer pointed out, for example, that if a pair of lights goes on and off in just the right sequence, we don't experience two separate flashing lights but a single light that appears to "jump" back and forth. You have probably seen this *phi phenomenon* in action on advertising signs that create the impression of a series of lights racing around a display. Movies provide another example. It would be incredibly boring to look one each of the thousands of still images contained one after another in a video recording. Yet when those same images appear on a screen at a particular rate, they combine to create a rich and seemingly seamless visual experience. To understand consciousness, then, said the Gestaltists, we have to study the whole "movie," not just its component parts.

Freud and Psychoanalysis

While Wundt and his colleagues in Leipzig were conducting scientific research on consciousness, Sigmund Freud was in Vienna, Austria, beginning to explore the unconscious. As a physician, Freud had presumed that all behavior and mental processes have *physical* causes somewhere in the nervous system. He began to question that assumption in the late 1800s, however, after encountering several patients who displayed a variety of physical ailments that had no apparent physical cause. After interviewing these patients using hypnosis and other methods, Freud concluded that the causes of these people's physical problems were not physical. The real causes, he said, were deep-seated problems that the patients had pushed out of consciousness (Friedman & Schustack, 2003). He eventually came to believe that all behavior—from everyday slips of the tongue to severe forms of mental disorder—is motivated by *psychological* processes, especially by mental conflicts that occur without our awareness, at an unconscious level. For nearly fifty years, Freud developed his ideas into a body of work known as *psychoanalysis*, which included a theory of personality and mental disorder, as well as a set of treatment methods. Freud's ideas have never been universally accepted, partly because they were based on a small number of medical cases, not on extensive laboratory experiments. Still, he was a groundbreaker whose theories have had a significant influence on psychology and many other fields.

William James and Functionalism

Scientific research in psychology began in North America not long after Wundt started his work in Germany. William James founded a psychology laboratory at Harvard University in the late 1870s, though it was used mainly to conduct demonstrations for his students (Schultz & Schultz, 2004). It was not until 1883 that G. Stanley Hall at Johns Hopkins University established the first psychology research laboratory in the United States. The first Canadian psychology research laboratory was established in 1889 at the University of Toronto by James Mark Baldwin, Canada's first modern psychologist and a pioneer in research on child development.

Like the Gestalt psychologists, William James rejected both Wundt's approach and Titchener's structuralism. He saw no point in breaking consciousness into component parts that never operate on their own. Instead, in accordance with Charles Darwin's theory of evolution, James wanted to understand how images, sensations, memories, and the other mental events that make up our flowing "stream of consciousness" *function* to help us adapt to our environment (James, 1890, 1892). This idea was consistent with an approach to psychology called *functionalism*, which focused on the role of consciousness in guiding people's ability to make decisions, solve problems, and the like.

James's emphasis on the functions of mental processes encouraged North American psychologists to look not only at how those processes work to our advantage but also at how they differ from one person to the next. Some of these psychologists began to measure individual differences in learning, memory, and other mental processes associated with intelligence, made recommendations for improving educational practices in the schools, and even worked with teachers on programs tailored to children in need of special help (Kramer, Bernstein, & Phares, 2014).

John B. Watson and Behaviorism

Besides fueling James's interest in the functions of consciousness, Darwin's theory of evolution led other psychologists—especially those in North America after 1900—to study animals as well as humans. These researchers reasoned that if all species evolved in similar ways, perhaps the behavior and mental processes of all species followed the same or similar laws, and if so, we can learn something about people by studying animals. They could not expect cats or rats or pigeons to introspect, so they watched what animals did when confronted with laboratory tasks such as finding the correct path through a maze. From these observations, psychologists made *inferences* about the animals' conscious experience and about the general laws of learning, memory, problem solving, and other mental processes that might apply to people as well.

John B. Watson, a psychology professor at Johns Hopkins University, agreed that the observable behavior of animals and humans is the most important source of scientific information for psychology. However, he thought it was utterly unscientific to use behavior as the basis for making inferences about consciousness, as structuralists and functionalists did—let alone about the unconscious, as Freudians did. In 1913, Watson published an article titled "Psychology as the Behaviorist Views It." In it, he argued that psychologists should ignore mental events and base psychology only on what they can actually see in overt behavior and in responses to known stimuli (Watson, 1913, 1919).

Watson's view, called *behaviorism*, recognized that consciousness exists, but it did not consider it worth studying because consciousness would always be private and therefore not observable by scientific methods. In fact, said Watson, preoccupation with consciousness would prevent psychology from ever being a true science. He believed that the most important determinant of behavior is *learning* and that it is through learning that animals and humans are able to adapt to their environments. Watson famously claimed that with enough control over the environment, he could create learning experiences that would make any infant into a doctor, a lawyer, or even a criminal.

The American psychologist B. F. Skinner was an early champion of behaviorism. From the 1930s until his death in 1990, Skinner worked on mapping out the details of how rewards and punishments shape, maintain, and change behavior through what he termed "operant conditioning." By conducting a *functional analysis of behavior*, he would explain, for example, how parents and teachers perhaps even unknowingly encourage children's tantrums by rewarding them with attention and how an addiction to gambling can result from the occasional and unpredictable rewards it brings.

Many psychologists were drawn to Watson's and Skinner's vision of psychology as the learning-based science of observable behavior. As such, behaviorism dominated psychological research from the 1920s through the 1960s, while the study of consciousness received less attention, especially in the United States. ("In Review: The Development of Psychology" summarizes behaviorism and the other schools of thought that have influenced psychologists in the past century.)

Psychology Today

Psychologists continue to study all kinds of overt behavior in humans and in animals. By the end of the 1960s, however, many had become dissatisfied with the limitations imposed by behaviorism (some, especially in Europe, had never accepted it in the first place). They grew uncomfortable about ignoring mental processes that might be important in more fully understanding behavior (e.g., Ericsson & Simon, 1994). The dawn of the computer age influenced these psychologists to think about mental activity in a new way—as information processing. Computers and rapid progress in computer-based biotechnology began to offer psychologists exciting new ways to study mental processes and the biological activity that underlies them. It is now possible to see what is happening in the brain when a person reads or thinks or makes decisions.

Armed with ever more sophisticated research tools, psychologists today are striving to do what Watson thought was impossible: to study mental processes with precision and scientific objectivity. In fact, there are probably now as many psychologists who study cognitive and biological processes as there are who study observable behaviors. So mainstream psychology has come full circle, once again accepting consciousness—in the form of cognitive processes—as a legitimate topic for scientific research and justifying the definition of psychology as the science of behavior and mental processes.

IN REVIEW

THE DEVELOPMENT OF PSYCHOLOGY

School of Thought	Early Advocates	Goals	Methods
Structuralism	Edward Titchener, trained by Wilhelm Wundt	To study conscious experience and its structure	Experiments; introspection
Gestalt psychology	Max Wertheimer	To describe the organization of mental processes: "The whole is different from the sum of its parts."	Observation of sensory-perceptual phenomena
Psychoanalysis	Sigmund Freud	To explain personality and behavior; to develop techniques for treating mental disorders	Study of individual cases
Functionalism	William James	To study how the mind works in allowing an organism to adapt to the environment	Naturalistic observation of animal and human behavior
Behaviorism	John B. Watson, B. F. Skinner	To study only observable behavior and explain behavior through learning principles	Observation of the relationship between environmental stimuli and behavioral responses

1. Darwin's theory of evolution had an especially strong influence on _____ ism and _____ ism .

2. Which school of psychological thought was founded by a European medical doctor? _____

3. In the history of psychology, _____ was the first school of thought to appear.

APPROACHES TO THE SCIENCE OF PSYCHOLOGY

Why don't all psychologists explain behavior in the same way?

We have seen that the history of psychology is, in part, a history of differing ways in which psychologists thought about, or "approached," behavior and mental processes. Today, psychologists no longer refer to themselves as structuralists or functionalists but the psychodynamic and behavioral approaches remain, along with some newer ones known as the *biological, evolutionary, cognitive,* and *humanistic approaches.* Some psychologists adopt just one of these approaches, but most are eclectic—they blend aspects of two or more approaches in an effort to understand more fully the behavior and mental processes in their subfield (e.g., Cacioppo et al., 2000). Some approaches to psychology are more influential than others these days, but we will review the main features of all of them so you can more easily understand why different psychologists may explain the same behavior or mental process in different ways.

The Biological Approach

As its name implies, the **biological approach** to psychology assumes that behavior and mental processes are largely shaped by biological processes. Psychologists who take this approach study the psychological effects of hormones, genes, and the activity of the nervous system, especially the brain. So if they are studying memory, they might try to identify the changes taking place in the brain as information is stored there (Figure 6.14, in the chapter on memory, shows an example of these changes). If they are studying thinking, they might look for patterns of brain activity associated with, say, making quick decisions or reading a foreign language.

The Biology of Emotion

Robert Levenson, a psychologist at the University of California at Berkeley, takes a biological approach to the study of social interactions. He measures heart rate, muscle tension, and other physical reactions as couples discuss problems in their relationships. He then looks for patterns of physiological activity in each of the partners (such as overreactions to criticism) that might be related to success or failure in resolving their problems.

University of California Berkeley

We discuss research in nearly every chapter of this book to show the enormous influence of the biological approach on psychology today. To help you better understand the terms and concepts used in that research, we have provided an appendix on the principles of genetics and a chapter on biological aspects of psychology.

The Evolutionary Approach

Biological processes also figure prominently in an approach to psychology based on Charles Darwin's 1859 book *On the Origin of Species*. Darwin argued that the forms of life we see today are the result of *evolution*—of changes in life forms that occur over many generations. He said that evolution occurs through **natural selection**, which promotes the survival of the fittest individuals. Those whose behavior and appearance allow them to withstand the elements, avoid predators, and mate are able to survive and produce offspring, who may have similar characteristics. Those less able to adjust (or *adapt*) to changing conditions are less likely to survive and reproduce. Most evolutionists today see natural selection operating at the level of genes, but the process is the same. Genes that result in characteristics and behaviors that are adaptive and useful in a certain environment will enable the creatures that inherit them to survive and reproduce, thereby

biological approach An approach to psychology in which behavior and behavior disorders are seen as the result of physical processes, especially those relating to the brain and to hormones and other chemicals.

natural selection The evolutionary mechanism through which Darwin said the fittest individuals survive to reproduce.

TRY THIS   Take a moment to jot down what you see in these clouds.

According to the psychodynamic approach to psychology, what we see in cloud formations and other vague patterns reflects unconscious wishes, impulses, fears, and other mental processes. In the personality chapter, we discuss the value of personality tests based on this assumption.

Jack Hollingsworth/Getty Images

passing those genes on to the next generation. According to evolutionary theory, many (but not all) of the genes that animals and humans possess today are the result of natural selection.

The **evolutionary approach** to psychology assumes that the *behavior and mental processes* of animals and humans today are also affected by evolution through natural selection. For example, psychologists who take this approach see cooperation as an adaptive survival strategy, aggression as a form of territory protection, and gender differences in mate selection preferences as reflecting different ways through which genes survive in future generations (Griskevicius et al., 2009). The evolutionary approach has generated a growing body of research (e.g., Buss, 2009; Confer et al., 2010); in later chapters, you will see how it is applied in relation to topics such as helping and altruism, mental disorders, temperament, and interpersonal attraction.

The Psychodynamic Approach

The **psychodynamic approach** to psychology offers a different slant on the role of inherited instincts and other biological forces in human behavior. Rooted in Freud's psychoanalysis, this approach assumes that our behavior and mental processes reflect constant and mostly unconscious psychological struggles deep within us (see Figure 1.4). Usually, these struggles involve conflict between the impulse to satisfy instincts (such as for food, sex, or aggression) and the need to follow the rules of civilized society. So psychologists taking a psychodynamic approach might see aggression, for example, as a case of primitive urges overcoming a person's defenses against expressing those urges. They would see anxiety, depression, or other disorders as overt signs of inner turmoil.

Freud's original theories are not as influential today as they once were (Mischel, 2004a), but you will encounter modern versions of the psychodynamic approach when we discuss theories of personality, psychological disorders, and psychotherapy.

The Behavioral Approach

The assumptions of the **behavioral approach** to psychology contrast sharply with those of the psychodynamic, biological, and evolutionary approaches. The behavioral approach is rooted in the behaviorism of Watson and Skinner, which, as we have seen, focused entirely on observable behavior and on how that behavior is *learned*. Accordingly, psychologists who take a strict behavioral approach concentrate on understanding how past experiences with rewards and punishments act on the "raw materials" provided by genes and evolution

evolutionary approach An approach to psychology that emphasizes the inherited, adaptive aspects of behavior and mental processes.

psychodynamic approach A view developed by Freud that emphasizes the interplay of unconscious mental processes in determining human thought, feelings, and behavior.

behavioral approach An approach to psychology emphasizing that human behavior is determined mainly by what a person has learned, especially from rewards and punishments.

Why Is He So Aggressive?

Psychologists who take a cognitive-behavioral approach suggest that behavior is not shaped by rewards and punishments alone. They say that children's aggressiveness, for example, is learned partly by being rewarded (or at least not punished) for aggression but also partly by seeing family and friends acting aggressively. Further, attitudes and beliefs about the value and acceptability of aggressiveness can be learned as children hear others talk about aggression as the only way to deal with threats, disagreements, and other conflict situations (e.g., Cooper, Gomez, & Buck, 2008; Wilkowski & Robinson, 2008).

Mary Kate Denny/PhotoEdit

cognitive approach A way of looking at human behavior that emphasizes research on how the brain takes in information, creates perceptions, forms and retrieves memories, processes information, and generates integrated patterns of action.

humanistic approach A perspective to psychology that focuses on how each person has a unique capacity to choose how to think and act.

to shape observable behavior into what it is today. So whether they are trying to understand a person's aggressiveness, fear of spiders, parenting methods, or drug abuse, behaviorists look mainly at that person's learning history. And because they believe that behavior problems develop through learning, behaviorists seek to eliminate problems by helping people replace bad habits with new and more appropriate ones.

Recall, though, that the peak of behaviorism's popularity passed precisely because it ignored everything but observable behavior. That criticism has had an impact on the many behaviorists who now apply their learning-based approach in an effort to understand thoughts, or cognitions, as well as observable behavior. Those who take this *cognitive-behavioral*, or *social-cognitive*, approach explore how learning affects the development of thoughts, attitudes, and beliefs and, in turn, how these learned cognitive patterns affect overt behavior.

The Cognitive Approach

The growth of the cognitive-behavioral perspective reflects the influence of a broader cognitive view of psychology. This **cognitive approach** focuses on how we take in, mentally represent, and store information; how we perceive and process that information; and how all these cognitive processes affect our behavior. Psychologists who take the cognitive approach study the rapid series of mental events—including those outside of awareness—that accompany observable behavior. So in analyzing, say, an aggressive incident in a movie theater line, these psychologists would describe the following series of information processing events: First, the aggressive person (1) *perceived* that someone has cut into the ticket line, then (2) *recalled* information stored in memory about appropriate social behavior, (3) *decided* that the other person's action was inappropriate, (4) *labeled* the person as rude and inconsiderate, (5) *considered* possible responses and their likely consequences, (6) *decided* that shoving the person is the best response, and (7) *executed* that response.

Psychologists who take a cognitive approach focus on these and other mental processes to understand many kinds of individual and social behaviors, from decision making and problem solving to interpersonal attraction and intelligence, to name but a few. In the situation just described, for example, the person's aggression would be seen as the result of poor problem solving, because there were probably several better ways to deal with the problem of line-cutting. The cognitive approach is especially important in the field of *cognitive science*, in which researchers from psychology, computer science, biology, engineering, linguistics, and philosophy study intelligent systems in humans and computers. Together, they try to discover the building blocks of cognition and determine how these components produce complex behaviors such as remembering a fact, recognizing objects, writing words, or making a decision.

The Humanistic Approach

Mental events play a different role in the **humanistic approach** to psychology (also known as the *phenomenological approach*). Psychologists who favor the humanistic perspective see behavior as determined primarily by each person's unique capacity to choose how to think and act. They don't see these choices as driven by instincts, biological processes, or rewards and punishments but rather by each individual's own perceptions of the world. So if you see the world as a friendly place, you are likely to be optimistic and secure. If you perceive it as full of hostile, threatening people, you will probably be defensive and fearful.

Like their cognitively oriented colleagues, psychologists who use a humanistic approach would see aggression in a theater line as stemming from a perception that aggression is justified. But where the cognitive approach leads psychologists to search for laws governing *all* people's thoughts and actions, humanistic psychologists try to

Cognitive Science at Work

Psychologists and other cognitive scientists are working on a "computational theory of the mind" in which they create computer programs and robotic devices that simulate how humans process information. In the chapter on cognition and language, we discuss their progress in creating "artificial intelligence" in computers that can help make medical diagnoses and perform other complex cognitive tasks, including the Internet searches you do using Google and other sophisticated web search engines.

Yoshikazu Tsuno/AFP/Getty Images

understand how each individual's unique experiences guide *that* person's thoughts and actions. In fact, many who prefer the humanistic approach claim that because no two people are exactly alike, the only way to understand behavior and mental processes is to focus on how they operate in each individual. Humanistic psychologists see people as essentially good, in control of themselves, and with an innate tendency to grow toward their highest potential.

The humanistic approach attracted attention in North America in the 1940s through the writings of Carl Rogers, a psychologist who trained in, but later rejected, the psychodynamic approach. We describe his views on personality and his psychotherapy methods in the chapters on personality and the treatment of psychological disorders. Another influential figure of the same era was Abraham Maslow, a psychologist who shaped and promoted the humanistic approach through his famous hierarchy-of-needs theory of motivation, which we describe in the chapters on motivation and emotion and personality. Today, the impact of the humanistic approach to psychology is less noticeable, partly because many psychologists find humanistic concepts and predictions too vague to be tested scientifically. It has, however, helped inspire the theories and research in positive psychology that are now becoming so popular (Snyder & Lopez, 2009). (For a summary of all the approaches we have discussed, see "In Review: Approaches to the Science of Psychology.")

APPROACHES TO THE SCIENCE OF PSYCHOLOGY

Approach	Characteristics
Biological	Emphasizes activity of the nervous system, especially of the brain; the action of hormones and other chemicals; and genetics
Evolutionary	Emphasizes the ways in which behavior and mental processes are adaptive for survival
Psychodynamic	Emphasizes internal conflicts, mostly unconscious, which usually pit sexual or aggressive instincts against environmental obstacles to their expression
Behavioral	Emphasizes learning, especially each person's experience with rewards and punishments; the *cognitive-behavioral approach* adds emphasis on learning by observation and the learning of certain ways of thinking
Cognitive	Emphasizes mechanisms through which people receive, store, retrieve, and otherwise process information
Humanistic	Emphasizes individual potential for growth and the role of unique perceptions in guiding behavior and mental processes

1. Teaching people to be less afraid of heights reflects the _____ approach.

2. Charles Darwin was not a psychologist, but his work influenced the _____ approach to psychology.

3. Assuming that people inherit mental disorders suggests a _____ approach.

Mary Whiton Calkins (1863–1930)

Mary Whiton Calkins studied psychology at Harvard University, where William James described her as "brilliant." Because she was a woman, though, Harvard refused to grant her a doctoral degree unless she received it through Radcliffe, which was then an affiliated school for women. She refused but went on to do research on memory and in 1905 became the first woman president of the American Psychological Association (APA). Margaret Washburn (1871–1939) encountered similar sex discrimination at Columbia University, so she transferred to Cornell and became the first woman to earn a doctorate in psychology. In 1921, she became the second woman president of the APA.

HUMAN DIVERSITY AND PSYCHOLOGY

How does your cultural background influence your behavior?

Today, the diversity seen in psychologists' approaches to their work is matched by the diversity in their own backgrounds. This was not always the case. As in other academic disciplines in the early twentieth century, most psychologists were white, middle-class men (Walker, 1991). Almost from the beginning, however, women and people of color were also part of the field (Schultz & Schultz, 2004). Throughout this book, you will find discussions of the work of their modern counterparts, whose contributions to research, service, and teaching have all increased, as has their representation in psychology. In the United States, women now constitute a majority of all working psychologists, and a majority of those earning doctoral degrees in psychology (Willyard, 2011). Moreover, about 25 percent of new doctoral degrees in psychology are being earned by members of ethnic minority groups (American Psychological Association, 2010; National Science Foundation, 2009). These numbers reflect continuing efforts by psychological organizations and governmental bodies, especially in the United States and Canada, to promote the recruitment, graduation, and employment of women and ethnic minorities in psychology.

The Impact of Sociocultural Diversity on Psychology

Another aspect of diversity in psychology lies in the wide range of people psychologists study and serve. This change is significant because most psychologists once assumed that all people are very much alike and that whatever principles emerged from research or treatment efforts with one group would apply to everyone, everywhere. They were partly right, because people around the world *are* alike in many ways. They tend to live in groups, have religious beliefs, and create rules, music, dances, and games. The principles of nerve cell activity or reactions to heat or a sour taste are likely the same in men and women everywhere, as is their recognition of a smile. But are all people's moral values, achievement motivation, or communication styles the same too? Would the results of research on white

Gilbert Haven Jones (1883–1966)

When Gilbert Haven Jones graduated from the University of Jena in Germany in 1909, he became one of the first African Americans to earn a doctorate in psychology. Many others were to follow, including J. Henry Alston, who was the first African American to publish research in a major U.S. psychology journal (Alston, 1920).

© Courtesy Wilberforce University/Archives & Special Collections

sociocultural factors Social identity and other background factors, such as gender, ethnicity, social class, and culture.

culture The accumulation of values, rules of behavior, forms of expression, religious beliefs, occupational choices, and the like for a group of people who share a common language and environment.

male college students in the midwestern United States apply to African American women or to people in Greece, Korea, Argentina, or Egypt? Not always. These and many other aspects of behavior and mental processes are affected by **sociocultural factors**, including people's gender, ethnicity, social class, and the culture in which they grow up. These variables create many significant differences in behavior and mental processes, especially from one culture to another (e.g., Shiraev & Levy, 2010).

Culture has been defined as the accumulation of values, rules of behavior, forms of expression, religious beliefs, occupational choices, and the like for a group of people who share a common language and environment (Fiske et al., 1998). Culture is an organizing and stabilizing influence. It encourages or discourages particular behaviors and thoughts; it also allows people to understand and know what to expect from others in that culture. It is a kind of group adaptation, passed along by tradition and example rather than by genes from one generation to the next (Castro & Toro, 2004). Culture determines, for example, whether children's education will focus on skill at hunting or reading, how close people stand during a conversation, and whether or not they form lines in public places.

Psychologists and anthropologists have found that cultures can differ in many ways (Cohen, 2009). They may have strict or loose rules governing social behavior. They might place great value on achievement or on self-awareness. Some seek dominance over nature; others seek harmony with it. Time is of great importance in some cultures but not in others. Psychologists have tended to focus on the differences between cultures that can best be described as individualist or collectivist (Triandis & Trafimow, 2001). As shown in Table 1.2, many people in *individualist* cultures, such as those typical of North America

TABLE **1.2** SOME CHARACTERISTICS OF BEHAVIOR AND MENTAL PROCESSES TYPICAL OF INDIVIDUALIST VERSUS COLLECTIVIST CULTURES

Psychologists and anthropologists have noticed that cultures can create certain general tendencies in behavior and mental processes among the people living in them (Bhagat et al., 2002). As shown here, individualist cultures tend to support the idea of placing one's personal goals before the goals of the extended family or work group, whereas collectivist cultures tend to encourage putting the goals of those groups ahead of personal goals. Remember, however, that these labels represent very rough categories. Cultures cannot be pigeonholed as being either entirely individualist or entirely collectivist, and not everyone raised in a particular culture always thinks or acts in exactly the same way (Na et al., 2010).

Variable	Individualist	Collectivist
Personal identity	Separate from others	Connected to others
Major goals	Self-defined; be unique; realize your personal potential; compete with others	Defined by others; belong; occupy your proper place; meet your obligations to others; be like others
Criteria for self-esteem	Ability to express unique aspects of the self; self-assurance	Ability to restrain the self and be part of a social unit; modesty
Sources of success and failure	Success comes from personal effort; failure is caused by external factors	Success is due to help from others; failure is due to personal faults
Major frame of reference	Personal attitudes, traits, and goals	Family, work group

and Western Europe, tend to value personal rather than group goals and achievement. Competitiveness to distinguish oneself from others is common in these cultures, as is a sense of isolation. By contrast, many people in *collectivist* cultures, such as Japan, tend to think of themselves mainly as part of their families or work groups. Cooperative effort aimed at advancing the welfare of these social units is highly valued, and although loneliness is seldom a problem, fear of rejection by the family or other group is common. Many aspects of U.S. culture—from self-reliant cowboy heroes and bonuses for "top" employees to the invitation to "help yourself" at a buffet table—reflect its tendency toward an individualist orientation (see Table 1.3).

A culture may be associated with a particular country, but most countries are actually *multicultural;* in other words, they host many *subcultures* within their borders. Often these subcultures are formed by people of various ethnic origins. The population of the United States, for instance, includes African Americans, Hispanic Americans, Asian Americans, and American Indians, as well as Americans whose families came from Italy, France, Germany, Britain, Poland, Brazil, India, Iraq, and many other places. In each of these groups, the individuals who identify with their cultural heritage tend to share behaviors, values, and beliefs based on their culture of origin, thus forming a *subculture*.

Like fish unaware of the water in which they swim, people often fail to notice how the culture or subculture in which they live shapes their thinking and behavior. Such influence may not be evident until people come in contact with other people whose culture or subculture has shaped different patterns. Consider hand gestures, for example. The "thumbs up" sign means that "everything is OK" to people in North America and Europe

TABLE 1.3   CULTURAL VALUES IN ADVERTISING

TRY THIS

The statements listed here appeared in advertisements in Korea and the United States. Those from Korea reflect collectivist values, whereas those from the United States emphasize a more individualist orientation (Han & Shavitt, 1994). See if you can tell which are which; then check at the bottom of page 24 for the answers. To follow up on this exercise, identify cultural values in ads you see in newspapers, magazines, billboards, television, and the Internet. By surfing the Internet or scanning international newspapers online, you can compare the values conveyed by ads in your culture with those in ads from other cultures.

1. "She's got a style all her own."

2. "You, only better."

3. "A more exhilarating way to provide for your family."

4. "We have a way of bringing people closer together."

5. "Celebrating a half-century of partnership."

6. "How to protect the most personal part of the environment: Your skin."

7. "Our family agrees with this selection of home furnishings."

8. "A leader among leaders."

9. "Make your way through the crowd."

10. "Your business success: Harmonizing with [company name]."

Source: Brehm, Kassin, & Fein (2005).

but is considered a rude gesture in Australia, Nigeria, and Bangladesh. And although in North America, making eye contact during social introductions is usually seen as a sign of interest or sincerity, it is likely to be considered rude in Japan. Even some of the misunderstandings that occur between men and women in the same culture can be traced to slight culturally influenced differences in their communication styles (Tannen, 2001, 2011). In the United States, for example, women's efforts to connect with others by talking are perceived by some men as "pointless" unless the discussion is aimed at solving a specific problem. As a result, women may feel frustrated and misunderstood by men who offer well-intentioned but unwanted advice instead of conversation.

For decades, the impact of culture on behavior and mental processes was of concern mainly to a relatively small group of researchers working in *cross-cultural psychology*. In the chapters ahead, however, you will see that psychologists in almost every subfield now look at how ethnicity, gender, age, and other sociocultural variables influence behavior and mental processes. In short, psychology strives to be the science of *all* behavior and mental processes, not just of those in the cultures where it began.

The Impact of Culture

Culture helps shape virtually every aspect of our behavior and mental processes, from how we dress to how we think to what we think is important. Because most people grow up immersed in a particular culture, they may not notice its influence on their thoughts and actions until—like these people who emigrated from Somalia to Lewiston, Maine—they encounter people whose culture has shaped them in different ways (Luna, Ringberg, & Peracchio, 2008; Markus, 2008; Masuda et al., 2008; Nisbett & Masuda, 2007; Varnum et al., 2008).

AP Images/Robert F. Bukaty

SUMMARY

Psychology is the science that seeks to understand behavior and mental processes and to apply that understanding in the service of human welfare.

The World of Psychology: An Overview

What is psychology and how did it grow?

The concept of "behavior and mental processes" is a broad one, encompassing virtually all aspects of what it means to be human. Some psychologists study and seek to alleviate problems that plague human life, while those working in *positive psychology* seek to understand happiness, optimism, human strengths, and the like.

Because the subject matter of psychology is so diverse, most psychologists work in different subfields within the discipline. For example, *biological psychologists*, also called physiological

psychologists, study topics such as the role played by the brain in normal and disordered behavior. *Cognitive psychologists*, some of whom prefer to be called experimental psychologists, focus on basic psychological processes such as learning, memory, and perception; they also study judgment, decision making, and problem solving. *Engineering psychology*, the study of human factors in the use of equipment, helps designers create better versions of that equipment. *Developmental psychologists* specialize in trying to understand the development of behavior and mental processes over a lifetime. *Personality psychologists* focus on characteristics that set people apart from one another and by which they can be compared. *Clinical psychologists* and *counseling psychologists* provide direct service to troubled people and conduct research on abnormal behavior. *Community psychologists* work to prevent mental disorders and to extend mental health services to those who need them. *Health psychologists* study the relationship between behavior and health and help promote healthy lifestyles. *Educational psychologists* conduct and apply research on teaching and learning, whereas *school psychologists* specialize in assessing and alleviating children's academic problems. *Social psychologists* examine questions regarding how people influence one another. *Industrial and organizational psychologists* study ways to increase efficiency and productivity in the workplace. *Quantitative psychologists* develop ways to analyze research data from all subfields. *Sport psychologists, forensic psychologists,* and *environmental psychologists* exemplify some of psychology's many other subfields.

Psychologists often work in more than one subfield and usually share knowledge with colleagues in many subfields. Psychologists also draw on and contribute to knowledge in other disciplines, such as computer science, economics, and law.

Psychologists use the methods of science to conduct research. This means that they perform experiments and use other scientific procedures to systematically gather and analyze information about psychological phenomena.

The founding of modern psychology is usually marked as 1879, when Wilhelm Wundt established the first psychology research laboratory. Wundt studied consciousness in a manner that was expanded by Edward Titchener into an approach he called *structuralism*. It was in the late 1800s, too, that Sigmund Freud, in Vienna, began his study of the unconscious, while in the United States, William James took the functionalist approach, suggesting that psychologists should study how consciousness helps us adapt to our environments. In 1913, John B. Watson founded *behaviorism*, arguing that to be scientific, psychologists should study only the behavior they can see, not private mental events. Behaviorism dominated psychology for decades, but psychologists are once again studying consciousness in the form of cognitive processes.

Approaches to the Science of Psychology

Why don't all psychologists explain behavior in the same way?

Psychologists differ in their approaches to psychology—that is, in their assumptions, questions, and research methods. Some adopt just one approach; most combine features of two or more approaches. Those adopting a *biological approach* focus on how physiological processes shape behavior and mental processes. Psychologists who prefer the *evolutionary approach* emphasize the inherited, adaptive aspects of behavior and mental processes. In the *psychodynamic approach*, behavior and mental processes are seen as reflecting struggles to resolve conflicts between raw impulses and the social rules that limit the expression of those impulses. Psychologists who take the *behavioral approach* view behavior as determined primarily by learning based on experiences with rewards and punishments. The *cognitive approach* assumes that behavior can be understood through analysis of the basic mental processes that underlie it. To those adopting the *humanistic approach*, behavior is controlled by the decisions that people make about their lives based on their perceptions of the world.

Human Diversity and Psychology

How does your cultural background influence your behavior?

Psychologists are diverse in their backgrounds and in their activities. Most of the prominent figures in psychology's early history were white males, but women and people of color made important contributions from the start and continue to do so.

Psychologists are increasingly taking into account the influence of culture and other sociocultural variables such as gender and ethnicity in shaping human behavior and mental processes.

TEST YOUR KNOWLEDGE

Select the best answer for each of the following questions. Then check your responses against the Answer Key at the end of the book.

1. The first research laboratory in psychology was established to study _____.
   a. consciousness
   b. the unconscious
   c. perceptual processes
   d. the collective unconscious

2. Dr. Gauzz believes that low-income families who live in crowded conditions are more likely to need mental health services. Therefore, she works to eliminate overcrowded high-rises for low-income families. Dr. Gauzz is most likely a(n) _____ psychologist.
   a. developmental
   b. industrial and organizational
   c. community
   d. engineering

3. Dr. Hemmings believes that human behavior is influenced by genetic inheritance, unconscious motivations, and environmental influences. Dr. Hemmings uses a(n) _____ approach.
   a. evolutionary
   b. eclectic
   c. humanistic
   d. behavioral

4. Solomon is a psychologist interested in conformity. He studies how the size of a group affects the amount of pressure that the group can exert on individuals. Solomon is most likely a _____ psychologist.
   a. personality
   b. clinical
   c. quantitative
   d. social

Answer key for Table 1.3: U.S. ads are numbers 1, 2, 6, 8, and 9.

5. You are marooned on a tropical island with a dangerous criminal. In your suitcase are four books on psychology. If you believe that the criminal's behavior is primarily due to unconscious conflicts, you should choose the book written by _____ to find more information.
   a. Sigmund Freud
   b. William James
   c. John Watson
   d. Wilhelm Wundt

6. Dr. Foreman studies what teachers actually do when they are teaching students to read. Dr. Foreman is most likely a(n) _____ psychologist.
   a. cognitive
   b. school
   c. educational
   d. community

7. Larry says that people act the way they have learned to act. He believes that if others stop rewarding a person's annoying behavior, that behavior will decrease. Larry most likely takes a(n) _____ approach to psychology.
   a. behavioral
   b. cognitive
   c. evolutionary
   d. humanistic

8. Marika just won a college scholarship because of her outstanding grades. If she is from a collectivist culture, she is most likely to say:
   a. "I've worked very hard for this honor and I appreciate the vote of confidence."
   b. "I had some tough times when I didn't think I would succeed, but this has made it all worthwhile."
   c. "I could not have won this award without the help of my teachers and family."
   d. "I am so happy that the committee recognized my hard work and perseverance and is rewarding it with this scholarship."

9. Dr. Rose, a cross-cultural psychologist, is most likely to find which behavior to be similar in all of the groups she studies?
   a. Striving for achievement
   b. Rules governing social behavior
   c. Styles of communication
   d. Recognition of a smile

10. Latisha is a forensic psychologist. You are most likely to find her working with a _____.
    a. physical therapist
    b. lawyer
    c. advertising company
    d. landscape architect

11. You have just graduated with a Ph.D. in human factors psychology and are now working at your first job. You are most likely to be _____.
    a. testing the personality traits of astronaut candidates
    b. helping to design a new video game console
    c. conducting group therapy with abused children
    d. designing research on racial prejudice

12. Psychology is best defined as the science of _____.
    a. behavior and mental processes
    b. psychological disorders and conditions
    c. personality development
    d. neurons and hormones

13. Research on the factors that lead people to be happy and satisfied with their lives is known as _____ psychology.
    a. developmental
    b. humanistic
    c. positive
    d. existential

14. The concepts of behavior and mental processes include
    a. personality traits
    b. sensory abilities
    c. intelligence
    d. all of the above

15. A major difference between psychologists and psychiatrists is that psychiatrists _____.
    a. have more training in psychological testing
    b. are medical doctors
    c. are more active in research
    d. all of the above

16. Ali argues that, compared to men, women's greater selectivity in choosing a mate is an adaptive strategy that makes it more likely that fathers will be good providers. This view is rooted in the _____ approach to psychology.
    a. evolutionary
    b. behavioral
    c. cognitive-behavioral
    d. humanistic

17. Today, the study of consciousness occurs mainly in the field of _____.
    a. psychoanalysis
    b. humanistic psychology
    c. functional analysis
    d. cognitive science

18. Paul tells his wife that she won't ever be able to understand him unless she can begin to understand his own unique view of the world. Without realizing it, Paul is expressing a basic principle of _____ psychology.
    a. psychodynamic
    b. cognitive-behavioral
    c. humanistic
    d. cognitive

19. Today, the majority psychologists in North America are _____.
    a. men
    b. women
    c. people of color
    d. psychoanalysts

20. People's gender, ethnicity, social class, religious beliefs, and the like are examples of the _____ variables that can affect behavior and mental processes.
    a. self-defined
    b. innate
    c. biological
    d. sociocultural

Research in Psychology

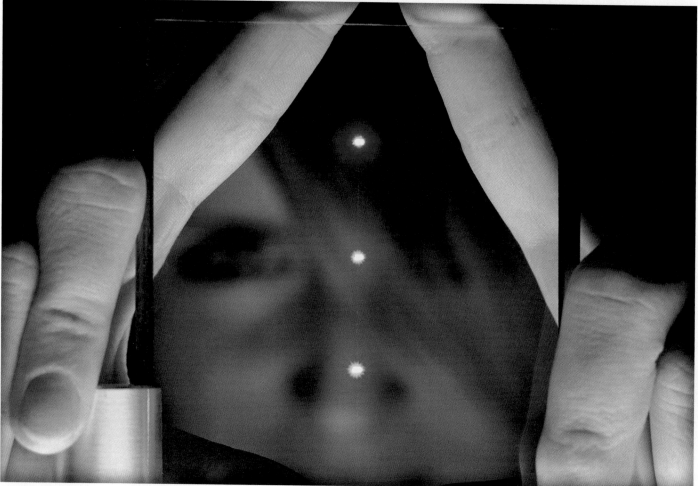

U. Bellhaeuser/ScienceFoto/Getty Images

Preview

Our goal in this chapter is to describe the research methods psychologists use to help answer their questions about behavior and mental processes. We will also describe the critical thinking processes that help psychologists form those questions and make sense of research results.

Francine Shapiro, a clinical psychologist in California, had an odd experience one day back in 1987. She was taking a walk and thinking about some distressing events when she noticed that her emotional reaction to them was fading away (Shapiro, 1989b). In trying to figure out why this should be, she realized that she had been moving her eyes from side to side. Could these eye movements have caused the change in her emotions? To test this possibility, she made more deliberate eye movements and found that the emotion-reducing effect was even stronger. Would the same thing happen to others? Curious, she first tested the effects of side-to-side eye movements with friends and colleagues and then with clients who had suffered traumatic experiences, such as sexual abuse, military combat, or rape. She asked these people to think about unpleasant experiences in their lives while keeping their eyes on her finger as she moved it rapidly back and forth in front of them. Like her, they found that during and after these eye movement sessions, their reactions to unpleasant thoughts faded away. They also reported that their emotional flashbacks, nightmares, fears, and other trauma-related problems decreased dramatically, often after only one session (Shapiro, 1989b).

Based on the success of these cases, Shapiro developed a treatment method she calls *eye movement desensitization and reprocessing,* or EMDR (Leeds, 2009; Shapiro, 1991, 2001; Shapiro & Forrest, 2004). She and her associates have trained more than 30,000 therapists in fifty-two countries to use EMDR in the treatment of an ever-widening range of anxiety-related problems in adults and children, from phobias and posttraumatic stress disorder to marital conflicts and skin rashes (e.g., Adúriz, Bluthgen, & Knopfler, 2009; Bloomgarden & Calogero, 2008; de Jongh et al., 2013; Gauvreau & Bouchard, 2008; Hase, Schallmayer, & Sack, 2008; Leer et al., 2013; Manfield & Shapiro, 2004; Marcus, 2008; Phillips et al., 2009; Rodenburg et al., 2009; Russell et al., 2007; Shapiro, 2005).

Suppose you had an anxiety-related problem. Would the popularity of EMDR be enough to convince you to try this treatment? If not, what would you want to know about EMDR before deciding? As a cautious person, you would probably ask some of the same questions that have also occurred to many scientists in psychology, such as these: Are the effects of EMDR caused by the treatment itself or by the faith that clients might have in any new treatment? And are EMDR's effects faster, stronger, and longer lasting than those of other treatments?

Raising tough questions about cause and effect, quality, and value is part of the process of *critical thinking.* Whether you are choosing a therapy method or an Internet provider, a college or a smartphone, critical thinking can guide you to ask the kinds of questions that lead to good decisions. But asking the right questions is not enough; you also have to try answering them. Critical thinking helps here, too, by prompting you to do some research on each of your options. For most people, this means asking the advice of friends or relatives, reading *Consumer Reports,* finding online reviews, studying a candidate's background, or the like. For psychologists, research means using scientific methods to gather information about behavior and mental processes.

In each chapter of this book, you will have the opportunity to think critically about many aspects of behavior and mental processes. In this chapter, we summarize five questions that will help you to do so in a systematic way, describe the scientific methods psychologists use in their research, and show how some of those methods have been applied in evaluating EMDR.

THINKING CRITICALLY ABOUT PSYCHOLOGY (OR ANYTHING ELSE)

How can critical thinking save you money?

Ask several friends and relatives if mental patients become more agitated when the moon is full, if psychics help the police solve crimes, and if people have suddenly burst into flames for no apparent reason. They will probably agree with at least one of these statements, even though not one of them is true. Perhaps you already knew that each of these statements is a myth, but don't feel too smug. At one time or another, we all accept things we are told simply because the information seems to come from a reliable source or because "everyone knows" it is true (Losh et al., 2003). If this were not the case, advertisers, politicians, salespeople, social activists, and others who seek our money, our votes, or our loyalty would not be as successful as they are. These people want you to believe their promises or claims without careful thought. In other words, they don't want you to think critically.

Uncritically accepting claims for the value of astrologers' predictions, get-rich-quick investment schemes, new therapies, or proposed government policies can be embarrassing, expensive, and dangerous. Critical thinkers carefully evaluate evidence for and against such claims before drawing a final conclusion.

"Doonesbury" © 1997 G. B. Trudeau. Reprinted with permission of Universal Uclick. All rights reserved.

They often get their wish. Millions of people around the world waste untold amounts of money every year on worthless predictions by online and telephone "psychics"; on bogus cures for cancer, heart disease, and arthritis; on phony degrees offered by nonexistent Internet "universities"; and on "miracle" defrosting trays, eat-all-you-want weight-loss pills, "effortless" exercise devices, and other consumer products that simply don't work. Millions more lose money to investment scams and fraudulent charity appeals (Cassel & Bernstein, 2007).

Critical thinking is the process of assessing claims and making judgments on the basis of reasonable evidence (Wade, 1988). One way to apply critical thinking to EMDR—or to any other topic—is by asking these five questions:

1. *What am I being asked to believe or accept?* In this case, the assertion to be examined is that EMDR reduces or eliminates anxiety-related problems.

2. *What evidence is available to support the assertion?* Francine Shapiro experienced a reduction in her own emotional distress following certain kinds of eye movements. Later, she found the same effect in others.

3. *Are there alternative ways of interpreting the evidence?* The dramatic effects Shapiro reported might not have been due to EMDR but to people's desire to overcome their problems or perhaps their desire to prove her right. And who knows? They might eventually have improved without any treatment. Even apparently remarkable evidence can't automatically be accepted as proof of an assertion until other plausible alternatives have been ruled out. The ruling-out process leads to the next step in critical thinking: conducting scientific research.

4. *What additional evidence would help evaluate the alternatives?* An ideal method for collecting further evidence about the value of EMDR would be to identify three groups of people who not only suffered anxiety-related problems of the same kind and intensity but also were alike in every other way except for the anxiety treatment they received. One group would receive EMDR, a second group would get an equally impressive but useless treatment, and a third group would get no treatment at all. Now suppose that the people in the EMDR group improved much more than those who got no treatment or the impressive but useless treatment. Results such as these would make it harder to explain away the improvements following EMDR as due to client motivation or the mere passage of time.

critical thinking The process of assessing claims and making judgments on the basis of well-supported evidence.

Taking Your Life in Your Hands?

Can microwave radiation from cell phones cause brain tumors? This question generates strong opinions, but the answer will only come from research based on critical thinking. Though there is no conclusive evidence that cell phones cause tumors (Hauri et al., 2014; Hsu et al., 2013; Inskip, Hoover, & Devesa, 2010; Szmigielski, 2013), some scientists see danger in short- and long-term exposure (Kesari et al., 2013; Samet et al., 2014; Volkow et al., 2011) and in prenatal and early postnatal exposure (Clinical Digest, 2011). Research on this issue continues.

© Antonio Guillem/Shutterstock.com

5. ***What conclusions are most reasonable?*** The research evidence collected so far has not yet ruled out alternative explanations for the effects of EMDR (e.g., Goldstein et al., 2000; Hertlein & Ricci, 2004; Hughes, 2006; Lilienfeld, 2011; Lohr et al., 2003; Spates & Rubin, 2012). And although those effects are often greater than the effects of no treatment at all, they appear to be no stronger than those of several other kinds of treatment (e.g., Bériault & Larivée, 2005; Bradley et al., 2005; Cook-Vienot & Taylor, 2012; Cvetek, 2008; Field & Cotrell, 2011; Ho & Lee, 2012; Lilienfeld & Arkowitz, 2007; Wanders, Serra, & de Jongh, 2008). So the only reasonable conclusions to be drawn at this point are that EMDR remains a controversial treatment, it seems to benefit some clients, and further research is needed in order to understand it.

Do these conclusions sound inconclusive? Critical thinking sometimes does seem indecisive. Like the rest of us, scientists in psychology would love to find quick, clear, and final answers to their questions, but to have scientific value, conclusions must be based on what the available evidence has the capacity to determine. So if the evidence about EMDR is limited in some way, conclusions about whether and why the treatment works have to be limited too. In the long run, though, critical thinking opens the way to understanding. You will sharpen your own critical thinking skills in each chapter to come in a "Thinking Critically" section that examines a particularly interesting issue in psychology. Each time, we urge you to use the same five questions we illustrated here about EMDR.

Critical Thinking and Scientific Research

Scientific research often begins with questions born of curiosity, such as "Can eye movements reduce anxiety?" Like many seemingly simple questions, this one is more complex than it first appears. How rapid are the eye movements? How long do they continue in each session, and how many sessions should there be? What kind of anxiety is to be treated, and how will we measure improvement? In other words, scientists have to ask *specific* questions in order to get meaningful answers.

Psychologists and other scientists clarify their questions about behavior and mental processes by phrasing them in terms of a **hypothesis**—a specific, testable statement about something they want to study. Hypotheses are precise, clearly worded statements that describe what researchers think may be true and how they will know if it is not. A hypothesis about EMDR might be "EMDR treatment causes significant reduction in anxiety." To make it easier to understand and evaluate their hypotheses, scientists employ **operational definitions**, which are descriptions of the precise operations or methods they

hypothesis In scientific research, a specific, testable proposition about a phenomenon.

operational definition A statement that defines the exact operations or methods used in research.

I Love It!

When we want something—or some-one—to be perfect, we may ignore all evidence to the contrary. This is one reason why people end up in faulty used cars—or in bad relationships. Psychologists and other scientists use special procedures, such as the double-blind methods described later in this chapter, to help keep *confirmation* bias from distorting the conclusions they draw from research evidence. We describe confirmation bias in more detail in the chapter on thought and language.

© wavebreakmedia/Shutterstock.com

will use in a research study. In other words, in an experiment, the researcher has to decide ahead of time exactly how each issue will be measured or manipulated. So, for our EMDR hypothesis, "EMDR treatment" might be operationally defined as a specific number of side-to-side eye movements per second over a particular period of time. And "significant reduction in anxiety" might be operationally defined as a decline of at least 10 points on a test that measures anxiety. The kind of treatment a client is given (say, EMDR versus no treatment) and the results of that treatment (the amount of anxiety reduction observed) are examples of research **variables**, the specific factors or characteristics that are manipulated and measured in research.

Scientists must also consider the value of the evidence they collect. They usually do this by evaluating its statistical reliability and validity. **Statistical reliability** (usually just called **reliability**) is the degree to which the data are stable and consistent. The **statistical validity** (usually just called **validity**) of data is the degree to which they accurately represent the topic being studied. For example, the first evidence for EMDR was based on Francine Shapiro's own experience with eye movements. If she had not been able to consistently repeat, or *replicate*, those effects in other people, one would have to question the reliability of such data. And if her clients' reports of reduced anxiety were not supported by, say, their overt behavior or the reports of their close relatives, one would have to doubt the validity of these data.

The Role of Theories

variable A factor or characteristic that is manipulated or measured in research.

statistical reliability (reliability) The degree to which test results or other research evidence occurs repeatedly.

statistical validity (validity) The degree to which evidence from a test or other research method measures what it is supposed to measure.

theory An integrated set of propositions that can be used to account for, predict, and even suggest ways of controlling certain phenomena.

After examining data from research, scientists may start to favor certain explanations as to why particular results occurred. Sometimes they organize their explanations into a **theory**, which is a set of statements designed to account for, predict, and even suggest ways of controlling certain phenomena. Shapiro's theory about the effects of EMDR suggests that eye movements may affect parts of the brain in which information about trauma or other unpleasant experiences is processed (Leeds, 2009; Shapiro & Forrest, 2004). Others (e.g., Lee, Taylor, & Drummond, 2006) suggest that EMDR may help troubled people think about stressful material in a more detached, less emotional way, perhaps as in a dream (Elofsson et al., 2008). In the chapter on introducing psychology, we review broader and more famous examples of explanatory theories, including Charles Darwin's theory of evolution and Sigmund Freud's theory of psychoanalysis.

Because theories are only tentative explanations, they must be examined scientifically using critical thinking. So although theories may be based on research results, they also generate new hypotheses that can be tested in research. The predictions of one

Theories of Prejudice

It is all too easy these days to spot evidence of prejudice against almost any identifiable group of people, especially minorities, but why does prejudice occur? The chapter on social psychology describes several theories, and the testing of these theories is an example of how theory and research go hand in hand. Without research results, there would be nothing to explain; without explanatory theories, the results might never be organized in a useful way. The knowledge generated by psychologists over the past century and a half has been based on this constant interaction of theory and research.

Keith Brofsky/Getty Images

psychologist's theory will be evaluated by other psychologists. If such research does not support a theory, the theory may need to be revised or abandoned.

The process of creating, evaluating, and revising psychological theories may not always lead to a single clear "winner." You will discover in the chapters ahead that there are several competing explanations for color vision, memory, sleep, aggression, eating disorders, and many other behaviors and mental processes. The conclusions we offer are based on what is known so far, and we always cite where there is need for new research. We do so because research often poses at least as many new questions as it answers. Data from one study might not apply to every situation or to all people. A treatment might be effective for mild depression in women, but it would have to be tested in more severe cases and with both sexes before drawing broader conclusions about the full extent of its value. Keep these points in mind the next time you hear a television personality confidently offering simple solutions to complex problems such as obesity or anxiety or presenting easy formulas for a happy marriage and perfect children. Such self-proclaimed experts—called "pop" (for *popular*) psychologists by the scientific community—may oversimplify issues, cite evidence for their views without concern for reliability or validity, and ignore evidence that contradicts their pet theories.

Psychological scientists must be more cautious, delaying judgments about behavior and mental processes until they have collected evidence. In evaluating theories and making conclusions, they are guided not only by the research methods described in the next section but also by the *law of parsimony* (also known as *simplicity*), summed up less scientifically as KISS ("Keep it simple, stupid"). The principle of parsimony is based on lessons from the long history of science. It suggests that when many alternative conclusions or several competing theories all offer convincing explanations of something, the simplest explanation is most often correct.

Throughout this book, you will see that research in psychology has created a large body of knowledge that is being put to good use in many ways. Let's now look at the scientific methods that psychologists use in their research and at some of the pitfalls that lie in their path.

RESEARCH METHODS IN PSYCHOLOGY

How do psychologists learn about people?

Like other scientists, psychologists try to achieve four main goals in their research: to *describe* a phenomenon, to *make predictions* about it, and to introduce enough *control* in their research to allow them to *explain* the phenomenon with some degree of confidence. Five research methods have proven especially useful for gathering the evidence needed to reach each of these goals. They include *observational methods, case studies, surveys, correlational studies,* and *experiments.*

Observational Methods: Watching Behavior

observational methods
Procedures for systematically watching behavior in order to summarize it for scientific analysis.

naturalistic observation The process of watching without interfering as a phenomenon occurs in the natural environment.

Sometimes, the best way to describe behavior is through **observational methods**, such as **naturalistic observation**, the process of watching without interfering as behavior occurs in the natural environment (Hoyle, Harris, & Judd, 2002). This method is especially valuable when more noticeable methods might alter the behavior you want to study. For example, if you ask people to keep track of how often they exercise, they might begin to exercise more than usual, so their reports might give a false impression of their typical behavior. Much of what we know about, say, gender differences in how children play and communicate with one another has come from psychologists' observations in classrooms and playgrounds. Observations of adults, too, have provided valuable insights into friendships, couple communication patterns, and even responses to terrorism (e.g., Mehl & Pennebaker, 2003a, 2003b).

Little Reminders

If you asked this man what he needs to use various computer programs efficiently, he might not think to mention the notes on his monitor that list his usernames and passwords. Accordingly, researchers in human factors and in industrial and organizational psychology usually arrange to watch employees at work rather than just asking them what they do, how they do it, and how they interact with machines and fellow employees (Barriera-Viruet et al., 2006; Dempsey, McGorry, & Maynard, 2005).

Turbo/Corbis

Observational methods can provide good information, but they are not without problems. For one thing, people may act differently if they know they're being watched (and research ethics usually require that they do know). To combat this problem, researchers try to observe people long enough so that they get used to the situation and begin to behave more naturally. Still, observations can be incomplete or misleading if observers are not well trained or if they report what they expect to see rather than what actually occurs. Further, even the best observational methods don't allow researchers to make conclusions about what causes the behavior being observed.

Case Studies: Taking a Closer Look

Observations are often an important part of **case studies**, which are intensive examinations of behavior or mental processes in a particular individual, group, or situation. Case studies can also include tests, interviews, and the analysis of letters, school transcripts, medical charts, or other written records. Case studies are especially useful when studying something that is new, complex, or relatively rare (Sacks, 2002). Francine Shapiro's EMDR treatment, for example, first attracted psychologists' attention through case studies of its remarkable effects on her clients (Shapiro, 1989b).

Case studies have played a special role in **neuropsychology**, an area of psychology that focuses on the relationships among brain activity, thinking, and behavior. Consider the case of Dr. P., a patient described by neurologist Oliver Sacks (1985). Dr. P. was a distinguished musician who began to show odd symptoms. He could not recognize familiar people or other objects when he viewed them. For instance, while he and his wife were at the neurologist's office, Dr. P. looked at his foot and mistook it for his shoe. When he rose to leave, he tried to lift off his wife's head as if it were a hat and put it on his own head. He could not name common objects in front of him, but he could describe what he saw. When shown a glove, for example, he said, "A continuous surface, infolded on itself. It appears to have … five outpouchings, if this is the word … a container of some sort." Only later, when he put it on his hand, did he exclaim, "My God, it's a glove!" (Sacks, 1985, p. 13). Using case studies such as this one, neuropsychologists have been able to describe which symptoms people have after different kinds of brain damage (Heilman & Valenstein, 2011). Eventually, neuropsychologists have tied specific disorders to certain types of injuries, poisons, and other causes (Lezak et al., 2012). In Dr. P.'s case, a large brain tumor caused his symptoms.

Case studies have limitations. They may not represent people in general and may contain only the evidence a particular researcher considered important (Loftus & Guyer, 2002). Nonetheless, when conducted and used with care, case studies can give a unique glimpse into new phenomena, and these discoveries give valuable raw material for innovative research that can address novel ideas more systematically.

case study A research method involving the intensive examination of some phenomenon in a particular individual, group, or situation.

neuropsychology An area of psychology that studies the relationships among brain activity, thinking, and behavior.

survey A research method that involves giving people questionnaires or special interviews designed to obtain descriptions of their attitudes, beliefs, opinions, and intentions

Surveys: Looking at the Big Picture

In contrast to the individual close-ups provided by case studies, surveys offer wide-angle views of large groups. In **surveys**, researchers use interviews or questionnaires to ask people about their behavior, attitudes, beliefs, opinions, or intentions. Just as politicians and advertisers rely on opinion polls to test the popularity of policies or products, psychologists use surveys to gather descriptive data on just about any behavior or mental process, from parenting practices to sexual behavior. However, the validity of survey data can depend on how questions are asked (Bhopal et al., 2004; Wahl, Svensson, & Hydén, 2010). In one survey study at a health clinic, patients were asked how often they experienced headaches, stomachaches, and other symptoms (Schwarz & Scheuring, 1992). When the wording of questions suggested that most people frequently experience such symptoms, patients said that they frequently experienced them, too. But when the wording suggested that people rarely experience these symptoms, respondents said that they seldom had such symptoms.

Designing Survey Research

TRY THIS How do people feel about whether gay men and lesbians should have the right to legally marry? To appreciate the difficulties of survey research, try writing a question about this issue that you think is clear enough and neutral enough to generate valid data. Then ask some friends whether or not they agree it would be a good survey question and why.

Rob Melnychuk/Digital Vision/Getty Images

Learning from Rare Cases

We can learn a great deal from studying individual cases such as Dr. Temple Grandin, whose autism has not prevented her from becoming a professor of animal science, a noted advocate for the humane treatment of livestock, a best-selling author, and a champion of the rights of people with autistic disorder. Other case studies have focused, for example, on people who can correctly identify the day of the week for any date in the past or the future or tell at a glance that, say, exactly 125 paper clips are scattered on the floor. By carefully studying such rare cases, cognitive psychologists are learning more about human mental capacities and how they might be maximized in everyone (Biever, 2009; Geddes, 2008).

Nancy Kaszerman/ZUMA/Corbis

correlational studies Research methods that examine relationships between variables in order to analyze trends in data, test predictions, evaluate theories, and suggest new hypotheses.

correlation In research, the degree to which one variable is related to another.

A survey's validity also depends on who is surveyed. If the people surveyed don't represent the views of all of the population you're interested in, survey results can be misleading (Gosling et al., 2004; Kraut et al., 2004). For example, if you were interested in Americans' views on how common ethnic prejudice is, you could come to the wrong conclusion if you surveyed only African Americans or only European Americans. To get a complete picture, you would want to survey people from many ethnic groups so that all opinions could be fairly represented.

Some limitations of the survey method are harder to avoid. For example, a poll conducted for the American Society for Microbiology (ASM) found that 92 percent of U.S. adults surveyed said that they always wash their hands after using public toilet facilities. However, watching thousands of people in public restrooms across the United States revealed that the figure is closer to 77 percent (Harris Interactive, 2007). In other words, people may be unwilling to admit undesirable or embarrassing things about themselves or they may say what they believe they *should* say about an issue (Uziel, 2010). And those who respond to a survey may hold views that differ from those who choose not to respond (Visser, Krosnick, & Lavrakas, 2000). Such a problem creates a *response bias*, meaning that a survey's results are skewed to rely too much on the views of responders while not fairly capturing views of non-responders (Hoyle, Harris, & Judd, 2002). Still, surveys are an efficient way to gather large amounts of data about people's attitudes, beliefs, or other characteristics.

Correlational Studies: Looking for Relationships

Data collected from naturalistic observations, case studies, and surveys help describe behavior and mental processes, but they can do more than that. We can examine these data to see how research variables are related, or correlated, with each other. For example, fear surveys show that most people have fears, but correlational analysis of those surveys also shows that the number of fears is related to age. Specifically, adults have fewer fears than do children (e.g., Kleinknecht, 1991). **Correlational studies** examine relationships between variables in order to describe research data more fully, test predictions, evaluate theories, and suggest new hypotheses about why people think and act as they do.

Correlation refers to both the strength and the direction of the relationship between two variables. A *positive correlation* means that the two variables increase together or decrease together. A *negative correlation* means that the variables move in opposite

A Severely Flawed Survey

Using survey methods like this, you could probably get whatever results you want! Psychologists work hard to write questions and use methods that maximize the validity of their surveys' results.

DILBERT: © Scott Adams/Dist. by United Feature Syndicate, Inc.

directions. For example, James Schaefer observed 4,500 customers in sixty-five bars and found that the tempo of the music playing was negatively correlated with the rate at which the customers drank alcohol. The slower the tempo, the faster the drinking (Schaefer et al., 1988). Does this mean that Schaefer could have worn a blindfold and predicted exactly how fast people were drinking by timing the music? Could he have plugged his ears and determined the musical tempo just by watching people's sip rates? No and no, because the accuracy of predictions made about one variable from knowing the other depends not only on the direction but also on the *strength* of the correlation. Only a perfect correlation between two variables would allow you to predict the exact value of one based on the other. The weaker a correlation, the less one variable can tell you about the other.

Psychologists describe the strength and direction of correlations with a number called a *correlation coefficient,* which can range from a high of 1.00 to a low of .00 (see the "Statistics in Psychological Research" appendix). If the correlation between two variables is *positive*— if they both move in the same direction—the correlation coefficient will have a plus sign in front of it. If there is a minus sign, the correlation is *negative,* and the two variables will move in opposite directions. The larger the correlation coefficient, the stronger the relationship between the two variables. The strongest possible relationship is indicated by either +1.00 or −1.00. A correlation of .00 indicates that there is no relationship between variables.

Correlation coefficients describe the results of correlational research to help evaluate hypotheses, but psychological scientists must be extremely careful when interpreting what correlations mean. The mere fact that two variables are correlated does not guarantee that one causes an effect on the other. And even if one variable actually does cause an effect on the other, a correlation coefficient can't tell us which variable is influencing which, or why (see Table 2.1). As an example of this important point, consider the question of how aggression develops. Correlational studies of observational data indicate that children who are in day care for more than thirty hours a week are more aggressive than those who stay at home with a parent. Does separation from parents cause the greater aggressiveness with which it is associated? It might, but psychologists must be careful about jumping to such a conclusion. What may seem an obvious explanation for a correlational relationship may not always be correct. Perhaps the aggressiveness seen in some children in day care has something to do with the children themselves or with what happens to them in day care, not just with separation from their parents.

One way scientists evaluate such alternative hypotheses is to conduct further correlational studies to look for trends that support or conflict with those hypotheses (Rutter, 2007; West, 2009). Further analysis of day-care research, for example, shows that the aggressiveness seen in preschoolers who spend a lot of time in day care is the exception, not the rule. Most children don't show any behavior problems, no matter how much time they have spent in day care. This more general trend suggests that whatever effect separation has, it may be different for different children in different settings,

TABLE 2.1   CORRELATION AND CAUSATION

TRY THIS   Look at the relationships described in the left-hand column, then ask yourself why the two variables in each case are correlated. Could one variable cause an effect on the other? If so, which is the cause, and how might it exert its effect? Could the relationship between the two variables be caused by a third one? If so, what might that third variable be? We suggest some possible explanations in the right-hand column. Can you think of others?

Correlation	Possible Explanations
The more sexual content U.S. teenagers reported watching on television, the more likely they were to begin having sex themselves in the following year (Collins et al., 2004).	Some teens' greater interest in sex may have led them to watch more sexually oriented shows and to become sexually active.
The number of drownings in the United States rises and falls during the year along with the amount of ice cream sold each month.	A third variable, the time of year, may explain the high consumption of ice cream and likelihood of water activities (Brenner et al., 2001).
In places where beer prices are increased, the number of new cases of sexually transmitted diseases falls among young people living in those places.	If price increases cause less beer consumption, people might stay sober enough to remember to use condoms during sex. The relationship could also be a coincidence, because prices don't always affect alcohol use. More research is required to understand this correlation.
A study found that the more antibiotics a woman has taken and the longer she has taken them, the greater is her risk of breast cancer (Velicer et al., 2004).	Long-term antibiotic use might have impaired the women's immune systems, but the cancer risk might also have been increased by the diseases for which the antibiotics were prescribed, not the drugs themselves. Obviously, much more research would be required before condemning the use of antibiotics.
The U.S. stock market rises during years when a team from the National Football Conference won the Super Bowl and falls when an American Conference team was the winner.	The so-called "Super Bowl Effect" has occurred in over 80 percent of Super Bowls through 2013; striking as this might seem, coincidence seems to be the most likely explanation.

causing some to express aggressiveness, others to show fear, and still others to be joyful. As described in the chapter on human development, psychologists are exploring this possibility by examining correlations between children's personality traits, qualities of different day-care programs, and reactions to day care (Belsky et al., 2007; Dupere, Leventhal, & Crosnoe, in press; NICHD Early Child Care Research Network, 2006a; Pluess & Belsky, 2010).

Throughout this book, you will see many more examples of how correlational studies help shed light on a wide range of topics in psychology (Rutter, 2007).

Experiments: Exploring Cause and Effect

The most direct way to test hypotheses and confirm cause-and-effect relationships between variables is to apply some control over those variables (Falk & Heckman, 2009). This kind of research usually takes the form of an experiment. An **experiment** is a type of study where a researcher controls one variable and then observes the effect of that manipulation on another variable, while holding all other variables constant.

Consider the experiment Francine Shapiro conducted to study the effects of EMDR. As illustrated in Figure 2.1, she first identified twenty-two people who were suffering the ill effects of traumas such as rape or war. These were her research participants. She then assigned each of the participants to be in one of two groups. Members of the first group received a single fifty-minute session of EMDR treatment. Members of the second group

experiment A study in which the researcher directly controls one variable and then observes the effect of that manipulation on another variable, while holding all other variables constant.

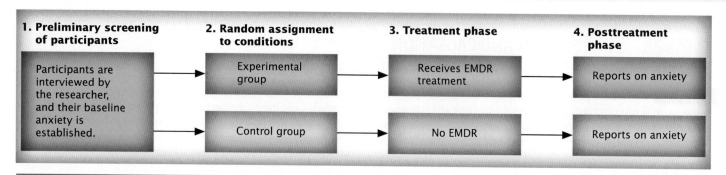

FIGURE 2.1

A Simple Two-Group Experiment

Ideally, the only difference between the experimental and control groups in experiments such as this one is whether the participants receive the treatment the experimenter wishes to evaluate. Under these ideal circumstances, at the end of the experiment, the best conclusion would be that any difference in the two groups' reported levels of anxiety would be due only to whether or not they received treatment.

experimental group In an experiment, the group that receives the experimental treatment.

control group In an experiment, the group that receives no treatment or provides some other baseline against which to compare the performance or response of the experimental group.

independent variable The variable directly controlled by the researcher in an experiment.

dependent variable In an experiment, the factor measured to see whether or not it has been affected by the independent variable.

confound In an experiment, any factor that affects the dependent variable, along with or instead of the independent variable.

received no EMDR treatment; instead, they focused on their unpleasant memories for eight minutes, without moving their eyes back and forth (Shapiro, 1989a).

The group assigned to receive an experimental treatment such as EMDR is called, naturally enough, the **experimental group**. The group not assigned to receive the treatment of interest is called the **control group**. Control groups provide baselines against which to compare the performance of other groups. In Shapiro's experiment, having a control group allowed her to measure how much change in anxiety could be expected from exposure to bad memories without EMDR treatment. Since people were assigned to the two groups by the experimenter, these groups should have been exactly the same before the experiment. Accordingly, any difference in anxiety between the groups afterward should have something to do with the EMDR treatment rather than with mere exposure to unpleasant memories.

Notice that Shapiro controlled one variable: whether or not her participants received EMDR. In an experiment, the name used for the variable controlled by the experimenter is the **independent variable**. It is called *independent* because the experimenter is free to adjust it at will, offering one, two, or three kinds of treatment, for example, or perhaps setting the length of treatment at one, five, or ten sessions. Notice, too, that Shapiro looked for the effects of treatment by measuring a different variable, her clients' anxiety level. This second variable is called the **dependent variable** because it is affected by, or depends on, the independent variable. So in Shapiro's experiment, the presence or absence of treatment was the independent variable, because she manipulated it. Her participants' anxiety level was the dependent variable, because she measured it to see how it was affected by treatment. (Table 2.2 describes the independent and dependent variables in other experiments.)

The results of Shapiro's experiment showed that participants who received EMDR treatment experienced a complete and nearly immediate reduction in anxiety related to their traumatic memories, whereas those in the control group showed no change (Shapiro, 1989a). You might conclude this difference suggests that EMDR caused the improvement. But look again at the structure, or design, of the experiment. The EMDR group's session lasted about fifty minutes, but members of the control group focused on their memories for only eight minutes. Would the people in the control group have improved, too, if they had spent fifty minutes focusing on their memories? We don't know, because the experiment did not compare methods of equal duration.

Anyone who conducts or relies on research must be on guard for such flaws in experimental design. So before drawing conclusions from research, experimenters must consider factors that might confound, or confuse, the interpretation of results. Any factor, such as differences in the length of treatment, that might have affected the dependent variable along with or instead of the independent variable can become a **confound**. When confounds are present, the experimenter cannot know whether the independent variable or the confound caused the results seen in the dependent variable.

TABLE 2.2   INDEPENDENT AND DEPENDENT VARIABLES

TRY THIS Fill in the names of the independent and dependent variables in each of these experiments (answers are at the bottom of page 38). Remember that the independent variable is set by the experimenter. The dependent variable is measured to learn how it was affected by the independent variable. How did you do on this task?

1. Children's reading skill is measured after taking either a special reading class or a standard reading class.

    The independent variable is _____.
    The dependent variable is _____.

2. College students' memory for German vocabulary words is tested after a normal night's sleep or a night of no sleep.

    The independent variable is _____.
    The dependent variable is _____.

3. Experiment title: "The effect of a daily walking program on elderly people's lung capacity."

    The independent variable is _____.
    The dependent variable is _____.

4. People's ability to avoid "accidents" in a driving simulator is tested before, during, and after talking on a cell phone.

    The independent variable is _____.
    The dependent variable is _____.

Let's examine three kinds of confounds: random variables, participants' expectations, and experimenter bias.

Random Variables

In an ideal research world, everything about the experimental and control groups would be the same except for what the experimenter did to the independent variable (such as whether or not they received treatment). In the real world, however, there may be other differences between the groups that reflect random variables (West, 2009). **Random variables** are uncontrolled, sometimes uncontrollable, factors such as the time of year when research takes place and differences in the participants' cultural backgrounds, personalities, life experiences, and sensitivity to stress, for example.

In fact, there are so many ways in which participants might vary from one another that it is usually impossible to form groups that are matched in all respects. Instead, experimenters simply flip a coin or use some other random process to assign each research participant to the experimental or control group. These procedures—called *random assignment* or **randomizing**—are presumed to distribute the impact of uncontrolled variables randomly (and probably about equally) across groups, thus minimizing the chance that these variables will distort the results of the experiment (Shadish, Cook, & Campbell, 2002).

Participants' Expectations: The Placebo Effect

After eight minutes of focusing on unpleasant memories, participants in the control group in Shapiro's experiment were instructed to begin moving their eyes from side to side. At that point they, too, said they began to experience a reduction in anxiety. Was this improvement caused by the eye movements themselves, or could it be that the instructions made the participants feel more confident that they were now getting "real" treatment? This question illustrates a second kind of confound: differences in what people *think* about the experimental situation. If participants who receive an impressive treatment expect that it will help them, they may try to improve in a different way than those in a control group who receive no treatment or a less impressive treatment. When improvement occurs as a result of a participant's knowledge and expectations, it is called the *placebo effect*. A

random variable In an experiment, a confound in which uncontrolled or uncontrollable factors affect the dependent variable, along with or instead of the independent variable.

randomizing Assigning participants in an experiment to various groups through a random process to ensure that random variables are evenly distributed among the groups.

Ever Since I Started Wearing This Titanium Necklace ...

Placebo-controlled experiments establish cause-effect relationships between treatments and outcomes with human participants. For example, many people swear that titanium bracelets and necklaces relieve the pain of sports injuries and even arthritis (Atkinson, 2006; Galdeira, 2006; Marchman, 2008; Siber, 2005). Phiten, the leading manufacturer and marketer of titanium accessories, touts glowing testimonials and a scientific-sounding explanation of the technology behind titanium's alleged effects but offers no evidence from placebo-controlled experiments to support their claims (Boyles, 2008; Wagg, 2008). Such experiments have already failed to support the value of "power balance" bracelets that are supposed to improve strength, flexibility, and balance (Underdown, 2011).

Gene J. Puskar/AP Images

placebo A physical or psychological treatment that contains no active ingredient but produces an effect because the person receiving it believes it will.

experimenter bias A confound that occurs when an experimenter unintentionally encourages participants to respond in a way that supports the experimenter's hypothesis.

double-blind design A research design in which neither the experimenter nor the participants know who is in the experimental group and who is in the control group.

placebo (pronounced "pluh-SEE-boh") is a treatment that contains nothing known to be helpful but that still produces benefits because the person receiving the treatment believes it will be beneficial.

How can researchers measure the extent to which a result is caused by the independent variable or by the placebo effect? Usually, they include a special control group that receives *only* a placebo treatment. Then they compare results for the experimental group, the placebo group, and a no-treatment group. In one quit-smoking study, for example, participants in a placebo group took sugar pills described by the experimenter as "fast-acting tranquilizers" that would help them learn to endure the stress of giving up cigarettes (Bernstein, 1970). These people did far better at quitting than those who got no treatment; in fact, they did as well as participants in the experimental group, who received extensive treatment. These results suggested that the success of the experimental group may have been due largely to the participants' expectations, not to the treatment methods.

Some studies suggest the same conclusion about the effects of EMDR, because significant anxiety reduction occurred in people who got a version of the treatment that did not involve eye movements or even focusing on traumatic memories (e.g., Nieuwenhuis et al., 2013; Seidler & Wagner, 2006; Servan-Schreiber et al., 2006; van den Hout & Engelhard, 2012). Other experiments have shown that EMDR can outperform placebo treatments, but the fact that its effects are often no better overall than those of other therapies has led some to conclude that EMDR should not have special status in the treatment of anxiety-related disorders (Bisson, 2007; Lilienfeld, 2011; Lilienfeld & Arkowitz, 2007; Lohr et al., 2003; Taylor, 2004).

Experimenter Bias

Another potential confound is **experimenter bias**, the unintentional effect that researchers may exert on their results. Robert Rosenthal (1966) was among the first to demonstrate a kind of experimenter bias called *experimenter expectancies*. His research participants were laboratory assistants whose job was to place rats in a maze. Rosenthal told some of the assistants that their rats were "maze-bright"; he told the others that their rats were "maze-dull." In fact, both groups of rats were randomly drawn from the same population and should have had about equal maze-learning capabilities. But the maze-bright animals learned the maze significantly faster than the maze-dull rats. Why? Rosenthal concluded that the results had nothing to do with the rats and everything to do with the experimenters. The only difference imposed onto the two groups of rats were that the assistants had different expectations about the rats. The assistants' belief in supposedly superior or inferior capabilities must have caused them to alter their training and handling techniques somehow. These slight differences may have speeded or slowed the animals' learning. Similarly, when therapists are asked to give different kinds of treatment to different groups of people in a therapy evaluation experiment, the therapists may do a slightly better job using the treatments they expected to work best. Even a slight unintentional difference could improve the effects of that treatment compared to the others.

To prevent experimenter bias from influencing results, experimenters may use a **double-blind design**. In this arrangement, both the research participants and those giving the treatments are unaware of ("blind") who gets the placebo. Only researchers who have no direct contact with participants have this information, and they do not reveal it until the experiment is over. The fact that double-blind studies of EMDR have not yet been conducted is another reason for caution in drawing conclusions about this treatment.

Answers to Table 2.2

1. Independent variable: type of reading class; dependent variable: reading skill. 2. Independent variable: amount of sleep; dependent variable: score on a memory test. 3. Independent variable: amount of exercise; dependent variable: lung capacity. 4. Independent variable: using or not using a cell phone; dependent variable: performance on a simulated driving task.

Keeping Experimenters "Blind"

TRY THIS Suppose that you are a sport psychologist conducting an experiment to evaluate two methods for reducing performance anxiety: standard coaching and a new relaxation-based technique. How might you create a double-blind design for this experiment? If you cannot, how might you try to keep coaches in the dark about which method is expected to produce better results?

Christopher Bissell / Stone / Getty Images

To sum up, experiments are vital tools for examining cause-and-effect relationships between variables, but like the other methods we have described (see "In Review: Methods of Psychological Research"), they are vulnerable to error. To maximize the value of experiments, psychologists try to eliminate as many confounds as possible. Then they replicate their work to ensure consistent results and temper their interpretation of those results to take into account the limitations or problems that remain.

IN REVIEW

METHODS OF PSYCHOLOGICAL RESEARCH

Method	Features	Strengths	Pitfalls
Observational methods (e.g., naturalistic observation)	observation of human or animal behavior in the environment in which it typically occurs	Provides descriptive data about behavior presumably uncontaminated by outside influences	Observer bias and participant self-consciousness can distort results
Case studies	Intensive examination of the behavior and mental processes associated with a specific person or situation	Provide detailed descriptive analyses of new, complex, or rare phenomena	May not provide a representative picture of phenomena
Surveys	Standard sets of questions asked of a large number of participants	Gather large amounts of descriptive data relatively quickly and inexpensively	Sampling errors, poorly phrased questions, and response biases can distort results
Correlational studies	Examine relationships between research variable	Can test predictions, evaluate theories, and suggest new hypotheses	Cannot confirm causal relationships between variables
Experiments	Manipulation of an independent variable and measurement of its effect on a dependent variable	Can establish a cause-and-effect relationship between independent and dependent variables	Confounds may prevent valid conclusions

1. The _____ method is most likely to use a double-blind design.

2. Research on a new treatment method is most likely to begin with _____.

3. Studying language by listening to people in public places is an example of _____ research.

Selecting Research Participants

Imagine that as a social psychologist, you want to study people's willingness to help each other. You have developed a method for testing helpfulness, but now you want a random sample of people to test. Take a minute to think about the steps necessary to select a truly random sample; then ask yourself how you might obtain a representative sample instead. Remember that although the names are similar, *random sampling* is not the same as *randomizing*. Random sampling is used in many kinds of research to ensure that the people studied are representative of some larger group. Randomizing is used in experiments to distribute participant characteristics as evenly as possible across various groups.

Jim West/The Image Works

sampling The process of selecting participants who are members of the population that the researcher wishes to study.

representative sampling A process for selecting research participants whose characteristics fairly reflect the characteristics of the population from which they were drawn.

random sampling The process of selecting a group of research participants from a population whose members all had an equal chance of being chosen.

biased sampling The process of selecting a group of research participants from a population whose members did not have an equal chance of being chosen.

Selecting Human Participants for Research

Visitors from another planet would be wildly mistaken if they tried to describe a typical earthling after meeting only Lady Gaga, Charlie Sheen, and a trained seal. Psychologists, too, can be led astray if the participants they encounter in their research are not typical of the people or animals about which they want to draw conclusions. Accordingly, a vital step in scientific research is selecting participants, a process called **sampling**.

If they want to make accurate statements about the behavior and mental processes of any large group, psychologists must conduct **representative sampling** of participants whose characteristics mirror the rest of that group in terms of age, gender, ethnicity, cultural background, socioeconomic status, sexual orientation, disability, and the like. In theory, a representative sample can be drawn at random from the entire population of interest. For example, psychologists could choose a representative sample of Canadians, Democrats, or any other group. Doing this would require putting hundreds of thousands—perhaps millions—of names into a computer, running a program to select participants randomly, and then tracking them down to invite them to take part in the research. This method would result in truly **random sampling**, because every single member of the population under study would have an equal chance of being chosen. (Any selection procedure that does not offer this equal chance is said to result in **biased sampling**.)

However, true random sampling is usually too expensive and time-consuming to be practical, so psychologists often find research participants in more conveniently available populations. The populations from which these *convenience samples* are drawn depend to some extent on the researcher's budget. They might include, for example, students enrolled in a course, students enrolled on a local campus, students who are willing to sign up for a study, or visitors to websites or Facebook groups. Ideally, this selection process will yield a sample that fairly represents the population from which it was drawn. However, scientists must realize that their conclusions might apply only to their samples (Kraut et al., 2004). Therefore, psychologists often conduct additional studies to determine whether their initial conclusions apply to other groups (APA Office of Ethnic Minority Affairs, 2000; Case & Smith, 2000).

LINKAGES How much of our behavior is due to genetics and how much to our environment? (A link to Biological Aspects of Psychology)

LINKAGES

PSYCHOLOGICAL RESEARCH METHODS AND BEHAVIORAL GENETICS

One of the most fascinating and difficult challenges in psychology is to find research methods that can help us understand the ways in which people's genetic inheritance (their biological *nature*) intertwines with environmental events and conditions before and after birth (often called *nurture*) to shape behavior and mental processes (Moffitt, Caspi, & Rutter, 2005). Consider Mark and John, identical twins who were both adopted at birth because their biological parents were too poor to care for them. John grew up with a married couple who made him feel secure and loved. Mark went from orphanage to foster home to hospital and, finally, back to his biological father's second wife. Thus, these genetically identical people lived in very different environments. Yet, when they met for the first time at the age of twenty-four, they discovered similarities that went far beyond physical appearance. They used the same aftershave lotion, smoked the same brand of cigarettes, used the same imported toothpaste, and liked the same sports. They had joined the military within eight days of each other, and their IQ scores were nearly identical. How had genetic influences operated in two different environments to shape such similarities?

Exploring questions such as these has taken psychologists into the field of **behavioral genetics**, the study of how genes shape behavior. They have discovered that most behavioral tendencies are likely to be influenced by interactions between the environment and many different genes. Accordingly, research in behavioral genetics is designed to explore how genetic and environmental factors act on each other to produce personality, mental ability, mental disorders, and patterns of behavior. Such research also seeks to identify which specific genes exert these influences.

Some behavioral genetics research takes the form of experiments, mainly on the selective breeding of animals (Suomi, 2004). For example, Stephen Suomi (1999) identified monkeys whose genes predisposed them to show strong or weak reactions to stress. He then mated strong reactors with other strong reactors and mated weak reactors with other weak reactors. Within a few generations, descendants of the strong-reactor pairs reacted much more strongly to stressors than did the descendants of the weak-reactor pairs. Selective-breeding experiments must be interpreted with caution, though, because animals do not inherit specific behaviors. Instead, they inherit differing sets of physical structures and capacities that make certain behaviors more likely or less likely.

Yet genes alone do not have a final say in these behavioral tendencies, since the behaviors can be altered by the environment (Grigorenko, 2002; Parker et al., 2006). For example, when Suomi (1999) placed young, highly stress-reactive monkeys with unrelated "foster mothers," he discovered that the foster mothers' own stress reactivity amplified or dampened the youngsters' genetically influenced behavioral tendencies. If stress-reactive monkeys were placed with stress-reactive foster mothers, they tended to be fearful of exploring their environments and had strong stress reactions. But if equally stress-reactive young monkeys had calm, supportive foster mothers, they appeared more eager to explore their environments and less upset by stressors than peers with stress-reactive foster mothers.

Research on behavioral genetics in humans must be interpreted with even greater care. Legal, moral, and ethical considerations obviously prohibit experiments on the selective breeding of people, so research in human behavioral genetics depends on correlational studies. Traditionally, these take the form of family studies, twin studies, and adoption studies (Plomin et al., 2008). Let's consider the logic of these behavioral genetics research methods. (The behavioral genetics appendix discusses basic principles of genetics and heredity that underlie these methods.)

In *family studies*, researchers look at whether close relatives are more likely than distant ones to show similar behavior and mental processes. If increasing similarity is associated with closer family ties, the similarities might be inherited. For example, family studies suggest a genetic basis for schizophrenia because this severe mental disorder appears much more often in the closest relatives of schizophrenics than in other people (see Figure 2.2). But remember that a correlation between variables does not establish that one is causing the other. Similar disorders might occur in close relatives due to environmental factors they

behavioral genetics The study of how genes and environment shape behavior.

have in common instead of or in addition to genetic ones. After all, close relatives tend to share both similar environments and similar genes. So family studies alone do not establish the role of genetic factors in mental disorders or other characteristics.

Twin studies explore the heredity-environment mix by comparing the similarities seen in identical twins with those of nonidentical pairs (Johnson et al., 2009). Twins usually share the same family environment as they grow up, and they may also be treated more similarly by parents and others. So if identical twins (whose genes are exactly the same) are more alike on some characteristic than nonidentical twins (whose genes are no more similar than those of other siblings), that characteristic may have a significant genetic component. As we learn in later chapters, this pattern of results holds for many characteristics, including some measures of intelligence and some mental disorders. As shown in Figure 2.2, for example, if one member of an identical twin pair develops schizophrenia, the chances are about 45 percent that the other twin will too. Those chances drop to about 17 percent if the twins are nonidentical.

FIGURE 2.2

Family and Twin Studies of Schizophrenia

The risk of developing schizophrenia, a severe mental disorder, is highest for the siblings and children of schizophrenia patients and lowest for those who are not genetically related to anyone with schizophrenia. Does this mean that schizophrenia is inherited? These results are consistent with that interpretation, but the question cannot be answered through family studies alone. Studies comparing identical and nonidentical twins also suggest genetic influence, but even twin studies cannot eliminate the role of environmental influences. Environmental factors, such as stressors that close relatives share, could also play an important role and may even contribute to the heritable epigenetic effects discussed later in this section (Crespi, 2008; Ivleva, Thaker, & Tamminga, 2008; Singh & O'Reilly, 2009; Tandon, Keshavan, & Nasrallah, 2008).

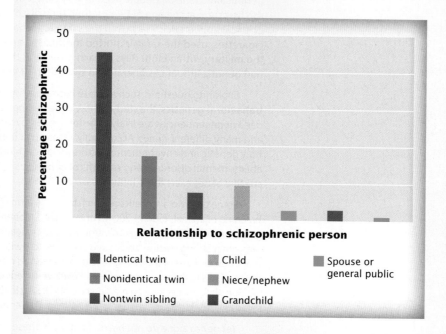

Adoption studies take scientific advantage of cases in which babies are adopted very early in life. The logic of these studies is that if adopted children's characteristics are more like those of their biological parents than of their adoptive parents, genetics may play a role in those characteristics. In fact, as you will read in the chapter on personality, traits of young adults who had been adopted at birth tend to be more like those of their biological parents than those of their adoptive parents. Adoption studies can be quite valuable when they focus on identical twins who, like Mark and John, were separated at or near birth. If identical twins show similarities after years of living in different environments, the role of heredity in those similarities is highlighted. Adoption studies of intelligence tend to support the role of genetics in variations in mental ability, but they show the impact of environmental influences too.

Family, twin, and adoption studies have played an important role in behavioral genetics research, but when you read in other chapters about the role of genes in personality, intelligence, mental disorders, and other features of behavior, remember this important point: Research on human behavioral genetics can tell us about the relative roles of heredity and environment in creating differences *among* individuals, but cannot determine the degree to which a *particular* person's behavior is due to heredity or environment. The two factors are too closely entwined in an individual to be separated that way. For example, the influence exerted on an adopted baby by its biological parents reflects not only their genetic legacy but also the environment they provided before the baby was born and between birth and the adoption.

(continued)

Twins and Behavioral Genetics

Like other identical twins, each member of this pair has identical genes. Twin studies and adoption studies help reveal the interaction of genetic and environmental influences in human behavior and mental processes. Cases in which identical twins who had been separated at birth are found to have similar interests, personality traits, and mental abilities suggest that these characteristics are significantly influenced by genetic factors.

Comstock/Getty Images/Thinkstock

Today, research methods in behavioral genetics have been shaped by procedures made possible by the Human Genome Project, which established the genetic code contained in the DNA that makes each human being unique (International Human Genome Sequencing Consortium, 2001; see the behavioral genetics appendix). This achievement has allowed behavioral geneticists and other scientists to pinpoint some of the genes that contribute to individual differences in disorders such as autism, learning disabilities, hyperactivity, and Alzheimer's disease, as well as to the normal variations in personality and cognitive abilities that we see all around us (Plomin et al., 2008). Finding the DNA differences responsible for certain personal attributes and behaviors has made it possible to better understand how heredity interacts with the environment during a person's life. As described in the behavioral genetics appendix, analysis of DNA, which can be collected by rubbing a cotton swab inside an individual's cheek, is being used not only in behavioral genetics research but also in medical clinics, where it can more precisely diagnose some medical problems, specify the best treatment option, and determine the likelihood of passing on a genetic defect to future offspring (Euhus & Robinson, 2013; Solomon & Muenke, 2012).

DNA does not tell the whole story of behavioral genetics, however. As we have already discussed, biological and psychological scientists study how people's genetic inheritance (DNA) interacts with the environments in which their genes operate (Champagne, 2009; Champagne & Mashoodh, 2009). This field of study, called **epigenetics**, describes how events within cells can alter the *functions* of genes, even though the genetic code itself—the chemical sequence coded in the DNA—remains unchanged (Gräff & Mansuy, 2008; Keverne & Curley, 2008; Lickliter, 2008). Research in epigenetics suggests that the cellular environment can not only affect the expression of an individual's genetic characteristics but may also create structural changes in genes that can potentially be passed on to future generations (Keverne & Curley, 2008; Lamm & Jablonka, 2008; Lickliter, 2008). Epigenetic effects—which can be triggered by many environmental influences, including diseases and stress—have been linked to individual differences in learning, memory, and brain development (Gräff & Mansuy, 2008; Keverne & Curley, 2008; Lickliter, 2008), and they may also play a role in the appearance of cognitive disorders such as Alzheimer's disease, mental disorders such as schizophrenia and depression, illnesses such as cancer, and health problems such as obesity (Akbarian, Beeri, & Haroutunian, 2013).

STATISTICAL ANALYSIS OF RESEARCH RESULTS

What does it mean when scientists say that a research finding is statistically significant?

Observational methods, case studies, surveys, correlational studies, and experiments generate mountains of numbers—known as **data**—that represent research results and provide the basis for drawing conclusions about them (Keselman et al., 2004). These data might represent scores on intelligence tests, levels of stress hormones in blood samples, tiny differences in the time required to detect visual signals, ratings of people's personality traits, or whatever else a psychologist might be studying. Like other scientists, psychologists use descriptive and inferential *statistics* to summarize data and interpret what they mean.

As the name implies, **descriptive statistics** are used to describe a set of data. For example, the performance of a group of students on a math test could be described statistically by the *mean,* or average, score of the group. The mean is determined by adding up all the scores and dividing the total by the number of scores. Describing the difference between the performance of men and women could be done by calculating the difference

epigenetics The study of potentially inheritable changes in gene expression that do not alter a cell's DNA.

data Numbers that represent research findings and provide the basis for conclusions.

descriptive statistics Numbers that summarize a set of research data.

between the mean scores for each gender. And, as mentioned earlier, when psychologists want to describe the relationship between two variables, they use a descriptive statistic called the correlation coefficient.

Inferential statistics are mathematical procedures that help psychologists make inferences—that is, draw conclusions from their data and make assumptions about the meaning of results. Suppose, for example, that a group of trauma victims scored an average of ten points lower on an anxiety test after being treated with EMDR and that the scores of victims in a no-treatment control group dropped by an average of seven points. Does the three-point difference between these two groups reflect the impact of EMDR, or could it have been caused by random factors that made EMDR appear more powerful than it actually is? Inferential statistics allow researchers to estimate the likelihood that the difference between the average scores of the two groups was caused by chance factors rather than being due to the impact of the differing treatment they received. Other inferential statistics can help psychologists decide how likely it is that a correlation between two variables is large enough to suggest a real underlying relationship versus the possibility that it is just a fluke.

When inferential statistics argue that a correlation coefficient or the difference between groups is larger than expected by chance alone, the scientists say that the result has **statistical significance**. Statistical significance alone does not guarantee final "proof," but signifies that a finding merits more attention, especially when those results have been repeated, or *replicated,* in separate studies. When thinking critically about research, then, evaluating evidence about hypotheses includes asking whether a researcher's results are statistically significant and repeatable. (For more details on descriptive and inferential statistics and how to calculate them, see the "Statistics in Psychological Research" appendix.)

Statistics and Research Methods as Tools in Critical Thinking

As you think critically about evidence for or against any hypothesis, you should ask some tough questions. Does the evidence come from a study whose design is free of major confounds and other flaws? Have the results been subjected to careful statistical analysis? Have the findings been replicated? Using your critical thinking skills to evaluate research designs and statistical methods becomes most important when you think about results that are dramatic or unexpected.

This point was well illustrated when Douglas Biklen (1990) began promoting a procedure called "facilitated communication" to help people with severe versions of autistic spectrum disorder (ASD) use language for the first time (we describe ASD in the chapter on psychological disorders). Biklen claimed that these people have coherent thoughts but cannot express them using traditional language. He reported case studies in which people with ASD were apparently able to answer questions and speak intelligently using a special keyboard, but only when assisted by a "facilitator" who physically supported their unsteady hands. Controlled experiments have repeatedly shown this claim to be groundless, however (Jacobson, Mulick, & Schwartz, 1995; Mostert, 2001; Randi, 2009; Wegner, Fuller, & Sparrow, 2003). The alleged communication abilities of these people disappeared under conditions in which the facilitator (1) did not know the question being asked of the participant or (2) could not see the keyboard (Delmolino & Romanczyk, 1995). The discovery that facilitators were—perhaps inadvertently (Spitz, 1997)—guiding participants' hand movements has allowed those who work with people affected by ASD to see facilitated communication in a different light. So when a doctor in Belgium recently claimed that a man who had been in a coma for twenty-three years was suddenly able to communicate via a computer keyboard, skeptics were quick to point out that the person "supporting" his arm was clearly also guiding it (Black, 2009). The claim was soon withdrawn (BBC News, 2010).

The role of experiments and other scientific research methods in understanding behavior and mental processes is so important that in each chapter to come we include a special feature called "Focus on Research Methods." These features describe in detail

inferential statistics A set of mathematical procedures that help psychologists make inferences about what their research data mean.

statistical significance Referring to a correlation, or a difference between two groups, that is larger than would be expected by chance.

The Social Impact of Research

The impact of research in psychology depends partly on the quality of the results and partly on how people feel about those results. Despite negative results of controlled experiments on facilitated communication, the Facilitated Communication Institute's website continues to announce training for the many professionals and relatives of people with autistic disorder who still believe in its value. The fact that some people ignore or even attack research results that challenge cherished beliefs reminds us that scientific research has always affected and been affected by the social and political values of the society in which it takes place (Lynn et al., 2003; Tavris, 2002).

Robin Nelson/PhotoEdit

the specific procedures used in a particularly interesting research study. We hope that as you read these sections, you will see how the research methods discussed in this chapter are applied in every subfield of psychology.

ETHICAL GUIDELINES FOR PSYCHOLOGISTS

Do psychologists deceive people when they do research?

Some years ago, newspaper headlines claimed that hair dye causes cancer. Hairdressers were alarmed at first, then angry. The information given to the public was less than accurate. Rats—not humans—had been used in the research, and the animals developed cancer only after drinking the hair dye. Later research showed that using hair dye does not significantly increase human cancer risk (Takkouche, Etminan, & Montes-Martinez, 2005).

Splashy headlines sell newspapers and attract advertisers, but all scientists have an ethical obligation not to manipulate, distort, or sensationalize their research results. The obligation to analyze and report research fairly and accurately is just one of the ethical standards that guide psychologists. Preserving the welfare and dignity of research participants is another. So although researchers *could* measure anxiety by putting a loaded gun to people's heads or study marital conflicts by telling one partner that the other has been unfaithful, those methods could be harmful and are therefore unethical.

Whatever the research topic, psychologists' top priority is to investigate it with the highest ethical standards. They must first find ways to protect participants from harm, then determine how best to gather data of potential benefit for everyone. To measure anxiety, for example, a psychologist might ask people to enter a situation that is anxiety provoking but not traumatic (for example, approaching a feared animal or sitting in a dark room). And research on marital conflict usually involves observing couples as they discuss controversial issues in their relationship.

Psychologists take very seriously the obligation to minimize any immediate discomfort or risk for research participants as well as the need to protect those participants from long-term harm. A key element of this process is to inform prospective research subjects about every aspect of a study that might influence their decision to participate, and to ensure that each person's involvement is voluntary. But what if the purpose of the study is to measure people's emotional reactions to being insulted? Participants might not react normally if they know ahead of time that an "insult" will be part of the experiment. When deception is necessary to create certain experimental conditions, ethical standards require the

Caring for Animals in Research

Psychologists are careful to protect the welfare of animal participants in research. They do not wish to see animals suffer, and undue stress on animals can provoke reactions that can act as confounds. For example, in a study of how learning is affected by food rewards, the researcher could starve animals to make them hungry enough to want rewards. But this would introduce discomfort, making it impossible to separate the effects of the rewards from the effects of starvation.

Will & Deni McIntyre/Science Source

researcher to "debrief" participants as soon as the study is over by revealing all relevant information about the research and correcting any misconceptions it created.

Government regulations in the United States, Canada, and many other countries require that any research involving human participants must be approved by an Institutional Review Board (IRB) whose members have no connection with the research. If a proposed study is likely to create risks or discomfort for participants, IRB members weigh the potential benefits of the work in terms of knowledge and human welfare against any potential harm.

The obligation to protect participants' welfare also extends to animals, which are used in a small percentage of psychological research projects (American Psychological Association Committee on Animal Research and Ethics, 2012). Psychologists study animals partly because their behavior is interesting and partly because research with animals can provide information that would be impossible or unethical to collect from humans. For example, researchers can randomly assign animals to live alone and then look at how these conditions affect later social interactions. The same thing could not ethically be done with people, but animal studies offer clues about how social isolation might affect humans (see the chapter on motivation and emotion).

Contrary to some claims, animals used in psychological research are not routinely subjected to extreme pain, starvation, or other inhumane conditions. Even in the small proportion of studies that require the use of electric shock, the discomfort created is mild, brief, and not harmful. High standards for the care and treatment of animal participants are outlined in the Animal Welfare Act, the National Institutes of Health's *Guide for the Care and Use of Laboratory Animals,* the National Institute of Mental Health's *Methods and Welfare Considerations in Behavioral Research with Animals,* the American Psychological Association's *Principles on Animal Use,* and other laws and regulations (APA Committee on Animal Research and Ethics, 2012). In the rare studies that require animals to undergo short-lived pain or other forms of moderate stress, legal and ethical standards require that funding agencies—as well as local IRB and other committees charged with monitoring animal research—first determine that the discomfort is highly justified by the expected benefits to human welfare.

The responsibility for conducting research in the most humane fashion is one aspect of the *Ethical Principles of Psychologists and Code of Conduct* developed by the American Psychological Association (2010). The main purpose of these standards is to protect and promote the welfare of society and those with whom psychologists work. For example, as teachers, psychology instructors should give students complete, accurate, and up-to-date coverage of each topic, not a narrow and biased point of view. Further, psychologists should perform only those services and use only those techniques for which they are adequately trained. Psychologists should not reveal personal information obtained from clients or research participants except in the most unusual of circumstances (see the chapter on treatment of psychological disorders). Finally, they should avoid situations in which a conflict of interest might impair their judgment or harm others. They should not, for example, have sexual relations with their clients, students, or employees.

Despite these guidelines, doubt and controversy arise in some cases about whether a proposed experiment or a particular practice, such as deceiving participants, is ethical. The American Psychological Association has published a two-volume handbook (Knapp, 2011a, b) and a casebook (Campbell et al., 2009) to help psychologists resolve such issues. The ethical principles themselves must continually be updated to deal with complex new questions—such as how to protect the confidentiality of e-mail communications—that psychologists face in their ever-expanding range of work (American Psychological Association, 2010; Hays, 2006; Pipes, Holstein, & Aguirre, 2005; Warmerdam et al., 2010).

LINKAGES

As noted in the chapter on introducing psychology, all of psychology's subfields are related to one another. Our discussion of behavioral genetics illustrates just one way in which the topic of this chapter, research in psychology, is linked to the subfield of biological psychology (see the chapter on biological aspects of psychology). The Linkages diagram shows ties to two other subfields as well, and there are many more ties throughout the book. Looking for linkages among subfields will help you see how they all fit together and help you better appreciate the big picture that is psychology.

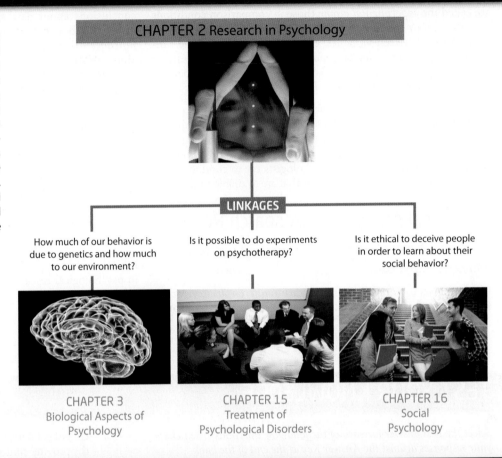

CHAPTER 2 Research in Psychology

LINKAGES

How much of our behavior is due to genetics and how much to our environment?

Is it possible to do experiments on psychotherapy?

Is it ethical to deceive people in order to learn about their social behavior?

CHAPTER 3
Biological Aspects of Psychology

CHAPTER 15
Treatment of Psychological Disorders

CHAPTER 16
Social Psychology

SUMMARY

Thinking Critically About Psychology (or Anything Else)

How can critical thinking save you money?

Critical thinking is the process of assessing claims and making judgments on the basis of well-supported evidence.

Often questions about behavior and mental processes are phrased in terms of *hypotheses* about *variables* that have been specified by *operational definitions*. Tests of hypotheses are based on objective, quantifiable evidence, or data, representing the variables of interest. If data are to be useful, they must be evaluated for *reliability* and *validity*.

Explanations of phenomena often take the form of a *theory*, which is a set of statements that can be used to account for, predict, and even suggest ways of controlling certain phenomena. Theories must be subjected to careful evaluation.

Research Methods in Psychology

How do psychologists learn about people?

Research in psychology, as in other sciences, focuses on four main goals: description, prediction, control, and explanation.

Observational methods such as *naturalistic observation* entail watching without interfering as behavior occurs in the natural environment. These methods can be revealing, but care must be taken to ensure that observers are unbiased and do not alter the behavior being observed.

Case studies are intensive examinations of a particular individual, group, or situation. They are useful for studying new or rare phenomena and for evaluating new treatments or training programs.

Surveys ask questions, through interviews or questionnaires, about behavior, attitudes, beliefs, opinions, and intentions. They provide an efficient way to gather large amounts of data from many people at a relatively low cost, but their results can be distorted if questions are poorly phrased, if answers are not given honestly, or if respondents do not constitute a representative sample of the population whose views are of interest.

Correlational studies examine relationships between variables in order to describe research data, test predictions, evaluate theories, and suggest hypotheses. Correlational studies are an important part of psychological research. However, the reasons behind the relationships they reveal cannot be established by correlational studies alone.

In *experiments,* researchers directly control an *independent variable* and observe the effect of that manipulation on a *dependent variable.* Participants receiving experimental treatment are called the *experimental group*; those in comparison conditions are called *control groups.* Experiments can reveal cause-and-effect relationships between variables, but researchers should use *randomizing* procedures, *placebo* conditions, *double-blind designs,* and other strategies to avoid being misled by *random variables,* participants' expectations, *experimenter bias,* and other *confounds.*

Psychologists' research can be limited if their *sampling* procedures do not give them a fair cross section of the population they want to study and about which they want to draw conclusions. Anything other than *random sampling* is said to be *biased sampling* of participants. In most cases, psychologists try to conduct *representative sampling* of the populations that are available to them.

Statistical Analysis of Research Results

What does it mean when scientists say that a research finding is "significant"?

Psychologists use *descriptive statistics* and *inferential statistics* to summarize and analyze data. Psychologists employ descriptive statistics such as the mean, or average, scores of various groups to characterize the typical score in each group and to summarize differences between groups. Inferential statistics guide conclusions about data and help determine if correlations or differences between group averages have reached *statistical significance*—that is, are larger than would be expected by chance alone. Although valuable for describing relationships, *correlations* alone cannot establish that two variables are causally related, nor can they determine which variable might affect which or why.

Scientific evaluation of research requires critical thinking to carefully assess the design and statistical analysis of even seemingly dramatic or desirable results.

Ethical Guidelines for Psychologists

Do psychologists deceive people when they do research?

Ethical guidelines promote the protection of humans and animals in psychological research. They also set the highest standards for behavior in all other aspects of psychologists' scientific and professional lives.

TEST YOUR KNOWLEDGE

Select the best answer for each of the following questions. Then check your responses against the Answer Key at the end of the book.

1. You are watching an infomercial that claims that if you drink liquefied seaweed twice a day, you will lose ten pounds a month. As a wise consumer who knows the five critical thinking questions listed in this chapter, you would FIRST say to yourself:
   a. "I don't know whether the person making the claim about the weight-loss effects of seaweed is a doctor or not."
   b. "The only evidence they present in support of their claim is one woman's personal experience."
   c. "I'll bet you also have to exercise to lose the ten pounds."
   d. "They are asking me to believe that I can lose ten pounds a month by drinking seaweed."

2. Dr. Lucas is interested in the effect of seeing colors on people's moods. She has participants complete a mood survey in either a bright red room or a stark white one. A participant's score on the mood survey is the researcher's _____.
   a. operational definition of mood
   b. random variable
   c. independent variable
   d. descriptive statistic

3. Case studies are used to _____.
   a. avoid a placebo effect
   b. determine the effects of an independent variable
   c. collect descriptive data
   d. provide control in an experiment

4. Before using survey results to support a hypothesis, we must be sure about which of the following?
   a. The questions are properly worded.
   b. The sample used is representative of the population of interest.
   c. The responses are not strongly biased by efforts to appear socially acceptable.
   d. All of the above.

5. When Dr. Beren compares the performance of his experimental group and his control group, he finds the difference in their scores to be statistically significant. This statement means that _____.
   a. the difference is larger than would be expected by chance
   b. he used descriptive statistics
   c. his results were confounded by random variables
   d. he used a double-blind method

6. Dr. Daneli believes that memory is aided by an increase in a brain chemical called serotonin. To avoid the possibility that experimenter bias might confound the results of an experiment aimed at testing this hypothesis, she should use a(n) _____ design.
   a. operational
   b. naturalistic
   c. random
   d. double-blind

7. In Dr. Daneli's experiment, Group A receives serotonin before taking a memory test, whereas Group B takes the same test without receiving serotonin. In this experiment, performance on the memory test is the _____ variable.
   a. dependent
   b. independent
   c. control
   d. random

8. Angelica designed an experiment to test the effects of praise on the sharing behavior of children. Children in Group A will be praised after they share; children in Group B will only be observed. Group A is the _____ group.
   a. control
   b. experimental
   c. operational
   d. random

9. José wants to know whether growing up in an abusive family causes children to become physically violent. Which of the following research methods would create the greatest ethical problems in trying to study this question scientifically?
   a. case studies
   b. experiments
   c. observations
   d. surveys

10. A correlation coefficient can tell us all of the following except the _____ of a relationship between two variables.
    a. strength
    b. direction
    c. existence
    d. cause

11. Your psychology professor asks you to learn about the smoking habits of all students on your campus. The most practical yet scientific way to get participants for your study would be to find a _____.
    a. random sample of all students
    b. random sample of smokers
    c. representative sample of all students
    d. representative sample of all nonsmokers

12. Why do psychologists follow ethical guidelines?
    a. Psychologists would not want the cost of participating in an experiment to be too high in comparison with the information to be gained.
    b. The American Psychological Association has set standards for psychologists to follow when conducting research and treating clients.
    c. Stress and pain could act as confounding variables in an experiment.
    d. All of the above.

13. Maria wanted to assess reactions to a new school rule requiring students to wear uniforms. She put the names of all 400 students enrolled in the school into a bag, drew out 25 names, and sent them a questionnaire. In this study, Maria used _____.
    a. biased sampling
    b. double-blind assignment
    c. random sampling
    d. random assignment

14. Tariq wants to test whether wearing magnets can relieve the pain from sports injuries. He recruits college athletes with knee injuries and randomly assigns them to wear either a magnet or an identical, but nonmagnetic, piece of metal on their injured knee. Tariq's use of the nonmagnetic metal in this experiment was to control for _____.
    a. the placebo effect
    b. random variables
    c. experimenter bias
    d. generalizability

15. Dr. Feelgood is conducting an experiment to determine if exercise can alleviate depression. Half of her participants rode a stationary bicycle for thirty minutes a day, while the other half did not exercise. At the end of a month, she gave each participant a test for depression. Which of the following is the operational definition of the dependent variable in this study?
    a. Being in the control group
    b. Being in the experimental group
    c. Riding a stationary bike thirty minutes each day for a month
    d. Participants' scores on the depression test

16. Choose the strongest correlation coefficient.
    a. $+.75$
    b. $-.99$
    c. $+.01$
    d. $-.01$

17. Biff has discovered a correlation of $-.83$ between the amount of time his fraternity brothers spend working out in the gym and the number of dates they have during the semester. Based on this information, Biff can correctly conclude that _____.
    a. when the men work out more, they also have more dates
    b. when the men work out more, they also have fewer dates
    c. working out increases dating
    d. working out decreases dating

18. Psychologists' first obligation in conducting research is to _____.
    a. avoid deceiving participants
    b. follow strict ethical standards
    c. find private rather than government grant support
    d. identify a representative sample of human or animal participants

19. To assure that people participate voluntarily in psychological research, psychologists must _____.
    a. pay them a reasonable participation fee, even if they drop out of the study later
    b. give them the right to sue for damages in the event something goes wrong
    c. tell them the true purpose of the study beforehand and let them ask questions
    d. inform them about everything that might influence their decision to participate

20. Assuring that any potential risks of research is outweighed by and justified by the potential benefits of that research is ultimately the job of the _____.
    a. researcher
    b. agency that funds the research
    c. institutional review board
    d. journal that publishes the research results

Biological Aspects of Psychology

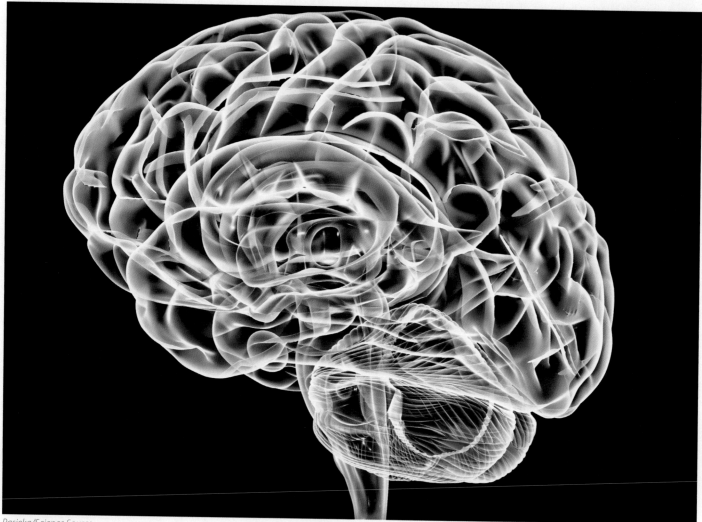

Pasieka/Science Source

Preview

TRY THIS Before you read the next sentence, close your eyes and touch your nose. This task is easy, but it is not simple. To get the job done, your brain used specific nerves to tell your eyelids to close. It used other nerves to tell your hand to extend a finger and then sent a series of messages that moved your arm in just the right direction until it received a message that your finger and your nose were in contact. This example illustrates that everything you do—including how you feel and think—is based on some kind of biological activity in your body, especially in your brain. This chapter tells the story of that activity, beginning with the neuron, one of the body's most basic biological units. We describe how neurons form systems capable of receiving and processing information and translate it into behavior, thoughts, and biochemical changes.

Biological factors are an intimate part of *all* behavior and mental processes. Brain cells, hormones, genes, and other body processes play a role in everything you think and feel and do, from the fleeting memory you had a minute ago to the anxiety or excitement or fatigue you felt last night to the eye movements you use to read these words. Biology does not reveal the whole story of psychology, but it tells an important part of it. Understanding the relationship between biology, behavior, and mental processes takes us into the realm of **biological psychology**—the study of cells, genes, and organs of the body and the physical and chemical changes involved in behavior and mental processes.

Studying the biology of behavior and mental processes also involves exploring the environment's role in influencing those processes. You will see later, for example, that the experiences we have in the environment can change the chemistry and even the structure of our brains. In this chapter we begin to consider in more detail the relationship between your body and your mind, between your brain and your behavior.

We will begin by considering the **nervous system**, the billions of cells that make up your brain, spinal cord, and nerves. The nervous system receives information, analyzes it, and sends messages from one part of the body to another. The combined activity of these cells helps you gather information, make decisions, and take action. Another system, the endocrine (pronounced "END-oh-krin") system, also helps direct body activities. It regulates internal activity of the body with glands that secrete chemicals, called *hormones,* into the bloodstream. Hormones affect energy consumption, reactions to stress, sexual functioning, and more. The nervous system and the endocrine system affect each other to coordinate activities of the body. Putting the pieces together about how all this happens is the next step in our understanding of the biology of our complex behavior.

CELLS OF THE NERVOUS SYSTEM

What are neurons, and what do they do?

The nervous system is a vast network of cells that tells you what is going on inside and outside your body and allows you to respond appropriately. For example, if you are jabbed with a pin, your nervous system gets the message and immediately causes you to flinch. But the nervous system can do far more than detect information and make responses. When information about the world reaches the brain, that information is *processed*—it is combined with information about past experiences and current wants and needs—to allow you to decide how to respond. Our exploration of the nervous system begins at the "bottom," with a description of its individual cells. Later we consider how these cells are organized to form the structures of the human nervous system.

biological psychology The psychological specialty focused on the physical and chemical changes that cause, and occur in response to, behavior and mental processes.

nervous system A complex combination of cells whose primary function is to allow an organism to gain information about what is going on inside and outside the body and to respond appropriately.

Three Functions of the Nervous System

The nervous system's three main functions are to receive information (input), integrate that information with past experiences (processing), and guide actions (output). When the alarm clock goes off, this person's nervous system, like yours, gets the message, recognizes what it means, decides what to do, and then takes action—by getting out of bed or perhaps hitting the snooze button.

© Paul Maguire/Shutterstock.com

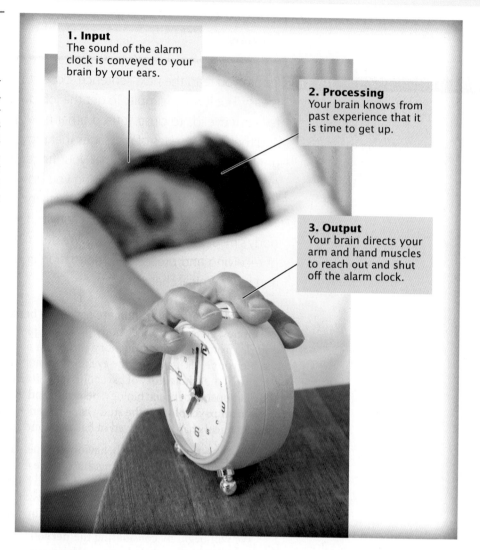

1. Input
The sound of the alarm clock is conveyed to your brain by your ears.

2. Processing
Your brain knows from past experience that it is time to get up.

3. Output
Your brain directs your arm and hand muscles to reach out and shut off the alarm clock.

Neurons

The nervous system is an information-processing system with three functions: input, processing, and output (see Figure 3.1). These functions are possible partly because the nervous system is made up of cells that communicate with each other. Two major types of cells, *neurons* and *glial cells*, allow the nervous system to carry out its complex signaling tasks efficiently. The specialized cells that send and receive signals are called **neurons**, or **nerve cells**.

Most of our discussion of brain cells concerns neurons, but glial cells are important, too. *Glial* means "glue," and scientists had long believed that glial cells did no more than hold neurons together. We now know, however, that **glial cells** also help neurons communicate by directing their growth, regulating their chemical environment, providing energy, adjusting blood flow, pruning connections among neurons, and secreting chemicals to help repair damage (Paolicelli et al., 2011; Petzold & Murthy, 2011). In fact, glial cells can do many of the functions of neurons, including releasing chemicals that influence neurons, responding to chemicals from neurons, and changing in response to experience (Barres, 2008; Zonouzi et al., 2011). Without glial cells, neurons could not function, and malfunctions in glial cells may play a role in problems ranging from recurring pain to depression and other mental disorders (Miller, 2005a).

Every cell in the body has an *outer membrane*, which acts kind of like the skin of your body, and every cell has a body that (with the exception of red blood cells) contains a core called the *nucleus*. Also inside each cell body are tiny "engines," called *mitochondria* (pronounced "my-toh-CON-dree-uh"), structures that help the cell generate and use energy.

neurons (or nerve cells) Fundamental units of the nervous system.

glial cells Cells in the nervous system that hold neurons together and help them communicate with one another.

FIGURE 3.2
The Neuron

Part (A B) shows fibers extending outward from the cell body of a neuron, which is a nervous system cell. These fibers, called *axons* and *dendrites*, are among the features that make neurons unique. Part (B) shows an enlarged drawing of the neuron's cell body. The cell body of a neuron includes an outer membrane, a nucleus, and mitochondria.

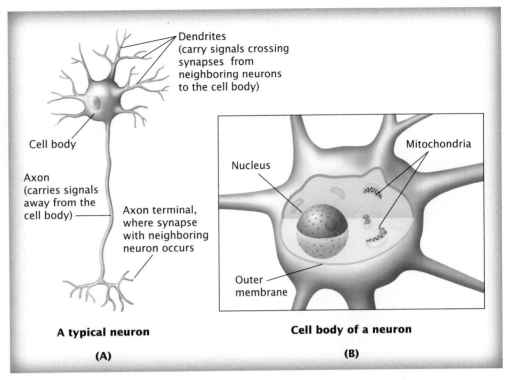

A typical neuron
(A)

Cell body of a neuron
(B)

Neurons are no different. A neuron's outer membrane acts like a screen, letting some substances pass in and out while blocking others. In the neuron's cell body, the nucleus carries genetic information that tells the cell what to do. And neurons' mitochondria turn oxygen and glucose into energy. This energy process is especially vital to brain cells, because although the human brain accounts for only 2 percent of body weight, it uses more than 20 percent of a body's oxygen. The human brain needs so much energy because its cells transmit signals among themselves to an even greater extent than do cells in the rest of the body.

Neurons use special structural and chemical features to communicate with each other. While neurons come in many shapes and sizes, they all have long, thin fibers that reach outward from the cell body like arms (see Part (A) in Figure 3.2). Communication between the cells can occur when these fibers are close to other neurons. The interweaving of these fibers with fibers from other neurons allows each neuron to be close to thousands or even hundreds of thousands of other neurons.

Fibers extending from the cell body are called *axons* and *dendrites*. As shown in Figure 3.2, each neuron generally has only one single **axon**, whose function is to carry signals away from the cell body. An axon may have many branches at its end, much like a tree has branches that reach to the sky. Axons can be short or long. In the brain, they may extend no more than a fraction of an inch, but the axon from your spine to your big toe is more than three feet long! **Dendrites** are the neuron fibers that receive signals from the axons of other neurons and carry those signals to the cell body. As you can see in Figure 3.2, whereas a neuron usually has just one axon, it can have many dendrites, each of which usually has many branches. Remember that *axons* carry signals *away* from the cell body, and *dendrites* *detect* those signals.

Action Potentials

The communication signal between neurons begins with an electrochemical pulse called an **action potential**, which shoots down the axon. This is an "all-or-nothing" affair: The cell either fires its action potential at full strength or it does not fire at all. Once a cell has fired, a very short recovery time called the **refractory period** follows, during which the cell cannot fire again. Even so, neurons are able to fire as often as 1,000 times per second. The speed of an action potential ranges from about 5 to 260 miles per hour and depends

axons Fibers that carry signals from the body of a neuron out to where communication occurs with other neurons.

dendrites Neuron fibers that receive signals from the axons of other neurons and carry those signals to the cell body.

action potential An abrupt wave of electrochemical changes traveling down an axon when a neuron becomes depolarized.

refractory period A short rest period between action potentials.

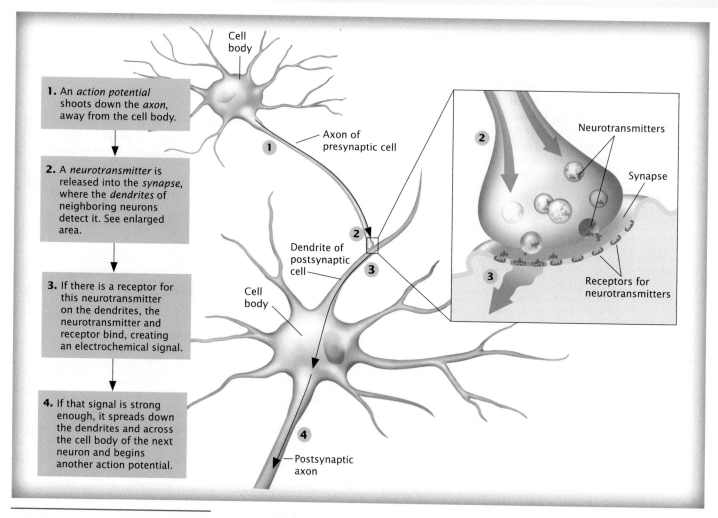

1. An *action potential* shoots down the *axon*, away from the cell body.

2. A *neurotransmitter* is released into the *synapse*, where the *dendrites* of neighboring neurons detect it. See enlarged area.

3. If there is a receptor for this neurotransmitter on the dendrites, the neurotransmitter and receptor bind, creating an electrochemical signal.

4. If that signal is strong enough, it spreads down the dendrites and across the cell body of the next neuron and begins another action potential.

Cell body

Axon of presynaptic cell

Dendrite of postsynaptic cell

Cell body

Postsynaptic axon

Neurotransmitters

Synapse

Receptors for neurotransmitters

FIGURE 3.3

Communication between Neurons

When stimulation of a neuron reaches a certain level, the neuron fires, sending an action potential shooting to the end of its axon and triggering the release of a neurotransmitter into the synapse. This stimulates neighboring neurons and may cause them to fire their own action potentials. A cell's receptors can also receive signals that have the opposite effect, making the cell less likely to fire.

neurotransmitters Chemicals that assist in the transfer of signals from one neuron to another.

synapses The tiny gaps between neurons across which they communicate.

receptors Sites on the surface of a cell that allow only one type of neurotransmitter to fit into them, triggering a chemical response that may lead to an action potential.

on the thickness or diameter of the axon—larger ones are faster—and on the presence of myelin (pronounced "MY-a-lin"). *Myelin* is a fatty substance that wraps around some axons like a stocking and speeds up action potentials. When a neuron fires, dendrites in the next cell detect the message and send the signal to their cell body.

Synapses and Communication Between Neurons

How do the dendrites detect a signal from another neuron? As shown in Figure 3.3, it works a little like the game of tag you may have played as a child. In this neural communication tag game, however, one neuron "sends" a tag without actually touching the next neuron. When an action potential reaches the ends of an axon's branches, it stimulates the release of a **neurotransmitter**. Neurotransmitters are chemicals that act as messengers between neurons. They're stored in little "bags" called *vesicles* (pronounced "VESS-ick-els"). Neurotransmitters flow across a tiny gap, less than a millionth of an inch wide, which separates the axon of one neuron and the dendrites of another. This is the *synaptic gap*, often referred to simply as the **synapse** (see Figure 3.4). Some nerve cells have direct electrical communication at specialized contact points called *gap junctions*, or *electrical synapses*. At these gap junctions, neurons can transfer either neurotransmitters or electrical signals. Electrical synapses allow clusters of neurons to fire together, and the strength of their activity can change in response to experience (Haas, Zavala, & Landiesman, 2011). As a result, electrical synapses may contribute to the process of learning. They may also be involved in epilepsy, a brain disorder in which large groups of neurons fire together and produce seizures (Dere & Zlomuzica, 2012).

When neurotransmitters cross a synapse and reach the dendrite of the next cell, they chemically fit, or bind, to proteins called **receptors**. Like a key fitting into the right lock, a neurotransmitter snugly binds to its own specific receptors but not to receptors for other neurotransmitters. Each receptor "recognizes" only one type of neurotransmitter. In the dendrite, this binding creates an electrochemical signal that is called a *postsynaptic potential* because it occurs *after* the neurotransmitter has crossed the synapse. The postsynaptic potential, in turn, passes the message to the cell body for the signaling process to continue.

Generally, more than one message must go to a cell to make it fire. Signals from groups of cells often arrive at the same postsynaptic cell at about the same time. The messages from these many cells may conflict with one another. Some messages tell the cell to fire, whereas others tell the cell not to fire. Whether it actually does fire depends on which kinds of signals are strongest and most numerous. In this way, axons, neurotransmitters, synapses, and dendrites allow nerve cells of the nervous system to communicate. If these components are damaged or disordered, however, problems occur. For example, spinal cord injuries may cut the neural communication lines that had once allowed people to feel and move their bodies. And when the myelin surrounding some axons is destroyed by a disorder known as *multiple sclerosis (MS)*, the result can disrupt vision, speech, balance, and other important functions.

Neurotransmitters are involved in every aspect of behavior and mental processes. You will see them involved, for example, in conveying pain messages, in creating the psychological effects of alcohol, and in providing the main targets for prescription drugs that treat schizophrenia and depression.

Organization of the Nervous System

Impressive as individual neurons are (see "In Review: Neurons, Neurotransmitters, and Receptors"), we can best understand their functions by looking at how they operate in groups called **neural networks**. The billions of neurons that make up the nervous system are organized into two main parts—the *central nervous system* and the *peripheral nervous system* (see Figure 3.5). These systems work together closely to coordinate behavior and

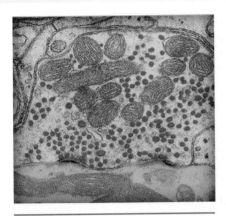

FIGURE 3.4
A Synapse

This photograph taken with an electron microscope shows part of a synaptic gap between two neurons, magnified 50,000 times. The ending of the first cell's axon is shaded green; the green ovals are mitochondria. The red spots are vesicles, which contain neurotransmitters. The synapse itself appears as the narrow gap between the first cell's green-shaded axon and the blue-shaded dendrite of the cell below.

A Damaged Nervous System

If axons, dendrites, or other components of the nervous system are damaged or disordered, serious problems can result. The spinal cord injury that this woman suffered in a car accident cut the neural communication lines that had allowed her to feel and move the lower part of her body.

Ariel Skelley/Corbis

neural networks Neurons that operate together to perform complex functions.

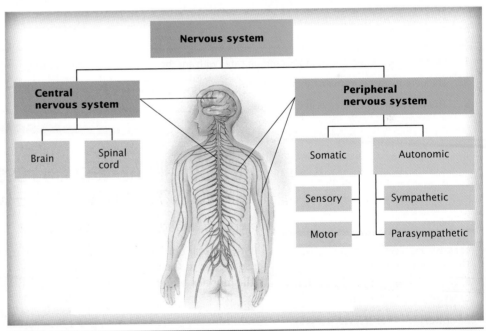

FIGURE 3.5
Organization of the Nervous System

The brain and spinal cord make up the bone-encased central nervous system (CNS), the body's central information processor, decision maker, and director of actions. The peripheral nervous system, which is not housed in bone, functions mainly to carry messages. The somatic subsystem of the peripheral nervous system transmits information to the CNS from the outside world and conveys instructions from the CNS to the muscles. The autonomic subsystem conveys messages from the CNS that alter the activity of organs and glands, and it sends information about that activity back to the brain.

mental processes, as we'll describe later on. The **central nervous system (CNS)** consists of the brain and spinal cord, which are encased in bone for protection. Like the chief executive officer in a company, the CNS receives information, processes it, and determines what actions should result (Banich, 2009). The **peripheral nervous system (PNS)** extends throughout the body and, like an e-mail or texting service, relays information to and from the brain.

NEURONS, NEUROTRANSMITTERS, AND RECEPTORS IN REVIEW

Part	Function	Type of Signal Carried
Axon	Carries signals away from the cell body	The action potential, an all-or-nothing electrochemical signal that shoots down the axon to vesicles at the tip of the axon, releasing neurotransmitters
Dendrite	Detects and carries signals to the cell body	The postsynaptic potential, an electrochemical signal moving toward the cell body
Synapse	An area for the transfer of signals between neurons, usually between axon and dendrite	Chemicals that cross the synapse and reach receptors on another cell or electrical impulses transferred from one cell to another
Neurotransmitter	A chemical released by one cell that binds to the receptors on another cell	A chemical message telling the next cell to fire or not to fire its own action potential
Receptor	Proteins on the cell membrane that receive chemical signals	Recognizes certain neurotransmitters, allowing it to begin a postsynaptic potential in the dendrite

In Review Questions

1. In most cases, when one neuron communicates with another, a _____ crosses the _____ between them.
2. The nervous system's main functions are to _____, _____, and _____ information.
3. The two main types of cells in the nervous system are _____ and _____.

THE PERIPHERAL NERVOUS SYSTEM: KEEPING IN TOUCH WITH THE WORLD

How do sights and sounds reach my brain?

The peripheral nervous system sends sensory information from the eyes, ears, and other sense organs to the CNS. The PNS also carries messages from the brain and spinal cord to the muscles, glands, and other parts of the body. Unlike the CNS, it is not protected by bone. To accomplish its relay tasks, the peripheral nervous system has two subsystems—the somatic nervous system and the autonomic nervous system.

The Somatic Nervous System

Imagine that you're at the beach. It's hot, and the ocean smells salty. An attractive stranger approaches, catching your eye. The stranger smiles. You smile in return. The stranger continues walking away. In these few seconds, your nervous system has been busy. You feel the warmth of the sun and smell the ocean because your **somatic nervous system (SNS)** takes in this sensory information and sends it to the central nervous system for processing. The CNS evaluates the warmth and the smells, sending messages through the somatic

---

central nervous system (CNS) The parts of the nervous system encased in bone; specifically, the brain and the spinal cord.

peripheral nervous system (PNS) The parts of the nervous system not housed in bone.

somatic nervous system (SNS) The subsystem of the peripheral nervous system that transmits information from the senses to the CNS and carries signals from the central nervous system to the muscles.

Is That Your Final Answer?

Which is the geographically largest U.S. state?: (a) Montana, (b) Texas, (c) Alaska, or (d) Wyoming? Like contestants on shows such as *Who Wants to Be a Millionaire*, you must rely on your central nervous system, and especially on the information-processing power of your brain, to understand the question, recognize the correct option, and direct movements of your vocal muscles to speak your answer. (The correct choice in this case is (c).)

Rolf Vennenbernd/dpa/Corbis

sensory neurons Cells in the nervous system that provide information to the brain about the environment.

motor neurons Cells in the nervous system that the brain uses to influence muscles and other organs to respond to the environment in some way.

autonomic nervous system A subsystem of the peripheral nervous system that carries messages between the central nervous system and the heart, lungs, and other organs and glands.

sympathetic nervous system The subsystem of the autonomic nervous system that readies the body for vigorous activity.

parasympathetic nervous system The subsystem of the autonomic nervous system that typically influences activity related to the protection, nourishment, and growth of the body.

nervous system to the muscles that allow you to turn over, sit up, or put on more sunscreen. **Sensory neurons** bring information into the brain. **Motor neurons** carry information from the part of the brain that directs motion.

The Autonomic Nervous System

The **autonomic nervous system** carries messages back and forth between the CNS and the heart, lungs, and other organs and glands. For example, the autonomic nervous system takes that passing stranger's "attractive" rating from the CNS and translates it into an increase in heart rate, pupil dilation, and perhaps a little blushing. This system is called "autonomic" (pronounced "aw-toh-NOM-ic") because its activities, including digestion and sweating, for example, are generally autonomous, or independent of your control. With training and practice, some people can use a technique called *biofeedback* to bring some of their involuntary responses, such as heart rate, under conscious (CNS) control.

As shown in Figure 3.5, the autonomic system has two subsystems of its own—the *sympathetic nervous system* and the *parasympathetic nervous system*. These two subsystems work like a seesaw on a playground. Generally, the **sympathetic nervous system** readies your body for action in the face of stress. The **parasympathetic nervous system** calms you down once the crisis has passed. So the *sympathetic nervous system spends* energy, whereas the *parasympathetic nervous system preserves* energy.

The functions of the autonomic nervous system may not get star billing, but you'd miss them if they were gone. Just as a racecar driver is nothing without a good pit crew, the somatic nervous system depends on the autonomic nervous system to get its job done. For example, when you want to move your muscles, you create a demand for energy. The autonomic nervous system fills the bill by increasing sugar fuels in the bloodstream. If you decide to stand up, you need increased blood pressure so that your blood does not flow out of your brain and settle in your legs. Again, the autonomic nervous system makes the adjustment. Disorders of the autonomic nervous system can make people sweat uncontrollably or faint whenever they stand up; they can also lead to other problems, such as an inability to have sex. We examine the autonomic nervous system in more detail in the chapter on motivation and emotion.

THE CENTRAL NERVOUS SYSTEM: MAKING SENSE OF THE WORLD

How is my brain "wired"?

The amazing speed and efficiency of the central nervous system—the brain and spinal cord—have prompted many people to compare it to the central processor in a computer. But the CNS does not simply function as a high-powered computer. It certainly isn't laid out as neatly, either (Lichtman & Denk, 2011; Poldrack, 2010). The layout of the brain is more like the map of a college campus. There are clusters of offices for the administrators in one place, clusters of faculty offices in another place, and classrooms in yet another. Some of the sidewalks or hallways that connect these clusters are wide; others are narrow. There are many different but connected ways to get to the same place. Like a campus with its office clusters, one way that the CNS has organized some neuron cell bodies is into globelike clusters called *nuclei* (pronounced "NUKE-lee-eye"; *nuclei* is the plural of *nucleus*). The sidewalks and hallways of the CNS are axons that travel together in bundles called *fiber tracts*, or *pathways*. The axon (hallway) from any given cell (office) may merge with and leave many *fiber tracts* (sidewalks) and send branches out to other tracts.

Let's consider a practical example of nervous system functioning to begin learning our way around the "campus" of the brain. It is 6 A.M. and your alarm clock goes off, creating the simple case of information processing illustrated in Figure 3.1. Your ears receive sensory input in the form of sound from the alarm. The sound is converted into neural signals and sent to the brain. Your brain compares these signals with previous experiences stored in memory and correctly associates the sound with "alarm clock." Your muscle-guiding output is not yet at peak performance, though, because your brain activity has not yet reached the waking state. So, you fumble to turn off the alarm, shuffle to the kitchen, and accidentally touch the coffeemaker's heating element. Things get more lively now. Heat energy activates sensory neurons in your fingers, generating action potentials that speed along fiber tracts going into the spinal cord and up to your brain. Your motor neurons are guided by the rapid, automatic responses of very basic brain systems that cause muscles in your arm to contract and quickly withdraw your hand.

The Spinal Cord

The **spinal cord** receives signals such as pain and touch from the senses and passes those signals to the brain. Neuron fibers within the cord also carry signals downward from the brain to the muscles. Some cells of the spinal cord can make simple decisions or direct simple movements without needing instructions from the brain. One example is known as a **reflex**, because the response to an incoming signal is directly "reflected" back out, as shown in Figure 3.6. Spinal reflexes, such as when your leg jerks after your doctor taps just below your knee, are very fast because they include few time-consuming synaptic links. Reflexes are simple and unlearned reactions to external stimuli, and they are *involuntary*; they can occur without instructions from the brain. Note that such an organization is an example of a *feedback system*. Your muscles have receptors that send information to the spinal cord to let it know how extended they are so that adjustments can be made for a smooth, contracting motion. Information about the consequences of an action goes back to the source of the action for further adjustment.

FIGURE 3.6
A Reflex Pathway

TRY THIS   Sit on a chair, cross one leg over the other, and then use the handle of a butter knife or some other solid object to gently tap your top knee, just below the kneecap, until you get a "knee jerk" reaction. Tapping your knee at just the right spot sets off an almost instantaneous sequence of events that begins with stimulation of sensory neurons that respond to stretch. When those neurons fire, their axons, which end within the spinal cord, cause spinal neurons to fire. This firing stimulates the firing of motor neurons with axons ending in your thigh muscles. As a result those muscles contract, causing a kicking motion of the lower leg and foot. Information about the knee tap and about what the leg has done also goes to your cerebral cortex, but the reflex is completed without waiting for guidance from the brain.

© iStock.com/101dalmatians

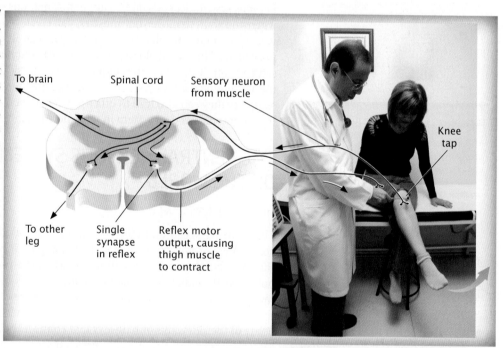

To brain   Spinal cord   Sensory neuron from muscle

Knee tap

To other leg   Single synapse in reflex   Reflex motor output, causing thigh muscle to contract

spinal cord The part of the central nervous system within the spinal column that relays signals from peripheral senses to the brain and conveys messages from the brain to the rest of the body.

reflexes Involuntary, unlearned feedback systems creating swift, automatic, and movements in response to external stimuli.

To make this system carry out the actions you want, though, you still need your brain. So, as reflexes occur, action potentials are also sent along fiber tracts to the brain. This way, your brain can choose to exert influence down the spinal cord. This influence explains why the strength of your knee-jerk reflex in a doctor's office can change depending on whether or not you watch the doctor tap your knee.

The Brain

When pain messages from a hot burner reach your brain, you may become aware of more than just being burned. You might also recall that you have burned yourself twice before in the past week and become annoyed at your carelessness. The brain is the most complex part in the central nervous system, and it is your brain's astonishing capacity for information processing that allows you to have these thoughts and feelings (Cacioppo & Decety, 2009).

The Hindbrain

You can see the major structures of the brain in Figure 3.7. The **hindbrain** lies just inside the skull and is actually a continuation of the spinal cord. Signals coming from the spinal cord reach the hindbrain first. Many vital autonomic functions, such as heart rate, blood pressure, and breathing, are controlled by nuclei in the hindbrain, particularly in an area called the **medulla oblongata** (pronounced "meh-DUH-lah ah-blon-GAH-da"), sometimes just called the **medulla**.

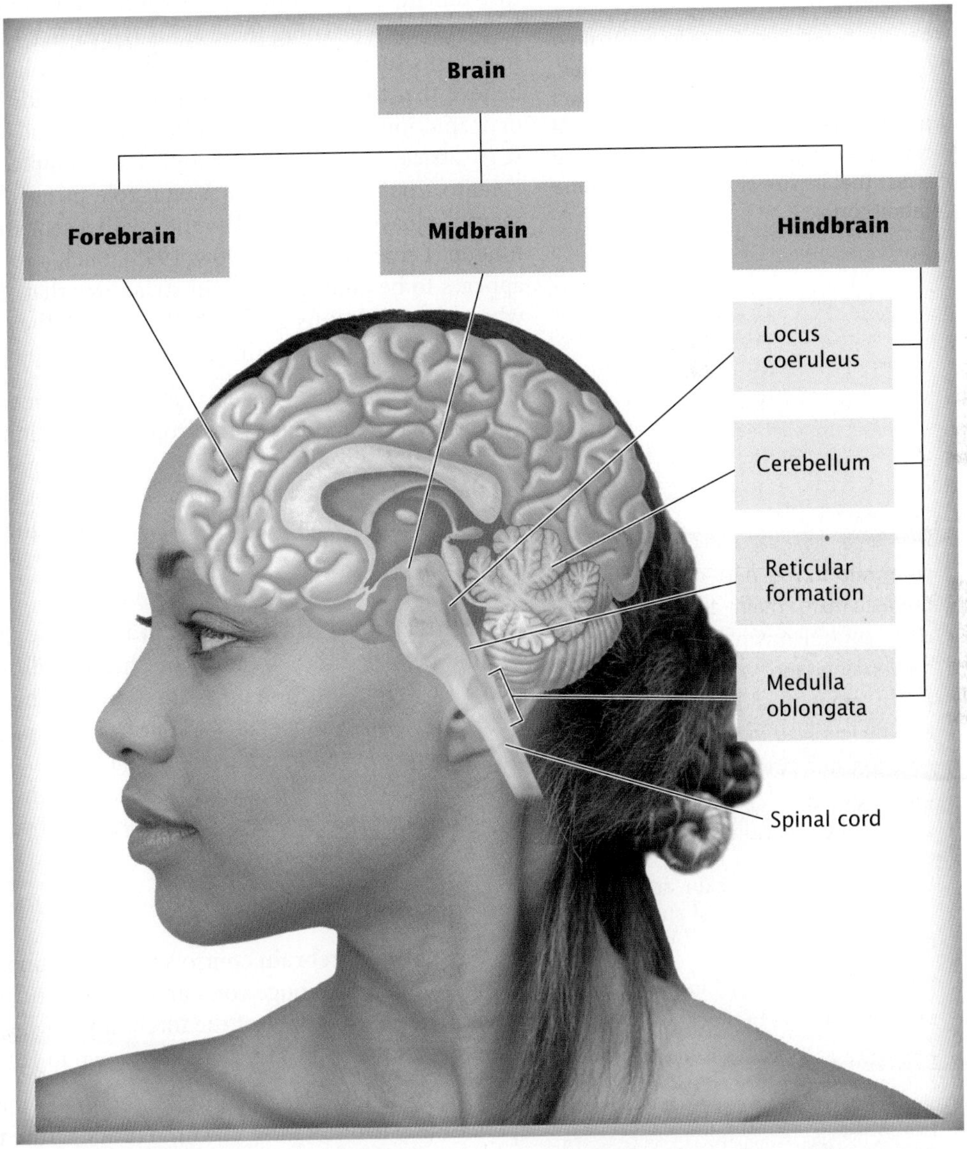

FIGURE 3.7
Major Structures of the Brain

This side view of a section cut down the middle of the human brain reveals the forebrain, midbrain, hindbrain, and spinal cord. Many of these subdivisions do not have clear-cut borders because they are all interconnected by fiber tracts. The anatomy of the mammalian brain reflects its evolution over millions of years. Newer structures (such as the cerebral cortex, which is the outer surface of the forebrain) that handle higher mental functions were built on older structures (such as the medulla oblongata) that coordinate heart rate, breathing, and other more basic functions.

© Blend Images/Shutterstock.com

hindbrain An extension of the spinal cord contained inside the skull where nuclei control blood pressure, heart rate, breathing, and other vital functions.

medulla oblongata (medulla) An area in the hindbrain that controls blood pressure, heart rate, breathing, and other vital functions.

reticular formation A network of cells and fibers threaded throughout the hindbrain and midbrain that gives alertness and arousal to the rest of the brain.

locus coeruleus A small nucleus in the reticular formation that is involved in directing attention.

A meshlike collection of cells called the **reticular formation** (*reticular* means "net-like") weaves through the hindbrain and up through the midbrain. This network helps promote alertness and arousal. Destroying the reticular system would put a person into a coma. Some of the fibers that carry pain signals from the spinal cord connect in the reticular formation and immediately arouse the brain from sleep.

Axons from a small nucleus within the reticular formation, the **locus coeruleus** (pronounced "LOH-kus seh-ROO-lee-us"), branch extensively, making contact with as many

A Field Sobriety Test

The cerebellum is involved in the balance and coordination required for walking. When the cerebellum's activity is impaired by alcohol, these skills are disrupted, which is why the police ask suspected drunk drivers to walk a straight line. The cerebellum's importance is suggested by the fact that its size is second only to the cerebral cortex.

Zuma Press, Inc./Alamy

cerebellum The part of the hindbrain whose main functions include controlling finely coordinated movements and storing memories about movement but which may also be involved in impulse control, emotion, and language.

midbrain A small structure between the hindbrain and forebrain that relays information from the eyes, ears, and skin and that controls certain types of automatic behaviors.

forebrain The most highly developed part of the brain; it is responsible for the most complex aspects of behavior and mental life.

thalamus A forebrain structure that relays signals from most sense organs to higher levels in the brain and plays an important role in processing and making sense out of this information.

hypothalamus A structure in the forebrain that regulates hunger, thirst, and sex drive.

as 100,000 other cells. The locus coeruleus (which means "blue spot" in Latin) is involved in directing attention, particularly toward new or important stimuli in the environment (Eldar, Cohen, & Niv, 2013). Changes in the locus coeruleus have been linked to depression, attention deficit hyperactivity disorder, sleep disorders, and posttraumatic stress disorder (Aston-Jones & Cohen, 2005).

The **cerebellum** (pronounced "sair-a-BELL-um") is also part of the hindbrain. Its function to control finely coordinated movements, such as threading a needle, has been known for a long time (Aso et al., 2010). We now know that the cerebellum may be important for higher-level behavior, too. The cerebellum helps us move our eyes as we track a moving target accurately (Krauzlis & Lisberger, 1991) and it may be the storehouse for well-rehearsed movements, such as those associated with dancing, playing a musical instrument, and athletics (McCormick & Thompson, 1984). The cerebellum might also be involved in learning these skills (Hardwick et al., 2012) and may add to uniquely human tasks such as language and abstract thinking (Mariën et al., 2013). Neuroscientists believe that the cerebellum is involved in additional activities as well, including memory, emotion, language, impulse control, and other higher-order cognitive processes (e.g., Strick, Dum, & Fiez, 2009). For example, the cerebellum is important in timing (Manto, 2008), which plays a vital role in normal speech, integrating moment-to-moment feedback about vocal sounds with a sequence of precise movements of the lips and tongue (Leiner, Leiner, & Dow, 1993). Such a role for the cerebellum may explain why it appears to be among the brain structures that show abnormal activity in young people who stutter (Watkins et al., 2008). In short, the cerebellum seems to be involved in both physical and cognitive agility.

Reflexes, feedback systems, and other basic processes are important in the hindbrain. For example, if blood pressure drops, heart action reflexively increases to make up for that decrease. If you stand up quickly, your blood pressure can drop so suddenly that you feel lightheaded until the hindbrain reflexively "catches up." You'll faint if the hindbrain does not activate the autonomic nervous system to increase your blood pressure.

The Midbrain

A small region called the **midbrain** lies above the hindbrain. If you focus your eyes on another person and then move your head, midbrain circuits allow you to move your eyes smoothly in the direction opposite from your head movement so you never lose eye contact. When you swing a bat, swat a mosquito, or jump rope, part of the midbrain and its connections to the forebrain allow you to produce those movements smoothly. When a car backfires and you turn your head to look in the direction of the sound, it is again the midbrain at work. Together, the midbrain and parts of the hindbrain other than the cerebellum are called the *brainstem*.

The Forebrain

In humans, the **forebrain** controls the most complex aspects of behavior and mental life. The forebrain is also huge compared to the hindbrain and midbrain, which it completely covers. The outer surface of the forebrain is a sheet of neurons called the *cerebral cortex*. Some structures of the forebrain are shown in Figure 3.8.

Two structures deep within the forebrain, the *hypothalamus* and the *thalamus*, help operate basic drives, emotion, and sensation. The **thalamus** acts as a relay station for pain and sense-organ signals (except smell) from the body to the upper levels of the brain. It also processes and makes sense of these signals. The **hypothalamus** lies under the thalamus (*hypo* means "under") and helps regulate hunger, thirst, and sex drives. The hypothalamus is well connected to the autonomic nervous system and to other parts of the brain. Damage to parts of the hypothalamus upsets normal appetite, thirst, and sexual behavior.

Can you set an "internal alarm clock" to wake up in the morning at whatever time you want? If you can, it is with the help of a remarkable part of your hypothalamus called the *suprachiasmatic nuclei* that contains the brain's own clock. The suprachiasmatic (pronounced

FIGURE 3.8
Major Structures of the Forebrain

The structures of the forebrain are covered by an outer "bark" known as the *cerebral cortex*. This diagram shows some of the structures that lie within the forebrain. The amygdala, the hippocampus, the hypothalamus, the septum, and portions of the cerebral cortex are all part of the limbic system.

© iStockphoto.com/juanestey

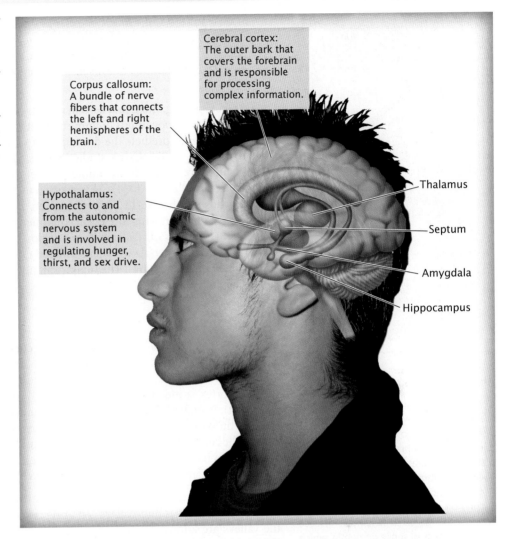

Corpus callosum: A bundle of nerve fibers that connects the left and right hemispheres of the brain.

Cerebral cortex: The outer bark that covers the forebrain and is responsible for processing complex information.

Hypothalamus: Connects to and from the autonomic nervous system and is involved in regulating hunger, thirst, and sex drive.

Thalamus

Septum

Amygdala

Hippocampus

amygdala A structure in the forebrain that, among other things, associates features of stimuli involved in memory and emotion.

hippocampus A structure in the forebrain associated with the formation of new memories.

"soo-prak-eye-as-MAT-ik") neurons operate on approximately a twenty-four-hour cycle, controlling daily biological rhythms such as waking and sleeping as well as cycles of body temperature. We discuss this brain area more in the chapter on consciousness.

Other parts of the forebrain, especially the **amygdala** (pronounced "ah-MIG-duh-luh") and the **hippocampus**, help regulate memory and emotion. The amygdala links emotional and certain other kinds of sensory information in memory, such as when a song or scent triggers the intensely rich recall of a lover's embrace (Paz & Pare, 2013). The amygdala also plays a role in fear and other emotions (Cunningham & Brosch, 2012; LeDoux, 1995; Whalen, 1998), connecting emotion to sensation. People who suffer from posttraumatic stress disorder have unusual amygdala activity (Shin, Rauch, & Pitman, 2006). The amygdala may also influence our sensitivity to other people (Corden et al., 2006). Brain scans show that the amygdala responds strongly when people view angry faces rather than neutral faces (Furmark et al., 2009). Such findings may explain why the amygdala and other nearby structures appear to be dysfunctional in people with autistic spectrum disorders, clinical conditions causing disruptions in the ability to relate to other people (Laupin et al., 2012) (see the chapter on psychological disorders). The amygdala, hippocampus, and some portions of the cerebral cortex are part of a group of brain structures called the *limbic system*, which regulates aspects of memory and emotion.

The most vital role of the hippocampus is in helping you form new memories. For example, a patient known as R. B. suffered a stroke (an interruption of blood flow in the brain) that damaged only his hippocampus. Although his intelligence remained above average and he could recall old memories, he was almost totally unable to build new ones (Squire, 1986). Damage to the hippocampus within a day of a mildly painful event seems to erase memories of the experience. However, if the damage occurs several days after the event, the memory remains. It seems that memories are not permanently stored in the hippocampus but instead are transferred from there to somewhere else in the brain.

It isn't surprising, then, that certain aspects of memory are related to the size and level of activity in the hippocampus (Zimmerman et al., 2008). For example, having a relatively small hippocampus predicts the development of severe memory problems in the elderly (Devanand et al., 2007). Other studies suggest that some people's physical responses to stress include a reduction in the number of neurons in the hippocampus (Caspi, Sugden, et al., 2003; Frodl et al., 2004). This effect was demonstrated in a study of people who had been close to the World Trade Center on 9/11. They showed less hippocampus volume, even three years after the event, than people who had been more distant (Ganzel et al., 2008). The loss of neurons in this region may help explain the memory problems that appear in some people who have suffered depression or posttraumatic stress disorder (Bremner et al., 2003, 2004). The hippocampus and memory also can be affected by disease (see Figure 3.9).

The Cerebral Cortex

On the surface of the forebrain is the **cerebral cortex**. The total area of the cerebral cortex is between one and two square feet, but it fits into the skull because it is wrinkled and folded. (You can wad up a T-shirt and fit it into a small bowl in much the same way.) The cerebral cortex is much larger in humans than in most other animals (dolphins are an exception). It analyzes information from all the senses and controls voluntary movement, abstract thinking, and the other most complex aspects of our behavior and mental processes. The cerebral cortex looks somewhat round and has a long groove down the middle creating two halves, called *cerebral hemispheres*. The **corpus callosum**, a massive bundle of more than a million fibers, connects the two hemispheres.

The folds of the cerebral cortex give the surface of the human brain its wrinkled appearance, its ridges and valleys. The ridges are called *gyri* (pronounced "JI-rye"), and the valleys are known as *sulci* (pronounced "SUL-sigh") or *fissures*. As you can see in Figure 3.10, we take advantage of several deep sulci to divide the cortex into four areas, called *lobes*: the frontal (front), parietal (top), occipital (back), and temporal (side). We use gyri and sulci as landmarks for describing the structure of the cortex, but the *functions* of the cortex do not stick to these boundaries. When divided according to function, the cortex includes areas of the sensory cortex, motor cortex, and association cortex.

The Sensory and Motor Cortex

Areas of the **sensory cortex** lie in parts of the parietal, occipital, and temporal lobes. Different regions of the sensory cortex receive information from different senses. Occipital lobe nerve cells called the *visual cortex* receive visual information. Temporal lobe nerve cells called the *auditory cortex* receive information from the ears. And information from the skin, such as sensations of touch, pain, and temperature, is received by cells in the parietal lobe. The skin-related areas are called the *somatosensory cortex* (*soma* is Greek for "body"). Information about skin sensations from neighboring parts of the body comes to neighboring parts of the somatosensory cortex. The places on the cortex where information from each area of skin arrives can be represented by the figure of a tiny person stretched out along the cortex (see Figure 3.11). This figure is called the *homunculus* (Latin for "little man"). Experience can change how the sensory cortex responds to sensory stimulation (Schaefer, Heinze, & Rotte, 2008). For example, if a limb is lost, the part of the sensory cortex that had been stimulated by that limb will now be stimulated by other regions of skin. Similarly, practicing a musical instrument will increase the number of sensory neurons that respond to touch (Hyde et al., 2009); the same thing happens when blind people learn to read Braille with their fingertips (Amedi et al., 2005).

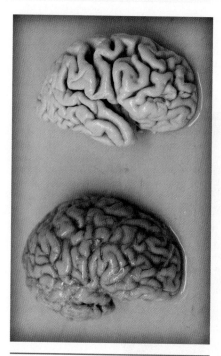

FIGURE 3.9
Alzheimer's Disease and the Brain

Compared to a normal brain (bottom), the brain of a person with Alzheimer's disease shows considerable degeneration in the cerebral cortex. The limbic system deteriorates, too (Callen et al., 2001). For example, the hippocampus of Alzheimer's patients is about 40 percent smaller on average than that of a person without the disease. Alzheimer's disease is a major cause of senile dementia, which involves the deterioration of cognitive capabilities.

Denis Balibouse/Reuters

cerebral cortex The outer surface of the brain.

corpus callosum A massive bundle of axons that connects the right and left cerebral hemispheres and allows them to communicate with each other.

sensory cortex The parts of the cerebral cortex that receive stimulus information from the senses.

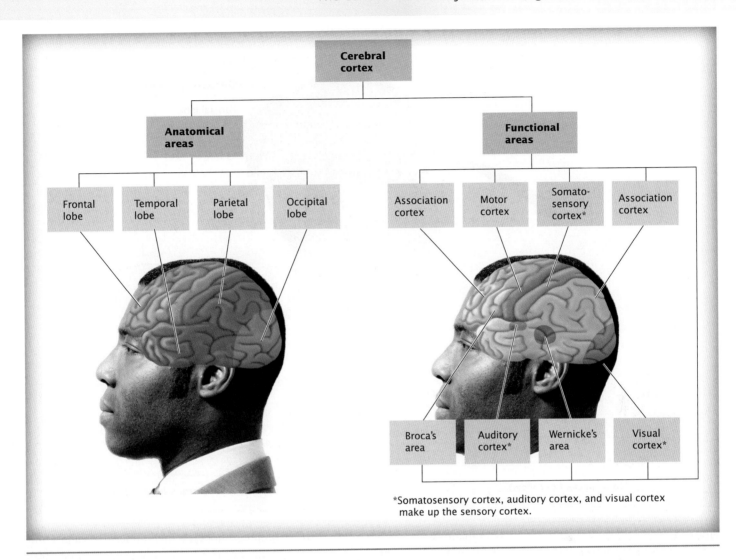

*Somatosensory cortex, auditory cortex, and visual cortex make up the sensory cortex.

FIGURE 3.10

The Cerebral Cortex (viewed from the left side)

The brain's ridges (gyri) and valleys (sulci) divide the cortex into four lobes: the frontal, parietal, occipital, and temporal. These terms describe where the regions are (the lobes are named for the skull bones that cover them), but the cortex is also divided in terms of function. These functional areas include the motor cortex (which controls movement), sensory cortex (which receives information from various senses), and association cortex (which integrates information). Also labeled are Wernicke's area and Broca's area, two regions that are found only on the left side of the cortex and that are vital to the interpretation and production of speech.

© photobank.ch/Shutterstock.com

motor cortex The part of the cerebral cortex whose neurons control voluntary movements in specific parts of the body.

In the frontal lobes, different specific neurons of the **motor cortex** control voluntary movements in each specific part of the body (Indovina & Sanes, 2001). The arrangement of the motor cortex is like that of the somatosensory cortex; the parts of the motor cortex that control hand movement are near parts of the sensory cortex that receive sensory information from the hands.

Seems easy, doesn't it? You have a map of your body parts in your cerebral cortex, and you activate cells in the hand region of the cortex if you want to move your hand. But, in fact, the process is quite complex. To grasp the handle of a coffeepot, for example, your cortex must first translate the pot's location into a position relative to your body—to your left or right, for example. Next, the cortex must determine which muscles must be contracted to produce the desired movement toward that exact position. Groups of neurons work together to produce just the right combinations of direction and force in particular muscle groups. Making these determinations involves many interconnected areas of the cortex, and the specific neurons involved can change over time (Gallivan, Cavina-Pratesi,

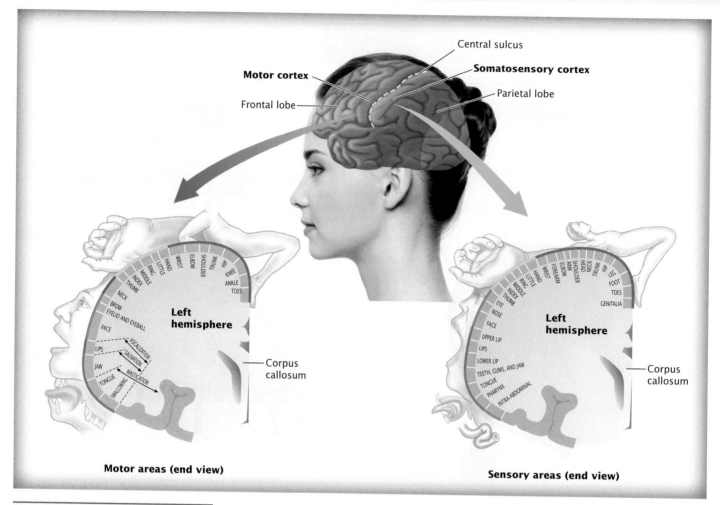

FIGURE 3.11

Motor and Somatosensory Cortex

The areas of the cortex that move parts of the body (motor cortex) and receive sensory input from body parts (somatosensory cortex) appear in both hemispheres of the brain. Here we show cross sections of only those on the left side, looking from the back of the brain toward the front. Areas receiving input from neighboring body parts, such as the lips and tongue, are near one another in the sensory cortex. Areas controlling movement of neighboring parts of the body, such as the foot and leg, occupy neighboring parts of the motor cortex. Notice that the size of these areas is uneven; the larger the area devoted to each body part, the larger that body part appears on the "homunculus."

Note: Did you notice the error in this classic drawing? The figure of the homunculus shows the right side of its body but its left hand and the left side of its face.

© Valua Vitaly/Shutterstock.com

& Culham, 2009; W. Wang et al., 2010). Computer models of neural networks show how these complex problem-solving processes might occur (Graziano, Taylor, & Moore, 2002; Krauzlis, 2002). ("In Review: Organization of the Brain" summarizes the major structures and functions of the brain.)

ORGANIZATION OF THE BRAIN
IN REVIEW

Major Division	Some Major Structures	Some Major Functions
Hindbrain	Medulla oblongata	Regulates breathing, heart rate, and blood pressure
	Reticular formation (also extends into midbrain)	Regulates alertness, arousal
	Cerebellum	Controls finely coordinated movements and certain cognitive processes
Midbrain	Various nuclei	Relays sensory signals to forebrain; creates automatic responses to certain stimuli, controls some aspects of eye movement

(continued)

ORGANIZATION OF THE BRAIN (CONT.)

Major Division	Some Major Structures	Some Major Functions
Forebrain	Thalamus	Interprets and relays sensory information
	Hypothalamus	Regulates hunger, thirst, and sex drives
	Amygdala	Connects certain sensations and emotions, especially with memory
	Hippocampus	Helps form new memories
	Cerebral cortex	Analyzes sensory information; controls voluntary movements, abstract thinking, and other complex cognitive activity
	Corpus callosum	Transfers information between the two cerebral hemispheres

In Review Questions

1. The oldest part of the brain is the _____.
2. Cells that operate as the body's twenty-four-hour "time clock" are found in the _____.
3. Memory problems seen in Alzheimer's disease are related to shrinkage of the _____.

Association Cortex

The parts of the cortex that do not directly receive specific sensory information or control specific movements are referred to as **association cortex.** The term *association* describes these areas well, because they receive input from more than one sense or input that combines sensory and motor information. For instance, these areas associate words with images. Association cortex appears in all lobes of the brain and forms a large percentage of the cerebral cortex in humans in particular. For this reason, damage to association areas can affect a wide range of mental abilities.

LINKAGES Where are the brain's language centers? (a link to Thought and Language)

Consider language. We rely on the auditory cortex to begin the process of understanding spoken language or the visual cortex for written language. Eventually, we need areas of the motor cortex to produce the speech or hand movements that express the language we want to get across. Putting all of this together in the complex activity known as language involves a network of neuron activity across many areas of association cortex. In the 1860s, a French surgeon named Paul Broca described the effects of damage to an area of association cortex in the left frontal lobe, near motor areas that control face muscles. This part of the cortex is now called *Broca's area* (see Figure 3.10). Damage to Broca's area causes *Broca's aphasia,* a language disorder where victims have difficulty getting words out, either by speaking or writing, and often making errors in grammar, though they can still understand fairly well the language that they hear or read.

Other language problems result from damage to a portion of association cortex described in the 1870s by a Polish neurologist named Carl Wernicke (pronounced "VER-nick-ee"). Figure 3.10 shows that, like Broca's area, *Wernicke's area* is on the left side of the brain, but it is in the temporal lobe, near the area of the sensory cortex that receives information from the ears. Wernicke's area also receives input from the visual cortex and is involved in the interpretation of both speech and written words. Damage to Wernicke's area produces complicated symptoms. Such patients have no hesitation to speak, but what they say often makes no sense, and they have a hard time understanding the meaning of words they hear or see.

association cortex The parts of the cerebral cortex that receive information from more than one sense or that combine sensory and motor information to perform complex cognitive tasks.

Language Areas of the Brain

TRY THIS Have you ever tried to write notes while you were talking to someone? You can probably write and talk at the same time because each of these language functions uses different association cortex areas. However, stop reading for a moment and try writing one word with your left hand and a different word with your right hand. If you had trouble, it is partly because you asked the same language area of your brain to do two things at once.

© iStockphoto.com/VikramRaghuvanshi

Case studies illustrate the different effects of damage to each area (Lapointe, 1990). In response to the request "Tell me what you do with a cigarette," a person with Wernicke's aphasia replied, "This is a segment of a pegment. Soap a cigarette." This speech came out easily, quickly, without effort, but without meaning. In response to the same request, a person with Broca's aphasia replied, "Uh.. uh.. cigarette [pause] smoke it." This speech was meaningful but not fluent; it was halting and awkwardly phrased. Surprisingly, when a person with Broca's aphasia sings, words may come easily and correctly. Apparently, words set to music are handled by one part of the brain and spoken words by another (Jeffries, Fritz, & Braun, 2003). Some speech therapists take advantage of this fact through "melodic intonation" therapy, which helps Broca's aphasia patients improve fluency by speaking in a singsong manner (Norton et al., 2009). This therapy is enhanced by noninvasive electrical stimulation of the right hemisphere, perhaps helping to compensate for damage to Broca's area in the left hemisphere (Vines, Norton, & Schlaug, 2011).

Other mental functions depend on somewhat different areas of association cortex. Areas in the *prefrontal cortex* at the front of the brain are involved in the complex processes necessary for the conscious control of thoughts and actions and for understanding our world (Fincham & Anderson, 2006; Koechlin & Hyafil, 2007). For example, these areas of association cortex allow us to understand sarcasm or irony—that is, when someone says one thing but means the opposite. In one study, people with prefrontal cortex damage listened to sarcastic stories such as this: "Joe came to work, and instead of beginning to work, he sat down to rest. His boss noticed his behavior and said, 'Joe, don't work too hard.'" Most people immediately realized that the boss was being sarcastic, but people with prefrontal brain damage did not (Shamay-Tsoory & Tomer, 2005).

FOCUS ON RESEARCH METHODS
THE CASE OF THE DISEMBODIED WOMAN

Neurologist Oliver Sacks described the case of "Christina," a woman who had somehow lost the ability to feel the position of her own body (Sacks, 1985). The case study gives important insights about biological aspects of psychology that could not be studied through controlled experiments. It shows, for example, that the sense known as *kinesthesia* (pronounced "kin-es-THEE-see-uh") not only tells us where our body parts are but also plays an important role in our sense of self.

Christina was a healthy young woman who entered a hospital in preparation for minor surgery. Before the surgery could be performed, however, she began to have difficulty holding onto objects. Then she had trouble moving. She would rise from bed and flop onto the floor like a rag doll. Christina seemed to have "lost" her body. She felt disembodied, like a ghost. On one occasion, for example, she became annoyed at a visitor for tapping her fingers on a tabletop. But it was Christina's fingers, not the visitor's, that were tapping. Her body was acting on its own, doing things she did not know about.

What was the researcher's question?

Christina could not walk or use her hands and arms. Why was a seemingly normal, healthy young woman falling and dropping things?

How did the researcher answer the question?

A psychiatrist at the hospital thought that Christina was suffering from *conversion disorder*, a condition in which psychological problems cause physical disabilities (see the chapter on psychological disorders). Unconvinced, Sacks studied Christina further.

What did the researcher find?

Sacks's examinations and tests revealed that Christina had lost all sensory feedback about her joints and muscle tone and the position of her limbs. She'd suffered a breakdown, or degeneration, of the sensory neurons that normally bring kinesthetic information to her brain. There was a biological reason that Christina could not walk or control her hands and arms.

(continued)

What do the results mean?

Sacks argued that the sense we have of our bodies is based not only partly on what we see but also partly on *proprioception* (sensing the self). Christina herself put it this way: "Proprioception is like the eyes of the body, the way the body sees itself. And if it goes, it's like the body's blind." With effort and determination, Christina eventually regained some ability to move about. For example, if she looked intently at her arms and legs, she could coordinate their movement more. She was able to leave the hospital and resume many normal activities, but Christina never recovered her sense of self. She still feels like a stranger in her own body.

What do we still need to know?

Notice that Christina's case study did not test any hypotheses about kinesthesia in the way an experiment might. It did, however, focus attention on how it feels to have lost this sense. It also highlighted a rare condition that, seldom discussed before Sacks reported it, has been observed more often in recent years, especially among people taking an excess of vitamin B6, also known as *pyridoxine*. Too much of this vitamin can damage sensory neurons (Dordain & Deffond, 1994). How and why vitamin B6 does such damage is unknown. Are there other causes of such a kinesthetic disorder? What treatments might best help? These questions remain to be answered.

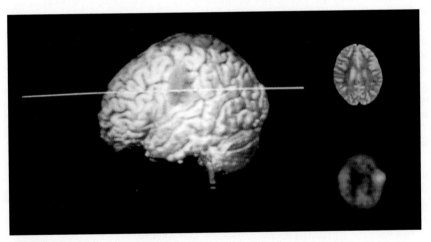

FIGURE 3.12

Combining a PET Scan and Magnetic Resonance Imaging

Researchers have superimposed images from PET scans and MRI to construct a three-dimensional view of the living brain. Here you can see the brain of a young girl with epilepsy. The picture of the outer surface of the brain is from the MRI. The pink area is from the PET scan and shows the source of epileptic activity. The images at the right are the MRI and PET images at one plane, or "slice," through the brain (indicated by the line on the brain at the left).

D. N. Levin, H. Xiaoping, K. K. Tan, S. Galhotra, C. A. Palizzare, G. T. Y. Chen, R. N. Beck, C. T. Chen, M. D. Cooper, J. F. Mullan, J. Hekmatpanah, & J. P. Spire (1989). The Brain: Integrated three-dimensional display of MR and PET images. Radiology, 172: 783-789.

Exporing the Brain

A variety of new techniques, combined with some older measures, give scientists ever better ways to study the brain and its activity (see Table 3.1). Each has different advantages and disadvantages. One of the earliest techniques, called the *electroencephalograph (EEG)*, measures general electrical activity of the brain. Electrodes are pasted on the scalp to detect the electrical fields resulting from the activity of billions of neurons (Figure 9.3 in the consciousness chapter shows how EEG can be used to record brain activity during sleep). Although this tool can associate rapidly changing electrical activity with changes in the activity of some brain surfaces, it cannot tell us exactly where the active cells are, and it can only reflect the activity of brain cells closest to the scalp.

A more recent technique, *PET* (for *positron emission tomography*), tries to locate brain cell activity by recording where radioactive blood sugar becomes concentrated after it is injected into the bloodstream. PET brain images show where the radioactive glucose goes in the brain as a person performs various tasks. Since the brain cells that fire action potentials should use the most glucose, PET brain scans essentially show which brain cells were most active during a task. For instance, PET studies have revealed that specific brain regions are activated when we look at fearful facial expressions or hear fearful voices (Pourtois et al., 2005) and that activity in these brain areas is modified in people with posttraumatic stress disorder (Murrough et al., 2011). PET scans can tell us a lot about where changes in brain activity occur, but they can't reveal details of the brain's physical structure.

Fortunately, we can get a detailed structural picture of what the brain physically looks like using *magnetic resonance imaging,* or *MRI*. MRI exposes the brain to a magnetic field and measures the resulting radiofrequency waves to make amazingly clear pictures of the brain's anatomical details (see Figure 3.12). *Functional MRI,* or *fMRI*, combines some advantages of PET and MRI, by detecting changes in blood flow and blood oxygen that suggest how active neurons are in each area of the brain, providing a sort of "moving picture" of brain functioning.

TABLE 3.1   TECHNIQUES FOR STUDYING HUMAN BRAIN FUNCTION AND STRUCTURE

Techniques	What It Shows	Advantages	Disadvantages
EEG (electroencephalograph) Electrodes are pasted to the outside of the head.	Lines that chart the summated electrical fields resulting from the activity of billions of neurons.	Detects very rapid changes in electrical activity, allowing analysis of stages of cognitive processing.	Poor spatial resolution of the source of electrical activity. Can only measure some brain activity.
PET (positron emission tomography) and SPECT (single-photon emission computed tomography) Radioactive substances, injected into the bloodstream, indicate activity in the brain.	An image of the amount and localization of any molecule that can be injected in radioactive form, such as neurotransmitters, drugs, or tracers for blood flow or glucose use (indicating specific changes in neuronal activity).	Allows functional and biochemical studies. Provides visual image corresponding to anatomy.	Requires exposure to low levels of radioactivity. Spatial resolution is better than EEG but poorer than MRI. Cannot follow rapid changes (faster than thirty seconds).
MRI (magnetic resonance imaging) A magnetic field measures radio frequency waves in the brain.	Traditional MRI provides high-resolution image of brain anatomy. Functional MRI (fMRI) provides images of changes in blood flow that indicate specific changes in neural activity. Another variant of MRI, diffusion tensor imaging (DTI), shows water flow in neural fibers, revealing the "wiring diagram" of neural connections in the brain.	Requires no exposure to radioactivity. Provides high spatial resolution of anatomical details (smaller than 1 mm). Provides high temporal resolution (less than one-tenth of a second).	Not safe for individuals with certain metals in their bodies, such as a pacemaker.
TMS (transcranial magnetic stimulation) Temporarily affects electrical activity of a small region of brain by exposing it to an intense magnetic field.	Studies normal function of a particular brain region by observing changes after TMS is applied to a specific location.	Shows which brain regions are necessary for given tasks.	Long-term safety not well established.
Optogenetics Genes are inserted into neurons to allow channels in the cell membranes to open or close in response to light, thus making action potentials more, or less, likely.	Allows scientists to manipulate brain activity by turning cells on or off by pointing a light on a brain area of interest	Shows how a person functions with or without the use of specific brain areas.	Long-term safety not well established. Invasive technique; requires placing genes into brain cells.

The newest techniques offer even deeper insight into brain activity, structure, and functioning. These techniques include a variant on fMRI called *diffusion tensor imaging (DTI)*, which traces the activity of axon pathways, and a procedure called *transcranial magnetic stimulation (TMS)*, which sets up magnetic fields outside the brain. These magnetic fields can either stimulate or disrupt neural activity (Glenberg, 2011; Lagopoulos & Malhi, 2008). Some researchers are studying brain functions by combining fMRI and TMS. For example, when one brain region is stimulated by TMS, and changes in activity are detected by fMRI in another region, this indicates that the two regions are functionally connected. Similarly, if the ability to perform a certain behavior is affected when TMS disrupts activity in a certain brain region, this suggests that the behavior is somehow controlled or influenced by that brain region (Muggleton, 2010). TMS may also have unexpected value in the treatment of depression and migraine headaches (O'Reardon et al., 2007).

A new technique, *optogenetics*, involves inserting genes of light-sensitive plants into brain cells of animals (Airan et al., 2009). The modified cells have channels in their cell membranes that open or close in response to light (Boyden et al., 2005; Wietek et al., 2014). The scientist then uses special lights that can actually penetrate through the skull and into the brain. When light strikes the genetically modified cells, their membrane channels allow electrically charged atoms to flow into or out of the cell. The result is that the cell becomes more or less likely to fire an action potential. In effect, the scientist can "turn on" or "turn off" brain cells just by shining a light on them! The results can be fascinating. For example, optogenetic work with mice has demonstrated that activating neurons within the hippocampus can create false memories; the mice remember things that never happened (Ramirez et al., 2013). Optogenetics has also begun to show how activity in certain brain areas may create or reduce psychological problems such as anxiety (Kim et al., 2013), and it holds promise for giving physicians new ways to treat diseases such as epilepsy (Bentley et al., 2013; Sukhotinsky et al., 2013).

THINKING CRITICALLY

WHAT CAN FMRI TELL US ABOUT BEHAVIOR AND MENTAL PROCESSES?

A picture may be worth a thousand words, but the pictures of brain activity offered by fMRI are generating millions of them. As of 2014, several thousand scientific articles have reported the results of fMRI scans taken while people engaged in various kinds of thinking or experienced various emotions. Neuroscientists who use brain-imaging techniques can now be found in psychology departments around the world, and, as described in other chapters, their work is changing the research landscape in cognitive, social, and abnormal psychology. Excitement over fMRI is not confined to scientists, however. Popular and scientific magazines routinely carry fMRI pictures that seem to "show" people's thoughts and feelings as they happen, and readers see claims made in these articles as more believable than those based on other kinds of data (Beck, 2010; McCabe & Castel, 2008). This may be one reason why some companies are able to make money by offering brain imaging services that can supposedly improve the quality of employee selection, lie detection, political campaign strategies, product design, and diagnosis of mental disorders (e.g., Ariely & Berns, 2010; Falk, Berkman, & Lieberman, 2012; Morin, 2011). Jurors, too, find evidence from fMRI scans extremely persuasive (McCabe, Castel, & Rhodes, 2011), even though research shows that it is not an effective method for detecting deception (Adelsheim, 2011; Ganis, et al., 2011). The editor of one scientific journal summed up this trend by saying that "a picture is worth a thousand dollars" (Farah, 2009).

What am I being asked to believe or accept?

In the early 1800s, similar excitement surrounded *phrenology*, a technique that involved measuring the bumps and depressions on the skull. It was claimed that these contours reflected the size of twenty-seven structures on the brain's surface that determine personality traits, mental abilities, talents, and other characteristics. Although wildly popular with the public (Benjamin & Baker, 2004), phrenology did not survive the critical thinking of nineteenth-century scientists, and the technique has long been discredited. Some scientists wonder whether fMRI is a twenty-first-century version of phrenology, at least in the sense that people might be accepting its value too readily. These scientists point out that although fMRI images can indicate where brain activity occurs as people think and experience emotion, there is no guarantee that this activity is *causing* the thoughts and feelings (Aldridge, 2005). Perhaps brain areas change their activity as a *reaction* to thoughts and feelings. Moreover, could it be that a brain area contributes to a mental task by changing how its nerve cells work, not whether they work more or less? Such questions challenge the assumption that increased energy use by a cell means that the cell is doing a more important job in support of some psychological function. These functions may not even "occur" in a particular brain structure or set of structures. It is easy to talk about "thinking" or "attention," but these psychological terms might not

(continued)

correspond to single biological processes that can be isolated and located by *any* technology (Miller, 2010). In short, critics claim that the results of fMRI scans can be misleading and that they don't necessarily tell us much about how the mind works (Uttal, 2003). Some believe that it would be better to focus on *how* the brain produces thoughts and feelings instead of searching for their locations (Poldrack, 2010).

What evidence is available to support the assertion?

When a participant in an fMRI experiment thinks or feels something, the colors in the scanned image of the brain change, much like the color changes you see on weather radar as a rainstorm intensifies or weakens. Looking at an fMRI scan, you see the brain areas that "light up" when a person experiences an emotion or performs a mental task are presumed to be the ones involved in that emotion or task.

These scans are not as precise as they seem, though, because fMRI doesn't measure brain cell activity directly. The colors shown in an fMRI scan reflect the flow of blood in the brain and the amount of oxygen the blood is carrying. Changes in blood flow and blood oxygen are *related* to changes in the firing rates of neurons (Kahn et al., 2013), but the relationship is complex; for example, the relationship differs from one brain region to another (Devonshire et al., 2011) and changes with age (Mohtasib et al., 2011). And changes in an fMRI signal can depend on how much neural firing was taking place before a stimulus appeared (Maandag et al., 2007; Perthen et al., 2008). Further, when brain cells process information, their firing rates may either increase or decrease (Gonsalves et al., 2005). If the increases and decreases in a particular brain region happen to cancel each other out, an fMRI scan will miss the neuronal activity taking place in that region (Glenberg, 2011). In fact, compared with the direct measurement of brain cell activity that can be done in research with animals, fMRI technology is still quite crude. It takes coordinated changes in millions of neurons to produce a detectable change in the fMRI signal.

Critics also argue that results of fMRI research can vary too much based on how experimenters interpret them. In a typical fMRI experiment, participants see some kind of display, such as pairs of photos, and then do various tasks. One task might be to press a button if the photos are exactly the same. A second task might be to press the button if objects in the photos are arranged in the same way. In this second task, a participant should press the button if one photo shows, say, a short man standing to the left of a tall woman and the other photo shows a small dog standing to the left of a giraffe. Both versions of the task require the participant to compare two images, but only the second of them requires considering whether things that look different are actually similar in some way. The fMRI scans taken during these tasks might show certain brain areas "lighting up" only during the second task. If so, the researcher would suggest that those areas are involved in recognizing *analogies*, or the similarities between apparently different things (Wharton et al., 2000). The researcher would base this conclusion on a computer program that compares fMRI scans taken during two tasks, subtracts all the "lighted" areas that are the same in both scans, and keeps only those that are different. But what the computer classifies as "different" depends on a rule that is set by the experimenter. If the experimenter programs the computer to display only big differences between the scans, not many "lit up" areas will remain after the comparison process. But if even tiny differences are allowed to count as "different," many more "lighted" areas will remain after the subtraction process. In our example, then, there could be large or small areas apparently associated with recognizing analogies, all depending on a rule set by the researcher.

These problems aside, critics wonder what it really means when fMRI research shows that certain brain areas appear activated during certain kinds of tasks or experiences. Their concern focuses on studies, such as one from the new field of *neuroeconomics*, which suggests that the neural basis of bad investment decisions is due to higher activity in a particular area of the brain (Kuhnen & Knutson, 2005). Other studies have used fMRI to identify the neural activity associated with trust, religious belief, political liberalism or conservatism, and even love (Amodio et al., 2007; Kapogiannis et al., 2009; Krueger et al., 2007). In this last study, on "the neural basis of romantic love" (Bartels & Zeki, 2000), investigators scanned people's brains as they looked at pictures of their romantic partners and compared these

(continued)

scans to those taken while the same people viewed nonromantic friends. According to the "difference" rule established by the experimenters, four brain areas were more active when viewing a romantic loved one than when viewing a friend. However, these same brain regions are active in many different emotions, so does the activity tell us anything specific about the neural basis of love? Critics of fMRI would say no.

Are there alternative ways of interpreting the evidence?

Supporters of fMRI disagree with those critics. They believe that the colorful areas seen on fMRI scans can provide information to answer important questions about behavior and mental processes. They point, for example, to fMRI research on brain mechanisms that help us appreciate what other people are feeling—that is, to experience empathy—and to learn by watching others.

These *mirror neuron mechanisms* were discovered accidentally by scientists who had been using surgical techniques to directly record the activity of monkeys' brain cells (Caggiano et al., 2009; Rizzolatti et al., 1996). They found that neurons in an area called F5 are activated not only when a monkey plans to reach for an object, such as a peanut, but also if the monkey sees an *experimenter* reach for a peanut (Glenberg, 2011)! After fMRI scanning became available, researchers could begin looking for mirror mechanisms in the human brain, and they did so with gusto: since 2003, more than 190 studies have used fMRI to study the mirror system in humans (Molenberghs et al., 2012). And in fact, some of the mirror systems they found in humans correspond to the F5 region in monkeys (Fizzolatti & Arbib, 1998) They are in other brain regions, too (Mukamel et al., 2010). One of them is *Broca's* area which, as described earlier, is an important component of our ability to speak. It makes sense that Broca's area contains a mirror mechanism, because language is a skill that we learn partly by imitation. The new fMRI findings suggest that Broca's area may also be important for many other skills that involve imitation. One study found that this area "lights up" when a guitar student learns chords by watching a professional guitarist (Buccino et al., 2004). Other fMRI research has found that mirror systems in other parts of the brain become active when a person sees someone experiencing emotion. For example, the brain area that is activated when you experience disgust (e.g., from the smell of rotten eggs) is also activated if you see a video in which someone else reacts to a smell with disgust (Wicker et al., 2003).

So fMRI can be uniquely useful, say its defenders. Without it, research on mirror neurons in humans could not have taken place. And because of it, we have evidence that the experience of empathy comes about because seeing the actions and emotions of others activates the same brain regions that would be active if we were doing or feeling the same things ourselves. Some fMRI studies have also found that malfunctioning mirror mechanisms are associated with the impairments in language development, imitative skills, and empathy seen in children diagnosed with autistic spectrum disorders (Dapretto et al., 2006; Perkins et al., 2010). Are all mirror functions affected in autistic spectrum disorders or just the emotional functions? This question is still being debated (Hamilton, 2013; see the chapter on psychological disorders).

What additional evidence would help evaluate the alternatives?

As technology continues to be refined, the quality of fMRI scans will improve, giving better images of where brain activity may occur. But the value of this scanning technology will depend on understanding of what it can and cannot tell us about how brain activity is related to behavior and mental processes. We also need more evidence about correlation and causation in fMRI research. For example, one study conducted fMRI scans on compulsive gamblers as they played a simple guessing game (Reuter et al., 2005). When they won the game, these people showed an unusually small amount of activity in a brain area that is normally activated by the experience of rewards, or pleasure. Noting the correlation between compulsive gambling and lower than normal activity in the reward area, the researchers suggested that an abnormality in the brain's reward mechanisms might be responsible for gambling addiction. But case studies also suggest that compulsive gambling appears in people taking a prescription drug that *increases* activity in reward areas—and that the gambling stops when the drug is discontinued (Abler et al., 2009; Cilia et al., 2008; Ferrara & Stacy, 2008).

(continued)

Exploring Brain Functions with fMRI

As a research participant performs a mental task, a functional magnetic resonance imaging scanner records blood flow and blood oxygen levels in her brain. The resulting computer analysis shows as "lit up" areas the parts of the brain that appear to be activated during the task, but critics doubt that fMRI scanning is as clear or accurate as its proponents suggest.

Image courtesy of Brad Sutton, Beckman Institute Biomedical Imaging Center, University of Illinois at Urbana-Champaign

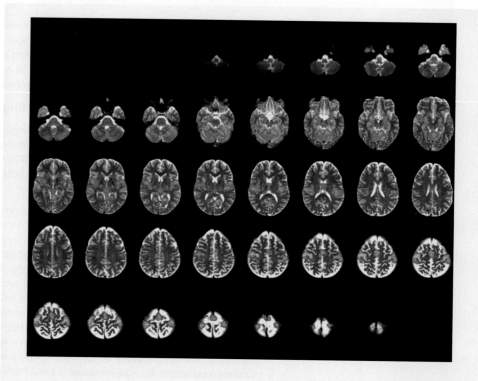

As noted in the research in psychology chapter, correlation does not guarantee causation. Is the brain activity reflected in fMRI scans causing the thoughts and feelings that take place during the scanning process? Possibly, but those thoughts and feelings might themselves be *caused* by activity elsewhere in the brain that affects the areas being scanned. The transcranial magnetic stimulation (TMS) and optogenetic procedures mentioned earlier might help identify causal versus correlational relationships in the brain. These methods temporarily disrupt neural activity in brain regions identified by fMRI as related to a particular kind of thought or feeling, so perhaps scientists can determine if those thoughts or feelings are temporarily disrupted when TMS or optogenetic activity occurs.

What conclusions are most reasonable?

A full understanding of fMRI requires continuing dialogue between those who dismiss the technique and those who sing its praises. To make this dialogue easier, a group of government agencies and private foundations has funded an fMRI Data Center (http://www.nitrc.org /projects/fmridatacenter). This facility stores information from fMRI experiments and makes it available to both critics and supporters of fMRI, who can review the research data, conduct their own analyses, and offer their own interpretations.

Such a process has been seen before in biological psychology. For example, when the EEG was invented in the 1920s, scientists had their first glimpse of brain cell activity, as reflected in the "brain waves" traced on a long sheet of paper rolling from the EEG machine. To many of these scientists, EEG must have seemed like a golden gateway to an understanding of the brain and its relationship to behavior and mental processes. EEG has, in fact, helped advance knowledge of the brain, but it certainly didn't solve all of its mysteries. The same will probably be true of fMRI. It is an exciting tool, and it offers previously undreamed-of images of brain structure and functioning, but it is unlikely on its own to explain just how the brain creates our behavior and mental processes. It seems reasonable to conclude, then, that those who question the use of fMRI to study psychological processes are right in calling for a careful analysis of the value of this important high-tech tool.

Although the meaning of fMRI data will remain a subject for debate, there is no doubt that brain-scanning techniques in general have opened new frontiers for biological psychology, neuroscience, and medicine. Much of our growing understanding of how and why behavior and mental processes occur is coming from research with these techniques (Poldrack, Halchenko, & Hanson, 2009).

The Divided Brain: Lateralization

A striking idea emerged from observations of people with damage to the language areas of the brain. Researchers noticed that when damage was limited to areas of the left hemisphere, there were impairments in the ability to use or understand language. Damage to corresponding parts of the right hemisphere usually did not have these effects. Could it be that the right and left halves of the brain serve different functions?

This concept was not entirely new. It had long been understood, for example, that most skin sensation and motor pathways cross over as they enter or leave the brain. As a result, the left hemisphere receives information from and controls movements of the right side of the body, and the right hemisphere receives input from and controls the left side of the body. However, both sides of the brain perform these functions. The fact that language areas, such as Broca's area and Wernicke's area, are found almost exclusively on the left side of the brain suggested that each hemisphere might show **lateralization**, also known as *lateral dominance*. That is, each might be specialized to perform some functions more efficiently than, and almost independently of, the other hemisphere (Stephan et al., 2003).

Split-Brain Studies

As far back as the late 1800s, scientists had wanted to test the hypothesis that the cerebral hemispheres might be specialized, but they had no techniques for doing so. Then, during the 1960s, Roger Sperry, Michael Gazzaniga, and their colleagues began to study *split-brain* patients—people who had undergone a surgical procedure in an attempt to control severe epilepsy. Before the surgery, their seizures began in one hemisphere and then spread to engulf the whole brain. As a last resort, surgeons isolated the two hemispheres from each other by severing the corpus callosum, the massive bundle of axons that connects the two hemispheres (see Figure 3.13).

After the surgery, researchers used a special apparatus to present visual images to only one side of these patients' split brains (see Figure 3.14). They found that severing the tie between the hemispheres had dramatically affected the way these people thought about and dealt with the world. For example, when the image of a spoon was presented to the left, language-oriented side of one patient's split brain, she could say what the spoon was; but when the spoon was presented to the right side of her brain, she could not describe the spoon in words. She still knew what it was, however. Using her left hand (controlled by the right hemisphere), she could pick out the spoon from a group of other objects by its shape. But when asked what she had just grasped, she replied, "A pencil." The right hemisphere recognized the object, but the patient could not describe it because the left (language) half of her brain did not see or feel it (Sperry, 1968).

Although the right hemisphere has no control over spoken language in split-brain patients, it does have important capabilities, including some related to nonspoken language. For example, a split-brain patient's right hemisphere can guide the left hand in spelling out words with Scrabble tiles (Gazzaniga & LeDoux, 1978). Thanks to this ability, researchers discovered that the right hemisphere of split-brain patients has self-awareness and normal learning abilities. In addition, it is superior to the left hemisphere on tasks dealing with spatial relations (especially drawing three-dimensional shapes) and at recognizing human faces.

Lateralization of Normal Brains

Sperry (1974) concluded from his studies that each hemisphere in the split-brain patient has its own "private sensations, perceptions, thoughts, and ideas all of which are cut off from the corresponding experiences in the opposite hemisphere. . . . In many respects each disconnected hemisphere appears to have a separate 'mind of its own'" (p. 7). But what about people whose hemispheres are connected normally? Are certain of their functions, such as mathematical reasoning or language skills, lateralized?

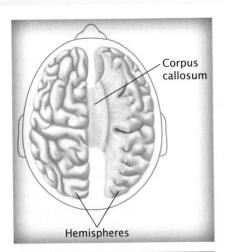

FIGURE 3.13
The Brain's Left and Right Hemispheres

Corpus callosum

Hemispheres

The brain's two hemispheres are joined by a core bundle of nerve fibers known as the *corpus callosum*. In this figure, the hemispheres are separated to reveal the corpus callosum. The two cerebral hemispheres look nearly the same but perform somewhat different tasks. For one thing, the left hemisphere receives sensory input from and controls movement on the right side of the body. The right hemisphere senses and controls the left side of the body.

lateralization (lateral dominance) The tendency for one cerebral hemisphere to excel at a particular function or skill compared with the other hemisphere.

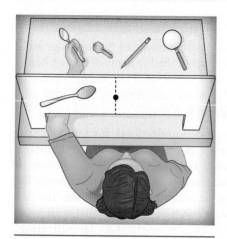

FIGURE 3.14
**Apparatus for Studying
Split-Brain Patients**

When the person stares at a dot in the center of the screen, images briefly presented on one side of the screen go to only one side of the brain. For example, a picture of a spoon presented on the left side of the screen goes to the right side of the brain. The right side of the brain can find the spoon and direct the left hand to touch it. However, because the language areas on the left side of the brain did not see the spoon, the person is unable to say what it is.

To find out, researchers presented images to just one hemisphere of people with normal brains and then measured how fast they could analyze information. If information is presented to one side of the brain, and if that side is specialized to analyze that type of information, a person's responses will be faster than if the information must first be transferred to the other hemisphere for analysis. These studies have confirmed that the left hemisphere has better language abilities than the right, whereas the right hemisphere has better spatial, artistic, and musical abilities (Springer & Deutsch, 1989).

Having two somewhat specialized hemispheres allows the brain to be more efficient in performing some tasks, particularly difficult ones, but the differences between the hemispheres should not be exaggerated. The corpus callosum usually integrates the functions of the "two brains," a role that is particularly important in tasks that require sustained attention (Rueckert et al., 1999). As a result, the hemispheres work so closely together, and each makes up so well for whatever lack of ability the other may have, that people are normally unaware that their brains are made up of two partly independent, somewhat specialized halves (Banich, 2009; Staudt et al., 2001).

Plasticity in the Central Nervous System

The central nervous system has a remarkable property called **neural plasticity** (also known as *neuroplasticity* or simply *plasticity*), which is the ability to strengthen neural connections at synapses as well as to establish new connections (Choquet & Triller, 2013). Plasticity depends partly on neurons and partly on glial cells (Lee & Silva, 2009), and it occurs throughout the central nervous system. Plasticity appears in the spinal cord, where simple reflexes can be modified by life experiences (Wolpaw & Chen, 2006), and also in the brain, where the connections between neurons are not only highly changeable but can change in a fraction of a second (Bikbaev & Manahan-Vaughan, 2008; Stettler et al., 2006). Plasticity in the brain is the basis of our ability to form new memories and learn new things (Ho, Lee, & Martin, 2011; Roberts et al., 2010). For example, more cells in the brain's motor cortex become involved in controlling hand movements in people who have learned to play a musical instrument. The process can be seen in brain-imaging studies; as non-musicians get better at making rhythmic finger movements, the amount of motor cortex devoted to this task increases (Munte, Altenmuller, & Jancke, 2002). MRI studies of individuals who were learning to juggle found an increase in the density of cortical regions associated with processing visual information about moving objects (Draganski et al., 2004).

Even more amazing is that merely *imagining* practicing these movements causes changes in the motor cortex (Pascual-Leone, 2001). Athletes have long engaged in exercises in which they visualize skilled sports movements; brain-imaging research reveals that this "mental practice" can change the brain (Olsson et al., 2008). Among trained opera singers, similar changes have been observed in brain areas that control vocalization (Kleber et al., 2010). Given the impact of these specific experiences, it is no wonder that more general cultural experiences, such as growing up in a collectivist versus individualist culture, can also affect the development of a person's brain (Park & Huang, 2010).

Repairing Brain Damage

There are limits to plasticity, though, especially in repairing damage in the brain and spinal cord. Unlike the skin or the liver, the adult central nervous system does not automatically replace damaged cells. As a result, most victims of severe stroke, Parkinson's disease, Alzheimer's disease, or spinal cord injury are permanently disabled in some way. Scientists are searching for ways to help a damaged central nervous system heal some of its own wounds.

One approach has been to transplant, or graft, tissue from the still-developing brain of a fetus into the brain of an adult animal. If the receiving animal doesn't reject

neural plasticity The ability to create new synapses and to change the strength of synapses.

it, the graft may send axons out into the brain and make functional connections. This treatment has reversed some animals learning difficulties, movement disorders, and other results of brain damage (Noble, 2000). The technique has also been used to treat a small number of people with Parkinson's disease—a disorder characterized by tremors, rigidity of the arms and legs, and poor balance (Barker et al., 2013). Some patients showed improvement for several years, though improvement faded for others, and some patients had serious side effects (Freed et al., 2001). Brain tissue transplants in humans are controversial because they require using tissue from aborted fetuses. As an alternative, some scientists have tried transplanting neural tissue from another species, such as pigs, into humans (Drucker-Colin & Verdugo-Diaz, 2004). Russian physicians even transplanted neural tissue from fruit flies into the brains of Parkinson's patients. The results helped, and there were no immediate side effects (Saveliev et al., 1997), but the patients' bodies eventually rejected the fruit fly neurons (Korochkin, 2000).

The most promising source of new neurons may be an individual's own tissues because these cells would not be rejected. This is a revolutionary idea, because it was once believed that after humans reached adulthood, the cells of the central nervous system stopped dividing, leaving each of us with a fixed set of neurons (Rakic, 2002). Then came research showing that adult cell division *can* take place in certain limited circumstances in the adult central nervous systems (Braun & Jessberger, 2014). This capacity exists because the adult human brain has some *neural stem cells*, a special kind of glial cells that are capable of dividing to form new tissue, including new neurons (English et al., 2013; Gage & Temple, 2013; Hsu et al., 2013). The process of creating new neurons is called *neurogenesis*.

This discovery has created both excitement and controversy. There is excitement because stem cells raise hope that damaged tissue may someday be replaced by cells created from a person's own body. There is controversy because it was at first believed that these stem cells could come only from human embryos, which must be destroyed in the process of harvesting the cells. That ethical concern is abating, however, now that researchers have demonstrated that stem cells can be harvested from a person's own bone marrow, the lining of the nose, skin cells, and other places (Vierbuchen et al., 2010), and then made to grow into brain cells. It has even been claimed that a simple acid bath can make body cells in an adult mouse revert back to simpler stem cells (Obokata et al., 2014a, 2014b). This claim has been under severe scrutiny (Cyranoski, 2014), but if validated—and proven successful in humans—the technique could provide an easy way to create completely compatible stem cells for anyone. The benefits of using stem cells in treating brain disorders could be substantial, especially for patients with spinal cord injuries, Parkinson's disease, and Alzheimer's disease (Karimi-Abdolrezaee & Eftekharpour, 2013; Nishimura & Takahashi, 2013; Wojda & Kuznicki, 2013).

There is still a long way to go before any of these experimental strategies can be routinely used in the clinic (Lindvall & Kokaia, 2010), and in any case, successfully generating new neurons is only half the battle. New cells' axons and dendrites would have to reestablish all the synaptic connections that had been lost to damage or disease. They may be able to do this (Weick, Liu, & Zhang, 2011), but the process is hampered in the central nervous system by glial cells that actively suppress new connections between newly sprouted axons and other neurons (Olson, 1997). Several central nervous system proteins, including one aptly named *Nogo*, have the same suppressant effect.

Despite these challenges, research is progressing to promote healing in damaged brains and spinal cords. For example, blocking the action of Nogo in mice and rats with spinal cord injuries allows surviving neurons to make new axonal connections and repair the damage (Harvey et al., 2009; Kastin & Pan, 2005). Other research with animals has shown that both spontaneous recovery and the effectiveness of brain-tissue transplants can be greatly enhanced by naturally occurring proteins

called *growth factors*, which promote the survival of neurons (Wu et al., 2009). Other scientists have begun to experiment with implantation of specially engineered neurons to encourage greater neuroplasticity (Boyden, 2011; Knöpfel et al., 2010; Li et al., 2011).

There are also things that patients themselves can do to promote the neural plasticity needed to restore lost central nervous system functions. Special mental and physical exercise programs appear useful in restructuring communication in the brains of stroke victims and spinal cord injury patients, thus reversing some forms of paralysis and improving some sensory and cognitive abilities (Bryck & Fisher, 2012; Kao et al., 2009).

He Was a Super Man

After suffering a spinal cord injury in 1995, *Superman* actor Christopher Reeve was told he would never again be able to move or feel his body. He refused to accept this gloomy prediction, and after years of devoted adherence to an exercise-oriented rehabilitation program, he regained some movement, and by the time of his death in 2004, he was able to feel sensations from most of his body (Blakeslee, 2002). Physicians and physical therapists hope to make such therapy programs even more effective in the future (Dunlop, 2008; Raineteau, 2008).

Neville Elder/Corbis

LINKAGES How do our brains change over a lifetime? (a link to Human Development)

LINKAGES

HUMAN DEVELOPMENT AND THE CHANGING BRAIN

Fortunately, most of the changes that take place in the brain are not the kind associated with damage and disease. How does the human brain change as we develop throughout our lives? Researchers are using PET and fMRI scans to begin to answer that question. For example, they have found that association areas of the cerebral cortex develop later than the sensory and motor cortexes do (Casey, Galvan, & Hare, 2005). There are also some interesting correlations between changes in neural activity and the behavior of newborns and infants. Among newborns, scans show that activity is relatively high in the thalamus but low in a portion of the forebrain related to smooth movement. This finding may be related to the way newborns move. They make random, sweeping movements of the arms and legs—much like patients with Huntington's disease, who have a hyperactive thalamus and a withering of the part of the forebrain that controls smooth movement (Chugani & Phelps, 1986). During the second and third months after birth, activity increases in many regions of the cortex. This change is correlated with the disappearance of certain reflexes, such as the grasping reflex. At eight or nine months of age, infants show increased frontal cortex activity, which correlates with the apparent beginnings of cognitive activity (Chugani & Phelps, 1986).

The brain continues to mature through adolescence, showing evidence of ever-more-efficient neural communication in its major fiber tracts (Gogtay et al., 2004; Lebel & Beaulieu, 2011; Thompson et al., 2000). However, research using diffusion tensor imaging reveals that the connections between the prefrontal cortex and other areas involved in judgment and decision making are not yet fully developed (Asato et al., 2010). Some researchers suggest that these underdeveloped connections may be related to the difficulties that many teenagers have in resisting dangerous peer influences and foreseeing the negative consequences of certain actions (Grosbras et al., 2007). These ideas are supported by fMRI studies of adolescents that correlate self-reports of poor impulse control with reduced activation of the lateral prefrontal cortex (Andrews-Hanna et al., 2011).

Most of the changes we have described reflect plasticity—changes in axons and synapses—not the appearance of new cells. After birth, the number of dendrites and synapses increases. Although different areas of the cortex sprout at different rates, the number of synapses can increase tenfold in the first year after birth (Huttenlocher, 1990). In fact, by the time children are six or seven years old, their brains have more dendrites than those of adults, and they use twice as much energy. In early adolescence, the number of dendrites and neural connections actually drops, so that the adult level is reached by about the age of fourteen. During childhood, the brain overproduces neural connections and then "prunes" the extra

(continued)

connections (Sowell et al., 2001). Figure 3.15 shows that as we grow, we develop more brain-power with less brain (Sowell et al., 2003).

FIGURE 3.15
Developmental Changes in the Cerebral Cortex

During childhood, the brain overproduces neural connections, establishes the usefulness of certain connections, and then "prunes" the extra connections. Overproduction of synapses, especially in the frontal cortex, may be essential for infants to develop certain intellectual abilities. The changes that occur in the brain during adolescence are particularly important, as this is when many psychiatric disorders first appear (Paus, Keshavan, & Giedd, 2008). Adolescence is also a time of adjusting to and (sometimes) resisting negative peer influences. Research suggests that functional connectivity among brain regions in early adolescence is correlated with resisting such influences (Grosbras et al., 2007).

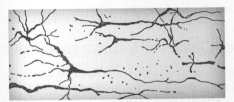

At birth

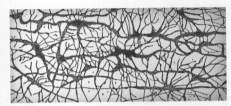

Six years old

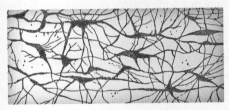

Fourteen years old

As already mentioned, the brain's plasticity allows it to restructure itself to form new connections throughout life (Hua & Smith, 2004; Kozorovitskiy et al., 2005). Genes apparently determine the basic pattern of growth and the major lines of connections. However, the details of the connections depend on experience, including how stimulating and interesting the environment is. For example, researchers have compared the brains of rats raised individually with only a boring view of their cages to the brains of rats raised with toys and playmates. The cerebral cortex of the rats from the enriched environment had more and longer dendrites as well as more synapses than did the cortex of animals raised alone in bare cages (Klintsova & Greenough, 1999). Furthermore, the number of synapses increased when old animals who had been living in boring cages were moved to an enriched environment. Such changes in the brain following increased environmental stimulation may help explain why the maze-learning ability of genetically "maze-dull" rats raised in stimulating cages can equal that of genetically "maze-bright" animals.

Researchers have not yet determined whether an enriched environment stimulates the development of new connections or slows down normal pruning. Also not known is whether animals that are moved from a stimulating environment to a boring one will lose synaptic connections. If existing findings apply to humans, however, they have implications for how we raise children and treat the elderly. It is surely the case that within the limits set by genetics, interactions with the world mold the brain itself (Chang & Merzenich, 2003; Dick et al., 2011; Holtmaat et al., 2006).

THE CHEMISTRY OF PSYCHOLOGY: NEUROTRANSMITTERS

How do biochemicals affect my mood?

We have already seen that neurons in the nervous system communicate with each other through chemical messengers called neurotransmitters. The neurotransmitters they use can differ from one set of nerve cells to another. A group of neurons that communicate using the same neurotransmitter is called a *neurotransmitter system*.

Promoting Research on Parkinson's Disease

Actor Michael J. Fox suffers from Parkinson's disease, a condition related to malfunctioning of dopamine systems in the brain. He founded the Michael J. Fox Foundation for Parkinson's Research to fund more research on treating, curing, and perhaps even preventing, Parkinson's disease.

Kevin Mazur/MJF/Getty Images

Certain neurotransmitter systems play a dominant role in particular functions, such as emotion or memory, and in particular problems, such as Alzheimer's disease.

Let's explore where some of these neurotransmitters operate in the brain and how they affect behavior and mental processes.

Three Classes of Neurotransmitters

Chemical neurotransmission was first demonstrated in 1921, and since then more than a hundred different neurotransmitters have been identified. The ones used in the nervous system fall into three main categories: *small molecules, peptides,* and *gases.*

Small Molecules

The most important of the small-molecule chemicals that act as neurotransmitters are acetylcholine, norepinephrine, serotonin, dopamine, GABA, and glutamate. *Acetylcholine* (pronounced "uh-see-tull-KOE-leen") was the first to be identified as a neurotransmitter. Among the many neurons that communicate using acetylcholine are those active in controlling movement of the body, in making memories, and in slowing the heartbeat and activating the digestive system. No wonder, then, that disruption of acetylcholine systems can result in a wide variety of problems, including the loss of memory and other mental powers seen in Alzheimer's disease.

Systems of neurons that use *norepinephrine* (pronounced "nor-eppa-NEF-rin") affect arousal, wakefulness, learning, and mood. This neurotransmitter is involved when your nervous system prepares you to fight or to run away from a threat. Changes in norepinephrine systems have also been implicated in depression.

The neurotransmitter *serotonin* (pronounced "sair-oh-TOE-nin") is similar to norepinephrine in that it is used in brain systems that affect both sleep and mood. Serotonin may also be involved in the appearance of aggressive and impulsive behaviors. Unlike norepinephrine, though, the amount of serotonin in your brain can be affected by what you eat. For example, eating carbohydrates can increase serotonin, and the increase in serotonin normally reduces the desire for carbohydrates. Some researchers suspect that malfunctions in serotonin systems can result in the mood and appetite problems seen in some types of obesity, premenstrual tension, and depression, including disorders in which depressed mood, suicidal tendencies, and impulsivity appear together (Bach-Mizrachi et al., 2006; McCloskey et al., 2009; Oquendo & Mann, 2000). Antidepressant medications such as Prozac, Zoloft, and Paxil appear to relieve some of the symptoms of depression by acting on serotonin systems to maintain proper functions of this neurotransmitter.

Dopamine (pronounced "DOPE-uh-meen") is a neurotransmitter that is important for movement. Malfunctions of dopamine systems contribute to movement disorders such as Parkinson's disease and the shakiness experienced by people who have it. Parkinson's has been treated with some success using drugs that enable neurons to use dopamine more efficiently and by implanting dopamine-using neurons (Chase, 1998; Connolly & Lang, 2014; Mendez et al., 2008). Permanently implanting an electrode that stimulates neurons in the brain's dopamine-influenced motor system not only offers an even more effective treatment but also carries a risk of surgical complications (Weaver et al., 2009). Other dopamine systems are involved in the experiencing of reward, or pleasure, which is vital in shaping and motivating behavior (Spanagel & Weiss, 1999). Animals will work very hard to receive a direct dose of dopamine to certain parts of the brain. These dopamine systems play a role in the rewarding properties of many drugs, including cocaine (Ciccocioppo, Sanna, & Weiss, 2001; Hyman, Malenka, & Nestler, 2006). Certain dopamine systems are also suspected to be partly responsible for the perceptual, emotional, and thought disturbances associated with schizophrenia, a severe mental disorder (Marenco & Weinberger, 2000).

GABA stands for gamma-amino butyric acid. Unlike most neurotransmitters, which excite neurons to fire action potentials, GABA *reduces* the likelihood that neurons will fire. In fact, it is the main neurotransmitter for slowing, or inhibiting, the brain's activity.

When you fall asleep, neurons that use GABA deserve part of the credit. Drugs that cause reduced neural activity often do so by amplifying the "braking" action of GABA. For example, alcohol's effect on GABA systems is partly responsible for the impairments in thinking, judgment, and motor skills that occur when people drink too much. Malfunctions of GABA systems contribute to severe anxiety and to *Huntington's disease*, an inherited disorder that causes its victims to suffer uncontrollable movement of the arms and legs along with a progressive loss of thinking abilities. Drugs that interfere with GABA's inhibitory effects produce intense repetitive electrical discharges, known as *seizures*. Researchers suspect that impaired GABA systems contribute to *epilepsy*, another brain disorder associated with seizures and convulsive movements. Repeated or sustained seizures can result in permanent brain damage. Drug treatments can reduce the frequency and severity of seizures but do not eliminate them and may cause undesirable side effects. An alternative treatment approach may someday come from the optogenetic techniques described earlier (Airan et al., 2009). There is evidence that this technique stops abnormal electrical activity in animal brain cells (Tonneson et al., 2009). It has already been used to prevent seizures in rats (Sukhotinsky et al., 2013), and is now being tested in primates (Bentley et al., 2013).

Glutamate (pronounced "GLOO-tuh-mate") is used by more neurons than any other neurotransmitter, and it also helps glial cells provide energy for neurons (Rouach et al., 2008). Glutamate is particularly important because it helps the brain strengthen its synaptic connections, allowing messages to more easily cross the gap between neurons. This strengthening process is necessary for normal development and may be at the root of learning and memory (Newpher & Ehlers, 2008). Yet overactivity of glutamate synapses can cause neurons to die, and is the main cause of the brain damage that occurs when oxygen is cut off from neurons during a stroke. Blocking glutamate receptors immediately after a brain trauma can prevent permanent brain damage (Colak et al., 2003). Glutamate may also contribute to the loss of brain cells that occurs in Alzheimer's disease (Cha et al., 2001).

Peptides

Hundreds of chemicals called *peptides* have been found to act as neurotransmitters. The first of these was discovered in the 1970s, when scientists were investigating *opiates*, such as heroin and morphine. Opiates can relieve pain, produce feelings of elation, and in high doses bring on sleep. After marking morphine with a radioactive substance, researchers traced where it became concentrated in the brain. They found that opiates bind to receptors that were not associated with any known neurotransmitter. Because it was unlikely that the brain had developed opiate receptors just in case a person might want to use morphine or heroin, researchers reasoned that the body must already contain a substance similar to opiates. This hypothesis led to the search for a naturally occurring, or endogenous, morphine, which was called *endorphin* (short for *endogenous morphine*). As it turned out, there are many natural opiate-like compounds. So the term *endorphins* refers to all neurotransmitters that can bind to the same receptors stimulated by opiates. Neurons in several parts of the brain use endorphins, including neuronal pathways that modify pain signals to the brain.

Gases

Our ideas of what neurotransmitters can be was radically altered following the discovery that *nitric oxide* and *carbon monoxide*—two toxic gases that contribute to air pollution—can act as neurotransmitters (Boehning & Snyder, 2003). When nitric oxide or carbon monoxide is released by a neuron, it spreads to nearby neurons, sending a signal that affects chemical reactions inside those neurons rather than binding to receptors on their surface. Nitric oxide is not stored in vesicles, as most other neurotransmitters are; it can be released from any part of the neuron. Nitric oxide appears to be one of the neurotransmitters responsible for such diverse functions as penile erection and the formation of memories—not at the same site, obviously.

In summary, neurotransmitters acting throughout the body link our biochemistry with every aspect of our behavior and mental processes. You will see other examples in the chapter on sensation and perception, where we describe some of the neurotransmitters that help convey pain messages. In the consciousness chapter, we consider how neurotransmitters are affected by alcohol and illegal drugs. In the chapter on psychological disorders, we discuss the role that neurotransmitters play in schizophrenia and depression, and in the chapter on the treatment of psychological disorders, we explore ways that prescription drugs act on neurotransmitters to alleviate the symptoms of those disorders. ("In Review: Classes of Neurotransmitters" lists the most important of these neurotransmitters and the consequences of malfunctioning neurotransmitter systems.)

CLASSES OF NEUROTRANSMITTERS   IN REVIEW

Neurotransmitter Class	Normal Function	Disorder Associated with Malfunction
Small Molecules		
Acetylcholine	Memory, movement	Alzheimer's disease
Norepinephrine	Mood, sleep, learning	Depression
Serotonin	Mood, appetite, impulsivity	Depression
Dopamine	Movement, reward	Parkinson's disease, schizophrenia
GABA	Sleep, movement	Anxiety, Huntington's disease, epilepsy
Glutamate	Memory	Damage after stroke
Peptides		
Endorphins	Pain control	No established disorder
Gases		
Nitric oxide	Memory	No established disorder

1. The main neurotransmitter for slowing, or inhibiting, brain activity is _____.

2. A group of neurons that use the same neurotransmitter is called a _____.

3. Which neurotransmitter's activity causes brain damage during a stroke?

THE ENDOCRINE SYSTEM: COORDINATING THE INTERNAL WORLD

How can my hormones help me in a crisis?

As we mentioned earlier, neurons are not the only cells that can use chemicals to communicate with one another in ways that affect behavior and mental processes. Another class of cells with this ability resides in the **endocrine system** (pronounced "EN-doh-krin"),

endocrine system Cells that form organs called glands and that communicate with one another by secreting chemicals called hormones.

which regulates functions ranging from stress responses to physical growth. The cells of endocrine organs, or **glands,** communicate by secreting chemicals, much as neurons do. In the case of endocrine organs, the chemicals are called **hormones.** Figure 3.16 shows the location and functions of some of the major endocrine glands.

FIGURE 3.16
Some Major Glands of the Endocrine System

Each of the glands shown releases its hormones into the bloodstream. Even the hypothalamus, a part of the brain, regulates the nearby pituitary gland by secreting hormones.

© iStockphoto.com/4x6;
Paul Radenfeld/Digital Vision/Getty Images

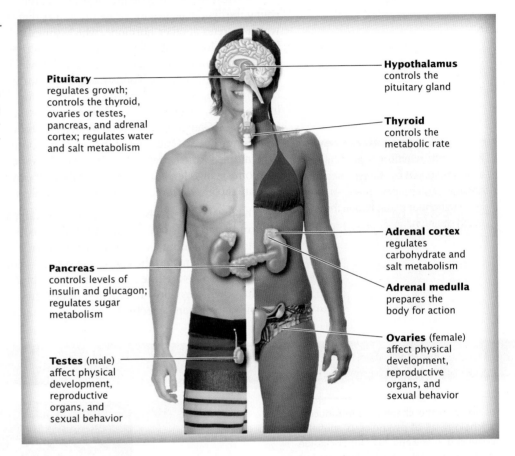

Pituitary
regulates growth; controls the thyroid, ovaries or testes, pancreas, and adrenal cortex; regulates water and salt metabolism

Pancreas
controls levels of insulin and glucagon; regulates sugar metabolism

Testes (male)
affect physical development, reproductive organs, and sexual behavior

Hypothalamus
controls the pituitary gland

Thyroid
controls the metabolic rate

Adrenal cortex
regulates carbohydrate and salt metabolism

Adrenal medulla
prepares the body for action

Ovaries (female)
affect physical development, reproductive organs, and sexual behavior

Hormones secreted from the endocrine organs are similar to neurotransmitters. In fact, many of these chemicals, including norepinephrine and the endorphins, act both as hormones and as neurotransmitters. However, whereas neurons release neurotransmitters into synapses, endocrine organs release their chemicals into the bloodstream, which carries them throughout the body. In this way, endocrine glands can stimulate cells with which they have no direct connection. But not all cells receive the hormonal message. Hormones, like neurotransmitters, can influence only cells with receptors capable of receiving them. Organs whose cells have receptors for a hormone are called *target organs.*

Each hormone acts on many target organs, producing coordinated effects throughout the body. For example, when the sex hormone *estrogen* is secreted by a woman's ovaries, it activates her reproductive system. It causes the uterus to grow in preparation for nurturing an embryo; it enlarges the breasts to prepare them for nursing; it stimulates the brain to enhance interest in sexual activity; and it stimulates the pituitary gland to release another hormone that causes a mature egg to be released by the ovary for fertilization. Male sex organs, called the *testes,* secrete *androgens,* which are sex hormones such as *testosterone.* Androgens stimulate the maturation of sperm, increase a male's motivation for sexual activity, and increase his aggressiveness (Romeo, Richardson, & Sisk, 2002).

The brain has ultimate control over the secretion of hormones. Through the hypothalamus, it controls the pituitary gland, which in turn controls endocrine organs in the body. The brain is also one of the target organs for most endocrine secretions. In fact, the brain creates some of the same hormones that are secreted in the endocrine system and uses them for neural communication (Melcangi et al., 2011). In summary, the endocrine system typically involves four elements:

glands Organs that secrete hormones into the bloodstream.

hormones Chemicals secreted by a gland into the bloodstream, which carries them throughout the body.

the brain, the pituitary gland, an endocrine organ, and the target organs, which include the brain. Each element in the system uses hormones to signal to the next element, and the secretion of each hormone is stimulated or suppressed by other hormones (Dubrovsky, 2005).

In stress hormone systems, for example, the brain controls the pituitary gland by signaling the hypothalamus to release hormones that stimulate receptors of the pituitary gland, which secretes another hormone, which stimulates another endocrine gland to secrete its hormones. More specifically, when the brain interprets a situation as threatening, the pituitary releases *adrenocorticotropic hormone (ACTH),* which causes the adrenal glands to release the hormone *cortisol* into the bloodstream. These hormones, in turn, act on cells throughout the body, including the brain. One effect of cortisol, for example, is to activate the emotion-related limbic system, making it more likely that you will remember stressful or traumatic events (Cahill & McGaugh, 1998). The combined effects of the adrenal hormones and the activation of the sympathetic system result in a set of responses called the **fight-flight reaction**, which, as mentioned earlier, prepares us for action in response to danger or other stress. With these hormones at high levels, the heart beats faster, the liver releases glucose into the bloodstream, fuels are mobilized from fat stores, and we usually enter a state of high arousal.

The hormones provide feedback to the brain, as well as to the pituitary gland. Just as a thermostat and furnace regulate heat, this feedback system regulates hormone secretion so as to keep it within a certain range. Feedback systems are just one illustration of how the nervous system and the endocrine system—both systems of communication between and among cells—are integrated to form the biological basis for a smoothly functioning self. Together, they allow interaction of our thoughts and emotions and provide us with the ability to respond effectively to life's challenges and opportunities.

fight-flight reaction A physical reaction triggered by the sympathetic nervous system that prepares the body to fight or to run from a threatening situation.

LINKAGES

As noted in the chapter on introducing psychology, all of psychology's subfields are related to one another. Our discussion of developmental changes illustrates just one way in which the topic of this chapter, the biological aspects of psychology, is linked to the subfield of developmental psychology, which is described in the chapter on human development. The Linkages diagram shows ties to two other subfields as well, and there are many more ties throughout the book. Looking for linkages among subfields will help you see how they all fit together and help you better appreciate the big picture that is psychology.

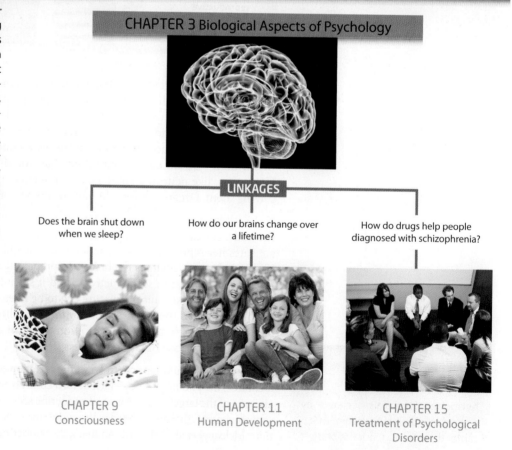

CHAPTER 3 Biological Aspects of Psychology

LINKAGES

Does the brain shut down when we sleep?

How do our brains change over a lifetime?

How do drugs help people diagnosed with schizophrenia?

CHAPTER 9
Consciousness

CHAPTER 11
Human Development

CHAPTER 15
Treatment of Psychological Disorders

SUMMARY

Biological psychology focuses on the biological aspects of our being, including the nervous system, which provide the physical basis for behavior and mental processes. The *nervous system* is a system of cells that allows an organism to gain information about what is going on inside and outside the body and to respond appropriately. Much of our understanding of the biological aspects of psychology has stemmed from research on animal and human nervous systems at levels ranging from single cells to complex organizations of cells.

Cells of the Nervous System

What are neurons, and what do they do?

The main units of the nervous system are cells called *neurons* (or *nerve cells*) and *glial cells*. Neurons are especially good at receiving signals from and transmitting signals to other neurons. Neurons have cell bodies and two types of fibers, called *axons* and *dendrites*. Axons usually carry signals away from the cell body, and dendrites usually carry signals to the cell body. Neurons can transmit signals because of the structure of these fibers, the excitable surface of some of the fibers, and the *synapses*, or gaps, between cells.

The membranes of neurons normally keep the distribution of electrically charged ions uneven between the inside of cells and the outside, creating an electrochemical force, or potential. The membrane surface of the axon can transmit a disturbance in this potential, called an *action potential*, from one end of the axon to the other. The speed of the action potential is fastest in neurons sheathed in *myelin*. Between firings there is a very brief rest, called a *refractory period*.

When an action potential reaches the end of an axon, the axon releases a chemical called a *neurotransmitter*. This chemical crosses the synapse and interacts with the postsynaptic cell at special sites called *receptors*. This interaction creates a *postsynaptic potential* that makes the postsynaptic cell more likely or less likely to fire an action potential of its own. So whereas communication within a neuron is electrochemical, communication between neurons is chemical. Because the fibers of neurons have many branches, each neuron can interact with thousands of other neurons. Each neuron constantly integrates signals received at its many synapses; the result of this integration determines how often the neuron fires an action potential.

Neurons are organized in *neural networks* of closely connected cells. Sensory systems receive information from the environment, and motor systems influence the actions of muscles and other organs. The two major divisions of the nervous system are the *central nervous system (CNS)*, which includes the brain and spinal cord, and the *peripheral nervous system (PNS)*.

The Peripheral Nervous System: Keeping in Touch with the World

How do sights and sounds reach my brain?

The peripheral nervous system has two components: the somatic nervous system and the autonomic nervous system.

The first component of the peripheral nervous system is the *somatic nervous system*, which transmits information from the senses to the CNS via *sensory neurons* and carries signals from the CNS via *motor neurons* to the muscles that move the skeleton.

The second component of the peripheral nervous system is the *autonomic nervous system*, whose two subsystems, the *sympathetic nervous system* and the *parasympathetic nervous system*, carry messages back and forth between the CNS and the heart, lungs, and other organs and glands.

The Central Nervous System: Making Sense of the World

How is my brain "wired"?

The CNS is laid out in interconnected groups of neuronal cell bodies, called nuclei, whose collections of axons travel together in fiber tracts, or pathways.

The *spinal cord* receives information from the peripheral senses and sends it to the brain; it also relays messages from the brain to the periphery. In addition, cells of the spinal cord can direct simple movements, called *reflexes*, without instructions from the brain.

The brain's major subdivisions are the *hindbrain, midbrain*, and *forebrain*. The hindbrain includes the *medulla oblongata*, the *locus coeruleus*, and the *cerebellum*. The *reticular formation* is found in both the hindbrain and the midbrain. The forebrain is the largest and most highly developed part of the brain; it includes many structures, including the *hypothalamus* and *thalamus*. A part of the hypothalamus called the suprachiasmatic nuclei maintains a clock that determines biological rhythms. Other forebrain structures include the *hippocampus*, and *amygdala*. Several of these structures form the limbic system, which plays an important role in regulating emotion and memory. The outer surface of the cerebral hemispheres is called the *cerebral cortex*; it is responsible for many of the higher functions of the brain, including speech and reasoning. The functional areas of the cortex include the *sensory cortex, motor cortex*, and *association cortex*.

A variety of new techniques, combined with some older measures, give scientists ever better ways to study the brain and its activity. These methods include the *electroencephalograph (EEG), PET (for positron emission tomography), magnetic resonance imaging (MRI), functional MRI (fMRI), diffusion tensor imaging (DTI), transcranial magnetic stimulation (TMS)*, and *optogenetics*.

The functions of the right and left hemispheres of the cerebral cortex show a certain degree of *lateralization*, or *lateral dominance*, which means they are somewhat specialized. In most people, the left hemisphere is more active in language and logical tasks and the right hemisphere is more active in spatial, musical, and artistic tasks. The hemispheres are connected through the *corpus callosum*, allowing them to operate in a co-ordinated fashion.

Neural plasticity in the central nervous system, the ability to strengthen neural connections at its synapses as well as to establish new synapses, forms the basis for learning and memory. Scientists are searching for ways to increase neural plasticity following brain damage, including through the use of neural stem cells.

The Chemistry of Psychology: Neurotransmitters

How do biochemicals affect my mood?

Neurons that use the same neurotransmitter form a neurotransmitter system.

There are three classes of neurotransmitters: small molecules, peptides, and gases. Acetylcholine systems in the brain influence memory processes and movement. Norepinephrine is released by neurons whose axons spread widely throughout the brain; it is involved in arousal, mood, and learning. Serotonin, another widespread neurotransmitter, is active in systems regulating mood and appetite. Dopamine systems are involved in movement, motivation, and higher cognitive activities. Both Parkinson's disease

and schizophrenia involve a disturbance of dopamine systems. Gamma-amino butyric acid (GABA) is an inhibitory neurotransmitter involved in anxiety and epilepsy. Glutamate is the most common excitatory neurotransmitter. It is involved in learning and memory and, in excess, may cause neuronal death. Endorphins are peptide neurotransmitters that affect pain pathways. Nitric oxide and carbon monoxide are gases that function as neurotransmitters.

The Endocrine System: Coordinating the Internal World

How can my hormones help me in a crisis?

Like nervous system cells, those of the *endocrine system* communicate by releasing a chemical that signals to other cells. However, the chemicals released by endocrine organs, or *glands*, are called *hormones* and are carried by the bloodstream to remote target organs. The target organs often produce a coordinated response to hormonal stimulation. One of these responses is the *fight-flight reaction*, which is triggered by adrenal hormones that prepare for action in times of stress. Hormones also affect brain development, contributing to sex differences in the brain and behavior. Feedback systems are involved in the control of most endocrine functions.

TEST YOUR KNOWLEDGE

Select the best answer for each of the following questions. Then check your responses against the Answer Key at the end of the book.

1. The nucleus of a cell _____, and the mitochondria _____.
   a. produces red blood cells; turn oxygen into glucose
   b. produces red blood cells; keep a stable chemical environment
   c. provides genetic information; turn oxygen into glucose
   d. provides genetic information; keep a stable chemical environment

2. A nurse has mixed up some test results on neurotransmitter function for several patients at the hospital where you work. To help her out, you tell her that the depressed patient's chart will probably show malfunctions in _____ systems and the Parkinson's patient's chart will probably show malfunctions in _____ systems.
   a. dopamine; norepinephrine
   b. dopamine; acetylcholine
   c. serotonin; dopamine
   d. acetylcholine; norepinephrine

3. Hannah had a stroke and oxygen was cut off from the neurons in her brain. This caused overactivity in _____ synapses, which led to brain damage.
   a. dopamine
   b. glutamate
   c. acetylcholine
   d. serotonin

4. Functional magnetic resonance imaging (fMRI) provides a way to _____.
   a. directly measure brain cell activity
   b. determine changes in blood flow and oxygen levels in various brain areas
   c. locate the causes of particular mental processes
   d. locate where certain emotions take place in the brain

5. As you switch on your favorite TV medical show, a doctor charges through the emergency room doors and tells a worried spouse that her husband has a neurological problem. "The nerves that carry signals to his muscles are not functioning," the doctor says, "which means the _____ nervous system has been damaged."
   a. central
   b. autonomic
   c. somatic
   d. sympathetic

6. Kalli finishes a difficult final exam, then hurries home and flops down on her bed to relax. As Kalli relaxes, her _____ nervous system becomes less active, whereas her _____ nervous system becomes more active.
   a. central; somatic
   b. somatic; central
   c. parasympathetic; sympathetic
   d. sympathetic; parasympathetic

7. Karena smells some cologne in a store, and suddenly remembers the emotions she had when her dad passed

away. He had worn that cologne. She was able to form this association partly because of the actions of the _____.
a. locus coeruleus
b. somatosensory cortex
c. amygdala
d. hypothalamus

8. A neuron's action potential shoots down its axon with greater speed when the _____.
a. axon is coated in myelin
b. refractory period is longer
c. neuron's diameter is smaller
d. neuron is in the brain

9. Jessica has severely damaged to her entire medulla. Most likely, Jessica _____.
a. is dead
b. will have memory problems
c. will have difficulty with fine motor movements
d. will not feel anything on the left side of her body

10. Damage in Lily's hindbrain caused her to lapse into a coma. The damage most likely occurred in the _____.
a. cerebellum
b. hippocampus
c. hypothalamus
d. reticular formation

11. Riley was an excellent pianist until he suffered brain damage. Now problems with fine motor skills make it impossible for him to play the piano. Riley most likely had damage to his _____.
a. cerebellum
b. hippocampus
c. hypothalamus
d. reticular formation

12. The hippocampus has been found to be significantly smaller in patients who are suffering from which of the following problems?
a. Parkinson's disease
b. Alzheimer's disease
c. Huntington's disease
d. an eating disorder

13. A woman was rushed to an emergency room with severely burned hands. She had picked up an iron because she couldn't tell it was hot, and she still doesn't feel pain from her burns. The neurologist who examined her concluded that the woman's _____ system is malfunctioning.
a. sensory
b. motor
c. autonomic
d. parasympathetic

14. Reginald has suffered damage to his occipital lobe. This means that Reginald will have difficulty _____.
a. feeling pain
b. moving his body
c. regulating body temperature
d. seeing

15. Elnora wants to hit a nail with a hammer so she can hang a picture on the wall. This involves voluntary movements that are controlled by neurons in the _____ cortex, which is located in the _____ lobe.
a. motor; frontal
b. motor; parietal
c. association; temporal
d. sensory; occipital

16. Roberto, an actor, is recovering following a freak accident on the set of his latest movie. When asked about the accident, Roberto, once a confident and fluent speaker, can now only say, "Noise… acting… hurts." The part of Roberto's brain most likely involved in this type of speech problem is _____ area.
a. Sperry's
b. Broca's
c. Wernicke's
d. Sylva's

17. Joe experienced such severe seizures that doctors had to sever his corpus callosum. Following surgery, a psychologist presented the left hemisphere of Joe's brain with a picture of a car and asked Joe what he saw. Most likely, Joe could _____.
a. correctly say "car"
b. not identify the car in words
c. only draw a car
d. not understand the question

18. Edie is 80 and has suffered a paralyzing stroke. Her doctors are likely to tell her that _____.
a. if she imagines moving her body, she can increase the number of neurons in her motor cortex
b. the Nogo protein will help regenerate nerve cells
c. neural stem cells will automatically repair the damage
d. mental and physical exercise programs can help reverse some of the effects of the stroke

19. Ted is creating a study sheet to help him learn the differences between neurotransmitters and hormones. Which of the following statements on his list is *not* correct?
a. Neurotransmitters travel through the bloodstream and hormones travel across synapses.
b. Both hormones and neurotransmitters stimulate only those cells and organs that have receptors for them.
c. Hormones and neurotransmitters regulate complex behaviors and mental processes.
d. Hormones operate mainly in the endocrine system; neurotransmitters operate mainly in the nervous system.

20. When Mitch saw a woman in danger of drowning, he jumped into the water to save her. Mitch's endocrine system readied him for this exertion by releasing _____ and other stress hormones into his bloodstream.
a. cortisol
b. GABA
c. glutamate
d. BABA

CHAPTER 4

Sensation and Perception

© Creativa/Shutterstock.com

Preview

You can understand what you read in this sentence because the lines and squiggles that make up its letters somehow become meaningful words. This "somehow" is what sensation and perception are all about. You translate incoming stimulation, such as the light bouncing off this page, into neural activity called *sensations*. Then you interpret these sensations as meaningful experiences called *perceptions*—in this case, as letters and words. These amazing processes are so quick and automatic that you probably take them for granted. In this chapter, we draw your attention to them. You will learn about how our sensory systems receive stimulation and how they encode that stimulation into patterns of nerve activity that the brain can decode. You will also discover how the brain interprets, or perceives, this information from your senses.

Years after Fred Aryee lost his right arm below the elbow in a boating accident, he could still "feel" sensations from his missing lower arm and hand. Once, his doctor asked Aryee to reach for a cup on the table in front of him with his right arm. When asked what he felt, Aryee said, "I feel my fingers clasping the cup" (Shreeve, 1993). People like Fred may also feel intense pain that seems to come from a lost limb (Glummarra et al., 2007; Ramachandran, 2008). Some people feel intense pain as a missing hand suddenly tightens into a fist, digging nonexistent fingernails into a phantom palm. Worse, they may not be able to "open" this hand to relieve the pain. To help such people, health workers can seat them in front of a mirror and angle the mirror to create the illusion that the amputated arm and hand have been restored. When these patients move their real hands while looking in the mirror, they not only "feel" movement in their phantom hands but can also "unclench" their phantom fists and stop their pain (Hsu & Cohen, 2013). This clever strategy arose from psychology research on how vision interacts with the sense of touch.

TRY THIS

To experience this kind of interaction yourself, sit across a table from someone and ask that person to stroke the tabletop while you stroke your own knee under the table in exactly the same way, in exactly the same direction. If you watch the person's hand as it strokes the table, you will soon experience the touch sensations coming from the table, not your knee! If the person's two hands do not move in sync, however, the illusion will not occur (Tsakiris & Haggard, 2005).

Where do "phantom limb" sensations and perceptions come from? Fred no longer has fingers to send messages to the brain, yet he experienced his "feeling" of the cup as real. Others who have lost, say, a left arm feel that they now have two right arms (Cipriani et al., 2011). These cases remind us that the "objective reality" we assume to be the same for everyone can actually differ from person to person (Bartoshuk, Fast, & Snyder, 2005). Just as someone can feel a hand that isn't actually "there," every individual's senses actively shape information about the outside world to create a personal reality.

SENSING AND PERCEIVING THE WORLD

What is the difference between sensation and perception?

Psychologists find it useful to distinguish between *sensation* (the stimulus message coming from the senses) and *perception* (the process of giving meaning to that message). You don't actually sense a cat lying on the sofa. You sense shapes and colors, the visual sensations. You then use your knowledge of the world to interpret, or perceive, these sensations as a cat. To be honest, it's impossible to draw a clear line between where sensation ends and perception begins, because interpreting sensations begins to some degree in the sense organs themselves. But psychologists make a distinction between sensation and perception nonetheless, in order to better organize our understanding of a very diverse set of processes.

To understand how sensory systems help us create reality, we need to consider some basic information about the senses. A **sense** is a system that translates outside information into activity in the nervous system. For example, your eyes convert light into neural activity that tells the brain something about the source of the light or about the objects reflecting it. Messages from the senses are called **sensations**. Sensations shape behaviors and mental processes by providing the vital link between the self and the world outside the brain.

sense A system that translates data from outside the nervous system into neural activity.

sensations Raw information from the senses.

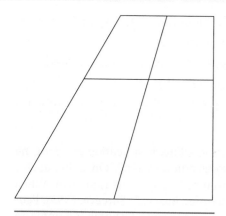

FIGURE 4.1
What do you see?

Perception is the process of using information and your understanding of the world to turn those sensations into meaningful experiences. Perception is more than a passive process of merely absorbing incoming data. For example, look at Figure 4.1. It contains only raw information about a series of intersecting lines, and so this is what your eyes help you "sense." But your perceptual system takes those data and automatically interprets them as an image of a rectangle, or perhaps a window frame, lying on its side. This act of perception is so quick and familiar that it may be difficult to appreciate the processes that allow you to turn sensory signals into your experience of reality. By shaping this experience, your perceptions influence your thoughts, feelings, and actions. But before you can perceive something, you must be able to sense it.

SENSORY SYSTEMS

How does information from my eyes and ears get to my brain?

Your senses gather information about the world by detecting various forms of energy, such as sound, light, heat, and physical pressure. Your eyes are specialized to be able to detect light energy, your ears detect the energy of sound, and your skin detects the energy of heat and pressure. Humans depend a lot on vision, hearing, and the skin senses to gain information about the world. Some animals depend more on smell and taste than we do. To your brain, "the world" also includes the rest of your body, so specific sensory systems provide information about the location and position of your body parts.

All senses detect information about stimuli, encode it into neural activity, and then send this encoded information to the brain. Figure 4.2 illustrates these basic steps in sensation. At each step, sensory information is "processed" in some way. So the information that arrives at one point in the system is not exactly the same information that goes to the next step.

The first step in most sensory systems involves **accessory structures**, which modify the incoming environmental stimuli (Step 1 in Figure 4.2). For example, the lens of the eye is an accessory structure that changes incoming light by focusing it. The flexible part of the ear that extends outside your head is an accessory structure that collects sound.

The second step in sensation is **transduction**, which is the process of converting incoming energy into neural activity (Step 2 in Figure 4.2). Your cell phone receives electromagnetic energy and transduces it into sounds. In much the same way, your ears receive sound energy and transduce it into neural activity that you recognize as voices and music. Transduction takes place in **neural receptors**, also called *sensory receptors*, which are specialized cells that can detect certain forms of energy. These receptors respond to incoming energy by changes in the firing of an action potential and release of neurotransmitters that send signals to neighboring cells. Sensory receptors respond best to *changes* in energy (Graziano et al., 2002). A constant level of stimulation usually produces **sensory adaptation**, or a decreasing responsiveness to the stimulus over time. This is the reason why the touch sensations you get from your glasses or wristwatch disappear shortly after you have put them on.

Sensory nerves carry information from receptors to the central nervous system—the spinal cord and the brain (Step 3 in Figure 4.2). For all the senses except smell, this information goes first to the brain's thalamus, which does initial processing before sending it on to the cerebral cortex (Step 4; Sherman, 2007). The most complex processing occurs in specialized areas of the sensory cortex (Step 5; Kanwisher, 2010).

Encoding Sensations: What Was That?

The neural activity created when neural receptors transduce incoming energy functions as a coded message about the stimulus that produced the energy. So our psychological experience of a stimulus, such as its brightness or color, is based on a corresponding feature of

perception The process through which people take raw sensations from the environment and give them meaning using knowledge, experience, and understanding of the world.

accessory structures Structures, such as the outer part of the ear, that modify a stimulus.

transduction The process of converting incoming physical energy into neural activity.

neural receptors Cells that are specialized to detect certain types of energy and convert it into neural activity.

sensory adaptation Decreasing responsiveness to an unchanging stimulus.

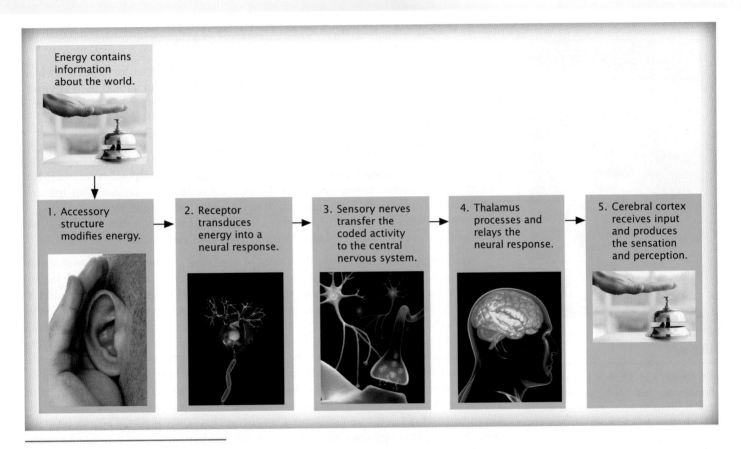

Energy contains information about the world.

1. Accessory structure modifies energy.

2. Receptor transduces energy into a neural response.

3. Sensory nerves transfer the coded activity to the central nervous system.

4. Thalamus processes and relays the neural response.

5. Cerebral cortex receives input and produces the sensation and perception.

FIGURE 4.2

Elements of a Sensory System

Objects in the world generate energy that is focused by accessory structures and detected by sensory receptors, which convert the energy into neural signals. The signals are then relayed through parts of the brain, which processes them into perceptual experiences.

© iStockphoto.com/AnthiaCumming; © Ilya Andriyanov/Shutterstock.com; James Steidl/Photos.com; Xiaofeng Luo/Photos.com; © fusebulb/Shutterstock.com

encoding Translation of the physical properties of a stimulus into a specific pattern of neural activity.

specific energy doctrine The discovery that stimulation of a particular sensory nerve provides codes for that sense, no matter how the stimulation takes place.

its physical energy, as encoded by neural receptors. In other words, **encoding** translates the physical properties of a stimulus, such as its shape or intensity, into a pattern of neural activity that represents those physical properties. When the brain organizes these neural patterns, you can make sense of the stimulus and decide whether you are looking at a white cat, a black dog, or a tall person.

To better appreciate the problem of encoding physical stimuli into neural activity, imagine that for your birthday you receive a Pet Brain. You are told that your Pet Brain is alive, but it does not respond when you open the box and talk to it. You remove it from the box and show it a hot-fudge sundae; no response. You show it pictures of other attractive brains; still no response. You are about to toss your Pet Brain in the trash when you suddenly realize that the two of you are not speaking the same language. If you want to communicate with your Pet Brain, the only way to do so is by sending it messages that can stimulate whatever sensory receptors that it happens to have. Then, to read its responses, you will have to record how it sends signals out, such as from its motor nerve cells.

Eagerly, you set up an electric stimulator and a recording device, but how do you describe a hot-fudge sundae to sensory nerves so that they pass on the right information to a brain? If you want the brain to perceive seeing a sundae, you should stimulate its optic nerve (the nerve from the eye to the brain) rather than its auditory nerve (the nerve from the ear to the brain). This idea is based on the **specific energy doctrine** (Norrsell, Finger, & Lajonchere, 1999), which says that stimulation of a particular sensory nerve provides codes for that one sense, no matter how the stimulation takes place. **TRY THIS** To experience this phenomenon, apply some pressure (be gentle!) to your closed eye; doing so will produce activity in the optic nerve so you will sense little spots of light.

Having chosen the optic nerve to send visual information, you must now develop a code for all the specific features of the sundae: the soft, white curves of the vanilla ice cream, the dark richness of the chocolate, the shiny, bright red of the round cherry on

What Is It?

In the split second before you recognized this stimulus as a hot-fudge sundae, sensory neurons in your visual system detected the light reflected off this page and transduced it into a neural code that your brain could interpret. The encoding and decoding process occurs so quickly and efficiently in all our senses that we are seldom aware of it. Later in this chapter, we describe how this remarkable feat is accomplished.

Ed Bock/Corbis

absolute threshold The minimum amount of stimulus energy that can be detected 50 percent of the time.

noise The spontaneous random firing of nerve cells that occurs because the nervous system is always active.

top. These dimensions must be coded in the language of nerve cell activity—that is, in the firing of action potentials.

In summary, the problem of encoding is solved by means of sensory systems, which allow the brain to receive detailed, accurate, and useful data about stimuli in its environment. If you succeed in creating the right coding system, your Pet Brain will finally know what a hot-fudge sundae looks like.

Absolute Thresholds: Is Something Out There?

How much stimulus energy does it take to trigger a conscious perceptual experience? Not much! Normal human vision can detect the light equivalent to a candle flame burning in the dark 30 miles away. The minimum detectable amount of light, sound, pressure, or other physical energy has traditionally been called the *absolute threshold*. Table 4.1 lists absolute thresholds for human vision, hearing, taste, smell, and touch.

Psychologists discovered these thresholds by exploring *psychophysics*, the relationship between *physical* energy in the environment and your *psychological experience* of that energy (e.g., Purves et al., 2011). In a typical absolute threshold experiment, you would sit in a dark laboratory. After your eyes got used to the darkness, a researcher would show you brief light flashes. These flashes would differ in brightness, or stimulus intensity. Each time, you'd be asked if you saw the light. Averaged over a large number of trials, the pattern of your correct detections would probably form a curve like the one shown in Figure 4.3. As you can see, the absolute threshold is not an all-or-nothing affair. A stimulus at an intensity of three, which is below the absolute threshold in the figure, will still be detected 20 percent of the time it occurs. Because of such variability, psychophysicists redefined the **absolute threshold** as the smallest amount of energy that can be detected 50 percent of the time. Why does a supposedly "absolute" threshold vary? The two most important reasons have to do with "noise" and our response bias.

In psychophysics, the term internal **noise** describes the random firing of cells in the nervous system that continues in varying amounts whether or not you are stimulated by physical energy. If the amount of internal noise happens to be high at a particular moment, your sensory systems might mistakenly interpret the noise as an external stimulus.

TABLE 4.1   SOME ABSOLUTE THRESHOLDS

Absolute thresholds can be amazingly low. Here are examples of the stimulus equivalents at the absolute threshold for the five primary senses. Set up the conditions for testing the absolute threshold for sound, and see if you can detect this minimal amount of auditory stimulation. If you can't hear it, the signal detection theory we discuss in this section may help explain why.

Human Sense	Absolute Threshold Is Equivalent to:
Vision	A candle flame seen at 30 miles on a clear night
Hearing	The tick of a watch under quiet conditions at 20 feet
Taste	One teaspoon of sugar in 2 gallons of water
Smell	One drop of perfume diffused into the entire volume of air in a six-room apartment
Touch	The wing of a fly falling on your cheek from a distance of 1 centimeter

Source: Galanter (1962).

The second source of variation in absolute threshold is **response bias**, also known as the **response criterion**, which reflects a person's willingness to respond to a stimulus. A person's *motivation*—wants and needs—as well as *expectations* affect response bias. For example, if you were punished for reporting that a faint light appeared when it did not, then you might be motivated to raise your response criterion. That is, you would report the light only when you were quite sure you saw it. Similarly, expecting a faint stimulus to occur lowers the response criterion. Suppose, for example, that you worked at an airport TSA checkpoint, examining security scans of people's handbags and luggage. The signal to be detected in this situation is a weapon. If there has been a recent terrorist attack or if the threat level has just been elevated, the airport will be on high alert. In that situation, you would lower your response criterion for deciding that a questionable object on the x-ray image might be a weapon. You will be more likely to detect a weapon if there is one, but you'll also be more likely to mistake, say, a hairdryer for a gun.

Signal Detection Theory

Once researchers understood that the detection of a stimulus depends on the combination of its physical energy, the effects of noise, and a person's response bias, they realized that measurement of absolute thresholds could never be more precise than the 50 percent rule mentioned earlier. So they abandoned the effort to pinpoint absolute thresholds and turned instead to signal detection theory.

Signal detection theory presents a mathematical model of how your personal sensitivity and response bias combine to determine your decision about whether or not a near-threshold stimulus occurred (Green & Swets, 1966). **Sensitivity** refers to your ability to detect a particular stimulus from a background of competing stimuli. It is influenced by internal noise, the intensity of the stimulus, and the capacity of your sensory systems. As already mentioned, response bias is the internal rule that you use in deciding whether to report a signal. How likely is it that an eyewitness can pick a criminal out of a lineup, or that an airport security guard will spot a weapon in a passenger's x-rayed luggage? Signal detection theory helps us understand and predict such responses more precisely (MacMillan & Creelman, 2004; Swets, 1996; Wixted & Mickes, 2014).

Judging Differences between Stimuli

Sometimes our task is not to detect a faint stimulus but to notice small changes in a stimulus or to decide whether two stimuli are the same or different. Musicians tuning up for a performance must discern whether a particular note played on one instrument matches the same note played by another instrument. When you repaint part of a wall, you have to judge whether the color of the new paint matches the old color. And when you are cooking, you have to decide whether your soup tastes any spicier after you've added some pepper.

Your ability to judge differences between stimuli depends on the strength of the stimuli you are dealing with. The weaker those stimuli are, the easier it is to detect small differences between them. For example, if you're comparing the weight of two oranges, you may be able to detect a difference of as little as a fraction of an ounce. But if you are comparing two boxes weighing around 50 pounds each, you might not notice a difference unless it is a pound or more.

An old law in psychology, named after German physiologist Ernst Weber (pronounced "VAY-ber"), describes how stimulus strength affects ability to detect differences. **Weber's law** states that the smallest detectable difference in stimulus energy is a constant fraction of the intensity of the stimulus. This smallest detectable difference is called the *difference*

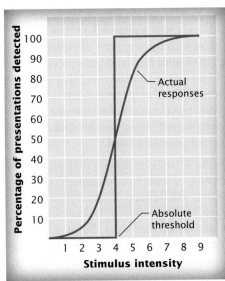

FIGURE 4.3
The Absolute Threshold

The curved line shows the relationship between the physical intensity of a signal and the chance that it will be detected. If the absolute threshold were truly absolute, or exact, all signals at or above a particular intensity would always be detected and no signals below that intensity would ever be detected (as shown by the red line). But this response pattern almost never occurs, so the "absolute" threshold is defined as the intensity at which the signal is detected 50 percent of the time.

response bias (response criterion) The internal rule a person uses to decide whether or not to report a stimulus.

signal detection theory A mathematical model of what determines a person's report of a near-threshold stimulus.

sensitivity The ability to detect a stimulus.

Weber's law A law stating that the smallest detectable difference in stimulus energy (just-noticeable difference) is a constant fraction of the intensity of the stimulus.

Detecting Vital Signals

According to signal detection theory, the likelihood that security screeners will detect the outline of a weapon appearing on x-ray images of luggage depends partly on the sensitivity of their visual systems and partly on their response criterion, their bias for responding to a questionable stimulus as a possible weapon. That bias, in turn, is affected by their expectations about how often weapons actually appear and by how motivated they are to look carefully for them. Airport security officials occasionally try to smuggle a simulated weapon through a checkpoint, not only to evaluate inspectors' performance but also to improve it by keeping their response criterion low enough to avoid missing real weapons (Fleck & Mitroff, 2007; McCarley et al., 2004; Wolfe et al., 2007; Wolfe & VanWert, 2010).

AP Images/Janet Hostetter

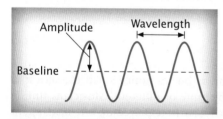

FIGURE 4.4
The Dimensions of a Wave

Wavelength is the distance from one peak of a wave to the next. *Frequency* is the number of complete waves, or cycles, that pass a given point in a given amount of time, such as one second. *Amplitude* is the height of a wave from baseline to peak.

just-noticeable difference (JND) The smallest detectable difference in stimulus energy. Also called difference threshold.

wavelength The distance between peaks in a wave of light or sound.

threshold, or **just-noticeable difference (JND)**. According to Weber's law, if an object weighs 25 pounds, the JND is only half a pound. So if you added a small container of yogurt to a grocery bag with three gallons of milk in it, you would not be able to tell the difference in weight. But candy snatchers beware: It takes a change of only two-thirds of an ounce to determine that someone has been into a 2-pound box of chocolates! The size of the just-noticeable difference differs for each sense. The human visual system, for example, is more sensitive than the taste system; that is why we will notice smaller differences in the brightness of a light than in, say, the saltiness of a salad.

The size of just-noticeable differences varies a bit among individuals, and as we age we tend to become less sensitive to stimulus differences. There are exceptions, however. If you like candy, you will be happy to know that Weber's fraction for sweetness stays fairly constant throughout life (Gilmore & Murphy, 1989). Weber's law does not hold when stimuli are very intense or very weak, but it does apply to complex, as well as simple, stimuli. We all tend to have our own personal JNDs that describe how much prices can increase before we notice or worry about the change. For example, if your JND for cost is .10, then you would surely notice, and perhaps protest, a 75-cent increase in a $2 bus fare. But the same 75-cent increase in your monthly rent would be less than a JND and thus unlikely to cause much notice or concern.

Sensory Energy

The sensory energies of light and sound vibrate as *waves* passing through space. These waves result from reflected light or from changes in air pressure caused when vocal cords and other objects move. The eye and ear detect the waves as light and sound, respectively. Waves of light and sound can be described in terms of wavelength, frequency, and amplitude, and these data determine what is sensed and perceived. **Wavelength** is the distance from one peak of the wave to the next. Wave **frequency** is the number of complete waves, or cycles, that pass a given point in a given amount of time. **Amplitude** is the height of the wave from baseline to peak (see Figure 4.4). Different wavelengths, frequencies, and amplitudes create different visual and sound experiences. Let's now consider how these physical properties of light and sound waves become sights and sounds.

SEEING

Why do some people need eyeglasses?

Soaring eagles have the incredible ability to see a mouse move in the grass from a mile away. Cats have special "reflectors" at the back of their eyes that help them see even in very dim light. Nature has provided each species with a visual system well adapted to its way of life. The human visual system is also adapted to do many things well. It combines great sensitivity with great sharpness, enabling us to see objects near and far, in day and at night. Our night vision is not as good as that of some animals, but our color vision is excellent. Not a bad trade-off if being able to experience a sunset's splendor is worth an occasional stumble in the dark.

Light

Light is a kind of energy called *electromagnetic radiation.* Most electromagnetic radiation, including x-rays, radio waves, television signals, Wi-Fi, and radar, is invisible to the human eye. In fact, as shown in Figure 4.5, the range, or spectrum, of *visible light* is just the tiny slice of electromagnetic radiation that vibrates at wavelengths from just under 400 nanometers to about 750 nanometers. (A *nanometer,* abbreviated *nm,* is a billionth of a meter.) It is correct to refer to light as either *light* waves or *light* rays.

Sensations of light depend on the intensity and wavelength of light waves. **Light intensity**, which refers to how much energy the light contains, is what you sense as the brightness of light, while what color you sense depends mainly on **light wavelength**.

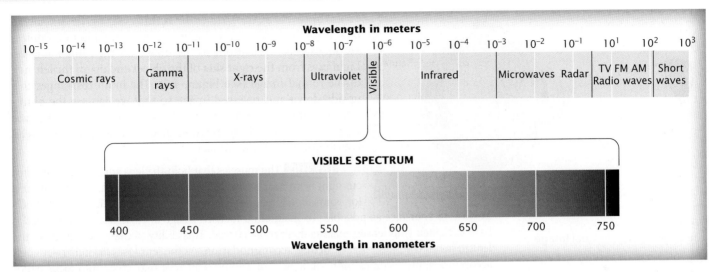

Wavelength in meters

VISIBLE SPECTRUM

Wavelength in nanometers

FIGURE 4.5

The Spectrum of Electromagnetic Energy

The human eye is sensitive to only a narrow range of electromagnetic wavelengths. To detect energy outside this range, we rely on radios, cell phones, TV sets, radar detectors, infrared night-vision scopes, and other electronic instruments that can "see" this energy, just as the eye sees visible light.

frequency The number of complete waves, or cycles, that pass a given point per unit of time.

amplitude The distance between the peak and the baseline of a wave.

light intensity A physical dimension of light waves that refers to how much energy the light contains and that determines our experience of its brightness.

light wavelength A physical dimension of light waves that refers to their length and that produces sensations of different colors.

cornea The curved, transparent, protective layer through which light rays enter the eye.

pupil An opening in the eye just behind the cornea through which light passes.

iris The part of the eye that gives it its color and adjusts the amount of light entering it.

lens The part of the eye directly behind the pupil.

At a given intensity, different wavelengths produce sensations of different colors. For instance, 440-nm light appears violet blue, and 700-nm light appears orange-ish red.

Focusing Light

The eye transduces light energy into neural activity. First, accessory structures of the eye modify incoming light rays. The light rays enter the eye by passing through a curved, transparent, protective layer called the **cornea**. As shown in Figure 4.6, light passes on through the **pupil**, an opening behind the cornea. The **iris**, which gives the eye its color, adjusts the amount of light allowed into the eye by constricting (reducing) or dilating (enlarging) the pupil. Directly behind the pupil is the **lens**.

Both the cornea and lens of the eye are curved so that they bend light rays. (A camera lens works the same way.) This bending process focuses light rays coming from various

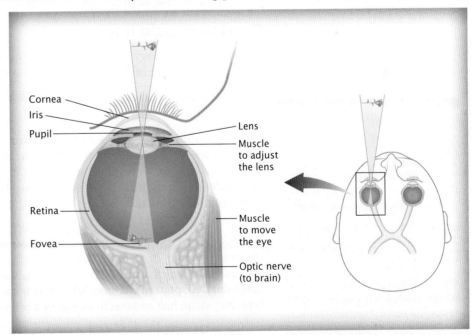

Cornea
Iris
Pupil
Lens
Muscle to adjust the lens
Retina
Fovea
Muscle to move the eye
Optic nerve (to brain)

FIGURE 4.6

Major Structures of the Eye

As shown in this top view of the eye, light rays bent by the combined actions of the cornea and the lens are focused on the retina, where the light energy is converted into neural activity. Nerve fibers from the retina combine to form the optic nerve, which leaves the back of the eye and continues to the brain.

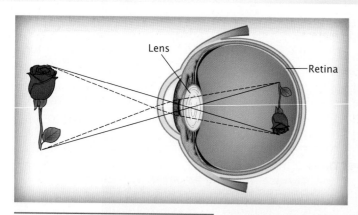

Lens

Retina

FIGURE 4.7

The Lens and the Retinal Image

To see objects as they are, your brain must rearrange the upside-down and reversed images that the lens focuses on the retina. If light rays are out of focus when they reach the retina, glasses usually correct the problem. In some older people, vision is impaired by cataracts, a condition in which a "cloudy" lens severely reduces incoming light. Cataracts can be cleared up with laser surgery or by replacing the natural lens with an artificial one (Snellingen et al., 2002).

angles into a sharp image onto the **retina**, which is the inner surface at the back of the eye. Light rays from the top of an object are focused at the bottom of the image on the retinal surface. Light rays from the right side of the object end up on the left side of the retinal image (see Figure 4.7). The brain rearranges this upside-down and reversed image so that we can see the object as it is. If the brain did not do so, as was claimed to be the case for one unfortunate lady (Haydon, 2013), you might have to read your newspaper upside down!

TRY THIS The muscles that hold the lens adjust its shape to focus light from near or far distances onto the retina. To illustrate this for yourself, try reading the next sentence while holding the book as close to your face as possible. To maintain a focused image at close range, your muscles have to tighten your lenses, making them more curved. This ability to change the shape of the lens to bend light rays is called **ocular accommodation**. As the lens loses flexibility with age, accommodation becomes more difficult. Converging light rays may come into focus either before or after they hit the retina, making images blurry. This is why older people may become "farsighted," seeing distant objects clearly but needing glasses for reading or close work. (For those who want to avoid glasses, a cell phone app has been developed with vision exercises that help train a stiffened lens to become more flexible again; Kaplan, 2014.)

A more common problem for people of all ages is "nearsightedness," in which close objects are clear but distant ones are blurry. This condition has a genetic component, but it may also be made more likely by environmental factors, such as when people spend more time looking at close-up images and less time gazing far away (French et al., 2013). These vision problems can usually be solved with glasses or contact lenses that add light-bending of their own. Other options include laser-assisted in-situ keratomileusis (LASIK) or photo-refractive keratectomy (PRK), eye surgeries that reshape or stretch the cornea (Shortt et al., 2013). These outpatient procedures change how the cornea bends light rays; thus the lens has to do less accommodation, eliminating the need for glasses or contacts.

Converting Light into Images

Converting light energy into neural activity occurs in the retina, using neurons that are actually an extension of the brain. The word *retina* is Latin for "net," and the retina is in fact an intricate network of cells (Masland, 2001).

Rods and Cones

Specialized cells in the retina called **photoreceptors** convert light energy into neural activity. There are two main types of photoreceptors: rods and cones. **Rods** and **cones** are retinal cells that are named for their shapes. These cells contain chemicals that respond to light. When light hits these chemicals, they break apart, creating a signal that can be transferred to the brain.

It takes time to rebuild these light-sensitive chemicals after they break down. This explains why you cannot see well when you come from bright sunshine into a dark room (Mahroo & Lamb, 2004). In the dark, as your rods build up their light-sensitive chemicals, your ability to see gradually increases. The increasing ability to see in the dark over time is called **dark adaptation** (Reuter, 2011). You become about 10,000 times more sensitive to light after about half an hour in a darkened room.

There are three kinds of light-sensitive chemicals in cones, and they provide the basis for color vision. Rods have only one kind of chemical, so they cannot discriminate colors. However, rods are more sensitive to light than cones, so they allow you to see in dim light, as on a moonlit night. It's only at higher light intensities that the cones, with their ability to detect colors, become most active. As a result, you might put on what looked like a matched pair of socks in a darkened bedroom only to go outside and discover that one is dark blue and the other is dark green.

retina The surface at the back of the eye onto which the lens focuses light rays.

ocular accommodation The ability of the lens to change its shape and bend light rays so objects are in focus.

photoreceptors Specialized cells in the retina that convert light energy into neural activity.

rods Photoreceptors in the retina that allow sight even in dim light but that cannot distinguish colors.

cones Photoreceptors in the retina that are less light sensitive than rods but that can distinguish colors.

dark adaptation The increasing ability to see in the dark as time passes.

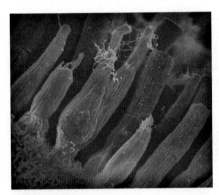

Rods and Cones

FIGURE 4.8

Find Your Blind Spot

TRY THIS There is a blind spot where the optic nerve exits the eye. To "see" your blind spot, cover your left eye and stare at the cross inside the circle. Move the page closer and farther away, and at some point the dot to the right should disappear from view. However, the vertical lines around the dot will probably look continuous, because the brain tends to fill in visual information at the blind spot (Spillmann et al., 2006). We are normally unaware of this "hole" in our vision because the blind spot of one eye is in the normal visual field of the other eye.

---

fovea A region in the center of the retina.

optic nerve A bundle of fibers that carries visual information to the brain.

blind spot The point at which the optic nerve exits the eyeball.

Cones are concentrated in the center of the retina in a circular region called the **fovea**, which is where the eye focuses incoming light. Differences in the density of cones in the fovea can lead to differences in visual *acuity,* or ability to see details (Beirne, Zlatkova, & Anderson, 2005). Decreases in cone density over time may also be partly to blame for some age-related losses in acuity (Song et al., 2011); in people with a condition known as *macular degeneration*, the cones die off altogether, causing blindness (Kent, 2014). New medical treatments may be able to treat such people by transplanting photoreceptors into the retina (Barber et al., 2013). There are no rods in the human fovea. With increasing distance from the fovea, though, the number of cones gradually decreases and the proportion of rods gradually increases. So if you are trying to detect a weak light, such as the light from a faint star, it is better to look slightly away from where you expect to see it. This focuses the weak light on the very light-sensitive rods outside the fovea. Because cones do not work well in low light, looking directly at the star will make it seem to disappear.

From the Retina to the Brain

If the eye simply transferred to the brain the images it focused on the retina, we would experience something like a slightly blurry photograph. Instead, the eye first sharpens visual images. How? The key lies in the interactions among cells of the retina.

Light rays pass through several layers of retinal cells before striking the rods and cones. Signals generated by the rods and cones then go back toward the surface of the retina, making connections with *bipolar cells* and *ganglion cells,* which allow the eye to begin analyzing visual information even before that information leaves the retina (Freeman, Rizzo, & Fried, 2011). Actually, ganglion cells can act as photoreceptors and detect a bit of light all by themselves, but this information seems to be used mainly for keeping our internal body clocks synchronized with the light and dark cycles of the world around us, as discussed in the chapter on consciousness (Münch & Kawasaki, 2013). When it comes to using light for conscious visual sensations, we rely on the photoreceptor work of rods and cones, and the information that they send into bipolar cells and ganglion cells. The axons of the ganglion cells bundle together to form the **optic nerve**, which then connects to the brain. Because there are no receptors for visual stimuli at the point where the optic nerve exits the eyeball, a **blind spot** is created, as Figure 4.8 shows.

After leaving the retina, about half the axons in the optic nerve cross over to the opposite side of the brain, creating a structure called the *optic chiasm*. (*Chiasm* means "cross" and is pronounced "KYE-az-um.") The axons from the inside half of each eye

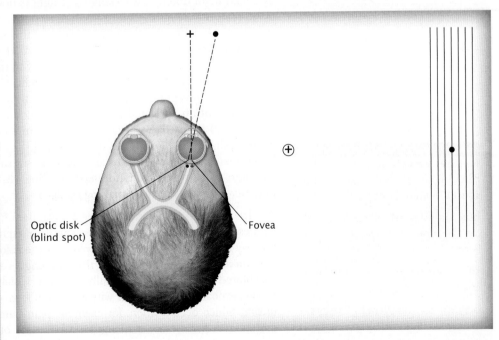

Optic disk
(blind spot)

Fovea

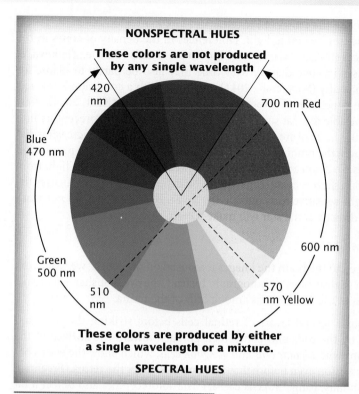

NONSPECTRAL HUES

These colors are not produced by any single wavelength

420 nm

700 nm Red

Blue 470 nm

600 nm

Green 500 nm

510 nm

570 nm Yellow

These colors are produced by either a single wavelength or a mixture.

SPECTRAL HUES

FIGURE 4.9
The Color Circle

Arranging colors according to their psychological similarities creates a color circle that predicts the result of additive mixing of two colored lights. For example, mixing equal amounts of pure green and pure red light will produce yellow, the color that lies at the midpoint of the line connecting red and green. (Note: nm stands for nanometers, the unit in which light wavelengths are measured.)

feature detectors Cells in the cerebral cortex that respond to a specific feature of an object.

hue The essential color determined by the dominant wavelength of light.

color saturation The purity of a color.

brightness The overall intensity of the wavelengths making up light.

(nearest to the nose) cross over. The axons from the outside half of each eye do not. So no matter where you look, all the visual information about the right half of the visual world goes to the left hemisphere of your brain and all the visual information from the left half of the visual world goes to the right hemisphere (Roth, Lora, & Heilman, 2002).

Beyond the optic chiasm, the ganglion cell axons continue into the brain itself, finally forming synapses in the thalamus. Neurons there send axons to connect to the primary visual cortex in the occipital lobe at the back of the brain. The primary visual cortex does initial processing of visual information, then sends that refined information to many association areas of the brain for more specialized processing (Dhruv et al., 2011).

Certain cells in the brain's cerebral cortex are called **feature detectors** because they respond to specific characteristics of objects in the visual world (Hubel & Wiesel, 1979; Jia et al., 2010). For example, one type of feature detector responds most to straight lines of light. Others respond to corners, to angles, or to some other feature. The combined responses of several types of feature-detecting cells help us sense the shapes of objects such as rectangles or triangles. Most people can also detect color. Let's explore how color vision works.

Seeing Color

Like beauty, color is in the eye of the beholder. Many animals see only shades of gray, even when they look at a rainbow, but for humans, color is a key feature of vision.

Wavelengths and Color Sensations

Each wavelength of light is sensed as a certain color. However, the eye rarely (if ever) encounters a "pure" light of a single wavelength. Sunlight, for example, is a mixture of all wavelengths of light. When sunlight passes through a water droplet, each different wavelength of light bends to a different degree, separating into a colorful rainbow. The spectrum of color found in the rainbow illustrates an important concept: The sensation produced by a *mixture* of different wavelengths of light is not the same as the sensations produced by separate wavelengths. Color sensation results from features of the wavelength mixtures striking the eye. The three separate aspects of this sensation are hue, color saturation, and brightness. These labels refer to the *psychological* dimensions of what we experience when the light arrives, and they correspond roughly to the light's physical properties. **Hue**, the essential "color," is determined by the dominant wavelength in the mixture of the light. Black, white, and gray are not hues because they do not have a dominant wavelength. **Color saturation** is related to the purity of color. A color is said to be more *saturated* (more pure) if just one wavelength is more intense (contains more energy) than other wavelengths. The yellow of a school bus and the red of a stop sign are saturated colors. When many other wavelengths are added in, we say that the color is *desaturated*. Pastels are colors that have been desaturated by adding whiteness. **Brightness** refers to the overall intensity of the wavelengths making up light.

The *color circle* shown in Figure 4.9 arranges hues according to their perceived similarities. Mix two different light wavelengths of equal intensity and the color you sense is midway between the two original colors on the color circle. This process is called *additive color mixing*, because the effects of the wavelengths are added together. Keep adding different colored lights and you eventually get white, which is the combination of all wavelengths. You are probably more familiar with a different form of color mixing, called *subtractive color mixing*, which occurs when, for example, paints are combined. Paint, like other physical objects, reflects certain wavelengths and absorbs others. Green paint is green because it

FIGURE 4.10
Individual Differences in Cone Types

These photographs show that people can differ widely from one another in the distribution of blue, green, and red cones in their retinas (Roorda & Williams, 1999). J. W., whose retina is shown at left, has an especially high population of red cones, whereas green cones predominate in A. N., whose retina is shown on the right. Both have normal color vision, but J. W. will be somewhat more sensitive to long wavelengths of light, whereas A. N. will be somewhat more sensitive to light of medium wavelengths.

Reprinted by permission from Nature. Roorda, A. & Williams, D. R. (1999). The arrangement of the three cone classes in the living human eye. Nature, 397, 520–522. Copyright © 1999 Macmillan Magazines Ltd.

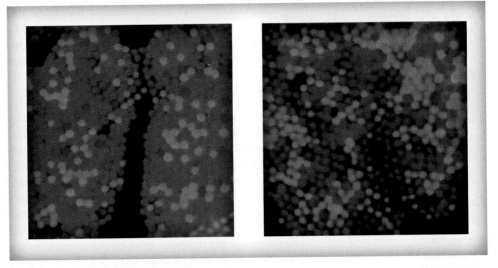

absorbs all wavelengths except wavelengths perceived as green. (White objects appear white because they reflect all wavelengths.) So if you keep combining different colored paints, all of the wavelengths will eventually be subtracted, resulting in black.

Theories of Color Vision

Psychologists have long tried to explain how color vision works, but only two theories have stood the test of time: trichromatic (or "three-color") theory and opponent-process theory.

The Trichromatic Theory of Color Vision

In the early 1800s, Thomas Young proved that mixing pure versions of blue, green, and red light in different ratios could produce any other color; Hermann von Helmholtz later confirmed these findings. The Young-Helmholtz theory of color vision is called the **trichromatic theory**.

Support for trichromatic theory comes from research on cones in the retina. There are three types of cones, each most sensitive to particular wavelengths. *Short-wavelength* cones respond most to light in the blue range. *Medium-wavelength* cones are most sensitive to light in the green range. *Long-wavelength* cones respond best to light in the reddish-yellow range, but by tradition they are known as "red" cones. No single cone by itself can signal the color of a light; it is the *ratio* of the activities of the three types of cones that determines the color you sense. As you can see in Figure 4.10, the exact mixture of these three cone types can differ from person to person. The trichromatic theory was applied in the creation of color television screens, which contain microscopic elements of red, green, and blue. A television broadcast excites these elements to varying degrees, mixing their colors to produce many other colors. You see color mixtures, not patterns of red, green, and blue dots, because the dots are too small and close together to be seen individually. However, with a magnifying glass you may be able to see similar pixels that make up the color photos in your local newspaper.

The Opponent-Process Theory of Color Vision

Although essentially correct, the trichromatic theory cannot explain some aspects of color vision, such as afterimages. To see an afterimage, stare at the black dot in the flag in Figure 4.11 for thirty seconds and then look at the black dot in the white space below it. What was yellow in the original image will be blue in the afterimage. What was green before will appear red, and what was black will now appear white.

This type of observation led Ewald Hering to offer another theory of color vision, called the **opponent-process theory**. Hering suggested that color-sensitive visual elements in the eye are arranged into three kinds of pairs and that the members of each pair

trichromatic theory A theory of color vision stating that information from three types of visual elements combines to produce the sensation of color.

opponent-process theory A theory of color vision stating that the visual elements that are sensitive to color are grouped into red-green, blue-yellow, and black-white pairs.

FIGURE 4.11

Afterimages Produced by the Opponent-Process Nature of Color Vision

TRY THIS Stare at the black dot in the flag for at least thirty seconds and then focus on the dot in the white space below it. The afterimage you will see can be explained by the opponent process theory of color vision. What colors appeared in the afterimage you saw?

oppose, or inhibit, each other. Each element signals one color or the other (red or green, blue or yellow, black or white), but never both. This theory explains color afterimages. When one member of an opponent pair is no longer stimulated, the other is activated. So in Figure 4.11, if the original image you look at is green, the afterimage will be red.

The Bottom Line on Color Vision

Together, the trichromatic and opponent-process theories encompass most of what we now know about the complex process of color vision. We see color because our three types of cones have different sensitivities to different wavelengths. We sense different colors when the three cone types are stimulated in different ratios. Because there are three types of cones, any color can be produced by mixing three pure wavelengths of light. But there is more to it than that. Cones connect to ganglion cells containing pairs of opposing elements that respond to different colors and inhibit each other. This arrangement provides the basis for afterimages. Therefore, the trichromatic theory explains color vision as it relates to rods and cones, whereas the opponent-process theory explains color vision as it relates to the ganglion cells. Both theories are needed to account for the complexity of color sensations (Jacobs, 2008).

Color vision also depends on what happens in the brain—especially in the cortex—where encoded color information from the retinas is assembled and processed (Conway, 2009; Gegenfurtner & Kiper, 2003; Heywood & Kentridge, 2003). As a result, certain kinds of brain damage can weaken or destroy color vision, even though all the cones in the retina are working normally (Bouvier & Engel, 2006).

Color Blindness

Cones normally contain three kinds of chemicals, each of which responds best to a particular wavelength of light. People who have cones containing only two of these three color-sensitive chemicals are described as *color blind* (Neitz & Neitz, 2011). They are not really blind to all color, but they discriminate fewer colors than do other people, as Figure 4.12 shows. Red-green color blindness, for example, means that reds and greens appear to be the same brownish-gray color. Color blindness is more common in men than in women. ("In Review: Seeing" summarizes our discussion of vision.)

FIGURE 4.12

Are You Color Blind?

TRY THIS Photograph A shows how this scene appears to people whose cones have all three types of color-sensitive chemicals. The other photos simulate how colors appear to people who are missing chemicals for long wavelengths (B), short wavelengths (C), or medium wavelengths (D). If any of these photos look to you just like the one at the upper left, you may have a form of color blindness.

Vienot, Brettel, Mollon–MNHN, CNRS

(A)   (B)

(C)   (D)

SEEING

Aspect of Sensory System	Elements	Key Characteristics
Energy	Visible light: electromagnetic radiation with a wavelength of about 400 nm to about 750 nm	The intensity, wavelength, and complexity of light waves determine the brightness, hue, and color saturation of visual sensations.
Accessory structures of the eye	Cornea, pupil, iris, lens	Light rays are bent to focus on the retina.
Conversion of visual stimuli to neural activity	Photoreceptors (rods and cones) in the retina	Rods are more sensitive to light than cones, but cones discriminate among colors. Sensations of color depend first on the cones, which respond differently to different light wavelengths, and then on processing by ganglion cells.
Pathway to the brain	Optic nerve to optic chiasm to thalamus to primary visual cortex	Neurons in the brain respond to particular aspects of the visual stimulus, such as shape.

In Review Questions

1. The ability to see in very dim light depends on photoreceptors called _____.

2. Color afterimages are best explained by the _____ theory of color vision.

3. Nearsightedness and farsightedness occur when images are not focused on the eye's _____.

HEARING

How would my voice sound on the moon?

In 1969, when Neil Armstrong became the first person ever to set foot on the moon, millions of people back on earth heard his radio transmission: "That's one small step for a man, one giant leap for mankind." But if Armstrong had been foolish enough to take off his space helmet and shout, "Whoo-ee! I can moonwalk!" not even an astronaut three feet away could have heard him. Why? Because he would have been speaking into airless, empty space. **Sound** is a repeating fluctuation—a rising and falling—in the pressure of a substance, such as air. Because the moon has almost no atmosphere and almost no air pressure, airborne sound cannot exist there.

Sound

Vibrations of an object produce the fluctuations in pressure that we experience as sound. When you speak, your vocal cords vibrate, causing fluctuations in air pressure that spread as sound waves. Figure 4.13 shows how these changes in air pressure can be described as sound waveforms. The waveforms are drawn in only two dimensions, but remember that sound waves actually move through the air in all directions. This is the reason that when people talk to each other during a movie or a lecture, others all around them are distracted by the conversation.

Just as the amplitude and wavelength of light waves affect our experience of light, characteristics of sound waves shape our experience of sound. The psychological experience we call **loudness** is determined by the amplitude, or height, of a sound wave. Greater amplitudes give louder sounds. Loudness is described in units called *decibels* (abbreviated *dB*). We define 0 dB as the minimum detectable sound for normal hearing. Every increase of 20 dB reflects a tenfold increase in the amplitude of sound waves. So the 40-dB sounds of an office are actually 10 times as intense as a 20-dB whisper; and traffic

sound A repetitive fluctuation in the pressure of a medium such as air.

loudness A psychological dimension of sound determined by the amplitude of a sound wave.

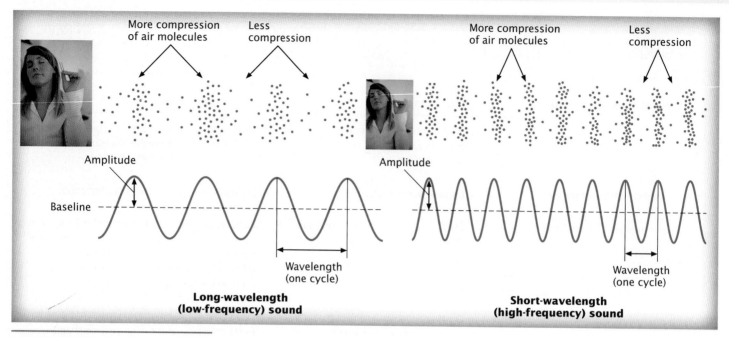

FIGURE 4.13

Sound Waves and Waveforms

Sound is created when objects, such as a tuning fork, vibrate. The vibration creates alternating regions of greater and lesser compression of air molecules, which can be represented as a waveform. The point of greatest compression is the peak of the wave. The lowest point of the wave is where compression is least. In each particular substance, or medium, such as air, a sound's wavelength (the distance between peaks) is related to its frequency (the number of waves per second). The longer the wavelength, the lower the sound frequency. The shorter the wavelength, the higher the frequency.

Daniel Krolls/Getty Images

TRY THIS

pitch How high or low a tone sounds; pitch depends on the frequency of a sound wave.

timbre The quality of a sound that identifies it.

pinna The crumpled part of the outer ear that collects sound waves.

middle ear The part of the ear that contains the hammer, anvil, and stirrup, which transmit sound from the tympanic membrane to the oval window.

noise of 100 dB is 10,000 times as intense as that whisper. The loudest musicians create sound intensity of 160 dB (Levine & Schefner, 1981).

The psychological dimension of **pitch**—how high or low a tone sounds—depends on the frequency of the sound wave. Frequency is the number of complete waves or cycles that pass a given point in one second. It is described in units called *hertz*, abbreviated *Hz* (for Heinrich Hertz, a nineteenth-century physicist). One cycle per second is 1 Hz. High-frequency waves are sensed as sounds of high pitch. The highest note on a piano has a frequency of about 4,000 Hz, and the lowest note has a frequency of about 50 Hz. Humans can hear sounds ranging from about 20 to 20,000 Hz.

Most sounds are a mixture of many frequencies and amplitudes, and this mixture creates a sound's **timbre** (pronounced "TAM-ber"), the psychological dimension of sound quality. Complex wave patterns added to the *fundamental*, or lowest, frequency of sound determine its timbre. The extra waves allow you to tell the difference between, say, a note played on a flute and the same note played on a clarinet.

The Ear

The human ear includes accessory structures that affect sound waves initially and transduction mechanisms that convert sound energy into neural activity. The visible part of the ear on the side of the head, called the **pinna**, collects sound waves in the outer ear. (People trying to hear a faint sound may cup a hand to their ear because this action tilts the pinna forward and enlarges the area that is collecting sound. Try this for a moment, and you will notice a clear difference in the sounds you hear.) The pinna funnels sound down through the ear canal. At the end of the ear canal, the sound waves reach the **middle ear** (see Figure 4.14). There they strike the **tympanic membrane**, a tightly stretched structure also known as the **eardrum**. The sound waves set up vibrations in the tympanic membrane. The *hammer*, the *anvil*, and the *stirrup*, three tiny bones named for their shapes, amplify these vibrations and direct them onto a smaller membrane called the *oval window*.

The Inner Ear

Sound vibrations passing through the oval window enter the inner ear, reaching the **cochlea** (pronounced "KOK-lee-ah"), where transduction occurs. The cochlea is rolled into a coiled spiral. (*Cochlea* comes from the Greek word for "snail.") A fluid-filled tube

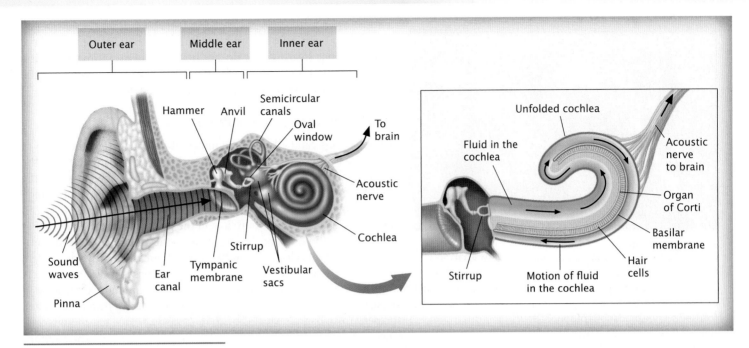

FIGURE 4.14
Structures of the Ear

The outer ear (pinna and ear canal) channels sound waves into the middle ear, where the vibrations of the tympanic membrane are amplified by the delicate bones that stimulate the cochlea. The close-up view of the cochlea shows how the vibrations of the stirrup set up vibrations in the fluid inside the cochlea. The coils of the cochlea are unrolled in this illustration to show the path of the fluid waves along the basilar membrane. Movements of the basilar membrane stimulate hair cells, which transduce the vibrations into changes in neural activity, which are sent along the acoustic nerve to the brain.

runs down its length. The **basilar membrane** forms the floor of this tube, as you can see in Figure 4.14. When a sound wave passes through the fluid in the tube, it makes the basilar membrane rise and fall like a bedsheet on a clothesline flapping in the wind (Ren, 2002). This movement, in turn, bends *hair cells* on the membrane. These hair cells make connections with fibers from the **acoustic nerve**, a bundle of axons that goes into the brain. Bending the hair cells stimulates the acoustic nerve, also known as the *auditory nerve*, which sends encoded signals to the brain about the amplitude and frequency of the sound waves (Griesinger, Richards, & Ashmore, 2005). These signals allow you to sense loudness, pitch, and timbre.

Deafness

The middle and inner ear are among the most delicate structures in the body, and damage to them can lead to impaired hearing or deafness. One form of deafness can be caused when the bones of the middle ear fuse together, preventing accurate conduction of vibrations (Stenfelt, 2011). This condition, called *conduction deafness,* can be treated by surgery to break the bones apart or to replace the natural bones with plastic ones (Manrique et al., 2014). Hearing aids that amplify incoming sounds can also help.

Nerve deafness results when the acoustic nerve or, more commonly, the hair cells that feed information to it, are damaged (Shepherd & McCreery, 2006). Hair-cell damage occurs gradually with age, but hair cells can be damaged earlier and more suddenly by very loud sounds, including amplified music (Sliwinska-Kowalska & Davis, 2012). High-intensity sounds actually rip the hair cells off the inner ear. Generally, any sound loud enough to produce ringing in the ears causes some damage. In humans, small amounts of damage gradually build up and can lead to significant hearing loss by middle age—as many older rock musicians (and their fans) later find out (Levine, 1999). Listening to music at high volume through headphones can also cause hearing loss (Petrescu, 2008; Vogel et al., 2009), which may explain the recent increase in hearing loss among adolescents (Shargorodsky et al., 2010).

Hair cells can be regenerated in chickens' ears (Cotanche, 1997), and a related kind of inner-ear hair cell has been regenerated in mammals (Malgrange et al., 1999). Scientists hope that human hair-cell regeneration might be possible by treating damaged areas with growth factors similar to those being used to repair damaged brain cells (Shepherd et al., 2005; see the chapter on biological aspects of psychology). Inserting genes that might stimulate the regrowth of damaged hair cells (Xia & Yin, 2013) and using stem cells to

tympanic membrane (eardrum) A tightly stretched membrane in the middle ear that generates vibrations that match the sound waves striking it.

cochlea A fluid-filled spiral structure in the inner ear in which auditory transduction occurs.

basilar membrane The floor of the fluid-filled duct that runs through the cochlea.

acoustic nerve The bundle of axons that carries messages from the hair cells of the cochlea to the brain.

Shaping the Brain

The brain region known as the primary auditory cortex is larger in trained musicians than in people whose jobs are less focused on fine gradations of sound. How much larger this area becomes is correlated with how long the musicians have studied their art. This finding reminds us that, as described in the chapter on biological aspects of psychology, the brain can literally be shaped by experience and other environmental factors.

Å © iStockphoto.com/mediaphotos

create new hair cells (Shi, Hu, & Edge, 2013) are two other promising approaches. Such efforts could revolutionize the treatment of nerve deafness, since hearing aids do not help. In the meantime, scientists have developed an artificial cochlea that can be implanted in the human ear to stimulate the acoustic nerve (Gaylor et al., 2013).

Auditory Pathways to the Brain

Before sounds can be heard, the information encoded in the firing of the many axons that make up the acoustic nerve must be sent to the brain for further analysis. This transmission process begins when the acoustic nerve conveys the information to the thalamus. From there, the information is relayed to the *primary auditory cortex,* an area in the temporal lobe of the brain. It is in the primary auditory cortex that information about sound is subjected to the most intense and complex analysis (Ciocca, 2008). Certain cells in the auditory cortex are differently specialized, much as different cells in the visual cortex show specialized responses to various aspects of light information. In the auditory cortex, different cells seem to fire most vigorously in response to sounds of particular frequencies; these are known as *preferred frequencies.* Each neuron in the acoustic nerve also has a "favorite," or characteristic, frequency, though each also responds to a range of frequencies, to some extent (Schnee et al., 2005). The auditory cortex examines the pattern of activity of many neurons to determine the frequency of a sound. This auditory analysis may be especially efficient in people who were deprived of visual experience because of blindness early in life (Stevens & Weaver, 2009).

Some parts of the auditory cortex are devoted to processing certain types of sounds. One part, for example, specializes in information from human speech (Belin, Zatorre, & Ahad, 2002); others are particularly responsive to sounds coming from animals, tools, or musical instruments (Lewis et al., 2005; Zatorre, 2003). Some specialization in the auditory cortex can be seen in brain scans. For example, fMRI scans of the auditory cortex look different in people who are listening to music and lyrics than to music alone (Brattico et al., 2011). Observing which brain areas become activated by which kind of sound has allowed researchers to detect whether a person is listening to words spoken by a familiar or unfamiliar voice and even to identify some details about what is being said (Formisano et al., 2008). The primary auditory cortex receives information from other senses as well. For example, it is activated when you watch someone say words (but not when the person makes other facial movements). This may reflect a biological basis for the lip-reading that helps you hear what people say (Campbell & Capek, 2008).

Encoding Sounds

Most people hear a wide range of sound intensities. The faintest sound that can be heard barely moves the ear's hair cells. Sounds more than a trillion times more intense can also be heard. Between these extremes, the auditory system encodes intensity in a simple way: The more intense the sound, the more rapid the firing of a given neuron. We're also very good at detecting differences between sound frequencies that allow us to hear differences in pitch (Shera, Guinan, & Oxenham, 2002). Information about frequency differences appears to be encoded in two ways: by their location on the basilar membrane and by the rate at which the auditory neurons fire.

As sound waves move down the basilar membrane, they reach a peak and then taper off, much like an ocean wave that crests and then dissolves. The waves produced by high-frequency sounds peak soon after they start down the basilar membrane. Waves produced by lower-frequency sounds peak farther down the basilar membrane. According to **place theory**, the greatest response by hair cells occurs at the peak of the wave. Because the location of the peak varies with the frequency of sound, it follows that hair cells at a particular place on the basilar membrane are most responsive to a particular frequency of sound. When cells with a particular characteristic frequency fire, we sense a sound of that frequency.

place theory A theory of hearing that states that hair cells at a particular place on the basilar membrane respond most to a particular frequency of sound.

But place theory cannot explain the encoding of very low frequencies (such as deep bass notes) because none of the acoustic nerve fibers have very low preferred frequencies. However, humans can hear frequencies as low as 20 hertz, so they must be encoded somehow. The answer appears to be *frequency matching*, a process in which certain neurons in the acoustic nerve fire each time a sound wave passes. So a sound wave whose frequency is 25 cycles per second would cause those neurons to fire 25 times per second. Frequency-matching theory is sometimes called the **volley theory** of frequency encoding because the outputs of many cells can combine to create a *volley* of firing.

The nervous system apparently uses more than one way to encode the range of audible frequencies. The lowest frequencies are encoded by frequency matching. Low to moderate frequencies are encoded by frequency matching as well as by the place on the basilar membrane where the wave peaks. And high frequencies are encoded solely by the place on the basilar membrane where the wave peaks. ("In Review: Hearing" summarizes the encoding process and other aspects of the auditory system.)

IN REVIEW

HEARING

Aspect of Sensory System	Elements	Key Characteristics
Energy	Sound: pressure fluctuations of air produced by vibrations	Amplitude, frequency, and complexity of sound waves determine the loudness, pitch, and timbre of sounds.
Accessory structures of the ear	Pinna, tympanic membrane, hammer, anvil, stirrup, oval window, basilar membrane	Changes in pressure produced by the original wave are amplified.
Conversion of sound frequencies into neural activity	Hair cells in the inner ear	Frequencies are encoded by the location of the hair cells receiving the greatest stimulation (place theory) and by the combined firing rate of neurons (volley theory).
Pathway to the brain	Acoustic nerve to thalamus to primary auditory cortex	Auditory cortex examines patterns of information from the auditory nerve, allowing us to sense loudness, pitch, and timbre.

In Review Questions

1. Sound energy is converted to neural activity in an inner ear structure called the _____.

2. Hearing loss due to damage to hair cells or the acoustic nerve is called _____.

3. How high or low a sound sounds is called _____ and is determined by the _____ of a sound wave.

Interaction of the Senses: Synesthesia

At the beginning of this chapter, we described the interaction of two senses, vision and touch, but there are many other kinds of interactions. For example, vision interacts with hearing. If a brief sound occurs just as lights are flashed, it can create the impression of more lights than there actually are (Shams, Kamitani, & Shimojo, 2000). Such interactions occur in everyone, but some people also report *synesthesia* (pronounced "sin-ess-THEE-zhuh"), a more unusual and stronger mixing of senses or of dimensions within senses (Ward, 2013). Some of these people say that they "feel" colors or sounds as touches or that they "taste" shapes or "smell" sounds; others say that they see certain colors, such as red, when they hear certain sounds, such as a trumpet or spoken words

volley theory A theory of hearing that states that the firing rate of an acoustic nerve matches a sound wave's frequency. Also called frequency-matching theory.

FIGURE 4.15
Synesthesia

In this experiment on synesthesia, a triangular pattern of Hs was embedded in a background of other letters, as shown at left. Most people find it difficult to detect the triangle, but J. C., a person with synesthesia, picked it out immediately because, as simulated at right, he saw the Hs as green, the Fs as yellow, and the Ps as red.

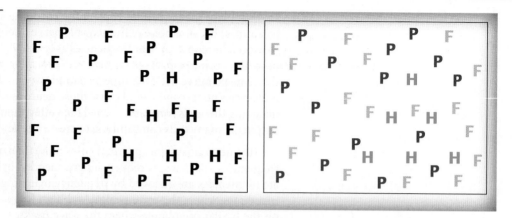

(Bargary et al., 2009). Though once dismissed as poetic delusions, many claims of synesthesia have been supported by scientific investigation (e.g., Hochel & Milán, 2008; see Figure 4.15).

Some researchers suggest that synesthesia occurs partly because brain areas that process one aspect of sensation (such as color) are near areas that process other aspects (such as the features of letters and numbers). Perhaps the synaptic connections between these neighboring areas are more extensive in people who experience synesthesia (Bargary & Mitchell, 2008; Wesson & Wilson, 2010). Synesthesia experiences are also associated with unusually wide-ranging activity in brain regions that process different kinds of sensory information (Hubbard & Ramachandran, 2005).

THE CHEMICAL SENSES: TASTE AND SMELL

Why can't I taste anything when I have a cold?

Some animals cannot see and some cannot hear, but all animals have some form of chemical sense. Chemical senses arise from the interaction of chemicals and receptors. **Olfactory perception**, also known as *olfaction*, or our **sense of smell**, detects chemicals that are airborne, or volatile. **Taste perception**, also known as *gustatory perception*, detects chemicals in solution that come into contact with receptors inside the mouth. These systems are connected.

Smell, Taste, and Flavor

If you have a stuffy nose, everything tastes like cardboard. Why? Because smell and taste act as two components of a single system known as *flavor* (Rozin, 1982). Most of the properties that make food taste good are actually odors detected by the olfactory system, not chemicals detected by the taste system. The scent and taste pathways converge in the *orbitofrontal cortex* of the brain (Rolls, 2006), perhaps explaining how smell and taste come to seem like one sensation.

Both tastes and odors prompt strong emotional responses. For tastes, the emotional reaction to bitterness or sweetness appears to be inborn (Mueller et al., 2005), but for most mammals, including humans, there are few other innate flavor preferences. Most of what we like to eat, and what we avoid, is based on the experiences we have had with various foods (Myers & Sclafani, 2006). Our emotional reactions to odors, too, are shaped by learning (Bartoshuk, 1991). In one study, people smelled a variety of odors while experiencing either pleasant or unpleasant tastes. Later, odors they had once rated as neutral were rated as pleasant if they had been paired with pleasant tastes (Barkat et al., 2008). Emotional reactions to smells can also be affected by expectations. Consider a study in which people sniffed an air sample that was described as coming from either cheddar cheese or body odor. Those who thought they were smelling body odor rated the air sample as more unpleasant than those who thought they were smelling cheese (de Araujo et al., 2005).

olfactory perception (sense of smell) The sense that detects chemicals that are airborne. Also called olfaction.

taste perception The sense that detects chemicals in solution that come into contact with receptors inside the mouth. Also called gustatory perception.

Variations in nutritional state also affect our experience of taste and flavor and our motivation to eat specific foods (Yeomans & Mobini, 2006). If we are deprived of food or don't get enough salt, then sweet or salty things taste better. Nutrition has a less direct influence on protein and fat intake. Protein and fat molecules have no particular taste or smell, so preferring or avoiding foods that contain these nutrients is based on associations between scent cues from other volatile substances in food and on the nutritional results of eating the foods (Bartoshuk, 1991; Schiffman et al., 1999).

We experience warm foods as sweeter, but temperature does not alter our experience of saltiness (Cruz & Green, 2000). Warming releases aromas that rise from the mouth into the nose and create more flavor sensations. This is why some people find hot pizza delicious and cold pizza disgusting. Spicy "hot" foods actually stimulate pain fibers in the mouth because they contain a substance called *capsaicin* (pronounced "kap-SAY-uh-sin") that stimulates pain-sensing neurons that are also stimulated by heat (Reyes-Escogido, Gonzalez-Mondragon, & Vazquez-Tzompantzi, 2011).

Our Sense of Smell

Pinching your nose makes it hard for you to smell odors, and putting a dilator strip on the bridge of your nose opens your nasal passages and intensifies odors (Raudenbush & Meyer, 2002). These effects occur because the nose (and the mouth, to some extent) acts as an accessory structure to collect airborne odor molecules and funnel them toward the olfactory sensory nerve cells (see Figure 4.16). As a result, odor molecules pass into the moist lining of the upper part of the nose—called the *mucous membrane*—and bind to receptors on the dendrites of olfactory neurons, causing a biochemical change. This change, in turn, leads to changes in the firing rates of these neurons, whose axons combine to form the *olfactory nerve* (Dionne & Dubin, 1994). It takes only a single molecule of an odorous substance to

Figure 4.16

The Olfactory System: The Nose and the Rose

Airborne odor molecules reach the olfactory area either through the nose or through an opening in the palate at the back of the mouth. This opening allows us to sample odors from our food as we eat. Nerve fibers pass directly from the olfactory area to the olfactory bulb in the brain, and from there signals pass to areas that are involved in emotion. This arrangement helps explain why odors often trigger strong emotional memories.

Ron Krisel/The Image Bank/Getty Images; © iStockphoto.com/ra3rn

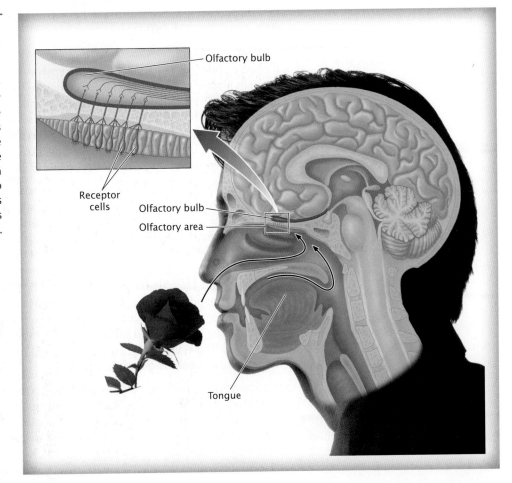

Olfactory bulb

Receptor cells

Olfactory bulb

Olfactory area

Tongue

cause a change in the activity of an olfactory neuron, but it takes about fifty such molecules before a human will detect the odor (Reed, 2004). The number of molecules needed to trigger an olfactory sensation can vary, however. For example, women are more sensitive to odors during certain phases of their menstrual cycles (Navarrete-Palacios et al., 2003).

Olfactory neurons are repeatedly replaced with new ones, as each lives only about two months (Ruitenberg & Vukovic, 2008). Scientists are especially interested in this process because, as noted in the chapter on biological aspects of psychology, most neurons cannot divide to create new ones. Understanding how new olfactory neurons are generated—and re-create appropriate connections in the brain—may someday help treat brain and spinal cord damage.

There are about a thousand different receptors for odors (Pinto, 2011) but there are even more possible odors in the world, and it seems that humans can discriminate over a trillion different ones (Bushdid et al., 2014). Any particular odor is sensed as a particular *pattern* of responses by these odorant receptors, and humans can discriminate among tens of thousands of different odors (Kajiya et al., 2001; Zou & Buck, 2006). So a rose, a pizza, and your favorite cologne each have a different smell because they stimulate their own unique patterns of activity in your odorant receptors. Scientists are just beginning to understand exactly how this odor encoding system works (Ma, 2007). This work has taken on special importance since the September 11, 2001, terrorist attacks in the United States. Researchers have intensified their efforts to develop an "electronic nose" capable of detecting odorants associated with guns and explosives (Thaler, Kennedy, & Hanson, 2001; Wilson & Baietto, 2011). Versions of these devices are in use at some airports. Elsewhere, electronic noses have been used to detect spoiled food (Abdullah et al., 2012) or assess air quality (Dentoni et al., 2012), and help doctors diagnose and treat patients. One electronic nose can "smell" the breath of asthma patients to predict who will respond to a medication (van der Schee et al., 2013). Other electronic noses detect cancers (Leunis et al., 2013), lung disease (Dragonieri et al., 2012), or liver failure (Wlodzimirow et al., 2013).

Unlike other senses, our sense of smell does not send its messages through the thalamus. Instead, axons from olfactory neurons in the upper nose extend straight up through a bony plate of the skull, directly into the brain, reaching a structure called the **olfactory bulb**, where odor processing continues (Kay & Sherman, 2007). Connections from the olfactory bulb spread throughout the brain (Zou, Li, & Buck, 2005), but they are especially plentiful in the amygdala, a part of the brain involved in emotional experience and learning (Su, Menuz, & Carlson, 2009). In humans, the amygdala is especially active in response to disgusting odors (Zald & Pardo, 1997).

The unique anatomy of the olfactory system may help account for the intense relationship between smells and emotion (Stevenson & Boakes, 2003). Smells tend to evoke emotional states, for example. Associations between particular odors and experiences—especially emotional experiences—are not weakened much by time or later experiences (Lawless & Engen, 1977). So catching a whiff of the cologne once worn by a lost loved one can reactivate intense feelings of love or sadness associated with that person. Odors can also bring back accurate memories of experiences linked with them, especially emotionally positive experiences (Engen, Gilmore, & Mair, 1991; Mohr et al., 2001). These special features of the olfactory system may account for the fact that losing the sense of smell can sometimes be an early sign of brain diseases that disrupt memory and emotion (Ruan et al., 2012). This is why doctors have developed special tests to identify even small changes in the sense of smell (Haxel et al., 2011).

Species ranging from humans to worms have remarkably similar neural mechanisms for sensing smell. And all mammals, including humans, have brain systems for detecting the source of smells by comparing the strength of sensory inputs reaching the left and right nostrils (Porter et al., 2005). Different species vary considerably, however, in their sensitivity to odor and in the degree to which they depend on it for survival. Humans have about 9 million olfactory neurons, compared with about 225 million in dogs, a

olfactory bulb A brain structure that receives messages regarding smell.

species far more dependent on smell to identify food, territory, and receptive mates. Dogs and many other species also have an accessory olfactory system that detects pheromones. **Pheromones** (pronounced "FAIR-oh-mohns") are chemicals that are released by one creature and when detected by another can shape the second animal's behavior or physiology (Swaney & Keverne, 2009). For example, when a male snake detects a chemical on the skin of a female snake, it is stimulated to court her. Other pheromones may be released during emotional states, such as fear, thereby alerting nearby animals of possible danger (Hauser et al., 2011).

The discovery of a possible human gene for pheromone receptors (Rodriguez et al., 2000) suggests that people may have a physiological basis for this type of social communication, but to date there are only limited examples of known pheromone influence on human behavior (Gelstein et al., 2011; Mildner & Buchbauer, 2013; Wyatt, 2009). For example, men have been shown to behave in more sexually oriented ways when around women who are ovulating (Haselton & Gildersleeve, 2011; Miller & Maner, 2010). Other research shows that women make more risky decisions while playing a computer game if they are first exposed to sweat samples taken from men who had been under stress (Haegler et al., 2010). Pheromones have also been shown to cause reproduction-related physiological changes in humans (Grammer, Fink, & Neave, 2005). Specifically, pheromonal signals secreted in women's perspiration can influence nearby women's menstrual cycles. As a result, women living together eventually tend to menstruate at about the same time (Stern & McClintock, 1998). Furthermore, odorants that cannot be consciously detected can nevertheless influence mood and stimulate activity in non-olfactory areas of the brain (e.g., Jacob et al., 2001).

Despite steamy ads for cologne and perfume, however, there is little or no evidence that humans give off or can detect pheromones that promote sexual behavior (Mast & Samuelsen, 2009). In one study, for example, exotic dancers reported that their income from customer tips increased during the ovulation phase of their menstrual cycles (Miller, Tyber, & Jordan, 2007), but the difference was probably not due to pheromones. During ovulation, females tend to speak in a more sexually alluring way (Pipitone & Gallup, 2008), to be more interested in erotic stimuli (Mass et al., 2008), and to be more receptive to courtship (Gueguen, 2008; Rosen & López, 2009). So it could well be that differences in their behavior, and not pheromones, were responsible for their higher tip income during ovulation (Miller, Tyber, & Jordan, 2007).

If a certain scent does enhance a person's readiness for sex, it is probably because the person has learned to associate that scent with previous sexual experiences. There are many other examples of people using olfactory information in social situations. For instance, after just a few hours of contact with their newborn babies, mothers can usually identify their infant by smell (Porter, Cernich, & McLaughlin, 1983). And if infants are breastfed, they can discriminate their own mother's odor from that of other breastfeeding women and appear to be comforted by it (Porter, 1991). Recognizing this odor may help establish the mother-infant bond discussed in the chapter on human development.

Our Sense of Taste

Our receptors for taste are in the taste buds, which are grouped together in structures called **papillae** (pronounced "puh-PILL-ee"). Normally, there are about 10,000 taste buds in a person's mouth, mostly on the tongue but also on the roof of the mouth and on the back of the throat. Unlike the many complexities of flavor, which combines the experiences of smell and taste, when it comes to human taste alone, we detect only a few basic sensations: sweet, sour, bitter, and salty. Each taste bud responds best to one or two of these categories (Zhang et al., 2003), but it responds weakly to others, too. Research has also revealed two additional taste sensations (Rolls, 1997). One, called *umami* (which means "delicious" in Japanese), enhances other tastes and is produced by certain proteins as well as by monosodium glutamate (MSG; Beauchamp, 2009). The other, called *astringent,* is the taste produced by tannins, which are found in tea and wine, for example. Activa

pheromones Chemicals that are released by one creature and detected by another, shaping the second creature's behavior or physiology.

papillae Structures in the mouth on which taste buds are grouped.

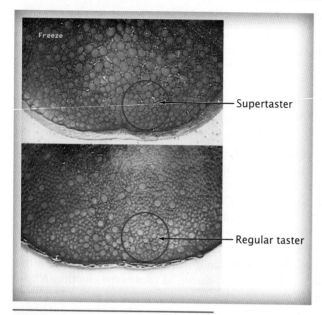

Supertaster

Regular taster

FIGURE 4.17
Are You a Supertaster?

TRY THIS The top photo shows papillae on the tongue of a "supertaster." If you don't mind a temporary stain on your mouth and teeth, you can look at your own papillae by painting the front of your tongue with a cotton swab soaked in blue food coloring. Distribute the dye by moving your tongue around and swallowing; then look into a magnifying mirror as you shine a flashlight on your tongue. The pink circles you see against the blue background are papillae, each of which has about six taste buds buried in its surface. Get several friends to do this test, and you will see that genes create wide individual differences in taste-bud density.

Linda Bartoshuk, Ph.D., Director of Human Research, Center for Smell and Taste, University of Florida

of each specific basic taste activates a correspondingly different set of brain areas (Chen et al., 2011; Rolls, 2009) and causes different patterns of blood flow to the face (Kashima & Hayashi, 2011).

About 25 percent of us are *supertasters*—individuals whose genes have given them an especially large number of papillae on their tongues (Bartoshuk, 2000; Hayes & Keast, 2011; see Figure 4.17). Supertasters are more sensitive than other people to bitterness, as revealed in their reactions to foods such as broccoli, soy products, and grapefruit.

Scientists are learning more and more about how foods interact with taste receptors to signal various tastes (e.g., Chandrashekar et al., 2006), and they are putting the information to good use. Understanding how we detect sweetness, for example, has led to new chemicals that fit into sweetness receptors and taste thousands of times sweeter than sugar. When used as artificial sweeteners, they offer new ways to enjoy good-tasting but low-calorie sweets. Interestingly, it turns out that the sensation of sweetness can bypass the traditional taste system altogether. Scientists have learned that food chemicals evaporate in our mouths as we eat, and some of the "volatile" compounds that result stimulate the smell system. This process can create a sweet taste sensation without involving the taste buds (Tieman et al., 2012). So, in part, you "taste" sweetness with your nose! Researchers are also looking into how taste is affected by other senses such as hearing. It appears, for example, that people may experience the taste of wine differently depending on the type of music they hear while drinking it (North, 2011). ("In Review: Smell and Taste" summarizes our discussion of these senses.)

IN REVIEW

SMELL AND TASTE

Aspect of Sensory System	Elements	Key Characteristics
Energy	Smell: volatile chemicals Taste: chemicals in solution	The amount, intensity, and location of the chemicals determine taste and smell sensations.
Structures of taste and smell	Smell: chemical receptors in the mucous membrane of the nose Taste: taste buds grouped in papillae in the mouth	Odor and taste molecules stimulate chemical receptors.
Pathway to the brain	Olfactory bulb and taste buds	Axons from the nose and mouth bypass the thalamus and extend directly to the olfactory bulb.

In Review Questions

1. The flavor of food arises from a combination of _____ and _____.

2. Emotion and memory are linked especially closely to our sense of _____.

3. Perfume ads suggest that humans are affected by _____ that increase sexual attraction.

SENSING YOUR BODY

Which is the largest organ in my body?

Some senses are not located in one place, such as in the eye or the ear. These are the *somatic senses,* also called *somatosensory systems,* and they are spread throughout the body. The **cutaneous senses** include the skin senses of touch, temperature, and pain. Another body sense, called *kinesthesia,* or *kinesthetic perception,* tells the brain where the parts of the body are. Kinesthetic perception is closely related to our sense of balance. Although balance is not strictly a somatosensory system, we describe it here.

Touch and Temperature

People can function and prosper without vision, hearing, or smell. But a person with no sense of touch might not survive. Without this sense, you could not even swallow food, because you could not tell where it was in your mouth and throat. You receive touch sensations through your skin, which is the body's largest organ. The skin covers nearly two square yards of surface area, weighs more than twenty pounds, and has hair virtually everywhere on it. The hairs on your skin do not sense anything, but they bend when contacted, creating pressure at their bases which stimulates touch receptors on and in the skin beneath them. Neural receptors in and just below the skin send the information from "touch" to the brain (Delmas, Hao, & Rodat-Despoix, 2011).

Encoding Touch Information

The sense of touch encodes information about two aspects of an object contacting the skin: its weight and its location. The *intensity* of the stimulus—how heavy it is—is encoded both by the firing rate of individual neurons and by the number of neurons stimulated. A heavy object triggers a higher rate of firing and stimulates more neurons than a light object. The brain "knows" where the touch occurs based on the *location* of the nerves that sense the touch information.

Touch information is organized so that signals from neighboring points on the skin stay next to one another as they travel from the skin through the spinal cord to the thalamus and on to the somatosensory cortex. So just as there is a map of the visual field in the brain, the area of cortex that receives touch information resembles a map of the surface of the body. As with the other senses, input from the left side of the body goes to the right side of the brain, and vice versa.

Adapting to Touch Stimuli

Continuous, unchanging input from all your touch neurons would provide a lot of unnecessary information. Once you get dressed, you don't need to be constantly reminded that you are wearing clothes. Thanks in part to the process of sensory adaptation described earlier, you don't continue to feel your clothes against your skin.

Changes in touch (as when your belt or shoe suddenly feels loose) provide the most important sensory information. The touch sense emphasizes these changes and acts to filter out the excess information. How? Typically, a touch neuron responds with a burst of firing when a stimulus is applied then quickly returns to its baseline firing rate, even though the stimulus may still be in contact with the skin. If the touch pressure increases, the neuron again responds by increasing its firing rate and then slowing down. A few neurons adapt more slowly, however, continuing to fire as long as pressure is applied. By attending to this input, you can sense a constant stimulus **TRY THIS** (try doing this by focusing on touch sensations from your clothes or shoes, or the surface you are sitting on).

Sensing Temperature

Some of the skin's sensory neurons respond to a change in temperature but not to simple contact. "Warm fibers" and "cold fibers" respond to specific temperature changes only.

Timing Is Everything

TRY THIS Some touch sensations depend on the timing of skin stimulation. You can experience this for yourself if you first try to feel the roughness of sandpaper by just placing your fingers on it. A much clearer sensation of roughness will appear if you slide your fingers over the surface (Hollins & Bensamaia, 2007). As you do so, the ridges that form your fingerprints vibrate in succession, activating special receptors in each ridge. Encoded messages about the timing of this sequence of activation tells the brain about the characteristics of the surface you are touching (Hartmann, 2009; Scheibert et al., 2009).

Ted Foxx/Alamy

cutaneous senses Senses including touch, temperature, pain, and kinesthetic perception that are spread throughout the body. Also called somatosensory systems.

A Girl Who Can't Feel Pain

Ashlyn Blocker, shown here being tested at age eleven, was born with a rare genetic disorder that prevented the development of pain receptors. As a result, she feels no pain if she is cut or bruised, if she bites her tongue while eating, or even if she is burned by hot soup or a hot stove. She only knows she has been injured if she sees herself bruised or bleeding, so she must find ways to protect herself from danger without the vital information provided by the pain system.

Erica Brough/The Gainesville Sun

However, many of these neural receptors respond not just to temperature but also to touch, so these sensations sometimes interact. For example, if you touch an object made up of alternating warm and cool sections, you'll have the sensation of intense heat (Thunberg, 1896, cited in Craig & Bushnell, 1994).

Pain

Touch can feel pleasurable, but if the intensity of touch stimulation increases too much, it can turn into a pain sensation. Pain tells you about the impact of the world on your body. It also has a distinctly negative emotional component that interrupts whatever you are doing (Eccleston & Crombez, 1999).

Pain as an Information Sense

The receptors for pain are free nerve endings that come from the spinal cord, enter the skin, and then simply end. Painful stimuli cause the release of chemicals that fit into these specialized receptors in pain neurons, causing them to fire. The axons of pain-sensing neurons release neurotransmitters not only near the spinal cord (thus sending pain information to the brain) but also near the skin (causing inflammation).

Two types of nerve fibers carry pain signals from the skin to the spinal cord. *A-delta fibers* carry signals that feel like sharp, pricking pain sensations; *C-fibers* carry signals that create a sensation of dull, continuous aches and burning sensations. When you stub your toe, for example, that immediate wave of sharp, intense pain is signaled by A-delta fibers, whereas that slightly delayed wave of gnawing, dull pain is signaled by C-fibers. When pain impulses reach the spinal cord, they form synapses with neurons that relay the pain signals to the thalamus and other parts of the brain. Different pain neurons are activated by different types and degrees of painful stimulation (Ploner et al., 2002).

Emotional Aspects of Pain

Specific pathways carry the emotional component of a painful stimulus to areas of the hindbrain, the reticular formation, and the cortex via the thalamus (Shackman et al., 2011). However, our overall emotional response depends greatly on our mood and how we think about the pain (e.g., Kirschneck et al., 2013; Miró, Huguet, & Jensen, 2014). In one study, some participants were told about the kind of painful stimulus they were to receive and when to expect it. Others were not informed. Those who knew what to expect objected less to the pain, even though the sensation was reported to be equally noticeable in both groups (Mayer & Price, 1982). People can lessen their emotional responses to pain by using pain-reducing strategies such as listening to music or focusing on pictures or distracting thoughts (e.g., Buhle et al., 2012; Simavli et al., 2013), especially if they expect these strategies to succeed (Bantick et al., 2002). Another emerging technology is "real-time functional MRI," a system that allows people to watch their own brain activity, live as it occurs, on a video display (Weiskopf, 2012). When people in pain view these images, they can learn movements, behaviors, or relaxation techniques that lessen activity in brain regions that process pain signals, and as they do so, they experience pain relief (Chapin, Bagarinao, & Mackey, 2013).

The Gate Control Theory of Pain

gate control theory of pain A theory suggesting the presence of a "gate" in the spinal cord that either permits or blocks the passage of pain impulses to the brain.

Pain is useful because it can protect you from harm. There are times, though, when enough is enough. Fortunately, the nervous system has several ways to control the experience of pain. One theory about how these mechanisms work is called the **gate control theory of pain** (Melzack & Wall, 1965). The theory suggests that a "gate" in the spinal cord either allows pain signals to reach the brain or stops them. Some

Itchy and Scratchy

The gate control theory of pain may partly explain why scratching relieves itching, because itch sensations involve activity in fibers located close to pain fibers (Andrew & Craig, 2001). Scratching itchy skin also activates brain regions related to reward (Vierow et al., 2009) and creates the temporary pleasure you get from doing so. Itch was once thought to result from low-level activity in pain neurons, but we now know that there are sensory pathways from the skin to the brain specifically dedicated to itch (Sun et al., 2009). Scientists are working on ways to block the spinal cord's response to itch signals from the skin. If they succeed, their methods may someday be applied in reducing the suffering of thousands of people afflicted with chronic itchiness (Gawande, 2008).

AJPhoto/Science Source

analgesia Reduction in the sensation of pain in the presence of a normally painful stimulus.

details of the original theory were incorrect, but it continues to guide medical efforts at pain management (Mendell, 2014). That's because there is evidence that natural mechanisms can indeed block pain sensations at the level of the spinal cord (DeLeo, 2006; Dickenson, 2002).

For example, input from other skin senses can come into the spinal cord at the same time the pain gets there and take over the pathways that the pain impulses would have used. This may be why we can temporarily relieve pain by rubbing the skin around a wound or using electrical stimulation or creams that produce temperature sensations (Henderson, 2008; Slavin, 2008). It also helps explain why scratching relieves itching; itchy sensations involve activity in fibers located close to pain fibers (Andrew & Craig, 2001; bin Saif et al., 2012).

Unfortunately, pain gates can sometimes be "left open." Chronic pain conditions can be caused by damage or inflammation in the peripheral nervous system that sensitizes incoming pain pathways, making them more likely to send pain signals to the brain (D'Mello & Dickenson, 2008). Gate control theory suggests a way to help individuals with these problems. One study focused on people with pain throughout their bodies caused by *neuropathy*, a condition that damages tiny nerves (Kessler & Hong, 2013). These patients reported reductions in their pain after receiving "whole body vibration therapy," a technique in which they stand on a rapidly vibrating platform for three-minute sessions three times a week for a month (Galea, 2012). Such findings suggest that the spinal pain gate was overwhelmed by the harmless non-painful vibration sensations, making it impossible for pain signals to enter.

The brain itself can close the gate to pain impulses by sending signals down the spinal cord. These messages from the brain block incoming pain signals at spinal cord synapses. The result is **analgesia**, a reduction in pain sensation in the presence of a normally painful stimulus. Aspirin and other *analgesic* drugs can dull pain sensations, but it may also be possible to help the brain close the pain gate without them. For example, research participants who received fifteen minutes of transcranial magnetic stimulation (see Table 3.1 in the chapter on biological aspects of psychology) found it easier to withstand a painful heat stimulus (Borckardt et al., 2007), and patients suffering from pain caused by brain damage are being helped by other brain-stimulation techniques (Arle & Shils, 2008).

Natural Analgesics

As described in the chapter on biology and behavior, natural opiates called *endorphins* play a role in the brain's ability to block pain signals. Endorphins are natural painkillers that act as neurotransmitters at many levels of the pain pathway. In the spinal cord, for example, they block the synapses of the fibers that carry pain signals. Endorphins may also relieve pain when the adrenal and pituitary glands secrete them into the bloodstream as hormones. The more endorphin receptors a person has inherited, the more pain tolerance that person has (Benjamin, Wilson, & Mogil, 1999).

Several conditions can cause the body to ease its own pain. For example, endorphins are released where inflammation occurs (Cabot, 2001). A spinal cord endorphin system is activated during the late stages of pregnancy, and the more endorphins a woman spontaneously generates, the less additional analgesia she needs during childbirth (Dabo et al., 2010). An endorphin system is also activated when people believe they are receiving a painkiller, even when they are not (Wager et al., 2011; Zubieta & Stohler, 2009); this may help explain some of the placebo effects described in the chapter on research in psychology (Stewart-Williams, 2004). The resulting pain inhibition is experienced in the part of the body where the person expected it to occur, but not elsewhere (Benedetti, Arduino, & Amanzio, 1999). Physical or psychological stress can also activate natural analgesic systems. Stress-induced release of natural analgesics may account for the fact that injured soldiers and athletes sometimes continue to perform in the heat of battle or competition with no apparent pain (Colloca & Benedetti, 2005).

THINKING CRITICALLY

DOES ACUPUNCTURE RELIEVE PAIN?

Acupuncture, a widely used 3,000-year-old Asian medical treatment, is said to relieve pain (Chon & Lee, 2013). The treatment is based on the idea that body energy, called *Qi,* flows along lines called *channels* that link the internal organs to places on the surface of the skin (Vincent & Richardson, 1986). According to this theory, there are fourteen main channels, and a person's health depends on the balance of energy flowing in them. Stimulating the channels by inserting fine needles into the skin and twirling them is said to restore a balanced flow of energy. The needles produce an aching and tingling sensation called *Teh-ch'i* at the site of stimulation and they relieve pain in distant, seemingly unrelated parts of the body (Liu & Akira, 1994; Yan et al., 1992).

What am I being asked to believe or accept?

Acupuncturists claim that twirling needles in the skin can relieve pain caused by everything from tooth extraction to cancer.

What evidence is available to support the assertion?

There is no scientific evidence for the existence of the energy channels proposed by acupuncturists (Wang, Kain, & White, 2008). However, there *is* evidence from functional magnetic resonance imaging (MRI) studies that stimulating acupuncture sites changes activity in brain regions related to pain sensory regulation (Zhang et al., 2009 Jiang et al., 2013). Numerous studies have also shown positive results in 50 to 80 percent of patients treated by acupuncture for various kinds of pain (e.g., Brinkhaus et al., 2006). One study found, for example, that acupuncture was more effective than an acupuncture-like placebo treatment in reducing the frequency of chronic migraine headaches (Li et al., 2012). A summary of eleven other headache studies found greater overall reductions in pain among patients who had been randomly assigned to receive acupuncture as compared to those randomly assigned to receive standard drug therapies (Linde et al., 2009). In another study, after acupuncture was added to a program of drugs and exercise, fibromyalgia patients had less pain, and the benefit remained at a three-month follow-up (Targino et al., 2008). Yet another study found that after receiving acupuncture, hospitalized infants needed less analgesic or sedative medications and showed improved eating and respiration (Gentry et al., 2011). Several studies have found that acupuncture reduces pain and nausea after surgeries, decreasing the need for pain-relieving drugs and reducing patients' distress (Cheong et al., 2013).

Are there alternative ways of interpreting the evidence?

Yes. Evidence about acupuncture might be interpreted as simply confirming that the body's pain-killing system can be stimulated by external means. Acupuncture may merely provide one activating method (Pariente et al., 2005); other methods might work just as well. For example, low-intensity laser beams applied to acupuncture sites can reduce arthritic knee pain even though no needles and no "true" acupuncture is used (Al Rashoud et al., 2013). There may even be other methods that are even more efficient than acupuncture (Petrovic et al., 2005; Ulett, 2003). We already know, for example, that successful placebo treatments for human pain appear to operate by activating the endorphin system.

What additional evidence would help evaluate the alternatives?

Placebo-controlled studies of acupuncture are needed, but it has been difficult to control for the placebo effect in acupuncture treatment, especially in double-blind fashion (e.g., Derry et al., 2006; Kaptchuk et al., 2006). How could a study be set up so that therapists would not know whether the treatment they are giving is acupuncture or not? What placebo treatment could look and feel like having a needle inserted and twirled in the skin? Some researchers have created single-blind placebo acupuncture using "sham" techniques in which the needles do not actually break the skin or are inserted but not twirled or are inserted in locations that should not, according to acupuncturists, have any effect on

(continued)

pain. In one study of "sham" techniques, research participants were indeed unable to tell whether they were getting genuine acupuncture (Enblom et al., 2008). So far, only a few studies have used sophisticated "sham" methods (e.g., Al Rashoud et al., 2013; Li et al., 2012), and some have found acupuncture to be no more effective than placebo methods (e.g., Cherkin et al., 2009; Haake et al., 2007; Linde et al., 2009). More controlled experiments could eventually reveal the degree to which placebo effects play a role in the results of acupuncture treatment.

Researchers must also learn more about what factors govern whether acupuncture will activate the endorphin system. Other important unknowns include the types of pain for which acupuncture is most effective, the types of patients who respond best, and the precise procedures that are most effective. Knowing more about the general relationship between internal pain-killing systems and external methods for stimulating them would also be valuable.

What conclusions are most reasonable?

Although acupuncture is no cure-all, in some circumstances it may help to relieve pain and reduce other unpleasant sensations like nausea. What we still don't know is exactly why this may be and through what mechanism any genuine effects might operate. Acupuncture remains a fascinating phenomenon, a treatment used on millions of people around the world. Some critics argue that further expenditures for acupuncture research are not warranted, but it seems likely that studies will continue. The quality of these studies' methodology and the nature of their results will determine whether acupuncture finds a more prominent place in Western medicine.

Sensing Body Position

Most sensory systems receive information from the outside world, such as the light reflected from a flower or the feeling of cool water. But as far as the brain is concerned, the rest of the body is "outside" too. You know about the position of your body and what each of its parts is doing only because sensory systems provide this information to your brain. Your sense of body movement and position is called **proprioception** (meaning "received from the self" and pronounced "pro-pree-oh-SEP-shun").

Kinesthetic Perception

In the biological aspects of psychology chapter, we describe the case of Christina, a woman who did not recognize her own body. She had lost her **kinesthetic perception** (pronounced "kin-es-THEH-tic"), which tells us where the parts of the body are in relation to one another. To better appreciate kinesthetic perception, try this: Close your eyes; then hold your arms out in front of you and touch your two index fingers together. You probably did this easily because your kinesthetic sense told you where each finger was with respect to your body. You depend on kinesthetic information to guide all your movements, from walking to complex athletic actions. These movement patterns become simple and fluid because with practice the brain uses kinesthetic information automatically. Normally, kinesthetic information comes primarily from **proprioceptors**, which are special receptors in the joints and muscles (Proske, 2006). These receptors send information to the brain about the stretching of muscles. When the position of the bones changes, receptors in the joints set off neural activity. This encoded information goes to the spinal cord and then to the thalamus, along with sensory information from the skin. Finally, it goes to the cerebellum and to the somatosensory cortex, both of which help coordinate movements (Longo & Haggard, 2010).

Balance

Have you ever been on a roller coaster? How did you feel when the ride ended? Your **sense of equilibrium**, sometimes called the **vestibular sense** (pronounced "ves-TIB-u-ler"), tells your brain about the position of your head (and, to some degree, the

TRY THIS

proprioception The sensory processes that tell us about the location of our body parts and what each is doing.

kinesthetic perception The proprioceptive sense that tells us where the parts of the body are with respect to one another.

proprioceptors Neural receptors that provide information about movement and body position.

sense of equilibrium (vestibular sense) The proprioceptive sense that provides information about the position of the head and its movements.

rest of your body) and about its general movements. You have probably heard it referred to as the *sense of balance.* People usually become aware of the sense of equilibrium only when they overstimulate it and become dizzy or experience motion sickness.

The organs for the vestibular sense are in the inner ear. As shown in Figure 4.14, each inner ear has two fluid-filled *vestibular sacs* that contain tiny, delicate crystals called *otoliths* ("ear stones") that rest on hair endings. There are also three arc-shaped tubes, called *semicircular canals,* and they, too, are filled with fluid. Tiny hairs extend into the fluid in the canals. When your head moves, the otoliths shift in the vestibular sacs and the fluid moves in the semicircular canals, stimulating hair endings. These responses to head movement activate neurons that travel along the acoustic nerve, signaling the brain about the amount and direction of head movement (Angelaki & Cullen, 2008). If the otoliths become displaced within the vestibular sacs, as they do in a condition called *benign paroxysmal positional vertigo,* or BPPV, the result can be intense spinning sensations (Fife, 2009). BPPV can sometimes be treated by having the patient lie down and make specific head movements that shift allow the otoliths to go back into their correct position (Bruintjes et al., 2014).

Neural connections from the vestibular system to the cerebellum help coordinate bodily movements. Connections to the part of the autonomic nervous system that affects the digestive system help create the nausea that may follow overstimulation of the vestibular system—by a roller-coaster ride, for instance. Finally, connections to the eye muscles produce *vestibular-ocular reflexes,* which cause your eyes to move opposite to your head movements. These reflexes allow you to focus on one spot even when your head is moving. You can experience these reflexes by having a friend spin you around on a stool for a while. When you stop, try to fix your gaze on one point in the room. You'll be unable to do so, because the excitation of the vestibular system will cause your eyes to move repeatedly in the direction opposite from the way you were spinning. Our vestibular reflexes adjust to the lack of gravity in outer space (Thornton, 2011), which is why astronauts returning to Earth have postural and movement difficulties until their vestibular systems readjust to gravity (Paloski, 1998). (See "In Review: Body Senses" for a summary of our discussion of touch, temperature, pain, and kinesthesia.)

TRY THIS

BODY SENSES

IN REVIEW

Sense	Energy	Conversion of Physical Energy to Nerve Activity	Pathways and Characteristics
Touch	Mechanical deformation of skin	Neural receptors in the skin (may be stimulated by hair on the skin)	Nerve endings respond to changes in weight (intensity) and location of touch.
Temperature	Heat	Sensory neurons in the skin	Changes in temperature are detected by warm-sensing and cool-sensing fibers. Temperature interacts with touch.
Pain	Increases with intensity of touch or temperature	Free nerve endings in or near the skin surface	Changes in intensity cause the release of chemicals detected by receptors in pain neurons. Some fibers convey sharp pain; others convey dull aches and burning sensations.

(continued)

BODY SENSES (CONT.)

Sense	Energy	Conversion of Physical Energy to Nerve Activity	Pathways and Characteristics
Kinesthetic perception	Mechanical energy of joint and muscle movement	Neural receptors in muscle fibers	Information from muscle fibers is sent to the spinal cord, thalamus, cerebellum, and cortex.
Sense of equilibrium	Mechanical energy of head movement	Neural receptors in the inner ear	Information about fluid moving in the semicircular canals is sent to the brain along the acoustic nerve.

In Review Questions

1. Gate control theory offers an explanation of why we sometimes do not feel _____.

2. Professional dancers look at the same spot as long as possible during repeated spins. They are trying to avoid the dizziness caused when the sense of _____ is overstimulated.

3. Without your sense of _____ you would not be able to swallow food without choking.

THE CASE OF THE MYSTERIOUS SPELLS

Early in this chapter, we discussed the specific energy doctrine, which says that each sensory system can send information to the brain only about its own sense, regardless of how the stimulation occurs. So gently pressing on your closed eye will send touch sensations from the skin on your eyelid and visual sensations from your eye. This doctrine applies even when stimulation of sensory systems arises from within the brain itself. The following case study illustrates an example in which spontaneous brain activity resulted in erotic sensations.

What was the researcher's question?

A thirty-one-year-old woman we'll call "Linda" reported that for many years, she had been experiencing recurring "spells" that began with what seemed like sexual sensations (Janszky et al., 2002). These "orgasm-like euphoric erotic sensations" were followed by a staring, unresponsive state in which she lost consciousness. The spells, which occurred without warning and in response to no obvious trigger, interfered severely with her ability to function normally in everyday life. Linda was examined by József Janszky, a neurologist, who suspected that she might be suffering from epilepsy, a seizure disorder in which nerve cells in the brain suddenly start firing uncontrollably. Seizures that activate the motor area of the cerebral cortex will cause uncontrollable movements, seizures that activate visual cortex will create the sensation of images, and so on. Could there be a specific brain region that, when activated by a seizure, cause the sensations of orgasm that are normally brought on by external stimulation?

How did the researcher answer the question?

It is not easy to study the neurological basis of sexual sensations because most people are understandably reluctant to allow researchers to monitor their sexual activity. In the process of diagnosing Linda's problem, Janszky had a unique opportunity to learn something about the origin of orgasmic sensations without intruding on his patient's privacy. His approach exemplifies the *case study* method of research. As described in the chapter on research in psychology, case studies

(continued)

focus intensively on a particular individual, group, or situation. Sometimes they lead to important insights about clinical problems or other phenomena that occur so rarely that they cannot be studied through surveys or controlled experiments. In this case, Janszky decided to study Linda's brain activity while she was actually having a spell. He reasoned that if the spells were caused by seizures in a specific brain region, it might be possible to eliminate the problem through surgery.

What did the researcher find?

Linda's brain activity was recorded during five of her spells, using electroen-cephalography (EEG), a method described in the chapter on biological aspects of psychology. During each spell, the EEG showed that she was having seizures in the right temporal lobe of her brain. A subsequent MRI of her brain revealed a small area of abnormal tissue in the same area of the right temporal lobe. The organization of nerve cells in abnormal brain tissue can make it easier for seizures to occur, so Linda was advised to have some tissue surgically removed from the problem area. After the surgery, her seizures stopped.

What do the results mean?

Janszky concluded that Linda had been having "localization-related epilepsy," meaning that her spells were seizures coming from a specific brain location. This conclusion was supported by the fact that she had right temporal lobe seizures on the EEG each time she had a spell. Her MRI showed an abnormality in the same region that commonly gives rise to seizures, and her spells disappeared after the abnormality was removed. Linda's case also led Janszky to suggest that the right temporal lobe may play a special role in creating the sensory experience of orgasm.

What do we still need to know?

Janszky's suggestion might be correct, meaning that activation of the right temporal cortex may be sufficient for the sensory experience of orgasm. But at least one important question remains: How specific is the linkage between activity in this brain region and the sensory experiences of orgasm? Could seizures in other brain regions cause similar experiences? Is right temporal cortex activity one of many ways to generate orgasm-like experiences, or is it necessary for these experiences? Answering this question would be easier if we knew whether Linda continued to experience orgasms during sexual activity. If she did, the implication would be that the area of right temporal lobe tissue that was removed was not necessary for the experience of orgasm. Unfortunately, Janszky's report is silent on this point, but future cases and further research will no doubt shed additional light on this fascinating sensory puzzle.

PERCEPTION

How do sensations become perceptions?

So far, we have explored how sensory information reaches the brain. Let's now consider the processes of perception that allow the brain to make sense of that information. These perceptual processes can sometimes make the difference between life and death. For example, at a traffic circle in Scotland, fourteen fatal accidents occurred in one year, partly because drivers did not slow down as they approached the circle. After warning signs failed to solve the problem, Gordon Denton, a British psychologist, found a clever solution. He recommended that white lines be painted across the road leading to the circle, in a pattern something like this:

/   /   /   /   /   / / / ///

Crossing these lines, which were spaced progressively more closely, gave drivers the impression that they were speeding up, so their automatic response was to slow down (Denton, 1980). During the fourteen months after Denton's idea was implemented, there were only two fatalities at the traffic circle! Similar kinds of striping patterns are now widely used throughout Britain and on approaches to some towns and intersections in the United States. Denton's solution depended partly on his knowledge of sensation but mostly on the principles of human perception.

Some perceptual tasks take attention and effort, as when a child struggles to recognize printed letters. But as experienced readers know, a lot of the perceptual work that transforms sensory information into meaningful experiences happens automatically without conscious awareness. To illustrate the workings of these complex processes, psychologists draw attention to *perceptual failures*—cases in which we perceive stimuli incorrectly (e.g., Ito, 2012; Witt, Linkenauger, & Proffitt, 2012). Just as drivers at the traffic circle incorrectly perceived themselves as speeding up, you will probably perceive the two lines in Figure 4.18 as differing in length, even though they are the same.

FIGURE 4.18
Misperceiving Reality

TRY THIS Measure lines A–C and A–B. They are exactly the same length, but you probably perceived A–C as longer. Why? Partly because your visual system tries to interpret all stimuli as three-dimensional, even when they are not. A three-dimensional interpretation of this drawing would lead you to see the two lines as the edges of two parallel paths, one of which ends closer to you than the other. Your eyes tell you that the two paths start at about the same point (the castle entrance), so you assume that the closer line must be the longer of the two.

Source: Gardner (1988).

ORGANIZING THE PERCEPTUAL WORLD

What determines how I perceive my world?

To further appreciate the wonder of the complicated perceptual work you do every day, imagine yourself driving on a busy road searching for Barney's Diner, an unfamiliar restaurant where you are to meet a friend. The roadside is crammed with signs of all shapes and colors, some flashing, some rotating. If you are ever to recognize the sign that says "Barney's Diner," you will have to impose some sort of organization on this overwhelming mixture of visual information. How do you do this? How do you know where one sign ends and another begins? And how do you know that an apparently tiny sign is not really tiny but just far away?

Principles of Perceptual Organization

Before you can recognize the Barney's Diner sign, your perceptual system must separate that sign from its background of lights, colors, letters, and other competing stimuli. Two basic principles—*figure ground perception* and *grouping*—guide this initial organization.

Figure and Ground

When you look at a complex scene or listen to a noisy environment, your perceptual apparatus automatically emphasizes certain features, objects, or sounds. These emphasized features become the **figure**. This part of the visual field has meaning, stands in front of the rest, and always seems to include contours or edges. These contours and edges separate

figure The part of the visual field that has meaning.

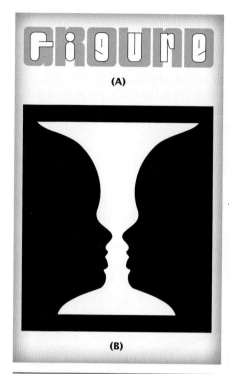

FIGURE 4.19
Reversible Images

These *reversible images* can be organized by your perceptual system in two ways. If you perceive Part A as the word "figure," the space around the letters becomes meaningless background. Now emphasize the word "ground," and what had stood out a moment ago now becomes background. In Part B, when you emphasize the white vase, the black profiles become background; if you organize the faces as the figure, what had been a vase now becomes background. We normally tend to see smaller, lower elements in a scene as figure and larger, higher elements as ground (Vecera, Vogel, & Woodman, 2002), but images like these don't allow us to use that rule of thumb.

ground The contourless part of the visual field; the background.

figure ground discrimination The ability to organize a visual scene so that it contains meaningful figures set against a less relevant ground.

the figure from the less relevant background, called the **ground** (Rubin, 1915; Zhang & von der Heydt, 2010). As you drive toward an intersection, a stop sign will become a figure that stands out clearly against the background of trees or buildings.

To experience your own **figure ground discrimination** ability, look at Figure 4.19. Notice that you can decide how to organize the stimuli in the drawings. You can repeatedly reverse figure and ground to see faces, then a vase, then faces again (4.19B) or to see the word *figure* or the word *ground* (4.19A). The fact that you can mentally manipulate these "reversible" images means that your perceptual systems are not just recording devices that passively absorb incoming sensations; you play an active part in organizing what you perceive. We also usually organize sensory stimulation into only one perceptual category at a time. This is why it is difficult to see both a vase and two faces—or the words *figure* and *ground*—at the same time.

Grouping

Why do certain parts of the world become figure and others become ground, even when nothing in particular stands out in the pattern of light that falls on the retina? The answer is that certain properties of stimuli lead you to group them together more or less automatically.

In the early 1900s, several German psychologists described the principles behind this grouping of stimuli. They argued that people perceive sights and sounds as organized wholes. These wholes, they said, are different from the sum of the individual sensations, just as a house is something other than a pile of bricks and wood and glass. Because the German word for figure or shape is *Gestalt* (pronounced "ge-SHTALT"), these researchers became known as *Gestalt psychologists*. Max Wertheimer, one of the founders of Gestalt psychology, proposed a number of principles that describe how the perceptual system "glues" raw sensations together in particular ways (Wagemans et al., 2012; Wertheimer, 1923):

1. *Proximity.* The closer objects or events are to one another, the more likely they are to be perceived as belonging together, as Figure 4.20(A) illustrates.

2. *Similarity.* Elements that are similar in size, color, orientation, and texture are perceived to be part of a group, as in Figure 4.20(B). This is why students wearing the same school colors at a stadium will be perceived as belonging together even if they are not seated close together.

3. *Continuity.* Sensations that appear to create a continuous form are perceived as belonging together, as in Figure 4.20(C).

4. *Closure.* We tend to mentally fill in missing parts of incomplete objects, as in Figure 4.20(D). The gaps are easy to see, but the tendency to link disconnected parts can be so strong that you may perceive faint connections that aren't actually there (Lleras & Moore, 2006).

5. *Simplicity.* We tend to group features of a stimulus in a way that provides the simplest interpretation of the world. You can see the simplicity principle in action in Figure 4.20(D), where it is simpler to see a single cube than an assortment of separate and unrelated arrows and Ys.

6. *Common fate.* Sets of objects that move in the same direction at the same speed are perceived together. So even though the individual birds in a flock are separated from each other as they fly, they will be perceived as a group. Choreographers and marching-band directors use this principle of common fate when they arrange for groups or subgroups of dancers or musicians to move in unison, causing the audience to perceive waves of motion or a single large moving object.

Stephen Palmer (1999) has identified three additional grouping principles:

1. *Synchrony.* Stimuli that occur at the same time are likely to be perceived as coming from the same source. For example, if you see a car up ahead stop violently at the same instant that you hear a crash, you will probably perceive these visual and auditory stimuli as part of the same event.

2. *Common region.* Stimuli located within some boundary tend to be grouped together. The boundary can be created by an enclosing perimeter, as in Figure 4.20(E), a region of color, or other factors.

3. *Connectedness.* Stimuli that are connected by other elements tend to be grouped together. In Figure 4.20(F), the circles connected by dotted lines seem to go together even though they are farther apart than some pairs of unconnected circles. Here, the principle of connectedness appears more important than the principle of proximity.

FIGURE 4.20

Gestalt Principles of Perceptual Grouping

We tend to perceive Part A as two groups of two circles plus one single circle rather than as, say, five circles. In Part B, we see two columns of Xs and two columns of Os, not four rows of XOXO. We see the X in Part C as being made out of two continuous lines, not a combination of the odd forms shown. In Part D, we fill gaps so as to perceive a hollow cube. In Part E, we tend to pair up dots in the same oval even though they are far apart. Part F shows that connected objects are grouped together.

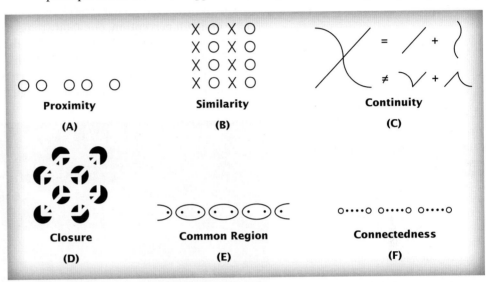

Why do we organize the world according to these grouping principles? One answer may be that they reflect the way stimuli are often organized in the natural world. Nearby elements are in fact more likely than separated elements to be part of the same object. Stimulus elements moving in the same direction at the same rate are also likely to be part of the same object. Your initial impression of the cube in Figure 4.20(D) reflects this *likelihood principle* in action. At first glance, you probably saw the cube as being below you rather than above you. This tendency makes adaptive sense, because boxes and other cube-shaped objects are more likely to be on the ground than hanging in midair.

Perception of Location and Distance

One of the most important perceptual tasks we face is to determine where objects and sound sources are located. This task involves knowing both their two-dimensional position (left or right, up or down) and their distance from us.

Two-Dimensional Location

Determining whether an object is to your right or your left appears to be simple. All the perceptual system has to do, it seems, is determine where the object's image falls on the retina. If the image falls on the center of the retina, then the object must be straight ahead. But when an object is, say, far to your right, and you focus its image on the center of your retina by turning your head and eyes toward it, you do not assume it is straight ahead. Instead, your brain calculates an estimate of the object's location by combining information about where an image strikes the retina with information about the movement of your eyes and head.

When it comes to locating the source of sounds, your brain depends on cues about differences in the information received by each of your ears. Sound waves coming toward the right side of your head will reach the right ear before reaching the left ear. Similarly, a sound coming toward the right side of your head will seem a little bit louder to the right ear than to the left ear, because your head blocks some of the sound to the left ear. The brain uses these slight differences in the timing and the intensity of a sound as cues to locate its source. Visual cues are often integrated with auditory cues to determine the exact identity and location of the sound source. However, there are times when the two senses produce conflicting impressions; in such cases, we tend to believe our eyes rather than our ears. This bias toward using visual information is known as *visual dominance*.

Depth Perception

We are able to experience the world in three-dimensional depth even though the visual information we receive from it is projected onto two-dimensional retinas. This is possible because of **depth perception**, our ability to perceive distance. Depth perception, in turn, is made possible by *stimulus cues* provided by the environment and also by the properties of our visual system (Anderson, 2003; Hildreth & Royden, 2011). To some extent, people perceive depth through the same cues that artists use to create the impression of depth and distance on a two-dimensional canvas. Figure 4.21 demonstrates several of these cues:

FIGURE 4.21

Stimulus Cues for Depth Perception

TRY THIS See if you can identify the cues of relative size, interposition, linear perspective, height in the visual field, textural gradient, and shadows that combine to create a sense of three-dimensional depth in this photograph. Notice, too, that sidewalk artist Kurt Wenner has used some of these same cues to create a dramatic illusion of depth in his drawing. (You can see more of Wenner's amazing work at http://www.kurtwenner.com/index.htm.)

Dies Irae. Copyright © Kurt Wenner, 1988

- One of the most important depth cues is *interposition*: Closer objects block the view of things farther away. This cue is illustrated in Figure 4.21 by the couple walking away from the camera. Because their bodies block out part of the buildings, we perceive them as being closer to us than the buildings are.

- You can see the principle of *relative size* operating in Figure 4.21 by measuring the images of that same couple and comparing it to the size of the man in the foreground. If two objects are assumed to be about the same size, the object producing a larger image on the retina is perceived as closer than the one producing a smaller image.

- Another cue comes from *height in the visual field*: On the ground, objects that are more distant are usually higher in the visual field than those that are nearby. Because the building in the center of Figure 4.21 is higher than the people in the restaurant, the building appears to be farther away from you. This is one reason why objects higher in the visual field are more likely to be interpreted as the background for objects that are lower in a scene (Vecera, Vogel, & Woodman, 2002).

depth perception Perception of distance, allowing us to experience the world in three dimensions.

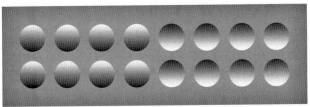

FIGURE 4.22
Light, Shadow, and Depth Perception

TRY THIS Shadows create three-dimensional impressions of bumps on the left side of this drawing and of dents on the right side. But if you turn the book upside down, the bumps will look like dents, and the dents will look like bumps. This reversal in depth perception occurs partly because people normally assume that illumination comes from above and interpret the pattern of light and shadow accordingly (Adams, Graf, & Ernst, 2004; Cook et al., 2008).

A Case of Depth Misperception

The runner in this photo is actually farther away than the man on the pitcher's mound. But because he is lower, not higher, in the visual field the runner appears smaller than normal rather than farther away (Vecera, Vogel, & Woodman, 2002).

AP images

TRY THIS

motion parallax A depth cue whereby a difference in the apparent rate of movement of different objects provides information about the relative distance of those objects.

eye convergence A depth cue that results when the eyes rotate to project the image of an object on each retina.

retinal disparity A depth cue based on the difference between the retinal images received by each eye.

■ The tiny figures near the center of Figure 4.21 are seen as very far away because they are near a point where the buildings on each edge of the plaza, like all parallel lines that recede into the distance, appear to converge toward a single point. This apparent *convergence* provides a cue called *linear perspective*. The closer together two converging lines are, the greater the perceived distance.

■ Notice that the street in Figure 4.21 fades into a hazy background. Increased distance usually produces less clarity, and this *reduced clarity* is interpreted as a cue for greater distance. Hazy, distant objects also tend to take on a bluish tone, which is why art students are taught to add a little blue when mixing paint for deep background features.

■ *Light and shadow* also contribute to the perception of three dimensions (Kingdom, 2003; Ramachandran, 1988). The buildings in Figure 4.21 are seen as three-dimensional, not flat, because of the shadows on some of their surfaces. Figure 4.22 shows a more dramatic example.

■ An additional stimulus-based depth cue comes from continuous changes across the visual field, called *gradients*. For example, a textural gradient is a graduated change in the texture, or "grain," of the visual field, as you can see in the plaza and the street in Figure 4.21. Texture appears more compact and less detailed as distance increases. As the texture of a surface changes across the retinal image, you perceive a change in distance.

An important visual depth cue that cannot be demonstrated in Figure 4.21, or in any other still image, comes from motion. You may have noticed, for example, that when you look out the side window of a moving car, objects nearer to you seem to speed across your visual field, whereas objects in the distance seem to move slowly, if at all. This difference in the apparent rate of movement is called **motion parallax**, and it provides cues to differences in the distance of various objects.

Some depth cues result from the way human eyes are built and positioned. Recall that to bring an image into focus on the retina, the lens of the eye changes shape, or *accommodates*. Information about the muscle activity involved is used by brain so that this *accommodation cue* helps create the perception of distance.

The depth cues described so far are called *monocular* cues because we can detect them with just one eye. There are also two *binocular* depth cues which are produced by the relative location of our two eyes. The first is **eye convergence**. Because each eye is located at a different place on the skull, the eyes must converge, or rotate inward, to project the same image on each retina. The closer the object, the more the eyes must converge. Eye muscles send information about this convergence to the brain, which processes it as a distance cue. You can experience this feedback from your eye muscles by holding up a finger at arm's length and then trying to keep it in focus as you move it toward your nose.

The second binocular cue occurs because each of our two eyes sees the world from a slightly different angle. The difference between these different retinal images is called **retinal disparity**, also known as *binocular disparity*. The difference, or disparity, between images decreases for objects that are far away and increases for objects that are nearby. The brain not only combines the two images of an object but also takes into account how much they differ. This information helps generate the impression of a single object that has a rich sense of depth as well as height and width and is located at a particular distance. Three-dimensional movies and some virtual reality systems use these *binocular cues* to create the appearance of depth in a two-dimensional stimulus. They show each eye an image of a scene as viewed from a slightly different angle.

In short, many cues—some present in the environment and in retinal images, others arising from the structure of the visual system—combine to give us a powerful and accurate sense of depth and distance.

Retinal Disparity and Distance

TRY THIS   There is a smaller difference, or disparity, between each eye's view of an object when the object is far away than when it is close by. The amount of this retinal disparity helps us estimate the object's distance from us. To see for yourself how retinal disparity changes with distance, hold a pen vertically about six inches in front of your nose; then close one eye and notice where the pen is in relation to the background. Now open that eye, close the other one, and notice how much the pen "shifts." These are the two different views your eyes have of the pen. Repeat this procedure while holding the pen at arm's length. Notice that there is now less disparity or "shift," because there is less difference in the angles from which your two eyes see the pen.

© Romulus Opriscan/Shutterstock.com

looming A motion cue whereby rapid expansion in the size of an image fills the available space on the retina.

stroboscopic illusion An illusion of motion that is created when we see slightly different images or slightly displaced lights flashed in rapid succession.

Perception of Motion

Sometimes the most important property of an object is its motion—how fast it is going and where it is heading. Many cues about motion come from *optical flow,* or the changes that take place in retinal images across the visual field. As in the case of depth perception, you automatically translate this two-dimensional information into a three-dimensional experience. One particularly meaningful pattern of optical flow is known as **looming,** the rapid expansion in the size of an image so that it fills the retina. When an image looms, there is an automatic tendency to perceive it as an approaching object. If the expansion is as fast to the right as to the left and as fast above as below, this information signals that the object is approaching the eyes directly. In other words, duck! One reason that young children are at high risk when crossing streets alone is that they may not yet perceive the danger posed by cars and other rapidly looming objects (Wann, Poulter, & Purcell, 2011).

We are lucky that movement of the retinal image isn't the only factor contributing to motion perception. If it were, everything in sight would appear to move every time you moved your eyes and head (Ölveczky, Baccus, & Meister, 2003). This doesn't happen, because as noted earlier, the brain receives and processes information about the motion of the eyes and head (Wexler, 2005). **TRY THIS** If you look around you right now, tables, chairs, and other stationary objects will not appear to move because your brain determines that all the movement of images on your retinas is due to the movement of your eyes and head (Goltz et al., 2003). But now close one eye and wiggle your open eyeball by gently pushing your lower eyelid. Because your brain receives no signals that your eye is being moved by its own muscles, everything in the room will appear to move.

When your body is moving, as in a car, the flow of visual information across the retina combines with information from the vestibular and touch senses to give you the experience of being in motion. If the car accelerates, you feel pressure from the back of the seat and feel your head tilting backward. Motion sickness may result if you perceive visual flow without appropriate sensations from other parts of the body, particularly the vestibular senses. This explains why you might feel nauseous while in a motion simulator or playing certain video games, especially those with virtual reality technology. The images suggest that you are moving through space when there is no real motion.

Other illusions of motion are more enjoyable. The most important of these occurs when still images appear, one at a time, in rapid succession, as they do on videos. Because each image differs slightly from the preceding one, the brain sees the objects in each image at one location for only a fraction of a second before they disappear and immediately reappear in a slightly different location. The entertaining result is the **stroboscopic illusion** of motion; when objects disappear and then quickly reappear nearby, the brain assumes that they have moved smoothly from one location to another. The same illusion is at work when it appears that flashing lights on a theater or casino sign are moving around the sign.

Perceptual Constancy

Suppose that one sunny day you are watching someone walking toward you along a tree-lined path. The visual sensations produced by this person are actually very strange. For one thing, the size of the image on your retinas keeps getting larger as the person gets closer. **TRY THIS** To see this for yourself, hold out a hand at arm's length and look at someone far away. The retinal image of that person will be so small that you can cover it with your hand. If you do the same thing when the person is three feet away, the retinal image will be too large to be covered by your hand, yet you will perceive the person as being closer now, not bigger. Similarly, as you watch the person pass from bright sunshine through the shadows of trees, your retinas receive images that shift back and forth from light to dark, but you perceive the person's coloring as staying the same.

These examples illustrate **perceptual constancy**, the perception that objects keep their size, shape, color, and other properties despite changes in their retinal image. Without this aspect of perception, you would experience the world as a place where solid objects continuously changed their properties.

Size Constancy

Why does an object's perceived size stay more or less constant, regardless of changes in the size of its retinal image? One reason is that the brain perceives a change in the distance of an object and automatically adjusts the perception of size (Combe & Wexler, 2010). Specifically, the *perceived size* of an object is equal to the size of the retinal image multiplied by the perceived distance (Holway & Boring, 1941). As an object moves closer, or as we move closer to it, the size of its retinal image increases yet the perceived distance decreases at the same rate. As a result the perceived size of the object remains constant. If a balloon is inflated in front of your eyes, perceived distance remains constant and the perceived size (correctly) increases as the size of the retinal image increases.

Shape Constancy

TRY THIS

The principles behind shape constancy are closely related to those of size constancy. To see shape constancy at work, close this book (remember what page you're on) and tilt it toward and away from you several times. The book will continue to look rectangular, even though the shape of its retinal image changes dramatically as you move it. Your brain automatically combines information about retinal images and distance as movement occurs. In this case, the distance information has to do with the difference in distance between the near and far edges of the book.

Brightness Constancy

TRY THIS

Even with dramatic changes in the amount of light striking an object, our perception of the object's brightness remains relatively constant (MacEvoy & Paradiso, 2001). To see this for yourself, place a piece of charcoal in sunlight and a piece of white paper in nearby shade. The charcoal will look very dark and the paper very bright, yet a light meter would tell you that much more light energy is reflected from the sun-bathed coal than from the shaded paper. The reason is partly that the charcoal is the darkest object relative to its sunlit background and the paper is the brightest object relative to its background of shade. As shown in Figure 4.23, the brightness of an object is perceived in relation to its background.

FIGURE 4.23
Brightness Contrast

TRY THIS At first glance, the inner rectangle on the left probably looks lighter than the inner rectangle on the right. But carefully examine the inner rectangles alone by covering their surroundings and you will see that both are of equal intensity. The brighter surround in the right-hand figure leads you to perceive its inner rectangle as relatively darker.

perceptual constancy The perception that objects retain the same size, shape, color, and other properties despite changes in their retinal image.

Size Illusions

Usually the visual perceptual system works automatically and perfectly to create correct impressions of depth, distance, and size. Sometimes, though, it can fail, resulting in *size illusions* such as the ones shown in Figure 4.24. Why does the monster that is placed higher in Figure 4.24(A) look larger than the lower one even though they are exactly the same size? The converging lines in the tunnel provide depth cues telling you that the higher monster is farther away. Because the retinal image of the "distant" monster is the

FIGURE 4.24

Three Size Illusions

These illusions are named for the scientists who described them. In Part A, a version of the Ponzo illusion, the upper monster looks bigger but is actually the same size as the lower one. In the Müller-Lyer illusion (Part B), both vertical lines are actually of equal length; in the Ebbinghaus illusion shown in Part C, both center circles are exactly the same size. To prove that you can't always believe your eyes, measure these drawings for yourself.

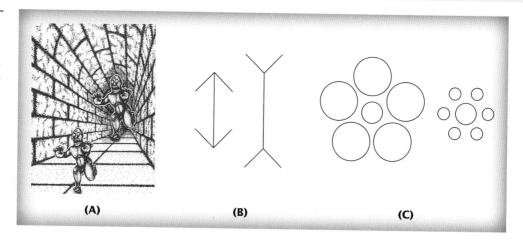

(A)   (B)   (C)

same size as the "closer" one, your perceptual system calculates that the more distant monster must be bigger. This shows the principle of size constancy at work: When two objects have retinal images of the same size, you perceive the one that seems farther away as larger. Now look at Figure 4.24(B). The two vertical lines are the same length, but the one on the right looks longer. Why? One possible reason is that the perceived length of an object is based on what frames it. When the frame is perceived as larger, as on the right side of Figure 4.24(B), the line segment within it is perceived as larger too (Rock, 1978). In Figure 4.24(C), the inner circle at the left looks smaller than the one at the right because, like the brightness of the center rectangles in Figure 4.23, the inner circles are judged in relation to what surrounds them. Because perception is based on many principles, and can be affected by many factors, illusions like these probably reflect the violation of more than one of them. (See "In Review: Principles of Perceptual Organization and Constancy.")

PRINCIPLES OF PERCEPTUAL ORGANIZATION AND CONSTANCY

IN REVIEW

Principle	Description	Example
Figure ground discrimination	Certain objects or sounds automatically become identified as figure, whereas others become meaningless background.	You see a person standing against a building, not a building with a person-shaped hole in it.
Grouping	Properties of stimuli lead us to automatically group them together. These include proximity, similarity, continuity, closure, simplicity, common fate, synchrony, common region, and connectedness.	People who are sitting together, or who are dressed similarly, are perceived as a group.
Depth perception	The world is perceived as three-dimensional, with help from stimulus cues such as relative size, height in the visual field, interposition, linear perspective, reduced clarity, light and shadow, and gradients, and from visual system cues such as accommodation, eye convergence, and retinal disparity.	A person who looks tiny and appears high in the visual field will be perceived as being of normal size, but at a great distance.
Perceptual constancy	Objects are perceived as constant in size, shape, color, and other properties despite changes in their retinal images.	A train coming toward you is perceived as getting closer, not larger; an advertising sign is perceived as rotating, not changing shape.

(continued)

PRINCIPLES OF PERCEPTUAL ORGANIZATION AND CONSTANCY (CONT.)

In Review Questions

1. The movement we see in videos is due to a perceptual illusion called _____.

2. People who have lost an eye also lose the ability to use _____ depth cues, two of which are called _____ and _____.

3. The grouping principle of _____ allows you to identify objects seen through a picket fence.

RECOGNIZING THE PERCEPTUAL WORLD

How do I recognize familiar people?

In discussing how people organize the perceptual world, we have set the stage for addressing one of the most vital questions that perception researchers must answer: How do we recognize what objects are? If you are driving in search of Barney's Diner, exactly what happens when your eyes finally locate the pattern of light that spells out its name?

To know that you have finally found what you've been looking for, your brain must analyze incoming patterns of information and compare them with information about the target that you have stored in memory. If the brain finds a match, recognition takes place. Once you recognize a stimulus as belonging to a particular category, your perception of that stimulus may never be the same again. Look at Figure 4.25. Do you see anything familiar? If not, turn to Figure 4.26; then look at Figure 4.25 again. You should now see it in an entirely new light. The difference between your "before" and "after" experiences is the difference between the sensory world before and after a perceptual match occurs and recognition takes place.

FIGURE 4.25
Categorizing Perceptions

TRY THIS   What do you see here? For the identity of this figure, turn to Figure 4.26.

FIGURE 4.26
Another Version of Figure 4.25

Now that you can identify a dog in this figure, it should be much easier to recognize when you look back at the original version.

How does this matching process occur? Some aspects of recognition begin at the "top." That is, they are based on applying knowledge, expectations, and other psychological factors. This phenomenon is called **top-down processing**, because it involves high-level, knowledge-based information. Other aspects of recognition begin at the "bottom," relying on specific detailed information from the sensory receptors and assembling them into a whole. This phenomenon is called **bottom-up processing**, because it begins with basic information units that serve as a foundation for recognition.

Bottom-Up Processing

All along the path from the eye to the brain, certain cells respond to selected features of a stimulus. The stimulus is first analyzed into these *basic features,* which are then recombined to create the perceptual experience.

What are these features? As mentioned earlier, certain cells specialize in responding to lines, edges, corners, and stimuli that have specific orientations in space (Hubel & Wiesel, 1979). For example, some cells in the cerebral cortex fire only in response to a diagonal line of light, so they act as *feature detectors* for diagonal lines. The analysis by such feature detectors early in the sensation-perception sequence may contribute to recognition of letters or judgments of shape. Other features seem to be detected and assembled farther down the visual pathway (Kubilius, Wagemans, & de Beeck, 2011). Color and motion are sensory features that appear to be analyzed separately in different parts of the brain before full perceptual recognition takes place (e.g., Levinthal & Franconeri, 2011). The brain also apparently analyzes patterns of light and darkness in the visual scene. Analyzing these patterns may help us perceive textural gradients, which in turn help us to judge depth and recognize the general shape of blurry images.

Psychologists know that feature analysis is involved in pattern recognition because they have been able to determine what type of object a person is looking at (e.g., a face versus a house) based on the pattern of activity occurring in visual processing areas of the person's brain (Haxby et al., 2001; Taylor & Downing, 2011).

Top-Down Processing

Bottom-up feature analysis can explain why you recognize the letters in a sign for Barney's Diner. But why is it that you can recognize the sign more easily if it appears where you were told to expect it rather than a block earlier? And why can you recognize it even if a few letters are missing from the sign? Top-down processing seems to be at work in those cases. In

top-down processing Aspects of recognition guided by higher-level cognitive processes and by psychological factors such as expectations.

bottom-up processing Aspects of recognition that depend first on information about stimuli that come up to the brain from the sensory systems.

top-down processing, people use their knowledge to make inferences, or "educated guesses," that help them recognize objects, words, or melodies, especially when sensory information is vague or ambiguous (DeWitt & Samuel, 1990; Rock, 1983). For example, once you knew that there was a dog in Figure 4.25, it became much easier for you to perceive one. Similarly, police officers find it easy to recognize familiar people on blurry security-camera videos, but it is much more difficult for them to identify strangers (Burton et al., 1999).

Top-down processing illustrates that our experiences create **schemas**, mental representations of what we know and expect about the world. Schemas can bias our perception to be more likely to recognize one specific pattern over another by creating a *perceptual set*—that is, a readiness to perceive a stimulus in a certain way. These expectations operate automatically, whether we are aware of them or not. For example, look again at Figure 4.20D. We see a hollow cube floating above the circles because once the closure principle has filled in the gaps, our experience tells us that the most likely interpretation of the resulting pattern of lines is a cube—even though it is not really there. Other perceptual sets are more conscious. For example, with deadly shooting incidents so much in the news, many people have become "set" to perceive ambiguous objects as weapons, especially in public places. A recent example occurred in Olympia, Washington, when police received a report of a man wearing a ski mask, carrying what appeared to be an assault rifle. A citywide manhunt ensued, and schools went into lockdown. The man had no idea about all the fuss until he noticed a helicopter tracking him. Police found that his "assault rifle" was actually an umbrella, and the "ski mask" just a black turtleneck and cap. Another misperceived umbrella caused a three-hour lockdown at a Carolina college after someone reported seeing a "gunman" near campus.

Expectancy can be shaped by the *context* in which a stimulus occurs. For example, we expect to see people, not gorillas, on a city street, so when a large gorilla escaped from Boston's Franklin Park zoo in 2003, a woman who saw him at a bus stop later said, "I thought it was a guy with a big black jacket and a snorkel on" (MacQuarrie & Belkin, 2003). Context has biasing effects for sounds as well as sights. When shots are heard on a downtown street, they are often perceived as a car backfiring. The same sounds heard at a shooting range would immediately be interpreted as gunfire.

Motivation is another aspect of top-down processing that can affect perception. For example, people tend to perceive desirable objects as being closer to them than less desirable ones (Balcetis & Dunning, 2010). They're also more likely to see objects as weapons if they feel angry or threatened (Baumann & DeSteno, 2010), and a very hungry person might at first misperceive a sign for "Burger's Body Shop" as indicating a place to eat (Radel & Clément-Guillotin, 2012). Similarly, perhaps you remember a time when an obviously incompetent referee incorrectly called a penalty on your favorite sports team. You knew the call was wrong because you clearly saw the other team's player at fault. But if you had been cheering for that other team, chances are good you would have agreed with the referee's call.

Top-Down and Bottom-Up Processing Together

Top-down and bottom-up processing usually work together to help us recognize the perceptual world (Förster, 2012). This interaction is beautifully illustrated by the process of reading. When the quality of the raw stimulus on the page is poor, as in Figure 4.27, top-down processes compensate to make continued reading possible. They allow you to fill in the gaps where words or letters are missing, or if they're shown backwards in a mirror, thus giving you a general idea of the meaning of the text (Duñabeitia, Molinaro, & Carreiras, 2011).

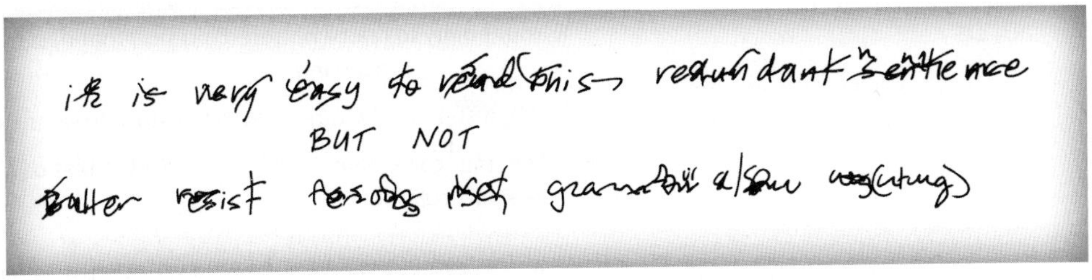

schemas Mental representations of what we know and expect about the world.

FIGURE 4.27
Interaction of Top-Down and Bottom-Up Processing

TRY THIS Which obscured line do you find easier to read: the first or the second? Top-down processing should help you read the obscured text on the first line. However, in the second line, the words are not related, so top-down processing cannot operate.

You can fill in the gaps because the world is *redundant;* it provides multiple clues about what is going on. So even if you lose or miss one stimulus in a pattern, other clues can help you recognize the pattern. There is so much redundancy in written language, for instance, that many of the words and letters you see are not needed. Fo- ex-mp-e, y-u c-n r-ad -hi- se-te-ce -it- ev-ry -hi-d l-tt-r m-ss-ng. Similarly, vision in three dimensions normally provides multiple cues to depth, making recognition of distance easy and clear. It is when many of these cues are eliminated that ambiguous stimuli create the sorts of depth illusions discussed earlier.

In hearing, too, top-down processing can compensate for ambiguous stimuli. In one experiment, participants heard strings of five words in meaningless order, such as "wet brought who socks some." There was so much background noise, however, that participants who heard this sequence could recognize only about 75 percent of the words (Miller, Heise, & Lichten, 1951). The words were then read to a second group of participants in a meaningful order (e.g., "who brought some wet socks"). The second group was able to recognize almost all of the words, even under the same noisy conditions. In fact, it took twice as much noise to reduce their performance to the level of the first group. Why? When the words were in meaningless order, only bottom-up processing was available. Recognizing one word was no help in identifying the next. Meaningful sentences, however, provided a more familiar context and allowed for some top-down processing. Hearing one word helped the listener make a reasonable guess (based on knowledge and experience) about the others. (See "In Review: Mechanisms of Pattern Recognition" for a summary of bottom-up and top-down processing.)

MECHANISMS OF PATTERN RECOGNITION

IN REVIEW

Mechanism	Description	Example
Bottom-up processing	Raw sensations from the eye or the ear are analyzed into basic features, such as edges, color, or movement; these features are then recombined at higher brain centers, where they are compared with stored information about objects or sounds.	You recognize a dog as a dog because its features—four legs, barking, panting—match your perceptual category for "dog."
Top-down processing	Knowledge of the world and experience in perceiving allow people to make inferences about the identity of stimuli, even when the quality of raw sensory information is low.	On a dark night, a small, vaguely seen blob pulling on the end of a leash is recognized as a dog because the stimulus occurs at a location where we would expect a dog to be.

In Review Questions

1. Your ability to read a battered old sign that has some letters missing is a result of _____ processing.

2. When stimulus features match the stimuli we are looking for, _____ takes place.

3. Schemas can create a _____ that makes us more likely to perceive stimuli in a particular way.

Culture, Experience, and Perception

We have been talking as if all aspects of perception work or fail in the same way for everyone everywhere. The truth is, though, that virtually all perceptual abilities are shaped to some extent by the sensory experiences we have or have not had. For example, people are better at judging the size and distance of familiar objects than of unfamiliar ones. Size and shape constancy, too, depend partly on the knowledge and experience that tell us that most solid objects do not suddenly change their size or shape. The experience-based nature of perception can also be seen in brightness constancy: You perceive charcoal to be darker than a sheet of writing paper partly because no matter how much light the charcoal reflects, you *know* charcoal is black. Experience even teaches us when to ignore certain stimulus cues (Yang & Kubovy, 1999). To fully experience the depth portrayed in a painting, for example, you have to ignore ridges, scratches, dust, or other texture cues from the canvas that would remind you of its flatness. And the next time you're watching TV, notice the indistinct reflections of objects in the room that appear on the screen. You've learned to ignore these reflections, so it will take a little effort to perceive them and a lot of effort to focus on them for long.

What if you hadn't had a chance to learn or practice these perceptual skills? One way to explore this question is through case studies of people who have been blind for decades and then have had surgery that restored their sight. It turns out that these people can immediately recognize simple objects and perceive movement, but they usually have problems with other aspects of perception. For example, M. M. had been blind from early childhood. When his vision was restored in his forties, he adjusted well overall, but he still has difficulty with depth perception and object recognition (Fine et al., 2003). Often, as people move toward or away from him, they appear to shrink or inflate. Identifying common objects can be difficult for him, and faces pose a particular challenge. To recognize individuals, he depends on features such as hair length or eyebrow shape. M. M. also has trouble distinguishing male faces from female ones and has great difficulty recognizing the meaning of facial expressions. He is unable to experience many of the perceptual illusions shown in this chapter, such as the closure illusion in Figure 4.20(D) or the size illusions in Figure 4.24. M. M.'s early blindness appears to have prevented his brain from fully developing the neural connections necessary for drawing accurate inferences about the visual world.

For the rest of us, too, the ability to experience perceptual illusions depends on our sensory history. People who grow up in significantly different sensory environments are likely to have noticeably different perceptual experiences (Caparos et al., 2012). For example, the size illusion shown in Figure 4.24(A) is strongest in the "carpentered world," where seeing straight lines is an everyday experience (Leibowitz et al., 1969). Responses to illusions such as this one are not as strong for people from rural areas of the Third World in which the visual environment contains more irregular and curved lines than straight ones (Coren & Girgus, 1978). Similarly, responses to depth cues in pictures and paintings differ in cultures that do and do not use such images to represent reality. People in the Me'n or the Nupa cultures of Africa, who have little experience with pictorial representation, have a more difficult time judging distances shown in pictures than do people in picture-oriented cultures (see Figure 4.28). These individuals also tend to have a harder time sorting pictures of three-dimensional objects into categories, even though they can easily sort the objects themselves (Derogowski, 1989). And residents of dense tropical rain forests, where most objects are seen over relatively short distances, may have some difficulty when asked to judge the distance of remote objects on an open plain (Turnbull, 1961). In other words, although the structure and principles of human perceptual systems tend to create generally similar views of the world for all of us, our perception of reality is also shaped by experience, including the experience of living in a particular culture (Chua, Boland, & Nisbett, 2005; Hedden et al., 2008).

TRY THIS

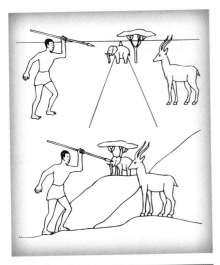

FIGURE 4.28
Culture and Depth Cues

People in various cultures were shown drawings like these and asked to judge which animal is closer to the hunter. Those in cultures that provide lots of experience with pictured depth cues choose the antelope, which is at the same distance from the viewer as the hunter. Those in cultures less familiar with such cues may choose the elephant, which, though closer on the page, is more distant when depth cues are considered.

LINKAGES How do infants perceive the world? (*a link to Human Development*)

PERCEPTION AND HUMAN DEVELOPMENT

LINKAGES

We have seen that perception is influenced by the knowledge and experience we gain over time, but what perceptual abilities do we start with? To learn about infants' perception, psychologists have studied two inborn patterns called habituation and dishabituation. Infants spend significantly less time looking at stimuli that are perceived to be unchanging. This is habituation. If they see a stimulus that is perceived to be new and different, they greatly increase their looking. This is dishabituation. Using the habituation/dishabituation technique, researchers have found that newborns can perceive differences in stimuli showing various amounts of black-and-white contrast but that they distinguish color differences very poorly, if at all (e.g., Bornstein, 2006). Other studies using the same methods have shown that newborns can perceive differences in the angles of lines (Slater et al., 1991). Taken together, these studies suggest that we are born with the basic components of feature detection.

Are we also born with the ability to combine features into perceptions of whole objects? This is still a matter of debate. We know that at one month, infants concentrate their gaze on one part of an object, such as the corner of a triangle (Goldstein, 2002). By two months, though, their eyes systematically scan around the edges of the object. This change suggests that they are now perceiving the pattern, or shape, of the object, not just its component features. However, other researchers have found that newborns show dishabituation (that is, they pay attention) when a familiar set of features are combined in a new way. So even newborns appear to notice and keep track of the ways some stimulus features are put together (Slater et al., 1991).

Infants may also be innately tuned to perceive at least one important complex pattern of features: the human face. In one study of newborns, patterns such as those in Figure 4.29 were moved slowly past the infants' faces (Johnson et al., 1991). The infants moved their heads and eyes to follow these patterns. But they tracked the facelike pattern shown on the left side of Figure 4.29 significantly farther than any of the nonfaces. The differences in tracking in this study and others indicate that infants can tell faces from nonfaces and are more interested in faces, or at least in facelike patterns (Cassia et al., 2008; Simion et al., 2003). Why should this be? Investigators who take an evolutionary approach suggest that interest in human faces is adaptive because it helps newborns focus on their only source of food and care. Further support for the evolutionary perspective comes from the finding that infants are also excellent at detecting potentially threatening stimuli, such as snakes (LoBue & DeLoache, 2010).

FIGURE 4.29

Infants' Perceptions of Human Faces

Newborns show significantly greater interest in the facelike pattern on the left than in either of the other patterns. Evidently some aspects of face perception are innate.

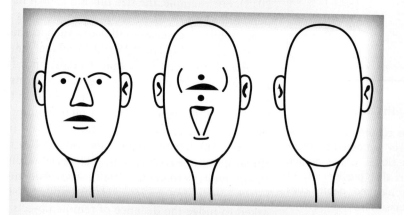

Other research on perceptual development suggests that our ability to accurately perceive depth and distance develops more slowly than our ability to recognize shapes (see Figure 4.30).

(*continued*)

For example, infants' ability to use binocular disparity and motion cues to judge depth appears to develop sometime after about three months of age (Yonas, Arterberry, & Granrud, 1987). They do not use textural gradients and linear perspective as cues to depth until they are five to seven months old (Arterberry, Craton, & Yonas, 1993; Bhatt & Bertin, 2001).

FIGURE 4.30
The Visual Cliff

The *visual cliff* is a glass-topped table that creates the impression of a sudden drop-off. A ten-month-old placed at what looks like the edge will calmly crawl across the shallow side to reach a parent but will hesitate and cry rather than crawl over the "cliff" (Gibson & Walk, 1960). Changes in heart rate show that infants too young to crawl also perceive the depth but are not frightened by it. Here is another example of the adaptive interaction of nature and nurture: Depth perception appears shortly after birth, but fear and avoidance of dangerous depth do not develop until an infant is old enough to crawl into trouble.

Mark Richards/PhotoEdit

In summary, there is little doubt that many of the basic building blocks of perception are present within the first few days after birth. The basics include such depth cues as accommodation, eye convergence, and information about movement (Arterberry & Yonas, 2000; Valenza & Bulf, 2007). Maturation of the visual system adds to these basics as time goes by. Over the first few months after birth, the eye's fovea gradually develops the number of cone cells necessary for high visual acuity and perception of fine details (Goldstein, 2002). Visual experience is also necessary. Experience teaches the infant to recognize unified patterns and objects and to interpret depth and distance cues and use them to move safely through the world (Bhatt & Quinn, 2011; Quinn & Bhatt, 2005). Like so many aspects of human psychology, perception is the result of a blending of heredity and environment. From infancy onward, the perceptual system creates a personal reality.

ATTENTION

Can you run out of attention?

Believe it or not, you still haven't found Barney's Diner! By now, you understand *how* you will recognize the right sign when you perceive it. But how can you be sure you *will* perceive it? The diner's sign will appear as one small piece of a sensory puzzle that also includes road signs, traffic lights, sirens, talk radio, and dozens of other stimuli. You can't perceive all of them at once. To find Barney's, you're going to have to be sure that the information you process includes the stimuli that will help you reach your goal. In short, you are going to have to pay attention.

Attention is the process of directing and focusing certain psychological resources to enhance perception, performance, and mental experience. We use attention to *direct* our sensory and perceptual systems toward certain stimuli, to *select* specific information for further processing, to *allocate* the mental energy required to do that processing, and to *regulate* the flow of resources necessary for performing a task or coordinating several tasks at once (Wickens & Carswell, 2012).

Psychologists have discovered three important characteristics of attention.

1. *Attention improves mental processing.* You often need to concentrate attention on a task to do your best at it.

attention The process of directing and focusing certain psychological resources to enhance perception, performance, and mental experience.

2. *Attention takes effort.* Prolonged concentration of attention can leave you drained (McNay, McCarty, & Gold, 2001). When you're already tired, focusing attention on anything becomes more difficult.

3. *Attention is limited.* When your attention is focused on reading this book, for instance, you will have less attention left over to listen to a conversation in the next room.

Directing Attention

TRY THIS

To experience the process of attention, try "moving it around" a bit. When you finish reading this sentence, look at something behind you, then face forward and notice the next sound you hear, then visualize your best friend, then focus on how your tongue feels. You just used attention to direct your perceptual systems toward different aspects of your external and internal environments. When you looked behind you, shifting attention involved *overt orienting*—pointing sensory systems at a particular stimulus. But you shifted attention to an image of your friend's face without having to move a muscle. This is called *covert orienting.* (We have heard a rumor that students sometimes use covert orienting to shift their attention from their lecturer to thoughts that have nothing to do with the lecture.)

How do you control, or allocate, your attention? Research shows that control over attention can be voluntary or involuntary (Yantis, 1993). *Voluntary,* or goal-directed, control over attention occurs when you purposely focus so that you can perform a task. Voluntary control reflects top-down processing because attention is guided by knowledge-based factors such as intention, beliefs, expectations, and motivation (e.g., Colzato et al., 2010; Liuzza et al., 2011; Pacheco-Unguetti et al., 2010). As people learn certain skills, they voluntarily direct their attention to information they once ignored (Zhang, Jiang, & He, 2012). For example, experienced drivers are better than new drivers are at noticing all that is going on around their vehicles, including events taking place far down the road (Koustanaï, Van Elslande, & Bastien, 2012).

When some aspect of the environment—such as a loud noise—diverts your attention, control is said to be *involuntary,* or stimulus driven. Stimulus characteristics that tend to capture attention include abrupt changes in lighting or color (such as flashing signs), movement, and the appearance of unusual shapes (Folk, Remington, & Wright, 1994). Engineering psychologists' findings about which stimuli are most likely to attract—and distract—attention have been used in the design of everything from websites to operator warning devices for airliners, nuclear power plants, and other complex systems (Clay, 2000; Hervet et al., 2011; Laughery, 1999). Other psychologists use the results of attention research to help design advertisements, logos, and product packaging that grab potential customers' attention.

As already mentioned, when we attend to some stimuli, we are less able to attend to others. In other words, attention is *selective.* It's like a spotlight that can illuminate only a part of the world at any particular moment. So if you focus intently on your reading or on a computer game, you may fail to perceive even dramatic changes in other parts of your environment (Hallett, Labert, & Regan, 2012). This phenomenon is called *inattentional blindness* (Mack, 2003; Mack & Rock, 1998). In one study, a researcher asked college students for directions to a campus building (Simons & Ambinder, 2005). During each conversation, two "workmen" carrying a large door passed between the researcher and the student. As the door hid the researcher from the student's view, one of the "workmen" took his place. This new person then resumed the conversation with the student as though nothing had happened. Amazingly, only half of the students noticed that they were suddenly talking to a new person! The rest had apparently been paying so much attention to the researcher's question or to the map he was showing that they did not notice what he looked like. Other studies have shown that most research participants can become so focused on their cell phone conversations or on their assigned task of counting the passes made during a basketball video that they fail to notice a clown riding by on a unicycle or a woman in a gorilla suit walking across the court (Hyman et al., 2010; Simons & Chabris, 1999).

FIGURE 4.31
Change Blindness

TRY THIS If you didn't immediately notice the difference between these photos, it was probably because you focused your attention on the similarity of their main features rather than on their specific elements. This common tendency results in blindness to a small, but obvious difference (Wilford & Wells, 2010; see page 136 for the answer). Just as we are usually unaware of our visual blind spot, we tend to be blind to inattentional blindness. We think we can see everything around us, but accidents are caused everyday because people sometimes fail to see what is right in front of their eyes (Galpin, Underwood, & Crundall, 2009). Fortunately, it may be possible to improve attentional skills through training and practice (Martens, 2011; Pollatsek, Romoser, & Fisher, 2011).

Dr. Ronald Rensink

Anyone can be affected by inattentional blindness. In one study, highly skilled doctors looking at computerized tomography scans of patients' chests were searching so intently for the presence of lung tumors that most of them failed to notice the image of a gorilla that researchers had superimposed onto the scans (Drew, Võ, & Wolfe, 2013)! Magicians take advantage of inattentional blindness when they use sudden movements or other attention-grabbing stimuli to draw our attention away from the actions that lie behind their tricks. To experience a type of inattentional blindness known as "change blindness," take a look at the photos in Figure 4.31.

Your search for Barney's Diner will be helped by your ability to overtly allocate attention to a certain part of the environment. It would be made even easier if Barney's had the only flashing sign on the road. As the most intense stimulus around you, it would attract your attention automatically. Psychologists describe this ability to search for targets rapidly and automatically as *parallel processing*. It is as if you can examine all nearby locations at once (in parallel) and rapidly detect the target no matter where it appears.

Dividing Attention

Often you can divide your attention efficiently enough to allow you to perform more than one activity at a time (Damos, 1992). You can drive a car, listen to the radio, sing along, and keep a beat by drumming on the steering wheel. However, your attention cannot be divided beyond a certain point without a loss in performance and mental-processing ability. For example, automobile drivers are much more likely to miss important signals, make errors in following directions, and react slowly to potentially dangerous situations when talking on a cell phone, even if it is a hands-free model (Reimer et al., 2010; Strayer & Drews, 2007). This is especially true if the conversation is an emotional one (Briggs, Hole, & Land, 2011). Distracted walking can be dangerous, too. The number of pedestrians killed or injured while listening to music on headphones more than tripled between 2004 and 2011 (Lichenstein et al., 2012). In other words, attention is a limited resource. If you try to spread it over too many targets, you "run out" of attention.

Still, it can sometimes be hard to keep your attention focused rather than divided. Look at the list of words in Figure 4.32 and as rapidly as possible call out *the color of the ink* in which each word is printed. *This Stroop task* (Stroop, 1935) is not easy, because your

The Dangers of Distracted Driving

Talking on any kind of phone—including hands-free models—can create inattentional blindness and distractions that impair driving and may contribute to accidents (e.g., Briggs, Hole, & Land, 2011; Hyman et al., 2010; Strayer & Drews, 2007). Twelve of the United States, the District of Columbia, Puerto Rico, Guam, the U.S. Virgin Islands, and many countries around the world have outlawed drivers' use of handheld cell phones. Forty–one states, the District of Columbia, Guam, and the U.S. Virgin Islands ban text messaging for all drivers (for the latest developments on this topic, visit http://distraction.gov).

© iStockphoto.com/nycshooter

BLUE GREEN
GREEN ORANGE
PURPLE ORANGE
GREEN BLUE
RED RED
GRAY GRAY
RED BLUE
BLUE PURPLE

FIGURE 4.32
The Stroop Task

TRY THIS Look at this list of words and as rapidly as possible call out the color of the *ink* in which each word is printed. How did you do?

brain automatically reads and processes the meanings of the familiar words in the list. These meanings then compete for attention with the responses you are supposed to give. To do well, you must focus on the ink color and not allow your attention to be divided between color and meaning. Children just learning to read have far less trouble with this task because they don't yet process the meanings of words as automatically as experienced readers do.

Although you can walk while talking or drive while listening to music, you would find it virtually impossible to read and talk at the same time. Why is it sometimes so easy and at other times so difficult to do two things at once (Connell & Lynott, 2010)? When one task is so automatic as to require little or no attention, it is usually easy to do something else at the same time (Schneider, 1985). Even when two tasks require attention, it may still be possible to perform them simultaneously if each taps into different kinds of attention (Wickens, 2002; Wickens et al., 1992). Some types of attention are devoted to perceiving incoming stimuli. Others handle making responses. This specialization allows a skilled pianist to use one kind of attention to read a new piece of music while using another kind of attention at the same time to press the correct keys. Apparently, the human brain can manage more than one type of attention and more than one spotlight of attention (Wickens, 1989). This notion of different types of attention also helps explain why an experienced driver can listen to the radio while steering safely. If two tasks require the same kind of attention, however, performance on both tasks will suffer (Just et al., 2001; Newman et al., 2007).

LINKAGES

As noted in the introductory chapter, all of psychology's subfields are related to one another. Our discussion of the development of perception illustrates just one way that the topic of this chapter, sensation and perception, is linked to the subfield of developmental psychology, which is described in the chapter on human development. The Linkages diagram shows ties to two other subfields, and there are many more ties throughout the book. Looking for linkages among subfields will help you see how they all fit together and help you better appreciate the big picture that is psychology.

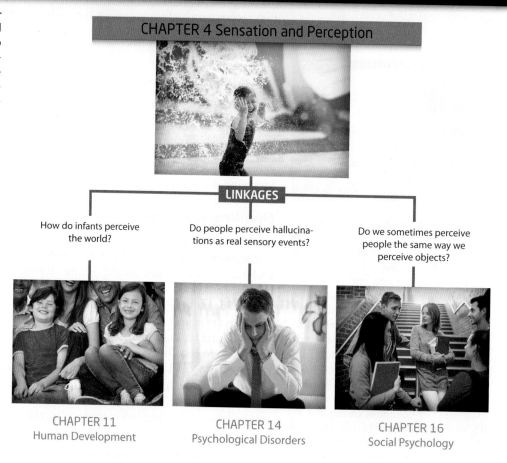

The difference between the photos in Figure 4.31 is that the top picture includes a clump of trees just to the left of the statue.

SUMMARY

Sensing and Perceiving the World

What is the difference between sensation and perception?

A **sense** is a system that translates information from outside the nervous system into neural activity. Messages from the senses are called **sensations**. **Perception** is the process through which people actively use knowledge and understanding of the world to interpret sensations as meaningful experiences.

Sensory Systems

How does information from my eyes and ears get to my brain?

Accessory structures collect and modify incoming energy from sensory stimuli. Then comes **transduction**, the process of converting that energy into neural activity. It is accomplished by sensory **neural receptors**, which are neural cells specialized to detect energy of some type. **Sensory adaptation** takes place when receptors continue to receive stimulation that does not change. Except in the case of smell, sensory neural activity is transferred through the thalamus, which relays it to the cerebral cortex. **Encoding** is the translation of the physical properties of a stimulus into patterns of neural activity that specifically identify those physical properties. It's the language the brain uses to describe sensations. Encoding is characterized by the *specific energy doctrine*: Stimulation of a particular sensory nerve provides codes for that one sense, no matter how the stimulation takes place.

The minimum amount of light, sound, pressure, or other physical energy that can be detected 50 percent of the time is called the **absolute threshold**. **Internal noise** is the spontaneous random firing of cells in the nervous system that occurs whether or not you are stimulated by physical energy. Your **response bias**, or **response criterion**, reflects your willingness to respond to a stimulus or ignore it. **Signal detection theory** addresses whether you will perceive a stimulus. **Sensitivity** refers to your ability to discriminate a stimulus from its background. **Weber's law** states that the smallest detectable difference in stimulus energy is a constant fraction of the intensity of the stimulus. This smallest detectable difference in a stimulus is called the difference threshold or **just-noticeable difference (JND)**. The distance from one peak of a sound wave or light wave to the next is its **wavelength**. Wave **frequency** is the number of complete waves, or cycles, that pass a given point per unit of time. **Amplitude** is the height of the wave from baseline to peak.

Seeing

Why do some people need eyeglasses?

Visible light is electromagnetic radiation with a wavelength of about 400 to about 750 nanometers. **Light intensity**, or the amount of energy in light, determines its brightness. Differing **light wavelengths** are sensed as different colors. Accessory structures of the eye include the **cornea**, the **pupil**, the **iris**, and the **lens**. Through **ocular accommodation** and other means, these structures focus light rays on the **retina**, the netlike structure of cells at the back of the eye.

Photoreceptors in the retina—**rods** and **cones**—convert light into neural activity. Rods and cones differ in shape, sensitivity to light, ability to discriminate colors, and distribution across the retina. Photoreceptors, especially rods, contribute to **dark adaptation**. The **fovea**, the area of highest acuity, has only cones, which are color sensitive. Rods are more sensitive to light but don't discriminate colors; they're distributed in areas around the fovea. From the photoreceptors, neural activity is transferred to bipolar cells and then to ganglion cells. A **blind spot** is created at the point where axons of ganglion cells leave the eye as a bundle of fibers called the **optic nerve**. Half of these fibers cross over at the optic chiasm. **Feature detectors** are cells in the cerebral cortex that respond to specific characteristics of objects in the visual field.

The color of an object depends on which of the wavelengths striking it are absorbed and which are reflected. The sensation of color has three psychological dimensions: **hue**, **color saturation**, and **brightness**.

According to the **trichromatic** (or Young-Helmholtz) **theory**, color vision results from the fact that the eye includes three types of cones, each of which is most sensitive to short, medium, or long wavelengths. Information from the three types combines to produce the sensation of color. According to the **opponent-process** (or Hering) **theory**, there are red-green, blue-yellow, and black-white visual elements and the members of each pair inhibit each other so that only one member of a pair may produce a signal at a time. Opponent-process theory explains color afterimages.

People who have cones containing only two of these three color-sensitive chemicals are described as *color blind*.

Hearing

How would my voice sound on the moon?

Sound is a repetitive fluctuation in the pressure of a medium such as air; it travels in waves. The frequency (which is related to wavelength) and amplitude of sound waves produce the psychological experiences of **pitch** and **loudness**, respectively. **Timbre**, the quality of sound, depends on complex wave patterns added to the basic frequency of sound. The energy from sound waves is collected and transmitted to the **cochlea** through a series of accessory structures, including the **pinna**, and components of the **middle ear**, including the **tympanic membrane**, the hammer, the anvil, the stirrup, and the oval window. Transduction occurs when sound energy stimulates hair cells on the **basilar membrane** of the cochlea, which in turn stimulate the **acoustic nerve**. Auditory information is relayed through the thalamus to the primary auditory cortex.

The intensity of a sound stimulus is encoded by the firing of auditory neurons. **Place theory** describes the encoding of high frequencies based on the place on the basilar membrane at which the sound wave peaks. Each neuron in the acoustic nerve is most sensitive to a specific frequency (its preferred frequency). According to **volley theory**, some frequencies may be matched by the firing rate of a group of neurons.

The Chemical Senses: Taste and Smell

Why can't I taste anything when I have a cold?

The chemical senses include smell (olfaction) and taste (gustatory perception). **Olfactory perception** (**sense of smell**) detects volatile chemicals that come into contact with olfactory receptors in the nose. **Taste perception**, also known as *gustatory perception,* detects chemicals in solution that come into contact with receptors inside the mouth. Smell and taste act as two components of a single system known as *flavor.* The scent and taste pathways converge in the *orbitofrontal cortex* of the brain. Olfactory signals are sent through the olfactory nerve to the **olfactory bulb** in the brain without passing through the thalamus. **Pheromones** are odors from one creature that change the physiology or behavior of another.

Taste perception detects chemicals that come into contact with taste receptors in **papillae** in the mouth, especially on the tongue. The basic taste sensations are sweet, sour, bitter, salty, umami, and astringent. The senses of smell and taste interact to produce flavor.

Sensing Your Body

Which is the largest organ in my body?

The **cutaneous senses**, also called somatosensory systems, include the skin senses and are related to proprioception. The skin senses detect touch, temperature, and pain. When they are mechanically stimulated, nerve endings in the skin generate touch sensations. Some nerve endings are sensitive to temperature and some respond to both temperature and touch.

Pain provides information about intense stimuli. Sharp pain is carried by A-delta fibers; dull, chronic pain is carried by C-fibers. The emotional response to pain depends on how the painful stimulus is interpreted. According to the **gate control theory of pain**, pain signals can be blocked on their way to the brain, sometimes by messages sent from the brain down the spinal cord, resulting in **analgesia**. Endorphins act at several levels in pain systems to reduce sensations of pain.

Proprioception includes **kinesthetic perception**, which provides information about the position of body parts with respect to one another, and the **sense of equilibrium**, or **vestibular sense** (balance), which provides information about the position of the head in space. This information is provided by **proprioceptors**, which are sensory receptors for movement and body position.

Perception

How do sensations become perceptions?

Perception is the knowledge-based interpretation of sensations. Much of this interpretation takes place automatically, but sometimes conscious effort is required to translate sensations into meaningful experience.

Organizing the Perceptual World

What determines how I perceive my world?

Our perceptual systems automatically engage in **figure ground discrimination** to sense the difference between **figure** and **ground**. They also automatically group stimuli into patterns on the basis of the Gestalt principles of proximity, similarity, continuity, closure, texture, simplicity, common fate, and three others known as synchrony, common region, and connectedness.

Depth perception depends partly on stimulus cues and partly on the physical structure of the visual system. Stimulus cues include relative size, height in the visual field, interposition, linear perspective, **motion parallax** reduced clarity, light and shadow, and textural gradients. Cues based on the structure of the visual system include **eye convergence** (movement of the eyes to focus on the same object), **retinal disparity** (due to each eye seeing the world from a slightly different angle), and accommodation (changes in the shapes of the lenses as objects are brought into focus).

The perception of motion results, in part, from the movement of stimuli across the retina. Expanding or **looming** stimulation is perceived as an approaching object. Movement of the retinal image is interpreted along with information about movement of the head, eyes, and other body parts to discriminate one's own movement from the movement of external objects. The **stroboscopic illusion** is a movement illusion arising when a series of slightly different still images is seen in rapid succession.

Because of **perceptual constancy**, the brightness, size, and shape of objects are seen as unchanging despite changes in the sensations received from those objects. Size constancy and shape constancy depend on the relationship between the retinal image of the object and one's knowledge-based perception of how far away the object is. Brightness constancy depends on the perceived relationship between the brightness of an object and its background.

Size illusions are distortions of reality that result when principles of perception are applied inappropriately. Many of these illusions occur when we misread depth cues or when we are overly influenced by the contexts (surroundings) in which visual stimuli appear.

Recognizing the Perceptual World

How do I recognize familiar people?

Both **bottom-up processing** and **top-down processing** contribute to our recognition of the world. Our ability to recognize objects is based on our capacity to match the pattern of sensations organized by the perceptual system with a pattern stored in our memory. Bottom-up processing occurs as the brain analyzes features, or combinations of features, such as form, color, motion, and depth. Top-down processing is influenced by our knowledge, expectations, and motivation. **Schemas** based on our past experiences can create a perceptual set; that is, a readiness or predisposition to perceive stimuli in certain ways. The context in which a stimulus appears can also create expectancies. Top-down and bottom-up processing commonly work together to create recognition. Top-down processing can fill in gaps in physical stimuli, in part because the environment provides redundant stimuli.

To the extent that the visual environments of people in different cultures differ, their perceptual experiences—and their responses to perceptual illusions—may differ as well. The ability to perceive color, basic shape features, and possibly the human face is present at or near birth. Other abilities, such the ability to recognize forms, develop later. Depth is also perceived early, but its meaning is learned later. Perceptual abilities are modified by both experience and maturation.

Attention

Can you run out of attention?

Attention is the process of focusing psychological resources to enhance perception, performance, and mental experience. We can

shift attention overtly (by moving the eyes, for example) or covertly (without any movement of sensory systems). Attention is selective; it is like a spotlight that illuminates different parts of the external environment or specific mental processes. Control over attention can be voluntary and knowledge-based or involuntary and driven by environmental stimuli. People can sometimes attend to two tasks at once, but there are limits to how much they can divide their attention.

TEST YOUR KNOWLEDGE

Select the best answer for each of the following questions. Then check your responses against the Answer Key at the end of the book.

1. Sandra reads English but not Chinese. So when she looks at a Chinese newspaper, there is more _____ than _____.
   a. sensation; perception
   b. perception; sensation
   c. perception; transduction
   d. sensation; transduction

2. As Jeremy listens to music on his iPod, sound waves are converted by his auditory system into neural signals. This process is called _____.
   a. attention
   b. transduction
   c. adaptation
   d. accommodation

3. In an experiment, Dante raises his hand each time he hears a tone through a set of headphones. The tone gets quieter and quieter until he fails to hear it half the time. After repeating the same procedure many times, the researcher ends the experiment because she has found Dante's _____.
   a. absolute threshold
   b. difference threshold
   c. internal noise
   d. response criterion

4. Jane is told that she will be paid $100 for each needle she can find in a haystack. According to signal detection theory, this information should _____ Jane's _____.
   a. raise; specificity
   b. lower; specificity
   c. raise; response criterion
   d. lower; response criterion

5. Matt finishes his can of soda as he walks across campus with Brad and Andy, and now he wants to slip the empty can into one of their open backpacks. Brad's pack has several heavy textbooks in it; Andy's contains only a notebook. Weber's law suggests that to avoid detection, Matt should put the can in _____ pack because the change in weight will be _____ than a just-noticeable difference.
   a. Andy's; less
   b. Brad's; less
   c. Andy's; more
   d. Brad's; more

6. Bianca wants Bruce to see the distant star she wishes on every night. Because the star is so faint, to have him see it she should have him look _____.
   a. directly at the star
   b. slightly away from where the star is expected to be
   c. at the star's reflection in a mirror
   d. at the star when there is a full moon

7. A projection-screen TV aims green, red, and blue lights at a screen. Because the TV can show a full range of colors by combining the green, red, and blue lights in differing amounts, it best illustrates the _____ theory of color vision.
   a. convergence
   b. frequency-matching
   c. opponent-process
   d. trichromatic

8. When Sarah stubbed her toe, she immediately began to rub it. According to the gate control theory of pain, the rubbing _____.
   a. shut down the brain's pain-sensing mechanisms
   b. released serotonin
   c. created an increase in pain tolerance
   d. created sensations that "took over" the pain pathways

9. Mick has been a rock musician for fifty years. The constant loud noise from his band has caused hair-cell damage, literally ripping off hair cells from his inner ear. We would expect that Mick now has _____.
   a. extremely acute hearing
   b. conduction deafness
   c. nerve deafness
   d. normal hearing loss for someone his age

10. Jeremy developed a disease that destroyed his thalamus. The only sense that was unaffected was _____.
    a. vision
    b. hearing
    c. touch
    d. smell

11. Your blind spot is located _____.
    a. where the optic nerve leaves the eye
    b. where visual fibers cross at the optic chiasm
    c. in the center of the fovea
    d. where accommodation takes place

12. In cooking school, Natalie studied flavor. She learned that the flavor of food can be altered by _____.
    a. changing its texture
    b. changing its temperature
    c. changing its color
    d. both a and b

13. Andrea cannot yet read but Lorraine can. They are each shown a list of color names (e.g., blue, red, yellow), but each word is printed in a color that doesn't match the word. They are asked to say the color of the ink each word is printed in, not the word itself. _____ will do better at this Stroop task because _____.
    a. Andrea; she can use top-down processing
    b. Lorraine; she is older
    c. Andrea; she will not be distracted by word meanings
    d. Lorraine; word meaning will help focus on the ink color

14. Ally has lost her sense of kinesthetic perception. She will most likely be unable to _____.
    a. know that her hand is raised without looking at it
    b. identify the flavor of her ice cream cone
    c. feel the warmth of the sun on her face
    d. feel pain

15. Shanelle likes the lights that appear to race around her Christmas tree as they flash on and off in sequence. This illusion is known as _____.
    a. motion parallax
    b. dishabituation
    c. the stroboscopic illusion
    d. texture gradient

16. Four swimmers practicing their synchronized swimming routine are perceived as a group because they are performing the same movements at the same speed. This is an example of _____.
    a. synchrony
    b. common fate
    c. orientation
    d. interposition

17. When you perceive an object as being closer to you because it blocks out part of the background, you are using the depth cue called _____.
    a. linear perspective
    b. reduced clarity
    c. interposition
    d. movement gradient

18. As Cliff walks out his front door, he sees a snowball coming straight at him. The retinal image of the snowball is increasing and he realizes that the snowball is approaching, not getting larger. This example illustrates _____.
    a. induced motion
    b. stroboscopic motion
    c. the movement gradient
    d. looming

19. Jeff and Larry were making chili. Jeff tasted the chili and thought it was perfectly seasoned. Then, while Jeff's back was turned, Larry added some more salt. When they sat down to eat Jeff immediately said the chili was too salty. Because he didn't know about the added salt, Jeff's perception must have been based on _____.
    a. top-down processing
    b. bottom-up processing
    c. pattern recognition
    d. selective attention

20. Although José appears to be listening as Rich talks about his new clothes, vacation plans, and exercise routine, José is thinking about the list of errands he has to run. José is _____.
    a. covertly orienting
    b. overtly orienting
    c. using parallel distributed processing
    d. using serial processing

Learning

© EpicStockMedia/Shutterstock.com

Preview

Live and learn. This simple phrase captures the idea that learning is a lifelong process that affects our behavior every day. Understanding how learning takes place is an important part of understanding ourselves. Sometimes learning involves one event signaling another, as when we learn to associate wailing sirens with ambulances. Other times learning depends on what happens after we do something—whether we receive praise or punishment, for example. But learning is more than these kinds of associations. What we think and how we feel about life's signals and consequences also have an impact on what we learn to do and not to do. Blend in practice and feedback about our behavior, mix well, and you have all the ingredients of the learning process.

Like most newborn babies, Jeffrey cried until he was fed. He awakened at 3 A.M. nearly every morning, hungry and crying for food. And as she had done every day since he was born, his mother would put on her slippers and walk down the tiled hallway to his bedroom. After a quick change of his diaper came the feeding. By the time he was four months old, Jeffrey would cry for about a minute and then quietly wait a few more minutes for his mother to arrive for his feeding. One particular morning, as his mother was halfway down the hall, she stopped in her tracks as she felt a sneeze coming. She pinched her nostrils together and the urge to sneeze passed. However, she noticed that Jeffrey had begun to cry again. This was unusual. She began to walk again and he quieted. Her scientific curiosity aroused, she walked a few steps, then stopped, then started, then stopped. She discovered that Jeffrey stopped crying when he heard her footsteps but resumed crying when the sound of footsteps stopped.

Jeffrey had learned a lot in the four months since his birth. He could anticipate events and predict outcomes based on the meaning of certain sounds. Like the rest of us, he showed an ability to learn about relationships in the environment and adjust to them. This adjustment to changes in the environment is called *adaptation*. Along with adaptation come expectations and predictions about what is and what is not likely to occur in our world.

The entire process of development, from birth to death, involves adapting to increasingly complex, ever-changing environments using continuously updated knowledge and skills gained through experience. This ability to adapt is especially impressive in humans, but it appears to varying degrees in every species. Charles Darwin highlighted the importance of adaptation in his theory of evolution, noting that individuals who do not adapt may not survive to reproduce. Many forms of adaptation follow the principles of learning.

Learning is a relatively permanent change in behavior or knowledge due to experience. We are born with some behaviors and knowledge, we acquire others automatically as we grow (through maturation), and we learn still others. In fact, learning plays a central role in most aspects of human behavior. If you want to know who you are and how you became the person you are today, examining what and how you have learned is a good place to start.

In this chapter, we first consider the simplest forms of learning—learning about sights, sounds, and other *stimuli* (the plural of *stimulus*). Then we examine the two major kinds of learning that involve associations between events—classical conditioning and operant conditioning. You will see that cognitive processes underlie some of the most complex forms of learning, such as the ability to learn from watching others. Some learning takes place consciously, as when you study for an exam, but you also learn many things without being aware that you are doing so. We conclude by discussing how research on learning might help people learn better.

LEARNING ABOUT STIMULI

Why do constant sounds seem to disappear?

In a changing world, our senses are constantly bombarded by massive amounts of information. If we tried to pay attention to every sight and sound, our information-processing systems would be overloaded, and we would be unable to focus on anything. People appear to be genetically tuned to attend to certain kinds of events, such as loud sounds, special tastes, or pain. *Novel* stimuli—things we have not experienced before—also tend to attract our attention.

learning The modification of preexisting behavior and understanding.

Learning to Live with It

People who move from a small town to a big city may at first be distracted by the din of traffic, low-flying aircraft, and other urban sounds, but after a while, the process of habituation makes all this noise far less noticeable.

Stock Connection/Superstock

By contrast, our response to *unchanging* stimuli decreases over time. This aspect of adaptation is a simple form of learning called **habituation**, and it can occur in relation to sights, sounds, smells, tastes, or touches. As described in the chapter on sensation and perception, it is through habituation that you eventually lose awareness of your glasses or your watch and that after being in a room for a while, you no longer smell its odor or hear its ticking clock. Habituation is especially important for adapting to initially startling but harmless events such as the repeated popping of balloons, but it occurs in some degree to all kinds of stimuli and in all kinds of animals, from simple sea snails to humans (Rankin et al., 2009; Thompson, 2009). After our response to a stimulus has habituated, it may quickly return if the stimulus changes or the situation changes. So you may become aware again of the ticking of a grandfather clock after the hourly chime has sounded because now, something in your environment has changed. The reappearance of your original response when a stimulus changes is called *dishabituation*. In the sensation and perception chapter, we described how habituation and dishabituation processes helped psychologists determine what babies notice, and fail to notice, as perceptual skills develop.

A second simple form of learning, called *sensitization*, appears as an increase in responsiveness to a stimulus. Sensitization occurs, for example, when people and animals show exaggerated responses to unexpected, potentially threatening sights or sounds, especially during periods of emotional arousal. So while breathlessly exploring a dark, spooky house, you might scream, run, or violently throw something in response to the unexpected creaking of a door.

Habituation and sensitization provide organisms with a useful way to adapt to their environments, but notice that these kinds of learning result from exposure to a single stimulus. Neither kind involves associating one stimulus with another, as when we learn that, say, dark clouds signal rain. For this reason, habituation and sensitization are referred to as *nonassociative learning* (Chance, 2009). These nonassociative processes cannot, by themselves, explain many of the behaviors and mental processes that are the focus of psychology. To better understand how learning affects our thoughts and behaviors, we have to consider forms of learning that involve noticing the associations between various stimuli, as well as between stimuli and responses. One major type of associative learning is called *classical conditioning.*

habituation Reduced responsiveness to a repeated stimulus.

CLASSICAL CONDITIONING: LEARNING SIGNALS AND ASSOCIATIONS

How did Russian dogs teach psychologists about learning?

At the first notes of the national anthem, an athlete's heart may start to pound because those sounds signal that the game is about to begin. A flashing red light on the instrument panel might raise your heart rate, too, because it means that something is wrong with your car. People are not born with these reactions. They have learned them by observing relationships, or *associations*, between events in the world. The experimental study of this kind of learning was begun, almost by accident, by Ivan Petrovich Pavlov.

Pavlov's Discovery

Pavlov is one of the best-known figures in psychology, but he was not a psychologist. He was a Russian physiologist who won the Nobel Prize in 1904 for his research on the digestive system of dogs. In the course of this research, Pavlov noticed a strange phenomenon. His dogs sometimes salivated, or drooled, when no food was present. For instance, they salivated when they saw the assistant who normally brought their food, even if he was empty-handed.

Pavlov devised a simple experiment to determine why salivation occurred without an obvious physical cause, such as food. First he performed an operation to divert a dog's saliva into a container so that the amount of salivation could be measured. Next he placed the dog in an apparatus similar to the one shown in Figure 5.1. The experiment had three phases.

In the first phase, Pavlov and his associates confirmed that when meat powder was placed in the dog's mouth, the dog automatically salivated (Anrep, 1920). They also confirmed that the dog did not automatically salivate in response to a musical tone. The researchers had now established the two basic components of Pavlov's experiment: (1) a quick automatic response and (2) a neutral stimulus that does not trigger that response.

In the second phase of Pavlov's experiment, the tone was sounded and then meat powder was placed in the dog's mouth. The dog salivated. This pairing of the tone and the meat powder was repeated several times. The tone always preceded the arrival of the meat powder, but had the dog learned that relationship? It had.

FIGURE 5.1

Apparatus for Measuring Conditioned Responses

Pavlov used this laboratory apparatus to precisely measure the amount of saliva flowing from a dog's mouth.

Bettmann/Corbis

FIGURE 5.2
Classical Conditioning

Before classical conditioning, putting meat powder on a dog's tongue produces salivation, but the sound of a tone—a neutral stimulus—brings only orienting responses such as turning toward the sound. During the process of conditioning, the tone is repeatedly paired with the meat powder. After classical conditioning, the tone alone is a conditioned stimulus, producing salivation.

© iStockphoto.com/joshblake; © Redshinestudio/ Shutterstock.com; Mark Raycroft/Minden Pictures/ Getty Images; © iStockphoto.com/yanzommer; © Soloviova Liudmyla/Shutterstock.com

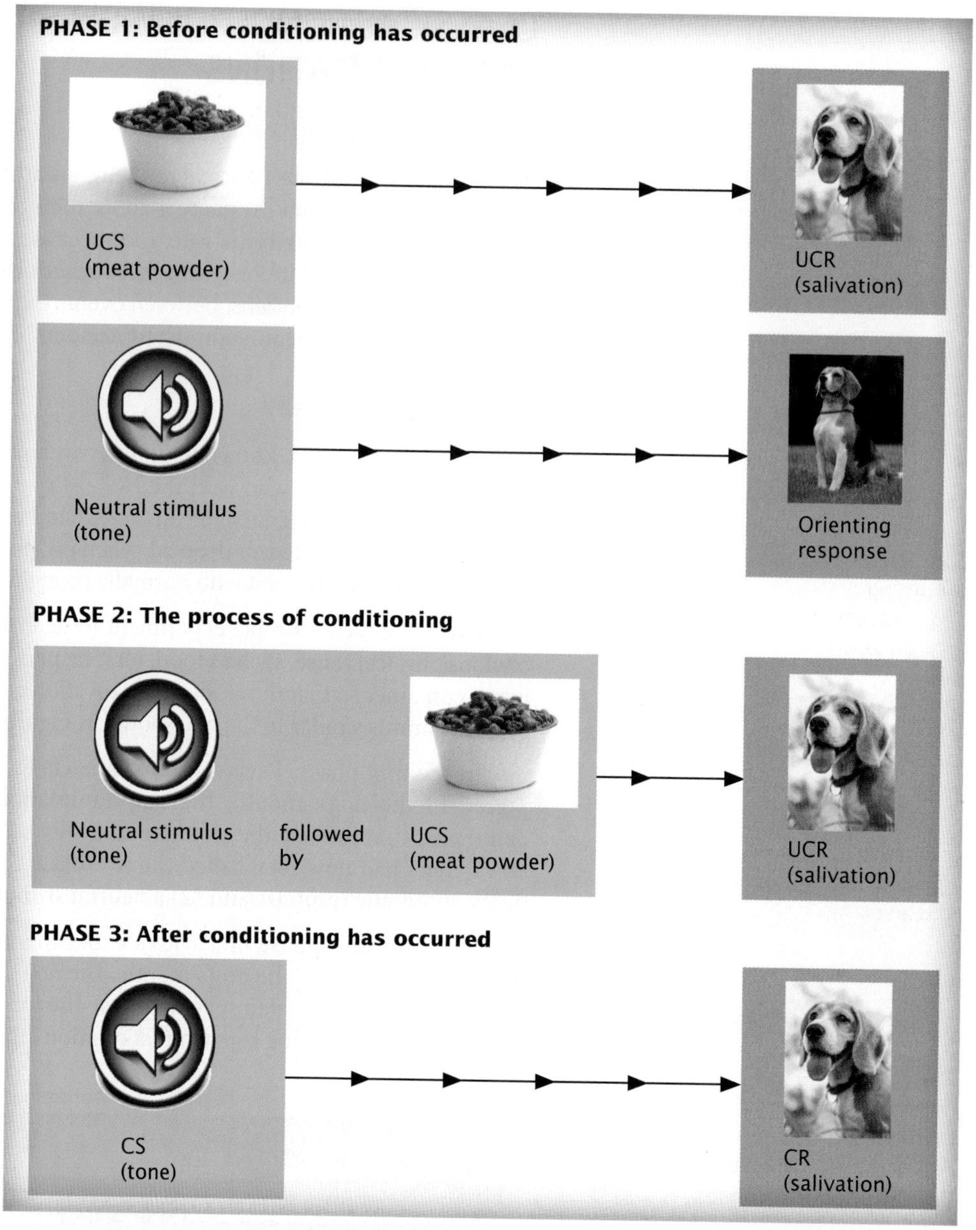

PHASE 1: Before conditioning has occurred

UCS (meat powder) → UCR (salivation)

Neutral stimulus (tone) → Orienting response

PHASE 2: The process of conditioning

Neutral stimulus (tone) followed by UCS (meat powder) → UCR (salivation)

PHASE 3: After conditioning has occurred

CS (tone) → CR (salivation)

classical conditioning A procedure in which a neutral stimulus is paired with a stimulus that triggers an automatic response until the neutral stimulus alone comes to trigger a similar response.

unconditioned stimulus (UCS) A stimulus that triggers a response without conditioning.

unconditioned response (UCR) The automatic, unlearned, reaction to a stimulus.

conditioned stimulus (CS) An originally neutral stimulus that now triggers a conditioned response.

conditioned response (CR) The response triggered by the conditioned stimulus.

In the third phase of the experiment, the tone was sounded but no meat powder was presented. The dog still salivated. The tone alone was now enough to trigger salivation. You may have seen a similar process if you regularly open pet food with an electric can opener. The sound of the opener probably brings your pet running (and salivating) because that sound means that food is on its way.

Pavlov's experiment demonstrated what we now call **classical conditioning**. In this procedure, a neutral stimulus is repeatedly paired with a stimulus that already triggers an automatic response. As a result of this pairing, the previously neutral stimulus itself comes to trigger a response that is similar to the automatic one. Figure 5.2 shows the basic elements of classical conditioning. The stimulus that naturally elicits a response without conditioning, such as the meat powder in Pavlov's experiment, is called the **unconditioned stimulus (UCS)**. The automatic, unlearned, response to this stimulus is called the **unconditioned response (UCR)**, in this case, salivation. After being paired with the unconditioned stimulus (meat powder), the previously neutral stimulus becomes the **conditioned stimulus (CS)** and the response it comes to trigger is a learned or **conditioned response (CR)**.

Conditioned Responses over Time: Extinction and Spontaneous Recovery

If you have ever been bitten by a barking dog, you might have learned to feel distress whenever you hear a dog's bark. The more bad experiences you have had with dogs, the stronger will be your learned distress in response to barking sounds. In the language of classical conditioning, continued pairings of a conditioned stimulus (CS/bark) with an unconditioned stimulus (UCS/bite) strengthen the conditioned response (CR/distress). The curve on the left side of Figure 5.3 shows an example: Repeated associations of a tone (CS) with meat powder (UCS) caused Pavlov's dogs to increase their salivation (CR) to the tone alone.

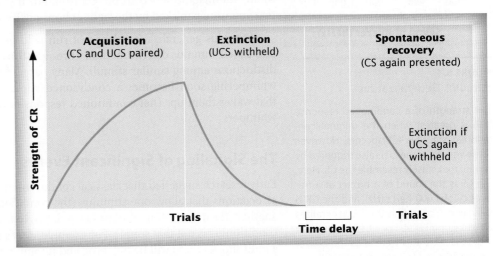

FIGURE 5.3

Changes over Time in the Strength of a Conditioned Response

As the conditioned stimulus (CS) and the unconditioned stimulus (UCS) are repeatedly paired during initial conditioning, the strength of the conditioned response (CR) increases. If the CS is then repeatedly presented without the UCS, the CR weakens—and eventually disappears—through a process called extinction. If the CS is presented again later on, a weaker version of the CR will reappear (Rescorla, 2004). This phenomenon, called spontaneous recovery, is only temporary, though. Unless the UCS is again paired with the CS, the recovered CR soon disappears.

What if the tone (CS) is repeatedly sounded but the meat powder (UCS) is no longer given? As you might expect, if the unconditioned stimulus is not paired with the conditioned stimulus at least now and then, the conditioned response will gradually disappear. This loss of the conditioned response is known as **extinction** (see the center section of Figure 5.3). The term is not entirely accurate, though. *Extinction* suggests that like the dinosaurs, the conditioned response has been wiped out, never to return. However, in this context we know that extinction merely suppresses a conditioned response but does not completely destroy it (Vurbic & Boutton, 2014). For instance, if the CS (tone) and the UCS (meat powder) are again paired after the conditioned response has been extinguished, that conditioned response will return to its original strength after as few as one or two trials. This quick relearning of a conditioned response after extinction is called **reconditioning**. Reconditioning takes much less time than the original conditioning, so it appears that extinction does not entirely erase the association between the conditioned stimulus and the conditioned response (Bouton, 1993, 2002; Myers & Davis, 2007).

The right side of Figure 5.3 provides more evidence for this conclusion. After a conditioned response has been extinguished it will temporarily reappear if the conditioned stimulus occurs again, even in a different situation (Neumann & Kitlertsirivatana, 2010). This is called **spontaneous recovery**, the temporary reappearance of a conditioned response after extinction (and without further CS-UCS pairings). In general, the longer the time between extinction and the reappearance of the CS, the stronger the recovered conditioned response (Devenport, 1998; Rescorla, 2005). Unless the UCS is again paired with the CS, extinction will reoccur and will further suppress the conditioned response (Leung & Westbrook, 2008). Still, even after many years, spontaneous recovery can create a ripple of emotion—a conditioned response—when we hear a song or catch a scent associated with a long-lost lover or a departed relative.

Stimulus Generalization and Discrimination

Once a conditioned stimulus is able to trigger a conditioned response, stimuli similar to the conditioned stimulus will also trigger some version of that response. This phenomenon, called **stimulus generalization**, is illustrated by the fact that a person who was

extinction The gradual disappearance of a conditioned response.

reconditioning The relearning of a conditioned response following extinction.

spontaneous recovery The temporary reappearance of a conditioned response after extinction.

stimulus generalization A process in which a conditioned response is triggered by stimuli similar to the original conditioned stimulus.

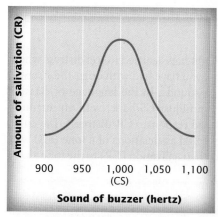

FIGURE 5.4
Stimulus Generalization

The strength of a conditioned response (CR) is greatest when the original conditioned stimulus (CS) occurs. However, some version of the CR is also triggered by stimuli that closely resemble the CS. Here, the CS is the sound of a buzzer at a frequency of 1,000 hertz (Hz), and the CR is salivation. Notice that the CR generalizes well to stimuli at 990 or 1,010 Hz, but that it gets weaker and weaker as the buzzer sounds less and less similar to the CS.

bitten by one particular dog may now show some fear of all dogs. Usually, the greater the similarity between a new stimulus and the original conditioned stimulus, the stronger the conditioned response will be. If the person was bitten by a small, curly-haired dog, fear responses would be strongest to other small dogs with similar types of hair. Figure 5.4 shows an example involving sounds.

Stimulus generalization has some obvious advantages. For example, it is important for survival that if you get sick after drinking sour-smelling milk, you now avoid dairy products that have a similar odor. Generalization would be a problem if it had no limits, however. You would probably be justifiably frightened if you found a lion in your living room, but imagine how disruptive it would be if your fear response generalized so widely that you were panicked by the sight of lions on TV or even by the word "lion" in a book.

Stimulus generalization does not run wild because it is usually balanced by a process called stimulus discrimination. Through **stimulus discrimination**, we learn to make distinctions among similar stimuli. Many parents find that the sound of their own baby whimpering soon becomes a conditioned stimulus, triggering a conditioned response that wakes them up. That conditioned response may not occur if a visiting friend's baby whimpers.

The Signaling of Significant Events

Early research suggested that classical conditioning involves nothing more than automatic associations that allow one stimulus (the conditioned stimulus, or CS) to substitute for another (the unconditioned stimulus, or UCS) in triggering a response. However, classical conditioning is not that simple. For example, a rat's unconditioned, automatic response to a mild shock (UCS) will be flinching and jumping. But the animal's conditioned response to the sound of a tone (CS) that always precedes shock will not be to flinch and jump but to freeze—much as it would if threatened by a predator (Domjan, 2005). In other words, classical conditioning allows the rat to prepare for an upcoming shock. Many psychologists now believe that classical conditioning provides a way for organisms to build *mental representations* of the relationships between events in their environment and expectancies about when such events will occur (Rescorla, 1988; Shanks, 1995; Sternberg & McClelland, 2012). These representations help us adapt and survive. When two events repeatedly take place together, we can predict that one will occur based on what we know about the other. Baby Jeffrey predicted his feeding from hearing his mother's footsteps. You have learned that a clear blue sky means dry weather, that too little sleep makes you irritable, that you can reach someone on the telephone by pressing certain buttons, and that yelling orders motivates some people and angers others.

What determines whether conditioned responses are learned? In general, these responses develop when one event *signals* the appearance of another. Other important factors are the timing, predictability, and intensity of the CS and UCS; the amount of attention that is devoted to them; and how easily the signals can be associated with other stimuli.

Timing

If your instructor always dismisses class at 9:59 and a bell rings at 10:00, the bell cannot prepare you for the dismissal. It comes too late to be a useful signal. For the same reason, classical conditioning works best when the conditioned stimulus comes before the unconditioned stimulus (called *forward conditioning*), rather than when the conditioned stimulus comes after the unconditioned stimulus (called *backward conditioning*). This timing makes sense for adaptation and survival, since it is more helpful to know when something important is going to occur before it happens. Indeed, the presence of food, predators, or other significant stimuli is most reliably signaled by smells, sounds, or other events that come just before their appearance (Einhorn & Hogarth, 1982).

It is logical that the brain should be "wired" to form associations most easily between things that occur at about the same time. How close together do they have to be? There is

stimulus discrimination A process through which people learn to differentiate among similar stimuli and respond appropriately to each one.

no one "best" interval for every situation. Classical conditioning can occur in some cases when the interval between the CS and the UCS is less than a second and in other cases when that interval is longer than a minute. It all depends on the particular CS, UCS, and UCR that are involved (Longo, Klempay, & Bitterman, 1964; Ross & Ross, 1971). However, classical conditioning will always be weaker if the interval between the CS and the UCS is longer than what is ideal for the stimuli and responses in a given situation.

Predictability

It is not enough for the CS merely to come before the UCS. Suppose your dogs, Moxie and Fang, have very different personalities. When Moxie growls, she sometimes bites, but sometimes she doesn't. Fang growls only before biting. Your conditioned fear response to Moxie's growl will probably occur slowly, because her growl does not reliably signal the danger of a bite. However, you are likely to quickly develop a classically conditioned fear response to Fang's growl. It always means that you are in danger of being bitten. Classical conditioning proceeds most rapidly when the CS *always* signals the UCS and only the UCS. Even if both dogs provide the same number of pairings of the CS (growl) and the UCS (bite), it is only with Fang that the CS *reliably* predicts the UCS (Rescorla, 1968).

Intensity

A conditioned response will be learned more rapidly if the UCS is strong. For example, a CS that acts as a predictive signal will be more rapidly associated with a strong shock (UCS) than with a weak one. As with the importance of timing and predictability, the effect of UCS strength on classical conditioning makes adaptive sense. It's more important to be prepared for major events than for minor ones.

Attention

An association between a pair of stimuli is most predictably learned when there are no other potentially distracting stimuli present (Jones & Haselgrove, 2011). In Pavlov's laboratory, just one conditioned stimulus, a tone, was linked to just one unconditioned stimulus, meat powder. In the natural environment, a wide variety of stimuli might be present just before a UCS occurs. Suppose you are at the beach. You're eating a hot dog, reading a magazine, listening to Katy Perry, digging your toes in the warm sand, and enjoying the smell of suntan lotion when you are surprised by the sting of a buzzing wasp. Which of these stimuli is most likely to become a conditioned stimulus that might later trigger discomfort? It depends partly on where you were focusing your attention at the moment you were stung. Because your attention was focused on the music or your reading, you might not have noticed the buzzing sound that preceded the sting (UCS). The stimulus you most closely attended to—the one you most fully perceived—is most likely to become a CS. In general, loud tones, bright lights, and other intense stimuli tend to get extra attention, so they are the ones most rapidly associated with an unconditioned stimulus. As long as it remains a reliable predictive signal, however, even a low-intensity CS will produce a reliable CR if repeatedly paired with a UCS (Jakubowska & Zielinski, 1978).

Biopreparedness

Certain kinds of signals or events are especially likely to become associated with other signals or events (Logue, 1985). Which stimulus becomes a conditioned stimulus for fear will depend not only on attention but also on whether the stimulus is a sight, a sound, or a taste and what kind of unconditioned stimulus follows it. The apparently natural tendency for certain events to become linked suggests that organisms are "biologically prepared" to develop certain conditioned associations (Öhman & Soares, 1993, 1998). This *biopreparedness* is seen in infants as young as fourteen months of age (LoBue & DeLoache, 2010).

The most dramatic example of the biopreparedness phenomenon is seen in conditioned taste aversions. In one study, rats were either shocked or made nauseous in the presence of a light, a buzzer, and flavored water. The rats formed only certain conditioned associations.

Taste Aversions

Humans can develop classically conditioned taste aversions, even to preferred foods. For example, Ilene Bernstein (1978) gave one group of cancer patients Mapletoff ice cream an hour before they received nausea-provoking chemotherapy. A second group ate this same kind of ice cream on a day they did not receive chemotherapy. A third group got no ice cream. Five months later, the patients were asked to taste several ice cream flavors. Those who had never tasted Mapletoff and those who had not eaten it in association with chemotherapy chose it as their favorite. Those who had eaten Mapletoff before receiving chemotherapy found it distasteful.

RubberBall/SuperStock

Animals that had been shocked developed a conditioned fear response to the light and the buzzer but not to the flavored water. Those that had been made nauseous developed a conditioned avoidance of the flavored water, but they showed no particular response to the light or buzzer (Garcia & Koelling, 1966). These results reflect an adaptive process. Nausea is more likely to be caused by something we eat or drink than by a noise or a light. So nausea is more likely to become a conditioned response to an internal stimulus, such as a flavor, than to an external stimulus. In contrast, the sudden pain of a shock is more likely to have been caused by an external stimulus, so it makes evolutionary sense that the organism should be "tuned" to associate shock or sudden pain with a sight or sound. In our beach example, it is more likely that you would have associated the pain of that wasp sting with the sight of the insect than with the taste of your hot dog.

Conditioned taste aversion shows that for certain kinds of stimuli, classical conditioning can occur even when there is a long delay between the CS (taste) and the UCS (sickness). The nausea caused by eating spoiled food may be delayed for minutes or hours, but people who have experienced food poisoning may never again eat the food that made them ill. Organisms that are biologically prepared to link taste signals with illness, even a delayed illness, are more likely to survive than organisms not so prepared.

Evidence from several sources suggests other ways in which animals and people are innately prepared to learn aversions to certain stimuli. For example, experiments with animals suggest that they are prone to learn the types of associations that are most common in or most relevant to their environments (Wilcoxon, Dragoin, & Kral, 1971). Birds are strongly dependent on their vision in searching for food and may develop taste aversions on the basis of visual stimuli. Coyotes and rats, more dependent on their sense of smell, tend to develop aversions related to odor. In humans, preparedness results in far more cases of conditioned fear of harmless dogs or snakes than of potentially more dangerous objects, such as electrical outlets or knives (Öhman & Mineka, 2001, 2003). We are also particularly likely to learn fear responses to people who are "different," such as members of other ethnic groups (Olsson et al., 2005).

Higher Order Conditioning

Once we learn that a conditioned stimulus (CS) signals the arrival of an unconditioned stimulus (UCS), the CS may operate as if it actually were that UCS. For instance, suppose that a child endures a painful medical procedure (UCS) at the doctor's office and the pain becomes associated with the doctor's white coat. The white coat might then become a conditioned stimulus (CS) that can trigger a conditioned fear response. Once the white coat is able to set off a conditioned fear response, the coat may take on some properties of an unconditioned stimulus. So, if the child later sees a white-coated pharmacist at the drugstore, that once-neutral store can become a conditioned stimulus for fear because it signals the appearance of a white coat, which in turn signals pain. When a conditioned stimulus (the white coat) acts like an unconditioned stimulus, creating conditioned stimuli (the drugstore) out of events associated with it, the process is called **higher order conditioning**. This process serves as an adaptive "early warning system." It prepares us for threatening events (UCS) that are signaled not only by a CS but also by associated events that precede—and thus predict—that CS.

Some Applications of Classical Conditioning

The principles of classical conditioning are summarized in "In Review: Basic Processes of Classical Conditioning." These principles have proven useful in many areas, including in recent efforts to use insects to help detect explosive material. In one study, for example, after the taste of sugar water was associated with the smell of a chemical used in certain explosives, wasps quickly developed a conditioned response to the smell alone. When several of these trained insects were placed in a plastic tube and brought near the target chemical, they displayed an

higher order conditioning A process through which a conditioned stimulus comes to signal another conditioned stimulus that is already associated with an unconditioned stimulus.

The Power of Higher Order Conditioning

Cancer patients may feel queasy when they enter a chemotherapy room because they have associated the room with nausea-producing treatment. Through higher order conditioning, almost anything associated with the room can also become a conditioned stimulus for nausea. One cancer patient who was flying out of town on a business trip became nauseated just by seeing her hospital from the air.

© Wei Ming/Shutterstock.com

immediate attraction to it (Rains, Utley, & Lewis, 2006). Researchers hope that it may someday be possible to use these so-called Wasp Hounds and other similar devices to detect explosives or drugs concealed in airline passengers' luggage (Tomberlin, Rains, & Sanford, 2008). Classical conditioning principles have also been applied in overcoming fears and understanding certain aspects of drug addiction (Xue et al., 2012).

Phobias

Phobias are intense, irrational fears of objects or situations—such as public speaking—that are not dangerous or that are less dangerous than the fear response would suggest. Classical conditioning often plays a role in the development of phobias (Bouton, Mineka, & Barlow, 2001; Waters, Henry, & Neumann, 2009). As mentioned earlier, a person frightened by a dog may learn a fear that is so intense and generalized that it leads the person to avoid all dogs and all situations in which dogs might be encountered. Classically conditioned fears can be very long lasting, especially when based on experiences with strong unconditioned stimuli. Combat veterans and victims of violent crime, terrorism, or other traumatic events may show intense fear responses to trauma-related stimuli for many years afterward.

Classical conditioning has also been used to treat phobias (see the chapter on treatment of psychological disorders). Joseph Wolpe (1958) was a pioneer in this effort. He showed that irrational fears could be relieved through *systematic desensitization,* a procedure that associates a new response, such as relaxation, with a feared stimulus. To treat a thunderstorm phobia, for instance, a therapist might first teach the client to relax

---

IN REVIEW

BASIC PROCESSES OF CLASSICAL CONDITIONING

Process	Description	Example
Acquisition	A neutral stimulus and an unconditioned stimulus (UCS) are paired. The neutral stimulus becomes a conditioned stimulus (CS), eliciting a conditioned response (CR).	A child learns to fear (conditioned response) the doctor's office (conditioned stimulus) by associating it with the automatic emotional reaction (unconditioned response) to a painful injection (unconditioned stimulus).
Stimulus generalization	A conditioned response is elicited not only by the conditioned stimulus but also by stimuli similar to the conditioned stimulus.	A child fears most doctors' offices and places that smell like them.
Stimulus discrimination	Generalization is limited so that some stimuli similar to the conditioned stimulus do not elicit the conditioned response.	A child learns that his mother's doctor's office is not associated with the unconditioned stimulus.
Extinction	The conditioned stimulus is presented alone, without the unconditioned stimulus. Eventually the conditioned stimulus no longer elicits the conditioned response.	A child visits the doctor's office several times for a checkup but does not receive a shot. Fear may eventually cease.

Review Questions

1. If a person with a conditioned fear of spiders is also frightened by the sight of creatures that look somewhat like spiders, the person is demonstrating stimulus _____.

2. Because of _____ , we are more likely to learn a fear of snakes than a fear of cars.

3. Feeling sad upon hearing a song associated with a long-lost relationship illustrates _____.

Predator Control through Conditioning

In the western United States, some ranchers lace a sheep carcass with enough lithium chloride to make wolves and coyotes nauseous (Pfister et al., 2003). The predators associate nausea with the smell and taste of sheep and afterward stay away from the ranchers' flocks. A similar program in India has greatly reduced the human death toll from tiger attacks. Stuffed dummies are connected to a shock generator and placed in areas where tigers have killed people. When the animals approach the dummies, they receive a shock (UCS). After learning to associate shock with the human form (CS), the tigers tend to avoid people (CR).

NHPA/Photoshot

law of effect A law stating that if a response made in the presence of a particular stimulus is rewarded, the same response is more likely to occur when that stimulus is encountered again.

operant conditioning A process in which responses are learned on the basis of their rewarding or punishing consequences.

operant A response that has some effect on the world.

reinforcer A stimulus event that increases the probability that the response immediately preceding it will occur again.

positive reinforcers Stimuli that strengthen a response if they follow that response.

negative reinforcers The removal of unpleasant stimuli.

deeply and then associate that relaxation with increasingly intense sights and sounds of thunderstorms presented on video (Öst, 1978). Because, as Wolpe (1958) noted, a person cannot be relaxed and afraid at the same time, the new conditioned response (relaxation) to thunderstorms replaces the old one (fear).

Drug Addiction

When people repeatedly use addictive drugs, their responses to the drugs become weaker. As already mentioned, this reduction in responsiveness to a repeated stimulus is called habituation. According to Richard Solomon's (1980) *opponent-process theory,* habituation is the result of two processes that balance each other, like a seesaw. The first process is a quick, automatic, involuntary response—essentially an unconditioned response (UCR) to the drug. The second—or opponent—process is a response that follows and counteracts the first. When a person is taking addictive drugs, this opponent response can be learned, or conditioned (McDonald & Siegel, 2004). So if the unconditioned response to a drug injection includes an increase in body temperature, the conditioned response will include an opponent process that reduces body temperature somewhat, creating the sensation of "chills." As the addict continues drug injections day after day, the learned opponent process ("chills") gets stronger and occurs sooner. As this CR strengthens, the rise in temperature caused by the drug gets smaller, resulting in habituation. In the same fashion, the intense pleasure first experienced as an unconditioned response to the drug begins to be weakened over time by an unpleasant opponent process (CR) that becomes faster and stronger. The addict begins to take larger drug doses in an effort to achieve the "high" once created by smaller doses. As described in the chapter on consciousness, people who display this pattern are said to have developed a *tolerance* for the drug.

The location where a drug is usually taken and the rituals that precede an injection (such as preparing the syringe) can become conditioned stimuli that trigger conditioned opponent-process responses even before the drug enters the bloodstream. These stimuli signal that the drug is coming, and the body begins to brace itself. But what if a person takes the drug in a new location or doesn't follow the usual ritual? According to opponent-process theory, in the absence of these conditioned environmental stimuli, the conditioned responses that normally dampen the user's unconditioned responses to the drug will not be as strong. As a result, the drug dose the addict took in the usual way yesterday might cause a potentially fatal overdose today (e.g., Siegel, 2005).

INSTRUMENTAL AND OPERANT CONDITIONING: LEARNING THE CONSEQUENCES OF BEHAVIOR

How do reward and punishment work?

Classical conditioning is an important form of learning, but you also learn many associations between responses and the stimuli that *follow* them, between behavior and its consequences. A child learns to say "please" and gets a piece of candy. A headache sufferer takes a pill and escapes pain. A dog "shakes hands" and earns a treat. Such actions are called *goal-directed* if the response is made with the outcome in mind, while they are called *habits* if the response occurs simply because the action has previously been rewarded in a similar situation (Balleine & Dickinson, 1998). The capacity for goal-directed action appears in children around the age of three (Klossek, Russell, & Dickinson, 2008) and develops early in the lives of other species, too (Hall et al., 2000).

From the Puzzle Box to the Skinner Box

While Pavlov was exploring classical conditioning in Russia, Edward L. Thorndike, an American psychologist, was studying the consequences of behavior and animal intelligence,

FIGURE 5.5
Thorndike's Puzzle Box

This photograph shows the kind of puzzle box used in Thorndike's research. His cats learned to open the door and reach food by stepping on a pedal, but the learning occurred gradually. Some cats actually took longer to get out of the box on one trial than on a previous trial.

Yale University Library

FIGURE 5.6
B. F. Skinner (1904–1990)

In the operant conditioning chamber shown here, the rat can press a bar to obtain food pellets from a tube. Operant and instrumental conditioning are similar in most respects, but they do differ in one way. Instrumental conditioning is measured by how long it takes for a response (such as a bar press) to occur. Operant conditioning is measured by the rate at which responses occur. In this chapter, the term operant conditioning refers to both.

Nina Leen/Time Life Pictures/Getty Images

including the ability to solve problems. For example, he placed a hungry cat in a *puzzle box* like the one in Figure 5.5. The cat had to learn some response—such as stepping on a pedal—to unlock the door and get food. During the first few trials in the puzzle box, the cat explored and prodded until it finally hit the pedal. The animal eventually solved the puzzle, but very slowly. It did not appear to understand, or suddenly gain insight into, the problem (Thorndike, 1898). After many trials, though, the cat solved the puzzle quickly each time it was placed in the box. What was it learning? Thorndike argued that any response (such as pacing or meowing) that did not produce a satisfying effect (opening the door) gradually became weaker, whereas any response (pressing the pedal) that did have a satisfying effect gradually became stronger. The cat's learning, said Thorndike, is governed by the **law of effect**. According to this law, if a response made to a particular stimulus is followed by a satisfying effect (such as food or some other reward), that response is more likely to occur the next time the stimulus occurs. In contrast, responses that produce discomfort are less likely to be performed again. Thorndike described this kind of learning as *instrumental conditioning* because responses are strengthened when they are instrumental in producing rewards (Thorndike, 1905).

About thirty years after Thorndike published his work, B. F. Skinner extended and formalized many of Thorndike's ideas. Skinner (1938) noted that during instrumental conditioning, an organism learns a response by *operating on* the environment. So he used the term **operant conditioning** to refer to the learning process in which behavior is changed by its consequences, specifically by rewards and punishments. The terms operant and instrumental conditioning are now used to refer to the same thing. To study operant conditioning, Skinner devised new tools. One of these was a small chamber that, over Skinner's objections, came to be known as the *Skinner box* (see Figure 5.6).

Basic Components of Operant Conditioning

The chamber Skinner designed allowed researchers to arrange relationships between a particular response and its consequences. If an animal pressed a lever in the chamber, for example, it might receive a food pellet. The researchers could then analyze how consequences affect behavior. It turned out that stimulus generalization, stimulus discrimination, extinction, spontaneous recovery, and other phenomena seen in classical conditioning also appear in operant conditioning. However, research in operant conditioning also focused on concepts known as operants, reinforcers, and discriminative conditioned stimuli.

Operants and Reinforcers

Skinner coined the term *operant,* or *operant response,* to distinguish the responses in operant conditioning from those in classical conditioning. In classical conditioning, the conditioned response does not affect whether or when the stimulus occurs. Pavlov's dogs salivated when a tone sounded. The salivation had no effect on the tone or on whether food was presented. In contrast, an **operant** has some effect on the world. It is a response that operates on the environment. When a dog stands whimpering by the front door and is then taken for a walk, it has made an operant response that influences when it will get to go outside.

A **reinforcer** is a stimulus that increases the probability that the operant behavior will occur again. There are two main types of reinforcers: positive and negative. **Positive reinforcers** strengthen a response if they are presented after that response occurs. The food that hungry pigeons received after pecking a response key in Skinner's training chamber was a positive reinforcer. Receiving the food increased the birds' key pecking. For people, positive reinforcers can include food, smiles, money, and other desirable outcomes. Presentation of a positive reinforcer after a response is called *positive reinforcement.* **Negative reinforcers** also strengthen responses because they are followed by the *removal* of unpleasant stimuli, such as pain or noise. For example, the disappearance of a headache

FIGURE 5.7
Positive and
Negative Reinforcement

TRY THIS Remember that behavior is strengthened through positive reinforcement when something pleasant or desirable occurs following the behavior. Behavior is strengthened through negative reinforcement when the behavior results in the removal or termination of something unpleasant. To see how these principles apply in your own life, list two examples of situations in which your behavior was affected by positive reinforcement and two in which you were affected by negative reinforcement.

Maria Deseo/PhotoEdit; Maria Deseo/PhotoEdit; © Jonathan Sammartino

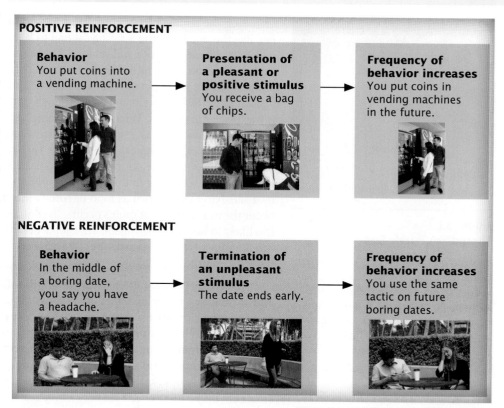

POSITIVE REINFORCEMENT

Behavior You put coins into a vending machine.

Presentation of a pleasant or positive stimulus You receive a bag of chips.

Frequency of behavior increases You put coins in vending machines in the future.

NEGATIVE REINFORCEMENT

Behavior In the middle of a boring date, you say you have a headache.

Termination of an unpleasant stimulus The date ends early.

Frequency of behavior increases You use the same tactic on future boring dates.

after you take a pain reliever acts as a negative reinforcer that makes you more likely to take that pain reliever in the future. When a response is strengthened by the removal of an unpleasant stimulus, the process is called *negative reinforcement*.

Notice that **reinforcement** always increases the likelihood of the behavior that came before it, whether the reinforcer is adding something pleasant or removing something unpleasant. Figure 5.7 shows this relationship.

Escape and Avoidance Conditioning

The effects of negative reinforcement can be seen in both escape conditioning and avoidance conditioning. **Escape conditioning** occurs when we learn responses that stop an unpleasant stimulus. The left-hand panel of Figure 5.8 shows an example from an animal laboratory, but escape conditioning operates in humans, too. Not only do we learn to take pills to stop pain, but some parents learn to stop their child's annoying demands for a toy by agreeing to buy it. And television viewers learn escape annoying commercials by muting the sound.

When an animal or a person responds to a signal in a way that *avoids* an aversive stimulus before it arrives, **avoidance conditioning** has occurred (see the right-hand sections of Figure 5.8). Avoidance conditioning is an important influence on everyday behavior. We go to work even when we would rather stay in bed, we stop at red lights even when we are in a hurry, we apologize for our mistakes even before they are discovered, and we stay away from feared or dangerous places. Each of these behaviors helps us avoid a negative consequence, such as lost pay, a traffic ticket, a scolding, or anxiety or injury.

Avoidance conditioning represents a marriage of classical and operant conditioning. If, as shown in Figure 5.8, a buzzer predicts shock (an unconditioned stimulus), the buzzer becomes a conditioned stimulus (CS). Through classical conditioning, the buzzer (now a CS) triggers a conditioned fear response (CR). Like the shock itself, conditioned fear is an unpleasant internal sensation. The animal then learns the instrumental response of jumping the barrier. The instrumental response (jumping) is reinforced because it reduces fear.

reinforcement The process through which a particular response is made more likely to recur.

escape conditioning The process of learning responses that stop an aversive stimulus.

avoidance conditioning The process of learning particular responses that avoid an aversive stimulus.

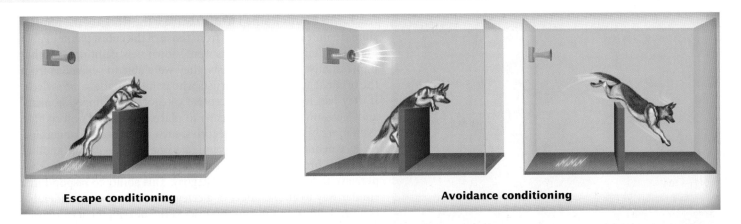

Escape conditioning

Avoidance conditioning

FIGURE 5.8
A Shuttle Box

A shuttle box has two sections that are usually separated by a barrier; its floor is an electric grid. Shock can be administered through the grid to either section. The left-hand panel shows escape conditioning, in which an animal learns to get away from a mild shock by jumping over the barrier when the electricity is turned on. The next two panels show avoidance conditioning. Here, the animal has learned to avoid shock altogether by jumping over the barrier when it hears a warning buzzer just before shock occurs.

Once learned, avoidance is a difficult habit to break, because avoidance responses continue to be reinforced by fear reduction (Solomon, Kamin, & Wynne, 1953). So even without the shock, animals may keep jumping over the barrier when the buzzer sounds because they never discover that avoidance is no longer necessary. The same is often true of people. Those who avoid escalators out of fear never get a chance to find out that they are safe. Others avoid potentially embarrassing social situations, but doing so also prevents them from learning how to be successful in those situations.

The study of avoidance conditioning has not only expanded our understanding of negative reinforcement but also has led some psychologists to consider more complex cognitive processes in operant learning. These psychologists suggest, for example, that in order for people to learn to avoid an unpleasant event (such as getting fired or paying a fine), they must have established an expectancy or other mental representation of that event. The role of such mental representations is emphasized in the cognitive theories of learning described later in this chapter.

Discriminative Conditioned Stimuli and Stimulus Control

The consequences of our behavior often depend on the situation we are in. Most people know that a flirtatious comment about someone's appearance may be welcomed on a date but not at the office. And even if you have been rewarded for telling jokes, you are not likely to do so during a funeral. In the language of operant conditioning, situations serve as **discriminative conditioned stimuli**, which are stimuli that signal whether reinforcement is available if a certain response is made. *Stimulus discrimination* occurs when an organism learns to make a particular response in the presence of one stimulus but not another. The response is then said to be under *stimulus control*. Stimulus discrimination allows people or animals to learn what is appropriate (reinforced) and inappropriate (not reinforced) in particular situations. For example, bears searching for food in Yosemite National Park campgrounds tend to break into minivans; it appears that they've learned that minivans are more likely than other vehicles to contain the goodies they are after (Breck, Lance, & Seher, 2009).

Stimulus generalization also occurs in operant conditioning. That is, an animal or person will perform a response in the presence of a stimulus that is similar to (but not exactly like) a stimulus that has signaled reinforcement in the past. The more similar the new stimulus is to the old one, the more likely it is that the response will be performed. Suppose you ate a wonderful meal at a restaurant called "Captain Jack's," which was decorated to look like the inside of a sailing ship. You might later be attracted to other restaurants with nautical names or with interiors that look something like the one where you had that great meal.

Stimulus generalization and stimulus discrimination complement each other. In one study, for example, pigeons received food for pecking at a response key, but only when they saw certain kinds of artwork (Watanabe, Sakamoto, & Wakita, 1995; see Figure 5.9). As a

discriminative conditioned stimuli Stimuli that signal whether reinforcement is available if a certain response is made.

result, these birds learned to *discriminate* the works of the impressionist painter Claude Monet from those of the cubist painter Pablo Picasso. Later, when the birds were shown new paintings by other impressionist and cubist artists, they were able to *generalize* from the original artists to other artists who painted in the same style, as if they had learned the conceptual categories of "impressionism" and "cubism." We humans learn to place people and objects into even more finely detailed categories, such as "honest," "dangerous," or "tax deductible." We discriminate one stimulus from another and then through generalization respond similarly to all those we perceive to be in a particular category. This ability to respond in a similar way to all members of a category can save us considerable time and effort, but it can also lead to the development of unwarranted prejudice against certain groups of people (see the chapter on social psychology).

FIGURE 5.9
Stimulus Discrimination

Pigeons reinforced for responding to the work of a particular painter learned to tell the difference between his paintings and those of other artists (Watanabe, Sakamoto, & Wakita, 1995).

Photo courtesy of Bruce E. Hesse, Ph.D., Department of Psychology and Child Development, California State University, Stanislaus

Forming and Strengthening Operant Behavior

Your daily life is full of examples of operant conditioning. You go to movies, parties, classes, and jobs primarily because doing so brings reinforcement. What is the effect of the type or timing of your reinforcers? How do you learn new behaviors? How can you get rid of old ones?

Shaping

Let's say you want to train your dog, Sugar, to sit and "shake hands." You figure that positive reinforcement should work, so you decide to give Sugar a treat every time she sits and shakes hands. But there's a problem with this plan. As smart as Sugar is, she may never make the desired response on her own, so you might never be able to give the reinforcer. The way around this problem is to shape Sugar's behavior. **Shaping** is the process of reinforcing *successive approximations*—that is, responses that come successively closer to the desired behavior. For example, you might first give Sugar a treat whenever she sits down. Next, you might reinforce her only when she sits and partially lifts a paw. Finally, you might reinforce only complete paw lifting. Eventually, you would require Sugar to perform the entire sit-lift-shake sequence before giving the treat. Shaping is a powerful tool. Animal trainers have used it to teach chimpanzees to roller-skate, dolphins to jump through hoops, and pigeons to play Ping-Pong (Coren, 1999).

Secondary Reinforcement

Operant conditioning often begins with the use of **primary reinforcers**, which are events or stimuli—such as food or water—that satisfy needs that are basic to survival. The effects of primary reinforcers are powerful and automatic. But constantly giving Sugar food as a reward can disrupt training, because she will stop to eat after every response. Also, once she gets full, food will no longer act as an effective reinforcer. To avoid these problems, animal trainers, parents, and teachers rely on the principle of secondary reinforcement.

Secondary reinforcers are previously neutral stimuli that take on reinforcing properties after being paired with stimuli that are already reinforcing. In other words, they are rewards that people or animals learn to like (Seo & Lee, 2009). If you say "Good girl!" just before feeding Sugar, those words will become reinforcing after a few pairings. "Good girl!" can then be used alone, without food, to reinforce Sugar's behavior. It helps if the words are again paired with food every now and then. Does this remind you of classical conditioning? It should, because the primary reinforcer (food) is an unconditioned stimulus. If the words "Good girl!" become a reliable signal for food, they will act as a conditioned stimulus (CS). For this reason, secondary reinforcers are sometimes called *conditioned reinforcers.*

shaping The reinforcement of responses that come successively closer to some desired response.

primary reinforcers Events or stimuli that satisfy physiological needs basic to survival.

secondary reinforcers Rewards that people or animals learn to like.

Getting the Hang of It

Learning to eat with a spoon is, as you can see, a hit-and-miss process at first. However, this child will learn to hit the target more and more often as the food reward gradually shapes a more efficient (and far less messy) pattern of behavior.

PureStock RF/Jupiter Images

The power of operant conditioning can be greatly increased by using secondary reinforcers. Consider the secondary reinforcer we call money. Some people will do almost anything for it despite the fact that it tastes terrible and won't quench your thirst. Its reinforcing power lies in its association with the many rewards it can buy. Smiles and other forms of social approval (such as the words "Good job!") are also important secondary reinforcers for human beings. However, secondary reinforcers can vary widely from person to person and culture to culture. Tickets to a rock concert may be an effective secondary reinforcer for some people but not for others. A ceremony honoring outstanding job performance might be strongly reinforcing in an individualist culture, but the same experience might be embarrassing for a person in a collectivist culture, where group cooperation is given greater value than personal distinction (Miller, 2001). When carefully chosen, however, secondary reinforcers can build or maintain behavior, even when primary reinforcement is absent for long periods.

Delay and Size of Reinforcement

Much of our behavior is learned and maintained because it is regularly reinforced. But many of us overeat, smoke, drink too much, or procrastinate, even though we know these behaviors are bad for us. We may want to eliminate them, but they are hard to change. We seem to lack self-control. If behavior is controlled by its consequences, why do we do things that are ultimately self-defeating?

Part of the answer lies in the timing of reinforcers. For example, the good feelings (positive reinforcers) that follow excessive drinking are immediate. But because hangovers and other negative consequences are usually delayed, their effects on future drinking are weakened. In other words, operant conditioning is stronger when reinforcers appear soon after a response occurs (Rachlin, 2000). Under some conditions, delaying a positive reinforcer for even a few seconds can decrease the effectiveness of positive reinforcement. The size of the reinforcer is also important. In general, conditioning is faster when the reinforcer is large than when it is small.

Reinforcement Schedules

When a *continuous reinforcement schedule* is in effect, a reinforcer is delivered every time a particular response occurs. This schedule can be helpful when teaching someone a new skill, but it can be impractical in the long run. Imagine how inefficient it would be, for example, if an employer had to deliver praise or pay following every little task employees performed all day long. In most cases, reinforcement is given only some of the time, on a *partial, or intermittent, reinforcement schedule*. Intermittent schedules are described in terms of when and how reinforcers are given. "When" refers to the number of responses that have to occur, or the amount of time that must pass, before a reinforcer will occur. "How" refers to whether the reinforcer will be delivered in a predictable or unpredictable way.

1. *Fixed-ratio (FR) schedules* provide reinforcement following a fixed number of responses. Rats might receive food after every tenth time they press the lever in a Skinner box (FR 10) or after every twentieth time (FR 20). Technicians working at computer help centers might be allowed to take a break after every fifth call they handle, or every tenth.

2. *Variable-ratio (VR) schedules* also call for reinforcement after a certain number of responses, but that number varies. As a result, it is impossible to predict which particular response will bring reinforcement. On a VR 30 schedule, for example, a rat will be reinforced after an *average* of thirty lever presses. This means that the reward sometimes comes after ten presses, sometimes after fifteen, and other times after fifty or more. Gambling offers humans a similar variable-ratio schedule. Casino slot machines pay off only after a frustratingly unpredictable number of button-pushes, averaging perhaps one in twenty.

3. *Fixed-interval (FI) schedules* provide reinforcement for the first response that occurs after some fixed time has passed since the last reward. On an FI 60 schedule,

Reinforcement Schedules on the Job

Make a list of all the jobs you have ever held, along with the reinforcement schedule on which you received your pay for each. Which of the four types of schedules (fixed ratio, fixed interval, variable ratio, or variable interval) was most common, and which was most satisfying to you?

Jim West/The Image Works

for instance, the first response after sixty seconds has passed will be rewarded, regardless of how many responses have been made during that interval. Some radio stations make use of fixed-interval schedules. Listeners who have won a call-in contest might have to wait at least ten days before they are eligible to win again.

4. *Variable-interval (VI) schedules* reinforce the first response after some period of time, but the amount of time varies unpredictably. So on a VI 60 schedule, the first response that occurs after an *average* of 60 seconds is reinforced, but the actual time between reinforcements might vary anywhere from 1 to 120 seconds or more. Police in Illinois and California have used a VI schedule to encourage seat belt use and careful driving. They stopped drivers at random times and awarded prizes to those who were buckled up and driving safely (Associated Press, 2007; Mortimer et al., 1988). Kindergarten teachers use VI schedules when they give rewards to children who are in their seats when a chime sounds at random intervals.

As shown in Figure 5.10, different **reinforcement schedules** produce different patterns of responding (Skinner, 1961). Both fixed-ratio and variable-ratio schedules produce especially high response rates overall. The reason, in both cases, is that the frequency of reward depends directly on the rate of responding.

Fixed-interval and variable-interval schedules generally produce lower response rates than ratio schedules. This makes perfect sense. Under a fixed-interval schedule, for example, it does not matter how many responses you make between one reward and the next. You will only be reinforced for the first response you make after a specified amount of time has passed. Because the timing of the reinforcement is so predictable, the rate of responding typically drops immediately after reinforcement and then increases as the time for another reward approaches. When teachers schedule quizzes on the same day each week, most students will study just before each quiz and then cease studying almost immediately afterward. Variable-interval schedules produce a slower, but steadier, response rate. Because one can never be sure how long it will be before the next response will be reinforced,

FIGURE 5.10
Results of Four Partial Reinforcement Schedules

These curves illustrate the patterns of behavior typically seen under different reinforcement schedules. The steeper the curve, the faster the response rate was. The thin, diagonal lines crossing the curves show when reinforcement was given. In general, the rate of responding is higher under ratio schedules than under interval schedules.

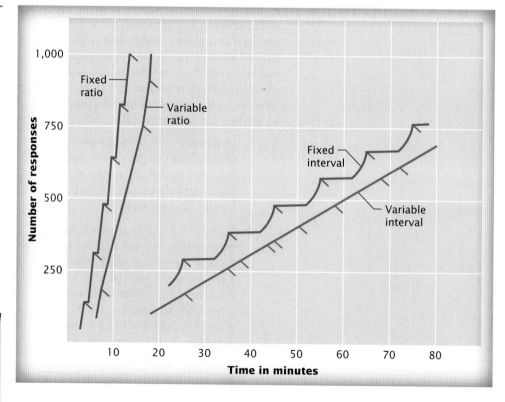

reinforcement schedules In operant conditioning, rules that determine how and when certain responses will be reinforced.

Superstition and Partial Reinforcement

Partial reinforcement helps sustain superstitious athletic rituals—such as a fixed sequence of actions prior to hitting a golf ball or shooting a free throw in basketball. If the ritual has preceded success often enough, failure to execute it may upset the player and disrupt performance. Former Oakland Athletics infielder Nomar Garciaparra tugged, loosened, and retightened each batting glove after every pitch. Those who watch sports have their superstitious rituals, too. One Pittsburgh Steelers football fan we know insists on wearing the same outfit while watching every game and eats a particular brand of lime-flavored corn chips because he believes this will ensure victory.

AP Images/Ben Margot

partial reinforcement effect A phenomenon in which behaviors learned under a partial reinforcement schedule are more difficult to extinguish than those learned on a continuous reinforcement schedule.

rewards will be maximized by responding at a regular, but not frantic, pace. This is why students whose teachers give unannounced "pop" quizzes on an unpredictable schedule are likely to study on a steady, regular basis just in case a quiz might occur at the next class (Kouyoumdjian, 2004). Variable-interval schedules also encourage the transformation of a goal-directed action (e.g., steady studying to do well on one professor's "pop" quizzes) into a habit that gains momentum from reinforcement and becomes, for example, a more general studying style (Nevin et al., 2001).

Schedules and Extinction

Ending the relationship between an operant response and its consequences weakens that response. In fact, failure to reinforce a response eventually extinguishes it. The response occurs less and less often and eventually may disappear. If you keep sending text messages to someone who never replies, you eventually stop trying. But extinction in operant conditioning does not erase learned relationships (Delamater, 2004). If a discriminative stimulus for reinforcement reappears some time after an operant response has been extinguished, that response may recur (spontaneously recover). And if it is reinforced again, the response will quickly return to its former level, as though extinction had never happened.

In general, behaviors learned under a partial reinforcement schedule are far more difficult to extinguish than those learned on a continuous reinforcement schedule. This phenomenon is called the **partial reinforcement effect**. Imagine, for example, that you are in a gambling casino, standing near a broken candy machine and a broken slot machine. You might deposit money in the broken candy machine once, but this behavior will probably stop (extinguish) very quickly. The candy machine should deliver its goodies on a continuous reinforcement schedule, so you can easily tell that it is not going to provide a reinforcer. But you know that slot machines give rewards on an unpredictable, intermittent schedule. So, you might put in coin after coin, unsure of whether the machine is broken or is simply not paying off at the moment.

Partial reinforcement helps explain why superstitious behavior is so resistant to extinction (Vyse, 2000). Suppose you had been out for a run just before hearing that you passed an important exam. The run did nothing to cause this outcome. The reward followed it through sheer coincidence. Still, for some people, this kind of *accidental reinforcement* can strengthen the behavior that appeared to "cause" good news (Mellon, 2009; Pronin et al., 2006). These people might decide that it is "lucky" to go running after taking an exam. Similarly, someone who wins the lottery or a sports bet while wearing a particular shirt may begin wearing the "lucky shirt" more often (Hendrick, 2003). Of course, if the person wears the shirt often enough, something good is bound to follow every now and then, thus further strengthening the superstitious behavior on a sparse partial schedule.

Why Reinforcers Work

What makes a reinforcer reinforcing? Research by biological psychologists suggests that reinforcers may exert particular effects on the brain. In a classic study on this point, James Olds and Peter Milner (1954) discovered that mild electrical stimulation of certain areas of the brain's hypothalamus can be a powerful reinforcer. Hungry rats will ignore food if they can press a lever that stimulates these "pleasure centers" (Olds, 1973). It has since been discovered that activation of certain brain systems that use the neurotransmitter dopamine is associated with the pleasure of many stimuli, including food, music, sex, and highly addictive drugs such as cocaine (e.g., Baik, 2013; Beierholm et al., 2013). Actions that produce unexpected rewards, such as gambling, also involve increased brain dopamine activity (Potenza, 2013). In fact, the same brain reward areas are activated whether we are receiving money or food rewards (Kim, Shimojo, &

O'Doherty, 2011). In short, complex and widespread patterns of brain activity are involved in our response to reinforcers, allowing us to enjoy them, to learn to want them, and to learn how to get them (e.g., Dreher et al., 2010; Pessiglione et al., 2006).

Punishment

Positive and negative reinforcement increase the frequency of a response, either by presenting something pleasurable (i.e., positive reinforcement) or by removing something that is unpleasant (i.e., negative reinforcement). In contrast, positive and negative **punishment** *reduce* the frequency of an operant behavior by presenting an unpleasant stimulus or removing a pleasant one (in other words, by increasing discomfort or reducing pleasure). Shouting "No!" and swatting your cat when it scratches your furniture is an example of positive punishment, because it *presents* an aversive stimulus following a response. Taking away a child's TV privileges because of rude behavior is called negative punishment because it *removes* a pleasurable stimulus (see Figure 5.11).

FIGURE 5.11
Two Kinds of Punishment

In positive punishment, an aversive, or unpleasant, stimulus follows a behavior. In negative punishment, sometimes called penalty, a pleasant stimulus is removed following a behavior. In either case, punishment decreases the chances that the behavior will occur in the future. Now you decide: When a toddler reaches toward an electric outlet and her father says "NO!" and gently taps her hand, is that punishment or negative reinforcement? If you said punishment, you're right, because it will reduce the likelihood of her touching outlets in the future.

Rob Wilkinson/Alamy; © Rob Byron/Shutterstock.com; © iStockphoto.com/akit; Exactostock/SuperStock; Tetra Images/Getty Images; Fotosearch/SuperStock

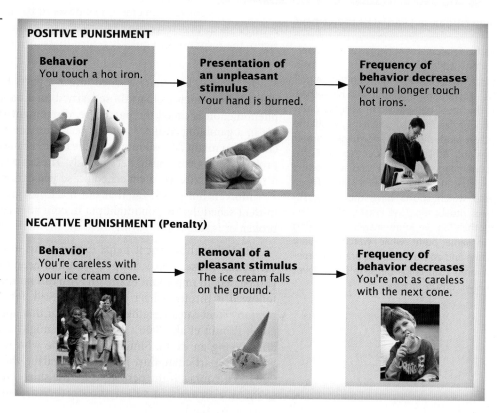

POSITIVE PUNISHMENT

Behavior
You touch a hot iron. → **Presentation of an unpleasant stimulus**
Your hand is burned. → **Frequency of behavior decreases**
You no longer touch hot irons.

NEGATIVE PUNISHMENT (Penalty)

Behavior
You're careless with your ice cream cone. → **Removal of a pleasant stimulus**
The ice cream falls on the ground. → **Frequency of behavior decreases**
You're not as careless with the next cone.

Punishment is often confused with negative reinforcement, but the two are quite different. Just remember that reinforcement of any type always *strengthens* behavior, whereas punishment always *weakens* behavior. If shock is *turned off* when a rat presses a lever, negative reinforcement occurs. It increases the probability that the rat will press the lever when shock occurs again. But if shock is *turned on* when the rat presses the lever, punishment occurs. The rat will be less likely to press the lever again.

Although punishment can change behavior, it has some drawbacks (Gershoff & Bitensky, 2007). First, it does not "erase" an undesirable behavior. It merely suppresses the behavior temporarily. In fact, people often repeat punished acts when they think they can do so without getting caught. Second, punishment can produce unwanted side effects. If you punish a child for swearing, the child may associate the punisher with the punishment and end up fearing you. Third, punishment is often ineffective unless it is given

punishment The presentation of an aversive stimulus or the removal of a pleasant one following some behavior.

immediately after the undesirable behavior and each time that behavior occurs. If a child gets into the cookie jar and enjoys a few cookies before being discovered and punished, the effect of the punishment will be greatly reduced. Fourth, physical punishment can become aggression, even abuse, if given in anger or with an object other than a hand (Zolotor et al., 2008). Fifth, because children tend to imitate what they see, frequent punishment may lead them to behave aggressively themselves (e.g., Taylor et al., 2010). Finally, punishment lets people know they have done something wrong, but it doesn't specify what they should do instead. An "F" on a term paper means that the assignment was poorly done, but the grade alone tells the student nothing about how to improve.

In the 1970s and 1980s, concerns over these drawbacks led many professionals to discourage parents from using spanking and some other forms of punishment with their children (Rosellini, 1998). More recent studies suggest, though, that occasional mild spanking can be an effective way to discipline children who are between three and thirteen years of age (e.g., Larzelere, 2000). Debate on this issue continues (e.g., Berlin et al., 2009; Kazdin & Benjet, 2003; Straus, 2005). Opponents point out that some youngsters who are spanked go on to show behavioral control problems, but proponents note that those same problems sometimes appear after children are given nonphysical punishments such as grounding, removing privileges, or being sent to their rooms (Larzelere, Cox, & Smith, 2010).

While some remain against spanking children under any circumstances (Gershoff, 2013), the results of an extensive review of the relevant research literature suggests that the long-term negative effects of spanking are minimal (Ferguson, 2013a). Indeed, the effects of spanking should be viewed in relation to when, where, and how it is used. For example, spanking is more common in some cultures and subcultures than in others (Runyan et al., 2010), and its negative effects, such as anxiety or aggressiveness, appear less likely to occur where it is a socially accepted form of discipline (Gershoff et al., 2010; Lansford et al., 2005). Further, occasional spanking may be least likely to harm children's development when it is used in combination with other disciplinary practices, such as requiring children to pay a penalty for their misdeeds, having them provide restitution to the victims of their actions, and making them aware of what they did wrong (Gunnoe & Mariner, 1997; Larzelere, 1996).

Punishment can even be therapeutic (Baumrind, Larzelere, & Cowan, 2002). As shown in Figure 5.12, for example, it can help children who suffer from certain developmental disorders or who purposely injure themselves (Flavell et al., 1982). So when properly used, punishment can be valuable, especially when a few guidelines are followed:

FIGURE 5.12
Life-Saving Punishment

This child suffered from chronic ruminative disorder, a condition in which he vomited everything he ate. At left, the boy was approximately one year old and had been vomiting for four months. At right is the same child thirteen days after punishment with electric shock had eliminated the vomiting response; his weight had increased 26 percent. He was physically and psychologically healthy when tested six months, one year, and two years later (Lang & Melamed, 1969).

University of Florida; University of Florida

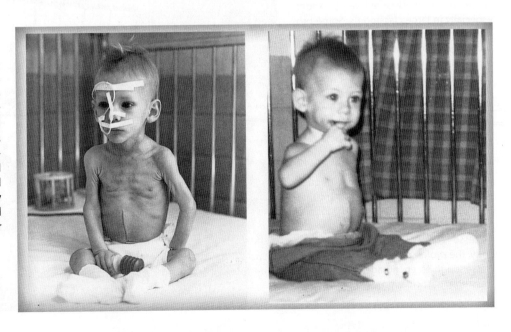

- Specify why punishment is being given, in order to prevent the development of a general fear of the punisher.

- Emphasize that the behavior, not the person, is being punished.

- Make the punishment immediate and noticeable enough to eliminate the undesirable response, without being abusive. A half-hearted "Quit it" may actually reinforce a child's misbehavior, because almost any attention is rewarding to some children. And once a child gets used to mild punishment, the parent may resort to punishment that is far more severe than would have been necessary if stern, but moderate, punishment had been used in the first place. (You may have witnessed this *escalation effect* in grocery stores or restaurants where children ignore their parents' initially weak efforts to stop their misbehavior.)

- Identify and positively reinforce more appropriate responses.

When these guidelines are not followed, the beneficial effects of punishment may be wiped out or may be only temporary. As prison systems demonstrate, punishment alone does not usually lead to rehabilitation because the punishment of confinement is not usually supplemented by efforts to teach and reinforce noncriminal lifestyles. Following their release, about two-thirds of U.S. prison inmates are rearrested for felonies or serious misdemeanors within three years, and about 50 percent will go back to prison (Cassel & Bernstein, 2007; U.S. Department of Justice, 2002).

Some Applications of Operant Conditioning

Although the principles of operant conditioning were originally worked out with animals in the laboratory, they are valuable for understanding human behavior in an endless variety of everyday situations. ("In Review: Reinforcement and Punishment" summarizes some key concepts of operant conditioning.) Effective use of reinforcements and punishments by parents, teachers, and peers is vital to helping children learn what is and is not appropriate behavior at the dinner table, in the classroom, or at a birthday party. People learn how to be "civilized" in their culture partly through experiencing positive and negative responses from others. And differing patterns of rewards and punishments for boys and girls underlie the development of behavior that fits culturally approved *gender roles*, a topic explored in more detail in the chapter on human development.

Speak Up!

Students are often reluctant to make comments or to ask or answer questions, especially in large classrooms. Some professors have used operant conditioning principles to help overcome this problem. In one introductory psychology course, classroom participation was reinforced with coinlike tokens that students could exchange for extra credit (Boniecki & Moore, 2003). The students responded faster to the professor's questions and offered many more comments and questions when this "token economy" was introduced. The frequency of student questions and comments dropped again when tokens were no longer given, but students continued their quick responses to the professor's questions. By that time, apparently, the professor's social reinforcement was enough to encourage this aspect of classroom participation.

Thomas Imo/Alamy

The scientific study of operant conditioning has been applied in many practical ways. For example, operant reinforcement of carpooling has been successful in reducing the number of cars on the road during big city rush hours (Ben-Elia & Ettema, 2011), and rewarding children for trying foods they once disliked has helped them learn to enjoy those foods (Cooke et al., 2011). Programs that combine the use of rewards and extinction (or carefully administered punishment) have helped improve the behavior of countless people with mental disorders, intellectual disability, and brain injuries, as well as preschoolers with behavioral and emotional disorders (e.g., Alberto, Troutman, & Feagin, 2002; Dickerson, Tenhula, & Green-Paden, 2005; Martin & Pear, 2010). These programs include establishing goal behaviors, choosing reinforcers and punishers, and developing a systematic plan for applying them to achieve desired changes. Many self-help books also incorporate the principles of positive reinforcement, recommending self-reward following each small victory in people's efforts to lose weight, stop smoking, avoid procrastination, or reach other goals (e.g., Grant & Kim, 2002; Rachlin, 2000).

When people cannot alter the consequences of a behavior, discriminative conditioned stimuli may help change their behavior. For example, many smokers find it easier to quit if they temporarily avoid bars and other places where there are powerful discriminative conditioned stimuli for smoking. Stimulus control can also help alleviate insomnia. Many insomniacs tend to use their beds for activities such as watching television, writing letters, reading magazines, worrying, and so on. Soon the bedroom becomes a discriminative stimulus for so many activities that relaxation and sleep become less and less likely. *Stimulus control therapy* encourages these people to use their beds only for sleeping, and perhaps sex, making it more likely that they will sleep better when in bed (Perlis et al., 2011).

IN REVIEW

REINFORCEMENT AND PUNISHMENT

Concept	Description	Example or Comment
Positive reinforcement	Increasing the frequency of a behavior by following it with the presentation of a positive reinforcer—a pleasant, positive stimulus or experience	You say "Good job!" after someone works hard to perform a task.
Negative reinforcement	Increasing the frequency of a behavior by following it with the removal of an unpleasant stimulus or experience	You learn to use the mute button on the TV remote control to remove the sound of an obnoxious commercial.
Escape conditioning	Learning to make a response that removes an unpleasant stimulus	A little boy learns that crying will cut short the time that he must stay in his room.
Avoidance conditioning	Learning to make a response that avoids an unpleasant stimulus	You slow your car to the speed limit when you spot a police car, thus avoiding being stopped and reducing the fear of a fine; very resistant to extinction.
Punishment	Decreasing the frequency of a behavior by either presenting an unpleasant stimulus (positive punishment) or removing a pleasant one (negative punishment)	You swat the dog after it steals food from the table or you take a favorite toy away from a child who misbehaves. A number of cautions should be kept in mind before using punishment.

In Review Questions

1. Taking a pill can relieve headache pain, so people learn to do so through the process of _____ reinforcement.

2. The "walk" sign that tells people it is safe to cross the street is an example of a _____ stimulus.

3. Response rates tend to be higher under _____ schedules of reinforcement than under _____ schedules.

LINKAGES   How are learned associations stored in memory? (a link to memory)

LINKAGES

NETWORKS OF LEARNING

Associations between conditioned stimuli and automatic responses or between responses and their consequences play an important role in learning, but how are they actually stored in the brain? No one yet knows for sure, but associative network models provide a good way of thinking about the process. As suggested in the chapter on memory, the associations we form among stimuli and events are represented in complex networks of connections among neurons in the brain. Consider the word "dog." As shown in Figure 5.13, each person's experience builds many associations to this word, and the strength of each association will reflect the frequency with which "dog" has been mentally linked to the other objects, events, and ideas in that person's life.

Using what they know about the laws of learning and the way neurons communicate and alter their connections, psychologists have developed computer models of how these associations are established (Messinger et al., 2001). These "neural network" models build on the observation that the brain uses many regions that work together across a widely dispersed system in order to accomplish mental tasks. Accordingly, many neural network models use the idea of distributed memory or distributed knowledge. These models suggest, for example, that your knowledge of "dog" does not lie in a single spot, or node, in your brain. Instead, that knowledge is distributed throughout the network of associations that connect the letters D, O, and G, along with other dog-related experiences. In addition, as shown in Figure 5.13, each of the interconnected nodes that make up your knowledge of "dog" is connected to many other nodes as well. So the letter D will be connected to "daisy," "danger," and many other concepts.

Neural network models of learning focus on how these connections develop through experience (Carasatorre & Ramírez-Amaya, 2013; Klingberg, 2010). For example, suppose you are learning a new word in a foreign language. Each time you read the word and associate it with its English equivalent, you strengthen the neural connections between the sight of the letters forming that word and all of the nodes activated when its English equivalent is brought to mind. Neural network models are sometimes called *connectionist* because they focus on how different parts of the network form connections with other parts. These models of learning predict how much the strength of each connection grows (in terms of the likelihood of neural communication between the two connected nodes) each time the two words are experienced together.

The details of various theories about how these connections grow are very complex, but a theme common to many of them is that the weaker the connection between two items, the greater the increase in connection strength when they are experienced together. So in a classical conditioning experiment, the connections between the nodes that characterize the

FIGURE 5.13

An Associative Network

Here is an example of a network of associations to the word "dog." Network theorists suggest that the connections shown here represent patterns of connections among nerve cells in the brain.

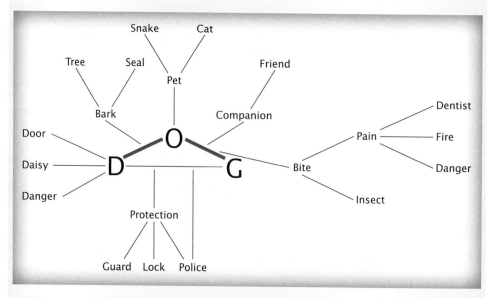

(continued)

conditioned stimulus and those that characterize the unconditioned stimulus will show the greatest increase in strength during the first few learning trials. Notice that this prediction nicely matches the typical learning curve shown in Figure 5.3 (Rescorla & Wagner, 1972). Further research using neural network models is likely to help us understand more about how we learn to recognize associations between the stimuli, responses, and events of our lives (e.g., Boden, 2006; Coutanche & Thompson-Schill, 2012).

COGNITIVE PROCESSES IN LEARNING

Can people learn to be helpless?

In the first half of the twentieth century, psychologists in North America tended to look at learning through the lens of behaviorism. Though they knew that mental representations, expectancies, and other cognitive processes can be involved in learning, they wanted to focus on studying the formation or modification of associations between observable stimuli and observable responses. Their research resulted in a rich set of learning principles based on classical and operant conditioning experiments.

In the decades since, however, psychologists have increasingly focused on exploring other, more complex forms of learning and the cognitive processes associated with them. These forms of learning include the development of concepts; of skill at communication, navigation, and tool use; and of abilities and behavior patterns formed by watching what others do (Blaisdell, Sawa, & Leising, 2006; Wasserman, 1993). Researchers in an area known as *comparative cognition,* for example, explore how cognitive processes in these more complex forms of learning may be seen in nonhumans as well as humans. How, they wonder, can food-storing birds hide, and then later retrieve, thousands of individual food items they need to survive over the winter? Their search might look random, but there is evidence that these birds form memories not only of where they have hidden something, but what they hid and when they hid it (Clayton & Dickinson, 1998; Suddendorf & Corballis, 2007). And although tool use was once thought to be a uniquely human form of adaptation, research by animal behaviorists has shown that chimpanzees, crows, sea otters, and other nonhuman animals have learned to use tools, too (e.g., Cheke et al., 2011; Goodall, 1964). It appears that nonhumans form mental representations, have expectations, and make generalizations that go beyond simply associating a particular response with a reward in an instrumental conditioning experiment (Asen & Cook, 2012; Blaisdell, Sawa, & Leising, 2006).

Examples of cognitive processes that affect learning include several phenomena, including learned helplessness, latent learning, cognitive maps, insight, and observational learning.

Learned Helplessness

Babies learn that crying attracts attention. Children learn how to make the TV louder. Adults learn what actions lead to success or failure in the workplace. People learn to expect that certain actions have certain consequences. But sometimes events are beyond our control. What happens when our actions have no effect on events, and especially when our escape or avoidance behaviors fail? If these circumstances last long enough, one result may be **learned helplessness**, a tendency to give up on efforts to control the environment (Overmier, 2002; Seligman, 1975).

Learned helplessness was first demonstrated in animals. As described earlier, dogs in a shuttle box will learn to jump over a partition to escape a shock (see Figure 5.8). But if the dogs first receive shocks that they cannot escape, they later do not even try to escape when the shock is turned on in the shuttle box (Overmier & Seligman, 1967). It is as if the animals had learned that "shock happens, and there is nothing I can do about it." Do people learn the same lesson?

learned helplessness A process in which a person or animal stops trying to exert control after experience suggests that no control is possible.

AN EXPERIMENT ON HUMAN HELPLESSNESS

What lessons do abused and neglected children learn about their ability to get what they need from the environment? Do they learn that even their best efforts result in failure? Do they give up even trying? Why would a student with above average ability tell a counselor, "I can't do math"? How do people develop an "I can't do it" attitude?

What was the researcher's question?

Can lack of control over the environment lead to helplessness in humans? Donald Hiroto (1974) conducted an experiment to test the hypothesis that people develop learned helplessness either after experiencing lack of control or after simply being told that their control is limited.

How did the researcher answer the question?

Hiroto (1974) randomly assigned research participants to one of three groups. One group heard a series of thirty bursts of loud, obnoxious noise and, like dogs receiving inescapable shock, had no way to stop it. A second group could control the noise by pressing a button to turn it off. The third group heard no noise at all. After this preliminary phase, all three groups heard eighteen additional bursts of noise, each preceded by a red warning light. During this second phase, all participants could prevent the noise if they pushed a lever quickly enough. However, they didn't know whether to push the lever left or right on any given trial. Before these new trials began, the experimenter told half the participants in each group that avoiding or escaping the noise depended on their skill. The other half were told that their success would be a matter of chance.

What did the researcher find?

The people who had previously experienced lack of control now failed to control noise on about four times as many trials as did those who had earlier been in control (50 percent versus 13 percent). This finding was similar to that of the research with dogs and inescapable shock. When the dogs were later placed in a situation in which they could escape or avoid shock, they did not even try. Humans, too, seem to use prior experiences to guide later efforts to try, or not to try, to control their environment.

Expectation of control, whether accurate or not, also had an effect on behavior. In Hiroto's study, those participants who expected that skill could control the noise exerted control on significantly more trials than did those who expected chance to govern the result. This outcome occurred regardless of whether the participants had experienced control before.

What do the results mean?

These results support Hiroto's hypothesis that people, like animals, tend to make less effort to control their environment when prior experience suggests that those efforts will be of no use. But unlike animals, humans need only be *told* that they have no control or are powerless in order for this same effect to occur.

Hiroto's (1974) results appear to show a general phenomenon. When prior experience leads people to *believe* that there is nothing they can do to change their lives or control their destiny, they may stop trying to improve their lot (Faulkner, 2001; Peterson, Maier, & Seligman, 1993). Instead, they may passively endure painful situations. Has this ever happened to you?

What do we still need to know?

Further research is needed on when and how learned helplessness affects people's thoughts, feelings, and actions. For example, could learned helplessness explain why some battered women remain with abusive partners? Could a soldier's sense of a lack of control during combat be at the root of a subsequent post-traumatic stress disorder (LoLordo & Overmier, 2011)? We do know that learned helplessness experiences are associated with the development of depression and other psychological disorders (Hammack, Cooper, & Lezak, 2012). Learned

(continued)

helplessness may increase a *pessimistic explanatory style*, such as occurs in people with depression (Peterson & Seligman, 1984). In this style of thinking, individuals explain away any good things that happen to them as temporary and due to chance, but they see the bad things as permanent and due to internal factors (e.g., lack of ability). This explanatory style has been linked with poor grades, inadequate sales performance, health problems, and other negative outcomes (Bennett & Elliott, 2002; Seligman & Schulman, 1986; Taylor, 2002).

By contrast, repeated success at controlling events may create a sense of "learned mastery" or "learned resourcefulness." Experiments suggest that animals are more resistant to learned helplessness tasks if they have first performed tasks in which their responses actually did determine what happened to them (Volpicelli et al., 1983). Such findings suggest that a learned sense of control may be enough to reduce learned helplessness effects. Some research suggests that, in rats at least, an expectation of control may depend on activity in the brain's medial prefrontal cortex. Chemicals that reduce nerve cell activity in this area tend to make learned helplessness more likely, whereas chemicals that stimulate medial prefrontal functioning tend to prevent learned helplessness (Amat et al., 2005). We do not yet know whether this brain area is equally important for human helplessness.

Whatever its biological basis, it is clear that a sense of control is important for humans. People with a history of successful control appear more likely than others to develop the *optimistic cognitive style*, hopefulness, and resilience that lead to even more success and healthier lives (Gillham, 2000; Zimmerman, 1990; see the chapter on health, stress, and coping). Accordingly, psychologists have been working on how best to help people minimize learned helplessness and maximize learned optimism in areas such as education, parenting, and psychotherapy (e.g., Jackson, Sellers, & Peterson, 2002). One option is "resiliency training" for children and adults at risk for depression or other problems (Bradshaw et al., 2007; Cardemil, Reivich, & Seligman, 2002; Waite & Richardson, 2004). Time will tell if such training leads to beneficial outcomes.

Latent Learning and Cognitive Maps

Decades ago, Edward Tolman conducted pioneering studies of cognitive processes in learning by watching rats trying to find their way through a complex maze to get food that was waiting for them at the end. At first, the rats took many wrong turns. But, over time, they made fewer and fewer mistakes. Behaviorists interpreted this result by saying that the rats learned a long chain of turning responses, because these responses were reinforced by getting food. But Tolman disagreed and offered evidence for a cognitive interpretation.

In one of his studies, three groups of rats were placed in the same maze once a day for several days (Tolman & Honzik, 1930). For Group A, food was placed at the end of the maze on each trial. As shown in Figure 5.14, these rats gradually improved their performance. Group B also ran the maze once a day, but there was never any food waiting for them. The animals in Group B continued to make many errors. Neither of these results is surprising.

The third group of rats, Group C, was the critical one. For the first ten days, they received no reinforcement for running the maze and continued to make many mistakes. Then, on the eleventh day, food was placed at the end of the maze for the first time. What do you think happened? On the day after receiving reinforcement, these rats made almost no mistakes (again, see Figure 5.14). In fact, their performance was as good as that of the group that had been reinforced every day. The single reinforcement trial on day 11 produced a dramatic change in their performance the next day.

Tolman argued that these results support two conclusions. First, because the rats in Group C improved their performance the first time they ran the maze after being reinforced, the reinforcement on day 11 could not have significantly affected their *learning* of the maze. Rather, the reinforcement simply changed their subsequent *performance*. They must have already learned the maze earlier as they wandered around making mistakes on their way to the end of the maze. These rats demonstrated **latent learning**—learning that had obviously occurred in the animal even though it was not evident when it first took place. (Latent learning occurs in humans, too; for example, after years of experience in

latent learning Learning that is not demonstrated at the time it occurs.

FIGURE 5.14
Latent Learning

This graph shows the average number of wrong turns that Tolman's rats made on their way to the end of a maze (Tolman & Honzik, 1930). Notice that when rats in Group C did not receive food reinforcement, they continued to make many errors. The day after first finding food at the end of the maze, however, they took almost no wrong turns! The reinforcement, argued Tolman, affected only the rats' performance; they must have learned the maze earlier, without reinforcement.

Matt Meadows/Photolibrary/Getty Images

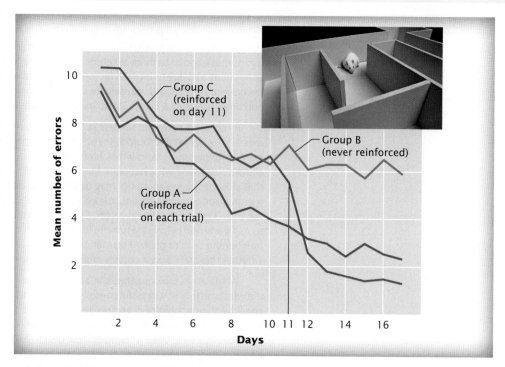

your neighborhood, you could probably tell a visitor that the corner drugstore is closed on Sundays, even if you had never tried to go there on a Sunday yourself.)

The second conclusion that Tolman drew from his data was that the rats' sudden improvement in performance after the first reinforcement trial could have occurred only if the rats had earlier developed a cognitive map of the maze. A **cognitive map** is a mental representation of some physical arrangement—in this case, a maze. How are such maps created? The hippocampus, a brain area associated with the formation of new memories, appears to play a special role. Scientists have discovered *place cells* in the rat hippocampus that fire only when particular locations in a maze are visited. When rats sleep after a maze-learning session, cells in the hippocampus "replay" the firing sequences and patterns that had occurred during the session, thus apparently strengthening, or *consolidating*, the maze's features in memory (Prerau et al., 2014; Suzuki, 2008).

Tolman could not have known about these specific processes, but he nevertheless concluded that cognitive maps develop naturally through experience, even in the absence of any overt response or reinforcement. Research on learning in the natural environment has supported this view. We develop mental maps of shopping malls and city streets even when we receive no direct reward for doing so (Tversky & Kahneman, 1991). Having such a map allows you to tell that neighborhood visitor exactly how to get to the corner drugstore from where you are standing.

Insight and Learning

Wolfgang Köhler was a psychologist whose work on the cognitive aspects of learning happened almost by accident. He was visiting Tenerife, one of the Canary Islands in the Atlantic Ocean, when World War I broke out in 1914. As a German citizen in territory controlled by Germany's enemy, Britain, Köhler was stuck on the island until the war ended in 1918. He put this time to good use by studying problem solving in a colony of local chimpanzees (Köhler, 1924).

For example, Köhler would put a chimpanzee in a cage and place a piece of fruit where the chimp could see it but not reach it. He sometimes hung the fruit too high to be reached or placed it on the ground too far outside the animal's cage to be retrieved. Many of the chimps overcame these obstacles easily. If the fruit was out of reach beyond the cage, some chimps looked around, found a long stick, and used it to rake in the fruit. Surprised that

cognitive map A mental representation of the environment.

IN THE BLEACHERS   By Steve Moore

OK, MAYBE WE COULD PLAY ONE QUICK GAME. THEY PROBABLY WON'T EVEN KNOW WE'RE HERE.

Despite the power of observational learning, some people just have to learn things the hard way.

IN THE BLEACHERS © 1999 Steve Moore. Reprinted with permission of Universal Uclick. All rights reserved.

the chimpanzees could solve these problems, Köhler tried more difficult tasks. Again, the chimps quickly got to the fruit. Like Tolman, Köhler became convinced that learning was likely to involve cognitive processes.

Three aspects of Köhler's observations convinced him that animals' problem solving does not have to depend exclusively on trial and error and the gradual associative learning from matching a response with a consequence. First, once a chimpanzee solved one type of problem, it would immediately do the same thing in a similar situation. In other words, it acted as if it understood the problem. Second, Köhler's chimpanzees rarely tried a solution that did not work. Apparently, the solution was not discovered randomly but "thought out" ahead of time and then acted out successfully. Third, the chimps often reached a solution quite suddenly. When confronted with a piece of fruit hanging from a string, for instance, a chimp would jump for it several times, then it would stop jumping, look up, and pace back and forth. Finally, it would run over to a wooden crate, place it directly under the fruit, and climb on top of it to reach the fruit. Once, when there were no other objects in the cage, a chimp went over to Köhler, dragged him by the arm until he stood beneath the fruit, and then started climbing up his back!

Köhler argued that the only explanation for these results was that the chimpanzees had experienced **insight**, a sudden understanding of a problem as a whole. Was he right? Possibly, but what Köhler saw as sudden insight might not have been so sudden. Other psychologists found that previous trial-and-error experience with objects, such as boxes and sticks, is necessary for "insight" in chimps (Birch, 1945). In fact, some psychologists argue that all known cases of "insight" by humans and nonhumans alike include a long history of experience with the objects that are used to solve the problem (Epstein et al., 1984; Kounios et al., 2006; Wynne, 2004). Others have suggested true insight seems to result from a "mental trial-and-error process" in which people (and perhaps certain other animals) envision a course of action, mentally simulate its results, compare it with the imagined outcome of other alternatives, and settle on the course of action most likely to aid complex problem solving and decision making (Klein, 1993). So although Köhler's work helped highlight the importance of cognitive processes in learning, questions remain about whether it demonstrated true insight in chimps.

Observational Learning: Learning by Imitation

People and animals learn a lot from personal experience, but they can also learn by observing what others do and what happens to them when they do it (e.g., Akins & Zentall, 1998; Mattar & Gribble, 2005). Learning by watching others—a kind of **observational learning**—is efficient and adaptive. In observational learning, we learn by what we see happen around us without having to experience it ourselves. Such "social learning" means that we don't have to find out for ourselves that a door is locked or an iron is hot if we have just seen someone else try the door or suffer a burn.

The biological basis for observational learning may lie partly in the activity of brain systems that help us predict what will happen when other people do something like walk on the thin ice of a recently frozen pond (Burke et al., 2010). It is also based partly on the operation of the brain's *mirror neurons* (Kilner & Lemon, 2013), which fire not only when we do something or experience something but also when we see someone else do or experience the same thing. This mirrored pattern of activity in our own brains makes it almost as though we are actually performing the observed action or having the observed experience. Mirror neurons are activated, for example, when we feel disgust upon seeing someone react to the taste of sour milk. They also probably fire when we imitate the correct pronunciation of foreign words or follow someone's example in using an unfamiliar tool.

Children are particularly influenced by the adults and peers who act as *models* for appropriate behavior. In a classic experiment, Albert Bandura showed nursery school children a film starring an adult and a large, inflatable, bottom-heavy Bobo doll (Bandura, 1965). The adult in the film punched the doll in the nose, kicked it, threw things at it, and hit its head with a hammer while saying things like "Sockeroo!" There were different endings to the film. Some children saw an ending in which the aggressive adult was called

insight A sudden understanding of what is required to solve a problem.

observational learning Learning how to perform new behaviors by watching others.

Learning by Imitation

TRY THIS Much of our behavior is learned by imitating others, especially those who serve as role models. To appreciate the impact of social learning in your life, list five examples of how your own actions, speech, appearance, or mannerisms have come to match those of a parent, a sibling, a friend, a teacher, or even a celebrity.

Rommel/Masterfile

a "champion" by a second adult and rewarded with candy and soft drinks. Some saw the aggressor scolded and called a "bad person." Some saw a neutral ending in which there was neither reward nor punishment. After the film, each child was allowed to play alone with a Bobo doll. The way they played in this and similar studies led to some important conclusions about learning and the role of cognitive factors in it.

Bandura found that children who saw the adult rewarded for aggression showed the most aggressive acts in play (see Figure 5.15). They had received *vicarious conditioning,*

FIGURE 5.15

Observational Learning

Bandura found that after observing an aggressive model, many children imitate the model's acts precisely, especially if the model's aggression was rewarded.

Source: Ross, L. A. et al. (1963). Imitation of film-mediated aggressive models. Journal of Abnormal and Social Psychology, 66, 3–11.

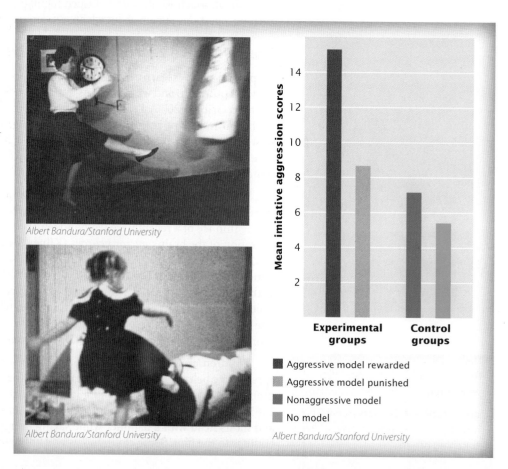

Albert Bandura/Stanford University

Albert Bandura/Stanford University

Albert Bandura/Stanford University

a kind of social observational learning through which a person is influenced by watching or hearing about the consequences of others' behavior. The children who had seen the adult punished for aggressive acts showed less aggression, but they still learned something. When later offered rewards for imitating all the aggressive acts they had seen in the film, these children displayed just as many of these acts as the children who had watched the adult being rewarded. Observational learning can occur even when there are no vicarious consequences; many children in the neutral condition also imitated the model's aggression.

Like direct reward and punishment, observational learning is a powerful force in the *socialization* process through which children learn about which behaviors are—and are not—appropriate in their culture (Bandura, 1999; Caldwell & Millen, 2009). For example, children show long-term increases in their willingness to help and share after seeing a demonstration of helping by a friendly, impressive model (Schroeder et al., 1995). Fears, too, can be learned partly by the sight of fearfulness in others (e.g., Broeren et al., 2011; Burstein & Ginsburg, 2010) and seeing other people behave dishonestly may lead observers to do the same (Gino, Ayal, & Ariely, 2009).

THINKING CRITICALLY

DOES WATCHING VIDEO VIOLENCE MAKE CHILDREN MORE VIOLENT?

If observational learning is important, then surely movies, video games, handheld and web-based videos, and television—and the violence they so often portray—must teach children a great deal. Psychologists have spent a great deal of time studying these media, and especially the possible effects of watching video images of violence. According to one recent estimate, the average child in the United States in 2013 spent about thirty-five hours a week watching television (Rothman, 2013). If true, that would be an increase of almost two hours a day compared to 2009 (Christakis & Garrison, 2009; Tandon et al., 2011). Much of what kids see on television is violent. In addition to the real-life violence in the news (Van der Molen, 2004), prime-time entertainment programs in the United States present an average of five acts of simulated violence per hour, and cartoons can be especially violent (American Psychological Association, 1993; Klein & Schiffman, 2011). As a result, the average child will see at least 8,000 murders and more than 100,000 other acts of violence before finishing elementary school and twice that number by age 18 (Annenberg Public Policy Center, 1999; Parents Television Council, 2006).

Psychologists have long worried that watching so much violence might be emotionally arousing, making viewers more likely to react violently to frustration (Huston & Wright, 1989). Some evidence suggests that exposure to media violence can trigger or amplify viewers' aggressive thoughts and feelings, thus increasing the likelihood that they will act aggressively (Anderson & Dill, 2000; Bushman, 1998). Televised violence might also provide models that viewers imitate, particularly if the violence is carried out by the "good guys" (Huesmann et al., 2003). Finally, prolonged viewing of violent TV programs might desensitize viewers, making them less distressed when they see others suffer, less likely to help them, and less disturbed about inflicting pain on others (Bushman & Anderson, 2009; Smith & Donnerstein, 1998).

What am I being asked to believe or accept?

For some time now, many have argued that watching video images of violence causes kids to behave violently (e.g., Anderson et al., 2003; Bushman & Gibson, 2011; Bushman & Huesmann, 2014). A National Academy of Sciences report concluded that "overall, the vast majority of studies, whatever their methodology, showed that exposure to television violence resulted in increased aggressive behavior, both contemporaneously and over time" (Reiss & Roth, 1993, p. 371). The American Psychological Association has repeatedly reached the same conclusion (American Psychological Association, 1993; Huesmann et al., 2003).

What evidence is available to support the assertion?

Three types of evidence back up the claim that watching violent video increases violent behavior. First, there are anecdotes and case studies. Children have poked one another in

(continued)

the eye after watching the Three Stooges appear to do so on television, and adults have claimed that watching TV shows prompted them to commit murders or other violent acts like those seen on the shows (Werner, 2003). The teenager who shot and killed twenty school-children and six adults in Newton, Connecticut on December 14, 2012, had been "obsessed" with violent video games and had developed a "score sheet" to tabulate "points" for killing victims (Lupica, 2013).

Second, correlational studies have found a strong link between watching violent programs and later acts of aggression and violence (Christakas & Zimmerman, 2007; Gentile et al., 2014; Johnson et al., 2002). A Canadian study found that children who watch more violent videos were more likely to bully and cyber-bully classmates (Beran et al., 2013). Another study tracked people from the time they were six or seven until they reached their early twenties. Those who watched more violent television as children were significantly more aggressive as adults (Huesmann et al., 1997, 2003) and more likely to engage in criminal activity (Huesmann, 1995). They were also more likely to use physical punishment on their own children, who themselves tended to behave more aggressive than average. Such results were found not only in the United States but also in Israel, Australia, Poland, the Netherlands, and even Finland, even though they have fewer violent TV shows (Centerwall, 1990; Huesmann & Eron, 1986).

Finally, experiments show that watching violent video sequences can cause an increase in aggressive behavior (e.g., Boxer et al., 2009; Huesmann & Taylor, 2006; Polman, de Castro & van Aken, 2008). In one study, groups of boys were assigned to watch either violent or nonviolent programs in a controlled setting, and then they played floor hockey (Josephson, 1987). The boys who had been assigned to watch the violent shows were more likely to behave aggressively on the hockey floor than the boys who had been told to watch nonviolent programs. This effect was greatest for boys who had the most aggressive tendencies to begin with. More extensive experiments in which children are exposed to carefully controlled types of television programs over long periods of time also found that being assigned to view more violent activity on television resulted in more aggressive behavior (Eron et al., 1972).

Are there alternative ways of interpreting the evidence?

To some, the evidence argues that media violence causes increases in aggressive and violent behavior, especially in children (Anderson et al., 2003). Others, however, suggest that the evidence is not conclusive and is open to qualifications and alternative interpretations (e.g., Ferguson et al., 2013; Thakkar, Garrison, & Christakis, 2006), or that increases in youth violence are due to other factors (Ferguson, San Miguel, & Hartley, 2009).

Anecdotal reports and case studies are certainly open to different interpretations. If people face imprisonment or execution for their violent acts, how believable are their claims that their actions were triggered by television programs? How many other people might say that the same programs made them less likely to be violent? Anecdotes alone do not provide a good basis for drawing final scientific conclusions.

What about the correlational evidence? As noted in the chapter on research in psychology, a correlation between two variables does not necessarily mean that one is causing the other. Both might be caused by a third factor. At least one possible "third factor" might account for the observed relationship between watching TV violence and acting aggressively: Certain people may enjoy violent themes and therefore both prefer to watch more violent TV programs and also choose to behave aggressively toward others. So personality could at least partly account for the observed correlations between watching violence and behaving aggressively (e.g., Aluja-Fabregat & Torrubia-Beltri, 1998; Steinberg & Monahan, 2011).

Further, video violence is just one of many influences that contribute to the learning of aggressive behavior (Kirsh, 2011). One study found, for example, that children who are more prone to violent behavior had been exposed not only to more video violence but also to more real violence in their neighborhoods and in their homes (Grabell et al., 2012).

As for the results of controlled experiments on the effects of televised violence, some researchers suggest that those effects may be short-lived and may not apply beyond the

(continued)

closetohome@ucomics.com

SMASH!

12-11   ©2003 John McPherson/Dist. by Universal Press Syndicate.   *McPherson*

**"I have HAD it with you two and your
violent video games!"**

The violence that may affect children's aggressive behavior is not always limited to what they see on television and video games.

experimental situation (Anderson, Lindsay, & Bushman, 1999; Browne & Hamilton-Giachritsis, 2005; Freedman, 2002). Who is to say, for example, whether an increase in aggressive acts during a hockey game has any later bearing on a child's tendency to commit an act of violence?

What additional evidence would help evaluate the alternatives?

By their nature, correlational studies of the role of TV violence in violent behavior can never be conclusive. As we've pointed out, a third, unidentified causal variable could always be responsible for the results. More important would be further evidence from controlled experiments in which equivalent groups of people were given different long-term "doses" of TV violence and its effects on their subsequent behavior were observed for many years. Such experiments could also explore the circumstances under which different people (for example, children versus adults) are affected by various forms of violence. However, conducting studies such as these would create an ethical dilemma. If watching violent television programs really does cause violent behavior, are psychologists justified in creating conditions that might lead some people to be more violent? If such violence occurred, would the researchers be responsible to the victims and to society? If some participants commit violent acts, should the researchers continue the experiment to establish a pattern or should they terminate the participation of those individuals? Difficulty in answering questions such as these is partly responsible for the use of short-term experiments and correlational designs in this research area, as well as for some of the remaining uncertainty about the effects of television violence.

One approach to this problem might be to conduct experiments in which children watch television shows that portray cooperative rather than violent behavior. If exposure to such *prosocial* programming were followed by significant increases in viewers' own prosocial behavior, it would strengthen—though still not prove—the argument that what children see on television can have a causal impact on their actions. Recent experiments have already shown that people who played prosocial video games were later more helpful than those who had played neutral games (Greitemeyer & Osswald, 2010), and showed greater empathy and less pleasure at others' misfortunes (Greitemeyer, Osswald, & Brauer, 2010; Um et al., 2011).

What conclusions are most reasonable?

The evidence collected so far reasonably argues that watching TV violence may be a cause of violent behavior, especially in some children and especially in boys (e.g., Anderson & Bushman, 2002a; Browne & Hamilton-Giachritsis, 2005; Bushman & Anderson, 2001). Playing violent video games may be another (e.g., Anderson et al., 2008, 2010). Some research suggests that violent video games may lead players to dehumanize other people, making them mere "targets" and releasing acts of real violence (e.g., Greitemeyer & McLatchie, 2011).

But a cause-and-effect relationship between watching TV violence or playing violent games and acting violently is not inevitable and may not always be long lasting (e.g., Ferguson & Kilburn, 2009, 2010; Ferguson et al., 2010; Savage & Yancey, 2008). Further, there are many circumstances in which the effect does not occur (Ferguson, 2009; Freedman, 1992, 2002). Parents, peers, and other environmental influences as well as personality factors may dampen or amplify the effect of watching televised violence or playing violent video games (Markey & Markey, 2010). So may the nature of the games themselves; aggressive behavior may be more strongly associated with games that feature competitiveness, difficulty, and a fast pace (Adachi & Willoughby, 2011). In addition, not every viewer interprets violence in the same way, and not everyone is equally vulnerable to its possible effects (e.g., Ferguson, 2009; Kirsh, 2011). The most vulnerable may be young boys, especially those who are the most aggressive or violence-prone in the first place, a trait that could well have been acquired by observing the behavior of parents or peers (Ferguson et al., 2010; Kirsh, 2011).

Still, the fact that violence on television and in video games *can* have a causal impact on violent behavior is reason for serious concern. Nevertheless, in June 2011, the U.S. Supreme Court ruled that free speech laws apply to video games, making it unconstitutional to regulate their sale to minors (Ferguson, 2013b). Public debate about the effects of violent television and video games will no doubt continue, as will controversy over what should and should not be aired on television and offered by video game manufacturers.

USING RESEARCH ON LEARNING TO HELP PEOPLE LEARN

What should teachers learn about learning?

The study of how people learn obviously has important implications for improved teaching in our schools and for helping people develop skills (Bjork & Linn, 2006; Halpern & Hakel, 2003; Li, 2005; Newcombe et al., 2009).

Active Learning

The importance of cognitive processes in learning is apparent in instructional methods that emphasize *active learning* (Bonwell & Eison, 1991). These methods take many forms, including, for example, small-group problem-solving tasks, discussion of "one-minute essays" written in class, use of student response devices ("clickers") or just "thumbs up" or "thumbs down" gestures to indicate agreement or disagreement with the instructor's lecture, and multiple-choice questions that give students feedback about their understanding of the previous fifteen minutes of a lecture (Goss Lucas & Bernstein, 2015). Students typically find classes that include active learning experiences to be interesting and enjoyable (Bruff, 2009; Moran, 2000; Murray, 2000). In addition, active learning methods help students go beyond memorizing isolated facts. These methods encourage students to think more deeply, to consider how new material relates to what they already know, and to apply it in new situations. This kind of thinking also makes the material easier to remember, which is why we have included so many opportunities for you to actively learn, rather than just passively read, the material in this book.

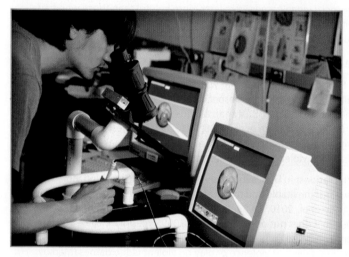

Virtual Surgery

Using a virtual reality system, this medical student can actively learn and practice eye surgery skills before working with real patients. Computer-based human body simulators are also giving new doctors active learning experience in emergency room diagnosis and treatment; heart, lung, and abdominal surgery; and other medical skills (e.g., Aggarwal, Cheshire, & Darzi, 2008; Heinrichs et al., 2008; Kanno et al., 2008; Kato, 2010; Tsang et al., 2008).

© *Hank Morgan/Science Photo Library/Science Source*

Studies of students in elementary schools, high schools, community colleges, and universities have found that compared with instructional techniques that are more passive, active learning approaches result in better test performance and greater class participation (e.g., Altman, 2007; Deslauriers, Schelew, & Wieman, 2011; Freeman et al., 2014; Karpicke & Blunt, 2011; Saville et al., 2006). In one study, a fifth-grade teacher spent some days calling only on students whose hands were raised. On other days, all students were required to answer every question by holding up a card with their response written on it. Scores on next-day quizzes and biweekly tests showed that students remembered more of the material covered on the active learning days than on the "passive" days (Gardner, Heward, & Grossi, 1994). In another study of two consecutive medical school classes taught by the same instructor, scores on the final exam were significantly higher when students learned mainly through small-group discussions and case studies than when they were taught mainly through lectures (Chu, 1994). Similarly, among adults being taught to use a new computer program, active learning with hands-on practice was more effective than passively watching a demonstration video (Kerr & Payne, 1994). Finally, high school and college students who passively listened to a physics lecture received significantly lower scores on a test of lecture content than did those who participated in a virtual reality lab that allowed them to interact with the physical forces covered in the lecture (Brelsford, 1993). Results like these have fueled the development of other science education programs that place students in virtual laboratory environments in which they actively manipulate materials and test hypotheses (e.g., Horwitz & Christie, 2000).

Despite the enthusiasm generated by active learning methods, rigorous experimental research is still needed to compare their short- and long-term effects with those of more traditional methods in teaching various kinds of course content (Alexander, Eaton, & Egan, 2010; Fiorella & Mayer, 2012; Moran, 2006). At least one study has shown that college students who learned about pathogens or electromechanical devices through the use of interactive computerized "adventure games" did not perform as well on exams as students who learned the same material using more conventional methods (Adams et al., 2011). Other studies have found standard textbooks superior to e-books and podcasts for delivering primary text material in college courses (Daniel & Woody, 2010; Woody, Daniel, & Baker, 2010). It may turn out that traditional teaching methods (including interesting lectures and engaging textbooks) are effective tools for presenting basic course material, but that active learning methods—including repeated testing and self-testing—may be superior to passive ones for helping students to retain, recall, and apply new information.

Skill Learning

The complex action sequences, or *skills,* that people learn to perform in everyday life develop through learning processes that include feedback and lots of practice (Ackerman, 2007). In fact, *practice*—the repeated performance of a skill—is critical to mastery (Howe, Davidson, & Sloboda, 1998). For perceptual-motor skills such as playing pool or piano, both physical and mental practice are beneficial (Druckman & Bjork, 1994). To be most effective, practice should continue past the point of correct performance until the skill can be performed automatically, with little or no attention. Feedback about the correctness of the response is also necessary. As with any learning process, the feedback should come soon enough to be effective but not so quickly that it interferes with the learner's efforts to learn independently.

Large amounts of guidance may produce very good performance during practice, but too much guidance may hurt later performance (Kluger & DeNisi, 1998; Wickens, 1992). For instance, coaching students about correct responses in math may impair their ability later to retrieve the correct response from memory on their own. Independent practice at retrieving previously learned responses or information requires more effort, but it is critical for skill development (Ericsson & Charness, 1994). There is little or no evidence to support "sleep learning" or similar schemes designed to make learning effortless (Druckman & Bjork, 1994). In short, "no pain, no gain."

Classrooms across Cultures

Many people have expressed concern that schools in the United States are not doing a very good job. A recent report by the Center on Education Policy found, for example, that nearly half of U.S. public schools failed to meet federal standards for adequate yearly progress (Usher, 2011). Further, the average performance of U.S. students on tests of reading, math, and other basic academic skills has tended to fall short of that of youngsters in other countries, especially Asian countries (Mullis et al., 2007; National Center for Education Statistics, 2002; Program for International Student Assessment, 2005). In one early comparison study, Harold Stevenson (1992) followed a sample of pupils in Taiwan, Japan, and the United States from the first grade, in 1980, to the eleventh grade, in 1991. In the first grade, the Asian students scored no higher than their U.S. peers on tests of mathematical aptitude and skills and they did not enjoy math more. However, by the fifth grade, the U.S. students had fallen far behind. Corresponding differences were seen in reading skills. More recent studies have found similar results (Mullis et al., 2004, 2007).

Some possible causes of these differences were found in the classroom itself (Rindermann & Ceci, 2009). In a typical U.S. classroom, teachers talked to students as a group, then students worked at their desks independently. Reinforcement or other feedback about performance on their work was usually delayed until the next day or not provided at all. In contrast, the typical Japanese classroom placed greater emphasis on cooperative work among students (Kristof, 1997). Teachers provided more immediate feedback on a one-to-one basis. And there was an emphasis on creating teams of students with varying abilities, an arrangement in which faster learners help teach slower ones. However, before concluding that the differences in performance are the result of social factors alone, we must consider

Reciprocal Teaching

Ann Brown and her colleagues (1992) demonstrated the success of reciprocal teaching, in which children take turns teaching each other. This technique, which is similar to the cooperative arrangements seen in Japanese education, has become increasingly popular in North American schools (Palincsar, 2003; Spörer, Brunstein, & Kieschke, 2009).

Payless Images/ Alamy

another important distinction: The Japanese children practiced more. They spent more days in school during the year and, on average, spent more hours doing homework.

Psychologists and educators are considering how various principles of learning can be applied to improve education. For example, anecdotal and experimental evidence suggests that some of the most successful educational techniques are those that apply basic principles of operant conditioning, offering frequent testing, positive reinforcement for correct performance, and immediate corrective feedback following mistakes (Oppel, 2000; Roediger, McDaniel, & McDermott, 2006).

Further, research in cognitive psychology suggests that students will retain more of what they learn if they study in several sessions distributed over time rather than in a single "cramming" session on the night before a test (e.g., Cepeda et al., 2009; Kramár et al., 2012; Rawson & Dunlosky, 2011). To encourage this kind of *distributed practice*, researchers say, teachers should give enough exams and quizzes (some unannounced, perhaps) that students will be reading and studying more or less continuously. And because learning is aided by repeated opportunities to use new information, these exams and quizzes should cover material from throughout the term, not just the material from recent classes (Karpicke, 2012). These recommendations are not necessarily popular with students, but there is good evidence that they promote long-term retention of course material (e.g., Bjork, 2001; Bjork & Linn, 2006).

LINKAGES

As noted in the introductory chapter, all of psychology's subfields are related to one another. Our discussion of associative network models illustrates just one way that the topic of this chapter, learning, is linked to the subfield of memory, which is described in the chapter by that name. The Linkages diagram shows ties to two other subfields, and there are many more ties throughout the book. Looking for linkages among subfields will help you see how they all fit together and help you better appreciate the big picture that is psychology.

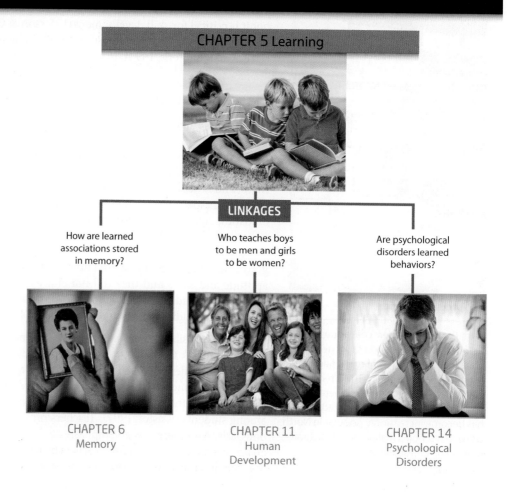

CHAPTER 5 Learning

LINKAGES

How are learned associations stored in memory?

Who teaches boys to be men and girls to be women?

Are psychological disorders learned behaviors?

CHAPTER 6
Memory

CHAPTER 11
Human
Development

CHAPTER 14
Psychological
Disorders

SUMMARY

Individuals adapt to changes in the environment through the process of *learning*, which is the modification, through experience, of preexisting behavior and understanding.

Learning about Stimuli

Why do constant sounds seem to disappear?

One of the simplest kinds of learning is **habituation**, which is reduced responsiveness to a repeated stimulus. A second kind of simple, nonassociative learning, called *sensitization*, appears as an increase in responsiveness to a stimulus.

Classical Conditioning: Learning Signals and Associations

How did Russian dogs teach psychologists about learning?

One form of learning is **classical conditioning**. It occurs when a previously neutral **conditioned stimulus**, or **CS** (such as a tone), is repeatedly paired with an **unconditioned stimulus**, or **UCS** (such as meat powder on a dog's tongue), which naturally brings about an **unconditioned response**, or **UCR** (such as salivation). Eventually the conditioned stimulus will elicit a response, known as the **conditioned response**, or **CR**, even when the unconditioned stimulus is not presented.

The strength of a conditioned response grows as CS-UCS pairings continue. If the UCS is no longer paired with the CS, the conditioned response eventually disappears; this is **extinction**. After extinction, the conditioned response may reappear if the CS is presented after some time; this is **spontaneous recovery**. In addition, if the conditioned and unconditioned stimuli are paired once or twice after extinction, **reconditioning** occurs; that is, the conditioned response regains much of its original strength.

Because of **stimulus generalization**, conditioned responses occur to stimuli that are similar, but not identical, to conditioned stimuli. Generalization is limited by **stimulus discrimination**, which prompts conditioned responses to some stimuli but not to others.

Classical conditioning involves learning that the CS is an event that predicts the occurrence of another event, the UCS. Many psychologists see the conditioned response as a means through which animals and people develop mental representations of the relationships between events. Classical conditioning works best when the conditioned stimulus precedes the unconditioned stimulus by intervals ranging from less than a second to a minute or more, depending on the stimuli involved. Conditioning is also more likely when the CS reliably signals the UCS. In general, the speed of conditioning increases as the intensity of the UCS increases. Which particular stimulus is likely to become a CS linked to a subsequent UCS depends partly on which stimulus was being attended to when the UCS occurred; more intense stimuli are more likely to attract attention. **Higher order conditioning** occurs when one conditioned stimulus signals a conditioned stimulus that is already associated with an unconditioned stimulus. Some stimuli become associated more easily than others; taste aversions provide illustrations that organisms seem to be biologically prepared to learn certain associations.

Classical conditioning plays a role in the development and treatment of phobias as well as in the development of drug tolerance and some cases of drug overdoses.

Instrumental and Operant Conditioning: Learning the Consequences of Behavior

How do reward and punishment work?

Learning occurs not only through associating stimuli but also through associating behavior with its consequences. Thorndike's **law of effect** holds that any response that produces satisfaction becomes more likely to occur again and that any response that produces discomfort becomes less likely to recur. Thorndike referred to this type of learning as instrumental conditioning. Skinner called the process **operant conditioning**.

An **operant** is a response that has some effect on the world. A **reinforcer** increases the probability that the operant preceding it will occur again. There are two types of reinforcers: **positive reinforcers**, desirable stimuli that strengthen a response if they are presented after that response occurs, and **negative reinforcers**, which are the removal of an unpleasant stimulus following some response. Both kinds of reinforcers strengthen the behaviors that precede them. When behavior is strengthened by a positive reinforcer, the process is called positive reinforcement. When behavior is strengthened by a negative reinforcer, the process is called negative reinforcement. **Escape conditioning** results when a behavior stops an unpleasant stimulus. **Avoidance conditioning** results when behavior prevents an unpleasant stimulus from occurring; it reflects both classical and operant conditioning. Behaviors learned through avoidance conditioning are hard to extinguish. **Discriminative conditioned stimuli** signal whether reinforcement is available for a particular behavior.

Complex responses can be learned through **shaping**, which involves reinforcing successive approximations of the desired response. **Primary reinforcers** are innately rewarding; **secondary reinforcers** are rewards that people or animals learn to like because of their association with primary reinforcers. In general, operant conditioning proceeds more quickly when the delay in receiving reinforcement is short rather than long and when the reinforcer is large rather than small. Reinforcement may be delivered on a continuous reinforcement schedule or on one of four types of partial, or intermittent, **reinforcement schedules**: fixed-ratio (FR), variable-ratio (VR), fixed-interval (FI), and variable-interval (VI) schedules. Ratio schedules lead to a rapid rate of responding. Behavior learned through partial reinforcement is very resistant to extinction; this phenomenon is called the **partial reinforcement effect**. Partial reinforcement is involved in superstitious behavior, which results when some action is followed by, but does not actually cause, a reinforcer.

Research in neuroscience suggests that reinforcers act as rewards largely because of their ability to create activity in "pleasure centers" in the hypothalamus as well as in other brain areas that use the chemical dopamine.

Punishment decreases the frequency of a behavior by following it either with an unpleasant stimulus (*positive punishment*) or with the removal of a pleasant one (*negative punishment*). Punishment can be useful when performed properly, but it can have drawbacks. It only suppresses behavior; fear of punishment may generalize to the person doing the punishing; it is ineffective when delayed; it can be physically harmful and may teach aggressiveness; and it teaches only what not to do, not what should be done to obtain reinforcement.

The principles of operant conditioning have been applied in many areas, from teaching social skills to treating sleep disorders.

Cognitive Processes in Learning

Can people learn to be helpless?

Cognitive processes—how people represent, store, and use information—play an important role in learning. **Learned helplessness** appears to result when people believe that their behavior has no effect on the world. Both animals and humans display **latent learning**. They also form **cognitive maps** of their environments, even in the absence of any reinforcement for doing so. Experiments on **insight** also suggest that cognitive processes play an important role in learning. The process of learning by watching others is a kind of **observational learning**, sometimes called "social learning." Some observational learning occurs through vicarious conditioning, in which a person is influenced by seeing or hearing about the consequences of others' behavior. Observational learning is more likely to occur when the observed model's behavior is seen to be rewarded. It is a powerful source of socialization.

Using Research on Learning to Help People Learn

What should teachers learn about learning?

Research on how people learn has implications for improved teaching and for the development of a wide range of skills. The degree to which learning principles such as immediate reinforcement are used in teaching varies considerably from culture to culture. The importance of cognitive processes in learning is seen in active learning methods designed to encourage people to think deeply about and apply new information instead of just memorizing isolated facts. Observational learning, practice, and corrective feedback play important roles in the learning of skills.

TEST YOUR KNOWLEDGE

Select the best answer for each of the following questions. Then check your responses against the Answer Key at the end of the book.

1. Which saying best reflects learning?
   a. "A watched pot never boils."
   b. "A stitch in time saves nine."
   c. "Once burned, twice shy."
   d. "If you will it, it is no dream."

2. In a classical conditioning experiment, a puff of air was blown into Ralph's eye and he automatically blinked. The experimenter then began flashing a green light just before presenting the puff of air. After many pairings of the green light and the puff of air, Ralph began to blink as soon as the green light appeared, whether or not the air puff followed. In this experiment, the green light is the
   a. unconditioned stimulus.
   b. conditioned stimulus.
   c. conditioned response.
   d. unconditioned response.

3. Suppose that the experimenter in the previous question continues presenting the green light but never again follows it with the puff of air. Ralph will soon _____ through the process of _____.
   a. blink faster; reconditioning
   b. stop blinking; extinction
   c. blink slower; stimulus control
   d. stop blinking; spontaneous recovery

4. Kim has gone out with both Alan and Brad this week. Even though she said she hates loud concerts, Alan took her to one, and she came home with a headache. Brad took her to a movie she had been wanting to see. According to _____, Kim would be more likely to date Brad in the future.
   a. the law of effect
   b. Premack's principle
   c. classical conditioning theory
   d. all of the above

5. After being bitten by a dog at a young age, Najla became fearful of all dogs. Now, when Najla sees a dog, her heart races and she feels like running away. Najla has developed _____ through _____ conditioning.
   a. habituation; operant
   b. habituation; classical
   c. a phobia; operant
   d. a phobia; classical

6. The idea that knowledge is located in many areas throughout the brain rather than in one particular place is a basic assumption of _____.
   a. neural network theories
   b. classical conditioning
   c. observational learning
   d. stimulus generalization

7. Because of birth defects, Justin, a four-year-old, has had to have a number of surgeries. As a result, just seeing a doctor or nurse in a surgical mask makes Justin fearful and tearful. At Halloween this year, Justin had the same reaction to children wearing masks. This is an example of _____.
   a. stimulus generalization
   b. stimulus discrimination
   c. vicarious learning
   d. observational learning

8. Laverne lost control and ate an entire coconut cream pie. Later that day she got the flu, complete with nausea and vomiting. After this experience, Laverne associated coconut cream pie with being sick, and now she can't even stand the smell of it. This is an example of _____, which supports the concept of _____.
   a. escape conditioning; spontaneous recovery
   b. discriminative conditioning; biopreparedness
   c. taste aversion; biopreparedness
   d. latent learning; spontaneous recovery

9. When baby Sally cries after being put to bed, her parents check to see that she is all right but otherwise they ignore her. After several evenings of this treatment, Sally's bedtime crying stopped. This is an example of _____.
   a. extinction
   b. habituation
   c. higher order conditioning
   d. shaping

10. Manuel has learned that every time he cleans his room, his mother makes his favorite dessert. This is an example of _____.
    a. classical conditioning
    b. operant conditioning
    c. negative reinforcement
    d. extinction

11. Loretta gets a backache every day, but if she sits in a hot bath, the pain goes away. So she decides to take a hot bath every day. She has learned to do this through _____.
    a. positive reinforcement
    b. negative reinforcement
    c. stimulus discrimination
    d. shaping

12. Doug hates to hear children misbehaving in the grocery store, so he always shops late at night when children are not present. Doug's choice of shopping time is an example of _____.
    a. escape conditioning
    b. avoidance conditioning
    c. shaping
    d. secondary reinforcement

13. Ten minutes before a movie starts, the theater is filled with people who are talking and laughing. As soon as the lights go out, everyone becomes quiet. Sudden darkness serves as a _____ in this example of operant conditioning.
    a. positive reinforcer
    b. negative reinforcer
    c. punishment
    d. discriminative conditioned stimulus

14. Craig wanted to teach his dog, JoJo, to sit up and beg using operant conditioning principles. He started by giving JoJo a treat when she was sitting. Next, he gave her a treat only if she was sitting and had raised one paw, and so on. This is an example of _____.
    a. stimulus discrimination
    b. stimulus generalization
    c. negative reinforcement
    d. shaping

15. When Jamey has washed the dinner dishes after five evening meals, his parents take him to the movies. Susan's dad occasionally gives her a dollar after she washes the dinner dishes. Jamey is on a _____ reinforcement schedule, and Susan is on a _____ schedule.
    a. fixed interval; variable interval
    b. fixed ratio; variable ratio
    c. variable ratio; fixed interval
    d. variable interval; fixed ratio

16. Which of the following is a potential problem with using punishment to change behavior?
    a. It can produce unwanted side effects.
    b. Frequent punishment can teach children to behave aggressively.
    c. It signals that inappropriate behavior occurred but doesn't indicate what should be done instead.
    d. These are all potential problems with using punishment.

17. Whenever Javier asked his next-door neighbor to turn down her loud music, she ignored him. Later, when a new neighbor moved in next door and began playing loud music, Javier did not even bother to complain. His case demonstrates _____.
    a. latent learning
    b. learned helplessness
    c. observational learning
    d. trial and error

18. When Kenzi got a flat tire not far from campus, he walked down the street to a service station he drove by every day but had never visited. The fact that he immediately knew where it was illustrates _____.
    a. insight learning
    b. observational learning
    c. latent learning
    d. vicarious learning

19. After watching a number of people petting and playing with a dog, Najla decides that dogs aren't as scary as she'd thought. The next day, at her neighbors' house, she pets their dog. Najla's fear has been reduced through _____.
    a. classical conditioning
    b. operant conditioning
    c. spontaneous recovery
    d. observational learning

20. Whether the skill you want to learn involves a foreign language, the words of a speech, or a golf swing, the most important thing you can do is _____.
    a. delay feedback until you have almost reached perfection
    b. read all you can about the task you want to learn
    c. engage in all the practice you can
    d. work in a group

Memory

Novastock/Stock Connection Blue/Alamy

Preview

Have you ever forgotten where you parked your car? Have you ever had a name on the tip of your tongue but couldn't quite recall it? Researchers in the field of memory explore these common experiences. They have found that memory is a complex system. You use different kinds of memory for storing different types of information, such as personal experiences, specific skills, and abstract concepts. They have also found that once information is stored in memory, recalling it can sometimes be difficult. In this chapter, you'll learn about some techniques that can help you to retrieve memories. Psychologists have used what they've learned about memory to create study techniques that really work!

Several years ago, an air traffic controller at Los Angeles International Airport cleared a US Airways flight to land on runway 24L. A couple of minutes later, the US Airways pilot radioed the control tower that he was on approach for runway 24L, but the controller did not reply because she was conversing with another pilot. After finishing that conversation, the controller told a Sky West commuter pilot to taxi onto runway 24L for takeoff, completely forgetting about the US Airways plane that was about to land on the same runway. The US Airways jet hit the commuter plane, killing thirty-four people. The controller's forgetting was so complete that she assumed the fireball from the crash was an exploding bomb. How could her memory have failed her at such a crucial time? This chapter will help you understand the nature of memory—how you form memories, how memory errors happen, and how you forget.

THE NATURE OF MEMORY

How does information turn into memories?

Memory is a funny thing. You might be able to remember the name of your first-grade teacher but not the name of someone you met five minutes ago. Mathematician John Griffith estimated that in an average lifetime, a person stores roughly five hundred times as much information as can be found in all the volumes of the *Encyclopaedia Britannica* (Hunt, 1982). Keep in mind, however, that although we retain a great deal of information, we also lose a great deal (Wixted, 2004). Consider Joshua Foer. In his book, *Moonwalking with Einstein: The Art and Science of Remembering Everything,* Foer (2011) describes his journey from forgetful science writer to U.S. Memory Champion but says that he still sometimes can't recall where he left his car keys. Memory is made up of many different abilities, some of which may be better than others from person to person and from time to time.

Memory plays a critical role in your life. Without it, you wouldn't know how to shut off your alarm, take a shower, get dressed, recognize objects, or communicate. You would be unaware of your own likes and dislikes. You would have no idea of who you are. The impressive capacity of human memory depends on the operation of a complex mental system.

Basic Memory Processes

In February 2002, prison warden James Smith lost his set of master keys to the Westville Correctional Facility. As a result, 2,559 inmates were kept under partial lockdown for eight days while the Indiana Department of Correction spent $53,000 to change locks in the affected areas. As it turned out, the warden had put the keys in his pocket when he went home, forgot he had done so, and reported the keys "missing" when they were not in their usual place in his office the next day (Associated Press, 2002). What went wrong? There are several possibilities. Memory depends on three basic processes: *encoding, storage,* and *retrieval* (see Figure 6.1). Our absent-minded warden might have had problems with any one of these processes.

First, information must be put into memory, a step that requires encoding. **Encoding** is a process that takes the information to be remembered and describes it in a form that our memory system can accept and use. We use *memory codes* to translate information from the senses into mental representations of that information. Codes for **auditory memory** (also known as **acoustic memory**) represent information as sequences of sounds, such as a tune or a rhyme. Codes for **visual memory** represent information as pictures, such as the image of your best friend's face. Codes for **semantic memory** represent the general meaning of an experience. So if you see a billboard that reads "Huey's Going-Out-of-Business Sale,"

encoding The process of putting information into a form that the memory system can accept and use.

auditory memory (acoustic memory) Mental representations of stimuli as sounds.

visual memory Mental representations of stimuli as pictures.

semantic memory Memory for generalized knowledge about the world.

FIGURE 6.1
Basic Memory Processes

Remembering something requires, first, that the information be encoded—put in a form that can be placed in memory. It must then be stored and, finally, retrieved, or recovered. If any of these processes fails, forgetting will occur.

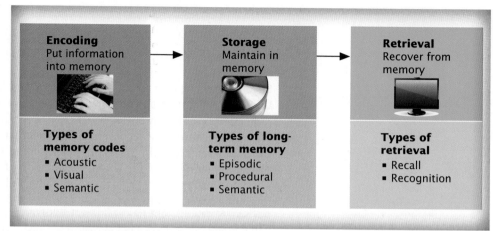

you might encode the sound of the words as if they had been spoken (acoustic encoding), the image of the letters as they were arranged on the sign (visual encoding), or the fact that you recently saw an ad for Huey's (semantic encoding). The type of encoding we use influences what we remember. Semantic encoding might allow you to remember the fact that an unfamiliar car was parked in your neighbors' driveway just before their house was robbed. If little or no other encoding took place, however, you might not be able to remember the make, model, or color of the car.

The second basic memory process is storage. **Storage** refers to the holding of information in your memory over time. When you recall a vacation you took in childhood or find that you can use a pogo stick many years after you last played with one, you are depending on the storage capacity of your memory.

The third memory process—retrieval—occurs when you find information stored in memory and bring it into conscious awareness. Retrieving stored information such as your address or telephone number is usually so fast and effortless that it feels automatic. The search-and-retrieval process becomes more noticeable, however, when you read a quiz question but cannot quite recall the information you need to answer it. Retrieval can take the form of either *recall* or *recognition*. To **recall** information, you have to retrieve it from memory on your own, without much help, such as when you answer an essay test question. In **recognition**, retrieval is aided by clues, such as when you have to select from among the correct response alternatives given on multiple-choice tests. Since recognition gives you more help, it tends to be easier than recall.

Types of Memory

When was the last time you made a phone call? Who was the first president of the United States? How do you keep your balance on roller skates? Answering each of these questions involves different aspects of memory. To answer the first question, you must remember a particular event in your life. To answer the second one, you have to recall general knowledge that is unlikely to be tied to a specific event. And the answer to the third question is easier to demonstrate than to describe. So how many types of memory are there? No one is sure, but most research suggests that there are at least three. Each type of memory is named for the kind of information it handles: *episodic, semantic,* and *procedural* (Rajaram & Barber, 2008).

Any memory of your experience of a specific event that happened while you were present is an **episodic memory** (Ezzyat & Davcachi, 2010; Tulving, 2005). It is a memory of an episode in your life. What you had for dinner yesterday, what you did last summer, or whether you've already told someone a story may be episodic memories (Gopie & MacLeod, 2009). Semantic memory refers to your generalized knowledge of the world—such as the fact that twelve items make a dozen—separate from a memory of experiencing a specific event. So if you were asked "Are wrenches pets or tools?" you could answer

storage The process of maintaining information in the memory system over time.

retrieval The process of finding information stored in memory.

recall Retrieving information stored in memory without much help from retrieval clues.

recognition Retrieving information stored in memory with the help of retrieval clues.

episodic memory Memory for events in one's own past.

How Does She Do That?

TRY THIS   As she practices, this youngster is developing procedural memories of how to ride a bike that may be difficult to put into words. To appreciate the special nature of procedural memory, try writing a step-by-step description of exactly how to tie a shoe.

Masterfile

procedural memory (procedural knowledge) A type of memory containing information about how to do things.

explicit memory Information retrieved through a conscious effort to remember something.

implicit memory The unintentional recollection and influence of prior experiences.

levels-of-processing model of memory A model that suggests that memory depends on the degree or depth to which we mentally process information.

maintenance rehearsal A memorization method that involves repeating information over and over to keep it in memory.

elaborative rehearsal A memorization method that relates new information to information already stored in memory.

using your semantic memory; you don't have to remember a specific episode in which you learned that wrenches are tools. As a general rule, people report episodic memories by saying, "I remember when . . ." whereas they report semantic memories by saying, "I know that . . ." (Tulving, 2000). Memory of how to do things, such as riding a bike, folding a map, or playing golf, is called **procedural memory**, or **procedural knowledge** (Cohen & Squire, 1980). Procedural memory often consists of a sequence of movements that are difficult or impossible to put into words. As a result, teachers of music, dance, cooking, woodworking, and other skills usually prefer to first show their students what to do rather than describe how to do it.

Many activities require all three types of memory. Consider the game of tennis. Knowing the official rules or the number of sets needed to win a match involves semantic memory. Remembering who served last requires episodic memory. And your skill in hitting the ball involves procedural memory.

Recalling these three kinds of memories can be either intentional or unintentional. When you deliberately choose to try to remember something, such as where you went on your last vacation, you are showing **explicit memory** when you access that information (Masson & McLeod, 1992). In contrast, **implicit memory** occurs when you unintentionally recall or otherwise show an influence of prior experiences (e.g., McDermott, 2002; Mulligan, 2012). For example, if you were to read this chapter twice, implicit memories from your first reading would help you to read it more quickly the second time. For the same reason, you can solve a puzzle faster if you have solved it in the past. This improvement of performance—often called *priming*—is automatic, and it occurs without conscious effort. In fact, people are often unaware that their actions have been influenced by previous events (see the chapter on consciousness). Have you ever found yourself disliking someone you just met but you didn't know why? The person might have triggered an implicit memory of a similar-looking person who once treated you badly. In such cases, we are usually unaware of any connection between the two individuals (Lewicki, 1992). Because some influential events cannot be recalled even when people try to do so, implicit memory has been said to involve "retention without remembering" (Roediger, Guynn, & Jones, 1995).

Models of Memory

We remember some information far better than other information. Suppose your friends throw a surprise party for you. When you enter the room, you might barely notice the flash of a camera. Later, you cannot recall it at all. And you might forget in a few seconds the name of a person you met at the party. But if you live to be a hundred, you might never forget where the party took place or how surprised and pleased you were. Why do some things stay in memory forever, whereas others barely make an impression? Five *models* of memory each provide a way to understand how memory works. Let's see what the levels-of-processing, transfer-appropriate processing, neural network processing, multiple memory systems, and information-processing models have to say about memory.

Levels of Processing

The **levels-of-processing model of memory** suggests that memory depends on the extent to which you encode and process information when you first encounter it (Craik & Lockhart, 1972). Consider, for example, the task of remembering a phone number you just heard on the radio. If you were unable to write it down, you would probably repeat the number over and over to yourself until you could find a pen or get to your phone. This repetition process is called **maintenance rehearsal**. It can be effective for encoding information temporarily, but what if you need to remember something for hours, months, or years? In that case, you would be better off using **elaborative rehearsal**, a process in which you relate new material to information you already have stored in memory. For example, instead of trying to remember a new person's name by simply repeating it to yourself, you could try thinking about how the name is related to something you know well. So if you are introduced to a man named Jim Crews, you might think, "He is as tall as my Uncle Jim, who always has a crew cut."

Study after study has shown that using elaborative rehearsal rather than maintenance rehearsal improves memory (Jahnke & Nowaczyk, 1998). Why? According to the levels-of-processing model of memory, when you use elaborative rehearsal you process material more "deeply" (Roediger, Gallo, & Geraci, 2002). The more you think about new information, organize it, and relate it to something you already know, the "deeper" the processing and the better your memory of the information becomes. Teachers use this idea when they ask students not only to define a new word but also to use it in a sentence. Figuring out how to use the new word takes deeper processing than merely defining it does. (The next time you come across an unfamiliar word in this book, don't just read its definition. Try to use the word in a sentence by coming up with an example of the concept that is related to your knowledge and experience.)

TRY THIS

Transfer-Appropriate Processing

Level of processing is not the only factor that affects memory (Baddeley, 1992). The **transfer-appropriate processing model of memory** suggests that another critical factor is the match between how we try to retrieve information and how we originally encoded it. For example, what do you think would happen to your performance on an exam if your instructor told you it would be in a multiple-choice format but then surprised you with an essay test? In a study about just such a situation, half the students in a class were told that their next exam would contain multiple-choice questions. The rest were told to expect essay questions. Only half the students actually got the type of exam they expected. These students did much better on the exam than those who took an unexpected type of exam. Apparently, in studying for the exam, each group used encoding strategies that were most appropriate to the type of exam they expected. Students who tried to retrieve the information in a way that didn't match their encoding method had a harder time (d'Ydewalle & Rosselle, 1978). Results such as these indicate that how well the encoding method aligns with the retrieval task is just as important as the depth of processing (Bauch & Otten, 2012; Mulligan & Picklesimer, 2012).

Neural Network Processing

A third way of thinking about memory is based on **neural network models of memory** (Avery, Dutt, & Krichmar, 2013; Lv et al., 2014). These models suggest that new experiences do more than provide specific facts that are stored and later retrieved one at a time. Those facts are also understood as they relate to each of the vast array of other facts that you already know. As a result, each new experience changes your overall understanding of the world and how it operates. For example, when you first arrived on campus, you learned lots of specific facts, such as where classes are held, how to get Wi-Fi access, and where to get the best pizza. Over time, these and many other facts about student life form a network of information that creates a more general understanding of how the whole system works. The development of this network makes experienced students not only more knowledgeable than new students but also more sophisticated. It allows them to, say, allocate their study time in order to do well in their most important courses and to plan a schedule that doesn't conflict with work commitments and maybe even avoids early morning classes—and certain professors.

Parallel distributed processing (PDP; Rumelhart & McClelland, 1986) is an example of such a neural network approach. PDP is a computational approach to brain function that seeks to model many aspects of the mind, including memory. A PDP model for memory sees each unit of knowledge as connected to every other unit. The connections between units become stronger as they are experienced together more frequently. In other words, your knowledge about the world is distributed across a network of associations that all operate at the same time, in parallel. The computations of such a PDP network allow you to be quick and efficient in drawing inferences and generalizations about the world, including how you get information that is not already in your knowledge base. For example, because of your network of associations, just seeing the word "chair" allows you to connect immediately to what a chair looks like, what it's used for, where it tends to be located, who might buy one, and how—such as through an Internet search—you can find one for sale (Sparrow, Liu, & Wegner, 2011). PDP models of memory explain this process very effectively.

transfer-appropriate processing model of memory A model that suggests that memory depends on how the encoding process matches up with what is later retrieved.
neural network models of memory Memory models in which new experiences are seen as changing one's overall knowledge base.

multiple memory systems model A model that suggests the existence of specialized and separated memory systems in the brain.

information-processing model of memory A model that suggests that information must pass through sensory memory, short-term memory, and long-term memory in order to become firmly embedded in memory.

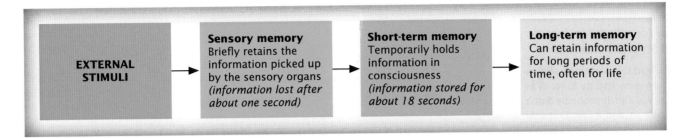

| Sensory memory | Short-term memory | Long-term memory |

EXTERNAL STIMULI → **Sensory memory** Briefly retains the information picked up by the sensory organs *(information lost after about one second)* → **Short-term memory** Temporarily holds information in consciousness *(information stored for about 18 seconds)* → **Long-term memory** Can retain information for long periods of time, often for life

FIGURE 6.2
Three Stages of Memory

This traditional information-processing model describes the three stages in the memory system.

Multiple Memory Systems

The **multiple memory systems model** suggests that the brain contains several relatively separate memory systems, each of which resides in a different area and each of which serves somewhat different purposes (Mizumori et al., 2004; Schacter, Wagner, & Buckner, 2000). Some evidence for the multiple memory systems approach comes from studies of people with brain damage (White, Packard, & McDonald, 2013). As described later, for example, damage to the hippocampus can leave people without explicit memory of doing a task, but their implicit memory allows their performance on that task to improve with practice (e.g., Warrington & Weiskrantz, 1970). Other research shows that inactivating the hippocampus with drugs causes massive disruption of explicit but not implicit memory processes (Frank, O'Reilly, & Curran, 2006).

Information Processing

The **information-processing model of memory** is the oldest and still probably the most influential and comprehensive memory model (Roediger, 1990). It suggests that for information to be firmly implanted in memory, it must pass through three stages of mental processing: sensory memory, short-term memory, and long-term memory (Atkinson & Shiffrin, 1968; see Figure 6.2).

In *sensory memory,* information from the senses—sights or sounds, for example—is held very briefly before being lost. But if information in sensory memory is attended to, analyzed, and encoded as a meaningful pattern, we say that it has been *perceived* (see the chapter on sensation and perception). Perceived information in sensory memory can now enter *short-term memory.* That information will disappear in less than twenty seconds, if nothing further is done with it. With additional processing, however, the information may be encoded into *long-term memory,* where it may remain indefinitely.

The act of reading illustrates all three stages of memory processing. As you read any sentence in this book, light energy reflected from the page reaches your eyes, where it is converted to neural activity and registered in your sensory memory. If you pay attention to these visual stimuli, your perception of the patterns of light can be held in short-term memory. This stage of memory links one moment in time with the next, holding the early parts of the sentence so that they can be integrated and understood as you read the rest of the sentence. As you read, you constantly recognize words by matching your perceptions of them with the patterns and meanings you have stored in long-term memory. In other words, all three stages of memory are necessary for you to understand a sentence.

Contemporary views of the information-processing model emphasize these constant interactions among sensory, short-term, and long-term memory. For example, sensory memory can be

Sensory Memory at Work

TRY THIS In a darkened room, ask a friend to hold a small flashlight and move it very slowly in a circle. You will see a moving point of light. If it appears to have a "tail," like a comet, that is your sensory memory of the light before it fades. Now ask your friend to move the light faster. You should now see a complete circle of light, because as the light moves, its impression on your sensory memory does not have time to fade before the circle is completed. A similar process allows us to see "sparkler circles."

© Jeff Lueders/Shutterstock.com

FIGURE 6.3

The Role of Long-Term Memory in Understanding New Information

TRY THIS   Read the paragraph shown here, then turn away and try to recall as much of it as you can. It probably didn't make much sense, and it was probably difficult to remember. But if you read it again after checking the footnote on page 188, the meaning will not only be clearer but it will now be much easier to remember (try it again!). Why? Because knowing the title of the paragraph allows you to retrieve from long-term memory what you already know about the topic (Bransford & Johnson, 1972).

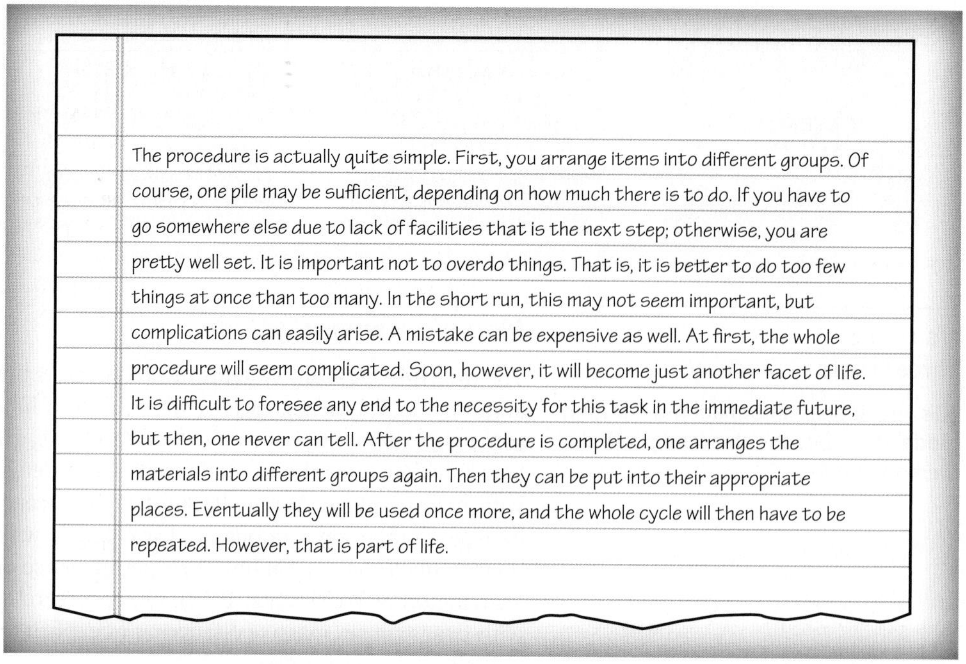

> The procedure is actually quite simple. First, you arrange items into different groups. Of course, one pile may be sufficient, depending on how much there is to do. If you have to go somewhere else due to lack of facilities that is the next step; otherwise, you are pretty well set. It is important not to overdo things. That is, it is better to do too few things at once than too many. In the short run, this may not seem important, but complications can easily arise. A mistake can be expensive as well. At first, the whole procedure will seem complicated. Soon, however, it will become just another facet of life. It is difficult to foresee any end to the necessity for this task in the immediate future, but then, one never can tell. After the procedure is completed, one arranges the materials into different groups again. Then they can be put into their appropriate places. Eventually they will be used once more, and the whole cycle will then have to be repeated. However, that is part of life.

thought of as that part of your knowledge base (or long-term memory) that is momentarily activated by information sent to the brain via the sensory nerves. And short-term memory can be thought of as that part of your knowledge base that is the focus of attention at any given moment (Cowan, 2011; Wagner, 1999). Like perception, memory is an active process, so what is already in long-term memory influences how new information is encoded (Cowan, 1988; Schacter, 2012). To understand this interaction better, try the exercise in Figure 6.3.

Which model offers the best explanation? There may not be a single "right" one. Each model makes important observations. The best conclusion is that more than one model may be required to understand memory. Psychologists find it useful to think of memory as both a sequential process, as suggested by the information-processing model, and as a parallel process, as suggested by neural network models such as parallel distributed processing. "In Review: Models of Memory" summarizes each of the five memory models we have described.

MODELS OF MEMORY   IN REVIEW

Model	Assumptions
Levels of processing	The more deeply material is processed, the better our memory of it.
Transfer-appropriate processing	Retrieval is improved when we try to recall material in a way that matches how the material was encoded.
Neural network	New experiences add to and alter our overall knowledge base; they are not separate, unconnected facts. Networks of associations allow us to draw inferences and make generalizations about the world.

(continued)

IN REVIEW

MODELS OF MEMORY (CONT.)

Model	Assumptions
Multiple memory systems	The brain contains relatively separate memory systems that serve somewhat different purposes.
Information processing	Information is processed in three stages: sensory memory, short-term memory, and long-term memory.

In Review Questions

1. The value of elaborative rehearsal over maintenance rehearsal has been cited as evidence for the _____ model of memory.

2. Deliberately trying to remember something means using your _____ memory.

3. Playing the piano uses _____ memory.

STORING NEW MEMORIES

What am I most likely to remember?

Storing information is critical to memory because we can retrieve only information that has been stored. According to the information-processing model, sensory memory, short-term memory, and long-term memory each provide a different type of storage. Let's take a closer look at these three memory systems in order to better understand how they work—and sometimes fail.

Sensory Memory

To recognize incoming information, the brain must analyze and compare it with what is already stored in long-term memory. This process is very quick, but it still takes time. The major function of **sensory memory** is to hold information long enough for it to be processed further (Nairne, 2003). This "holding" function is the job of the **sensory registers**, which act as temporary storage bins. There is a separate register for each of the senses. Each register can store a nearly complete representation of a sensory stimulus, but it can do so only briefly, often for less than one second (Eysenck & Keane, 2005).

Sensory memory helps us experience a smooth flow of information, even if that flow is interrupted. To see this for yourself, move your head and eyes slowly from left to right. It may seem as though your eyes are moving smoothly, like a movie camera scanning a scene, but that's not what is happening. Your eyes fixate at one point for about one-fourth of a second and then rapidly jump to a new position. You perceive smooth motion because you hold the scene in your visual sensory register (also known as your **iconic memory**) until your eyes fixate again. Similarly, when you listen to someone speak, your auditory sensory register allows you to experience a smooth flow of information, even though there are actually short silences between or within words.

The fact that sensory memories fade quickly if they are not processed further is actually an adaptive characteristic of the memory system (Baddeley, 1998). You simply cannot deal with all of the sights, sounds, odors, tastes, and touch sensations that come to your sense organs at any given moment. Using **selective attention**, you focus your mental resources on only some of the stimuli around you, thus controlling what information is processed further in short-term memory.

sensory memory A type of memory that is very brief but lasts long enough to connect one impression to the next.

sensory registers Memory systems that briefly hold incoming information.

iconic memory The sensory register for visual information.

selective attention The process of focusing mental resources on only part of the stimulus field.

Short-Term Memory and Working Memory

The sensory registers allow your memory system to develop a representation of a stimulus. However, they can't perform the more thorough analysis needed if the information is going to be used in some way. That function is accomplished by short-term memory and working memory.

Short-term memory (STM) is the part of your memory system that stores limited amounts of information for up to about twenty seconds. When you check the building directory to see which floor your new dentist's office is on, and then keep that number in mind as you press the correct elevator button, you are using short-term memory. **Working memory** is the part of the memory system that allows us to mentally work with, or manipulate, the information being held in short-term memory. When you mentally calculate what time you have to leave home in order to have lunch on campus, return a library book, and still get to class on time, you are using working memory.

TRY THIS

Short-term memory is actually a component of working memory, and together these memory systems allow us to do many kinds of mental work (Baddeley, 2003). Suppose you're buying something for eighty-three cents. You go through your change and pick out two quarters, two dimes, two nickels, and three pennies. To do this you use both short-term memory and working memory to remember the price, retrieve the rules of addition from long-term memory, and keep a running count of how much change you have so far. Now try to recall how many windows there are on the front of the house or apartment where you grew up. In answering this question, you probably formed a mental image of the building. You used one kind of working-memory process to form that image and then you maintained the image in short-term memory while you "worked" on it by counting the windows. So working memory has at least two components: *maintenance* (holding information in short-term memory) and *manipulation* (working on that information).

Encoding in Short-Term Memory

Encoding information in short-term memory is much more elaborate and varied than encoding in the sensory registers (Brandimonte, Hitch, & Bishop, 1992; Logie, 2011). Acoustic encoding (by sound) seems to dominate. This conclusion comes from research on the mistakes people make when encoding information in short-term memory, which tend to involve the substitution of similar sounds. For instance, Robert Conrad (1964) showed people strings of letters and asked them to repeat the letters immediately. Among their most common mistakes was the replacement of the correct letter with another that sounded like it. So if the correct letter was *C*, it was often replaced with a *D, P,* or *T*. The participants made these mistakes even though the letters were presented visually, without any sound. Studies in several cultures have also shown that items are more difficult to remember if they sound similar. For example, native English speakers do less well when they try to remember a string of letters like *ECVTGB* (which all have similar sounds) than when trying to remember one like *KRLDQS* (in which there are different sounds).

short-term memory (STM) A stage of memory in which information normally lasts less than twenty seconds; a component of working memory.

working memory Memory that allows us to mentally work with, or manipulate, information being held in short-term memory.

immediate memory span The maximum number of items a person can recall perfectly after one presentation of the items.

Encoding in short-term memory is not always acoustic, however. Information in short-term memory also can be encoded visually, semantically, and even kinesthetically (in terms of physical movements; Best, 1999). In one study, deaf people were shown a list of words and then asked to immediately write down as many as they could remember (Shand, 1982). When these participants made errors, they wrote words expressed through similar *hand movements* in American Sign Language rather than words that *sounded* similar to the correct words. Apparently, these individuals had encoded the words on the basis of the movements they would use when making the signs for them.

Storage Capacity of Short-Term Memory

How much information can you hold in short-term memory? The simple, classic test presented in Figure 6.4 will help you determine your **immediate memory span**, which is the largest number of items you can recall perfectly after one presentation. If your memory span is like most people's, you can repeat six or seven items from the test in this figure. Further, you should

The title of the paragraph in Figure 6.3 is "Washing Clothes."

The Capacity of Short-Term Memory

TRY THIS Here is a test of your immediate memory span (Howard, 1983). Ask someone to read to you the numbers in the top row at the rate of about one per second, then try to repeat them back in the same order. Then try the next row and the one after that, until you make a mistake. Your immediate memory span is the maximum number of items you can repeat back perfectly.

```
9 2 5
8 6 4 2
3 7 6 5 4
6 2 7 4 1 8
0 4 0 1 4 7 3
1 9 2 2 3 5 3 0
4 8 6 8 5 4 3 3 2
2 5 3 1 9 7 1 7 6 8
8 5 1 2 9 6 1 9 4 5 0
9 1 8 5 4 6 9 4 2 9 3 7
```

come up with about the same result whether you use digits, letters, words, or virtually anything else (Pollack, 1953). George Miller (1956) noticed that studies using many different tasks always seemed to show the same limit on the ability to process information. This "magic number," which is seven plus or minus two, appears to be the immediate memory span or capacity of short-term memory, at least for most adults in laboratory settings. In addition, the "magic number" refers not only to discrete elements, such as words or digits, but also to *chunks,* meaningful groupings of information that are produced by a process called **chunking** (Gilchrist & Cowan, 2012; Mathy & Feldman, 2012).

To see the difference between discrete elements and chunks, read the following letters to a friend, pausing at each dash: *FB-ILO-LM-TVN-BCB-MW.* The chances are very good that your friend will not be able to repeat this string of letters perfectly. Why? There are fifteen letters, which exceeds most people's immediate memory span. Now, give your friend the test again, but group the letters like this: *FBI-LOL-MTV-NBC-BMW.* Your friend will probably repeat the string easily. Although the same fifteen letters are involved, they will be processed as only five meaningful chunks of information.

The Power of Chunking

Chunks of information can be quite complex. If you heard someone say, "The boy in the red shirt kicked his mother in the shin," you could probably repeat the sentence perfectly. Yet it contains twelve words and forty-three letters. How can you repeat the sentence so effortlessly? The answer is that you are able to build bigger and bigger chunks of information (Ericsson & Staszewski, 1989). In this case, you might represent "the boy in the red shirt" as one chunk of information rather than as six words or nineteen new letters. Similarly, "kicked his mother" and "in the shin" represent separate chunks of information.

Learning to use bigger and bigger chunks of information can improve short-term memory. In fact, children's short-term memories improve partly because they gradually become able to hold more chunks in memory and also because they get better at grouping information into chunks (Cowan, 2010; Servan-Schreiber & Anderson, 1990). Adults also can greatly increase the capacity of their short-term memory by using more efficient chunking (Zhang & Luck, 2011). For example, after extensive training, one college student increased his immediate memory span from seven to eighty digits (Neisser, 2000a), and experienced waiters often use chunking techniques to remember the details of numerous dinner orders without taking notes (Bekinschtein, Cardozo, & Manes, 2008). So although the capacity of short-term memory is more or less constant (from five to nine chunks of meaningful information), the size of those chunks can vary tremendously.

Duration of Short-Term Memory

Why don't you remember every phone number you ever called or every conversation you ever had? The answer is that unless you do something to retain it, information in short-term memory is soon forgotten. This feature of short-term memory is adaptive because it gets rid of a lot of useless information; indeed, there are rare cases of people whose inability to forget interferes with their ability to concentrate (Parker, Cahill, & McGaugh, 2006; Storm, 2011). But losing information from short-term memory can also be inconvenient. You may have discovered this if you ever spotted an interesting web address on TV, got distracted before you visited it, and then forgot it.

chunking Organizing individual stimuli so that they will be perceived as larger units of meaningful information.

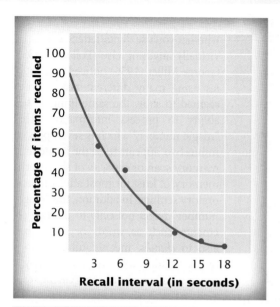

FIGURE 6.5
Forgetting in Short-Term Memory

This graph shows the percentage of items recalled after various intervals during which rehearsal was prevented. Notice that forgetting was virtually complete after a delay of eighteen seconds.

Source: Data from Peterson & Peterson (1959).

Brown-Peterson distractor technique A method for determining how long unrehearsed information remains in short-term memory.

long-term memory (LTM) The stage of memory that researchers believe has an unlimited capacity to store new information.

How long does information remain in short-term memory if you don't keep rehearsing it? John Brown (1958) and Lloyd and Margaret Peterson (1959) devised the **Brown-Peterson distractor technique** to measure the duration of short-term memory when no rehearsal is allowed. In this procedure, participants are presented with a group of three letters, such as *GRB*. They then count backward by threes from some number until they get a signal. Counting serves as a distraction that prevents the participants from rehearsing the letters. At the signal, they stop counting and try to recall the letters. By varying the number of seconds spent counting backward, the experimenter can determine how much forgetting takes place over time. As you can see in Figure 6.5, information in short-term memory is forgotten rapidly: After only twenty seconds or so, participants can remember almost nothing. Evidence from other such experiments also suggests that unrehearsed information can be held in short-term memory for no more than about twenty seconds. However, if the information is rehearsed or processed further in some other way, it may be encoded into long-term memory.

Long-Term Memory

When most of us talk about memory, we're usually referring to long-term memory. **Long-term memory (LTM)** is the part of the memory system where encoding and storage capabilities can produce memories that last a lifetime.

Encoding in Long-Term Memory

Sometimes information is encoded into long-term memory even if we don't try to memorize it (Ellis, 1991; Hoffman, Bein, & Maril, 2011). However, putting information into long-term memory is often the result of more elaborate and effortful processing that usually involves *semantic encoding*. As we mentioned earlier, semantic encoding often leaves out details in favor of the more general underlying meaning of the information.

In a classic study, Jacqueline Sachs (1967) demonstrated the dominance of semantic encoding in long-term memory. Her participants first listened to tape recordings of people speaking. She then showed them sets of similar sentences and asked them to say which contained the exact wording heard on the tape. Participants did well at this task when tested immediately, using mainly short-term memory. However, after twenty-seven seconds, they couldn't be sure which of two sentences they had heard. For example, they could not remember whether they had heard "He sent a letter about it to Galileo, the great Italian scientist" or "A letter about it was sent to Galileo, the great Italian scientist." They didn't do as well after the delay because they had to recall information from long-term memory, where they had encoded the general meaning of what they had heard, but not the exact wording.

Perhaps you are thinking, "So what?" After all, the two sentences mean the same thing. Unfortunately, when people encode the general meaning of information they hear or read, they can make mistakes about the details (Brewer, 1977). For example, after listening to a list of words such as *cold, white, ice, winter, frosty, blizzard, frozen, drift, flurries, parka, shovel, skis, sled,* and *flakes,* people often remember having heard the related word "snow" even though it was not presented (Gallo, 2006; Roediger & McDermott, 1995). This kind of false memory can be a problem when recalling exact words is important—such as in the courtroom, during business negotiations, and in agreements between students and teachers about course requirements. Later in this chapter, we show that such mistakes occur partly because people encode into long-term memory not only the general meaning of information but also what they think and assume about that information (McDermott & Chan, 2006).

Counterfeiters depend on the fact that people encode the general meaning of visual stimuli rather than specific details. For example, look at Figure 6.6 and find the correct drawing of a U.S. penny (Nickerson & Adams, 1979). Research shows that most people from the United States are unsuccessful at this task. People from other countries do poorly at recognizing their country's coins, too (Jones, 1990). This research has prompted the U.S. Department of the Treasury to begin using more distinctive drawings on the paper currency it distributes.

FIGURE 6.6
Encoding into Long-Term Memory

TRY THIS Which is the correct image of a U.S. penny? (See page 192 for answers.)

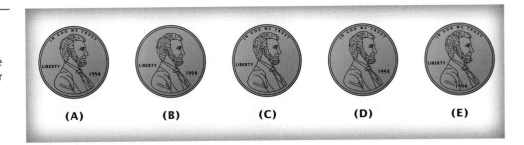

(A)   (B)   (C)   (D)   (E)

Storage Capacity of Long-Term Memory

The capacity of long-term memory is extremely large. In fact, it may be unlimited (Matlin, 1998). There is no way to prove this, but we do know that people store vast quantities of information in long-term memory that can be remembered remarkably well after long periods of time (Seamon, Punjabi, & Busch, 2010). For example, people are amazingly accurate at recognizing the faces of their high school classmates after having not seen them for over twenty-five years (Bruck, Cavanagh, & Ceci, 1991). They also do surprisingly well on tests of a foreign language or algebra fifty years after having formally studied these subjects (Bahrick et al., 1994; Bowers, Mattys, & Gage, 2009).

But long-term memories can become distorted. Are you old enough to remember where were you were and what you were doing when you heard about the 9/11 terrorist attacks on the United States? If so, you may be quite sure you can answer correctly, but if you are like the students tested in one study, your memories of 9/11 may not be entirely correct (Hirst et al., 2009; Talarico & Rubin, 2003). Most of the students whose memories had been substantially distorted over time were unaware that this distortion had occurred. In fact, they were very confident that their reports were accurate. Later, we will see that such overconfidence can also appear in courtroom testimony by eyewitnesses to crime.

Distinguishing between Short-Term and Long-Term Memory

Some psychologists argue that short-term memory and long-term memory have different features and obey different laws (Cowan, 1988; Talmi et al., 2005). ("In Review: Storing New Memories" summarizes the characteristics of these systems.) Evidence that information is transferred from short-term memory to a distinct storage system comes primarily from experiments on recall.

A Remarkable Memory

TRY THIS Using only his long-term memory, Franco Magnani created amazingly accurate paintings of his hometown in Italy even though he had not seen it for more than 30 years (Sacks, 1992). People like Magnani display *eidetic imagery*, commonly called *photographic memory*. About 5 percent of school-age children have eidetic imagery, but it is extremely rare in adults (Haber, 1979). You can test yourself for eidetic imagery by drawing a detailed picture or map of a place that you know well but have not seen recently, then comparing your version with a photo or map of the same place. How did you do?

Franco Magnani, www.francomagnani.com; Exploratorium, www.exploratorium.edu, photo by Susan Schwartzenberg

Magnani's painting

Photo of the same scene

TRY THIS

You can conduct your own recall experiment by reading aloud a list of words at a slow pace (about one word every two seconds). After reading the list just once, look away and write down as many of the words as you can, in any order. Here is a list you can use: *desk, frame, carburetor, flag, grill, book, urn, candle, briefcase, screen, tree, soup, ocean, castle, monster, bridge.* Did you notice anything about which words you remembered and which ones you forgot? If you are like most people, your recall depended partly on where each word appeared on the list—its serial position. As shown in the serial-position curve in Figure 6.7, memory researchers have found that recall tends to be very good for the first two or three words in a list. This result is called the **primacy effect**. The probability of recall decreases for words in the middle of the list and then rises dramatically for the last few words. The ease of recalling words near the end of the list is called the **recency effect**. The primacy effect may reflect the rehearsal that puts early words into long-term memory. The recency effect may occur because the last few words are still in short-term memory when you try to recall the list (Glanzer & Cunitz, 1966; Koppenaal & Glanzer, 1990).

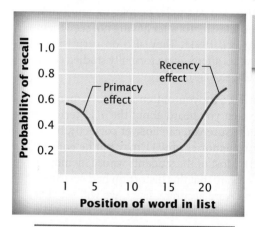

FIGURE 6.7
A Serial-Position Curve

This curve shows the probability of recalling items that appear at various serial positions in a list. Generally, the first several items and the last several items are most likely to be recalled (Silverman, 2012).

STORING NEW MEMORIES

IN REVIEW

Storage System	Function	Capacity	Duration
Sensory memory	Briefly holds representations of stimuli from each sense for further processing	Large: absorbs all sensory input from a particular stimulus	Less than one second
Short-term and working memory	Hold information in awareness and manipulate it to accomplish mental work	Five to nine distinct items or chunks of information	About eighteen seconds
Long-term memory	Stores new information indefinitely	Unlimited	Unlimited

In Review Questions

1. If you looked up a phone number but forgot it before you could call it, the information was probably lost from _____ memory.

2. The capacity of short-term memory is about _____ to _____ items.

3. Encoding is usually _____ in short-term memory and _____ in long-term memory.

RETRIEVING MEMORIES

How do I retrieve stored memories?

Most people have trouble remembering things at one time or another. Have you ever been unable to recall the name of a song or movie star, only to think of it the next day? Remembering requires not only the encoding and storing of information but also the ability to bring it into consciousness. In other words, you have to be able to *retrieve* it.

Retrieval Cues and Encoding Specificity

Retrieval cues are stimuli that help you retrieve information from long-term memory. As mentioned earlier, these cues make recognition tasks (such as multiple-choice tests) easier than recall tasks (such as essay exams).

primacy effect A characteristic of memory in which recall is particularly good for the first two or three items in a list.

recency effect A characteristic of memory in which recall is particularly good for the last few items in a list.

retrieval cues Stimuli that allow or help people to recall information.

Answer for Figure 6.6: Drawing A shows the correct penny image.

Context-Dependent Memories

The key to retrieval cues is that they are more effective when they tap into information that was encoded at the time of learning (Tulving, 1983). This rule is known as the **encoding specificity principle**. Because long-term memories are often encoded in terms of their general meaning, cues that trigger the meaning of the stored information tend to work best. For example, imagine that you have learned a long list of sentences. One of them was either (1) "The man lifted the piano" or (2) "The man tuned the piano." Now suppose that on a later recall test, you were given the retrieval cue "something heavy." This cue would probably help you to remember the first sentence (because you probably encoded something about the weight of a piano as you read it) but not the second sentence (because it has nothing to do with weight). Similarly, the cue "makes nice sounds" would probably help you recall the second sentence but not the first (Barclay et al., 1974; Goh & Lu, 2012).

Context and State Dependence

Have you ever taken a test in a classroom other than the one where you learned the material for that test? If so, was your performance affected? Research has shown that people tend to recall more of what they have learned when they're in the place where they learned it (Smith & Vela, 2001). Why? Because if they have encoded features of the environment where the learning occurred, these features can later act as retrieval cues (Richardson-Klavehn & Bjork, 1988). Smells are especially effective retrieval cues (Toffolo, Smeets, & van den Hout, 2012). In one experiment, people studied a series of photos while in the presence of a particular odor. Later, they reviewed a larger set of photos and tried to recognize the ones they had seen earlier. Half of the people were exposed to the original odor while taking the recognition test. The rest were tested in the presence of another odor. Those who smelled the same odor during learning and testing did significantly better on the recognition task than those who were tested in the presence of a different odor. The matching odor served as a powerful retrieval cue (Cann & Ross, 1989).

Context-specific memory, also known as **context-specific learning**, refers to memories that are helped or hindered by similarities or differences in environmental context. Police and prosecutors sometimes ask eyewitnesses to revisit the scene of a crime because they hope that being there will provide retrieval cues that can improve the accuracy of eyewitness testimony (e.g., Campos & Alonso-Quecuty, 2006). This context-specificity effect is not always strong (Smith, Vela, & Williamson, 1988), but some students do find it helpful to study for a test in the classroom where the test will be given.

encoding specificity principle A principle stating that the ability of a cue to aid retrieval depends on how well it taps into information that was originally encoded.

context-specific memory (context-specific learning) Memories that are helped or hindered by similarities or differences between the contexts in which they are learned and recalled.

Sometimes we also encode information about how we felt during a learning experience, and this information, too, can act as a retrieval cue. When our internal state influences retrieval, we have a **state-dependent memory**, also known as **state-dependent learning**. For example, if people learn new material while under the influence of marijuana, they tend to recall it better if they are tested on the material while under the influence of marijuana (Eich et al., 1975). Similar effects have been found with alcohol and other psychoactive drugs (Eich, 1989; Overton, 1984), although memory is best when people aren't using any drugs during encoding or retrieval. Mood states, too, can affect memory (Eich & Macaulay, 2000). College students are more likely to remember pleasant events when they're feeling good at the time of recall (Bower, 1981; Eich & Macaulay, 2006). Negative events are more likely to be recalled when people are feeling sad or angry (Lewinsohn & Rosenbaum, 1987). These *mood congruency* effects are strongest when people try to recall personally meaningful episodes (Eich & Metcalfe, 1989). The more meaningful the experience, the more likely it is that the memory has been colored by their mood. (See "In Review: Factors Affecting Retrieval from Long-Term Memory.")

FACTORS AFFECTING RETRIEVAL FROM LONG-TERM MEMORY

IN REVIEW

Process	Effect on Memory
Encoding specificity	Retrieval cues are effective only to the extent that they tap into information that was originally encoded.
Context-specific memory	Retrieval is most successful when it occurs in the same environment where the information was originally learned.
State-dependent memory	Retrieval is most successful when people are in the same physiological or psychological state as when they originally learned the information.

In Review Questions

1. Stimuli called _____ help you recall information stored in long-term memory.
2. If it is easier to remember something in the place where you learned it, you have _____ learning.
3. The tendency to remember the last few items in a list is called the _____ effect.

Retrieval from Semantic Memory

The retrieval situations we have discussed so far are relevant to episodic memory—our memory for events. But how do we retrieve information from semantic memory, where we store our general knowledge about the world? Researchers studying this question typically ask participants general knowledge questions, such as (1) Are fish minerals? (2) Is a beagle a dog? (3) Do birds fly? and (4) Does a car have legs? As you might imagine, most people answer such questions correctly. But by measuring how long it takes to answer them, psychologists gain important clues about how semantic memory is organized and how we retrieve information from it.

Semantic Networks

One view of semantic memory suggests that virtually everything we know about, including concepts such as "bird" or "animal," is represented in a dense network of associations (Churchland, 1989). Figure 6.8 presents just a tiny part of what our *semantic memory*

state-dependent memory (state-dependent learning) Memory that is helped or hindered by similarities or differences in a person's internal state during learning versus recall.

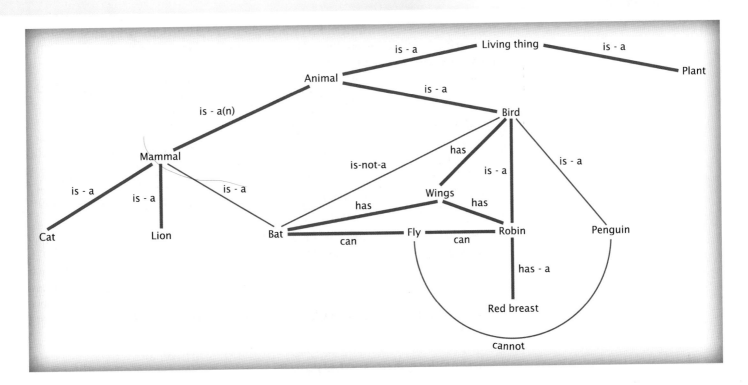

FIGURE 6.8
Semantic Memory Networks

This drawing represents just a small part of a network of semantic associations. Semantic network theories of memory suggest that networks like these allow us to retrieve specific pieces of previously learned information, draw conclusions about how concepts are related, and make new inferences about the world.

network might look like. In general, semantic network theories suggest that information is retrieved from memory through the principle of **spreading activation** (Medin, Ross, & Markman, 2001). In other words, when you think about some concept, it becomes activated in the network and this activation begins to "spread" down all the paths that are related to it. So if you are asked if a robin is a bird, the concepts of both "robin" and "bird" will become activated and the spreading activation from each will intersect somewhere in these paths. When they do, you know what answer to give.

Some associations in the network are stronger than others, as illustrated by the thicker lines between some concepts in Figure 6.8. For instance, you probably have a stronger association between "bat" and "wings" than between "bat" and "mammal." Spreading activation travels faster along stronger paths than along weaker ones. As a result, you'd probably respond more quickly to "Can a bat fly?" than to "Is a bat a mammal?"

Because of the tight organization of semantic networks and the speed at which activation spreads through them, we can gain access to an enormous body of knowledge about the world quickly and effortlessly. We can retrieve not only facts we have learned from others but also knowledge that allows us to draw our own conclusions and inferences (Matlin, 1998). For example, imagine answering these two questions: (1) Is a robin a bird? and (2) Is a robin a living thing? You can probably answer the first question "directly," because you probably learned this fact at some point in your life. However, you may never have consciously thought about the second question, so answering it requires some inference. Figure 6.8 illustrates the path to that inference. Because you know that a robin is a bird, a bird is an animal, and animals are living things, you infer that a robin must be a living thing. As you might expect, however, it takes slightly longer to answer the second question than the first.

Retrieving Incomplete Knowledge

Figure 6.8 shows that concepts such as "bird" or "living thing" are represented in semantic memory as unique sets of features or attributes. As a result, there may be times when you can retrieve some features of a concept from your semantic network but not enough of them to identify the concept. For example, you might know that there is an animal that has

spreading activation In semantic network theories of memory, a principle that explains how information is retrieved.

wings, can fly, and is not a bird and yet you might not be able to retrieve its name (Connor, Balota, & Neely, 1992). When this happens, you are retrieving *incomplete knowledge*. (The animal in question is a bat.)

You've probably experienced a particular example of incomplete knowledge called the *tip-of-the-tongue phenomenon* (Schwartz & Metcalfe, 2011). In a typical experiment on this phenomenon, participants listen to dictionary definitions and then are asked to name the word being defined (Brown & McNeill, 1966). If they can't recall the correct word, they are asked if they can recall any feature of it, such as its first letter or how many syllables it has. People are surprisingly good at this task, indicating that they are able to retrieve at least some knowledge of the word (Brennen et al., 1990). Most people experience the tip-of-the-tongue phenomenon about once a week; older people tend to experience it more often than younger people (Brown, 1991; Brown & Nix, 1996).

Another example of retrieving incomplete knowledge is the *feeling-of-knowing experience,* which some researchers study by asking trivia questions (Reder & Ritter, 1992). When research participants cannot answer a question, they are asked to say how likely it is that they could recognize the correct answer among several options. Again, people are remarkably good at this task. Even though they cannot recall the answer, they can retrieve enough knowledge to determine whether the answer is actually stored in their memory (Costermans, Lories, & Ansay, 1992).

CONSTRUCTING MEMORIES

How accurate are my memories?

Our memories are affected by what we experience but also by what we already know about the world in general and about the particular culture and family in which we live (Ross & Wang, 2010; Simpson, Rholes, & Winterheld, 2010). We use that existing knowledge to organize the new information we encounter, and we fill in gaps in that information as we encode and retrieve it (Schwabe, Nader, & Pruessner, 2014). These processes are called *constructive memory.*

Constructive Memory

TRY THIS   Here is a photo of the office used in the Brewer & Treyens (1981) study. Ask a friend to examine it for a minute or so (cover this caption). Then close the book and ask whether each of the following items appeared in the office: chair, wastebasket, bottle, typewriter, coffeepot, and book. If your friend reports having seen a wastebasket or a book, you will have demonstrated constructive memory.

Courtesy Professor William F. Brewer. From Brewer, W. F., & Treyens, J. C. (1981). Role of schemata in memory for places. Cognitive Psychology, 13, 207-230.

In one study of constructive memory, undergraduates were asked to wait for several minutes in a graduate student's office (Brewer & Treyens, 1981). Later, they were asked to recall everything that was in the office. Most of the students mistakenly "remembered" seeing books, even though there were none. Apparently, the general knowledge that graduate students read many books influenced the participants' memory of what was in the room (Roediger, Meade, & Bergman, 2001). In another study, participants read one of two versions of a story about a man and woman at a ski lodge. One version ended with the man proposing marriage to the woman. The second version was identical until the end, when instead of proposing, the man sexually assaulted the woman. A few days after reading the story, all the participants were asked what they remembered from it. Those who had read the "proposal" version recalled nice things about the man, such as that he wanted the woman to meet his parents. Those who read the "assault" version recalled negative things, such as that the man liked to drink a lot. However, neither kind of information had actually been part of the original story. The participants had "recalled" memories of the man that they had constructed in accordance with their overall impression of him (Carli, 1999).

FOCUS ON RESEARCH METHODS
I COULD SWEAR I HEARD IT!

By constructing our own versions of what we have seen and heard, we may remember an event differently from the way it actually happened. These errors, called *false memories,* can occur in relation to anything from the objects present in a room to the identity of an armed robber (Clancy et al., 2000).

What was the researchers' question?

How easy is it for people to form false memories? Henry Roediger and Kathleen McDermott (1995) addressed this question in an experiment to test for false memories as people recalled lists of words that had been read to them.

How did the researchers answer the question?

On each of sixteen trials, college students heard a different list of words. Each list related to a particular theme. For example, the "cold" list contained fifteen words such as *sleet, slush, frost, white, snow,* and so on. Yet the list's theme word—in this case, *cold*—was not included. In half of these trials, the students were simply asked to recall as many words as possible from the list they had just heard. But in the other half, the students did math problems instead of trying to recall the words. Once all sixteen lists had been presented, the students were given a new list of words and asked to say which of them they recognized as having been on the lists they had heard earlier. Some of the words on this new list were theme words, such as *cold*, that had not been presented earlier. Would the students "remember" hearing these theme words on the list even though they hadn't? And if so, how confident would they be about their "memory" of these words?

What did the researchers find?

The students falsely, but confidently, recognized the theme words from twelve of the sixteen lists. In fact, theme words were falsely recognized as often as listed words were correctly recognized. As you might expect, the chance of accurately recognizing the listed words was greater when the students had been allowed to recall them shortly after hearing them. However, false memory of never-presented theme words occurred in both conditions.

What do the results mean?

The results of this study suggest that the participants could not always distinguish words they had heard from those they had not heard. Why? The never-presented theme words "belonged" with the lists of presented words and apparently were "remembered" because they fit logically into the gaps in the students' memories. In short, the students' knowledge of words that *should* have been included on the lists created a "memory" that they *were* presented.

(continued)

What do we still need to know?

Studies such as this one make it clear that memory is constructive and that memory distortion and inaccuracy are very common (e.g., Arndt, 2012; Otgaar et al., 2012; Zhu et al., 2012). In fact, even people with highly superior memory for the events of their lives still have many false memories and do not realize it (Patihis et al., 2013). With appropriate feedback, people may be able to recognize and correct false memories (Clark et al., 2012; Leding, 2012), but exactly how the distortion process works and why false memories seem so real is still unclear. Perhaps the more frequently we recall an event, as when students were allowed to rehearse some lists, the stronger our belief is that we have recalled it accurately. There is also evidence that merely thinking about certain objects or events or hearing sounds or seeing photos associated with them appears to make false memories of them more likely (Garry & Gerrie, 2005; Henkel, Franklin, & Johnson, 2000). And there are times when, after watching someone else do something, we form the false memory that we have done that same thing ourselves (Lindner et al., 2010). This phenomenon may involve the activity of mirror neurons, which are discussed in the chapter on biological aspects of psychology. Questions about how false memories are created lead to even deeper questions about the degree to which our imperfect memory processes might distort our experiences of reality. Is there an objective reality, or do we each experience our own version of reality?

Constructive Memory and Neural Network Models

Neural network models of memory offer one way of explaining how semantic and episodic information become integrated in constructive memories. As mentioned earlier, these models suggest that newly learned facts alter our general knowledge of the world. These network models focus on how memory creates associations between different specific facts. Let's say, for example, that your own network "knows" that your friend Joe is a male European American business major. It also "knows" that Claudia is a female African American student, but it has never learned her major. Now suppose that every other student you know is a business major. In this case, the connection between "students you know" and "business majors" would be so strong that you would conclude that Claudia is a business major, too. You would be so confident in this belief that it would take overwhelming evidence for you to change your mind (Rumelhart & McClelland, 1986). In other words, you would have constructed a memory about Claudia.

Neural networks of memory also create *spontaneous generalizations*. So if your friend tells you that Claudia just bought a new car, you would know without asking that like all other cars you have experienced, it has four wheels. This is a spontaneous generalization from your knowledge base. Spontaneous generalizations are obviously helpful, but they can also create significant errors if the network is based on limited or biased experience with a class of objects or people.

If it occurs to you that prejudice based on ethnicity or other personal characteristics can result from spontaneous generalization errors, you're right (Greenwald & Banaji, 1995). Researchers are actually encouraged by this aspect of neural network models, though, because it accurately reflects human thought and memory. Virtually all of us make spontaneous generalizations about males, females, European Americans, African Americans, the young, the old, and many other categories (Rudman et al., 1999). Is prejudice, then, a process that we have no choice in or control over? Not necessarily. Relatively unprejudiced people tend to recognize that they are making generalizations and consciously try to ignore or suppress them (Amodio et al., 2004).

Schemas

Neural network models also help us understand constructive memory, because these models explain how *schemas* guide memory. As described in the chapters on social psychology and thought and language, **schemas** are mental representations of categories of objects, places, events, and people. For example, most North Americans have a schema for *baseball game*, so simply hearing these words is likely to activate entire clusters of information in

Neural Network Models and Constructive Memory

If you hear that "our basketball team won last night," your schema about basketball might prompt you to encode, and later retrieve, the fact that the players were men. Such spontaneous, though often incorrect, generalizations associated with neural network models of memory help explain the appearance of constructive memories.

AP Images/Phil Klein

schemas Mental representations of categories of objects, places, events, and people.

long-term memory, including the rules of the game and images of players, bats, balls, a green field, summer days, and perhaps hot dogs and stadiums. The generalized knowledge contained in schemas provides a basis for making inferences about new information during the encoding stage. So, if you hear that a baseball player was injured, your schema about baseball might prompt you to encode the incident as game related, even though the cause was not mentioned. Later, you are likely to recall the injury as having occurred during a game (see Figure 6.9 for another example).

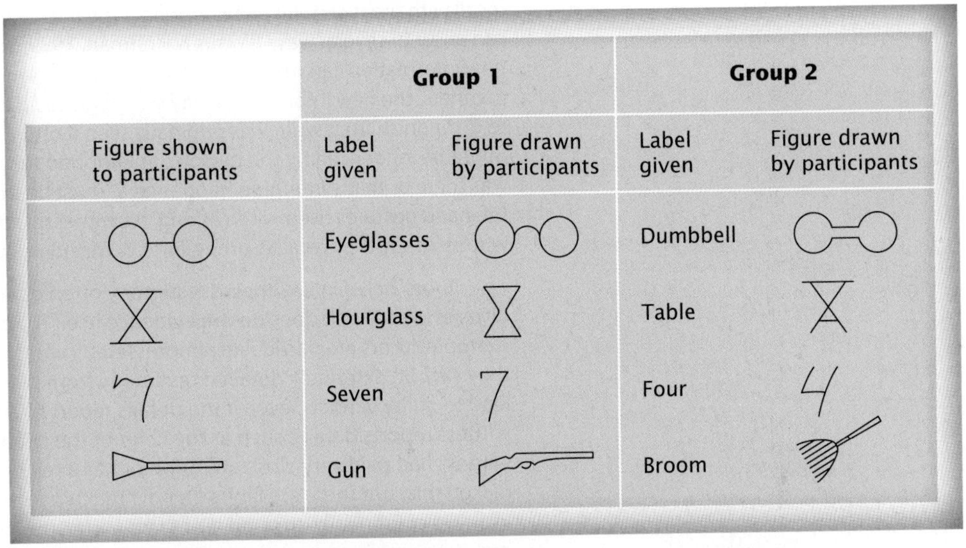

FIGURE 6.9
The Effect of Schemas on Recall

In a classic experiment, people were shown figures like these, along with labels designed to activate certain schemas (Carmichael, Hogan, & Walter, 1932). For example, when showing the top figure, the experimenter said either "This resembles eyeglasses" or "This resembles a dumbbell." When the participants were later asked to draw these figures from memory, their drawings tended to resemble the items mentioned by the experimenter. In other words, their memory had been altered by the schema-activating labels.

Figure shown to participants	Group 1		Group 2	
	Label given	Figure drawn by participants	Label given	Figure drawn by participants
⊙—⊙	Eyeglasses	⊙⊙	Dumbbell	⊙—⊙
⋈	Hourglass	⋈	Table	⋈
7	Seven	7	Four	4
⊢——	Gun	(gun)	Broom	(broom)

LINKAGES How accurate is eyewitness testimony? (a link to Sensation and Perception)

LINKAGES

MEMORY, PERCEPTION, AND EYEWITNESS TESTIMONY

There are few situations in which accurate retrieval of memories is more important—and constructive memory is more dangerous—than when an eyewitness testifies in court about a crime. Let's consider the accuracy of eyewitness memory and how it can be distorted.

The presence of an eyewitness can be a key factor in deciding to prosecute an alleged criminal (Flowe, Mehta, & Ebbesen, 2011), and in the courtroom it is the most compelling evidence a lawyer can provide. Nevertheless, eyewitnesses often make mistakes (Brewer & Wells, 2011; Police Executive Research Forum, 2013; Roediger, Wixted, & DeSoto, 2012). In 1984, for example, North Carolina college student Jennifer Thompson confidently identified Ronald Cotton as the man who had raped her at knifepoint. Mainly on the basis of Thompson's testimony, Cotton was convicted of rape and sentenced to life in prison. He was released eleven years later, when DNA evidence revealed that he was innocent (and identified another man as the rapist). The eyewitness/victim's certainty had convinced a jury, but her memory had been faulty (O'Neill, 2000).

Like the rest of us, eyewitnesses can remember only what they perceive, and they can perceive only what they attend to (Backman & Nilsson, 1991). We have already seen in the chapter on sensation and perception that perception is an active process in which we interpret what our senses tell us. Eyewitness perceptions can also be affected by physiological arousal and many other factors (Gallo, 2013; Hope et al., 2012). All these influences affect the memory that an eyewitness may form. So when witnesses are asked to report as accurately as possible what they saw or heard, no matter how hard they try to be accurate, there are limits to how valid their reports can be (e.g., Fahsing, Ask, & Granhag, 2004).

(continued)

For example, hearing new information about a crime (including in the form of a lawyer's question) can alter a witness's memory (Belli & Loftus, 1996; Wells & Quinlivan, 2009). Experiments show that when witnesses are asked "How fast were the cars going when they *smashed into* each other?" they are likely to recall a higher speed than when asked "How fast were the cars going when they *hit* each other?" (Loftus & Palmer, 1974; see Figure 6.10). There is also evidence that an object mentioned during questioning about an incident is often mistakenly remembered as having been there during the incident (e.g., Broaders & Goldin-Meadow, 2010). So if a lawyer says that a screwdriver was lying on the ground when it was not, witnesses may recall with great certainty having seen it (Ryan & Geiselman, 1991). This *misinformation effect* can occur in several ways (Loftus & Hoffman, 1989; Steblay et al., 2014). In some cases, hearing new information can make it harder to retrieve the original memory (Tversky & Tuchin, 1989). In others, the new information may be integrated into the old memory, making it impossible to distinguish from what was originally seen (Loftus, 1992). In still others, an eyewitness report might be influenced by the person's assumption that if a lawyer or police officer says an object was there or that something happened, it must be true (Chan, Thomas, & Bulevich, 2009). Even the hand gestures used when asking eyewitnesses to report a memory can change what the witnesses say they recall (Gurney, Pine, & Wiseman, 2013).

Jurors' belief in a witness's testimony often depends at least as much on how the witness gives evidence as it does on the evidence itself (Leippe, Manion, & Romanczyk, 1992). For example, jurors are particularly impressed by witnesses who give lots of details about what they saw. So extremely detailed testimony from prosecution witnesses are more likely to lead to guilty verdicts, even if the details reported are irrelevant (Bell & Loftus, 1989). When a witness reports details, such as the color of the criminal's shoes, jurors may assume that the witness had paid very close attention or has a really good memory. This assumption seems reasonable, but there are limits on how much people can pay attention to, particularly when they are emotionally aroused and the crime happens quickly. Witnesses whose attention was drawn to details such as shoe color might not have accurately perceived the criminal's facial features (Backman & Nilsson, 1991; Perfect, Andrade, & Syrett, 2012). So the fact that an eyewitness reports many details doesn't guarantee that all of them were remembered correctly.

Even when judges and juries know about the many factors that can affect eyewitness recall (Houston et al., 2013), they may be guided by other factors instead. For example, jurors tend to believe witnesses who respond quickly to questions (Oeberst, 2012) or otherwise appear confident about their testimony (Leippe, Manion, & Romanczyk, 1992). Unfortunately, research shows that witnesses' confidence is frequently much higher than their accuracy (Devilly et al., 2007; Dobolyi & Dodson, 2013; Luna & Martín-Luengo, 2012). In some cases, repeated exposure to misinformation and the repeated recall of that misinformation can lead witnesses to feel certain

FIGURE 6.10

The Impact of Questions on Eyewitness Memory

After seeing a filmed traffic accident, people were asked, "About how fast were the cars going when they (smashed into, hit, or contacted) each other?" As shown here, the witnesses' responses were influenced by the verb used in the question. "Smashed" was associated with the highest average speed estimates. A week later, people who heard the "smashed" question remembered the accident as being more violent than did people in the other two groups (Loftus & Palmer, 1974).

Aspix/Alamy ; Ashley Cooper/Corbis

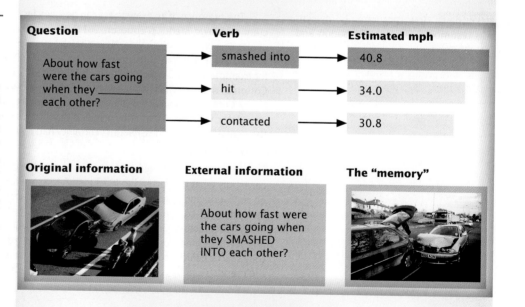

Question	Verb	Estimated mph
About how fast were the cars going when they _____ each other?	smashed into	40.8
	hit	34.0
	contacted	30.8

Original information

External information

About how fast were the cars going when they SMASHED INTO each other?

The "memory"

(continued)

about their testimony even when—as in the Jennifer Thompson case—it may not be correct (Foster et al., 2012; Frenda, Nichols, & Loftus, 2011; Roediger, Jacoby, & McDermott, 1996).

The accuracy of eyewitness memory can also be affected by how police lineups or certain other criminal identification procedures are set up (e.g., Brewer & Wells, 2011; Laudan, 2012; Wells, Memon, & Penrod, 2006; Wells, Steblay, & Dysart, 2012). For example, in one study, eyewitnesses were more accurate in identifying a criminal when viewing suspects standing together in a lineup, as opposed to viewing them one at a time. However, the witnesses were (wrongly) more confident in their identifications when they had seen the suspects one at a time (Dobolyi & Dodson, 2013). In another study, participants watched a videotaped crime and then tried to identify the criminal from a set of photographs (Wells & Bradfield, 1999). None of the photos showed the person who had committed the crime, but some participants nevertheless identified one of them as the criminal they saw on tape. When these mistaken participants were led to believe that they had correctly identified the criminal, they became even more confident in the accuracy of their false identification (Semmler, Brewer, & Wells, 2004; Wells, Olson, & Charman, 2003). These incorrect but confident witnesses became more likely than other participants to claim that it had been easy for them to identify the criminal from the photos because they had had a good view of him and had paid careful attention to him.

According to the Death Penalty Information Center (2014), 143 people, including Ronald Cotton, have been released from U.S. prisons since 1973 after DNA tests or other evidence revealed that they had been falsely convicted—mostly on the basis of faulty eyewitness testimony. Research on memory and perception helps explain how such miscarriages of justice can occur, and it has also been guiding efforts to prevent such errors in the future. In 1999, the U.S. Department of Justice officially acknowledged the potential for errors in eyewitness evidence as well as the dangers of asking witnesses to identify suspects from lineups and photo arrays. The result was *Eyewitness Evidence: A Guide for Law Enforcement* (U.S. Department of Justice, 1999), the first-ever guide for police and prosecutors involved in obtaining eyewitness evidence. The guide warned that asking witnesses leading questions about what they saw could distort their memories. It also suggested ways to avoid witness mistakes. For example, it pointed out that false identifications are less likely if witnesses viewing a lineup are told that the criminal they saw might not be included (Humphries, Holliday, & Flowe, 2012; Quinlivan et al., 2012; Wells & Olson, 2003). Research on other methods for improving the accuracy of eyewitness testimony continues on several fronts (e.g., Ahola, 2012; Clark, 2012a, 2012b; Gronlund, Wixted, & Mickes, 2013; Newman & Loftus, 2012).

This is exactly the sort of biased police lineup that *Eyewitness Evidence: A Guide for Law Enforcement* (U.S. Department of Justice, 1999) is designed to avoid. Based on research in memory and perception, this guide recommends that no suspect should stand out from all the others in a lineup, that witnesses should not assume that the real criminal is in the lineup, and that they should not be encouraged to "guess" when making an identification.

Tom Cheney The New Yorker Collection/The Cartoon Bank

"Thank you, gentlemen—you may all leave except for No. 3."

It's All Coming Back to Me

This grandfather hasn't fed an infant for decades, but his memory of how to do it is not entirely gone. He showed some "savings"; it took him less time to relearn the skill than it took him to learn it initially. In fact, sometimes previously forgotten information is later recalled in exquisite, accurate detail, a phenomenon called *hypermnesia* (Erdelyi, 2010).

© Istock.com/elkor

FIGURE 6.11
Ebbinghaus's Curve of Forgetting

TRY THIS List 30 words, selected at random from a dictionary, and spend a few minutes memorizing them. After an hour has passed, write down as many words as you can remember, but don't look at the original list again. Test yourself again eight hours later, a day later, and two days later. Now look at the original list and see how well you did on each recall test. Ebbinghaus found that most forgetting occurs during the first nine hours after learning, especially during the first hour. If this was not the case for you, why do you think your results were different?

relearning method A method for measuring forgetting.

decay theory A description of forgetting as the gradual disappearance of information from memory.

FORGETTING

What causes me to forget things?

The frustrations of forgetting—where you left your cell phone, the answer to a test question, an anniversary—are apparent to most people nearly every day (Neisser, 2000b). Let's look more closely at the nature of forgetting and what causes it.

How Do We Forget?

Hermann Ebbinghaus, a German psychologist, began the systematic study of memory and forgetting in the late 1800s, using only his own memory as his laboratory. He read aloud a list of nonsense syllables (such as *POF, XEM,* and *QAL*) at a constant pace and then tried to recall them.

Ebbinghaus devised a special **relearning method** to measure how much he forgot over time. He compared the number of repetitions (or trials) it took him to learn a list of items and the number of trials needed to relearn that same list later. Any reduction in the number of relearning trials represents the *savings* from one learning to the next. If it took Ebbinghaus ten trials to learn a list and another ten trials to relearn it, there would be no savings. Forgetting would have been complete. If it took him ten trials to learn the list and only five trials to relearn it, there would be a savings of 50 percent.

Ebbinghaus's research produced two lasting discoveries. One is the shape of the forgetting curve shown in Figure 6.11. Even when psychologists substitute words, sentences, and stories for nonsense syllables, the forgetting curve shows the same large initial drop in memory, followed by a more moderate decrease over time (Slamecka & McElree, 1983; Wixted, 2004). Of course, we remember sensible stories better than nonsense syllables, but the shape of the curve is the same no matter what type of material is involved (Davis & Moore, 1935). Even the forgetting of events from daily life tends to follow Ebbinghaus's forgetting curve (Thomson, 1982).

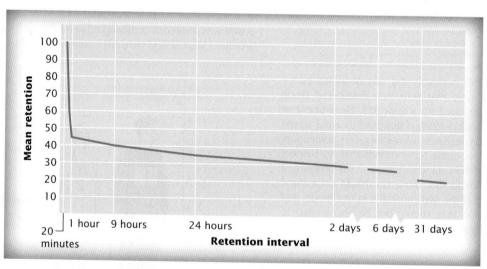

Ebbinghaus also discovered just how long-lasting "savings" in long-term memory can be. Psychologists now know from the method of savings that information about everything from algebra to bike riding is often retained for decades (Matlin, 1998). So although you may forget something you have learned if you do not use the information, it is very easy to relearn the material if the need arises, indicating that the forgetting was not complete (Hall & Bahrick, 1998).

Why Do We Forget?

We have seen how forgetting occurs, but *why* does it happen? In principle, one of two processes can be the cause (Best, 1999). One process is described by **decay theory**, which

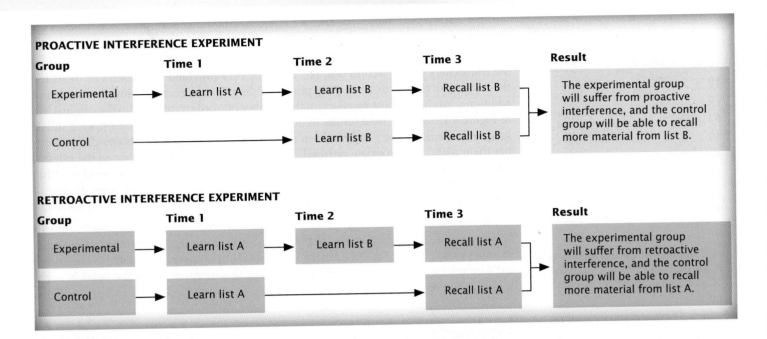

FIGURE 6.12
Procedures for
Studying Interference

To remember the difference between the two types of interference, note that prefixes *pro* and *retro* indicate directions in time. Pro means "forward," and retro means "backward." In proactive inhibition, previously learned material "comes forward" to interfere with new learning; retroactive inhibition occurs when new information goes back to interfere with the recall of past learning.

interference The process through which storage or retrieval of information is impaired by the presence of other information.

retroactive inhibition A cause of forgetting whereby new information placed in memory interferes with the ability to recall information already in memory.

proactive inhibition A cause of forgetting whereby previously learned information interferes with the ability to remember new information.

suggests that information gradually disappears from memory. Decay occurs in memory in much the same way that the inscription on a ring or bracelet wears away and fades over time. Forgetting might also occur because of **interference**, a process in which other information impairs either the storage or the retrieval of the information that was to be remembered (Healy et al., 2010; Robertson, 2012). Interference might occur because one piece of information actually displaces other information, pushing it out of memory. It might also occur because one piece of information makes storing or recalling other information more difficult.

Memory for an item in short-term memory decreases consistently over the course of about twenty seconds if it isn't rehearsed or thought about. So decay appears to play the main role in forgetting in short-term memory. But interference through displacement also matters. Like the top of a desk, short-term memory can hold only so much. Once it is full, adding additional items tends to make others "fall off" and become unavailable (Haberlandt, 1999). Displacement is one reason why the web address you just saw is likely to drop out of short-term memory if you see another one immediately afterward. Rehearsal prevents displacement by continually reentering the same information into short-term memory.

Unlike the situation in short-term memory, the forgetting that occurs from long-term memory appears to be more directly tied to interference (Raaijmakers & Jakab, 2013). Sometimes the interference is due to **retroactive inhibition**, in which learning new information interferes with our ability to recall older information (Miller & Laborda, 2011; Wixted, 2005). Interference can also occur because of **proactive inhibition**, a process by which old information interferes with our ability to learn or remember newer information (Wright, Katz, & Ma, 2012). Retroactive inhibition would help explain why studying French vocabulary this term might make it more difficult to remember the Spanish words you learned last term. And because of proactive inhibition, the French words you are learning now might make it harder to learn German vocabulary next term. Figure 6.12 outlines the types of experiments used to study the influence of each form of interference in long-term memory.

Does interference push information out of memory or does it merely make it harder to retrieve the information? To find out, Endel Tulving and Joseph Psotka (1971) presented people with lists of words that represented a particular category. For example, there was a "buildings" list (e.g., *hut, cottage, cabin, hotel*) and a geographical features list (e.g., *cliff, river, hill, volcano*). Some people learned a list and then recalled as many of its words as possible. Other groups learned one list and then learned up to five additional lists before trying to recall the first one.

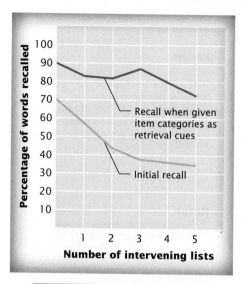

FIGURE 6.13
Retrieval Failures and Forgetting

Tulving and Psotka (1971) found that people's ability to recall a list of items was strongly affected by the number of other lists they learned before being tested on the first one.

The results were dramatic. As the number of additional lists increased, the number of words that people could recall from the original list decreased. This finding reflected strong retroactive inhibition; the new lists were interfering with recall of the first one. Then the researchers gave a second test, but this time they provided a retrieval cue by telling the category of the words (such as "types of buildings") to be recalled. Now the number of additional lists had almost no effect on the number of words recalled from the original list, as Figure 6.13 shows. These results indicate that the words from the first list were still in long-term memory: They had not been pushed out, but the participants couldn't remember them without appropriate retrieval cues. In short, faulty retrieval caused the original forgetting. Putting more and more information in long-term memory may be like putting more and more items in a suitcase or a refrigerator. Although none of the items disappear, it becomes increasingly difficult to find the one you are looking for (Malmberg et al., 2012).

Some theorists have suggested that all forgetting from long-term memory is due to retrieval failure (Ratcliff & McKoon, 1989). Does this mean that everything in long-term memory remains there for life, even if you cannot always (or ever) recall it? No one knows for sure yet, but as described in the next section, this question lies at the heart of some highly controversial court cases.

THINKING CRITICALLY

CAN TRAUMATIC MEMORIES BE REPRESSED, THEN RECOVERED?

In 1989, Eileen Franklin told California police that when she looked into her young daughter's eyes one day, she suddenly remembered seeing her father kill her childhood friend more than 20 years earlier. On the basis of her testimony about this memory, her father, George Franklin, Sr., was sent to prison for murder (Loftus & Ketcham, 1994).

What am I being asked to believe or accept?

Other cases have also resulted in imprisonment as adults claim to have recovered childhood memories of physical or sexual abuse. The juries in these trials accepted the claim that memory of shocking events can be *repressed,* or pushed into an inaccessible corner of the mind where subconscious processes keep it out of awareness for decades, yet potentially subject to accurate recall (Hyman, 2000). Jurors are not the only ones who have accepted claims of a **repressed memory** phenomenon. Some years ago a large American news organization reported that the United States had illegally used nerve gas during the war in Vietnam. This story was based, in part, on a Vietnam veteran's account of recovered memories of having been subjected to a nerve gas attack.

What evidence is available to support the assertion?

First, as discussed in the chapter on consciousness, a lot of mental activity occurs outside of awareness (Kihlstrom, 1999). Second, research on implicit memory shows that our behavior can be influenced by information of which we are not aware (Betch et al., 2003; Kouider & Dupoux, 2005). Third, research on *motivated forgetting* suggests that people may sometimes be able to suppress information willfully, so that it is no longer accessible on a later memory test (Anderson & Levy, 2009; Bailey & Chapman, 2012). Even suppressing one's emotional reactions to events can interfere with memories of those events (Richards & Gross, 2000). And people appear more likely to forget unpleasant rather than pleasant events (Erdelyi, 1985; Lynn et al., 2014). One psychologist kept a detailed record of his daily life over a six-year period. When he later tried to recall these experiences, he remembered more than half of the positive events but only a third of the negative ones (Waagenaar, 1986). In another study, 38 percent of women who had been brought to a hospital when they were children because of sexual abuse did not report the incident when they were interviewed as adults (Williams, 1994). Fourth, retrieval cues can help people recall memories that had previously

(continued)

repressed memory A painful memory that is said to be kept out of consciousness by psychological processes.

been inaccessible to conscious awareness (Andrews et al., 2000; Landsdale & Laming, 1995). For example, these cues have helped soldiers remember for the first time the circumstances under which they had been wounded many years before (Karon & Widener, 1997). Finally, there is the confidence with which people report recovered memories; they say they are just too vivid to be anything but real.

Are there alternative ways of interpreting the evidence?

Skeptical psychologists agree that subconscious memory and retrieval processes exist (Kihlstrom, 1999), and that, sadly, child abuse and other traumas are too common. Nevertheless, some of these psychologists conclude that the available evidence is not strong enough to support the conclusion that traumatic memories are likely to be repressed and then accurately recalled years later. For one thing, several studies have confirmed that memories of childhood events are no more accurate overall when people are adults than when they were still children (Brainerd, 2013). Any memory purportedly "recovered" in adulthood, then, could easily be a distorted or constructed memory (Clancy et al., 2000; Hyman, 2000; Loftus, 1998). Our recall of past events is affected by what happened at the time, what we knew beforehand, and everything we have experienced since. The people in the study mentioned earlier who "remembered" nonexistent books in an office inadvertently used their prior knowledge of what is usually in graduate students' offices to construct a false memory of seeing books. Similarly, that Vietnam veteran's "recovered memory" of a nerve gas attack appears to have had no basis in fact; the news organization that published the story later retracted it.

As we saw in the Focus on Research Methods section, false memories—distortions of actual events and the recall of events that didn't actually happen—can be just as vivid as real, accurate memories, and people can be just as confident about them (Brainerd & Reyna, 2005; Loftus, 2004; Roediger & McDermott, 2000). Most of us have experienced everyday versions of false memories. It is not unusual to "remember" turning off the coffeemaker or mailing the rent check, only to discover later that we didn't. Researchers have demonstrated that false memories can occur in relation to more emotional events, too. For example, a teenager named Chris was given descriptions of four incidents from his childhood and asked to write about each of them every day for five days (Loftus, 1997a). One of these incidents—being lost in a shopping mall at age five—never really happened. Yet Chris eventually "remembered" this event, and even added many details about the mall and the stranger whose hand he was supposedly found holding. He also rated this (false) memory as being more vivid than two of the other three (real) incidents he wrote about. Similar results occurred with about half of 77 child participants in other case studies (Porter, Yuille, & Lehman, 1999).

The same pattern of results has appeared in formal experiments about planting emotion-laden false memories (Hyman & Pentland, 1996; Loftus & Pickrell, 1995). Researchers have been able to create vivid and striking (but completely false) memories of events that people thought they experienced when they were one day old (DuBreuil, Garry, & Loftus, 1998). And some people will begin to avoid a certain food after researchers create in them a false memory of having been ill after eating that food as a child (Bernstein & Loftus, 2009a; Geraerts et al., 2008a). In other experiments, children who were repeatedly asked about a nonexistent trauma (getting a hand caught in a mousetrap) eventually developed a clear and unshakable false memory of experiencing it (Ceci et al., 1994). Results like these have led to concern that inaccurate reports and false memories might be made more likely by the use of repeated questioning and anatomically correct dolls during interviews with children about whether they have been touched inappropriately by an adult (Poole, Bruck, & Pipe, 2011).

Studies have found that people who are prone to fantasy, who easily confuse real and imagined stimuli, and who tend to have lapses in attention and memory are more likely than others to develop false memories and possibly more likely to report the recovery of repressed memories (e.g., Fuentemilla et al., 2009; McNally, 2003; McNally et al., 2005; Wilson & French, 2006). Two other studies have found that women who have suffered physical or sexual abuse are more likely to falsely remember words on a laboratory recall test (Bremner, Shobe, & Kihlstrom, 2000; Zoellner et al., 2000). This tendency appears strongest among abused women who show signs of posttraumatic stress disorder (Bremner, Shobe, & Kihlstrom, 2000). Another study found that the tendency to have false memories during a word recall task was greater in

(continued)

women who reported recovered memories of sexual abuse than in nonabused women or in those who had always remembered the abuse they suffered (Clancy et al., 2000).

Why would anyone "remember" a trauma that did not actually occur? Elizabeth Loftus (1997b) suggests that popular books about repressed memory may lead people to believe that anyone who experiences guilt, depression, low self-esteem, over-emotionality, or virtually any other psychological problem is harboring repressed memories of abuse. This message may be reinforced and elaborated by certain therapists, particularly those who specialize in using guided imagination, hypnosis, and other methods to "help" clients recover repressed memories (Lindsay et al., 2004; McHugh, 2009). In so doing, these therapists may influence their clients to construct false memories by encouraging them to imagine experiencing events that might never have actually occurred or that occurred only in a dream (Mazzoni & Loftus, 1996; Olio, 1994). As one client described her therapy, "I was rapidly losing the ability to differentiate between my imagination and my real memory" (Loftus & Ketcham, 1994, p. 25). To such therapists, a client's failure to recover memories of abuse or refusal to accept that they exist is evidence of denial of the truth (Loftus, 1997a; Tavris, 2003).

Exploring Memory Processes

Elizabeth Loftus (at center) is shown here with her students. Loftus and other cognitive psychologists have demonstrated mechanisms through which false memories can be created. They have shown, for example, that false memories appear even in research participants who are told about them and asked to avoid them (McDermott & Roediger, 1998). Their work has helped focus scientific scrutiny on reports of recovered memories, especially those arising from contact with therapists who assume that most people have repressed memories of abuse.

Courtesy of Elizabeth Loftus

The possibility that recovered memories might actually be false memories has led to dismissed charges or not-guilty verdicts for defendants in some repressed memory cases. In other cases, previously convicted defendants have been released. (George Franklin's conviction was overturned, but only after he spent five years in prison.) Many families (including George Franklin's) filed lawsuits against hospitals and therapists. In 1994, California winery executive Gary Ramona received $500,000 in damages from two therapists who had "helped" his daughter recall his alleged sexual abuse of her. Similar cases in Wisconsin and Illinois have more recently resulted in multimillion dollar judgments against therapists who had "found" their patients' lost memories (Heller, 2011; Loftus, 1998).

What additional evidence would help evaluate the alternatives?

Evaluating reports of recovered memories would be easier if we had more information about whether it is possible for people to repress memories of traumatic events. If it is possible, we also need to know how common it is and how accurate recovered memories might be. So far, we know that some people apparently forget intense emotional experiences but that most people's memories of them are vivid and long lasting (Alexander et al., 2005; Henckens et al., 2009; Porter & Peace, 2007). Some of these memories are called *flashbulb memories* because they preserve particular experiences in great detail (Brown & Kulik, 1977; McGaugh, 2003). In other words, evidence suggests that negative emotional information is retained as long, and as accurately, as any other information (Nørby, Lange, & Larsen, 2010).

(continued)

In fact, many people who live through trauma are *unable* to forget it, though they wish they could (Henig, 2004). In the sexual abuse study mentioned earlier, for example (Williams, 1994), 62 percent of the victims recalled as adults the trauma that had been documented in their childhoods. A similar study of a different group of adults found that about 92 percent of them recalled the abuse that had been documented in their childhoods (Alexander et al., 2005; Goodman et al., 2003). The true recall figures might actually be even higher in such studies, because some people who remember abuse may not wish to talk about it. In any case, additional studies like these—studies that track the fate of memories in known abuse cases—would not only help estimate the prevalence of this kind of forgetting but also might offer clues as to the kinds of people and events most likely to be associated with it.

It would also be valuable to know more about the processes through which repression might occur. Is there a mechanism that specifically pushes traumatic memories out of awareness and then keeps them at a subconscious level for long periods? Despite some suggestive results (e.g., Anderson & Levy, 2009; DePrince & Freyd, 2004), cognitive psychologists have so far not found reliable evidence for such a mechanism (Bulevich et al., 2006; Geraerts et al., 2006; Loftus, 1997a; McNally, 2003).

What conclusions are most reasonable?

LINKAGES Do forgotten memories remain in the subconscious? (a link to Consciousness)

An objective reading of the research evidence suggests that the recovery of traumatic memories is at least possible but that the implantation of false memories is also possible—and has been demonstrated repeatedly in controlled experiments. With this in mind, it is not easy to decide whether any particular case is an instance of recovered memory or false memory, especially when there is no objective corroborating evidence to guide the decision (Belli, 2012).

The intense conflict between those who uncritically accept claims of recovered memories and those who are more wary about the accuracy of such claims reflects a fundamental disagreement about evidence (Tavris, 2003). To many therapists who deal daily with victims of sexual abuse and other traumas, clients' reports constitute stronger proof of recovered memories than do the results of laboratory experiments. Client reports are viewed with considerably more skepticism by psychologists who engage in, or rely on, empirical research on the processes of memory and forgetting (Loftus, 2003, 2004; Pope, 1998). They would like to have additional sources of evidence, including from research on brain activity "signatures" that might someday distinguish true memories from false ones (e.g., Bernstein & Loftus, 2009b; Rissman, Greely, & Wagner, 2010; Slotnick & Schacter, 2004).

So people's responses to claims of recovered memory may be determined by the relative weight that they assign to reports of personal experiences versus evidence from controlled experiments. Still, the apparent ease with which false memories can be created should lead judges, juries, and the general public to exercise great caution before accepting unverified memories of traumatic events as the truth. At the same time, we should not automatically reject the claims of people who appear to have recovered memories (Geraerts et al., 2007; McNally & Geraerts, 2009). Perhaps the wisest course is to use all the scientific and circumstantial evidence available to carefully and critically examine claims of recovered memories while keeping in mind the possibility that constructive memory processes might have influenced those memories (Alison, Kebbell, & Lewis, 2006; Geraerts et al., 2007). This careful scientific approach is vital if we are to protect the rights of those who report recovered memories as well as those who face accusations arising from them (Geraerts et al., 2008b).

BIOLOGICAL BASES OF MEMORY

How does my brain change when I store a memory?

Many psychologists who study memory focus on explicit and implicit mental processes (e.g., Rubin et al., 2011; Schott et al., 2005). Others explore the physical, electrical, and chemical changes that take place in nerve cells when people encode, store, and retrieve information (e.g., Goldinger & Papesh, 2012; Kuhl, Bainbridge, & Chun, 2012; Linden et al., 2012; Prepau et al., 2014).

The Biochemistry of Memory

As described in the chapter on biological aspects of psychology, brain cells communicate at synapses, which are places where an axon from one cell meets with the dendrites of another. This communication uses chemicals called *neurotransmitters* that axons release into the synapses. The formation and storage of new memories are associated with at least two kinds of changes in synapses.

The first kind of change occurs when stimulation from the environment promotes the formation of *new* synapses. Scientists can actually see this process occur. As shown in Figure 6.14, repeatedly sending signals across a particular synapse increases the number of special little branches, called *spines,* that appear on the receiving cell's dendrites (Enriquez-Barreto et al., 2014; Roberts et al., 2010; Stepanyants & Escobar, 2011). The second kind of change occurs as new experiences change how *existing* synapses operate. For example, when two neurons fire at the same time and together stimulate a third neuron, that other neuron will later be more responsive than before to stimulation by either neuron alone (Sejnowski, Chattarji, & Stanton, 1990). This process of "sensitizing" synapses is called *long-term potentiation* (Fidzinski et al., 2012; Lisman, Yasuda, & Raghavachari, 2012). Other patterns of electrical stimulation can weaken synaptic connections, a process called *long-term depression* (Malenka, 1995). Changes in the sensitivity of synapses might account for the development of conditioned responses and other types of learning and for the operation of working memory.

In the brain's hippocampus (see Figure 6.15), such changes may be particularly likely at synapses using the neurotransmitter *glutamate* (Malenka & Nicoll, 1999). Other neurotransmitters, such as *acetylcholine,* also play important roles in memory formation (e.g., Furey, Pietrini, & Haxby, 2000; Li et al., 2003). The memory problems seen in conditions such as Alzheimer's disease appear related to disruptions in the activity of these neurons in the hippocampus (e.g., Ferrarini et al., 2014; Leal & Yassa, 2013). It is not surprising, then, that drugs designed to treat Alzheimer's disease seem to work by affecting synapses that use glutamate or acetylcholine (Schneider, 2013).

In summary, research has shown that the formation of memories is associated with changes in many individual synapses that, together, strengthen and improve the communication in networks of neurons.

FIGURE 6.14
Building Memories

These models are based on electron microscope images of synapses in the brain. The model on the left shows that before signals were repeatedly sent across the synapse, just one spine (shown in white) appears on this part of the dendrite. Afterward, as shown in the other model, there are two spines, which help improve communication across the synapse. The creation and changing of many individual synapses in the brain appear to underlie the formation and storage of new memories.

Courtesy of Professor Dominique Muller

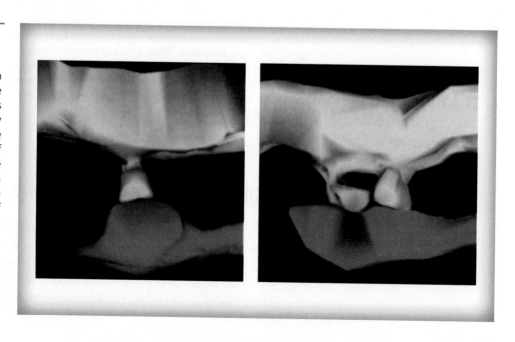

FIGURE 6.15
Brain Structures Involved in Memory

Combined neural activity in many parts of the brain allows us to encode, store, and retrieve memories. The complexity of the biological bases of these processes is underscored by research showing that different aspects of a memory—such as the sights and sounds of some event—are stored in different parts of the cerebral cortex.

© iStockphoto.com/GlobalStock

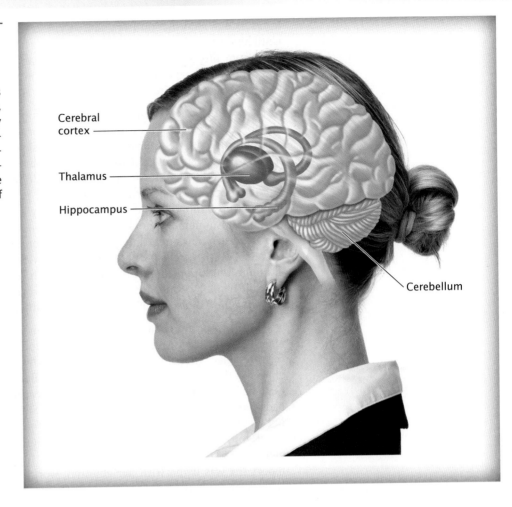

Cerebral cortex

Thalamus

Hippocampus

Cerebellum

Brain Structures and Memory

LINKAGES Where are memories stored? (a link to Biological Aspects of Psychology)

Are the biochemical processes involved in memory concentrated in certain brain regions, or are they distributed throughout the brain? Research suggests that memory involves both specialized regions where various types of memories are formed and widespread areas for storage (Takashima et al., 2006).

The Impact of Brain Damage

Studies of how brain injuries affect memory give hints about which parts of the brain are involved in various kinds of memory. For example, damage to the hippocampus, nearby parts of the cerebral cortex, and the thalamus often cause **anterograde amnesia**, a loss of ability to form new memories for events after the injury (Zhuang et al., 2011).

The case of Henry Molaison (once known only as H. M.; Eichenbaum, 2013) provides a striking example of anterograde amnesia (Milner, 1966). When H. M. was twenty-seven years old, part of his hippocampus was surgically removed to help stop his frequent epileptic seizures. After the operation, his long-term and short-term memory appeared normal, but something was wrong. Two years later, he still believed that he was twenty-seven. When his family moved into a new house, he couldn't remember the new address or how to get there. When his uncle died, he grieved in a normal way, but later asked why his uncle had not visited him. He had to be repeatedly reminded of the death, and each time, H. M. began to mourn all over again. The surgery had apparently destroyed the mechanism that

anterograde amnesia A loss of memory for events that occur after a brain injury.

transfers new information from short-term to long-term memory (Annese, et al., 2014). Until his death in 2008, H. M. lived in a nursing home, where his only long-term memories were from fifty years earlier, before the operation. He was still unable to recall events and facts he had experienced since then—not even the names of people he saw every day (Hathaway, 2002; Squire, 2009).

Although patients with damage to the hippocampus may not form new episodic memories, they may still form implicit memories. For example, H. M.'s performance on a complicated puzzle improved steadily over several days of practice, just as it does with normal people, and eventually he became almost perfect. But each time he tried the puzzle, he said he had never seen it before (Cohen & Corkin, 1981). Even people without a hippocampus can form certain kinds of memories. For example, Clive Wearing, a pianist whose hippocampus was destroyed by a viral infection, has only a few seconds of short-term memory, but he can still play pieces he'd learned before the infection. He can also learn new ones, though he has no memory of doing so (Sacks, 2007). The same is true of P. M., a cellist with a similar condition (Finke, Esfahani, & Ploner, 2013). So although the hippocampus is needed to form new episodic memories, it appears that implicit memory, procedural memory, and working memory can all form using other brain regions (Budson, 2009; Touzani, Puthanveettil, & Kandel, 2007).

Retrograde amnesia involves loss of memory formed prior to a brain injury (Kapur, 1999). A person with this type of amnesia would have trouble remembering anything that took place in the months or years before the injury. In 1994, head injuries from a car crash left thirty-six-year-old Perlene Griffith-Barwell with retrograde amnesia so severe that she forgot virtually everything she had learned about everything and everyone she had known over the previous twenty years. She thought she was still sixteen and did not recognize her husband, Malcolm, or her four children. She said, "The children were sweet, but they didn't seem like mine," and she "didn't feel anything" for Malcolm. Her memories of the previous twenty years never fully returned. She is divorced, but at last report she was living with her children, working in a bank, and planning to remarry (Echo News, 2000).

Unlike Perlene, most people with retrograde amnesia after brain trauma gradually recover their memories (Riccio, Millin, & Gisquet-Verrier, 2003). The most distant events are recalled first, then the person gradually regains memory for events leading up to the injury. Recovery is seldom complete, however, and the person may never remember the last few seconds before the injury. One man received a severe blow to

A Famous Case of Retrograde Amnesia

After Ralf Schumacher slammed his race car into a wall during the U.S. Grand Prix in June of 2004, he sustained a severe concussion that left him with no memory of the crash. Retrograde amnesia is relatively common following concussions, so if you ride a bike or a motorcycle, wear that helmet!

Paul Gilham/Getty Images

retrograde amnesia A loss of memory for events that occurred prior to a brain injury.

the head after being thrown from his motorcycle. Upon regaining consciousness, he thought he was eleven years old. Over the next three months, he slowly recalled more of his life. He remembered when he was twelve, thirteen, and so on—right up until the day of the accident. But he was never able to remember what happened just before the accident (Baddeley, 1982). Those final events were probably never transferred into long-term memory (Dudai, 2004).

The appearance of retrograde amnesia following a blow to the head has led researchers to suggest that as memories are transferred into long-term memory, they are initially unstable and therefore vulnerable to disruption (Dudai, 2004). It may take minutes, hours, days, or even longer before these memories are fully solidified, or *consolidated* (Donegan & Thompson, 1991). Such consolidation processes may depend on movement of electrochemical impulses within clusters of neurons in the brain (Taubenfeld et al., 2001). Accordingly, conditions that suppress nerve cell activity in the brain may also disrupt the transfer of information into long-term memory. These conditions include anesthetic drugs, poisoning by carbon monoxide or other toxins, and strong electrical impulses such as those in the electroconvulsive therapy that is sometimes used to treat cases of severe depression (see the chapter on treatment of psychological disorders).

Multiple Storage Areas

Obviously, the hippocampus does not permanently store long-term memories (Bayley, Hopkins, & Squire, 2003; Rosenbaum et al., 2000). If it did, H. M. would not have retained memories from the years before part of his hippocampus was removed. The hippocampus and thalamus send nerve impulses to the cerebral cortex, and it is in and around the cortex that long-term semantic and episodic memories are probably stored—but not just in one place (Levy, Bayley, & Squire, 2004; Ranganath, 2010). As described in the chapter on biological aspects of psychology, different regions of the cortex receive messages from different senses. Specific aspects of an experience are probably stored in or near these regions. For example, damage to the auditory association cortex disrupts memory for sounds (Colombo et al., 1990). A memory, however, involves more than one sensory system. Even in the simple case of a rat remembering a maze, the experience of the maze involves vision, smell, movements, and emotions, each of which may be stored in different regions of the brain (Gallagher & Chiba, 1996). So memories are both localized and distributed. Certain brain areas store specific aspects of each remembered event, but many brain systems are involved in experiencing a whole event (Brewer et al., 1998; Kensinger & Corkin, 2004). For example, the cerebellum (see Figure 6.15) is involved in the storage of procedural knowledge, such as dance steps and other movements.

What happens in the brain as we retrieve memories? Brain imaging studies show that the hippocampus and various regions of the cerebral cortex are active during memory retrieval (e.g., Andrews-Hanna, Saxe, & Yarkoni, 2014; McDermott, Szpunar, & Christ, 2009; Wing, Marsh, & Cabeza, 2013). There is also evidence to suggest that retrieving memories of certain experiences, such as a conversation or a tennis game, reactivates the sensory and motor regions of the brain that had been involved during the event itself (Danker & Anderson, 2010; Nyberg et al., 2001). Research shows, too, that when people or animals recall a stored emotional (fear-related) memory, that memory may have to be stored again. During this biological restorage process known as *reconsolidation*, it may be either strengthened or distorted (e.g., Dudai, 2004; Inda, Muravieva, & Alberini, 2011; Schiller et al., 2010).

Cognitive neuroscientists are trying to determine whether different patterns of brain activity occur with the storage and retrieval of accurate versus inaccurate memories (Bäuml & Samenieh, 2012; Bernstein & Loftus, 2009b; Urbach et al., 2005). Another line of investigation concerns the ability to think about the future (Atance & O'Neill, 2001; Szpunar, 2010). Scientists have found, for example, that patients with amnesia due to damage to the medial temporal lobe are not only unable to recollect the past, but they also cannot vividly envision future events, such as their next birthday party (Hassabis et al., 2007; Maguire & Hassabis, 2011). It appears from neuroimaging studies that the same brain regions involved in remembering are important for envisioning, too (Szpunar, Watson, & McDermott, 2007; Szpunar, Chan, & McDermott, 2009).

IMPROVING YOUR MEMORY

How can I remember more information?

Some questions remain about what memory is and how it works, but the results of memory research offer many valuable guidelines to help people improve their memories. For example, the physiological arousal that accompanies walking and other exercise appears to promote the storage and retrieval of memories (Lin et al., 2012; Salas, Minakata, & Kelemen, 2011), and as noted in the consciousness chapter, a good night's sleep can help consolidate the memories you formed during the day (Payne et al., 2012; Simmons, 2012). More specific memory enhancement strategies are based on the elaboration of incoming information and especially on linking new information to what you already know.

Mnemonic Strategies

One way to improve your memory is to use mnemonic strategies (pronounced "nee-MON-ik"). **Mnemonic strategies** are ways to put information into an organized framework in order to remember it more easily. To remember the names of the Great Lakes, for example, you could use the acronym HOMES (for Huron, Ontario, Michigan, Erie, and Superior). Verbal organization is the basis for many mnemonic strategies. You can link items by weaving them into a story, a sentence, or a rhyme. To help customers remember where they left their cars, some large parking lots have replaced traditional section

Mnemonic Strategies

You can improve your memory by using mnemonic strategies, but make sure they are easy to remember!

© S.Harris/www.sciencecartoonsplus.com

"YOU SIMPLY ASSOCIATE EACH NUMBER WITH A WORD, SUCH AS 'TABLE' AND 3,476,029"

mnemonic strategies Methods for organizing information in order to remember it.

designations such as "A1" or "G8" with the names of colors, months, or animals. Customers can then tie the location of their cars to information already in long-term memory—for example, "I parked in the month of my mother's birthday." And which do you think would be easier to remember: 1-800-438-4357 or 1-800-GET-HELP? Obviously, the more meaningful "get help" number is more memorable (Topolinski, 2011), and there are Web sites that can help you translate any phone number into words or a phrase.

TRY THIS

A simple but powerful mnemonic strategy is called the *method of loci* (pronounced "LOW-sigh"), or the "method of places." To use this method, first think about a set of familiar locations. Use your home, for example. You might imagine walking through the front door, around all four corners of the living room, and through each of the other rooms. Next, imagine that each item you want to remember is in one of these locations. Creating vivid or unusual images of how the items appear in each location seems to be particularly effective (Kline & Groninger, 1991). For example, tomatoes smashed against the front door or bananas hanging from the bedroom ceiling might be helpful in recalling these items on a grocery list. Whenever you want to remember a new list, you can create new images using the same locations in the same order.

Guidelines for More Effective Studying

The success of mnemonic strategies demonstrates again the importance of relating new information to knowledge already stored in memory. All mnemonic systems require that you have a well-learned body of knowledge (such as locations) that can be used to provide a framework, or context, for organizing incoming information.

When you want to remember complex material, such as a textbook chapter, the same principle applies. You can improve your memory for text material by first creating an outline or other overall context for learning, rather than by just reading and rereading (Glover et al., 1990). Repetition may *seem* effective because it keeps material in short-term memory, but for retaining information over long periods, repetition alone tends to be ineffective, no matter how much time you spend on it (Bjork, 1999). In short, "work smarter, not harder."

In addition, spend your time wisely. **Distributed practice** is much more effective than **massed practice** for learning and retaining new information. If you are going to spend 10 hours studying for a test, you will be much better off studying for ten 1-hour blocks, separated by periods of sleep and other activity. "Cramming" for one 10-hour block will not be as successful (Rohrer & Pashler, 2007). By scheduling more study sessions, you will stay fresh and be able to think about the material from a new perspective during each session. This method will remind you of the previously studied material and help you elaborate on the material, as in elaborative rehearsal, and thus remember it better (Benjamin & Tullis, 2010; Cepeda et al., 2009).

Elaborative rehearsal may also explain why, as mentioned in the learning chapter, students develop better long-term memory for course material if they are tested in a series of exams, each of which includes material presented during the entire course so far, as compared to a program of non-cumulative exams that cover only a specific part of the course (Lawrence, 2013). Apparently, the opportunity to encode, store, and retrieve the same material several times—and relate it to an ever-growing knowledge base in the process—creates more enduring memories.

You should also practice retrieving what you have learned by testing yourself repeatedly. For example, instead of simply rereading a section of a chapter, close the book and try to jot down the section's main points from memory. Both laboratory and classroom studies have found that students' exam performance is clearly better after self-testing than after merely reading and rereading the material they are trying to learn (e.g., Bugg & McDaniel, 2012; Hartwig & Dunlosky, 2012; Karpicke & Smith, 2012; Nunes & Weinstein, 2012; Roediger et al., 2011). Taking practice tests has been shown to have many benefits. It can

distributed practice Learning new information in many study sessions that are spaced across time.

massed practice Trying to learn complex new information in a single long study period.

help you study, store, and retrieve information in ways that match the task you will face when taking real tests. Practice tests also tell you what you know and what you don't know, so you can decide if you are ready for the real test or whether you need to study certain topics more thoroughly (Roediger, Putnam, & Smith, 2011). It is for reasons like these that we have included self-tests following each "In Review" table and at the end of every chapter of this book.

Reading a Textbook

More specific advice for remembering textbook material comes from a study that examined how successful and unsuccessful college students approached their reading (Whimbey, 1976). Unsuccessful students tended to read the material straight through. They did not slow down when they reached a difficult section. They kept going even when they did not understand what they were reading. In contrast, successful college students monitored their understanding, reread difficult sections, and periodically stopped or reviewed what they had learned. (This book's "In Review" features are designed to help you do that.) In short, effective learners engage in a deep level of processing. They are active learners. They think of each new fact in relation to other material, and they develop a context in which many new facts can be organized effectively.

Research on memory suggests two specific guidelines for reading a textbook. First, make sure that you understand what you are reading before moving on (Herrmann & Searleman, 1992). Second, try the *PQ4R method* (Thomas & Robinson, 1972). PQ4R stands for six activities to engage in when you read a chapter: *preview, question, read, reflect, recite,* and *review*. These activities are designed to increase the depth to which you process the information you read and should be done as follows:

1. *Preview.* Begin by skimming the chapter. Look at the section headings and any boldfaced or italicized terms. Get a general idea of what material will be discussed, the way it is organized, and how its topics relate to one another and to what you already know. Some people find it useful to survey the entire chapter once and then survey each major section a little more carefully before reading it in detail.

2. *Question.* Before reading each section, ask yourself what content will be covered and what information you should be getting from it.

3. *Read.* Read the text, but think about the material as you read. Are the questions you raised earlier being answered? Do you see the connections between and among the topics?

4. *Reflect.* As you read, think of your own examples—and create visual images—of the concepts and phenomena you encounter. Ask yourself what the material means and consider how each section relates to other sections in the chapter and other chapters in the book (this book's Linkages features are designed to promote this kind of reflection).

5. *Recite.* At the end of each section, recite the major points. Resist the temptation to be passive and say, "Oh, I'll remember that." Be active. Put the ideas into your own words by reciting them aloud to yourself (MacLeod et al., 2010) or by summarizing the material in a mini-lecture to a friend or study partner.

6. *Review.* When you reach the end of the chapter, review all of its material. You should now see connections not only within each section but also among sections. The objective is to see how the material is organized. Once you grasp that organization, the individual facts will be far easier to remember.

By following these procedures, you will learn and remember the material better. You will also save yourself considerable time.

Understand and Remember

Research on memory suggests that students who simply read their textbooks won't remember as much as those who read for understanding using strategies such as the PQ4R method. Further, memory for the material is likely to be better if you read and study it over a number of weeks rather than in one marathon session on the night before a test.

David Fischer/Photodisc/Getty Images

Lecture Notes

Students and employees often have to learn and remember material from lectures or other presentations. Taking notes will help, but effective note taking is a learned skill that improves with practice (Pauk & Owens, 2010). Research on memory suggests some simple strategies for taking and using notes effectively.

Recognize first that in note taking, more is not necessarily better. Taking detailed notes on everything requires that you pay close attention to unimportant as well as important content, leaving little time for thinking about the material. Note takers who concentrate on expressing the major ideas in relatively few words remember more than those who try to catch every detail (Pauk & Owens, 2010). In short, the best way to take notes is to think about what is being said. Draw connections with other material in the presentation. Then summarize the major points clearly and concisely (Kiewra, 1989).

Once you have a set of lecture notes, review them as soon as possible after the lecture so that you can fill in missing details. (Remember: Most forgetting from long-term memory occurs during the first hour after learning.) When the time comes for serious study, use your notes as if they were a chapter in a textbook. Write a detailed outline. Think about how various points are related. Once you have organized the material, the details will make more sense and will be much easier to remember. ("In Review: Improving Your Memory" summarizes tips for studying.)

IN REVIEW

IMPROVING YOUR MEMORY

Goal	Helpful Techniques
Remembering lists of items	■ Use mnemonic strategies. ■ Look for meaningful acronyms. ■ Try the method of loci.
Remembering textbook material	■ Follow the PQ4R system. ■ Allocate your time to allow for distributed practice. ■ Read actively, not passively. ■ Test yourself repeatedly as you read.
Taking lecture notes	■ Take notes, but record only the main points. ■ Think about the overall organization of the material. ■ Review your notes as soon after the lecture as possible in order to fill in missing points.
Studying for exams	■ Write a detailed outline of your lecture notes rather than passively reading them.

In Review Questions

1. Using mnemonic strategies and the PQ4R system to better remember course material are examples of the value of _____ rehearsal.

2. "Cramming" illustrates _____ practice that usually leads to _____ long-term retention than _____ practice.

3. To minimize forgetting, you should review lecture notes _____ after a lecture ends.

LINKAGES

As noted in the introductory chapter, all of psychology's subfields are related to one another. Our discussion of eyewitness testimony illustrates just one way that the topic of this chapter, memory, is linked to the subfield of sensation and perception, as discussed in the chapter by that name. The Linkages diagram shows ties to two other subfields, and there are many more ties throughout the book. Looking for linkages among subfields will help you see how they all fit together and help you better appreciate the big picture that is psychology.

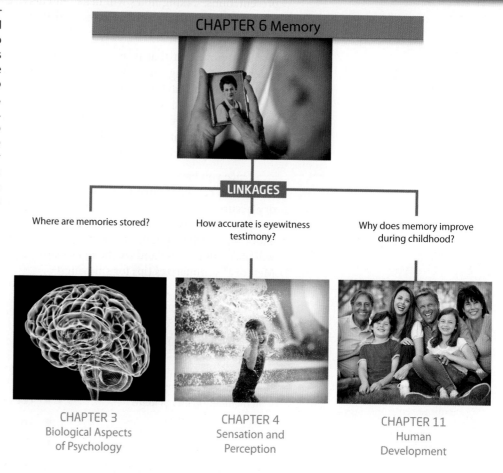

CHAPTER 6 Memory

LINKAGES

Where are memories stored?   How accurate is eyewitness testimony?   Why does memory improve during childhood?

CHAPTER 3
Biological Aspects of Psychology

CHAPTER 4
Sensation and Perception

CHAPTER 11
Human Development

SUMMARY

The Nature of Memory

How does information turn into memories?

Human memory depends on a complex mental system. There are three basic memory processes. **Encoding** transforms stimulus information into some type of mental representation. Codes for **auditory** (or **acoustic) memory** represent information as sounds, codes for **visual memory** represent information as images, and codes for semantic memory represent information as general meanings. **Storage** maintains information in the memory system over time. **Retrieval** is the process of gaining access to previously stored information.

Most psychologists agree that there are at least three types of memory. **Episodic memory** refers to memory for specific events in a person's life. **Semantic memory** refers to generalized knowledge about the world. **Procedural memory**, or **procedural knowledge**, refers to information about how to do things. Research on memory focuses on **explicit memory**, the information we retrieve through a conscious effort to remember something, and **implicit memory**, the unintentional recollection and influence of prior experiences.

Five models of memory have guided most research. The **levels-of-processing model of memory** suggests that the most important determinant of memory is how extensively information is encoded or processed when it is first received. In general, **elaborative rehearsal** is more effective than **maintenance rehearsal** in learning new information, because it represents a deeper level of processing. According to the **transfer-appropriate processing model of memory**, the critical determinant of memory is not how deeply information is encoded but whether the processes used during retrieval match those used during encoding. **Neural network models of memory**, such as parallel distributed processing (PDP) models, suggest that new experiences not only provide specific information but also become part of (and alter) a whole network of associations. The **multiple memory systems model** suggests that the brain contains several relatively separate memory systems. The **information-processing model of memory** suggests that for information to become firmly embedded in memory, it must pass through three stages of processing: sensory memory, short-term memory, and long-term memory.

Storing New Memories

What am I most likely to remember?

Sensory memory maintains information about incoming stimuli in the **sensory registers**, such as in **iconic memory**, for a very brief time. **Selective attention**, which focuses mental resources on only part of the stimulus field, controls what information in the sensory registers is actually perceived and transferred to short-term memory.

Working memory is a system that allows us to store, organize, and manipulate information in order to think, solve problems, and make decisions. The storage, or maintenance, component of working memory is referred to as **short-term memory (STM)**. Various memory codes can be used in short-term memory, but acoustic codes seem to be used in most verbal tasks. Studies of the **immediate memory span** indicate that the capacity of short-term memory is approximately seven meaningful groupings of information, created by **chunking**. Studies using the **Brown-Peterson distractor technique** show that information in short-term memory is usually forgotten in about twenty seconds or so if it is not rehearsed.

Long-term memory (LTM) normally results from semantic encoding, which means that people tend to encode the general meaning of information, not the surface details, into long-term memory. The capacity of long-term memory to store new information is extremely large and perhaps unlimited. The appearance of a **primacy effect** and a **recency effect** suggests that short-term and long-term memory may be distinct systems.

Retrieving Memories

How do I retrieve stored memories?

Retrieval cues help people remember things that they would otherwise not be able to recall. The effectiveness of retrieval cues follows the **encoding specificity principle**: Cues help retrieval only if they match some feature of the information that was originally encoded. All else being equal, memory may be better when we attempt to retrieve information in the same environment in which it was learned; this is called **context-specific memory**, or **context-specific learning**. When our internal state can affect retrieval, we have a **state-dependent memory**, or **state-dependent learning**. Researchers usually study retrieval from semantic memory by examining how long it takes people to answer general knowledge questions. It appears that ideas are represented as associations in a dense semantic memory network and that the retrieval of information occurs by a process of **spreading activation**. Each concept in the network is represented as a unique collection of features or attributes. The tip-of-the-tongue phenomenon illustrates the retrieval of incomplete knowledge.

Constructing Memories

How accurate are my memories?

In the process of constructive memory, people use generalized knowledge, or **schemas**, to fill in gaps in the information they encode and retrieve. PDP models provide one explanation of how people make spontaneous generalizations about the world.

Eyewitnesses can remember only what they perceive, and they can perceive only what they attend to. As a result, eyewitness testimony is often much less accurate than witnesses—and jurors—think it is.

Forgetting

What causes me to forget things?

In his research on long-term memory and forgetting, Ebbinghaus devised a **relearning method** to measure the amount of time that is saved when previously learned material is learned again after a delay. He found that most forgetting from long-term memory occurs during the first hour after learning and that savings can be extremely long lasting. **Decay theory** and **interference** describe two mechanisms of forgetting. There is evidence of both decay and interference in short-term memory; it appears that most forgetting from long-term memory is due to interference caused by either **retroactive inhibition** or **proactive inhibition**. There is considerable controversy over the possibility of **repressed memory** of traumatic events, especially about whether recovered memories of such events are more likely to be true recollections or false, constructed ones.

Biological Bases of Memory

How does my brain change when I store a memory?

Research has shown that memories can result from new synapses forming in the brain and improved communication at existing synapses. Studies of **anterograde amnesia**, **retrograde amnesia**, and other consequences of brain damage provide information about the brain structures involved in memory. For example, the hippocampus and thalamus are known to play a role in the formation of memories. These structures send nerve impulses to the cerebral cortex, and it is there that memories are probably stored. Memories appear to be both localized and distributed throughout the brain.

Improving Your Memory

How can I remember more information?

Mnemonic strategies are methods that can be used to remember things better. One of the simplest but most powerful mnemonic strategies is the method of loci. It is useful because it provides a context for organizing material effectively. Another key memory strategy is to space out your study sessions over time. This **distributed practice** is much more effective than **massed practice** ("cramming"), in which you try to learn a lot of information all at once. The key to remembering textbook material is to read actively rather than passively. One way to do this is to follow the PQ4R method: preview, question, read, reflect, recite, and review. Similarly, to take lecture notes or to study them effectively, organize the points in a meaningful outline and think about how each main point relates to the others.

TEST YOUR KNOWLEDGE

Select the best answer for each of the following questions. Then check your responses against the Answer Key at the end of the book.

1. Ludwig had an extraordinary memory for sound. Even when he lost his hearing in his later years, he was still able to create beautiful music. This demonstrates his well-developed _____ codes.
   a. acoustic
   b. visual
   c. semantic
   d. auditory

2. Henry is talking about his high school graduation ceremony. He remembers that his parents and grandparents were there and that afterward they gave him a laptop computer. Henry's memory of this event is both _____ and _____.
   a. semantic; explicit
   b. episodic; explicit
   c. semantic; implicit
   d. episodic; implicit

3. Riesa was uncomfortable when she was introduced to her roommate's cousin. She was not aware of it, but the cousin reminded her of a hated classmate in elementary school. This incident provides an example of the operation of _____ memory.
   a. procedural
   b. semantic
   c. implicit
   d. anterograde

4. Raquel was still studying ten minutes before her test. As she entered the classroom, she kept repeating the last sentence she had read: "Henry VIII had six wives." She was using _____ to keep this information in mind.
   a. elaborative rehearsal
   b. maintenance rehearsal
   c. the method of loci
   d. spreading activation

5. In a memory study, half the students in a class were told to expect multiple-choice questions on their upcoming exam and the other half was told to expect essay questions. Students did better if they got the type of exam they expected, which is consistent with the _____ model of memory.
   a. levels-of-processing
   b. transfer-appropriate processing
   c. parallel distributed processing
   d. information-processing

6. Reepal listens as her father describes a party the family is planning. She also smells popcorn from the kitchen, hears the radio playing, notices flashes of lightning outside, and feels too warm in her sweater. Yet Reepal is able to transfer the information about the party to her short-term memory, primarily because of _____.
   a. elaborative rehearsal
   b. implicit memory cues
   c. selective attention
   d. transfer-appropriate processing

7. Larry was thrilled when he met the girl of his dreams at the mall. She told him her phone number before she left, but if Larry doesn't use any rehearsal methods, he will remember the number for only about _____.
   a. one second
   b. twenty seconds
   c. one minute
   d. five minutes

8. Remembering your bank account number (2171988) as your birthday (February 17, 1988) is an example of _____.
   a. chunking
   b. the Brown-Peterson distractor technique
   c. the PQ4R method
   d. the method of loci

9. Lisbeth's mother once told her to remember that "the nail that stands out will get pounded down." But when Lisbeth tried to tell a friend about this saying, she remembered it as "if you stand out too much you'll get in trouble." Her problem in recalling the exact words is probably due to the fact that encoding in long-term memory is usually _____.
   a. acoustic
   b. visual
   c. semantic
   d. state dependent

10. Nesta had made a list of twenty CDs that she wanted to check out of the library, but she forgot to bring it with her. Nesta is most likely to remember the CDs that were at the _____ of the list.
    a. beginning
    b. middle
    c. end
    d. beginning and end

11. Janetta has been studying for tomorrow's test while drinking strong caffeinated coffee. A friend tells Janetta that her test score can be improved if she takes advantage of state-dependent memory by _____.
    a. drinking strong, caffeinated coffee just before the test
    b. doing the rest of her studying where the test will be given
    c. avoiding any kind of coffee just before the test
    d. using mnemonic strategies to remember key terms

12. Molly, a high school student, knows that she knows the name of her kindergarten teacher, but she can't quite remember it when asked. This experience is called _____.
    a. constructive memory block
    b. sensory memory impairment
    c. the tip-of-the-tongue phenomenon
    d. anterograde amnesia

13. When asked if there was a fever thermometer in her doctor's office, Careen says she remembers seeing one, even though it wasn't actually there. This is an example of _____, which is influenced by _____.
    a. the tip-of-the-tongue phenomenon; schemas
    b. the tip-of-the-tongue phenomenon; selective attention
    c. constructive memory; schemas
    d. constructive memory; selective attention

14. The use of DNA evidence has had what effect on the U.S. legal system's view of eyewitness testimony?
    a. It has had generally convinced witnesses to change their minds.
    b. It has demonstrated that eyewitness testimony, though not always accurate, is much better than anyone thought it was.
    c. It has revealed that eyewitness testimony has put many people in prison for crimes they did not commit.
    d. It has had little effect.

15. Robin memorized the names of all of the U.S. presidents when she was ten. Two years later, she had forgotten most of them, so she was pleasantly surprised that she could learn them a second time much more quickly than the first. This faster relearning time is an example of what Ebbinghaus called _____.
    a. mnemonic strategies
    b. state dependence
    c. context dependence
    d. savings

16. Berean studied French during his first year at college and then started learning Spanish in his second year. Now he is having difficulty remembering his Spanish vocabulary because the French words keep popping into his mind. This is an example of _____.
    a. retrograde amnesia
    b. anterograde amnesia
    c. retroactive inhibition
    d. proactive inhibition

17. When her brother said he had gotten a job in a bookstore, Danielle immediately assumed it would be a large room with books along the walls, a magazine section, a children's section, and cash registers near the door. But he had been hired by an online store, so Danielle was wrong. Her mistaken assumptions occurred because of _____, which is/are predicted by the model of memory.
    a. spontaneous generalizations; a neural network
    b. spontaneous generalizations; information-processing
    c. constructive memory; depth of processing
    d. semantic memory; transfer-appropriate

18. Jerry, a factory worker, suffered a brain injury when a steel beam fell on his head. Jerry cannot remember anything that has happened since the accident. Jerry is experiencing _____ amnesia.
    a. retrograde
    b. anterograde
    c. proactive
    d. retroactive

19. The brain area Jerry (above) most likely damaged was the _____.
    a. visual cortex
    b. corpus callosum
    c. cerebellum
    d. hippocampus

20. Loretta wanted to remember a list of important memory researchers, so she pictured them all visiting her apartment. She imagined Elizabeth Loftus playing video games in the living room, Hermann Ebbinghaus napping in the bathtub, Henry Roediger and Kathleen McDermott dancing in the kitchen, and so on. Loretta is using the memory strategy called _____.
    a. the method of loci
    b. procedural memorization
    c. encoding cues
    d. context dependence

Thought and Language

Chris Rout/Alamy

Preview

"Say what you mean, and mean what you say." This is good advice, but following it isn't always easy, partly because our thoughts don't always come to us in clear, complete sentences. We have to construct those sentences—using the language we've learned—from the words, images, ideas, and other mental material in our minds. Often, the material's complexity makes it difficult to accurately express what we're thinking. We all manage to do it, but with varying degrees of success. In this chapter, we explore what thoughts are, what language is, and how people translate one into the other. We also consider how thinking guides decision making and problem solving.

Dr. Joyce Wallace, a New York City physician, was having trouble figuring out what was the matter with a forty-three-year-old patient, "Laura McBride." Laura reported pain in her abdomen, aching muscles, irritability, occasional dizzy spells, and fatigue (Rouéché, 1986). The doctor's first hypothesis was iron-deficiency anemia, a condition in which there is not enough oxygen-carrying hemoglobin in the blood. There was some evidence to support this idea. A physical examination revealed that Laura's spleen was a bit enlarged, and blood tests showed low hemoglobin and high production of red blood cells, suggesting that her body was attempting to compensate for lost hemoglobin. However, other tests revealed normal iron levels. Perhaps she was losing blood through internal bleeding, but other tests ruled that out. Had Laura been vomiting blood? She said no. Blood in the urine? No. Abnormally heavy menstrual flow? No.

As Dr. Wallace puzzled over the problem, Laura's condition worsened. She reported more intense pain, cramps, shortness of breath, and loss of energy. Her blood was becoming less and less capable of sustaining her, but if it was not being lost, what was happening to it? Finally, the doctor looked at a smear of Laura's blood on a microscope slide. What she saw indicated that a poison was destroying Laura's red blood cells. What could it be? Laura spent most of her time at home, and her teenage daughters, who lived with her, were perfectly healthy. Dr. Wallace asked herself, "What does Laura do that the girls do not?" She repairs and restores paintings. Paint. Lead! She might be suffering from lead poisoning! When the next blood test showed a lead level seven times higher than normal, Dr. Wallace had found the answer at last.

To unravel this medical mystery, Dr. Wallace relied on her ability to think, solve problems, and make judgments and decisions. She put these vital cognitive abilities to use in weighing the pros and cons of various hypotheses and in reaching decisions about what tests to order and how to interpret them. In consulting with the patient and other physicians, she relied on another remarkable human cognitive ability: *language*. Let's take a look at what psychologists have discovered about these complex mental processes and how to measure them. We begin by examining a general framework for understanding human thinking and then go on to look at some specific cognitive processes.

BASIC FUNCTIONS OF THOUGHT

What good is thinking, anyway?

Thinking involves five main operations or functions: describing, elaborating, deciding, planning, and guiding action. Figure 7.1 shows how these functions can be organized into a *circle of thought*.

The Circle of Thought

Consider how the circle of thought operated in Dr. Wallace's case. It began when she received information about Laura's symptoms that allowed her to *describe* the problem. Next,

FIGURE 7.1
The Circle of Thought

The circle of thought begins as our sensory systems receive information from the world. Our perceptual system describes and elaborates this information, which is represented in the brain in ways that allow us to make decisions, formulate plans, and guide our actions. As those actions change our world, we receive new information, which begins another journey around the circle of thought.

© Umberto Shtanzman/Shutterstock.com

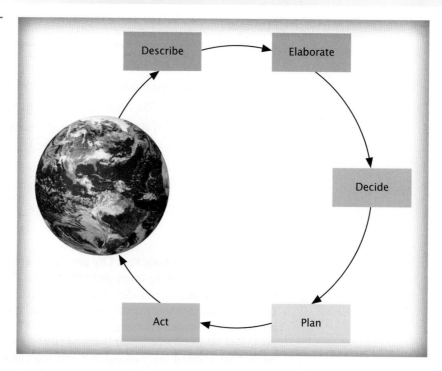

FIGURE 7.2
An Information-Processing Model

Some stages in the information-processing model depend heavily on both short-term and long-term memory and require some attention—that limited supply of mental resources required for information processing to be carried out efficiently (Oberauer & Hein, 2012).

Dr. Wallace *elaborated* on this information by using her knowledge, experience, and powers of reasoning to consider what disorders might cause such symptoms. Then she made a *decision* to investigate a possible cause, such as anemia. To pursue this decision, she came up with a *plan*—and then *acted* on that plan. But the circle of thought did not stop there. Information from the blood test gave new descriptive information, from which Dr. Wallace elaborated further to reach another decision, create a new plan, and guide her next action. Each stage in the circle of thought was also influenced by her overall intention—in this case, to find and treat her patient's problem.

The processes making up the circle of thought usually occur so quickly and are so complex that slowing them down for careful analysis might seem impossible. Some psychologists approach this difficult task by studying thought processes as if they were part of a computer-like information-processing system. An **information-processing system** receives information, represents the information with symbols, and then manipulates those symbols (e.g., Anderson, Bothell et al., 2004). In an information-processing model, **thinking** is defined as the manipulation of mental representations. Figure 7.2 shows how an information-processing model might describe the sequence of mental events that make up one trip around the circle of thought.

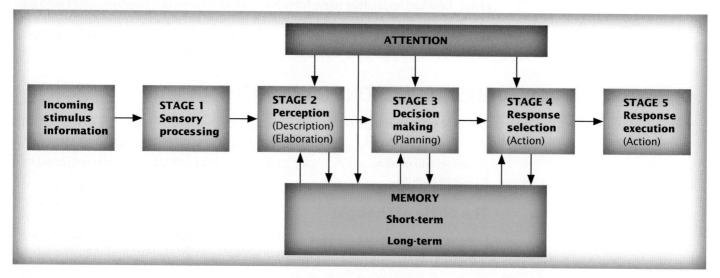

"Automatic" Thinking

The sensory, perceptual, decision-making, response-planning, and action components of the circle of thought can occur so rapidly that—as when playing a fast-paced video game—we may only be aware of the incoming information and our quick response to it. In such cases, our thinking processes become so well practiced that they are virtually automatic (Charlton & Starkey, 2011).

© ostill/Shutterstock.com

information-processing system Mechanisms for receiving information, representing it with symbols, and manipulating it.

thinking The manipulation of mental representations.

reaction time The time between the presentation of a stimulus and an overt response to it.

In the first stage, information about the world reaches your brain through the senses we discussed in the chapter on sensation and perception. This stage does not require attention. In the second stage, you must perceive and recognize the information—processes that do require attention. Also in this stage, you consciously elaborate information using the short-term and working-memory processes described in the memory chapter. These processes allow you to think about new information in relation to knowledge stored in your long-term memory. Once the information has been elaborated in this way, you must decide what to do with it. This third stage—decision making—demands attention, too. Your decision might be to store the information or to take some action. If the decision is to act, it is at this stage that you plan what to do. In the fourth and fifth stages, the action is carried out. Your action usually affects the environment, providing new information that is "fed back" to the system for processing in the ongoing circle of thought.

Measuring Information Processing

"Elliot," an intelligent and successful young businessman, had a cancerous tumor removed from the front of his brain. After surgery, his normally sharp reasoning and decision-making abilities failed. He made a series of reckless, impulsive business moves that put him into bankruptcy (Damasio, 1994). The brain damage that Elliot suffered appeared to have mainly affected the decision-making and response selection stages of information processing. Analyzing the effects of brain damage is just one method scientists use to study the details of how the entire information-processing sequence normally works and what can interfere with it.

Mental Chronometry

Drivers and video game players know that there is always a slight delay between seeing a red light or a "bad guy" and hitting the brakes or firing the laser gun. The delay occurs because each of the processes described in Figure 7.2 takes some time. Psychologists began the laboratory study of thinking by exploring *mental chronometry*, the timing of mental events (Posner, 1978). Specifically, they examined **reaction time**, the time elapsing between the presentation of a stimulus and the appearance of an overt response to it. Reaction time, they reasoned, should give us an idea of how long it takes for all the processes shown in Figure 7.2 to occur. In a typical reaction time experiment, a person is asked to say a word or to push a button as rapidly as possible after a stimulus appears. Even in such simple situations, several factors influence reaction times (Wickens, Gordon-Becker, & Liu, 2004).

One such factor is the *complexity* of the decision. The more options we have in responding to a set of stimuli, the longer the reaction time. The tennis player who knows that her opponent usually serves to a particular spot on the court will have a simple decision to make when the serve is completed and will react rapidly. But if she faces an opponent whose serve is less predictable, her reaction will be slower, because a more complex decision about which way to move is now required.

Expectancy, too, affects reaction time. People respond faster to stimuli that they expect and more slowly to stimuli that surprise them. So your reaction time will be shorter when braking for a traffic light that you knew might turn red than when dodging a ball thrown at you unexpectedly. Reaction time is also influenced by *stimulus-response compatibility*. If the relationship between a set of stimuli and possible responses is a natural or compatible one, reaction time will be fast. If not, reaction time will be slower (see Figure 7.3). Finally, in any reaction time task, there is a *speed-accuracy trade-off*. If you attempt to respond quickly, errors increase. If you try for an error-free performance, reaction time increases (Wickens & Carswell, 2006). At a track meet, for example, contestants who try too hard to anticipate the starting gun may have especially quick starts but may also have especially frequent false starts that disqualify them.

FIGURE 7.3
Stimulus-Response Compatibility

TRY THIS Imagine standing in front of an unfamiliar stove when a pot starts to boil over. Your reaction time in turning down the heat will be quicker on the stove shown in the left photo, because each knob is positioned to indicate the burner it controls. There is compatibility between the source of the stimulus and the location of the response. The stove in the right photo shows far less compatibility. Here, which knob you should turn is not as obvious, so your reaction time will be slower. Are there devices in your own house or apartment that lack stimulus-response compatibility? If so, how would you redesign them?

Courtesy of BadDesigns.com

Research on reaction time helped establish the time required for information processing to occur, but reaction times alone cannot provide a detailed picture of what goes on between the presentation of a stimulus and the execution of a response. They do not tell us, for example, whether we respond more quickly to an expected stimulus because we perceive it faster or because we make a decision about it faster. To analyze mental events more directly, psychologists have turned to other methods, such as neuroimaging.

Neuroimaging

Using positron emission tomography (PET), functional magnetic resonance imaging (fMRI), and other neuroimaging techniques described in the chapter on biological aspects of psychology, cognitive neuroscientists can watch the activity occurring in the brain during information processing (e.g., Karuza, Emberson, & Aslin, 2014; Price, 2012). In one study, for example, participants performed a task that required complex problem-solving skills. The brain's frontal lobe was especially active when this task was still relatively new and difficult, as shown by the red-shaded areas in Figure 7.4. As the participants learned the skills, however, frontal lobe activity decreased. When the task was well learned, the hippocampus became especially active (see the green-shaded areas in Figure 7.4). Activation in the hippocampus suggests that the participants were no longer struggling with a problem-solving task but instead were drawing upon memory systems.

Other studies of brain activity during the performance of cognitive tasks have also found that the frontal lobes are especially important for making decisions and solving problems (Wallis, Anderson, & Miller, 2001; Yarkoni et al., 2005), so it is no wonder that damage to Elliot's frontal area disrupted his decision-making and impulse-control abilities.

FIGURE 7.4
Watching People Think

Cognitive psychologists and other cognitive neuroscientists have found ways to watch brain activity as information processing takes place. These fMRI pictures show activity in two "slices" of the brain of a research participant who was practicing a complex problem-solving task. The areas shown in red were activated early in the learning process. As skill developed, the areas shown in green became activated.

From Cognitive Psychology and Its Implications, 5e by John R. Anderson © 2000 by Worth Publishers and W. H. Freeman and Company. Used with permission.

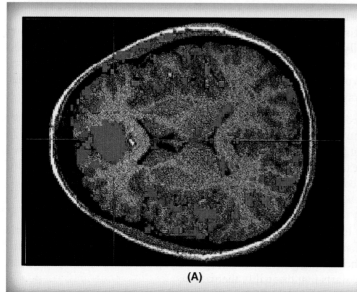

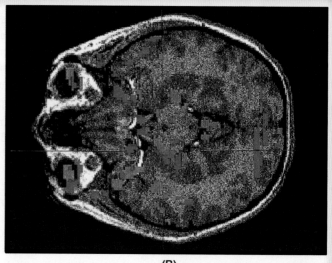

(A)   (B)

MENTAL REPRESENTATIONS: THE INGREDIENTS OF THOUGHT

What are thoughts made of?

Just as measuring, stirring, and baking are only part of the story of cookie making, describing the processes of thinking tells only part of the story behind the circle of thought. Psychologists usually describe the ingredients of thought as information. But that is like saying that you make cookies with "stuff." What specific forms can information take in our minds? Cognitive psychologists have found that information can be mentally represented in many ways, including as concepts, propositions, schemas, scripts, mental models, images, and cognitive maps. Let's explore these ingredients of thought and how people manipulate them as they think.

Concepts

When you think about anything—dogs, happiness, sex, movies, pizza—you are manipulating a basic ingredient of thought called concepts. **Concepts** are categories of objects, events, or ideas with common properties. Some concepts, such as "round" and "red," are visual and concrete. Concepts such as "truth" and "justice" are more abstract and harder to define. To have a concept is to recognize the properties, or features, that tend to be shared by members of a category. For example, the concept of "bird" includes such properties as having feathers, laying eggs, and being able to fly. The concept of "scissors" includes such properties as having two blades, a connecting hinge, and a pair of finger holes. Concepts allow you to relate each object or event you encounter to a category that you already know. Using concepts, you can say, "No, that is not a dog," or "Yes, that is a car." Concepts also make it possible for you to think logically. If you have the concepts "whale" and "bird," you can decide whether a whale is a bird without having either creature in the room with you.

Types of Concepts

Some concepts—called *formal concepts*—clearly define objects or events by a set of rules and properties, so that every member of the concept has all of the concept's defining properties and nonmembers do not. For instance, the concept "square" can be defined as "a shape with four equal sides and four right-angle corners." Any object that does not have all of these features is simply not a square. Formal concepts are often used to study concept learning in the laboratory because the members of these concepts can be neatly defined (Trabasso & Bower, 1968).

TRY THIS   Now stop reading for a moment and make a list of the features that define the concepts "home" or "game." You might have said that "home" is the place where you live and that a "game" is a competition between players. However, some people define "home" as the place where they were born, and almost everyone thinks of solitaire as a card game even though it involves only one player. These are just two examples of *natural concepts*. Unlike formal concepts, natural concepts don't have a fixed set of defining features. Instead, natural concepts have a set of typical or *characteristic* features, and members don't need to have all of them. For example, the ability to fly is a characteristic feature of the natural concept "bird," but an ostrich is still a bird even though it can't fly. It is a bird because it has enough other characteristic features of "bird" (such as feathers and wings). Having just one bird property is not enough, though. A snake lays eggs and a bat can fly, but neither animal is a bird. It is usually a combination of properties that defines a concept. In most situations outside the laboratory, people are thinking about natural rather than formal concepts. These natural concepts include object categories, such as "bird" or "house." They also include abstract idea categories, such as "honesty" or "justice," and goal-related categories, such as "things to pack for my vacation" (Barsalou, 1993).

The boundaries of a natural concept are fuzzy, so some members are better examples of it than others. A robin, a chicken, an ostrich, and a penguin are all birds. But a robin is a better example of the bird concept than the others, because it is closer to what most people

concepts Categories of objects, events, or ideas that have common properties.

A Natural Concept

A space shuttle and a hot-air balloon are two examples of the natural concept "aircraft," but most people think of the space shuttle, with its wings, as the better example. A prototype of the concept is probably an airplane. Members of natural concepts share a kind of "family resemblance" that helps us recognize items that belong in the same category, even if they are not identical.

NASA; © BenC/Shutterstock.com

have learned to think of as a typical bird. A member of a natural concept that possesses all or most of its characteristic features is called a **prototype**. The robin is a *prototypical* bird. The more prototypical of a concept something is, the more quickly you can decide whether it is an example of the concept. This is the reason people can answer just a little more quickly when asked "Is a robin a bird?" than when asked "Is a penguin a bird?" With practice, most of us get very good at using natural concepts to organize our thinking about the world (Wahlheim, Finn, & Jacoby, 2012). And, because prototypes are fundamental to the way we perceive and understand the world, understanding the nature of people's prototypes can have great practical value. For example, smokers—particularly young male smokers—are at greater risk for long-term cigarette use if their prototype for "smoker" includes traits such as "smart and independent" (Piko, Bak, & Gibbons, 2007). This is why health psychologists' anti-smoking programs often include efforts to create in smokers' minds a more negative prototype of the "typical smoker."

Propositions

We often combine concepts in units known as propositions. A **proposition** is a mental representation that expresses a relationship between concepts. Propositions can be true or false. Suppose you hear someone say that your friend Heather broke up with her boyfriend Jason. Your mental representation of this event will include a proposition that links your concepts of "Heather" and "Jason" in a particular way. This proposition could be diagrammed (in an unscientific way) as follows: Heather → dumped → Jason.

The arrows indicate that this statement is a proposition rather than a sentence. Propositions can be expressed as sentences, but they are actually general ideas that can be conveyed in any number of specific ways. In this case, the words "Jason was dumped by Heather" and "Heather is not willing to date Jason anymore" would all express the same proposition. If you later discovered that it was Jason who caused the breakup, the diagram of your proposition about the event would change to reflect this new information, shown here as reversed arrows: Heather ← dumped ← Jason.

Schemas, Scripts, and Mental Models

We organize the basic units of our thought in increasingly complex ways, and doing so allows us to see how these units are linked. For example, sets of propositions are often so closely associated that they form more complex mental representations called *schemas.*

prototype A member of a natural concept that possesses all or most of its characteristic features.

proposition A mental representation that expresses a relationship between concepts.

Does this person look like a millionaire to you? Our schemas tell us what to expect about objects, places, events, and people, but those expectations can sometimes be wrong. This was dramatically illustrated in October 1999 when Gordon Elwood died. The Medford, Oregon, man, who dressed in rags and collected cans, left over $9 million to charity (McMahon, 2000).

© iStock.com/Anna Bryukhanova

As mentioned in the chapters on sensation and perception, memory, and human development, **schemas** are generalizations that we develop about categories of objects, places, events, and people. Our schemas help us understand the world. If you borrow a friend's car, your "car" schema will give you a good idea of where the accelerator and brake are, and how to raise and lower the windows. Schemas also generate expectations about objects, places, events, and people—telling us that stereo systems have speakers, that picnics occur in the summer, that rock concerts are loud, and so on.

Scripts

Schemas about familiar activities, such as going to a restaurant, are known as **scripts** (Anderson, 2000). Your "restaurant" script represents the sequence of events you can expect when you go out to eat (see Figure 7.5). That script tells you what to do when you are in a restaurant and helps you understand stories involving restaurants (Whitney, 2001). Scripts also shape your interpretation of events. For example, on your first day of high school, you no doubt assumed that the person standing at the front of the class was a teacher, not a security guard or a janitor.

If our scripts are violated, however, it is easy to misinterpret events. In one case, a heart attack victim in London lay for nine hours in the hallway of an apartment building after an ambulance crew smelled alcohol on his breath and assumed he was "sleeping it off." The crew's script for what happens in the poorer sections of big cities told them that someone slumped in a hallway is drunk, not sick. Because script-violating events are unexpected, our reactions to them tend to be slower and less effective than our reactions to expected events. Your "grocery shopping" script, for example, probably includes pushing a cart, putting items in it, going to the checkout stand, paying, and leaving. But suppose you are at the back of the store when a robber near the entrance fires a gun and shouts at the manager to open the safe. People sometimes ignore these script-violating events, interpreting gunshots as a car backfiring and shouted orders as "someone fooling around" (Raisig et al., 2010). Others simply freeze, unsure of what to do or not realizing that they could call the police on their cell phones.

Mental Models

The relationships among concepts can be organized not only as schemas and scripts but also as **mental models** (Johnson-Laird, 1983). For example, suppose someone

---

schemas Generalizations about categories of objects, places, events, and people.

scripts Mental representations of familiar sequences of activity.

mental models Sets of propositions that represent people's understanding of how things look and work.

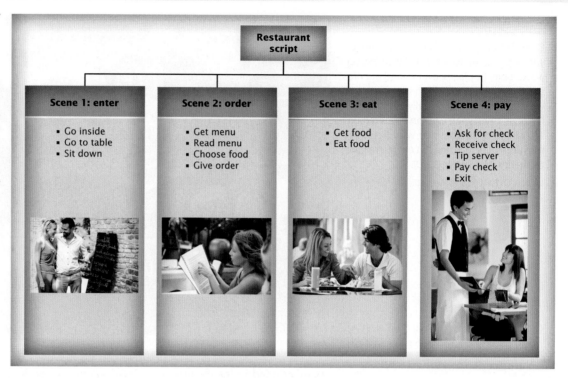

FIGURE 7.5

Following a Script: Eating at a Restaurant

Schemas about what happens in restaurants and how to be-have in them take the form of scripts, represented here in four "scenes." Scripts guide our actions in all sorts of fa-miliar situations and also help us understand descriptions of events occurring in those sit-uations (e.g., "Our service was really slow").

Source: Whitney (2001).

© iStocko.com/andrearoad; ©iStock.com/webphotographeer; © Monkey Business Images/Shutterstock.com; © Phil Date/Shutterstock.com

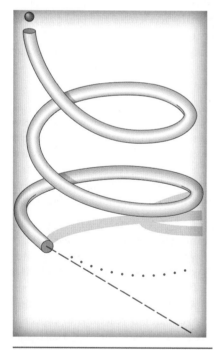

FIGURE 7.6

Applying a Mental Model

TRY THIS Try to imagine the path that the ball will follow when it leaves the curved tube. In one study, most people drew the incorrect (curved) path indicated by the dotted line, rather than the correct (straight) path indicated by the dashed line (McCloskey, 1983). Their error was based on the construction of a faulty mental model of the behavior of physical objects.

tells you, "My living room has blue walls, a white ceiling, and an oval window across from the door." You will mentally represent this information as propositions about how the concepts "wall," "blue," "ceiling," "white," "door," "oval," and "window" are related. However, you will also combine these propositions to create in your mind a three-dimensional model of the room. As more information about the world becomes avail-able, either from existing memories or from new information we receive, our mental models become more complete.

Accurate mental models are excellent guides for thinking about, and interacting with, many of the things we encounter every day (Johnson-Laird, 2010). If our mental models are incorrect, however, we are likely to make mistakes (e.g., Michael, Garry, & Kirsch, 2012; see Figure 7.6). For example, college students conduct more effective online searches while shopping or consulting academic databases if their mental models of search engines recognize that those search engines require precise search terms. Students who think that human operators read and interpret the meaning of the search terms they enter are less likely to use precise terms and thus less likely to get useful results (Holman, 2011). Similarly, people who hold an incorrect mental model of how physical illness is cured might stop taking their antibiotic medication when their symptoms begin to disappear, well before the bacteria causing those symptoms have been eliminated (Medin, Ross, & Markman, 2001). Others overdose on medication because according to their faulty mental model, "if taking three pills a day is good, taking six would be even better."

Images and Cognitive Maps

Think about how your best friend would look in a clown suit. The mental picture you just got illustrates that thinking often involves the manipulation of **images**—mental repre-sentations of visual information. We can manipulate these images in a way that is similar to manipulating the objects themselves (Reed, 2000; Trickett, Trafton, & Schunn, 2009; see Figure 7.7). Our ability to think using images extends beyond the manipulation of stimuli such as those in Figure 7.7. We also create mental images that serve as mental models of descriptions we hear or read (Mazoyer et al., 2002). For example, you probably created an image a minute ago when you read about that blue-walled room.

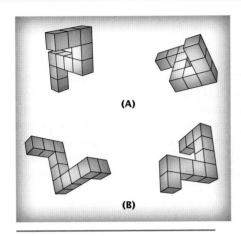

FIGURE 7.7
Manipulating Images

TRY THIS Are these pairs of objects the same or different? To decide, you will have to rotate one member of each pair. Manipulating mental images, like manipulating actual objects, takes time, so the speed of your decision will depend on how far you have to mentally rotate one object to line it up with the other for comparison. (The top pair matches; the bottom pair does not.)

The same thing happens when someone gives you directions to a new pizza place in town. In this case, you scan your **cognitive map**—a mental model of familiar parts of your world—to find the location. In doing so, you use a mental process similar to the visual process of scanning a Google map (Anderson, 2000; Hölscher, Tenbrink, & Wiener, 2011; Taylor & Tversky, 1992). Manipulating images on a different cognitive map would help you if a power failure left your home pitch dark. Even though you couldn't see a thing, you could still find a flashlight or a candle because your cognitive map would show the floor plan, furniture placement, door locations, and other physical features of your home. You would not have this mental map in a hotel room or an unfamiliar house; there, you would have to walk slowly, arms outstretched, to avoid wrong turns and painful collisions. In the chapter on learning, we describe how experience shapes cognitive maps that help animals navigate mazes and people navigate shopping malls. ("In Review: Ingredients of Thought" summarizes the ways we mentally represent information.)

IN REVIEW

INGREDIENTS OF THOUGHT

Ingredient	Description	Examples
Concepts	Categories of objects, events, or ideas with common properties; basic building blocks of thought	"Square" (a formal concept); "game" (a natural concept)
Propositions	Mental representations that express relationships between concepts; can be true or false	Assertions such as "The cow jumped over the moon."
Schemas	Sets of propositions that create generalizations and expectations about categories of objects, places, events, and people	A schema might suggest that all grandmothers are elderly, have gray hair, and bake a lot of cookies.
Scripts	Schemas about familiar activities and situations that guide behavior in those situations	You pay before eating in fast-food restaurants and after eating in fancier restaurants.
Mental models	Representations of how concepts relate to each other in the real world; can be correct or incorrect	Mistakenly assuming that airflow around an open car will send thrown objects upward, a driver tosses a lighted cigarette butt overhead, causing it to land in the back seat.
Images	Mental representations of visual information	Hearing a description of your blind date creates a mental picture of him or her.
Cognitive maps	Mental representations of familiar parts of the world	You can get to class by an alternate route even if your usual route is blocked by construction.

images Mental representations of visual information.

cognitive map A mental model that represents familiar parts of the environment.

In Review Questions

1. Thinking is the manipulation of _____.

2. Arguments over what is "fair" occur because "fairness" is a _____ concept.

3. Your _____ of "hotel room" would lead you to expect yours to include a bathroom.

THINKING STRATEGIES

Do people always think logically?

We have seen that our thinking capacity is based largely on our ability to manipulate mental representations—the ingredients of thought—much as a baker manipulates the ingredients of cookies. The baker's food-processing system combines and transforms these ingredients into a delicious treat. Our information-processing system combines, transforms, and elaborates mental representations in ways that allow us to engage in reasoning, problem solving, and decision making. Let's begin our discussion of these thinking strategies by considering **reasoning**: the process through which we generate and evaluate arguments, as well as reach conclusions about them.

Formal Reasoning

Astronomers tell us that the temperature at the core of the sun is about 27 million degrees Fahrenheit. How do they know this? They can't put a temperature probe inside the sun, so their estimate is based on *inferences* from other things that they know about the sun and about physical objects in general. For example, telescopic observations allowed astronomers to calculate the energy coming from one small part of the sun. They then used what geometry told them about the surface area of spheres to estimate the sun's total energy output. Further calculations told them how hot a body would have to be to generate that much energy.

In other words, astronomers' estimates of the sun's core temperature are based on **formal reasoning** (also called *logical reasoning*)—the process of following a set of rigorous steps intended to reach valid, or correct, conclusions. Some of these steps included applying specific mathematical formulas to existing data in order to generate new data. Such formulas are examples of **algorithms**—systematic methods that always reach a correct solution to a problem if a correct solution exists.

The astronomers also followed the rules of **logic**, a set of statements that provide a formula for drawing valid conclusions about the world. For example, each step in the astronomers' thinking took the form of if-then propositions: if we know how much energy comes from one part of the sun's surface and if we know how big the whole surface is, then we can calculate the total energy output. You use the same logical reasoning processes when you conclude, for example, that if your friend José is two years older than you are, then his twin brother, Juan, will be two years older, too. This kind of reasoning is called *deductive reasoning*, because it takes a general rule (e.g., twins are the same age) and applies it to deduce conclusions about specific cases (e.g., José and Juan).

Most of us try to use logical or deductive reasoning to reach valid conclusions and avoid invalid ones. However, even when our logic is perfect, we can make mistakes if we base our reasoning on false assumptions. Likewise, correct assumptions combined with faulty logic can lead to errors. Do you think the following example leads to a valid conclusion?

Assumption 1: *All women want to be mothers.*

Assumption 2: *Jill is a woman.*

Conclusion: *Jill wants to be a mother.*

If you said that the first assumption is not necessarily correct, you're right. Now consider this example:

Assumption 1: *All gun owners are people.*

Assumption 2: *All criminals are people.*

Conclusion: *All gun owners are criminals.*

Here, the assumptions are correct but the logic is faulty. According to the rules of logic, if "all As are B" and "all Cs are B," it does not follow that "all As are C." So it is true that all gun owners are people and that all criminals are people, but it does not follow that all gun owners are criminals.

reasoning The process by which people generate and evaluate arguments and reach conclusions about them.

formal reasoning A set of rigorous procedures for reaching valid conclusions.

algorithms Systematic procedures that cannot fail to produce a correct solution to a problem.

logic A system of formulas for drawing valid conclusions.

informal reasoning The process of evaluating a conclusion based on the evidence available to support it.

heuristics Mental shortcuts or rules of thumb.

So logical reasoning can fail because assumptions are wrong or because the logic applied to those assumptions is wrong. Psychologists have discovered that both kinds of pitfalls can lead people to make errors in logical reasoning. This finding is one reason that misleading advertisements or speeches can still attract sales and votes (Cialdini, 2007).

Informal Reasoning

Using the rules of formal logic to deduce answers about specific cases is an important kind of reasoning, but it is not the only kind. A second kind, **informal reasoning**, comes into play when we are trying to assess the *believability* of a conclusion based on the evidence available to support it. Informal reasoning is also known as *inductive reasoning*, because its goal is to induce a general conclusion to appear on the basis of specific facts or examples. Psychologists use informal reasoning when they design experiments and other research methods whose results will provide evidence for (or against) their hypotheses. Judges and jurors use informal reasoning when weighing evidence for the guilt or innocence of a defendant. Doctors use this type of thinking when they try to decide why a patient has a headache. And air crash investigators use it in their efforts to discover and eliminate the causes of aviation accidents.

Formal reasoning is guided by algorithms, or formulas, but there are no foolproof methods for informal reasoning. For instance, how many white swans would you have to see before concluding that all swans are white? Fifty? A hundred? A million? Formal logic would require that you observe every swan in existence. A more practical approach is to base your conclusion on the number of observations that some mental rule of thumb leads you to believe is enough. In other words, you would take a mental shortcut to reach a conclusion that is probably, but not necessarily, correct (there are, in fact, black swans). Such mental shortcuts are called **heuristics** (pronounced "hyoor-IST-ix").

Suppose that you are about to leave home but can't find your watch. Applying an algorithm would mean searching in every possible location, room by room, until you find the watch. But you can reach the same outcome more quickly by using a heuristic—that is, by searching only where your experience suggests you might have left the watch. In short, heuristics are often valuable in guiding judgments about which events are probable or which hypotheses are likely to be true. These "rules of thumb" are easy to use and frequently work well.

However, heuristics can also bias our thinking and result in errors. Suppose that your rule of thumb is to vote for all the candidates in a particular political party instead of researching the views of each candidate. You might help elect someone with whom you strongly disagree on some issues. The extent to which heuristics are responsible for important errors in judgment and decision making is a matter of continuing research and debate by cognitive psychologists (e.g., Deng & Sloutsky, 2012; Hilbert, 2012; Keysar, Hayakawa, & An, 2012; Weaver, Vandello, & Bosson, 2012), and awareness of their potentially biasing influences has caused reexamination of decision-making processes in many fields, including medicine and economics (e.g., Handgraaf & Van Raaij, 2005; Kahneman & Shane, 2005; Slovic et al., 2005).

Pitfalls in Logical Reasoning

"Elderly people cannot be Antarctic explorers; this is an elderly man; therefore, he cannot be an Antarctic explorer." The logic is correct, but because the first statement is wrong, so is the conclusion. In 1929, Norman Vaughan reached the South Pole as part of Richard Byrd's team of Antarctic explorers. Here he is in 1994, at the age of 88, after climbing Antarctica's Mount Vaughan, a mountain named for him.

Gordon Wiltsie/National Geographic Creative

Formal reasoning follows the rules of logic, but there are no foolproof rules for informal reasoning, as this fool demonstrates.

Amos Tversky and Daniel Kahneman (1974; 1993) have described three potentially problematic heuristics that often affect people's judgments. These are the *anchoring heuristic* (also known as *anchoring bias*), the *representativeness heuristic,* and the *availability heuristic.*

The Anchoring Bias

People use the **anchoring bias** (or **anchoring heuristic**) when they estimate the probability of some event by adjusting their existing estimate rather than starting from scratch, on the basis of new information (Furnham & Boo, 2011; Rottenstreich & Tversky, 1997). This strategy sounds reasonable, but their existing estimate biases their final judgment. So even if new information suggests that their first estimate is way off, people may not adjust that estimate enough. It is as if they have dropped a "mental anchor" that keeps them from drifting too far from their original judgment. For example, suppose you think that the chance of being mugged in Los Angeles is 90 percent, but then you see evidence to suggest that the figure is closer to 1 percent. Since you started your estimate at 90 percent, though, you might reduce your original estimate only to, say, 80 percent, so your new estimate would still be quite inaccurate. The anchoring heuristic presents a challenge for defense attorneys in U.S. criminal courts because the prosecution presents its evidence first. Once this evidence has created the impression that a defendant is guilty, some jurors mentally anchor to that impression and may not be swayed much by defense evidence to the contrary (Greene & Loftus, 1998; Hogarth & Einhorn, 1992). In a similar way, first impressions of people are not easily shifted by later evidence (see the chapter on social psychology).

The Representativeness Heuristic

People use the **representativeness heuristic** when they conclude that something belongs in a certain class based on how similar it is to other items in that class. For example, consider this personality sketch:

> *Tom W. is of high intelligence although lacking in true creativity. He has a need for order and clarity and for neat and tidy systems in which every detail finds its appropriate place. His writing is rather dull and mechanical, occasionally enlivened by somewhat corny puns and by flashes of imagination of the sci-fi type. He has a strong drive for competence. He seems to have little feeling and little sympathy for other people and does not enjoy interacting with others. Self-centered, he nonetheless has a deep moral sense.*

Do you think Tom is majoring in computer science or psychology? Research by Kahneman and Tversky (1973; Tversky & Kahneman, 1974) showed that most people would choose *computer science.* But this answer would probably be wrong. True, the description given is more similar to the prototypical computer science major than to the prototypical psychology major. However, there are many more psychology majors than computer science majors in the world. So there are probably more psychology majors than computer science majors who match this description. In fact, almost any personality sketch is more likely to describe a psychology major than a computer science major.

The representativeness heuristic affects many real-life judgments and decisions. For example, when jurors hear an expert witness presenting technical or scientific evidence, they are supposed to consider only the validity of the evidence itself, not the characteristics of the person presenting it. However, they're more likely to be persuaded by the evidence if the witness looks and acts in ways that are representative of the "expert" category (Bornstein & Greene, 2011; McAuliff, Kovera, & Nuñez, 2008). (See the chapter on social psychology for more on the role of communicator characteristics in persuasion.)

The Availability Heuristic

People use the **availability heuristic** when they judge the likelihood of an event or the correctness of a hypothesis by how easy it is to think of that event or hypothesis (Tversky & Kahneman, 1974). In other words, they tend to choose the hypothesis or predict the event

Anchoring to a Price

The anchoring heuristic operates in many bargaining situations. The asking price of this house, for example, has probably anchored the sellers' perception of its value. As a result, they may be reluctant to accept a lower price, even if their sales agent suggests that they should. The buyers' judgment of the house's value will also be anchored to some extent by the seller's asking price. Even if the buyers discover that the house needs some repairs, they are more likely to offer 90 percent of the price rather than 50 percent.

Jason Homa/The Image Bank/Getty Images

anchoring bias (anchoring heuristic) A shortcut in the thought process that involves adding new information to existing information to reach a judgment.

representativeness heuristic A mental shortcut that involves judging whether something belongs in a given class on the basis of its similarity to other members of that class.

availability heuristic A mental shortcut through which judgments are based on information that is most easily brought to mind.

that is most mentally "available," much as they might select the box of cereal that happens to be at the front of a supermarket shelf. Although the availability heuristic tends to work well, it too can lead to biased judgments—especially when the mental availability of events doesn't match their actual frequency (Morewedge, Gilbert, & Wilson, 2005). For example, news reports about shark attacks and urban shootings lead many people to overestimate how often these memorable but relatively rare events actually occur (Courtenay, Smith, & Gladstone, 2012; Ungemach, Chater, & Stewart, 2009). As a result, people may suffer undue anxiety over swimming in the ocean or being in certain cities (Bellaby, 2003). Similarly, many students stick with their first responses to multiple-choice test questions because it is especially easy to recall those galling occasions on which they changed a right answer to a wrong one. Research shows, though, that an answer that is changed in light of further reflection is more likely to be correct than incorrect (Kruger, Wirtz, & Miller, 2005; Skinner, 2009).

The three heuristics we have presented represent only a few of the many mental shortcuts that people use more or less automatically in making judgments in daily life (Todd & Gigerenzer, 2007), and they describe only some of the biases and limitations that operate in human reasoning. Other biases and limitations are described in the following sections, as we consider two important goals of thinking: problem solving and decision making.

PROBLEM SOLVING

What's the best way to solve a problem?

Suppose that you're lost, you don't have a cell phone or a GPS, and there's nobody around to ask for directions. You have a *problem*. The circle of thought suggests that the most efficient approach to solving it would be to first diagnose the problem in the elaboration stage, then formulate a plan for solving it, then execute the plan, and finally evaluate the results to determine whether the problem remains (Bransford & Stein, 1993). But people's problem-solving efforts are not always so systematic. This is one reason why medical tests are sometimes given unnecessarily, diseases are sometimes misdiagnosed, and auto parts are sometimes replaced when there is nothing wrong with them (Mamede et al., 2010).

Strategies for Problem Solving

When you're trying to get from one place to another, the best path may not necessarily be a straight line. In fact, obstacles may require going in the opposite direction to get around them. So it is with problem solving. Sometimes the best strategy doesn't involve mental steps aimed straight at your goal. Psychologists have identified a variety of strategies that people use when solving a problem (Marewski & Schooler, 2011). For example, when a problem is especially difficult, it can sometimes be helpful to allow it to "incubate" by setting it aside for a while. A solution that once seemed out of reach may suddenly appear after you have been thinking about other things. The benefits of *incubation* probably arise from forgetting incorrect ideas that may have been blocking the path to a correct and possibly creative solution (Koppel & Storm, 2014). Other effective problem-solving strategies are more direct.

One of these strategies is called *means-end analysis*. It involves continuously asking where you are in relation to your final goal and then deciding on the means by which you can get one step closer to that goal (Newell & Simon, 1972). In other words, rather than trying to solve the problem all at once, you identify a subgoal that will take you toward a solution (this process is also referred to as *decomposition*). After reaching that subgoal, you identify another one that will get you even closer to the solution, and you continue this step-by-step process until the problem is solved. Some students apply this approach to the problem of writing a major term paper. The task might seem overwhelming at first, but their first subgoal is simply to write an outline of what they think the paper should cover. When the outline is complete, they decide whether a paper based on it will satisfy the assignment. If it will, the next subgoal might be to search the library and the Internet for information about each section. If they decide that this information is adequate, the next subgoal would be to write a rough draft of the introduction, and so on.

Simply knowing about problem-solving strategies, such as decomposition, is not enough. As described in the chapter on motivation and emotion, people must believe that the effort required is worth the rewards it can bring.

Working Backward to Forge Ahead

Whether you are organizing a family vacation or preparing to sail alone around the world, as sixteen-year-old Laura Dekker did, working backward from the final goal through all the steps necessary to reach that goal is a helpful approach to solving complex problems.

Jerry Lampen/epa/Corbis

A second strategy in problem solving is to *work backward.* Many problems are like a tree. The trunk is the information you are given; the solution is a twig on one of the branches. If you work forward by taking the "givens" of the problem and trying to find the solution, it's easy to branch off in the wrong direction. Sometimes the more efficient approach is to start at the twig end and work backward (Galotti, 1999b). Consider the problem of planning a climb to the summit of Mount Everest. The best strategy is to figure out, first, what equipment and supplies are needed at the highest camp on the night before the attempt to reach the summit, then how many people are needed to stock that camp the day before, then how many people are needed to supply those who must stock the camp, and so on until a plan for the entire expedition is established. People often overlook the working-backward strategy because it runs counter to the way they have learned to think. It is hard to imagine that the first step in solving a problem could be to assume that you have already solved it. It is partly because of failure to apply this strategy that climbers sometimes die on Everest (Krakauer, 1997).

A third problem-solving strategy is trying to find *analogies,* or similarities, between today's problem and others you have encountered before. A supervisor may discover that a seemingly hopeless problem between co-workers can be resolved by the same compromise that worked during a recent family squabble. Of course, to take advantage of analogies, you must first recognize the similarities between current and previous problems. Then you will be in a position to recall the solution that worked before. Unfortunately, most people are surprisingly poor at seeing the similarities between new and old problems (Anderson, 2000). They tend to concentrate on the surface features that make problems appear different. But, research shows that if you practice focusing on the ways in which different problems may have similarities, you can get better at this skill over time, leading to better problem-solving success in new situations (Nokes-Malach et al., 2013).

FOCUS ON RESEARCH METHODS

PROBLEM-SOLVING STRATEGIES IN THE REAL WORLD

How do people use the problem-solving strategies we have described to solve real-world problems? To explore this question, researchers have reconstructed problem-solving strategies associated with major inventions and scientific discoveries (Klahr & Simon, 1999; Weber, 1992).

What was the researcher's question?

On December 17, 1903, Wilbur and Orville Wright successfully flew the first heavier-than-air flying machine. Gary Bradshaw (1993a, 1993b) was interested in identifying the problem-solving strategies that led to this momentous event. He found that 49 individuals or teams

(continued)

had worked on the problem of heavier-than-air flight, but only the Wright brothers were successful. In fact, it took them only four years to develop the airplane, whereas others worked for decades without success. Bradshaw asked himself how the Wright brothers solved the problem of creating a heavier-than-air flying machine when so many others had failed?

How did the researcher answer the question?

Bradshaw compared the written records left by all the individuals and teams who had worked on an airplane design. Using this *comparative case study* method, he was able to see patterns in the ways they approached the flying machine problem.

What did the researcher find?

Bradshaw found several factors that might have contributed to the Wright brothers' success. First, as bachelors, they had a lot of spare time to work on their designs. Second, they owned a bicycle shop, so they were familiar with lightweight but sturdy structures. Third, they were brothers who had a good working relationship. And finally, as mechanics, they were good with their hands. Were any of these features directly responsible for their successful invention of the airplane?

Perhaps, but Bradshaw's use of the comparative case study method revealed that everyone else working on the problem of flight shared at least one of these features with the Wright brothers. For instance, an engineer named Octave Chanute was good with his hands and familiar with lightweight, sturdy structures. And two other pairs of brothers had worked together to try to invent a flying machine.

However, Bradshaw found one feature that was unique to the Wright brothers' approach. Of all the inventors working on the problem, only the Wrights spent considerable time and energy testing aircraft components before field-testing complete machines. This feature was important because even the best designs of the day flew for only a few seconds—far too briefly to reveal what was working and what was not. As a result, inventors had to guess about what to fix and often ended up with an "improved" model that was worse than the previous one.

What do the results mean?

Bradshaw's comparative case study method suggested that the problem-solving strategy of decomposition was the basis for the Wright brothers' success. By testing components, they were able to collect the information they needed to develop an efficient propeller, improve the shape of the wings for maximum lift, and refine other vital components of their aircraft.

What do we still need to know?

Decomposition is a strategy often seen in the laboratory, and as demonstrated by the case of the Wright brothers, it is a potentially important aspect of major inventions and discoveries beyond the laboratory. But is decomposition, or means-end analysis, used in other real-world settings as well? To find out, researchers will need to conduct additional studies of the mental strategies people use as they attempt to solve problems ranging from how to install a new computer to how to efficiently search the Internet.

Obstacles to Problem Solving

The failure of the Wright brothers' competitors to use decomposition is just one example of the obstacles that problem solvers encounter every day. Difficulties frequently occur at the start, during the diagnosis stage, when a person forms and then tests hypotheses about a problem.

As a case in point, consider this true story: John Gatiss was in the kitchen of his rented house in Cheltenham, England, when he heard a faint "meowing" sound. Worried that a kitten had become trapped somewhere, he called for the fire brigade to rescue the animal. The sound seemed to be coming from the electric stove, so the rescuers dismantled it, disconnecting the power cord in the process. The sound stopped, but everyone assumed that wherever the kitten was, it was now too frightened to meow. The search was reluctantly abandoned and the stove was reconnected. Four days later, however, the meowing began anew. This time, Gatiss and his landlord called the Royal Society for the Prevention of Cruelty to Animals (RSPCA), whose inspectors heard the kitten in distress and asked the fire brigade to come back. They spent the next three days searching for the cat. First, they dismantled parts of the kitchen walls and ripped up the floorboards. Next, they called in plumbing and drainage specialists, who used cables tipped with fiber-optic cameras to search remote cavities where a kitten might hide. Rescuers then brought in a disaster search team, which tried to find the kitten with acoustic and ultrasonic equipment normally used to locate victims trapped under earthquake debris. Not a sound was heard. Increasingly concerned about how much longer the kitten could survive, the fire brigade tried to coax it from hiding with the finest-quality fish, but to no avail. Suddenly, there was a burst of "purring" that, to everyone's surprise (and the landlord's dismay), was traced by the ultrasonic equipment to the clock in the electric stove! Later, the landlord commented that everyone assumed Gatiss's original hypothesis was correct—that the "meowing" came from a cat trapped in the kitchen. "I just let them carry on. If there is an animal in there, you have to do what it takes. The funniest thing was that it seemed to reply when we called out to it" (*London Daily Telegraph*, 1998).

How could fifteen fire-rescue workers, three RSPCA inspectors, four drainage workers, and two acoustics experts waste eight days and cause thousands of dollars in damage to a house in pursuit of a nonexistent kitten? The answer lies in the fact that they, like the rest of us, were prone to the four main obstacles to efficient problem solving described in the following sections.

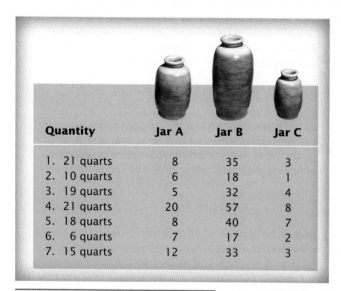

FIGURE 7.8
The Jar Problem

TRY THIS   The task here is to come up with the number of quarts of water shown in the first column by using jars with the capacities shown in the next three columns. Each line represents a different problem and you have an unlimited supply of water for each one. Try to solve all seven problems without looking at the answers in the text.

Melvyn Longhurst/Alamy

Quantity	Jar A	Jar B	Jar C
1. 21 quarts	8	35	3
2. 10 quarts	6	18	1
3. 19 quarts	5	32	4
4. 21 quarts	20	57	8
5. 18 quarts	8	40	7
6. 6 quarts	7	17	2
7. 15 quarts	12	33	3

Multiple Hypotheses

Often we begin to solve a problem with only a hazy notion of which hypotheses to test. Suppose you heard a strange sound in your kitchen. It could be caused by several different things, but which hypotheses should you test, and in what order?

People have a difficult time working with more than two or three hypotheses at a time (Mehle, 1982). The limited capacity of short-term memory may be part of the reason (Halford et al., 2005). As discussed in the memory chapter, a person can hold only about seven chunks of information in short-term memory. Because a single hypothesis, let alone two or three, might include more than seven chunks, it may be difficult or impossible to keep them all in mind at once. Further, the availability and representativeness heuristics may lead people to choose the hypothesis that comes most easily to mind and seems most likely to fit the circumstances (Tversky & Kahneman, 1974). That hypothesis may be wrong, though, meaning that the correct hypothesis is never considered (Bilalić, McLeod, & Gobet, 2010). Mr. Gatiss diagnosed what he heard as distressed meowing because it sounded more like a kitten than a clock and because it was easier to imagine an animal trapped behind the stove than a suddenly faulty clock inside it.

Mental Sets

Sometimes people are so blinded by one hypothesis or strategy that they stick with it even when better alternatives should be obvious. This is a clear case of the anchoring heuristic at work. Once Gatiss reported hearing a "trapped kitten," his description created an assumption that everyone else accepted and no one challenged. Figure 7.8 shows a problem-solving situation in which such errors often appear. The first problem in the figure is to come up with 21 quarts of liquid by using 3 jars that have capacities of 8, 35, and 3 quarts, respectively. Before you read any further, try to solve this problem and all the others listed in Figure 7.8.

FIGURE 7.9

The Nine-Dot Problem

TRY THIS Draw four straight lines that run through all nine dots on the page without lifting your pen or pencil from the paper. Figure 7.11 shows how to go beyond mental sets to solve this problem.

FIGURE 7.10

An Example of Functional Fixedness

TRY THIS Before reading further, look at this image and ask yourself how you would fasten together two strings that are hanging from the ceiling but are too far apart for you to grasp at the same time. Several tools are available, yet most people don't think of attaching, say, a hammer to one string and swinging it like a pendulum until it can be reached while holding the other string. This solution is not obvious because we tend to fixate on the hammer's function as a tool rather than as a weight. People are more likely to solve this problem if the tools are scattered around the room. If the hammer is in a toolbox, its function as a tool is emphasized, and functional fixedness becomes nearly impossible to break.

© Bill Altman

mental set The tendency for old patterns of problem solving to persist.

functional fixedness The tendency to think about familiar objects in familiar ways.

How did you do? You probably figured out that the solution to the first problem is to fill Jar B to its capacity of 35 quarts, and then use its contents to fill Jar A to its capacity of 8 quarts, leaving 27 quarts in Jar B. Finally, you pour from Jar B to fill Jar C twice, leaving 21 quarts in Jar B [$27 - (2 \times 3) = 21$]. You probably found that a similar solution worked for each problem. In fact, by the time you reached Problem 7, you might have developed a **mental set**, a tendency for old patterns of problem solving to persist (Luchins, 1942; Sweller & Gee, 1978). If so, your mental set probably caused you to use the same old formula (B − A − 2C) even though a simpler one (A + C) would have worked just as well. Figures 7.9 and 7.11 show another way in which mental sets can restrict our perception of the possible solutions to a problem.

Another restriction on problem solving may come from experience with objects. Once people become familiar with using an object for one purpose, they may be blinded to other ways of using it. Long experience may produce **functional fixedness**, a tendency to use familiar objects in familiar rather than creative ways (German & Barrett, 2005). Figure 7.10 provides an example. An incubation strategy often helps to break mental sets.

Ignoring Negative Evidence

On September 26, 1983, Lt. Col. Stanislav Petrov was in command of a secret facility that analyzed information from Russian early-warning satellites. Suddenly alarms went off as computers found evidence that five U.S. missiles were being launched toward Russia. Tension between the two countries was high at the time, so based on the availability heuristic, Petrov hypothesized that a nuclear attack was under way. He was about to alert his superiors to launch a counterattack on the United States when it occurred to him that if this were a real nuclear attack, it would involve many more than five missiles. Fortunately for everyone, he realized that the "attack" was a false alarm (Hoffman, 1999). As this near-disaster shows, the *absence* of symptoms or events can sometimes provide important evidence for or against a hypothesis. Compared with evidence that is present, however, symptoms or events that do not occur are less likely to be noticed (Hunt & Rouse, 1981). People have a difficult time using the absence of evidence to help eliminate hypotheses from consideration (Hyman, 2002). In the "trapped kitten" case, when the "meowing" stopped for several days after the stove was unplugged and reconnected, rescuers assumed that the animal was frightened into silence. They ignored the possibility that their hypothesis was incorrect in the first place.

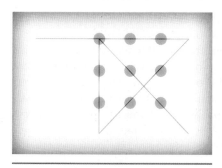

FIGURE 7.11
A Creative Solution to the
Nine-Dot Problem

TRY THIS Many people find problems
like this difficult because mental sets create artificial limits on the range of solutions. In this case, the mental set involves
the tendency to draw within the frame of
the dots. As shown here, however, there
are other possibilities.

confirmation bias The tendency
to pay more attention to evidence
in support of one's hypothesis
about a problem than to evidence
that refutes that hypothesis.

Confirmation Bias

Anyone who has had a series of medical tests knows that diagnosis is not a one-shot affair. Instead, physicians choose their first hypothesis on the basis of observed symptoms—perhaps the most dramatic or obvious ones—and then order tests or evaluate additional symptoms to support or eliminate that hypothesis (Kwan et al., 2012; Trillin, 2001). This process can be distorted by a **confirmation bias**: Humans have a strong bias to confirm rather than reject a hypothesis they have chosen, even in the face of strong evidence against the hypothesis (Aronson, Wilson, & Akert, 2005; Groopman, 2007; Mendel et al., 2011). In other words, people are quite willing to perceive and accept data that support their hypothesis, but they tend to ignore information that is inconsistent with it (Groopman, 2000). Confirmation bias may be seen as a form of the anchoring heuristic. Once you've "anchored" to your first hypothesis, you may be reluctant to abandon it. The would-be rescuers of John Gatiss's "trapped kitten" were so intent on their efforts to pinpoint its location that they never stopped to question its existence. Similarly, as described in the chapter on social psychology, we tend to look for and pay extra attention to information that is consistent with our first impressions of other people. This tendency can create positive or negative bias in, say, a teacher's views of children's cognitive abilities or an interviewer's judgments of a job candidate's skills (Jussim & Eccles, 1992; Reich, 2004).

Confirmation bias can also serve to perpetuate and intensify differences of opinion. People often get their news from media outlets that support their own political views, and they pay more attention to areas of discord than to areas of agreement when talking to individuals who hold differing views (Jern, Chang, & Kemp, 2014; Wojcieszak & Price, 2010). With this phenomenon in mind, some psychologists have developed programs designed to reduce the confirmation bias that can impair communication on "hot button" issues (Lilienfeld, Ammirati, & Landfield, 2009). Confirmation bias is also a concern in criminal cases because it can lead people to see evidence as "proving" a suspect's guilt even though that suspect might actually be innocent (Kassin, Dror, & Kukucka, 2013). The National Academy of Science's *Committee on Identifying the Needs of the Forensic Sciences Community* (2009) has pointed out that such cognitive biases have led to wrongful arrests and convictions in the United States criminal justice system, and has made recommendations for procedures aimed at avoiding such outcomes.

Building Problem-Solving Skills

How do experts in any field avoid some of the obstacles that normally limit problem solving? What do they bring to a situation that a beginner does not? Knowledge based on experience is particularly important (Mayer, 1992). One way that they develop this knowledge is through deliberate practice, solving progressively more difficult problems and forming ever more accurate mental models over a long period of time (Campitelli & Gobet, 2008, 2011; Plant & Stanton, 2012). Using that knowledge, experts frequently proceed by looking for similarities or analogies between current and past problems. Their experience makes experts better than beginners at identifying the common principles that underlie seemingly different problems. Experts' superior ability to link information about a new problem to what they already know (Anderson, 1995) also allows them to organize information about a problem into manageable and memorable *chunks,* a process described in the chapter on memory (Jaušovec & Jaušovec, 2012). By chunking many elements of a problem into a smaller number of units, experts are better than beginners at visualizing problems clearly and efficiently (Reingold et al., 2001). Their experience also helps experts to stay calm while working on a problem, thus reducing the emotion-related disruptions in cognitive skills often seen in nonexperts under stress (Decety, Yang, & Cheng, 2010; Worthy et al., 2011).

It is no wonder, then, that experts are often better problem solvers than beginners, but their expertise also carries a danger: Extensive experience may create mental sets. Top-down, knowledge-driven processes can bias experts toward seeing what they expect or want to see and prevent them from seeing a problem in new ways (Dror, 2011). As in the case of the "trapped kitten," confirmation bias sometimes prevents experts from appreciating that a proposed solution is incorrect. Several studies have shown that although experts may be more confident in their solutions (Payne, Bettman, & Johnson, 1992), they are not always more accurate than others in such areas as medical diagnosis, accounting, pilot judgment, and predicting political events (Sibbald, Panisko, & Cavalcanti, 2011; Stiegler et al., 2012; Tetlock, 2006). In other words, there is a fine line between using past experience and being trapped by it. Experience alone does not ensure excellence at problem solving, and practice may not make perfect. (For a summary of problem solving and its pitfalls, see "In Review: Solving Problems.")

		IN REVIEW
SOLVING PROBLEMS		

Steps	Pitfalls	Remedies
Define the problem.	Inexperience: the tendency to see each problem as unique.	Gain experience and practice in seeing the similarity between present problems and previous problems.
Form hypotheses about solutions.	Availability heuristic: the tendency to recall the hypothesis or solution that is most available to memory.	Force yourself to write down and carefully consider many different hypotheses.
	Anchoring bias, or mental set: the tendency to anchor on the first solution or hypothesis and not adjust your beliefs in light of new evidence or failures of the current approach.	Break the mental set, stop, and try a fresh approach.
Test hypotheses.	The tendency to ignore negative evidence.	In evaluating a hypothesis, consider the things you should see (but don't) if the hypothesis is true.
	Confirmation bias: the tendency to seek only evidence that confirms your hypothesis.	Look for disconfirming evidence that, if found, would show your hypothesis to be false.

In Review Questions

1. People stranded without water could use their shoes to collect rain, but they may not do so because of an obstacle to problem solving called _____.

2. Because of the _____ heuristic, once sellers set a value on their house, they may refuse to take much less for it.

3. If you tackle a massive problem one small step at a time, you are using an approach called _____.

Problem Solving by Computer

Researchers have created artificial limbs, retinas, cochleas, and even hearts to help people with disabilities move, see, hear, and live more normally. They are also developing artificial brains in the form of computer systems that not only see, hear, and manipulate objects but also reason and solve problems. These systems are the product of research in **artificial intelligence (AI)**, a field that seeks to develop computers that imitate the processes of human perception and thought.

artificial intelligence (AI) The field that studies how to program computers to imitate the products of human perception, understanding, and thought.

Symbolic Reasoning and Computer Logic

Chess-playing artificial intelligence systems have won games against the world's best chess masters. This result is not surprising, because chess is a clearly defined, logical game at which computers can perform effectively. However, it is precisely their reliance on logic and formulas that accounts for the shortcomings of all the artificial intelligence systems developed so far (Dowe & Hernández-Orallo, 2012). For example, these systems are successful only in narrowly defined fields, not in general problem solving. This limitation stems from the fact that AI systems are based on logical symbolic manipulations that depend on if-then rules. Unfortunately, it is difficult to tell a computer how to recognize the "if" condition in the real world (Dreyfus & Dreyfus, 1988). Consider this simple if-then rule: "If it is a clock, then set it." Humans recognize all kinds of clocks because we are good at using the natural concept of "clock," but computers are still not very good at forming natural concepts. Doing so requires putting into the same category many examples that have very different physical features, from your bedside digital alarm clock to London's Big Ben. The fact that computers cannot yet do this allows online businesses to protect themselves from potentially dangerous computer programs that pose as human customers. So when ordering something online, you may be shown a set of distorted, odd-looking letters and numbers and then be asked to type them. By doing so, you are proving that you are a human being, not a computer.

Neural Network Models

Recognizing the problems posed by the need to teach computers to form natural concepts, many researchers in AI have moved toward a connectionist, or neural network, approach. This approach uses computers to simulate the information processing taking place at many different but interconnected locations in the brain. Neural network models have helped researchers develop computers that are able to recognize voices, understand speech, read print, guide missiles, and perform many other complex tasks (Ashcraft, 2006). Some of the newest of these computer systems are even capable of recognizing and expressing certain basic emotions (e.g., D'Mello & Graesser, 2010; Velik, 2010; Yang & Wang, 2011).

Applications of connectionist research in AI are all around us. It is being used to improve the speech recognition software that allows us to interact with our smartphones and GPS navigation systems through voice commands (Nasoz, Lisetti, & Vasilakos, 2010). Apple has even attempted to create a sense of humor for Siri, the assistance service in its iPhone (Fowler, Sherr, & Troianovski, 2011). Other AI systems help people with disabilities and medical conditions to remain more independent (e.g., Boger & Mihailidis, 2011; Chittaro et al., 2011). Still others have been used to improve on human decision making; AI systems have been found superior to humans in making decisions in areas ranging from judging meat quality and running credit checks to detecting credit card fraud, and diagnosing and prescribing treatment for various medical conditions (e.g., Başçiftçi & Hatay, 2011; Chen et al., 2012; Faisal, Taib, & Ibrahim, 2012; Keleş, Keleş, & Yavuz, 2011; Wong et al., 2012).

"Intelligent" Internet search engines such as Google are also based on neural network models, as are the systems that guide you to the news items, films, books, and other material that your previous online activity suggests will be of greatest interest to you. Artificial intelligence systems are also at the heart of interactive learning programs that not only present course material but adjust the content and pace of instruction to match each student's abilities and understanding (e.g., Bakardjieva & Gercheva, 2011; Corbett et al., 2010; Gaudioso, Montero, & Hernandez-del-Olmo, 2012; Hsu, & Ho, 2012). Some researchers are even hoping to develop computers that can grade papers and evaluate other complex student work (Nehm Ha, & Mayfield, 2012; Nehm & Haertig, 2012).

Artificial Intelligence

Artificial intelligence systems such as IBM's Deep Blue have been able to win chess games against the world's best competitors, and AI researchers hope to have the same success someday against champion players of the ancient Chinese board game called Go (Harré et al., 2011). Still, even the most sophisticated computers cannot perceive and think about the world in general anywhere near as well as humans can. Some observers believe that this situation will eventually change as progress in computer technology—and a deepening understanding of human cognitive processes—leads to dramatic breakthroughs in artificial intelligence.

Unfortunately, however, most computer models of neural networks still fall well short of the capacities of the human perceptual system. For example, computers are slow to learn how to classify visual patterns, which has led to disappointment in efforts to develop computerized face recognition systems capable of identifying terrorists and other criminals in public places (Feder, 2004; Fleuret et al., 2011). But even though neural networks are far from perfect "thinking machines," they are sure to play an important role in psychologists' efforts to build ever more intelligent systems and to better understand the principles of human problem solving (Gamez, 2008; Schapiro & McClelland, 2009).

One approach to overcoming the limitations of both computers and humans is to have them work together in ways that create a better outcome than either could achieve alone. In medical diagnosis, for example, the human's role is to establish the presence and nature of a patient's symptoms. The computer then combines this information in a completely unbiased way to identify the most likely diagnosis (Roy et al., 2009; Swets, Dawes, & Monahan, 2000). This kind of human-machine teamwork can also help in the assessment of psychological problems (Kramer, Bernstein, & Phares, 2014).

Creative Thinking

One of the greatest challenges in the development of artificial intelligence will be to program devices that can think and solve problems as creatively as humans. Consider the case that opened this chapter. It was Dr. Wallace's knowledge of the chemicals in paint—which has no obvious connection to human body chemistry—that led her to figure out what was causing Laura McBride's illness. Computers are still not nearly as good as humans are at recognizing that information from one area can be used to solve a problem in a seemingly unrelated area. The ability to blend knowledge from many different domains is only one aspect of the creative thinking that humans display every day. People demonstrate **creativity** by producing original but useful solutions to all sorts of challenges (Simonton, 1999, 2004, 2012; Sternberg & Grigorenko, 2004a).

How do we know when people are thinking creatively? Psychologists have defined *creativity* as mental activity that can be inferred from performance on certain tests, as well as from the writings, computer programs, artwork, and other products resulting from the creative process (Sternberg & Dess, 2001). To measure creativity, some psychologists have generated tests of **divergent thinking**—the ability to think along many paths to generate multiple solutions to a problem (Diakidoy & Spanoudis, 2002). The Consequences Test is an example. It contains items such as "Imagine all of the things that might possibly happen if all national and local laws were suddenly abolished" (Guilford, 1959). Divergent-thinking tests are scored by counting the number of sensible responses that a person can give to each item and how many of these responses differ from those given by most people.

Only sensible responses to creativity tests are counted, because creativity involves divergent thinking that is appropriate for a given problem or situation. To be productive rather than just weird, a creative person must be firmly anchored in reality, understand society's needs, and learn from the experience and knowledge of others (Sternberg & Lubart, 1992). Theresa Amabile has identified three kinds of cognitive and personality characteristics necessary for creativity (Amabile, 1996; Amabile, Hennessey, & Grossman, 1986):

1. *Expertise* in the field of endeavor, which is directly tied to what a person has learned. For example, a painter or composer must know the paints, techniques, or instruments available.

Thinking Outside the Box

Psychological scientists are finding that people tend to think less creatively while in confined spaces or when their movements are restricted (Ambrosini, Sinigaglia, & Costantini, 2012; Goldin-Meadow & Beilock, 2010; Leung et al., 2012). Perhaps the boundaries that limit physical movement create psychological boundaries that—like the mental sets and functional fixedness discussed earlier—limit the options we consider when solving problems and developing new ideas. With this possibility in mind, many businesses today work with environmental psychologists to design workplaces that avoid the physical confinements of traditional office cubicles.

James Brittain/Corbis

creativity The capacity to produce original solutions or novel compositions.

divergent thinking The ability to generate many different solutions to a problem.

2. A set of *creative skills,* including persistence at problem solving, capacity for divergent thinking, ability to break out of old problem-solving habits (mental sets), and willingness to take risks. Amabile believes that training can influence many of these skills, some of which are closely linked to the strategies for problem solving discussed earlier.

3. The *motivation* to pursue creative work for internal reasons, such as satisfaction, rather than for external reasons, such as prize money. In fact, Amabile and her colleagues found that external rewards can deter creativity. They asked groups of children and adults to produce creative projects such as paintings or stories. Some were simply asked to work on these projects. Others were told that the projects would be judged for creativity and excellence and that rewards would be given or winners announced. Experts, who had no idea which products were created by which group, judged those from the "reward" group to be significantly less creative. Similar effects have been found in other studies (Byron & Khazanchi, 2012; Deci, Koestner, & Ryan, 2001; Murayama et al., 2010), though under some circumstances, rewarding people's creativity can strengthen it—in much the same way that positive reinforcement strengthens any other behavior (Eisenberger & Rhoades, 2001; Eisenberger & Shanock, 2003).

Is creativity inherited? To some extent, perhaps it is (Kéri, 2009; Lykken, 1998a), but evidence suggests that the social, economic, and political environment in which a person grows and lives also influences creative behavior (Amabile, 2001; Nakamura & Csikszentmihalyi, 2001). Do you have to be smart to be creative? Creativity does appear to require a certain degree of intelligence (Sternberg, 2001). For example, longitudinal studies have shown that individuals identified as particularly smart in adolescence were up to eight times more likely than other people to show creativity as adults by patenting inventions or producing scientific publications (Park, Lubinski, & Benbow, 2008; Wai, Lubinski, & Benbow, 2005). But you don't have to be a genius to be creative (Simonton, 1984, 2002; Sternberg, 2001). In fact, although correlations between scores on creativity tests and intelligence tests are almost always positive, they are relatively modest (Kim, 2008; Simonton, 1999). This finding is not surprising, because creativity involves divergent thinking about many solutions to a problem. As described later, high scores on most intelligence tests require **convergent thinking**, which uses logic and knowledge to narrow down the number of possible solutions to a problem. One result of research on this topic has been to see intelligence and creativity in the same person as contributing to the broader trait of *wisdom* (Baltes & Smith, 2008; Callahan, 2011; Sternberg, 2010).

The biological aspects of creativity are being investigated through the use of fMRI technology, which can identify the amount and location of brain activity that accompanies creative thinking (Chermahini & Hommel, 2010; Dietrich & Kanso, 2010). Other researchers are exploring the possibility of teaching creativity (e.g., Gupta et al., 2012; Jarosz, Colflesh, & Wiley, 2012). If it is successful, their work may someday enable all of us to think more creatively about life's problems, and perhaps about life in general (Glăveanu, 2012).

DECISION MAKING

How can I become a better decision maker?

Paper or plastic? Do I watch TV or study for the test? Should I get out of this relationship? Is it time to start thinking about a nursing home for Mom? Life is full of decisions. Some are quick and easy to make; others are painfully difficult and require considerable time, planning, and mental effort. Even carefully considered decisions can lead to undesirable outcomes, though, because the world is an uncertain place. Decisions made when the outcome is uncertain are called *risky decisions* or *decisions under uncertainty.* Chance aside, psychologists have discovered reasons why human decisions sometimes lead to unsatisfactory outcomes (Chandler & Pronin, 2012; Gifford, 2011). Let's consider some of these reasons.

convergent thinking The ability to apply the rules of logic and what one knows about the world to narrow down the possible solutions to a problem.

Analyzing your choices and the possible outcomes of each takes some time and effort, but the results are usually worth it. Like Dilbert's boss, many people prefer to make decisions more impulsively, and although their decisions sometimes turn out well, they often don't (Gladwell, 2005; Myers, 2004; Rubenwolf & Spörrle, 2011).

DILBERT: © Scott Adams/Dist. by United Feature Syndicate, Inc.

Evaluating Options

Suppose that you have to decide whether to pursue an academic major you love but that is less likely to lead to steady employment, or to choose a less interesting major that almost guarantees a high-paying job. The fact that each option has positive and negative features certainly complicates the decision making, doesn't it? Deciding which car to buy, which college to attend, or even how to spend the evening are all examples of choices that require you to weigh several options. Such choices are often based on the positive or negative value, or **utility**, that you place on each feature of each option. Listing the pros and cons of each option is a good way to keep them all in mind as you think about your decisions. You also have to estimate the probabilities and risks associated with the possible outcomes of each choice. For example, you must consider how likely it is that job opportunities in your chosen major will have faded by the time you graduate. In studying risky decision making, psychologists begin with the assumption that the best decision maximizes *expected value*. The **expected value** of a decision is the average benefit you could expect to receive if the decision were repeated on several occasions.

Biases and Flaws in Decision Making

Most people think of themselves as logical and rational, but in making decisions about everything from giving up smoking to investing in the stock market, they don't always act in ways that maximize expected value (Farmer, Patelli, & Zovko, 2005; Shiller, 2001; Tessari et al., 2011). Why not?

Gains, Losses, and Probabilities

For one thing, our pain over losing a certain amount is usually greater than the pleasure we feel after gaining the same amount (Kermer et al., 2006). This phenomenon is called *loss aversion* (Dawes, 1998; McGraw et al., 2010; Tversky & Kahneman, 1991). Because of loss aversion, you might go to more trouble to collect a $100 debt than to win a $100 prize. In addition, the value of a gain may not depend on the amount of the gain but on what you start with. Suppose you could have a $10 gift certificate from a restaurant but you would have to drive 10 miles to pick it up. This gain has the same monetary value as having an extra $10 added to your paycheck. However, most people tend to behave as if the difference between $0 and $10 is greater than the difference between, say, $300 and $310. So a person who won't drive across town after work to earn a $10 bonus on next week's paycheck might gladly make the same trip to pick up a $10 gift certificate. Understanding these biases and how they affect people's purchasing patterns and other economic decisions has proven so important that Daniel Kahneman received the 2002 Nobel Prize in economics for his research in this area.

People are also biased in how they think about probability. For example, we tend to overestimate the probability of rare events and to underestimate the probability of frequent ones (Kahneman & Tversky, 1984). This bias tends to be especially strong in relation to risky decisions (Glaser et al., 2012; Huber, 2012) and helps explain why people gamble in casinos and enter lotteries. The odds are against them and the decision to gamble has

utility In decision making, any subjective measure of value.

expected value The total benefit to be expected of a decision if it were repeated on several occasions.

a negative expected value, but because people overestimate the probability of winning, they associate a positive expected value with gambling. In one study, not even a course that highlighted gambling's mathematical disadvantages could change university students' gambling behavior (Williams & Connolly, 2006). The tendency to overestimate rare events is amplified by the availability heuristic: vivid memories of rare gambling successes and the publicity given to lottery winners encourage people to recall gains rather than losses.

Sometimes a bias in estimating probability costs more than money. For example, many people underestimate the risk of HIV and other sexually transmitted diseases and thus continue to engage in unprotected sex (Specter, 2005). And after the September 11, 2001, terrorist attacks on the United States, the risks of flying seemed so high that many more people than usual chose to travel by car instead. Yet driving is more dangerous overall than flying, so the decision to drive may actually have increased the risk of death, especially if stress associated with the attacks made drivers less careful (Su et al., 2008). With more cars on the road, there were 353 more traffic fatalities in the last three months of 2001 than there were during the same period in previous years (Gigerenzer, 2004). Similar bias in risk perception leads many people to buy a big, heavy sport utility vehicle that makes them feel safe, even though the chances of serious injury in an SUV are actually greater than in a minivan or family sedan (Gladwell, 2004). Their heightened sense of safety may even lead some SUV drivers to drive less carefully, which further increases the risk of injury (Bener et al., 2008; Thomas & Walton, 2007).

Another bias in estimating probability is called the *gambler's fallacy:* People believe that the probability of future events in a random process will change depending on past events. This belief is false. For example, if you flip a coin and it comes up heads ten times in a row, what is the likelihood of tails on the next flip? Although some people think otherwise, the chance that it will come up tails on the eleventh flip is still 50 percent, just as it was for the first ten flips. Yet many gamblers continue feeding a slot machine that has not paid off much for hours, because they wrongly believe it is "due."

Poor decision making can also stem from the human tendency to be unrealistically confident in the accuracy of our predictions. Baruch Fischoff and Donald MacGregor (1982) devised a clever way to study this bias. People were asked whether they believed a certain event would occur and then were asked to say how confident they were about their prediction. For example, they were asked whether a particular sports team would win an upcoming game. After the events were over, the accuracy of the people's forecasts was compared with their level of confidence. Sure enough, their confidence in their predictions was consistently greater than their accuracy. Investors, too—including professional stockbrokers—are usually confident about what to buy and sell even though many of their decisions turn out to be bad ones (Puetz & Ruenzi, 2011). Overconfidence operates even when people make predictions concerning the accuracy of their own memories (Bjork, 1999). The moral of the story is to be wary when people express confidence that a forecast or decision is correct. They will be wrong more often than they think.

How Biased Are We?

Almost everyone makes decisions that they later regret, but these outcomes may not entirely be due to biased thinking about gains, losses, and probabilities. Some decisions are not intended to maximize expected value but rather to satisfy other goals, such as minimizing expected loss, producing a quick and easy resolution, or preserving a moral principle (Arkes & Ayton, 1999; Galotti, 2007; McCaffery & Baron, 2006). Often decisions depend not just on how likely we are to gain or lose a particular amount of something but also on what that something is. A decision that could cost or save a human life may be made differently than one that could cost or gain a few dollars, even though the probabilities of each outcome are exactly the same in both cases.

The "goodness" or "badness" of decisions can be difficult to measure. Many decisions depend on personal values (utilities), which vary from person to person and across cultures (Weber & Morris, 2010; Yates, 2010). People in individualist cultures, for example,

A Highly Unlikely Outcome

Casinos and lotteries attract business by creating memorable images of big winners. They know that people's gambling and ticket buying will be influenced by the availability heuristic and the tendency to overestimate the probability of rare events. Did you ever notice that casino and lottery ads and websites never show or talk about the millions of players who lost money or whose tickets were worthless (McMullan & Miller, 2009)?

Jupiterimages/Photos.com

Justice Is Served

Decision making can be affected by many factors, including motivational states such as hunger (e.g., Bos, van Baaren, & Dijksterhuis, 2011; Eskine, Kacinik, & Prinz, 2011). One study found, for example, that judges' courtroom decisions tended to be more lenient just after they had eaten, and became progressively harsher as the judges got hungrier (Danziger, Levav, & Avnaim-Pessoa, 2011).

Rich Legg/Getty Images

may tend to assign high utilities to attributes that promote personal goals, whereas people in collectivist cultures might place greater value on attributes that bring group harmony and the approval of family and friends (Markus, Kitayama, & Heiman, 1996; Varnum et al., 2010).

LINKAGES

GROUP PROCESSES IN PROBLEM SOLVING AND DECISION MAKING

LINKAGES
Do groups solve problems more effectively than individuals? (a link to Social Psychology)

Problem solving and decision making often take place in groups. The factors that influence an individual's problem solving and decision making continue to operate when the individual is in a group, but group interactions also shape the outcome.

When groups are trying to make a decision, for example, they usually begin by considering the preferences or opinions stated by various members. Not all of these views have equal influence. Views that are shared by the greatest number of group members will have the greatest impact on the group's final decision (Tindale & Kameda, 2000). This means that extreme proposals or opinions will usually have less effect on group decisions than those that are more representative of the majority's views.

This is not always the case, though. Through a process called *group polarization*, discussions sometimes result in decisions that are more extreme than group members would make individually (Baron, Branscombe, & Byrne, 2008). Two mechanisms appear to underlie group polarization. First, most arguments presented during the discussion favor the majority view and most criticisms are directed at the minority view. In fact, confirmation bias leads group members to seek additional information that supports the majority position (Minson & Mueller, 2012; Schulz-Hardt et al., 2000). In this atmosphere, those who favor the majority view find it reasonable to adopt an even stronger version of it (Kassin, Fein, & Markus, 2010). Second, once some group members begin to agree that a particular decision is desirable, other members may try to associate themselves with it, perhaps by suggesting an even more extreme version (Kassin, Fein, & Markus, 2010).

(continued)

Are people better at problem solving and decision making when they work in groups or on their own? Research shows that shared decision making about health treatments can improve medical care outcomes and lower costs (Lee & Emanuel, 2013). However, two heads are not always better than one. This is one of the questions about human thinking that social psychologists study. In a typical experiment, a group of people is asked to solve a problem like the one in Figure 7.8 or to decide the guilt or innocence of the defendant in a fictional court case. Each person is asked to work alone and then to join with the others to try to agree on a decision. These studies have found that when problems have solutions that can be easily demonstrated to everyone, groups will usually outperform individuals at solving them (Laughlin, 1999). When problems have less obvious solutions, groups may be somewhat better at solving them than their average member but usually no better than their most talented member (Hackman, 1998). And because of phenomena such as *social loafing* and *groupthink* (discussed in the social psychology chapter), people working in a group are often less productive than people working alone (Cheshire & Antin, 2010; Williams & Sommer, 1997).

Other research suggests that a critical element in successful group problem solving is the sharing of individual members' unique information and expertise (e.g., Kohn, Paulus, & Choi, 2011; Puvathingal & Hantula, 2012). For example, when asked to diagnose an illness, groups of physicians were much more accurate when they pooled their knowledge (Larson et al., 1998). However, *brainstorming,* a popular strategy that supposedly encourages group members to generate new and innovative solutions to a problem, may actually produce fewer or less creative ideas than are generated by individuals working alone (Baumeister & Bushman, 2008). This result may occur because comments from other group members may interfere with some members' ability to think clearly and creatively (Nijstad, Stroebe, & Lodewijkx, 2003). Further, some participants in a brainstorming session may be reluctant to offer an idea, even a good one, for fear it will be rejected or ridiculed by the group (Mojzisch & Schulz-Hardt, 2010). To prevent these problems, some brainstorming groups are specifically instructed to come up with as many ideas as possible, without regard for quality or anything else, just to ensure that as many ideas as possible are considered (Paulus, Kohn, & Arditti, 2011). Following these procedures has been shown to elevate the level of performance by brainstorming groups significantly above what is typically found in such groups (Nemeth et al., 2004). Other researchers arrange for brainstorming groups to meet electronically using computer-based communication systems that allow group members to offer suggestions without being identified or interrupted yet still give everyone access to the ideas of all the other members. The levels of trust and the patterns of communication that develop in these groups appear comparable to those seen in face-to-face groups (Wilson, Straus, & McEvily, 2006), and because electronic brainstorming allows people to think more clearly and express themselves without fear, these groups may actually perform as well or better than those that meet in person (Englemann, Tergan, & Hesse, 2010).

As they work to solve a problem, group members experience their own thoughts as concepts, propositions, images, or other mental representations. How does each member share these private events to help the group perform its task? The answer lies in the use of language.

One disadvantage of brainstorming sessions is that running comments and bizarre ideas from some group members can interfere with the creative process in others (Nijstad, Stroebe, & Lodewijkx, 2003).

DILBERT: © Scott Adams/Dist. by United Feature Syndicate, Inc.

LANGUAGE

How do babies learn to talk?

Our language abilities are usually well integrated with our memory, thinking, and other cognitive abilities (Boroditsky & Gaby, 2010). This integration allows us to use language to express everything from simple requests to abstract principles. We can speak about our thoughts and memories, think about what people tell us, and interact with each other in meaningful ways (Majid et al., 2011). We can create stories that pass on cultural information and traditions from one generation to the next. In fact, as described in the chapter on biological aspects of psychology, our brains process language so effectively that it is only when strokes or other forms of damage interfere with the brain's language areas that we are reminded that language is a very special kind of cognitive ability (Bedny et al., 2011; Kohnert, 2004; Stephens, Silbert, & Hasson, 2010).

The Elements of Language

A **language** has two basic elements: *symbols,* such as words, and *rules,* called **grammar,** for combining those symbols. With our knowledge of approximately 50,000 to 100,000 words (Miller, 1991), we humans can create and understand an infinite number of sentences. All of the sentences ever spoken are built from just a few dozen categories of sounds. The power of language comes from the way these rather unimpressive raw materials are organized according to certain rules. This organization occurs at several levels.

From Sounds to Sentences

Organization occurs first at the level of sounds. A **phoneme** is the smallest unit of sound that affects the meaning of speech. Changing a phoneme changes the meaning of a spoken word, much as changing a letter in a printed word changes its meaning. *Tea* has a meaning different from *sea,* and *sight* is different from *sigh.*

Although changing a phoneme affects the meaning of speech, phonemes themselves are not meaningful. We combine them to form a higher level of organization: morphemes. A **morpheme** is the smallest unit of language that has meaning. For example, because they have meaning, *dog* and *run* are morphemes; but so are prefixes such as *un-* and suffixes such as *-ed* because they, too, have meaning, even though they cannot stand alone.

Words are made up of one or more morphemes. Words, in turn, are combined to form phrases and sentences according to a set of grammatical rules called **syntax.** According to English syntax, a subject and a verb must be combined to form a sentence, adjectives typically appear before the nouns that they modify, and so on. Compare the following sentences:

Fatal accidents deter careful drivers.

Snows sudden floods melting cause.

The first sentence makes sense, but the second sentence violates English syntax. If the words were reordered, however, they would produce the perfectly acceptable sentence "Melting snows cause sudden floods."

Even if you use English phonemes combined in proper ways to form morphemes strung together according to the laws of English syntax, you may still not end up with an acceptable sentence. Consider the sentence "Rapid bouquets deter sudden neighbors." It somehow sounds right, but it is nonsense. Why? It has syntax, but it ignores the set of rules, called **semantics,** that govern the meaning of words and sentences. For example, because of its meaning, the noun *bouquets* cannot be modified by the word *rapid.*

Surface Structure and Deep Structure

In 1965, Noam Chomsky started a revolution in how we study language. He argued that if linguists looked only at the sentences people produce, they would never uncover all the

language Symbols (and a set of rules for combining them) that are used as a means of communicating.

grammar A set of rules for combining the symbols, such as words, used in a given language.

phoneme The smallest unit of sound that affects the meaning of speech.

morpheme The smallest unit of language that has meaning.

syntax The set of rules that govern the formation of phrases and sentences in a language.

semantics Rules governing the meaning of words and sentences.

Making sure that the surface structures we create accurately convey the deep structures we intend is one of the greatest challenges people face when communicating through language.

Danny Shanahan/The New Yorker Collection/www .cartoonbank.com

principles underlying language. Without looking deeper into language, he said, they could not explain, for example, why the sentence "This is my old friend" can have more than one meaning. Nor could they account for the similar meaning conveyed by such seemingly different sentences as "Don't give up just because things look bad" and "It ain't over till it's over."

To take these aspects of language into account, Chomsky chose a more abstract level of analysis. He suggested that behind the strings of words people produce, which he called **surface structures**, there is a **deep structure**, an abstract representation of the relationships expressed in a sentence. For example, the surface structure "The shooting of the psychologist was terrible" can represent either of two deep structures: (1) that the psychologist had terrible aim or (2) that it was terrible that someone shot the psychologist. Chomsky's analysis of deep and surface structures was important because it encouraged psychologists to analyze not just verbal behavior and grammatical rules but also mental representations.

Understanding Speech

When someone speaks to you in your own language, your sensory, perceptual, and other cognitive systems reconstruct the sounds of speech in a way that allows you to detect, recognize, and understand what the person is saying. The process may seem effortless, but it involves amazingly complex feats of information processing. Despite these challenges, humans can instantly recognize and understand the words and sentences produced by almost anyone speaking a familiar language. In contrast, even the best voice recognition software must learn to recognize words spoken by a new voice, and even then it may make many mistakes.

Scientists have yet to discover all the details about how people overcome the challenges of understanding speech, but some general answers are emerging. Just as we recognize objects by analyzing their visual features (as discussed in the chapter on sensation and perception), it appears that humans identify and recognize the specific—and changing—features of the sounds created when someone speaks. And as in visual perception, this *bottom-up processing* of stimulus features combines with *top-down processing* guided by knowledge-based factors, such as context and expectation, to aid understanding

surface structures The order in which words are arranged in sentences.

deep structure An abstract representation of the underlying meaning of a given sentence.

Understanding Spoken Language

The top-down perceptual processes described in the sensation and perception chapter help explain why people speaking an unfamiliar language seem to produce a continuous stream of abnormally rapid speech. The problem is that you don't know where each word starts and stops. Without any perceived gaps, the sounds of speech run together, creating the impression of rapid-fire "chatter." People unfamiliar with your language think you are speaking extremely fast, too!

eddie linssen / Alamy

(Samuel, 2001). For example, knowing the general topic of conversation helps you to recognize individual words that might otherwise be hard to understand (Cole & Jakimik, 1978). People also use the visual cues provided by looking at a speaker's face, especially in noisy or distracting settings (Golumbic et al., 2013). This ability to use context is especially helpful for people with hearing impairments or when trying to understand what someone is saying at a loud party or in other noisy environments (Davis, Johnsrude, et al., 2005).

Learning to Speak: Stages of Language Development

Children the world over develop language with impressive speed; the average six-year-old already has a vocabulary of about 13,000 words (Pinker, 1994). But acquiring language involves more than just learning vocabulary. We also have to learn how words are combined and how to produce and understand sentences. Psychologists who study the development of language have found that the process begins in the earliest days of a child's life and follows some predictable steps (Parise & Csibra, 2012; Saffran, Senghas, & Trueswell, 2001).

The First Year

In their first year, infants become more and more attuned to the sounds that will be important in acquiring their native language (DePaolis, Vihman, & Nakai, 2013; Gomez et al., 2014). In fact, this early experience with language appears to be vital. Without it, language development can be impaired (Mayberry & Lock, 2003). The first year is also the time when babies begin to produce particular kinds of **infant vocalizations**, called **babblings**, patterns of meaningless sounds that first resemble speech. These alternating consonant and vowel sounds (such as "bababa," "dadada," and "mamimamima") appear at about four months of age, once the infant has developed the necessary coordination of the tongue and mouth. Though meaningless to the baby, babblings are a delight to parents. Infants everywhere begin with the same set of babbling sounds, but at about nine months of age, they begin to produce only the sounds that occur in the language they hear the most. At about the same time, their babbling becomes more complex and begins to sound like "sentences" in the babies' native language (Goldstein, King, & West, 2003). Infants who hear English, for example, begin to shorten some of their vocalizations to "da," "duh," and "ma." They use these sounds to convey joy, anger, interest, and other messages in specific contexts and with obvious purpose (Blake & de Boysson-Bardies, 1992).

By ten to twelve months of age, babies can understand several words—certainly more words than they can say (Fenson et al., 1994). Proper names and object words—such as *mama, daddy, cookie, doggy,* and *car* in English-speaking cultures—are among the earliest words they understand. These are also the first words children are likely to say when they begin to talk at around twelve months of age (some talk a little earlier and some a little later). Infants acquire nouns for simple object categories (*dog, flower*) before they acquire more general nouns (*animal, plant*) or more specific names (*collie, rose*) (Rosch et al., 1976).

Of course, these early words do not sound exactly like adult language. English-speaking babies usually reduce them to a shorter, easier form, like "duh" for *duck* or "mih" for *milk*. Children make themselves understood, however, by using gestures, voice tones, facial expressions, and endless repetitions (Özçalışkan & Dimitrova, 2013). Once they have a word for an object, they may "overextend" it to cover more ground. So they might use *doggy* to refer to cats, bears, and horses; they might use *fly* for all insects and perhaps for other small things such as raisins and M&Ms (Clark, 1983, 1993). Children make these "errors" because their vocabularies are limited, not because they fail to notice the difference between dogs and cats or because they want to eat flies (Fremgen & Fay, 1980; Rescorla, 1981). Being around people who don't understand these overextensions encourages children to learn and

infant vocalizations Early sounds, such as babblings, made by babies.

babblings Repetitions of syllables; the first sounds infants make that resemble speech.

Getting Ready to Talk

Long before they say their first words, babies are getting ready to talk. Laboratory studies show that even six-month-olds tend to look longer at faces whose lip movements match the sounds of spoken words. This tendency reflects babies' abilities to focus on, recognize, and discriminate the sounds of speech, especially in their native language. These abilities are crucial to the development of language (Lewkowicz & Hansen-Tift, 2012; Mayberry, Lock, & Kazmi, 2002).

Marilyn Conway/Getty Images

use more precise words (Markman, 1994). During this period, children build vocabularies one word at a time. They also use their limited vocabulary one word at a time. They cannot yet put words together into sentences. Their language skills will blossom during the years from two to four, and the richness of the vocabulary they eventually develop will be influenced by the richness of the language that they hear and the encouragement they receive for their earliest efforts to communicate using both words and gestures (Goldstein & Schwade, 2008; Özçalışkan & Dimitrova, 2013; Rowe & Goldin-Meadow, 2009).

The Second Year

The **one-word stage** of speech lasts for about six months. Then, some time around eighteen months of age, children's vocabularies expand dramatically (Gleitman & Landau, 1994). They may learn several new words each day, and by the age of two, most youngsters can use 50 to well over 100 words. They also start using two-word combinations to form efficient little sentences. These two-word sentences are called "telegraphic" because, like telegrams or text messages, they are brief and to the point, leaving out anything that is not absolutely essential. So if she wants her mother to give her a book, a twenty-month-old might first say, "Give book," then "Mommy give," and if that does not work, "Mommy book." The child also uses rising tones to indicate a question ("Go out?") and emphasizes certain words to indicate location ("Play *park*") or new information ("*Big* car").

Three-word sentences come next, and though still telegraphic, they are more nearly complete: "Mommy give book." The child's sentences begin to have the subject-verb-object form typical of adult sentences. Other words and word endings begin appearing, too. In English, these include the suffix -*ing*, the prepositions *in* and *on*, the plural -*s*, and irregular past tenses such as "It broke," and "I ate" (Brown, 1973; Dale, 1976). Children learn to use the suffix -*ed* for the past tense ("I walked"), but often overapply this rule to irregular verbs that they had previously used correctly, saying, for example, "It breaked," "It broked," or "I eated" (Marcus, 1996). Children also expand their sentences with adjectives, although at first they make some mistakes. For example, they are likely to use both *less* and *more* to mean "more" (Smith & Sera, 1992).

The Third Year and Beyond

By age three or so, children begin to use auxiliary verbs ("Adam is going") and to ask questions using what, where, who, and why. They begin to put together clauses to form complex sentences ("Here's the ball I was looking for"). By age five, children have acquired most of the grammatical rules of their native language.

How Is Language Acquired?

LINKAGES   How do we learn to speak? (a link to Human Development)

Despite all that has been learned about the steps children follow in acquiring language, mystery and debate still surround the question of just how they do it. We know that children pick up the specific content of language from the speech they hear around them: English children learn English; French children learn French. But how do children come to follow the rules of grammar?

Conditioning, Imitation, and Rules

Perhaps children learn grammar because their parents reward them for using it. This idea sounds reasonable, but observational research suggests that positive reinforcement (which we describe in the learning chapter) is not the main character in the story of language acquisition. Parents are usually more concerned about what is said than about its grammatical form (Hirsch-Pasek, Treiman, & Schneiderman, 1984). So when the little boy with chocolate crumbs on his face says, "I not eat cookie," his mother is more likely to respond, "Yes, you did" than to ask the child to say, "I did not eat the cookie" and then praise him for his grammatical correctness.

one-word stage A stage of language development during which children tend to use one word at a time.

Learning through imitation appears to be more influential. Children learn grammar most rapidly when adult models demonstrate the correct form in the course of conversation (Zimmerman et al., 2009). For example:

Child: *Mommy fix.*

Mother: *Okay, Mommy will fix the truck.*

Child: *It breaked.*

Mother: *Yes, it broke.*

But if children learn grammar by imitation, why do children who at one time said "I went" later say "I goed"? Adults don't use this form of speech, so neither imitation nor reward can account for its sudden appearance. It appears more likely that children analyze for themselves the underlying patterns in the language they hear around them and then learn the rules governing those patterns (Bloom, 1995).

Biological Bases for Language Acquisition

The ease with which children the world over discover these patterns and develop language has led some to argue that language acquisition is at least partly innate, or automatic. Chomsky (1965) proposed that we are born with a built-in universal grammar, a mechanism that allows us to identify the basic dimensions of language (Baker, 2002; Chomsky, 1986; Nowak, Komarova, & Niyogi, 2001). According to this view, a child's universal grammar might tell the child that word order is important to the meaning of a sentence. In English, for example, word order tells us who is doing what to whom (the sentences "Heather teased Jason" and "Jason teased Heather" contain the same words, but they have different meanings). In Chomsky's view, then, we don't entirely learn language—we develop it as genetic predispositions interact with experience (Li & Bartlett, 2012). So a child's innate assumption that word order is important to grammar would change if the child heard language in which word order did not have much effect on the meaning of a sentence.

Those who disagree with Chomsky argue that language development comes about from the development of more general sensory, perceptual, and cognitive skills, not just unique, language-specific mechanisms (e.g., Bates, 1993; Gogate & Hollich, 2010; Goldstein et al., 2010). In other words, they say, we don't inherit a single, specific "grammar gene" (White, 2006). Still, other evidence supports the existence of biological factors in language acquisition (Peltola et al., 2012). For example, the unique properties of the human mouth and throat, the language-related brain regions described in the chapter on biological aspects of psychology, and genetic research all suggest that humans are innately "prewired," or biologically programmed, for language (Buxhoeveden et al., 2001; Dehaene-Lambertz et al., 2010; Lai et al., 2001). So even though a single gene does not fully bestow us with language capacity, certain genes do seem to affect brain development in ways that help make language possible (Sia, Clem, & Huganir, 2013). And researchers are beginning to uncover genetic mechanisms behind some speech and language disorders (e.g., Amarillo et al., 2014; Bates et al., 2011; Fisher, 2005). In addition, there appears to be a period in childhood during which we can learn language more easily than at any other time (Ridley, 2000). The existence of this *critical period* is supported by evidence from tragic cases in which children spent their early years isolated from human contact and the sound of adult language. Even after years of therapy and language training, these individuals are not able to combine ideas into sentences (Rymer, 1993). Such cases suggest that in order to acquire the complex features of language, we must be exposed to speech before a certain age.

Bilingualism

Does trying to learn two languages at once, even before the critical period for language learning is over, impair the learning of either? Research suggests just the opposite. Like some children in any situation, the early language of children from a bilingual environment may be confused or delayed, but they eventually show enhanced performance in each language (Bialystok & Craik, 2010; de Houwer, 1995; Garcia-Sierra et al., 2011). Early

Learning a Second Language

As these international students are discovering, people who learn a second language as adults do so more slowly, and with less proficiency, than younger people (Johnson & Newport, 1989; Patkowski, 1994) and virtually never learn to speak it without an accent (Lenneberg, 1967). Still, the window of opportunity for learning a second language remains open long after the end of the critical period in childhood during which first-language acquisition must occur (Hakuta, Bialystok, & Wiley, 2003).

ZUMA Press, Inc. / Alamy

exposure to more than one language appears to help the brain maintain flexibility in recognizing the sounds and patterns of speech that monolingual children normally lose.

There is also some evidence that balanced bilinguals—those who have roughly equal mastery of two languages in childhood—enjoy some more general advantages in cognitive flexibility, concept formation, and creativity. Also, bilingual school-age children may be better at learning non-language topics when that learning rests heavily on the use of language (Kaushanskaya, Gross, & Buac, 2014). It is as if learning more than one language offers a person a slightly different perspective on thinking and that this dual perspective makes the brain more flexible and better able to learn new things (Bialystok & Craik, 2010; Krizman et al., 2012; Kroll, Bobb, & Hoshino, 2014; Poulin-Dubois et al., 2011). This flexibility may start very early; even six-month-old children in bilingual homes seem to have greater learning and memory capacity than is the case among infants in monolingual homes (Brito & Barr, 2013). Bilinguals also have an easier time than other people do in learning a third language later in life, even if the grammar of the new language is very different from the ones they already know (Kaushanskaya, 2009). The flexibility of thought developed by bilingual children also seems to provide a sort of *cognitive reserve* in old age, which may protect against the loss of cognitive abilities that is sometimes associated with aging, and may even delay the onset of Alzheimer's disease (Bialystok, Craik, & Luk, 2012; Craik, Bialystok, & Freedman, 2010; Luk et al., 2011).

CAN NONHUMANS USE LANGUAGE? THINKING CRITICALLY

We have said that our ability to acquire and use language helps set humans apart from all other creatures. Yet those creatures, too, use symbols to communicate. Bees perform a dance that tells other bees where they found sources of nectar, killer whales signal one another as they hunt in groups, and the grunts and gestures of chimpanzees signify varying desires and emotions. These forms of communication do not necessarily have the grammatical characteristics of language, however. Are any nonhumans capable of learning language?

What am I being asked to believe or accept?

Over the past forty years, several researchers have claimed that nonhumans can master language. Chimpanzees and gorillas have been the most popular targets of study (e.g., Beran, Smith, & Perdue, 2013) because at maturity they are estimated to have intelligence similar to two- or three-year-old human children, who are usually well on their way to learning language. Dolphins have also been studied because they have a complex communication system and exceptionally large brains relative to their body size (Janik, 2013; Pack & Herman, 2007; Reiss & Marino, 2001). It would seem that if these animals were unable to learn language, their general intelligence could not be blamed. Instead, failure would be attributed to the absence of a genetic makeup that permits language learning.

What evidence is available to support the assertion?

Whether nonhuman mammals can learn to use language is not a simple question, for at least two reasons. First, language is not just communication, but defining just when animals are exhibiting that "something different" is a source of debate. A key factor that seems to set human language apart from the gestures, grunts, chirps, whistles, or cries of other animals is grammar—a formal set of rules for combining words, permitting the creation of an unlimited number of messages. Also, because of their anatomical structures, nonhuman mammals cannot "speak" in the same way that we humans do (Lieberman, 1991; Nishimura et al., 2003). To test these animals' ability to learn language, investigators must devise novel ways to allow them to communicate.

(continued)

David and Ann Premack taught a chimp, Sarah, to communicate by placing differently shaped chips, each symbolizing a word, on a magnetic board (Premack, 1971). Lana, a chimpanzee studied by Duane Rumbaugh (1977), learned to communicate by pressing keys on a specially designed computer. A simplified version of American Sign Language (ASL) has been used by Beatrice and Allen Gardner with the chimp Washoe, by Herbert Terrace with Nim Chimpsky (a chimp named after Noam Chomsky), and by Penny Patterson with a gorilla named Koko. Kanzi, a bonobo, or pygmy chimpanzee, studied by Sue Savage-Rumbaugh (1990; Savage-Rumbaugh et al., 1993), learned to recognize spoken words and to communicate by both gesturing and pressing word symbol keys on a computer that would "speak" them. Kanzi was a special case: He learned to communicate by listening and watching as his mother, Matata, was being taught and then used what he had learned to interact with her trainers.

Studies of these animals suggested that they could use combinations of words to refer to things that were not present. Washoe, Lana, Sarah, Nim, and Kanzi all mastered between 130 and 500 words. Their vocabulary included names for concrete objects, such as *apple* or *me*; verbs, such as *tickle* and *eat*; adjectives, such as *happy* and *big*; and adverbs, such as *again*. The animals combined the words to express wishes such as "You tickle me" or "If Sarah good, then apple." Sometimes their expressions referred to things in the past. When an investigator called attention to a wound that Kanzi had received, the animal responded with "Matata hurt," referring to a disciplinary bite his mother had recently given him (Savage-Rumbaugh, 1990). Finally, all these animals seemed to enjoy their communication tools and used them spontaneously to interact with their caretakers and with other animals.

Most of the investigators mentioned here have argued that their animals mastered a crude grammar (Premack & Premack, 1983; Savage-Rumbaugh, Shanker, & Taylor, 2001). For example, if Washoe wanted to be tickled, she would gesture, "You tickle Washoe." But if she wanted to do the tickling, she would gesture, "Washoe tickle you." The correct placement of object and subject in these sentences suggested that Washoe was following a set of rules for word combination—in other words, a grammar (Gardner & Gardner, 1978). Louis Herman and his colleagues documented similar grammatical sensitivity in dolphins, who rarely confused subject-verb order in following instructions given by human hand signals (Herman, Richards, & Wolz, 1984). Furthermore, Savage-Rumbaugh observed several hundred instances in which Kanzi understood sentences he had never heard before. Once, for example, while his back was turned to the speaker, Kanzi heard the sentence "Jeanie hid the pine needles in her shirt." He turned around, approached Jeanie, and searched her shirt to find the pine needles. His actions would seem to indicate that he understood this new sentence the first time he heard it.

Animal Language?

As demonstrated here by Nim Chimpsky, several chimpanzees and gorillas have been taught American Sign Language (ASL). Nim died in 2000 at the age of twenty-six, but Koko, the gorilla trained by Penny Patterson, is still with us. In one Internet chat session, Patterson relayed online questions to Koko in ASL, and a typist sent back Koko's signed responses. This procedure left some questioners wondering whether they were talking to Koko or to her trainer. (You can decide for yourself by reading the transcript of the session at www.koko.org/world/talk_aol.html.)

Susan Kuklin/Science Source

(continued)

Are there alternative ways of interpreting the evidence?

Many of the early conclusions about primate language learning were challenged by Herbert Terrace and his colleagues (1979) in their investigation of Nim and by other critics' responses to other cases. For example, Terrace noticed many characteristics of Nim's communications that seemed quite different from a child's use of language.

First, he said, Nim's sentences were always very short. For example, Nim could combine two or three gestures but never used strings that conveyed more sophisticated messages. The ape was never able to say anything equivalent to a three-year-old child's "I want to go to Wendy's for a hamburger, OK?" Others have noted that even the most intelligent of primates are unable to master the full grammatical possibilities of either ASL or specially developed artificial languages (Fitch & Hauser, 2004). Further, apes don't point at things, as humans do from a young age as they develop language and use it in joint communication (e.g., Tomasello, 2006). Second, Terrace questioned whether the animals' use of language demonstrated the spontaneity, creativity, and expanding complexity characteristic of children's language. Many of the animals' sentences were requests for food, tickling, baths, pets, and other pleasurable objects and experiences. Is such behavior really any different from the kind of behavior shown by the family dog who learns to sit up and beg for table scraps? Other researchers also pointed out that chimps are not naturally predisposed to associate seen objects with heard words, as human infants are (Savage-Rumbaugh et al., 1983). Finally, Terrace questioned whether experimenter bias influenced the reports of the chimps' communications. Consciously or not, experimenters who want to conclude that chimps learn language might tend to ignore strings of symbols that violate grammatical order or to reinterpret ambiguous strings so that they make grammatical sense. If Nim sees someone holding a banana and signs, "Nim banana," the experimenter might assume that the word order is correct and means "Nim wants the banana" rather than, for example, "That banana belongs to Nim," in which case the word order would be wrong.

Critics also point out that the results presented in support of animal language capabilities are usually only samples of an animal's behavior. They say that the unedited sequences of an animal's signing or other behavior presents a picture that is far more repetitious, chaotic, and random than one might expect on the basis of the selected samples (Aitchison, 2008).

What additional evidence would help evaluate the alternatives?

Studies of animals' ability to learn language are expensive and take many years. As a result, the amount of evidence in the area is small—just a handful of studies, each based on a few animals. Obviously, more data are needed from more studies that use a common methodology.

It is important, too, to study the extent to which limits on the length of primates' spontaneous sentences result from limits on short-term and working memory (Savage-Rumbaugh & Brakke, 1996). If memory is in fact the main limiting factor, then the failure to produce progressively longer sentences does not necessarily reflect an inability to master language.

Research on how primates might spontaneously acquire language by listening and imitating, as Kanzi did, as well as naturalistic observations of communications among primates in their natural habitat, would also help scientists better understand primates' capacity to communicate (Savage-Rumbaugh, Shanker, & Taylor, 2001; Sevcik & Savage-Rumbaugh, 1994).

What conclusions are most reasonable?

There is still no full agreement about whether our sophisticated mammalian cousins can learn language. Two things are clear, however. First, whatever the chimp, gorilla, and dolphin have learned is a much more primitive and limited form of communication than that learned by children. Second, their level of communication does not do justice to their overall intelligence; these animals are smarter than their "language" production suggests. In short, the evidence to date favors the view that humans have language abilities that are unique (e.g., Povinelli & Bering, 2002; Zuberbühler, 2005), but that under the right circumstances and with the right tools, some nonhuman creatures can communicate using abstract symbols (e.g., Gillespie-Lynch et al., 2011; Lyn et al., 2011).

LINKAGES

As noted in the introductory chapter, all of psychology's subfields are related to one another. Our discussion of group problem solving illustrates just one way that the topic of this chapter—thought and language—is linked to the subfield of social psychology, which is described in the chapter by that name. The Linkages diagram shows ties to two other subfields, and there are many more ties throughout the book. Looking for linkages among subfields will help you see how they all fit together and help you better appreciate the big picture that is psychology.

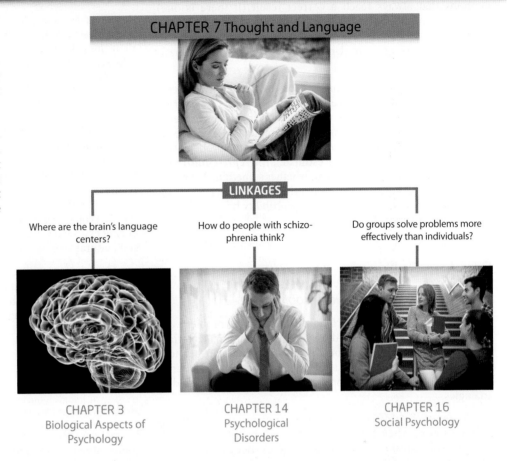

CHAPTER 7 Thought and Language

LINKAGES

Where are the brain's language centers?

How do people with schizo-phrenia think?

Do groups solve problems more effectively than individuals?

CHAPTER 3
Biological Aspects of Psychology

CHAPTER 14
Psychological Disorders

CHAPTER 16
Social Psychology

SUMMARY

Basic Functions of Thought

What good is thinking, anyway?

The five core functions of thought are describing, elaborating, deciding, planning, and guiding action. Many psychologists think of the components of this circle of thought as constituting an *information-processing system* that receives, represents, transforms, and acts on incoming stimuli. *Thinking*, then, is defined as the manipulation of mental representations by this system.

Mental Representations: The Ingredients of Thought

What are thoughts made of?

Mental representations take the form of concepts, propositions, schemas, scripts, mental models, images, and cognitive maps. *Concepts* are categories of objects, events, or ideas with common properties. They may be formal or natural. Formal concepts are

precisely defined by the presence or absence of certain features. Natural concepts are fuzzy; no fixed set of defining properties determines membership in a natural concept. A member of a natural concept that displays all or most of the concept's characteristic features is called a *prototype*.

Propositions are assertions that state how concepts are related. Propositions can be true or false. *Schemas* serve as generalized mental representations of concepts and generate expectations about them. *Scripts* are schemas about familiar sequences of events or activities. Experience creates accurate or inaccurate *mental models* that help guide our understanding of and interaction with the world. Mental *images* may also be manipulated when people think. *Cognitive maps* are mental representations of familiar parts of one's world.

Thinking Strategies

Do people always think logically?

By combining and transforming mental representations, our information-processing system makes it possible for us to engage in *reasoning*, to solve problems, and to make decisions. **Formal reasoning** seeks valid conclusions through the application of rigorous procedures. It is guided by **algorithms**, systematic methods that always reach a correct result (if there is one). To reach a sound conclusion, people should consider both the truth and falsity of their assumptions and whether the argument follows the rules of **logic**. Unfortunately, people are prone to logical errors.

People use **informal reasoning** to assess the validity of a conclusion based on the evidence supporting it. Errors in informal reasoning often stem from the use of **heuristics**, which are mental shortcuts or rules of thumb. Three important heuristics are the **anchoring bias** or **anchoring heuristic** (estimating the probability of an event by adjusting an earlier estimate), the **representativeness heuristic** (basing conclusions about whether something belongs in a certain class on how similar it is to other items in that class), and the **availability heuristic** (estimating probability by how available an event is in memory).

Problem Solving

What's the best way to solve a problem?

Steps in problem solving include diagnosing the problem and then planning, executing, and evaluating a solution. Especially when solutions are not obvious, problem solving can be aided by incubation and the use of strategies such as means-end analysis (also called decomposition), working backward, and finding analogies.

Many of the difficulties that people experience in solving problems arise when they are dealing with hypotheses. People do not easily consider multiple hypotheses. Because of **mental sets**, they may stick to one hypothesis even when it is incorrect, and because of **functional fixedness**, they may miss opportunities to use familiar objects in unusual ways. People may be reluctant to revise or change hypotheses on the basis of new data, partly because **confirmation bias** focuses their attention on evidence that supports their hypotheses. They may also fail to use the absence of symptoms or events as evidence in solving problems. Problem solving ability can be improved through deliberate practice.

Some specific problems can be solved by computer programs developed by researchers in the field of **artificial intelligence (AI)**. There are two approaches to AI. One focuses on programming computers to imitate the logical manipulation of symbols that occurs in human thought; the other (involving connectionist, or neural network, models) attempts to imitate the connections among neurons in the human brain.

Tests of **divergent thinking** are used to measure differences in **creativity**. In contrast, intelligence tests require **convergent thinking**. Although creativity and intelligence are not highly correlated, creative behavior requires a certain amount of intelligence, along with expertise in a creative field, skill at problem solving and divergent thinking, and motivation to pursue a creative endeavor for its own sake.

Decision Making

How can I become a better decision maker?

Decisions are sometimes difficult because there are too many alternatives and too many features of each alternative to consider all at once. Furthermore, decisions often involve comparisons of subjective **utility**, not of objective value. Decision making is also complicated by the fact that the world is unpredictable, which makes decisions risky.

People should act in ways that maximize the **expected value** of their decisions. They often fail to do so because losses are perceived differently from gains of equal size and because people tend to overestimate the probability of rare events, underestimate the probability of frequent events, and feel overconfident about the accuracy of their forecasts. The gambler's fallacy leads people to believe that events in a random process are affected by previous events. People also make decisions aimed at goals other than maximizing expected value; these goals may be determined by personal and cultural factors.

Group decisions tend to show group polarization, the selection of more extreme outcomes than would have been chosen by the average group member. Group performance in problem solving and decision making can be effective, but depending on the problem and the people involved, it may be less efficient than when individuals work alone.

Language

How do babies learn to talk?

Language consists of words or word symbols and rules for their combination—a **grammar**. Spoken words are made up of **phonemes**, which are combined to make **morphemes**. Combinations of words must have both **syntax** (grammar) and **semantics** (meaning). Behind the word strings, or **surface structures**, is an underlying representation, or **deep structure**, that expresses the relationship among the ideas in a sentence. Ambiguous sentences occur when one surface structure reflects two or more deep structures. To understand language generally and conversations in particular, people use their knowledge of the context and of the world. In addition, understanding is guided by nonverbal cues.

Children develop grammar according to an orderly pattern. **Infant vocalizations**, such as **babblings**, come first, then a **one-word stage** of speech, and then two-word sentences. Next come three-word sentences and certain grammatical forms that appear in a somewhat predictable order. Once children learn certain regular verb forms and plural endings, they may overgeneralize rules. Children acquire most of the grammatical rules of their native language by the time they are five years old.

Both conditioning and imitation play a role in a child's acquisition of language, but neither can provide a complete explanation of how children acquire grammar. Humans may be biologically programmed to learn language. In any event, it appears that language must be learned during a certain critical period if normal language is to occur.

TEST YOUR KNOWLEDGE

Select the best answer for each of the following questions. Then check your responses against the Answer Key at the end of the book.

1. Thinking is defined as the manipulation of _____.
   a. concepts
   b. mental models
   c. heuristics
   d. mental representations

2. While trying to describe an unusual bird he saw on his walk, Jarrod asks his friend to "think of a robin, but with blue tips on the wings and a tuft of hair on the head. That's what it looked like." Because "bird" is a _____ concept, Jarrod began with the image of a robin, which is the _____ of "bird." He hoped that his description would allow his friend to develop a _____ of the bird he saw.
   a. formal; concept; prototype
   b. natural; image; concept
   c. natural; prototype; mental model
   d. visual; mental model; script

3. Clint is frustrated. His uncle has been winning at checkers all night. During the next game he is going to base his strategy on an algorithm, not a heuristic. What problem will this strategy cause?
   a. Clint will not win the game.
   b. Clint and his uncle may be playing the same game of checkers for a long time.
   c. Clint will be ignoring overall probabilities.
   d. The representativeness heuristic will bias Clint's choice of strategy.

4. Alicia agreed to go to dinner and a movie with Adam but was surprised and angry when Adam expected her to pay for her half of the evening's expenses. Adam and Alicia apparently had different _____ for what is supposed to happen on a date.
   a. mental models
   b. propositions
   c. images
   d. scripts

5. Stephanie has worked for hours on a biochemistry problem without success. She decides to put it aside and work on her psychology homework in the hope that a solution might occur to her while she is thinking about something else. Stephanie is trying the _____ strategy to solve her problem.
   a. decomposition
   b. incubation
   c. working backward
   d. analogies

6. Ebony wanted to leave a note for her husband but couldn't find a pen, so she wrote the note with her lipstick. Ebony was able to overcome the obstacle to problem solving called _____.
   a. absence of information
   b. multiple hypotheses
   c. confirmation bias
   d. functional fixedness

7. Dr. Sand is sure that Ahmed has appendicitis and as a result he pays more attention to test results that are consistent with appendicitis than to results that suggest a different problem. Dr. Sand has fallen victim to _____.
   a. functional fixedness
   b. a mental model
   c. confirmation bias
   d. the availability heuristic

8. While playing a dominos game, Richard drew a tile at random and got a "double blank," which costs the most points during the first two rounds. At the start of the third round, he says, "There is no way I will draw the double blank tile next time!" Richard is being influenced by _____.
   a. the gambler's fallacy
   b. loss aversion
   c. a disregard of negative evidence
   d. confirmation bias

9. The fact that children learning language sometimes make errors, such as saying "I goed" instead of "I went," has been used to suggest which of the following?
   a. There is a critical period in language development.
   b. Children are born with a knowledge of grammar.
   c. Children do not learn language entirely through imitation.
   d. Speech is learned mainly through imitation.

10. Children who spend their early years isolated from human contact and the sound of adult language are unable to develop adult language skills despite extensive training efforts later. This phenomenon best provides evidence for the notion that _____.
    a. there is a critical period in language development
    b. children are born with a language acquisition device
    c. there are no fixed stages in language acquisition
    d. speech is acquired only through imitation

11. "All monsters are ugly. The Creature from the Black Lagoon is a monster. Therefore, the Creature is ugly." Together, these three statements are an example of _____.
    a. a premise
    b. a proposition
    c. a natural concept
    d. formal reasoning

12. When traveling by air to and from her hometown, Elisa always connects through Chicago's O'Hare airport, so she knows it well. On her last trip, even though she had only 35 minutes to make her connecting flight at a gate she had never used before, she had a _____ that helped her take the most efficient route to the correct gate.
    a. mental model
    b. schema
    c. cognitive map
    d. prototype

13. Theresa Amabile identified cognitive and personality characteristics necessary for creativity. Which of the following is not one of these characteristics?
    a. Capacity for focusing on the most important element in a problem, which is tied to convergent thinking.
    b. Expertise in the field of endeavor, which is tied to learning.
    c. A set of creative skills, including the capacity for divergent thinking.
    d. The motivation to pursue creative work for internal reasons.

14. Gulla was concerned about flying because he thought that the odds of being in a plane crash were around 1 in 100. Even after a pilot told him that the odds were actually less than 1 in a million, Gulla still believes that the chances of a crash are about 1 in 1,000. His new estimate is still far too high, suggesting that he has been affected by _____.
    a. confirmation bias
    b. the availability heuristic
    c. the representativeness heuristic
    d. the anchoring heuristic

15. The words "basket" and "casket" mean different things because of a single _____.
    a. syntax
    b. phoneme
    c. pivot word
    d. proposition

16. Matt cannot solve a difficult design problem for his architecture class. If he decides to use the problem-solving strategy called decomposition, Matt will _____.
    a. break the problem into smaller pieces and deal with each part separately
    b. begin with the finished design and work backwards to achieve it
    c. put the problem aside for a while and return to it later
    d. use an algorithm to plot all possible solutions

17. Seven-year-old Nunes speaks Hindi at home and English at school. His language skills will probably be _____ his classmates who speak only one language.
    a. inferior to
    b. superior to
    c. equal to
    d. less-developed than

18. Doris speaks no Spanish, so when she went to Mexico, she had the impression that everyone there speaks much faster than she does. This impression was probably caused by the fact that when listening to Spanish, she was unable to use _____ to identify individual words.
    a. bottom-up processing
    b. schemas
    c. top-down processing
    d. prototypes

19. When Wanda invites Tanya to join her in a cup of coffee Tanya laughs and says "That would have to be a very big cup!" She could make this joke by focusing on the _____ of Wanda's invitation.
    a. unconscious meaning
    b. deep structure
    c. surface structure
    d. context

20. Scientists who claim that nonhuman animals can use language base their assertions partly on the animals' ability to learn _____.
    a. chess
    b. American sign language
    c. typing skills
    d. basic human speech sounds

Intelligence

Cathy Melloan / Alamy

Preview

Intelligence tests are used to guide decisions about which children need special education, which job applicants should be hired, which students will be admitted to college, which individuals should be classified as gifted or intellectually disabled, and whether mental functioning has been impaired by head injury or disease. Intelligence tests have even been used to determine who is eligible for the death penalty. With so many important decisions being based on the results of intelligence tests, it is no wonder that there is controversy about them. In theory, these tests measure intelligence, but what does that mean? What, exactly, is "intelligence," where does it come from, and how good are the tests that are designed to measure it? These are some of the questions that we explore in this chapter.

People who are good at using and understanding language and skilled at thinking, problem solving, and decision making are likely to be seen as *intelligent*. But intelligence is not limited to these abilities alone. Over the years, psychologists studying people in various cultures around the world have proposed that the concept of "intelligence" is a broad umbrella that can include many different kinds of attributes and abilities, from rapidly processing information to having a good sense of direction or displaying polished social skills (e.g., Berry & Bennett, 1992; Gardner, 1999; Hunt, 1983; Kush, Spring, & Barkand, 2012; Meyer & Salovey, 1997; Sternberg, Lautrey, & Lubart, 2003). We can't use x-rays or brain scans to see intelligence, so we have to draw conclusions about people's intelligence from what can be observed and measured in their actions (Borkenau et al., 2004). This usually means looking at scores on tests designed to measure intelligence.

TESTING FOR INTELLIGENCE

How is intelligence measured?

What, exactly is *intelligence?* The answer is hard to pin down. Though there is no single, universally accepted definition, most psychologists agree that **intelligence** includes three main characteristics: (1) abstract thinking or reasoning abilities, (2) problem-solving abilities, and (3) the capacity to acquire knowledge (Gottfredson, 1997b; Snyderman & Rothman, 1987). Standard tests of intelligence measure some of these characteristics, but they don't address all of them. That is why some psychologists argue that these tests fail to provide a complete picture of someone's intelligence in its broadest sense. Others say that broadening the definition of intelligence too much makes it meaningless. Still others suggest dropping the term altogether in favor of the more descriptive and less emotionally charged concept of *cognitive ability*. To better understand the controversy, let's look at how standard intelligence tests were created, what they are designed to measure, and how well they do their job. Later, we will consider some alternative intelligence tests that have been proposed by those who find fault with traditional ones.

A Brief History of Intelligence Tests

The story of modern intelligence tests begins in France in 1904, when the French government appointed a psychologist named Alfred Binet (pronounced "bee-NAY") to a committee whose job was to identify, study, and provide special educational programs for children who were not doing well in school. As part of his work, Binet developed a set of test items that provided the model for today's intelligence tests. Binet assumed that reasoning, thinking, and problem solving all depend on intelligence, so he looked for tasks that would highlight differences in children's ability to do these things (Binet & Simon, 1905). His test included tasks such as unwrapping a piece of candy, repeating numbers or sentences from memory, and identifying familiar objects (Rogers, 1995).

Binet also assumed that children's abilities increase with age. With this in mind, he tried out his test items on children of various ages and, in later versions of his test, categorized each item according to the age at which the typical child could respond correctly. For example, a "six-year-old item" was one that half of six-year-olds could answer. In other words, Binet's test contained a set of *age-graded* items. It measured a child's "mental level"—later called **mental age**—by determining the age level of the most-advanced items a child could consistently answer correctly. Children whose mental age equaled their actual age, or *chronological age,* were considered to be of "regular" intelligence (Schultz & Schultz, 2000).

At about the time Binet published his test, Lewis Terman at Stanford University began to develop an English-language version that has come to be known as the **Stanford-Binet Intelligence Scale** (Terman, 1906, 1916). Table 8.1 gives examples of the kinds of items included on the Stanford-Binet test. Terman added items to measure the intelligence of adults and, following a formula devised by William Stern (1914), revised the scoring procedure. Mental age was divided by chronological age, and the result, multiplied

intelligence Personal attributes that center around skill at information processing, problem solving, and adapting to new or changing environments.

mental age A score corresponding to the age level of the most-advanced items a child could answer correctly on Alfred Binet's first intelligence test.

Stanford-Binet Intelligence Scale A test for determining a person's intelligence quotient, or IQ.

TABLE 8.1   THE STANFORD-BINET INTELLIGENCE SCALE

Here are samples of the types of items included on Lewis Terman's original Stanford-Binet Intelligence Scale. As in Alfred Binet's test, an age level was assigned to each item.

Age	Task
2	Place geometric shapes into corresponding openings; identify body parts; stack blocks; identify common objects.
4	Name objects from memory; complete analogies (e.g., fire is hot; ice is ___); identify objects of similar shape; answer simple questions (e.g., "Why do we have schools?").
6	Define simple words; explain differences (e.g., between a fish and a horse); identify missing parts of a picture; count out objects.
8	Answer questions about a simple story; identify absurdities (e.g., in statements such as "John had to walk on crutches because he hurt his arm"); explain similarities and differences among objects; tell how to handle certain situations (e.g., finding a stray puppy).
10	Define more difficult words; give explanations (e.g., about why people should wait their turn to be served in a store); list as many words as possible; repeat six-digit numbers.
12	Identify more difficult verbal and pictured absurdities; repeat five-digit numbers in reverse order; define abstract words (e.g., *sorrow*); fill in a missing word in a sentence.
14	Solve reasoning problems; identify relationships among points of the compass; find similarities in apparently opposite concepts (e.g., "high" and "low"); predict the number of holes that will appear when folded paper is cut and then opened.
Adult	Supply several missing words for incomplete sentences; repeat six-digit numbers in reverse order; create a sentence using several unrelated words (e.g., *forest, businesslike,* and *dismayed*); describe similarities between concepts (e.g., "teaching" and "business").

by 100, was called the *intelligence quotient* (*IQ*). So a child whose mental age and chronological age were equal would have an IQ of 100, which defined an expected "average" intelligence. A ten-year-old who scored at the mental age of a twelve-year-old would have an IQ of $12/10 \times 100 = 120$. In the ensuing years, the term *IQ test* has come to be applied to any test designed to measure intelligence on an objective, standardized scale.

This scoring method allowed testers to rank people on IQ, which was seen as an important advantage by Terman and others who promoted the test in the United States. Unlike Binet—who believed that intelligence improved with education and training—they saw intelligence as a fixed and inherited entity, and so they said IQ tests could pinpoint who did and who did not have a suitable "amount" of intelligence. These beliefs were controversial because they were not supported by empirical evidence and in some instances served to reinforce prejudices against certain people. In other words, enthusiasm for testing outpaced understanding of what was being tested.

For example, in 1917, as the United States moved closer to entering World War I, the government asked a team of psychologists to develop the first group-administered intelligence tests to assess the cognitive abilities of military recruits. One of these tests, called the Army Alpha test, presented arithmetic problems, verbal analogies (e.g., hot is to cold as high is to ___), and general knowledge questions to all recruits who could read English. The Army Beta test was developed for recruits who could not read or speak English; it presented nonverbal tasks, such as visualizing three-dimensional objects and solving mazes. Unfortunately, the verbal tests contained items that were unfamiliar to many recruits. Further, the tests were often given under stressful conditions in crowded rooms where instructions were

Coming to America

Early in the twentieth century, immigrants to the United States, including these new arrivals at Ellis Island in New York harbor, were tested for both physical and mental weaknesses. Especially for those who could not read, speak, or understand English, the intelligence tests they took tended to greatly underestimate their intellectual capacity. Today, psychologists recognize that cognitive abilities are developed partly through education and experience (Cronbach, 1975; Lohmann, 2004; Martinez, 2000), and they take much greater care in administering and interpreting intelligence tests.

Records of the Public Health Service/National Archives

not always audible or (for those who did not speak English) understandable. Nevertheless, when 47 percent of the recruits scored at a mental age of thirteen years or lower (Yerkes, 1921), some psychologists incorrectly concluded that these recruits—even those who did not speak English—lacked normal intelligence (Brigham, 1923).

In the late 1930s, David Wechsler (1939, 1949) developed new tests designed to improve on the earlier ones in three important ways. First, the new tests included both verbal and nonverbal subtests. Second, these tests were designed so that success depended less on having formal schooling. Third, each subtest was scored separately, resulting in a profile that described an individual's performance on all subtests. Special versions of these tests were developed for adults (the Wechsler Adult Intelligence Scale, WAIS) and for children (the Wechsler Intelligence Scale for Children, WISC).

Intelligence Tests Today

Today's revised editions of the Wechsler tests and the Stanford-Binet Intelligence Scale are the most widely used, individually administered intelligence tests. The Wechsler Adult Intelligence Scale (WAIS IV; Wechsler, 2008) contains fifteen subtests that include items such as remembering a series of digits, solving arithmetic problems, defining vocabulary words, understanding and answering general-knowledge questions, assembling blocks, solving visual puzzles, and completing unfinished pictures. Scores on these subtests can be grouped to indicate a person's performance on each of four intellectual factors: mental processing speed, memory ability, perceptual skills, and understanding of verbal information. A full-scale IQ can be calculated by combining scores on all four of these factors. The latest edition of the Wechsler Intelligence Scale for Children (WISC-IV; Wechsler, 2003) yields four similar index scores, along with an overall IQ (see Figure 8.1).

Like the WISC-IV, the fifth edition of the Stanford-Binet (SB5; Roid, 2003) also consists of ten main subtests. However, the SB5 subtests are designed to measure five different abilities: *fluid reasoning* (e.g., completing verbal analogies), *knowledge* (e.g., defining words, detecting absurdities in pictures), *quantitative reasoning* (e.g., solving math problems),

FIGURE 8.1

Items Similar to Those on the Wechsler Intelligence Scale for Children (WISC-IV)

The WISC-IV is made up of ten standard and five supplemental subtests, grouped into four clusters. The *perceptual reasoning* cluster includes tasks, such as those shown here, that involve assembling blocks, solving mazes, and reasoning about pictures. Tests in the *verbal comprehension* cluster require defining words, explaining the meaning of sentences, and identifying similarities between words. Tests in the *working memory* cluster ask children to recall a series of numbers, put a random sequence of numbers into logical order, and the like. The *processing speed* cluster tests children's ability to search for symbols on a page and to decode simple coded messages.

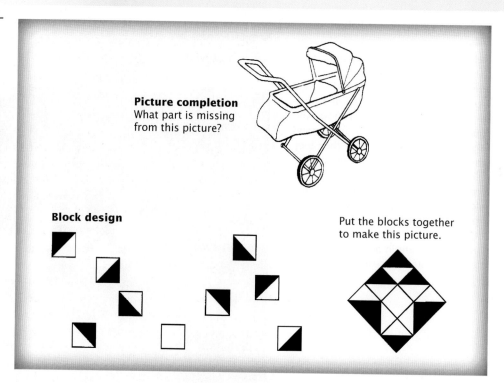

visual-spatial processing (e.g., assembling a puzzle), and *working memory* (e.g., repeating a sentence). Each of these five abilities is measured by one verbal and one nonverbal subtest, so it is possible to calculate a score for each of the five abilities, a total score on all the verbal tests, a total score on all the nonverbal tests, and an overall score for all ten tests combined.

Calculating IQ

IQs are no longer calculated by dividing mental age by chronological age. If you take an IQ test today, the points you earn for each correct answer are added up. That total score is then compared with the scores earned by other people. The average score obtained by people at each age level is assigned an IQ value of 100. Other scores are given IQ values that reflect how far each score deviates from that average. If you do better on the test than the average person in your age group, you will receive an IQ above 100; how far above depends on how much better than average you do. Similarly, a person scoring below the age-group average will have an IQ below 100. This procedure is based on a well-documented aspect of many characteristics: Most people's scores fall in the middle of the range of possible scores, creating a bell-shaped curve that approximates the normal distribution shown in Figure 8.2.

FIGURE 8.2

The Normal Distribution of IQ Scores in a Population

When IQs in the general population are plotted on a graph, a bell-shaped curve appears. The average IQ of any given age group is 100. Half are higher than 100, and half are lower than 100. Approximately 68 percent of the IQs of any age group fall between 84 and 116; about 16 percent fall below 84, and about 16 percent fall above 116.

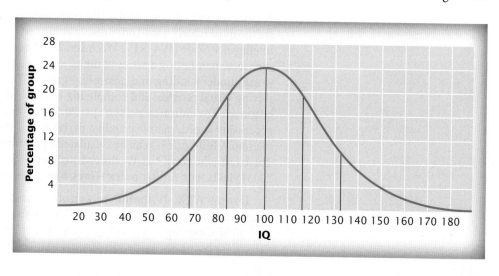

(The statistics appendix provides a fuller explanation of the normal distribution and how IQ tests are scored.) As a result of this scoring method, your **intelligence quotient (IQ)**, reflects your relative standing within a population of your age.

EVALUATING INTELLIGENCE TESTS

How good are IQ tests?

We have said that no intelligence test can accurately measure all aspects of what various people think of as intelligence. So just what does your IQ say about you? Can it predict your performance in school or on the job? Is it a fair summary of your cognitive abilities? To answer questions such as these scientifically, we must measure the quality of the tests that yield IQs, using the same criteria that apply to tests of personality, language skills, driving, or anything else. Let's review these criteria and then see how they are used to evaluate IQ tests.

A **test** is a systematic procedure for observing behavior in a standard situation and describing it with the help of a numerical scale or system of categories (Cronbach, 1990). Tests are *standardized,* meaning that they present the same tasks, under similar conditions, to each person who takes them. Standardization helps ensure that test results will not be significantly affected by factors such as who gives and scores the test. Because the biases of those giving and scoring a test are minimized, a standardized test is said to be *objective.* Test scores can be used to calculate **norms**, which are descriptions of the frequency of particular scores. Norms tell us, for example, what percentage of high school students obtained each possible score on a college entrance exam. They also allow us to say whether a particular IQ or entrance-exam score is above or below the average score. Any test, including IQ tests, should fairly and accurately measure a person's performance. The two most important things to know about when determining the value of a test are its *statistical reliability* and *validity.*

Defining Statistical Reliability

If you stepped on a scale, checked your weight, stepped off, stepped back on, and found that your weight had increased by twenty pounds, you would know it was time to buy a new scale. A good scale, like a good test, must have **statistical reliability**; in other words, the results must be repeatable or stable. The test must measure the same thing in the same way every time it is used. Let's suppose you receive a very high score on a test of reasoning, but when you take the same test the next day, you get a very low score. Your reasoning ability probably didn't change much overnight, so the test is probably unreliable. The higher the reliability of a test, the less likely it is that its results will be affected by temperature, hunger, or other random and irrelevant changes in the environment or the test taker.

Defining Statistical Validity

Most scales reliably measure your weight, giving you about the same reading day after day. But what if you use these readings as a measure of your height? This far-fetched example illustrates that a reliable scale reading can be incorrect, or invalid, if it is misinterpreted. The same is true of tests. Even the most reliable test might not provide a correct, or valid, measure of intelligence, of anxiety, of typing skill, or of anything else if those are not the things the test really measures. In other words, we can't say that a test itself is "valid" or "invalid." Instead, **statistical validity** refers to the degree to which test scores are interpreted appropriately and used properly (American Educational Research Association, American Psychological Association, & National Council on Measurement in Education, 1999; Messick, 1989). As in our scale example, a test can be valid for one purpose but invalid for another.

Researchers evaluate the statistical reliability of a test by obtaining two sets of scores on the same test from the same people. They then calculate a correlation coefficient between the two sets of scores (see the introductory chapter). When the correlation is high

---

intelligence quotient (IQ) An index of intelligence that reflects the degree to which a person's score on an intelligence test deviates from the average score of others in the same age group.

test A systematic procedure for observing behavior in a standard situation and describing it with the help of a numerical scale or a category system.

norms Descriptions of the frequency at which particular scores occur, allowing scores to be compared statistically.

statistical reliability The degree to which a test can be repeated with the same results.

statistical validity The degree to which test scores are interpreted correctly and used appropriately.

If only measuring intelligence were this easy!

J.B. Handelsman The New Yorker Collection/The Cartoon Bank

and positive (usually above +.80), the test is considered reliable. Evaluating a test's statistical validity usually means calculating a correlation coefficient between test scores and something else. What that "something else" is depends on what the test is designed to measure. Suppose, for example, you wanted to know if a creativity test is valid for identifying creative people. You could do so by computing the correlation between people's scores on the creativity test and experts' judgments about the quality of those same people's artistic creations. If the correlation is high, the test has high validity as a measure of creativity.

The Statistical Reliability and Validity of Intelligence Tests

The statistical reliability of intelligence tests is generally evaluated on the basis of their stability, or consistency. The statistical validity of intelligence tests is usually based on their accuracy in guiding statements and predictions about people's cognitive abilities.

How Reliable Are Intelligence Tests?

IQs obtained before the age of seven are only moderately correlated with scores on intelligence tests given later (e.g., Fagan, Holland, & Wheeler, 2007). There are two key reasons. First, the test items used with very young children are different from those used with older children. Second, cognitive abilities change rapidly in the early years (see the chapter on human development). During the school years, IQs tend to remain stable (Allen & Thorndike, 1995; Mayer & Sutton, 1996). So for teenagers and adults, the reliability of intelligence tests is high, as seen in correlation coefficients that are generally between +.85 and +.95 (Deary et al., 2000, 2004).

Of course, a person's score may vary from one occasion to another if there are significant changes in the person's motivation, anxiety, health, or other factors. Overall, though, modern IQ tests usually provide exceptionally consistent results, especially compared with most other kinds of mental tests.

How Valid Are Intelligence Tests?

If everyone agreed on exactly what intelligence is (having a good memory, for example), we could evaluate the statistical validity of IQ tests simply by correlating people's IQs with their performance on various tasks (in this case, memory tasks). IQ tests whose scores correlated most highly with scores on memory tests would be the most valid measures of intelligence. But because psychologists do not fully agree on a single definition of intelligence, they don't have a single standard against which to compare intelligence tests. Therefore, the validity of intelligence tests is best examined by correlating IQ test scores with a variety of performance measures. Because intelligence is always displayed in the course of specific tasks and specific social, educational, and work situations, psychologists assess the validity of intelligence tests for specific purposes.

The results of their research suggest that intelligence test scores are most valid for assessing aspects of intelligence that are related to schoolwork, such as abstract reasoning and understanding verbal material. Their validity—as measured by correlating IQs with high school grades—is reasonably good, about +.50 (Brody & Erlichman, 1998). Scores on tests that focus more specifically on reasoning skills show even higher correlations with school performance (Kuncel, Hezlett, & Ones, 2004; Lohman & Hagen, 2001). For example, the correlation between people's intelligence test scores and the level of education they achieve ranges from +.60 to +.80 (e.g., Colom & Flores-Mendoza, 2007; Judge, Ilies, & Dimotakis, 2010; Lynn & Mikk, 2007).

There is also evidence that employees who score high on verbal and mathematical reasoning tests tend to perform better at work than those who earn lower scores (e.g., Arneson, Sackett, & Beatty, 2011; Kuncel & Hezlett, 2010), especially if their jobs require complex reasoning and judgment skills (Schmidt & Hunter, 2004). One study kept track of people for 70 years and found that those who had high IQs as children tended to be

IQ and Job Performance

IQ is a reasonably good predictor of the ability to learn job-relevant information and to deal with unpredictable, changing aspects of the work environment—characteristics that are needed for success in complex jobs such as this one.

Justin Sullivan/Getty Images

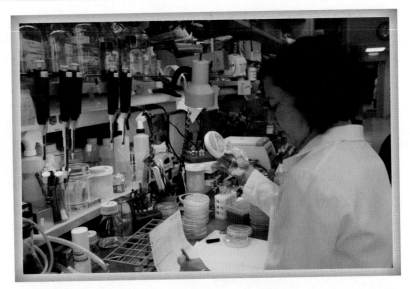

well above average in terms of academic and financial success in adulthood (Oden, 1968; Terman & Oden, 1947). IQs also appear to be highly correlated with performance on routine tasks such as following instructions on medicine labels and using reference material (Gottfredson, 1997b, 2004).

So, in summary, by the standard measures for judging psychological tests, scores on intelligence tests have good reliability and good validity for predicting success in school and in many life situations and occupations (Firkowska-Mankiewicz, 2011; Sackett, Borneman, & Connelly, 2008).

How Fair Are IQ Tests?

As noted earlier, IQ is not a perfect measure of how "smart" a person is. For example, the average intelligence of children appears to have risen in recent decades, but some psychologists suggest that this may be partly due to the use of deviation scores instead of the old MA/CA × 100 formula for calculating IQ (McDonald, 2010). Further, because intelligence tests do not measure the full array of cognitive abilities, a particular test score tells only part of the story, and even that part may be distorted. Many factors other than cognitive ability, including self-control and reactions to the testing situation, can affect test performance (Chapell et al., 2005; Duckworth, Quinn, & Tsukayama, 2012; Onyper et al., 2011). So if children are suspicious of strangers and adults and fear making mistakes, they may become anxious and fail even to try answering certain questions, thus artificially lowering their IQ scores (Fagan, 2000). Scores may also be depressed artificially if individuals are not motivated to take a particular test (Duckworth et al., 2011).

Test scores can also be affected by anxiety, physical disabilities, and language differences and other cultural barriers (Fagan, 2000; Steele, 1997). For example, consider this multiple-choice question: Which is most similar to a xylophone? (violin, tuba, drum, marimba, piano). No matter how intelligent children are, if they have never seen an orchestra or learned about these instruments, they may miss this question. Accordingly, test designers have developed sophisticated procedures to detect and eliminate obviously biased questions. Furthermore, because intelligence tests now include more than one scale, areas that are most influenced by culture, such as vocabulary, can be assessed separately from areas that are less influenced by cultural factors.

However, the solutions to many of the technical problems in intelligence tests have not resolved the controversy over the fairness of intelligence *testing*. The debate continues partly because the results of intelligence tests can have important consequences. Some students who score well above average on these tests may receive advanced educational opportunities that set them on the road to further high achievement. Those whose relatively low test scores identify them as having special educational needs may find themselves in separate classes that isolate them from other students and carry negative social labels. Obviously, the social consequences of testing can be evaluated separately from the quality of the tests themselves; but those consequences cannot be ignored, especially if they tend to affect some groups more than others.

LINKAGES How does excessive emotional arousal affect scores on cognitive ability tests? (a link to Motivation and Emotion)

EMOTIONALITY AND THE MEASUREMENT OF INTELLIGENCE

LINKAGES

What noncognitive factors might influence scores on tests of intelligence and other cognitive abilities? One of the most important factors is emotional arousal. As described in the chapter on motivation and emotion, people tend to perform best when their arousal level is moderate. Too little arousal tends to result in decreased performance, and so does too much. People whose overarousal impairs their ability to do well in testing situations are said to suffer from *test anxiety*.

Some of these people fear that they will do poorly on the test and that others will think they are "stupid." Some may have other unrealistic thoughts, such as that they must be perfect (Eum & Rice, 2011). When people with test anxiety approach a testing situation, they may experience physical symptoms such as heart palpitations and sweating, as well as negative thoughts such as "I am going to blow this exam" (Chapell et al., 2005). In the most severe cases of test anxiety, individuals may be so distressed that they are unable to complete a test.

Test anxiety may affect up to 40 percent of elementary school students and about the same percentage of college students. It is seen in both males and females (Baghurst & Kelley, 2013; Devine et al., 2012). High test anxiety is correlated with lower IQ, but even among people with high IQ, those who experience severe test anxiety tend to do poorly on tests such as college entrance exams. Test-anxious elementary school students are likely to receive low grades and to perform poorly on evaluated tasks and on those that require new learning (Campbell, 1986). Some children with test anxiety refuse to attend school or "play sick" on test days, creating a vicious circle that further harms their performance on standardized achievement tests.

Anxiety, frustration, and other emotions may also be at work in a testing phenomenon that Claude Steele and his colleagues have identified as *stereotype threat* (Steele & Aronson, 2000). According to Steele, concern over negative stereotypes about the cognitive abilities of the group to which they belong can impair the performance of some women and some members of ethnic minorities. As a result, the test scores they earn, in laboratory settings at least, may underestimate those abilities (e.g., Cadinu et al., 2005; Mazerolle et al., 2012; Murphy, Steele, & Gross, 2007; Schmader, 2010). In one study, bright African American students read test instructions designed to make them more sensitive to negative stereotypes about the intelligence of their ethnic group. These students performed less well on a standardized test than equally bright African American students whose sensitivity to the stereotypes had not been increased (Steele & Aronson, 2000). In another study, women with good math skills were randomly assigned to one of two groups. The first group was given information intended to create concern over the stereotype that women aren't as good as men at math. In fact, they were told that men usually do better than women on the difficult math test they were about to take. The second group was not given this information. The women in the second group performed much better on the test than those in the first. In fact, their performance was equal to that of men who took the same test (Spencer, Steele, & Quinn, 1997).

Studies such as these suggest that stereotype threat can lead to reduced scores on tests—possibly by impairing test preparation and test-taking strategies (e.g., Appel, Kronberger, & Aronson, 2011; Mangels et al., 2012; Martiny et al., 2012; Robinson-Cimpian et al., 2014). However, other research on the performance of females and minority group members on high-stakes tests has found no such effects or only a weak effect (e.g., Cullen, Waters, & Sackett, 2006; Fischer & Massey, 2007; Grand et al., 2011). It may be that some people—such as girls whose parents reject gender stereotypes—are more resistant to stereotype threat than others (Tomasetto, Alparone, & Cadinu, 2011). In any case, the extent to which stereotype threat

(continued)

impairs performance on cognitive abilities tests in real-world settings remains uncertain (Stoet & Geary, 2012).

Test anxiety is associated with lower performance on cognitive ability tests (e.g., Gass & Curiel, 2011), but it does not appear to decrease the accuracy of predictions made on the basis of the tests' scores (Reeve & Bonaccio, 2008; Wicherts & Scholten, 2010). In other words, if people's performance is hampered by anxiety in a testing situation, it may be hampered in other stressful situations as well. The good news for people who suffer from test anxiety is that counseling centers at most colleges and universities have effective programs for dealing with it (Brown et al., 2011; Nemati, 2013).

These and other research findings indicate that the relationship between anxiety and test performance is complex, but one generalization seems to hold true: People who are severely test-anxious do not perform to the best of their ability on intelligence tests (Lang & Lang, 2010).

IQ As a Measure of Inherited Ability

Concern over the fairness of intelligence tests is based partly on what many people assume to be true about these tests. A good intelligence test, they believe, should be able to see through the surface ripples created by an individual's cultural background, experience, and motivation to discover the innate cognitive abilities that lie beneath. But years of study have led psychologists to conclude that intelligence is a *developed ability,* influenced partly by genetics but also by educational, cultural, and other life experiences that shape the very knowledge, reasoning, and other skills that intelligence tests measure (e.g., Hunt, 2012; Nisbett et al., 2012; Plomin & Spinath, 2004; Rattan, Good, & Dweck, 2012). For example, when brighter, more curious children ask more questions of their parents and teachers, they are generating a more enriching environment for themselves. Their innate abilities are allowing these children to take better advantage of their environment (Scarr, 1997; Scarr & Carter-Saltzman, 1982). The parents of these children are likely to be bright too. If so, their own biologically influenced intelligence probably helped them acquire resources that enrich their children's environment. That enriched environment helps develop the children's intelligence, so these children are favored by both heredity and environment.

Psychologists have explored the influence of genetics on individual differences in intelligence by comparing the correlation between the IQs of people who have differing degrees of similarity in their genetic makeup and environment. For example, they have examined the IQs of identical twins—pairs with exactly the same genes—who were separated when very young and raised in different environments. They have also examined the IQs of identical twins raised together.

These studies find, first, that hereditary factors are strongly related to IQ. When identical twins who were separated at birth and adopted by different families are tested many years later, the correlation between their scores is usually at least +.60 (e.g., Bouchard, 1999). That is, if one twin scores high on an IQ test, the other probably will too; if one twin's IQ is low, the other's is likely to be low as well. However, studies of IQ correlations also highlight the importance of the environment (Scarr, 1998). Consider any two people—twins, siblings, or unrelated children—brought up together in a foster home. No matter what the degree of genetic similarity in these pairs, the correlation between their IQs is higher if they share the same home than if they are raised in different environments, as Figure 8.3 shows (Scarr & Carter-Saltzman, 1982).

The role of environmental influences is also seen in the results of studies that compare children's IQs before and after environmental changes such as adoption (van IJzendoorn & Juffer, 2005). Generally, when children from relatively impoverished backgrounds were adopted into homes offering a more enriching intellectual environment—including interesting materials and experiences, as well as a supportive, responsive adult—they show twelve- to eighteen-point increases in their IQs (e.g., Capron & Duyme, 1989;

FIGURE 8.3
Correlations of IQ Scores

The correlation in IQ between pairs increases with increasing similarity in heredity or environment.

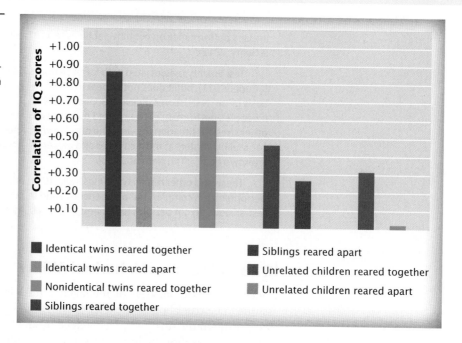

Identical twins reared together

Identical twins reared apart

Nonidentical twins reared together

Siblings reared together

Siblings reared apart

Unrelated children reared together

Unrelated children reared apart

Nisbett et al., 2012; Weinberg, Scarr, & Waldman, 1992; Zhai, Brooks-Gunn, & Waldfogel, 2011; Zhai, Raver, & Jones, 2012).

A study of French children who were adopted soon after birth demonstrates the importance of both genetic and environmental influences. These children were tested after years of living in their adopted homes. Children whose biological parents were from upper socioeconomic groups (in which higher IQs are more common) had higher IQs than children whose biological parents came from lower socioeconomic groups, regardless of the socioeconomic status of the adoptive homes (Capron & Duyme, 1989, 1996). These findings were supported by data from the Colorado Adoption Project (Cardon & Fulker, 1993; Cardon et al., 1992), and they suggest that a genetic component of children's cognitive abilities continues to exert an influence even in their adoptive environment.

Programs designed to enhance young children's school readiness and academic ability have also been associated with improved scores on tests of intelligence and academic success (Bulotsky-Shearer, Dominguez, & Bell, 2012; McWayne et al., 2012; Neisser et al., 1996). The same is true of enrichment programs that focus on musical training and improving memory capacity (e.g., Moreno et al., 2011; Morrison & Chein, 2011; Shipstead, Redick, & Engle, 2012). These early intervention programs may be partly responsible for the steady increase of children's average IQs mentioned earlier (Flynn, 1999; Neisser, 1998).

Some researchers have concluded that the influence of heredity and environment on differences in cognitive abilities appears to be roughly equal. Others see a somewhat larger role for heredity (Herrnstein & Murray, 1994; Loehlin, 1989; Plomin, 1994), and they are working to identify specific groups of genes that might be associated with variations in cognitive abilities (Posthuma & de Geus, 2006). However, the effects of genetics and the environment are intertwined in complex ways, so the influence of either factor may change across developmental stages, in particular situations, and across some cultures (Kan et al., 2013; Tucker-Drob et al., 2011). It is also important to understand that estimates of the relative contributions of heredity and environment apply only to groups, not to individuals. It would not be correct to say that about 50 percent of your IQ is inherited and about 50 percent learned. It is far more accurate to say that about half of the *variability* in the IQs of a group of people can be attributed to hereditary influences. The other half can be attributed to environmental influences and measurement error. Intelligence provides yet another example of nature and nurture working together to shape human behavior and mental processes.

Research on genetic and environmental influences can help us understand the differences we see *among* people in terms of cognitive abilities and other characteristics, but it cannot tell us how strong each influence is in any *particular* person, including in this person.

Leo Cullum The New Yorker Collection/The Cartoon Bank

Group Differences in IQ

Much of the controversy over the roles played by genes and the environment in intelligence has been sparked by efforts to explain differences in the average IQs seen in particular groups of people. For example, the average IQ of Asian Americans is typically the highest among the various ethnic groups in the United States, followed, in order, by European Americans, Hispanic Americans, and African Americans (e.g., Fagan, 2000; Herrnstein & Murray, 1994; Lynn, 2006). Similar patterns appear on a number of other tests of cognitive ability and achievement (e.g., Koretz, Lynch, & Lynch, 2000; Sackett et al., 2001). Further, the average IQ of people from high-income areas in the United States and elsewhere is consistently higher than that of people from low-income communities with the same ethnic makeup (McLoyd, 1998; Rowe, Jacobson, & Van den Oord, 1999).

To understand these differences and where they come from, we must remember two things. First, group scores are just that; they do not describe individuals. Although the mean IQ of Asian Americans is higher than the mean IQ of European Americans, there will still be large numbers of European Americans who score well above the Asian American mean and large numbers of Asian Americans who score below the European American mean (see Figure 8.4).

Second, increases in average IQ in recent decades, and other similar findings, suggest that inherited characteristics are not necessarily fixed. As already mentioned, a favorable environment can improve a child's performance somewhat, even if the inherited influences on that child's IQ are negative (Humphreys, 1984). There is also evidence that living in an impoverished environment can impair the development of cognitive skills (Turkheimer et al., 2003) and that environmental influences can magnify the effects of genetic influences (Bates, Lewis, & Weiss, 2013).

Socioeconomic Differences

We have already mentioned that there is a positive correlation between socioeconomic status (SES) and scores on IQ and other cognitive ability tests (e.g., Sackett et al., 2009). Why should this be? Four factors seem to be involved. First, parents' jobs and status depend on characteristics related to their own intelligence. This intelligence is partly determined by a genetic component that in turn contributes to their children's IQ. Second, parents' income affects their children's environment in ways that can increase or decrease IQ (Bacharach & Baumeister, 1998; Suzuki & Valencia, 1997). Third, motivational differences may play a role. Parents in upper- and middle-income families tend to provide more financial and psychological support for their children's motivation to succeed and excel in academic endeavors (Erikson et al., 2005; Nelson-LeGall & Resnick, 1998). As a result, children from

LINKAGES How does motivation affect IQ scores? (a link to Motivation and Emotion)

FIGURE 8.4

A Representation of Ethnic Group Differences in IQ Scores

The average IQ of Asian Americans is about four to six points higher than the average IQ of European Americans, who average twelve to fifteen points higher than African Americans and Hispanic Americans. Notice, though, that there is much more variation *within* these groups than there is among their average scores.

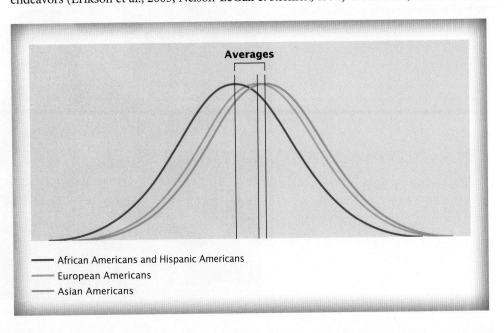

Averages

— African Americans and Hispanic Americans
— European Americans
— Asian Americans

middle- and upper-income families may exert more effort in testing situations and therefore obtain higher scores (Bradley-Johnson, Graham, & Johnson, 1986; Robbins et al., 2004; Zigler & Seitz, 1982). Fourth, because colleges, universities, and businesses usually select people who score high on various cognitive ability tests, those with higher IQs—who tend to do better on such tests—may have greater opportunities to earn more money (Sackett et al., 2001).

Ethnic Differences

Some experts have argued that the average differences in IQ among ethnic groups in the United States are due at least partly to heredity (Rowe, 2005; Rushton & Jensen, 2005). Remember, though, that the existence of hereditary differences among individuals *within* groups does not indicate whether differences *between* groups result from similar genetic causes (Lewontin, 1976). As shown in Figure 8.4, variation within ethnic groups is much greater than variation among the mean scores of those groups (Zuckerman, 1990).

We must also take into account the significantly different environments in which average children in various ethnic groups grow up. To take only the most blatant evidence, recent Census Bureau figures show 27.2 percent of African American families and 25.6 percent of Hispanic American families living below the poverty level, compared with 11.7 percent of Asian American families and 9.7 percent of European American families (Gabe, 2013). Compared with European Americans, African Americans are more likely to have parents with less extensive educational backgrounds and to have less access to good nutrition, health care, and schools (Evans, 2004; W. J. Wilson, 1997). All of these conditions are likely to pull down scores on intelligence tests (e.g., Englund, Luckner, & Whaley, 2004; Lemos et al., 2011). Cultural factors may also contribute to differences among the average scores of various ethnic groups. For example, those differing averages may partly reflect differences in the degree to which parents in each group tend to encourage their children's academic achievement (Ryan et al., 2010; Steinberg, Dornbusch, & Brown, 1992).

The influence of environmental factors on the average black-white difference in IQ is supported by data from adoption studies. One such study involved African American children from disadvantaged homes who were adopted by middle- to upper-class European American families in the first years of their lives (Scarr & Weinberg, 1976). When measured

Helping with Homework

There are differences in the average IQs of European Americans and African Americans, but these differences are due in large measure to various environmental, social, and other nongenetic factors.

Andy Sacks/Stone/Getty Images

a few years later, the mean IQ of these children was 110. A comparison of this mean score with that of nonadopted children from similar backgrounds suggests that the new environment raised the children's IQs at least ten points. A ten-year follow-up study of these youngsters showed that their average IQ was still higher than the average of African American children raised in disadvantaged homes (Weinberg, Scarr, & Waldman, 1992).

As discussed in the chapter on human development, cultural factors may also contribute to differences among the mean scores of various ethnic groups. For example, those differing averages may partly reflect differences in the degree to which parents in each group tend to encourage their children's academic achievement (Al-Fadhli & Kersen, 2010; Ryan et al., 2010; Steinberg, Dornbusch, & Brown, 1992).

In short, it appears that some important nongenetic factors decrease the mean scores of African American and Hispanic American children. Whatever heredity might contribute to children's performance, under the right conditions it may be possible for them to improve.

Conditions That Can Raise IQ

As noted, environmental conditions can help or deter cognitive development (see the chapter on human development). For example, lack of caring attention or of normal intellectual stimulation can inhibit a child's mental growth. Low test scores have been linked to poverty, chaos, and noise in the home; poor schools; and inadequate nutrition and health care (Alaimo, Olson, & Frongillo, 2001; Kwate, 2001; Morrissey et al., 2014). Can the effects of bad environments be reversed? Not always, but efforts to intervene in the lives of children and enrich their environments have had some limited success. Conditions for improving children's performance include rewards for progress, encouragement of effort, and creation of expectations for success.

In the United States, the best-known attempt to enrich children's environments is Project Head Start, a set of programs established by the federal government in the 1960s to help preschoolers from lower-income backgrounds. In some of these programs, teachers visit the home and work with the child and parents on cognitive skills. In others, the children attend classes in nursery schools. Some programs emphasize health and nutrition and family mental health and social skills as well. Head Start has brought measurable benefits to children's health (Abbot-Shim, Lambert, & McCarty, 2003; Spernak et al., 2006), as well as improvements in their academic, intellectual, and language skills (e.g., Bierman, Domitrovich, et al., 2008; Bierman, Nix, et al., 2008).

Project Head Start

This teacher is working in Project Head Start, a U.S. government program designed to enrich the academic environments of preschoolers from lower-income backgrounds and improve their chances of succeeding in grade school.

Mark Richard/PhotoEdit

Do the gains achieved by preschool enrichment programs last? Although program developers sometimes claim long-term benefits (e.g., Christensen et al., 2014), these claims are disputed (e.g., Caputo, 2004; Mehr et al., 2013). Various findings from more than a thousand such programs are often contradictory, but the effect on IQ typically diminishes after a year or two (Woodhead, 1988). A study evaluating two of the better preschool programs concluded that their effects are at best only temporary (Locurto, 1991). These fading effects reflect the fact that IQ describes a person's performance compared with others of the same age. To keep the same IQ, a child must keep improving at the same rate as other children in the same age group (Kanaya, Scullin, & Ceci, 2003). So IQ will drop from year to year in children whose rate of cognitive growth falls behind that of their age-mates. This slowing in the cognitive growth rate is often seen when children leave special preschool programs and enter the substandard schools that often serve the poor (Finn-Stevenson & Zigler, 1999; Zigler & Muenchow, 1992).

Some beneficial effects have also been seen in programs such as the Abecedarian Project (Ramey, 1992). Children at risk for intellectual disabilities were identified while they were still in the womb. They then received five years of intense interventions to improve their chances of academic success. When they started school, children in this enrichment program had IQs that were seven points higher than those of at-risk children who were not in the program. At age twelve, they still scored higher on IQ tests, but the size of the difference at that time was just five points. Clear benefits in educational achievement, income, and social-emotional outcomes were still evident nearly two decades later (Campbell et al., 2012).

The primary benefit of early-enrichment programs probably lies in improving children's attitudes toward school (Woodhead, 1988). This can be an important benefit because, especially in borderline cases, children with favorable attitudes toward school may be less likely to be held back or placed in special education classes. Avoiding these experiences may in turn help children retain positive attitudes about school and enter a cycle in which gains due to early enrichment are maintained and amplified on a long-term basis.

THINKING CRITICALLY
ARE INTELLIGENCE TESTS UNFAIRLY BIASED AGAINST CERTAIN GROUPS?

We have seen that intelligence tests can have great value but also that IQ can be negatively affected by poverty, inferior educational opportunities, and other environmental factors. So there is concern that members of ethnic minorities and other disadvantaged groups have not had an equal chance to develop the knowledge and skills that are required to achieve high scores on IQ tests.

What am I being asked to believe or accept?

Some critics claim that standard intelligence tests are not fair. They argue that a disproportionately large number of people in some ethnic minority groups receive low scores on intelligence tests for reasons that are unrelated to cognitive ability, job potential, or other criteria that the tests are supposed to predict (Helms, 1997; Kwate, 2001; Neisser et al., 1996). They say that using ability and aptitude measures to make decisions about people—such as assigning them to particular jobs or special classes—may unfairly deprive members of some ethnic minority groups of equal employment or educational opportunities.

What evidence is available to support the assertion?

Research reveals several possible sources of bias in tests of cognitive abilities. First, as noted earlier, noncognitive factors such as anxiety, lack of motivation, or distrust can impair test performance and may put certain individuals at a disadvantage. For example, children from some minority groups may be less motivated to perform well on standardized tests and less

(continued)

likely to trust the adult tester (Steele, 1997). So differences in test scores may partly reflect motivational or emotional differences among various groups, not intellectual ones.

Second, many intelligence test items still reflect the vocabulary and experiences of the dominant middle-class culture in the United States. Individuals who are less familiar with the knowledge and skills valued by that culture will not score as well as those who are more familiar with them. Not all cultures value the same things, however (Sternberg & Grigorenko, 2004b). A study of Cree Indians in northern Canada revealed that words and phrases associated with *competence* included "good sense of direction"; at the *incompetent* end of the scale was the phrase "lives like a white person" (Berry & Bennett, 1992). A European American might not perform well on a Cree intelligence test based on these criteria. In fact, as illustrated in Table 8.2, poor performance on a culture-specific test is probably due more to unfamiliarity with culture-based concepts than to lack of cognitive ability. Compared with more traditional measures, "culture-fair" tests—such as the Universal Nonverbal Intelligence Test—that reduce dependence on oral skills do produce smaller differences between native English speakers and English-language learners (Bracken & McCallum, 1998).

TABLE 8.2   AN INTELLIGENCE TEST?

TRY THIS Take a minute to answer each of the following questions on this "intelligence test," and check your answers against the key at the bottom of page 277. If, like most people, you are unfamiliar with the material being tested by these rather obscure questions, your score will probably be low. Would it be fair to say, then, that you are not very intelligent?

1. What fictional detective was created by Leslie Charteris?
2. What dwarf planet travels around the sun every 248 years?
3. What vegetable yields the most pounds of produce per acre?
4. What was the infamous pseudonym of broadcaster Iva Toguri d'Aquino?
5. What kind of animal is Dr. Dolittle's pushmi-pullyu?

Third, some tests may reward individuals who interpret questions as expected by the test designer. Conventional intelligence tests have clearly defined "right" and "wrong" answers. Yet a person may interpret test questions in a manner that is "intelligent" or "correct" but that produces a "wrong" answer. For example, when one child was asked, "In what way are an apple and a banana alike?" he replied, "They both give me diarrhea." And when Liberian rice farmers were asked to sort objects, they tended to put a knife in the same group as vegetables. This was the clever way to do it, they said, because the knife is used to cut vegetables. When asked to sort the objects as a "stupid" person would, the farmers grouped the cutting tools together, the vegetables together, and so on, as most North Americans would (Segall et al., 1990). In other words, the fact that people don't give the answer that the test designer was looking for does not mean that they *can't* (which is why well-trained test administrators would ask for another answer before moving on).

Are there alternative ways of interpreting the evidence?

This same evidence might be interpreted as showing that although intelligence tests do not provide a pure measure of innate cognitive ability, they do provide a fair picture of whether a person has developed the skills necessary to succeed in school or in certain jobs. When some people have had more opportunity than others to develop their abilities, the difference will be reflected in their IQs. From this point of view, intelligence tests are fair measures of the cognitive abilities developed by people living in a society that, unfortunately, contains some unfair elements. In other words, the tests may be accurately detecting knowledge and skills

(*continued*)

that are not represented equally in all groups, but this doesn't mean that the tests discriminate *unfairly* among those groups.

To some observers, concern over cultural bias in intelligence tests stems from a tendency to think of IQ as a measure of innate ability. These psychologists suggest instead that intelligence tests are measuring ability that is developed and expressed in a cultural context—much as athletes develop the physical skills needed to play certain sports (Lohman, 2004). Eliminating language and other cultural elements from intelligence tests, they say, would eliminate a vital part of what the term *intelligence* means in any culture (Sternberg, 2004). This may be why "culture-fair" tests do not predict academic achievement as well as conventional intelligence tests do (Aiken, 1994; Lohman, 2005). Perhaps familiarity with the culture reflected in intelligence tests is just as important for success at school or work in that culture as it is for success on the tests themselves. After all, the ranking among groups on measures of academic achievement is similar to the ranking for average IQs (Sue & Okazaki, 1990).

What additional evidence would help evaluate the alternatives?

If the problem of test bias is really a reflection of differences between various groups' opportunities to develop their cognitive skills, it will be important to conduct research on interventions that can reduce those differences. Making "unfair" cultures fairer by enhancing the skill development opportunities of traditionally disadvantaged groups should lead to smaller differences between groups on tests of cognitive ability (Martinez, 2000). It will also be important to find better ways to encourage members of disadvantaged groups to take advantage of those opportunities (Sowell, 2005).

At the same time, alternative tests of cognitive ability must also be explored, particularly those that include assessment of problem-solving skills and other abilities not measured by most intelligence tests (e.g., Sternberg & Kaufman, 1998). If new tests show smaller between-group differences than traditional tests but have equal or better predictive validity, many of the issues discussed in this section will have been resolved. So far, efforts in this direction have not been successful.

What conclusions are most reasonable?

The effort to reduce unfair cultural biases in tests is well founded, but "culture-fair" tests will be of little benefit if they fail to predict academic or occupational success as well as traditional tests do (Anastasi & Urbina, 1997; Sternberg, 1985). Whether one considers this situation good or bad, fair or unfair, the fact remains that it is important for people to have the information and skills that are valued by the culture in which they live and work. So it seems reasonable to continue using conventional cognitive ability tests as long as they accurately measure the skills and knowledge that people need for success in their culture.

In other words, there is probably no value-free, experience-free, or culture-free way to measure the construct known as intelligence when that construct is defined by the behaviors that a culture values and that are developed through experience in that culture (Sternberg, 1985, 2004). This conclusion has led some researchers to worry less about how cultural influences might "contaminate" tests of innate cognitive abilities and to focus instead on how to help people develop the abilities that are required for success in school and society. As mentioned earlier, if more attention were focused on combating poverty, poor schools, inadequate nutrition, lack of health care, and other conditions that result in lower average IQs and reduced economic opportunities for certain groups of people, many of the reasons for concern about test bias might be eliminated.

The Bottom Line on IQ Tests

IQ tests have been criticized for being biased and for labeling people on the basis of scores or profiles. ("In Review: Influences on IQ" lists the factors that can shape IQ.) "Summarizing" a person with a score on an IQ test does indeed run the risk of oversimplifying reality and making errors. But intelligence tests can also *prevent* errors. Specifically, they can reduce the chances that inaccurate stereotypes, false preconceptions, and faulty generalizations will influence important educational and employment decisions. For example, boredom or lack of motivation at school might make a child appear mentally slow or perhaps even intellectually disabled. But a test of cognitive abilities conducted under the right conditions is likely to reveal the child's potential. The test can prevent the mistake of moving a child of average intelligence to a class for children with intellectual disabilities. And as Alfred Binet had hoped, intelligence tests have been enormously helpful in identifying children who need special educational attention. So despite their limitations and potential for bias, IQ tests can minimize the likelihood of assigning children to remedial work they do not need or to advanced work they cannot yet handle.

IN REVIEW

INFLUENCES ON IQ

Source of Effect	Description	Examples of Evidence for Effect
Genetics	Genes appear to play a significant role in differences among people on intelligence test performance.	The IQs of siblings who share no common environment are positively correlated. There is a greater correlation between scores of identical twins than between those of nonidentical twins.
Environment	Environmental conditions interact with genetic inheritance. Nutrition, medical care, sensory and intellectual stimulation, educational experiences, interpersonal relations, and influences on motivation are all significant features of the environment.	IQs have risen among children who are adopted into homes that offer a stimulating, enriching environment. Correlations between IQs of identical twins reared together are higher than for those reared apart.

1. Intelligence is influenced by both _____ and _____.
2. Children living in poverty tend to have _____ IQs than those in middle-income families.
3. IQs of children whose parents encourage learning tend to be _____ than those of children whose parents do not.

DIVERSITY IN INTELLIGENCE

Is there more than one type of intelligence?

Intelligence test scores can tell us some things—and predict some things—about people, but we have seen that they don't tell the whole story of intelligence. Let's see how diverse intelligence can be by looking at some of the ways in which psychological scientists have approached it.

The Psychometric Approach

Standard intelligence tests are associated with **psychometrics**, the scientific study and measurement of knowledge, abilities, attitudes, personality, and other psychological characteristics. The **psychometric approach** to intelligence focuses on the *products of*

psychometrics The scientific study and measurement of knowledge, abilities, attitudes, personality, and other psychological characteristics.

psychometric approach A way of studying intelligence that emphasizes analysis of the products of intelligence, especially scores on intelligence tests.

Answers to Table 8.2: (1) Simon Templar; (2) Pluto; (3) cabbage; (4) Tokyo Rose; (5) a two-headed llama.

intelligence, including scores on IQ tests. Researchers taking this approach ask whether intelligence is one general trait or a bundle of more specific abilities. The answer matters, because if intelligence is a single trait, then an employer might assume that someone with a low IQ could not do any tasks well. But if intelligence is composed of many abilities that are somewhat independent of one another, then a poor showing in one area—say, imagining the rotation of objects in space—would not rule out good performance in others, such as understanding information or solving mathematical word problems.

Early in the twentieth century, the writings of statistician Charles Spearman began the modern debate about the nature of intelligence. Spearman noticed that scores on almost all tests of cognitive abilities were positively correlated (Spearman, 1904, 1927). That is, people who did well on one test also tended to do well on all of the others. Spearman concluded that these correlations were created by general cognitive ability, which he called **g**, for *general intelligence*, and a group of special intelligences, which he collectively referred to as **s**. The s factors, he said, are the specific information and skills needed for particular tasks. Raymond B. Cattell (1963) agreed with Spearman, but his own factor analyses suggested two kinds of g. **Fluid intelligence**, he said, is the basic power of reasoning and problem solving. **Crystallized intelligence**, in contrast, involves specific knowledge gained as a result of applying fluid intelligence. It produces, for example, a good vocabulary and familiarity with the multiplication tables.

After decades of research and debate, most psychologists today agree that there is a positive correlation among various tests of cognitive ability, a correlation that is attributed to the g factor (e.g., Carroll, 1993; Frey & Detterman, 2004). Further, it appears that the g factor can be measured by many different groups of cognitive tests, even if the tests in each group are entirely different (Johnson et al., 2004). However, the brain probably does not contain some unified "thing" corresponding to what people call intelligence. Instead, cognitive abilities appear to be organized in "layers," beginning with as many as fifty or sixty narrow and specific skills that can be grouped into seven or eight more general ability factors, all of which combine into g, the broadest and most general of all (e.g., Carroll, 1993; Kievit et al., 2012; Lubinski, 2004; Unsworth et al., 2014). Understanding g and how it arises is a major goal of research in cognitive psychology and brain research (e.g., Bouchard, 2014; Garlick, 2002; Hampshire et al., 2012; Reynolds, 2013).

Intelligence as Information Processing

As described in the chapter on thought and language, many cognitive psychologists see the brain as an information-processing system that receives and works on information in ways that allow us to think, remember, and engage in other cognitive activities. When applied to the concept of intelligence, this **information-processing model** focuses on identifying the mental *processes* involved in intelligent behavior, not the abilities that result in test scores and other *products* of intelligence. Researchers taking this information-processing approach ask, What mental operations are necessary to perform intellectual tasks? What aspects depend on past learning, and what aspects depend on attention, working memory, and processing speed? Are there individual differences in these processes that correlate with measures of intelligence? More specifically, are measures of intelligence related to differences in the amount of attention people have available for basic mental processes or in the speed of those processes?

As discussed in the chapter on sensation and perception, attention represents a pool of resources or mental energy. When people perform difficult tasks or perform more than one task at a time, they must call on greater amounts of these resources. Early research by Earl Hunt (1980) suggests that people with greater intellectual ability have more attentional resources available. There is also evidence of a positive correlation between IQ and performance on tasks requiring attention, such as silently counting the number of words in the "animal" category while reading a list of varied terms aloud (Stankov, 1989).

Another possible link between differences in information processing and differences in intelligence relates to processing speed. Perhaps more intelligent people just have "faster

g A general intelligence factor that Charles Spearman postulated as accounting for positive correlations between people's scores on all sorts of cognitive ability tests.

s A group of special abilities that Charles Spearman saw as accompanying general intelligence (g).

fluid intelligence The basic power of reasoning and problem solving.

crystallized intelligence The specific knowledge gained as a result of applying fluid intelligence.

information-processing model An approach to the study of intelligence that focuses on mental operations, such as attention and memory, that underlie intelligent behavior.

brains." When a task is complex, having a "fast brain" might reduce the chance that information will fade from memory before it can be used (Jensen, 1993; Larson & Saccuzzo, 1989). With this view in mind, some researchers have attempted to measure various aspects of intelligence by looking at activity in particular parts of the brain (e.g., Colom, Jung, & Haier, 2006; Gläscher et al., 2010; Koten et al., 2009).

Evidence that better performance on intellectual tasks is related to more efficient information processing (Koten et al., 2009; Neubauer & Fink, 2009; Rypma & Prabhakaran, 2009) highlights the role of brain processes in intelligence, but it probably doesn't tell the whole story. Other research suggests that only a portion of the variation seen in people's performance on cognitive abilities tests can be accounted for by differences in their speed of access to long-term memory, the capacity of short-term and working memory, or other information-processing abilities (Baker, Vernon, & Ho, 1991; Friedman et al., 2006; Miller & Vernon, 1992).

The Triarchic Theory of Intelligence

Robert Sternberg's *triarchic theory* of intelligence (1988b, 1999) proposes three different types of intelligence: analytic, creative, and practical. *Analytic intelligence,* the kind that is measured by traditional intelligence tests, would help you solve a physics problem; *creative intelligence* is what you would use to compose music; and you would draw on *practical intelligence* to figure out what to do if you were stranded on a lonely road during a blizzard.

Sternberg recognizes that analytic intelligence is important for success at school and in other areas, but he argues that universities and employers should not select people solely on the basis of tests of this kind of intelligence (Sternberg, 1996; Sternberg & Williams, 1997). Why? Because the tasks posed by tests of analytic intelligence are often of little interest to the people taking them and typically have little relationship to their daily experience. For one thing, each task is usually clearly defined and comes with all the information needed to find the one right answer (Neisser et al., 1996), a situation that seldom occurs in the real world. The practical problems people face every day are generally of personal interest and are related to more common life experiences. That is, they are ill defined and do not contain all the information necessary to solve them, they typically have more than one correct solution, and there may be several paths to a solution (Sternberg et al., 1995).

Brainpower and Intelligence

The information-processing model of intelligence suggests that people with the most rapid information processors—the "fastest" brains—should do best on cognitive ability tests, including intelligence tests and college entrance exams. Research suggests that there is more to intelligent behavior than sheer processing speed, though.

Stephen Collins/Science Source

It is no wonder, then, that some children who do poorly in school may nevertheless show high degrees of practical intelligence, including—as in the case of Brazilian street children—the ability to live by their wits in hostile environments (Carraher, Carraher, & Schliemann, 1985). Some racetrack bettors whose IQs are as low as 82 are experts at predicting race odds at post time by combining many different kinds of complex information about horses, jockeys, and track conditions (Ceci & Liker, 1986). In these particular cases, practical intelligence appears almost unrelated to the analytic intelligence measured by traditional cognitive tests, but research with larger populations shows that there is actually a significant correlation between the two (Gottfredson, 2003).

Sternberg's theory is important because it extends the concept of intelligence into areas that most psychologists have traditionally not examined and because it emphasizes what intelligence means in everyday life. The theory is so broad, however, that many parts of it are difficult to test. For example, methods for measuring practical "street smarts" have been proposed (Sternberg, 2001; Sternberg et al., 1995), but they remain controversial (Brody, 2003; Gottfredson, 2003). Sternberg and his colleagues have also developed new intelligence tests designed to assess analytic, practical, and creative intelligence (see Figure 8.5), and they offer evidence that scores on these tests can predict success in college and at some jobs at least as well as standard intelligence tests (Sternberg & Kaufman, 1998; Sternberg & Rainbow Project, 2006). Other researchers have questioned this interpretation (Brody, 2003). The value of these newer tests, they say, may be due in part to the correlation between practical and analytic intelligence. To some extent, the newer tests may be measuring the same thing as the older ones (Gottfredson, 2003).

FIGURE 8.5
Testing for Practical and Creative Intelligence

TRY THIS Robert Sternberg argues that traditional tests measure mainly analytic intelligence. Here are sample items from tests he developed to test both practical and creative intelligence. Try answering them before you check the answers at the bottom of page 283. How did you do?

PRACTICAL

1. Think of a problem that you are currently experiencing in real life. Briefly describe the problem, including how long it has been present and who else is involved (if anyone). Then describe three different practical things you could do to try to solve the problem. *(Students are given up to 15 minutes and up to 2 pages.)*

2. Choose the answer that provides the **best** solution, given the specific situation and desired outcome.

   John's family moved to Iowa from Arizona during his junior year in high school. He enrolled as a new student in the local high school two months ago but still has not made friends and feels bored and lonely. One of his favorite activities is writing stories. What is likely to be the most effective solution to this problem?

   A. Volunteer to work on the school newspaper staff.

   B. Spend more time at home writing columns for the school newsletter.

   C. Try to convince his parents to move back to Arizona.

   D. Invite a friend from Arizona to visit during Christmas break.

3. This question asks you to use information about everyday things. Read the question carefully and choose the best answer.

   Mike wants to buy two seats together and is told there are pairs of seats available only in Rows 8, 12, 49, and 95–100. Which of the following is not one of his choices for the total price of the two tickets?

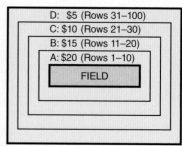

   A. $10.   **B.** $20.   **C.** $30.   **D.** $40.

FIGURE 8.5 (*continued*)

CREATIVE

1. Suppose you are the student representative to a committee that has the power and the money to reform your school system. Describe your ideal school system, including buildings, teachers, curriculum, and any other aspects you feel are important.
    (Students are given up to 15 minutes and up to 2 pages.)

2. Each question has a "Pretend" statement. You must suppose that this statement is true. Decide which word goes with the third underlined word in the same way that the first two underlined words go together.

    Colors are audible.

    flavor is to *tongue* as *shade* is to

    A. ear.   **B.** light.   **C.** sound.   **D.** hue.

3. First, read how the operation is defined. Then, decide what is the correct answer to the question.

    There is a new mathematical operation called **flix.**
    It is defined as follows:

    $$A \text{ flix } B = A + B, \text{ if } A > B$$

    but $A \text{ flix } B = A \times B, \text{ if } A < B$

    and $A \text{ flix } B = A / B, \text{ if } A = B$

    How much is 4 flix 7?

    A. 28.   **B.** 11.   **C.** 3.   **D.** −11.

Multiple Intelligences

Some people whose IQs are only average, or even below average, may have exceptional ability in certain specific areas. One child whose IQ was just 50 could correctly state the day of the week for any date between 1880 and 1950 (Scheerer, Rothmann, & Goldstein, 1945). He could also play melodies on the piano by ear and sing Italian operatic pieces he had heard. In addition, he could spell—forward or backward—any word spoken to him and could memorize long speeches, although he had no understanding of what he was doing.

Cases such as this are part of the evidence cited by Howard Gardner in support of his theory of *multiple intelligences* (Gardner, 1993, 2002). To study intelligence, Gardner focuses on how people learn and use symbol systems such as language, mathematics, and music. He asks, Do these systems all require the same abilities and processes, the same "intelligence"? According to Gardner, the answer is no. All people, he says, possess a number of intellectual potentials, or intelligences, each of which involves a somewhat different set of skills. Biology provides raw capacities; cultures provide symbolic systems—such as language—to use those raw capacities. Although the intelligences normally interact, they can function with some independence, and individuals may develop certain intelligences further than others. ("In Review: Approaches to Intelligence" summarizes Gardner's theory, along with the other views of intelligence we have discussed.)

The specific intelligences that Gardner (1999) proposes are (1) *linguistic* intelligence (reflected in good vocabulary and reading comprehension), (2) *logical-mathematical*

A Musical Prodigy?

According to Gardner's theory of multiple intelligences, skilled artists, athletes, and musicians—such as the young flutist shown here—display forms of intelligence not assessed by standard intelligence tests.

Comstock Images/Alamy

intelligence (as indicated by skill at arithmetic and certain kinds of reasoning), (3) *spatial* intelligence (seen in the ability to visualize relationships among objects in the environment), (4) *musical* intelligence (as in abilities involving rhythm, tempo, and sound identification), (5) *body-kinesthetic* intelligence (reflected in skill at dancing, athletics, and eye-hand coordination), (6) *intrapersonal* intelligence (displayed by self-understanding), (7) *interpersonal* intelligence (seen in the ability to understand and interact with others), and (8) *naturalistic* intelligence (the ability to see patterns in nature). Other researchers have suggested that people also possess *emotional* intelligence, which involves the capacity to perceive, use, understand, and manage their emotions (Meyer & Salovey, 1997; Salovey & Grewal, 2005). Gardner says that traditional intelligence tests sample only the first three of these intelligences, mainly because these are the forms of intelligence most valued in school. To measure intelligences not tapped by standard tests, Gardner suggests collecting samples of children's writing, assessing their ability to appreciate or produce music, and obtaining teacher reports of their strengths and weaknesses in athletic and social skills (Gardner, 1991).

Gardner's view of intelligence is appealing, partly because it allows virtually everyone to be highly intelligent in at least one way. However, his critics argue that including athletic or musical skill dilutes the validity and usefulness of the intelligence concept, especially as it is applied in school and in many kinds of jobs. They suggest that intrapersonal, interpersonal, body-kinesthetic, and naturalistic abilities are best described as collections of specific skills. Therefore, it makes more sense to speak of, say, "interpersonal skills" rather than "interpersonal intelligence." At the moment, Gardner's theory lacks the empirical evidence necessary to challenge other, more established theories of intelligence (Klein, 1997; Waterhouse, 2006a, 2006b). This is true in part because there are still no dependable measures of the various intelligences he proposes (Lubinski & Benbow, 1995; Visser, Ashton, & Vernon, 2006). Until and unless such measures are developed, say Gardner's critics, his theory will be of little scientific value.

APPROACHES TO INTELLIGENCE

IN REVIEW

Approach	Method	Key Findings or Propositions
Psychometric	Define the structure of intelligence by examining factor analyses of the correlations between scores on tests of cognitive abilities.	Performance on many tests of cognitive abilities is highly correlated, but this correlation, represented by g, reflects a bundle of abilities, not just one trait.

(continued)

IN REVIEW
APPROACHES TO INTELLIGENCE (CONT.)

Approach	Method	Key Findings or Propositions
Information processing	Understand intelligence by examining the mental operations involved in intelligent behavior.	The speed of basic cognitive processes and the amount of attentional resources available make significant contributions to performance on intelligence tests.
Sternberg's triarchic theory	Understand intelligence by examining the information processing involved in thinking, changes with experience, and effects in different environments.	There are three distinct kinds of intelligence: analytic, creative, and practical. Intelligence tests measure only analytic intelligence, but creative intelligence (which involves dealing with new problems) and practical intelligence (which involves adapting to one's environment) may also be important to success in school and at work.
Gardner's theory of multiple intelligences	Understand intelligence by examining test scores, information processing, biological and developmental research, the skills valued by different cultures, and exceptional people.	Biology provides the capacity for eight distinct "intelligences": linguistic, logical-mathematical, spatial, musical, body-kinesthetic, intrapersonal, interpersonal, and naturalistic.

In Review Questions

1. The concepts of fluid and crystallized intelligence developed from research on the _____ approach to intelligence.

2. Using fMRI scanning to relate memory skills to intelligence reflects the _____ approach to intelligence.

3. Which theory of intelligence highlights the fact that some people with low IQs can still succeed at complex tasks of daily living?

FOCUS ON RESEARCH METHODS
TRACKING COGNITIVE ABILITIES OVER THE LIFE SPAN

LINKAGES Which research designs are best for studying changes in cognitive abilities as people age? (a link to Research in Psychology)

As described in the chapter on human development, significant changes in cognitive abilities occur from infancy through adolescence, but development does not stop there. One major study has focused specifically on the changes in cognitive abilities that occur during adulthood.

What was the researchers' question?

The researchers began by asking what appears to be a relatively simple question: How do adults' cognitive abilities change over time?

(continued)

Answers to Figure 8.5: Practical (2) A, (3) B. Creative: (2) A, (3) A.

How did the researchers answer the question?

Answering this question is extremely difficult because findings about age-related changes in cognitive abilities depend to some extent on the methods that are used to observe those changes. None of the methods include true experiments, because psychologists cannot randomly assign people to be a certain age and then give them mental tests. So changes in cognitive abilities must be explored through a number of other research designs.

One of these, the *cross-sectional study,* compares data collected at the same point in time from people of different ages. However, cross-sectional studies contain a major confounding variable: Because people are born at different times, they may have had very different educational, cultural, nutritional, and medical experiences. This confounding variable is referred to as a *cohort effect.* Suppose that two cohorts, or age groups, are tested on their ability to imagine the rotation of an object in space. The cohort born around 1940 might not do as well as the one born around 1980, but does the difference reflect declining spatial ability in the older people? It might, but it might also be due in part to the younger group's greater experience with video games and other spatial tasks. In other words, differences in experience, and not just age, could account for differences in ability between older and younger people in a cross-sectional study.

Changes associated with age can also be examined through *longitudinal studies,* in which people are repeatedly tested as they grow older. But longitudinal designs, too, have some built-in problems. For one thing, fewer and fewer members of an age cohort can be tested over time as death, physical disability, relocation, and lack of interest reduce the sample size. Researchers call this problem the *mortality effect.* Further, the remaining members are likely to be the healthiest in the group and may also have retained better mental powers than the dropouts. As a result, longitudinal studies may underestimate the degree to which abilities decline with age. Another confounding factor can come from the *history effect.* Here, some event—such as a reduction in health care benefits for senior citizens—might have an effect on cognitive ability scores that is mistakenly attributed to age. Finally, longitudinal studies may be confounded by *testing effects,* meaning that participants may improve over time because of what they learn during repeated testing procedures.

As part of the Seattle Longitudinal Study of cognitive aging, K. Warner Schaie (1993) developed a research design that measures the impact of the confounding variables we have discussed and allows corrections to be made for them. In 1956, Schaie identified a random sample of five thousand members of a health maintenance organization (HMO) and invited some of them to volunteer for his study. The volunteers, who ranged in age from twenty to eighty, were given a set of intelligence tests designed to measure certain primary mental abilities (PMA). The cross-sectional comparisons allowed by this first step were, of course, confounded by cohort effects. To control for those effects, the researchers retested the same participants seven years later, in 1963. This design allowed the researchers to compare the size of the *difference* in PMA scores between, say, the twenty-year-olds and twenty-seven-year-olds tested in 1956 with the size of the *change* in PMA scores for these same people as they aged from twenty to twenty-seven and from twenty-seven to thirty-four. Schaie reasoned that if the size of the longitudinal change was about the same as the size of the cross-sectional difference, the cross-sectional difference could probably be attributed to aging, not to the era in which the participants were born.

To measure the impact of testing effects, the researchers randomly drew a new set of participants from their original pool of five thousand. These people were of the same age range as the first sample, but they had not yet been tested. If people from the first sample did better on their second PMA testing than the people of the same age who now took the PMA for the first time, a testing effect would be suggested. To control for history effects, the researchers examined the scores of people who were the same age in different years. For example, they compared people who were thirty in 1956 with those who were thirty in 1963, people who were forty in 1956 with those who were forty in 1963, and so on. If PMA scores were the same for people of the same age no matter what year they were tested, it is unlikely that events that happened in any particular year would have influenced test results. The researchers tested participants multiple times between 1956 and 1999 (Gerstorf et al., 2011). On each occasion, they retested some previous participants and tested others for the first time.

(continued)

The Voice of Experience

Even in old age, people's crystallized intelligence may remain intact. Their extensive storehouse of knowledge, experience, and wisdom makes older people a valuable resource for the young.

© Konstantin Sutyagin/Shutterstock.com

What did the researchers find?

The results of the Seattle Longitudinal Study and other, more limited longitudinal studies suggest a reasonably consistent conclusion: Unless people are impaired by Alzheimer's disease or other brain disorders, most of their cognitive abilities usually decline very slightly between early adulthood and old age. Some aspects of crystallized intelligence, which depends on retrieving information and facts about the world from long-term memory, may remain robust well into old age. Other components of intelligence, however, may have failed quite noticeably by the time people reach sixty-five or seventy. Fluid intelligence, which involves rapid and flexible manipulations of ideas and symbols, is the most likely to decline (Bugg et al., 2006; Gilmore, Spinks, & Thomas, 2006; Schaie, 1996). The decline shows up in the following areas:

1. *Working memory.* The ability to hold and organize material in working memory declines beyond age fifty or sixty, particularly when attention must be redirected (e.g., Fandakova et al., 2014).

2. *Processing speed.* There is a general slowing of all mental processes (e.g., Manard et al., 2014; Stawski, Silwinski, & Hofer, 2013).

3. *Organization.* Older people seem to be less likely to solve problems by adopting specific strategies, or mental shortcuts (Charness, 2000). The tests carried out by older people tend to be more random and haphazard (Young, 1971). This result may occur partly because many older people are out of practice at solving such problems.

4. *Flexibility.* Older people tend to be less flexible than younger people in problem solving (Johnco, Wuthrich, & Rapee, 2013).

5. *Control of attention.* The ability to direct or control attention declines with age (Kramer et al., 1999). Older adults tend to be overwhelmed by distracting information, which may help account for many of the cognitive problems accompanying aging (Gazzaley et al., 2005).

What do the results mean?

This study indicates that different kinds of cognitive abilities change in different ways throughout our lifetimes. In general, there is a gradual, continual accumulation of knowledge about the world, some systematic changes in the limits of cognitive processes, and changes

(continued)

in the way those processes are carried out. This finding suggests that a general decline in cognitive abilities during adulthood is neither inevitable nor universal (Richards et al., 2004).

What do we still need to know?

There is an important question that Schaie's study doesn't answer: Why do age-related changes in cognitive abilities occur? Some researchers suggest that these changes are largely due to a decline in the speed and accuracy with which older people process information (Li et al., 2004; Salthouse, 2000). If this interpretation is correct, it would explain why some older people are less successful than younger ones at tasks that require rapidly integrating several pieces of information in working memory prior to making a choice or a decision.

It is also vital to learn why some people do *not* show declines in cognitive abilities, even when they reach their eighties. By understanding the biological and psychological factors responsible for these exceptions to the general rule, we might be able to reverse or delay some of the intellectual consequences of growing old.

Unusual Intelligence

Psychologists' understanding of intelligence has been advanced by studying people whose intelligence is unusual—especially the gifted and the intellectually disabled (Robinson, Zigler, & Gallagher, 2000).

Giftedness

People who show remarkably high levels of accomplishment in particular areas are often referred to as gifted (Guénolé et al., 2013). Giftedness is typically measured by school achievement. A child's potential for high achievement is usually measured by intelligence tests, but researchers warn that it is risky to predict academic potential from a single measure, such as IQ (Hagen, 1980; Lohman & Hagen, 2001; Thorndike & Hagen, 1996).

For one thing, not all people with unusually high IQs become famous and successful in their chosen fields, although they are more likely than others to do so. One of the best-known studies of the intellectually gifted was conducted by Lewis Terman and his colleagues (Oden, 1968; Terman & Oden, 1947, 1959). This study began in 1921 with the identification of more than 1,500 boys and girls whose IQs were very high—most higher than 135 by age ten. Periodic interviews and tests over the next seventy years revealed that few, if any, became world-famous scientists, inventors, authors, artists, or composers. But only eleven failed to graduate from high school, and more than two-thirds graduated from college—this at a time when completing a college education was relatively rare, particularly for women. Ninety-seven went on to earn Ph.D.s; ninety-two, law degrees; and fifty-seven, medical degrees. In 1955, their median family income was well above the national average (Terman & Oden, 1959).

In general, people with higher IQs were physically and mentally healthier than the general population and appeared to have led happier lives (Ali et al., 2013; Cronbach, 1996). Several more recent studies also show that people with higher IQs tend to live longer (e.g., Deary & Batty, 2011; Ghirlanda, Enquist, & Lind, 2014; Hagger-Johnson et al., 2012), perhaps because they have the reasoning and problem-solving skills that lead them to take better care of themselves and avoid danger (e.g., Calvin et al., 2011; Deary & Der, 2005b; Hall et al., 2009; see the Focus on Research Methods section in the chapter on health, stress, and coping).

In other words, higher IQs tend to predict greater success in life (Lubinski et al., 2006; Simonton & Song, 2009), but an extremely high IQ does not guarantee special distinction. Some research suggests that gifted children are not fundamentally different kinds of people. They just have more of the same basic cognitive abilities seen in all children (Dark & Benbow, 1993; Singh & O'Boyle, 2004). Other work suggests that gifted people may be different in other ways, too, such as having unusually intense curiosity or motivation to master certain tasks or areas of intellectual endeavor (e.g., Lubinski et al., 2001; Nicpon & Pfeiffer, 2011). Whatever the case, there is broad support for the idea that giftedness is something that can and should be encouraged and developed (Dai, Swanson, & Cheng, 2011; Subotnik, Olszewski-Kubilius, & Worrell, 2011).

Intellectual Disability

intellectual development disorder Defined in DSM-5 as an IQ at or below 70, starting in childhood, and affecting a person's ability to function as compared to other people of the same age.

People whose IQs are lower than about 70 and who fail to display the skills at daily living, communication, and other tasks that are expected of those their age were once described as mentally retarded (American Psychiatric Association, 1994). They might now more often be said to be mentally challenged or to have a developmental disability, an intellectual disability, or a developmental delay (Schalock et al., 2009). The new Diagnostic and Statistical Manual (DSM-5, American Psychiatric Association) describes these people as having an **intellectual development disorder**. This diagnosis is given not only on the basis of a low measured IQ, but also on whether that measurement was made in childhood and whether there is evidence of impairment in day-to-day functioning. As a result, people in this very broad category differ greatly in their cognitive abilities and in their ability to function independently in daily life (see Table 8.3).

TABLE 8.3 CATEGORIES OF INTELLECTUAL DISABILITY

These categories are approximate. Especially at the upper end of the scale, many intellectually disabled people can learn to handle tasks well beyond what their IQ might have predicted. Thus, a given IQ score does not automatically guarantee a certain level of function in society. Many people with IQs lower than 70 can function adequately in their communities and so would not be diagnosed with an intellectual development disorder.

Level of Intellectual Disability	IQ Range	Characteristics
Mild	50–70	A majority of all intellectually disabled people. Many live independently, marry, and maintain skilled employment with training. May have difficulty with academics, abstract reasoning, risk evaluation, and problem solving. May need support for complex tasks such as home organization, money management, child care, and health care.
Moderate	35–49	With extended training and time, some people can manage personal needs (hygiene, eating) and household tasks independently. May maintain employment with limited responsibilities, but could need help with ancillary job-related duties (scheduling, transportation, money management), as well as with other personal responsibilities such as health care, social judgments, communication, and decision making.
Severe	20–34	Can participate in household tasks with ongoing training and supervision. Most need support for much of their self-care. Relationships usually limited to family and caregivers. Speech is usually limited to simple vocabulary, focused on immediate circumstances. Most require constant supervision.
Profound	Below 20	Dependent on caregivers for self-care and for household tasks, but may be able to participate in some tasks if assisted. Motor and sensory impairments limit many goal-directed actions. Sometimes can understand simple verbal communication, but self-expression is mostly nonverbal. Can often enjoy close familial and caregiver relationships. Require constant supervision.

The Eagle Has Landed

In February 2000, Richard Keebler, twenty-seven, became an Eagle Scout, the highest rank in the Boy Scouts of America. His achievement is notable not only because only 4 percent of all Scouts reach this pinnacle but also because Keebler has Down syndrome. As we come to better understand the potential, not just the limitations, of people with intellectual disabilities, their opportunities and their role in society will continue to expand.

Photo by Fraser Hale. Copyright St. Petersburg Times. Reprinted with permission.

Some cases of intellectual disability have a clearly identifiable cause. The best-known example is *Down syndrome*, which occurs when an abnormality during conception results in an extra copy of chromosome 21 (Kleschevnikov et al., 2012). Children with Down syndrome typically have IQs in the range of 40 to 55, though some may score higher than that. There are also several inherited causes of intellectual disability. The most common of these is *fragile X syndrome,* a defect on chromosome 23 (known as the *X chromosome*) (Hunter et al., 2014). More rarely, intellectual disability is caused by inheriting *Williams syndrome* (a defect on chromosome 7) or by inheriting a gene for *phenylketonuria,* or PKU (which causes the body to create toxins out of milk and other foods). Intellectual disability can also result from environmental causes, such as exposure to German measles (rubella), alcohol, or other toxins before birth; oxygen deprivation during birth; and head injuries, brain tumors, and infectious diseases (such as meningitis or encephalitis) in childhood (U.S. Surgeon General, 1999).

Psychosocial intellectual disability refers to the 30 to 40 percent of (usually mild) cases of intellectual disability that have no obvious genetic or environmental cause (American Psychiatric Association, 1994). These cases appear to result from a complex and as yet unknown interaction between heredity and environment that researchers are continuing to explore (Croen, Grether, & Selvin, 2001; Spinath, Harlaar et al., 2004).

People who have mild intellectual disability differ from other people in three important ways (Campione, Brown, & Ferrara, 1982):

1. They perform certain mental operations more slowly, such as retrieving information from long-term memory. When asked to repeat something they have learned, they are not as quick as a person of normal intelligence.

2. They know fewer facts about the world. It is likely that this deficiency is a consequence of the problem listed next.

3. They are not very good at using certain mental strategies that may be important in learning and problem solving. For example, they do not remember to rehearse material that must be held in short-term memory, even though they know how to do so.

Despite such difficulties, the cognitive abilities of intellectually disabled people can be improved to some extent. One program that emphasized positive parent-child communications began when the children were as young as two and a half years old. It helped children with Down syndrome to eventually master reading skills at a second-grade level, providing the foundation for further achievement (Rynders & Horrobin, 1980; Turkington, 1987). However, designing effective programs for children who are intellectually disabled is complicated by the fact that learning does not depend on cognitive skills alone. It also depends on social and emotional factors, including where children learn. Much debate has focused on *mainstreaming* and *inclusive education*, which involve teaching children with disabilities, including those who are intellectually disabled, in regular classrooms alongside children without disabilities. A number of studies comparing the cognitive and social skills of children who have been mainstreamed and those who were separated show few significant differences overall. However, it does appear that students at higher ability levels may gain more from being mainstreamed than their less mentally able peers. There are also advantages for them in terms of self-esteem, friendships, and social support (e.g., Huck, Kemp, & Carter, 2010; Mills et al., 1998; Pati, 2011; Vianello & Lanfranchi, 2011).

psychosocial intellectual disability
Cases of mild cognitive disability for which there is no obvious genetic or environmental cause.

LINKAGES

As noted in the chapter on introducing psychology, all of psychology's many subfields are related to one another. Our discussion of test anxiety illustrates just one way in which the topic of this chapter, intelligence, is linked to the subfield of motivation and emotion (which is the focus of the chapter by that name). The Linkages diagram shows ties to two other subfields as well, and there are many more ties throughout the book. Looking for linkages among subfields will help you see how they all fit together and better appreciate the big picture that is psychology.

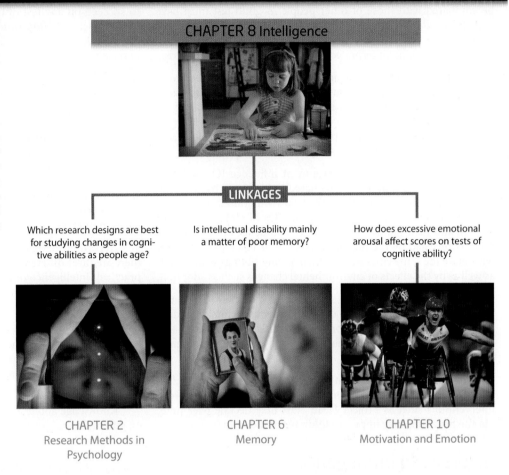

CHAPTER 8 Intelligence

LINKAGES

Which research designs are best for studying changes in cognitive abilities as people age?

Is intellectual disability mainly a matter of poor memory?

How does excessive emotional arousal affect scores on tests of cognitive ability?

CHAPTER 2
Research Methods in Psychology

CHAPTER 6
Memory

CHAPTER 10
Motivation and Emotion

SUMMARY

Intelligence refers to the capacity to perform higher mental processes, such as reasoning, remembering, understanding, problem solving, and decision making.

Testing for Intelligence

How is intelligence measured?

Psychologists have not reached a consensus on how best to define intelligence. A working definition describes **intelligence** in terms of reasoning, problem solving, and dealing with changing environments.

Alfred Binet's pioneering test of intelligence included questions that required reasoning and problem solving of varying levels of difficulty, graded by age and resulting in a **mental age** score. Lewis Terman developed a revision of Binet's test that became known as the **Stanford-Binet Intelligence Scale**; it included items designed to assess the intelligence of adults as well as children and became the model for IQ tests. David Wechsler's tests remedied some of the deficiencies of the earlier IQ tests. Made up of subtests, some of which have little verbal content, these tests allowed testers to generate scores for different aspects of cognitive ability.

The Stanford-Binet and Wechsler tests are the most popular individually administered intelligence tests. Both include subtests and provide scores for parts of the test, as well as an overall score. For example, in addition to a full-scale IQ, the Wechsler tests yield scores for verbal comprehension, perceptual reasoning, working memory, and processing speed. Currently, a person's **intelligence quotient**, or **IQ**, reflects how far that person's performance on the test deviates from the average performance of people in the same age group. An average performance is assigned an IQ of 100.

Evaluating Intelligence Tests

How good are IQ tests?

A **test** has two key advantages over other techniques of evaluation. First, they are standardized, which means that the conditions surrounding a test are as similar as possible for everyone who takes it. Second, they produce scores that can be compared with **norms**, thus allowing people's strengths or weaknesses in various areas to be compared with those of other people. A good test must have **statistical reliability**, which means that the results for each person are consistent, or stable. **Statistical validity** refers to the degree to which test scores are interpreted appropriately and used properly.

Intelligence tests are reasonably reliable, and they do a good job of predicting academic success. However, these tests assess only some of the abilities that might be considered aspects of intelligence, and they tend to favor people most familiar with middle-class culture. Nonetheless, this familiarity is important for academic and occupational success.

Both heredity and the environment influence IQ, and their effects interact. The influence of heredity is shown by the high correlation between the IQs of identical twins raised in separate households and by the similarity in the IQs of children adopted at birth and their biological parents. The influence of the environment is revealed by the higher correlation of IQs among siblings who share the same environment than among siblings who do not, as well as by the effects of environmental changes such as adoption.

Average IQs differ across socioeconomic and ethnic groups. These differences appear to be due to numerous factors, including differences in educational opportunity, motivation to achieve, family support for cognitive development, and other environmental conditions.

An enriched environment sometimes raises preschool children's IQs. Initial gains in cognitive performance that result from interventions such as Project Head Start may decline over time, but the programs may improve children's attitudes toward school.

Diversity in Intelligence

Is there more than one type of intelligence?

Researchers have taken several approaches to understanding the concept of intelligence. Based on the field of **psychometrics**, the **psychometric approach** to intelligence attempts to analyze the structure of intelligence by examining correlations between tests of cognitive ability. Because scores on almost all tests of cognitive ability are positively correlated, Charles Spearman concluded that such tests measure a general factor of mental ability, called **g**, as

well as more specific factors, called **s**. As a result of factor analysis, other researchers have concluded that intelligence is not a single general ability but a collection of abilities and subskills needed to succeed on any test of intelligence. Raymond B. Cattell distinguished between **fluid intelligence**, the basic power of reasoning and problem solving, and **crystallized intelligence**, the specific knowledge gained as a result of applying fluid intelligence. Modern psychometric theories of intelligence describe it as a hierarchy that is based on a host of specific abilities that fit into about eight groups that themselves combine into a single, general category of cognitive ability.

The **information-processing model** of intelligence focuses on the processes underlying intelligent behavior. Varying degrees of correlation have been found between IQ and measures of the flexibility and capacity of attention and between IQ and measures of the speed of information processing. This model has helped deepen our understanding of the processes that create individual differences in intelligence.

According to Robert Sternberg's triarchic theory of intelligence, there are three different types of intelligence: analytic, creative, and practical. Intelligence tests typically focus on analytic intelligence, but recent research has suggested ways to assess practical and creative intelligence too.

Howard Gardner's approach to intelligence suggests that biology equips us with the capacities for multiple intelligences that can function with some independence—specifically, linguistic, logical-mathematical, spatial, musical, body-kinesthetic, intrapersonal, interpersonal, and naturalistic intelligences.

Knowledge about intelligence has been expanded by research on giftedness and intellectual disabilities. Gifted people, those with very high IQs, tend to be healthier and more successful, but they are not necessarily geniuses. People are considered to have an intellectual development disorder if as children they have IQs below about 70 and if their functioning is less than expected for people their age. Some cases of intellectual disability have a known cause; in **psychosocial intellectual disability**, the mix of genetic and environmental causes is unknown. Compared with people of normal intelligence, intellectually disabled people process information more slowly, know fewer facts, and are deficient at knowing and using mental strategies. Despite such difficulties, the cognitive skills of some intellectually disabled people can be improved to some extent.

TEST YOUR KNOWLEDGE

Select the best answer for each of the following questions. Then check your responses against the Answer Key at the end of the book.

1. Binet's intelligence test was developed to _____.
   a. identify children who needed special educational programs
   b. help the armed forces make appropriate assignments of recruits
   c. identify which immigrants were mentally defective and thus should not be allowed into the United States
   d. help employers decide which employees were most appropriate for the available jobs

2. Jonah's parents are told that their son has an IQ of 100. According to the intelligence test scoring method used today, this means that Jonah _____.
   a. has a mental age that is higher than his chronological age
   b. scored higher than half the children in his age group
   c. is considered to be a gifted child
   d. shows about average skill at divergent thinking

3. Like all other applicants to medical school, Lavinia took the MCAT admission test. Later, researchers compared all the successful applicants' medical school grades with

their MCAT scores. The researchers were obviously trying to measure the MCAT's _____.
a. statistical reliability
b. standardization
c. statistical validity
d. norms

4. When Jerrica first took the Handy Dandy Intelligence test, her score was 140. When she took the same test six weeks later, her score was only 102. If other people showed similarly changing score patterns, the Handy Dandy Intelligence test would appear to lack _____.
a. statistical reliability
b. statistical validity
c. standardization
d. norms

5. Research shows that today's standardized intelligence tests _____.
a. have good reliability and reasonably good validity for predicting success in school
b. do not do a good job of predicting success on the job
c. are not correlated with performance on "real-life" tasks
d. measure the full array of cognitive abilities

6. There are two sets of twins in the Mullis family. Louise and Lanie are identical twins; Andy and Adrian are not. According to research on heredity and intelligence, which pair of twins is likely to show the most similarity in IQs?
a. Andy and Adrian, because they are male siblings.
b. Andy and Adrian, because they are fraternal twins.
c. Louise and Lanie, because they are female siblings.
d. Louise and Lanie, because they are identical twins.

7. Rowena is mildly intellectually disabled, but she is attending regular classes at a public school. Rowena most likely _____ and she will _____ from being mainstreamed.
a. knows fewer facts about the world than others; benefit
b. knows fewer facts about the world than others; not benefit
c. learns just as fast as other children, but forgets it faster; not benefit
d. has little or no potential for employment; benefit

8. Betsey took an intelligence test that included items requiring her to say what she would do if she were stranded in a large city with no money and how she would teach music to children who had no musical instruments. This test was most likely based on _____.
a. Sternberg's triarchic theory of intelligence
b. Gardner's concept of multiple intelligences
c. Terman's giftedness theory
d. The Wechsler Adult Intelligence Scale

9. Your cousin Alix is enrolled in a preschool program for "at-risk" children designed to enrich his learning environment. Based on research on programs such as Project Head Start, you tell his parents that the program will most likely positively influence Alix's _____, but

might have little or no influence on his _____ in the long-term.
a. attitudes toward school; IQ
b. IQ; attitudes toward school
c. spatial ability; mathematical ability
d. mathematical ability; spatial ability

10. Mrs. Linder, a high school teacher, believes that students who are good at math will also be good in English, history, and music. Mrs. Linder most likely subscribes to the _____ theory of intelligence.
a. g
b. triarchic
c. genetic
d. multiple intelligences

11. Eugene, 77, is retired now, but he has worked crossword puzzles every day since he was a teenager. He no longer finishes the puzzles as quickly as he used to, but he can complete more difficult puzzles. Eugene's puzzle performance reflects the fact that his _____ intelligence has remained relatively intact.
a. spatial
b. fluid
c. crystallized
d. flexible

12. Although many successful musical artists don't appear to have "book smarts," they certainly have the "street smarts" needed to succeed in the music industry. Which theory of intelligence best accounts for this observation?
a. g theory
b. triarchic theory
c. information processing theory
d. crystallized intelligence theory

13. Dr. Armstrong is conducting an experiment on the possible effects of stereotype threat on women's math test performance. Which of the following independent variables would Dr. Armstrong manipulate in his experiment?
a. age of the participants
b. age and ethnic background of the participants
c. information about alleged sex differences in math ability
d. sex of the participants

14. Differences in the average IQ scores of various ethnic groups
a. are not statistically significant.
b. reflect mainly genetic differences.
c. reflect mainly differing environmental factors.
d. reflect both genetic and environmental factors.

15. If the influence of heredity and environment on differences in intelligence is about equal, it would mean that _____.
a. about 50 percent of your IQ is inherited and 50 percent learned
b. about half of the IQ variability seen in a group of people is attributed to heredity
c. about half of the IQ variability seen in a group of people is attributed to environment
d. both b and c are correct

16. Today, your IQ score would be determined by
    a. the total number of test items you answered correctly.
    b. how much your score deviates from others of the same age.
    c. dividing your mental age by your chronological age and multiplying by 100.
    d. dividing your chronological age by your mental age and multiplying by 100.

17. People whose scores on intelligence tests identify them as gifted are more often
    a. troubled during their teenage years.
    b. troubled during adulthood.
    c. world famous for some achievement.
    d. more successful than the average person.

18. Paul has a terrible time with academic exams, but he is a great dancer and a highly skilled mechanic who can take apart, repair, and fix almost anything. The _____ approach would be most likely to label these skills as intelligent?
    a. psychometric
    b. triarchic
    c. multiple intelligence
    d. information processing

19. _____ is an important environmental influence on children's IQ scores.
    a. Parents' socioeconomic status
    b. Parents' support for children's motivation to succeed at school
    c. Parents' age and marital status
    d. both a and b are correct

20. Research on intelligence has established that _____.
    a. once set by genetics, intelligence cannot change much
    b. once set by environmental factors, intelligence cannot change much
    c. environmental factors can improve or impair intelligence test performance
    d. environmental factors can impair IQ scores, but not improve them

Consciousness

© sheff/Shutterstock.com

Preview

Have you ever "spaced out" while driving on a boring highway? Has your mind wandered far and wide during a dull lecture? These experiences contrast sharply with how it feels to focus your attention on playing a video game or to concentrate on a complicated recipe, but all of them represent differing versions of consciousness. In this chapter, we delve into both "normal" and altered states of consciousness. Most of the altered states—sleep, dreaming, hypnosis, meditation—differ psychologically and physiologically from normal waking consciousness. We will examine how they differ, and we will also look at the effects of psychoactive drugs, which, in addition to altering consciousness, have complex physiological effects.

In an old *Sesame Street* episode, Ernie is trying to find out whether Bert is asleep or awake. Ernie observes that Bert's eyes are closed, and comments that Bert usually closes his eyes when he is asleep. Ernie also notes that Bert doesn't respond to pokes when he's asleep, so naturally he delivers a few pokes. At first, Bert doesn't respond, but after being poked a few times, he awakes, very annoyed, and yells at Ernie for waking him. Ernie then informs Bert that he just wanted to let him know that it was time for his nap.

Doctors face a similar situation in dealing with the more than 30 million people each year who receive general anesthesia during surgery. These patients certainly seem unresponsive, but there's no reliable way of knowing whether they actually are unconscious (Alkire, Hudetz, & Tononi, 2008). It turns out that about 1 in 500 people may retain some degree of consciousness during surgical procedures (Pandit et al., 2013). In rare cases, patients actually are aware of surgical pain and remember the trauma. Although their surgical wounds heal, these people may be psychologically scarred by the experience and may even show symptoms of posttraumatic stress disorder (Leslie et al., 2010). To reduce the possibility of operating on someone who appears unconscious but may not be, some physicians suggest monitoring patients' brain activity during every surgery (Jameson & Sloan, 2006). Unfortunately, even this precaution may not eliminate the problem in every case (Avidan et al., 2011).

If people can be aware yet appear to be unconscious, you can see how difficult it can be to define consciousness (Sarà & Pistoia, 2009). One way that medical doctors chose to define consciousness is awareness that is demonstrated by an ability to recall an experience (Schwender et al., 1995). Psychologists use a somewhat broader definition: **Consciousness** is generally defined as your awareness of the outside world and of your mental processes, thoughts, feelings, and perceptions (Metzinger, 2000; Zeman, 2001). Let's see how this definition applies as we explore the scope of consciousness and various states of consciousness.

Keeping an Eye Out

Humans are not the only creatures capable of processing information while apparently unconscious. While ducks sleep, one hemisphere of their brains can process visual information from an eye that remains open. Birds positioned where they are most vulnerable to predators, such as at the end of a row, may spend twice as much time in this "alert" sleep than do birds in more protected positions (Rattenborg, Lima, & Amlaner, 1999).

© David Welling/Animals Animals

consciousness The awareness of external stimuli and our own mental activity.

consciousness state The characteristics of consciousness at any particular moment.

THE SCOPE OF CONSCIOUSNESS

Can unconscious thoughts affect your behavior?

Mental activity changes constantly. The features of consciousness at any instant—what reaches your awareness, the decisions you make, and so on—make up what is called your **consciousness state** at that moment (Tassi & Muzet, 2001). Possible *states of consciousness* include coma, deep sleep, hypnosis, meditation, daydreaming, and alert wakefulness. Consciousness can also be altered by drugs and other influences.

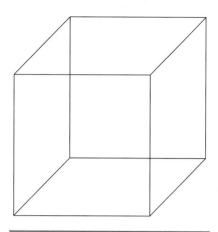

FIGURE 9.1

The Necker Cube

Each of the two squares in the Necker cube can be perceived as either the front or rear surface of the cube. Try to see the cube switch back and forth between these two orientations. Now try to see only one orientation. You probably cannot maintain the whole cube in consciousness for longer than about three seconds before it "flips" from one orientation to the other.

conscious level The level of consciousness at which mental activities accessible to awareness occur.

nonconscious level The level of consciousness at which reside processes that are totally inaccessible to conscious awareness.

preconscious level The level of consciousness at which reside mental events that are not currently conscious but can become conscious at will.

unconscious The term used to describe a level of mental activity said by Freud to contain unacceptable sexual, aggressive, and other impulses of which an individual is unaware.

Consciousness States

Consciousness states can be viewed as different points along a scale or continuum of consciousness (Cavanna et al., 2011). For example, suppose you're aboard an airliner flying from New York to Los Angeles. The pilot calmly scans instrument displays while talking to an air traffic controller. In the seat next to you, a lawyer finishes her second cocktail while planning a courtroom strategy. Across the aisle, a young father gazes out the window, daydreaming, while his small daughter sleeps in his lap, dreaming dreams of her own. All these people are experiencing different states of consciousness. Some states are active and some are passive. The daydreaming father lets his mind wander, passively noticing images, memories, and other mental events that come to mind. Like the pilot, the lawyer actively directs her mental processes. In her case, though, as she evaluates various options and considers their likely outcomes, she is altering her state of consciousness by sipping alcohol.

Generally, people spend most of their time in a *waking* consciousness state. Mental processing in this state varies with changes in attention or arousal (Taylor, 2002). While reading, for example, you may temporarily ignore sounds around you. Similarly, if you're upset or bored or talking on a cell phone, you may tune out important cues from the environment, making it dangerous to perform complex activities, such as driving a car.

Levels of Consciousness

The events and mental processes that you are aware of at any given moment are said to exist at the **conscious level**. For example, look at the Necker cube in Figure 9.1. If you're like most people, you can hold the cube in one orientation for only a few seconds before the other version "pops out" at you. The version that you experience at any moment is at your conscious level of awareness for that moment.

Some events, however, cannot be experienced consciously. For example, you are not directly aware of your brain regulating your blood pressure or controlling the dilation of the pupils in your eyes (Laeng, Sirois, & Gredebäck, 2012). Mental processes that control our biological functions occur at the **nonconscious level**, totally removed from conscious awareness. People can learn to alter a nonconscious process through *biofeedback training*, receiving information about their biological processes in order to control them. Usually special equipment is required, but you can approximate a biofeedback session by having a friend take your pulse at one-minute intervals while you sit quietly. First, establish a baseline pulse, then imagine a peaceful scene or think about lowering your pulse rate. Then ask your friend to softly say whether your pulse is higher or lower compared with the baseline. After four or five minutes of having this information "fed back" to you, you will probably be able to keep your pulse rate below the original baseline. Yet the pulse-regulating processes themselves remain out of consciousness.

Some mental events are not conscious but can become conscious or can influence conscious experience. These mental events make up the *cognitive unconscious* (Reber, 1992), which includes the preconscious and the subconscious. Mental events that are outside awareness but that can easily be brought into awareness are said to exist at the **preconscious level**. What did you have for dinner last night? The information you needed to answer this question probably wasn't already in your conscious awareness, but it was at the preconscious level. So when you read the question, you could answer it immediately. Similarly, when you play trivia games, you draw on your large storehouse of preconscious memories to come up with obscure facts.

Other mental activities can alter thoughts, feelings, and actions but are more difficult to bring into awareness. Sigmund Freud suggested that these **unconscious** activities, especially those involving unacceptable sexual and aggressive urges, are actively kept out of consciousness. Most psychologists do not accept Freud's view, but they still

Research shows that some surgery patients can hear, and later comply with, instructions or suggestions given while they were under anesthesia, even though they have no memory of what they were told (Bennett, Giannini, & Davis, 1985). People also have physiological responses to emotionally charged words even when they are not paying attention to them (Von Wright, Anderson, & Stenman, 1975). These and other similar studies provide evidence for the operation of subconscious mental processing (Deeprose & Andrade, 2006).

Reprinted by permission of International Creative Management, Inc. Copyright © 1996 by Berkeley Breathed. Cartoon first appeared in The Washington Post.

use the term *unconscious,* or **subconscious,** to describe mental activity that influences us in various ways but that occurs outside of awareness (Dijksterhuis & Nordgren, 2006).

Mental Processing without Awareness

A fascinating demonstration of mental processing without awareness was provided by an experiment with patients who had surgery under general anesthesia. After their operations but while the patients were still unconscious from the anesthesia, a recording of fifteen word pairs was played over and over for them in the recovery room. After regaining consciousness, the patients could not say what words were on the recording or even whether a recording had been played at all. However, when given one word from each of the word pairs and asked to say the first word that came to mind, the patients came up with the other member of the word pair from the recording (Cork, Kihlstrom, & Hameroff, 1992).

Even when conscious and alert, you sometimes process and use information without being aware of it (Fu, Fu, & Dienes, 2008; Mudrick et al., 2011). In one study, participants watched a computer screen as an X flashed in one of four locations. The task was to indicate as quickly as possible where the X appeared. The location of the X seemed to vary randomly, but actually followed a set of complex rules. (One such rule was "If the X moves horizontally twice in succession, its next move will be vertical.") Participants' responses became progressively faster and more accurate. Then, unknown to the participants, the rules were abandoned and the X appeared in *truly* random locations. Instantly, participants' accuracy and speed deteriorated. Apparently, the participants had learned the rules without knowing what they were, and this learning improved performance! However, even when offered $100 to state the rules that had guided the location sequence, they could not do so, nor were they sure that any such rules existed (Lewicki, 1992).

Visual processing without awareness may even occur in some blind people. When blindness is caused by damage only to the brain's primary visual cortex, pathways from the eyes are still connected to other brain areas that process visual information (Garrido, 2012). Such connections may permit visual processing without awareness—a condition called *blindsight* (Stoerig & Cowey, 1997). People who experience blindsight say they see nothing, but if forced to guess, they may still locate visual targets, identify the direction of moving images, reach for objects, name the color of lights, and even discriminate happy from fearful faces (Azzopardi & Hock, 2011; Cowey, 2010a). The same blindsight phenomenon has been created in visually normal volunteers using magnetic brain stimulation to temporarily disable the primary visual cortex (Allen, Sumner, & Chambers, 2014).

Research on *priming* also demonstrates mental processing without awareness. In a typical priming study, people respond faster or more accurately to the stimuli they have seen before, even if they do not consciously recall those stimuli (Abrams & Greenwald, 2000; Breuer et al., 2009; Kouider & Dupoux, 2005). In one study, for example, people

subconscious Another term that describes the mental level at which influential but normally inaccessible mental processes take place.

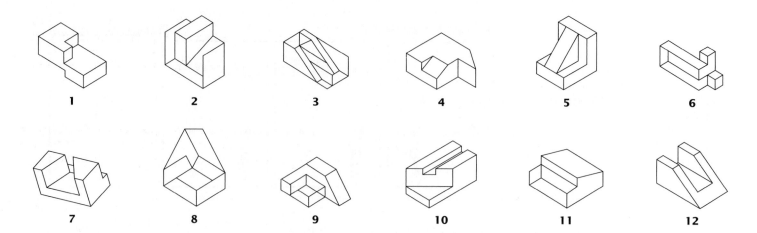

FIGURE 9.2
Stimuli Used in a Priming Experiment

TRY THIS Look at these figures and decide, as quickly as you can, whether each can actually exist. Priming studies show that this task would be easier for figures you have seen in the past, even if you don't recall seeing them. How did you do? The correct answers appear at the bottom of page 301.

looked at figures like those in Figure 9.2. They had to decide which figures could possibly exist in three-dimensional space and which could not. Participants were better at classifying pictures they had seen before, even when they couldn't remember seeing them (Schacter et al., 1991). Some priming effects are short lived, but others can last for years (Mitchell, 2006).

To some degree, decisions and choices we make in our everyday lives may be guided by mental processes without our awareness (e.g., Hassin, 2013; Galdi, Arcuri, & Gawronski, 2008; Mealor & Dienes, 2012). For example, your "lucky" choice of the fastest-moving supermarket checkout line might seem to have been based on nothing more than a hunch, a gut feeling, or intuition, but previous visits to that store might have given you useful information that you didn't know you had about the various clerks (Adolphs et al., 2005). In a laboratory study that supports this notion, people watched videotaped television commercials while the changing stock prices of fictional companies crawled across the bottom of the screen. Later, these people were asked to choose which of these companies they liked best. They couldn't recall anything they had seen about the companies' stock, so they had to make their choice on the basis of their gut reaction to the company names. Nevertheless, their choices were not random; they more often chose companies whose stock prices had been rising rather than those whose stock had been falling (Betch et al., 2003).

THINKING CRITICALLY

CAN SUBLIMINAL MESSAGES CHANGE YOUR BEHAVIOR?

The research we have described shows that we don't always have to be aware of information in order for it to affect us. How strong can this influence be? In 1957, an adman named James Vicary claimed that a New Jersey theater flashed messages such as "buy popcorn" and "drink Coke" on a movie screen, too briefly to be noticed, while customers watched the movie *Picnic*. He said that these messages caused a 15 percent rise in sales of Coca-Cola and a 58 percent increase in popcorn sales. Can messages perceived at a *subliminal* level—that is, below conscious awareness—act as a form of "mind control"? Many people seem to think so. Each year, they spend millions of dollars on video and audio products whose subliminal messages are promised to help people lose weight, raise self-esteem, quit smoking, make more money, or achieve other goals.

What am I being asked to believe or accept?

LINKAGES Can subliminal messages help you lose weight? (a link to Sensation and Perception)

Two types of claims have been made about subliminal stimuli. The more general one is that subliminal stimuli influence people's behavior. A second, more specific claim is that subliminal stimuli effectively change people's buying habits, political opinions, self-confidence, and other complex attitudes and behaviors, without their awareness or consent.

(continued)

What evidence is available to support the assertion?

Evidence that subliminal messages can affect conscious judgments comes in part from laboratory studies that present visual stimuli too briefly to be perceived consciously. In one such study, participants saw slides showing people performing ordinary acts such as washing dishes. Unknown to the participants, each slide was preceded by a subliminal exposure to a photo of "positive" stimuli (such as a child playing) or "negative" stimuli (such as a monster). Later, participants rated the people on the visible slides that had been preceded by a positive subliminal photo as being more likable, polite, friendly, successful, and reputable (Krosnick et al., 1992). The subliminal photos not only affected participants' liking of the people they saw but also shaped beliefs about their personalities.

In another study, participants were exposed to subliminal presentations of slides showing snakes, spiders, flowers, and mushrooms. Even though the slides were impossible to perceive at a conscious level, participants who were afraid of snakes or spiders showed physiological arousal (and reported feeling fear) in response to slides of snakes and spiders (Öhman & Soares, 1994).

The results of studies such as these support the notion that subliminal information can have an impact on judgments and emotion, but they say little or nothing about the value of subliminal recordings for achieving self-help goals. In fact, no laboratory evidence exists to support the effectiveness of these recordings. Their promoters offer only the reports of satisfied customers.

Are there alternative ways of interpreting the evidence?

Many claims for subliminal advertising—including the New Jersey movie theater case—have been unmasked as publicity stunts using phony data (Haberstroh, 1995; Pratkanis, 1992). And testimonials from satisfied customers could be biased by what these people would like to believe about the subliminal recordings they bought. In one study designed to test this possibility, half the participants were told that they would hear recordings containing subliminal messages for improving memory. The rest were told that the subliminal messages would promote self-esteem. However, half the participants in the memory group actually got self-esteem messages, and half of the self-esteem group actually got memory messages. Regardless of which version they received, participants who thought they had heard memory enhancement messages reported improved memory; those who thought they had received self-esteem messages said their self-esteem had improved (Pratkanis, Eskenazi, & Greenwald, 1994). In other words, the effects of the recordings were determined by the listeners' expectations, not by the subliminal content of the recordings. These results suggest that customers' reports about the value of subliminal self-help recordings may reflect placebo effects based on optimistic expectations rather than the effects of subliminal messages.

What additional evidence would help evaluate the alternatives?

The effectiveness of self-help recordings and other subliminal products must be evaluated through further experiments, such as the one just mentioned, that carefully control for expectations. Those who support and sell subliminal-influence methods are responsible for conducting those experiments, but as long as customers are willing to buy subliminal products on the basis of testimonials alone, scientific evaluation efforts will probably come only from those interested in protecting consumers from fraud.

What conclusions are most reasonable?

The available evidence suggests that subliminal perception occurs but that it has no potential for "mind control" (Greenwald, Klinger, & Schuh, 1995). Subliminal effects are usually small and short-lived, and they mainly affect simple judgments and general measures of overall arousal. The effects also tend to be related to temporary conditions such as fatigue or motivation (Bermeitinger et al., 2009). For example, a subliminal message about a beverage is more likely to influence a person who is thirsty than one who is not (Karremans, Stroebe, & Klaus, 2006). As for subliminal messages aimed at long-term behavior change, most researchers agree that such messages have no special power to create needs, goals, skills, or actions (Pratkanis & Aronson, 2001; Randolph-Seng & Mather, 2009; Strahan et al., 2005). In fact, advertisements, political speeches, and other messages that we *can* perceive consciously have far stronger persuasive effects.

SUBLIMINAL MESSAGES IN POPULAR MUSIC

Would the persuasive power of subliminal messages be increased if they were presented at normal speed but in reverse, so that we could not understand them consciously? According to numerous websites, this is how secret messages have been hidden in the recorded music of Lady Gaga, Marilyn Manson, Eminem, Nine Inch Nails, Pink Floyd, the Rolling Stones, and hundreds of other performers. Some contend that these "back masked" *subliminal* messages caused listeners to commit suicide or murder. However, for this claim to be true, subliminal backward messages would have to be perceived at some level of consciousness.

What was the researchers' question?

There is no clear evidence that secret backward messages exist in most of the music cited. However, John R. Vokey and J. Don Read (1985) wondered if any backward messages had existed, could they be perceived and understood while the music was playing forward. They also asked whether such a message would affect a listener's behavior.

How did the researchers answer the question?

First, Vokey and Read made tape recordings of a person reading portions of the Twenty-third Psalm and Lewis Carroll's poem "Jabberwocky." This poem includes many nonsense words, but it follows the rules of grammar (e.g., "Twas brillig, and the slithy toves …"). The recordings were then played backward to college students, who judged whether what they heard would have been meaningful or nonsensical if played forward.

What did the researchers find?

When the students heard the readings being played backward, they could not discriminate sense from nonsense. They could not tell the difference between declarative sentences and questions. They couldn't even identify the original material on which the recordings were based. In short, the participants couldn't understand the backward messages at a conscious level. Could they do so subconsciously? To find out, the researchers asked the participants to sort the backward statements they heard into one of five categories: nursery rhymes, Christian, satanic, pornographic, or advertising. They reasoned that if some sort of meaning could be subconsciously understood, the participants might sort the statements nonrandomly. Yet participants did no better at this task than random chance would predict.

Perhaps backward messages might influence people's behavior even if the messages were not perceived consciously. To check on this possibility, Vokey and Read (1985) conducted another study. This time, they presented a backward version of a message whose sentences contained homophones (words that sound alike but have two spellings and two different meanings, such as "feat" and "feet"). When heard in the normal forward direction, such messages affect people's spelling of ambiguous words that are read aloud to them at a later time. (For example, they tend to spell out f-e-a-t rather than f-e-e-t if they had previously heard the sentence "It was a great feat of strength.") This example of priming occurs even if people do not recall having heard the message. After hearing a *backward* version of the message, however, the participants in this study did not produce the expected spelling bias.

What do the results mean?

It wasn't possible for the participants to understand meaning in the backward messages at a subconscious level. It seems that backward messages are not consciously or unconsciously understood, nor do they influence behavior (Vokey, 2002).

What do we still need to know?

Why does the incorrect idea persist that backward messages can influence behavior? Beliefs and suspicions do not simply disappear in the face of contrary scientific evidence (Vyse, 2000; Winer et al., 2002). Perhaps such evidence needs to be publicized more widely in order to lay the misconceptions to rest. Perhaps, though, some people so deeply want to believe in the existence and power of backward messages in popular music that such beliefs will forever grip folk myth in Western culture.

Cultures differ in their definitions of which altered states of consciousness are approved and which are inappropriate. Here we see members of a Brazilian spirit possession cult in various stages of trance and, in Peru, a Moche curandero, or "curer," attempting to heal an ailing patient by using fumes from a potion—and a drug from the San Pedro cactus—to put himself in an altered state of consciousness.

Nacho Doce/Reuters /Landov; Nathan Benn/National Geographic Creative

Altered States of Consciousness

When changes in mental processes are great enough for you or others to notice significant differences in how you function, you are said to have entered an **altered state of consciousness**. In an altered state, mental processing shows distinct changes unique to that state. Cognitive processes or perceptions of yourself or the world may change, and normal inhibitions or self-control may weaken (Vaitl et al., 2005).

The phrase *altered states of consciousness* recognizes waking consciousness as the most common state, a baseline against which altered states are compared. However, this is not to say that waking consciousness is universally considered more normal, proper, or valued than other states. In fact, judgments about the status and meaning of certain states of consciousness vary considerably across cultures (Ward, 1994).

Consider, for instance, *hallucinations,* which are perceptual experiences (such as hearing voices) that occur without sensory stimulation from the outside world. In the United States, hallucinations are usually viewed as so undesirable that even if they are caused by nothing more than an eye disorder people may be ashamed to seek the medical help they need to solve the problem (Menon et al., 2003). If mental patients hallucinate, they may feel such stress or self-blame and so choose not to report their hallucinations (Karidi et al., 2014). Those who do report them tend to be considered more disturbed and may receive more drastic treatments than patients who keep their hallucinations to themselves (Wilson et al., 1996). Among the Moche of Peru, however, hallucinations have a culturally approved place. When someone experiences illness or misfortune, a healer conducts an elaborate ritual to find causes and treatments. During the ceremony, the healer takes mescaline, a drug that causes hallucinations. These hallucinations are thought to give the healer spiritual insight into the patient's problems (de Rios, 1992). In many other tribal cultures, too, purposeful hallucinations are respected, not rejected (Grob & Dobkin de Rios, 1992).

In other words, states of consciousness differ not only in their characteristics but also in their value to members of particular cultures. In the sections that follow, we describe some of the most interesting altered states of consciousness, beginning with the most common one: sleep.

SLEEPING AND DREAMING

Does your brain go to sleep when you do?

According to ancient myths, sleepers lose control of their minds and flirt with death as their souls wander freely. Early researchers thought sleep was a time of mental inactivity, but sleep is actually an active, complex state (Hobson, 2005).

Stages of Sleep

Sleep researchers study the brain's electrical activity during sleep using an *electroencephalograph (EEG)*. EEG recordings, often called *brain waves,* vary in height (amplitude)

altered state of consciousness A condition that exists when changes in mental processes are extensive enough to produce noticeable differences in psychological and behavioral functioning.

Answers for Figure 9.2: Figures 1, 4, 5, 7, 10, and 12 can exist in three-dimensional space.

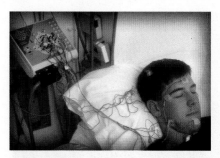

A Sleep Lab

The electroencephalograph (EEG) allows scientists to record brain activity through electrodes attached to the scalp. The development of this technology in the 1950s opened the door to the scientific study of sleep.

Hank Morgan-Rainbow/Science Faction/Corbis

LINKAGES Does the brain shut down when we sleep? (a link to Biological Aspects of Psychology)

FIGURE 9.3
EEG during Sleep

EEG recordings of brain wave activity show three relatively distinct stages of sleep. Notice the regular patterns of brain waves that occur just before a person goes to sleep, followed by even slower waves as sleep becomes deeper in non-REM stages N1 through N3. In REM (rapid eye movement) sleep, the frequency of brain waves increases dramatically. In some ways the brain waves of REM sleep resemble patterns seen in people who are awake.

NREM (non-rapid eye movement) sleep Sleep stages N1, N2, and N3; they are accompanied by gradually slower and deeper breathing; a calm, regular heartbeat; reduced blood pressure; and slower brain waves. (Stage N3 is called slow-wave sleep.)

REM (rapid eye movement) sleep The stage of sleep during which muscle tone decreases dramatically but the EEG resembles that of someone who is awake.

and speed (frequency) as behavior or mental processes change. The brain waves of an awake, alert person are irregular, small, and closely spaced; that is, high frequency and low amplitude. A relaxed person with closed eyes shows more rhythmic brain waves occurring at slower speeds, about eight to twelve cycles per second (cps). During a normal night's sleep, your brain waves show distinctive and systematic changes in amplitude and frequency as you pass through various stages of sleep (Shatzmiller, 2010; Silber et al., 2007).

Non-REM Sleep

Imagine that you are participating in a sleep study. You're hooked up to an EEG and various monitors, and a video camera watches as you sleep through the night. If you were to view the results, here's what you'd see: At first, you are relaxed, with your eyes closed, but you are still awake. At this point, your muscle tone and eye movements are normal and your EEG shows the slow brain waves associated with relaxation. Then, as you drift into sleep, your breathing deepens, your heartbeat slows, and your blood pressure falls. Over the next half-hour, you descend through three stages of sleep—N1, N2, and N3—that are characterized by even slower brain waves with even higher amplitude (see Figure 9.3). Together, these three stages are called **NREM**, or **non-REM sleep** because they do not include the rapid eye movements (REM) described in the next section (Iber et al., 2007). The deepest of the NREM stages, N3, is also known as *slow-wave sleep*. When you reach stage N3, it's quite difficult to wake up. If you were roused from this stage of deep sleep, you'd be groggy and slow to answer questions.

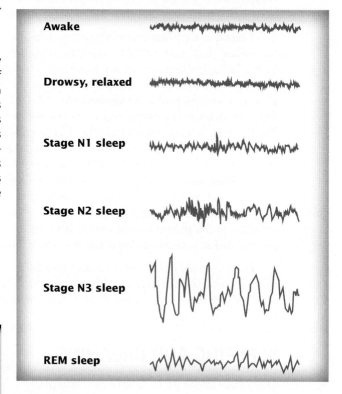

REM Sleep

After thirty to forty-five minutes in stage N3, you quickly return to stage N2 and then enter a unique stage in which your eyes move rapidly under your closed eyelids. This is called **REM (rapid eye movement) sleep**, or paradoxical sleep. It's called paradoxical because its characteristics contain a paradox, or contradiction. In REM sleep, your EEG looks like an awake, alert person, and your physiological arousal—heart rate, breathing, and blood pressure—is also similar to when you are awake. However, most of your muscles are nearly paralyzed. Thus, REM sleep and NREM sleep are very different types of sleep (Silber et al., 2007).

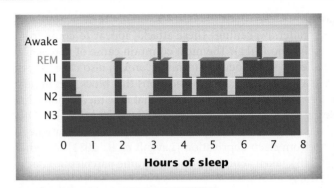

FIGURE 9.4
A Night's Sleep

During a typical night, a sleeper goes through this sequence of EEG stages. Notice that sleep is deepest during the first part of the night and shallower later on, when REM sleep (highlighted in orange here) becomes more prominent.

Stimulus Control Therapy

Insomnia can often be reduced through a combination of relaxation techniques and stimulus control therapy, in which the person goes to bed only when sleepy and gets out of bed if sleep does not come within fifteen to twenty minutes. The goal is to have the bed become a stimulus associated with sleeping, and perhaps sex, but not with reading, eating, watching television, worrying, or anything else that is incompatible with sleep (Edinger et al., 2001).

Jupiterimages/Getty Images

insomnia A sleep disorder in which a person does not get enough sleep to feel rested.

narcolepsy A daytime sleep disorder in which a person suddenly switches from an active waking state into REM sleep.

A Night's Sleep

Most people pass through the cycle of sleep stages four to six times each night. Each cycle lasts about ninety minutes, but the pattern of stages and length of the stages change somewhat. Early in the night, most time is spent in NREM with only a few minutes in REM (see Figure 9.4). As sleep continues, though, it is dominated by stage N2 and REM sleep, from which sleepers finally awaken. Sleep patterns change with age. An infant averages thirteen hours of sleep a day (Williams, Zimmerman, & Bell, 2013), but a seventy-year-old sleeps only about six hours (Roffwarg, Muzio, & Dement, 1966). Elderly people also tend to wake more often during the night than younger people do (Floyd, 2002; Roenneberg et al., 2007). The "architecture," or composition of sleep, also changes with age. REM accounts for half of a newborn's sleep but less than 25 percent in young adults and even less in the elderly (Darchia, Campbell, & Feinberg, 2003). Elderly people spend more time in N1 and N2, the lighter stages of sleep (Espiritu, 2008). Though the National Sleep Foundation (www.sleepfoundation.org) recommends that most adults should sleep seven to nine hours each night, individual needs vary widely. Some people feel rested after four hours of sleep, while others of similar age need ten hours or more (Clausen, Sersen, & Lidsky, 1974).

Sleep Disorders

Most people have sleep-related problems at some time (Silber, 2001). These can range from grogginess after a late night out to occasional nights of tossing and turning to more serious and long-term *sleep disorders* that affect perhaps 70 million people in the United States alone (Institute of Medicine, 2006; Morin et al., 2009).

The most common sleep disorder is **insomnia**, in which people feel fatigue during waking hours because they do not get enough sleep to feel rested. If, for a month or more, you have difficulty getting to sleep or staying asleep, you may be suffering from insomnia. Besides being tiring, insomnia may cause mental distress, health problems, and impairments in daily functioning (Hamilton et al., 2007; Rajaratnam et al., 2011). Fatigue-related workplace accidents and errors are estimated to cost the U.S. economy $31.1 billion annually (Shahly et al., 2012), and a study in Norway found that people with insomnia were nearly five times more likely than others to develop a permanent work disability (Sivertsen et al., 2009). Overall, people with insomnia are three times more likely to show a mental disorder than those with no sleep complaints (Ohayon & Roth, 2003). Insomnia is especially associated with depression and anxiety disorders (Baglioni et al., 2010). It is not clear from such correlations, however, whether insomnia causes mental disorders, mental disorders cause insomnia, or some other factor causes both.

Some medications may relieve insomnia temporarily (Saper & Scammell, 2013); however, they may have unwanted side effects, reduce REM sleep, and lead to dependency and increased sleeplessness down the line (Curry, Eisenstein, & Walsh, 2006; Poyares et al., 2004). In the long run, an approach including learning-based treatments is best (Neubauer, 2013). Such treatments include the cognitive behavior therapy methods described in the chapter on treatment of psychological disorders, and the progressive relaxation training techniques mentioned in the chapter on health, stress, and coping (Bootzin & Epstein, 2011). Both of these treatments promote better sleeping by reducing anxiety, tension, and other stress reactions (Bernstein, Borkovec, & Hazlett-Stevens, 2000; Jacobs et al., 2004). Short daytime naps and moderate evening exercise also help some people fall sleep more easily and sleep better, with better mood and performance the next day (Tanaka et al., 2001).

Narcolepsy is a disturbing daytime sleep disorder that is typically first seen in people between fifteen and twenty-five years old (Dyken & Yamada, 2005; Zeman et al., 2004). People with narcolepsy suddenly enter REM sleep directly from a waking state, often as they laugh or experience another emotional state (Ahmed & Thorpy, 2011). Because of the

Sudden Infant Death Syndrome (SIDS)

In SIDS cases, seemingly healthy infants stop breathing while asleep in their cribs. All the causes of SIDS are not known, but health authorities now urge parents to ensure that infants sleep on their backs, as this baby demonstrates.

JGI/Blend Images/Corbis

sleep apnea A sleep disorder in which a person briefly but repeatedly stops breathing during the night.

sudden infant death syndrome (SIDS) A disorder in which a sleeping baby stops breathing, does not awaken, and dies.

sleepwalking A phenomenon that starts primarily in NREM sleep, especially in stage N3, and involves walking while asleep.

loss of muscle tone in REM, narcoleptics may have *cataplexy,* meaning that they collapse and remain briefly immobile even after awakening. These attacks appear to come from the brain's lateral hypothalamus (Nishino, 2011). The most common cause of narcolepsy appears to be the absence or deficiency of the neurotransmitter *orexin,* also called *hypocretin* (Caylak, 2009; Miyagawa et al., 2008). Because medications that block orexin help insomnia sufferers fall asleep (Herring et al., 2012), it is hoped that new medications that mimic orexin will make narcolepsy sufferers feel more alert (Mieda & Sakuri, 2013). One helpful medication is modafinil, taken in the morning, since this helps both the fatigue in narcolepsy and in those suffering from sleep deprivation (Lavault et al., 2011). Another drug, gamma hydroxybutyrate (GHB), taken at night, reduces daytime narcoleptic attacks of fatigue (Boscolo-Berto et al., 2011).

People who suffer from **sleep apnea** briefly stop breathing hundreds of times each night, waking each time long enough to resume breathing. In the morning, they don't recall the awakenings, but they feel tired and tend to have headaches, learning difficulties, and reduced attention (Jackson, Howard, & Barnes, 2011). The daytime fatigue and inattention caused by sleep apnea also increase the risk for accidents (Tregear et al., 2009). In one tragic case, two members of a train crew—both of whom had apnea—fell asleep on the job, resulting in a crash that killed two people (Pickler, 2002). Sleep apnea also increases risks for stroke and high blood pressure (Barone & Kriefer, 2013). Apnea has many causes, including genetic predisposition, obesity, problems with brain mechanisms that control breathing, and compression of the windpipe (White & Younes, 2013). Effective treatments include weight loss and use of sleep masks like CPAP (continuous positive airway pressure) to help keep breathing passages open (Antonescu-Turcu & Parthasarathy, 2010). In some cases, surgery may widen the air passageway in the upper throat (Lin et al., 2013).

In cases of **sudden infant death syndrome (SIDS)**, sleeping infants stop breathing and die. SIDS is the most common cause of unexpected infant death in Western countries (Hunt & Hauck, 2006). In the United States, it strikes about six of every ten thousand infants (Balayla, Azoulay, & Abenhaim, 2011), especially very low birthweight babies, usually when they are two to four months old (Smith & White, 2006; Vernacchio et al., 2003).

Some SIDS cases may be caused by exposure to cigarette smoke, problems with brain systems that regulate breathing, or genetic factors (e.g., Klintschar & Heimbold, 2012; Machaalani, Say, & Waters, 2011; Trachtenberg et al., 2012). However, the most important causes may be related to how and where infants sleep at night (Moon & Fu, 2012). SIDS rates appear to be lower in some countries where infants and parents sleep in the same bed (Li, Petitti, et al., 2003) but higher in others, including the United States and Ireland (McGarvey et al., 2006; Ostfeld et al., 2006). The differing risks may have to do with the kinds of bedding used or with sleeping position. Correlational evidence suggests that about half of apparent SIDS cases might actually be accidental suffocations that occur when infants sleep face down on a soft surface. In the United States, for example, SIDS may be particularly common when caregivers place babies in the face-down position (e.g., Dwyer & Ponsonby, 2009). The danger of the face-down position is especially great for babies who don't usually sleep in that position, who are not breastfed, or who don't sleep with a pacifier in their mouths (Vennemann et al., 2009a, 2009b). In 1992, a new health campaign was started, called "back to sleep," in which doctors urged parents to be sure their babies sleep face up (Task Force on Sudden Infant Death Syndrome, 2011). Since then, the number of infants dying from SIDS in the United States and United Kingdom has dropped by 50 to 90 percent (Moon, Horn, & Hauk, 2007).

Sleepwalking occurs in NREM sleep, affecting up to 14 percent of children and 4 percent of adults (Remulla & Guilleminault, 2004). By morning, most sleepwalkers have forgotten their travels and their sometimes bizarre activities. One sleepwalking man had no recollection of tying his four-month-old daughter to a clothesline in his attic (Pillmann, 2009). Sleepwalking has been associated with several possible causes, including genetic predisposition, sleep deprivation, and the side effects of some drugs (Zadra et al., 2013). Walking around while asleep can lead to injury, so affected individuals are advised to remove fall risks in the bedroom. Otherwise, there are no consistently effective medical treatments for sleepwalking (Harris & Grunstein, 2009), although sleepwalkers who also have sleep apnea often find relief for both conditions by wearing a CPAP mask at night (Guilleminault et al., 2005). Most children simply outgrow the problem. One adult sleepwalker was cured when his wife blew a whistle whenever he began a nighttime stroll (Meyer, 1975). Despite myths to the contrary, waking a sleepwalker is not harmful.

Nightmares are frightening REM dreams that occur in 4 to 8 percent of the general population. Adult women report more nightmares than men (Schredl & Reinhard, 2011), and they are especially common in people who suffer from posttraumatic stress disorder following military combat, torture, rape, or other horrific events (e.g., Hinton et al., 2009). Drugs have proved helpful in reducing the frequency of nightmares (Aurora et al., 2010), as has imagery therapy, in which people repeatedly imagine new and less frightening outcomes to their nightmares (Hansen et al., 2013). **Sleep terror disorder** (also known as **night terrors**) involves frightful dream images during stage N3 sleep (Derry et al., 2009). Sleepers often awaken from a night terror with a bloodcurdling scream and remain intensely afraid for up to 30 minutes, yet they may not recall the episode in the morning (Snyder et al., 2008). Sleep terror disorder is especially common in children, but adults can suffer milder versions, and it appears to be partly inherited (Nguyen et al., 2008). The condition is sometimes treatable with drugs or psychotherapy (Jan et al., 2004; Sadeh 2005).

In **REM behavior disorder**, sleepers enter REM sleep without the near-paralysis that normally accompanies it (Arnulf, 2012). As a result, they can act out their dreams. If the dreams are violent, the disorder can be dangerous to the dreamer or those nearby (Schenck, Gittings, & Colussi-Mas, 2009). One nine-year-old boy in New York City was seriously injured when he jumped from a third-floor window while dreaming that his parents were being murdered. In another case, a man shot his wife to death while dreaming that burglars were invading their home (de Bruxelles, 2009). Although he was acquitted of murder charges, most defendants who offer a REM behavior disorder or sleepwalking defense are convicted (Lyon, 2009). REM behavior disorder, which sometimes occurs in tandem with daytime narcolepsy (Billiard, 2009; Schenck & Mahowald, 1992), can be caused by the side effects of medication (Morrison, Frangulyan, & Riha, 2011), and in one case was caused by a brain tumor (Zambelis, Paparrigopoulos, & Soldatos, 2002). Most often, REM behavior disorder has no obvious cause at first, but over many years the affected person may go on to develop Parkinson's disease or other similar brain disorders (Zanigni et al., 2011). Fortunately, prescription drugs are usually effective in treating REM behavior disorder (Ramar & Olson, 2013).

Why Do People Sleep?

People need a certain amount of uninterrupted sleep to function normally. In fact, most living creatures sleep. In trying to understand why people sleep, psychologists have studied what sleep does for us and how the brain shapes the characteristics of sleep (Siegel, 2005).

Sleep as a Circadian Rhythm

Humans and almost all animals display cycles of behavior and physiology that repeat about every 24 hours (Mazzoccoli, 2011). These patterns are called **circadian rhythms** (also known as **human biological rhythms**). (*Circadian,* pronounced "sir-KAY-dee-en," comes from the Latin *circa dies,* meaning "about a day.") Longer and shorter rhythms also occur, but they are less common.

Circadian rhythms are linked to signals such as the light of day and the dark of night (Ohta, Yamazaki, & McMahon, 2005). However, most of these rhythms continue even when no time signals are available. People living for months without external light and dark cues maintain daily rhythms in sleeping and waking, eating, urination, hormone release, and other physiological functions. Under such conditions, these cycles repeat about every twenty-four hours (Czeisler et al., 1999).

nightmares Frightening dreams that take place during REM sleep.

sleep terror disorder (night terrors) The occurrence of horrific dream images during N3 sleep, followed by a rapid awakening and a state of intense fear.

REM behavior disorder A sleep disorder in which the decreased muscle tone normally seen in REM sleep does not appear, thus allowing dreams to be acted out.

circadian rhythm (human biological rhythm) A cycle, such as waking and sleeping, that repeats about once a day.

The Cost of Jet Lag

Twice a year, exhibitors freshly arrived from around the world groggily set up displays at Asia's largest jewelry show. Then they try to wait on customers while keeping track of their treasures. Taking advantage of these jet-lagged travelers' inattentiveness, thieves steal millions of dollars' worth of merchandise at every show (Fowler, 2004).

Jodi Cobb/National Geographic Creative

Trying to change our sleep-wake cycle can create problems. A common example is air travel across several time zones, which may cause **jet lag**, a pattern of fatigue, irritability, inattention, and sleeping problems that can last for several days (Weingarten & Collop, 2013). The traveler's body feels ready to sleep at the wrong time for the new location. It tends to be easier to stay awake longer than usual than to go to sleep earlier than usual. That explains why jet lag symptoms are usually more intense after a long eastward trip (when time is lost) than after a long westward journey (when time is gained; Doane et al., 2010; Lemmer et al., 2002). Symptoms similar to those of jet lag also occur when workers repeatedly change between day and night shifts, or when people who try to go to sleep early on a Sunday night after a weekend of later-than-usual bedtimes (Czeisler et al., 2005; Di Milia, 2006). For these people, Monday morning "blues" may actually be symptoms of a disrupted sleep-wake cycle (Yang & Spielman, 2001).

The timing of circadian sleep rhythms varies from person to person. Most people fall into one of two patterns (Roenneberg et al., 2007)—some have a natural tendency to stay up later at night ("owls") while others normally tend to wake up earlier in the morning ("larks"). These different *chronotypes* may occur because of "clock genes," genetic codes that help set the daily peaks and valleys in a person's sleepiness and wakefulness, hormone levels, and body temperature (Zhang et al., 2011). These clock genes appear less effective, though, when people have disorders such as Alzheimer's disease, depression, and certain cancers (Kishi et al., 2011; Yang et al., 2011; Yesavage et al., 2011), perhaps helping to explain why sleep may be disrupted in certain illnesses.

Because our sleep-wake rhythms stay about the same even without external cues about light and dark, we must have an internal biological clock that keeps track of time. This clock is in the *suprachiasmatic nuclei (SCN)* of the hypothalamus (Honma et al., 2012), as shown in Figure 9.5. The SCN receives light information from a special set of photoreceptors in the eyes and then sends signals to hindbrain areas that initiate sleep or wakefulness (Reinoso-Suárez, de Andrés, & Garzón, 2011). When animals with SCN damage receive transplanted SCN cells, their circadian rhythms become like those of the donor animal (Menaker & Vogelbaum, 1993). SCN neurons appear to respond to the hormone vasopressin (Yamaguchi et al, 2013) and also regulate the release of the hormone *melatonin* (Hardeland, 2013). Melatonin rises during periods of darkness, and appears to be important in maintaining circadian rhythms (Zawilska, Skene, & Arendt, 2009). Many symptoms associated with jet lag and other disruptions in sleep-wake cycles can be prevented or treated by taking melatonin (Brown et al., 2009), although for some people,

jet lag Fatigue, irritability, inattention, and sleeping problems caused by air travel across several time zones.

FIGURE 9.5

Sleep, Dreaming, and the Brain

This diagram shows the location of some of the brain structures thought to be involved in sleep and dreaming, as well as in other altered states discussed later in the chapter. For example, one area near the suprachiasmatic nuclei acts as a "master switch" to promote sleep (Saper, Chou, & Scammell, 2001). If it is damaged, sleep may be nearly impossible. Another nearby area promotes wakefulness; individuals with damage to this area sleep virtually all the time (Salin-Pascual et al., 2001).

© iStockphoto.com/GlobalStock

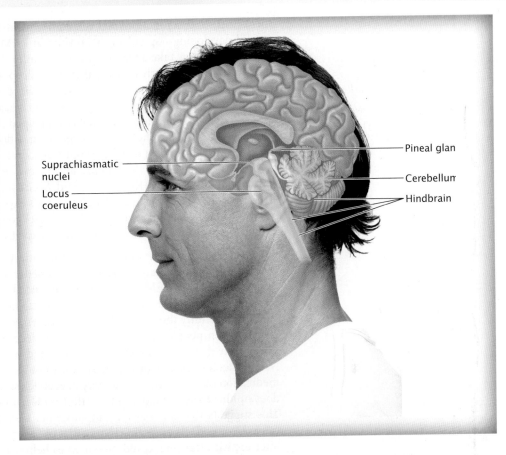

such as commercial airline crewmembers, regular use is not recommended (Simons & Valk, 2009). It may also be possible to reduce jet lag through diet, exercise, and exposure to natural lighting conditions upon daytime arrival or to dim light upon nighttime arrival (Armstrong, 2006; Edwards, Reilly, & Waterhouse, 2009; Evans, Elliott, & Gorman, 2009).

The Value of Sleep

One way to explore what sleep does for us is to study what happens when we are prevented from sleeping. After being deprived of sleep, people don't need to make up every hour of lost sleep. Instead, they sleep about 50 percent more than usual, then wake up feeling rested. But their "recovery" night includes an unusually high percentage of REM sleep (Feinberg & Campbell, 1993). And if people are deprived *only* of REM sleep, they compensate even more specifically. In one study, sleep subjects were awakened whenever their EEGs showed REM. When allowed to sleep normally the next night, they "rebounded," nearly doubling the percentage of time spent in REM (Dement, 1960). Such research suggests we have a specific need for REM sleep, perhaps because it has its own special functions. What might those functions be? There are several interesting possibilities.

One idea is that REM improves the functioning of neurons that use norepinephrine (Siegel & Rogawski, 1988), a neurotransmitter released by cells in the *locus coeruleus* (pronounced "lo-kus seh-ROO-lee-us"; see Figure 9.5). During waking hours, the locus coeruleus affects alertness and mood. But neurons respond less to norepinephrine if it is released continuously for too long. REM sleep deprivation causes unusually high norepinephrine levels and decreased daytime alertness (Mallick and Singh, 2011). Researchers suggest that because the locus coeruleus is almost completely inactive during REM sleep, REM helps restore sensitivity to norepinephrine and thus its ability to keep us alert (Steriade & McCarley, 1990).

REM sleep may help your brain "consolidate" what you learned from the day before, by improving the connections that form between nerve cells in the brain (Diekelmann &

Born, 2010). Such a function might explain why infants and young children—whose brains are still developing—spend so much time in REM sleep, or why preschoolers appear to learn better if they take afternoon naps (Mednick, 2013). Evidence for such a mechanism includes animal research showing that REM sleep increases neural connections after new learning experiences (Frank et al., 2001; Scullin & McDaniel, 2010). Also, memory for a learning task is improved when odors or other sensory cues present during the task again appear in REM sleep, suggesting that REM helped make memories stronger (Rudoy et al., 2009). So, if your psychology class meets in a flower garden, a vase of fragrant roses next to your bed at night may help your test scores the next day (Bendor, 2013)! Evidence also suggests that REM sleep deprivation slows the creation of nerve cell connections formed during learning (Kim, Mahmoud, & Grover, 2005). Such findings argue that REM sleep may help to solidify and absorb the day's experiences and skills (Fenn, Nusbaum, & Margoliash, 2003; Ishikawa et al., 2006; Stickgold, James, & Hobson, 2000). There is evidence, too, that REM sleep may improve daytime creativity (Cai et al., 2009).

Other studies have found that information, including emotional information or certain aspects of language, is remembered better and longer when followed immediately by sleep, especially REM sleep (e.g., Djonlagic et al., 2009; Gaskell et al., 2014; Payne & Kensinger, 2010). Even sixty- to ninety-minute naps in which REM sleep occurs can be enough to solidify the learning of visual information (Mednick, Nakayama, & Stickgold, 2003). When people are deprived of REM sleep, their performance at a skill they had learned the day before suffers when compared with people who were either deprived of NREM sleep or had slept normally (Karni et al., 1994). However, if people are given a medication that increases the activity of acetylcholine in the brain, REM sleep deprivation does not have the same disruptive effect on learning (Aleisa, Alzoubi, & Alkadhi, 2011). This suggests that the learning impairments seen after REM sleep deprivation may be caused by its effects on brain circuits that use acetylcholine. If REM sleep deprivation can interfere with learning, could it be used to help people forget traumatic events? Some researchers have suggested that sleep deprivation immediately after a trauma might reduce the risk of posttraumatic stress disorder (Wagner et al., 2006), but others disagree (van der Helm et al., 2011). Further research will be needed to evaluate this claim.

What are the effects of total **sleep deprivation**? People who go without sleep for as long as a week usually don't suffer serious long-term effects. However, extended sleeplessness does lead to fatigue, irritability, memory problems, and inattention (van der Kloet et al., 2012). Even short-term sleep deprivation—a common condition among busy adolescents and adults—can take its toll (Caldwell, 2012; Lim & Dinges, 2010). For example, sleep deprivation can reduce the ability of the body's immune system to fight off colds (Cohen et al., 2009), and serious mistakes in patient care are more likely when doctors work sleep-disrupting extended hospital shifts than when they work more normal hours (Lockley et al., 2007). By one estimate, sleep deprivation was involved in 23.7 percent of all workplace accidents in the United States (Shahly et al., 2012). For example, thirty-two passengers were injured on March 24, 2014, when a Chicago Transit Authority train slammed into a station at the end of the line because the train operator had fallen asleep. She had been overtired after working a lot of overtime (Esposito & Rossi, 2014). Most fatal car crashes in the United States occur during the "fatigue hazard" hours of midnight to 6 a.m. (Coleman, 1992), and sleepiness resulting from long work shifts or other causes is a major factor in up to 25 percent of all auto accidents (Barger et al., 2005; Filtness, Reyner, & Horne, 2012). Young drivers (ages seventeen to twenty-four) who sleep less are more likely to get into a car accident, too, especially on weekends (Martiniuk et al., 2013). Fatigue has also been identified as a major cause of car accidents in Asia, South America, and Europe (Abe et al., 2010; de Pinho et al., 2006; Pizza et al., 2010; Sagaspe et al., 2010). The fact that "sleepy driving" can be as dangerous as drunk driving led the state of New Jersey to expand the definition of reckless driving to include "driving while fatigued" (i.e., having had no sleep in the previous twenty-four hours). Fatigue also plays a role in many injuries suffered by sleepy young children at play or in day care (Boto et al., 2011). Learning and performance on IQ tests are also impaired after sleep deprivation (Gruber et al., 2010; Yoo et al., 2007), but certain parts of the cerebral cortex actually increase their activity

sleep deprivation A condition in which people do not get enough sleep; it may result in reduced cognitive abilities, inattention, and increased risk of accidents.

when a sleep-deprived person faces a learning task, so we're able to compensate for a while (Drummond et al., 2000).

Scientists are looking for drugs that can combat the effects of sleep deprivation, but there seems to be no substitute for sleep itself. It appears to help restore the body and the brain for future activity and to help consolidate memories of newly learned facts (Korman et al., 2007; Racsmány, Conway, & Demeter, 2010; Walker & Stickgold, 2006). The restorative function is especially associated with NREM sleep, which would help explain why most people get their NREM sleep in the first part of the night (see Figure 9.4).

IN REVIEW

SLEEP AND SLEEP DISORDERS

Sleep Disorders	Characteristics	Possible Causes
NREM (non–rapid eye movement) Stage N3 is also called slow-wave sleep	Includes the deepest stages of sleep, characterized by slowed heart rate and breathing, reduced blood pressure, and low-frequency, high-amplitude brain waves	Refreshes body and brain; consolidates memory
REM (rapid eye movement) sleep	Characterized by eye movements, waking levels of heart rate, breathing, blood pressure, and brain waves, but near-paralysis in muscles	Restores sensitivity to norepinephrine, thus improving waking alertness; creates and solidifies nerve cell connections; consolidates memories and new skills
Insomnia	Difficulty (lasting at least a month) in falling asleep or staying asleep	Worry, anxiety
Narcolepsy	Sudden switching from a waking state to REM sleep	Absence or deficiency in orexin (*hypocretin*)
Sleep apnea	Frequent episodes of interrupted breathing while asleep	Genetic predisposition, obesity, faulty breathing-related brain mechanisms, windpipe compression
Sudden infant death syndrome (SIDS)	Interruption of an infant's breathing, resulting in death	Genetic predisposition, faulty breathing-related brain mechanisms, exposure to cigarette smoke
Sleepwalking	Engaging in walking or other waking behaviors during NREM sleep	Genetic predisposition, drug side effects, and sleep deprivation
Nightmares	Frightening dreams during REM sleep	Stressful or traumatic events or experiences
Sleep terror disorder (night terrors)	Frightening dream images during NREM sleep	Stressful or traumatic events or experiences
REM behavior disorder	Lack of paralysis during REM sleep allows dreams to be enacted, sometimes with harmful consequences	Malfunction of brain mechanism normally creating REM paralysis

In Review Questions

1. Jet lag occurs because of a disruption in a traveler's _____.

2. The importance of NREM sleep is suggested by its appearance _____ in the night.

3. The safest sleeping position for babies is _____.

Dreams and Dreaming

We have seen that the brain is active in all sleep stages (for a summary of our discussion, see "In Review: Sleep and Sleep Disorders"). Some of this brain activity during sleep produces the storylike experiences known as **dreaming**. Dreams may be as short as a few seconds or last for many minutes. They may be organized or chaotic, realistic or fantastic, peaceful or exciting (Schredl, 2010).

Some dreaming occurs during NREM sleep, but most dreams—and the most bizarre and vivid ones—happen in REM (Dement & Kleitman, 1957; Eiser, 2005). Even when they seem to make no sense, dreams may contain a certain kind of logic. For example, people can tell the difference between written dream reports whose sentences had been randomly rearranged and those that had been left alone (Stickgold, Rittenhouse, & Hobson, 1994). And although dreams often involve one person transforming into another or one object turning into another object, it is rare that objects become people or vice versa (Cicogna et al., 2006).

Daytime activities affect dream content (Blagrove et al., 2011). In one study, an unusually high number of animal characters appeared in the dreams reported by people who had just attended an animal rights conference (Lewis, 2008). In another, people with health problems reported more dreams that included illness or injury (King & DiCicco, 2007), and several studies have found that dream images of violence, terrorism, and disaster became more common in the days and weeks following the September 11, 2001, terrorist attacks in the United States (Bulkeley & Kahan, 2008). Sounds and odors influence dreams, too. In one study, sleeping research participants were exposed to the smell of roses or rotten eggs. Those who had smelled the roses reported happier dreams than those who had smelled the rotten eggs (Schredly et al., 2010). It is even possible to intentionally direct dream content. This is called **lucid dreaming**, because the sleeper is aware of dreaming while it occurs (Stumbrys et al., 2012).

Research leaves little doubt that everyone dreams during every night of normal sleep (e.g., Saurat et al., 2011; Voss et al., 2011). Whether you remember a dream depends on how you sleep and wake up. You'll remember more if you awaken abruptly and lie quietly while writing or recording your recollections.

Why do we dream? Theories abound. Some see dreaming as a process through which all species with complex brains analyze and consolidate information that is personally important or has survival value (Payne & Nadel, 2004; Zadra, Desjardins, & Marcotte, 2006). This view is supported by the fact that most mammals have REM sleep, and they are probably dreaming when they do. Such a conclusion was suggested with researchers studying sleep in cats. When the animals had damage to the neurons that cause REM sleep paralysis, the cats ran around and attacked or seemed alarmed by unseen objects, presumably the images from dreams (Winson, 1990).

Sigmund Freud (1900), whose ideas we describe more in the chapter on personality, argued that dreams are a disguised form of *wish fulfillment,* a way to satisfy unconscious urges or resolve unconscious conflicts that are too upsetting to deal with consciously. For example, a person's sexual desires might appear in a dream as the rhythmic motions of a horseback ride. Conflicting feelings about a parent might appear as a dream about a fight. Seeing his patients' dreams as a "royal road to a knowledge of the unconscious," Freud interpreted their meaning as part of his psychoanalytic therapy methods (see the chapter on the treatment of psychological disorders).

In contrast, the *activation-synthesis theory* describes dreams as meaningless by-products of REM sleep (Eiser, 2005; Hobson, 1997). According to this theory, random signals from the hindbrain occur during REM sleep, and these signals *activate* the brain's cerebral cortex. Dreams may result when the cortex tries to make sense of

dreaming The production during sleep of storylike sequences of images, sensations, and perceptions that last from several seconds to many minutes; it occurs mainly during REM sleep.

lucid dreaming Being aware that a dream is a dream while it is occurring.

these random signals, using stored memories and current feelings to *synthesize* something more coherent. From this perspective, dreams represent the brain's attempt to impose sensibility onto meaningless stimulation during sleep (Bernstein & Roberts, 1995; Tierney, 2009).

Even if dreams arise from random brain activity, their content may show something psychologically significant (Bulkeley & Domhoff, 2010). Some psychologists see dreams as giving people a chance to review and address some of the problems they face during waking hours (Cartwright, 1993). This view is supported by evidence suggesting that people's current concerns can affect both the content of their dreams and the way in which dreams are organized and recalled (e.g., Domhoff & Schneider, 2008). However, neuroimaging studies show that while we are in REM sleep, brain areas involved in emotion tend to be overactivated, whereas those areas controlling logical thought tend to be suppressed (Miyauchi et al., 2009). In fact, as we reach deeper sleep stages and then enter REM sleep, logical thinking subsides and unusual perceptions increase (Fosse, Stickgold, & Hobson, 2001). This is probably why dreams rarely provide realistic, logical solutions to our problems (Blagrove, 1996).

HYPNOSIS

Can you be hypnotized against your will?

The word *hypnosis* comes from the Greek word *hypnos,* meaning "sleep." However, hypnotized people are not sleeping. Even those who say afterward that their bodies felt "asleep" also report that their minds were active and alert. **Hypnosis** has been defined as an altered state of consciousness that is brought on by special techniques and produces responsiveness to suggestions for changes in experience and behavior (Kirsch, 1994a). Most hypnotized people do not feel forced to follow the hypnotist's instructions. They simply see no reason to refuse (Hilgard, 1965). In fact, the more that people want to cooperate with the hypnotist, the more likely it is they will experience hypnosis (Lynn et al., 2002). People cannot be hypnotized against their will.

Experiencing Hypnosis

Hypnosis often begins with suggesting that the person feels relaxed and sleepy. The hypnotist then gradually focuses the person's attention on a particular and often monotonous set of stimuli, such as a swinging pendant. The hypnotist asks that the individual ignore everything else and imagine certain feelings.

There are tests to measure **hypnotic susceptibility**, the degree to which people respond to hypnotic suggestions (Kumar & Farley, 2009). In general, they show that about 10 percent of adults are difficult or impossible to hypnotize (Hilgard, 1982). At the other extreme are people whose hypnotic experiences are so vivid that they can't tell the difference between images the hypnotist asked them to imagine and images shown on a screen (Bryant & Mallard, 2003). Brain scans of people who are highly susceptible to hypnosis may show unusually active interactions between attention-regulating regions of cerebral cortex, even in a normal waking state of consciousness (Hoeff et al., 2013). Perhaps this is why hypnotically susceptible people typically differ from others in having a better ability to focus attention and ignore distractions (e.g., Iani et al., 2006). They also tend to have more active imaginations (Spanos, Burnley, & Cross, 1993), a tendency to fantasize (Lynn & Rhue, 1986), a capacity for processing information quickly and easily (Dixon, Brunet, & Laurence, 1990), a tendency to be suggestible (Kirsch & Braffman, 2001), and positive attitudes and expectations about hypnosis (Benham et al., 2006; Fassler, Lynn, & Knox, 2008).

Inducing Hypnosis

In the late 1700s, Austrian physician Franz Anton Mesmer used a forerunner of hypnosis to treat physical disorders. His procedure, known as mesmerism, included elaborate trance-induction rituals, but we now know that hypnosis can be induced far more easily, often simply by staring at an object, as this woman did.

© iStockphoto.com/AtnoYdur

hypnotic susceptibility The degree to which a person responds to hypnotic suggestion.

hypnosis A phenomenon that is brought on by special techniques and is characterized by varying degrees of responsiveness to suggestions for changes in a person's behavior and experiences.

FIGURE 9.6
Hypnotic Age Regression

TRY THIS Here are the signatures of two adults before hypnotically induced age regression (top of each pair) and while age regressed (bottom of each pair). The lower signature in each pair looks less mature, but was the change due to hypnosis? To find out, ask a friend to sign a blank sheet of paper, first as usual, and then as if he or she were five years old. If the two signatures look significantly different, what does this say about the cause of certain age-regression effects?

state theories of hypnosis Theories proposing that hypnosis creates an altered state of consciousness.

nonstate theories of hypnosis Theories, such as role theory, proposing that hypnosis does not create an altered state of consciousness.

The results of hypnosis are fascinating. People told that their eyes are locked shut may struggle unsuccessfully to open them. They may appear deaf or blind or insensitive to pain. They may seem to forget their own names. Some claim to remember forgotten things. Others show *age regression,* seeming to recall or reenact their childhoods (see Figure 9.6). Hypnotic effects can be extended for hours or days through *posthypnotic suggestions,* which are instructions about how to behave after hypnosis has ended (such as smiling whenever someone says "Paris"). Some individuals show *posthypnotic amnesia,* an inability to recall what happened while they were hypnotized, even after being told what happened (Sutcher, 2008; Wark, 2008).

Ernest Hilgard (1965, 1992) described the main changes that people display during hypnosis. First, hypnotized people *tend not to begin actions on their own,* waiting instead for the hypnotist's instructions. One participant said, "I was trying to decide if my legs were crossed, but I couldn't tell, and didn't quite have the initiative to move to find out" (Hilgard, 1965). Second, hypnotized people tend to ignore all but the hypnotist's voice and whatever it points out: Their *attention is redistributed.* Third, hypnosis *enhances the ability to fantasize.* Participants more vividly imagine a scene or relive a memory. Fourth, hypnotized people *readily take on roles.* They more easily act as though they were people of a different age or sex than nonhypnotized people do. Fifth, hypnotized individuals show *reduced reality testing.* They tend not to question whether statements are true, and they are more willing to accept distortions of reality. So a hypnotized person might shiver in a warm room if a hypnotist says it is snowing.

Explaining Hypnosis

Hypnotized people look and act differently from nonhypnotized people (Hilgard, 1965). Do these differences indicate an altered state of consciousness?

Advocates of **state theories of hypnosis** say that they do. They point to the changes in brain activity that occur during hypnosis (Burgmer et al., 2013) and to the dramatic effects that hypnosis can produce, including insensitivity to pain and the disappearance of warts (Noll, 1994). They also note that there are slight differences in the way hypnotized and nonhypnotized people carry out suggestions. In one study, hypnotized people and those pretending to be hypnotized were told to run their hands through their hair whenever they heard the word "experiment" (Orne, Sheehan, & Evans, 1968). The pretenders did so only when the hypnotist said the cue word. Hypnotized participants complied no matter who said it. Another study found that hypnotized people complied more often than pretenders with a posthypnotic suggestion to mail postcards to the experimenter (Barnier & McConkey, 1998).

By contrast, there are also several **nonstate theories of hypnosis.** Supporters of *role theory,* for example, maintain that hypnosis is not a special state of consciousness. They point out that some of the changes in brain activity associated with hypnosis can also be created by other means (McGeown et al., 2012; Mohr, Binkofski, et al., 2005). Advocates for the role theory of hypnosis suggest that hypnotized people are simply complying with the demands of a situation that asks them to act out a special social role (Kirsch, 1994b). From this perspective, hypnosis just gives a socially acceptable reason to follow someone's suggestions, much as a checkup at your doctor's office provides a socially acceptable reason to remove your clothing on request. Support for role theory comes from several sources. First, nonhypnotized people sometimes show behaviors like some that are seen with hypnosis. For example, contestants on television game shows and reality shows do lots of odd, silly, disgusting, or even dangerous things without first being hypnotized. Second, laboratory studies show that motivated but nonhypnotized volunteers can duplicate many aspects of hypnotic behavior, from arm rigidity to age regression (Dasgupta et al., 1995; Mazzoni et al., 2009; Orne & Evans, 1965). Other studies have found that people rendered blind or deaf by hypnosis can

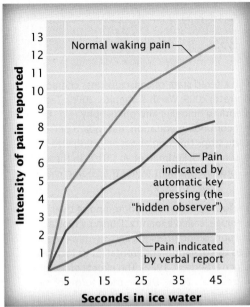

FIGURE 9.7
Reports of Pain in Hypnosis

This graph compares the intensity of pain reported by three groups of participants while one of their hands was immersed in ice water. The orange line represents nonhypnotized participants. The blue line represents hypnotized participants who were told they would feel no pain. The purple line shows the reports of hypnotized participants who were told they would feel no pain but were asked to press a key if "any part of them" felt pain. The key pressing by this "hidden observer" suggests that under hypnosis, the experience of pain was dissociated from conscious awareness.

still see or hear, even though their actions and beliefs suggest that they cannot (Bryant & McConkey, 1989). Still others indicate that people's responses to hypnotic suggestions can vary from one occasion to the next, depending on situational factors (Fassler, Lynn, & Knox, 2008).

Hilgard's (1992) *dissociation theory* blends role and state theories. He suggested that hypnosis is not one specific state but a general condition that temporarily reorganizes or breaks down our normal control over thoughts and actions (Holmes et al., 2005). By this view, hypnosis creates a *dissociation*, meaning a split in consciousness (Hilgard, 1979). Dissociation allows body movements normally under voluntary control to occur on their own and normally involuntary processes (such as overt reactions to pain) to be controlled voluntarily. This relaxation of control depends on a social agreement between the hypnotized person and the hypnotist to share control. In other words, people usually decide for themselves how to act or what to attend to, perceive, or remember. During hypnosis, the hypnotist is given permission to control some of these experiences and actions. Compliance with a social role may tell part of the story, Hilgard said, but hypnosis also leads to significant changes in mental processes.

Support for Hilgard's theory comes from brain-imaging studies showing that the ability to dissociate certain mental processes is greater in people who are more hypnotically susceptible (Bob, 2008; Egner, Jamieson, & Gruzelier, 2005). Dissociation was also demonstrated behaviorally by asking hypnotized participants to keep a hand in ice water (Hilgard, Morgan, & MacDonald, 1975). They were told that they would feel no pain but were asked to press a key with their other hand if "any part of them" felt pain. The results are shown in Figure 9.7. The participants' oral reports indicated almost no pain, but their key-pressing told a different story. Hilgard concluded that a "hidden observer" was reporting on pain that was reaching these people but that had been separated, or dissociated, from conscious awareness (Hilgard, 1977).

Applications of Hypnosis

Whatever hypnosis is, it has proven useful, especially in relation to pain (Patterson, 2010). Functional magnetic resonance imaging (fMRI) studies of hypnotized pain patients show reduced activity in brain regions that normally process the emotional aspects of pain (Vanhaudenhuyse et al., 2009). For some people, hypnosis can block the pain of dental work (Gow, 2010), childbirth (Landolt & Milling, 2011), burns (Askay et al., 2007), and surgery (Hammond, 2008). For others, hypnosis has been shown to relieve chronic pain from arthritis, nerve damage, migraine headaches, and cancer (Stewart, 2005), help eliminate diarrhea (Tan, Hammond, & Joseph, 2005), reduce chemotherapy related nausea and vomiting (Richardson et al., 2007), limit surgical bleeding (Gerschman, Reade, & Burrows, 1980), and speed up postoperative recovery (Astin, 2004). Hypnosis has even helped reduce stress-related hair loss (Willemsen & Vanderlinden, 2008)!

Some applications of hypnosis remain quite controversial (Loftus & Davis, 2006). For example, hypnotic age regression is claimed to help people recover lost memories. One problem with this claim, however, is that the memories of past events reported by age-regressed individuals are not as accurate as those of nonhypnotized individuals (Lynn, Myers, & Malinoski, 1997). Similarly, it is doubtful that hypnosis truly helps most witnesses recall the details of a crime. In fact, their positive expectations about the value of hypnosis may lead them to unintentionally distort or reconstruct memories of what they saw and heard (Garry & Loftus, 1994; Wells & Olson, 2003). Being hypnotized may also make witnesses more confident about even inaccurate reports.

Surgery under Hypnosis

Bernadine Coady of Wimblington, England, has a condition that makes general anesthesia dangerous for her. In April 1999, she faced a foot operation that would have been extremely painful without anesthesia. She arranged for a hypnotherapist to help her through the procedure, but when he failed to show up, she was forced to rely on self-hypnosis as her only anesthetic. She said she imagined the pain as "waves lashing against a sea wall … [and] going away, like the tide." Coady's report that the operation was painless is believable because, in December 2000, she had the same operation on her other foot, again using only self-hypnosis for pain control (Morris, 2000).

© Masons News Service

LINKAGES   Can meditation relieve stress? (a link to Health, Stress, and Coping)

MEDITATION, HEALTH, AND STRESS
LINKAGES

Meditation uses a set of techniques to create an altered state of consciousness characterized by inner peace and tranquility (Chiesa & Serretti, 2009; Walsh & Shapiro, 2006). Techniques to achieve a meditative state differ, depending on belief and philosophy (e.g., Eastern meditation, Sufism, yoga, or prayer). In the most common meditation methods, a person focuses attention on just one thing until he or she stops thinking about anything else and experiences nothing but "pure awareness" (Benson, 1975; Perlman et al., 2010). In this way, the individual becomes more fully aware of the present moment rather than being caught up in the past or the future.

To organize their attention, meditators may focus on the sound or tempo of their breathing or slowly repeat a soothing word or phrase, called a mantra. During a typical meditation session, breathing, heart rate, muscle tension, blood pressure, and oxygen consumption decrease, whereas blood flow in the brain to the thalamus and frontal lobes increases (Cahn & Polich, 2006; Newberg et al., 2001; Wallace & Benson, 1972). The effects of meditation on the brain are complex (Austin, 2006; Hölzel et al., 2011). During most forms of meditation, EEG activity is similar to that seen in a relaxed, eyes-closed, waking state (see Figure 9.3). Meditation is also associated with increased activity of dopamine (Kjaer et al., 2002), a neurotransmitter involved in the experience of reward or pleasure, and fMRI scans show that during meditation, activity increases in brain areas involved in concentrated attention (Brefczynski-Lewis et al., 2007; Hölzel et al., 2011). Neuroimaging studies have shown, too, that meditation is associated with increased connectivity among brain cells (Luders et al., 2011; Moyer et al., 2011).

Some people claim that meditation improves awareness and understanding of themselves and their environment. It is also associated with better immune system function, reductions in high blood pressure and anxiety, improved sleep, longer life span, and better performance in everything from work to tennis (e.g., Dakwar & Levin, 2009; Goyal et al., 2014; Lee et al., 2009; MacLean et al., 2010; Schutte & Malouff, 2014;). Even a brief meditation session makes it easier to quit smoking (Tang, Tang, & Posner, 2013). More generally, meditators' scores on personality tests indicate increases in overall mental health, happiness, self-esteem, and social openness (e.g., Hofmann, Grossman, & Hinton, 2011; Tang et al., 2007). We still do not know exactly how meditation produces these benefits, though its activation of dopamine brain systems may be an important part of the story. Whatever the mechanism, it is probably not unique to meditation. Many of the benefits associated with meditation have also been reported in with biofeedback, hypnosis, tai chi, or just relaxing (Bernstein et al., 2000; Beyerstein, 1999; Wang, Collet, & Lau, 2004).

PSYCHOACTIVE DRUGS

How do drugs affect the brain?

The altered states we have discussed so far serve a biological need (sleep) or rely on the chemistry of the brain and body (hypnosis and meditation). Other altered states are brought on by outside agents, namely drugs. Every day most people in the world use drugs that alter brain activity and consciousness (Levinthal, 2001). For example, 80 to 90 percent of people in North America use caffeine, the stimulant found in coffee, tea, and energy drinks. A *drug* is a chemical that is not required for normal physiological functioning yet has an effect on the body. You may say that you "need" a cup of coffee in the morning, but you'll still wake up without it; accordingly, the caffeine in coffee is defined as a drug. Drugs whose effects on the brain alter consciousness and

meditation A set of techniques used to focus on the "present moment," which create an altered state of consciousness characterized by inner peace and tranquility

other psychological processes are called **psychoactive drugs** (Julien, 2008). The study of psychoactive drugs is called **psychopharmacology**.

Psychopharmacology

Most psychoactive drugs affect the brain by changing the behavior of neurotransmitters or receptors, topics we describe in the chapter on biological aspects of psychology. To create their effects, psychoactive drugs must cross the **blood-brain barrier**, a feature of blood vessels in the brain that prevents some substances from entering brain tissue (Urquhart & Kim, 2009). If a drug can pass this barrier, its psychoactive effects depend on several factors, such as with which neurotransmitter systems the drug interacts, how the drug affects those neurotransmitters and their receptors, and the psychological functions normally affected by the brain systems that use those neurotransmitters.

Drugs can affect neurotransmitters or their receptors through several mechanisms. As mentioned in the biological aspects of psychology chapter, neurotransmitters fit into their own receptors (see Figure 9.8). Some drugs, such as morphine, are similar enough to a particular neurotransmitter to fool its receptors. These drugs, called **agonists**, bind to receptors and imitate, or mimic, the effects of the normal neurotransmitter. Other drugs, called **antagonists**, are similar enough to a neurotransmitter to occupy its receptors but cannot mimic its effects. When they bind to receptors, they prevent the normal neurotransmitter from binding. Still other drugs work by increasing or decreasing the release of a specific neurotransmitter. Finally, some drugs work by speeding or slowing the *removal* of a neurotransmitter from synapses.

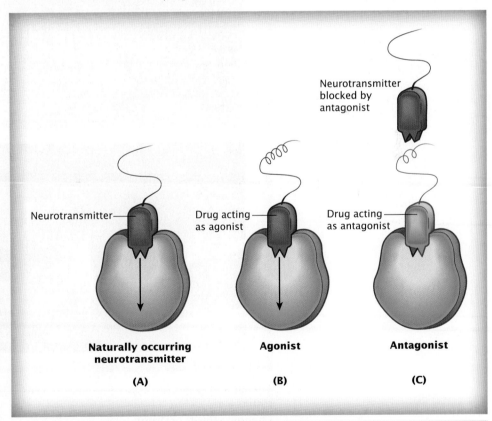

psychoactive drugs Chemical substances that act on the brain to create psychological effects.

psychopharmacology The study of psychoactive drugs and their effects.

blood-brain barrier A characteristic of blood vessels in the brain that prevents some substances from entering brain tissue.

agonists Drugs that bind to a receptor and mimic the effects of the neurotransmitter that normally fits that receptor.

antagonists Drugs that bind to a receptor and prevent the normal neurotransmitter from binding.

FIGURE 9.8

Agonists and Antagonists

In Part A, a molecule of neurotransmitter interacts with a receptor on a neuron's dendrite by fitting into and stimulating it. Part B shows a drug molecule acting as an agonist, affecting the receptor in the same way a neurotransmitter would. Part C depicts an antagonist drug molecule blocking a natural neurotransmitter from reaching and acting on the receptor.

Predicting a psychoactive drug's effects on behavior is complicated. For one thing, most of these drugs interact with many neurotransmitter systems. Also, the nervous system may compensate for a given drug's effects. For instance, repeated exposure to a drug that blocks receptors for a certain neurotransmitter often leads to an increase in the number of receptors available to accept that neurotransmitter.

The Varying Effects of Drugs

The chemical properties that give drugs their medically desirable main effects, such as pain relief, often create undesirable side effects as well.

Drug Abuse

One side effect may be the potential for abuse. **Drug abuse** (sometimes called a **substance use disorder**) is a pattern of use that causes serious social, legal, or interpersonal problems for the user (American Psychiatric Association, 2013). Of course, as a culture changes, which drugs cause a person social and legal problems may also change, as Figure 9.9 illustrates.

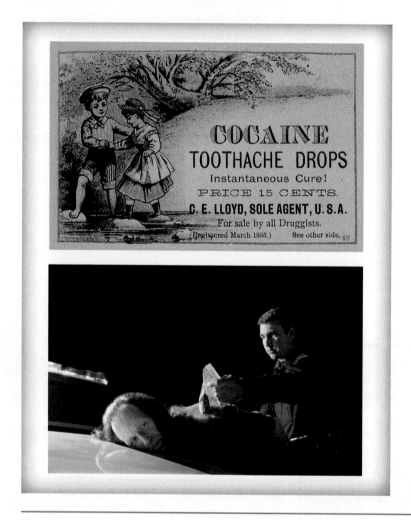

FIGURE 9.9
Changing Views of Drugs

The legal and social status of a drug can vary across cultures and over time (Weiss & Moore, 1990). For example, in the United States cocaine was once a respectable, commercially available drug; today it is illegal. Marijuana, once illegal throughout the United States, is now legal in some states. Meanwhile, alcohol, which is legal in the United States and many other nations, is banned in countries such as Kuwait, Iran, and Saudi Arabia.

The William H. Helfand Collection, New York Academy of Medicine; Thinkstock/Getty Images

drug abuse (substance use disorder) The use of psychoactive drugs in ways that deviate from cultural norms and cause serious problems for the user.

Substance abuse can lead to psychological or physical *dependence*. People displaying *psychological dependence* on a drug will continue to use it even though it has harmful effects. They need the drug for a sense of well-being and become preoccupied with getting the drug if it is no longer available. However, they can still function without the drug. Psychological dependence can occur with or without addiction. **Addiction** (also known as *physical dependence*) is a physiological state in which there is not only a strong craving for the drug but also in which using the drug becomes necessary to prevent the unpleasant experience of **drug withdrawal** (sometimes called a *withdrawal syndrome*). Withdrawal symptoms vary depending on the drug, but they often include an intense desire for the drug and physical effects often opposite to those of the drug itself. Eventually, drug use may produce **drug tolerance**, a condition in which increasingly larger drug doses are required to produce the same effects. With the development of drug tolerance, many addicts need the drug just to prevent the negative effects of not taking it. However, a craving for the positive effects of drugs is mainly what keeps addicts coming back to them (Blum et al., 2011).

You may be tempted to think of "addicts" as being different from the rest of us, but we should not underestimate the ease with which drug dependence can develop in any person. Physical dependence develops gradually and may do so without our awareness. In fact, scientists believe that the changes in the brain that underlie addiction may be similar to those that occur during learning (Koob & Kreek, 2007; Nestler, 2001; Ross & Peselow, 2009). All addictive drugs stimulate the brain's "pleasure centers," regions that are sensitive to the neurotransmitter dopamine (Quintero, 2013). Activity of neurons in these areas creates intensely pleasurable feelings, including those associated with a good meal, "runner's high," gambling, or sex (Haber & Knutson, 2010; Reuter et al., 2005). When addictive drugs affect dopamine regulation in these "pleasure centers," they, too, produce tremendously rewarding effects in most people. In fact, the changes created in the brain by drug addiction can remain long after drug use ends (Diana, Spiqa, & Acquas, 2006), which is one reason that people who succeed in giving up addictive drugs may still be in danger of relapse even years later. The risk of relapse is also elevated because of epigenetic effects (see the introductory chapter); for some people, exposure to addictive drugs changes gene expression such that the pleasure a drug creates becomes more intense as use continues (Ponomarev, 2013).

Expectations and Drug Effects

Drug effects are not determined by biochemistry alone (Crombag & Robinson, 2004). The *expectations* we learn through experience with drugs and/or drug users also play a role (Pollo & Benedetti, 2009; Siegel, 2005). So just expecting to drink alcohol, for example, can create neural activity in the same brain areas that are affected by actually drinking it (Gundersen et al., 2008). Several experiments have shown that research participants who consume nonalcoholic drinks that they *think* contain alcohol are likely to behave in line with their expectations about alcohol's effects. So they tend to feel drunk and to become more aggressive, more interested in violent and sexual material, and more easily sexually aroused (Darkes & Goldman, 1993; George & Marlatt, 1986; Lang et al., 1975). And because they know that alcohol impairs memory, these participants are more vulnerable to developing false memories about a crime they witnessed on videotape (Assefi & Garry, 2003). The effects of expectancy are not limited to alcohol. Other research shows that people may feel and act "high" after smoking a cigarette that they believe contains marijuana, even if it doesn't (Metrik et al., 2009).

We build expectations about drug effects in part by watching how other people, especially parents, react to drugs (Cranford et al., 2010; Sher et al., 1996). Such expectations can influence how much of a drug a user will consume. Of course, what a person sees can differ from one individual and culture to the next, so drug effects vary greatly throughout the world (Lin, Smith, & Ortiz, 2001; MacAndrew & Edgerton, 1969). In the United States, for example, drinking alcohol is often associated with uninhibited behavior, including impulsiveness, anger, violence, and sexual promiscuity. But these effects are not seen in all cultures. In Bolivia's Camba culture, for example, people sometimes engage in extended bouts of drinking a brew that is 89 percent alcohol (178 proof). During these binges, the

addiction Development of a physical need for a psychoactive drug.

drug withdrawal A set of symptoms associated with ending the use of an addictive substance.

drug tolerance A condition in which increasingly larger drug doses are needed to produce a given effect.

Camba repeatedly pass out, wake up, and start drinking again—all the while maintaining friendly social relations.

In short, the effects of psychoactive drugs are complex and variable. Let's now consider several major categories of psychoactive drugs that people use primarily to produce altered states of consciousness. They include depressant drugs, stimulating drugs, opiates, hallucinogenic drugs, and dissociative drugs.

CNS Depressant Drugs

Drugs such as alcohol and barbiturates are called **CNS depressant drugs** because they reduce or depress activity in the central nervous system (CNS), mainly in the brain. They do so partly by increasing the effects of the neurotransmitter GABA. As described in the chapter on biological aspects of psychology, GABA reduces the activity of neurons in various brain circuits. So if a drug increases the amount of GABA available, activity in those circuits will be lower than usual, creating feelings of relaxation, drowsiness, and sometimes depression (Hanson & Venturelli, 1995).

Alcohol

The most common CNS depressant drug by far is alcohol. In the United States, more than 100 million people drink it, and alcohol is equally popular worldwide (Leigh & Stacy, 2004; Swendsen et al., 2012). Alcohol affects several neurotransmitters, including glutamate, serotonin, and GABA (Daglish & Nutt, 2003; Enoch, 2003; Vinod et al., 2006). Alcohol also enhances the effect of endorphins, the body's natural painkillers. The fact that endorphins produce a sense of well-being may explain why people initially feel "high" when drinking alcohol. It may also explain why drugs that block endorphins effectively reduce alcohol cravings and relapse rates in recovering alcoholics (Soyka, 2013). Alcohol's pleasurable effects are partly due to its interaction with the dopamine systems that are part of the brain's reward mechanisms (Morikawa & Morrisett, 2010). Prolonged alcohol use can have lasting effects on the brain's ability to regulate dopamine levels (Tiihonen et al., 1995). Dopamine agonists reduce alcohol cravings and the effects of alcohol withdrawal (Swift et al., 2010).

Alcohol affects some brain regions more than others. It depresses activity in the locus coeruleus, an area that, as described in our discussion of sleep, normally helps activate the cerebral cortex (Koob & Bloom, 1988). The resulting reduction in cortical activity, in turn, may cause cognitive changes that can cause a loosening of control over normally inhibited behaviors (Casbon et al., 2003). Some drinkers begin talking loudly, acting silly, or telling others what they think of them. Emotional reactions range from giddy happiness to despair. Normally shy people may become impulsive or violent (Giancola & Corman, 2007). Alcohol also impairs the hippocampus, making it more difficult to process information and form new memories (Anderson et al., 2012). Chronic alcohol use appears to damage the hippocampus permanently, making it smaller and less functional in heavy drinkers as compared to nondrinkers (Beresford et al., 2006; McClintick et al., 2013). Elsewhere in the brain, alcohol's suppression of the cerebellum causes poor motor coordination, including difficulty in walking (Rogers et al., 1986). Excessive use can permanently damage the cerebellum (Manto, 2012). Alcohol's ability to depress hindbrain mechanisms required for breathing and heartbeat is probably why very high doses become fatal.

As mentioned earlier, some effects of alcohol—such as anger and aggressiveness—depend on not only biochemical factors but also learned expectations (Goldman, Darkes, & Del Boca, 1999; Kushner et al., 2000). Other effects—especially disruptions in motor coordination, speech, and thought—result from biochemical factors alone. These biological effects depend on the amount of alcohol the blood carries to the brain. It takes the liver about an hour to break down one ounce of alcohol (the amount in one typical drink), so alcohol has milder effects if consumed slowly (Zakhari, 2006). Faster drinking or drinking on an empty stomach speeds absorption of alcohol into the blood and heightens its effects. Even after allowing for differences in average male and female body weight, metabolic differences allow male bodies to tolerate somewhat greater amounts of alcohol. So a given quantity of alcohol may have a stronger effect on the average woman than on

CNS depressant drugs Psychoactive drugs that inhibit the functioning of the central nervous system.

Drinking and Driving Don't Mix

Though practice makes it seem easy, driving a car is a complex information-processing task. As described in the chapter on thought and language, such tasks require constant vigilance, quick decisions, and skillful execution of responses. Alcohol can impair all these processes, as well as the ability to judge the degree of impairment—thus making drinking and driving a deadly combination that results in almost 11,000 deaths each year in the United States alone (National Highway Traffic Safety Administration, 2010).

Luis Santana/Photos.com

the average man (York & Welte, 1994). Overindulgence by either sex results in unpleasant physical hangover effects that are not effectively prevented or relieved by aspirin, bananas, vitamins, coffee, eggs, exercise, fresh air, honey, pizza, herbal remedies, more alcohol, or any of dozens of other "surefire" hangover cures (Pittler, Verster, & Ernst, 2005).

Genetics helps determine the biochemical effects of alcohol (Rietschel & Treutlein, 2013). Evidence suggests that some people have a genetic predisposition toward alcohol dependence (Kimura & Higuchi, 2011), though the genes involved have not yet been identified. Other groups (the Japanese, for example) may have inherited metabolic characteristics that enhance the adverse effects of alcohol, possibly inhibiting the development of alcohol abuse (Iwahashi et al., 1995).

Barbiturates

Sometimes called "downers" or sleeping pills, *barbiturates* are highly addictive. In small doses, their psychoactive effects include relaxation, mild pleasure, loss of muscle coordination, and reduced attention. Higher doses cause deep sleep, but continued use actually distorts sleep patterns (Zammit, 2007), so long-term use of barbiturates as sleeping pills may be unwise. Overdoses can be fatal. Withdrawal symptoms are among the most severe for any drug and can include intense agitation, violent outbursts, seizures, hallucinations, and even sudden death.

GHB

Gamma hydroxybutyrate (GHB) is a naturally occurring substance similar to the neurotransmitter GABA (Drasbek, Christensen, & Jensen, 2006; Wong, Gibson, & Snead, 2004). As mentioned earlier, it is sometimes used by physicians in the treatment of narcolepsy. However, a laboratory-manufactured version of GHB (also known as "G") has become a popular "club drug," meaning that it is often used at nightclubs, concerts, raves, or dance parties (Gahlinger, 2004). GHB is known for creating relaxation, feelings of elation, loss of inhibitions, and increased sex drive (Schuman-Oliver et al., 2011). It can also cause nausea and vomiting, headaches, memory loss, dizziness, loss of muscle control or paralysis, breathing problems, loss of consciousness, and even death—especially when combined with alcohol or other drugs (Miotto et al., 2001; Stillwell, 2002). As with other CNS depressants, long-term use of GHB can lead to dependence (Carter et al., 2006). Dependent users who abruptly stop taking the drug may experience withdrawal symptoms that can include seizures, hallucinations, agitation, coma, or death (Van Noorden et al., 2009).

Flunitrazepam

A drug related to the prescription medications Xanax and Valium, *flunitrazepam* has been used by physicians to treat insomnia, but those who abuse it risk becoming dependent, and acute intoxication can be fatal (Druid, Holmgren, & Ahlner, 2001). Flunitrazepam relaxes muscles, produces sedation, but also impairs decision making and may cause a person to forget the drug experience. This amnesic effect, combined with the drug's reputation for making people more willing to engage in sex (Britt & McCance-Katz, 2005), makes it one of several club drugs, including GHB, that are used in drug-facilitated sexual assault or "date rape" (Beynon et al., 2008).

CNS Stimulating Drugs

Whereas depressants slow down central nervous system activity, **CNS stimulating drugs** speed it up. Amphetamines, cocaine, caffeine, and nicotine are all examples of CNS stimulating drugs.

Amphetamines

Often called "uppers" or "speed," *amphetamines* increase the release of norepinephrine and dopamine into synapses, affecting sleep, learning, and mood (Bonci et al., 2003; Kolb et al., 2003). Amphetamines also slow the removal of both substances at synapses, leaving more of them there, ready to work. The increased activity at these neurotransmitters' receptors results in alertness, arousal, and appetite suppression. These effects are amplified by the fact that amphetamines also reduce activity of the inhibitory neurotransmitter GABA (Vlachou & Markou, 2010). Amphetamines' rewarding properties are probably associated with their effect on dopamine activity, because taking dopamine antagonists reduces amphetamine use (Higley et al., 2011).

Amphetamine abuse usually begins after taking these drugs to lose weight, increase alertness, stay awake, or "get high." Repeated use leads to anxiety and insomnia. Continued use often causes heart problems, brain damage, movement disorders, confusion, paranoia, nonstop talking, and psychological and physical dependence (Rusyniak, 2011). In some cases, symptoms of amphetamine abuse are almost identical to those of paranoid schizophrenia (Salo, Ravizza, & Fassbender, 2011), a serious mental disorder linked to dopamine malfunction.

Cocaine

Like amphetamines, *cocaine* increases norepinephrine and dopamine activity and decreases GABA activity, so it produces many amphetamine-like effects (Ciccarone, 2011; Vlachou & Markou, 2010). Cocaine has a particularly powerful and rapid effect on dopamine activity and so is remarkably addictive (Wise & Kiyatkin, 2011). In fact, most drugs with rapid onset and short duration are more addictive than others (Kato, Wakasa, & Yamagita, 1987), which helps explain why *crack*—a purified, fast-acting, highly potent, smokable form of cocaine—is especially addictive (Falck, Wang, & Carlson, 2007). In the United States, about 5.3 million people over the age of twelve have used cocaine and about 1.1 million have used crack at least once in the last year (Substance Abuse and Mental Health Services Administration, 2009).

Cocaine stimulates self-confidence, a sense of well-being, and optimism. Continued use brings nausea, overactivity, insomnia, paranoia, a sudden depressive "crash," hallucinations, sexual dysfunction, and seizures (Lacayo, 1995). However, every time it is used, immediate effects on the heart and brain are unpredictable; even small doses can cause a fatal heart attack or stroke (Maraj, Figueredo, & Lynn, 2010). Using cocaine during pregnancy harms the fetus (Hurt et al., 1995) and is known to leave lasting cognitive and behavioral problems for the child (Salisbury et al., 2009). Nonetheless, many of the severe, long-term behavioral problems seen in "cocaine babies" may stem from poverty and

Deadly Drug Use

Singer Whitney Houston's death in 2012 was due in part to her chronic use of cocaine. She joined a long list of celebrities (including Corey Monteith, Lisa Robin Kelly, Amy Winehouse, Chris Kelley, Heath Ledger, and Phillip Seymour Hoffman) and an even longer list of non-celebrities whose lives have been destroyed by the abuse of alcohol, cocaine, or other addictive drugs.

Ian West/PA Photos /Landov

CNS stimulating drugs Psychoactive drugs that increase behavioral and mental activity.

neglect after birth and not just the mother's cocaine use (Ackerman, Riggins, & Black, 2010). Early intervention can reduce some of the effects of both cocaine and the hostile environment that confronts cocaine babies (Bada, 2012).

Caffeine

Caffeine may be the world's most popular drug. It is found in chocolate, many soft drinks, tea, and coffee, which is consumed worldwide more than any other beverage except water (Butt & Sultan, 2011). A typical cup of coffee has 58 to 259 mg of caffeine, and even "decaffeinated" coffee may contain up to 15.8 mg (McCusker, Goldberger, & Cone, 2003; McCusker et al., 2006). Energy drinks have up to 505 mg per can (Reissig, Strain, & Griffiths, 2009). Caffeine reduces drowsiness, can create temporary improvements in cognitive performance, including problem solving and vigilance (Snel & Lorist, 2011). In modest quantities, caffeine may help people form memories. In one study, participants viewed a series of images, then received either caffeine or a placebo. The next day, those who had received mild to moderate elevations in their caffeine levels performed better when trying to remember the images they had seen. Those who had the highest caffeine levels did not do as well, suggesting that a "medium" dose may work best (Borota et al., 2014). Indeed, at high doses, caffeine causes anxiety and tremors. People can develop tolerance to caffeine, and it is physically addictive (Ogawa & Ueki, 2007; Strain et al., 1994). Withdrawal symptoms—including headache, fatigue, anxiety, shakiness, and craving—appear on the first day of abstinence and last about a week (Silverman et al., 1992). Caffeine may also slightly raise the risk of breast cancer in women (Jiang, Wu, & Jiang, 2013). Whereas heavy caffeine use may increase the risk of miscarriage, stillbirth, or having a low birth weight baby (Kuczkowski, 2009), it is unclear if mild to moderate caffeine use poses a pregnancy risk (Jahanfar & Jaafar, 2013). Moderate daily use may cause slight increases in blood pressure (Geleijnse, 2008), but otherwise appears to have few, if any, negative effects (e.g., Lopez-Garcia et al., 2008; Winkelmayer et al., 2005). Caffeine consumption may even be associated with a decreased risk of developing Alzheimer's disease (Marques et al., 2011).

Nicotine

A powerful autonomic nervous system stimulant, *nicotine* is the main psychoactive ingredient in tobacco. It enhances the action of acetylcholine (Penton & Lester, 2009) and increases the availability of glutamate, the brain's primary excitatory neurotransmitter (Liechti & Markou, 2008). It also activates the brain's dopamine-related pleasure systems (Herman et al., 2014). Nicotine has many psychoactive effects, including elevated mood and improved memory and attention (Domino, 2003; Ernst et al., 2001).

Like cocaine, nicotine can be physically addictive (White, 1998), and teenagers who smoke cigarettes are more likely to go on to use illegal addictive drugs (Mayet et al., 2011). Some people are more vulnerable to nicotine addiction than others (Hiroi & Scott, 2009), and the tendency to become physically dependent on nicotine appears to be at least partly inherited (Russo et al., 2011). Nicotine doesn't create the "rush" noted in many drugs of abuse, yet quitting smoking causes a potent withdrawal syndrome, with craving, irritability, anxiety, reduced heart rate, and lower activity in the brain's reward pathways (Epping-Jordan et al., 1998; Hughes, Higgins, & Bickel, 1994). This is partly why smoking tobacco can be a difficult habit to break (Crane, 2007). Today, so-called electronic cigarettes are touted as a safer alternative to tobacco cigarettes, but their safety remains in question (Palazzolo, 2013). Use of various forms of smokeless nicotine replacement may help some people quit smoking (Stead et al., 2012), as can medications such as varenicline and buproprion (Carson et al., 2013). An antismoking vaccine is being proposed as well (Fahim, Kesser, & Kalnik, 2013). By whatever means, quitting is worthwhile. Although smoking is a major risk factor for death from cancer, heart disease, and respiratory disorders, smokers who quit before the age of thirty-five have long-term mortality rates similar to those who never smoked (Centers for Disease Control and Prevention, 2008, 2011a).

MDMA

The stimulant "ecstasy," or *MDMA* (short for methylenedioxymethamphetamine)—also known as "XTC," "clarity," "essence," "E," and "Adam"—is another club drug that is popular on college campuses in the United States. MDMA acts on dopamine pathways in the brain (Schenk, Gittings, & Colussi-Mas, 2011), so it leads to some of the same effects as those produced by cocaine and amphetamines (Steele, McCann, & Ricaurte, 1994). These include emotional changes with a sense of well-being, increased sex drive, and a feeling of greater closeness to others. Undesirable effects of MDMA may include dry mouth, hyperactivity, jaw muscle spasms that may result in "lockjaw," elevated blood pressure, fever, and dangerous heart rhythms (Baylen & Rosenberg, 2006). Hallucinations from MDMA are probably because MDMA acts as a serotonin agonist and it increases serotonin release (Green, Cross, & Goodwin, 1995). On the day after using MDMA, people often report muscle aches, fatigue, depression, and poor concentration.

MDMA does not appear to be physically addictive, but it is dangerous and potentially deadly, especially when taken by women (Liechti, Gamma, & Vollenweider, 2001; National Institute on Drug Abuse, 2000). It permanently damages the brain (Sarkar & Schmued, 2010), killing serotonin-sensitive and dopamine-using neurons. As you might expect, the danger of brain damage increases with higher doses and continued use. MDMA users may develop the symptoms of panic disorder, with intense anxiety and a sense of impending death (see the chapter on psychological disorders). When given to pregnant animals, MDMA produces permanent behavioral changes in their offspring (Thompson et al., 2009). Research on humans and nonhumans indicates that many of the MDMA's effects remain even after its use is discontinued (Kalechstein et al., 2007; Smith, Tivarus, et al., 2006).

Opiates

The **opiates** (opium, morphine, heroin, and codeine) are unique in their capacity for inducing sleep and relieving pain (Julien, 2008). *Opium*, which comes from the poppy plant, relieves pain and creates feelings of euphoria and relaxation (Cowan et al., 2001). One of its most active ingredients, *morphine*, was first isolated in the early 1800s. It is used worldwide for pain relief. Percocet, Vicodin, and OxyContin are some common morphine-like drugs. *Heroin* is made from morphine but is three times more powerful, causing intensely pleasurable reactions. Opiates have complex effects on consciousness (Gruber, Silveri, & Yurgelun-Todd, 2007). Drowsy, cloudy feelings occur because opiates depress activity in some areas of the cerebral cortex. They also create excitation in other parts, causing some users to experience euphoria, or elation (Bozarth & Wise, 1984). Opiates exert many of their effects by stimulating the receptors normally stimulated by endorphins, the body's own painkillers. This action "tricks" the brain into an exaggerated activation of its pain-killing and mood-altering systems (Julien, 2008).

Opiates are highly addictive, largely because of their actions on the dopamine reward system (Kreek et al., 2009), but also partly because they affect both glutamate and GABA receptors in a way that changes how nerve cells communicate with each other (Dacher & Nugent, 2011). It may be, then, that opiates alter neurons so that they come to require the drug (Christie, 2008). Beyond the hazard of addiction itself, heroin addicts risk death through overdoses, contaminated drugs, or AIDS contracted through sharing needles (Hser et al., 2001).

Hallucinogenic Drugs

Hallucinogenic drugs, also called *psychedelic drugs*, create a loss of contact with reality and alter other aspects of emotion, perception, and thought. They can cause distortions in body image (the user may feel gigantic or tiny), loss of identity (uncertainty about who one actually is), dreamlike fantasies, and hallucinations. Because these effects resemble many severe forms of mental disorder, hallucinogenic drugs are also called *psychotomimetics* ("mimicking psychosis").

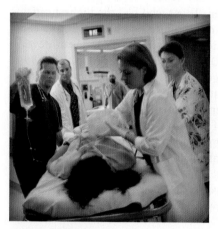

Another Drug Danger

Oxycodone, a morphine-like drug prescribed by doctors under the label OxyContin, is popular among recreational substance abusers. It was designed as a timed-release painkiller, but when people crush OxyContin tablets and then inject or inhale the drug, they get a much stronger and potentially lethal dose, especially when they are also using other drugs such as alcohol or cocaine (Cone et al., 2004). Deaths from OxyContin abuse have been on the rise in the United States in recent years (Centers for Disease Control and Prevention, 2011b).

Stockbyte/Thinsktock

opiates Psychoactive drugs that produce both sleep-inducing and pain-relieving effects.

hallucinogenic drugs Psychoactive drugs that alter consciousness by producing a temporary loss of contact with reality and changes in emotion, perception, and thought.

LSD

One of the most powerful hallucinogenic drugs is *lysergic acid diethylamide* (LSD). It was first synthesized from a rye fungus by Swiss chemist Albert Hofmann. In 1938, after Hofmann accidentally ingested a tiny amount of the substance, he discovered the drug's strange effects in the world's first LSD "trip" (Julien, 2008). LSD hallucinations can be quite bizarre. Time may seem distorted, sounds may cause visual sensations, and users may feel as if they have left their bodies. LSD's hallucinations may stem from its ability to stimulate a specific type of serotonin receptor (Halberstadt & Geyer, 2011). This possibility is supported by evidence that serotonin antagonists reduce LSD's hallucinatory effects (Passie et al, 2008). The strangeness of LSD hallucinations may occur because the drug activates slightly different brain areas than those activated when we are correctly sensing the world around us (Iaria et al., 2010).

The effects of LSD on a particular person are unpredictable. Unpleasant hallucinations and delusions can occur during a person's first—or two hundredth—LSD experience. Although LSD is not addictive, tolerance to its effects does develop. Some users suffer lasting side effects, including severe short-term memory loss, paranoia, violent outbursts, nightmares, and panic attacks (Gold, 1994). Sometimes "flashbacks" can occur, in which a person suddenly returns to an LSD-like state of consciousness weeks or even years after using the drug.

Ketamine

Ketamine is an anesthetic used by veterinarians to ease pain in animals (Hirota, 2006; Robakis & Hirsch, 2006), but because it also has hallucinogenic effects, it is used as a recreational drug known as "Special K." Its effects include dissociative feelings that create an "out-of-body" or "near-death" experience. Ketamine intoxication can create thought problems similar to those seen in schizophrenia (Neill et al., 2011), and long-term use causes lasting memory impairments (Venâncio et al., 2011), probably because the drug damages memory-related brain structures such as the hippocampus (Jevtovic-Todorovic et al., 2001).

Marijuana

A mixture of crushed leaves, flowers, and stems from the hemp plant (*Cannabis sativa*) makes up *marijuana*. The active ingredient is *tetrahydrocannabinol* (THC) (Fisar, 2009). When inhaled, THC is absorbed in minutes by many organs, including the brain (Martin-Santos et al., 2010), and it continues to affect consciousness for a few hours (O'Leary et al., 2002). THC tends to collect in fatty deposits of the brain and reproductive organs, where it can remain for weeks. Low doses of marijuana may initially create restlessness and hilarity, followed by a dreamy, carefree relaxation, an expanded sense of space and time, more vivid sensations, food cravings, and subtle changes in thinking (Kelly et al., 1990).

For some time now, marijuana has been legally prescribed by physicians in the District of Columbia, in several U.S. states, and in Canada and several other countries, and has been successful in the treatment of asthma, glaucoma, epilepsy, chronic pain, and nausea from cancer chemotherapy; it may even help in treating some types of cancer (Grevdanus et al., 2013). While opponents of medical marijuana point to its possible health and safety risks and argue that other medications may be equally effective and less dangerous (e.g., Campbell et al., 2001; Fox et al., 2004; Hall & Degenhardt, 2003), some U.S. states are bypassing the medical debate by legalizing the sale, purchase, and use of marijuana for any purpose, including recreation.

Even if marijuana becomes legal everywhere, controversy over its use will likely continue. Proponents argue that, unlike tobacco, marijuana does not harm the lungs (Sidney, Feng, & Kertesz, 2011). Opponents point to findings that withdrawal from marijuana may be accompanied by increases in anxiety, depression, irritability, restlessness, and aggressiveness (Allsop et al., 2011; Levin et al., 2010). And because marijuana interacts with the same dopamine and opiate receptors as heroin (Cadoni et al., 2013), some researchers speculate that, like tobacco, marijuana may act as a "gateway" to using more addictive drugs (Mayet et al., 2012). Others point out, though, that the rewarding effects of sex and chocolate occur by activating these same receptors, and that those pleasures are not generally viewed as gateways to drug addiction.

Regardless of whether marijuana is addicting or leads to opiate use, like all drugs, it can create problems, including in the cardiovascular and immune systems (Hall & Degenhardt, 2009; Jayanthi et al., 2010). Marijuana also disrupts memory formation, making it difficult to carry out mental or physical tasks and, despite many users' impressions, it actually reduces creativity (Bourassa & Vaugeois, 2001). Because marijuana disrupts muscle coordination, driving under its influence is dangerous (Asbridge, Hayden, & Cartwright, 2012). Marijuana easily reaches a developing fetus, and while the risk to a pregnancy is not clear (Jaques et al., 2013), pregnant women's use of marijuana has been associated with behavioral problems in their children (Day, Leech, & Goldschmidt, 2011). Finally, long-term use can lead to psychological dependence (Stephens, Roffman, & Simpson, 1994) as well as to impairments in reasoning and memory that last for months or years after marijuana use stops (Sofuoglu, Sugarman, & Carroll, 2010).

These effects are especially strong in people who start using marijuana before the age of fifteen (Fontes et al., 2011). In fact, heavy use by teenagers has been associated with smaller than normal volume in brain areas involved in emotion and memory as well as with the later appearance of anxiety, depression, and other even more serious symptoms of mental disorder (e.g., Moore et al., 2007; Yücel et al., 2008). Some research suggests that frequent marijuana users also show lower IQ scores as individuals move from childhood to adulthood (Meier et al., 2012). Still, these correlations cannot establish cause and effect. For example, some research suggests that the relationship between marijuana use and lower IQ may be caused by a third factor, such as educational or socioeconomic status (Rogeberg, 2013).

Further complicating the scientific and legal controversy surrounding marijuana is the recent emergence of several forms of "legal pot." These synthetic substances, such as "spice" and "K2," are being marketed as marijuana alternatives, and because their chemical makeup differs from the THC molecules they mimic, they are not yet illegal. Nevertheless, these compounds and their effects are not well understood, and so potential new dangers arise for users each time a new one is synthesized.

("In Review: Major Classes of Psychoactive Drugs" summarizes our discussion of these substances.)

MAJOR CLASSES OF PSYCHOACTIVE DRUGS   IN REVIEW

Drug	Trade/Street Name	Main Effects	Potential for Physical/ Psychological Dependence
CNS Depressant Drugs			
Alcohol	"booze"	Relaxation, anxiety reduction, sleep	High/high
Barbiturates	Seconal, Tuinal, Nembutal ("downers")	Relaxation, anxiety reduction, sleep	High/high
GHB	"G," "jib," "scoop," "GH buddy"	Relaxation, euphoria	High/high

(continued)

MAJOR CLASSES OF PSYCHOACTIVE DRUGS (CONT.)

Drug	Trade/Street Name	Main Effects	Potential for Physical/ Psychological Dependence
Flunitrazepam	"R2," "roofie," "roach"	relaxation, impaired decision making, memory loss	High/high
CNS Stimulating Drugs			
Amphetamines	Benzedrine, Dexedrine, Methadrine ("speed," "uppers," "ice")	Alertness, euphoria	Moderate/high
Cocaine	"coke," "crack"	Alertness, euphoria	Moderate to high/high
Caffeine		Alertness	Moderate/ moderate
Nicotine	"smokes," "coffin nails"	Alertness	High (?)/high
MDMA	"ecstasy," "clarity"	Hallucinations	Low/(?)
Opiates			
Opium		Euphoria	High/high
Morphine	Percodan, Demerol	Euphoria, pain control	High/high
Heroin	"junk," "smack"	Euphoria, pain control	High/high
Hallucinogenic Drugs			
LSD/ketamine	"acid"/"special K"	Altered perceptions, hallucinations	Low/low
Marijuana (cannabis)	"pot," "dope," "reefer," "weed"	Euphoria, relaxation	Low/moderate

In Review Questions

1. Physical dependence on a drug is a condition more commonly known as _____ .

2. Drugs that act as antagonists _____ the interaction of neurotransmitters and receptors.

3. Drug effects are determined partly by what we learn to _____ the effects to be.

LINKAGES

As noted in the introductory chapter, all of psychology's subfields are related to one another. Our discussion of meditation, health, and stress illustrates just one way that the topic of this chapter, consciousness, is linked to the subfield of health psychology, which is described in the chapter on health, stress, and coping. The Linkages diagram shows ties to two other subfields, and there are many more ties throughout the book. Looking for linkages among subfields will help you see how they all fit together and help you better appreciate the big picture that is psychology.

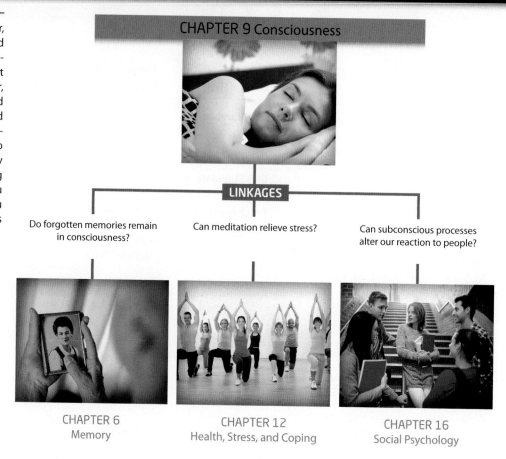

CHAPTER 9 Consciousness

LINKAGES

Do forgotten memories remain in consciousness?

Can meditation relieve stress?

Can subconscious processes alter our reaction to people?

CHAPTER 6
Memory

CHAPTER 12
Health, Stress, and Coping

CHAPTER 16
Social Psychology

SUMMARY

Consciousness can be defined as awareness of the outside world and of one's own thoughts, feelings, perceptions, and other mental processes.

The Scope of Consciousness

Can unconscious thoughts affect your behavior?

A person's **consciousness state** is constantly changing. When the changes are particularly noticeable, they are called **altered states of consciousness**. Examples of altered states include sleep, hypnosis, meditation, and some drug-induced conditions. Cultures differ in the value they place on particular states of consciousness.

Differing levels of consciousness are described as variations in awareness of your own mental functions. The **preconscious level** includes mental activities that are outside awareness but that can easily be brought to the **conscious level**. **Subconscious** and **unconscious** mental activity is said to involve thoughts, memories, and processes that are more difficult to bring to awareness. Mental processes that cannot be brought into awareness are said to occur at the **nonconscious level**.

Awareness is not always required for mental operations. For example, research on priming shows that people's responses to stimuli speed up and improve as stimuli are repeated, even when there is no conscious memory of which stimuli are old and which are new. And some decisions that seem intuitive may be guided by information that is outside of awareness.

Sleeping and Dreaming

Does your brain go to sleep when you do?

Sleep is an active and complex state. Different stages of sleep are defined on the basis of changes in brain activity (as measured by an electroencephalograph, or EEG) and physiological arousal. Sleep normally begins with stage N1 sleep and progresses gradually through stage N2 to stage N3 sleep. The deepest stage of this **NREM (non-rapid eye movement)** sleep is also called slow-wave sleep. After passing back to stage N2, people enter **REM (rapid eye movement) sleep**, or paradoxical sleep. The sleeper passes through these stages several times each night, gradually spending more time in stage N2 and REM sleep later in the night.

Sleep disorders can disrupt the natural rhythm of sleep. Among the most common is **insomnia**, a condition in which one has trouble falling asleep or staying asleep. **Narcolepsy** produces sudden daytime sleeping episodes. In cases of **sleep apnea**, people briefly but repeatedly stop breathing during sleep. **Sudden infant death syndrome (SIDS)** may be due to brain abnormalities or accidental suffocation. **Sleepwalking** happens most frequently during childhood. **Nightmares** and **sleep terror disorder (night terrors)** involve different kinds of frightening dreams. **REM behavior disorder** is potentially dangerous because it allows people to act out REM dreams.

The cycle of waking and sleeping is a natural **circadian rhythm** or **human biological rhythm**, controlled by the suprachiasmatic nuclei of the brain. **Jet lag** can be one result of disrupting the normal sleep-wake cycle.

The purpose of sleep is still unclear. NREM sleep may aid bodily rest and repair. REM sleep may help maintain activity in brain areas that provide daytime alertness or it may allow the brain to "check circuits," eliminate useless information, and solidify learning from the previous day. **Sleep deprivation** leads to fatigue, irritability, and inattention and is a major factor in poor decision making, learning and memory difficulties, and traffic accidents.

Dreaming is the production of storylike sequences of images, sensations, and perceptions that occur during sleep. Most dreams occur during REM sleep. Evidence from research on **lucid dreaming** suggests that people may be able to control their own dreams. Some claim that dreams are the meaningless by-products of brain activity, but our recall of dreams may still have psychological significance.

Hypnosis

Can you be hypnotized against your will?

Hypnosis is a well-known but still poorly understood phenomenon. Tests of **hypnotic susceptibility** suggest that some people cannot be hypnotized and that others are hypnotized easily. Hypnotized people tend to focus attention on the hypnotist and passively follow instructions. They become better at fantasizing and role taking. They may exhibit apparent age regression, experience posthypnotic amnesia, and obey posthypnotic suggestions.

State theories of hypnosis see hypnosis as a special state of consciousness. **Nonstate theories of hypnosis** such as role theory suggest that hypnosis creates a special social role that frees people to act in unusual ways. **Dissociation theory** combines aspects of role and state theories, suggesting that hypnotized individuals enter into a social contract with the hypnotist to allow normally integrated mental processes to become dissociated and to share control over these processes. Hypnosis is useful in the control of pain and the reduction of nausea associated with cancer chemotherapy.

Meditation is a set of techniques designed to create an altered state of consciousness characterized by inner peace and increased awareness. The consistent practice of meditation has been associated with reductions in stress-related problems such as anxiety and high blood pressure.

Psychoactive Drugs

How do drugs affect the brain?

Psychoactive drugs affect the brain, changing consciousness and other psychological processes. **Psychopharmacology** is the field that studies drug effects and their mechanisms. Psychoactive drugs exert their effects primarily by influencing specific neurotransmitter systems and hence certain brain activities. To reach brain tissue, drugs must cross the **blood-brain barrier**. Drugs that mimic the receptor effects of a neurotransmitter are called **agonists**; drugs that block the receptor effects of a neurotransmitter are called **antagonists**. Some drugs alter the release or removal of specific neurotransmitters, thus affecting the amount of neurotransmitter available for receptor effects.

Adverse effects such as **drug abuse (substance use disorder)** often accompany the use of psychoactive drugs. Psychological dependence, **addiction** (physical dependence), **drug tolerance**, and symptoms of **drug withdrawal** (withdrawal syndrome) may result. Drugs that produce dependence share the property of directly stimulating certain dopamine-sensitive areas of the brain known as pleasure centers. The consequences of using a psychoactive drug depend both on how the drug affects neurotransmitters and on the user's expectations.

Alcohol, barbiturates, GHB, and flunitrazepam are examples of **CNS depressant drugs**. They reduce activity in the central nervous system, often by enhancing the action of inhibitory neurotransmitters. They have considerable potential for producing both psychological and physical dependence.

CNS stimulating drugs, such as amphetamines and cocaine, increase behavioral and mental activity mainly by increasing the action of dopamine and norepinephrine. These drugs can produce both psychological and physical dependence. Caffeine, one of the world's most popular stimulants, may also create dependence. Nicotine is a potent stimulant. And MDMA, which has both stimulant and hallucinogenic properties, is one of several psychoactive drugs that can permanently damage brain tissue.

Opiates such as opium, morphine, and heroin are highly addictive drugs that induce sleep and relieve pain.

LSD and marijuana are examples of **hallucinogenic drugs**, or psychedelic drugs. They alter consciousness by producing a temporary loss of contact with reality and changes in emotion, perception, and thought.

TEST YOUR KNOWLEDGE

Select the best answer for each of the following questions. Then check your responses against the Answer Key at the end of the book.

1. Tyrrell is undergoing biofeedback training to help him regulate his blood pressure, a bodily function typically regulated at which level of consciousness?
   a. Nonconscious
   b. Preconscious
   c. Subconscious
   d. Unconscious

2. Dr. Eplort is staying in a cave for several months with no external light cues and no way to keep time. He goes to sleep when he feels sleepy and gets up when he is awake. Dr. Eplort will most likely sleep _____.
   a. fewer hours than he did before
   b. more hours than he did before
   c. about the same as he did before
   d. on a varying and unpredictable schedule

3. Zandra knew nothing about art, and during her first semester on campus she had not noticed the framed Rembrandt prints in the hallway of her classroom building. But when she took an art appreciation class the next semester, she found that the paintings she liked best were those same Rembrandt images. Her preference was most likely affected by _____.
   a. the prosopagnosia effect
   b. supraliminal perception
   c. priming
   d. visual masking

4. Edie has purchased a tape that contains subliminal messages designed to help her lose weight. According to the Thinking Critically section in this chapter, Edie's success in losing weight most likely depends on _____.
   a. the content of the subliminal messages
   b. her expectation that the subliminal messages will help
   c. how relaxed the subliminal messages make her feel
   d. the number of times the subliminal messages occur

5. Mitch noticed that after his friends smoked marijuana, they soon began giggling, acting silly, and singing "We're Off to See the Wizard." After he smoked marijuana himself for the first time, he found himself doing the very same things. Mitch's specific responses to marijuana were most likely due to _____.
   a. an altered state of consciousness
   b. reversion to a preconscious state
   c. priming
   d. learned expectations

6. The telephone rang several hours after Leroy fell asleep. It takes Leroy a while to locate the phone, and he is so groggy when he answers that in the morning, he can't remember who called or what was said. When the phone rang, Leroy was most likely in _____ sleep.
   a. stage N1
   b. stage N2
   c. stage N3
   d. REM

7. Alan's wife is concerned because he often gets out of bed during the night and acts out his dreams. One night he boxed with an invisible opponent, and last night he was fighting a phantom bull. Alan most likely would be diagnosed as having _____.
   a. sleep apnea
   b. narcolepsy
   c. REM behavior disorder
   d. sleep terror disorder

8. The "back to sleep" program, which advises parents to have their babies sleep face up, has greatly reduced the incidence of _____ in the United States.
   a. SIDS
   b. sleep terror disorder
   c. REM behavior disorder
   d. insomnia

9. Dr. Franklin was flying from Los Angeles to Paris, where he was to give a speech shortly after arrival. To minimize the effects of jet lag, his physician would most likely recommend that Dr. Franklin should _____.
   a. be sure to sleep eight hours a night for at least a week before his trip
   b. take melatonin
   c. stay awake for 24 hours before departure, then sleep throughout the flight
   d. reverse his sleep-wake cycle for a week before departure

10. Sleep research suggests that REM sleep may be important for all of the following *except* _____.
    a. improving the functioning of neurons that use norepinephrine
    b. improving the connections that form between nerve cells in the brain
    c. restoring the body's and brain's energy stores for the next day's activity
    d. establishing memories of emotional information

11. According to the activation-synthesis theory, dreams _____.
    a. help our brains analyze and consolidate information
    b. satisfy unconscious urges and resolve unconscious conflicts
    c. are hallucinations
    d. are meaningless, random by-products of REM sleep

12. Lavonne, a hypnotist, wanted to present a dramatic demonstration of hypnosis. Which of the following people should she select as her hypnotic subject?
    a. Alex, who is easily distracted.
    b. Bobbi, who doesn't believe in hypnosis.
    c. Dellena, whose imagination is limited.
    d. Carl, who is good at focusing his attention.

13. Hypnosis has been especially effective in _____.
    a. connecting with past lives
    b. improving memory
    c. pain control
    d. lowering cholesterol

14. Norman has been meditating for over a year. By now, according to this chapter, we would expect Norman to _____.
    a. be less anxious
    b. need less sleep to feel refreshed
    c. have a better memory
    d. daydream more

15. Candice was given morphine to ease the pain of back surgery. Her doctor explained that morphine occupies the same receptors and has the same effect as endorphins, the body's natural painkillers. In other words, morphine is an endorphin _____.
    a. reuptake blocker
    b. placebo
    c. antagonist
    d. agonist

16. Vincent has been using heroin for some time, and now he finds that he needs larger amounts of the drug to achieve the same effect he used to get from smaller doses. Vincent is experiencing _____.
    a. drug tolerance
    b. learned expectations
    c. withdrawal
    d. synaptic potential

17. Which of the following is true about alcohol?
    a. A given amount of alcohol will affect a man more than a woman.
    b. Alcohol's effects are the same whether it is consumed slowly or quickly.
    c. There are no genetic predispositions toward alcohol abuse.
    d. Dopamine agonists reduce alcohol cravings.

18. A woman is brought to a hospital emergency room after an apparent date rape. Which of the following drugs would her doctor suspect was used by her attacker?
    a. Amphetamine
    b. Marijuana
    c. Flunitrazepam
    d. LSD

19. Abel took a drug to reduce the pain in his broken arm. The drug Abel took to reduce his pain would be classified as a(n) _____.
    a. depressant
    b. opiate
    c. hallucinogen
    d. stimulant

20. Yeh is doing research for a term paper about legalizing the use of marijuana in the United States. If her research is accurate, she is likely to learn all of the following *except* which one?
    a. Marijuana has been used successfully in treating asthma, glaucoma, chronic pain, and nausea from chemotherapy.
    b. Marijuana increases memory function and creativity.
    c. It is legal to grow and use marijuana for medicinal purposes in many U.S. states.
    d. Doctors have found that marijuana may help treat some types of cancer.

CHAPTER 10

Motivation and Emotion

Julian Finney/Getty Images

Preview

When your clock goes off in the morning, do you jump out of bed, eager to face the day, or do you bury your head in the blankets? Once you're at your job or on campus, do you always do your best, or do you work just hard enough to get by? Are you generally happy? Do you sometimes worry or feel sad? In this chapter, we explore the physical, mental, and social factors that motivate behavior in areas ranging from eating to sexuality to achievement. We also examine what emotions are and how they are expressed.

Think of a famous person you admire—maybe a business or technology innovator like Steve Jobs, an inspiring leader like Martin Luther King, an athlete like Serena Williams, or an actor like Denzel Washington. As with these people, success probably came to the person you chose only after years of great effort and unwavering determination. Why do some people work so hard in the face of daunting challenges and tough competition and rise to the top of their fields? For that matter, why do any of us try to excel, to perform acts of kindness, to look for food, to take dancing lessons, to go bungee jumping, to become violent, or to act in any other particular way? Why do some people go all out to reach a goal whereas others make only half-hearted efforts and quit at the first obstacle?

Questions about "why" behavior occurs are questions about **motivation**, the processes that give behavior its energy, direction, intensity, and persistence (Figner & Weber, 2011; Reeve, 2009). Like the study of *how* people and other animals behave and think, the puzzle of *why* they do so has intrigued psychologists for decades. Part of the motivation for behavior is to feel certain emotions, such as the joy of finishing a race or becoming a parent. Motivation also affects emotion, as when hunger makes you more likely to be annoyed by people around you. In this chapter, we review several aspects of motivation and the features and value of emotions.

Motivation and Emotion

The link between motivation and emotion can be seen in many situations. For example, being motivated to win the U.S. National Spelling Bee creates strong emotions, as we see in this winning contestant. And the link works both ways. Often, emotions create motivation, as when anger leads a person to become aggressive toward a child or when love leads a person to provide for that child.

Kamenko Pajic/Upi/Landov

CONCEPTS AND THEORIES OF MOTIVATION

Where does motivation come from?

Suppose that a woman works two jobs, never goes to parties, wears used clothes, drives an old car, eats food left behind by others, ignores charity appeals, and keeps her house at sixty degrees all winter. Why does she do these things? You could suggest a separate explanation for each of these behaviors, or you could suggest a **motive**, a reason or purpose that provides a single explanation for all of them. That unifying motive might be the woman's desire to save as much money as possible. This example illustrates that motivation itself cannot be directly observed. We have to infer, or presume, that motivation is present based on what we can observe.

Sources of Motivation

Human motivation stems from five main sources. First, we are motivated by *physiological factors*, such as when hormones or certain areas of the brain influence sexual interest. Second, our behavior is motivated by *needs*, such as food, water, or sleep. *Emotional factors* provide a third source of motivation. Panic, fear, anger, love, envy, and hatred influence behaviors ranging from selfless giving to brutal murder (Terburg, Aarts, & van Honk, 2012; van de Ven, Zeelenberg, & Pieters, 2011). *Cognitive factors* are a fourth source of motivation. These include perceptions of the world, beliefs about what you can and cannot do, the amount of choice or control you think you have in particular situations, and expectations about how others will respond to the behaviors you are considering (e.g., Johnson & Fujita, 2012; Laurin, Kay, & Fitzsimons, 2012; Witt, Linkenauger, & Proffitt, 2012). For example, some contestants who try for stardom on talent shows such as *American Idol* seem utterly confident in their ability to sing despite being painfully wrong. Finally, motivation stems from *social and environmental factors* (Neville, 2012). These include the influence of parents, teachers, siblings, friends, television, and other sociocultural forces. Have you ever bought a jacket, tried a new hairstyle, or gotten a tattoo, not because you really liked it but because it was in fashion at the time? And think about all the times when deadlines and demands from teachers or parents or bosses led you to spend time doing things that you might not otherwise have done. These are examples of how social factors can affect almost all human behavior.

No one source of motivation fully explains all aspects of why people behave as they do, but psychologists combine them in various ways to formulate four main theories of

motivation The influences that account for the initiation, direction, intensity, and persistence of behavior.

motive A reason or purpose for behavior.

motivation. These include the *instinct doctrine, drive reduction theory, arousal theory,* and *incentive theory.* Each theory has helped account for some aspects of behavior.

Instinct Doctrine and Its Descendants

In the early 1900s, many psychologists explained motivation in terms of the **instinct doctrine**, which highlights the instinctive nature of behavior. **Instinctive behaviors** are automatic, involuntary, and unlearned behavior patterns consistently "released" or triggered by particular stimuli (Tinbergen, 1989). For example, the male stickleback fish instantly attacks when it sees the red underbelly of another male. Such behaviors in non-human species were originally called *fixed-action patterns* because they are unlearned, genetically coded responses to specific "releaser" stimuli.

William McDougall (1908) argued that human behavior, too, is instinctive. He began by listing eighteen human instinctive behaviors that included self-assertion, reproduction, pugnacity (eagerness to fight), and gregariousness (sociability). Within a few years, McDougall and other theorists named over 10,000 instinctive behaviors, prompting one critic to say that his colleagues had "an instinct to produce instincts" (Bernard, 1924). The problem was that instincts had become meaningless labels that described behavior without explaining it. Saying that people gamble because of a gambling instinct or work hard because of a work instinct explains nothing about why these behaviors appear in some people and not others or about how they develop. Applying the instinct doctrine to human motivation also seemed problematic because people display few, if any, instinctive fixed-action patterns.

Today, psychologists continue to investigate the role played by inborn tendencies in human motivation. Their work has been stimulated partly by research on a number of human behaviors that are present at birth. Among these are the sucking, grasping, and other reflexes discussed in the human development chapter, as well as apparent dislike of bitter tastes (Steiner et al., 2001) and enjoyment of sweet ones (Booth et al., 2010). Further, as discussed in the chapter on learning, humans appear to be biologically prepared to learn to fear snakes and other potential dangers (e.g., Öhman et al., 2012). But psychologists' thinking about instinctive behavior is more sophisticated now than it was a century ago. For one thing, they recognize that inborn tendencies are more flexible than early versions of the instinct doctrine suggested. It turns out that so-called fixed-action patterns—even the simple ones shown by baby chicks as they peck at seeds—actually vary quite a bit among individuals and can be modified by experience (Deich, Tankoos, & Balsam, 1995). Accordingly, these tendencies are now often referred to as *modal action patterns.* They recognize, too, that even though certain behaviors reflect inborn motivational tendencies, those behaviors may or may not actually appear, depending on each individual's experience. So although we might be biologically "programmed" to learn to fear snakes, that fear won't develop if we never see a snake. In other words, motivation can be influenced by inherited tendencies, but that doesn't mean that all motivated behavior is genetically determined.

By emphasizing the possible evolutionary roots of human behavior, modern versions of the instinct doctrine focus on the ultimate, long-term reasons behind much of what we do. Psychologists who take an evolutionary approach to behavior suggest that a wide range of behavioral tendencies have evolved because over the centuries they were adaptive for individual survival in particular circumstances. Those who possessed and expressed these adaptive predispositions were more likely than others to live to produce children. We are descendants of these human survivors, so to the extent that their behavioral predispositions were transmitted genetically, we should have inherited similar predispositions. Evolutionary psychologists also argue that many aspects of human social behavior—including helping, aggression, and the choice of sexual or marriage partners—are motivated by inborn factors, especially by the desire to maximize our genetic contribution to the next generation (Kenrick, 2012). We may not be consciously aware of this desire (Hassin, 2013), so you're more likely to hear someone say "I can't wait to have children" than to hear them say "I want to pass on my genes."

instinct doctrine A view that behavior is motivated by automatic, involuntary, and unlearned responses.

instinctive behaviors Innate, automatic dispositions to respond in particular ways to specific stimuli.

The Instinct Doctrine and Mate Selection

The evolutionary approach suggests, for example, that people's choice of a marriage partner or sexual mate is influenced by the consequences of the choices made by their ancestors over countless generations. For instance, research in many different cultures shows that both men and women express a strong preference for a long-term partner who is dependable, emotionally stable, and intelligent—characteristics that create a good environment for having and raising children (Buss et al., 1990). But evolutionary psychologists also point to sex differences in mating preferences and strategies. They argue that since women can produce fewer children in their lifetimes than men can, they may be more psychologically invested in their children's survival and development. This greater investment might motivate women to be choosier than men in selecting mates.

It takes some time to assess resource-related characteristics (he drives an expensive car, but can he afford it?), which is why, according to an evolutionary view, women are more likely than men to prefer a period of courtship before sex. Research suggests that men tend to be less selective because they want to start a sexual relationship sooner than women (Buss, 2004b; Buss & Schmitt, 1993). Their eagerness to engage in sex early in a relationship is seen as reflecting their evolutionary ancestors' tendency toward opportunistic sex as way to maximize their genetic contribution to the next generation. Evolutionary psychologists suggest that a desire to produce as many children as possible motivates men's attraction to women whose fertility and good health are signaled by factors generally associated with physical beauty, such as clear skin and a low waist-to-hip ratio (Buss, 2009).

Research support for such ideas includes preference ratings from several thousand people in more than three dozen cultures, showing that men generally prefer physical attractiveness and good health in prospective mates, and that women generally prefer mates with higher levels of social status and financial resources (March & Bramwell, 2012; Shackelford, Schmitt, & Buss, 2005).

Critics argue that such preferences stem from cultural traditions, not genetic predispositions. Among the Zulu of South Africa, where women are expected to build houses, carry water, and perform other physically demanding tasks, men tend to value maturity and ambition in a mate more than women do (Buss, 1989). The fact that women have been systematically denied economic and political power in many cultures may account for their tendency to rely on the security and economic power provided by men (Eagly, Wood, & Johannesen-Schmidt, 2004; Silverstein, 1996). Indeed, an analysis of data from thirty-seven cultures showed that women valued potential mates' access to resources far more in cultures that sharply limited women's reproductive freedom and educational opportunities (Kasser & Sharma, 1999). Evolutionary theorists agree that cultural forces and traditions shape behavior, but they focus on how evolutionary factors might contribute to these forces and traditions, including the relative ease with which certain gender roles and mate preferences emerge (e.g., Geher, Camargo, & O'Rourke, 2008). For instance, whereas men are generally more willing to engage in casual sex than women, this tendency is more often seen in cultures where there is more pressure to have many children, and less likely where there is more emphasis on social and economic gender equality (Schmitt, 2005).

Evolution at Work?

The marriage of Donald Trump to Melania Knauss-Trump, a former model who is twenty-four years his junior, illustrates the worldwide tendency for older men to often prefer younger women and for younger women to prefer older men. This tendency has been interpreted as evidence supporting an evolutionary explanation of mate selection, but skeptics see social and economic forces at work in establishing these preference patterns.

Craig Barritt/Getty Images

Drive Reduction Theory

Like the instinct doctrine, the drive reduction theory of motivation emphasizes internal factors, but it focuses mainly on how such factors maintain homeostasis. **Homeostasis** (pronounced "ho-me-oh-STAY-sis") is the tendency to make constant adjustments to maintain body temperature, blood pressure, and other physiological systems at a steady level, or *equilibrium*—much as a thermostat functions to maintain a constant temperature in a house.

homeostasis The tendency for physiological systems to remain stable by constantly adjusting themselves in response to change.

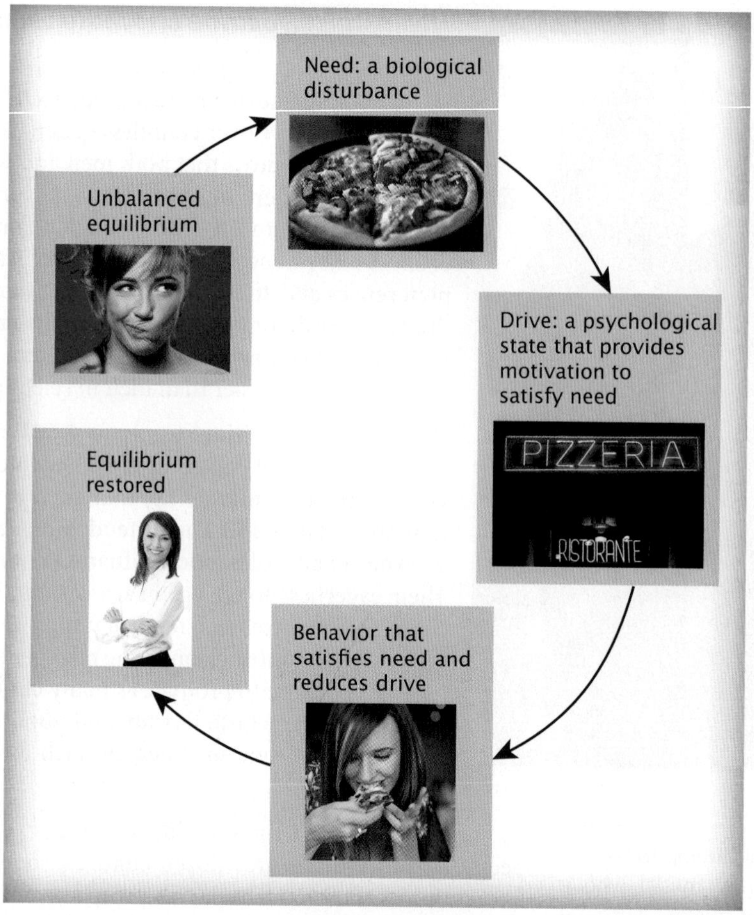

FIGURE 10.1
Drive Reduction Theory and Homeostasis

The mechanisms of homeostasis regulate your body temperature and food and water intake, among other things. For example, when you don't have enough nutrients in your bloodstream, an unbalanced equilibrium is created and your body develops a need for food. This biological disturbance leads to your drive to find something to eat, perhaps by ordering a pizza. After eating satisfies your need for food, your equilibrium is restored.

© Hywit Dimyadi/Shutterstock.com; © Lana K/Shutterstock.com; Vincenzo Lombardo/Photodisc/Getty Images; iStockphoto/Thinkstock; amana productions inc/Getty Images

Need: a biological disturbance

Unbalanced equilibrium

Drive: a psychological state that provides motivation to satisfy need

PIZZERIA
RISTORANTE

Equilibrium restored

Behavior that satisfies need and reduces drive

drive reduction theory A theory that motivation arises from imbalances in homeostasis.

needs Biological requirements for well-being.

drive A psychological state that arises from an imbalance in homeostasis and prompts action to fulfill a need.

primary drives Drives that arise from basic biological needs.

secondary drives Stimuli that take on the motivational properties of primary drives through learning.

According to **drive reduction theory**, any imbalances in homeostasis create **needs**, which are biological requirements for well-being. To respond, the brain tries to restore homeostasis by creating a psychological state called **drive**—a feeling that prompts an organism to take action to meet the need, and thus create homeostatic balance. For example, if you have had nothing to drink for some time, the chemical balance of your body fluids changes, creating a physiological need for water. A consequence of this need is a drive—thirst—motivating you to find and drink water. After you drink, the need for water is met, so the drive to drink is reduced. In other words, drives push people to satisfy needs, thus reducing the drives. Remember, in this formulation, a *need* is a *biological requirement*, and a *drive* is the *psychological state* that may help address it. The cycle is shown in Figure 10.1.

Early drive reduction theorists described two types of drives. **Primary drives** stem from physiological needs, such as a need for food or water. People do not have to learn these basic needs or the primary drives to satisfy them (Hull, 1951). However, we learn other drives through experience. These learned **secondary drives** motivate us to act as if we have unmet basic needs. For example, as we learn to associate money with buying things that satisfy primary drives for food, shelter, and so on, having money becomes a secondary drive. Having too little money then motivates many behaviors—from hard work to stealing—to get more funds (Nordgren & Chou, 2011).

Arousal Theory

Drive reduction theory can account for many motivated behaviors, but not all of them. Consider curiosity, for example. Monkeys, dogs, cats, and rats will work hard simply to enter a new environment, especially if it is complex and has new objects to explore and manipulate (Loewenstein, 1994). And most humans, too, can't resist checking out whatever is new and unusual. We go to a new play, watch builders work, surf the Internet, and travel the world just to see what there is to see. People also ride roller coasters, skydive,

Arousal and Personality

People whose ideal, or optimal, level of arousal is high are more likely to smoke, drink alcohol, engage in frequent sexual activity, listen to loud music, eat "hot" foods, and do other things that are stimulating, novel, and risky (Farley, 1986; Zuckerman, 1993). Those whose optimal level of arousal is lower tend to take fewer risks and behave in ways that are less stimulating. As discussed in the personality chapter, differences in optimal arousal may help shape other characteristics, such as whether we tend to be introverted or extraverted.

Terje Rakke/The Image Bank/Getty Images

drive race cars, and do many other things that do not reduce any known drive (e.g., Bergman & Kitchen, 2009; Hsee, Yang, & Wang, 2010).

In fact, far from reducing a drive, such behaviors seem to increase **physiological arousal**—the body's general level of activation. Physiological arousal is reflected in heart rate, muscle tension, brain activity, blood pressure, and other bodily systems (Plutchik & Conte, 1997). It is usually low during deep sleep, but physiological arousal can also be lowered by meditation, relaxation techniques, and depressant drugs. Increased arousal tends to occur in response to hunger, thirst, stimulant drugs, and stimuli that are intense, sudden, new, or unexpected. Because people sometimes try to reduce their arousal and sometimes try to increase it, some psychologists have suggested that motivation is tied to the regulation of physiological arousal.

Specifically, **arousal theory** suggests that we are motivated to behave to keep or restore an ideal, or *optimal level*, of arousal (Hebb, 1955). Too much arousal can hurt performance, as when test anxiety interferes with some students' ability to recall what they studied. Overarousal can also cause athletes to "choke" so badly that they miss an easy catch or a simple shot (Balk et al., 2013; Buelow & Frakey, 2013). Underarousal, too, can cause problems, as you probably know if you have ever tried to work, drive, or study when you are sleepy. So we try to increase arousal when it is too low, such as when we're bored, and decrease it when it is too high, such as when we're stressed or overstimulated. How much arousal is "just right"? The answer may not be the same for all people. People appear to differ in their optimal level of arousal (Zabel et al., 2009; Zuckerman, 1984). These differences in optimal arousal may stem from inherited differences in the nervous system (e.g., Derringer et al., 2010; Eysenck, 1990a) and may motivate boldness, shyness, and many other personality traits and behavioral tendencies.

Incentive Theory

Instinct, drive reduction, and arousal theories of motivation all focus on internal processes that prompt us to behave in certain ways. In contrast, **incentive theory** emphasizes how external stimuli motivate behavior. According to this view, people are pulled toward behaviors that bring positive incentives (maximizing pleasure) and are pushed away from behaviors with negative incentives (minimizing pain). For example, as described in the learning chapter, operant conditioning occurs because we're more likely to repeat actions that are followed by positive outcomes rather than by negative ones. According to incentive theory, differences in behavior from one person to another or from one situation to another can be traced to the incentives available and the value a person places on those incentives at the time. If you expect that some behavior (such as buying a lottery ticket or apologizing for a mistake) will lead to a valued outcome (winning money or reducing guilt), you will be motivated to engage in that behavior (Bastian, Jetten, & Fasoli, 2011; Cooke et al., 2011).

The value of incentives can be influenced by inborn physiological factors such as hunger and thirst as well as by cognitive and social factors (e.g., Chein et al., 2011; DeVoe & Iyengar, 2010). As an example of physiological influences, consider that food is a more motivating incentive when you are hungry than when you're full. As for cognitive and social influences, notice that the value of some things we eat—such as communion wafers or diet shakes—isn't determined by hunger or flavor but by what our culture has taught us about spirituality, health, or attractiveness. Perhaps you have also noticed that what early drive reduction theorists called *primary drives* reappear in incentive theory as unlearned influences on an incentive's value. *Secondary drives* reappear as learned influences on the value of incentives.

Intrinsic and Extrinsic Motivation

Suppose that you decide to learn a new language, write a book, start an exercise program, or volunteer at a homeless shelter. Like almost everything else we do, these decisions can be based on intrinsic motivation or extrinsic motivation (Deci et al., 2001; Ryan & Deci, 2000).

physiological arousal A general level of activation reflected in several physiological systems.

arousal theory A theory that people are motivated to maintain what is an optimal level of arousal for them.

incentive theory A theory that people are pulled toward behaviors that offer positive incentives and pushed away from behaviors associated with negative incentives.

The Hidden Cost of Reward

We might expect that when people receive money, trophies, prizes, and other extrinsic rewards for doing something, they would be more motivated to continue doing it. As described in the learning chapter, this may be true as long as the rewards continue, but external rewards can undermine intrinsic motivation and may result in poorer performance over time (Pulfrey, Buchs, & Butera, 2011). The adverse effect of extrinsic motivation on intrinsic motivation has been called *the hidden cost of reward* (Lepper & Greene, 1978).

© iStockphoto.com/Kolbz

intrinsic motivation Engaging in behavior simply for the feelings of pleasure, satisfaction, or sense of competence or independence it brings.

extrinsic motivation Engaging in behavior in order to obtain an external reward or avoid a penalty or other undesirable consequence.

Intrinsic motivation would lead you to do these things simply to experience the pleasure and satisfaction of doing them, and especially to enjoy the feelings of competence and autonomy (independence) they bring (Przbylski et al., 2011). When intrinsically motivated to do something, you're likely to explain your behavior by saying, "I enjoy it" or "It's interesting." But you might do those same things because of **extrinsic motivation**, in which case your actions would be aimed at achieving some external goal, such as pleasing or impressing other people, qualifying for a better job, alleviating a health problem, or making money. In such cases, you would probably explain your behavior in a different way, perhaps by saying, "It's a good way to get a raise" or "My parents insisted." And, of course, there are many cases in which behavior is based on both intrinsic and extrinsic motivation. For example, many people decide to get in shape not only to experience a sense of accomplishment and autonomy but also to become more physically attractive to others.

It isn't always easy to tell whether someone's behavior is based on intrinsic or extrinsic motivation, and sometimes we may not be sure what motivates our own behavior. Psychologists have discovered some clues, however (Vansteenkiste et al., 2009). For example, when people are intrinsically motivated—doing things mainly for the sake of doing them—they tend to show greater energy, persistence, and creativity, more enjoyment, and better learning than when they are motivated mainly by extrinsic rewards such as money or grades (Ryan & Deci, 2000). So you are more likely to understand this chapter, think actively about its contents, and enjoy reading it if you're motivated by intrinsic, rather than extrinsic, factors (Vansteenkiste et al., 2005). This is one reason that students who take courses because they *want* to often do better—and enjoy class more—than those who take courses because they *have* to.

What happens if a person who is intrinsically motivated to engage in an activity—painting or singing or woodworking, say—begins to receive an extrinsic reward for it? If the extrinsic motivation is added to the intrinsic motivation, you might expect to see super-high motivation and performance, but that is not what typically happens. Instead, the longer people receive extrinsic rewards for doing something that had been intrinsically motivated, the less intrinsic motivation they show later on (e.g., Deci, Koester, & Ryan, 1999; Murayama et al., 2010).

So although creating extrinsic motivation with rewards and punishments is a vital tool to shape all kinds of behavior, in some situations it creates some hidden costs (Lepper & Greene, 1978). Extrinsic rewards can dampen intrinsic motivation and interfere with learning. If you have been learning French just for fun, but are now offered a lot of money for doing well in the course, the fun might disappear and the arousal associated with worrying about the next test might impair your performance. Even if it doesn't, the prospect of getting that reward might change what and how you learn. Because extrinsically motivated students tend to focus on test scores, final grades, and other external rewards rather than on really trying to understand and apply course material, they tend to be passive learners (Vansteenkiste et al., 2005). As described in the learning and memory chapters, passive learners may be at a disadvantage because they depend on superficial reading and rote memorization rather than more active learning methods.

Yet another hidden cost of relying on extrinsic motivation in education is that it can undermine students' capacity to be independent learners (Lepper, 1983; Ryan, 1993). After years of receiving rewards for doing well on tests, students may become dependent on them. Over time, the learning process becomes little more than just a process of studying for tests. Questions about whether, when, and how long to study come to be regulated by the test schedule rather than by interest or curiosity. As a result, when students ask teachers if the final exam will cover the entire course, they may really be asking when they can stop trying to remember what they learned for previous exams.

Not all extrinsic rewards bring hidden costs (Cameron, 2001; Deci et al., 1999). Research shows that these costs are most likely for rewards that are both expected (announced in advance) and tangible (money, food, or prizes). The costs are less likely when rewards are unexpected and intangible, such as a sincere compliment from a respected teacher, colleague, or boss. Unfortunately, expected and tangible rewards are exactly the kinds that are most commonly used in schools and workplaces (Kohn, 1993).

"In Review: Sources, Theories, and Types of Motivation" summarizes our discussion of the basic concepts and principles of motivation. These concepts and principles have helped to guide research on motivated behaviors such as eating, sex, and work, which we consider in the sections that follow.

IN REVIEW
SOURCES, THEORIES, AND TYPES OF MOTIVATION

Sources of Motivation

Source	Examples
Physiological factors	Activity of hormones or brain cells
Needs	Food, water, or sleep
Emotional factors	Feelings, such as happiness, sadness, fear, anger, surprise, or disgust
Cognitive factors	Perceptions and beliefs about yourself and the consequences of your actions
Social and environmental factors	Influence of other people or situations

Theories of Motivation

Theory	Main Points
Instinct doctrine	Innate biology produces instinctive behaviors.
Drive reduction	Behavior is guided by biological needs and learned ways of reducing drives that arise from those needs.
Arousal	People seek to maintain an optimal level of physiological arousal, which differs from person to person. Maximum performance occurs at optimal arousal levels.
Incentive	Behavior is guided by the lure of rewards and the threat of punishment. Cognitive factors influence expectations of the value of various rewards and the likelihood of attaining them.

Types of Motivation

Type	Examples
Intrinsic	Doing things for the sake of enjoyment, satisfying curiosity, or feeling competent or independent
Extrinsic	Doing things to get money, prizes, or other external rewards

In Review Questions

1. The fact that some people like roller coasters and other scary amusement park rides has been cited as evidence for the_____ theory of motivation.

2. Evolutionary theories of motivation are modern outgrowths of theories based on _____.

3. The value of incentives can be affected by _____, _____, and _____ factors.

HUNGER AND EATING

What makes me start eating and stop eating?

At first glance, eating seems to be a simple example of homeostasis and drive reduction theory at work. You're motivated to eat when you get hungry. Much as a car needs gasoline, you need fuel from food, so you eat. If so, what bodily mechanism is the "gauge" to signal the need for food? What determines which foods you eat, and how you know when to stop? Answers to these questions involve complex interactions between the brain and the rest of the body, but they also involve learning, social, and environmental factors.

Biological Signals for Hunger and Satiation

A variety of mechanisms operate to create **hunger**, the general state of wanting to eat, and **satiation** (pronounced "say-she-EH-shun"), the satisfaction of hunger. Satiation leads to **satiety** (pronounced "seh-TYE-a-tee"), a state in which we no longer want to eat.

Signals from the Gut

The stomach seems a logical source for hunger and satiety signals. You have probably felt hunger pangs from an "empty" stomach and felt "stuffed" after overeating. In fact, the stomach does contract during hunger pangs, and increased pressure in the stomach can reduce appetite (Cannon & Washburn, 1912; Houpt, 1994). But people who have lost their stomachs due to illness still get hungry and eat normal amounts of food (Janowitz, 1967). So while stomach cues clearly can affect eating, they appear to operate mainly when you are very hungry or very full. The small intestine also regulates eating (Maljaars et al., 2008). It is lined with cells that detect the presence of nutrients and send neural signals to the brain about the need to eat (Capasso & Izzo, 2008). Part of the signaling process even involves bacteria that normally live in a healthy gastrointestinal system. These "gut" microorganisms generate chemicals in response to the food they encounter (Stilling, Dinan, & Cryan, 2014). Psychologists are just starting to study this chemical signaling, but the process appears to have far-reaching consequences, affecting digestion and a desire to eat or stop eating, as well as influencing emotions, learning, and stress responses (Cryan & Dinan, 2012; Li et al., 2009; Ridaura et al., 2013).

Signals from the Blood

Still, the most important signals about the body's fuel level and nutrient needs are sent to the brain from the blood. The brain's ability to "read" blood-borne signals about the body's nutritional needs was discovered when researchers deprived rats of food for a long period and then injected some of the rats with blood from rats that had just eaten. When offered food, the injected rats ate little or nothing (Davis et al., 1969). Something in the injected blood of the well-fed animals apparently signaled the hungry rats' brains that there was no need to eat. What was that satiety signal? Research has shown that the brain constantly monitors both the level of food nutrients absorbed into the bloodstream from the stomach and the level of hormones released into the blood in response to those nutrients (Burdakov, Karnani, & Gonzalez, 2013; Parker & Bloom, 2012).

The nutrients that the brain monitors include *glucose* (the main form of sugar used by body cells), *fatty acids* (from fats), and *amino acids* (from proteins). When the level of blood glucose drops, eating increases sharply (Chaput & Tremblay, 2009; Mogenson, 1976). The brain also monitors hormone levels to regulate hunger and satiety. For example, when a lack of nutrients is detected by the stomach, the hormone *ghrelin* is released into the bloodstream and acts as a "start eating" signal when it reaches the brain (Pradhan, Samson, & Sun, 2013). When glucose levels rise, the pancreas releases *insulin,* a hormone that most body cells need in order to use the glucose they receive. Insulin itself may also provide a satiety signal by acting directly on brain cells (Brüning et al., 2000; Lakhi, Snow, & Fry, 2013).

hunger The general state of wanting to eat.

satiation The satisfaction of a need such as hunger.

satiety The condition of no longer wanting to eat.

The hormone *leptin* (from the Greek word for "thin") appears to be a key satiety signal to the brain (Fève & Bastard, 2012). Unlike glucose and insulin, whose satiety signals help us know when to end a particular meal, leptin appears to be involved mainly in the long-term regulation of body fat (Huang & Li, 2000). The process works like this: cells that store fat normally have genes that produce leptin. As the fat supply in these cells increases, leptin enters the blood and reduces food intake (Tamashiro & Bello, 2008). Mice with defects in these genes make no leptin and are obese (Bouret, Draper, & Simerly, 2004). When these animals are given leptin injections, though, they rapidly lose weight and body fat but not muscle tissue (Forbes et al., 2001). Leptin injections can also produce the same changes in normal animals (Priego et al., 2010). Some cases of human obesity are due to leptin dysregulation (e.g., Müller et al., 2009), but for most of us, leptin is not a "magic bullet" against obesity. Although leptin injections help those rare people whose fat cells make no leptin (Kelesidis et al., 2010), this treatment is far less effective in people who are obese due to eating a high-fat diet (Heymsfield et al., 1999). In these far more common cases of obesity, the brain appears to have become less sensitive to leptin's satiety signals (e.g., Lustig et al., 2004).

Hunger and the Brain

LINKAGES How does the brain know when we are hungry? (a link to Biological Aspects of Psychology)

Many brain areas help control eating. The hypothalamus in particular may play a primary role in detecting and reacting to blood signals about the need to eat. The hypothalamus influences both how much food is taken in and how quickly its energy is used, or metabolized.

Some regions of the hypothalamus detect ghrelin, leptin, and insulin; these regions generate signals that either increase hunger and reduce energy expenditure or reduce hunger and increase energy expenditure (Créptin et al., 2014; Kanoski et al., 2013). At least twenty neurotransmitters convey these signals to networks in various parts of the hypothalamus and in the rest of the brain (Cota et al., 2006; Woods et al., 2000).

Activity in a part of the neural network that passes through the *ventromedial nucleus* in the hypothalamus tells an animal that there is no need to eat. So if a rat's ventromedial nucleus is stimulated, the animal will stop eating (Kent et al., 1994). However, if the ventromedial nucleus is destroyed, the animal will eat much more than usual and maintain a much higher body weight.

In contrast, the *lateral hypothalamus* participates in networks that tell an animal to start eating. So when the lateral hypothalamus is stimulated, rats begin to eat huge quantities, even if they have just had a large meal (Stanley et al., 1993). When the lateral hypothalamus is destroyed, however, rats stop eating almost entirely.

One Fat Mouse

After surgical damage to its ventromedial nucleus, this mouse ate enough to triple its body weight. Results such as this initially led many psychologists to conclude that food intake is regulated by a combination of "start-eating" signals from the lateral hypothalamus and "stop-eating" signals from the ventromedial nucleus. We now know that the regulation process is far more complex and involves more than just these two brain regions.

Richard Howard Photography

Decades ago, these findings led to the idea that these two hypothalamic regions interact to maintain some homeostatic level, or *set point,* based on food intake, body weight, or other eating-related signals (Powley & Keesey, 1970). According to set-point theory, each individual has a "fat thermostat" set by genetics, either at birth or shortly thereafter, to maintain a certain body weight (Keesey, 1980; Keesey & Powley, 1975). So normal animals eat until their set point is reached, then stop eating until desirable intake falls below the set point (Cabanac & Morrissette, 1992).

This theory was too simplistic, however. Researchers found that rats with damage to the lateral hypothalamus would still eat very tasty foods, even though the damage never healed (Teitelbaum & Stellar, 1954). It appears that the brain's control of eating involves more than just the interaction of a "stop-eating" and a "start-eating" area (Winn, 1995). For example, the *paraventricular nucleus* in the hypothalamus is also important. As with the ventromedial nucleus, stimulating the paraventricular nucleus reduces food intake. Damaging it makes animals obese (Leibowitz, 1992). In addition, hunger—and the eating of particular types of food—is related to the effects of various neurotransmitters on certain brain cells. One neurotransmitter, *neuropeptide Y,* stimulates increased carbohydrate eating (Kishi & Elmquist, 2005; Kuo et al., 2007). Another one, *serotonin,* suppresses carbohydrate intake. *Galanin* motivates eating of high-fat food (Krykouli et al., 1990), and *enterostatin* reduces it (Lin et al., 1998). *Endocannabinoids* stimulate eating in general, especially tasty foods (e.g., DiPatrizio, Astarita et al., 2011). They affect the same hypothalamic receptors as the active ingredient in marijuana does, which may explain "the munchies," a sudden hunger that marijuana use may create (Cota et al., 2003). *Peptide YY3–36* causes a feeling of fullness and reduced food intake (Batterham et al., 2002, 2003).

In short, several brain regions and chemicals regulate hunger and food selection. These internal regulatory processes are themselves affected by the physical environment (e.g., what foods are available), past experiences with foods, and, for humans, social and cultural traditions about eating.

Flavor, Sociocultural Experience, and Food Selection

Eating is powerfully affected by food's *flavor*—the combination of taste and smell. In general, we eat more when differently flavored foods are served, as in a multicourse meal, than when only one food is served (Berry, Beatty, & Klesges, 1985; Remick, Polivy, & Pliner, 2009). Apparently the flavor of a food becomes less enjoyable as more of it is eaten (Swithers & Hall, 1994). In one study, participants rated how much they liked four kinds of food, then they ate one of the foods and rated all four again. The participants gave the food they had just eaten a lower rating the second time, but their liking increased for all the other foods (Johnson & Vickers, 1993). A similar finding occurred when just the shape of pasta was varied; recently eaten shapes were liked less than new ones (Rolls, Rowe, & Rolls, 1982).

The appearance and smell of certain foods also affect eating. These signals come to elicit conditioned physiological responses—including the secretion of saliva, digestive juices, and insulin—in anticipation of eating those foods (see the learning chapter for more on conditioned responses). So merely seeing a pizza on television may prompt you to order one. And if a delicious-looking cookie comes your way, you don't have to be hungry to start eating it. In fact, many people who have just pronounced themselves "full" after a huge holiday meal still manage to find room for an appetizing dessert. In other words, we eat not just to satisfy nutritional needs but also because of *appetite*, the desire to experience enjoyment (Zheng et al., 2009).

Eating is stimulated by other signals, too. Do you usually eat while reading or watching television? If so, you may find that merely settling down with a book or your favorite show can trigger a desire for a snack, even if you just finished dinner! This happens partly because situations associated with eating in the past can become signals to stimulate eating in the future (Epstein et al., 2009). Learned social rules and cultural traditions also influence eating. In North American culture, having lunch at noon, munching popcorn at movies, and eating hot dogs at ball games are common examples of how certain social situations can lead us to eat particular items at particular times.

How much you eat may also depend on what others do. Politeness or custom might prompt you to try foods you might otherwise avoid. Generally, the mere presence of others, especially friends and family, but even strangers, tends to increase the amount we eat and how long we eat (De Castro, 1990, 1994; Redd & de Castro, 1992). Most people consume 60 to 75 percent more food when they are with others than when eating alone (Clendenen, Herman, & Polivy, 1995), and the same effect occurs in other species, from monkeys to chickens (Galloway et al., 2005; Keeling & Hurink, 1996). If others stop eating, we may do the same even if we're still hungry—especially if we want to impress them with our self-control (Herman, Roth, & Polivy, 2003). And people who are trying to diet are more likely to relapse when they're with others who eat without restraint (Grilo, Shiffman, & Wing, 1989).

Celebrations, holidays, vacations, and even daily family interactions often revolve around food and what some call a *food culture* (Rozin, 2007). Food use and selection varies widely across cultures. For example, chewing coca leaves is popular in the Bolivian

Bon Appetit!

TRY THIS The definition of delicacy differs from culture to culture. Most people in the United States are unlikely to sit down to a plate of grasshoppers or mealworms, but 80 percent of the world's population enjoys eating one or more of over 1,000 different insects (e.g., Ekpo, 2011; Gahukar, 2011) that provide a rich source of protein and essential amino acids (Melo et al., 2011). To appreciate your own food culture, make a list of foods that are traditionally valued by your family or cultural group but that people from other groups do not (or might even be unwilling to) eat.

© Chad Zuber/Shutterstock.com

highlands but illegal in the United States (Burchard, 1992). Many westerners find insects called palm weevils disgusting (Springer & Belk, 1994), but they are a food delicacy in Papua New Guinea (Paoletti, 1995), whereas the beef those same westerners enjoy is morally repugnant to devout Hindus in India. Even within the same culture, different groups may have sharply contrasting food traditions. Squirrel brains won't be found on most dinner tables in the United States, but some people in the rural American South consider them a tasty treat. In short, eating serves functions beyond nutrition—functions that help to remind us of who we are and with whom we identify.

Unhealthy Eating

Problems in the processes that regulate hunger and eating may cause *eating disorders* such as anorexia nervosa, bulimia, or binge eating disorder. While not considered an eating disorder, obesity can occur from too much food intake and is a significant health problem.

Obesity

The World Health Organization (WHO, 2002) defines **obesity** as a condition in which a person's body mass index (BMI) is greater than 30 (Yanovski & Yanovski, 2002). You can determine your BMI by dividing your weight by the square of your height. So someone who is 5 feet 2 inches and weighs 164 pounds would be classified as obese, as would someone 5 feet 10 inches who weighs 207 pounds. People with a BMI of 25 to 29.9 may be "overweight" but not obese. (Keep in mind, though, that a given volume of muscle weighs more than the same volume of fat, so very muscular individuals may have an elevated BMI without being overweight.)

Obesity is a major health problem (Koh, Blakey, & Roper, 2014). Using the BMI criterion, about 36 percent of adults in the United States are obese, as are about 17 percent of children and adolescents (Centers for Disease Control and Prevention, 2014). These percentages are even higher among the poor and members of some ethnic minority groups (Centers for Disease Control and Prevention, 2014; Ogden et al., 2014). Obesity has become so common that commercial jets have to burn excess fuel to carry heavier loads, the U.S. Coast Guard has reduced the number of passengers that boats are allowed to carry, the parents of obese young children have trouble finding car safety seats to fit them, and the funeral industry has had to offer larger coffins and purchase wider hearses (e.g., Associated Press, 2011; Nolin, 2011; Trifiletti et al., 2006). Though the problems of overweight and obesity are especially severe in the United States, they are growing worldwide. An analysis of data from 106 countries in Asia, Europe, South America, and Africa—comprising about 88 percent of the world's population—found that 23.2 percent of adults are overweight and another 10 percent are obese. Projections suggest that by 2030, over 1 *billion* obese people will be living in these countries (Kelly et al., 2008).

Obesity increases the risk of death (Flegal et al., 2013), with life expectancy reduced by an average of six to seven years (Haslam & James, 2005), in part by creating more risk of Type 2 diabetes, respiratory disorders, high blood pressure, cancer, heart attack, and stroke (Centers for Disease Control and Prevention, 2014). The medical and other costs of obesity in the workplace are more than $73.1 billion per year (Finkelstein et al., 2010). Obesity, especially in adolescence, is also associated with anxiety and depression (e.g., Bell et al., 2011; Gariepy, Nitka, & Schmitz, 2010), though it is not yet clear whether the relationship is causal, and if it is, which condition might be causing which problem (Hilbert et al., 2014; Saguy, 2013).

Possible causes for our current obesity epidemic include big portion sizes in restaurants—especially fast-food outlets—the prevalence of high-fat foods, and reduced physical activity (e.g., Mozaffarian et al., 2011; Wansink & Wansink, 2010). These are important factors, because body weight is determined by a combination of food intake and energy output (Keesey & Powley, 1986). Obese people get more energy from food than their body metabolizes, or "burns up." The excess energy, measured in calories, is stored as fat. Obese

obesity A condition in which a person is severely overweight.

people tend to eat above-average amounts of high-calorie tasty foods but below-average amounts of less-tasty foods (Kauffman, Herman, & Polivy, 1995). Further, they may be less active than lean people, a pattern that often starts in childhood (Jago et al., 2005; Marshall et al., 2004; Strauss & Pollack, 2001). Spending long hours watching television or playing video games is a major cause of the inactivity seen in overweight children (e.g., Bickham et al., 2013), which may partly explain why children who have a TV in their bedrooms are more likely to be overweight than those who don't (Gilbert-Diamond et al., 2014).

In short, inadequate physical activity combined with overeating—especially of the high-fat foods so common in most Western cultures—has a lot to do with obesity (Arsenault et al., 2010). But not everyone who is inactive and eats a high-fat diet becomes obese, and some obese people are as active as lean people, so other factors must also exist (Blundell & Cooling, 2000; Parsons, Power, & Manor, 2005). Some people probably have a genetic predisposition toward obesity (e.g., Frayling et al., 2007; Llewellyn et al., 2014). For example, although most obese people have the genes to make leptin, they may not be sensitive to its weight-suppressing effects, perhaps because of differing genetic codes for leptin receptors in the hypothalamus. Brain-imaging studies also suggest that obese people's brains may be slower to "read" satiety signals coming from their blood, thus causing them to continue eating when leaner people would have stopped (Morton et al., 2006; Thorens, 2008). They may also be more sensitive to the rewards of eating (Stice et al., 2011). These genetic factors may help explain obese people's tendency to eat more, accumulate fat, and feel hungrier than lean people. Also, chronic intake of a high-fat, high-sugar "western" diet may not only increase weight but also cause problems in memory and other cognitive processes that may in turn affect regulation of food intake (Kanoski & Davidson, 2011).

Other factors affecting obesity include learning from the examples set by parents who overeat (Hood et al., 2000), too little parental control over what and how much children eat (Cooper & Warren, 2011; Johnson & Birch, 1994), impulsivity (Churchill, Jessop, & Sparks, 2008), or over-responsiveness to high-fat "comfort foods" (Hofmann et al., 2010; Troisi & Gabriel, 2011). Many people eat more when under stress, a reaction that may be especially extreme in those who become obese (Dallman et al., 2003; Friedman & Brownell, 1995).

Most people, especially those who are obese, find it easier to gain weight than to lose it and keep it off (Jain, 2005; McTigue et al., 2003). For this we can probably blame our evolutionary ancestors who—like nonhuman animals in the wild today—could not always count on food being available. Those who survived lean times were the ones whose genes created tendencies to build and maintain fat reserves (King, 2013). These "thrifty genes" are adaptive in famine-plagued environments but now may be harmful and even deadly in affluent societies where overeating is unnecessary and fast food is on every corner. Further, if people starve themselves to lose weight, their bodies learn to burn calories more slowly. This drop in metabolism saves energy and fat reserves and slows weight loss (Leibel, Rosenbaum, & Hirsch, 1995). Restricted eating also activates the brain's "pleasure centers" when a hungry person even looks at energy-rich food (Siep et al., 2009), making restraint that much more difficult. It is no wonder, then, that health experts warn that we should not try to lose a great deal of weight quickly by dramatically cutting food intake (Carels et al., 2008).

Researchers keep looking for safe and effective medications to treat obesity (Yanovski & Yanovski, 2014). The drugs now available act either to suppress appetite or increase fat burning (e.g., Gilbert et al., 2012; Witkamp, 2011), and millions of people take them (Neovius & Narbro, 2008). A more radical approach is *bariatric surgery*, which restructures the stomach and intestines so that less food energy is absorbed and stored (Hamad, 2004; Vetter et al., 2009). Bariatric surgery can be effective (Courcoulas et al., 2013), but due to its costs and risks—postoperative mortality rates range from 0.1 to 2 percent (Skroubis et al., 2011; Steele et al., 2011)—it is recommended only for extreme cases of obesity that are not helped by more conservative treatments.

Unhappy Meals

TRY THIS A report from the Feeding Infants and Toddlers Study found that toddlers in the United States prefer French fries to any other vegetable, that one in five babies eats candy every day, and that 44 percent of babies consume sugary drinks (Fox et al., 2004). Children's preference for high-fat fast food is so well learned that when children in one experiment were given identical foods wrapped either in plain paper or in paper bearing the logo of a popular fast-food restaurant, they rated the restaurant-branded food as tasting better (Robinson et al., 2009). Changing these habits and preferences will not be easy, but the need to do so is obvious and urgent. Take a look at the nutrition information on packages of your favorite foods. If the fat and sugar content seems excessive, make a list of some alternative choices that might make your eating habits healthier.

The food passionates/Corbis

Thin Is In

In Western cultures today, thinness is a much sought-after ideal, especially among young women. This ideal is seen in fashion models as well as in beauty pageant contestants, whose body mass index has decreased from the "normal" range of 20 to 25 in the 1920s to an "undernourished" 18.5 in recent years (Rubinstein & Caballero, 2000; Voracek & Fisher, 2002). In the United States, 35 percent of normal-weight girls—and 12 percent of underweight girls!—begin dieting when they are as young as age nine or ten. Correlational studies suggest that the efforts of many of these children to lose weight may have come in response to criticism from family members (Barr Taylor et al., 2006a; Schreiber et al., 1996); for some, the result is anorexia. To combat the problem, some fashion shows have established a minimum BMI for all models, and Israel bans the use of underweight models in advertising (New Israeli Law, 2012).

Jack Guez/Afp/Getty Images

---

anorexia nervosa An eating disorder characterized by self-starvation and dramatic weight loss.

bulimia An eating disorder that involves eating massive quantities of food, then eliminating it by self-induced vomiting or laxatives.

No single anti-obesity treatment is a safe, effective solution that works for everyone. Even when people lose weight through diet and exercise and have a strong desire to maintain their healthier behaviors, many people regain what they lost (Burnette & Finkel, 2012; Gipson et al., 2014). To achieve the kind of weight loss that is most likely to last, obese people are advised to make gradual lifestyle changes in addition to (or instead of) seeking medical solutions. These changes can be as simple as limiting the number of available foods, eating from smaller plates, buying lower-fat foods in smaller packages, and fasting one day a week (Levitsky, Iyer, & Pacanowski, 2012). The most effective weight-loss programs include components designed to reduce food intake, change eating habits and attitudes toward food, and increase energy expenditure through regular exercise (Bell et al., 2011; Dombrowski et al., 2014; Shamah et al., 2012). Exercise is especially important because it burns calories while raising metabolism instead of lowering it, as reducing food intake alone does (Curioni & Lourenço, 2005).

Of course, the ultimate remedy for obesity is prevention, which will require parents and others to promote exercise and healthy eating habits in children from an early age.

Anorexia Nervosa

In stark contrast to the problem of obesity is the eating disorder known as **anorexia nervosa**. It is characterized by some combination of self-starvation, self-induced vomiting, excessive exercise, and laxative use that results in weight loss to below 85 percent of normal (Kaye et al., 2000). Anorexia affects about 0.5 to 1 percent of young people in the United States, and it is a significant problem in many other industrialized nations as well (Currin, 2005; Hoek, 2006; Hudson et al., 2007). About 95 percent of those who suffer from anorexia are young women. People with anorexia often feel hungry, and many are obsessed with food and its preparation yet they refuse to eat. Anorexic self-starvation causes serious, often irreversible, physical damage, including reduction in bone density that increases the risk of fractures (Grinspoon et al., 2000). The health dangers may be especially high in anorexic dancers, gymnasts, and other female athletes, who are at risk for stress fractures and heart problems (e.g., Van Durme, Goossens, & Braet, 2012). It is estimated that from 4 to 30 percent of those suffering severe anorexia eventually die of starvation, biochemical imbalances, or suicide; their death rate is six to twelve times higher than the death rate for other young women (National Association of Anorexia Nervosa and Associated Disorders, 2002; Suokas et al., 2013).

Anorexia has been attributed to many factors, including genetic predispositions, hormonal and other biochemical imbalances, social influences, and psychological problems (e.g., Kaye et al., 2013; Treat & Viken, 2010; Wasylkiw, MacKinnon, MacLellan, 2012). Those psychological factors may include a self-punishing, perfectionistic personality and a culturally reinforced obsession with thinness and attractiveness (e.g., American Psychological Association Task Force on the Sexualization of Girls, 2007; Juarascio et al., 2011; Steinglass et al., 2012). People with anorexia appear to be afraid of being fat and take that worry to dangerous extremes. Many still view themselves as fat or misshapen even as they waste away.

Drugs, hospitalization, and psychotherapy are all used to help relieve anorexia (Herpertz et al., 2011). In many cases, treatment brings recovery and the maintenance of normal weight (e.g., Brewerton & Costin, 2011a, b; Steinglass et al., 2012), but more effective treatments and early intervention methods are still needed.

Bulimia

Like anorexia, the eating disorder called bulimia (pronounced "bu-LEE-mee-uh") involves an intense fear of being fat, but the person may be thin, normal in weight, or even overweight. **Bulimia** (also referred to as *bulimia nervosa*) involves eating huge amounts of food (say, several boxes of cookies, a half-gallon of ice cream, and a bucket of fried chicken) and then getting rid of the food through self-induced vomiting or strong laxatives. These "binge-purge" episodes may occur as often as twice a day (Weltzin et al., 1995).

Bulimia shares many features with anorexia (Fairburn et al., 2008). For instance, most bulimics are women, and like anorexia, bulimia usually begins with a desire to be slender. However, most people with bulimia see their eating habits as problematic, whereas most people with anorexia do not (Eddy et al., 2008). Also, bulimia is usually not life threatening (Thompson, 1996). It has consequences, however, that include dehydration, nutritional problems, and intestinal damage (e.g., Abraham & Kellow, 2011; Li et al., 2011; Mehler, 2011). Many people with bulimia develop dental problems from the acids in vomit (Schlueter et al., 2012). Frequent vomiting and the insertion of objects to cause it can also damage the throat.

In the United States about 1 to 3 percent of adolescent and college-age women have bulimia (Hudson et al., 2007), a figure that has remained fairly stable since the early 1990s (Crowther et al., 2008). A combination of factors contributes to bulimia, including perfectionism, high achievement orientation, low self-esteem, stress, a cultural preoccupation with being thin, and emotional problems (de Souza, Mussap, & Cummins, 2010). Problems in the brain's satiety mechanisms may also be involved (e.g., Stice, Marti, & Durant, 2011; Zalta & Keel, 2006). Treatment for bulimia, which typically includes individual or group psychotherapy and, sometimes, antidepressant drugs, helps most people with this disorder (e.g., Brewerton & Costin, 2011a, b; Herpertz et al., 2011).

Binge Eating Disorder

Individuals with **binge eating disorder** engage in food binges but do not display the purging pattern seen in bulimia. Unlike "compulsive overeating," people with binge eating disorder do not feel a general desire to overeat and do not usually fantasize about food. Instead, they experience episodes in which they suddenly and uncontrollably eat huge quantities of food, usually in less than two hours, several times a week (Hudson et al., 2006). It appears that individuals with binge eating disorder are more likely than those with anorexia or bulimia to have problems such as depression, anxiety disorders, and substance abuse (Swanson et al., 2011). There is some evidence, too, that binge eating disorder may run in families, though the nature of any genetic influences is not yet clear (Trace et al., 2013). Nongenetic factors likely play some role, though, since the binge behavior is more common after people "recover" from a very restrictive diet (Tuschl, 1990). The lifetime risk of binge eating disorder may be about 2 percent in the United States (Smink, van Hoeken, & Hoek, 2013). Prescription medications combined with psychotherapy represent the best currently available treatment options, though results are mixed (Brownley et al., 2007; Reas & Grilo, 2014; Wilson, 2011).

For a summary of the processes involved in hunger and eating, see "In Review: Major Factors Controlling Hunger and Eating."

IN REVIEW
MAJOR FACTORS CONTROLLING HUNGER AND EATING

Theory	Stimulate Eating	Inhibit Eating
Biological factors	Hormones released into the bloodstream provide signals that stimulate eating. Signals in the blood such as ghrelin and glucose affect neurons in the hypothalamus and stimulate eating, including hungers for specific kinds of foods, such as fats and carbohydrates. The lateral nucleus of the hypothalamus may be a "hunger center" that monitors these hormonal signals in the blood.	Hormones released into the bloodstream provide signals that inhibit eating. Signals in the blood such as leptin and insulin affect neurons in the hypothalamus and inhibit eating. The ventromedial nucleus of the hypothalamus may be a "satiety center" that monitors these hormonal signals in the blood.

(continued)

MAJOR FACTORS CONTROLLING HUNGER AND EATING (CONT.)

Theory	Stimulate Eating	Inhibit Eating
Nonbiological factors	Sights and smells of particular foods elicit eating because of prior associations. Family customs and social occasions often include norms for eating in particular ways.	Values in contemporary U.S. society encourage thinness and thus can inhibit eating.

In Review Questions

1. People may eat when they are "full," suggesting that eating is not controlled by _____ alone.

2. People who binge and purge have an eating disorder called _____. Those who only binge have a disorder called _____.

3. The best strategy for lasting weight loss includes regular _____ as well as improved eating habits.

SEXUAL BEHAVIOR

How often does the average person have sex?

Unlike food, sex is not necessary for an individual's survival, but it improves the chances that a person's genes will make it to the next generation. The many factors that shape sexual motivation and behavior differ in strength across species. These factors can include physiology, evolutionary forces, learned behavior, and physical and social environments. For example, one species of desert bird requires adequate sex hormones, a suitable mate, and a particular environment before it engages in sexual behavior. As long as the dry season lasts, it shows no interest in sex, but within ten minutes of the first rainfall, the birds vigorously court and copulate.

Rainfall is obviously much less influential as a sexual trigger for humans. In fact, people show an amazing diversity of *sexual scripts,* the step-by-step sequences of thoughts and events that lead to sexual behavior (Simon & Gagnon, 1986). Surveys of college-age men and women have identified 122 specific acts, 34 different tactics, and 237 stated reasons surrounding their efforts to have sex (Greer & Buss, 1994; Meston & Buss, 2007). What actually happens during sex? The matter is exceedingly difficult to address scientifically, partly because most people are reluctant to allow researchers to observe their sexual behavior. Many won't even answer questions about their sexual practices. Yet having valid information about the nature of human sexual behavior is a vital first step for psychologists and other scientists who study such topics as individual differences in sexuality, gender differences in sexual motivation and behavior, sources of sexual orientation, disturbances of sexual functioning, and pathways through which AIDS and other sexually transmitted diseases reach new victims. This information can also help people think about their own sexual behavior in relation to trends in the general population.

The Biology of Sex

Observations in Masters and Johnson's laboratory led to important findings about the **sexual response cycle,** the pattern of physiological arousal before, during, and after sexual activity (see Figure 10.2). Masters and Johnson (1966) found that men show one primary pattern of sexual response but women display at least three different patterns from time to time. In both men and women, the first, or *excitement,* phase begins with sexually stimulating input from the environment or from one's own thoughts. Further stimulation leads to intensified excitement in the second, or *plateau,*

binge eating disorder A pattern of sudden, recurrent episodes of eating huge amounts of food, but without purging.

sexual response cycle The pattern of arousal before, during, and after sexual activity.

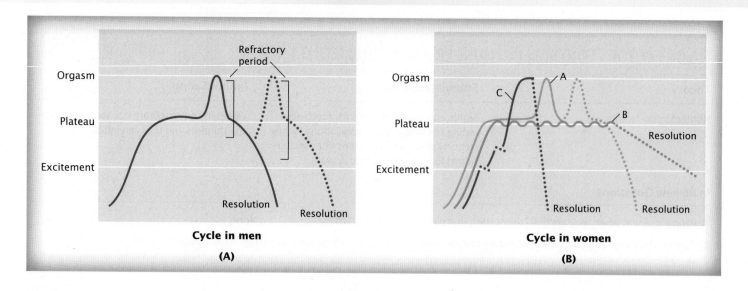

FIGURE 10.2
The Sexual Response Cycle

Masters and Johnson (1966) found that men show one primary pattern of sexual response, depicted in Part A, and that women display at least three different patterns from time to time—labeled A, B, and C in Part B.

A SURVEY OF HUMAN SEXUAL BEHAVIOR

The first extensive studies of sexual behavior in the United States were done in the 1950s and 1960s by Alfred Kinsey (Kinsey, Pomeroy, & Martin, 1948; Kinsey et al., 1953) and William Masters and Virginia Johnson (1966). In the Kinsey studies, volunteers answered questions about their sexual practices, whereas Masters and Johnson actually recorded volunteers' **sexual arousal**, their physiological responses during natural or artificial sexual stimulation in a laboratory. Together, these pioneering studies broke new ground to explain human sexuality.

However, the people who volunteered for them were probably not a representative sample of the adult population. So the results and conclusions drawn from them might not apply to people in general. Further, the data are now so old that they may not reflect sexual practices today. Unfortunately, results of more recent surveys, such as reader polls in *Cosmopolitan* and other magazines, are flawed because their samples are also not representative (Davis & Smith, 1990).

What was the researchers' question?

Is it possible to gather data about sexual behavior that are more representative and therefore more applicable to people in general? A team of researchers at the University of Chicago believe it is, so they undertook the National Health and Social Life Survey, the first extensive survey of sexual behavior in the United States since the Kinsey studies (Laumann et al., 1994).

How did the researchers answer the question?

This survey included important design features that had been neglected in most other surveys of sexual behavior. First, the study did not depend on self-selected volunteers. The researchers sought out a particular sample of 3,432 people who ranged in age from 18 to 59. Second, the sample was carefully constructed so as to reflect the sociocultural diversity of the U.S. population in terms of gender, ethnicity, socioeconomic status, geographical location, and the like. Third, unlike previous surveys that had relied on mail-in responses from participants, the Chicago study was based on face-to-face interviews. This approach made it easier to ensure that the participants understood each question and allowed them to explain their responses. To encourage honesty, the researchers let participants answer some of the survey's questions anonymously by placing written responses in a sealed envelope.

(continued)

sexual arousal Physiological arousal that arises from sexual contact or erotic thoughts.

What did the researchers find?

For one thing, the researchers found that people in the United States have sex less often and with fewer partners than many had assumed. For most, sex occurs about once a week and almost always with the partner with whom they share a stable relationship. About a third of the participants reported having had sex only a few times (or not at all) in the preceding year. And, in contrast to various celebrities' splashy tales of dozens, even hundreds, of sexual partners per year, the average male survey participant had had only six sexual partners in his entire life. The average female respondent reported a lifetime total of two. Further, the survey data suggested that people in committed, one-partner relationships had the most frequent and the most satisfying sex. And although a wide variety of specific sexual practices were reported, the overwhelming majority of heterosexual couples said that they tend to engage mainly in penis-vagina intercourse. Many of these findings are consistent with the results of more recent surveys conducted by other researchers (e.g., National Center for Health Statistics, 2007).

What do the results mean?

The Chicago survey challenges some of the cultural and media images of sexuality in the United States. In particular, it suggests that people in the United States may be more sexually conservative than one might think on the basis of magazine reader polls and the testimony of guests on daytime talk shows.

What do we still need to know?

Many questions remain. The Chicago survey did not ask about some of the more controversial aspects of sexuality, such as the effects of pornography or the role in sexual activity of sexual fetishes such as shoes or other clothing. Had the researchers asked about such topics, their results might have painted a different picture. Further, because the Chicago survey focused on people in the United States, it told us little or nothing about the sexual practices, traditions, and values of people in the rest of the world.

The Chicago team continued to conduct interviews after their initial effort to fill in the picture about sexual behavior in the United States and around the world (Youm & Laumann, 2002). They found, for example, that nearly one-quarter of U.S. women prefer to achieve sexual satisfaction without partners of either sex. And although people in the United States tend to engage in a wider variety of sexual behaviors than do those in Britain, people in the United States appear to be less tolerant of disapproved sexual practices (Laumann & Michael, 2000; Michael et al., 1998). They have found, too, that although sexual activity declines with advancing age, it by no means disappears. Between 26 and 33 percent of people in the 75 to 95 age group—especially men—reported that they were still sexually active (e.g., Hyde et al., 2010).

Other researchers have found a number of consistent gender differences in sexuality (Basson, 2001; Schmitt et al., 2012). For example, men are more likely than women to mistake another person's friendliness for sexual interest (Perilloux, Easton, & Buss, 2012). This may be because men tend to have a stronger interest in and desire for sex than women, whereas women are more likely than men to associate sexual activity with love and to be affected by cultural and situational influences on sexual attitudes and behavior (e.g., Diamond, 2008; Petersen & Hyde, 2010). Many such differences are actually quite small, and, according to some studies, not necessarily significant (Conley et al., 2011).

The results of even the best survey methods—like those of the best of all other research methods—usually raise many questions. When do people get interested in sex, and why? How do they express these desires, and why? What determines their sexual likes and dislikes? How do learning and sociocultural factors modify the biological forces that seem to provide the raw material of human sexual motivation? These are some of the questions about human sexual behavior that a survey cannot easily or accurately explore (Benson, 2003).

phase. If stimulation continues, the person reaches the third, or *orgasmic*, stage. Although orgasm lasts only a few seconds, it provides an intensely pleasurable release of physical and psychological tension. The *resolution* phase follows, during which the person returns to a state of relaxation. At this point, men enter a *refractory period*, during which they are temporarily unable to be aroused. Women are capable of immediately repeating the cycle if stimulation continues.

People's motivation to engage in sexual activity is influenced by **sex hormones**. Three classes of hormones are most directly related to sexual behavior: **estrogens, progestational hormones** (also called **progestins**), and **androgens**. The main estrogen is *estradiol*, the main progestin is *progesterone*, and the main androgen is *testosterone*. Each sex hormone flows in the blood of both sexes, but males have relatively more androgens than estrogens or progestins, and women have relatively more estrogens and progestins than androgens.

Sex hormones have both *organizing* and *activating* effects on the brain. The organizing effects are permanent changes in the brain that influence the brain's response to hormones. The activating effects are temporary behavioral changes that last only as long as the level of a sex hormone is elevated, such as in the ovulation phase of the monthly menstrual cycle. In mammals, including humans, the organizing effects of hormones occur around the time of birth. It is then that certain brain areas are sculpted into a "female-typical" or "male-typical" pattern. For example, a brain area called *BnST* is generally larger in men than in women. Its possible role in some aspects of human sexuality was suggested by a study that compared the brains of men with a male gender identity to those of male-to-female transsexuals (genetic males who feel like women and may request surgery and hormone treatments to create more feminine bodies). The BnST was larger in the male-identified men than in the transsexuals. In fact, the transsexuals' BnST was about the size usually seen in women (Zhou et al., 1995). This result has not been replicated in more recent research, however (Savic & Aryer, 2011).

Rising levels of sex hormones during puberty activate increased sexual desire and interest in sexual behavior. Generally, estrogens stimulate females' sexual interest, especially in more masculine-looking men, and increase the accuracy of their judgments of men's sexual orientation (Durante et al., 2012; Roney & Simmons, 2008; Rule et al., 2011). Androgens raise males' sexual interest (Davidson, Camargo, & Smith, 1979), but they may also do so in females (Sherwin & Gelfand, 1987). The activating effects of hormones are also seen in reduced sexual motivation and behavior among people whose hormone-secreting ovaries or testes have been removed for medical reasons. Injections of hormones help restore these people's sexual interest and activity (Sherwin, Gelfand, & Brender, 1985).

Generally, hormones affect sexual desire, not the physical ability to have sex (Wallen & Lovejoy, 1993). This fact may explain why castration (removal of the testes) does not prevent sex crimes by male offenders. Men with low testosterone levels due to medical problems or castration show less sexual desire but still have erections in response to erotic stimuli (Kwan et al., 1983). So a sex offender treated by chemical or physical castration might be less likely to seek out sex, but he would still respond as before to his favorite sexual stimuli (Wickham, 2001).

Social and Cultural Factors in Sexuality

Human sexuality is shaped not only by hormones but also by a lifetime of learning and thinking. For example, children learn some of their sexual attitudes and behaviors as part of the development of *gender roles*, as described in the human development chapter. The specific attitudes and behaviors they learn depend partly on the nature of gender roles in their culture (Petersen & Hyde, 2010).

There are also differences in what women and men find sexually arousing. For example, in many cultures, men are far more interested in and responsive to erotic visual images than women are (e.g., Petersen & Hyde, 2010). A biological basis for this difference

sex hormones Chemicals in the blood that organize and motivate sexual behavior.

estrogens Feminine hormones that circulate in the bloodstream.

progestational hormones (progestins) Feminine hormones that circulate in the bloodstream.

androgens Masculine hormones that circulate in the bloodstream.

was investigated in a study that scanned the brain activity of males and females while they looked at erotic photographs (Hamann et al., 2004). The men showed greater activity in the amygdala and hypothalamus than the women did. But even though there were gender differences in brain activity, the male and female participants rated the photos as equally attractive and sexually arousing. In another study, when men reported sexual arousal in response to erotic films, they showed signs of physiological arousal, too. For women, self-reports of sexual arousal were not strongly correlated with signs of physiological arousal (Chivers et al., 2004). Further, though men and women both show more sexual arousal to more intensely erotic films, the level of women's arousal may not depend as much as men's does on whether the actors are males or females (Chivers, Seto, & Blanchard, 2007). A third study found that women were aroused by a wider range of sexual stories than men were (Suschinsky & Lalumière, 2011).

These are just a few examples of the fact that a complex mixture of factors produces sexuality. Each person's learning history, cultural background, and perceptions of the world interact so deeply with such a wide range of physiological processes that—as in many other aspects of human behavior and mental processes—it is impossible to separate their influence on sexuality. Nowhere is this point clearer than in the case of sexual orientation.

Sexual Orientation

Sexual orientation refers to the nature of a person's enduring emotional, romantic, or sexual attraction to others (American Psychological Association, 2002a; Ellis & Mitchell, 2000). The most common sexual orientation is **heterosexuality**, in which the attraction is to members of the opposite sex. When attraction focuses on members of one's own sex, the orientation is called **homosexuality**, more specifically, gay (for men) and lesbian (for women). **Bisexuality** refers to the orientation of people who are attracted to members of both sexes. Sexual orientation involves feelings that may or may not be translated into corresponding patterns of sexual behavior (Pathela et al., 2006). For example, some people whose orientation is gay, lesbian, or bisexual may have sex only with opposite-sex partners. Similarly, people whose orientation is heterosexuality may have had one or more same-sex encounters.

In many cultures, heterosexuality has long been regarded as a moral norm, and homosexuality has been cast as a disease, a mental disorder, or even a crime (Hooker, 1993). Yet there is no good evidence that efforts to alter the sexual orientation of gay men and lesbians—using psychotherapy, brain surgery, or electric shock—are effective (American Psychiatric Association, 1999; American Psychological Association, 2008; King, Smith, & Bartlett, 2004). In 1973, the American Psychiatric Association dropped homosexuality from the *Diagnostic and Statistical Manual of Mental Disorders*, thus ending its official status as a form of psychopathology. The same change was made by the World Health Organization in its *International Classification of Diseases* in 1993, by Japan's psychiatric organization in 1995, and by the Chinese Psychiatric Association in 2001.

Nevertheless, some people still disapprove of homosexuality. Gays, lesbians, and bisexuals are often the victims of discrimination and even hate crimes, so many are reluctant to let their sexual orientation be known. It is difficult, therefore, to obtain an accurate picture of the mix of heterosexual, gay, lesbian, and bisexual orientations in a population. In the Chicago sex survey mentioned earlier, 1.4 percent of women and 2.8 percent of men identified themselves as exclusively gay or lesbian (Laumann et al., 1994). These figures are much lower than the 10 percent found earlier in Kinsey's studies. However, the Chicago survey's face-to-face interviews did not allow respondents to give anonymous answers to questions about sexual orientation. Some suggest that if anonymous responses had been permitted, the prevalence figures for gay, lesbian, and bisexual orientations would have been higher (Bullough, 1995). In fact, studies that have allowed anonymous responding estimate that gay, lesbian, and bisexual people make up between 2 and 21 percent of the population in the United States, Canada, and Western Europe (e.g., Aaron et al., 2003; Hayes et al., 2012; Savin-Williams, 2006).

heterosexuality Sexual desire or behavior that is focused on members of the opposite sex.

homosexuality Sexual desire or behavior that is focused on members of one's own sex.

bisexuality Sexual desire or behavior that is focused on members of both sexes.

WHAT SHAPES SEXUAL ORIENTATION?

The question of where sexual orientation comes from is a topic of intense debate in scientific circles, on talk shows, in Internet chat rooms, and in everyday conversations.

What am I being asked to believe or accept?

Some people believe that genes exert a major influence on our sexual orientation. According to this view, we do not learn or choose a sexual orientation but rather are born with a strong predisposition to develop a particular orientation.

What evidence is available to support the assertion?

In 1995, a report by a respected research group suggested that one kind of sexual orientation—namely, that of gay men—is associated with a particular gene on the X chromosome (Hu et al., 1995). This specific finding was not supported by later studies (Rice et al., 1999), but other research in behavioral genetics strongly suggests that some kind of genetic influence must affect sexual orientation in humans (e.g., Kendler et al., 2000; Rice, Friberg, & Gavrilets, 2012). One study examined pairs of monozygotic male twins (whose genes are identical), pairs of dizygotic, or nonidentical, twins (whose genes are no more alike than those of any pair of brothers), and pairs of adopted brothers (who are genetically unrelated). To participate in this study, at least one brother in each pair had to be gay. As it turned out, the other brother was also gay or bisexual in 52 percent of the identical twin pairs but in only 22 percent of the non-identical pairs and in just 11 percent of the adoptive pairs (Bailey & Pillard, 1991). Similar findings are seen in male identical twins raised apart, where a shared sexual orientation cannot be due a shared environment (Whitam, Diamond, & Martin, 1993). Studies of female sexual orientation have yielded similar results (Bailey & Benishay, 1993; Bailey, Dunne, & Martin, 2000).

Sex hormones may provide another biological influence on sexual orientation. In adults, different levels of these hormones are not generally associated with different sexual orientation. However, hormonal differences during prenatal development might be involved (Lippa, 2003; Mustanski et al., 2002). For example, one study found that women—but not men—who had been exposed to high levels of androgens during fetal development were much more likely to report bisexual or homosexual behaviors or fantasies than were their relatives of the same sex who had not been exposed (Meyer-Bahlburg et al., 2008).

Another line of research focuses on the possibility that previous pregnancies might permanently affect a woman's hormones in ways that influence the sexual orientation of her next child (Blanchard, 2001). Some evidence for this hypothesis comes from a study showing that the more older biological brothers a man has, the higher is the probability he will have a homosexual orientation (Bogaert & Skorska, 2011). These results appear to reflect mainly hormonal rather than mainly environmental influences, because the number of *nonbiological*

A Committed Relationship, with Children

Like heterosexual relationships, gay and lesbian relationships can be brief and stormy or stable and long lasting (Kurdek, 2005). These gay men are committed to each other for the long haul, as evidenced by their decision to adopt two children together. The strong role of biological factors in sexual orientation is seen in research showing that these children's orientation will not be influenced much, if at all, by that of their adoptive parents (e.g., Patterson, 2004, 2009; Pennington & Knight, 2011).

ONOKY - Fabrice LEROUGE/Brand X Pictures/Getty Images

(continued)

(adopted) brothers that the men had was not predictive of their sexual orientation. Further, because sexual orientation in women appeared not to be predicted by the number and gender of their older biological siblings, it was at first thought that the hormonal consequences of carrying male fetuses might only influence males' sexual orientation. The picture is not that simple, though. Other researchers have found that women's sexual orientation, too, is related to the number of older biological brothers they have (McConaghy et al., 2006), and still others have reported a relationship between men's sexual orientation and the number of older biological sisters they have (Francis, 2008; Vasey & VanderLaan, 2007). We don't yet know exactly how prenatal hormonal influences might operate to affect sexual orientation, but studies of nonhuman animals have found that such influences alter the structure of the hypothalamus, a brain region known to underlie some aspects of sexual functioning (Swaab & Hofman, 1995).

Finally, a biological basis for sexual orientation is suggested by the fact that sexual orientation is not predicted by environmental factors. For example, the sexual orientation of children's caregivers has little or no effect on those children's own orientation. Several studies have shown that children adopted by homosexual parents are no more or less likely to display a homosexual orientation than are children raised by heterosexual parents (e.g., Anderssen, Amlie, & Ytteroy, 2002; Bailey et al., 1995).

Are there alternative ways of interpreting the evidence?

Like all correlational data, correlations between genetics and sexual orientation are open to alternative interpretations. As discussed in the introductory chapter, a correlation describes the strength and direction of the relationship between two variables, but it does not guarantee that one variable actually influences the other. Consider again the data showing that the brothers who shared the most genes (identical twins) were also most likely to share a gay orientation. What they shared was probably not a "gay gene" but rather a set of genes that influenced the boys' activity levels, emotionality, aggressiveness, and the like. One example is gender conformity/nonconformity in childhood, the tendency for children to either conform or not conform to the behaviors, interests, and appearance that are typical for their gender in their culture. Such general aspects of their temperaments or personalities in childhood—and other people's reactions to them—could influence the emergence in later life of a particular sexual orientation (Bem, 2000). In other words, sexual orientation could arise as a reaction to the way people respond to a genetically determined but nonsexual aspect of personality. The influence of prenatal hormone levels could also influence sexual orientation by shaping aggressiveness or other nonsexual aspects of behavior.

It is also important to look at behavioral genetics evidence for what it can tell us about the role of *environmental* factors in sexual orientation. When we read a study showing that 52 percent of the time, both members of identical-twin pairs have a gay, lesbian, or bisexual orientation, it is easy to ignore the fact that the sexual orientation of the twin pair members *differed* in 48 percent of the cases. Viewed in this way, the results suggest that genes do not tell the entire story of sexual orientation. In other words, it is not determined by unlearned, genetic forces alone. As described in the chapter on biological aspects of psychology, the brains and bodies we inherit are quite responsive to environmental influences. In fact, the behaviors we engage in and the experiences we have often result in physical changes in the brain and elsewhere (Wang et al., 1995). For example, physical changes occur in the brain's synapses as we form new memories. So differences seen in the brains of adults with differing sexual orientations could be the effect, not the cause, of their behavior or experiences.

What additional evidence would help evaluate the alternatives?

Much more evidence is needed regarding the role of genes in shaping sexual orientation. We also have a lot to learn about the extent to which genes and hormones shape physical and psychological characteristics that lead to various sexual orientations. In studying these topics, researchers will want to learn more about the genetic makeup, mental style, and behavioral characteristics of people with different sexual orientations. Are there personality characteristics associated with particular sexual orientations? If so, do those characteristics have a strong genetic component? To what extent are heterosexuals, gays, lesbians, and bisexuals similar—and different—in terms of biases, coping skills, developmental histories, and the like (Bailey,

(continued)

Dunne, & Martin, 2000)? The more we learn about sexual orientation in general, the easier it will be to interpret data relating to its origins.

Yet even classifying sexual orientation is not simple, because people do not always fall into sharply defined categories (Thompson & Morgan, 2008; Worthington et al., 2008). Should a man who identifies himself as gay be considered bisexual because he occasionally has heterosexual daydreams? What sexual orientation label would be appropriate for a forty-year-old woman who experienced a few lesbian encounters in her teens but has engaged in exclusively heterosexual sex since then? Progress in understanding the origins of sexual orientation would be enhanced by a generally accepted system for describing and defining all facets of exactly what is meant by the term *sexual orientation* (Klein, 1990; Stein, 1999).

What conclusions are most reasonable?

The evidence available so far suggests that genetic factors, possibly including effects on prenatal hormones, create differences in the brains of people with different sexual orientations. However, the manner in which a person expresses a genetically influenced sexual orientation will be profoundly shaped by what that person learns through social and cultural experiences. In short, as with other psychological phenomena, sexual orientation reflects the complex interplay of both genetic and nongenetic mechanisms—of both nature and nurture.

ACHIEVEMENT MOTIVATION

Why do some people try harder than others to succeed?

The next time you visit someone's home or office, notice the mementos displayed. Perhaps there are framed diplomas and awards, trophies and ribbons, and photos of children and grandchildren. These badges of achievement affirm that a person has accomplished tasks that merit approval or establish worth. Much of human behavior is motivated by a desire for approval, admiration, and a sense of achievement—in short, for esteem—from others and from within. In this section, we examine two of the most common avenues to esteem: achievement in general and achievement in one's work.

Need for Achievement

Many athletes who already hold world records still train intensely; many people who have built multimillion-dollar businesses still work fourteen-hour days. What motivates these people? One answer is **achievement motivation** (also called the **need for achievement**)—the desire to do well in relation to some standard of excellence (McClelland et al., 1953; Murray, 1938). People with high achievement motivation seek to master tasks—such as sports, business ventures, occupational skills, intellectual puzzles, or artistic creation—and feel intense satisfaction from doing so. They work hard at striving for excellence, enjoy themselves in the process, and take great pride in achieving at a high level. For individuals with low achievement motivation, standards of excellence tend to create avoidance as well as anxiety, worry, and the anticipation of shame (Bjornebekk, Gjesme, & Ulriksen, 2011).

Individual Differences

How do people with strong achievement motivation differ from others? To find out, researchers gave children a test to measure their need for achievement (Figure 10.3 shows a test for adults) and then asked them to play a ring-toss game. Most of the children who scored low on the need-for-achievement test stood either so close to the ring-toss target that they couldn't fail or so far away that they could not succeed. In contrast, children scoring high on the need-for-achievement test stood at a moderate distance from the target, making the game challenging but not impossible (McClelland, 1958).

Experiments with adults and children suggest that people with high achievement needs tend to set challenging but realistic goals. They actively seek success, take risks when necessary, can wait for rewards, and are intensely satisfied when they do well (Mayer & Sutton, 1996). Yet if they feel they have tried their best, people with high achievement

FIGURE 10.3
Assessing Achievement Motivation

This picture is similar to those included in the Thematic Apperception Test, or TAT (Morgan & Murray, 1935). The strength of people's achievement motivation is inferred from the stories they tell about TAT pictures. A response like "The boy is thinking about playing his violin in concert at Carnegie Hall" would be seen as reflecting high achievement motivation.

Palm/Rsch/Redferns/Getty Images

motivation are not too upset by failure. Those with low achievement motivation also like to succeed, but instead of joy, success tends to bring them relief at having avoided failure (Winter, 1996). Indeed, there is some evidence that the differing emotions—such as anticipation versus worry—that accompany the efforts of people with high and low achievement motivation can affect how successful those efforts will be (Pekrun et al., 2009).

Differences in achievement motivation also appear in the kinds of goals people go after when they are in achievement-related situations (Corker & Donnellan, 2012; Molden & Dweck, 2000). Some, known as *learning goals,* focus on developing competence (Dweck, 1999; Pintrich, 2003). People pursuing learning goals play golf, take piano lessons, work on puzzles or problems, go to school, and so on, mainly to get better at those activities (Spinath & Steinmayr, 2012). They realize that they may not yet have the skill needed to achieve at a high level, so they learn by watching others and by struggling on their own rather than immediately asking for help (Mayer & Sutton, 1996). They seek help only if they feel they really need it, preferring to ask for explanations, hints, and other forms of task-related information, so as not to lose out on the challenge of the situation (Roussel, Elliot, & Feltman, 2011). In contrast, *performance goals* focus on demonstrating competence to others. People who pursue performance goals tend to seek information about how well they have done compared to others, and not so much about how to improve their performance (Butler, 1998). When they seek help, it is usually to ask for the "right answer" rather than for tips on how to find the answer themselves. Since their primary goal is to display competence, people with performance goals tend to avoid new challenges if they are not confident that they will succeed, and they tend to quit in response to failure (Grant & Dweck, 2003).

Development of Achievement Motivation

Achievement motivation develops in early childhood under the influence of both genetic and environmental factors. As described in the personality chapter, children inherit general behavioral tendencies, such as impulsiveness and emotionality, and these tendencies may support or undermine the development of achievement motivation. The motivation to achieve is also shaped by what children learn from watching and listening to others, especially their parents and teachers (Hughes et al., 2012; Kim, Schaller, & Kim, 2010). Evidence for the influence of parental teachings about achievement comes from a study in which young boys were given a task so difficult that they were sure to fail. Fathers whose sons scored low on achievement motivation tests often became annoyed as they watched their boys work on the task, discouraged them from continuing, and interfered or even completed the task themselves (Rosen & D'Andrade, 1959). A much different response pattern emerged among parents of children who scored high on tests of achievement motivation. Those parents tended to (1) encourage the child to try difficult tasks, especially new ones; (2) give praise and other rewards for success; (3) encourage

Helping Them Do Their Best

Learning-oriented goals are especially appropriate in classrooms, where students typically have little knowledge of the subject matter. This is why most teachers tolerate errors and reward gradual improvement. They do not usually encourage performance goals, which emphasize doing better than others and demonstrating immediate competence (Reeve, 1996). Still, to help students do their best in the long run, teachers may also promote performance goals. The proper combination of both kinds of goals may be more motivating than either kind alone (Barron & Harackiewicz, 2001; Byron & Khazanchi, 2012).

michaeljung/Fotolia

achievement motivation (need for achievement) The degree to which a person establishes specific goals, cares about meeting them, and experiences satisfaction by doing so.

the child to find ways to succeed rather than merely complaining about failure; and (4) prompt the child to go on to the next, more difficult challenge (McClelland, 1985).

The ways in which children learn to think about themselves is another important factor in achievement motivation. Those who are optimistic, confident in their abilities, expect to succeed, and think of achievement situations as challenges rather than threats are more likely to develop high achievement motivation than children who are pessimistic about their abilities, threatened by achievement situations, and expect to fail (Dweck, 1999; Law, Elliot, & Murayama, 2012).

These cognitive habits affect children's behavior in achievement situations, but the habits are themselves affected by the outcome of previous achievement efforts. Strong achievement motivation is more likely to develop in children who have experienced the pride that follows success at facing challenges and meeting standards of excellence. Achievement motivation is likely to be lower in those who have experienced embarrassment or shame following unsuccessful achievement efforts—especially if their failures have been met with ridicule (Stipek, 1983).

Cultural factors can also influence the development of achievement motivation. For example, subtle messages about a culture's view of the importance and value of achievement often appear in the books children read, the stories they hear, and the programs they see on television (Hong & Lin-Siegler, 2011). Does the story's main character work hard and overcome obstacles, thus creating expectations of a payoff for persistence? Or does a lazy main character drift aimlessly and then win the lottery, suggesting that rewards come randomly, regardless of effort? And if the main character succeeds, is it the result of personal effort, as is typical of stories in individualist cultures? Or is success based on ties to a cooperative and supportive group, as is typical of stories in collectivist cultures? These themes appear to act as blueprints for reaching one's goals. It is not surprising, then, that ideas about achievement motivation differ from culture to culture. In one study, individuals from Saudi Arabia and from the United States were asked to comment on short stories describing people succeeding at various tasks. Saudis tended to see the people in the stories as having succeeded because of the help they got from others, whereas Americans tended to attribute success to the internal characteristics of each story's main character (Zahrani & Kaplowitz, 1993).

Children raised in environments that support the development of strong achievement motivation tend not to give up on difficult tasks—even if all the king's horses and all the king's men do!

Al Ross/The New Yorker/wwwCartoonBank,com

"Maybe they didn't try hard enough."

Achievement and Success in the Workplace

In the workplace, there is usually more concern with employees' motivation to work hard during business hours than with their general level of achievement motivation. In fact, employers tend to set up jobs consistent with their ideas about how intrinsic and extrinsic motivations combine to shape employees' performance (Riggio, 1989). Employers who see workers as lazy, dishonest, and lacking in ambition tend to offer highly structured, heavily supervised jobs. They give the employees little say in deciding what to do or how to do it. These employers assume that workers are motivated mainly by extrinsic rewards—especially money or job security. So they are often surprised when some employees are dissatisfied with their jobs and show little motivation to work hard, in spite of good pay and benefits (Diener & Seligman, 2004; Igalens & Roussel, 1999).

If good pay and benefits alone don't bring job satisfaction and the desire to excel on the job, what does? In Western cultures, low worker motivation appears to come largely from negative thoughts and feelings about having little or no control over the work environment (Rosen, 1991). Compared with those in highly structured jobs, workers tend to be happier, more satisfied, and more productive if they are (1) encouraged to participate in decisions about how work should be done; (2) given problems to solve, without being told how to solve them; (3) taught more than one skill; (4) given individual responsibility; and (5) given public recognition, not just money, for good performance (Fisher, 2000).

What is the best way to encourage work motivation? Allowing people to set and achieve clear goals is one way to increase both job performance and job satisfaction (Abramis, 1994; Locke & Latham, 2002). Goals that most effectively maintain work motivation have several features (Katzell & Thompson, 1990). First, they are personally meaningful. Thus, if a high-level administrator tells employees that their goal should be to increase production, workers might feel unfairly burdened and not particularly motivated. Second, effective goals tend to be challenging, but not impossible. Moderately difficult goals provide the best opportunity for fairly testing one's skills and for experiencing pride and satisfaction when the goals are met (Trope, 1975, 1983). Third, goals that involve interpersonal competition tend to be effective, especially for workers with high achievement motivation. For example, some automakers have teams of designers compete, not necessarily for money, but for the honor of having "their" new model chosen to be manufactured and sold throughout the world. Similarly, students with high achievement motivation often improve their academic performance by forming study groups whose members compete for the best grades. For such people, knowing that others are vying to achieve the same goal as they are tends to create strong intrinsic motivation, even when there are few if any extrinsic rewards at stake (Harackiewicz & Elliot, 1993; Harackiewicz, Sansone, & Manderlink, 1985). Fourth, effective goals are specific and concrete (Locke & Latham, 2002). Thus, a goal of "doing better" is usually not a strong motivator, whereas a specific target, such as increasing sales by 10 percent, is far more motivating. Finally, goals are most effective if management supports the workers' own goal setting, offers special rewards for reaching goals, and gives encouragement for renewed efforts after failure (Kluger & DeNisi, 1998).

To summarize, motivating jobs offer personal challenges, independence, and both intrinsic and extrinsic rewards. They provide enough satisfaction to feel excitement and pleasure in working hard. They inspire workers to be passionate about work, not merely driven by it (Burke & Fiksenbaum, 2009). For employers, the rewards are more productivity, less absenteeism, and fewer resignations (Ilgen & Pulakos, 1999).

Achievement and Well-Being

Some people believe that the more they achieve and the more money and other material goods they gain as a result, the happier they will be. Do you agree? Researchers studying *positive psychology* (Seligman et al., 2005; Mongrain & Anselmo-Mathews, 2012) have become interested in the systematic study of what it actually takes to achieve happiness, or, more formally, well-being (McNulty & Fincham, 2012). **Well-being** (also known as **subjective well-being**) is a combination of a cognitive judgment of satisfaction with life, the frequent experiencing of positive moods and emotions, and the relatively infrequent experiencing of unpleasant moods and emotions (Diener, 2012).

Goal Setting and Achievement Motivation

Clear and specific goals motivate the most persistent achievement efforts on the job and in other areas, too (Locke & Latham, 2002). These people are more likely to stick with their exercise program if they pursue the goal of "losing twenty pounds" or "doing aerobics three times a week" rather than a vague goal of "getting in shape." Similarly, you are more likely to keep reading this chapter if your goal is to "read the motivation section of the motivation and emotion chapter today" than if it is to "do some studying." Clarifying your goal makes it easier to know when you have reached it and when it is time to take a break. Without clear goals, a person can be more easily distracted by fatigue, boredom, or frustration and more likely to give up too soon.

Purestock/Thinkstock

well-being (subjective well-being) A cognitive judgment of satisfaction with life, the frequent experiencing of positive moods and emotions, and the relatively infrequent experiencing of unpleasant moods and emotions.

Research on well-being indicates that, as you might expect, people living in extreme poverty or in war-torn or politically chaotic countries are less happy than people in better circumstances (Sacks, Stevenson, & Wolfers, 2013). And people everywhere react to good or bad events with corresponding changes in mood. Making progress toward a goal, for example, can boost well-being (Klug & Maier, 2014). By contrast, as described in the chapter on health, stress, and coping, severe or long-lasting stressors—such as the death of a loved one—can lead to psychological and physical problems. But although events do have an impact, the depressing or elevating effects of major changes, such as being promoted or fired or even being imprisoned, seriously injured, or disabled tend not to last as long or be as intense as we might think they would (Abrantes-Pais et al., 2007; Mathieu & Gosling, 2012). In other words, how happy you are may have less to do with what happens to you than you might expect.

Most event-related changes in mood subside within days or weeks, and most people then return to their previous level of happiness (Suh, Diener, & Fujita, 1996). Even when events create permanent changes in circumstances, most people adapt by changing their expectancies and goals, not by radically and permanently changing their baseline level of happiness (e.g., Smith et al., 2009; Sussman & Shafir, 2011). For example, people may be thrilled after getting a big salary increase, but as they get used to having more money, the thrill fades, and they may eventually feel just as underpaid as before. In fact, although there are exceptions (Fujita & Diener, 2005; Lucas, 2007), most people's level of well-being tends to be remarkably stable over their lives. This stable baseline may be related to temperament or personality and may function like the homeostatic processes that maintain body temperature or weight (Lykken, 1999). Like many other aspects of temperament, our baseline level of happiness may be affected by genetics. Twin studies have shown, for example, that individual differences in happiness are more strongly associated with inherited personality characteristics than with environmental factors such as money, popularity, or physical attractiveness (Lykken, 1999; Tellegen et al., 1988).

Beyond inherited tendencies, the things that appear to matter most in generating happiness are having close social ties (such as friends and a satisfying marriage or partnership) and social support in general, being religious, having relatively high status and respect within a group, fitting in with one's culture, and having the resources necessary to make progress toward one's goals (e.g., Adams, 2012; Anderson et al., 2012; Fischer & Boer, 2011; Oishi, Schimmack, & Diener, 2012). So you don't have to be a smart, rich, physically attractive high achiever to be happy.

These results are consistent with the views expressed over many centuries by philosophers, psychologists, and wise people in all cultures (e.g., Ekman et al., 2005). As discussed in the personality chapter, for example, Abraham Maslow (1970) noted that when people in Western cultures experience unhappiness and psychological problems, those problems may reflect a *deficiency orientation*. This orientation encourages us to seek happiness by trying to acquire the goods and status we don't have—but think we need—rather than by appreciating life itself and the material and nonmaterial riches we already have. The trap inherent in this orientation is that as we struggle to get more money, status, power, or the other things that we think will bring happiness, we may become more unhappy if what we get is never "enough." Indeed, the old saying that "life is a journey, not a destination" suggests that we are more likely to find happiness by being fully engaged in what we are *doing*—a state that some positive psychologists call *flow* (Hektner, Schmidt, & Csikszentmihalyi, 2007)—rather than by focusing on what we are or are not *getting*.

RELATIONS AND CONFLICTS AMONG MOTIVES

Which motives move me most?

It is far too early to tell whether research on well-being will help channel people's achievement motivation toward a more balanced set of goals, but there is no doubt that people will continue striving to meet whatever needs they perceive to be important. What are those needs?

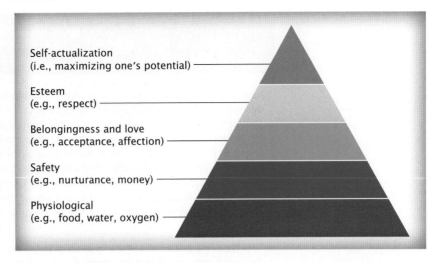

Self-actualization (i.e., maximizing one's potential)

Esteem (e.g., respect)

Belongingness and love (e.g., acceptance, affection)

Safety (e.g., nurturance, money)

Physiological (e.g., food, water, oxygen)

Maslow's Hierarchy

Abraham Maslow (1970) was an influential psychologist who argued that human behavior is affected by a hierarchy, or ranking, of five classes of needs, or motives (see Figure 10.4). He reasoned that needs at lower levels of the hierarchy must be at least partially satisfied before people can be motivated by the ones at higher levels. From the bottom to the top of Maslow's hierarchy, these five motives are as follows:

1. *Physiological*, such as the need for food, water, oxygen, and sleep.

2. *Safety*, such as the need to be cared for as a child and to have a secure income as an adult.

3. *Belongingness and love*, such as the need to be part of groups and to participate in affectionate sexual and nonsexual relationships.

4. *Esteem*, such as the need to be respected as a useful, honorable individual.

5. *Self-actualization*, which means reaching one's full potential. People motivated by this need explore and enhance relationships with others; follow interests for intrinsic pleasure rather than for money, status, or esteem; and are concerned with issues affecting all people, not just themselves.

Maslow's hierarchy has been very influential over the years, partly because the needs associated with basic survival and security do generally take precedence over those related to self-enhancement or personal growth (Baumeister & Leary, 1995; Oishi et al., 1999). But critics see the hierarchy as too simplistic (Hall, Lindzey, & Campbell, 1998; Kenrick et al., 2010; Neher, 1991). It doesn't predict or explain, for example, the motivation of people who starve themselves to draw attention to political or moral causes. Further, people may not have to satisfy one kind of need before addressing others; we can seek to satisfy several needs at once. Finally, the ordering of needs within the survival/security and enhancement/growth categories differs from culture to culture, suggesting that there may not be a single, universal hierarchy of needs.

To address some of the problems in Maslow's theory, Clayton Alderfer (1969) proposed *existence, relatedness, growth (ERG) theory,* which places human needs into just three categories: *existence needs* (such as for food and water), *relatedness needs* (e.g., for social interactions and attachments), and *growth needs* (such as for developing one's capabilities). Unlike Maslow, Alderfer doesn't propose that needs must be satisfied in a particular order. Instead, he sees needs in each category as rising and falling from time to time and situation to situation. When a need in one area is fulfilled (or even if it is frustrated), a person will be motivated to pursue some other needs. For example, if a breakup frustrates relatedness needs, a person might focus on existence or growth needs by eating more or volunteering to work late.

CONFLICTING MOTIVES AND STRESS

As in the case of hunger strikes, in which the desire to promote a cause is pitted against the desire to eat, human motives sometimes conflict. The usual result is some degree of discomfort. For example, imagine that you are alone and bored on a Saturday night and you think about going out for a snack. What are your motives? Hunger might play a part, and so might the prospect of the increased physiological arousal that a change of scene will provide. Even sexual motivation might be involved, as you consider the chances of meeting someone exciting in the convenience store. But safety-related motives may also kick in: Is your neighborhood safe enough to go out alone? An esteem motive might come into play, too, making you hesitate to be seen on your own on a weekend night (Krieglmeyer et al., 2010).

These are just a few of the motives that may shape even a trivial decision. When the decision is more important, the number and strength of motivational pushes and pulls are often greater, creating far more internal conflict and indecision. There are four basic types of motivational conflicts (Elliot, 2008; Miller, 1959):

1. **Approach-approach conflicts.** When we must choose only one of two desirable activities—say, going to a movie or to a concert—an *approach-approach conflict* exists.

2. **Avoidance-avoidance conflicts.** An *avoidance-avoidance conflict* arises when we must select one of two undesirable alternatives. Someone forced either to sell the family home or to declare bankruptcy faces an avoidance-avoidance conflict.

3. **Approach-avoidance conflicts.** If someone you dislike had tickets to your favorite group's sold-out concert and invited you to come along, what would you do? When a particular event or activity has both attractive and unattractive features, an *approach-avoidance conflict* is created.

4. **Multiple approach-avoidance conflicts.** Suppose you must choose between two jobs. One offers a high salary in a well-known company but requires long work hours and moving to a miserable climate. The other boasts advancement opportunities, fringe benefits, and a better climate, but doesn't pay as much and requires an unpredictable work schedule. This is an example of a *multiple approach-avoidance conflict,* in which two

A Stressful Conflict

TRY THIS   Think back to when you were deciding which college to attend. Was the decision easy and obvious or did it create a motivational conflict? If there was a conflict, was it an approach-approach, approach-avoidance, or multiple approach-avoidance conflict? What factors were most important in deciding how to resolve the conflict, and what emotions and signs of stress did you experience during and after the decision-making process?

PhotosIndia.com LLC/Alamy

(continued)

or more alternatives each have both positive and negative features. Such conflicts are the most difficult to resolve, partly because the features of each option may not be easy to compare. For example, how many dollars a year does it take to compensate you for living in a bad climate?

The difficulties associated with resolving each of these conflicts can create stress, a topic explored in the chapter on health, stress, and coping (Krosch, Figner, & Weber, 2012). During motivational conflicts, people are often tense, irritable, and more vulnerable than usual to physical and psychological problems. These reactions are especially likely when no choice is obviously "right," when varying motives have approximately equal strength, and when a choice can have serious consequences (as in decisions about marrying, splitting up, or placing an elderly parent in a nursing home). Some people may spend a long time agonizing over these conflicts, whereas others may make a choice quickly, impulsively, and thoughtlessly, simply to end the discomfort of uncertainty. Even after resolving the conflict on the basis of careful thought, people may continue to experience stress responses, such as worrying about whether they made the right decision or blaming themselves for bad choices. These and other consequences of conflicting motives sometimes lead to depression or other serious disorders.

The emotions associated with motivational conflicts provide just one example of the close links between motivation and emotions. Motivation can intensify emotions, as when hunger leads a normally calm person to angrily complain about slow service at a restaurant. But emotions can also create motivation. Happiness, for example, is an emotion that people want to feel (e.g., Bryant & Veroff, 2006), so they engage in whatever behaviors—studying, artwork, investing, beachcombing—they think will achieve it. Similarly, as an emotion that most people want to avoid, anxiety motivates many behaviors, from leaving the scene of an accident to staying away from poisonous snakes. But sometimes, as when facing a stressful job interview or agreeing to a painful medical procedure, people are motivated to endure anxiety or other unpleasant emotions because they believe that doing so will eventually lead to a desired goal (Tamir, 2009). Let's take a closer look at emotions.

THE NATURE OF EMOTIONS

How do feelings differ from thoughts?

Everyone seems to agree that joy, sorrow, anger, fear, love, and hate are emotions. However, it is often hard to identify the shared features that make these experiences emotions rather than, say, thoughts or impulses.

Defining Characteristics and Dimensions

Most psychologists in Western cultures tend to see emotions as organized psychological and physiological reactions to significant life events (Izard, 1993). These reactions are partly private, or *subjective*, experiences and partly measurable patterns of behavior and physiological arousal. The subjective experience of emotions has several characteristics:

1.   Emotions are usually *temporary*. In other words, they tend to have relatively clear beginnings and ends and a relatively short duration. Moods, by contrast, tend to last longer.

2.   Emotions can feel *positive*, as in joy, or *negative*, as in sadness. They can also be a mixture of both, as in the bittersweet feelings of watching one's child leave for the first day of kindergarten (Larsen et al., 2004).

3.   Emotions vary in intensity. You can feel pleased, happy, or ecstatic. You can also feel mildly disappointed, sad, or deeply depressed (Shidlovski & Hassin, 2011).

Winners and Losers

Emotional experiences depend in part on our interpretation of situations and how those situations relate to our goals. A single event—the announcement of the results of this wrestling match—triggered drastically different emotional reactions in the contestants, depending on whether they perceived it as making them the winner or the loser.

Dimitri Iundt/TempSport/Corbis Sports/Corbis

4. Emotion is triggered partly by thoughts, especially by a *mental assessment* of how a situation relates to your goals. The same event can bring on different emotions depending on what it means to you. An exam score of 75 percent may thrill you if your best previous score had been 50 percent, but it may upset you if you had never before scored below 90 percent.

5. Emotion *alters thought processes,* often by directing attention toward some things and away from others. Negative emotions tend to narrow attention, and positive emotions tend to broaden it (Ford et al., 2010; Fredrickson et al., 2008). Anxiety about terrorism, for example, narrows our attention to focus on potential threats in airports and other public places (e.g., Nobata, Hakoda, & Ninose, 2010).

6. Emotion brings on an *action tendency,* a motivation to behave in certain ways. Grieving parents' anger, for example, might motivate them to try to harm their child's killer. But for other parents, grief might lead them to form an organization dedicated to preventing similar crimes and bringing more criminals to justice.

7. Emotional experiences are *passions* that you feel, whether you want to or not. You have some control over emotions, though, because they depend partly on how you view situations (Gross, 2001). For example, you can reduce your emotional reaction to a car accident by reminding yourself that no one was hurt and that you are insured. Still, you can't just *decide* to have an emotion; instead, you "fall in love" or "explode in anger" or are "overcome by grief."

In other words, the subjective aspects of emotions are experiences that are both triggered by the thinking self and felt as happening to the self. The extent to which we are "victims" of our passions versus rational controllers of our emotions is a central dilemma of human existence.

The objectively measurable aspects of emotions include learned and innate *expressive displays* and *physiological responses.* Expressive displays—such as a smile or a frown—communicate feelings to others. Physiological responses—changes in heart rate, for example—provide the biological adjustments needed to perform actions generated by the emotional experience. If you throw a temper tantrum, for instance, your heart must deliver additional oxygen and fuel to your muscles.

In summary, **emotions** are temporary experiences with positive, negative, or mixed qualities (Larsen & Green, 2013). People experience emotions with varying intensity as

emotions Temporary positive or negative experiences that are felt as happening to the self, that are generated partly by interpretation of situations, and that are accompanied by learned and innate physical responses.

happening to the self, generated in part by a mental assessment of situations, and accompanied by both learned and innate physical responses. Through emotions, whether they mean to or not, people communicate their internal states and intentions to others. Emotions often disrupt thinking and behavior, but they also trigger and guide thinking and organize, motivate, and sustain behavior and social relations (Izard, 2007).

Where do our emotions come from? There are two main sources: our biology and our thoughts. Let's consider what psychologists have discovered about how these sources operate, separately and together, to create emotional experiences.

The Biology of Emotions

The biological systems described in the chapter on biological aspects of psychology play a major role in emotions. In the *central nervous system,* numerous brain areas are involved in generating emotions as well as in our experience of those emotions (Wilson-Mendenhall, Barrett, & Barsalou, 2013). The *autonomic nervous system* gives rise to many of the physiological changes associated with emotional arousal.

Brain Mechanisms

Three main principles describe how brain processes contribute to emotions. First, activity in the *limbic system,* especially in the *amygdala,* is central to emotions (Kensinger & Corkin, 2004; Phelps & LeDoux, 2005). Normal functioning in the amygdala appears critical to the ability to learn emotional associations, recognize emotional expressions, detect personally relevant information, and perceive emotionally charged words (e.g., Cunningham & Brosch, 2012). For example, victims of a disease that destroys only the amygdala are unable to judge other people's emotional states by looking at their faces (Adolphs, Tranel, & Damasio, 1998).

TRY THIS
A second aspect of the brain's involvement in emotions is seen in its control over our emotional and nonemotional facial expressions (Rinn, 1984; Szameitat et al., 2010). Take a moment to look in a mirror, and put on your best fake smile. The voluntary facial movements you just made, like all voluntary movements, are controlled by the brain's *pyramidal motor system,* a system that includes the motor cortex. However, a smile that expresses genuine happiness is involuntary. That kind of smile, like the other facial movements associated with emotions, is governed by the *extrapyramidal motor system,* which depends on areas beneath the cortex. Brain damage can disrupt either system. People with pyramidal motor system damage show normal facial expressions during genuine emotion, but they cannot fake a smile. In contrast, people with damage to the extrapyramidal system can pose facial expressions at will, but they may remain straight-faced even when feeling genuine joy or profound sadness (Hopf, Muller, & Hopf, 1992).

A third aspect of the brain's role in emotions is revealed by research on the two sides, or hemispheres, of the cerebral cortex. For example, after suffering damage to the right, but not the left, hemisphere, people no longer laugh at jokes, even though they can still understand their words, the logic (or illogic) underlying them, and their punch lines (Critchley, 1991). Further, when people are asked to name the emotions shown in slides of facial expressions, blood flow increases in the right hemisphere more than in the left hemisphere (Gur, Skolnic, & Gur, 1994). But smiling while experiencing a positive emotion is correlated with greater activity in the *left* side of the brain (Davidson et al., 1990). When an area of one patient's left hemisphere was stimulated, she began to smile, then laugh (Fried et al., 1998). She attributed her emotional expression to the situation ("You guys are just so funny … standing around"). Similarly, brain-imaging studies conducted while sports fans watched their favorite team in action have revealed greater activation in the left hemisphere when the team is winning and more activation in the right hemisphere when the team is losing (Park et al., 2009). And there's evidence that the experience of anger or depression is associated with greater brain activity on the right side than on the left (Carver & Harmon-Jones, 2009; Herrington et al., 2010).

The fact that different brain areas appear to be involved in displaying and experiencing positive and negative emotions (e.g., Harmon-Jones, 2004) makes it difficult to map the exact roles the two hemispheres play in emotion. Generally, however, most aspects of emotions—the experiencing of negative emotion, the perception of any emotion exhibited in faces or other stimuli, and the facial expression of any emotion—depend more on the right hemisphere than on the left (Heller, Nitschke, & Miller, 1998; Kawasaki et al., 2001).

If the right hemisphere is relatively dominant in emotions, which side of the face would you expect to be somewhat more involved in expressing emotions? If you said the left side, you are correct, because, as described in the chapter on biological aspects of psychology, movements of each side of the body are controlled by the opposite side of the brain.

Mechanisms of the Autonomic Nervous System

The autonomic nervous system (ANS) triggers many of the physiological changes that go with emotions (Vernet, Robin, & Dittmar, 1995; see Figure 10.5). If your hands get cold and clammy when you are nervous, it is because the ANS has increased perspiration and decreased the blood flow in your hands.

As described in the chapter on biological aspects of psychology, the ANS carries information between the brain and most body organs—the heart and blood vessels, the digestive system, and so on. Each of these organs is active on its own, but input from the

FIGURE 10.5
The Autonomic Nervous System

TRY THIS Emotional responses involve activation of the autonomic nervous system, which is organized into sympathetic and parasympathetic subsystems. Which of the bodily responses shown here do you associate with emotional experiences?

Peter Kindersley/Stockbyte/Getty Images

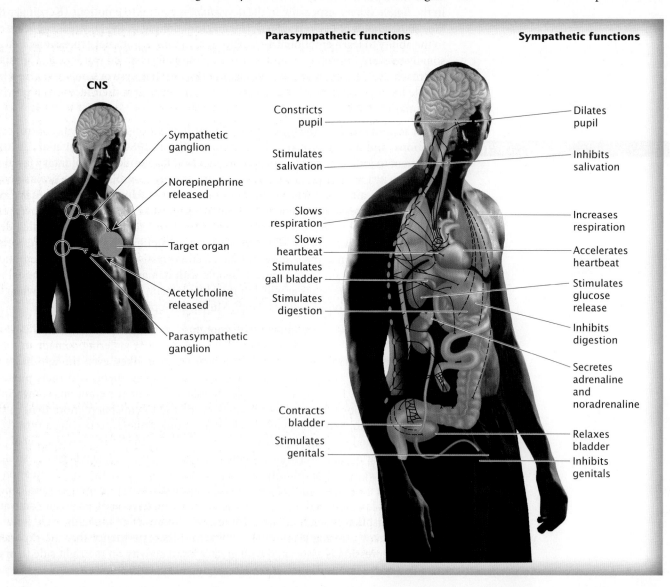

ANS can increase or decrease that activity. By doing so, the ANS coordinates the functioning of these organs to meet the body's general needs and prepare the body for change (Porges, Doussard, & Maita, 1995). If you are aroused to take action, such as running to catch a bus, you need more glucose to fuel your muscles. The ANS frees needed energy by stimulating the secretion of glucose-generating hormones and promoting blood flow to the muscles.

Figure 10.5 shows that the autonomic nervous system is organized into two parts: the sympathetic nervous system and the parasympathetic nervous system. Emotions can activate either part, both of which send axon fibers to each organ in the body. Generally, the sympathetic and parasympathetic fibers have opposite effects on these *target organs*. Axons from the **parasympathetic nervous system** release the neurotransmitter *acetylcholine* onto target organs, leading to activity related to the protection, nourishment, and growth of the body. Axons from the **sympathetic nervous system** release a different neurotransmitter, *norepinephrine*, onto target organs, helping prepare the body for vigorous activity. When one part of the sympathetic system is stimulated, other parts are activated "in sympathy" with it (Gellhorn & Loofbourrow, 1963). The result is the **fight-flight reaction** (also called the **fight-or-flight syndrome**), a pattern of increased heart rate and blood pressure, rapid or irregular breathing, dilated pupils, perspiration, dry mouth, increased blood sugar, "goose bumps," and other changes that help prepare the body to confront or run from a threat.

You cannot consciously experience the brain mechanisms that alter the activity of your autonomic nervous system. This is why most people cannot exert direct, conscious control over blood pressure or other aspects of ANS activity. However, you can do things that have indirect effects on the ANS. For example, to create autonomic arousal of your sex organs, you might imagine an erotic situation. To raise your blood pressure, you might hold your breath or strain your muscles. And to lower your blood pressure, you can lie down, relax, and think calming thoughts.

THEORIES OF EMOTION

Are emotions in the heart, in the head, or both?

Are the physiological responses associated with emotions enough to create an emotional experience? Or are those responses the *result* of emotional experiences that begin in the brain? And how do our mental interpretations of events affect our emotional reactions to them? For over a century now, psychologists have worked to answer these questions. In the process, they developed a number of theories that explain emotions mainly in terms of biological or cognitive factors. The main biological theories are those of William James and Walter Cannon. The most prominent cognitive theories are those of Stanley Schachter and Richard Lazarus. Let's review these theories, along with some research designed to evaluate them.

James's Peripheral Theory

Suppose you are camping in the woods when a huge bear wanders into camp. You might be afraid and run for your life, but would you run because you're afraid or are you afraid because you run? This was the example and question posed by William James, one of the first psychologists to offer a formal account of how physiological responses relate to emotional experience. He argued that you are afraid because you run. Your running and the physiological responses associated with it, he said, follow directly from your perception of the bear.

At first, James's claim sounds ridiculous; it would be silly to run from something unless you already feared it. James concluded otherwise after examining his own mental processes. He felt that once you strip away all physiological responses—such as changes in heart rate, breathing, and other peripheral nervous system activity—nothing remains of

parasympathetic nervous system The subsystem of the autonomic nervous system that typically influences activity related to the protection, nourishment, and growth of the body.

sympathetic nervous system The subsystem of the autonomic nervous system that readies the body for vigorous activity.

fight-flight reaction (fight-or-flight syndrome) Physical reactions triggered by the sympathetic nervous system that prepare the body to fight or flee a threatening situation.

an emotion's experience (James, 1890). Without these responses, he said, you would feel no fear, because it is the experiencing of physiological responses that creates fear and other emotions. The same argument was made by Carle Lange, a Danish physician, so James's view is sometimes called the *James-Lange theory* of emotion. It is also known as a *peripheral theory* of emotion, because it emphasizes activity in the peripheral nervous system, not in the central nervous system, as the main cause of emotional experience.

Observing Peripheral Responses

According to James, the first step in the creation of an emotional experience occurs when perception affects the cerebral cortex. The brain interprets a situation and automatically directs a unique set of physiological changes, such as increased heart rate, sinking stomach, perspiration, and certain patterns of blood flow. It is the act of being *aware* of this pattern of bodily changes, said James, that constitutes the experience of an emotion. According to this view, each particular emotion is created by a particular pattern of physiological responses.

Notice that according to James's theory, emotional experience is not generated by the brain alone. There is no special "emotion center" in the brain where neuron activity directly creates an experience of emotion. If this theory is accurate, it might account for the difficulty we sometimes have in knowing our true feelings: we must figure out what emotions we feel by perceiving small differences in specific physiological response patterns (Katkin, Wiens, & Öhman, 2001).

Evaluating James's Theory

Indeed, certain emotional states are associated with particular patterns of autonomic changes (e.g., Damasio et al., 2000; Dunn et al., 2010; Harrison et al., 2010). For example, blood flow to the hands and feet increases in anger and decreases with fear (Levenson, Ekman, & Friesen, 1990). Thus fear truly does involve "cold feet"; anger does not. When we feel disgust, there is increased muscle activity but no change in heart rate. Differing patterns of autonomic activity occur even when people just mentally relive emotional experiences (Ekman, Levenson, & Friesen, 1983). These emotion-specific patterns of physiological activity occur in widely different cultures (Levenson et al., 1992). Further, people who are more keenly aware of physiological changes in their bodies are likely to experience emotions more intensely than those who are less aware of such changes (Schneider, Ring, & Katkin, 1998; Wiens, Mezzacappa, & Katkin, 2000). It may even be that the "gut feelings" that cause us to approach or avoid certain situations might come from physiological changes that we perceive without conscious awareness (Katkin, Wiens, & Öhman, 2001; Winkielman & Berridge, 2004).

Different patterns of autonomic activity are also related to specific emotional facial expressions. In one study, research participants were told to make a series of facial movements that, when combined, would create the appearance of sadness, fear, happiness, anger, or some other emotion (Levenson, Ekman, & Friesen, 1990). Making these movements led to autonomic changes that resembled those normally accompanying emotions. Also, almost all participants reported feeling the emotion associated with the expression they created, even though they couldn't see their own expressions and didn't realize that they had made an "emotional" face.

Do You Feel It, Too?

Other studies have confirmed these results (Schnall & Laird, 2003) and have also shown that emotional feelings can be eased by relaxing facial muscles (Duclos & Laird, 2001). Even our ability to understand emotional information seems to be due in part to the facial movements we make in response to that information. For example, when people's faces are immobilized by injections of botulinum toxin-A (Botox) they find it more difficult to understand the meaning of emotional reading material (Havas et al., 2010).

A variation on James's theory, called the *facial feedback hypothesis,* suggests that facial movements provide enough information to cause an emotional feeling (Ekman & Davidson, 1993). If so, it might explain why posed facial expressions create the emotions normally associated with them. Try taking advantage of this notion yourself. The next time you want to cheer yourself up, it might help to smile—even though you don't feel like it (Fleeson, Malanos, & Achille, 2002)! And be aware that even unintentional facial expressions may trigger an emotion. For example, the involuntary frown caused by the brightness of the sun has been shown to make people feel more aggressive (Marzoli et al., 2013).

Lie Detection

The idea that different patterns of physiological activity are associated with different emotions forms the basis for most lie detection techniques. If people experience anxiety or guilt when they lie, specific patterns of autonomic physiological activity accompanying these emotions should be detectable on instruments, called *polygraphs,* that record heart rate, breathing rate, and perspiration (Granhag & Stromwall, 2004; Iacono & Patrick, 2006).

To identify the perpetrator of a crime using the *control question test,* a polygraph tester might ask questions specific to the crime, such as "Did you stab someone on May 31, 2014?" Responses to such *relevant questions* are then compared with responses to *control questions,* such as "Have you ever lied to get out of trouble?" Innocent people might have lied at some time in the past and might feel guilty when asked about it, but they should have no reason to feel guilty about what they did on May 31, 2014. Accordingly, an innocent person should have a stronger emotional response to control questions than to relevant questions (Rosenfeld, 1995). Another approach, called the *directed lie test,* compares a person's physiological reactions when asked to lie about something and when telling what is known to be the truth. Finally, the *guilty knowledge test* seeks to determine whether a person reacts in a notable way to information about a crime that only the guilty party would know (Ben-Shakhar, Bar-Hillel, & Kremnitzer, 2002).

Most people have emotional responses when they lie, but the accuracy of polygraphs is not perfect. Some studies suggest that polygraphs detect 90 percent of lying individuals (e.g., Gamer et al., 2006; Honts & Quick, 1995), while others find that polygraphs mislabel up to 40 percent of truthful people as guilty liars (Ben-Shakhar & Furedy, 1990; Saxe & Ben-Shakhar, 1999). The inconsistency occurs partly because polygraph results are not just based on whether a person is truthful. What people think about the act of lying and about the value of the test can also matter. For example, people who believe that lying is ok and who don't trust polygraphs are not likely to have emotion-linked physiological responses while lying during the test. However, an innocent person who believes in such tests and who thinks that "everything always goes wrong" might show a large fear response when asked about a crime, thus wrongly indicating "guilt" (Lykken, 1998b).

So although polygraphs do catch some liars, most agree that a guilty person can "fool" a polygraph lie detector and that some innocent people can be mislabeled as guilty (Ruscio, 2005). After reviewing the relevant research literature, a panel of distinguished psychologists and other scientists in the United States expressed serious reservations about the value of polygraph tests in detecting deception and argued against their use as evidence in court or in employee screening and selection (Committee to Review the Scientific Evidence on the Polygraph, 2003). Scientists are working on several alternative lie-detecting techniques, including those that focus on brain activity, impose high cognitive demands during interrogation interviews, spring surprising questions, or ask people to draw pictures about their experiences. Such alternative measures do not depend on a link between deception and autonomic nervous system responses (Farah et al., 2014; Langelben & Moriarty, 2013; ten Brink, Stimson, & Carney, 2014).

Searching for the Truth

Polygraph tests have limited accuracy, and so do the alternative lie detection methods designed to improve on them (Ganis et al., 2011; Porter & Brinke, 2010). However, they may intimidate people who believe that they are foolproof. In one small town police station, which had no polygraph, a burglar confessed to his crime when a kitchen colander was placed on his head and attached by wires to a copy machine (Shepherd, Kohut, & Sweet, 1989).

Guy Bell/Alamy

Cannon's Central Theory

James said that the experience of emotions depends on feedback from physiological responses occurring outside the brain, but Walter Cannon disagreed (Cannon, 1927).

According to Cannon, you feel fear at the sight of a wild bear even before you start to run because, he argued, emotional experience starts in the brain.

According to Cannon's *central theory* of emotions (called the *Cannon-Bard theory*, in recognition of Philip Bard's contribution), information about emotional situations goes first to the thalamus. The thalamus then sends signals to the autonomic nervous system and—at the same time—to the cerebral cortex, where emotion becomes conscious. So when you see a bear, the brain receives sensory information about it, interprets that information as a bear, and then creates the experience of fear while at the same time sending messages to your heart, lungs, and legs to get you out of the situation. According to Cannon's theory, then, there is a *direct* experience of emotion in the central nervous system, whether or not the brain receives feedback about responses in other parts of the body.

Updating Cannon's Theory

Research after Cannon's time showed that the thalamus is not the "seat" of emotion, as he had suggested. Still, the thalamus does participate in emotional processing (Lang, 1995). For example, studies of humans and laboratory animals show that the emotion of fear can be generated by connections from the thalamus to the amygdala (Anderson & Phelps, 2000; LeDoux, 1995). The implication is that strong emotions can bypass the cortex without requiring conscious thought to activate them. This process may explain why it is so difficult to overcome an intense fear, or phobia, even if we consciously know the fear is irrational.

An updated version of Cannon's theory suggests that activity in certain brain areas is experienced as either enjoyable or aversive, and produces the pleasure or discomfort of emotion. In humans, these areas connect extensively throughout the brain (Fossati et al., 2003). As a result, representation of emotions in the brain probably involves widely distributed neural circuits, not a narrowly localized emotion "center" (Derryberry & Tucker, 1992; West et al., 2010).

Cognitive Theories of Emotion

Suppose you are about to be interviewed for your first job or go out on a blind date or take your first ride in a hot-air balloon. In such situations, it is not always easy to be sure of what you are feeling. Is it fear, excitement, anticipation, worry, happiness, dread, or what? Stanley Schachter suggested that the emotions we experience are shaped partly by how we interpret the arousal we feel. His cognitive theory of emotions is known as the *Schachter-Singer theory* in recognition of the contributions of Jerome Singer. The theory took shape in the early 1960s, when many psychologists were questioning the validity of James's theory of emotion. Schachter argued that the theory was essentially correct but needed a few modifications (Cornelius, 1996).

According to the Schachter-Singer theory, emotions result from a combination of feedback from the body's responses and our interpretation of what caused those responses. So cognitive interpretation comes into play twice: first, when you perceive the situation that leads to bodily responses and second, when you interpret those responses as a particular emotion. Schachter said that a given pattern of physiological responses can be interpreted in many different ways and so might yield many different emotions. According to Schachter, then, the emotion you experience when that bear approaches your campsite might be fear, excitement, astonishment, or surprise, depending on how you label your bodily reactions (Schachter & Singer, 1962).

Schachter also argued that how we label arousal depends on **attribution**, or what we think caused an event. We attribute our physiological arousal to different emotions depending on the information we have about the situation. For example, if you watch the final seconds of a close ball game, you might attribute your racing heart, rapid breathing, and perspiration to excitement. But you might attribute the same physiological reactions to anxiety if you are waiting for a big exam to begin. Schachter predicted that our emotional

attribution The process of explaining the cause of some event.

Labeling Arousal

Schachter's cognitive theory of emotion predicts that these people will attribute their physiological arousal to the game they are watching and will label their emotion as "excitement." Further, as described in the chapter on health, stress, and coping, the emotions they experience will also depend partly on their cognitive interpretation of the outcome (Lazarus & Folkman, 1984). Those who see their team's defeat as a disaster will experience more negative emotions than those who think of it as a challenge to improve.

ZUMA Press/ZUMAPRESS/Newscom

experiences will be less intense if we attribute arousal to a nonemotional cause. So if you notice your heart pounding before an exam but say to yourself, "Sure my heart's pounding—I just drank five cups of coffee!" then you should feel "wired" from caffeine but not afraid or worried. This prediction has received some support (Mezzacappa, Katkin, & Palmer, 1999; Sinclair et al., 1994), but other aspects of Schachter's theory have not.

Few researchers today fully accept the Schachter-Singer theory, but it did stimulate an enormous amount of research, including research on **excitation transfer theory**. This theory focuses on a phenomenon in which physiological arousal from one experience carries over to affect emotions in a new situation (Eskine, Kacinik, & Prinz, 2012; Reisenzein, 1983; Zillmann, 1984). For example, people who have been aroused by physical exercise become angrier when provoked and experience more intense sexual feelings around an attractive person than do people who have been less physically active (Allen et al., 1989). Physiological arousal from fear, like arousal from exercise, can also enhance emotions, including sexual feelings. One study of this transfer took place in Canada, near a deep river gorge. The gorge could be crossed either by a shaky, swinging bridge or by a more stable wooden structure. A female researcher asked men who had just crossed each bridge to respond to a questionnaire that included pictures from the TAT, the projective test described in Figure 10.3. The amount of sexual content in the stories these men wrote about the pictures was much higher among those who met the woman after crossing the more dangerous bridge compared to those who had crossed the stable bridge. Furthermore, they were more likely to rate the researcher as attractive and to attempt to contact her afterward (Dutton & Aron, 1974). When the person giving out the questionnaire was a male, however, the type of bridge crossed had no impact on sexual imagery. You might be wondering whether the men who crossed the dangerous bridge were simply more adventurous than other men regarding both bridge crossing and heterosexual encounters. To check this possibility, the researchers repeated the study, but with one change. This time, the woman approached the men farther down the trail, long after physiological arousal from the bridge crossing had subsided. Now the apparently adventurous men were no more likely than others to rate the woman as attractive. So it was probably excitation transfer, not differing amounts of adventurousness, that produced the original result.

Schachter focused on the way we interpret our bodily responses to events. Other cognitive theorists have argued that it is our interpretations of the events themselves that are most important in shaping emotional experiences. For example, as we mentioned earlier, a person's emotional reaction to receiving exam results can depend partly on whether the score is seen as a sign of improvement or as a disaster. According to Richard Lazarus's (1966, 1991) *cognitive appraisal theory* of emotion, these differing reactions can be best explained by how we think exam scores, job interviews, blind dates, bear sightings, and other events will affect our personal well-being. According to Lazarus, the process of cognitive appraisal, or evaluation, begins when we decide whether an event matters to us; that is, do we even care about it? If we don't, as might be the case when an exam doesn't count toward our grade, we are unlikely to have an emotional experience when we get the results. If the event is relevant to our health, well-being, status, self-esteem, goals, or finances (or those of a loved one) we will probably have a significant emotional reaction to it. That reaction will be positive or negative, said Lazarus, depending on whether we interpret the event as advancing our personal goals or as threatening to harm us or block our progress. The *specific* emotion we experience depends on our individual goals, needs, personal and cultural standards, expectations, and experiences. As a result, a second-place finisher in a marathon race might experience bitter disappointment at having "lost," whereas someone at the back of the pack may be thrilled just to have completed the race.

excitation transfer theory The theory that physiological arousal stemming from one situation is carried over to and enhances emotional experience in an independent situation.

More recently, researchers have developed cognitive theories of emotion that depart from Schachter's in some new directions. In the *conceptual act model* of emotion, for instance, *core affect*—pleasant or unpleasant feelings—is distinguished from *emotion*. According to this model, emotion results when we impose on a feeling a *category label* (e.g., guilt, shame, anger, or resentment) that our cultural and language training has taught us to use (Barrett & Kensinger, 2010; Barrett, Mesquita, & Gendron, 2011). For instance, if you succeed at an important task and attribute the success to your own efforts, then you'll likely feel pride. But, if you attribute that same success to the help of another person, then you'll more likely feel gratitude. Similarly, if you fail at an important task and attribute your failure to your own mistakes or lack of effort, then you'll probably feel guilt or shame. If you attribute that same failure to the interference of another person, then you are more likely to feel anger. Models like this one are valuable because they incorporate research on language and culture in an effort to better understand the labeling processes involved in human emotional experience.

"In Review: Theories of Emotion" summarizes key elements of the theories we have discussed. Research on these theories suggests that both bodily responses (including facial responses) and the cognitive interpretation of those responses add to emotional experience. So does cognitive appraisal of events themselves. In addition, the brain can apparently generate emotional experience independent of physiological arousal. So emotions are probably both in the heart and in the head (including the face). Some basic emotions—fear and anger, for example—probably occur directly within the brain, whereas the many more complex shades of emotions—such as hope, pride, shame, guilt, and disappointment—probably arise from attributions, categorization, and other cognitive interpretations of physiological responses (Barrett et al., 2013; Dębiec & LeDoux, 2009).

THEORIES OF EMOTIONS
IN REVIEW

Theory	Source of Emotions	Example
James-Lange	Emotions are created by awareness of specific patterns of peripheral (autonomic) responses.	Anger is associated with increased blood flow in the hands and feet; fear is associated with decreased blood flow in these areas.
Cannon-Bard	The brain generates direct experiences of emotions.	Stimulation of certain brain areas can create pleasant or unpleasant emotions.
Cognitive (Schachter-Singer, Lazarus)	Cognitive interpretation of events and of physiological reactions to events shapes emotional experiences.	Autonomic arousal can be experienced as anxiety or excitement, depending on how it is labeled. A single event can lead to different emotions, depending on whether it is perceived as threatening or challenging.

In Review Questions

1. Research showing that there are pleasure centers in the brain has been cited in support of the _____ theory of emotions.

2. The use of polygraphs in lie detection is based on the _____ theory of emotions.

3. The process of attribution is most important to _____ theories of emotions.

COMMUNICATING EMOTION

Which emotional expressions are innate and which are learned?

So far, we have described emotions and how people experience them. Let's now consider how people communicate emotions to one another.

One way they do this is, of course, through words. Some people describe their feelings relatively simply, and mainly in terms of pleasantness or unpleasantness; others include information about the intensity of their emotions (Barrett et al., 2001, 2007). In general, women are more likely than men to talk about their emotions and the complexity of their feelings (Barrett et al., 2000). Humans also communicate emotion through touch (Thompson & Hampton, 2011), body movement and posture (de Gelder et al., 2004; Hadjikhani & de Gelder, 2003), tone of voice (Simon-Thomas et al., 2009), and especially through facial movements and expressions.

Imagine a woman watching television. You can see her face but not what she sees on the screen. She might be deep in complex thought, perhaps comparing her investment decisions with those of the experts being interviewed on CNBC. Or she might be thinking of nothing at all as she loses herself in a rerun of *CSI*. In other words, you can't tell much about what she is thinking just by looking at her. But if the TV program creates an emotional experience, you will be able to make a reasonably accurate guess about which emotion she is feeling based on her facial expressions. The human face can create thousands of different expressions, and people—especially females—are good at detecting them (McClure, 2000; Rennels & Cummings, 2013; Zajonc, 1998). Observers can see even very small facial movements: a twitch of the mouth can carry a lot of information (Ambadar, Schooler, & Cohn, 2005; Ekman, 2009). Are emotional facial expressions innate or are they learned? And how are they used in communicating emotion?

Innate Expressions of Emotion

Charles Darwin noticed that some facial expressions seem to be universal (Darwin, 1872). He proposed that these expressions are genetically determined, passed on biologically from one generation to the next. The facial expressions seen today, said Darwin, are those that have been most effective over the centuries for telling others something about how a person is feeling, and thus what they are likely to say and do next (Shariff & Tracey, 2011). If someone is scowling with teeth clenched, for example, you will probably assume that the person is angry, and you won't choose that particular moment to ask for a loan (Marsh, Ambady, & Kleck, 2005).

Infants provide one source of evidence that some facial expressions are innate. Newborns do not have to be taught to grimace in pain, to smile in pleasure, or to blink when startled (Balaban, 1995). Even blind infants, who cannot imitate adults' expressions, show the same emotional expressions as do sighted infants (Goodenough, 1932). These emotional facial expressions help to provide caregivers with accurate information about babies' conditions and needs (Izard et al., 1980; Huebner & Izard, 1988).

Another line of evidence for innate facial expressions comes from studies showing that for the most basic emotions, people in all cultures show similar facial responses to similar emotional stimuli (Hejmadi, Davidson, & Rozin, 2000; Matsumoto & Willingham, 2006). Participants in these studies looked at photographs of people's faces and then tried to name the emotion each person was feeling. The pattern of facial movements we call a smile, for example, is universally related to positive emotions. Sadness is almost always accompanied by slackened muscle tone and a "long" face. Likewise, in almost all cultures, people contort their faces in a similar way when shown something they find disgusting. And a furrowed brow is frequently associated with frustration or unpleasantness (Ekman, 1994).

Anger is also linked with a facial expression recognized by almost all cultures. One study examined the ceremonial masks seen in eighteen Western and non-Western cultures

What Are They Feeling?

TRY THIS People's emotions are usually "written on their faces." Jot down what emotions you think these people are feeling, and then look at the answer shown at the bottom of page 370 to see how well you "read" their emotions.

AP Images/Ken Ruinard/Anderson Independent-Mail

The Universal Smile

The idea that some emotional expressions are inborn is supported by the fact that the facial movement pattern we call a smile is related to happiness, pleasure, and other positive emotions in cultures throughout the world.

Tom Cockrem/Lonely Planet Images/Getty Images; Craig Lovell/Photoshot

(Aronoff, Barclay, & Stevenson, 1988). In all these cultures, angry, threatening masks contained similar elements, such as triangular eyes and diagonal lines on the cheeks. In particular, angular and diagonal elements carry the impression of threat. "Scary" Halloween pumpkins tend to include these patterns, too.

Social and Cultural Influences on Emotional Expression

Not all basic emotional expressions are innate or universal (Ekman, 1993; Jack et al., 2012). Some are learned through contact with a particular culture, and all of them, even innate expressions, are flexible enough to change in certain social situations (Fernández-Dols & Ruiz-Belda, 1995; Merluzzi, 2014; Todorov & Porter, 2014). For example, facial expressions become more intense and change more frequently when people are imagining social scenes as opposed to solitary scenes (Fridlund et al., 1990). Similarly, facial expressions in response to odors tend to be more intense when others are watching than when people are alone (Jancke & Kaufmann, 1994).

Further, although some basic emotional facial expressions are recognized by all cultures (Hejmadi, Davidson, & Rozin, 2000), even these can be interpreted differently depending on body language and environmental cues (Gendron et al., 2014b). For example, research participants interpreted a particular expression as disgust when it appeared on the face of a person who was holding a dirty diaper, but that same expression was seen as anger when it was digitally superimposed on a person in a fighting stance (Aviezer et al., 2008).

There is a certain degree of cultural variation when it comes to recognizing some emotions (Kayyal & Russell, 2013; Russell, 1995). In one study, Japanese and North Americans agreed about which facial expressions signaled happiness, surprise, and sadness, but they frequently disagreed about which faces showed anger, disgust, and fear (Matsumoto & Ekman, 1989). Members of cultures such as the Fore of Papua New Guinea agree even less with people in Western cultures on the labeling of facial expressions (Russell, 1994). People from different cultures may also differ in the way they interpret emotions expressed by tone of voice, or by a combination of vocal and facial cues (Gendron et al., 2014a; Mesquita & Frijda, 1992; Tanaka et al., 2010). An example is provided by a study showing that Taiwanese participants were best at recognizing a sad tone of voice, whereas Dutch participants were best at recognizing happy tones (Van Bezooijen, Otto, & Heenan, 1983).

People learn how to express some emotions by following cultural rules. Suppose you say, "I just bought a new car," and your friends stick their tongues out at you. In North America, such a display may mean they are envious or resentful. But in some parts of China, it expresses surprise. Even smiles can vary as people learn to use them to communicate feelings. Paul Ekman and colleagues categorized seventeen types of smiles, including "false smiles," which fake enjoyment, and "masking smiles," which hide unhappiness. They named the smile that occurs with real happiness the *Duchenne smile* (pronounced "doo-SHEN"), after the French researcher who first noticed a difference between spontaneous, happy smiles and posed ones. A genuine Duchenne smile includes contractions of the muscles around the eyes (creating a distinctive skin wrinkle there) plus contractions of the muscles that raise the lips and cheeks. Few people can correctly mimic the muscle contractions around the eyes during a posed smile, so this feature can distinguish "lying smiles" from genuine ones (Frank, Ekman, & Friesen, 1993).

Learning about Emotions

The effects of learning are seen in a child's growing range of emotional expressions. Although infants begin with a set of innate emotional responses, they soon learn to imitate facial expressions and use them to express a wide range of emotions. In time, these expressions become more precise and personalized, so that a particular expression conveys a clear message to anyone who knows that person well.

The photo on page 369 shows the wife and daughter of a U.S. Army soldier waving goodbye as his unit departs for training prior to deployment in a war zone. Their emotions probably included sadness, anxiety, worry, dread, uncertainty, hope, and perhaps anger.

If facial expressions are too personalized, however, no one will know what the expressions mean and so they will not cause others to respond. Operant shaping, described in the chapter on learning, probably helps keep emotional expressions within certain limits. If you could not see other people's facial expressions or observe their responses to yours, you might show fewer, or less intense, facial signs of emotion. In fact, as congenitally blind people grow older, their facial expressions tend to become less animated (Izard, 1977; Matsumoto & Willingham, 2009).

As children grow, they learn an *emotion culture*—rules that govern what emotions are appropriate in what circumstances and what emotional expressions are allowed (Chen, Kennedy, & Zhou, 2012). These rules can vary between genders and from culture to culture (e.g., Matsumoto et al., 2005; Tsai, Levenson, & McCoy, 2006). For example, TV news cameras showed that men in the U.S. military being deployed to a war zone tended to keep their emotions in check as they said goodbye to wives, girlfriends, and parents. However, many male soldiers in Italy—where mother-son ties are particularly strong—wailed with dismay and wept openly as they left. In a laboratory study, when viewing a distressing movie with a group of peers, Japanese students exerted much more control over their facial expressions than did North American students. When they watched the film while alone, however, the Japanese students' faces showed the same emotional expressions as those of the North American students (Ekman, Friesen, & Ellsworth, 1972).

Emotion cultures shape how people describe and categorize feelings, resulting in both similarities and differences across cultures (Russell, 1991). At least five of the seven basic emotions listed in an ancient Chinese book called the *Li Chi*—joy, anger, sadness, fear, love, liking, and dislike—are considered primary emotions by most Western theorists. Yet even though English has more than five hundred emotion-related words, some emotion words in other languages have no English equivalent. Similarly, other cultures have no equivalent for some English emotion words.

Learning about emotions appears to be crucial to social development. Evidence from humans and rhesus monkeys suggests that impaired ability to recognize and imitate others' facial expressions is associated with poor social adjustment and, possibly, some forms of autistic spectrum disorder (e.g., Kothari et al., 2013; Poljac, Poljac, & Wagemans, 2013; Tseng et al., 2013).

Social Referencing

Facial expressions, tone of voice, body postures, and gestures can do more than communicate emotion. They can also influence other people's behavior, especially people who are not sure what to do (e.g., Blechert et al., 2012; Howell & Shepperd, 2012). An inexperienced chess player, for instance, might reach out to move the queen, catch sight of a spectator's pained expression, and infer that another move would be better. Poker players often rely on their opponents' telltale facial expressions for cues about whether to bet, and how much (Schlicht et al., 2010). The process of letting another person's emotional state guide our own behavior is called *social referencing* (Campos, 1980). This process begins early; even three-month-old infants will look in the direction in which an adult's eyes have moved (Hood, Willen, & Driver, 1998).

The visual-cliff studies described in the sensation and perception chapter have been used to create an uncertain situation for infants. To reach its mother, an infant in these experiments must cross the visual cliff. If the apparent drop-off is very small or very large, there is no doubt about what to do. One-year-olds crawl across in the first case and stay put in the second case. However, if the apparent drop-off is just large enough (say, two feet) to create uncertainty, the infant relies on its mother's facial expressions to decide what to do. In one study, mothers were asked to make either a fearful or a joyful face. When the mothers made a fearful face, no infant crossed the glass floor. But when they made a joyful face, most infants crossed (Sorce et al., 1981). This result showed the adaptive value of sending, and receiving, emotional communications.

LINKAGES

As noted in the introductory chapter, all psychology subfields are related to one another. Our discussion of motivational conflicts and stress illustrates just one way that the topic of this chapter, motivation and emotion, is linked to the subfield of health psychology, discussed in the chapter on health, stress, and coping. The Linkages diagram shows ties to two other subfields, and there are many more ties throughout the book. Looking for linkages among subfields will help you see how they fit together and help you better appreciate the big picture of psychology.

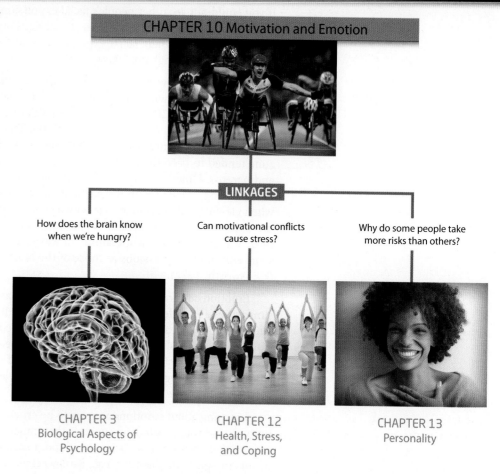

CHAPTER 10 Motivation and Emotion

LINKAGES

How does the brain know when we're hungry?

Can motivational conflicts cause stress?

Why do some people take more risks than others?

CHAPTER 3
Biological Aspects of Psychology

CHAPTER 12
Health, Stress, and Coping

CHAPTER 13
Personality

SUMMARY

Motivation refers to factors that influence the initiation, direction, intensity, and persistence of behavior. Emotions and motivation are often linked: motivation can influence emotions, and people are often motivated to seek certain emotions.

Concepts and Theories of Motivation

Where does motivation come from?

Focusing on a *motive* often reveals a single theme within apparently diverse behaviors. The many sources of motivation fall into five categories: physiological factors, needs, emotional factors, cognitive factors, and social factors.

An early argument held that motivation is based on *instinctive behaviors*—automatic, involuntary, and unlearned action patterns consistently "released" by particular stimuli. Modern versions of this *instinct doctrine* are seen in evolutionary accounts of helping, aggression, mate selection, and other aspects of social behavior. *Drive reduction theory* is based on *homeostasis*, a tendency to maintain equilibrium in a physical or behavioral process. When

disruption of equilibrium creates *needs* of some kind, people are motivated to reduce the resulting *drives* by behaving in some way that satisfies the needs and restores balance. *Primary drives* are unlearned; *secondary drives* are learned. According to the *arousal theory* of motivation, people are motivated to behave in ways that maintain a level of *physiological arousal* that is optimal for their functioning. Finally, *incentive theory* highlights behaviors that are motivated by attaining desired stimuli (positive incentives) and avoiding undesirable ones (negative incentives).

When behavior is based mainly on *intrinsic motivation*, it occurs simply for the pleasure and satisfaction that it brings. Behavior based mainly on *extrinsic motivation* is aimed at an external goal such as winning a prize or avoiding a penalty.

Hunger and Eating

What makes me start eating and stop eating?

Eating is controlled by a complex mixture of learning, culture, and biochemistry. The desire to eat *(hunger)* and the satisfaction (satiation) of that desire (satiety) that leads us to stop eating depend on signals from the gut and from blood-borne substances such as glucose, fatty acids, amino acids, insulin, and leptin. Activity in the ventromedial nucleus of the hypothalamus results in satiety, whereas activity in the lateral hypothalamus results in hunger. Other areas of the hypothalamus, such as the paraventricular nucleus, are also involved. Further, several neurotransmitters act in various regions of the hypothalamus to motivate the eating of certain types of foods. Eating may also be influenced by the flavor of food and by the pleasure it can bring. Food selection is influenced by many factors, including social contexts and cultural traditions.

Obesity has been linked to overconsumption of certain kinds of foods, low energy metabolism, genetic factors, and even viruses. People suffering from **anorexia nervosa** starve themselves. Those who suffer from **bulimia** engage in binge eating, followed by purging through self-induced vomiting or laxatives. Those with **binge eating disorder** engage in food binges, but do not purge.

Sexual Behavior

How often does the average person have sex?

Sexual motivation and behavior result from a rich interplay of biology and culture. Sexual stimulation produces a **sexual response cycle**, a predictable physiological pattern of **sexual arousal** before, during, and after sexual activity. **Sex hormones**, which include male hormones (**androgens**) and female hormones (**estrogens** and **progestational hormones**, or **progestins**), occur in different relative amounts in both sexes. They can have organizing effects, which create physical differences in the brain, and activating effects, which temporarily increase the desire for sex.

Gender-role learning, educational experiences, media influences, and family dynamics are examples of cultural factors that can bring about variations in sexual attitudes and behaviors. Sexual orientation—**heterosexuality**, **homosexuality** (gay or lesbian), or **bisexuality**—is increasingly viewed as a sociocultural variable that affects many other aspects of behavior and mental processes. Although undoubtedly shaped by a lifetime of learning, sexual orientation appears to have strong biological roots.

Achievement Motivation

Why do some people try harder than others to succeed?

People gain esteem from achievement in many areas, including the workplace. The motive to succeed is called **achievement motivation**, or the **need for achievement**. Individuals with high achievement motivation strive for excellence, persist despite failures, and set challenging but realistic goals.

Workers are most satisfied when they are working toward their own goals and getting concrete feedback. Jobs that offer clear and specific goals, a variety of tasks, individual responsibility, and other intrinsic rewards are the most motivating. People tend to have a characteristic level of happiness, or **well-being**, that is not necessarily related to the attainment of money, status, or other material goals.

Relations and Conflicts among Motives

Which motives move me most?

People's behavior reflects many motives, some of which may be in conflict. Maslow proposed a hierarchy of five types of human motives, from meeting basic physiological needs to attaining self-actualization. Motives at the lowest levels, according to Maslow, must be at least partially satisfied before people can be motivated by higher-level goals. Alderfer's three-level version does not assume that needs must be met in a particular order.

Four types of motivational conflict have been identified: approach-approach, avoidance-avoidance, approach-avoidance, and multiple approach-avoidance conflicts. These conflicts act as stressors, and people caught in them often experience physical and psychological problems.

The Nature of Emotions

How do feelings differ from thoughts?

Emotions are temporary experiences with negative or positive qualities that are felt with some intensity as happening to the self, are generated in part by interpretation of a situation, and are accompanied by both learned and innate physical responses.

Several brain mechanisms are involved in emotions, including the amygdala in the limbic system. The expression of emotions through involuntary facial movement is controlled by the extrapyramidal motor system. Voluntary facial movements are controlled by the pyramidal motor system. The brain's right and left hemispheres play somewhat different roles in emotions. In addition to specific brain mechanisms, both the **sympathetic nervous system** and the **parasympathetic nervous system**, which are divisions of the autonomic nervous system, are involved in physiological changes that accompany emotional activation. The **fight-flight reaction** (or **fight-or-flight syndrome**), for example, follows from activation of the sympathetic nervous system.

Theories of Emotion

Are emotions in the heart, in the head, or both?

James said that peripheral physiological responses are the primary source of emotions and that awareness of these responses creates emotional experience. James's peripheral theory is supported by evidence that, at least for several basic emotions, physiological responses are distinguishable enough for emotions to be generated in this way. Distinct facial expressions are linked to particular patterns of physiological change.

Cannon's central theory of emotions proposes that emotional experience is independent of bodily responses and that there is a direct experience of emotions based on activity of the central nervous system. Updated versions of this theory suggest that various parts of the central nervous system may be involved in different emotions and different aspects of emotional experience. Some pathways in the brain, such as the pathway from the thalamus to the amygdala, allow strong emotions to occur before conscious thought can take place. Specific parts of the brain appear to be responsible for the feelings of pleasure or pain in emotions.

Cognitive theories of emotions include the Schachter-Singer theory. It suggests that physiological responses are primary sources of emotion but that interpretation of these responses in light of the situation is required to label the emotion. This interpretation process depends on **attribution**. Attributing arousal from one situation to stimuli in another situation is explained by **excitation transfer theory**, which suggests that physiological arousal stemming from one situation can intensify the emotion experienced in a second situation. Other cognitive theorists such as Lazarus have argued that emotional experience is significantly affected by how we interpret events themselves, not just by how we interpret physiological responses to those events.

Communicating Emotion

Which emotional expressions are innate, and which are learned?

In humans, emotions can be communicated by words, voice tones, postures, bodily movements, and facial movements and expressions.

Darwin suggested that certain facial expressions of emotions are innate and universal and that these expressions evolved because they effectively communicate one creature's emotional condition to other creatures. Some facial expressions of basic emotions do appear to be innate, and certain facial movements are universally associated with certain emotions.

Other emotional expressions are learned, and even innate expressions are modified by learning and social contexts. As children grow, they learn an emotion culture, the rules of emotional expression appropriate to their culture. Accordingly, the same emotion may be communicated by different facial expressions in different cultures. Especially in ambiguous situations, one person's emotional expressions may serve to guide another person's behavior, a phenomenon called **social referencing**.

TEST YOUR KNOWLEDGE

Select the best answer for each of the following questions. Then check your responses against the Answer Key at the end of the book.

1. Although most researchers do not believe in instinct theories of motivation, psychologists who advocate _____ theory argue that many aspects of human behavior are motivated by efforts to pass on our genes to the next generation.
   a. drive reduction
   b. evolutionary
   c. arousal
   d. incentive

2. Steve is cold, so he turns up the thermostat in his house. As soon as it starts to get too warm, the thermostat shuts off the furnace. This process is similar to the biological concept of _____.
   a. homeostasis
   b. secondary drive
   c. incentive
   d. arousal

3. Lisbeth and Harriet work as instructors in an exercise class. After class, Lisbeth prefers to go home and read quietly, whereas Harriet is ready to party. Which theory of motivation *best* explains the difference between these two women?
   a. Drive reduction
   b. Instinct
   c. Evolutionary
   d. Arousal

4. Monica wants her daughter to get high grades, so she offers her $10 for each A that she earns and $5 for each B. Monica appears to believe in the _____ theory of motivation.
   a. drive reduction
   b. incentive
   c. evolutionary
   d. arousal

5. Ahmed is desperate to lose weight. To keep from eating, he buys an electrical device that allows him to stimulate various areas of his brain. Which areas should he stimulate if he wants his brain to help him reduce food intake?
   a. Ventromedial nucleus and paraventricular nucleus
   b. Lateral hypothalamus and ventromedial nucleus
   c. Lateral hypothalamus and paraventricular nucleus
   d. Thalamus and pineal gland

6. Ronia is on a diet—again! She is *most* likely to eat less food if she _____.
   a. eats only with friends, never alone
   b. eats only one or two kinds of food at each meal
   c. changes her food culture
   d. focuses on the flavor of what she eats

7. Dr. Stefan is working in the emergency room when a very dehydrated young woman comes in. She is of normal weight, but a medical exam reveals nutritional imbalances and intestinal damage. The woman is *most* likely suffering from _____.
   a. anorexia nervosa
   b. bulimia
   c. binge eating disorder
   d. ventromedial disorder

8. The University of Chicago's National Health and Social Life Survey found that people in the United States _____.
   a. are more sexually active than previously thought
   b. have sex more often if they are not in an exclusive relationship
   c. have sex less often and with fewer people than previously thought
   d. do not enjoy sex very much

9. According to the Thinking Critically section of this chapter, sexual orientation is *most* likely influenced by _____.
   a. prenatal hormones
   b. genetic factors
   c. sociocultural learning
   d. all of the above

10. Edwina wants her son, Egbert, to develop high achievement motivation and to be successful in life. According to research on the need for achievement, Edwina should do all of the following *except* _____.
    a. encourage Egbert to try difficult tasks
    b. encourage Egbert to avoid failure at all costs
    c. give praise and rewards for success
    d. read achievement-oriented stories to him

11. Liang wants his employees to work hard. As a psychologist specializing in motivation, you tell Liang that the *best* way to increase employees' performance is to _____.
    a. increase their pay and benefits
    b. allow them to set their own goals
    c. remind them regularly of the need to do better
    d. keep all tasks as simple as possible

12. According to Maslow, which of the following would you *most* likely do first if you were shipwrecked on a desert island?
    a. Look for food and fresh water
    b. Look for shelter
    c. Start keeping a diary
    d. Build a fire

13. Jill would like to send her son to an expensive private school, but this would create a financial hardship for her. Jill is faced with a(n) _____ motivational conflict.
    a. approach-approach
    b. avoidance-avoidance
    c. approach-avoidance
    d. multiple approach-avoidance

14. Which of the following is *not* a characteristic associated with emotions? They _____.
    a. tend to last a relatively short time
    b. can be triggered by thoughts
    c. are always intense
    d. can motivate behavior

15. When people are afraid to do something, they are said to have "cold feet." The fact that fear is associated with decreased blood flow to the feet and hands supports _____ theory of emotion.
    a. James's peripheral
    b. Cannon's central
    c. Schachter's cognitive
    d. Lazarus's cognitive

16. After she finished a vigorous workout, Lydia saw Thaddeus walk into the gym and instantly fell in love. This is an example of _____, which is consistent with _____ theory of emotion.
    a. social referencing; James's
    b. social referencing; Schachter's
    c. excitation transfer; James's
    d. excitation transfer; Schachter's

17. When Yatsira saw someone trying to open her car door while she was stopped at a light, her heart raced and at the exact same time she felt fear. This is *most* consistent with _____ theory of emotion.
    a. James's
    b. Cannon's
    c. Schachter's
    d. Lazarus's

18. As Jarrod got older, he learned that he could not express his anger by throwing his toys. Jarrod is learning _____.
    a. to use facial feedback
    b. Darwin's universal rules
    c. to use social referencing
    d. his emotion culture

19. Suppose that some friendly space aliens landed in your backyard. They tell you they want to learn how to communicate their emotions so that humans will understand them. What should you focus on teaching them?
    a. Body postures
    b. Facial movements
    c. Hand gestures
    d. Voice inflections

20. Sam is unsure how to react to a comment from one of his friends, so he glances at his girlfriend, Diane, to see what her reaction is. In doing so, he is using _____.
    a. facial feedback
    b. social referencing
    c. attribution
    d. excitation transfer

CHAPTER 11

Human Development

© Monkey Business Images/Shutterstock.com

Preview

Infancy, childhood, adolescence, adulthood, and old age. These words can be read in seconds, but the stages they represent take a lifetime to play out. The story of development is different for each of us, but there are some common threads, too, and developmental psychologists are exploring them. In this chapter, we describe what they have discovered so far about how people change and grow over the course of their lives.

When he was eight years old, Jelani Freeman came home from school to find that his mentally ill mother was gone. She never came back. His father, whom he had never met, was in prison, so social workers arranged for him to live in a foster home. Over the next ten years he lived in six of them, in a series of slum neighborhoods in Rochester, New York. A few attempts were made to reunite him with his mother, but because of her mental condition, these reunions did not last long. His final placement, for a year and a half, was with an older sister who took him in on a foster-care basis but told him he would have to leave when he turned eighteen. As a teenager, his grades slipped, as did his school attendance, and when he asked a high school counselor about taking a college entrance examination, she told him the exam was for students who value education. Jelani took the test anyway and did well enough to get into college in Buffalo, New York, taking out loans, finding financial aid, and working several part-time jobs. After graduation, he won an internship at the U.S. Senate in Washington, DC, and then went on to complete a master's degree in history and then a law degree. Why did Jelani succeed, when the odds were so heavily against him from the beginning?

Developmental psychologists try to answer questions like these. They ask how and why some children are more resilient to stress than others, why some develop into well-adjusted, socially competent, caring individuals while others become murderers, or why some adolescents go on to win honors in college while others drop out of high school. They explore how genetics and the environment affect development through infancy, childhood, and adolescence, and analyze the extent to which development is a product of what we arrive with at birth—our inherited, biological *nature*—and the extent to which it is a product of what the world provides—the *nurture* of the environment. They explore the times when certain kinds of behavior first appear and how those behaviors change with age. They look into how development in one area, such as moral reasoning, relates to development in other areas, such as aggressive behavior. Developmental psychologists attempt to discover whether everyone develops at the same rate and if not, whether slow starters ever catch up to early bloomers. They also study the development that occurs over the years of adulthood and try to determine how these changes are related to earlier abilities and the events of life. In short, **developmental psychology** is concerned with the course and causes of developmental changes over a person's entire lifetime.

This chapter focuses on many of these changes, beginning with the physical and biological changes that take place from the moment of conception to the moment of birth.

EXPLORING HUMAN DEVELOPMENT

What does "genetic influence" mean?

Philosophical arguments about how nature and nurture affect development are centuries old. In the 1690s, British empiricist philosopher John Locke wrote about the importance of nurture. He argued that what happens in childhood profoundly and permanently affects an individual. Empiricists saw the newborn as a blank slate, or *tabula rasa*. Adults write on that slate, said Locke, as they teach children about the world and how to behave in it. About seventy years later, French philosopher Jean-Jacques Rousseau argued just the opposite, claiming that children are capable of discovering how the world operates and how they should behave without instruction from adults. Rousseau wrote that children should be allowed to grow as nature commands, with little guidance or pressure from parents.

The first American psychologist to study systematically the role of nature in behavior was Arnold Gesell (pronounced "geh-ZELL"). In the early 1900s, Gesell observed children of all ages. He found that motor skills —such as standing and walking, picking up a cube, and throwing a ball— develop in a fixed sequence of stages in all children, as illustrated in Figure 11.1. Gesell argued that the order of the stages and the ages when they appear are decided by nature, mostly unaffected by nurture. Only under extreme conditions, such as famine, war, or poverty, he claimed, might children deviate from their biologically programmed timetable. This type of natural growth or change, which unfolds in a fixed

developmental psychology The psychological specialty that documents the course of people's social, emotional, moral, and intellectual development over the life span.

FIGURE 11.1
Motor Development

When did you start walking? The left end of each bar indicates the age at which 25 percent of infants were able to perform a particular behavior; 50 percent of the babies were performing the behavior at the age indicated by the vertical line in the bars; the right end indicates the age at which 90 percent could do so (Frankenberg & Dodds, 1967). Although different infants, especially in different cultures, achieve milestones of motor development at slightly different ages, all infants—regardless of their ethnicity, social class, or temperament—achieve them in the same order.

Design Pics/Kelly Redinger/Getty Images; Elyse Lewin/The Image Bank/Getty Images; Mastering_Microstock/Shutterstock; Liz Banfield/Photolibrary/Getty Images; Rayes/Digital Vision/Jupiterimages; Ryan McVay/The Image Bank/Getty Images; Blend Images - KidStock/Brand X Pictures/Getty Images

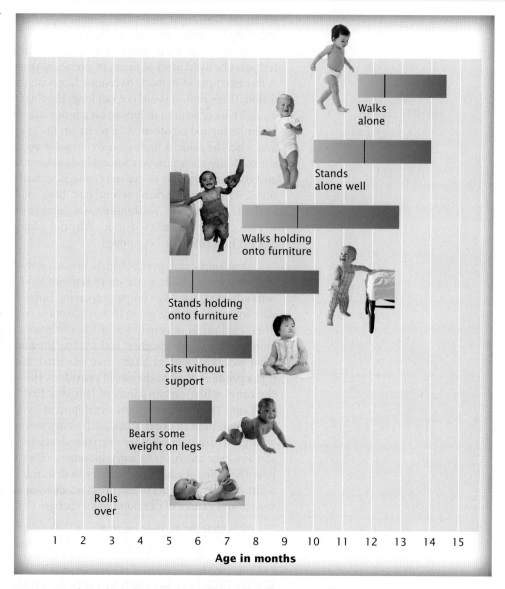

sequence relatively independent of the environment, is called **maturation**. The broader term *development* encompasses not only maturation but also the behavioral and mental processes that are influenced by learning.

John B. Watson disagreed with Gesell's views. He argued that the environment, not nature, shapes development. As described in the introductory chapter, Watson founded the behaviorist approach to psychology. In the early 1900s, he began conducting experiments with children, from which he concluded that children learn *everything*, from skills to fears. In his words, "There is no such thing as an inheritance of capacity, talent, temperament, mental constitution and characteristics. These things … depend on training that goes on mainly in the cradle" (Watson, 1925, pp. 74–75).

It was Swiss psychologist Jean Piaget (pronounced "pee-ah-ZHAY") who first suggested that nature and nurture work together and that their influences are inseparable and interactive. Through a series of books published from the 1920s until his death in 1980, Piaget influenced the field of developmental psychology more than any other person before or since (Flavell, 1996).

Understanding Genetic Influence

Most developmental psychologists now accept Piaget's idea that both nature and nurture contribute to development. Guided by research in *behavioral genetics*, the study of

maturation Natural growth or change triggered by biological factors independent of the environment.

how genes affect behavior, they explore how genes and the environment influence specific aspects of development (Loehlin, 2010). Their studies have demonstrated that nature and nurture jointly affect development in two ways. First, nature and nurture operate together to make all people *similar* in some ways. For example, because of nature we achieve motor development milestones in the same order and at roughly the same rate. But supportive nurture, in the form of proper nutrition and exercise, is also necessary to allow normal maturation to unfold. Second, nature and nurture operate together to make each person *unique*. The nature of inherited genes and the nurture of diverse family and cultural environments produce differences among individuals in athletic abilities, intelligence, speech patterns, personality, and many other dimensions (e.g., Benjamin & Taylor, 2010; Bleidorn et al., 2010; Boutwell et al., 2011; Hopwood et al., 2011; Nigg, Nikolas, & Burt, 2010).

Nature and Nurture Entwined

The combined effects of nature and nurture are illustrated in this family photo of Eli and Peyton Manning and their father, Archie Manning. The effect of nature on their athleticism could be seen in the fact that both boys weighed over twelve pounds at birth and were built like athletes, even as toddlers. The influence of nurture on their success—both are quarterbacks in the National Football League (NFL)—came about partly through the fact that their father was an NFL quarterback too. Their family life revolved around sports; they were tossing a football at the age of three—and honing their skills with help from their father's coaching.

Charles Eshelman/FilmMagic/Getty Images

Genes and the Environment

Just how much nature and nurture contribute varies from one characteristic to another. For some characteristics, such as physical size and appearance, nature's influence is so strong that only extreme environmental conditions affect them. For example, 80 to 95 percent of the differences in height that we see among people are due to their genes. Less than 20 percent of the differences are due to prenatal or postnatal diet, early illness, or other growth-stunting environmental factors. Nature's influence on other characteristics, such as intelligence or personality, is less strong. These complex traits are influenced by genes and by many environmental factors as well.

It is impossible for researchers to separate the influences that nature and nurture exert on such complex traits, partly because heredity and environment are forever intertwined (Perovic & Radenovic, 2011). For instance, highly intelligent biological parents give their children genes related to high intelligence, and typically provide a stimulating environment too. Heredity and environment also influence each other. The environment promotes or hampers the expression of an individual's abilities, and those inherited abilities affect the individual's environment (e.g., Mitchell et al., 2014). For example, a stimulating environment full of toys, books, and lessons encourages children's mental development and increases the chances that their full inherited intelligence will emerge. At the same time, more-intelligent children seek out environments that are more stimulating, ask more questions, draw more attention from adults, and ultimately learn more from these experiences.

In short, heredity creates *predispositions* that interact with environmental influences, including family and teachers, books and computers, and friends and random events (Caspi et al., 2002). This interaction produces the developmental outcomes we see in individuals (e.g., Lahey et al., 2011; Tucker-Drob & Harden, 2012a, 2012b). So Michael Jordan, Michael Phelps, Michael Douglas, and Michael Moore differ from one another and from other men because of both their genes and their experiences. Let's now consider how it all begins.

BEGINNINGS

Why should pregnant women stay away from tobacco and alcohol?

Nowhere are the intertwined contributions of heredity and environment clearer than during the eventful nine months before birth, when a single fertilized egg develops into a functioning newborn infant.

Prenatal Development

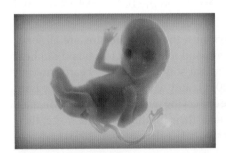

A Fetus at Twelve Weeks

In this photo of a fetus at three months after conception, the umbilical cord and placenta are clearly visible. At this point in prenatal development, the fetus can kick its legs, curl its toes, make a fist, turn its head, squint, open its mouth, swallow, and take a few "breaths" of amniotic fluid.

Zuber / Custom Medical Stock Photo

The process of development begins when sperm from a father-to-be fertilizes the egg of a mother-to-be and forms a brand-new cell. Most human cells contain forty-six chromosomes, arranged in twenty-three matching pairs. Each chromosome hosts thousands of **genes**, the biochemical units of heredity that govern the development of an individual. Genes, in turn, are made of **DNA (deoxyribonucleic acid)**. The DNA in genes provides coded messages that serve as blueprints to construct a physical human being, including eye color, height, blood type, inherited disorders, and the like. All of this information fits in less space than the period that ends this sentence.

New cells in the body are constantly being produced by the division of existing cells. Most cells divide through *mitosis*, a process in which the cell's chromosomes duplicate themselves so that each new cell contains copies of the twenty-three pairs of chromosomes in the original cell.

A different kind of cell division, called *meiosis*, occurs in the formation of a male's sperm cells and a female's egg cells. In meiosis, the chromosome pairs are not copied, but are randomly split and rearranged, leaving each new sperm and egg cell with just one member of each chromosome pair, or twenty-three *single* chromosomes. No two of these special new cells are quite the same, and none contains an exact copy of the person who produced it. So, at conception, when a male's sperm penetrates and *fertilizes* the female's ovum, a truly new cell is formed. The fertilized cell, called a *zygote,* carries the usual twenty-three pairs of chromosomes, but half of each pair comes from the mother and half from the father. The zygote represents a unique heritage—a complete genetic code for a new person that combines randomly selected aspects from both parents. The zygote divides first into copies of itself; then it continues to divide into billions of specialized cells to form a complete new human being (see the behavioral genetics appendix).

Stages of Prenatal Development

The first two weeks after conception are the *germinal stage* of development. By the end of this stage, the cells of the dividing zygote have formed an **embryo**. In the *embryonic stage* of development, the embryo quickly forms a heart, nervous system, stomach, esophagus, and ovaries or testes. By two months after conception, when the embryonic stage ends, the embryo looks decidedly human, with eyes, ears, nose, jaw, mouth, and lips. The tiny arms have elbows, hands, and stubby fingers and the legs have knees, ankles, and toes.

The seven-month period remaining until birth is the *fetal stage* of prenatal development. During this stage, the various organs grow and start to function. By the end of the third month, the **fetus** can kick, make a fist, turn its head, open its mouth, swallow, and frown. In the sixth month, the eyelids, which have been sealed, open. The fetus is now capable of making sucking movements and has taste buds, eyebrows, eyelashes, and a well-developed grasp.

By the end of the seventh month, the organ systems, though immature, are all functional. In the eighth and ninth months, fetuses can respond to light and touch and can hear what is going on outside. They can remember a particular sound or melody heard a month earlier (Dirix et al., 2009; Granier-Deferre et al., 2011), and when hearing an unpleasant sound, they may respond with movements like those of a crying newborn (Gingras, Mitchell, & Grattan, 2005). They can also learn. When they hear their mother's familiar voice, their heart beats a little faster, but it slows if they hear a stranger (Kisilevsky et al., 2003).

Prenatal Risks

During prenatal development, a spongy organ called the *placenta* appears and attaches itself to the mother's uterus through an *umbilical cord*. (The cord is detached at birth, but you can see where yours was by looking at your navel.) The placenta sends nutrients from the mother to the developing baby and carries away waste. It also screens out many potentially harmful substances, including most bacteria. This screening is imperfect, however: gases, microorganisms, and some drugs pass through. Damage can occur if the baby's mother uses certain drugs, is exposed to some toxic substances such as mercury, or has certain illnesses while organs form in the embryonic stage (Koger, Schettler, & Weiss, 2005).

chromosomes Structures in every biological cell that contain genetic information in the form of genes.

genes Hereditary units, located on chromosomes, that contain biological instructions inherited from both parents, providing the blueprint for physical development.

DNA (deoxyribonucleic acid) The molecular structure of a gene that provides the genetic code.

embryo The developing individual from two weeks to two months after fertilization.

fetus The developing individual from the third month after conception until birth.

A Rare Multiple Birth

When Nadya Suleman delivered eight babies on January 26, 2009, it was only the second time that octuplets have been known to survive for more than a few hours. The infants remained at severe risk for a considerable time, though, because they were premature and underweight (the heaviest was 3 pounds, 4 ounces, and the lightest only 1 pound, 8 ounces).

AP Images/Ron Siddle

teratogens Harmful substances, such as alcohol and other drugs, that can cause birth defects.

critical period An interval during which certain kinds of growth must occur if development is to proceed normally.

fetal alcohol syndrome A pattern of defects found in babies born to women who abused alcohol during pregnancy.

Harmful external substances that invade the womb and result in birth defects are called **teratogens**. Teratogens especially matter in the embryonic stage, because it is a **critical period** in prenatal development, a time during which certain kinds of development must occur if they are going to occur at all. If the heart, eyes, ears, hands, and feet do not appear during the embryonic stage, they cannot form later on. If they form incorrectly, the defects will be permanent. So even before a mother knows she is pregnant, her embryo can be damaged by teratogens. For example, a baby whose mother had rubella (German measles) during the third or fourth week after conception has a 50 percent chance of being born blind, deaf, intellectually disabled, or having a malformed heart. But, if the mother had rubella later in the pregnancy, after the infant's eyes, ears, brain, and heart have formed, such defects are less likely. Unlike earlier stages of pregnancy, during the fetal stage, teratogens affect a baby's size, behavior, intelligence, and health rather than the formation of organs and limbs.

Defects due to teratogens are most likely to appear when the negative effects of nature and nurture combine. The worst-case scenario is when a genetically vulnerable infant receives a strong dose of a damaging substance during a critical period of prenatal development (Huizink, Mulder, & Buitelaar, 2004; Van den Bergh & Marcoen, 2004).

Of special concern are the effects of drugs on infants' development. Pregnant women who use substances such as cocaine create a substantial risk for their fetuses, which do not yet have the enzymes necessary to break down the drugs. "Cocaine babies" or "crack babies" may be born premature, underweight, tense, and fussy (Tronick et al., 2005). They may also suffer delayed physical growth and motor development (Shankaran et al., 2011) and they are more likely to have behavioral and learning problems (Levine et al., 2012). However, other aspects of their cognitive abilities are not necessarily different from those of any baby born into an impoverished environment (Behnke et al., 2006; Jones, 2006). How well these crack babies ultimately do depends on how supportive their childhood environments turn out to be (e.g., Ackerman, Riggins, & Black, 2010).

Alcohol is another potent teratogen. It affects infants' brain development (Sayal et al., 2009) and can cause stunted growth, developmental delay, fine motor dysfunction, and genetic abnormalities (Day, 2012). Almost half the children born to mothers who abuse alcohol will develop **fetal alcohol syndrome**, a pattern of defects that includes intellectual disability (O'Leary et al., 2013). Even drinking a glass or two of wine a day can produce a baby with decreased intellectual functioning (Roussotte et al., 2012). Bouts of heavy drinking triple the odds that the child will develop alcohol-related problems by age twenty-one (Baer et al., 2003; Landgren et al., 2010). The effects of prenatal exposure to alcohol are even more severe when combined with the effects of other environmental toxins, such as air pollution (Arruda et al., 2011).

Smoking also affects a developing fetus. Smokers' babies often have respiratory problems, allergies, irritability, and attention problems, and a greater risk for nicotine addiction, insulin resistance, and behavioral problems in adolescence and adulthood (Espy et al., 2011; Tanaka & Miyake, 2011; Thiering et al., 2011; Verhagen et al., 2011). Worse, they may be born prematurely, and they are usually underweight.

The risk of low birth weight and later complications is also higher when mothers, during the first six months of their pregnancy, experience significant stress or depression, or get the flu (Brown et al., 2005; Hay et al., 2010; Khashan et al., 2008). Babies who are premature and/or underweight—for whatever reason—more often have cognitive, emotional, and behavioral problems that continue throughout their lives (Doyle & Anderson, 2010; Evrard et al., 2011; Kerstjens et al., 2011; Nosarti et al., 2012; Rogers et al., 2012). However, mild degrees of maternal anxiety or depression (DiPietro et al., 2006) or anxiety that occurs later during the pregnancy (Davis & Sandman, 2010; DiPietro et al., 2010) may actually advance development of the fetus and infant. Fortunately, mental or physical problems resulting from a harmful prenatal factor affect fewer than 10 percent of babies born in Western nations.

A Baby's-Eye View of the World

The top photograph simulates what a mother looks like to her infant at three months of age. Although their vision is blurry, infants particularly seem to enjoy looking at faces.

Nelson, C. A. (1987). The recognition of facial expressions in the first two years of life: Mechanisms of development. Child Development, 58, 889–909.

The Newborn

Determining what newborns can see, hear, or do is a fascinating and frustrating challenge for researchers in developmental psychology. Babies are difficult to study because they sleep about 70 percent of the time. When they are not sleeping, they are drowsy, crying, awake, and active, or awake and inactive. It is only when they are in this latter state, which is infrequent and lasts only a few minutes, that psychologists can assess infants' abilities. To do so, they may show infants objects or pictures and record where they look and for how long. They film the infants' eye movements and pupil dilations, and note changes in heart rates, sucking rates, brain waves, body movements, and skin conductance (a measure of sweat that accompanies emotion) when objects are shown or sounds are made. From studies using these techniques, researchers have pieced together a fair picture of what infants can see and hear (e.g., Gredebäck, Johnson, & von Hofsten, 2009; Taylor & Herbert, 2013).

Vision and Other Senses

Infants can see at birth, but their vision is blurry. Researchers estimate that newborns have 20/300 eyesight. In other words, an object 20 feet away looks only as clear as it would if viewed from 300 feet by an adult with normal vision. The reason infants' vision is so limited is that their eyes and brains are not fully developed. Newborns' eyes are smaller than those of adults, and the cells in the fovea—the area in each eye on which images are focused—are fewer and far less sensitive. Infant eye movements are slow and jerky. And pathways from the eyes to the brain are inefficient, as is the processing of visual information within the brain.

Although infants cannot see small objects across the room, they can see large objects up close—the distance at which most interactions with caregivers take place. Infants look longest at moving objects, especially those that have large elements, clear contours, and a lot of contrast—all of which are features of the human face (Farroni et al., 2005; Turati, 2004).

Newborns actively use their senses to explore the world around them. At first, they attend to sights and sounds for only short periods. Gradually, their attention spans lengthen and their exploration becomes more systematic. In the first two months, they focus only on the edges of objects, but after that, they scan whole objects (Banks & Salapatek, 1983). Then, when they see an object, they get all the information they can from it before going on to something new (Hunter & Ames, 1988). Newborns stare at human faces longer than other figures (Valenza et al., 1996). They are particularly interested in eyes, as shown in their preference for faces that are looking directly at them (Farroni et al., 2002). Over time, older infants switch to look more at mouths, especially when a person is talking or making expressions (Frank, Vul, & Saxe, 2012; Tenenbaum et al., 2013). They look longer at faces showing happy emotions (Kim & Johnson, 2013). Soon, they become more able to recognize faces when the face is moving and talking (Guellaï, Coulon, & Streri, 2011).

At two or three days of age, newborns can hear soft voices and notice differences between tones about one note apart on the musical scale (Aslin, Jusczyk, & Pisoni, 1998). In addition, they turn their heads toward sounds (Clifton, 1992). But their hearing is not as sharp as that of adults until well into childhood. This condition is not merely a hearing problem; it also reflects an inability to listen selectively to some sounds over others (Bargones & Werner, 1994). As infants grow, they develop sensory capacities and the skill to use them.

Infants pay special attention to speech. When they hear someone talking, they open their eyes wider and search for the speaker. Infants also prefer certain kinds of speech. They like rising tones spoken by women or children (Sullivan & Horowitz, 1983). They also like high-pitched, exaggerated, and expressive speech. In other words, they like to hear the "motherese," or "baby talk," used by most adults in all cultures when talking to babies. They even seem to learn language faster when they hear baby talk (Thiessen, Hill, & Saffran, 2005).

Newborns also like certain smells and tastes more than others. When given something sweet to drink, they suck longer and slower, pause for shorter periods, and smile and lick their lips (Ganchrow, Steiner, & Daher, 1983). They also prefer the flavors of food consumed by their mothers during pregnancy (Warren, 2011). When they smell their mother's breast, newborns become quiet, open their eyes, and try to suck (Doucet et al., 2007, 2009). Within a few days after birth, breastfed babies prefer the odor of their own mother's breast milk to that of another mother (Porter et al., 1992). In the presence of their mother's body odors, in fact, babies' preference for looking at faces (and eyes) is heightened (Durand et al., 2013).

Reflexes and Motor Skills

In the first weeks and months after birth, babies show involuntary, unlearned reactions called **reflexes**. These swift, automatic movements occur in response to external stimuli. Figure 11.2 illustrates the *grasping reflex,* one of more than twenty reflexes that have been observed in newborn infants. Another is the *rooting reflex,* whereby the infant turns its mouth toward a finger or nipple that touches its cheek. And the newborn exhibits the *sucking reflex* in response to anything that touches its lips. Many of these reflexive behaviors evolved because they help infants survive. The absence of reflexes in a newborn signals problems in nervous system development. So does a failure of reflexes to disappear during the first three or four months, when brain development allows the infant to control muscles voluntarily.

Voluntary control permits motor skill development, so the infant starts to roll over, sit up, crawl, stand, and walk. Until recently, most developmental psychologists accepted Gesell's view that except under extreme environmental conditions, these motor abilities occur spontaneously as the central nervous system and muscles mature. Research demonstrates, however, that maturation does not tell the whole story, even in normal environments (Thelen, 1995).

Consider the fact that many babies today aren't learning to crawl on time—or at all. Why? One reason has to do with the "Back to Sleep" campaign, launched in 1995 to prevent sudden infant death syndrome (see the chapter on consciousness). This public health campaign urges parents to put sleeping babies on their backs and not face down. The campaign has been successful, but researchers have discovered that many babies who were never placed on their tummies went directly from sitting to toddling, skipping the crawling stage but reaching all other motor milestones on schedule (Kolata & Markel, 2001). In contrast, the "Prone to Play" campaign, which began in 2001, advised parents to place awake babies in a prone (face down) position to encourage play and learning. Babies of parents who followed this advice did show earlier than expected skill at rolling, crawling on their abdomens, and crawling on all fours, but their ability to walk did not appear unusually early (Kuo et al., 2008).

Observation of infants as they learn to crawl has shown that it happens gradually. It takes the development of enough muscle strength to support the abdomen—and some active experimentation. Six infants in one study tried various crawling techniques—moving backward, moving one limb at a time, using the arms only, and so on (Freedland & Bertenthal, 1994). After a week or two of trial and error, all six infants arrived at the same method: moving the right arm and left leg together, then the left arm and right leg. This pattern turned out to be the best way to get around quickly without tipping over. Such observations suggest that as infants' strength increases, they try various motor patterns and select the ones that work best (Nelson, 1999).

In other words, motor development results from a combination of maturation and experience. It does not reflect an entirely automatic sequence that is genetically etched in the brain. Yet again, we see that nature and nurture affect each other. The brain controls developing behavior, but its own development is affected by experience, including efforts to build motor skills.

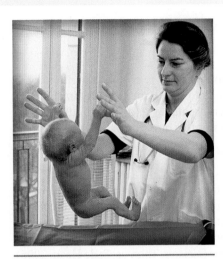

FIGURE 11.2
Reflexes in the Newborn

When a finger is pressed into a newborn's palm, the grasping reflex causes the infant to hold on tightly enough to suspend its entire weight. And when a newborn is held upright over a flat surface, the stepping reflex leads to walking movements.

Petit Format/J. DaCunha/Science Source

reflexes Simple, involuntary, unlearned behaviors directed by the spinal cord without instructions from the brain.

INFANCY AND CHILDHOOD: COGNITIVE DEVELOPMENT

How do babies think?

In less than ten years, a tiny infant becomes a person who can read a book, write a poem, and argue logically for a new computer. What leads to the dramatic shifts in thinking, knowing, and remembering that occur between early infancy and later childhood? Researchers studying *cognitive development* try to answer this question.

Changes in the Brain

One factor that underlies the cognitive leaps of infancy and childhood is brain development. When infants are born, they already have a full quota of brain cells, but the neural networks connecting cells are immature. With time, connections get more complex and then, with pruning, more efficient. As different brain areas develop more complex and efficient neural networks, new cognitive abilities appear (Nelson, Thomas, & de Haan, 2006).

In the first few months of infancy, the cerebellum is the most mature area of the brain. Its early maturation allows infants to display simple associative abilities, such as sucking more when they see their mother's face or hear her voice. Between six and twelve months of age, neurological development in the medial temporal lobe of the forebrain may help make it possible for infants to remember and imitate an action or to recognize an object. Neurological development in the frontal lobes, which occurs later in childhood, allows higher cognitive functions such as reasoning. In other words, brain structures provide the "hardware" for cognitive development. How does the "software" of thinking develop, and how does it modify the "wiring" of the brain's "hardware"? These questions have been pursued by many developmental psychologists, beginning with Jean Piaget.

The Development of Knowledge: Piaget's Theory

Piaget dedicated his life to a search for the origins of intelligence and the factors that lead to changes in knowledge over the life span. He was the first to chart the journey from the simple reflexes of newborns to the complex understandings of adolescents. Although his theory turned out to be incomplete (and in some ways incorrect), his ideas about cognitive development are still useful and still guide research.

Intensive observations of infants (including his own) and extensive interviews with children led Piaget to propose that cognitive development proceeds in a series of distinct periods. He believed that all children's thinking goes through the same periods, in the same order, without skipping. (Table 11.1 outlines these periods.) According to Piaget, infants' thinking is different from children's thinking, which is different from adolescents' thinking. He said that children are not just miniature adults and that they are not less intelligent than adults; they just think in completely different ways at different periods of development. In other words, entering each period involves a *qualitative* change from whatever preceded it, much as a caterpillar is transformed into a butterfly.

Building Blocks of Development

To explain how infants and children move to ever higher levels of understanding and knowledge, Piaget introduced the concept of *schemas* as the basic units of knowledge, the building blocks of intellectual development. As noted in other chapters, **schemas** are the generalizations that form as people experience the world. Schemas, in other words, organize past experiences and provide a framework for understanding future experiences.

At first, infants form simple schemas. For example, a sucking schema combines their experiences of sucking into images of what objects can be sucked on (bottles, fingers, pacifiers) and what kinds of sucking can be done (soft and slow, speedy and vigorous). Later, children form more complex schemas, such as a schema for tying a knot or making a bed. Still later, adolescents form schemas about what it is to be in love.

schemas Mental representations of what we know and expect about the world.

TABLE 11.1   PIAGET'S PERIODS OF COGNITIVE DEVELOPMENT

According to Piaget, a predictable set of features characterizes each period of children's cognitive development. The ages associated with the stages are approximate; Piaget realized that some children move through the periods slightly faster or slower than others.

Period	Abilities and Achievements
Sensorimotor	
Birth–2 years	Infants discover aspects of the world through their sensory impressions, motor activities, and coordination of the two. They learn to differentiate themselves from the external world. They learn that objects exist even when they are not visible and that these objects are independent of the infants' own actions. Infants gain some appreciation of cause and effect.
Preoperational	
2–4 years	Children cannot yet manipulate and transform information in logical ways, but they now can think in images and symbols.
4–7 years	They become able to represent something with something else, acquire language, and play games of pretend. Intelligence at this stage is said to be intuitive because children cannot make general, logical statements.
Concrete operational	
7–11 years	Children can understand logical principles that apply to concrete external objects. They can appreciate that certain properties of an object remain the same, despite changes in appearance, and they can sort objects into categories. They can appreciate the perspective of another viewer. They can think about two concepts (such as longer and wider) at the same time.
Formal operational	
Over 11 years	Only adolescents and adults can think logically about abstractions, can speculate, and can consider what might or what ought to be. They can work in probabilities and possibilities. They can imagine other worlds, especially ideal ones. They can reason about purely verbal or logical statements. They can relate any element or statement to any other, manipulate variables in a scientific experiment, and deal with proportions and analogies. They can reflect on their own activity of thinking.

Two related processes guide this development: assimilation and accommodation. In **assimilation**, children take in information about new objects by trying out existing schemas and finding schemas that new objects will fit. They *assimilate* new objects into existing schemas. So when an infant gets a squeaker toy, he sucks on it, assimilating it into the sucking schema he developed with his bottle and pacifier. In the same way, a toddler who sees a butterfly for the first time may assimilate it into her "birdie" schema because, like a bird, it's colorful and it flies. Now suppose an older toddler encounters a large dog. How she assimilates this new experience depends on her existing dog schema. If she has had positive experiences with the family dog, she will have a positive schema, and, expecting the dog to behave like her pet, she greets it happily. In other words, past experiences affect what and how children think about new ones.

Sometimes, like Cinderella's stepsisters squeezing their oversized feet into the glass slipper, people distort information about a new object to make it fit an existing schema. When squeezing won't work, though, people are forced to change, or *accommodate*, their schemas to the new objects. In **accommodation**, the person tries out familiar schemas on a new object, finds that the schemas cannot be made to fit the object, and changes the schemas so that they will fit (see Figure 11.3). So when the infant discovers that the squeaker toy is more fun when it makes a noise, he accommodates his sucking schema

assimilation The process of taking in new information about objects by using existing schemas on objects that fit those schemas.

accommodation The process of modifying schemas when they do not work on new objects.

FIGURE 11.3
Accommodation

Because the bars of the crib are in the way, this child discovers that her schema for grasping and pulling objects toward her will not work. So she adjusts, or accommodates, her schema to achieve her goal.

© George S. Zimbel

sensorimotor period According to Piaget, the first period of cognitive development, when the infant's mental activity is confined to sensory perception and motor skills.

object permanence The knowledge that an object exists even when it is not in view.

preoperational period According to Piaget, the second period of cognitive development, during which children begin to understand, create, and use symbols that represent things that are not present.

and starts munching on the squeaker instead. When the toddler realizes that butterflies are not birds because they don't have beaks and feathers, she accommodates her "birdie" schema to include two kinds of "flying animals"—birds and butterflies. And if the child with the positive "doggie" schema meets a snarling stray, she discovers that her original schema does not extend to all dogs and refines it to distinguish between friendly dogs and aggressive ones.

Sensorimotor Development

Piaget (1952) called the first stage of cognitive development the **sensorimotor period**, a time when mental activity is confined to schemas about sensory functions, such as seeing and hearing, and schemas about motor skills, such as grasping and sucking. Piaget believed that during the sensorimotor period, infants can only form schemas of objects and actions that are present—things they can see, hear, or touch. They cannot think about absent objects, he said, because they cannot act on them. For infants, then, thinking *is* doing. They do not lie in the crib thinking about their mother or teddy bear, because they are not yet able to use schemas as *mental representations* of objects and actions that are not present.

The sensorimotor period ends when infants do become able to form such mental representations. At that point, they can think about objects or actions when the objects are not visible or the actions are not occurring. This milestone, according to Piaget, frees the child from the here and now of the sensory environment. It allows for the development of thought. One sign of this milestone is the child's ability to find a hidden object. This behavior reflects the infant's knowledge that an object exists even if it cannot be seen, touched, or sucked. Piaget called this knowledge **object permanence**.

Piaget concluded that before infants acquire knowledge of object permanence, they do not search for objects out of sight. For infants, out of sight is literally out of mind. He found evidence of object permanence when infants are four to eight months old. At this age, for the first time, they recognize a familiar object even if part of it is hidden: they know it's their bottle even if they can see only the nipple peeking out under the blanket. Infants now have some primitive mental representations of objects. If an object is completely hidden, however, they will not search for it.

Several months later, infants will search briefly for a hidden object, but their search is random and ineffective. Not until they are about eighteen to twenty-four months old, said Piaget, do infants appear able to picture and follow events in their minds. They look for the object in places other than where they saw it last, sometimes in entirely new places. According to Piaget, their concept of object permanence is now fully developed. They have a mental representation of the object that is completely separate from their immediate perception of it.

Preoperational Development

According to Piaget, the **preoperational period** follows the sensorimotor stage of development. During the first half of the period, children between the ages of two and four begin to understand, create, and use *symbols* that represent things that aren't present. They draw, pretend, and talk.

Using and understanding symbols opens up a new world for two- to four-year-olds. At two, for the first time, children play "pretend." They make their fingers "walk" or "shoot" and use a spoon to make a bridge. By the age of three or four, children can symbolize complex roles and events as they play "house," "doctor," or "superhero." They also can use drawing symbolically: pointing to their scribble, they might say, "This is Mommy and Daddy and me going for a walk."

During the second half of the preoperational period, according to Piaget, four- to seven-year-olds begin to make intuitive guesses about the world as they try to figure out how things work. However, Piaget observed that they cannot tell the difference between imagination and reality. For example, children in this age range might claim that dreams are real and take

Testing for Conservation

conservation The ability to recognize that the important properties of substances or objects, such as quantity, volume, or weight, remain constant despite changes in shape, length, or position.

concrete operations According to Piaget, the third period of cognitive development, during which children can learn to count, measure, add, and subtract.

formal operations According to Piaget, the fourth period of cognitive development, characterized by the ability to engage in hypothetical thinking.

place outside of themselves as "pictures on the window," "a circus in the room," or "something from the sky." And they believe that inanimate objects are alive and have intentions, feelings, and consciousness: "Clouds go slowly because they have no legs"; "Flowers grow because they want to"; and "Empty cars feel lonely." Children in the preoperational period are also *egocentric*: they assume that their own view of the world is shared by everyone else. (This helps explain why they stand between you and the TV screen and assume you can still see it or ask "What's this?" as they look at a picture book in the back seat of the car you're driving.)

Children's thinking at this period is so dominated by what they can see and touch for themselves that they do not realize something is the same if its appearance is changed. In one study, preoperational children thought that a cat wearing a dog mask was actually a dog because that's what it looked like (DeVries, 1969). These children do not yet have what Piaget called **conservation**, the ability to recognize that important properties of a substance or a person remain the same despite changes in shape or appearance.

In a test of conservation, Piaget showed children water from each of two equal-sized glasses being poured into either a tall, thin glass or a short, wide one. They were then asked if one glass contained more water than the other. Children at the preoperational period of development said that one glass (usually the taller one) contained more. They were dominated by the evidence of their eyes. If the glass looked bigger, then they thought it contained more.

Children at this period do not understand the logic of *reversibility*—that if you just poured the water from one container to another, you can pour it back into the original container and it will be the same amount. Nor do they understand the concept of *complementarity*—that one glass is taller but narrower and the other is shorter but wider. They focus on only one dimension at a time—the most obvious or important one—and make their best guess. In fact, Piaget named this time *preoperational* because children at this stage do not yet understand logical mental *operations* such as reversibility and complementarity.

Concrete and Formal Operational Thought

At around the age of six or seven, Piaget observed, children develop conservation. When they do, they enter what he called the period of **concrete operations**. Now, he said, they can count, measure, add, and subtract. Their thinking is no longer dominated by the appearance of things. They can use simple logic and perform simple mental manipulations and mental operations on things. They can sort objects into classes (such as tools, fruit, and vehicles) or series (such as largest to smallest) by systematic searching and ordering.

Still, children in the concrete operational period can use logical operations only for real, concrete objects, such as sticks, glasses, tools, and fruit—not on abstract concepts, such as justice or freedom. They can reason only about what *is*, not about what is *possible*. The ability to think logically about abstract ideas comes in the next period of cognitive development, as children enter adolescence. This new stage is called the **formal operational** period, and it is marked by the ability to engage in hypothetical thinking, including the imagining of logical consequences. For example, adolescents who have reached this level can consider various strategies for finding a part-time job and recognize that some methods are more likely to succeed than others. They can form general concepts and understand the impact of the past on the present and the present on the future. They can question social institutions, think about the world as it might be and ought to be, and consider the consequences and complexities of love, work, politics, and religion. They can think logically and systematically about symbols and propositions.

Piaget explored adolescents' formal operational abilities by asking them to do science experiments that involved forming and investigating hypotheses. Only about half the people in Western cultures reach the formal operational level necessary to succeed in Piaget's experiments (Kuhn & Franklin, 2006). People who have not studied science and math at a high school level are less likely to do well in those experiments (Keating, 1990). Adults are more likely to use formal operations for problems based on their own occupations; this is one reason that people who think logically at work may still fall for a home-repair or investment scam (Cialdini, 2001).

Thinking about the Future

Once they have reached the formal operational stage, many young people become involved in politics because, for the first time, they can think about the consequences of differing approaches to government and which approach might support their emerging ideals.

David Bacon/Report Digital-Rea/Redux Pictures

Modifying Piaget's Theory

Piaget's observations and demonstrations of children's cognitive development are vivid and fascinating. He was right to point out that significant shifts in children's thinking occur with age and that thinking becomes more systematic, consistent, and integrated over time. He said that children actively explore and construct knowledge, not passively receive it from the environment, and this view strongly shapes contemporary views of child development. Piaget's work also inspired experiments to test his ideas (Marti & Rodriguez, 2012). The results of these experiments suggest that Piaget's theory needs some modification.

New Views of Infants' Cognitive Development

Since Piaget's time, psychologists have used new ways to measure what is going on in infants' minds. They use infrared photography to record infants' eye movements, time-lapse photography to detect slight hand movements, and special equipment to measure infants' sucking rates. Their research shows that infants know a lot more—and know it sooner—than Piaget ever thought they did (Franchak & Adolph, 2012; Onishi & Baillargeon, 2005; Roseberry et al., 2011).

For example, it turns out that infants in the sensorimotor period are doing more than just sensing and moving; they are thinking, judging people's reliability, and developing preferences as well (e.g., Carey, 2009; Saxe, Tzelnic, & Carey, 2007; Téglás et al., 2011). And they aren't just experiencing isolated sights and sounds but combining these experiences (Vouloumanos et al., 2009). In one study, for example, infants were shown two different videotapes at the same time, while the soundtrack for only one of them came from a speaker placed between the two TV screens. The infants tended to look at the video that matched the soundtrack—for example, at a toy bouncing in synch with a tapping sound, at Dad's face when his voice was on the audio, or at an angry face when an angry voice was heard (Soken & Pick, 1992). Infants remember, too (Rovee-Collier & Cuevas, 2009). Babies as young as two to three months of age can recall a mobile that was hung over their crib a few days before (Rovee-Collier, 1999; see Figure 11.4).

Young babies even seem to have a kind of object permanence. Piaget required infants to demonstrate object permanence by making effortful responses, such as removing a cover that had been placed over an object. Today, researchers recognize that finding a hidden object under a cover requires several abilities: mentally representing the hidden object, figuring out where it might be, and pulling off the cover. Piaget's tests did not allow for the possibility that infants know a hidden object still exists but don't yet have the skill to find it. When researchers have created situations in which infants merely have to stare to indicate that they know where an object is hidden, even infants have demonstrated this cognitive ability, especially when the object is a familiar one (Baillargeon, 2008; Bertenthal, Longo, & Kenny, 2007; Shinskey & Munakata, 2005). And when experimenters

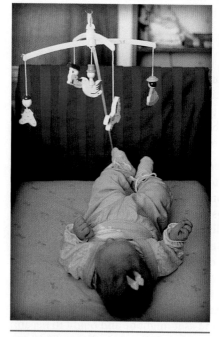

FIGURE 11.4
Infant Memory

This infant has learned to move a mobile by kicking her left foot, which is connected to the mobile by a ribbon. Even a month later, the baby will show recognition of this particular mobile by kicking more vigorously when she sees it than when she sees another one.

Busch Campus, Rutgers University

simply turn off the lights in a room, infants as young as five months of age may reach for now-unseen objects in the dark (Clifton on et al., 1991).

Developmental psychologists generally agree that infants develop some mental representations earlier than Piaget suggested. However, they disagree about whether this knowledge is "programmed" in infants (Spelke et al., 1992), whether it develops quickly through interactions with the world (Baillargeon, 1995, 2008), or whether it is constructed by combining old schemas into new ones (Fischer & Bidell, 1991).

New Views of Developmental Periods

Contemporary researchers have also shown that changes from one developmental period to the next are less consistent and global than Piaget thought. For example, three-year-olds can sometimes make the distinction between physical and mental events; they know the characteristics of real dogs versus pretend dogs (Woolley, 1997). And they are not always egocentric (Wallace, Allan, & Tribol, 2001). In one study, children of this age knew that a white card, which looked pink to them because they were wearing rose-colored glasses, looked white to someone who was not wearing the glasses (Liben, 1978). Preoperational children can even succeed at conservation tasks if they are allowed to count the number of objects or have been trained to focus on relevant dimensions such as number, height, and width (Gelman & Baillargeon, 1983).

Taken together, these studies suggest that children's knowledge and mental strategies develop at different ages in different areas and in "pockets" rather than at global levels of understanding (Sternberg, 1989). Knowledge in particular areas is demonstrated sooner in children who are given specific experience in those areas or who are faced with very simple questions and tasks. So children's reasoning depends not only on their general level of development but also on (1) how easy the task is; (2) how familiar they are with the objects involved; (3) how well they understand the language being used; and (4) what experiences they have had in similar situations (Siegal, 1997). Research has also shown that the level of a child's thinking varies from day to day and may even shift when the child solves the same problem twice in the same day (Siegler, 1994; 2006).

In summary, psychologists today tend to think of cognitive development in terms of rising and falling "waves," not fixed periods (Siegler, 2006). It appears that children systematically try out many different solutions to problems and gradually come to select the best of them.

Information Processing During Childhood

An alternative to Piaget's theory of cognitive development is based on the concept of information processing described in the chapters on memory and on thought and language. The **information-processing model** describes cognitive activities in terms of how people take in information, use it, and remember it. Developmental psychologists taking this approach focus on gradual quantitative changes in children's mental capacities rather than on qualitative advances or stages in development.

LINKAGES   Why does memory improve during childhood? (a link to Memory)

As children get older, information-processing skills gradually get better, and they can do more complex tasks faster and more easily (Duan, Dan, & Shi, 2013; Rose, Feldman, et al., 2012). Older children have longer attention spans. They take in information and shift their attention from one task to another more rapidly. (This may be how they manage to do homework while watching TV.) They are also more efficient in processing information once it is received (Miller & Vernon, 1997). Children's memory storage capacity also improves (Bauer & Fivush, 2013). Preschoolers can keep only two or three pieces of information in mind at the same time; older children can hold four or five. And compared with younger children, older children are better at choosing problem-solving strategies that fit the task they are facing (Schwenck, Bjorklund, & Schneider, 2009; Siegler, 2006).

information processing model A view of cognitive development which focuses on the processes of taking in, remembering or forgetting, and using information.

We don't yet know exactly what causes these increases in children's attention, information processing, and memory capacities. A full explanation will undoubtedly include both nature—specifically, maturation of the brain (Munakata, Snyder, & Chatham, 2012), and nurture—including attention training and increased familiarity with the information that is to be processed and memorized (Bryck & Fisher, 2012; Immordino-Yang, Christodoulou, & Singh, 2012). Researchers have noticed that children's cognitive abilities improve dramatically when they are dealing with familiar rather than unfamiliar material. In one experiment, Mayan children in Mexico lagged behind their age-mates in the United States on standard memory tests of pictures and nouns. But they did a lot better when researchers gave them a more familiar task, such as recalling miniature objects in a model of a Mayan village (Rogoff & Waddell, 1982).

Better memorization strategies may also help explain why children's memories improve. To a great extent, children learn these strategies in school. They learn how to memorize and how to study. They learn to place information into categories and to use other memory aids to help them remember it. After about age seven, schoolchildren are also better at remembering more complex and abstract information. Their memories are more accurate, extensive, and well organized. The knowledge they have accumulated allows them to draw more inferences and integrate new information into a more complete network of facts. (See "In Review: Milestones of Cognitive Development in Infancy and Childhood.")

MILESTONES OF COGNITIVE DEVELOPMENT IN INFANCY AND CHILDHOOD

IN REVIEW

Age*	Achievement	Description
3–4 months	Maturation of senses	Immaturities that limit the newborn's vision and hearing are overcome.
	Voluntary movement	Reflexes disappear, and infants begin to gain voluntary control over their movements.
12–18 months	Mental representation	Infants can form images of objects and actions in their minds.
	Object permanence	Infants understand that objects exist even when out of sight.
18–24 months	Symbolic thought	Young children use symbols to represent things that are not present in their pretend play, drawing, and talk.
4 years	Intuitive thought	Children reason about events, real and imagined, by guessing rather than by engaging in logical analysis.
6–7 years	Concrete operations; Conservation	Children can apply simple logical operations to real objects. For example, in conservation they recognize that important properties of a substance, such as number or amount, remain constant despite changes in shape or position.
7–8 years	Information processing	Children can remember more information; they begin to learn strategies for memorization.

In Review Questions

1. Research in cognitive development suggests that children form mental representations _____ than Piaget thought they did.

2. Recognizing that changing the shape of clay doesn't change the amount of clay is evidence of a cognitive ability called _____.

3. The appearance of object permanence signals the end of the _____ period.

*These ages are approximate; they indicate the order in which children first reach these milestones of cognitive development rather than the exact ages.

DEVELOPMENT AND MEMORY

TRY THIS

LINKAGES What happens to our memories of infancy? (a link to Memory)

The ability to remember facts, figures, pictures, and objects improves as we get older and more expert at processing information. But take a minute right now and try to recall anything that happened to you when you were, say, one year old. Most people can accurately recall a few memories from age five or six but remember virtually nothing from before the age of three (e.g., Bauer & Larkina, 2013; Davis, Gross, & Hayne, 2008; Howe, 2013).

Psychologists have not yet found a fully satisfactory explanation for this "infantile amnesia." Some have suggested that young children lack the memory encoding and storage processes described in the chapter on memory. Yet children of two or three can clearly recall experiences that happened weeks or even months earlier (Bauer, 2006; Cleveland & Reese, 2008). Others suggest that infantile amnesia occurs because very young children lack a sense of self. Because they don't even recognize themselves in the mirror, they may not have a framework for organizing memories about what happens to them (Howe, 2003, 2011). However, this explanation would hold for only the first two years or so, because after that children do recognize their own faces and even their recorded voices (Legerstee, Anderson, & Schaffer, 1998).

Another possibility is that early memories, though "present," are implicit rather than explicit. As mentioned in the memory chapter, *implicit memories* can affect our emotions and behavior even when we do not consciously recall them. However, children's implicit memories of their early years, like the *explicit memories* that they create on purpose, are quite limited. One study found that when ten-year-old children were shown photographs of preschool classmates they hadn't seen in five years, the children had little implicit or explicit memory of them (Newcombe & Fox, 1994). But, adults correctly identify 90 percent of photographs of high-school classmates they have not seen for thirty years (Bahrick, Bahrick, & Wittlinger, 1975).

Other explanations of infantile amnesia suggest that our early memories are lost because in early childhood we don't yet have language skills to talk about—and thus solidify—memories. This possibility was explored in a study in which two- to three-year-old children played with a machine that supposedly could shrink toys (Simcock & Hayne, 2002). Six months later, they were asked what they remembered about this event. If they had not yet developed language at the time they played with the machine, the children could say little or nothing about the experience when asked about it later. However, most of these same children could correctly identify pictures of the machine and act out what they had done with it. It appears that they had memories of the event that could be recalled nonverbally but not in words (Richardson & Hayne, 2007). Another idea is that early experiences tend to be fused into *generalized event representations,* such as "going to Grandma's" or "playing at the beach," so it becomes difficult to recall specific events.

Some researchers believe that adults have difficulty accessing early memories because when they were very young children they lacked the emotional knowledge necessary for interpreting, representing, organizing, and retrieving information about the events they experienced (Wang, 2008). Still other researchers believe that infantile amnesia is due partly to the ways that people are asked about their early memories and that specialized questioning techniques might allow retrieval of early memories that are normally unavailable (Jack & Hayne, 2007; Wang & Peterson, 2014).

Research on hypotheses such as these may someday unravel the mystery of infantile amnesia.

Culture and Cognitive Development

To explain cognitive development, Piaget focused on the physical world of objects. Russian psychologist Lev Vygotsky (pronounced "vah-GOT-skee") focused on the social world of people. He viewed cognitive abilities as due to cultural history. The child's mind, said Vygotsky, grows by contact with other minds. It is through interaction with parents, teachers, and other representatives of their culture that children learn the ideas of that culture (Vygotsky, 1991).

Vygotsky's followers have studied the effects of the social world on children's cognitive development—especially how participation in social routines affects children's developing knowledge of the world (Gauvain, Beebe, & Zhao, 2011). In Western societies, those routines include shopping, eating at McDonald's, going to birthday parties, and attending religious services. In other cultures they might include helping to make pottery, going hunting, and weaving baskets (Larson & Verma, 1999). Quite early, children develop mental representations, called *scripts,* for these activities (see the chapter on thought and language). By the time they are three, children can describe routine activities quite accurately (Nelson, 1986). Scripts, in turn, affect children's knowledge and understanding of cognitive tasks (Saxe, 2004). For example, in cultures in which pottery making is important, children display conservation about the mass of objects sooner than children do in other cultures (Gardiner & Kosmitzki, 2005).

Children's cognitive abilities are also influenced by the language of their culture. Korean and Chinese children, for instance, show exceptional ability at adding and subtracting large numbers (Miller et al., 1995). As third-graders, they do three-digit problems in their heads (such as 702 minus 125) that peers in the United States would labor to solve. The difference may stem in part from the clear and explicit words that Asian languages use for the numbers from eleven to nineteen. In English, the meaning of the words *eleven* and *twelve,* for instance, is not as clear as the Asian *ten-one* and *ten-two.* Moreover, Asians use the abacus and a metric system of measurement, both of which center around the number ten. Korean math textbooks emphasize this tens structure by presenting ones digits in red, tens in blue, and hundreds in green. Above all, for children in Asian cultures, educational achievement, especially in mathematics, is strongly encouraged (Naito & Miura, 2001). In short, children's cognitive development is affected in ways large and small by the culture they live in (Broesch et al., 2011; Gauvain et al., 2011).

Individual Variations in Cognitive Development

Even within a single culture, some children are mentally advanced, whereas others lag behind their peers. Why? As already suggested, heredity is an important factor, but experience also plays a role. To explore how significant that role is, psychologists have studied the cognitive development of children raised in many different environments.

Cognitive development is seriously delayed if children are raised in environments where they are deprived of the everyday sights, sounds, and feelings provided by pictures

Babies at Risk

The cognitive development of infants raised in this understaffed Russian orphanage will be permanently impaired if they are not given far more stimulation in the orphanage or, better yet, are adopted into a loving family before they're six months of age (Becket et al., 2006; Kreppner et al., 2007). It's likely that they'll suffer from reduced brain metabolism and reduced activity in regions associated with higher cognitive functions, memory, and emotion (McLaughlin et al., 2011; Nelson, 2007).

Josef Polleross/The Image Works

and books, by conversation and loving interaction with family members, and even by television, radio, and the Internet. Children subjected to this kind of severe deprivation show significant impairment in intellectual development by the time they are two or three years old. "Genie" was one such child. When rescued at age fourteen, she weighed only fifty-nine pounds. The only things she could say were "stop it" and "no more." Investigators discovered that she had spent her life confined to a small bedroom, harnessed to a potty chair during the day and caged in a crib at night. She had not been permitted to hear or make many sounds. Although scientists and therapists worked intensively with Genie in the years after her rescue, she never learned to speak in complete sentences, and she remains in an adult care facility (James, 2008).

Cognitive development may also be impaired by less extreme conditions of deprivation, including the neglect, malnourishment, noise, and chaos that occur in some homes. One study of the effects of poverty found that by the time they were five years old, children raised in poverty scored nine points lower on IQ tests than did children in families whose incomes were at twice the poverty level—even after the researchers had controlled for other variables, such as family structure and parents' education (Duncan, Brooks-Gunn, & Klebanov, 1994; Marcus Jenkins et al., 2013). These differences continue as poor children enter school (Cushon et al., 2011). Children who remain in poverty have lower IQs and poorer school achievement (Duncan, Morris, & Rodrigues, 2011; Siegler, 2003). They also have more learning disabilities (Bigelow, 2006), are less engaged in school (Teachman, 2008), and score lower on neurocognitive tests (Farah et al., 2006). One study of more than 10,000 children found that the economic status of the family into which a child is born is a much better predictor of the child's cognitive development than are physical risk factors such as low birth weight (Jefferis, Power, & Hertzman, 2002). It is no wonder then that lower average IQs are seen in countries where higher numbers of children are living in poverty (Weiss, 2007).

When Does Stimulation Become Overstimulation?

A child's cognitive development is enhanced by a stimulating environment, but can there be too much stimulation? In the face of an avalanche of electronic media aimed specifically at babies and toddlers, some people are beginning to wonder (Zimmerman & Christakis, 2007; Zimmerman, Christakis, & Neltzoff, 2007). These stimulating media include computer "lapware," such as this baby is enjoying, videos and DVDs for even the tiniest infants, and, of course, television programs such as *Teletubbies*. We don't yet know how all this well-intentioned electronic stimulation is affecting young children, but there is some evidence that passively watching videos may not promote learning in infants and toddlers (DeLoache et al., 2010), and the American Academy of Pediatrics (2011) recommends that children under the age of two should remain "screen free" because they don't yet understand what they're seeing.

LWA/Photographer's Choice/Getty Images

In families with incomes above the poverty line, children's cognitive development is still related to their surroundings and experiences. Parents often make the difference between a child getting A's or C's. To help children achieve those A's, adults can expose them from the early years to a variety of interesting materials and experiences—though not too many to be overwhelming (Cook, Goodman, & Schulz, 2011; van Schijndel et al., 2010). Children's cognitive development is enhanced when parents read and talk to them, encourage and help them explore, and actively teach them (Gottfried, 1997; Raikes et al., 2006)—in short, when they provide both support and challenge for a child's talents (Yeung, Linver, & Brooks-Gunn, 2002). Children benefit as well from early access to a computer (Fish et al., 2008). In one study, third-graders who had a computer but not a TV in their bedroom scored 10 to 20 points higher on tests of math, reading, and language than children who had a TV but no computer (Borzekowski & Robinson, 2005).

To improve the cognitive skills of children who do not get these kinds of stimulation, developmental psychologists have provided some children with extra lessons, educational materials, and contact with caring adults (e.g., van der Kooy-Hofland et al., 2012). In the United States, the most comprehensive effort of this sort is Project Head Start, a federally funded preschool program for poor children. Many smaller, more intensive programs are offered by state and local agencies. Such programs do enhance children's cognitive abilities (Tucker-Drob, 2012; Welsh et al., 2010), and some effects can last into adulthood (Campbell et al., 2012). Music lessons can also promote children's cognitive development, especially verbal memory (Ho, Cheung, & Chan, 2003; Moreno et al., 2011). Internet access, too, has been related to improved reading scores and school grades among poor children (Jackson et al., 2011). Even electronic games, although they are no substitute for adult attention, can provide opportunities for school-age children to hone spatial skills (Blumberg et al., 2013). There are limits, however. An excess of computer gaming has been associated with reduced academic achievement as well as with some physical and behavioral problems (Desai et al., 2010; Weis & Cerankosky, 2010).

INFANCY AND CHILDHOOD: SOCIAL AND EMOTIONAL DEVELOPMENT

How do infants become attached to their caregivers?

Life for the child is more than learning about objects, doing math problems, and getting good grades. It is also about social relationships and emotional reactions. From the first months onward, infants are sensitive to those around them (Geangu et al., 2010; Mumme & Fernald, 2003), and they are both attracted by and attractive to other people—especially parents and other caregivers.

During the first hour or so after birth, mothers gaze into their infants' eyes and give them gentle touches (Klaus & Kennell, 1976). This is the first chance for the mother to show her *bond* to her infant—an emotional tie that begins even before the baby is born (Feldman et al., 2007). Psychologists once believed that this immediate contact was critical—that the mother-infant bond would never be strong if the opportunity for early interaction was missed. Research has revealed, however, that although skin-to-skin contact with the infant immediately after birth increases the mother's positive behavior with the infant and the length of time she breastfeeds (e.g., Bigelow et al., 2010, 2013; Moore et al., 2012), such interaction is not a requirement for a close relationship (Myers, 1987). Mothers and fathers, whether biological or adoptive, gradually form close attachments to their infants by interacting with them day after day.

As the mother gazes at her baby, the baby gazes back. By the time infants are two days old, they recognize—and like—their mother's face. They will suck more vigorously in order to see an image of her face than to see a stranger's (Walton, Bower, & Bower, 1992). Soon, they begin to respond to the mother's facial expressions as well. By the time they are a year old, children use their mothers' emotional expressions to guide their own behavior in uncertain situations (Hertenstein & Campos, 2004; Saarni, 2006). As mentioned in the chapter on motivation and emotion, this phenomenon is called *social referencing*. If the mother looks frightened when a stranger approaches, for example, the child is more likely to avoid the stranger. Research on infants' brain activity suggests that they

Forming a Bond

Mutual eye contact, exaggerated facial expressions, and shared "baby talk" are an important part of the early social interactions that promote an enduring bond of attachment between parent and child.

© Daniel M. Nagy/Shutterstock.com

pay particular attention to signs of fear and other negative emotions in adults (Leppänen & Nelson, 2012). This tendency may explain why, as described in the chapter on learning, observation of other people's reactions can sometimes lead to the development of fears and even phobias.

Infants communicate feelings as well as recognize them. Before they can speak, infants use gestures to show their caregivers that they are feeling happy, mad, sad, scared, sleepy, or cold (Vallotton, 2008).

Individual Temperament

From the moment infants are born, they differ from each other. Some are happy, active, and vigorous; they splash, thrash, and wriggle. Others lie still most of the time. Some infants eagerly approach new objects; others turn away or fuss. Some infants whimper; others kick, scream, and wail. Characteristics such as these make up an infant's temperament. **Temperament** refers to the infant's individual style and frequency of expressing needs and emotions; it is constitutional, biological, and genetically based. Although temperament mainly reflects nature's effect on the beginning of an individual's personality, it can also be affected by prenatal environment, including—as noted earlier—a mother's smoking, drug use, and stress during pregnancy (Blair et al., 2011; Davis et al., 2011; Sandman et al., 2011, 2012). Maternal stress after birth also affects a baby's temperament. For example, breastfed infants who ingest more of the stress-related hormone cortisol tend to have more fearful temperaments (Glynn et al., 2007). And if mothers of babies with negative temperaments continue to experience stress, the babies tend to express even more negative emotion during the next five years (Pesonen et al., 2008).

Babies seem to fall into one of three main temperament patterns (Thomas & Chess, 1977). Most common are *easy babies,* who get hungry and sleepy at predictable times, react to new situations cheerfully, and seldom fuss. *Difficult babies* are irregular and irritable. The third group, *slow-to-warm-up babies,* react warily to new situations but eventually enjoy them.

Traces of early temperamental characteristics weave their way from birth throughout childhood and into adulthood. Easy infants usually stay easy (Zhou et al., 2004) and tend not to develop conduct problems (Lahey et al., 2008); difficult infants often remain difficult, sometimes developing attention and aggression problems in childhood (Else-Quest et al., 2006; Miner & Clarke-Stewart, 2008). Timid toddlers tend to become shy preschoolers, restrained and inhibited eight-year-olds, somewhat anxious teenagers, and shy and cautious young adults (Caspi, Harrington et al., 2003; Rothbart, 2011). These individuals tend to marry at a later age than their more outgoing peers (Caspi, Elder, & Bem, 1988). However, in temperament, as in cognitive development, nature interacts with nurture (Jaffari-Bimmel et al., 2006; Kiff, Lengua, & Zalewski, 2011). Events and influences that occur between infancy and adulthood can help to stabilize an individual's temperament or shift its development in one direction or the other.

One source of influence may be the degree to which an infant's temperament matches the parents' personal styles and what they want and expect from their baby. When the match is a good one, parents tend to support and encourage the infant's behavior, thus increasing the chances that temperamental qualities will be stable. Consider the temperament patterns of Chinese American and European American children. At birth, Chinese American infants are calmer, less changeable, less excitable, and more easily comforted when upset than European American infants (Kagan et al., 1994). This tendency toward self-control is reinforced by Chinese culture. Compared with European American parents, Chinese parents are less likely to reward and stimulate infants' babbling and smiling and more likely to maintain close control of their young children. The children, in turn, are more dependent on their mothers and less likely to play by themselves. They are less vocal, noisy, and active than European American children (Smith & Freedman, 1983), and as preschoolers they show far more impulse control, including the ability to wait their turn (Sabbagh et al., 2006).

temperament An individual's basic, natural disposition that is evident from infancy.

FIGURE 11.5
Wire and Terry Cloth "Mothers"

These are the two types of artificial mothers used in Harlow's research. Although baby monkeys received milk from the wire mother, they spent most of their time with the terry cloth version, and they clung to it when frightened.

Nina Leen/Time Life Pictures/Getty Images

attachment A deep, affectionate, close, and enduring relationship with a person with whom a baby has shared many experiences.

attachment theory The idea that children form a close attachment to their earliest caregivers and that this attachment pattern can affect aspects of the children's later lives.

Temperamental differences between children in different ethnic groups show the combined contributions of nature and nurture. Mayan infants, for example, are relatively inactive from birth. The Zinacantecos, a Mayan group in southern Mexico, reinforce this innate predisposition toward restrained motor activity by tightly wrapping infants and by nursing at the slightest sign of movement (Greenfield & Childs, 1991). This combination of genetic predisposition and cultural reinforcement is adaptive. Quiet infants do not kick off their covers at night, which is important in the cold highlands where they live. Inactive infants are able to spend long periods on their mothers' backs as the mothers work. And infants who do not walk until they understand some language do not wander into the open fire at the center of the house. This adaptive interplay of innate and cultural factors in temperament operates in all cultures.

Nature and nurture combine to influence individual differences within cultures, too. Many studies show that children are more likely to show aggressiveness, anxiety, depression, or academic and social problems if they suffer the "double whammy" of starting life with a difficult temperament and then grow up in a harsh, insensitive, unsupportive, or anxiety-provoking family environment (e.g., Bates, Schermerhorn, & Petersen, 2012; Crawford, Schrock, & Woodruff-Borden, 2011; Engle & McElwain, 2011). For example, children who had both timid temperaments and mothers who were unsupportive, negative, or depressed were more likely to remain fearful, to be socially withdrawn, to have more negative moods, and to have difficulty controlling negative emotions (Hane et al., 2008; Lewis-Morrarty et al., 2012). However, if a difficult or shy baby is lucky enough to have patient parents who allow their baby to respond to new situations and changes in daily routines at a more relaxed pace, the baby is likely to become less difficult or shy over time. Children are least likely to have problems if they have an easy temperament and their parents do not display harshness and psychological problems (Derauf et al., 2011).

The Infant Grows Attached

As infants and caregivers respond to one another in the first year, the infant begins to form an **attachment**—a deep, affectionate, close, and enduring relationship—to these important figures. **Attachment theory** was first developed by John Bowlby, a British psychoanalyst who drew attention to the importance of attachment after he observed children who had been orphaned in World War II. These children's depression and other emotional scars led Bowlby to propose a theory about the importance of developing a strong attachment to one's primary caregivers—a tie that normally keeps infants close to those caregivers and, therefore, safe (Bowlby, 1973). Soon after Bowlby first described his theory, researchers in the United States began to investigate how such attachments are formed and what happens when they fail to form or are broken by loss or separation. The most dramatic of these studies was conducted with monkeys by psychologist Harry Harlow.

Motherless Monkeys—and Children

Harlow (1959) separated newborn monkeys from their mothers and raised them in cages containing two artificial mothers. One "mother" was made of wire with a rubber nipple from which the infant could get milk (see Figure 11.5). It provided food but no physical comfort. The other artificial mother had no nipple but was made of soft, comfortable terry cloth. If attachments form entirely because caregivers provide food, the infants would be expected to prefer the wire mother. In fact, they spent most of their time with the terry cloth mother. And when they were frightened, the infants immediately ran to their terry cloth mother and clung to it. Harlow concluded that the monkeys were motivated by the need for comfort. The terry cloth mother provided feelings of softness and cuddling, which were things the infants needed when they sensed danger.

Harlow also investigated what happens when attachments do not form. He isolated some monkeys from all social contact from birth. After a year of this isolation, the monkeys showed dramatic disturbances. When visited by normally active, playful monkeys, they withdrew to a corner, huddling or rocking. These monkeys' problems continued into adulthood. As adults, they were unable to have normal sexual relations. When some of the females became pregnant through artificial means, their maternal behaviors were woefully inadequate. In most cases, these mothers ignored their infants. When the infants became distressed, the mothers physically abused and sometimes even killed them.

Humans who spend their first few years without a consistent caregiver react in a similar manner. Like Harlow's deprived monkeys, children raised in orphanages staffed by neglectful caregivers tend not to develop attachments to those caregivers, become withdrawn and constantly rocking (Holden, 1996; Zeanah et al., 2005, 2009). In one study, researchers observed the behavior of four-year-old children who had been in a poorly staffed orphanage for at least eight months before being adopted (Chisholm, 1997). Compared with children who had been adopted before they were four months old, the late-adopted children were found to have many more serious problems. Depressed or withdrawn, they stared blankly, demanded attention, and could not control their tempers. Although they interacted poorly with their adoptive mothers, they were friendly with strangers, usually trying to cuddle and kiss them. At age six, a third of late-adopted children still showed no preference for their parents or any tendency to look to them when stressed (Rutter, O'Connor, & ERA Study Team, 2004). Other studies have found that children who spent their first year in such orphanages displayed antisocial behavior and other long-term social and behavioral problems (Hawk & McCall, 2011). Neuroscientists suggest that the problems seen in isolated primates—as well as in humans—are the result of developmental brain dysfunction and damage brought on by a lack of touch and body movement in infancy, and by the absence of early play, conversation, and other social experiences in childhood (Kalcher-Sommersguter et al., 2011; Wiik et al., 2011; Wismer, Fries et al., 2005, 2008). These problems are less likely if orphanage caregivers receive social-emotional training (McCall et al., 2013).

Forming an Attachment

Fortunately, most infants do have a consistent caregiver, usually the mother, to whom they form an attachment. They quickly learn to recognize her and distinguish her from a stranger. Even at three months, some infants vocalize more to their mothers than to a stranger. By six or seven months, infants prefer the mother to anyone else. They crawl after her, call out to her, hug her, climb into her lap, protest when she leaves, and brighten when she returns (Ainsworth & Marvin, 1995). After an attachment has formed, separation from the mother for even thirty minutes can be a stressful experience (Cassidy, 2008). Babies who recognize and prefer their mothers even earlier—at three months—may be especially bright: they tend to get better grades in school and complete more years of education (Roe, 2001).

Infants also develop attachments to fathers, but usually a little later (Arsalidou et al., 2010; Lamb, 1997). Father-infant interaction is also less frequent than mother-infant interaction, and most studies show that it has a somewhat different nature (Lamb & Lewis, 2010). Mothers tend to feed, bathe, dress, cuddle, and talk to their infants, whereas fathers are more likely to play with, jiggle, and toss them, especially sons.

Variations in Attachment

How much closeness and contact an infant seeks with a parent depends to some extent on the infant. Babies who are ill, tired, or slow to warm may need more closeness. Closeness also depends in part on the parent. An infant whose parent has been absent or unresponsive may need more closeness than one whose parent is accessible and responsive.

Researchers have studied the differences in infants' **attachment behavior** in a special situation that simulates the natural comings and goings of parents and infants—the so-called *Strange Situation* (Ainsworth et al., 1978). Testing occurs in an unfamiliar playroom where the infant interacts with the mother and an unfamiliar woman in brief episodes: the infant plays with the mother and the stranger, the mother leaves the baby with the stranger

attachment behavior Actions such as crying, smiling, vocalizing, and gesturing that help bring an infant into closer proximity to its caretaker.

for a few minutes, the mother and the stranger leave the baby alone in the room briefly, and the mother returns.

These sessions show that most infants display a *secure attachment* to their mothers (Thompson, 2006). In the unfamiliar room, the infant uses the mother as a home base, leaving her side to explore or play but returning periodically for comfort or contact. Securely attached children tolerate brief separation from mothers, but are happy to see them return, and receptive to the mothers' offers of contact. These mother-child pairs tend to interact well from early in life, and the mothers tend to be sensitive and responsive (DeWolff & van Ijzendoorn, 1997).

Some infants, however, form *insecure attachments*. If the relationship is *avoidant*, infants avoid or ignore the mother when she approaches or returns after a brief separation. If the relationship is *ambivalent*, the infant is upset when the mother leaves, but when she returns the child acts angry and rejects the mother's efforts at contact; when picked up, the child squirms to get down. If the relationship is *disorganized*, the infant's behavior is inconsistent, disturbed, and disturbing; the child may begin to cry again after the mother has returned and provided comfort or may reach out for the mother while looking away from her (Moss et al., 2004).

Patterns of child care and attachment vary widely in different parts of the world (Rothbaum, Morelli, & Rusk, 2010). In northern Germany, for example, where parents are quite strict, the proportion of infants who display avoidant attachments is much higher than in the United States (Grossman et al., 2008; Spangler, Fremmer-Bombik, & Grossman, 1996). It used to be common for kibbutz babies in Israel to sleep in infant houses away from their parents, but they were found to be more likely to show insecure attachments and other related problems (Aviezer et al., 1999). The practice is unusual now. In Japan, where mothers are expected to be completely devoted to their children and are seldom apart from them, even at night, children develop an attachment relationship that emphasizes harmony and union (Rothbaum, Pott, et al., 2000). These attachment patterns differ from the secure type that is most common in the United States: with their parents' encouragement, U.S. children balance closeness and proximity with exploration and autonomy.

In all countries, the likelihood that children will develop a secure attachment depends on the mother's attentiveness; if the mother is sensitive and responsive to the baby's needs and signals, a secure attachment is more likely; if she is rejecting or neglecting, the child's attachment is more likely to be insecure (Bakermans-Kranenburg, van IJzendoorn, & Juffer, 2008; Nievar & Becker, 2008).

Consequences of Attachment Patterns

The nature of a child's attachment to caregivers can have long-term and far-reaching effects). For example, an infant's secure attachment continues into young adulthood—and probably throughout life—unless it is disrupted by the loss of a parent, abuse by a family member, chronic depression in the mother, or certain other severe negative events (e.g., Mattanah, Hancock, & Brand, 2004; Weinfield, Sroufe, & Egeland, 2000). A secure attachment to the mother is also reflected in relationships with other people. Children who are securely attached receive more positive reactions from other children as toddlers (Fagot, 1997) and have better relations with peers in middle childhood and adolescence (Dykas & Cassidy, 2011; Lucas-Thompson & Clarke-Stewart, 2007; McElwain, Booth-LaForce, & Wu, 2011). Securely attached children also require less contact, guidance, and discipline from teachers, and are less likely to seek excessive attention, to act impulsively or aggressively, to express frustration, to become distracted, or to display helplessness or anxiety (see the chapter on learning; Davies et al., 2013; Fearon et al., 2010; Groh et al., 2012; Kochanska & Kim, 2013). Their teachers like them more, expect more of them, and rate them as more competent (Diener et al., 2008). Children who do not form secure attachments, in contrast, risk developing anxiety and depression (Kerns & Brumariu, 2013) and are more likely to behave aggressively and violently later in life (Ogilvie et al., 2014; Savage, 2014).

Why should this be? According to Bowlby, securely attached children develop positive relationships with other people because they develop mental representations, or *internal working models,* of the social world that lead them to expect that everyone else will respond to them in the same positive ways as their parents do. But secure attachment at the age of one doesn't guarantee a life of social competence and emotional well-being. In one study, researchers found that attachment security was stable from infancy to adolescence only for children whose mothers were supportive and sensitive at both age periods (Beijersbergen et al, 2012). If parents become neglectful or rejecting as the result of marital strife, divorce, or depression, for example, the secure attachments are likely to disintegrate, and the child may begin to have problems (Thompson, 2006). So although a secure attachment alone does not predict long-term sociability and well-being, in concert with continuing supportive care, it sets the stage for positive psychological growth.

THINKING CRITICALLY

DOES DAY CARE HARM THE EMOTIONAL DEVELOPMENT OF INFANTS?

With about 65 percent of U.S. mothers working outside of the home (U.S. Department of Labor, 2012), how does such daily separation affect their children, especially infants (Clarke-Stewart & Allhusen, 2005)? Some argue that putting infants in day care with a nanny or child care center damages the quality of mother-child relations and increases the child's risk for psychological problems (Gallagher, 1998). Other researchers question whether day care alone causes such problems (Stein et al., 2013; Zachrisson et al., 2013).

What am I being asked to believe or accept?

The claim is that daily separations created by day care damage the formation of an attachment between the mother and infant and harm the infant's emotional development.

What evidence is available to support the assertion?

There is clear evidence that separation from the mother is painful for young children. If separation lasts a week or more, children who have formed an attachment to their mother tend to protest, then become apathetic and mournful (Robertson & Robertson, 1971). But day care does not involve such lasting separations. Research has shown that infants who are in day care do form attachments to their mothers. In fact, they prefer their mothers to their daytime caregivers (Lamb & Ahnert, 2006).

Are these attachments as secure as the attachments formed by infants whose mothers do not work outside the home? An answer may be suggested by comparing how infants react to brief separations from mothers in the Strange Situation. A review of about twenty such studies revealed that infants in full-time day care were somewhat more likely to be classified as insecurely attached. About 36 percent of them were classified as insecure; only 29 percent of the infants who were not in full-time day care were counted as insecure (Clarke-Stewart, 1989). These results might suggest that day care could harm infants' attachments to mothers.

Are there alternative ways of interpreting the evidence?

Perhaps factors other than day care could explain the difference between infants in day care and those at home with their mothers. One such factor could be the method that was used to assess attachment. Infants in these studies were judged insecure if they did not run to their mothers after a brief separation in the Strange Situation. But maybe infants who experience daily separations from their mothers during day care feel more comfortable in the Strange Situation and therefore seek out less closeness with their mothers. A second factor concerns the possible differences between the infants' mothers. Perhaps mothers who value independence in themselves and in their children are more likely to be working and to place their children in day care, whereas mothers who emphasize closeness with their children are more likely to stay home.

(continued)

What additional evidence would help evaluate the alternatives?

Finding insecure attachment to be more common among the infants of working mothers does not, by itself, demonstrate that day care is harmful. To judge the effects of day care, we must consider other measures of emotional adjustment as well. If infants in day care showed consistent signs of impaired emotional relations in other situations (at home, for example) and with other caregivers (such as the father), this evidence would support the argument that day care harms children's emotional development. We should also statistically control for differences in the behavior and attitudes of parents who do and do not put their infants in day care and then look for differences in their children.

In fact, this research design has already been employed. In 1990, the U.S. government started funding for a study of infant day care in ten sites around the country. The psychological and physical development of more than 1,300 randomly selected infants was tracked from birth through age three. The results have shown that when factors such as parents' education, income, and attitudes were statistically controlled, infants in day care were no more likely to have emotional problems or to be insecurely attached to their mothers than infants not in day care. However, in cases in which infants were in poor-quality day care with insensitive, unresponsive caregivers, and in which mothers were insensitive to their babies' needs at home, the infants were less likely to develop a secure attachment to their mothers (Belsky et al., 2007; NICHD Early Child Care Research Network, 2005, 2006a). A 2011 follow-up on the children in this study found that the ones who experienced both poor care at home and in day care also had the most behavior problems as preschoolers (Watamura et al., 2011).

What conclusions are most reasonable?

Based on available evidence, the most reasonable conclusion appears to be that day care by itself does not lead to insecure attachment. But if that day care is of poor quality, it can worsen a risky situation at home and increase the likelihood that infants will have problems forming a secure attachment to their mothers.

Relationships with Parents and Peers

Erik Erikson (1968) described the first year of life as a time when infants develop a feeling of trust (or mistrust) about the world. According to his theory, an infant's first year represents the first of eight stages of lifelong psychosocial development (see Table 11.2). Each stage focuses on an issue, or "crisis," that is especially important at that time of life. Erikson believed that the ways that people resolve these crises shape their personalities and social relationships. Resolving a crisis in a positive way provides the foundation for characteristics such as trust, independence, initiative, or industry. But if the crisis is not resolved positively, according to Erikson, the person will be psychologically troubled and cope less effectively with later crises. In Erikson's theory, trusting caregivers during infancy forms the bedrock for all future social and emotional development.

The Effects of Day Care

Parents are understandably concerned that leaving their infants in a day-care center might interfere with the mother-infant attachment or other aspects of their children's development. Research shows that most infants in day care do form healthy bonds with their parents but that if children spend many hours in day care between infancy and kindergarten, they are more likely to have behavior problems in school, such as talking back to the teacher or getting into fights (NICHD Early Child Care Research Network, 2001, 2006b). Some employers try to help parents build attachments with their infants by providing on-site day care or letting employees keep their babies with them while working (Armour, 2008).

Bob Mahoney/The Image Works

TABLE 11.2   ERIKSON'S STAGES OF PSYCHOSOCIAL DEVELOPMENT

In each of Erikson's stages of development, a different psychological issue presents a new crisis for the person to resolve. The person focuses attention on that issue and by the end of the period has worked through the crisis and resolved it either positively, in the direction of healthy development, or negatively, hindering further psychological development.

Age	Central Psychological Issue or Crisis
First Year	**Trust versus mistrust** Infants learn to trust that their needs will be met by the world, especially by the mother—or they learn to mistrust the world.
Second year	**Autonomy versus shame and doubt** Children learn to exercise will, make choices, and control themselves—or they become uncertain and doubt that they can do things by themselves.
Third to fifth year	**Initiative versus guilt** Children learn to initiate activities and enjoy their accomplishments, acquiring direction and purpose—or, if they are not allowed initiative, they feel guilty for their attempts at becoming independent.
Sixth year through puberty	**Industry versus inferiority** Children develop a sense of industry and curiosity and are eager to learn—or they feel inferior and lose interest in the tasks before them.
Adolescence	**Identity versus role confusion** Adolescents come to see themselves as unique and integrated persons with an ideology—or they become confused about what they want out of life.
Early adulthood	**Intimacy versus isolation** Young people become able to commit themselves to another person—or they develop a sense of isolation and feel they have no one in the world but themselves.
Middle age	**Generativity versus stagnation** Adults are willing to have and care for children and to devote themselves to their work and the common good—or they become self-centered and inactive.
Old age	**Integrity versus despair** Older people enter a period of reflection, becoming assured that their lives have been meaningful and becoming ready to face death with acceptance and dignity—or they are in despair about their unaccomplished goals, failures, and ill-spent lives.

After children form strong emotional attachments to their parents, their next psychological task is to develop a more independent relationship with them. In Erikson's theory, this task is reflected in the second stage (again, see Table 11.2). Children begin to exercise their wills, to be more independent from parents, and begin activities on their own. According to Erikson, children who are not allowed to exercise their wills or start their own activities will feel uncertain about doing things for themselves and guilty about seeking independence. The extent to which parents allow or encourage their children's independence is related to their parenting style.

socialization The process by which parents, teachers, and others teach children the skills and social norms necessary to be well-functioning members of society.

Parenting Styles

Most parents try to channel children's impulses into socially accepted outlets and teach them the skills and rules needed to function in their culture. This process is called **socialization.**

European American parents tend to use one of four **parenting styles** (Baumrind, 1991; Maccoby & Martin, 1983). **Authoritarian parents** tend to be strict, punishing, and unsympathetic. They value obedience from children and try to curb the children's wills and shape their children's behavior to meet a set standard. They do not encourage independence. They are detached and seldom praise their kids. In contrast, **permissive parents** give children complete freedom with little discipline. **Authoritative parents** fall between these two extremes. They reason with their children, encouraging give and take. They allow children increasing responsibility as they get better at making decisions. They are firm but understanding. They set limits but also encourage independence. Their demands are reasonable, rational, and consistent. **Uninvolved parents** (also known as **rejecting-neglecting parents**) are indifferent to their children. They invest as little time, money, and effort in their children as possible, focusing on their own needs before their children's. These parents often fail to monitor their children's activities, particularly when the children are old enough to be out of the house alone.

Research shows that these parenting styles are consistently related to young children's social and emotional development (e.g., Eisenberg, Fabes, & Spinrad, 2006; Erath et al., 2011; Parke & Buriel, 2006). Authoritarian parents tend to have children who are unfriendly, distrustful, and withdrawn. These children have more behavioral problems, show less remorse or acceptance of blame after doing something wrong, and more often cheat in school (Eisenberg, Fabes, & Spinrad, 2006; Paulussen-Hoogeboom et al., 2008). Children of permissive parents tend to be immature, dependent, and unhappy; they are likely to have tantrums or to ask for help when they encounter even slight difficulties. Children raised by authoritative parents tend to do best. They are more often friendly, cooperative, self-reliant, and socially responsible (Ginsburg et al., 2009). They do better in school, enjoy greater popularity, and show better psychological adjustment in the event of parental divorce (Hinshaw et al., 1997; Steinberg et al., 1994).

The results of all these parenting studies are limited in several ways. First, they are based on correlations, which, as discussed in the chapter on research in psychology, do not prove causation. Finding consistent correlations between parents' and children's behavior does not establish that the parents are *causing* the differences seen in their children. Socialization is a two-way street: Parents' behavior is shaped by their children, too. Children's temperament, size, and appearance may influence how parents treat them (Ganiban et al., 2011; Lipscomb et al., 2011). Some developmental psychologists even suggest that it is not the parents' socialization practices that influence children but rather how the children perceive discipline—as stricter or more lenient than what an older sibling received, for example (Reiss et al., 2000).

A second limitation of parenting studies is that the correlations between parenting styles and children's behavior, though statistically significant, are usually not terribly large (Ho, Bluestein, & Jenkins, 2008) and therefore do not apply to every child in every family. In fact, research shows that the effects of parents' socialization can differ depending on their children's temperament. The gentle parental guidance that has a noticeable effect on a child with a fearful temperament might have far less impact on a child whose temperament is less fearful (Kochanska, Aksan, & Joy, 2007). Similarly, harsh authoritarian parenting seems to disrupt emotion regulation and the development of conscience in children who are temperamentally fearful (Feng et al., 2008; Schwartz & Bugental, 2004).

Parenting Styles and Culture

Yet another limitation of parenting studies is that most of them were conducted with European American families. Is the impact of various parenting styles different in other ethnic groups and other cultures? Possibly. Parents in Latino cultures in Mexico, Puerto Rico, and Central America and in Asian cultures in China and India, for example, tend to be influenced by a collectivist tradition in which family and community interests are emphasized over individual goals. Children in these cultures are expected to respect and obey their elders and to do less of the questioning, negotiating, and arguing that is encouraged—or at least allowed—in many middle-class European and European American families (Greenfield, Suzuki, & Rothstein-Fisch, 2006; Parke & Buriel, 2006). When parents from these cultures immigrate to the United States, they bring their authoritarian

parenting styles The varying patterns of behavior—ranging from permissive to authoritarian—that parents display as they interact with and discipline their children.

authoritarian parents Parents who are firm, punitive, and unsympathetic.

permissive parents Parents who give their children complete freedom and lax discipline.

authoritative parents Parents who reason with their children and are firm but understanding.

uninvolved parents (rejecting-neglecting parents) Parents who invest as little time, money, and effort in their children as possible.

Parent-Training Programs

Parenting styles are determined by many factors, including genetics (Klahr & Burt, 2014), and research on how different styles affect children's behavior has helped shape parent-training programs based on the learning principles described in the chapter on learning and on the social-cognitive and humanistic approaches described in the chapter on personality. These programs are designed to teach parents authoritative methods that can avoid scenes like this.

Ulrich Baumgarten/Getty Images

parenting style with them. There is evidence, though, that the authoritarian discipline often seen in Asian American, Hispanic American, and African American families does not have the same negative consequences for young children's behavior as it does in European American families (Chao & Tseng, 2002; Slade & Wissow, 2004). For example, Chinese children tend to believe that their mothers (and teachers) are motivated to teach them to behave well rather than to control them and so they feel more positive than European American children do about authoritarian disciplinary techniques such as shaming, imparting guilt, and withdrawing love (Helwig et al., 2013; Zhou, Lam, & Chan, 2012). By contrast, European American parents are more likely to use authoritarian discipline to keep children in line and break their wills. In countries such as India and Kenya, where physical punishment tends to be an accepted form of discipline, punishment is associated with less aggression and anxiety than in Thailand and China, where it is rarely used (Lansford et al., 2005). These findings require us to view parenting styles in a cultural context—no one style is universally "best" (Parke & Buriel, 2006).

Peer Friendships and Popularity

Social development over childhood occurs in a world that broadens to include siblings, playmates, and classmates. Relationships with other children start early (Hay, Caplan, & Nash, 2011). By two months of age, infants engage in mutual gazing. By six months, they vocalize and smile at each other. By eight months, they prefer to look at another child rather than at an adult (Bigelow et al., 1990). In other words, even infants are interested in other people, but it's a long journey from interest to intimacy.

Observations of two-year-olds show that the most they can do with their peers is to look at them, imitate them, and exchange—or grab—toys. By age four, they begin to play "pretend" together, agreeing about roles and themes (Coplan & Arbeau, 2011). This kind of play is important because it provides a new context for communicating desires and feelings and offers an opportunity to form first "friendships" (Dunn & Hughes, 2001). In the school years, peer interaction becomes more frequent, complex, and structured. Children play games with rules, join teams, tutor each other, and cooperate—or compete—in achieving goals. Friends become more important and friendships longer lasting as school-age children find that friends are a source of companionship, stimulation, support, and affection (Hartup & Stevens, 1997). In fact, companionship and fun are the most important aspects of friendship for children at this age. Psychological intimacy does not enter the picture until adolescence (Parker et al., 2001).

Friends help children establish a sense of self-worth (Harter, 2012). Through friendships, children compare their own strengths and weaknesses with those of others in a supportive and accepting atmosphere. Some children have more friends than others. When children are asked to nominate the classmates they like the best and the least, those who get the most votes—the *popular children*—tend to be the ones who are friendly, assertive, and who communicate well; they help set the rules for their group and use positive social behavior, such as helping others. They attract more attention, especially from other popular kids (Lansu, Cillessen, & Karremans, 2013). Especially in early adolescence, children who are athletic, arrogant, or aggressive may also be popular, if their aggressiveness is not too extreme (Asher & McDonald, 2011).

About 10 percent of schoolchildren have no friends. Some, known as *rejected children*, are actively disliked, either because they are too aggressive or because they are anxious and socially unskilled. Others, called *neglected children,* are seldom mentioned in peer nominations; they are isolated, quiet, and withdrawn but not necessarily

Children's Friendships

Although relationships with peers may not always be this friendly, they are often among the closest and most positive in a child's life. Friends are more interactive than nonfriends; they smile and laugh together more, pay closer attention to equality in their conversations, and talk about mutual goals. Having at least one close friend in childhood predicts good psychological functioning later on (Laursen et al., 2007; Parker et al., 2001).

David Grossman/Science Source

disliked. Friendless children tend to do poorly in school and usually have psychological and behavior problems later in life (Asher & Hopmeyer, 2001; Ladd & Troop-Gordon, 2003). Having even one close, stable friend may protect schoolchildren from such problems (Laursen et al., 2007; Parker et al., 2001). Overall, the single most important factor in determining children's popularity may be the *social skills* they learn from childhood to adolescence (Rubin, Bukowski, & Parker, 2006).

Social Skills

Changes in peer interactions and relationships over childhood show children's increasing social talents and understanding. Social skills, like cognitive skills, are learned (Rubin et al., 2006).

One important social skill is the ability to engage in sustained, responsive interactions. These interactions require cooperation, sharing, and taking turns—behaviors that first appear in the preschool years. A second social skill that children learn is the ability to detect and correctly interpret other people's emotional signals as well as understand the causes of emotion (Weimer, Sallquist, & Bolnick 2012). Much as children's school performance depends on processing academic information, their social performance depends on processing emotional information.

A related set of social skills includes being able to feel what another person is feeling, or *empathy*, and to comfort or help others in distress. Children whose social skills include these abilities tend to be the most popular in their peer groups (Izard et al., 2001; Rubin et al., 2006). Children without these skills tend to be rejected or neglected; they may become bullies or the victims of bullies.

Bullying has attracted intense attention in recent years, not only because its victims often experience reduced self-esteem and depression (Messias, Kindrick, & Castro, 2014; Zwierzynska, Wolke, & Lereya, 2013; van Geel, Vedder, & Tanilon, 2014), but also because some of the victims have committed suicide or sought revenge through school shootings and other violent acts. A bully's aggression can take the form of hitting, pushing, threatening, or taunting, but can also involve spreading rumors and other forms of harassment, including cyberbullying, in which communications through Internet devices are used to torment victims (Patchin & Hinduja, 2012; Wolak et al., 2006). Combating the problem is not easy and increasingly is becoming a legal matter. As of 2013, every state in the United States except Montana has anti-bullying laws (Hinduja & Patchin, 2013).

Parents, other adults, and even older siblings can help children develop adaptive social skills by engaging them in "pretend" play and other prosocial activities and by encouraging constructive expression of emotion (Eisenberg, Fabes, & Spinrad, 2006; Ladd, 2005). Empathy may start early in childhood. When a baby spontaneously cries and fusses, a six-month-old nearby typically orients toward the infant by leaning, gesturing, or touching, and making concerned facial expressions and vocalizations (Davidov et al., 2013).

The ability to control one's emotions and behavior—an ability known as **self-regulation**—is another social skill that develops in childhood (Rothbart & Bates, 2006; Thompson, Lewis, & Calkins, 2008). In the first few years of life, children learn to calm or console themselves by sucking their thumbs or cuddling their favorite blanket (Posner & Rothbart, 2000). Later they learn more-sophisticated self-regulation strategies. These include waiting for something they want rather than crying or grabbing for it (Eisenberg et al., 2004), counting to ten in order to control anger, planning ahead to avoid a problem (e.g., getting on the first bus to avoid a disliked peer), and recruiting social support (e.g., casually joining a group of big kids to walk past a playground bully). Children who regulate their emotions poorly tend to have anxiety and do not recover well from stressful events. They become emotionally overaroused when they see someone in distress and are often unsympathetic and unhelpful (Eisenberg et al., 2006). Further, boys whose emotions are easily aroused and have difficulty regulating this arousal become less and less popular with their peers and may develop problems with aggressiveness (e.g., Eisenberg et al., 2004, 2009).

self-regulation The ability to control one's emotions and behavior.

EXPLORING DEVELOPING MINDS

Children's ability to make sense of other people's behavior depends on understanding the thinking behind another person's actions. Critical to this understanding is the recognition that what other people think may be wrong. For more than twenty years, researchers have argued that children under four years of age cannot understand other people's mental states because they do not yet have a "theory of mind." This argument was based on studies in which children were asked questions about other people's beliefs (e.g., Baron-Cohen, Leslie, & Frith, 1985). In one study, children were shown a simple little drama starring two dolls, "Sally" and "Anne." First, Sally puts a marble in her basket and then leaves the stage. While Sally is away, Anne takes the marble out of Sally's basket and puts it into her own box. Then Sally returns to get her marble, and the child is asked where Sally will look for it. To correctly predict that Sally will look in the basket where she last saw the marble, the children in this study would have to recognize that Sally has a false belief about its location. Even though they know where the marble really is, they will have to be able to "read Sally's mind," realize what she must be thinking, and say "she'll look in her basket." However, most children under the age of four ignore the fact that Sally thinks the marble is still in her basket and say that she'll look in Anne's box.

What was the researcher's question?

Renee Baillargeon (pronounced "by-ar-ZHAN") wondered, though, whether the inability of these young children to recognize what others are thinking reflected a true lack of a "theory of mind" or was the result of using research methods that were not sensitive enough to detect its existence. So her research question was whether more specialized methods might reveal that even children under four can understand that other people's behavior is affected by their mental states, including false beliefs and false perceptions.

How did the researcher answer the question?

Instead of requiring children to answer questions about other people's behavior, Baillargeon used a more creative and potentially more sensitive method to probe young children's knowledge. She reasoned that infants' tendency to look longer at certain events indicates that those events violate their expectations about the world, so she showed infants various events and then carefully measured the amount of time they spent looking at them.

Baillargeon used this method to measure the ability of fifteen-month-old infants to predict where a woman would look for a toy, depending on whether she had a true or a false belief about the toy's location (Onishi & Baillargeon, 2005). Each infant first watched the woman play with a toy watermelon slice for a few seconds, then hide it inside a green box. Next, the woman watched the toy being moved from the green box to a yellow box. Then she left the scene, and while she was gone the toy was put back into the green box. When she came back, she looked for the toy by reaching either into the green box or the yellow box. Baillargeon reasoned that if the infants expected the woman to search for the toy on the basis of her false belief that it was still in the yellow box, they would look longer at her if she violated their expectation by searching in the green box instead. This would suggest that they were thinking "Hey, how could she know the toy had been moved? I expected her to look where she last saw it!" But if, as earlier studies had suggested, the infants really had no "theory of mind," they would ignore the woman's false belief and expect her to look in the green box, where they knew the toy now lay. If the woman did that, they would not pay any special attention to her action.

What did the researcher find?

The results of this study showed that, contrary to what would be expected from previous research, the infants did look longer when the woman looked for the toy in the green box.

What do the results mean?

These results argue that children under the age of four do have a "theory of mind." When evaluated using appropriate research methods, these young children demonstrate an ability

(continued)

to recognize that other people's beliefs and perceptions can be false, that those beliefs and perceptions can differ from the child's own, and that these mental states affect the other person's behavior (Baillargeon, Scott, & He, 2010).

What do we still need to know?

Among other things, it would be good to know more about the extent of infants' understanding of mental states. Does it appear in other situations? Baillargeon has begun to explore this question. In one study, infants viewed a scene in which a woman looked for a doll with blue pigtails. She could look in either a plain box or in a box that had a blue tuft of hair sticking out from under its lid (Song & Baillargeon, 2008). The infants knew that the doll was in the plain box, but they stared longer when the woman looked in that box first; this suggested that they expected her to be misled by the blue tuft of hair and to falsely perceive it as belonging to the doll. In another study, Baillargeon investigated whether infants know that new information can correct an adult's false belief (Song et al., 2008). In this case, infants watched an adult hide a ball in a box while another adult watched. After the first adult left the scene, the second adult moved the ball from the box to a cup. When the first adult returned, the second adult told her "The ball is in the cup!" Infants stared longer if the adult searched for the ball in the box despite this corrective information. Those who saw her reach for the cup did not pay special attention, suggesting that they expected her to do so once her false belief had been corrected.

What other mental states can infants understand (Palmquist & Jaswal, 2012)? Do they also realize that other people's behavior can be influenced by goals, intentions, emotions, and even by the fairness or unfairness of a situation (LoBue, Nichida et al., 2011; Sloane, Baillargeon, & Premack, 2012; Warneken et al., 2011)? How soon after birth does a "theory of mind" develop? These are among the dozens of additional questions that remain for future research in this fascinating area of developmental psychology (Woodward, 2009).

Gender Roles

An important aspect of understanding other people is knowing about social roles, including those linked to being male or female. All cultures establish expectations about **sex roles**—also known as **gender roles**—which are the general patterns of work, appearance, and behavior associated with being a man or a woman (Blakemore, Berenbaum, & Liben, 2009). Gender roles appear in every culture, but they are more pronounced in some cultures than in others. One analysis revealed, for example, that where smaller differences in social status exist between males and females, gender-role differences are smaller as well (Wood & Eagly, 2002). In North America, some roles—such as homemaker and firefighter—have traditionally been tied to gender, although these traditions are weakening. Research by Deborah Best suggests that although children show gender-role expectations earliest in Muslim countries (where the differences in roles are perhaps most extreme), children in all twenty-five countries she studied eventually developed them (Best, 1992; Williams & Best, 1990).

Gender roles endure because they are deeply rooted in both nature and nurture. Small physical and behavioral differences between boys and girls appear early and tend to increase over time. For example, girls tend to speak and write earlier, with better grammar and spelling than boys (Halpern, 2012). Girls read emotions at younger ages than boys (Dunn et al., 1991) and more often ask for or offer help (Benenson & Koulnazarian, 2008). Girls play more with dolls, interact more with caregivers, and show gender-stereotyped activities during play (for example, pretending to "cook" in a kitchen area) (Alexander & Saenz, 2012; Fausto-Sterling, Coll, & Lamarre, 2012). Boys tend to be more skilled at manipulating objects, building three-dimensional forms, and mentally manipulating complex figures and pictures (Choi & Silverman, 2003; Newhouse, Newhouse, & Astur, 2007). They spend more time playing with blocks, vehicles, and tools (Alexander & Saenz, 2012; Fausto-Sterling,

LINKAGES Who teaches boys to be men and girls to be women? (a link to Learning)

Learning Gender Roles

In every culture, socialization by parents and others typically encourages the interests, activities, and other characteristics traditionally associated with a child's own gender.

Superstudio/The Image Bank/Getty Images

Coll, & Lamarre, 2012). They are more physically active and aggressive and are more inclined to hit objects or people (Baillargeon et al., 2007; Card et al., 2008; Ostrov, 2006). They play in larger groups and spaces and enjoy noisier, more strenuous physical games (Fabes, Martin, & Hanish, 2003; Rose & Rudolph, 2006).

Biological Factors

A biological contribution to male-female differences is suggested by several lines of evidence. First, studies show sex differences in anatomy, hormones, and brain organization and functioning (Geary, 2010; Ruble, Martin, & Berenbaum, 2006). Second, cross-cultural research reveals consistent gender patterns at an early age, despite differing socialization practices (Baillargeon et al., 2007; Simpson & Kenrick, 1997). Third, research with non-human primates finds sex differences that parallel those seen in human children. Young female animals prefer playing with dolls, and young male animals prefer playing with a toy car, for example (Alexander & Hines, 2002; Williams & Pleil, 2008). Fourth, research in behavioral genetics shows that genes exert a moderate influence on the appearance of gender-typed behaviors (Iervolino et al., 2005).

Social Factors

Socialization influences gender roles, partly by exaggerating sex differences that may already exist (Hyde, 2005, 2007). From birth, boys and girls are treated differently (Lobue & DeLoache, 2011). Adults usually play more gently with, and talk more to, infants they believe to be girls than infants they believe to be boys (Culp, Cook, & Housley, 1983). They often give their daughters dolls and tea sets, their sons trucks and tools. They tend to encourage boys to achieve, compete, and explore; to control their feelings; to be independent; and to assume personal responsibility. They more often encourage girls to be expressive, nurturing, reflective, dependent, domestic, obedient, and unselfish (Blakemore et al., 2009; Ruble, Martin, & Berenbaum, 2006). Parents spend more time vocalizing to daughters than to sons (Fausto-Sterling, Coll, & Lamarre, 2012) and engage in more physical play with boys and more reading activities with girls (Leavell et al., 2012). In short, parents, teachers, and television role models consciously or accidentally pass on their ideas about "appropriate" behaviors for boys and girls (Else-Quest et al., 2010; Parke & Buriel, 2006; Ruble et al., 2006).

They also convey information about gender-appropriate interests (Wood & Eagly, 2012). For example, sixth-grade girls and boys express equal interest in science and earn the same grades. Yet parents underestimate their daughters' interest in science, believe that science is difficult for them, and are less likely to give them scientific explanations when working on a physics task (Tenenbaum & Leaper, 2003) or visiting a science museum (Crowley et al., 2001; Leinhardt & Knutson, 2004). They do not encourage their daughters to select science courses in school (Tenenbaum, 2009). Additionally, even though girls have the same aptitudes as boys (Schmidt, 2011), they may choose not to enter technical fields in which they feel, or have been taught, that they do not belong (Diekman et al., 2010; Good, Rattan, & Dweck, 2012).

Children also pick up ideas about gender-appropriate behavior from their peers (Martin et al., 2013). For example, boys tend to be better than girls at computer or video games (Greenfield, 1994). However, this difference stems partly from the fact that boys encourage and reward each other for skilled performance at these games more than girls do (Law, Pellegrino, & Hunt, 1993). Children are also more likely to play with children of the same sex and in gender-typical ways on the playground than they are in private, at home, or in the classroom (Luria, 1992; Martin & Ruble, 2009). An analysis of 143 studies of sex differences in aggression showed that boys acted significantly and consistently more aggressively than girls, but especially so when they knew they were being watched (Hyde, 1986). Among girls, aggression is less obvious; it is usually "relational aggression" that shows up in nasty words or social exclusion, not punching (Benenson et al., 2011; Crick et al., 2004; McAndrew, 2014).

gender roles (sex roles) Patterns of work, appearance, and behavior that a society associates with being male or female.

Human Development

In short, social and cultural training tends to support and amplify any biological predispositions that distinguish boys and girls. Gender roles reflect a mix of nature and nurture.

Parents' efforts to deemphasize gender roles in their children's upbringing may be helping to reduce the size of sex differences in areas such as verbal and quantitative skills. And their efforts may be changing children's ideas about gender roles. One recent study found that four- to eight-year-old children tended to think of gender roles as personal choices rather than social imperatives (Conry-Murray, & Turiel, 2012). However, evolutionary psychologists suggest that some sex differences are unlikely to change much; for example, males' greater ability to visualize the rotation of objects in space and females' greater ability to read facial expressions (Quinn & Liben, 2008). Evolutionary psychologists see these differences as deeply rooted reflections of gender-related hunting versus child-rearing duties that were adaptive eons ago for the survival of both sexes (Buss, 2004a; Geary, 2010). Others have suggested that such differences result from prenatal exposure to male or female hormones that shape brain development in different ways (Halpern, 2012; Vuoksimaa et al., 2010). Still others see gender differences as reflecting social inequality, not just biological destiny (Wood & Eagly, 2002). Whatever the cause of gender differences, it is important to remember that most of them are quite small (Ardila et al., 2011; Hyde, 2005). (Gender roles and other elements of early development are summarized in "In Review: Social and Emotional Development during Infancy and Childhood.")

SOCIAL AND EMOTIONAL DEVELOPMENT DURING INFANCY AND CHILDHOOD   IN REVIEW

Age	Relationships with Parents	Relationships with Other Children	Social Understanding
Birth–2 years	Infants form an attachment to the primary caregiver.	Play focuses on toys, not on other children.	Infants respond to emotional expressions of others.
2–4 years	Children become more independent and no longer need their parents' constant attention.	Toys are a way of eliciting responses from other children.	Young children can recognize emotions of others.
4–10 years	Parents actively socialize their children.	Children begin to cooperate, compete, play games, and form friendships with peers.	Children learn social rules (such as politeness) and roles (such as being a male or female).

In Review Questions

1. As part of their social development, children learn _____, which tell them what patterns of appearance and behavior are associated with being male or female.

2. Teaching children to talk quietly in a restaurant is part of the process called _____.

3. Strict rules and the threat of punishment are typical of _____ parenting.

Risk and Resilience

resilience A quality allowing children to develop normally in spite of severe environmental risk factors.

Family instability, child abuse, homelessness, parental unemployment, poverty, substance abuse, and domestic violence put many children at risk for various difficulties in social and emotional development (Ackerman, Brown, & Izard, 2004; Karevold et al., 2009). Children vary in how well they ultimately adjust to these stressors. Even when the odds are against them, some children are left virtually unscathed by even the most dangerous risk factors. These children are said to be resilient. **Resilience** is a characteristic that permits successful development in the face of significant challenge. It has been studied throughout the world in a variety of adverse situations, including war, natural disaster, family violence, child maltreatment, and poverty. This research has consistently identified certain qualities in children and their environments that are associated with resilience. Specifically, resilient children tend to be intelligent and to have easy temperaments, high self-esteem, talent, and faith (Masten 2013). They are cheerful, focused, and persistent in completing a task (Wills et al., 2001). They also typically have significant relationships with a warm and authoritative parent, with someone in their extended family, or with other caring adults outside the family, at school, or in clubs or religious organizations (Rutter, 2006). In addition, they have genes that direct optimal regulation of serotonin, a neurotransmitter that, as described in the chapter on biological aspects of psychology, plays a role in mood and stress-related responses (Kim-Cohen & Gold, 2009). There appear to be long-term benefits for resilient kids who faced adversity in childhood. When they confront new problems later in life, they adapt better than people who had experienced little or no childhood difficulty (Luthar & Barkin, 2012; Masten & Tellegen, 2012). They also appear to have better long-term mental health outcomes than those who experienced either *extreme* adversity or *no* adversity (Seery, 2011).

ADOLESCENCE

What threatens adolescents' self-esteem?

The years of middle childhood usually pass smoothly as children busy themselves with schoolwork, hobbies, friends, and clubs. But in adolescence, things change dramatically. All adolescents undergo significant changes in size, shape, and physical capacities. In Western cultures, many adolescents also experience huge changes in their social lives, reasoning abilities, and views of themselves.

Changes in Body, Brain, and Thinking

A sudden spurt in physical growth is a visible signal that adolescence has begun. This growth spurt peaks at about age twelve for girls and at about age fourteen for boys (Tanner, 1978; see Figure 11.6). Suddenly, adolescents find themselves in new bodies. At around the

FIGURE 11.6
Physical Changes in Adolescence

At about ten and a half years of age, girls begin their growth spurt, and by age twelve, they are taller than their male peers. When boys, at about twelve and a half years of age, begin their growth spurt, they usually grow faster and for a longer period of time than girls. Adolescents may grow five inches in a year. Sexual characteristics develop too. The ages at which these changes occur vary across individuals, but the sequence of changes is the same.

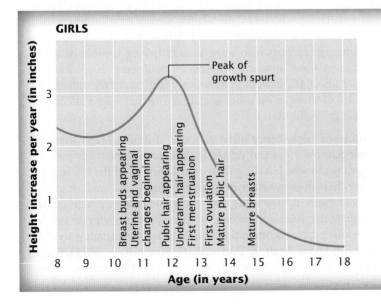

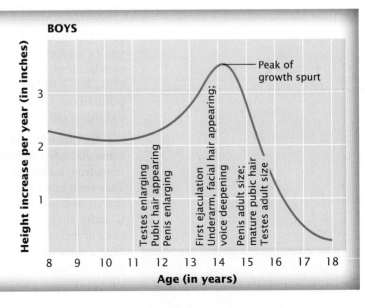

Digital Connections

Compared to adults and children, adolescents spend more time online and communicating electronically to stay in touch with people in their social networks (Reich, Subrahmanyam, & Espinoza, 2012; Valkenburg & Peter, 2007a, 2009). About a third of them believe that online communication is more effective than in-person conversation for disclosing intimate personal information. We do not yet know what (if any), long-term effects the constant use of social media might have on adolescents' cognitive functioning and academic performance, or whether it has positive or negative effects on the size of young people's social networks, their feelings of well-being, or their closeness to friends.

Britt Erlanson/Cultura/Getty Images

peak of the growth spurt, menstruation begins in females and live sperm are produced in males. This condition of being able to reproduce is called **puberty**.

These dramatic changes in teenagers' bodies are accompanied by significant changes in their brains, especially in parts of the frontal lobes known as the prefrontal cortex (Kuhn, 2006; Spear, 2000). These areas are vital to the ability to think flexibly, to act appropriately in challenging situations, and to juggle multiple pieces of information. They are also involved in skills such as planning and organization, controlling impulses, and allocating attention.

In Western cultures, the changes of *early adolescence*, from approximately ages eleven to fourteen, can be disorienting. Adolescents—especially early-maturing girls—may have depression, insomnia, or other psychological problems (Johnson et al., 2006; Mendle, Turkheimer, & Emery, 2007; Ohring, Graber, & Brooks-Gunn, 2002). This is also when eating disorders may first appear (Wilson et al., 1996). As sex hormones and pleasure-related brain systems become more active, sexual interest stirs and the prospect of smoking or using alcohol or illegal drugs becomes more appealing (Patton et al., 2004; Reyna & Farley, 2006). Opportunities to do these things increase because adolescents may spend more time with peers than family, be more influenced by peers, and take more risks and seek out more novel sensations than either younger children or adults (Harden, Quinn, & Tucker-Drob, 2012; Steinberg, 2008).

Much of this risk-taking seems to be due to the different rates at which parts of the adolescent brain develop. The areas of prefrontal cortex involved in planning and impulse control do not finish developing until long after the emotional and reward-related areas of the limbic system do (Chein et al., 2011; Steinberg, 2008; Vetter-O'Hagen & Spear, 2012). So, as one researcher put it, the teenage brain is like a car with a good gas pedal but a weak brake (Ritter, 2007). Adolescents can make rational decisions and appreciate right versus wrong, but when confronted with stressful or emotional decisions, they may act impulsively, without fully understanding or analyzing the consequences of their actions. Especially when with peers, teens may take risks despite clearly recognizing the dangers involved (Smith, Chein, & Steinberg, 2014). Of course, a certain amount of adolescent risk-taking and sensation-seeking is normal. In fact, adolescents who engage in moderate risk-taking tend to be more socially competent than those who take no risks or extreme risks (Spear, 2000).

Some of the problems of adolescence appear as young people begin to face threats to *self-esteem*—a sense of being worthy, capable, and deserving of respect (Harter, 2012). Adolescents are especially vulnerable if other stressors occur at the same time (DuBois et al., 1992; Kling et al., 1999). The switch from elementary school to middle school is particularly challenging (Eccles, Lord, & Buchanan, 1996; Wigfield et al., 2006). Declining grades are especially likely among students who were already having trouble in school or who don't have confidence in their own abilities (Eccles & Roeser, 2003; Rudolph et al., 2001). But grades do not affect self-esteem in all teens; many base their self-esteem primarily on what others think of them or on other social factors that might affect their feelings of self-worth (Crocker & Wolfe, 2001).

The changes and pressures of adolescence often play out at home. Many teens become discontented with their parents' rules and values, leading to arguments over everything from taking out the garbage to who left the gallon of milk on top of the refrigerator. They want more control over their lives, whether it involves going to the mall or getting tattoos or body piercings—especially if they think that their friends enjoy such control (Daddis, 2011). Serious conflicts may lead adolescents—especially those who do not feel close to their parents—to serious problems, including running away, pregnancy, stealing, drug use, or suicide (Goldstein, Davis-Kean, & Eccles, 2005; Klahr et al., 2011). Fortunately, although the bond with parents weakens during early to mid-adolescence, most adolescents and young adults maintain fairly good relationships with parents (e.g., McGue

puberty The condition of being able, for the first time, to reproduce.

Mothers Too Soon?

More than half of the U.S. adolescents who become pregnant elect to keep their babies and become single mothers. These young women and their children are likely to face special academic, social, and other problems. For this reason, support programs for teenage mothers have been developed, and a number of them have reported some success in three areas: alleviating the mothers' symptoms of depression, increasing the mothers' parenting capabilities, and achieving the mothers' educational goals (Cox et al., 2008; Sadler et al., 2007).

Ebby May/The Image Bank/Getty Images

et al., 2005; Moore, 2005). That's a good thing, because adolescents who maintain positive relationships with parents are better adjusted in early adulthood and show less depression, anxiety, suicidal behavior, drug abuse, or criminal activity (Ogilvie et al., 2014; Raudino, Fergusson, & Horwood, 2013).

Love and Sex in Adolescence

Nearly half of fifteen-year-olds and 70 percent of eighteen-year-olds in North America have romantic relationships (Collins & Steinberg, 2006), and about a third of sixteen-year-olds and half of seventeen-year-olds in the United States are sexually active (Guttmacher Institute, 2013). Teens who have sex differ from those who do not (Huibregtse et al., 2011). They hold less conventional attitudes and values and are more likely to smoke, use alcohol and other drugs (National Center on Addiction and Substance Abuse, 2004), be aggressive, and have attention problems in school (Schofield et al., 2008). They also spend more unsupervised time after school (Cohen & Steele, 2002), they are more likely to belong to peer groups with socially deviant behavioral norms (diNoia & Schinke, 2008), they are more likely to have sexually active best friends (Jaccard, Blanton, & Dodge, 2005), and they are more likely to live in poverty (Belsky, Schlomer, & Ellis, 2012). Their parents tend to be less educated, less likely to exert control over them, less supportive, and less able to talk openly (Price & Hyde, 2011). The typical pairing of sexually active heterosexual teens is a "macho" male and a "girly" female (Udry & Chantala, 2003). Adolescents who showed poor self-control skills as children are the ones most likely to take greater sexual risks, such as having multiple partners and not using condoms (Atkins, 2008; Raffaelli & Crockett, 2003).

Teenage sexual activity is associated with declining interest in academic achievement and in school generally (Frisco, 2008), sexually transmitted diseases, and unwanted pregnancies. Teenage girls have the highest rates of sexually transmitted diseases of any age group (Forhan et al., 2009). About half of the 19 million cases of sexually transmitted diseases reported each year occur in adolescents (Malhotra, 2008); these cases include about one-fourth of all teenage girls (Contemporary Sexuality, 2008; Hampton, 2008).

Nearly 18 percent of teenage girls in the United States get pregnant before they reach age nineteen, and about 415,000 of them become teenage mothers (Martin et al., 2011; Perper & Manlove, 2009). The teens most likely to become pregnant are those with little confidence in themselves or in their educational futures (Chandra et al., 2008; Young et al., 2004). A teenage pregnancy can create problems for the mother, the baby, and others in the family. For one thing, the mother is less likely to complete high school (Perper, Peterson, & Manlove, 2010). The education of younger siblings may be affected, too, because they may have to take time away from schoolwork to help care for the baby. These siblings are also at increased risk for drug and alcohol use and, for sisters, of becoming pregnant themselves (East & Jacobson, 2001; Monstad, Propper, & Salvanesvc, 2011). The baby is less likely than an older mother's child to survive its first year (Phipps, Blume, & DeMonner, 2002). This danger may occur partly because teenage parents tend to be less positive and stimulating with their children than older parents and are more likely to abuse them (Brooks-Gunn & Chase-Lansdale, 2002). The children of teenage parents are also more likely to develop behavior problems and to do poorly in school than children whose parents are older (Hoffman, 2008; Moffitt, 2002).

Violent Adolescents

Some people respond to the challenges of adolescence with violence. The roots of teenage violence lie partly in genetic factors (e.g., Cicchetti, Rogosch, & Thibodeau, 2012; Latendresse et al., 2011). Among the other factors that increase the risk of violent behavior in adolescence are insecure attachments, fearlessness, low intelligence, lack of empathy, lack of emotional self-regulation, aggressiveness, and moral disengagement (e.g., Eisenberg et al., 2004; Marceau et al., 2013; Ogilvie et al., 2014, Pepler et al., 2008). Gender is another important factor (Baxendale, Cross, & Johnston, 2012). Worldwide, the rate of homicide committed by males is more than thirty times higher than the rate for females (Cassel & Bernstein, 2007).

Several environmental factors are also associated with increased risk of youth violence, including maternal depression, rejection, living in violent neighborhoods (Herrenkohl et al., 2004), involvement with delinquent gangs or antisocial peers (Burt, McGue, & Iacono, 2009; Rutter, 2003), poverty (Strohschein, 2005), malnutrition (Liu et al., 2004), and exposure to violent television and video games (Comstock & Scharrer, 2006; Nicoll & Kieffer, 2005). Peers are particularly influential. Adolescent violence is also more likely when children grow up witnessing family violence, clashing with siblings, or experiencing physical abuse (Cicchetti, Rogosch, & Thibodeau, 2012; Ehrensaft et al., 2003; Noland et al., 2004).

Despite the potential problems of adolescence, most teens in Western cultures are not violent and do not experience major personal turmoil or family conflicts. So although most parents and teachers seem to believe that adolescence is a time of "storm and stress" (Hines & Paulson, 2007), research suggests that more than half of today's teens find adolescence relatively trouble-free (Arnett, 1999, 2007b; Chung, Flook, & Fuligni, 2009). Only about 15 percent of the adolescents studied experience serious distress (Steinberg, 1990). Most adolescents cope well with the changes puberty brings and soon find themselves in the midst of perhaps the biggest challenge of their young lives: preparing themselves for the transition to young adulthood.

Identity and Development of the Self

In many less economically developed nations today, as in the United States in the nineteenth century, early adolescence ends at around age fifteen. This age marks the onset of adulthood—a time when work, parenting, and grown-up responsibilities begin. In modern North America, the transition from childhood to adulthood often lasts well into the twenties. Adolescents spend a lot of time being students or trainees. This lengthened adolescence has created special problems—among them, the matter of finding or forming an identity.

Forming a Personal and Ethnic Identity

Preschool children asked to describe themselves often mention a favorite or habitual activity: "I watch TV" or "I play sports." At eight or nine, children identify themselves by giving facts such as gender, age, name, physical appearance, and their likes and dislikes. They may still describe themselves by what they do, but they include how well they do it compared to others. Then, at about age eleven, children begin to describe themselves by social relationships, personality traits, and other general, stable psychological qualities such as "smart" or "friendly" (Sakuma, Endo, & Muto, 2000; Shaffer, 1999). By the end of adolescence, self-descriptions emphasize personal beliefs, values, and moral standards (Harter, 2012). These changes in the way children and adolescents describe themselves suggest changes in how they think about themselves (Davis-Kean, Jager, & Collins, 2009). As they become more self-conscious, they gradually develop a personal identity as unique individuals.

Their personal identity includes an **ethnic identity**—the part of identity that reflects the racial, religious, or cultural group to which the person belongs (French et al., 2006; Quintana, 2010). In melting-pot nations such as the United States, some members of ethnic minorities may identify with their ethnic group—Chinese, Mexican, or Italian, for example—even more than with their national citizenship. Children are aware of ethnic cues such as skin color before they are three years old. Minority-group children notice these cues earlier than other children and prefer to play with children from their own group (Milner, 1983). In high school, most students hang out with members of their own ethnic group. They tend not to know classmates in other ethnic groups as well, seeing them more as members of groups than as individuals (Steinberg, Dornbusch, & Brown, 1992). A positive ethnic identity adds to self-esteem, partly because seeing their own group as superior makes people feel good about themselves and creates positive attitudes about education

ethnic identity The part of a person's identity that reflects the racial, religious, or cultural group to which that person belongs.

Hanging Out, Separately

TRY THIS Ethnic identity is that part of our personal identity that reflects the racial, religious, or cultural group to which we belong. Ethnic identity often leads people to interact mainly with others who share that same identity. To what extent is this true of you? You can get a rough idea by jotting down the ethnicity of all the people you chose to spend time with over the past week or so.

Bill Aron/PhotoEdit

(Fiske, 1998; Fuligni, Witkow, & Garcia, 2005). Adolescents with a strong ethnic identity are more likely to do well academically and less likely to break the law, become depressed, or be adversely affected by racial discrimination (e.g., Adelabu, 2008; Mandara et al., 2009; Neblett et al., 2012). Parents and other mentors play a major role in developing adolescents' ethnic identity by imparting cultural traditions, instilling pride in ethnic heritage, and preparing children for hardships that can be a part of minority status (Hurd et al., 2012; Seaton et al., 2012). Daily contact with others from one's ethnic group is also related to positive ethnic identity (Yip, Douglass. & Shelton, 2013).

As described in the chapter on social psychology, the same processes that create ethnic identity can also sow the seeds of ethnic prejudice, but such prejudice is not inevitable. Adolescents who regularly interact with members of other ethnic groups usually develop more mature ethnic identities and express more favorable attitudes toward people of other ethnicities (Phinney, Jacoby, & Silva, 2007).

Facing the Identity Crisis

Identity formation is the central task of adolescence in Erikson's theory of psychosocial development. According to Erikson (1968), events of late adolescence—graduating from high school, going to college, forming new relationships—challenge an adolescent's self-concept and trigger an **identity crisis** (see Table 11.2). In this crisis, the adolescent must develop the self-image of a unique person by pulling together self-knowledge acquired earlier. According to Erikson, if infancy, childhood, and early adolescence brought trust, autonomy, initiative, and industry, adolescents will resolve the identity crisis positively and develop feelings of self-confidence and competence. However, if infancy and childhood created feelings of mistrust, shame, guilt, and inferiority, adolescents will be confused about their identity and goals.

In Western cultures there is some limited empirical support for Erikson's ideas about the identity crisis. In late adolescence, young people do consider alternative identities (Roberts, Walton, & Viechtbauer, 2006; Waterman, 1982). They may "try out" being rebellious, studious, or detached as they attempt to resolve questions about sexuality, self-worth, industriousness, and independence, but late adolescence is also a time when many people become more aware of their obligations to their families (Fuligni & Pedersen, 2002). By the time they are twenty-one, about half of the adolescents studied have resolved the identity crisis in a way that is consistent with their self-image and the historical era in which they are living. They enter young adulthood with self-confidence. They are basically the same people they were when they entered adolescence, but they now have more mature attitudes and behavior, more consistent goals and values, and a clearer idea of who they are (Savin-Williams & Demo, 1984). For those who fail to resolve identity issues—either because they avoided the identity crisis by accepting the identity their parents set for them or because they postponed dealing with the crisis and remain uncommitted and lacking in direction—there are often problems ahead (Lange & Byrd, 2002).

Moral Development

Adolescents are able to develop an identity partly because, according to Piaget's theory, they have entered the period of *formal operations,* which allows them to think logically and reason about abstract concepts. Adolescents often find themselves applying these advanced cognitive skills to questions of morality.

Kohlberg's Stages of Moral Reasoning

To examine how people think about morality, Lawrence Kohlberg asked them to explain how they would resolve certain moral dilemmas. Perhaps the most famous of these is the "Heinz dilemma," in which people decide whether a man named Heinz should steal a rare and unaffordable drug to save his wife's life. By posing dilemmas such as this one, Kohlberg found that the reasons given for moral choices change systematically and consistently with

identity crisis The phase during which an adolescent attempts to develop an integrated self-image as a unique person by pulling together self-knowledge acquired during childhood.

TABLE 11.3   KOHLBERG'S STAGES OF MORAL REASONING

Kohlberg's stages of moral reasoning describe differences in how people think about moral issues. Some researchers have suggested that the changes seen from stage to stage are partly attributable to developments in the brain that allow greater cognitive complexity and empathy (van den Bos et al., 2011). Here are some examples of answers that people at different stages of development might give to the "Heinz dilemma" described in the text. This dilemma is more realistic than you might think. In 1994, a man was arrested for robbing a bank after being turned down for a loan to pay for his wife's cancer treatments.

Stage	What Is Right?	Should Heinz Steal the Drug?
Preconventional		
1.	Obeying and avoiding punishment from a superior authority	"Heinz should not steal the drug because he will be jailed."
2.	Making a fair exchange, a good deal	"Heinz should steal the drug because his wife will repay him later."
Conventional		
3.	Pleasing others and getting their approval	"Heinz should steal the drug because he loves his wife and because she and the rest of the family will approve."
4.	Doing your duty, following rules and social order	"Heinz should steal the drug for his wife because he has a duty to care for her," or "Heinz should not steal the drug because stealing is illegal."
Postconventional		
5.	Respecting rules and laws but recognizing that they may have limits	"Heinz should steal the drug because life is more important than property."
6.	Following universal ethical principles such as justice, reciprocity, equality, and respect for human life and rights	"Heinz should steal the drug because of the principle of preserving and respecting life."

preconventional level Moral reasoning that is not based on the conventions or rules that guide social interactions in a society.

moral development The growth of an individual's understanding of the concepts of right and wrong.

conventional level Moral reasoning that reflects a concern about other people as well as the belief that morality consists of following rules and conventions.

postconventional level Moral reasoning that reflects moral judgments based on personal standards or universal principles of justice, equality, and respect for human life.

age (Kohlberg & Gilligan, 1971). Young children make moral judgments that differ from those of older children, adolescents, or adults. Kohlberg argued that moral reasoning develops in six stages, summarized in Table 11.3. These stages, he said, are not tightly linked to chronological age. Instead, there is a range of ages for reaching each stage, and not everyone reaches the highest level.

Stage 1 and Stage 2 moral judgments, which are most typical of children under age nine, tend to be selfish. Kohlberg called this the **preconventional level** of moral reasoning because it is not based on the conventions or rules that often guide social interactions in society. People at this level of **moral development** are mainly concerned with avoiding punishment or following rules when it is to their own advantage. At the **conventional level** of moral reasoning, Stages 3 and 4, people care about other people. They think that morality consists of following rules and conventions such as duty to the family, marriage vows, and country. The moral reasoning of children and adolescents from nine to nineteen is most often at this level. Stages 5 and 6 represent the highest level of moral reasoning, which Kohlberg called the **postconventional level** because it occurs after conventional reasoning. Moral judgments at this level are based on personal standards or universal principles of justice, equality, and respect for human life, not just demands of authority figures or society. People who have reached this level view rules and laws as arbitrary but respect them because they protect human welfare. They believe that individual rights sometimes justify violating laws that have become destructive. People do not usually reach this level until sometime in young adulthood—if at all. Studies of Kohlberg's stages have generally supported the sequence he proposed (Turiel, 2006).

Limitations of Kohlberg's Stages

Do Kohlberg's stages appear across cultures? In general, yes. Forty-five studies in twenty-seven cultures from Alaska to Zambia showed that people do tend to make upward progress through Kohlberg's stages, without reversals, although Stages 5 and 6 did not always appear (Gibbs et al., 2007; Snarey & Hooker, 2006; Turiel, 2006). Further, the moral judgments made in some cultures do not always fit neatly into Kohlberg's stages. For example, some people in collectivist cultures, such as Papua New Guinea, Taiwan, and Israeli kibbutzim, explained their answers to moral dilemmas by pointing to the importance of the community. And people in India included in their moral reasoning the importance of acting in accordance with one's caste (social class) and with maintaining personal purity (Shweder et al., 1994). As in other areas of cognitive development, culture plays a significant role in shaping moral judgments (Abarbanell & Hauser, 2010; Rai & Fiske, 2011).

Gender may also play a role. Carol Gilligan (1982, 1993) suggested that Kohlberg's research documented mainly the abstract, impersonal concept of justice typically seen in males. When Gilligan asked people about moral conflicts, the majority of men focused on justice, but only half of the women did. The other half focused on caring. This finding supports Gilligan's belief that for North American women, the moral ideal is to protect enduring relationships and fulfill human needs. This gender difference has not been found consistently, however (Jaffee & Hyde, 2000). In fact, it appears that men and women sometimes use either approach to moral reasoning (Johnston, 1988). The tendency for women to focus on caring more than men do and for men to focus on justice more than women do appears most clearly when they resolve real-life moral issues that they have personally experienced (Jaffe & Hyde, 2000). However, when asked about hypothetical moral dilemmas, there is no substantial difference in how men and women reason (Jaffe & Hyde, 2000; Walker, 2006).

Taken together, research in different countries shows that moral ideals are neither absolute nor universal. Moral development is apparently an adaptation to the moral world and the specific situations in which people find themselves. Formal operational reasoning may be necessary for people to reach the highest level of moral reasoning, but formal operational reasoning alone is not enough. To some extent, at the highest levels, moral reasoning is a product of culture and history, of situations, and of people's emotions and goals in those situations (e.g., Almås et al., 2010; Amit & Greene, 2012; Feinberg et al., 2012; Hussar & Horvath, 2011; Teper, Inzlicht, & Page-Gould, 2011).

ADULTHOOD

What developmental changes occur in adulthood?

Development does not end at adolescence. Adults, too, go through transitions and experience physical, cognitive, and social changes. It has been suggested that adulthood emerges as early as age eighteen (Arnett, 2000), but for our purposes, adulthood can be divided into three periods: *early adulthood* (ages twenty to thirty-nine), *middle adulthood* (ages forty to sixty-five), and *late adulthood* (beyond age sixty-five).

Physical Changes

In early adulthood, physical growth continues. Shoulder width, height, and chest size increase, and people continue to develop athletic abilities. By their mid-thirties, nearly everyone shows some hearing impairment, but for most people, the years of early adulthood are the prime of life.

In middle adulthood, physical changes slowly emerge. The most common involve the further loss of sensory sharpness (Fozard et al, 1977). People become less sensitive to light, less accurate at perceiving differences in distance, and slower and less able at seeing details. Increased farsightedness is common among people in their forties, so they may need reading glasses. By their early fifties, women usually experience **menopause**, the shutdown of reproductive capability. Estrogen and progesterone levels drop, and the menstrual cycle eventually ceases.

Most people are well into late adulthood before body functions show noticeable impairment. However, inside the body, bone mass dwindles. Men shrink about an inch in height and women about two inches as their posture changes and cartilage disks between the spinal vertebrae thins. Older adults tend to go to sleep earlier but may awaken more often through the night to use the bathroom (Park et al., 2002). Changes in the walls of arteries may lead to heart disease. The digestive system becomes less efficient. Both digestive disorders and heart disease sometimes result from problems of diet—too little fluid, too little fiber, too much fat—and inactivity. In addition, the brain shrinks. The flow of blood to the brain slows. As in earlier years, many of these changes can be delayed or diminished by a healthy diet and exercise (Brach et al., 2003; Larson et al., 2006).

Cognitive Changes

Adulthood is marked by increases as well as decreases in cognitive abilities. Reaction times become slower and more variable (Deary & Der, 2005a), and although abilities that involve intensive information processing begin to decline in early adulthood, those that depend on accumulated knowledge and experience increase and don't begin to decline until old age, and some individuals never experience this decline. In fact, older adults may function as well as or better than younger adults in situations that tap their long-term memories and well-learned skills (Campbell, Hasher, & Thomas, 2010; Worthy et al., 2011). The experienced teacher may deal with an unruly child more skillfully than the new teacher, and the senior lawyer may understand the implications of a new law better than the recent graduate. Their years of accumulating and organizing information can make older adults practiced, skillful, and wise.

Early and Middle Adulthood

Until age sixty at least, important cognitive abilities improve. During this period, adults do better on tests of vocabulary, comprehension, and general knowledge—especially if they use these abilities in their daily lives or engage in enriching activities such as travel or reading (Park, 2001). Young and middle-aged adults learn new information and new skills and remember old information and hone old skills. In fact, it is in their forties through their early sixties that people tend to put in the best performance of their lives on complex mental tasks such as reasoning, verbal memory, and vocabulary (Schaie & Willis, 2010).

The nature of thought may also change during adulthood. Adult thought is often more complex and adaptive than adolescent thought (Labouvie-Vief, 1992). Unlike adolescents, adults more often see both possibilities and problems in a course of action—in deciding whether to start a new business, back a political candidate, move to a new city, or change jobs. Middle-aged adults are more expert than adolescents or young adults at making rational decisions and at relating logic and abstractions to actions, emotions, social issues, and personal relationships (Tversky & Kahneman, 1981). As they appreciate these relationships, their thought becomes more global, more concerned with broad moral and practical issues (Labouvie-Vief, 1982). It has been suggested that this kind of thinking reflects a stage of cognitive development that goes beyond Piaget's formal operational period (Lutz & Sternberg, 1999). In this period, people's thinking becomes *dialectical,* which means they understand that knowledge is relative, not absolute. They realize that what is seen as wise today might have been thought foolish in the past. They see life's contradictions as an inevitable part of reality, and tend to weigh solutions rather than just accepting the first one that springs to mind (Grossmann et al., 2010).

menopause The cessation of a woman's reproductive capacity.

Late Adulthood

After the age of sixty-five or so, some intellectual abilities decline noticeably (Verhaeghen, 2013). Generally, these are abilities that require intense mental effort, such as rapid and flexible manipulation of ideas and symbols, and active thinking and reasoning (Baltes, 1994; Bugg et al., 2006; Gilmore, Spinks, & Thomas, 2006; see Figure 11.7). Older adults do just as well as younger ones at tasks they know well, such as naming familiar objects (Radvansky, 1999). But, when doing an unfamiliar task or solving a new complex problem, older adults are generally slower and less effective than younger ones (Craik & Rabinowitz, 1984). When faced with complex problems, older people apparently suffer from having too much information to sift through (Gazzaley et al., 2005). They have trouble considering, choosing, and executing solutions (Peters et al., 2007). As people age, they grow less efficient at organizing the elements of a problem and at holding and mentally manipulating more than one idea at a time. They have difficulty doing tasks that require them to divide their attention between two activities and are slower at shifting their attention back and forth between those activities (Verhaeghen, 2011; Wasylyshyn, Verhaeghen, & Sliwinski, 2011). If older adults have enough time, though, and if they can separate the two activities and choose appropriate problem-solving strategies, they can perform as well as younger adults (Hawkins, Kramer, & Capaldi, 1993; Lemaire, 2010).

Usually, the loss of intellectual abilities is slow and need not cause severe problems (Bashore & Ridderinkhof, 2002). The memory difficulties often seen among older adults relate more to *episodic memory* (e.g., remembering what they had for lunch yesterday) than to *semantic memory* (remembering general information, such as the capital of Italy) (Mousavi-Nasab et al., 2012; Nilsson, 1996). In other words, everyday abilities that involve verbal processes are likely to remain intact into advanced old age (Freedman, Aykan, & Martin, 2001; Schaie & Willis, 2010). There is one way, though, in which older adults' declining memories can have negative effects: They may be more likely than younger adults to recall false information as being true (Schmitz, Dehon, & Peigneux, 2013), making some of them prone to victimization by scam artists. So the more warnings they hear about a false medical claim—such as that shark cartilage supposedly cures arthritis—the more familiar it becomes, and the more likely they are to believe it. As described in the chapter on memory, younger people are also vulnerable to memory distortions, but they are more likely to remember that false information is false, even when it is familiar.

The decline in cognitive abilities in old age, as well as the rate of that decline, is partly due to genetics (Finkel et al., 2009; Kremen & Lyons, 2011; Reynolds et al., 2005), but

FIGURE 11.7

Mental Abilities over the Life Span

Mental abilities collectively known as "fluid" intelligence—speed and accuracy of information processing, for example—begin to decline quite early in adult life (Tucker-Drob, 2011). Changes in these biologically based aspects of thinking are usually not noticeable until late adulthood, however. "Crystallized" abilities learned over a lifetime—such as reading, writing, comprehension of language, and professional skills—decline too, but later and at a slower pace (Finkel et al., 2007; Li et al., 2004).

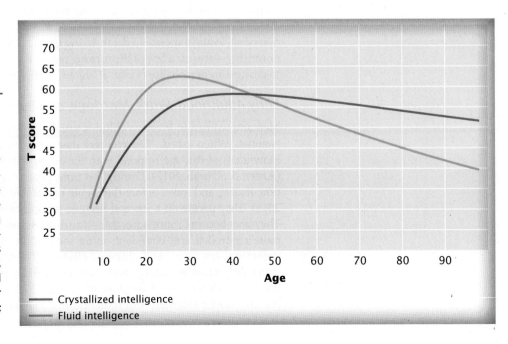

— Crystallized intelligence
— Fluid intelligence

Staying Alert, Staying Active, Staying Alive

Sisters Alcantara, Claverine, and Nicolette of the School Sisters of Notre Dame convent were in their eighties or nineties when this photo was taken. They stayed alert by reading, solving puzzles, playing cards, and participating in vocabulary quizzes. The nuns at this convent are participating in a study of aging and the brain.

Steve Liss/Time & Life Pictures/Getty Images

other factors are important too. The risk of cognitive decline is significantly lower for people who are healthy and psychologically flexible and who have a high level of education, income, and occupation. Cognitive decline is slower among those who eat a healthy diet (Lourida et al., 2013; Morris et al., 2006), had a lifetime of mentally stimulating activities (Vemuri et al., 2014), live with mentally able spouses or companions (Chodosh et al., 2002), and had high IQ and activity levels in adolescence (Morris et al., 2006; Yaffe et al., 2009). Continued mental exercise—such as doing puzzles, painting, and having intellectually stimulating conversations with friends—can also help older adults think and remember effectively and creatively (e.g., Wilson et al., 2012). Practice at memory and other information-processing tasks may even lead to some improvement in skills that had been impaired by old age and disuse (Gross & Rebok, 2011; Kelly et al., 2014). Maintaining physical fitness through dancing or other forms of aerobic exercise has been associated with better maintenance of skills on a variety of mental tasks, including those involving reaction time, reasoning, and divided attention (Baker et al., 2010; Kelly et al., 2014; Smith et al., 2010). And a life full of organized activities and opportunities to interact with lots of different people—not just family members—seems best for preventing decline in cognitive abilities (Hertzog et al., 2009; Keller-Cohen et al., 2004).

A major threat to cognitive abilities in late adulthood is dementia, and the most common cause is from Alzheimer's disease (Oboudiyat et al., 2013). As the disease progresses, parts of the brain deteriorate, leaving even the brightest minds dysfunctional (Defina et al., 2013). People with Alzheimer's may become emotionally flat, less oriented, and mentally vacant (Dillon et al., 2013). They usually die about three to seven years after being diagnosed (Todd et al., 2013). The age of onset and rate of decline may depend on several factors (Tejada-Vera, 2013), such as intelligence (Fritsch et al., 2005), gender (Wilson, Scherr, et al., 2007), education (Wilson, Scherr, et al., 2007), vulnerability to stress (Wilson et al., 2011), physical activity (Buchman et al., 2012), and vascular health (Reitz et al., 2010). For reasons still not clear, women tend to deteriorate more slowly than men (Mielke, Vemuri, & Rocca, 2014).

Social Changes

Adulthood is a time when changes occur in social relationships and positions. These changes do not come in neat, predictable stages but instead follow various paths, depending on individual experiences. Transitions—such as divorcing, being fired, going back to school, remarrying, losing a spouse to death, being hospitalized, getting arrested, moving back home, or retiring—are just a few of the turning points that can redirect a person's life path and lead to changes in personality (Caspi & Shiner, 2006; Roberts, Helson, & Klohnen, 2002).

Early Adulthood: Work, Marriage, and Parenthood

Men and women in Western cultures usually enter a period of *emerging adulthood* in their twenties. When asked, "Do you feel that you have reached adulthood?" the majority of individuals of this age respond with the ambiguous "in some ways yes, in some ways no" (Arnett & Schwab, 2012). During this time, people explore life's possibilities through education, dating, and travel before they settle into stable adult roles and responsibilities (Arnett, 2013). They decide on a job and become preoccupied with careers (Srivastava et al., 2003). They also become more agreeable—warm, generous, and helpful (Srivastava et al., 2003); more controlled and confident; more socially dominant, conscientious, and emotionally stable; and less angry and alienated (Roberts & Mroczek, 2008). Still, by age twenty-five, about 20 percent of young adults still live with their parents, and just under half are still financially dependent (Cohen et al., 2003). Many young adults in their twenties also become more concerned with romantic love. Having reached the sixth of Erikson's stages of psychosocial development listed in Table 11.2 (intimacy versus isolation), they begin to focus on forming mature relationships based on sexual intimacy, friendship, or mutual intellectual stimulation. The result may be marriage or another kind of committed relationship.

Just how willing and able people are to make intimate commitments may depend on their earlier attachment relationships (Birnbaum et al., 2006; Nosko et al., 2011; Oriña et al., 2011). Young adults' views of intimate relationships parallel the patterns of infant attachment that we described earlier (Broussard & Cassidy, 2010; Campbell et al., 2005). If their view reflects a secure attachment, they tend to feel valued and worthy of support and affection; they develop closeness easily. Their relationships are characterized by joy, trust, and commitment. If their view reflects an insecure attachment, however, they tend to be preoccupied with relationships and may feel misunderstood, underappreciated, and worried about being abandoned. Their relationships are often negative, obsessive, and jealous. Alternatively, they may be aloof and unable to trust or to commit themselves to a partner; they may be more prone to infidelity (DeWall et al., 2011). Overall, young adults whose parents have been accepting and supportive tend to develop warm and supportive romantic relationships (Hatton et al., 2009; Salvatore et al., 2011).

For many young adults, becoming a parent marks entry into a major new developmental phase (Palkovitz, Copes, & Woolfolk, 2001). This milestone may come earlier for young adults from lower income backgrounds, who are more likely to be in full-time jobs and less likely to live at home (Cohen et al., 2003). Often, satisfaction with marriage or partnership declines once a baby is born (Doss et al., 2009; Gilbert, 2006), and nearly half of all marriages break under the strain (National Center for Health Statistics, 2011). Young mothers may feel especially dissatisfied—particularly if they resent the constraints infants bring, if they see careers as important, if infants are temperamentally difficult, if partnerships are not strong, or if partners are unsupportive (Cowan & Cowan, 2009; Hogan & Msall, 2002; Jokela, 2010). When a father does not do his share of child care, both mothers and fathers are dissatisfied (Levy-Shiff, 1994). The ability of young parents to provide adequate care for a baby is related to their own attachment histories. New mothers whose attachments to their own mothers were secure tend to be more responsive to their infants, and the infants, in turn, are more likely to develop secure attachments to them (Adam, Gunnar, & Tanaka, 2004; Behrens, Hesse, & Main, 2007).

The challenges of young adulthood are complicated by the nature of family life today (Halpern, 2005: Howe, 2012). In the mid- to late twentieth century, about half of North American households consisted of married couples in their twenties and thirties—a breadwinner husband and a homemaker wife—raising at least two children together. This description now applies to only about one-fifth of households (Lofquist et al., 2012). Today, more people live together without getting married (Fry & Cohn, 2011); parents are older because young adults delay marriage and wait longer to have children. Many become parents without marrying (Hertz, 2006). About 40 percent of births are to unmarried women (Child Trends, 2011). Most of these women become pregnant "the old-fashioned way," but some take advantage of technological advances that allow them to conceive through in vitro fertilization (Hahn & DiPietro, 2001; Parke et al., 2012). Many gay men and lesbians are becoming parents too. Some estimates suggest that at least 4 million families in the United States are headed by openly gay or lesbian adults who became parents by retaining custody of children born in a previous heterosexual marriage, by adopting children, or by having children through artificial insemination or surrogacy (Goldberg, 2010; Patterson, 2002).

Whether homosexual or heterosexual, the 60 percent of mothers who hold full-time jobs outside the home often find demands of children and career pulling them in opposite directions. Devotion to jobs leaves many mothers with guilt about spending too little time with their children (Booth et al., 2002), but placing too much emphasis on home life may reduce their productivity at work and threaten their advancement. This stressful balancing act can lead to anxiety, frustration, and conflicts at home and on the job. It affects fathers too. Husbands of employed women are more involved in child care (Pleck, 2004) and can

The "Sandwich" Generation

During their midlife transition, many people feel "sandwiched" between generations—pressured by the social, emotional, and financial needs of their children on one side and the needs of their aging parents on the other.

Fuse/Getty Images

"When I was your age, I was an adult."

Most people in their sixties want their offspring to be independent, so they may have mixed feelings toward children who continue to need financial support during an extended period of "emerging adulthood" (Kloep & Hendry, 2010; Pillemer & Suitor, 2002).

William Haefeli/The New Yorker Collection/The Cartoon Bank

generativity The concern of adults in midlife with generating something enduring.

be effective parents (Parke, 2002), but mothers still do most child care and housework (Coltrane & Adams, 2008).

Nearly half of all marriages in the United States end in divorce, creating yet another set of challenges for adults (Clarke-Stewart & Brentano, 2006; U.S. Census Bureau, 2012). People who divorce face many unanticipated stressors, including money problems, changes in living circumstances and working hours, loneliness, anxiety, and, for custodial parents, a dramatic increase in housework and child-care tasks (Amato, 2010; Clarke-Stewart & Brentano, 2006). In short, the changes seen in families and family life over the past several decades have made it more challenging than ever to successfully navigate the years of early adulthood.

Middle Adulthood: Reappraising Priorities

Around age forty, people go through a *midlife transition* during which they may rethink and modify their lives. Many feel invigorated and liberated; some may feel upset and have a "midlife crisis" (Beck, 1992; Levinson et al., 1978). The contrast between youth and middle age may be especially upsetting for men who matured early in adolescence and were sociable and athletic rather than intellectual (Block, 1971). Women who chose a career over a family may hear a biological clock ticking out their last childbearing years. Women who have had children, however, become more independent and confident and more oriented toward achievement and events outside the family (Helson & Moane, 1987). For both men and women, the emerging sexuality of teenage children, an empty nest as children leave home, or the declining health of a parent may precipitate a crisis.

Following the midlife transition, the middle years of adulthood often bring satisfaction and happiness (Mroczek & Spiro, 2005). Many people become concerned with producing something to outlast them (Sheldon & Kasser, 2001; Zucker, Ostrove, & Stewart, 2002). Erikson called this concern a crisis of **generativity** because people focus on producing or generating something. Making this kind of social investment tends to be associated with better adult adjustment (Snarey, 1994; Wilt et al., 2010). If people do not resolve this crisis, he suggested, they stagnate.

In their fifties, most people become grandparents (Smith & Drew, 2002), though they may find it hard to see themselves as no longer young (Karp, 1991). Recent trends toward decreased family size, longer life expectancy, and the rise of single-parent families and maternal employment increase the potential for grandparents to play larger roles in the lives of their grandchildren (Dunifon, 2013). But spending lots of time caring for young grandchildren can be stressful for some at this age, and may increase depression and reduce life satisfaction (Hayslip, King & Jooste, 2008; Lee, Colditz et al., 2003). Overall, the degree of happiness and healthiness people experience during middle adulthood depends on how much control they feel they have over their work, finances, marriages, children, and sex lives as well as on their personality characteristics, how many years of education they completed, and what kind of jobs they have (Azar, 1996; Griffin, Mroczek, & Spiro, 2006).

Late Adulthood: Retirement and Restriction

Most people between sixty-five and seventy-five years of age think of themselves as middle-aged, not old (Kleinspehn-Ammerlahn, Kotter-Grühn, & Smith, 2008). They are active and influential politically and socially, and often physically vigorous. Ratings of life satisfaction and self-esteem are, on average, as high in old age as during any other period of adulthood (Charles, Mather, & Carstensen, 2003; Stone, 2010). Men and women who have been employed usually retire from their jobs during this period. They adjust most easily to retirement if they are prepared for it and view it as a choice (Adams & Rau, 2011; Moen et al., 2000; Swan, 1996). Retirement doesn't need to mean giving up on life. In fact, in many ways the current generation of retirees has transformed retirement into a more active, engaged stage of life (Shultz & Wang, 2011).

Still Going Strong

At the age of eighty-four, actor and Academy Award–winning director Clint Eastwood is a famous example of the many people whose late adulthood is healthy and vigorous. And he is not slowing down. His acting remains as riveting as ever, and the films he directs continue to attract huge audiences and critical acclaim.

Castle Rock Pictures/ZUMAPRESS/Newscom

Today, more people than ever are reaching old age. Those over age seventy-five constitute a group that is twenty-five times larger than it was a century ago. In fact, 100,000 people in the United States are over age 100, and the U.S. Census Bureau predicts that number will rise to 834,000 by 2050 (Volz, 2000). Old age is not necessarily a time of loneliness and desolation, but can be a time when people generally become more inward looking, cautious, and conforming (Reedy, 1983). It is a time when people develop coping strategies that increasingly take into account the limits of their control; people in this age group begin to accept what they cannot change, such as chronic health problems (Urry & Gross, 2010). One such coping strategy is to direct attention to positive thoughts, activities, and memories (Charles, Mather, & Carstensen, 2003; Mather et al., 2004). In fact, when older adults are asked to look at pictures of faces portraying various emotions, they spend more time looking at happy faces; people of college age look longer at fearful faces (Isaacowitz et al., 2006).

Compared to younger adults, older people remember a larger proportion of positive events (Brassen et al., 2012; Charles, 2011; Mather & Carstensen, 2005) and report less anger in response to interpersonal conflicts (Charles & Carstensen, 2008). In late adulthood, people find relationships more satisfying, supportive, and fulfilling than earlier in life. As they sense that time is running out, they value positive interactions and become selective about social partners. So although they interact with others less frequently, older adults enjoy these interactions more (Carstensen, 1997). As long as they have a network of at least three close relatives or friends, they are usually content (Litwin & Shiovitz-Ezra, 2006).

The many changes associated with adolescence and adulthood are summarized in "In Review: Milestones of Adolescence and Adulthood."

Death and Dying

With the onset of old age, people become aware that death is approaching. They watch friends disappear. They may feel their health failing, their strength waning, and intellectual capabilities declining. A few years or a few months before death, people may experience a gradual decline or a sharper **terminal drop** in mental functioning (Gerstorf et al., 2011; MacDonald, Hultsch, & Dixon; 2011).

The awareness of impending death brings about the last psychological crisis, according to Erikson's theory. During this stage, people evaluate their lives and accomplishments and see them as meaningful (leading to a feeling of integrity) or meaningless (leading to a feeling of despair). They tend to become more philosophical and reflective. They attempt to put their lives into perspective. They revisit old memories, resolve past conflicts, and integrate past events. They may also become more interested in the religious and spiritual side of life. This "life review" may trigger anxiety, regret, guilt, despair, even suicide (Anderson & Conwell, 2002). But it may also help people face their own deaths and the deaths of others with a feeling of peace and acceptance (Steinhauser et al., 2008; Torges, Stewart, & Nolen-Hoeksema, 2008).

Even the actual confrontation with death does not have to bring despair and depression. When death finally is imminent, old people strive for a death with dignity, love, affection, physical contact, and no pain (Schulz, 1978). As they think about death, they are comforted by their religious faith, their achievements, and the love of their friends and family.

Longevity

Facing death with dignity and openness helps us complete the life cycle with meaningfulness, but most of us want to live as long as possible. How can we do so? Much of what gives long life may be genetic (Chung et al., 2010; Dykiert et al., 2012) and gender-related. Women live longer than men, on average. Longevity is also related to personality traits such

terminal drop A sharp decline in mental functioning that tends to occur in late adulthood, a few months or years before death.

MILESTONES OF ADOLESCENCE AND ADULTHOOD

Age	Physical Changes	Cognitive Changes	Social Events and Psychological Changes
Early adolescence (11–15 years)	Puberty brings reproductive capacity and marked bodily changes.	Formal operations and principled moral reasoning become possible for the first time. (This occurs only for some people.)	Social and emotional changes result from growing sexual awareness; adolescents experience mood swings, physical changes, and conflicts with parents.
Late adolescence (16–19 years)	Physical growth continues.	Formal operations and principled moral reasoning become more likely.	An identity crisis accompanies graduation from high school.
Early adulthood (20–39 years)	Physical growth continues.	Increases continue in knowledge, problem-solving ability, and moral reasoning.	People choose a job and often a mate; they may become parents.
Middle adulthood (40–65 years)	Size and muscle mass decrease; fat increases; eyesight declines; reproductive capacity in women ends.	Thought becomes more complex, adaptive, and global.	Midlife transition may lead to change; for most, the middle years are satisfying.
Late adulthood (over 65 years)	Height decreases; organs become less efficient.	Reasoning, mathematical ability, comprehension, novel problem solving, and memory may decline.	Retirement requires adjustments; people look inward; awareness of death precipitates life review.

In Review Questions

1. The greatest threat to cognitive abilities in late adulthood is _____ disease.

2. Adolescents' _____ identity may be more defining than their national citizenship.

3. Not stealing because "I might get caught" reflects the _____ stage of moral reasoning.

as conscientiousness as a child (Friedman & Martin, 2011) and curiosity as an adult (Boyle et al., 2009; Swan & Carmelli, 1996). People with higher IQs and faster reaction times tend to live longer, too (Deary & Der, 2005b), as do those who typically experienced happiness, enthusiasm, contentment, and other forms of *positive affect* as adults (Carstensen et al., 2011; Ong, 2010; Pressman & Cohen, 2007). Having a sense of purpose in life is also associated with longer lifespans (Hill & Turiano, 2014). Certain age-related life events— such as whether women have children later in life or whether men have experienced hair loss—can act as environmental cues that affect people's perceptions of their ages and the aging process (Hsu, Chung, & Langer, 2010). In one study, adults who had more positive self-perceptions when they were in their fifties and sixties lived seven and a half years longer than those with less positive self-perceptions. This factor was more predictive of longevity than were health problems such as high blood pressure, high cholesterol, smoking, lack of exercise, or being overweight (Levy et al., 2002). Remaining more socially engaged and having a network of good friends, even more than close family ties, is also related to longer life (Giles et al., 2005; Poon, 2008; Shankar et al., 2011). Further, people live longer if they don't smoke, don't drink heavily, restrict caloric intake, engage in regular physical and mental exercise, and have a sense of control over life (Infurna, Gerstorf, & Zarit, 2011; Kahlbaugh et al., 2011; Poon, 2008; Sun et al., 2010). So eat your veggies, stay physically fit, and continue to think actively—not just to live longer later but also to live better now.

LINKAGES

As noted in the introductory chapter, all of psychology's subfields are related to one another. Our discussion of infantile amnesia illustrates just one way that the topic of this chapter, human development, is linked to the subfield of memory, which is discussed in the chapter on memory. The Linkages diagram shows ties to two other subfields, and there are many more ties throughout the book. Looking for linkages among subfields will help you see how they all fit together and help you better appreciate the big picture that is psychology.

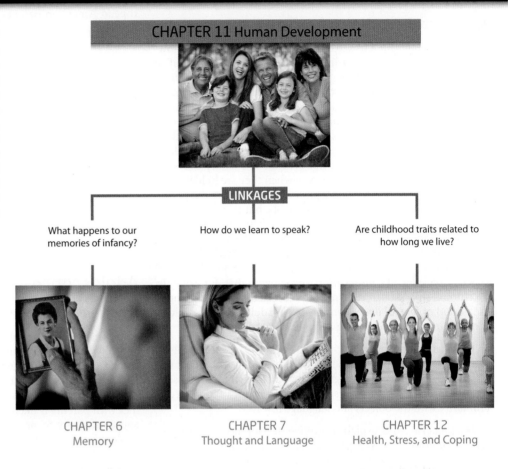

CHAPTER 11 Human Development

LINKAGES

What happens to our memories of infancy?

How do we learn to speak?

Are childhood traits related to how long we live?

CHAPTER 6
Memory

CHAPTER 7
Thought and Language

CHAPTER 12
Health, Stress, and Coping

SUMMARY

Developmental psychology is the study of the course and causes of systematic, sequential, age-related changes in mental abilities, social relationships, emotions, and moral understanding over the lifespan.

Exploring Human Development

What does "genetic influence" mean?

A central question in developmental psychology concerns the relative influences of nature and nurture. Gesell stressed nature in his theory of development, proposing that development is ***maturation***—the natural unfolding of abilities with age. Watson took the opposite view, claiming that development is learning, as shaped by the external environment. In his theory of cognitive development, Piaget described how nature and nurture work together. Today we accept the notion that both nature and nurture affect development and ask not whether but how and to what extent each contributes. Research in behavioral genetics shows that complex traits, such as intelligence and personality, are influenced by many genes, as well as by many environmental factors.

Beginnings

Why should pregnant women stay away from tobacco and alcohol?

Development begins with the union of an ovum and a sperm to form a zygote, which develops into an ***embryo***. ***Genes***, which consist of **DNA (*deoxyribonucleic acid*)**, make up the ***chromosomes*** that are in each body cell. The embryonic stage is a ***critical period*** for development, a time when certain organs must develop properly or they never will. The development of organs at this stage is permanently affected by harmful ***teratogens*** such as tobacco, alcohol, or other drugs. After the embryo develops into a ***fetus***, adverse conditions may harm the infant's size, behavior, intelligence, or health. Babies born to women who drink heavily are at risk for ***fetal alcohol syndrome***.

Newborns have limited but effective senses of vision, hearing, taste, and smell. They exhibit many ***reflexes***—swift, automatic responses to external stimuli. Motor development proceeds as the nervous system matures and muscles grow and as the infant experiments with and selects the most efficient movement patterns.

Infancy and Childhood: Cognitive Development

How do babies think?

Cognitive development refers to the development of thinking, knowing, and remembering. According to Piaget, *schemas* are modified through the complementary processes of *assimilation* (fitting new objects or events into existing schemas) and *accommodation* (changing schemas when new objects will not fit existing schemas). During the *sensorimotor period*, infants progress from using only their senses and simple reflexes to forming mental representations of objects and actions. As a result, the child becomes capable of thinking about objects that are not present. The ability to recognize that objects continue to exist even when they are hidden from view is what Piaget called *object permanence*. During the *preoperational period*, children can use symbols, but they do not have the ability to think logically and rationally. Their understanding of the world is intuitive. When children develop the ability to think logically about concrete objects, they enter the period of *concrete operations*. At this time, they can solve simple problems and have a knowledge of *conservation,* recognizing that, for example, the amount of a substance is not altered when its shape changes. The period of *formal operations* begins in adolescence and allows thinking and logical reasoning about abstract ideas.

Today, developmental psychologists believe that new levels of cognition do not appear in sharply separated stages of global understanding but emerge more gradually, and that children's reasoning can be affected by factors such as task difficulty and degree of familiarity with the objects and language involved.

Psychologists who explain cognitive development in terms of the *information processing model* have documented age-related improvements in children's attention, their abilities to explore and focus on features of the environment, and their memories. "Infantile amnesia" leaves us with virtually no memory of events from before the age of three. Several explanations have been suggested, but this phenomenon is not yet fully understood.

The specific content of cognitive development, including the development of scripts, depends on the cultural context in which children live. How fast children develop cognitive abilities depends to some extent on how stimulating and supportive their environments are. Children growing up in poverty are likely to have delayed or impaired cognitive abilities.

Infancy and Childhood: Social and Emotional Development

How do infants become attached to their caregivers?

From the early months onward, infants and their caregivers respond to each other's emotional expressions. Most infants can be classified as having easy, difficult, or slow-to-warm-up *temperaments*. Whether they retain these temperamental styles depends to some extent on their parents' expectations and demands. According to *attachment theory*, infants form a deep, long-lasting emotional *attachment* to their mothers or other primary caregivers. Their *attachment behavior* may reflect secure or insecure attachment. The process of *socialization* begins as parents teach their children the skills and rules needed in their culture, using *parenting styles* described as *authoritarian, permissive, authoritative,* or *uninvolved* (*rejecting-neglecting*). Among European American parents, those with authoritative styles tend to have more competent and cooperative children. Patterns of parental socialization depend on cultural and other circumstances.

Over the childhood years, interactions with peers evolve into cooperative and competitive encounters; friendships become more important. Changes in children's relationships are based in part on their growing social competence. Children become increasingly able to interpret and understand social situations and emotional signals. They begin to express empathy and sympathy and to engage in the *self-regulation* of their emotions and behaviors. They also learn social rules and roles, including those related to gender. *Gender roles*, also known as *sex roles*, are based both on biological differences between the sexes and on implicit and explicit socialization by parents, teachers, and peers. Children who lead successful lives despite such adversities as family instability, child abuse, homelessness, poverty, or war are described as having *resilience*.

Adolescence

What threatens adolescents' self-esteem?

Adolescents undergo significant changes not only in size, shape, and physical capacity but also, typically, in their social lives, reasoning abilities, and views of themselves. *Puberty* brings about physical changes that lead to psychological changes. Early adolescence is a period of shaky self-esteem. It is also a time when conflict with parents is likely to arise and when closeness with friends and conformity to peer group norms are likely to emerge. Later adolescence focuses on finding an answer to the question, "Who am I?" Events such as graduating from high school and going to college challenge the adolescent's self-concept, precipitating an *identity crisis*. To resolve this crisis, the adolescent must develop an integrated self-image as a unique person, an image that often includes *ethnic identity*. *Moral development* progresses from *preconventional* to *conventional* and (possibly) *postconventional levels*. Principled moral judgment—shaped by gender and culture—becomes possible for the first time.

Adulthood

What developmental changes occur in adulthood?

Physical, cognitive, and social changes occur throughout adulthood. During middle adulthood, changes begin that include decreased sharpness of the senses, increased risk of heart disease, and declining fertility (*menopause* in women). Nevertheless, most people do not experience major health problems until late adulthood.

The cognitive changes that occur in early and middle adulthood are generally positive, including improvements in reasoning and problem-solving ability. In late adulthood, some intellectual abilities decline—especially those involved in tasks that are unfamiliar, complex, or difficult. Other abilities, such as recalling facts or making wise decisions, tend not to decline.

In their twenties, young adults make choices about occupations and form intimate commitments. By the end of their thirties, they settle down and decide what is important. They become concerned with *generativity*—with producing something that will outlast them. Sometime around age forty, adults experience a midlife transition, which may or may not be a crisis. The forties and fifties are often a time of satisfaction. In their sixties, people contend with the issue of retirement. They generally become more inward looking, cautious, and conforming. In their seventies, eighties, and beyond, people confront their own mortality. They may become more philosophical and reflective as they review their lives. A few years or months before death, many experience a sharp decline in mental functioning, known as *terminal drop*. Still, they strive for a death with dignity, love, and no pain.

Death is inevitable, but healthy diets, exercise, conscientiousness and curiosity, and a sense of control over one's life are associated with living longer and happier lives. Older adults feel better and live longer if they receive attention from other people, maintain an open attitude toward new experiences, and keep their minds active.

TEST YOUR KNOWLEDGE

Select the best answer for each of the following questions. Then check your response against the Answer Key at the end of the book.

1. Ralph read an article that described intelligence as 50 percent heritable. Ralph can reasonably conclude that
   a. half of his intelligence came from his genes and half from his environment.
   b. about half of the variation in intelligence among groups of people can be accounted for by genetic influences.
   c. about half of a person's intelligence can be changed by environmental influences.
   d. about half the population got their intelligence from their genes alone.

2. When she became pregnant, Alyse was advised to quit smoking, but she didn't. As a result, her baby is more likely to be born _____.
   a. mentally retarded
   b. with facial deformities
   c. underweight
   d. with an irritable temperament

3. When Tyrone was a newborn, his parents brought him home from the hospital and always laid him on his back, especially at night. As Tyrone grew, he began to roll over, sit up, pull himself up on furniture, and walk. He skipped the crawling stage. Tyrone's physical development is the result of _____.
   a. behavioral genetics alone
   b. maturation alone
   c. environmental influences alone
   d. maturation and environmental influences

4. Keshawn is one month old. He is most likely to look longest at _____.
   a. a nearby human face
   b. small figures on the wallpaper
   c. a ribbon hanging above his crib
   d. colorful figures

5. At six months of age, Jacob still demonstrates the grasping and rooting reflexes. This could signal that Jacob
   a. has advanced motor skills.
   b. has muscles that cannot support his body.
   c. has a problem with nervous system development.
   d. needs less environmental stimulation than the average baby.

6. When two-year-old Jesse sees a scuba diver emerge on the beach, he says "Big fish!" According to Piaget, Jesse used _____ to try to understand the new stimulus of a scuba diver.
   a. assimilation
   b. accommodation
   c. object permanence
   d. conservation

7. Adriana is crying because her teddy bear, Boyd, has fallen off the table and landed face down. She insists that her mother put a bandage on Boyd's nose. According to Piaget's theory, Adriana is most likely in the stage of _____ cognitive development.
   a. sensorimotor
   b. preoperational
   c. concrete operational
   d. formal operational

8. Renee Baillargeon's research focused on infants' understanding about the mental states of other people and how those states affect behavior. Baillargeon found that infants
   a. looked longer at "possible" events that they had experienced many times.
   b. looked longer at events that violated their expectations about other people's beliefs.
   c. do not yet have a "theory of mind" and thus are unable to anticipate what others might do.
   d. can recognize the effects of people's true beliefs but are unable to recognize the effects of false beliefs.

9. According to research on information processing and memory, when you try to recall your first birthday, you are likely to
   a. recall a general schema of "birthday" as well as details about your first one.
   b. be unable to recall anything about your first birthday due to infantile amnesia.
   c. recall information about your first birthday if you are shown pictures of yourself taken that day.
   d. recall information about the birthday if you hear a tape recording of your party.

10. Tara is a difficult baby. She is irritable, sleeps at irregular intervals, and cries at unpredictable times. According to research on temperament, compared to babies with other temperaments, Tara will be more likely to
   a. outgrow her difficult temperament and become an easier child.
   b. remain difficult in childhood and may display aggressiveness.
   c. develop a dependent relationship with her parents.
   d. become independent and especially successful in school.

11. Harlow's research with infant monkeys and artificial mothers demonstrated that
   a. the monkeys became attached to the "mothers" that fed them.
   b. the monkeys became attached to the "mothers" that provided contact comfort.
   c. attachment is innate and not learned.
   d. "mothering" is innate and not learned.

12. When young Habib's mother drops him off at the day care center, he always cries when she leaves. When his mother returns and lifts him up, Habib tries to squirm away. Habib is demonstrating a(n) _____ attachment to his mother.
   a. secure
   b. anxious insecure
   c. avoidant insecure
   d. ambivalent insecure

13. Sam and Alex are both age sixteen and want to drive to a rock concert in a big city that is five hours away. Sam's parents explain that it is too dangerous for him to drive that distance and to be in a major city without an adult. They offer to drive him and Alex to the concert. Alex's parents tell him to drive their car and stay in the city overnight if he wishes. According to Baumrind's research, Sam's parents are displaying a(n) _____ style of parenting, whereas Alex's parents are displaying a(n) _____ style.
   a. authoritative; authoritarian
   b. authoritarian; authoritative
   c. authoritative; permissive
   d. authoritarian; permissive

14. Five-year-old Peng has a new preschool teacher who wants to get to know him, so she asks him "tell me about yourself." Peng is most likely to say
   a. I am Asian.
   b. I am Tommy's friend.
   c. I am the fastest runner in class.
   d. I play basketball.

15. Ludmilla recently graduated from high school but can't decide whether to attend a local community college or work full time. She doesn't know what career she would like to pursue, and she is also uncertain whether she should stay with her current boyfriend. According to Erikson, Ludmilla is most likely experiencing the psychosocial crisis characterized by _____ ,
   a. trust versus mistrust
   b. initiative versus guilt
   c. identity versus role confusion
   d. integrity versus despair

16. Louise is sixteen and having a difficult time with adolescence. She became sexually active two years ago and doesn't worry about using condoms or other safe sex practices. Louise is most likely to
   a. hold conventional attitudes and values and feel ashamed of herself.
   b. avoid smoking and drinking alcohol.
   c. have average or better grades at school.
   d. have parents who are not highly educated.

17. Jeanine and Helen are in a drugstore when Jeanine suggests that they steal some candy. Helen says that they should not steal the candy because they might get caught and put into jail. According to Kohlberg's theory, Helen is at the _____ stage of moral reasoning.
   a. preconventional
   b. conventional
   c. postconventional
   d. universal

18. In the past ten years Vernon has gained weight, especially around the middle. He also now needs glasses. If he is typical of most people his age, Vernon has most likely reached _____.
   a. adolescence
   b. early adulthood
   c. middle adulthood
   d. late adulthood

19. Verna is fifty years old. Based on developmental research, we would assume that Verna
   a. has less general knowledge than younger people.
   b. has a more limited vocabulary than younger people.
   c. understands that knowledge is relative, not absolute.
   d. is experiencing a slow but steady decay of all of her cognitive skills.

20. Patrice is eighty years old and has recently been unable to understand what she reads. She can't make sense of her checkbook, even though she was once an expert accountant. Her health is deteriorating, and her strength is waning. Patrice is most likely experiencing _____.
   a. cognitive dissonance
   b. terminal drop
   c. the crisis of initiative versus guilt
   d. androgyny

CHAPTER 12

Health, Stress, and Coping

© Andrey Popov/Shutterstock.com

Preview

People in North America are living longer than ever. In fact, those over 75 constitute the fastest-growing age group in the United States. Will you join them one day? To some extent, the answer lies in your genes, but how long you live is also determined in large measure by how you behave, how you think, and what stressors you face. Health care psychologists explore how illness and death are related to these behavioral, psychological, and social factors, and they apply their research to preventing illness and promoting health. They develop programs to help people make lifestyle changes that can lower their risk of illness and premature

Running for Your Life

Health psychologists have developed programs to help people increase exercise, stop smoking, eat healthier diets, and make other lifestyle changes that can lower their risk of illness and death. They have even helped bolster community blood supplies by finding ways to make blood donation less stressful (Bonk, France, & Taylor, 2001).

Lori Adamski Peek/The Image Bank/Getty Images

health care psychology (health psychology) A field focused on understanding how psychological factors affect health and illness and which interventions help maintain health and combat illness.

death. And they study how stress affects people's mental and physical health. The immune system's response to stress is particularly important. In this chapter, you will learn about several kinds of stressors, how people respond to them, and the relationship between stress reactions and illness. You will also discover what you can do to protect your own health and change risky behaviors that may affect it.

In Bangor, Maine, where snow and ice have paralyzed the community, Angie's headache gets worse as her four-year-old daughter and six-year-old son start bickering again. The daycare center and elementary school are closed, so Angie must stay home from her job at the grocery store. She probably couldn't have gotten there anyway, because the buses have stopped running. During the latest storm, the power went out, and the house is now almost unbearably cold; the can of spaghetti Angie opens is nearly frozen. Worry begins to creep into her head: "If I can't work, how will I pay for rent and daycare?" Her parents have money problems, too, so they can't offer financial help, and her ex-husband rarely makes his child support payments. On top of everything else, Angie is coming down with the flu.

How do people manage such adversity, and what are its consequences for them? Psychologists who study questions such as these have established a specialty known as **health care psychology** (also called **health psychology**), "a field within psychology devoted to understanding psychological influence on how people stay healthy, why they become ill, and how they respond when they do get ill" (Taylor, 1999, p. 4).

HEALTH PSYCHOLOGY

What do health care psychologists do?

The themes underlying health care psychology date back to ancient times. For thousands of years, in many cultures around the world, people have believed that their mental state, their behavior, and their health are linked. Today, there is scientific evidence to support this belief (Antoni & Lutgendorf, 2007; Schneiderman, 2004; Taylor, 2002). Stress affects health through its impact on psychological and physical processes. Research has also associated anger, hostility, pessimism, depression, and hopelessness with physical illnesses. Traits such as optimism are associated with good health. Similarly, poor health has been linked to behavioral factors such as lack of adequate sleep or exercise, eating too much fat and sugar, sleep deprivation, smoking, and abuse of alcohol and other drugs (e.g., Mente et al., 2009; Pressman, Gallagher, & Lopez, 2013; van Dam et al., 2008). Good health has been associated with behaviors such as regular exercise and following medical advice.

Health psychology has become increasingly prominent in North America, in part because of changing patterns of illness. Until the middle of the twentieth century, acute infectious diseases such as influenza, tuberculosis, and pneumonia were the major causes of illness and death in the United States and Canada. With these deadly diseases now tamed, chronic illnesses—such as coronary heart disease, cancer, and diabetes—have joined stroke, accidents, and injury as leading causes of disability and death (Heron, 2007). Compared with acute diseases, these chronic diseases develop more slowly and are more strongly associated with people's psychological makeup, lifestyle, and environment (Centers for Disease Control and Prevention, 2008; see Table 12.1). The psychological and behavioral factors that contribute to illness can be changed by intervention programs that promote exercising, healthy eating, and quitting smoking (e.g., Kohn, Blakey, & Roper, 2014; Taylor et al., 2014). In fact, about half of the deaths in the United States remain due to preventable health-risk behaviors (Khot et al., 2003; Mokdad et al., 2004).

Yet as few as 3 percent of people in the United States follow a lifestyle that includes maintaining a healthy weight, getting regular exercise, eating a healthy diet, getting eight hours of sleep, and not smoking (Reeves & Rafferty, 2005). One goal of health psychology is to help people understand the role they can play in controlling their own health and life expectancy (Nash et al., 2003; Nicassio, Meyerowitz, & Kerns, 2004). For example,

TABLE **12.1   BEHAVIORS THAT AFFECT SOME OF THE LEADING CAUSES OF DEATH IN THE UNITED STATES**

This table shows five of the leading causes of death in the United States today and behavioral factors that contribute to their development (Jemal et al., 2005; Kochanek et al., 2011).

Cause of Death	Excessive Alcohol Consumption	Tobacco Smoking	Unhealthy Diet	Inadequate Exercise	Inadequate Sleep
Heart disease	x	x	x	x	x
Cancer	x	x	x		
Chronic lung diseases		x			x
Stroke	x	x	x	?	x
Accidents and injury	x	x			x

Source: Data from National Vital Statistics Reports, Centers for Disease Control and Prevention (Kochanek, 2011).

health care psychologists have been active in educating people about the warning signs of cancer, heart disease, and other serious illnesses; encouraging them to engage in self-examinations; and emphasizing the importance of seeking medical attention while lifesaving treatment is still possible. Health care psychologists also study and help people understand the role stress plays in physical health and illness. And clinical health care psychologists help individuals cope as effectively as possible with cancer, diabetes, heart disease, and many other kinds of serious and chronic illness.

UNDERSTANDING STRESS AND STRESSORS

How do psychological stressors affect physical health?

You have probably heard that death and taxes are the only two things guaranteed in life. If there is a third, it surely must be stress. Stress is woven into the fabric of life. No matter how wealthy, powerful, attractive, or happy you might be, stress happens. It comes in many forms: a difficult exam, an automobile accident, a trauma of some kind, standing in a long line, reading about frightening world events, or just having a day when everything goes wrong. Some stress experiences, such as waiting to be with that special person, can be stimulating, motivating, and even desirable, but when circumstances begin to exceed our ability to cope with them, the result can be stress that creates physical, psychological, and behavioral problems. Stress in the workplace, for example, costs U.S. businesses more than $150 billion each year due to employee absenteeism, reduced productivity, and health care costs (Chandola, Brunner, & Marmot, 2006; Schwartz, 2004).

stress The process of adjusting to circumstances that disrupt or threaten to disrupt a person's daily functioning.

stressors Events or situations to which people must adjust.

stress reactions Physical and psychological responses to stressors.

Stress is the negative emotional and physiological process that occurs as individuals try to adjust to or deal with stressors. **Stressors**, in turn, are events and situations (such as exams or accidents) that disrupt or threaten to disrupt a person's daily functioning and sense of well-being. **Stress reactions** are the physical, psychological, and behavioral responses (such as nausea, anxiety, or avoidance) that occur in the face of stressors (Taylor, 2002).

Some of us are more strongly affected by stressors than others, and we may be more strongly affected on some occasions than on others. Why? As described in more detail later, several *mediating factors* influence the relationship between people and their

FIGURE 12.1
The Process of Stress

Stressful events, stress reactions, and stress mediators are all important components of the stress process. Notice that the process involves many two-way relationships. For example, if a person has effective coping skills, stress responses will be less severe. Having milder stress responses can act as a "reward" that strengthens those skills. Further, as coping skills (such as refusing unreasonable demands) improve, certain stressors (such as a boss's unreasonable demands) may become less frequent.

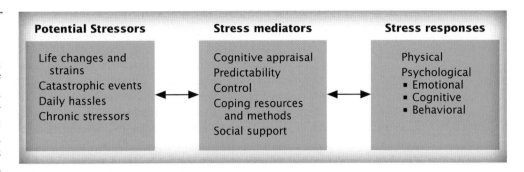

Potential Stressors	Stress mediators	Stress responses
Life changes and strains Catastrophic events Daily hassles Chronic stressors	Cognitive appraisal Predictability Control Coping resources and methods Social support	Physical Psychological • Emotional • Cognitive • Behavioral

environments. These mediating factors include (1) the extent to which we can *predict* and *control* our stressors; (2) how we *interpret* the threat involved; (3) the *social support* we get; and (4) our *skills* for coping with stress. Mediating factors can either minimize or magnify a stressor's impact. In other words, as shown in Figure 12.1, stress is not a specific event but a transaction between people and their environments. It is a *process* in which the nature and intensity of our responses depend on what stressors occur and how they are affected by factors such as the way we think about them and how much confidence we have in our coping skills and resources.

Psychological Stressors

Most stressors have both physical and psychological components. Because these components overlap, it's often difficult to separate them for analysis. For example, students are challenged by psychological demands to do well in their courses as well as by physical fatigue resulting from a heavy load of classes and maybe a job and family responsibilities, too. So although we focus here on psychological stressors, remember that physical stressors almost always accompany them (Rios & Zautra, 2011).

Any event that forces a person to change or adapt can be a psychological stressor. Even pleasant events can be stressful. For example, a vacation is supposed to be relaxing and a wedding is supposed to be wonderful, but both can also be exhausting. And a promotion that brings higher pay can also bring new pressures (Schaubroeck, Jones, & Xie, 2001). Still, circumstances that are unpleasant, threatening, and difficult to cope with usually produce the most adverse psychological and physical effects (e.g., Kiecolt-Glaser et al., 2005). These circumstances include catastrophic events, life changes and strains, chronic stressors, and daily hassles.

Coping with Catastrophe

Catastrophic events such as terrorism, explosions, hurricanes, and plane crashes are stressors that can be psychologically devastating for victims, their families, and rescue workers.

Reuters/Marco Dormino/Minustah/Landov

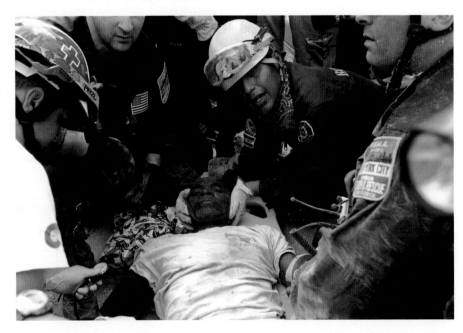

Catastrophic events are sudden, unexpected, potentially life-threatening experiences or traumas. Physical or sexual assault, military combat, natural disasters, terrorist attacks, and accidents fall into this category (e.g., Besser et al., 2014; Grimm et al., 2014). *Life changes* and *strains* include divorce, illness in the family, difficulties at work, moving to a new house, and other circumstances that create demands to which people must adjust (see Table 12.2). *Chronic stressors*—those that continue over a long period of time—include such circumstances as living under the threat of terrorism, having a serious illness (or caring for someone who does), being unable to earn a decent income, living in a high-crime urban neighborhood, being the victim of discrimination, and even enduring years of academic pressure (e.g., Fuller-Rowell, Evans, & Ong, 2012; Lederbogen et al., 2011; Lovell, Moss, & Wetherell, 2012). Finally, *daily hassles* involve irritations, pressures, and annoyances that may not be major stressors by themselves but whose effects add up to become significant (Almeida, 2005; Evans & Wener, 2006). The frustrations of daily commuting in heavy traffic, for example, can become so intense for some drivers that they display a pattern of aggression called "road rage."

Measuring Stressors

Which stressors are the most harmful? To study stress more precisely, psychologists have tried to measure the impact of particular stressors. In 1967, Thomas Holmes and Richard Rahe (pronounced "ray") pioneered the effort to find a standard way of measuring the stress in a person's life. Working on the assumption that both positive and negative changes produce stress, they asked a large number of people to rate—in terms of *life-change units (LCUs)*—the amount of change and demand for adjustment caused by events such as divorcing, being fired, retiring, losing a loved one, or becoming pregnant. On the basis of these ratings, Holmes and Rahe (1967) created the *Social Readjustment Rating Scale (SRRS)*. People taking the SRRS receive a stress score equal to the sum of the LCUs for all the stressful events they've recently experienced. Numerous studies have shown that people scoring high on the SRRS and other life-change scales are more likely to suffer physical illness, mental disorder, or other problems than those with lower scores (e.g., Monroe, Thase, & Simons, 1992).

TABLE 12.2   THE UNDERGRADUATE STRESS QUESTIONNAIRE

Here are some items from the Undergraduate Stress Questionnaire (Crandall, Priesler, & Aussprung, 1992), which asks students to indicate whether various stressors have occurred in their lives during the previous week. Has this stressful event happened to you at any time during the last week? If it has, please check the space next to it. If it has not, please leave it blank.

1. _____	Assignments in all classes due the same day
2. _____	Having roommate conflicts
3. _____	Lack of money
4. _____	Trying to decide on major
5. _____	Can't understand your professor
6. _____	Stayed up late writing a paper
7. _____	Sat through a boring class
8. _____	Went into a test unprepared
9. _____	Parents getting divorced
10. _____	Incompetence at the registrar's office

Source: Crandall, Priesler, & Aussprung (1992).

A Daily Hassle

Relatively minor daily hassles can combine to create significant physical and psychological stress responses. The frustrations of daily commuting in heavy traffic, for example, can become so intense for some drivers that they may display a pattern of anger and aggression called "road rage." Aggressive driving, including road rage, has been cited in as many as 56 percent of all fatal automobile accidents in the United States, and has resulted in thousands of injuries (AAA Foundation for Traffic Safety, 2009; Rathbone & Huckabee, 1999).

Jose Luis Pelaez Inc/Blend Images/Getty Images

Other researchers wondered, though, whether life changes alone tell the whole story about the impact of stressors. Accordingly, some investigators have used face-to-face interviews to more precisely measure stressors and their impact (e.g., Dohrenwend et al., 1993). Others developed scales such as the *Life Experiences Survey* (*LES*) (Sarason, Johnson, & Siegel, 1978), which measure not just which life events occurred but also people's perceptions of how positive or negative the events were and how well they were able to cope with the events. The LES also allows respondents to write in and rate any stressors they have experienced that are not on the printed list. This individualized approach can capture the differing impact and meaning that certain experiences might have for men compared with women and for members of various cultural groups. Divorce, for example, may have different meanings to people of different religious backgrounds. And members of some ethnic groups may experience stressors, such as prejudice and discrimination, that are not felt by other groups (e.g., Flores et al., 2010; Yip, Gee, & Takeuchi, 2008).

The timing of stressors matters, too; those that occur early in life can have especially enduring consequences. For example, experiencing the stress of poverty, trauma, or other adversities during early childhood is associated with an increased risk of developing heart disease, arthritis, certain cancers, and other health problems in adulthood, even for people who by then had achieved middle or upper class socioeconomic status (Chan et al., 2011; Rooks et al., 2012). These long-lasting effects occur partly because early life stressors affect the brain as well as the heart and the immune system, and may affect the early basic structuring of these systems in a way that sets the stage for poor stress-coping abilities later on in life (Mitchell et al., 2014; Taylor, 2010).

STRESS RESPONSES

How do people react to stressors?

Physical and psychological stress reactions often occur together, especially as stressors become more intense. Furthermore, one type of stress response can set off a stress response in another dimension. For example, a physical stress reaction such as mild chest pains might trigger the psychological stress response of worrying about a heart attack. Still, it's useful to consider each category of stress responses one at a time.

Physical Responses

If you have experienced a near-accident or some other sudden, frightening event, you know that the physical responses to stressors can include rapid breathing, increased heartbeat and blood pressure, sweating, and perhaps shakiness. These reactions make up a general pattern known as the **fight-flight reaction**. As described in the chapters on biological aspects of psychology and on motivation and emotion, the fight-flight reaction allows the body to be prepared either to face or to flee an immediate threat. Once a danger passes, fight-flight responses subside (Gump et al., 2005).

When stressors last longer or recovery from stressors is slow, however, a fight-flight reaction is just the start of a long sequence of events. Observation of animals and humans led Hans Selye (pronounced "SELL-yay") to suggest that this extended sequence of physical stress responses follows a consistent pattern. He called this sequence the **general adaptation syndrome**, or **GAS** (Selye, 1956, 1976). The GAS occurs in three stages (see Figure 12.2), and it is activated by efforts to adapt to any physical or psychological stressor.

The first stage, called the *alarm reaction,* involves a version of the fight-flight reaction. The alarm reaction to a mild stressor, such as an overheated room, might be no more than changes in heart rate, breathing, and sweating that help the body regulate its temperature. More severe stressors prompt more dramatic alarm reactions, rapidly mobilizing the body's adaptive energy, much as a burglar alarm alerts the police to take action (Kiecolt-Glaser et al., 1998).

fight-flight reaction Physical reactions triggered by the sympathetic nervous system that prepare the body to fight or to run from a threatening situation.

general adaptation syndrome (GAS) A three-stage pattern of responses triggered by the effort to adapt to stressors.

FIGURE 12.2

The General Adaptation Syndrome

Hans Selye found that physical reactions to stressors include an initial alarm reaction followed by resistance and then exhaustion. During the alarm reaction, the body's resistance to stress temporarily drops below normal as it absorbs a stressor's initial impact. Resistance increases and then levels off in the resistance stage, but it ultimately declines if the exhaustion stage is reached.

Source: Adapted from Selye (1975).

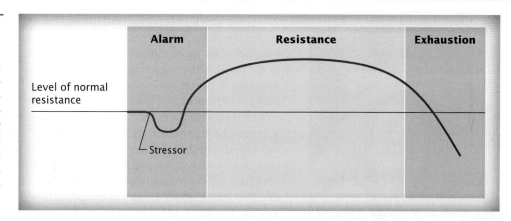

Alarm reactions are controlled by the sympathetic nervous system through interactions involving the brain, various body organs, and glands. These interactions make up the *sympatho-adreno-medullary (SAM) system*. As shown on the right side of Figure 12.3, stressors trigger a process that begins when the brain's hypothalamus activates the sympathetic branch of the autonomic nervous system (ANS), which stimulates the medulla (inner part) of the adrenal glands. The adrenals, in turn, secrete *catecholamines*

FIGURE 12.3

Organ Systems Involved in the General Adaptation Syndrome

Stressors produce a variety of physiological responses that begin in the brain and spread to organs throughout the body. For example, the pituitary gland triggers the release of painkilling endorphins. It also stimulates the release of corticosteroids, which help resist stress but also tend to suppress the immune system. Some of these substances may interact with sex hormones to create different physical stress responses and coping methods in men and women (Taylor, Klein et al., 2000; Taylor et al., 2006).

Michael Sharkey/Taxi/Getty Images

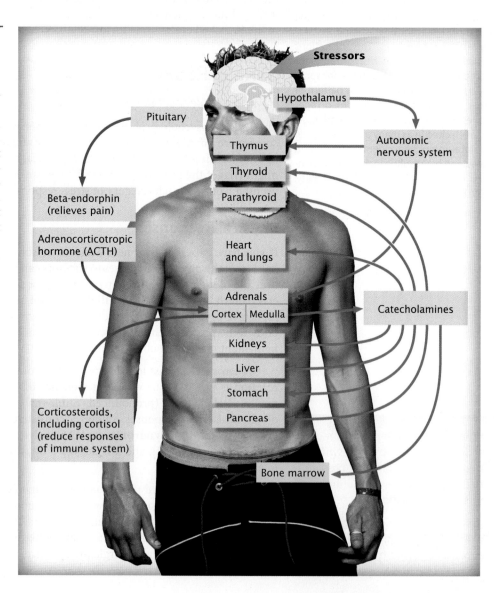

(pronounced "kat-uh-KOH-luh-meens")—especially adrenaline and noradrenaline—which circulate in the bloodstream, affecting the liver, kidneys, heart, lungs, and other organs. This action causes increases in blood pressure, muscle tension, blood sugar, and pupil size, along with other physical changes that provide the energy and resources that may be needed to respond to stressors. Even brief exposure to a stressor may cause major changes in these coordinated regulatory body systems (Stoney et al., 2002).

As shown on the left side of Figure 12.3, stressors also activate the *hypothalamic-pituitary-adrenocortical (HPA) system,* in which the hypothalamus stimulates the pituitary gland in the brain. The pituitary, in turn, secretes hormones such as adrenocorticotropic hormone (ACTH). Among other things, ACTH stimulates the cortex (outer surface) of the adrenal glands to secrete *corticosteroids such as cortisol*; these hormones release the body's energy supplies and fight excessive inflammation. Even little daily hassles can cause SAM activation and cortisol release (Stawski et al., 2013). The pituitary gland also triggers the release of *endorphins,* which act as natural painkillers.

Together, these stress systems generate the energy that may be needed to respond to an emergency. The more stressors there are and the longer they last, the more resources the body may need to spend in responding to them. If the stressors persist, the second stage of Selye's GAS may occur. In this *resistance stage,* obvious signs of the initial alarm reaction fade as the body settles in to resist the stressor on a long-term basis. The drain on adaptive energy is less during the resistance stage compared with the alarm stage, but the body is still working hard to cope with stress.

This continued campaign of biochemical resistance is costly. It slowly but surely uses up the body's reserves of adaptive resources. As this happens, the body enters the third GAS stage, the stage of *exhaustion.* In extreme cases, such as prolonged exposure to freezing temperatures, the result is death. More commonly, the exhaustion stage brings signs of physical wear and tear. Especially hard hit are organ systems that were weak to begin with or that were heavily involved in the resistance process. For example, if adrenaline and cortisol (which help fight stressors during the resistance stage) remain elevated for an extended time, the result can be damage to the heart and blood vessels; suppression of the body's disease-fighting immune system; and vulnerability to illnesses such as heart disease, high blood pressure, arthritis, colds, and flu (e.g., Robles, Glaser, & Kiecolt-Glaser, 2005). Selye referred to illnesses caused or worsened by stressors as **diseases of adaptation**.

Psychological Responses

Selye's widely influential model focused mainly on physiological aspects of stress responses. But stressors also create a variety of psychological responses, including changes in emotion and cognition (thinking) and accompanying changes in behavior.

Emotional Changes

The physical stress responses we have described are commonly accompanied by emotional stress responses. If someone pulls out a gun and demands your money, you will most likely have physiological reactions, such as a spike in heart rate, but you'll also feel some strong emotion—probably fear, maybe anger. In describing stress, people tend to say, "I was angry and frustrated!" rather than "My heart rate increased and my blood pressure went up." In other words, we tend to mention the emotional changes that stress may bring.

In most cases, emotional stress reactions fade soon after the stressors are gone or coped with effectively. Even severe emotional stress responses ease eventually. However, if stressors continue for a long time or if many of them occur in a short time, emotional stress reactions may persist. When people don't have a chance to recover their emotional equilibrium, they feel tense, irritable, short-tempered, or anxious, and they may experience increasingly intense feelings of fatigue, depression, and hopelessness. These reactions can become severe enough to be diagnosed as major depressive disorder, generalized anxiety disorder, or other stress-related problems discussed in the chapter on psychological disorders.

diseases of adaptation Illnesses caused or worsened by stressors.

Cognitive Changes

In the busy, noisy intensive care unit of a London hospital, a doctor misplaced a decimal point while calculating the amount of morphine that a one-day-old premature baby should receive. The child died of an overdose (Davies, 1999). Reductions in the ability to concentrate, think clearly, or remember accurately are typical cognitive stress reactions (e.g., Liston, McEwen, & Casey, 2009; Morgan et al., 2006). These problems appear partly because of *ruminative thinking*, the repeated intrusion of thoughts about stressful events (Lyubomirsky & Nolen-Hoeksema, 1995). Ruminative thoughts about relationship problems, for example, can interfere with studying for a test. A related phenomenon is *catastrophizing*, which means dwelling on and overemphasizing the possible negative consequences of events. During exams, college students who are anxious about tests might say to themselves, "I'm falling behind" or "Everyone is doing better than I am." As catastrophizing or ruminative thinking impairs memory and other aspects of cognitive functioning, resulting feelings of anxiety and other emotional arousal add to the total stress response, further hampering performance (Beilock et al., 2004).

Overarousal created by stressors can also interfere with our ability to adapt to new or difficult situations (Schwabe & Wolf, 2011) because one effect of overarousal is to narrow the scope of attention. When people don't attend to the entire situation and don't consider enough solutions to complex problems (Craske, 1999), they may make one or more of the problem-solving errors described in the chapter on thought and language. People under stress are more likely to cling to *mental sets*, which are well-learned (but not always efficient) approaches to problems. Stress may also intensify *functional fixedness*, the tendency to use objects for only one purpose. Victims of hotel fires, for example, sometimes die trapped in their rooms because in the stress of the moment it did not occur to them to use a piece of furniture to break open a window (Renner & Beversdorf, 2010).

Stressors may also impair decision making (Mather & Lighthall, 2012). Under stress, people who normally consider all aspects of a situation before making a decision may act impulsively and sometimes foolishly. High-pressure salespeople take advantage of this stress response by creating time-limited offers or by telling indecisive customers that others are waiting to buy the item they are considering (Cialdini, 2001).

Behavioral Responses

Clues about people's physical and emotional stress reactions come from changes in how they look, act, or talk. Strained facial expressions, a shaky voice, tremors, and jumpiness are common behavioral stress responses.

Even more obvious behavioral stress responses appear as people try to escape or avoid stressors (Atalay & Meloy, 2011). They may turn to alcohol, overeat (especially high-fat "comfort" foods), begin or increase smoking, and either sleep too much or skimp on sleep

Stress for $500, Alex

The negative effects of stress on memory, thinking, decision making, and other cognitive functions are often displayed by players on TV game shows such as *Jeopardy!*, *Who Wants to Be a Millionaire*, and *Survivor*. Under the intense pressure of time, competition, and the scrutiny of millions of viewers, contestants may make mistakes that seem ridiculous to those calmly watching at home.

Amanda Edwards/Getty Images Entertainment/ Getty Images

in favor of late-night socializing. These tactics may provide temporary relief but at the cost of negative health consequences (Cohen et al., 2009; Tsenkova, Boylan, & Ryff, 2013). In the face of severe or long-lasting stress, some people quit their jobs, drop out of school, or even attempt suicide. After the global economic downturn in 2008, for example, suicide rates went up around the world (Chang et al., 2013). Natural disasters are examples of particularly severe and sometimes long-lasting stressors that can challenge our coping skills (Musa et al., 2014). In the month after Hurricane Katrina struck the U.S. Gulf Coast in 2005, more than double the normal number of calls were placed from the affected area to the National Suicide Prevention Hotline, and stress-related mental health problems remained long after the storm's immediate effects abated (Kessler et al., 2008; Roberts et al., 2010). Aggression is another common behavioral response to stressors. All too often, this response is directed at members of one's own family (Hellmuth & McNulty, 2008; Polusny & Follette, 1995). So areas devastated by hurricanes and other natural disasters are likely to see not only an increase in suicides but also significant increases in reports of domestic violence (Curtis, Miller, & Berry, 2000). Even "everyday" stressors can tempt us to resort to escape or avoidance tactics. Unfortunately, as discussed in the chapter on learning, such behaviors deprive us of a chance to learn more adaptive ways of coping with stressful events and situations, including those typically encountered in college life (Cooper et al., 1992).

LINKAGES When do stress responses become mental disorders? (a link to Psychological Disorders)

STRESS AND PSYCHOLOGICAL DISORDERS
LINKAGES

Physical and psychological stress responses sometimes appear together in patterns known as *burnout* and *posttraumatic stress disorder*. **Burnout** is an increasingly intense pattern of physical and psychological dysfunction in response to a continuous flow of stressors or to chronic stress (Maslach, 2003). As burnout nears, previously reliable workers or once-attentive spouses become indifferent, disengaged, impulsive, or accident-prone. They miss work frequently, oversleep, perform their jobs poorly, abuse alcohol or other drugs, and become irritable, suspicious, withdrawn, and depressed (Beck et al., 2013; Taylor, 2002). Burnout is particularly common among those who do "people work," such as teachers, doctors, and nurses and those who perceive themselves as being treated unjustly by employers (Barnard & Curry, 2012; Dyrbye et al., 2014; Hoobler & Brass, 2006).

Posttraumatic stress disorder (PTSD) is a different pattern of severe negative reactions to a traumatic event. Among its characteristics are anxiety, irritability, jumpiness, inability to concentrate or work productively, sexual dysfunction, intrusive thoughts and images, and difficulty in social and family relationships. PTSD sufferers also experience sleep disturbances, intense startle responses to noise or other sudden stimuli, long-term suppression of their immune systems, and elevated risk of coronary heart disease (e.g., Hagenaars et al., 2010; Kubzansky et al., 2009; Rutkowski et al., 2010). In one study, children with PTSD due to a terrorist incident still showed elevated heart rate and blood pressure seven years later (Pfefferbaum et al., 2014). Neuroimaging studies reveal that PTSD symptoms are accompanied by noticeable changes in brain functioning and even in brain structure (Kitayama et al., 2005). The most common feature of PTSD is reexperiencing the trauma through nightmares or vivid memories. In rare cases, *flashbacks* occur in which the person behaves for minutes, hours, or days as if the trauma were occurring again.

Posttraumatic stress disorder is often associated with events such as war, rape, terrorism, natural disasters, assault, or abuse in childhood, but researchers believe that some PTSD symptoms can be triggered by any major stressor, such as a car accident, being stalked, or living in a community that is threatened by terrorism or serial killers (Cormer et al., 2014; Diamond et al., 2010; Marshall, Miles, & Stewart, 2010; Schulden et al., 2006). PTSD usually appears immediately following a trauma, but all of its symptoms may not appear until weeks later (Andrews et al., 2007). Many people affected by PTSD require professional help, although some seem to recover without it (Bradley et al., 2005; Perkonigg et al., 2005). For most, improvement takes time; one summary analysis of research found that 56 percent of people who developed PTSD

(continued)

burnout A pattern of physical and psychological dysfunctions in response to continuous stressors.

posttraumatic stress disorder (PTSD) A pattern of adverse reactions following a traumatic event, commonly involving reexperiencing the event through nightmares or vivid memories.

Life Hanging in the Balance

Symptoms of burnout and posttraumatic stress disorder (PTSD) often plague firefighters, police officers, emergency medical personnel, and others who are repeatedly exposed to time pressure, trauma, danger, and other stressors (Fullerton, Ursano, & Wang, 2004; Perrin et al., 2007). PTSD can also occur following a single catastrophic event, such as the earthquake and tsunami that caused devastation in Japan in 2011.

Camera Press/Dan Chung/Guardian/Redux

continued to display symptoms forty months later (Morina et al., 2014). For nearly all, the support of family and friends is vital to recovery (Foa et al., 2005).

Not everyone who endures a trauma will go on to experience PTSD, even after severe trauma (Breslau et al., 2005). In fact, some people report enhanced psychological growth after surviving a trauma (Zoellner & Maercker, 2006). Health psychologists are working to discover what protective factors operate in these individuals and whether those factors can be strengthened through PTSD treatment and prevention programs (e.g., Cacioppo, Reis, & Zautra, 2011; Cornum et al., 2011; Shalev et al., 2012; Tedeschi & McNally, 2011).

Stress plays a role in the development of many other psychological disorders, including depression, certain anxiety disorders, and schizophrenia spectrum disorders (e.g., Cutrona et al., 2005). We emphasize this point in the chapter on psychological disorders, especially in relation to the *diathesis-stress model* of psychopathology. This model suggests that some people may be predisposed to develop certain disorders but that whether or not these disorders actually appear depends on the frequency, nature, and intensity of the stressors such people encounter.

STRESS MEDIATORS

Why doesn't everyone react to stressors in the same way?

The various ways that different people interact with particular stressors can be seen in many areas of life. The stress of combat, for example, is partly responsible for the errors in judgment and decision making that lead to "friendly fire" deaths and injuries in almost every military operation (Adler, 1993). But not everyone in combat makes these mistakes. Why not? And why does one individual survive and even thrive under the same circumstances that lead another to break down, give up, and burn out?

Answers may lie in *psychobiological models,* which examine the interaction of both psychological as well as biological factors in the stress process (Cyranowski et al., 2011; Folkman et al., 2000; Kidd, Hamer, & Steptoe, 2011; Suls & Rothman, 2004; Taylor, 2002). These models emphasize that (as shown in Figure 12.1) the impact of stressors depends not only on the actual stressors themselves but also on several important *mediating factors* (Bonanno, 2005; Kemeny, 2003).

How Stressors Are Perceived

As described in the chapter on sensation and perception, our view of the world depends partly on how we interpret data from our senses. Similarly, our physical and psychological reactions to stressors depend somewhat on how we think about them, a process known as *cognitive appraisal.* A potential stressor usually has a stronger negative impact on people who perceive it as a threat than on people who see it as a challenge (Lazarus, 1999; Maddi & Khoshaba, 2005). This may be why people who are deeply engaged in and passionate about their stressful jobs are less likely than their coworkers to suffer burnout (Vallerand et al., 2010).

Evidence for the effects of cognitive factors on stress responses comes from surveys and experiments. In one of the first laboratory demonstrations of these effects, Richard Lazarus gave differing instructions to three groups of students who were about to watch a film showing bloody industrial accidents (Lazarus et al., 1965). One group (the "intellectualizers") was told to remain mentally detached from the gruesome scenes; a second group (the "denial" group) was instructed to think of the scenes as unreal; and a third group (the "unprepared" group) was told nothing about the film. As Figure 12.4 shows, the intensity of physiological arousal during the film, as measured by sweat gland activity, depended on how the viewers were instructed to think about the film. The unprepared students were more upset than either of the other two groups. In a more recent study, students who were first trained to see the threatening aspects of information showed more emotional arousal to a stressful video than those who had been trained to see information as nonthreatening (Wilson et al., 2006). Similarly, physical and psychological symptoms associated with the stress of airport noise, of being diagnosed with a serious illness, of learning about toxins in local soil, or of living with terrorism threats are more common in people who engage in more catastrophic thinking about these problems (e.g., Bryant & Guthrie, 2005; Lerner et al., 2003; Speckhard, 2002). Those who hold a more optimistic outlook in general tend to show milder stress responses and better health outcomes (de Moor et al., 2006; Taylor et al., 2003).

The influence of cognitive factors is somewhat less important as stressors become extreme. For example, patients who have a sense of control over chronic pain are more likely than other patients to remain physically active, but this difference does not hold if the pain is severe (Jensen & Karoly, 1991). Still, even the impact of major stressors, such as a natural disaster or a divorce, may be less severe for those who think of them as challenges to be overcome. In other words, many stressful events are not inherently stressful; their impact depends partly on how people perceive them. An important part of this appraisal is the degree to which the stressors are perceived to be predictable and controllable, or at least manageable.

FIGURE 12.4

Cognitive Influences on Stress Responses

Richard Lazarus and his colleagues found that students' physiological stress reactions to a film showing bloody industrial accidents were affected by the way they thought about what they saw. Those who had been instructed to remain detached from the film (the "intellectualizers") or to think of it as unreal (the "denial" group) were less upset—as measured by sweat gland activity—than those in an "unprepared" group. These results were among the first to show that people's cognitive appraisals of stressors can affect their responses to those stressors.

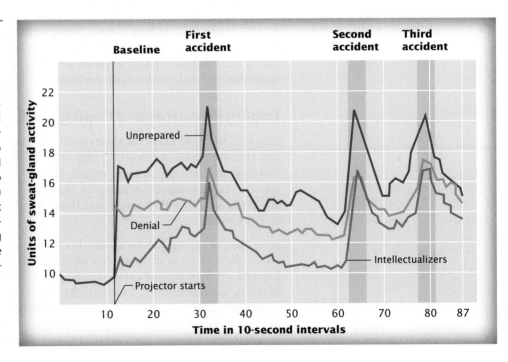

Predictability and Control

Why is the threat of terrorism so terrorizing? A key reason is because knowing that a stressor might occur but being uncertain whether or when it will occur tends to increase the stressor's impact (Lerner et al., 2003; Sorrentino & Roney, 2000). In other words, *unpredictable* stressors tend to have more impact than those that are predictable (Lazarus & Folkman, 1984; Pham, Taylor, & Seeman, 2001), especially when the stressors are intense and relatively brief. For example, people whose spouses have died suddenly tend to display more immediate disbelief, anxiety, and depression than those who have had weeks or months to prepare for the loss (Schulz et al., 2001; Swarte et al., 2003). Still, predictability does not provide total protection against stressors. Research with animals shows that predictable stressors can be even more damaging than unpredictable ones if they occur over long periods of time (Abbott, Schoen, & Badia, 1984).

The *perception of control* is also a powerful mediator of the effects of stressors. If people feel they have some control over stressors, those stressors usually have less impact (e.g., Johnson & Krueger, 2005; Smith et al., 2008). For example, studies of several thousand employees in the United States, Sweden, and the United Kingdom have found that those who felt they had little or no control over their work environment were more likely to suffer heart disease and other health problems than workers with a high degree of perceived control (Bosma et al., 1997; Cheng et al., 2000; Spector, 2002). And at many hospitals, it is now standard procedure to help patients manage or control the stress of emergency treatment or the side effects of surgery by providing preparatory information about what to expect during and after a medical procedure, teaching relaxation skills, and allowing patients to control the administration of their pain medication. These strategies have all been shown to help people heal faster and go home sooner (Broadbent et al., 2003; Chamberlin, 2000; Gordon et al., 2005).

Simply *believing* that a stressor is controllable (even if it isn't) can also reduce its impact. In one study, participants with panic disorder inhaled a mixture of oxygen and carbon dioxide that typically causes a panic attack (Sanderson, Rapee, & Barlow, 1989). Half the participants were led to believe (falsely) that they could control the concentration of the mixture. Compared with those who believed that they had no control, significantly fewer of the "in-control" participants experienced full-blown panic attacks during the session, and their panic symptoms were fewer and less severe.

People who feel they have no control over negative events appear especially prone to physical and psychological problems. They often experience feelings of helplessness and hopelessness that in turn may promote depression or other mental disorders (Sarin, Abela, & Auerbach, 2005; Whang et al., 2009). It's even been suggested that a perceived lack of control partly explains why people in lower socioeconomic groups are at somewhat elevated risk for early death (Stringhini et al., 2010; Trumbetta et al., 2010).

Coping Resources and Coping Methods

People usually suffer fewer ill effects from a stressor if they have adequate coping resources and effective coping methods. *Coping resources* include, among other things, the money and time to deal with stressful events. For example, the physical and psychological responses you experience if your car breaks down tend to be more negative if you are broke and pressed for time than if you have the money for repairs and the freedom to take a day off from work.

Effective coping methods can also reduce the impact of stressors (Cote & Pepler, 2002). Most of these methods can be classified as either problem-focused or emotion-focused. *Problem-focused* coping methods involve efforts to change or eliminate a source of stress, whereas *emotion-focused* techniques attempt to control the negative emotional consequences of stressors (Folkman et al., 1986). Many people use both kinds of coping. For example, you might deal with the problem of noise from a nearby factory by forming a community action group to push for tougher noise-reduction laws and at the same time

TABLE 12.3 WAYS OF COPING

Coping is defined as cognitive and behavioral efforts to manage specific demands that people perceive as taxing their resources (Folkman et al., 1986). This table illustrates two major approaches to coping measured by Folkman and Lazarus's (1988) Ways of Coping Questionnaire: problem-focused and emotion-focused. Ask yourself which approach you usually take when faced with stressors. Now rank the coping skills under each major approach in terms of how often you tend to use each. Do you rely on just one or two? Or do you adjust your coping strategies to fit different kinds of stressors?

Coping Skills	Example
Problem-focused coping	
Confronting	"I stood my ground and fought for what I wanted."
Seeking social support	"I talked to someone to find out more about the situation."
Planful problem solving	"I made a plan of action and I followed it."
Emotion-focused coping	
Self-controlling	"I tried to keep my feelings to myself."
Distancing	"I didn't let it get to me; I tried not to think about it too much."
Positive reappraisal	"I changed my mind about myself."
Accepting responsibility	"I realized I brought the problem on myself."
Escape/avoidance (wishful thinking)	"I wished that the situation would go away or somehow be over with."

Source: Adapted from Folkman et al. (1986).

calm your anger when noise occurs by mentally focusing on the group's efforts to improve the situation (Folkman & Moskowitz, 2000; Hatfield et al., 2002). Susan Folkman and Richard Lazarus (1988) devised a widely used questionnaire to assess the specific ways in which people cope with stressors; Table 12.3 shows some examples from their questionnaire.

Particularly when a stressor is difficult to control, it is sometimes helpful to fully express and think about the emotions you are experiencing in relation to the stressful event (Niederhoffer & Pennebaker, 2002; Stanton & Low, 2012). In one program designed to promote this kind of emotional expression, also known as *emotional disclosure*, people spend thirty to sixty minutes a day for several days writing or talking about their thoughts and feelings about past or present stressors. Laboratory studies have shown this emotional coping strategy to significantly reduce psychological and physical stress responses (Petrie et al., 2004; Willmott et al., 2011). Its benefits have been observed outside the laboratory, too. People recovering from their first heart attack who were asked to write about their emotions were less likely to have future heart symptoms or hospitalizations than those who had not been assigned to this emotional coping strategy task (Willmott et al., 2011). Even wound healing appears to go faster in people who have been asked to write about their emotional reactions to their health problems (Koschwanez et al., 2013). Some individuals who use humor to help them cope also show better adjustment and milder physiological reactivity to stressful events (Martin, 2001; Moran, 2002).

Social Support

Has a good friend comforted or reassured you during troubled times? If so, you have
experienced the value of *social support* in easing the impact of stressful events. Social support consists of emotional, tangible, or informational resources provided by other people.
These people might help eliminate a stressor (by, say, fixing your car), suggest how to deal
with the stressor (by recommending a good mechanic), or reduce a stressor's impact by
providing companionship and reassurance (Sarason, Sarason, & Gurung, 1997). The people you can depend on for support make up your network of **social support** (Burleson,
Albrecht, & Sarason, 1994).

The stress-reducing effects of social support have been documented in people dealing with a wide range of stressors, including cancer, stroke, military combat, loss of loved
ones, natural disasters, arthritis, AIDS, and even ethnic discrimination (e.g., Antoni &
Lutgendorf, 2007; Penner, Dovidio, & Albrecht, 2001; Smyth et al., 2014; Weihs, Enright,
& Simmens, 2008). Social support can have health benefits, too. For example, students who
get emotional support from friends show better immune system functioning than those
with less-adequate social support (Cohen & Herbert, 1996). This may be why people with
strong social support are less vulnerable to colds and flu during exams and other periods
of high academic stress (Pressman et al., 2005; Taylor, Dickerson, & Klein, 2002). Having
strong social support is also associated with faster recovery from surgery or illness, possibly
because helpful friends and family members encourage patients to follow medical advice
(Brummett et al., 2005; Taylor, 2002). Even people with cancer do better if they have strong
social support (Hughes et al., 2014; Yoo et al., 2014). People in stronger social networks—
especially those filled with happy people—tend to be happier than those in weaker networks
and may even enjoy better mental functioning in old age (Fowler & Christakis, 2008; Gleibs
et al., 2011). According to some researchers, having inadequate social support can be as dangerous as smoking, obesity, or lack of exercise in that it nearly doubles a person's risk of dying
from disease, suicide, or other causes (Kiecolt-Glaser & Newton, 2001; Rutledge et al., 2004).

Exactly how social support brings about its positive effects is not entirely clear. We
do know that people who receive more social support in response to stressors display patterns of brain activation that differ from those with less support (Eisenberger et al., 2013).
These data suggest support-related differences in the mental processing of stressors, but
what might those differences be? James Pennebaker (1995, 2000) has suggested that social
support may help prevent illness by providing the person under stress with an opportunity
to express pent-up thoughts and emotions. Pennebaker and other researchers suggest that
keeping important things to yourself is itself a stressor (e.g., Dalgleish, Hauer, & Kuyken,
2008; Srivastava et al., 2009). In a laboratory experiment, for example, participants

social support The friends and
social contacts on whom one can
depend for help and support.

who were asked to deceive an experimenter showed elevated physiological arousal (Pennebaker & Chew, 1985). Further, if the spouses of people who die as the result of an accident or suicide do not or cannot confide their feelings to others, they're especially likely to develop physical illness during the year following the death (Pennebaker & O'Heeron, 1984). Disclosing (even anonymously) the stresses and traumas one has experienced is associated with enhanced immune functioning, reduced physical symptoms, and decreased use of health services (e.g., Campbell & Pennebaker, 2003; Epstein, Sloan, & Marx, 2005; Pachankis & Goldfried, 2010). This may explain why support groups for a wide range of problems such as bereavement, overeating, and alcohol and drug abuse tend to promote participants' physical health (Taylor et al., 2002).

Research in this area is made more challenging by the fact that the relationship between social support and the impact of stressors is not a simple one. For one thing, the quality of social support can influence the ability to cope with stress, but the reverse may also be true: your ability to cope may determine the quality of the social support you receive (McLeod, Kessler, & Landis, 1992). People who complain endlessly about stressors but never do anything about them may discourage social support, whereas those with an optimistic, action-oriented approach may attract support.

Second, *social support* refers not only to your relationships with others but also to the recognition that others care and will help (Demaray & Malecki, 2002). Some relationships in a seemingly strong social network can be stormy, fragile, or shallow, resulting in interpersonal conflicts that can have an adverse effect on health (Ben-Ari & Gil, 2002; Malarkey et al., 1994).

Third, the quality of social support can alter its effectiveness. For example, children coping with the 2011 Japan tsunami showed more-severe stress effects if their parents suddenly became more protective, less willing to give them independence, and more often emphasized life's dangers (Cobham & McDermott, 2014). The quality of social support can have longer-term effects, too. In one study, people who viewed their marriages as supportive and positive were less likely than other married people to have developed harmful plaque in their coronary arteries (Uchino, Smith, & Berg, 2014).

Evidently, both in the short term and in the long term, having the right kind of social support appears to be what matters. In fact, having too much support or the wrong kind of support can be as bad as not having enough (Reynolds & Perrin, 2004). Dangerous behaviors such as smoking or overeating, for example, can be harder to give up if one's social support consists largely or entirely of smokers or overeaters (Christakis & Fowler, 2007). People whose friends and family overprotect them from stressors may have fewer opportunities to learn effective coping strategies. They may also lose confidence in the strategies they have and thus put less energy into their coping efforts. If the efforts of people in a social support network become annoying, disruptive, or interfering, they can actually increase stress and intensify psychological and physical problems (Gleason et al., 2008; Newsom et al., 2008). It has even been suggested that among people under intense stress, the benefits of having a large social support network may be offset by the dangers of catching a cold or the flu from people in that network (Hamrick, Cohen, & Rodriguez, 2002).

Finally, the value of social support may depend on the kind of stressor being encountered. So although having a friend nearby might reduce the impact of some stressors, it might amplify the impact of others. In one study, participants who were about to make a speech experienced the task as more threatening—and showed stronger physical and psychological stress responses—when a friend was with them than when they were waiting alone (Stoney & Finney, 2000).

Stress, Personality, and Gender

The impact of stress on health appears to depend not only on how people think about particular stressors but also to some extent on how they think about and react to the world in general. For instance, stress-related health problems tend to be especially common among people whose "disease-prone" personalities lead them to (1) try to ignore stressors when possible; (2) perceive stressors as long-term, catastrophic threats that they brought on themselves; and (3) be pessimistic about their ability to overcome stressors (e.g., Penninx et al., 2001; Roy et al., 2010; Suinn, 2001).

Other cognitive styles, such as those characteristic of "disease-resistant" personalities, help insulate people from the ill effects of stress. These people tend to think of stressors as temporary challenges to be overcome, not catastrophic threats. And they don't constantly blame themselves for causing these stressors. One particularly important component of the "disease-resistant" personality seems to be *dispositional optimism,* the belief or expectation that things will work out positively (Folkman & Moskowitz, 2000; Pressman & Cohen, 2005; Rosenkranz et al., 2003; Taylor, Kemeny et al., 2000). Optimistic people tend to live longer (Giltay et al., 2004, 2006) and to have more resistance than pessimists to colds and other infectious diseases (e.g., Boyce & Wood, 2011; Pressman & Cohen, 2005; Segerstrom & Sephton, 2010), which helps explain why optimistic students experience fewer physical symptoms at the end of the academic term (e.g., Ebert, Tucker, & Roth, 2002).

Optimistic older adults show different activation patterns in certain brain regions when shown distressing images, suggesting that optimism may affect activity of brain systems involved in regulating negative emotions (Bangen et al., 2013). Optimistic coronary bypass surgery patients tend to heal faster and stay healthier than pessimists (Scheier et al., 1989, 1999), perceive their quality of life following coronary surgery to be higher (Fitzgerald et al., 1993), and respond better to treatments for post-operative depression (Tindle et al., 2012) than do patients with less optimistic outlooks. And among HIV-positive men, dispositional optimism has been associated with lower psychological distress, fewer worries, and lower perceived risk of acquiring full-blown AIDS (Johnson & Endler, 2002). These effects appear in part due to optimists' tendency to use challenge-oriented, problem-focused coping strategies that attack stressors directly, in contrast to pessimists' tendency to use emotion-focused coping strategies, such as denial and avoidance (Brenes et al., 2002; Moskowitz et al., 2009). They also tend to be happier than pessimists, a tendency associated not only with less intense and less dangerous physiological responses to stressors but also with greater success in life (e.g., Lyubomirsky, King, & Diener, 2005).

Indeed, like optimism, happiness and other positive emotions and traits, such as hope, resilience, conscientiousness, and curiosity, have been associated with better health and longer life (Challen, Machin, & Gillham, 2014; Cohen et al., 2003a; Friedman et al., 2014; Ong et al., 2006; Xu & Roberts, 2010). For example, a long-term study of Catholic nuns found that those who wrote with the most positive emotional style when they were young lived longer than those whose writing contained less positive emotions (Danner, Snowden, & Friesen, 2001). Studies like these represent a new line of research in health psychology that focuses on investigating and promoting the positive emotions, behaviors, and cognitive styles associated with better health (Kashdan & Rottenberg, 2010; Seligman, Steen, et al., 2005).

Gender may also play a role in responses to stressors (Tomova et al., 2014). In a review of 200 studies of stress responses and coping methods, Shelley Taylor and her colleagues found that males under stress tended to get angry, avoid stressors, or both, whereas females were more likely to help others and to make use of social support (Taylor, Klein et al., 2000; Taylor et al., 2002). Further, in the face of equally intense stressors, men's physical responses tend to be more intense than women's (Stoney & Matthews, 1988). This is not true in every case, of course (Smith et al., 2008), but why should gender differences show up at all? Though the learning of the gender roles that we discuss in the human development chapter surely plays a part (Eagly & Wood, 1999), Taylor proposes that women's "tend and befriend" style differs from the "fight-flight" pattern often seen in men partly because of gender differences in how hormones combine under stress. Consider, for example, oxytocin (pronounced "ox-see-TOH-sin"), a hormone released in both sexes in response to stressors, including social stressors. Taylor suggests that oxytocin interacts differently with male and female sex hormones: in men, it amplifies physical responses to stress, but it reduces those responses in women (Light et al., 2005). This gender difference could lead to the more intense emotional and behavioral stress responses typical of men, and it might be partly responsible for men's greater vulnerability to heart disease and other stress-related illnesses (Kajantie & Phillips, 2006). If that is the case, gender differences in stress responses may help explain why women in industrialized societies live an average of five to ten years longer than men (Hoyert, Kung, & Smith, 2005; Kajantie, 2008). The role of gender-related hormones in responding to stress is supported by the fact that there are few (if any) gender differences in children's responses to stress. Those differences begin to appear only around adolescence, when sex hormone differences become pronounced (Allen & Matthews, 1997).

FOCUS ON RESEARCH METHODS

PERSONALITY AND HEALTH

The way people think and act in the face of stressors, the ease with which they attract social support, and their tendency to be optimists or pessimists are but a few aspects of *personality*.

What was the researchers' question?

Are there other personality characteristics that protect or threaten people's health? This was the question asked by Howard Friedman and his associates (Friedman, 2000; Friedman et al., 1995a, 1995b). In particular, they tried to identify aspects of personality that increase the likelihood that people will die prematurely from heart disease, high blood pressure, or other chronic diseases.

LINKAGES Are childhood traits related to how long we live? (a link to Personality)

How did the researchers answer the question?

Friedman suspected that an answer might lie in the results of the Terman Life Cycle Study of Intelligence. As described in the chapter on thought and language, the study was originally designed to measure the long-term development of 1,528 gifted California children (856 boys and 672 girls) who were nicknamed the "Termites," after Louis Terman, the research team leader (Terman & Oden, 1947).

Starting in 1921, and every five to ten years thereafter, the team gathered information about the Termites' personality traits, social relationships, stressors, health habits, and many other variables. The data were collected through questionnaires and interviews with the Termites themselves as well as with their teachers, parents, and other family members. By the early 1990s, about half of the Termites had died. It was then that Friedman realized that the Terman Life Cycle Study could shed light on the relationship between personality and health, because the personality traits identified in the Termites could be related to how long they lived. So he examined the Termites' death certificates, noting the dates and causes of death, and then looked for associations between their personalities and the length of their lives.

What did the researchers find?

Friedman and his colleagues found that one of the most important predictors of long life was a dimension of personality known as *conscientiousness*, or social dependability (described in the personality chapter). Termites who in childhood had been seen as truthful, prudent, reliable, hard working, and humble tended to live longer than those whose parents and teachers had identified them as impulsive and lacking in self-control.

Friedman also examined the Terman Life Cycle Study for what it suggested about the relationship between health and social support. In particular, he compared Termites whose parents had divorced or who had been in unstable marriages themselves with those who grew up in stable homes and who had stable marriages. He discovered that people who had experienced parental divorce during childhood or who themselves had unstable marriages died an average of four years earlier than those whose close social relationships had been less stressful.

(continued)

What do the results mean?

Did these differences in personality traits and social support actually cause some Termites to live longer than others? Friedman's research is based mainly on correlational analyses, so it was difficult for the investigators to draw conclusions about what caused the relationships they observed. Still, Friedman and his colleagues searched the Terman data for clues to mechanisms through which personality and other factors might have exerted a causal influence on how long the Termites lived (Peterson et al., 1998). For example, they evaluated the hypothesis that conscientious, dependable Termites who lived socially stable lives might have followed healthier lifestyles than those who were more impulsive and socially stressed. They found that people in the latter group did, in fact, tend to eat less healthy diets and were more likely to smoke, drink to excess, or use drugs. But health behaviors alone did not fully account for their shorter average life spans. Another possible explanation is that conscientiousness and stability in social relationships reflect a general attitude of caution that goes beyond eating right and avoiding substance abuse. Friedman found some support for this idea in the Terman data. Termites who were impulsive or low on conscientiousness were somewhat more likely to die from accidents or violence than those who were less impulsive.

What do we still need to know?

The Terman Life Cycle Study does not provide final answers about the relationship between personality and health. However, it has generated some important clues and a number of intriguing hypotheses to be evaluated in research with more representative samples of participants. Some of that research has already taken place and tends to confirm Friedman's findings about conscientiousness (e.g., Hampson et al., 2006; Kern & Friedman, 2008; Roberts et al., 2009). Further, Friedman's decision to reanalyze a set of data on psychosocial development as a way of exploring issues in health care psychology stands as a fine example of how a creative researcher can pursue answers to complex questions that are difficult or impossible to study via controlled experiments.

Our discussion of personality and other factors that can alter the impact of stressors should make it obvious that what is stressful for a given individual is not determined fully and simply by predispositions, coping styles, or situations (see "In Review: Stress Responses and Stress Mediators"). Even more important are interactions between the person and the situation, the mixture of each individual's coping resources with the specific characteristics of the situations encountered.

IN REVIEW

STRESS RESPONSES AND STRESS MEDIATORS

Category	Examples
Responses	
Physical	The fight-flight reaction involves increased heart rate, respiration, and muscle tension as well as sweating and dilated pupils. Activation of SAM and HPA systems releases catecholamines and corticosteroids. Organ systems involved in prolonged resistance to stressors eventually break down.
Psychological	*Emotional* examples include anger, anxiety, depression, and other emotional states. *Cognitive* examples include inability to concentrate or think logically, ruminative thinking, and catastrophizing. *Behavioral* examples include aggression and escape/avoidance tactics (including suicide attempts) and health-risk behaviors.
Mediators	
Appraisal	Thinking of a difficult new job as a challenge will create less discomfort than focusing on the threat of failure.

(continued)

STRESS RESPONSES AND STRESS MEDIATORS (CONT.)

Category	Examples
Predictability	A tornado that strikes without warning may have a more devastating emotional impact than a long-predicted hurricane.
Control	Repairing a disabled spacecraft may be less stressful for the astronauts doing the work than for their loved ones on earth, who can do nothing to help.
Coping resources and methods	Having no effective way to relax after a hard day may prolong tension and other stress responses.
Social support	Having no one to talk to about a rape or other trauma may amplify the negative impact of the experience.

In Review Questions

1. The friends and family we can depend on to help us deal with stressors are called our _____ network.

2. Fantasizing about winning money is a(n) _____ focused way of coping with financial stress.

3. Sudden, extreme stressors may cause psychological and behavioral problems known as _____.

THE PHYSIOLOGY AND PSYCHOLOGY OF HEALTH AND ILLNESS

How does stress affect your immune system?

Several studies mentioned so far show that people under stress are more likely than less-stressed people to develop infections. Other research shows that they are also more likely to experience flare-ups of the latent viruses responsible for oral herpes (cold sores) or genital herpes (Cohen & Herbert, 1996). In the following sections we focus on some of the ways that these and other illnesses are related to the impact of stress on the immune system and other body systems.

LINKAGES Can stress give you the flu? (a link to Biological Aspects of Psychology)

Stress, Illness, and the Immune System

On March 19, 1878, at a seminar at the Académie de Médecine in Paris, Louis Pasteur showed his distinguished audience three chickens. One bird had been raised normally and was healthy. A second bird had been intentionally infected with bacteria but given no other treatment; it was also healthy. The third chicken that Pasteur presented was dead. It had been infected with the same bacteria as the second bird, but it had also been physically stressed by being exposed to cold temperatures; as a result, the bacteria had killed it (Kelley, 1985).

Research conducted since Pasteur's time has greatly expanded our knowledge about how stressors affect the body's reaction to disease and has expanded our notions of stress to include not only environmental factors but also psychological and social ones. **Psychoneuroimmunology** is the field that examines the interaction of psychological and physiological processes that strengthen or weaken the body's ability to defend itself against disease (Ader, 2001).

The Immune System and Illness

psychoneuroimmunology The field that examines the interaction of psychological and physiological processes affecting the body's ability to defend itself against disease.

immune system The body's first line of biological defense against invading substances and microorganisms.

inflammation An immune system response that combats infectious agents and helps to heal injuries.

The body's first line of biological defense against invading substances and microorganisms is the **immune system**. The immune system is perhaps as complex as the nervous system, and it contains as many cells as the brain (Guyton, 1991). Some of these cells are in organs such as the thymus and spleen and lymph nodes, whereas others circulate in the bloodstream, entering tissues throughout the body. Components of the immune system kill or inactivate foreign or harmful substances in the body, such as viruses and bacteria (Simpson, Hurtley, & Marx, 2000). **Inflammation** (seen externally as swelling and redness

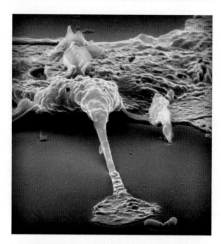

The Body's Internal Defense System

A patrolling immune system cell sends out an extension known as a pseudo-pod to engulf and destroy a bacterial cell before alerting more defenders. These immune cells are able to squeeze out of the bloodstream and enter organs, where they destroy foreign cells.

Boehringer Ingelheim International GmbH/photo Lennart Nilsson, The Incredible Machine, National Geographic Society/Scanpix

around a wound) is an immune system response that helps to fight infectious agents and promote the healing of injuries. However, if this inflammatory response is prolonged or excessive it can promote or worsen asthma, coronary artery disease, diabetes, some cancers, and other chronic conditions (Chiang et al., 2012; Cohen et al., 2012).

If our immune systems are impaired, we are left more vulnerable to colds, mononucleosis, and many other infectious diseases (Potter & Zautra, 1997). Even the healing of wounds is slower when we experience psychological stress (Broadbent & Koschwanez, 2012). The human immunodeficiency virus (HIV) disables the immune system, leading to AIDS and leaving the HIV-infected person defenseless against other infections or cancers. The immune system can also become overactive, with devastating results. Many chronic, progressive diseases—including arthritis, diabetes, and lupus erythematosus—are now recognized as *autoimmune disorders*. In these cases, cells of the immune system begin to attack and destroy normal body cells (Oldenberg et al., 2000; Wang & Zheng, 2013).

An important aspect of the human immune system is the action of the white blood cells, called *leukocytes* (pronounced "LU-koh-sites"). These cells are formed in the bone marrow and serve as the body's mobile defense units. Leukocytes are called to action when foreign substances are detected. Among the varied types of leukocytes are *B-cells*, which produce *antibodies* to fight foreign toxins; *T-cells*, which kill other cells; and *natural killer cells*, which destroy a variety of foreign organisms and are particularly important in fighting viruses and tumors. The brain can influence the immune system indirectly by altering the secretion of adrenal hormones, such as cortisol, that modify the circulation of T-cells and B-cells. The brain can also influence the immune system directly by connecting with the immune organs, such as the thymus, where T-cells and B-cells are stored (Felten et al., 1991; Maier & Watkins, 2000).

The Immune System and Stress

A wide variety of stressors can lead to suppression of the immune system (Vitlic, Lord, & Phillips, 2014). The effects are especially strong in the elderly (Penedo & Dahn, 2004), but they occur in everyone (Kiecolt-Glaser & Glaser, 2001; Kiecolt-Glaser et al., 2002). One study showed that as first-year law students participated in class, took exams, and experienced other stressful aspects of law school, they showed a decline in several measures of immune functioning (Segerstrom et al., 1998). Similarly, decreases in natural killer cell activity have been observed in both men and women following the deaths of their spouses (Irwin et al., 1987), and a variety of immune system impairments have been found in people suffering the effects of prolonged marital conflict, divorce, unemployment, lack of social support, loneliness, or extended periods of caring for elderly relatives (e.g., Cohen et al., 2007; Kiecolt-Glaser et al., 2003, 2005; Sbarra, Law, & Portley, 2011). The link between stress and the immune system may even cross generations. Animal studies show that when a pregnant mother experiences stress, her offspring show changes in their immune systems, suggesting that prenatal stress exposure can play a role in immune-related disorders such as allergies (Veru et al., 2014).

The relationship between stress and the immune system can be critical to people who are HIV positive but do not have AIDS. Because their immune systems are already vulnerable, further stress-related impairments might be life threatening. Research indicates that psychological stressors are associated with the progression of HIV-related illnesses (e.g., Antoni et al., 2000; Gore-Felton & Koopman, 2008). Unfortunately, people with HIV (and AIDS) face a particularly heavy load of immune-suppressing psychological stressors, including uncertainty about the future. A lack of perceived control and resulting depression and anxiety can further magnify their stress responses (e.g., Sewell et al., 2000).

Stress, Illness, and the Cardiovascular System

Earlier we mentioned the role of the sympatho-adreno-medullary (SAM) system in mobilizing the body's defenses during times of threat. Because the SAM system is linked to the cardiovascular system, its repeated activation in response to stressors has been linked to the development of coronary heart disease (CHD), high blood pressure (hypertension), and stroke. For example, adults in a nationwide sample who reported the strongest and longest-lasting worry about terrorism after the 9/11 attacks on New York City and Washington, D.C., were three times more likely than less worried people to develop heart problems over the next three years. Even those who reported the most intense temporary distress right after 9/11 were at elevated risk of developing heart problems over those same three years (Holman et al., 2008). Less severe stressors—such as long-term exposure to airport noise—can also increase the risk of heart disease (Correia et al., 2013).

Some cardiac problems occur sooner after stress exposure, especially if the stressor is severe, which may explain why heart attacks are more common in the weeks immediately following the death of a spouse (Carey et al., 2014). The link between CHD and physical stress responses appears especially close in people whose stress responses are especially strong. For example, among healthy young adult research participants, those whose blood pressure rose most dramatically in response to a mild stressor or a series of stressors were the ones most likely to develop hypertension later in life (Light et al., 1999; Matthews et al., 2004).

THINKING CRITICALLY

DOES HOSTILITY INCREASE THE RISK OF HEART DISEASE?

Health care psychologists see hostility as characterized by suspiciousness, resentment, frequent anger, antagonism, and distrust of others (Krantz & McCeney, 2002; Williams, 2001). The identification of hostility as a risk factor for coronary heart disease and heart attack may be an important breakthrough in understanding these illnesses, which remain among the chief causes of death in the United States and most other Western nations. But is hostility as dangerous as health care psychologists suspect?

What am I being asked to believe or accept?

Many researchers claim that individuals who display hostility—especially when it is accompanied by irritability and impatience—increase their risk for coronary heart disease and heart attack (e.g., Bunde & Suls, 2006; Compare et al., 2014; Krantz & McCeney, 2002; Smith et al., 2007). This risk, they say, is independent of other risk factors such as heredity, diet, smoking, and drinking alcohol.

What evidence is available to support the assertion?

There is evidence that hostility and heart disease are related, but scientists are still not sure about what causes the relationship. In one study, over 1000 people with known heart disease answered questions about how much hostility they experience in their attitudes and behavior. Those who reported more hostility at the start of the study later had more heart attacks, strokes, or deaths as compared to those who had reported less hostility (Wong et al., 2013). Some suggest that the risk of coronary heart disease and heart attack is elevated in hostile people because these people tend to be unusually reactive to stressors, especially when challenged. During interpersonal conflicts, for example, people predisposed to hostile behavior display not only overt hostility but also unusually large increases in blood pressure, heart rate, and other aspects of autonomic reactivity (Brondolo et al., 2003; Suls & Wan, 1993). In addition, it takes hostile individuals longer than normal to get back to their resting levels of autonomic functioning (Gerin et al., 2006). Like a driver who damages a car's engine by pressing the accelerator and applying the brakes at the same time, these "hot reactors" may create excessive wear and tear on the heart's arteries as their increased heart rate forces blood through tightened vessels (Johnston, Tuomisto, & Patching, 2008). Increased sympathetic nervous system activation not only puts stress on the coronary arteries but also leads to surges of stress-related hormones from the adrenal glands. High levels of these hormones are associated with increases in cholesterol and other fatty substances that are deposited in arteries and contribute to coronary heart disease (Bierhaus et al., 2003; Stoney & Hughes, 1999). Some studies show that cholesterol levels are elevated in the blood of hostile people (Sahebzamani et al., 2013).

Hostility may affect heart disease risk less directly as well, through its impact on social support. Some evidence suggests that hostile people get fewer benefits from social support (Lepore, 1995). Failing to use this support—and possibly offending potential supporters in the process—may intensify the impact of stressful events on hostile people. The result may be increased anger, antagonism, and, ultimately, additional stress on the cardiovascular system.

(continued)

You Can't Fire Me—I Quit!

For a time, researchers believed that anyone who displayed the pattern of aggressiveness, competitiveness, and nonstop work known as Type A behavior was at increased risk for heart disease (Friedman & Rosenman, 1974). More recent research, however, has led to the hypothesis that the danger lies not in these characteristics alone but in hostility, which is seen in some, but not all, Type A people.

Christopher Robbins/Photodisc/Getty Images

Are there alternative ways of interpreting the evidence?

Studies suggesting that hostility causes coronary heart disease are not true experiments. Researchers cannot manipulate the independent variable by creating hostility in randomly selected people in order to assess its effects on heart health. Accordingly, we have to consider other possible explanations of the observed relationship between hostility and heart disease.

For example, some researchers suggest that higher rates of heart problems among hostile people are not due entirely to the impact of hostility on blood pressure, heart rate, and hormone surges. Since a high-sugar diet contributes to heart disease (Yang et al., 2014) and may also be associated with negative attitudes (Möttus et al, 2013), perhaps dietary choices could be the link between poor heart health with hostile behavioral tendencies. It may also be that a genetically determined tendency toward autonomic reactivity increases the likelihood of both hostility and heart disease (Cacioppo et al., 1998; Krantz et al., 1988). If this is the case, then the fact that hostility and coronary heart disease often appear in the same people might reflect not just the effects of hostility but also a third factor—autonomic reactivity—that contributes to both of them.

It has also been suggested that hostility may be only one of many traits linked to heart disease. Depressiveness, hopelessness, pessimism, anger, and anxiety may be involved, too (e.g., Kubzansky, Davidson, & Rozanski, 2005; Nicholson, Fuhrer, & Marmot, 2005; Roy et al., 2010; Suls & Bunde, 2005).

What additional evidence would help evaluate the alternatives?

Research on the role these other traits may play in heart disease will be vital, and some of that work has already been done. One way to test whether hostile people's higher rates of heart disease are related specifically to their hostility or to a more general tendency toward intense physiological arousal is to examine how these individuals react to stress when they are not angry. Some researchers have done this by observing the physiological reactions of hostile people during the stress of surgery. One study found that even under general anesthesia, such people show unusually strong autonomic reactivity (Krantz & Durel, 1983). Because these patients were not conscious, it appears that oversensitivity to stressors, not hostile thinking, caused their exaggerated stress responses. This possibility is supported by research showing that individuals who have strong blood pressure responses to stressors also show different patterns of brain activity during stress than other people do (Gianaros et al., 2005).

What conclusions are most reasonable?

Most studies continue to find that among generally healthy people, those who are hostile—especially men—are at greater risk for heart disease and heart attacks than other people (Compare et al., 2014; Mathews, 2013; Wong et al., 2014). However, the picture is complex; it appears that many interacting factors affect the relationship between hostility and heart problems (Sloan et al., 2010).

A more elaborate psychobiological model may be required—one that takes into account that (1) some individuals may be biologically predisposed to react to stress with hostility and increased cardiovascular activity, each of which can contribute to heart disease; (2) hostile people help create and maintain stressors through aggressive thoughts and actions, which can provoke others to be aggressive; and (3) hostile people are more likely than others to smoke, drink alcohol to excess, overeat, fail to exercise, and engage in other heart-damaging behaviors (Kiecolt-Glaser, 2010).

We must also keep in mind that the relationship between heart problems and hostility may not be universal. Although this relationship appears to hold for women as well as men and for individuals in various ethnic groups (e.g., Nakano & Kitamura, 2001; Olson et al., 2005; Yoshimasu et al., 2002), final conclusions must await further research that examines the relationship between hostility and heart disease in other cultures (Finney, Stoney, & Engebretson, 2002).

PROMOTING HEALTHY BEHAVIOR

Who is most likely to adopt a healthy lifestyle?

Health care psychologists are deeply involved in the development of smoking cessation programs, in campaigns to discourage young people from taking up smoking, in anti-alcoholism efforts, in the prevention of skin cancer through sun safety education, in promoting regular exercise, in encouraging health care workers to wear protective masks and

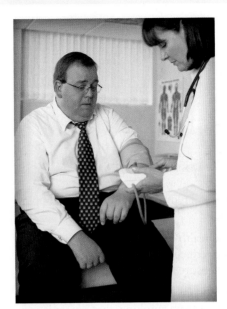

Doctor's Orders

Despite physicians' instructions, many patients fail to take their blood pressure medication and continue to eat an unhealthy diet. Noncompliance with medical advice is especially common when cultural values and beliefs conflict with that advice. Aware of this problem, health care psychologists are developing culture-sensitive approaches to health promotion and disease prevention (Kazarian & Evans, 2001).

Digital Vision/Getty Images

follow other safety practices, and in the fight against the spread of HIV and AIDS (e.g., Albarracín et al., 2008; Grant & Hofmann, 2011; Lally et al., 2010; Lichtenstein, Zhu, & Tedeschi, 2010; Lombard et al., 2010; Tybur et al., 2011). They are also working to identify individuals who are at elevated risk for disease because of genetic predispositions or exposure to stressors early in life.

In addition, health care psychologists help promote early detection of disease. Encouraging women to perform breast self-examinations and men to do testicular self-examinations are just two examples of health care psychology programs that can save thousands of lives each year (Taylor, 2002). Health care psychologists have also explored the reasons why some people fail to follow public health recommendations or doctors' orders that are vital to the control of diabetes, heart disease, lung cancer, AIDS, high blood pressure, and various childhood diseases (Gardner et al., 2010; Griffin & Harris, 2011; Sieverding, Decker, & Zimmermann, 2010). Understanding these reasons and finding ways to encourage better adherence to medical advice could speed recovery, prevent unnecessary suffering, and save many lives (Howell & Shepperd, 2012; Rhodes, Warburton, & Bredin, 2009).

Efforts to reduce, eliminate, or prevent behaviors that pose health risks and to encourage healthy behaviors are called **health promotion** (Smith, Orleans, & Jenkins, 2004). For example, health care psychologists have developed programs that teach children as young as nine to engage in healthy behaviors and avoid health-risk behaviors. School systems now offer a variety of these programs, including those that give children and adolescents the skills necessary to turn down cigarettes, drugs, and unprotected sex (e.g., Layzer, Rosapep, & Barr, 2014). Methods to help young adults quit smoking appear on social media as well as in other venues (Ramo, Liu, & Prochaska, 2014). Health care psychologists have also brought healthy lifestyle campaigns into workplaces, and some are involved in creating video games designed to promote better health (Peng, 2009; Thompson et al., 2010). They teach stress-management techniques, too (Tuomilehto et al., 2001). These programs can create savings in future medical treatment costs (Blumenthal et al., 2002) and better health for those who participate (Orth-Gomér et al., 2009).

Even modest lifestyle changes can have profound effects. In one long-term study, adults who engaged in mild exercise for fifteen minutes a day had an average life expectancy that was three years longer than those who weren't physically active; every additional fifteen minutes of daily physical activity was associated with a further 4 percent reduction in mortality (Wen et al., 2011). Increased exercise is also associated with reduced health risks among children and adolescents (Ekelund et al., 2012).

Health Beliefs and Health Behaviors

Health care psychologists also try to understand the social, educational, and cognitive factors that lead people to engage in health-endangering behaviors and that can interfere with efforts to adopt healthier lifestyles (e.g., Berkman, Falk, & Lieberman, 2011; Chiou, Yang, & Wan, 2011; Fitzsimons & Finkel, 2011; Moffitt et al., 2011; Peters et al., 2010). Their research has led to intervention programs that seek to change these patterns of thinking or at least take them into account (e.g., Freimuth & Hovick, 2012; Knauper et al., 2011; Kwan et al., 2012; Petrie & Weinman, 2012). In one study, for example, women who avoid thinking about the risks of breast cancer were more likely to get a mammogram screening after receiving health information that was tailored to their cognitive styles (Williams-Piehota et al., 2005).

This cognitive approach to health care psychology can be seen in various *health-belief models*. Irwin Rosenstock (1974) developed one of the most influential and extensively tested of these models (e.g., Aspinwall & Duran, 1999). He based his model on the assumption that people's decisions about health-related behaviors (such as smoking) are guided by four main factors:

1. Perceiving a *personal threat* of risk for getting a specific illness. (Do you believe that *you* will get lung cancer from smoking?)

2. Perceiving the seriousness of the illness and the consequences of having it. (How serious do you think lung cancer is? What will happen to you if you get it?)

health promotion The process of altering or eliminating behaviors that pose risks to health and, at the same time, fostering healthier behavior patterns.

LIFELONG SMOKERS HAVE A ONE-IN-TWO CHANCE OF DYING FROM SMOKING-RELATED DISEASE.

IT'LL NEVER HAPPEN TO ME.

THE ODDS OF WINNING THE POWERBALL LOTTERY ARE 80 MILLION TO ONE.

THIS COULD BE MY LUCKY DAY!

As described in the chapter on thought and language, humans tend to underestimate the likelihood of common outcomes and overestimate the likelihood of rare events. When this tendency causes people to ignore the dangers of smoking and other health-risk behaviors, the results can be disastrous.

Reprinted by permission, Steve Kelley, The Times-Picayune, New Orleans

3. Believing that changing a particular behavior will reduce the threat. (Will stopping smoking prevent *you* from getting lung cancer?)

4. Comparing the *perceived costs* of changing a health-risk behavior and the *benefits expected* from making that change. (Will the reduced risk of getting cancer in the future be worth the discomfort and loss of pleasure from not smoking?)

According to this health-belief model, people most likely to quit smoking would be those who believe that they are at risk for getting cancer from smoking, that cancer is serious and life threatening, and that the benefits of reducing cancer risks are greater than the costs of quitting (McCaul et al., 2006).

Other cognitive factors are the focus of other health-belief models (Ng et al., 2012). For example, people generally do not try to quit smoking unless they believe they can succeed. So *self-efficacy,* the belief that you are able to perform some behavior, is an additional consideration in making decisions about health behaviors (Armitage, 2005; Bandura, 1992). A related factor is the *intention* to engage in a healthy behavior (Albarracín et al., 2001; Webb & Sheeran, 2006).

Health-belief models have been useful in predicting a variety of health behaviors, including exercise (McAuley, 1992), safe-sex practices (Fisher, Fisher, & Rye, 1995), adherence to doctors' orders (Bavat et al., 2013), and having routine vaccinations and mammograms (Brewer et al., 2007).

Changing Health Behaviors: Stages of Readiness

Changing health-related behaviors depends not only on a person's health beliefs but also on that person's readiness to change. According to one model, successful change occurs in five stages (Prochaska, DiClemente, & Norcross, 1992; Schumann et al., 2005):

1. *Precontemplation:* The person does not perceive a health-related problem and has no intention of changing anytime soon.

2. *Contemplation:* A problem behavior has been identified and the person is seriously thinking about changing it.

3. *Preparation:* The person has a strong intention to change and has made specific plans to do so.

4. *Action:* The person is engaging successfully in behavior change.

5. *Maintenance:* The healthy behavior has continued for at least six months and the person is using newly learned skills to prevent relapse, or "backsliding."

These stages may actually overlap somewhat; for example, some "precontemplators" might actually be starting to contemplate change (Herzog & Blagg, 2007). The road from precontemplation through maintenance can be a bumpy one (Prochaska, 1994). Usually, people relapse and go through the stages repeatedly until they finally achieve stability in the healthy behavior they desire (Polivy & Herman, 2002). Smokers, for example, typically require three to four cycles through the stages over several years before they finally reach the maintenance stage (Piasecki, 2006).

TABLE 12.4   STEPS FOR COPING WITH STRESS

Many successful programs for systematically coping with stress guide people through several steps and are aimed at removing stressors that can be changed and improving responses to stressors that cannot be changed (Taylor, 2002).

Step	Task
1. Assessment	Identify the sources and effects of stress.
2. Goal setting	List the stressors and stress responses to be addressed. Designate which stressors can and cannot be changed.
3. Planning	List the specific steps to be taken to cope with stress.
4. Action	Implement coping plans.
5. Evaluation	Determine the changes in stressors and stress responses that have occurred as a result of coping methods.
6. Adjustment	Alter coping methods to improve results if necessary.

Programs for Coping with Stress and Promoting Health

Improving people's stress-coping skills is an important part of health care psychologists' health promotion work (e.g., Keogh, Bond, & Flaxman, 2006; Sbarra, Smith, & Mehl, 2012). Let's consider a few specific procedures and programs associated with this effort.

Planning to Cope

Just as people with extra money in the bank have a better chance of weathering a financial crisis, those with effective coping skills have a better chance of escaping some of the more harmful effects of intense stress. Like family money, the ability to handle stress appears to come naturally—perhaps even genetically—to some individuals (Caspi et al., 2010). We know from animal studies, for example, that one of the brain's neurotransmitters acts on the amygdala to decrease the anxiety associated with acute stress (Ciccoippo et al., 2014). Perhaps variations between people in the activity of this system may be reflected in individual differences in the ability to cope with stress. Effective coping strategies can be learned, too. Programs for teaching these strategies include several stages, which are summarized in Table 12.4.

Bear in mind, though, that no one coping method is right for everyone or every stressor. For example, denying the existence of an uncontrollable stressor may be fine in the short run but may lead to problems if no other coping method is used. Similarly, people who rely entirely on active, problem-focused coping might handle controllable stressors well but find themselves nearly helpless in the face of uncontrollable ones (Murray & Terry, 1999). The most successful stress managers may be those who can adjust their coping methods to the demands of changing situations, differing stressors, and cultural traditions (Chen, 2012; Chen & Miller, 2012; Sheppes et al., 2011; Taylor, 2002).

Developing Coping Strategies

Strategies for coping with stress can be cognitive, emotional, behavioral, or physical. *Cognitive coping strategies* involve changing the way we think. These changes include thinking more calmly, rationally, and constructively in the face of stressors and may lead to a more hopeful outlook. For example, students with heavy course loads may experience anxiety, confusion, discouragement, lack of motivation, and the desire to run away from it all. Frightening, catastrophizing thoughts (such as "What if I fail?") magnify these stress responses. Cognitive coping strategies replace catastrophic thinking with thoughts that cast stressors as challenges, not threats (Ellis & Bernard, 1985). This substitution process is called *cognitive restructuring* (Lazarus, 1971; Meichenbaum, 1977). It involves first identifying upsetting thoughts (such as "I'll never figure this out!") and then developing and practicing

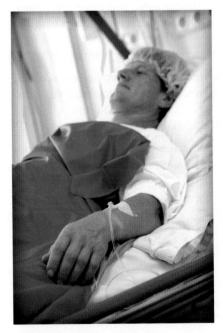

Dealing with Chemotherapy

Progressive relaxation training (Jacobson, 1938) involves briefly tensing groups of muscles throughout the body, one at a time, then releasing the tension and focusing on the resulting feelings of relaxation. It can be used to ease a variety of health-related problems, including the anxiety, physiological arousal, and nausea associated with cancer chemotherapy (Bernstein, Borkovec, & Hazlette-Stevens, 2000).

Medioimages/Photodisc/Getty Images

LINKAGES How can people manage stress? (a link to Treatment of Psychological Disorders)

TRY THIS

more constructive thoughts to use when under stress (such as "All I can do is the best I can"). Cognitive coping doesn't eliminate stressors, of course, but it can help us to perceive them as less threatening and therefore less disruptive (Antoni et al., 2000; Chesney et al., 2003).

Finding social support is an effective *emotional coping strategy*. As mentioned earlier, feeling that you are cared about and valued by others can be a buffer against the ill effects of stressors, which can lead to enhanced immune functioning (Kiecolt-Glaser & Newton, 2001) and quicker recovery from illness (Taylor, 2002).

Behavioral coping strategies involve changing behavior in order to minimize the negative impact of stressors. Time management is one example. If it seems that you are always pressed for time, try developing a time management plan. The first step is to use a calendar or day planner to record how you spend each hour of each day in a typical week. Next, analyze the information you have recorded. Locate when and how you might be wasting time and how you might use your time more efficiently. Then set out a schedule for the coming week and stick to it. Make adjustments in subsequent weeks as you learn more realistic ways to manage your time. Time management can't create more time, but it can help control catastrophizing thoughts by providing reassurance that there is enough time for everything and a plan for handling all that you have to do.

Physical coping strategies can be used to alter the undesirable physical responses that occur before, during, or after the appearance of stressors. The most common physical coping strategy is some form of drug use. Prescription medications are sometimes an appropriate coping aid, especially when stressors are severe and acute, such as the sudden death of one's child. However, people who rely on prescribed or nonprescription drugs, including alcohol, to help them face stressors may come to believe that their ability to cope is due to the drug, not to their own skill. This belief can make people more and more psychologically dependent on the drug. Further, the drug effects that blunt stress responses may also interfere with the ability to apply other coping strategies. The resulting loss of perceived control over stressors may make those stressors even more threatening and disruptive.

Nonchemical methods of reducing physical stress reactions and improving stress coping include progressive relaxation training (Bernstein, Borkovec, & Hazlette-Stevens, 2000), physical exercise (Houser et al., 2013), biofeedback (Wells et al., 2012), yoga (Köhn et al., 2013), meditation (Goyal et al., 2014), and tai chi (Davidson et al., 2003), among others (Taylor, 2002).

"In Review: Methods for Coping with Stress" summarizes our discussion of methods for coping with stress.

IN REVIEW

METHODS FOR COPING WITH STRESS

Type of Coping Method	Examples
Cognitive	Thinking of stressors as challenges rather than as threats; avoiding perfectionism
Emotional	Seeking social support; getting advice
Behavioral	Implementing a time-management plan; where possible, making life changes to eliminate stressors
Physical	Progressive relaxation training; exercise; meditation

In Review Questions

1. Catastrophizing thoughts are best overcome through _____ coping strategies.
2. The first step in coping with stress is to _____ the sources and effects of your stressors.
3. True or false: It is best to rely on only one good coping strategy. _____

LINKAGES

As noted in the introductory chapter, all of psychology's subfields are related to one another. Our discussion of how stressors can lead to the development of mental disorders illustrates just one way that the topic of this chapter—health, stress, and coping—is linked to the subfield of abnormal psychology, which is described in the chapter on psychological disorders. The Linkages diagram shows ties to two other subfields, and there are many more ties throughout the book. Looking for linkages among subfields will help you see how they all fit together and help you better appreciate the big picture that is psychology.

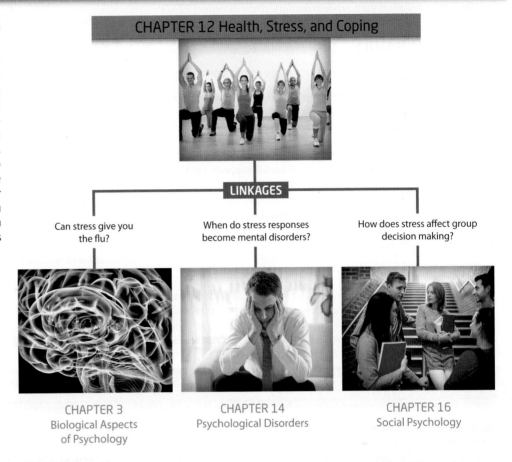

CHAPTER 12 Health, Stress, and Coping

LINKAGES

Can stress give you the flu?

When do stress responses become mental disorders?

How does stress affect group decision making?

CHAPTER 3
Biological Aspects of Psychology

CHAPTER 14
Psychological Disorders

CHAPTER 16
Social Psychology

SUMMARY

Health Psychology

What do health care psychologists do?

Recognition of the link between stress and illness and of the role of behaviors such as smoking in increasing the risk of illness prompted the development of **health care psychology** (or **health psychology**). Health care psychologists work to understand how psychological factors are related to physical disease and to help people behave in ways that prevent or minimize disease and promote health.

Understanding Stress and Stressors

How do psychological stressors affect physical health?

Stress is an ongoing, interactive process that takes place as people adjust to and cope with their environment. **Stressors** are physical or psychological events or situations to which people must adjust. Psychological stressors include catastrophic events, life changes and strains, chronic stressors, and daily hassles. Stressors can be measured by tests such as the Social Readjustment Rating Scale (SRRS) and the Life Experiences Survey (LES), but scores on such tests

provide only a partial picture of the stress in a person's life. **Stress reactions** are physical and psychological responses to stressors.

Stress Responses

How do people react to stressors?

Physical and psychological stress responses can occur alone or in combination, and the appearance of one can often stimulate others.

Physical stress responses include changes in heart rate, respiration, and many other processes that are part of a pattern known as the **general adaptation syndrome**, or **GAS**. The GAS has three stages: alarm (or **fight-flight reaction**), resistance, and exhaustion. The GAS helps people resist stress, but if activated for too long it can lead to impairment of immune system functions as well as to physical illnesses; Selye called such illnesses **diseases of adaptation**.

Psychological stress responses can be emotional, cognitive, or behavioral. Anxiety, anger, and depression are among the most common emotional stress reactions. Cognitive stress reactions include ruminative thinking, catastrophizing, and disruptions in the ability to think clearly, remember accurately, and solve problems efficiently.

Behavioral stress responses include irritability, aggression, absenteeism, engaging in health-damaging behaviors, and even suicide attempts. Severe or long-lasting stressors can lead to **burnout** or to psychological disorders such as **posttraumatic stress disorder (PTSD)**.

Stress Mediators

Why doesn't everyone react to stressors in the same way?

The key to understanding stress appears to lie in observing how particular people interact with specific stressors. Stressors are likely to have greater impact if an individual perceives them as threats or if they are unpredictable, uncontrollable, or unmanageable. The people most likely to react strongly to a stressor are those whose coping resources, coping methods, and **social support** are inadequate or perceived as inadequate.

The Physiology and Psychology of Health and Illness

How does stress affect your immune system?

Psychoneuroimmunology is the field that examines the interaction of psychological and physiological processes that affect the body's ability to defend itself against disease. When a person is under stress, some of the hormones released from the adrenal glands, such as cortisol, reduce the effectiveness of the cells of the **immune system** (T-cells, B-cells, and natural killer cells), which use **inflammation** and other responses in combating foreign invaders, such as viruses and cancer cells.

People who are hostile appear to be at greater risk for heart disease than other people. The heightened reactivity to stressors that these people experience may damage their cardiovascular systems.

Promoting Healthy Behavior

Who is most likely to adopt a healthy lifestyle?

The process of altering or eliminating health-risk behaviors and encouraging healthy behaviors is called **health promotion**. People's health-related behaviors are partly guided by their beliefs about health risks and what they can do about them.

The process of changing health-related behaviors appears to involve several stages, including precontemplation, contemplation, preparation, action, and maintenance. Understanding which stage people are in and helping them move through these stages is an important task in health care psychology.

To cope with stress, people must identify the stressors affecting them and develop a plan for coping with these stressors. Important coping skills include cognitive restructuring, acting to minimize the number or intensity of stressors, and using progressive relaxation training and other techniques for reducing physical stress reactions.

TEST YOUR KNOWLEDGE

Select the best answer for each of the following questions. Then check your response against the Answer Key at the end of the book.

1. Health research statistics show that your great-grandparents' generation was most likely to die from _____ diseases, whereas your own generation is most likely to die from _____ diseases.
   a. infectious; infectious
   b. chronic; chronic
   c. infectious; chronic
   d. chronic; infectious

2. Stephanie married a wonderful guy, moved to a new city, and took a great new job, all in the same month. We would expect her to _____.
   a. display physical and/or psychological stress responses
   b. experience little stress, because these are all desirable changes
   c. experience little stress, because these are not chronic stressors
   d. experience physical stress responses only

3. Doug lives next to a family that includes several teenagers. He is forever reminding them not to run across his front lawn. Their loud music often keeps him awake at night, and their cars are parked so that it is hard for him to back out of his driveway. These stressors can best be classified as _____.
   a. life changes and strains
   b. traumatic
   c. catastrophic
   d. daily hassles

4. Aaron's sympathetic nervous system is engaged in the fight-flight reaction. Which stage of the general adaptation syndrome (GAS) is he experiencing?
   a. Alarm
   b. Resistance
   c. Exhaustion
   d. Precontemplative

5. Bill and Ellen's car breaks down and it takes two hours for help to arrive. According to Shelley Taylor's research on stress and gender, Bill is likely to _____, and Ellen is likely to _____.
   a. get angry; get angry, too
   b. be supportive of Ellen; be supportive of Bill
   c. get angry; seek and offer support
   d. seek and offer support; get angry

6. Enrico finds that no matter what else he is doing, he can't stop thinking about all the stressful events in his life. Enrico is experiencing _____.
   a. catastrophizing
   b. cognitive restructuring
   c. functional fixedness
   d. ruminative thinking

7. Caitlin just failed her high school math test. She says to herself, "Mom is going to be furious with me! She will probably ground me, which means I won't be able to go to the prom. If I don't go to the prom, I will be a social outcast, and no one will talk to me. I'll never have any friends or find a partner, and no one will ever love me!" This is an example of _____.
   a. cognitive restructuring
   b. catastrophizing
   c. posttraumatic stress disorder
   d. the fight-or-flight syndrome

8. Dr. Zarro finds that one of her patients, Juan, has a disease-resistant personality. This means that Juan is likely to _____.
   a. ignore his stressors
   b. be optimistic
   c. blame himself for his stressors
   d. ruminate about his stressors

9. Shane occasionally experiences flashbacks involving vivid recollections of his wartime experiences. Flashbacks are associated with _____.
   a. generalized anxiety disorder
   b. posttraumatic stress disorder
   c. the general adaptation syndrome
   d. the fight-flight reaction

10. When Robin didn't get the promotion he had been hoping for, he tried to laugh it off. He went out with friends and jokingly told them that it is all for the best because the promotion would have forced him to buy a lot of new clothes. Robin was using _____ coping strategies.
    a. problem-focused
    b. social-focused
    c. emotion-focused
    d. posttraumatic

11. Postsurgical patients who are allowed to adjust their own levels of pain medication tend to use less medication than patients who must ask for it. This phenomenon is consistent with research showing that _____.
    a. social support can mediate stress
    b. predictable stressors are easier to manage
    c. the perception of control reduces the impact of stressors
    d. thinking of stressors as threats amplifies their effects

12. Laton, the head of human resources at his company, knows that the employees have stressful jobs. He schedules group picnics and lunches to help employees get better acquainted. Laton is trying to ease the employees' stressors by _____.
    a. promoting cognitive restructuring
    b. improving social support
    c. increasing employees' sense of control
    d. helping employees think of their stressors as challenges rather than threats

13. The Focus on Research Methods section of this chapter described the relationship between personality and life expectancy. Researchers have found _____.
    a. no significant relationship between the two
    b. that conscientiousness was associated with longer life
    c. that social relationships had no impact on longevity
    d. that impulsiveness was associated with longer life

14. Porter has a flu virus. Research on the immune system shows that Porter's _____ will be especially important in working to fight off this virus.
    a. red blood cells
    b. adrenal medulla
    c. natural killer cells
    d. macrophages

15. Fred is at high risk for coronary heart disease. As his friend, you tell him that current research suggests that he could lower his risk if he _____.
    a. takes up fishing as a hobby
    b. works at being less hostile
    c. reduces his workload
    d. restructures his thinking about stress

16. When Larry is diagnosed with arthritis, he is very upset. His stress reactions are likely to be reduced *most* if Larry _____.
    a. goes to a spa to try to ignore the situation
    b. keeps his worries to himself
    c. focuses all his attention on worrying about his medical condition
    d. joins an arthritis support group

17. According to Rosenstock's health-belief model, which of the following would *most* help Bridgit decide to quit smoking?
    a. Perceiving a personal threat of getting cancer from her smoking
    b. Knowing that smoking causes cancer
    c. Knowing that quitting can lower people's risk of cancer
    d. Carefully reading the statistics on smoking and health in general

18. Amanda is severely overweight. She knows that for her health's sake, she needs to limit her caloric intake, but she loves to eat and has made no specific plans to go on a diet. Amanda is at the _____ stage of readiness to change a health-risk behavior.
    a. precontemplation
    b. contemplation
    c. preparation
    d. maintenance

19. Sayumi is trying to control her stress. In response to a hurtful comment from a friend, Sayumi thinks to herself, "Don't jump to conclusions; he probably didn't mean it the way it sounded," instead of "That jerk! Who does he think he is?" Sayumi is using the coping strategy of _____.
    a. cognitive restructuring
    b. emotional restructuring
    c. catastrophizing
    d. contemplation

20. Loretta, a marriage counselor, finds her job very stressful. She has found that physical coping strategies help her the most. This means that Loretta most likely _____.
    a. constantly reminds herself about the good she is doing
    b. organizes a support group for therapists
    c. practices progressive relaxation every evening
    d. works on her time-management plan

Personality

Tom Grill/Corbis

Preview

If you've ever been stuck in heavy traffic, you have probably noticed differences in how drivers deal with the situation. Some are tolerant and calm; others become so cautious that they worsen the congestion; still others react with such impatience and anger that they may trigger a shouting match or cause an accident. Variations in how people handle traffic jams and other frustrating situations reflect just one aspect of their personalities—the consistent patterns of thinking, feeling, and behaving that make each person different from (and in some ways similar to) others. In this chapter, we examine four views of personality and review some of the personality tests psychologists have developed to measure and compare people's personalities. We also look at how our personalities interact with the situations in which we find ourselves. For example, being late for an important meeting might change the way in which you would normally handle being in a traffic jam. We also describe some of the ways that personality theory and research are being applied in areas such as diagnosing psychological disorders and screening potential employees.

Take out your wallet, look through it, and select the four most important things you carry with you. One person we know picked a driver's license, a credit card, a friend's phone number, and a witty prediction from a fortune cookie. The driver's license describes his physical traits. The credit card represents information about his buying history and responsibility in paying debts. His friends provide support, affection, and intimacy. And the fortune cookie prediction says something about his wishes, beliefs, or hopes. In other words, the selected items form a crude personality sketch.

There is no universally accepted definition, but psychologists generally view **personality** as the unique pattern of enduring thoughts, feelings, and actions that characterize a person. Personality research, in turn, seeks to understand how and why our consistent patterns of thinking, emotion, and behavior make each of us different in some ways and alike in others (Schultz & Schultz, 2013).

To gain a full understanding of just one individual's personality, a researcher would have to learn about many things, including the person's developmental experiences and cultural influences, genetic and other biological characteristics, perceptual and other information-processing habits and biases, typical patterns of emotional expression, and social skills. Psychologists also want to know about personality in general, such as how it develops and changes across the life span. They ask why some people are usually optimistic whereas others are usually pessimistic and whether people respond consistently or inconsistently from one situation to the next.

The specific questions psychologists ask and the methods they use to investigate personality often depend on which of the four main approaches to personality they take. These are the *psychodynamic, trait, social-cognitive,* and *humanistic* approaches.

THE PSYCHODYNAMIC APPROACH

How did paralyzed patients lead Freud to psychoanalysis?

Some people think that personality reveals itself in behavior alone. A person with an "obnoxious personality," for example, shows it by acting obnoxiously. But is that all there is to personality? Not according to Sigmund Freud. As a physician in Vienna, Austria, during the 1890s, Freud specialized in treating "neurotic" disorders. These were physical ailments, such as blindness or paralysis, for which there was no physical cause. Often, hypnosis could alleviate or remove these ailments. One patient sleepwalked on legs that were paralyzed during the day. Such cases led Freud to argue for *psychic determinism*, the idea that personality and behavior are determined more by psychological factors than by biological conditions or current events (Carducci, 2009). He proposed that people may not know why they feel, think, or act the way they do because they are partly controlled by an unconscious portion of personality—a part of which they are normally unaware (Friedman & Schustack, 2009; Funder, 2007). From these ideas Freud created **psychoanalytic theory**, a theory of personality that also led to a way of treating psychological disorders. Freud's theory became the basis of the **psychodynamic approach** to personality, which assumes that various unconscious psychological processes interact to determine our thoughts, feelings, and behavior (Engler, 2014).

TRY THIS

Founder of Psychoanalytic Theory

Here is Sigmund Freud with his daughter, Anna, who became a psychoanalyst herself and eventually developed a revised version of her father's theories.

Mary Evans/Sigmund Freud Copyrights/The Image Works

personality The pattern of psychological and behavioral characteristics by which each person can be compared and contrasted with other people.

psychoanalytic theory Freud's view that human behavior and personality are determined largely by psychological factors, many of which are unconscious.

psychodynamic approach A view developed by Freud that emphasizes unconscious mental processes in explaining human thought, feelings, and behavior.

FIGURE 13.1

A Freudian View of Personality Structure

According to Freud, some parts of the personality are conscious, whereas others are unconscious. Between these levels is the preconscious, which Freud saw as the home of memories and other material that we are not usually aware of but that we can easily bring into consciousness.

Source: Adapted from Liebert & Spiegler (1994). Photos (*clockwise from left*): © Eduardo Fuentes Guevara/iStockphoto; © Ana de Sousa/Shutterstock; © Jaimie Duplass/Shutterstock; © iStockphoto.com/edfuentesg; © Ana de Sousa/Shutterstock.com; © Jaimie Duplass/Shutterstock.com

---

id According to Freud, a personality component containing basic instincts, desires, and impulses with which all people are born.

pleasure principle The operating principle of the id, which guides people toward whatever feels good.

ego According to Freud, the part of the personality that makes compromises and mediates conflicts between and among the demands of the id, the superego, and the real world.

reality principle The operating principle of the ego, which takes into account the constraints of the social world.

superego According to Freud, the component of personality that tells people what they should and should not do.

defense mechanisms Unconscious tactics that either prevent threatening material from surfacing or disguise it when it does.

The Structure of Personality

Freud concluded that people have certain basic impulses or urges, related not only to food and water but also to sex and aggression. Freud described these impulses and urges with a German word that translates as "instinct," but he did not believe that they are all inborn and unchangeable, as the word *instinct* might imply (Ryckman, 2013). He did argue, though, that our desires for love, knowledge, security, and the like arise from more basic impulses. He said that each of us faces the task of figuring out how to satisfy basic urges in a world that often frustrates our efforts. Our personality develops, he claimed, as we struggle with that task, and it is reflected in the ways we go about satisfying a range of urges.

Id, Ego, and Superego

Freud described the personality as having three major components: the id, the ego, and the superego (Cervone & Pervin, 2013; see Figure 13.1). The **id** represents the inborn, unconscious portion of the personality where life and death instincts reside. The *life instincts* promote positive, constructive behavior; the *death instincts* are responsible for human aggression and destructiveness (Fiest et al., 2013). The id operates on the **pleasure principle**, seeking immediate satisfaction of both kinds of instincts, regardless of society's rules or the rights and feelings of others. The hungry person who pushes to the front of the line at Burger King would be satisfying an id-driven impulse.

As parents, teachers, and others place ever greater restrictions on the expression of id impulses, a second part of the personality, called the *ego* (or "self"), emerges from the id. The **ego** is responsible for organizing ways to get what a person wants in the real world, as opposed to the fantasy world of the id. Operating on the **reality principle**, the ego makes compromises as the id's demands for immediate satisfaction run into the practical realities of the social world. The ego would influence that hungry person at Burger King to wait in line and think about what to order rather than risk punishment by pushing ahead.

As children gain experience with the rules and values of society, they tend to adopt them. This process of *internalizing* parental and cultural values creates the third component of personality. It is called the **superego**, and it tells us what we should and should not do. The superego becomes our moral guide, and it is just as relentless and unreasonable as the id in its demands to be obeyed. The superego would make the person at Burger King feel guilty for even thinking about violating culturally approved rules about waiting in line.

Conflicts and Defenses

Freud described the inner clashes among id, ego, and superego as *intrapsychic*, or *psychodynamic, conflicts*. He believed that each individual's personality is shaped by the number, nature, and outcome of these conflicts. Freud said that the ego's main job is to prevent the anxiety or guilt that would arise if we became conscious of socially unacceptable id impulses, especially those that would violate the superego's rules (Schultz & Schultz, 2013). Sometimes the ego guides sensible actions, as when people ask for help once they realize they have a drinking problem. However, the ego also uses **defense mechanisms**, which are unconscious tactics that protect against anxiety and guilt by either preventing threatening material from surfacing or disguising it when it does (Feist et al., 2013; see Table 13.1).

Stages of Personality Development

Freud proposed that during childhood, personality evolves through several stages of **psychosexual development**. Failure to resolve the conflicts that appear at any of these stages can leave a person *fixated*—that is, unconsciously preoccupied with the area of pleasure associated with that stage. Freud believed that the stage at which a person became fixated in childhood can be seen in the person's adult personality characteristics.

TABLE 13.1   EGO DEFENSE MECHANISMS

TRY THIS According to Freud, defense mechanisms prevent anxiety or guilt in the short run. They may also help us choose creative or adaptive actions in potentially upsetting situations (e.g., Kim, Zeppenfeld, & Cohen, 2014). But ego defense mechanisms may cause difficulties when we use them to avoid dealing with the source of our problems, which can make those problems worse in the long run. Try listing some incidents in which you or someone you know might have used each of the defenses described here. What questions would a critical thinker ask to determine whether these behaviors were unconscious defense mechanisms or actions motivated by conscious intentions?

Defense Mechanism	Description
Repression	Unconsciously pushing threatening memories, urges, or ideas from conscious awareness: a person may experience loss of memory of unpleasant events.
Rationalization	Attempting to make actions or mistakes seem reasonable: the reasons or excuses given (e.g., "I spank my children because it is good for them") sound rational, but they are not the real reasons for the behavior.
Projection	Unconsciously attributing one's own unacceptable thoughts or impulses to another person: instead of recognizing that "I hate him," a person may feel that "He hates me."
Reaction formation	Defending against unacceptable impulses by acting opposite to them: sexual interest in a married co-worker might appear as strong dislike instead.
Sublimation	Converting unacceptable impulses into socially acceptable actions and perhaps symbolically expressing them: sexual or aggressive desires may appear as artistic creativity or devotion to athletic excellence.
Displacement	Deflecting an impulse from its original target to a less threatening one: anger at one's boss may be expressed through hostility toward a clerk, a family member, or even a pet.
Denial	Simply discounting the existence of threatening impulses: a person may vehemently deny ever having had even the slightest degree of physical attraction to a person of the same sex.
Compensation	Striving to make up for unconscious impulses or fears: a business executive's extreme competitiveness might be aimed at compensating for unconscious feelings of inferiority.

TRY THIS Which of Freud's ego defense mechanisms is operating here? (Check the answer at the bottom of page 462).

Dilbert © 2003 Scott Adams. Used by permission of Universal Uclick. All rights reserved

psychosexual development Periods of personality development in which, according to Freud, internal and external conflicts focus on particular issues.

oral stage The first of Freud's psychosexual stages, in which the mouth is the center of pleasure.

The Oral Stage

In Freud's theory, a child's first year or so is called the **oral stage** because the mouth—which infants use to eat and to explore everything from toys to their own hands and feet—is the center of pleasure during this period. Personality problems arise, said Freud, when oral needs are either neglected or overindulged. For example, early or late weaning from breastfeeding or bottle-feeding may leave a child fixated at the oral stage. The resulting adult characteristics may range from overeating or childlike dependence (late weaning) to the use of "biting" sarcasm (early weaning).

The Oral Stage

According to Freud, personality develops in a series of psychosexual stages. At each stage, a different part of the body becomes the primary focus of pleasure. This baby would appear to be in the oral stage.

Big Cheese Photo RF/Jupiterimages

anal stage The second of Freud's psychosexual stages, in which the focus of pleasure shifts from the mouth to the anus.

phallic stage The third of Freud's psychosexual stages, in which the focus of pleasure shifts to the genital area.

Oedipal complex The notion that young boys' impulses involve sexual feelings for the mother and the desire to eliminate the father.

Electra complex The notion that young girls develop an attachment to the father and compete with the mother for the father's attention.

latency period The fourth of Freud's psychosexual stages, in which sexual impulses become dormant and the child focuses on education and other matters.

genital stage The fifth and last of Freud's psychosexual stages, when sexual impulses reappear at the conscious level during adolescence.

The Anal Stage

The **anal stage** occurs during the second year, when the child's ego develops to cope with parental demands for socially appropriate behavior. For example, in most Western cultures, toilet training clashes with the child's freedom to have bowel movements at will. Freud said that if toilet training is too harsh or begins too early, it can produce an anal fixation that leads, in adulthood, to stinginess or excessive neatness (symbolically withholding feces). If toilet training is too late or too lax, however, the result could be a kind of anal fixation that is reflected in adults who are disorganized or impulsive (symbolically expelling feces).

The Phallic Stage

According to Freud, between the ages of three and five the focus of pleasure shifts to the genital area. Because he emphasized the psychosexual development of boys, Freud called this period the **phallic stage** (*phallus* is another word for penis). It is during this stage, he claimed, that the boy experiences sexual feelings for his mother and a desire to eliminate, or even kill, his father, with whom the boy competes for the mother's affection. Freud called this set of impulses the **Oedipal complex** because it reminded him of the plot of the classical Greek play *Oedipus Rex*. (In the play, Oedipus unknowingly kills his father and marries his mother.) The boy's fantasies create so much fear, however, that the ego represses his incestuous desires and leads him to "identify" with his father and try to be like him. In the process, the child's superego begins to develop.

According to Freud, a girl begins the phallic stage with a strong attachment to her mother. However, when she realizes that boys have penises and girls don't, she supposedly develops *penis envy* and transfers her love to the father. (This sequence has been called the **Electra complex** because it echoes the plot of *Electra*, another classical Greek play, but Freud never used this term.) To avoid her mother's disapproval, the girl identifies with and imitates her, thus forming the basis for her own superego.

Freud believed that unresolved conflicts during the phallic stage create a fixation that is reflected in many kinds of adult problems. These problems can include difficulties with authority figures and an inability to maintain a stable love relationship.

The Latency Period

As the phallic stage draws to a close and its conflicts are coped with by the ego, there is an interval of psychological peace. During this **latency period**, which lasts through childhood, sexual impulses stay in the background as the youngster focuses on education, same-sex peer play, and the development of social skills.

The Genital Stage

During adolescence, when sexual impulses reappear at the conscious level, the genitals again become the focus of pleasure. Thus begins what Freud called the **genital stage**, which lasts for the rest of the person's life. The quality of relationships and the degree of fulfillment experienced during this final stage, he claimed, are influenced by how intrapsychic conflicts were resolved during the earlier stages.

Variations on Freud's Personality Theory

Freud's ideas—especially those concerning infantile sexuality and the Oedipal complex—were (and still are) controversial. Even many of Freud's followers did not entirely agree with him. Some of these followers are known as *neo-Freudian* theorists because they

The defense mechanism illustrated in the cartoon on page 461 is displacement.

employed many aspects of Freud's theory but developed their own approaches. Others are known as *ego psychologists* because their theories focus more on the ego than on the id (Engler, 2014).

Neo-Freudian Theorists

An Early Feminist

After completing medical school at the University of Berlin in 1913, Karen Horney (1885–1952) trained as a Freudian psychoanalyst. She accepted some aspects of Freud's views, including the idea of unconscious motivation, but she eventually developed her own neo-Freudian theory. She saw the need for security as more important than biological instincts in motivating infants' behavior.

Bettmann/Corbis

Carl Jung (pronounced "YOONG") was the most prominent of Freud's early followers to chart his own theoretical course. In developing his ideas about *analytic psychology*, Jung (1916) argued that people are born with a general life force that (in addition to a sex drive) includes a drive for creativity, for growth-oriented resolution of conflicts, and for the productive blending of basic impulses with real-world demands. Jung did not identify specific stages in personality development. He suggested instead that people gradually develop differing degrees of *introversion* (a tendency to reflect on one's own experiences) or *extraversion* (a tendency to focus on the social world) along with differing tendencies to rely on specific psychological functions, such as thinking or feeling. The combination of these tendencies and functions, said Jung (1933), creates personalities that show distinctive and predictable patterns of behavior.

Alfred Adler, once a loyal follower of psychoanalysis, came to believe that the power behind the development of personality comes not from id impulses but from an innate desire to overcome infantile feelings of helplessness and gain some control over the environment. Other prominent neo-Freudians emphasized social relationships in the development of personality. Some, including Erik Erikson, Erich Fromm, and Harry Stack Sullivan, argued that once biological needs are met, the attempt to meet social needs (to feel protected, secure, and accepted, for example) is the main force that shapes personality. According to these theorists, the strategies that people use to meet social needs, such as dominating other people or being dependent on them, become core features of their personalities.

The first feminist personality theorist, Karen Horney (pronounced "HORN-eye"), challenged Freud's view that women's lack of a penis causes them to envy men and feel inferior to them. Horney (1937) argued that it is men who envy women. Realizing that they cannot bear children, males see their lives as having less meaning and substance than women's. Horney called this condition *womb envy,* and she felt that it led men to belittle women. She believed that when women feel inferior, it is because of cultural factors—such as the personal and political restrictions that men have placed on them—not because of penis envy (Hergenhahn & Olson, 2011; Larsen & Buss, 2005).

Contemporary Psychodynamic Theories

Today, some of the most influential psychodynamic approaches to personality focus on *object relations*—that is, on how early relationships, particularly with parents, affect how people perceive and relate to other people later in life (Cervone & Pervin, 2013). According to object relations theorists, early relationships between infants and their love objects (usually the mother and other primary caregivers) are vital influences on the development of personality (e.g., Klein, 1975; Kohut, 1984; Sohlberg & Jansson, 2002). These relationships, they say, shape our thoughts and feelings about social relationships in later life (Funder, 2012).

A close cousin of object relations theory is called *attachment theory* because it focuses specifically on the early attachment process that we describe in the chapter on human development. Ideally, infants form a secure bond, or attachment, to their mothers, gradually tolerate separation from this "attachment object," and eventually develop the ability to relate to others as independent, secure individuals (Ainsworth & Bowlby, 1991). Attachment theorists have studied how variations in the nature of this early bond are related to differences in people's personalities, self-images, identities, security, and social relationships in adolescence, adulthood, and even old age (e.g., Fraley et al., 2013; Mikulincer, Shaver, & Berant, 2013; Simpson, Collins, & Salvatore, 2014). One study, for example, found that insecure attachment during infancy was associated with less-happy romantic relationships later on (Tomlinson et al., 2010). Others have found that people who had had insecure attachments showed much stronger physiological reactions to interpersonal conflicts than did people whose attachments had been secure (Powers et al., 2006), and that people with insecure early attachments were less likely than those with secure attachments to be helpful when encountering a person in distress (Mikulincer & Shaver, 2005). People with insecure attachment styles are also more at risk for psychological disorders (Palitsky, et al., 2013).

Further evidence about the influence of attachment comes from a long-term study of children diagnosed with severe heart disease. The children whose mothers had not been securely attached to their own mothers tended to show more anxiety and other emotional difficulties in the years after the diagnosis than did those whose mothers had been more securely attached (Berant, Mikulincer, & Shaver, 2008). Also, cancer patients with insecure attachment styles appear to trust their physicians less and to be less satisfied with treatment (Holwerda et al., 2013). In short, attachment theorists suggest that people who miss the opportunity to become securely attached may suffer significant disturbances in their later relationships (Esbjørn et al., 2013), including in relationships with their own children.

Evaluating the Psychodynamic Approach

Freud's personality theory may be the most comprehensive and influential psychological theory ever proposed, and it is still influential worldwide (Osnos, 2011). His ideas have shaped a wide range of psychotherapy techniques (see the chapter on treatment of psychological disorders) and stimulated the development of several personality assessments, including the projective personality measures described later in this chapter. Research on cognitive processes supports some of Freud's ideas. For example, people do use several of the defense mechanisms Freud described (Diehl et al., 2014), although these may not always operate at an unconscious level. There's also evidence that our thoughts and actions can be influenced by events and experiences that we don't recall (Bargh et al., 2012) and possibly by emotions we don't consciously experience (Williams et al., 2009). Some researchers believe that unconscious processes can also affect our health (Goldenberg et al., 2008; Krieger et al., 2010). Research confirms that early experiences do influence brain development, and some researchers have suggested this line of inquiry may eventually identify the neurological underpinnings of some of the drives (e.g., libido) proposed by Freud (Engler, 2014).

However, Freud's theories have several weaknesses. For one thing, his conclusions about personality are based almost entirely on case studies of a few individuals. As discussed in the introductory chapter, conclusions drawn from case studies may not apply to people in general. Freud's sample of cases was certainly not representative of people in general. Most of his patients were upper-class Viennese women who not only had psychological problems but were raised in a society that considered the discussion of sex to be uncivilized. Second, Freud's theory reflected Western European and North American cultural values, which may or may not be helpful in understanding people in other cultures (Schultz & Schultz, 2013). For example, the concepts of ego and self that are so central to Freud's personality theory are based on the self-oriented values of individualist cultures. These values may be less central to personality development in collectivist cultures, such as those of Asia and South America (Park & Kitayama, 2012).

Freud's conclusions may have been distorted by other biases as well. Some Freud scholars believe he might have (perhaps unconsciously) modified reports of what happened during therapy to better fit his theory (Schultz & Schultz, 2013). He may also have asked leading questions that influenced patients to "recall" events from their childhoods that never happened (Carducci, 2009). Today, as described in the memory chapter, there are similar concerns that some patients who recover allegedly repressed memories about childhood sexual abuse may actually be reporting false memories implanted by therapists (Patihis, Tingen, & Loftus, 2013).

Other critics have noted that Freud's theories focus too much on men's psychosexual development and largely ignore women (Engler, 2014; Feist et al., 2013). His notion that females envy male anatomy has also been attacked. In the tradition of Horney, some contemporary neo-Freudians have proposed theories that focus specifically on the psychosexual development of women (Miletic, 2002).

Finally, as judged by modern standards, Freud's theory is not very scientific. His definitions of id, ego, unconscious conflict, and other concepts lack the precision required to allow researchers to test these ideas scientifically (Funder, 2012). Further, his belief that unconscious desires drive most human behavior ignores evidence showing that much of that behavior goes beyond impulse gratification. For example, the conscious drive to attain personal, social, and spiritual goals is an important determinant of behavior, as is learning from others.

Some of the weaknesses in Freudian theory have been addressed by theorists who have altered some of Freud's concepts and devoted more attention to social influences on personality. Attempts have also been made to increase precision and objectivity in the measurement of psychodynamic concepts (e.g., Barber, Crits-Christoph, & Paul, 1993). Research on concepts from psychodynamic theory is, in fact, becoming more sophisticated and increasingly reflects interest in subjecting psychodynamic principles to empirical tests (e.g., Betan & Westen, 2009; Roffman & Gerber, 2008). For example, researchers are exploring the brain activities that accompany some of the mental operations that are central to Freud's theories (Bernstein, 2011). Still, the psychodynamic approach is better known for generating hypotheses about personality than for scientifically testing them. Accordingly, this approach to personality is now much less influential in mainstream psychology than it was in the past (Feist et al., 2013; Schultz & Schultz, 2013).

THE TRAIT APPROACH

What personality traits are most basic?

You might describe the personality of someone you know well with just a few statements. For example, you might say,

> He's a really caring person, and very outgoing. He's generous with his time, and he works very hard at everything he does. Yet sometimes I think he also lacks self-confidence. He always gives in to other people's demands because he wants to be accepted by them.

In other words, most people describe others by referring to the kind of people they are ("outgoing"); to the thoughts, feelings, and actions that are most typical of them ("caring," "lacks self-confidence"); or to their needs ("wants to be accepted"). Together, these statements describe **personality traits**—the tendencies that help direct how a person usually thinks and behaves (Cervone & Pervin, 2013).

The trait approach to personality makes three main assumptions:

1. Personality traits are relatively stable, and therefore predictable, over time. So a gentle person tends to stay that way day after day, year after year (Cervone & Pervin, 2013).

2. Personality traits are relatively stable across situations, and they can explain why people act in predictable ways in many different situations. A person who is competitive at work will probably also be competitive on the tennis court or at a party (Roberts, Woods, & Caspi, 2008).

3. People differ in how much of a particular personality trait they possess; no two people are exactly alike on all traits. The result is an endless variety of unique personalities.

In short, psychologists who take the **trait approach** see personality as a combination of stable internal characteristics that people display consistently over time and across

personality traits A set of stable characteristics that people display over time and across situations.

trait approach A perspective on personality that views it as the combination of stable characteristics that people display over time and across situations.

FIGURE 13.2

Two Personality Profiles

TRY THIS Trait theory describes personality in terms of the strength of particular dimensions, or traits. Here are trait profiles for Bob, a computer engineer, and Ted, a stock trader. Compared with Ted, Bob is about equally industrious, more generous, and less nervous, extraverted, and aggressive. Just for fun, score yourself to indicate how strong you think you are on each of the listed traits. Trait theorists suggest that it should be easy for you to do this, because virtually everyone displays a certain amount of almost any personality characteristic.

Source: From McCrae & John, "An Introduction to the five-factor model and its applications," Journal of Personality vol 60 (pp. 175–215). John Wiley & Sons, 1992; © gyn9037/Shutterstock.com; © Monkey Business Images/Shutterstock.com

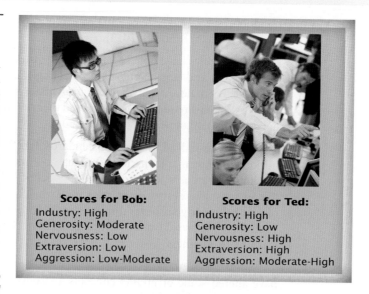

Scores for Bob:
Industry: High
Generosity: Moderate
Nervousness: Low
Extraversion: Low
Aggression: Low-Moderate

Scores for Ted:
Industry: High
Generosity: Low
Nervousness: High
Extraversion: High
Aggression: Moderate-High

situations (Pervin, Cervone, & John, 2005). Trait theorists try to measure the relative strength of the many personality characteristics that they think may be present in everyone (see Figure 13.2).

Early Trait Theories

Today's trait theories of personality are largely based on the work of Gordon Allport, Raymond Cattell, and Hans Eysenck. Allport spent 30 years searching for the traits that combine to form personality. When he looked at the nearly 18,000 dictionary terms used to describe human behavior (Allport & Odbert, 1936; John, Naumann, & Soto, 2008), he noticed clusters of terms that refer to the same thing. For example, *hostile, nasty,* and *mean* all convey a similar meaning. To better understand this clustering, think of a close relative and jot down all the personality traits that describe this person. If you are like most people, you were able to capture your relative's personality using only a few trait labels. Allport believed that the set of labels that describe a particular person reflects that person's *central traits*—those that are usually obvious to others and that organize and control behavior in many different situations. Central traits are roughly equivalent to the descriptive terms used in letters of recommendation (*reliable* or *distractible,* for example) that are meant to tell what can be expected from a person most of the time (Schultz & Schultz, 2009). Allport also believed that people possess *secondary traits*—those that are more specific to certain situations and control far less behavior. "Dislikes crowds" is an example of a secondary trait.

Selecting a Jury

Some psychologists employ trait theories of personality in advising prosecution or defense attorneys about which potential jurors are most likely to be sympathetic to their side of a court case.

© iStockphoto.com/Moodboard_Images

Allport's research helped lay the foundation for modern research on personality traits. His focus on the uniqueness of each personality made it difficult to draw conclusions about the structure of personality in general (Barenbaum & Winter, 2008), but some researchers today continue to employ a modern version of Allport's approach (e.g., Caldwell, Cervone, & Rubin, 2008).

In contrast, British psychologist Raymond Cattell was interested in the personality traits that people share. He used a mathematical technique called *factor analysis* to study which traits are correlated with one another. Factor analysis can reveal, for example, whether people who are moody are also likely to be anxious, rigid, and unsociable. Cattell found sixteen clusters of traits that he believed make up the basic dimensions, or factors, of personality, and he measured their strength across individuals using a test called the Sixteen Personality Factor Questionnaire, or 16PF (Cattell, Eber, & Tatsuoka, 1970).

The Five-Factor Personality Model

Building on the work of Allport and Cattell, factor analytic research by many of today's trait theorists suggests that personality is organized around just five basic dimensions (McCrae & Costa, 2004, 2008). The dimensions of this **five-factor (or Big Five) personality model** have been given slightly different labels by different researchers, but the most widely used names are *openness, conscientiousness, extraversion, agreeableness,* and *neuroticism* (see Table 13.2). The fact that some version of the Big Five factors reliably appears in many countries and cultures provides evidence that these factors may indeed represent the most important components of human personality (De Fruyt et al., 2009; McCrae, Terracciano, & Profiles of Cultures Project, 2005). Some researchers have used MRI and other scanning techniques to see if activities in specific brain regions are associated with each of these factors (DeYoung et al., 2010), but these efforts are controversial and have not yielded clear results (Liu et al., 2013).

Many trait theorists consider the emergence of the five-factor personality model to be a major breakthrough in examining the personalities of all people, regardless of where they live or the nature of their economic, social, and cultural backgrounds (Carver & Scheier, 2004; John, Naumann, & Soto, 2008). The model also allows researchers to describe in a precise way the similarities and differences in people's personalities and to explore how these factors are related to everything from personality disorders and political beliefs to substance abuse, academic and occupational performance, happiness, physical well-being, driving skills, and even voting behavior (e.g., Adrian et al., 2011; Boyce & Wood, 2011; Boyce et al., 2010; Chiaburu et al., 2011; Cuperman & Ickes, 2009; Friedman, Kern, & Reynolds, 2010; Hughes et al., 2012; Mottus, Kuh, & Deary, 2013; Vianello, Robusto, & Anselmi, 2010; Vecchione et al., 2011).

five-factor personality model (Big Five model) A view based on studies using factor analysis that suggests the existence of five basic components of human personality: openness, conscientiousness, extraversion, agreeableness, and neuroticism.

TABLE 13.2 DIMENSIONS OF THE FIVE-FACTOR PERSONALITY MODEL

Here is a list of the adjectives that define the Big Five personality factors. You can more easily remember these factors by noting that the first letters of their names spell the word *ocean*.

Dimension	Defining Descriptors
Openness	Artistic, curious, imaginative, insightful, original, wide interests, unusual thought processes, intellectual interests
Conscientiousness	Efficient, organized, planful, reliable, thorough, dependable, ethical, productive
Extraversion	Active, assertive, energetic, outgoing, talkative, gesturally expressive, gregarious
Agreeableness	Appreciative, forgiving, generous, kind, trusting, noncritical, warm, compassionate, considerate, straightforward
Neuroticism	Anxious, self-pitying, tense, emotionally unstable, impulsive, vulnerable, touchy, prone to worry

Source: Adapted from McCrae & John (1992).

Animal Personalities

The idea that personality can be described using five main dimensions may hold for some animals as well as humans. The five animal dimensions differ from (but are still related to) human traits. For example, hyenas differ among themselves in terms of dominance, excitability, agreeableness (toward people), sociability (toward each other), and curiosity. Some of these same traits have been observed in a wide variety of other species, including sheep, langurs, orangutans, chipmunks, and chimpanzees (e.g., Bell & Sih, 2007; Martin & Réale, 2008; Michelena et al., 2009; Weinstein, Capitanio, & Gosling, 2008). Dog and cat lovers often report such traits in their pets, too (e.g., Ley, Bennett, & Coleman, 2009). Researchers have even begun to develop personality tests for nonhuman primates, dogs, and other animals (Freeman et al., 2013).

uwesSERENGETI/ Alamy

Biological Trait Theories

While some personality theorists study the basic dimensions of personality, others explore the biological factors that shape and influence those dimensions.

Eysenck's Biological Trait Theory

The biological basis for personality was emphasized in the work of British psychologist Hans Eysenck (pronounced "EYE-sink"). Like other trait theorists who helped lay the groundwork for the five-factor personality model, Eysenck used factor analysis to study personality. His research led him to focus on two main personality dimensions known as *introversion-extraversion* and *emotionality-stability* (Eysenck, 1990a, 1990b; Deary & Bedford, 2011):

1. ***Introversion-extraversion.*** Extraverts are sociable and outgoing, enjoy parties and other social activities, take risks, and love excitement and change. Introverts tend to be quiet, thoughtful, and reserved, enjoying solitary pursuits and avoiding social involvement.

2. ***Emotionality-stability*** (also often called ***neuroticism***). At one extreme of this dimension are people who exhibit such characteristics as moodiness, restlessness, worry, anxiety, and other negative emotions. People at the opposite end are calm, even-tempered, relaxed, and emotionally stable.

According to Eysenck, personality can be described in terms of where a person falls along these two dimensions. For example, an introverted but stable person is likely to be controlled and reliable. An introverted but emotional person is likely to be rigid and anxious (see Figure 13.3). Eysenck's personality dimensions do seem to be related to particular behaviors. For example, college students' levels of neuroticism, extraversion, and psychoticism (a third dimension described by Eysenck) have been shown to be related to the students' passion for Internet use and how much they reveal about themselves online (Tosun & Lajunen, 2009, 2010)

FIGURE 13.3
Eysenck's Personality Dimensions

TRY THIS According to Eysenck, varying degrees of emotionality-stability and introversion-extraversion combine to produce predictable trait patterns. The traits appearing in the four sections created by crossing these two personality dimensions roughly define the four basic temperaments identified centuries ago by the ancient Greek physician Hippocrates: melancholic (sad), choleric (hot-tempered), phlegmatic (slow and lethargic), and sanguine (optimistic). Which section of the figure do you think best describes your personality traits? How about those of a friend or a relative? Did you find it any easier to place other people's personalities in a particular section than it was to place your own personality? If so, why do you think that might be?

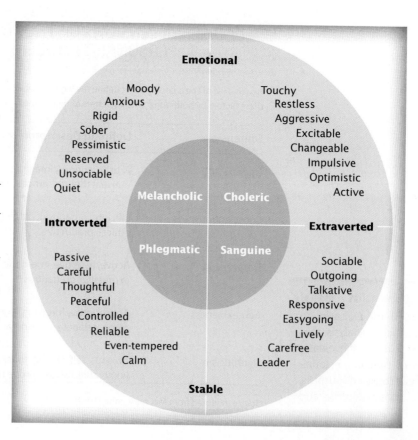

LINKAGES Why do some people take more risks than others? (a link to Motivation and Emotion)

Eysenck argued that the variations in personality characteristics that we see among individuals can be traced to inherited biological differences. These biological differences, he said, create differences in people's typical levels of physiological arousal and in their sensitivity to stress and other environmental stimulation. For example, people who inherit a nervous system that normally operates below some ideal level of arousal will always be on the lookout for excitement, change, and social contact in order to increase their arousal. As a result, they will be *extraverted*. In contrast, people whose nervous system is normally "overaroused" will tend to avoid excitement, change, and social contact in order to reduce arousal to their ideal level. In short, they will be *introverted*. What about the emotionality-stability dimension? Eysenck said that people who fall toward the stability side have nervous systems that are relatively insensitive to stress; those who are more emotional have nervous systems that react more strongly to stress.

Gray's Reinforcement Sensitivity Theory

Jeffrey Gray, another British psychologist, agrees with Eysenck about the two basic dimensions of personality but offers a different explanation of how biology underlies them (Johnson et al., 2012; Gray & McNaughton, 2002). According to Gray's *reinforcement sensitivity theory*, differences among people along the dimensions of introversion-extraversion and emotionality-stability originate in the brain regions that influence how sensitive people are to different kinds of events. These regions are called the behavioral approach system and the flight or freeze system (Johnson et al., 2012).

The *behavioral approach system (BAS)* affects people's sensitivity to rewards and their motivation to seek these rewards. The BAS has been called a "go" system because it is responsible for how impulsive or uninhibited a person is. The *flight or freeze system (FFS)* affects how sensitive people are to punishment (Smillie, Pickering, & Jackson, 2006). The FFS is a "stop" system that is responsible for how fearful or inhibited a person is (Bijttebier et al., 2009). Gray sees extraverts as having a sensitive reward system (BAS) and an insensitive punishment system (FFS). Introverts are just the opposite: they are relatively insensitive to rewards but highly sensitive to punishment. Emotionally unstable people are much more sensitive to both rewards and punishments than are those who are emotionally stable. One study found that individual differences in the FFS versus BAS systems predicted the heights that various mountaineers were able to reach in their attempts to scale Mount Everest. Those with greater reward responsiveness (a BAS feature) and less pre-climb anxiety (a FFS feature) were more likely to reach the summit (Feldman et al., 2013).

Gray's theory has its critics (e.g., Jackson, 2003; Matthews, 2008), but it is now more widely accepted than Eysenck's theory—primarily because it is supported by more data (e.g., Revelle, 2008) and it seems more consistent with what neuroscientists have learned about brain structures and neurotransmitters and how they operate (e.g., Joseph et al., 2009; Read et al., 2010).

THINKING CRITICALLY

ARE PERSONALITY TRAITS INHERITED?

Gray's reinforcement sensitivity theory is one of several biologically oriented explanations of the origins of personality traits (e.g., Loehlin & Martin, 2013; Turkheimer, Pettersson, & Horn, 2014). A related approach explores the role of genetics in these traits (e.g., Loehlin, 2011; Terracciano et al., 2010). For example, consider a pair of identical twins who were separated at five weeks of age and did not meet for thirty-nine years. Both drove Chevrolets, chain-smoked the same brand of cigarettes, had divorced a woman named Linda, were remarried to a woman named Betty, had sons named James Allan, had dogs named Toy, enjoyed similar hobbies, and had served as sheriff's deputies (Tellegen et al., 1988).

(continued)

What am I being asked to believe or accept?

Cases like this suggest that some core aspects of personality might be partly or even largely inherited (Ekehammar et al., 2010; Turkheimer & Harden, 2014).

What evidence is available to support the assertion?

Other evidence for this assertion comes from the many anecdotal cases in which children seem to "have" their parents' or grandparents' bad temper, generosity, or shyness. Systematic studies have also found moderate but significant correlations between children's personality test scores and those of their parents and siblings (Turkheimer et al., 2014).

Even stronger evidence comes from studies around the world that compare identical twins raised together, identical twins raised apart, nonidentical twins raised together, and nonidentical twins raised apart (Turkheimer et al. 2014). Whether they are raised apart or together, identical twins (who have exactly the same genes) tend to be more alike in personality than nonidentical twins (whose genes are no more similar than those of other siblings). This research also shows that identical twins are more alike than nonidentical twins in general temperament, such as how active, sociable, anxious, and emotional they are, and where they fall on various other personality dimensions (e.g., Kandler, et al., 2010; Johnson et al., 2009). Using such twin studies, behavioral geneticists have concluded that about 50 percent of the differences among people in terms of personality traits are due to genetic factors (Caspi, Roberts, & Shiner, 2005; Kreuger et al., 2008).

Are there alternative ways of interpreting the evidence?

Family resemblances in personality could reflect inheritance or social influence. So an obvious alternative interpretation of this evidence might be that family similarities come not from common genes but from a shared environment (Rentfrow, 2010). Children learn many rules, skills, and behaviors by watching parents, siblings, and others; perhaps they learn their personalities as well (Funder, 2007). And the fact that nontwin siblings are less alike than twins may well result from what is called a *nonshared environment* (Plomin, 2004). Nonshared factors include, for example, a child's place in the family birth order; differences in the way parents treat each of their children; and accidents, illnesses, or events that alter a particular child's life or health (Loehlin, 2011). Nontwins are more likely than twins, especially identical twins, to experience these nonshared environmental factors.

What additional evidence would help evaluate the alternatives?

One way to evaluate the extent to which personality is inherited would be to locate genes that are associated with certain personality characteristics (Ebstein, 2006). Genetic differences have already been tentatively associated with certain behavior disorders, but most behavioral genetics researchers doubt that there are direct links between particular genes and particular personality traits (Caspi, Roberts, & Shiner, 2005; Kreuger & Johnson, 2008).

Another way to evaluate the role of genes in personality is to study people in infancy, before the environment has had a chance to exert its influence. If the environment were entirely responsible for personality, newborns should be essentially alike. However, as discussed in the chapter on human development, infants show immediate differences in activity level, sensitivity to the environment, the tendency to cry, and interest in new stimuli (Olino et al., 2013; Slutske et al., 2012). These differences in *temperament* suggest biological and perhaps genetic influences.

To evaluate the relative contributions of nature and nurture beyond infancy, psychologists have examined the personality characteristics of adopted children. If adopted children are more like their biological than their adoptive parents, this suggests the influence of heredity in personality. If they are more like their adoptive families, a strong role for environmental factors in personality is suggested. In actuality, adopted children's personalities tend to resemble the personalities of their biological parents and siblings more closely than they do those of the families in which they are raised (Turkeheimer et al., 2014).

Other research seeks to determine more clearly which aspects of the environment are most important in shaping personality (Turkheimer & Waldron, 2000). So far, the evidence suggests that personality is not influenced very strongly by elements of the shared environment—such

(continued)

Family Resemblance

Do children inherit personality traits in the same direct way as they inherit facial features, coloration, and other physical characteristics? Research in behavioral genetics suggests that personality is the joint product of genetically influenced behavioral tendencies and the environmental conditions each child encounters.

© wavebreakmedia ltd/Shutterstock.com

as socioeconomic status—that equally affect all children in the same family. However, nonshared environmental influences, at home and elsewhere, may be very important in personality development (Loehlin, 2011). We need to know more about the exact impact on personality development of nonshared environmental factors that may be different for twins and nontwin siblings

What conclusions are most reasonable?

Even those researchers who strongly support genetic theories of personality caution that we should not replace "simple-minded environmentalism" with the equally incorrect view that personality is almost completely biologically determined (Loehlin, 2010). It is pointless to talk about heredity *versus* environment as causes of personality, because nature and nurture always intertwine to exert joint and simultaneous influences (Kreuger & Johnson, 2008). For example, we know that genetic factors affect the environment in which people live (e.g., their families) and how they react to that environment, but as discussed in the introductory chapter, research in epigenetics has shown that environmental factors can influence which of a person's genes are activated (or "expressed") and how much those genes affect the person's behavior (Cole, 2013; Manuck & McCaffery, 2014). The impact of epigenetics on personality research is illustrated by the recent finding that the chromosomes that contain our genes get slightly shorter in older people with more pessimistic personalities (Ikeda et al., 2014).

In short, we can draw only tentative conclusions about the origins of personality differences. The evidence available so far suggests that genetic influences do appear to contribute significantly to the differences among people in many personality traits (DeYoung et al., 2007; Vernon et al., 2008). As noted earlier, though, there is no evidence of a specific gene directly responsible for a specific personality trait (Manuck & McCaffery, 2014). The genetic contribution to personality most likely comes as genes influence people's nervous systems and general predispositions toward certain temperaments (Alliey-Rodriquez et al., 2011; Blom et al., 2011). Temperamental factors (e.g., emotionality and sociability) then interact with environmental factors, such as family experiences, to produce specific features of personality (Slutske, et al. 2012). For example, a child's ability to control or regulate emotions appears to be strongly determined by heredity. Children who are less able to regulate their emotions might play less with other children, withdraw more from social interactions, and thereby fail to learn important social skills (Spinrad et al., 2006). These experiences and tendencies, in turn, might foster the self-consciousness and shyness seen in introverted personalities. Genes also appear to influence people's emotional responses to specific events, such as how they respond to socioeconomic adversity or other negative environmental conditions (Cole et al., 2011).

Notice, though, that genetic predispositions toward particular personality characteristics may or may not be expressed in behavior, depending on whether the environment supports or stifles them. Changes in genetically predisposed traits are not only possible but may actually be quite common as children grow (Cacioppo et al., 2000). So even though there is a strong genetic basis for shyness, many children learn to overcome this tendency and become quite outgoing (Volbrecht & Goldsmith, 2010). In summary, rather than inheriting specific traits, people appear to inherit the behavioral and emotional raw materials out of which their personalities are shaped by the world.

Evaluating the Trait Approach

The trait approach, and especially the five-factor personality model, tends to dominate contemporary research in personality. Yet there are several problems and weaknesses associated with this approach.

Trait theories seem better at describing people than at understanding them. It is easy to say, for example, that Marilyn is nasty because she has a strong hostility trait; but other factors, such as the way people treat her, could also be responsible. In other words, trait theories say a lot about how people behave, but they don't always explain why (Funder, 2012). Nor do trait theories say much about how traits are related to the thoughts and feelings that precede, accompany, and follow behavior. Do introverts and extraverts decide to act as they do? Can they behave otherwise? And how do they feel about their actions and experiences? Some personality psychologists are linking their research with that of cognitive psychologists in an effort to better understand how thoughts and emotions influence, and are influenced by, personality traits (Jackson et al., 2012; Shoda & LeeTiernan, 2002). And as noted earlier, other psychologists are studying the roles played by genes, brain structures, and neurotransmitters in the individual differences we see among people's personality traits (e.g., Carver et al., 2011; Loehlin & Martin, 2011).

The trait approach has also been criticized for offering a short list of traits that provides, at best, a fixed and rather shallow description of personality that fails to capture how traits combine to form a complex and dynamic individual (Boag, 2011; Funder, 2012). There are questions, too, about whether there really are exactly five core dimensions of personality. Some evidence suggests, for example, that there might be a sixth dimension known as *honesty and humility* (Lee, Ogunfowora, & Ashton, 2005). Whatever the number turns out to be, some personality researchers doubt that these dimensions are exactly the same in all cultures (Gurven et al., 2013). Finally, even if some version of the five-factor personality model proves to be correct and universal, its factors are not all-powerful. Situations, too, affect behavior. For instance, eating sweet-tasting food can (at least temporarily) lead people to describe themselves as more agreeable and helpful to others (Meier et al., 2011). And people high in extraversion are not always sociable. Whether they behave sociably depends, in part, on where they are and who else is present.

In fairness, early trait theorists such as Allport acknowledged the importance of situations in influencing behavior, but it is only recently that consideration of interactions between people and situations has become an important part of trait-based approaches to personality. This change is largely the result of research conducted by psychologists who have taken a social-cognitive approach to personality, which we describe next.

THE SOCIAL-COGNITIVE APPROACH

Do we learn our personalities?

To social-cognitive researchers, psychodynamic theories place too much emphasis on unconscious forces in personality, and trait theories presume more consistency in people's behavior than there really is. In contrast, researchers who take a **social-cognitive approach** see personality as the full set of behaviors that people have acquired through *learning* and that they then display in particular situations (Cervone & Pervin, 2013). Some aspects of this approach reflect the view of traditional behaviorists, namely that all behavior is learned through classical and operant conditioning (see the chapter on learning). However, the social-cognitive approach expands that view by emphasizing (1) the role played by *learned patterns of thinking* in guiding behavior; and (2) the fact that personality is learned in social situations as people observe and interact with other people (Bandura & Walters, 1963; Cervone & Pervin, 2013). The social-cognitive approach is sometimes called the *social-learning approach* because it defines personality as the sum of the behaviors and cognitive habits that develop as people learn through experience in the social world. Social-cognitive theorists are interested in how our thinking affects our behavior as well as how our behavior and its consequences affect our thinking and our future actions (Mischel & Shoda, 2008; Shoda & Mischel, 2006).

Prominent Social-Cognitive Theories

The most prominent social-cognitive theories were developed by Julian Rotter, Albert Bandura, and Walter Mischel.

social-cognitive approach The view that personality reflects learned patterns of thinking and behavior.

self-efficacy According to Bandura, the learned expectation of success in given situations.

Rotter's Expectancy Theory

Julian Rotter (1982) argued that learning creates cognitions known as *expectancies* and that these expectancies guide behavior. According to Rotter, a person's decision to engage in a behavior is determined by (1) what the person expects to happen following the behavior; and (2) the value the person places on the outcome. For example, people spend a lot of money on new clothes for job interviews because past learning leads them to expect that doing so will help get them the job, and they place a high value on having the job. To Rotter, then, behavior is shaped by the positive or negative consequences it brings and by the expectancy that a particular behavior will be rewarded or punished (Mischel, Shoda, & Smith, 2004).

Personality researchers influenced by Rotter have suggested that in addition to learning expectancies about particular behaviors in particular situations, we also learn more general expectancies, especially about how life's good and bad outcomes are controlled (e.g., Phares, 1976). Some people (called *internals*) come to expect that most events are controlled by their own efforts. These people assume, for example, that what they achieve and the rewards they receive are determined by what they themselves do. Others (*externals*) tend to expect events to be controlled by external forces over which they have no control. So when externals succeed, they tend to believe that their success was based on chance or other forces outside themselves.

Research on differences in generalized expectancies does show that they are correlated with differences in behavior. For example, when threatened by a hurricane or other natural disaster, internals—in accordance with their belief that they can control what happens to them—are more likely than externals to buy bottled water and make other preparations (Sattler, Kaiser, & Hittner, 2000). Internals tend to work harder than externals at staying physically healthy and as a result may be healthier (Stürmer, Hasselbach, & Amelang, 2006). For instance, children with an internal control orientation are less likely than externals to become obese in later life (Gale, Batty, & Deary, 2008). Internals are less likely to drink alcohol or, if they do drink, are less likely to drive while intoxicated (Cavaiola & Desordi, 2000). They are also more careful with money and better than externals at bargaining or negotiating (Lim, Teo, & Loo, 2003; Shalvi, Simone, & Ritov, 2010). As college students, internals tend to be better informed about their courses and about what they need to do to get a high grade than externals are. This may help to account for why internals tend to get better grades and graduate sooner (Dollinger, 2000; Hall, Smith, & Chia, 2008).

Bandura and Reciprocal Determinism

In his social-cognitive theory, Albert Bandura (1999, 2011) sees personality as shaped by the ways that thoughts, behavior, and the environment interact and influence one another. He points out that whether people learn through direct experience with rewards and punishments or through watching what happens to others, their behavior creates changes in their environment. Observing these changes, in turn, affects how they think, which then affects their behavior, and so on in a constant web of mutual influence that Bandura calls *reciprocal determinism* (see Figure 13.4).

An especially important cognitive element in this system of mutual influence is perceived **self-efficacy**, the learned expectation of success. Bandura argued that what we do and what we try to do are heavily affected by our perceptions or beliefs about our chances of success at a task. People with a high perceived self-efficacy believe that they can successfully do things regardless of past failures or current obstacles. So the higher your perceived self-efficacy is in a particular task, the greater your actual accomplishments are likely to be (Joët, Usher, & Bressoux, 2011; Richardson, Abraham, & Bond, 2012). For example, research in twenty-six countries found that students' self-efficacy in mathematics was significantly related to their mathematical achievement (Williams & Williams, 2010). (Perhaps you recall the classic children's story *The Little Engine That Could:* Trying to get up a steep hill, the scared little engine starts by saying "I think I can, I think I can" and ends up saying "I know I can, I know I can." And it did.)

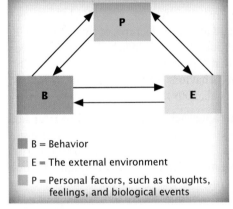

B = Behavior

E = The external environment

P = Personal factors, such as thoughts, feelings, and biological events

FIGURE 13.4
Reciprocal Determinism

Bandura's notion of reciprocal determinism suggests that thoughts, behavior, and the environment are constantly affecting each other. For example, a person's hostile thoughts might lead to hostile behavior, which generates even more hostile thoughts. At the same time, the hostile behavior offends others, thus creating a threatening environment that causes the person to think and act in even more negative ways. As increasingly negative thoughts alter the person's perceptions of the environment, that environment seems to be more threatening than ever (e.g., Bushman et al., 2005).

Source: From A. Bandura, "The Assessment and Predictive Generality of Self-Precepts of efficacy," Journal of Behavior Therapy and Experimental Psychiatry vol 13 (pp. 195–199).

Self-efficacy interacts with expectancies about the outcome of behavior in general, and the result of this interplay helps shape a person's psychological well-being (Srimathi & Kiran, 2011). So if a person has low self-efficacy and believes that people have little effect on the world, apathy may result. But if a person with low self-efficacy believes that *other* people are enjoying the benefits of their efforts, the result may be self-criticism and depression.

Mischel's Cognitive/Affective Theory

Social-cognitive theorists argue that learned beliefs, feelings, and expectancies characterize each individual and make that individual different from other people. Walter Mischel calls these characteristics *cognitive person variables*. He argues that they outline the dimensions along which individuals differ (Mischel, 2009; Mischel & Shoda, 2008).

According to Mischel, these are the most important cognitive person variables:

1. *Encodings*: the person's beliefs about the environment and other people

2. *Expectancies*: including self-efficacy and what results the person expects will follow from various behaviors

3. *Affects*: feelings and emotions

4. *Goals and values*: the things a person believes in and wants to achieve

5. *Competencies and self-regulatory plans*: the things the person can do and the ability to thoughtfully plan behaviors (Engler, 2014)

To predict how a person might behave in a particular situation, says Mischel, we need to know about these cognitive person variables and about the features of that situation. In short, the person and the situation interact to produce behavior. Mischel's ideas have been called an "if-then" theory because he proposes that *if* people encounter a particular situation, *then* they will engage in the characteristic behaviors (called *behavioral signatures*) that they typically show in this situation (Smith et al., 2009).

Mischel was once highly critical of the trait approach to personality, but later said that his own theory is generally consistent with it. In fact, the concept of behavioral signatures resembles the concept of traits. However, Mischel still argues that trait theorists underestimate the power of situations to alter behavior and do not pay enough attention to the cognitive and emotional processes that underlie people's overt actions. Despite their remaining differences, most advocates of the trait and social-cognitive approaches have come to focus on the similarities between their views (Cervone, 2005; Funder, 2008). This search for similarities has helped clarify the relationship between personal and situational variables and how they affect behavior under various conditions. Many of the conclusions that have emerged are consistent with Bandura's concept of reciprocal determinism:

1. Personal dispositions (which include traits and cognitive person variables) influence behavior only in relevant situations. The trait of anxiousness, for example, may predict anxiety, but mainly in situations in which an anxious person feels threatened.

2. Personal dispositions can lead to behaviors that alter situations that in turn promote other behaviors. For example, a hostile child can trigger aggression in others and thus start a fight.

3. People choose to be in situations that are in accord with their personal dispositions. Introverts, for instance, are likely to choose quiet environments, whereas extraverts tend to seek out livelier, more social circumstances (Beck & Clark, 2009).

4. Personal dispositions are more important in some situations than in others. Where many different behaviors would be appropriate—at a picnic, for example—what people do can usually be predicted from their dispositions (extraverts will probably play games and socialize while introverts will probably watch from the sidelines).

The Impact of Situations

Like the rest of us, Dwayne "The Rock" Johnson behaves differently in different situations, including when acting in his movies or wrestling, and when not "on stage." Mischel's theory of personality emphasizes that the interactions between particular people and specific situations are vitally important in determining behavior.

Universal Pictures/Photofest; Axel Schmidt/AFP/ DDP/Getty Images

However, in situations such as a funeral, where fewer options are socially acceptable, personal dispositions will not differentiate one person from another; everyone is likely to be quiet and somber.

Today, social-cognitive theorists are attempting to discover how cognitive person variables develop, how they relate to stress and health, and how they interact with situational variables to affect behavior.

Evaluating the Social-Cognitive Approach

The social-cognitive approach to personality is valuable because it blends concepts from behavioral learning theory with those of cognitive psychology and applies them to socially important topics such as aggression, the effects of mass media on children, and the development of techniques that enhance personal control over behavior. Social-cognitive principles have also been translated into cognitive-behavioral treatment procedures (Ryckman, 2013; see the chapter on treatment of psychological disorders).

The social-cognitive approach has not escaped criticism, however. Psychodynamic theorists point out that social-cognitive theories leave no role for unconscious thoughts and feelings in determining behaviors (e.g., Westen et al., 2008). Some trait theory advocates complain that social-cognitive theorists focus more on explaining why traits are unimportant than on why situations are important and argue that they have failed to identify what it is about specific situations that brings out certain behaviors (Sherman, Nave, & Funder, 2012). The social-cognitive approach has also been faulted for offering only a set of limited theories that share certain common assumptions about the nature of personality, rather than presenting a general theory of personality (Feist et al., 2013). Finally, some critics feel that the social-cognitive approach cannot capture the complexities, richness, and uniqueness that are inherent in human personality (Carver & Scheier, 2012). For these critics, a far more attractive alternative is offered by the humanistic approach to personality.

THE HUMANISTIC PSYCHOLOGY APPROACH

Is everyone basically good?

humanistic psychology approach The view that personality develops in accordance with each person's unique perceptions of the world.

self-actualization The reaching of one's fullest potential; the complete realization of a person's talents, faculties, and abilities.

The **humanistic psychology approach** to personality focuses on mental capabilities that set humans apart: self-awareness, creativity, planning, decision making, and responsibility. Those who adopt the humanistic approach see human behavior as motivated mainly by an innate drive toward growth that prompts each of us to fulfill a unique potential and thus achieve an ideal state known as **self-actualization** (Goldstein, 1939). Like the planted

What Is Reality?

Each of these people has a different perception of what happened during the play that started this argument—and each is sure he is right! Disagreement about the "same" event illustrates *phenomenology*, each person's unique perceptions of the world. The humanistic psychology approach holds that these perceptions shape personality and guide behavior. As described in the sensation and perception chapter, our perceptions are often influenced by top-down processing. In this case, expectations and motivation stemming from differing loyalties are likely to influence reality—and reactions—for each team's players, coaches, and fans.

AP Images/Paul Spinelli

seed whose natural potential is to become a flower, people are seen as naturally inclined toward goodness, creativity, love, and joy. Humanistic psychologists argue that to explain people's actions, it is more important to understand their view of the world than their instincts, traits, or learning experiences. To humanists, every individual's worldview is a bit different, and it is this unique *phenomenology* (pronounced "feh-nah-men-AHL-oh-gee"), or way of perceiving and interpreting the world, that shapes personality and guides behavior (Schultz & Schultz, 2013). Because of its emphasis on the importance of looking at people's perceptions, this approach to personality is also sometimes called the *phenomenological approach*.

Prominent Humanistic Theories

The best-known humanistic theories of personality are those of Carl Rogers and Abraham Maslow.

Rogers's Self Theory

In his extensive writings, Carl Rogers (1961, 1970, 1980) emphasized the **actualizing tendency**, which he described as an innate inclination toward growth and fulfillment that motivates all human behavior (Raskin & Rogers, 2001). To Rogers, personality is the expression of that actualizing tendency as it unfolds in each person's uniquely perceived reality (Schultz & Schultz, 2013).

The centerpiece of Rogers's theory is the *self*, the part of experience that a person identifies as "I" or "me." According to Rogers, those who accurately experience the self—with all its preferences, abilities, fantasies, shortcomings, and desires—are on the road to self-actualization. When experiences of the self become distorted, however, progress toward self-actualization is likely to be slowed or stopped.

Rogers saw personality development beginning early, as children learn to need others' approval, or *positive regard*. Evaluations by parents, teachers, and others soon begin to affect children's self-evaluations. When evaluations by others are in agreement with a child's self-evaluations, the child reacts in a way that matches, or is *congruent* with, self-experience. The child not only feels others' positive regard but also evaluates the self as "good" for having earned approval. This positive self-experience becomes part of a **self-concept**, the way one thinks of oneself. Unfortunately, things may not always go so smoothly. If

actualizing tendency An innate inclination toward growth and fulfillment that motivates all human behavior.

self-concept The way one thinks of oneself.

"Just remember, son, it doesn't matter whether you win or lose—unless you want Daddy's love."

Parents aren't usually this obvious about creating conditions of worth, but according to Rogers, the message gets through in many more subtle ways.

Pat Byrnes The New Yorker Collection/Cartoon Bank.com

The Joys of a Growth Orientation

According to Maslow's theory of personality, the key to personal growth and fulfillment lies in focusing on what we have, not on what we lack or have lost. Liz Heywood, a successful horse trainer, author, activist, and speaker, has never let the loss of her left leg slow her down.

Photo by Scott Huffman

conditions of worth According to Rogers, circumstances in which an individual experiences positive regard from others only when displaying certain behaviors or attitudes.

a pleasurable self-experience is evaluated negatively by others, the child must either do without positive regard or reevaluate the experience. So a little boy who is teased by his father for playing with dolls might have a distorted self-experience—deciding, perhaps, that "I don't like dolls" or that "Feeling good is bad."

In other words, Rogers suggested that personality is shaped partly by the actualizing tendency and partly by others' evaluations. In this way, people come to like what they are "supposed" to like and behave as they are "supposed" to behave. This socialization process helps people get along in society but may require that they suppress their self-actualizing tendencies and distort their experiences. Rogers argued that psychological discomfort, anxiety, or mental disorder can result when the feelings people experience or express are *incongruent,* or at odds, with their true feelings.

Incongruence is likely, Rogers said, when parents and teachers lead children to believe that their personal worth depends on displaying the "right" attitudes, behaviors, and values. These **conditions of worth** are created whenever *people* are evaluated instead of their behavior. For example, parents who find their child drawing on the wall are not likely to say, "I love you, but I don't approve of this behavior." They are more likely to shout, "Bad boy!" or "Bad girl!" This reaction suggests that the child is lovable and worthwhile only when well behaved. As a result, the child's self-experience is not, "I like drawing on the wall but Mom and Dad don't approve," but instead, "Drawing on the wall is bad and I am bad if I like it, so I don't like it." The child may eventually show overly neat and tidy behaviors that do not reflect the real self but rather are part of an ideal self that was dictated by the parents.

As with Freud's concept of superego, conditions of worth are first set up by external pressure but eventually become part of the person's belief system. To Rogers, then, rewards and punishments are important in personality development not just because they shape behavior but also because they so easily create distorted self-perceptions and incongruence (Roth et al., 2009).

Maslow's Growth Theory

Like Rogers, Abraham Maslow (1954, 1971) viewed personality as expressing a basic human tendency toward growth and self-actualization. In fact, Maslow saw self-actualization as not just a human capacity, but as the highest on a hierarchy of needs, as described in the chapter on motivation and emotion. Yet, said Maslow, people are often distracted from seeking self-actualization because they focus on lower-level needs.

Maslow argued that most people seem controlled by a *deficiency orientation,* a preoccupation with perceived needs for material things. Ultimately, he said, deficiency-oriented people see life as meaningless, disappointing, and boring, so they may start to behave in problematic ways. For example, in trying to satisfy a need for love, people may focus on what love gives them (security), not on what they can give to someone else. This deficiency orientation may lead a person to be jealous and focus on what is missing in relationships; as a result, the person may never truly experience love or security.

In contrast, those with a *growth orientation* experience satisfaction from what they have, what they are, and what they can do, instead of focusing on what's missing. This orientation opens the door to what Maslow called *peak experiences,* in which people feel joy, and even ecstasy, in the mere fact of being alive, being human, and knowing that they are utilizing their fullest potential.

Evaluating the Humanistic Approach

The humanistic approach to personality is consistent with the way many people view themselves. It focuses on immediate experience and emphasizes each person's uniqueness. The best-known application of the humanistic approach is the client-centered therapy of Carl Rogers, which is discussed in the chapter on treatment of psychological disorders. The humanistic approach has also inspired other therapies as well as short-term personal-growth experiences such as sensitivity training and encounter groups that are designed to help people become more aware of themselves and how they relate to others (e.g., Cain & Seeman, 2002). Rogers' perspective has also been incorporated into interventions designed to help people live healthier lives, including by giving up smoking and exercising more (Suarez & Mullins, 2008). Further, the humanistic approach fits well with the rapidly growing field of *positive psychology,* which, as described in the chapter on motivation and emotion, focuses on well-being and other positive aspects of human thought and feelings (Compton & Hoffman, 2012; Snyder, Lopez, & Pedrotti, 2010).

Yet to some, the humanistic approach is naive, romantic, and unrealistic. Are all people as inherently good and "growth oriented" as this approach suggests? Critics wonder about that assumption, and they also fault humanists for paying too little attention to the role of inherited characteristics, learning, situational influences, and unconscious motivation in shaping personality. Further, the idea that personality development is directed only by an innate growth potential is seen by many as an oversimplification. So, too, is the humanistic assumption that all human problems stem from blocked self-actualization. Personality researchers also see many humanistic concepts as too vague to be tested empirically. Accordingly, the humanistic approach has not been popular among those who conduct empirical research to learn about personality (Cervone & Pervin, 2010). That may begin to change, though, as an explosion of research in positive psychology leads to new humanistically oriented theories that better lend themselves to empirical evaluation (e.g., Burton et al., 2006; Cohn et al., 2009; Waugh, Fredrickson, & Taylor, 2008).

Finally, humanists' tendency to define ideal personality development in terms of personal growth, independence, and self-actualization has been criticized for emphasizing culture-specific concepts about mental health that may not apply outside Western individualist cultures (Heine & Buchtel, 2009). As discussed in the next section, the foundations of humanistic self theories may be in direct conflict with the values of non-Western collectivist cultures.

"In Review: Major Approaches to Personality" summarizes key features of the humanistic approach and those of the other approaches we described. Which approach is most accurate? There is no simple answer to that question, partly because each approach emphasizes different aspects of personality. Instead, a full understanding of the origins and development of personality may come only by recognizing the roles of all the factors that various approaches have shown to be important. Some psychologists are working on theoretical models that take this promising integrative approach (Mayer, 2005; McAdams & Pals, 2006).

MAJOR APPROACHES TO PERSONALITY
IN REVIEW

Approach	Basic Assumptions about Behavior	Typical Research Method
Psychodynamic	Determined by largely unconscious intrapsychic conflicts	Case studies
Trait	Determined by traits or needs	Analysis of tests for basic personality dimensions

(continued)

IN REVIEW
MAJOR APPROACHES TO PERSONALITY (CONT.)

Approach	Basic Assumptions about Behavior	Typical Research Method
Social-cognitive	Determined by learning, cognitive factors, and specific situations	Analysis of interactions between people and situations
Humanistic	Determined by innate growth tendency and individual perception of reality	Studies of relationships between perceptions and behavior

In Review Questions

1. Tests that measure the five-factor model's dimensions of personality are based on the _____ approach to personality.

2. The role of learning is most prominent in the _____ approach to personality.

3. Object relations and attachment theories are modern variants on _____ personality theories.

LINKAGES   Does culture determine personality? (a link to Human Development)

LINKAGES
PERSONALITY, CULTURE AND HUMAN DEVELOPMENT

Western cultures tend to encourage people to "stand up for yourself" or "blow your own horn" to "get what you have coming to you." In middle-class North America, the values of achievement and personal distinction are taught to children, particularly boys, early in life (Matsumoto & Juang, 2011). North American children are encouraged to feel uniquely special and to have self-esteem, partly because of a culturally based association of these characteristics with happiness, popularity, and academic achievement. Whether self-esteem is the cause or the result of these good outcomes (Baumeister, Masicampo, & Twenge, 2013), children who display these values tend to receive praise for doing so.

As a result of this cultural training, many people in North America and Europe develop personalities based on a sense of high self-worth. In one study (Markus & Kitayama, 1997), 70 percent of a sample of U.S. students believed that they were superior to their peers. In addition, 60 percent believed that they were in the top 10 percent on a wide variety of personal attributes! This tendency toward self-enhancement is evident as early as age four.

Many Western personality theorists see a sense of independence, uniqueness, and self-esteem as fundamental to mental health. As noted in the chapter on human development, for example, Erik Erikson included the emergence of personal identity and self-esteem as part of normal psychosocial development. Middle-class North Americans who fail to value and strive for independence, self-promotion, and unique personal achievement may be seen as having a personality disorder, some form of depression, or other psychological problems.

Are these ideas based on universal truths about personality development or do they reflect the values of the cultures that generated them? It's certainly clear that people in many non-Western cultures develop personal orientations that are quite different from those of North Americans and Europeans (Kitayama, 2013; Matsumoto & Juang, 2011). In China and Japan, for example, an independent, unique self is not emphasized nearly as much as it is in North America (Kitayama et al., 2009). Children there are encouraged to develop and maintain pleasant, respectful relations with others but not to stand out from the crowd, because doing so might make others seem inferior by comparison. So, whereas children in the United States

(continued)

hear that "the squeaky wheel gets the grease" (meaning that you don't get what you want unless you ask for it), Japanese children are warned that "the nail that stands up gets pounded down" (meaning that it is not a good idea to draw attention to yourself). From a very young age, they are taught to be modest, to play down the value of personal contributions, and to appreciate the joy and value of group work (Kitayama & Uchida, 2003).

The goal of esteem building is clear these days in many children's activities at school and in some team sports, too, which are designed either to eliminate competition or (as in this case) assure that everyone feels like winners. The same goal is reflected in daycare centers, summer camps, and other children's programs with names such as Starkids, Little Wonders, Superkids, and Precious Jewels.

Leo Cullum The New Yorker Collection/The Cartoon Bank

"We lost!"

In contrast to the *independent* self system common in individualist cultures such as Great Britain, Switzerland, and the United States, cultures with a more collectivist orientation (such as Brazil, China, Japan, and Nigeria) promote an *interdependent* self system through which people see themselves as a fraction of the social whole. Each person has little or no meaningful definition without reference to the group. These differences in self systems may produce differences in what gives people a sense of well-being and satisfaction (Han et al., 2013). For example, in the United States, a sense of well-being is usually associated with having *positive* attributes, such as intelligence, creativity, competitiveness, persistence, and so on. In Japan and other Asian countries, feelings of well-being are more likely to be associated with having no *negative* attributes (Ruby et al., 2012). Studies of thousands of people all over the world indicate that in collectivist cultures, life satisfaction is associated with having social approval and harmonious relations with others. In individualist cultures, life satisfaction is associated with having high self-esteem and good feelings about one's own life (Uchida et al., 2001).

Culture and Personality

TRY THIS   In individualist cultures, most children learn early that personal distinction is valued by parents, teachers, and peers. In collectivist cultures, having a strong sense of self-worth may be seen as less important. In other words, the features of "normal" personality development vary from culture to culture. Make a list of the core values you've learned. Which of them are typical of individualist cultures, which are typical of collectivist cultures, and which reflect a combination of both?

© iStockphoto.com/Mari

Because cultural factors shape ideas about how the ideal personality develops, it's important to evaluate approaches to personality in terms of how well they apply to cultures other than the one in which they were developed (Markus & Kitayama, 2010). Their applicability to males and females must be considered as well. Even within North American cultures, for example, there are gender differences in the development of self-esteem. Females tend to show an interdependent self system, achieving their sense of self and self-esteem from attachments to others. By contrast, males' self-esteem tends to develop in relation to personal achievement, in a manner more in keeping with an independent self system (Cross & Madson, 1997). Cross-gender and cross-cultural differences in the nature and determinants of a sense of self highlight the widespread effects of gender and culture on the development of many aspects of human personality (Heine & Ruby, 2010; Matsumoto & Juang, 2011).

PERSONALITY DEVELOPMENT OVER TIME

Psychologists have long wondered how people's personalities differ, but they also want to know how those differences begin. Some search for answers in infants' differing temperaments. As noted in the chapter on human development, temperament is reflected in the unlearned, generalized patterns of emotional expression and other behavior that people show from birth (Buss, 1997).

What was the researchers' question?

Can young children's temperaments predict their personality characteristics and behaviors as adults?

How did the researchers answer the question?

To try to answer this question, Avshalom Caspi and his colleagues have conducted a longitudinal study that assessed the same people at several different times in their lives (Caspi et al., 1995; Caspi, Harrington et al., 2003; Slutske et al., 2012). The research sample included all the children born in Dunedin, New Zealand, between April 1972 and March 1973—a total of about 1,000 people. When these children were three years old, research assistants observed them in a standard situation and rated them on a number of dimensions, including the degree to which they showed explosive or uncontrolled behavior, interacted easily with others, or acted withdrawn and unresponsive. These observations were used to place each child into one of five temperament categories: *undercontrolled* (irritable, impatient, emotional), *inhibited* (shy, fearful, easily distracted), *confident* (eager to perform, responsive to questions), *reserved* (withdrawn, uncomfortable), and *well adjusted* (friendly, well controlled). The children were observed and categorized again when they were three, five, seven, and nine years old. If it occurs to you that seeing a child at one point in life might bias an observer's ratings of that child later on, you are right. To ensure that ratings would not be influenced by this kind of observer bias, the researchers arranged for different people to make the ratings at each point in time. These ratings indicated that the children's temperaments stayed about the same over the years from age three to age nine.

When the research participants were between the ages eighteen and thirty-two, they were interviewed. Some interviews explored involvement in risky and unhealthy behaviors, such as excessive drinking, violent criminal activities, unprotected sex, unsafe driving habits, or pathological gambling. At one point, the participants took a standard personality test and were rated by friends on the Big Five personality dimensions. To avoid bias, interviewers had no information about the participants' childhood temperaments. The primary question was whether temperament assessed in childhood predicted personality traits and behavior problems in adulthood.

What did the researchers find?

Adult personality and behavior characteristics were in fact different across the five original childhood temperament groups. For example, the average test scores of twenty-six-year-olds who had been classified as "undercontrolled" in childhood showed that they were more alienated, uninhibited, and stressed, and reported many more negative emotions than the other temperament groups. Participants who had been "inhibited" at age three scored much lower as adults on social potency and positive emotionality than other participants. Further, people who had been classified as "confident" or "well adjusted" as children tended to be better adjusted and more extraverted at age twenty-six than people who had been classified as "inhibited" or "reserved." These findings held true for males and females alike.

There were also correlations between childhood temperament and risky behavior in young adulthood. For example, "undercontrolled" children were about twice as likely as

(*continued*)

others to develop personalities associated with violence, excessive drinking, and other health-endangering behaviors (Caspi, Harrington et al., 2003). These individuals were also more likely to have serious gambling problem at both ages twenty-one and thirty-two (Slutske et al., 2012).

What do the results mean?

Such research results suggest that we can make relatively accurate predictions about people's personalities and behaviors as adults if we know about their temperaments as children (e.g., Glenn et al., 2007). But as critical thinkers, we must be careful not to overstate the strength of these results. Although the correlations between temperament and personality or problematic behaviors were statistically significant, they were also relatively small. Not all children classified as "undercontrolled" at age three turned out to be aggressive or violent at eighteen. So it is more accurate to say that personality may be influenced and shaped by temperament but is not completely determined by it (Clark & Watson, 2008; Roberts, Walton, & Viechtbauer, 2006).

What do we still need to know?

Valuable as it is, this research leaves a number of unanswered questions about the relationship between temperament and personality (Shanahan et al., 2012). For example, why is there a connection between temperament as a child and personality as an adult? The link is probably a complex one involving both nature and nurture (Hampson, 2008). Caspi and his colleagues (1989) offered one explanation that draws heavily on social-cognitive theories, especially Bandura's notion of reciprocal determinism. They proposed that long-term consistencies in behavior result from the mutual influence that temperament and environmental events have on one another (Friedman et al., 2012). For example, people may put themselves in situations that reinforce their temperament. So undercontrolled people might choose to spend time with people who accept (and even encourage) rude or impolite behavior. When such behavior does bring negative reactions, the world seems that much more hostile, and the undercontrolled people become even more aggressive and negative. Caspi and his colleagues see the results of their studies as evidence that this process of mutual influence between personality and situations can continue over a lifetime (Caspi, Harrington et al., 2003).

ASSESSING PERSONALITY

How do psychologists measure personality?

We all want to know something about our own personality and other people's, too, so it is no wonder that various kinds of personality assessments are widely available in newspapers and magazines and on the Internet. For example, there is a website called Tweet-Psych that offers personality profiles of frequent Twitter users based on the content of their tweets. Information available on Facebook has also been used to assess various personality dimensions (Back et al., 2010), but psychologists usually assess and describe personality using information from four main sources (Funder, 2007): *life outcomes* (such as records of education, income, or marital status), *situational tests* (observations of behavior in situations designed to measure personality), *observer ratings* (judgments about a person made by friends or family; Oltmanns & Turkheimer, 2009), and *self-reports* (responses to interviews and personality test items). Data gathered through these methods assist in employee selection, in the diagnosis of psychological disorders, in making predictions about a convict's or mental patient's dangerousness, and in other situations involving risky decisions (Kramer, Bernstein, & Phares, 2014; Meyer et al., 2001).

Life outcomes, observer ratings, and situational tests make it possible to directly assess many aspects of personality and behavior, including how often, how effectively, and how consistently various actions occur (Funder, 2012). *Interviews* provide information about personality from the person's own point of view. Some interviews are *open-ended,* meaning that questions are tailored to the intellectual level, emotional state, and special needs of the person being assessed. Others are *structured,* meaning that the interviewer asks a fixed set of questions about specific topics in a particular order. Structured interviews are routinely used in personality research because they are sure to cover matters of special interest to the researcher.

Personality tests offer a way to gather self-report information that is more standardized and economical than interviews. To be useful, however, a personality test must be reliable and valid. As described in the chapter on thought and language, *reliability* refers to how stable or consistent the results of a test are; *validity* reflects the degree to which test scores are interpreted appropriately and used properly in making inferences about people. The many personality tests available today are traditionally classified as either *projective* or *nonprojective.*

Projective Personality Measures

Projective personality measures contain items or tasks that are ambiguous, meaning that they can be perceived in many different ways. People taking projective tests might be asked to draw a house, a person, a family, or a tree; to fill in the missing parts of incomplete pictures or sentences; to say what they associate with particular words; or to report what they see in a drawing or picture. Projective techniques are sometimes used in personality research, but they are far more popular among psychodynamically oriented clinical psychologists, who use them to assess their clients' personality characteristics and psychological disorders (Schultz & Schultz, 2013). These psychologists believe that people's responses to projective tests are guided by unconscious needs, motives, fantasies, conflicts, or other hidden aspects of personality.

One widely used projective test, called the *Thematic Apperception Test (TAT)* is described in the chapter on motivation and emotion as a measure of need for achievement. Henry Murray and Christina Morgan developed this test to assess the needs they saw as the basis of personality. Another well-known projective test, the *Rorschach Inkblot Test,* uses a series of ten inkblots similar to the one in Figure 13.5. The respondent is asked to tell what the blot might be, and then to explain why.

Those who support projective testing claim that using ambiguous test items makes it hard for respondents to figure out what is being measured or what the "best" answers should be. They argue, therefore, that these tests can measure aggressive and sexual impulses and other personality features that people might want to conceal. Advocates of projective measures also point to specific cases in which projective tests have shown acceptable reliability and validity, such as in the assessment of achievement motivation with the TAT (Schultheiss, 2013).

Nonetheless, most researchers agree that projective personality measures, especially the Rorschach, are much less reliable and valid than the nonprojective personality measures described next (Garb et al., 2005; Wood et al., 2010). In fact, because of their generally poor ability to predict behavior, projective measures often add little information about people beyond what might be inferred from interviews or other sources (Hunsley, Lee, & Wood, 2003).

Nonprojective Personality Measures

Nonprojective personality measures, also known as *objective personality measures,* ask clear questions about a person's thoughts, feelings, or behavior (such as "Do you like to go to parties?"). The answers are used to draw conclusions about the individual's personality. These self-report tests are usually set up in a multiple-choice or true-false format

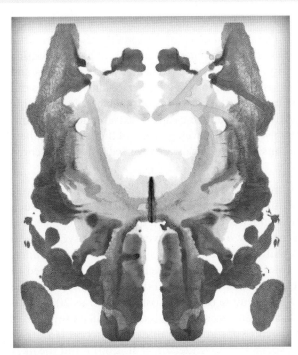

FIGURE 13.5

The Rorschach Inkblot Test

TRY THIS People taking the Rorschach test are shown ten patterns similar to this one and asked to tell what the blot looks like and why. Jot down what you see in this blot and why, and then compare your responses to those of some friends. Most methods of scoring this test focus on (1) what part of the blot the person responds to; (2) what details, colors, or other features determine each response; (3) the content of responses (such as seeing animals, maps, or body parts); and (4) the popularity or commonness of the responses.

Charlotte Miller

projective personality measures Tests made up of relatively unstructured stimuli in which responses are seen as reflecting the individuals' unconscious needs, fantasies, conflicts, thought patterns, and other aspects of personality.

nonprojective personality measures Tests that list clear, specific questions, statements, or concepts to which people are asked to respond.

that allows them to be given to many people at once, much like the academic tests used in many classrooms. A different approach has been taken by personality researchers who assess personality characteristics on the basis of computerized analysis of people's writing style, including how formal it is and how often they use particular kinds of words and phrases (e.g., Yarkoni, 2010). As in the classroom, nonprojective personality measures can be scored by machine and then compared with the responses of other people. So before interpreting your score on a nonprojective personality measure of extraversion, for example, a psychologist would compare it to a *norm*, or the average score of thousands of others of your age and gender. You would be considered unusually extraverted only if you scored well above that norm.

Some nonprojective personality measures focus on one particular trait, such as optimism (Carver & Scheier, 2002). Others measure a small group of related traits, such as empathy and social responsibility (Penner & Orom, 2009). Still other nonprojective tests measure the strength of a wider variety of traits to reveal general psychological functioning. For example, the third edition of the *Neuroticism Extraversion Openness Personality Inventory*, or *NEO-PI-3* (McCrae, Harwood & Kelly, 2011), is designed to measure the Big Five personality traits described earlier. Table 13.3 shows how the test's results are presented. The NEO-PI-3 is quite reliable (Costa & McCrae, 2008), and people's scores on its various scales have been successfully used to predict a number of criteria, including performance on specific jobs and overall career success (Conte & Gintoft, 2005; Zhao & Seibert, 2006), social status (Anderson et al., 2001), and the likelihood that a person will engage in criminal activities or risky sexual behaviors (Miller et al., 2004).

TABLE 13.3   SAMPLE SUMMARY OF RESULTS FROM THE NEO-PI-3

The NEO-PI-3 assesses the Big Five personality dimensions (McCrae & Costa, 2010). In this example of the results that a person might receive, the five factors scored are (from the top row to the bottom row) neuroticism, extraversion, openness, agreeableness, and conscientiousness. Because people with different NEO profiles tend to have different psychological problems, this test has been used to aid in the diagnosis of personality disorders (Trull & Sher, 1994).

Compared with the responses of other people, your responses suggest that you can be described as:

☐ Sensitive, emotional, and prone to experience feelings that are upsetting.	☒ Generally calm and able to deal with stress but you sometimes experience feelings of guilt, anger, or sadness.	☐ Secure, hardy, and generally relaxed even under stressful conditions.
☐ Extraverted, outgoing, active, and high-spirited. You prefer to be around people most of the time.	☐ Moderate in activity and enthusiasm. You enjoy the company of others but you also value privacy.	☒ Introverted, reserved, and serious. You prefer to be alone or with a few close friends.
☐ Open to new experiences. You have broad interests and are very imaginative.	☐ Practical but willing to consider new ways of doing things. You seek a balance between the old and the new.	☒ Down-to-earth, practical, traditional, and pretty much set in your ways.
☐ Compassionate, good-natured, and eager to cooperate and avoid conflict.	☒ Generally warm, trusting, and agreeable, but you can sometimes be stubborn and competitive.	☐ Hardheaded, skeptical, proud, and competitive. You tend to express your anger directly.
☒ Conscientious and well organized. You have high standards and always strive to achieve your goals.	☐ Dependable and moderately well organized. You generally have clear goals but are able to set your work aside.	☐ Easygoing, not very well organized, and sometimes careless. You prefer not to make plans.

FIGURE 13.6

The MMPI-2-RF: Clinical Scales and Sample Profiles

A score of 50 on the clinical scales of the MMPI-2-RF is average. Scores at or above 65 mean that the person's responses on that scale are more extreme than at least 95 percent of the normal population. The red line on this chart represents the MMPI-2-RF profile of a twenty-six-year-old married man. It is characteristic of a person who is about average in most ways, but who believes that other people are against him, are "out to get him," or are a threat to him. The clinical scales abbreviated in the figure are as follows:

RCd: Demoralization—General unhappiness and dissatisfaction

RC1: Somatic Complaints—Diffuse physical health complaints

RC2: Low Positive Emotions—Lack of positive emotional responsiveness

RC3: Cynicism—Beliefs that express distrust and a generally low opinion of others

RC4: Antisocial Behavior—Rule breaking and irresponsible behavior

RC6: Ideas of Persecution—Beliefs that others pose a threat to oneself

RC7: Dysfunctional Negative Emotions—Maladaptive anxiety, anger, irritability

RC8: Aberrant Experiences—Unusual perceptions or thoughts

RC9: Hypomanic Activation—Overactivation, aggression, impulsivity, and grandiosity

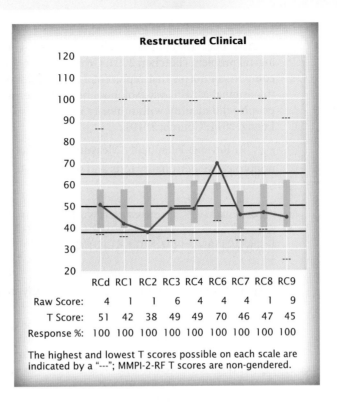

	RCd	RC1	RC2	RC3	RC4	RC6	RC7	RC8	RC9
Raw Score:	4	1	1	6	4	4	4	1	9
T Score:	51	42	38	49	49	70	46	47	45
Response %:	100	100	100	100	100	100	100	100	100

The highest and lowest T scores possible on each scale are indicated by a "---"; MMPI-2-RF T scores are non-gendered.

When the goal of personality assessment is to diagnose psychological disorders, the most commonly used nonprojective measure is the *Minnesota Multiphasic Personality Inventory*, better known as the *MMPI* (Butcher, 2006). The original 566-item true-false test, developed in the 1930s at the University of Minnesota by Starke Hathaway and J. C. McKinley, has been revised and updated as the MMPI-2-RF (restructured form; Ben-Porath & Tellegen, 2008).

The MMPI is organized into groups of items called *clinical scales*. Certain patterns of responses to the items on these scales have been associated with people who display particular psychological disorders or personality characteristics. It also contains several *validity scales*. Responses to these scales detect whether respondents are distorting their answers, misunderstanding the items, or being uncooperative. For example, someone who responds "true" to items such as "I never get angry" may not be giving honest answers to the test as a whole.

To interpret the meaning of MMPI results, a person's scores on the clinical scales are plotted as a *profile* (see Figure 13.6). This profile is then compared with the profiles of people who are known to have certain personality characteristics or problems. It is presumed that people taking the MMPI share characteristics with people whose profiles are most similar to their own. So although a high score on a particular clinical scale, such as depression, might suggest a problem in that area, interpreting the MMPI usually focuses on the overall pattern in the clinical scale scores—particularly on the combination of two or three scales on which a person's scores are unusually high.

The MMPI clinical scales appear to be reliable and valid (Forbey & Ben-Porath, 2008), but even the latest editions of the test are far from perfect measurement tools (Rouse, 2007; Selbom & Bagby, 2010). A particular pattern of MMPI scale scores does not guarantee the presence of a particular disorder (Leising & Zimmerman, 2011). The validity of MMPI interpretations may be particularly suspect when—because of cultural factors—the perceptions, values, and experiences of the test taker differ significantly from those of the test developers and the people with whom the respondent's results are compared. So although

LINKAGES Can personality tests be used to diagnose mental disorders? (a link to Psychological Disorders)

an MMPI profile might look like that of someone with a mental disorder, the profile might actually reflect the culture-specific way the person interpreted the test items, not a psychological problem (Butcher, 2004; Groth-Marnat, 1997). Even though the MMPI-2-RF uses comparison norms that represent a more culturally diverse population than did those of the original MMPI, psychologists must still be cautious when interpreting the profiles of people who identify with minority subcultures (Butcher, 2004; Cheung, van de Vijver, & Leong, 2011; Church, 2010).

"In Review: Personality Measures" summarizes the characteristics of projective and nonprojective personality tests and some of their advantages and disadvantages.

PERSONALITY MEASURES

IN REVIEW

Type of Test	Characteristics	Advantages	Disadvantages
Projective	Ambiguous stimuli create maximum freedom of response; scoring is relatively subjective	"Correct" answers not obvious; designed to tap unconscious impulses; flexible use	Reliability and validity lower than those of nonprojective tests
Nonprojective	Written format; quantitatively scored	Efficiency, standardization	Subject to deliberate distortion

In Review Questions

1. Projective personality measures are based on the _____ approach to personality.

2. The NEO-PI-3 and the MMPI-2-RF are examples of _____ tests.

3. Most personality researchers use _____ tests in their work.

Personality Tests and Employee Selection

How good are nonprojective personality measures at selecting people for jobs? Most industrial and organizational psychologists see them as valuable tools for selecting good employees. Tests such as the MMPI (and even some projective measures) are sometimes used to help guide hiring decisions (Matyas, 2004), but large organizations usually choose nonprojective measures that are designed to measure the Big Five personality dimensions or related characteristics (Barrick & Mount, 2012; Kuncel, Ones, & Sackett, 2010). Several researchers have found significant relationships between scores on the Big Five dimensions and measures of job performance and effective leadership (Detrick & Chibnall, 2013; Motowidlo, Brownlee, & Schmit, 2008; Sitser, van der Linden & Born, 2013). A more general review of studies involving thousands of people has shown that nonprojective personality measures are of value in helping businesses reduce theft, absenteeism, and other disruptive employee behaviors (e.g., Iliescu, Ilie, & Ispas, 2011; Kuncel et al., 2010).

Still, personality tests are not perfect predictors of workplace behavior (Sackett & Schmitt, 2012). Many of them measure traits that may be too general to predict specific aspects of job performance (Berry, Sackett, & Wiemann, 2007; Furnham, 2001). Also, some researchers have raised questions about the validity and usefulness of the tests used (Van Iddekinge et al., 2012), and job applicants do sometimes engage in faking to increase the chances they will be hired (Galić, & Jerneić, 2013; Griffin & Wilson, 2012). By contrast, some features of the work situation may better predict employee behavior than do personality measures (Gupta, Ganster, & Kepes, 2013). Further, some employees see personality measures as an invasion of privacy. They worry that test results in their personnel files might be misinterpreted and hurt their chances for promotion or jobs elsewhere. Lawsuits have resulted in a ban on using personality tests to select U.S. federal employees. Concerns about privacy and other issues surrounding personality testing led the American Psychological Association and related organizations to publish joint ethical standards on the development, distribution, and use of all psychological tests (American Educational Research Association, American Psychological Association, & National Council on Measurement in Education, 1999; American Psychological Association, 2002b). The goal is not only to improve the reliability and validity of tests but also to ensure that their results are properly used and do not infringe on individuals' rights (Turner et al., 2001).

LINKAGES

As noted in the introductory chapter, all of psychology's subfields are related to one another. Our discussion of personality, culture, and human development illustrates just one way that the topic of this chapter, personality, is linked to the subfield of developmental psychology, which is described in the chapter on human development. The Linkages diagram shows ties to two other subfields, and there are many more ties throughout the book. Looking for linkages among subfields will help you see how they all fit together and help you better appreciate the big picture that is psychology.

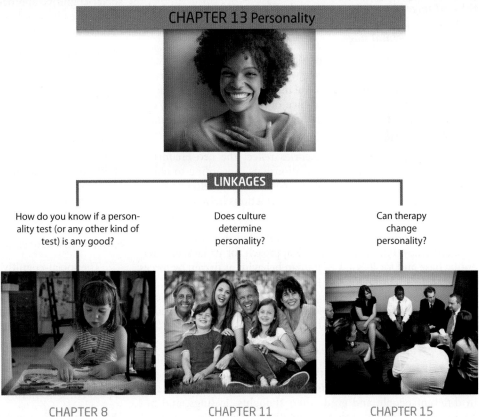

CHAPTER 13 Personality

LINKAGES

How do you know if a personality test (or any other kind of test) is any good?

Does culture determine personality?

Can therapy change personality?

CHAPTER 8
Intelligence

CHAPTER 11
Human Development

CHAPTER 15
Treatment of Psychological Disorders

SUMMARY

Personality refers to the unique pattern of psychological and behavioral characteristics by which each person can be compared and contrasted with other people. The four main theoretical approaches to personality are the psychodynamic, trait, social-cognitive, and humanistic approaches.

The Psychodynamic Approach

How did paralyzed patients lead Freud to psychoanalysis?

The *psychodynamic approach*, pioneered by Freud, assumes that personality arises out of unconscious psychological processes that interact to determine our thoughts, feelings, and behavior. According to Freud's *psychoanalytic theory*, personality has three components—the *id*, which operates according to the *pleasure principle*; the *ego*, which operates according to the *reality principle*; and the *superego*, which internalizes society's rules and values. The ego uses *defense mechanisms* to prevent unconscious conflicts among these components from becoming conscious and causing anxiety or guilt.

Freud proposed that the focus of conflict changes as the child passes through stages of *psychosexual development*. These include the *oral stage*, the *anal stage*, the *phallic stage* (during which the *Oedipal complex* or the *Electra complex* occurs), the *latency period*, and the *genital stage*.

Many of Freud's followers developed new theories that differed from his. Among these theorists were Jung, Adler, and Horney. They tended to downplay the role of instincts and the unconscious, emphasizing instead the importance of conscious processes, ego functions, and social and cultural factors. Horney also challenged the male-oriented nature of Freud's original theory.

Current psychodynamic theories reflect the neo-Freudians' emphasis on family and social relationships. According to object relations and attachment theorists, personality development depends mainly on the nature of early interactions between individuals and their caregivers.

The psychodynamic approach is reflected in many forms of psychotherapy, but critics fault the approach for its lack of a scientific base and for its view of human behavior as driven by forces that are difficult or impossible to measure.

The Trait Approach

What personality traits are most basic?

The *trait approach* assumes that personality is made up of stable internal *personality traits* that appear at varying strengths in different people and guide their thoughts, feelings, and behavior. Allport believed that personality is created by a small set of central traits and a larger number of secondary traits in each individual. Allport studied unique patterns of traits, whereas later researchers such as Cattell used factor analysis to explore common traits or core dimensions of personality. Most recently, these factor analyses have identified five basic dimensions of personality, collectively referred to as the *five-factor*, or *Big Five, personality model*. These dimensions—openness, conscientiousness, extraversion, agreeableness, and neuroticism—have been found in many different cultures and may arise partly from inherited differences in temperament and other biological factors that provide the raw materials from which each personality is molded by experience. These biological factors are the focus of trait theories proposed by Eysenck and by Gray.

The trait approach has been criticized for being better at describing personality than at explaining it, for failing to consider mechanisms that motivate behavior, and for underemphasizing the role of situational factors. Nevertheless, the trait approach—particularly the five-factor personality model—currently dominates the field.

The Social-Cognitive Approach

Do we learn our personalities?

The *social-cognitive approach* assumes that personality is a set of unique patterns of thinking and behavior that a person acquires through learning and then displays in particular situations. The social-cognitive approach has expanded on traditional behavioral approaches by emphasizing the role of cognitive factors, such as observational learning, in personality development.

Rotter's theory focuses on expectancies that guide behavior, and it generated interest in assessing general beliefs about whether rewards occur because of personal efforts (internal control) or chance (external control). Bandura believes that personality develops largely through cognitively mediated learning, including observational learning. He sees personality as reciprocally determined by interactions among cognition, environmental stimuli, and behavior. *Self-efficacy*—the belief in one's ability to accomplish a given task—is an important determinant of behavior. Mischel emphasizes the importance of situations and their interactions with cognitive person variables in determining behavior. According to Mischel, we must look at both cognitive person variables and situational variables in order to understand human consistencies and inconsistencies.

The social-cognitive approach has led to new forms of psychological treatment and many other applications. However, critics of this approach consider even its latest versions to be incapable of capturing all the unlearned factors that some psychologists see as important in personality.

The Humanistic Approach

Is everyone basically good?

The *humanistic psychology approach*, also called the *phenomenological approach*, is based on the assumption that personality is determined by the unique ways that each individual views the world. These perceptions form a personal version of reality and guide people's behavior as they strive to reach *self-actualization*, their fullest potential.

Rogers believed that personality development is driven by an innate **actualizing tendency**, but also that one's **self-concept** is shaped by social evaluations. He proposed that the **conditions of worth** that parents and others impose interfere with personal growth and can lead to psychological problems. Maslow saw self-actualization as the highest in a hierarchy of needs. Personality development is healthiest, he said, when people have a growth orientation rather than a deficiency orientation.

The humanistic approach has been used in certain forms of psychotherapy, in parent training, and in group experiences designed to enhance personal growth. This approach has considerable popularity, but it has been faulted for being too idealistic, for failing to explain personality development, for being vague and unscientific, and for underplaying cultural differences in "ideal" personalities.

Many people in the individualist cultures of North America and Europe are taught to believe in the importance of self-worth and personal distinction. This independent self system contrasts with the interdependent self system that is often fostered in collectivist cultures, in which the self is defined mainly in relation to family or other groups. Contrasting definitions of the self in different cultures and among males versus females tend to exert differing influences on the development of personality.

Research suggests that temperament in childhood may influence personality development into adulthood.

Assessing Personality

How do psychologists measure personality?

Personality is usually assessed through some combination of life outcomes, observer ratings, situational tests, and self-reports. To be useful, personality assessments must be both reliable and valid.

Based on psychodynamic theories, **projective personality measures** present ambiguous stimuli in an attempt to tap unconscious personality characteristics. Two popular projective tests are the TAT and the Rorschach. In general, projective personality measures are less reliable and valid than nonprojective personality measures.

Nonprojective personality measures, also known as objective measures, usually present clear, direct items; their scores can be compared with group norms. The NEO-PI-3 and the MMPI-2-RF are examples of nonprojective personality measures.

Nonprojective personality measures are often used to identify which people are best suited for certain occupations. Although such tests can be helpful in this regard, those who use them must be aware of the tests' limitations and take care not to violate the rights of test respondents.

TEST YOUR KNOWLEDGE

Select the best answer for each of the following questions. Then check your responses against the Answer Key at the end of the book.

1. When psychologists talk about the unique pattern of enduring psychological and behavioral characteristics by which each person can be compared and contrasted with other people, they are referring to _____.
   a. motivation
   b. personality
   c. reciprocal determinism
   d. conditions of worth

2. As Jared is jostled by a passerby, he thinks, "I'd like to hit that guy!" Freud would say that this impulse comes from Jared's _____, which operates on the _____ principle.
   a. id; pleasure
   b. id; reality
   c. ego; pleasure
   d. ego; reality

3. Nine-year-old Jeffrey has just bounded into the room with his latest artistic creation. He chatters about his friends at school and how much he likes reading and working math problems. According to Freud, Jeffrey is most likely in the _____ stage of psychosexual development.
   a. oral
   b. anal
   c. phallic
   d. latency

4. Elizabeth's therapist suggests that Elizabeth's inability to trust her boyfriend could stem from her parents' neglecting her when she was a child. This therapist most likely follows the _____ theory of personality.
   a. reciprocal deterministic
   b. social-cognitive
   c. humanistic
   d. object relations

5. Oscar strives to be the best at everything he does. He believes that he is successful because he is intelligent, works hard, and never gives up. Oscar most likely has a(n) _____ self system.
   a. independent
   b. interdependent
   c. reciprocal
   d. growth-oriented

6. Which of the following is *not* a common criticism of Freud's psychodynamic approach to personality?
   a. His sample of patients was small and unrepresentative of the general population.
   b. His theory reflects Western European and North American cultural values.
   c. The theory was not developed scientifically and thus is subject to bias.
   d. The theory was not comprehensive and has had little influence on psychology.

7. Rajeem believes that he is unique because no one else has exactly the same combination of internal characteristics (such as high intelligence, low sociability, average creativity) that he does. In other words, Rajeem believes in the _____ approach to personality.
   a. psychodynamic
   b. trait
   c. social-cognitive
   d. humanistic

8. A politician is described by her critics as dishonest, intelligent, industrious, extraverted, aggressive, generous, and charming. This method of describing personality most closely matches _____ model of personality.
   a. Eysenck's biological trait
   b. Rotter's expectancy
   c. Allport's trait
   d. the five-factor

9. Tamerika has been described as high in openness, low in conscientiousness, high in extraversion, high in agreeableness, and high in neuroticism. This description reflects _____ model of personality
   a. Eysenck's biological trait
   b. Rotter's expectancy
   c. Allport's trait
   d. the five-factor

10. David is very sociable and tends to seek out situations in which other people are appreciative of his work and his jokes. He is usually happy and loves to try new activities, such as bungee jumping. According to Gray, David has an active _____ system.
    a. external control
    b. internal control
    c. behavioral approach
    d. flight or freeze system

11. According to the Thinking Critically section of this chapter, research on the question of whether or not personality is inherited concludes that _____.
    a. there are specific genes for specific personality traits
    b. there are genetic predispositions toward particular personality characteristics
    c. the environment is the strongest influence on personality development
    d. personality is essentially determined by the age of six months

12. Sandy believes that if she works hard, she will be rewarded. So when she gets a D on her psychology test, she decides that she didn't study hard enough. When she wins the "Outstanding Senior of the Month" award, she believes that she earned it. According to one type of social-cognitive personality theory, Sandy would be described as _____.
    a. internal
    b. external
    c. deficiency oriented
    d. growth oriented

13. Darma was standing in line at a movie theater, thinking about how her boyfriend had dumped her, when she was accidentally shoved from behind. She shouted "Hey! Back off, you jerks!" This prompted angry comments from the people behind her, which made Darma even angrier, so she refused to move forward in line. This case is an example of _____.
    a. conditions of worth
    b. growth orientation
    c. reciprocal determinism
    d. internal locus of control

14. At college basketball games, Melinda jumps up and down and yells and screams continuously. Otherwise, however, she is a quiet person who chooses peaceful environments without much social stimulation. She finds that when she is around other people, they often become quiet, too. Melinda's personality can best be explained by _____ theory.
    a. psychodynamic
    b. Allport's trait
    c. Rotter's expectancy
    d. Mischel's person-situation

15. Rolf believes that his children's personalities are shaped by the way he rewards and punishes them. His wife, Jena, believes that the children were born with an innate drive toward growth and that their personalities are shaped by their unique perceptions of the world. Rolf's beliefs most closely match the _____ approach to personality, and Jena's most closely match the _____ approach.
    a. psychodynamic; trait
    b. social-cognitive; trait
    c. social-cognitive; humanistic
    d. psychodynamic; humanistic

16. When Lizzie finger-paints on the wall, her mother gets angry and shouts, "You are a very bad girl!" Rogers would say that Lizzie's mother is creating _____.
    a. growth-oriented development
    b. deficiency-oriented development
    c. conditions of worth
    d. psychodynamic conflicts

17. Ruben is preoccupied with what is missing from his life. He has a good job and just got a raise, but he still feels underpaid. He has a great wife, but he wishes she were more attractive. He bought a new car, but he just saw a better one that has become his latest obsession. Maslow would say that Ruben is controlled by _____.
    a. growth orientation
    b. deficiency orientation
    c. conditions of worth
    d. self-actualization

18. Which of the following techniques would a psycho-dynamic psychologist be most likely to use to assess personality?
    a. Behavioral observations
    b. Nonprojective personality measures
    c. Measurements of physiological activity
    d. Projective personality measures

19. Paul is an undercontrolled eight-year-old who regularly has tantrums. The longitudinal study described in this chapter's Focus on Research Methods section would suggest that, when Paul is an adult, he will most likely _____.
    a. join the military or live in some other highly structured environment
    b. have outgrown his lack of control
    c. be more aggressive than most other men
    d. keep jobs longer than most other men

20. Peggy is responsible for hiring new employees for her company. To guide her selections, she decides to use _____, which have been shown to have value in screening out employees who are likely to be unreliable or dishonest.
    a. structured interviews
    b. nonprojective personality measures
    c. projective personality measures
    d. life outcome measures

CHAPTER 14

Psychological Disorders

© Dragon Images/Shutterstock.com

Preview

Do you know someone who collects odd objects, or believes in things that most people don't, or dresses in strange or even shocking ways? Is this person crazy or just eccentric? When does oddness become abnormality? When does sadness become depression? What are psychological disorders? In this chapter, we describe the major categories of psychological disorders, discuss some of their possible causes, consider how they have been explained over the centuries, and examine their role in the insanity defense.

José is a fifty-five-year-old electronics technician. A healthy and vigorous father of two adult children, he was forced to take medical leave because of a series of sudden, uncontrollable panic attacks in which dizziness, a racing heart, sweating, and other terrifying symptoms made him fear that he was about to die. José is suffering from a psychological disorder, also called a *mental disorder* or *psychopathology.* **Psychopathology** involves patterns of thought, emotion, and behavior that are maladaptive, disruptive, or uncomfortable either for the person affected or for others.

Psychological disorders appear in every country in the world, and the number of people who are affected is staggering (Alonso et al., 2013; Farmer et al., 2013; Kessler et al., 2012). Surveys reveal that each year in the United States alone, over 85 million people, or about 27 percent of the adult population, show some form of mental disorder and that as many as 46 percent have had a disorder at some point in their lives (Alonso et al., 2013; National Institute of Mental Health [NIMH], 2014; see Figure 14.1). In addition, about 13 percent of U.S. children show a significant mental disorder each year. About three-quarters of adult disorders first appear by age twenty-four; half begin as early as fourteen (Merikangas et al., 2010; NIMH, 2014; Twenge et al., 2010).

Individuals experiencing a severe mental disorder spend an average of 136 days out-of-role, meaning that students are not going to school, employees are not going to work, and full-time parents are unable to care for their families (Alonso et al., 2013). These rates of mental disorder have remained steady in recent years and are seen in all segments of society. As described later, though, some disorders are more prevalent in males or in females or in certain ethnic groups (NIMH 2014; Zahn-Waxler, Shirtcliff, & Marceau, 2008). The actual prevalence may be higher than the survey percentages suggest, because major studies have examined fewer than half of all known psychological disorders. In short, psychological disorders are very costly in human suffering, wasted potential, economic burden, and lost resources (Alonso et al., 2013; Kessler, 2012; Kessler, Chiu et al., 2008). You can learn more about the latest surveys conducted by the World Health Organization at the homepage of the World Mental Health Survey Initiative.

FIGURE 14.1

Annual Incidence of Specific Psychological Disorders

Several large-scale surveys of adults in the United States revealed that 27 percent of them experience some form of mental disorder in any given year and that almost half of them have displayed a disorder at some time in life. The data shown here summarize these findings by category of disorder. The same general patterns appear among the more than 400 million people worldwide who suffer from some form of psychological disorder (Farmer et al., 2013; Kessler et al., 2012; NIMH, 2014).

psychopathology Patterns of thinking and behaving that are maladaptive, disruptive, or uncomfortable for the affected person or for others.

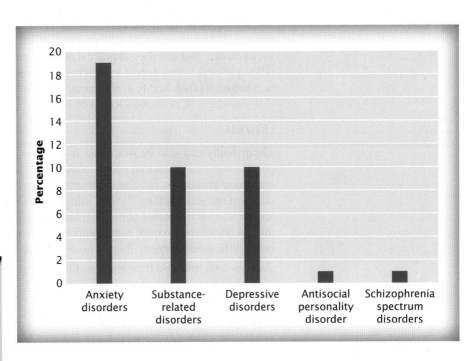

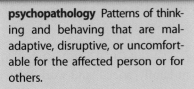

Is This Person Abnormal?

Whether unusual individuals are labeled "abnormal" and perhaps given treatment for psychological disorders depends on a number of factors, including how abnormality is defined by the culture in which they live, who is most directly affected by their behavior, and how much distress they suffer or cause.

Xinhua / eyevine Xinhua / eyevine/eyevine/Redux

DEFINING PSYCHOLOGICAL DISORDERS

How do psychologists define abnormal behavior?

A California woman's husband dies. In her grief, she stays in bed all day, weeping, refusing to eat, at times holding "conversations" with him. In India, a Hindu holy man on a pilgrimage rolls along the ground for more than 1,000 miles of deserts and mountains, in all kinds of weather, until he reaches the sacred place he seeks. In London, an artist randomly scratches parked cars as part of his "creative process" (Telegraph Correspondent, 2005). One third of U.S. adults believe in UFOs, 14 percent say they have seen one (Associated Press, 2007), and hundreds claim to have been abducted by space aliens (Clancy, 2005). These examples and countless others raise the question of where to draw the line between normality and abnormality, between eccentricity and mental disorder.

What Is Abnormal?

The criteria for judging whether people's thinking, emotions, or behaviors are abnormal have been called the "three D's": deviance, distress, and dysfunction. Each criterion has value but also some flaws.

Deviance

If we define *normality* as what most people do, then the criterion for abnormality becomes *statistical infrequency,* or that which is deviant, meaning unusual or rare. By this criterion, the few people who believe that space aliens steal their thoughts would be judged as abnormal; the many people who worry about becoming victims of crime or terrorism would not. But statistical infrequency alone is a poor criterion for abnormality because it would define as abnormal any rare quality or characteristic, including creative genius or world-class athletic ability. Further, the infrequency criterion implies that conformity with the majority is normal, so equating rarity with abnormality may result in the oppression of nonconformists who express unusual or unpopular views or ideas. Finally, just how rare must a behavior be in order to call it "abnormal"? The dividing line is not easy to locate.

A related criterion for abnormality is the violation of social norms, the cultural rules that tell us how we should and shouldn't behave in various situations, especially in relation to others. According to this *norm violation* criterion, when people behave in ways that are unusual enough or disturbing enough to violate social norms, they may be described as abnormal. However, norm violation alone is an inadequate measure of abnormality. For one thing, some norm violations are better characterized as eccentric or illegal than as abnormal. People who seldom bathe or who stand too close during conversation violate social norms, but are they abnormal or merely annoying? Further, whose norms are we talking about? Social norms vary across cultures, subcultures, and historical eras, so certain behaviors that qualify as abnormal in one part of the world might be perfectly acceptable elsewhere (Chentsova-Dutton & Tsai, 2007).

Distress

Abnormality can also be described in terms of *personal suffering*. In fact, experiencing distress is the criterion that people often use in deciding that their psychological problems are severe enough to require treatment. But personal suffering alone is not an adequate criterion for abnormality. For one thing, it does not take into account the fact that people are sometimes distressed about characteristics (such as being gay or lesbian) that are not mental disorders. Second, some people display serious psychological disorders but experience little or no distress. Those who sexually abuse children, for example, create far more distress in victims and their families than they suffer themselves.

Dysfunction

A final criterion for abnormality is *impaired functioning*, which means having difficulty in fulfilling appropriate and expected roles in family, social, and work-related

Situational Factors in Defining Abnormality

TRY THIS   Men in Delhi, India, can take advantage of outdoor urinals like this one. In some countries, it is even acceptable for men to urinate against buildings on city streets. In the United States and many other places, though, males who urinate anywhere other than the relative privacy of a men's room are considered to be deviant and might even be arrested for indecent exposure. In other words, situational factors can determine whether a particular behavior is labeled "normal" or "abnormal." Make a list of the reasons you would give for, or against, calling these men "abnormal." Which criteria for abnormality did you use?

Mark A. Johnson/Alamy

situations (Üstün & Kennedy, 2009). For example, it is normal for people to experience sadness at one time or another, but if their sadness becomes so intense or long lasting that it interferes with their ability to hold a job or care for their children, it is likely to be considered abnormal. It isn't quite fair, though, to call someone abnormal just because they are dysfunctional. Their dysfunction might be caused by physical illness, by an overwhelming but temporary family problem, or by a variety of things other than a psychological disorder. Further, some people who display significant psychological disorders are still able to function reasonably well at school, at work, or at home.

Behavior in Context: A Practical Approach

Obviously, no single criterion fully defines abnormality. So mental health practitioners and researchers tend to adopt a *practical approach* that combines aspects of all the criteria we've described. They consider the *content* of behavior (that is, what the person does), the sociocultural *context* in which the person's behavior occurs, and the *consequences* of the behavior for that person and for others.

They also recognize that the definition of behavior that is "appropriate," "expected," and "functional" depends on age, gender, culture, and the particular situation and historical era in which people live. For example, a short attention span and unemployment are considered normal in a two-year-old but inappropriate and problematic in an adult. In some countries, expressing certain emotions is considered more appropriate for women than for men. So kisses, tears, and long embraces are common when women in North America greet each other after a long absence; men tend to simply shake hands or hug briefly. And because of cultural differences, hearing a dead relative's voice calling from the afterlife would be more acceptable in certain American Indian tribes than among, say, the families of suburban Toronto. Situational factors are important as well. Falling to the floor and "speaking in tongues" is considered appropriate and even desirable during the worship services of some religious groups; but the same behavior would be seen as inappropriate (and possibly a sign of disorder) in a college classroom. Finally, judgments about behavior are shaped by changes in social trends and cultural values. At one time, the American Psychiatric Association listed homosexuality as a mental disorder, but it dropped this category from its official list of disorders in 1973. In taking this step, it was responding to changing views of sexual orientation prompted in part by the political and educational efforts of gay and lesbian rights groups.

In summary, it is difficult (and probably impossible) to define with certainty a specific set of behaviors that everyone, everywhere, will agree constitutes abnormality. Instead, the practical approach sees abnormality as including those patterns of thought, behavior, and emotion that lead to suffering and significantly impair people's ability to function as expected within their culture (Nordsletten, & Mataix-Cols, 2012).

EXPLAINING PSYCHOLOGICAL DISORDERS

What causes abnormality?

It is one thing to define psychological disorders; it is quite another to explain each of them. Centuries ago, explanations of abnormal behavior focused on gods or demons. Disordered people were seen either as innocent victims of evil spirits or as social or moral deviants suffering supernatural punishment. In Europe during the late Middle Ages, for example, it was widely believed that people who engaged in threatening or unusual behavior were controlled by the devil or other evil beings. Supernatural explanations of psychological disorders are still invoked today in many cultures around the world, including certain ethnic and religious subcultures in North America (Chentsova-Dutton & Tsai, 2007; Legare & Gelman, 2008). Other explanations have focused on mental incompetence, weak character, personal choices, illness or other physical problems, faulty learning, and difficult social conditions.

An Exorcism

The exorcism being performed by this Buddhist monk in Thailand is designed to cast out the evil forces that are seen as causing this child's disorder. Supernatural explanations of mental disorder remain influential among religious groups in many cultures and subcultures around the world (Fountain, 2000). Awareness of this influence in the United States and Europe has increased recently after cases in which people have died during exorcism rituals (e.g., Christopher, 2003; Radford, 2005).

Jean Leo Dugast/Sygma/Corbis

Explanations of psychological disorders tend to influence a society's attitudes and responses toward the people who display them (Blease, 2012; Fontaine, 2009). Where disorder is seen as a sign that a person is evil, that person may be the target of anger and punishment, but in societies in which the cause of disorder is thought to be demonic possession, the person may be the object of sympathy and might be offered an exorcism ceremony. If abnormality is viewed as a personal decision to behave in odd ways, those who do so are likely to be avoided, isolated, and ignored, but if psychological problems are assumed to be caused by illness or learned habits, troubled people are likely to receive drugs or to be offered programs designed to teach more appropriate behaviors. The view of psychological disorders that is most prevalent in a given society is often driven by the ways in which those disorders are portrayed in the news and entertainment media (Lewison et al., 2012; Sarrett, 2011).

The Biopsychosocial Approach

Today, most mental health researchers in Western cultures attribute the appearance of psychopathology to a combination of three main causes: biological factors, psychological processes, and sociocultural contexts. For many decades, there was controversy over which of these three causes was most important, but it is now widely agreed that they can all be important. Most researchers have adopted a **biopsychosocial approach** in which mental disorders are seen as caused by the combination and interaction of biological, psychological, and sociocultural factors, each of which contributes in varying degrees to particular problems in particular people (e.g., Kendler et al., 2011; Nolen-Hoeksema & Watkins, 2011; Wright et al., 2013).

Biological Factors

The biological factors thought to be involved in causing mental disorders include physical illnesses and disruptions or imbalances of bodily processes. This view of psychological disorders has a long history. For example, Hippocrates, a physician in ancient Greece, said that psychological disorders result from imbalances among four *humors*, or bodily fluids (blood, phlegm, black bile, and yellow bile). In ancient Chinese cultures, psychological disorders were seen as arising from an imbalance of *yin* and *yang*, the dual forces of the universe flowing in the physical body.

biopsychosocial approach Viewing mental disorders as resulting from a combination of biological, psychological, and sociocultural factors.

As the biologically oriented view gained prominence in Western cultures after the Middle Ages, special hospitals for the insane were established throughout Europe. Treatment in these early *asylums* consisted mainly of physical restraints, laxative purges, bleeding of "excess" blood, and induced vomiting. Cold baths, fasts, and other physical discomforts were also used in efforts to "shock" patients back to normality.

The biologically oriented view, sometimes called the *medical model,* also gave rise to the concept of abnormality as *mental illness.* Today the medical model is also sometimes called a *neurobiological model* because it explains psychological disorders in terms of particular disturbances in the anatomy and chemistry of the brain and in other biological processes, including genetic influences (e.g., Schlaepfer & Nemeroff, 2012; Williams, 2008). Neuroscientists and others who employ a neurobiological model investigate these disorders as they would investigate any physical illness, seeing problematic symptoms stemming primarily from an underlying illness that can be diagnosed, treated, and cured. This model is widely accepted in Western cultures today; most people tend to seek medical doctors and hospitals for the diagnosis and treatment of psychological disorders (Wang et al., 2011).

Visiting Bedlam

As shown in William Hogarth's portrayal of "Bedlam" (slang for a hospital in London formerly known as St. Mary Bethlehem), most asylums of the 1700s were little more than prisons. Notice the well-dressed visitors. In those days, the public could buy tickets to look at mental patients, much as people go to the zoo today.

"The Interior of Bedlam," from 'A Rake's Progress,' by William Hogarth, 1763

Psychological Processes

The biological factors we have described are constantly influencing and being influenced by a variety of psychological processes, such as our wants, needs, and emotions; our learning experiences; and our way of looking at the world. The roots of the **psychological model** of mental disorders can be found in ancient Greek literature and drama dealing with *psyche,* or mind, and especially with the problems people experience as they struggle to resolve inner conflicts or to overcome the effects of stressful events.

These ideas took center stage in the late 1800s, when Sigmund Freud challenged the assumption that psychological disorders had only physical causes. As described in the chapter on personality, Freud viewed psychological disorders as resulting mainly from the effects of unresolved, mostly unconscious clashes between people's inborn impulses and the limits placed on those impulses by the environment. These conflicts, he said, begin early in childhood. Today's versions of this *psychodynamic approach* focus less on instinctual urges and more on the role of attachment and other early interpersonal relationships, but they retain the basic idea that internal conflicts can cause psychological disorders (Barber et al., 2013; Levy & Ablon, 2009).

psychological model A view in which mental disorder is seen as arising from psychological processes.

LINKAGES Are psychological disorders learned behaviors? (a link to Learning)

Other theories discussed in the personality chapter suggest other psychological processes that contribute to the appearance of mental disorders. For example, *social-cognitive* theorists, also known as *social-learning* theorists, see most psychological disorders as the result of past learning and current situations. These theorists say that just as people learn to avoid touching hot stoves after being burned by one, bad experiences in school or a dental office can "teach" people to fear such places. Social-cognitive theorists also emphasize the effects of expectancies and other mental processes (e.g., Johnson-Laird, Mancini, & Gangemi, 2006). They see depression, for example, as stemming from negative events, such as losing a job, and from learned patterns of thoughts about these events, such as "I never do anything right."

According to the *humanistic,* or phenomenological, approach to personality, behavior disorders appear when a person's natural tendency toward healthy growth is blocked, usually by a failure to be aware of and to express true feelings. When this happens, the person's perceptions of reality become distorted. The greater the distortion, the more serious the psychological disorder.

Sociocultural Context

LINKAGES How do societies define what is abnormal? (a link to Social Psychology)

Together, neurobiological and psychological factors can go a long way toward explaining many forms of mental disorder. Still, they focus mainly on causes residing within the individual. The **sociocultural perspective** on disorder emphasizes the importance of examining the individual's environment, including the social and cultural factors that form the context of abnormal behavior. Looking for causes of disorders in this *sociocultural context* means paying attention to **sociocultural factors** such as gender, age, and marital status; the physical, social, and economic situations in which people live; and the cultural values, traditions, and expectations in which they are immersed (Alcantara & Gone, 2014; Appignanesi, 2009; Sue & Sue, 2008). Sociocultural context influences not only what is and is not labeled "abnormal" but also who displays what kind of disorder.

Consider gender, for instance. The greater tolerance in many cultures for the open expression of emotional distress among women but not men may contribute to the fact that women report higher rates of depression than men do (Nolen-Hoeksema, 2012). Similarly, the view held in many cultures that excessive alcohol consumption is less appropriate for women than for men is a sociocultural factor that may set the stage for rates of alcohol abuse that are higher in men than women (Graham et al., 2011; Timko, Finney, & Moos, 2005).

Sociocultural factors also influence the form that abnormality takes (Kyrios et al., 2001). For example, depression is considered a *culture-general* disorder because it appears virtually everywhere in the world. However, specific symptoms tend to differ depending on a person's cultural background (Alcantara & Gone, 2014; Whaley & Hall, 2009). In Western cultures, where the emotional and physical components of disorders are generally viewed separately, symptoms of depression tend to revolve around despair and other signs of emotional distress (Kleinman, 1991). But in China and certain other Asian cultures where emotional and physical experiences tend to be viewed as one, depressed people are as likely to report stomach or back pain as to complain of sadness (Nakao & Yano, 2006; Weiss et al., 2009; Ryder et al., 2008).

There are also *culture-specific* forms of disorder. For instance, Puerto Rican and Dominican Hispanic women sometimes experience *ataques de nervios* ("attacks of nerves"), a unique way of reacting to stress that includes heart palpitations, shaking, shouting, nervousness, depression, and possibly fainting or seizure-like episodes (Lizardi, Oquendo, & Graver, 2009). In Asia, Khmer refugees sometimes suffer from panic-related fainting spells known as *kyol goeu* (Hinton, Um, & Ba, 2001). And genital retraction syndromes are occasionally observed in a number of places around the world. In Southeast Asia, southern China, and Malaysia, men suffering from *koro* fear that their penis will shrivel, retract into the body, and cause death (Dzokoto & Adams, 2005; Garlipp, 2008). In females the fear relates to shriveling of the breasts.

In short, sociocultural factors create differing stressors, social roles, opportunities, experiences, and avenues of expression for different groups of people. They also help shape the disorders and symptoms to which certain categories of people are prone, and they even affect responses to treatment (e.g., Hopper & Wanderling, 2000).

sociocultural perspective Explaining mental disorders in ways that emphasize the role of factors such as gender and age, physical situations, cultural values and expectations, and historical era.

sociocultural factors Characteristics or conditions that can influence the appearance and form of maladaptive behavior.

diathesis-stress model The notion that psychological disorders arise when a predisposition for a disorder combines with sufficient amounts of stress to trigger symptoms.

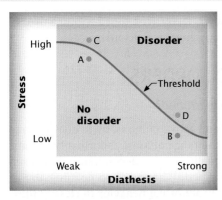

FIGURE 14.2
Diathesis, Stress, and Disorder

The diathesis-stress model's explanations suggest that psychological disorders can result from many combinations of predisposition and stress. Point D shows disorder stemming from a strong predisposition and relatively little stress. At Point C, disorder resulted from a weak predisposition but a lot of stress. Points A and B represent blends of diathesis and stress that are not potent enough to trigger disorder.

The Diathesis-Stress Model as an Integrative Explanation

The biopsychosocial approach is currently the most comprehensive and influential way of explaining psychological disorders. It is prominent partly because it encompasses so many important causal factors, including biological imbalances, genetically inherited characteristics, brain damage, psychological traits, socioculturally influenced learning experiences, stressful life events, and many more.

But how do all these factors actually interact to create disorder? Most researchers who study psychopathology believe that inherited characteristics, biological processes, learning experiences, and sociocultural forces combine to create a predisposition, or *diathesis* (pronounced "dye-ATH-uh-sis"), for psychological disorders. Whether a person eventually develops symptoms of disorder, they say, depends on the nature and amount of stress the person encounters (Elwood et al., 2009; Roisman et al., 2012). For example, a person may have inherited a biological tendency toward depression or may have learned depressing patterns of thinking, but these predispositions might not result in a depressive disorder unless the person is faced with a severe financial crisis or suffers the loss of a loved one. If major stressors don't occur or if the person has good stress-coping skills, depressive symptoms may never appear or may be relatively mild (Canli et al., 2006).

So according to the **diathesis-stress model**, biological, psychological, and sociocultural factors can predispose us toward a psychological disorder, but it takes a certain amount of stress to actually trigger it. For those with a strong diathesis, relatively mild stress might be enough to create a problem. Those whose predisposition is weaker might not show signs of disorder until stress becomes extreme or prolonged (see Figure 14.2). Another way to think about the diathesis-stress model is in terms of *risk:* The more risk factors for a disorder a person has—whether they take the form of genetic tendencies, personality traits, cultural traditions, or stressful life events—the more likely it is that the person will display a form of psychological disorder associated with those risk factors.

Table 14.1 shows how a particular case of psychopathology might be explained by various biopsychosocial factors and how it might be summarized in terms of diathesis

TABLE 14.1   EXPLAINING PSYCHOPATHOLOGY

Here are the factors that would be highlighted by the biopsychosocial approach in the case of José, the man described at the beginning of this chapter. At the bottom is a summary of how these factors might be combined within a diathesis-stress framework.

Explanatory Domain	Possible Contributing Factors
Neurobiological/medical	José may have a genetic tendency toward anxiety, an endocrine dysfunction, a neurotransmitter imbalance, a brain tumor, or some other biological disorder.
Psychological: psychodynamic	José has unconscious conflicts and desires. Instinctual impulses are breaking through ego defenses into consciousness, causing panic.
Psychological: social-cognitive	José interprets physical stress symptoms as signs of serious illness or impending death. His panic is rewarded by stress reduction when he stays home from work.
Psychological: humanistic	José fails to recognize his genuine feelings about work and his place in life, and he fears expressing himself.
Sociocultural	A culturally based belief that "a man should not show weakness" amplifies the intensity of stress reactions and delays José's decision to seek help.
Diathesis-stress summary	José has a biological (possibly genetic) predisposition to be overly responsive to stressors. The stress of work and extra activity exceeds his capacity to cope and triggers panic as a stress response.

and stress. Later, you'll see these same biopsychosocial factors combined within a diathesis-stress framework to explain a number of other psychological disorders.

CLASSIFYING PSYCHOLOGICAL DISORDERS

How many psychological disorders have been identified?

Although definitions of abnormality differ within and across cultures, there does seem to be a set of behavior patterns that roughly defines the range of most abnormality in most cultures. The majority of these behavior patterns qualify as disorders because they result in impaired functioning, a main criterion of the practical approach to defining abnormality. It has long been the goal of those who study abnormal behavior to classify these patterns into a set of precise diagnostic categories. Ideally, establishing these categories should make it easier to diagnose which disorder a particular person is displaying and thus which treatment method would be most appropriate.

Diagnoses are also important for research on the causes of psychopathology. If researchers can accurately classify people into particular disorder categories, they will have a better chance of spotting genetic features, biological abnormalities, cognitive processes, and environmental experiences that people in the same category might share. Finding that people in one category share a set of features that differs from those shared by people in other categories could provide clues about which features are related to the development of each disorder.

Seeking to create a standardized way to diagnose psychological disorders, in 1952 the American Psychiatric Association published the first edition of what has become a heavily relied upon North American diagnostic classification system, the *Diagnostic and Statistical Manual of Mental Disorders (DSM)*. The manual has grown in size over the years; the current edition, DSM-5, was released in 2013 and includes over 300 specific diagnostic labels (American Psychiatric Association, 2013). Mental health professionals outside North America diagnose mental disorders using classification systems that appear in the tenth edition of the World Health Organization's *International Classification of Diseases (ICD-10)* and its companion volume, the International Classification of Functioning, Disability, and Health (ICF). The ICD-10 is scheduled to be replaced by the ICD-11 by 2017. To facilitate international communication and cross-cultural research with respect to psychopathology, efforts are under way to remove any inconsistencies between the DSM and the ICD (Kupfer & Regier, 2010; Löwe et al., 2008), and the DSM-5 lists ICD code numbers alongside the DSM diagnostic codes. (The latest information about DSM-5 and the upcoming edition of the *ICD* is available at the websites of the American Psychiatric Association and the World Health Organization.)

A Classification System: The *DSM-5*

In the *DSM-5,* the American Psychiatric Association has attempted to describe the patterns of thinking, emotion, and behavior that define various mental disorders. For each disorder, the *DSM-5* provides specific criteria outlining the conditions that must be present before a person is given that diagnostic label (see Table 14.2).

Not everyone is happy with the latest version of the DSM. Some quarrel with the decisions its authors made about how to define certain disorders. Other critics say that the DSM-5 just continues the long tradition of focusing diagnosis only on people's weaknesses and problems while ignoring their character strengths, virtues, prosocial values, and other psychological resources upon which they can potentially build during treatment. Some researchers in the field of *positive psychology* have even offered comprehensive lists of human strengths and values from which diagnosticians can choose (Diener, 2013; Kobau et al., 2011; Seligman, 2011).

TABLE 14.2 THE DIAGNOSTIC AND STATISTICAL MANUAL OF MENTAL DISORDERS (DSM) OF THE AMERICAN PSYCHIATRIC ASSOCIATION

The fifth edition (DSM-5) lists the following major categories of mental disorders:

Neurodevelopmental Disorders. Includes problems in normal social and behavioral development ranging from attention deficit hyperactivity and communication disorders to autism spectrum disorders (severe impairment in social, behavioral, and language development), specific learning disorders, and intellectual disability (previously known as mental retardation; see the chapter on intelligence).

Schizophrenia Spectrum and Other Psychotic Disorders. Severe conditions characterized by abnormalities in thinking, perception, emotion, movement, and motivation that greatly interfere with daily functioning. Problems involve false beliefs (delusions) and false perceptions (hallucinations).

Bipolar and Related Disorders. Severe disturbances of mood and activity patterns, especially episodes of overexcitement (mania), and alternating episodes of mania and depression (bipolar disorder).

Depressive Disorders. Problems that take the form of moderate to severely depressed mood for significant periods, including, among others, major depressive disorder, persistent depressive disorder, disruptive mood dysregulation disorder, and premenstrual dysphoric disorder.

Anxiety Disorders. Disorders involving specific fears (phobias), panic attacks, generalized feelings of dread, and severe social anxiety.

Obsessive-Compulsive and Related Disorders. Includes rituals of thought and action associated with combating anxiety (obsessive-compulsive disorder) or perceived bodily flaws (body dysmorphic disorder), as well as other problematic patterns such as hoarding.

Trauma- and Stressor-Related Disorders. Problems caused by traumatic events, such as natural disasters, sexual assault, or military combat (posttraumatic stress disorder); also includes a wide range of adjustment disorders involving failure to adjust to or deal well with such stressors as divorce, financial problems, family discord, or other stressful life events (see the chapter on health, stress, and coping).

Dissociative Disorders. Psychologically caused problems of consciousness and self-identification—for example, loss of memory (dissociative amnesia) or the development of more than one identity (dissociative identity disorder).

Somatic Symptom and Related Disorders. Physical symptoms such as paralysis and blindness that have no physical cause (conversion disorder), unusual preoccupation with physical health or with nonexistent physical problems (e.g., illness anxiety disorder, somatic symptom disorder), and false mental disorders that are intentionally produced to satisfy some psychological need (factitious disorder).

Feeding and Eating Disorders. Patterns of eating too little (anorexia nervosa), binge eating followed by self-induced vomiting (bulimia and binge-eating disorder), and problems associated with abnormal elimination, persistent regurgitation, or eating non-food substances.

Elimination Disorders. Problems involving inability to hold urine (enuresis) or feces (encopresis) after the age at which these skills are considered developmentally appropriate.

Sleep-Wake Disorders. Problems involving inability to sleep at night (insomnia disorder) or to stay awake during the day, breathing-related problems such as sleep apnea, and problems in the timing of sleep-wake cycles (see the chapter on consciousness).

Sexual Dysfunctions. Problems associated with painful or otherwise unsatisfactory sexual activity, including premature ejaculation or reduced arousal.

Gender Dysphoria. Problems associated with gender incongruence, including aversion to one's gender and identification with an alternate gender.

Disruptive, Impulse-Control, and Conduct Disorders. Problems in emotional and behavioral self-control, often first appearing in childhood, including those such as oppositional defiant disorder, conduct disorder, stealing (kleptomania), and fire setting (pyromania).

(continued)

TABLE 14.2   THE DIAGNOSTIC AND STATISTICAL MANUAL OF MENTAL DISORDERS (DSM) OF THE AMERICAN PSYCHIATRIC ASSOCIATION (CONT.)

Substance-Related and Addictive Disorders. Psychological, behavioral, physical, social, or legal problems caused by use of a variety of chemical substances, including alcohol, heroin, cocaine, amphetamines, painkillers, hallucinogens, marijuana, and tobacco. Also includes compulsive gambling (known as gambling disorder).

Neurocognitive Disorders. Problems caused by deterioration of the brain due to aging, disease, drugs or other chemicals, or other causes. These problems can appear as an inability to "think straight" (delirium) or as loss of memory and other intellectual functions (e.g., mild cognitive impairment, dementia).

Personality Disorders. Diagnostic labels given to individuals who show longstanding behavior patterns that are unsatisfactory to them or that disturb other people. These patterns may involve unusual suspiciousness, unusual ways of thinking, self-centeredness, shyness, overdependency, excessive concern with neatness and detail, or overemotionality, among others.

Paraphilic Disorders. Problems associated with attraction to sexual situations involving socially or legally inappropriate activities or targets (e.g., children, unwilling partners, or exposing oneself to strangers).

Source: From the Diagnostic and Statistical Manual of Mental Disorders, Text Revision, Fourth Edition. American Psychiatric Association.

Evaluating the Diagnostic System

How good is the diagnostic system? There has not yet been extensive research on the DSM-5 version, but so far, it appears that the strengths and weaknesses of DSM-5 are similar to those of DSM-IV. One way to evaluate any diagnostic system is to consider *interrater reliability,* the degree to which different mental health professionals agree on what diagnostic label a particular person should have. Research shows that the reliability of the *DSM-5* is acceptable or high for categories such as anxiety disorders, bipolar disorder, some childhood disorders, and schizophrenia spectrum disorders, but much lower for others such as major depressive disorder and some personality disorders (Regier et al., 2013). Overall, interrater agreement appears highest when diagnosis is based on structured interviews that systematically address each area of functioning and provide uniform guidelines for interpreting people's responses (Narrow et al., 2013).

Do diagnostic labels give accurate information that guides correct inferences about people? This *validity* question is difficult to answer because accuracy can be judged in different ways. A diagnosis could be evaluated, for example, on how well it predicts a person's behavior or perhaps on whether the person is helped by treatment that has helped others in the same diagnostic category. Though evidence does support the validity of most criteria in the DSM-5 (Clarke et al., 2013; Zoellner et al., 2013), there is still room for improvement. In an effort to increase diagnostic validity, the National Institute of Mental Health has organized an initiative to identify underlying factors (such as emotion regulation or neurobiological processes) that operate across many types of psychopathology and also to focus on observable behaviors rather than diagnostic labels. Known as the NIMH Research Domain Criteria (RDoC), this new system would allow researchers and clinicians to communicate about individuals' behavior on the basis of factors that may have more validity than the DSM-5 labels (Cuthbert & Kozak, 2013). Other researchers are exploring the question of whether there is a common feature in all forms of psychopathology. This so-called "p factor" refers to a single dimension that is suspected to be a fundamental part of the structure of psychopathology and that may be associated with a history of family problems, early problems in brain functioning, life impairments, and troubled childhoods (Caspi et al., 2014).

Any diagnostic system is bound to be imperfect, however (Cuthbert & Kozak, 2013, because, first, people's problems often do not fit neatly into a single category. For example, a person may suffer both anxiety and depression (e.g., Waszczuk et al., 2014). Second, the same symptom (such as sleep difficulty) can appear as part of more than one disorder. Third, although the DSM provides many useful diagnostic criteria, some of them—such as "clinically significant impairment"—are open to judgment and interpretation. When mental health professionals must decide for themselves whether a particular person's symptoms fit a particular diagnosis, personal bias can creep into the system (Narrow et al., 2013). All of these factors may lead to misdiagnosis in some cases. Concern over this possibility has grown as the nations of North America and Western Europe have become increasingly multicultural. Diagnosticians in these countries are meeting more people whose cultural backgrounds they may not fully understand and whose behavior they may misinterpret (Broekman et al., 2011; Crowther, Lipworth, & Kerridge, 2011).

Some people whose behavior differs enough from cultural norms to cause annoyance feel that society should tolerate their "neurodiversity" instead of giving them a diagnostic label (Kapp et al., 2013; Langan, 2011; Mackenzie & Watts, 2011). In the same vein, Thomas Szasz (pronounced "zaws") and other critics have argued that the entire process of labeling people instead of describing problems is dehumanizing because it ignores people's strengths and the features that make each individual unique (e.g., McElvaney, 2011; Perry, 2011; Snyder & Lopez, 2007; Szasz, 2003). According to Szasz, calling people "schizophrenics," for example, may actually encourage the behaviors associated with these labels, undermine the confidence of clients and therapists about a person's chances for improvement, and may even force people—especially those who hold noncomformist or politically unpopular views—to undergo unnecessary treatment (Dickinson & Hurley, 2012; Szasz, 2009). Though most mental health professionals disagree with Szasz on this last point, his arguments are worth noting because psychiatric diagnosis has indeed been used in the past, and even in some countries today, to suppress social dissent or unpopular beliefs and lifestyles.

In summary, it is unlikely that any diagnostic system will ever satisfy everyone. No shorthand label can fully describe a person's problems or predict exactly how that person will behave. All that can be reasonably expected of a diagnostic system is that it provides informative general descriptions of the types of problems displayed by people who have been placed in various categories (Regier et al., 2013).

THINKING CRITICALLY
IS PSYCHOLOGICAL DIAGNOSIS BIASED?

Some researchers and clinicians worry that problems with the reliability and validity of the diagnostic system are due partly to bias in its construction and use (Koukopoulos, Sani, & Ghaemi, 2013; Nemeroff et al., 2013). Beyond the concerns that people may have symptoms that span more than one preconceived diagnosis, the very criteria used for diagnosing disorders may not be appropriate for all people if they were based on research that focused on only one gender, one ethnic group, or one age group. Moreover, diagnosticians, like other people, hold expectations and make assumptions about males versus females and about individuals from differing cultures or ethnic groups. Such cognitive biases could color their judgments and might lead them to apply diagnostic criteria in ways that are slightly but significantly different from one case to the next (e.g., Caetano, 2011; During et al., 2011; Lewis-Fernández et al., 2010).

(continued)

What am I being asked to believe or accept?

Here we focus on ethnicity as a possible source of bias in diagnosing psychopathology. It is of special interest because there is evidence that like social class and gender, ethnicity is an important sociocultural factor in the development of mental disorder. The assertion to be considered is that clinicians in the United States base their diagnoses partly on a client's ethnic background and more specifically that bias affects these clinicians' diagnoses of African Americans.

What evidence is available to support the assertion?

Several facts suggest the possibility of ethnic bias in psychological diagnosis. For one thing, African Americans receive the diagnosis of schizophrenia more frequently than European Americans do (Chien & Bell, 2008). And certain kinds of odd symptoms tend to be diagnosed as a mood disorder in European Americans but as schizophrenia in African Americans (Gara et al., 2012; Schwartz & Feisthamel, 2009). Further, relative to their presence in the general population, African Americans are overrepresented in public mental hospitals, where the most serious forms of disorder are seen, and underrepresented in private hospitals and outpatient clinics, where less severe problems are treated (Barnes, 2004; Miehls, 2011). African Americans are also more likely than European Americans to be discharged from mental hospitals without a definite diagnosis, suggesting that clinicians have more difficulty in diagnosing their disorders (Sohler & Bromet, 2003). Emergency room physicians, too, appear less likely to recognize psychiatric disorders in African American patients than in patients from other groups (Kunen et al., 2005).

There is also evidence that members of ethnic minorities, including African Americans, are underrepresented in research on psychopathology (Iwamasa, Sorocco, & Koonce, 2002). This lack of minority representation may leave clinicians less aware of sociocultural factors that could influence diagnosis. For example, they might more easily misinterpret an African American's unwillingness to trust a European American diagnostician as evidence of paranoid symptoms (Whaley, 2001, 2011).

Are there alternative ways of interpreting the evidence?

Differences among ethnic groups in diagnosis or treatment do not automatically indicate bias based on ethnicity. Perhaps there are real differences in psychological functioning among different ethnic groups. If African Americans are exposed to more risk factors for disorder, including poverty, violence, and other major stressors than other groups are, they could be especially vulnerable to more serious forms of mental disorder (Plant & Sachs-Ericsson, 2004; Turner & Lloyd, 2004). And poverty, not diagnostic bias, could be responsible for the fact that African Americans are more often seen at less expensive public hospitals than at more expensive private ones. Finally, there is no guarantee that diagnostic criteria would be significantly different if more African Americans had been included in psychopathology research samples.

What additional evidence would help evaluate the alternatives?

So do African Americans actually display more signs of mental disorder than other groups do, or do diagnosticians just perceive them as more disordered? One way of approaching this question is to conduct experiments in which diagnosticians assign labels to clients on the basis of case histories, test scores, and the like. In some studies, the cases are selected so that pairs of clients show about the same amount of disorder but one member of the pair is described as European American and the other as African American. In other studies, the same case materials, described as representing either African American or European American clients, are presented to different diagnosticians. Bias in diagnosis would be suggested if, for example, the clinicians saw patients who were described as African American as more seriously disordered than others.

Most studies of this type have found little or no ethnic bias (e.g., Angold et al., 2002; Kales et al., 2005a, 2005b). These results are difficult to interpret, however, because the diagnosticians might have been aware of the purpose of the study and so might have gone out of their way to be unbiased (Abreu, 1999; Gushue, 2004). In fact, researchers *have* found evidence of some diagnostic bias against African Americans when clinicians were unaware of the purpose of the research (e.g., Baskin, Bluestone, & Nelson, 1981; Jones, 1982). But bias can result in

(continued)

underdiagnosis as well as overdiagnosis. One review of research found that African American children exhibited more signs of attention deficit/hyperactivity disorder than European American children did, yet were given that diagnosis less often (Miller, Nigg, & Miller, 2009). In another study, socially disruptive African American youngsters were less likely than disruptive European American adolescents to be diagnosed with conduct disorder (Pottick et al., 2007). These results suggest that some diagnosticians might believe that a certain amount of over-activity, inattention, and misbehavior is to be expected of African Americans and that this behavior is therefore "normal" for them.

Bias has also appeared in studies aimed at identifying the factors that influence clinicians' judgments following extensive interviews with patients. For example, one hospital study found that in arriving at their diagnoses, psychiatrists were more likely to attribute halluci-nations and paranoid thinking to African American patients than to non–African American patients and they were more likely to attribute symptoms of depressive disorders to non–African Americans (Trierweiler et al., 2000). Another study showed that after being diagnosed with schizophrenia, African Americans were more likely than European Americans to be hospitalized, even when symptoms were about equally severe (Rost et al., 2011).

As noted earlier, some of these differences could reflect ethnic differences in the rate of disorder in the population. However, when people were interviewed in their own homes as part of large-scale mental health surveys, the diagnosis of schizophrenia was given only slightly more often to African Americans than to European Americans (Robins & Regier, 1991; Snowden & Cheung, 1990). So the presence of ethnic bias is suggested, at least for some diag-noses, for patients who are evaluated in mental hospitals but not necessarily for those who are interviewed in their own homes (Trierweiler et al., 2000, 2005).

What conclusions are most reasonable?

Just as the DSM is imperfect, so are the people who use it. As described in the chapters on social psychology and on thought and language, cognitive biases and stereotypes affect human thinking to some extent in virtually every social situation. It is not surprising, then, that they operate in diagnosis as well. Diagnostic bias does not necessarily reflect deliberate discrimination, however. Like the processes of prejudice discussed in the social psychology chapter, diagnostic bias based on ethnicity can operate unconsciously, without the diagnos-tician's being aware of it (Abreu, 1999; Boysen, 2009). So no matter how precisely research-ers specify the criteria for assigning diagnostic labels, biases and stereotypes are likely to threaten the objectivity of the diagnostic process (Poland & Caplan, 2004; Trierweiler et al., 2000).

Minimizing diagnostic bias requires a better understanding of it. Diagnosticians should focus more intently than ever on the fact that their concepts of "normality" and "abnormality" are affected by sociocultural values that a given client might not share (Kales et al., 2006; Whaley & Hall, 2009). They must also become more aware that the same cognitive shortcuts and biases that affect everyone else's thinking and decision-making can impair their own clinical judgments (Lopez, 1989). In fact, research on memory, problem solving, decision making, social attributions, and other aspects of culture and cognition may hold the key to reducing bias in the diagnosis of psychological disorders. Meanwhile, perhaps the best way to counteract clinicians' cognitive shortcomings is to teach them to base their diagnoses solely on standard diagnostic criteria and decision rules rather than just relying on their (potentially biased) clinical impressions (Akin & Turner, 2006; Kramer, Bernstein, & Phares, 2014).

We don't have space to cover all of the DSM-5 categories, so we will focus on several of the most prevalent and socially significant examples. As you read, try not to catch "medi-cal student's disease." Just as medical students often think that they have the symptoms of every illness they read about, some psychology students worry that certain aspects of their behavior (or that of a relative or friend) might reflect a mental disorder. A related phe-nomenon has been called *cyberchondria* (Hart & Björgvinsson, 2010; Vasconcellos-Silva et al., 2010) because people's worries so often stem from their unguided use of the Internet to learn about psychiatric disorders (Norr, Capron, & Schmidt, 2014). Just remember that

It's a Long Way Down

Almost everyone is afraid of something, but between 9 and 15 percent of people in the United States have a specific phobia in which fear interferes significantly with daily life (Kessler & Wang, 2008). For example, people with acrophobia (fear of heights) would not do well in a job that requires being in this high position.

Louie Psihoyos/Latitude/Corbis

TABLE 14.3	SOME PHOBIAS

Phobia, the Greek word for "morbid fear," refers to *Phobos,* the Greek god of terror. The names of most phobias begin with the Greek word for the feared object or situation.

Name	Feared Stimulus
Acrophobia	Heights
Aerophobia	Flying
Claustrophobia	Enclosed places
Cynophobia	Dogs
Entomophobia	Insects
Gamophobia	Marriage
Gephyrophobia	Crossing a bridge
Hematophobia	Blood
Kenophobia	Empty rooms
Melissophobia	Bees
Ophidiphobia	Snakes
Xenophobia	Strangers

everyone has problems sometimes. Before deciding that you or someone you know has a serious disorder or needs psychological help, consider whether the content, context, and functional impairment associated with the behavior would qualify it as abnormal according to the criteria of the practical approach.

ANXIETY DISORDERS

What is a phobia?

If you've ever been tense before an exam, a date, or a job interview, you have some idea of what anxiety feels like. An increased heart rate, sweating, rapid breathing, dry mouth, and a sense of dread are all common features of anxiety. Brief episodes of moderate anxiety are a normal part of life for most people. But when anxiety is so intense and long-standing that it disrupts a person's daily functioning, it can create **anxiety disorders** (Morrison & Heimberg, 2013).

Types of Anxiety Disorders

Here, we discuss three types of anxiety disorders: *specific phobia, generalized anxiety disorder,* and *panic disorder. Together, anxiety disorders* are the most common psychological disorders in North America; about 29 percent of the adults and 25 percent of children and adolescents in the United States will have an anxiety disorder at some point in their lives (Kessler et al., 2009; National Institute of Mental Health, 2014).

Phobia

An intense, irrational fear of an object or situation that is not likely to be dangerous is called a **phobia**. DSM-5 includes the diagnoses of *specific phobia, social anxiety disorder (social phobia),* and *agoraphobia.* Examples of **specific phobias** are shown in Table 14.3 and include fear and avoidance of heights, blood, animals, automobile or air travel, and other specific stimuli and situations. In most developed nations, they are the most prevalent anxiety disorders, affecting 9 to 15 percent of adults and children (e.g., Burstein et al., 2011; Kessler & Wang, 2008; National Institute of Mental Health, 2014).

Social anxiety disorder (social phobia) involves anxiety about being criticized by others or acting in a way that is embarrassing or humiliating. Though many of us may have such anxiety to some degree, in a social phobia the discomfort is so intense and persistent that it impairs a person's normal functioning. Common social phobias include fear of public speaking or performance ("stage fright"), fear of eating in front of others, and fear of using public rest rooms. *Generalized social phobia* is a particularly severe form of social phobia in which fear occurs in virtually all social situations (Jacobs et al., 2009; Mineka & Zinbarg, 2006; Noyes & Hoehn-Saric, 2006). Sociocultural factors can alter the form of social phobias. For example, in Japan, where cultural training emphasizes group-oriented values and goals, a common social phobia is *taijin kyofusho,* fear of embarrassing those around you (Essau et al., 2012; Kleinknecht, 1994).

Agoraphobia is a strong fear of being away from a safe place, such as home; of being away from a familiar person, such as a spouse or close friend; or of being in crowds or in other situations that are difficult to leave. Because people who suffer from agoraphobia prefer to stay at home, thus avoiding the intense anxiety associated with shopping, driving, or using public transportation, the condition is sometimes wrongly called a fear of "open spaces." Many individuals who display agoraphobia have a history of panic attacks, which we describe later (Fava et al., 2008). In Western cultures, agoraphobia is more often reported by women, many of whom are totally homebound by the time they seek help. Although agoraphobia occurs less frequently than specific phobias (affecting only about 1.4 percent of adults and about 2.4 percent of children and adolescents in the United States), it is the phobia that most often leads people to seek treatment—mainly because it so severely disrupts everyday life (National Institute of Mental Health, 2014).

Generalized Anxiety Disorder

Strong and long-lasting anxiety that is not focused on any particular object or situation marks **generalized anxiety disorder**. Because the problem occurs in virtually all situations and because the person cannot pinpoint its source, this disorder is sometimes called *free-floating anxiety* and is essentially a disorder of worry (Ouimet, Covin, & Dozois, 2012). For weeks at a time, the person feels anxious and preoccupied, sure that some disaster is about to occur. The person becomes jumpy and irritable and cannot sleep soundly. Fatigue, inability to concentrate, and physiological signs of anxiety are also common. Generalized anxiety disorder affects about 3 percent of adults in the United States in any given year and about 6 percent of the population at some point in their lives (Hollander & Simeon, 2008; Kessler & Wang, 2008; NIMH, 2014). It is more common in women, often accompanying other problems such as depression or substance abuse (Ouimet et al., 2012).

Panic Disorder

For some people, anxiety takes the form of **panic disorder**. Like José, whom we met at the beginning of this chapter, people suffering from panic disorder experience recurrent, terrifying *panic attacks* that seem to come without warning or obvious cause. These attacks are marked by intense heart palpitations, pressure or pain in the chest, sweating, dizziness, and feeling faint. Often, victims believe they are having a heart attack. They may worry so much about having panic episodes that they limit their activities to avoid possible embarrassment (Kinley et al., 2009). As noted earlier, the fear of experiencing panic attacks may lead to agoraphobia as the person begins to fear and avoid places where help won't be available should panic recur (Koerner, Vorstenbosch, & Antony, 2012). Panic disorder may last for years, during which periods of improvement may be followed by recurrence. As many as 30 percent of the U.S. population have experienced at least one panic attack within the past year, but full-blown panic disorder is seen in only about 2 to 3 percent of the population in any given year (Hollander & Simeon, 2008; Kessler, Chiu et al., 2006; NIMH, 2014).

OBSESSIVE-COMPULSIVE AND RELATED DISORDERS

What are obsessive rituals?

Obsessive-compulsive disorder (OCD) affects about 1 percent of the U.S. population in any given year and about 2 to 3 percent of the world population at some time in their lives (Worden & Tolin, 2014; NIMH, 2014). People displaying OCD are plagued by persistent, upsetting, and unwanted thoughts—called **obsessions**—that often focus on the possibility of infection, contamination, or doing harm to themselves or others. They don't actually carry out harmful acts, but the obsessive thoughts motivate repetitive behaviors—called **compulsions**—that the person believes will prevent infection, aggressive acts, or other events associated with the obsessions (Noyes & Hoehn-Saric, 2006). Common compulsions include rituals such as checking locks; repeating words or numbers; counting things; or arranging objects "just so." Obsessions and compulsions are much more intense than the familiar experience of having a thought or tune running "in the back of your mind" or rechecking a door to see that it is locked. In OCD, the obsessions and compulsions are intense, disturbing, and often strange intrusions that can severely impair daily activities (Morillo, Belloch, & Garcia-Soriano, 2007). Many of those who display OCD recognize that their thoughts and actions are irrational, but they still experience severe anxiety if they try to interrupt their obsessions or give up their compulsive rituals.

Other forms of obsessive-compulsive disorder can appear as obsessive preoccupation with the perceived infidelity of a partner (obsessional jealousy), extreme hoarding of possessions, persistent hair-pulling, nail- or lip-biting, and skin-picking. In another form of OCD called **body dysmorphic disorder**, the person is intensely distressed about an imagined abnormality of the skin, hair, face, or other bodily area. They may become preoccupied with the imagined deformity or imperfection, avoid social contacts, become dysfunctional, and even seek unnecessary corrective surgery (Hartmann et al., 2014; Veale, 2009).

anxiety disorders Conditions in which intense feelings of fear and dread are long-standing or disruptive.

phobia An anxiety disorder that involves strong, irrational fear of an object or situation that does not objectively justify such a reaction.

specific phobias Phobias that involve fear and avoidance of specific stimuli and situations such as heights, blood, and certain animals.

social anxiety disorder (social phobia) Strong, irrational fears related to social situations.

agoraphobia A strong fear of being alone or away from the safety of home.

generalized anxiety disorder A condition that involves long-lasting anxiety that is not focused on any particular object or situation.

panic disorder Anxiety in the form of sudden, severe panic attacks that appear without obvious cause.

obsessive-compulsive disorder (OCD) A disorder in which a person becomes obsessed with certain thoughts or feels a compulsion to do certain things.

obsessions Persistent, upsetting, and unwanted thoughts that interfere with daily life and may lead to compulsions.

compulsions Repetitive behaviors that interfere with daily functioning but are performed in an effort to prevent dangers or events associated with obsessions.

body dysmorphic disorder An obsessive-compulsive disorder characterized by intense distress over imagined abnormalities of the skin, hair, face, or other areas of the body.

A Cleaning Compulsion

Obsessive-compulsive disorder is diagnosed when a culturally expected degree of cleanliness turns into an obsessive preoccupation with germs and a life-disrupting compulsion to clean things. Learning and stress appear to play the major role in shaping and triggering this and other obsessive-compulsive disorders, but biological factors, including genetically inherited characteristics and problems in certain neurotransmitter systems, may result in an oversensitive nervous system and a predisposition toward anxiety.

© R.Ashrafov/Shutterstock.com

Causes of Anxiety and Obsessive-Compulsive Disorders

As with all the forms of psychopathology we will consider, the exact causes of anxiety disorders are a matter of some debate. However, there is good evidence that biological, psychological, and social factors all contribute (Coelho & Purkis, 2009; McKay & Storch, 2014). The exact nature and combination of causal factors varies from one anxiety disorder to the next. For example, the brain regions involved in panic disorder are not identical to those involved in social or other forms of anxiety disorder (Young, Wu, & Menon, 2012; Zhou et al., 2010), and the learning experiences that contribute to specific phobias may differ from those that contribute to agoraphobia.

Biological Factors

Most anxiety and obsessive-compulsive disorders appear to run in families, suggesting that these disorders are influenced by genes (Taylor, 2014). This influence is seen in the fact that if one identical twin has an anxiety disorder, the other twin (who shares the same genes) is also more likely to have an anxiety disorder than is the case in nonidentical twin pairs (Taylor, 2014). Some inherited predispositions may be rather specific. One study found that identical twins are more likely than other siblings to share phobias about small animals and social situations but not about heights or enclosed spaces (Skre et al., 2000). The degree of genetic influence on anxiety disorders is moderate, however (Hollander & Simeon, 2008), and varies among disorders. For instance, genes may play a stronger role in early-onset panic disorder and generalized anxiety disorder than in specific phobias (Bolton et al., 2006; Distel et al., 2008).

Many researchers are trying to identify the specific genes or gene combinations involved in anxiety and obsessive-compulsive disorders. For example, a number of genes have been suggested as contributing to OCD, including two variations of the SLlC6A4 gene (Saiz et al., 2008). This work is difficult, though, because the mere presence of a gene doesn't necessary predict the appearance of a disorder. Rather, genes are often "switched on" or "switched off" by environmental triggers (Uddin et al., 2010). The genes or gene combinations that may be involved in anxiety disorders may exert their influence through their effects on the brain's neurotransmitter systems. For instance, excessive activity of norepinephrine circuits in certain parts of the brain has been linked with panic disorder, and dysregulation of serotonin has been associated with obsessive-compulsive disorder and social anxiety disorder (Lanzenberger et al., 2007). The role of these neurotransmitters is also suggested by the fact that medications that affect them are often effective in the treatment of OCD and various anxiety disorders (Bartz & Hollander, 2006).

Psychological and Environmental Factors

Biological predispositions combine with environmental stressors and psychological factors—especially cognitive processes and learning—to cause most anxiety and obsessive-compulsive disorders (e.g., Hudson & Rapee, 2009; Leppänen & Nelson, 2012; Nugent et al., 2011). Abuse or other stressful experiences in childhood are also associated with increased risk of developing an anxiety disorder, particularly panic disorder (Brook & Schmidt, 2008; Safren et al., 2002). The effects of abuse, natural disasters, war, terrorist attacks, and other extreme environmental stressors can also be seen in the appearance of *trauma- and stressor-related disorders* such as posttraumatic stress disorder (American Psychiatric Association, 2013). The impact of learning on anxiety disorders can be seen in families in which parents don't socialize much, tend to be suspicious of others, and exaggerate life's everyday dangers. These parents might unwittingly promote social anxiety in their children—especially in those with a tendency toward shyness or anxiety (Eley et al., 2010)—by being overly protective and controlling, and thus influencing them to interpret social situations as threatening (Essex et al., 2010).

Learned ways of thinking play their part, too. Many people suffering from anxiety disorders exaggerate dangers in their environment, thereby creating an unrealistic expectation that bad things are going to happen (Cisler & Koster, 2010; Lissek et al., 2014).

This expectation leads them to dwell on and be constantly on the lookout for negative events. In addition, they tend to underestimate their own capacity for dealing with threatening events, thus triggering anxiety and desperation when feared events do occur (Beck & Emery, 1985). Their lack of perceived control, in turn, can lead these people to avoid or overreact to threatening situations. Consider how panic attacks develop. They may seem to come out of nowhere, but in fact subtle symptoms of physical arousal may set the stage (Meuret et al., 2011). It is the person's sensitivity to and cognitive interpretation of those symptoms that can make an attack actually develop (Domschke et al., 2010). In fact, experiments have shown that panic attacks are less likely in panic disorder patients who believe they can control the source of their discomfort (Koerner et al., 2012). These and other research results suggest that cognitive factors play an important role in panic disorder as well as in specific phobias, social anxiety disorder, generalized anxiety disorder, and OCD.

LINKAGES Can we learn to become "abnormal"? (a link to Learning)

LINKAGES

ANXIETY AND OBSESSIVE-COMPULSIVE DISORDERS AND LEARNING

Money troubles, illness, final exams, unhappy relationships, and other problems can create worry and anxiety, especially for people who are under stress from other sources or feel incapable of dealing with their problems. As upsetting thoughts about these problems become more persistent, anxiety increases. If doing something such as cleaning the kitchen temporarily relieves the anxiety, that action may be strengthened through the process of negative reinforcement (see the chapter on learning). But cleaning can't eliminate the obsessive thoughts, so when they return, the cleaning may begin again. Eventually, cleaning or other actions may become compulsive, endlessly repeated rituals that keep the person trapped in a vicious circle of anxiety (Worden & Tolin, 2014). Based on this kind of analysis, social-cognitive theorists see obsessive-compulsive disorder as a learned pattern sparked by distressing thoughts and maintained by operant conditioning (Abramowitz et al., 2006).

They also see phobias as partly due to learning, especially to classical conditioning and observational learning. The object of the phobia becomes a conditioned aversive stimulus through association with a traumatic event that acts as an unconditioned stimulus (Olatunji, 2006; Stein, 2006). Fear of dogs, for example, may result from a dog attack. Observing or hearing about other people's bad experiences can produce the same result: most people who fear flying have never been in a plane crash. Fears can even develop after seeing scary movies or TV shows (Askew, Kessock-Philip, & Field, 2008). Once the fear is learned, avoidance of the feared object or situation prevents the person from finding out that the fear is exaggerated. This cycle of avoidance helps explain why many fears don't disappear on their own (Lovibond et al., 2009).

Biological Preparedness

TRY THIS Being predisposed to learn to fear snakes and other potentially dangerous stimuli makes evolutionary sense. Like other animals, humans who rapidly learn a fear response to objects or situations that they see frightening their parents or peers are more likely to survive to pass on their genes to the next generation. Are there things you are especially afraid of? If so, list them and make a note of how you think these fears developed. How many of them appear to have "survival value"?

Photo reproduced with permission of Susan Mineka

(continued)

Why are phobias involving snakes and spiders so common, even though people are seldom harmed by them? And why are there so few cases of phobias about electrical shocks, even though lots of people receive accidental shocks? The answer may be that people are *biologically prepared* to learn to fear and avoid things that had the potential to harm their evolutionary ancestors. This idea is supported by laboratory research (Hamm, Vaitl, & Lang, 1989). In one study, a group of Swedish psychologists created conditioned fear reactions to certain stimuli by associating photographs of those stimuli with electrical shocks (Öhman, Dimberg, & Öst, 1985). Their volunteer participants developed approximately equal conditioned anxiety reactions to photos of houses, human faces, and snakes. Later, however, when the participants were shown the photos alone, their conditioned reaction to snakes remained long after their response to houses and faces had faded. Similar results have also occurred in experiments with monkeys (Mühlberger et al., 2006; Zinbarg & Mineka, 1991). If a monkey sees another monkey behaving fearfully in the presence of a snake, it quickly develops a strong and persistent fear of snakes. However, if the snake is entwined in flowers, the observer monkeys come to fear only the snake, not the flowers. So the fear conditioning appears to be selective, focusing only on potentially dangerous creatures such as snakes or crocodiles (Mühlberger et al., 2006; Zinbarg & Mineka, 1991) and not on harmless objects.

Learning is obviously important in the development of fear, but learning principles alone cannot explain why exposure to certain stimuli causes anxiety disorders in some people and not in others (Field, 2006). Why is it, for example, that some survivors of the 9/11 terrorist attacks developed phobias (or posttraumatic stress disorder) and others did not? As suggested by the diathesis-stress approach, the impact of people's experiences is heightened or dampened by other factors, such as their genetic and biological vulnerability or resilience to stress, their previous experiences with frightening events, their expectations and other cognitive habits, and the social support and other conditions that follow the trauma (Bryant et al., 2010; Leyro, Zvolensky, & Bernstein, 2010; Mineka & Zinbarg, 2006; Nugent et al., 2011). In short, learning—including the learning that supports the development of anxiety and obsessive-compulsive disorders—occurs more quickly among those who are biologically and psychologically prepared for it.

SOMATIC SYMPTOM AND RELATED DISORDERS

Can mental disorder cause blindness?

A young athlete was suffering fainting spells that prevented her from competing in track and field events. Doctors found no physical problems, and it was only after a program of stress management that her symptoms disappeared and she was able to rejoin her team (Lively, 2001). Sometimes people show symptoms of a *somatic,* or bodily, disorder even though there is nothing physically wrong to cause the symptoms. When psychological problems take somatic form, they are called **somatic symptom disorders**.

One type of somatic symptom disorder called **illness anxiety disorder** (once known as *hypochondriasis*) involves a strong, unjustified fear that one has or might get cancer, heart disease, AIDS, or some other serious medical problem. This fear prompts people with illness anxiety disorder to make frequent visits to doctors, where they report numerous symptoms. Their preoccupation with illness often leads these people to become "experts" on their most feared diseases, sometimes by endlessly searching health-related websites (Taylor & Asmundson, 2008). Other people whose disorders fall in this category make dramatic but vague reports about a multitude of physical problems; some may complain of severe, often constant pain (typically in the neck, chest, or back) all with no obvious physical cause. The classic example of disorders in this category is **conversion disorder**, a condition in which a person appears to be (but is not) blind, deaf, paralyzed, or insensitive to pain in various parts of the body. (An older term for this disorder was *hysteria.*) Conversion disorders are rare; less than 1 percent of adults experience them, and they are more common in women than men (American Psychiatric Association, 2013; Feinstein, 2011). Although they can occur at any point in life, conversion disorders usually appear in adolescents or young adults.

somatic symptom disorders Psychological problems in which a person shows the symptoms of a physical disorder for which there is no physical cause.

illness anxiety disorder A strong, unjustified fear of physical illness.

conversion disorder A somatic symptom disorder in which a person appears to be (but actually is not) blind, deaf, paralyzed, or insensitive to pain.

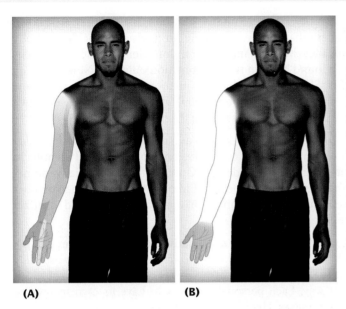

(A)   **(B)**

FIGURE 14.3
Glove Anesthesia

In a form of conversion disorder called *glove anesthesia*, lack of feeling stops abruptly at the wrist (Part B). But as indicated by the overlapping colors in Part A, the nerves of the hand and arm blend, so if they were actually impaired, part of the arm would also lose sensitivity. Other neurologically impossible symptoms of conversion disorder include sleepwalking at night on legs that are "paralyzed" during the day.

Dylan Ellis/The Image Bank/Getty Images

Conversion disorders differ from true physical disabilities in several ways. First, they tend to appear when a person is under severe stress. Second, they often help reduce that stress by allowing the person to avoid unpleasant situations. Third, the symptoms may be neurologically impossible or improbable, as Figure 14.3 illustrates. Finally, the person may show surprisingly little concern about what most people would think was a rather serious problem. One college student, for example, experienced visual impairment that began each Sunday evening and became total blindness by Monday morning. Her vision would begin to return on Friday evenings and was fully restored in time for weekend social activities. She expressed no particular concern over her condition (Holmes, 1991).

Can people who display a conversion disorder actually see, hear, or move, even though they act as if they cannot? Observations and experiments suggest that they can. Supposedly paralyzed people have been seen to sleepwalk, and supposedly blind or deaf people make use of sights and sounds to guide their behavior (e.g., Blake, 1998; Grosz & Zimmerman, 1970). But this does not mean that they are consciously faking. In fact, conversion disorder is diagnosed only when the symptoms are *not* being faked. Rather than destroying sensory or motor ability, the conversion process may prevent the person from being aware of information that the brain is processing (Bryant & Das, 2012).

Biological, psychological, and social factors have all been suggested as contributing to somatic symptom disorders. Some cases, for example, may be related to childhood experiences in which a person learns that symptoms of physical illness bring special attention and care (Abramowitz & Braddock, 2006; Feinstein, 2011). Others, including conversion disorder, may be triggered by severe stressors (Ovsiew, 2006). Cognitive factors come into play, too. When given information about their health, people who display illness anxiety disorder are strongly biased to focus on threat-confirming information but to ignore reassuring information (Eifert, Zvolensky, & Louis, 2008). Abnormal serotonin functioning has also been associated with illness anxiety disorder, and various combinations of neurochemical and social skill deficits appear to accompany conversion disorder and body dysmorphic disorder (Eifert, Zvolensky, & Louis, 2008).

Based on such findings, many researchers have adopted a diathesis-stress approach to explaining somatic symptom disorders. The results of their work suggest that certain people may have biological and psychological traits that make them especially vulnerable to these disorders, particularly when combined with a history of physical illness (Suls & Howren, 2012). Among these traits are self-consciousness and oversensitivity to physical sensations. If such people experience a number of long-lasting stressors, intense emotional conflicts, or severe traumas, they are more likely than others to display physical symptoms in association with negative emotional arousal (Abramowitz & Braddock, 2006; Siti, 2004).

Sociocultural factors may also shape somatic symptom disorders. In some Asian, Latin American, and African cultures, it is common for people to experience severe headaches and other physical symptoms in association with psychological or interpersonal conflicts (Weiss et al., 2009). In North America such conflicts are more likely to be accompanied by anxiety or depression (Brislin, 1993). Genetic factors appear to play only a minor role in somatic symptom disorders.

DISSOCIATIVE DISORDERS

What disorders create sudden memory loss?

Have you ever been driving all day on a boring highway and suddenly realized that you had almost no memory of what happened during the past half-hour? This common experience does not signal a mental disorder, but when disruptions in a person's memory, consciousness, or identity are more intense and long lasting, they are known as **dissociative disorders.** These disruptions can come on gradually, but they usually occur suddenly and last from a few hours to many years. Consider the case of eighteen-year-old "Jane Doe," who was found lying in the fetal position outside a New York City youth shelter in October 2009. She claimed to have no memory of her name, where she came from, or how she got where she was (Moore, 2009). After her picture was shown on national television, a viewer identified her as Kacie Peterson.

Kacie displayed a severe form of a disorder known as a **dissociative amnesia,** which is characterized by sudden loss of memory for (or confusion about) personal identity. In some cases, the person adopts an entirely new identity. Other forms of dissociative amnesia also involve sudden loss of memory about personal information but the person does not leave home or create a new identity. These conditions are rare, but they tend to attract intense publicity because they are so dramatic.

The most famous dissociative disorder is **dissociative identity disorder (DID)**, known in earlier editions of the DSM (and still commonly called) *multiple personality disorder (MPD)*. A person with DID appears to have more than one identity, each of which speaks and acts in a different way. Each personality seems to have its own memories, wishes, and (often conflicting) impulses. Here is a case example:

> *Mary, a pleasant and introverted 35-year-old social worker, was referred to a psychiatrist for hypnotic treatment of chronic pain. At an early interview she mentioned the odd fact that though she had no memory of using her car after coming home from work, she often found that it had been driven 50 to 100 miles overnight. It turned out that she also had no memory of large parts of her childhood. Mary rapidly learned self-hypnosis for pain control, but during one hypnotic session, she suddenly began speaking in a hostile manner. She told the doctor her name was Marian and that it was "she" who had been taking long evening drives. She also called Mary "pathetic" for "wasting time" trying to please other people. Eventually, six other identities emerged, some of whom told of having experienced parental abuse in childhood. (Spitzer et al., 1994)*

During the 1970s, there was a minor "epidemic" of DID, as well as an increase in the number of alternative personalities per case; some patients reported over forty of them (Castelli, 2009). This upsurge in DID may have occurred because clinicians were looking for it more carefully or because the conditions leading to it became more prevalent, but it may have also been influenced by movies such as *Sybil* and by tell-all books written by people who had been diagnosed with DID (Kihlstrom, 2005). These media influences may have increased the status of DID as a socioculturally approved method of expressing distress (Hacking, 1995).

There is a great deal of controversy over how dissociative disorders develop (Boysen & Van Bergen, 2014). Psychodynamic theorists see massive repression of traumatic events as the basis for creating "new personalities" who act out otherwise unacceptable impulses or recall otherwise unbearable memories (Maldonado & Spiegel, 2008; Ross, 1997). Social-cognitive theorists focus on the fact that everyone is capable of behaving in different ways depending on the circumstances (e.g., rowdy in a bar, quiet in a museum). In rare cases, they say, this variation can become so extreme that a person feels like and is perceived by others as a "different person." Further, sudden memory loss or unusual behavior may be rewarded if they allow a person to escape unpleasant situations, responsibilities, or punishment for misbehavior (Lilienfeld & Lynn, 2003; Lilienfeld et al., 2009). Among other possible contributing factors are habitual errors in thinking and memory, difficulties in controlling attention, and problems in the daily sleep-wake cycle (Lynn et al., 2012; vander Kloet et al., 2012).

Research available so far suggests four conclusions. First, memory loss and other forms of dissociation are real phenomena that can be extreme. Second, many people displaying DID have experienced events they want to forget or avoid. Most (some clinicians

dissociative disorders Conditions involving sudden and usually temporary disruptions in a person's memory, consciousness, or identity.

dissociative amnesia A psychological disorder marked by a sudden loss of memory for one's own name, occupation, or other identifying information.

dissociative identity disorder (DID) A dissociative disorder in which a person appears to have more than one identity, each of which behaves in a different way.

"Would it be possible to speak with the personality that pays the bills?"

By dropping the label *multiple personality disorder*, the DSM downplayed the idea that some people harbor multiple personalities that can easily be "contacted" through hypnosis or drugs. The new label, *dissociative identity disorder*, suggests instead that a dissociation, or separation, between one's memories and other aspects of identity can be so dramatic that people experiencing it may come to believe that they have more than one personality.

Leo Cullum/The New Yorker Collection/Cartoonbank

believe all) have suffered severe, unavoidable, persistent abuse in childhood (Foote et al., 2006; Kihlstrom, 2005). Third, like Mary, most affected people appear to be skilled at self-hypnosis, through which they can induce a trance-like dissociative state. Fourth, most found that they could escape the trauma of abuse (at least temporarily) by creating "new personalities" to deal with stress (Spiegel, 1994; van der Hart et al., 2005).

However, not all abused children display DID, and some cases of DID may indeed be triggered by media stories or by therapists who expect to see alternative personalities and use hypnosis and other methods that encourage clients to display them (McHugh, 2009; Rieber, 2006). For example, it now appears that "Sybil's" famous story about having sixteen personalities was untrue (Nathan, 2011). This evidence has led some skeptics to question the very existence of multiple personalities (Lynn et al., 2012). They point to research showing, for example, that people who display DID may be more aware than they think they are of the memories and actions of each apparent identity (Allen, 2002; Allen & Iacono, 2001; Canaris, 2008). Even those who argue for the existence of DID concede that it is quite rare (American Psychiatric Association, 2013).

Research on the existence and effects of repressed memories (discussed in the memory chapter) is sure to have an impact on our understanding of (and the controversy over) the causes of DID. ("In Review: Anxiety, Obsessive-Compulsive, Somatic Symptom, and Dissociative Disorders" presents a summary of our discussion of these topics.)

IN REVIEW

ANXIETY, OBSESSIVE-COMPULSIVE, SOMATIC SYMPTOM, AND DISSOCIATIVE DISORDERS

Disorder	Subtypes	Major Symptoms
Anxiety Disorders	Specific Phobias	Intense, unreasonable, and disruptive fear of objects or situations.
	Generalized Anxiety Disorder	Excessive anxiety not focused on a specific situation or object; free-floating anxiety.
	Panic Disorder	Repeated attacks of intense fear involving physical symptoms such as faintness, dizziness, and nausea.
Obsessive-Compulsive and Related Disorders	Obsessive-Compulsive Disorder	Persistent ideas or worries accompanied by ritualistic behaviors performed to neutralize anxiety-driven thoughts.
	Body Dysmorphic Disorder	Rituals of thought and action associated with perceived bodily flaws.
	Hoarding Disorder	Problematic retention of possessions caused by a perceived need to save them and distress associated with discarding them.
Somatic Symptom and Related Disorders	Conversion Disorder	A loss of physical ability (e.g., vision, hearing) that is related to psychological factors.
	Illness Anxiety Disorder	Preoccupation with or belief that one has a serious illness in the absence of any physical evidence.

(continued)

ANXIETY, OBSESSIVE-COMPULSIVE, SOMATIC SYMPTOM, AND DISSOCIATIVE DISORDERS (CONT.)

Disorder	Subtypes	Major Symptoms
Dissociative Disorders	Dissociative Amnesia	Sudden loss of memory.
	Dissociative Identity Disorder (Multiple Personality Disorder)	Appearance within the same person of two or more distinct identities, each with a unique way of thinking and behaving.

In Review Questions

1. Concern that it may be triggered by media stories or therapists' suggestions has made _____ the most controversial of the dissociative disorders.

2. A person who sleepwalks but is not able to walk when awake is showing signs of _____.

3. Panic disorder is sometimes associated with another anxiety disorder called _____.

DEPRESSIVE AND BIPOLAR DISORDERS

How common is depression?

Everyone's mood, or *affect,* tends to rise and fall from time to time. However, when people experience long periods of extreme moods such as wild elation or deep depression, when they shift from one extreme to another, and especially when their moods are not consistent with the events around them, they are said to show **depressive disorders** (sometimes also called *mood disorders* or *affective disorders)* or *bipolar disorders.*

Depressive Disorders

Depression can range from occasional, normal "down" periods to episodes severe enough to require hospitalization. A person suffering **major depressive disorder** feels sad and overwhelmed, typically losing interest in activities and relationships and taking pleasure in nothing (American Psychiatric Association, 2013). Despite the person's best efforts, anything from conversation to bathing can become an unbearable, exhausting task. Changes in eating habits resulting in weight loss or weight gain often accompany major depression. There may also be disturbed sleeping or excessive sleeping. Problems in working, concentrating, making decisions, and thinking clearly are also common, as are symptoms of an accompanying anxiety disorder or physical illness (Cuijpers et al., 2012; Suls, & Howren, 2012). In extreme cases, depressed people may express false beliefs, or **delusions**, worrying, for example, that government agents are planning to punish them. Major depression may come on suddenly or gradually. It may consist of a single episode, or of repeated periods of depression (Klein, 2010). These episodes can last weeks or months; the average length of the first episode is four to nine months (Durand & Barlow, 2006). Exaggerated feelings of inadequacy, worthlessness, hopelessness, or guilt are common in major depression (Klein, 2010). Here is a case example:

> *Mr. J. was a fifty-one-year-old industrial engineer…. Since the death of his wife five years earlier, he had been suffering from continuing episodes of depression marked by extreme social withdrawal and occasional thoughts of suicide…. He drank, and when thoroughly intoxicated would plead to his deceased wife for forgiveness. He lost all capacity for joy…. Once a gourmet, he now had no interest in food … and could barely*

depressive disorders Conditions in which a person experiences extremes of moods for long periods, shifts from one extreme mood to another, and experiences moods that are inconsistent with events.

major depressive disorder A condition in which a person feels sad and hopeless for weeks or months, often losing interest in all activities and taking pleasure in nothing.

delusions False beliefs, such as those experienced by people suffering from schizophrenia or severe depression.

manage to engage in small talk. As might be expected, his work record deteriorated markedly. Appointments were missed and projects haphazardly started and left unfinished. (Davison & Neale, 1990, p. 221)

In other cases, the depth of depression is not so extreme (de Graaf et al., 2010). In a less severe pattern of depression called **persistent depressive disorder**, the person shows the sad mood, lack of interest, and loss of pleasure associated with major depressive disorder but less intensely and for a longer period. Mental and behavioral disruptions are also less severe.

Depressive disorders occur at some time in the lives of about 17 percent of people in North America and Europe; in any given year, about 7 percent of these populations are experiencing them (American Psychiatric Association, 2013; Cuijpers et al., 2012). Unfortunately, depression is becoming more common, both in the United States and elsewhere. The World Health Organization estimates that if current trends continue, depression will become the second leading cause of disability and premature death in developed countries (Kessler, 2012; World Health Organization, 2012). The incidence of these disorders varies considerably across cultures and subcultures, however. For example, they occur at much higher rates in urban Ireland than in urban Spain, or in China (Judd et al., 2002; Lee et al., 2007), and at higher rates in countries with the highest average incomes (Kessler, 2012). There are gender differences in some cultures, too. In North America and Europe, women are two to three times more likely than men to experience major depressive disorder (Kessler & Wang, 2008), but this difference does not appear in the less economically developed countries of the Middle East, Africa, and Asia (Ayuso-Mateos et al., 2001; World Health Organization, 2003). Depression can occur at any age, but it peaks in late adolescence or young adulthood and again in old age (American Psychiatric Association, 2013).

Depression often occurs in combination with other psychological disorders and medical conditions; it is especially likely to be diagnosed along with posttraumatic stress disorder, obsessive-compulsive disorder, and various anxiety disorders, as well as with substance-related and addictive disorders, physical disabilities, and obesity, and during recovery from heart attack (e.g., Rosen-Reynoso et al., 2011).

Suicide and Depression

Suicide is associated with a variety of psychological disorders, but it is most closely tied to depressive disorders (Balázs et al., 2006; Holma et al., 2010). In fact, thinking about suicide is a symptom of depressive disorders. When suicidal thoughts combine with hopelessness about the future, which is another depressive symptom, a suicide attempt is much more likely to occur. Indeed, the rate of suicide among those with major depressive disorder is 3.4 percent overall, but 7 percent for males and as high as 15 percent for those who have been hospitalized for depression (Pompili et al., 2008; Van Orden et al., 2010).

In 2010, the year for which the most recent data are available, more than 38,000 people in the United States committed suicide, and over 1 million people attempted it (Centers for Disease Control and Prevention, 2014). Suicide was the tenth leading cause of death in the United States that year. Compared with the United States, the suicide rate is nearly twice as high in some northern and eastern European countries and Japan and only about half as high in countries with stronger religious prohibitions against suicide, such as Greece, Italy, Ireland, and the nations of the Middle East (Ono et al., 2008; World Health Organization, 2003).

Suicide rates differ considerably depending on sociocultural factors such as age, gender, and ethnicity. In the United States, suicide is most common among people sixty-five and older, especially males (Centers for Disease Control and Prevention, 2014; Warner, 2010). However, since 1950, suicide among adolescents has tripled. And though the rate has begun to level off in the last decade (Centers for Disease Control and Prevention, 2014), it is still the third leading cause of death, after accidents and homicides, among fifteen- to

persistent depressive disorder A pattern of depression in which the person shows the sad mood, lack of interest, and loss of pleasure associated with major depressive disorder but to a lesser degree and for a longer period.

twenty-four-year-olds (Centers for Disease Control and Prevention, 2014). Suicide is the second leading cause of death among college students; about 10,000 try to kill themselves each year and about 1,000 actually do so. These figures are much higher than for young people in general but much lower than for the elderly (NIMH, 2009). Women attempt suicide three times as often as men, but men are four times as likely to actually kill themselves (Centers for Disease Control and Prevention, 2014). The gender difference is even greater among people who have been diagnosed with depressive disorders. In this group, the male suicide rate of 65 per 100,000 is ten times higher than the rate for women (Blair-West et al., 1999; Centers for Disease Control and Prevention, 1999b). The suicide rate for men who are eighty-five or older is 55 per 100,000, which is more than ten times higher than for women in this age group (Centers for Disease Control and Prevention, 2004).

Suicide rates also differ across ethnic groups. Among males in the United States, for example, the overall rate for American Indians is 15.1 per 100,000, compared with 13.9 for European Americans, 5.7 for Asian Americans, 4.9 for Hispanic Americans, and 5.0 for African Americans. The same pattern of ethnic differences appears among women, though the actual rates are much lower (NIMH, 2009).

Predicting who will commit suicide is difficult. For one thing, suicidal thoughts are common. About 3 percent of all adults and as many as 10 percent of college students report having had such thoughts during the past year (Dawe, 2008; Kessler, Berglund, Borges et al., 2005). Still, hundreds of research studies provide some predictive guidelines (Liu & Miller, 2014; Smyth & MacLachian, 2005). In the United States, at least, suicide is most likely among European American males, especially those who are older than forty-five, single or divorced, and living alone. Extended unemployment increases the suicide risk for this group (Joska & Stein, 2008; Inoue et al., 2006). The risk is also heightened among people diagnosed with a mood disorder, anxiety disorder, or schizophrenia (e.g., Khan et al., 2002; Rihmer, 2001). Among the elderly, suicide is most common in males who suffer depression over health problems (e.g., Brown, Bongar, & Cleary, 2004). The risk is higher, too, in people who have made a specific plan, given away possessions, and are impulsive (Centers for Disease Control and Prevention, 2004; Kohli et al., 2010). Certain genetic risk factors combined with a history of child abuse may further increase the likelihood of a suicide attempt (Murphy et al., 2011). A previous suicide attempt may not always be a good predictor of eventual suicide, because such attempts may have been help-seeking gestures, not failed efforts to die (Nock & Kessler, 2006). In fact, although about 10 percent of unsuccessful attempters try again and succeed, most people who commit suicide had made no prior attempts (Clark & Fawcett, 1992).

You may have heard that people who talk about suicide will never try it. This is a myth (Shneidman, 1987). In fact, those who say they are thinking of suicide are much more likely than other people to attempt suicide. Most suicides are preceded by some kind of warning, whether direct ("I think I'm going to kill myself") or vague ("Sometimes I wonder if life is worth living"). Failure to recognize or respond to warning signs is common, even among psychologists (Fowler, 2012; Valuck et al., 2007). So although not everyone who threatens suicide follows through, if you suspect that someone you know is thinking about suicide, encourage the person to contact a mental health professional or a crisis hotline. If the danger is immediate, make the contact yourself and ask for advice about how to respond. Many suicide attempts—including those triggered by other suicides in the same town or school—can be prevented by social support and other forms of help for people at high risk (Centers for Disease Control and Prevention, 2014; Mann et al., 2005). For more information, visit suicide-related websites, such as that of the American Association of Suicidology.

Bipolar Disorders

bipolar disorders Conditions in which a person alternates between the two emotional extremes of depression and mania.

mania An elated, active emotional state.

The alternating appearance of two emotional extremes, or poles, characterizes **bipolar disorders**. In these disorders, episodes of depression alternate with **mania**, which is an extremely agitated and usually elated emotional state. During periods of mania, people tend to be overly optimistic, boundlessly energetic, certain of having extraordinary powers and abilities, and bursting with all sorts of ideas. They are irritated by anyone who tries to reason with them or "slow them down," and they may make impulsive and unwise decisions, including spending their life savings on foolish schemes; they can even become a danger to themselves or to others (Goldberg & Burdick, 2008; Ketter, 2010).

There are two versions of bipolar disorder, known as bipolar I and bipolar II. In *bipolar I disorder,* episodes of mania may alternate with periods of depression (Ghaemi, 2008). Sometimes periods of relatively normal mood separate these extremes (Tohen et al., 2003). This pattern has also been called *manic depression.* Compared with major depressive disorder, bipolar disorder is less common. It occurs in only about 1 percent of adults, and it affects men and women about equally. Another 1 percent of adults display *bipolar II disorder,* in which major depressive episodes alternate with episodes known as *hypomania,* which are less severe than the manic phases seen in bipolar I disorder (Merikangas et al., 2007). Either version can severely disrupt a person's ability to work or manage social relationships (American Psychiatric Association, 2013). Slightly more common is a pattern of milder mood swings known as **cyclothymic disorder**. Like depressive disorders, bipolar disorders are extremely disruptive to a person's ability to work or maintain social relationships, and they are often accompanied by anxiety disorders or substance abuse (Andreescu et al., 2007; Ghaemi, 2008). "In Review: Depressive and Bipolar Disorders" summarizes the main types of disorders affecting mood and activity.

IN REVIEW

DEPRESSIVE AND BIPOLAR DISORDERS

Type	Typical Symptoms	Related Features
Major Depressive Disorder	Deep sadness, feelings of worthlessness, changes in eating and sleeping habits, loss of interest and pleasure.	Lasts weeks or months; may occur in repeating episodes; severe cases may include delusions.
Persistent Depressive Disorder	Similar to major depression but less severe and longer lasting.	Hospitalization usually not necessary.
Bipolar Disorder	Alternating extremes of mood from deep depression to mania and back.	Manic episodes include impulsivity, unrealistic optimism, high energy, severe agitation.
Cyclothymic Disorder	Similar to bipolar disorder but less severe.	Hospitalization usually not necessary.

In Review Questions

1. The risk of suicide is associated with _____ more than with any other disorder.

2. Cyclothymic disorder is a less severe version of _____.

3. Women are _____ likely than men to try suicide, but men are _____ likely to succeed.

LINKAGES Are some psychological disorders inherited? (a link to Biological Aspects of Psychology)

cyclothymic disorder A bipolar disorder characterized by an alternating pattern of mood swings that is less extreme than that of bipolar I or II disorder.

Causes of Depressive and Bipolar Disorders

Research on the causes of depressive and bipolar disorders has focused on biological, psychological, and sociocultural risk factors. The more of these risk factors people have, the more likely they are to experience a depressive or bipolar disorder.

Biological Factors

Because some depressive disorders seem to run in families, it has long been suspected that genetic factors are involved in causing them (Gotlib, Joorman, & Foland-Ross, 2014). The role of genetics is suggested by the results of twin studies and family studies (Cuijpers et al., 2012; Fullerton et al., 2010). For example, bipolar disorder is much more likely to be seen in both members of genetically identical twin pairs than in nonidentical twins (Smoller, 2008). Family studies also show that those who are closely related to people with bipolar disorder are more likely than others to develop the disorder themselves (Althoff et al., 2005; Serretti et al., 2009). Major depressive disorder, too, is more likely to occur in both members of identical twins than in both members of nonidentical twins (Kendler et al., 2009; Levinson, 2006). Findings such as these suggest that genetic influences tend to be stronger for depressive and bipolar disorders (especially for bipolar I disorder and severe, early-onset depression) than for most other disorders.

Researchers have identified certain genetic variations that affect vulnerability to depressive and bipolar disorders. These include genes on chromosome 13 that are involved in the operation of the neurotransmitter serotonin (Hariri et al., 2005; Jacobs et al., 2006; Wilhelm et al., 2006). But genetic variations alone do not cause depressive and bipolar disorders. Rather, genes appear to act along with other biological, psychological, and environmental factors. For example, a version of the serotonin transporter gene appears to increase the likelihood that high amounts of stress will trigger depression (Caspi et al., 2010). Researchers in the field of epigenetics are investigating how genes associated with depressive and bipolar disorders can be "turned on" or "turned off" by environmental factors (Butcher, Mineka, & Hooley, 2010; Levinson et al., 2007).

Other biological factors that may contribute to these disorders include dysfunction of brain regions that are involved in mood, problems with the activity of certain brain neurotransmitter systems, changes in the endocrine system, disruption of biological rhythms, and altered development in brain areas such as the frontal lobes and hippocampus (e.g., Alloy et al., 2011; Butcher et al., 2010; Nurnberger et al., 2014). All of these conditions may themselves be influenced by genetics (Caspi et al., 2010).

Many brain regions are involved in mood, including the prefrontal cortex, the hippocampus, the amygdala, and other parts of the limbic system (Blumberg et al., 2003; MacQueen et al., 2003). How these regions are involved in depressive and bipolar disorders is not yet clear (e.g., Singh et al., 2013), but some researchers expect that particular disorders will eventually be shown to reflect problems in particular brain regions (Busatto, 2013; Savitz, Price, & Drevets, 2014). Some of the same brain regions, and many of the same genes, may also be involved in anxiety disorders, which may explain why depressive and anxiety disorders often occur together (Middeldorp et al., 2005; Vialou et al., 2014).

A role for the neurotransmitters norepinephrine, serotonin, and dopamine in depressive and bipolar disorders was suggested decades ago, when scientists discovered that drugs capable of altering these substances also relieved these disorders. However, the precise nature of the relationship between neurotransmitters and depression, for example, is still not fully understood. So despite what drug companies' advertisements might suggest, no one really knows exactly what "chemical imbalance" exists in the brains of depressed people (Sharp & Cowen, 2011).

Depressive disorders have also been related to malfunctions of the endocrine system, especially the subsystem involved in the body's responses to stress. For example, research shows that as many as 70 percent of depressed people secrete abnormally high levels of the stress hormone cortisol (Dinan, 2001; Posener et al., 2000). Studies of identical twins also suggest that higher levels of cortisol are associated with depression (Dinan, 2001; Wichers et al., 2008). Another hormone, oxytocin, is higher in individuals with depression and bipolar disorder, though the significance of this finding is not yet clear (Turan et al., 2013).

The cycles of mood swings seen in bipolar disorders and in recurring episodes of major depressive disorder suggest that these disorders may be related to stressful triggering events (Hammen, 2005; Keller & Nesse, 2006). They may also be related to disturbances in the body's biological clock, which is described in the chapter on consciousness (Griesauer et al., 2014; Salgado-Delgado et al., 2011). This second possibility seems especially likely in the 15 percent of depressed people who consistently experience a calendar-linked pattern

Treating SAD

Seasonal affective disorder (SAD) can often be relieved by exposure to full-spectrum light for as little as a couple of hours a day (Terman & Terman, 2005).

© iStock.com/kbwills

of depressive episodes known as *seasonal affective disorder (SAD)*. During months of shorter daylight, these people slip into severe depression, accompanied by irritability and excessive sleeping (Durand & Barlow, 2006; Vyssoki et al., 2012). Their depression tends to lift as daylight hours lengthen (Faedda et al., 1993). Disruption of biological rhythms is also suggested by the fact that many depressed people tend to have trouble sleeping, partly because during the day their biological clocks may be telling them it is the middle of the night. Resetting the biological clock through methods such as sleep deprivation or light stimulation has relieved depression in many cases (Lavoie et al., 2009).

Psychological and Social Factors

Researchers have come to recognize that the biological factors involved in depressive and bipolar disorders always operate in combination with psychological and social factors (Cuijpers et al., 2012). As mentioned earlier, the very nature of depressive symptoms can depend on the culture in which a person lives. Biopsychosocial explanations for these disorders also emphasize the impact of social isolation, anxiety, and negative thinking; other psychological and emotional responses triggered by stressful events such as trauma; and the impact of cultural factors. For example, the higher rate of depression among females—especially poor ethnic-minority single mothers—has been attributed to their greater exposure to stressors of all kinds (Nolen-Hoeksema, 2006; Siddique et al., 2012). Environmental stressors affect men, too, which may be one reason that gender differences are smaller in countries in which men and women face equally stressful lives (Bierut et al., 1999).

A number of social-cognitive theories suggest that the way that people think about stressors affects the likelihood of depressive disorders. One such theory is based on the *learned helplessness* research described in the chapter on learning. Just as animals become inactive and appear depressed when they have no control over negative events (El Yacoubi et al., 2003), humans may experience depression as a result of feeling incapable of controlling their lives, especially stressors confronting them (Alloy et al., 2008; Seligman, 1991). But most of us have limited control, so why aren't we all depressed? The ways that people learn to think about events in their lives may hold the key. For example, Aaron Beck's cognitive theory of depression suggests that depressed people develop mental habits of (1) blaming themselves when things go wrong; (2) focusing on and exaggerating the negative side of events; and (3) jumping to overly generalized, pessimistic conclusions. Such cognitive habits, says Beck, are errors that lead to depressing thoughts and other depression symptoms (Beck, 2008). Depressed people, in fact, do tend to think about significant negative events in ways that are likely to increase or prolong depression (e.g., Gotlib et al., 2004; Morris, Ciesla & Garber, 2008).

Severe, long-lasting depression is especially likely among people who blame their lack of control or other problems on a permanent, generalized lack of personal competence rather than on a temporary condition or some external cause (Seligman et al., 1988). This *negative attributional style* may be another important cognitive factor in depression (Alloy et al., 2006; Ball et al., 2008). Are depressed people's unusually negative beliefs about themselves actually helping to cause their depression or are they merely symptoms of it? To answer this question, some studies have assessed the attributional styles of large samples of nondepressed people and then kept in touch with them to see whether individuals with negative self-beliefs are more likely to become depressed when stressors occur. These longitudinal studies suggest that a negative attributional style is, in fact, a risk factor for depression, not just a result of being depressed. In one study, for example, adolescents who held strong negative self-beliefs were more likely than other youngsters to develop depression when faced with stress later in life (Lewinsohn, Joiner, & Rohde, 2001).

Social-cognitive theorists also suggest that whether depression continues or worsens depends in part on how people respond once they start to feel depressed. People who continuously dwell on negative events, on why they occur, and even on being depressed are likely to feel more and more depressed (e.g., Just & Alloy, 1997; McMurrich & Johnson, 2008). Research by Susan Nolen-Hoeksema (2012; McLaughlin & Nolen-Hoeksema,

2011) suggests that this *ruminative style* is especially characteristic of women and may help explain gender differences in the frequency of depression. She found that when men start to feel sad, they tend to use a *distracting style*, engaging in activity that distracts them from their concerns and helps bring them out of their depressed mood (Nolen-Hoeksema, 2012).

Notice that social-cognitive explanations of depression are consistent with the diathesis-stress approach (Hankin & Abramson, 2001). These explanations suggest that certain cognitive styles serve as a predisposition (or diathesis) that makes a person vulnerable to depression, which is made even more likely by stressors. As suggested in the chapter on health, stress, and coping, the depressing effects of these stressors are likely to be magnified by lack of social support, inadequate coping skills, and the presence of other stressful conditions, such as poverty (e.g., Nikulina, Widom, & Czaja, 2011; Stice, Ragan, & Randall, 2004).

Given the number and complexity of biological, psychological, social, and situational factors potentially involved in causing depressive and bipolar disorders, the diathesis-stress approach appears to be an especially appropriate guide to future research (Kendler, Gardner, & Prescott, 2006). Indeed, some researchers are integrating the various factors into predictive and causal models. For instance, Kenneth Kendler and his colleagues have described specific sets of risk factors for depression in women that appear at five developmental stages, including childhood, early adolescence, late adolescence, adulthood, and in the year preceding the diagnosis of depression (Kendler, Gardner, & Prescott, 2006).

In the final analysis, it may turn out that each subtype of depressive and bipolar disorder is caused by a unique combination of factors. The challenge for researchers is to identify these subtypes and map out their causal ingredients (American Psychiatric Association, 2013; Eshel & Roiser, 2010).

SCHIZOPHRENIA SPECTRUM AND OTHER PSYCHOTIC DISORDERS

Is schizophrenia the same as "split personality"?

Schizophrenia (pronounced "skit-so-FREE-nee-uh") is a pattern of severely disturbed thinking, emotion, perception, and behavior that seriously impairs the ability to communicate and relate to others, and disrupts most other aspects of daily life (Green & Horan, 2010; Hooley, 2010). It appears in a wide range, or spectrum, of severity, and its designation as *psychotic* reflects the fact that its various forms are among the most severe and disabling of all mental disorders. (*Psychosis* refers to conditions that leave people "out of touch with reality" or unable to function in society.)

Schizophrenia's core symptoms are seen virtually everywhere in the world, though in less than 1 percent of the population (American Psychiatric Association, 2013). In the United States, it appears about equally in various ethnic groups, but like most disorders, it tends to be diagnosed more frequently in economically disadvantaged populations. It is seen about equally in men and women, although in women it may appear later in life, be less severe, and respond better to treatment (Aleman, Kahn, & Selten, 2003; American Psychiatric Association, 2013).

Schizophrenia tends to develop in adolescents or young adults. In about three out of four cases, symptoms start gradually over a few years; in other cases, the onset is more rapid. Longitudinal studies suggest that about 40 percent of people diagnosed with schizophrenia improve with treatment and function reasonably well; the rest continue to show symptoms that permanently impair their functioning (Harrow & Jobe, 2005; Jobe & Harrow, 2010) and— especially for those with a drug abuse problem—may lead to homelessness (Timms, 2005). A strong predictor of treatment outcome is *premorbid adjustment,* which refers to the level of functioning a person had achieved before schizophrenia symptoms first appeared. Improvement is more likely in those who had reached

schizophrenia A pattern of severely disturbed thinking, emotion, perception, and behavior that constitutes one of the most serious and disabling of all mental disorders.

higher levels of education and employment and who had supportive relationships with family and friends (Keshavan et al., 2005; Rabinowitz et al., 2002).

As described in the next section, schizophrenia symptoms can vary widely from person to person, and the severity of symptoms can range from mild to extreme.

Symptoms of Schizophrenia

The main problems seen in people with schizophrenia relate to thinking—both how they think and what they think (Heinrichs, 2005). Indeed, the very word *schizophrenia,* or "split mind," refers to the oddities of schizophrenic thinking, including a splitting of normally integrated mental processes, such as thoughts and feelings. So the person may giggle while talking about sad events and claiming to feel unhappy. Contrary to common usage, schizophrenia does not refer to the "split personality" seen in dissociative identity disorder (multiple personality disorder).

Schizophrenic thought and language are often disorganized, as illustrated in the following letter that arrived in the mail several years ago:

Dear Sirs:

Pertaining to our continuing failure to prosecute violations of minor's rights to sovereign equality which are occurring in gestations being compromised by the ingestion of controlled substances, … the skewing of androgyny which continues in female juveniles even after separation from their mother's has occurred, and as a means of promulflagitating my paying Governor Hickel of Alaska for my employees to have personal services endorsements and controlled substance endorsements, … the Iraqi oil being released by the United Nations being identified as Kurdistanian oil, and the July, 1991 issue of the Siberian Review spells President Eltsin's name without a letter y.

People with schizophrenia may create *neologisms,* or new words, that are usually nonsensical and have meaning only to the person speaking them. The word "promulflagitating" in the preceding letter is one example. The letter also illustrates *loose associations,* the tendency for one thought to be logically unconnected or only loosely connected to the next. In the most severe cases, thought becomes just a jumble known as *word salad.* For example, one patient was heard to say, "Upon the advisability of held keeping, environment of the seabeach gathering, to the forest stream, reinstatement to be placed, poling the paddleboat, of the swamp morass, to the forest compensation of the dunce" (Lehman, 1967, p. 627).

The content of schizophrenic thinking is also disturbed. Often it includes a bewildering assortment of *delusions* (false beliefs), especially *delusions of persecution.* Some patients believe that space aliens or government agents are trying to steal their internal organs, and they may interpret everything from TV commercials to casual hand gestures as part of the plot. Delusions that such common events are somehow related to oneself are called *ideas of reference. Delusions of grandeur* may also appear; one young man was convinced that the president of the United States was trying to contact him for advice. Other types of delusions include *thought broadcasting,* in which patients believe that their thoughts can be heard by others; *thought blocking* or *thought withdrawal,* the belief that someone is either preventing thoughts or "stealing" them as they appear; and *thought insertion,* the belief that other people's thoughts are appearing in one's own mind. Some patients believe that their behavior is being controlled by others; in one case, a man claimed that the CIA had placed a control device in his brain. Such delusions tend to be deeply entrenched and resistant to change, no matter how strong the evidence against them (Minzenberg et al., 2008; Woodward et al., 2006).

Hallucinations, or false perceptions that are not caused by sensory stimuli from the environment, are common in schizophrenia. Often, schizophrenic hallucinations emerge as voices. These voices may sound like an overheard conversation or they may urge the person

hallucinations False or distorted perceptions of objects or events.

LINKAGES   Do people perceive hallucinations as real sensory events? (a link to
Sensation and Perception)

to do or not to do things. Sometimes they comment on, narrate, or (most often) criticize the person's actions. Hallucinations can also involve the experience of nonexistent sights, smells, tastes, and touch sensations. The brain areas activated during hallucinations are related to those that respond to real sights and sounds (Simons et al., 2010).

People with schizophrenia often say that they cannot focus their attention. They may feel overwhelmed as they try to attend to everything at once. Various perceptual disorders may also appear. The person may feel detached from the world and see other people as flat cutouts. The body may feel like a machine or parts of it may seem to be dead or rotting. Emotional expression is often muted—a pattern called *flat affect*. But when people with schizophrenia do display emotion, it is often exaggerated or inappropriate (Kring et al., 2011; Kring & Caponigro, 2010), For example, they may cry for no apparent reason or fly into a rage in response to a simple question.

Some people with schizophrenia are quite agitated, constantly fidgeting, grimacing, or pacing the floor in ritualized patterns. Others become so withdrawn that they move very little. Lack of motivation and poor social skills, deteriorating personal hygiene, and an inability to function in everyday situations are other common characteristics of schizophrenia.

The Schizophrenia Spectrum

Researchers have made some useful distinctions among various forms of schizophrenia. One of these distinctions involves the presence of positive versus negative symptoms. Disorganized thoughts, delusions, and hallucinations are sometimes called *positive symptoms* of schizophrenia, because they appear as undesirable *additions* to a person's mental life (Iancu et al., 2005; Smith et al., 2006). In contrast, the absence of pleasure and motivation, lack of emotion, social withdrawal, reduced speech, and other deficits seen in schizophrenia are sometimes called *negative symptoms,* because they appear to *subtract* elements from normal mental life (Batki et al., 2008). Many patients exhibit both positive and negative symptoms, but when the negative symptoms are stronger, schizophrenia generally has a more severe course, including long-term disability and relative lack of response to treatment (e.g., Kirkpatrick et al., 2006; Milev et al., 2005; Prikryl et al., 2006).

Yet another way of categorizing schizophrenia symptoms focuses on whether they are *psychotic* (e.g., hallucinations or delusions), *disorganized* (e.g., incoherent speech, chaotic behavior, or inappropriate affect), or *negative* (e.g., lack of speech or motivation). The fact that, like positive and negative symptoms, these dimensions of schizophrenia are to some extent independent from one another suggests to some researchers that each symptom cluster or dimension may ultimately be traceable to different causes that may require different treatments (Jones & Meaden, 2012).

The schizophrenia spectrum also includes other diagnoses that share features with schizophrenia. For example, people diagnosed with *schizoaffective disorder* show symptoms of both schizophrenia and depression. *Schizophreniform disorder* is characterized by schizophrenia-like symptoms that do not last as long as those typically seen in schizophrenia, and in *delusional disorder*, symptoms mainly involve a persistent pattern of false beliefs.

Causes of Schizophrenia

The search for causes of schizophrenia has been more intense than for any other psychological disorder. The findings so far confirm one thing for certain: as with other disorders, biological, psychological, and sociocultural factors combine to cause or worsen all forms of schizophrenia (Sullivan, Kendler, & Neale, 2003; Tandon, Nasrallah, & Keshaven, 2009).

Biological Factors

Research in behavioral genetics shows that schizophrenia runs in families (Gottesman et al., 2010). If one person in a family is diagnosed with schizophrenia, the risk that another family member will receive the same diagnosis increases in proportion with their genetic similarity (Kasper & Papadimitriou, 2009). Even if they are adopted by families in which there is no schizophrenia, the children of parents with schizophrenia are ten times more likely to develop schizophrenia than adopted children whose biological parents do not have schizophrenia (Kety et al., 1994; Tienari et al., 2003). But even though identical twins have virtually identical genes, the appearance of schizophrenia in one of them does not guarantee that the other will be diagnosed as well. In fact, the rate of shared diagnosis is only about 50 percent, which suggests that genetics alone cannot explain the disorder. Further, it is unlikely that a single gene transmits schizophrenia (Plomin & McGuffin, 2003; Pogue-Geile, & Yokley, 2010). Rather, several genes on several chromosome pairs are probably involved, and probably combine with nongenetic factors to cause the disorder. Researchers in the field of epigenetics are studying how environmental factors alter the expression of genes associated with schizophrenia (Akbarian, 2010; Pogue-Geile, & Yokley, 2010).

The search for biological factors in schizophrenia also focuses on a number of abnormalities in the structure, functioning, and chemistry of the brain that tend to appear in people with schizophrenia (e.g., Grace, 2010; Lynall et al., 2010; Meyer-Lindenberg, 2010; Rasmussen et al., 2010; van Haren et al., 2012). For example, as shown in Figure 14.4, brain-imaging studies have compared schizophrenia patients with other mental patients (Salgado-Pineda et al., 2010). Many patients with schizophrenia (especially those who display mostly negative symptoms) have less tissue in areas of the brain that are involved in emotional expression, thinking, and information processing—functions that are disordered in schizophrenia (e.g., Arango et al., 2012; Goto, Yang, & Otani, 2010; Rimol, Nesvåg et al., 2012; Ursu et al., 2011). There is also evidence that worsening symptoms are associated with continued tissue loss in these areas (Ho et al., 2003). Patients with mainly positive symptoms tend to have essentially normal-looking brains (Andreasen, 1997).

Researchers are also investigating the possibility that abnormalities in brain chemistry—especially in neurotransmitter systems that use dopamine—play a role in causing or intensifying the symptoms of schizophrenia (Javitt & Kantrowitz, 2009; Tan et al., 2007). Because drugs that block the brain's dopamine receptors often reduce the hallucinations, disordered thinking, and other positive symptoms of schizophrenia, some investigators speculate that schizophrenia results from excess dopamine. Other research suggests that excessive activity in dopamine systems may be related to the appearance of these positive symptoms (Buchsbaum et al., 2006; Winterer, 2006). However, the relationship between dopamine and schizophrenia may be more complex than that. For example, it may be that changes in the ratio of dopamine to other neurochemicals, particularly in the region of the thalamus, are involved in the difficulties experienced by people with schizophrenia in distinguishing genuine sights and sounds from those produced by neural "noise" within the brain (Buchsbaum et al., 2006; Winterer, 2006).

FIGURE 14.4
Brain Abnormalities in Schizophrenia

Here is a magnetic resonance imaging (MRI) comparison of the brains of identical twins. The schizophrenic twin (photo at right) has greatly enlarged ventricles (see arrows) and correspondingly less brain tissue, including in the hippocampal area, a region involved in memory and emotion. The same results appeared in fourteen other identical-twin pairs. By contrast, no significant differences appeared between members of a seven-pair control group of normal identical twins (Suddath et al., 1990). These results support the idea that brain abnormalities are associated with schizophrenia and, because identical twins have the same genes, that such abnormalities may stem from nongenetic factors (Baare et al., 2001).

National Institute of Mental Health

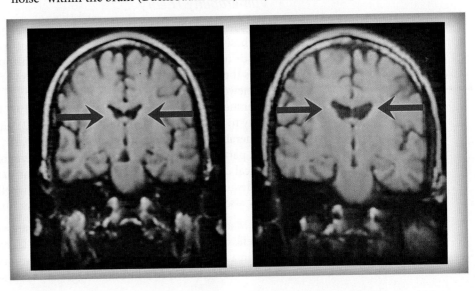

Some researchers are integrating genetic and environmental explanations for schizophrenia by looking for *neurodevelopmental* abnormalities (e.g., Meyer et al., 2005; Rapoport, Addington, & Frangou, 2005). Perhaps, they say, some disorders in the schizophrenia spectrum arise from disruptions in brain development during the period from before birth through childhood, when the brain is growing and its various functions are maturing (King, St-Hilaire, & Heidkamp, 2010; Walker et al., 2010). For instance, pre-natal exposure to physical trauma, flu, or other infections is associated with increased risk for developing schizophrenia (e.g., Brown & Derkits, 2010; Subotnik et al., 2006). The expression of a genetically transmitted predisposition for brain abnormality may be enhanced by environmental factors such as maternal drug use during pregnancy, oxygen deprivation or other complications during birth, or childhood malnutrition (Sørensen et al., 2003; NIMH, 2008b). For example, as mentioned earlier, smaller-than-normal prefrontal lobes and other brain structures appear to constitute an inherited predisposition for schizophrenia. However, reduced brain growth alone is not sufficient to cause the disorder. When only one member of an identical-twin pair has schizophrenia, both tend to have unusually small brains, but the schizophrenic twin's brain in each pair is the smaller of the two (Baare et al., 2001). This finding suggests that some environmental influence caused degeneration in an already underdeveloped brain, making it even more prone to function abnormally.

Psychological and Sociocultural Factors

Psychological processes and sociocultural influences can contribute to the appearance of schizophrenia and influence its course (Kealy, 2005; Vahia & Cohen, 2009). Among the factors cited are dysfunctional cognitive habits, the stress of urban living, the stigma of being labeled with a severe mental disorder, being an immigrant, and exposure to stressful family communication patterns (e.g., Henry, von Hippel, & Shapiro, 2010; Mueser & Jeste, 2009). For example, criticism by family members—sometimes called *expressed emotion*—is associated with more severe symptoms (Nomura et al., 2005; Polanczyk et al., 2010). And if individuals with schizophrenia live with relatives who are critical, unsupportive, or emotionally overinvolved, they're especially likely to relapse following initial improvement (Hooley, 2004). Family members' negative attitudes may be a source of stress that actually increases the chances that disruptive or odd behaviors will persist or worsen (Rosenfarb et al., 1995). Keep in mind, though, that the strange and often disturbing behavior of a family member with schizophrenia can place tremendous strain on the rest of the family, making it harder for them to remain helpful and supportive (Kymalainen et al., 2006; Rosenfarb, Bellack, & Aziz, 2006). In any case, patients who are helped to cope with potentially damaging family influences tend to have better long-term outcomes (Bustillo et al., 2001; Velligan et al., 2000).

Vulnerability Theory

All the causal theories of schizophrenia we have outlined are consistent with the diathesis-stress approach, which assumes that stress activates a person's predisposition for disorder (Stahl, 2007). ("In Review: Schizophrenia Spectrum Disorders" summarizes these theories, as well as the symptoms of schizophrenia.) In fact, a diathesis-stress framework forms the basis for the *vulnerability theory* of schizophrenia (Cornblatt & Erlenmeyer-Kimling, 1985; Zubin & Spring, 1977). This theory suggests that (1) vulnerability to schizophrenia is mainly biological; (2) different people have differing degrees of vulnerability; (3) vulnerability is influenced partly by genetic influences on development and partly by abnormalities that arise from environmental risk factors; and (4) psychological components, such as exposure to poor parenting, a high-stress environment, or inadequate coping skills, may help determine whether schizophrenia actually appears and may also influence its course (van Os, Kenis, & Rutten, 2010; Wearden et al., 2000).

Many different blends of vulnerability and stress can lead to schizophrenia. People whose genetic characteristics or prenatal experiences leave them vulnerable to developing schizophrenia may be especially likely to do so if they are later exposed to learning experiences, family conflicts, or other stressors that trigger and maintain schizophrenic patterns of thought and action. Those same experiences and stressors would not be expected to lead to schizophrenia in people who are less vulnerable to developing the disorder. In other words, schizophrenia is a highly complex spectrum of related disorders (Kirkpatrick et al., 2001; Lenzenweger, McLachlan, & Rubin, 2007) whose origins appear to lie in numerous biological, psychological, and sociocultural domains, some of which are yet to be discovered (Gilmore, 2010).

SCHIZOPHRENIA SPECTRUM DISORDERS   IN REVIEW

Aspect	Key Features
Common Symptoms	
Disorders of thought	Disturbed content, including delusions; disorganization, including loose associations, neologisms, and word salad.
Disorders of perception	Hallucinations or false perceptions; poorly focused attention.
Disorders of emotion	Flat affect; inappropriate tears, laughter, or anger.
Possible Causes	
Biological	Genetics; abnormalities in brain structure; abnormalities in dopamine systems; neuro-developmental problems.
Psychological and sociocultural	Learned maladaptive behavior; disturbed patterns of family communication.

In Review Questions

1. The _____ approach forms the basis of the vulnerability theory of schizophrenia.

2. Hallucinations are _____ symptoms of schizophrenia; lack of emotion is a _____ symptom.

3. Patients with schizophrenia who were able to finish school are _____ likely to show improvement.

PERSONALITY DISORDERS

Which personality disorder often leads to crime?

Personality disorders are long-standing, relatively inflexible ways of behaving that are not so much severe mental disorders as dysfunctional styles of living (McMurran, 2012). Some psychologists view these disorders as habitual interpersonal strategies (Kiesler, 1996) or as extreme, rigid, and maladaptive expressions of personality traits (Widiger, 2008). In order to be labeled as personality disorders rather than just, say, annoying or unsatisfactory lifestyles, they must be judged by a diagnostician to have reached a level of severity that affects all areas of functioning and, beginning in childhood or adolescence, create problems for those who display them and for others (American Psychiatric Association, 2013).

The ten personality disorders listed in DSM-5 are grouped into three clusters that share certain features (see Table 14.4). The *odd-eccentric* cluster (Cluster A) includes paranoid,

personality disorders Long-standing, inflexible ways of behaving that become styles of life that create problems for the person affected and/or others.

TABLE 14.4   PERSONALITY DISORDERS

Here are brief descriptions of the ten personality disorders listed in DSM-5.

	Type	Typical Features
Cluster A (odd-eccentric)	Paranoid	Suspiciousness and distrust of others, all of whom are assumed to be hostile.
	Schizoid	Detachment from social relationships; restricted range of emotion.
	Schizotypal	Detachment from and great discomfort in social relationships; odd perceptions, thoughts, beliefs, and behaviors.
Cluster B (dramatic-erratic)	Histrionic	Excessive emotionality and preoccupation with being the center of attention, emotional shallowness, overly dramatic behavior.
	Narcissistic	Exaggerated ideas of self-importance and achievements, preoccupation with fantasies of success, arrogance.
	Borderline	Lack of stability in interpersonal relationships, self-image, and emotion; impulsivity; angry outbursts; intense fear of abandonment; recurring suicidal gestures.
	Antisocial	Shameless disregard for and violation of other people's rights.
Cluster C (anxious-fearful)	Dependent	Helplessness, excessive need to be taken care of, submissive and clinging behavior, difficulty in making decisions.
	Obsessive-compulsive	Preoccupation with orderliness, perfection, and control.
	Avoidant	Inhibition in social situations, feelings of inadequacy, oversensitivity to criticism.

schizoid, and schizotypal personality disorders. People diagnosed as having *schizotypal personality disorder,* for example, display some of the peculiarities seen in schizophrenia but are not disturbed enough to be labeled as having schizophrenia. The *dramatic-erratic* cluster (Cluster B) includes the histrionic, narcissistic, borderline, and antisocial personality disorders. The main characteristics of *narcissistic personality disorder,* for example, are an exaggerated sense of self-importance, extreme sensitivity to criticism, a constant need for attention, and a tendency to arrogantly overestimate personal abilities and achievements. Finally, the *anxious-fearful* cluster (Cluster C) includes dependent, obsessive-compulsive, and avoidant personality disorders. *Avoidant personality disorder,* for example, is similar to social anxiety disorder in the sense that people labeled with this disorder tend to be "loners" with a long-standing pattern of avoiding social situations and of being particularly sensitive to criticism or rejection.

Personality disorder diagnoses are controversial, partly because people with these diagnoses sometimes produce more distress in others than in themselves, so the role of social and moral judgment in deciding who is disordered comes into play (McMurran, 2012). In addition, the overlap among symptoms of some of the personality disorders makes diagnosis difficult (Widiger, Livesley, & Clark, 2009). Studies that use symptom checklists or other behavioral measures to diagnose these disorders, as well as those that use molecular genetic data, generally identify either three or four clusters, not always what

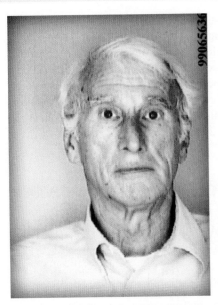

A Classic Case of Antisocial Personality Disorder

Alfred Jack Oakley meets women through personal ads, claiming to be a millionaire movie producer, pilot, and novelist. In reality, he is a penniless con artist who uses his smooth-talking charm to gain the women's trust so he can steal from them. In January 2000, after being convicted of stealing a Florida woman's Mercedes, Oakley complimented the prosecutor's skills and the jury's wisdom and claimed remorse. The judge appeared to see through this ploy ("I don't believe there is a sincere word that ever comes out of your mouth"), but it was still effective enough to get Oakley probation instead of jail time!

Hillsborough County Sheriff, Tampa, Florida

antisocial personality disorder A long-term, persistent pattern of impulsive, selfish, unscrupulous, even criminal behavior.

would be expected according to DSM-5 (Fossati et al., 2006; Livesley, 2005). Some critics have suggested that there is gender bias in the application of diagnoses—pointing to the fact that women are labeled as borderline much more often than men, while men are labeled as antisocial more often than women (Bjorklund, 2006; Boggs et al., 2009). Even the stability of personality disorders over the lifetime has been questioned (Durbin & Klein, 2006).

The most serious, costly, and intensively studied personality disorder is **antisocial personality disorder**. It is marked by a long-term pattern of irresponsible, impulsive, unscrupulous, and sometimes criminal behavior, beginning in childhood or early adolescence (Hare, Neumann, & Widiger, 2012; Moreira et al., 2014). In the nineteenth century, the pattern was called *moral insanity* because the people displaying it appear to have no morals or common decency. Later, people in this category were called *psychopaths* or *sociopaths* (Coid & Ullrich, 2010; Hare & Newmann, 2009). The current "antisocial personality" label used in DSM-5 more accurately portrays them as troublesome but not "insane" by the legal standards we discuss later (Skeem et al., 2011). About 3 percent of men and about 1 percent of women in the United States fall into this diagnostic category (American Psychiatric Association, 2013; Hodgins, 2007).

At their least troublesome, these people are a nuisance. They are often charming, intelligent "fast talkers" who borrow money and fail to return it; they are arrogant, selfish manipulators who "con" people into doing things for them, usually by lying and taking advantage of the decency and trust of others. At their most troublesome, people with this disorder are criminals, sometimes violent ones. Persistent violent offenders, most of whom have antisocial personality disorder, make up less than 5 percent of the male population, but they commit over 50 percent of violent crimes (Hodgins, 2007). A hallmark of those displaying antisocial personality is a lack of anxiety, remorse, or guilt, whether they have wrecked a borrowed car or killed an innocent person (Gray et al., 2003; Hare & Newmann, 2009).

No method has yet been found for permanently altering the behavior of individuals with antisocial personality disorder (Hare et al., 2012). Research suggests that the best hope for dealing with them is to identify their antisocial personalities early, before the most treatment-resistant traits are fully developed (Compton et al., 2005; Diamantopoulou, Verhulst, & van der Ende, 2010). Fortunately, these individuals tend to become less active and dangerous after about age forty (Hare et al., 2012). If, as sometimes happens, people with milder forms of antisocial personality disorder also have a certain degree of conscientiousness, they may become successful in socially acceptable roles, often in the world of politics or business (Mullins-Sweatt, et al., 2010).

You might wonder whether terrorists and suicide bombers should be classified as antisocial personalities—after all, they exhibit violent and disruptive behavior in the extreme. Some terrorists do exhibit the characteristics of antisocial personality disorder, but most do not (Martens, 2004). Acts of terrorism are probably better explained from the perspective of social and political psychology—terrorists are spurred to take extreme destructive measures by political and religious ideologies during intense group conflict (Saucier et al., 2009). In short, the psychology of group conflict and war might better explain the terrorism of today, just as it might have explained the terrifying behavior of Japanese kamikaze pilots during World War II.

There are numerous theories about the causes of antisocial personality disorder. Some research suggests a genetic predisposition (Arseneault et al., 2003; Larsson, Andershed, & Lichtenstein, 2006), possibly in the form of abnormal brain development, impaired neurological functioning, deficits in the ability to encode or recall emotional information, or chronic underarousal of both the autonomic and central nervous systems (e.g., Craig et al., 2009; Crozier et al., 2008; Raine et al., 2005; Visser et al., 2010). This underarousal may render people less sensitive to punishment and more likely to seek excitement than is normally the case (Fowles & Dindo, 2009; Gao et al., 2010). Broken homes, rejection by parents, poor discipline, lack of good parental models, lack of attachment to early caregivers, impulsivity, conflict-filled childhoods, and poverty have all been suggested as psychological and sociocultural factors that contribute to the development of antisocial personality disorder (e.g., Caspi et al., 2004; Lahey et al., 1995; Lyman & Gudonis, 2005). The biopsychosocial approach suggests that antisocial personality disorder results when these psychosocial and environmental conditions combine with a genetic predisposition to low arousal and the sensation seeking and impulsivity associated with it (Beach, et al., 2010; Diamantopoulou, Verhulst, & van der Ende, 2010).

FOCUS ON RESEARCH METHODS
EXPLORING LINKS BETWEEN CHILD ABUSE AND ANTISOCIAL PERSONALITY DISORDER

Exploring Links between Child Abuse and Antisocial Personality Disorder

One of the most prominent environmental factors associated with the more violent forms of antisocial personality disorder is the experience of abuse in childhood (MacMillan et al., 2001). However, most of the studies that have found a relationship between childhood abuse and antisocial personality disorder have been potentially biased (Monane, Leichter, & Lewis, 1984; Rosenbaum & Bennett, 1986). People with antisocial personalities—especially those with criminal records—are likely to make up stories of abuse to shift the blame for their behavior onto others. Even if their reports were accurate, however, most of these studies didn't compare the abuse histories of antisocial people with those of a control group from similar backgrounds who did not become antisocial. This research design flaw has made it almost impossible to separate the effects of reported child abuse from the effects of poverty or other factors that might also have contributed to the development of antisocial personality disorder.

What was the researcher's question?

Can childhood abuse cause antisocial personality disorder? To help answer this question and to correct some of the flaws in earlier studies, Cathy Widom (1989) used a *prospective* research design. They first found cases of childhood abuse and then followed the affected people over time to look at the effects of that abuse on adult behavior.

How did the researcher answer the question?

Widom began by identifying 416 adults whose backgrounds included official records of their having been physically or sexually abused before the age of eleven. She then explored the stories of these people's lives as told in police and school records as well as in a two-hour diagnostic interview. To reduce experimenter bias and distorted reporting, Widom made sure that the interviewers did not know the purpose of the study and that the respondents were told only that the study's purpose was to talk to people who had grown up in an urban area of the midwestern United States in the late 1960s and early 1970s. Widom also selected a comparison group of 283 people who had no histories of abuse but who were similar to the abused sample in terms of age, gender, ethnicity, hospital of birth, schools attended, and area of residence. Her goal was to obtain a nonabused control group that had been exposed to approximately the same environmental risk factors and socioeconomic conditions as the abused children.

What did the researcher find?

First, Widom (1989) tested the hypothesis that exposure to abuse in childhood is associated with criminality and/or violence in later life. She found that 26 percent of the abused youngsters went on to commit juvenile crimes, 29 percent were arrested as adults, and 11 percent committed violent crimes. These percentages were significantly higher than the figures for the nonabused group. The correlations between criminality and abuse were higher for males

(continued)

than for females and higher for African Americans than for European Americans. And overall, victims of physical abuse were more likely to commit violent crimes as adults than were victims of sexual abuse.

Next, Widom tested the hypothesis that childhood abuse is associated with the development of antisocial personality disorder (Luntz & Widom, 1994). She found that the abused group did show a significantly higher rate of antisocial personality disorder (13.5 percent) than the comparison group (7.1 percent). The apparent role of abuse in antisocial personality disorder was particularly pronounced in men, and it remained strong even when other factors—such as age, ethnicity, and socioeconomic status—were accounted for in the statistical analyses. One other factor—failure to graduate from high school—was also strongly associated with the appearance of antisocial personality, regardless of whether childhood abuse had occurred.

What do the results mean?

Widom's research supported earlier studies in finding an association between childhood abuse and criminality, violence, and antisocial personality disorder. Further, although her study did not permit a firm conclusion that abuse alone causes antisocial personality disorder, the data from its prospective design added strength to the argument that abuse may be an important causal factor (Widom, 2000). This interpretation is supported by the results of research by other investigators (Dudeck et al., 2007; Jaffee et al., 2004; McGrath, Nilsen, & Kerley, 2011). Finally, Widom's work offers yet another reason (as if more reasons were needed) why it is so important to prevent the physical and sexual abuse of children. The long-term consequences of such abuse can be tragic not only for its immediate victims but also for those victimized by the criminal actions and antisocial behavior of some abused children as they grow up (Weiler & Widom, 1996; Widom, Czaja, & Dutton, 2008).

What do we still need to know?

Widom's results suggest that child abuse can have a broad range of effects, all of which can derail normal childhood development. It is not yet clear, though, how abuse combines with other risk factors such as genetics or differences in neurocognitive functioning. More research is obviously needed to discover whether antisocial personality disorder stems from abuse itself, from one of the factors accompanying it, or from some specific combination of known and still-unknown risk factors (Beach et al., 2010). The importance of combined and interacting risk factors is suggested by the fact that abuse is often part of a larger pool of experiences, such as exposure to deviant models, social rejection, and poor supervision. For instance, child abuse might increase the likelihood of encountering stressful events later in life (Horwitz et al., 2001), thus creating a general vulnerability to a variety of psychological disorders, including antisocial personality disorder (Scott, Smith, & Ellis, 2010). Until we understand how all these potentially causal pieces fit together, we will not fully understand the role childhood abuse plays in the chain of events leading to antisocial personality disorder.

We need to know more, too, about why such a small percentage of the abused children in Widom's sample displayed violence, criminal behavior, and antisocial personality disorder. These results raise the question of which genetic characteristics or environmental experiences serve to protect children from at least some of the devastating effects of abuse (Flores, Cicchetti, & Rogosch, 2005; Rind, Tromovitch, & Bauserman, 1998). As described in the chapter on human development, some clues have already been found, but a better understanding of what these protective elements are might go a long way toward the development of programs to prevent antisocial personality disorder.

SOME ADDITIONAL PSYCHOLOGICAL DISORDERS

How do children's disorders differ from adults' disorders?

The disorders described so far represent some of the most common and socially disruptive psychological problems. Several others are mentioned in other chapters. In the chapter on consciousness, for example, we discuss insomnia, apnea, night terrors, and other sleep-wake disorders; intellectual disability is covered in the chapter on intelligence; and posttraumatic stress disorder is described in the chapter on health, stress, and coping. Here we consider two other significant psychological problems: neurodevelopmental disorders and substance-related and addictive disorders.

Neurodevelopmental Disorders

The physical, cognitive, emotional, and social changes that occur in childhood—and the stress associated with them—can create or worsen psychological disorders in children. Stress can do the same in adults, but the neurodevelopmental disorders seen in childhood are not just miniature versions of adult psychopathology. Because children's development is still incomplete and because their capacity to cope with stress is limited, children are often vulnerable to special types of disorders. The DSM lists many neurodevelopmental disorders seen in infants, children, and adolescents, but the majority of them can be placed in two broad categories: externalizing disorders and internalizing disorders (Phares, 2014).

Externalizing Disorders

The *externalizing,* or *undercontrolled,* category includes behaviors that disturb people in the child's environment. Lack of control shows up as *conduct disorders* in about 2 to 9 percent of children and adolescents, mostly boys, and appears most frequently at around eleven or twelve years of age (Merikangas et al., 2010; Nock et al., 2006). Conduct disorders are characterized by a relatively stable pattern of aggression, disobedience, destructiveness, inappropriate sexual activity, academic failure, and other problematic behaviors (Frick & Nigg, 2012; Petitclerc & Tremblay, 2009). Often these behaviors involve criminal activity, pursued without remorse or empathy for victims, and they may signal the development of antisocial personality disorder (Lahey et al., 2005; Pardini, Frick, & Moffitt, 2010).

There may be a genetic predisposition toward externalizing disorders. For example, many children who display conduct disorder have parents who display antisocial personality disorder (Gelhorn et al., 2005). Children who are temperamentally inclined toward high activity levels and lack of concern for other people's feelings are at greater risk for externalizing disorders (Anastassiou-Hadjicharalambous & Warden, 2008; Pardini et al., 2010). There is no doubt, though, that parental and peer influences as well as academic problems at school combine with genetic factors to shape the antisocial behavior of these children (e.g., Brody et al., 2011; Giles et al., 2011; Jaffee et al., 2012; Lahey et al., 2011; Weitzman, Rosenthal, & Liu, 2011).

Another kind of externalizing problem, *attention deficit hyperactivity disorder* (*ADHD*), is seen in up to 8 percent of children and in about 4 percent of adults, mainly boys and men (Bloom & Cohen, 2007; Merikangas et al., 2010). An ADHD diagnosis is given to children who are more impulsive, more inattentive, or both, than other children their age (Feldman & Reiff, 2014). Many of these children also have great difficulty sitting still or otherwise controlling their physical activity. They appear to be less able than other children to recognize emotions in others and to regulate their own emotions (Da Fonseca et al., 2009; Musser et al., 2011). Their impulsiveness and lack of self-control contribute to significant impairments in learning and to an astonishing ability to annoy and exhaust those around them. Children diagnosed with ADHD also tend to perform poorly on tests of attention, memory, decision making, and other information-processing tasks. As a result, ADHD is being increasingly viewed as more than just "bad behavior" (Halperin & Schulz, 2006; Krain & Castellanos, 2006).

Like so many other disorders, ADHD appears to result from the interaction of a genetic predisposition and environmental influences. The genes involved may be those that regulate dopamine, a neurotransmitter important in the functioning of the attention system (Bush, 2010; Gilden & Marusich, 2009; Waldman & Gizer, 2006). Other factors, such as brain damage, poisoning from lead or other household substances, and low birth weight may also play causal roles (Hudziak et al., 2005; Nigg, 2010; Nikolas & Burt, 2010). In some cases, problems in parenting may increase the risk for ADHD (Clarke et al., 2002). Exactly how all these factors might combine is still not clear.

Also uncertain is exactly what constitutes hyperactivity. Cultural standards about acceptable activity levels in children vary, so a "hyperactive" child in one culture might be considered merely "active" in another. In fact, when mental health professionals from four cultures used the same rating scale to judge hyperactivity in a videotaped sample of children's behavior, the Chinese and Indonesians rated the children as significantly more hyperactive than did their U.S. and Japanese colleagues (Jacobson, 2002; Mann et al., 1992). And as mentioned earlier, there is evidence that African American children are diagnosed with ADHD only about two-thirds as often as European American children even when they have at least as many symptoms (Miller, Nigg, & Miller, 2009). Such findings remind us that sociocultural factors can be important determinants of what is expected or acceptable and thus what is considered abnormal.

Internalizing Disorders

The second broad category of child behavior problems involves *internalizing*, or *overcontrol*. Children in this category experience significant distress, especially depression and anxiety, and may be socially withdrawn (Luby, 2010). Those displaying *separation anxiety disorder*, for example, constantly worry that they will be lost, kidnapped, or injured or that some harm may come to a parent, usually the mother (Orgilés et al., 2009, 2011). The child clings desperately to the parent, and becomes upset or sick at the prospect of separation (Brand et al., 2011; Kossowsky et al., 2012). Refusal to go to school, sometimes called "school phobia," is often the result (Bahali, & Tahiroğlu, 2010; Iwata, Hazama, & Nakagome, 2012). Children who are temperamentally shy or withdrawn are at higher risk for internalizing disorders, but these disorders are also associated with environmental factors, including rejection or bullying by peers, and (especially for girls) being raised by a single parent (Phares, 2014).

Autism Spectrum Disorder

A few childhood disorders, including *autism spectrum disorder*, do not fall into either the externalizing or internalizing category. Children diagnosed with this disorder show deficits in communication and impaired social relationships. They also often show repetitive patterns of behavior (such as spinning objects) and unusual preoccupations and interests (American Psychiatric Association, 2013). This disorder is conceptualized as a spectrum disorder, such that some individuals are able to function relatively well and others show severe impairments (American Psychiatric Association, 2013). Estimates of the prevalence of autism spectrum disorder are consistently around 1 percent (American Psychiatric Association, 2013). It is diagnosed four times as often in boys than in girls (Kogan et al., 2009).

The children who show severe levels of impairment would have received a diagnosis of *autistic disorder* in DSM-IV. The earliest signs of severe autism spectrum disorder usually occur within the first thirty months after birth; these babies show little or no evidence of forming an attachment to their caregivers. Language development is seriously disrupted in most of these children; half of them never learn to speak at all. Individuals who display higher functioning or a less severe autism spectrum disorder would have been diagnosed with *Asperger's disorder* with DSM-IV. These individuals are able to function adaptively and, in some cases, independently as adults (Pexman et al., 2011).

Possible biological roots of autism spectrum disorder include genetic factors (e.g., Hallmayer et al., 2011; Sandin et al., 2014; St. Pourcain et al., 2010) or neurodevelopmental abnormalities that affect language and communication (Baron-Cohen, Knickmeyer, & Belmonte, 2005; Minshew & Williams, 2007). Researchers studying these biological factors are especially interested in the activity of *mirror neurons* in the brain. As described in the chapter on biological aspects of psychology, these neurons are activated when we see other people's actions, such as smiling, frowning, or showing disgust. Because they are in the areas of our own brain that control these same actions, activity in mirror neurons helps us to understand how the other person might be feeling and to empathize with those feelings. The functioning of mirror neurons appears disturbed in people with autism,

Active or Hyperactive?

TRY THIS Normal behavior for children in one culture might be considered hyperactive in other cultures. Do people in the same culture disagree on what is hyperactive? To find out, ask two or three friends to join you in observing a group of children at a playground, a schoolyard, a park, or some other public place. Ask your friends to privately identify which children they would label as "hyperactive" and then count how many of their choices agree with yours and with others in your group.

© Cherry-Merry/Shutterstock.com

which may help explain why these individuals seem to operate with little appreciation for what others might be thinking or feeling (Welsh et al., 2009; Williams et al., 2006). This explanation has not been confirmed, however, (Yang-Teng et al., 2010), and other possible causal factors are also being investigated, including the effects of drugs, environmental chemicals, and infectious agents. Hypotheses that autism spectrum disorder is caused by cold and unresponsive parents or by vaccinations have been rejected by the results of scientific research (Dietert, Dietert, & DeWitt, 2011; Doja & Roberts, 2006).

Neurodevelopmental disorders seen in childhood differ from adult disorders not only because the patterns of behavior are distinct but also because their early onset disrupts development. To take just one example, children whose separation anxiety causes spotty school attendance may not only fall behind academically but also may fail to form the relationships with other children that promote normal social development (Wood, 2006). Some children never make up for this deficit. They may drop out of school and risk a life of psychiatric disorders, poverty, crime, and violence (Bahali, & Tahiroğlu, 2010; Doobay, 2008). Moreover, children depend on others to get help for their psychological problems, but all too often those problems may go unrecognized or untreated. For some, the long-term result may be adult forms of mental disorder. This is particularly tragic because early diagnosis and appropriate intervention can lead to significant improvement in childhood disorders (Ingersoll, 2011; Kurita, 2012).

Substance-Related and Addictive Disorders

Childhood disorders, especially externalizing disorders, often lead to substance-related disorders in adolescence and adulthood. The DSM-5 defines **substance-related disorders** as the use of alcohol or other psychoactive drugs for months or years in ways that harm the user or others. These disorders create major political, economic, social, and health problems worldwide. The substances involved most often are alcohol and other depressants (such as barbiturates), opiates (such as heroin), stimulants (such as cocaine or amphetamines), hallucinogenic drugs (such as LSD), and tobacco. About half of the world's population uses at least one psychoactive substance, and about two-thirds of people in the United States report that alcohol or drug addiction has affected them, their families, or their close friends (Leamon, Wright, & Myrick, 2008; Swendsen et al., 2012).

One effect of using some substances (including alcohol, heroin, and amphetamines) is **addiction** (also known as *dependence*), a physical need for the substance. Even when people with a substance use disorder do not become addicted, some may overuse, or *abuse* a drug, because it may give temporary self-confidence, enjoyment, or relief from tension. In other words, people can become psychologically dependent on psychoactive drugs without becoming physiologically addicted to them. But people who are psychologically dependent on a drug often have problems that are at least as serious as those of people who are addicted and that may be even more difficult to treat.

In the consciousness chapter, we describe how consciousness is affected by a wide range of psychoactive drugs. Here, we focus more specifically on the problems associated with the use and abuse of alcohol, heroin, and cocaine.

Alcohol Use Disorder

According to national surveys in the United States, 3.1 percent of the adult population abuse alcohol or are dependent on it in any given year, and 14 percent of adults have had these problems at some time in their lives (Kessler & Wang, 2008; Leamon, Wright, & Myrick, 2008). In previous versions of the DSM, *alcohol abuse* (a pattern of continuous or intermittent drinking with negative consequences) was distinguished from *alcohol dependence* (an addiction that almost always causes severe social, physical, and other problems). In DSM-5, the disorders of alcohol abuse and alcohol dependence were combined into an overarching diagnosis of *alcohol use disorder* (American Psychiatric Association, 2013). Males outnumber females in this category three to one, but the problem is on the rise among women and teenagers of both genders (Grucza et al., 2008). Alcohol use disorder

substance-related disorders Problems involving the use of psychoactive drugs for months or years in ways that harm the user or others.

addiction Development of a physical need for a psychoactive drug.

is greater among European Americans and American Indians than among African Americans and Hispanics; it is lowest among Asians (Substance Abuse and Mental Health Services Administration, 2007). Prolonged overuse of alcohol can result in life-threatening liver damage, impaired cognitive abilities, vitamin deficiencies that can lead to severe and permanent memory loss, and a host of other physical ailments (Reid et al., 2012).

Alcohol use disorder, commonly referred to as **alcoholism**, is a serious problem that is implicated in 40 to 50 percent of all automobile accidents, murders, and rapes (Butcher et al., 2010). Alcohol use disorder also figures prominently in child abuse and in elevated rates of hospitalization and absenteeism from work (Freisthler, 2011; Lawder et al., 2011; Lidwall & Marklund, 2011). Children growing up in families in which one or both parents abuse alcohol are more likely than other children to develop a host of psychological disorders, including substance-related disorders (Jones, 2007; Odgers et al., 2008). And as described in the chapter on human development, children of mothers who abused alcohol during pregnancy may be born with fetal alcohol syndrome. In short, alcohol use disorder carries a huge cost in personal suffering, medical expenditures, lost productivity, and shortened lifespans.

The biopsychosocial approach suggests that alcohol use disorder stems from a combination of genetically influenced characteristics (including inherited aspects of temperament such as impulsivity, a taste for novelty, and emotionality) and what people learn in their social and cultural environments. For example, the children of people with alcoholism are more likely than others to develop alcoholism themselves, and if the children are identical twins, both are at increased risk for alcoholism, even when raised apart (Reid et al., 2012). It is still unclear just what might be inherited or which genes are involved. One possibility involves inherited abnormalities in the brain's neurotransmitter systems or in the body's metabolism of alcohol (Reid et al., 2012). Males with alcoholism do tend to be less sensitive than other people to the effects of alcohol—a factor that may contribute to greater consumption (Graham et al., 2011; Vetter-O'Hagen, Carlinskaya, & Spear, 2009). Now that the human genome has been decoded, researchers are focusing on specific chromosomes as the possible location of genes that predispose people to—or protect them from—the development of alcoholism (e.g., Bierut et al., 2012). However, the genetics of addiction are highly complex; there is probably not a single gene for alcoholism (Reid et al., 2012). As with other disorders, alcoholism arises as many genes interact with each other and with environmental events, including parental influences. For example, one study found that boys whose fathers had alcoholism were at elevated risk for alcoholism, but not if the father's genetically identical *twin* had alcoholism (Jacob et al., 2003). In these cases, something in the boys' nonalcoholic family environment had apparently moderated whatever genetic tendency toward alcoholism they might have inherited.

Youngsters typically learn to drink by watching parents and peers (Abar, 2012). Their observations help shape their expectations, such as that alcohol will make them feel good and help them to cope with stressors (Schell et al., 2005). But alcohol use becomes a problem if drinking is a person's main coping strategy (National Institute on Alcohol Abuse and Alcoholism, 2001). The importance of learning is supported by evidence that alcoholism is more commonly reported among ethnic and cultural groups in which frequent drinking tends to be socially approved, such as the Irish and English, than among religious or ethnic groups in which all but moderate drinking tends to be discouraged, such as Jews, Italians, and Chinese (Koenig, Haber, & Jacob, 2011; Ryan & Hout, 2011; Schwartz et al., 2011). Moreover, different forms of social support for drinking can result in different consumption patterns within a cultural group (Biron, Banberger, & Noyman, 2011; McKay et al., 2011). For example, one study found significantly more drinking among Japanese men living in Japan (where social norms for male drinking are most permissive) compared with Japanese men living in Hawaii or California, where excessive drinking is less strongly supported (Kitano et al., 1992). Learning may also help explain why rates of alcoholism are higher than average among bartenders, cocktail servers, and others who work where alcohol is available and drinking is socially reinforced or even expected (Fillmore & Caetano, 1980). (Of course, it is also possible that attraction to alcohol led some of these people into such jobs in the first place.)

alcoholism A pattern of drinking that may lead to addiction and that almost always causes severe social, physical, and other problems.

Heroin Use Disorder and Cocaine Use Disorder

Like people with alcoholism, those who develop a substance-related disorder involving heroin or cocaine suffer many serious health problems as a result of both the drugs themselves and the poor eating and health habits related to use of those drugs. The risk of death from overdose, contaminated drugs, AIDS (contracted through shared needles), or suicide is also always present. Drug dependence tends to be more prevalent among males, especially young males (Compton et al., 2007; Reid et al., 2012).

Continued use or overdoses of cocaine can cause problems ranging from nausea and hyperactivity to paranoid thinking, sudden depressive "crashes," and even death. Cocaine use has been on the decline since 1985, but it is still a serious problem. Surveys indicate that 7.7 percent of high school seniors in the United States have used cocaine at some time in their lives, and millions more teens and adults still use it on occasion (Johnston et al., 2004). The widespread availability of crack, a powerful and relatively cheap form of cocaine, has made it one of the most dangerous and addicting of all drugs. Pregnant women who use cocaine are much more likely than nonusers to lose their babies through spontaneous abortion, placental detachment, early fetal death, or stillbirth.

Addiction to heroin and cocaine appears in about 4 percent of the adult population in the United States (Compton et al., 2005) and is mainly a biological process brought about by the physical effects of the drugs (Kalivas & Volkow, 2005; Phillips et al., 2003). Explaining why people first use these drugs is more complicated. Beyond the obvious and immediate pleasure these drugs provide, the causes of initial drug use are less well established than the reasons for alcohol abuse. Some research has identified structural abnormalities in the brains of people who become addicted to stimulant drugs (Ersche et al., 2012). Another line of research suggests that there might be a genetic tendency toward behavioral compulsions that predisposes some people to abuse many kinds of drugs (Fernández-Serrano et al., 2012; Koob & Volkow, 2010; Reid et al., 2012). One study supporting this idea found a link between alcoholism in biological parents and drug abuse in the sons they had given up for adoption (Cadoret et al., 1995). The same study also found a link between antisocial personality traits in biological parents and antisocial acts—including drug abuse—in the sons they had put up for adoption.

A number of psychological and environmental factors have been proposed as promoting initial drug use (Vedel & Emmelkamp, 2012). These include seeing parents use drugs, being abused in childhood, using drugs to cope with stressors or to ease anxiety or depression, associating drug use with pleasant experiences, seeking popularity, caving in to peer pressure, and thrill seeking (Ferguson & Meehan, 2011; García-Montes et al., 2009; Rudolph et al., 2011; Tucker et al., 2011). Research has not yet established why continued drug use occurs in some people and not in others, but, again, it is likely that a biological predisposition interacts with psychological processes and stressors that play out their roles in specific social and cultural contexts.

MENTAL ILLNESS AND THE LAW

Can insanity protect criminals from punishment?

Have you wondered why the word *insanity* doesn't appear in our definition of *mental disorder* or in the DSM-5 categories we have described? The reason is that *insanity* is a legal term, not a medical diagnosis or psychological term (Torry & Billick, 2010). For example, John Hinckley, Jr., was found *not guilty by reason of insanity* for his attempted assassination of President Ronald Reagan in 1981. This verdict reflected U.S. laws and rules that protect people with severe psychological disorders when they are accused of crimes (Cassel & Bernstein, 2007). Many other countries around the world have similar laws (Goldstein, Morse, & Packer, 2013).

This protection takes two forms. First, under certain conditions, people designated as mentally ill may be protected from criminal prosecution. If at the time of trial individuals accused of crimes are unable to understand the proceedings and charges against them or

Assessment of Mental Competence

Andrea Yates admitted to drowning her five children in the bathtub of her Houston, Texas, home in 2001. She had twice tried to kill herself in previous years, and she was reportedly depressed at the time of the murders. Accordingly, she pleaded not guilty by reason of insanity. The first legal step in deciding her fate was to confine her in a mental institution to assess her mental competency to stand trial. Following the testimony of psychologists who examined her, she was found competent and ultimately sentenced to life in prison. Her conviction was overturned on appeal, though, and at a second trial in 2006, she was found not guilty by reason of insanity and committed to a mental hospital.

AP Images/Brett Coomer, Pool

help their attorneys to prepare a defense, they are declared *mentally incompetent* to stand trial. When that happens, defendants are sent to a mental institution for treatment until they are judged to be mentally competent (Zapf & Roesch, 2011). If they are still not competent after some specified period—two years, in many cases—defendants may be ruled permanently ineligible for trial and either committed to a mental institution or released. Release is rare, however, because most defendants who are unable to meet competency standards have mental disorders that are serious enough to pose a danger to themselves or others.

Second, the mentally ill may be protected from punishment. In most U.S. states, defendants may be judged not guilty by reason of insanity if at the time of the crime mental illness prevented them from (1) understanding what they were doing; (2) knowing that what they were doing was wrong; and (3) resisting the impulse to do wrong. The first two of these criteria relate to a person's ability to think clearly and are called the *M'Naghton rule,* for the defendant in the 1843 case that established it. The third criterion, which relates to the defendant's emotional state during a crime, is known as the *irresistible impulse test.* All three criteria were combined in a rule proposed by the American Law Institute in 1962—a rule that is now followed in about one-third of U.S. states: "A person is not responsible for criminal conduct if at the time of such conduct as a result of mental disease or defect he lacks substantial capacity either to appreciate the criminality (wrongfulness) of his conduct or to conform his conduct to the requirements of law" (p. 66).

After the Hinckley verdict, the U.S. Congress passed the Insanity Defense Reform Act, which eliminated the irresistible impulse criterion from the definition of insanity in federal cases. About 75 percent of the U.S. states have passed similar or related reform laws (Giorgi-Guarnieri et al., 2002); in about half the states, these laws require the use of some version of the narrower M'Naghton rule (American Psychiatric Association, 2003). Whatever criteria are used, when defendants plead insanity, judges and juries must decide whether these people should be held responsible for criminal acts. Defendants who are judged not guilty by reason of insanity and who still display a psychological disorder are usually required to receive treatment, typically through commitment to a hospital, until judged to be cured or no longer dangerous. Thirteen U.S. states have laws allowing jurors to find defendants *guilty but mentally ill.* These defendants are supposed to receive treatment while in prison, though they seldom do (Cassel & Bernstein, 2007). A second reform already noted is that federal courts no longer use the irresistible-impulse criterion in defining insanity. Third, federal courts and some state courts now require defendants to prove that they were insane at the time of their crime, rather than requiring the prosecution to prove that the defendants were sane.

Critics of insanity rules complain that these rules allow criminals to "get away with murder." Actually, such outcomes are rare. Insanity pleas occur in only 1 out of every 200 felony cases in the United States, and they are successful in only 2 of every 1,000 attempts (American Psychiatric Association, 2003). Even the few defendants found not guilty by reason of insanity in the United States may be hospitalized for at least as long as they would have spent in prison had they been found guilty (Roesch, Zapf, & Hart, 2010). Those with the most severe disorders may never be released. John Hinckley, Jr., has been in Saint Elizabeth's Hospital in Washington, D.C., since 1982, and in spite of his annual efforts to be released and court approval for longer visits with his mother outside the hospital, he is unlikely to be freed anytime soon.

In summary, society is constantly seeking the proper balance between protecting the rights of defendants and protecting society from dangerous criminals. In the process, the sociocultural values that shape our views about what is abnormal also influence judgments about the extent to which abnormality should relieve people of responsibility for criminal behavior (O'Connell, 2011)

LINKAGES

As noted in the introductory chapter, all of psychology's subfields are related to one another. Our discussion of how mental disorders might be learned illustrates just one way that the topic of this chapter, psychological disorders, is linked to the subfield of learning, which is discussed in the chapter by that name. The Linkages diagram shows ties to two other subfields, and there are many more ties throughout the book. Looking for linkages among subfields will help you see how they all fit together and help you better appreciate the big picture that is psychology.

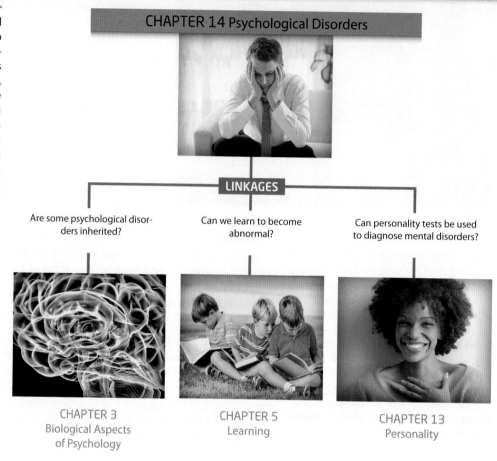

CHAPTER 14 Psychological Disorders

LINKAGES

Are some psychological disorders inherited?

Can we learn to become abnormal?

Can personality tests be used to diagnose mental disorders?

CHAPTER 3
Biological Aspects of Psychology

CHAPTER 5
Learning

CHAPTER 13
Personality

SUMMARY

Psychopathology involves patterns of thinking, feeling, and behaving that are maladaptive, disruptive, or distressing, either for the person affected or for others.

Defining Psychological Disorders

How do psychologists define abnormal behavior?

Some psychological disorders show considerable similarity across cultures, but the definition of abnormality is largely determined by social and cultural factors. The criteria for judging abnormality include deviance (statistical infrequency and norm violations), distress (personal suffering), and dysfunction. Each of these criteria is flawed to some extent. The practical approach, which considers the content, context, and consequences of behavior, emphasizes the question of whether individuals show impaired functioning in fulfilling the roles appropriate for particular people in particular settings, cultures, and historical eras.

Explaining Psychological Disorders

What causes abnormality?

At various times and places, abnormal behavior has been attributed to the action of gods or the devil. Mental health professionals in Western cultures rely on a **biopsychosocial approach**, which attributes mental disorders to the interaction of biological, psychological, and **sociocultural factors**. Biological factors, such as brain chemistry, are highlighted by the medical or *neurobiological model* of disorder. The **psychological model** focuses on processes such as inner conflicts, maladaptive learning experiences, or blocked personal growth. The **sociocultural perspective** helps explain disorder by focusing on the social relations, social support, and cultural and subcultural factors that form the context of abnormality. The **diathesis-stress model** suggests that biological, psychological, and sociocultural characteristics create predispositions for disorder that are translated into symptoms in the face of sufficient amounts of stress.

Classifying Psychological Disorders

How many psychological disorders have been identified?

The dominant system for classifying abnormal behavior in North America is the fifth edition of the *Diagnostic and Statistical Manual of Mental Disorders* (DSM-5) of the American Psychiatric Association. It includes more than 300 specific categories of mental disorder. Diagnosis helps identify the features, causes, and most effective methods of treating various psychological disorders. Research on the reliability and validity of the DSM shows that it is a useful but not perfect classification system.

Anxiety Disorders

What is a phobia?

Long-standing and disruptive patterns of anxiety characterize **anxiety disorders**. The most prevalent type of anxiety disorder is **phobia**, a category that includes **specific phobias, social anxiety disorder (social phobia)**, and **agoraphobia**. Other anxiety disorders are **generalized anxiety disorder**, which involves nonspecific anxiety, and **panic disorder**, which brings unpredictable attacks of intense anxiety.

Obsessive-Compulsive and Related Disorders

What are obsessive rituals?

Obsessive-compulsive disorder (OCD) is characterized by uncontrollable repetitive thoughts called **obsessions** and ritualistic actions called **compulsions**. Obsessional jealousy and **body dysmorphic disorder** also fall in this category.

The most influential explanations of anxiety and obsessive-compulsive disorders suggest that they may develop when a biological predisposition for strong anxiety reactions combines with fear-enhancing thought patterns and learned anxiety responses. Many anxiety disorders appear to develop in accordance with the principles of classical and operant conditioning and with those of observational learning. People may be biologically prepared to learn fear of certain objects and situations.

Somatic Symptom and Related Disorders

Can mental disorder cause blindness?

Somatic symptom disorders appear as physical problems that have no apparent physical cause or as intense preoccupation with physical illness or deformity. They include **conversion disorder**, which involves problems such as blindness, deafness, and paralysis that have no apparent physical cause, as well as **illness anxiety disorder**, an unjustified concern over being or becoming ill.

Dissociative Disorders

What disorders create sudden memory loss?

Dissociative disorders involve rare conditions such as **dissociative amnesia**, which involves sudden and severe memory loss, and **dissociative identity disorder (DID)**, or multiple personality disorder, in which a person appears to have two or more identities. There is considerable controversy about the origins of dissociative identity disorder.

Depressive and Bipolar Disorders

How common is depression?

Depressive disorders are quite common and involve extreme moods that may be inconsistent with events. **Major depressive disorder** is marked by feelings of inadequacy, worthlessness, and guilt; in extreme cases, **delusions** may also occur. **Persistent depressive disorder** includes similar but less severe symptoms that persist for a long period. Suicide is often related to these disorders.

Alternating periods of depression and **mania** characterize **bipolar disorders**; there are more intense manic phases in bipolar I disorder than in bipolar II disorder. These disorders are also known as manic depression. **Cyclothymic disorder**, an alternating pattern of less extreme mood swings, is a slightly more common variant.

Depressive and bipolar disorders have been attributed to biological causes such as genetic inheritance, disruptions in neurotransmitter and endocrine systems, and irregularities in biological rhythms. These factors interact with stressors and psychological factors such as maladaptive patterns of thinking. A predisposition toward some of these disorders may be inherited, although their appearance is probably determined by a diathesis-stress process.

Schizophrenia Spectrum and Other Psychotic Disorders

Is schizophrenia the same as "split personality"?

Schizophrenia is perhaps the most severe and puzzling disorder of all. Among its symptoms are problems in thinking, perception (often including **hallucinations**), attention, emotion, movement, motivation, and daily functioning. Positive symptoms of schizophrenia include hallucinations or disordered speech; negative symptoms can include withdrawal, immobility, and the absence of affect.

Genetic influences, neurotransmitter problems, abnormalities in brain structure and functioning, and neurodevelopmental abnormalities are biological factors implicated in schizophrenia. Psychological factors such as maladaptive learning experiences and disturbed family interactions can affect the severity and course of this disorder. Diathesis-stress explanations, including vulnerability theory, provide a promising framework for research into the multiple causes of schizophrenia.

Personality Disorders

Which personality disorder often leads to crime?

Personality disorders are long-term patterns of maladaptive behavior that create discomfort for the person with the disorder and/or other peoples. These include odd-eccentric types (paranoid, schizoid, and schizotypal personality disorders), anxious-fearful types (dependent, obsessive-compulsive, and avoidant personality disorders), and dramatic-erratic types (histrionic, narcissistic, borderline, and antisocial personality disorders). **Antisocial personality disorder** is marked by impulsive, irresponsible, and unscrupulous behavior patterns that often begin in childhood. Childhood abuse may be related to the appearance of this potentially dangerous personality disorder.

Some Additional Psychological Disorders

How do children's disorders differ from adults' disorders?

Neurodevelopmental disorders seen in childhood can be categorized as externalizing conditions (such as conduct disorders or attention deficit hyperactivity disorder) and internalizing disorders, in which children show overcontrol and experience distress (as in separation anxiety disorder). Some childhood disorders do not fall into either category. In autism spectrum disorder, which can be the most severe of these, children show limitations in their social connections and their use of language.

Substance-related disorders involving alcohol and other drugs affect millions of people. **Addiction** to and psychological dependence on these substances contribute to disastrous personal and social problems, including physical illnesses, accidents, and crime. Genetic factors probably create a predisposition for **alcoholism**, but learning, cultural traditions, and other nonbiological processes are also important. Stress reduction, imitation, thrill seeking, and social maladjustment have been proposed as important factors in drug addiction, as has genetic predisposition; but the exact causes of initial use of these drugs are unknown.

Mental Illness and The Law

Can insanity protect criminals from punishment?

"Insanity" is a legal term, not a psychiatric diagnosis. Current rules protect people accused of crimes from prosecution or punishment if they are declared mentally incompetent at the time of their trials or if they were legally insane at the time of their crimes. Defendants judged not guilty by reason of insanity and who still display a psychological disorder are usually required to receive treatment until they are judged to be cured or no longer dangerous. Those found guilty but mentally ill are supposed to receive treatment in prison.

TEST YOUR KNOWLEDGE

Select the best answer for each of the following questions. Then check your responses against the Answer Key at the end of the book.

1. According to the statistics on psychopathology, _____ percent of people in the United States experience a mental disorder in their lifetimes.
   a. less than 5 percent
   b. approximately 25 percent
   c. almost 50 percent
   d. over 75 percent

2. Babette, a successful opera singer, believes that aliens could snatch her at any time if she isn't wearing her lucky charm. She is constantly worried and insists that the stage be rimmed with foil to ward off evil spirits. According to which criterion of abnormality would Babette *not* be considered abnormal?
   a. Statistical
   b. Norm violation
   c. Practical
   d. Personal suffering

3. Herman murdered a man who bumped into him in a bar. In order to be found not guilty by reason of insanity, the jury would have to find that he _____.
   a. was under the influence of alcohol when he committed the crime
   b. is currently insane
   c. was insane when he committed the crime
   d. knew the crime was wrong but did it anyway

4. Roberta and Rhonda are identical twins who inherited identical predispositions for depression. Roberta has lived an easy life and has not developed any depressive symptoms. Rhonda, who has been divorced and lost several jobs over the years, has been diagnosed with major depression. The difference between these twins is most consistent with the _____ approach to abnormality.
   a. neurobiological
   b. psychological
   c. sociocultural
   d. diathesis-stress

5. Dr. Kramer, an American psychiatrist, is evaluating a patient who came to a hospital for treatment. In his report he indicates that the patient meets all the standard criteria for major depressive disorder. Dr. Kramer is probably using _____ to evaluate the patient.
   a. the M'Naghton rule
   b. norm violation criteria
   c. insanity criteria
   d. DSM-5

6. Kat stopped going to classes because of worry that she will embarrass herself by saying something silly. She takes her meals to her dorm room so that no one will see her eat. According to the DSM-5, Kat is probably displaying _____.
   a. agoraphobia
   b. simple phobia
   c. generalized anxiety disorder
   d. social anxiety disorder

7. Terraba had a difficult time driving to work. Every time she went over a bump she had to drive back around to make sure that she had not run over anything. This occurred ten or twelve times each day, so Terraba was always late for everything. Terraba appears to be suffering from _____.
   a. specific phobia
   b. panic attacks
   c. obsessive-compulsive disorder
   d. generalized anxiety disorder

8. Conversion disorder is characterized by _____.
   a. impairment of movement or sensory ability with no apparent physical cause
   b. severe pain with no apparent physical cause
   c. fear of becoming seriously ill
   d. frequent, vague complaints of physical symptoms

9. Tomas has been suffering severe back pain for several weeks, but extensive medical tests reveal no physical problem. Tomas appears to be displaying _____.
   a. a somatic symptom disorder
   b. schizophrenia
   c. body dysmorphic disorder
   d. obsessive-compulsive disorder

10. When Jennifer, a newspaper reporter, disappeared while covering a crime story that put her under constant threat, everyone assumed she had been kidnapped. But she was found several months later, now married and calling herself Emily, working as a waitress in a city 1,000 miles from her home. She had no memory of her previous life, even after being reunited with her parents. Jennifer would most likely be diagnosed as displaying _____.
   a. dissociative amnesia
   b. dissociative identity disorder
   c. paranoia
   d. schizophrenia

11. Over the past three months, Barb has been feeling very sad; she has been sleeping as much as fifteen hours a day and has gained thirty pounds. Debbie, too, feels very low, but she can barely sleep and has lost both her appetite and fifteen pounds. Both Barb and Debbie have symptoms of _____.
   a. obsessive-compulsive disorder
   b. depression
   c. bipolar disorder
   d. illness anxiety disorder

12. Suicide is closely tied to depression. Studies of suicide in the United States have found that _____.
   a. people who talk about suicide typically don't attempt suicide
   b. older males who are living alone are the most likely to commit suicide
   c. suicide rates are about the same across ethnic groups and gender
   d. depressed women almost never actually attempt suicide

13. Carlisle has been very depressed. He can't face his responsibilities and often spends days at a time in bed. A psychologist who adopts the social-cognitive approach would be most likely to see this depression as caused by Carlisle's _____.
   a. attributional style
   b. brain chemicals
   c. unconscious conflicts
   d. blocked growth tendencies

14. As you sit down next to a messy-looking man on a bus, he says, "Ohms vibrate orange and dishwrings obvious dictionary." As he continues talking in this manner, you begin to suspect that he is displaying _____, a _____ symptom of _____.
   a. anxiety; negative; obsessive-compulsive disorder
   b. delusion; positive; schizophrenia
   c. delusion; negative; schizophrenia
   d. flat affect; negative; depression

15. Juan can't explain why, but he worries constantly that something terrible is going to happen to him. This vague feeling of impending doom is associated with a diagnosis of _____.
   a. conversion disorder
   b. specific phobia
   c. social phobia
   d. generalized anxiety disorder

16. Forty-year-old Richard believes that he was ordered by God to save the world. He is suspicious of other people because he thinks they want to prevent him from fulfilling his mission. He is unable to keep a job because he is angry and argumentative most of the time. Richard would most likely be diagnosed as displaying _____.
   a. persistent depressive disorder
   b. dissociative identity disorder
   c. schizophrenia
   d. body dysmorphic disorder

17. Al is charming and intelligent, but he has always been irresponsible, impulsive, and unscrupulous. None of his girlfriends knows he is dating other women. He borrows money from friends and doesn't pay them back. He doesn't care about anyone else, including his family. Al would probably be diagnosed as displaying _____ personality disorder.
   a. antisocial
   b. narcissistic
   c. passive-aggressive
   d. inadequate

18. Cathy Widom's research study, discussed in the Focus on Research Methods section of this chapter, found that there was a relationship between antisocial personality disorder and _____.
   a. narcissistic personality disorder
   b. schizophrenia
   c. high intelligence
   d. being abused in childhood

19. Angelo drinks alcohol until he passes out. Unable to hold a job or take care of himself, Angelo is diagnosed as having a substance-related disorder. Research on alcoholism suggests that Angelo's problems are caused by _____.
   a. a single inherited gene
   b. a culture that did not tolerate drinking
   c. having parents with alcoholism
   d. a combination of genetic and environmental factors

20. Aaron is an infant who shows no signs of attachment to his parents. He dislikes being held and doesn't smile or laugh. Aaron's symptoms are most consistent with _____.
   a. infantile schizophrenia
   b. autism spectrum disorder
   c. antisocial personality disorder
   d. an externalizing disorder of childhood

Treatment of Psychological Disorders

© iStock.com/Alina555

Preview

In old Hollywood movies, such as *The Dark Past or The Three Faces of Eve*, troubled people find instant cures when a psychotherapist helps them discover an unconscious memory that holds the key to their psychological disorder. Somewhat more realistic versions of psychotherapy have been presented in movies and television shows such as *Good Will Hunting, The Sopranos,* and *In Treatment.* Yet even these portrayals do not convey what psychotherapy is really like, and even the best of them tell only part of the story of how psychological disorders can be treated. In this chapter, we describe a wide range of treatment options, including methods based on psychodynamic, humanistic, behavioral, and biological theories of psychological disorders. We also consider research on the effectiveness of treatment and methods for preventing disorders.

In the chapter on psychological disorders, we described José, an electronics technician who had to take medical leave from his job because of his panic attacks. After four months of diagnostic testing turned up no physical problems, José's physician suggested that he see a psychologist. José resisted at first, insisting that his condition was not "just in his head," but he eventually began psychological treatment. Within a few months, his panic attacks had ceased and José had returned to all his old activities. After the psychologist helped him reconsider his workload, José decided to take early retirement from his job in order to pursue more satisfying work at his home-based computer business.

José's case is common. During any given year in the United States alone, about 15 percent of adults and about 21 percent of children and adolescents are receiving some form of treatment for psychological disorders, including substance use problems (Costello, Copeland, & Angold, 2011; McGorry et al., 2011). In fact, you probably know someone who has received treatment for a psychological disorder (Connor-Greene, 2001). Treatment can be expensive in the short run but saves money in the long run because it typically reduces a person's need for later mental and physical health services (Lambert, 2013). The most common targets of treatment in adults are problems involving anxiety, mood, impulse control, substance abuse, or some combination of these (Kessler & Ustun, 2011). Many people also seek treatment for problems that are not officially diagnosed as disorders, such as relationship conflicts or difficulties associated with grief, divorce, retirement, or other life transitions. The most common treatment targets in children are hyperactivity, oppositional behavior, anxiety, and affective disorders (Phares, 2014).

BASIC FEATURES OF TREATMENT

What features do all treatment techniques have in common?

Psychotherapy is the treatment of psychological disorders through psychological methods. All types of psychotherapy share certain basic features. These common features include a *client* or *patient*, a professionally trained *therapist* or other agent who works to help the client, and a *special therapeutic relationship* between the client and the therapist. In addition, all forms of treatment are based on some *theory* about the causes of the client's problems (Antony & Barlow, 2010). The presumed causes can range from magic spells to infections, and everything in between (Corey, 2008). These theories form the basis of *treatment procedures* for dealing with the client's problems. So traditional healers combat supernatural forces with ceremonies and prayers, medical doctors treat chemical imbalances with medications, and psychologists focus on altering psychological processes through psychotherapy.

People can receive treatment as inpatients or outpatients. *Inpatients* are treated while living in a hospital or other institution. They enter these institutions—voluntarily or

psychotherapy The treatment of psychological disorders through talking and other psychological methods.

Medieval Treatment Methods

Methods used to treat psychological disorders have always been related to the presumed causes of those disorders. In medieval times, when abnormal behavior was associated with demonic possession, physician-priests tried to make the victim's body an uncomfortable place for evil spirits. In this depiction, demons are shown fleeing as an afflicted person's head is placed in an oven.

Stock Montage

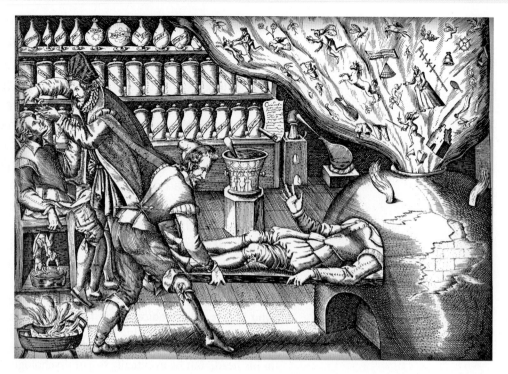

involuntarily—because their impairments are severe enough to create a threat to their own well-being or that of others. Depending on their level of functioning, inpatients may stay in the hospital for a few days or weeks or (in rare cases) several years. Their treatment almost always includes prescription medication. *Outpatients* receive psychotherapy and/or prescription medications while living in the community. Outpatients tend to have fewer and less severe symptoms than inpatients and function better in social and occupational situations (Hybels et al., 2008; Pottick et al., 2008).

Those who provide psychological treatment are a diverse group (Robiner, 2006). **Psychiatrists** are medical doctors who complete specialty training in the treatment of mental disorders. Like other physicians, they are authorized to prescribe medication for the relief of psychological problems. **Psychologists** who offer psychotherapy have usually completed a doctoral degree in clinical or counseling psychology, often followed by additional specialized training. Except in Louisiana and New Mexico, and in the U.S. military and the Indian Health Service, psychologists in the United States are not legally authorized to prescribe medication (Heiby, DeLeon, & Anderson, 2008). Other therapy providers include *clinical social workers, marriage and family therapists,* and *licensed professional counselors,* all of whom typically hold master's degrees in their respective fields. They provide treatment in many settings, including hospitals, clinics, and private practice. *Psychiatric nurses, substance abuse counselors,* members of the clergy working as *pastoral counselors,* and a host of *paraprofessionals* also provide therapy services, often as part of a hospital or outpatient treatment team (Kramer, Bernstein, & Phares, 2014).

The overall goal of treatment is to help troubled people change their thinking, feelings, and behavior in ways that relieve discomfort, promote happiness, and improve functioning as parents, students, employees, and the like. More specific goals and the methods chosen to reach them are included in a treatment plan that the therapist and client develop together. The details of this plan depend on the nature of the client's problems, preferences, financial circumstances, and the time available for treatment (Johnson, 2003). They also depend on the therapist's training and qualifications, theoretical leanings, methodological preferences, and the degree to which the therapist is guided by the results of experimental research on treatment. Let's consider several forms of

psychiatrists Medical doctors who have completed special training in the treatment of mental disorders.

psychologists Among therapists, those with advanced training in clinical or counseling psychology.

Freud's Consulting Room

During psychoanalytic sessions, Freud's patients lay on this couch, free associating or describing dreams and events in their lives, while he sat in the chair behind them. (The couch is now on display at the Freud Museum in London, which you can visit online at www.freud.org.uk.) According to Freud, even apparently trivial actions may carry messages from the unconscious. Forgetting a dream or missing a therapy appointment might reflect a client's unconscious resistance to treatment. Even accidents may be meaningful. Freud might have said that a waiter who spilled hot soup on an older male customer was acting out unconscious aggressive impulses against a father figure.

Geraint Lewis/Alamy

psychoanalysis A method of psychotherapy that seeks to help clients gain insight into and work through unconscious thoughts and emotions presumed to cause psychological problems.

psychotherapy, each of which is based on psychodynamic, humanistic, behavioral, or cognitive behavioral explanations of mental disorder.

Although we describe different approaches in separate sections, keep in mind that the majority of mental health professionals describe themselves as *eclectic* therapists. In other words, they might lean toward one set of treatment methods, but when working with particular clients or particular problems they may employ other methods as well (Lambert, 2013).

PSYCHODYNAMIC PSYCHOTHERAPY

How did Freud get started as a therapist?

The field of formal psychotherapy began in the late 1800s when, as described in the personality chapter, Sigmund Freud established the psychodynamic approach to personality and mental disorders. Freud's method of treatment, **psychoanalysis**, was aimed at understanding unconscious conflicts and how they affect people. Almost all forms of psychotherapy reflect some of Freud's ideas, including (1) his one-to-one treatment method; (2) his search for relationships between an individual's life history and current problems; (3) his emphasis on thoughts, emotions, and motivations in treatment; and (4) his focus on the patient-therapist relationship. We'll describe Freud's original methods first and then consider some more recent treatments that are rooted in his psychodynamic approach.

Classical Psychoanalysis

Classical psychoanalysis developed mainly out of Freud's medical practice. He was puzzled by people who came to him suffering from "hysterical" ailments, such as blindness, paralysis, or other disabilities that had no physical cause (see our discussion of *conversion disorders* in the chapter on psychological disorders). Freud tried to cure these individuals with hypnotic suggestions, but he found this method to be only partially and temporarily successful. Later, he asked hypnotized patients to recall events that might have caused their symptoms. Eventually, however, he stopped using hypnosis and merely had patients lie on a couch and report whatever thoughts, memories, or images came to mind. Freud called this process *free association.*

Freud's "talking cure" produced surprising results. He was struck by how many patients reported memories of childhood sexual abuse, usually by a parent or other close relative (Esterson, 2001). Although these allegations were probably accurate (DeMause, 1987), Freud eventually concluded that his patients' memories of abuse were actually unconscious childhood wishes and fantasies that resulted in hysterical symptoms.

As a result, Freud's psychoanalysis came to focus on an exploration of the unconscious and the conflicts raging within it. Classical psychoanalytic treatment aims first to help troubled people gain *insight* into their problems by recognizing unconscious thoughts and emotions. Then they are encouraged to discover, or *work through,* the many ways in which those unconscious elements continue to motivate maladaptive thinking and behavior in everyday life. The treatment may require as many as three to five sessions per week, usually over several years. Generally, the psychoanalyst is compassionate but emotionally neutral as the patient slowly develops an understanding of how past conflicts influence current problems (Gabbard, 2004).

To gain glimpses of the unconscious—and of the sexual and aggressive impulses he believed reside there—Freud looked for meaning in his patients' free associations, their dreams, their everyday behaviors, and their relationship with him. He believed that hidden beneath the obvious or *manifest content* of dreams is *latent content* that reflects the wishes, impulses, and fantasies that the dreamer's defense mechanisms keep out of consciousness during waking hours. He focused also on what have become known as "Freudian slips" of the tongue and other seemingly insignificant but potentially meaningful behaviors. So if

A Play Therapy Session

Modern versions of psychodynamic treatment include fantasy play and other techniques that make the approach more useful with children. A child's behavior and comments while playing with puppets representing family members, for example, are seen as a form of free association that the therapist hopes will reveal important unconscious material, such as fear of abandonment (Booth & Lindaman, 2000; Carlson, Watts, & Maniacci, 2006). Some therapists encourage child clients to play video games during therapy sessions. This allows them to observe the children's behaviors, draw inferences about their attitudes, and enhance the therapeutic relationship (Ceranoglu, 2010a, 2010b).

AMELIE-BENOIST / BSIP /Alamy

a patient mistakenly used the name of a former girlfriend while talking about his wife, Freud might wonder if the patient unconsciously regretted his marriage. Similarly, when patients expressed dependency, hostility, or even love toward him, Freud saw it as an unconscious process in which childhood feelings and conflicts about parents and other significant people were being transferred to the therapist. Analysis of this *transference*, this "new edition" of the patient's childhood conflicts and current problems, became another important psychoanalytic method (Gabbard, 2004). Freud believed that focusing on the transference allows patients to see how old conflicts haunt their lives and helps them resolve these conflicts.

Contemporary Variations on Psychoanalysis

Classical psychoanalysis is still practiced, but not as much as it was several decades ago (Kaner & Prelinger, 2007; Wolitzky, 2011). This decline is due in part to the growth of several alternative forms of treatment, including several variations on classical psychoanalysis developed by neo-Freudian theorists (Barber et al., 2013). As noted in the personality chapter, these theorists placed less emphasis than Freud did on the past and on unconscious impulses driven by the id. They focused instead on the role played by social relationships in people's problems and on how the power of the ego can be harnessed to solve them (Gray, 2005). Psychotherapists who adopt various neo-Freudian treatment methods tend to take a much more active role than classical analysts do, in particular by directing a patient's attention to evidence of certain conflicts in social relationships.

Many of these methods have come to be known as *short-term psychodynamic psychotherapy* because they aim to provide benefits in far less time than is required in classical psychoanalysis (Levenson, 2003; Messer & Kaplan, 2004; Rawson, 2006). However, virtually all modern psychodynamic therapies still focus attention on unconscious as well as conscious aspects of mental life, on the impact of internal conflicts, and on transference analysis as key elements in treatment (Safran, 2012). In a particularly popular short-term psychodynamic approach known as *object relations therapy,* the powerful need for human contact and support takes center stage (Greenberg & Mitchell, 2006). Object relations therapists believe that most of the problems for which people seek treatment ultimately stem from their relationships with others, especially their mothers or other early caregivers. (The term *object* usually refers to a person who has emotional significance for the client.) Accordingly, these therapists work to create a nurturing relationship in which a person's problems can be understood and corrected (Kahn & Rachman, 2000; Wallerstein, 2002). This relationship provides a "second chance" to receive the support that might have been missing in infancy and to counteract some of the consequences of maladaptive early attachment patterns. For example, object relations therapists take pains to show that they will not abandon their clients, as might have happened to these people in the past. *Interpersonal therapy* is rooted partly in neo-Freudian theory as well (Sullivan, 1954). Often used in cases of depression, it focuses on helping people explore and overcome the problematic effects of interpersonal events that occur after early childhood, such as the loss of a loved one, conflicts with a parent or a spouse, job loss, or social isolation (e.g., Weissman, Markowitz, & Kierman, 2007).

With their focus on interpersonal relationships rather than instincts, their emphasis on people's potential for self-directed problem solving, and their reassurance and emotional supportiveness, contemporary variants on classical psychoanalysis have helped the psychodynamic approach retain its influence among some mental health professionals (Barber et al., 2013; Safran, 2012).

HUMANISTIC PSYCHOTHERAPY

Why won't some therapists give advice?

Whereas some therapists revised Freud's ideas, others developed radical new therapies based on the humanistic approach to personality, which we described in the personality chapter. *Humanistic psychologists*, sometimes called *phenomenologists*, view people as capable of consciously controlling their own actions and taking responsibility for their decisions (Schneider & Längle, 2012). Most humanistic therapists believe that human behavior isn't motivated by inner conflicts but by an innate drive toward growth that is guided by the way people perceive their world. Disordered behavior, they say, reflects a blockage in natural growth brought on by distorted perceptions or lack of awareness about feelings. Accordingly, humanistic therapy operates on the following assumptions:

1. Treatment is an encounter between equals, not a "cure" given by an expert. It's a way to help clients restart their natural growth and feel and behave in more genuine ways.

2. Clients will improve on their own, given the right therapeutic conditions. These ideal conditions promote clients' awareness, acceptance, and expression of their feelings and perceptions.

3. Ideal conditions in therapy can best be established through a therapeutic relationship in which clients are made to feel accepted and supported as human beings, no matter how problematic or undesirable their behavior may be. The client's experience of this relationship brings beneficial changes. (Notice that this assumption is shared with object relations and some other forms of brief psychodynamic therapy.)

4. Clients must remain responsible for choosing how they will think and behave.

Of the many humanistically oriented treatments in use today, the most influential are *client-centered therapy*, developed by Carl Rogers (1951), and *Gestalt therapy*, developed by Frederick and Laura Perls.

Client-Centered Therapy

Carl Rogers was trained in psychodynamic therapy methods during the 1930s, but he soon began to question their value. He especially disliked being a detached expert whose task is to "figure out" the client. Eventually convinced that a less formal approach would be more effective, Rogers allowed his clients to decide what to talk about, and when, without direction, judgment, or interpretation by the therapist (Raskin & Rogers, 2005). This approach, now called **client-centered therapy** or **person-centered therapy**, relies on the creation of a relationship that reflects three intertwined therapist attitudes: unconditional positive regard, empathy, and congruence.

Unconditional Positive Regard

The attitude Rogers called **unconditional positive regard** consists of treating the client as a valued person, no matter what. This attitude is communicated through the therapist's willingness to listen without interrupting and to accept what is said without evaluating it. The therapist doesn't have to approve of everything the client says or does but must accept it as reflecting that client's view of the world. Because Rogerian therapists trust clients to solve their own problems, they rarely give advice (Merry & Brodley, 2002). Doing so, said Rogers, would send clients an unspoken message that they are incompetent, making them less confident and more dependent on help.

Empathy

In addition, client-centered therapists try to see the world as the client sees it. In other words, the therapist tries to develop **empathy**, an emotional understanding of what the

---

client-centered therapy (person-centered therapy) A type of therapy in which the client decides what to talk about, and when, without direction, judgment, or interpretation from the therapist.

unconditional positive regard In client-centered therapy, the therapist's attitude that expresses caring for and acceptance of the client as a valued person.

empathy In client-centered therapy, the therapist's attempt to appreciate how the world looks from the client's point of view.

Client-Centered Therapy

Carl Rogers believed that people in successful client-centered therapy become more self-confident, more aware of their feelings, more accepting of themselves, more comfortable and genuine with other people, more reliant on self-evaluation than on the judgments of others, and more effective and relaxed.

Bettmann/Corbis

client might be thinking and feeling. Like other skillful interviewers, they engage in active listening—making eye contact with the client, nodding in recognition as the client speaks, and giving other signs of careful attention. They also use *reflection*, a paraphrased summary of the client's words that emphasizes the feelings and meanings that appear to go along with them. Reflection confirms that the therapist has understood what the client has said, conveys the therapist's interest in hearing it, and helps the client to be more aware of the thoughts and feelings being expressed. Here is an example:

> **Client:** This has been such a bad day. I've felt ready to cry any minute, and I'm not even sure what's wrong!
>
> Therapist: You really do feel so bad. The tears just seem to well up inside, and I wonder if it is a little scary to not even know why you feel this way.

Notice that, in rephrasing the client's statements, the therapist reflected back not only the obvious feelings of sadness but also the fear in the client's voice. Most clients respond to empathic reflection by elaborating on their feelings. This client went on to say, "It *is* scary, because I don't like to feel in the dark about myself. I have always prided myself on being in control."

Empathic listening tends to be so effective in promoting self-understanding and awareness that it is used across a wide range of therapies (Corsini & Wedding, 2005). Even beyond the realm of therapy, people who are thought of as easy to talk to are usually "good listeners" who reflect back the important messages they hear from others.

Congruence

Rogerian therapists also try to convey **congruence** (sometimes called *genuineness*) by acting in ways that are consistent with their feelings during therapy. For example, if they are confused by what a client has said, they say so instead of trying to pretend that they always understand everything. When the therapist's unconditional positive regard and empathy are genuine, the client is able to see that relationships can be built on openness and honesty. Ideally, this experience will help the client become more congruent, or genuine, in other relationships.

Gestalt Therapy

Another form of humanistic treatment was developed by Frederick S. (Fritz) Perls and his wife, Laura Perls. A European psychoanalyst, Frederick Perls was greatly influenced by Gestalt psychology, which focused on the idea that people actively organize their perceptions of the world. As a result, he believed that (1) people create their own versions of reality; and (2) people's natural psychological growth continues only as long as they perceive, remain aware of, and act on their true feelings. Growth stops and symptoms of mental disorder appear, said Perls, when people are not aware of all aspects of themselves (Perls, 1969; Perls, Hefferline, & Goodman, 1951).

Like client-centered therapy, **Gestalt therapy** seeks to create conditions in which clients can become more unified, self-aware, and self-accepting and thus ready to grow again. However, Gestalt therapists use more direct and dramatic methods than do Rogerians. Often working with groups, Gestalt therapists prod clients to become aware of feelings and impulses that they have disowned and to discard feelings, ideas, and values that are not really their own. For example, the therapist or other group members might point out inconsistencies between what clients say and how they behave. Gestalt therapists pay particular attention to clients' gestures and other forms of "body language" that appear to conflict with what the clients are saying (Kepner, 2001). The therapist may also ask clients to engage in imaginary dialogues with other people, with parts of their own personalities, and even with objects (Elliott, Watson, & Goldman, 2004a, 2004b). Like a shy person who can be socially outgoing only while at a costume party, clients often find that these dialogues help them get in touch with and express their feelings (Woldt & Toman, 2005).

congruence In client-centered therapy, a consistency between the way therapists feel and the way they act toward clients.

Gestalt therapy An active form of humanistic treatment that seeks to create conditions in which clients can become more unified, more self-aware, and more self-accepting.

Over the years, client-centered and other forms of humanistic therapy have declined in popularity (Watson, 2011), but Carl Rogers's contributions to psychotherapy remain significant and influential (Cook, Biyanova, & Coyne, 2009). In particular, many other treatment approaches have incorporated his emphasis on the importance of the therapeutic relationship in bringing about change (Elliott et al., 2013). Gestalt therapy, too, remains on the therapy scene; some psychologists now combine Perls's techniques with concepts from Eastern philosophy to help clients develop greater self-awareness and self-acceptance (Barnard & Curry, 2011; Schanche et al., 2011).

BEHAVIOR THERAPY AND COGNITIVE BEHAVIOR THERAPY

Can we learn to conquer fears?

Psychodynamic and humanistic approaches to therapy assume that if clients gain insight or self-awareness about underlying problems, the symptoms created by those problems will disappear. Behavior therapists emphasize a different kind of self-awareness: they help clients think about psychological problems as *learned behaviors* that can be changed without first searching for hidden meanings or unconscious causes (Miltenberger, 2011; Spiegler & Guevremont, 2009). For example, suppose you have a panic attack every time you leave home and find relief only when you return. Making excuses when friends invite you out temporarily eases your anxiety but does nothing to solve the problem. Could you reduce your fear without first searching for its underlying meaning? Behavior therapists say yes. So instead of focusing on the possible meaning of your anxiety, they would begin by helping you identify the learning principles that have served to create and maintain it. They would then guide you in learning more adaptive responses in anxiety-provoking situations.

These goals are based on the behavioral approach to psychology in general and on the social-cognitive approach to personality and disorder in particular. As described in the personality chapter, social-cognitive theorists see learning as the basis of both normal personality and most behavior disorders. According to this perspective, disordered behavior and thinking are examples of the maladaptive actions and thoughts that the client has developed through the processes described in the chapter on learning. For example, behavior therapists believe that fear of being in open spaces, in crowds, or away from home (agoraphobia) stems from classically conditioned associations between being away from home and having panic attacks. The problem is partly maintained, they say, through operant conditioning: Staying home and making excuses for doing so is rewarded by reduced anxiety.

Some behavior therapists also emphasize that fears and other problems are maintained by what we think about situations and about ourselves. As discussed later, these *cognitive behavior* therapists focus their treatment efforts on changing maladaptive thoughts as well as problematic behaviors. In short, behavior therapists believe that if problems can be created through prior learning experiences, they can be eliminated through new learning experiences. So whether phobias and other problems are based on events in childhood or were learned more recently, behavior therapists address them by arranging for their clients to have beneficial new experiences.

The notion of applying learning principles in order to change troublesome overt behavior has its roots in the work of John B. Watson, Ivan Pavlov, and others who studied the learned nature of fear in the 1920s. It also stems from B. F. Skinner's research on the impacts of reward and punishment on behavior. In the late 1950s and early 1960s, researchers began to use classical conditioning, operant conditioning, and observational learning techniques in a systematic way to create treatment programs designed to eliminate fears, improve the behavior of disruptive schoolchildren and mental patients, and deal with many other problems (Fishman, Rego, & Muller, 2011). By 1970, behavioral treatment had

Existential Therapy

Additional forms of humanistic therapy were developed by Rollo May (1969), Viktor Frankl (1963), and Irwin Yalom (1980). Their methods were based on existential philosophy, which highlights such uniquely human concerns as our freedom to choose our actions, being responsible for those actions, feeling alone in the world, trying to find meaning and purpose in our lives, and confronting the prospect of death (Yalom, 2002). *Existential therapy* is designed to help people accept and deal with these concerns head-on rather than to continue ignoring or avoiding them. Because people can feel lost, alone, and unsure of life's meaning without displaying serious behavior problems, existential therapists consider their approach as applicable to anyone, whether officially diagnosed with some form of mental disorder or not.

Zigy Kaluzny/Stone/Getty Images

become a popular alternative to psychodynamic and humanistic methods (Miltenberger, 2011). The most notable features of behavioral treatment include the following:

1. **Development of a productive therapist-client relationship.** As in other therapies, this relationship enhances clients' confidence that change is possible and makes it easier for them to speak openly and to cooperate in and benefit from treatment (Emmelkamp, 2013).

2. **A careful listing of the behaviors and thoughts to be changed** (Umbreit et al., 2006). This assessment and the establishment of specific treatment goals sometimes replace the formal diagnosis used in some other therapy approaches. So, instead of treating "depression" or "obsessive-compulsive disorder," behavior therapists work to change the specific thoughts, behaviors, and emotional reactions that lead people to receive these diagnostic labels.

3. **A therapist who acts as a teacher/assistant** by providing learning-based treatments, giving "homework" assignments, and helping the client make specific plans for dealing with problems rather than just talking about them (Kazantizis et al., 2010).

4. **Continuous monitoring and evaluation of treatment,** and constant adjustments to any procedures that do not seem to be effective (Farmer & Nelson-Gary, 2005). Because ineffective procedures are soon altered or abandoned, behavioral treatment tends to be one of the briefer forms of therapy.

Behavioral treatment can take many forms. By tradition, those that rely mainly on classical conditioning principles are usually referred to as **behavior therapy**. Those that focus on operant conditioning methods are usually called **behavior modification**, or *applied behavior analysis* (Miltenberger, 2011). Behavioral treatment that focuses on changing thoughts as well as overt behaviors is called **cognitive behavior therapy**. These methods, especially cognitive behavior therapy, have become increasingly influential in recent years (Hollon & Beck, 2013; Schueller, Muñoz, & Mohr, 2013). Newer cognitive behavior therapies, such as *acceptance and commitment therapy (ACT)* and *mindfulness training*, have a history in alternative medicine and are supported by a strong evidence base (Dimidjian & Linehan, 2009; Hayes & Lillis, 2014; Swain et al., 2013).

Techniques for Modifying Behavior

The most commonly used behavioral treatment methods include *systematic desensitization therapy, modeling, positive reinforcement, extinction, aversion conditioning, and punishment.*

Systematic Desensitization Therapy

Joseph Wolpe (1958) developed one of the first behavioral methods for helping clients to overcome phobias and other forms of anxiety. In his **systematic desensitization therapy**, the client remains relaxed while visualizing a series of anxiety-provoking stimuli. Wolpe believed that this process gradually weakens the learned association between anxiety and the feared object until the fear disappears.

Wolpe first helped his clients learn to relax, often using the *progressive relaxation training* procedures described in the chapter on health, stress, and coping. While relaxed, clients would be asked to imagine the easiest item on a *desensitization hierarchy*, a list of increasingly fear-provoking situations. As treatment progressed, clients imagined each item in the hierarchy, one at a time, moving to a more difficult item only after learning to imagine the previous one without distress. For example, a client who feared flying might begin by imagining airline ads in the newspaper, then imagine people on a TV show boarding an airliner, then imagine boarding a flight, being seated during takeoff, and so on. Wolpe found that once clients could remain calm as they imagined being in feared situations, they were better able to deal with those situations in real life later on.

LINKAGES Can people learn their way out of a disorder? (a link to Learning)

behavior therapy Treatments that use classical conditioning principles to change behavior.

behavior modification Treatments that use operant conditioning methods to change behavior.

cognitive behavior therapy Learning-based treatment methods that help clients change the way they think as well as the way they behave.

systematic desensitization therapy A behavioral method for treating anxiety in which clients visualize a graduated series of anxiety-provoking stimuli while remaining relaxed.

Virtual Desensitization

This client fears spiders. She is wearing a virtual reality display that, under the therapist's careful control, creates the visual experience of seeing spiders of various sizes at varying distances. After learning to tolerate these realistic images without anxiety, clients are better able to fearlessly face the situations they once avoided.

Thierry Berrod/Mona Lisa Production/Science Source

It turns out, though, that desensitization can be especially effective when it slowly and carefully presents clients with real, rather than imagined, hierarchy items (e.g., Choy, Fyer, & Lipsitz, 2007; Tryon, 2005). This *in vivo*, or "real life," desensitization was once difficult to arrange or control, especially in treating fear of heights, highway driving, or flying, for example. Today, however, *virtual reality graded exposure* makes it possible for clients to "experience" vivid, precisely graduated versions of feared situations without actually being exposed to the real thing. In one early study of this approach, clients who feared heights wore a virtual reality helmet that gave the impression of standing on bridges of gradually increasing heights, on outdoor balconies on higher and higher floors, and in a glass elevator as it slowly rose forty-nine stories (Rothbaum et al., 1995). The same virtual reality technology has been used successfully in the treatment of fears caused by spiders, dentistry, air travel, social interactions, public speaking, and posttraumatic stress disorder (e.g., North, North, & Burwick, 2008; Powers et al., 2010; Rothbaum, 2006; Safir & Wallach, 2012; Winerman, 2005).

Modeling

In **modeling** treatments, clients learn important skills by watching other people perform desired behaviors (Bidwell & Rehfeldt, 2004). For example, modeling can teach fearful clients how to respond fearlessly and confidently. In one case study, a therapist showed a spider-phobic client how to calmly kill spiders with a fly swatter and then assigned her to practice this skill at home with rubber spiders (MacDonald & Bernstein, 1974). This combination of fearless demonstrations and firsthand practice, called *participant modeling*, is one of the most powerful treatments for fear (e.g., Bandura, Blanchard, & Ritter, 1969; Zinbarg & Griffith, 2008).

Modeling is also a major part of *assertiveness training* and *social skills training*, which help clients learn how to deal with people more comfortably and effectively. Social skills training has been used to help children interact more effectively with peers, to help social-phobic singles make conversation on dates, to reduce loneliness in adults, and to help rebuild mental patients' ability to have normal conversations with people outside a hospital setting (e.g., Lin et al., 2008; Masi et al., 2011). In **assertiveness training**, the therapist helps clients learn to express their feelings and stand up for their rights in social situations (Alberti & Emmons, 2008). So instead of sheepishly agreeing to be seated at an undesirable restaurant table, clients learn to be comfortable making "I-statements," such as "I would rather sit over there, by the window." Notice that *assertiveness* does not mean aggressiveness; instead, it involves clearly and directly expressing both positive and negative feelings and standing up for one's own rights while respecting the rights of others (Alberti & Emmons, 2008; Patterson, 2000). Assertiveness training is often done in groups and involves both modeling and role playing of specific situations (Duckworth, 2009). For example, group assertiveness training has helped wheelchair-bound adults and students with learning disabilities to more comfortably handle the socially awkward situations in which they sometimes find themselves (Eamon, 2008).

Positive Reinforcement

modeling A behavior therapy method in which desirable behaviors are demonstrated for clients.

assertiveness training A set of methods for helping clients learn to express their feelings and stand up for their rights in social situations.

positive reinforcement Presenting a positive reinforcer (reward) after a desired response.

Behavior therapists also use **positive reinforcement** to alter problematic behaviors and teach new skills in cases ranging from childhood tantrums and juvenile delinquency to schizophrenia and substance abuse (Lussier et al., 2006; Virués-Ortega, 2010). Employing operant conditioning principles, they set up *contingencies,* or rules, that specify the behaviors to be strengthened through reinforcement. In one pioneering study, children with autistic disorder, who typically speak very little, were given grapes, popcorn, or other

FIGURE 15.1

Positive Reinforcement for a Child with Autistic Disorder

During each pretreatment baseline period, a child with autistic disorder rarely said "please," "thank you," or "you're welcome," but he began to make such statements once the therapist demonstrated them, then reinforced the child for saying them. Did modeling and reinforcement actually cause the change? Probably, because each type of response did not start to increase until the therapist began demonstrating it.

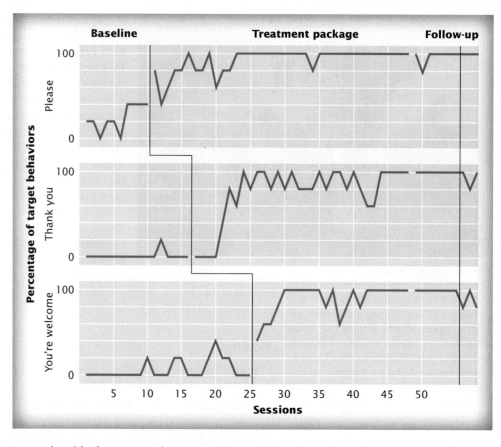

token economy program A system for improving the behavior of clients in institutions by rewarding desirable behaviors with tokens that can be exchanged for various rewards.

extinction The gradual disappearance of a conditioned response.

flooding An exposure technique for reducing anxiety that keeps a client in a feared but harmless situation.

implosive therapy An exposure technique in which clients are helped to imagine being kept in a feared but harmless situation.

items they liked in return for saying "please," "thank you," and "you're welcome" while exchanging crayons and blocks with a therapist. After the therapist modeled the desired behavior by saying the appropriate words at the appropriate times, the children began to say these words on their own. Their use of language also began to appear in other situations, and, as shown in Figure 15.1, the new skills were still evident six months later (Matson et al., 1990).

When working with severely disturbed or intellectually disabled clients in institutions or with juveniles who display emotional or behavioral disorders in residential facilities, behavior therapists sometimes establish a **token economy program**, which is a system for reinforcing desirable behaviors with points or coinlike tokens that can be exchanged later for snacks, access to television, or other rewards (Kazdin, 2008; Matson & Boisjoli, 2009). The goal is to shape more adaptive behavior patterns that will continue outside the institution (Miltenberger, 2011).

Extinction

Just as reinforcing desirable behaviors can make them more likely to occur, failing to reinforce undesirable behaviors can make them less likely to occur, a process known as **extinction**. Treatment methods that use extinction change behavior slowly but offer a valuable way of reducing inappropriate behavior in children and adolescents and in intellectually disabled or seriously disturbed adults (Xue et al., 2012). For example, a client who gets attention by disrupting a classroom, damaging property, or violating hospital rules might be placed in a quiet, boring "time out" room for a few minutes to eliminate reinforcement for misbehavior (Kaminski et al., 2008; Kazdin, 2008).

Extinction can also reduce some learned fears (e.g., Liu et al., 2014), forming the basis of a fear-reduction treatment called **flooding**, in which clients are kept in a feared but harmless situation and are not permitted to use their normally rewarding escape strategies (O'Donohue, Fisher, & Hayes, 2003). **Implosive therapy** is a related method in which the therapist helps the client to vividly imagine being in the feared situation

Treating Fear through Flooding

Flooding is designed to extinguish anxiety by allowing it to occur without the harmful consequences the person dreads. These clients' fear of flying is obvious here, just before takeoff, but it is likely to diminish during and after an uneventful flight. Like other behavioral treatments, flooding is based on the idea that phobias and other psychological disorders are learned and can thus be "unlearned." Some therapists prefer more gradual exposure methods similar to those of in vivo desensitization, which start with situations that are lower on the client's fear hierarchy (Back et al., 2001; Fava et al., 2001).

Westend61/Getty Images

by describing it at length and in great detail. A client undergoing flooding or implosive therapy might be overwhelmed with fear at first, but after an extended period of exposure to the feared stimulus (a frog, say) without experiencing pain, injury, or any other dreaded result, the association between the feared stimulus and the fear response gradually weakens and the conditioned fear response is extinguished (Hauner et al., 2012; Öst et al., 2001; Powers et al., 2010). In one early study, twenty clients who feared needles were exposed for two hours to the sight and feel of needles, including by having mild finger pricks, harmless injections, and blood samplings (Öst, Hellström, & Kåver, 1992). Afterward, all but one of these clients were able to have a blood sample drawn without experiencing significant anxiety.

Because they continuously expose clients to feared stimuli, flooding and other similar methods are also known as *exposure techniques*. Although often highly effective, these methods do cause considerable distress, much like immediately exposing a fearful client to the most difficult item on a desensitization hierarchy. Therefore, some therapists prefer more gradual exposure therapy methods, especially when treating fear that is not focused on a specific stimulus (Berry, Rosenfield, & Smits, 2009).

Aversion Therapy

Some unwanted behaviors, such as excessive gambling or using addictive drugs, can become so habitual and temporarily rewarding that they must be made less attractive if a client is to have any chance of giving them up. Methods for reducing the appeal of certain stimuli are known as *aversion therapy*. The name reflects the fact that these methods rely on a classical conditioning process called **aversion conditioning** to associate shock, nausea, or other physical or psychological discomfort with undesirable stimuli, thoughts, or actions (e.g., Bordnick et al., 2004).

Because aversion conditioning is unpleasant and uncomfortable, because it may not work with all clients (Flor et al., 2002), and because its effects are often temporary, most behavior therapists use this method relatively rarely, only when it is the best treatment choice, and only long enough to allow the client to learn more appropriate alternative behaviors.

Punishment

Sometimes the only way to eliminate a dangerous or disruptive behavior is to punish it with an unpleasant but harmless stimulus, such as a shouted "No!" or a mild electric shock. Unlike aversion conditioning, in which the unpleasant stimulus occurs along with the behavior that is to be eliminated (a classical conditioning approach), **punishment** is an operant conditioning technique; it presents the unpleasant stimulus *after* the undesirable behavior occurs.

Before using electric shock or other forms of punishment, behavior therapists are required by ethical and legal guidelines to ask themselves several important questions: Have all other methods failed? Would the client's life be in danger without treatment? Has an ethics committee reviewed and approved the procedures? Has the adult client or a child client's parent or guardian agreed to the treatment (Kazdin, 2008)? When the answer to these questions is yes, punishment can be an effective, sometimes life-saving, treatment—as in the case illustrated in Figure 5.12 in the chapter on learning. Like extinction and aversion conditioning, though, punishment works best when it is used just long enough to eliminate undesirable behavior and is combined with other behavioral methods designed to reward more appropriate behavior (Hanley et al., 2005).

aversion conditioning A method for reducing unwanted behaviors by using classical conditioning principles to create a negative response to some stimulus.

punishment The presentation of an aversive stimulus or the removal of a pleasant one following some behavior.

Cognitive Behavior Therapy

Like psychodynamic and humanistic therapists, most behavior therapists recognize that depression, anxiety, and many other behavior disorders can stem from how clients think about themselves and the world. And like other therapists, most behavior therapists try to change clients' troublesome ways of thinking, not just their overt behavior. Unlike other therapists, however, behavior therapists rely on learning principles to help clients change the way they think. Their methods are known collectively as *cognitive behavior therapy* (Hollon & Beck, 2013). Suppose, for example, that a client has good social skills but suffers intense anxiety around other people. In a case like this, social skills training would obviously be unnecessary. Instead, the behavior therapist would use cognitive behavioral methods designed to help the client identify habitual thoughts (such as "I shouldn't draw attention to myself") that create awkwardness and discomfort in social situations. Once these cognitive obstacles are brought to light, the therapist describes new and more adaptive ways of thinking and encourages the client to learn and practice them. As these cognitive skills develop (e.g., "I have as much right to give my opinion as anyone else"), it becomes easier and more rewarding for clients to let these new thoughts guide their behavior (Beck, 2005). Cognitive behavior therapy approaches such as these are increasingly common and influential in psychological treatment (Hollon & Beck, 2013; Hayes & Lillis, 2014).

Rational-Emotive Behavior Therapy

A prominent form of cognitive behavior therapy is **rational-emotive behavior therapy (REBT)**, developed by Albert Ellis (1962, 2014). REBT aims first at identifying unrealistic and self-defeating thoughts, such as "I must be loved or approved of by everyone" or "I must always be competent to be worthwhile." After the client learns to recognize such thoughts and to see how they can cause problems, the therapist uses suggestions, encouragement, and logic to help the client replace maladaptive thoughts with more realistic and beneficial ones. The client is then given "homework" assignments to try these new ways of thinking in everyday situations. Here is part of an REBT session with a woman who suffered from panic attacks. She has just said that it would be "terrible" if she had an attack in a restaurant and that people "should be able to handle themselves!"

> **Therapist:** The reality is that … "shoulds" and "musts" are the rules that other people hand down to us, and we grow up accepting them as if they are the absolute truth, which they most assuredly aren't.
>
> **Client:** You mean it is perfectly okay to, you know, pass out in a restaurant?
>
> **Therapist:** Sure!
>
> **Client:** But … I know I wouldn't like it to happen.
>
> **Therapist:** I can certainly understand that. It would be unpleasant, awkward, inconvenient. But it is illogical to think that it would be terrible, or … that it somehow bears on your worth as a person.
>
> **Client:** What do you mean?
>
> **Therapist:** Well, suppose one of your friends calls you up and invites you back to that restaurant. If you start telling yourself, "I might panic and pass out and people might make fun of me and that would be terrible," … you might find you are dreading going to the restaurant, and you probably won't enjoy the meal very much.
>
> **Client:** Well, that is what usually happens.
>
> **Therapist:** But it doesn't have to be that way…. The way you feel, your reaction … depends on what you choose to believe or think, or say to yourself. (Masters et al., 1987)

Cognitive behavior therapists use many techniques related to REBT to help clients learn to think in more adaptive ways (e.g., Lang et al., 2012; Lau et al., 2011;

rational-emotive behavior therapy (REBT) A treatment designed to identify and change illogical, self-defeating thoughts that lead to anxiety and other symptoms of disorder.

Albert Ellis

Rational-emotive behavior therapy (REBT) focuses on altering the self-defeating thoughts that Ellis believed underlie people's behavior disorders. Ellis argued, for example, that students do not get upset because they fail a test but because they have learned to believe that failure is a disaster that indicates they are worthless. Many of Ellis's ideas have been incorporated into various forms of cognitive behavior therapy, and they helped Ellis himself to deal rationally with the health problems he encountered prior to his death in 2007 (Ellis, 1997).

Jim Kahnweiler/jimkphotographics.com

Macleod & Mathews, 2012). Techniques aimed at replacing upsetting thoughts with alternative thinking patterns are described by behaviorists as *cognitive restructuring* (Dobson & Hamilton, 2009). They help clients plan calming thoughts to use during exams, tense conversations, and other anxiety-provoking situations. These thoughts might include "OK, stay calm, you can handle this. Just focus on the task, and don't worry about being perfect." Sometimes, these techniques are expanded to include *stress inoculation training,* in which clients imagine being in a stressful situation and then practice newly learned cognitive skills to remain calm (Meichenbaum, 2009; Sheehy & Horan, 2004).

Beck's Cognitive Therapy

Behavior therapists seek a different kind of cognitive restructuring when they use Aaron Beck's **cognitive therapy** (Beck, 1976, 1995, 2005, 2011; Clark & Beck, 2012). Beck's treatment approach is based on the idea that certain psychological problems—especially those related to depression and anxiety but also those related to personality disorders and schizophrenia (Beck et al., 2007; Beck et al., 2008)—can be traced partly to errors in logic and false beliefs. These include *catastrophizing* (e.g., "If I fail my driver's test the first time, I'll never pass it, and that'll be the end of my social life"), *all-or-none thinking* (e.g., "Everyone ignores me"), and *personalization* (e.g., "I know those people are laughing at me"). Beck refers to these errors and beliefs as *cognitive distortions* (Beck, Freeman, & Davis, 2007). They occur so quickly and automatically that the client never stops to consider that they might not be true (see Table 15.1).

Cognitive therapy takes an active, organized, problem-solving approach in which therapists first help clients learn to identify the errors in logic, false beliefs, and other cognitive distortions that precede anxiety, depression, conduct problems, eating disorders, and other psychological problems (Hollon & Beck, 2013). Then, much as in the five-step critical thinking system illustrated throughout this book, these thoughts and beliefs are considered as hypotheses to be tested, not as "facts" to be uncritically accepted (Hollon & DiGiuseppe, 2011). In other words, the therapist and client become a team of "investigators" as they plan ways to test beliefs such as "I'm no good around the house." For example, they might agree on tasks that the client will attempt as "homework"—such as cleaning the basement, hanging a picture, or cutting the grass. Success at accomplishing even one of these tasks provides concrete evidence to challenge a false belief about incompetence that has supported feelings of depression or anxiety, thus helping to reduce them (Beck et al., 1992; Mullin, 2000).

As described in the chapter on psychological disorders, however, depression, anxiety, and some other disorders may not entirely be due to specific thoughts or beliefs about specific situations. Sometimes they stem from a more general cognitive style that leads

TRY THIS

cognitive therapy An organized problem-solving approach in which the therapist actively collaborates with clients to help them notice how certain negative thoughts precede anxiety and depression.

TABLE 15.1   SOME EXAMPLES OF NEGATIVE THINKING

Here are a few examples of the kinds of thoughts that cognitive behavior therapists believe underlie anxiety, depression, and other behavior problems. After reading this list, try writing an alternative thought that clients could use to replace each of these ingrained cognitive habits. Then jot down a "homework assignment" that you would recommend to help clients challenge each maladaptive statement and thus develop new ways of thinking about themselves.	"I shouldn't draw attention to myself." "I will never be any good at this." "It will be so awful if I don't know the answer." "Everyone is smarter than I am." "Nobody likes me." "I should be able to do this job perfectly." "What if I panic?" "I'll never be happy." "I should have accomplished more by this point in my life."

A Circle of Friends

Some of the advantages of group therapy are also applied in *self-help* groups for problems such as alcohol and drug addiction, childhood sexual abuse, cancer, overeating, overspending, bereavement, compulsive gambling, and schizophrenia (Humphreys, 2004; Kurtz, 2004). Hundreds of thousands of local chapters enroll 10 to 15 million participants in the United States and about half a million in Canada (Harwood & L'Abate, 2010). Some participants meet solely on the Internet (Tan, 2008; Tillfors et al., 2008).

© Andresr/Shutterstock.com

people to expect that the worst will always happen to them and to assume that negative events occur because they are completely and permanently incompetent and worthless (Beck & Alford, 2009). So cognitive behavior therapists also work with clients to develop more generally optimistic ways of thinking and to reduce their tendency to blame themselves for negative outcomes (Persons, Davidson, & Tompkins, 2001). In some cases, cognitive restructuring is combined with skill training, techniques for managing anxiety, and practice in using logical thinking, all of which are designed to help clients experience success and develop confidence in situations in which they had previously expected to fail (Bryant et al., 2008).

Some cognitive therapists have also encouraged clients to use traditional Eastern practices such as meditation (see the chapter on consciousness) to help monitor problematic thoughts. This combined approach is called *mindfulness-based cognitive therapy* (Hofmann et al., 2010; Ma & Teasdale, 2004). It has been helpful in cases of depression (Meadows et al., 2014) and in helping to prevent relapse in people battling substance use disorders (Bowen et al., 2014; Witkiewitz et al., 2014). Research in the field of positive psychology suggests that the effects of cognitive behavior therapy may be enhanced through exercises designed to promote positive emotions—such as identifying and using personal strengths and making a list of things that have gone well each day (Seligman, Berkowitz, et al., 2005; Seligman, Rashid, & Parks, 2006).

GROUP, FAMILY, AND COUPLES THERAPY

How does group psychotherapy differ from individual therapy?

The one-on-one methods of psychodynamic, humanistic, and behavioral treatment we have described are often adapted for use with groups of clients or with family units (Burlingame, Strauss, & Joyce, 2013; Kaslow, 2011).

Group Psychotherapy

Group psychotherapy refers to the treatment of several clients under the guidance of a therapist who encourages helpful interactions among group members. Many groups are organized around one type of problem (such as alcoholism) or one type of client (such as adolescents). In most cases, six to twelve clients meet with their therapist at least once a week for about two hours. All group members agree to hold confidential everything that occurs within these sessions.

Group psychotherapy offers features that are not found in individual treatment (Burlingame, Strauss, & Joyce, 2013). First, it allows the therapist to observe clients interacting with one another. Second, groups encourage their members to talk about themselves and explore their feelings. As they listen to each other, clients often feel less alone because they realize that other people are struggling with difficulties they can relate to as well. This realization tends to raise each client's expectations for improvement, a factor that is important in all forms of treatment. Third, group members can boost one another's self-confidence and self-acceptance as they come to trust and value one another. Fourth, clients learn from one another. They share ideas for solving problems and give one another honest feedback about their attitudes and behavior. Fifth, perhaps through mutual modeling, the group experience makes clients more sensitive to other people's needs, motives, and messages. Finally, group psychotherapy allows clients to try out new skills in a supportive environment. So although the procedures and techniques employed in group psychotherapy may reflect one or more of the theoretical orientations we have described in relation to individual therapy (Burlingame, Strauss, & Joyce, 2013), the impact of the treatment is thought to be enhanced by the nature and strength of the group itself.

group psychotherapy Psychotherapy involving six to twelve unrelated individuals.

family therapy A type of treatment involving two or more clients from the same family.

couples therapy A form of therapy that focuses on improving communication between partners.

- Always begin wih something positive when stating a problem.
- Maintain a focus on the present or the future; don't review all previous examples of the problem or ask "why" questions such as "Why do you always...?"
- Talk about observable events; don't make inferences about them (e.g., say "I get angry when you interrupt me" rather than "Stop trying to make me feel stupid").

FIGURE 15.2
Some "Rules for Talking" in Couples Therapy

TRY THIS Many forms of couples therapy help partners improve communication by establishing rules such as the ones listed here. Think about your own experience in relationships or your observations of heterosexual or homosexual couples as they interact, and then write down some rules you would add to this list. Why do you think it would be important for couples to follow the rules on your list?

Nancy Sheehan / Photo Edit

Family and Couples Therapy

As its name implies, **family therapy** involves treatment of two or more individuals from the same family. One of these, often a troubled adolescent or child, is the initially identified client. Whether family therapy is based on psychodynamic, humanistic, or cognitive behavioral approaches, the family is usually considered as a functioning unit known as a *family system*. As with group psychotherapy, the family therapy format gives the therapist a chance to see how the initially identified client interacts with others, thus providing a basis for discussion of topics that are important to each family member. And as with group psychotherapists, family therapists usually have special training that helps them understand how the problems of individual family members affect and are affected by problems in the complex interactions taking place within the family system as a whole (Kaslow, 2011; Sexton et al., 2013). Ultimately, the client in family therapy is the family itself, and treatment involves as many members as possible (Doherty & McDaniel, 2014). In fact, the goal of family therapy is not just to ease the identified client's problems but also to create greater harmony and balance within the family by helping each member understand family interaction patterns and the problems they create (Blow & Timm, 2002).

In **couples therapy**, improving communication between partners is one of the most important targets of treatment (Long & Andrews, 2011). Discussions in couples therapy sessions typically focus on identifying the miscommunication or lack of communication that interferes with the couples' happiness and intimacy (Sexton et al., 2013). Often the sessions revolve around learning to abide by certain "rules for talking" (see Figure 15.2). For some therapists, helping couples become closer also means helping them express emotions more honestly and be more accepting of one another (Gurman, 2011). One version of couples therapy focuses on strengthening the bond between partners by teaching them how to deal with their unsolvable problems and recover from their fights by making at least five times as many positive statements as negative ones (Gottman, Driver, & Tabares, 2002). Some therapists even offer preventive treatment to couples who are at risk for relationship problems (Gottman, Gottman, & Shapiro, 2010). ("In Review: Approaches to Psychological Treatment" summarizes key features of the main approaches to treatment that we have discussed so far.)

APPROACHES TO PSYCHOLOGICAL TREATMENT

IN REVIEW

Dimension	Classical Psychoanalytic	Contemporary Psychodynamic	Humanistic	Behavioral/Cognitive Behavioral
Nature of the human being	Driven by sexual and aggressive urges	Driven by the need for human relationships	Has free will, choice, and capacity for self-actualization	Is a product of social learning and conditioning; behaves on the basis of experience
Therapist's role	Neutral; helps client explore meaning of free associations and other material from the unconscious	Active; develops relationship with client as a model for other relationships	May be active or nondirective; facilitates client's growth	Active, action oriented; teacher/trainer helps client replace undesirable thoughts and behaviors
Focus	Unresolved unconscious conflicts from the distant past	Understanding the past but focusing on current relationships	Here and now; focus on immediate experience	Current behavior and thoughts; may not need to know original causes to create change

(continued)

APPROACHES TO PSYCHOLOGICAL TREATMENT (CONT.)

Dimension	Classical Psychoanalytic	Contemporary Psychodynamic	Humanistic	Behavioral/Cognitive Behavioral
Goals	Psychosexual maturity through insight; strengthening of ego functions	Correcting effects of early attachment failures; developing satisfying intimate relationships	Expanded awareness; fulfillment of potential; self-acceptance	Changes in thinking and behavior in particular classes of situations; better self-management
Typical methods	Free association; dream analysis, analysis of transference	Analysis of interpersonal relationships, including the client-therapist relationship	Reflection-oriented interviews convey unconditional positive regard, empathy, and congruence; exercises to promote self-awareness	Systematic desensitization, flooding, implosive therapy, modeling, assertiveness and social skills training, positive reinforcement, extinction, aversion conditioning, punishment, cognitive restructuring

In Review Questions

1. Object relations therapy and interpersonal therapy are both contemporary examples of the _____ approach to psychological treatment.

2. Imagining increasingly fear-provoking stimuli while relaxed is a treatment method called _____.

3. Reflection is an interviewing technique associated mainly with the _____ approach to treatment.

EVALUATING PSYCHOTHERAPY

How effective is psychotherapy?

Twenty years ago, a consumer magazine's survey suggested that most clients believe that psychotherapy is effective (Consumer Reports, 1995; Seligman, 1996), but confirming that effectiveness through scientific research has been challenging and controversial.

LINKAGES Can therapy change personality? (a link to Personality)

The value of psychotherapy was first widely questioned in 1952, when British psychologist Hans Eysenck reviewed studies in which thousands of clients had received either traditional psychodynamic therapy, various other therapies, or no treatment. To the surprise and dismay of many therapists, Eysenck (1952) found that the percentage of clients who improved following any kind of psychotherapy was actually lower than among people who received no treatment.

Critics argued that Eysenck was wrong (e.g., Bergin, 1971; de Charms, Levy, & Wertheimer, 1954; Luborsky, 1972). They claimed that he had ignored studies supporting the value of psychotherapy and had misinterpreted the data. In fact, when some of these critics reviewed treatment successes and failures themselves, they concluded that psychotherapy tends to be *more* helpful than no treatment (e.g., Bergin, 1971).

Debate over Eysenck's findings and the contradictory reports that followed them highlight several reasons why it is so hard to answer the apparently simple question of whether psychotherapy works. For one thing, there is the problem of how to measure improvement in psychotherapy. Should we focus on psychological test results, behavioral observations, interviews, or a combination of all three? Different measurements may tell somewhat different stories about improvement, making it difficult for researchers to

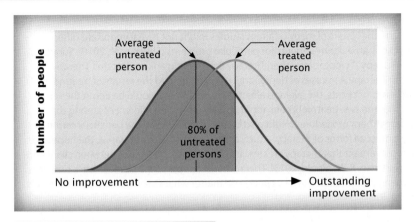

FIGURE 15.3

An Analysis of Psychotherapy's Effects

These curves show the results of a large-scale analysis of the effects of psychotherapy. Notice that on average, people who received therapy were better off than 80 percent of troubled people who did not. The overall effectiveness of psychotherapy has also been confirmed in an analysis of 90 treatment outcome studies (Shadish et al., 2000) and in other research reviews (Nathan & Gorman, 2007; Weisz & Kazdin, 2010).

compare or combine the results of different studies and draw conclusions about the overall effectiveness of treatment (Achenbach, 2011; De Los Reyes, 2011; Wampold et al., 2011).

The question of effectiveness is further complicated by the broad range of clients, therapists, and treatments involved in psychotherapy. Clients differ in the problems they present, in their motivation to solve those problems, and in the amount of stress and social support present in their environments (Petrie & Weinman, 2012; Price & Anderson, 2012). Therapists differ, too, not only in skill, experience, and personality but also in which of the hundreds of available treatment procedures they decide to use and for how long (Barkham et al., 2006; Norcross, Beutler, & Levant, 2005; Owen, 2013; Tracey et al., 2014;). In addition, differences in the nature and quality of the client-therapist relationship from one case to another can significantly alter the course of treatment, the clients' belief in the procedures, and their willingness to cooperate (Bohart & Wade, 2013). Because clients' responses to psychotherapy can be influenced by all of these factors, results from any particular treatment evaluation study might not tell us much about how well different therapists using different methods would do with other kinds of clients and problems (Lambert, 2013).

In short, the question of whether psychotherapy "works" is difficult (if not impossible) to answer scientifically in a way that applies to all therapies for all disorders. However, several research reviews (e.g., Antony & Barlow, 2010; Lambert, 2013; Norcross, 2011; Weisz & Kazdin, 2010) have suggested that, in general, psychotherapy does work (see Figure 15.3).

THINKING CRITICALLY

ARE ALL FORMS OF THERAPY EQUALLY EFFECTIVE?

As you might imagine, most therapists agree that psychotherapy is effective, and most believe that the theoretical approach and treatment methods *they* use work better than those of other therapists (Mandelid, 2003).

What am I being asked to believe or accept?

They can't all be right, of course, and some researchers claim that all of them are wrong. These researchers argue that the success of psychotherapy doesn't have much to do with theories about the causes of behavior disorder, or even with the specific treatment methods used in treatment. All approaches, they say, are equally effective. This has been called the "Dodo Bird Verdict," named after the *Alice in Wonderland* creature who when called on to judge who had won a race answered, "Everybody has won and all must have prizes" (Duncan, 2002; Luborsky, Singer, & Luborsky, 1975).

What evidence is available to support the assertion?

Evidence exists to suggest that there are no significant differences in the overall effectiveness of psychodynamic, humanistic, and behavioral therapies. Statistical analyses that combine the results of a large number of therapy studies show that the three approaches are associated with about the same degree of success (e.g., Keefe et al., 2014; Luborsky, Rosenthal, & Diguer, 2003; Shadish et al., 2000; Weisz, McCarty, & Valeri, 2006).

Are there alternative ways of interpreting the evidence?

Those who question the Dodo Bird Verdict say that evidence in its favor is based on statistical methods that cannot detect genuine differences among treatments (Barlow, 2010). Statistical

(continued)

analyses that average the results of many different studies might not reveal important differences in the impact of particular treatments for particular problems (Ehlers et al., 2010). Suppose, for example, that Therapy A works better than Therapy B in treating anxiety but that Therapy B works better than Therapy A in cases of depression. If you combined the results of treatment studies with both kinds of clients, the average effects of each therapy would be about the same, making it appear that the two treatments are about equally effective. Differences among the effects of specific treatment procedures might also be overshadowed by the beneficial *common factors* shared by almost all forms of therapy—such as the support of the therapist, the hope and expectancy for improvement that therapy creates, and the trust that develops between client and therapist (Laska, Gurtman, & Wampold, 2013). Therapists whose personal characteristics can motivate clients to change might promote that change no matter what specific therapeutic methods they use (Owen, 2013).

What additional evidence would help evaluate the alternatives?

Debate is likely to continue over whether, on average, all forms of psychotherapy are about equally effective, but to many researchers, this is the wrong question. They argue that it's pointless to compare the effects of psychodynamic, humanistic, and behavioral methods in general. It is more important, they say, to address what Gordon Paul called the "ultimate question" about psychotherapy: "What treatment, by whom, is most effective for this individual with that specific problem, under what set of circumstances?" (Paul, 1969).

What conclusions are most reasonable?

Statistical analyses show that various treatment approaches appear about equally effective overall. But this does not mean that every psychotherapy experience will be equally helpful. Potential clients must realize that the success of their treatment can still be affected by how severe their problems are, by the quality of the therapeutic relationship they form with a therapist, by their motivation to change, and by the appropriateness of the therapy methods chosen for their problems (Haque & Waytz, 2012; Hatfield et al., 2010).

Like those seeking treatment, many clinical psychologists are eager for more specific scientific evidence about the effectiveness of particular therapies for particular kinds of clients and disorders. These empirically oriented clinicians are concerned that, all too often, therapists' choices of therapy methods depend more heavily on personal preferences or current fads and trends rather than on objective evidence of effectiveness (Lambert, 2013; Lilienfeld et al., 2013). Empirically oriented psychotherapists believe that advocates of any treatment—whether it is object relations therapy or systematic desensitization—must demonstrate that its benefits are the result of the treatment itself and not just of the passage of time, the effects of repeated assessment, the client's motivation and personal characteristics, or other confounding factors (Chambless & Hollon, 1998). In other words, these clinicians advocate **evidence-based practice**, in which practitioners make decisions about which methods to use based mainly on the results of empirical evidence about the effectiveness of those methods. A movement to use evidence-based practice has also appeared in the medical and dental professions (Diamond, 2014; Richards, 2013; Sniderman et al., 2013).

Empirically oriented clinicians also want to see evidence that the benefits of treatment are clinically significant. To be *clinically significant,* therapeutic changes must be great enough to make the feelings and actions of treated clients similar to those of people who have not experienced these clients' disorders (Crits-Christoph et al., 2008; Kazdin, 2011). For example, a reduction in treated clients' scores on an anxiety test might be *statistically significant*, but the change would not be clinically significant unless those clients now feel and act more like people without an anxiety disorder (see Figure 15.4). The need to demonstrate clinical significance has become more important than ever as increasingly cost-conscious clients and their health insurance companies decide whether and how much to pay for various psychotherapy services. The most scientific way to evaluate treatment effects is through studies in which clients are randomly assigned to various treatments or control conditions and their progress is measured objectively.

evidence-based practice The selection of treatment methods based mainly on empirical evidence of their effectiveness.

FIGURE 15.4
Clinical Significance

Evaluations of psychological treatments must consider the clinical, as well as statistical, significance of observed changes. The shaded area of this graph shows the range of deviant behaviors per minute displayed at home by normal boys. The solid line shows the average rate of deviant behaviors for boys in an operant conditioning treatment for severe behavior problems. The improvement following reinforcement of appropriate behavior was not only statistically significant (compared with the pretreatment baseline) but also clinically significant, in as much as the once-deviant behavior came to resemble that of normal boys.

Source: G.R. Patterson. "Intervention for Boys with Conduct Problems: Multiple Settings, Treatments, And Criteria". Journal Of Consulting And Clinical Psychology, vol. 42, p. 476. American Psychological Association.

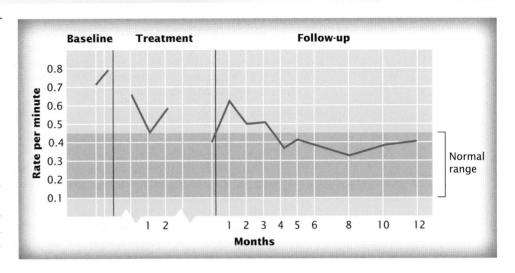

FOCUS ON RESEARCH METHODS

WHICH THERAPIES WORK BEST FOR WHICH PROBLEMS?

To help clinicians select treatment methods on the basis of this kind of empirical evidence, the Society of Clinical Psychology (a division of the American Psychological Association) created a task force in 1993, called the Task Force on Promotion and Dissemination of Psychological Procedures.

What was the researchers' question?

The question addressed by this task force was "What therapies have proven themselves most effective in treating various kinds of psychological disorders?"

How did the researchers answer the question?

Working with other empirically oriented clinical psychologists, this task force examined thousands of studies that evaluated the psychotherapy methods used for treating mental disorders, marital distress, and health-related behavior problems in children, adolescents, and adults.

What did the researchers find?

The task force found that a number of treatments—known as **empirically supported therapies**, or **ESTs**—had been validated by controlled experimental research (Chambless & Ollendick, 2001; DeRubeis & Crits-Christoph, 1998; Kendall & Chambless, 1998; Norcross, 2001, 2002). These therapies were called "efficacious and specific" and "well-established" if they had been found superior to no treatment or to some alternative treatment in at least two randomized clinical trials (RCTs). RCTs are experiments in which clients are randomly assigned to different treatment or control conditions. Also included in this "well established" category were treatments supported by scientific measures in a large number of carefully conducted case studies. Treatments were called "probably efficacious" if they had been supported by at least one RCT or by a smaller number of rigorously evaluated case studies. Finally, treatments were labeled "possibly efficacious" if they had been supported only by a mixture of data from single-case studies or other nonexperimental designs (Chambless & Ollendick, 2001).

Years later, another APA task force was asked to update experimental research on treatment effectiveness and to integrate that knowledge with what clinical expertise can tell us about treating people from various sociocultural backgrounds in real-world treatment

(continued)

empirically supported therapies (ESTs) Treatments for psychological disorders whose effectiveness has been validated by controlled experimental research.

settings. The goal was to seek consensus among researchers *and* clinicians about which specific treatments, and which specific clinical practices, are most likely to lead to improvements in mental health. The result was the establishment of guidelines for *evidence-based practice (EBP) in psychology* (APA Presidential Task Force on Evidence-Based Practice, 2006). Table 15.2 contains some examples of what the EBP task force found.

What do the results mean?

The authors of the original report on empirically supported therapies, the authors of the more recent EBP guidelines, and psychologists who support their efforts argue that by relying on analysis of experimental research and other high-quality clinical studies, they have scientifically evaluated various treatments. They have generated a list of methods from which consumers—and clinicians who want to conduct an evidence-based practice—can choose with confidence when dealing with specific disorders (e.g., Kazdin, 2011; Lambert, 2013). They also suggest that many of the *treatment manuals* that guided therapists in psychotherapy outcome experiments can help other clinicians deliver evidence-based therapies exactly as they were intended (e.g. Beintner, Jacobi, & Schmidt, 2014).

Not everyone agrees with the conclusions or recommendations of the two APA task forces (see Norcross, 2011). Critics note, first, that treatments missing from the latest list of effective therapies haven't necessarily been discredited. Some of those treatments might not yet have been studied thoroughly enough or validated in relation to the efficacy criteria selected by the task force (Lantz, 2004; Westen & Morrison, 2001). These critics also have doubts about the value of some of those criteria. They point to research showing that had the first task force used different outcome criteria, it might have reached different (and perhaps less optimistic) conclusions about the value of some empirically supported treatments (Bradley et al., 2005; Thompson-Brenner, Glass, & Westen, 2003). Critics argue further that the first list of effective therapies was based on research that may not be relevant to clinicians working in the real world of clinical practice. They note that experimental studies of psychotherapy have focused mainly on relatively brief treatments for highly specific disorders, even though most clients' problems tend to be far more complex (Westen & Bradley, 2005). These studies also focused on the therapeutic procedures used rather than on the characteristics and interactions of therapists and clients (Bohart & Wade, 2013). This emphasis on procedure is a problem, critics say, because the outcome of therapy in these experiments might have been strongly affected by client-therapist factors, such as whether the random pairing of clients and therapists resulted in a match or a mismatch on certain personal characteristics. In real clinical situations, clients and therapists are not usually paired up at random (Goldfried & Davila, 2005; Hill, 2005). Finally, because therapists participating in experimental research were required to follow standard treatment manuals, they were not free to adapt treatment methods to the needs of particular clients, as they normally would do (Lambert, 2013). Perhaps, say critics, when there is less experimental control over the treatment situation, all therapies really are about equally effective, as suggested by the statistical analyses of outcome research we mentioned earlier (Shadish et al., 2000; Smith, Glass, & Miller, 1980). In short, these critics reject the idea of creating lists of effective therapies as useful guides.

The APA's evidence-based task force was created partly in response to these concerns, and its practice guidelines are based on results not just from randomized clinical trials but also from less-rigorous studies of therapy and the therapeutic relationship and from clinicians' experiences in real-world treatment settings (Norcross, 2011).

What do we still need to know?

The effort to develop evidence-based practice in clinical psychology represents an important step in responding to Paul's (1969) "ultimate question" about psychotherapy: "What treatment, by whom, is most effective for this individual with that specific problem, under what set of circumstances?" We still have a long way to go to answer all aspects of this question, but empirically oriented clinical psychologists are determined to do so (e.g., Karlin & Cross, 2014; Youn, Kraus, & Castonguay, 2012).

There remains a significant divide, though, between those who would base treatment decisions mainly on the outcome of controlled experimental research and those who feel that the guidance provided by research results must be interpreted and adjusted in light of clinical judgment and experience. The work of the evidence-based task force shows that clinical researchers and clinical practitioners are looking for common ground. It remains to be seen if they will be able to bridge the gap between them in a way that makes the best use of both domains of knowledge in the service of clients' welfare (Grossman & Walfish, 2014).

TABLE 15.2   EXAMPLES OF EVIDENCE-BASED PRACTICE THERAPIES THAT WORK FOR SELECTED DISORDERS

Treatments listed here as having "strong" research support are those that meet the criteria originally defined as "well established" in the original APA Task Force Report (Chambless et al., 1998). Those listed as having "modest" research support are comparable to those defined earlier as "probably efficacious." Therapies appear in the "controversial research support" column either because outcome research on them has produced mixed results or because the reason that they work is still uncertain. For more information on evidence-based practice and research-supported psychological treatments, visit the website of the Society of Clinical Psychology. Information on evidence-based therapies for children and adolescents can be found by searching the Internet for "effective child therapy." There are also reviews of empirical research aimed at identifying potentially harmful therapies (Barlow, 2010; Lilienfeld, 2007; Norcross, et al., 2010).

Problem	Strong Research Support	Modest Research Support	Controversial Research Support
Major depression	Behavior therapy/behavior activation Cognitive behavior therapy Cognitive therapy Interpersonal therapy Problem-solving therapy	Acceptance and commitment therapy Short-term psychodynamic therapy Behavioral couples therapy	
Specific phobia	Exposure therapies Cognitive behavior therapy		Psychoanalytic treatment
Panic disorder		Applied relaxation	
Generalized anxiety disorder	Cognitive and behavior therapies		
Obsessive-compulsive disorder	Exposure and response prevention Cognitive therapy	Acceptance and commitment therapy	
Posttraumatic stress disorder	Prolonged exposure Cognitive processing therapy Present-centered therapy	Stress inoculation	Eye movement desensitization and reprocessing (EMDR)
Schizophrenia	Social skills training Cognitive behavior therapy Assertive community treatment Family psychoeducation Social learning/token economy programs Cognitive remediation	Cognitive adaptation training Illness management and recovery Acceptance and commitment therapy	
Alcohol use disorder	Motivational interviewing Motivational enhancement therapy (MET) MET plus cognitive behavior therapy Behavioral couples therapy	Moderate drinking therapy Prize-based contingency management	
Mixed substance use disorders	Motivational interviewing Motivational enhancement therapy (MET) MET plus cognitive behavior therapy Prize-based contingency management Seeking safety	Friends care program Guided self-change	
Borderline personality disorder	Dialectical behavior therapy	Mentalization-based treatment Schema-focused therapy	Transference-focused therapy

Source: http://www.div12.org/PsychologicalTreatments/index.html.

Though the combinations of treatment methods and therapist and client characteristics that are best suited to solving particular psychological problems have not yet been mapped out, a few notable trends have emerged. For example, when differences in the effectiveness of different treatments occur in comparative studies of adult psychotherapy, they tend to reveal a small to moderate advantage for behavioral and cognitive behavioral methods—especially in the treatment of phobias and certain other anxiety disorders (e.g., Antony & Barlow, 2010; Chaker, Hofmann, & Hoyer, 2010; Craske & Barlow, 2008; Hollon, Stewart, & Strunk, 2006; Houben, Wiers, & Jansen, 2011; Mochizuki-Kawai et al., 2010; Tolin, 2010), and in the prevention and treatment of eating disorders (Hendricks & Thompson, 2005; Wilson et al., 2010). The same overall trend holds true in the treatment of child and adolescent clients (Carr, 2009; Kazak et al., 2010; Kendall et al., 2008). Cognitive methods appear to be less effective, however, at dealing with severe disorders such as schizophrenia (Morrison et al., 2012). Psychodynamic methods are still quite controversial. As shown in Table 15.2, interpersonal therapy and short-term psychodynamic therapy have received strong and modest support, respectively, for the treatment of depression, but some studies have found this approach no more effective overall than placebo or other methods (Shedler, 2010; Smit et al., 2012).

The client-therapist relationship seems to play a significant role in the success of many forms of treatment (e.g., Norcross, 2011; Zuroff & Blatt, 2006). Certain people seem to be particularly effective in forming productive human relationships. Even without formal training, these people can sometimes be as helpful as professional therapists because of personal qualities that are inspiring, healing, and soothing to others (Hill & Lent, 2006; Ronnestad & Ladany, 2006). These qualities may help account for the success of many kinds of therapy.

In summary, the Dodo Bird Verdict is probably incorrect, and it is certainly incomplete. Although different treatments can be equally effective in addressing some disorders, empirical research shows that for other disorders, certain therapies are more effective than others. That research provides valuable guidelines for matching treatments to disorders, but it doesn't guarantee success. The outcome of any given case will also be affected by characteristics of the client, characteristics of the therapist, and the nature of the therapeutic relationship that develops between them (Baldwin & Imel, 2013; Bohart & Wade, 2013). The challenge now is to combine research on empirically supported therapy methods with research on the common factors they share and create a picture of the effectiveness of psychotherapy methods that is based on both sets of data (Messer, 2004; Westen & Bradley, 2005). Such a comprehensive view would be a useful guide for clinicians practicing today and an ideal training model for the clinicians of tomorrow.

Given what is known so far, potential clients should choose a treatment approach and a therapist based on (1) suggestions from empirical research about the best treatment for their particular problem; (2) the treatment approach, methods, and goals the person finds most comfortable and appealing; (3) information about the potential therapist's "track record" of clinically significant success with a particular method for treating problems similar to those the person faces; and (4) the likelihood of forming a productive relationship with the therapist. This last consideration assumes special importance when the client and the therapist do not share similar social or cultural backgrounds.

Sociocultural Factors in Therapy

Sociocultural differences between clients and therapists—in religious faith, gender, age, ethnicity, sexual orientation, socioeconomic background, and the like—can sometimes create miscommunication or mistrust (Seeley, 2006). If it does, their working relationship and the clients' motivation to change may both be impaired (Vasquez, 2007; Wintersteen, Mensinger, & Diamond, 2005). Suppose, for example, that a therapist suggests that a client's insomnia is a reaction to stress, but the client is sure that it comes as punishment for having offended a long-dead ancestor. That client may not easily accept a treatment based on the principles of stress management (Wohl, 1995). Similarly, a therapist who believes that people should

Preparing for Therapy

Special pretreatment orientation programs may be offered to clients who, because of sociocultural factors, are unfamiliar with the rules and procedures of psychotherapy. These programs provide a preview of what psychotherapy is, how psychotherapy can help, and what the client is expected to do to make it more effective (Reis & Brown, 2006; Swartz, Zuckoff et al., 2007).

Rhoda Sidney/PhotoEdit

confront and overcome life's problems might run into trouble when treating people whose cultural or religious training encourages the calm acceptance of these problems (Sue et al., 2009). In such cases, the result may be much like two people singing a duet using the same music but different lyrics (Martinez et al., 2005; Martinez-Taboas, 2005).

In the United States, cultural clashes may contribute to the underuse of mental health services by new immigrants and several minority populations (Comas-Diaz, 2014; Thurston & Phares, 2008). Accordingly, there are efforts being made to ensure that sociocultural differences do not deprive people of treatment they may need (Cabral & Smith, 2011; Richards & Bergin, 2000). For example, virtually all mental health training programs in North America seek students from traditionally underserved minority groups, in hopes of maintaining a diverse workforce of psychotherapists (e.g., Meredith & Baker, 2007; Rogers & Molina, 2006; Vasquez & Jones, 2006). Also, some U.S. states require clinical psychologists to take courses on how culture affects therapy in order to qualify for their licenses (Rehm & DeMers, 2006). Cultural diversity training is also required for graduate students in clinical and counseling psychology training programs accredited by the American Psychological Association (Commission on Accreditation, 2008; Smith, Constantine et al., 2006). Such training helps clinicians appreciate, for example, that it may be considered impolite in some cultures to make eye contact with a stranger. Armed with this information, a therapist is more likely to realize that people from those cultures are not necessarily depressed, lacking in self-esteem, or overly submissive just because they look at the floor during an interview. In the meantime, many minority clients are likely to encounter a therapist from a differing background, so researchers are examining the value of matching therapeutic techniques with clients' culturally based expectations and preferences (Meyer, Zane, & Cho, 2014).

There is no guarantee that cultural diversity training for therapists improves treatment results (Shin et al., 2005), but it can help (Sue & Sue, 2012). Though all therapists will not be equally effective with clients of all sociocultural backgrounds, cultural diversity training offers a way to improve therapists' *cultural competence,* an extension of Carl Rogers's concept of empathy. When therapists appreciate the client's view of the world, it is easier for them to set goals that are in harmony with that view (Comas-Diaz, 2014). Minimizing misunderstanding and miscommunication is one of the many ethical obligations that therapists assume when working with clients (Tomes, 1999). Let's consider some others.

Rules and Rights in the Therapeutic Relationship

Psychotherapy can be an intensely emotional experience, and the relationship established with a therapist can profoundly influence a client's life. Professional ethics and common sense require the therapist to ensure that this relationship does not harm the client. For example, the American Psychological Association's *Ethical Principles of Psychologists and Code of Conduct* forbids a sexual relationship between therapist and client during treatment and for at least two years afterward because of the harm it can cause the client (American Psychological Association, 2002b; Sonne, 2012). Even after two years have passed, therapists may not ethically pursue a sexual relationship with a former client unless they can demonstrate that the relationship is not exploitative or otherwise harmful to that client. Laws in some U.S. states prohibit therapists from *ever* having a sexual relationship with a former client.

The APA's ethical standards also require therapists to keep strictly confidential everything a client says in therapy. Confidentiality is one of the most important features of a successful therapeutic relationship. It allows the client to reveal unpleasant or embarrassing

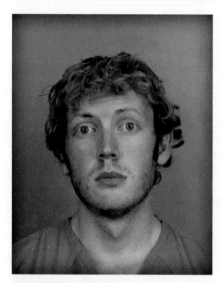

Rights of the Mentally Ill

On July 20, 2012, James Holmes, a former graduate student at the University of Colorado, fired several weapons in a local movie theater, killing twelve people and injured seventy others. A university psychiatrist who had been treating him had previously notified campus police that he could be a threat to other people, but the danger was apparently not clear enough to hospitalize him. Cases such as his are frustrating to mental health professionals, who must always balance the rights of patients against those of the public.

Handout/Getty Images

impulses, behaviors, or events without fear that this information will be repeated to anyone else. Professionals do sometimes consult with one another about a client, but each is required not to reveal information to outsiders (including members of an adult client's family) without the client's consent. The APA's code of ethics even includes standards for protecting confidentiality for the growing number of clients who seek psychological services via *telehealth* or *e-health* channels, which include telephone, Skype, FaceTime, e-mail, or online links (Aguilera & Munoz, 2011; Ragusea, 2012; Slone, Reese, & McClellan, 2012; Yuen et al., 2012). One of these standards requires therapists to inform clients that others might be able to gain access to their electronic communication and that no formal client-therapist relationship exists in e-mail exchanges (Van Allen & Roberts, 2011).

Professional standards about confidentiality are backed up in most U.S. states and in federal courts by laws that recognize that information revealed in therapy—like information given to a priest, a lawyer, or a physician—is privileged communication. This means that a therapist can refuse—even in court—to answer questions about a client or to provide personal notes or recordings from therapy sessions (Fisher, 2012). In special circumstances therapists may be legally required to violate confidentiality (Donner et al., 2008), including when (1) a client is so severely disturbed or suicidal that hospitalization is needed; (2) a client uses his or her mental condition and history of therapy as part of a defense in a courtroom trial; (3) the therapist must defend against a client's charge of malpractice; (4) a client reveals information about sexual or physical abuse of a child; and (5) the therapist believes a client may commit a violent act against a specific person.

Several U.S. states now have laws that make a therapist liable for failing to take steps to protect those who are threatened with violence by the therapist's clients (Bersoff, 2008; Werth, Welfel, & Benjamin, 2009). Other states allow therapists more discretion in warning or protecting potential victims (Carson & Bull, 2003).

Other laws protect people in the United States from being committed to mental hospitals without good cause (Lareau, 2013). Before people can be forcibly committed, the state must provide "clear and convincing" evidence that they are not only mentally ill but also gravely disabled or an "imminent danger" to themselves or others. While hospitalized, patients have the right to receive treatment, but they also have the right to refuse certain forms of treatment (Carson & Bull, 2003). These rules are designed to protect hospitalized mental patients from abuse, neglect, or exploitation, but the right to refuse treatment does not extend to hospitalized patients who pose a danger to themselves or others (Manahan, 2004).

Hospitalized patients who do not pose such dangers—including those whose dangerous impulses are being suppressed by prescription medications—have the right to be subjected to minimal restriction of their freedom (Bell, 2005). Accordingly, they are released from mental hospitals, usually with a supply of medication that they are to take on their own. Unfortunately, not all these patients follow doctors' orders. Andrew Goldstein was not considered dangerous as long as he took his antipsychotic medication, but after being released from a New York City mental hospital in December 1998, he stopped doing so. About two weeks later, Goldstein pushed Kendra Webdale to her death under the wheels of a subway train (Perlin, 2003). Cases such as these put the staff at mental health facilities in a bind—they worry about being sued if they keep patients unnecessarily confined or if someone is harmed by a patient they have released too soon (Bonta, Blaise, & Wilson, 2014). In an effort to strike a balance between the rights of mental patients and those of the public, several states now have laws requiring outpatient treatment for people who are dangerous when not medicated. The New York statute is known as Kendra's Law (Appelbaum, 2005).

BIOLOGICAL TREATMENTS

Is electric shock still used to treat psychological disorders?

So far, we have described psychological approaches to the treatment of mental disorders. But there are also biological treatments, primarily offered by psychiatrists and other medical doctors, who often work in cooperation with psychologists. Today, biological treatments for psychological problems mainly involve prescription medications. As late as the mid-1900s, however, the most common biological treatments for severe psychological disorders were brain surgery and electric shock.

Psychosurgery

Psychosurgery involves treating mental disorders by using procedures that destroy brain tissue. Among the first to try these procedures was a Portuguese neurosurgeon, António Egas Moniz. In 1935, he developed a technique, called *prefrontal lobotomy*, in which small holes are drilled in the front of the skull and a sharp instrument is inserted and moved from side to side to cut connections between the prefrontal cortex and the rest of the brain (Freeman & Watts, 1942; Moniz, 1948). Moniz's theory was that emotional reactions in disturbed people become exaggerated due to neural processes in the frontal lobes, and he believed that the lobotomy disrupts these processes. During the 1940s and 1950s, psychosurgery became almost routine in the treatment of schizophrenia, depression, anxiety, aggressiveness, and obsessive-compulsive disorder (Valenstein, 1980). However, brain surgery carries a risk of complications and is sometimes fatal. Further, its benefits are uncertain, and some problems it can create, including epilepsy, may be irreversible (Balon, 2004). Today, psychosurgery is performed rarely, when all else has failed, and it focuses on much smaller brain areas than those involved in lobotomies (Helmes & Velamoor, 2009; Mathern & Miller, 2013).

A different type of brain surgery is performed as part of *deep brain stimulation (DBS)*. This procedure places electrodes in the brain to provide pulses of electricity to specified target areas (Oluigbo, Salma, & Rezal, 2012). The amount of electricity delivered is adjusted over time, based on how a person responds to treatment. DBS was first used to treat movement disorders such as Parkinson's disease (Yu & Neimat, 2008), but it has also proven helpful in people whose severe depression or obsessive-compulsive disorder did not respond to other therapies (Mohr et al., 2011; Williams & Okun, 2013).

In yet another surgical procedure, called *vagal nerve stimulation (VNS)*, a pacemaker-like device is implanted in the upper chest and attached by thin wires to the vagus nerve in the neck (Christancho et al., 2011). Signals from this stimulated nerve are carried into the brain, where they are effective not only in reducing seizures in patients with epilepsy (Patel et al., 2013) but also in treating some forms of depression (Mohr et al., 2011).

Electroconvulsive Shock Therapy

Another form of biological treatment is based on work in the 1930s by a Hungarian physician named Ladislaus von Meduna. He used a drug to induce convulsions in people with schizophrenia. He believed—incorrectly—that because schizophrenia and epilepsy sometimes (though rarely) occur in the same person, epileptic-like seizures might combat schizophrenia. In 1938, Italian physicians Ugo Cerletti and Lucio Bini created seizures by passing an electric current through the brains of patients with schizophrenia. During the next twenty years or so, this procedure, called **electroconvulsive shock therapy** (**ECT**), became a routine treatment for schizophrenia, depression, and sometimes mania. Many patients improved at first, but their problems often reappeared. The benefits of ECT also had to be weighed against side effects such as memory loss, confusion, speech disorders, and, in some cases, death due to cardiac arrest (Lickey & Gordon, 1991; Shiwach, Reid, & Carmody, 2001).

Today, ECT is given mainly to people with severe depression (and occasionally mania) who do not respond to medication (de Macedo-Soares et al., 2005; Payne & Prudic, 2009; Weiner & Falcone, 2011). It can be quite effective (e.g., Martínez-Amorós et al., 2012), though a high percentage of patients experience a return of depression after a few months (Huuhka et al., 2012). They sustain benefits longer if their course of ECT is followed by psychotherapy (Brakemeier et al., 2013). Although the use of ECT is less common now than it was in the 1950s in the United States (Case et al., 2013), it is given more frequently

Hospital Restraints

Here are examples of the chains, straitjackets, belts, and covered bathtubs that were used to restrain disruptive patients in North American and European mental hospitals in the 1800s and well into the 1900s. These devices were gentle compared with some of the methods endorsed in the late 1700s by Benjamin Rush. Known as the father of American psychiatry, Rush advocated curing patients by frightening or disorienting them—for example, by placing them in a coffin-like box that was then briefly immersed in water.

The Medical History Museum of the University of Zürich

psychosurgery Surgical procedures that destroy tissue in small regions of the brain in an effort to treat psychological disorders.

electroconvulsive shock therapy (ECT) A brief electric shock administered to the brain, usually to reduce severe depression that does not respond to medication treatments.

Electroconvulsive Shock Therapy (ECT)

Approximately 100,000 individuals in the United States receive ECT each year (Payne & Prudic, 2009). ECT remains a controversial treatment (Breggin, 2007). Critics point to fears of possible brain damage, but proponents say the benefits of ECT for certain patients outweigh its potential dangers.

Will McIntyre/Science Source

than coronary bypass operations, appendectomies, and tonsillectomies (Mathew, Amiel, & Sackeim, 2005). This is despite the fact that scientists are still unsure why ECT works (e.g., Perrin et al., 2012; Shorter & Healy, 2007) and that there is still uncertainty about the degree to which repeated ECT causes lasting effects on the brain or on cognitive functions (Abbott et al., 2014; Bergsholm et al., 2012).

In an effort to minimize ECT side effects, doctors today give patients an anesthetic so that they are unconscious before the shock is delivered, along with a muscle relaxant to prevent bone fractures during convulsions. Also, the shock now lasts only about half a second and is usually delivered to only one side of the brain (Magid et al., 2013). In contrast to the dozens of treatments administered decades ago, patients now receive only about six to twelve shocks, one approximately every two days (Shorter & Healy, 2007).

Magnetic seizure therapy (MST) may offer an even safer option than ECT because it induces seizures through timed pulses of magnetic energy, not electrical shocks (Zyss et al., 2010). MST appears effective in treating depression, but its effects may not be as long-lasting as those of traditional ECT (Allan & Ebmeier, 2011; Kayser et al., 2011). A newer procedure called *repetitive transcranial magnetic stimulation (rTMS)*, manages to excite brain cells without causing a seizure. In this technique, a strong magnet is placed on specific regions of the head, creating an electrical field that activates brain cells beneath the magnet. Research suggests that the use of rTMS over certain brain areas can result in some improvement in depression, auditory hallucinations, and posttraumatic stress disorder (Karsen, Watts, & Holtzheimer, 2014; Ren et al., 2014). It is still unclear, however, if there are any harmful side effects of rTMS (Muller, Pascual-Leone, & Rotenberg, 2012), so it is not yet widely available for use.

Psychoactive Medications

The use of ECT declined after the 1950s, in part because psychoactive medications had begun to emerge as more convenient and effective treatment alternatives. In the chapters on biological aspects of psychology and on consciousness, we discuss the effects of psychoactive drugs on neurotransmitter systems, autonomic activity, emotions, thinking, and behavior. Here, we describe their role in combating schizophrenia, depression, mania, and anxiety.

Antipsychotic Medications

Antipsychotics reduce the intensity of psychotic symptoms such as hallucinations, delusions, paranoid suspiciousness, disordered thinking, and confused speech in many mental patients, especially those with schizophrenia. A widely used category of antipsychotics is known as the *phenothiazines* (pronounced "fee-noh-THIGH-uh-zeens"). The first of these, chlorpromazine (marketed as Thorazine in the United States and as Largactil in Canada and the United Kingdom), was especially popular. Another antipsychotic, haloperidol (Haldol), is about as effective as the phenothiazines but creates less sedation (Julien, 2005) and is used frequently today (Joy, Adams, & Lawrie, 2006). Patients who do not respond to one medication may respond to another (Schatzberg, Cole, & DeBattista, 2007). Between 60 and 70 percent of psychiatric patients receiving these medications show improvement, though fewer than 30 percent respond well enough to live successfully on their own (Rothschild, 2010). Together, haloperidol and the phenothiazines are sometimes referred to as *neuroleptics*.

In some people, neuroleptics cause side effects, ranging from dry mouth and sedation to symptoms similar to those of Parkinson's disease, including muscle rigidity, tremors, and slowed movement. Some of these side effects can be treated with medication, but not always. Some people who take neuroleptics develop an often irreversible movement disorder, called *tardive dyskinesia* (TD) (Blumberger et al., 2014). The symptoms of TD include uncontrollable, repetitive actions, often involving twitching of the face, thrusting of the tongue, and sometimes flailing of the arms and legs (Aquino & Lang, 2014).

antipsychotics Medications that relieve the symptoms of schizophrenia and other severe psychological disorders.

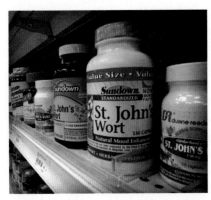

A Natural Cure?

St. John's wort, an herbal remedy, has become a popular nonprescription treatment for depression. One of its active ingredients, *hypericin*, may affect neurotransmitters in the brain, much as do psychoactive medications such as Prozac or Zoloft. One double-blind, placebo-controlled study showed St. John's wort to be no more effective than a placebo for treating major depression (Hypericum-Depression Trial Study Group, 2002), though others have suggested that it helps in cases of milder depression (e.g., Hammerness, Basch, & Ulbricht, 2003; Szegedi et al., 2005). Final conclusions about the safety and effectiveness of St. John's wort must await the results of further research.

Mario Tama/Getty Images

Most of the newer antipsychotic medications are known as *atypical antipsychotics*. Examples include clozapine, olanzapine, quetiapine, risperidal, ziprasidone, and aripiprazole. They are called *atypical* mainly because they are less likely to cause movement disorders (Forand, DeRubeis, & Amsterdam, 2013). Although probably no more effective overall than the neuroleptics, atypical antipsychotics are often better tolerated and so are considered a "first line" antipsychotic medication choice (Meltzer, 2013). Atypical antipsychotics have helped many patients who did not respond to neuroleptics (Rothschild, 2010). Unfortunately, some of their possible side effects require the treating doctor to monitor patients carefully, sometimes with blood tests and other studies (Meyer, 2007; Stöllberger, Huber, & Finsterer, 2005).

Antidepressant Medications

Soon after antipsychotics appeared, they were joined by **antidepressants**, a class of medications that is now widely used to relieve the symptoms of depression (Forand et al., 2013). There are several types of antidepressants. The *monoamine oxidase inhibitors (MAOIs)* were used to treat depression, especially when accompanied by anxiety and panic (Julien, 2008). Medications in another category, the *tricyclic antidepressants (TCAs)*, were prescribed even more often than MAOIs because they worked better with fewer side effects.

Today, however, there are newer options that are tolerated even better (Undurraga & Baldessarini, 2012). The most popular of these are *selective serotonin reuptake inhibitors (SSRIs)*, of which fluoxetine (Prozac) was the first example. Introduced in 1986, fluoxetine quickly became the most widely used antidepressant medication in North America (Brambilla et al., 2005). Its popularity was because it is as effective as older medications but in most cases has fewer and milder side effects—mainly weight gain, sexual dysfunction, and gastrointestinal problems (e.g., Magni et al., 2013). Many other SSRIs are in common use now as well (Deshauer et al., 2008), and even newer examples of antidepressants have been developed (Stahl et al., 2013), including venlafaxine (Effexor), desvenlafaxine (Pristiq), duloxetine (Cymbalta), buproprion (WelButrin), mirtazapine (Remeron), and trazodone (Desyrel).

There is some debate about the benefits of antidepressants (Davis et al., 2011; Ioannidis, 2008). For example, whereas about 50 to 70 percent of patients who take antidepressant drugs experience improved mood, greater physical activity, increased appetite, and better sleep, others do not (Baghai, Möller, & Rupprecht, 2006; Craighead & Dunlap, 2014). And drug trials comparing their effects to those of placebos have shown a shrinking advantage for these medications over the last thirty years (Khin et al., 2011; Undurraga & Baldessarini, 2012). Does this mean that the newer antidepressants do not work as well as the older ones? Not necessarily. True, depressed people who received placebo treatment have been doing better in more recent drug trials than in previous ones (Schalkwijk et al., 2014), but more research will be needed to determine whether this change might reflect changes in the research designs and statistical analyses used in the newer studies.

Unfortunately, only about 10 to 20 percent of people suffering the most severe psychotic depression show good improvement with antidepressant medication alone (Fournier et al., 2010). An analysis of pharmaceutical companies' clinical trial data submitted to the U.S. Food and Drug Administration by the makers of six widely prescribed antidepressant medications showed that in 57 percent of the trials, antidepressant medications did only a little better than placebo at relieving severe depression (Kirsch et al., 2002; Kirsch, Scoboria, & Moore, 2002). A more recent study found similar results when comparing the effects of newer antidepressants and placebos (Kirsch, 2009). Final conclusions must await better research, though, because there are far too few well-designed placebo controlled studies on medications for the most severe forms of depression (Wijkstra et al., 2013). For now, defenders of antidepressant medications argue that even relatively small effects are better than none (e.g., Baldwin, 2011), whereas critics contend that those effects are too small to

antidepressants Medications that reduce symptoms of depression.

matter, especially when viewed in light of these drugs' high cost and potential side effects (Ioannidis, 2008). Fortunately, some antipsychotic medications appear to help people with depression, even severe psychotic depression, when they do not respond to antidepressant medication alone (e.g., Gabriel, 2013; Nelson et al., 2014; Thase, 2011, 2013).

Lithium and Anti-Seizure Medications

The mineral salt lithium carbonate, when taken regularly, prevents both the depression and the mania associated with bipolar disorder in some people (Rybakowski, 2014). Without lithium, the typical person with bipolar disorder has a manic episode about every fourteen months and a depressive episode about every seventeen months (American Psychiatric Association, 2000); with lithium, attacks of mania occur as rarely as every nine years (Geddes et al., 2004; Ketter, 2010). Lithium may be particularly valuable in lowering the risk of suicide in people with bipolar disorder (Cipirani et al., 2013). The lithium dosage must be carefully controlled, however, because taking too much can cause vomiting, nausea, tremor, fatigue, slurred speech, and, with severe overdoses, coma or death (Johnson, 2002).

In recent years, some antiseizure medications (such as divalproex [Depakote] or lamotrigine [Lamictal]) have emerged as effective alternatives to lithium in treating bipolar disorder (Selle et al., 2014; Vieta & Valentí, 2013). For some individuals, these medications may be better tolerated, less dangerous at higher doses, and easier to regulate than lithium (Ketter, 2010; Schatzberg et al., 2007).

Tranquilizing Medications (Anxiolytics)

During the 1950s, a new class of medications called **tranquilizers** was shown to reduce mental and physical tension and the symptoms of anxiety. The first of these, meprobamate (Miltown or Equanil), acts somewhat like barbiturate sleeping pills, meaning that overdoses can cause sleep and even death. Because they do not pose this danger, the *benzodiazepines*—particularly chlordiazepoxide (Librium) and diazepam (Valium)—became a popular worldwide choice for anxiety (Stevens & Pollack, 2005). Over time, these and other anti-anxiety medications, also called **anxiolytics** (pronounced "ang-zee-oh-LIT-ix"), became the most widely prescribed and used of all legal drugs (Stevens & Pollack, 2005). Anxiolytics (whose name means "breaking anxiety apart") have an immediate calming effect and so can help reduce the symptoms of generalized anxiety and posttraumatic stress disorder.

One of the benzodiazepines, alprazolam (Xanax), has become especially popular for helping to relieve the acute anxiety experienced in panic disorder and agoraphobia (Verster & Volkerts, 2004). In some people, though, the benzodiazepines can also cause sleepiness, lightheadedness, and impaired memory and thinking. They can also be quite addictive (Lader, 2011). Combining these medications with alcohol can have additive, and potentially fatal, effects (Chouinard, 2004). Further, suddenly discontinuing benzodiazepines after heavy or long-term use can cause severe withdrawal symptoms, including seizures and worsening anxiety (Lemoine et al., 2006).

While benzodiazepines help reduce anxiousness, they are less helpful in preventing it. An alternative anxiolytic called buspirone (BuSpar) is better at preventing anxiousness. Its effects may not occur for days or weeks after treatment begins, but buspirone can ultimately equal diazepam in reducing generalized anxiety (Gorman, 2003; Rickels & Rynn, 2002). Further, it does not seem to promote dependence, it causes less interference with thinking, and it does not interact so much with alcohol.

Perhaps because anxiety is often accompanied by depression, many antidepressants are also helpful in treating problems such as panic disorder, social phobia, obsessive-compulsive disorder, and posttraumatic stress disorder (e.g., Julien, 2005; Nutt, 2005b). Table 15.3 lists the effects and side effects of some of the psychoactive medications we have described.

tranquilizers (anxiolytics) Medications that reduce tension and symptoms of anxiety.

TABLE 15.3 A SAMPLING OF PSYCHOACTIVE MEDICATIONS USED FOR TREATING PSYCHOLOGICAL DISORDERS

Psychoactive medications have been successful in reducing symptoms of many psychological disorders, but there are limits to their usefulness. They can have troublesome side effects and some may create dependence, especially after years of use (e.g., Breggin, 2008). Further, medications do not "cure" mental disorders (National Institute of Mental Health, 1995), and their effects are not always strong (Kirsch et al., 2002). It is of concern, then, that public perceptions of drug benefits have become unrealistic, leading many people to choose drug treatment over psychotherapies that might offer a more permanent solution to their psychological problems (Mackenzie et al., 2014).

Chemical Name	Trade Name	Effects and Side Effects
For Schizophrenia Spectrum Disorders: Antipsychotics		
Chlorpromazine	Thorazine	Reduce hallucinations, delusions, incoherence, jumbled thought processes; but may cause movement-disorder side effects, including tardive dyskinesia.
Haloperidol	Haldol	
Clozapine	Clozaril	Reduces psychotic symptoms; causes no movement disorders but carries some risk of rare serious blood disease.
Risperidone	Risperdal	Reduces positive and negative psychotic symptoms without risk of blood disease.
Ziprasidone	Geodon	Reduces positive and negative psychotic symptoms without causing weight gain.
Aripiprazole	Abilify	Reduces positive and negative psychotic symptoms without weight gain and with few side effects; can also be effective in some cases of depression.
For Depressive and Bipolar Disorders: Antidepressant Medications and Mood Elevators		
Tricyclics		
Imipramine	Tofranil	Act as antidepressants but also have anti-panic action; cause sleepiness and other moderate side effects; potentially dangerous if taken with alcohol.
Amitriptyline	Elavil, Amitid	
Other Antidepressant Medications		
Fluoxetine	Prozac	
Clomipramine	Anafranil	
Fluvoxamine	Luvox	
Sertraline	Zoloft	All have antidepressant, anti-panic, and anti-obsessive action.
Escitalopram	Lexapro	
Paroxetine	Paxil	
Citalopram	Celexa	
Other Medications		
Lithium carbonate	Carbolith, Lithizine	Calms mania and reduces mood swings of bipolar disorder; overdose harmful, potentially deadly.
	Depakote	
Divalproex	Lamictal	Effective against mania with fewer side effects.
Lamotrigine		Effective in delaying relapse in bipolar disorder; most benefits associated with depression.
For Anxiety Disorders: Tranquilizing Medications (Anxiolytics)		
Benzodiazepines		
Chlordiazepoxide Diazepam	Librium Valium	Act as potent anxiolytics for generalized anxiety, panic, stress; extended use may cause physical dependence and withdrawal syndrome if abruptly discontinued.
Alprazolam	Xanax	Also has antidepressant effects; often used in agoraphobia; has high potential for addiction.
Clonazepam	Klonopin	Often used in combination with other anxiolytics for panic disorder.
Other Anti-Anxiety Agents		
Buspirone	BuSpar	Has slow-acting anti-anxiety action; no known dependence problems.

Human Diversity and Medication

Medications are designed to benefit everyone in the same way, but it turns out that the same psychoactive medication dose can have significantly different effects in each sex and in people from various ethnic groups. For example, Caucasians must take significantly higher doses than Asians of the benzodiazepines, haloperidol, clozapine, lithium, and possibly the tricyclic antidepressants in order to obtain equally beneficial effects (Hull et al., 2001; Ng et al., 2005). In addition, African Americans may show a faster response to tricyclic antidepressants than European Americans and may respond to lower doses of lithium (Chaudhry et al., 2008). There is also some evidence that, compared with European Americans, African Americans and Hispanic Americans might require higher doses of antipsychotics to get the same benefits (Citrome et al., 2005). Some of these ethnic differences may be related to genetically regulated differences in drug metabolism (Kato & Serretti, 2010; Zhang, Lencz, & Malhotra, 2010), whereas others may be due to dietary practices and other sociocultural factors (Bakare, 2008).

Males and females may respond in about the same way to tricyclic antidepressants (Wohlfarth et al., 2004), but women may maintain higher blood levels of these and other therapeutic medications and may show better response to antipsychotics (Hildebrandt et al., 2003; Salokangas, 2004). Women also may be more vulnerable to antipsychotics' adverse side effects, such as tardive dyskinesia (Yarlagadda et al., 2008), but less prone to the cholesterol-related side effects of medications for bipolar disorder (Vemuri et al., 2011). These gender differences in medication response appear less related to estrogen than to other hormonal or body-composition differences between men and women, such as the ratio of body fat to muscle (Dawkins & Potter, 1991; Salokangas, 2004). Continued research on these and other dimensions of human diversity will undoubtedly lead to more effective and safer medications for everyone (Thompson & Pollack, 2001; Vemuri et al., 2011).

Medications and Psychotherapy

Despite their success in treating psychological disorders, psychoactive medications can have drawbacks. As we have seen, some can result in dependence, and side effects can range from minor problems such as the thirst and dry mouth caused by some antidepressants to movement disorders such as tardive dyskinesia caused by some neuroleptics. Although the most serious side effects are relatively rare, some are irreversible, and it is impossible to predict in advance who will develop them. For example, although a clear causal link has not yet been confirmed, the U.S. National Institute of Mental Health (NIMH) and regulatory agencies in Canada and Britain have issued warnings about the danger of suicidal behavior in children and adolescents who are given Prozac and similar antidepressants (National Institute of Mental Health, 2004; Olfson, Marcus, & Shaffer, 2006; Stone et al., 2009). There is also concern about how effective psychoactive medications truly are, dampening the enthusiasm that once led many clinical psychologists to seek prescription privileges (Greenberg, 2010).

So which is better: medications or psychotherapy? Although occasionally a study shows that one form of treatment or the other is more effective, neither has been shown to be clearly superior overall for treating problems such as anxiety disorders and major depressive disorder (Forand et al., 2013; Huhn et al., 2014; Stewart & Harkness, 2012). For example, studies of treatment for severe depression have found that antidepressants, behavior therapy, cognitive behavior therapy, and interpersonal psychotherapy are equally effective (e.g., Butler et al., 2006; Dimidjian et al., 2006; Stewart & Harkness, 2012). Cognitive behavior therapy and medications are equally effective in phobias (e.g., Clark et al., 2003; Davidson et al., 2004), panic disorder (Barlow, 2007), generalized anxiety disorder (Mitte, 2005a), and obsessive-compulsive disorder (Kozak, Liebowitz, & Foa, 2000).

What about combining medications and psychotherapy? Research suggests that doing so can sometimes be helpful (Addington, Piskulic, & Marshall, 2010). Combined

There is concern that we rely too heavily on medications to treat psychological problems, partly because of pharmaceutical ads that fuel consumer demand (Albee, 2002; Breggin, 2008). In one case, for example, increasing doses of medication failed to stop a patient with paranoid schizophrenia from repeatedly escaping from a mental hospital. The problem was solved without drugs, though, after a psychologist discovered that the man's escapes were motivated by his fear of calling his mother on "bugged" hospital phones, and he was allowed to use a telephone at a nearby shopping mall (Rabasca, 1999).

Frank Cotham/Cartoon Bank.com

"I medicate first and ask questions later."

treatment is recommended in cases of bipolar disorder (Vieta et al., 2011) and produces slightly better results than either psychotherapy or medications alone in people suffering from severe, long-term depression (Hegerl, Plattner, & Moller, 2004). The combination of medications and psychotherapy has also been shown to be more effective than either method alone in treating attention deficit hyperactivity disorder, childhood anxiety disorders, obsessive-compulsive disorder, alcoholism, stammering, eating disorders, compulsive sexual behavior, posttraumatic stress disorder, and panic disorder (e.g., Barlow, 2007; Flament, Bissada, & Spettigue, 2012; Sheerin, Seim, & Spates, 2012; Walkup et al., 2008).

The combined approach may be especially useful for people who are initially too distressed to benefit much from psychotherapy. A related approach, already shown to be successful with people who had been taking medications for panic disorder and depression, is the use of psychotherapy to prevent relapse and to make further progress as medications are discontinued (e.g., Dobson et al., 2008; Klein et al., 2004). Evidence also suggests that a drug called D-cycloserine might be helpful in preventing the reappearance of fears being extinguished through exposure techniques or other forms of behavior therapy (Choy, Fyer, & Lipsitz, 2007; Norberg, Krystal, & Tolin, 2008). And when combined with cognitive behavior therapy, D-cycloserine also shows promise for treating obsessive-compulsive disorder, posttraumatic stress disorder, generalized anxiety, and schizophrenia (Cain et al., 2014; Difede et al., 2014; Hoffman, Fang, & Gutner, 2014; Mataix-Cols et al., 2014).

It has recently been suggested that certain hormones may enhance the effects of psychotherapy. Of particular interest is oxytocin, a hormone that may help play a role in developing social connections early in life (MacDonald et al., 2013). Scientists are exploring the question of whether combining oxytocin with psychotherapy might amplify treatment benefits for disorders that involve troubled social relationships. Some studies have found, for example, that the use of oxytocin in conjunction with evidence-based psychological treatments has been associated with symptom improvement in autism spectrum disorder and depression (Harris & Carter, 2013; MacDonald et al., 2013).

However, combining medication with psychotherapy may not always be the best approach. One early study compared the effects of a form of in vivo desensitization called *gradual exposure* and an anti-anxiety medication (Xanax) in the treatment of agoraphobia. Clients who received gradual exposure alone showed better short- and long-term benefits than those who received either the medication alone or a combination of the medication and gradual exposure (Echeburua et al., 1993). A more conservative strategy for treating most cases of anxiety and depression is to begin with cognitive or interpersonal psychotherapy (which have no major negative side effects) and then add or switch to medication if psychotherapy alone is ineffective (Forand et al., 2013). Often, people who do not respond to one method will be helped by the other (Heldt et al., 2006). Someday, research may offer better guidelines about who should be treated with psychotherapy alone, medication alone, or a combination of the two (Hollon et al., 2005; Practice Guidelines, 2011).

LINKAGES

BIOLOGICAL ASPECTS OF PSYCHOLOGY AND THE TREATMENT OF PSYCHOLOGICAL DISORDERS

LINKAGES How do psychoactive medications work? (a link to Biological Aspects of Psychology)

Human feelings, thoughts, and actions—whether normal or abnormal—are ultimately the result of biological processes, especially those involving neurotransmitters and their receptors in the brain. Because different neurotransmitters are especially prominent in particular circuits or regions of the brain, altering the functioning of particular neurotransmitter systems can have relatively specific psychological and behavioral effects.

Let's consider some of the ways that therapeutic psychoactive medications affect neurotransmitters and their receptors. Some therapeutic medications cause neurons to fire, whereas others reduce, or inhibit, firing. For example, benzodiazepines (e.g., Valium and Xanax) exert their anti-anxiety effects by helping the inhibitory neurotransmitter GABA bind to receptors and thus suppress neuron firing. This increased inhibitory effect acts as a sort of braking system that slows the activity of GABA-sensitive neurons involved in the experience of anxiety. However, benzodiazepines also slow the action of all neural systems that use GABA, including those associated with motor activity and mental processing, which are spread throughout the brain. The result is the decreased motor coordination and clouded thinking that can appear as the side effects of the benzodiazepines. It might soon be possible to develop medications that will bind only to certain kinds of GABA receptors and thus greatly reduce these side effects (Gorman, 2005).

LINKAGES How do medications help people who suffer from schizophrenia? (a link to Biological Aspects of Psychology)

Other therapeutic medications are receptor antagonists (see Figure 9.8 in the consciousness chapter), acting to block the receptor site normally used by a particular neurotransmitter. Most antipsychotics, for example, exert their effects by blocking receptors for dopamine, a neurotransmitter that is important for movement, as described in the chapter on biological aspects of psychology. Blocking dopamine seems to reduce the jumbled thinking of many schizophrenia patients, but it can create problems—including tardive dyskinesia—in the movement systems that are also controlled by dopamine.

Some psychoactive medications exert a therapeutic influence by affecting the amount of a neurotransmitter available to act on receptors. One way for such an effect to occur is by slowing a process called *reuptake*, through which the neurotransmitter would normally return to the brain cell from which it was released. The tricyclic antidepressants, for example, operate by slowing the reuptake of norepinephrine. Prozac, Anafranil, and some other antidepressants are called *selective serotonin reuptake inhibitors (SSRIs)* because they slow the reuptake of serotonin. Others, such as Effexor, slow the reuptake of both serotonin and norepinephrine.

COMMUNITY PSYCHOLOGY

How can we prevent psychological disorders?

It has long been argued that even if psychologists and psychiatrists knew exactly how to treat every psychological problem, there would never be enough mental health professionals to help everyone in need (Albee, 1968, 2006). A study by the World Health Organization

Community Mental Health Efforts

Professional and nonprofessional staff members at community mental health centers provide traditional therapy and mental health education as well as walk-in facilities and hotlines for people who are suicidal or in crisis because of rape or domestic violence. They also offer day treatment to former mental patients, many of whom are homeless.

Geri Engberg/The Image Works

community psychology An approach to minimizing or preventing psychological disorders by promoting social change and community mental health programs.

found, for example, that even individuals with severe mental health problems often do not receive the psychological services they need (Alonso, Chatterji, & He, 2013). One study revealed that the treatment situation is especially dire in poorer countries where only about 11 percent of psychologically troubled individuals had received treatment for their disorders. In "high-income" countries such as the United States and Belgium, the figure was about 60 percent (Wang et al., 2007; see also Gonzalez et al., 2010). Even in high-income countries, though, mental health problems are more common among individuals who are poor, so the people who most need psychological treatment are often the ones least likely to receive it (van Oort et al., 2011).

Recognition of this treatment access problem helped fuel the rise of **community psychology**, which seeks to treat people in their local communities, raise people's awareness and understanding of mental health problems, and work for social changes that can prevent psychological disorders (Jorm, 2012; Nelson & Prilleltensky, 2004).

One aspect of community psychology, the *community mental health movement,* appeared during the 1960s as an attempt to make treatment available to people in their own communities. As antipsychotics became available and as concern grew that patients were not improving (and might be getting worse) after years of confinement in mental hospitals, thousands of these patients were released. The plan was for them to receive medications and other mental health services in newly funded community mental health centers. This *deinstitutionalization* process spared patients the boredom and isolation of the hospital environment, but the mental health services available in the community never matched the need for them (Dalton et al., 2013). Some former hospital patients and many people whose disorders might once have sent them to mental hospitals are now living in halfway houses and other community-based facilities where they receive *psychosocial rehabilitation.* These community support services are not designed to "cure" them but to help them cope with their problems and develop the social and occupational skills necessary for semi-independent living (Coldwell & Bender, 2007). Too many others with severe psychological disorders did not receive or respond to rehabilitation and are to be found enduring the dangers of homelessness on city streets or of confinement in jails and prisons (Luhrmann, 2008; Smith & Sederer, 2009).

Community psychology also attempts to prevent psychopathology by addressing unemployment, poverty, overcrowded substandard housing, and other stressful social situations that may put vulnerable people at greater risk for some disorders (Dalton et al., 2013; Fagan et al., 2009). Less ambitious but perhaps even more significant are efforts to detect psychological problems in their earliest stages and keep those problems from becoming worse. Some examples include encouraging positive lifestyle changes (Walsh, 2011), prevention of depression and suicide and posttraumatic stress disorder (Gates et al., 2012; Gillham et al., 2007; Shalev et al., 2012); programs (including Project Head Start) that help preschoolers whose backgrounds hurt their chances of doing well in school and put them at risk for failure and delinquency (Foster et al., 2006; Shaw et al., 2006); and identification of children who are at risk for disorder because of parental divorce, poverty, or because they are rejected or victimized at school (e.g., Cappella et al., 2012; Martinez & Forgatch, 2001). Other interventions are designed to head off conduct problems, anxiety disorders, or schizophrenia in children and adults (McGilloway et al., 2012; Neil & Christensen, 2009; Rapee et al., 2005); to prevent domestic violence, dating violence, and child abuse (Miller et al., 2012; Whitaker et al., 2006); and to promote health consciousness in ethnic minority communities (Borg, 2002).

LINKAGES

As noted in the introductory chapter, all of psychology's subfields are related to one another. Our discussion of the psychopharmacology of medication illustrates just one way that the topic of this chapter, treatment of psychological disorders, is linked to the subfield of biological psychology, which is described in the chapter on biological aspects of psychology. The Linkages diagram shows ties to two other subfields, and there are many more ties throughout the book. Looking for linkages among subfields will help you see how they all fit together and help you better appreciate the big picture that is psychology.

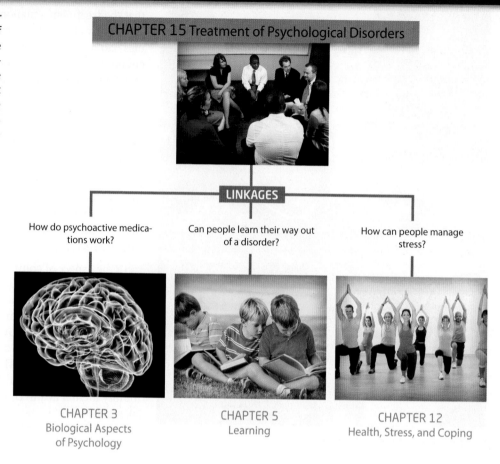

CHAPTER 15 Treatment of Psychological Disorders

LINKAGES

How do psychoactive medications work?

Can people learn their way out of a disorder?

How can people manage stress?

CHAPTER 3
Biological Aspects
of Psychology

CHAPTER 5
Learning

CHAPTER 12
Health, Stress, and Coping

SUMMARY

Basic Features of Treatment

What features do all treatment techniques have in common?

Psychotherapy is usually based on psychodynamic, humanistic, or behavioral theories of personality and behavior disorder. Many therapists employ elements of more than one approach. The biological approach uses medications and other physical treatment methods.

All forms of treatment include a client, a therapist, a theory of behavior disorder, a set of treatment procedures suggested by the theory, and a special relationship between the client and therapist. Therapy may be offered to inpatients and outpatients in many different settings by **psychologists, psychiatrists**, and other helpers. The goal of treatment is to help people change their thinking, feelings, and behavior so that they will be happier and function better.

Psychodynamic Psychotherapy

How did Freud get started as a therapist?

Psychodynamic psychotherapy began with Freud's **psychoanalysis**, which seeks to help clients gain insight into unconscious conflicts and impulses and then to explore how those factors have created disorders. Exploration of the unconscious is aided by the use of free association, dream interpretation, and related methods. Some variations on psychoanalysis retain most of Freud's principles but are typically shorter in duration and tend to stress social and interpersonal factors, such as early relationships with caregivers.

Humanistic Psychotherapy

Why won't some therapists give advice?

Humanistic psychotherapy helps clients become more aware of discrepancies between their feelings and their behavior. According to the humanistic approach, these discrepancies are at the root of behavior disorders and can be resolved by the client once they are brought to light in the context of a genuine, trusting relationship with the therapist.

Therapists using Rogers's **client-centered therapy**, also known as **person-centered therapy**, help mainly by adopting attitudes toward the client that express **unconditional positive regard**, **empathy**, and **congruence** to create a nonjudgmental atmosphere. Therapists employing the **Gestalt therapy** of Fritz and Laura Perls use more active techniques than Rogerian therapists, often pointing out inconsistencies between what clients say and how they behave.

Behavior Therapy and Cognitive Behavior Therapy

Can we learn to conquer fears?

Behavior therapy and **behavior modification** apply learning principles to eliminate undesirable behavior patterns and strengthen more desirable alternatives. The methods they employ include **systematic desensitization therapy**, **modeling**, **assertiveness training** and social skills training, **positive reinforcement** (sometimes within a **token economy program**), **extinction** techniques (such as **flooding** or **implosive therapy**), **aversion conditioning**, and **punishment**.

Many behavior therapists also employ **cognitive behavior therapy** to help clients alter the way they think as well as the way they behave. Among the specific cognitive behavioral methods are **rational-emotive behavior therapy (REBT)**, cognitive restructuring, stress inoculation training, and **cognitive therapy**.

Group, Family, and Couples Therapy

How does group psychotherapy differ from individual therapy?

Therapists of all theoretical persuasions offer **group psychotherapy**, **family therapy**, and **couples therapy**. These forms of treatment take advantage of relationships in the group, family, or couple to enhance the effects of treatment.

Evaluating Psychotherapy

How effective is psychotherapy?

Research has found that clients who receive psychotherapy are better off than most clients who receive no treatment, but that no single approach is uniformly better than all others for all clients and problems. Still, some methods appear effective enough in the treatment of particular disorders to have been listed as **empirically supported therapies (ESTs)** that can guide **evidence-based practice**. The outcome of treatment is also affected by the characteristics of the client and the therapist and the relationship that develops between them. Several factors, including personal preferences, must be considered when choosing a form of treatment and a therapist. The effects of cultural differences in the values and goals of therapist and client have also attracted increasing attention. In all forms of treatment and under all but the most exceptional circumstances, the client's rights include the right to confidentiality.

Biological Treatments

Is electric shock still used to treat psychological disorders?

Biological treatment methods seek to relieve psychological disorders by physical or pharmaceutical means. **Psychosurgery** procedures once involved mainly prefrontal lobotomy; when used today, usually as a last resort, they focus on more limited areas of the brain.

Electroconvulsive shock therapy (ECT) involves passing an electric current through the patient's brain, usually in an effort to relieve severe depression. Today, the most prominent form of biological treatment involves psychoactive medications, including those with **antipsychotic**, **antidepressant**, or **tranquilizing (anxiolytic)** effects. Psychoactive medications appear effective in many cases, but critics point out that a number of undesirable side effects are associated with these medications. Medications may be no more effective than some forms of psychotherapy for many people. Combining medication and psychotherapy may help in some cases and in the treatment of certain disorders, but their joint effect may be no greater than the effect of either one alone.

Community Psychology

How can we prevent psychological disorders?

The realization that there will never be enough therapists to treat all who need help prompted the development of **community psychology**. Community mental health programs and efforts to prevent mental disorders are the two main elements of community psychology.

TEST YOUR KNOWLEDGE

Select the best answer for each of the following questions. Then check your responses against the Answer Key at the end of the book.

1. Claudia's therapist asks her to talk about whatever thoughts, memories, or ideas come into her mind. He asks her not to "edit" any of her thoughts. This technique is called _____ and is part of _____ therapy.
   a. reflection; psychodynamic
   b. reflection; humanistic
   c. free association; psychodynamic
   d. free association; humanistic

2. Vicki tells Dr. Denter, her therapist, that she is very happy in her marriage. Dr. Denter points out that as she says this, she is clenching her fist. He asks her to have a dialogue with herself by "becoming" her fist and saying what it would say to her. Dr. Denter is most likely a _____ therapist.
   a. Gestalt
   b. psychodynamic
   c. behavior
   d. cognitive

3. Melinda is a licensed clinical psychologist, which means she probably has _____.
   a. a doctoral degree in psychology
   b. a psychodynamic approach to therapy
   c. the right to prescribe medications in most U.S. states
   d. a medical degree

4. A primary aim of classical psychoanalysis is to _____.
   a. help clients get in touch with their current feelings
   b. help clients gain insight into their unconscious conflicts
   c. replace clients' problematic behaviors with more desirable behaviors
   d. teach clients new ways of thinking

5. Dr. Margent listens as her client, Eric, talks at length about his problems at work, including the fact that he hates his job, often sneaks out early, sometimes ignores his manager's instructions, and generally avoids working hard. Dr. Margent doesn't interrupt or criticize him but often rephrases what he says to be sure she understands it. Dr. Margent is using methods most closely associated with _____ therapy.
   a. psychodynamic
   b. behavioral
   c. client-centered
   d. cognitive-behavioral

6. Carl's therapist is helping him overcome his fear of heights by imagining increasingly frightening images while he is relaxed. The therapist is using methods known as _____.
   a. assertion training
   b. systematic desensitization therapy
   c. flooding
   d. modeling

7. Shanobi is tearfully telling a friend that she is depressed and does not know why. Her friend says, "You seem so unhappy, and maybe a bit scared, too." The friend's response is most like which method used in client-centered therapy?
   a. sympathy
   b. empathy
   c. reflection
   d. actualization

8. Rebecca is convinced that she will never get the promotion she wants because she "is just not good at job interviews." Her therapist asks her to close her eyes and say the first thing that comes into her mind as she thinks about her job. He also asks Rebecca for details of the dreams she has been having lately. Rebecca's therapist appears to prefer the _____ approach to treatment.
   a. behavioral
   b. cognitive behavioral
   c. Gestalt
   d. psychodynamic

9. Brandon complains that he has an intense need to touch all four walls of any room he enters for the first time. His therapist suggests that Brandon might have learned this compulsive behavior because it helped him avoid anxiety. The therapist appears to favor the _____ approach to treatment.
   a. psychodynamic
   b. humanistic
   c. behavioral
   d. neurobiological

10. Your friend Rallo is considering entering psychotherapy, but he wonders if it will help. Based on the research you read about in this chapter, you tell Rallo that _____.
    a. therapy does not help the average client
    b. therapy helps the average client
    c. humanistic therapies are most effective overall
    d. there is no experimental research on the effectiveness of therapy

11. According to the American Psychological Association's *Ethical Principles of Psychologists and Code of Conduct,* a therapist may reveal information learned about a client during therapy if _____.
    a. the client's employer requests this information in confidence
    b. the client drops out of therapy
    c. the client is suicidal and needs immediate hospitalization
    d. the therapist feels it will do no harm

12. Juanita is trying to influence her state legislature to pass laws that will help prevent psychological problems caused by malnutrition, overcrowding, and homelessness. She is most likely a _____ psychologist.
    a. behavioral
    b. community
    c. humanistic
    d. psychodynamic

13. Rafer's intense fear of spiders greatly interferes with his job as a forest ranger. His therapist suggests that he stay in a room full of harmless spiders until he feels no further anxiety. This therapy technique is known as _____.
    a. flooding
    b. punishment
    c. systematic desensitization therapy
    d. aversion conditioning

14. Sally constantly tells herself that she is "worthless" and "will never succeed at anything." Her therapist helps her practice new thoughts such as "I'm as good as the next person" and "I am going to try my best." Her therapist is using the technique of _____, which is part of _____ therapy.
    a. free association; psychodynamic
    b. reflection; humanistic
    c. stress inoculation; behavioral
    d. cognitive restructuring; cognitive behavior

15. Lucinda is experiencing severe depression that leaves her unable to enjoy life. She has not responded to psychotherapies or antipsychotic medication. Lucinda would be a candidate for _____.
    a. neuroleptic medications
    b. ECT
    c. aversion conditioning
    d. cognitive restructuring

16. Therapeutic medications can work in many ways, but *not* by _____.
    a. increasing the amount of neurotransmitters released in the brain
    b. decreasing the amount of neurotransmitters released in the brain
    c. blocking the action of neurotransmitters in the brain
    d. changing the kind of neurotransmitters released by neurons in the brain

17. An important common element in the success of many forms of psychotherapy is _____.
    a. the client-therapist relationship
    b. randomly assigning therapists to clients
    c. having a therapist trained in a variety of therapeutic methods
    d. having appropriate assessment methods to measure outcomes

18. When prescribing neuroleptic medications for schizophrenia, psychiatrists must consider that patients may _____.
    a. become addicted to them
    b. become insensitive to them after an extended period of time
    c. develop tardive dyskinesia
    d. experience hallucinations after extensive use

19. Jon's therapist has prescribed anxiolytics for him. Jon is probably being treated for _____.
    a. depression
    b. an anxiety disorder
    c. schizophrenia
    d. somatoform disorder

20. Which of the following is *not* an advantage of group psychotherapy?
    a. It allows the therapist to observe clients interacting with one another.
    b. Clients learn from one another.
    c. Clients improve more quickly.
    d. Clients feel less alone.

CHAPTER 16

Social Psychology

© wavebreakmedia/Shutterstock.com

Preview

If you are like most people, there is probably at least one thing you do in private that you would never do when someone else is around. The tendency to behave differently when others are present is just one aspect of social psychology. This chapter describes many other ways that the presence and behavior of other people affect our own thoughts and actions and how we, in turn, affect the thoughts and actions of others. It explores how perception, learning, memory, thinking, and emotion occur in relation to other people; how people think about themselves and others; why we may like one person but dislike another; how people form and change attitudes; and why and how we judge other people, sometimes in biased ways. Social pressure, ranging from unspoken social rules to commands for obedience, is another concern of social psychologists. The chapter also reviews some of the helpful, cooperative, competitive, and aggressive ways in which people behave toward one another in the workplace and in other social situations. Finally, it considers group decision making and other group processes.

On April 15, 2013, Tamerlan and Dzhokhar Tsarnaev, two brothers who had lived in the United States for most of their lives, left powerful backpack bombs among hundreds of spectators near the finish line of the Boston Marathon. When the bombs exploded, 3 people were killed and 264 others were injured. Similar acts of terrorism have cost the lives of many thousands of people in the United States and around the world. Almost all of the questions that can be asked about terrorism relate to human behavior. For example, what could lead someone to try to kill and injure innocent people because of political or religious beliefs? Why do firefighters, police officers, emergency medical workers, and other first responders risk their own lives to save the lives of terrorism victims? Why do some people flee the scene of an attack, while others stay to tend to wounded strangers? Is there any reason to hope that the hatred, distrust, and extremism that underlie terrorist attacks can someday be reduced or eliminated?

We may never have final answers to such questions as these, but some partial answers may lie in the study of **social psychology**, the scientific investigation of how people's thoughts and feelings influence their behavior toward others and how the behavior of others influences people's own thoughts, feelings, and behavior. In this chapter, we focus on several topics in social psychology, including **social cognition**, the mental processes associated with how people perceive and react to other individuals and groups (Fiske & Taylor, 2008), and group and interpersonal behaviors such as conformity, aggression, and helping. One important aspect of social cognition is how it affects the way we see ourselves.

SOCIAL INFLUENCES ON THE SELF

How do we compare ourselves with others?

Each of us lives in both a personal and a social world. This means that although you experience your thoughts and feelings as your own, they have been strongly influenced by other people.

The thoughts, feelings, and beliefs about what characteristics you have and who you are make up your **self-concept**. Although your self-concept is unique to you, it is a product of your social and cultural environment. In the chapters on human development and personality, we describe how each individual develops within a cultural context and how collectivist and individualist cultures emphasize different core values and encourage contrasting definitions of the self. As you will see in this chapter, culture also provides the context for **self-esteem**, the evaluations you make of your worth as a human being (Crocker & Canevello, 2012). Let's look at how self-esteem develops.

Social Comparison

People spend a lot of time thinking about themselves, trying to evaluate their own perceptions, opinions, values, abilities, and so on (Epstude & Mussweiler, 2009). Self-evaluation involves two distinct types of questions: those that can be answered objectively and those that cannot (Festinger, 1954). You can determine your height or weight by measuring it, but for other types of questions—about your creativity or attractiveness, for example—there are no objective criteria. According to Leon Festinger's theory of **social comparison**,

---

social psychology The subfield of psychology that explores the effects of the social world on the behavior and mental processes of individuals and groups.

social cognition Mental processes associated with people's perceptions of and reactions to other people.

self-concept The way one thinks of oneself.

self-esteem The evaluations people make about their worth as human beings.

social comparison Using other people as a basis of comparison for evaluating oneself.

people evaluate themselves in relation to others. When you use others as a basis for evaluating how intelligent, athletic, interesting, or attractive you are, you engage in social comparison (Dijkstra, Gibbons, & Buunk, 2010; Freund & Kasten, 2012).

Who serves as your basis of comparison? Festinger said that people usually look to others who are similar to themselves. For example, if you are curious about how good you are at swimming or science, you'll probably compare yourself with people who are at about your own level of experience and ability, not with Olympic champions or Nobel Prize winners (Aronson, Wilson, & Akert. 2013). The categories of people you feel you belong to and usually compare yourself with are called your **reference groups**.

The performance of individuals in your reference groups can affect your self-esteem (Crocker & Canevello, 2012). If being good at science is important to you, for example, knowing that someone in your reference group always scores much higher than you on science tests can lower your self-esteem. To protect their self-esteem and make themselves feel better, people sometimes compare themselves with those who are not as good, a strategy called *downward social comparison.* They may also sometimes engage in *upward social comparison,* in which they compare themselves with people who are doing much better than they are (John, Lowenstein & Rick, 2014). At first glance, this might not seem sensible, but upward social comparison can create optimism about improving our own situations (Wheeler & Suls, 2007). We may tell ourselves "If they can do it, so can I!" (Buunk, Peiró, & Griffioen, 2007). Or we might tell ourselves that the superior performer is not really similar enough to be in our reference group or even that the ability in question is not that important to us (Dijkstra, Gibbons, & Buunk, 2010).

An unfavorable comparison of your own status with that of others can produce a sense of *relative deprivation*—the belief that no matter how much you are getting in terms of recognition, status, money, and other rewards, it is less than you deserve (Kassin, Fein, & Markus, 2014). The concept of relative deprivation explains why employees become dissatisfied when they consider themselves underpaid or underappreciated in comparison to their coworkers (Ren, Bolino, Shaffer, & Kraimer, 2013). When large groups of people experience relative deprivation, political unrest may follow (de la Sablonnière, Tougas, & Lortie-Lussier, 2009). It is likely, for example, that resentment over U.S. prosperity and global influence plays a role in creating the hatred that leads some people to engage in terrorist attacks against the United States (Brewer, 2010).

FOCUS ON RESEARCH METHODS

SELF-ESTEEM AND THE ULTIMATE TERROR

Why is self-esteem so important to so many people? An intriguing answer to this question comes from the *terror management theory* proposed by Jeff Greenberg, Tom Pyszczynski, and Sheldon Solomon (Solomon, Greenberg, & Pyszczynski, 2004). This theory is based on the notion that humans are the only creatures capable of thinking about the future and realizing that we will all eventually die. Terror management theory suggests that humans cope with anxiety, including the terror that thoughts about death might bring, by developing a variety of self-protective psychological strategies. One strategy is to establish and maintain high self-esteem (Greenberg, Solomon, & Arndt, 2008; Pyszczynski et al., 2010).

What was the researchers' question?

In a series of experiments, Greenberg and his colleagues (1992) asked whether high self-esteem serves as a buffer against anxiety—specifically, the anxiety brought on by thoughts about death and pain.

(continued)

reference groups Categories of people with whom individuals compare themselves.

How did the researchers answer the question?

About 150 students at several North American universities participated in these studies, each of which followed a similar format. The first step was to temporarily alter the participants' self-esteem. To do so, the researchers gave the students feedback about a personality or intelligence test they had taken earlier in the semester. Half the participants received positive feedback designed to increase their self-esteem. The other half received feedback that was neutral—it was neither flattering nor unflattering. (Measurements showed that the positive feedback actually did create higher self-esteem than the neutral feedback.) In the next phase of each experiment, the researchers used either a film about death or the (false) threat of a mild electric shock to provoke some anxiety in half the participants in the positive-feedback group and half the participants in the neutral-feedback group. The amount of anxiety created was measured by the participants' self-reports or by monitoring galvanic skin resistance (GSR), a measure of perspiration in the skin that reflects anxiety-related physiological arousal (Dawson, Schell, & Filion, 2000).

What did the researchers find?

Self-reports and GSR measures revealed that participants in all three experiments were significantly less upset by an anxiety-provoking experience (the death film or the threat of shock) if they had first received esteem-building feedback about their previous test performance. Other studies have reported similar findings (Schmeichel et al., 2009).

What do the results mean?

The researchers concluded that their results support the notion that self-esteem can act as a buffer against anxiety and other negative feelings. This conclusion would help explain why people are so eager to maintain or enhance their self-esteem (Leary, 2010; Loughnan et al., 2011): we don't like to feel anxious, and increased self-esteem reduces most people's anxiety.

What do we still need to know?

These results certainly support terror management theory, but by themselves they're not broad enough to confirm all of its assumptions. For example, the theory also predicts that when people are sensitized to the threat of death, they will seek to protect themselves by suppressing thoughts of death and by doing things that increase the approval and support of others in their society (Baka, Derbis, & Maxfield, 2012; Goncalves Portelinha et al., 2012). Consistent with this prediction, people have been found to make larger contributions to charity after being made more aware of their own mortality (Wade-Benzoni et al., 2012). Similarly, dramatic increases in volunteering for charity work occurred after the terrorist attacks of 9/11 (Penner, Brannick et al., 2005).

But not everyone reacts with prosocial behavior when sensitized to the threat of death. The greatest increase in prosocial behavior following reminders about death appears in people who value prosocial behavior (Joireman & Durell, 2007). In other people, those same reminders may be followed by a *reduction* in humanitarian concerns (Hirschberger, 2009). Social psychologists would like to know more about how people's values and personality characteristics are related to the strategies they adopt when dealing with the threat of death.

Researchers also wonder whether terror management theory offers the best explanation of why high self-esteem reduces anxiety. Perhaps people value self-esteem not because it makes them less afraid of death but simply because it is a flattering indicator (a sort of "sociometer") of their acceptance by others (Leary, 2010). According to sociometer theory, people want to have high self-esteem because it tells them that they are liked and accepted. Perhaps the goal of acceptance evolved because people who were excluded from the protective circle of their group were not likely to survive to reproduce. Compared with terror management theory, sociometer theory is certainly a simpler and more plausible explanation of the desire for high self-esteem, but is it the best explanation? Both theories make similar predictions about the effects of self-esteem on anxiety, so it will take additional research to evaluate their relative merits.

Social Identity Theory

TRY THIS Take a moment to complete the following sentence: I am a(n) _____. Did you fill the blank with something like "good athlete" or "honor student," or did you insert something like "woman" or "Hispanic American?" The first type of response reflects *personal identity*, something about one's individuality, while the second reflects **social identity**, the beliefs we hold about the groups to which we belong. Our social identity is therefore a part of our self-concept (Hogg, 2012).

Our social identity permits us to feel part of a larger whole (Bryant & Cummins, 2010). We see its importance in the pride people feel when a member of their family graduates from college or when a local team wins a big game (Kassin, Fein, & Markus, 2014). In wars between national, ethnic, or religious groups, individuals sacrifice and sometimes die for the sake of their group identity (Swann et al., 2014). A group identity is also one reason people donate money to those in need, support friends in a crisis, and display other forms of prosocial behavior. Many factors may affect the strength of our group identity. For instance, thinking about the challenges and difficulties our own group has overcome tends to strengthen our identification with that group (Ersner-Hershfield et al., 2010). As we shall see later, however, defining ourselves in terms of a group identity can foster an "us versus them" mentality that sets the stage for prejudice, social discrimination, intergroup conflict, and even terrorism (Hogg & Adelman, 2013).

SOCIAL PERCEPTION

Do we perceive people and objects in similar ways?

LINKAGES Do we sometimes perceive people the same way we perceive objects? (a link to Sensation and Perception)

There's a story about a company president who was having lunch with a man being considered for an executive position. When the man salted his food without first tasting it, the president decided not to hire him. The reason, she explained, was that the company had no room for a person who acted before collecting all relevant information. The candidate lost his chance because of the president's **social perception**, the processes through which people interpret information about others, form impressions of them, and draw conclusions about the reasons for their behavior. In this section, we examine how and why social perception influences our thoughts, feelings, and actions.

The Role of Schemas

The ways in which we perceive people follow many of the same laws that govern how we perceive objects, including the Gestalt principles discussed in the chapter on sensation and perception (Macrae & Quadflieg, 2010). Consider Figure 16.1. Consistent with Gestalt principles, most people would describe it as "a square with a notch in one side," not as eight straight lines (Woodworth & Schlosberg, 1954). The reason is that they interpret new information using the mental representations, or **schemas**, that they already have about squares (Aronson, Wilson, & Akert, 2013). In other words, they interpret this diagram as a square with a slight modification.

We have schemas about people, too, and they can affect our perceptions. For one thing, schemas influence what we pay attention to and what we ignore. We tend to process information about another person more quickly if it confirms our beliefs about that person's gender or ethnic group, for example, than if it violates those beliefs (Betz & Sekaquaptewa, 2012; Carlston, 2010). Schemas also influence what we remember about others (Carlston, 2010). In one study, if people thought a woman they saw in a video was a waitress, they recalled that she had a beer with dinner and owned a TV set. Those who thought she was a librarian remembered that she was wearing glasses and liked classical music (Cohen, 1981). We also tend to remember people who violate our schemas. In another study, researchers showed pictures of men and women and told a little story about each, including whether the pictured people had cheated on their romantic partners. Many people hold schemas suggesting that women are kinder and less self-centered than men, so participants were better at remembering pictures of cheating women than of cheating

FIGURE 16.1

A Schema-Plus-Correction

People who see an object like this tend to use a preexisting mental representation (their schema of a square) and then correct or modify it in some way (here, with a notch).

May I Help You?

Schemas help us quickly categorize people and respond appropriately to them, but schemas can also create narrow-mindedness and (as we shall see later) social prejudice. If this woman does not fulfill your schema—your mental representation—of how carpenters are supposed to look, you might be less likely to ask her for advice on your home improvement project. One expert carpenter who manages the hardware department of a large home improvement store told us that most customers walk right past her in order to ask the advice of one of her less-experienced male clerks.

Tanya Constantine/Blend Images/Alamy

men (Kroneisen & Bell, 2013). Schemas can also affect our judgment about the actions of others (Moskowitz, 2005). For instance, people may be less likely to blame a defendant in a rape case if their schema about rape victims includes the myth that their appearance or behavior makes them partially responsible for being attacked (Eyssel & Bohner, 2011).

In other words, our schemas about people influence our perceptions of them through the top-down processing that is discussed in the chapter on sensation and perception. And just as schemas help us read sentences that contain words with missing letters, they also allow us to efficiently "fill in the blanks" about people. Our schemas tell us, for example, that someone wearing a store uniform or name tag is likely to know where merchandise is located, so we usually approach that person for assistance. Accurate schemas help us categorize people quickly and respond appropriately in social situations, but if schemas are incorrect they can create false expectations and errors in judgment about people that can lead to narrow-mindedness and even prejudice.

First Impressions

Our schemas about people act as lenses that alter our first impressions of them. Those impressions, in turn, affect both our later perceptions of their behavior and our reactions to it. First impressions are formed quickly, usually change slowly, and typically have a long-lasting influence. No wonder they're so important in the development of social relations (Kassin, Fein, & Markus, 2014). How do people form impressions of other people? And why are these impressions so resistant to change?

Forming Impressions

TRY THIS Think about your first impression of a close friend. It was probably formed quickly, because existing schemas create a tendency to automatically assume a great deal about a person on the basis of limited information (Uleman & Saribay, 2013). In fact, people can make surprisingly accurate judgments about a person's trustworthiness, competence, or leadership abilities after seeing a person's face for only a tenth of a second (Rule et al., 2011; Willis & Todorov, 2006). First impression judgments become even more accurate after as little as one minute of exposure to a new person (Ames et al., 2010), and although our judgments of more attractive people tend to be more accurate—perhaps because we spend more time looking at them (Lorenzo, Biesanz, & Human, 2010; Stirrat & Perrett, 2010)—we are not influenced by appearance alone. We're often swayed, too, by a person's handshake or use of language (Bernieri & Petty, 2011; Douglas & Sutton, 2010). And a distinctive or unusual name, for example, might cause us to draw inferences about the person's religion, ethnicity, food preferences, or temperament (Gebauer, Leary, & Neberich, 2011). Clothing or hairstyle might lead us to make assumptions about political views or taste in music (Brown et al., 2013). These inferences and assumptions may or may not be accurate. How many turned out to be true in your friend's case?

social identity The beliefs we hold about the groups to which we belong.

social perception The processes through which people interpret information about others, draw inferences about them, and develop mental representations of them.

schemas Generalizations about categories of objects, places, events, and people.

Noticeable features or actions help shape our impressions of others. Those impressions may or may not be correct (Biesanz et al., 2011; Human & Biesanz, 2012; Vartanian et al., 2012).

Self-Fulfilling Prophecies in the Classroom

If teachers inadvertently spend less time helping children who at first seem "dull," those children may not learn as much, thus fulfilling the teachers' expectations. If this girl has not impressed her teacher as being very bright, how likely do you think it is that she will be called on during class?

Ableimages/Iconica/Getty Images

One schema has a particularly strong influence on first impressions: We tend to assume that the people we meet have attitudes and values similar to our own (Srivastava, Guglielmo, & Beer, 2010). So all else being equal, we're inclined to like other people. However, even a small amount of negative information can change our minds. Why? The main reason is that most of us don't expect other people to act negatively toward us. When unexpected negative behaviors do occur, they capture our attention and lead us to believe that these behaviors reflect something negative about the other person (Aronson, Wilson, & Akert, 2013). As a result, negative information attracts more attention and carries more weight than positive information in shaping first impressions (Dickter & Gyurovski, 2012).

Self-Fulfilling Prophecies

Another reason first impressions tend to be stable is that we often do things that cause others to confirm our impressions (Madon et al., 2011). If teachers expect particular students to do poorly in mathematics, those students may sense this expectation, exert less effort, and perform below their ability level in that teacher's class, and perhaps in later years (de Boer, Bosker, & van der Werf, 2010; Michael, Garry, & Kirsch, 2012). And if mothers expect their young children to abuse alcohol eventually, those children may be more likely to do so than the children of mothers who didn't convey that expectation (Madon et al., 2006). When, without our awareness, schemas cause us to subtly lead people to behave in line with our expectations, a **self-fulfilling prophecy** is at work.

Self-fulfilling prophecies also help maintain our judgments about groups. If you assume that people in a certain social group are snobby, you might be defensive or even hostile when you encounter them. If they react to your behavior with hostility and anger, their behavior would fulfill your prophecy and strengthen the impression that created it (Kassin, Fein, & Markus, 2014).

Explaining Behavior: Attribution

So far, we have examined how people form impressions about other people's characteristics. But our perceptions of others also include our explanations of their behavior. People tend to form ideas about why people (including themselves) behave as they do and about what behavior to expect in the future (Baumeister & Bushman, 2014; Shafto, Goodman, & Frank, 2012). Psychologists use the term **attribution** to describe the process we go through to explain the causes of behavior (including our own).

Suppose a classmate borrows your lecture notes but fails to return them. You could attribute this behavior to many causes, from an emergency situation to selfishness. Which of these explanations you choose is important, because it will help you *understand* your classmate's behavior, *predict* what will happen if this person asks to borrow something in the future, and decide how to *control* the situation should it arise again. Similarly, whether a person attributes a partner's nagging to temporary stress or to loss of affection can influence whether that person will work on the relationship or end it.

People usually attribute behavior in a particular situation to either internal causes (characteristics of the person) or external causes (characteristics of the situation). For example, if you thought your classmate's failure to return your notes was due mainly to lack of consideration or laziness, you would be making an *internal attribution*. If you thought that the oversight was due mainly to preoccupation with a family crisis, you would be making an *external attribution*. Similarly, if you failed an exam, you could explain it by concluding that you're not very smart (internal attribution) or that your work schedule left you too little time to study (external attribution). The attribution that you make might determine how much you study for the next exam or even whether you decide to stay in school.

Errors in Attribution

Most people are usually logical in their attempts to explain behavior (Aronson, Wilson, & Akert, 2013). However, they are also prone to *attributional errors* that can distort their view of behavior (Baumeister & Bushman, 2014).

self-fulfilling prophecy A process in which an initial impression causes us to bring out behavior in another that confirms the impression.

attribution The process of explaining the causes of people's behavior, including our own.

Why Are They Helping?

Attributional biases are more common in some cultures than in others. In one study, students in an individualist culture were more likely than those in a collectivist culture to explain acts of helping as being due to internal causes such as kindness or the enjoyment of helping (Miller & Bersoff, 1994).

Zute Lightfoot/Alamy

The Fundamental Attribution Error

North American psychologists have paid special attention to the **fundamental attribution error**, a tendency to over-attribute the behavior of others to internal factors (Kassin, Fein, & Markus, 2014). Imagine that you receive an e-mail that contains lots of errors in spelling and grammar. If you are like most people, you'll probably attribute these errors to an internal cause and infer that the writer isn't very smart, or at least not very careful (Vignovic & Thompson, 2010). In doing so, however, you might be ignoring possible external factors, such as the possibility that the writer didn't have time to proofread the message or is not a native English speaker.

The *ultimate attribution error* is a related attributional bias. Here, we attribute the positive actions of people from a different ethnic or social group to external causes, such as easy opportunities, whereas we attribute their negative actions to internal causes, such as dishonesty (Pettigrew, 2001). The ultimate attribution error also causes people to see good deeds done by those in their own group as due to kindness or other internal factors and bad deeds as stemming from external causes, such as unemployment or a bad economy. In this way, the ultimate attribution error helps create and maintain people's negative views of other groups and positive views of their own group (Pettigrew, 2001).

These attributional biases may not be universal (Li et al., 2012). For example, research suggests that the fundamental attribution error and the ultimate attribution error are less likely to appear among people in collectivist cultures such as India, China, Japan, and Korea than among people in the individualist cultures of North America and Europe (Heine, 2010). And even within individualist cultures, some people hold a stronger individualist orientation than others. So some people in these cultures are more likely than others to make attribution errors (Li et al., 2012; Miller, 2001).

Other Attributional Errors

People are less likely to make internal attributions when explaining their own behavior. In fact, people tend to show the **actor-observer effect**: that is, we often attribute other people's behavior to internal causes but attribute our own behavior to external factors, especially when our behavior is inappropriate or inadequate (Baumeister & Bushman, 2014). For example, when Australian students were asked why they sometimes drive too fast, they focused on circumstances, such as being late, but saw other people's dangerous driving as a sign of aggressiveness or immaturity (Harré, Brandt, & Houkamau, 2004). Similarly, when you're driving too slowly, the reason is that you are looking for an address, not that you are a big loser like that jerk who crawled along in front of you yesterday.

The actor-observer effect occurs mainly because people have different kinds of information about their own behavior and the behavior of others. When *you* are in a situation—giving a speech, perhaps—the information most available to you is likely to be external and situational, such as the temperature of the room and the size of the audience. You also have a lot of information about other external factors, such as the amount of time you had to prepare your talk or the upsetting conversation you had this morning. If your speech is disorganized and boring, you can easily attribute it to one or all of these external causes. But when you observe someone else, the most obvious information in the situation is *that person*. You don't know what happened to that person last night or this morning, so you're likely to attribute the quality of the performance to stable, internal characteristics (Moskowitz & Gill, 2013).

fundamental attribution error A bias toward attributing the behavior of others to internal factors.

actor-observer effect The tendency to attribute other people's behavior to internal causes while attributing one's own behavior to external causes.

Of course, people don't always attribute their own behavior to external forces. In fact, whether they do so often depends on whether the outcome is positive or negative. In one study, when people were asked to explain their good and bad online shopping experiences, they tended to take personal credit for positive outcomes (such as finding bargains) but blamed the computer for problems such as receiving the wrong merchandise (Moon, 2003). In other words, these people showed a **self-serving bias**, the tendency to take personal credit for success but to blame external causes for failure (Alston et al., 2013). This bias has been found in almost all cultures, but as with the fundamental attribution error, it is usually more pronounced among people from individualistic Western cultures than among those from collectivist Eastern cultures (Mezulis et al., 2004).

The self-serving bias occurs, in part, because people are motivated to maintain their self-esteem, and ignoring negative information about themselves is one way to do so. If you just failed an exam, it's painful to admit that the exam was fair. Like the other attributional biases we have discussed, self-serving bias helps people think about their failures and shortcomings in ways that protect their self-esteem (Sanjuán & Magallares, 2013). These self-protective cognitive biases can help us temporarily escape unpleasant thoughts and feelings, but they may also create a distorted view of reality that can lead to other problems. One such problem is *unrealistic optimism,* the tendency to believe that good things (such as financial success or having a gifted child) are likely to happen to you but that bad things (such as accidents or illness) are not (Shepperd et al., 2013). Unrealistic optimism tends to persist even when there is strong evidence against it and can lead to potentially harmful behaviors. For example, people who are unrealistically optimistic about their health may not bother to exercise, may ignore information about how to prevent heart disease, or may underestimate the risks of engaging in unsafe sex (Ferrer et al., 2012). ("In Review: Some Biases in Social Perception" summarizes the common cognitive biases discussed here.)

Attributional Bias

Men whose thinking is colored by the ultimate attribution error might assume that women who succeed at tasks associated with traditional male roles are just lucky and that men succeed at those tasks because of their skill (Deaux & LaFrance, 1998). When this attributional bias is in operation, people who are perceived as belonging to an outgroup, whether on the basis of their sex, age, sexual orientation, religion, ethnicity, or other characteristics, may be denied fair evaluations and equal opportunities.

© Bob Daemmrich/The Image Works

self-serving bias The tendency to attribute one's successes to internal characteristics while blaming one's failures on external causes.

SOME BIASES IN SOCIAL PERCEPTION

IN REVIEW

Bias	Description
Importance of first impression	Ambiguous information is interpreted in line with a first impression, and the initial schema is recalled better and more vividly than any later correction to it. Actions based on this impression may bring out behavior that confirms it.
Fundamental attribution error	The tendency to over-attribute the behavior of others to internal factors.
Actor-observer bias	The tendency to attribute our own behavior to external causes and to attribute the behavior of others to internal factors.
Self-serving bias	The tendency to attribute one's successes to internal factors and one's failures to external factors.
Unrealistic optimism	The tendency to believe that good things will happen to us but that bad things will not.

In Review Questions

1. The fundamental attribution error appears to be somewhat less likely to occur among people in _____ cultures.

2. First impressions form _____, but tend to change _____.

3. If you believed that immigrants' successes are due to government help but that their failures are due to laziness, you would be committing the _____ error _____.

ATTITUDES

Do attitudes always determine behavior?

Our views about health, safety, or any other topic reflect our attitudes. An **attitude** is our tendency to think, feel, or act in positive or negative ways about the world around us. Social psychologists have long viewed attitudes as having three components (Banaji & Heiphetz, 2010). The *cognitive* component is a set of beliefs about the attitude object. The emotional, or *affective*, component includes feelings about the object. The *behavioral* component is the way people act toward the object.

We can hold attitudes about almost anything, but they are usually focused on other people, such as a spouse, on groups of people (such as the elderly), on social or political issues such as abortion or term limits, or on events and activities such as art exhibitions or sports (Fabrigar & Wegener, 2010). Attitudes help guide how we react to other people, which causes and politicians we support, which products we choose to buy, and countless other daily decisions.

Forming Attitudes

People's attitudes about objects begin to appear in early childhood and continue to emerge throughout life. How do these attitudes form? Genetics may influence some attitudes to an extent (Albarricín & Vargas, 2010), but social learning—what children learn from their parents and others—appears to play the major role in attitude formation. Children learn not only the names of objects but also what they should believe and feel about them and how they should act toward them. For example, a parent may teach a child not only that snakes are reptiles but also that they should be feared and avoided. So as children learn concepts such as "reptile" or "work," they learn attitudes about those concepts, too (Aronson, Wilson, & Akert, 2013).

Classical and operant conditioning can also shape attitudes (Baron, Byrne, & Branscombe, 2006). Advertisers pair up enjoyable music or sexy images with the products they want to sell (Pratkanis & Aronson, 2001; Walther & Langer, 2008), and parents, teachers, and peers reward children for stating particular views. The *mere-exposure effect* is influential as well. All else being equal, more frequent exposure to an object produces a more positive attitude toward it (deZilva, Mitchell, & Newell, 2013). One study found, for example, that the more often European children and teens saw an ad for a particular brand of cigarettes, the more they liked the brand, even if they didn't smoke (Morgenstern, Isensee, & Hanewinkel, 2012). The mere-exposure effect helps explain why commercials and political ads are aired over and over and why some rock bands won't include new songs in a live concert until their fans have repeatedly heard and come to like the recorded versions.

Changing Attitudes

The nearly $170 billion a year spent on advertising in the United States alone provides just one example of how people constantly try to change our attitudes. There are many others, including the persuasive messages of groups concerned with abortion or gun control or recycling—and don't forget about friends and family members who want you to think the way they do.

Two Routes to Attitude Change

Whether a persuasive message succeeds in changing attitudes depends mainly on three factors: (1) the person communicating the message; (2) the content of the message; and (3) the person receiving it (Albarracín & Vargas, 2010). The **elaboration likelihood model** of attitude change provides a framework for understanding when and how these

---

attitude A tendency toward a particular cognitive, emotional, or behavioral reaction to objects in one's environment.

elaboration likelihood model A model of attitude change suggesting that people can change their attitudes through a central route (by considering an argument's content) or through a peripheral route (by relying on irrelevant persuasion cues).

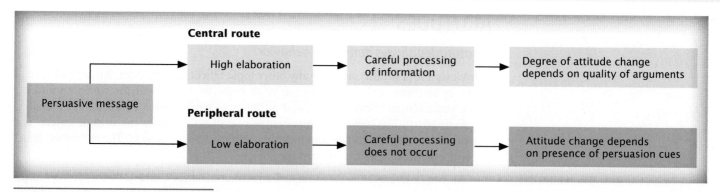

FIGURE 16.2

The Elaboration Likelihood Model of Attitude Change

The central route to attitude change involves carefully processing and evaluating a message's content (high elaboration). The peripheral route involves little processing and evaluation of message content (low elaboration) and relies instead on persuasion cues such as the attractiveness of the person making the argument (Cacioppo, Petty, & Crites, 1993).

factors affect attitude change (Petty & Briñol, 2012). As shown in Figure 16.2, the model is based on the idea that persuasive messages can change people's attitudes through one of two main routes.

The first is called the *peripheral route* because when it is activated, we devote little attention to the central content of the persuasive message. We tend to be affected instead by peripheral, or surrounding, persuasion cues, such as the confidence, attractiveness, or other characteristics of the person who delivers the message. These persuasion cues influence attitude change even though they may have nothing to do with the logic or accuracy of the message itself. Commercials in which movie stars or other attractive non-experts endorse pain relievers or denture cleaners encourage the peripheral route to attitude change.

By contrast, when the *central route* is activated, the core content of the message becomes more important than the communicator's characteristics in determining attitude change. A person following the central route uses logical steps—such as those outlined in the Thinking Critically sections of this book—to analyze the content of the persuasive message, including the validity of its claims, whether it leaves out important information, alternative interpretations of evidence, and so on.

What determines which route people will follow? One factor is a person's *need for cognition*, the desire to think things through (Douglas, Sutton, & Stathi, 2010). People with a strong need for cognition are more likely than others to follow a central route to attitude change. Personal involvement with a message's content is another important factor. People are more likely to activate the central route when thinking about topics that are personally relevant (Petty & Briñol, 2012). Suppose, for example, that you hear someone arguing for the cancellation of all student loans in Chile. This message might persuade you through the peripheral route if it comes from someone who looks attractive and sounds intelligent. However, if the message proposes eliminating student loans at your own school, you're more likely to follow the central route. You might still be persuaded, but only if the logic of the message is clear and convincing. This is why celebrity endorsements tend to be more effective when the products being advertised are relatively unimportant to the audience.

Persuasive messages are not the only means of changing attitudes. Another approach is to get people to act in ways that are inconsistent with their attitudes in the hope that they will adjust those attitudes to match their behavior. Often, such adjustments do occur, and Leon Festinger proposed a theory to explain why.

Cognitive Dissonance Theory

cognitive dissonance theory A theory that attitude change is driven by efforts to reduce tension caused by inconsistencies between attitudes and behaviors.

According to his **cognitive dissonance theory**, people want their thoughts, beliefs, and attitudes to be in harmony with one another and with their behavior (Festinger, 1957). People

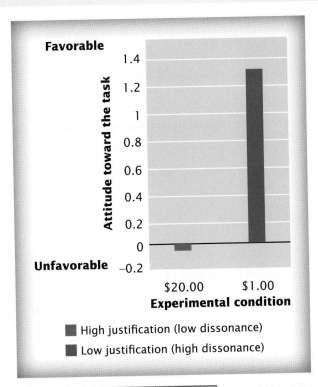

FIGURE 16.3

Cognitive Dissonance and Attitude Change

According to cognitive dissonance theory, the $20 that people were given to say that a boring task was enjoyable provided them with a clear justification for lying. Having been paid to lie, they should experience little dissonance between what they said and what they felt about the task. And in fact their attitude toward the task was not positive. However, people who received only $1 had little justification to lie so they reduced their dissonance mainly by displaying a more positive attitude toward the task.

experiencing inconsistency, or *dissonance*, among these elements, become anxious and are motivated to make them more consistent (Harmon-Jones, 2010; Gawronski, 2012). For example, someone who believes that "smoking is dangerous" but who must also admit that "I smoke" would be motivated to reduce the resulting dissonance. Because it is often difficult to change well-established behavior, people usually reduce cognitive dissonance by changing attitudes that are inconsistent with the behavior. So rather than quit smoking, the smoker might decide that smoking is not so dangerous after all.

In one of the first studies of cognitive dissonance, Festinger and his colleague Merrill Carlsmith asked people to turn pegs in a pegboard, a very dull task (Festinger & Carlsmith, 1959). Later, some of these people were asked to persuade a person who was waiting to participate in the study that the task was "exciting and fun." Some were told that they would be paid $1 to tell this lie. Others were promised $20. After they had talked to the waiting person, their attitudes toward the dull task were measured. Figure 16.3 shows and explains the surprising results. The people who were paid just $1 to lie liked the dull task more than those who were paid $20 (Festinger & Carlsmith, 1959).

Hundreds of other experiments have also found that when people publicly engage in behaviors that are inconsistent with their privately held attitudes, they're likely to change their attitudes to be consistent with their behavior (Cooper, Mirabile, & Scher, 2005). Attitude-behavior inconsistency is likely to change attitudes when (1) the inconsistency causes some distress or discomfort in a person; and (2) changing attitudes will reduce that discomfort. But why should attitude-behavior inconsistency cause discomfort in the first place? There is considerable debate among attitude researchers about this question (Harmon-Jones, Amodio, & Harmon-Jones, 2009). Currently, the most popular of several possible answers is that discomfort results when people's positive self-concept (e.g., "I am honest") is threatened by recognizing that they have done something inconsistent with that self-concept. For example, if they have encouraged another person to do something that they themselves didn't believe in or that they themselves wouldn't do, this inconsistency makes most people feel uncomfortable. So they change their attitudes to reduce or eliminate the discomfort (Stone & Fernandez, 2008). In other words, if people can persuade themselves that they really believe in what they've said or done, the inconsistency disappears, their positive self-concept is restored, and they can feel good about themselves again. One study suggests that people can experience the same result, at least for a little while, just by washing their hands (Lee & Schwarz, 2010). Perhaps this cleansing represents a fresh start and creates a greater sense of moral superiority (Zhong, Strejcek, & Sivanathan, 2010).

The circumstances that lead to cognitive dissonance may be different in the individualist cultures of Europe and North America than in collectivist cultures such as those in Japan and China. In individualist cultures, dissonance typically arises from behaving in a manner inconsistent with one's own beliefs because this behavior causes self-doubt. But in collectivist cultures, dissonance typically arises when such behavior causes people to worry about what others think of them (Imada & Kitayama et al., 2010). Cultural values also help shape dissonance-reducing strategies. For example, people from individualistic cultures can reduce the unpleasant feelings that accompany dissonance by affirming their value as unique individuals, whereas people from collectivist cultures can reduce the same kind of feelings by affirming the value of the groups to which they belong (Hoshino-Browne et al., 2005). ("In Review: Forming and Changing Attitudes" summarizes some of the main processes through which attitudes are formed and changed.)

FORMING AND CHANGING ATTITUDES

Type of Influence	Description
Social learning and conditioning	Attitudes are usually formed through observing how others behave and speak about an attitude object, as well as through classical and operant conditioning.
Elaboration likelihood model	People change attitudes through either a central or peripheral route, depending on factors such as personal involvement.
Cognitive dissonance	Holding inconsistent cognitions can motivate attitude change.

In Review Questions

1. According to the elaboration likelihood model, people are more likely to pay close attention to the content and logic of a persuasive message if the _____ route to attitude change has been activated.

2. Holding attitudes that are similar to those of your friends illustrates the importance of _____ in attitude formation.

3. According to cognitive dissonance theory, we tend to reduce conflict between attitudes and behaviors by changing our _____.

PREJUDICE AND STEREOTYPES

How does prejudice develop?

All of the principles behind impression formation, attribution, and attitudes come together in prejudice and stereotypes. **Stereotypes** are the perceptions, beliefs, and expectations a person has about members of a particular group. They are schemas about entire groups of people (Dovidio & Gaertner, 2010). Usually, they involve the false assumption that all members of a group share the same characteristics. The characteristics that make up the stereotype can be positive, but more often they are negative. The most prevalent and powerful stereotypes focus on observable personal attributes, particularly ethnicity, gender, and age (Bodenhausen & Richeson, 2010).

The stereotypes people hold can be so ingrained that their effects on behavior can be automatic and unconscious (Dovidio et al., 2009; Stepanikova, Triplett, & Simpson, 2011). In one study, for example, European American and African American participants played a video game in which white or black men suddenly appeared on a screen holding an object that might be a weapon (Correll et al., 2002; see Figure 16.4). The participants had to immediately "shoot" armed men but not unarmed ones. Under this time pressure, participants' errors were not random. If they "shot" an unarmed man, he was more likely to be black; when they failed to "shoot" an armed man, he was more likely to be white. These differences appeared in both European American and African American participants, but were most pronounced among those who held the strongest cultural stereotypes about blacks.

Stereotyping often leads to **prejudice**, which is a positive or negative attitude toward an individual based simply on that individual's membership in some group (Biernat & Danaher, 2013). The word *prejudice* means "prejudgment." Many theorists believe that prejudice, like other attitudes, has cognitive, affective, and behavioral components. The cognitive component of prejudice is stereotyped thinking. The affective component includes people's hatred, admiration, anger, and other feelings about stereotyped groups. The behavioral component of prejudice involves **social discrimination**, which is differing treatment of individuals who belong to different groups. Prejudiced thinking can be quite complex. For instance, most people are prejudiced in favor of attractive people in general, but in a competitive situation they tend to be prejudiced against the best-looking individuals of the same sex (Agthe, Spörrle, & Maner, 2010, 2011).

stereotypes False assumptions that all members of some group share the same characteristics.

prejudice A positive or negative attitude toward people in certain groups.

social discrimination Differential treatment of people in certain groups; the behavioral component of prejudice.

FIGURE 16.4
The Impact of Stereotypes on Behavior

TRY THIS When these men suddenly appeared on a video screen, participants were supposed to "shoot" them, but only if they appeared to be armed (Correll et al., 2002). Stereotypes about whether white men or black men are more likely to be armed significantly affected the errors made by participants in firing their video game "weapons." Similar results appeared in a sample of police officers, although they were not as quick as civilians were to "shoot" an unarmed black man (Correll et al., 2007). Cover these photos with a pair of index cards, then ask a few friends to watch as you show each photo, one at a time, for just an instant, before covering it again. Then ask your friends to say whether either man appeared to be armed. Was one individual more often seen as armed? If so, which one?

University of Chicago

Theories of Prejudice and Stereotyping

Prejudice and stereotyping may occur for several reasons. Let's consider three explanatory theories, each of which has been supported by research and accounts for many instances of stereotyping and prejudice.

Motivational Theories

Prejudice meets certain needs and increases the sense of security for some people. This idea was first proposed by Theodor W. Adorno and his associates more than sixty years ago (Adorno et al., 1950), and it is still seen as a major cause of prejudice (Goodnight et al., 2013; Hehman et al., 2012; Huang et al., 2011). Researchers suggest that prejudice is especially likely among people who display a personality trait called *authoritarianism*. Authoritarianism is composed of three main elements: (1) acceptance of conventional or traditional values; (2) willingness to unquestioningly follow the orders of authority figures; and (3) an inclination to act aggressively toward individuals or groups identified by authority figures as threats to the person's values or well-being. In fact, people with an authoritarian orientation tend to view the world as a threatening place (Sibley & Duckitt, 2013). One way to protect themselves from the threats they perceive all around them is to strongly identify with people like themselves—their *ingroup*—and to reject, dislike, and maybe even punish people who are members of *outgroups*, groups that are different from their own (Thomsen, Green, & Sidanius, 2008). Looking down on and discriminating against members of these outgroups—gay men and lesbians, African Americans, or Muslims, for example—may help authoritarian people feel safer and better about themselves (MacInnis et al., 2013; Onraet & Van Heil, 2014).

Another motivational explanation of prejudice involves the concept of social identity, discussed earlier. Recall that whether or not they display authoritarianism, most people are motivated to identify with their ingroup and tend to see it as better than other groups (Abrams & Hogg, 2010). As a result, members of an ingroup often see all members of outgroups as less attractive and less socially acceptable than members of the ingroup and may thus treat them badly (Brewer, 2010). In other words, prejudice may result when people's motivation to enhance their own self-esteem causes them to disrespect other people.

Cognitive Theories

Stereotyping and prejudice may also result from the thought processes that people use in dealing with the world. There are so many other people, so many situations in which we meet them, and so many behaviors that others might display that we cannot possibly attend to and remember them all. Therefore, when people encounter other people, especially for the first time, they must use schemas and other cognitive shortcuts to organize and make sense of their social world (Penner & Dovidio, 2014). Often these cognitive processes provide accurate and useful summaries of what to expect from other people, but sometimes they lead to inaccurate stereotypes (Lewis et al., 2012).

For example, one effective way to deal with social complexity is grouping people into *social categories*. Rather than remembering every detail about everyone we have ever encountered, we tend to put other people into categories such as doctor, senior citizen, Republican, student, Italian, and the like (Biernat & Danaher, 2013). To further simplify perception of these categories, we tend to see group members as quite similar to one another. In fact, members of one ethnic group may find it harder to distinguish among specific faces in other ethnic groups than in their own (Anthony, Cooper, & Mullen, 1992; Michel et al., 2006). People also tend to assume that all members of a different group hold the same beliefs and values and that those beliefs and values differ from those of their own group (Gaertner, Dovidio, & Houlette, 2010; Waytz & Young, 2012). And because particularly noticeable stimuli tend to draw a lot of attention, rude behavior by even a few members of an easily identified ethnic group may lead people to see an *illusory correlation* between rudeness and ethnicity (Meiser & Hewstone, 2010). As a result, they may incorrectly believe that all members of that group are rude. Finally, many people—especially those at lower levels of cognitive ability—seem to have a need for *cognitive closure*, meaning

Schemas and Stereotypes

The use of schemas to assign certain people to certain categories can be helpful when deciding who is a customer and who is a store employee, but it can also lead to inaccurate stereotypes. After 9/11, many people began to think of all Muslims as potential terrorists and to discriminate against them.

Jessica Rinaldi/Reuters/Landov

that they prefer to decide quickly and once and for all what they think about everyone in a particular group (Hodson & Busseri, 2012; Roets & Hiel, 2011). Satisfying this need saves them the time and effort it would take to consider individuals as individuals (Rubin, Paolini, & Crisp, 2010).

Learning Theories

Like other attitudes, prejudice can be learned. Some prejudice is learned as a result of personal conflicts with members of particular groups, but people also develop negative attitudes toward groups with whom they have had little or no contact. Learning theories suggest that children can pick up prejudices just by watching and listening to parents, peers, and others (Castelli, Zogmaister, & Tomelleri, 2009; Rutland, Killen, & Abrams, 2010). Evolutionary forces may even have created a kind of biopreparedness (described in the learning chapter) that makes us especially likely to affiliate with our own group and to learn to fear people who are strangers or who look different from us (Kelly et al., 2007; Lewis & Bates, 2010; Park, 2012). The media also portray certain groups in ways that teach stereotypes and prejudice (Kassin, Fein, & Markus, 2014). For example, one study found that European American characters in popular television shows tend to behave more negatively toward African American characters than toward other European Americans. This study also found that watching these shows can elevate viewers' prejudice against African Americans in general (Weisbuch, Pauker, & Ambady, 2009). No wonder so many young children already know about the supposed negative characteristics of certain groups long before they ever meet members of those groups (Baron & Banaji, 2006; Degner & Wentura, 2010).

Reducing Prejudice

The cognitive and learning theories of prejudice and stereotyping suggest that members of one group are often ignorant of, or misinformed about, the characteristics of people in other groups (Dovidio, Gaertner, & Kawakami, 2010). However, simply providing accurate information to prejudiced people and encouraging them to be less prejudiced can actually increase prejudice (Legault, Gutsell, & Inzlicht, 2011). Encouraging people to ignore ethnic differences does not seem to reduce prejudiced attitudes, either (Apfelbaum et al., 2010).

The **contact hypothesis** provides a more promising approach. It states that stereotypes and prejudice toward a group will decrease as contact with that group increases (Hodson & Hewstone, 2013). Before 1954, most black and white schoolchildren in the United States knew very little about one another because they went to separate schools. Then the Supreme Court declared that segregated public schools should be prohibited. In doing so, the court created a real-life test of the contact hypothesis.

Did the desegregation of U.S. schools confirm that hypothesis? In a few schools, integration was followed by a decrease in prejudice, but in many places, either no change occurred or prejudice actually increased (Pettigrew et al., 2011). However, these results did not necessarily disprove the contact hypothesis. In-depth studies of schools with successful desegregation suggested that contact alone was not enough. Integration usually reduced prejudice only when certain social conditions were created (Pettigrew et al., 2011). First, members of the two groups had to be of roughly equal social and economic status. Second, school authorities had to promote cooperation and interdependence between ethnic groups by having members of the two groups work together on projects that required reliance on one another to achieve success. Third, the contact between group members had to occur on a one-to-one basis. It was only when *individuals* got to know each other that the errors contained in stereotypes became apparent. Finally, the members of each group had to be seen as typical and not unusual in any significant way. When these four conditions were met, the children's attitudes toward one another became more positive (Deeb et al., 2011).

A teaching strategy called the *jigsaw technique* helps create these conditions (Aronson & Patnoe, 2011). The strategy calls for children from several ethnic groups to work in teams to complete a task, such as writing a report about a famous person in history. Each child learns a separate piece of information about this person, such as place of birth or greatest

contact hypothesis The idea that stereotypes and prejudice toward a group will diminish as contact with the group increases.

achievement, then provides this information to the team (Aronson, 2004). Studies show that children from various ethnic groups who take part in the jigsaw technique and other cooperative learning experiences display substantial reductions in prejudice while also facilitating learning (Aronson & Patnoe, 2011; Doymus, Karacop, & Simsel, 2010). The success reported in these studies has greatly increased the popularity of cooperative learning exercises in U.S. classrooms. Such exercises may not eliminate all aspects of ethnic prejudice in children, but they seem to be a step in the right direction.

Can friendly, cooperative, interdependent contact reduce the more entrenched forms of prejudice seen in adults? It may (Hodson, 2011). One study found that the prejudicial attitudes of first-year college students weakened more if their roommate was from a different ethnic group rather than from the students' own ethnic group (Shook & Fazio, 2008). Another showed that when equal-status adults from different ethnic groups work jointly toward a common goal, bias and distrust can be reduced, particularly among those in ethnic majority groups (Pettigrew et al., 2011). This is especially true if they come to see themselves as members of the same group rather than as belonging to opposing groups (al Ramiah & Hewstone, 2013). The challenge to be met in creating such cooperative experiences in the real world is that the participants must be of equal status, a challenge made more difficult in many countries by the status differences that still exist between ethnic groups (Kenworthy et al., 2006).

In the final analysis, contact can provide only part of the solution to the problems of stereotyping, prejudice, and social discrimination. To reduce ethnic prejudice, we must develop additional techniques to address the social cognitions and perceptions that lie at the core of bigotry and hatred toward people who are different from ourselves (Amodio & Devine, 2009; Bigler & Liben, 2007).

Fighting Ethnic Prejudice

Negative attitudes about members of ethnic groups are often based on negative personal experiences or on the negative experiences and attitudes people hear about from others. Cooperative contact between equals can help promote mutual respect and reduce ethnic prejudice (Fischer, 2011; Hodson, 2011; Vezzali & Giovannini, 2011).

Robert Brenner/PhotoEdit

LINKAGES Can we ever be unbiased about anyone? (a link to Consciousness)

LINKAGES Can subliminal stimuli influence our judgments about people? (a link to Perception)

THINKING CRITICALLY

IS ETHNIC PREJUDICE TOO INGRAINED EVER TO BE ELIMINATED?

Overt ethnic prejudice has decreased dramatically in the United States over the past fifty to sixty years. Four decades ago, fewer than 40 percent of European Americans said they would vote for an African American presidential candidate (Dovidio & Gaertner, 1998); in 2008, an African American president was elected. Despite these changes, research in social psychology suggests that more subtle aspects of prejudice and discrimination may remain as entrenched in the United States today as they were a couple of decades ago (Bonilla-Silva & Dietrich, 2011).

What am I being asked to believe or accept?

Some psychologists claim that even people who see themselves as unprejudiced and who disavow ethnic stereotypes and discrimination may, without realizing it, hold negative stereotypes about ethnic outgroups and, in certain situations, display prejudice and discriminatory behavior (Dovidio et al., 2009; Penner & Dovidio, 2014; Sabin et al., 2009).

What evidence is available to support the assertion?

Evidence for this assertion focuses primarily on prejudice against dark-skinned people by light-skinned people. It comes, first, from studies testing the theory of *aversive racism* (Hodson, Dovidio, & Gaertner, 2010). This theory holds that even though many people of European descent consider ethnic prejudice unacceptable or aversive, they still sometimes display it—especially when they can do so without admitting, even to themselves, that they are prejudiced (Gaertner & Dovidio, 1986; Kunstman & Plant, 2008).

In one test of this theory (Hodson, Dovidio, & Gaertner, 2010), white participants read a story about a robbery. There were no eyewitnesses, but police had arrested a known troublemaker whose DNA linked him to the crime. For half participants, the story described the suspect as white; the other half read that he was black. If they were allowed to consider the DNA evidence, both groups were equally likely to say the suspect was guilty, suggesting that

(continued)

racial prejudice was not operating. However, some participants had been told that the DNA evidence was inadmissible in court, so they had to ignore it. These participants were more likely to judge black rather than white suspects guilty and to recommend harsher punishments for the black criminals.

A second line of evidence for the entrenched nature of prejudice comes from research showing that many people hold negative stereotypes about ethnic minorities but are unaware that they do so. This kind of prejudice is often called *implicit* (Biernat & Danaher, 2013; Penner & Dovidio, in press). In contrast, people with *explicit* prejudice are aware of their negative attitudes toward particular groups, and so can choose to control their bias (Dovidio & LaFrance, 2013; Penner et al., 2013). An example of implicit bias appeared in a study of physicians who were not conscious of their bias against African Americans, yet were found to behave more negatively toward their African American patients (Penner et al., 2013). The doctors' behavior caused these patients, in turn, to react negatively toward the doctors (Blair et al., 2013).

Other researchers have used the priming procedures described in the chapter on consciousness to activate unconscious thoughts and feelings that can alter people's reactions to stimuli without their awareness (Lybarger & Monteith, 2011). In one study, white participants were exposed to subliminal presentations of pictures of black individuals (Chen & Bargh, 1997). The participants were not consciously aware that they had seen these pictures, but when they interacted with a black man soon afterward, those who had been primed with the pictures acted more negatively toward him and saw him as more hostile than people who had not been primed. Other studies suggest it is also possible to prime unconscious negative stereotypes about other groups, including women and people who are overweight (Glick & Fiske, 2001; Degner & Wentura, 2009). All of these findings suggest that stereotypes may be so well learned and so ingrained in people that they may be activated automatically and without conscious awareness (Amodio & Devine, 2009).

Are there alternative ways of interpreting the evidence?

The evidence presented so far suggests that it may be impossible to eliminate ethnic prejudice because everyone harbors implicit negative bias about various groups. But the evidence does not necessarily mean that such biases will affect everyone in the same way. For example, it could be that they have a greater impact on people who are more overtly prejudiced and less concerned about displaying that prejudice.

What additional evidence would help evaluate the alternatives?

One way to evaluate this possibility is to compare the responses of prejudiced and unprejudiced people in various experimental situations. In one mock-trial study, for example, overtly prejudiced white jurors recommended the death penalty more often for black defendants than for white defendants found guilty of the same crime. Low-prejudice white jurors showed this bias only when they believed that a black member of the jury also favored giving the death penalty (Dovidio et al., 1997). Priming studies, too, show that although negative stereotypes can be primed in both prejudiced and unprejudiced people, it is easier to do in people who openly display their ethnic bias (Amodio & Devine, 2010). Furthermore, activation of these stereotypes may be less likely to affect the conscious attitudes and behavior of unprejudiced people. So when unconscious stereotypes are activated in unprejudiced people, the effects tend to appear in subtle ways, such as in facial expressions or other nonverbal behaviors (e.g., Vanman et al., 2004).

What conclusions are most reasonable?

Taken together, research evidence presents a mixed picture regarding the possibility of eliminating ethnic prejudice. True, ethnic prejudice may be so ingrained in some people that they may hold nonconscious or implicit bias and stereotypes, but it may still be possible to eliminate even nonconscious stereotypes (e.g., Devine et al., 2012; Gervais & Norenzayan, 2012; Luguri, Napier, & Dovidio, 2012). It also appears that when apparently unprejudiced people are made aware of their negative beliefs about some target group, they will actively work to prevent those beliefs from influencing their behavior toward members of that group (Woodcock & Monteith, 2013).

INTERPERSONAL ATTRACTION

What factors affect who likes whom?

Research on prejudice suggests some of the reasons why people may come to dislike or even hate other people. An equally fascinating aspect of social cognition is why people like or love other people. Folklore tells us that "opposites attract" but also that "birds of a feather flock together." Each statement is partly true, but neither is entirely accurate in all cases. We begin our coverage of interpersonal attraction by discussing the factors that draw people toward one another. We then examine how liking sometimes develops into more intimate relationships.

Proximity and Liking

TRY THIS Research on environmental factors in attraction suggests that, barring bad first impressions, the more often we make contact with someone—as neighbors, classmates, or co-workers, for example—the more we tend to like that person (Preciado et al., 2012). Does this principle apply in your life? To find out, think about how and where you met each of your closest friends. If you can think of cases in which proximity did not lead to liking, what do you think interfered with the formation of friendship?

© iStockphoto.com/Blend_Images

Keys to Attraction

Whether you like someone or not depends partly on situational factors and partly on personal characteristics.

The Environment

One of the most important determinants of attraction is simple physical proximity (Clark & Lemay, 2010). As long as you do not initially dislike a person, your liking for that person will increase with additional contact (Kassin, Fein, & Markus, 2014). This proximity phenomenon—another example of the *mere-exposure effect* mentioned earlier—helps account for why next-door neighbors are usually more likely to become friends than people who live farther from one another. Chances are, most of your friends are people you met as neighbors, co-workers, or classmates (Reis et al., 2011).

The circumstances under which people first meet also influence attraction. You are much more likely to be attracted to a stranger if you meet in comfortable, rather than uncomfortable, physical conditions (IJzerman & Semin, 2009). Similarly, if you receive a reward in the presence of a stranger, the chances are greater that you will like that stranger, even if the stranger is not the one giving the reward (Clark & Pataki, 1995). At least among strangers, then, liking can occur through associating someone with something pleasant. But, there are limits. One study found that pairing positive stimuli with pictures of someone of the opposite sex did not increase attraction to that person if it was known that the person was already involved in a romantic relationship (Korayni, Gast, & Rothermund, 2013).

Similarity

People also tend to like those they perceive as similar to themselves on variables such as appearance, age, religion, smoking or drinking habits, being a "morning" or "evening" person, or their use of language (Clark & Lemay, 2010; Ireland et al., 2011; MacKinnon, Jordan, & Wilson, 2011). Similarity in attitudes is another important influence on attraction (Baumeister & Bushman, 2014).

An especially good predictor of liking is similarity in attitudes about mutual acquaintances, because in general, people prefer relationships that are *balanced*. As illustrated in Figure 16.5, if Meagan likes Abigail, the relationship is balanced as long as they agree on their evaluation of a third person, regardless of whether they like or dislike that third person. However, the relationship will be imbalanced if Meagan and Abigail disagree on their evaluation of a third person.

One reason why we like people whose attitudes are similar to our own is that we expect such people to think highly of us (Condon & Crano, 1988). It's hard to

"HE'S PERFECT. WE HAVE LOADS OF THE SAME APPS."

TRY THIS Similarity can take many forms. How many apps do you and your closest friends have in common?

S. Harris/ScienceCartoonsPlus.com

Here are some common examples of balanced and imbalanced relationships among three people. The plus and minus signs refer to liking and disliking, respectively. Balanced relationships are comfortable and harmonious; imbalanced ones often bring conflict.

© Palmer Kane LLC /Shutterstock.com; rphotos/ Photos.com; © iStockphoto.com/Mazdaguy03

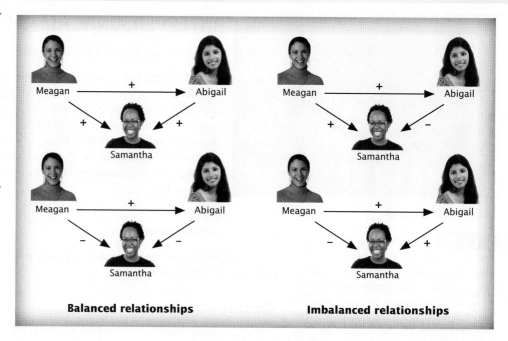

Balanced relationships   **Imbalanced relationships**

say, though, whether attraction is a cause or an effect of similarity. For example, you might like someone because his attitudes are similar to yours, but it is also possible that as a result of liking him, your attitudes will become more similar to his (Davis & Rusbult, 2001). Even if your own attitudes do not change, you may change your perceptions of the liked person's attitudes such that those attitudes now seem more similar to yours (Aronson. Wilson & Akert, 2013).

Physical Attractiveness

Physical characteristics are another important factor in attraction, particularly in the early stages of a relationship (Leary, 2010; Platek & Singh, 2010). From preschool through adulthood, physical attractiveness is a key to popularity with members of both sexes (Finkel & Baumeister, 2010). Consistent with the **matching hypothesis** of interpersonal attraction, however, people tend to date, marry, or form other committed relationships with those who are similar to themselves in physical attractiveness (Finkel & Baumeister, 2010). One possible reason for this is that although people tend to be most attracted to those with the greatest physical appeal, they also want to avoid being rejected by such individuals. So it may be compromise and not preference that leads people to pair off with those who are roughly equivalent to themselves in physical attractiveness (Kavanagh, Robins, & Ellis, 2010).

Intimate Relationships and Love

There is much about intimate relationships that psychologists do not and may never understand, but they are learning all the time (Clark & Grote, 2013). For example, evolutionary psychologists suggest that men and women employ different strategies to ensure the survival of their genes and that each gender looks for different attributes in a potential mate (Buss, 2013; Foster, 2013). The physical appearance of a partner tends to be more important to men than to women, whereas a partner's intelligence tends to be more important to women than to men (Buss, 2008; see Figure 16.6). Women also tend to be more influenced than men are by a potential mate's economic and social status. In one study, for instance, women rated men as being far more attractive when the men were seen to own a luxury automobile rather than an ordinary one. Men's ratings of women's attractiveness was not related to the kind of car she owned (Dunn & Searle, 2010).

matching hypothesis The notion that people are most likely to form committed relationships with those who are similar to themselves in physical attractiveness.

FIGURE 16.6
Sex Differences in Date and Mate Preferences

Evolutionary psychologists suggest that men and women have developed different strategies for selecting sexual partners (e.g., Buss, 2004b; Kenrick, Neuberg, & Cialdini, 2005). These psychologists say that women became more selective than men because they can have relatively few children and want a partner who is best able to help support those children. So when asked about the intelligence of people they would choose for one-night stands, dating, and sexual relationships, women preferred much smarter partners than men did. Only when the choices concerned steady dating and marriage did the men's preference for bright partners equal that of the women (Eastwick & Finkel, 2008). Critics suggest, however, that these sex differences reflect learned social norms and expected gender-specific behaviors (Eagly & Wood, 1999; Miller, Putcha-Bhagavatula, & Pedersen, 2002).

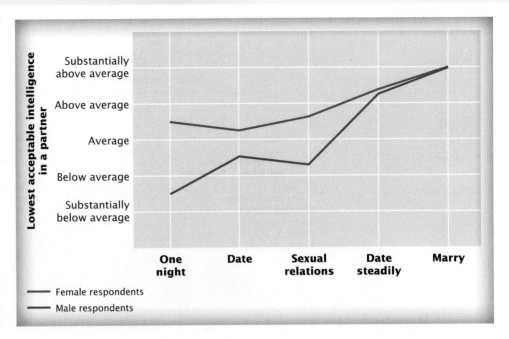

Intimate Relationships

Eventually, people who are attracted to each other usually become *interdependent,* which means that one person's thoughts, emotions, and behaviors affect the thoughts, emotions, and behaviors of the other (Clark & Lemay, 2010). Interdependence is one of the defining characteristics of intimate relationships (Clark & Grote, 2013).

Another key component of successful intimate relationships is *commitment,* which is the extent to which each person is psychologically attached to the relationship and wants to remain in it (Amodio & Showers, 2005). People feel committed to a relationship when they are satisfied with the rewards they receive from it, when they have invested significant tangible and intangible resources in it, and when they have few attractive alternative relationships available to them (Bui, Peplau, & Hill, 1996; Lydon, Fitzsimons, & Naidoo, 2003).

Analyzing Love

Although some people think love is simply a strong form of liking, research suggests that romantic love and liking are quite separate emotions, at least in the sense that they are associated with differing patterns of brain chemistry and brain activity (Hsia & Schweinle, 2012). And although romantic love and sexual desire are often experienced together, they too seem to be separate emotions associated with different patterns of physiological arousal (Acevedo & Aron, 2014). Further, most theorists agree that there are several different types of love (Berscheid, 2010). One widely accepted view distinguishes between passionate (romantic) love and companionate love (Berscheid, 2011). *Passionate love* is intense, arousing, and marked by both strong physical attraction and deep emotional attachment. Sexual feelings are intense, and thoughts of the other intrude on each person's awareness frequently. *Companionate love* is less arousing but psychologically more intimate. It is marked by mutual concern for the welfare of the other and a willingness to disclose personal information and feelings (Berscheid, 2010). People who experience companionate love seem especially satisfied with their lives (Kassin, Fein, & Markus, 2014).

Robert Sternberg (2009) has offered an even broader analysis of love. According to his *triangular theory,* the three basic components of love are passion, intimacy, and commitment (see Figure 16.7). Various combinations of these components result in various types of love. For example, Sternberg suggests that *romantic love* involves a high degree of passion and intimacy yet lacks substantial commitment to the other person. *Companionate love* is

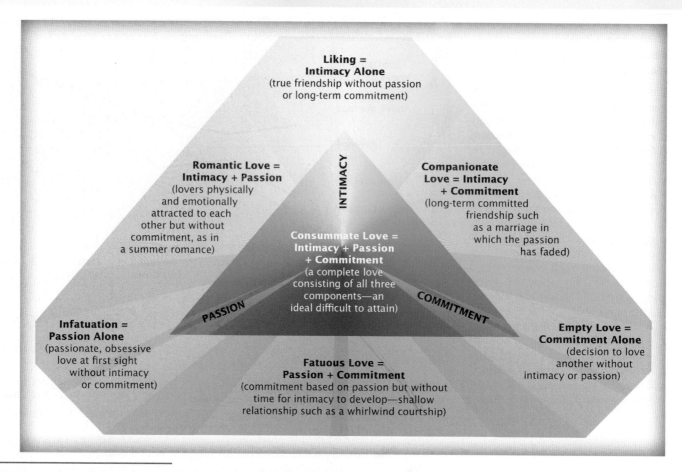

FIGURE 16.7

A Triangular Theory of Love

According to Sternberg (2009), different types of love result when the three basic components in his triangular theory occur in different combinations. The size of the triangle of love increases as love increases, and its shape is determined by the relative strength of each basic component.

marked by a great deal of intimacy and commitment but little passion. *Consummate love* is the most complete and satisfying. It is the most complete because it includes a high level of all three components. It is the most satisfying because the relationship is likely to fulfill many of the needs of each partner. More recently, Sternberg advanced a "duplex theory" of love by pairing his triangular theory with a second one that focuses on love as a story. This second theory is based on the fact that in Western cultures, at least, it appears that the success of a relationship depends not just on its perceived characteristics but also on the degree to which those characteristics fit each partner's ideal story of love, such as that of a prince and princess, or a pair of business partners, for example (Sternberg, 2009).

Cultural factors have a strong influence on the way people think about love and marriage. In North America and Western Europe, for example, the vast majority of people believe that they should love the person they marry. By contrast, in India and Pakistan, about half the people interviewed in a survey said they would marry someone they did not love if that person had other qualities that they desired (Levine et al., 1995). In Russia, only 40 percent of respondents said that they married for love. Most reported marrying because of loneliness, shared interests, or an unplanned pregnancy (Baron & Byrne, 1994). Many such cultural differences in the role of love in marriage are likely to continue, but others seem to be disappearing (Hatfield & Rapson, 2006).

SOCIAL INFLUENCE

What social rules shape our behavior?

So far, we have considered social cognition, the mental processes associated with people's perceptions of, and reactions to, other people. Let's now explore *social influence*, the process through which individuals and groups directly and indirectly influence a person's thoughts, feelings, and behavior. Research has shown, for example, that suicide rates increase following

Clothing and Culture

The social norms that guide how people dress and behave in various situations are part of the culturally determined socialization process described in the chapter on human development. The process is the same worldwide. Parents, teachers, peers, religious leaders, and others communicate their culture's social norms to children, but differences in those norms result in quite different behaviors from culture to culture.

C3899 Sandra Gaetke Deutsche Presse-Agentur/ Newscom

well-publicized suicides (Chen et al., 2010; Collings & Kemp, 2010) and that murder rates increase after well-publicized homicides (Jamieson, Jamieson, & Romer, 2003). Do these correlations mean that media coverage of violence triggers similar violence? As described in the chapter on learning, televised violence can play a causal role in aggressive behavior, but there are other reasons to believe that murders or suicides stimulate imitators when they become media events. For one thing, many of the people who kill themselves after a widely reported suicide are similar to the original victim in some respect (Cialdini, 2008). For example, after German television reported a story about a young man who committed suicide by jumping in front of a train, there was a dramatic increase in the number of young German men who committed suicide in the same way (Schmidtke & Hafner, 1988). This phenomenon—known as "copycat" violence—illustrates the effects of social influence.

Social Norms

The most common yet subtle form of social influence is communicated through social norms. **Social norms** are learned, socially based rules that tell people what they should or should not do in various situations (Hogg, 2010). Parents, teachers, members of the clergy, peers, and other agents of culture transmit these social norms (Schmidt & Tomasello, 2012). Because of the power of social norms, people often follow them automatically. In North America and the United Kingdom, for example, social norms tell us that we should get in line to buy a movie ticket rather than crowd around the box office window. They also lead us to expect that others will do the same. By informing people of what is expected of them and others, social norms make social situations clearer, more predictable, and more comfortable (Schultz et al., 2007).

Robert Cialdini (2007) has described social norms as either descriptive or injunctive. *Descriptive norms* indicate how most other people actually behave in a given situation. They tell us what actions are common in the situation and thereby implicitly give us permission to act in the same way. The fact that most people do not cross a street until the green light or "walk" sign appears is an example of a descriptive norm. *Injunctive norms* give more specific information about the actions that others find acceptable and those that they find unacceptable. Subtle pressure exists to behave in accordance with these norms. A sign that reads "Do not cross on red" or the person next to you saying the same thing is an example of an injunctive norm (Ecker & Buckner, 2014; Simons-Morton,

social norms Learned, socially based rules that prescribe what people should or should not do in various situations.

Deindividuation

Robes, hoods, and group rituals help create deindividuation in these members of the Ku Klux Klan by focusing their attention on membership in their organization and its values. The hoods also hide their identities, which reduces their sense of personal responsibility and accountability and makes it easier for them to engage in hate crimes and other cowardly acts of bigotry. Deindividuation operates in other groups, too, ranging from lynch mobs and terrorist cells to political protesters, urban rioters, and even members of so-called "flash mobs." Through deindividuation, people appear to become "part of the herd," and they may do things that they might not do on their own (Spears et al., 2001).

David Leeson/The Image Works

deindividuation A psychological state occurring in group members that results in loss of individuality and a tendency to do things not normally done when alone.

conformity Changing one's behavior or beliefs to match those of others, generally as a result of real or imagined (though unspoken) group pressure.

compliance Adjusting one's behavior because of a direct request.

et al., 2014). Sometimes both kinds of norms operate at the same time. There is evidence, for example, that how much college students use tobacco and alcohol is influenced both by how much they think other students drink and smoke (descriptive norms) and whether they think that their close friends approve of these behaviors (injunctive norms) (Etcheverry & Agnew, 2008; Neighbors et al., 2008).

One particularly powerful social norm is *reciprocity,* the tendency to respond to others as they have acted toward you (Cialdini & Griskevicius, 2010). Restaurant servers often take advantage of this social norm by leaving some candy with the bill. Customers who receive this gift tend to reciprocate by leaving a larger tip than customers who don't get candy (Strohmetz et al., 2002). The strength of the reciprocity norm appears to increase when people are reminded of their own mortality. In one study, when people were exposed to themes about dying, the size of the tip they left for a server was more strongly associated with the level of service they received—larger tips for good service, smaller tips for poor service (Schindler, Reinhard, & Stahlberg, 2013). This finding is consistent with the terror management theory we discussed earlier.

Though the reciprocity norm probably exists in every culture, other social norms are less universal (Adam, Shirako, & Maddux, 2010; Miller, 2001). For instance, people around the world differ greatly in terms of the physical distance they keep between themselves and others while talking. People from South America usually stand much closer to each other than do people from North America. And as suggested in the chapter on psychological disorders, behavior that is considered normal and friendly in one culture may be seen as offensive or even abnormal in another.

The social influence exerted by social norms creates orderly social behavior, but social influence can also lead to a breakdown in order. For example, **deindividuation** is a psychological state in which a person becomes "submerged in the group" and loses the sense of individuality (Baumeister & Bushman, 2014). When people experience deindividuation, they become emotionally aroused and feel intense closeness with their group. This increased awareness of group membership may lead people to follow the group's social norms, even if those norms promote antisocial behavior (Reimann & Zimbardo, 2011). Normally mild-mannered adults may throw rocks at police during political protests, and youngsters who would not ordinarily commit hate crimes have done so as part of gangs. Such behavior—whether physical or verbal—becomes more extreme as people feel less identifiable, as they often do in crowds, in dark environments, or online (Naquin, Kurtzberg, & Belkin, 2010; Zhong, Bohns, & Gino, 2010). An analysis of newspaper accounts of lynchings in the United States over a 50-year period showed that larger lynch mobs were more savage and vicious than smaller ones (Mullen, 1986). Deindividuation provides an example of how, given the right circumstances, quite normal people can engage in destructive, even violent behavior.

Conformity and Compliance

When people change their behavior or beliefs to match those of other members of a group, they are said to conform. **Conformity** occurs as a result of unspoken group pressure, real or imagined (Forsyth, 2013). You probably have experienced group pressure when everyone around you stands to applaud a performance that you thought was not particularly great. You may conform by standing as well, though no one told you to do so; the group's behavior creates a silent but influential pressure to follow suit. **Compliance**, in contrast, occurs when people adjust their behavior because of a request. The request can be clear and direct, such as "Please do me a favor," or it can be more subtle, as when someone simply looks at you in a way that lets you know that the person needs a favor.

Conformity and compliance are usually generated by spoken or unspoken social norms. In a classic experiment, Muzafer Sherif (1937) charted the formation of a group norm by taking advantage of a visual illusion: if you look at a fixed point of light in a pitch-dark room, the light will appear to move. Estimates of how far the light seems to move tend to stay the same over time if an observer is alone. But when Sherif tested several people at once, asking each person to say aloud how far the light moved on repeated trials,

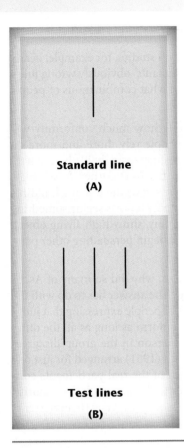

FIGURE 16.8

Types of Stimulus Lines Used in Experiments by Asch

TRY THIS Participants in Asch's experiments saw a new set of lines like these on each trial. The middle line in Part B matches the one in Part A, but when several of Asch's assistants claimed that a different line matched, so did many of the participants. Try re-creating this experiment with four friends. Secretly ask three of them to say that the test line on the left matches the standard line, then show this drawing to all four. Did the fourth person conform to the group norm? If not, do you think it was something about the person, the length of the incorrect line chosen, or both that led to nonconformity? Would conformity be more likely if the first three people had chosen the test line on the right? (Read on for more about this possibility.)

their estimates tended to converge; they had established a group norm. Even more important, when individuals who had been in the group were later tested alone, they continued to be influenced by this norm.

In another classic experiment, Solomon Asch (1956) explored what people do when faced with a norm that is obviously wrong. The participants in this experiment saw a standard line like the one in Figure 16.8(A); then they saw a display like that in Figure 16.8(B). Their task was to pick out the line in the display that was the same length as the one they had first been shown.

Each participant performed this task in a small group of people who posed as fellow participants but who were actually the experimenter's assistants. There were two conditions. In the control condition, the real participant responded first. In the experimental condition, the participant did not respond until after the other people did. The experimenter's assistants chose the correct response on six trials, but on the other twelve trials they all gave the same, obviously incorrect response. So on twelve trials, each participant was confronted with a "social reality" created by a group norm that conflicted with the physical reality created by what the person could clearly see. Only 5 percent of the participants in the control condition ever made a mistake during this easy perceptual task. However, among participants who heard the assistants' incorrect responses before giving their own, about 70 percent made at least one error by conforming to the group norm. An analysis of 133 studies conducted in seventeen countries reveals that conformity in Asch-type situations has declined somewhat in the United States since the 1950s but that it still occurs (Cialdini et al., 2001).

Why Do People Conform?

Why did so many people in Asch's experiment give incorrect responses when they were capable of near-perfect performance? One possibility, called *public conformity*, is that they didn't really believe in their responses but gave them simply because it was the socially desirable thing to do. Another possibility is that the participants experienced *private acceptance*. Perhaps they used the other people's responses as a guide, became convinced that their own perceptions were wrong, and actually changed their minds. Which possibility is more likely? Morton Deutsch and Harold Gerard (1955) reasoned that if people still conformed even when the other group members couldn't hear their response, then Asch's findings must reflect private acceptance, not just public conformity. Actually, although conformity does decrease when people respond privately, it doesn't disappear (Deutsch & Gerard, 1955). So people sometimes say things in public that they don't believe in, but hearing other people's responses also appears to influence their private beliefs (Moscovici, 1985). Such effects may not be long lasting, however. One study found that private conformity to a group's opinion lasted for no more than three days after an Asch-like experiment (Huang, Kendrick, & Yu, 2014).

Why are group norms so powerful? Research suggests several influential factors (Forsyth, 2013). First, people are motivated to be correct, and group norms provide information about what is right and wrong. Second, people want others to like them, so they may seek favor by conforming to the social norms that those others have established (Hewlin & Faison, 2009). Third, conforming to group norms may increase a person's sense of self-worth, especially if the group is valued or prestigious (Cialdini & Goldstein, 2004). The process may occur without our awareness (Lakin & Chartrand, 2003). For example, observations of interviews by former talk show host Larry King revealed that he tended to imitate the speech patterns of high-status guests but not low-status ones (Gregory & Webster, 1996). Finally, social norms affect the distribution of social rewards and punishments (Cialdini, 2008). From childhood on, people in many cultures learn that going along with group norms is good and earns rewards. (These positive outcomes presumably help compensate for not always saying or doing exactly what we please.) People also learn that breaking a norm may bring punishments ranging from scoldings for small transgressions to imprisonment for violation of social norms that have been translated into laws.

When Do People Conform?

People do not always conform to group influence. In the Asch studies, for example, nearly 30 percent of the participants did not go along with the assistants' obviously wrong judgments. Countless experiments have probed the question of what combinations of people and circumstances do and do not lead to conformity.

Ambiguity, or uncertainty, is important in determining how much conformity will occur. As the features of a situation become less clear, people rely more and more on others' opinions, and conformity to a group norm becomes increasingly likely (Forsyth, 2013). You can demonstrate this aspect of conformity on any street corner. First, create an ambiguous situation by having several people look at the sky or the top of a building. When passersby ask what is going on, be sure everyone excitedly reports seeing something interesting but fleeting—perhaps a faint flashing light or a tiny, shiny high-flying object. If you are especially successful, conforming newcomers will begin persuading other passersby that there is something fascinating to be seen.

TRY THIS

If ambiguity contributes so much to conformity, though, why did so many of Asch's participants conform to a judgment that was clearly wrong? The answer has to do with the *unanimous* nature of the group's judgment and the number of people expressing that judgment. Specifically, people experience intense pressure to conform as long as all the other group members agree with each other. If even one other person in the group disagrees with the majority view, conformity drops greatly. When Asch (1951) arranged for just one assistant to disagree with the others, fewer than 10 percent of the real participants conformed. Once unanimity is broken, it becomes much easier to disagree with the majority, even if the other nonconformist does not agree with the person's own view (Baumeister & Bushman, 2014).

Conformity also depends on the *size of the majority.* Asch (1955) demonstrated this phenomenon by varying the number of assistants in the group from one to fifteen. Conformity to incorrect social norms grew as the number of people in the group increased. However, most of the growth in conformity occurred as the size of the majority rose from one to about three or four members. This effect probably occurs because pressure to conform has already reached a peak after someone has heard three or four people agree. Hearing more people confirm the majority view has little additional social impact (Latané, 1981).

Conformity can also occur through *minority influence,* by which a minority of group members influences the behavior or beliefs of the majority (Hogg, 2010). This phenomenon is less common than majority influence, but when members of a numerical minority

Mass Conformity

The faithful who gather at Mecca, at the Vatican, and at other holy places around the world exemplify the power of religion and other social forces to produce conformity to group norms.

Nabeel Turner/The Image Bank/Getty Images; AP Images/L'Osservatore Romano

are established group members, agree with one another, and persist in their views, they can be influential (Hogg, 2010; Mucchi-Faina & Pagliaro, 2008). Perhaps because the views of a numerical minority are examined especially carefully by the rest of the group (Crano, 2012), minority-influenced change often takes a while. Even then, the amount of change tends to be small (Crano, 2012) and is most likely to occur when those in the minority are perceived by the majority to be loyal group members (Crano & Seyranian, 2009).

Does gender affect conformity? Early research suggested that women conform more than men, but the gender difference stemmed mainly from the fact that the tasks used in those studies were often more familiar to men than to women. This fact is important because people are especially likely to conform when they are faced with an unfamiliar situation (Kassin, Fein & Markus, 2014). Those studies also usually required people to make their responses aloud so that everyone knew if they had conformed or not. When the experimental tasks are equally familiar to both genders and when people can make their responses privately, no male-female differences in conformity are found. Accordingly, it has been suggested that gender differences in public conformity are based not on a genuine difference in reactions to social pressure but rather on men's desire to be seen as strong and independent and women's desire to be seen as cooperative (Hogg, 2010; Kenrick, Neuberg, & Cialdini, 2010).

Creating Compliance

In the experiments just described, the participants experienced psychological pressure to conform to the views or actions of others even though no one specifically asked them to do so. In contrast, *compliance* involves changing what you say or do because of a direct request.

How is compliance brought about? Many people believe that the direct approach is always best: if you want something, ask for it. But salespeople, political strategists, social psychologists, and other experts have learned that often the best way to get something is to ask for something else. Three examples of this strategy are the foot-in-the-door technique, the door-in-the-face technique, and the lowball technique (Cialdini & Griskevicius, 2010).

The *foot-in-the-door technique* works by getting a person to agree to small requests and then working up to larger ones. This technique was well illustrated in a study in which a woman asked strangers to keep an eye on her shopping bag while she stepped away for a few minutes. The strangers were twice as likely to agree to do this favor if the woman had first asked them "what time is it?" Apparently, by granting that first small favor they become much more likely to do a somewhat larger one (Dolinski, 2012).

Why should granting small favors lead to the granting of larger ones? First, people are usually far more likely to comply with a request that doesn't cost much in time, money, effort, or inconvenience. Second, complying with a small request makes people think of themselves as being committed to the cause or issue involved (Burger & Guadagno, 2003). This occurs through the processes of self-perception and cognitive dissonance discussed earlier (Cialdini & Griskevicius, 2010). Doing the first favor changes the way that people see themselves, that is, as people who are likely to do favors for others (Forsyth, 2013).

The foot-in-the-door technique can be amazingly effective. Steven Sherman (1980) created a 700 percent increase in the rate at which people volunteered to work for a charity simply by first getting them to say that in a hypothetical situation they would volunteer if asked. For some companies, the foot in the door is a request that potential customers merely answer a few questions; the request to buy something comes later. Others offer a small gift, or "door opener," as salespeople call it. Acceptance of the gift not only gives the salesperson a foot in the door but also may activate the reciprocity norm: many people who get something for free feel obligated to reciprocate by buying something, especially if the request to do so is delayed for a while (Cialdini & Griskevicius, 2010; Guadagno et al., 2001).

The *door-in-the-face technique* offers a second effective way of obtaining compliance (Cialdini, 2008). This strategy begins with a request for a favor that is likely to be refused.

Promoting Compliance

Have you ever been asked to sign a petition favoring some political, social, or economic cause? Supporters of these causes know that people who comply with this small request are the best people to contact later with requests to do more. Complying with larger requests is made more likely because it's consistent with the signer's initial commitment to the cause. If you were contacted after signing a petition, did you agree to donate money or become a volunteer?

EdBockStock/Shutterstock.com

The person making the request then concedes that this favor was too much to ask and substitutes a lesser alternative, which is what the person really wanted in the first place! Because the person appears willing to compromise and because the second request seems small in comparison with the first one, it is more likely to be granted than if it had been made at the outset. The door-in-the-face strategy is at the heart of bargaining among political groups and between labor and management (Ginges et al., 2007).

The third method, called the *lowball technique,* is commonly used by car dealers and other businesses (Forsyth, 2013). The first step in this strategy is to get people to say that they will do something, such as purchase a car. Once this commitment is made, the cost of fulfilling it is increased, often because of an "error" in computing the car's price. Why do buyers end up paying much more than originally planned for "lowballed" items? Apparently, once people commit themselves to do something, they feel obligated to follow through, especially when the initial commitment was made in public and when the person who obtained that commitment also makes the higher-cost request (Burger & Cornelius, 2003).

OBEDIENCE

How far will people go in obeying authority?

Compliance involves a change in behavior in response to a request. In the case of **obedience**, the behavior change comes in response to a *demand* from an authority figure (Sanderson, 2010). In the 1960s, Stanley Milgram developed a laboratory procedure at Yale University to study obedience. For his first experiment, he used newspaper ads to find forty male volunteer participants. They ranged in age from twenty to fifty, lived in the local community, and included professionals, white-collar businessmen, and unskilled workers (Milgram, 1963).

Imagine you are one of the people who answered the ad. When you arrive for the experiment, you join a fifty-year-old man who has also volunteered and has been scheduled for the same session. The experimenter explains that the purpose of the experiment is to examine the effects of punishment on learning. One of you—the "teacher"—will help the "learner" remember a list of words by administering an electric shock whenever the learner makes a mistake. Then the experimenter turns to you and asks you to draw one of two cards out of a hat. Your card says, "TEACHER." You think to yourself that this must be your lucky day.

Now the learner is taken into another room and strapped into a chair, and, as illustrated in Figure 16.9, electrodes are attached to his arm. You are shown a shock generator with thirty switches. The experimenter explains that the switch on the far left administers a mild, 15-volt shock and that each succeeding switch increases the shock by 15 volts. The one on the far right delivers 450 volts. The far left section of the shock generator is labeled "Slight shock." Looking across the panel, you see "Moderate shock," "Very strong shock," and at the far right, "Danger—severe shock." The last two switches are ominously labeled "XXX." The experimenter explains that you, the teacher, will begin by reading a list of word pairs to the learner. Then you will go through the list again, presenting just one word of each pair. The learner will have to say which word went with it. After the first mistake, you are to throw the switch to deliver 15 volts of shock. Each time the learner makes another mistake, you are to increase the shock by 15 volts.

You begin, following the experimenter's instructions. But after the learner makes his fifth mistake and you throw the switch to give him 75 volts, you hear a loud moan. At 90 volts, the learner cries out in pain. At 150 volts, he screams and asks to be let out of the experiment. You look to the experimenter, who says, "Proceed with the next word."

No shock was actually delivered in Milgram's experiments. The learner was always an employee of the experimenter, and the moans and other sounds of pain came from a prerecorded tape. But you do not know that. What would you do in this situation? Suppose you continue and eventually deliver 180 volts. The learner screams that he cannot

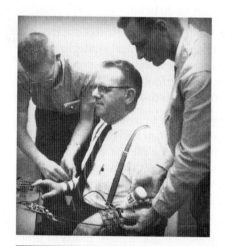

FIGURE 16.9
**Studying Obedience
in the Laboratory**

In this photograph from Milgram's original experiment, a man is being strapped into a chair with electrodes on his arm. Although participants in the experiment didn't know it, the man was actually the experimenter's assistant and received no shock.

From the film Obedience © 1968 by Stanley Milgram, © renewed 1993 by Alexandra Milgram, and distributed by Alexander Street Press. Permission granted by Alexandra Milgram

obedience Changing behavior in response to a demand from an authority figure.

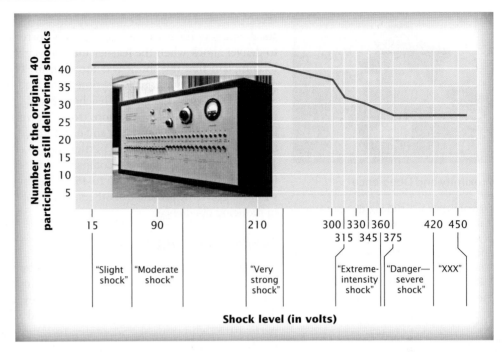

stand the pain any longer and starts banging on the wall. The experimenter says, "You have no other choice; you must go on." Would you continue? Would you keep going even when the learner begged to be let out of the experiment and then fell silent? Would you administer 450 volts of potentially deadly shock to an innocent stranger just because an experimenter demanded that you do so? Figure 16.10 shows that only five participants in Milgram's experiment stopped before 300 volts and that twenty-six out of forty (65 percent) went all the way to the 450-volt level. The decision to continue was difficult and stressful for the participants. Many protested repeatedly. But each time the experimenter told them to continue, they did so.

Factors Affecting Obedience

Milgram had not expected so many people to deliver such apparently intense shocks. Was there something about his procedure that produced this high level of obedience? To find out, Milgram and other researchers varied the original procedure in a number of ways and discovered that the degree of obedience was affected by several aspects of the situation and procedure.

Experimenter Status and Prestige

Perhaps the experimenter's status as a Yale University professor helped produce high levels of obedience in Milgram's original experiment (Blass & Schmitt, 2001). To test this possibility, Milgram rented an office in a rundown building in Bridgeport, Connecticut. He then placed a newspaper ad for research sponsored by a private firm. There was no mention of Yale. In all other ways, the experimental procedure was identical to the original.

Under these less impressive circumstances, the level of obedience dropped, but not as much as Milgram expected: 48 percent of the participants continued to the maximum level of shock, compared with 65 percent in the original study. Milgram concluded that people are willing to obey orders to do great harm to another person even when the authority making the demand is not especially reputable or prestigious.

The Behavior of Other People

To study how the behavior of fellow participants might affect obedience, Milgram (1965) created a situation in which there appeared to be three teachers. Teacher 1 (in reality, a

Proximity and Obedience

Milgram's research showed that close physical proximity to an authority figure is one of several factors that can enhance obedience to authority (Rada & Rogers, 1973). This proximity principle is used in the military, where no one is ever far away from the authority of a higher-ranking person.

US Marines Photo/Alamy

May I Take Your Order?

In February 2004, the managers of four fast-food restaurants in Boston received calls from someone claiming to be a police detective on the trail of a robbery suspect. The caller said the suspect might be one of the restaurant's employees and told the managers to strip search all of them for evidence of guilt. The calls turned out to be hoaxes, but every manager obeyed this bizarre order, apparently because it appeared to come from a legitimate authority. In two similar cases, residents of a special needs school were given unnecessary electric shock treatments on the telephoned orders from a hoaxer, and hospital nurses obeyed medical treatment orders given by a teenager who claimed to be a doctor (Associated Press, 2007a; Kenrick, Neuberg, & Cialdini, 2010).

Photodisc/Getty Images

research assistant) read the words to the learner. Teacher 2 (another research assistant) stated whether the learner's response was correct. Teacher 3 (the actual participant) was to deliver shock when the learner made mistakes. At 150 volts, when the learner began to complain that the shock was too painful, Teacher 1 refused to participate any longer and left the room. The experimenter asked him to come back, but he refused. The experimenter then instructed Teachers 2 and 3 to continue by themselves. The experiment continued for several more trials. However, at 210 volts, Teacher 2 said that the learner was suffering too much and also refused to participate further. The experimenter then told Teacher 3 (the actual participant) to continue the procedure. In this case, only 10 percent of the participants (compared with 65 percent in the original study) continued to deliver shock all the way up to 450 volts. In other words, as research on conformity would suggest, the presence of others who disobey appears to be the most powerful factor in reducing obedience.

The Behavior of the Learner

A recent reanalysis of data from Milgram's obedience studies (Packer, 2008) found that although the supposedly shocked learner's increasingly intense expressions of pain had no effect on whether the participants disobeyed the experimenter, the learner's stated desire to be released from the experiment did affect disobedience. In fact, among those participants who refused to continue to shock the learner, almost 37 percent of them disobeyed at the 150-volt level, which was when the learner first said he wanted to be released from the experiment. So it appears that perceiving a victim's pain does not reduce obedience to authority but being reminded of a victim's right to be released from the experiment does.

Personality Characteristics

Were the participants in Milgram's original experiment heartless creatures who would have given strong shocks even if there had been no pressure on them to do so? Quite the opposite; most of them were nice people who were influenced by experimental situations to behave in apparently antisocial ways. A more recent illustration of this phenomenon occurred among a few soldiers who were assigned to guard or interrogate prisoners in Afghanistan and Iraq.

Still, not everyone is equally obedient to authority. For example, people who display what we described earlier as *authoritarianism* are more likely than others to obey an experimenter's instructions to shock the learner (Blass, 2000; Dambrun & Valnetine, 2010). Further support for this idea comes from findings that German soldiers who may have obeyed orders to kill Jews during World War II displayed more authoritarianism than other German men of the same age and background (Steiner & Fahrenberg, 2000). In contrast, a more recent study that repeated Milgram's experimental procedures (Burger, 2009) found that the participants who were less likely to obey orders to harm the learner were also the ones who were concerned about others and predisposed to have *empathy*—that is, to understand or experience another person's emotional state (Davis, 1994). On the other hand, people who score higher on neuroticism, a personality dimension discussed in the personality chapter, are more likely to be obedient in a Milgram-type situation (Zeigler-Hill et al., 2013).

Evaluating Obedience Research

How relevant are Milgram's fifty-year-old obedience studies today? Consider the obedience to authority that operated on 9/11, when some people returned to their offices in the World Trade Center after hearing an ill-advised public address announcement telling them to do so. Most of these people died as a result. Similar kinds of obedience continue to be observed in experiments conducted in many countries, from Europe to the Middle East, with female as well as male participants, and even in simulated game shows and lifelike virtual environments (Beauvious, Courbat, & Oberelé, 2012; Burger, 2009; Dambrun & Valentine, 2010). In short, people may be as likely to obey orders today as they were when Milgram conducted his research (Blass, 2004, 2009; Burger, 2009). Nevertheless, there is still debate over the ethics and meaning of Milgram's work.

Questions About Ethics

LINKAGES Is it ethical to deceive people to learn about their social behavior? (a link to Research Methods in Psychology)

Although the "learners" in Milgram's experiment suffered no discomfort, the participants did. Milgram (1963) observed participants "sweat, stutter, tremble, groan, bite their lips, and dig their fingernails into their flesh" (p. 375). Against the potential harm inflicted by Milgram's experiments stand the potential gains. For example, people who learn about Milgram's work often take his findings into account when deciding how to act in social situations (Sherman, 1980). But even if social value has come from Milgram's studies, a question remains: Was it ethical for Milgram to treat his participants as he did?

In the years before his death in 1984, Milgram defended his experiments (e.g., Milgram, 1977). He argued that the way he dealt with his participants after the experiment prevented any lasting harm. For example, he explained to them that the learner did not experience any shock; in fact, the learner came in and chatted with each participant. On a later questionnaire, 84 percent of the participants said that they had learned something important about themselves and that the experience had been worthwhile. Still, the committees charged with protecting human participants in research today would be unlikely to approve Milgram's experiments as they were originally done, and less controversial ways to study obedience have now been developed (Blass, 2004; Elms, 2009).

Questions About Meaning

Do Milgram's dramatic results mean that most people are putty in the hands of authority figures and that most of us would blindly follow inhumane orders from our leaders? Some critics have argued that Milgram's results cannot be interpreted in this way because his participants knew they were in an experiment and may simply have been playing a cooperative role. If so, the social influence processes identified in his studies may not explain obedience in the real world today (Berkowitz, 1999).

In fact, it has been proposed that what looks like blind obedience in Milgram's experiments might be better explained by the *social identity theory* we described earlier (Reicher, Haslam, & Smith, 2012). According to this interpretation, when participants administered what they thought were severe shocks it could have been because they identified more strongly with the experimenter and the scientific community he represented than with the person they were supposedly shocking. When the research was not associated with Yale and when others refused to continue, participants might have identified more with the learner than with the experimenter and so were less willing to continue. This line of reasoning offers quite a different perspective on why people sometimes follow brutal orders. These people may simply see themselves and their leaders as part of the same group and their willingness to follow orders reflects the conscious pursuit of that group's goals. This alternative explanation of Milgram's results has yet to be directly tested, but that will surely happen in the near future.

Most psychologists believe, however, that Milgram demonstrated a basic truth about human behavior—namely, that under certain circumstances people are capable of unspeakable acts of brutality toward other people (Benjamin & Simpson, 2009). Sadly, examples abound. And one of the most horrifying aspects of human inhumanity—whether it is the Nazis' campaign of genocide against Jews seventy years ago or the campaigns of terror under way today—is that the perpetrators are not necessarily demented, sadistic fiends. Most of them are normal people who have been prompted by economic, political, or religious influences and the persuasive power of their leaders to behave in a demented and fiendish manner (Skitka, 2010). (For a summary of Milgram's results, plus those of studies on conformity and compliance, see "In Review: Types of Social Influence.")

In short, inhumanity can occur even without pressure to obey. A good deal of people's aggressiveness toward other people appears to come from within. Let's consider human aggressiveness and some of the circumstances that influence its expression.

	IN REVIEW
TYPES OF SOCIAL INFLUENCE	

Type	Definition	Key Findings
Conformity	A change in behavior or beliefs to match those of others	In cases of ambiguity, people develop a group norm and then adhere to it. Conformity occurs because people want to be right, because they want to be liked by others, and because conformity to group norms is usually reinforced. Conformity usually increases with the ambiguity of the situation as well as with the unanimity and size of the majority.
Compliance	Adjusting one's behavior because of a direct request	Compliance increases with the foot-in-the-door technique, which begins with a small request and works up to a larger one. The door-in-the-face procedure can also be used. After making a large request that is denied, the person substitutes a less extreme alternative that was desired all along. The lowball approach also elicits compliance. An oral commitment for something is first obtained, then the person claims that only a higher-cost version of the original request will suffice.
Obedience	A change in behavior in response to an explicit demand, typically from an acknowledged authority figure	People may inflict great harm on others when an authority demands that they do so. Even when people obey orders to harm another person, they often agonize over the decision. People are most likely to disobey orders to harm someone else when they see another person disobey.

In Review Questions

1. Joining the end of a ticket line is an example of _____, whereas forming two lines when a theater employee requests it is an example of _____.

2. Seeing someone disobey a questionable order makes people _____ likely to obey the order themselves.

3. Pricing your used car for more than you expect to get but then agreeing to reduce it to make a sale is an example of the _____ approach to gaining compliance.

AGGRESSION

Are people born aggressive?

Aggressive behavior, more commonly known as **aggression**, is any action intended to harm another person (DeWall, Anderson, & Bushman, 2013). It is all too common. About 1.6 million violent crimes are committed each year in the United States alone, including nearly 90,000 rapes and about 15,000 murders (U.S. Census Bureau, 2012). In fact, homicide is the third leading cause of death for people in the United States between the ages of 15 and 24 (Heron, 2007). One of the most disturbing aspects of these figures is that about 85 percent of all murder victims knew their assailants and that over 70 percent of rapists were romantic partners, friends, relatives, or acquaintances of their victims (U.S. Department of Justice, 2007). Further, as many as one-third of married people and a significant proportion of dating couples in the United States have engaged in aggressive acts toward each other that range from pushing, shoving, and slapping to beatings and the threatened or actual use of weapons (Cornelius & Resseguie, 2007; Durose et al., 2005).

aggressive behavior (aggression)
An act that is intended to harm another person.

Why Are People Aggressive?

Sigmund Freud proposed that aggression is an instinctive biological urge that builds up in everyone and must be released. Evolutionary psychologists offer a different view, suggesting that in prehistoric times, aggression helped people compete for mates, thus ensuring the survival of their genes in the next generation (Liddle, Shackelford, & Weekes–Shackelford, 2012; Malamuth & Addison, 2001). Through natural selection, they say, aggressive tendencies have been passed on through countless generations.

Evolutionary theories of aggression are popular, but even evolutionary theorists recognize that "nature" alone cannot fully account for aggression. "Nurture," in the form of environmental factors, also plays a role in when and why people are aggressive. We know this partly because there are large differences in aggression from culture to culture. The murder rate in Venezuela, for example, is more than nine times higher than it is in the United States, and the U.S. murder rate is about three times as high as the rate in Canada or the United Kingdom (United Nations Office on Drugs and Crime, 2010). These data suggest that even if aggressive *impulses* are universal, the appearance of aggressive *behavior* reflects the influence of both nature and nurture, including the degree to which people learn to control aggressive tendencies (DeWall, Anderson, & Bushman, 2013). No equation can predict exactly when people will be aggressive, but research has revealed a number of important biological, learning, and environmental factors that combine in various ways to produce aggression in various situations.

Genetic and Biological Mechanisms

There is strong evidence for hereditary influences on aggression, especially in nonhuman animals (Bushman & Huesmann, 2010). In one study, the most aggressive members of a large group of mice were interbred and then the most aggressive of their offspring were interbred. After this procedure was followed for twenty-five generations, the resulting animals would immediately attack any mouse put in their cage. Continuous inbreeding of the least aggressive members of the original group produced animals that were so nonaggressive that they would refuse to fight even when attacked (Lagerspetz & Lagerspetz, 1983). Research that rated the aggressiveness of human twins who had been raised together or apart suggests that there is a genetic component to aggression in people as well (Hudziak et al., 2003; Vierikko et al., 2006). However, other research suggests that people do not necessarily inherit the tendency to be aggressive. Instead, they may inherit certain aspects of temperament, such as impulsiveness, or certain aspects of brain chemistry that in turn make aggression more likely (Alia-Klein et al., 2009; Eisenberger et al., 2007; Hennig et al., 2005).

Several parts of the brain influence aggression (Carré, Murphy, & Hariri, 2013). One of these is the limbic system, which includes the amygdala, the hypothalamus, and related areas. Damage to these structures may produce *defensive aggression,* which includes heightened aggressiveness toward stimuli that are not usually threatening or a decrease in the responses that normally inhibit aggression (Coccaro, 1989; Siever, 2008). The cerebral cortex may also be involved in aggression (e.g., Pietro et al., 2000; Séguin & Zelazo, 2005). Hormones such as *testosterone*—the masculine hormone that is present in both sexes—may also play an important role in aggression (Carré, Murphy, & Hariri, 2013). Aggressive behavior increases or decreases dramatically with the amount of testosterone in the human bloodstream. This may be because people with high levels of testosterone have more difficulty controlling their impulses (Mehta & Beer, 2010). Criminals who commit violent crimes have higher levels of testosterone than those whose crimes are nonviolent (Schiltz, Witzel, & Bogerts, 2011), and murderers with higher levels of testosterone are more likely than others to have planned their crimes before committing them (Dabbs, Riad, & Chance, 2001).

Testosterone's most significant and durable influence may be through its impact on early brain development. One natural test of this hypothesis occurred when pregnant women were given testosterone in an attempt to prevent miscarriage. As a result, their children were exposed to high doses of testosterone during prenatal development. Figure 16.11 shows that these children grew up to be more aggressive than their same-sex siblings who

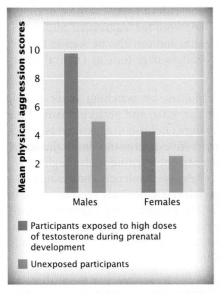

FIGURE 16.11

Testosterone and Aggression

In the study illustrated here, the children of women who had taken testosterone during pregnancy to prevent miscarriage became more aggressive than the mothers' other children of the same sex who had not been exposed to testosterone during prenatal development. This outcome appeared in both males' and females' development (Reinisch, Ziemba-Davis, & Sanders, 1991).

were not exposed to testosterone during prenatal development (Reinisch, Ziemba-Davis, & Sanders, 1991). Another study found that men who had been exposed to high levels of testosterone before birth were more likely than other men to be aggressive toward their female partners (Cousins, Fugere, & Franlin, 2009). Still other research has linked low levels of the neurotransmitter serotonin with high levels of impulsive aggression in both humans and nonhuman animals (Bushman & Bartholow, 2010; Carver, Johnson, & Joormann, 2008). It is not yet clear, though, whether the low serotonin level is a cause or a consequence of aggression (Kassin, Fein, & Markus, 2008). Aggression may vary in relation to other biological factors, too. For example, married couples have been found to show more aggression when blood sugar levels drop (Bushman et al., 2014).

Aggression can also be influenced by drugs that affect the central nervous system. For example, even relatively small amounts of alcohol can greatly increase some people's aggressiveness (Gallagher et al., 2014; Shorey et al., 2013). Canadian researchers have found that in almost 70 percent of the acts of aggression they studied, the aggressors had been drinking alcohol. And the more alcohol the aggressors consumed, the more aggressive they were (Wells, Graham, & West, 2000). No one knows exactly why alcohol increases aggression, but research suggests that the drug may affect areas of the brain that normally inhibit aggressive responses (Bartholow & Heinz, 2006; Graham et al., 2006; Lau, Pihl, & Peterson, 1995).

Learning and Cultural Mechanisms

Biological factors may increase or decrease the likelihood of aggression, but cross-cultural research makes it clear that learning also plays a role. Aggressive behavior is much more common in individualist than in collectivist cultures, for example (Oatley, 1993). Cultural differences in the expression of aggression appear to stem partly from differing cultural values (Cohen, 1998). For example, the Utku (an Inuit culture) view aggression in any form as a sign of social incompetence. In fact, the Utku word for "aggressive" also means "childish" (Oatley, 1993). The effects of culture on aggression can also be seen in the fact that the amount of aggression in a given culture changes over time as cultural values change (Matsumoto, 2000).

In addition, people can learn aggressive responses by watching other people (Bushman & Huesmann, 2014). Children, in particular, learn and perform many of the aggressive responses they see modeled by others. Bandura's Bobo-doll experiments, which are described in the chapter on learning, provide impressive demonstrations of the power of observational learning. The significance of observational learning is also highlighted by studies described in that chapter on the effects of televised violence. For example, the amount of violent content eight-year-olds watch on television predicts aggressiveness in these children even fifteen years later (Bushman & Huesmann, 2010; Huesmann et al., 2003). Fortunately, not everyone who sees aggression becomes aggressive. Individual differences in temperament, the modeling of nonaggressive behavior by parents, and other factors can reduce the effects of violent television.

Reward or punishment can also alter the frequency of aggressive acts. People become more aggressive when rewarded for aggressiveness and less aggressive when punished for aggression (Bushman & Bartholow, 2010). In short, a person's life experiences, including culturally transmitted teachings, combine with daily rewards and punishments to influence whether, when, and how aggressive acts occur (Bettencourt et al., 2006; Bushman & Bartholow, 2010).

Aggression and Video Games

Some scientists claim that violent video games may increase aggressiveness in those who play them (Anderson & Gentile, 2008; DeWall, Anderson, & Bushman, 2013; DeLisi et al., 2013). In fact, some argue that violent games can produce even more aggression than violent television can because games allow players to practice simulated aggression and have it rewarded by reaching the games' next level (e.g., Bushman & Anderson, 2007; Lin, 2013).

Following Adult Examples

Learning to express aggression is especially easy for children who live in countries plagued by war or sectarian violence because they see aggressive acts modeled for them all too often.

Mario Tama/Getty Images

Claims like these are supported by the results of more than a hundred correlational studies and laboratory experiments. This research suggests that playing video games not only increase players' aggressive thoughts, feelings, and actions, but may make them less likely to help others and less sensitive to other people's pain and suffering.

Is exposure to violent video games actually causing greater aggressiveness or is it just that more aggressive people are the ones inclined to play them (Rieger et al., 2014)? Skeptical scientists point out that correlational studies do not allow us to draw conclusions about cause and effect. Even laboratory experiments have been criticized because their highly controlled methods may not reflect—and their results may therefore not apply to— the game-playing that goes on in the real world (Ferguson, 2010; Goldstein, 2001). Further, some of these experiments have found *no* effect of violent video games on aggression (e.g., Ferguson & Rueda, 2010). Some psychological scientists argue, too, that even if there is a statistically significant cause-and-effect relationship between violent video game-playing and aggression, it is not very strong when compared to the impact of other social forces, such as what children learn when they see their families and friends behaving aggressively (Ferguson & Kilburn, 2010; Sherry, 2001). Given the evidence available so far, it seems reasonable to say that violent video games probably do have some impact on the people who play them, but additional research will be required to determine its exact nature and intensity (Gentile et al., 2014).

When Are People Aggressive?

In general, people are more likely to be aggressive when they are both physically aroused and experiencing a strong emotion such as anger (DeWall, Anderson, & Bushman, 2013). People tend either to lash out at those who make them angry or to displace, or redirect, their anger toward children, pets, or other defenseless targets. However, aggression can also be made more likely by other forms of emotional arousal. One emotion that has long been considered to be a major cause of aggression is *frustration*, which occurs when we are prevented from reaching some goal.

Frustration and Aggression

Suppose that a friend interrupts your studying for an exam by asking to borrow a book. If things have been going well that day and you are feeling confident about the exam, you will probably be friendly and helpful. But what if you are feeling frustrated because your friend's visit was the fifth interruption in the last hour? Under these emotional circumstances, you may react aggressively, perhaps snapping at your startled visitor for bothering you.

Your aggressiveness in this situation would be predicted by the **frustration-aggression hypothesis**, which suggests that frustration leads to aggression (Dollard et al., 1939). Research on this hypothesis has shown that it is too simple and too general, however. For one thing, frustration sometimes produces depression and withdrawal, not aggression (Berkowitz, 1998). In addition, not all aggression is preceded by frustration (Berkowitz, 1994).

After many years of research, Leonard Berkowitz suggested two modifications designed to increase the accuracy of the frustration-aggression hypothesis. First, he proposed that it may be stress in general, not just frustration, that is involved in aggression. Stress, he said, produces a readiness for aggression that may or may not be translated into aggressive behavior (Berkowitz, 1998). Once this readiness exists, however, aggression can be more easily triggered by environmental stimuli. The triggering stimuli might be guns or knives, televised scenes of people arguing, violent song lyrics, or other cues associated with aggression. In other words, neither stress alone nor environmental cues alone are enough to set off aggression. When combined, however, they often do. Support for this aspect of Berkowitz's theory has been quite strong (DeWall, Anderson, & Bushman, 2013).

Second, Berkowitz argues that the direct cause of most kinds of aggression is negative feelings, or *negative affect* (Berkowitz, 1998). Research suggests that the more negative affect people experience, regardless of what caused it, the stronger is their readiness to be aggressive. Participants in one study experienced negative affect caused by the pain of immersing their hands in ice water. They became more aggressive than participants in a control group whose hands were in water of room temperature (Berkowitz, 1998).

Generalized Arousal

Imagine that you have just jogged for three miles. You are hot, sweaty, and out of breath, but you are not angry. Still, the physiological arousal caused by jogging may increase the probability that you will become aggressive if, say, a passerby shouts an insult (Zillmann, 1988). Why? The answer lies in a phenomenon described in the chapter on motivation and emotion: Arousal from one experience may carry over to an independent situation, producing what is called *excitation transfer*. So the physiological arousal caused by jogging may intensify your reaction to an insult (Harrison, 2003).

LINKAGES What role does arousal play in aggression? (a link to Motivation and Emotion)

By itself, however, generalized arousal does not lead to aggression. It is most likely to produce aggression when the situation contains some reason, opportunity, or target for aggression (Zillmann, 2003). In one study, for example, people engaged in two minutes of vigorous exercise. Then they had the opportunity to deliver an electrical shock to another person. The participants chose high levels of shock only if they were first insulted (Zillmann, Katcher, & Milavsky, 1972). Apparently, the arousal resulting from the exercise made aggression more likely; the insult "released" it.

Other research suggests that men who are aroused by watching violent pornography may be more likely to commit rape or other forms of aggression against women. In one experiment, for example, male participants were told that a person in another room (actually the experimenter's assistant) would be performing a learning task and that they were to administer an electric shock every time the person made a mistake. The intensity of shock could be varied (as in the Milgram studies, no shock actually reached the assistant), but participants were told that changing the intensity would not affect the speed of learning. So the shock intensity (and presumed pain) that they chose to administer was considered to be a measure of aggression. Before the learning trials began, some participants watched a film in which several men had sex with the same woman, against her will. These participants' aggressiveness toward women during the learning experiment

frustration-aggression hypothesis A proposition stating that frustration always leads to some form of aggressive behavior.

environmental psychology The study of the effects of the physical environment on people's behavior and mental processes.

was greater than that of men who did not watch the film (Donnerstein, 1984). There was no parallel increase in aggression against other men, indicating that the violent pornography didn't create a generalized increase in aggression but did create an increase in aggressiveness directed toward women.

Such effects do not appear in all men, however (Ferguson & Hartley, 2009; Seto, Maric, & Barbaree, 2001). One study of about 2,700 men in the United States found that men who are not hostile toward women and who rarely have casual sex showed little, if any, change in sexual aggressiveness after viewing aggressive pornography. In contrast, among men who are high in promiscuity and hostility, watching aggressive pornography was followed by a dramatic increase in the chances that these men would engage in sexual aggression (Malamuth, Addison, & Koss, 2000; Malamuth, Hald, & Koss, 2012). In fact, 72 percent of the men who frequently used pornography and were high in promiscuity and hostility had actually engaged in sexually aggressive acts (see Figure 16.12). Viewing pornography appears to have similar effects on convicted sex offenders who have been placed on probation or released on parole, and the effects are especially pronounced among those who had committed the most serious sex crimes (Kingston et al., 2008).

These findings support the notion that aggression is not caused solely by a person's characteristics or by the particular situation a person is in. Instead, the occurrence and intensity of aggression are determined by the joint influence of individual characteristics and environmental circumstances (Ferguson & Dyck, 2012; Klinesmith, Kasser, & McAndrew, 2006).

Environmental Influences on Aggression

The link between stress, arousal, and the likelihood of aggressive behavior suggests that stressful environmental conditions can create enough arousal to make aggressive behavior more likely (Bushman & Bartholow, 2010). This possibility is one of the research topics in **environmental psychology**, the study of the relationship between people's physical environment and their behavior (Bell et al., 2000). One aspect of the environment that clearly affects social behavior is the weather, especially temperature. High temperatures are a source of stress: as Figure 16.13 indicates, murder and other violent crimes are most likely to occur during the hottest months of the year (Anderson & DeLisi, 2011; Bushman, Wang, & Anderson, 2005). Athletes tend to behave more aggressively in hotter weather, and even hearing words associated with high temperatures—such as "boiling" or "roasting"—is associated with increased aggressiveness (Dewall & Bushman, 2009; Larrick et al., 2011).

Aggressiveness is also associated with noisy environments, especially if the noise is unpredictable and irregular (Bushman & Bartholow, 2010), and with living in crowded and unpleasant conditions such as those often found in prisons and some psychiatric hospitals (Baumeister & Bushman, 2014; Yuma, 2010).

ALTRUISM AND PROSOCIAL BEHAVIOR

What motivates people to help one another?

Acts of terrorism provide horrifying examples of human behavior at its worst. But like all tragedies, they draw responses that provide inspiring examples of human behavior at its best. For example, in the moments just after the 2013 Boston Marathon bombing, Carlos Arrendondo, a spectator at the race, ran to the side of a severely injured young man and saved the man's life by using his own clothes to make a tourniquet to stop the bleeding, then stayed with the man until medical help arrived (CNN April 17, 2013). Arrendondo ignored the possibility that he himself could have been killed had another bomb exploded nearby. In the following days, police officers, medical personnel, and others came to Boston from all over the United States to help survivors.

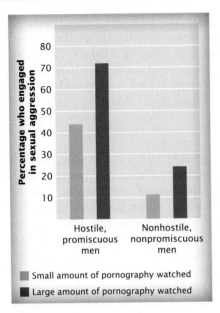

FIGURE 16.12
Pornography and Sexual Aggression

By itself, extensive exposure to pornography does not increase most men's sexual aggressiveness. Such aggressiveness is much more likely, however, among men who not only view or read a lot of pornography but also are hostile toward women and are sexually promiscuous (Malamuth, 1998).

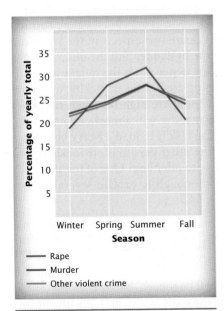

FIGURE 16.13
Temperature and Aggression

Studies from around the world indicate that aggressive behaviors are most likely to occur during the hottest months of the year. These studies support the hypothesis that environmental factors can affect aggression.

A Young Helper

Even before their second birthday, some children offer help to those who are hurt or crying by snuggling, patting, or offering food or even their own teddy bears. Their helpful actions are shaped by the norms established by their families and the broader culture (Grusec & Goodnow, 1994).

© iStockphoto.com/RuslanDashinsky

Actions such as these are examples of **prosocial behavior**, also known as **helping behavior**, which is defined as any act that is intended to benefit another person. Helping can range from picking up dropped packages to donating a kidney. Closely related to prosocial behavior is **altruism**, an unselfish concern for another's welfare (Penner, Dovidio, et al., 2005). Let's consider some of the reasons behind helping and altruism, along with some of the conditions under which people are most likely to help others.

Why Do People Help?

The tendency to help others begins early in life, although at first it is not automatic. Children have to learn to be helpful (Pettygrove et al., 2013). In most cultures, very young children usually help others only when they are asked to do so or are offered a reward (Grusec, Davidov, & Lundell, 2002). Still, observational studies have shown that many children as young as eighteen months will spontaneously help a friend, a family member, or even a stranger (e.g., Dunfield & Kuhlmeier, 2010; Hepach, Vaish, & Tomasello, 2012). As they grow older, children use helping to gain social approval, and their efforts at assisting others become more elaborate. The role of social influence in the development of helping is seen as children follow the examples set by people around them (McCullough & Tabak, 2010). In addition, children are usually praised and given other rewards for helpfulness but are scolded for selfishness. Eventually most children come to believe that being helpful is good and that they are good when they are helpful. By the late teens, people often assist others even when no one is watching and no one will know that they did so (Grusec, Davidov, & Lundell, 2002).

There are a number of possible reasons why people help even when they cannot expect any external rewards for doing so. Let's consider some of the most prominent ones.

Arousal: Cost-Reward Theory

The **arousal: cost-reward theory** proposes that people find the sight of a victim distressing and anxiety-provoking and that this experience motivates them to do something to reduce the unpleasant arousal (Dovidio et al., 2006; Piliavin et al., 1981). Before rushing to a victim's aid, however, the bystander will first evaluate two aspects of the situation: the costs associated with helping and the costs (to the bystander and the other person) of not helping. Whether the bystander actually helps depends on the outcome of this evaluation (Dovidio et al., 1991). If the costs of helping are low (as in picking up someone's dropped grocery bag) and the costs of not helping are high (as when the other person is physically unable to do this alone), the bystander will almost certainly help. However, if the costs of helping are high (as when the task is to load a heavy box into a car) and the costs of not helping are low (as when the other person is obviously strong enough to do the job alone), the bystander is unlikely to offer help. One of the strengths of the arousal: cost-reward theory is that it is broad enough to explain several factors that affect assistance.

One such factor is the *clarity of the need for help* (McCullough & Tabak, 2010). In a laboratory study of this factor, undergraduate students waiting alone in a campus building saw what appeared to be an accident involving a window washer. The man screamed as he and his ladder fell to the ground, then he clutched his ankle and groaned in pain. All the students looked out of the window to see what had happened, but only 29 percent of them did anything to help. Other students witnessed the same "accident" but with one important added element: the man said he was hurt and needed help. In this case, more than 80 percent of the participants came to his aid (Yakimovich & Saltz, 1971). Why so many? Apparently, this one additional cue eliminated any uncertainty about whether assistance was needed. The man's more obvious need for assistance served to raise the perceived costs of not helping him, thus making helping more likely.

If this laboratory study seems unrealistic, consider the March 2000 case of a sixty-two-year-old woman in Darby, Pennsylvania. She was walking to the grocery store when she was pushed from behind by an attacker. She fended him off and then did her shopping as usual.

prosocial behavior (helping behavior) Any act that is intended to benefit another person.

altruism An unselfish concern for another's welfare.

arousal: cost-reward theory A theory attributing people's prosocial behavior to their efforts to reduce unpleasant arousal in the face of someone's need or suffering, while also considering the costs involved.

It was only when she got home and her daughter saw the handle of a knife protruding from her back that she realized that the assailant had stabbed her! No one in the grocery store said anything to her about the knife, let alone offered to help. Why? The most likely explanation is that the woman did nothing to suggest that assistance was necessary.

The *presence of others* also has a strong influence on the tendency to help. Somewhat surprisingly, however, their presence tends to make assistance less likely (Garcia et al., 2002). For example, twelve people in Richmond, California, simply watched as a fifteen-year-old girl was beaten and gang-raped outside her high school homecoming dance ("Dozen People Watched," 2009). The next year, in New York City, a man was stabbed while trying to help a woman who was being attacked. As the man lay bleeding to death on the sidewalk, at least twenty-five people walked by without trying to help him (ABC News, 2010). Whenever such cases are publicized, journalists and social commentators express dismay about the cold, uncaring attitudes that seem to exist among people who live in big cities.

That description may apply to some people, but research stimulated by such cases has revealed a social phenomenon that offers a different explanation of why all those passersby took no action to help. This phenomenon, called the **bystander effect**, makes an individual less likely to help in an emergency when there are many other people present (Snyder & Dwyer, 2013). Why does the bystander effect occur? One explanation is that each witness assumes someone else will take responsibility for helping the victim. This *diffusion of responsibility* among all the witnesses leaves each witness feeling less obligated to help and thus lowers the perceived cost of not helping (Dovidio et al., 2006; Dovidio & Penner, 2001). So if you're ever in need of help, especially in a crowd, it is important not only to actually ask for help, but also to tell a specific onlooker to take specific action (e.g., "You, in the yellow shirt, please call an ambulance!").

The degree to which the presence of other people will suppress the tendency to help may depend on who those other people are. When they are strangers, perhaps poor communication interferes with assistance. Many people have difficulty speaking to strangers, particularly in an emergency, and without speaking, they have difficulty knowing what the others intend to do. According to this logic, if people are with friends rather than strangers, they should be less embarrassed, more willing to discuss the problem, and more likely to help.

No Diffusion of Responsibility Here

TRY THIS Although people are sometimes callous and indifferent to the plight of others in emergencies, they are sometimes just the opposite. This September 2011 photo shows bystanders lifting a burning car to reach a motorcyclist who had been trapped underneath it after a collision. In light of our previous discussion, make a list of the social, personality, cultural, and situational factors that might have prevented diffusion of responsibility in this case and led these people to risk their lives to pull the injured man to safety.

AP Images/Chris Garff

bystander effect A phenomenon in which the chances that someone will help in an emergency decrease as the number of people present increases.

Creating Empathy

The amount of empathy a person feels for you can depend on several factors, including the words you choose when asking for help (Guéguen & Lamy, 2011), whether you physically touch the other person while asking (Schirmer et al., 2011), whether you're a member of the same social ingroup (Cikara, Botvinik, & Fiske, 2011; Cikara, Bruneau, & Saxe, 2011), and whether the person sees you as a potential threat (Agthe, Spörrle, & Maner, 2010; van de Ven, Zeelenberg, & Pieters, 2010). The person's actual or perceived socioeconomic status can also be influential (Ma, Wang, & Han, 2011; Rucker, Dubois, & Galinsky, 2011; Stellar et al., 2012).

Dougal Waters/Photographer's Choice RF/Getty Images

empathy-altruism helping theory A theory suggesting that people help others because they feel empathy toward them.

In a study designed to test this idea, an experimenter left a research participant in a waiting room, either alone, with a friend, with a stranger, or with a stranger who was actually the experimenter's assistant (Latané & Rodin, 1969). The experimenter then stepped behind a curtain into an office. For a few minutes, she could be heard opening and closing the drawers of her desk, shuffling papers, and so on. Then there was a loud crash and she screamed, "Oh, my god—my foot, I—I can't move it. Oh, my ankle—I can't get this—thing off me." Then the participant heard her groan and cry.

Would the participant go behind the curtain to offer assistance? Once again, people were most likely to help if they were alone. When one other person was present, participants were more likely to communicate with one another and offer help if they were friends than if they were strangers. When the stranger was the experimenter's assistant—who had been instructed not to help—very few participants offered to help. Other studies have confirmed that bystanders' tendency to help increases when they know one another (Rutkowski, Gruder, & Romer, 1983).

Empathy-Altruism Helping Theory

Sometimes, costs and rewards are not the major causes of a decision to help or not help. **Empathy-altruism helping theory** considers some of these situations. This theory suggests that people are more likely to engage in altruistic, or unselfish, assistance—even at a high cost—if they feel empathy toward the person in need (Batson, 2010). In one experiment illustrating this phenomenon, students listened to a recorded interview in which a young woman told how her parents had died in an automobile accident, leaving no life insurance (Batson et al., 1997). She said that she was trying to take care of her younger brother and sister while going to college but that time and money were so tight that she might have to quit school or give up her siblings for adoption. None of this was true, but the participants were told that it was. Before hearing the recording, half the participants were given information about the woman that would increase their empathy for her; the other half were not. After listening to the recording, all participants were asked to help the woman raise money for herself and her siblings. Consistent with the empathy-altruism helping theory, more participants in the empathy group offered to help than did those in the control group.

Were the students who offered help in this experiment being utterly unselfish or could there have been other reasons for their apparent altruism? This is a hotly debated question. Some researchers dispute the claim that this study illustrated truly altruistic helping. They suggest instead that people help in such situations for more selfish reasons, such as relieving the distress they experienced after hearing of the woman's problems (Maner et al., 2002). The final verdict on this question is not yet in.

Evolutionary Theory

The evolutionary approach to psychology offers yet another way to explain prosocial behavior. According to this approach, many human social behaviors are a reflection of actions that contributed to the survival of our prehistoric ancestors (Maner & Kenrick, 2010). At first glance, it might not seem reasonable to apply evolutionary theory to prosocial behavior and altruism, because helping others at the risk of our own well-being does not appear adaptive. If we die while trying to save others, it will be their genes, not ours, that will survive. In fact, according to Darwin's concept of the "survival of the fittest," helpers—and their genes—should have disappeared long ago. Today's evolutionary theorists suggest, however, that Darwin's thinking about natural selection focused too much on the survival of the fittest *individuals* and not enough on the survival of their genes in *others*. Accordingly, the concept of survival of the fittest has been replaced by the concept of *inclusive fitness*, the survival of one's genes in future generations (Hamilton, 1964; West & Gardner, 2010). Because we share genes with our relatives, helping—or even dying for—a cousin, a sibling, or (above all) our own child increases the likelihood that at least some of our genetic characteristics will be passed on to the next generation through the beneficiary's future reproduction (Buck, 2011). So *kin selection,* or helping a relative survive, may produce genetic benefits for the helper even if it provides no personal benefits (Krebs, 2005).

There is considerable evidence that kin selection occurs among birds, squirrels, and other animals. The more closely the animals are related, the more likely they are to risk their lives for one another. Studies in a wide variety of cultures show the same pattern of prosocial behavior among humans (Krebs, 2005). For example, people in the United States have been three times as likely to donate a kidney to a relative as to a nonrelative (Borgida, Conner, & Monteufel, 1992).

Biopsychosocial Factors in Prosocial Behavior

However, helpfulness is not found in every member of every family. These differences could be the result of many factors, one of which is genetics. It is unlikely that a single "altruism gene" will ever be found, but it does appear that sets of genes do indirectly influence the likelihood of helping behavior (Thompson, Hurd, & Crespi, 2013). For example, there are slight genetic differences among people in how their brain cells respond to certain neurotransmitters, such as dopamine. Further, genetic differences in dopamine receptor systems have been associated with differences in prosocial behavior (Knafo, Israel, & Ebstein, 2011).

Other brain chemicals may also influence helping. One of these is *oxytocin,* a chemical that is made and released by certain cells of the brain's hypothalamus, and that also can act as a hormone in the endocrine system (Carter, 2014; Ganten & Pfaff, 2012). One study looked at the relationship between oxytocin and people's willingness to help a person who had been excluded from a game (Riem et al., 2013). They found that higher oxytocin levels were associated with more prosocial behavior, but only among people who had had positive relationships with their parents in childhood. Here is yet another example of the interaction of nature and nurture in many kinds of social behaviors, including helping.

"In Review: Prosocial Behavior" summarizes the three main theories of why people help and the conditions under which they are most likely to do so, but other factors may be at play as well. Let's briefly consider some of these.

Personality and Prosocial Behavior

To put it simply, it appears that people with certain personality traits are more likely than others to be helpful. Consider, for example, the Christians who risked their lives to save Jews from the Nazi Holocaust during World War II. Researchers interviewed these rescuers many years later and compared their personalities with those of people who had a chance to save Jews but did not do so (Fagin-Jones & Midlarsky, 2007; Oliner & Oliner, 1988). The rescuers were found to have more empathy, more concern about others, a greater sense of responsibility for their own actions, and greater confidence that their efforts would succeed. Louis Penner and his associates (Penner, 2002; Penner & Finkelstein, 1998) have found that these kinds of personality traits predict a broad range of helping, from how quickly bystanders intervene in an emergency to how much time volunteers spend helping AIDS patients. Consistent with the arousal: cost-reward theory, these personality characteristics are correlated with people's estimates of the costs of helping and not helping. For example, empathic individuals usually estimate the costs of not helping as high, and people who are confident about their ability to help usually rate the costs of helping as low (Penner et al., 1995).

Environmental Factors and Prosocial Behavior

The setting in which people live can affect how willing they are to be helpful. Research conducted in several countries has shown that people in urban areas are generally less helpful than those in rural areas (Aronson, Wilson, & Akert, 2013). Why? The explanation probably has more to do with the stressors found in cities than with city living itself. For example, one study of twenty-four U.S. cities showed that the greater a city's size and density (number of people per square mile), the less likely people were to help others. Helping was also much less likely in cities where stressful environmental conditions exist (e.g., population density, noise) and were greatest (Levine, Reysen, & Ganz, 2008). One possible explanation is that crowding, noise, and other urban stressors create too much stimulation. To reduce this stimulation, people may pay less attention to their surroundings, including less attention to individuals who need help (Anker & Feeley, 2011). Another explanation is that stressful environments create bad moods—and generally speaking, people in bad moods are less likely to help than people who feel good (Brethel-Haurwitz & Marsh, 2014; Forgas, Dunn, & Granland, 2008).

PROSOCIAL BEHAVIOR
IN REVIEW

Theory	Basic Premise	Important Variables
Arousal: cost-reward	People help others in order to reduce the unpleasant arousal caused by another person's distress. They attempt to minimize the costs of doing this.	Factors that affect the costs of helping and of not helping.
Empathy-altruism	People sometimes help others for unselfish reasons if they feel empathy for a person in need. They are motivated by a desire to increase another person's well-being.	The amount of empathy that one person feels for another.
Evolutionary	People help relatives because it increases the chances that the helper's genes will survive in future generations.	The biological relationship between the helper and the recipient of help.

In Review Questions

1. If you could save only one person from a burning house, the _____ theory of prosocial behavior would predict that it would be your own child rather than, say, a grandparent.

2. Are you more likely to receive help in a nearly empty bus or in a crowded bus terminal?

3. People who have empathy for others are _____ likely to be helpful

COOPERATION, COMPETITION, AND CONFLICT

What's the best way to help people cooperate?

Helping is one of several ways in which people *cooperate* with one another. **Cooperation** is any type of behavior in which people work together to attain a common goal (Dovidio et al., 2006). For example, several law students might form a study group to help one another pass a difficult exam. But people can also engage in **competition**, trying to attain a goal for themselves while denying that goal to others. So those same students might later compete with one another for a single job opening at a prestigious law firm. Finally, **conflict** results when one person or group believes that another stands in the way of their achieving a goal. When the students become attorneys and represent opposing parties in a legal dispute, they will be in conflict. One way in which psychologists have learned about all three of these behaviors is by studying social dilemmas (Kassin, Fein, & Markus, 2014).

Social Dilemmas

Social dilemmas are situations in which an action that brings rewards for the individual will, if widely adopted, produce negative consequences for the group (Baumiester & Bushman, 2014). For instance, during a drought, individual homeowners are better off in the short run if they water their lawns as often as necessary to keep the grass from dying, but if everyone ignores local water restrictions, there will be no drinking water for anyone

cooperation Any type of behavior in which people work together to attain a goal.

competition Any type of behavior in which individuals try to attain a goal while denying others access to that goal.

conflict What occurs when a person or group believes that another person or group interferes with the attainment of a goal.

social dilemmas Situations in which actions that produce rewards for one individual will produce negative consequences for all if they are adopted by everyone.

Cooperation, Competition, Conflict, and Cash

Cooperation, competition, and conflict can all be seen on *Survivor*, a television series in which people try to win money by staying the longest in some remote location. Early on, contestants cooperate with members of their own teams, but as more and more people are eliminated, even team members compete with one another. When only two people remain, each stands in the way of the other's goal of winning, so they are in direct conflict.

CBS Photo Archive/Getty Images

in the long run. Social psychologists have studied situations like this by conducting experiments using the two-person "prisoner's dilemma" game.

The Prisoner's Dilemma Game

The **prisoner's dilemma game** is based on a scenario in which two people are separated for questioning immediately after being arrested on suspicion of having committed a serious crime (Bornstein, 2002). The prosecutor believes they are guilty but doesn't have enough evidence to convict them. Each prisoner can either confess or not, but they are told that if they both refuse to confess, each will be convicted of a minor offense and will be jailed for one year. If they both confess, the prosecutor will recommend a five-year sentence for each. However, if one prisoner remains silent and the other confesses to what they did, the prosecutor will allow the confessing prisoner to go free, whereas the other will serve the maximum ten-year sentence.

Each prisoner faces a dilemma. Obviously, the strategy that will guarantee the best *mutual* outcome—short sentences for both prisoners—is cooperation. In other words, neither should confess. But the prisoner who remains silent runs the risk of receiving a long sentence if the other prisoner confesses. Further, the prisoner who confesses will benefit if the other prisoner doesn't talk. In other words, each prisoner has an incentive to compete for freedom by confessing. But if they *both* compete and confess, each will end up going to jail for longer than if they had kept quiet.

In the typical prisoner's dilemma experiment, two people sit at separate control panels. Each of them has a red button and a black button, one of which is to be pushed on each of many trials. Pressing the black button is a cooperative response. Pressing the red button is a competitive response. For example, on a given trial, if both participants press their black buttons, each wins $5. If both press their red buttons, they earn only $1. However, if one player presses the red button and the other presses the black button, the one who pressed the red button will win $10, and the other will win nothing.

Over the course of the experiment, the combined winnings of the players are greatest if each presses the black button—that is, if they cooperate. By pressing the black button, however, a player becomes open to exploitation, because on any trial, the other might press the red button and take all the winnings. So each player stands to benefit the most individually by pressing the red button occasionally.

What happens when people play this game? Overall, there is a strong tendency to respond competitively. People find it difficult to resist the competitive choice on any given trial (Kanazawa & Fontaine, 2013). This choice wins them more money on that trial, but in the long run, they gain less than they would have gained through cooperation.

If acting competitively leads to smaller rewards in the long run, why do people persist in competing? There seem to be two reasons (Komorita, 1984). First, winning more than an opponent does seem to be rewarding in itself. In the prisoner's dilemma game, many people want to outscore an opponent even if the result is that they win less money overall (Insko, Wildschut, & Cohen, 2013). Second, and more important, once several competitive responses are made, the competition seems to feed on itself (Kassinove et al., 2002). Each person becomes distrustful of the other, and cooperation becomes increasingly difficult. The more competitive one person acts, the more competitive the other becomes (McClintock & Liebrand, 1988).

Promoting Cooperation

Communication can reduce people's tendency to act competitively (Pavitt et al., 2007). Unfortunately, however, not all communication increases cooperation, just as not all contact between ethnic groups reduces prejudice. If the communication takes the form of a threat, people may interpret the threat itself as a competitive response and become more likely

prisoner's dilemma game A social dilemma scenario in which mutual cooperation guarantees the best mutual outcome.

to respond competitively (Gifford & Hine, 1997). Furthermore, the communication must be relevant. In one social dilemma study, cooperation increased only when people spoke openly about the dilemma and how they would be rewarded for various responses. Praising one another for past cooperation was most beneficial (Orbell, van de Kragt, & Dawes, 1988).

Interpersonal Conflict

Though social psychologists are applying research on cooperation to help people work more closely together in school, on the job, and in the community, humans do not always cooperate. Conflict is especially likely when people are involved in a *zero-sum game*. This is a situation in which one person's gains are subtracted from the other person's resources. It is called *zero-sum* because when you add up the gains and losses, the result is zero. Election campaigns, lawsuits over a deceased relative's estate, and competition between children for a toy are all examples of zero-sum games.

Interpersonal conflicts can be difficult to resolve and can easily escalate (De Dreu, 2010). This is because, first, people in conflict invest so much time, effort, and commitment in establishing their own point of view that being asked to adjust it in order to compromise seems to be asking too much (Yarenell & Neff, 2013). Second, people often see the problem as due to the other person's hostility or selfishness rather than to an honest difference of opinion (Samuelson & Messick, 1995). Faulty communication is a third reason for the persistence of interpersonal conflicts. Such miscommunication can start a cycle of increasingly provocative actions in which each person believes the other is being aggressive and unfair (Pruitt & Carnevale, 1993). Fourth, there is a tendency to believe that the other person is not really interested in reaching a settlement. This view may become a self-fulfilling prophesy; each side may begin to behave in ways that actually bring about the uncooperative behavior expected from the other side, and the end result may be increasing conflict and eventually, a stalemate (Kennedy & Pronin, 2008).

GROUP PROCESSES

What makes a good leader?

Although Western industrialized cultures tend to emphasize individuals over groups, the fact remains that most important decisions and efforts by governments and businesses in those cultures and elsewhere are made by groups, not individuals (Forsyth, 2013). Sometimes groups function very well. Perhaps you recall the extraordinary teamwork of emergency workers and volunteers that led to dramatic rescues of people trapped by flood waters after Hurricane Sandy struck the Northeast coast of the United States in 2012. At other times, though, groups malfunction, resulting in poor performance and bad and sometimes disastrous decisions. To begin to understand why, let's consider some of the social psychological processes that often occur in groups to alter the behavior of individuals and the quality of their collective efforts.

The Presence of Others

The term **social facilitation** describes circumstances in which the presence of other people can improve performance (Aiello & Douthitt, 2001). For example, people pedal a bicycle faster when there is a competitor, even a virtual one (Snyder, Anderson-Hanley, & Arciero, 2012). This improvement does not always occur, however. In fact, having other people present sometimes hurts performance, a process known as **social interference**. For decades, these results seemed contradictory; then Robert Zajonc (pronounced "ZYE-onze") suggested that both effects could be explained by one process: arousal.

The presence of other people, said Zajonc, increases a person's general level of arousal or motivation (Zajonc, 1965). Why? One reason is that being watched by others increases

Social Facilitation

Premier athletes like Victoria Azarenka are able to perform at their best even though large crowds are present. In fact, the crowds probably help them do well, because the presence of others tends to increase arousal, which enhances the performance of familiar and well-learned skills, such as tennis strokes. However, arousal created by an audience tends to interfere with the performance of unfamiliar and poorly developed skills. This is one reason that professional athletes who show flawless grace in front of thousands of fans are likely to freeze up or blow their lines in front of a small production crew when trying for the first time to tape a TV ad or a public service announcement.

epa/Ahmad Yusni/Landov

our sense of being evaluated, producing worry, which in turn increases emotional arousal (Penner & Craiger, 1992; Uziel, 2007). Arousal increases the tendency to perform those behaviors that are most *dominant*—the ones you know best. This tendency can either help or hinder performance. When you are performing an easy, familiar task, such as riding a bike, increased arousal due to the presence of others should allow you to ride even faster than normal. But when a task is hard or unfamiliar—such as trying new dance steps or playing a newly learned piano piece in front of an audience—the most dominant responses may be incorrect and cause performance to suffer. In other words, the impact of other people on performance depends on whether the task is easy or difficult. It can depend, too, on how people interpret the performance situation. For example, they tend to do better if they see the performance as a chance to show off their skill rather than as an attempt to avoid looking incompetent (Feinberg & Aiello, 2010).

What if a person is not merely in the presence of others but is working with them on some task? In these situations, people often exert less effort than when performing alone, a phenomenon called **social loafing** (Forsyth & Burnette, 2010). Whether the task is pulling on a rope, clapping as loudly as possible, or working together on a class project, people tend to work harder when alone than with others (Price, Harrison, & Gavin, 2006; van Dick et al., 2009). Research in industrial and organizational psychology suggests that social loafing is most likely when large groups work on the same task (making each member's contribution harder to evaluate), when the group is not closely knit, and when members feel they are not being rewarded according to their performance (Mefoh & Nwanosike, 2012; Pearsall, Christian, & Ellis, 2010). Social loafing is less likely when group members like each other and identify with the group and its goals (Hoigaard, Säfvenbom, & Tonnessen, 2006). It is also reduced when harder-working members of a group punish the social loafers with criticism or other negative consequences (Barclay, 2006).

Group Leadership

The role of group leaders is especially important when social loafing and other obstacles threaten to impair the effectiveness of group efforts. A good leader can help a group pursue its goals, but a bad one can get in the way of a group's functioning (Forsyth & Burnette, 2010). What makes a good leader? Psychologists once thought that the personalities of good and bad leaders were about the same, but we now know that certain personality traits often distinguish effective from ineffective leaders. For example, researchers have found that, in general, effective leaders are intelligent, conscientious, success oriented, flexible, and confident (Foti & Hauenstein, 2007; Ones, Dilchert, &Viswesvaran, 2012).

Having particular personality traits does not guarantee good leadership ability, however. People who are effective leaders in one situation may be ineffective in another (Chemers, 2000; Ng, Ang, & Chan, 2008). This is because effective leadership also depends on the characteristics of the group members, the task at hand, and, most important, the interaction between these factors and the leader's style (Van Kleef et al., 2010; Yun, Faraj, & Sims, 2005).

For many years, leadership research focused on two main types of leaders. The first type, called **task-motivated leaders**, provides close supervision, lead by giving orders, and generally discourage group discussion (Yukl & Van Fleet, 1992). Their style may make them unpopular. The second type, called **relationship-motivated leaders**, provide loose supervision, asks for group members' ideas, and are generally concerned with subordinates' feelings. They are usually well liked by the group, even when they must discipline a group member (Kassin, Fein, & Markus, 2014). More recently, additional leadership styles have been identified. One of these styles is seen in *transactional leaders*, whose actions depend on the actions of those they lead. They reward those who behave as the leader wishes and they correct or punish those who don't. There are also *transformational* or *charismatic leaders* (Hogg, 2010). These people concentrate on creating a vision of the group's goals, inspiring others to pursue that vision, and giving their followers reason to respect and admire them.

Do men or women make better leaders? Research by Alice Eagly and her colleagues at first found that, overall, men and women are equally capable leaders (e.g., Eagly & Carli,

social facilitation A phenomenon in which the presence of others improves a person's performance.

social interference A reduction in performance due to the presence of other people.

social loafing Exerting less effort when performing a group task than when performing the same task alone.

task-motivated leaders Leaders who provide close supervision, lead by giving directions, and generally discourage group discussion.

relationship-motivated leaders Leaders who provide loose supervision, ask for group members' ideas, and are generally concerned with subordinates' feelings.

2007). It also looked as though men tend to be more effective when success requires a task-motivated leader, and that women tend to be more effective when success requires a more relationship-motivated leader. In other words, it appeared that people of each gender tend to be most effective when they are acting in a manner consistent with gender-role traditions (Wang et al., 2013). Perhaps the reason was that some people did not like female leaders who act in a "masculine" manner or occupy leadership positions traditionally held by men (Eagly, Makhijani, & Klonsky, 1992).

A somewhat different picture of gender and leadership has emerged from Eagly's more recent research. For one thing, she found that females are generally more likely than males to display a transformational leadership style. Further, when women display a transactional style, they tend to be more encouraging than transactional male leaders, focusing more on using rewards rather than punishments to modify group members' behaviors. Finally, and in contrast to earlier findings, Eagly's results now suggest that women may be slightly more effective leaders overall than men (Ayman, Korabik, & Morris, 2009; Eagly & Sczesny, 2009).

LINKAGES

BIOLOGICAL AND SOCIAL PSYCHOLOGY

LINKAGES Can we "see" prejudice in the brain (a link to Biological Aspects of Psychology)

Research in social psychology was once thought to be entirely separate from research on the biological processes that underlie social behavior (Heatherton & Wheatley, 2010). Social psychologists believed it was impossible to reduce complex social psychological processes to the firing of neurons or the secretion of hormones. For their part, biological psychologists, more commonly known as *neuroscientists,* viewed the study of social psychology as having little, if any, relevance to the understanding of, say, behavioral genetics or the functioning of the nervous system. Over the past two decades, however, scientists in both subfields have begun to take a closer look at each other's research and at how their subfields are linked. The result has been the emergence of a field of study known as **social neuroscience** or *social cognitive neuroscience* (Lieberman, 2012). Researchers in this field focus on the influence of social processes on biological processes and on the influence of biological processes, including genetics, on social psychological phenomena (e.g., Bilderbeck et al., 2014; Cikara & Van Bavel, 2014; Mikolajczak et al., 2010).

For example, using brain-scanning technology, researchers have found that European Americans who are prejudiced against African Americans show significantly more activity in the amygdala—a structure involved in emotion—when looking at pictures of black people than when looking at pictures of white people (Cunningham et al., 2004; Phelps et al., 2000). They have also found that while watching other people in distress, people's patterns of brain activity are quite different depending on whether they are feeling empathy for the distressed person (Decety, 2011). Other studies have identified a relationship between brain development during childhood and people's later ability to take the perspectives of others (van den Bos et al., 2011). Studies such as these are shedding light on the biological aspects of empathy, and they may eventually lead to a broader understanding of the factors influencing people's motivation to help each other.

At the same time, social factors can affect biological processes, including the ways our genes express themselves (Cole, 2009). The study of the effects of social environments on gene expression has been called "social genomics" (Slavich & Cole, 2013). This research has shown, for example, that programs that reduce a person's social stress can affect which of that person's genes are turned on and off (Antoni et al., 2012). Social factors can also have many health-related biological consequences. As discussed in the chapter on health, stress, and coping, the availability and quality of a person's social support network can affect biological processes ranging from blood pressure to the healing of wounds (Gouin et al., 2008, 2010; Kiecolt-Glaser, 2009). So the psychological pain of social rejection can appear not only in words ("she broke my heart," or "he hurt my feelings") but also in activation of brain regions that normally process physical pain (Eisenberger, 2012). Both marital distress and loneliness can impair the disease-fighting immune system (Cole, 2013; Jarmeka et al., 2013a, 2013b).

In short, social cognitive neuroscience is creating a better understanding of the linkages among social, cognitive, and biological phenomena as well as a better understanding of complex social and physiological processes.

social neuroscience A specialty that focuses on the influence of social processes on biological processes and on the influence of biological processes on social psychological phenomena.

LINKAGES

As noted in the introductory chapter, all of psychology's subfields are related to one another. Our discussion of social neuroscience illustrates just one way that the topic of this chapter, social psychology, is linked to the subfield of biological psychology, which is discussed in the chapter on biological aspects of psychology. The Linkages diagram shows ties to two other subfields, and there are many more ties throughout the book. Looking for linkages among subfields will help you see how they all fit together and help you better appreciate the big picture that is psychology.

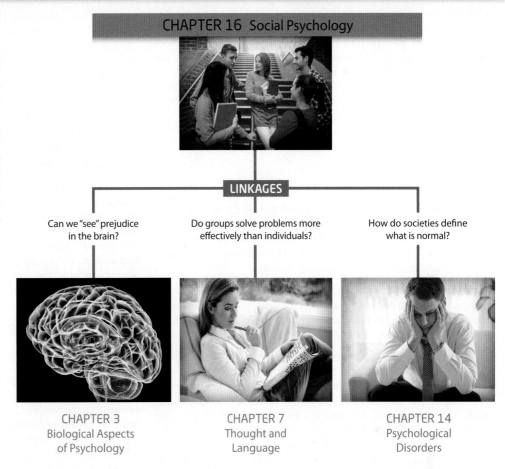

CHAPTER 16 Social Psychology

LINKAGES

Can we "see" prejudice in the brain?

Do groups solve problems more effectively than individuals?

How do societies define what is normal?

CHAPTER 3
Biological Aspects
of Psychology

CHAPTER 7
Thought and
Language

CHAPTER 14
Psychological
Disorders

SUMMARY

Social cognition, the mental processes through which people perceive and react to others, is one aspect of **social psychology**, the study of how people influence and are influenced by other people. Through social cognition, each person creates a unique perception of reality.

Social Influences on the Self

How do we compare ourselves with others?

People's social and cultural environments affect their thoughts and feelings about themselves, including their **self-concept** and their **self-esteem**. When people have no objective criteria by which to judge themselves, they look to others as the basis for **social comparison**. Such comparison can affect self-evaluation or self-esteem. Categories of people that are regularly used for social comparison are known as **reference groups**.

A person's **social identity** is formed from beliefs about the groups to which the person belongs. Social identity affects the beliefs we hold about ourselves, our self-concept. Social identity permits people to feel that they are part of a larger group, generating loyalty and sacrifice from group members but also potentially creating bias and social discrimination toward people who are not members of the group.

Social Perception

Do we perceive people and objects in similar ways?

Social perception concerns the processes by which people interpret information about others, form impressions of them, and draw conclusions about the reasons for their behavior. **Schemas**, the knowledge about people and social situations that we carry into social interactions, affect what we pay attention to, what we remember, and how we judge people and events.

First impressions are formed easily and quickly, in part because people apply existing schemas to their perceptions of others. First impressions change slowly because once we form an impression about another person, we try to maintain it. Schemas, however, can create **self-fulfilling prophecies**, leading us to act in ways that bring out behavior in others that is consistent with our expectations of them.

Attribution is the process of explaining the causes of people's behavior, including our own. Observers tend to attribute behavior to causes that are either internal or external to the actor. Attributions are also affected by biases that systematically distort our view of behavior. The most common attributional biases are the *fundamental attribution error* (and its cousin, the ultimate attribution error), the *actor-observer effect*, and the *self-serving bias*. Personal and cultural factors can affect the extent to which people exhibit these biases.

Attitudes

Do attitudes always determine behavior?

An *attitude* is the tendency to respond positively or negatively to a particular object. Attitudes affect a wide range of behaviors. Most social psychologists see attitudes as composed of three components: cognitive components (beliefs), affective components (feelings), and behavioral components (actions).

Attitudes can be learned through modeling as well as through classical or operant conditioning. They are also subject to the mere-exposure effect: all else being equal, people develop greater liking for a new object the more often they are exposed to it.

The effectiveness of a persuasive message in changing attitudes is influenced by the characteristics of the person who communicates the message, by its content, and by the audience receiving it. The *elaboration likelihood model* suggests that attitude change can occur through either the peripheral or the central route, depending on a person's ability to carefully consider an argument and their motivation to do so. Accordingly, different messages will produce attitude change under different circumstances. Another approach is to change a person's behavior in the hope that attitudes will be adjusted to match the behavior. *Cognitive dissonance theory* holds that if inconsistency between attitude and behavior creates discomfort related to a person's self-concept, the attitude may change in order to reduce the conflict.

Prejudice and Stereotypes

How does prejudice develop?

Stereotypes often lead to *prejudice* and *social discrimination*. Motivational theories of prejudice suggest that some people have a need to dislike people who differ from themselves. This need may stem from the trait of authoritarianism as well as from a strong social identity with one's ingroup. In either case, feeling superior to members of outgroups helps these people feel better about themselves. As a result, ingroup members tend to discriminate against outgroups. Cognitive theories suggest that people categorize others into groups in order to reduce social complexity. Learning theories maintain that stereotypes, prejudice, and discriminatory behaviors can be learned from parents, peers, and the media. The *contact hypothesis* proposes that intergroup contact can reduce prejudice and lead to more favorable attitudes toward the stereotyped group, but only if the contact occurs under specific conditions, such as equal status between groups.

Interpersonal Attraction

What factors affect who likes whom?

Interpersonal attraction is affected by many variables. Physical proximity is important because it allows people to meet. The situation in which they meet is important because positive or negative aspects of the situation tend to be associated with the other person. Characteristics of the other person are also important. Attraction tends to be greater when two people share similar attitudes and personal characteristics. Physical appearance plays a role in attraction; initially, attraction is strongest to those who are most physically attractive. But for long-term relationships, the *matching hypothesis* applies: people tend to choose others whose physical attractiveness is about the same as theirs.

Two key components of successful intimate relationships are interdependence and mutual commitment. Sternberg's triangular theory suggests that love is a function of three components: passion, intimacy, and commitment. Varying combinations of these three components create qualitatively different types of love. Marital satisfaction depends on communication, the perception that the relationship is equitable, the couple's ability to deal effectively with conflict and anger, and agreement on important issues in the marriage.

Social Influence

What social rules shape our behavior?

Social norms establish the rules for what should and should not be done in a particular situation. One particularly powerful norm is reciprocity, the tendency to respond to others as they have acted toward us. *Deindividuation* is a psychological state in which people temporarily lose their individuality, their normal inhibitions are relaxed, and they may perform aggressive or illegal acts that they would not do otherwise.

When behavior or beliefs change as the result of unspoken or implicit group pressure, *conformity* has occurred. When the change is the result of a request, *compliance* has occurred. People tend to follow the normative responses of others, and groups create norms when none already exist. People sometimes display public conformity without private acceptance; at other times, the responses of others have an impact on private beliefs. People conform because they want to be right, because they want to be liked, and because they tend to be rewarded for conformity. People are most likely to conform when the situation is unclear as well as when others in the group are in unanimous agreement. Up to a point, conformity usually increases as the number of people holding the majority view grows larger. Effective strategies for creating compliance include the foot-in-the-door technique, the door-in-the-face procedure, and the lowball approach.

Obedience

How far will people go in obeying authority?

Obedience involves complying with an explicit demand from an authority figure. Research by Milgram indicates that obedience is likely even when obeying an authority appears to result in pain and suffering for another person. Obedience declines when the status of the authority figure declines, when others are observed to disobey, and if a victim asks to be released. Some people are more likely to obey orders than others. Because participants in Milgram's studies experienced considerable stress, the experiments have been questioned on ethical grounds. Nevertheless, his research showed that people do not have to be psychologically disordered to inflict pain on others.

Aggression

Are people born aggressive?

Aggressive behavior (*aggression*) is an act intended to harm another person. Freud saw aggression as due partly to instincts. More recent theories attribute aggressive tendencies to genetic and evolutionary factors, brain dysfunctions, and hormonal influences. Learning is also important; people learn to display aggression by watching others and by being rewarded for aggressive behavior. There are wide cultural differences in the occurrence of aggression.

A variety of emotional factors play a role in aggression. The *frustration-aggression hypothesis* suggests that frustration can lead to aggression, particularly in the presence of cues that invite or promote aggression. Arousal from sources unrelated to aggression, such as exercise, can also make aggressive responses more likely, especially if aggression is already a dominant response in that situation. Research in *environmental psychology* suggests that factors such as high temperature and crowding increase the likelihood of aggressive behavior, particularly among people who are already angry.

Altruism and Prosocial Behavior

What motivates people to help one another?

Humans often display *prosocial behavior* (*helping behavior*) and *altruism*. There are three major theories of why people help others. According to the *arousal: cost-reward theory*, people help in order to reduce the unpleasant arousal they experience when others are in distress. Their specific reaction to a suffering person depends on the costs associated with helping or not helping. Helping is most likely when the need for help is clear and when diffusion of responsibility is not created by the presence of other people—a phenomenon called the *bystander effect*. Environmental and personality factors also affect willingness to help others. The *empathy-altruism helping theory* suggests that helping can be truly unselfish if the helper feels empathy for the person in need. Finally, evolutionary theory suggests that humans have an innate tendency to help others, especially relatives, because doing so increases the likelihood that family genes will survive.

Cooperation, Competition, and Conflict

What's the best way to help people cooperate?

Cooperation is any type of behavior in which people work together to attain a goal; *competition* exists whenever individuals try to attain a goal while denying others access to that goal. Interpersonal or intergroup *conflict* occurs when one person or group believes that another stands in the way of reaching some goal. Psychologists study conflict by observing behavior in *social dilemmas,* situations in which behavior that benefits individuals in the short run may spell disaster for an entire group in the long run.

Group Processes

What makes a good leader?

People's behavior is affected by the mere presence of other people. By enhancing one's most likely behavior in a situation, the presence of others sometimes creates *social facilitation* (which improves performance) and sometimes creates *social interference* (which impairs performance). When people work in groups, they often exert less effort than when alone, a phenomenon called *social loafing*. Effective group leaders tend to score high on emotional stability, agreeableness, and conscientiousness. In general, they are also intelligent, success oriented, flexible, and confident. *Task-motivated leaders* provide close supervision, lead by giving orders, and generally discourage group discussion. *Relationship-motivated leaders* provide loose supervision, ask for group members' ideas, and are generally concerned with subordinates' feelings. Transactional leaders focus on rewarding or correcting group members' performance, and transformational leaders tend to lead by example, thus inspiring good performance.

A specialty called *social neuroscience* focuses on the influence of social processes on biological processes and on the influence of biological processes on social psychological phenomena.

TEST YOUR KNOWLEDGE

Select the best answer for each of the following questions. Then check your responses against the Answer Key at the end of the book.

1. Jack was accepted to a top graduate school in social psychology after completing college with honors and having his senior research paper published. As he reads the biographies of Leon Festinger, Theodor Adorno, Elliot Aronson, and other famous social psychologists, he thinks about all of the things each of them accomplished and contrasts that with his own career, which is just beginning. Jack is engaging in _____.
   a. social facilitation
   b. social interference
   c. upward social comparison
   d. social discrimination

2. One of the assumptions of terror management theory is that _____.
   a. having high self-esteem helps reduce the impact of thoughts about death
   b. people who engage in terrorism have antisocial personalities
   c. it is better to dwell on negative thoughts than to avoid them
   d. people cope better with terrifying thoughts when they do not seek social support

3. When Rowland first met Jacob, Jacob wasn't feeling well and threw up on Rowland's shoes. According to research on first impressions, we would expect Rowland to _____.
   a. feel sorry for Jacob and thus have a positive first impression of him
   b. develop a negative impression of Jacob because of the negative first experience with him
   c. have an initial negative impression that will become positive later, no matter what Jacob does
   d. have a positive first impression of Jacob because he is a male

4. Gena is in a bad mood because she is convinced that she won't like her blind date, Pat. When Pat arrives, he is outgoing and considerate, but Gena is short-tempered and rude to him. Soon Pat becomes irritable and ends the date early. Gena's prediction that she wouldn't have a good time came true mainly because of _____.
   a. cognitive dissonance
   b. prejudice
   c. a self-fulfilling prophecy
   d. the fundamental attribution error

5. "I earned an A on my history test because I studied hard and I'm smart, but I failed my philosophy test because its questions were poorly worded and the teacher doesn't like me." This statement is an example of _____.
   a. the actor-observer effect
   b. the fundamental attribution error
   c. a self-fulfilling prophecy
   d. a self-serving bias

6. Richard is listening to a student government leader suggest that professors on campus should stop giving grades. Richard is most likely to be convinced if the speaker _____.
   a. introduces a famous celebrity who supports this idea
   b. circulates a petition in support of the idea
   c. presents evidence that eliminating grades will not hurt students' job prospects
   d. is personable and funny

7. Rachel and Matteus listen to a boring lecture. Afterward, Rachel is offered $100 and Matteus is offered $1 to tell the lecturer's next class that the lecture was interesting and fun. Both agree to do so. According to cognitive dissonance theory, we would expect real attitude change about the lecture to occur in _____.
   a. Rachel, but not Matteus
   b. Matteus, but not Rachel
   c. both Rachel and Matteus
   d. neither Rachel nor Matteus

8. In an attempt to reduce prejudice between ethnic groups at Lincoln School, the principal asks members of all groups to help build a new playground. Prejudice would be most likely to decrease as a result if _____.
   a. teams from each ethnic group competed to see which could work the fastest
   b. one member of each group was appointed to a committee to lead the project
   c. members of all the groups worked together in teams to complete various parts of the playground
   d. members of each ethnic group wore the same kind of T-shirt

9. Rhona, a pretty woman with conservative political views, has just moved into an apartment building on campus. All else being equal, which neighbor will Rhona probably like the most?
   a. Jill, whose hair color, height, and weight are similar to Rhona's
   b. Shauna, president of the Young Conservatives club
   c. Patrice, president of the Young Liberals club
   d. Yolanda, who comes from Rhona's home town

10. Giorgio and Louisa share their thoughts, hopes, and daily worries. They plan to stay married throughout their lifetime, and they enjoy an active and satisfying sex life. According to Sternberg's theory, Giorgio and Louisa are experiencing _____ love.
   a. consummate
   b. companionate
   c. temporary
   d. romantic

11. When her best friend stopped by with a Christmas gift, Jen was upset because she had nothing to give in return. Jen was uncomfortable because she _____.
   a. experienced deindividuation
   b. engaged in social loafing
   c. made the ultimate attribution error
   d. could not follow the reciprocity norm

12. In Harper Lee's novel *To Kill a Mockingbird*, an angry mob tries to lynch a prisoner. The prisoner's attorney, Atticus Finch, and his young daughter, "Scout," talk to the crowd, calling people by name, and reminding them that they know their families. Soon the mob disperses, no longer a faceless crowd but a group of identifiable individuals. Atticus and Scout disrupted the phenomenon of _____.
   a. diffusion of responsibility
   b. deindividuation
   c. situational ambiguity
   d. social facilitation

13. Shawn's teacher doesn't keep track of her students' performance when they work in groups, so Shawn does not put as much effort into his group project as he does into his individual project. Shawn is exhibiting _____.
    a. a self-serving bias
    b. social facilitation
    c. social loafing
    d. diffusion of responsibility

14. Keyonna thought that the play she had just seen was boring, but everyone else seemed to like it. At the closing curtain, the audience gave the actors a standing ovation. Keyonna stood up and applauded too, even though she didn't believe the actors deserved it. Keyonna's behavior in this situation is an example of _____.
    a. conformity
    b. compliance
    c. obedience
    d. a self-fulfilling prophecy

15. Colleen knows she should take a day off from work to study for a big exam, but she also knows her boss won't like it. So she first asks for the entire week off. When the boss refuses, she asks for the one day off instead and he agrees. Colleen used the _____ approach to gain her boss's compliance.
    a. foot-in-the-door
    b. door-in-the-face
    c. lowball
    d. peripheral

16. Which of the following is not a major factor in determining whether or not a person will obey an order?
    a. The status of the authority figure giving the order.
    b. The personality characteristics of the person receiving the order.
    c. The presence of another person who disobeys the order.
    d. The gender of the person given the order.

17. Leonard is upset because he just can't get his new iPhone to work. When his roommate comes home and accidentally knocks over Leonard's glass of lemonade, Leonard becomes abusive, screaming at his roommate and throwing books and pillows at him. This is an example of the _____ theory of aggression.
    a. frustration-aggression
    b. generalized arousal
    c. authoritarian
    d. biological

18. While shopping, Lenora falls and breaks her ankle. She is most likely to receive help from a stranger if she _____.
    a. is in a quiet area where only a few people saw her fall
    b. is in the midst of a large crowd
    c. is in a large city
    d. doesn't ask for help

19. Which of the following summarizes the evolutionary view of prosocial behavior?
    a. People feel good when they help others.
    b. People help others in order to improve the chance that some of their genes will survive in future generations.
    c. People are motivated to protect others if the costs of helping are outweighed by the benefits.
    d. People are helpful because it improves everyone's chances of survival.

20. One of the most important ways to promote cooperation between people is to _____.
    a. improve communication
    b. improve conflict-relevant communication
    c. punish non-conflict relevant communication
    d. increase arousal in each person

CHAPTER 17

Industrial and Organizational Psychology

© wavebreakmedia/Shutterstock.com

Preview

If you've ever had a full-time or part-time job, you know that work involves more than just doing certain tasks and collecting a paycheck. Many job-related experiences—including the characteristics of coworkers and supervisors, the nature of the work, and the pleasures and stressors found in the workplace—have significant effects on employees and the organizations that hire them. Understanding the impact of these experiences is just one aspect of the subfield known as *industrial and organizational (I/O) psychology*. In this chapter, we explore this growing subfield by reviewing how I/O psychologists conduct their research and how they apply that research to improve the performance and welfare of workers and the organizations that employ them.

Suppose that you are the manager of a large department store. You want to hire someone to head up the cosmetics department, but you're not sure how to find the best person for the job. How can you attract applicants with the necessary skills? How will you know which of them would be the best choice? Should you rely on interviews with the candidates, or should you also give them some psychological tests? Perhaps you decide to do both, but how do you choose the interview questions and tests? How should you interpret the results? And what happens after you've made your hiring decision? How will you train, motivate, supervise, and reward employees so that they perform at their best and are happy in their work? And how will you determine if your procedures have met your goals? To address problems such as these, many human resources managers and other organizational executives seek the help of *industrial and organizational (I/O) psychologists*. We briefly mentioned I/O psychology in the introductory chapter; here we describe it in more detail, including a summary of what I/O psychologists do and some of the ways their work has benefited organizations and employees.

AN OVERVIEW OF INDUSTRIAL AND ORGANIZATIONAL PSYCHOLOGY

What do industrial and organizational psychologists do?

Psychology is the science of behavior and mental processes. The subfield of **industrial and organizational (I/O) psychology** is the science of behavior and mental processes in workplace settings. I/O psychologists conduct scientific research on all sorts of people-oriented workplace topics, such as what personality traits predict good performance under stress, what social factors cause conflict in work groups, and how people feel about the organizations in which they work. I/O psychologists are also hands-on practitioners who help organizations apply research findings to problems such as matching employees to jobs and improving cooperation in workplace teams. The link between scientific research and professional practice can be especially strong in I/O psychology, because the workplace provides both a natural laboratory for studying psychological questions and a setting in which research-based answers can be applied and evaluated.

I/O psychologists address two main goals in their research and practice. First, they *promote effective job performance* by employees and thus create better performance by the organization as a whole. Second, they contribute to human welfare by *improving the health, safety, and well-being of employees*. This second goal is important by itself, but it is also related to the first one. Effective organizations are those whose employees are not only capable of performing their jobs well but are also healthy and well adjusted in the workplace.

industrial and organizational (I/O) psychology The science of behavior and mental processes in the workplace.

Entering I/O Psychology

Some graduates pursue careers in I/O psychology after completing a master's degree program, but salaries and opportunities are better for those with a Ph.D. For example, virtually all I/O psychologists who are hired as college or university professors have completed a doctoral degree. Master's or doctoral training in I/O psychology is available at more than 100 universities in the United States, about 10 in Canada, and more than 80 in other countries.

© Yuri Arcurs/Shutterstock.com

I/O psychology emerged early in the 1900s as psychologists began to apply laboratory findings about topics such as learning, memory, and motivation to solve practical problems in the workplace. In fact, some of the first I/O psychologists studied under experimental psychologists. For example, Hugo Münsterberg and James McKeen Cattell, both widely considered as instrumental in the founding of I/O psychology, studied under Wilhelm Wundt in Germany. Elsie Oschrin Bregman, a pioneer in the study of employment testing, was a student of Edward L. Thorndike at Columbia University (Katzell & Austin, 1992; Koppes, 1997; Landy, 1992). Research and applications in I/O psychology continue to be influenced by laboratory research in many of psychology's subfields, including cognitive psychology, personality, motivation and emotion, health psychology, and especially social psychology. And many I/O psychologists study work-related behavior in the laboratory as well as in the workplace (Parasuraman, 2011). The work of I/O psychologists is also shaped by findings in fields beyond psychology, including business management, marketing, economics, engineering, statistical theory, and medicine.

Like psychologists in other subfields, I/O psychologists hold graduate degrees in their specialty. The popularity of I/O psychology has grown rapidly in recent decades, both in North America and throughout the industrialized world (Spector, 2003). About 53 percent of I/O psychologists work in the private sector. Another 34 percent are professors in college or university departments of psychology, business, or related fields. About 8 percent are research scientists in the public sector, including in government agencies, and about 5 percent work in non-profit companies (Khanna & Medsker, 2013). Let's consider some of the specific kinds of work that I/O psychologists do in these various settings.

ASSESSING PEOPLE, JOBS, AND JOB PERFORMANCE

How do industrial and organizational psychologists match employees to jobs?

If you apply for a job with a large corporation or government agency, you will probably be given one or more standardized tests of mental ability or personality, as well as assessments of your knowledge and skills to help determine whether you have the "right stuff" for the job you seek. These assessment programs are usually designed by I/O psychologists. In fact, the most typical request that I/O psychologists receive from organizations is to develop or conduct some sort of assessment procedure. Accordingly, the creation and evaluation of new and better assessment devices is one of the main areas for scientific research in I/O psychology. This kind of work aligns I/O psychology closely with the field of psychological measurement, or *psychometrics*, so the two subfields have long overlapped.

Knowledge, Skills, Abilities, and Other Characteristics

Industrial and organizational assessments are often used to describe the human attributes necessary for doing jobs successfully. Those attributes are referred to collectively as *KSAOs*, which stands for *knowledge, skill, ability, and other personal characteristics. Knowledge* refers to what a person knows. *Skill* refers to how good a person is at doing a particular task. *Ability* is defined as a person's more general capacities in areas such as thinking, physical coordination, or interpersonal functioning. Skills and abilities are closely related; some researchers consider skills to be the products of inherent abilities (Muchinsky, 2003). *Other personal characteristics* can be almost anything else about a person, including attitudes, personality traits, physical characteristics, preferences, or values.

Job Analysis

How do organizations know which KSAOs are important for which jobs? The answer lies in **job analysis**, in which I/O psychologists collect information about particular jobs and job requirements. This job-analysis information is then used to guide decisions about whom to hire and what kind of training is needed to succeed at a particular job (Brannick & Levine, 2002). There are two major approaches to job analysis. The *job-oriented approach* describes the tasks involved in doing a job, such as wiring circuit boards, creating a computer database, or driving a truck. In organizations that emphasize teamwork, the job-oriented approach to job analysis might also include asking each team member to describe their coworkers' tasks as well as their own (Brannick, Levine, & Morgeson, 2007). The *person-oriented approach* describes the KSAOs needed to do those job tasks (see Table 17.1).

Some job analyses take one approach or the other, but many provide information about both tasks and KSAOs. A job-analysis report can be a relatively brief and superficial description, a microscopically detailed examination, or anything in between. The approach taken and the level of detail included in a job analysis depend mainly on how the report will be used. When the analysis will guide the hiring of employees, it should contain enough detail to make clear what needs to be done in a particular job. Having these details spelled out also helps the organization establish and maintain fair hiring practices. The person-oriented approach is the most useful one for these purposes, because it describes the KSAOs the employer should be looking for in the new employee.

job analysis The process of collecting information about jobs and job requirements that is used to guide hiring and training decisions.

TABLE **17.1**   KNOWLEDGE, SKILL, ABILITY, AND OTHER PERSONAL CHARACTERISTICS (KSAOs)

Here are examples of the kinds of KSAOs required for successful performance by people working in two different jobs. Just for fun, try writing KSAOs for your job as a student and for your teacher's job, too.

Job Title	Knowledge	Skill	Ability	Other
Secretary	Knowledge of office procedures	Skill in using a word-processing program	Ability to communicate with others	Willingness to follow instructions
Plumber	Knowledge of county building codes	Skill in using a wrench	Good hand-eye coordination	Willingness to work in dirty environments

Job analysis can also help organizations recognize the need to train employees, and it can help establish the kind of training required. Suppose you have five job openings, but when you test candidates for hiring or promotion, too few of them have the KSAOs that a job analysis says are necessary for success in these positions. Obviously, some training will be needed, and because the job analysis lists specific KSAOs, you can use that analysis to determine exactly what the training should include. Suppose a job analysis reveals that people in a particular computer sales position have to be familiar with the Linux operating system. You would need to provide Linux training for all individuals hired for that position unless they already knew that operating system.

Questionnaires that ask current employees to describe their jobs are the most common tool for job analysis. Other methods include assigning specially trained job analysts to observe people as they do their jobs or even to perform those jobs themselves (Dierdorff & Wilson, 2003). If the goals of job analysis include comparing one job with another, I/O psychologists might use an instrument such as the *Position Analysis Questionnaire,* or *PAQ* (McCormick, Jeanneret, & Mecham, 1972). The 189 items on the PAQ can describe almost any job in terms of a particular set of characteristics, or dimensions, such as the degree to which a job involves communicating with people, lifting heavy objects, or doing mental arithmetic. The results of thousands of job analyses have been collected in the U.S. Department of Labor's Occupational Information Network, or O*NET (Peterson et al., 2001). This computer database contains analyses of approximately 1,100 groups of jobs, including the KSAOs and tasks involved in each, and how each job fits into the larger organizational picture. O*NET is an excellent source of information about occupations for anyone who is in the process of choosing a career, and you can access it online.

Measuring Employee Characteristics

LINKAGES   What methods are used to select good employees? (a link to Personality)

I/O psychologists use many instruments to measure a person's knowledge, skill, ability, and other characteristics. These instruments range from simple paper-and-pencil tests (an arithmetic test for a sales clerk, for example) to several days of hands-on activities that simulate the tasks required of a midlevel manager. Some assessments are used to select new employees, others are designed to choose employees for promotion, and still others are meant to determine how well employees are doing their jobs at the moment. The three main methods used to measure employee characteristics are psychological tests, "structured" job applicant interviews, and assessment center exercises.

Psychological Tests

The tests that I/O psychologists most often use to measure general mental ability and skill are the standard intelligence tests described in the chapter on intelligence. These tests are relatively inexpensive and easy to administer, and they do a reasonably good job at predicting people's performance in a wide variety of occupational tasks (e.g., Jansen & Vinkenburg, 2006; Kuncel & Hezlett, 2010; Rooy et al., 2006). In addition, job applicants might take *situational judgment tests (SJTs),* in which they read about or watch videos of simulated workplace situations, such as a conflict between coworkers, then rate which of several responses would be best or describe what they would do in a similar situation (Sackett & Lievens, 2008). Information provided by SJTs supplements cognitive and personality tests and provides an additional perspective from which to predict an applicant's eventual job performance (Lievens, Peeters, & Schollaert, 2008). Tests of job-relevant knowledge—such as basic accounting principles or stock-trading rules—may also be used to confirm that an individual is familiar with the procedures and other information necessary to do well at a particular job.

Finally, personality tests measure a variety of other employee characteristics. As described in the personality chapter, some such tests provide information about personality dimensions that may be relevant to hiring decisions. For example, a person's score on *conscientiousness* (i.e., reliability and industriousness) has been linked to job performance across many occupations (Dudley et al., 2006; Thoreson et al., 2003). You might assume that more conscientious workers display better job performance, but I/O psychologists have found that this is true only up to a point. It turns out that employees who are either the least conscientious *or* who are overly conscientious tend not to perform as well as workers whose conscientiousness is high but not extreme. This "too much of a good thing" effect (Carter et al., 2013; Pierce & Aguinis, 2013) has also appeared in relation to extraversion (Grant, 2013). Some employers also use personality-related *integrity tests*, which ask about moral values, tendencies, temptations, and history that might make employees more likely to steal or engage in other disruptive acts (e.g., Berry, Sackett, & Wiemann, 2007; Wanek, Sackett, & Ones, 2003). Unfortunately, it is relatively easy to give false or misleading responses on these tests, and there is evidence that applicants may do so (van Hooft & Born, 2012; Zickar, Gibby, & Robie, 2004).

Job Applicant Interviews

Job applicant interviews are intended to determine a job applicant's suitability for a job. They tend to be preferred by both employers and employees (Hausknecht, Day, & Thomas, 2004). Interviews usually take place in person, though some are conducted by telephone, videoconferencing, or e-mail. As discussed in the personality chapter, interviews can be structured or unstructured (open ended). In a *structured interview,* the interviewer prepares a list of specific topics or even specifically worded questions to be covered in a particular order (Campion, Palmer, & Campion, 1997; Chapman & Zweig, 2005). In *unstructured interviews,* the course of a conversation is more spontaneous and variable. Following some interviews, especially structured ones, the candidate's responses will be rated on a set of dimensions, such as product knowledge, clarity of expression, or poise. After other interviews, the interviewer's subjective impression of the candidate is used to make a yes-or-no judgment about the candidate's suitability for the job.

Research consistently shows that structured interviews are far more effective than unstructured interviews in leading to good hiring decisions (e.g., Huffcutt & Arthur, 1994; Wiesner & Cronshaw, 1988). The difference is due largely to the fact that structured interviews focus specifically on job-related knowledge and skills—especially interpersonal skills—whereas unstructured interviews do not (Huffcutt et al., 2001). Further, lack of structure makes it easier for personal bias, observational errors, and misinterpretations to enter the hiring picture; ratings from an unstructured interview might have more to do with the interviewer's personal bias about a candidate than with the candidate's objective qualifications. Finally, lack of structure can also create unfairness because different candidates might not necessarily be asked the same set of questions or be given the same chance to "show their stuff."

Assessment Centers

An **assessment center** is an extensive set of exercises designed to determine an individual's suitability for a particular job. Performance is usually judged by a team of raters (Spychalski et al., 1997). Assessment centers are often used to hire or promote managers, but they can be employed in relation to other positions as well. A typical assessment center consists of two to three days of exercises that simulate various aspects of a job. The *in-basket test* is a typical assessment center exercise for managers. Candidates are seated at a desk and asked to imagine that they have just taken over a new management job. On the desk is the "previous manager's" overflowing in-basket, containing correspondence, memos, phone messages, and other items. The candidate's task is to go through all this material and write on the back of each item what action should be taken to deal with it and how soon. Later, experts read what the candidate has written and assign an appropriateness score to each action. For example, candidates who prioritize tasks well—taking immediate action on critical matters and delaying action on less-important ones—would receive higher scores than those who, say, deal with each task in the order in which it is encountered, regardless of its importance.

A Matter of Degree

When hiring employees for some jobs, organizations often rely on credentials rather than knowledge tests. For example, an undergraduate degree in any major may be enough to qualify for some white-collar jobs because people assume that college graduates have enough general knowledge and "mental horsepower" to succeed. For jobs in medicine, law, accounting, engineering, and other specialty fields, candidates' knowledge is assumed if they have completed a particular degree program or earned a particular license. These assumptions are usually correct, but credentials alone do not always guarantee competence.

© iStockphoto.com/StockLib; Thinkstock Images/Photos.com

assessment center An extensive set of exercises designed to determine an individual's suitability for a particular job.

Other assessment center exercises measure interpersonal skills. The job candidate might be asked to play the role of a manager who is working with others to solve a problem or who must discipline a problem employee. As in the in-basket test, each candidate is given a score on the knowledge, skills, abilities, and other job-relevant characteristics displayed during each exercise.

The evaluation team reviews and discusses the candidate's total score on the assessment center exercises and reaches a group decision about the person's suitability for a particular position. Research shows that assessment centers work well. For example, the assessment center scores earned by first-year college students predict their performance as teachers several years after graduation (Shechtman, 1992). Assessment centers also predict the performance of police officers, pilots, and managers, among others (Dayan, Kasten, & Fox, 2002; Lievens et al., 2003; McEvoy & Beatty, 1989). However, assessment centers can be expensive and time-consuming. Further, performance scores on assessment centers correlate relatively strongly with applicants' performance on interviews and cognitive tests. With these factors in mind, some researchers suggest using assessment centers only as a second step in the selection process, and only for applicants whose interview and test scores are neither high enough nor low enough to guide a final hiring decision (Dayan, Fox, & Kasten, 2008).

Measuring Job Performance

Almost all employees of medium to large organizations receive an annual **job performance** appraisal, which, much like a student's report card, provides an evaluation of how well they are doing in various aspects of their work. Organizations use these appraisals to guide decisions about salary raises and bonuses for employees and about whether to keep, promote, or fire particular individuals. The appraisals are also used to give employees feedback on the quality and quantity of their work (Rynes, Gerhart, & Parks, 2005). This feedback function of job performance appraisals is important because it helps employees recognize what they are doing right and what they need to do differently to reach their own goals and promote the goals of the organization.

Establishing Performance Criteria

One of the most important roles for I/O psychologists in designing job performance appraisal systems is to help establish *criteria*, or benchmarks, that define what the organization means by "good" or "poor" performance (see Table 17.2). These criteria can be theoretical or actual. A *theoretical criterion* is a statement of what we mean by good (or poor) performance, in theory. A theoretical criterion for good teaching, for example, might be "promotes student learning." This criterion certainly sounds reasonable, but notice that it does not specify how we would measure it in order to decide whether a particular teacher is actually promoting student learning. So we also need an *actual criterion,* which specifies what we should measure to determine whether the theoretical criterion has been met. An actual criterion for good teaching might be defined in terms of students' performance on a standardized test of what their teacher has taught them. If, on average, the students reach or exceed some particular score, the teacher will have satisfied one of the school district's criteria for good teaching.

Keep in mind, though, that the match between theoretical criteria and actual criteria is never perfect. The actual criterion chosen should provide a sensible way to assess the theoretical criterion, but the actual criterion may be flawed. For one thing, actual criteria are usually incomplete. There is more to good teaching than just ensuring that students earn a particular score on a particular test. The teacher may have done a great (or poor) job at teaching material that did not happen to be covered on that test. Second, the actual criterion can be affected by factors other than the employee's performance. Perhaps students' scores on a standardized test were affected partly by the work of a good (or poor) teacher they had before their current teacher was hired. I/O psychologists are sensitive to these problems, and they usually recommend basing job performance appraisals on several actual criteria, not just one.

job performance A measure of how well employees are doing in various aspects of their work, usually recorded in an annual appraisal.

TABLE 17.2	EXAMPLES OF THEORETICAL AND ACTUAL CRITERIA

Here are some theoretical and actual criteria for several kinds of jobs. Notice that theoretical criteria tend to be rather vague, so for purposes of job performance appraisals, they must be backed up by actual criteria. By evaluating employees on how well they have reached actual criteria, organizations can decide whether the theoretical criteria have been met, and they can act accordingly. Think about the kinds of jobs you have had in your life or that you might like to have, and try to develop your own set of fair, appropriate theoretical and actual criteria for performance in these jobs.

Job	Theoretical Criterion	Actual Criterion
Architect	Design buildings	Number of buildings designed
Car salesperson	Sell cars	Number of cars sold per month
Police officer	Fight crime	Number of arrests made per month
Roofer	Install roofs	Square feet of shingles installed per month
Scientist	Make scientific discoveries	Number of articles published in scholarly journals

I/O psychologists also distinguish between different *types* of performance. They focus in particular on three basic dimensions of performance. The first of these, *task performance*, is what we generally think of when we hear the phrase "job performance" and refers to how well employees complete their job-related tasks and handle their duties and responsibilities. The second dimension, *organizational citizenship behaviors (OCBs)*, are "extra-role behaviors," which includes things like chipping in to help a coworker meet a crucial deadline. The third dimension, *counterproductive work behaviors (CWBs)*, are negative behaviors that harm the organization; these can range from stealing office supplies to sabotaging other workers' performance. Most supervisors tend to emphasize task performance and CWBs, but OCBs are also an important component of performance in organizations (Rotundo & Sackett, 2002).

Methods of Performance Appraisal

The information used in job performance appraisals can come from objective measures and subjective measures.

Objective Measures

Objective measures of job performance include counting the frequency of certain behaviors or the results of those behaviors. The number of calls made by a telemarketer, the number of computers shipped out by a factory worker, and the total value of items sold each month by a shoe store employee are examples of objective measures of job performance. Objective measures of problematic behaviors might include the number of days employees are absent, how often they arrive late, or the number of complaints filed against them (Roth, Huffcutt, & Bobko, 2003). Objective appraisal measures may be especially valuable because they can link theoretical criteria with actual performance criteria. If the theoretical criterion for good performance as a salesperson is to sell a company's products, the most closely linked actual criterion would be an objective count of the number of those products sold per month.

Objective methods of job performance are not right for all jobs, however, because some performance criteria cannot be evaluated by counting things. For example, it would make no sense to evaluate a teacher's job performance by counting the number of students taught per year. Teachers usually have no control over their class size, and in any case, an enrollment count tells us nothing about what the students learned. Similarly, a salesperson might have sold twenty cars last month, but it would also be important to know how this was accomplished. If the person used unethical or high-pressure tactics that angered customers and harmed the organization's reputation, the sales count tells only part of the story of this employee's performance. In other words, except for the simplest jobs, objective measures may fail to assess all the aspects of performance that are of interest to an organization.

Subjective Measures

I/O psychologists sometimes recommend that objective performance measures be supplemented or sometimes even replaced by subjective measures. *Subjective measures* of job performance tend to focus on a supervisor's judgments about various aspects of an employee's work (Rynes, Gerhart, & Parks, 2005). Typically, the supervisor records these judgments on a graphic rating form or a behavior-focused rating form.

Graphic rating forms list several criterion-related dimensions of job performance and provide a space for the supervisor to rate each employee's performance on each dimension, using a scale ranging from, say, 1 to 10 or from *poor* to *excellent* (see Figure 17.1). These graphic ratings can be valuable, but they reflect the supervisor's subjective judgment. So, as in unstructured interviews, factors other than the employee's performance can influence the results (Peretz & Fried, 2012; Wong & Kwong, 2005). For example, most graphic ratings reflect *leniency error,* meaning that supervisors tend to use only the top of the scale. As a result, most employees in most organizations receive ratings of "satisfactory" or better. Many supervisors also show errors based on a *halo effect,* meaning that they tend to give the same rating on every dimension of job performance. So if Tasha receives an "outstanding" rating on one dimension, such as promptness, she will probably be rated at or near "outstanding" on all the others. Similarly, if Jack is rated as only

FIGURE 17.1

A Graphic Rating Form Used in Subjective Job Performance Appraisal

Supervisors often use graphic rating forms like this one in subjective job performance appraisals. The ratings are based on the supervisor's personal experience with the employee and on subjective impressions of that employee's work.

Rate employee on each dimension on the left by checking the appropriate box corresponding to the level of performance for the past year.

Dimension

Customer service	☐ Poor	☐ Fair	☐ Satisfactory	☐ Above satisfactory	☐ Outstanding
Management of time	☐ Poor	☐ Fair	☐ Satisfactory	☐ Above satisfactory	☐ Outstanding
Professional appearance	☐ Poor	☐ Fair	☐ Satisfactory	☐ Above satisfactory	☐ Outstanding
Teamwork	☐ Poor	☐ Fair	☐ Satisfactory	☐ Above satisfactory	☐ Outstanding
Work quality	☐ Poor	☐ Fair	☐ Satisfactory	☐ Above satisfactory	☐ Outstanding
Work quantity	☐ Poor	☐ Fair	☐ Satisfactory	☐ Above satisfactory	☐ Outstanding

"satisfactory" on one scale, such as product knowledge, he will probably get "satisfactory" ratings on the rest of them.

To some extent, these rating tendencies may just reflect reality. After all, most people try to do their jobs well and may do about equally well (or equally poorly) in various aspects of their work (Balzer & Sulsky, 1992; Solomonson & Lance, 1997). However, when using graphic rating forms, supervisors may not carefully discriminate between those aspects of job performance that are satisfactory from those that need improvement. Further, many tend to "go easy" on their employees, especially if they like them, if they want to curry favor with them for some reason, or if they want to appear "politically correct" (Harber et al., 2012; Judge & Cable, 2011). Such bias can result in favoritism in which supervisors inflate ratings beyond what an employee's performance deserves (Rynes, Gerhart, & Parks, 2005). Supervisors who are biased against certain employees based on gender, ethnicity, or other factors may give those employees undeservedly low ratings (Heilman & Haynes, 2008; Stauffer & Buckley, 2005).

To help minimize the errors and bias associated with graphic rating forms, I/O psychologists developed *behavior-focused rating forms,* which ask supervisors to rate employees on specific actions rather than on general overviews of performance (Smith & Kendall, 1963). These forms contain lists of *critical incidents* that illustrate different levels of performance—from "extremely effective" to "extremely ineffective"—on important job dimensions (Flanagan, 1954). A critical incident list relating to customer relations, for example, might include "listens patiently," "tries to reach a compromise," "coldly states store policy," and "angrily demands that complaining customers leave." Once these behavior-focused forms are constructed, supervisors choose which incidents are most typical of each employee.

Behavior-based rating forms help supervisors and their employees come to a better understanding of what is meant by "good" and "poor" performance. However, these forms don't appear to eliminate the impact of supervisor bias and error (Bernardin & Beatty, 1984; Latham et al., 1993). Accordingly, some employers assess employees' job performance on the basis of ratings by peers and subordinates as well as supervisors. These "360-degree" ratings are designed to provide a broader and potentially less biased picture of an employee's performance (Oh & Berry, 2009). (See "In Review: Assessing People, Jobs, and Job Performance" for a summary of these topics.)

			IN REVIEW
ASSESSING PEOPLE, JOBS, AND JOB PERFORMANCE			
Target of Assessment	**Typical Purpose**	**What Is Assessed**	**Examples**
Employees	Employee selection	Knowledge, skill, ability, and other personal characteristics (KSAOs)	Tests of ability, achievement, or personality; structured or unstructured interviews; assessment centers requiring simulated job tasks
Jobs	Matching employees to jobs; identifying training needs	Job tasks and personal attributes needed for the job	Job-oriented analysis (identifies required tasks); person-oriented analysis (identifies KSAOs required for success)

(continued)

	IN REVIEW
ASSESSING PEOPLE, JOBS, AND JOB PERFORMANCE (CONT.)	

Target of Assessment	Typical Purpose	What Is Assessed	Examples
Job performance	Feedback on performance; decisions about retention, salary adjustments, or promotion	Work activities and/or products; supervisors' reports	Evaluating employees' work in relation to theoretical and actual criteria as measured by objective (counting) or subjective (rating) methods

In Review Questions

1. Lists of critical incidents are contained in _____-focused employee rating forms.

2. A potential employer might use a two-day _____ to measure your skill at the job you want.

3. In general, _____ interviews are more useful in employee selection than _____ interviews.

RECRUITING AND SELECTING EMPLOYEES

How do organizations find good employees?

So far, we've described some of the assessment methods that I/O psychologists have developed to help organizations hire, train, and evaluate employees. Let's now consider the role of I/O psychology in finding candidates for employment and in selecting the right people for each job.

Recruitment Processes

People are usually an organization's most valuable assets because people are ultimately responsible for achieving an organization's goals. So it is no wonder that there is intense competition among organizations to recruit the "best and brightest" employees. It is a disciplined competition, however. There is no point in hiring this year's top ten accounting graduates if your organization needs only two new accountants. So the first step in effective recruiting is to determine what employees are needed and then go after the best people to fill those needs.

Determining employment needs means more than just counting empty chairs, though. Analyses by I/O psychologists help organizations determine how many people are needed in each position at the moment and how many will be needed in the future. Suppose, for example, that a computer company anticipates a 20 percent growth in business over the next five years. That growth will require a 20 percent increase in the number of customer service representatives, but how many new representatives should be hired each month? An I/O psychologist's analysis would help answer this question by taking into account not only the growth projections but also estimates of how many representatives quit their jobs each year and whether the existing ratio of customer service employees to customers is too high, too low, or just about right for efficient operation. In making recommendations about recruitment plans, I/O psychologists must also consider the intensity of demand for employees in various occupations. More active recruitment plans will be necessary to attract the best people in high-demand areas (see Table 17.3).

TABLE 17.3   FAST-GROWING OCCUPATIONS

Here are the ten fastest growing occupations listed in the U.S. Bureau of Labor *Statistics Occupational Out-look Handbook* (U.S. Bureau of Labor Statistics, 2014). I/O psychologists must take such trends into account when making recommendations about where to make the strongest efforts at recruiting new employees. More information about these job categories is available on the Bureau of Labor Statistics website.

Occupation	Percent Employment Change, 2012–2022
Industrial/Organizational psychologists	53
Personal and home care aides	49
Home health aides	48
Insulation workers, mechanical	47
Interpreters and translators	46
Diagnostic medical sonographers	46
Helpers—brickmasons, blockmasons, stonemasons, and tile and marble setters	43
Occupational therapy assistants	43
Genetic counselors	41
Physical therapist assistants	41

Once employment needs are established and the competitive landscape has been explored, the next step in recruitment is to persuade people with the right kinds of knowledge, skills, ability, and other characteristics to apply for the jobs to be filled. Common methods for identifying and attracting candidates include posting jobs on recruitment websites; newspaper advertising; interviewing graduating seniors on college campuses; seeking referrals from current employees; working with employment agencies, recruitment consultants, and private "head-hunting" firms; and accepting walk-in applications from job seekers who appear on their own. The recruitment methods used for any particular job will depend on how easy or difficult it is to attract high-quality applicants and on the importance of the position in the organization. For relatively low-level positions requiring few skills, it may be possible to rely on walk-in applicants to fill available positions. Much more effort and several different recruitment methods may be required in order to attract top-notch candidates for higher-level jobs that demand extensive experience and skill.

Selection Processes

Selecting the right employee for a particular job is generally a matter of using the results of tests, interviews, and assessment centers to find the best fit between each candidate's characteristics and the tasks and characteristics that a job analysis has identified as necessary for successful performance. This matching strategy would suggest that a candidate who is better at written communication than at computer skills would do better in, say, the public relations department than at the computer help desk.

Is this strategy the best way to select employees? Usually, but one job of I/O psychologists is to learn if the characteristics that are supposed to predict success at particular jobs are, in fact, associated with success. To do so, they conduct *validity studies*, which are research projects that analyze how well a particular test, interview, or other assessment method predicts employees' actual job performance (Chan, 2005). For example, on the basis of a job analysis conducted years ago, a department store might require applicants for sales clerk positions to pass a test of mental arithmetic. A validity study could determine whether performance on that test is actually related to sales clerks' performance. The easiest way to conduct this study would be to ask a representative sample of the store's sales clerks to take the arithmetic test, then compute the correlation between their test scores and some objective or subjective performance criterion, such as monthly sales figures or a supervisor's ratings. If those who score highest on the test also do best at their job, the arithmetic test can be seen as valid for predicting job performance. If not, it may be that for clerks using today's computerized sales terminals, mental arithmetic is no longer as important to job success as it was in the past.

A large body of results from I/O psychology research is available to tell organizations which types of tests and other assessments are most valid in predicting performance in which types of jobs. These results save organizations a great deal of time and money because they eliminate the need to conduct their own validity studies for each assessment device they use in selecting employees for every job they want to fill.

Legal Issues in Recruitment and Selection

The United States and many other countries have laws requiring that an organization's hiring, firing, and promotion processes should not discriminate against anyone based on characteristics that have nothing to do with job performance. Such laws are intended to protect all employees and job candidates against unfair discrimination. U.S. laws—including the Civil Rights Act, the Americans with Disabilities Act, and the Age Discrimination in Employment Act—have also created special safeguards for several *protected classes,* including women, Asians, Blacks, Hispanics, American Indians, and other groups. Together, these laws make it illegal for employers in the United States to discriminate in hiring or promotion on the basis of a candidate's age, ethnicity, gender, national origin, disability, or religion. Many states, cities, and counties—and some other countries, such as Canada, Spain, and Denmark—also prohibit discrimination based on sexual orientation.

In 1978, I/O psychologists helped the U.S. government create its *Uniform Guidelines on Employee Selection Procedures,* a document that outlines the procedures organizations must use to ensure fairness in hiring and promotion. The most important element of these guidelines is the requirement that personnel decisions be based solely on job-related criteria. This means that in choosing new employees, for example, organizations should hire people whose knowledge, skill, ability, and other characteristics match the KSAO requirements previously established by the job-analysis process described earlier. The guidelines also state that organizations should use only test scores and other assessment data that validation studies have established as good predictors of job performance.

TRAINING EMPLOYEES

What kind of training do employees need?

Every year, organizations in the industrialized world spend billions on training their employees (Thompson et al., 2002); in the United States alone, the figure is more than $126 billion each year (Paradise, 2007). I/O psychologists are directly involved in establishing the need for training, designing training methods and content, and evaluating the outcome of training efforts (Salas et al., 2012). Some I/O psychologists actually conduct training programs, but in most cases these programs are delivered by professional trainers and/or by experts on the training topics involved.

Ensuring Equal Opportunity

Affirmative Action (AA) is an important element of the U.S. government's *Uniform Guidelines on Employee Selection Procedures*. A major goal of AA was to encourage organizations to actively seek out job applicants from underrepresented minority groups and in the process ensure that qualified minority candidates are not overlooked. Critics claim, though, that AA establishes quota systems in which certain percentages of people from particular groups must be hired or promoted even if they are not all well qualified. AA has thus become a controversial aspect of employment law.

Comstock/Stockbyte/Getty Images

Assessing Training Needs

To help organizations identify which employees need what kind of training, I/O psychologists typically carry out a *training needs assessment* that takes into account the organization's job categories, work force, and goals (Blanchard & Thacker, 2007; Goldstein, 1993; Salas et al., 2012). One aspect of this assessment involves looking at job-analysis reports. As mentioned earlier, the need for training is indicated when job analyses reveal that certain jobs require knowledge, skills, or abilities that employees do not have or that should be strengthened. A second aspect of a training needs assessment is to give employees a chance to describe the training they would like to have. This information often emerges from *personal development plans* created by employees and their supervisors. These plans usually include an evaluation of the person's strengths and weaknesses. The weaknesses identified suggest where training might be useful, especially for employees who are motivated to improve their skills (Klein, Noe, & Wang, 2006). For example, if the supervisor notes that an individual is awkward when making presentations, a course in public speaking might be worthwhile. Finally, I/O psychologists will look at the goals of the organization. If those goals include reducing workplace accidents or improving communication with international customers, then training in safety procedures or foreign-language skills would be in order.

Designing Training Programs

In designing organizational training programs, I/O psychologists are mindful of the basic principles that govern the learning and remembering of new information and skills. These principles, which are described in the learning and memory chapters, guide efforts to promote *transfer of training, feedback, training in general principles, overlearning,* and *sequencing.*

Transfer of Training

The most valuable training programs teach knowledge and skills that generalize, or transfer, to the workplace. If employees don't apply what they learn to improve job performance, then training efforts will have been wasted. Because promoting *transfer of training* is not always easy, I/O psychologists develop written materials and active learning exercises that both clarify the link between training and application and give employees experience at

Staying Goofy

Training programs for employees who portray cartoon characters at major theme parks emphasize the general principle that the organization's goal is to create a fantasy world for customers. This aspect of training helps the employees understand why it is important to follow the rule of remaining in character at all times. A carefully cultivated fantasy world would be disrupted if children were to see "Mickey Mouse" or "Bugs Bunny" holding his headgear under his arm while smoking a cigarette!

© *John Neubauer/PhotoEdit*

applying new knowledge and skills in simulated work situations. So trainees might first complete reading assignments, attend lectures, and watch videos illustrating effective approaches to dealing with customer complaints or defusing an office conflict. Then they might form groups to role-play using these approaches in a variety of typical workplace scenarios. These experiences enhance transfer of training, especially when the trainees' newly learned skills are supported and rewarded by their coworkers and supervisors (Kontoghiorghes, 2004).

Feedback

People learn new skills faster when they receive *feedback* on performance (Smither, London, & Reilly, 2005). In organizational training, this feedback usually comes from the trainer and/or other trainees. It takes the form of positive reinforcement following progress, constructive suggestions following errors or failure, and constant encouragement to continue the effort to learn. For example, after one trainee has role-played a new way to deal with an irate customer or a disgruntled employee, the trainer might play a videotape of the effort so that everyone can offer comments, compliments, and suggestions for improvement.

Training in General Principles

People tend to learn better and remember more of what they learn when they can see new information in a broader context—in other words, when they have some insight into how the information or skill they are learning fits into a bigger picture (Baldwin & Ford, 1988). We specifically designed the Linkages sections in this book to promote this kind of learning. In organizational settings, the "big picture" approach takes the form of *training in general principles,* which teaches not only how to do things in particular ways but also why it is important to do so. When training new customer service agents at a hotel, a bank, or an airline, for example, trainers often provide an orientation to the basic characteristics of these businesses, including how competitive they are. Understanding their company's need to survive intense competition will help employees recognize the importance of courtesy training in determining whether a customer remains a customer or goes elsewhere.

Overlearning

Practice makes perfect in all kinds of teaching and training. I/O psychologists emphasize the need for employees to practice using the information and skills learned in a training program until they reach a high level of performance. In fact, many training programs encourage employees to continue practicing until they are not only highly competent but are also able to perform the skill or use the information automatically without having to think much about it. This *overlearning* is seen in many everyday situations, most notably among experienced drivers, who can easily get from one place to another without paying much attention to the mechanics of steering, braking, and turning. Athletes and musicians, too, practice until their skills seem to unfold on their own. In the workplace, overlearning can save time and improve efficiency. For example, members of an experienced medical team can perform surgery using skills and information that, through overlearning, have become second nature to them. They do not have to stop and think about how critical tasks must be done; they simply do them (Driskell, Willis, & Copper, 1992).

Sequencing

Is it better to cram organizational training into one or two long, intense sessions over a single weekend or to schedule it in several shorter sessions over a longer period of time? Intense, *massed training* is certainly less expensive and less disruptive to employees' work schedules than *distributed training.* However, as described in the memory chapter, we know that people don't retain as much after massed practice ("cramming") as they do after distributed practice (Bjork, 1999; Donovan & Radosevich, 1999). Among other problems, massed training, like massed practice, can create boredom, inattention, and fatigue, all of which interfere with the learning and retention of new material. As most students can appreciate, an employee might remain motivated and interested during a one-hour training session but will probably be exhausted and inattentive by the end of an eight-hour training marathon. With this in mind, organizational training programs are set up using a distributed schedule whenever possible.

Evaluating Training Programs

Did a training program produce enough benefits to the organization to make it worth the time and money it cost? Should it be repeated? If so, should it be refined in some way? I/O psychologists conduct research on these important evaluation questions (Salas et al., 2012). As described in the introductory chapter, controlled experiments offer a way to draw reasonably strong cause-effect conclusions about the impact of a training program. In such experiments, a sample of employees who need training would be randomly selected and then randomly assigned either to receive training or to spend an equivalent amount of time away from their jobs pursuing some alternative activity. The value of the training program could then be measured in terms of the size of the difference in job performance between the trained (experimental) group and the untrained (control) group. However, organizations rarely ask for experimental research on their training programs. Most of them merely hope that what seemed to be valuable training did, in fact, deliver information and skills that employees will remember and use to improve their job performance. Accordingly, evaluation tends to focus on nonexperimental designs using criteria such as employees' reactions to training, what they remember about it, and the changes in behavior that follow it.

Evaluation Criteria

The first kind of evaluation criteria, called *training-level criteria,* includes data collected immediately after a training session. Trainees are typically asked to fill out questionnaires about how much they liked the training and how valuable they felt it was. Training sessions that receive low ratings on enjoyment, value, and effectiveness are not likely to be repeated, at least not in the same format. But just as some effective teachers may not be immediately appreciated by their students, some effective training programs may receive low post-session ratings. A complete evaluation should consider other criteria as well.

A second class of evaluation criteria, called *trainee-learning criteria,* includes information about what trainees actually learned from the training program. These criteria are usually measured by a test similar to a college final exam that is designed to determine each trainee's knowledge and skill in the areas covered by the training. In some cases, alternative forms of this test are given to the trainees before and after training to assess how much improvement has taken place.

Finally, *performance-level criteria* measure the degree to which the knowledge and skills learned in training transferred to the employees' workplace behavior. If employees now know how to do a better job on the assembly line or at the hotel's front desk but do not apply this knowledge to improve their performance, the training program has not been successful. Organizations often evaluate training on the basis of criteria such as number or quality of products produced, frequency of customer complaints, or number of sales made. Significant improvements following training might be a result of that training, but because so few organizations conduct controlled experimental evaluations of training, drawing this conclusion is often risky. The improvement might have had less to do with the training than with some other uncontrolled factor, such as a downturn in the economy that motivated employees to work harder in an effort to keep their jobs.

Most I/O psychologists recommend evaluating training programs on as many criteria as possible, because the apparent value of training can depend on which criteria you consider (Sitzmann et al., 2008). A program that looks great on one criterion might be dismal on another. In particular, many programs that get high employee ratings on enjoyment, value, and other training-level criteria fail to show effectiveness in terms of increased productivity, efficiency, or other performance-level criteria (Alvarez, Salas, & Garofano, 2004; May & Kahnweiler, 2000). For example, one training program that was designed to improve employees' interviewing skills received high ratings from the trainees, who showed improved interviewing during training. Unfortunately, these skills did not transfer to real interview situations (Campion & Campion, 1987). ("In Review: Recruiting, Selecting, and Training Employees" summarizes our discussion of these topics.)

RECRUITING, SELECTING, AND TRAINING EMPLOYEES   **IN REVIEW**

Process	Methods
Recruitment	Perform hiring needs assessment; place ads on websites and in newspapers; contact employment agencies; conduct campus interviews; solicit nominations from current employees; accept walk-in applications
Selection	Measure candidates' knowledge, skill, ability, and other personal characteristics using interviews, tests, and assessment centers; conduct validation studies to ensure that these KSAO criteria predict job success
Training	Conduct training needs assessment; design training to promote transfer of training, feedback, understanding of general principles, overlearning, and distributed training; evaluate training in terms of employee ratings of the experience and improvement in employee performance

In Review Questions

1. Employees tend to remember more from a training program when it is set up on a _____ rather than a _____ schedule.

2. Depending on walk-in applications is usually acceptable when hiring _____-level employees.

3. Assuring that your hiring criteria actually predict employees' job performance requires a _____.

EMPLOYEE MOTIVATION

What motivates employees to do their best?

In the chapter on motivation and emotion, we discuss some of the reasons why people engage in certain behaviors. These include biological, emotional, cognitive, and social factors that influence the direction, intensity, and persistence of behavior (Reeve, 1996; Spector, 2003). These factors are as important in the workplace, too (Nye et al., 2012). We can see motivation affecting the *direction* of work-related behavior in people's decisions about whether to work and what kind of job to seek. The effect of motivation on the *intensity* of work can be seen in how often an employee misses work, shows up late, works overtime, or goes beyond the call of duty. Motivation is also reflected in a worker's *persistence* at a task. Some employees give up as soon as difficulties arise, perhaps not bothering to pursue information if it is hard to find. Others keep trying, using every strategy possible until their efforts are successful.

Let's consider three theories that have been used by I/O psychologists to better understand employee motivation. One theory focuses on general factors that can affect behavior in the workplace and all other areas of life, too. The others highlight factors that are more specifically associated with motivation in the workplace.

ERG Theory

In the motivation and emotion chapter, we describe Abraham Maslow's (1943, 1970) theory, in which human behavior is seen as based on a hierarchy of needs or motives. These range from such basic biological needs as food and water to higher needs, such as esteem and self-actualization (see Figure 10.4). According to Maslow's theory, people must at least partially satisfy needs at the lower levels of the hierarchy before they will be motivated by higher-level goals. This is not always true, though. Hunger strikers, for example, ignore their need for food in order to pursue a protest that brings them closer to self-actualization.

To address some of the problems in Maslow's theory, Clayton Alderfer (1969) proposed **existence, relatedness, growth (ERG) theory**, which places human needs into three rather than five categories. *Existence needs* are things such as food and water that are necessary for survival. *Relatedness needs* include the need for social contact, especially having satisfying interactions with and attachments to others. *Growth needs* are those involving the development and use of a person's capabilities. These three categories of needs range from the most concrete (existence) to the most abstract (growth), but unlike the hierarchy of needs theory, ERG theory does not suggest that needs must be satisfied in any particular order. Instead, the strength of people's needs in each category is seen as rising and falling from time to time and from situation to situation. If a need in one area is fulfilled or frustrated, a person will be motivated to pursue some other needs. For example, after a relationship breakup frustrates relatedness needs, a person might focus on existence or growth needs by eating more or volunteering to work late. Similarly, losing a job frustrates growth needs, so a laid-off employee might focus on relatedness needs by seeking the social support of friends. Finally, a person obsessed with work-related growth needs might ignore those friends until after a big project is completed and it is time to party.

I/O psychologists apply ERG theory in the workplace by helping organizations recognize when employees' motivation to pursue job-related growth needs may be impaired because other need categories are frustrated or unfulfilled. For example, as we describe later, many organizations allow flexible working hours in the hope that employees will be more motivated on the job once they can more easily satisfy family-oriented relatedness needs.

Expectancy Theory

A second approach to employee motivation is similar in many respects to Julian Rotter's (1954, 1982) expectancy theory, which we discuss in the personality chapter. It seeks to explain how cognitive processes affect the impact of salary, bonuses, and other rewards on employees' behavior (Vroom, 1964). The main assumption of **expectancy theory** in the workplace is that employees behave in accordance with (1) what results they expect their actions to bring; and (2) how much they value those results. For example, the motivation to put out extra effort will increase if (1) employees expect a bonus for doing so; and (2) the bonus is valued enough to be worth the effort. Both expectancy and value are a matter of individual perception, though, so it is difficult to use expectancy theory to predict employee motivation by considering outcomes alone. If some workers don't believe that a supervisor will actually provide a bonus for extra work or if certain individuals are not strongly focused on money, the prospect of a bonus may not be equally motivating for all employees.

Workplace tests provide strong support for expectancy theory. One review of seventy-seven studies showed that how hard employees work and the quality of their work are strongly related to their expectancies about rewards and the value they place on those rewards (Van Eerde & Thierry, 1996). In other words, people tend to work hard when they believe it will be worth it to do so. Part of the task of industrial and organizational psychologists is to help organizations make employees feel that the effort needed for high performance is worthwhile.

existence, relatedness, growth (ERG) theory A theory of motivation that focuses on employees' needs at the levels of existence, relatedness, and growth.

expectancy theory A theory of workplace motivation in which employees are seen as acting in accordance with expected results and with how much they value those results.

In an ideal workplace, the goals of employees and employers are aligned. When they are not, a worker's motivation can suffer.

Goal-Setting Theory

A third approach to employee motivation, called **goal-setting theory**, focuses on the idea that workplace behavior is affected partly by people's general needs and expectations, but also by their intentions to achieve specific goals. These goals can be short term, such as finishing a report by the end of the week, or long term, such as earning a promotion within the next two years. A basic prediction of goal-setting theory is that employees will be motivated to choose, engage in, and persist at behaviors that take them closer to their goals.

Goal-setting theory has proven quite useful in motivating employees. There is evidence that arranging for employees to spend some time setting specific goals can lead to better job performance (Locke & Latham, 1990). Many organizations encourage their employees to engage in goal-setting activities (Yearta, Maitlis, & Briner, 1995), but I/O psychologists remind managers that some goals are more useful than others. The most motivating goals tend to be those that are (1) chosen, or at least accepted, by employees; (2) difficult enough to be challenging but not so difficult as to be impossible; and (3) specific enough (e.g., "increase sales by 10 percent") to allow employees to keep track of their progress and know when they have succeeded (Latham, 2004; Locke, 2000; Wegge & Haslam, 2005).

JOB SATISFACTION

Is pay the most important factor in job satisfaction?

Success in achieving workplace goals is one of many factors that can affect **job satisfaction**, the degree to which people like or dislike their jobs. Like other attitudes described in the chapter on social psychology, job satisfaction is made up of cognitive, emotional, and behavioral components (Schleicher, Watt, & Greguras, 2004). The cognitive component of job satisfaction includes *beliefs* about the job, such as "this job is too demanding" or "this job always presents new challenges." The emotional component includes positive or negative *feelings* about the job, such as boredom, excitement, anxiety, or pride. The behavioral component of job satisfaction is reflected in how people act in relation to their work, perhaps showing up early and staying late or maybe taking every opportunity to avoid work by calling in "sick."

Measuring Job Satisfaction

I/O psychologists assess employees' attitudes about their jobs in general (a *global approach*) and about various aspects of it (a *facet approach;* see Table 17.4). In most cases, job satisfaction is measured using questionnaires. Some questionnaires, such as the Job in General Scale (Cooper-Hakim & Viswesvaran, 2005), take a global approach. Others, such as the Job Satisfaction Survey (Spector, 1985), are designed to assess attitudes about several job facets, including pay, promotion, benefits, coworkers, and supervision (see Figure 17.2).

goal-setting theory A theory of workplace motivation focused on the idea that employees' behavior is shaped by their intention to achieve specific goals.

job satisfaction The degree to which people like or dislike their jobs.

TABLE 17.4   FACETS OF JOB SATISFACTION

Here are the results of a Gallup poll in which workers in the United States reported on their attitudes toward various facets of their jobs. Notice that workers tend to have differing attitudes about differing facets. For example, workers can be satisfied with their coworkers and supervisors but not satisfied with their salaries. How do you feel about your own job as "student"? Try listing those aspects of "studenting" that give you the most satisfaction, then take a poll among your student friends to see which aspects of their studentship give them the most satisfaction.

TRY THIS

Facet	Percent Satisfied
Relationships with coworkers	94
Physical safety conditions of work	92
Flexibility of hours	90
Amount of work	88
Job security	87
Supervisor	84
Recognition received at work	81
Amount of vacation time	79
Salary	75
Promotion opportunities	68
Health insurance	64
Retirement plan	62

Factors Affecting Job Satisfaction

Satisfaction with a job in general or with its various aspects can vary widely from one person to the next, even when people do the same job in the same organization (e.g., Schleicher, Watt, & Greguras, 2004; Staw & Cohen-Charash, 2005). In other words, some employees may like jobs or aspects of jobs that others hate. I/O psychologists have studied several environmental and personal factors that can influence people's job satisfaction (Chudzikowski et al., 2009; Sonnentag, 2012). Among the environmental factors are the requirements of the job, how much it pays, and how it affects workers' lives outside of the workplace. Among the personal factors are workers' attachment styles, gender, age, and ethnicity (e.g., Richards & Schat, 2011).

Job Requirements

Some jobs, such as those of assembly line workers, involve performing the same, relatively simple tasks again and again throughout the workday. Other jobs, such as those in management, are more complex, requiring workers to perform a different set of tasks each day, often in response to unpredictable requests or demands. Is the complexity of a job related

FIGURE 17.2

Pay Satisfaction Subscale from the Job Satisfaction Survey

Here are just four items from the pay satisfaction subscale of the Job Satisfaction Survey (Spector, 1985). As its name implies, this subscale focuses on employees' attitudes about the pay they receive in their jobs. Other subscales assess attitudes toward other job facets, such as promotion opportunities, benefits, co-workers, and supervisors.

Source: Paul E. Spector.

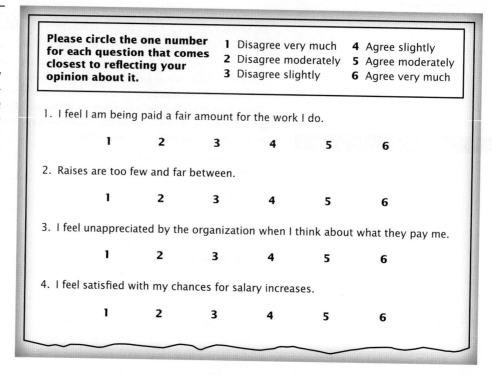

to workers' job satisfaction? In general, yes. People tend to be more satisfied with jobs that are more complex (Fried & Ferris, 1987; Melamed, Fried, & Froom, 2001). As described in the chapter on motivation and emotion, this higher satisfaction may relate to the fact that more complex jobs tend to be more interesting, more challenging, and more likely to create a sense of responsibility and control in setting and achieving goals (Maynard, Joseph, & Maynard, 2006). However, not everyone responds to complex jobs in the same way (Jex et al., 2002). A complex job may create dissatisfaction among people who don't have the knowledge, skills, abilities, or other characteristics to do it successfully (Hackman & Oldham, 1980). Even individuals who have the necessary knowledge and skills may be dissatisfied with a complex job if their personality characteristics lead them to prefer simpler, less intellectually demanding work (Loher et al., 1985).

Salary

Many workers feel underpaid, but as discussed in the motivation and emotion chapter, higher salaries alone do not necessarily lead to higher levels of job satisfaction (Igalens & Roussel, 1999). One study of recent college graduates found a correlation of only +.17 between starting salary and overall job satisfaction (Brasher & Chen, 1999). A main reason for this low correlation is that a substantial salary may not compensate for other unsatisfactory aspects of a job, such as poor working conditions or lack of respect from supervisors. In fact, knowing that salary and pay raise decisions are made in a fair way can be more important to job satisfaction than the amount of money employees receive (Liao & Rupp, 2005; Simons & Roberson, 2003). As a result, students working at low-paying jobs may be more satisfied than executives who earn six-figure salaries. The student's satisfaction may come from knowing that everyone doing the same job is getting the same pay, whereas the executive may experience *relative deprivation,* the perception that others are unfairly receiving more benefits for the same or lesser effort (see the social psychology chapter).

Work-Family Conflict

Compared to many years ago, the number of two-career couples and single-parent families has increased in the industrialized world (Vespa, Lewis, & Kreider, 2013). With this increase comes more conflict between the demands of a job and the demands of family life (O'Driscoll, Brough, & Kalliath, 2006; ten Brummelhuis & Bakker, 2012). A common example of this conflict is when the need to care for a sick child or attend a child's school play interferes with a parent's work responsibilities. For both men and women, the amount of conflict between the demands of job and family is strongly and consistently related to job satisfaction (e.g., Ford, Heinen, & Langkamer, 2007; Lapierre & Allen, 2006). I/O psychologists help organizations deal with this source of job dissatisfaction by developing *family-friendly work policies* that help employees balance work and family responsibilities. For example, *flextime* is a policy that allows parents to work an eight-hour day but frees them from the standard nine-to-five schedule. One parent can come to work at, say, 9:30 a.m. after taking the children to school and then stay on the job beyond 5:00 p.m. to complete an eight-hour day. The other parent can start work at, say, 7:30 a.m. and then leave early to pick up the children from school.

Gender, Age, and Ethnicity

The many studies that have compared job satisfaction in men and women have found few, if any, differences—even when the men and women compared were doing quite different jobs (e.g., Moncrief et al., 2000). Job satisfaction is related to age, though. Older workers tend to be more satisfied than younger ones, but the picture may be a bit more complicated than that (Clark, Oswald, & Warr, 1996; Hedge, Borman, & Lammlein, 2006). For example, among people who enter the world of work immediately after high school or community college, job satisfaction may at first be quite high but may soon begin to decline, especially among males. Satisfaction ratings then tend to increase slowly but steadily from about age thirty until retirement. This pattern may occur because young workers with relatively little education may find themselves in jobs that not only are poorly paid but also offer few of the features associated with job satisfaction, such as complexity, control over time, or opportunity to set goals and tasks (White & Spector, 1987).

Some studies of workers in the United States have found slightly higher job satisfaction among whites than among nonwhites (e.g., Jones & Schaubroeck, 2004; Tuch & Martin, 1991), but others have found no differences (e.g., Brush, Moch, & Pooyan, 1987). In fact, when comparisons are made across groups doing the same jobs, ethnicity does not appear to be a major factor in job satisfaction. Culture can have an influence though (Benton & Overtree, 2012). For example, one study found that job satisfaction among workers in the United States tends to be related to internal factors, such as feeling stimulated and challenged by their jobs, while satisfaction among workers in China may be related more to external factors, such as being offered new opportunities or satisfying the requests of their employers (Chudzikowski et al., 2009).

Minimizing Work-Family Conflict

TRY THIS To help working couples deal with the demands of work and family obligations, many organizations have adopted family-friendly programs and policies, including workplace daycare services and the availability of flexible work schedules (flex time). These programs and policies have been associated with higher levels of job satisfaction and less absenteeism among employees with children (Baltes et al., 1999; Scandura & Lankau, 1997). *Fortune* magazine publishes an annual issue listing the best U.S. companies to work for. Look through this year's issue to see what kinds of family-friendly policies these companies have created.

© michaeljung/Shutterstock.com

IS JOB SATISFACTION GENETIC?

In the chapter on motivation and emotion, we mention that people's overall level of happiness, or subjective well-being, may be determined partly by genetic influences. Could those same influences operate in the workplace in relation to job satisfaction?

What am I being asked to believe or accept?

Richard Arvey and his colleagues (1989) have suggested that differences in job satisfaction reflect genetic predispositions toward liking or not liking a job.

What evidence is available to support the assertion?

People's temperament and personality are certainly influenced by genetics. Research in I/O psychology shows that these genetically influenced personality characteristics are related to people's job satisfaction (Illies & Judge, 2003). In one study, for example, hostility and other personality traits measured in adolescence were found to be significantly related to job satisfaction up to fifty years later (Judge, Heller, & Mount, 2002). Because personality is relatively stable across the life span, the link between personality and job satisfaction may explain why changing jobs has very little effect on job satisfaction. In fact, research suggests a "honeymoon-hangover" effect, in that job satisfaction often rises immediately after starting a new job, but then tends to decrease quickly to about the same level as it was at the previous job (Boswell, Boudreau, & Tichy, 2005). These data suggest that job satisfaction is at least indirectly shaped by inherited predispositions.

However, Arvey and his colleagues (1989) conducted what may be the only direct investigation of the role of genetics in job satisfaction. They selected thirty-four pairs of genetically identical twins who had been separated and raised in different environments. They then arranged for these people to complete a job satisfaction questionnaire. The questionnaire responses showed a strong positive correlation between the twins' job satisfaction; if one twin was satisfied, the other one tended to be satisfied, too. If one was dissatisfied, the other twin tended to be dissatisfied as well. The researchers suggested that because the members of each twin pair had been raised in different environments, genetic factors were at least partly responsible for creating the observed similarity in job satisfaction ratings.

Are there alternative ways of interpreting the evidence?

These results suggest a strong genetic influence, but they could have been affected by factors other than a genetic predisposition to be satisfied or dissatisfied with a job. For example, although the twins grew up in different home environments, their work environments might have been quite similar, and it may have been those similar work environments that produced similar satisfaction ratings. Why would separated twins have similar work environments? For one thing, the innate abilities, interests, behavioral tendencies, or physical characteristics that identical twins might share could have led them into similar kinds of jobs. Some pairs might have selected jobs that tend to be satisfying, whereas other pairs might have taken jobs that tend to be less satisfying. A pair of bright, athletic, or musically

Genes may play a role in job satisfaction, but other factors are surely at work as well.

talented twins might have found it possible to have complex, interesting, and challenging jobs and to enjoy a high level of satisfaction. A less fortunate set of twins may have been unable to qualify for the kind of job they might want and may have settled for more routine work that leaves them feeling dissatisfied. In other words, it may be that genes don't shape job satisfaction itself but do help shape characteristics that influence people's access to satisfying work.

What additional evidence would help evaluate the alternatives?

One way to assess the impact of job characteristics on the high correlation in twins' job satisfaction ratings is to look at the nature of the twins' jobs. When Arvey and his colleagues (1989) did this, they found that the twins did tend to hold jobs that were similar in several ways, including overall job complexity and some of the skills required. A more complete assessment of the jobs and job environments would be needed, however, to determine the strength of these nongenetic factors in creating positively correlated job satisfaction ratings.

It will also be important to look for specific genes that might be associated with job satisfaction. Research has already linked job satisfaction with two specific genetic markers associated with the activity of the neurotransmitters dopamine and serotonin (Song, Li, & Arvey, 2011), and this line of research will undoubtedly continue.

What conclusions are most reasonable?

Research in I/O psychology suggests that individual differences in job satisfaction are probably related to workers' characteristics, some of which are influenced by genetics. However, the precise mechanisms through which genetics might affect job satisfaction are not yet clear (Ilies & Judge, 2003). It is most likely that job satisfaction, like so many other aspects of behavior and mental processes, is shaped by both genetic and environmental influences. So there is no single reason why people differ in terms of job satisfaction. How satisfied we are with our work can be predicted to some extent by job characteristics and to some extent by personal characteristics (Gerhart, 2005), but the outcome in a given case is ultimately a matter of who does what job in what organization.

Consequences of Job Satisfaction

Organizations spend a lot of time, money, and effort to try to maintain a reasonable level of job satisfaction among their employees. They do so, if for no other reason, because job satisfaction is linked to a variety of positive consequences for individuals, their coworkers, and their organizations (Harter et al., 2010). Dissatisfaction with a job can lead to numerous negative consequences.

Job Performance

Research shows that people who are satisfied with their jobs tend to be more motivated, work harder, and perform better than employees who are dissatisfied (e.g., Fisher, 2003; Judge et al., 2001). The positive correlation between job satisfaction and performance makes sense, and though a correlation alone cannot confirm that satisfaction is causing good performance, it is certainly consistent with that conclusion (Harrison, Newman, & Roth, 2006). It's possible, though, that people who perform better feel more satisfied with their jobs as a result (Jacobs & Solomon, 1977).

Organizational Citizenship Behavior

organizational citizenship behavior (OCB) A willingness to go beyond formal job requirements in order to help coworkers and/or the organization.

Job satisfaction is also associated with **organizational citizenship behavior (OCB)**, a willingness to go beyond formal job requirements in order to help coworkers and/or the organization (Ilies, Scott, & Judge, 2006; Organ, Podsakoff, & MacKenzie, 2006). As in the case of job performance, it is difficult to determine whether job satisfaction causes increased organizational citizenship behavior or whether engaging in OCB causes increased job satisfaction. Further, OCB may reflect factors other than job satisfaction, such as personality characteristics (Chiaburu et al., 2011). And some cases of OCB might occur as part of a strategy designed to get a pay raise or promotion or reach some other personal goal. In one study, for example, employees who believed it would help their chances for promotion engaged in high levels of OCB before being promoted, then reduced their OCB afterward (Hui, Lam, & Law, 2000).

Turnover

Every organization must deal with a certain amount of *turnover*, or loss of employees. Some turnover is involuntary, as in cases of disability or dismissal, but much of it is voluntary (Harman et al., 2007). Some employees simply quit, and they tend to be employees whose job satisfaction is low (e.g., Griffeth, Hom, & Gaertner, 2000). However, in order to avoid unemployment, few dissatisfied workers quit until and unless they have found another job (Kammeyer-Mueller et al., 2005). So the relationship between job dissatisfaction and turnover is strongest when people are able to find other jobs (Trevor, 2001). When alternative employment is unavailable, even dissatisfied workers tend to stay put.

Absenteeism

You might expect that absenteeism, like voluntary turnover, would be strongly related to low job satisfaction. However, the correlation between job satisfaction and attendance is surprisingly weak (Farrell & Stamm, 1988). True, there is a tendency for dissatisfied employees to be absent more frequently than those who are satisfied, but other factors, including personal or family illness, work-family conflicts, and the financial consequences of missing work are far more important in determining who shows up and who doesn't (Dalton & Mesch, 1991; Erickson, Nichols, & Ritter, 2000).

Aggression and Counterproductive Work Behavior

Job dissatisfaction is one cause of workplace aggression as well as of theft and other forms of *counterproductive work behavior (CWB)*. Assaults or murders involving co-workers or supervisors are rare (Barling, Dupre, & Kelloway, 2009; LeBlanc, Dupre, & Barling, 2006), but theft, computer hacking, and other forms of CWB by employees and former employees are commonplace. Employee theft in the United States alone costs organizations billions of dollars each year (Brown, 2010; Gatewood & Feild, 2001). In fact, employees steal more from their employers than do shoplifters (Hollinger et al., 1996; Rob, 2012). The direct and indirect costs of other forms of counterproductive work behavior, such as sabotage, working slowly, or doing jobs incorrectly, are staggering. But the true cost of CWB can be hard to determine because so much of it goes unnoticed (Bennett & Robinson, 2000).

LINKAGES How do stressors affect job performance? (a link to Health, Stress, and Coping)

As illustrated in Figure 17.3, it is often stress in the workplace that leads to job dissatisfaction and negative emotions, such as anger and anxiety (e.g., Spector, Fox, & Domalgaski, 2006). These emotions, in turn, can result in CWB, especially among employees who feel they have been treated unfairly or have little or no control over stressors (Aquino, Tripp, & Bies, 2006; Penney & Spector, 2005; Whitman et al., 2012). Why does lack of control matter? As described in the chapter on health, stress, and coping, when people feel they have control over the work situation, they are more likely to perceive stressors as challenges to be overcome and to try constructive means of doing so. Suppose, for example, that a supervisor suddenly assigns a difficult task to an employee, who must complete it by the next day or face serious consequences. If the employee senses enough control over the situation to complete the task on time, this stressful assignment is likely to be perceived as a challenge to be mastered. If the employee doesn't have that sense of control

FIGURE 17.3

Job Satisfaction and Counterproductive Work Behavior

Workplace stressors can lead to job dissatisfaction, which leads to negative emotions and counterproductive work behavior, especially among employees who feel mistreated and unable to control stressors.

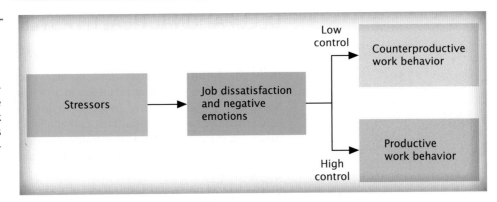

and believes it is impossible to meet the deadline, this stressful assignment will probably create dissatisfaction and negative emotions, such as resentment. This person is at elevated risk for engaging in counterproductive work behavior directed at the supervisor, the organization, or other employees.

LINKAGES What causes workplace aggression? (a link to Social Psychology)

AGGRESSION IN THE WORKPLACE   LINKAGES

In the chapter on social psychology, we describe a number of biological, psychological, and environmental factors that appear to be responsible for creating and/or triggering human aggression and violence. These factors operate in the workplace, too, but aggression between or against workers differs in some ways from violence outside of the workplace (Hershcovis et al., 2007).

About 70 percent of workplace homicides are committed against employees by strangers (U.S. Department of Justice, 2011). Despite well-publicized cases of disgruntled employees killing coworkers or supervisors, employees actually commit only about 21 percent of workplace homicides and less than 10 percent of workplace assaults (U.S. Department of Justice, 2011). Convenience store clerks, taxi drivers, and others who deal directly with the public, handle money, and work alone at night are the employees at greatest risk to be victims of workplace aggression (LeBlanc, Dupre, & Barling, 2006). Most aggression against these people is *instrumental aggression*, meaning that the aggressor's intent is not necessarily to injure but to achieve a goal such as getting money or other valuables (Merchant & Lundell, 2001). Though the perpetrator often uses a weapon to intimidate the employee, these aggressive incidents do not usually result in physical injury.

Most cases of injury in the workplace occur in the course of aggressive assaults on doctors, nurses, and other health care workers, sales clerks, bartenders, and food servers by patients or customers (Büssing & Höge, 2004; LeBlanc & Barling, 2004). Often these injuries occur under stressful circumstances—such as during emergency room treatment—in which pain, anger, fatigue, and frustration lead to an impulsive, emotional, aggressive outburst. In contrast to instrumental aggression, the perpetrator's intent in these cases is to injure the employee victim.

Aggression in the workplace is typically verbal, and the result is usually resentment and hurt feelings, not bruised bodies (Barling, Dupre, & Kelloway, 2009; Grubb et al., 2005). Like road-rage incidents, employee-to-employee aggression is often the by-product of an impulsive outburst under time pressure or other stressful conditions, such as workplace injustices or abusive supervision (Berry, Ones, & Sackett, 2007; Inness, Barling, & Turner, 2005). Sometimes, though, this form of aggression reflects a continuing attempt by one employee to control others through intimidation or bullying (Bies, Tripp, & Kramer, 1997; Grubb et al., 2005).

OCCUPATIONAL HEALTH PSYCHOLOGY

How can workplace accidents be prevented?

In the chapter on health, stress, and coping, we defined *health psychology* as a field devoted to understanding psychological factors in how people stay healthy, why they become ill, and how they respond when they do get ill (Taylor, 2002). **Occupational health psychology** is concerned with psychological factors that affect the health, safety, and well-being of employees in the workplace. I/O psychologists help promote the goals of occupational health psychology by consulting with organizations about ways to reduce threats to employees posed by undue stress, accidents, and hazards. Their success in this enterprise is reflected in the fact that today, most workplaces are safer and healthier than employees' own homes (National Safety Council, 2004).

Physical Conditions Affecting Health

Many physical conditions in the workplace have the potential to cause illness and injury (Lund et al., 2006). Accordingly, in the United States, the Occupational Safety and Health Administration (OSHA) establishes regulations designed to minimize employees' exposure to hazards arising from sources such as infectious agents, toxic chemicals, or dangerous machinery. For example, to guard against the spread of AIDS, U.S. doctors, dentists, nurses, and other health care workers have been asked to follow a set of safety procedures called *universal precautions*, which include wearing disposable gloves when drawing blood, giving injections, or performing dental procedures and discarding needles and other sharp objects into special sealed containers.

These procedures may be effective in reducing the spread of disease, but health care workers do not always follow them, possibly because of heavy workloads and lack of encouragement from supervisors (McDiarmid & Condon, 2005). I/O psychologists play a role in this aspect of occupational health psychology by promoting organizational support for following proper safety procedures and by designing safety training that employees will actually use in the workplace (Smith-Crowe, Burke, & Landis, 2003). They also help protect employees' health by creating reminders to be careful on the job and by consulting with organizations to minimize stressors that can lead to illness or injury.

One of these stressors comes in the form of jobs that require performing specific movements in the same way over long periods of time, such as turning a screwdriver or making cut after cut in pieces of plastic. Eventually, these movements can create *repetitive strain injuries*, in which joints become inflamed, sometimes producing permanent damage. The most familiar of these injuries is *carpal tunnel syndrome*, a condition of the wrist that produces pain, numbness, and weakness in the fingers. Although often associated with using a computer keyboard or mouse, carpal tunnel syndrome can be caused by many other activities involving the fingers and wrist. Psychologists have been involved in two approaches to preventing repetitive strain injuries. First, as we describe in the introductory chapter, those working in *engineering psychology* (also called *human factors psychology*) consult with industrial designers to create tools and equipment that are less physically stressful to use. As a result, people who perform typing tasks for many hours each day now usually place a pad in front of their keyboard that provides support and helps keep their wrists from twisting. Second, I/O psychologists are working with organizations to ensure that employees whose jobs require repetitive actions be allowed to take breaks that are long enough and frequent enough to rest the body parts at risk for strain injuries. These psychologists are also working with employees to ensure that they follow the recommended break schedule.

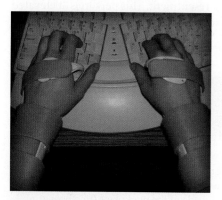

Doing It Over and Over

TRY THIS Performing the same movements on the job hour after hour and day after day can lead to *repetitive strain injuries*. This employee's keyboard movements resulted in a painful and potentially disabling condition called *carpal tunnel syndrome*. Wearing a wrist brace can reduce the pain somewhat, but I/O and engineering psychologists know that improved wrist support for keyboard users can help prevent the problem in the first place. To appreciate the impact of psychologists' consultation efforts, browse some online computer equipment catalogs, such as geeks.com or tigerdirect.com, and calculate the percentage of keyboards, mice, and other devices that have been designed to minimize the possibility of repetitive strain injuries.

Lanica Klein/Photos.com

occupational health psychology A field concerned with psychological factors that affect the health, safety, and well-being of employees.

Work Schedules, Health, and Safety

The arrangements mentioned earlier that allow employees to adjust their working hours are but one part of a more general trend away from the traditional nine-to-five workday. As many organizations expand their hours of service, including to twenty-four hours a day, seven days a week, more and more employees are on the job during what once would have been considered "odd hours." They may work at night or on weekends and follow shift patterns once associated mainly with hospitals, law enforcement, and factories. Others are working more than eight hours a day but less than five days a week, and in the face of staffing cutbacks, still others may be working more than forty hours a week. Whether undertaken by choice or by assignment, these nontraditional work schedules can create stress and fatigue that can adversely affect employees' health.

Staying Sharp

I/O psychologists' research on the negative impact of extended work shifts has led to organizational and U.S. government rules requiring rest breaks at fixed intervals for commercial airline pilots, long-haul bus and truck drivers, and others whose jobs require constant attention to complex tasks and systems. The rules also limit the total number of hours these employees can work in any twenty-four-hour period.

Walter Hodges/keepsake/Corbis

Rotating Shift Work

The negative effects of such schedules can be especially great among employees who change work shifts from week to week, rotating from evenings to days to nights, for example (Demerouti et al., 2004). As we describe in the chapter on consciousness, these shift changes disrupt employees' *circadian rhythms* of eating, sleeping, and wakefulness, resulting in a number of unpleasant mental and physical symptoms. A major problem with working night shifts, for example, is fatigue, irritability, and reduced cognitive sharpness resulting from difficulty in getting to sleep or staying asleep during the day (Morrissette, 2013). Some shift workers also experience upset stomachs and other symptoms of digestive distress (Rouch et al., 2005). These problems may be far less troubling for workers whose night shift assignments last long enough that they can get used to their "backward" schedule (Barton & Folkard, 1991), but rotating shift work can also be disruptive to employees' social relationships and may create work-family conflicts (Barnes-Farrell et al., 2008). Absenteeism, too, may increase, especially among younger workers who are new to shift work, and burnout and earlier retirement may be more common among workers on rotating shifts than among those on fixed schedules (Shen & Dicker, 2008).

Long Shifts and Long Weeks

Many organizations now have longer-than-normal work shifts. For example, some have set up ten-hour shifts that allow employees to work forty hours in four days, thus creating an extra day off. Others have replaced three 8-hour work shifts with a more efficient system of two 12-hour shifts that allows workers even more time off. Many employees like these arrangements, so longer shifts can lead to greater job satisfaction and better job performance (Baltes et al., 1999).

However, extended workdays may create health and performance problems for some workers in some jobs (Lamberg, 2004). This possibility is suggested by research on drivers of intercity buses. Those who drove longer routes that required being on the road for up to fourteen hours a day with few rest breaks tended to use stimulants to stay alert, drink alcohol to counteract the stimulants after arrival, and experience sleep disturbances, various physical symptoms, and anxiety and fatigue. They were also more likely than drivers with shorter shifts to be involved in accidents (Raggatt, 1991).

There are also dangers in requiring employees to work more than forty-eight hours per week, especially when those employees would prefer not to do so. These involuntary extensions of the work week have been associated with a number of employee health problems, particularly heart disease (Sparks et al., 1997). Accordingly, nations of the European Union have adopted regulations setting work weeks at a maximum of forty-eight hours. So far, there are no such governmental regulations in the United States.

Stress, Accidents, and Safety

Though most accidents occur outside the workplace, workplace safety is still a major focus of organizations and, therefore, of I/O psychologists (Barling & Frone, 2004). In just one recent year, 4,628 workers were killed and nearly 3 million others were injured on the job in the United States alone (U.S. Bureau of Labor Statistics, 2012). Motor vehicle accidents account for nearly half of all workplace fatalities. Falls and equipment accidents account for about another third of these deaths.

Longer-than-normal work shifts and extended work weeks are just one source of the occupational stress contributing to the fatigue, inattention, cognitive impairment, sleepiness, and other problems that elevate the risk of workplace accidents (Caldwell, 2012). I/O psychologists have identified many other individual and organizational factors that contribute to stress-related accidents. These include, for example, lack of clear instructions, heavy workloads, concern about job security, sexual harassment or ethnic discrimination, burnout, and workplace bullying (e.g., Berdahl & Moore, 2006; Hoel, Faragher, & Cooper, 2004; Schabracq, 2003; Sparks, Faragher, & Cooper, 2001). Accidents are also more likely when the *climate of safety* in the workplace is poor, meaning that there is a lack of safety training, too little supervisory emphasis on following safety rules, and a tendency for workers to ignore those rules (Griffin & Neal, 2000). Accidents are least common in organizations that create a *total safety culture* by providing adequate safety training for employees, conducting thorough and frequent safety inspections, and ensuring that supervisors consistently communicate the need for and value of safety (Newnam, Griffin, & Mason, 2008; Wallace, Popp, & Mondore, 2006).

WORK GROUPS AND WORK TEAMS

Do groups need supervision to work well?

A great deal of workplace activity is accomplished by groups of individuals working together. I/O psychologists have been at the forefront of efforts to help organizations maximize the effectiveness and efficiency of work groups and work teams (e.g., Barsade & Gibson, 2012; Ormiston & Wong, 2012; Shuffler, DiazGranados, & Salas, 2011). A **work group** is defined as at least two people who interact with one another as they perform the same or different tasks. The four servers waiting on customers during the dinner shift at a restaurant would be an example of a work group. A **work team** is a special kind of work group in which (1) each member's activities are coordinated with and depend on the activities of other members; (2) each member has a specialized role; and (3) members are working to accomplish a common goal (West, Borrill, & Unsworth, 1998). The entire staff on duty during the restaurant's dinner shift would be considered a work team. All members of the team are working on the same task with the same goal in mind—namely, to successfully serve customers as quickly and efficiently as possible. Further, each team member has a specialized role: greeters seat customers, servers take orders and deliver the food prepared by the cooks, and managers monitor progress, direct employees, and fill in at various tasks as needed. Whether it involves food service, brain surgery, automobile repair, or other workplace activities, an effective work team performs like the proverbial well-oiled machine.

Autonomous Work Groups

In most organizations, work groups and work teams operate in a traditional way, meaning that as in the case of a restaurant or grocery store, all workers report to a manager

work group At least two people who interact with one another as they perform the same or different workplace tasks.

work team A work group in which the members' specialized activities are coordinated and interdependent as they work toward a common goal.

Medical Teamwork

The doctors, nurses, and technicians who join forces to perform surgery are a perfect example of a work team. Everyone on the surgical team is devoted to the same goal of completing a successful operation, but each performs a somewhat different task in a coordinated way under the direction of the surgeon, who acts as the team leader.

Jupiterimages/Photos.com

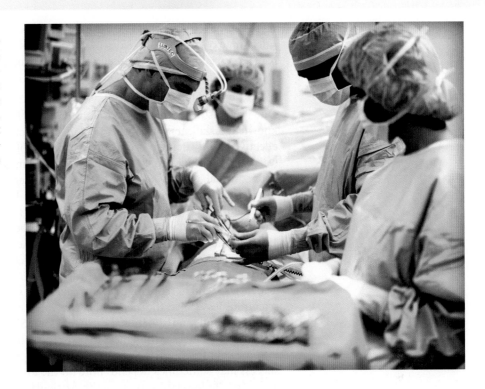

who directs and supervises their activities. However, a growing number of organizations today are establishing **autonomous work groups (AWGs)** that manage themselves and do not report to anyone for routine daily supervision. Instead, once AWGs are given a work assignment, it is up to them to determine how best to accomplish their goal and then work together to achieve it. The classic example of AWGs can be seen in the manufacturing sector. Automobiles and other consumer products were once built on long assembly lines by large numbers of workers who each performed only one small part of the process before passing the product on to another worker, who performed the next step. In AWGs, however, each member rotates among jobs, such that everyone is involved in every aspect of assembly from time to time. The team members also design and order their own tools, conduct their own product inspections to ensure quality and performance, and even participate in hiring and firing decisions. Many brands of automobiles and other large pieces of equipment are now assembled in AWG factories that feature a series of workstations where perhaps half a dozen employees assemble the entire product or a substantial portion of it.

AWGs have benefits for employees and for organizations. In one comparison study, employees in AWG factories reported higher levels of job satisfaction than did employees of traditional factories (Cordery, Mueller, & Smith, 1991). Further, the productivity of AWGs has been shown to be at least as good as and sometimes better than traditional arrangements despite the fact that AWG facilities don't need as many supervisors and thus cost less to run (Hoegl & Parboteeah, 2006; Stewart, 2006).

Group Leadership

Workplace groups almost always have leaders. Even in AWGs, leaders tend to emerge (Taggar, Hackett, & Saha, 1999), although the leadership roles may sometimes be shared by more than one person (Uhl-Bien, Marion, & McKelvey, 2007). And AWGs are themselves embedded in organizations that operate through a leadership hierarchy (Kaiser, Hogan, & Craig, 2008). At each level, designated leaders direct or supervise the activities of others, set group and organizational objectives, figure out how individual employees can best contribute to

autonomous work groups (AWGs)
Self-managed employee groups that do not report to anyone for routine daily supervision.

those objectives, and make sure employees perform the tasks assigned to them. Let's consider some of the characteristics of good leaders, how good leaders behave, and how they relate to various members of their work groups and work teams.

What Makes a Good Leader?

One way to study leadership is to look at lots of leaders to see whether particular kinds of knowledge, skill, ability, or other personal characteristics are associated with those who are effective and those who are ineffective. Much of what social and I/O psychologists have learned about the KSAOs of effective leaders comes from their research on managers (e.g., Peterson et al., 2003; Zaccarco, 2007). That research suggests that some characteristics are seen by almost everyone as necessary for good leadership. For example, a large study of leadership effectiveness in sixty-two countries found that being intelligent, trustworthy, and team-oriented were universally rated as important traits of good leaders (House et al., 1999). These results are supported by other studies showing that intelligence is consistently important for competent managerial performance (Chemers, Watson, & May, 2000; Judge, Colbert, & Ilies, 2004). In other words, smarter leaders tend to be better leaders. Good leaders also tend to score high on agreeableness, emotional stability, extraversion, and conscientiousness (Silverthorne, 2001). The value of other leadership traits can depend on social, cultural, and situational factors (Hoyt, Simon, & Innella, 2011; Livingston et al., 2012). For instance, a willingness to take risks tends to be seen as a positive leadership trait in some countries and as a negative trait in others (House et al., 1999). Further, a leader's success may sometimes depend more on the loyalty, organizational citizenship behaviors, and other "followership" traits of the particular people they lead than on their leadership style (Popper, 2011).

How Do Good Leaders Behave?

Another way to study leadership is to explore the things that effective and ineffective leaders do. The foundation for this research was provided by the Ohio State Leadership Studies, which began in 1945. The first step in this extensive program was to collect 1,800 critical incidents of effective and ineffective leader behavior. An example of "effective" leadership might be a situation in which a manager suggested that a troubled employee transfer to a less-demanding job; an example of "ineffective" leadership might be a situation in which a manager shouted at an employee who questioned the leader's decision. These and other studies have revealed that specific kinds of leader behaviors can have profound effects on group members and organizations. For example, one study found that army platoons led by active and involved leaders were especially effective under combat conditions (Bass et al., 2003). The Ohio State researchers identified two dimensions on which leaders typically vary. The first, called *consideration*, is the degree to which a leader shows concern for the welfare of employees, including friendly and supportive behavior that makes the workplace more pleasant. The second dimension, called *initiating structure*, is the degree to which a leader coordinates employee efforts by assigning tasks and clarifying expectations so that group members know what is required of them to perform well.

The relationship-motivated leaders described in the social psychology chapter tend to be high on the consideration dimension, whereas the task-motivated leaders described there tend to be high on the initiating-structure dimension. Where managers fall on each of these dimensions of leadership style can have important effects on employees (Eagly, Johannesen-Schmidt, & van Engen, 2003; Keller, 2006; Zaccarco, 2007). In one study, workers in a truck-manufacturing plant were asked to rate their immediate supervisors on the dimensions of consideration and initiating structure (Fleishman & Harris, 1962). These ratings were then related to the number of complaints these employees filed against their supervisors and the rate at which they quit their jobs (voluntary turnover). There were more grievances and much higher turnover among employees whose supervisors had been rated low on consideration than among those whose supervisors had been rated high on consideration. More grievances were also filed by employees whose supervisors were high on initiating structure, but there is more to that part of the story. The highest rates of grievance and turnover occurred among employees whose supervisors were not only high on initiating structure but also low on consideration. As long as supervisors were high on consideration, they could be high on initiating structure without creating a lot of grievances and turnover. In other words, it is possible for a leader to be firm but fair, thus promoting maximum performance with a minimum of complaints and employee losses.

Leader-Member Interactions

Are leadership styles like the relatively stable traits described in the personality chapter? Do they create consistent leadership behaviors toward all group members in all situations? Some leaders might fit this description, but **leader-member exchange (LMX) theory** suggests that as leaders gain experience with their groups over time, most of them tend to adopt different styles with two different kinds of subordinates (Dansereau, Graen, & Haga, 1975; Naidoo et al., 2011). Leaders tend to offer the most consideration and best treatment to subordinates who make up the employee *ingroup*. These individuals tend to be the best performers and are seen by the leader as competent, trustworthy, loyal, and dependable (Bauer & Green, 1996). As such, ingroup members' opinions and requests tend to carry more weight with the leader than do those of *outgroup* employees, who are seen by the leader as less competent, less reliable, and potentially expendable. Ingroup members may also benefit from having "inside" information from the leader, more helpful mentoring, and perhaps even inflated performance evaluations (Duarte, Goodson, & Klich, 1993; Scandura & Schriesheim, 1994). Leaders give outgroup employees less opportunity to influence decisions and tend to supervise them by giving high structure and low consideration (Dansereau, Graen, & Haga, 1975).

More than eighty studies of leader-member interaction patterns support the existence of employee ingroups and outgroups. They also confirm the tendency for ingroup members to experience more job satisfaction and less occupational stress and to more often engage in organizational citizenship behaviors (Ilies, Nahrgang, & Morgeson, 2007; Schyns, 2006). By comparison, the job satisfaction and performance of outgroup members is likely to suffer, especially if they feel that the organizational climate is unjust (Hooper & Martin, 2007).

Traditional leadership models are based on situations in which there is face-to-face interaction among team members and leaders. Do these models apply equally well to "virtual teams" whose members communicate electronically (Zigurs, 2003)? Industrial and organizational psychologists are beginning to investigate this question, and the results of their research on *e-leadership* will undoubtedly expand our understanding of leadership as it operates in today's increasingly technology-driven workplaces.

Researchers have also begun to explore the idea of *shared leadership*, an organizational structure that focuses less on formally defined leadership roles and more on the informal structure that describes how things happen naturally in work teams (Carter & DeChurch, 2012; Contractor et al., 2012). People in a shared leadership framework do not assume that one person must hold the majority of influence in a team. Such a framework may be especially useful for understanding teams in which there is no overall "leader," as is often the case when groups of equally distinguished scientists from various fields work together on a single project. Shared leadership models may also be particularly relevant in workplaces where interdependent individuals work in groups whose membership frequently changes (Carter & DeChurch, 2012).

leader-member exchange (LMX) theory A theory suggesting that leaders tend to supervise ingroup and outgroup employees in different ways.

FOCUS ON RESEARCH METHODS

CAN PEOPLE LEARN TO BE CHARISMATIC LEADERS?

Some people's leadership abilities are so effective that they are described as *charismatic*. A *charismatic leader* is one who inspires followers to embrace a vision of success and make extraordinary efforts to achieve things they would not have done on their own (Bass & Riggio, 2006; Erez et al., 2008). Charismatic leaders such as Martin Luther King, Jr., and Sir Winston Churchill captured the imaginations of their followers. Dr. King led the fight for civil rights in the 1960s, inspiring countless thousands of followers to overcome entrenched opposition and personal danger to achieve the long-sought goal of equality under the law for African Americans. Prime Minister Churchill rallied the British people to resist and overcome the effects of Nazi air attacks during the darkest days of 1940 and throughout World War II. It has long been assumed that charismatic leadership is a by-product of a charismatic personality, not something one can learn.

What was the researchers' question?

I/O psychologists wonder, though, whether that assumption is correct. Might it be possible to train leaders to be charismatic, and if so, how would such training affect the job satisfaction and performance of those leaders' employees? Julian Barling, Tom Weber, and E. Kevin Kelloway (1996) addressed these questions by designing and evaluating a charisma-building training program for corporate managers.

How did the researchers answer the question?

Their study was conducted in twenty branches of a large Canadian banking corporation. The managers of these branches were randomly assigned to either a charisma training group or a control group that received no training. Two weeks before training began and five months after it was completed, the people working for each manager filled out a questionnaire, which included rating their manager's charisma. They also reported on their own level of job satisfaction. The financial performance of each branch office was measured before and after training, too.

Charisma training was delivered in five sessions over a three-month period. At the first session, managers met as a group to spend an entire day learning what makes charismatic leaders charismatic and practicing these behaviors in order to increase their own charisma. In the next four sessions, managers worked individually with one of the researchers, receiving additional training, getting feedback on performance, and setting goals for further progress.

What did the researchers find?

All the results indicated that this training program had a positive impact on managers' charisma. First, branch employees' ratings showed that managers in the training group were now more charismatic. There was a small decline in charisma for those in the control group. Second, employees who worked for the managers who had received charisma training reported higher levels of job satisfaction after training was over than did those who worked for the untrained managers. Finally, the financial performance of the trained managers' branches increased, whereas that of the untrained group decreased somewhat.

What do the results mean?

This charisma training program may not have produced a Martin Luther King, Jr., or a Winston Churchill, but its impact supports the notion that charisma can be taught, at least to some extent (Frese, Beimel, & Schoenborn, 2003). The trained managers became more charismatic and more effective than their untrained colleagues, suggesting that charisma involves behavior that can be learned by people with many different personality characteristics.

A Charismatic Leader

Apple founder Steve Jobs was considered by many to exemplify the kind of leader whose charisma inspires followers to accomplish what they might not otherwise have done.

Zuma Press, Inc./Alamy

(continued)

What do we still need to know?

The findings of this study are encouraging, but we should be cautious in interpreting them. For one thing, the changes seen in the trained managers might have been due to factors other than the training itself. As described in the introductory chapter, improvements following almost any treatment may be due partly or largely to placebo effects or other factors that create positive expectations among research participants. If the managers expected to be better at their jobs as a result of training and if their subordinates expected them to be better managers, it could have been these expectations rather than the training that caused the behavior changes and/or the increased charisma ratings. Even the improved financial performance could have been the result of expectation-driven efforts by managers and employees to do better, efforts that had nothing to do with the training itself. Interpreting the results of this experiment would have been easier if members of the untrained group had participated in some sort of placebo program that, like the charisma training, would have raised their expectations and those of their employees.

Even if the training program actually was responsible for the improvements seen, it would be important to know whether its effects would last beyond the five-month follow-up period. If it does have long-term effects, it would then be important to evaluate charisma training with leaders in other kinds of organizations and at other levels of leadership. It will take time and a lot of research to explore these matters, but if charisma can indeed be taught, we may someday see candidates for political office lining up to learn it.

LINKAGES

As noted in the introductory chapter, all of psychology's subfields are related to one another. Our discussion of aggression in the workplace illustrates just one way that the topic of this chapter, industrial and organizational psychology, is linked to the subfield of social psychology, which is covered in the chapter by that name. The Linkages diagram shows ties to two other subfields, and there are many more ties throughout the book. Looking for linkages among subfields will help you see how they all fit together and help you better appreciate the big picture that is psychology.

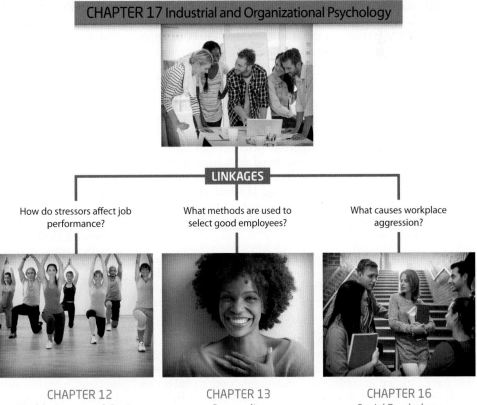

CHAPTER 17 Industrial and Organizational Psychology

LINKAGES

How do stressors affect job performance?

What methods are used to select good employees?

What causes workplace aggression?

CHAPTER 12
Health, Stress, and Coping

CHAPTER 13
Personality

CHAPTER 16
Social Psychology

SUMMARY

An Overview of Industrial and Organizational Psychology

What do industrial and organizational psychologists do?

Industrial and organizational (I/O) psychology is the science of behavior and mental processes in the workplace. I/O psychologists study the psychology of the workplace and apply psychological research to enhance the performance of employees and organizations and improve the health, safety, and well-being of employees. I/O psychology grew out of experimental psychology early in the twentieth century as psychologists began to apply laboratory research to workplace problems.

Assessing People, Jobs, and Job Performance

How do industrial and organizational psychologists match employees to jobs?

The development and evaluation of methods for assessing employees, jobs, and job performance is one of the main areas for scientific research in I/O psychology. The human attributes necessary for doing jobs successfully are referred to collectively as KSAOs, which stands for knowledge, skill, ability, and other personal characteristics.

A **job analysis** is the assessment of jobs and job requirements. It may be job oriented (describing job tasks), person oriented (describing the KSAOs necessary to perform job tasks), or both. Organizations use job analysis information for many purposes, including employee hiring and training.

The three main methods used to measure employee characteristics are psychological tests, job applicant interviews, and assessment centers. Tests can focus on employees' knowledge, ability, skill, and other characteristics, such as personality traits. A job applicant interview is designed to determine an applicant's suitability for a job. It can be structured or unstructured, but structured interviews are far more effective in selecting successful employees than unstructured interviews, in which questions are not organized ahead of time. An **assessment center** is an extensive battery of exercises used to determine whether a person is suited for a particular job.

Most organizations give an annual **job performance** appraisal to all employees. Much like a school report card, these appraisals describe how well a person is doing in several job domains. Performance is measured in relation to general (theoretical) criteria as well as in relation to more specific (actual) criteria.

Objective measures of job performance rely on counting behaviors or the results of behaviors. These measures are valuable, but they are not appropriate for evaluating performance in jobs that have little or no objectively measurable output. Subjective measures can be used in any job situation, but because they rely on supervisor ratings of performance, these measures may be distorted by judgment bias or error.

Recruiting and Selecting Employees

How do organizations find good employees?

I/O psychologists frequently use assessment tools to help hire people who will be best able to succeed in particular jobs. The first step in effective recruiting is to determine what employees are needed and then attract applicants to fill those needs, using employment agencies, Internet and print advertising, and campus visits; encouraging nominations from current employees; and accepting walk-in applications.

The I/O approach to hiring uses scientific principles to match jobs to the KSAOs of applicants. Establishing the KSAO requirements of a job helps determine which employee assessment tools will be most appropriate, and validation studies may be used to confirm that particular scores on the chosen assessments actually predict success on the job. Many industrialized countries have established laws and regulations that bar discrimination in hiring, firing, or promotion based on ethnicity, age, gender, or any other characteristics that have nothing to do with job performance.

Training Employees

What kind of training do employees need?

I/O psychologists help organizations establish the need for training, design training methods and content, and evaluate the outcome of training. Using a training needs assessment, organizations determine what training employees need in order to perform their jobs safely and well. Training needs assessments can focus on what KSAOs are required for specific jobs, on what training employees say they need, and on the objectives of the organization, such as improving production and decreasing accidents.

The design of training programs is guided by research on the processes through which people acquire new information and skills. These principles are translated into employee training that emphasizes transfer of training (applying new skills to the workplace), feedback (providing reinforcement for progress and guidance and encouragement following errors), training in general principles (providing "big picture" information to show the relevance of training), overlearning (practicing new skills until they become automatic), and sequencing (distributing training over time to improve learning and retention). A training program can be evaluated in terms of how trainees felt about the training (training-level criteria), what trainees actually learned during training (trainee learning criteria), and/or the degree to which trainees used what was learned during training in doing their jobs (performance-level criteria).

Employee Motivation

What motivates employees to do their best?

Motivation in the workplace refers to factors that influence the direction, intensity, and persistence of employees' behavior. Three theories of motivation have special workplace applications. **Existence, relatedness, growth (ERG) theory** divides human needs into existence needs (e.g., for food and water), relatedness needs (e.g., social contact), and growth needs (the development and use of one's capabilities). It suggests that the strength of each type of need affects workers' motivation to do their jobs well. According to *expectancy theory,* employees work hard if they perceive it to be in their best interest to do so. *Goal-setting theory* describes workers' motivation as stemming mainly from their desire to achieve short- and long-term goals. According to this theory, organizations should help employees set clear, specific goals that are challenging but not impossible.

Job Satisfaction

Is pay the most important factor in job satisfaction?

Job satisfaction is a cluster of attitudes that reflect the degree to which people like their jobs. It is usually assessed using questionnaires that ask employees to say how they feel about their jobs in general (the global approach) or about pay, supervision, or other specific job components (the facet approach). I/O psychologists have studied several environmental and personal factors that can influence people's job satisfaction. Among the environmental factors are the requirements of the job, how much it pays, and how it affects workers' lives outside the workplace. Among the personal factors are workers' gender, age, and ethnicity. For the most part, complex jobs tend to be more satisfying than simple jobs. Salary itself may be a less important factor in job satisfaction than the fairness of the salary system. Excessive work-family conflict can reduce job satisfaction. Because of temperament and experience, some individuals may have a tendency to be more satisfied with their jobs than others.

Job satisfaction has been associated with better job performance and with **organizational citizenship behavior (OCB)**, but it isn't clear whether satisfaction is a cause or an effect of these attributes. Job dissatisfaction is clearly at work in causing people to quit their jobs (turnover), but it has a smaller effect on absenteeism. Job dissatisfaction can also lead to aggression and counterproductive work behavior (CWB) such as theft or sabotage. CWB is especially likely among dissatisfied employees who work under conditions of high stress and low perceived control.

Occupational Health Psychology

How can workplace accidents be prevented?

Occupational health psychology is concerned with psychological factors that affect the health, safety, and well-being of employees. A number of physical conditions in the workplace can affect health, including infectious agents, toxic chemicals, dangerous machinery, and stressors such as the need to perform repetitive actions.

Work schedules, too, can have an impact on health and well-being. Rotating shift work, extended shifts, and longer-than-normal work weeks have been associated with a variety of problems ranging from fatigue and sleeping problems to substance abuse and increased risk of heart disease. Reduction of workplace accidents can be accomplished not only by reducing occupational stressors but also by promoting a climate of safety. Workplace accidents are least frequent in organizations that provide rigorous safety training, conduct frequent safety inspections, and encourage adherence to safety procedures.

Work Groups and Work Teams

Do groups need supervision to work well?

A **work group** is a collection of people who interact on the job, whereas a **work team** is a group in which members depend on one another as they work at specialized yet coordinated tasks aimed at accomplishing a common goal. Unlike traditional, closely supervised work teams, **autonomous work groups (AWGs)** are assigned tasks and then given the freedom to manage themselves, solve their own problems, and even influence hiring and firing decisions, all of which tend to result in greater job satisfaction among team members.

Leaders direct or supervise the activities of others, set group and organizational objectives, and ensure that employees perform their assigned tasks. Certain characteristics tend to be universally seen as desirable leadership attributes; others may not be seen as ideal in all cultures. Two dimensions of leadership style—consideration and initiating structure—have been found to have strong effects on employees' performance and job satisfaction. **Leader-member exchange (LMX) theory** suggests that leaders adopt different styles toward ingroup and outgroup employees. Charismatic leaders have the ability to influence and inspire employees to accomplish things they would not have done on their own. Charisma in leaders tends to promote job satisfaction in employees, and there is evidence that some aspects of charisma can be taught.

TEST YOUR KNOWLEDGE

Select the best answer to each of the following questions. Then check your responses against the Answer Key at the end of the book.

1. I/O psychologists _____.
   a. conduct research on behavior and mental processes in the workplace
   b. focus mainly on improving the efficiency of employees
   c. focus mainly on the development of intelligence and personality tests
   d. work mainly for government agencies

2. Donald Crump's new business has grown so quickly that he needs to hire more employees. The first thing that Mr. Crump should do is _____.
   a. interview all applicants
   b. create psychological profiles of the best applicants
   c. conduct a job analysis of each open position
   d. identify the salary for each position

3. You have been hired to conduct a job analysis at a local fast-food chain. After completing your analysis, you conclude that the job requires cooking hamburgers. What type of job analysis have you performed?
   a. Job oriented
   b. Person oriented
   c. Analysis oriented
   d. Performance oriented

4. Jobs require individuals with specific knowledge, skill, ability, and other personal characteristics. These KSAOs are identified by a detailed study called a _____.
   a. job assessment study
   b. job analysis
   c. KSAO-ometry
   d. computer-aided assessment

5. Attributes or characteristics necessary to successfully perform a job are called _____.
   a. compensable factors
   b. critical factors
   c. KSAOs
   d. essential functions

6. Larry Recruiter is interviewing potential employees at an on-campus job fair. To find the most appropriate candidate for his job opening, Larry should use _____ interviews.
   a. unstructured
   b. panel
   c. structured
   d. inferential

7. A large company is most likely to select high-level managers using mainly _____.
   a. assessment centers
   b. unstructured interviews
   c. letters of recommendation
   d. personality tests

8. Performance appraisal information can be used for _____.
   a. employee development
   b. decisions about pay increases
   c. evaluating the need for new training
   d. all of the above

9. Consider the job of "student." Which of the following is a theoretical criterion for this job?
   a. The number of A's earned in a three-year period
   b. The total value of scholarships obtained over a three-year period
   c. Engaging in scholarly activities
   d. The number of clubs joined

10. Which of the following reflects a subjective measure of a teacher's job performance?
    a. The average of student ratings on a course evaluation questionnaire
    b. The average size of the teacher's classes
    c. The number of courses taught
    d. The frequency of being late for class

11. Ruth is evaluating all of the employees in her department. To be as fair as possible, she uses behavior-focused ratings. This means that Ruth will _____.
    a. interview each employee in an unstructured way.
    b. give each employee global ratings in areas such as efficiency and honesty.
    c. rate employees on their handling of critical incidents in their job.
    d. observe each employee's performance for one day.

12. Organizations hope that employees will apply to their jobs what they learn during training. This process is called _____.
    a. response discrimination
    b. transfer of training
    c. application management
    d. training to learn

13. _____ training is more efficient, but _____ training is more effective in the long run.
    a. Part; whole
    b. Whole; part
    c. Massed; distributed
    d. Distributed; massed

14. Which of the following aspects of employee training is *not* usually done by I/O psychologists?
    a. Conducting a training needs assessment
    b. Delivering the training
    c. Designing the training
    d. Evaluating the training

15. The need for water is an example of a _____ need in Maslow's hierarchy of needs theory and of a(n) _____ need in Alderfer's ERG theory of employee motivation.
    a. physiological; relatedness
    b. safety; existence
    c. safety; growth
    d. physiological; existence

16. According to the _____ approach to job satisfaction, people can be satisfied with some aspects of their jobs and dissatisfied with other aspects of their jobs.
    a. global
    b. facet
    c. ERG
    d. expectancy

17. If Eric is satisfied with his job, he most likely _____.
    a. earns a lot of money
    b. feels that his company's promotion and salary decisions are fair
    c. has a job that does not require complex thinking
    d. works alone with few distractions

18. Which of the following statements about counterproductive work behavior (CWB) is correct?
    a. Employees steal more from their employers than do shoplifters.
    b. Dissatisfied employees are much more likely to be absent from work than satisfied employees.
    c. Employees are more likely to engage in CWB if they feel in control of their work.
    d. Assaulting a coworker is as common as stealing from a coworker.

19. Five students in an advertising class jointly prepare a sixty-second commercial, each taking a separate production role. The quality of the commercial determines the project grade for all five students. These five students constitute a _____.
    a. work group but not a work team
    b. work team
    c. group-think
    d. nominal group

20. Which leadership theory emphasizes the relationship between the leader and individual group members rather than between the leader and the group as a whole?
    a. Leader-member exchange theory
    b. Vroom-Yetton model
    c. Leader behavior theory
    d. Path-goal theory

Neuropsychology

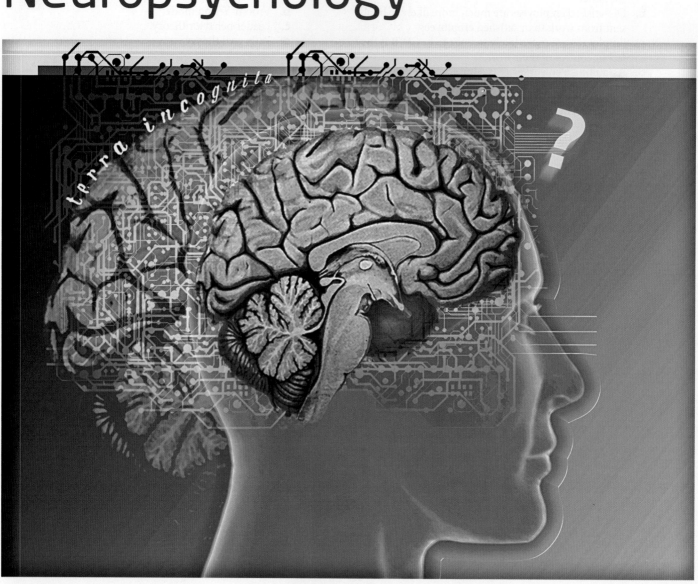

Daniel Matzenbacher/Alamy

Preview

Something was wrong with Max. He put away his car keys, his wallet, and a pair of dress shoes in their usual places, but when he tried looking for them later, he had no idea where they were. "You're just getting forgetful," his wife teased. But at breakfast one morning, he used a piece of bacon to stir his coffee. Then, mistaking a candle on the table for a glass of juice, he tried to drink it, and he used a pancake as a napkin, wiping his mouth with it before placing it on his lap. He seemed puzzled by these mistakes. His wife took him to a doctor. Suppose you were that doctor. How could you know what was wrong with Max? You could consider many possibilities. Maybe he is choosing to be silly to annoy his wife. But if he is not acting oddly on purpose, where does the problem lie? Perhaps his mind is being affected by a problem in his brain. The problem might affect his memory systems, but it might also be affecting attention or some other psychological function. Of course, the problem might be something less specific. Perhaps he has just been working too hard or is having a reaction to a medication or some sort of dietary deficiency. He might be experiencing depression, or maybe an unrecognized infection is affecting his ability to remember and concentrate.

Understanding what the problem is for someone like Max, exactly where it is, and how it affects a person's behavior and mental processes takes us into the realm of *neuropsychology*. In this chapter, we will describe how neuropsychology developed, what it has revealed about the relationship between brain functions and psychological functions, and how neuropsychologists study patients on a case-by-case basis. We will also describe some of the most interesting examples of what can go wrong in the brain and how these problems can affect people's thoughts, actions, and abilities.

FOUNDATIONS OF NEUROPSYCHOLOGY

What is neuropsychology and how did it develop?

Neuropsychology is the subfield of psychology whose goal is to explore and understand the relationships among brain processes, human behavior, and psychological functioning. *Neuropsychologists* study how brain systems, and disruptions of those systems, affect a wide range of human abilities, including cognitive functions (such as language, memory, attention, mathematical, and visual-spatial skills), motor functions (such as walking or threading a needle), emotional functions (such as the ability to express emotions and understand other people's emotional expressions), and social functions (such as daily interactions with others). They study, too, how the brain affects personality and psychological disorders such as depression.

The field of neuropsychology rests on two main assumptions. The first is that many complicated mental tasks, such as memory or decision making, involve numerous subtasks that can be tested and studied separately (Lezak, Loring, & Howieson, 2004). For example, as described in earlier chapters, the ability to form a new memory usually requires a person to be awake, to pay attention, to receive sensations, to perceive those sensations, to form mental representations of that information, to be motivated to remember the information, and to have the language or other verbal skills necessary to express the information when it is retrieved from memory. If any of these subtasks fail, a person's memory function would fail in any number of everyday situations. With this assumption about subtasks in mind, neuropsychologists must not only figure out what complicated mental tasks a person can and cannot do but also identify the failure of one or more subtasks that may be at the root of the problem.

The second main assumption of neuropsychology is that different psychological processes are controlled by different brain regions or by different combinations of brain regions

neuropsychology The subfield of psychology whose goal is to explore and understand the relationships among brain processes, human behavior, and psychological functioning.

(Fodor, 1983; Sternberg, 2011). Neuropsychologists use this assumption to draw conclusions about each patient they examine. After deciding what psychological processes are impaired, they work backward to infer what brain region or combinations of regions may not be working properly. This "working backward" approach is valuable, because many kinds of brain damage or disease are too subtle to be identified by physical examination or by various brain-scanning procedures (Nadeau & Crosson, 1995). Also, this approach helps implicate which areas of known brain damage may be symptomatic and which may not be so.

Using these two main assumptions, some neuropsychologists conduct research on how the human brain controls and organizes separate parts of complicated mental activities. These scientists, known as *experimental neuropsychologists,* most often study people with brain damage, but they sometimes do research on people with normal brains too. Their aim is to add to our knowledge of brain functioning among people in general. **Clinical neuropsychologists** use this knowledge to try to understand the problems that appear in a particular patient, such as Max. They look for the best way to examine a person so as to determine the likelihood and location of brain dysfunction by learning what psychological processes are impaired and exactly how they are impaired (Lezak et al., 2012). Most clinical neuropsychologists are to be found in hospitals and other health care settings, where they work with physicians to test people with brain damage (Johnson-Green & Collins, 2011).

For example, think back to our friend Max. He was tested by a clinical neuropsychologist. She showed Max a long series of simple drawings of common objects and asked him to name each one. Experimental neuropsychological research on large numbers of people provided *norms* that told her what kind of performance she could expect on this test from people of Max's age and educational background. She could then compare his performance with these norms. As you might expect, Max's responses were not normal. For example, looking at the drawing of a pencil, he said he saw "a long, narrow protrusion of some kind." He called a paper clip "an object curling into itself." For eyeglasses, he said, "That's two circular devices suspended together." Clearly he was not naming things well— but why? Could his vision be bad? No, because his descriptions were visually accurate, and he could correctly read words in small print. He could also produce reasonably accurate copies of the drawings, even though he could not always name the objects in them. These findings meant that he had sensed and perceived the drawings' shapes, angles, and spatial relationships. Did Max have a general problem with memory, as his wife suggested? To test that idea, the neuropsychologist read him lists of words and later asked him to recall them. He did about as well on this memory test as most people of his age and level of education, so his memory seemed normal. The neuropsychologist next considered whether Max was no longer able to understand the concepts represented in the drawings. But this possibility was ruled out when he correctly defined the words *pencil, paper clip,* and *eyeglasses.* So he knew about these objects, and when examples of them were placed into his hands while he was blindfolded, he could name them instantly. So Max could recognize these objects through his sense of touch but not through his sense of vision.

Why? The neuropsychologist concluded that Max still had normal function in brain systems that process basic visual sensations but that something was wrong with the brain systems that normally convert those sensations into recognizable visual perceptions. This problem is called a *visual agnosia* (pronounced "ag-NOH-zhuh"), and it can occur when parts of the temporal lobes on both sides of the brain do not work properly (Devinsky, Farah & Barr, 2008). Max's physician used that information to focus his medical care on those brain regions.

Max's case illustrates several important aspects of what neuropsychologists have learned about how the brain operates. Let's review some of what they have discovered and how these discoveries occurred.

A Brief History of Neuropsychology

Max's case shows **localization of function**, the idea that specific psychological functions can be affected by damage to specific brain areas. This concept might seem obvious to you, especially if you have read about the brain in the chapters on biological aspects of psychology,

clinical neuropsychologists Neuropsychologists who use tests and other methods to try to understand neuropsychological problems and intact functions in individual patients.

localization of function The idea that specific psychological functions can be affected by damage to specific brain areas.

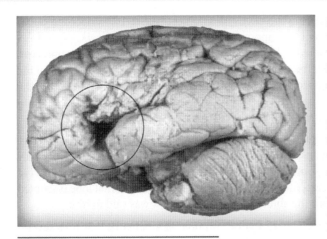

FIGURE 18.1
Tan's Brain

When Tan died, surgeon Paul Broca discovered severe damage in the left frontal lobe of the cerebral cortex, just in front of the primary motor cortex. Now called Broca's area, it is involved with the ability to produce normal speech.

From Corsi, P., ed. The Enchanted Loom. New York: Oxford University Press, 1991. Musée Dupuytren, Paris. Photo courtesy of Dr. Jean-Louis Signoret

sensation and perception, and consciousness. But this "commonsense" notion was born amidst considerable debate (Tyler & Malessa, 2000), some of which continues today. Indeed, for centuries, philosophers and scientists have speculated on the role of different brain areas in different psychological functions (Eling, 2008; Kaitaro, 2001).

Early in the 1800s, the dominant view was that the brain worked more or less as a single organ, and that no one part was more important than any other in the control of mental life. An anatomist named Franz Gall disagreed with this view, arguing instead that different brain areas each controlled particular aspects of cognitive function (Zola-Morgan, 1995). Some of Gall's ideas turned out to be correct, and his legacy would be more widely honored except for the fact that Gall also mistakenly believed that brain areas, like muscles, get bigger as people use them. He believed, too, that each brain area is associated with personality traits, such as honesty or love or aggressiveness. Fatal to his legacy, Gall claimed that as brain areas grew larger, there would be corresponding bumps in the skull just above them. He created a map showing which brain areas were supposedly controlling which traits, and he used it to assess a person's psychological makeup by measuring the bumps on the skull. Gall's approach, known as *phrenology*, was a hit with the public because it promised a simple way to measure personality (Benjamin & Baker, 2004). But assessing personality by feeling people's skulls was a far-fetched and easily refuted notion. Thus, Gall's scientific colleagues dismissed virtually everything he said about the brain's role in psychology, and the ridicule heaped on phrenology tainted any claims of localization of function.

Everything changed in 1861 when a famous and widely respected French surgeon, Paul Broca, examined a hospitalized patient whose leg had gangrene, a serious deep-tissue infection. (In this era before antibiotics, gangrene often required amputation.) It so happened that many years earlier, this patient had had a **stroke** (also called a **cerebral infarct**)—a condition in which one of the blood vessels to the brain is blocked, causing permanent damage to the brain. The stroke left the patient unable to say anything but the word *tan*, which became the staff's nickname for him. Despite his speech difficulties, "Tan" could apparently understand most spoken language because he easily followed verbal commands. Before anything could be done about Tan's gangrene, he died, and Broca ordered an autopsy. It showed a small **lesion**, or area of damage, in the left frontal lobe of Tan's brain (see Figure 18.1). Broca wondered if this lesion was related to Tan's speech problems. But, if so, how could such a small lesion create such a major and specific problem? Not long afterward, Broca requested an autopsy on another patient who had had language problems similar to Tan's and discovered a brain lesion in the same place as Tan's.

If lesions in this particular spot were somehow linked to these patients' language disorders, the previously dismissed idea of localization of function might be correct. Indeed, a particular brain area could be involved in controlling a particular function such as speech (Broca, 1861, 1865). This is precisely what Broca proposed when he shared his observations in a lecture to the Anthropological Society of Paris. And because, unlike Gall, Broca held such high status in the scientific community, his support of localization of function made it a respectable idea. The resulting explosion of brain research in the past century and a half has established that localization exists and is more complex than anyone in Broca's time had guessed.

Modules and Networks

Modern approaches to localization of function rest on the idea that the brain is organized into discrete regions called **modules**, each of which adds its own unique kind of analysis of the information it receives (Fodor, 1983; Sternberg, 2011). According to a *modularity* view, each module, located in a unique brain area, acts somewhat like a circuit board in a computer. That is, a module does not itself "control" any particular function, but it adds a needed piece to complete a larger puzzle that allows speech or some other function to occur. The analysis performed by a particular module can be used in many kinds of brain functions. And each

stroke (cerebral infarct) A loss of blood supply to some part of the brain, resulting in brain damage that disrupts some aspect of behavior or mental processes.

lesion An area of damaged tissue in the brain.

modules Regions of the brain that perform their own unique kind of analysis of the information they receive.

brain function—whether it is detecting the edges of an object or making a decision about something—is accomplished through the support of a different team, or *network,* of modules (Sporns, 2011). It is as if a brain were the head of a company with a vast array of employees, each with a specific skill, which can be organized and reorganized from one moment to the next into many different work teams to perform many different tasks. In this way, some of the same brain areas might be used in many different psychological tasks, but the exact combination of which areas are used and when may still differ from one function to another.

Speaking and understanding language, for example, involves a network of modules in several brain areas (Friederici, 2011). This means that damage to any part of the network may affect a person's language ability in some way, but the exact effect will depend on which part of the network is damaged. In Tan's case, for example, the lesion in his left frontal lobe disrupted his ability to speak but left him with the ability to understand what was said to him.

The brain regions used in language are a good example of a network that uses several modules. One of the interesting consequences of organizing a system in this way is the potential for a *disconnection syndrome.* Such syndromes occur when different modules in a network, though themselves intact, are prevented from interacting (Geschwind, 1968). A classic example is *alexia without agraphia,* which literally means inability to read while still being able to write (Sheldon, Malcolm, & Barton, 2008). The brain damage shown in Figure 18.2 could produce this kind of disconnection syndrome. Here, there is damage to the left occipital lobe, causing loss of vision, but only for what is on the right side of the visual field. The patient can still see the left side of the visual field. However, there is also damage to the corpus callosum, which connects the left and right hemispheres of the brain. The damaged area of the corpus callosum would have allowed visual information from the left side of the world to cross from the right hemisphere into the left hemisphere, but now this pathway is blocked. Because the language-producing regions of the left hemisphere are intact, the person can still talk and write normally but can see only what lies in the left visual field. That information goes to the right hemisphere, but because it cannot cross into the left hemisphere, where most language functions reside, people with this disconnection syndrome cannot read what they have written. In effect, the visual processing of the words is disconnected from the brain regions that are needed to extract the meaning of the words they see.

Lesion Analysis

Much as Broca did so long ago, one way that experimental neuropsychologists today still study localization of function is by observing the results of brain damage. This activity is sometimes called *lesion analysis* (Aharonov et al., 2003). To get an idea of how lesion analysis works, suppose that a man with normal mathematical ability has a stroke that damages an area of his left parietal lobe (see Figure 3.10 in the chapter on biological aspects of psychology for the location of this area). Afterward, like other people with similar brain damage, he can no longer do math. Do these observations require us to decide that math ability is localized in the left parietal lobe? Not necessarily. Critical thinking gives other possibilities too.

For example, we have already seen that complex psychological functions often require cooperation of many modules in different brain areas. So although mathematical ability may suffer after damage to the left parietal lobe, it may also be affected by damage to other regions in a "mathematics" network. Experimental neuropsychologists explore this possibility by studying the changes in math ability seen in large numbers of people with damage to different brain regions. If they find that math ability is affected by left parietal lobe damage but nowhere else, they would be more confident in asserting that mathematical disability is localized in that area. If they find that damage in other areas also affects math ability, they would realize that this ability may depend on a widely distributed set of brain areas.

Neuropsychologists can also learn how people function when a brain area stops working for reasons other than from a brain area being destroyed. It is now possible to "shut off" a brain area using a technique called *transcranial magnetic stimulation (TMS)* (Dayan et al., 2013). In this procedure, a powerful magnet is held at a specified area of a person's head, and after adjusting certain parameters, specific areas of the brain's cortex can be inactivated

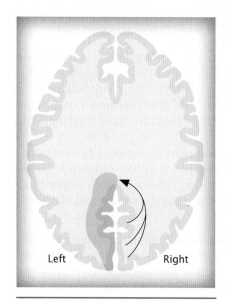

FIGURE 18.2
Alexia without Agraphia

This is a classic example of a disconnection syndrome. Brain damage (in darker blue) has occurred in the left occipital lobe and part of the corpus callosum. As a result, no visual information can enter the left hemisphere. The left-hemisphere brain regions that create writing are intact, so the patient can write. But because feedback from the visual system cannot get back to the language-processing systems of the left hemisphere, the patient cannot read what he or she has written.

for a time. In this way, a brain module can be reversibly taken out of the networks in which it participates. By observing how a person behaves during the time that TMS has created temporary dysfunction of specific brain modules, experimental neuropsychologist can in effect perform a kind of "reversible" lesion analysis (Sternberg, 2011).

But lesion analysis must also clarify just what function it is that has been damaged. For example, doing a mathematical calculation might require you to use several abilities, such as recognizing numbers and symbols, remembering the rules of addition or multiplication, keeping many numbers in your head as you do calculations, and being able to read or hear a math problem and report your answer. So if a brain lesion makes it hard for you to talk, you would not be able to answer the question "How much is 2 plus 2?" But this may not mean that there is anything wrong with your mathematical ability.

To help figure out exactly what problems a brain-damaged patient actually has, experimental neuropsychologists look at a complex mental task, such as reading or doing math, and—in light of research from sensation, perception, and cognitive psychology—try to identify all the abilities that a person's brain must combine to succeed at that task. They then try to determine which of these abilities are actually separate, or *dissociated*, perhaps because they are based on using different brain modules in particular brain regions. One way to establish a dissociation between abilities is to study which components of a mental task are affected by which kinds of brain damage. An important example of dissociated abilities is described in the chapter on biological aspects of psychology. Damage to a particular area in the left frontal lobe disrupts a person's ability to speak fluently but leaves the person able to understand most of what others say (remember Broca's patient, "Tan"?). Damage to a different area in the left temporal lobe does the opposite, leaving the person able to speak easily but unable to understand what others are saying. We will discuss these conditions again later in this chapter. ("In Review: Foundations of Neuropsychology" summarizes milestones in the history of neuropsychology.)

IN REVIEW

FOUNDATIONS OF NEUROPSYCHOLOGY

Principle	Main Figure or Era	Key Ideas
Localization of function	Franz Gall, early 1800s Paul Broca, mid-1800s	The idea that a specific psychological function could depend on a specific brain area
Modularity	Late 1900s	A revision of localization in which each brain area performs different, unique computations, which contribute to various psychological functions
Networks	Late 1900s	A perspective suggesting that different complex psychological functions rely on unique combinations of brain modules
Lesion analysis	1800s to the present	An approach to experimental neuropsychology in which psychological functions are linked to particular brain areas by studying patients with damage to those areas and comparing these people with people who have damage elsewhere or no damage

1. A person who studies individual patients to determine what kind of brain damage each one happens to have is called a _____.

2. The case of "Tan" helped establish the principle of _____.

3. In alexia without agraphia, the brain areas that control reading and writing are intact but cannot interact. This condition is called a _____.

Neuropsychological Assessment

So far we have discussed how the brain is organized and how neuropsychologists study ways in which its functioning is related to behavior and behavior problems. Let's now consider how they decide when a person has such problems. Consider memory, for example. Everyone forgets things sometimes, even such familiar things as the name of your roommate's brother or where you left your car keys. But how much forgetfulness is normal and how much does it take to be labeled as excessive or problematic?

LINKAGES   What psychological tests are used in diagnosing neuropsychological disorders? (a link to Intelligence)

To answer this question, neuropsychologists typically conduct a **neuropsychological assessment** by giving patients a large number of tests designed to measure a wide range of mental functions, such as general intelligence, memory, reading, motor coordination, naming pictures, and finding targets in a visual display. Some neuropsychologists prefer to use an individualized set of assessments uniquely tailored to each patient (Blakesley et al., 2009). In this way, they hope to measure the specific problems that a particular patient is most likely to have. Another approach is to give patients a standardized test battery, a predetermined set of tests that are designed to complement one another and comprehensively address all aspects of psychological functioning (Kane, 1991). Many such test batteries have been carefully prepared and validated. Among the best-known examples are the Halstead-Reitan Battery, the Wechsler Adult Intelligence Scale, and the Luria-Nebraska Neuropsychology Battery. Standardized batteries offer the advantage of giving each patient the same tests in the same way, but they don't allow the neuropsychologist to tailor testing to focus on a patient's particular problems or unique situation. Accordingly, most clinical neuropsychologists start with a standard test battery and then administer additional tests that are particularly relevant to each case.

By giving a variety of tests, a clinical neuropsychologist can study many different areas of a person's psychological functioning and also measure each area separately. Analyzing the overall pattern of results may help pinpoint where the brain difficulties lie. But results of neuropsychological testing, like those of personality testing, intelligence testing, and academic testing, must be interpreted with caution. Many factors, such as age, education, and cultural background, can affect a person's performance on neuropsychological tests. With this in mind, each patient's performance on these tests must be compared with established averages, or norms. These norms may be based on test performance of large numbers of people of the patient's own age, educational level, and cultural background but who have no known brain damage. Norms also give clinical neuropsychologists an idea of how often normal people's scores vary from the average and by how much. Having this information helps establish whether a score that looks deviant at first glance is actually as unusual as it seems. Norms can also reveal when what seems like a minor deficit is actually quite unusual and indicative of a potential problem.

MECHANISMS OF BRAIN DYSFUNCTION

What are the main causes of brain damage or dysfunction?

We have been talking a lot about brain damage, so you may wonder how brains get hurt.

Cerebral Infarcts

neuropsychological assessment Testing a patient's intelligence, memory, reading, motor coordination, and other cognitive and sensory functions in an effort to locate problems in the brain responsible for neuropsychological symptoms.

Strokes, also known as cerebral infarcts, are a common source of brain damage. The brain receives all the oxygen, sugar (glucose), and other nutrients it needs from the rich supply of blood flowing through it (see Figure 18.3). But brain cells cannot store much of this energy, so they must have a supply of fresh blood at all times (Acker & Acker, 2004). If a vessel bringing blood into some part of the brain becomes blocked, the brain tissue in that part of the brain will die, and that is called a cerebral infarct. When someone's behavior or mental processes are affected by a cerebral infarct, that person is said to have had a stroke, sometimes also called a *cerebrovascular accident (CVA)*. Even very tiny strokes can cause disabling symptoms if they take place in vital brain areas, but cerebral infarcts in less vital areas may cause few, if any, symptoms.

FIGURE 18.3
The Brain's Blood Supply

TRY THIS Blood reaches the brain either through the carotid arteries on either side of the neck or through vertebral arteries entering through the base of the skull. Once in the brain, these arteries branch into the anterior cerebral artery, the middle cerebral artery, and the posterior cerebral artery. Each artery provides blood to specific brain areas. As a result, a blockage in each particular blood vessel damages a specific, predictable part of the brain. Review the chapter on biological aspects of psychology to remind yourself of what functions are associated with each area of the cerebral cortex. Then make a list of the functions that would most likely be affected by blockage in each of the arteries shown in this figure.

Jupiterimages/Photos.com

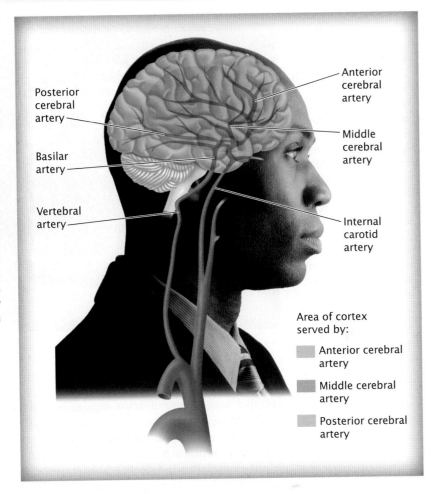

Strokes can be quite dangerous. In fact, stroke is the fourth leading cause of death in the United States (Towfighi & Saver, 2011). They tend to occur as people get older, but even children can have them (Katsetos, Smith, & Scott, 2009). Unlike heart attacks, in which blood flow to the heart muscle is disrupted, a stroke usually involves little or no pain because there are no pain receptors in brain tissue. So a stroke victim may not immediately realize that anything is wrong (Jenkinson, Preston, & Ellis, 2011). The resulting delay in seeking medical attention can be costly, because treatments that can reverse the effects of a stroke must be used as soon as possible (Kurz, Kurz, & Farbu, 2013).

Like explosions that break windows a block away, strokes affect not only the area in which brain tissue has died but also the surrounding area. Fortunately, if cells in the area around a stroke have not actually died, they may start working again (Rosso & Samson, 2013), allowing people to recover all or part of their lost functions. The amount of recovery depends on many factors, including the quality and speed of medical treatment, how large the stroke is and where it is located, the health of the remaining blood vessels and brain tissue, the quantity of salvageable tissue, the degree to which the remaining nervous system can reorganize along its original lines, and the kinds of rehabilitation programs undertaken after the stroke (Heiss, 2012; Rosso & Samson, 2013). To help the brain heal itself, some scientists are experimenting with chemicals that stimulate existing cells and blood vessels to grow (Yu et al., 2012); others are inserting stem cells into the brain to replace damaged tissue (Gutiérrez-Fernández, 2013). Electrical brain stimulation is also being studied as a way to enhance stroke recovery (Sandrini & Cohen, 2013). As described in the chapter on biological aspects of psychology, though, restoring functions lost to a stroke takes more than just restoring cells in damaged brain areas. The new cells must also somehow reestablish the right connections with other brain cells (Kalluri & Dempsey, 2008; Liu et al., 2009).

Traumatic Brain Injury in Sports

Traumatic brain injuries known as *concussions* are a risk in football and other contact sports (Gilchrist et al., 2011; Hamalainen, 2012; O'Rourke, 2011). The short-term effects of a concussion may include nausea, confusion, and problems with vision and memory. The long-term effects can be even more problematic (DeKosky, Ikonomovic, & Gandy, 2010). Some players develop symptoms similar to those of Alzheimer's disease (Hamalainen, 2012). Others suffer depression, and some develop a form of amyotrophic lateral sclerosis, or Lou Gehrig's disease (Bartholet, 2012). There is hope that better helmets and more restrictive rules about helmet-to-helmet contact will reduce the number of concussions among football players at every level, from high school to the NFL.

© iStockphoto.com/jpbcpa

Traumatic Brain Injury

Another major cause of brain damage is **traumatic brain injury (trauma)** (Heegaard, 2007). Trauma creates an impact on the brain, such as when a person's head is struck by something or when the head moves suddenly or is thrown violently against some object. Traumatic events such as these can cause damage because the brain is not firmly attached to the skull. Instead, it floats within it, suspended in a bath of **cerebrospinal fluid**. So when the head violently accelerates or decelerates, the soft globe of brain bounces back and forth inside the skull, bumping up against bone and causing nerve fibers in many areas to stretch and tear (Meaney & Smith, 2011).

The amount of brain damage resulting from trauma depends greatly on the amount of force involved in such situations and whether repeated brain traumas occur (Mannix et al., 2013). Further, unlike in strokes, where only the area in or near a disrupted blood supply is likely to be affected, the damage and disruption caused by trauma may be widespread. So whereas stroke patients may show very specific kinds of neuropsychological deficits, sometimes with striking dissociations between functions that are lost and those that are preserved, people with head injuries may show deficits that are far more diffuse, harder to specify, and involve many aspects of functioning (Wade, 2004), including cognitive and psychiatric problems (Stern et al., 2011; Whyte et al., 2011). This may explain why we know much more about the neuropsychological symptom patterns that follow strokes than we do about those following brain traumas. Greater attention has been paid lately to the hypothesis that repeated brain traumas in sports concussions may lead to progressive cognitive decline that worsen after the brain injuries (Noble & Hesdorffer, 2013), a condition known in the early 20th century as *dementia pugilistica* and now more commonly called *chronic traumatic encephalopathy* (CTE) (Levin & Bhardwaj, 2013). Recovery from traumatic brain injury is more likely in people who had completed more education prior to their injury, but it is not yet clear why this is so (Schneider et al., 2014).

Neurodegenerative Diseases

Unlike the sudden symptoms that result from brain damage caused by stroke, other brain problems develop gradually. One way that slowly developing symptoms may appear is with **neurodegenerative diseases,** processes that gradually damage brain cells

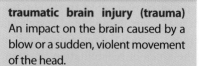

traumatic brain injury (trauma) An impact on the brain caused by a blow or a sudden, violent movement of the head.

cerebrospinal fluid A clear liquid that surrounds and buffers the brain against vibration.

neurodegenerative diseases Conditions in the brain that result in a gradual loss of nerve cells and of the cognitive or other functions in which those cells are normally involved.

over longer periods of time (Mayeux, 2003). Three of the most prominent examples of neurodegenerative diseases are Alzheimer's disease, Parkinson's disease, and frontotemporal degeneration. Each type of neurodegenerative disease affects a particular kind of brain cell or cells in a particular area of the brain, causing them to be the first to stop working properly (Cummings, 2003) and leaving the victim without the mental or physical functions those cells had once supported. The pattern of symptoms resulting from each neurodegenerative disease is different enough that neuropsychological assessment of a patient can lead to a diagnosis of which disease is affecting that patient (Brun, 2007; Miller, 2007).

Some kinds of neurodegeneration appear to be caused by infections, nutritional deficiencies, or genetic abnormalities, but despite intense research, we are still not sure about the specific causes of most such diseases. ("In Review: Mechanisms of Brain Dysfunction" summarizes the major causes of brain injury and dysfunction.)

MECHANISMS OF BRAIN DYSFUNCTION

IN REVIEW

Brain Problem	Onset	Underlying Process	Symptoms
Cerebral infarct (stroke)	Sudden	Blood flow is blocked in some part of the brain.	Specific to the area of the brain that is destroyed
Traumatic brain injury (trauma)	Sudden	Brain moves back and forth inside the skull.	Often nonspecific, diffuse
Neurodegenerative disease (neurodegeneration)	Gradual	A subset of neuron cell types becomes diseased and stops working properly.	Specific to the types of brain cells affected

1. The brain floats in a bath of _____ inside the skull.

2. The brain needs a constant flow of fresh _____ at all times.

3. Strokes rank as the number _____ cause of death in the United States.

NEUROPSYCHOLOGICAL DISORDERS

What disorders can be caused by brain damage or dysfunction?

Let's now take a closer look at the **syndromes**, or patterns of symptoms, that clinical neuropsychologists often see in patients after a stroke, trauma, or neurodegenerative disease. These syndromes are referred to as *neuropsychological disorders* and include amnestic disorders, consciousness disturbances, perceptual disturbances, disorders of language and communication, disorders of movement, and disorders involving dementia.

Amnestic Disorders

Amnestic disorders involve memory loss (often called *amnesia*). Concerns about memory often bring people to clinical neuropsychologists for evaluation. These people are concerned partly because they rely heavily on memory, so any threat to its integrity can be very upsetting. But patients also tend to focus on memory problems because we have a tendency to interpret almost any psychological deficit as being related to memory (Lezak, Loring, & Howieson, 2004). As in Max's case, for example, people who develop trouble naming objects may say they are "forgetting" words, even though the problem

LINKAGES What disorders are caused by damage to brain areas involved in memory? (a link to Memory)

syndrome A pattern of symptoms associated with a specific disorder.

amnestic disorders Neuropsychological disorders that involve memory loss.

might actually be one of language or visual recognition. Many older individuals, too, seek neuropsychological assessment because of worry that even minor forgetfulness might be an early sign of Alzheimer's disease. We discuss this disease in the section on dementia, but memory loss can occur in other neuropsychological syndromes too (Lucas, 2005).

For example, the ability to create new long-term memories can be impaired by damage in the brain's medial temporal lobes ("medial" means toward the middle of the brain), especially in the hippocampus (Ando et al., 2008; de Haan et al., 2006; Rosenbaum et al., 2008). Consider the famous case of Henry Molaison, known for much of his life as patient H.M. to protect his identity (Scoville & Milner, 1957). In 1953, as a twenty-seven-year-old man, his epilepsy was so severe that he had brain surgery in an effort to stop his seizures. The surgery removed parts of both his left and right temporal lobes, including parts of the hippocampus on both sides. This radical treatment helped control his seizures, but it left H.M. with a dense amnestic syndrome that persisted until he died at age of eighty-two in 2008 (Squire, 2009; see Figure 18.4). Although he was able to recall most details of his life from before the surgery, after surgery he had difficulty forming new memories. In other words, as discussed in the memory chapter, he had **anterograde amnesia**. When he met someone new, he was unable

FIGURE 18.4
H. M.'s Brain Surgery

H. M. underwent surgery that removed the hippocampus, the amygdala, and part of the association cortex from both temporal lobes. As shown in these MRI scans comparing an intact brain with H. M.'s brain after surgery, H. M. had some hippocampus (H) but no entorhinal cortex (EC). In this image, (V) refers to the lateral ventricle, (f) refers to the fornix, (PH) refers to the parahippocampal cortex, and (Cer) refers to the cerebellum.

Courtesy Dr. Suzanne Corkin, Massachusetts Institute of Technology. Copyright © 1997 Society for Neuroscience. J. Neurosci., May 15, 1997, 17(10):3964-3979

anterograde amnesia A loss of memory for events that occur after a brain injury.

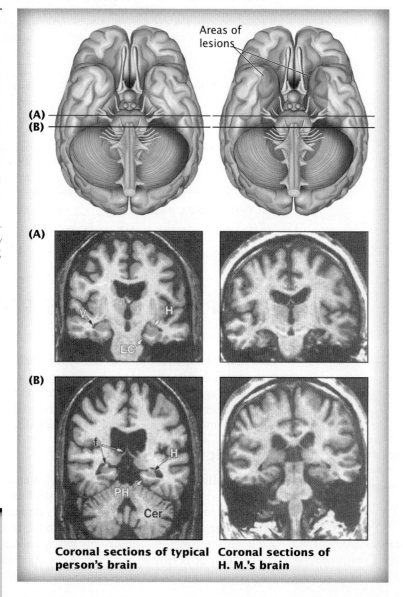

Coronal sections of typical person's brain   **Coronal sections of H. M.'s brain**

FIGURE 18.5
Memory without Awareness

People with amnesia from medial temporal lobe damage may still learn from the experiences that they otherwise cannot recall. This stimulus shows a degraded version of a drawing. Using stimuli similar to these, participants with amnesia first saw a very degraded version, then one less so, then less, and so on until they could name the item. Patients with amnesia were able to name items earlier if they had seen them before, even when they could not recall having seen them.

Source: From Snodgrass, J. G., and Feenan, K. "Priming effects in picture fragment completion: support for the perceptual closure hypothesis." Journal of Experimental Psychology: General vol. 119 (p.280).

Korsakoff's syndrome An amnestic condition in people whose thiamine (vitamin B1) level is depleted by inadequate nutrition or alcoholism.

confabulation A characteristic of some neuropsychological disorders in which patients report false memories.

to recall the meeting moments later, so the person seemed to be a stranger no matter how many times they met again. Similarly, new words he heard over the years—such as *computer, video, cell phone,* and *Jacuzzi*—never made it into his vocabulary. He wasn't even able to remember that time was passing, so he had few clues that he was getting older; to a great extent, he was mentally stuck in the 1950s.

Many of H.M.'s other mental capacities remained largely intact, however, providing a striking example of the dissociation that can occur between abilities lost and those spared after brain damage. He had good language function; he recognized objects; he thought and reasoned; he remained intelligent, pleasant, and sociable; and he carried on very normal-sounding conversations. Yet, he was quite aware of his memory problem. He put it as follows: "Right now, I'm wondering, have I done or said something amiss? You see, at this moment everything looks clear to me, but what happened just before? That's what worries me. It's like waking from a dream. I just don't remember" (Milner, 1970, p. 37).

H.M. was carefully studied for years, and the lessons learned from him prompted research on memory loss in other people after medial temporal lobe damage. When other people have amnesia caused by damage to the hippocampus, just like H.M., they also have difficulty remembering the new experiences or events of their lives. But also like H.M., it turns out that these individuals can still learn new skills and habits as a result of their new experiences. When they do a task over and over, they get better at it, meaning that they do form some kind of a memory. Nonetheless, they have no awareness of this learning and do not recall the experiences that led to it (see Figure 18.5).

Anterograde amnesia and other amnestic syndromes can be caused by events other than surgery in the hippocampus and medial temporal lobe. For example, certain brain infections, such as herpes encephalitis, tend to damage these same parts of the brain and create an amnestic syndrome similar to that of H.M. (Ando et al., 2008; Baringer, 2008). Strokes, too, can sometimes damage these regions, though they are usually on just one side of the brain, so the amnestic syndrome is less often seen. Finally, as described later, these regions, and the memory functions they normally perform, can also be impaired by Alzheimer's disease (Colliott, Hamelin, & Sarazin, 2013).

The hippocampus is not the only brain area involved in memory. For example, as described in the chapter on biological aspects of psychology, the thalamus processes information from all the senses except smell and sends it on to the cerebral cortex for more analysis. But some parts of the thalamus are also part of the brain's *limbic system,* an interconnected set of structures that includes the hippocampus (see Figure 18.6). When strokes in the thalamus damage their limbic connections, memory loss can occur (Pergola et al. 2012). One part of the thalamus, the medial dorsal (middle and top) thalamus, is damaged when people have **Korsakoff's syndrome** (Butters, 1981), a condition in people whose thiamine (vitamin B1) is depleted by poor nutrition or alcoholism. Running low on thiamine is dangerous because this vitamin is needed to process glucose (sugar) for energy. Nerve cells of the medial dorsal thalamus are especially dependent on this function of thiamine (Marti, Singleton, & Hiller-Sturmhofel, 2003), so if thiamine deficiency is severe, nerve cells there are more likely to die than in other brain regions (Hazell et al., 2013). The result is anterograde amnesia, plus an added unusual feature: **confabulation**, or the creation of false memories, both spontaneously and in response to questions (Borsutzky et al., 2008; Butters, 1981). These individuals believe that they have had experiences that they have not actually had, and they "recall" them as if they were real. Research with other confabulating patients suggests that this condition may also occur following damage to certain prefrontal brain regions (Nieuwenhuis & Takashima, 2011). Other amnestic syndromes do not usually produce confabulation, so when clinical neuropsychologists test patients with severe anterograde amnesia and find confabulation too, they may suspect medial dorsal thalamic amnesia or prefrontal amnesia.

FIGURE 18.6
The Limbic System

A number of closely connected structures form the limbic system, which controls many aspects of motivation and emotion.

Monika Gete/Moment Open/Getty Images

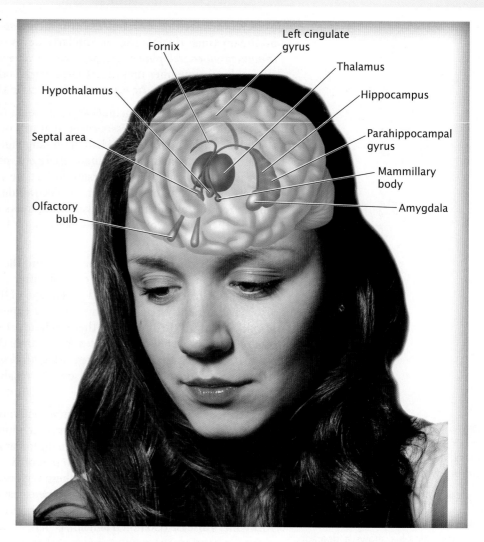

Consciousness Disturbances

Sometimes brain problems cause **consciousness disturbances**, impairing a person's awareness of the world around them (Bruno et al., 2011). One such problem occurs when there is disruption or damage to the **reticular formation**, also known as the *reticular activating system (RAS)*. The RAS is a long, tubelike structure stretching from the base of the brain upward, eventually splitting into both sides of the thalamus. As its name implies, the RAS normally serves to increase and decrease arousal in the rest of the brain and is partly responsible for our daily cycles of wakefulness and sleep (Yeo, Chang, & Jang, 2013). If the RAS is severely damaged, the result can be an unconscious state known as a *coma*. People with lesser amounts of RAS damage may enter a *persistent vegetative state (PVS)* or a *minimally conscious state (MCS)* (Gosseries et al., 2011). Unlike patients in comas, people in a PVS or MCS may open their eyes and appear to wake up in the day and close their eyes and appear to sleep at night. They may also show more automatic movements than coma patients. For example, when food is put in the mouth of someone in a PVS or MCS, chewing movements may occur, and sounds and touches may trigger facial expressions. But though EEG and brain PET scans sometimes show isolated activity in some areas of these individuals' brains—including activity in response to familiar sounds (Cruse et al., 2011; Heiss, 2012)—most patients seem unaware or poorly aware of their environment. The chances for recovery are often poor after significant RAS damage.

consciousness disturbances Neuropsychological disorders in which there are impairments in the ability to be aware of the world.

reticular formation A collection of cells and fibers in the hindbrain and midbrain that are involved in arousal and attention.

Even if the RAS is working properly to stimulate the rest of the brain, consciousness can be impaired if there are widespread disruptions in the functioning of both sides of the cerebral cortex, where other aspects of awareness are controlled (Stevens & Bhardwaj, 2006). Impairment of both sides of the cortex is most commonly caused by drugs such as alcohol or sleeping pills, but other causes include fever, seizures, chemical imbalances in the blood, hormonal disorders, and infections that have spread to the blood (Posner et al., 2007).

Other disturbances of consciousness have more complex and changing effects. People with **delirium**, for example, alternate between abnormally reduced and abnormally elevated levels of consciousness (Gofton, 2011). These patients may appear sleepy and "out of it" one minute and then far too attentive the next, as shown by reactions to any little sight and sound. Impairments often also appear in many mental functions, usually including poor attention, poor memory, and disorientation. People with delirium may experience hallucinations (hearing sounds or seeing things that are not really there) or agitation for no clear reason. Common causes of delirium include fever, poisons, infections affecting the bloodstream, and medication side effects. Delirium may signal a medical emergency, but usually its psychological effects go away when the underlying medical cause is corrected or ends on its own (Skrobik, 2009).

Neuropsychological testing of people in delirium is difficult (Milisen et al., 2006). Their attention and awareness can vary, sometimes dramatically, during testing. In general, performance on almost any test is very poor, probably because patients with delirium cannot pay attention well enough to cooperate with the testing process. Indeed, their typical pattern of performance on neuropsychological tests is that there is no pattern—everything may look impaired.

Still other consciousness disturbances involve problems not in people's level of consciousness but in the nature or content of their consciousness. For example, a person may have a stroke that causes total paralysis of one side of the body, but the person may not know that they cannot move (Vocat, Saj, & Vuilleumier, 2013). This condition is called *anosognosia* (pronounced "an-oh-sug-NOH-zhuh"), which means an absence of knowledge of disease (Long, Reger, & Adams, 2013). In such cases, brain damage not only impairs functioning but also decreases the ability to know about the impairment. This makes sense because the brain is the organ that we use to figure out when something is wrong. So if you have pain in your arm, sensory neurons tell the brain about it. But if the brain itself is hurt, it has nowhere to send its message!

People can have anosognosia for a variety of problems, from paralysis to blindness to amputation of a limb (McGlynn & Schacter, 1989). It is also sometimes seen in association with neurodegenerative dementias (Morris & Mograbi, 2013). Anosognosia is more likely after damage to the right side of the brain (Vocat et al., 2010). Anosognosia is relatively common, occurring, for example, in more than 25 percent of all stroke cases (Starkstein et al., 1992). An unfortunate result is that these patients may not be motivated to get the prompt medical attention needed to limit the amount of damage that a stroke can cause. Anosognosia usually fades over time, but when it does persist, it impairs patients' cooperation with rehabilitative treatments. They don't recognize that something is wrong, so they don't understand why treatment is necessary. Also, many doctors do not know about anosognosia, so they may fail to diagnose a problem since the patient does not complain about anything (Fowler et al., 2013). There may be ways to improve awareness of neurological deficits, though. In one case, a man was unaware of the sudden and bizarre involuntary movements he had been making for several years. He could not see these movements, even when looking at himself in a mirror, but when he watched himself on videotape, he instantly saw the problem (Shenker et al., 2004).

delirium Periods of abnormally impaired or abnormally elevated levels of consciousness.

CAN SOMEONE BE PARTIALLY PARALYZED AND NOT KNOW IT?

In anosognosia, a person denies a neurological deficit because she or he does not know that a problem exists. This phenomenon was first described long ago in strokes that caused *hemiparesis,* a weakness or partial paralysis affecting just one side of the body (Babinski, 1914). Skeptics argue that people with hemiparesis are still fully capable of knowing that they are partially paralyzed but that this knowledge would be so upsetting that they simply cannot admit it, even to themselves. According to this argument, anosognosia is not true unawareness but an unconscious mental process similar to the ego defense mechanism that Freud called *denial* (see the chapter on personality).

What am I being asked to believe or accept?

Arguing against these skeptics are those who say that anosognosia occurs because the brain damage that causes hemiparesis also damages the brain areas that are needed to know that something is wrong. As a result, patients who seem unaware of hemiparesis or other problems are, in fact, truly unaware of them (Heilman, Barrett, & Adair, 1998; McGlynn & Schacter, 1989).

What evidence is available to support the assertion?

Those who believe that anosognosia is genuine unawareness argue that if it were due to an ego defense mechanism, patients should deny any and all potentially upsetting deficits. Yet evidence shows that some hemiparesis patients, for example, are aware that an arm is weak but not that a leg is weak (Berti, Ladavas, & Corti, 1996; Bisiach et al., 1986). Others are aware that they have a speech problem but not limb weakness (Bisiach et al., 1986; Breier et al., 1995), and some are aware of blindness but unaware of limb paralysis (Prigatano et al., 2011).

Another problem with the ego defense mechanism argument is that anosognosia occurs more often after right-sided brain damage, which causes left hemiparesis, than it does after left-sided brain damage causes right hemiparesis. Weakness on either side should be upsetting and both should cause anosognosia by the denial hypothesis. In fact, because most people are right-handed, weakness on the right side of the body might be even more upsetting and so *more* likely to result in psychologically motivated denial.

Additional evidence against the ego defense mechanism hypothesis comes from finding that anosognosia can occur even when there is no threat of permanent paralysis. In a procedure pioneered by June Wada (Strauss & Wada, 1983), patients being evaluated for possible brain surgery had an anesthetic injected into one side of the brain at a time (Adair et al., 1995; Gilmore et al., 1992). This *Wada test* temporarily "turns off" either the brain's left hemisphere or the right hemisphere but causes no brain damage. When the right hemisphere was "turned off" in this way, participants became paralyzed in the left arm and leg. When asked about their experience, they recalled most details correctly, but most of them showed anosognosia—that is, they said that they did not notice any weakness. When the left hemisphere was anesthetized, though, the patients not only became weak on the right side but also later reported awareness of it. These data are hard to explain due to ego defense mechanisms because once participants had recovered from their left-side paralysis, why would they be motivated to deny that it had occurred?

Are there alternative ways of interpreting the evidence?

A problem with the Wada test is that it is difficult to compare patient experiences during left-versus right-brain anesthesia. The reason is that speech areas are on the left side of the brain, so people are usually unable to speak when their left hemisphere is "turned off," However, this doesn't happen on the right side. The only way to do a direct comparison of the experience of left- versus right-hemisphere inactivation is to ask questions after the anesthetic has worn off. If it were possible for patients to talk during the left-hemisphere inactivation, perhaps they would show anosognosia because at that particular moment, there could be enough distress to motivate denial.

(continued)

The psychological denial interpretation is supported by research decades ago in patients who had a stroke causing hemiparesis (Weinstein & Kahn, 1955). When their families were interviewed, those patients who, before their stroke, had tended to cope with stress through denial were also the ones most likely to deny their hemiparesis. Patients who did not show anosognosia were described by their families as less likely to have previously used denial as a coping strategy. These data implied that denial of hemiparesis could be an exaggeration of one's typical stress-coping tendencies. Also, patients who denying weakness sometimes show implicit awareness of it, such as changing the way they walk after one leg becomes weak (Fotopoulou et al., 2010). Some argue from such an observation that, at some level, such patients actually "know" they are weak, even if it is not conscious.

What additional evidence would help evaluate the alternatives?

The results of family report studies might be affected by *retrospective bias.* That is, if family members know that their relative is denying hemiparesis, they might more often recall similar episodes of denial in the relative's past and forget about when the patient coped with stress in other ways.

One way around the problem of retrospective bias would be to do a *prospective* study in which a large group of individuals is identified, their typical stress-coping tendencies are assessed, and then they are contacted on a regular basis for many years. The ego defense mechanism hypothesis would be supported in such a study if the people in the group who were most likely to use denial as a coping mechanism are also the ones most likely to display anosognosia following a stroke.

Implicit "awareness" of deficits may not necessarily mean that psychological denial is otherwise preventing "explicit awareness" in anosognosia patients. Instead, such observations may merely be another example of how, as described in the consciousness chapter, some of the brain systems that monitor body functions operate outside of our awareness (Prigitano 2013).

What conclusions are most reasonable?

Some individuals who suffer neurological deficits probably do use denial or other psychological defense mechanisms to avoid facing distress, but the evidence best argues that most cases of anosognosia reflect a true lack of awareness of neurological deficit.

Perceptual Disturbances

As described in the chapter on sensation and perception, the brain must organize, recognize, and interpret the information we receive from our eyes, ears, and other senses if we are to make sense of the world. These vital perceptual functions depend on the normal operation of specific brain areas. For example, visual information from the eyes goes to the thalamus and is then analyzed further in the cerebral cortex of the occipital lobe. From there, visual information is sent along two pathways. Along each of these pathways are a series of connected cortical regions that do more specialized analyses, giving us different aspects of visual perception (Ungerleider & Mishkin, 1982; see Figure 18.7). The pathway leading down toward the temporal lobe has been called the "what" system because the brain activity along this pathway helps us decide what we see—a dog or a car, for example. The pathway going up toward the parietal lobe has been called the "where" system because it analyzes object location and where objects are in relation to one another. This system helps us understand, for example, that the dog is sitting inside a car. Damage to our perceptual systems can result in **perceptual disturbances**.

For example, damage to the "what" pathway can cause *visual agnosia* (Barton, 2011). As in the case of Max, individuals with visual agnosia may see objects in the world, describe them, and even draw them, but they cannot use their vision to identify what they see (Rubens & Benson, 1971). So such a patient can correctly define the word *apple* and, based on how it feels, correctly state when one has been placed in their hand. In other

perceptual disturbances Neuro-psychological disorders in which there are impairments in the ability to organize, recognize, interpret, and make sense of incoming sensory information.

FIGURE 18.7
"What" versus "Where"
Visual Pathways

Research suggests that visual information reaching the primary visual cortex
is sent along two separate but parallel
systems. The "where" system focuses on
an object's location in space and how it
is moving. The "what" system determines
the identity of the object.

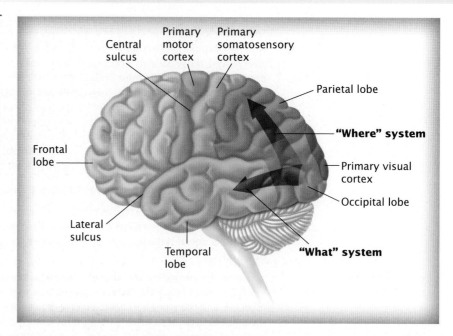

words, these patients still know what apples and other objects are, but they can no longer
link visual images of these objects to the brain systems where that knowledge is stored.

Some visual agnosia patients cannot name anything they see. For others, the problem
is only for categories of objects (Bauer & Demery, 2003). For example, some people appear
to have visual agnosia only for manufactured objects, such as cars, books, or drinking
glasses, but can still see and identify a tree, a dog, or any other living thing (Riddoch et al.,
2008). In other cases, only manufactured objects can be named on sight (Riddoch et al.,
2008; Thomas & Forde, 2006). Such observations suggest that recognition of natural versus
manufactured objects must be based on different brain processing.

Visual agnosias can be even more specific. For example, there may be a brain system that is specialized for visual recognition of faces (Susilo et al., 2013). People with
prosopagnosia (pronounced "proh-suh-pag-NOH-zhuh") can't recognize faces on sight,
even very familiar ones, such as the patient's own face in a photo or mirror (Barton,
2011). Most people with prosopagnosia have damage to both temporal lobes of the brain
(Valdés-Sosa et al., 2011), but sometimes, right-sided damage alone causes this syndrome
(Gainotti, 2013). Interestingly, while prosopagnosia patients may not be able to say if a
face is familiar or not, they still show changes in fMRI and EEG to faces of people they
should know as compared to people they do not know, implying that recognition may
still exist at a "covert" level (Simon et al., 2011).

In a different kind of face-related perceptual disturbance, people can recognize
faces but they believe that a familiar person has been replaced by an "imposter." This
false belief is known as *Capgras syndrome* (pronounced "KAHP-grah"), recognizing the
French psychiatrist who first reported it (Capgras & Reboul-Lachaux, 1923). The damage seen in Capgras syndrome tends to be in the temporal lobes, disconnecting brain
areas that help recognize faces from those that help us to have a sense of familiarity
(Ramachandran, 1998). Capgras delusions are often permanent, but in at least one case
they were cured by antiseizure medication (Shenker, 2013).

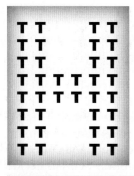

FIGURE 18.8
A "Global-Local" Stimulus

TRY THIS People with simultanagnosia
have difficulty seeing an H in this stimulus but see the Ts easily. Try showing this
pattern to several friends. Unless any of
them are suffering a similar neuropsychological disorder, you should be able to
confirm that they will report seeing both
the little Ts and the larger letter H.

As you might expect, brain damage in the "where" system affects visual perception
of the spatial location of objects and how they are related to one another. An interesting example is called *simultanagnosia* (pronounced "sih-MUL-tun-ag-NOH-zhuh")
(Wolpert, 1924), wherein a person may see parts of a visual scene but not the whole
scene. In a sense, a person with simultanagnosia sees the "trees" but not the "forest."
So if such a patient saw the pattern in Figure 18.8, he or she could see all "Ts" but not
the larger letter "H" formed by the smaller letters.

One patient described her perceptions as follows (Shenker, 2005):

Examiner: What do you see?

Patient: I see T, T, T, T, . . . Do I keep going?

Examiner: Anything else?

Patient: T, T, T, T, . . . lots of Ts.

Examiner: Are there any other letters?

Patient: No.

Examiner: Is there an H?

Patient: No, just Ts.

Examiner: Is there a big letter?

Patient: No, I don't see one.

Examiner: Is there a big letter H?

Patient: No.

Examiner: Do the little letters together form the shape of a big letter H?

Patient: I don't see how.

Examiner: (*outlines the H with finger*) Do you see how this is a big H?

Patient: I don't see an H.

Simultanagnosia is often caused by dysfunction in the brain's parietal lobes (Barton, 2011). Damage to parietal regions can also sometimes cause *hemineglect*. This condition involves difficulty in seeing, responding to, or acting on information coming from either the right or, more often, the left side of the world (Heilman, Watson, & Valenstein, 2003). The side of space that is neglected is usually opposite the side of parietal lobe damage. A person with hemineglect may ignore food on one side of a dinner plate, fail to put makeup on one side of the face, or pay no attention to voices on one side of the room. As shown in Figure 18.9, when asked to draw a picture of, say, a flower or a clock, only half a drawing may be completed.

Hemineglect cannot be simply a lack of sensory input from one side of space. For patients with left hemineglect, the very concept of "leftness" seems lost, and so the left side of the world gets ignored (Bisiach, Capitani, & Tansini, 1979). Such a process is easy to demonstrate in some patients. An examiner may hold up one hand on each side of a patient's visual field and ask the patient to say when fingers are wiggling. In many cases of hemineglect, patients may correctly report when fingers are seen moving on the right *or* on the left, as long as the wiggling is only on one side at a time. But when wiggling is on both sides, patients may see it only on the side they do not ignore. These cases show that some hemineglect patients can *see* both sides of space but are simply more likely to *attend* to one side. The tendency to do so can be reduced, though. In one study, patients were aware of the once-neglected side of space while listening to music evoking positive emotions (Soto et al., 2009). New techniques using electrical brain stimulation also may help (Müri et al., 2013).

Some patients with hemineglect also have sensory problems. They may be blind in their left visual field, for example. It may seem surprising, but we know that even in some of these patients, the tendency to ignore one side of space cannot be due to sensory loss. For example, patients with left hemineglect may not respond to the sound of a voice coming from the left. Is it because of a problem in their left ear? No, because sound is heard by both ears. Also, left hemineglect patients may ignore the left side of an object even if the entire object appears in their right visual field.

FIGURE 18.9

Examples of Neglect on a Drawing Test

When shown pictures like those at left and asked to draw them, patients with hemineglect often leave out details from the neglected side of the object.

FOCUS ON RESEARCH METHODS

STUDYING HEMINEGLECT

Showing that hemineglect is not explained by sensory problems alone can be tricky. After all, in many cases of hemineglect, the brain damage that caused it also caused a loss of sensation from the same side. Also, most tests for hemineglect rely on giving a person some kind of sensory information to respond to. How can one show that hemineglect is not due to a sensory problem if you can only test for it by having people respond to sensory inputs?

What was the researcher's question?

Edoardo Bisiach (Bisiach, Luzzatti, & Perani, 1979) reasoned that if hemineglect was truly a problem with understanding that a particular side of space exists, then this problem should persist even for a scene that exists only in one's imagination.

How did the researcher answer the question?

Bisiach tested patients who had right brain damage and left-sided hemineglect. He created shapes that looked a bit like clouds. The shapes passed behind a vertical slit so that as the image moved, patients could peak at only a small "slice" of it at a time (see Figure 18.10). So, the only way to see the whole shape was to imagine all the "slices" assembled in the mind's eye. Patients were shown two of these passing images at a time, one at the top part of the slit and the other at the bottom. Sometimes, the two shapes were identical; sometimes, their left sides were different, and sometimes, only their right sides were different. The patients had to decide whether the two shapes were same or different.

What did the researcher find?

Patients with left-sided hemineglect could say when the shapes were different if the right sides were mismatched, but not if the left sides were different.

What do the results mean?

Because of the slit, the patients could not see the left and right sides of the images at the same time. So, their failure to notice differences on only the left side could not be from an inability to see the left side. Instead, these results mean that hemineglect occurred when patients ignored a particular side of space for an image assembled into imagery alone.

What do we still need to know?

Different kinds of hemineglect are produced by damage in different parts of the brain (Watson & Heilman, 1979). So it is not clear whether Bisiach's patients, who had parietal lobe damage, are representative of all hemineglect patients. Also, all Bisiach's cloud stimuli were visual. Would the same results appear in research using imagined touches or sounds, for example?

FIGURE 18.10
Studying Hemineglect

Here are examples similar to the cloud-like shapes used by Edoardo Bisiach and his colleagues (1979) to explore whether hemineglect is a sensory problem. Hemineglect patients could see only vertical slices of these shapes as the patterns passed behind a narrow vertical slit. So to "see" these shapes as whole patterns and to decide whether pairs of patterns were the same or different, they had to build an image of each pattern in their minds.

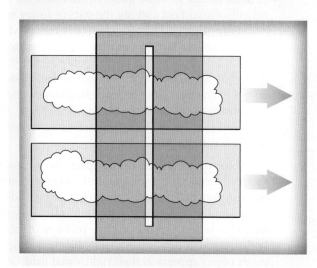

LANGUAGE DISORDERS AND THE BRAIN

LINKAGES How does damage to the brain affect language abilities? (a link to Biological Aspects of Psychology)

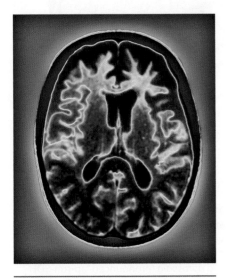

FIGURE 18.11
Frontotemporal Degeneration

In frontotemporal degeneration, a relatively limited part of the brain can become extremely shrunken, as shown here.

Zephyr/Science Source

language disorders (aphasias) Neuropsychological disorders in which there are disruptions in the ability to speak, read, write, and understand language.

Broca's aphasia A language disorder in which there is a loss of fluent speech.

Wernicke's aphasia A language disorder in which there is a loss of ability to understand written or spoken language and to produce sensible speech.

Dysfunction of brain regions that normally support the ability to speak, read, write, and understand language causes **language disorders**, also called **aphasias** (pronounced "uh-FAY-zhuhz"). In this section, we discuss several subtypes of aphasias (Caplan, 2003a), each caused by dysfunction in different parts of the brain's language network.

Most aphasias occur as a result of damage to the left side of the brain, often from stroke or trauma but sometimes from a neurodegenerative disease process called *primary progressive aphasia (PPA)* (Gorno-Tempini et al., 2011). While some cases of PPA are due to a form of Alzheimer's disease (Kirshner, 2012), many are caused by a disease called *frontotemporal degeneration (FTD)*, a condition that gradually kills nerve cells in the brain's temporal or frontal lobes, often on one side more than on the other (Davies & Kipps, 2011; see Figure 18.11). The result may remind you of a stroke in the sense that FTD may affect a limited specific brain area, but unlike the sudden symptoms of a stroke, FTD symptoms develop gradually over years. If FTD is focused on the brain's language-related regions, the result is PPA. Let's consider where these language-related brain regions are, what they normally do, and what else can happen when their functioning is disrupted.

As described in the chapter on biological aspects of psychology, the brain uses several areas to make language possible. These interconnected regions work together as a network, and each must work properly to use and understand language. For example, it appears that *Broca's area* is vital to our ability to translate thoughts into words or writing meaningful to others. Damage to Broca's area (see Figure 18.12) causes **Broca's aphasia**, characterized by a loss of language fluency (Burns & Fahy, 2010). That is, people with Broca's aphasia cannot produce language smoothly and easily. Instead, they speak in a halting, sputtering manner, with great effort and often much frustration. There may be other features as well, including a change in the kinds of words that individuals produce (Benson & Geschwind, 1971). Most of the words that Broca's aphasia patients produce refer to concrete objects, such as *book, pillow,* or *water,* rather than words that refer to abstract ideas such as *justice, art,* or *weather.* These patients also tend to use more nouns and verbs, leaving out articles, adjectives, and adverbs. This style of word usage is called "telegraphic," recalling the bygone telegram era when people had to pay for each letter of a sent message (rekindled by smartphone texting, where an economy of letters spares finger movements!). Thus, a Broca's aphasia patient who once would have said, "Please give me the spoon," might now say simply, "Give spoon." Sometimes Broca's aphasic patients make naming mistakes, called *paraphasias.* In Broca's aphasia, paraphasias tend to be *phonemic paraphasias,* errors in how a word sounds (e.g., call a pen a "peb"). Finally, people with Broca's aphasia may show *agrammatism,* meaning reduced understanding of grammar (Johnson & Cannizzaro, 2009; Caplan, 2003a, 2003b). So, they may not understand that the sentences *The boy hit the girl* and *The girl was hit by the boy* have the same meaning.

People with aphasia caused by damage to *Wernicke's area* (see Figure 18.12) have a different language problem. This area is needed to extract the meaning of language-related sensory information, so if its functioning is disrupted, people may not understand what they read or what others say (Goodglass & Kaplan, 1982). So to a person with **Wernicke's aphasia**, other people's speech can seem to be nonsense, making the world a suddenly strange place where everyone *else* has a problem. Unlike in Broca's aphasia, in Wernicke's aphasia people speak fluently and easily. But *what* they say is far from normal. They make *semantic paraphasias,* naming errors by using the wrong words (e.g., trying to name a pen, calling it a "book"). Unlike Broca's aphasia, in Wernicke's aphasia people use lots of adverbs, adjectives, and articles but fewer nouns and verbs. So the speech of a Wernicke's aphasia patient may sound incomprehensible. For example, when attempting to describe a picture of a woman and her children in the kitchen, a Wernicke's aphasia patient may say, "Over here is the top of the rest for the other rapid if am a many red sitters." The speech of Wernicke's aphasia patient may sound so disorganized that it can seem like the "word salad" of some people with schizophrenia (Sambunaris & Hyde, 1994; see the chapter on psychological disorders). Yet because the patients do not recognize their problems, people with Wernicke's aphasia are often puzzled when others do not seem to understand them.

(continued)

FIGURE 18.12
The Wernicke-Geschwind Model of Aphasia

The Wernicke-Geschwind model of aphasia accounts for many (but not all) of the findings associated with the major aphasias. The pathways shown in Part A transmit information when a participant is instructed to repeat a spoken word. The image shown in Part B traces the flow of information when the person is asked to read a written word out loud.

© iStockphoto.com/Cameron Whitman

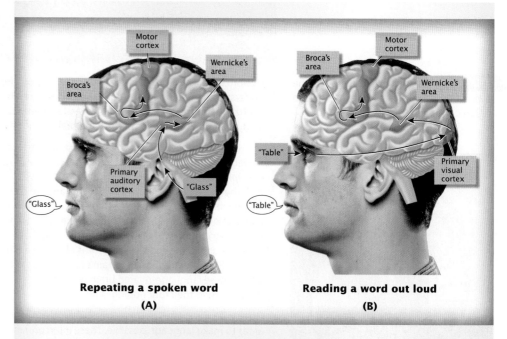

Repeating a spoken word
(A)

Reading a word out loud
(B)

When brain damage causes language disorders, the injury is usually in the brain's left cerebral hemisphere, but right hemisphere damage can also affect communication. In general, people with right-hemisphere damage can still form words well and understand the words they hear and read. However, they may have problems using or understanding *prosody*, or tone of voice (Ross & Monnot, 2008). This problem, called *aprosodia* (pronounced "ap-ruh-SOH-dee-uh"), can take several forms (Ross, 1981, 2006). For example, damage to the right frontal lobe can cause *expressive aprosodia*, such that a person speaks in such a monotone that they need to say something like "I am angry" to convey how they are feeling (Ghacibeh & Heilman, 2003). However, such a patient may still understand and use prosody heard as other people speak. By contrast, people with damage to the right temporal and parietal regions may have a *receptive aprosodia;* they can use tone of voice correctly when they speak but have difficulty understanding it in others. So if someone were to say sarcastically, "Well, that was really smart," meaning just the opposite, a person with receptive aprosodia may miss the sarcasm, note only the words themselves, and say, "Thanks!"

Disorders of Movement Control

The brain's motor pathways are "wired" to muscles in ways that allow us to move our limbs and body, but the knowledge of how to do so in order to accomplish our goals effectively is not built in to that system (Goldenberg, 2013). Using silverware, pedaling a bicycle, sucking on a straw, or swinging a hammer are just a few examples of the many coordinated movements that we must learn from experience. A network of brain areas control such learned motor skills by instructing the brain's motor control centers to make the movements needed for each action sequence (see Figure 18.13). These brain areas give you the function of *praxis*, the ability to tell the motor system the combinations of movements needed for a specific learned task. When brain damage disrupts this process, the result is called **apraxia** (pronounced "uh-PRAK-see-uh"), an inability to do a learned skilled movement not due to weakness, a sensory problem, or a state of general confusion.

There are different types of apraxia (Heilman & Gonzalez-Rothi, 2003; Pearce, 2009). In *ideational apraxia*, individual movements are done right, but in the wrong order. For example, the person may open a tube of toothpaste, wet the toothbrush, squeeze paste onto the brush, insert the brush in the mouth, and move the brush in the mouth correctly. But she might put the brush in her mouth before putting paste on it, or she might squeeze the tube before unscrewing the cap.

apraxia Neuropsychological disorder in which there are impairments in the ability to perform or coordinate a previously learned motor skills.

FIGURE 18.13
The Initiation of
Voluntary Movement

A network of brain regions is involved in
initiating voluntary movements.

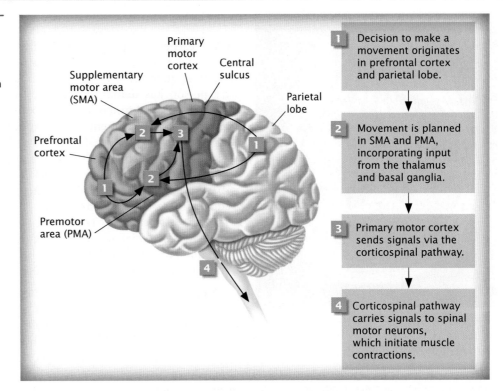

FIGURE 18.13
The Initiation of
Voluntary Movement

A network of brain regions is involved in
initiating voluntary movements.

1 Decision to make a movement originates in prefrontal cortex and parietal lobe.

2 Movement is planned in SMA and PMA, incorporating input from the thalamus and basal ganglia.

3 Primary motor cortex sends signals via the corticospinal pathway.

4 Corticospinal pathway carries signals to spinal motor neurons, which initiate muscle contractions.

A more common apraxia is *ideomotor apraxia*, which involves difficulties not in the sequence of skilled movements but in movements themselves (Wheaton & Hallett, 2007). Such a patient may try to do each step in toothbrushing in order but has difficulty positioning the hand to hold the brush, or timing the limb motions to do the actual tooth brushing. Such a person may use a finger or body part as if it were a tool, perhaps brushing with the finger itself. In such cases, the person cannot seem to figure out how to use the actual tool they once utilized with ease (see Figure 18.14).

FIGURE 18.14
An Example of Apraxic
Motor Behavior

When imitating the movements involved
in using a common object, an individual
with apraxia may mistakenly use an arm or
a leg to represent that object. So instead
of showing how they would move in order
to use a tool, they act as if their limb is the
tool itself.

*Source: From Banich M. T. Cognitive Neuroscience
and Neuropsychology, 2nd ed. (p. 179). Copyright ©
2004 Cengage Learning.*

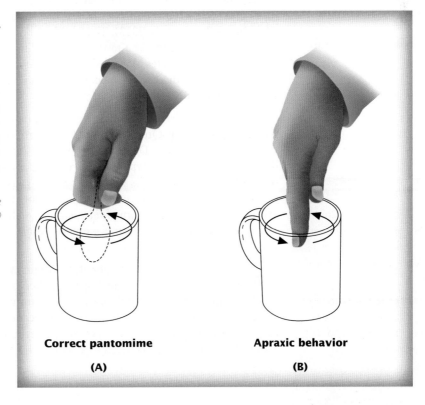

Correct pantomime

(A)

Apraxic behavior

(B)

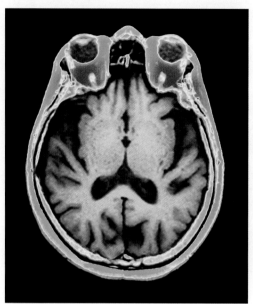

FIGURE 18.15
Brain Atrophy in Alzheimer's Disease

Alzheimer's disease causes some brain cells to stop working and eventually die, whereas other brain cells may be unaffected. Where brain cells die off, the cortex shrinks, leaving gaping spaces.

Zephyr/Science Source

dementia Neuropsychological disorders in which there are significant and disruptive impairments in memory, as well as in perceptual ability, language, or learned motor skills.

Alzheimer's disease Dementia resulting from a neurodegenerative disease characterized by the loss of cognitive functions.

Dementia

We saw earlier that people with delirium had alertness that was too high or low, and many psychological abilities may fail at once. Delirium usually stops some time after the toxin or other cause of delirium disappears. When we say a person has **dementia**, however, alertness remains mostly normal, yet many other mental functions are impaired (Dekosky et al., 2008). In dementia, there is a decline in memory and other areas of psychological functioning such as perceptual ability, language, or learned motor skills. By convention, to use the word "dementia," these impairments must be interfering with one's ability to function at work, in social situations, or in everyday tasks such as driving, cooking, or handling finances. In most cases, but not all, dementia is gradual, progressive, and irreversible. DSM-5, the fifth edition of the *American Psychiatric Association's Diagnostic and Statistical Manual* (2013), refers to dementia as *major neurocognitive disorder*, but whatever the name, about 35.6 million people worldwide have this problem, and that number is expected to more than double by the year 2030 (Prince et al., 2013).

A condition known as *mild cognitive impairment* (*MCI*) may precede some kinds of dementia (Petersen, 2011) (in DSM-5, MCI is termed *minor neurocognitive disorder*). In *amnestic MCI,* for example, a person develops memory problems to a certain degree, but no other deficits, and the person can maintain daily functioning. People with amnestic MCI may or may not get worse, but some do progress into dementia (Runtti et al., 2013). Identifying people in this relatively early stage of memory loss is important because following the so-called Mediterranean diet, and a diet rich in antioxidants, appears to slow cognitive decline at this stage (Shah, 2013). Medications are also being evaluated that may help to stabilize memory and delay full-fledged dementia (Karakaya et al., 2013).

Alzheimer's Disease

Dementia is often caused by a progressive neurodegenerative disease, and between 60 to 80 percent of the time, that disease is **Alzheimer's disease** (Alzheimer's Association, 2014; Fratiglioni & Qiu, 2009). In the United States, about 5.2 million people have Alzheimer's disease, costing $203 billion a year and incalculable personal suffering (Thies, Bleiler, & Alzheimer's Association, 2013). The likelihood of Alzheimer's disease doubles about every five years after age sixty. As a result, over 5 million people over age sixty-five have this disease in the United States alone (Alzheimer's Association, 2014). With more people living longer, Alzheimer disease is expected to affect 65.7 million people worldwide by the year 2030 (Gulland, 2012).

Alzheimer's disease was first described in 1907 by the German neurologist Alois Alzheimer (Devi & Quitschke, 1999). He reported the case of a forty-six-year-old woman, "Frau Auguste Deter," with a type of "senility" (see Figure 18.15), and after she died, he described two types of microscopic abnormalities in her brain. First, he saw dead and dying nerve cells that had become twisted and misshapen, what we now call *neurofibrillary tangles*. Second, he saw abnormal debris lying outside of nerve cells. We now call this finding *amyloid plaque*. To this day, a definitive autopsy diagnosis of Alzheimer's disease requires neurofibrillary tangles and amyloid plaque (Nelson, Braak, & Markesbery, 2011).

In an Alzheimer's disease patient, the brain areas that develop neurofibrillary tangles fail to work properly, thus causing the patient's symptoms. But before neurofibrillary tangles cause symptoms, amyloid plaques accumulate diffusely in the patient's brain (Vos et al., 2013). According to the "amyloid cascade hypothesis," the cause of Alzheimer's disease lies in the toxic process of creating amyloid plaques (Krstic & Knuesel, 2013). We all develop some of this plaque as we get older, but in Alzheimer's disease patients, amyloid plaque is much more abundant. Other scientists are looking at mitochondria of brain cells as a cause for Alzheimer's disease. Mitochondria give energy to cells by using oxygen and sugar from the blood supply. Some scientists argue that mitochondria dysfunction may be the initial defect causing the brain damage of Alzheimer's disease (Swerdlow, 2011). This argument is supported by findings that foods high in antioxidants, which are substances that help bypass the dysfunctioning mitochondria, may help delay Alzheimer's disease (Shah, 2013).

Some areas of the cerebral cortex are more affected than others in Alzheimer's patients (Jacobs et al., 2012), leading to the neuropsychological symptoms of the disease (Peña-Casanova et al., 2013). One brain area affected is the temporal lobes, and in particular the hippocampus (Teipel et al, 2013), causing reduced ability to form new memories. Old memories, already formed and stored elsewhere, usually remain intact until the disease's later stages. So as in the case of H.M., Alzheimer's disease patients may remember details from early adulthood but not an event from yesterday. But, because the temporal lobes also help interpret visual sensations, patients with Alzheimer's disease may develop visual agnosia and so may not recognize the objects they see.

The parietal lobes are also affected. Dysfunction there can affect spatial perceptions, so a patient may get lost. Many Alzheimer's patients can get lost so easily that they may wander away from where they live (Rolland et al., 2007). Language problems also occur, especially *anomia*, meaning it is hard to name objects even if they know what the objects are. Many Alzheimer's patients may also develop apraxia, a problem we discussed earlier, making it hard to do learned motor skills such as using a hammer or a spoon.

There is still no way to prevent Alzheimer's disease (Friedrich, 2014). Medications help Alzheimer's disease patients to some degree, but the benefits remain slight, and more effective new treatments are still needed (Schneider, 2013). Meanwhile, the cognitive decline in Alzheimer's disease is lessened some by staying physically active (Sattler et al., 2011) and mentally active (Ballard et al., 2011).

Vascular Dementia

As we have already seen, a loss of blood supply to the brain can damage brain tissue. When this brain damage leads to dementia, we call this **vascular dementia** (O'brien, 2011). Sometimes a loss of blood supply to the brain occurs in tiny blood vessels, damaging a small amount of brain tissue. Such injuries may not cause symptoms at first, especially if vital areas are not affected. But if many such small injuries occur, more and more brain tissue is lost, and the cumulative effect can be an impairment of memory and other psychological functions (Fisher, 1989).

Vascular dementia is second only to Alzheimer's disease as a common cause of dementia (Korczyn, Vakhapova, & Grinberg, 2012). The two conditions may occur in the same individual (Honjo, Black, S. & Cerhoeff, 2012), but the symptoms of vascular dementia may differ from those of Alzheimer's disease (Knopman, 2006). Vascular dementia patients show memory loss, including forgetting of recent events, but in contrast to Alzheimer's disease, the hippocampus may be well preserved. So vascular dementia patients may still be able to form new memories. Why, then, do they have difficulty recalling new material? In some cases, the answer may be that they have more of a problem retrieving recent memories than in forming them. This subtle difference highlights the importance of careful neuropsychological assessment. Differences between vascular dementia and other dementias have also been found in the appearance of deficits such as aphasia, apraxia, and dyslexia (Topakian & Aichner, 2008).

vascular dementia A form of dementia caused by multiple restrictions of the brain's blood supply.

Treating Dementia

It is helpful for physicians to know what form of dementia a patient has in order to prescribe the correct medication and help families plan for the future (Leifer, 2009). Choosing the right drug at the right time can help patients enjoy a better quality of life for a longer time and may delay the need for nursing home care (Geldmacher et al., 2003). Accordingly, it would be ideal if Alzheimer's disease and other dementias could be diagnosed even before their symptoms appear. Scientists are working to develop early diagnostic clues using molecular tests and brain imaging (Ballard et al., 2011), analysis of EEG brain waves (Gasser et al., 2008), refined neuropsychological assessment batteries (De Santi et al., 2008), and observation of various behavioral changes (Caputo et al., 2008).

Progress in the development of new medications and early diagnostic tests leads many researchers to hope that instead of just stopping or slowing the progress of dementia, it may someday be possible to reverse its course, allowing some patients to once again enjoy more normal cognitive functioning (Lacor, 2007). And as discussed in the human development chapter, the appearance of dementia may be delayed or prevented in those who spend their lives engaged in stimulating mental activity, interactions with friends, and healthy eating and exercise (Fratiglioni & Qiu, 2009). ("In Review: Major Neuropsychological Disorders" summarizes the various dysfunctions discussed here.)

IN REVIEW
MAJOR NEUROPSYCHOLOGICAL DISORDERS

Syndrome	Type of Difficulty	Areas of Brain Malfunction
Apraxia	Making learned skilled movements even if not weak or confused	Usually left cerebral hemisphere parietal or frontal lobes
Visual	Attaching meaning to visual	Temporal lobes, often bilateral
Anosognosia	Becoming aware of the loss of neurological function	Usually right cerebral hemisphere
Hemineglect	Paying attention to one side of space	Usually right parietal lobe
Aphasia	Using language as a communication system	Usually left cerebral hemisphere
Aprosodia	Using tone of voice as a communication tool	Usually right cerebral hemisphere
Dementia	Memory and at least one other psychological ability that are severe enough to impair functioning	Variable, depending on the cause of the dementia

1. A patient who has become forgetful but has no problems in other areas of cognitive function may be said to have _____.

2. A dementia patient whose hippocampus is relatively intact and can still form new memories probably has _____ dementia.

3. A patient with thiamine deficiency who is forgetful but makes up memories and believes they are real probably has _____.

LINKAGES

As noted in the introductory chapter, all of psychology's subfields are related to one another. Our discussion of language disorders illustrates just one way in which the topic of this chapter, neuropsychology, is linked to the subfield of biological psychology, which is described in the chapter on biological aspects of psychology. The Linkages diagram shows ties to two other subfields, and there are many more ties throughout the book. Looking for linkages among subfields will help you see how they all fit together and help you better appreciate the big picture that is psychology.

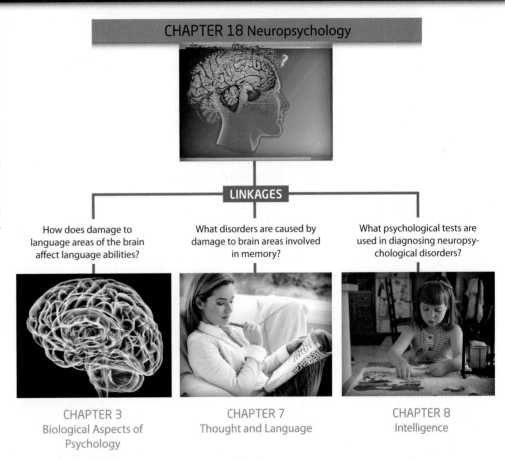

CHAPTER 18 Neuropsychology

LINKAGES

How does damage to language areas of the brain affect language abilities?

What disorders are caused by damage to brain areas involved in memory?

What psychological tests are used in diagnosing neuropsychological disorders?

CHAPTER 3
Biological Aspects of Psychology

CHAPTER 7
Thought and Language

CHAPTER 8
Intelligence

SUMMARY

Neuropsychology is the subfield of psychology whose goal is to explore and understand the relationships among brain processes, human behavior, and psychological functioning.

Foundations of Neuropsychology

What is neuropsychology and how did it develop?

There are two main assumptions in neuropsychology. The first is that complicated mental tasks such as memory involve many subtasks that can be studied separately. The second is that different psychological processes are controlled by different brain regions or different combinations of brain regions. Experimental neuropsychologists use these assumptions as they conduct research on how the brain controls and organizes human mental activity. *Clinical neuropsychologists* use the results of neuropsychological research to try to understand the nature and location of brain disorders seen in individual patients.

Neuropsychology's early history focused on debates over *localization of function*, the idea that specific psychological functions are governed by specific parts of the brain. Early evidence for this notion was dismissed by serious scientists, but by the 1860s, localization of function began to be accepted, and it now forms the basis for much of what we know about neuropsychological functioning.

Recent theories of localization center on the idea that the brain is organized into *modules*, each of which performs its own unique analysis of information and works together with varying combinations of other modules throughout the brain to perform all aspects of behavior and mental processes.

Experimental neuropsychologists use *lesion* analysis to try to understand the complexities of localization of function; they look at how damage (lesions) in particular places in the brain relate to the appearance of particular problems.

Clinical neuropsychologists use a wide variety of *neuropsychological assessment* methods to help determine the nature of a patient's neuropsychological problems and even to suggest where in the brain the problem may lie. These tests may consist of a standardized group of instruments, such as the Halstead-Reitan Battery, or they may be an individualized combination of tests chosen by the neuropsychologist with a particular patient in mind. In most cases, a standard battery is followed by some additional individualized tests.

To develop their skills, clinical neuropsychologists typically earn a Ph.D. in clinical psychology with a focus on neuropsychology and then complete a postdoctoral internship.

Mechanisms of Brain Dysfunction

What are the main causes of brain damage and dysfunction?

Brain dysfunctions can be caused by a number of conditions.

One of the main causes of brain damage and dysfunction is a *cerebral infarct* (*stroke*), which occurs when the blood supply to a part of the brain is blocked, causing the death of brain cells in that region and the loss of that brain region's ability to exercise its normal control over some aspect of behavior or mental processing. Strokes can be disabling and sometimes deadly.

Damage and dysfunction can also result from *traumatic brain injury* (*trauma*), a sudden impact on the brain caused by a blow to the head, sudden and violent head movements, or other events that literally shake the brain inside the skull. The amount of damage and dysfunction following such events depends mainly on the amount of force involved and the degree to which the impact is cushioned by the action of the *cerebrospinal fluid*.

Neurodegeneration is the gradual process of damage to brain cells caused by *neurodegenerative diseases* such as Alzheimer's, Parkinson's, and Huntington's or by infections, nutritional deficiencies, or genetic abnormalities.

Neuropsychological Disorders

What disorders can be caused by brain damage or dysfunction?

The *syndromes,* or patterns of symptoms, associated with stroke, trauma, and neurodegenerative diseases appear as several kinds of neuropsychological disorders.

The hallmark of *amnestic disorders* is some significant disruption or loss of memory, as seen in conditions such as *anterograde amnesia,* in which new memories do not form, and *Korsakoff's*

psychosis (*Korsakoff's syndrome*), in which memory distortions and *confabulations* are caused by a lack of thiamine.

In *consciousness disturbances,* a person's normal awareness of the world is impaired. These conditions can range from loss of consciousness, as in coma or persistent vegetative state (which may result from damage to the *reticular formation*), to *delirium,* in which the patient alternates between reduced and elevated degrees of consciousness. In cases of anosognosia, a person may be paralyzed on one side of the body but have no awareness of the problem.

People who experience *perceptual disturbances* may become unable to understand what objects, or certain categories of objects, are by looking at them (visual agnosia), may be unable to recognize faces (prosopagnosia), or have difficulty assembling the specific parts of a visual scene into a coherent whole (simultanagnosia). Patients with a perceptual disorder called hemineglect ignore one half of the world.

Language disorders usually result from damage to language areas on the left side of the brain and take the form of *aphasias,* in which the ability to speak or understand language is disrupted. The many forms of aphasia include *Broca's aphasia,* in which people can no longer speak fluently, and *Wernicke's aphasia,* which makes it difficult for people to understand what they read or hear, and although they can speak fluently, their speech makes little or no sense. Damage in the right side of the brain can result in aprosodia, the loss of ability to use tone of voice to express one's meaning or to understand the meaning of other people's speech.

Apraxias involve the inability to perform various motor skills or the inability to perform those skills in the correct order.

Patients with *dementia* suffer gradually more significant and, usually, irreversible, loss of many mental functions, including impairment of memory, perception, language, and motor skills. It is usually caused by progressive neurodegenerative disorders such as *Alzheimer's disease,* though in *vascular dementia,* the cause is restrictions of the brain's blood supply. A condition known as mild cognitive impairment may precede the appearance of some forms of dementia.

TEST YOUR KNOWLEDGE

Select the best answer for each of the following questions. Then check your responses against the Answer Key at the end of the book.

1. Dr. Boar is an experimental neuropsychologist, whereas Dr. Yemas is a clinical neuropsychologist. This means that Dr. Boar's work will most likely involve _____ ; and Dr. Yemas's work will most likely involve _____ .
   a. adding to the knowledge about general brain function; applying knowledge of brain function to specific patients
   b. adding to the knowledge about general brain function; adding to the knowledge about general brain function
   c. applying knowledge of brain function to specific patients; adding to the knowledge about general brain function
   d. applying knowledge of brain function to specific patients; applying knowledge of brain function to specific patients

2. The idea that feeling the bumps on a person's head can tell you about that person's psychological makeup, originated from the idea that _____ .
   a. much-used areas of the brain shrink because they become more efficient at processing
   b. the brain is a homogenous organ that works in a unified fashion
   c. different areas of the brain perform different functions
   d. both a and b

3. Broca's area _____ .
   a. is not related to a specific place in the brain but is used as a general descriptor for people experiencing any language impairment
   b. was identified when people experiencing language difficulties were found to have lesions in the left frontal part of the brain
   c. is a brain module used in all language functions in the brain
   d. directs the network responsible for language within the brain

4. When an experimental neuropsychologist performs lesion analysis, this means that she is _____ .
   a. looking for the one brain module that is responsible for the patient's neurological problem
   b. looking for a dissociation between abilities
   c. performing brain surgery to look at particular lesions in the brain
   d. looking for general information about how normal brains work

5. Damian was having extreme difficulty remembering anything. His mother, worried about his memory, took him to the doctor to find out if his memory lapses were normal. The neuropsychologist evaluating Damian will most likely give him _____ .
   a. a battery of psychometric tests and compare his scores with established norms
   b. a battery of psychometric tests and compare his scores with those of people with memory disorders
   c. an individualized set of psychometric tests, which will be normed only for Damian
   d. a clinical interview in which he asks Damian to identify changes in his own memory functioning

6. Jerry suddenly was unable to speak and felt "funny." His doctor's diagnosis was that Jerry had suffered a stroke. This means that _____ .
   a. Jerry had experienced some type of brain trauma
   b. Jerry was experiencing pain in his brain
   c. a blood vessel in Jerry's brain was blocked
   d. parts of Jerry's brain temporarily stopped functioning

7. When Roselle was diagnosed with a neurodegenerative disease, she didn't understand what was happening. Her doctor explained that _____ .
   a. some blood vessels in her brain were blocked, killing brain tissue
   b. the nerve cells of her brain had become too easily excitable
   c. her brain had bumped against bone, causing microscopic tears
   d. diseased brain neurons had stopped functioning correctly

8. Mickey cannot remember people he just met, but he still remembers his childhood. He also remembers that he was at the fateful Cubs baseball game when Steve Bartman interfered with the outfielder's catching of a fly ball. However, Mickey has never been to Chicago and was not at that game, despite what he believes he remembers. Mickey will most likely be diagnosed _____ .
   a. with Alzheimer's disease
   b. as having had a stroke
   c. with a brain infection such as herpes encephalitis
   d. with Korsakoff's syndrome

9. When Betty was told that her mother was experiencing delirium, it was explained that this means that her mother _____ .
   a. probably would remain in a persistent vegetative state
   b. could have both impaired and elevated levels of consciousness from time to time
   c. had a problem caused by being very upset and nervous
   d. would be likely to show signs of brain trauma

10. Rachel did not seek medical care when she had a stroke because her brain was damaged in such a way that she had no knowledge of the damage. In other words, Rachel experienced _____ .
    a. aphasia
    b. anterograde amnesia
    c. anosognosia
    d. a deficiency in thiamine

11. When a patient experiences visual agnosia, it is often due to damage to the "what" pathway. This damage is most likely to be in the _____ lobe.
    a. thalamic
    b. parietal
    c. temporal
    d. frontal

12. Tracy was diagnosed with prosopagnosia. This means that Tracy will be unable to identify _____ .
    a. an apple she is holding
    b. manufactured objects
    c. the sound of a familiar voice
    d. people's faces

13. When Robin experienced a stroke, she had significant damage to her right parietal lobe. She now ignores everything in the left side of space. Robin is showing symptoms of _____ .
    a. hemineglect
    b. simultanagnosia
    c. aphasia
    d. anosognosia

14. A study described in the Focus on Research Methods section of this chapter was able to establish that patients with hemineglect _____ .
    a. ignore one side of space in a manner that is not explained by sensory loss
    b. are no longer able to imagine scenes under any circumstances
    c. can use only concrete visual stimuli
    d. do not experience sensory deficits

15. Alex had a language problem. He could speak, but not in a normal manner. He could use only a limited number of simple and concrete words. For example, when he wanted his wife to purchase applesauce when she went to the grocery store, he was only able to say, "Applesauce buy." A neuropsychologist would most likely look for damage to _____ in Alex's brain.
    a. Wernicke's area
    b. Broca's area
    c. the occipital lobe
    d. the corpus callosum

16. Allana also had a language problem. Her speech also was not normal. However, when she wanted her husband to purchase applesauce from the grocery store, she said "From flowing flowery in a with the shrubs buy over the other." We know that Allana is not schizophrenic, so we would infer that she has damage to _____.
    a. Wernicke's area
    b. Broca's area
    c. the occipital lobe
    d. corpus callosum

17. A neurological deficit in which people have difficulty reading the letters that they themselves wrote is known as _____.
    a. anosognosia
    b. aprosodia
    c. alexia without agraphia
    d. corpus callosumania

18. Alfreda said to her husband, "I am very angry with you." However, she said it in a monotone that did not really suggest she was expressing anger. It was as though she had e-mailed him this information. A neuropsychologist would suspect Alfreda is experiencing _____.
    a. hemineglect
    b. simultanagnosia
    c. Alzheimer's disease
    d. aprosodia

19. Fred's problem in remembering things was slowly becoming more apparent. In addition, he had to stop playing golf because he could no longer swing his club correctly. Yet he remained alert and attentive. His wife brought him to a neuropsychologist because Fred, a skilled accountant, could no longer even balance their checkbook. Fred most likely will be diagnosed with _____.
    a. dementia
    b. delirium
    c. aphasia
    d. apraxia

20. Research on Alzheimer's disease has found that _____.
    a. the number of people diagnosed with Alzheimer's disease decreases after age eighty
    b. memory loss is the only significant symptom
    c. patients with Alzheimer's have a different brain pathology than those experiencing normal aging
    d. the disease begins with dysfunction in the dopamine neurotransmitter network

ANSWER KEY
Answers to In Review Questions

The questions at the bottom of each chapter's In Review charts are listed here, followed in parentheses by the correct answers. The questions are grouped under each chapter's title and by the name and page number of the In Review chart in which they appear.

Chapter 1 Introducing Psychology

In Review: The Development of Psychology (p. 15)

1. Darwin's theory of evolution had an especially strong influence on _____ism and _____ism. (functional; behavior)
2. Which school of psychological thought was founded by a European medical doctor? _____ (psychoanalysis)
3. In the history of psychology, _____ was the first school of thought to appear. (structuralism)

In Review: Approaches to the Science of Psychology (p. 20)

1. Teaching people to be less afraid of heights reflects the _____ approach. (behavioral)
2. Charles Darwin was not a psychologist, but his work influenced the _____ approach to psychology. (evolutionary)
3. Assuming that people inherit mental disorders suggests a _____ approach. (biological)

Chapter 2 Research in Psychology

In Review: Methods of Psychological Research (p. 39)

1. The _____ method is most likely to use a double-blind design. (experimental)
2. Research on a new treatment method is most likely to begin with _____. (case studies)
3. Studying language by listening to people in public places is an example of _____ research. (naturalistic observation)

Chapter 3 Biological Aspects of Psychology

In Review: Neurons, Neurotransmitters, and Receptors (p. 56)

1. In most cases, when one neuron communicates with another, a _____ crosses the _____ between them. (neurotransmitter; synapse)
2. The nervous system's main functions are to _____, _____, and _____ information. (receive; process; act on)
3. The two main types of cells in the nervous system are _____ and _____. (neurons; glial cells)

In Review: Organization of the Brain (p. 64)

1. The oldest part of the brain is the _____. (hindbrain)
2. Cells that operate as the body's twenty-four-hour "time clock" are found in the _____. (hypothalamus)
3. Memory problems seen in Alzheimer's disease are related to shrinkage of the _____ (hippocampus)

In Review: Classes of Neurotransmitters (p. 80)

1. The main neurotransmitter for slowing, or inhibiting, brain activity is _____. (GABA)

2. A group of neurons that use the same neurotransmitter is called a _____. (neurotransmitter system)
3. Which neurotransmitter's activity causes brain damage during a stroke? _____ (glutamate)

Chapter 4 Sensation and Perception

In Review: Seeing (p. 99)

1. The ability to see in very dim light depends on photoreceptors called _____. (rods)
2. Color afterimages are best explained by the _____ theory of color vision. (opponent-process)
3. Nearsightedness and farsightedness occur when images are not focused on the eye's _____. (retina)

In Review: Hearing (p. 103)

1. Sound energy is converted to neural activity in an inner ear structure called the _____. (cochlea [or basilar membrane])
2. Hearing loss due to damage to hair cells or the auditory nerve is called _____. (nerve deafness)
3. How high or low a sound sounds is called _____ and is determined by the _____ of a sound wave. (pitch; frequency)

In Review: Smell and Taste (p. 108)

1. The flavor of food arises from a combination of _____ and _____. (taste; smell)
2. Emotion and memory are linked especially closely to our sense of _____. (smell)
3. Perfume ads suggest that humans are affected by _____ that increase sexual attraction. (pheromones)

In Review: Body Senses (p. 114)

1. Gate control theory offers an explanation of why we sometimes do not feel _____. (pain)
2. Professional dancers look at the same spot as long as possible during repeated spins. They are trying to avoid the dizziness caused when the sense of _____ is overstimulated. (equilibrium)
3. Without your sense of _____, you would not be able to swallow food without choking. (touch)

In Review: Principles of Perceptual Organization and Constancy (p. 124)

1. The movement we see in videos is due to a perceptual illusion called _____. (the stroboscopic illusion)
2. People who have lost an eye also lose the ability to use _____ depth cues, two of which are called _____ and _____. (binocular; eye convergence; retinal disparity)
3. The grouping principle of _____ allows you to identify objects seen through a picket fence. (closure)

In Review: Mechanisms of Pattern Recognition (p. 128)

1. Your ability to read a battered old sign that has some letters missing is a result of _____ processing. (top-down)

2. When stimulus features match the stimuli we are looking for, _____ takes place. (recognition)

3. Schemas can create a _____ that makes us more likely to perceive stimuli in a particular way. (perceptual set)

Chapter 5 Learning

In Review: Basic Processes of Classical Conditioning (p. 149)

1. If a person with a conditioned fear of spiders is also frightened by the sight of other creatures that look somewhat like spiders, the person is demonstrating stimulus _____. (generalization)

2. Because of _____, we are more likely to learn a fear of snakes than a fear of cars. (biopreparedness)

3. Feeling sad upon hearing a song associated with a long-lost relationship illustrates _____. (spontaneous recovery)

In Review: Reinforcement and Punishment (p. 161)

1. Taking a pill can relieve headache pain, so people learn to do so through the process of _____ reinforcement. (negative)

2. The "walk" sign that tells people it is safe to cross the street is an example of a _____ stimulus. (discriminative conditioned)

3. Response rates tend to be higher under _____ schedules of reinforcement than under _____ schedules. (ratio; interval)

Chapter 6 Memory

In Review: Models of Memory (p. 184)

1. The value of elaborative rehearsal over maintenance rehearsal has been cited as evidence for the _____ model of memory. (levels-of-processing)

2. Deliberately trying to remember something means using your _____ memory. (explicit)

3. Playing the piano uses _____ memory. (procedural)

In Review: Storing New Memories (p. 190)

1. If you looked up a phone number but forgot it before you could call it, the information was probably lost from _____ memory. (short-term)

2. The capacity of short-term memory is about _____ to _____ items. (five; nine)

3. Encoding is usually _____ in short-term memory and _____ in long-term memory. (acoustic; semantic)

In Review: Factors Affecting Retrieval from Long-Term Memory (p. 192)

1. Stimuli called _____ help you recall information stored in long-term memory. (retrieval cues)

2. If it is easier to remember something in the place where you learned it, you have _____ memory. (context-dependent)

3. The tendency to remember the last few items in a list is called the _____ effect. (recency)

In Review: Improving Your Memory (p. 213)

1. Using mnemonic strategies and the PQ4R system to better remember course material are examples of the value of _____ rehearsal. (elaborative)

2. "Cramming" illustrates _____ practice that usually leads to _____ long-term retention than _____ practice. (massed; poorer [or less]; distributed)

3. To minimize forgetting, you should review lecture notes _____ after a lecture ends. (immediately [or as soon as possible])

Chapter 7 Thought and Language

In Review: Ingredients of Thought (p. 227)

1. Thinking is the manipulation of _____. (mental representations)

2. Arguments over what is "fair" occur because "fairness" is a _____ concept. (natural)

3. Your _____ of "hotel room" would lead you to expect yours to include a bathroom. (schema)

In Review: Solving Problems (p. 237)

1. People stranded without water could use their shoes to collect rain, but they may not do so because of an obstacle to problem solving called _____. (functional fixedness)

2. Because of the _____ heuristic, once sellers set a value on their house, they may refuse to take much less for it. (anchoring)

3. If you tackle a massive problem one small step at a time, you are using an approach called _____. (decomposition or means-end analysis)

Chapter 8 Intelligence

In Review: Influences on IQ (p. 275)

1. Intelligence is influenced by both _____ and _____. (heredity; environment)

2. Children living in poverty tend to have _____ IQs than those in middle-class families. (lower)

3. IQs of children whose parents encourage learning tend to be _____ than those of children whose parents do not. (higher)

In Review: Approaches to Intelligence (p. 280)

1. The concepts of fluid and crystallized intelligence developed from research on the _____ approach to intelligence. (psychometric)

2. Using fMRI scanning to relate memory skills to intelligence reflects the _____ approach to intelligence. (information processing)

3. Which theory of intelligence highlights the fact that some people with low IQs can still succeed at complex tasks of daily living? (triarchic)

Chapter 9 Consciousness

In Review: Sleep and Sleep Disorders (p. 307)

1. Jet lag occurs because of a disruption in a traveler's _____. (circadian rhythms [or sleep-wake cycle])

2. The importance of NREM sleep is suggested by its appearance _____ in the night. (early)

3. The safest sleeping position for babies is _____. (face up)

In Review: Major Classes of Psychoactive Drugs (p. 322)

1. Physical dependence on a drug is a condition more commonly known as _____. (addiction)

2. Drugs that act as antagonists _____ the interaction of neurotransmitters and receptors. (block)

3. Drug effects are determined partly by what we learn to _____ the effects to be. (expect)

Chapter 10 Motivation and Emotion

In Review: Sources, Theories, and Types of Motivation (p. 335)

1. The fact that some people like roller coasters and other scary amusement park rides has been cited as evidence for the _____ theory of motivation. (optimal arousal)

2. Evolutionary theories of motivation are modern outgrowths of theories based on _____. (the instinct doctrine)

3. The value of incentives can be affected by _____, _____, and _____ factors. (physiological [or biological]; cognitive; social)

In Review: Major Factors Controlling Hunger and Eating (p. 342)

1. People may eat when they are "full," suggesting that eating is not controlled by _____ alone. (hunger)

2. People who binge and purge have an eating disorder called _____. Those who only binge have a disorder called _____. (bulimia; binge eating disorder)

3. The best strategy for lasting weight loss includes regular _____, as well as improved eating habits. (exercise)

In Review: Theories of Emotion (p. 366)

1. Research showing that there are pleasure centers in the brain has been cited in support of the _____ theory of emotions. (Cannon-Bard)

2. The use of polygraphs in lie detection is based on the _____ theory of emotions. (James-Lange)

3. The process of attribution is most important to _____ theories of emotions. (cognitive)

Chapter 11 Human Development

In Review: Milestones of Cognitive Development in Infancy and Childhood (p. 388)

1. Research in cognitive development suggests that children form mental representations _____ than Piaget thought they did. (earlier)

2. Recognizing that changing the shape of clay doesn't change the amount of clay is evidence of a cognitive ability called _____. (conservation)

3. The appearance of object permanence signals the end of the _____ period. (sensorimotor)

In Review: Social and Emotional Development During Infancy and Childhood (p. 406)

1. As part of their social development, children learn _____, which tell them what patterns of appearance and behavior are associated with being male or female. (gender roles)

2. Teaching children to talk quietly in a restaurant is part of the process called _____ (socialization)

3. Strict rules and the threat of punishment are typical of _____ parenting. (authoritarian)

In Review: Milestones of Adolescence and Adulthood (p. 420)

1. The greatest threat to cognitive abilities in late adulthood is _____ disease. (Alzheimer's)

2. Adolescents' _____ identity may be more defining than their national citizenship. (ethnic)

3. Not stealing because "I might get caught" reflects the _____ stage of moral reasoning. (preconventional)

Chapter 12 Health, Stress, and Coping

In Review: Stress Responses and Stress Mediators (p. 444)

1. The friends and family we can depend on to help us deal with stressors are called our _____ network. (social support)

2. Fantasizing about winning money is a(n) _____-focused way of coping with financial stress. (emotion)

3. Sudden, extreme stressors may cause psychological and behavioral problems known as _____. (posttraumatic stress disorder)

In Review: Methods for Coping with Stress (p. 452)

1. Catastrophizing thoughts are best overcome through _____ coping strategies. (cognitive)

2. The first step in coping with stress is to _____ the sources and effects of your stressors. (identify)

3. True or false: It is best to rely on only one good coping strategy. _____ (false)

Chapter 13 Personality

In Review: Major Approaches to Personality (p. 476)

1. Tests that measure the five-factor model's dimensions of personality are based on the _____ approach to personality. (trait)

2. The role of learning is most prominent in the _____ approach to personality. (social-cognitive)

3. Object relations and attachment theories are modern variants on _____ personality theories. (psychodynamic)

In Review: Personality Measures (p. 484)

1. Projective personality measures are based on the _____ approach to personality. (psychodynamic)

2. The NEO-PI-3 and the MMPI-2-RF are examples of _____ tests. (nonprojective)

3. Most personality researchers use _____ tests in their work. (nonprojective)

Chapter 14 Psychological Disorders

In Review: Anxiety, Obsessive-Compulsive, Somatic Symptom, and Dissociative Disorders (p. 512)

1. Concern that it may be triggered by media stories or therapists' suggestions has made _____ the most controversial of the dissociative disorders. (dissociative identity disorder)

2. A person who sleepwalks but is not able to walk when awake is showing signs of _____. (conversion disorder)

3. Panic disorder is sometimes associated with another anxiety disorder called _____. (agoraphobia)

In Review: Depressive and Bipolar Disorders (p. 515)

1. The risk of suicide is associated with _____ more than with any other symptom of disorder. (depression)

2. Cyclothymic disorder is a less severe version of _____. (bipolar disorder)

3. Women are _____ likely than men to try suicide, but men are _____ likely to succeed. (more; more)

In Review: Schizophrenia Spectrum Disorders (p. 523)

1. The _____ approach forms the basis of the vulnerability theory of schizophrenia. (diathesis-stress)

2. Hallucinations are _____ symptoms of schizophrenia; lack of emotion is a symptom. (positive; negative)

3. Patients with schizophrenia who were able to finish school are _____ likely to show improvement. (more)

Chapter 15 Treatment of Psychological Disorders

In Review: Approaches to Psychological Treatment (p. 553)

1. Object relations therapy and interpersonal therapy are both contemporary examples of the _____ approach to psychological treatment. (psychodynamic)

2. Imagining increasingly fear-provoking stimuli while relaxed is a treatment method called _____. (systematic desensitization)

3. Reflection is an interviewing technique associated mainly with the _____ approach to treatment. (humanistic [or nondirective])

Chapter 16 Social Psychology

In Review: Some Biases in Social Perception (p. 584)

1. The fundamental attribution error appears to be somewhat less likely to occur among people in _____ cultures. (collectivist)

2. First impressions form _____, but tend to change _____. (quickly; slowly)

3. If you believed that immigrants' successes are due to government help but that their failures are due to laziness, you would be committing the _____ error. (ultimate attribution)

In Review: Forming and Changing Attitudes (p. 587)

1. According to the elaboration likelihood model, people are more likely to pay close attention to the content and logic of a persuasive message if the _____ route to attitude change has been activated. (central)

2. Holding attitudes that are similar to those of your friends illustrates the importance of _____ in attitude formation. (learning)

3. According to cognitive dissonance theory, we tend to reduce conflict between attitudes and behaviors by changing our _____. (attitudes)

In Review: Types of Social Influence (p. 606)

1. Joining the end of a ticket line is an example of _____, whereas forming two lines when a theater employee requests it is an example of _____. (conformity; compliance)

2. Seeing someone disobey a questionable order makes people _____ likely to obey the order themselves. (less)

3. Pricing your used car for more than you expect to get but then agreeing to reduce it to make a sale is an example of the _____ approach to gaining compliance. (door-in-the-face)

In Review: Prosocial Behavior (p. 616)

1. If you could save only one person from a burning house, the _____ theory of prosocial behavior would predict that it would be your own child rather than, say, a grandparent. (evolutionary)

2. Are you more likely to receive help in a nearly empty bus or in a crowded bus terminal? _____. (a nearly empty bus)

3. People who have empathy for others are _____ likely to be helpful. (more)

Chapter 17 Industrial/Organizational Psychology

In Review: Assessing People, Jobs, and Job Performance (p. 635)

1. Lists of critical incidents are contained in _____-focused employee rating forms. (behavior)

2. A potential employer might use a two-day _____ to measure your skill at the job you want. (assessment center)

3. In general, _____ interviews are more useful in employee selection than _____ interviews. (structured; unstructured)

In Review: Recruiting, Selecting, and Training Employees (p. 642)

1. Employees tend to remember more from a training program when it is set up on a _____ rather than a _____ schedule. (distributed; massed)

2. Depending on walk-in applications is usually acceptable when hiring _____-level employees. (low)

3. Assuring that your hiring criteria actually predict employees' job performance requires a _____. (validation study)

Chapter 18 Neuropsychology

In Review: Foundations of Neuropsychology (p. 669)

1. A person who studies individual patients to determine what kind of brain damage each one happens to have is called a _____. (clinical neuropsychologist)

2. The case of "Tan" helped to establish the principle of _____. (localization of function)

3. In alexia without agraphia, the brain areas that control reading and writing are intact but cannot interact. This condition is called a _____. (disconnection syndrome)

In Review: Mechanisms of Brain Dysfunction (p. 673)

1. The brain floats in a bath of _____ inside the skull. (cerebrospinal fluid)

2. The brain needs a constant flow of fresh _____ all the time. (blood)

3. Cerebrovascular accidents rank as the number _____ cause of death in the United States. (four)

In Review: Major Neuropsychological Disorders (p. 688)

1. A patient who has become forgetful but has no problems in other areas of cognitive function may be said to have _____. (mild cognitive impairment)

2. A dementia patient whose hippocampus is relatively intact and can still form new memories probably has _____ dementia. (non-Alzheimer)

3. A patient with thiamine deficiency who is forgetful but makes up memories and believes they are real probably has _____. (Korsakoff's syndrome)

Test Your Knowledge Answer Key

Chapter 1

1c, 2c, 3b, 4d, 5a, 6c, 7a, 8c, 9d, 10b, 11b, 12a, 13c, 14d, 15b, 16a, 17d, 18c, 19b, 20d

Chapter 2

1d, 2a, 3c, 4d, 5a, 6d, 7a, 8b, 9b, 10d, 11c, 12d, 13c, 14a, 15d, 16b, 17b, 18b, 19d, 20c

Chapter 3

1c, 2c, 3b, 4b, 5c, 6d, 7c, 8a, 9a, 10d, 11a, 12b, 13a, 14d, 15a, 16b, 17b, 18d, 19a, 20a

Chapter 4

1a, 2b, 3a, 4d, 5b, 6b, 7d, 8d, 9c, 10d, 11a, 12b, 13c, 14a, 15c, 16b, 17c, 18d, 19b, 20a

Chapter 5

1c, 2b, 3b, 4a, 5d, 6a, 7a, 8c, 9a, 10b, 11b, 12b, 13d, 14d, 15b, 16d, 17b, 18c, 19d, 20c

Chapter 6

1a, 2b, 3c, 4b, 5a, 6c, 7b, 8a, 9c, 10d, 11a, 12c, 13c, 14c, 15d, 16d, 17a, 18b, 19d, 20a

Chapter 7

1d, 2c, 3b, 4d, 5b, 6d, 7c, 8a, 9c, 10a, 11d, 12c, 13c, 14d, 15b, 16a, 17b, 18c, 19c, 20b

Chapter 8

1a, 2B, 3c, 4a, 5c, 6d, 7a, 8a, 9a, 10a, 11b, 12b, 13c, 14d, 15d, 16b, 17d, 18b, 19d, 20c

Chapter 9

1a, 2b, 3c, 4b, 5d, 6c, 7c, 8a, 9b, 10c, 11d, 12d, 13c, 14a, 15d, 16a, 17D, 18c, 19b, 20b

Chapter 10

1b, 2a, 3d, 4b, 5a, 6b, 7b, 8c, 9d, 10b, 11c, 12a, 13c, 14c, 15a, 16d, 17b, 18d, 19b, 20b

Chapter 11

1b, 2c, 3d, 4a, 5c, 6a, 7c, 8b, 9a, 10B, 11b, 12d, 13c, 14d, 15C, 16d, 17a, 18c, 19c, 20b

Chapter 12

1c, 2a, 3d, 4a, 5c, 6d, 7b, 8b, 9b, 10c, 11c, 12b, 13b, 14c, 15b, 16d, 17a, 18a, 19a, 20c

Chapter 13

1b, 2a 3d, 4d, 5a, 6d, 7b, 8c, 9d, 10c, 11b, 12a, 13c, 14d, 15c, 16c, 17b, 18d, 19c, 20b

Chapter 14

1b, 2b, 3c, 4d, 5d, 6d, 7c, 8a, 9a, 10a, 11b, 12b, 13a, 14b, 15d, 16c, 17a, 18d, 19d, 20b

Chapter 15

1c, 2a, 3a, 4b, 5c, 6b, 7c, 8d, 9c, 10b, 11c, 12b, 13a, 14d, 15b, 16d, 17a, 18c, 19b, 20c

Chapter 16

1c, 2a, 3b, 4c, 5d, 6c, 7b, 8c, 9b, 10a, 11d, 12b, 13c, 14a, 15b, 16d, 17a, 18a, 19b, 20b

Chapter 17

1a, 2c, 3a, 4b, 5c, 6c, 7a, 8d, 9c, 10a, 11c, 12b, 13c, 14b, 15d, 16b, 17b, 18a, 19b, 20a

Chapter 18

1a, 2c, 3b, 4a, 5a, 6c, 7d, 8d, 9b, 10c, 11c, 12d, 13a, 14a, 15b, 16a, 17c, 18d, 19a, 20c

APPENDIX A
Statistics in Psychological Research

Understanding and interpreting the results of psychological research depend on *statistical analyses,* which are methods for describing and drawing conclusions from data. The chapter on research in psychology introduced some terms and concepts associated with *descriptive statistics*—the numbers that psychologists use to describe and present their data—and with *inferential statistics*—the mathematical procedures they use to help draw conclusions from data and to make inferences about what those data mean. Here, we present more details about these statistical analyses to help you evaluate research results.

DESCRIBING DATA

To illustrate our discussion, consider a hypothetical experiment on the effects of incentives on performance. The experimenter presents a list of mathematics problems to two groups of participants. Each group must solve the problems within a fixed time, but for each correct answer, the low-incentive group is only paid ten cents, whereas the high-incentive group gets one dollar. The hypothesis to be tested is the **null hypothesis**, the assertion that the independent variable directly manipulated by the experimenter will have no effect on the dependent variable measured by the experimenter. In this case, the null hypothesis is that the size of the incentive (the independent variable) will not affect performance on the mathematics task (the dependent variable).

Assume that the experimenter has gathered a representative sample of participants, assigned them randomly to the two groups, and done everything possible to avoid the confounds and other research problems we discussed in the chapter on research in psychology. The experiment has been run, and the psychologist now has the data: a list of the number of correct answers given by each participant in each group. Now comes the first task of statistical analysis: describing the data in a way that makes them easy to understand.

The Histogram

The simplest way to describe the data is with something like Table 1, which just lists all the numbers. After examining the table, you might conclude that the high-incentive group did better than the low-incentive group, but this is not immediately obvious. The difference might be even harder to see if more participants had been involved and if the scores included three-digit numbers. If a picture is "worth a thousand words," then a better way to present the same data is in a picture-like graphic called a **histogram** (see Figure 1).

Making a histogram is simple. First, divide the scale for measuring the dependent variable (in this case, the number of correct answers) into a number of categories, or "bins." The bins in our example are 1–2, 3–4, 5–6, 7–8, and 9–10. Next, sort the raw data into the appropriate bin. (For example, the score of a participant who had 5 correct answers would go into the 5–6 bin, a score of 8 would go into the 7–8 bin, and so on.) Finally, for each bin, count the number of scores in that bin and draw a bar up to the height of that number on the vertical axis of a graph. The resulting set of bars makes up the frequency histogram.

Because we want to compare the scores of two groups, there are separate histograms in Figure 1: one for the high-incentive group and one for the low-incentive group. Now the difference between groups that was difficult to see in Table 1 stands out more clearly, doesn't it? High scores were more common among people in the high-incentive group than among those in the low-incentive group.

null hypothesis A testable statement that the independent variable manipulated by the experimenter will have no effect on the dependent variable measured by the experimenter.

histogram A graphic presentation of data that consists of a set of bars, each of which represents how frequently different scores or values occur in a data set.

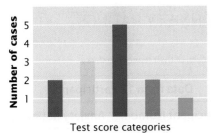

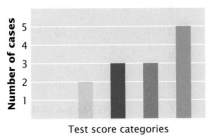

FIGURE 1
Histograms

The height of each bar of a histogram represents the number of scores falling within each range of score values. The pattern formed by these bars gives a visual image of how research results are distributed.

TABLE 1	A SIMPLE DATA SET

Here are the test scores obtained by thirteen participants performing under low-incentive conditions and thirteen participants performing under high-incentive conditions.

Low Incentive	High Incentive
4	6
6	4
2	10
7	10
6	7
8	10
3	6
5	7
2	5
3	9
5	9
9	3
5	8

Histograms and other pictures of data help to visualize and understand the "shape" of research results, but to analyze those results statistically, we need to use other ways of handling the data that make up these graphic presentations. For example, before we can say whether two histograms are different statistically or just visually, the data they represent must be summarized by *descriptive statistics*.

Descriptive Statistics

The three most important descriptive statistics are *measures of central tendency*, which describe the typical score in a set of data; *measures of variability*, which describe the spread, or dispersion, among the scores in a set of data; and *correlation coefficients*, which describe relationships between variables.

Measures of Central Tendency

In the research in psychology chapter, we described a treatment called eye movement desensitization and reprocessing (EMDR). Suppose you wanted to test whether EMDR affects fear of the dark. You find participants by giving volunteers an anxiety test and end up collecting the eleven self-ratings of anxiety listed on the left side of Table 2. What is the typical score, the *central tendency*, that best describes the anxiety level of this group of people? You can chose from three measures to capture this typical score: the mode, the median, and the mean.

mode A measure of central tendency that is the value or score that occurs most frequently in a data set.

The **mode** is the value or score that occurs most frequently in a data set. You can find it by simply counting how many times each score appears. On the left side of Table 2, the mode is 50, because the score of 50 occurs more often than any other. Notice, however,

TABLE 2   A SET OF PRETREATMENT ANXIETY RATINGS

Here are scores representing people's self-ratings, on a 1–100 scale, of their fear of the dark.

Data from 11 Participants		Data from 12 Participants	
Participant Number	Anxiety Rating	Participant Number	Anxiety Rating
1	20	1	20
2	22	2	22
3	28	3	28
4	35	4	35
5	40	5	40
6	45 (Median)	6	45 (Median = 46[a])
7	47	7	47
8	49	8	49
9	50	9	50
10	50	10	50
11	50	11	50
		12	100

Measures of central tendency Mode = 50 Median = 45 Mean = 436/11 = 39.6	**Measures of central tendency** Mode = 50 Median = 46 Mean = 536/12 = 44.7
Measures of variability Range = 30 Standard deviation = 11.064	**Measures of variability** Range = 80 Standard deviation = 19.763

[a] When there is an uneven number of scores, the exact middle of the list lies between two numbers. The median is the value halfway between those numbers.

that in this data set the mode is actually an extremely high score. Sometimes the mode acts like a microphone for a small but vocal minority that, though speaking loudest or most frequently, may not represent the views of the majority.

Unlike the mode, the median takes all scores into account. The **median** is the halfway point in a set of data. When scores are arranged from lowest to highest, half the scores fall above the median, and half fall below it. For the scores on the left side of Table 2, the halfway point—the median—is 45.

The third measure of central tendency is the **mean**, which is the *arithmetic average* of a set of scores. When people talk about the "average" in everyday conversation, they are usually referring to the mean. To find the mean, add the scores and divide by the number of scores. For the data on the left side of Table 2, the mean is 436/11 = 39.6.

Like the median (and unlike the mode), the mean reflects all the data to some degree, not just the most frequent data. Notice, however, that the mean reflects the actual values of all the scores, whereas the median gives each score equal weight, whatever its value. This

median A measure of central tendency that is the halfway point in a set of data: Half the scores fall above the median and half fall below it.

mean A measure of central tendency that is the arithmetic average of the scores in a set of data.

Descriptive statistics are valuable for summarizing research results, but we must evaluate them carefully before drawing conclusions about what they mean. Given this executive's reputation for uncritical thinking, you can bet that Dogbert's impressive-sounding restatement of the definition of *median* will win him an extension of his pricey consulting contract.

DILBERT © 1994 Scott Adams. Used By permission of UNIVERSAL UCLICK. All rights reserved.

distinction can have a big effect on how well the mean and median represent the scores in a particular set of data. Suppose that you add to your sample a twelfth participant, whose anxiety rating is 100. When you reanalyze the anxiety data (see the right side of Table 2), the median hardly changes, because the new participant counts as just one more score. However, when you compute the new mean, the actual *amount* of the new participant's rating is added to everyone else's ratings; as a result, the mean jumps 5 points. As this example shows, the median is sometimes a better measure of central tendency than the mean because the median is less sensitive to extremely high or extremely low scores. But because the mean is more representative of the values of all the data, it is often a preferred measure of central tendency.

Measures of Variability

The variability (also known as *spread* or *dispersion*) in a set of data is described by statistics known as the *range* and the *standard deviation*. The **range** is simply the difference between the highest and the lowest scores in a data set (it would be 30 for the data on the left side of Table 2 and 80 for the data on the right side). In contrast, the **standard deviation (SD)** measures the average difference between each score and the mean of the data set. So the standard deviation tells us how much the scores in a data set vary, or differ from one another. The more variable the data are, the higher the standard deviation will be. For example, the SD for the eleven participants on the left side of Table 2 is 11.064, but it rises to 19.763 once that very different twelfth score is added on the right side.

The Effect of Variability

TRY THIS   Suppose that on your first day as a substitute teacher at a new school, you are offered either of two classes. The mean IQ score in both classes is 100, but the standard deviation (SD) of scores is 16 in one class and 32 in the other. Before you read the next sentence, ask yourself which class you would choose if you wanted an easy day's work or if you wanted a tough challenge. (A higher standard deviation means more variability, so students in the class with the SD of 32 will vary more in ability, thus creating a greater challenge for the teacher.)

Education Images/Contributor/Universal Images Group/Getty Images

TABLE 3   CALCULATING THE STANDARD DEVIATION

The standard deviation of a set of scores reflects the average degree to which those scores differ from the mean of the set..

Raw Data	Difference from Mean = D	D²
2	$2 - 4 = -2$	4
2	$2 - 4 = -2$	4
3	$3 - 4 = -1$	1
4	$4 - 4 = 0$	0
9	$9 - 4 = 5$	25
Mean = 20/5 = 4		$\Sigma D^2 = 34$

$$\text{Standard deviation} = \sqrt{\frac{\Sigma D^2}{N}} = \sqrt{\frac{34}{5}} = \sqrt{6.8} = 2.6$$

Note: Σ means "the sum of."

To see how the standard deviation is calculated, consider the data in Table 3. The first step is to compute the mean of the set—in this case, 20/5 = 4. Second, calculate the difference, or *deviation* (D), of each score from the mean by subtracting the mean from each score, as in column 2 of Table 3. Third, find the average of these deviations. Notice, though, that if you calculated this average by finding the arithmetic mean, you would sum the deviations and find that the negative deviations exactly balance the positive ones, resulting in a mean difference of 0. Obviously, there is more than zero variation around the mean in the data set. So, instead of employing the arithmetic mean, you compute the standard deviation by first squaring the deviations (which, as shown in column 3 of Table 3, removes any negative values). You then add up these squared deviations, divide the total by N, and then take the square root of the result.

The Normal Distribution

Now that we have described histograms and reviewed some descriptive statistics, let's reexamine how these methods of representing research data relate to some of the concepts discussed elsewhere in the book.

In most subfields in psychology, when researchers collect many measurements and plot their data in histograms, the resulting pattern often resembles the one shown for the low-incentive group in Figure 1. That is, the majority of scores tend to fall in the middle of the distribution, with fewer and fewer scores occurring toward the extremes. As more and more data are collected, and as smaller and smaller bins are used (perhaps containing only one value each), histograms tend to smooth out until they resemble the bell-shaped curve, also known as the **normal distribution**, or *normal curve*. When a distribution of scores follows a truly normal curve, its mean, median, and mode all have the same value. Furthermore, if the curve is normal, we can use its standard deviation to describe how any particular score stands in relation to the rest of the distribution.

IQ scores provide an example. They are distributed in a normal curve, with a mean, median, and mode of 100 and an SD of 16—as shown in Figure 2. In such a distribution, half of the population has an IQ above 100 and half below 100. The shape of a true normal curve is that 68 percent of the area under it lies in a range within one standard deviation above and below the mean. So, for IQ scores, this means that 68 percent of the population has an IQ somewhere between 84 (100 minus 16) and 116 (100 plus 16). Of the remaining 32 percent of the population,

range A measure of variability that is the difference between the highest and the lowest values in a data set.

standard deviation (SD) A measure of variability that is the average difference between each score and the mean of the data set.

normal distribution A dispersion of scores such that the mean, median, and mode all have the same value.

FIGURE 2
The Normal Distribution

Many kinds of research data approximate the balanced, or symmetrical, shape of the normal curve, in which most scores fall toward the center of the range.

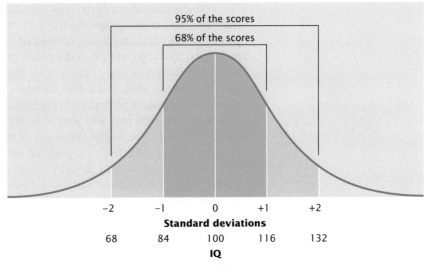

The normal distribution of IQ

half falls more than 1 SD above the mean and half falls more than 1 SD below the mean. Thus, 16 percent of the population has an IQ above 116 and 16 percent scores below 84.

The normal curve is also the basis for percentiles. A **percentile** refers to the percentage of people or observations that fall below a given score in a normal distribution. In Figure 2, for example, the mean score (which is also the median) lies at a point below which 50 percent of the scores fall. Thus the mean of a normal distribution is at the 50th percentile. What does this say about IQ? If you score 1 SD above the mean, your score is at a point above which only 16 percent of the population falls. This means that 84 percent of the population (100 percent minus 16 percent) must be below that score; so this IQ score is at the 84th percentile. A score at 2 SDs above the mean is at the 97.5 percentile, because only 2.5 percent of the scores are above it in a normal distribution.

Scores may also be expressed in terms of their distance in standard deviations from the mean, producing what are called **standard scores**. A standard score of 1.5, for example, is 1.5 standard deviations from the mean.

Correlation

Histograms and measures of central tendency and variability describe certain characteristics of one dependent variable at a time. However, psychologists often want to describe the relationship between two variables. Measures of correlation are frequently used for this purpose. We discussed the interpretation of the **correlation coefficient** in the chapter on research in psychology; here we describe how to calculate it.

Recall that correlations are based on the relationship between two numbers that are associated with each participant or observation. The numbers might represent, say, a person's height and weight or the IQ scores of a parent and child. Table 4 contains this kind of data for four participants from our incentives study who took the test twice. (As you may recall from the chapter on intelligence, the correlation between their scores would be a measure of test-retest reliability.)

The formula for computing the Pearson product-moment correlation, or r, is as follows:

$$r = \frac{\Sigma(x - M_x)(y - M_y)}{\sqrt{\Sigma(x - M_x)^2 \, \Sigma(y - M_y)^2}}$$

where:

x = each score on variable 1 (in this case, test 1)
y = each score on variable 2 (in this case, test 2)
M_x = the mean of the scores on variable 1
M_y = the mean of the scores on variable 2

percentile A value that indicates the percentage of people or observations that fall below a given point in a normal distribution.

standard scores Values that indicate the distance, in standard deviations, between a given score and the mean of all the scores in a data set.

correlation coefficient A statistic, r, that summarizes the strength and direction of a relationship between two variables.

The main function of the denominator (bottom part) in this formula is to ensure that the coefficient ranges from +1.00 to −1.00, no matter how large or small the values of the variables being correlated. The "action element" of this formula is the numerator (or top part). It is the result of multiplying the amounts by which each of two observations (x and y) differ from the means of their respective distributions (M_x and M_y). Notice that, if the two variables "go together" (so that if one score is large, the score it is paired with is also large, and if one is small, the other is also small), then both scores in each pair will tend to be above the mean of their distribution or both of them will tend to be below the mean of their distribution. When this is the case, $x - M_x$ and $y - M_y$ will both be positive, or they will both be negative. In either case, when you multiply one of them by the other, their product will always be positive, and the correlation coefficient will also be positive. If, on the other hand, the two variables go opposite to one another (such that when one score in a pair is large, the other is small), one of them is likely to be smaller than the mean of its distribution, so that either $x - M_x$ or $y - M_y$ will have a negative sign and the other will have a positive sign. Multiplying these differences together will always result in a product with a negative sign, and r will be negative as well.

Now compute the correlation coefficient for the data presented in Table 4. The first step (step a in the table) is to compute the mean (M) for each variable. M_x turns out to be 3 and M_y is 4. Next, calculate the numerator by finding the differences between each x and y value and its respective mean and by multiplying them (as in step b of Table 4). Notice that, in this example, the differences in each pair have like signs, so the correlation coefficient will be positive. The next step is to calculate the terms in the denominator; in this case, as shown in steps c and d in Table 4, they have values of 18 and 4. Finally, place all the terms in the formula and carry out the arithmetic (step e). The result in this case is an r of +.94, a high and positive correlation suggesting that performances on repeated tests are very closely related. A participant doing well the first time is very likely to do well again; a person doing poorly at first will probably do no better the second time.

TABLE 4   CALCULATING THE CORRELATION COEFFICIENT

Though it appears complex, calculation of the correlation coefficient is quite simple. The resulting r reflects the degree to which two sets of scores tend to be related, or to co-vary.

Participant	Test 1	Test 2	$(x - M_x)(y - M_y)$[(b)]
A	1	3	$(1-3)(3-4) + (-2)(-1) = +2$
B	1	3	$(1-3)(3-4) = (-2)(-1) = +2$
C	4	5	$(4-3)(5-4) = (1)(1) = +1$
D	6	5	$(6-3)(5-4) = (3)(1) = +3$
	[(a)]$M_x = 3$	$M_y = 4$	$\Sigma(x - M_x)(y - M_y) = +8$

[(c)]$\Sigma(x - M_x)^2 = 4 + 4 + 1 + 9 = 18$

[(d)]$\Sigma(y - M_y)^2 = 1 + 1 + 1 + 1 = 4$

$$^{(e)}r = \frac{\Sigma(x - M_x)(y - M_y)}{\sqrt{\Sigma(x - M_x)^2\,\Sigma(y - M_y)^2}} = \frac{8}{\sqrt{18 \times 4}} = \frac{8}{\sqrt{72}} = \frac{8}{8.48} = +.94$$

INFERENTIAL STATISTICS

To help interpret the meaning of correlations and the other descriptive statistics that flow from research results, psychological scientists rely on *inferential statistics*. For example, inferential statistics allowed many researchers to conclude that the benefits of EMDR are not great enough when compared with other treatment options to recommend it as a first choice in cases of anxiety.

Inferential statistics use certain rules to evaluate whether a correlation or a difference between group means is a significant finding or might have occurred just by chance. Suppose that a group of people treated with EMDR showed a mean decrease of 10 points on a posttreatment anxiety test, whereas the scores of a no-treatment control group decreased by a mean of 7 points. Does this 3-point difference between the groups' means reflect the impact of EMDR, or could it have been caused by random factors that made EMDR appear more powerful than it actually is? Traditionally, psychologists have answered questions such as this by using statistical tests to estimate how likely it is that an observed difference was due to chance alone (Krueger, 2001).

Differences Between Means: The *t* Test

One of the most important tools of inferential statistics is the *t* test. It allows a researcher to ask how likely it is that the difference between two means occurred by chance rather than being caused by the independent variable. When the *t* test or other inferential statistic says that the probability of chance effects is small enough (usually less than 5 percent), we say the results are *statistically significant*. Conducting a *t* test of statistical significance requires the use of three descriptive statistics.

The first part of the *t* test is the size of the observed effect, the difference between the means. Recall that the mean is calculated by summing a group's scores and dividing that total by the number of scores. In the example shown in Table 1, the mean of the high-incentive group is 94/13, or 7.23, and the mean of the low-incentive group is 65/13, or 5. So the difference between the means of the high- and low-incentive groups is 7.23 − 5 = 2.23.

Second, we have to know the standard deviation of scores in each group. If the scores in a group are quite variable, the standard deviation will be large, meaning that chance may have played a large role in the results obtained. The next replication of the study might generate quite a different set of group scores. But, if the scores in a group are all very similar, then the standard deviation will be small, suggesting that the same result would likely occur for that group if the study were repeated. In other words, the apparent *difference* between groups is more likely to be statistically significant when each group's standard deviation is small. If variability is high enough that the scores of two groups overlap, the mean difference, though large, may not be statistically significant. (In Table 1, for example, some people in the low-incentive group actually did better on the math test than some in the high-incentive group.)

Third, we need to take the sample size, known as *N*, into account. The larger the number of participants or observations, the more likely it is that an observed difference between means is significant. This is so because, with larger samples, random factors within a group—the unusual performance of a few people who were sleepy or anxious or hostile, for example—are more likely to be canceled out by the majority, who better represent people in general. The same effect of sample size can be seen in coin tossing. If you toss a quarter five times, you might not be too surprised if heads comes up 80 percent of the time. If you get 80 percent heads after 100 tosses, however, you might begin to suspect that this is probably not due to chance alone and that some other effect, perhaps some bias in the coin, is significant in producing the results. (For the same reason, even a relatively small correlation coefficient—between diet and grades, say—might be statistically significant if it was based on 50,000 students. As the number of participants increases, it becomes less likely that the correlation reflects the influence of a few oddball cases.)

To summarize, as the differences between the means get larger, as N increases, and as standard deviations get smaller, t increases. This increase in t raises the researcher's confidence in the significance of the difference between means.

Let's now calculate the t statistic and see how it is interpreted. The formula for t is:

$$t = \frac{(M_1 - M_2)}{\sqrt{\dfrac{(N_1 - 1)S_1^2 + (N_2 - 1)S_2^2}{N_1 + N_2 - 2}\left(\dfrac{N_1 + N_2}{N_1 N_2}\right)}}$$

where:

M_1 = mean of group 1
M_2 = mean of group 2
N_1 = number of scores or observations for group 1
N_2 = number of scores or observations for group 2
S_1 = standard deviation of group 1 scores
S_2 = standard deviation of group 2 scores

Despite appearances, working through this formula is quite simple. The numerator consists of the difference between the two group means; t will get larger as this difference gets larger. The denominator contains an estimate of the standard deviation of the *differences* between group means; in other words, it suggests how much the difference between group means would vary if the experiment were repeated many times. Because this estimate is in the denominator, the value of t will get smaller as the standard deviation of group differences gets larger. For the data in Table 1,

$$t = \frac{(M_1 - M_2)}{\sqrt{\dfrac{(N_1 - 1)S_1^2 + (N_2 - 1)S_2^2}{N_1 + N_2 - 2}\left(\dfrac{N_1 + N_2}{N_1 N_2}\right)}}$$

$$= \frac{7.23 - 5}{\sqrt{\dfrac{(12)(5.09) + (12)(4.46)}{24}\left(\dfrac{26}{169}\right)}}$$

$$= \frac{2.23}{\sqrt{.735}} = 2.60 \text{ with 24 df}$$

To determine what a particular t means, we must use the value of N and a special statistical table called, appropriately enough, the t *table*. We have reproduced part of the t table in Table 5.

First, we have to find the computed values of t in the row corresponding to the **degrees of freedom (df)** associated with the experiment. In this case, degrees of freedom are simply $N_1 + N_2 - 2$ (or two less than the total sample size or number of scores). Because our experiment had 13 participants per group, df = 13 + 13 - 2 = 24. In the row for 24 df in Table 5, you will find increasing values of t in each column. These columns correspond to decreasing p values, the probabilities that the difference between means occurred by chance. If an obtained t value is equal to or larger than one of the values in the t table (on the correct df line), then the difference between means that generated that t is said to be significant at the .10, .05, or .01 level of probability.

Suppose, for example, that an obtained t (with 19 df) was 2.00. Looking along the 19 df row, you find that 2.00 is larger than the value in the .05 column. This allows you to say that the probability that the difference between means occurred by chance was no greater than .05, or 5 in 100. If the t had been less than the value in the .05 column, the probability

degrees of freedom (df) The total sample size or number of scores in a data set, less the number of experimental groups.

TABLE 5   THE *t* TABLE

This table allows the researcher to determine whether an obtained *t* value is statistically significant. If the *t* value is larger than the one in the appropriate row in the .05 column, the difference between means that generated that *t* score is usually considered statistically significant.

df	*p* Value		
	.10 (10%)	.05 (5%)	.01 (1%)
4	1.53	2.13	3.75
9	1.38	1.83	2.82
14	1.34	1.76	2.62
19	1.33	1.73	2.54
22	1.32	1.71	2.50
24	1.32	1.71	2.49

of a chance result would have been greater than .05. As noted earlier, when an obtained *t* is not large enough to exceed *t* table values at the .05 level, at least, it is not usually considered statistically significant. The *t* value from our experiment was 2.60, with 24 df. Because 2.60 is greater than all the values in the 24 df row, the difference between the high- and low-incentive groups would have occurred by chance less than 1 time in 100. In other words, the difference is statistically significant.

Positive outcomes on tests of statistical significance are important, but they do not necessarily prove that a difference is important or "real" or that a particular treatment is effective or ineffective. Accordingly, psychologists who specialize in quantitative methods recommend that research findings be evaluated using other statistical analysis methods too (e.g., Kileen, 2005; Kline, 2004; Krueger, 2001). Whatever the methods, though, psychological scientists are more confident in, and pay the most attention to, correlations or other research findings that statistical analyses suggest are robust and not flukes.

Beyond the *t* Test

Many experiments in psychology are considerably more complex than simple comparisons between two groups. They often involve three or more experimental and control groups. Some experiments also include more than one independent variable. For example, suppose we had been interested not only in the effect of incentive size on performance but also in the effect of problem difficulty. We might then create six groups whose members would perform easy, moderate, or difficult problems and would receive either low or high incentives.

In an experiment like this, the results might be due to the size of the incentive, the difficulty of the problems, or combined effects (known as the *interaction*) of the two. Analyzing the size and source of such effects is often accomplished by using procedures known as *analysis of variance*. The details of analysis of variance are beyond the scope of this book. For now, note that the statistical significance of each effect is influenced by the size of the differences between means, by standard deviations, and by sample size in much the same way as we described for the *t* test. For more detailed information about how analysis of variance and other inferential statistics are used to understand and interpret the results of psychological research, consider taking courses in research methods and statistical or quantitative methods.

SUMMARY

Psychological research generates large quantities of data. Statistics are methods for describing and drawing conclusions from data.

Describing Data

Researchers often test the *null hypothesis,* the assertion that the independent variable will have no effect on the dependent variable.

Graphic representations such as *histograms* provide visual descriptions of data, making the data easier to understand.

Numbers that summarize a set of data are called descriptive statistics. Data can be described by three main types of descriptive statistics: a measure of central tendency, which describes the typical value of a set of data; a measure of variability, which describes the spread, or dispersion, among scores; and a *correlation coefficient*, which describes relationships between variables.

Measures of central tendency include the *mean, median,* and *mode*; variability is typically measured by the *range* and by the *standard deviation*. Sets of data often follow a *normal distribution*, which means that most scores fall in the middle of the range, with fewer and fewer scores occurring as one moves toward the extremes. In a truly normal distribution, the mean, median, and mode are identical. When a set of data shows a normal distribution, a data point can be cited in terms of a *percentile*, which indicates the percentage of people or observations falling below a certain score, and in terms of *standard scores*, which indicate the distance, in standard deviations, between any score and the mean of the distribution.

Inferential Statistics

Researchers use inferential statistics to quantify the probability that conducting the same experiment again would yield similar results.

One inferential statistic, the *t* test, assesses the likelihood that differences between two means occurred by chance or reflect the impact of an independent variable. Performing a *t* test requires using the difference between the means of two sets of data, the standard deviation of scores in each set, and the number of observations or participants. Interpreting a *t* test requires that *degrees of freedom* also be taken into account. When the *t* test indicates that the experimental results had a low probability of occurring by chance, the results are said to be statistically significant.

When more than two groups must be compared, researchers typically rely on analysis of variance in order to interpret the results of an experiment.

APPENDIX B
Behavioral Genetics

Think about some trait that distinguishes you from other people, a trait on which you feel you are well above or well below average. Perhaps you would think about your skill at sports, languages, or music, or maybe your fearfulness, sociability, or other aspects of your personality. Have you ever wondered what made you the way you are? If you are shy, for example, it is easy to come up with possible environmental explanations. You might be shy because as a child you had few chances to meet new kids or because you had embarrassing or unpleasant experiences when you did meet them. Maybe you have shy parents who served as the role models you imitated. Such environmental explanations are reasonable, but it is also possible that you inherited a tendency toward shyness from your parents. It is even more likely that both inheritance and environment shaped your shyness.

Topics such as these are studied by researchers in the field of *behavioral genetics*, the study of how genes affect behavior. These researchers have developed methods to explore genetic, as well as environmental, origins of behavioral differences among people. The results of behavioral genetics research make it clear that heredity has a significant influence, not just on shyness but on personality more generally, on cognitive abilities, on psychological disorders, and on many other aspects of human behavior and mental processes. However, behavioral genetics is just as much the study of environment as of genetics. In the process of trying to disentangle genetic from environmental factors, researchers have made several important discoveries about the impact of the environment.

In this appendix, we discuss behavioral genetics in more detail than we did in the chapter on research in psychology. We begin with a review of the biochemical mechanisms underlying genetics and heredity. We then offer a brief history of genetic research in psychology, followed by a discussion of what research on genetic influences can and cannot tell us about the origins of human differences. Finally, we describe some findings from behavioral genetics research that illuminate several important aspects of human behavior and mental processes.

THE BIOLOGY OF GENETICS AND HEREDITY

What does it mean to say that someone has inherited a physical feature or behavioral trait? The answer lies in **genetics**, the biology of inheritance. The story begins with the biochemistry of human cells, and tiny structures called chromosomes, found in every cell of your body. Most human cells have forty-six chromosomes, arranged in twenty-three matching pairs. These **chromosomes** are like long, thin strands made up of thousands of segments, called genes. **Genes** are the biochemical units of heredity. Each gene guides the development of an individual by telling a cell how to make different proteins. Genes are made of **DNA (deoxyribonucleic acid)**—a grouping of sugar, phosphate, and four kinds of nitrogen-containing molecules twisted around each other in a double spiral (see Figure 1).

The exact mechanism by which genes work remains a subject of intensive research. Here's what we know so far. The structure of a gene—as seen in the particular order in which the four nitrogen-containing molecules are arranged in that segment of DNA—determines, through the production of *RNA (ribonucleic acid)*, which proteins the gene says to produce. (A typical gene may produce any one of several proteins, depending on other factors.) Protein molecules, in turn, form the physical structure of each cell and also direct the activity of the cell. So DNA essentially uses a coded message to provide a

genetics The biology of inheritance.

chromosomes Long, thin structures in every biological cell that contain genetic information.

genes The biological instructions, inherited from both parents and located on the chromosomes, that provide the blueprint for physical development.

DNA (deoxyribonucleic acid) The material that makes up chromosomes and provides the genetic code.

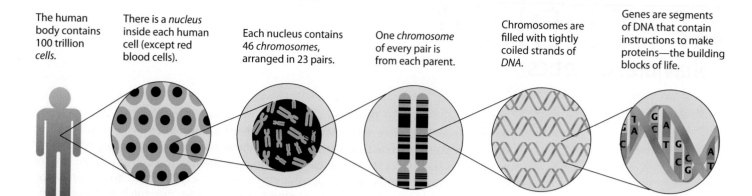

The human body contains 100 trillion *cells*.

There is a *nucleus* inside each human cell (except red blood cells).

Each nucleus contains 46 *chromosomes*, arranged in 23 pairs.

One *chromosome* of every pair is from each parent.

Chromosomes are filled with tightly coiled strands of *DNA*.

Genes are segments of DNA that contain instructions to make proteins—the building blocks of life.

FIGURE 1

Genetic Building Blocks

Only about 3 percent of DNA contains genes, though some of the rest of it affects how and when each gene actually works to guide the production of proteins. Together, genes and non-gene material in DNA essentially determine all the inherited aspects of our physical bodies and influence many of our behavioral characteristics, too.

Source: "Genetic Building Blocks" from Time, January 17, 1994.

polygenic traits Characteristics that are determined by more than one gene.

genotype The full set of genes, inherited from both parents, contained in twenty-three pairs of chromosomes.

phenotype How an individual looks and acts, which depends on how inherited characteristics interact with the environment.

blueprint for constructing and controlling every physical aspect of a human being, including eye color, height, blood type, inherited disorders, and the like—and all in less space than the period that ends this sentence.

New cells are constantly being produced when existing cells divide. Usually, the body's cells divide through a process called *mitosis*, in which the cell's chromosomes duplicate themselves so that each new cell exactly contains copies of the twenty-three pairs of chromosomes in the original.

A different kind of cell division occurs when a male's sperm cells or a female's egg cells (called *ova*) are formed. This type of cell division is called *meiosis*. In meiosis, chromosome pairs are not copied. Instead, they randomly split up and rearrange themselves, leaving each new sperm and egg cell with just one member of each chromosome pair, or twenty-three single chromosomes. No two of these special new cells are quite the same, and none contains an exact copy of the person who produced it. So at conception, when a male's sperm cell fertilizes the female's ovum, a truly new cell is formed. This fertilized cell, called a *zygote*, carries twenty-three pairs of chromosomes—half of each pair from the mother and half from the father. The zygote represents a unique heritage, a complete genetic code for a new person using genes from each parent. As described in the chapter on human development, the zygote divides first into copies of itself and later into the trillions of specialized cells to form a new human being.

Not all genes express themselves in the person who carries them. *Dominant* genes are outwardly expressed whenever they are present. *Recessive* genes are expressed only when they are paired with a similar gene from the other parent. For example, phenylketonuria (PKU)—a disorder seen in about 1 in 10,000 newborns—is caused by a recessive gene. When inherited from both parents, the protein from this gene disrupts the body's ability to control phenylalanine, an amino acid found in milk and other foods. As a result, phenylalanine is converted into a toxic substance that can cause severe intellectual disability. (Discovery of this genetic defect made it possible to prevent such disability in children with PKU simply by making sure they did not consume foods high in phenylalanine.) PKU is one of more than 4,000 single-gene disorders, but in fact, relatively few human characteristics are controlled by just one gene. Most characteristics are **polygenic traits**, meaning that they are affected by many genes. Even a person's eye color and height are affected by more than one gene.

The genes contained in the forty-six chromosomes inherited from parents make up an individual's **genotype**. Because identical twins develop from one fertilized egg cell, they are said to be *monozygotic*; they have exactly the same genotype. So why aren't all identical twins exactly alike? Because they do not have exactly the same environment. An individual's **phenotype** is the set of observable characteristics that result from the combination of heredity and environment. In twins and nontwins alike, the way people actually look and act is influenced by the combination of genes they carry, as well as by environmental factors—in other words, by both nature and nurture.

A BRIEF HISTORY OF GENETIC RESEARCH IN PSYCHOLOGY

The field now known as behavioral genetics began in the late 1800s with the work of Sir Francis Galton. A cousin of Charles Darwin, Galton was so impressed with Darwin's book on evolution that he decided to study heredity in the human species, especially as it relates to human behavior. Galton suggested the family, twin, and adoption study designs that remain mainstays of human behavioral genetics research today. He even coined the phrase *nature-nurture* to refer to genetic and environmental influences. Galton's most famous behavioral genetics study was one in which he showed that genius runs in families. Unfortunately, Galton went too far in interpreting the evidence from this family study when he concluded that "nature prevails enormously over nurture" (Galton, 1883, p. 241). As noted in the chapter on research in psychology, family members can be similar to each other because of environmental, as well as hereditary, factors. Galton failed to take into account the fact that similarity among family members in characteristics such as genius could be traced to the environments family members share, to their shared genes, or both. Yet, Galton's work helped focus psychologists' interest on the influence of genetics and on the effort to separate nature from nurture to learn why people resemble or differ from each other.

The first two studies aimed at separating nature and nurture by studying twins and adoptees were conducted in 1924. Both focused on IQ, and both suggested that genetics make important contributions to intelligence. However, two factors limited research on the influence of genetics on behavior and mental processes. The first factor was the dominant impact of John B. Watson's behaviorism in the 1920s. As mentioned in the introductory chapter, behaviorism suggested that we are only what we learn. In 1925, Watson insisted that "there is no such thing as an inheritance of capacity, talent, temperament, mental constitution and characteristics. These things again depend on training that goes on mainly in the cradle" (Watson, 1925, pp. 74–75). The second factor that discouraged attention to human genetics was *eugenics*, the notion that the human race can be improved by promoting the reproduction of those with "desirable" traits and reducing reproduction by less "desirable" people. This social philosophy had become mainstream thinking in the United States, Great Britain, and elsewhere. It led to compulsory sterilization of those deemed "unfit" and reached its extreme in Germany under the Nazi regime of Adolf Hitler. The idea that certain groups of people were "genetically inferior" led to the Holocaust during World War II, a campaign of genocide during which millions of Jews and other allegedly "inferior" people were killed.

Genetic research on human behavior shrank to a trickle during the 1930s and 1940s. Then, animal research led to the 1960 publication of the first behavioral genetics textbook (Fuller & Thompson, 1960) and renewed interest in human genetics. In 1963, an influential article reviewed family, twin, and adoption findings and concluded that genetic factors are an important influence on IQ (Erlenmeyer-Kimling & Jarvik, 1963). Around that time, the first adoption study of schizophrenia showed a strong genetic contribution to that disorder (Heston, 1966).

In the early 1970s, however, interest in human behavioral genetics among psychologists faded again, this time because of reactions to two publications. The first was a paper by Arthur Jensen, in which he said that differences in average IQ between blacks and whites might be partly due to genetic factors (Jensen, 1969). The second was a book by Richard Herrnstein, in which he argued that genetics might contribute to social class differences (Herrnstein, 1973). The public and scientific furor over these publications—which included branding the authors as racists—inhibited genetic research in psychology, even though very few behavioral geneticists had studied ethnic or class differences. It was some time until major genetic studies were again conducted in psychology.

Today most psychologists recognize the role of both genetics and environment in behavior and mental processes, including the controversial area of cognitive abilities. By 1992 the American Psychological Association selected behavioral genetics as one of two themes best representing the past, present, and especially the future of psychological research (Plomin & McClearn, 1993). To some, though, the study of human behavioral genetics still carries a taint of racism and class elitism. Such concerns were resurrected by *The Bell Curve,* a book arguing for a role of genetics in ethnic differences in intelligence, and subsequent implications for social class structure (Herrnstein & Murray, 1994). Fortunately, reaction to that book has re-emphasized the need to balance the roles of both nature and nurture in psychology.

THE FOCUS OF RESEARCH IN BEHAVIORAL GENETICS

Much of the controversy about behavioral genetics and about nature and nurture in general comes from misunderstandings about what behavioral genetics researchers study and, more specifically, what it means to say that genes influence behavior.

For one thing, behavioral genetics is the study of genetic and environmental factors that are responsible for *differences* among individuals or groups of individuals, not for the characteristics of a single individual. Consider height, for example. Identical twins are much more similar in height than are fraternal twins (who share no more genes than other siblings), and individuals who are genetically related but raised separately are just as similar in height as are relatives who are raised together. Further, genetically unrelated individuals who are raised together are no more similar in height than random pairs of individuals. These data suggest, not surprisingly, that height is highly *heritable.* This means that much of the *variability* in height that we see among people—actually about 80 percent of it—can be explained by genetic differences among them rather than by environmental differences. (It does not mean that a person who is six feet tall grew 80 percent of that height because of genes and the other 20 percent because of environment!) It also follows that if a person is, say, shorter than average, genetic reasons are probably the primary cause. We say "probably" because finding a genetic influence on height involves referring only to the origins of average individual differences in the population. So although the difference in people's heights is attributable mainly to genetic factors, a particular person's height could be due mainly to an early illness or other growth-stunting environmental factors. For example, Hattie and Samantha Peters, a pair of identical twins, were exposed to a rare condition in their mother's womb that deprived Samantha of vital nutrients. As a result, Hattie is 5 feet 4 inches tall, but Samantha is only 4 feet 8 inches (Taggart, 2004).

To see how the logic of behavioral genetics applies to conclusions about psychological characteristics, suppose a researcher found that the heritability of a certain personality trait is 50 percent. This result would mean that approximately half of the differences among people on that trait are attributable to genetic factors. It would not mean that each person inherits half of the trait and gets the other half from environmental influences. As in our height example, behavioral geneticists want to know how much variability among people can be accounted for by genetic and environmental factors. The results of their research allow generalizations about the influence of nature and nurture on certain characteristics, but those generalizations do not necessarily apply to the origin of a particular person's characteristics.

Another misconception about genetic influences is that they are "hard-wired" and so their effects are inevitable. Instead, in most cases, a particular genetic makeup does not guarantee that a person will develop a particular condition, but only that the person's *chance* of developing that condition is higher or lower. Further, complex traits—intelligence, for example—are influenced by many genes, as well as by many environmental factors. So genetic influence means just that—influence. Genes can affect a trait without completely determining whether or not it will appear.

THE ROLE OF GENETIC FACTORS IN PSYCHOLOGY

In the following sections, we consider behavioral genetics research results that tell a little more of the story about how genes can have an impact on behavior and mental processes.

Genetic Influences over the Life Span

One particularly interesting finding about genetic influences on general cognitive ability is that these influences accumulate throughout a life span (Finkel & Reynolds, 2014). Thus, the proportion of individual differences (variance) in IQ scores that can be explained by genetic factors increases from 40 percent in childhood to 60 percent in adolescence and young adulthood and then to 80 percent later in life. This increase in the magnitude of genetic influence can be seen, for example, in the expanding difference between IQ correlations for identical twins and those for fraternal twins: Identical twins become more similar in IQ over the life span, whereas fraternal twins become less similar as the years go by. This finding is all the more interesting in light of the common assumption that environmental influences become increasingly important as accidents, illnesses, and other experiences accumulate throughout life.

How can it be that genetic influences become more important over time? One possible explanation is that, as discussed later, genetic predispositions lead people to select, and even create, environments that foster the continued development of their genetically influenced abilities.

Genes Affecting Multiple Traits

Behavioral genetics research has also revealed that genes affecting one trait can sometimes affect others as well. For example, it appears that the same genetic factors that affect anxiety also affect depression (Kendler, Neale, et al., 1992; Kendler et al., 2003). So if we could identify specific genes responsible for genetic influences on anxiety, we would expect to find that the same genes were associated with the appearance of depression. Similarly, genetic factors affecting substance dependence are highly correlated with genetic factors affecting antisocial behavior and impulsive style (Kendler et al., 2003; Krueger et al., 2002).

A similar finding has emerged for cognitive ability and scholastic achievement. Tests of scholastic achievement show almost as much genetic influence as do tests of cognitive ability. Moreover, tests of scholastic achievement correlate substantially with tests of cognitive ability. To what extent is a common set of genes responsible for this overlap? Research suggests that the answer is "almost entirely." It appears that the genes that influence performance on mental ability tests are the same ones that influence students' performance at school (Wadsworth, 1994).

Identifying Genes Related to Behavior

One of the most exciting developments in behavioral genetics involves identifying specific genes responsible for genetic influences in psychology. For example, in the case of PKU discussed earlier, there are hundreds of rare, single-gene disorders that affect behavior. One of these is *Huntington's disease*, an ultimately fatal disease that involves loss of motor control and progressive damage to the central nervous system. Huntington's disease emerges only in adulthood, beginning with personality changes, forgetfulness, and other behavioral problems. It is caused by a single dominant gene whose identification in 1983 made it possible to determine who will get this disease—even though the biochemical mechanisms underlying the disorder are still not fully understood and prevention is not yet possible.

Researchers are also tracking down the several genes involved in the appearance of Alzheimer's disease. (As described in the chapter on biological aspects of psychology, this disease causes memory loss and increasing confusion in many older people.) One of these, a gene that predicts risk for late-onset Alzheimer's disease, was identified in 1993. This gene increases the risk for Alzheimer's disease as much as thirty times (Farrer et al., 1997), but its presence is neither necessary nor sufficient for the disease to appear. In fact, this gene's influence is different depending on what part of the world a person lives in (Crean et al., 2011). Thus, many people with Alzheimer's disease do not have the gene, many people with the gene do not have the disease, and the gene's effect must interact with other factors as well. Nonetheless, this gene's discovery marks a process in which specific genes—or regions of DNA near specific genes—are being identified as influencing disorders and psychological traits.

Progress in identifying specific genes in humans has been slow, in part because research ethics and common sense prevent use of selective breeding. Accordingly, human studies have lacked the statistical power needed to detect subtle but potentially important genetic influences on behavior. However, the more powerful genetic research techniques available in studies of animals have identified several genes associated, for example, with fearfulness (Saiz et al., 2008), sensitivity to drugs such as alcohol (Wall et al., 2005), and various aspects of learning and memory (Wahlsten, 1999). In most cases, however, such associations are tendencies rather than certainties—they are indicators that are not necessarily definitive.

Today's efforts to identify genes related to human behavior are being aided by advances flowing from the Human Genome Project, which in early 2001 succeeded in identifying the sequence of most of the 3 billion "letters" of DNA in the human genome. One of the most surprising findings of that project so far is that the human genome appears to contain only about 20,000 to 25,000 genes—less than half the number expected, and a number that is similar to the estimates for animals such as mice and worms (International Human Genome Sequencing Consortium, 2004). Does this smaller-than-expected number of human genes mean that there are too few to influence all aspects of human behavior, and that the environment (nurture) must be even more important than we thought in this regard? Not necessarily. It may be that the greater complexity seen in human behavior versus, say, mouse behavior stems not from the number of genes we have but from the greater complexities in how we decode our genes into proteins. Human genes, more than the genes of other species, are spliced in alternative ways, giving us a greater variety of proteins. It may be that this more subtle variation in genes—not the number of genes—creates the differences between mice and people. Such a possibility has important implications for behavioral genetics because if the obvious differences between humans and other species are due to subtle DNA differences, then individual differences *within* our species—in other words, among people—are likely to involve genetic factors that are even more subtle and hard to find.

Fortunately, new techniques make it possible to detect DNA differences for many thousands of genes simultaneously. These techniques help to identify genes related to behavior, a process that will fill in the causal picture about a variety of characteristics and disorders that are influenced by many genes and many environmental factors. But it might not just be the actions of multiple genes that have a major impact on behavior. It might also be a gene-environment interaction—the combination of a specific gene in a specific environment—that has the greatest influence on behavior. Examples of such interactions appear in research by Avshalom Caspi and his colleagues (Caspi et al., 2002; Caspi et al., 2003; Jaffee et al., 2007). In one study, they found that children living in an environment in which there is abuse or other maltreatment were at increased risk for displaying antisocial behavior in later life. But the at-risk children who also had a particular gene did not become antisocial. It was as if the gene protected them against this common consequence of childhood maltreatment. A second study showed that, although depression and suicide are often associated with stressful life events, variation in a particular gene could predict whether people became depressed and suicidal in response to such events (Caspi et al., 2003). Understanding how multiple genes combine to influence behavior and analyzing gene-environment interactions will continue to be active and exciting areas of research in behavioral genetics.

BEHAVIORAL GENETICS AND ENVIRONMENTAL INFLUENCES

As suggested earlier, research on genetic influences in psychology has also provided some of the best evidence for the importance of environmental influences. It has shown that even though genetic influences are important, they cannot explain everything about human behavior.

For example, twin and adoption studies demonstrate the importance of genetic factors in schizophrenia, and as a result, many researchers are looking for the specific genes responsible. Enthusiasm for genetic explanations of schizophrenia makes it easy to forget, however, that environmental factors can be at least as important as genes. As described in the chapter on psychological disorders, when one member of an identical-twin pair is schizophrenic, the chances are about 40 percent that the other member of the pair is also schizophrenic, a rate that is much higher than the 1 percent rate of schizophrenia in the general population. This result surely means that there is a strong genetic contribution to schizophrenia, but it also indicates that schizophrenia must be strongly influenced by the environment. After all, most of the time, the identical twin of a person with schizophrenia will not show the disorder. Such differences within pairs of identical twins can be due only to the operation of environmental factors.

In fact, research generally suggests that genetic factors account for only about half of the variance among individuals for psychological characteristics such as personality and psychopathology. Therefore, at least half of the variance among individuals on these characteristics must be due to environmental factors. Such environmental—or more properly, *nongenetic*—factors span everything other than genetic inheritance. They include such biological factors as prenatal events, nutrition, and illnesses, as well as more traditional environmental factors such as parenting, schooling, and peer influences.

In short, one of the most important findings emerging from behavioral genetics research concerns the environment, not genetics. Research suggests that the most important environmental influences are likely to be those that different family members do not share (Plomin, Asbury, & Dunn, 2001). Psychologists want to find out more about these *nonshared factors* and how they act to create differences in children—twins or not—who grow up in the same family.

So far, research on this topic has shown that children may grow up in the same family yet experience quite different environments, especially in relation to their parents (Brody, 2004). Siblings perceive that their parents treat them very differently—and observational studies back up these perceptions of differential treatment (Plomin, Asbury, & Dunn, 2001). Even events such as parental divorce, which would seem to be shared equally by all children in the family, are experienced differently by each child, depending especially on age, personality, and the nature of the relationship with each parent.

Research is also beginning to focus on environmental influences beyond the family—such as relationships with teachers or friends—which are even more likely than home-related

TRY THIS

factors to vary among siblings. If you have a brother or sister, think about a psychological trait on which you and your sibling differ—confidence, for example. Why do you think you two are different on that trait? Perhaps one of you experienced a loss of self-confidence when faced with a demanding grade-school teacher or after being betrayed by a childhood friend. Did such differing experiences occur randomly and thus make you more confident or less confident than your sibling? Or do you think that differences in your genetic makeups helped bring about these different experiences? Remember, unless you and your sibling are identical twins, you share only about 50 percent of your genes. Perhaps genetically influenced differences between the two of you—in emotionality or other aspects of temperament, for example—caused parents, peers, and others to respond to each of you differently. This brings us to a key major discovery about the environment that has emerged from research on behavioral genetics: Environmental influences associated with differences between siblings might actually be the *result* of genetic differences between the siblings.

Most of the measures used by psychologists to assess what might be thought of as environmental factors have now been shown to be influenced by genetic factors (Plomin & Bergeman, 1991). These include measures such as adolescents' ratings of how their parents treated them, observations of parent-child interactions, and questionnaires about life events and social support. If scores on measures such as these reflected only environmental factors, then the scores of identical twins should be no more similar to each other than those of fraternal twins. Also, there should be little similarity in environmental–experience measures for genetically related individuals who grew up in different families.

But results reported by behavioral geneticists defy such expectations. For example, parents differ in how responsive they are to their children, but such differences in responsiveness correlate with the children's intelligence—a trait that has a clear genetic component. So, as described in the chapters on intelligence and human development, parental responsiveness affects cognitive development, and—as behavioral genetics research suggests—children's inherited intellectual abilities in turn can alter their parent's responsiveness. In other words, parents tend to be more responsive to bright children who ask lots of questions and are interested in the answers.

Outside the family, too, genetic factors also play a role in generating environmental experiences. For example, research on the characteristics of children's peer groups shows that children tend to choose their friends—and to be chosen as friends—partly based on genetically influenced traits, such as mental ability and temperament (Manke et al., 1995). Several studies also suggest that genetic factors can increase or decrease the likelihood of family conflicts and other social stressors that threaten one's physical and psychological well-being (Karevold et al., 2009; Reiss et al., 2000). In addition, genetic influences on personality can account for the genetic effects seen in adults' reports about their family environments when growing up (Krueger, Markon, & Bouchard, 2003).

An important implication of genetic influences on environmental events is that measuring the impact of family relationships, peer influences, and other environmental factors on behavior and mental processes may be less straightforward than at first it may seem. A measure that is aimed at assessing an "environmental" factor may also be affected by the genetic characteristics of the people being studied.

Clearly, in human development, nature and nurture work together. Children select, modify, and create environments that are correlated with their genetic inclinations. As developmental psychologists have long argued, children are not formless blobs of raw clay passively molded by the environment. Rather, they are active participants and architects in their experiences. The new findings we have described here suggest that genetics plays an important role in those experiences.

SUMMARY

Behavioral genetics is the study of how genes affect behavior.

The Biology of Genetics and Heredity

Research on the ways in which nature and nurture interact to shape behavior and mental processes requires knowledge of *genetics*, the biology of inheritance. The genetic code that transmits characteristics from one generation to the next is contained in the *DNA (deoxyribonucleic acid)* that makes up the *genes* that in turn make up *chromosomes*. Dominant genes are expressed whenever they are present; recessive genes are expressed only when inherited from both parents. Most human characteristics are controlled by more than one gene; they are *polygenic traits*. The genes in a person's forty-six chromosomes make up the *genotype*. The *phenotype*—how people actually look and act—is influenced by genes and the environment.

A Brief History of Genetic Research in Psychology

Sir Francis Galton's work in the nineteenth century helped to stimulate psychologists' interest in the influence of genetics on behavior. The popularity of research in this area has waxed and waned over the years, but today most psychologists recognize the role of genetic, as well as environmental, influences on many aspects of behavior and mental processes.

The Focus of Research in Behavioral Genetics

Behavioral genetics research identifies the genetic and environmental factors responsible for differences among individuals, not for the characteristics of a particular person. Although genes can influence a trait, they may not completely determine whether that trait appears.

The Role of Genetic Factors in Psychology

Genetic factors probably influence, to some extent, every aspect of behavior and mental processes.

Genetic influences on general cognitive ability appear to increase over time, possibly because genetic predispositions lead people to select and even create environments that foster the continued development of abilities that are in line with those predispositions.

Genes that affect one trait, such as anxiety, can sometimes also affect other traits, such as depression.

Current research in behavioral genetics, aided by findings from the Human Genome Project, is identifying specific genes responsible for specific characteristics—especially rare, single-gene disorders such as Huntington's disease. It is also illuminating gene-environment interactions.

Behavioral Genetics and Environmental Influences

Research in behavioral genetics has actually provided evidence for the importance of environmental influences, too, because the research shows that genetics alone cannot account for such characteristics as intelligence, personality, and psychological disorders. Some of the most important environmental influences are likely to be those that members of the same family do not share. In short, neither nature nor nurture is conducting the performance of the other: They are playing a duet.

REFERENCES

AAA Foundation for Traffic Safety. (2009). *Aggressive Driving: Research Update.* Washington, D.C.: Author.

Aaron, D. J., Chang, Y.-F., Markovic, N., & LaPorte, R. E. (2003). Estimating the lesbian population: A capture-recapture approach. *Journal of Epidemiology and Community Health, 57,* 207–209.

Abar, C. C. (2012). Examining the relationship between parenting types and patterns of student alcohol-related behavior during the transition to college. *Psychology of Addictive Behaviors, 26*(1), 20–29. doi:10.1037/a0025108.

Abarbanell, L., & Hauser, M. D. (2010). Mayan morality: An exploration of permissible harms. *Cognition, 115*(2), 207–224. doi:10.1016/j.cognition.2009.12.007.

Abbott, B. B., Schoen, L. S., & Badia, P. (1984). Predictable and unpredictable shock: Behavioral measures of aversion and physiological measures of stress. *Psychological Bulletin, 96,* 45–71.

Abbott, C. C., Gallegos, P., Rediske, N., Lemke, N. T., & Quinn, D. K. (2014). A review of longitudinal electroconvulsive therapy: Neuroimaging investigations. *Journal of Geriatric Psychiatry & Neurology, 27*(1), 33–46.

Abbot-Shim, M., Lambert, R., & McCarty, F. (2003). A comparison of school readiness outcomes for children randomly assigned to a Head Start program and the program's wait list. *Journal of Education for Students Placed at Risk, 8,* 191–214.

ABC News, April 28, 2010. Why homeless hero Hugo Tale-Yax died on NYC street. http://abcnews.go.com/Health/Wellness/dying-good-samaritan-hugo-alfredo-tale-yax-symptom/story? Retrieved March 24, 2014.

Abdullah, A. H., Adom, A. H., Shakaff, A. Y. M., Ahmad, M. N., Zakaria, A., Saad, F. S. A. Isa, C. M. N. C., Masnan, M. J., & Kamarudin, L. M. (2012). Hand-held electronic nose sensor selection system for basal stamp rot (BSR) disease detection. *Intelligent Systems, Modelling and Simulation, 2,* 737–742.

Abdallah, S. A., l-Shatti, L. A., Alhajraf, A. F., Al-Hammad, N., & Al-Awadi, B. (2013). The detection of foodborne bacteria on beef: The application of the electronic nose. *Springerplus, 2,* 687.

Abe, T., Komada, Y., Nishida, Y., Hayashida, K., & Inoue, Y. (2010). Short sleep duration and long spells of driving are associated with the occurrence of Japanese drivers' rear-end collisions and single-car accidents. *Journal of Sleep Research, 19*(2), 310–316.

Abler, B., Hahlbrock, R., Unrath, A., Gron, G., & Kassubek, J. (2009). At-risk for pathological gambling: Imaging neural reward processing under chronic dopamine agonists. *Brain,132,* 2396–2402.

Abraham, S., & Kellow, J. (2011). Exploring eating disorder quality of life and functional gastrointestinal disorders among eating disorder patients. *Journal of Psychosomatic Research, 70*(4), 372–377.

Abramis, D. J. (1994). Work role ambiguity, job satisfaction, and job performance: Meta-analyses and review. *Psychological Reports, 75,* 1411–1433.

Abramowitz, J. S., & Braddock, A. E. (2006). Hypochondriasis: Conceptualization, treatment, and relationship to obsessive-compulsive disorder. *Psychiatric Clinics of North America, 29,* 503–519.

Abrams, D., & Hogg, M. A. (2010). Social identity and self-categorization In J. F. Dovidio, M. Hewstone, P. Glick, & V. M. Esses (Eds.), *The SAGE handbook of prejudice, stereotyping and discrimination.* London: Sage.

Abrams, R. L., & Greenwald, A. G. (2000). Parts outweigh the whole (word) in unconscious analysis of meaning. *Psychological Science, 11,* 118–124.

Abrantes-Pais, F. de N., Friedman, J. K., Lovallo, W. R., & Ross, E. D. (2007). Psychological or physiological: Why are tetraplegic patients content? *Neurology, 69,* 261–267.

Abreu, J. M. (1999). Conscious and unconscious African American stereotypes: Impact on first impression and diagnostic ratings by therapists. *Journal of Consulting and Clinical Psychology, 67,* 387–393.

Acevedo, B. P., & Aron, A. P. (2014). Romantic love, pair-bonding, and the dopaminergic reward system. In M. Mikulincer, P. R. Shaver (Eds), *Mechanisms of social connection: From brain to group* (pp. 55–69). Washington, DC: American Psychological Association.

Achenbach, T. M. (2011). Definitely more than measurement error: But how should we understand and deal with informant discrepancies? *Journal of Clinical Child and Adolescent Psychology, 40,* 80–86.

Acker, T., & Acker, H. (2004). Cellular oxygen sensing need in CNS function: Physiological and pathological implications. *Journal of Experimental Biology, 207*(Pt. 18), 3171–3188.

Ackerman, B. P., Brown, E. D., & Izard, C. E. (2004). The relations between contextual risk, earned income, and the school adjustment of children from economically disadvantaged families. *Developmental Psychology, 40,* 204–216.

Ackerman, J. P., Riggins, T., & Black, M. M. (2010). A review of the effects of prenatal cocaine exposure among school-aged children. *Pediatrics, 125,* 554–565.

Ackerman, P. L. (2007). New developments in understanding skilled performance. *Current Directions in Psychological Science, 16,* 235–239.

Adachi, P. J., & Willoughby, T. (2011). The effect of violent video games on aggression: Is it more than just the violence? *Aggression and Violent Behavior 16,* 55–62. doi:10.1016/j.avb.2010.12.002.

Adair, J. C., Gilmore, R. L., Fennell, E. B., Gold, M., & Heilman, K. M. (1995). Anosognosia during intracarotid barbiturate anesthesia: Unawareness or amnesia for weakness. *Neurology, 45*(2), 241–243.

Adam, E. K., Gunnar, M. R., & Tanaka, A. (2004). Adult attachment, parent emotion, and observed parenting behavior: Mediator and moderator models. *Child Development, 75,* 110–122.

Adam, H., Shirako, A., & Maddux, W. W. (2010). Cultural variance in the interpersonal effects of anger in negotiations. *Psychological Science (Sage Publications Inc.), 21*(6), 882–889. doi:10.1177/0956797610370755.

Adams, D. M., Mayer, R. E., MacNamara, A., Koenig, A., & Wainess, R. (2011). Narrative games for learning: Testing the discovery and narrative hypotheses. *Journal of Educational Psychology,* doi:10.1037/a0025595.

Adams, G. A., & Rau, B. L. (2011). Putting off tomorrow to do what you want today planning for retirement. *American Psychologist, 66*(3), 180–192. doi:10.1037/a0022131.

Adams, N. (2012). Skinner's Walden Two: An anticipation of positive psychology? *Review of General Psychology, 16*(1), 1–9. doi:10.1037/a0026439

Adams, W. J., Graf, E. W., & Ernst, M. O. (2004). Experience can change the "light from above" prior. *Nature Neuroscience, 7,* 1057–1058.

Adank, P., Hagoort, P., & Bekkering, H. (2010). Imitation improves language comprehension. *Psychological Science, 21*(12), 1903–1909. doi:10.1177/0956797610389192.

Addington, J., Piskulic, D., & Marshall, C. (2010). Psychosocial Treatments for Schizophrenia. *Current Directions in Psychological Science, 19*(4), 260–263. doi:10.1177/0963721410377743.

Adelabu, D. H. (2008). Future time perspective, hope, and ethnic identity among African American adolescents. *Urban Education, 43,* 347–360.

Adelsheim, C. (2011). Functional magnetic resonance detection of deception: Great as fundamental research, inadequate as substantive evidence. *Mercer Law Review, 62*(3), 885–908.

Ader, R. (2001). Psychoneuroimmunology. *Current Directions in Psychological Science, 10,* 94–98.

Adler, T. (1993, March). Bad mix: Combat stress, decisions. *APA Monitor,* p. 1.

Adolphs, R., Tranel, D., & Damasio, A. R. (1998). The human amygdala in social judgment. *Nature, 393*(6684), 470–474.

Adolphs, R., Tranel, D., Koenigs, M., & Damasio, A. R. (2005). Preferring one taste over another without recognizing either. *Nature Neuroscience, 8,* 860–861.

Adorno, T. W., Frenkel-Brunswik, E., Levinson, D. J., & Sanford, R. N. (1950). *The authoritarian personality.* New York: Harper & Row.

Aduriz, M.E., Bluthgen, C. & Knopfler, C. (2009). Helping child flood victims using group EMDR intervention in Argentina: Treatment outcome and gender differences. *International Journal of Stress Management. 16,* 138–153.

Aggarwal, R., Cheshire, N., & Darzi, A. (2008). Endovascular simulation-based training. *Surgeon, 6*(4), 196–197.

Agthe, M., Spörrle, M., & Maner, J. K. (2010). Don't hate me because i'm beautiful: Anti-attractiveness bias in organizational evaluation and decision making. *Journal of Experimental Social Psychology, 46*(6), 1151–1154.

Agthe, M., Spörrle, M., & Maner, J. K. (2011). Does being attractive always help? Positive and negative effects of attractiveness on social decision making. *Personality and Social Psychology Bulletin, 37*(8), 1042–1054.

Aguiler, A., & Munoz, R. F. (2011). Text messaging as an adjunct to CBT in low-income populations: A usability and feasibility pilot study. *Professional Psychology: Research and Practice, 42,* 472–478.

Aharonov, R., Segev, L., Meilijson, I., & Ruppin, E. (2003). Localization of function via lesion analysis. *Neural Computation, 15*(4), 885–913.

Ahmed. I., & Thorpy, M. (2010). Clinical features, diagnosis and treatment of narcolepsy. *Clinics in Chest Medicine, 31*(2), 371–381.

Ahola, A. (2012). How reliable are eyewitness memories? Effects of retention interval, violence of act, and gender stereotypes on observers' judgments of their own memory regarding witnessed act and perpetrator. *Psychology, Crime & Law, 18*(5), 491–503. doi:10.1080/1068316X.2010.509316.

Aiello, J. R., & Douthitt, E. A. (2001). Social facilitation from Triplett to electronic performance monitoring. *Group Dynamics, 5,* 163–180.

Aiken, L. R. (1994). *Psychological testing and assessment* (8th ed.). Boston: Allyn & Bacon.

Ainsworth, M. D. S., Blehar, M. D., Waters, E., & Wall, S. (1978). *Patterns of attachment: A psychological study of the Strange Situation.* Hillsdale, NJ: Erlbaum.

Ainsworth, M. D. S., & Bowlby, J. (1991). An ethological approach to personality development. *American Psychologist, 46,* 333–341.

Ainsworth, M. D. S., & Marvin, R. S. (1995). On the shaping of attachment theory and research: An interview with Mary D. S. Ainsworth (Fall 1994). *Monographs of the Society for Research in Child Development, 60,* 3–21.

Airan, R. D., Thompson, K. R., Fenno, L. E., Bernstein, H., & Deisseroth, K. (2009). Temporally precise in vivo control of intracellular signaling. *Nature, 458,* 1025–1029. Epub 2009 Mar 1018.

Aitchison, J. (2008). Chimps, children, and creoles: The need for caution. In V. Clark, P. Eschholz, A. Rosa, & B. L. Simon (Eds.,) *Language: Introductory readings* (7th Ed., pp. 61–75). New York: Palgrave MacMillan.

Akbarian, S. (2010). The molecular pathology of schizophrenia: Focus on histone and DNA modifications. *Brain Research Bulletin, 83,* 103–107. doi:10.1016/j.brainresbull.2009.08.018.

Akbarian, S., Beeri, M. S., & Haroutunian, V. (2013). Epigeneitc determinants of healthy and diseased brain aging and cognition. *JAMA Neurology, 70*(6), 711–718.

Akin, W. M., & Turner, S. M. (2006). Toward understanding ethnic and cultural factors in the interviewing process. *Psychotherapy: Theory, Research, Practice, Training, 43,* 50–64.

Akins, C. K., & Zentall, T. R. (1998). Imitation in Japanese quail: The role of reinforcement of demonstrator responding. *Psychonomic Bulletin and Review, 5,* 694–697.

Alaimo, K., Olson, C. M., & Frongillo, E. A., Jr. (2001). Food insufficiency and American school-aged children's cognitive, academic, and psychosocial development. *Pediatrics, 108,* 44–53.

Albarracín, D., Durantini, M. R., Allison, E., Gunnoe, J. B., & Leeper, J. (2008). Beyond the most willing audiences: A meta-intervention to increase exposure to HIV-prevention programs by vulnerable populations. *Health Psychology, 27,* 638–644.

Albarracín, D., Johnson, B. T., Fishbein, M., & Muellerleile, P. A. (2001). Theories of reasoned action and planned behavior as models of condom use: A meta-analysis. *Psychological Bulletin, 127,* 142–161.

Albarracín, D., & Vargas, P. (2010). Attitudes and persuasion: From biology to social responses to persuasive intent. In S. T. Fiske, D. T. Gilbert, & G. Lindzey (Eds.), *Handbook of social psychology* (5th ed., Vol. 2, pp. 394–427). Hoboken, NJ: Wiley.

Albee, G. W. (1968). Conceptual models and manpower requirements in psychology. *American Psychologist, 23,* 317–320.

Albee, G. W. (2002). Just say no to psychotropic drugs! *Journal of Clinical Psychology, 58,* 635–648.

Albee, G. W. (2006). Historical overview of primary prevention of psychopathology. *Journal of Primary Prevention, 27,* 449–456.

Alberti, R., & Emmons, M. (2008). *Your perfect right: Assertiveness and equality in your life and relationships* (9th ed.). Atascadero, CA: Impact Publishers.

Alberto, P. A., Troutman, A. C., & Feagin, J. R. (2002). *Applied behavior analysis for teachers* (6th ed.). Englewood Cliffs, NJ: Prentice Hall.

Alcantara, C., & Gone, J. P. (2014). Multicultural issues in the clinical interview and diagnostic process. In F. T. L. Leong, L. Comas-Diaz, G. C. Nagayama Hall, V. C. McLoyd, & J. E. Trimble (Eds.), *APA handbook of multicultural psychology, Vol. 2: Applications and training* (pp. 153–163). Washington, DC: American Psychological Association.

Alderfer, C. P. (1969). An empirical test of a new theory of human needs. *Organizational Behavior and Human Performance, 4,* 142–175.

Aldridge, J. W. (2005). Interpreting correlation as causation? *Science, 308*(5724), 954.

Aleisa, A. M., Alzoubi, K. H., & Alkadhi, K. A. (2011). Post-learning REM sleep deprivation impairs long-term memory: Reversal by acute nicotine treatment. *Neuroscience Letters, 499*(1), 28–31.

Aleman, A., Kahn, R. S., & Selten, J.-P. (2003). Sex differences in the risk of schizophrenia: Evidence from meta-analysis. *Archives of General Psychiatry, 60,* 565–571.

Alexander, G., Eaton, I., & Egan, K. (2010). Cracking the code of electronic games: Some lessons for educators. *Teachers College Record, 112*(7), 1830–1850.

Alexander, G. M., & Hines, M. (2002). Sex differences in response to children's toys in non-human primates (*Cercopithecus aethiops sabaeus*). *Evolution and Human Behavior, 23,* 467–479.

Alexander, G. M., & Saenz, J. (2012). Early androgens, activity levels and toy choices of children in the second year of life. *Hormones and Behavior, 62,* 500–504.

Alexander, K. W., Quas, J. A., Goodman, G. S., Ghetti, S., Edelstein, R. S., Redlich, A. D., et al. (2005). Traumatic impact predicts long-term memory for documented child sexual abuse. *Psychological Science, 16,* 33–40.

Ali, A., Ambler, G., Strydom, A., Rai, D., Cooper, C., McManus, S., Weich, S., Meltzer, H., Dein, S., & Hassiotis, A. (2013). The relationship between happiness and intelligent quotient: the contribution of socio-economic and clinical factors. *Psychological Medicine, 43*(6), 1303–1312.

Alia-Klein, N., Goldstein, R. Z., Tomasi, D., Woicik, P. A., et al. (2009). Neural mechanisms of anger regulation as a function of genetic risk for violence. *Emotion, 9,* 385–396.

Alison, L., Kebbell, M., & Lewis, P. (2006). Considerations for experts in assessing the credibility of recovered memories of child sexual abuse: The importance of maintaining a case-specific focus. *Psychology, Public Policy, and Law, 12,* 419–441.

Alkire, M. T., Hudetz, A. G., & Tononi, G. (2008). Consciousness and anesthesia. *Science, 322,* 876–880.

Allan, C. L., & Ebmeier, K. P. (2011). The use of ECT and MST in treating depression. *International Review of Psychiatry, 23*(5), 400–412.

Allen, C. P., Sumner, P., & Chambers, C. D. (2014). The timing and neuroanatomy of conscious vision as revealed by TMS-induced blindsight. *Journal of Cognitive Neuroscience.* Epub January 6, 2014.

Allen, J. B., Kenrick, D. T., Linder, D. E., & McCall, M. A. (1989). Arousal and attraction: A response-facilitation alternative to misattribution and negative-reinforcement models. *Journal of Personality and Social Psychology, 57,* 261–270.

Allen, J. J. B. (2002). The role of psychophysiology in clinical assessment: ERPs in the evaluation of memory. *Psychophysiology, 39,* 261–280.

Allen, J. J. B., & Iacono, W. G. (2001). Assessing the validity of amnesia in dissociative identity disorder: A dilemma for the DSM and the courts. *Psychology, Public Policy and Law, 7,* 311–344.

Allen, M. T., & Matthews, K. A. (1997). Hemodynamic responses to laboratory stressors in children and adolescents: The influences of age, race and gender. *Psychophysiology, 34,* 329–339.

Allen, S. R., & Thorndike, R. M. (1995). Stability of the WPPSI-R and WISC-III factor structure using cross-validation of covariance structure models. *Journal of Psychoeducational Assessment, 13,* 3–20.

Alloy, L. B., Abramson, L. Y., Cogswell, A., Hughes, M. E., & Iacoviello, B. M. (2008). Cognitive vulnerability to depression: Implications for prevention. In M. T. Tsuang, W. S. Stone, & M. J. Lyons (Eds.) *Recognition and prevention of major mental and substance use disorders* (pp. 97–113). Arlington, VA: American Psychiatric Publishing.

Alloy, L. B., Bender, R. E., Whitehouse, W. G., Wagner, C. A., Liu, R. T., Grant, D. A., & ... Abramson, L. Y. (2011). High Behavioral Approach System (BAS) sensitivity, reward responsiveness, and goal-striving predict first onset of bipolar spectrum disorders: A prospective behavioral high-risk design. *Journal of Abnormal Psychology,121,* 339–351. doi:10.1037/a0025877

Allport, G. W., & Odbert, H. S. (1936). Trait names: A psycholexical study. *Psychological Monographs, 47*(1, Whole No. 211).

Allsop, D. J., Norberg, M. M., Copeland, J., Fu, S., & Budney, A. J. (2011). The Cannabis Withdrawal Scale development: Patterns and predictors of cannabis withdrawal and distress. *Drug and Alcohol Dependence, 119*(1–2), 123–129.

Almeida, D. M. (2005). Resilience and vulnerability to daily stressors assessed via diary methods. *Current Directions in Psychological Science, 14,* 64–68.

Alonso, J., Chatterji, S., He, Y., & Kessler, R. C. (2013). Burdens of mental disorders: The approach of the World Mental Health Surveys. In J. Alonso, S. Chatterji, & Y. He (Eds.), *The burdens of mental health disorders: Global perspectives from the WHO World Mental Health Surveys* (pp. 1–6). New York: Cambridge University Press.

Al Rashoud, A. S., Abboud, R. J., Wang, W., & Wigderowitz, C. (2013). Efficacy of low-level laser therapy applied at acupuncture points in knee osteoarthritis: A randomised double-blind comparative trial. *Physiotherapy.* Epub November 15, 2013.

Alston, J. H. (1920). Spatial condition of the fusion of warmth and cold in heat. *American Journal of Psychology, 31,* 303–312.

Alston, L. L., Kratchmer, C., Jeznach, A., Bartlett, N. T., Davidson, P. R., & Fujiwara, E. (2013). Self-serving episodic memory biases: Findings in the repressive coping style. *Frontiers in Behavioral Neuroscience, 7,* 717.

Althoff, R. R., Faraone, S. V., Rettew, D. C., Morley, C. P., & Hudziak, J. J. (2005). Family, twin, adoption, and molecular genetic studies of juvenile bipolar disorder. *Bipolar Disorders, 7*, 598–609.

Altman, W. S. (2007, January 4). *In-class writing as a teaching tool: An evaluation.* Poster presented at the National Institute on the Teaching of Psychology, St. Pete Beach, FL.

Aluja-Fabregat, A., & Torrubia-Beltri, R. (1998). Viewing of mass media violence, perception of violence, personality and academic achievement. *Personality and Individual Differences, 25*, 973–989.

Alvarez, K., Salas, E., & Garofano, C. M. (2004). An integrated model of training evaluation and effectiveness. *Human Resource Development and Review, 3*, 385–416.

Alzheimer's Association. (2009). 2009 Alzheimer's disease facts and figures. *Alzheimer's & Dementia: The Journal of the Alzheimer's Association, 5*(3), 234–70.

Alzheimer's Association. (2014). 2014 Alzheimer's disease facts and figures. *Alzheimer's and Dementia, 10*, 1–67.

Amabile, T. M. (1996). *Creativity in context: Update to "The Social Psychology of Creativity."* Boulder, CO: Westview.

Amabile, T. M. (2001). Beyond talent: John Irving and the passionate craft of creativity. *American Psychologist, 56*, 333–336.

Amabile, T. M., Hennessey, B. A., & Grossman, B. S. (1986). Social influences on creativity: The effects of contracted-for reward. *Journal of Personality and Social Psychology, 50*, 14–23.

Amarillo, I. E., Li, W. L., Li, X., Vilain, E., & Kantarci, S. (2014). De novo single exon deletion of AUTS2 in a patient with speech and language disorder: A review of disrupted AUTS2 and further evidence for its role in neurodevelopmental disorders. *American Journal of Medical Genetics, Part A., 164*(4), 958–965.

Amat, J., Baratta, M. V., Paul, E., Bland, S. T., Watkins, L. R., & Maier, S. F.(2005). Medial prefrontal cortex determines how stressor controllability affects behavior and dorsal raphe nucleus. *Nature Neuroscience 8*, 365–371.

Amato, P. R. (2010). Research on Divorce: Continuing Trends and New Developments. *Journal of Marriage and Family, 72*, 650–666.

Ambadar, Z., Schooler, J. W., & Cohn, J. F. (2005). Deciphering the enigmatic face. *Psychological Science, 16*, 403–410.

Ambrosini, E., Sinigaglia, C., & Costantini, M. (2012). Tie my hands, tie my eyes. *Journal of Experimental Psychology: Human Perception and Performance, 38*(2), 263–266. doi:10.1037/a0026570

Amedi, A., Merabet, L. B., Bermpohl, F., & Pascual-Leone, A. (2005). The occipital cortex in the blind. *Current Directions in Psychological Science, 14*, 306–311.

American Academy of Pediatrics: Council On Communications and Media. (2011). Media Use by Children Younger Than 2 Years. *Pediatrics, 128*, 1040–1045.

American Educational Research Association, American Psychological Association, & National Council on Measurement in Education. (1999). *Standards for educational and psychological testing.* Washington, DC: American Educational Research Association.

American Psychiatric Association. (1994). *Diagnostic and statistical manual of mental disorders* (4th ed.). Washington, DC: American Psychiatric Association.

American Psychiatric Association. (1999). Position statement on psychiatric treatment and sexual orientation. *American Journal of Psychiatry, 156*, 1131.

American Psychiatric Association. (2000). *Diagnostic and statistical manual of mental disorders* (4th ed., text rev.). Washington DC: Author.

American Psychiatric Association. (2003). *The insanity defense.* Retrieved May 26, 2004, from http://www.psych.org/public_info/insanity.cfm.

American Psychiatric Association (2013). *Diagnostic and statistical manual of mental disorders: Fifth edition (DSM-5).* Washington, DC: American Psychiatric Publishing.

American Psychological Association. (1993). *Violence and youth: Psychology's response.* Washington: DC: American Psychological Association.

American Psychological Association. (2002a). *Answers to your questions about sexual orientation and homosexuality.* Retrieved December 13, 2004, from http://www.apa.org/pubinfo/answers.html#whatis.

American Psychological Association. (2002b). Ethical principles of psychologists and code of conduct. *American Psychologist, 57*, 1060–1073.

American Psychological Association. (2008). *Answers to your questions: For a better understanding of sexual orientation and homosexuality.* Washington, DC: Author.

American Psychological Association. (2009). Medical cost offset. In *Resources for practicing psychologists: The practice directorate.* Retrieved April 23, 2009, from http://www.apa.org/ practice/offset3.html.

American Psychological Association (2010). *Ethical principles of psychologists and code of conduct (including 2010 amendments).* Washington, D.C.: APA.

American Psychological Association (2010). *Race/Ethnicity of doctorate recipients in psychology in the past 10 years.* Washington, D.C.: APA Center for Workforce Studies.

American Psychological Association Committee on Animal Research and Ethics. (2009). *Research with animals in psychology.* Retrieved from http://www.apa.org/science/animal2.html.

American Psychological Association Presidential Task Force on Evidence-Based Practice. (2006). Evidence-based practice in psychology. *American Psychologist, 61*, 271–285.

American Psychological Association Task Force on the Sexualization of Girls. (2007). *Report of the APA Task Force on the Sexualization of Girls.* Washington, DC: American Psychological Association.

Ames, D. R., Kammrath, L. K., Suppes, A., & Bolger, N. (2010). Not so fast: The (not-quite-complete) dissociation between accuracy and confidence in thin-slice impressions. *Personality and Social Psychology Bulletin, 36*, 264–277.

Amodio, D. M., & Devine, P. G. (2009). On the functions of implicit prejudice and stereotyping: Insights from social neuroscience. In R. E. Petty, R. H. Fazio, & P. Briñol (Eds.), *Attitudes: Insights from the new wave of implicit measures* (pp. 192–229). Hillsdale, NJ: Erlbaum.

Amodio, D. M., & Devine, P. G. (2010). Control in the regulation of intergroup bias. In R. R. Hassin, K. N. Ochsner, & Y. Trope (Eds.), *Self control in society, mind, and brain* (pp. 49–75). New York: Oxford University Press.

Amodio, D. M., Harmon-Jones, E., Devine, P. G., Curtin, J. J., Hartley, S. L., & Covert, A. E. (2004). Neural signals for the detection of unintentional race bias. *Psychological Science, 15*, 88–93.

Amodio, D. M., Jost, J. T., Master, S. L., & Yee, C. M. (2007). Neurocognitive correlates of liberalism and conservatism. *Nature Neuroscience, 10*, 1246–1247.

Amodio, D. M., & Lieberman, M. D (2009). Pictures in our heads: Contributions of fMRI to the study of prejudice and stereotyping. In T. D. Nelson, (Ed.), *Handbook of prejudice, stereotyping, and discrimination* (pp. 347–365). New York: Psychology Press.

Amodio, D. M., & Showers, C. J. (2005). "Similarity breeds liking" revisited: The moderating role of commitment. *Journal of Social and Personal Relationships, 22*, 817–836.

Anastasi, A., & Urbina, S. (1997). *Psychological testing* (7th ed.). Upper Saddle River, NJ: Prentice Hall.

Anastassiou-Hadjicharalambous, X., & Warden, D. (2008). Physiologically indexed and self perceived affective empathy in conduct-disordered children high and low on callousunemotional traits. *Child Psychiatry and Human Development, 39*, 503–517.

Anderson, A., & Conwell, Y. (2002). Doctors study why elderly so prone to suicide. *American Journal of Geriatric Psychiatry.* Retrieved June 7, 2009, from http://www.stopgettingsick.com/templates/news_template.cfm/6086.

Anderson, A. K., & Phelps, E. A. (2000). Expression without recognition: Contributions of the human amygdala to emotional communication. *Psychological Science, 11*, 106–111.

Anderson, A. K., & Phelps, E. A. (2001). Lesions of the human amygdala impair enhanced perception of emotionally salient events. *Nature, 411*, 305–309.

Anderson, B. L. (2003). The role of occlusion in the perception of depth, lightness, and opacity. *Psychological Review, 110*(4), 785–801.

Anderson, C., Kraus, M. W., Galinsky, A. D., & Keltner, D. (2012). The local-ladder effect: Social status and subjective well-being. *Psychological Science, 23*, 764. doi: 10.1177/0956797611434537.

Anderson, C. A., Berkowitz, L., Donnerstein, E., Huesmann, L. R., Johnson, J. D., Linz, D., et al. (2003). The influence of media violence on youth. *Psychological Science in the Public Interest, 4*, 81–110.

Anderson, C. A., & Bushman, B. J. (2002a). Human aggression. *Annual Review of Psychology, 53*, 27–51.

Anderson, C. A., & Bushman, B. J. (2002b). Media violence and the American public revisited. *American Psychologist, 57*, 448–450.

Anderson, C. A., & DeLisi, M. (2011). Implications of global climate change for violence in developed and developing countries. In J. P. Forgas, A. W. Kruglanski, K. D. Williams (Eds.), *The psychology of social conflict and aggression* (pp. 249–265). New York: Psychology Press.

Anderson, C. A., & Dill, K. E. (2000). Video games and aggressive thoughts, feelings, and behavior in the laboratory and in life. *Journal of Personality and Social Psychology, 78*, 772–790.

Anderson, C. A., & Gentile, D. A. (2008). Media violence, aggression, and public policy. In E. Borgida & S. Fiske (Eds.), *Beyond common sense: Psychological science in the courtroom* (pp. 281–300). Malden, MA: Blackwell.

Anderson, C. A., Lindsay, J. J., & Bushman, B. J. (1999). Research in the psychological laboratory: Truth or triviality? *Current Directions in Psychological Science, 8*, 3–9.

Anderson, C. A., Sakamoto, A., Gentile, D. A., Ihori, N., Shibuya, A. Yukawa, S., Naito, M., & Kobayashi, K. (2008). Longitudinal effects of violent video games on aggression in Japan and the United States. *Pediatrics, 122*, 1067–1072.

Anderson, C. A., Shibuya, A., Ihori, N., Swing, E. L., Bushman, B. J., Sakamoto, A., & Saleem, M. (2010). Violent video game effects on aggression, empathy, and prosocial behavior in Eastern and Western countries: A meta-analytic review. *Psychological Bulletin, 136*(2), 151–173. doi:10.1037/a0018251.

Anderson, J. R. (1995). *Learning and memory: An integrated approach.* New York: Wiley.

Anderson, J. R. (2000). *Cognitive psychology and its implications* (5th ed). New York: Worth.

Anderson, J. R., Bothell, D., Byrne, M. D., Douglass, S., Lebiere, C., & Qin, Y. (2004). An integrated theory of the mind. *Psychological Review, 111,* 1036–1060.

Anderson, M. C., & Levy, B. J. (2009). Suppressing unwanted memories. *Current Directions in Psychological Science, 18,* 189–194.

Anderson, M. L., Nokia, M. S., Govindaraju, K. P., & Shors, T. J. (2012). Moderate drinking? Alcohol consumption significantly decreases neurogenesis in the adult hippocampus. *Neuroscience, 224,* 202–209.

Anderssen, N., Amlie, C., & Ytteroy, E. A. (2002). Outcomes for children with lesbian or gay parents: A review of studies from 1978 to 2000. *Scandinavian Journal of Psychology, 43,* 335–351.

Andersson, G. (2009). Using the Internet to provide cognitive behaviour therapy. *Behaviour Research and Therapy, 47,* 175–180.

Ando, Y., Kitayama, H., Kawaguchi, Y., & Koyanagi, Y. (2008). Primary target cells of herpes simplex virus type 1 in the hippocampus. *Microbes & Infection, 10*(14/15), 1514–1523.

Andrade, J., Deeprose, C., & Barker, I. (2008). Awareness and memory function during paediatric anaesthesia. *British Journal of Anaesthesia, 100,* 389–396.

Andreasen, N.C. (1997). The evolving concept of schizophrenia: From Kraepelin to the present and future. *Schizophrenia Research, 28,* 105–109.

Andreasen, N. C., & Pierson, R. (2008). The role of the cerebellum in schizophrenia. *Biological Psychiatry, 64,* 81–88.

Andreescu, C., Lenze, E. J., Dew, M. A., Begley, A. E., Mulsant, B. H., et al. (2007). Effect of comorbid anxiety on treatment response and relapse risk in late-life depression. *British Journal of Psychiatry, 190,* 344–349.

Andrew, D., & Craig, A. D. (2001). Spinothalamic lamina I neurons selectively sensitive to histamine: A central neural pathway for itch. *Nature Neuroscience, 4,* 72–77.

Andrews, B., Brewin, C., Ochera, J., Morton, J., Bekerian, D. A., Davies, G. M., & Mollon, P. (2000). The timing, triggers, and quality of recovered memories in therapy. *British Journal of Clinical Psychology, 39,* 11–26.

Andrews, B., Brewin, C. R., Philpott, R., & Stewart, L. (2007). Delayed-onset posttraumatic stress disorder: A systematic review of the evidence. *American Journal of Psychiatry, 164,* 1319–1326.

Andrews-Hanna, J. R., Mackiewicz Seghete, K. L., Claus, E. D., Burgess, G. C., Ruzic, L., & Banich, M. T. (2011). Cognitive control in adolescence: neural underpinnings and relation to self-report behaviors. *PLoS One 6*(6):e21598.

Andrews-Hanna, J. R., Saxe, R., & Yarkoni, T. (2014). Contributions of episodic retrieval and mentalizing to autobiographical thought: Evidence from functional neuroimaging, resting-state connectivity, and fMRI meta-analyses. *Neuroimage.* Epub January 31, 2014.

Angelaki, D. E., & Cullen, K. E. (2008). Vestibular system: The many faces of a multimodal sense. *Annual Review of Neuroscience, 31,* 125–150.

Angold, A., Erkanli, A., Farmer, E. M. Z., Fairbank, J. A., Burns, B. J., Keeler, G., & Costello, E. J. (2002). Psychiatric disorder, impairment, and service use in rural African American and white youth. *Archives of General Psychiatry, 59,* 893–901.

Anker, A. E., & Feeley, T. (2011). Are nonparticipants in prosocial behavior merely innocent bystanders? *Health Communication, 26*(1), 13–24.

Annenberg Public Policy Center. (1999). *The 1999 state of children's television report: Programming for children over broadcast and cable television.* Washington, DC: Annenberg Public Policy Center.

Annese, J., Schenker-Ahmed, N. M., Bartsch, H., Maechler, P., Sheh, C., Thomas, N., Kayano, J., Ghatan, A., Bresler, N., Frosch, M. P., Klaming, R., & Corkin, S. (2014). Postmortem examination of patient H. M.'s brain based on histological sectioning and digital 3D reconstruction. *Nature Communications, 5,* Epub January 28, 2014.

Anrep, G. V. (1920). Pitch discrimination in the dog. *Journal of Physiology, 53,* 367–385.

Anshel, M. (1996). Coping styles among adolescent competitive athletes. *Journal of Social Psychology, 136,* 311–323.

Anthony, T., Cooper, C., & Mullen, B. (1992). Cross-racial facial identification: A social cognitive integration. *Personality & Social Psychology Bulletin, 18,* 296–301.

Antonescu-Turcu, A. & Parthasarathy, S. (2010). CPAP and bi-level PAP therapy: new and established roles. *Respiratory Care, 55*(9), 1216–1229.

Antoni, M. H., Cruess, D. G., Cruess, S., Lutgendorf, S., Kumar, M., Ironson, G., et al. (2000). Cognitive-behavioral stress management intervention effects on anxiety, 24-hr urinary norepinephrine output, and t-cytotoxic/suppressor cells over time among symptomatic HIV-infected gay men. *Journal of Consulting and Clinical Psychology, 68,* 31–45.

Antoni, M. H., & Lutgendorf, S. (2007). Psychosocial factors and disease progression in cancer. *Current Directions in Psychological Science, 16,* 42–46.

Antoni, M. H., Lutgendorf, S. K., Blomberg, B., Carver, C. S., Lechner, S., Diaz, A., Stagl, J., Arevalo, J. M. G., & Cole, S. W. (2012). Cognitive-behavioral stress management reverses anxiety-related leukocyte transcriptional dynamics. *Biological Psychiatry, 71,* 366–372.

Antony, M. M., & Barlow, D. H. (2010). *Handbook of assessment and treatment planning for psychological disorders* (2nd ed.). New York: Guilford.

APA Office of Ethnic Minority Affairs. (2000). *Guidelines for research in ethnic minority communities.* Washington, DC: American Psychological Association.

Apfelbaum, E. P., Pauker, K., Sommers, S. R., & Ambady, N. (2010). In blind pursuit of racial equality? *Psychological Science, 21*(11), 1587–1592. doi:10.1177/0956797610384741.

Appel, M., Kronberger, N., & Aronson, J. (2011). Stereotype threat impairs ability building: Effects on test preparation among women in science and technology. *European Journal of Social Psychology, 41*(7), 904–913. doi:10.1002/ejsp.835.

Appelbaum, P. S. (2005). Assessing Kendra's Law: Five years of outpatient commitment in New York. *Psychiatric Services, 56,* 791–792.

Appignanesi, L. (2009). *Mad, bad, and sad: A history of women and mind doctors.* New York: W. W. Norton.

Aquino, C. C., & Lang, A. E. (2014). Tardive dyskinesia syndromes: Current concepts. *Parkinsonism & Related Disorders, 20*(Supplement 1), S113–117.

Aquino, K., Tripp, T. M., & Bies, R. J. (2006). Getting even or moving on? Power, procedural justice, and types of offense as predictors of revenge, forgiveness, reconciliation, and avoidance in organizations. *Journal of Applied Psychology, 91,* 653–668.

Arango, C., Rapado-Castro, M., Reig, S., Castro-Fornieles, J., González-Pinto, A., Otero, S., & Desco, M. (2012). Progressive brain changes in children and adolescents with first-episode psychosis. *Archives Of General Psychiatry, 69*(1), 16–26.

Ardila, A., Rosselli, M., Matute, E., & Inozemtseva, O. (2011). Gender differences in cognitive development. *Developmental Psychology, 47*(4), 984–990. doi:10.1037/a0023819.

Ariely, D., & Berns, G. S. (2010). Neuromarketing: The hope and hype of neuroimaging in business. *Nature Reviews Neuroscience, 11*(4), 284–292. doi:10.1038/nrn2795.

Arkes, H. R., & Ayton, P. (1999). The sunk cost and Concorde effects: Are humans less rational than lower animals? *Psychological Bulletin, 125,* 591–600.

Arle, J. E., & Shils, J. L. (2008). Motor cortex stimulation for pain and movement disorders. *Neurotherapeutics, 5*(1), 37–49.

Armitage, C. J. (2005). Can the theory of planned behavior predict the maintenance of physical activity? *Health Psychology, 24,* 235–245.

Armour, S. (2008, March 31). Day care's new frontier: Your baby at your desk. *USA Today.*

Armstrong, L. E. (2006). Nutritional strategies for football: Counteracting heat, cold, high altitude, and jet lag. *Journal of Sports Sciences, 24*(7), 723–740.

Arndt, J. (2012). The influence of forward and backward associative strength on false recognition. *Journal of Experimental Psychology. Learning, Memory & Cognition, 38*(3), 747–756. doi:10.1037/a0026375

Arneson, J. J., Sackett, P. R., & Beatty, A. S. (2011). Ability-performance relationships in education and employment settings: Critical tests of the more-is-better and the good-enough hypotheses. *Psychological Science, 22*(10), 1336–1342. doi:10.1177/0956797611417004.

Arnett, J. J. (1999). Adolescent storm and stress, reconsidered. *American Psychologist, 54,* 317–326.

Arnett, J. J. (2000). Emerging adulthood: A theory of development from the late teens through the twenties. *American Psychologist, 55,* 469–480.

Arnett, J. J. (2007). Suffering, selfish, slackers? Myths and reality about emerging adults. *Journal of Youth & Adolescence, 36*(1), 23–29.

Arnett, J. J. (2011). Emerging adulthood(s): The cultural psychology of a new life stage. In L. A. Jensen (Ed.), *Bridging cultural and developmental psychology: New syntheses in theory, research, and policy.* New York: Oxford University Press.

Arnett, J. J. (2013). Emerging adulthood. In R. Biswas-Diener & E. Diener (Eds.), Noba Textbook Series: *Psychology.* Champaign, IL: DEF Publishers.

Arnett, J. J., & Schwab, J. (2012). *The Clark University Poll of Emerging Adults: Thriving, Struggling, & Hopeful.* Worcester, MA: Clark University.

Arnulf, I. (2012). REM sleep behavior disorder: Motor manifestations and pathophysiology. *Movement Disorders, 27*(6), 677–689.

Aronoff, J., Barclay, A. M., & Stevenson, L. A. (1988). The recognition of threatening stimuli. *Journal of Personality and Social Psychology, 54,* 647–655.

Aronson, E. (2004). Reducing hostility and building compassion: Lessons from the jigsaw classroom. In A. G. Miller (Ed.), *The social psychology of good and evil* (pp. 469–488). New York: Guilford Press.

Aronson, E., & Patnoe, S. (2011). *Cooperation in the classroom: The jigsaw method* (3rd ed.). London: Pinter & Martin, Ltd.

Aronson, E., Wilson, T., & Akert, R. (2010). *Social psychology* (7th ed.). Upper Saddle River, NJ: Prentice Hall.

Aronson, E., Wilson, T., & Akert, R. (2013). *Social psychology* (8th ed.). Boston: Pearson.

Aronson, E., Wilson, T. D., & Akert, R. M. (2005). *Social psychology* (5th ed.). Upper Saddle River, NJ: Prentice Hall.

Arruda, M., Guidetti, V., Galli, F., de Albuquerque, R., & Bigal, M. (2011). Prenatal exposure to tobacco and alcohol are associated with chronic daily headaches at childhood: A population-based study. *Arquivos de Neuro-Psiquiatria, 69*(1), 27–33. doi:10.1590/S0004–282X2011000100007.

Arsalidou, M., Barbeau, E. J., Bayless, S. J., & Taylor, M. J. (2010). Brain responses differ to faces of mothers and fathers. *Brain & Cognition, 74*(1), 47–51. doi:10.1016/j.bandc.2010.06.003.

Arsenault, B. J., Rana, J. S., Lemieux, I., Despres, J.-P., et al. (2010). Physical inactivity, abdominal obesity and risk of coronary heart disease in apparently healthy men and women. *International Journal of Obesity, 34,* 340–347.

Arseneault, L., Moffitt, T. E., Caspi, A., Taylor, A., et al. (2003). Strong genetic effects on crosssituational antisocial behavior among 5-year-old children according to mothers, teachers, examiner-observers, and twins' self-reports. *Journal of Child Psychology and Psychiatry, 44,* 832–848.

Arterberry, M. E., Craton, L. G., & Yonas, A. (1993). Infants' sensitivity to motion-carried information for depth and object properties. In C. Granrud (Ed.), *Visual perception and cognition in infancy. Carnegie Mellon symposia on cognition* (pp. 215–234). Hillsdale, NJ: Erlbaum.

Arvey, R. D., Bouchard, T. J., Segal, N. L., & Abraham, L. M. (1989). Job satisfaction: Environmental and genetic components. *Journal of Applied Psychology, 74,* 187–192.

Asato, M. R., Terwilliger, R., Woo, J., & Luna, B. (2010). White matter development in adolescence: A DTI study. *Cerebral Cortex, 5,* 5. doi:10.1093/cercor/bhp282.

Asbridge, M., Hayden, J. A., & Cartwright, J. L. (2012). Acute cannabis consumption and motor vehicle collision risk: Systematic review of observational studies and meta-analysis. *BMJ, 344,* e536.

Asch, S. E. (1951). Effects of group pressure upon the modification and distortion of judgments. In H. Guetzkow (Ed.), *Groups, leadership, and men* (pp. 177–190). Pittsburgh, PA: Carnegie Press.

Asch, S. E. (1955). Opinions and social pressure. *Scientific American, 193,* 31–35.

Asch, S. E. (1956). Studies of independence and conformity: A minority of one against a unanimous majority. *Psychological Monographs, 70,* 1–70.

Asen, Y., & Cook, R. G. (2012). Discrimination and Categorization of Actions by Pigeons. *Psychological Science (Sage Publications Inc.), 23*(6), 617–624. doi:10.1177/0956797611433333

Ashcraft, M. H. (2006). *Cognition* (4th ed.). Upper Saddle River, NJ: Prentice Hall.

Asher, S. R., & Hopmeyer, A. (2001). Loneliness in childhood. In G. Bear, K. Minke, & A. Thomas (Eds.), *Children's needs II: Psychological perspectives.* Silver Spring, MD: National Association of School Psychologists.

Asher, S. R., & McDonald, K. L. (2011). The behavioral basis of acceptance, rejection, and perceived popularity. In K. H. Rubin, W. M. Bukowski, & B. Laursen (Eds.), *Handbook of Peer Interactions, Relationships, and Groups* (pp. 232–248). New York: Guilford Press.

Askay, S. W., Patterson, D. R., Jensen, M. P., & Sharar, S. R. (2007). A randomized controlled trial of hypnosis for burn wound care. Rehabilitation *Psychology, 52*(3), 247–253.

Askew, C., Kessock-Phillip, H., & Field, A. P. (2008). What happens when verbal threat information and vicarious learning combine. *Behavioural and Cognitive Psychotherapy, 36,* 491–505.

Aslin, R. N., Jusczyk, P. W., & Pisoni, D. B. (1998). Speech and auditory processing during infancy: Constraints on and precursors to language. In W. Damon (Ed.), *Handbook of child psychology* (5th ed., pp. 147–198). New York: Wiley.

Aso, K., Hanakawa, T., Aso, T., & Fukuyama, H. (2010). Cerebro-cerebellar interactions underlying temporal information processing. *Journal of Cognitive Neuroscience, 4,* 4.

Aspinwall, L. G., & Duran, R. E. F. (1999). Psychology applied to health. In A. M. Stec & D. A. Bernstein (Eds.), *Psychology: Fields of application* (pp. 17–38). Boston: Houghton Mifflin.

Assefi, S. L., & Garry, M. (2003). Absolut® memory distortions: Alcohol placebos influence misinformation effect. *Psychological Science, 14,* 77–80.

Associated Press. Dozen people watched gang rape, police say. (2009, October 27). Retrieved from http://www.youtube.com/watch?v=vwxiCVVGnZ8.

Associated Press. (2002, March 9). Odds and ends. *Naples Daily News.* Retrieved August 27, 2003, from http://www.nctimes.net/news/2002/20020313/ wwwwn.html.

Associated Press. (2007, December 17). Excellent driving, now pull over: California cops to reward motorists with $5 Starbucks cards.

Associated Press. (2007a). Officials investigating prank call that led to shock treatments at special needs school. December 18.

Associated Press. (2007b). Kansas store video captures five shoppers stepping over dying stabbing victim. July 3.

Associated Press. (2007). Poll: One-Third of Americans Believe in Ghosts, UFOs. Retrieved from http://www.foxnews.com/story/0,2933,305277,00.html

Associated Press. (2011). Obesity rise prompts Washington ferry capacity change. *The Daily Astorian.* Retrieved from http://www.dailyastorian.com/business/obesity-rise-prompts-washington-ferry-capacity-change/article_6859103c-2cc9-11e1-b9c0-001871e3ce6c.html

Astin, J. A. (2004). Mind-body therapies for the management of pain. *Clinical Journal of Pain, 20,* 27–32.

Aston-Jones, G., & Cohen, J. D. (2005). An integrative theory of locus coeruleus-norepinephrine function: Adaptive gain and optimal performance. *Annual Review of Neuroscience, 28,* 403–450.

Atalay, A., & Meloy, M. G. (2011). Retail therapy: A strategic effort to improve mood. *Psychology & Marketing, 28,* 638–660. doi:10.1002/mar.20404

Atance, C. M., & O'Neill, D. K. (2001). Episodic future thinking. *Trends in Cognitive Science, 5,* 533–539.

Atkins, R. (2008). The association of childhood personality on sexual risk taking during adolescence. *Journal of School Health, 78*(11), 594–600.

Atkinson, J. (2006, August). Shake it off. *GQ: Gentlemen's Quarterly, 76*(8), 87–92.

Atkinson, R. C., & Shiffrin, R. M. (1968). Human memory: A proposed system and its control processes. In K. Spence (Ed.), *The psychology of learning and motivation* (Vol. 2, pp. 89–195). New York: Academic Press.

Aurora, R. N., Zak, R. S., Auerbach, S. H., Casey, K. R., Chowdhuri, S., Karippot, A., Maganti, R. K., Ramar, K., Kristo, D. A., Bista, S. R., Lamm, C. I., Morgenthaler, T. I., & Standards of Practice Committee, American Academy of Sleep Medicine. (2010). Best practice guide for the treatment of nightmare disorder in adults. *Journal of Clinical Sleep Medicine, 6*(4):389–401.

Austin, J. (2006). *Zen-Brain reflections.* Cambridge, MA, US: MIT Press.

Avery, M. C., Dutt, N., & Krichmar, J. L. (2013). A large-scale neural network model of the influence of neuromodulatory levels on working memory and behavior. *Frontiers in Computational Neuroscience, 7,* 133.

Avidan, M. S., Jacobsohn, E., Glick, D., Burnside, B. A., Zhang, L., Villafranca, A., Karl, L., Kamal, S., Torres, B., O'Connor, M., Evers, A.S., Gradwohl, S., Lin, N., Palanca, B. J., and Mashour, G. A., for the BAG-RECALL Research Group. (2011). Prevention of intraoperative awareness in a high-risk surgical population. *New England Journal of Medicine, 365*(7), 591–600.

Aviezer, O., Sagi, A., Joels, T., & Ziv, Y. (1999). Emotional availability and attachment representations in kibbutz infants and their mothers. *Developmental Psychology, 35,* 811–821.

Ayman, R. , Korabik, K., & Morris, S. (2009). Is transformational leadership always perceived as effective? Male subordinates' devaluation of female transformational leaders. *Journal of Applied Social Psychology, 39,* 852–879.

Ayuso-Mateos, J. L., Vazquez-Barquero, J. L., Dowrick, C., Lehtinen, V., Dalgard, O. S., Casey, P., et al. (2001). Depressive disorders in Europe: Prevalence figures from the ODIN study. *British Journal of Psychiatry, 179,* 308–316.

Azar, B. (1996, November). Project explores landscape of midlife. *APA Monitor,* p. 26.

Azzopardi, P., & Hock, H. S. (2011). Illusory motion perception in blindsight. *Proceedings Of The National Academy Of Sciences Of The United States Of America, 108*(2), 876–881. doi:10.1073/pnas.1005974108.

Babinski, J. (1914). Contribution a l'etude dies troubles mentaux dans l'hemiplegie organique cerebrale (anosognosia). *Reveu Neurologie (Paris), 27,* 845–847.

Bacharach, V. R., & Baumeister, A. A. (1998). Direct and indirect effects of maternal intelligence, maternal age, income, and home environment on intelligence of preterm, low-birth-weight children. *Journal of Applied Developmental Psychology, 19,* 361–375.

Bach-Mizrachi, H., Underwood, M. D., Kassir, S. A., Bakalian, M. J., Sibille, E., Tamir, H., et al. (2006). Neuronal tryptophan hydroxylase mRNA expression in the human dorsal and median raphe nuclei: Major depression and suicide. *Neuropsychopharmacology: Official Publication of the American College pf Neuropsychopharmacology, 31,* 814–824.

Back, M. D., Stopfer, J. M., Vazire, S., Gaddis, S., et al. (2010). Facebook profiles reflect actual personality, not self-idealization. *Psychological Science, 21,* 372–374. doi:10.1177/0956797609360756

Back, S. E., Dansky, B. S., Carroll, K. M., Foa, E. B., & Brady, K. T. (2001). Exposure therapy in the treatment of PTSD among cocaine-dependent individuals: Description of procedures. *Journal of Substance Abuse Treatment, 21,* 35–45.

Backman, L., & Nilsson, L. (1991). Effects of divided attention on free and cued recall of verbal events and action events. *Bulletin of the Psychonomic Society, 29,* 51–54.

Bada, H. S., Bann, C. M., Whitaker, T. M., Bauer, C. R., Shankaran, S., Lagasse, L., Lester, B. M., Hammond, J., & Higgins, R. (2012). Protective factors can mitigate behavior problems after prenatal cocaine and other drug exposures. *Pediatrics, 130*(6), e1479–e1488.

Baddeley, A. (1982). *Your memory: A user's guide.* New York: Macmillan.

Baddeley, A. (1992). Working memory. *Science, 255,* 556–559.

Baddeley, A. (1998). *Human memory: Theory and practice.* Boston: Allyn & Bacon.

Baddeley, A. D. (2003). Working memory: Looking back and looking forward. *Nature Reviews Neuroscience, 4,* 829–839.

Badhwar, A., Lerch, J. P., Hamel, E., & Sled, J. G. (2013). Impaired structural correlates of memory in Alzheimer's disease mice. *Neuroimage Clinical, 3,* 290–300.

Baer, J. S., Sampson, P. D., Barr, H. M., Connor, P. D., & Streissguth, A. P. (2003). A 21-year longitudinal analysis of the effects of prenatal alcohol exposure on young adult drinking. *Archives of General Psychiatry, 60,* 377–385.

Baghai, T, C, Möller, H. J., & Rupprecht, R. (2006). Recent progress in pharmacological and non-pharmacological treatment options of major depression. *Current Pharmacology Design, 12*(4), 503–515.

Baghurst, T., & Kelley, B. C. (2013). An examination of stress in college students over the course of a semester. *Health Promotion Practice.* Epub November 14, 2013.

Baglioni, C., Spiegelhalder, K., Lombardo, C., & Riemann, D. (2010). Sleep and emotions: A focus on insomnia. *Sleep Medicine Reviews, 14,* 227–238. Epub 2010 Feb. 6.

Bahali, K., & Tahiroğlu, A. (2010). Okul Reddi: Klinik Özellikler, Tani ve Tedavi. (Turkish). *Current Approaches in Psychiatry / Psikiyatride Guncel Yaklasimlar, 2*(3), 362–383.

Bahrick, H. P., Bahrick, P. O., & Wittlinger, R. P. (1975). Fifty years of memory for names and faces: A cross-cultural approach. *Journal of Experimental Psychology: General, 104,* 54–75.

Bahrick, H. P., Hall, L. K., Noggin, J. P., & Bahrick, L. E. (1994). Fifty years of language maintenance and language dominance in bilingual Hispanic immigrants. *Journal of Experimental Psychology: General, 123,* 264–283.

Baik, J. H. (2013). Dopamine signaling in reward-related behaviors. *Frontiers in Neural Circuits, 7,* 152.

Bailey, J. M., & Benishay, D. S. (1993). Familial aggregation of female sexual orientation. *American Journal of Psychiatry, 150,* 272–277.

Bailey, J. M., Bobrow, D., Wolfe, M., & Mikach, S. (1995). Sexual orientation of adult sons of gay fathers. *Developmental Psychology, 31*(1), 124–129.

Bailey, J. M., Dunne, M. P., & Martin, N. G. (2000). Genetic and environmental influences on sexual orientation and its correlates in an Australian twin sample. *Journal of Personality and Social Psychology, 78,* 524–536.

Bailey, J. M., & Pillard, R. C. (1991). A genetic study of male sexual orientation. *Archives of General Psychiatry, 48,* 1086–1096.

Bailey, K., & Chapman, P. (2012). When can we choose to forget? An ERP study into item-method directed forgetting of emotional words. *Brain & Cognition, 78*(2), 133–147. doi:10.1016/j.bandc.2011.11.004.

Baillargeon, R. (1995). Physical reasoning in infancy. In M. S. Gazzaniga (Ed.), *The cognitive neurosciences* (pp. 181–204). Cambridge, MA: MIT Press.

Baillargeon, R. (2008). Innate ideas revisited: For a principle of persistence in infants' physical reasoning. *Perspectives on Psychological Science, 3*(1), 2–13.

Baillargeon, R., Scott, R. M., & He, Z. (2010). False-belief understanding in infants. *Trends in Cognitive Science,* 110–118.

Baillargeon, R. H., Zoccolillo, M., Keenan, K., Cote, S., et al. (2007). Gender differences in physical aggression: A prospective population-based survey of children before and after 2 years of age. *Developmental Psychology, 43,* 13–26.

Baillargeon, R. H., Zoccolillo, M., Keenan, K., Côté, S., Pérusse, D., Wu, H.-X., Boivin, M., & Tremblay, R. E. (2007). Gender differences in physical aggression: A prospective population-based survey of children before and after 2 years of age. *Developmental Psychology, 43,* 13–26.

Baka, L., Derbis, R., & Maxfield, M. (2012). The anxiety-buffering properties of cultural and subcultural worldviews: Terror management processes among juvenile delinquents. *Polish Psychological Bulletin, 43,* 1–11. doi:10.2478/v10059-012-0001-x.

Bakardjieva, T., & Gercheva, G. (2011). Knowledge Management and e-Learning—An Agent-Based Approach. *World Academy Of Science, Engineering & Technology,* 663–666.

Bakare, M. O. (2008). Effective therapeutic dosage of antipsychotic medications in patients with psychotic symptoms: Is there a racial difference? *BMC Research Notes, 1,* 25.

Baker, J. L., Olsen, L. W., & Sørensen, T. I. A. (2007). Childhood body-mass index and the risk of coronary heart disease in adulthood. *The New England Journal of Medicine, 357,* 2229–2237.

Baker, L. D., Frank, L. L., Foster-Schubert, K., Green, P. S., et al. (2010). Effects of aerobic exercise on mild cognitive impairment: A controlled trial. *Archives of Neurology, 67,* 71–79.

Baker, L. T., Vernon, P. A., & Ho, H. (1991). The genetic correlation between intelligence and speed of information processing. *Behavior Genetics, 21,* 351–367.

Baker, M. C. (2002). *The atoms of language: The mind's hidden rules of grammar.* New York: Basic Books.

Bakermans-Kranenburg, M. J., van IJzendoorn, M. H., & Juffer, F. (2008). Less is more: Meta-analytic arguments for the use of sensitivity-focused interventions. In F. Juffer, M. J. Bakermans-Kranenburg, & M. H. van IJzendoorn (Eds.), *Promoting positive parenting: An attachment-based intervention* (pp. 59–74). New York: Taylor & Francis Group/Lawrence Erlbaum Associates.

Balaban, M. T. (1995). Affective influences on startle in five-month-old infants: Reactions to facial expressions of emotion. *Child Development, 66*(1), 28–36.

Balayla, J., Azoulay, L., & Abenhaim, H. A. (2011). Maternal marital status and the risk of stillbirth and infant death: a population-based cohort study on 40 million births in the United States. *Women's Health Issues, 21*(5), 361–365.

Balázs, J., Benazzi, F., Rihmer, Z., Annamaria, A., Akiskal, K. K., et al. (2006). The close link between suicide attempts and mixed (bipolar) depression: Implications for suicide prevention. *Journal of Affective Disorders, 91,* 133–138.

Balcetis, E., & Dunning, D. (2006). See what you want to see: Motivational influences on visual perception. *Journal of Personality and Social Psychology, 91,* 612–625.

Baldwin, D. S. (2011). Where is the room for improvement in the drug treatment of depression and anxiety? *Human Psychopharmacology: Clinical and Experimental, 26,* 1–3.

Baldwin, S. A., & Imel, Z. E. (2013). Therapist effects: Finds and methods. In M. J. Lambert (Ed.), *Bergin and Garfield's handbook of psychotherapy and behavior change* (6th ed.) (pp. 258–297). Hoboken, NJ: Wiley.

Baldwin, T. T., & Ford, J. K. (1988). Transfer of training: A review and directions for future research. *Personnel Psychology, 41,* 63–105.

Balk, Y. A., Adriaanse, M. A., de Ridder, Denise, T. D., & Evers, C. (2013). Coping under pressure: Employing emotion regulation strategies to enhance performance under pressure. *Journal of Sport & Exercise Psychology, 35*(4), 408–418.

Ball, H. A., McGuffin, P., & Farmer, A. E. (2008). Attributional style and depression. *British Journal of Psychiatry, 192,* 275–278.

Ballard, C., Gauthier, S., Corbett, A., Brayne, C., Aarsland, D., & Jones, E. (2011). Alzheimer's disease. *Lancet, 377*(9770), 1019–1031.

Ballard, C., Khan, Z., Clack, H., & Corbett, A. (2011). Nonpharmacological treatment of Alzheimer disease. *Canadian Journal of Psychiatry, 56*(10), 589–595.

Balleine, B. W., & Dickinson, A. (1998). Goal-directed instrumental action: contingency and incentive learning and their cortical substrates. *Neuropharmacology, 37,* 407–419.

Balon, R. (2004). Developments in treatment of anxiety disorders: Psychotherapy, pharmacotherapy, and psychosurgery. *Depression and Anxiety, 19,* 63–76.

Baltes, B. B., Briggs, T. E., Huff, J. W., Wright, J. A., & Neumann, G. A. (1999). Flexible and compressed workweek schedules: A meta-analysis of their effects on work-related criteria. *Journal of Applied Psychology, 84,* 496–513.

Baltes, P. B. (1994, August). *Life-span developmental psychology: On the overall landscape of human development.* Address presented at the annual meeting of the American Psychological Association, Los Angeles.

Baltes, P. B., & Smith, J. (2008). The fascination of wisdom: Its nature, ontogeny, and function. *Perspectives on Psychological Science, 3,* 56–64.

Balzer, W. K., & Sulsky, L. M. (1992). Halo and performance appraisal research: A critical examination. *Journal of Applied Psychology, 77,* 975–985.

Banaji, M., Lemm, K. M., & Carpenter, S. J. (2001). The social unconscious. In A. Tesser & N. Schwarz (Eds.), *Blackwell handbook of social psychology: Intraindividual processes* (pp. 134–158). Oxford, UK: Blackwell.

Bandstra, E. S., Morrow, C. E., Accornero, V. H., Mansoor, E., Xue, L., & Anthony, J. C. (2011). Estimated effects of in utero cocaine exposure on language development through early adolescence. *Neurotoxicology and Teratology, 33,* 25–35.

Bandura, A. (1965). Influence of a model's reinforcement contingencies on the acquisition of imitative responses. *Journal of Personality and Social Psychology, 1,* 589–595.

Bandura, A. (1992). Self-efficacy mechanism in psychobiologic functioning. In R. Schwarzer (Ed.), *Self-efficacy: Thought control of action* (pp. 355–394). Washington, DC: Hemisphere.

Bandura, A. (1999). Social cognitive theory of personality. In L. Pervin & O. John (Eds.), *Handbook of personality: Theory and research* (2nd ed., pp. 154–196). New York: Guilford.

Bandura, A., Blanchard, E. B., & Ritter, B. (1969). The relative efficacy of desensitization and modeling approaches for inducing behavioral, affective, and attitudinal changes. *Journal of Personality and Social Psychology, 13,* 173–199.

Bandura, A., & Walters, R. H. (1963). *Social learning and personality development*. New York: Holt, Rinehart & Winston.

Bangen, K. J., Bergheim, M., Kaup, A. R., Mizakhanjan, H., Wierenga, C. E., Jeste, D. V., & Eyler, L. T. (2013). Brains of optimistic older adults respond less to fearful faces. *Journal of Neuropsychiatry and Clinical Neuroscience*. Epub November 26, 2013.

Banich, M. T. (2009). Executive function: The search for an integrated account. *Psychological Science, 18*, 89–94.

Banks, M. S., & Salapatek, P. (1983). Infant visual perception. In P. H. Mussen (Ed.), *Handbook of child psychology: Vol. 2. Infancy and developmental psychobiology* (pp. 435–571). New York: Wiley.

Bantick, S. J., Wise, R. G., Ploghaus, A., Clare, S., Smith, S. M., & Tracey, I. (2002). Imaging how attention modulates pain in humans using functional MRI. *Brain, 125*, 310–319.

Barber, A. C., Hippert, C., Duran, Y., West, E. L., Bainbridge, J. W., Warre-Cornish, K., Luhmann, U. F., Lakowski, J., Sowden, J. C., Ali, R. R., & Pearson, R. A. (2013). Repair of the degenerate retina by photoreceptor transplantation. *Proceedings of the New York Academy of Sciences, 110*(1), 354–359.

Barber, J. P., Muran, J. C., McCarthy, K. S., & Keefe, J. E. (2013). Research on dynamic therapies. In M. J. Lambert (Ed.), *Bergin and Garfield s handbook of psychotherapy and behavior change* (6th ed.) (pp. 443–494). Hoboken, NJ: Wiley.

Barclay, J. R., Bransford, J. D., Franks, J. J., McCarrell, N. S., & Nitsch, K. (1974). Comprehension and semantic flexibility. *Journal of Verbal Learning and Verbal Behavior, 13*, 471–481.

Barclay, P. (2006). Reputational benefits for altruistic punishment. *Evolution and Human Behavior, 27*, 325–344.

Bargary, G., Barnett, K. J., Mitchell, K. J., & Newell, F. N. (2009). Colored-speech synaesthesia is triggered by multisensory, not unisensory, perception. *Psychological Science, 20*, 529–533.

Barger, L. K., Cade, B. E., Ayas, N. T., Cronin, J. W., Rosner, B., Speizer, F. E., et al. (2005). *New England Journal of Medicine, 352*, 125–134.

Bargh J. A., Schwader, K. L., Hailey, S. E., Dyer R. L., & Boothby E. J. (2012). Automaticity in social-cognitive processes. *Trends in Cognitive Science, 16*, 593–605.

Bargones, J. Y., & Werner, L. A. (1994). Adults listen selectively; infants do not. *Psychological Science, 5*, 170–174.

Baringer, J. R. (2008). Herpes simplex infections of the nervous system. *Neurology Clinics, 26*, 657–674.

Barkat, S., Poncelet, J., Landis, B. N., Rouby, C., & Bensafi, M. (2008). Improved smell pleasantness after odor-taste associative learning in humans. *Neuroscience Letters, 434*, 108–112.

Barker. R. A., Barrett, J., Mason, S. L., & Björklund, A. (2013). Fetal dopaminergic transplantation trials and the future of neural grafting in Parkinson's disease. *Lancet Neurology, 12*(1), 84–91.

Barkham, M., Connell, J., Stiles, W. B., Miles, J. N. V., Margison, F., Evans, C., et al. (2006). Dose-effect relations and responsive regulation of treatment duration: The good enough level. *Journal of Consulting and Clinical Psychology, 74*, 160–167.

Barling, J., Dupré, K. E., & Kelloway, E. K. (2009). Predicting workplace aggression and violence. *Annual Review of Psychology, 60*, 671–692.

Barling, J., & Frone, M. R. (Eds.). (2004). *The psychology of workplace safety*. Washington, DC: APA Books.

Barling, J., Weber, T., & Kelloway, E. K. (1996). Effects of transformational leadership training on attitudinal and financial outcomes: A field experiment. *Journal of Applied Psychology, 81*, 827–832.

Barlow, D. H. (2006). Psychotherapy and psychological treatments: The future. *Clinical Psychology: Science and Practice, 13*, 216–220.

Barlow, D. H. (2007). *Clinical handbook of psychological disorders*. New York: Guilford.

Barlow, D. H. (2010). The dodo bird–again–and again. *The Behavior Therapist, 33*, 15–16.

Barlow, D. H., Gorman, J. M., Shear, M. K., & Woods, S. W. (2000). Cognitive-behavioral therapy, imipramine, or their combination for panic disorder: A randomized controlled trial. *Journal of the American Medical Association, 283*, 2529–2536.

Barnard, L., & Curry, J. (2012). The relationship of clergy burnout to self-compassion and other personality dimensions. *Pastoral Psychology, 61*, 149–163. doi:10.1007/s11089-011-0377-0

Barnard, L. K., & Curry, J. F. (2011). Self-compassion: Conceptualizations, correlates, & interventions. *Review of General Psychology, 15*(4), 289–303. doi:10.1037/a0025754.

Barnes, A. (2004). Race schizophrenia, and admission to state psychiatric hospitals. *Administration and Policy in Mental Health, 31*, 241–252.

Barnes-Farrell, J. L., Davies-Schuls, K., McGonagle, A., Walsh, B., Di Milia, L., Fischer, F. M., Hobbs, B. B., Kaliterna, L., & Tepas, D. (2008). What aspects of shiftwork influence off-shift well-being of healthcare workers? *Applied Ergonomics, 39*, 589–596.

Barnier, A. J., & McConkey, K. M. (1998). Posthypnotic responding away from the hypnotic setting. *Psychological Science, 9*, 256–262.

Baron, A. S., & Banaji, M. R. (2006). The development of implicit attitudes. *Psychological Science 17*, 53–58.

Baron, R. A., & Byrne, D. (1994). *Social psychology: Understanding human interaction* (7th ed.). Boston: Allyn & Bacon.

Baron, R. A., Byrne, D., & Branscombe, N. R. (2006). *Social psychology* (11th ed.). Boston: Allyn & Bacon.

Baron-Cohen, S., Knickmeyer, R. C., & Belmonte, M. K. (2005). Sex differences in the brain: Implications for explaining autism. *Science, 310*, 819–823.

Baron-Cohen, S., Leslie, A. M., & Frith, U. (1985). Does the autistic child have a "theory of mind"? *Cognition, 21*, 37–46.

Barone, D. A., & Krieger, A. C. (2013). Stroke and obstructive sleep apnea: A review. *Current Atherosclerosis Reports, 15*(7), 334–338.

Barr Taylor, C., Bryson, S., Celio Doyle, A. A., Luce, K. H., Cunning, D., Abascal, L. B., et al. (2006a). The adverse effect of negative comments about weight and shape from family and siblings on women at high risk for eating disorders. *Pediatrics, 118*, 731–738.

Baare, W. F. C., van Oel, C. J., Hushoff, H. E., Schnack, H. G., et al. (2001). Volumes of brain structures in twins discordant for schizophrenia. *Archives of General Psychiatry, 58*, 33–40.

Barres, B. A. (2008). The mystery and magic of glia: A perspective on their roles in health and disease. *Neuron, 60*(3), 430–440.

Barrett, L. F. (2013). Psychological construction: The Darwinian approach to the science of emotion. *Emotion Review, 5*(4), 379–389.

Barrett, L. F., Gross, J., Christensen, T. C., & Benvenuto, M. (2001). Knowing what you're feeling and knowing what to do about it: Mapping the relation between emotion differentiation and emotion regulation. *Cognition and Emotion, 15*, 713–724.

Barrett, L. F., Lane, R. D., Sechrest, L., & Schwartz, G. E. (2000). Sex differences in emotional awareness. *Personality and Social Psychology Bulletin, 26*, 1027–1035.

Barrett, L. F., Mesquita, B., & Gendron, M. (2011). Context in emotion perception. *Current Directions in Psychological Science, 20*(5) 286–290. doi:10.1177/0963721411422522.

Barrett, L. F., Mesquita, B., Ochsner, K. N., & Gross, J. J. (2007). The experience of emotion. *Annual Review of Psychology, 58*, 373–403.

Barrick, M. R., & Mount, M. K. (2012). Nature and use of personality in selection. In N. Schmitt (Ed.) *The Oxford handbook of personnel assessment and selection*. (pp. 225–251). New York: Oxford University Press.

Barriera-Viruet, H., Sobeih, T. M., Daraiseh, N., & Salem, S. (2006). Questionnaires vs observational and direct measurements: A systematic review. *Theoretical Issues in Ergonomics Science, 7*(3), 261–284.

Barron, K. E., & Harackiewicz, J. M. (2001). Achievement goals and optimal motivation: Testing multiple goal models. *Journal of Personality and Social Psychology, 80*, 706–722.

Barsade, S. G., & Gibson, D. E. (2012). Group affect: Its influence on individual and group outcomes. *Current Directions In Psychological Science, 21*, 119–123. doi:10.1177/0963721412438352.

Barsalou, L. W. (1993). Flexibility, structure, and linguistic vagary in concepts: Manifestations of a compositional system of perceptual symbols. In A. F. Collins, S. E. Gathercole, M. A. Conway, & P. E. Morris (Eds.), *Theories of memory* (pp. 29–102). Hillsdale, NJ: Erlbaum.

Bartels, A., & Zeki, S. (2000). The neural basis of romantic love. *Neuroreport, 11*, 3829–3834.

Bartholow, B. D., & Heinz, A. (2006). Alcohol and aggression without consumption: Alcohol cues, aggressive thoughts, and hostile perception bias. *Psychological Science, 17*, 30–37.

Barton, J., & Folkard, S. (1991). The response of day and night nurses to their work schedules. *Journal of Occupational Psychology, 64*, 207–218.

Barton, J. J., Cherkasova, M. V., Press, D. Z., Intriligator, J. M., & O'Connor, M. (2004). Perceptual functions in prosopagnosia. *Perception, 33*(8), 939–956.

Bartoshuk, L. M. (1991). Taste, smell, and pleasure. In R. C. Bollef (Ed.), *The hedonics of taste* (pp. 15–28). Hillsdale, NJ: Erlbaum.

Bartoshuk, L. M. (2000). Comparing sensory experiences across individuals: Recent psychophysical advances illuminate genetic variation in taste perception. *Chemical Senses, 25*, 447–460.

Bartoshuk, L. M., Fast, K., & Snyder, D. J. (2005). Differences in our sensory worlds: Invalid comparisons with labeled scales. *Current Directions in Psychological Science, 14*, 122–125.

Bartz, J. A., & Hollander, E. (2006). Is obsessive-compulsive disorder an anxiety disorder? *Progress in Neuro-Psychopharmacology & Biological Psychiatry, 30*, 338–352.

Başçiftçi, F., & Hatay, Ö. (2011). Reduced-rule based expert system by the simplification of logic functions for the diagnosis of diabetes. *Computers In Biology & Medicine, 41*(6), 350–356. doi:10.1016/j.compbiomed.2011.03.012.

Bashore, T. R., & Ridderinkhof, K. R. (2002). Older age, traumatic brain injury, and cognitive slowing: Some convergent and divergent findings. *Psychological Bulletin, 128,* 151–198.

Baskin, D., Bluestone, H., & Nelson, M. (1981). Ethnicity and psychiatric diagnosis. *Journal of Clinical Psychology, 37,* 529–537.

Bass, B. M., Avolio, B. J., Jung, D. I., & Berson, Y. (2003). Predicting unit performance by assessing transformational and transactional leadership. *Journal of Applied Psychology, 88,* 207–218.

Bass, B. M., & Riggio, R. E. (2006). *Transformational leadership* (2nd ed.). Mahwah, NJ: Erlbaum.

Basson, R. (2001). Human sex-response cycles. *Journal of Sex and Marital Therapy, 27,* 33–43.

Basson, R. (2002). Women's sexual desire—disordered or misunderstood? *Journal of Sex and Marital Therapy, 28,* 17–28.

Basson, R. (2003). Commentary on "In the mood for sex—The value of androgens." *Journal of Sex and Marital Therapy, 29,* 177–179.

Bastian, B., Jetten, J., & Fasoli, F. (2011). Cleansing the soul by hurting the flesh: The guilt-reducing effect of pain. *Psychological Science, 22*(3), 334–335. doi:10.1177/0956797610397058.

Bates, E. (1993, March). *Nature, nurture, and language development.* Paper presented at the biennial meeting of the Society for Research in Child Development, New Orleans.

Bates, J. E., Schermerhorn, A. C., & Petersen, I. T. (2012). Temperament and parenting in developmental perspective. In M. Zentner & R. L. Shiner (Eds.), *Handbook of Temperament* (pp. 425–441). New York: Guilford Press.

Bates, T. C., Lewis, G. J., & Weiss, A. (2013). Childhood socioeconomic status amplifies genetic effects on adult intelligence. *Psychological Science, 24,* 2111–2116.

Bates, T. C., Luciano, M., Medland, S. E., Montgomery, G. W., Wright, M. J., & Martin, N. G. (2011). Genetic variance in a component of the Language Acquisition Device: ROBO1 polymorphisms associated with phonological buffer deficits. *Behavior Genetics, 41*(1), 50–57. doi:10.1007/s10519-010-9402-9.

Batki, S. L., Leontieva, L., Dimmock, J. A., & Ploutz-Snyder, R. (2008). Negative symptoms are associated with less alcohol use, craving, and "high" in alcohol dependent patients with schizophrenia. *Schizophrenia Research, 105,* 201–207.

Batson, C. D. (2010). Empathy-induced altruistic motivation. In M. Mikulincer & P. Shaver (Eds.), *Prosocial motives, emotions, and behavior: The better angels of our nature* (pp. 15–34). Washington, DC: American Psychological Association.

Batson, C. D., Sager, K., Garst, E., & Kang, M. (1997). Is empathy-induced helping due to self-other merging? *Journal of Personality and Social Psychology, 73,* 495–509.

Batterham, R. L., Cohen, M. A., Ellis, S. M., Le Roux, C. W., Withers, D. J., Frost, G. S., et al. (2003). Inhibition of food intake in obese subjects by peptide YY3–36. *New England Journal of Medicine, 349,* 941–948.

Batterham, R. L., Cowley, M. A., Small, C. J., Herzog, H., Cohen, M. A., Dakin, C. L., et al. (2002). Gut hormone PYY3–36 physiologically inhibits food intake. *Nature, 418,* 650–654.

Bauch, E. M., & Otten, L. J. (2012). Study-test congruency affects encoding-related brain activity for some but not all stimulus materials. *Journal of Cognitive Neuroscience, 24*(1), 183–195. doi:10.1162/jocn_a_00070

Bauer, P., & Fivush, R. (2013). *The Wiley handbook on the development of children's memory.* Hoboken, NJ: Wiley-Blackwell.

Bauer, P. J. (2006). Event memory. In W. Damon & R. M. Lerner (Series Eds.) & D. Kuhn & R. Siegler (Vol. Eds.), *Handbook of child psychology: Vol. 2. Cognition, perception, and language* (6th ed., pp. 373–345). New York: Wiley.

Bauer, P. J., & Larkina, M. (2013). Childhood amnesia in the making: Different distributions of autobiographical memories in children and adults. *Journal of Experimental Psychology: General.* Epub August 12, 2013.

Bauer, R. M., & Demery, J. A. (2003). Agnosia. In K. M. Heilman & E. Valenstein (Eds.), *Clinical neuropsychology* (4th ed.). New York: Oxford.

Bauer, T. N., & Green, S. G. (1996). Development of leader-member exchange: A longitudinal test. *Academy of Management Journal, 39,* 1538–1567.

Baumann, S., Meyer, M., & Jäncke, L. (2008). Enhancement of auditory-evoked potentials in musicians reflects an influence of expertise but not selective attention. *Journal of Cognitive Neuroscience, 20*(12), 2238–2249.

Baumeister, H., & Härter, M. (2007). Mental disorders in patients with obesity in comparison with healthy probands. *International Journal of Obesity, 31,* 1155–1164.

Baumeister, R., & Bushman, B. (2008). *Social psychology and human nature.* Belmont, CA: Wadsworth.

Baumeister, R., & Bushman, B. (2014). *Social psychology & human nature* (3rd ed.). Belmont, CA: Cengage Learning.

Baumeister, R. F. (2010). The self. In R. Baumeister & E. Finkel (Eds.) *Advanced social psychology: The state of the science* (pp. 139–176). New York: Oxford.

Baumeister, R. F., & Leary, M. R. (1995). The need to belong: Desire for interpersonal attachments as a fundamental human motivation. *Psychological Bulletin, 117*(3), 497–529.

Baumeister, R. F., Masicampo, E. J., & Twenge, J. M. (2013). The social self. In H. Tennen, J. Suls, & I. B. Weiner (Eds.), *Handbook of psychology, Vol. 5: Personality and social psychology, 2nd ed.* (pp. 247–273). Hoboken, NJ: John Wiley & Sons Inc.

Baumeister, R. J. & Bushman, B. J. (2011). *Social psychology and human nature* (2nd Ed.) Belmont, CA: Cengage.

Bäuml, K. T., & Samenieh, A. (2012). Selective memory retrieval can impair and improve retrieval of other memories. *Journal of Experimental Psychology: Learning, Memory, and Cognition, 38*(2), 488–494. doi:10.1037/a0025683

Baumrind, D. (1991). Effective parenting during the early adolescent transition. In P. A. Cowan & E. M. Hetherington (Eds.), *Family transition* (pp. 111–163). Hillsdale, NJ: Erlbaum.

Baumrind, D., Larzelere, R. E., & Cowan, P. A. (2002). Ordinary physical punishment: Is it harmful? Comment on Gershoff. *Psychological Bulletin, 128,* 580–589.

Baxendale, S., & Johnston, C. (2012). A review of the evidence on the relationship between gender and adolescents' involvement in violent behavior. *Aggression and Violent Behavior, 17,* 297–310.

Bayat, F., Shojaeezadeh, D., Baikpour, M., Heshmat, R., Baikpour, M., & Hosseini, M. (2013). The effects of education based on extended health belief model in type 2 diabetic patients: A randomized controlled trial. *Journal of Diabetes and Metabolic Disorders, 12*(1), 45.

Baylen, C. A., & Rosenberg, H. (2006). A review of the acute subjective eff ects of MDMA/ecstasy. *Addiction, 101,* 933–947.

Bayley, P. J., Hopkins, R. O., & Squire, L. R. (2003). Successful recollection of remote autobiographical memories by amnesic patients with medial temporal lobe lesions. *Neuron, 38,* 135–144.

BBC News (2010). Belgian coma 'writer' Rom Houben can't communicate. http://news.bbc.co.uk/2/hi/8526017.stm

Beach, S. R. H., Brody, G. H., Gunter, T. D., Packer, H., Wernett, P., & Philibert, R. A. (2010). Child maltreatment moderates the assiciation of MAOA with symptoms of depression and antisocial disorder. *Journal of Family Psychology, 24*(1), 12–20. doi:10.1037/a0018074.

Beauchamp, G. K. (2009). Sensory and receptor responses to umami: An overview of pioneering work. *American Journal of Clinical Nutrition, 90,* S723–S727.

Beauvois, J. L., Courbet, D. D., & Oberlé, D. D. (2012). The prescriptive power of the television host. A transposition of Milgram's obedience paradigm to the context of TV game show. *European Review of Applied Psychology 62*(3), 111–119.

Becerra, T. A., von Ehrenstein, A. S., Heck, J. E., Olsen, J., Arah, A. A., Jeste, S. S., Rodriguez, M., & Ritz, B. (2014). Autism spectrum disorders and race, ethnicity, and nativity: A population-based study. *Pediatrics, 134*(1), e63–e71.

Beck, A. T. (1976). *Cognitive therapy and the emotional disorders.* New York: International Universities Press.

Beck, A. T. (1995). Cognitive therapy: A 30-year retrospective. In S. O. Lilienfeld (Ed.), *Seeing both sides: Classic controversies in abnormal psychology* (pp. 303–311). Pacific Grove, CA: Brooks/Cole. (Original work published 1991.)

Beck, A. T. (2005). The Current State of Cognitive Therapy: A 40-Year Retrospective. *Archives of General Psychiatry, 62,* 953–959. doi:10.1001/archpsyc.62.9.953

Beck, A. T. (2008). The evolution of the cognitive model of depression and its neurobiological correlates. *American Journal of Psychiatry, 165,* 969–977.

Beck, A. T., & Alford, B. A. (2009). *Depression: Causes and treatment.* Philadelphia, PA: University of Pennsylvania Press.

Beck, A. T., & Dozois, D. A. (2011). Cognitive Therapy: Current Status and Future Directions. *Annual Review of Medicine, 62,* 397–409. doi:10.1146/annurev-med- 052209-100032

Beck, A. T., & Emery, G. (1985). *Anxiety disorders and phobias: A cognitive perspective.* New York: Basic Books.

Beck, A. T., Freeman, A., & Davis, D. D. (2007). *Cognitive therapy of personality disorders.* New York: Guilford.

Beck, A. T., Rector, N. A., Stolar, N., & Grant, P. (2008). *Schizophrenia: Cognitive theory, research, and therapy.* New York: Guilford.

Beck, A. T., Sokol, L., Clark, D., Berchick, R., & Wright, F. (1992). A crossover study of focused cognitive therapy for panic disorder. *American Journal of Psychiatry, 149,* 778–783.

Beck, D. M. (2010). The appeal of the brain in the popular press. *Perspectives on Psychological Science, 5*(6), 762–766. doi:10.1177/1745691610388779.

Beck, J., Gerber, M., Brand, S., Pühse, U., & Holsboer-Trachsler, E. (2013). Executive function performance is reduced during occupational burnout but can recover to the level of healthy controls. *Journal of Psychiatric Research, 47*(11), 1824–1830.

Beck, J. S. (2005). *Cognitive therapy for challenging problems: What to do when the basics don't work.* New York: Guilford.

Beck, L. A., & Clark, M. S. (2009). Choosing to enter or avoid diagnostic social situations. *Psychological Science, 20,* 1175–1181.

Beck, M. (1992, December 7). The new middle age. *Newsweek,* 50–56.

Beckett, C., Maughan, B., Rutter, M., Castle, J., Colvert, E., Groothues, C., et al. (2006). Do the effects of early severe deprivation on cognition persist into early adolescence? Findings from the English and Romanian adoptees study. *Child Development, 77,* 696–711.

Bedny, M., Pascual-Leone, A., Dodell-Feder, D., Fedorenko, E., & Saxe, R. (2011). Language processing in the occipital cortex of congenitally blind adults. *PNAS Proceedings of the National Academy of Sciences of the United States of America, 108*(11), 4429–4434. doi:10.1073/pnas.1014818108.

Behnke, M., Eyler, F. D., Warner, T. D., Garvan, C. W., Hou, W., & Wobie, K. (2006). Outcome from a prospective, longitudinal study of prenatal cocaine use: Preschool development at 3 years of age. *Journal of Pediatric Psychology, 31*(1), 41–49.

Behrens, K. Y., Hesse, E., & Main, M. (2007). Mothers' attachment status as determined by the Adult Attachment Interview predicts their 6-year-olds' reunion responses: A study conducted in Japan. *Developmental Psychology, 43,* 1553–1567.

Beierholm, U., Guitart-Masip, M., Economides, M., Chowdhury, R., Düzel, E., Dolan, R., & Dayan, P. (2013). Dopamine modulates reward-related vigor. *Neuropsychopharmacology, 38*(8), 1495–503.

Beijersbergen, M. D., Juffer, F., Bakermans-Kranenburg, M. J., & van IJzendoorn, M. H. (2012). Remaining or becoming secure: Parental sensitive support predicts attachment continuity from infancy to adolescence in a longitudinal adoption study. *Developmental Psychology, 48,* 1277–1282.

Beintner, I., Jacobi, C., & Schmidt, U. H. (2014). Participation and outcome in manualized self-help for bulimia nervosa and binge eating disorder. A systematic review and metaregression analysis. *Clinical Psychology Review, 34*(2), 158–176.

Bell, S. (2005). What does the "right to health" have to offer mental health patients? *International Journal of Law and Psychiatry, 28,* 141–153.

Beilock, S. L., Kulp, C. A., Holt, L. E., & Carr, T. H. (2004). More on the fragility of performance: Choking under pressure in mathematical problem solving. *Journal of Experimental Psychology: General, 133,* 584–600.

Beirne, R. O., Zlatkova, M. B., & Anderson, R. S. (2005). Changes in human short-wavelength-sensitive and achromatic resolution acuity with retinal eccentricity and meridian. *Visual Neuroscience, 22,* 79–86.

Belin, P., Zatorre, R. J., & Ahad, P. (2002). Human temporal-lobe response to vocal sounds. *Brain Research and Cognitive Brain Research, 13,* 17–26.

Bell, A. M., & Sih, A. (2007). Exposure to predation generates personality in threespined sticklebacks (*Gasterosteus aculeatus*). *Ecology Letters, 10,* 828–834.

Bell, A. S. (2011). A critical review of ADHD diagnostic criteria: What to address in the DSM-V. *Journal of Attention Disorders, 15*(1), 3–10. doi:10.1177/1087054710365982.

Bell, B. E., & Loftus, E. F. (1989). Trivial persuasion in the courtroom: The power of (a few) minor details. *Journal of Personality and Social Psychology, 56,* 669–679.

Bell, P. A., Greene, T. C., Fisher, J. D., & Baum, A. (2000). *Environmental psychology* (5th ed.). Belmont, CA: Wadsworth.

Bellaby, P. (2003). Communication and miscommunication of risk: Understanding UK parents' attitudes to combined MMR vaccination. *British Medical Journal, 327,* 725–728.

Belli, R. F. (2012). Epilogue: Continuing points of contention in the recovered memory debate. *Nebraska Symposium on Motivation, 58,* 243–255.

Belli, R. F., & Loftus, E. F. (1996). The pliability of autobiographical memory: Misinformation and the false memory problem. In D. C. Rubin (Ed.), *Remembering our past: Studies in autobiographical memory* (pp. 157–179). New York: Cambridge University Press.

Belsky, D. W., Moffitt, T. E., & Caspi, A. (2013). Genetic in population health science: Strategies and opportunities. *American Journal of Public Health, 103,* S73–S83.

Belsky, J., Schlomer, G.L., & Ellis, B.J. (2012). Beyond cumulative risk: Distinguishing harshness and unpredictability as determinants of parenting and early life history strategy. *Developmental Psychology, 48,* 662–673.

Belsky, J., Vandell, D. L., Burchinal, M., Clarke-Stewart, K. A., McCartney, K., Owen, M. T., & The NICHD Early Child Care Research Network. (2007). Are there long-term effects of early child care? *Child Development, 74,* 681–701.

Bem, D. J. (2000). Exotic becomes erotic: Interpreting the biological correlates of sexual orientation. *Archives of Sexual Behavior, 29*(6), 531–548.

Ben-Ari, A., & Gil, S. (2002). Traditional support systems: Are they sufficient in a culturally diverse academic environment? *British Journal of Social Work, 32,* 629–638.

Ben-David, K., & Rossidis, G. (2011). Bariatric surgery: Indications, safety and efficacy. *Current Pharmaceutical Design, 17*(12), 1209–1217.

Bender, D., & Lösel, F. (2011). Bullying at school as a predictor of delinquency, violence and other anti-social behaviour in adulthood. *Criminal Behaviour and Mental Health, 21,* 99–106.

Bendor, D. (2013). Play it again, brain. *Science, 342*(6158), 574–575.

Benedetti, F., Arduino, C., & Amanzio, M. (1999). Somatotopic activation of opioid systems by target-directed expectations of analgesia. *Journal of Neuroscience, 19,* 3639–3648.

Ben-Elia, E., & Ettema, D. (2011). Changing commuters' behavior using rewards: A study of rush-hour avoidance. *Transportation Research Part F: Traffic Psychology and Behaviour, 14*(5), 354–368. doi:10.1016/j.trf.2011.04.003.

Benenson, J., Markovits, H., Thompson, M., & Wrangham, R. (2011). Under threat of social exclusion, females exclude more than males. *Psychological Science, 22*(4), 538–544.

Benenson, J. F., & Koulnazarian, M. (2008). Sex differences in help-seeking appear in early childhood. *British Journal of Developmental Psychology, 26,* 163–169.

Bener, A., Al Maadidb, M. G. A., Özkanc, T., Al-Bastb, D. A. E., Diyabb, K. N., & Lajunenc, T. (2008). The impact of four-wheel drive on risky driver behaviours and road traffic accidents. *Transportation Research Part F: Traffic Psychology and Behaviour, 11,* 324–333.

Benjamin, A. S., & Tullis, J. (2010). What makes distributed practice effective? *Cognitive Psychology, 61*(3), 228–247. doi:10.1016/j.cogpsych.2010.05.004.

Benjamin, K., Wilson, S. G., & Mogil, J. S. (1999). Sex differences in supraspinal morphine analgesia are dependent on genotype. *Journal of Pharmacology and Experimental Therapeutics, 289,* 1370–1375.

Benjamin, L. T., Jr. (2000). The psychology laboratory at the turn of the 20th century. *American Psychologist, 55,* 318–321.

Benjamin, L. T., Jr., & Baker, D. (2004). *From séance to science: A history of the profession of psychology in America.* Belmont, CA: Wadsworth.

Benjamin, L. T., Jr., & Simpson, J. A. (2009). The power of the situation: The impact of Milgram's obedience studies on personality and social psychology. *American Psychologist, 64,* 12–19.

Benjamin, S., & Taylor, W. D. (2010). Nature and nurture: Genetic influences and gene-environment interactions in depression. *Current Psychiatry Reviews, 6*(2), 82–90. doi:10.2174/157340010791196484.

Bennett, H. L., Giannini, J. A., & Davis, H. S. (1985). Nonverbal response to intraoperational conversation. *British Journal of Anaesthesia, 57,* 174–179.

Bennett, K. K., & Elliott, M. (2002). Explanatory style and health: Mechanisms linking pessimism to illness. *Journal of Applied Social Psychology, 32,* 1508–1526.

Bennett, R. J., & Robinson, S. L. (2000). Development of a measure of workplace deviance. *Journal of Applied Psychology, 85,* 349–360.

Ben-Porath, Y. S., & Tellegen, A. (2008). *Minnesota multiphasic personality inventory-2-RF.* San Antonio, TX: Pearson Assessment.

Ben-Shakhar, G., & Furedy, J. J. (1990). *Theories and applications in the detection of deception: A psychophysiological and international perspective.* New York: Springer-Verlag.

Ben-Shakhar, G., Bar-Hillel, M., & Kremnitzer, M. (2002). Trial by polygraph: Reconsidering the use of the guilty knowledge technique in court. *Law & Human Behavior, 26,* 527–541.

Benson, D. F., & Geschwind, N. (1971). Aphasia and related cortical disturbances. In A. B. Baker & L. H. Baker (Eds.), *Clinical neurology.* New York: Harper & Row.

Benson, E. (2003). Sex: The science of sexual arousal. *Monitor on Psychology, 34,* 50.

Benson, H. (1975). *The relaxation response.* New York: Morrow.

Benton, J. M., & Overtree, C. E. (2012). Multicultural office design: A case example. *Professional Psychology: Research and Practice, 43,* 265–269. doi:10.1037/a0027443.f

Bentley, J. N., Chestek, C., Stacey, W. C., & Patil, P. G. (2013). Optogenetics in epilepsy. *Neurosurgical Focus, 34*(6), E4.

Beran, M. J., Smith, J. D., & Perdue, B. M. (2013). Language-trained chimpanzees (Pan troglodytes) name what they have seen but look first at what they have not seen. *Psychological Science, 24*(5), 660–666.

Beran, T. N., Mishna, F., Hetherington, R., & Shariff, S. (2013). Do children who bully their peers also play violent video games? A Canadian national study. *Journal of School Violence, 12*(4), 297–318.

Berant, E., Mikulincer, M., & Shaver, P. R. (2008). Mothers' attachment style, their mental health, and their children's emotional vulnerabilities: A 7-year study of children with congenital heart disease. *Journal of Personality, 76,* 31–65.

Berdahl, J. L., & Moore, C. (2006). Workplace harassment: Double jeopardy for minority women. *Journal of Applied Psychology, 91,* 426–436.

Beresford, J., & Blades, M. (2006). Children's identification of faces from lineups: The effects of lineup presentation and instructions on accuracy. *Journal of Applied Psychology, 91,* 1102–1113.

Bergin, A. E. (1971). The evaluation of therapeutic outcomes. In A. E. Bergin, & S. L. Garfield (Eds.), *Handbook of psychotherapy and behavior change: An empirical analysis* (pp. 217–270). New York: Wiley.

Bergman, T. J., Kitchen, D. M. (2009). Comparing responses to novel objects in wild baboons (*Papio ursinus*) and geladas (*Theropithecus gelada*). *Animal Cognition, 12*(1), 63–73.

Bergsholm, P. (2012). Patients' perspectives on electroconvulsive therapy: A reevaluation of the review by Rose et al on memory loss after electroconvulsive therapy. *Journal of ECT, 28*(1), 27–30.

Bériault, M., & Larivée, S. (2005). French review of EMDR efficacy: Evidences and controversies. *Revue de Psychoéducation, 34,* 355–396.

Berkowitz, L. (1994). Is something missing? Some observations prompted by the Cognitive-neoassociationist view of anger and emotional aggression. In L. R. Huesmann (Ed.), *Human aggression: Current perspectives* (pp. 35–60). New York: Plenum.

Berkman, E. T., Falk, E. B., & Lieberman, M. D. (2011). In the trenches of real-world self-control: Neural correlates of breaking the link between craving and smoking. *Psychological Science, 22*(4), 498–506. doi:10.1177/0956797611400918.

Berkowitz, L. (1998). Affective aggression: The role of stress, pain, and negative affect. In R. G. Geen & E. Donnerstein (Eds.), *Human aggression* (pp. 49–72). San Diego: Academic Press.

Berkowitz, L. (1999). Evil is more than banal: Situationism and the concept of evil. *Personality and Social Psychology Review, 3,* 246–253.

Berlin, L. J., Ispa, J. M., Fine, M. A., Malone, P. S., et al. (2009). Correlates and consequences of spanking and verbal punishment for low-income white, African American, and Mexican American toddlers. *Child Development, 80,* 1403–1420.

Bermeitinger, C., Goelz, R., Johr, N., Neumann, M., Ecker, U. K. H., & Doerr, R. (2009). The hidden persuaders break into the tired brain. *Experimental Social Psychology, 45*(2), 320–326.

Bernard, L. L. (1924). *Instinct.* New York: Holt, Rinehart & Winston.

Bernardin, H. J., & Beatty, R. W. (1984). *Performance appraisal: Assessing human behavior at work.* Boston: Kent.

Bernieri, F. J., & Petty, K. N. (2011). The influence of handshakes on first impression accuracy. *Social Influence, 6,* 78–87. doi:10.1080/15534510.2011.566706.

Bernstein, D. A. (1970). The modification of smoking behavior: A search for effective variables. *Behaviour Research and Therapy, 8,* 133–146.

Bernstein, D. A., Borkovec, T. D., & Hazlett-Stevens, H. (2000). *Progressive relaxation training: A manual for the helping professions* (2nd ed.). New York: Praeger.

Bernstein, D. M., & Loftus, E. F. (2009a). The consequences of false memories for food preferences and choices. *Perspectives on Psychological Science, 4,* 135–139.

Bernstein, D. M., & Loftus, E. F. (2009b). How to tell if a particular memory is true or false. *Perspectives in Psychological Science, 4,* 370–374.

Bernstein, D. M., & Roberts, B. (1995). Assessing dreams through self-report questionnaires: Relation with past research and personality. *Dreaming: Journal of the Association for the Study of Dreams, 5,* 13–27.

Bernstein, I. L. (1978). Learned taste aversions in children receiving chemotherapy. *Science, 200,* 1302–1303.

Bernstein, W. M. (2011). *A basic theory of psychoanalysis.* London, England: Karnac Books.

Berry, A. C., Rosenfield, D., & Smits, J. A. J. (2009). Extinction retention predicts improvement in social anxiety symptoms following exposure therapy. *Depression and Anxiety, 26,* 22–27.

Berry, C. M., Ones, D. S., & Sackett, P. R. (2007). Interpersonal deviance, organizational deviance, and their common correlates: A review and meta- analysis. *Journal of Applied Psychology, 92,* 409–423.

Berry, C. M., Sackett, P. R., & Wiemann, S. (2007). A review of recent developments in integrity test research. *Personnel Psychology, 60,* 271–301.

Berry, J. W., & Bennett, J. A. (1992). Cree conceptions of cognitive competence. *International Journal of Psychology, 27,* 73–88.

Berry, S. L., Beatty, W. W., & Klesges, R. C. (1985). Sensory and social influences on ice cream consumption by males and females in a laboratory setting. *Appetite, 6,* 41–45.

Berscheid, E. (2011). Love and compassion: Caregiving in adult close relationships. In S. Brown, M. Brown, & L. Penner (Eds.), *Self-interest and beyond: Toward a new understanding of human caregiving.* New York: Oxford University Press.

Berscheid, E. (2010). Love in the fourth dimension. *Annual Review of Psychology, 61,* 1–26.

Bersoff, D. N. (2008). *Ethical conflicts in psychology* (4th ed.). Washington, DC: American Psychological Association.

Bertenthal, B. I., Longo, M. R., & Kenny, S. (2007). Phenomenal permanence and the development of predictive tracking in infancy. *Child Development, 78*(1), 350–363.

Berti, A., Ladavas, E., & Corti, M. D. (1996). Anosognosia for hemiplegia, neglect dyslexia, and drawing neglect: Clinical findings and theoretical implications. *Journal of the International Neuropsychological Association, 2,* 426–440.

Besser, A., Zeigler-Hill, V., Pincus, A. L., & Neria, Y. (2013). Pathological narcissism and acute anxiety symptoms after trauma: A study of Israeli civilians exposed to war. *Psychiatry, 76*(4), 381–397.

Best, D. (1992, June). *Cross-cultural themes in developmental psychology.* Paper presented at workshop on cross-cultural aspects of psychology. Western Washington University, Bellingham.

Best, J. B. (1999). *Cognitive psychology* (5th ed.). Belmont, CA: Brooks/Cole.

Betan, E. J., & Westen, D. (2009). Countertransference and personality pathology: Development and clinical application of the Countertransference Questionnaire. In R. A. Levy & J. S. Ablon (Eds.), *Handbook of evidence-based psychodynamic psychotherapy: Bridging the gap between science and practice* (pp. 179–197). New York: Humana Press.

Betch, T., Hoffman, K., Hoffrage, U., & Plessner, H. (2003). Intuition beyond recognition: When less familiar events are liked more. *Experimental Psychology, 50,* 49–54.

Bettencourt, B. A., Talley, A., Benjamin, A. J., & Valentine, J. (2006). Personality and aggressive behavior under provoking and neutral conditions: A meta-analytic review. *Psychological Bulletin. 132,* 751–777.

Betz, D., & Sekaquaptewa, D. (2012). My fair physicist? Feminine math and science role models demotivate young girls. *Social Psychological and Personality Science.* doi:dx.doi.org/10.1177/1948550612440735.

Beyerstein, B. L. (1999). Pseudoscience and the brain: Tuners and tonics for aspiring superhumans. In S. Della Sala (Ed.), *Mind myths: Exploring popular assumptions about the mind and brain* (pp. 59–82). Chichester, UK: Wiley.

Beynon, C. M., McVeigh, C., McVeigh, J., Leavey, C., & Bellis, M. A. (2008). The involvement of drugs and alcohol in drug-facilitated sexual assault: A systematic review of the evidence. *Trauma Violence & Abuse, 9*(3), 178–188.

Bhagat, R. S., Kedia, B. L., Harveston, P. D., & Triandis, H. C. (2002). Cultural variations in the cross-border transfer of organizational knowledge: An integrative framework. *Academy of Management Review, 27,* 204–221.

Bhatt, R. S., & Bertin, E. (2001). Pictorial cues and three-dimensional information processing in early infancy. *Journal of Experimental Child Psychology, 80,* 315–332.

Bhatt, R. S., & Quinn, P. C. (2011). How does learning impact development in infancy? The case of perceptual organization. *Infancy, 16*(1), 2–38.

Bhopal, R., Vettini, A., Hunt, S., Wiebe, S., Hanna, L., & Amos, A. (2004). Review of prevalence data in, and evaluation of methods for cross cultural adaptation of, UK surveys on tobacco and alcohol in ethnic minority groups. *British Medical Journal, 328,* 76.

Bialystok, E., & Craik, F. M. (2010). Cognitive and linguistic processing in the bilingual mind. *Current Directions in Psychological Science, 19*(1), 19–23. doi:10.1177/0963721409358571.

Bialystok, E., Craik, F. M., & Luk, G. (2012). Bilingualism: consequences for mind and brain. *Trends in Cognitive Sciences, 16*(4), 240–250. doi:10.1016/ j.tics.2012.03.001.

Bickham, D. S., Blood, E. A., Walls, C. E., Shrier, L. A., & Rich, M. (2013). Characteristics of screen media use associated with higher BMI in young adolescents. *Pediatrics, 131*(5), 935–941.

Bidwell, M. A., & Rehfeldt, R. A. (2004). Using video modeling to teach a domestic skill with an embedded social skill to adults with severe mental retardation. *Behavioral Interventions, 19,* 263–274.

Bierhaus, A., Wolf, J., Andrassy, M., Rohleder, N., Humpert, P. M., Petrov, D., et al. (2003). A mechanism converting psychosocial stress into mononuclear cell activation. *Proceedings of the National Academy of Sciences, 100,* 1920–1925.

Bierman, K. L., Domitrovich, C. E., Nix, R. L., Gest, S. D., et al. (2008). Promoting academic and social-emotional school readiness: The Head Start REDI program. *Child Development, 79,* 1802–1817.

Bierman, K. L., Nix, R. L., Greenberg, M. T., Blair, C., & Domitrovich, C. E. (2008). Executive functions and school readiness intervention: Impact, moderation, and mediation in the Head Start REDI program. *Development and Psychopathology, 20,* 821–843.

Biernat, M., & Danaher, K. (2013). Prejudice. In H. Tennen, J. Suls, & I. B. Weiner (Eds.), *Handbook of psychology, Vol. 5: Personality and social psychology* (2nd ed.) (pp. 341–367). Hoboken, NJ: John Wiley & Sons Inc.

Bierut, L. J., Goate, A.M., Breslau, N., et al. (2012). ADH1B is associated with alcohol dependence and alcohol consumption in populations of European and African ancestry. *Molecular Psychiatry, 17,* 445–450.

Bierut, L. J., Heath, A. C., Bucholz, K. K., Dinwiddie, S. H., Madden, P. A., Statham, D. J., et al. (1999). Major depressive disorder in a community-based twin sample: Are there different genetic and environmental contributions for men and women? *Archives of General Psychiatry, 56,* 557–563.

Bies, R. J., Tripp, T. M., & Kramer, R. M. (1997). At the breaking point: Cognitive and social dynamics of revenge in organizations. In R. A. Giacalone & J. Greenberg (Eds.), *Antisocial behavior in organizations* (pp. 18–36). Thousand Oaks, CA: Sage.

Biesanz, J. C., Human, L. J., Paquin, A., Chan, M., Parisotto, K. L., Sarracino, J., & Gillis, R. L. (2011). Do we know when our impressions of others are valid? Evidence for realistic accuracy awareness in first impressions of personality. *Social Psychological and Personality Science, 2,* 452–459. doi:10.1177/1948550610397211.

Biever, C. (2009, January 3). Interview: Inside the savant mind. *New Scientist, 200*(2688), 40–41.

Bigelow, A., MacLean, J., Wood, C., & Smith, J. (1990). Infants' responses to child and adult strangers: An investigation of height and facial configuration variables. *Infant Behavior and Development, 13,* 21–32.

Bigelow, A. E., Littlejohn, M., Bergman, N., & McDonald, C. (2010). The relation between early mother-infant skin-to-skin contact and later maternal sensitivity in South African mothers of low birth weight infants. *Infant Mental Health Journal, 31,* 358–377.

Bigelow, B. J. (2006). There's an elephant in the room: The impact of early poverty and neglect on intelligence and common learning disorders in children adolescents, and their parents. *Developmental Disabilities Bulletin, 34,* 177–215.

Bigler, R., & Liben, L. (2007). Developmental intergroup theory: Explaining and reducing children's social stereotyping and prejudice. *Current Directions in Psychological Science, 16,* 162–166.

Bijttebier, P., Beck, I., Claes, L., & Vandereycken, W. (2009). Gray's reinforcement sensitivity theory as a framework for research on personality-psychopathology associations. *Clinical Psychology Review, 5,* 421–430.

Bikbaev, A., & Manahan-Vaughan, D. (2008). Relationship of hippocampal theta and gamma oscillations to potentiation of synaptic transmission. *Frontiers in Neuroscience, 2*(1), 56–63.

Biklen, D. (1990). Communication unbound: Autism and praxis. *Harvard Educational Review, 60,* 290–314.

Bilalić, M., McLeod, P., & Gobet, F. (2010). Th e mechanism of the *Einstellung* (set) effect: A pervasive source of cognitive bias. *Current Directions in Psychological Science, 19,* 111–115.

Bilderbeck, A. C., Brown, G. D. A., Read, J., Woolrich, M., Cowen, P. J., Behrens, T. E. J., & Rogers, R. D. (2014). Serotonin and social norms: Tryptophan depletion impairs social comparison and leads to resource depletion in a multiplayer harvesting game. *Psychological Science, 25*(7), 1303–1313.

Billiard, M. (2009). REM sleep behavior disorder and narcolepsy. *CNS and Neurological Disorders—Drug Targets, 8,* 264–270.

bin Saif, G. A., Papoiu, A. P., Banari, L. L., McGlone, F. F., Kwatra, S. G., Chan, Y. H., & Yosipovitch, G. G. (2012). The pleasurability of scratching an itch: A psychophysical and topographical assessment. *British Journal of Dermatology, 166*(5), 981–985. doi:10.1111/j.1365-2133.2012.10826.x.

Binet, A., & Simon, T. (1905). Methodes nouvelles pour le diagnostic du niveau intellectuel des anormaux. *L' Annee Psychologique, 11,* 191–244.

Birnbaum, G. E., Reis, H. T., Mikulincer, M., Gillath, O., & Orpaz, A. (2006). When sex is more than just sex: Attachment orientations, sexual experience, and relationship quality. *Journal of Personality & Social Psychology, 91,* 929–943.

Birch, H. G. (1945). The relation of previous experience to insightful problem solving. *Journal of Comparative Psychology, 38,* 367–383.

Biron, M., Bamberger, P. A., & Noyman, T. (2011). Work-related risk factors and employee substance use: Insights from a sample of Israeli blue-collar workers. *Journal of Occupational Health Psychology, 16*(2), 247–63. doi:10.1037/a0022708

Bisiach, E., Capitani, E., & Tansini, E. (1979). Detection from left and right hemifields on single and double simultaneous stimulation. *Perceptual and Motor Skills, 48* (3, Pt. 1), 960.

Bisiach, E., Vallar, G., Perani, D., Papagano, C., & Berti, A. (1986). Unawareness of disease following lesions of the right hemisphere: Anosognosia for hemiplegia and anosognosia for hemianopia. *Neuropsychologia, 24,* 471–482.

Bisson, J. I. (2007). Eye movement desensitisation and reprocessing reduces PTSD symptoms compared with fluoxetine at six months post-treatment. *Evidence-Based Mental Health, 10*(4), 118.

Bjork, R. A. (1999). Assessing our own competence: Heuristics and illusions. In D. Gopher & A. Koriat (Eds.), *Attention and performance XVII. Cognitive regulation of performance: Interaction of theory and application* (pp. 435–459). Cambridge: MIT Press.

Bjork, R. A. (2001, March). How to succeed in college: Learn how to learn. *American Psychological Society Observer, 14,* 9.

Bjork, R. A., & Linn, M. C. (2006, March). The science of learning and the learning of science: Introducing desirable difficulties. *American Psychological Society Observer, 19,* 29, 39.

Bjorklund, P. (2006). No man's land: Gender bias and social constructivism in the diagnosis of borderline personality disorder. *Issues in Mental Health Nursing, 27,* 3–23.

Bjornebekk, G., Gjesme, T., & Ulriksen, R. (2011). Achievement motives and emotional processes in children during problem-solving: Two experimental studies of their relation to performance in different achievement goal conditions. *Motivation and Emotion, 35,* 351–367.

Black, R. (2009, November 27). Bioethicist questions whether Belgian coma patient Rom Houben is communicating. *New York Daily News.* Retrieved from http://www.nydailynews.com/lifestyle/health/2009/11/27/2009-11-27_bioethicist_questions_whether_belgian_coma_patient_rom_houben_is_communicating.html

Blagrove, M. (1996). Problems with the cognitive psychological modeling of dreaming. *Journal of Mind and Behavior, 17,* 99–134.

Blagrove, M., Fouquet, N. C., Henley-Einion, J. A., Pace-Schott, E. F., Davies, A. C., Neuschaffer, J. L., & Turnbull, O. H. (2011). Assessing the Dream-Lag Effect for REM and NREM Stage 2 Dreams. *PLoS One, 6*(10), e26708.

Blair, G. (2011). Japan's suicide rate is expected to rise after triple disasters in March. *BMJ, 343,* d5839.

Blair, M. M., Glynn, L. M., Sandman, C. A., & Davis, E. (2011). Prenatal maternal anxiety and early childhood temperament. *Stress: The International Journal on the Biology of Stress, 14*(6), 644–651.

Blair-West, G. W., Cantor, C. H., Mellsop, G. W., & Eyeson-Annan, M. L. (1999). Lifetime suicide risk in major depression: Sex and age determinants. *Journal of Affective Disorders, 53,* 171–178.

Blaisdell, A. P., Sawa, K., & Leising, K. J. (2006). Causal reasoning in rats. *Science, 311,* 1020–1022.

Blake, J., & de Boysson-Bardies, B. (1992). Patterns in babbling: A cross-linguistic study. *Journal of Child Language, 19,* 51–74.

Blake, R. (1998). What can be "perceived" in the absence of visual awareness? *Current Directions in Psychological Science, 6,* 157–162.

Blakeslee, S. (2001, August 28). Therapies push injured brains and spinal cords into new paths. *New York Times.*

Blakeslee, S. (2002, September 22). Exercising toward repair of the spinal cord. *New York Times.* Retrieved from http://www.nytimes.com/2002/09/22/us/exercising-toward-repair-of-the-spinal-cord.html.

Blakesley, R. E., Mazumdar ,S., Dew, M. A., Houck, P. R., Tang, G., Reynolds, C. F. 3rd, & Butters, M. A. (2009). Comparisons of methods for multiple hypothesis testing in neuropsychological research. *Neuropsychology, 23*(2), 255–264.

Blakemore, J. E. O., Berenbaum, S. A., & Liben, L. S. (2009). *Gender development.* New York: Taylor & Francis.

Blanchard, P. N., & Thacker, J. W. (2007). *Effective training: Systems, strategies, and practices.* Upper Saddle River, NJ: Pearson Prentice Hall.

Blanchard, R. (2001). Fraternal birth order and the maternal immune hypothesis of male homosexuality. *Hormones and Behavior, 40,* 105–114.

Blass, T. (2000). The Milgram paradigm 35 years later: Some things we know about obedience to authority. In T. Blass (Ed.), *Current perspectives on the Milgram paradigm* (pp. 35–59). Mahwah, NJ: Erlbaum.

Blass, T., & Schmitt, C. (2001). The nature of perceived authority in the Milgram paradigm: Two replications. *Current Psychology: Developmental, Learning, Personality, Social, 20,* 115–121.

Blease, C. (2012). Mental health illiteracy? Perceiving depression as a disorder. *Review Of General Psychology, 16*(1), 59–69. doi:10.1037/a0026494.

Blechert, J., Sheppes, G., Di Tella, C., Williams, H., & Gross, J. J. (2012). See what you think: Reappraisal modulates behavioral and neural responses to social stimuli. *Psychological Science, 23*(4), 346–353. doi:10.1177/0956797612438559

Bleidorn, W., Kandler, C., Hülsheger, U. R., Riemann, R., Angleitner, A., & Spinath, F. M. (2010). Nature and nurture of the interplay between personality traits and major life goals. *Journal Of Personality And Social Psychology, 99*(2), 366–379. doi:10.1037/a0019982.

Block, J. A. (1971). *Lives through time.* Berkeley: Bancroft Books.

Blom, R. M., Samuels, J. F., et al. (2011). Association between a serotonin transporter promoter polymorphism (5HTTLPR) and personality disorder traits in a community sample. *Journal of Psychiatric Research, 45,* 1153–1159.

Bloom, B., & Cohen, R. A. (2007). *Summary health statistics for U.S. children: National Health Interview Survey, 2006.* Washington, D C: National Center for Health Statistics.

Bloom, L. (1995). *The transition from infancy to language: Acquiring the power of expression*. New York: Cambridge University Press.

Bloomgarden, A., & Calogero, R. M. (2008). A randomized experimental test of the efficacy of EMDR treatment on negative body image in eating disorder inpatients. *Eating Disorders, 16*(5), 418–427.

Blow, A. J., & Timm, T. M. (2002). Promoting community through family therapy: Helping clients develop a network of significant social relationships. *Journal of Systematic Therapies, 21,* 67–89.

Blum, K., Liu, Y., Shriner, R., & Gold, M. S. (2011). Reward circuitry dopaminergic activation regulates food and drug craving behavior. *Current Pharmaceutical Design, 17*(12), 1158–1167.

Blumberg, F. C., Altschuler, E. A., Almonte, D. E., & Mileaf, M. I. (2013). The impact of recreational video game play on children's and adolescents' cognition. *New Directions for Child and Adolescent Development*, No. 139, 41–50.

Blumberg, H. P., Leung, H.-C., Skudlarski, P., Lacadie, C. M., Fredericks, C. A., Harris, B. C., et al. (2003). A functional magnetic resonance imaging study of bipolar disorder: State- and trait-related dysfunction in ventral prefrontal cortices. *Archives of General Psychiatry, 60,* 601–609.

Blumberger, D. M., Mulsant, B. H., Kanellopoulos, D., Whyte, E. M., Rothschild, A. J., Flint, A. J., & Meyers, B. S. (2013). The incidence of tardive dyskinesia in the study of pharmacotherapy for psychotic depression. *Journal of Clinical Psychopharmacology, 33*(3), 391–397.

Blumenthal, J. A., Babyak, M., Wei., J., O'Conner, C., Waugh, R., Eisenstein, E., et al. (2002). Usefulness of psychosocial treatment of mental stress-induced myocardial ischemia in men. *American Journal of Cardiology, 89,* 164–168.

Blundell, J. E., & Cooling, J. (2000). Routes to obesity: Phenotypes, food choices, and activity. *British Journal of Nutrition, 83,* S33–S38.

Boag, S. (2011). Explanation in personality psychology: "Verbal magic" and the five-factor model. *Philosophical Psychology, 24,* 223–243.

Bob, P. (2008). Pain, dissociation and subliminal self-representations. *Consciousness and Cognition, 17,* 355–369.

Boden, M. A. (2006). *Computer models of mind.* Cambridge, UK: Cambridge University Press.

Bodenhausen, G. V., & Richeson, J. A. (2010). Prejudice, stereotyping, and discrimination. In R. F. Baumeister, E. J. Finkel (Eds.), *Advanced social psychology: The state of the science* (pp. 341–383). New York: Oxford University Press.

Boehning, D., & Snyder, S. H. (2003). Novel neural modulators. *Annual Review of Neuroscience, 26,* 105–131.

Bogaert, A. F., & Skorska, M. (2011). Sexual orientation, fraternal birth order, and the maternal immune hypothesis: A review. *Frontiers in Neuroendocrinology, 32*(2), 247–254.

Boger, J., & Mihailidis, A. (2011). The future of intelligent assistive technologies for cognition: Devices under development to support independent living and aging-with-choice. *Neurorehabilitation, 28*(3), 271–280. doi:10.3233/NRE-2011-0655.

Boggs, C. D., Morey, L. C., Skodol, A. E., Shea, M. T., et al. (2009). Differential impairment as an indicator of sex bias in DSM-IV criteria for four personality disorders. *Personality Disorders: Theory, Research, and Treatment*, special volume, 61–68.

Bohart, A. C., & Wade, A. G. (2013). The client in psychotherapy. In M. J. Lambert (Ed.), *Bergin and Garfield's handbook of psychotherapy and behavior change* (6th ed.) (pp. 219–257). Hoboken, NJ: Wiley.

Bohner, G., Erb, H.-P., & Siebler, F. (2008). Information processing approaches to persuasion: Integrating assumptions from the dual- and single-processing perspectives. In W. B. Crano & R. Prislin (Eds.), *Attitudes and persuasion* (pp. 161–188). New York: Psychology Press.

Bolton, D., Eley, T. C., O'Connor, T. G., Perrin, S., & Rabe-Hesketh, S., et al. (2006). Prevalence and genetic and environmental influences on anxiety disorders in 6-year-old twins. *Psychological Medicine, 36,* 335–344.

Bonanno, G. A. (2005). Resilience in the face of potential trauma. *Current Directions in Psychological Science, 14,* 135–138.

Bonci, A., Bernardi, G., Grillner, P., & Mercuri, N. B. (2003). The dopamine- containing neuron: Maestro or simple musician in the orchestra of addiction? *Trends in Pharmacological Science, 24,* 172–177.

Boniecki, K. A., & Moore, S. (2003). Breaking the silence: Using a token economy to reinforce classroom participation. *Teaching of Psychology, 30,* 224–227.

Bonilla-Silva, E., & Dietrich, D. (2011). The sweet enchantment of color-blind racism in Obamerica. *Annals of the American Academy of Political and Social Science, 634,* 190–206.

Bonk, V. A., France, C. R., & Taylor, B. K. (2001). Distraction reduces self-reported physiological reactions to blood donation in novice donors with a blunting coping style. *Journal of Psychosomatic Medicine, 63,* 447–452.

Bonta, J., Blaise, J., & Wilson, H. A. (2014). A theoretically informed meta-analysis of the risk for general and violent recidivism for mentally disordered offenders. *Aggression and Violent Behavior.* Epub ahead of print, April 30. http://dx.doi.org/10.1016/j.avb.2014.04.014.

Bonwell, C. C., & Eison, J. A. (1991). *Active learning: Creating excitement in the classroom.* Washington, DC: George Washington University.

Boot, W. R., Blakely, D. P., & Simons, D. J. (2011). Do action video games improve perception and cognition? *Frontiers in Psychology, 2,* 226.

Booth, C. B., Clarke-Stewart, K. A., Vandell, D. L., McCartney, K., & Owen, M. T. (2002). Child-care usage and mother-infant "quality time." *Journal of Marriage and the Family, 64,* 16–26.

Booth, D. A., Higgs, S., Schneider, J., & Klinkenberg, I. (2010). Learned liking versus inborn delight: Can sweetness give sensual pleasure or is it just motivating? *Psychological Science, 21*(11), 1656–1663.

Booth, P. B., & Lindaman, S. L. (2000). Theraplay as a short-term treatment for enhancing attachment in adopted children. In H. G. Kaduson & C. E.Schaefer (Eds.) *Short Term Play Therapy for Children.* New York: The Guilford Press.

Bootzin, R. R., & Epstein D. R. (2011). Understanding and treating insomnia. *Annual Review of Clinical Psychology, 7,* 435–458.

Borckardt, J. J., Smith, A. R., Reeves, S. T., Weinstein, M., Kozel, F. A., Nahas, Z., Shelley, N., Branham, R. K., Thomas, K. J., & George, M.S. (2007). Fifteen minutes of left prefrontal repetitive transcranial magnetic stimulation acutely increases thermal pain thresholds in healthy adults. *Pain Research and Management,* 12(4), 287–290.

Bordnick, P. S., Elkins, R. L., Orr, T. E., Walters, P., & Thyer, B. A. (2004). Evaluating the relative effectiveness of three aversion therapies designed to reduce craving among cocaine abusers. *Behavioral Interventions, 19,* 1–24.

Borg, M. B., Jr. (2002). The Avalon Garden Men's Association: A community health psychology case study. *Journal of Health Psychology, 7,* 345–357.

Borgida, E., Conner, C., & Monteufel, L. (1992). Understanding living kidney donors: A behavioral decision-making perspective. In S. Spacapan & S. Oskamp (Eds.), *Helping and being helped* (pp. 183–212). Newbury Park, CA: Sage.

Borkenau, P., Mauer, N., Riemann, R., Spinath, F. M., & Angleitner, A. (2004). Thin slices of behavior as cues of personality and intelligence. *Journal of Personality and Social Psychology, 86,* 599–614.

Bornstein, B. H., & Greene, E. (2011). Jury decision making: Implications for and from psychology. *Current Directions in Psychological Science, 20*(1), 63–77. doi:10.1177/0963721410397282.

Bornstein, G. (2002). The intergroup Prisoner's Dilemma game as a model of intergroup conflict. In C. von Hofsten, L. Bäckman (Eds.), *Psychology at the turn of the millennium, Vol. 2: Social, developmental, and clinical perspectives* (pp. 347–360). Florence, KY: Taylor & Frances/Routledge.

Bornstein, M. H. (2006). Hue categorization and color naming: Physics to sensation to perception. In N. J. Pitchford & C. P. Biggum (Eds.), *Progress in Color Studies: Volume II. Psychological Aspects.* Amsterdam: John Benjamins.

Boroditsky, L., & Gaby, A. (2010). Remembrances of times east: Absolute spatial representations of time in an Australian Aboriginal community. *Psychological Science, 21*(11), 1635–1639. doi:10.1177/0956797610386621.

Borota, D., Murray, E., Keceli, G., Chang, A., Watabe, J. M., Ly, M., Toscano, J. P., & Yassa, M. A. (2014). Post-study caffeine administration enhances memory consolidation in humans. *Nature Neuroscience.* Epub January 12, 2014.

Borsutzky, S., Fujiwara, E., Brand, M., & Markowitsch, H. J. (2008). Confabulations in alcoholic Korsakoff patients. *Neuropsychologia, 46*(13), 3133–3143.

Borzekowski, D. L., & Robinson, T. N. (2005). The remote, the mouse, and the no. 2 pencil: The household media environment and academic achievement among third grade students. *Archives of Pediatric Adolescent Medicine, 159*(7), 607–613.

Bos, M. W., van Baaren, R. B., & Dijksterhuis, A. (2011). Food for thought? *Neuropsychoeconomics Conference Proceedings,* 26.

Boscolo-Berto, R., Viel, G., Montagnese, S., Raduazzo, D. I., Ferrara, S. D., & Dauvilliers. Y. (2011). Narcolepsy and effectiveness of gamma-hydroxybutyrate (GHB): A systematic review and meta-analysis of randomized controlled trials. *Sleep Medicine Reviews,* Nov 3, 2011 [Epub ahead of print].

Bosma, H., Marmot, M. G., Hemingway, H., Nicholson, A. C., Brunner, E., & Stansfeld, S. A. (1997). Low job control and risk of coronary heart disease in Whitehall II (prospective cohort) study. *British Medical Journal, 314,* 558–565.

Boswell, W. R., Bourdreau, J. W., & Tichy, J. (2005). The relationship between employee job change and satisfaction: The Honeymoon-Hangover effect. *Journal of Applied Psychology, 90*(5), 882–892.

Boto, L. R., Crispim, J. N., de Melo, I. S., Juvandes, C., Rodrigues, T., Azeredo, P., & Ferreira R. (2011). Sleep deprivation and accidental fall risk in children. *Sleep Medicine,* November 4, 2011 [Epub ahead of print].

Botwinick, J. (1961). Husband and father-in-law: A reversible figure. *American Journal of Psychology, 74,* 312–313.

Bouchard, T. J. (2014). Genes, evolution and intelligence. *Behavioral Genetics.* Epub March 7, 2014.

Bourassa, M., & Vaugeois, P. (2001). Effects of marijuana use on divergent thinking. *Creativity Research Journal, 13,* 411–416.

Bouret, S. G., Draper, S. J., & Simerly, R. B. (2004). Trophic action of leptin on hypothalamic neurons that regulate feeding. *Science, 304,* 108–110.

Bouton, M., Mineka, S., & Barlow, D. (2001). A modern learning theory perspective on the etiology of panic disorder. *Psychological Review, 107,* 4–32.

Bouton, M. E. (1993). Context, time, and memory retrieval in the interference paradigms of Pavlovian learning. *Psychological Bulletin, 114,* 80–99.

Bouton, M. E. (2002). Context, ambiguity, and unlearning: Sources of relapse after behavioral extinction. *Biological Psychiatry, 52,* 976–986.

Boutwell, B. B., Franklin, C. A., Barnes, J. C., & Beaver, K. M. (2011). Physical punishment and childhood aggression: The role of gender and gene–environment interplay. *Aggressive Behavior, 37*(6), 559–568. doi:10.1002/ab.20409.

Bouvier, S. E., & Engel, S. A. (2006). Behavioral deficits and cortical damage loci in cerebral achromatopsia. *Cerebral Cortex, 16*(2), 183–191.

Bowen, S., Witkiewitz, K., Clifasefi, S. L., Grow, J., Chawla, N., Hsu, S. H., Carroll, H. A., Harrop, E., Collins, S. E., Lustyk, M. K., & Larimer, M. E. (2014). Relative efficacy of mindfulness-based relapse prevention, standard relapse prevention, and treatment as usual for substance use disorders: A randomized clinical trial. *JAMA Psychiatry,* Epub March 19, 2014

Bower, G. H. (1981). Mood and memory. *American Psychologist, 36,* 129–148.

Bower, J. M., & Parsons, L. M. (2003). Rethinking the "lesser brain." *Scientific American, 289,* 50–57.

Bowers, J. S., Mattys, S. L., & Gage, S. H. (2009). Preserved implicit knowledge of a forgotten childhood language. *Psychological Science, 20,* 1064–1069.

Bowlby, J. (1973). *Attachment and loss: Vol. 2. Separation.* New York: Basic Books.

Boxer, P., Huesmann, L. R., Bushman, B. J., O'Brien, M., & Moceri, D. (2009). The role of violent media preference in cumulative developmental risk for violence and general aggression. *Journal of Youth & Adolescence, 38*(3), 417–428.

Boyce, C. J., Brown, G. A., & Moore, S. C. (2010). Money and happiness: Rank of income, not income, affects life satisfaction. *Psychological Science, 21*(4), 471–475. doi:10.1177/0956797610362671.

Boyce, C. J., & Wood, A. M. (2011). Personality prior to disability determines adaptation: Agreeable individuals recover lost life satisfaction faster and more completely. *Psychological Science, 22*(11), 1397–1402. doi:10.1177/0956797611421790.

Boyd, S. T. (2006). The endocannabinoid system. *Pharmacotherapy, 26*(12 Pt. 2), 218S–221S.

Boyden, E. S. (2011, July 1). The birth of optogenetics: An account of the path to realizing tools for controlling brain circuits with light. *The Scientist: Magazine of the Life Sciences.* Retrieved from http://the-scientist.com/2011/07/01/the-birth- of-optogenetics/.

Boyle, P. A., Barnes, L. L., Buchman, A. S., & Bennett, D. A. (2009). Purpose in life is associated with mortality among community-dwelling older persons. *Psychosomatic Medicine, 71,* 574–579.

Boyles, S. (2008, October 14). Phiten necklace: Red Sox secret weapon? Some athletes are true believers in the power of titanium. Retrieved January 15, 2009, from http://www.webmd.com/pain-management/news/20081014/phiten- necklace-red -sox-secret-weapon.

Boysen, G. A. (2009). A review of experimental studies of explicit and implicit bias among counselors. *Journal of Multicultural Counseling and Development, 37,* 240–249.

Boysen, G. A., & VanBergen, A. (2014). Simulation of multiple personalities: A review of research comparing diagnosed and simulated dissociative identity disorder. *Clinical Psychology Reviews, 34*(1), 14–28.

Bozarth, M. A., & Wise, R. A. (1984). Anatomically distinct opiate receptor fields mediate reward and physical dependence. *Science, 224,* 516–518.

Bracken, B. A., & McCallum, R. S. (1998). *Universal Nonverbal Intelligence Test (UNIT).* Boston: Riverside.

Brach, J. S., FitzGerald, S., Newman, A. B., Kelsey, S., Kuller, L., VanSwearingen, J. M., & Kriska, A. M. (2003). Physical activity and functional status in community-dwelling older women. *Archives of Internal Medicine, 163,* 2565–2571.

Bradley, R., Greene, J., Russ, E., Dutra, L., & Westen, D. (2005). A multidimensional meta-analysis of psychotherapy for PTSD. *American Journal of Psychiatry, 162,* 214–227.

Bradley-Johnson, S., Graham, D. P., & Johnson, C. M. (1986). Token reinforcement on WISC-R performance for white, low-socioeconomic, upper and lower elementary-school-age students. *Journal of School Psychology, 24,* 73–79.

Bradshaw, G. L. (1993a). Why did the Wright brothers get there first? Part 1. *Chemtech, 23*(6), 8–13.

Bradshaw, G. L. (1993b). Why did the Wright brothers get there first? Part 2. *Chemtech, 23*(7), 16–22.

Brainerd, C. J. (2013). Developmental reversals in false memory: A new look at the reliability of children's evidence. *Current Directions in Psychological Science, 22*(5), 335–341.

Brainerd, C. J., & Reyna, V. F. (2005). *The science of false memory.* New York: Oxford University Press.

Brakemeier, E. L., Merkl, A., Wilbertz, G., Quante, A., Regen, F., Bührsch, N., van Hall, F., Kischkel, E., Danker-Hopfe, H., Anghelescu, I., Heuser, I., Kathmann, N., & Bajbouj, M. (2013). Cognitive-behavioral therapy as continuation treatment to sustain response after electroconvulsive therapy in depression: A randomized controlled trial. *Biological Psychiatry,* Epub December 12, 2013.

Brambilla, P., Cipriani, A., Hotopf, M., & Barbul, C. (2005). Side-effect profile of fluoxentine in comparison with other SSRIs, tricyclic, and newer antidepressants: A meta-analysis of clinical trial data. *Pharmacopsychiatry, 38,* 69–77.

Brand, S., Wilhelm, F. H., Kossowsky, J., Holsboer-Trachsler, E., & Schneider, S. (2011). Children suffering from separation anxiety disorder (SAD) show increased HPA axis activity compared to healthy controls. *Journal of Psychiatric Research, 45*(4), 452–459. doi:10.1016/j.jpsychires.2010.08.014

Brandimonte, M. A., Hitch, G. J., & Bishop, D. V. M. (1992). Influence of short-term memory codes on visual image processing: Evidence from image transformation tasks. *Journal of Experimental Psychology: Learning, Memory, and Cognition, 18,* 157–165.

Brannick, M., & Levine, E. (2002). *Job analysis.* Thousand Oaks: CA: Sage.

Brannick, M. T., Levine, E. L., & Morgeson, F. P. (Eds.) (2007). *Job and work analysis, second edition: Methods, research, and applications for human resource management.* Thousand Oaks, CA: Sage.

Bransford, J. D., & Johnson, M. K. (1972). Contextual prerequisites for understanding: Some investigations of comprehension and recall. *Journal of Verbal Learning and Verbal Behavior, 11,* 717–726.

Bransford, J. D., & Stein, B. S. (1993). *The ideal problem solver* (2nd ed.). New York: Freeman.

Brasher, E. E., & Chen, P. Y. (1999). Evaluation of success criteria in job search: A process perspective. *Journal of Occupational and Organizational Psychology, 72,* 57–70.

Brassen, S., Gamer, M., Peters, J., Gluth, S., & Büchel, C. (2012, May 4). Don't look back in anger! Responsiveness to missed chances in successful and nonsuccessful aging. *Science, 336*(6081), 612–614. Published online first: http://www.sciencemag.org/content/336/6081/612.short.

Brattico, E., Alluri, V., Bogert, B., Jacobsen, T., Vartiainen, N., Nieminen, S., & Tervaniemi, M. (2011). A functional MRI study of happy and sad emotions in music with and without lyrics. *Frontiers in Psychology,* Epub December 1, 2011.

Braun, S. M., & Jessberger, S. (2014). Review: Adult neurogenesis and its role in neuropsychiatric disease, brain repair and normal brain function. *Neuropathology & Applied Neurobiology, 40*(1), 3–12.

Breck, S. W., Lance, N., & Seher, V. (2009). Selective foraging for antrhopogenic resources by black bears: Minivans in Yosemite National Park. *Journal of Mammology, 90*(5), 1041–1044.

Brefczynski-Lewis, J. A., Lutz, A., Schaefer, H. S., Levinson, D. B., & Davidson, R. J. (2007). Neural correlates of attentional expertise in long-term meditation practitioners. *Proceedings of the National Academies of Science, 104,* 11483–11488.

Breggin, P. R. (2007). *Brain-disabling treatments in psychiatry: Drugs, electroshock, and the psychopharmaceutical complex* (2nd ed.). New York: Springer Publishing.

Breggin, P. R. (2008). *Medication madness: True stories of mayhem, murder, and suicide caused by psychiatric drugs.* New York: St. Martin's Press.

Brehm, S., Kassin, S., & Fein, S. (2005). *Social psychology* (6th ed.). Boston, MA: Houghton-Mifflin.

Breier, J. I., Adair, J. C., Gold, M., Fennell, E. B., Gilmore, R. L., & Heilman, K. M. (1995). Dissociation of anosognosia for hemiplegia and aphasia during left-hemisphere anesthesia. *Neurology, 45,* 65–67.

Brelsford, J. W. (1993). Physics education in a virtual environment. In *Proceedings of the 37th Annual Meeting of the Human Factors and Ergonomics Society.* Santa Monica, CA: Human Factors.

Bremner, J. D., Shobe, K. K., & Kihlstrom, J. F. (2000). False memories in women with self-reported childhood sexual abuse. *Psychological Science, 11,* 333–337.

Bremner, J. D., Vythilingam, M., Vermetten, E., Caccarino, V., & Charney, D. S. (2004). Deficits in hippocampal and anterior cingulate functioning during verbal declarative memory encoding in midlife major depression. *American Journal of Psychiatry, 161,* 637–645.

Bremner, J. D., Vythilingam, M., Vermetten, E., Southwick, S. M., McGlashan, T., Nazeer, A., et al. (2003). MRI and PET study of deficits in hippocampal structure and function in women with childhood sexual abuse and posttraumatic stress disorder. *American Journal of Psychiatry, 160*, 924–932.

Brenes, G. A., Rapp, S. R., Rejeski, W. J., & Miller, M. E. (2002). Do optimism and pessimism predict physical functioning? *Journal of Behavioral Medicine, 25*, 219–231.

Brennan, F. X., & Charnetski, C. J. (2000). Explanatory style and Immunoglobulin A (IgA). *Integrative Physiological & Behavioral Science, 35*, 251–255.

Brennen, T., Baguley, T., Bright, J., & Bruce, V. (1990). Resolving semantically induced tip-of-the-tongue states for proper nouns. *Memory & Cognition, 18*, 339–347.

Brenner, R. A., Trumble, A. C., Smith, G. S., Kessler, E. P., & Overpeck, M. D. (2001). Where children drown, United States, 1995. *Pediatrics, 108*, 85–89.

Breslau, N., Reboussin, B. A., Anthony, J. C., & Storr, C. L. (2005). The structure of posttraumatic stress disorder: Latent class analysis in 2 community samples. *Archives of General Psychiatry, 62*, 1343–1351.

Brethel-Haurwitz, K. M., & Marsh, A. A. (2014). Geographical differences in subjective well-being predict extraordinary altruism. *Psychological Science, 25*, 762–771.

Breuer, A. T., Masson, M. E., Cohen, A. L., & Lindsay, D. S. (2009). Long-term repetition priming of briefly identified objects. *Journal of Experimental Psychology: Learning, Memory, and Cognition, 35*, 487–498.

Brewer, J. B., Zhao, Z., Desmond, J. E., Glover, G. H., & Gabriel, J. D. E. (1998). Making memories: Brain activity that predicts how well visual experience will be remembered. *Science, 281*, 1185–1187.

Brewer, M. B. (2010). Intergroup relations. In R. F. Baumeister, E. J. Finkel (Eds.), *Advanced social psychology: The state of the science* (pp. 535–571). New York: Oxford University Press.

Brewer, N., & Wells, G. L. (2011). Eyewitness identification. *Current Directions In Psychological Science, 20*(1), 24–27. doi:10.1177/0963721410389169.

Brewer, N. T., Chapman, G. B., Gibbons, F. X., Gerrard, M., McCaul, K. D., & Weinstein, N. D. (2007). *Health Psychology, 26*, 136–145.

Brewer, W. F. (1977). Memory for the pragmatic implications of sentences. *Memory & Cognition, 5*, 673–678.

Brewer, W. F., & Treyens, J. C. (1981). Role of schemata in memory for places. *Cognitive Psychology, 13*, 207–230.

Brewerton, T. D., & Costin, C. (2011a). Long-term outcome of residential treatment for anorexia nervosa and bulimia nervosa. *Eating Disorders: The Journal of Treatment & Prevention, 19*(2), 132–144. doi:10.1080/10640266.2011.551632

Brewerton, T. D., & Costin, C. (2011b). Treatment results of anorexia nervosa and bulimia nervosa in a residential treatment program. *Eating Disorders: The Journal of Treatment & Prevention, 19*(2), 117–131. doi:10.1080/10640266.2011.551629

Briggs, G. F., Hole, G. J., & Land, M. F. (2011). Emotionally involving telephone conversations lead to driver error and visual tunnelling. *Transportation Research Part F: Traffic Psychology and Behaviour, 14*(4), 313–323. doi:10.1016/j.trf.2011.02.004.

Brigham, C. C. (1923). *A study of American intelligence.* Princeton, NJ: Princeton University Press.

Brinkhaus, B., Witt, C. M., Jena, S., Linde, K., Streng, A., Wagenpfeil, S., et al. (2006). Acupuncture in patients with chronic low back pain: A randomized controlled trial. *Archives of Internal Medicine, 166*, 450–457.

Brislin, R. (1993). *Understanding culture's influence on behavior.* Fort Worth: Harcourt, Brace, Jovanovich.

Brito, N., & Barr, R. (2013). Flexible memory retrieval in bilingual 6-month-old infants. *Developmental Psychobiology*, Epub December 7, 2013.

Britt, G. C., & McCance-Katz, E. F. (2005). A brief overview of the clinical pharmacology of "club drugs." *Substance Use and Misuse, 40*(9–10), 1189–1201.

Broadbent, E., & Koschwanez, H. E. (2012). The psychology of wound healing. *Current Opinion in Psychiatry, 25*(2), 135–140.

Broadbent, E., Petrie, K. J., Alley, P. G., & Booth, R. J. (2003). Psychological stress impairs early wound repair following surgery. *Psychosomatic Medicine, 65*, 865–869.

Broaders, S. C., & Goldin-Meadow, S. (2010). Truth is at hand: How gesture adds information during investigative interviews. *Psychological Science, 21*(5), 623–628. doi:10.1177/0956797610366082.

Broca, P. (1861). Remarques sur le siege de la faculte de la porle articulee, suives d'une observation d'aphemie (perte de parole). *Bulletin Societie Anatomie, 36*, 330–357.

Broca, P. (1865). Sur la faculté du langage articulé. *Bulletin Societe Anthropologie Paris, 6*, 337–393.

Brody, G. H., Beach, S. R. H., Chen, Y., Obasi, E., Philibert, R. A., Kogan, S. M. (2011). Perceived discrimination, serotonin tranporter linked polymorphic region status, and the development of conduct problems. *Development and Psychopathology, 23*, 617–627. doi:10.1017/S0954579411000046.

Brody, N. (2003). Construct validation of the Sternberg Triarchic Abilities Test: Comment and reanalysis. *Intelligence, 31*, 319–330.

Brody, N., & Ehrlichman, H. (1998). *Personality psychology: The science of individuality.* Upper Saddle River, NJ: Prentice Hall.

Broekman, B. P., Niti, M., Nyunt, M., Ko, S., Kumar, R., & Ng, T. (2011). Validation of a brief seven-item response bias-free Geriatric Depression Scale. *The American Journal of Geriatric Psychiatry, 19*(6), 589–596. doi:10.1097/JGP.0b013e3181f61ec9.

Broeren, S., Lester, K. J., Muris, P., & Field, A. P. (2011). They are afraid of the animal, so therefore I am too: Influence of peer modeling on fear beliefs and approach-avoidance behaviors towards animals in typically developing children. *Behaviour Research and Therapy, 49*(1), 50–57. doi:10.1016/j.brat.2010.11.001.

Broesch, T., Callaghan, T., Henrich, J., Murphy, C., & Rochat, P. (2011). Cultural variations in children's mirror self-recognition. *Journal Of Cross-Cultural Psychology, 42*(6), 1018–1029. doi:10.1177/0022022110381114.

Brondolo, E., Rieppi, R., Erickson, S. A., Bagiella, E., Shapiro, P. A., McKinley, P., & Sloan, R. P. (2003). Hostility, interpersonal interactions, and ambulatory blood pressure. *Psychosomatic Medicine, 65*, 1003–1011.

Brook, C. A., & Schmidt, L. A. (2008). Social anxiety disorder: A review of environmental factors. *Neuropsychiatric Disease and Treatment, 4*, 123–143.

Brooks-Gunn, J., & Chase-Lansdale, P. L. (2002). Adolescent parenthood. In M. H. Bornstein (Ed.), *Handbook of parenting* (2nd ed.). Mahwah, NJ: Erlbaum.

Broussard, E. R., & Cassidy, J. (2010). Maternal perception of newborns predicts attachment organization in middle adulthood. *Attachment & Human Development, 12*(1/2), 159–172. doi:10.1080/14616730903282464.

Brown, A. (2010). Reduce Employee Theft Be proactive. Not reactive. *Alaska Business Monthly, 26*(1), 68–69.

Brown, A. S. (2004). *The déjà vu experience.* New York: Psychology Press.

Brown, A. S., Begg, M. D., Gravenstein, S., Schaefer, C. A., Wyatt, R. J., Bresnahan, M., et al. (2005). Serologic evidence of prenatal influenza in the etiology of schizophrenia. *Obstetrical and Gynecological Survey, 60*, 77–78.

Brown, A. S., & Derkits, E. J. (2010). Prenatal infection and schizophrenia: A review of epidemiologic and translational studies. *American Journal of Psychiatry, 167*, 261–280.

Brown, A. S., & Nix, L. A. (1996). Age-related changes in the tip-of-the-tongue experience. *American Journal of Psychology, 109*, 79–91.

Brown, A. S., Schaefer, C. A., Quesenberry, C. P., Jr., Liu, L., Babulas, V. P., & Susser, E. S. (2005). Maternal exposure to toxoplasmosis and risk of schizophrenia in adult offspring. *American Journal of Psychiatry, 162*, 767–773.

Brown, G. M., Pandi-Perumal, S. R., Trakht, I., & Cardinali, D. P. (2009). Melatonin and its relevance to jet lag. *Travel Medicine and Infectious Disease, 7*(2):69–81.

Brown, J. (1958). Some tests of the decay theory of immediate memory. *Quarterly Journal of Experimental Psychology, 10*, 12–21.

Brown, L. A., Forman, E. M., Herbert, J. D., Hoffman, K. L., Yuen, E. K., & Goetter, E. M. (2011). A randomized controlled trial of acceptance-based behavior therapy and cognitive therapy for test anxiety: A pilot study. *Behavior Modification, 35*(1), 31–53.

Brown, L. M., Awad, G. H., Preas, E. J., Allen, V., Kenney, J., Roberts, S., & Lusk, L. (2013). Investigating prejudice toward men perceived to be Muslim: Cues of foreignness versus phenotype. *Journal of Applied Social Psychology, 43*(Suppl 2), E237–E245.

Brown, L. M., Bongar, B., & Cleary, K. M. (2004). A profile of psychologists' views of critical risk factors for completed suicide in older adults. *Professional Psychology: Research and Practice, 35*, 90–96.

Brown, R., & Kulik, J. (1977). Flashbulb memories. *Cognition, 5*, 73–99.

Brown, R., & McNeill, D. (1966). The "tip-of-the-tongue" phenomenon. *Journal of Verbal Learning and Verbal Behavior, 5*, 325–337.

Brown, R. A. (1973). *First language.* Cambridge: Harvard University Press.

Brown, S. L., Nesse, R. M., Vinokur, A. D., & Smith, D. M. (2003). Providing social support may be more beneficial than receiving it: Results from a prospective study of mortality. *Psychological Science, 14*, 320–327.

Browne, K. D., & Hamilton-Giachritsis, C. (2005). The influence of violent media on children and adolescents: A public health approach. *Lancet, 365*, 702–710.

Brownley, K. A., Berkman, N. D., Sedway, J. A., Lohr, K. N., & Bulik, C. M. (2007). Binge eating disorder treatment: A systematic review of randomized controlled trials. *International Journal of Eating Disorders, 40*(4), 337–348.

Bruce, D., Wilcox-O'Hearn, L. A., Robinson, J. A., Phillips-Grant, K., Francis, L., & Smith, M. C. (2005). Fragment memories mark the end of childhood amnesia. *Memory & Cognition, 33*, 567–76.

Bruck, M., Cavanagh, P., & Ceci, S. J. (1991). Fortysomething: Recognizing faces at one's 25th reunion. *Memory and Cognition, 19*, 221–228.

Bruff, D. (2009). *Teaching with classroom response systems: Creating active learning environments.* San Francisco: Jossey-Bass.

Bruintjes, T. D., Companjen, J., van der Zaag-Loonen, H. J., & van Benthem, P. P. (2014). A randomised sham-controlled trial to assess the long-term effect of the Epley manoeuvre for treatment of posterior canal BPPV. *Clinical Otolaryngology.* Epub January 18, 2014.

Brumfield, B. (2013). After decades in prison over murders, DNA evidence frees 2 New York men. *CNN,* February 9, 2014.

Brummett, B. H., Mark, D. B., Siegler, I. C., Williams, R. B., Babyak, M. A., Clapp-Channing, N. E., & Barefoot, J. C. (2005). Perceived social support as a predictor of mortality in coronary patients: Effects of smoking, sedentary behavior, and depressive symptoms. *Psychosomatic Medicine, 67,* 40–45.

Brun, A. (2007). Identification and characterization of frontal lobe degeneration: Historical perspective on the development of FTD. *Alzheimer Disease & Associated Disorders, 21*(4), S3–S4.

Bruning, J. C., Gautam, D., Burks, D. J., Gillette, J., Schubert, M., Orban, P. C., & … Kahn, C. (2000). Role of Brain Insulin Receptor in Control of Body Weight and Reproduction. *Science, 289*(5487), 2122.

Bruno, M. A., Vanhaudenhuyse, A., Thibaut, A., Moonen, G., & Laureys, S. (2011). From unresponsive wakefulness to minimally conscious PLUS and functional locked-in syndromes: recent advances in our understanding of disorders of consciousness. *Journal of Neurology, 258*(7), 1373–1384.

Brush, D. H., Moch, M. K., & Pooyan, A. (1987). Individual demographic differences and job satisfaction. *Journal of Occupational Behaviour, 8,* 139–155.

Bryant, F. B., & Veroff, J. (2006). *The process of savoring: A new model of positive experience.* Mahwah, NJ: Erlbaum.

Bryant, J., & Cummins, R, G. (2010). The effects of outcome of mediated and live sporting events on sports fans' self- and social identities. In H. L. Hundley & A. Billings (Eds.), *Examining identity in sports media* (pp. 217–238). Thousand Oaks, CA: Sage.

Bryant, R. A., & Das, P. (2012). The neural circuitry of conversion disorder and its recovery. *Journal Of Abnormal Psychology, 121*(1), 289–296. doi:10.1037/a0025076.

Bryant, R. A., Felmingham, K. L., Falconer, E. M., Benito, L. P., Dobson-Stone, C., Pierce, K. D. (2010). Preliminary evidence of the short allele of the serotonin transporter gene predicting poor response to cognitive behavior therapy in posttraumatic stress disorder. *Biological Psychiatry, 67,* 1217–1219. doi:10.1016/j.biopsych.2010.03.016.

Bryant, R. A., & Guthrie, R. M. (2005). Maladaptive appraisals as a risk factor for posttraumatic stress. *Psychological Science, 16,* 749–752.

Bryant, R. A., & Mallard, D. (2003). Seeing is believing: The reality of hypnotic hallucinations. *Consciousness and Cognition, 12,* 219–230.

Bryant, R. A., & McConkey, K. M. (1989). Hypnotic blindness: A behavioral and experiential analysis. *Journal of Abnormal Psychology, 98,* 71–77.

Bryant, R. A., Moulds, M. L., Guthrie, R. M., Dang, S. T., Mastrodomenico, J., Nixon, R. D. V., et al. (2008). A randomized controlled trial of exposure therapy and cognitive restructuring for posttraumatic stress disorder. *Journal of Consulting and Clinical Psychology, 76,* 695–703.

Bryck, R. L., & Fisher, P. A. (2012). Training the brain: Practical applications of neural plasticity from the intersection of cognitive neuroscience, developmental psychology, and prevention science. *American Psychologist, 67*(2), 87–100. doi:10.1037/a0024657.

Buccino, G., Vogt, S., Ritzl, A., Fink, G. R., Zilles, K., Freund, H. J., et al. (2004). Neural circuits underlying imitation learning of hand actions: An event-related fMRI study. *Neuron, 42,* 323–334.

Buchman, A. S. Boyle, P. A., Yu, L., Shah, R. C., Wilson, R. S., & Bennett, D. A. (2012) Total daily physical activity and the risk of AD and cognitive decline in older adults. *Neurology, 78*(17), 1323–1329. doi:10.1212/WNL.0b013e3182535d35 Published online before print. Retrieved from http://www.neurology.org/content/78/17/1323.abstract?etoc.

Buchsbaum, M. S., Christian, B. T., Lehrer, D. S., Narayanan, T. K., Shi, B., et al. (2006). D2/D3 dopamine receptor binding with (F–18) fallypride in thalamus and cortex of patients with schizophrenia. *Schizophrenia Research, 85,* 232–244.

Buck, R. (2011). Communicative genes in the evolution of empathy and altruism. *Behavior Genetics, 41*(6), 876–888.

Budson, A. E. (2009). Understanding memory dysfunction. The Neurologist, 15, 71–79.

Buelow, M. T., & Frakey, L. L. (2013). Math anxiety differentially affects WAIS-IV arithmetic performance in undergraduates. *Archives of Clinical Neuropsychology, 28*(4), 356–362.

Bugental, D. B., & Grusec, J. E. (2006). Socialization processes. In W. Damon & R. M. Lerner (Series Eds.) & N. Eisenberg (Vol. Ed.), *Handbook of child psychology: Vol. 3. Social, emotional, and personality development* (6th ed.). New York: Wiley.

Bugg, J. M., & McDaniel, M. A. (2012). Selective benefits of question self-generation and answering for remembering expository text. *Journal of Educational Psychology,* doi:10.1037/a0028661

Bugg, J. M., Zook, N. A., DeLosh, E. L., Davalos, D. B., & Davis, H. P. (2006). Age differences in fluid intelligence: Contributions of general slowing and frontal decline. *Brain and Cognition, 62*(1), 9–16.

Buhle, J. T., Stevens, B., L., Friedman, J. J., & Wager, T. D. (2012). Distraction and placebo: Two separate routes to pain control. *Psychological Science.* doi:10.1177/0956797611427919.

Bui, K.-V. T., Peplau, L. A., & Hill, C. T. (1996). Testing the Rusbult model of relationship commitment and stability in a 15–year study of heterosexual couples. *Personality and Social Psychology Bulletin, 22,* 1244–1257.

Buka, S. L., Shenassa, E. D., & Niaura, R. (2003). Elevated risk of tobacco dependence among offspring of mothers who smoked during pregnancy: A 30–year prospective study. *American Journal of Psychiatry, 160,* 1978–1984.

Bulevich, J. B., Roediger, H. L., Balota, D. A., & Butler, A. C. (2006). Failures to find suppression of episodic memories in the think/no-think paradigm. *Memory and Cognition, 34,* 1569–1577.

Bulkeley, K., & Domhoff, G. W. (2010). Detecting meaning in dream reports: An extension of a word search approach. *Dreaming, 20*(2), 77–95.

Bulkeley, K., & Kahan, T. L. (2008). The impact of September 11 on dreaming. *Consciousness and Cognition, 17,* 1248–1256.

Bullough, V. L. (1995, August). Sex matters. *Scientific American,* 105–106.

Bulotsky-Shearer, R. J., Dominquez, X., & Bell, E. R. (2012). Preschool classroom behavioral context and school readiness outcomes for low-income children: A multilevel examination of child- and classroom-level influences. *Journal of Educational Psychology, 104,* 421.

Bunde, J., & Suls, J. (2006). A quantitative analysis of the relationship between the Cook-Medley hostility scale and traditional coronary artery disease risk factors. *Health Psychology, 25,* 493–500.

Burchard, R. E. (1992). Coca chewing and diet. *Current Anthropology, 33*(1), 1–24.

Burdakov, D., Karnani, M. M., & Gonzalez, A. (2013). Lateral hypothalamus as a sensor-regulator in respiratory and metabolic control. *Physiology & Behavior, 121,* 117–124.

Burger, J. M. (2009). Replicating Milgram: Would people still obey today? *American Psychologist, 64,* 1–11.

Burger, J. M., & Cornelius, T. (2003). Raising the price of agreement: Public commitment and the lowball compliance procedure. *Journal of Applied Social Psychology, 33,* 923–934.

Burgmer, M., Kugel, H., Pfleiderer, B., Ewert, A., Lenzen, T., Pioch, R., Pyka, M., Sommer, J., Arolt, V., Heuft, G., & Konrad, C. (2013). The mirror neuron system under hypnosis—brain substrates of voluntary and involuntary motor activation in hypnotic paralysis. *Cortex, 49*(2), 437–445.

Burke, C. J., Tobler, P. N., Baddeley, M., & Schultz, W. (2010). Neural mechanisms of observational learning. *Proceedings Of The National Academy Of Sciences Of The United States Of America, 107*(32), 14431–14436.

Burke, R. J., & Fiksenbaum, L. (2009). Work motivations, work outcomes, and health: Passion versus addiction. *Journal of Business Ethics, 84*(Suppl. 2), 257–263.

Burleson, B. R., Albrecht, T. L., & Sarason, I. G. (Eds.). (1994). *Communication of social support: Messages, interactions, relationships, and community.* Thousand Oaks, CA: Sage.

Burlingame, G. M., & Baldwin, S. (2011). Group therapy. In J. C. Norcross, G. R. VandenBos, & D. K. Freedheim (Eds.), *History of psychotherapy: Continuity and change* (pp. 505–515). Washington, D.C.: American Psychological Association.

Burlingame, G. M., Strauss, B., & Joyce, A. S. (2013). Change mechanisms and effectiveness of small group treatments. In M. J. Lambert (Ed.), *Bergin and Garfield's handbook of psychotherapy and behavior change* (pp. 640–689). Hoboken, NJ: Wiley.

Burnette, J. L., & Finkel, E. J. (2012). Buffering against weight gain following dieting setbacks: An implicit theory intervention. *Journal of Experimental Social Psychology, 48*(3), 721–725.

Burns, M. S., & Fahy, J. (2010). Broca's area: rethinking classical concepts from a neuroscience perspective. *Topics in Stroke Rehabilitation, 17*(6), 401–410.

Burstein, M., & Ginsburg, G. S. (2010). The effect of parental modeling of anxious behaviors and cognitions in school-aged children: An experimental pilot study. *Behaviour research and Therapy, 48*(6), 506–515. doi:10.1016/j.brat.2010.02.006.

Burt, S. A., McGue, M., & Iacono, W. G. (2009). Nonshared environmental mediation of the association between deviant peer affiliation and adolescent externalizing behaviors over time: Results from a cross-lagged monozygotic twin differences design. *Developmental Psychology, 45,* 1752–1760.

Burton, A. M., Wilson, S., Cowan, M., & Bruce, V. (1999). Face recognition in poor-quality video: Evidence from security surveillance. *Psychological Science, 10,* 243–248.

Burton, K. D., Lydon, J. E., D'Alessandro, D. U., & Koestner, R. (2006). The differential effects of intrinsic and identified motivation on well-being and performance: Prospective, experimental, and implicit approaches to self-determination theory. *Journal of Personality and Social Psychology, 91,* 750–762.

Busatto, G. F. (2013). Structural and functional neuroimaging studies in major depressive disorder with psychotic features: A critical review. *Schizophrenia Bulletin, 39*(4), 776–786.

Bushdid, C., Magnasco, M. O., Vosshall, L. B., & Keller, A. (2014). Humans can discriminate more than 1 trillion olfactory stimuli. *Science, 343*(6177), 1370–1372.

Bushman, B., & Bartholow, B. D. (2010). Aggression In R. Baumeister & E. Finkel (Eds.) *Advanced social psychology: The state of the science* (pp. 303–340). New York: Oxford.

Bushman, B. J. (1998). Priming effects of media violence on the accessibility of aggressive constructs in memory. *Personality and Social Psychology Bulletin, 24,* 537–545.

Bushman, B. J., & Anderson, C. A. (2007). Measuring the strength of the effect of violent media on aggression. *American Psychologist, 62,* 253–254.

Bushman, B. J., & Anderson, C. A. (2009). Comfortably numb: Desensitizing effects of violent media on helping others. *Psychological Science, 20,* 273–277.

Bushman, B. J., Bonacci, A. M., Pedersen, W. C., Vasquez, E. A., & Miller, N. (2005). Chewing on it can chew you up: Effects of rumination on triggered displaced aggression. *Journal of Personality and Social Psychology, 88,* 969–983.

Bushman, B. J., DeWall, C. N., Pond, R. S., & Hanus, M. D. (2014). Low glucose relates to greater aggression in married couples. *Proceedings of the National Academy of Sciences,* Epub April 14, 2014.

Bushman, B. J., & Gibson, B. (2011). Violent video games cause an increase in aggression long after the game has been turned off. *Social Psychological and Personality Science, 2*(1), 29–32.

Bushman, B. J., & Huesmann, L. R. (2010). Aggression. In S. T. Fiske, D. T. Gilbert, & G. Lindzey (Eds.), *Handbook of social psychology* (5th ed., Vol. 2, pp. 833–863). Hoboken, NJ: Wiley.

Bushman, B. J., & Huesmann, L.R. (2014). Twenty-five years of research on violence in digital games and aggression: A reply to Elson and Ferguson. *European Psychologist. 19*(1), 47–55.

Bushman, B. J., & Huesmann, L. (2014). Twenty-five years of research on violence in digital games and aggression revisited: A reply to Elson and Ferguson (2013). *European Psychologist, 19*(1), 47–55.

Bushman, B. J., Wang, M. C., & Anderson, C. A. (2005). Is the curve relating temperature to aggression linear or curvilinear? Assaults and temperature in Minneapolis reexamined. *Journal of Personality and Social Psychology, 89,* 62–66.

Buss, A. H. (1989). Personality as traits. *American Psychologist, 44,* 1378–1388.

Buss, A. H. (1997). Evolutionary perspectives on personality traits. In R. Hogan, J. Johnson, & S. Briggs (Eds.), *Handbook of personality psychology* (pp. 345–366). San Diego: Academic Press.

Buss, D. M. (2004a). *Evolutionary psychology: The new science of the mind* (2nd ed.). Boston: Allyn & Bacon.

Buss, D. M. (2004b). *The evolution of desire: Strategies of human mating.* New York: Basic Books.

Buss, D. M. (2008). *Evolutionary psychology: The new science of the mind* (3rd ed.). Boston: Allyn & Bacon.

Buss, D. M. (2009). The great struggles of life: Darwin and the emergence of evolutionary psychology. *American Psychologist, 64,* 140–148.

Buss, D. M. (2013). The science of human mating strategies: An historical perspective. *Psychological Inquiry, 24*(3), 171–177.

Buss, D. M., Abbott, M., Angleitner, A., Biaggio, A., et al. (1990). International preferences in selecting mates. *Journal of Cross-Cultural Psychology, 21,* 5–47.

Buss, D. M., & Schmitt, D. P. (1993). Sexual strategies theory: An evolutionary perspective on human mating. *Psychological Review, 100,* 204–232.

Büssing, A., & Höge, A. (2004). Aggression and violence against home care workers. *Journal of Occupational Health Psychology, 9,* 206–219.

Butcher, J. N. (2004). Personality assessment without borders: Adaptation of the MMPI-2 across cultures. *Journal of Personality Assessment, 83*(2), 90–104.

Butcher, J. N. (2006). *MMPI-2: A practitioner's guide.* Washington, DC: American Psychological Association.

Butcher, J. N., Mineka, S., & Hooley, J. M. (2010). *Abnormal psychology* (14th ed.). Boston: Allyn & Bacon.

Butler, A. C., Chapman, J. E., Forman, E. M., & Beck, A. T. (2006). The empirical status of cognitive-behavioral therapy: A review of meta-analyses. *Clinical Psychology Review, 26,* 17–31.

Butler, R. (1998). Information seeking and achievement motivation in middle childhood and adolescence: The role of conceptions of ability. *Developmental Psychology, 35,* 146–163.

Butt, M. S., & Sultan, M. T. (2011). Coffee and its consumption: benefits and risks. *Critical Reviews in Food Science and Nutrition,* 51(4), 363–373.

Butters, N. (1981). The Wernicke-Korsakoff syndrome: A review of psychological, neuropathological and etiological factors. *Currents in Alcohol, 8,* 205–232.

Buunk, A. P., Peiró, J. M., & Griffioen, C. (2007). A positive role model may stimulate career-oriented behavior. *Journal of Applied Social Psychology, 37,* 1489–1500.

Buxhoeveden, D. P., Switala, A. E., Roy, E., Litaker, M., & Casanova, M. F. (2001). Morphological differences between minicolumns in human and nonhuman primate cortex. *American Journal of Physical Anthropology, 115,* 361–371.

Byron, K., & Khazanchi, S. (2012). Rewards and creative performance: A meta-analytic test of theoretically derived hypotheses. *Psychological Bulletin, 138*(4), 809–830. doi:10.1037/a0027652.

Bystrova, K., Ivanova, V., Edhborg, M., Matthiesen, A. S., Ransjö-Arvidson, A. B., Mukhamedrakhimov, R., Uvnäs-Moberg, K., & Widström, A. M. (2009). Early contact versus separation: Effects on mother-infant interaction one year later. *Birth, 36,* 97–109.

Cabanac, M., & Morrissette, J. (1992). Acute, but not chronic, exercise lowers the body weight set-point in male rats. *Physiology and Behavior, 52*(6), 1173–1177.

Cabot, P. J. (2001). Immune-derived opioids and peripheral antinociception. *Clinical and Experimental Pharmacology and Physiology, 28,* 230–232.

Cabral, R. R., & Smith, T. B. (2011). Racial/ethnic matching of clients and therapists in mental health services: A meta-analytic review of preferences, perceptions, and outcomes. *Journal of Counseling Psychology, 58*(4), 537–554. doi:10.1037/a0025266.

Cacioppo, J. T., Berntson, G. G., Sheridan, J. F., & McClintock, M. K. (2000). Multilevel integrative analyses of human behavior: Social neuroscience and the complementing nature of social and biological approaches. *Psychological Bulletin, 126,* 829–843.

Cacioppo, J. T., & Decety, J. (2009). What are the brain mechanisms on which psychological processes are based? *Perspectives on Psychological Science, 4,* 10–18.

Cacioppo, J. T., Petty, R. E., & Crites, S. L. (1993). Attitude change. In V. S. Ramachandran (Ed.), *Encyclopedia of human behavior* (pp. 261–270). San Diego: Academic Press.

Cacioppo, J. T., Poehlmann, K. M., Kiecolt-Glaser, J. K., Malarkey, W. B., Burleson, M. H., Berntson, G. G., & Glaser, R. (1998). Cellular immune responses to acute stress in female caregivers of dementia patients and matched controls. *Health Psychology, 17,* 182–189.

Cacioppo, J. T., Reis, H. T., & Zautra, A. J. (2011). Social resilience: The value of social fitness with an application to the military. *American Psychologist, 66*(1), 43–51. doi:10.1037/a0021419.

Cadinu, M., Maass, A., Rosabianca, A., & Kiesner, J. (2005). Why do women underperform under stereotype threat? *Psychological Science, 16,* 572–578.

Cadoni, C., Simola, N., Espa, E., Fenu, S., & Di Chiara, G. (2013). Strain dependence of adolescent Cannabis influence on heroin reward and mesolimbic dopamine transmission in adult Lewis and Fischer 344 rats. *Addiction Biology,* Epub August 20, 2013.

Cadoret, R. J., Yates, W. R., Troughton, E., Woodworth, G., & Stewart, M. A. (1995). Adoption study demonstrating two genetic pathways to drug abuse. *Archives of General Psychiatry, 52,* 42–52.

Caetano, R. (2011). There is potential for cultural and social bias in DSM-V. *Addiction, 106*(5), 885–887. doi:10.1111/j.1360-0443.2010.03308.x.

Caggiano, V., Fogassi, L., Rizzolatti, G., Thier, P., & Casile, A. (2009). Mirror neurons differentially encode the peripersonal and extrapersonal space of monkeys. *Science, 324,* 403–406.

Cahill, S. P., Carrigan, M. H., & Frueh, B. C. (1999). Does EMDR work? And if so, why?: A critical review of controlled outcome and dismantling research. *Journal of Anxiety Disorders, 13,* 5–33.

Cahn, B. R., & Polich, J. (2006). Meditation states and traits, EEG, ERP, and neuroimaging studies. *Psychological Bulletin, 132,* 180–211.

Cai, D. J., Mednick, S. A., Harrison, E. M., Kanady, J. C., & Mednick, S. C. (2009). REM, not incubation, improves creativity by priming associative networks. *Proceedings of the National Academy of Sciences, 106,* 10130–10134.

Cain, C. K., McCue, M., Bello, I., Creedon, T., Tang, D. I., Laska, E., & Goff, D. C. (2014). d-Cycloserine augmentation of cognitive remediation in schizophrenia. *Schizophrenia Research, 153*(1–3), 177–183.

Cain, D. J., & Seeman, J. (Eds.). (2002). *Humanistic psychotherapies: Handbook of research and practice.* Washington, DC: APA Books.

Caldwell, C. A., & Millen, A. E. (2009). Social learning mechanisms and cumulative cultural evolution: Is imitation necessary? *Psychological Science, 20,* 1478–1483.

Caldwell, J. A. (2012). Crew schedules, sleep deprivation, and aviation performance. *Current Directions in Psychological Science, 21*(2), 85–89. doi:10.1177/ 0963721411435842

Caldwell, T. L., Cervone, D., & Rubin, L. H. (2008). Explaining intra-individual variability in social behavior through idiographic assessment: The case of humor. *Journal of Research in Personality 42,* 1229–1242.

Callahan, C. M. (2011). The "multiples" of Howard Gardner, Joseph Renzulli, and Robert Sternberg. *Gifted Child Quarterly, 55*(4), 300–301. doi:10.1177/0016986211421871.

Callen, D. J. A., Black, S. E., Gao, F., Caldwell, C. B., & Szalai, J. P. (2001). Beyond the hippocampus: MRI volumetry confirms widespread limbic atrophy in AD. *Neurology, 57,* 1669–1674.

Calvin, C. M., Batty, G., Lowe, G. O., & Deary, I. J. (2011). Childhood intelligence and midlife inflammatory and hemostatic biomarkers: The National Child Development Study (1958) cohort. *Health Psychology, 30*(6), 710–718. doi:10.1037/a0023940.

Cameron, J. (2001). Negative effects of reward on intrinsic motivation: A limited phenomenon: Comment on Deci, Koestner, and Ryan. *Review of Educational Research, 71,* 29–42.

Campbell, F. A., Pungello, E. P., Burchinal, M., Kainz, K., Pan, Y., Wasik, B. H., Barbarin, O. A., Sparling, J. J., & Ramey, C. T. (2012). Adult outcomes as a function of an early childhood educational program: An Abecedarian Project follow-up. *Developmental Psychology, 48,* 1033–1043. doi:10.1037/a0026644

Campbell, F. A., Pungello, E. P., Miller-Johnson, S., Burchinal, M., & Ramey, C. T. (2001). The development of cognitive and academic abilities: Growth curves from an early childhood educational experiment. *Developmental Psychology, 37,* 231–242.

Campbell, K. L, Hasher, L., & Thomas, R. C. (2010). Hyper-binding: A unique age effect. *Psychological Science, 21,* 399–405. doi:10.1177/0956797609359910.

Campbell, L., Simpson, J. A., Boldry, J., & Kashy, D. A. (2005). Perceptions of conflict and support in romantic relationships: The role of attachment anxiety. *Journal of Personality and Social Psychology, 88,* 510–531.

Campbell, L., Vasquez, M., Behnke, S., & Kinscherff, R. (2009). *APA ethics code commentary and case illustrations.* Washington, DC: American Psychological Association.

Campbell, R., & Capek, C. (2008). Seeing speech and seeing sign: Insights from a fMRI study. *International Journal of Audiology, 47*(Suppl. 2), S3–S9.

Campbell, R. S., & Pennebaker, J. W. (2003). The secret life of pronouns: Flexibility in writing style and physical health. *Psychological Science, 14,* 60–65.

Campbell, S. B. (1986). Developmental issues. In R. Gittelman (Ed.), *Anxiety disorders of childhood* (pp. 24–57) New York: Guilford Press.

Campion, M. A., & Campion, J. E. (1987). Evaluation of an interviewee skills training program in a natural field experiment. *Personnel Psychology, 40,* 676–691.

Campion, M. A., Palmer, D. K., & Campion, J. E. (1997). A review of structure in the selection interview. *Personnel Psychology, 50,* 655–702.

Campione, J. C., Brown, A. L., & Ferrara, R. A. (1982). Mental retardation and intelligence. In R. J. Sternberg (Ed.), *Handbook of human intelligence* (pp. 392–490). Cambridge: Cambridge University Press.

Campitelli, G., & Gobet, F. (2008). The role of practice in chess: A longitudinal study. *Learning & Individual Differences, 18*(4), 446–458. doi:10.1016/j.lindif.2007.11.006.

Campos, J. J. (1980). Human emotions: Their new importance and their role in social referencing. *Research and Clinical Center for Child Development, 1980–81 Annual Report,* 1–7.

Campos, L., & Alonso-Quecuty, M. L. (2006). Remembering a criminal conversation: Beyond eyewitness testimony. *Memory, 14,* 27–36.

Canaris, J. (2008). An analysis of the efficacy of extinction as an intervention in the modification of switching in patients with dissociative identity disorder. *Disseration Abstracts International: Section B: Sciences and Engineering,* p. 3255.

Canli, T., Qui, M., Omura, K., Congdon, E., Haas, B. W., Amin, Z., et al. (2006). Neural correlates of epigenesist. *Proceedings of the National Academy of Sciences, 103,* 16033–16038.

Cann, A., & Ross, D. A. (1989). Olfactory stimuli as context cues in human memory. *American Journal of Psychology, 102,* 91–102.

Cannon, W. B. (1927). *Bodily changes in pain, hunger, fear and rage—An account of recent researches into the function of emotional excitement.* New York: Appleton.

Cannon, W. B., & Washburn, A. L. (1912). An explanation of hunger. *American Journal of Physiology, 29,* 444–454.

Caparos, S., Ahmed, L., Bremner, A. J., de Fockert, J. W., Linnell, K. J., & Davidoff, J. (2012). Exposure to an urban environment alters the local bias of a remote culture. *Cognition, 122*(1), 80–85. doi:10.1016/j.cognition.2011.08.013.

Capasso, R., Izzo, A. A. (2008). Gastrointestinal regulation of food intake: General aspects and focus on anandamide and oleoylethanolamide. *Journal of Neuroendocrinology, 20*(Suppl. 1), 39–46.

Capgras, J., & Reboul-Lachaux, J. (1923). Illusion des << sosies >> dans un delire systematise chronique ["Doppelganger" delusion in chronic persistent delirium]. *Bulletin de la Société Clinique de Médecine Mentale, 2,* 6–16.

Caplan, D. (2003a). Aphasic syndromes. In K. M. Heilman & E. Valenstein (Eds.), *Clinical neuropsychology* (4th ed.). New York: Oxford.

Caplan, D. (2003b). Syntactic aspects of language disorders. In K. M. Heilman & E. Valenstein (Eds.), *Clinical neuropsychology* (4th ed.). New York: Oxford University Press.

Cappella, E., Hamre, B. K., Kim, H. Y., Henry, D. B., Frazier, S. L., Atkins, M. S., & Schoenwald, S. K. (2012). Teacher consultation and coaching within mental health practice: Classroom and child effects in urban elementary schools. *Journal of Consulting and Clinical Psychology.* doi:10.1037/a0027725.

Capron, C., & Duyme, M. (1989). Assessment of effects of socio-economic status on IQ in a full cross-fostering study. *Nature, 340,* 552–553.

Capron, C., & Duyme, M. (1996). Effect of socioeconomic status of biological and adoptive parents on WISC-R subtest scores of their French adopted children. *Intelligence, 22,* 259–276.

Caputo, M., Monastero, R., Mariani, E., Santucci, A., Mangialasche, F., Camarda, R., Senin, U., & Mecocci, P. (2008). Neuropsychiatric symptoms in 921 elderly subjects with dementia: a comparison between vascular and neurodegenerative types. *Acta Psychiatrica Scandinavica, 117*(6), 455–464.

Carasatorre, M., & Ramírez-Amaya, V. (2013). Network, cellular, and molecular mechanisms underlying long-term memory formation. *Current Topics in Behavioral Neuroscience, 15,* 73–115.

Card, N. A., Stucky, B. D., Sawalani, G. M., & Little, T. D. (2008). Direct and indirect aggression during childhood and adolescence: A meta-analytic review of gender differences, intercorrelations, and relations to maladjustment. *Child Development, 79,* 1185–1229.

Cardemil, E. V., Reivich, K. J., & Seligman, M. E. P. (2002). The prevention of depressive symptoms in low-income minority middle school students [Electronic version.] *Prevention and Treatment, 5,* art. 8.

Cardon, L. R., & Fulker, D. W. (1993). Genetics of specific cognitive abilities. In R. Plomin & G. McClearn (Eds.), *Nature, nurture, and psychology* (pp. 99–120). Washington, DC: American Psychological Association.

Cardon, L. R., Fulker, D. W., DeFries, J. C., & Plomin, R. (1992). Multivariate genetic analysis of specific cognitive abilities in the Colorado Adoption Project at age 7. *Intelligence, 16,* 383–400.

Carducci, B. (2009). *The psychology of personality.* Malden, MA: Wiley-Blackwell.

Cardwell, M. S. (2013). Video media-induced aggressiveness in children. *Southern Medical Journal, 106*(9), 513–517.

Carels, R. A., Young, K. M., Coit, C., Clayton, A. M., Spencer, A., & Hobbs, M. (2008). Can following the caloric restriction recommendations from the Dietary Guidelines for Americans help individuals lose weight? *Eating Behaviors, 9,* 328–335.

Carey, I. M., Shah, S. M., Dewilde, S., Harris, T., Victor, C. R., & Cook, D. G. (2014). Increased Risk of Acute Cardiovascular Events After Partner Bereavement: A Matched Cohort Study. *JAMA Internal Medicine,* Epub February 24, 2014.

Carey, S. (2009). *The origin of concepts.* New York: Oxford University Press.

Carlbring, P., & Smit, F. (2008). Randomized trial of Internet-delivered self-help with telephone support for pathological gamblers. *Journal of Consulting and Clinical Psychology, 76,* 1090–1094.

Carli, L. L. (1999). Cognitive reconstruction, hindsight, and reactions to victims and perpetrators. *Personality and Social Psychology Bulletin, 25,* 966–979.

Carlson, J., Watts, R. E., & Maniacci, M. (2006). Play therapy. In J. Carlson, R. E. Watts, & M. Maniacci (Eds.), *Adlerian therapy: Theory and practice* (pp. 227–248). Washington, DC: American Psychological Association.

Carlston, D. (2010). Social cognition. In R. Baumeister & E. Finkel (Eds.) *Advanced social psychology: The state of the science* (pp. 63–99). New York: Oxford.

Carmichael, L. L., Hogan, H. P., & Walter, A. A. (1932). An experimental study of the effect of language on the reproduction of visually perceived form. *Journal of Experimental Psychology, 15,* 73–86.

Carpenter, J. T. (2004). EMDR as an integrative psychotherapy approach: Experts explore the paradigm prism. *Psychotherapy Research, 14,* 135–136.

Carr, A. (2009). The effectiveness of family therapy and systemic interventions for child-focused problems. *Journal of Family Therapy, 31,* 3–45.

Carraher, T. N., Carraher, D., & Schliemann, A. D. (1985). Mathematics in the streets and in the schools. *British Journal of Developmental Psychology, 3,* 21–29.

Carré, J. M., Murphy, K. R., & Hariri, A. R. (2013). What lies beneath the face of aggression? *Social Cognitive and Affective Neuroscience, 8*(2), 224–229.

Carrington, D. (2010). Insects could be the key to meeting food needs of growing global population. *The Observer,* July 31, 2010.

Carroll, J. B. (1993). *Human cognitive abilities: A survey of factor-analytic studies.* New York: Cambridge University Press.

Carson, D., & Bull, R. (Eds.). (2003). *Handbook of psychology in legal contexts* (2nd ed.). Hoboken, NJ: Wiley.

Carson, K. V., Brinn, M. P., Robertson, T. A., To-A-Nan, R., Esterman, A. J., Peters, M., & Smith, B. J. (2013). Current and emerging pharmacotherapeutic options for smoking cessation. *Substance Abuse, 7*, 85–105.

Carstensen, L. (1997, August). *Psychology and the aging revolution: Changes in social needs and social goals across the lifespan.* Paper presented at the annual convention of the American Psychological Association.

Carstensen, L. L.,Turan, B., Scheibe, S., Ram, N., Ersner-Hershfield, H., Samanez-Larkin, G. R. Brooks, K. P., & Nesselroade, J. R. (2011). Emotional experience improves with age: Evidence based on over 10 years of experience sampling. *Psychology and Aging, 26*, 21–33.

Carter, D. R., & DeChurch, L. A. (2012). Networks: The way forward for collectivistic leadership research. *Industrial and Organizational Psychology: Perspectives on Science and Practice, 5*, 412–415.

Carter, G. L., Campbell, A. C., & Muncer, S. (2014). The dark triad personality: Attractiveness to women. *Personality and Individual Differences, 56*, 57–61.

Carter, L. P., Richards, B. D., Mintzer, M. Z., & Griffiths, R. R. (2006). Relative abuse liability of GHB in humans: A comparison of psychomotor, subjective, and cognitive effects of supratherapeutic doses of triazolam, pentobarbital, and GHB. *Neuropsychopharmacology, 31*(11), 2537–2551.

Carter, N. T., Dalal, D. K., Boyce, A. S., O'Connell, M. S., Kung, M.-C., & Delgado, K. (2013). Uncovering curvilinear relationships between conscientiousness and job performance: How theoretically appropriate measurement makes an empirical difference. *Journal of Applied Psychology*, Epub November 4, 2013.

Carter, S. E. (2014). Oxycotin pathways and the evolution of human behavior. *Annual Review of Psychology, 65*, 17–39.

Cartwright, R. D. (1993). Who needs their dreams? The usefulness of dreams in psychotherapy. *Journal of the American Academy of Psychoanalysis, 21*(4), 539–547.

Carver, C., & Scheier, M. F. (2012). *Perspectives on personality* (7th ed.). Upper Saddle River, NJ: Pearson Education.

Carver, C. S., & Connor-Smith, J. (2010). Personality and coping. *Annual Review of Psychology,61*, 679–704.

Carver, C. S., & Harmon-Jones, E. (2009). Anger is an approach-related aff ect: Evidence and implications. *Psychological Bulletin, 135*, 183–204.

Carver, C. S., Johnson, S. L., & Joormann, J. (2008). Serotonergic function, two-mode models of self-regulation, and vulnerability to depression: What depression has in common with impulsive aggression. *Psychological Bulletin, 134*, 912–943.

Carver, C. S., Johnson, S. L., Joormann, J., Kim, Y., & Nam, J. Y. (2011). Serotonin transporter polymorphism interacts with childhood adversity to predict aspects of impulsivity. *Psychological Science, 22*, 589–595.

Casbon, T. S., Curtin, J. J., Lang, A. R., & Patrick, C. J. (2003). Deleterious effects of alcohol intoxication: Diminished cognitive control and its behavioral consequences. *Journal of Abnormal Psychology, 112*, 476–487.

Case, B. G., Bertollo D. N., Laska, E. M., Price, L. H., Siegel, C. E., Olfson, M., & Marcus, S. C. (2013). Declining use of electroconvulsive therapy in United States general hospitals. *Biological Psychiatry, 73*(2), 119–126.

Case, L., & Smith, T. B. (2000). Ethnic representation in a sample of the literature of applied psychology. *Journal of Consulting and Clinical Psychology, 68*, 1107–1110.

Casey, B. J., Galvan, A., & Hare, T. A. (2005). Changes in cerebral functional organization during cognitive development. *Current Opinion in Neurobiology, 15*, 239–244.

Caspi, A., Bem, D. J., & Elder, G. H., Jr. (1989). Continuities and consequences of interactional styles across the life course. *Journal of Personality, 57*, 375–406.

Caspi, A., Elder, G. H., & Bem, D. J. (1988). Moving away from the world: Life-course patterns of shy children. *Developmental Psychology, 24*, 824–831.

Caspi, A., Harrington, H., Milne, B., Amell, J. W., Theodore, R. F., & Moffitt, T. E. (2003). Children's behavioral styles at age 3 are linked to their adult personality traits at age 26. *Journal of Personality, 71*, 495–513.

Caspi, A., Henry, B., McGee, R. O., Moffitt, T. E., & Silva, P. A. (1995). Temperamental origins of child and adolescent behavior problems: From age 3 to Age 15. *Child Development, 66*, 55–68.

Caspi, A., Houts, R. M., Belsky, D. W., Goldman-Mellor, S. J., Harrington, H. Israel, S., . . . & Moffitt, T. E. (2014). The p factor: One general psychopathology factor in the structure of psychiatric disorders? *Clinical Psychological Science, 2*, 119–137.

Caspi, A., McClay, J., Moffitt, T. E., Mill, J., Martin, J., Craig, I. W., et al. (2002). Role of genotype in the cycle of violence in maltreated children. *Science, 297*, 851–854.

Caspi, A., Moffitt, T. E., Morgan, J., Rutter, M., Taylor, A., Arseneault, L., et al. (2004). Maternal expressed emotion predicts children's antisocial behavior problems: Using monozygotic-twin differences to identify environmental effects on behavioral development. *Developmental Psychology, 40*, 149–161.

Caspi, A., Roberts, B. W., & Shiner, R. L. (2005). Personality development: Stability and change. *Annual Review of Psychology, 56*, 453–484.

Caspi, A., & Shiner, R. L. (2006). Personality development. In W. Damon & R. M. Lerner (Series Eds.) & N. Eisenberg (Vol. Ed.), *Handbook of child psychology: Vol. 3. Social, emotional, and personality development* (6th ed., pp. 300–365). New York: Wiley.

Caspi, A., & Silva, P. A. (1995). Temperamental qualities at age 3 predict personality traits in young adulthood: Longitudinal evidence from a birth cohort. *Child Development, 66*, 468–498.

Caspi, A., Sugden, K., Moffitt, T. E., Taylor, A., Craig, I. W., Harrington, H., et al. (2003). Influence of life stress on depression: Moderation by a polymorphism in the 5-HTT gene. *Science, 301*, 386–389.

Cassel, E., & Bernstein, D. A. (2007). *Criminal behavior* (2nd ed.). Mahwah, NJ: Erlbaum.

Cassia, V. M., Valenza, E., Simion, F., & Leo, I. (2008). Congruency as a non-specific perceptual property contributing to newborns' face preference. *Child Development, 79*(4), 807–820.

Cassidy, J. (2008). The nature of the child's ties. In J. Cassidy & P. R. Shaver (Eds.), *Handbook of attachment: Theory, research, and clinical applications* (2nd ed., pp. 3–22). New York: Guilford Press.

Castelli, J. (2009). Life after MPD/DID: An article on multiple personality disorder and child abuse. *Mental Health Matters.* Retrieved from http://www.mental-health -matters. com/index.php?option=com_content&view=article&id=364: life-after -mpddid-anarticle-on-multiple-personality-disorder-and-child- abuse&catid=77 :dissociativeidentity&Itemid=2086.

Castelli, L., Zogmaister, C., & Tomelleri, S. (2009). Th e transmission of racial attitudes within the family. *Developmental Psychology, 45*, 586–591.

Castro, L., & Toro, M. A. (2004).The evolution of culture: From primate social learning to human culture. *Proceedings of the National Academy of Sciences, 101*, 10235–10240.

Cattell, R. B., Eber, H. W., & Tatsuoka, M. (1970). *Handbook for the sixteen personality factor questionnaire (16PF).* Champaign, IL: Institute for Personality Testing.

Cavaiola, A. A., & Desordi, E. G. (2000). Locus of control in drinking driving offenders and nonoffenders. *Alcoholism Treatment Quarterly, 18*, 63–73.

Cavanna, A. E., Shah, S., Eddy, C. M., Williams, A., & Rickards, H. (2011). Consciousness: A neurological perspective. *Behavioural Neurology, 24*(1), 107–116.

Caylak, E. (2009). Th e genetics of sleep disorders in humans: Narcolepsy, restless legs syndrome, and obstructive sleep apnea syndrome. *American Journal of Medical Genetics A, 149A*, 2612–2626.

Ceci, S. J., Huffman, M. L. C., Smith, E., & Loftus, E. F. (1994). Repeatedly thinking about a non-event: Source misattributions among preschoolers. *Consciousness and Cognition, 3*, 388–407.

Ceci, S. J., & Liker, J. K. (1986). A day at the races: A study of IQ, expertise, and cognitive complexity. *Journal of Experimental Psychology: General, 115*, 255–266.

Centers for Disease Control and Prevention. (1999b). *Suicide deaths and rates per 100,000.* Retrieved December 7, 2004, from http://www.cdc.gov/ncipc/data /us9794/suic.htm.

Centers for Disease Control and Prevention. (2002a). *Suicide and self-inflicted injury.* Retrieved June 30, 2009, from http://www.cdc.gov/nchs/fastats/suicide.htm.

Centers for Disease Control and Prevention. (2004). Web-based injury statistics query and reporting system (WISQARS). Retrieved December 7, 2004, from http:// www.cdc.gov/ ncipc/wisquars.

Centers for Disease Control and Prevention. (2006). WISQARS website and "Fatal Injury Reports." Retrieved February 8, 2006, from http://www.cdc.gov/ncipc/wisqars/.

Centers for Disease Control and Prevention. (2008). Deaths: Final Data for 2005. *National Vital Statistics Reports, 56*, 1–121.

Centers for Disease Control and Prevention. (2009a). *Preventing teen pregnancy: An update in 2009.* Retrieved from http://www.cdc.gov/reproductivehealth /AdolescentReproHealth/AboutTP.htm#b.

Centers for Disease Control and Prevention. (2009b). Preventing teen pregnancy: An update in 2009. Retrieved June 10, 2009, from http://www.cdc.gov / reproductivehealth/AdolescentReproHealth/AboutTP.htm#b.

Centers for Disease Control and Prevention. (2010). Trends in the prevalence of sexual behaviors: National Youth Risk Behavior Survey: 1991–2009. Retrieved September 14, 2012 from http://www.cdc.gov/healthyyouth/yrbs/pdf/us_ sexual_trend_yrbs.pdf

Centers for Disease Control and Prevention. (2011a). Quitting smoking among adults—United States, 2001–2010. *Morbidity and Mortality Weekly, 60*, 1513–1519.

Centers for Disease Control And Prevention. (2011b). Drug Overdose Deaths—Florida, 2003–2009. *Morbidity and Mortality Weekly Report, 60*, 869–905.

Centers for Disease Control and Prevention. (2012). Youth suicide. Retrieved July 24, 2012 from http://www.cdc.gov/violenceprevention/pub/youth_suicide.html on July 24, 2012.

Centers for Disease Control and Prevention. (2014a). Overweight and obesity. http:// www.cdc.gov/obesity/data/facts.html. Updated April 24, 2014.

Centers for Disease Control and Prevention. (2014b). Suicide: Consequences. Retrieved from http://www.cdc.gov/violenceprevention/suicide/consequences.html

Centerwall, L. (1990). Controlled TV viewing and suicide in countries: Young adult suicide and exposure to television. *Social Psychiatry and Social Epidemiology, 25,* 149–153.

Cepeda, N. J., Coburn, N., Rohrer, D., Wixted, J. T., Mozer, M. C., & Pashler, H. (2009). Optimizing distributed practice: Theoretical analysis and practical implications. *Experimental Psychology, 56*(4), 236–246. doi:10.1027/1618-3169.56.4.236

Ceranoglu, T. (2010a). Star Wars in psychotherapy: Video games in the office. *Academic Psychiatry: The Journal of the American Association of Directors of Psychiatric Residency Training and the Association for Academic Psychiatry, 34*(3), 233–236.

Ceranoglu, T. (2010b). Video games in psychotherapy. *Review of General Psychology, 14*(2), 141–146. doi:10.1037/a0019439.

Cervone, D. (2005). Personality architecture: Within-person structures and processes. *Annual Review of Psychology, 56,* 423–452.

Cervone, D., & Pervin, L. (2010). *Personality: Theory and research.* (11th ed). Danvers, MA: Wiley.

Cervone, D., & Pervin, L. A. (2013). *Personality: Theory and Research* (12th ed.). Hoboken, NJ: Wiley.

Cha, J. H., Farrell, L. A., Ahmed, S. F., Frey, A., Hsiao-Ashe, K. K., Young, A. B., et al. (2001). Glutamate receptor dysregulation in the hippocampus of transgenic mice carrying mutated human amyloid precursor protein. *Neurobiological Disorders, 8,* 90–102.

Chaker, S., Hofmann, S. G., & Hoyer, J. (2010). Can a one-weekend group therapy reduce fear of blushing? Results of an open trial. *Anxiety, Stress & Coping, 23*(3), 303–318. doi:10.1080/10615800903075132.

Challen, A. R., Machin, S. J., & Gillham, J. E. (2014). The UK Resilience Programme: A school-based universal nonrandomized pragmatic controlled trial. *The Journal of Consulting and Clinical Psychology, 82*(1), 75–89.

Chamberlin, J. (2000). Easing children's psychological distress in the emergency room. *Monitor on Psychology, 31,* 40–42.

Chambless, D. L., & Hollon, S. D. (1998). Defining empirically supported therapies. *Journal of Consulting and Clinical Psychology, 66,* 7–18.

Chambless, D. L., & Ollendick, T. H. (2001). Empirically supported psychological treatments. *Annual Review of Psychology, 52,* 685–716.

Champagne, F. A. (2009). Beyond nature vs. nurture: Philosophic insights from molecular biology. *Association for Psychological Science Observer, 22*(3), 27–28.

Champagne, F. A. (2010). Early adversity and developmental outcomes: Interaction between genetics, epigenetics, and social experiences across the life span. *Perspectives on Psychological Science, 5*(5), 564–574. doi:10.1177/1745691610383494.

Champagne, F. A., & Mashoodh, R. (2009). Genes in context: Gene-environment interplay and the origins of individual diff erences in behavior. *Current Directions in Psychological Science, 18,* 127–131.

Chan, D. (2005). Current directions in personnel selection research. *Current Directions in Psychological Science, 14,* 220–223.

Chan, J. C. K., Thomas, A. K., & Bulevich, J. B. (2009). Recalling a witnessed event increases eyewitness suggestibility: The reversed testing effect. *Psychological Science, 20,* 66–73.

Chan, M., Chen, E, Hibbert, A. S., Wong, J. H. K., Miller, G. E. (2011). Implicit measures of early-life family conditions: relationships to psychosocial characteristics and cardiovascular disease risk in adulthood. *Health Psychology, 30,* 570–578.

Chance, P. (2009). *Learning and behavior* (6th ed.). Belmont, CA: Wadsworth.

Chandler, J. J., & Pronin, E. (2012). Fast thought speed induces risk taking. *Psychological Science, 23*(4), 370–374. doi:10.1177/0956797611431464.

Chandola, T., Brunner, E., & Marmot, M. (2006). Chronic stress at work and the metabolic syndrome: Prospective study. *British Medical Journal, 332,* 521–525.

Chandra, A., Martino, S., Collins, R., Elliott, M., et al. (2008). Does watching sex on television predict teen pregnancy? Findings from a national longitudinal survey of youth. *Pediatrics, 122,* 1047–1054.

Chandrashekar, J., Hoon, M. A., Ryba, N. J., & Zuker, C. S. (2006). The receptors and cells for mammalian taste. *Nature, 444*(7117), 288–294.

Chang, E. F., & Merzenich, M. M. (2003). Environmental noise retards auditory cortical development. *Science, 300,* 498–502.

Chang, S. S., Stuckler, D., Yip, P., & Gunnell, D. (2013). Impact of 2008 global economic crisis on suicide: Time trend study in 54 countries. *BMJ, 347,* f5239.

Chao, R. K., & Tseng, V. (2002). Parenting of Asians. In M. H. Bornstein (Ed.), *Handbook of parenting: Vol. 4. Social conditions and applied parenting* (2nd ed., pp. 59–93). Mahwah, NJ: Erlbaum.

Chapell, M. S., Blanding, Z. B., Silverstein, M. E., Takahashi, M., et al. (2005). Test anxiety and academic performance in undergraduate and graduate students. *Journal of Educational Psychology, 97,* 268–274.

Chapin, H., Bagarinao, E., & Mackey, S. (2012). Real-time fMRI applied to pain management. *Neuroscience Letters, 520*(2), 174–181.

Chapman, D. Z., & Zweig, D. I. (2005). Developing a nomological network for interview structure: Antecedents and consequences of the structured selection interview. *Personnel Psychology, 58,* 673–702.

Chaput, J.-P., & Tremblay, A. (2009). The glucostatic theory of appetite control and the risk of obesity and diabetes. *International Journal of Obesity, 33,* 46–53.

Charles, S. T. (2011). Emotional experience and regulation in later life. In K. W. Schaie & S. L. Willis (Eds.), *Handbook of the Psychology of Aging* (7th ed., pp. 295–310). San Diego, CA: Academic Press/Elsevier Science.

Charles, S. T., & Carstensen, L. L. (2008). Unpleasant situations elicit different emotional responses in younger and older adults. *Psychology and Aging, 23,* 495–504.

Charles, S. T., Mather, M., & Carstensen, L. L. (2003). Aging and emotional memory: The forgettable nature of negative images for older adults. *Journal of Experimental Psychology: General, 132,* 310–324.

Charlton, S. G., & Starkey, N. J. (2011). Driving without awareness: The effects of practice and automaticity on attention and driving. *Transportation Research: Part F, 14*(6), 456–471. doi:10.1016/j.trf.2011.04.010

Charman, S. D., Wells, G. L., & Joy, S. W. (2011). The dud effect: Adding highly dissimilar fillers increases confidence in lineup identifications. *Law and Human Behavior, 35*(6), 479–500. doi:10.1007/s10979-010-9261-1.

Charness, N. (2000). Can acquired knowledge compensate for age-related declines in cognitive efficiency? In S. H. Qualls & N. Abeles (Eds.), *Psychology and the aging revolution: How we adapt to longer life* (pp. 99–117). Washington, DC: American Psychological Association.

Chase, T. N. (1998). The significance of continuous dopaminergic stimulation in the treatment of Parkinson's disease. *Drugs, 55*(Suppl. 1), 1–9.

Chaudhry, I. B., Neelam, K., Duddu, V., & Husain, N. (2008). Ethnicity and psychopharmacology. *Journal of Psychopharmacology, 22,* 673–680.

Chein, J., Albert, D., O'Brien, L., Uckert, K., & Steinberg, L. (2011). Peers increase adolescent risk taking by enhancing activity in the brain's reward circuitry. *Developmental Science, 14*(2), F1–F10. doi:10.1111/j.1467-7687.2010.01035.x

Cheke, L. G., Bird C. D., Clayton N. S. (2011). Tool-use and instrumental learning in the Eurasian jay (Garrulus glandarius), *Animal Cognition, 14,* 441–455.

Chemers, M. M. (2000). Leadership research and theory: A functional integration. *Group Dynamics, 4,* 27–43.

Chemers, M. M., Watson, C. B., & May, S. T. (2000). Dispositional affect and leadership effectiveness: A comparison of self-esteem, optimism, and efficacy. *Personality and Social Psychology Bulletin, 26,* 267–277.

Chen, E., & Miller, G. E. (2012). "Shift-and-persist" strategies: Why low socioeconomic status isn't always bad for health. *Perspectives on Psychological Science, 7,* 135–158. doi:10.1177/1745691612436694

Chen, M., & Bargh, J. A. (1997). Nonconscious behavioral confirmation processes: The self-fulfilling consequences of automatic stereotype activation. *Journal of Experimental Social Psychology, 33,* 541–560.

Chen, S. H., Kennedy, M., Zhou, Q. (2012). Parents' Expression and Discussion of Emotion in the Multilingual Family: Does Language Matter? *Perspectives on Psychological Science, 7,* 365–383, doi:10.1177/1745691612447307

Chen, Y., Hsu, C., Liu, L., & Yang, S. (2012). Constructing a nutrition diagnosis expert system. *Expert Systems With Applications, 39*(2), 2132–2156. doi:10.1016/j.eswa.2011.07.069.

Chen, Y., Tsai, P, Chen, P, Fan, C., Hung, G. C. & Cheng, A. T. A. (2010). Effect of media reporting of the suicide of a singer in Taiwan: The case of Ivy Li. *Social Psychiatry and Psychiatric Epidemiology, 45,* 363–369.

Cheng, Y., Kawachi, I., Coakley, E. H., Schwartz, J., & Colditz, G. (2000). Association between psychosocial work characteristics and health functioning in American women: Prospective study. *British Medical Journal, 320,* 1432–1436.

Chentsova-Dutton, Y. E., & Tsai, J. L. (2007). Cultural factors influence the expression of psychopathology. In S. O. Lilienfeld, & W. T. O'Donohue (Eds.), *The great ideas of clincial Science: 17 principles that every mental health professional should understand* (pp. 375–396). New York: Routledge/Taylor & Francis Group.

Cheong, K. B., Zhang, J. P., Huang, Y., & Zhang, Z. J. (2013). The effectiveness of acupuncture in prevention and treatment of postoperative nausea and vomiting— A systematic review and meta-analysis. *PLoS One, 8*(12), e82474.

Cherkin, D. C., Sherman, K. J., Avins, A. L., Erro, J. H., et al. (2009). A randomized trial comparing acupuncture, simulated acupuncture, and usual care for chronic low back pain. *Archives of Internal Medicine, 169,* 858–866.

Chermahini, S., & Hommel, B. (2010). The (b)link between creativity and dopamine: Spontaneous eye blink rates predict and dissociate divergent and convergent thinking. *Cognition, 115*(3), 458–465. doi:10.1016/j.cognition.2010.03.007.

Cheshire, C., & Antin, J. (2010). None of us is as lazy as all of us. *Information, Communication & Society, 13*(4), 537–555. doi:10.1080/13691181003639858.

Chesney, M. A., Chambers, D. B., Taylor, J. M., Johnson, L. M., & Folkman, S. (2003). Coping effectiveness training for men living with HIV: Results from a randomized clinical trial testing a group-based intervention. *Psychosomatic Medicine, 65,* 1038–1046.

Cheung, F. M., van de Vijver, F. R., & Leong, F. L. (2011). Toward a new approach to the study of personality in culture. *American Psychologist, 66*(7), 593–603. doi:10.1037/a0022389.

Chiaburu, D. S., Oh, I.-S., Berry, C. M., Li, N., & Gardner, R. G. (2011). The five- factor model of personality traits and organizational citizenship behaviors: A meta-analysis. *Journal of Applied Psychology, 96*(6), 1140–1166. doi:10.1037/a0024004.

Chiang, J. J., Eisenberger, N. I., Seeman, T. E., & Taylor, S. E. (2012). Negative and competitive social interactions are related to heightened proinflamatory cytokine activity. *Proceedings of the National Academy of Sciences*, online, Jan 23, 2012.

Chien, P. L., & Bell, C. C. (2008). Racial differences in schizophrenia. *Directions in Psychiatry, 28,* 297–304.

Chiesa, A., & Serretti, A. (2009). A systematic review of neurobiological and clinical features of mindfulness meditations. *Psychological Medicine*, 40, 1249–1252. Epub 2009 Nov 27.

Chiou, W., Yang, C., & Wan, C. (2011). Ironic effects of dietary supplementation: Illusory invulnerability created by taking dietary supplements licenses health- risk behaviors. *Psychological Science, 22*(8), 1081–1086. doi:10.1177/0956797611416253.

Chisholm, K. (1997, June). Trauma at an early age inhibits ability to bond. *APA Monitor,* 11.

Chittaro, L., Carchietti, E., De Marco, L., & Zampa, A. (2011). Personalized emergency medical assistance for disabled people. *User Modeling And User- Adapted Interaction, 21*(4–5), 407–440. doi:10.1007/s11257-010-9092-2.

Chivers, M. L., Rieger, G., Latty, E., & Bailey, J. M. (2004). A sex difference in the specificity of sexual arousal. *Psychological Science, 15,* 736–744.

Chivers, M. L., Seto, M. C., & Blanchard, R. (2007). Gender and sexual orientation differences in sexual response to sexual activities versus gender of actors in sexual films. *Journal of Personality and Social Psychology, 93,* 1108–1121.

Chodosh, J., Reuben, D. B., Albert, M. S., & Seeman, T. E. (2002). Predicting cognitive impairment in high-functioning community-dwelling older persons: MacArthur studies of successful aging. *Journal of the American Geriatrics Society, 50*(6), 1051–1060.

Choi, J., & Silverman, I. (2003). Processes underlying sex differences in route- learning strategies in children and adolescents. *Personality and Individual Differences, 34,* 1153–1166.

Chomsky, N. (1965). *Aspects of the theory of syntax.* Cambridge, MA: MIT Press.

Chomsky, N. (1986). *Knowledge of language: Its nature, origin, and use.* New York: Praeger.

Chon, T. Y., & Lee, M. C. (2013). Acupuncture. *Mayo Clinic Proceedings,88*(10), 1141–1146.

Choquet, D., & Triller, A. (2013). The dynamic synapse. *Neuron, 80*(3), 691–703.

Chouinard, G. (2004). Issues in the clinical use of benzodiazepines: Potency, withdrawal, and rebound. *Journal of Clinical Psychiatry, 65*(Suppl. 5), 7–21.

Choy, Y., Fyer, A. J., & Lipsitz, J. D. (2007). Treatment of specific phobia in adults. *Clinical Psychology Review, 27,* 266–286.

Christakis, D. A., & Garrison, M. M. (2009). Preschool-aged children's television viewing in child care settings. *Pediatrics, 124,* 1627–1632.

Christakas, D. A., & Zimmerman, F. J. (2007). Violent television viewing during preschool is associated with antisocial behavior during school age. *Pediatrics, 120,* 993–999.

Christakis, N. A., & Fowler, J. R. (2007). The spread of obesity in a large social network over 32 years. *New England Journal of Medicine, 357,* 370–379.

Christancho, P., Christancho, M., Baltuch, G.H., et al. (2011). Effectiveness and safety of vagus nerve stimulation for severe treatment-resistant depression in clinical practice after FDA approval: outcomes at 1 year. *Journal of Clinical Psychiatry, 72,* 1376–1382.

Christensen, D. L., Schieve, L. A., Devine, O., & Drews-Botsch, C. (2014). Socioeconomic status, child enrichment factors, and cognitive performance among preschool-age children: Results from the Follow-Up of Growth and Development Experiences study. *Research in Developmental Disabilities*, Epub March 24, 2014.

Christie, M. J. (2008). Cellular neuroadaptations to chronic opioids: Tolerance, withdrawal and addiction. *Journal of Pharmacology, 154*(2). 384–396.

Christopher, K. (2003). Autistic boy killed during exorcism. *Skeptical Inquirer, 27*(6), 11.

Chu, J. (1994). Active learning in epidemiology and biostatistics. *Teaching and Learning in Medicine, 6,* 191–193.

Chua, H. F., Boland, J. E., & Nisbett, R. E. (2005). Cultural variation in eye movements during scene perception. *Proceedings of the National Academy of Sciences, 102,* 12629–12633.

Chudzikowski, K., Demel, B., Mayrhofer, W., Briscoe, J. P., Unite, J., Milikić, B., & Zikic, J. (2009). Career transitions and their causes: A country-comparative perspective. *Journal of Occupational & Organizational Psychology, 82*(4), 825–849.

Chugani, H. T., & Phelps, M. E. (1986). Maturational changes in cerebral function in infants determined by 18FDG positron emission tomography. *Science, 231,* 840–843.

Chung, G. H., Flook, L., & Fuligni, A. J. (2009). Daily family conflict and emotional distress among adolescents from Latin American, Asian, and European backgrounds. *Developmental Psychology, 45,* 1406–1415.

Chung, W., Dao, R., Chen, L., & Hung, S. (2010). The role of genetic variants in human longevity. *Ageing Research Reviews, 9 Suppl 1,* S67–S78.

Church, A. T. (2001). Personality measurement in cross-cultural perspective. *Journal of Personality, 69*(6), 979–1006.

Church, A. T. (2010). Current perspectives in the study of personality across cultures. *Perspectives on Psychological Science, 5*(4), 441–449. doi:10.1177/1745691610375559.

Churchill, S., Jessop, D., & Sparks, P. (2008). Impulsive and/or planned behaviour: Can impulsivity contribute to the predictive utility of the theory of planned behaviour? *British Journal of Social Psychology, 47,* 631–646. doi:10.1348/ 014466608X284434.

Churchland, P. M. (1989). *A neurocomputational perspective: The nature of mind and the structure of science.* Cambridge, MA: MIT Press.

Cialdini, R. B. (2001). *Influence: Science and practice* (4th ed.). Boston: Allyn & Bacon.

Cialdini, R. (2007). *Influence: Sciences and Practice* (5th ed.). New York: Allyn & Bacon.

Cialdini, R. B., & Goldstein, N. J. (2004). Social influence: Compliance and conformity. *Annual Review of Psychology, 55,* 591–621.

Cialdini, R. C. (2008). *Influence: Science and practice* (5th ed) Boston, MA: Allyn & Bacon.

Cialdini, R. C., & Griskevicius. (2010). Social Influence In R. Baumeister & E. Finkel (Eds.) *Advanced social psychology: The state of the science* (pp. 385–418). New York, NY: Oxford.

Ciccarone, D. (2011). Stimulant abuse: Pharmacology, cocaine, methamphetamine, treatment, attempts at pharmacotherapy. *Primary Care, 38*(1), 41–58.

Cicchetti, D., Rogosch, F. A., & Thibodeau, E. L. (2012). The effects of child maltreatment on early signs of antisocial behavior: Genetic moderation by tryptophan hydroxylase, serotonin transporter, and monoamine oxidase A genes. *Development and Psychopathology, 24*(3):907–928.

Ciccoippo, R., deGugliemo, G., Hansson, A. C., Ubaldi, M., Kallupi, M., Cruz, M. T., Oleata, C. S., Heilig, M., & Roberto, M. (2014). Restraint stress alters nociception/orphanin FQ and CRF systems in the rat central amygdala: Significance for anxiety-like behaviors. *The Journal of Neuroscience, 34*(2), 363–372.

Ciccocioppo, R., Sanna, P. P., & Weiss, F. (2001). Cocaine-predictive stimulus induces drug-seeking behavior and neural activation in limbic brain regions after multiple months of abstinence: Reversal by D1 antagonists. *Proceedings of the National Academy of Sciences, 98,* 1976–1981.

Cicogna, P. C., Occhioneroa, M., Natalea, V., & Espositoa, M. J. (2006). Bizarreness of size and shape in dream images. *Consciousness and Cognition, 16,* 381–390.

Cikara, M., Botvinick, M. M., & Fiske, S. T. (2011). Us versus them: Social identity shapes neural responses to intergroup competition and harm. *Psychological Science, 22*(3), 306–313. doi:10.1177/0956797610397667.

Cikara, M., Bruneau, E. G., & Saxe, R. R. (2011). Us and them: Intergroup failures of empathy. *Current Directions in Psychological Science 20*(3) 149–153. doi:10.1177/ 0963721411408713.

Cikara, M., & Van Bavel, J. J. (2014). The Neuroscience of intergroup relations An integrative review. *Perspectives on Psychological Science, 9,* 245–274.

Cilia, R., Siri, C., Marotta, G., Isaias, I. U., De Gaspari, D., Canesi, M., Pezzoli, G., & Antonini, A. (2008). Functional abnormalities underlying pathological gambling in Parkinson disease. *Archives of Neurology, 65,* 1604–1611.

Ciocca, V. (2008). The auditory organization of complex sounds. *Frontiers in Bioscience, 13,* 148–169.

Cipriani, A., Hawton, K., Stockton, S., & Geddes, J. R. (2013). Lithium in the prevention of suicide in mood disorders: Updated systematic review and meta-analysis. *BMJ,* Epub June 27, 2013.

Cipriani, G., Picchi, L., Vedovello. M., Nuti, A., & Fiorino, M. D. (2011). The phantom and the supernumerary phantom limb: historical review and new case. *Neuroscience Bulletin, 27*(6), 359–365.

Cisler, J. M., & Koster, E. H. W. (2010). Mechanisms of attentional biases toward threat in anxiety disorders: An integrative review. *Clinical Psychology Review, 30,* 203–216.

Citrome, L., Jaffe, A., Levine, J., & Lindenmayer, J. (2005). Dosing of quetiapine in schizophrenia: How clinical practice differs from registration studies. *Journal of Clinical Psychiatry, 66,* 1512–1516.

Clancy, S. A. (2005). *Abducted: How people come to believe they were kidnapped by aliens.* Cambridge, MA: Harvard University Press.

Clancy, S. A., Schacter, D. L., McNally, R. J., & Pittman, R. K. (2000). False recognition in women reporting recovered memories of sexual abuse. *Psychological Science, 11,* 26–31.

Clark, A., Nash, R. A., Fincham, G., & Mazzoni, G. (2012). Creating non-believed memories for recent autobiographical events. *Plos ONE, 7*(3), doi:10.1371/journal.pone.0032998

Clark, A., Oswald, A., & Warr, P. (1996). Is job satisfaction U-shaped in age? *Journal of Occupational and Organizational Psychology, 69,* 57–81.

Clark, D. A., & Beck, A. T. (2012). *The anxiety and worry workbook: The cognitive behavioral solution.* New York: Guilford Press.

Clark, D. C., & Fawcett, J. (1992). Review of empirical risk factors for evaluation of the suicidal patient. In B. Bongar (Ed.), *Suicide: Guidelines for assessment, management, and treatment* (pp. 16–48). New York: Oxford University Press.

Clark, D. M., Ehlers, A., McManus, F., Hackmann, A., Fennell, M.,Campbell, H., Flower, T., Davenport, C., & Louis, B. (2003). Cognitive therapy versus fluoxetine in generalized social phobia: A randomized placebo-controlled trial. *Journal of Consulting and Clinical Psychology, 71,* 1058–1067.

Clark, E. V. (1983). Meanings and concepts. In P. H. Mussen, J. H. Flavell, & E. M. Markman (Eds.), *Handbook of child psychology: Vol. 3. Cognitive development* (4th ed., pp. 787–840). New York: Wiley.

Clark, E. V. (1993). *The lexicon in acquisition.* Cambridge: Cambridge University Press.

Clark, L. A., & Watson, D. (2008). Temperament: An organizing paradigm for trait psychology. In O. John, R. Robins, & L. Pervin (Eds.), *Handbook of personality: Theory and research* (3rd ed., pp. 265–286). New York: Guilford.

Clark, M. S., & Grote, N. K. (2013). Close relationships. In H. Tennen, J. Suls & I. B. Weiner (Eds.), *Handbook of psychology, Vol. 5: Personality and social psychology* (2nd ed.) (pp. 329–339). Hoboken, NJ: John Wiley & Sons Inc.

Clark, M. S., & Lemay, E. A., Jr. (2010). Close relationships. In S. T. Fiske, D. T. Gilbert, & G. Lindzey (Eds.), *Handbook of social psychology* (5th ed., Vol. 2, pp. 898–940). Hoboken, NJ: Wiley.

Clark, M. S., & Pataki, S. P. (1995). Interpersonal processes influencing attraction and relationships. In A. Tesser (Ed.), *Advanced social psychology* (pp. 283–332). New York: McGraw-Hill.

Clark, S. E. (2012a). Costs and benefits of eyewitness identification reform: Psychological science and public policy. *Perspectives in Psychological Science, 7*(3), 238–259. doi:10.1177/1745691612459584

Clark, S. E. (2012b). Eyewitness identification reform: Data, theory, and due process. *Perspectives on Psychological Science, 7*(3), 279–283. doi:10.1177/1745691612444136

Clarke, D. E., Narrow, W. E., Regier, D. A., Kuramotoa, S. J., Kupfer, D. J., Kuhl, E. A., . . . & Kraemer, H.C. (2013). *DSM-5* field trials in the United States and Canada, Part I: Study design, sampling strategy, implementation, and analytic approaches. *American Journal of Psychiatry, 170,* 43–58.

Clarke, L., Ungerer, J., Chahoud, K., Johnson, S., Stiefel, I. (2002). Attention deficit hyperactivity disorder is associated with attachment insecurity. *Clinical Child Psychology and Psychiatry, 7,* 179–198.

Clarke-Stewart, A., & Allhusen, V. (2005). *What we know about childcare.* Cambridge, MA: Harvard University Press.

Clarke-Stewart, A., & Brentano, C. (2006).*'Til divorce do us part: Causes and consequences of marital separation for children and adults.* New Haven, CT: Yale University Press.

Clarke-Stewart, K. A. (1989). Infant day care: Maligned or malignant? *American Psychologist, 44,* 266–273.

Clausen, J., Sersen, E., & Lidsky, A. (1974). Variability of sleep measures in normal subjects. *Psychophysiology, 11,* 509–516.

Clay, R. A. (2000). Often, the bells and whistles backfire. *Monitor on Psychology, 31,* 64–65.

Clayton N. S., & Dickinson A. (1998). Episodic-like memory during cache recovery by scrub-jays. *Nature, 395,* 272–278.

Clendenen, V. I., Herman, C. P., & Polivy, J. (1995). Social facilitation of eating among friends and strangers. *Appetite, 23,* 1–13.

Cleveland, E. S., & Reese, E. (2008). Children remember early childhood: Long-term recall across the offset of childhood amnesia. *Applied Cognitive Psychology, 22*(1), 127–142.

Clifton, R. K. (1992). The development of spatial hearing in human infants. In L. A. Werner & E. W. Rubel (Eds.), *Developmental psychoacoustics* (pp. 135–157). Washington, DC: American Psychological Association.

Clifton, R. K., Rochat, P., Litovsky, R., & Perris, E. (1991). Object representation guides infants' reaching in the dark. *Journal of Experimental Psychology: Human Perception and Performance, 17,* 323–329.

Clinical Digest. Early exposure to mobile phones affects children's behaviour. (2011). *Nursing Standard, 25*(21), 17.

CNN US. April 17, 2013 Boston Marathon heroes: running to help. http://www.cnn .com/2013/04/16/us/boston-heroes/ Retrieved march 24, 2014.

Cobham, V. E., & McDermott, B. (2014). Perceived parenting change and child posttraumatic stress following a natural disaster. *Journal of Child and Adolescent Psychopharmacology, 24*(1), 18–23.

Coccaro, E. F. (1989). Central serotonin and impulsive aggression. *British Journal of Psychiatry, 155,* 52–62.

Coelho, C. M., & Purkis, H. (2009). The origins of specific phobias: Influential theories and current perspectives. *Review of General Psychology, 13,* 335–348.

Cofer, L. F., Grice, J., Palmer, D., Sethre-Hofstad, L., & Zimmermann, K. (1992, June 20–22). *Evidence for developmental continuity of individual differences in morningness-eveningness.* Paper presented at the annual meeting of the American Psychological Society, San Diego, CA.

Cohen, A. (2009). Many forms of culture. *American Psychologist, 64,* 194–204.

Cohen, C. E. (1981). Person categories and social perception: Testing some boundaries of the processing effects of prior knowledge. *Journal of Personality and Social Psychology, 40,* 441–452.

Cohen, D. (1998). Culture, social organization, and patterns of violence. *Journal of Personality and Social Psychology, 75,* 408–419.

Cohen, F., Kemeny, M. E., Zegans, L. S., Johnson, P., Kearney, K. A., & Strites, D. P. (2007). Immune function declines with unemployment and recovers after stressor termination. *Psychosomatic Medicine, 69,* 225–234.

Cohen, G. L., & Steele, C. M. (2002). A barrier of mistrust: How negative stereotypes affect cross-race mentoring. In J. Aronson (Ed.), *Improving academic achievement: Impact of psychological factors on education* (pp. 303–327). San Diego, CA: Academic Press.

Cohen, N. J., & Corkin, S. (1981). The amnesic patient H. M.: Learning and retention of a cognitive skill. *Neuroscience Abstracts, 7,* 235.

Cohen, N. J., & Squire, L. R. (1980). Preserved learning and retention of pattern analyzing skills in amnesia: Dissociation of knowing how and knowing that. *Science, 210,* 207–210.

Cohen, P., Kasen, S., Chen, H., Hartmark, C., & Gordon, K. (2003). Variations in patterns of developmental transitions in the emerging adulthood period. *Developmental Psychology, 39,* 657–669.

Cohen, S., Doyle, W. J., Alper, C. M., Janicki-Deverts, D., & Turner, R. B. (2009). Sleep habits and susceptibility to the common cold. *Archives of Internal Medicine, 169,* 62–67.

Cohen, S., Doyle, W. J., Turner, R. B., Alper, C. M., & Skoner, D. P. (2003a). Emotional style and susceptibility to the common cold. *Psychosomatic Medicine, 65,* 652–657.

Cohen, S., Doyle, W. J., Turner, R., Alper, C. M., & Skoner, D. P. (2003b). Sociability and susceptibility to the common cold. *Psychological Science, 14,* 389–395.

Cohen, S., & Herbert, T. B. (1996). Health psychology: Psychological factors and physical disease from the perspective of human psychoneuroimmunology. *Annual Review of Psychology, 47,* 113–142.

Cohen, S., Janicki-Deverts, D., Doyle, W. J., Miller, G. E., Frank, E., Rabin, B. S., & Turner, R. B. (2012). Chronic stress, glucocorticoid receptor resistance, inflammation, and disease risk. *Proceedings of the National Academy of Sciences of the United States of America, 109,* 5995–5999. doi:10.1073/pnas.1118355109.

Cohen, S., & Pressman, S. D. (2006). Positive affect and health. *Current Directions in Psychological Science, 15,* 122–125.

Coid, J. & Ullrich, S. (2010). Antisocial personality disorder is on a continuum with psychopathy. *Comprehensive Psychiatry, 51,* 426–433.

Colak, A., Soy, O., Uzun, H., Aslan, O., Barut, S., Belce, A., et al. (2003). Neuroprotective effects of GYKI 52466 on experimental spinal cord injury in rats. *Journal of Neurosurgery, 98,* 275–281.

Coldwell, C. M., & Bender, W. S. (2007). The effectiveness of assertive community treatment for homeless populations with severe mental illness: A meta-analysis. *American Journal of Psychiatry, 164,* 393–399.

Cole, R. A., & Jakimik, J. (1978). Understanding speech: How words are heard. In G. Underwood (Ed.), *Strategies of information processing* (pp. 67–116). London: Academic Press.

Cole, S. W. (2009). Social regulation of human gene expression. *Current Directions in Psychological Science, 18,* 132–137.

Cole, S. W. (2013). Social regulation of human gene expression: Mechanisms and implications for public health. *American Journal of Public Health, 103,* S84–S92.

Cole, S. W., Arevalo, J. M. G. Manu, K., Telzer, E. H., Kiang, L., Bower, J. E., Irwin, M. R. & Fuligni, A. J. (2011). Antagonistic pleiotropy at the human IL6 promoter confers genetic resilience to the pro-inflammatory effects of adverse social conditions in adolescence *Developmental Psychology, 47,* 1173–1180.

Coleman, D. (1992). Why do I feel so tired? Too little, too late. *American Health, 11*(4), 43–46.

Collings, S. C., & Kemp, C. G. (2010). Death knocks, professional practice, and the public good: The media experience of suicide reporting in New Zealand., *Social Science and Medicine, 71,* 244–248.

Collins, R. L., Elliott, M. N., Berry, S. H., Kanouse, D. E., Kunkel, D., Hunter, S. B., et al. (2004). Watching sex on television predicts adolescent initiation of sexual behavior. *Pediatrics, 114,* e280–e289.

Collins, S. E., & Spelman, P. J. (2013). Associations of descriptive and reflective injunctive norms with risky college drinking. *Psychology of Addictive Behaviors, 27*(4), 1175–1181.

Collins, W. A., & Steinberg, L. (2006). Adolescent development in interpersonal context. In W. Damon & R. M. Lerner (Series Eds.) & N. Eisenberg (Vol. Ed.), *Handbook of child psychology: Vol. 3, Social, emotional, and personality development* (pp. 1003–1068). Hoboken, NJ: Wiley.

Colliott, O., Hamelin, L., & Sarazin, M. (2013). Magnetic resonance imaging fort diagnosis of early Alzheimer's disease. *Revue Neurologique, 169*(70), 724–728.

Colloca, L., & Benedetti, F. (2005). Placebos and painkillers: Is mind as real as matter? *Nature Reviews Neuroscience, 6,* 545–552.

Colom, R., & Flores-Mendoza, C. E. (2007). Intelligence predicts scholastic achievement irrespective of SES factors: Evidence from Brazil. *Intelligence, 35,* 243–251.

Colom, R., Jung, R. E., & Haier, R. J. (2006). Distributed brain sites for the g-factor of intelligence. *Neuroimage, 31,* 1359–1365.

Colombo, M., D'Amato, M. R., Rodman, H. R., & Gross, C. G. (1990). Auditory association cortex lesions impair auditory short-term memory in monkeys. *Science, 247,* 336–338.

Coltrane, S., & Adams, M. (2008). *Gender and families* (2nd ed.). Lanham, MD: Rowman & Littlefield.

Colzato, L. S., Beest, I., van den Wildenberg, W. M., Scorolli, C., Dorchin, S., Meiran, N., & Hommel, B. (2010). God: Do I have your attention? *Cognition, 117*(1), 87–94. doi:10.1016/j.cognition.2010.07.003.

Comas-Diaz, L. (2014). Multicultural psychotherapy. In F. T. L. Leong, L. Comas-Diaz, G. C. Nagayama Hall, V. C. McLoyd, & J. E. Trimble (Eds.), *APA handbook of multicultural psychology, Vol. 2: Applications and training* (pp. 419–441). Washington, DC: American Psychological Association.

Combe, E., & Wexler, M. (2010). Observer movement and size constancy. *Psychological Science, 21*(5), 667–675. doi:10.1177/0956797610367753.

Commission on Accreditation. (2008). *Guidelines and principles for accreditation of programs in professional psychology.* Washington, DC: American Psychological Association.

Committee on Identifying the Needs of the Forensic Sciences Community. (2009). *Strengthening Forensic Science in the United States: A Path Forward.* Washington, D.C. National Academies Press.

Committee to Review the Scientific Evidence on the Polygraph. (2003). *The polygraph and lie detection.* Washington, DC: National Academies Press.

Compare, A., Mommersteeg, P. M., Faletra, F., Grossi, E., Pasotti, E., Moccetti, T., & Auricchio, A. (2014). Personality traits, cardiac risk factors, and their association with presence and severity of coronary artery plaque in people with no history of cardiovascular disease. *Journal of Cardiovascular Medicine,* Epub February 26, 2014.

Compton, W. C., & Hoffman, E. (2012). *Positive psychology: The science of happiness and flourishing.* Belmont, CA: Cenage Learning.

Compton, W. M., Conway, K. P., Stinson, F. S., Colliver, J. D., & Grant, B. F. (2005). Prevalence, correlates, and comorbidity of DSM-IV antisocial personality syndromes and alcohol and specific drug use disorders in the United States: Results from the national epidemiologic survey on alcohol and related conditions. *Journal of Clinical Psychiatry, 66,* 677–685.

Compton, W. M., Thomas, Y. F., Stinson, F. S., & Grant, B. F. (2007). Prevalence, correlates, disability, and comorbidity of DSM-IV drug abuse and dependence in the United States: Results from the National Epidemiologic Survey on Alcohol and Related Conditions. *Archives of General Psychiatry, 164,* 566–576.

Comstock, G., & Scharrer, E. (2006). Media and popular culture. In W. Damon & R. M. Lerner (Series Eds.) & K. A. Renninger & I. E. Sigel (Vol. Eds.), *Handbook of child psychology: Vol. 4. Child psychology in practice* (6th ed., pp. 817–863). Hoboken, NJ: Wiley.

Condon, J. W., & Crano, W. D. (1988). Inferred evaluation and the relationship between attitude similarity and interpersonal attraction. *Journal of Personality and Social Psychology, 54,* 789–797.

Cone, E. J., Fant, R. V., Rohay, J. M., Caplan, Y. H., Ballina, M., Reder, R. F., et al. (2004). Oxycodone involvement in drug abuse deaths: II. Evidence for toxic multiple drug-drug interactions. *Journal of Analytical Toxicology, 28,* 616–624.

Confer, J. C., Easton, J. A., Fleischman, D. S., Goetz, C. D., Lewis, D.M.G., Perilloux, C., & Buss, D. M. (2010). Evolutionary psychology: Controversies, questions, prospects, and limitations. *American Psychologist, 65,* 110–126.

Conley, T. D., Moors, A. C., Matsick, J. L., Ziegler, A., & Valentine, B. A. (2011). Women, men, and the bedroom: Methodological and conceptual insights that narrow, reframe, and eliminate gender differences in sexuality. *Current Directions In Psychological Science, 20*(5), 296–300. doi:10.1177/0963721411418467.

Connell, L., & Lynott, D. (2010). Look but don't touch: Tactile disadvantage in processing modality-specific words. *Cognition, 115*(1), 1–9. doi:10.1016/j.cognition.2009.10.005.

Connolly, B. S., & Lang, A. E. (2014). Pharmacological treatment of Parkinson disease, *JAMA, 311*(16), 1670–1683.

Connor, L. T., Balota, D. A., & Neely, J. H. (1992). On the relation between feeling of knowing and lexical decision: Persistent subthreshold activation of topic familiarity? *Journal of Experimental Psychology: Learning, Memory, and Cognition, 18,* 544–554.

Connor-Greene, P. A. (2001). Family, friends, and self: The real-life context of an abnormal psychology class. *Teaching of Psychology, 28,* 210–212.

Conrad, R. (1964). Acoustic confusions in immediate memory. *British Journal of Psychology, 55,* 75–84.

Conry-Murray, C., & Turiel, E. (2012). Jimmy's baby doll and Jenny's truck: Young children's reasoning about gender norms. *Child Development, 83*(1), 146–158. doi:10.1111/j.1467–8624.2011.01696.x.

Consumer Reports. (1995, November). Mental health: Does therapy help? *Consumer Reports,* pp. 734–739.

Conte, J. M., & Gintoft, J. N. (2005). Polychronicity, big five personality dimensions, and sales performance. *Human Performance, 18,* 427–444.

Contemporary Sexuality. (2008, May). CDC: One in four teens has an STI. *Contemporary Sexuality, 42*(5), 11–12.

Contractor, N. S., DeChurch, L. A., Carson, J., Carter, D., & Keegan, B. (2012). The topology of collective leadership. *Leadership Quarterly, 6,* 994–1011.

Conway, B. R. (2009). Color vision, cones, and color-coding in the cortex. *Neuroscientist, 15,* 274–290.

Cook, C., Goodman, N. D., & Schulz, L. E. (2011). Where science starts: Spontaneous experiments in preschoolers' exploratory play. *Cognition, 120*(3), 341–349. doi:10.1016/ j.cognition.2011.03.003.

Cook, J. M., Biyanova, T., & Coyne, J. C. (2009). Influential psychotherapy figures, authors, and books: An Internet survey of over 2,000 psychotherapists. *Psychotherapy: Theory, Research, Practice, Training, 46,* 42–51. doi:10.1037/a0015152

Cook, N. D., Yutsudo, A., Fujimoto, N., & Murata, M. (2008). Factors contributing to depth perception: Behavioral studies on the reverse perspective illusion. *Spatial Vision, 21*(3–5), 397–405.

Cooke, L. J., Chambers, L. C., Añez, E. V., Croker, H. A., Boniface, D., Yeomans, M. R., & Wardle, J. (2011). Eating for Pleasure or Profit: The Effect of Incentives on Children's Enjoyment of Vegetables. *Psychological Science, 22*(2), 190–196. doi:10.1177/0956797610394662.

Cook-Vienot, R., & Taylor, R. J. (2012). Comparison of eye movement desensitization and reprocessing and biofeedback/Stress inoculation training in treating test anxiety. *Journal of EMDR Practice and Research, 6,* 62–72.

Cooper, A., Gomez, R., & Buck, E. (2008). The relationships between the BIS and BAS, anger and responses to anger. *Personality and Individual Differences, 44*(2), 403–413.

Cooper, J., Mirabile, R., & Scher, S. J. (2005). Actions and attitudes: The theory of cognitive dissonance. In T. Brock & M. Green (Eds.), *Persuasion: Psychological insights and perspectives* (2nd ed., pp. 63–79). Thousand Oaks, CA: Sage Publications, Inc.

Cooper, M.J., & Warren, L. (2011). The relationship between body weight (body mass index) and attachment history in young women. *Eating Behaviors, 12,* 94–96.

Cooper, M. L., Russell, M., Skinner, J. B., Frone, M. R., & Mudar, P. (1992). Stress and alcohol use: The moderating effects of gender, coping, and alcohol expectancies. *Journal of Abnormal Psychology, 101,* 139–152.

Cooper-Hakim, A., & Viswesvaran, C. (2005). The construct of work commitment: Testing an integrative framework. *Psychological Bulletin, 131*(2), 241–259.

Coplan, R. J., & Arbeau, K. A. (2011). Peer interactions and play in early childhood. In K. H. Rubin, W. M. Bukowski, & B. Laursen (Eds.), *Handbook of peer interactions, relationships, and groups* (pp. 143–161). New York: Guilford Press.

Corbett, A., Kauffman, L., MacLaren, B., Wagner, A., & Jones, E. (2010). A cognitive tutor for genetics problem solving: Learning gains and student modeling. *Journal of Educational Computing Research, 42*(2), 219–239. doi:10.2190/EC.42.2.e.

Corden, B., Critchley, H. D., Skuse, D., & Dolan, R. J. (2006). Fear recognition ability predicts differences in social cognitive and neural functioning in men. *Journal of Cognitive Neuroscience, 18,* 889–897.

Cordery, J. L., Mueller, W. S., & Smith, L. M. (1991). Attitudinal and behavioral effects of autonomous group working: A longitudinal field study. *Academy of Management Journal, 34,* 464–476.

Coren, S. (1999). Psychology applied to animal training. In A. Stec & D. Bernstein (Eds.), *Psychology: Fields of application.* Boston: Houghton Mifflin.

Coren, S., & Girgus, J. S. (1978). *Seeing is deceiving: The psychology of visual illusions.* Hillsdale, NJ: Erlbaum.

Corey, G. (2008). *Theory and practice of counseling and psychotherapy* (8th ed.). Belmont, CA: Brooks/Cole.

Cork, R. C., Kihlstrom, J. F., & Hameroff, S. R. (1992). Explicit and implicit memory dissociated by anesthetic technique. *Society for Neuroscience Abstracts, 22,* 523.

Corker, K. S., & Donnellan, M.B. (2012). Setting lower limits high: The role of boundary goals in achievement motivation. Journal of Educational Psychology, 104, 138–149.

Cornblatt, B., & Erlenmeyer-Kimling, L. E. (1985). Global attentional deviance in children at risk for schizophrenia: Specificity and predictive validity. *Journal of Abnormal Psychology, 94,* 470–486.

Cornelius, R. R. (1996). *The science of emotion.* Upper Saddle River, NJ: Prentice Hall.

Cornelius, T. L., & Resseguie, N. (2007). Primary and secondary prevention programs for dating violence: A review of the literature. *Aggression and Violent Behavior, 12,* 364–375.

Cornum, R., Matthews, M. D., & Seligman, M. E., P. (2011). Comprehensive soldier fitness: Building resilience in a challenging institutional context. *American Psychologist, 66*(1), 4–9. doi:10.1037/a0021420.

Correia, A. W., Peters, J. L., Levy, J. I., Melly, S., & Dominici, F. (2013). Residential exposure to aircraft noise and hospital admissions for cardiovascular diseases: Multi-airport retrospective study. *BMJ, 347,* f5561.

Correll, J., Park, B., Judd, C. M., & Wittenbrink, B. (2002). The police officer's dilemma: Using ethnicity to disambiguate potentially threatening individuals. *Journal of Personality and Social Psychology, 83,* 1314–1329.

Correll, J., Park, B., Judd, C. M., Wittenbrink, B., et al. (2007). Across the thin blue line: Police officers and racial bias in the decision to shoot. *Journal of Personality and Social Psychology, 92,* 1006–1023.

Corsini, R. J., & Wedding, W. (Eds.). (2005). *Current psychotherapies* (7th ed.). Belmont, CA: Thomson Brooks/Cole.

Costa, P., & McCrae, R. (2008). Th e NEO inventories. In R. P. Archer & S. R. Smith, (Eds), *Personality assessment* (pp. 213–245). New York: Routledge/Taylor & Francis.

Costello, E. J., Copeland, W., & Angold, A. (2011). Trends in psychopathology across the adolescent years: What changes when children become adolescents, and when adolescents become adults? *Journal of Child Psychology and Psychiatry, 52,* 1015–1025.

Costermans, J., Lories, G., & Ansay, C. (1992). Confidence level and feeling of knowing in question answering: The weight of inferential processes. *Journal of Experimental Psychology: Learning, Memory, and Cognition, 18,* 142–150.

Cota, D., Marsicano, G., Lutz, B., Vicennati, V., Stalla, G. K., Pasquali, R., & Pagotto, U. (2003). Endogenous cannabinoid system as a modulator of food intake. *International Journal of Obesity, 27,* 289–301.

Cota, D., Proulx, K., Smith, K. A. B., Kozma, S. C., Thomas, G., Woods, S. C., et al. (2006). Hypothalamic mTOR signaling regulates food intake. *Science, 312,* 927–930.

Cotanche, D. A. (1997). Hair cell regeneration in the avian cochlea. *Annals of Otology, Rhinology, and Laryngology Supplement, 168,* 9–15.

Cote, J. K., & Pepler, C. (2002). A randomized trial of a cognitive coping intervention for acutely ill HIV-positive men. *Nursing Research, 51,* 237–244.

Courcoulas, A. P., Christian, N. J., Belle, S. H., Berk, P. D., Flum, D. R., Garcia, L., Horlick, M., Kalarchian, M. A., King, W. C., Mitchell, J. E., Patterson, E. J., Pender, J. R., Pomp, A., Pories, W. J., Thirlby, R. C., Yanovski, S. Z., Wolfe, B. M., & Longitudinal Assessment of Bariatric Surgery (LABS) Consortium. (2013). Weight change and health outcomes at 3 years after bariatric surgery among individuals with severe obesity. *JAMA, 310*(22), 2416–2425.

Courtenay, G., Smith, D. R., & Gladstone, W. (2012). Occupational health issues in marine and freshwater research. *Journal of Occupational Medicine & Toxicology, 7*(1), 1–11. doi:10.1186/1745-6673-7-4.

Cousins, A. J., Fugère, M. A., & Franklin, M. (2009). Digit ratio (2D:4D), mate guarding, and physical aggression in dating couples. *Personality and Individual Differences, 46,* 709–713.

Coutanche, M. N., & Thompson-Schill, S. L. (2012). Reversal without remapping: What we can (and cannot) conclude about learned associations from training-induced behavior changes. *Perspectives On Psychological Science, 7*(2), 118–134. doi:10.1177/1745691611434211

Cowan, D. T., Allan, L. G., Libretto, S. E., & Griffiths, P. (2001). Opiod drugs: A comparative survey of therapeutic and "street" use. *Pain, 2,* 193–203.

Cowan, N. (1988). Evolving concepts of memory storage, selective attention, and their mutual constraints within the human information-processing system. *Psychological Bulletin, 104,* 163–191.

Cowan, N. (2010). The magical mystery four: How is working memory capacity limited, and why? *Current Directions in Psychological Science, 19*(1) 51–57. doi:10.1177/0963721409359277.

Cowan, N. (2011). The focus of attention as observed in visual working memory tasks: Making sense of competing claims. *Neuropsychologia, 49,* 1401–1406.

Cowan, P. A., & Cowan, C. P. (2009). How working with couples fosters childrens development: From prevention science to public policy. In M. Schulz, M. K. Pruett, P. Kerig, & R. D. Parke (Eds.), *Strengthening couple relationships for optimal child development* (pp. 211–228). Washington, DC: American Psychological Association.

Cowey, A. (2010a). The blindsight saga. *Experimental Brain Research, 200*(1), 3–24.

Cowey, A. (2010b). Visual system: how does blindsight arise? *Current Biology, 20*(17), R702–R704.

Cox, J. E., Buman, M., Valenzuela, J., Joseph, N. P., Mitchell, A., & Woods, E. R. (2008). Depression, parenting attributes, and social support among adolescent mothers attending a teen tot program. *Journal of Pediatric & Adolescent Gynecology, 21*(5), 275–281.

Craig, A. D. (2009). How do you feel—now? The anterior insula and human awareness. *Nature Reviews Neuroscience, 10*(1), 59–70.

Craighead, W. E., & Dunlop, B. W. (2014). Combination psychotherapy and antidepressant medication treatment for depression: for whom, when, and how. *Annual Review of Psychology, 65,* 267–300.

Craik, F., Bialystok, E., & Freedman, M. (2010). Delaying the onset of Alzheimer disease: bilingualism as a form of cognitive reserve. *Neurology, 75*(19), 1726–1729.

Craik, F. I. M., & Lockhart, R. S. (1972). Levels of processing: A framework for memory research. *Journal of Verbal Learning and Verbal Behavior, 11,* 671–684.

Craik, F. I. M., & Rabinowitz, J. C. (1984). Age differences in the acquisition and use of verbal information. In H. Bouma & D. G. Bouwhuis (Eds.), *Attention and performance* (Vol. 10, pp. 471–499). Hillsdale, NJ: Erlbaum.

Crandall, C. S., Preisler, J. J., & Aussprung, J. (1992). Measuring life event stress in the lives of college students: The Undergraduate Stress Questionnaire (USQ). *Journal of Behavioral Medicine, 15,* 627–662.

Crane, R. (2007). The Most Addictive Drug, the Most Deadly Substance: Smoking Cessation Tactics for the Busy Clinician. *Primary Care: Clinics in Office Practice, 34*(1), 117–135.

Cranford, J. A., Zucker, R. A., Jester, J. M., Puttler, L. I., & Fitzgerald, H. E. (2010). Parental alcohol involvement and adolescent alcohol expectancies predict alcohol involvement in male adolescents. *Psychology of Addictive Behaviors, 24*(3), 386–396.

Crano, W. D. (2012). *The rules of influence: Winning when you're in the minority.* New York: St Martin's Press.

Crano. W. D., & Seyranian, V. (2009). How minorities prevail: The context/comparisonleniency contract model. *Journal of Social Issues, 65,* 335–363.

Craske, M. G. (1999). *Anxiety disorders: Psychological approaches to theory and treatment.* Boulder, CO: Westview Press.

Crawford, N. A., Schrock, M., & Woodruff-Borden, J. (2011). Child internalizing symptoms: Contributions of child temperament, maternal negative affect, and family functioning. *Child Psychiatry and Human Development, 42,* 53–64.

Crean, R. D., Crane, N. A., & Mason, B. J. (2011). An evidence based review of acute and long-term effects of cannabis use on executive cognitive functions. *Journal of Addiction Medicine, 5*(1), 1–8.

Crean, S., Ward, A., Mercaldi, C. J., Collins, J. M., Cook, M. N., Baker, N. L. & Arrighi, H. M. (2011). Apolipoprotein E ε4 prevalence in Alzheimer's disease patients varies across global populations: a systematic literature review and meta-analysis. *Dementia and Geriatric Cognitive Disorders, 31,* 20–30.

Crépin, D., Benomar, Y., Riffault, L., Amine, H., Gertler, A., & Taouis, M. (2014). The over-expression of miR-200a in the hypothalamus of ob/ob mice is linked to leptin and insulin signaling impairment. *Molecular & Cellular Endocrinology, 384*(1–2), 1–11.

Crespi, B. (2008). Genomic imprinting in the development and evolution of psychotic spectrum conditions. *Biological Reviews, 83*(4), 441–493.

Crick, N. R., Ostrov, J. M., Appleyard, K., Jansen, E. A., & Casas, J. F. (2004). Relational aggression in early childhood: "You can't come to my birthday party unless. . . ." In M. Putallaz & K. L. Bierman (Eds.), *Aggression, antisocial behavior, and violence among girls: A developmental perspective* (pp. 71–89). New York: Guilford Press.

Cristancho, P., Cristancho, M. A., Baltuch, G. H., Thase, M. E., & O'Reardon, J. P. (2011). Effectiveness and safety of vagus nerve stimulation for severe treatment-resistant major depression in clinical practice after FDA approval: Outcomes at 1 year. *Journal of Clinical Psychiatry, 72*(10), 1376–1382.

Critchley, E. M. (1991). Speech and the right hemisphere. *Behavioural Neurology, 4*(3), 143–151.

Crits-Christoph, P., Gibbons, M. B. C., Ring-Kurtz, S., Gallop, R., Stirman, S., Present, J., Temes, C., & Goldstein, L. (2008). Changes in positive quality of life over the course of psychotherapy. *Psychotherapy: Theory, Research, Practice, Training, 45,* 419–430.

Crocker, J., & Canevello, A. (2012). Self and identity: Dynamics of persons and their situations. In K. Deaux, M. Snyder (Eds.), *The Oxford handbook of personality and social psychology* (pp. 263–286). New York: Oxford University Press.

Crocker, J., & Wolfe, T. (2001). Contingencies of self-worth. *Psychological Review, 108,* 593–623.

Croen, L. A., Grether, J. K., & Selvin, S. (2001). The epidemiology of mental retardation of unknown cause. *Pediatrics, 107,* 86.

Crombag, H. S., & Robinson, T. E. (2004). Drugs, environment, brain, and behavior. *Current Directions in Psychological Science, 13,* 107–111.

Cronbach, L. J. (1975). Five decades of public controversy over mental testing. *American Psychologist, 30,* 1–14.

Cronbach, L. J. (1990). *Essentials of psychological testing* (5th ed.). New York: Harper & Row.

Cross, S. E., & Madson, L. (1997). Models of the self: Self-construals and gender. *Psychological Bulletin, 122,* 5–37.

Cross-National Collaborative Group. (2002). The changing rate of major depression: Cross-national comparisons. *Journal of the American Medical Association, 268,* 3098–3105.

Crowley, K., Callanan, M. A., Tenenbaum, H. R., & Allen, E. (2001). Parents explain more often to boys than to girls during shared scientific thinking. *Psychological Science, 12,* 258–261.

Crowther, H., Lipworth, W., & Kerridge, I. (2011). Evidence-based medicine and epistemological imperialism: narrowing the divide between evidence and illness. *Journal of Evaluation In Clinical Practice, 17*(5), 868–872. doi:10.1111/ j.1365-2753.2011.01723.x.

Crowther, J. H., Sanftner, J., Bonifazi, D. Z., & Shepherd, K. L. (2001). The role of daily hassles in binge eating. *International Journal of Eating Disorders, 29,* 449–454.

Crozier, J. C., Dodge, K. A., Fontaine, R. G., Lansford, J. E., et al. (2008). Social information processing and cardiac predictors of adolescent antisocial behavior. *Journal of Abnormal Psychology, 117,* 253–267.

Cruse, D., Chennu, S., Chatelle, C., Bekinschtein, T. A., Fernández-Espejo, D., Pickard, J. D., Laureys, S., Owen, A. M. (2011). Bedside detection of awareness in the vegetative state: a cohort study. *Lancet, 378*(9809), 2088–2094.

Cruz, A., & Green, B. G. (2000). Thermal stimulation of taste. *Nature, 403,* 889–892.

Cryan, J. F., & Dinan, T. G. (2012). Mind-altering microorganisms: The impact of the gut microbiota on brain and behavior. *Nature Reviews Neuroscience, 13*(10), 701–712.

Cuijpers, P., vanStraten, A., Driessen, E., vanOppen, P., Bockting, C., & Andersson, G. (2012). Depression and dysthymic disorders. In P. Sturmey & M. Hersen (Eds.), *Handbook of evidence-based practice in clinical psychology, Vol 2: Adult disorders* (pp. 243–284). Hoboken, NJ: Wiley.

Cullen, M. J., Waters, S. D., & Sackett, P. R. (2006). Testing stereotype threat theory predictions for math-identified and non-math-identified students by gender. *Human Performance, 19*(4), 421–440.

Culp, R. E., Cook, A. S., & Housley, P. C. (1983). A comparison of observed and reported adult-infant interactions: Effects of perceived sex. *Sex Roles, 9,* 475–479.

Cummings, J. L. (2003). Toward a molecular neuropsychiatry of neurodegenerative diseases. *Annals of Neurology, 54*(2), 147–154.

Cunningham, W. A., & Brosch, T. (2012). Motivational salience: Amygdala tuning from traits, needs, values, and goals. *Current Directions In Psychological Science, 21*(1), 54–59. doi:10.1177/0963721411430832.

Cunningham, W. A., Johnson, M. K., Raye, C. L., Gatenby, J. C., Gore, J. C., & Banaji, M. R. (2004). Separable neural components in the processing of black and white faces. *Psychological Science, 15,* 806–813.

Cuperman, R., & Ickes, W. (2009). Big Five predictors of behavior and perceptions in initial dyadic interactions: Personality similarity helps extraverts and introverts but hurts "disagreeables." *Journal of Personality and Social Psychology, 97,* 667–684.

Curioni, C. C., & Lourenço, P. M. (2005). Long-term weight loss after diet and exercise: A systematic review. *International Journal of Obesity, 29,* 1168–1174.

Currin, L., Schmidt, U., Treasure, J., & Jick, H. (2005). Time trends in eating disorder incidence. *British Journal of Psychiatry, 186,* 132–135.

Curry, D. T., Eisenstein, R. D., & Walsh, J. K. (2006). Pharmacologic management of insomnia: Past, present, and future. *Psychiatric Clinics of North America, 29,* 871–893.

Curtis, T., Miller, B. C., & Berry, E. H. (2000). Changes in reports and incidence of child abuse following natural disasters. *Child Abuse & Neglect, 24,* 1151–1162.

Cushon, J. A., Vu, L. H., Janzen, B. L., & Muhajarine, N. (2011). Neighborhood poverty impacts children's physical health and well-being over time: Evidence from the Early Development Instrument. *Early Education & Development, 22,* 183–205. doi:10.1080/10409280902915861

Cuthbert, B. N., & Kozak, M. J. (2013). Constructing constructs for psychopathology: The NIMH research domain criteria. *Journal of Abnormal Psychology, 122*(3), 928–937.

Cutrona, C. E., Russell, D. W., Brown, P. A., Clark, L. A., Hessling, R. M., & Gardner, K. A. (2005). Neighborhood context, personality, and stressful life events as predictors of depression among African American women. *Journal of Abnormal Psychology, 114,* 3–15.

Cvetek, R. (2008). EMDR treatment of distressful experiences that fail to meet the criteria for PTSD. *Journal of EMDR Practice and Research, 2*(1), 2–14.

Cyranoski, D. (2014). Accusations pile up amidst Japan's stem-cell controversy. *Nature,* Epub, May 7, 2014.

Cyranowski, J. M., Hofkens, T. L., Swartz, H. A., & Gianaros, P. J. (2011).Thinking about a close relationship differentially impacts cardiovascular stress responses among depressed and nondepressed women. *Health Psychology, 30,* 276–284, 2011.

Czeisler, C. A., Duffy, J. F., Shanahan, T. L., Brown, E. N., Mitchell, J. F., Rimmer, D. W., et al. (1999). Stability, precision, and near 24-hour period of the human circadian pacemaker. *Science, 284,* 2177–2181.

Czeisler, C. A., Walsh, J. K., Roth, T., Hughes, R. J., Wright, K. P., Kingsbury, L., et al. (2005). Modafinil for excessive sleepiness associated with shift-work sleep disorder. *New England Journal of Medicine, 353,* 476–486.

Dabbs, J. M., Jr., Riad, J. K., & Chance, S. E. (2001). Testosterone and ruthless homicide. *Personality and Individual Differences, 31,* 599–603.

Dabo, F., Nyberg, F., Qin Zhou, Sundström-Poromaa, I., & Akerud, H. (2010). Plasma levels of beta-endorphin during pregnancy and use of labor analgesia. *Reproductive Sciences, 17*(8), 742–747.

Dacher, M., & Nugent, F. S. (2011). Opiates and plasticity. *Neuropharmacology, 61*(7), 1088–1096.

Daddis, C. (2011). Desire for increased autonomy and adolescents' perceptions of peer autonomy: "Everyone else can; why can't I?" *Child Development, 82,* 1310–1326.

Da Fonseca, D., Seguier, V., Santos, A., Poinso, F., & Deruelle, C. (2009). Emotion understanding in children with ADHD. *Child Psychiatry and Human Development, 40,* 111–121.

Daglish, M. R., & Nutt, D. J. (2003). Brain imaging studies in human addicts. *European Neuropsychopharmacology, 13,* 453–458.

Dai, D., Swanson, J., & Cheng, H. (2011). State of research on giftedness and gifted education: A survey of empirical studies published during 1998–2010 (April). *Gifted Child Quarterly, 55*(2), 126–138. doi:10.1177/0016986210397831.

Dakwar, E., & Levin, F. R. (2009). The emerging role of meditation in addressing psychiatric illness, with a focus on substance use disorders. *Harvard Review of Psychiatry, 17,* 254–267.

Dale, P. S. (1976). *Language and the development of structure and function.* New York: Holt, Rinehart & Winston.

Dalgleish, T., Hauer, B., & Kuyken, W. (2008). The mental regulation of autobiographical recollection in the aftermath of trauma. *Current Directions in Psychological Science, 17,* 259–263.

Dallman, M. F., Pecoraro, N., Akana, S. F., La Fleur, S. E., Gomez, F., Houshyar, H., et al. (2003). Chronic stress and obesity: A new view of "comfort food." *Proceedings of the National Academies of Science, 100,* 11696–11701.

Dalton, D. R., & Mesch, D. J. (1991). On the extent and reduction of avoidable absenteeism: An assessment of absence policy provisions. *Journal of Applied Psychology, 76,* 810–817.

Dalton, J. H., Hill, J., Thomas, E., & Kloos, B. (2013). Community psychology. In D. K. Freedheim, & I. B. Weiner (Eds.), *Handbook of psychology, Vol 1: History of psychology* (2nd ed.) (pp. 468–487). Hoboken, NJ: Wiley.

Damasio, A. R. (1994). *Descartes' error.* New York: Putnam.

Damasio, A. R., Grabowski, T. J., Bechara, A., Damasio, H., Ponto, L. L. B., Parvizi, J., & Hichwa, R. D. (2000). Subcortical and cortical brain activity during the feeling of self-generated emotions. *Nature Neuroscience, 3,* 1049–1056.

Dambrun, M., & Valentiné, E., (2010). Reopening the study of extreme social behaviors: Obedience to authority within an immersive video environment, *European Journal of Social Psychology, 40,* 760–773.

Damos, D. (1992). *Multiple task performance.* London: Taylor & Francis.

Danevova, V., Kvetnansky, R., & Jezova, D. (2013). Kinetics of oxytocin response to repeated restraint stress and/or chronic cold exposure. *Hormone Metabolism Research, 45*(12), 845–848.

Daniel, D. B., & Woody, W. D. (2010). They hear, but do not listen: Retention for podcasted material in a classroom context. *Teaching of Psychology, 37*(3), 199–203. doi:10.1080/00986283.2010.488542.

Danker, J. F., & Anderson, J. R. (2010). The ghosts of brain states past: Remembering reactivates the brain regions engaged during encoding. *Psychological Bulletin, 136,* 87–102.

Danner, D. D., Snowden, D. A., & Friesen, W. V. (2001). Positive emotions in early life and longevity findings from the nun study. *Journal of Personality and Social Psychology, 80,* 804–813.

Dansereau, F., Jr., Graen, G., & Haga, W. J. (1975). A vertical dyad linkage approach to leadership with formal organizations. *Organizational Behavior and Human Performance, 13,* 46–78.

Danziger, S., Levav, J., & Avnaim-Pessoa, L. (2011). Extraneous factors in judicial decisions. *PNAS Proceedings of the National Academy of Sciences of the United States of America, 108*(17), 6889–6892. doi:10.1073/pnas.1018033108.

Dapretto, M., Davies, M. S., Pfeifer, J. H., Scott, A. A., Sigman, M., Bookheimer, S. Y., et al. (2006). Understanding emotions in others: Mirror neuron dysfunction in children with autism spectrum disorders. *Nature Neuroscience, 9,* 28–30.

Darchia, N., Campbell, I. G., & Feinberg, I. (2003). Rapid eye movement density is reduced in the normal elderly. *Sleep, 26,* 973–977.

Dark, V. J., & Benbow, C. P. (1993). Cognitive differences among the gifted: A review and new data. In D. K. Detterman (Ed.), *Current topics in human intelligence* (Vol. 3, pp. 85–120). Norwood, NJ: Ablex.

Darkes, J., & Goldman, M. S. (1993). Expectancy challenge and drinking reduction. *Journal of Clinical and Consulting Psychology, 61,* 344–353.

Darwin, C. E. (1872). *The expression of the emotions in man and animals.* London: John Murray.

Dasgupta, A. M., Juza, D. M., White, G. M., & Maloney, J. F. (1995). Memory and hypnosis: A comparative analysis of guided memory, cognitive interview, and hypnotic hypermnesia. *Imagination, Cognition, and Personality, 14*(2), 117–130.

Davidov, M., Zahn-Waxler, C., Roth-Hanania, R., & Knafo, A. (2013). Concern for others in the first year of life: Theory, evidence, and avenues for research. *Child Development Perspectives, 7,* 126–131.

Davidson, J. M., Camargo, C. A., & Smith, E. R. (1979). Effects of androgen on sexual behavior in hypogonadal men. *Journal of Clinical Endocrinological Metabolism, 48,* 955–958.

Davidson, J. R., Foa, E. B., Huppert, J. D., Keefe, F. J., Franklin, M. E., Compton, J. S., et al. (2004). Fluoxetine, comprehensive cognitive behavioral therapy, and placebo in generalized social phobia. *Archives of General Psychiatry, 61,* 1005–1013.

Davidson, R. J., Ekman, P., Saron, C., Senulis, J., & Friesen, W. V. (1990). Approach-withdrawal and cerebral asymmetry: Emotional expression and brain physiology: I. *Journal of Personality and Social Psychology, 58,* 330–341.

Davidson, R. J., Pizzagalli, D., Nitschke, J. B., & Putnam, K. (2002). Depression: Perspectives from affective neuroscience. *Annual Review of Psychology, 53,* 545–574.

Davies, C. (1999, April 21). Junior doctor is cleared in baby overdose death. *London Daily Telegraph,* p. 2.

Davies, G. G., Tenesa, A. A., Payton, A. A., Yang, J. J., Harris, S. E., Liewald, D. D., & Deary, I. J. (2011). Genome-wide association studies establish that human intelligence is highly heritable and polygenic. *Molecular Psychiatry, 16*(10), 996–1005. doi:10.1038/mp.2011.85.

Davies, P. T., Sturge-Apple, M. L., Bascoe, S. M., & Cummings, E. M. (2013). The legacy of early insecurity histories in shaping adolescent adaptation to interparental conflict. *Child Development, 85*(1), 338–354.

Davies, R. R., & Kipps, C. M. (2011). Lobar atrophy in frontotemporal dementia: diagnostic and prognostic implications. *Current Alzheimer Research, 8*(3), 261–265.

Davis, E., Glynn, L. M., Waffarn, F., & Sandman, C. A. (2011). Prenatal maternal stress programs infant stress regulation. *Journal of Child Psychology and Psychiatry, 52*(2), 119–129. doi:10.1111/j.1469-7610.2010.02314.x.

Davis, E. P., & Sandman, C. A. (2010). The timing of prenatal exposure to maternal cortisol and psychosocial stress is associated with human infant cognitive development. *Child Development, 81,* 131–148.

Davis, J. A., & Smith, T. W. (1990). *General social surveys, 1972–1990: Cumulative codebook.* Chicago: National Opinion Research Center.

Davis, J. D., Gallagher, R. J., Ladove, R. F., & Turansky, A. J. (1969). Inhibition of food intake by a humoral factor. *Journal of Comparative and Physiological Psychology, 67,* 407–414.

Davis, J. L., & Rusbult, C. (2001). Attitude alignment in close relationships. *Journal of Personality and Social Psychology, 81,* 65–84.

Davis, J. M., Giakas, W. J., Qu, J., Prasad, P., & Leucht, S. (2011). Should we treat depression with drugs or psychological interventions? A reply to Ioannidis. *Philosophy, Ethics, and Humanities in Medicine, 6,* 8.

Davis, K., Desrocher, M., & Moore, T. (2011). Fetal Alcohol Spectrum Disorder: A review of neurodevelopmental findings and interventions. *Journal of Developmental and Physical Disabilities, 23*(2), 143–167. doi:10.1007/s10882-010-9204-2.

Davis, M., Myers, K. M., Ressler, K. J., & Rothbaum, B. O. (2005). Facilitation of extinction of conditioned fear by D-cycloserine. *Current Directions in Psychological Science, 14,* 214–219.

Davis, M., Ressler, K., Rothbaum, B. O., & Richardson, R. (2006). Effects of D-cycloserine on extinction: Translation from preclinical to clinical work. *Biological Psychiatry, 60,* 369–375.

Davis, M. H. (1994). *Empathy: A social psychological approach.* Madison, WI: Brown and Benchmark.

Davis, M. H., Johnsrude, I. S., Hervais-Adelman, A., Taylor, K., & McGettigan, C. (2005). Lexical information drives perceptual learning of distorted speech: Evidence from the comprehension of noise-vocoded sentences. *Journal of Experimental Psychology: General, 134,* 222–241.

Davis, N., Gross, J., & Hayne, H. (2008). Defining the boundary of childhood amnesia. *Memory, 16*(5), 465–474.

Davis, R. A., & Moore, C. C. (1935). Methods of measuring retention. *Journal of General Psychology, 12,* 144–155.

Davis-Kean, P. E., Jager, J., & Collins, W. A. (2009). The self in action: An emerging link between self-beliefs and behaviors in middle childhood. *Child Development Perspectives, 3,* 184–188.

Davison, G. C., & Neale, J. M. (1990). *Abnormal psychology* (5th ed.). New York: Wiley.

Dawe, I. C. (2008). Suicide and homicide. In R. L. Glick, J. S. Berlin, A. B. Fishkind, & S. L. Zeller (Eds.). *Emergency psychiatry: Principles and practice* (pp. 149–159). Philadelphia: Wolters Kluwer Health/Lippincott Williams & Wilkins. doi:10.1073/pnas.1118653109

Dawes, R. M. (1998). Behavioral decision making and judgment. In D. Gilbert, S. T. Fiske, & G. Lindzey (Eds.), *Handbook of social psychology* (Vol. 1, 4th ed., pp. 497–549). Boston: McGraw-Hill.

Dawkins, K., & Potter, W. (1991). Gender differences in pharmacokinetics and pharmacodynamics of psychotropics: Focus on women. *Psychopharmacology Bulletin, 27,* 417–426.

Dawson, M., Schell, A. M., & Filion, D. L. (2000). The electodermal system. In J. Cacioppo, L. Tassinary, & G. Bernston (Eds.), *Handbook of psychophysiology* (2nd ed., pp. 200–222). New York: Cambridge University Press.

Day, N. L., Leech, S. L., & Goldschmidt, L. (2011). The effects of prenatal marijuana exposure on delinquent behaviors are mediated by measures of neurocognitive functioning. *Neurotoxicology and Teratology, 33*(1), 129–136.

Day, S. M. (2012). Alcohol consumption during pregnancy: The growing evidence. *Developmental Medicine & Child Neurology, 54,* 200.

Dayan, E., Censor, N., Buch, E. R., Sandrini, M., & Cohen, L. G. (2013). Noninvasive brain stimulation: From physiology to network dynamics and back. *Nature Neuroscience, 16*(7), 838–844.

Dayan, K., Fox, S., & Kasten, R. (2008). The preliminary employment interview as a predictor of assessment center outcomes. *International Journal of Selection and Assessment, 16,* 102–111.

Dayan, K., Kasten, R., & Fox, S. (2002). Entry-level police candidate assessment center: An efficient tool or a hammer to kill a fly? *Personnel Psychology, 55,* 827–849.

de Araujo, I. E., Rolls, E. T., Velazco, M. I., Margot, C., & Cayeux, I. (2005). Cognitive modulation of olfactory processing. *Neuron, 46,* 671–679.

Deary, I. J., & Batty, G. (2011). Intelligence as a predictor of health, illness; and death. In R. J. Sternberg, S. Kaufman, R. J. Sternberg, S. Kaufman (Eds.) , *The Cambridge handbook of intelligence* (pp. 683–707). New York, NY: Cambridge University Press.

Deary, I. J., & Bedford, A. (2011). Some origins and evolution of the EPQ-R (short form) neuroticism and extraversion items. *Personality and Individual Differences, 50,* 1213–1217.

Deary, I. J., & Der, G. (2005a). Reaction time, age, and cognitive ability: Longitudinal findings from age 16 to 63 years in representative population samples. *Aging, Neuropsychology, and Cognition, 12,* 187–215.

Deary, I. J., & Der, G. (2005b). Reaction time explains IQ's association with death. *Psychological Science, 16*(1), 64–69.

Deary, I. J., Whalley, L. J., Lemmon, H., Crawford, J. R., & Starr, J. M. (2000). The stability of individual differences in ability from childhood to old age: Follow up of the 1932 Scottish mental survey. *Intelligence, 28,* 49–55.

Deary, I. J., Whiteman, M. C., Starr, J. M., Whalley, L. J., & Fox, H. C. (2004). The impact of childhood intelligence on later life: Following up the Scottish mental surveys of 1932 and 1947. *Journal of Personality and Social Psychology, 86,* 130–147.

Death Penalty Information Center. (2012, March 29). Facts about the death penalty. Retrieved from http://www.deathpenaltyinfo.org/documents/FactSheet.pdf.

Deaux, K., & LaFrance, M. (1998). Gender. In D. T. Gilbert, S. T. Fiske, & G. Lindzey (Eds.), *Handbook of social psychology* (4th ed., Vol. 1, pp. 778–828). New York: McGraw-Hill.

Dębiec, J., & LeDoux, J. (2009). The amygdala and the neural pathways of fear. In P. Shiromani, T. Keane, & J. E. LeDoux (Eds.), *Post-Traumatic Stress Disorder: Basic Science and Clinical Practice.* Totowa, NJ: Humana Press, pp. 23–38.

de Boer, H., Bosker, R. J., & van der Werf, M. P. C. (2010). Sustainability of teacher expectation bias effects on long-term student performance. *Journal of Educational Psychology, 102,* 168–179.

de Bruxelles, S. (2009, November 18). Sleepwalker accidentally killed wife during nightmare, prosecutors say. *London Times*

De Castro, J. M. (1990). Social facilitation of duration and size but not rate of the spontaneous meal intake of humans. *Physiology and Behavior, 47,* 1129–1135.

Decety, J. (2011). Neuroscience of empathic responding. In S. Brown, M. Brown, & L. Penner (Eds.), *Self-interest and beyond: Toward a new understanding of human.* New York: Oxford University Press

Decety, J., Yang, C., & Cheng, Y. (2010). Physicians down-regulate their pain empathy response: An event-related brain potential study. *Neuroimage, 50*(4), 1676–1682. doi:10.1016/j.neuroimage.2010.01.025.

de Charms, R., Levy, J., & Wertheimer, M. (1954). A note on attempted evaluations of psychotherapy. *Journal of Clinical Psychology, 10,* 233–235.

Deci, E. L., Koestner, R., & Ryan, R. M. (1999a). A meta-analytic review of experiments examining the effects of extrinsic rewards on intrinsic motivation. *Psychological Bulletin, 125,* 627–668.

Deci, E. L., Koestner, R., & Ryan, R. M. (1999b). The undermining effect is a reality after all—Extrinsic rewards, task interest, and self-determination: Reply to Eisenberger, Pierce, and Cameron (1999) and Lepper, Henderlong, and Gingras (1999). *Psychological Bulletin, 125,* 692–700.

Deci, E. L., Koestner, R., & Ryan, R. M. (2001). A meta-analytic review of experiments examining the effects of extrinsic rewards on intrinsic motivation. *Psychological Bulletin, 125,* 627–668.

De Dreu, C. K. W. (2010). Social conflict. In S. T. Fiske, D. T. Gilbert, & G. Lindzey (Eds.), *Handbook of social psychology* (5th ed., Vol. 2, pp. 883–1023). Hoboken, NJ: Wiley.

Deeb, I., Segall, G., Birnbaum, D., Ben-Eliyahu, A., & Diesendruck, G. (2011). Seeing isn't believing: The effect of intergroup exposure on children's essentialist beliefs about ethnic categories. *Journal of Personality and Social Psychology, 101*(6), 1139–1156. doi:10.1037/a0026107.

Deeprose, C., & Andrade, J. (2006). Is priming during anesthesia unconscious? *Consciousness and Cognition, 15,* 1–23.

Defina, P. A., Moser, R. S., Glenn, M., Lichtenstein, J. D., & Fellus, J. (2013). Alzheimer's Disease Clinical and Research Update for Health Care Practitioners. *Journal of Aging Research.* Epub September 4, 2013.

De Fruyt, F., De Bolle, M., McCrae, R. R., Terracciano, A. & Costa, P. T., Jr. (2009). Assessing the universal structure of personality in early adolescence: The NEO-PI-R and NEO-PI-3 in 24 cultures. *Assessment, 16,* 301–311.

de Gelder, B., Snyder, J., Greve, D., Gerard, G., & Hadjikhani, N. (2004). Fear fosters flight: A mechanism for fear contagion when perceiving emotion expressed by a whole body. *Proceedings of the National Academy of Sciences, 101,* 16701–16706.

Degner, J., & Wentura, D. (2009). Not everybody likes the thin and despises the fat: One's weight matters in the automatic activation of weight-related social evaluations. *Social Cognition, 27,* 202–221.

Degner, J., & Wentura, D. (2010). Automatic prejudice in childhood and early adolescence. *Journal of Personality and Social Psychology, 98,* 356–374.

de Gonzalez, A., Hartge, P., Cerhan, J. R., Flint, A. J., Hannan, L., MacInnis, R. J., & .. Hoppin, J. A. (2010). Body-mass index and mortality among 1.46 million White adults. *New England Journal of Medicine, 363*(23), 2211–2219. doi:10.1056/ NEJMoa1000367.

de Graaf, L. E., Huibers, M. J. H., Cuijpers, P., & Arntz, A. (2010). Minor and major depression in the general population: Does dysfunctional thinking play a role? *Comprehensive Psychiatry, 51,* 266–274.

de Groot, J. H. B., Smeets, M. A. M., Kaldewaij, A., Duijndam, M. J. A., & Semin, G. R. (2012). Chemosignals communicate human emotions. *Psychological Science, 23,* 1417–1424.

de Haan, M., Mishkin, M., Baldeweg, T., & Vargha-Khadem, F. (2006). Human memory development and its dysfunction after early hippocampal injury. *Trends in Neurosciences, 29*(7), 374–381.

Dehaene-Lambertz, G. G., Montavont, A. A., Jobert, A. A., Allirol, L. L., Dubois, J. J., Hertz-Pannier, L. L., & Dehaene, S. S. (2010). Language or music, mother or Mozart? Structural and environmental influences on infants' language networks. *Brain & Language, 114*(2), 53–65. doi:10.1016/j.bandl.2009.09.003.

de Houwer, A. (1995). Bilingual language acquisition. In P. Fletcher & B. MacWhinney (Eds.), *The handbook of child language* (pp. 219–250). Cambridge, MA: Blackwell.

Deich, J. D., Tankoos, J., & Balsam, P. D. (1995). Systematic changes in gaping during the ontogeny of pecking in ring doves (*Streptopelia risoria*). *Developmental Psychobiology, 28,* 147–163.

De Jongh, A., Ernst, R., Marques, L., & Hornsveld, H. (2013). The impact of eye movements and tones on disturbing memories involving PTSD and other mental disorders. *Journal of Behavior Therapy and Experimental Psychiatry, 44*(4), 477–483.

DeKosky, S. T., Kaufer, D. I., Hamilton, R. L., Wolk, D. A., Lopez, O. L. (2008). The Dementias. In W. G. Bradley, R. B. Daroff, G. M. Fenichel, & J. Jamkovic (Eds). *Bradley: Neurology in Clinical Practice, 5th Edition.* Philadelphia, PA: Butterworth, Heinemann, Elsevier.

Delamater, A. R. (2004). Experimental extinction in Pavlovian conditioning: Behavioural and neuroscience perspectives. *Quarterly Journal of Experimental Psychology, 57B,* 97–132.

de la Sablonnière, R., Tougas, F., & Lortie-Lussier, M. (2009). Dramatic social change in Russia and Mongolia: Connecting relative deprivation to social identity. *Journal of Cross-Cultural Psychology, 40,* 327–348.

DeLeo, J. A. (2006). Basic science of pain. *Journal of Bone and Joint Surgery (American), 88*(Suppl. 2), 58–62.

DeLisi, M., Vaughn, M. G., Gentile, D. A., Anderson, C. A., & Shook, J. J. (2013). Violent video games, delinquency, and youth violence: New evidence. *Youth Violence and Juvenile Justice, 11*(2), 132–142.

Delmas, P., Hao, J. & Rodat-Despoix, L. (2011). Molecular mechanisms of mechanotransduction in mammalian sensory neurons. *Nature Review Neuroscience, 12*(3), 139–153.

Delmolino, L. M., & Romanczyk, R. G. (1995). Facilitated communication: A critical review. *Behavior Therapist, 18,* 27–30.

DeLoache, J. S., Chiong, C., Sherman, K., Islam, N., Vanderborght, M., Troseth, G. L., & O'Doherty, K. (2010). Do babies learn from baby media? *Psychological Science, 21*(11), 1570–1574. doi:10.1177/0956797610384145.

De Los Reyes, A. (2011). More than measurement error: Discovering meaning behind informant discrepancies in clinical assessments of children and adolescents, *Journal of Clinical Child and Adolescent Psychology, 40,* 1–9.

DeMause, L. (1987). Schreber and the history of childhood. *The Journal of Psychohistory, 15,* 423–430.

de Macedo-Soares, M. B., Moreno, R. A., Rigonatti, S. P., & Lafer, B. (2005). Efficacy of electroconvulsive therapy in treatment-resistant bipolar disorder: A case series. *Journal of ECT, 21,* 31–34.

Demaray, M. K., & Malecki, C. K. (2002). Critical levels of perceived social support associated with student adjustment. *School Psychology Quarterly, 17,* 213–241.

Dement, W. (1960). The effect of dream deprivation. *Science, 131,* 1705–1707.

Dement, W., & Kleitman, N. (1957). Cyclic variations in EEG during sleep and their relation to eye movements, body motility and dreaming. *Electroencephalography and Clinical Neurophysiology, 9,* 673–690.

Demerouti, E., Geurts, S. A. E., Bakker, A. B., & Euwema, M. (2004). The impact of shiftwork on work-home conflict, job attitudes, and health. *Ergonomics, 47,* 987–1002.

de Moor, J. S., de Moor, C. A., Basen-Engquist, K., Kudelka, A., Bevers, M. W., & Cohen, L. (2006). Optimism, distress, health-related quality of life, and change in cancer antigen 125 among patients with ovarian cancer undergoing chemotherapy. *Psychosomatic Medicine, 68,* 555–562.

Dempsey, P. G., McGorry, R. W., & Maynard, W. S. (2005). A survey of tools and methods used by certified professional ergonomists. *Applied Ergonomics, 36*(4), 489–503.

DeNeve, J-E., Diener, E., Tay, L., & Xuereb, C. (2013). The objective benefits of subjective well-being. In J. F. Helliwell, R. Layard, & J. Sachs (Eds.), *World happiness report 2013. Volume 2.* (pp. 54–79). New York: UN Sustainable Network Development Solutions Network.

Deng, W., & Sloutsky, V. M. (2012). Carrot eaters or moving heads: Inductive inference is better supported by salient features than by category labels. *Psychological Science, 23*(2), 178–186. doi:10.1177/0956797611429133.

Dentoni, L., Capelli, L., Sironi, S., Del Rosso, R., Zanetti, S., & Della Torre, M. (2012). Development of an electronic nose for environmental odour monitoring. *Sensors, 12*(11), 14363–14381.

DePaolis, R. A., Vihman, M. M., & Nakai, S. (2013). The influence of babbling patterns on the processing of speech. *Infant Behavior & Development, 36*(4), 642–649.

de Pinho, R. S., da Silva-Júnior, F. P., Bastos, J. P., Maia, W. S., de Mello, M. T., de Bruin, V. M., & de Bruin, P. F. (2006). Hypersomnolence and accidents in truck drivers: A cross-sectional study. *Chronobiology International, 23*(5):963–971.

DePrince, A. P., & Freyd, J. J. (2004). Forgetting trauma stimuli. *Psychological Science, 15,* 488–492.

Derauf, C., LaGasse, L., Smith, L., Newman, E., Shah, R., Arria, A., Huestis, M., Haning, W., Strauss, A., Della Grotta, S., Dansereau, L., Lin, H., & Lester, B. (2011). Infant temperament and high-risk environment relate to behavior problems and language in toddlers. *Journal of Developmental and Behavioral Pediatrics, 32,* 125–135.

Dere, E., & Zlomuzica, A. (2012). The role of gap junctions in the brain in health and disease. *Neurosci Biobehav Rev 36* (1):206–217.

de Rios, M. D. (1992). Power and hallucinogenic states of consciousness among the Moche: An ancient Peruvian society. In C. A. Ward (Ed.), *Altered states of consciousness and mental health: A cross cultural perspective.* Newbury Park, CA: Sage.

Derogowski, J. B. (1989). Real space and represented space: Cross-cultural perspectives. *Behavior and Brain Sciences, 12,* 51–73.

Derringer, J., Krueger, R. F., Dick, D. M., Saccone, S., Grucza, R. A., Agrawal, A., & .. Bierut, L. J. (2010). Predicting sensation seeking from dopamine genes: A candidate-system approach. *Psychological Science, 21*(9), 1282–1290. doi:10.1177/0956797610380699.

Derry, C. J., Derry, S., McQuay, H. J., & Moore, R. A. (2006). Systematic review of systematic reviews of acupuncture published 1996–2005. *Clinical Medicine, 6,* 381–386.

Derry, C. P., Harvey, A. S., Walker, M. C., Duncan, J. S., & Berkovic, S. F. (2009). NREM arousal parasomnias and their distinction from nocturnal frontal lobe epilepsy: A video EEG analysis. *Sleep, 32*(12), 1637–1644.

Derryberry, D., & Tucker, D. M. (1992). Neural mechanisms of emotion. *Journal of Consulting and Clinical Psychology, 60,* 329–338.

DeRubeis, R. J., & Crits-Christoph, P. (1998). Empirically supported individual and group psychological treatments for adult mental disorders. *Journal of Consulting and Clinical Psychology, 66,* 37–52.

Desai, R., Krishnan-Sarin, S., Cavallo, D., & Potenza, M. (2010). Video-gaming among high school students: health correlates, gender differences, and problematic gaming. *Pediatrics, 126*(6), e1414-e1424.

De Santi, S., Pirraglia, E., Barr, W., Babb, J., Williams, S., Rogers, K., Glodzik, L. Brys, M., Mosconi, L., Reisberg, B., Ferris, S., & de Leon, M. J. (2008). Robust and conventional neuropsychological norms: Diagnosis and prediction of age-related cognitive decline. *Neuropsychology, 22,* 469–484.

Deshauer, D., Moher, D., Fergusson, D., Moher, E., Sampson, M., & Grimshaw, J. (2008). Selective serotonin reuptake inhibitors for unipolar depression: a systematic review of classic long-term randomized controlled trials. *CMAJ, 178*(10), 1293–1301.

Deslauriers, L., Schelew, E., & Wieman, C. (2011). Improved Learning in a Large-Enrollment Physics Class. *Science, 332*(6031), 862–864. doi:10.1126/science.1201783.

de Souza, M., Mussap, A. J., & Cummins, R. A. (2010). Primary and secondary control over eating behaviors. *Eating Behaviors,* doi:10.1016/ j.eatbeh.2010.05.002.

Detrick, P., & Chibnall, J. T. (2013). Revised NEO Personality Inventory normative data for police officer selection. *Psychological Services, 10,* 372–377.

Deutsch, M., & Gerard, H. B. (1955). A study of normative and informative social influences on individual judgments. *Journal of Abnormal and Social Psychology, 51,* 629–636.

Devanand, D. P., Pradhaban, G., Liu, X., Khandji, A., De Santi, S., Segal, S., et al. (2007). Hippocampal and entorhinal atrophy in mild cognitive impairment: Prediction of Alzheimer's disease. *Neurology, 68,* 828–836.

Devenport, L. D. (1998). Spontaneous recovery without interference: Why remembering is adaptive. *Animal Learning and Behavior, 26,* 172–181.

Devi, G., & Quitschke, W. (1999). Alois Alzheimer, neuroscientist (1864–1915). *Alzheimer Disease and Associated Disorders, 13*(3), 132–137.

Devilly, G. J., Varker, T., Hansen, K., & Gist, R. (2007). An analogue study of the eff ects of psychological debriefing on eyewitness testimony. *Behaviour Research and Therapy, 45,* 1245–1254.

Devine, A., Fawcett, K., Szűcs, D., & Dowker, A. (2012). Gender differences in mathematics anxiety and the relation to mathematics performance while controlling for test anxiety. *Behavioral & Brain Functions, 8,* 33.

Devine, P. G., Forscher, P. S., Austin, A. J., & Cox, W. L. (2012). Long-term reduction in implicit race bias: A prejudice habit-breaking intervention. *Journal of Experimental Social Psychology, 48*(6), 1267–1278.

Devinsky, O., Farah, M. J., & Barr ,W. B. (2008). Chapter 21 Visual agnosia. In P. J. Vinken & G. W. Bruyn (Eds). *Handbook of Clinical Neurology, 88,* 417–27.

DeVoe, S. E., & Iyengar, S. S. (2010). Medium of exchange matters: What's fair for goods is unfair for money. *Psychological Science, 21*(2), 159–162. doi:10.1177/ 0956797609357749.

Devonshire, I. M., Papadakis, N. G., Port, M., Berwick, J., Kennerley, A. J., Mayhew, J. E., & Overton, P. G. (2011). Neurovascular coupling is brain region-dependent. *Neuroimage.*

DeVries, R. (1969). Constancy of generic identity in the years three to six. *Monographs of the Society for Research in Child Development, 34*(3), 1–67.

DeWall, C., Anderson, C. A., & Bushman, B. J. (2013). Aggression. In H. Tennen, J. Suls, I. B. Weiner (Eds.), *Handbook of psychology, Vol. 5: Personality and social psychology* (2nd ed.) (pp. 449–466). Hoboken, NJ: John Wiley & Sons Inc.

DeWall, C., Lambert, N. M., Slotter, E. B., Pond, R. r., Deckman, T., Finkel, E. J., & Fincham, F. D. (2011). So far away from one's partner, yet so close to romantic alternatives: Avoidant attachment, interest in alternatives, and infidelity. *Journal of Personality and Social Psychology, 101*(6), 1302–1316. doi:10.1037/a0025497.

DeWall, C. N., & Bushman, B. J. (2009). Hot under the collar in a lukewarm environment: Words associated with hot temperature increase aggressive thoughts and hostile perceptions *Journal of Experimental Social Psychology, 45,* 1045–1047.

DeWitt, L. A., & Samuel, A. G. (1990). The role of knowledge-based function in music perception. *Journal of Experimental Psychology: General, 119,* 123–144.

DeWolff, M. S., & van IJzendoorn, M. H. (1997). Sensitivity and attachment: A meta-analysis on parental antecedents of infant attachment. *Child Development, 68,* 571–591.

DeYoung, C. G., Hirsh, J. B., Shane, M. S., Papademetris, X. Rajeevan, N. & Gray, J. R. (2010). Testing predictions from personality neuroscience: Brain structure and the big five. *Psychological Science, 21*(6), 820–828. doi:10.1177/0956797610370159.

DeYoung, C. G., Quilty, L. C., & Peterson, J. B. (2007). Between facets and domains: 10 aspects of the Big Five. *Journal of Personality and Social Psychology, 93*(5), 880–896.

de Zilva, D., Mitchell, C. J., & Newell, B. R. (2013). Eliminating the mere exposure effect through changes in context between exposure and test. *Cognition and Emotion, 27*(8), 1345–1358.

Dhruv, N. T, Tailby, C., Sokol, S. H., and Lennie, P. (2011). Multiple adaptable mechanisms early in the primate visual pathway. *Journal of Neuroscience, 31*(42), 15016–15025.

Dhurandhar, N. V., Israel, B. A., Kolesar, J. M., Mayhew, G. F., Cook, M. E., & Atkinson, R. L. (2000). Increased adiposity in animals due to a human virus. *International Journal of Obesity, 24,* 989–996.

Diakidoy, I. N., & Spanoudis, G. (2002). Domain specificity in creativity testing: A comparison of performance on a general divergent-thinking test and a parallel, content-specific test. *Journal of Creative Behavior, 36,* 41–61.

Diamantopoulou, S., Verhulst, F. C., & van der Ende, J. (2010). Testing developmental pathways to antisocial personality problems. *Journal of Abnormal Child Psychology, 38,* 91–103.

Diamond, G. A. (2014). Randomized trials, observational registries, and the foundations of evidence-based medicine. *American Journal of Cardiology,* Epub February 1, 2014.

Diamond, G. M., Lipsitz, J. D., Fajerman, Z., & Rozenblat, O. (2010). Ongoing traumatic stress response (OTSR) in Sderot, Israel. *Professional Psychology: Research and Practice, 41,* 19–25.

Diamond, L. M. (2008). *Sexual fluidity: Understanding women's love and desire.* Cambridge, MA: Harvard University Press.

Diana, M., Spiga, S., & Acquas, E. (2006). Persistent and reversible morphine withdrawal– induced morphological changes in the nucleus accumbens. *Annals of the New York Academy of Sciences, 1074,* 446–457.

Dick, D. M., Meyers, J. L., Latendresse, S. J., Creemers, H. E., Lansford, J. E., Pettit, G. S., & Huizink, A. C. (2011). CHRM2, Parental monitoring, and adolescent externalizing behavior: Evidence for gene-environment interaction. *Psychological Science, 22*(4), 481–489. doi:10.1177/0956797611403318.

Dickenson, A. H. (2002). Gate control theory of pain stands the test of time. *British Journal of Anaesthesia, 88*(6), 755–757.

Dickerson, F. B., Tenhula, W. N., & Green-Paden, L. D. (2005). The token economy for schizophrenia: Review of the literature and recommendations for future research. *Schizophrenia Research, 75,* 405–416.

Dickinson, T., & Hurley, M. (2012). Exploring the antipathy of nursing staff who work within secure healthcare facilities across the United Kingdom to young people who self-harm. *Journal of Advanced Nursing, 68*(1), 147–158. doi:10.1111/j. 1365-2648.2011.05745.x.

Dickter, C., & Gyurovski, I. (2012). The effects of expectancy violations on early attention to race in an impression-formation paradigm. *Social Neuroscience, 7*(3), 240–251.

Diehl, M., Chui, H., Hay, E. L., Lumley, M. A., Grühn, D., & Labouvie-Vief, G. (2014). Change in coping and defense mechanisms across adulthood: Longitudinal findings in a European American sample. *Developmental Psychology, 50*(2), 634–648.

Diekelmann, S. & Born, J. (2010). The memory function of sleep. *Nature Reviews, Neuroscience, 11*(2), 114–126.

Diekman, A. B., Brown, E. R., Johnston, A. M., & Clark, E. K. (2010). Seeking congruity between goals and roles: A new look at why women opt out of science, technology, engineering, and mathematics careers. *Psychological Science, 21*(8), 1051–1057. doi:10.1177/0956797610377342.

Diener, E. (2000). Subjective well-being: The science of happiness and a proposal for a national index. *American Psychologist, 55,* 34–43.

Diener, E. (2012). New findings and future directions for subjective well-being research. *American Psychologist, 67*(8), 590–597.

Diener, E. (2013). The remarkable changes in the science of subjective well-being. *Perspectives on Psychological Science, 8*(6), 663–666.

Diener, E., & Seligman, M. E. P. (2004). Beyond money: Towards an economy of well-being. *Psychological Science in the Public Interest, 5,* 1–31.

Diener, M. L., Isabella, R. A., Behunin, M. G., & Wong, M. S. (2008). Attachment to mothers and fathers during middle childhood: Associations with child gender, grade, and competence. *Social Development, 17,* 84–101.

Dierdorff, E. C., & Ellington, K. J. (2008). It's the nature of the work: Examining behavior-based sources of work-family conflict across occupations. *Journal of Applied Psychology, 93,* 883–892.

Dierdorff, E. C., & Wilson, M. A. (2003). A meta-analysis of job analysis reliability. *Journal of Applied Psychology, 88,* 635–646.

Dietert, R. R., Dietert, J. M., & DeWitt, J. C. (2011). Environmental risk factors for autism. *Emerging Health Threats, 4,* 1–11. doi:10.3402/ehtj.v4i0.7111.

Dietrich, A., & Kanso, R. (2010). A review of EEG, ERP, and neuroimaging studies of creativity and insight. *Psychological Bulletin, 136*(5), 822–848. doi:10.1037/a0019749.

Difede, J., Cukor, J., Wyka, K., Olden, M., Hoffman, H., Lee, F. S., & Altemus, M. (2014). D-cycloserine augmentation of exposure therapy for post-traumatic stress disorder: A pilot randomized clinical trial. *Neuropsychopharmacology, 39*(5), 1052–1058.

Dijksterhuis, A., & Nordgren, L. F. (2006). A theory of unconscious thought. *Perspectives on Psychological Science, 1,* 95–109.

Dijkstra, P., Gibbons, F. X. & Buunk, A. P. (2010). Social comparison theory In J. Maddux & J. Tangney (Eds.) *Social psychological foundations of clinical psychology* (pp. 195–211). New York, NY: Guilford Press.

Dillon, C., Serrano, C. M., Castro, D., Leguizamón, P. P., Heisecke, S. L., & Taragano, F. E. (2013). Behavioral symptoms related to cognitive impairment. *Neuropsychiatric Disease and Treatment, 9,* 1443–1455.

Dimidjian, S., & Linehan, M. M. (2009). Mindfulness practice. In W. T. O'Donohue & J. E. Fisher (Eds.), *General principles and empirical supported techniques of cognitive behavior therapy* (pp. 425–434). Hoboken, NJ: Wiley

Dimidjian, S., Hollon, S. D., Dobson, K. S., Schmaling, K. B., Kohlenberg, R. J., Addis, M. E., et al. (2006). Randomized trial of behavioral activation, cognitive therapy, and antidepressant medication in the acute treatment of adults with major depression. *Journal of Consulting and Clinical Psychology, 74,* 658–670.

Di Milia, L. (2006). Shift work, sleepiness, and long distance driving. *Transportation Research, 9,* 278–285.

Dinan, T. G. (2001). Novel approaches to the treatment of depression by modulating the hypothalamic-pituitary-adrenal axis. *Human Psychopharmacology: Clinical and Experimental, 16,* 89–93.

diNoia, J., & Schinke, S. P. (2008). HIV risk-related attitudes, interpersonal influences, and intentions among at-risk urban, early adolescent girls. *American Journal of Health Behavior, 32*(5), 497–507.

Dionne, V. E., & Dubin, A. E. (1994). Transduction diversity in olfaction. *Journal of Experimental Biology, 194,* 1–21.

DiPatrizio, N. V., Astarita, G., Schwartz, G., Xiaosong, L., & Piomelli, D. (2011). Endocannabinoid signal in the gut controls dietary fat intake. *Proceedings Of The National Academy Of Sciences Of The United States Of America, 108*(31), 12904–12908. doi:10.1073/pnas.1104675108.

DiPatrizio, N. V., & Simansky, K. J. (2008). Activating parabrachial cannabinoid CB-sub-1 receptors selectively stimulates feeding of palatable foods in rats. *Journal of Neuroscience, 28*(39), 9702–9709.

DiPietro, J. A., Kivlighan, K. T., Costigan, K. A., Rubin, S. E., Shiffler, D. E., Henderson, J. L., & Pillion, J. P. (2010). Prenatal antecedents of newborn neurological maturation. *Child Development, 81,* 115–130.

DiPietro, J. A., Novak, M. F., Costigan, K. A., Atella, L. D., & Reusing, S. P. (2006). Maternal psychological distress during pregnancy in relation to child development at age two. *Child Development, 77,* 573–587.

Dirix, C. E. H., Nijhuis, J. G., Jongsma, H. W., & Hornstra, G. (2009). Aspects of fetal learning and memory. *Child Development, 80,* 1251–1258.

Distel, M. A., Vink, J. M., Willemsen, G., Middeldorp, C. M., Merckelbach, H. G. J., & Boomsma, D. I. (2008). Heritability of self-reported fear. *Behavioral Genetics, 38,* 24–33.

Dixon, M., Brunet, A., & Laurence, J.-R. (1990). Hypnotizability and automaticity: Toward a parallel distributed processing model of hypnotic responding. *Journal of Abnormal Psychology, 99,* 336–343.

Djonlagic, I., Rosenfeld, A., Shohamy, D., Myers, C., et al. (2009). Sleep enhances category learning. *Learning and Memory, 16,* 751–755.

D'Mello, R., & Dickenson, A. H. (2008). Spinal cord mechanisms of pain. *British Journal of Anesthesiology, 101*(1), 8–16.

D'Mello, S. K., & Graesser, A. (2010). Multimodal semi-automated affect detection from conversational cues, gross body language, and facial features. *User Modeling And User-Adapted Interaction, 20*(2), 147–187. doi:10.1007/s11257-010-9074-4.

Doane, L.D., Kremen, W.S., Eaves, L.J., Eisen, S.A., Hauger, R., Hellhammer, D., Levine, S., Lupien, S., Lyons, M.J., Mendoza, S., Prom-Wormley, E., Xian, H., York, T.P., Franz, C.E., & Jacobson, K.C. (2010). Associations between jet lag and cortisol diurnal rhythms after domestic travel. *Health Psychology, 29*(2), 117–123.

Dobolyi, D. G., & Dodson, C. S. (2013). Eyewitness confidence in simultaneous and sequential lineups: A criterion shift account for sequential mistaken identification overconfidence. *Journal of Experimental Psychology, Applied, 19*(4), 345–357.

Dobson, & Hamilton, K. E. (2009). Cognitive restructuring: Behavioral tests of negative cognitions. In W. T. O'Donohue & J. E. Fisher (Eds.), *General principles and empirically supported techniques of cognitive behavior therapy* (pp. 194–198). Hoboken, NJ: Wiley and Sons.

Dobson, K. S., Hollon, S. D., Dimidjian, S.,Schmaling, K. B., Kohlenberg, R. J., Gallop, R. J., Rizvi, S. L., Gollan, J. K., Dunner, D. L., & Jacobson, N. S. (2008). Randomized trial of behavioral activation, cognitive therapy, and antidepressant medication in the prevention of relapse and recurrence in major depression. *Journal of Consulting and Clinical Psychology, 76,* 468–477.

Doherty, W. J., & McDaniel, S. H. (2014). Family therapy. In G. R. VandenBos, E. Meidenbauer, & J. Frank-McNeil (Eds.), *Psychotherapy theories and techniques* (pp. 155–163). Washington, DC: American Psychological Association.

Dohrenwend, B. P., Raphael, K. G., Schwartz, S., Stueve, A., & Skodol, A. (1993). The structured event probe and narrative rating method for measuring stressful life events. In L. Goldenberger & S. Breznitz (Eds.), *Handbook of stress: Theoretical and clinical aspects* (2nd ed.). New York: The Free Press.

Doja, A., & Roberts, W. (2006). Immunizations and autism: a review of the literature. *The Canadian Journal of Neurological Sciences. Le Journal Canadien des Sciences Neurologiques, 33,* 341–346.

Dolinski, D. (2012). The nature of the first small request as a decisive factor in the effectiveness of the foot-in-the-door technique. *Applied Psychology: An International Review, 61*(3), 437–453.

Dollard, J., Doob, L., Miller, N., Mowrer, O. H., & Sears, R. R. (1939). *Frustration and aggression.* New Haven, CT: Yale University Press.

Dollinger, S. J. (2000). Locus of control and incidental learning: An application to college students. *College Student Journal, 34,* 537–540.

Dombrowski, S. U., Knittle, K., Avenell, A., Araújo-Soares, V., & Sniehotta, F. F. (2014). *BMJ,* Epub May 14, 2014.

Domhoff , G. W., & Schneider, A. (2008). Studying dream content using the archive and search engine on DreamBank.net. *Consciousness and Cognition, 17,* 1238–1247.

Domino, E. F. (2003). Effects of tobacco smoking on electroencephalographic, auditory evoked and event related potentials. *Brain and Cognition, 53,* 66–74.

Domjan, M. (2005). Pavlovian conditioning: A functional perspective. *Annual Review of Psychology, 56,* 179–206.

Domschke, K., Stevens, S., Pfl eiderer, B., & Gerlach, A. L. (2010). Interoceptive sensitivity in anxiety and anxiety disorders: An overview and integration of neurobiological findings. *Clinical Psychology Review, 30,* 1–11.

Donegan, N. H., & Thompson, R. F. (1991). The search for the engram. In J. L. Martinez Jr. & R. P. Kesner (Eds.), *Learning and memory: A biological view* (2nd ed., pp. 3–58). San Diego, CA: Academic Press.

Donner, M. B., VandeCreek, L., Gonsiorek, J. C., & Fisher, C. B. (2008). Balancing confidentiality: Protecting privacy and protecting the public. *Professional Psychology: Research and Practice, 39,* 369–376.

Donnerstein, E. (1984). Pornography: Its effects on violence against women. In N. M. Malamuth & E. Donnerstein (Eds.), *Pornography and sexual aggression.* New York: Academic Press.

Donovan, J. J., & Radosevich, D. J. (1999). A meta-analytic review of the distribution of practice effect: Now you see it, now you don't. *Journal of Applied Psychology, 84,* 795–805.

Doobay, A. F. (2008). School refusal behavior associated with separation anxiety disorder: A cognitive-behavioral approach to treatment. *Psychology in The Schools, 45*(4), 261–272.

Dordain, G., & Deffond, D. (1994). Pyridoxine neuropathies: Review of the literature. *Therapie, 49*(4), 333–337.

Doss, B. D., Rhoades, G. K., Stanley, S. M., & Markman, H. J. (2009). The effect of the transition to parenthood on relationship quality: An 8-year prospective study. *Psychological Bulletin, 96,* 601–619.

Doucet, S., Soussignan, R., Sagot, P., & Schaal, B. (2007). The "smellscape" of mother's breast: Effects of odor masking and selective unmasking on neonatal arousal, oral, and visual responses. *Developmental Psychobiology, 49,*129–138.

Doucet, S., Soussignan, R., Sagot, P., & Schaal, B. (2009). The secretion of areolar (Montgomery's) glands from lactating women elicits selective, unconditional responses in neonates. *PLoS ONE 4*, e7579.

Douglas, K. M., & Sutton, R. M. (2010). By their words ye shall know them: Language abstraction and the likeability of describers. *European Journal of Social Psychology, 40*, 366--374. doi:10.1002/ejsp.634.

Douglas, K. M., Sutton, R. M., & Stathi, S. (2010). Why I am less persuaded than you: People's intuitive understanding of the psychology of persuasion. *Social Influence, 5*(2), 133–148. doi:10.1080/15534511003597423.

Dovidio, J., Piliavin, J., Schroeder, D., & Penner, L. (2006). *The social psychology of prosocial behavior.* Mahwah, NJ: Lawrence Erlbaum.

Dovidio J. F., & Gaertner S. L. (1998). On the nature of contemporary prejudice: The causes, consequences, and challenges of aversive racism. In Eberhardt J., Fiske S. T. (Eds.), *Confronting racism: The problem and the response* (pp. 3–32). Newbury Park, CA: Sage.

Dovidio, J. F., & Gaertner, S. L. (2010). Intergroup bias. In S. T. Fiske, D. T. Gilbert, & G. Lindzey (Eds.), *Handbook of social psychology* (5th ed., Vol. 2, pp. 1084–1121). Hoboken, NJ: Wiley.

Dovidio, J. F., Gaertner, S. L., & Kawakami, K. (2010). Racism. In J. F. Dovidio, M. Hewstone, P. Glick, & V. M. Esses (Eds.), *The SAGE handbook of prejudice, stereotyping and discrimination* (pp. 312–327). London: Sage.

Dovidio, J. F., Kawakami, K., Smoak, N., & Gaertner, S. L. (2009). The roles of implicit and explicit processes in contemporary prejudice. In R. E. Petty, R. H. Fazio, & P. Brinol (Eds.), *Attitudes: Insights from the new implicit measures* (pp. 165–192). New York: Psychology Press.

Dovidio, J. F., & LaFrance, M. (2013). Race, ethnicity, and nonverbal behavior. In J. A. Hall & M. Knapp (Eds.), *Nonverbal communication* (pp. 671–696). The Hague, The Netherlands: DeGruyter-Mouton.

Dovidio, J. F., & Penner, L. A. (2001). Helping and altruism. In G. Fletcher & M. Clark (Eds.), *Blackwell handbook of social psychology: Interpersonal processes* (pp. 162–195). Boston: Blackwell.

Dovidio, J. F., Piliavin, J. A., Gaertner, S. L., Schroeder, D. A., & Clark, R. D., III. (1991). The arousal: Cost-reward model and the process of intervention: A review of the evidence. In M. Clark (Ed.), *Review of personality and social psychology: Vol. 12. Prosocial behavior* (pp. 86–118). Newbury Park, CA: Sage.

Dovidio, J. F., Smith, J. K., Donnella, A. G., & Gaertner, S. L. (1997). Racial attitudes and the death penalty. *Journal of Applied Social Psychology, 27*, 1468–1487.

Dowe, D. L., & Hernández-Orallo, J. (2012). IQ tests are not for machines, yet. *Intelligence, 40*(2), 77–81. doi:10.1016/j.intell.2011.12.001.

Doyle, J. (2005). *True witness: Cops, courts, science, and the battle against misidentification.* New York: Palgrave Macmillan.

Doyle, L., & Anderson, P. (2010). Adult outcome of extremely preterm infants. *Pediatrics, 126*(2), 342–351.

Doymus, K., Karacop, A., & Simsek, U. (2010). Effects of jigsaw and animation techniques on students' understanding of concepts and subjects in electrochemistry. *Educational Technology Research and Development, 58*, 671–691.

Draganski, B., Gaser, C., Busch, V., Schuierer, G., et al. (2004). Neuroplasticity: Changes in grey matter induced by training. *Nature, 427*, 311–312.

Dragonieri, S., Van Der Schee, M. P., Massaro, T., Schiavulli, N., Brinkman, P., Pinca, A., Carratú, P., Spanevello, A., & Resta, O. (2012). An electronic nose distinguishes exhaled breath of patients with Malignant Pleural Mesothelioma from controls. *Lung Cancer, 75*(3), 326–331.

Drasbek, K. R., Christensen, J., & Jensen, K. (2006). Gamma-hydroxybutyrate—A drug of abuse. *Acta Neurologica Scandinavica, 114*, 145–156.

Dreher, J.-C., Kohn, P., Kolachana, B., Weinberger, D. R., & Berman, K. F. (2010). Variation in dopamine genes influences responsivity of the human reward system. *Proceedings of the National Academy of Sciences, 106*, 617–622.

Drew, T., Võ, M. L., Wolfe, J. M. (2013). The invisible gorilla strikes again: Sustained inattentional blindness in expert observers. *Psychological Sciences, 24*(9), 1848–1853

Dreyfus, H. L., & Dreyfus, S. E. (1988). Making a mind versus modeling the brain: Intelligence back at a branchpoint. In S. R. Graubard (Ed.), *The artificial intelligence debate* (pp. 15–44). Cambridge: MIT Press.

Driskell, J. E., Willis, R., & Copper, C. (1992). Effect of overlearning on retention. *Journal of Applied Psychology, 77*, 615–622.

Dror, I. E. (2011). The paradox of human expertise: Why experts get it wrong. In Kapur, N. (Ed.), *The paradoxical brain.* Cambridge University Press.

Drucker-Colin, R., & Verdugo-Diaz, L. (2004). Cell transplantation for Parkinson's disease: Present status. *Cellular and Molecular Neurobiology, 24*, 301–316.

Druckman, D., & Bjork, R. A. (1994). *Learning, remembering, believing: Enhancing human performance.* Washington, DC: National Academy Press.

Drug Enforcement Adminstration, US Department of Justice. (2010). Herbal high-legal synthetic cannabinoids produce illicit marijuana effects: Spice, k2 and other "legal" products sold as marijuana alternatives. Available at: www.wyptac.org/upload/DEA%20K2%20Fact%20Sheet.pdf. Accessed May 31, 2011.

Druid, H., Holmgren, P., & Ahlner, J. (2001). Flunitrazepam: an evaluation of use, abuse and toxicity. *Forensic Science International, 122*, 136–141.

Drummond, S. P., Brown, G. G., Gillin, J. C., Stricker, J. L., Wong, E. C., & Buxton, R. B. (2000). Altered brain response to verbal learning following sleep deprivation. *Nature, 403*, 655–657.

Duan, X., Dan, Z., & Shi, J. (2013). The speed of information processing of 9- to 13-year-old intellectually gifted children. *Psychological Reports, 112*, 20–32.

DuBois, D. L., Portillo, N., Rhodes, J. E., Silverthorn, N., & Valentine, J. C. (2011). How effective are mentoring programs for youth? A systematic assessment of the evidence. *Psychological Science in the Public Interest, 12*(2), 57–91. doi:10.1177/1529100611414806.

Duckworth, A. L., Quinn, P. D., & Tsukayama, E. (2012). What No Child Left Behind leaves behind: The roles of IQ and self-control in predicting standardized achievement test scores and report card grades. *Journal of Educational Psychology, 104*(2), 439–451. doi:10.1037/a0026280

Duckworth, M. P. (2009). Assertiveness skills and the management of related factors. In W. T. O'Donohue & J. E. Fisher (Eds.), *General principles and empirically supported techniques of cognitive behavior therapy* (pp. 124–132). Hoboken, NJ: Wiley and Sons.

Dunfield, K. A., & Kuhlmeier, V. A. (2010). Intention-mediated selective helping in infancy. *Psycholoigcal Science, 21*, 523–527. doi:10.1177/ 0956797610364119.

Dunn, M. J., & Searle, R. (2010). Effect of manipulated prestige-car ownership on both sex attractiveness ratings. *British Journal Of Psychology, 101*(1), 69–80. doi:10.1348/000712609X417319.

Duarte, N. T., Goodson, J. R., & Klich, N. R. (1993). How do I like thee? Let me appraise the ways. *Journal of Organizational Behavior, 14*, 239–249.

DuBois, D. L., Felner, R. D., Brand, S., Adan, A. M., & Evans, E. G. (1992). A prospective study of life stress, social support, and adaptation in early adolescence. *Child Development, 63*, 542–557.

DuBreuil, S. C., Garry, M., & Loftus, E. F. (1998). Tales from the crib: Memories of infancy. In S. J. Lynn, & K. M. McConkey (Eds.), *Truth in memory* (pp. 137–160). New York: Guilford.

Dubrovsky, B. O. (2005). Steroids, neuroactive steroids and neurosteroids in psychopathology. *Progress in Neuropsychopharmacology and Biological Psychiatry, 29*, 169–192.

Duckitt, J. (2006). Differential effects of right-wing authoritarianism and social dominance orientation on outgroup attitudes and their mediation by threat from and competitiveness to outgroups. *Personality and Social Psychology Bulletin, 32*, 684–696.

Duckworth, A., Quinn, P. D., Lynam, D. R., Loeber, R., & Stouthamer-Loeber, M. (2011). Role of test motivation in intelligence testing. *PNAS Proceedings of the National Academy of Sciences of the United States of America, 108*(19), 7716–7720. doi:10.1073/pnas.1018601108.

Duclos, S. E., & Laird, J. D. (2001). The deliberate control of emotional experience through control of expressions. *Cognition and Emotion, 15*, 27–56.

Dudai, Y. (2004). The neurobiology of consolidations, or, how stable is the engram? *Annual Review of Psychology, 55*, 51–86.

Dudeck, M., Spitzer, C., Stopsack, M., Freyberger, H. J., & Barnow, S. (2007). Forensic inpatient male sexual offenders: The impact of personality disorders and childhood sexual abuse. *Journal of Forensic Psychiatry and Psychology, 18*, 494–506.

Dudley, N. M., Orvis, K. A., Lebeicki, J. E., & Cortina, J. M. (2006). A meta-analytic investigation of conscientiousness in the prediction of job performance: Examining the intercorrelations and the incremental validity of narrow traits. *Journal of Applied Psychology, 91*, 40–57.

Dumas, L., Lepage, M., Bystrova, K., Matthiesen, A. S., Welles-Nyström, B., & Widström, A. M. (2013). Influence of skin-to-skin contact and rooming-in on early mother-infant interaction: A randomized controlled trial. *Clinical Nursing Research, 22*, 310–336.

Duñabeitia, J. A., Molinaro, N., & Carreiras, M. (2011). Through the looking-glass: Mirror reading. *NeuroImage, 54*, 3004–3009. doi:10.1016/j.neuroimage. 2010.10.079.

Duncan, B. L. (2002). The legacy of Saul Rosenzweig: The profundity of the dodo bird. *Journal of Psychotherapy Integration, 12*(1), 32–57.

Duncan, G. J., Brooks-Gunn, J., & Klebanov, P. K. (1994). Economic deprivation and early childhood development. *Child Development, 65*, 296–318.

Duncan, G. J., Morris, P. A., & Rodrigues, C. (2011). Does money really matter? Estimating impacts of family income on young children's achievement with data from random-assignment experiments. *Developmental Psychology, 47*, 1263–1279.

Dunifon, R. (2013). The influence of grandparents on the lives of children and adolescents. *Child Development Perspectives, 7*, 55–60.

Dunlop, S. (2008). Activity-dependent plasticity: Implications for recovery after spinal cord injury. *Trends in Neurosciences, 31*(8), 410–418.

Dunn, J., & Hughes, C. (2001). "I got some swords and you're dead!": Violent fantasy, antisocial behavior, friendship, and moral sensibility in young children. *Child Development, 72*, 491–505.

Dupere, V., Leventhal, T., & Crosnoe, R. (in press). Understanding the positive role of neighborhood socioeconomic advantage in achievement: The contributions of the home, child care, and school environments. *Developmental Psychology*.

Durand, K., Baudouin, J-Y., Lewkowicz, D. J., Goubet, N., & Schaal, B. (2013). Eye-catching odors: Olfaction elicits sustained gazing to faces and eyes in 4-month-old infants. *PLOS ONE, August 28*. DOI: 10.1371/journal.pone.0070677

Durand, M. V., & Barlow, D. H. (2006). *Essentials of abnormal psychology*. Belmont, CA: Wadsworth.

Durante, K. M., Griskevicius, V., Simpson, J. A., Cantú, S. M., & Li, N. P. (2012). Ovulation leads women to perceive sexy cads as good dads. *Journal of Personality and Social Psychology, 103*, 292–305. doi:10.1037/a0028498

Durbin, C. E., & Klein, D. N. (2006). Ten-year stability of personality disorders among outpatients with mood disorders. *Journal of Abnormal Psychology, 115*, 75–84.

During, E. H., Elahi, F. M., Taleb, O., Moro, M., & Baubet, T. (2011). A critical review of dissociative trance and possession disorders: Etiological, diagnostic, therapeutic, and nosological issues. *Canadian Journal of Psychiatry, 56*(4), 235–242.

Durose, M. R., Harlow, C. W., Langan, P. A., Motivans, M., Rantala, R. R., & Smith, E. L. (2005). *Family violence statistics*. Washington, DC: Bureau of Justice Statistics.

Dutton, D. G., & Aron, A. P. (1974). Some evidence for heightened sexual attraction under conditions of high anxiety. *Journal of Personality and Social Psychology, 30*, 510–517.

Dweck, C. S. (1999). *Self-theories: Their role in motivation, personality, and development*. Philadelphia: Psychology Press.

Dwyer, T., & Ponsonby, A. L. (2009). Sudden infant death syndrome and prone sleeping position. *Annals of Epidemiology, 19*, 245–249.

d'Ydewalle, G., & Rosselle, H. (1978). Text expectations in text learning. In M. M. Gruneberg, P. E. Morris, & R. N. Sykes (Eds.), *Practical aspects of memory*. Orlando, FL: Academic Press.

Dykas, M. J., & Cassidy, J. (2011). Attachment and the processing of social information across the life span: Theory and evidence. *Psychological Bulletin, 137*(1), 19–46. doi:10.1037/a0021367.

Dyken, M. E., & Yamada, T. (2005). Narcolepsy and disorders of excessive somnolence. *Primary Care, 32*, 389–413.

Dykiert, D., Bates, T. C., Gow, A. J., Penke, L., Starr, J. M., & Deary, I. J. (2012). Predicting mortality from human faces. *Psychosomatic Medicine, 74*, 560–566. Published online: doi:10.1097/PSY.0b013e318259c33f.

Dyrbye, L. N., West, C. P., Satele, D., Boone, S., Tan, L., Sloan, J., & Shanafelt, T. D. (2014). Burnout among U.S. Medical students, residents, and early career physicians relative to the general U.S. population. *Academic Medicine, 89*(3), 443–451.

Dzokoto, V. A., & Adams, G. (2005). Understanding genital-shrinking epidemics in West Africa: Koro, Juju, or mass psychogenic illness? *Culture, Medicine, and Psychiatry, 29*, 53–78.

Eagly, A., & Carli, L. (2007). *Through the labyrinth: The truth about how women become leaders*. Boston: Harvard Business School Press.

Eagly, A. H., Johannesen-Schmidt, M. C., & van Engen, M. L. (2003). Transformational, transactional, and laissez-faire leadership styles: A meta-analysis comparing women and men. *Psychological Bulletin, 129*, 569–591.

Eagly, A. H., Makhijani, M. G., & Klonsky, B. G. (1992). Gender and evaluation of leaders: A meta-analysis. *Psychological Bulletin, 111*, 3–22.

Eagly, A. H., & Sczesny, S. (2009). Stereotypes about women, men, and leaders: Have times changed? In M. Barreto, M. Ryan, & M. Schmitt (Eds.), *The glass ceiling in the 21st century: Understanding barriers to gender equality* (pp. 21–47). Washington, DC: American Psychological Association.

Eagly, A. H., & Wood, W. (1999). The orgins of sex diffrences in human behavior: Evolved dispositions versus social roles. *American Psychologist, 54*, 408–423.

Eagly, A. H., Wood, W., & Johannesen-Schmidt, M. C. (2004). Social role theory of sex differences and similarities: Implications for the partner preferences of women and men. In A. H. Eagly, A. E. Beall, & R. J. Sternberg (Eds.), *The psychology of gender* (2nd ed., pp. 269–295). New York: Guilford Press.

Eamon, M. K. (2008). *Empowering vulnerable populations: Cognitive-behavioral interventions*. Chicago, IL: Lyceum Books.

East, P. L., & Jacobson, L. J. (2001). The younger siblings of teenage mothers: A follow-up of their pregnancy risk. *Developmental Psychology, 37*, 254–264.

Eastwick, P. W., & Finkel, E. J. (2008). Sex differences in mate preferences revisited: Do people know what they initially desire in a romantic partner? *Journal of Personality and Social Psychology, 94*, 245–264.

Ebert, S. A., Tucker, D. C., & Roth, D. L. (2002). Psychological resistance factors as predictors of general health status and physical symptom reporting. *Psychology Health & Medicine, 7*, 363–375.

Ebstein, R. B. (2006). The molecular genetic architecture of human personality: Beyond self-report questionnaires. *Molecular Psychiatry, 11*, 427–445.

Eccles, J., Lord, S., & Buchanan, C. M. (1996). School transitions in early adolescence: What are we doing to our young people? In J. A. Graber, J. Brooks-Gunn, & A. C. Peterson (Eds.), *Transitions through adolescence: Interpersonal domains and context* (pp. 251–284). Mahwah, NJ: Erlbaum.

Eccles, J. S., & Roeser, R. W. (2003). Schools as developmental contexts. In G. Adams & D. Beizonsky (Eds.), *Blackwell handbook of adolescence* (pp. 129–148). Malden, MA: Blackwell.

Eccleston, C., & Crombez, G. (1999). Pain demands attention: A cognitive-affective model of the interruptive function of pain. *Psychological Bulletin, 125*, 356–366.

Echeburua, E., de Corral, P., Garcia Bajos, E., & Borda, M. (1993). Interactions between self-exposure and alprazolam in the treatment of agoraphobia without current panic: An exploratory study. *Behavioural and Cognitive Psychotherapy, 21*, 219–238.

Echo News. (2000). Car crash mum tells of fight to rebuild her life. March 17. Retrieved from May 17, 2009, at http://archive.echo-news.co.uk/2000/3/17/ 206088.html.

Ecker, A. H., & Buckner, J. D. (2014). Cannabis use behaviors and social anxiety: The roles of perceived descriptive and injunctive social norms. *Journal of Studies on Alcohol and Drugs, 75*(1), 74–82.

Eddy, K. T., Dorer, D. J., Franko, D. L., Tahilani, K., Thompson-Brenner, H., & Herzog, D. B. (2008). Diagnostic crossover in anorexia nervosa and bulimia nervosa: Implications for DSM-V. *American Journal of Psychiatry, 165*, 245–250.

Edinger, J. D., Wohlgemuth, W. K., Radtke, R. A., Marsh, G. R., & Quillian, R. E. (2001). Cognitive behavioral therapy for treatment of chronic primary insomnia. *American Medical Association, 285*, 1856–1864.

Edwards, B. J., Reilly, T., & Waterhouse, J. (2009). Zeitgeber-effects of exercise on human circadian rhythms: What are alternative approaches to investigating the existence of a phase-response curve to exercise? *Biological Rhythm Research, 40*(1), 53–69.

Edwards, R. R., Campbell, C., Jamison, R. N., & Wiech, K. (2009). The neurobiological underpinnings of coping with pain. *Psychological Science, 18*, 237–241.

Egner, T., Jamieson, G., & Gruzelier, J. (2005). Hypnosis decouples cognitive control from conflict monitoring processes of the frontal lobe. *Neuroimage, 27*, 969–978.

Ehlers, A., Bisson, J., Clark, D. M., Creamer, M., et al. (2010). Do all psychological treatments really work the same in posttraumatic stress disorder? *Clinical Psychology Review, 30*, 269–276.

Ehrensaft, M. K., Cohen, P., Brown, J., Smailes, E., et al. (2003). Intergenerational transmission of partner violence: A 20-year prospective study. *Journal of Consulting and Clinical Psychology, 71*, 741–753.

Eich, E. (1989). Theoretical issues in state dependent memory. In H. L. Roediger & F. I. M. Craik (Eds.), *Varieties of memory and consciousness*. Hillsdale, NJ: Erlbaum.

Eich, E., & Macaulay, D. (2000). Are real moods required to reveal mood-congruent and mood-dependent memory? *Psychological Science, 11*, 244–248.

Eich, E., & Metcalfe, J. (1989). Mood dependent memory for internal versus external events. *Experimental Psychology: Learning, Memory, and Cognition, 15*, 443–455.

Eich, J. E., Weingartner, H., Stillman, R. C., & Gillin, J. C. (1975). State dependent accessibility of retrieval cues in the retention of a categorized list. *Journal of Verbal Learning and Verbal Behavior, 14*, 408–417.

Eichenbaum, H. (2013). What H.M. taught us. *Journal of Cognitive Neuroscience, 25*(1), 14–21.

Eid, M., & Larsen, R. J. (Eds.) (2008). *The science of subjective well-being*. New York, NY: Guilford Press.

Eiden, R. D., Schuetze, P., Colder, C. R., & Veira, Y. (2011). Maternal cocaine use and mother-toddler aggression. *Neurotoxicology and Teratology, 33*, 360–369.

Eifert, G. H., Zvolensky, M. J., & Louis, A. (2008). Somatoform disorders: Nature, psychological processes, and treatment strategies. In J. E. Maddux & B. A. Winstead (Eds.). *Psychopathology: Foundations for a contemporary understanding* (2nd ed., pp. 307–325). New York: Routledge/Taylor & Francis Group.

Einhorn, H., & Hogarth, R. (1982). Prediction, diagnosis and causal thinking in forecasting. *Journal of Forecasting, 1*, 23–36.

Eisenberg, N., Fabes, R. A., & Spinrad, T. L. (2006). Prosocial development. In W. Damon & R. M. Lerner (Series Eds.) & N. Eisenberg (Vol. Ed.), *Handbook of child psychology: Vol. 3. Social, emotional, and personality development* (6th ed.). New York: Wiley.

Eisenberg, N., Spinrad, T. L., Fabes, R. A., Reiser, M., et al. (2004). The relations of effortful control and impulsivity to children's resiliency and adjustment. *Child Development, 75*, 25–46.

Eisenberg, N., Valiente, C., Spinrad, T. L., Cumberland, A., et al. (2009). Longitudinal relations of children's effortful control, impulsivity, and negative emotionality to their externalizing, internalizing, and co-occurring behavior problems. *Developmental Psychology, 45*, 988–1008.

Eisenberger, N.I. (2012). Broken hearts and broken bones: A neural perspective on the similarities between social and physical pain. *Current Directions in Psychological Science, 21*, 42–47.

Eisenberger, N. I. (2013). An empirical review of the neural underpinnings of receiving and giving social support: implications for health. *Psychosomatic Medicine, 75*(6), 545–556.

Eisenberger, N. I., Way, B. M., Taylor, S. E., Welch, W. T., & Lieberman, M. D. (2007). *Biological Psychiatry, 61*, 1100–1108.

Eisenberger, R., & Rhoades, L. (2001). Incremental effects of reward on creativity. *Journal of Personality and Social Psychology, 81*, 728–741.

Eisenberger, R., & Shanock, L. (2003). Rewards, intrinsic motivation, and creativity: A case study of conceptual and methodological isolation. *Creativity Research Journal, 15*, 121–130.

Eiser, A. S. (2005). Physiology and psychology of dreams. *Seminars in Neurology, 25*, 97–105.

Ekehammar, B., Akrami, N., Hedlund, L. E., Yoshimura, K., Ono, Y., Ando, J., & Yamagata, S. (2010). The generality of personality heritability: Big-Five trait heritability predicts response time to trait items. *Journal of Individual Differences, 31*, 209–214.

Ekelund, U., Luan, J., Sherar, L. B., Esliger, D. W., Griew, P., & Cooper, A. (2012). Moderate to vigorous physical activity and sedentary time and cardiometabolic risk factors in children and adolescents. *JAMA: Journal Of The American Medical Association, 307*(7), 704–712.

Ekman, P. (1994). Strong evidence for universals in facial expressions: A reply to Russell's mistaken critique. *Psychological Bulletin, 115*(2), 268–287.

Ekman, P. (2009). Lie catching and micro expressions. In C. W. Martin (Ed.), *The philosophy of deception* (pp. 118–138). New York: Oxford University Press.

Ekman, P., & Davidson, R. J. (1993). Voluntary smiling changes regional brain activity. *Psychological Science, 4*(5), 342–345.

Ekman, P., Davidson, R. J., Ricard, M., & Alan, W. B. (2005). Buddhist and psychological perspectives on emotions and well-being. *Current Directions in Psychological Science, 14*, 59–63.

Ekman, P., Friesen, W. V., & Ellsworth, P. (1972). *Emotion in the human face: Guidelines for research and a review of findings*. New York: Pergamon Press.

Ekman, P., Levenson, R. W., & Friesen, W. V. (1983). Autonomic nervous system activity distinguishes among emotions. *Science, 221*, 1208–1210.

Ekpo, K. E. (2011). Nutritional and biochemical evaluation of the protein quality of four popular insects consumed in Southern Nigeria. *Archives of Applied Science Research, 3*(6), 24–40.

Eldar, E., Cohen, J. D., & Niv, Y. (2013). The effects of neural gain on attention and learning. *Nature Neuroscience, 16*(8), 1146–1153.

Eley, T. C., Napolitano, M., Lau, J. Y. F., & Gregory, A. M. (2010). Does childhood anxiety evoke maternal control? A genetically informed study. *The journal of child psychology and psychiatry, 51:7*, 772–779. doi:10.1111/j.1469-7610.2010.02227.x.

Eling, P. (2008). Cerebral localization in the Netherlands in the nineteenth century: Emphasizing the work of Aletta Jacobs. *Journal of the History of the Neurosciences, 17*(2), 175–194.

Elliot, A. J. (Ed.). (2008). *Handbook of approach and avoidance motivation*. New York: Psychology Press.

Ellis, A. (1997). Using rational emotive behavior therapy techniques to cope with disability. *Professional Psychology: Research and Practice, 28*, 17–22.

Elliott, R., Greenberg, L. S., Watson, J, Timulak, L., & Freire, E. (2013). Research on humanistic-experiential psychotherapies. In M. J. Lambert (Ed.), *Bergin and Garfield's handbook of psychotherapy and behavior change* (6th ed.) (pp. 495–538). Hoboken, NJ: Wiley.

Elliott, R., Watson, J. C., & Goldman, R. N. (2004a). Empty chair work for unfinished interpersonal issues. In R. Elliott & J. Watson (Eds.), *Learning emotion-focused therapy: The process-experiential approach to change* (pp. 243–265). Washington, DC: American Psychological Association.

Elliott, R., Watson, J. C., & Goldman, R. N. (2004b). Two-chair work for conflict splits. In R. Elliott & J. Watson (Eds.), *Learning emotion-focused therapy: The process-experiential approach to change* (pp. 219–241). Washington, DC: American Psychological Association.

Ellis, A., & Bernard, M. E. (1985). *Clinical applications of rational-emotive therapy*. New York: Plenum.

Ellis, A. (1962). *Reason and emotion in psychotherapy*. New York: Lyle Stuart.

Ellis, A. (2014). Rational emotive behavior therapy. In G. R. VandenBos, E. Meidenbauer, & J. Frank-McNeil (Eds.), *Psychotherapy theories and techniques* (pp. 289–298). Washington, DC: American Psychological Association.

Ellis, A., & Bernard, M. E. (1985). *Clinical applications of rational-emotive therapy*. New York: Plenum.

Ellis, A. L., & Mitchell, R. W. (2000). Sexual orientation. In L. T. Szuchman & F. Muscarella (Eds.), *Psychological perspectives on human sexuality* (pp. 196–231). New York: Wiley.

Ellis, N. R. (1991). Automatic and effortful processes in memory for spatial location. *Bulletin of the Psychonomic Society, 29*, 28–30.

Elms, A. C. (2009). Obedience lite. *American Psychologist, 64*, 32–36.

Elofsson, U. O. E., von Schèele, B., Theorell, T., & Söndergaard, H. P. (2008). Physiological correlates of eye movement desensitization and reprocessing. *Journal of Anxiety Disorders, 22*(4), 622–634.

Else-Quest, N. M., Hyde, J. S., Goldsmith, H. H., & Van Hulle, C. A. (2006). Gender differences in temperament: A meta-analysis. *Psychological Bulletin, 132*, 33–72.

Else-Quest, N. M., Hyde, J. S., & Linn, M. C. (2010). Cross-national patterns of gender differences in mathematics: A meta-analysis. *Psychological Bulletin, 136*, 103–127.

Elwood, L. S., Hahn, K. S., Olatunji, B., O., & Williams, N. L. (2009). Cognitive vulnerabilities to the development of PTSD: A review of four vulnerabilities and the proposal of an integrative vulnerability model. *Clinical Psychology Review, 29*, 87–100.

El Yacoubi, M., Bouali, S., Popa, D., Naudon, L., Leroux-Nicollet, I., Hamon, M., et al. (2003). Behavioral, neurochemical, and electrophysiological characterization of a genetic mouse model of depression. *Proceedings of the National Academy of Sciences, 100*, 6227–6232.

Emmelkamp, P. M. G. (2013). Behavior therapy with adults. In M. J. Lambert (Ed.), *Bergin and Garfield's handbook of psychotherapy and behavior change* (6th ed.) (pp. 343–392). Hoboken, NJ: Wiley.

Enblom, A., Hammar, M., Steineck, G., & Börjeson, S. (2008). Can individuals identify if needling was performed with an acupuncture needle or a non- penetrating sham needle? *Complementary Therapies in Medicine, 16*(5), 288–294.

Engelhardt, C. R., Bartholow, B. D., Kerr, G. T., & Bushman, B. J. (2011). This is your brain on violent video games: Neural desensitization to violence predicts increased aggression following violent video game exposure. *Journal of Experimental Social Psychology, 47*(5), 1033–1036.

Engen, T., Gilmore, M. M., & Mair, R. G. (1991). Odor memory. In T. V. Getchell et al. (Eds.), *Taste and smell in health and disease*. New York: Raven Press.

Engle, J. M., & McElwain, N. L. (2011). Parental reactions to toddlers' negative emotions and child negative emotionality as correlates of problem behavior at the age of three. *Social Development, 20*, 251–271.

Englemann, T., Tergan, S., & Hesse, F. (2010). Evoking knowledge and information awareness for enhancing computer-supported collaborative problem solving. *Journal of Experimental Education, 78*(2), 268–290.

Engler, B. (2014). *Personality theories* (9th ed.). Belmont, CA: Cengage Learning.

English, D., Sharma, N. K., Sharma, K., & Anand, A. (2013). Neural stem cells-trends and advances. *Journal of Cellular Biochemistry, 114*(4), 764–772.

Englund, M. M., Luckner, A. E., Whaley, G. L., & Egeland, B. (2004). Children's achievement in early elementary school: Longitudinal effects of parental involvement, expectations, and quality of assistance. *Journal of Educational Psychology, 96*(4), 723–730.

Enoch, M. A. (2003). Pharmacogenomics of alcohol response and addiction. *American Journal of Pharmacogenomics, 3*, 217–232.

Enriquez-Barreto. L., Cuesto, G., Dominguez-Iturza, N., Gavilán, E., Ruano, D., Sandi, C., Fernández-Ruiz, A., Martín-Vázquez, G., Herreras, O., & Morales, M. (2014). Learning improvement after PI3K activation correlates with de novo formation of functional small spines. *Frontiers in Molecular Neuroscience, 6*, 54

Epping-Jordan, M. P., Watkins, S. S., Koob, G. F., & Markou, A. (1998). Dramatic decreases in brain reward function during nicotine withdrawal. *Nature, 393*, 76–79.

Epstein, E. M., Sloan, D. M., & Marx, B. P. (2005). Getting to the heart of the matter: Written disclosure, gender, and heart rate. *Psychosomatic Medicine, 67*, 413–419.

Epstein, L. H., Temple, J. L., Roemmich, J. N., & Bouton, Mark E. (2009). Habituation as a determinant of human food intake. *Psychological Review, 116*, 384–407.

Epstein, R., Kirshit, C. E., Lanza, R. P., & Rubin, C. L. (1984). "Insight" in the pigeon: Antecedents and determinants of an intelligent performance. *Nature, 308*, 61–62.

Epstude, K., & Mussweiler, T. (2009). What you feel is how you compare: How comparisons influence the social induction of affect. *Emotion, 9*, 1–14.

Erdelyi, M. (2010). The ups and downs of memory. *American Psychologist, 65*(7), 623–633. doi:10.1037/a0020440.

Erdelyi, M. H. (1985). *Psychoanalysis: Freud's cognitive psychology*. San Francisco: Freeman.

Erez, A., Misangyi, V. F., Johnson, D. E., LePine, M. A., & Halverson, K. C. (2008). Stirring the hearts of followers: Charismatic leadership as the transferal of affect. *Journal of Applied Psychology, 93*, 602–616.

Erickson, K. I., Colcombe, S. J., Wadhwa, R., Scalf, P. E., Kim, J. S., et al. (2007). Training-induced plasticity in older adults: Effects of training on hemispheric asymmetry. *Neurobiology of Aging, 28*, 272–283.

Erickson, R. J., Nichols, L., & Ritter, C. (2000). Family influences on absenteeism: Testing an expanded process model. *Journal of Vocational Behavior, 57*, 246–272.

Ericsson, K. A., & Charness, N. (1994). Expert performance: Its structure and acquisition. *American Psychologist, 49*, 725–747.

Ericsson, K. A., & Staszewski, J. (1989). Skilled memory and expertise: Mechanisms of exceptional performance. In D. Klahr & K. Kotovsky (Eds.), *Complex information processing: The impact of Herbert A. Simon*. Hillsdale, NJ: Erlbaum.

Erikson, E. H. (1968). *Identity: Youth and crisis*. New York: Norton.

Erikson, R., Goldthorpe, J. H., Jackson, M., Yaish, M., & Cox, D. R. (2005). On class differentials in educational attainment. *Proceedings of the National Academy of Sciences, 102*, 9730–9733.

Ernst, M., Matochik, J. A., Heishman, S. J., Van Horn, J. D., Jons, P. H., Henningfield, J. E., & London, E. D. (2001). Effect of nicotine on brain activation during performance of a working memory task. *Proceedings of the National Academy of Sciences, 98*, 4728–4733.

Eron, L. D., Huesmann, L. R., Lefkowitz, M. M., & Walder, L. O. (1972). Does television violence cause aggression? *American Psychologist, 27*(4), 253–263.

Ersche, K. D., Jones, P., Williams, G. B., Turton, A. J., Robbins, T. W., & Bullmore, E. T. (2012). Abnormal brain structure implicated in stimulant drug addiction. *Science, 335*(6068), 601–604. doi:10.1126/science.1214463.

Ersner-Hershfield, H., Galinsky, A. D., Kray, L. J., & King, B. G. (2010). Company, country, connections: Counterfactual origins increase organizational commitment, patriotism, and social investment. *Psychological Science, 21*(10), 1479–1486. doi:10.1177/0956797610382123.

Esbjørn, B. H., Pedersen, S. H., Daniel, S. I., Hald, H. H., Holm, J. M., & Steele, H. (2013). Anxiety levels in clinically referred children and their parents: Examining the unique influence of self-reported attachment styles and interview-based reflective functioning in mothers and fathers. *British Journal of Clinical Psychology, 52*, 394–407.

Eshel, N., & Roiser, J. P. (2010). Reward and punishment processing in depression. *Biological Psychiatry, 68*, 118–124.

Eskine, K. J., Kacinik, N. A., & Prinz, J. J. (2011). A bad taste in the mouth: Gustatory disgust influences moral judgment. *Psychological Science, 22*(3), 295–299. doi:10.1177/0956797611398497.

Eskine, K. J., Kacinik, N. A., & Prinz, J. J. (2012). Stirring images: Fear, not happiness or arousal, makes art more sublime. *Emotion*, doi:10.1037/a0027200

Espiritu, J. R. D. (2008). Aging-Related Sleep Changes. *Clinics in Geriatric Medicine, 24*(1), 1–14.

Esposito, S., & Rossi, R. (2014). CTA operator awoke "when she hit," dozed off before, BTSB says. *Chicago Sun-Times*, March 27, 2014.

Espy, K. A., Fang, H., Johnson, C., Stopp, C., Wiebe, S. A., & Respass, J. (2011). Prenatal tobacco exposure: Developmental outcomes in the neonatal period. *Developmental Psychology, 47*, 153–169.

Essau, C. A., Sasagawa, S., Chen, J., & Sakano, Y. (2012). Taijin kyofusho and social phobia symptoms in young adults in England and in Japan. *Journal of Cross-Cultural Psychology, 43*(2), 219–232. doi:10.1177/0022022110386372.

Essex, M. J., Klein, M. H., Slattery, M. J., Goldsmith, H. H., & Kalin, N. H. (2010). Early risk factors and developmental pathways to chronic high inhibition and social anxiety disorder in adolescence. *American Journal of Psychiatry, 167*, 40–46.

Esterson, A. (2001). The mythologizing of psychoanalytic history: Deception and self-deception in Freud's account of the seduction theory episode. *History of Psychiatry, 12*, 329–352.

Etcheverry, P. E., & Agnew, C. R. (2008). Romantic partner and friend influences on young adult cigarette smoking: Comparing close others' smoking and injunctive norms over time. *Psychology of Addictive Behaviors, 22*, 313–325.

Euhus, D. M., & Robinson, L. (2013). Genetic predisposition syndromes and their management. *Surgical Clinics of North America, 93* (2), 341–62.

Eum, K., & Rice, K. G. (2011). Test anxiety, perfectionism, goal orientation, and academic performance. *Anxiety Stress Coping, 24*(2), 167–178.

Evans, G. W. (2004). The environment of childhood poverty. *American Psychologist, 59*, 77–92.

Evans, G. W., Ricciuti, H. N., Hope, S., Schoon, I., et al. (2010). Crowding and cognitive development: The mediating role of maternal responsiveness among 36-month-old children. *Environment and Behavior, 42*, 135–148.

Evans, G. W., & Wener, R. E. (2006). Rail commuting duration and passenger stress. *Health Psychology, 25*, 408–412.

Evans, J. A., Elliott, J. A., & Gorman, M. R. (2009). Dim nighttime illumination accelerates adjustment to timezone travel in an animal model. *Current Biology, 19*(4), R156–R157.

Evrard, D., Charollais, A., Marret, S., Radi, S., Rezrazi, A., & Mellier, D. (2011). Cognitive and emotional regulation developmental issues in preterm infants 12 and 24 months after birth. *European Journal of Developmental Psychology, 8*(2), 171–184. doi:10.1080/17405620903504538.

Eysenck, H. J. (1952). The effects of psychotherapy: An evaluation. *Journal of Consulting Psychology, 16*, 319–324.

Eysenck, H. J. (1990a). Biological dimensions of personality. In L. A. Pervin (Ed.), *Handbook of personality: Theory and research* (pp. 244–276). New York: Guilford.

Eysenck, H. J. (1990b). Genetic and environmental contributions to individual differences: The three major dimensions of personality. *Journal of Personality, 58*, 245–261.

Eysenck, M. W., & Keane, M. T. (2005). *Cognitive psychology: A student's handbook* (5th ed.). East Sussex, UK: Psychology Press.

Eyssel, F. & Bohner, G. (2011). Schema effects of rape myth acceptance on judgments of guilt and blame in rape cases: The role of perceived entitlement to judge. *Journal of Interpersonal Violence, 26*, 1579–1605.

Ezzyat, Y., & Davachi, L. (2010). What constitutes an episode in episodic memory? *Psychological Science, 22*(2), 243–252. doi:10.1177/0956797610393742.

Fabes, R. A., Martin, C. L., & Hanish, L. D. (2003). Young children's qualities in same-, other-, and mixed-sex peer groups. *Child Development, 74*, 921–932.

Fabrigar, L. R. & Wegener, D. T. (2010). Attitude structure In R. Baumeister & E. Finkel (Eds.) *Advanced social psychology The state of the science* (pp. 177–216). New York, NY: Oxford.

Faedda, G., Tondo, L., Teicher, M., Baldessarini, R., Gelbard, H., & Floris, G. (1993). Seasonal mood disorders: Patterns of seasonal recurrence in mania and depression. *Archives of General Psychiatry, 50*, 17–23.

Fagan, A. A., Hanson, K., Hawkins, J. D., & Arthur, M. S. (2009). Translational research in action: Implementation of the Communities That Care prevention system in 12 communities. *Journal of Community Psychology, 37*, 809–829.

Fagan, J. F. (2000). A theory of intelligence as processing. *Psychology, Public Policy, and Law, 26*, 168–179.

Fagan, J. F., Holland, C. R., & Wheeler, K. (2007). The prediction, from infancy, of adult IQ and achievement. *Intelligence, 35*, 225–231.

Fagin-Jones, S., & Midlarsky, E. (2007). Courageous altruism: Personal and situational correlates of rescue during the Holocaust. *The Journal of Positive Psychology, 2*, 136–147.

Fagot, B. I. (1997). Attachment, parenting, and peer interactions of toddler children. *Developmental Psychology, 33*, 489–499.

Fahim, R. E., Kessler, P. D., & Kalnik, M. W. (2013). Therapeutic vaccines against tobacco addiction. *Expert Review of Vaccines, 12*(3), 333–342.

Fahsing, I. A., Ask, K., & Granhag, P. A. (2004). Th e man behind the mask: Accuracy and predictors of eyewitness off ender descriptions. *Journal of Applied Psychology, 89*, 722–729.

Fairburn, C. G. (Ed.). (2008). *Cognitive behavior therapy and eating disorders*. New York: Guilford.

Faisal, T., Taib, M., & Ibrahim, F. (2012). Adaptive Neuro-Fuzzy Inference System for diagnosis risk in dengue patients. *Expert Systems With Applications, 39*(4), 4483–4495. doi:10.1016/j.eswa.2011.09.140.

Falck, R. S., Wang, J., & Carlson, R. G. (2007). Crack cocaine trajectories among users in a midwestern American city. *Addiction, 102*, 1421–1431.

Falk, A., & Heckman, J. J. (2009). Lab experiments are a major source of knowledge in the social sciences. *Science, 326*, 535–538.

Falk, E., Berkman, E., & Lieberman, M. (2012). From neural responses to population behavior: neural focus group predicts population-level media effects. *Psychological Science, 23*(5), 439–445.

Fandakova, Y., Sander, M. C., Werkle-Bergner, M., & Shing, Y. L. (2014). Age differences in short-term memory binding are related to working memory performance across the lifespan. *Psychology & Aging, 29*(1), 140–149.

Farah, M. J. (2009). A picture is worth a thousand dollars. *Journal of Cognitive Neuroscience, 21*, 623–624.

Farah, M. J., Hutchinson, J. B., Phelps, E. A., & Wagner, A. D. (2014). Functional MRI-based lie detection: scientific and societal challenges. *Nature Reviews Neuroscience 15*(2), 123–131.

Farah, M. J., Shera, D. M., Savage, J. H., Betancourt, L., Giannetta, J. M., Brodsky, N. L., Malmud, E. K., & Hurt, H. (2006). Childhood poverty: Specific associations with neurocognitive development. *Brain Research, 1110*, 166–174.

Farley, F. (1986). The big T in personality. *Psychology Today, 20,* 44–52.

Farlow, M. R. (2009). Treatment of mild cognitive impairment (MCI). *Current Alzheimer Research, 6*(4), 362–367.

Farmer, J. D., Patelli, P., & Zovko, I. I. (2005). The predictive power of zero intelligence in financial markets. *Proceedings of the National Academy of Sciences, 102,* 2254–2259.

Farmer, R. F., Kosty, D. B., Seeley, J. R., Olino, T. M., & Lewinsohn, P. M. (2013). Aggregation of lifetime Axis I psychiatric disorders through age 30: Incidence, predictors, and associated psychosocial outcomes. *Journal of Abnormal Psychology, 122,* 573–586.

Farmer, R. F., & Nelson-Gray, R. (2005). *Personality-guided behavior therapy.* Washington, DC: American Psychological Association.

Farrell, D., & Stamm, C. L. (1988). Meta-analysis of the correlates of employee absence. *Human Relations, 41,* 211–227.

Farrer, L. A., Cupples, L. A., Haines, J. L., Hyman, B., Kukull, W. A., Mayeux, R., Myers, R. H., Pericak-Vance, M. A., Risch, N., & van Duijn, C. N. (1997). Effects of age, sex, and ethnicity on the association between apolipoprotein E genotype and Alzheimer disease: A meta-analysis. *JAMA, 278,* 1349–1356.

Farrington, D P., Loeber, R., Stallings, R., & Ttofi, M. (2011). Bullying perpetration and victimization as predictors of delinquency and depression in the Pittsburgh Youth Study. *Journal of Aggression, Conflict and Peace Research, 3,* 74–81.

Farroni, T., Csibra, G., Simion, F., & Johnson, M. H. (2002). Eye contact detection in humans from birth. *Proceedings of the National Academy of Sciences, 99,* 9602–9605.

Farroni, T., Johnson, M. H., Menon, E., Zulian, L., Faraguna, D., & Csibra, G. (2005). Newborns' preference for face-relevant stimuli: Effects of contrast polarity. *Proceedings of the National Academy of Sciences, 102,* 17245–17250.

Fassler, O., Lynn, S. J., & Knox, J. (2008). Is hypnotic suggestibility a stable trait? *Consciousness and Cognition, 17,* 240–253.

Faulkner, M. (2001). The onset and alleviation of learned helplessness in older hospitalized people. *Aging & Mental Health, 5,* 379–386.

Fausto-Sperling, A., Coll, C. G., & Lamarre, M. (2012). Sexing the baby: Part 1—What do we really know about sex differentiation in the first three years of life? *Social Science & Medicine,* 1684–1692.

Fava, G. A., Grandi, S. Rafanelli, C., Ruini, C., Conti, S., & Bellurado, P. (2001). Long-term outcome of social phobia treated by exposure. *Psychological Medicine, 31,* 899–905.

Fava, G. A., Rafanelli, C., Tossani, E., & Grandi, S. (2008). Agoraphobia is a disease: A tribute to Sir Martin Roth. *Psychotherapy and Psychosomatics, 77,* 133–138.

Fearon, R. P., Bakermans-Kranenburg, M. J., Van IJzendoorn, M. H., Lapsley, A.-M., & Roisman, G. I. (2010). The significance of insecure attachment and disorganization in the development of children's externalizing behavior: A meta-analytic study. *Child Development, 81,* 435–456.

Feder, B. J. (2004, May 31). Technology strains to find menace in the crowd. *The New York Times,* p. C1.

Feinberg, J. M., & Aiello, J. R. (2010). The effect of challenge and threat appraisals under evaluative presence. *Journal of Applied Social Psychology, 40,* 2071–2104.

Feinberg, L., & Campbell, I. G. (1993). Total sleep deprivation in the rat transiently abolishes the delta amplitude response to darkness: Implications for the mechanism of the "negative delta rebound." *Journal of Neurophysiology, 70*(6) 2695–2699.

Feinberg, M., Willer, R., Antonenko, O., & John, O. (2012). Liberating reason from the passions: overriding intuitionist moral judgments through emotion reappraisal. *Psychological Science, 23,* 788–795.

Feinstein, A. (2011). Conversion disorder: advances in our understanding. *CMAJ: Canadian Medical Association Journal, 183*(8), 915–920. doi:10.1503/cmaj.110490

Feist, J., Feist, G. J., & Roberts, T. A. (2013). *Theories of personality* (8th ed.). New York: McGraw-Hill.

Feldman, G., Zayfert, C., Sandoval, L., Dunn, E., & Cartreine, J. A. (2013). Reward responsiveness and anxiety predict performance of Mount Everest climbers. *Journal of Research In Personality, 47,* 111–115.

Feldman, H. M., & Reiff, M. I. (2014). Attention deficit–hyperactivity disorder in children and adolescents. *New England Journal of Medicine, 370,* 838–846.

Feldman, R., Weller, A., Zagoory-Sharon, O., & Levine, A. (2007). Evidence for a neuroendocrinological foundation of human affiliation: Plasma oxytocin levels across pregnancy and the postpartum period predict mother-infant bonding. *Psychological Science, 18,* 965–970.

Feldman Barrett, L., & Kensinger, E. A. (2010). Context is routinely encoded during emotion perception. *Psychological Science (Sage Publications Inc.), 21*(4), 595–599. doi:10.1177/0956797610363547

Felten, D. L., Cohen, N., Ader, R., Felten, S. Y., Carlson, S. L., & Roszman, T. L. (1991). Central neural circuits involved in neural-immune interactions. In R. Ader (Ed.), *Psychoneuroimmunology* (2nd ed.). New York: Academic Press.

Feng, X., Shaw, D. S., Kovacs, M., Lane, T., O'Rourke, F. E., & Alarcon, J. H. (2008). Emotion regulation in preschoolers: The roles of behavioral inhibition, maternal affective behavior, and maternal depression. *Journal of Child Psychology and Psychiatry, 49,* 132–141.

Fenn, K. M., Nusbaum, H. C., & Margoliash, D. (2003). Consolidation during sleep of perceptual learning of spoken language. *Nature, 425,* 614–616.

Fenson, L., Dale, P. S., Reznick, J. S., & Bates, E. (1994). Variability in early communicative development. *Monographs of the Society for Research in Child Development, 59,* 173.

Ferguson, C. J. (2009). Violent video games: Dogma, fear, and pseudoscience. *Skeptical Inquirer, 33,* 38–43.

Ferguson, C. J. (2010). Blazing angels or resident evil? Can violent video games be a force for good? *Review of General Psychology, 14,* 122–140.

Ferguson, C. J. (2013a). Spanking, corporal punishment and negative long-term outcomes: A meta-analytic review of longitudinal studies. *Clinical Psychology Review, 33*(1), 196–208.

Ferguson, C. J. (2013b). Violent video games and the Supreme Court: Lessons for the scientific community in the wake of Brown v. Entertainment Merchants Association. *American Psychologist, 66*(2), 57–74.

Ferguson, C. J., & Dyck, D. (2012). Paradigm change in aggression research: The time has come to retire the General Aggression Model. *Aggression & Violent Behavior, 17,* 220–228. doi:10.1016/j.avb.2012.02.007.

Ferguson, C. J., Garza, A., Jerabeck, J., Ramos, R., & Galindo, M. (2013). Not worth the fuss after all? Cross-sectional and prospective data on violent video game influences on aggression, visuospatial cognition and mathematics ability in a sample of youth. *Journal of Youth & Adolescence, 42*(1), 109–122.

Ferguson, C. J., & Hartley, R. D. (2009). The pleasure is momentary . . . the expense damnable? The influence of pornography on rape and sexual assault. *Aggression and Violent Behavior, 14,* 323–329.

Ferguson, C. J., & Kilburn, J. (2009). The public health risks of media violence: A meta-analytic review. *Journal of Pediatrics, 154,* 759–763.

Ferguson, C. J., & Kilburn, J. (2010). Much ado about nothing: The misestimation and overinterpretation of violent video game eff ects in Eastern and Western nations: Comment on Anderson et al. (2010). *Psychological Bulletin, 136,* 174–178.

Ferguson, C. J., & Meehan, D. C. (2011). With friends like these…: Peer delinquency influences across age cohorts on smoking, alcohol and illegal substance use. *European Psychiatry, 26*(1), 6–12. doi:10.1016/j.eurpsy.2010.09.002

Ferguson,C. J., Olson, C. K., Kutner, L. A., & Warner, D. E. (2010). Violent video games, catharsis seeking, bullying, and delinquency: A multivariate analysis of eff ects. *Crime and Delinquency, 56,* 1–21.

Ferguson, C. J., & Rueda, S. M. (2010). The hitman study: Violent video game exposure effects on aggressive behavior, hostile feelings, and depression. *European Psychologist, 15,* 99–108.

Ferguson, C. J., San Miguel, C., & Hartley, R. D. (2009). A multivariate analysis of youth violence and aggression: The influence of family, peers, depression, and media violence. *Journal of Pediatrics, 155*(6), 904–908.

Fernández-Dols, J.-M., & Ruiz-Belda, M.-A. (1995). Are smiles a sign of happiness? Gold medal winners at the Olympic Games. *Journal of Personality and Social Psychology, 69,* 1113–1119.

Fernández-Serrano, M., Perales, J., Moreno-López, L., Pérez-García, M., & Verdejo-García, A. (2012). Neuropsychological profiling of impulsivity and compulsivity in cocaine dependent individuals. *Psychopharmacology, 219*(2), 673–683. doi:10.1007/s00213-011-2485-z

Ferrara, J. M., & Stacy, M. (2008). Impulse-control disorders in Parkinson's disease. *CNS Spectrums, 13*(8), 690–698.

Ferrarini, L., van Lew, B., Reiber, J. H., Gandin, C., Galluzzo, L., Scafato, E., Frisoni, G. B., Milles, J., & Pievani, M. (2014). Hippocampal atrophy in people with memory deficits: results from the population-based IPREA study. *International Psychogeriatrics,* Epub February 13, 2014.

Ferrer, R. A., Klein, W. P., Zajac, L. E., Sutton-Tyrrell, K., Muldoon, M. F., & Kamarck, T. W. (2012). Unrealistic optimism is associated with subclinical atherosclerosis. *Health Psychology, 31*(6), 815–820.

Festinger, L. (1954). A theory of social comparison processes. *Human Relations, 7,* 117–140.

Festinger, L. (1957). *A theory of cognitive dissonance.* Evanston, IL: Row, Petersen.

Festinger, L., & Carlsmith, J. M. (1959). Cognitive consequences of forced compliance. *Journal of Abnormal and Social Psychology, 58,* 203–210.

Fève, B., & Bastard, J. P. (2012). From the conceptual basis to the discovery of leptin. *Biochimie, 94*(10), 2065–2068.

Fidzinski, P., Wawra, M., Bartsch, J., Heinemann, U., & Behr, J. (2012). High-frequency stimulation of the temporoammonic pathway induces input-specific long-term potentiation in subicular bursting cells. *Brain Research, 1430*:1–7. doi:10.1016/j.brainres.2011.10.040.

Field, A., & Cotrell, D. (2011). Eye movement desensitization and reprocessing as a therapeutic intervention for traumatized children and adolescents: a systematic review of the evidence for family therapists. *Journal of Family Therapy, 33,* 374–388.

Field, A. P. (2006). Is conditioning a useful framework for understanding the development and treatment of phobias? *Clinical Psychology Review, 26,* 857–875.

Fife, T. D. (2009). Benign paroxysmal positional vertigo. *Seminars in Neurology, 29*(5), 500–508.

Figner, B., & Weber, E. U. (2011). Who takes risks when and why?: Determinants of risk taking. *Current Directions in Psychological Science, 20*(4), 211–216. doi 10.1177/0963721411415790.

Fillmore, K. M., & Caetano, R. (1980, May 22). *Epidemiology of occupational alcoholism.* Paper presented at the National Institute on Alcohol Abuse and Alcoholism's Workshop on Alcoholism in the Workplace, Reston, VA.

Filtness, A. J., Reyner, L. A., & Horne, J. A. (2012). Driver sleepiness—Comparisons between young and older men during a monotonous afternoon simulated drive. *Biological Psychology, 89*(3), 580–583. doi:10.1016/j.biopsycho.2012.01.002.

Fincham, J. M., & Anderson, J. R. (2006). Distinct roles of the anterior cingulated and the prefrontal cortex in the acquisition and performance of a cognitive skill. *Proceedings of the National Academy of Sciences, 103,* 12941–12946.

Fine, I., Wade, A. R., Brewer, A. A., May, M. G., Goodman, D. F., Boynton, G. M., et al. (2003). Long-term deprivation affects visual perception and cortex. *Nature Neuroscience, 6,* 915–916.

Finke, C., Esfahani, N. E., & Ploner, C. J. (2013). Preservation of musical memory in an amnesic professional cellist. *Current Biology, 22,* R591-R592.

Finkel, D., & Reynolds, C. A. (2014). *Behavior Genetics of Cognition Across the Lifespan.* New York: Springer.

Finkel, D., Reynolds, C. A., McArdle, J. J., Hamagami, F., & Pedersen, N. L. (2009). Genetic variance in processing speed drives variation in aging of spatial and memory abilities. *Developmental Psychology, 45,* 820–834.

Finkel, D., Reynolds, C. A., McArdle, J. J., & Pedersen, N. L. (2007). Age changes in processing speed as a leading indicator of cognitive aging. *Psychology and Aging, 22*(3), 558–568.

Finkel, E. & Baumeister, R. F. (2010). Attraction and rejection In R. Baumeister & E. Finkel (Eds.) *Advanced social psychology: The state of the science* (pp. 419–459). New York, NY: Oxford.

Finkelstein, E. A., DiBonaventura, M., Burgess, S. M., & Hale, B. C. (2010). The costs of obesity in the workplace. *Journal Of Occupational & Environmental Medicine, 52*(10), 971–976. doi:10.1097/JOM.0b013e3181f274d2.

Finney, M. L., Stoney, C. M., & Engebretson, T. O. (2002). Hostility and anger expression in African American and European American men is associated with cardiovascular and lipid reactivity. *Psychophysiology, 39,* 340–349.

Finn-Stevenson, M. & Zigler, E. (1999). *Schools of the 21st century: Linking child care and education.* Boulder, CO: Westview Press.

Fiorella, L., & Mayer, R. E. (2012). Paper-based aids for learning with a computer-based game. *Journal of Educational Psychology,* doi:10.1037/a0028088

Firkowska-Mankiewicz, A. (2011). Adult careers: Does childhood IQ predict later life outcome?. *Journal of Policy and Practice in Intellectual Disabilities, 8*(1), 1–9. doi:10.1111/j.1741–1130.2011.00281.x.

Fisar, Z. (2009). Phytocannabinoids and endocannabinoids. *Current Drug Abuse Review, 2,* 51–75.

Fischer, K. W., & Bidell, T. (1991). Constraining nativist inferences about cognitive capacities. In S. Carey & R. Gelman (Eds.), *The epigenesis of mind: Essays on biology and cognition* (pp. 199–235). Hillsdale, NJ: Erlbaum.

Fischer, M. J. (2011). Interracial contact and changes in the racial attitudes of White college students. *Social Psychology of Education, 14,* 547–574. doi:10.1007/s11218-011-9161-3.

Fischer, M. J., & Massey, D. S. (2007). The effects of affirmative action in higher education. *Social Science Research, 36*(2), 531–549.

Fischer, R., & Boer, D. (2011). What is more important for national well-being: Money or autonomy? A meta-analysis of well-being, burnout, and anxiety across 63 societies. *Journal Of Personality & Social Psychology, 101*(1), 164–184.

Fischoff, B., & MacGregor, D. (1982). Subjective confidence in forecasts. *Journal of Forecasting, 1,* 155–172.

Fish, A. M., Li, X., McCarrick, K., Butler, S. T., et al. (2008). Early childhood computer experience and cognitive development among urban low-income preschoolers. *Journal of Educational Computing Research, 38,* 97–113.

Fisher, C. D. (2000). Mood and emotion while working: Missing pieces of job satisfaction? *Journal of Organizational Behavior, 21,* 185–202.

Fisher, C. D. (2003). Why do lay people believe that satisfaction and performance are correlated? Possible sources of a commonsense theory. *Journal of Organizational Behavior, 24,* 753–777.

Fisher, C. M. (1989). Binswanger's encephalopathy: A review. *Journal of Neurology, 236*(2), 65–79.

Fisher, M. A. (2012). Confidentiality and record keeping. In S. J. Knapp, M. C. Gottlieb, M. M. Handelsman, & L. D. VandeCreek (Eds.), *APA handbook of ethics in psychology, Vol. 1: Moral foundations and common themes* (pp. 333–375). Washington, DC: American Psychological Association.

Fisher, S. E. (2005). Dissection of molecular mechanisms underlying speech and language disorders. *Applied Psycholinguistics, 26,* 111–128.

Fisher, S. P., Foster, R. G., & Peirson, S. N. (2013). The circadian control of sleep. *Handbook of Experimental Pharmacology,* (217), 157–183.

Fisher, W. A., Fisher, J. D., & Rye, B. J. (1995). Understanding and promoting AIDS-preventive behavior: Insights from the theory of reasoned action. *Health Psychology, 14,* 255–264.

Fishman, D. B., Rego, S. A., & Muller, K. L. (2011). Behavioral theories of psychotherapy. In J. C. Norcross, G. R. VandenBos, & D. K. Freedheim (Eds.), *History of psychotherapy: Continuity and change* (pp. 101–140). Washington, D.C.: American Psychological Association.

Fiske, A. P., Kitayama, S., Markus, H. R., & Nisbett, R. E. (1998). The cultural matrix of social psychology. In D. T. Gilbert, S. T. Fiske, & G. Lindzey (Eds.), *Handbook of social psychology* (Vol. 2, 4th ed., pp. 915–981). Boston: McGraw-Hill.

Fiske, S., & Taylor, S. (2008). *Social cognition, from brains to culture.* New York: McGraw-Hill.

Fiske, S. T. (2010). Venus and Mars or down to Earth: Stereotypes and realities of gender differences. *Perspectives on Psychological Science, 5*(6), 688–692. doi:10.1177/1745691610388768.

Fitzgerald, T. E., Tennen, H., Affect, G. S., & Pransky, G. (1993). The relative importance of dispositional optimism and control appraisals in quality of life after coronary artery bypass surgery. *Journal of Behavioral Medicine, 16,* 25–43.

Fitzsimons, G. M., & Finkel, E. J. (2011). Outsourcing self-regulation. *Psychological Science, 22*(3), 369–375. doi:10.1177/0956797610397955.

Flament, M., Bissada, H., & Spettigue, W. (2012). Evidence-based pharmacotherapy of eating disorders. *International Journal of Neuropsychopharmacology, 15,* 189–207.

Flanagan, J. C. (1954). The critical incident technique. *Psychological Bulletin, 51,* 327–358.

Flavell, J. E., Azrin, N., Baumeister, A., Carr, E., Dorsey, M., Forehand, R., et al. (1982). The treatment of self-injurious behavior. *Behavior Therapy, 13,* 529–554.

Flavell, J. H. (1996). Piaget's legacy. *Psychological Science, 7,* 200–203.

Fleck, M. S., & Mitroff, S. R. (2007). Rare targets are rarely missed in correctable search. *Psychological Science, 18*(11), 943–947.

Fleeson, W., Malanos, A. B., & Achille, N. M. (2002). An intraindividual process approach to the relationship between extraversion and positive affect: Is acting extraverted as "good" as being extraverted? *Journal of Personality & Social Psychology, 83,* 1409–1422.

Flegal, K. M., Kit, B. K., Orpana, H., & Graubard, B. I. (2013). Association of all-cause mortality with overweight and obesity using standard body mass index categories: a systematic review and meta-analysis. *JAMA, 309*(1), 71–82.

Fleishman, E. A., & Harris, E. F. (1962). Patterns of leadership behavior related to employee grievances and turnover. *Personnel Psychology, 15,* 43–56.

Fleuret, F., Li, T., Dubout, C., Wampler, E. K., Yantis, S., & Geman, D. (2011). Comparing machines and humans on a visual categorization test. *PNAS Proceedings of the National Academy of Sciences of the United States of America, 108*(43), 17621–17625. doi:10.1073/pnas.1109168108.

Flor, H., Birbaumer, N., Herman, C., Ziegler, S., & Patrick, C. J. (2002). Aversive Pavlovian conditioning in psychopaths: Peripheral and central correlates. *Psychophysiology, 39,* 505–518.

Flores, E., Cicchetti, D., & Rogosch, F. A. (2005). Predictors of resilience in maltreated and nonmaltreated Latino children. *Developmental Psychology, 41,* 338–351.

Flores, E., Tschann, J. M., Dimas, J. M., Pasch, L. A., & de Groat, C. L. (2010). Perceived racial/ethnic discrimination, posttraumatic stress symptoms, and health risk behaviors among Mexican American adolescents. *Journal of Counseling Psychology, 57,* 264–273.

Flowe, H. D., Mehta, A., & Ebbesen, E. B. (2011). The role of eyewitness identification evidence in felony case dispositions. *Psychology, Public Policy, And Law, 17*(1), 140–159. doi:10.1037/a0021311.

Floyd, J. A. (2002). Sleep and aging. *Nursing Clinics of North America, 37,* 719–731.

Flynn, J. T. (1999). Searching for justice: The discovery of IQ gains over time. *American Psychologist, 54,* 5–20.

Foa, E. B., Cahill, S. P., Boscarino, J. A., Hobfoll, S. E., Lahad, M., McNally, R. J., et al. (2005). Social, psychological, and psychiatric interventions following terrorist attacks: Recommendations for practice and research. *Neuropsychopharmacology, 30,* 1806–1817.

Fodor, J. A. (1983). Modularity of mind: An essay on faculty psychology. Cambridge, MA: MIT Press.

Foer, J. (2011). *Moonwalking with Einstein: The Art and Science of Remembering Everything*. New York: Penguin Press.

Folk, C. L., Remington, R. W., & Wright, J. H. (1994). The structure of attentional control: Contingent attentional capture by apparent motion, abrupt onset, and color. *Journal of Experimental Psychology: Human Perception and Performance, 20,* 317–329.

Folkman, S., & Lazarus, R. (1988). *Manual for the ways of coping questionnaire*. Palo Alto, CA: Consulting Psychologists Press.

Folkman, S., Lazarus, R., Dunkel-Shetter, C., DeLongis, A., & Gruen, R. (1986). Dynamics of a stressful encounter: Cognitive appraisal, coping, and encounter outcomes. *Journal of Personality and Social Psychology, 50,* 992–1003.

Folkman, S., & Moskowitz, J. T. (2000). Stress, positive emotion, and coping. *Current Directions in Psychological Science, 9,* 115–118.

Fontaine, K. L. (2009). *Mental health nursing*. Upper Saddle River, NJ: Pearson/ Prentice Hall.

Fontes, M. A., Bolla, K. I., Cunha, P. J., Almeida, P. P., Jungerman, F., Laranjeira, R. R., Bressan, R. A., & Lacerda, A. L. (2011). Cannabis use before age 15 and subsequent executive functioning. *British Journal of Psychiatry, 198*(6), 442–447.

Foote, B., Smolin, Y., Kaplan, M., Legatt, M. E., & Lipschitz, D. (2006). Prevalence of dissociative disorders in psychiatric outpatients. *American Journal of Psychiatry, 163,* 623–629.

Forand, N. R., DeRubeis, R. J., & Amsterdam, J. D. (2013). Combining medication and psychotherapy in the treatment of major mental disorders. In M. J. Lambert (Ed.), *Bergin and Garfield's handbook of psychotherapy and behavior change* (6th ed.) (pp. 735–774). Hoboken, NJ: Wiley.

Forbes, D., Phelps, A., & McHugh, T. (2001). Treatment of combat-related nightmares using imagery rehearsal: A pilot study. *Journal of Traumatic Stress, 14,* 433–442.

Ford, B. Q., Tamir, M., Brunyé, T. T., Shirer, W. R., Mahoney, C. R., & Taylor, H. A. (2010). Keeping your eyes on the prize: Anger and visual attention to threats and rewards. *Psychological Science, 21*(8), 1098–1105. doi:10.1177/ 0956797610375450.

Ford, M. T., Heinen, B. A., & Langkamer, K. L. (2007). Work and family satisfaction and conflict: A meta-analysis of cross-domain relations. *Journal of Applied Psychology, 92,* 57–80.

Forgas, J. P., Dunn, E., & Granland, S. (2008). Are you being served. . . ? An unobtrusive experiment of affective influences on helping in a department store. *European Journal of Social Psychology, 38,* 333–342.

Forhan, S. E., Gottlieb, S. L., Sternberg, M. R., Xu, F., et al. (2009). Prevalence of sexually transmitted infections among female adolescents aged 14 to 19 in the United States. *Pediatrics, 124,* 1505–1512.

Formisano, E., De Martino, F., Bonte, M., & Goebel, R. (2008). "Who" is saying "what?" Brain-based decoding of human voice and speech. *Science, 322*(5903), 970–973.

Förster, J. (2012). GLOMOsys: The how and why of global and local processing. *Current Directions in Psychological Science, 21*(1), 15–19. doi:10.1177/ 0963721411429454.

Forsyth, D., & Burnette, J. (2010). Group processes In R. Baumeister & E. Finkel (Eds.), *Advanced social psychology: The state of the science* (pp. 495–534). New York: Oxford.

Forsyth, D. R. (2013). Social inlfuence and group behavior. In Tennen, H., Suls, J., & Weiner, I. B. (Eds.). *Handbook of psychology, Vol. 5: Personality and social psychology* (2nd ed.). Hoboken, NJ: John Wiley & Sons Inc.

Fossati, P., Hevenor, S. J., Graham, S. J., Grady, C., Keightley, M. L., Craik, F., & Mayberg, H. (2003). In search of the emotional self: An FMRI study using positive and negative emotional words. *American Journal of Psychiatry, 160,* 1938–1945.

Fosse, R., Stickgold, R., & Hobson, J. A. (2001). Brain-mind states: Reciprocal variation in thoughts and hallucinations. *Psychological Science, 12,* 30–36.

Foster, E. M., Jones, D., & the Conduct Problems Prevention Research Group. (2006). Can a costly intervention be cost-effective? An analysis of violence prevention. *Archives of General Psychiatry, 63,* 1284–1291.

Foster, J. L., Huthwaite, T., Yesberg, J. A., Garry, M., & Loftus, E. F. (2012). Repetition, not number of sources, increases both susceptibility to misinformation and confidence in the accuracy of eyewitnesses. *Acta Psychologica, 139*(2), 320–326. doi:10.1016/j.actpsy.2011.12.004.

Foster, V. (2013). Exploring the evolution of human mate preference. *Science, 342*(6162), 1060–1061.

Foti, R. J., & Hauenstein, N. M. A. (2007). Pattern and variable approaches in leadership emergence and effectiveness. *Journal of Applied Psychology, 92,* 347–355.

Fotopoulou, A., Pernigo, S., Maeda, R., Rudd, A., & Kopelman, M. A. (2010). Implicit awareness in anosognosia for hemiplegia: Unconscious interference without conscious re-representation. *Brain, 133*(Part 12), 3564–3577.

Fountain, J. W. (2000, November 28). Exorcists and exorcisms proliferate across U.S. *New York Times*. Retrieved from http://www.rickross.com/reference/general/general315.html

Fournier, J. C., DeRubeis, R. J., Hollon, S. D., Dimidjian, S., et al. (2010). Antidepressant drug effects and depression severity: A patient-level meta-analysis. *Journal of the American Medical Association, 303,* 47–53.

Fowler, E. A., Hart, S. R., McIntosh, R. D., & Sala, S. D. (2013). Health professionals are unaware of anosognosia. *Cognitive Neuroscience, 4*(3–4), 208–209.

Fowler, G. A. (2004, March 4). Calling all jewel thieves. *Wall Street Journal*, p. B1.

Fowler, G. A., Sherr, I., & Troianovski, A. (2011, October 15). Are Smartphones Becoming Smart Alecks?. *Wall Street Journal—Eastern Edition*. pp. A1–A12.

Fowler, J. (2012). Suicide risk assessment in clinical practice: Pragmatic guidelines for imperfect assessments. *Psychotherapy, 49*(1), 81–90. doi:10.1037/a0026148.

Fowler, J. R., & Christakis, N. A. (2008). Dynamic spread of happiness in a large social network: Longitudinal analysis over 20 years in the Framingham Heart Study. *British Medical Journal, 337,* a2533.

Fowles, D. C., & Dindo, L. (2009). Temperament and psychopathy: A dual-pathway model. *Current Directions in Psychological Science, 18,* 179–183.

Fox, M. K., Pac, S., Devaney, B., & Jankowski, L. (2004). Feeding infants and toddlers study: What foods are infants and toddlers eating? *Journal of the American Dietetic Association, 104*(Suppl 1), s22–30.

Fozard, J., Wolf, E., Bell, B., Farland, R., & Podolsky, S. (1977). Visual perception and communication. In J. Birren & K. Schaie (Eds.), *Handbook of the psychology of aging*. New York: Van Nostrand Reinhold.

Fraley, R. C., Roisman, G. I., Booth-LaForce, C., Owen, M. T., & Holland, A. S. (2013). Interpersonal and genetic origins of adult attachment styes: A longitudinal study from infancy to early adulthood. *Journal of Personality and Social Psychology, 104,* 817–838.

Franchak, J. M., & Adolph, K. E. (2012). What infants know and what they do: Perceiving possibilities for walking through openings. *Developmental Psychology*, doi:10.1037/a0027530.

Francis, A. M. (2008). Family and sexual orientation: The family-demographic correlates of homosexuality in men and women. *Journal of Sex Research, 45*(4), 371–377.

Frank, D. A., Augustyn, M., Knight, W. G., Pell, T., & Zuckerman, B. (2001). Growth, development, and behavior in early childhood following prenatal cocaine exposure: A systematic review. *Journal of the American Medical Association, 285,* 1613–1625.

Frank, M. C., Vul, E., & Saxe, R. (2012). Measuring the development of social attention using free-viewing. *Infancy, 17,* 355–375.

Frank, M. G., Ekman, P., & Friesen, W. V. (1993). Behavioral markers and recognizability of the smile of enjoyment. *Journal of Personality and Social Psychology, 64*(1), 83–93.

Frankenberg, W. K., & Dodds, J. B. (1967). The Denver developmental screening test. *Journal of Pediatrics, 71,* 181–191.

Frankenhuis, W. E., & de Weerth, C. (2013). Does early-life exposure to stress shape or impair cognition? *Current Directions in Psychological Science, 22*(5), 407.

Frank, M. J., O'Reilly, R. C., & Curran, T. (2006). When memory fails, intuition reigns: Midazolam enhances implicit inference in humans. *Psychological Science, 17,* 700–707.

Frankl, V. (1963). *Man's search for meaning*. New York: Washington Square Press.

Fratiglioni, L., & Qiu, C. (2009). Prevention of common neurodegenerative disorders in the elderly. *Experimental Gerontology, 44*(1–2), 46–50.

Frayling, T. M., Timpson, N. J., Weedon, M. N., Zeggini, E., Freathy R. M., Lindgren, C. M., Perry, J. R. B., Elliott, et al. (2007). A common variant in the FTO gene is associated with body mass index and predisposes to childhood and adult obesity. *Science, 316,* 889–894.

Fredrickson, B. L., & Cohn, M. A. (2008). Positive emotions. In M. Lewis, J. M. Haviland-Jones, L. Barrett, M., Lewis, J. M. Haviland-Jones, L. Barrett (Eds.) , *Handbook of emotions* (3rd ed.) (pp. 777–796). New York, NY US: Guilford Press.

Freed, C. R., Greene, P. E., Breeze, R. E., Tsai, W. Y., DuMouchel, W., Kao, R., et al. (2001). Transplantation of embryonic dopamine neurons for severe Parkinson's disease. *New England Journal of Medicine, 344,* 710–719.

Freedland, R. L., & Bertenthal, B. I. (1994). Developmental changes in interlimb coordination: Transition to hands-and-knees crawling. *Psychological Science, 5,* 26–32.

Freedman, J. L. (1992). Television violence and aggression: What psychologists should tell the public. In P. Suedfeld & P. E. Tetlock (Eds.), *Psychology and social policy*. New York: Hemisphere.

Freedman, J. L. (2002). *Media violence and its effect on aggression: Assessing the scientific evidence*. Toronto, Ontario, Canada: University of Toronto Press.

Freedman, V. A., Aykan, H., & Martin, L. G. (2001). Aggregate changes in severe cognitive impairment among older Americans: 1993 and 1998. *Journal of Gerontology, 56B,* S100–S111.

Freeman, D., Rizzo, J., & Fried, S. (2011). Encoding visual information in retinal ganglion cells with prosthetic stimulation. *Journal of Neural Engineering, 8*(3), 035005.

Freeman, H., Gosling. S. D., & Schapiro, S. J. (in press). Methods for assessing personality in non-human primates. In A. Weiss, J. King, & L. Murray (Eds.), *Personality and Behavioral Syndromes in Nonhuman Primates.* New York: Springer

Freeman, S., Eddy, S., McDonough, M., Smith, M., Okoroafor, N., Jordt, H., & Wenderoth, M. P. (2014). Active learning increases student performance in science, engineering, and mathematics. *Proceedings of the New York Academy of Sciences of the United States of America, 111*(23), 8410–8415.

Freeman, W., & Watts, J. W. (1942). *Psychosurgery.* Springfield, IL: Thomas.

Freimuth, V. S., & Hovick, S. R. (2012). Cognitive and emotional health risk perceptions among people living in poverty. *Journal of Health Communication, 17,* 303–318. doi:10.1080/10810730.2011.626505

Freisthler, B. (2011). Alcohol use, drinking venue utilization, and child physical abuse: Results from a pilot study. *Journal of Family Violence, 26,* 185–193. doi:10.1007/s10896-010-9352-2

Fremgen, A., & Fay, D. (1980). Overextensions in production and comprehension: A methodological clarification. *Journal of Child Language, 7,* 205–211.

French, A. N., Ashby, R. S., Morgan, I. G., & Rose, K. A. (2013). Time outdoors and the prevention of myopia. *Experimental Eye Research, 114,* 58–68.

French, S. E., Seidman, E., Allen, L., & Aber, J. L. (2006). The development of ethnic identity during adolescence. *Developmental Psychology, 42,* 1–10.

Frenda, S. J., Nichols, R. M., & Loftus, E. F. (2011). Current issues and advances in misinformation research. *Current Directions In Psychological Science (Sage Publications Inc.), 20*(1), 20–23. doi:10.1177/0963721410396620.

Frese, M., Beimel, S., & Schoenborn, S. (2003). Action training for charismatic leadership: Two evaluations of studies of a commercial training module on inspirational communication of a vision. *Personnel Psychology, 56,* 671–697.

Freud, S. (1900). The interpretation of dreams. In J. Strachey (Ed.), *The standard edition of the complete psychological works of Sigmund Freud* (Vol. 8). London: Hogarth Press.

Freund, P., & Kasten, N. (2012). How smart do you think you are? A meta-analysis on the validity of self-estimates of cognitive ability. *Psychological Bulletin, 138,* 296–321. doi:10.1037/a0026556.

Frick, P., & Nigg, J. (2012). Current issues in the diagnosis of attention deficit hyperactivity disorder, oppositional defiant disorder, and conduct disorder. *Annual Review of Clinical Psychology, 8,* 77–107.

Fridlund, A., Sabini, J. P., Hedlund, L. E., Schaut, J. A., Shenker, J. I., & Knauer, M. J. (1990). Audience effects on solitary faces during imagery: Displaying to the people in your head. *Journal of Nonverbal Behavior, 14*(2), 113–137.

Fried, I., Wilson, C. L., MacDonald, K. A., & Behnke, E. J. (1998). Electric current stimulates laughter. *Nature, 391,* 650.

Fried, Y., & Ferris, G. R. (1987). The validity of the job characteristics model: A review and meta-analysis. *Personnel Psychology, 40,* 287–322.

Friederici, A, D. (2011). The brain basis of language processing: from structure to function. *Physiological Reviews, 91*(4), 1357–1392.

Friedman, H., Kern, M. L., Hampson, S. E., & Duckworth, E. (2014). A new life-span approach to conscientiousness and health: Combining the pieces of the causal puzzle. *Developmental Psychology, 50*(5), 1377–1389.

Friedman, H. S. (2000). Long-term relations of personality and health: Dynamisms, mechanisms, tropisms. *Journal of Personality, 68,* 1089–1107.

Friedman, H. S., Kern, M. L., Hampson, S. E., & Duckworth, A. L. (2012). A new lifespan approach to conscientiousness and health: Combining the pieces of the causal puzzle. *Developmental Psychology,* Epub Oct 12, 2012.

Friedman, H. S., Kern, M. L. & Reynolds, C. A. (2010). Personality and health, subjective well-being, and longevity. *Journal of Personality, 78,* 179–216.

Friedman, H. S., & Martin, L. R. (2011). The Longevity Project: Surprising discoveries for health and long life from the landmark eight-decade study. New York: Hudson Street Press.

Friedman, H. S., & Schustack, M. (2009). *Personality: Classic theories and modern research* (4th ed.). Boston: Allyn & Bacon.

Friedman, H. S., & Schustack, M. W. (2003). *Personality: Classic theories and modern research.* Boston: Allyn & Bacon.

Friedman, H. S., Tucker, J. S., Schwartz, J. E., Martin, L. R., Tomlinson-Keasey, C., Wingard, D. L., & Criqui, M. H. (1995a). Childhood conscientiousness and longevity: Health behaviors and cause of death. *Journal of Personality and Social Psychology, 68,* 696–703.

Friedman, H. S., Tucker, J. S., Schwartz, J. E., Tomlinson-Keasey, C., Martin, L. R., Wingard, D. L., & Criqui, M. H. (1995b). Psychosocial and behavioral predictors of longevity: The aging and death of the "Termites." *American Psychologist, 50,* 69–78.

Friedman, M., & Rosenman, R. H. (1974). *Type A behavior and your heart.* New York: Knopf.

Friedman, M. A., & Brownell, K. D. (1995). Psychological correlates of obesity: Moving to the next research generation. *Psychological Bulletin, 117*(1), 3–20.

Friedman, N. P., Miyake, A., Corley, R. P., Young, S. E., et al. (2006). Not all executive functions are related to intelligence. *Current Directions in Psychological Science, 17,* 172–179.

Friedrich, M. J. (2014). Researchers test strategies to prevent Alzheimer's disease. *JAMA, 311*(16), 1596–1598.

Frisco, M. L. (2008). Adolescents' sexual behavior and academic attainment. *Sociology of Education, 81*(3), 284–311.

Fritsch, T., Smyth, K. A., McClendon, M. J., Ogrocki, P. K., Santillan, C., et al. (2005). Associations between dementia/mild cognitive impairment and cognitive performance and activity levels in youth. *Journal of the American Geriatrics Society, 53,* 1191–1196.

Frodl, T., Meisenzahl, E. M., Zill, P., Baghai, T. Rujescu, D. Leinsinger, G., et al. (2004). Reduced hippocampal volumes associated with the long variant of the serotonin transporter polymorphism in major depression. *Archives of General Psychiatry, 61,* 177–183.

Fry, R., & Cohn, D. (2011). Living together: The economics of cohabitation. *Social & Demographic Trends.* Washington, DC: Pew Research Center. Retrieved from: Fuligni, A. J., Witkow, M., & Garcia, C. (2005). Ethnic identity and the academic adjustment of adolescents from Mexican, Chinese, and European backgrounds. *Developmental Psychology, 41,* 799–811.

Fu, Q., Fu, X., & Dienes, Z. (2008). Implicit sequence learning and conscious awareness. *Consciousness and Cognition, 17,* 185–202.

Fuentemilla, L., Camara, E., Munte, T. F., Kramer, U. M., et al. (2009). Individual differences in true and false memory retrieval are related to white matter brain microstructure. *Journal of Neuroscience, 29,* 8698–8703.

Fujita, F., & Diener, E. (2005). Life satisfaction set point: Stability and change. *Journal of Personality and Social Psychology, 88,* 158–164.

Fuligni, A. J., & Pedersen, S. (2002). Family obligation and the transition to young adulthood. *Developmental Psychology, 38*(5), 856–868.

Fuligni, A. J., Witknow, M., & Garcia, C. (2005). Ethnic identity and the academic adjustment of adolescents from Mexican, Chinese, and European backgrounds. *Developmental Psychology, 41,* 799–811.

Fuller-Rowell, T. E., Evans, G. W., & Ong, A. D. (2012). Poverty and health: The mediating role of perceived discrimination. *Psychological Science, 23,* 734–739. doi:10.1177/0956797612439720.

Fullerton, C. S., Ursano, R. J., & Wang, L. (2004). Acute stress disorder, posttraumatic stress disorder, and depression in disaster or rescue workers. *American Journal of Psychiatry, 161,* 1370–1376.

Fullerton, J. M., Donald, J. A., Mitchell, P. B., & Schofield, P. R. (2010). Two-dimensional genome scan identifies multiple genetic interactions in bipolar affective disorder. *Biological Psychiatry, 67,* 478–486.

Funder, D. C. (2007). *The personality puzzle* (4th ed.). New York: Norton.

Funder, D. (2008). Persons, situations, and person-situation interactions. In O. John, R. Robins, & L. Pervin (Eds.), *Handbook of personality: Theory and research* (3rd ed., pp. 568–582). New York: Guilford.

Funder, D. C. (2012a). *The personality puzzle* (6th ed.). New York: W.W. Norton.

Funder, D. C. (2012b). Accurate personality judgment. *Current Directions in Psychological Science, 21,* 177–182. doi:10.1177/0963721412445309

Furey, M. L., Pietrini, P., & Haxby, J. V. (2000). Cholinergic enhancement and increased selectivity of perceptual processing during working memory. *Science, 290,* 2315–2319.

Furmark, T., Henningsson, S., Appel, L., Ahs, F., Linnman, C., Pissiota, A., et al. (2009). Genotype over-diagnosis in amygdala responsiveness: Affective processing in social anxiety disorder. *Journal of Psychiatry and Neuroscience, 34*(1), 30–40.

Furnham, A. (2001). Personality and individual differences in the workplace: Person-organization-outcome fit. In R. Hogan & B. Roberts (Eds.), *Personality psychology in the workplace* (pp. 223–251). Washington, DC: American Psychological Association.

Furnham, A., & Boo, H. (2011). A literature review of the anchoring effect. *Journal of Socio-Economics, 40*(1), 35–42. doi:10.1016/j.socec.2010.10.008.

Gabbard, G. O. (2004). *Long-term psychodynamic psychotherapy: A basic text.* Washington DC: American Psychiatric Association.

Gabe, T. (2013). Poverty in the United States: 2012. *U.S. Congressional Research Service.*

Gabriel, A. (2013). Risperidone, quetiapine, and olanzapine adjunctive treatments in major depression with psychotic features: A comparative study. *Neuropsychiatric Disease Treatment, 9,* 485–492.

Gaertner, S. L., Dovidio, J. F., & Houlette, M. (2010). Social categorization. In J. F. Dovidio, M. Hewstone, P. Glick, & V. M. Esses (Eds.), *The SAGE handbook of prejudice, stereotyping, and discrimination* (pp. 526–543) London: Sage.

Gage, F. H., & Temple, S. (2013). Neural stem cells: Generating and regenerating the brain. *Neuron, 80*(3), 588–601.

Gahlinger, P. M. (2004). Club drugs: MDMA, gamma-hydroxybutyrate (GHB), Rohypnol, and ketamine. *American Family Physician, 69*(11), 2619–2626.

Gahukar, R. T. (2011). Entomophagy and human food security. *International Journal of Tropical Insect Science, 31*(3), 129–144. doi:10.1017/S1742758411000257.

Gainotti, G. (2013). Is the right anterior temporal variant of prosopagnosia a form of "associative prosopagnosia" or a form of "multimodal person recognition disorder"? *Neuropsychology Review, 23*(2), 99–110.

Galanter, E. (1962). Contemporary psychophysics. In R. Brown (Ed.), *New directions in psychology* (Vol. 1). New York: Holt, Rinehart, Winston.

Galdeira, K. (2006, October). Phiten power. *Hawaii Business, 52*(4), 52–54.

Galdi, S., Arcuri, L., & Gawronski, B. (2008). Automatic mental associations predict future choices of undecided decision-makers. *Science, 321*, 1100–1102.

Gale, C. R., Booth, T., Mõttus, R., Kuh, D., & Deary, I. J. (2013). Neuroticism and extraversion in youth predict mental wellbeing and life satisfaction 40 years later. *Journal of Research in Personality, 47*(6), 687–697

Gale, C., R., Batty, G., & Deary, I. J. (2008). Locus of control at age 10 years and health outcomes and behaviors at age 30 years: The 1970 British cohort study. *Psychosomatic Medicine, 70*, 397–403.

Galea, M. P. (2012). Physical modalities in the treatment of neurological dysfunction. *Clinical Neurology & Neurosurgery, 114*(5), 483–488.

Galić, Z., & Jernেić, Ž. (2013). Measuring faking on five-factor personality questionnaires: The usefulness of communal and agentic management scales. *Journal of Personnel Psychology, 12*, 115–123.

Gallagher, K. E., Lisco, C. G., Parrott, D. J., & Giancola, P. R. (2014). Effects of thought suppression on provoked men's alcohol-related physical aggression in the laboratory. *Psychology of Violence, 4*(1), 78–89.

Gallagher, M. (1998, January 26). Day careless. *National Review, 50*(1), 37–43.

Gallagher, M., & Chiba, A. A. (1996). The amygdala and emotion. *Current Opinions in Neurobiology, 6*(2), 221–227.

Gallivan, J. P. Cavina-Pratesi, C., & Culham, J. C. (2009). Is that within reach? fMRI reveals that the human superior parieto-occipital cortex encodes objects reachable by the hand. *The Journal of Neuroscience, 29*, 4381–4391.

Gallo, D. A. (2006). *Associative illusions of memory.* New York: Psychology Press.

Gallo, D. S. A. (2013). Retrieval expectations affect false recollection: Insights from a criterial recollection task. *Current Directions in Psychological Science, 22*(4), 316–323.

Galloway, A. T., Addessi, E., Fragaszy, D. M., & Visalberghi, E. (2005). Social facilitation of eating familiar food in tufted capuchins (*Cebus appella*): Does it involve behavioral coordination? *International Journal of Primatology, 26*, 181–189.

Gallup, G. G., Jr., & Frederick, D. A. (2010). The science of sex appeal: An evolutionary perspective. *Review of General Psychology, 14*(3), 240–250.

Galotti, K. M. (1999a). Making a "major" real-life decision: College students choosing an academic major. *Journal of Educational Psychology, 91*, 379–387.

Galotti, K. M. (1999b). *Cognitive psychology in and out of the laboratory* (2nd ed.). Belmont, CA: Brooks/Cole.

Galpin, A., Underwood, G., & Chapman, P. (2008). Sensing without seeing in comparative visual search. *Consciousness and Cognition, 17*, 672–687.

Gamer, M., Rill, H.-G., Vossel, G., & Gödert, H. W. (2006). Psychophysiological and vocal measures in the detection of guilty knowledge. *International Journal of Psychophysiology, 60*, 76–87.

Gamez, D. (2008). Progress in machine consciousness. *Consciousness and Cognition, 17*, 887–910.

Ganchrow, J. R., Steiner, J. E., & Daher, M. (1983). Neonatal facial expressions in response to different qualities and intensities of gustatory stimuli. *Infant Behavior and Development, 6*, 189–200.

Ganiban, J. M., Ulbricht, J., Saudino, K. J., Reiss, D., & Neiderhiser, J. M. (2011). Understanding child-based effects on parenting: Temperament as a moderator of genetic and environmental contributions to parenting. *Developmental Psychology, 47*, 676–692.

Ganis, G., Rosenfeld, J., Meixner, J., Kievit, R. A., & Schendan, H. E. (2011). Lying in the scanner: Covert countermeasures disrupt deception detection by functional magnetic resonance imaging. *Neuroimage, 55*(1), 312–319. doi:10.1016/j.neuroimage.2010.11.025.

Ganten, D., & Pfaff, D. (2012). *Neurobiology of oxytocin.* Berlin: Springer.

Ganzel, B. L., Kim, P., Glover, G. H., & Temple, E. (2008). Resilience after 9/11: Multimodal neuroimaging evidence for stress-related change in the healthy adult brain. *NeuroImage, 40*(2), 788–795.

Ganzel, B. L., Morris, P. A., & Wethington, E. (2010). Allostasis and the human brain: Integrating models of stress from the social and life sciences. *Psychological Review, 117*, 134–174.

Gao, Y., Raine, A., Venables, P. H., Dawson, M. E., & Mednick, S. A. (2010). Association of poor childhood fear conditioning and adult crime. *American Journal of Psychiatry, 167*, 56–60.

Gara, M. A., Vega, W. A., Arndt, S. Escamilla, M., Fleck, D. E., Lawson, W. B., Lesser, I., Neighbors, H. W., Wilson, D. R., Arnold, L. M., & Strakowski, S. M. (2012). Influence of patient race and ethnicity on clinical assessment in patients with affective disorders. Published online first: *Arch Gen Psychiatry.* 2012;69:593–600. doi:10.1001/archgenpsychiatry.2011.2040 Retrieved from: http://archpsyc.jamanetwork.com/article.aspx?articleid=1151017

Garb, H. N., Wood, J. M., Lilienfeld, S. O., & Nezworski, T. (2005). Roots of the Rorschach controversy. *Clinical Psychology Review, 25,* 97–118.

Garcia, J., & Koelling, R. A. (1966). Relation of cue to consequences in avoidance learning. *Psychonomic Science, 4,* 123–124.

Garcia, S. M., Weaver, K., Moskowitz, G. B., & Darley, J. M. (2002). Crowded minds: The implicit bystander effect. *Journal of Personality and Social Psychology, 83,* 843–853.

García-Montes, J. M., Zaldívar-Basurto, F., López-Ríos, F., & Molina-Moreno, A. (2009). The role of personality variables in drug abuse in a Spanish university population. *International Journal of Mental Health & Addiction, 7*(3), 475–487. doi:10.1007/s11469-007-9144-y

Garcia-Sierra, A., Rivera-Gaxiola, M., Percaccio, C. R., Conboy, B. T., Romo, H., Klarman, L., & Kuhl, P. K. (2011). Bilingual language learning: An ERP study relating early brain responses to speech, language input, and later word production. *Journal of Phonetics, 39*(4), 546–557. doi:10.1016/j.wocn.2011.07.002.

Gardiner, H. W., & Kosmitzki, C. (2005). *Lives across cultures: Cross-cultural human development* (3rd ed.). Needham Heights, MA: Allyn & Bacon.

Gardner, B., Davies, A., McAteer, J., & Michie, S. (2010). Beliefs underlying UK parents' views towards MMR promotion interventions: A qualitative study. *Psychology, Health & Medicine, 15*(2), 220–230. doi:10.1080/13548501003623963.

Gardner, H. (1993). *Multiple intelligences: The theory in practice.* New York: Basic Books.

Gardner, H. (1999). Are there additional intelligences? The case for naturalist, spiritual, and existential intelligences. In J. Kane (Ed.), *Education, information and transformation: Essays on learning and thinking* (pp. 111–131). Englewood Cliffs, NJ: Prentice Hall.

Gardner, H. (2002). *Learning from extraordinary minds.* Mahwah, NJ: Erlbaum.

Gardner, M. (1988). *The second* Scientific American *book of mathematical puzzles and diversions.* Chicago: University of Chicago Press.

Gardner, R. A., & Gardner, B. T. (1978). Comparative psychology and language acquisition. *Annals of the New York Academy of Sciences, 309,* 37–76.

Gardner, R., Heward, W. L., & Grossi, T. A. (1994). Effects of response cards on student participation and academic achievement: A systematic replication with inner-city students during whole-class science instruction. *Journal of Applied Behavior Analysis, 27,* 63–71.

Gariepy, G., Nitka, D., & Schmitz, N. (2010). The association between obesity and anxiety disorders in the population: A systematic review and meta-analysis. *International Journal of Obesity, 34,* 407–419.

Garlick, D. (2002). Understanding the nature of general intelligence: The role of individual differences in neural plasticity as an explanatory mechanism. *Psychological Review, 109,* 116–136.

Garlipp, P. (2008). Koro–a culture-bound phenomenon: Intercultural psychiatric implications. *German Journal of Psychiatry, 11,* 21–28.

Garrido, M. I. (2012). Brain connectivity: The feel of blindsight. *Current Biology, 22*(15), R599–600.

Garry, M., & Gerrie, M. P. (2005). When photographs create false memories. *Current Directions in Psychological Science, 14,* 321–325.

Garry, M., & Loftus, E. (1994). Pseudomemories without hypnosis. *International Journal of Clinical and Experimental Hypnosis, 42,* 363–373.

Gaskell, M. G., Warker, J., Lindsay, S., Frost, R., Guest, J., Snowdon, R., & Stackhouse, A. (2014). Sleep underpins the plasticity of language production. *Psychological Science,* Epub June 3, 2014.

Gass, C. S., & Curiel, R. E. (2011). Test anxiety in relation to measures of cognitive and intellectual functioning. *Archives of Clinical Neuropsychology, 26*(5), 396–404.

Gasser, U. S., Rousson, V., Hentschel, F., Sattel, H., & Gasser, T. (2008). Alzheimer disease versus mixed dementias: An EEG perspective. *Clinical Neurophysiology, 119*(10), 2255–2259.

Gates, M. A., Holowka, D. W., Vasterling, J. J., Keane, T. M., Marx, B. P., & Rosen, R. C. (2012). Posttraumatic stress disorder in veterans and military personnel: Epidemiology, screening, and case recognition. *Psychological Services.* doi:10.1037/a0027649.

Gatewood, R. D., & Feild, H. S. (2001). *Human resource selection* (5th ed.). Fort Worth, TX: Harcourt.

Gaudioso, E., Montero, M., & Hernandez-del-Olmo, F. (2012). Supporting teachers in adaptive educational systems through predictive models: A proof of concept. *Expert Systems With Applications, 39*(1), 621–625. doi:10.1016/ j.eswa.2011.07.052.

Gauvain, M., Beebe, H., & Zhao, S. (2011). Applying the cultural approach to cognitive development. *Journal of Cognition and Development, 12,* 121–133.

Gauvreau, P., & Bouchard, S. (2008). Preliminary evidence for the efficacy of EMDR in treating generalized anxiety disorder. *Journal of EMDR Practice and Research, 2*(1), 26–40.

Gawande, A. A. (2008, June 30). The itch. *New Yorker.* Retrieved from http://www .newyorker.com/reporting/2008/06/30/080630fa_fact_gawande?currentPage=all

Gawronski, B. (2012). Back to the future of dissonance theory: Cognitive consistency as a core motive. *Social Cognition, 30*(6), 652–668.

Gaylor, J. M., Raman, G., Chung, M., Lee, J., Rao, M., Lau, J., Poe, D. S. (2013). Cochlear implantation in adults: A systematic review and meta-analysis. *JAMA Otolaryngology—Head & Neck Surgery, 139*(3), 265–272.

Gazzaley, A., Cooney, J. W., Rissman, J., & D'Esposito, M. (2005). Top-down suppression deficit underlies working memory impairment in normal aging. *Nature Neuroscience 8,* 1298–1300.

Gazzaniga, M. S., & LeDoux, J. E. (1978). *The integrated mind.* New York: Plenum.

Geangu, E., Benga, O., Stahl, D., & Striano, T. (2010). Contagious crying beyond the first days of life. *Infant Behavior & Development, 33*(3), 279–288. doi:10.1016/j. infbeh.2010.03.004.

Geary, D. C. (2000). Evolution and proximate expression of human paternal investment. *Psychological Bulletin, 126,* 55–77.

Geary, D. C. (2010). *Male, female: The evolution of human sex differences* (2nd ed.). Washington, DC: American Psychological Association.

Gebauer, J., Leary, M., & Neberich, W. (2011). Unfortunate first names: Effects of name-based relational devaluation and interpersonal neglect. *Social Psychological and Personality Science.* doi:http://dx.doi.org/10.1177/1948550611431644.

Geddes, J. R., Burgess, S., Hawton, K., Jamison, K., & Goodwin, G. M. (2004). Long-term lithium therapy for bipolar disorder: Systematic review and meta-analysis of randomized controlled trials. *American Journal of Psychiatry, 161,* 217–222.

Geddes, L. (2008, June 7). Are autistic savants made not born? *New Scientist, 198*(2659), 10.

Gegenfurtner, K. R., & Kiper, D. C. (2003). Color vision. *Annual Review of Neuroscience, 26,* 181–206.

Geher, G., Camargo, M. A., & O'Rourke, S. D. (2008). Mating intelligence: An integrative model and future research directions. In G. Geher & G. Miller (Eds.), *Mating intelligence: Sex, relationships, and the mind's reproductive system* (pp. 395–424). Mahwah, NJ: Erlbaum.

Geldmacher, D. S., Provenzano, G., McRae, T., Mastey, V., & Ieni, J. R. (2003). Donepezil is associated with delayed nursing home placement in patients with Alzheimer's disease. *Journal of the American Geriatric Society, 51,* 937–944.

Geleijnse, J. M. (2008). Habitual coffee consumption and blood pressure: An epidemiological perspective. *Vascular Health Risk Management, 4,* 963–970.

Gellhorn, E., & Loofbourrow, G. N. (1963). *Emotions and emotional disorders.* New York: Harper & Row.

Gelhorn, H. L., Stallings, M. C., Young, S. E., Corley, R. P., Rhee, S. H., & Hewitt, J. K. (2005). Genetic and environmental influences on conduct disorder: symptom, domain and full-scale analyses. *Journal of Child Psychology and Psychiatry, 46,* 580–591.

Gelman, R., & Baillargeon, R. (1983). A review of some Piagetian concepts. In P. H. Mussen (Ed.), *Handbook of child psychology* (Vol. 3, pp. 167–230). New York: Wiley.

Gelstein, S., Yeshurun, Y., Rozenkrantz, L., Shushan, S., Frumin, I., Roth, Y., & Sobel, N. (2011). Human tears contain a chemosignal. *Science, 331*(6014), 226–230.

Gendron, M., Roberson, D., van der Vyver, J. M., & Barrett, L. F. (2014a). Cultural relativity in perceiving emotion from vocalizations. *Psychological Science, 25*(4), 911–920.

Gendron, M., Roberson, D., van der Vyver, J. M., Marietta, J., & Barrett, L., F. (2014b). Perceptions of emotion from facial expressions are not culturally universal: Evidence from a remote culture. *Emotion 14*(2), 251–262.

Gentile, D. A., Dongdong, L., Khoo, A., Prot, S., & Anderson, C. A. (2014). Mediators and moderators of long-term effects of violent video games on aggressive behavior: Practice, thinking, and action. *JAMA Pediatrics, 168*(5), 450–457.

Gentile, D. A., Li, D., Khoo, A., Prot, S., & Anderson, C. A. (2014). Mediators and moderators of long-term effects of violent video games on aggressive behavior: Practice, thinking, and action. *JAMA Pediatrics, 168,* 450–457.

Gentry, K. R., McGinn, K. L., Kundu, A., & Lynn, A. M. (2011). Acupuncture therapy for infants: a preliminary report on reasons for consultation, feasibility, and tolerability. *Paediatric Anaesthesia.* Epub December 6, 2011.

George, M. S., Anton, R. F., Bloomer, C., Teneback, C., Drobes, D. J., Lorberbaum, J. P., et al. (2001). Activation of prefrontal cortex and anterior thalamus in alcoholic subjects on exposure to alcohol-specific cues. *Archives of General Psychiatry, 58,* 345–352.

George, W. H., & Marlatt, G. A. (1986). The effects of alcohol and anger on interest in violence, erotica, and deviance. *Journal of Abnormal Psychology, 95,* 150–158.

Geraerts, E., Bernstein, D. M., Merckelbach, H., Linders, C., Raymaekers, L., & Loftus, E. F. (2008a). Lasting false beliefs and their behavioral consequences. *Psychological Science, 19,* 749–753.

Geraerts, E., Lindsay, D. S., Merckelbach, H., Jelicic, M., Raymaekers, L., Arnold, M. M., & Schooler, J. W. (2008b). Cognitive mechanisms underlying recovered-memory experiences of childhood sexual abuse. *Psychological Science, 20,* 92–98.

Geraerts, E., Schooler, J. W., Merckelbach, H., Jelicic, M., Hauer, B. J. A., & Ambadar, Z. (2007). The reality of recovered memories: Corroborating continuous and discontinuous memories of childhood sexual abuse, *Psychological Science, 18,* 564–568.

Geraerts, E., Smeets, E., Jelicic, M., Merckelbach, H., & van Heerden, J. (2006). Retrieval inhibition of trauma-related words in women reporting repressed or recovered memories of childhood sexual abuse. *Behaviour Research and Therapy, 44,* 1129–1136.

Gerhart, B. (2005). The (affective) dispositional approach to job satisfaction: Sorting out the policy implications. *Journal of Organizational Behavior, 26,* 79–97.

Gerin, W., Davidson, K. W., Christenfeld, N. J. S., Goyal, T., & Schwartz, J. E. (2006). The role of angry rumination and distraction in blood pressure recovery from emotional arousal. *Psychosomatic Medicine, 68,* 64–72.

German, T. P., & Barrett, H. C. (2005). Functional fixedness in a technologically sparse culture. *Psychological Science, 16*(1), 1–5.

Gerschman, J. A., Reade, P. C., & Burrows, G. D. (1980). Hypnosis and dentistry. In G. D. Burrows & L. Dennerstein (Eds.), *Handbook of hypnosis and psychosomatic medicine.* New York: Elsevier.

Gershoff, E. T. (2013). Spanking and child development: We know enough now to stop hitting our children. *Child Development Perspectives, 7*(3), 133–137.

Gershoff, E. T., & Bitensky, S. H. (2007). The case against corporal punishment of children: Converging evidence from social science research and international human rights law and implications for U.S. public policy. *Psychology, Public Policy, and Law, 13,* 231–272.

Gershoff, E. T., Grogan-Kaylor, A., Lansford, J. E., Chang, L., Zelli, A., Deater-Deckard, K., & Dodge, K. A. (2010). Parent discipline practices in an international sample: Associations with child behaviors and moderation by perceived normativeness. *Child Development, 81,* 487–502.

Gerstorf, D., Ram, N., Hoppmann, C., Willis, S. L., & Schaie, K. (2011). Cohort differences in cognitive aging and terminal decline in the Seattle Longitudinal Study. *Developmental Psychology, 47*(4), 1026–1041. doi:10.1037/a0023426.

Gervais, W. M., & Norenzayan, A. (2012). Reminders of secular authority reduce believers' distrust of atheists. *Psychological Science, 23,* 483–491. doi:10.1177/ 0956797611429711.

Geschwind, N. (1968). Disconnexion syndromes in animals and man. *Brain, 88,* 237–294.

Ghacibeh, G A. & Heilman, K. M. (2003). Progressive affective aprosodia and prosoplegia. *Neurology, 60*(7), 1192–1194.

Ghaemi, S. N. (2008). *Mood disorders* (2nd ed.). Philadelphia: Wolters Kluwer Health/ Lippincott, Williams & Wilkins.

Ghirlanda, S., Enquist, M., & Lind, J. (2014). Coevolution of intelligence, behavioral repertoire, and lifespan. *Theoretical Population Biology, 91,* 44–49.

Gianaros, P. J., May, J. C., Siegle, G. J., & Jennings, J. R. (2005). Is there a functional neural correlate of individual differences in cardiovascular reactivity? *Psychosomatic Medicine, 67,* 31–39.

Giancola, P. R., & Corman, M. D. (2007). Alcohol and aggression: A test of the attention-allocation model. *Psychological Science, 18,* 649–655.

Gibbs, J. C., Basinger, K. S., Grime, R. L., & Snarey, J. R. (2007). Moral judgment development across cultures: Revisiting Kohlberg's universality claims. *Developmental Review, 27,* 443–500.

Gibson, E. J., & Walk, R. D. (1960). The visual cliff. *Scientific American, 202,* 64–71.

Gifford, R. (2011). The dragons of inaction: Psychological barriers that limit climate change mitigation and adaptation. *American Psychologist, 66*(4), 290–302. doi:10.1037/a0023566.

Gifford, R., & Hine, D. (1997). Toward cooperation in the commons dilemma. *Canadian Journal of Behavioural Science, 29,* 167–178.

Gigerenzer, G. (2004). Dread risk, September 11, and fatal traffic accidents. *Psychological Science, 15,* 286–287.

Gilbert, D. T. (2006). *Stumbling on happiness.* New York: Knopf.

Gilbert, J., Gasteyger, C., Raben, A., Meier, D., Astrup, A., & Sjödin, A. (2012). The effect of tesofensine on appetite sensations. *Obesity (Silver Spring, Md.)*, *20*(3), 553–561. doi:10.1038/oby.2011.197.

Gilbert-Diamond, D., Li, Z., Adachi-Mejia, A. M., McClure, A. C., & Sargent, J. D. (2014). Association of a television in the bedroom with increased adiposity gain in a nationally representative sample of children and adolescents. *JAMA Pediatrics*, *168*(5), 427–434.

Gilboa-Schechtman, E., & Foa, E. B. (2001). Patterns of recovery from trauma: The use of intraindividual analysis. *Journal of Abnormal Psychology*, *110*, 392–400.

Gilchrist, D., & Cowan, N. (2012). Chunking. In: V.S. Ramachandran (Ed.) *Encyclopedia of Human Behavior*, 2nd Ed, vol. 1, pp 476–483. San Diego: Academic Press.

Gilden, D. L., & Marusich, L. R. (2009). Contraction of time in attention-deficit hyperactivity disorder. *Neruopsychology*, *23*, 265–269.

Giles, L., Davies, M., Whitrow, M., Warin, M., & Moore, V. (2011). Maternal depressive symptoms and child care during toddlerhood relate to child behavior at age 5 years. *Pediatrics*, *128*, e78–e84.

Giles, L. C., Glonek, G. F., Luszcz, M. A., & Andrews, G. R. (2005). Effect of social networks on 10-year survival in very old Australians: The Australian Longitudinal Study of Aging. *Journal of Epidemiology and Community Health*, *59*, 574–579.

Gillespie-Lynch, K., Greenfield, P. M., Lyn, H., & Savage-Rumbaugh, S. (2011). The role of dialogue in the ontogeny and phylogeny of early symbol combinations: A cross-species comparison of bonobo, chimpanzee, and human learners. *First Language*, *31*(4), 442–460. doi:10.1177/0142723711406882.

Gillham, J. E., Reivich, K. J., Freres, D. R., Chaplin, T. M., Shatté, A. J., Samuels, B., et al. (2007). School-based prevention of depressive symptoms: A randomized controlled study of the effectiveness and specificity of the Penn Resiliency Program. *Journal of Consulting and Clinical Psychology*, *75*, 9–19.

Gilligan, C. (1982). *In a different voice: Psychological theory and women's development*. Cambridge, MA: Harvard University Press.

Gilligan, C. (1993). Adolescent development reconsidered. In A. Garrod (Ed.), *Approaches to moral development: New research and emerging themes*. New York: Teachers College Press.

Gilmore, G. C., Spinks, R. A., & Thomas, C. W. (2006). Age effects in coding tasks: Componential analysis and test of the sensory deficit hypothesis. *Psychology and Aging*, *21*, 7–18.

Gilmore, J. H. (2010). Understanding what causes schizophrenia: A developmental perspective. *American Journal of Psychiatry*, *167*, 8–10.

Gilmore, M. M., & Murphy, C. (1989). Aging is associated with increased Weber ratios for caffeine, but not for sucrose. *Perception and Psychophysics*, *46*, 555–559.

Gilmore, R. L., Heilman, K. M., Schmidt, R. P., Fennell, E. M., & Quisling, R. (1992). Anosognosia during Wada testing. *Neurology*, *42*(4), 925–927.

Gilmore, G. C., Spinks, R. A., & Thomas, C. W. (2006). Age effects in coding tasks: Componential analysis and test of the sensory deficit hypothesis. *Psychology and Aging*, *21*, 7–18.

Giltay, E. J., Kamphuis, M. H., Kalmijn, S., Zitman, F. G., & Kromhout, D. (2006). Dispositional optimism and the risk of cardiovascular death: The Zutphen elderly study. *Archives of Internal Medicine*, *166*, 431–436.

Ginges, J., Atran, S., Medin, D., & Shikaki, K. (2007). Sacred bounds on rational resolution of violent political conflict. *Proceeedings of the National Academy of Sciences*, *104*, 7357–7360.

Gingras, J. L., Mitchell, E. A., & Grattan, K. E. (2005). Fetal homologue of infant crying. *Archives of Disease in Childhood: Fetal and Neonatal Edition*, *90*, F415–F418.

Gino, F., Ayal, S., & Ariely, D. (2009). Contagion and diff erentiation in unethical behavior: Theeffect of one bad apple on the barrel. *Psychological Science*, *20*, 393–398.

Ginsburg, K. R., Durbin, D. R., Garcia-Espana, J. F., Kalicka, E. A., & Winston, F. K. (2009). Associations between parenting styles and teen driving, safety-related behaviors, and attitudes. *Pediatrics*, *124*, 1040–1051.

Giorgi-Guarnieri, D., Janofsky, J., Keram, E., Lawsky, S., Merideth, P., Mossman, D., et al. (2002). AAPL practice guideline for forensic psychiatric evaluation of defendants raising the insanity defense. *Journal of the American Academy of Psychiatry and the Law*, *30*(Suppl. 2), S1–S40.

Gipson, C. D., Kupchik, Y. M., & Kalivas, P. W. (2014). Rapid, transient synaptic plasticity in addiction. *Neuropharmacology*, *76*, 276–286.

Gladwell, M. (2004, January 12). Big and bad. *New Yorker*, 28–33.

Gladwell, M. (2005). *Blink: The power of thinking without thinking*. New York: Little, Brown.

Gladwell, M. (2008). *Outliers: The story of success*. New York: Little Brown.

Glanzer, M., & Cunitz, A. (1966). Two storage mechanisms in free recall. *Journal of Verbal Learning and Verbal Behavior*, *5*, 351–360.

Glaser, C., Trommershäuser, J., Mamassian, P., & Maloney, L. T. (2012). Comparison of the distortion of probability information in decision under risk and an equivalent visual task. *Psychological Science*, *23*(4), 419–426. doi:10.1177/ 0956797611429798.

Glǎveanu, V. (2012). Habitual creativity: Revising habit, reconceptualizing creativity. *Review of General Psychology*, *16*(1), 78–92. doi:10.1037/a0026611.

Gleason, M. E. J., Iida, M., Shrout, P. E., & Bolger, N. (2008). Receiving support as a mixed blessing: Evidence for dual effects of support on psychological outcomes. *Journal of Personality and Social Psychology*, *94*, 824–838.

Gleibs, I. H., Haslam, C., Jones, J. M., Alexander Haslam, S. S., McNeill, J., & Connolly, H. (2011). No country for old men? The role of a "Gentlemen's Club" in promoting social engagement and psychological well-being in residential care. *Aging & Mental Health*, *15*(4), 456–466. doi:10.1080/13607863.2010.536137.

Gleitman, L., & Landau, B. (1994). *The acquisition of the lexicon*. Cambridge: MIT Press.

Glenberg, A. M. (2011). Introduction to the Mirror Neuron Forum. *Perspectives on Psychological Science*, *6*(4), 363–368. doi:10.1177/1745691611412386.

Glenn, A. L., Raine, A., Venables, P. H., & Mednick, S. A. (2007). Early temperamental and psychophysiological precursors of adult psychopathic personality. *Journal of Abnormal Psychology*, *116*(3), 508–518.

Glick, P. T., & Fiske, S. T. (2001). Ambivalent sexism. In M. Zanna (Ed.), *Advances in experimental social psychology* (Vol. 33, pp. 115–188). New York: Academic Press.

Glover, J. A., Krug, D., Dietzer, M., George, B. W., & Hannon, M. (1990). "Advance" advance organizers. *Bulletin of the Psychonomic Society*, *28*, 4–6.

Glummarra, M. J., Gibson, S. J., Georgiou-Karistianis, N., & Bradshaw, J. L. (2007). Central mechanisms in phantom limb perception: The past, present and future. *Brain Research Reviews*, *54*(1), 219–232.

Glynn, L. M., Davis, E. P., Schetter, C. D., Chicz-DeMet, A., Hobel, C. J., & Sandman, C. A. (2007). Postnatal maternal cortisol levels predict temperament in healthy breastfed infants. *Early Human Development*, *83*, 675–681.

Gofton, T. E. (2011). Delirium: a review. *Canadian Journal of Neurological Sciences*, *38*(5), 673–680.

Gogate, L. J., & Hollich, G. (2010). Invariance detection within an interactive system: A perceptual gateway to language development. *Psychological Review*, *117*(2), 496–516. doi:10.1037/a0019049.

Gogtay, N., Giedd, J. N., Lusk, L., Hayashi, K. M., Greenstein, D., Vaituzis, A. C., Nugent, T. F., III, Herman, D. H., Clasen, L. S., Toga, A. W., Rapoport, J. L., & Thompson, P. M. (2004). Dynamic mapping of human cortical development during childhood through early adulthood. *Proceedings of the National Academy of Sciences*, *101*, 8174–8179.

Goh, W. D., & Lu, S. X. (2012). Testing the myth of the encoding–retrieval match. *Memory & Cognition*, *40*(1), 28–39. doi:10.3758/s13421–011–0133–9.

Gold, M. S. (1994). The epidemiology, attitudes, and pharmacology of LSD use in the 1990s. *Psychiatric Annals*, *24*(3), 124–126.

Goldberg, A. E. (2010). *Lesbian and gay parents and their children: Research on the family life cycle*. Washington, DC: American Psychological Association Press.

Goldberg, J. F., & Burdick, K. E. (Eds.) (2008). *Cognitive dysfunction in bipolar disorder*. Washington, DC: American Psychiatric Association Publishing.

Goldenberg, G. (2013). Apraxia—The cognitive side of motor control. *Cortex*, ePub September 12, 2013.

Goldenberg, J. L., Arndt, J., Hart, J., & Routledge, C. (2008). Uncovering an existential barrier to breast self-exam behavior. *Journal of Experimental Social Psychology*, *44*, 260–274.

Goldfriend, M. R., Glass, C. R., & Arnkoff, D. B. (2011). Integrative approaches to psychotherapy. In J. C. Norcross, G. R. VandenBos, & D. K. Freedheim (Eds.), *History of psychotherapy: Continuity and change* (pp. 269–296). Washington, D.C.: American Psychological Association.

Goldin-Meadow, S., & Beilock, S. L. (2010). Action's influence on thought: The case of gesture. *Perspectives on Psychological Science*, *5*(6), 664–674. doi:10.1177/1745691610388764.

Goldinger, S. D., & Papesh, M. H. (2012). Pupil dilation reflects the creation and retrieval of memories. *Current Directions in Psychological Science*, *21*(2) 90–95. doi:10.1177/0963721412436811.

Goldman, M. S., Darkes, J., & Del Boca, F. K. (1999). Expectancy meditation of biopsychosocial risk for alcohol use and alcoholism. In I. Kirsch (Ed.), *How expectancies shape experience* (pp. 233–262). Washington, DC: American Psychological Association.

Goldstein, A. J., de Beurs, E., Chambless, D. L., & Wilson, K. A. (2000). EMDR for panic disorder with agoraphobia: Comparison with waiting list and credible attention-placebo control conditions. *Journal of Consulting and Clinical Psychology*, *68*(6), 947–956.

Goldstein, A. M., Morse, S. J., & Packer, I. K. (2013). Evaluation of criminal responsibility. In R. K. Otto & I. B. Weiner (Eds.), *Handbook of psychology, Vol. 11: Forensic psychology* (2nd ed.) (pp. 440–472). Hoboken, NJ: Wiley.

Goldstein, E. B. (2002). *Sensation and perception* (6th ed.). Pacific Grove CA: Wadsworth.

Goldstein, I., & Rosen, R. C. (Eds.). (2002). Guest editors' introduction: Female sexuality and sexual dysfunction. *Archives of Sexual Behavior, 31,* 391.

Goldstein, I. L. (1993). *Training in organizations: Needs assessment, development, and evaluation* (3rd ed.). Monterey, CA: Brooks/Cole.

Goldstein, J. (2001, October 26–27). *Does playing violent video games cause aggressive behavior?* Paper presented at the University of Chicago Cultural Policy Center conference "Playing by the Rules: The Cultural Policy Challenges of Video Games," Chicago. Retrieved from http://culturalpolicy.uchicago.edu/conf-2001/papers/goldstein.html

Goldstein, J. M., Jerram, M., Abbs, B., Whitfield-Gabrieli, S., & Makris, N. (2010). Sex differences in stress response circuitry activation dependent on female hormonal cycle. *Journal of Neuroscience, 30,* 431–438.

Goldstein, K. (1939). *The organism.* New York: American Book.

Goldstein, M., Peters, L., Baillie, A., McVeagh, P., Minshall, G., & Fitzjames, D. (2011). The effectiveness of a day program for the treatment of adolescent anorexia nervosa. *International Journal of Eating Disorders, 44*(1), 29–38. doi:10.1002/eat.20789.

Goldstein, M. H., King, A. P., & West, M. J. (2003). Social interaction shapes babbling: Testing parallels between birdsong and speech. *Proceedings of the National Academy of Sciences, 100,* 8030–8035.

Goldstein, M. H., Schwade, J., Briesch, J., & Syal, S. (2010). Learning while babbling: Prelinguistic object-directed vocalizations indicate a readiness to learn. *Infancy, 15*(4), 362–391. doi:10.1111/j.1532–7078.2009.00020.x.

Goldstein, M. H., & Schwade, J. A. (2008). Social feedback to infants' babbling facilitates rapid phonological learning. *Psychological Science, 19,* 515–523.

Goldstein, S. E., Davis-Kean, P. E., & Eccles, J. S. (2005). Parents, peers, and problem behavior: A longitudinal investigation of the impact of relationship perceptions and characteristics on the development of adolescent problem behavior. *Developmental Psychology, 41,* 401–413.

Goltz, H. C., DeSouza, J. F. X., Menon, R. S., Tweed, D. B., & Vilis, T. (2003). Interaction of retinal image and eye velocity in motion perception. *Neuron, 39,* 569–576.

Golumbic, E.Z., Cogan, G.B., Schroeder, C.E., & Poeppel, D. (2013). Visual input enhances selective speech envelope tracking in auditory cortex at a "cocktail party." *The Journal of Neuroscience, 33,* 1417–1426.

Gomez, D. M., Berent, I., Benavides-Varelaa, S., Bion, R.A.H., Cattarossi, L., Nespor, M., & Mehler, J. (2014). Language universals at birth. *Proceedings of the National Academy of Sciences, doi: 10.1073/pnas.1318261111, March 31, 2014.*

Goncalves Portelinha, I., Verlhiac, J., Meyer, T., & Hutchison, P. (2012). Terror management and biculturalism: When the salience of cultural duality affects worldview defense in the face of death. *European Psychologist, 17,* 237–245. doi:10.1027/1016–9040/a000111.

Gonsalves, B. D., Kahn, I., Curran, T., Norman, K. A., & Wagner, A. D. (2005). Memory strength and repetition suppression: Multimodal imaging of medial temporal cortical contributions to recognition. *Neuron, 47,* 751–761.

Gonzalez, H. M., Vega, W. A., Williams, D. R., Tarraf, W., et al. (2010). Depression care in the United States: Too little for too few. *Archives of General Psychiatry, 67,* 37–46.

Good, C., Rattan, A., & Dweck, C. S. (2012). Why do women opt out? Sense of belonging and women's representation in mathematics. *Journal of Personality and Social Psychology, 102*(4), 700–717. doi:10.1037/a0026659.

Goodall, J. (1964). Tool-using and aimed throwing in a community of free-living chimpanzees. *Nature, 201,* 1264–1266.

Goodenough, F. L. (1932). Expression of the emotions in a blind-deaf child. *Journal of Abnormal and Social Psychology, 27,* 328–333.

Goodglass, H., & Kaplan, E. (1982). *The assessment of aphasia and related disorders* (2nd ed.). Philadelphia: Lea & Febiger.

Goodman, G. S., Ghetti, S., Quas, J. A., Edelstein, R. S., Alexander, K. W., Redlich, A. D., et al. (2003). A prospective study of memory for child sexual abuse: New findings relevant to the repressed-memory controversy. *Psychological Science, 14,* 113–118.

Goodman, W. K., Foote, K. D., Greenberg, B. D., Ricciuti, N., et al. (2010). Deep brain stimulation for intractable obsessive compulsive disorder: Pilot study using a blinded, staggered-onset design. *Biological Psychiatry, 67,* 535–542.

Goodnight, B. L., Cook, S. L., Parrott, D. J., & Peterson, J. L. (2013). Effects of masculinity, authoritarianism, and prejudice on antigay aggression: A path analysis of gender-role enforcement. *Psychology of Men and Masculinity.* Epub December 23, 2013.

Gopie, N., & MacLeod, C. M. (2009). Destination memory: Stop me if I've told you this before. *Psychological Science (Wiley-Blackwell), 20*(12), 1492–1499. doi:10.1111/j.1467–9280.2009.02472.x.

Gordon, D. B., Dahl, J. L., Miaskowski, C., McCarberg, B., Todd, K. H., Paice, J. A., et al. (2005). American Pain Society recommendations for improving the quality of acute and cancer pain management: American Pain Society Quality of Care Task Force. *Archives of Internal Medicine, 165,* 1574–1580.

Gore-Felton, C., & Koopman, C. (2008). Behavioral mediation of the relationship between psychosocial factors and HIV disease progression. *Psychosomatic Medicine 70,* 569–574.

Gorman, J. M. (2003). Treating generalized anxiety disorder. *Journal of Clinical Psychiatry, 64*(Suppl. 2), 24–29.

Gorman, J. M. (2005). Benzodiazepines: Taking the good with the bad and the ugly. *CNS Spectrums, 10,* 14–15.

Gorno-Tempini, M. L., Hillis, A. E., Weintraub, S., Kertesz, A., Mendez, M., Cappa, S. F., Ogar, J. M., Rohrer, J. D., Black, S., Boeve, B. F., Manes, F., Dronkers, N. F, Vandenberghe, R., Rascovsky, K., Patterson, K., Miller, B. L, Knopman, D. S., Hodges, J. R., Mesulam, M. M., & Grossman, M. (2011). Classification of primary progressive aphasia and its variants. *Neurology. 76*(11), 1006–1114.

Gosling, S. D., & Jones, A. C. (2012) Dog personality questionnaire. Available at https://survey.psy.utexas.edu/API/dpq4.php.

Gosling, S. D., Vazire, S., Srivastava, S., & John, O. P. (2004). Should we trust web-based studies? A comparative analysis of six preconceptions about Internet questionnaires. *American Psychologist, 59,* 93–104.

Goss Lucas, S., & Bernstein, D. A. (2005). *Teaching psychology: A step by step guide.* Mahwah, NJ: Erlbaum.

Gosseries, O., Bruno, M. A., Chatelle, C., Vanhaudenhuyse, A., Schnakers, C., Soddu, A., & Laureys, S. (2011). Disorders of consciousness: what's in a name? *NeuroRehabilitation. 28*(1), 3–14.

Gotlib, I. H., Joorman, J., & Foland-Ross, L. C. (2014). Understanding familial risk for depression: A 25-year perspective. *Perspectives on Psychological Science, 9*(1), 94–108.

Gotlib, I. H., Krasnoperova, E., Yue, D. N., & Joorman, J. (2004). Attentional biases for negative interpersonal stimuli in clinical depression. *Journal of Abnormal Psychology, 113,* 127–135.

Goto, Y., Yang, C. R., & Otani, S. (2010). Functional and dysfunctional synaptic plasticity in prefrontal cortex: Roles in psychiatric disorders. *Biological Psychiatry, 67,* 199–207.

Gottesman, I. I., Laursen, T. M., Bertelsen, A., & Mortensen, P. B. (2010). Severe mental disorders in offspring with 2 psychiatrically ill parents. *Archives of General Psychiatry, 67,* 252–257.

Gottfredson, L. S. (1997a). Mainstream science on intelligence: An editorial with 52 signatories, history, and bibliography. *Intelligence, 24,* 13–23.

Gottfredson, L. S. (1997b). Why g matters: The complexity of everyday life. *Intelligence, 24,* 79–132.

Gottfredson, L. S. (2003). Dissecting practical intelligence theory: Its claims and evidence. *Intelligence, 31,* 343–397.

Gottfredson, L. S. (2004). Intelligence: Is it the epidemiologists' elusive "fundamental cause" of social class inequalities in health? *Journal of Personality and Social Psychology, 86,* 174–199.

Gottfried, A. W. (1997, June). Parents' role is critical to children's learning. *APA Monitor,* 24.

Gottman, J., Gottman, J., & Shapiro, A. (2010). A new couples approach to interventions for the transition to parenthood. In M.S. Schulz, M. K. Pruett, P. K. Kerig, & R. D. Parke (Eds.), *Strengthening couple relationships for optimal child development* (pp. 165–179). Washington, DC: American Psychological Association.

Gottman, J. M., Driver, J., & Tabares, A. (2002). Building the sound marital house: An empirically derived couple therapy. In A. S. Gurman & N. S. Jacobson (Eds.), *Clinical handbook of couple therapy* (3rd ed., pp. 373–399). New York: Guilford Press.

Gouin, J.-P., Carter, C. S., Pournajafi-Nazarloo, H., Glaser, R., et al. (2010). Marital behavior, oxytocin, vasopressin, and wound healing. *Psychoneuroendocrinology, 35,* 1082–1090

Gouin, J.-P., Kiecolt-Glaser, J. K., Malarkey, W. B., & Glaser, R. (2008). The influence of anger expression on wound healing. *Brain, Behavior, and Immunity, 22,* 699–708.

Gow, A. J., Johnson, W., Pattie, A., Brett, C. E., Roberts, B., Starr, J. M., & Deary, I. J. (2011). Stability and change in intelligence from age 11 to ages 70, 79, and 87: The Lothian Birth Cohorts of 1921 and 1936. *Psychology and Aging, 26,* 232–240.

Gow, M. A. (2010). Dental extractions and immediate implant placements using hypnosis in place of traditional local anaesthetics. *Contemporary Hypnosis, 27*(4), 268–277.

Goyal, M., Singh, S., Sibinga, E. S., Goyal, M., Singh, S., Sibinga, E. M. S., Gould, N. F., Rowland-Seymour, A., Sharma, R., Berger, Z., Sleicher, D., Maron, D. D., Shihab, H. M., Ranasinghe, P. D., Linn, S., Saha, S. Bass, E. B., & Haythornthwaite, J. A. (2014). Meditation programs for psychological stress and well-being: A systematic review and meta-analysis. *JAMA Internal Medicine.* ePub January 6, 2014.

Grabell, A., Thomas, A., Bermann, E., & Graham-Bermann, S. A. (2012). The associations between community violence, television violence, intimate partner violence, parent–child aggression, and aggression in sibling relationships of a sample of preschoolers. *Psychology of Violence, 2*(2), 165–178.

Grace, A. A. (2010). Ventral hippocampus, interneurons, and schizophrenia: A new understanding of the pathophysiology of schizophrenia and its implications for treatment and prevention. *Current Directions in Psychological Science, 19*(4), 232–237. doi:10.1177/0963721410378032.

Gräff, J., & Mansuy, I. M. (2008). Epigenetic codes in cognition and behaviour. *Behavioural Brain Research, 192*(1), 70–87.

Graham, K., Bernards, S., Knibbe, R., Kairouz, S., Kuntsche, S., Wilsnack, S. C., . . . & Gmel, G. (2011). Alcohol-related negative consequences among drinkers around the world. *Addiction, 106,* 1391–1405.

Graham, K., Osgood, D. W., Wells, S., & Stockwell, T. (2006). To what extent is intoxication associated with aggression in bars? A multilevel analysis. *Journal of Studies on Alcohol, 67,* 382–390.

Grammer, K., Fink, B., & Neave, N. (2005). Human pheromones and sexual attraction. *European Journal of Obstetrics, Gynecology, and Reproductive Biology, 118,* 135–142.

Grand, J. A., Ryan, A., Schmitt, N., & Hmurovic, J. (2011). How far does stereotype threat reach? The potential detriment of face validity in cognitive ability testing. *Human Performance, 24*(1), 1–28. doi:10.1080/08959285.2010.518184.

Granhag, P.-A., & Stromwall, L. (2004). *The detection of deception in forensic contexts.* New York: Cambridge University Press.

Granier-Deferre, C., Bassereau, S., Ribeiro, A., Jacquet, A.-Y., & DeCasper, A. J. (2011). A melodic contour repeatedly experienced by human near-term fetuses elicits a profound cardiac reaction one month after birth. *PLoS One, 6,* e17304.

Grant, A. M. (2013). Rethinking the extraverted sales ideal: The ambivert advantage. *Psychological Science,* 1024–1030.

Grant, A. M., & Hofmann, D. A. (2011). It's not all about me : Motivating hand hygiene among health care professionals by focusing on patients. *Psychological Science, 22*(12), 1494–1499. doi:10.1177/0956797611419172.

Grant, H., & Dweck, C. S. (2003). Clarifying achievement goals and their impact. *Journal of Personality and Social Psychology, 85,* 541–553.

Grant, J. E., & Kim, S. W. (2002). *Stop me because I can't stop myself: Taking control of impulsive behavior.* New York: McGraw-Hill.

Gray, J. A. (1991). Neural systems, emotions, and personality. In J. Madden, IV (Ed.), *Neurobiology of learning, emotion, and affect* (pp. 272–306). New York: Raven Press.

Gray, J. A., & McNaughton, N. (2000). *The neuropsychology of anxiety: An enquiry into the functions of the septohippocampal system* (2nd ed.). New York: Oxford University Press.

Gray, N. S., MacCulloch, M. J., Smith, J., Morris, M., & Snowden, R. J. (2003). Forensic psychology: Violence viewed by psychopathic murderers. *Nature, 423,* 497.

Gray, P. (2005). *The ego and analysis of defense.* Northvale, NJ: Aronson.

Graziano, M. S., Taylor, C. S., & Moore, T. (2002). Complex movements evoked by microstimulation of precentral cortex. *Neuron, 34,* 841–851.

Gredebäck, G., Johnson, S., & von Hofsten, C. (2009). Eye tracking in infancy research. *Developmental Neuropsychology, 35,* 1–19.

Green, D. M., & Swets, J. A. (1966). *Signal detection theory and psychophysics.* New York: Wiley.

Green, M. F., & Horan, W. P. (2010). Social cognition in schizophrenia. *Current Directions in Psychological Science, 19*(4), 243–248. doi:10.1177/0963721410377600.

Green, R. A., Cross, A. J., & Goodwin, G. M. (1995). Review of the pharmacology and clinical pharmacology of 3,4-methylenedioxymethamphetamine (MDMA or "ecstacy"). *Psychopharmacology, 119,* 247–260.

Greenberg, J., Solomon, S., Pyszczynski, T., & Rosenblatt, A. (1992). Why do people need self-esteem? Converging evidence that self-esteem serves an anxiety-buffering function. *Journal of Personality and Social Psychology, 63,* 913–922.

Greenberg, J. R., & Mitchell, S. A. (1983). *Object relations in psychoanalytic theory.* Cambridge, MA: Harvard University Press.

Greenberg, J. R., & Mitchell, S. A. (2006). *Object relations in psychoanalytic theory.* Cambridge, MA: Harvard University Press.

Greenberg, R. P. (2010). Prescriptive authority in the face of research revelations. *American Psychologist, 65,* 136–137.

Greene, E. & Loftus, E. F. (1998). Psycholegal research on jury damage awards. *Current Directions in Psychological Science, 7,* 50–54.

Greenfield, P. M. (1994). Video games as cultural artifacts. *Journal of Applied Developmental Psychology, 15,* 3–12.

Greenfield, P. M., & Childs, C. P. (1991). Developmental continuity in biocultural context. In R. Cohen & A. W. Siegel (Eds.), *Context and development* (pp. 135–159). Hillsdale, NJ: Erlbaum.

Greenfield, P. M., Suzuki, L. K., & Rothstein-Fisch, C. (2006). Cultural pathways through human development. In W. Damon & R. M. Lerner (Series Eds.) & K. A. Renninger & I. E. Sigel (Vol. Eds.), *Handbook of child psychology: Vol. 4. Child psychology in practice* (6th ed.). New York: Wiley.

Greenwald, A. G. (2010). Under what conditions does intergroup contact improve intergroup harmony? In M. Gonzales, C. Tavris, & J. Aronson (Eds.) *The scientist and the humanist: A festschrift in honor of Elliot Aronson* (pp. 269–283). New York: Psychology Press.

Greenwald, A. G., & Banaji, M. R. (1995). Implicit social cognition: Attitudes, self-esteem, and stereotypes. *Psychological Review, 102,* 4–27.

Greenwald, A. G., Klinger, M. R., & Schuh, E. S. (1995). Activation by marginally perceptible ("subliminal") stimuli: Dissociation of unconscious from conscious cognition. *Experimental Psychology: General, 124*(1), 22–42.

Greer, A. E., & Buss, D. M. (1994). Tactics for promoting sexual encounters. *Journal of Sex Research, 31*(3), 185–201.

Gregory, S. W., & Webster, S. (1996). A nonverbal signal in voices of interview partners effectively predicts communication accommodation and social status perceptions. *Journal of Personality and Social Psychology, 70,* 1231–1240.

Greitemeyer, T. (2010). Exposure to music with prosocial lyrics reduces aggression: First evidence and test of the underlying mechanism. *Journal of Experimental Social Psychology,* doi:10.1016/j.jesp.2010.08.005.

Greitemeyer, T., & McLatchie, N. (2011). Denying humanness to others: A newly discovered mechanism by which violent video games increase aggressive behavior. *Psychological Science, 22*(5), 659–665. doi:10.1177/0956797611403320.

Greitemeyer, T., & Osswald, S. (2010). Effects of prosocial video games on prosocial behavior. *Journal of Personality and Social Psychology, 98,* 211–221.

Greitemeyer, T., Osswald, S., & Brauer, M. (2010). Playing prosocial video games increases empathy and decreases shadenfreude. *Emotion, 10*(6), 796–802. doi:10.1037/a0020194.

Greydanus, D. E., Hawver, E. K., Greydanus, M. M., & Merrick, J. (2013). Marijuana: Current concepts. *Frontiers in Public Health, 1,* 42, eCollection 2013.

Griesauer, I., Diao, W., Ronovsky, M., Elbau, I., Sartori, S., Singewald, N., & Pollak, D. D. (2014). Circadian abnormalities in a mouse model of high trait anxiety and depression. *Annals of Medicine,* Epub January 10, 2014.

Griesinger, C. B., Richards, C. D., & Ashmore, J. F. (2005). Fast vesicle replenishment allows indefatigable signalling at the first auditory synapse. *Nature, 435,* 212–215.

Griffeth, R. W., Hom, P. W., & Gaertner, S. (2000). A meta-analysis of antecedents and correlates of employee turnover: Update, moderator tests, and research implications for the next millennium. *Journal of Management, 26,* 463–488.

Griffin, B., & Wilson, I. G. (2012). Faking good: Self-enhancement in medical school applicants. *Medical Education, 46,* 485–490.

Griffin, D. W., & Harris, P. R. (2011). Calibrating the response to health warnings: Limiting both overreaction and underreaction with self-affirmation. *Psychological Science, 22,*(5), 572–578. doi:10.1177/0956797611405678.

Griffin, M. A., & Neal, A. (2000). Perceptions of safety at work: A framework for linking safety climate to safety performance, knowledge, and motivation. *Journal of Occupational Health Psychology, 5,* 347–358.

Griffin, P. W., Mroczek, D. K., & Spiro, A. (2006). Variability in affective change among aging men: Longitudinal findings from the VA Normative Aging Study. *Journal of Research in Personality, 40,* 942–965.

Grigorenko, E. L. (2002). In search of the genetic engram of personality. In D. Cervone & W. Mischel (Eds.), *Advances in personality science* (pp. 29–82). New York: The Guilford Press.

Grilo, C., Shiffman, S., & Wing, R. (1989). Relapse crises and coping among dieters. *Journal of Consulting And Clinical Psychology, 57*(4), 488–495.

Grimm, A., Hulse, L., Preiss, M., & Schmidt, S. (2014). Behavioural, emotional, and cognitive responses in European disasters: results of survivor interviews. *Disasters, 38*(1), 62–83.

Grinspoon, S., Thomas, E., Pitts, S., Gross, E., Mickley, D., Killer, K., et al. (2000). Prevalence and predictive factors for regional osteopenia in women with anorexia nervosa. *Annals of Internal Medicine, 133,* 790–794.

Griskevicius, V., Tybur, J. M., Gangestad, S. W., Perea, E. F., Shapiro, J. R., & Kenrick, D. T. (2009). Aggress to impress: Hostility as an evolved context-dependent strategy. *Journal of Personality and Social Psychology, 96,* 980–994.

Grob, C., & Dobkin de Rios, M. (1992). Adolescent drug use in cross-cultural perspective. *Journal of Drug Issues, 22*(1), 121–138.

Groh, A. M., Roisman, G. I., van IJzendoorn, M. H., Bakermans-Kranenburg, M. J., & Fearon, R. P. (2012). The significance of insecure and disorganized attachment for children's internalizing symptoms: A meta-analytic study. *Child Development, 83,* 591–610.

Gronlund, S. D., Wixted, J. T., & Mickes, L. (2014). Evaluating eyewitness identification procedures using receiver operating characteristic analysis. *Current Directions in Psychological Science, 23*(1), 3–10.

Groopman, J. (2000, January 24). Second opinion. *The New Yorker,* pp. 40–49.

Groopman, J., (2005, May 2). A model patient. *The New Yorker,* 48–54.

Groopman, J. (2007, January 29). What's the trouble? *The New Yorker*, 36–41.

Grosbras, M. H., Jansen, M., Leonard, G., McIntosh, A., et al. (2007). Neural mechanisms of resistance to peer influence in early adolescence. *Journal of Neuroscience, 27*, 8040–8045.

Gross, A. L., & Rebok, G. W. (2011). Memory training and strategy use in older adults: Results from the ACTIVE study. *Psychology and Aging, 26*, 503–517.

Gross, J. J. (2001). Emotion regulation in adulthood: Timing is everything. *Current Directions in Psychological Science, 10*, 214–219.

Grossman, L., & Walfish, S. (Eds.) (2014). *Translating psychological research into practice.* New York: Springer.

Grossmann, I., Na, J., Varnum, M. E. W., Park, D. C., et al. (2010). Reasoning about social conflicts improves into old age. *Proceedings of the National Academy of Sciences, 107*, 7246–7250.

Grossmann, K., Grossmann, K. E., Kindler, H., & Zimmermann, P. (2008). A wider view of attachment and exploration: The influence of mothers and fathers on the development of psychological security from infancy to young adulthood. In J. Cassidy & P. R. Shaver (Eds.), *Handbook of attachment: Theory, research, and clinical applications* (2nd ed., pp. 857–879). New York: Guilford Press.

Grosz, H. I., & Zimmerman, J. (1970). A second detailed case study of functional blindness: Further demonstration of the contribution of objective psychological data. *Behavior Therapy, 1*, 115–123.

Groth-Marnat, G. (1997). *Handbook of psychological assessment* (3rd ed.). New York: Wiley.

Grubb, P. L., Roberts, R. K., Swanson, N. G., Burnfield, J. L., & Childress, J. H. (2005). Organizational factors and psychological aggression: Results from a nationally representative sample of US companies. In V. Bowie, B. S. Fisher, & C. L. Cooper (Eds.), *Workplace violence: Issues, trends, strategies* (pp. 37–59). Portland, OR: Willan Publishing.

Gruber, J., Mauss, I. B., & Tamir, M. (2011). A dark side of happiness? How, when, and why happiness is not always good. *Perspectives On Psychological Science, 6*(3), 222–233.

Gruber, R., Laviolette, R., Deluca, P., Monson, E., et al. (2010). Short sleep duration is associated with poor performance on IQ measures in healthy school-age children. *Sleep Medicine, 11*, 289–294. Epub 2010 Feb 13.

Gruber, S. A., Silveri, M. M., & Yurgelun-Todd, D. A. (2007). Neuropsychological consequences of opiate use. *Neuropsychology Review, 17*, 299–315.

Grucza, R. A., Bucholz, K. K., Rice, J. P., & Beirut, L. J. (2008). Secular trends in the lifetime prevalence of alcohol dependence in the United States: A re-evaluation. *Alcoholism: Clinical and Experimental Research, 32*, 763–770.

Grusec, J. E., Davidov, M., & Lundell, L. (2002). Prosocial and helping behavior. In P. K. Smith & C. H. Hart (Eds.), *Blackwell handbook of childhood social development* (pp. 457–474). Malden, MA: Blackwell.

Grusec, J. E., & Goodnow, J. J. (1994). Impact of parental discipline methods on the child's internalization of values. *Developmental Psychology, 30*, 4–19.

Guadagno, R. E., Asher, T., Demaine, L. J., & Cialdini, R. B. (2001). When saying yes leads to saying no: Preference for consistency and the reverse foot-in-the-door effect. *Personality and Social Psychology Bulletin, 27*, 859–867.

Gueguen, N. (2008). The receptivity of women to courtship solicitation across the menstrual cycle: A field experiment. *Biological Psychology, 80*(3), 321–324.

Guéguen, N., & Lamy, L. (2011). The effect of the word "love" on compliance to a request for humanitarian aid: An evaluation in a field setting. *Social Influence, 6*(4), 249–258. doi: http://dx.doi.org/10.1080/15534510.2011.627771.

Guellaï, B., Coulon, M., & Streri, A. (2011). The role of motion and speech in face recognition at birth. *Visual Cognition, 19*, 1212–1233.

Guénolé, F., Louis, J., Creveuil, C., Baleyte, J. M., Montlahuc, C., Fourneret, P., & Revol, O. (2013). Behavioral profiles of clinically referred children with intellectual giftedness. *BioMed Research International*, Epub July 10, 2013.

Guilford, J. P. (1959). Traits of creativity. In H. H. Anderson (Ed.), *Creativity and its cultivation* (pp. 142–161). New York: Harper & Row.

Guilleminault, C., Kirisoglu, C., Bao, G., Arias, V., et al. (2005). Adult chronic sleepwalking and its treatment based on polysomnography. *Brain, 128*, 1062–1069.

Guilleminault, C., Palombini, L., Pelayo, R., & Chervin, R. D. (2003). Sleepwalking and sleep terrors in prepubertal children: What triggers them? *Pediatrics, 111*, 17–25.

Gulland, A. (2012). Number of people with dementia will reach 65.7 million by 2030, says report. *British Medical Journal, 344*, e2604.

Gump, B. B., Reihman, J., Stewart, P., Lonky, E., & Darvill, T. (2005). Terrorism and cardiovascular responses to acute stress in children. *Health Psychology, 24*, 594–600.

Gundersen, H., Specht, K., Gruner, R., Ersland, L., & Hugdahl, K. (2008). Separating the effects of alcohol and expectancy on brain activation during an fMRI working memory study. *Neuroimage, 42*, 1587–1596.

Gunderson, E. W., Kirkpatrick, M. G., Willing, L. M., Holstege, C. P. (2013). Substituted cathinone products: A new trend in "bath salts" and other designer stimulant drug use. *Journal of Addiction Medicine, 7*(3), 153–162.

Gunnoe, M. L., & Mariner, C. L. (1997). Toward a developmental-contextual model of the effects of parental spanking on children's aggressoin. *Archives of Pediatrics and Adolescent Medicine, 151*, 768–775.

Gupta, N., Ganster, D. C., & Kepes, S. (2013). Assessing the validity of sales self-efficacy: A cautionary tale. *Journal of Applied Psychology, 98*, 690–700.

Gupta, N., Jang, Y., Mednick, S. C., & Huber, D. E. (2012). The road not taken: Creative solutions require avoidance of high-frequency responses. *Psychological Science, 23*(3), 288–294. doi:10.1177/0956797611429710.

Gur, R. C., Skolnic, B. E., & Gur, R. E. (1994). Effects of emotional discrimination tasks on cerebral blood flow: Regional activation and its relation to performance. *Brain and Cognition, 25*(2), 271–286.

Gurman, A. S. (2011). Couple therapies. In S. B. Messer & A. S. Gurman (Eds.), *Essential psychotherapies: Theory and practice* (3rd ed.) (pp. 1–39). New York: Guilford.

Gurney, D. J., Pine, K. J., & Wiseman, R. (2013). The gestural misinformation effect: Skewing eyewitness testimony through gesture. *American Journal of Psychology, 126*(3), 301–314.

Gurven, M., von Rueden, C., Massenkoff, M., Kaplan, H., & Marino. L. V. (2013). How universal is the Big Five? Testing the five-factor model of personality variation among forager–farmers in the Bolivian Amazon. *Journal of Personality and Social Psychology, 104*, 354–370.

Gushue, G. V. (2004). Race, color-blind racial attitudes, and judgments about mental health: A shifting standards perspective. *Journal of Counseling Psychology, 51*, 398–407.

Gutiérrez-Fernández, M., Rodríguez-Frutos, B., Ramos-Cejudo, J., Otero-Ortega, L., Fuentes, B. & Díez-Tejedor, E. (2013). Stem cells for brain repair and recovery after stroke. *Expert Opinion on Biological Therapy*, 13(11), 1479–1483.

Guttmacher Institute. (2013). Facts on American teens' sexual and reproductive health. Retrieved from http://www.guttmacher.org/pubs/FB-ATSRH.html

Guyton, A. C. (1991). *Textbook of medical physiology* (8th ed.). Philadelphia: Saunders.

Haake, M., Müller, H.-H., Schade-Brittinger, C., Basler, H. D., Schäfer, H., Maier, C., Endres, H. G., Trampisch, H. J., & Molsberger, A. (2007). German acupuncture trials (GERAC) for chronic low back pain: Randomized, multicenter, blinded, parallel-group trial with 3 groups. *Archives of Internal Medicine, 167*, 1892–1898.

Haas, J. S., Zavala, B., & Landisman, C. E. (2011). Activity-dependent long-term depression of electrical synapses. *Science 334* (6054):389–393.

Haber, R. N. (1979). Twenty years of haunting eidetic imagery: Where's the ghost? *The Behavioral and Brain Sciences, 2*, 583–629.

Haber, S. N., & Knutson, B. (2010). The reward circuit: Linking primate anatomy and human imaging. *Neuropsychopharmacology, 35*, 4–26.

Haberlandt, K. (1999). *Human memory: Exploration and application*. Boston: Allyn & Bacon.

Haberstroh, J. (1995). *Ice cube sex: The truth about subliminal advertising*. South Bend, IN: Cross Cultural Publications/Crossroads.

Hacking, I. (1995). *Rewriting the soul: Multiple personality and the sciences of memory*. Princeton, NJ: Princeton University Press.

Hackman, J. R. (1998). Why don't teams work? In R. S. Tindale, J. Edwards, & E. J. Posavac (Eds.), *Applications of theory and research on groups to social issues*. New York: Plenum.

Hackman, J. R., & Oldham, G. R. (1980). *Work redesign*. Reading, MA: Addison-Wesley.

Hadjikhani, N., & de Gelder, B. (2003). Seeing fearful body expressions activates the fusiform cortex and amygdale. *Current Biology, 13*, 2201–2205.

Haegler, K., Zernecke, R., Kleemann, A. .M., Albrecht, J., Pollatos, O., Brückmann, H., and Wiesmann, M. (2010). No fear no risk! Human risk behavior is affected by chemosensory anxiety signals. *Neuropsychologia, 48*(13), 3901–3908.

Hagen, E. P. (1980). *Identification of the gifted*. New York: Teachers College Press.

Hagenaars, M. A., Brewin, C. R., van Minnen, A., Holmen, E. A., & Hoogduin, K. A. L. (2010). Intrusive images and intrusive thoughts as different phenomena: Two experimental studies. *Memory, 18* (1), 76–84. doi:10.1080/09658210903476522.

Hagger-Johnson, G., Mõttus, R., Craig, L. A., Starr, J. M., & Deary, I. J. (2012). Pathways from childhood intelligence and socio-economic status to late-life cardiovascular disease risk. *Health Psychology*, doi:10.1037/a0026775.

Hahn, C.-S., & DiPietro, J. A. (2001). In vitro fertilization and the family: Quality of parenting, family functioning, and child psychosocial adjustment. *Developmental Psychology, 37*, 37–48.

Hakuta, K., Bialystok, E., & Wiley, E. (2003). Critical evidence: A test of the critical-period hypothesis for second language acquisition. *Psychological Science, 14*, 31–38.

Halberstadt AL, & Geyer MA. (2011). Multiple receptors contribute to the behavioral effects of indoleamine hallucinogens. *Neuropharmacology, 61*(3), 364–381.

Halford, G. S., Baker, R., McCredden, J. E., & Bain, J. D. (2005). How many variables can humans process? *Psychological Science, 16*(1), 70–76.

Hall, C., Smith, K., & Chia, R. (2008). Cognitive and personality factors in relation to timely completion of a college degree. *College Student Journal, 42,* 1087–1098.

Hall, C. B., Lipton, R. B., Sliwinski, M., Katz, M. J., et al. (2009). Cognitive activities delay onset of memory decline in persons who develop dementia. *Neurology, 73,* 356–361.

Hall, C. S., Lindzey, G., & Campbell, J. P. (1998). *Theories of personality* (4th ed.). New York: Wiley.

Hall, W., & Degenhardt, L. (2003). Medical marijuana initiatives: Are they justified? How successful are they likely to be? *CNS Drugs, 17,* 689–697.

Hall, W., & Degenhardt, L. (2009). Adverse health effects of non-medical cannabis use. *Lancet, 374,* 1383–1391.

Hall, W.G. Moore Arnold, H., & Myers, K. P. (2000). The acquisition of an appetite. *Psychological Science, 11,* 101–105.

Hallett, C., Lambert, A., & Regan, M. A. (2012). Text messaging amongst New Zealand drivers: Prevalence and risk perception. *Transportation Research: Part F, 15*(3), 261–271. doi:10.1016/j.trf.2011.12.002.

Hallmayer, J., Cleveland, S., Torres, A., Phillips, J., Cohen, B., Torigoe, T., & Risch, N. (2011). Genetic heritability and shared environmental factors among twin pairs with autism. *Archives Of General Psychiatry, 68*(11), 1095–1102. doi:10.1001/archgenpsychiatry.2011.76.

Halperin, J. M., & Schulz, K. P. (2006). Revisiting the role of the prefrontal cortex in the pathophysiology of attention-deficit/hyperactivity disorder. *Psychological Bulletin, 132,* 560–581.

Halpern, D. F. (2005). Psychologyret at the intersection of work and family: Recommendations for employers, working families, and policymakers. *American Psychologist, 60,* 397–409.

Halpern, D. F. (2012). *Sex differences in cognitive abilities* (4th ed.). New York: Psychology Press.

Halpern, D. F., & Hakel, M. D. (2003). *Applying the science of learning to university teaching and beyond: New directions for teaching and learning.* San Francisco: Jossey-Bass.

Hamad, G. G. (2004). The state of the art in bariatric surgery for weight loss in the morbidly obese patient. *Clinics in Plastic Surgery, 31,* 591–600.

Hamann, S., Herman, R. A., Nolan, C. L., & Wallen, K. (2004). Men and women differ in amygdala response to sexual stimuli. *Nature Neuroscience, 7,* 411–416.

Hamilton, A. F. de C. (2013). Reflecting on the mirror neuron system in autism: A systematic review of current theories. *Developmental Cognitive Neuroscience, 3,* 91–105.

Hamilton, N. A., Gallagher, M. W., Preacher, K. J., Stevens, N., Nelson, C. A., Karlson, C., & McCurdy, D. (2007). Insomnia and well-being. *Journal of Consulting and Clinical Psychology, 75,* 939–946.

Hamilton, W. D. (1964). The evolution of social behavior: Parts I and II. *Journal of Theoretical Biology 7,* 1–52.

Hamm, A. O., Vaitl, D., & Lang, P. J. (1989). Fear conditioning, meaning, and belongingness: A selective association analysis. *Journal of Abnormal Psychology, 98,* 395–406.

Hammack, S. E., Cooper, M. A., & Lezak, K. R. (2012). Overlapping neurobiology of learned helplessness and conditioned defeat: implications for PTSD and mood disorders. *Neuropharmacology, 62*(2), 565–575.

Hammad, T. A., Laughren, T., & Racoosin, J. (2006). Suicidality in pediatric patients treated with antidepressant drugs. *Archives of General Psychiatry, 63,* 332–339.

Hammen, C. (2005). Stress and depression. *Annual Review of Clinical Psychology, 1,* 293–319.

Hammerness, P., Basch, E., & Ulbricht, C. (2003). St. John's wort: A systematic review of adverse effects and drug interactions for the consultation psychiatrist. *Journal of Consultation Liaison Psychiatry, 44*(4), 271–282.

Hammond, D. C. (2008). Hypnosis as sole anesthesia for major surgeries: Historical & contemporary perspectives. *American Journal of Clinical Hypnosis, 51*(2), 101–121.

Hampshire, A., Highfield, R. R., Parkin, B. L., & Owen, A. M. (2012). Fractioning human intelligence. *Neuron, 76*(6), 1225–1237.

Hampson, S. E. (2008). Mechanisms by which childhood personality traits influence adult well-being. *Current Directions in Psychological Science, 17,* 264–268.

Hampson, S. E., Goldberg, L. R., Vogt, T. M., & Dubanoski, J. P. (2006). Forty years on: Teachers' assessments of children's personality traits predict self-reported health behaviors and outcomes at midlife. *Health Psychology, 25,* 57–64.

Hampton, T. (2008). Researchers seek ways to stem STDs. *Journal of the American Medical Association, 299*(16), 1888–1889.

Hamrick, N., Cohen, S., & Rodriguez, M. S. (2002). Being popular can be healthy or unhealthy: Stress, social network diversity, and incidence of upper respiratory infection. *Health Psychology, 21,* 294–298.

Han, S., Northoff, G., Vogeley, K., Wexler, B. E., Kitayama, S., & Varnum, M. E. W. (2013). A cultural neuroscience approach to the biosocial nature of the human brain. *Annual Review of Psychology, 64,* 335–359.

Han, S., & Shavitt, S. (1994). Persuasion and culture: Advertising appeals in individualist and collectivist societies. *Journal of Experimental Social Psychology, 30,* 326–350.

Handgraaf, M. J. J., & van Raaij, W. F. (2005). Fear and loathing no more: The emergence of collaboration between economists and psychologists. *Journal of Economic Psychology, 28,* 387–391.

Hane, A. A., Cheah, C., Rubin, K. H., & Fox, N. A. (2008). The role of maternal behavior in the relation between shyness and social reticence in early childhood and social withdrawal in middle childhood. *Social Development, 17,* 795–811.

Hankin, B. L., & Abramson, L. Y. (2001). Development of gender differences in depression: An elaborated cognitive vulnerability-transactional stress theory. *Psychological Bulletin, 127,* 773–796.

Hanley, G. P., Piazza, C. C., Fisher, W. W., & Maglieri, K. A. (2005). On the effectiveness of and preference for punishment and extinction components of function-based interventions. *Journal of Applied Behavior Analysis, 38,* 51–65.

Hansen, K., Höfling, V., Kröner-Borowik, T., Stangier, U., & Steil, R. (2013). Efficacy of psychological interventions aiming to reduce chronic nightmares: A meta-analysis. *Clinical Psychology Review, 33*(1), 146–155.

Hanson, G., & Venturelli, P. J. (1995). *Drugs and society* (4th ed.). Boston: Jones & Bartlett.

Haque, O., & Waytz, A. (2012). Dehumanization in medicine: Causes, solutions, and functions. *Perspectives on Psychological Science, 7*(2), 176–186. doi:10.1177/1745691611429706.

Harackiewicz, J. M., & Elliot, A. J. (1993). Achievement goals and intrinsic motivation. *Journal of Personality and Social Psychology, 65,* 904–915.

Harber, K. D., Gorman, J. L., Gengaro, F. P., Butisingh, S., Tsang, W., & Ouellette, R. (2012). Students' race and teachers' social support affect the positive feedback bias in public schools. *Journal Of Educational Psychology,* doi:10.1037/a0028110.

Hardeland, R. (2013). Chronobiology of melatonin beyond the feedback to the suprachiasmatic nucleus-consequences to melatonin dysfunction. *International Journal of Molecular Sciences, 14*(3), 5817–5841.

Harden, K., Quinn, P. D., & Tucker-Drob, E. M. (2012). Genetically influenced change in sensation seeking drives the rise of delinquent behavior during adolescence. *Developmental Science, 15*(1), 150–163. doi:10.1111/j.1467-7687. 2011.01115.x.

Hardwick, R. M., Rottschy, C., Miall, R. C., & Eickhoff, S. B. (2012). A quantitative meta-analysis and review of motor learning in the human brain. *Neuroimage, 67,* 283–97.

Hare, R. D., & Newmann, C. S. (2009). Psychopathy: Assessment and forensic implications. *Canadian Journal of Psychiatry, 54,* 791–802.

Hare, R. D., Neumann, C. S., & Widiger, T. A. (2012). Psychopathy. In T. A. Widiger (Ed.), *The Oxford handbook of personality disorders* (pp. 478–504). New York: Oxford University Press.

Hariri, A. R., Drabant, E. M., Munoz, K. E., Kolachana, B. S., Mattay, V. S., Egan, M. F., et al. (2005). A susceptibility gene for affective disorders and the response of the human amygdala. *Archives of General Psychiatry, 62,* 146–152.

Harlow, H. F. (1959, June). Love in infant monkeys. *Scientific American,* pp. 68–74.

Harman, W. S., Lee, T. W., Mitchell, T. R., Felps, W., & Ownes, B. P. (2007). The psychology of voluntary turnover. *Current Directions in Psychological Science, 16,* 51–54.

Harmon-Jones, E. (2004). On the relationship of frontal brain activity and anger: Examining the role of attitude toward anger. *Cognition and Emotion, 18,* 337–361.

Harmon-Jones, E., Amodio, D. M., & Harmon-Jones, C. (2009). Action-based model of dissonance: A review, integration, and expansion of conceptions of cognitive confl ict. In M. Zanna (Ed.), *Advances in experimental social psychology* (Vol. 41, pp. 119–166). San Diego: Academic Press.

Harmon-Jones, E. (2010). Decisions, action, and neuroscience: A contemporary perspective on cognitive dissonance. In M. Gonzales, C. Tavris, & J. Aronson (Eds.) *The scientist and the humanist: A festschrift in honor of Elliot Aronson* (pp. 109–131). New York: Psychology Press.

Harré, M. S., Bossomaier, T. T., Gillett, A. A., & Snyder, A. A. (2011). The aggregate complexity of decisions in the game of Go. *European Physical Journal B—Condensed Matter, 80*(4), 555–563. doi:10.1140/epjb/e2011-10905-8.

Harré, N., Brandt, T., & Houkamau, C. (2004). An examination of the actor-observer effect in young drivers' attributions for their own and their friends' risky driving. *Journal of Applied Social Psychology, 34,* 806–824.

Harris, J. C., & Carter, C. S. (2013). Therapeutic interventions with oxytocin: Current status and concerns. *Journal of the American Academy of Child and Adolescent Psychiatry, 52,* 998–1000.

Harris Interactive. (2007). Handwashing survey fact sheet. Retrieved January 22, 2009, from http://www.asm.org/ASM.

Harrison, D. A., Newman, D. A., & Roth, P. L. (2006). How important are job attitudes? Meta-analytic comparisons of integrative behavioral outcomes and time sequences. *Academy of Management Journal, 49*, 305–325.

Harrison, K. (2003). Fitness and excitation. In J. Bryant, & D. Roskos-Ewoldsen (Eds.), *Communication and emotion: Essays in honor of Dolf Zillmann* (pp. 473–489). Mahwah, NJ: Erlbaum.

Harrison, N., Gray, M., Gianaros, P., & Critchley, H. (2010). The embodiment of emotional feelings in the brain. *The Journal Of Neuroscience: The Official Journal Of The Society For Neuroscience, 30*(38), 12878–12884.

Harrow, M., & Jobe, T. H. (2005). Longitudinal studies of outcome and recovery in schizophrenia and early interventions: Can they make a difference? *Canadian Journal of Psychiatry, 50*, 879–880.

Hart, J., & Björgvinsson, T. (2010). Health anxiety and hypochondriasis: Description and treatment issues highlighted through a case illustration. *Bulletin of The Menninger Clinic, 74*(2), 122–140.

Harter, J. K., Schmidt, F. L., Asplund, J. W., Killham, E. A., & Agrawal, S. (2010). Causal impact of employee work perceptions on the bottom line of organizations. *Perspectives On Psychological Science, 5*(4), 378–389. doi:10.1177/1745691610374589.

Harter, S. (2012). *The construction of the self* (2nd ed.). New York: Guilford Press.

Hartmann, A. S., Blashill, A. J., Greenberg, J. L., & Wilhelm, S. (2014). Body dysmorphic disorder. In E. A. Storch & D. McKay (Eds.), *Obsessive-compulsive disorder and its spectrum: A life-span approach* (pp. 141–162). Washington, DC: American Psychological Association.

Hartmann, M. J. (2009). Active touch, exploratory movements, and sensory prediction. *Integrative and Comparative Biology, 49*(6), 681–690.

Hartup, W. W., & Stevens, N. (1997). Friendships and adaptation in the life course. *Psychological Bulletin, 121,* 355–370.

Hartwig, M. K., & Dunlosky, J. (2012). Study strategies of college students: Are self-testing and scheduling related to achievement? *Psychonomic Bulletin & Review, 19*(1), 126–134. doi:10.3758/s13423–011–0181–y.

Harvey, P. A., Lee, D. H. S., Qian, F., Weinreb, P. H., & Frank, E. (2009). Blockade of Nogo receptor ligands promotes functional regeneration of sensory axons after dorsal root crush. *Journal of Neuroscience, 29*, 6285–6295.

Harwood, T. M., & L'Abate, L. (2010). *Self-help in mental health: A critical review.* New York: Springer.

Hase, M., Schallmayer, S., & Sack, M. (2008). EMDR reprocessing of the addiction memory: Pretreatment, posttreatment, and 1-month follow-up. *Journal of EMDR Practice and Research, 2*(3), 170–179.

Haselton, M. G., & Gildersleeve, K. (2011). Can men detect ovulation? *Current Directions in Psychological Science, 20*(2), 87–92. doi:10.1177/0963721411402668.

Haslam, D. W., & James, W. P. T. (2005). Obesity. *Lancet, 366*(9492), 1197–1209.

Hassin, R. R. (2013). Yes it can: On the functional abilities of the human unconscious. *Perspectives on Psychological Science, 8,* 195–207.

Hassabis, D., Kumaran, D., Vann, S. D., & Maguire, E. A. (2007). Patients with hippocampal amnesia cannot imagine new experiences. *Proceedings of the National Academy of Sciences of The United States of America, 104*(5), 1726–1731. doi:10.1073/pnas.0610561104.

Hatfield, D., McCullough, L., Frantz, S. B., & Krieger, K. (2010). Do we know when our clients get worse? an investigation of therapists' ability to detect negative client change. *Clinical Psychology & Psychotherapy, 17*(1), 25–32.

Hatfield, E., & Rapson, R. L. (2006). Passionate love, sexual desire, and mate selection: Cross-cultural and historical perspectives. In P. Noller & J. Feeney (Eds.), *Close relationships: Functions, forms and processes* (pp. 227–243). Hove, England: Psychology Press/Taylor & Francis.

Hatfield, J., Job, R. F. S., Hede, A. J., Carter, N. L., Peploe, P., Taylor, R., & Morrell, S. (2002). Human response to environmental noise: The role of perceived control. *International Journal of Behavioral Medicine, 9,* 341–359.

Hathaway, W. (2002, December 22). Henry M: The day one man's memory died. *Hartford Courant.*

Hatton, H., Conger, R. D., Larsen-Rife, D., & Ontai, L. (2009). An integrative and developmental perspective for understanding romantic relationship quality during the transition to parenthood. In M. S. Schulz, M. K. Pruett, P. K. Kerig, & R. D. Parke (Eds.), *Strengthening couple relationships for optimal child development: Lessons from research and intervention.* Washington, DC: American Psychological Association Press.

Hauner, K., Mineka, S., Voss, J., & Paller, K. (2012). Exposure therapy triggers lasting reorganization of neural fear processing. *Proceedings of the National Academy of Sciences of the United States of America, 109,* 9203–9208.

Hauri, D.D., Spycher, B., Huss, A., Zimmermann, F., Grotzer, M., von der Weid, N., Spoerri, A., Kuehni, C.E., & Röösli, L., for the Swiss National Cohort and the Swiss Paediatric Oncology Group. (2014). Exposure to Radio-Frequency Electromagnetic Fields From Broadcast Transmitters and Risk of Childhood Cancer: A Census-based Cohort Study. *American Journal of Epidemiology, doi: 10.1093/aje/kwt442.*

Hauser, R., Wiergowski, M., Kaliszan, M., Gos, T., Kernbach-Wighton, G., Studniarek, M., Jankowski, Z., and Namieśnik, J. (2011). Olfactory and tissue markers of fear in mammals including humans. *Medical Hypotheses, 77*(6), 1062–1067.

Havas, D. A., Glenberg, A. M., Gutowski, K. A., Lucarelli, M. J., & Davidson, R. J. (2010). Cosmetic use of botulinum toxin-A affects processing of emotional language. *Psychological Science, 21*(7), 895–900. doi:10.1177/0956797610374742.

Hawk, B. N., & McCall, R. B. (2011). Specific extreme behaviors of postinstitutionalized Russian adoptees. *Developmental Psychology, 47*, 732–738.

Hawkins, H. L., Kramer, A. R., & Capaldi, D. (1993). Aging, exercise, and attention. *Psychology and Aging, 7,* 643–653.

Haxby, J. V., Gobbini, M. I., Furey, M. L., Ishai, A., et al. (2001). Distributed and overlapping representations of faces and objects in ventral temporal cortex. *Science, 293,* 2425–2430.

Haxel, B. R., Bertz-Duffy, S., Faldum, A., Trellakis, S., Stein, B., Renner, B., Kobal, G., Letzel, S., Mann, W. J., and Muttray, A. (2011). The Candy Smell Test in clinical routine. *American Journal of Rhinology and Allergy, 25*(4), e145–e148.

Hay, D. F., Pawlby, S., Waters, C. S., Perra, O., & Sharp, D. (2010). Mothers' antenatal depression and their children's antisocial outcomes. *Child Development, 81,* 149–165.

Hay, D. H., Caplan, M., & Nash, A. (2011). The beginnings of peer relations. In K. H. Rubin, W. M. Bukowski, & B. Laursen (Eds.), *Handbook of peer interactions, relationships, and groups* (pp. 121–142). New York: Guilford Press.

Haydon, H. (2013). A woman whose world has literally been turned upside down has baffled scientists studying her rare condition. *The Sun.* March 14, 2013.

Hayes, J., Chakraborty, A. T., McManus, S., Bebbington, P., Brugha, T., Nicholson, S., & King, M. (2012). Prevalence of same-sex behavior and orientation in England: Results from a national survey. *Archives of Sexual Behavior, 41*(3), 631–639. doi:10.1007/s10508–011–9856–8

Hayes, J. E. & Keast, R. S. (2011). Two decades of supertasting: Where do we stand? *Physiology & Behavior, 104*(5), 1072–1074.

Hayes, S. C., & Lillis, J. (2014). Acceptance and commitment therapy. In G. R. VandenBos, E. Meidenbauer, & J. Frank-McNeil (Eds.), *Psychotherapy theories and techniques* (pp. 3–8). Washington, DC: American Psychological Association.

Haynes, S. R., Cohen, M. A., & Ritter, F. E. (2009). Designs for explaining intelligent agents. *International Journal of Human-Computer Studies, 67*(1), 90–110.

Hays, K. F. (2006). Being fit: The ethics of practice diversification in performance psychology. *Professional Psychology: Research and Practice, 37,* 223–232.

Hayslip, B., King, J. K., & Jooste, J. L. (2008). Grandchildren's difficulties and strengths impact the mental health of their grandparents. In B. Hayslip & P. Kaminski (Eds.), *Parenting the custodial grandchild: Implications for clinical practice* (pp. 53–74). New York: Springer.

Hazell, A. S., Wang, D., Oanea, R., Sun, S., Aghourian, M., & Yong, J. J. (2013). Pyrithiamine-induced thiamine deficiency alters proliferation and neurogenesis in both neurogenic and vulnerable areas of the rat brain. *Metabolic Brain Disease,* epub October 1, 2013.

Healy, M., Campbell, K. L., Hasher, L., & Ossher, L. (2010). Direct evidence for the role of inhibition in resolving interference in memory. *Psychological Science, 21*(10), 1464–1470. doi:10.1177/0956797610382120.

Heatherton, T. F. & Wheatley, T. (2010). Social neuroscience.). In R. Baumiester & E. Finkel (Eds.) *Advanced social psychology: The state of the science* (pp. 575–612). New York, NY: Oxford.

Hebb, D. O. (1955). Drives and the C. N. S. (conceptual nervous system). *Psychological Review, 62,* 243–254.

Hedden, T., Ketay, S., Aron, A., Markus, H. R., & Gabrieli, J. D. E. (2008). Cultural influences on neural substrates of attentional control. *Psychological Science 19,* 12–17.

Hedge, J. W., Borman, W. C., & Lammlein, S. E. (2006). *The aging workforce: Realities, myths, and implications for organizations.* Washington, DC: American Psychological Association.

Heegaard, W. (2007). Traumatic brain injury. *Emergency Medicine Clinics of North America, 25*(3), 655–678.

Hegerl, U., Plattner, A., & Moller, H. J. (2004). Should combined pharmaco- and psychotherapy be offered to depressed patients? A qualitative review of randomized clinical trials from the 1990s. *European Archives of Psychiatry and Clinical Neuroscience, 254,* 99–107.

Hehman, E., Gaertner, S. L., Dovidio, J. F., Mania, E. W., Guerra, R., Wilson, D. C., & Friel, B. M. (2012). Group status drives majority and minority integration preferences. *Psychological Science, 23,* 46–52. doi:10.1177/0956797611423547.

Heiby, E. M., DeLeon, P. H., & Anderson, T. (2008). A debate on prescription privileges for psychologists. In D. N. Bersoff (Ed.), *Ethical conflicts in psychology* (4th ed., pp. 370–375). Washington, DC: American Psychological Association.

Heilman, K. M., Barrett, A. M., & Adair, J. C. (1998). Possible mechanisms of anosognosia: A defect in self-awareness. *Philosophical Transactions of the Royal Society of London: Series B. Biological Sciences, 353*(1377), 1903–1909.

Heilman, K. M., & Gonzalez-Rothi, L. (2003). Apraxia. In K. M. Heilman & E. Valenstein (Eds.), *Clinical neuropsychology* (4th ed.). New York: Oxford University Press.

Heilman, K. M., & Valenstein, E. (2011). *Clinical neuropsychology,* 5th ed. Oxford University Press.

Heilman, K. M., Watson, R. T., & Valenstein, E. (2003). Neglect and related disorders. In K. M. Heilman & E. Valenstein (Eds.), *Clinical neuropsychology* (4th ed.). New York: Oxford University Press.

Heilman, M. E., & Haynes, M. C. (2008). Subjectivity in the appraisal process: A facilitator of gender bias in work settings. In E. Borgida & S. T. Fiske (Eds.), *Beyond common sense: Psychological science in the courtroom* (pp. 127–155). Malden: Blackwell Publishing.

Heine, S. J. (2010) Cultural psychology In R. Baumeister & E. Finkel (Eds.) *Advanced social psychology: The state of the science* (pp. 665–696). New York, NY: Oxford.

Heine, S. J., & Buchtel, E. A. (2009). Personality: The universal and the culturally specific. *Annual Review of Psychology, 60,* 369–394.

Heine, S. J., & Ruby, M. B. (2010). Cultural psychology. *Wiley Interdisciplinary Reviews: Cognitive Science, 1,* 254–266.

Heinrichs, R. W. (2005). The primacy of cognition in schizophrenia. *American Psychologist, 60,* 229–242.

Heinrichs, W. L., Youngblood, P., Harter, P. M., & Dev, P. (2008). Simulation for team training and assessment: Case studies of online training with virtual worlds. *World Journal of Surgery, 32*(2), 161–170.

Heiss, W. D. (2012a). The ischemic penumbra: How does tissue injury evolve? *Annals of the New York Academy of Sciences, 1268,* 26–34.

Heiss, W. D. (2012b). PET in coma and in vegetative state. *European Journal of Neurology, 19*(2), 207–211.

Hejmadi, A., Davidson, R. J., & Rozin, P. (2000). Exploring Hindu Indian emotion expressions: Evidence for accurate recognition by Americans and Indians. *Psychological Science, 11,* 183–187.

Hektner, J. M., Schmidt, J. A., & Csikszentmihalyi, M. (2007). *Experience sampling method: Measuring the quality of everyday life.* Thousand Oaks, CA: Sage Publications, Inc.

Heldt, E., Manfro, G. G., Kipper, L., Blaya, C., Isolan, L., & Otto, M. W. (2006). One-year follow-up of pharmacotherapy-resistant patients with panic disorder treated with cognitive-behavior therapy: Outcome and predictors of remission. *Behaviour Research and Therapy, 44,* 657–665.

Heller, M. (2011, March 12). Parents make history with $1M false memory award. Retrieved from http://www.onpointnews.com/NEWS/Parents-Make-History -With-$1M-False-Memory-Award.html.

Heller, W., Nitschke, J. B., & Miller, G. A. (1998). Lateralization in emotion and emotional disorders. *Current Directions in Psychological Science, 7,* 26–32.

Hellmuth, J. C., & McNulty, J. K. (2008). Neuroticism, marital violence, and the moderating role of stress and behavioral skills. *Journal of Personality and Social Psychology, 95,* 166–180.

Helmes, E., & Velamoor, V. R. (2009). Long-term outcome of leucotomy on behaviour of people with schizophrenia. *International Journal of Social Psychiatry, 55,* 64–70.

Helms, J. E. (1997). The triple quandary of race, culture, and social class in standardized cognitive ability testing. In D. P. Flanagan, J. L. Genshaft, & P. L. Harrison (Eds.), *Contemporary intellectual assessment: Theories, tests, and issues* (pp. 517–532). New York: Guilford Press.

Helson, R., & Moane, G. (1987). Personality change in women from college to midlife. *Journal of Personality and Social Psychology, 53,* 176–186.

Helwig, C. C., To, S., Wang, Q., Liu, C., & Yang, S. (2013). Judgments and reasoning about parental discipline involving induction and psychological control in China and Canada. *Child Development.* Epub November 6, 2013.

Henckens, M. J. A. G., Hermans, E. J., Pu, Z., Joels, M., & Fernandez, G. (2009). Stressed memories: How acute stress affects memory formation in humans. *Journal of Neuroscience, 29,* 10111–10119.

Henderson, J. M. (2008). Peripheral nerve stimulation for chronic pain. *Current Pain and Headache Reports, 12*(1), 28–31.

Hendrick, B. (2003, May 8). Exam day rituals help students feel lucky. *Naples Daily News.*

Hendricks, P. S., & Thompson, J. K. (2005). An integration of cognitive-behavioral therapy and interpersonal psychotherapy for bulimia nervosa: A case study using the case formulation method. *International Journal of Eating Disorders, 37,* 171–174.

Henig, R. (2004, April 4). The quest to forget. *New York Times,* p. 32.

Henkel, L. A., Franklin, N., & Johnson, M. K. (2000). Cross-modal source monitoring, confusion between perceived and imagined events. *Journal of Experimental Psychology: Learning, Memory and Cognition, 26,* 321–335.

Hennig, J., Reuter, M., Netter, P., Burk, C., & Landt, O. (2005). Two types of aggression are differentially related to serotonergic activity and the A779C TPH polymorphism. *Behavioral Neuroscience, 119,* 16–25.

Henry, J. D., von Hippel, C., & Shapiro, L. (2010). Stereotype threat contributes to social difficulties in people with schizophrenia. *British Journal Of Clinical Psychology, 49*(1), 31–41.

Hepach, R., Vaish, A., & Tomasello, M. (2012). Young children are intrinsically motivated to see others helped. *Psychological Science.* Published online before print July 31, 2012, doi:10.1177/0956797612440571.

Hergenhahn, B. R., & Olson, M. (2007). *Introduction to theories of personality* (7th ed.). Upper Saddle River, NJ: Prentice Hall.

Herman, A. I., Devito, E. E., Jensen, K. P., & Sofuoglu, M. (2014). Pharmacogenetics of nicotine addiction: Role of dopamine. *Pharmacogenomics, 15*(2), 221–234.

Heron, M. P. (2007). Deaths: Leading causes for 2004. *National Vital Statistics Reports, 56*(5), 1–96.

Herrenkohl, T., Hill, K., Chung, I.-J., Guo, J., et al. (2004). Protective factors against serious violent behavior in adolescence: A prospective study of violent children. *Social Work Research, 27,* 179–191.

Herring, W. J., Snyder, E., Budd, K., Hutzelmann, J., Snavely, D., Liu, K., Lines, C., Roth, T., & Michelson, D. (2012). Orexin receptor antagonism for treatment of insomnia: A randomized clinical trial of suvorexant. *Neurology, 79*(23), 2265–2274.

Herrington, J. D., Heller, W., Mohanty, A., Engels, A. S., et al. (2010). Localization of asymmetric brain function in emotion and depression. *Psychophysiology, 11,* 11.

Herman, C. P., Roth, D. A., & Polivy, J. (2003). Effects of the presence of others on food intake: A normative interpretation. *Psychological Bulletin, 129,* 873–886.

Herman, L. M., Richards, D. G., & Wolz, J. P. (1984). Comprehension of sentences by bottlenosed dolphins. *Cognition, 16,* 129–219.

Herpertz, S., Hagenah, U., Vocks, S., von Wietersheim, J., Cuntz, U., Zeeck, A., & Wagstaff, K. (2011). The diagnosis and treatment of eating disorders. *Deutsches Ärzteblatt International, 108*(40), 678–685.

Herrmann, D. J., & Searleman, A. (1992). Memory improvement and memory theory in historical perspective. In D. Herrmann, H. Weingartner, A. Searlman, & C. McEvoy (Eds.), *Memory improvement: Implications for memory theory.* New York: Springer-Verlag.

Herrnstein, R. J., & Murray, C. (1994). *The bell curve: Intelligence and class structure in American life.* New York: Free Press.

Hershcovis, M. S., Turner, N., Barling, H., Arnold, K. A., Dupré, K. E., Innes, M., LeBlanc, M. M., & Sivanathan, N. (2007). Predicting workplace aggression: A meta-analysis. *Journal of Applied Psychology, 92,* 228–238.

Hertenstein, M. J., & Campos, J. J. (2004). The retention effects of an adult's emotional displays on infant behavior. *Child Development, 75,* 585–613.

Hertlein, K., & Ricci, R. J. (2004). A systematic research synthesis of EMDR studies: Implementation of the platinum standard. *Trauma, Violence, and Abuse, 5,* 285–300.

Hertzog, C., Kramer, A. F., Wilson, R. S., & Lindenberger, U. (2009). Enrichment eff ects on adult cognitive development: Can the functional capacity of older adults be preserved and enhanced? *Psychological Science in the Public Interest, 9,* 1–65.

Hervet, G., Guérard, K., Tremblay, S., Chtourou, M. S. (2011). Is banner blindness genuine? Eye tracking internet text advertising. *Applied Cognitive Psychology, 25*(5), 708–716. doi:10.1002/acp.1742.

Herzog, T. A., & Blagg, C. O. (2007). Are most precontemplators contemplating smoking cessation? Assessing the validity of the stages of change. *Health Psychology, 26,* 222–231.

Hesselink, J. M., & Kopsky, D. J. (2011). Enhancing acupuncture by low dose naltrexone. *Acupuncture Medicine, 29*(2), 127–130.

Hewlin, J., & Faison, P. (2009). Wearing the cloak: Antecedents and consequences of creating facades of conformity. *Journal of Applied Psychology, 94,* 727–741.

Heymsfield, S. B., Greenberg, A. S., Fujioa, K., Dixon, R. M., Kushner, R., Hunt, T., et al. (1999). Recombinant leptin for weight loss in obese and lean adults. *Journal of the American Medical Association, 282,* 1568–1575.

Heywood, C. A., & Kentridge, R. W. (2003). Achromatopsia, color vision, and cortex. *Neurology Clinics, 21,* 483–500.

Higley, A. E., Kiefer, S. W., Li, X., Gaál, J., Xi, Z. X., & Gardner, E. L. (2011). Dopamine D(3) receptor antagonist SB-277011A inhibits methamphetamine self-administration and methamphetamine-induced reinstatement of drug-seeking in rats. *European Journal of Pharmacology, 659*(2–3), 187–192.

Hilbert, A., Braehler, E., Haeuser, W., & Zenger, M. (2014). Weight bias internalization, core self-evaluation, and health in overweight and obese persons. *Obesity, 22*(1), 79–85.

Hilbert, M. (2012). Toward a synthesis of cognitive biases: How noisy information processing can bias human decision making. *Psychological Bulletin, 138*(2), 211–237. doi:10.1037/a0025940.

Hildebrandt, M. G., Steyerberg, E. W., Stage, K. B., Passchier, J., Kragh-Soerensen, P., and the Danish University Antidepressant Group. (2003). Are gender differences important for the clinical effects of antidepressants? *American Journal of Psychiatry, 160,* 1643–1650.

Hildreth, E. C., & Royden, C. S. (2011). Integrating multiple cues to depth order at object boundaries. *Attention, Perception, and Psychophysics, 73*(7), 2218–2235.

Hilgard, E. R. (1965). *Hypnotic susceptibility.* New York: Harcourt, Brace & World.

Hilgard, E. R. (1977). *Divided consciousness: Multiple controls in human thought and action.* New York: Wiley.

Hilgard, E. R. (1979). *Personality and hypnosis: A study of imaginative involvement.* Chicago: University of Chicago Press.

Hilgard, E. R. (1982). Hypnotic susceptibility and implications for measurement. International *Journal of Clinical and Experimental Hypnosis, 30,* 394–403.

Hilgard, E. R. (1992). Divided consciousness and dissociation. *Consciousness and Cognition, 1,* 16–31.

Hilgard, E. R., Morgan, A. H., & MacDonald, H. (1975). Pain and dissociation in the cold pressor test: A study of "hidden reports" through automatic key-pressing and automatic talking. *Journal of Abnormal Psychology, 84,* 280–289.

Hill, C. (2005). Therapist techniques, client involvement, and the therapeutic relationship: Inextricably intertwined in the therapy process. *Psychotherapy: Theory, Research, Practice, Training, 42,* 431–442.

Hill, C. E., & Lent, R. W. (2006). A narrative and meta-analytic review of helping skills training: Time to revive a dormant area of inquiry. *Psychotherapy: Theory, Research, Practice, Training, 43,* 154–172.

Hill, P. L., & Turiano, N. A. (2014). Purpose in life as a predictor of mortality across adulthood. *Psychological Science,* Epub May 8, 2014.

Hinduja, S., & Patchin, J. W. (2013). A brief review of state cyberbullying laws and policies.http://www.cyberbullying.us/Bullying_and_Cyberbullying_Laws.pdf

Hines, A. R., & Paulson, S. E. (2007). Parents' and teachers' perceptions of adolescent storm and stress: Relations with parenting and teaching styles. *Family Therapy, 34*(2), 63–80.

Hinshaw, S. P., Zupan, B. A., Simmel, C., Nigg, J. T., & Melnick, S. (1997). Peer status in boys with and without attention-deficit hyperactivity disorder: Predictions from overt and covert antisocial behavior, social isolation, and authoritative parenting beliefs. *Child Development, 68,* 880–896.

Hinton, D., Um, K., & Ba, P. (2001). Kyol goeu ("wind overload") Part I: A cultural syndrome of orthostatic panic among Khmer refugees. *Transcultural Psychiatry, 38,* 403–432.

Hinton, D. E., Hinton, A. L., Pich, V., Loeum, J. R., & Pollack, M. H. (2009). Nightmares among Cambodian refugees: The breaching of concentric ontological security. *Culture Medicine and Psychiatry, 33,* 219–265.

Hiroi, N., & Scott, D. (2009). Constitutional mechanisms of vulnerability and resilience to nicotine dependence. *Molecular Psychiatry, 14,* 653–667.

Hirota, K. (2006). Special cases: Ketamine, nitrous oxide and xenon. *Best Practice and Research: Clinical Anaesthesiology, 20*(1), 69–79.

Hiroto, D. S. (1974). Locus of control and learned helplessness. *Journal of Experimental Psychology, 102,* 187–193.

Hirschberger, G. (2009). Compassionate callousness: A terror management perspective on prosocial behavior. In M. Mikulincer & P. Shaver (Eds.), *Prosocial motives, emotions, and behavior: The better angels of our nature,* 201–219. Washington, DC: American Psychological Association.

Hirsch-Pasek, K., Treiman, R., & Schneiderman, M. (1984). Brown and Hanlon revisited: Mothers' sensitivity to ungrammatical forms. *Journal of Child Language, 11,* 81–88.

Hirst, W., Phelps, E. A., Buckner, R. L., Budson, A. E., Cuc, A., Gabrieli, J. E., & . . . Vaidya, C. J. (2009). Long-term memory for the terrorist attack of September 11: Flashbulb memories, event memories, and the factors that influence their retention. *Journal of Experimental Psychology: General, 138*(2), 161–176. doi:10.1037/ a0015527

Ho, B.-C., Andreasen, N. C., Nopoulos, P., Arndt, S., Magnotta, V., & Flaum M. (2003). Progressive structural brain abnormalities and their relationship to clinical outcome: A longitudinal magnetic resonance imaging study early in schizophrenia. *Archives of General Psychiatry, 60,* 585–594.

Ho, C., Bluestein, D. N., & Jenkins, J. M. (2008). Cultural differences in the relationship between parenting and children's behavior. *Developmental Psychology, 44,* 507–522.

Ho, M. S. K., & Lee, C. W. (2012). Cognitive behaviour therapy versus eye movement desensitization and reprocessing for post-traumatic disorder–Is it all in the homework then?. *Revue Européenne de Psychologie Appliquée/European Review of Applied Psychology, 62*(4), 253–260.

Ho, V., Lee, J., & Martin, K. (2011). The cell biology of synaptic plasticity. *Science, 334*(6056), 623–628.

Ho, Y.-C., Cheung, M., & Chan, A. S. (2003). Music training improves verbal but not visual memory: Cross-sectional and longitudinal explorations in children. *Neuropsychology, 17,* 439–450.

Hobson, J. (1997). Dreaming as delirium: A mental status analysis of our nightly madness. *Seminar in Neurology, 17,* 121–128.

Hobson, J. A. (2005). Sleep is of the brain, by the brain and for the brain. *Nature, 437,* 1254–1256.

Hochel, M., & Milán, E. G. (2008). Synaesthesia: The existing state of affairs. *Cognitive Neuropsychology, 25,* 93–111.

Hodgins, S. (2007). Persistent violent offending: What do we know? *British Journal of Psychiatry, 190 (supplement),* s12–s14.

Hodson, G. (2011). Do ideologically intolerant people benefit from intergroup contact? *Current Directions in Psychological Science, 20*(3), 154–159. doi:10.1177/ 0963721411409025.

Hodson, G., & Busseri, M. A. (2012). Bright minds and dark attitudes: Lower cognitive ability predicts greater prejudice through right-wing ideology and intergroup conflict. *Psychological Science,* Published online in advance of publication. doi:10.1177/0956797611421206.

Hodson, G., Dovidio, J. F., & Gaertner, S. L. (2010). The aversive form of racism. In J. Chin (Ed.), *The psychology of prejudice and discrimination: A revised and condensed edition* (pp. 1–13). Santa Barbara, CA: Praeger/ABC-CLIO.

Hoeft, F., Gabrieli, J. D., Whitfield-Gabrieli, S., Haas, B. W., Bammer, R., Menon, V., & Spiegel, D. (2012). Functional brain basis of hypnotizability. *Archives of General Psychiatry, 69*(10), 1064–1072.

Hoegl, M., & Parboteeah, K. P. (2006). Autonomy and teamwork in innovative projects. *Human Resource Management, 45,* 67–79.

Hoek, H. W. (2006). Incidence, prevalence and mortality of anorexia nervosa and other eating disorders. *Current Opinion in Psychiatry, 19*(4), 389–394.

Hoel, H., Faragher, B., & Cooper, C. L. (2004). Bullying is detrimental to health, but all bullying behaviors are not necessarily equally damaging. *British Journal of Guidance and Counseling, 32,* 367–387.

Hoen, P. W., Denollet, J., de Jonge, P., & Whooley, M. A. (2013). Positive affect and survival in patients with stable coronary heart disease: Findings from the Heart and Soul Study. *Journal of Clinical Psychiatry, 74*(7), 716–722.

Hofferth, S. L. (2010). Home media and children's achievement and behavior. *Child Development, 81,* 1598–1619.

Hoffman, D. (1999, February 11). When the nuclear alarms went off, he guessed right. *International Herald Tribune,* p. 2.

Hoffman S. D. (2008). *Kids having kids: Economic costs and social consequences of teen pregnancy.* Washington, DC: Urban Institute Press.

Hoffman, Y., Bein, O., & Maril, A. (2011). Explicit memory for unattended words: The importance of being in the "no." *Psychological Science, 22*(12), 1490–1493.

Hofmann, S. G., Fang, A., & Gutner, C. A. (2014). Cognitive enhancers for the treatment of anxiety disorders. *Restorative Neurology & Neuroscience, 32*(1), 183–195.

Hofmann, S. G., Grossman, P., & Hinton, D. E. (2011). Loving-kindness and compassion meditation: Potential for psychological interventions. *Clinical Psychology Review, 31*(7), 1126–1132. doi:10.1016/j.cpr.2011.07.003.

Hofmann, W., can Koningsbruggen, G. M., Stroebe, W., Ramanathan, S., & Aarts, H. (2010). As pleasure unfolds: Hedonic responses to tempting food. *Psychological Science, 21*(12), 1863–1870. doi:10.1177/0956797610389186.

Hogan, D. P., & Msall, M. E. (2002). Family structure and resources and the parenting of children with disabilities and functional limitations. In J. G. Borkowski, S. L. Ramey, & M. Bristol-Power (Eds.), *Parenting and the child's world* (pp. 311–328). Mahwah, NJ: Erlbaum.

Hogarth, R. M., & Einhorn, H. J. (1992). Order effects in belief updating: The belief adjustment model. *Cognitive Psychology, 24,* 1–55.

Hogg, M. A. (2010). Influence and leadership In S. T. Fiske, D. T. Gilbert, & G. Lindzey (Eds.), *Handbook of social psychology* (5th ed., Vol 2, pp. 1166–1207). Hoboken, NJ: Wiley.

Hogg, M. A. (2012). Social identity and the psychology of groups. In M. R. Leary, J. Tangney (Eds.), *Handbook of self and identity* (2nd ed.) (pp. 502–519). New York: Guilford Press.

Hogg, M. A., & Adelman, J. (2013). Uncertainty–identity theory: Extreme groups, radical behavior, and authoritarian leadership. *Journal of Social Issues, 69*(3), 436–454.

Hoigaard, R., Säfvenbom, R., & Tonnessen, F. E. (2006). The relationship between group cohesion, group norms, and perceived social loafing in soccer teams. *Small Group Research, 37,* 217–232.

Holden, C. (1996). Small refugees suffer the effects of early neglect. *Science, 274,* 1076–1077.

Hollander, E., & Simeon, D. (2008). Anxiety disorders. In R. E. Hales, S. C. Yudofsky, & G. O. Gabbard (Eds.), *Textbook of psychiatry* (pp. 505–567). Alexandria, VA: American Psychiatric Association.

Hollinger, R. C., Dabney, D. A., Lee, G., Hayes, R., Hunter, J., & Cummings, M. (1996). *1996 national retail security survey final report.* Gainesville: University of Florida.

Hollins, S. S. & Bensmaia, S. J. (2007). The coding of roughness. *Canadian Journal of Experimental Psychology, 61,* 184–195.

Hollon, S. D., & Beck, A. T. (2013). Cognitive and cognitive-behavioral therapies. In M. J. Lambert (Ed.), *Bergin and Garfield's handbook of psychotherapy and behavior change* (6th ed.) (pp. 393–442). Hoboken, NJ: Wiley.

Hollon, S. D., & DiGiuseppe, R. (2011). Cognitive theories of psychotherapy. In J. C. Norcross, G. R. VandenBos, & D. K. Freedheim (Eds.), *History of psychotherapy: Continuity and change* (pp. 203–241). Washington, DC: American Psychological Association.

Hollon, S. D., Jarrett, R. B., Nienbeg, A. A., Thase, M. E., Trivendi, M., et al. (2005). Psychotherapy and medication in the treatment of adult and geriatric depression: Which monotherapy or combined therapy? *Journal of Clinical Psychiatry, 66,* 455–468.

Hollon, S. D., Stewart, M. O., & Strunk, D. (2006). Enduring effects for cognitive behavior therapy in the treatment of depression and anxiety. *Annual Review of Psychology, 57,* 285–315.

Holma, K. M., Melartin, T. K., Haukka, J., Holma, I.A.K., Sokero, T. P., & Isometsa, E. T. (2010). Incidence and predictors of suicide attempts in DSM-IV major depressive disorder: A five-year prospective study. *American Journal of Psychiatry, 167,* 801–808.

Holman, E. A., Silver, R. C., Poulin, M., Andersen, J., Gil-Rivas, V., & McIntosh, D. N. (2008). Terrorism, acute stress, and cardiovascular health: A 3-year national study following the September 11th attacks. *Archives of General Psychiatry, 65,* 73–80.

Holman, L. (2011). Millennial students' mental models of search: Implications for academic librarians and database developers. *Journal of Academic Librarianship, 37*(1), 19–27.

Holmes, D. S. (1991). *Abnormal psychology.* New York: HarperCollins.

Holmes, E. A., Brown, R. J., Mansell, W., Fearon, R. P., Hunter, E. C. M., Frasquilho, F., & Oakley, D. A. (2005). Are there two qualitatively distinct forms of dissociation? A review and some clinical implications. *Clinical Psychology Review, 25*(1), 1–23.

Holmes, T. H., & Rahe, R. H. (1967). The Social Readjustment Rating Scale. *Journal of Psychosomatic Research, 11,* 213–218.

Hölscher, C., Tenbrink, T., & Wiener, J. M. (2011). Would you follow your own route description? Cognitive strategies in urban route planning. *Cognition, 121*(2), 228–247. doi:10.1016/j.cognition.2011.06.005.

Holtmaat, A., Wilbrecht, L., Knott, G. W., Welker, E., & Svoboda, K. (2006). Experience-dependent and cell-type-specific spine growth in the neocortex. *Nature, 441,* 979–983.

Holway, A. H., & Boring, E. G. (1941). Determinants of apparent visual size with distance variant. *American Journal of Psychology, 54,* 21–37.

Holwerda, N., Sanderman, R., Pool, G., Hinnen, C., Langendijk, J. A., Bemelman, W. A., Hagedoorn, M., & Sprangers, M. A. (2013). Do patients trust their physician? The role of attachment style in the patient-physician relationship within one year after a cancer diagnosis. *Acta Oncology, 52,* 110–117.

Hölzel, B. K., Lazar, S. W., Gard, T., Schuman-Olivier, Z., Vago, D. R., & Ott, U. (2011). How does mindfulness meditation work? Proposing mechanisms of action from a conceptual and neural perspective. *Perspectives on Psychological Science, 6*(6), 537–559.

Hong, H., & Lin-Siegler, X. (2011). How learning about scientists' struggles influences students' interest and learning in physics. *Journal Of Educational Psychology,* doi:10.1037/a0026224.

Honjo, K., Black, S. E., & Cerhoeff, N. P. (2012). Alzheimer's disease, cerebrovascular disease, and the β-amyloid cascade. *Canadian Journal of Neurological Sciences, 39*(6), 712–728.

Honma, S., Ono, D., Suzuki, Y., Inagaki, N., Yoshikawa, T., Nakamura, W., & Honma, K. (2012). Suprachiasmatic nucleus: Cellular clocks and networks. *Progress in Brain Research, 199,* 129–141.

Honts, C. R., & Quick, B. D. (1995). The polygraph in 1996: Progress in science and the law. *North Dakota Law Review, 71,* 997–1020.

Hoobler, J. M., & Brass, D. J. (2006). Abusive supervision and family undermining as displaced aggression. *Journal of Applied Psychology, 91,* 1125–1133.

Hood, B. M., Willen, J. D., & Driver, J. (1998). Adult's eyes trigger shifts of visual attention in human infants. *Psychological Science, 9,* 131–134.

Hood, M. Y., Moore, L. L., Sundarajan-Ramamurti, A., Singer, M., Cupples, L. A., & Ellison, R. C. (2000). Parental eating attitudes and the development of obesity in children: The Framingham children's study. *International Journal of Obesity, 24,* 1319–1325.

Hooker, E. (1993). Reflections of a 40-year exploration: A scientific view on homosexuality. *American Psychologist, 48,* 450–453.

Hooley, J. M. (2004). Do psychiatric patients do better clinically if they live with certain kinds of families? *Current Directions in Psychological Science, 13,* 202–205.

Hooley, J. M. (2010). Social factors in schizophrenia. *Current Directions in Psychological Science, 19*(4), 238–242. doi:10.1177/0963721410377597.

Hooper, D. T., & Martin, R. (2007). Measuring perceived LMX variability within teams and its impact on procedural justice climate. In A. Glendon, B. M. Thompson, B. Myors, A. Glendon, B. M. Thompson, B. Myors (Eds.) , *Advances in organisational psychology* (pp. 249–267). Bowen Hills, QLD Australia: Australian Academic Press.

Hope, L., Lewinski, W., Dixon, J., Blocksidge, D., & Gabbert, F. (2012). Witnesses in action: The effect of physical exertion on recall and recognition. *Psychological Science.* Advance online publication. doi:10.1177/0956797611431463.

Hopf, H. C., Muller, F. W., & Hopf, N. J. (1992). Localization of emotional and volitional facial paresis. *Neurology, 42*(10), 1918–1923.

Hopper, K., & Wanderling, J. (2000). Revisiting the developed versus developing country distinction in course and outcome in schizophrenia: Results from ISoS, the WHO Collaborative Followup Project. *Schizophrenia Bulletin, 26,* 835–846.

Hopwood, C. J., Donnellan, M., Blonigen, D. M., Krueger, R. F., McGue, M., Iacono, W. G., & Burt, S. (2011). Genetic and environmental influences on personality trait stability and growth during the transition to adulthood: A three-wave longitudinal study. *Journal of Personality and Social Psychology, 100*(3), 545–556. doi:10.1037/a0022409.

Horney, K. (1937). *Neurotic personality of our times.* New York: Norton.

Horwitz, A. V., Widom, C. S., McLaughlin, J., & White, H. R. (2001). Th e impact of childhood abuse and neglect on adult mental health: A prospective study. *Journal of Health and Social Behavior, 42,* 184–201.

Horwitz, P., & Christie, M. A. (2000). Computer-based manipulatives for teaching scientific reasoning: An example. In M. J. Jacobson & R. B. Kozuma (Eds.), *Innovations in science and mathematics education: Advanced designs for technologies of learning* (pp. 163–191). Mahwah, NJ: Erlbaum.

Hoshino-Browne, E., Zanna, A. S., Spencer, S. J., Zanna, M. P., Kitayama, S., & Lackenbauer, S. (2005). On the cultural guises of cognitive dissonance: The case of Easterners and Westerners. *Journal of Personality and Social Psychology, 89,* 294–310.

Houben, K., Wiers, R., & Jansen, A. (2011). Getting a grip on drinking behavior: Training working memory to reduce alcohol abuse. *Psychological Science, 22*(7), 968–975.

Houpt, T. R. (1994). Gastric pressure in pigs during eating and drinking. *Physiology and Behavior, 56*(2), 311–317.

House, R. J., Hanges, P. J., Ruiz-Quintanilla, S. A., Dorfman, P. W., Javidan, M., Dickson, M., et al. (1999). Cultural influences on leadership and organizations: Project GLOBE. In W. H. Mobley, M. J. Gessner, & V. Arnold (Eds.), *Advances in global leadership* (Vol. 1, pp. 171–233). Stamford, CT: JAI.

Houser, M. M., Rosen, L., Seagrave, M. P., Grabowski, D., Matthew, J. D., & Craig, W. A. (2013). Exercise heart rate monitors for anxiety treatment in a rural primary care setting: A pilot study. *Family Medicine, 45*(9), 615–621.

Houston, K. A., Hope, L., Memon, A., & Don Read, J. (2013). Expert testimony on eyewitness evidence: In search of common sense. *Behavioral Sciences and the Law, 31*(5), 637–651.

Howard, D. V. (1983). *Cognitive psychology.* New York: Macmillan.

Howe, M. J. A., Davidson, J. W., & Sloboda, J. A. (1998). Innate talent: Reality or myth? *Behavioral and Brain Sciences, 21,* 399–442.

Howe, M. L. (2003). Memories from the cradle. *Current Directions in Psychological Science, 12,* 62–65.

Howe, M. L. (2011). *Nature of early memory: An adaptive theory of the genesis and development of memory.* Oxford, England: Oxford University Press.

Howe, M. L. (2013). Memory development: Implications for adults recalling childhood experiences in the courtroom. *Nature Reviews Neuroscience, 14*(12), 869–876.

Howe, T. (2012). *Marriage and families in the 21st century.* Malden, MA: Wiley-Blackwell.

Howell, J. L., & Shepperd, J. A. (2012). Reducing information avoidance through affirmation. *Psychological Science, 23*(2), 141–145. doi:10.1177/0956797611424164.

Hoyert, D. L., Kung, H.-C., & Smith, B. L. (2005). Deaths: Preliminary data for 2003. *National Vital Statistics Reports, 53,* 1–48.

Hoyle, R. H., Harris, M. J., & Judd, C. M. (2002). *Research methods in social relations.* Belmont, CA: Wadsworth.

Hoyt, C. L., Simon, S., & Innella, A. N. (2011). Taking a turn toward the masculine: The impact of mortality salience on implicit leadership theories. *Basic and Applied Social Psychology, 33,* 374–381. doi:10.1080/01973533.2011.614173.

Hsee, C. K., Yang, A., X., & Wang, L. (2010). Idleness aversion and the need for justifiable busyness. *Psychological Science, 21*(7), 926–930. doi:10.1177/ 0956797610374738.

Hser, Y. I., Hoffman, V., Grella, C. E., & Anglin, M. D. (2001). A 33-year follow-up of narcotics addicts. *Archives of General Psychiatry, 58,* 503–508.

Hsia, J. F., & Schweinle, W. E. (2012). Psychological definitions of love. In M. A. Paludi (Ed.), *The psychology of love (Vols. 1–4)* (pp. 15–17). Santa Barbara, CA: Praeger/ABC-CLIO.

Hsu, C., & Ho, C. (2012). The design and implementation of a competency-based intelligent mobile learning system. *Expert Systems With Applications, 39*(9), 8030–8043. doi:10.1016/j.eswa.2012.01.130.

Hsu, E., & Cohen S. P. (2013). Postamputation pain: Epidemiology, mechanisms, and treatment. *Journal of Pain Research, 6,* 121–136.

Hsu, L. M., Chung, J., & Langer, E. J. (2010). The influence of age-related cues on health and longevity. *Perspectives on Psychological Science, 5*(6), 632–648. doi:10.1177/1745691610388762.

Hsu, M. H., Syed-Abdul, S., Scholl, J., Jian, W. S., Lee, P., Iqbal, U., & Li, Y. C. (2013). The incidence rate and mortality of malignant brain tumors after 10 years of intensive cell phone use in Taiwan. *European Journal of Cancer Prevention, 22*(6), 596–598.

Hsu, Y. C., Chen, S. L., Wang, D. Y., & Chiu, I. M. (2013). Stem cell-based therapy in neural repair. *Biomedical Journal, 36*(3), 98–105.

Hu, S., Patatucci, A. M. L., Patterson, C., Li, L., Fulker, D. W., Cherny, S. S., et al. (1995). Linkage between sexual orientation and chromosome Xq28 in males but not females. *Nature Genetics, 11,* 248–256.

Hua, J. Y., & Smith, S. J. (2004). Neural activity and the dynamics of central nervous system development. *Nature Neuroscience, 7,* 327–332.

Huang, J. Y., Sedlovskaya, A., Ackerman, J. M., & Bargh, J. A. (2011). Immunizing against prejudice: Effects of disease protection on attitudes toward out-groups. *Psychological Science, 22*(12), 1550–1556. doi:10.1177/0956797611417261.

Huang, L., & Li, C. (2000). Leptin: A multifunctional hormone. *Cell Research, 10,* 81–92. doi:10.1016/j.chb.2010.03.014.

Huang, Y., Kendrick, K. M., & Yu, R. (2014). Conformity to the opinions of other people lasts for no more than 3 days. *Psychological Science, 25*(7), 1388–1393.

Hubbard, E. M., & Ramachandran, V. S. (2005). Neurocognitive mechanisms of synesthesia. *Neuron, 48,* 509–520.

Hubel, D. H., & Wiesel, T. N. (1979). Brain mechanisms of vision. *Scientific American, 241,* 150–162.

Huber, O. (2012). Risky decisions: Active risk management. *Current Directions in Psychological Science, 21*(1), 26–30. doi:10.1177/0963721411422055.

Huck, S., Kemp, C., & Carter, M. (2010). Self-concept of children with intellectual disability in mainstream settings. *Journal of Intellectual and Developmental Disability, 35*(3), 141–154. doi:10.3109/13668250.2010.489226.

Hudson, J. I., Hiripi, E., Pope, H. G., Jr, & Kessler, R. C. (2007). The prevalence and correlates of eating disorders in the National Comorbidity Survey replication. *Biological Psychiatry, 61,* 348–358.

Hudson, J. I., Lalonde, J. K., Berry, J. M., Pindyck, L. J., Bulik, C. M., Crow, S. J., McElroy, S. L., Laird, N. M., Tsuang, M. T., Walsh, B. T., Rosenthal, N. R., & Pope, H. G. Jr. (2006). Binge-eating disorder as a distinct familial phenotype in obese individuals. *Archives of General Psychiatry, 63*(3), 313–319.

Hudson, J. L., & Rapee, R. M. (2009). Familial and social environments in the eitology and maintenance of anxiety disorders. In M. M. Antony & M. B. Stein (Eds.), *Oxford handbook of anxiety and related disorders* (pp. 173–189). New York: Oxford University Press.

Hudziak, J. J., Derks, E. M., Althoff, R. R., Rettew, D. C., & Boomsma, D. I. (2005). The genetic and environmental contributions to attention deficit hyperactivity disorder as measured by the Conners' Rating Scales—Revised. *American Journal of Psychiatry, 162,* 1614–1620.

Hudziak, J. J., van Beijsterveldt, C. E. M., Bartels, M., Rietveld, M. J. H., Rettew, D. C., Derks, E. M., et al. (2003). Individual differences in aggression: Genetic analyses by age, gender, and informant in 3-, 7-, and 10-year-old Dutch twins. *Behavior Genetics, 33,* 575–589.

Huebner, R. R., & Izard, C. E. (1988). Mothers responses to infants facial expressions of sadness, anger, and physical distress. *Motivation and Emotion, 12,* 185–196.

Huesmann, L. R. (1998). The role of social information processing and cognitive schema in the acquisition and maintenance of habitual aggressive behavior. In R. G. Geen & E. Donnerstein (Eds.), *Human aggression.* San Diego: Academic Press.

Huesmann, L. R., & Eron, L. D. (1986). *Television and the aggressive child: A cross-national comparison.* Hillsdale, NJ: Erlbaum.

Huesmann, L. R., Moise, J., Podolski, C., & Eron, L. (1997, April). *Longitudinal relations between early exposure to television violence and young adult aggression: 1977–1992.* Paper presented at the annual meeting of the Society for Research in Child Development, Washington, DC.

Huesmann, L. R., Moise-Titus, J., Podolski, C., & Eron, L. D. (2003). Longitudinal relations between children's exposure to TV violence and their aggressive and violent behavior in young adulthood: 1977–1992. *Developmental Psychology, 39,* 201–221.

Huesmann, L. R., & Taylor, L. D. (2006). The role of media violence in violent behavior. *Annual Review of Public Health, 27,* 393–415.

Huffcutt, A. I., & Arthur, W. (1994). Hunter and Hunter (1984) revisited: Interview validity for entry-level jobs. *Journal of Applied Psychology, 79,* 184–190.

Huffcutt, A. I., Conway, J. M., Roth, P. L., & Stone, N. J. (2001). Identification and meta-analytic assessment of psychological constructs measured in employment interviews. *Journal of Applied Psychology, 86,* 897–913.

Hughes, B. M. (2006). Lies, damned lies, and pseudoscience: The selling of eye movement desensitization and reprocessing (EMDR). *PsycCritiques, 51,* 10.

Hughes, D., Rowe, M., Batey, M., & Lee, A. (2012). A tale of two sites: Twitter vs. Facebook and the personality predictors of social media usage. *Computers in Human Behavior, 28,* 561–569. doi:10.1016/j.chb.2011.11.001.

Hughes, J. R., Higgins, S. T., & Bickel, W. K. (1994). Nicotine withdrawal versus other drug withdrawal syndromes: Similarities and dissimilarities. *Addiction, 89*(11), 1461–1470.

Hughesa, R., Jaremkaa, L. M., Alfanoc, C. M., Glasera, R., Povoskis, S. P., Liparig, A. M., Agneseg, D. M., Farrarg, W. B., Yeeg, L. D., Carson III, W. E., Malarkeya, W. B., & Kiecolt-Glasera, J. K. (2014). Social support predicts inflammation, pain, and depressive symptoms: Longitudinal relationships among breast cancer survivors. *Psychoneuroendocrinology, 42,* 38–44.

Huhn, M., Tardy, M., Spineli, L. M., Kissling, W., Förstl, H., Pitschel-Walz, G., Leucht, C., Samara, M., Dold, M., Davis, J. M., & Leucht, S. (2014). *JAMA Psychiatry,* Published online April 30, 2014. doi:10.1001/jamapsychiatry.2014.112.

Hui, C., Lam, S. S. K., & Law, K. K. S. (2000). Instrumental values of organizational citizenship behavior for promotion: A field quasi-experiment. *Journal of Applied Psychology, 85,* 822–828.

Huibregtse, B., Bornovalova, M., Hicks, B., McGue, M., & Iacono, W. (2011). Testing the role of adolescent sexual initiation in later-life sexual risk behavior: A longitudinal twin design. *Psychological Science, 22*(7), 924–933.

Huizink, A. C., Mulder, E. J. H., & Buitelaar, J. K. (2004). Prenatal stress and risk for psychopathology. *Psychological Bulletin, 130,* 115–142.

Hull, C. L. (1951). *Essentials of behavior.* New Haven, CT: Yale University Press.

Hull, S. A., Cornwell, J., Harvey, C., Eldridge, S., & Bare, P. O. (2001). Prescribing rates for psychotropic medication amongst east London general practices: Low rates where Asian populations are greatest. *Family Practice, 18,* 167–173.

Human, L. J., & Biesanz, J. C. (2012). Accuracy and assumed similarity in first impressions of personality: Differing associations at different levels of analysis. *Journal of Research in Personality, 46,* 106–110. doi:10.1016/j.jrp.2011.10.002.

Humphreys, L. G. (1984). General intelligence. In C. R. Reynolds & R. T. Brown (Eds.), *Perspectives on bias in mental testing.* New York: Plenum.

Humphreys, K. (2004). *Circles of recovery: Self-help organizations for addictions.* New York: Cambridge University Press.

Humphries, J. E., Holliday, R. E., & Flowe, H. D. (2012). Faces in motion: Age-related changes in eyewitness identification performance in simultaneous, sequential, and elimination video lineups. *Applied Cognitive Psychology, 26*(1), 149–158. doi:10.1002/acp.1808.

Hunsley, J., Lee, C. M., & Wood, J. M. (2003). Controversial and questionable assessment techniques. In S. O. Lilienfeld & S. J. Lynn (Eds.), *Science and pseudoscience in clinical psychology* (pp. 39–76). New York: Guilford Press.

Hunt, C. B. (1980). Intelligence as an information processing concept. *British Journal of Psychology, 71,* 449–474.

Hunt, C. E., & Hauck, F. R. (2006). Sudden infant death syndrome. *Canadian Medical Association Journal, 174,* 1861–1869.

Hunt, E. (1983). On the nature of intelligence. *Science, 219,* 141–146.

Hunt, E. (2012). What makes nations intelligent? *Perspectives on Psychological Science, 7*(3), 284–306. doi:10.1177/1745691612442905.

Hunt, M. (1982). *The universe within.* New York: Simon & Schuster.

Hunt, R., & Rouse, W. B. (1981). Problem solving skills of maintenance trainees in diagnosing faults in simulated power plants. *Human Factors, 23,* 317–328.

Hunter, J., Rivero-Arias, O., Angelov, A., Kim, E., Fotheringham, I., & Leal, J. (2014). Epidemiology of fragile X syndrome: A systematic review and meta-analysis. American *Journal of Medical Genetics. Part A,* Epub April 3, 2014.

Hunter, M. A., & Ames, E. W. (1988). A multifactor model of infants' preferences for novel and familiar stimuli. In C. Rovee-Collier & L. P. Lipsitt (Eds.), *Advances in infancy research* (Vol. 5, pp. 69–91). Norwood, NJ: Ablex.

Hurd, N. M., Sánchez, B., Zimmerman, M. A., & Caldwell, C. H. (2012). Natural mentors, racial identity, and educational attainment among African American adolescents: Exploring pathways to success. *Child Development, 83*, 1196–1212.

Hurt, H., Brodsky, N. L., Betancourt, L., & Braitman, L. E. (1995). Cocaine-exposed children: Follow-up through 30 months. *Journal of Developmental and Behavioral Pediatrics, 16*(1), 29–35.

Hussar, K. M., & Horvath, J. C. (2011). Do children play fair with mother nature? Understanding children's judgments of environmentally harmful actions. *Journal of Environmental Psychology, 31*(4), 309–313. doi:10.1016/j.jenvp.2011.05.001.

Huston, A. C., & Wright, J. C. (1989). The forms of television and the child viewer. In G. Comstock (Ed.), *Public communication and behavior* (Vol. 2, pp. 103–159). San Diego: Academic Press.

Huttenlocher, P. R. (1990). Morphometric study of human cerebral cortex development. *Neuropsychologia, 28*, 517–527.

Huuhka, K., Viikki, M., Tammentie, T., Tuohimaa, K., Björkqvist, M., Alanen, H. M., Leinonen, E., & Kampman, O. (2012). One-year follow-up after discontinuing maintenance electroconvulsive therapy. *Journal of ECT, 28*(4), 225–228.

Hwang, K. (2009). The development of indigenous counseling in contemporary Confucian communities. *The Counseling Psychologist, 37*(7), 930–943. doi:10.1177/ 0011000009336241.

Hybels, C. F., Pieper, C. F., Blazer, D. G., & Steffens, D. C. (2008). The course of depressive symptoms in older adults with comorbid major depression and dysthymia. *American Journal of Geriatric Psychiatry, 16*, 300–309.

Hyde, J. S. (2005). The gender similarities hypothesis. *American Psychologist, 60*, 581–592.

Hyde, J. S. (2007). New directions in the study of gender similarities and differences. *Current Directions in Psychological Science, 16*, 259–263.

Hyde, J. S., & Durik, A. M. (2000). Gender differences in erotic plasticity–Evolutionary or sociocultural forces? Comment on Baumeister (2000). *Psychological Bulletin, 126*, 375–379.

Hyde, K. L., Lerch, J., Norton, A., Forgeard, M., Winner, E., Evans, A. C., & Schlaug, G. (2009). Musical training shapes structural brain development. *The Journal of Neuroscience, 29*, 3019–3025.

Hyde, Z., Flicker, L., Hankey, G. J., Almeida, O. P., McCaul, K. A., Chubb, S., & Yeap, B. B. (2010). Prevalence of sexual activity and associated factors in men aged 75 to 95 years. *Annals Of Internal Medicine, 153*(11), 693–702.

Hyman, I. E., Jr. (2000). The memory wars. In U. Neisser & I. E. Hyman, Jr. (Eds.), *Memory observed* (2nd ed., pp. 374–379). New York: Worth.

Hyman, I. E., Jr., Boss, S. M., Wise, B. M., McKenzie, K. E., & Caggiano, J. M. (2010). Did you see the unicycling clown? Inattentional blindness while walking and talking on a cell phone. *Applied Cognitive Psychology, 24*, 597–607. doi:10.1002/ acp.1638

Hyman, I. E., Jr., & Pentland, J. (1996). The role of mental imagery in the creation of false childhood memories. *Journal of Memory and Language, 35*, 101–117.

Hyman, R. (2002). Why and when are smart people stupid? In R. J. Sternberg (Ed.), *Why smart people can be so stupid* (pp. 1–23). New Haven, CT: Yale University Press.

Hyman, S. E., Malenka, R. C., & Nestler, E. J. (2006). Neural mechanisms of addiction: The role of reward-related learning and memory. *Annual Review of Neuroscience, 29*, 565–598.

Hypericum Depression Trial Study Group. (2002). Effect of *Hypericum perforatum* (St. John's wort) in major depressive disorder: A randomized, controlled trial. *Journal of the American Medical Association, 287*, 1.

Iacono, W. G., & Patrick, C. J. (2006). Polygraph ("lie detector") testing: Current status and emerging trends. In I. B. Weiner & A. K. Hess (Eds.), *The handbook of forensic psychology* (3rd ed., pp. 552–588). Hoboken, NJ: Wiley.

Iancu, I., Poreh, A., Lehman, B., Shamir, E., & Kotler, M. (2005). The positive and negative symptoms questionnaire: A self-report in schizophrenia. *Comprehensive Psychiatry, 46*, 61–66.

Insko, C. A., Wildschut, T., & Cohen, T. R. (2013). Interindividual–intergroup discontinuity in the prisoner's dilemma game: How common fate, proximity, and similarity affect intergroup competition. *Organizational Behavior And Human Decision Processes, 120*(2), 168–180.

Iani, C., Ricci, F., Ghem, E., & Rubichi, S. (2006). Hypnotic suggestion modulates cognitive conflict: The case of the flanker compatibility effect. *Psychological Science, 17*, 721–727.

Iaria, G., Fox, C. J., Scheel, M., Stowe, R. M., & Barton, J. J. (2010). A case of persistent visual hallucinations of faces following LSD abuse: a functional Magnetic Resonance Imaging study. *Neurocase, 16*(2), 106–18.

Iber, C., Ancoli-Israel, S., Chesson, A., & Quan, S. F. (2007). *The AASM Manual*

Iervolino, A. C., Hines, M., Golombok, S. E., Rust, J., & Plomin, R. (2005). Genetic and environmental influences on sex-typed behavior during the preschool years. *Child Development, 76*, 826–840.

Igalens, J., & Roussel, P. (1999). A study of the relationships between compensation package, work motivation, and job satisfaction. *Journal of Organizational Behavior, 20*, 1003–1025.

IJzerman, H., & Semin, G. R. (2009). Th e thermometer of social relations: Mapping social proximity on temperature. *Psychological Science, 20*, 1214–1220.

Ikeda, A., Schwartz, J., Peters, J. L., Baccarelli, A. A., Hoxha, M., Dioni, L., Spiro, A., Sparrow, D., Vokronas, P., & Kubzanski, L. D. (2014). Pessimistic orientation in relation to telomere length in older men: The VA Normative Aging Study. *Psychoneuroendocrinology, 42*, 68–76.

Ilgen, D. R., & Pulakos, E. D. (Eds.). (1999). *The changing nature of performance: Implications for staffing, motivation, and development.* San Francisco, CA: Jossey-Bass.

Ilies, R., & Judge, T. A. (2003). On the heritability of job satisfaction: The mediating role of personality. *Journal of Applied Psychology, 88*, 750–759.

Ilies, R., & Judge, T. A. (2013). On the heritability of job satisfaction: The mediating role of personality. *Journal of Applied Psychology, 88*, 750–759.

Ilies, R., Nahrgang, J. D., & Morgeson, F. P. (2007). Leader-member exchange and citizenship behaviors: A meta-analysis. *Journal of Applied Psychology, 92*, 269–277.

Ilies, R., Scott, B. A., & Judge, T. A. (2006). The interactive effects of personal traits and experienced states on intraindividual patterns of citizenship behavior. *Academy of Management Journal, 49*, 561–575.

Iliescu, D., Ilie, A., & Ispas, D., (2011). Examining the Criterion-Related Validity of the Employee Screening Questionnaire: A Three-Sample Investigation *International Journal of Selection and Assessment, 19*, 222–228.

Imada, T., & Kitayama, S. (2010). Social eyes and choice justification: Culture and dissonance revisited. *Social Cognition, 28*(5), 589–608.

Immordino-Yang, M. H., Christodoulou, J. A., & Singh, V. (2012). Rest is not idleness: Implications of the brain's default mode for human development and education. *Perspectives on Psychological Science, 7*, 352–364. *doi:10.1177/1745691612447308.*

Inda, M., Muravieva, E. V., & Alberini, C. M. (2011). Memory retrieval and the passage of time: From reconsolidation and strengthening to extinction. *Journal of Neuroscience, 31*(5), 1635–1643. doi:10.1523/JNEUROSCI.4736–10.201.

Indovina, I., & Sanes, J. N. (2001). On somatotopic representation centers for finger movements in human primary motor cortex and supplementary motor area. *Neuroimage, 13*, 1027–1034.

Ingersoll, B. (2011). Recent advances in early identification and treatment of autism. *Current Directions in Psychological Science, 20*(5), 335–339. doi:10.1177/ 0963721411418470.

Inness, M., Barling, J., & Turner, N. (2005). Understanding supervisor-targeted aggression: A within-person, between-jobs design. *Journal of Applied Psychology, 90*, 731–739.

Inskip, P., Hoover, R., & Devesa, S. (2010). Brain cancer incidence trends in relation to cellular telephone use in the United States. *Neuro-Oncology, 12*(11), 1147–1151.

Institute of Medicine. (2006, April 5). *Sleep disorders and sleep deprivation: An unmet public health problem* [Press release]. Retrieved September 26, 2006, from http:// www.iom.edu/ CMS/3740/23160/33668.aspx.

International Human Genome Sequencing Consortium. (2001). Initial sequencing and analysis of the human genome. *Nature, 409*, 860–921.

Ioannidis, J. P. (2008). Effectiveness of antidepressants: An evidence myth constructed from a thousand randomized trials? *Philosophy, Ethics, and Humanities in Medicine, 3*, 14.

Ireland, M. E., Slatcher, R. B., Eastwick, P. W., Scissors, L. E., Finkel, E. J., & Pennebaker, J. W. (2011). Language style matching predicts relationship initiation and stability. *Psychological Science, 22*(1), 39–44. doi:10.1177/0956797610392928.

Irwin, M., Daniels, M., Smith, T., Bloom, E., & Weiner, H. (1987). Impaired natural killer cell activity during bereavement. *Brain, Behavior, and Immunity, 1*, 98–104.

Isaacowitz, D. M., Wadlinger, H. A., Goren, D., & Wilson, H. R. (2006). Selective preference in visual fixation away from negative images in old age: An eye-tracking study. *Psychology and Aging, 21*, 40–48.

Ishikawa, A., Kanayama, Y., Matsumura, H., Tsuchimochi, H., Ishida, Y., & Nakamura, S. (2006). Selective rapid eye movement sleep deprivation impairs the maintenance of long-term potentiation in the rat hippocampus. *European Journal of Neuroscience, 24*, 243–248.

Ito, T., Tiede, M., & Ostry, D. J. (2009). Somatosensory function in speech production. *Proceedings of the National Academy of Sciences, 106*, 1245–1248.

Ivleva, E., Thaker, G., & Tamminga, C. (2008). Comparing genes and phenomenology in the major psychoses: Schizophrenia and bipolar 1 disorder. *Schizophrenia Bulletin, 34*(4), 734–742.

Iwadare, Y., Usami, M., Suzuki, Y., Ushijima, H., Tanaka, T., Watanabe, K., Kodaira, M., & Saito, K. (2011). Posttraumatic symptoms in elementary and junior high school children after the 2011 Japan earthquake and tsunami: Symptom severity and recovery vary by age and sex. *Journal of Pediatrics*, Epub January 2, 2014.

Iwahashi, K., Matsuo, Y., Suwaki, H., Nakamura, K., & Ichikawa, Y. (1995). CYP2E1 and ALDH2 genotypes and alcohol dependence in Japanese. *Alcoholism Clinical and Experimental Research, 19*(3), 564–566.

Iwamasa, G. Y., Sorocco, K. H., & Koonce, D. A. (2002). Ethnicity and clinical psychology: A content analysis of the literature. *Clinical Psychology Review, 22*, 932–944.

Iwata, M., Hazama, G., & Nakagome, K. (2012). Depressive state due to isolated adrenocorticotropic hormone deficiency underlies school refusal. *Psychiatry & Clinical Neurosciences, 66*(3), 243–244. doi:10.1111/j.1440-1819.2012.02322.x

Izard, C., Fine, S., Schultz, D. Mostow, A., Ackerman, B., & Youngstrom, E. (2001). Emotion knowledge as a predictor of social behavior and academic competence in children at risk. *Psychological Science, 12*, 18–23.

Izard, C. E. (1977). *Human emotions*. New York: Plenum.

Izard, C. E. (1993). Four systems for emotion activation: Cognitive and noncognitive development. *Psychological Review, 100*, 68–90.

Izard, C. E. (2007). Basic emotions, natural kinds, emotion schemas, and a new paradigm. *Perspectives on Psychological Science, 2*, 260–280.

Izard, C. E., Huebner, R. R., Risser, D., McGinnes, G., & Dougherty, L. (1980). The young infant's ability to reproduce discrete emotion expressions. *Developmental Psychology, 16*, 132–140.

Jaccard, J., Blanton, H., & Dodge, T. (2005). Peer influences on risk behavior: An analysis of the effects of a close friend. *Developmental Psychology, 41*, 135–147.

Jack, F., & Hayne, H. (2007). Eliciting adults' earliest memories: Does it matter how we ask the question? *Memory, 15*(6), 647–663.

Jack, R. E., Garrod, O. G. B., Yu, H., Caldarac, R., & Schyns, P. G. (2012). Facial expressions of emotion are not culturally universal. www.pnas.org/cgi/doi/10.1073/pnas.1200155109.

Jackson, B., Sellers, R. M., & Peterson, C. (2002). Pessimistic explanatory style moderates the effect of stress on physical illness. *Personality & Individual Differences, 32*, 567–573.

Jackson, C. J. (2003). Gray's Reinforcement Sensitivity Theory: A psychometric critique. *Personality and Individual Differences, 34*, 533–544.

Jackson, J. J., Thoemmes, F., Jonkmann, K., Lüdtke, O., & Trautwein, U. (2012). Military training and personality trait development: Does the military make the man, or does the man make the military? *Psychological Science, 23*, 270–277. doi:10.1177/0956797611423545.

Jackson, L. A., von Eye, A., Fitzgerald, H. E., Witt, E. A., Zhao, Y., & Fitzgerald, H. E. (2011). Internet use, videogame playing and cell phone use as predictors of children's body mass index (BMI), body weight, academic performance, and social and overall self-esteem. *Computers in Human Behavior, 27*, 599–604.

Jackson, M. L., Howard, M. E., & Barnes, M. (2011). Cognition and daytime functioning in sleep-related breathing disorders. *Progress in Brain Research, 190*, 53–68.

Jacob, S., Kinnunen, L. H., Metz, J., Cooper, M., & McClintock, M. K. (2001). Sustained human chemosignal unconsciously alters brain function. *Neuroreport, 12*, 2391–2394.

Jacob, T., Waterman, B., Heath, A., True, W., Bucholz, K. K., Haber, R., et al. (2003). Genetic and environmental effects on offspring alcoholism: New insights using an offspring-of-twins design. *Archives of General Psychiatry, 60*, 1265–1272.

Jacobs, G. D., Pace-Schott, E. F., Stickgold, R., & Otto, M. W. (2004). Cognitive behavior therapy and pharmacotherapy for insomnia: A randomized controlled trial and direct comparison. *Archives of Internal Medicine, 164*, 1888–1896.

Jacobs, G. H. (2008). Primate color vision: A comparative perspective. *Vision Neuroscience, 25*(5–6), 619–631.

Jacobs, H. I., van Boxtel, M. P., Gronenschild, E. H., Williams, V. J., Burgmans, S., Uylings, H. B., Jolles, J., and Verhey, F. R. (2012). Patterns of gray and white matter changes in individuals at risk for Alzheimer's disease. *Current Alzheimer Research, 9*(9), 1097–1105.

Jacobs, M., Snow, J., Geraci, M., Vythilingam, M., Blair, R. J. R., et al. (2009). Association between level of emotional intelligence and severity of anxiety in generalized social phobia. *Journal of Anxiety Disorders, 22*, 1487–1495.

Jacobs, N., Kenis, G., Peeters, F., Derom, C., Vlietinck, R., & van Os, J. (2006). Stress-related negative affectivity and genetically altered serotonin transporter function: Evidence of synergism in shaping risk of depression. *Archives of General Psychiatry, 63*, 989–996.

Jacobs, R., & Solomon, T. (1977). Strategies for enhancing the prediction of job performance from job satisfaction. *Journal of Applied Psychology, 62*, 417–421.

Jacobson, E. (1938). *Progressive relaxation*. Chicago: University of Chicago Press.

Jacobson, J. W., Mulick, J. A., & Schwartz, A. A. (1995). A history of facilitated communication. *American Psychologist, 50*, 750–765.

Jacobson, K. (2002). ADHD in cross-cultural perspective: Some empirical results. *American Anthropologist, 104*, 283–286.

Jaffari-Bimmel, N., Juffer, F., van IJzendoorn, M. H., Bakermans-Kranenburg, M. J., & Mooijaart, A. (2006). Social development from infancy to adolescence: Longitudinal and concurrent factors in an adoption sample. *Developmental Psychology, 42*(6), 1143–1153.

Jaffee, S., & Hyde, J. S. (2000). Gender differences in moral orientation: A meta-analysis. *Psychological Bulletin, 126*, 703–726.

Jaffee, S. R., Caspi, A., Moffitt, T. E., & Taylor, A. (2004). Physical maltreatment to antisocial child: Evidence of an environmentally mediated process. *Journal of Abnormal Psychology, 113*, 44–55.

Jaffee S. R., Caspi A., Moffitt T. E., Polo-Tomas M., Taylor A. (2007). Individual, family, and neighborhood factors distinguish resilient from non-resilient maltreated children: a cumulative stressors model. *Child Abuse and Neglect, 31*, 231–253.

Jaffee, S. R., Hanscombe, K. B., Haworth, C. A., Davis, O. P., & Plomin, R. (2012). Chaotic homes and children's disruptive behavior: A longitudinal cross-lagged twin study. *Psychological Science, 23*, 643–650. doi:10.1177/0956797611431693

Jago, R., Baranowski, T., Baranowski, J. C., Thompson, D., & Greaves, K. A. (2005). BMI from 3-6 y of age is predicted by TV viewing and physical activity, not diet. *International Journal of Obesity, 29*, 557–564.

Jahanfar, S., & Jaafar, S. H. (2013). Effects of restricted caffeine intake by mother on fetal, neonatal and pregnancy outcome. *The Cochrane Database of Systemic Reviews, 2*, CD006965.

Jahnke, J. C., & Nowaczyk, R. H. (1998). *Cognition*. Upper Saddle River, NJ: Prentice Hall.

Jain, A. (2005). Treating obesity in individuals and populations. *British Medical Journal, 331*, 1387–1390.

Jakubowska, E., & Zielinski, K. (1978). Stimulus intensity effects on the acute extinction of the CER in rats. *Acta Neurobiologica Experimentalis, 38*, 1–10.

James, S. D., (2008, May 7). Wild child speechless after tortured life. Retrieved from http://abcnews.go.com/Health/story?id=4804490&page=1#.T6_6k1Iuh8E.

James, W. (1890). *Principles of psychology*. New York: Holt.

James, W. (1892). *Psychology: Briefer course*. New York: Holt.

Jameson, L. C., & Sloan, T. B. (2006). Using EEG to monitor anesthesia drug effects during surgery. *Journal of Clinical Monitoring and Computers, 20*, 445–472.

Jamieson, P., Jamieson, K. H., & Romer, D. (2003). The responsible reporting of suicide in print journalism. *American Behavioral Scientist, 46*, 1643–1660.

Jan, J. E., Freeman, R. D., Wasdell, M. B., & Bomben, M. M. (2004). 'A child with severe night terrors and sleep-walking responds to melatonin therapy'. *Developmental Medicine and Child Neurology, 46*(11), 789.

Jancke, L., & Kaufmann, N. (1994). Facial EMG responses to odors in solitude and with an audience. *Chemical Senses, 19*(2), 99–111.

Janik, V. M. (2013). Cognitive skills in bottlenose dolphin communication. *Trends in Cognitive Sciences, 17*(4), 157–159.

Janowitz, H. D. (1967). Role of gastrointestinal tract in the regulation of food intake. In C. F. Code (Ed.), *Handbook of physiology: Alimentary canal 1*. Washington, DC: American Physiological Society.

Jansen, P. G., & Vinkenburg, C. J. (2006). Predicting managerial career success from assessment center data: A longitudinal study. *Journal of Vocational Behavior, 68*, 253–266.

Janszky, J., Szucs, A., Halasz, P., Borbely, C., et al. (2002). Orgasmic aura originates from the right hemisphere. *Neurology, 58*, 302–304.

Jaques, S. C., Kingsbury, A., Henshcke, P., Chomchai, C., Clews, S., Falconer, J., Abdel-Latif, M. E., Feller, J. M., Oei, J. L. (2013). Cannabis, the pregnant woman and her child: Weeding out the myths. *Journal of Perinatology*. Epub January 23, 2014.

Jaremka, L. M., Fagundes, C. P., Peng, J., Bennett, J. M., Glaser, R., Malarkey, W. B., & Kiecolt-Glaser, J. K. (2013). Loneliness promotes inflammation during acute stress. *Psychological Science, 24*(7), 1089–1097.

Jaremka, L. M., Glaser, R., Malarkey, W. B., & Kiecolt-Glaser, J. K. (2013). Marital distress prospectively predicts poorer cellular immune function. *Psychoneuroendocrinology, 38*(11), 2713–2719.

Jarosz, A., Colflesh, G., and Wiley, J. (2012). Uncorking the muse: Alcohol intoxication facilitates creative problem solving. *Consciousness and Cognition, 21*(1), 487–493 DOI: 10.1016/j.concog.2012.01.002

Jaušovec, N., & Jaušovec, K. (2012). Working memory training: Improving intelligence—Changing brain activity. *Brain & Cognition, 79*(2), 96–106. doi:10.1016/j.bandc.2012.02.007.

Javitt, D. C., Kantowitz, J., & Lajtha, A. (Eds.) (2009). *Handbook of neurochemistry and molecular neurobiology: Schizophrenia* (3rd ed.). New York: Springer.

Jayanthi, S., Buie, S., Moore, S., Herning, R. I., et al. (2010). Heavy marijuana users show increased serum apolipoprotein C-III levels: Evidence from proteomic analyses. *Molecular Psychiatry, 15*, 101–112.

Jefferis, B. M. J. H., Power, C., & Hertzman, C. (2002). Birth weight, childhood socioeconomic environment, and cognitive development in the 1958 British birth cohort study [Electronic version]. *British Medical Journal, 325*, 305.

Jeffries, K. J., Fritz, J. B., & Braun, A. R. (2003). Words in melody: An H(2)15O PET study of brain activation during singing and speaking. *Neuroreport, 14*, 749–754.

Jemal, A., Ward, E., Hao, Y., & Thun, M. (2005). Trends in the leading causes of death in the United States, 1970–2002. *Journal of the American Medical Association, 294*, 1255–1259.

Jenkinson, P. M., Preston, C., & Ellis, S. J. (2011). Unawareness after stroke: a review and practical guide to understanding, assessing, and managing anosognosia for hemiplegia. *Journal of Clinical and Experimental Neuropsychology, 33*(10), 1079–1093.

Jensen, A. R. (1993). Why is reaction time correlated with psychometric g? *Current Directions in Psychological Science, 2*, 53–55.

Jensen, M., & Karoly, P. (1991). Control beliefs, coping eff orts, and adjustment to chronic pain. *Journal of Consulting and Clinical Psychology, 59*, 431–438.

Jern, A., Chang, K. K., & Kemp, C. (2014). Belief polarization is not always irrational. *Psychological Review, 121*, 206–224.

Jevtovic-Todorovic, V., Wozniak, D. F., Benshoff, N. D., & Olney, J. W. (2001). A comparative evaluation of the neurotoxic properties of ketamine and nitrous oxide. *Brain Research, 895*, 264–267.

Jex, S. M., Adams, G. A., Elacqua, T. C., & Bachrach, D. G. (2002). Type A as a moderator of stressors and job complexity: A comparison of achievement strivings and impatience-irritability. *Journal of Applied Social Psychology, 32*, 977–996.

Jia, H., Rochefort, N. L., Chen, X., & Konnerth, A. (2010). Dendritic organization of sensory input to cortical neurons *in vivo. Nature, 464*, 1307–1312.

Jiang, Y., Wang, H., Liu, Z., Dong, Y., Dong, Y., Xiang, X., Bai, L., Tian, J., Wu, L., Han, J., & Cui, C. (2013). Manipulation of and sustained effects on the human brain induced by different modalities of acupuncture: An fMRI study. *PLoS One, 8*(6), e66815.

Jiang, W., Wu, Y., & Jiang, X. (2013). Coffee and caffeine intake and breast cancer risk: An updated dose-response meta-analysis of 37 published studies. *Gynecologic Oncology, 129*(3), 620–629.

Jobe, T. H., & Harrow, M. (2010). Schizophrenia course, long-term outcome, recovery, and prognosis. *Current Directions in Psychological Science, 19*(4), 220–225. doi:10.1177/0963721410378034.

Joët, G., Usher, E. L., & Bressoux, P. (2011). Sources of self-efficacy: An investigation of elementary school students in France. *Journal of Educational Psychology, 103*(3), 649–663. doi:10.1037/a0024048.

John, L. K., Loewenstein, G., & Rick, S. I. (2014). Cheating more for less: Upward social comparisons motivate the poorly compensated to cheat. *Organizational Behavior and Human Decision Processes, 123*(2), 101–109.

John, O., Naumann, L., & Soto, C. (2008). Paradigm shift to the integrative big five trait taxonomy: History, measurement, and conceptual issues, In O. John, R. Robins, & L. Pervin (Eds.), *Handbook of personality: Theory and research* (3rd ed. pp., 114–158). New York: Guilford.

Johnco, C., Wuthrich, V. M., & Rapee, R. M. (2013). The role of cognitive flexibility in cognitive restructuring skill acquisition among older adults. *Journal of Anxiety Disorders, 27*(6), 576–584.

Johnson, D. & Cannizzaro, M. S. (2009). Sentence comprehension in agrammatic aphasia: History and variability to clinical implications. *Clinical Linguistics and Phonetics, 23*(1), 15–37.

Johnson, E. O., Roth, T., Schultz, L., & Breslau, N. (2006). Epidemiology of DSM-IV insomnia in adolescence: Lifetime prevalence, chronicity, and an emergent gender difference. *Pediatrics, 117*, 247–256.

Johnson, G. (2002). Comments on lithium toxicity. *Australian and New Zealand Journal of Psychiatry, 36*, 703.

Johnson, I. R., & Fujita, K. (2012). Change we can believe in: Using perceptions of changeability to promote system-change motives over system-justification motives in information search. *Psychological Science, 23*(2), 133–140. doi:10.1177/0956797611423670.

Johnson, J., & Vickers, Z. (1993). Effects of flavor and macronutrient composition of food servings on liking, hunger and subsequent intake. *Appetite, 21*(1), 25–39.

Johnson, J. G., Cohen, P., Smailes, E. M., Kasen, S., & Brook, J. S. (2002). Television viewing and aggressive behavior during adolescence and adulthood. *Science, 295*, 2468–2471.

Johnson, J. M., & Endler, N. S. (2002). Coping with human immunodeficiency virus: Do optimists fare better? *Current Psychology: Developmental, Learning, Personality, Social, 21*, 3–16.

Johnson, J. S., & Newport, E. L. (1989). Critical period effects in second language learning. *Cognitive Psychology, 21*, 60–99.

Johnson, M. A., Dziurawiec, S., Ellis, H., & Morton, J. (1991). Newborns' preferential tracking of face-like stimuli and its subsequent decline. *Cognition, 4*, 1–19.

Johnson, S. L. (2003). *Therapist's guide to clinical intervention: The 1-2-3's of treatment planning.* San Diego, CA: Academic Press.

Johnson, S. L., & Birch, L. L. (1994). Parents' and children's adiposity and eating style. *Pediatrics, 94*, 653–656.

Johnson, S. L., Edge, M. D., Holmes, M. K., & Carver, C. S. (2012). The behavioral activation system and mania. *Annual Review of Clinical Psychology, 8*, 243–267.

Johnson, W., McGue, M., & Krueger, R. F. (2005). Personality stability in late adulthood: A behavioral genetic analysis. *Journal of Personality, 73*, 523–551.

Johnson, W., Turkheimer, E., Gottesman, I. I., & Bouchard, T. J., Jr. (2009). Beyond heritability: Twin studies in behavioral research. *Current Directions in Psychological Science, 18*, 217–220.

Johnson-Greene, D. & Collins, K. C. (2011). Characteristics of American Psychological Association Division 40 (clinical neuropsychology) Fellows. *Clinical Neuropsychology, 25*(8), 1378–1385.

Johnson-Laird, P. N. (1983). *Mental models: Toward a cognitive science of language, inference, and consciousness.* Cambridge, MA: Harvard University Press.

Johnson-Laird, P. N. (2010). Mental models and human reasoning. *Proceedings of the National Academy of Sciences, 107*, 18243–18250.

Johnson-Laird, P. N., Mancini, F., & Gangemi, A. (2006). A hyper-emotion theory of psychological illnesses. *Psychological Review, 113*, 822–841.

Johnston, D. W., Tuomisto, M. T., & Patching, G. R. (2008). The relationship between cardiac reactivity in the laboratory and in real life. *Health Psychology, 27*, 34–42.

Johnston, K. (1988). Adolescents' solutions to dilemmas in fables: Two moral orientations. In C. Gilligan, J. V. Ward, J. M. Taylor, & B. Bardige (Eds.), *Mapping the moral domain: A contribution to psychological theory and education.* Cambridge: Harvard University Press.

Johnston, L. D., O'Malley, P. M., Bachman, J. G., & Schulenberg, J. E. (2004). *Monitoring the Future national survey results on drug use, 1975–2003. Vol. 1. Secondary school students* (NIH Publication No. 04–5507). Bethesda, MD: National Institute on Drug Abuse.

Joireman, J., & Durell, B. (2007). Self-transcendent values moderate the impact of mortality salience on support for charities. *Personality and Individual Differences, 43*, 779–789.

Jokela, M. (2010). Characteristics of the first child predict the parents' probability of having another child. *Developmental Psychology, 46*, 915–926.

Jones, A. (2007). Maternal alcohol abuse/dependence, children's behavior problems, and home environment: Estimates from the national longitudinal survey of youth using propensity score matching. *Journal of Studies on Alcohol and Drugs, 68*(2), 266–275.

Jones, C., & Meaden, A. (2012). Schizophrenia. In P. Sturmey & M. Hersen (Eds.), *Handbook of evidence-based practice in clinical psychology, Vol 2: Adult disorders* (pp. 221–242). Hoboken, NJ: Wiley.

Jones, E. E. (1982). Psychotherapists' impressions of treatment outcome as a function of race. *Journal of Clinical Psychology, 38*, 722–731.

Jones, G. V. (1990). Misremembering a common object: When left is not right. *Memory & Cognition, 18*, 174–182.

Jones, H. E. (2006). Drug addiction during pregnancy. *Current Directions in Psychological Science, 15*, 126–130.

Jones, J. R., & Schaubroeck, J. (2004). Mediators of the relationship between race and organizational citizenship behavior. *Journal of Managerial Issues, 16*, 505–527.

Jones, P. M., & Haselgrove, M. (2011). Overshadowing and associability change. *Journal of Experimental Psychology: Animal Behavior Processes, 37*, 287–299.

Jorm, A. F. (2012). Mental health literacy: Empowering the community to take action for better mental health. *American Psychologist, 67*(3), 231–243. doi:10.1037/a0025957.

Joseph, J. E., Liu, X., Jiang, Y., Lynam, D., & Kelly, T. (2009). Neural correlates of emotional reactivity in sensation seeking. *Psychological Science, 20*, 215–223.

Josephson Institute, Center for Youth Ethics (2012). Report Card on the ethics of American youth: Violence, bullying and high-risk behavior. Retrieved from: http://charactercounts.org/programs/reportcard/

Josephson, W. L. (1987). Television violence and children's aggression: Testing the priming, social script, and disinhibition predictions. *Journal of Personality and Social Psychology, 53*, 882–890.

Joska, J. A., & Stein, D. J. (2008). Mood disorders. In R. E. Hales, S. C. Yudofsky, & G. O. Gabbard (Eds.), *Textbook of psychiatry* (pp. 457–503). Washington, DC: American Psychiatric Publishing.

Joy, C. B., Adams, C. E., & Lawrie, S. M. (2006). Haloperidol versus placebo for schizophrenia. *Cochrane Database of Systemic Reviews, 18*(4), CD003082.

Juarascio, A., Forman, E., Timko, C., Herbert, J., Butryn, M., & Lowe, M. (2011). Implicit internalization of the thin ideal as a predictor of increases in weight, body dissatisfaction, and disordered eating. *Eating Behaviors, 12*(3), 207–213.

Judd, F. K., Jackson, H. J., Komiti, A., Murray, G., Hodgins, G., Fraser, C. (2002). High prevalence disorders in urban and rural communities. *Australian and New Zealand Journal of Psychiatry, 36,* 104–113.

Judge, T. A., & Cable, D. M. (2011). When it comes to pay, do the thin win? The effect of weight on pay for men and women. *Journal of Applied Psychology, 96,* 95–112. doi:10.1037/a0020860.

Judge, T. A., Colbert, A. E., & Ilies, R. (2004). Intelligence and leadership: A quantitative review and test of theoretical propositions. *Journal of Applied Psychology, 89,* 542–552.

Judge, T.A., Heller, D., & Mount, M. K. (2002). Five-factor model of personality and job satisfaction: A meta-analysis. *Journal of Applied Psychology, 87,* 530–541.

Judge, T. A., Ilies, R., & Dimotakis, N. (2010). Are health and happiness the product of wisdom? The relationship of general mental ability to educational and occupational attainment, health, and well-being. *Journal of Applied Psychology, 95,* 454–468.

Judge, T. A., Thoresen, C. J., Bono, J. E., & Patton, G. K. (2001). The job satisfaction-job performance relationship: A qualitative and quantitative review. *Psychological Bulletin, 127,* 376–407.

Julien, R. M. (2005). *A primer of drug action* (10th ed.). New York: Worth.

Julien, R. M. (2008). *A primer of drug action* (11th ed.). New York: Worth.

Jung, C. G. (1916). *Analytical psychology.* New York: Moffat.

Jung, C. G. (1933). *Psychological types.* New York: Harcourt, Brace and World.

Jussim, L., & Eccles, J. S. (1992). Teacher expectations: II. Construction and reflection of student achievement. *Journal of Personality and Social Psychology, 63,* 947–961.

Just, M. A., Carpenter, P. A., Keller, T. A., Emery, L., Zajac, H., & Thulborn, K. R. (2001). Interdependence of nonoverlapping cortical systems in dual cognitive tasks. *Neuroimage, 14,* 417–426.

Just, N., & Alloy, L. B. (1997). The response styles theory of depression: Tests and an extension of the theory. *Journal of Abnormal Psychology, 106,* 221–229.

Kagan, J. R., Snidman, N., Arcus, D., & Resnick, J. S. (1994). *Galen's prophecy: Temperament in human nature.* New York: Basic Books.

Kahn, E., & Rachman, A. W. (2000). Carl Rogers and Heinz Kohut: A historical perspective. *Psychoanalytic Psychology, 17,* 294–312.

Kahn, I., Knoblich, U., Desai, M., Bernstein, J., Graybiel, A. M., Boyden, E. S., Buckner, R. L., & Moore, C. I. (2013). Optogenetic drive of neocortical pyramidal neurons generates fMRI signals that are correlated with spiking activity. *Brain Research, 1511,* 33–45.

Kahneman, D., & Shane, F. (2005). A model of heuristic judgment. In K. Holyoak & R. G. Morrison (Eds.), *The Cambridge handbook of thinking and reasoning* (pp. 267–293). New York: Cambridge University Press.

Kahneman, D., & Tversky, A. (1973). On the psychology of prediction. *Psychological Review, 80,* 237–251.

Kaiser, R. B., Hogan, R., & Craig, S. B. (2008). Leadership and the fate of organizations. *American Psychologist, 63,* 96–110.

Kaitaro, T. (2001). Biological and epistemological models of localization in the nineteenth century: From Gall to Charcot. *Journal of Historical Neuroscience, 10*(3), 262–276.

Kajantie, E. (2008). Physiological stress response, estrogen, and the male-female mortality gap. *Current Directions in Psychological Science, 17,* 348–352.

Kajantie, E. J., & Phillips, D. I. W. (2006). The effects of sex and hormonal status on the physiological response to acute psychosocial stress. *Psychoneuroendocrinology, 31,* 151–178.

Kajiya, K., Inaki, K., Tanaka, M., Haga, T., Kataoka, H., & Touhara, K. (2001). Molecular bases of odor discrimination: Reconstitution of olfactory receptors that recognize overlapping sets of odorants. *Journal of Neuroscience, 21,* 6018–6025.

Kalcher-Sommersguter, E., Preuschoft, S., Crailsheim, K., & Franz, C. (2011). Social competence of adult chimpanzees (Pan troglodytes) with severe deprivation history: I. An individual approach. *Developmental Psychology, 47*(1), 77–90. doi:10.1037/a0020783.

Kalechstein, A. D., De La Garza, R., II, Mahoney, J. J., III, Fantegrossi, W. E., & Newton, T. F. (2007). MDMA use and neurocognition: A meta-analytic review. *Psychopharmacology* (Berlin), *189,* 531–537.

Kales, H. C., DiNardo, A. R., Blow, F. C., McCarthy, J. F., et al. (2006). International medical graduates and the diagnosis and treatment of late-life depression. *Academic Medicine, 81,* 171–175.

Kales, H. C., Neighbors, H. W., Blow, F. C., Taylor, K. K., et al. (2005a). Race, gender, and psychiatrists' diagnosis and treatment of major depression among elderly patients. *Psychiatric Services, 56,* 721–728.

Kales, H. C., Neighbors, H. W., Valenstein, M., Blow, F. C., et al. (2005b). Effect of race and sex on primary care physicians' diagnosis and treatment of late-life depression. *Journal of the American Geriatrics Society, 53,* 777–784.

Kalivas, P. W., & Volkow, N. D. (2005). The neural basis of addiction: A pathology of motivation and choice. *American Journal of Psychiatry, 162,* 1403–1413.

Kalluri, H. S., & Dempsey, R. J. (2008). Growth factors, stem cells, and stroke. *Neurosurgery Focus, 24*(3–4), E14.

Kaminski, J. W., Valle, L. A., Filene, J. H., & Boyle, C. L. (2008). A meta-analytic review of components associated with parent training program effectiveness. *Journal of Abnormal Child Psychology, 36,* 567–589.

Kammeyer-Mueller, J. D., Wanberg, C. R., Glomb, T. M., & Ahlburg, D. (2005). The role of temporal shifts in turnover processes: It's about time. *Journal of Applied Psychology, 90,* 644–658.

Kan, K. J., Wicherts, J. M., Dolan, C. V., & van der Maas, H. L. J. (2013). On the nature and nurture of intelligence and specific cognitive abilities: The more heritable, the more culture dependent. *Psychological Science, 24,* 2420–2428.

Kanaya, T., Scullin, M. H., & Ceci, S. J. (2003). The Flynn effect and U.S. policies. *American Psychologist, 58,* 778–790.

Kanazawa, S., & Fontaine, L. (2013). Intelligent people defect more in a one-shot prisoner's dilemma game. *Journal of Neuroscience, Psychology, and Economics, 6*(3), 201–213.

Kandler, C., Bleidorn, W., Riemann, R., Spinath, F. M., Thiel, W., & Angleitner, A. (2010). Sources of cumulative continuity in personality: A longitudinal multiple-rater twin study. *Journal of Personality Social Psychology, 98,* 995–1008.

Kane, R. L. (1991). Standardized and flexible batteries in neuropsychology: an assessment update. *Neuropsychology Review, 2*(4), 281–339.

Kaner, A., & Prelinger, E. (2007). *The craft of psychodynamic psychotherapy* (2nd ed.). Lanham, MD: Jason Aronson Publishers.

Kanno, T., Mitsugi, M., Sukegawa, S., Hosoe, M., & Furuki, Y. (2008). Computer-simulated bi-directional alveolar distraction osteogenesis. *Clinical Oral Implants Research, 19*(12), 1211–1218.

Kanoski, S. E., & Davidson, T. L. (2011). Western diet consumption and cognitive impairment: Links to hippocampal dysfunction and obesity. *Physiology & Behavior, 103*(1), 59–68.

Kanoski, S. E., Fortin, S. M., Ricks, K. M., & Grill, H. J. (2013). Ghrelin signaling in the ventral hippocampus stimulates learned and motivational aspects of feeding via PI3K-Akt signaling. *Biological Psychiatry, 73*(9), 915–923.

Kanwisher, N. (2010). Functional specificity in the human brain: A window into the functional architecture of the mind. *Proceedings of The National Academy of Sciences of The United States of America, 107*(25), 11163–11170. doi:10.1073/pnas.1005062107.

Kao, T., Shumsky, J. S., Murray, M., & Moxon, K. A. (2009). Exercise induces cortical plasticity after neonatal spinal cord injury in the rat. *Journal of Neuroscience, 29,* 7549–7557.

Kaplan, J. A (2014). GlassesOff app claims to eliminate need for reading glasses. *FoxNews.com.* Published January 23, 2014.

Kapogiannis, D., Barbey, A. K., Su, M., Zamboni, G., Krueger, F., & Grafman, J. (2009). Cognitive and neural foundations of religious belief. *Proceedings of the National Academy of Sciences, 106,* 4876–4881.

Kapp, S. K., Gillespie-Lynch, K., Sherman, L. E., & Hutman, T. (2013). Deficit, difference, or both? Autism and neurodiversity. *Developmental Psychology, 49,* 59–71.

Kaptchuk, T. J., Stason, W. B., Legedza, A. R. T., Schnyer, R. N., et al. (2006). Sham device vs. inert pill: Randomised controlled trial of two placebo treatments. *British Medical Journal, 332,* 391–397.

Kapur, N. (1999). Syndromes of retrograde amnesia: A conceptual and empirical synthesis. *Psychological Bulletin, 125,* 800–825.

Karakaya, T, Fuber, F., Schroder, J. & Pantel, J. (2013). Pharmacological treatment of mild cognitive impairment as a prodromal syndrome of Alzheimer´s disease. *Current Neuropharmacology, 11*(1), 102–108.

Karevold, E., Røysamb, E., Ystrom, E., & Mathiesen, K. S. (2009). Predictors and pathways from infancy to symptoms of anxiety and depression in early adolescence. *Developmental Psychology, 45,* 1051–1060.

Karidi M.V., Vasilopoulou D., Savvidou E., Vitoratou S., Rabavilas A.D., Stefanis C.N. (2014). Aspects of perceived stigma: The stigma inventory for mental illness, its development, latent structure and psychometric properties. *Comprehensive Psychiatry; 55,* 1620–1625.

Karimi-Abdolrezaee, S., & Eftekharpour, E. (2013). Stem cells and spinal cord injury repair. *Advances in Experimental Medicine & Biology, 760,* 53–73.

Karlin, B. E., & Cross, G. (2014). From the laboratory to the therapy room: National dissemination and implementation of evidence-based psychotherapies in the U.S. Department of Veterans Affairs Health Care System. *American Psychologist, 69*(1), 19–33.

Karlsgodt, K. H., Daqiang, S., & Cannon, T. D. (2010). Structural and functional brain abnormalities in schizophrenia. *Current Directions in Psychological Science, 19*(4), 226–231. doi:10.1177/0963721410377601.

Karni, A., Meyer, G., Adams, M., Turner, R., & Ungerleider, L. G. (1994). The acquisition and retention of a motor skill: A functional MRI study of long-term motor cortex plasticity. *Abstracts of the Society for Neuroscience, 20,* 1291.

Karon, B. P., & Widener, A. J. (1997). Repressed memories and World War II: Lest we forget. *Professional Psychology: Research and Practice, 28*(4), 338–340.

Karp, D. A. (1991). A decade of reminders: Changing age consciousness between fifty and sixty years old. In B. B. Hess & E. W. Markson (Eds.), *Growing old in America* (pp. 67–92). New Brunswick, NJ: Transaction.

Karpicke, J. D. (2012). Retrieval-Based Learning: Active Retrieval Promotes Meaningful Learning. *Current Directions In Psychological Science (Sage Publications Inc.), 21*(3), 157–163. doi:10.1177/0963721412443552.

Karpicke, J. D., & Blunt, J. R. (2011). Retrieval practice produces more learning than elaborative studying with concept mapping. *Science, 331*(6018), 772–775. doi:10.1126/science.1199327.

Karpicke, J. D., & Smith, M. A. (2012). Separate mnemonic effects of retrieval practice and elaborative encoding. *Journal Of Memory And Language,* doi:10.1016/j.jml.2012.02.004

Karremans, J. C., Stroebe, W., & Claus, J. (2006). Beyond Vicary's fantasies: The impact of subliminal priming and brand choice. *Journal of Experimental Social Psychology, 42,* 792–798.

Karsen, E. F., Watts, B.V., & Holtzheimer, P. E. (2014). Review of the effectiveness of transcranial magnetic stimulation for post-traumatic stress disorder. *Brain Stimulation, 7*(2), 151–157.

Karuza, E. A., Emberson, L. L., & Aslin, R. N. (2013). Combining fMRI and behavioral measures to examine the process of human learning. *Neurobiology of Learning & Memory, 109C,* 193–206.

Kashima, H., & Hayashi, N. (2011). Basic taste stimuli elicit unique responses in facial skin blood flow. *PLoS One, 6*(12), e28236.

Kaslow, F. W. (2011). Family therapy. In J. C. Norcross, G. R. VandenBos, & D. K. Freedheim (Eds.), *History of psychotherapy: Continuity and change* (pp. 497–504). Washington, DC: American Psychological Association.

Kasper, S., & Papadimitriou, G. N. (Eds.) (2009). *Schizophrenia* (2nd ed.). New York: Informa Health Care.

Kasser, T., & Sharma, Y. S. (1999). Reproductive freedom, educational equality, and females' preference for resource-acquisition characteristics in mates. *Psychological Science, 10,* 374–377.

Kassin, S., Fein, S., & Markus, H. (2008). *Social psychology* (9th ed). Boston: Houghton-Mifflin.

Kassin, S. M., Dror, I. E., & Kukucka, J. (2013). The forensic confirmation bias: Problems, perspectives, and proposed solutions. *Journal of Applied Research in Memory and Cognition, 2,* 42–52.

Kassin, S. M., Fein, S., & Markus, H. R. (2010). *Social psychology* (8th ed.). Belmont, CA: Wadsworth.

Kassinove, H., Roth, D., Owens, S., & Fuller, J. (2002). Effects of trait anger and anger expression style on competitive attack responses in a wartime prisoner's dilemma game. *Aggressive Behavior, 28*(2), 117–125.

Kastin, A. J., & Pan, W. (2005). Targeting neurite growth inhibitors to induce CNS regeneration. *Current Pharmaceutical Design, 11,* 1247–1253.

Katkin, E. S., Wiens, S., & Öhman, A. (2001). Nonconscious fear conditioning, visceral perception, and the development of gut feelings. *Psychological Science, 12,* 366–370.

Kato, M., & Serretti, A. (2010). Review and meta-analysis of antidepressant pharmacogenetic findings in major depressive disorder. *Molecular Psychiatry, 15,* 473–500. Epub 2008 Nov 4.

Kato, P. M. (2010). Video games in health care: Closing the gap. *Review Of General Psychology, 14*(2), 113–121. doi:10.1037/a0019441.

Kato, S., Wakasa, Y., & Yamagita, T. (1987). Relationship between minimum reinforcing doses and injection speed in cocaine and pentobarbital self-administration in crab-eating monkeys. *Pharmacology, Biochemistry, and Behavior, 28,* 407–410.

Katsetos, C., Smith, E. R., & Scott, R. M. (2009). Cerebrovascular disorders in children. In A. Legido & J. H. Piatt (Eds.), *Clinical Pediatric Neurosciences, Elk Grove Village* (1st ed.). American Academy of Pediatrics, 171–215.

Katzell, R. A., & Austin, J. T. (1992). From then to now: The development of industrial-organizational psychology in the United States. *Journal Of Applied Psychology, 77*(6), 803–835. doi:10.1037/0021–9010.77.6.803.

Katzell, R. A., & Thompson, D. E. (1990). Work motivation: Theory and practice. *American Psychologist, 45,* 144–153.

Kauffman, N. A., Herman, C. P., & Polivy, J. (1995). Hunger-induced finickiness in humans. *Appetite, 24,* 203–218.

Kaushanskaya, M. (2009). The bilingual advantage in novel word learning. *Psychonomic Bulletin and Review, 16,* 705–710.

Kaushanskaya, M., Gross, M., & Buac, M. (2014). Effects of classroom bilingualism on task-shifting, verbal memory, and word learning in children. *Developmental Science,* Epub February 27, 2014.

Kavanagh, P. S., Robins, S. C., & Ellis, B. J. (2010). The mating sociometer: A regulatory mechanism for mating aspirations. *Journal of Personality and Social Psychology, 99,* 120–132.

Kawasaki, H., Adolphs, R., Kaufman, O., Damasio, H., Damasio, A. R., Granner, M., et al. (2001). Single-neuron responses to emotional visual stimuli recorded in human ventral prefrontal cortex. *Nature Neuroscience, 4,* 15–16.

Kay, L. M., & Sherman, S. (2007). An argument for an olfactory thalamus. *Trends In Neurosciences, 30*(2), 47–53. doi:10.1016/j.tins.2006.11.007.

Kaye, W. H., Klump, K. L., Frank, G. K., & Strober, M. (2000). Anorexia and bulimia nervosa. *Annual Review of Medicine, 51,* 299–313.

Kaye, W. H., Wierenga, C. E., Bailer, U. F., Simmons, A. N., & Bischoff-Grethe, A. (2013). Nothing tastes as good as skinny feels: The neurobiology of anorexia nervosa. *Trends in Neurosciences, 36*(2), 110–120.

Kayser, S., Bewernick, B. H., Grubert, C., Hadrysiewicz, B. L., Axmacher, N., & Schlaepfer, T. E. (2011). Antidepressant effects, of magnetic seizure therapy and electroconvulsive therapy, in treatment-resistant depression. *Journal of Psychiatry Research, 45*(5), 569–576.

Kayyal, M. H., & Russell, J. A. (2013). Americans and Palestinians judge spontaneous facial expressions of emotion. *Emotion, 13*(5), 891–904.

Kazak, A. E., Hoagwood, K., Weisz, J. R., Hood, K., Kratochwill, T. R., Vargas, L. A., & Banez, G. A. (2010). A meta-systems approach to evidence-based practice for children and adolescents. *American Psychologist, 65*(2), 85–97. doi:10.1037/a0017784.

Kazantzis, N., Lampropoulos, G. K., & Deane, F. P. (2005). A national survey of practicing psychologists' use and attitudes toward homework in psychotherapy. *Journal of Consulting and Clinical Psychology, 73,* 742–748.

Kazarian, S. S., & Evans, D. R. (Eds.). (2001). *Handbook of cultural health psychology.* New York: Academic Press.

Kazdin, A. E. (2008). *Behavior modification in applied settings* (6th ed.). Long Grove, IL: Waveland Press.

Kazdin, A. E. (2011). Evidence-based treatment research: Advances, limitations, and next steps. *American Psychologist, 66,* 685–698.

Kazdin, A. E., & Benjet, C. (2003). Spanking children: Evidence and issues. *Current Directions in Psychological Science, 12,* 99–103.

Kealy, E. M. (2005). Variations in the experience of schizophrenia: A cross-cultural review. *Journal of Social Work Research and Evaluation, 6,* 47–56.

Keating, D. P. (1990). Adolescent thinking. In S. S. Feldman & G. R. Elliott (Eds.), *At the threshold: The developing adolescent* (pp. 4–89). Cambridge, MA: Harvard University Press.

Keefe, J. R., McCarthy, K. S., Dinger, U., Zilcha-Mano, S., & Barber, J. P. (2014). *Clinical Psychology Review, 34*(4), 309–323.

Keeling, L. J., & Hurink, J. F. (1996). Social facilitation acts more on the consummatory phase on feeding behaviour. *Animal Behaviour, 52,* 11–15.

Keesey, R. E. (1980). A set-point analysis of the regulation of body weight. In A. J. Stunkard (Ed.), *Obesity* (pp. 144–165). Philadelphia: Saunders.

Keesey, R. E., & Powley, T. L. (1986). The regulation of body weight. *Annual Review of Psychology, 37,* 109–133.

Keesey, R. E., & Powley, T. L. (1975). Hypothalamic regulation of body weight. *American Scientist, 63,* 558–565.

Keleş, A., Keleş, A., & Yavuz, U. (2011). Expert system based on neuro-fuzzy rules for diagnosis breast cancer. *Expert Systems With Applications, 38*(5), 5719–5726. doi:10.1016/j.eswa.2010.10.061.

Kelesidis, T., Kelesidis, L., Chou, S., & Mantzoros, C. S. (2010). The role of leptin in human physiology: Emerging clinical applications. *Annals of Internal Medicine, 152,* 93–100.

Keller, M. C., & Nesse, R. M. (2006). The evolutionary significance of depressive symptoms: Different adverse situations lead to different depressive symptom patterns. *Journal of Personality and Social Psychology, 91,* 316–330.

Keller, R. T. (2006). Transformational leadership, initiating structure, and substitutes for leadership: A longitudinal study of research and development project team performance. *Journal of Applied Psychology, 91,* 202–210.

Keller-Cohen, D., Toler, A., Miller, D., Fiori, K., & Bybee, D. (2004, August). *Social contact and communication in people over 85.* Paper presented at the convention of the American Psychological Association, Honolulu, HI.

Kelley, K. W. (1985). Immunological consequences of changing environmental stimuli. In G. P. Moberg (Ed.), *Animal stress.* Bethesda, MD: American Physiological Society.

Kelly, D. J., Quinn, P. C., Slater, A. M., Lee, K., Ge, L., & Pascalis, O. (2007). The other-race effect develops during infancy: Evidence of perceptual narrowing. *Psychological Science 18,* 1084–1089.

Kelly, M. E., Loughrey, D., Lawlor, B. A., Robertson, I. H., Walsh, C., & Brennan, S. (2014). The impact of cognitive training and mental stimulation on cognitive and everyday functioning of healthy older adults: A systematic review and meta-analysis. *Ageing Research Reviews, 15,* 28–43.

Kelly, T., Yang, W., Chen, C.-S., Reynolds, K., & He, J. (2008). Global burden of obesity in 2005 and projections to 2030. *International Journal of Obesity, 32,* 1431–1437.

Kelly, T. H., Foltin, R. W., Emurian, C. S., & Fischman, M. W. (1990). Multidimensional behavioral effects of marijuana. *Progress in Neuro-Psychopharmacology and Biological Psychiatry, 14,* 885–902.

Kemeny, M. E. (2003). The psychobiology of stress. *Current Directions in Psychological Science, 12,* 124–129.

Kendall, P. C., & Chambless, D. L. (Eds.). (1998). Special section: Empirically supported psychological therapies. *Journal of Consulting and Clinical Psychology, 66,* 3–167.

Kendall, P. C., Hudson, J. L., Gosch, E., Flannery-Schroeder, E., & Suveg, C. (2008). Cognitive-behavioral therapy for anxiety disordered youth: A randomized clinical trial evaluating child and family modalities. *Journal of Consulting and Clinical Psychology, 76,* 282–297.

Kendler, K. S., Eaves, L. J., Loken, E. K., Pedersen, N. L., Middeldorp, C. M., Reynolds, C., & .. Gardner, C. O. (2011). The impact of environmental experiences on symptoms of anxiety and depression across the life span. *Psychological Science, 22*(10), 1343–1352. doi:10.1177/0956797611417255.

Kendler, K. S., Fisk, A., Gardner, C. O., & Gatz, M. (2009). Delineation of two genetic pathways to major depression. *Biological Psychiatry, 65,* 808–811.

Kendler, K. S., Gardner, C. C., & Dick, D. M. (2011). Predicting alcohol consumption in adolescence from alcohol-specific and general externalizing genetic risk factors, key environmental exposures and their interaction. *Psychological Medicine: A Journal of Research in Psychiatry and the Allied Sciences, 41*(7), 1507–1516. doi:10.1017/S003329171000190X

Kendler, K. S., & Neale, M. C. (2009). "Familiality" or heritability? *Archives of General Psychiatry, 66,* 452–453.

Kendler, K. S., Thornton, L. M., Gilman, S. E., & Kessler, R. C. (2000). Sexual orientation in a U.S. national sample of twin and non-twin sibling pairs. *American Journal of Psychiatry, 157,* 1843–1846.

Kennedy, K. A., & Pronin, E. (2008). When disagreement gets ugly: Perceptions of bias and the escalation of conflict. *Personality and Social Psychology Bulletin, 34,* 833–848.

Kenrick, D., Neuberg, S., & Cialdini, R. (2005). *Social psychology: Unraveling the mystery* (3rd ed). Boston: Pearson.

Kenrick, D., Neuberg, S., & Cialdini, R. (2007). *Social psychology: Goals in interaction* (4th ed.). Upper Saddle River, NJ: Pearson.

Kenrick, D. T. (2012). Evolutionary theory and human social behavior. In P. A. M. Van Lange, A. W. Kruglanski, & E. T. Higgins (Eds.), *Handbook of Theories of Social Psychology (Vol. 1).* Thousand Oaks, CA: Sage Publications Ltd.

Kenrick, D. T., Griskevicius, V., Neuberg, S. L., & Schaller, M. (2010). Renovating the pyramid of needs: Contemporary extensions built upon ancient foundations. *Perspectives On Psychological Science, 5*(3), 292–314. doi:10.1177/1745691610369469.

Kensinger, E. A., & Corkin, S. (2004). Two routes to emotional memory: Distinct neural processes for valence and arousal. *Proceedings of the National Academy of Sciences, 101,* 3310–3315.

Kent, D. L. (2014). Age-related macular degeneration: Beyond anti-angiogenesis. *Molecular Vision, 20,* 46–55.

Kent, S., Rodriguez, F., Kelley, K. W., & Dantzer, R. (1994). Reduction in food and water intake induced by microinjection of interleukin-1b in the ventromedial hypothalamus of the rat. *Physiology and Behavior, 56*(5), 1031–1036.

Kenworthy, J. B., Turner, R. N., Hewstone, M., & Voci, A. (2006). Intergroup contact: When does it work, and why. In J. Dovidio, P. Glick, & L. Rudman (Eds.), *On the nature of prejudice: Fifty years after Allport.* Boston, MA: Blackwell.

Keogh, E., Bond, F. W., & Flaxman, P. E. (2006). Improving academic performance and mental health through a stress management intervention: Outcomes and mediators of change. *Behaviour Research and Therapy, 44,* 339–357.

Kepner, J. (2001). Touch in Gestalt body process psychotherapy: Purpose, practice, and ethics. *Gestalt Review, 5,* 97–114.

Keri, S. (2009). Genes for psychosis and creativity: A promoter polymorphism of the neuregulin 1 gene is related to creativity in people with high intellectual achievement. *Psychological Science, 20,* 1070–1073.

Kermer, D. A., Driver-Linn, E., Wilson, T. D., & Gilbert, D. T. (2006). Loss aversion is an affective forecasting error. *Psychological Science, 17,* 649–653.

Kern, M. L., & Friedman, H. S. (2008). Do conscientious individuals live longer? A quantitative review. *Health Psychology, 27,* 505–512.

Kerns, K.A. & Brumariu, L.E. (2013). Is insecure parent–child attachment a risk factor for the development of anxiety in childhood or adolescence? *Child Development Perspectives, 8,* 12–17.

Kerr, M. P., & Payne, S. J. (1994). Learning to use a spreadsheet by doing and by watching. *Interacting with Computers, 6,* 3–22.

Kerstjens, J. M., de Winter, A. F., Bocca-Tjeertes, I. F., ten Vergert, E. J., Reijneveld, S. A., & Bos, A. F. (2011). Developmental delay in moderately preterm-born children at school entry. *The Journal of Pediatrics, 159*(1), 92–98. doi:10.1016/j.jpeds.2010.12.041.

Kesari, K. K., Siddiqui, M. H., Meena, R., Verma, H. N., & Kumar, S. (2013) Cell phone radiation exposure on brain and associated biological systems. *Indian Journal of Experimental Biology, 51,* 187–200.

Keselman, H. J., Othman, A. R., Wilcox, R. R., & Fradette, K. (2004). The new and improved two-sample t test. *Psychological Science, 15,* 47–51.

Keshavan, M. S., Diwadkar, V. A., Montrose, D. M., Rajarethinam, R., & Sweeny, J. A. (2005). Premorbid indicators and risk for schizophrenia: A selective review and update. *Schizophrenia Research, 79,* 45–57.

Kessler, N. J., & Hong, J. (2013). Whole body vibration therapy for painful diabetic peripheral neuropathy: A pilot study. *Journal of Body Work and Movement Therapies, 17*(4), 518–522

Kessler, R., Avenevoli, S., Costello, E., Georgiades, K., Green, J., Gruber, M., & Merikangas, K. (2012). Prevalence, persistence, and sociodemographic correlates of DSM-IV disorders in the National Comorbidity Survey Replication Adolescent Supplement. *Archives Of General Psychiatry, 69*(4), 372–380.

Kessler, R. C., Berglund, P., Borges, G., Nock, M., & Wang, P. S. (2005). Trends in suicide ideation, plans, gestures, and attempts in the United States, 1990–1992 to 2001–2003. *Journal of the American Medical Association, 293,* 2487–2495.

Kessler, R. C., Chiu, W. T., Jin, R., Ruscio, A. M., Shear, K., & Walters, E. E. (2006). The epidemiology of panic attacks, panic disorder, and agoraphobia in the National Comorbidity Survey Replication. *Archives of General Psychiatry, 63,* 415–424.

Kessler, R. C., Galea, S., Gruber, M. J., Sampson, N. A., Ursano, R. J., & Wessely, S. (2008). Trends in mental illness and suicidality after Hurricane Katrina. *Molecular Psychiatry, 13,* 374–384.

Kessler, R. C., Ruscio, A., Shear, K., & Wittchen, H.-U. (2009). Epidemiology of anxiety disorders. In M. M. Antony & M. B. Stein (Eds.), *Oxford handbook of anxiety and related disorders* (pp. 19–33). New York: Oxford University Press.

Kessler, R. C., & Ustun, T. B. (Eds.) (2011). *The WHO World Mental Health Surveys: Global perspectives on the epidemiology of mental disorders.* New York: Cambridge University Press.

Kessler, R. C., & Wang, P. S. (2008). The descriptive epidemiology of commonly occurring mental disorders in the United States. *Annual Review of Public Health, 29,* 115–129.

Ketter, T. A. (2010). *Handbook of diagnosis and treatment of bipolar disorders.* Arlington, VA: American Psychiatric Publishing.

Kety, S. S., Wender, P. H., Jacobsen, B., Ingraham, L. J., Jansson, L., Faber, B., & Kinney, D. K. (1994). Mental illness in the biological and adoptive relatives of schizophrenic adoptees. *Archives of General Psychiatry, 51,* 442–455.

Keverne, E. B., & Curley, J. P. (2008). Epigenetics, brain evolution and behaviour. *Frontiers in Neuroendocrinology, 29*(3), 398–412.

Keysar, B., Hayakawa, S. L., & An, S. (2012). The foreign-language effect: Thinking in a foreign tongue reduces decision biases. *Psychological Science, 23*(6), 661–668. doi:10.1177/0956797611432178.

Khan, A., Leventhal, R. M., Khan, S., & Brown, W. A. (2002). Suicide risk in patients with anxiety disorders: A meta-analysis of the FDA database. *Journal of Affective Disorders, 69,* 183–190.

Khann, C., Medsker, G.J., & Ginter, R. (2013). *2012 income and employment survey results for the Society for Industrial and Organizational Psychology [Technical report].* Bowling Green, OH: Society for Industrial and Organizational Psychology.

Khashan, A. S., McNamee, R., Abel, K. M., Pedersen, M. G., Webb, R. T., Kenny, L. C., Mortensen, P. B., & Baker, P. N. (2008). Reduced infant birthweight consequent upon maternal exposure to severe life events. *Psychosomatic Medicine, 70,* 688–694.

Khin, N. A., Chen, Y. F., Yang, Y., Yang, P., & Laughren, T. P. (2011). Exploratory analyses of efficacy data from major depressive disorder trials submitted to the U.S. Food and Drug Administration in support of new drug applications. *Journal of Clinical Psychiatry, 72*(4), 464–472.

Khot, U. N., Khot, M. B., Bajzer, C. T., Sapp, S. K., Ohman, E. M., Brener, S. J., et al. (2003). Prevalence of conventional risk factors in patients with coronary heart disease. *Journal of the American Medical Association, 290,* 898–904.

Kidd, T., Hamer, M., & Steptoe, A. (2011). Examining the association between adult attachment style and cortisol responses to acute stress. *Psychoneuroendocrinology, 36*, 771–779. doi:10.1016/j.psyneuen.2010.10.014

Kiecolt-Glaser, J. K. (2009). Psychoneuroimmunology psychology's gateway to the biomedical future. *Perspectives in Psychological Science, 4*, 367–369.

Kiecolt-Glaser, J. K. (2010). Stress, food, and inflammation: Psychoneuroimmunology and nutrition at the cutting edge. *Psychosomatic Medicine, 72*, 365–369.

Kiecolt-Glaser, J. K., & Glaser, R. (2001). Stress and immunity: Age enhances the risks. *Current Directions in Psychological Science, 10*, 18–21.

Kiecolt-Glaser, J. K., Loving, T. J., Stowell, J. R., Malarkey, W. B., Lemeshow, S., Dickinson, S. L., et al. (2005). Hostile marital interactions, proinflammatory cytokine production, and wound healing. *Archives of General Psychiatry, 62*, 1377–1384.

Kiecolt-Glaser, J. K., McGuire, L., Robles, T. F., & Glaser, R. (2002). Psychoneuroimmunology: Psychological influences on immune function and health. *Journal of Consulting & Clinical Psychology, 70*, 537–547.

Kiecolt-Glaser, J. K., & Newton, T. L. (2001). Marriage and health: His and hers. *Psychological Bulletin, 127*, 472–503.

Kiecolt-Glaser, J. K., Page, G. G., Marucha, P. T., MacCallum, R. C., & Glaser, R. (1998). Psychological influences on surgical recovery: Perspectives from psychoneuroimmunology. *American Psychologist, 11*, 1209–1218.

Kiecolt-Glaser, J. K., Preacher, K. J., MacCallum, R. C., Atkinson, C., Malarkey, W. B., & Glaser, R. (2003). Chronic stress and age-related increases in the proinflammatory cytokine IL-6. *Proceedings of the National Academy of Sciences, 100*, 9090–9095.

Kiesler, D. J. (1996). *Contemporary interpersonal theory and research.* New York: Wiley.

Kievit, R. A., van Rooijen, H., Wicherts, J. M., Waldorp, L. J., Kan, K.-J., Scholte, H. S., & Borsboom, D. (2012). Intelligence and the brain: A model-based approach. *Cognitive Neuroscience, 3*, 89–97.

Kiewra, K. A. (1989). A review of note-taking: The encoding storage paradigm and beyond. *Educational Psychology Review, 1*, 147–172.

Kiff, C. J., Lengua, L. J., & Bush, N. R. (2011). Temperament variation in sensitivity to parenting: Predicting changes in depression and anxiety. *Journal of Abnormal Child Psychology, 39*, 1199–1212.

Kiff, C. J., Lengua, L. J., & Zalewski, M. (2011). Nature and nurturing: Parenting in the context of child temperament. *Clinical Child And Family Psychology Review, 14*(3), 251–301. doi:10.1007/s10567-011-0093-4.

Kihlstrom, J. F. (1999). The psychological unconscious. In L. Pervin & O. John (Eds.), *Handbook of personality* (pp. 424–442). New York: Guilford.

Kihlstrom, J. F. (2005). Dissociative disorders. *Annual Review of Clinical Psychology, 1*, 227–253.

Kihlstrom, J. F. (2012). Unconscious processes. In D. Reisberg (Ed.), *Oxford handbook of cognitive psychology.* Oxford: Oxford University Press.

Kilner, J. M., & Lemon, R. N. (2013). What we know currently about mirror neurons. *Current Biology, 23*(23), R1057–R1062.

Kim, E., Zeppenfeld, V., & Cohen, D. (2014). Sublimation, culture, and creativity. *Journal of Personality and Social Psychology, 105*(4), 639–666.

Kim, E. Y., Mahmoud, G. S., & Grover, L. M. (2005). REM sleep deprivation inhibits LTP in vivo in area CA1 of rat hippocampus. *Neuroscience Letters, 388*, 163–167.

Kim, H., Shimojo, S. and O'Doherty, J. P. (2011). Overlapping responses for the expectation of juice and money rewards in human ventromedial prefrontal cortex *Cerebral Cortex, 21*, 769–776.

Kim, H. I., & Johnson, S. P. (2013). Do young infants prefer an infant-directed face or a happy face? *International Journal of Behavioral Development, 37*, 125–130.

Kim, J., Schallert, D. L., & Kim, M. (2010). An integrative cultural view of achievement motivation: Parental and classroom predictors of children's goal orientations when learning mathematics in Korea. *Journal Of Educational Psychology, 102*(2), 418–437. doi:10.1037/a0018676.

Kim, K. (2008). Meta-analyses of the relationship of creative achievement to both IQ and divergent thinking test scores. *The Journal of Creative Behavior, 42*(2), 106–130. doi:10.1002/j.2162–6057.2008.tb01290.x.

Kim, S.-Y., Adhikari, A., Lee, S. Y., Marshel, J. H., Kim, C. K., Mallory, C. S., Lo, M., Pak, S., Mattis, J., Lim, B. K., Malenka, R. C., Warden, M. R., Neve, R., Tye, K. M., & Deisseroth, K. (2013). Diverging neural pathways assemble a behavioural state from separable features in anxiety. *Nature, 496*(7444), 219–223.

Kim-Cohen, J., & Gold, A. L. (2009). Measured gene-environment interactions and mechanisms promoting resilient development. *Current Directions in Psychological Science, 18*, 138–142.

Kimura, M. & Higuchi, S. (2011). Genetics of alcohol dependence. *Psychiatry and Clinical Neurosciences, 65*(3), 213–25.

King, B. M. (2013). The modern obesity epidemic, ancestral hunter-gatherers, and the sensory/reward control of food intake. *American Psychologist, 68*(2), 88–96.

King, D. B., & DiCicco, T. L. (2007). The relationships between dream content and physical health, mood, and self-construal. *Dreaming, 17*, 127–139.

King, M., Smith, G., & Bartlett, A. (2004). Treatments of homosexuality in Britain since the 1950s—an oral history: The experience of professionals. *British Medical Journal, 328*, 429–432. doi:10.1136/bmj.37984.496725.EE

King, S., St-Hilaire, A., & Heidkamp, D. (2010). Prenatal factors in schizophrenia. *Current Directions in Psychological Science, 19*(4), 209–213. doi:10.1177/0963721410378360.

Kingdom, F. A. (2003). Color brings relief to human vision. *Nature Neuroscience, 6*, 641–644.

Kingsbury, K., & McLeod, K. (2008, June 30). Postcard: Gloucester. *Time, 8.*

Kingston, D. A., Fedoroff, P., Firestone, P., Curry, S., & Bradford, J. (2008). Pornography use and sexual aggression: The impact of frequency and type of pornography use on recidivism among sexual offenders. *Aggressive Behavior, 34*, 341–351.

Kinley, D. J., Cox, B. J., Clara, I., Goodwin, R. D., & Sareen, J. (2009). Panic attacks and their relation to psychological and physical functioning in Canadians: Results from a nationally representative sample. *Canadian Journal of Psychiatry, 54*, 113–118.

Kinsey, A. C., Pomeroy, W. B., & Martin, C. E. (1948). *Sexual behavior in the human male.* Philadelphia: Saunders.

Kinsey, A. C., Pomeroy, W. B., Martin, C. E., & Gebhard, P. H. (1953). *Sexual behavior in the human female.* Philadelphia: Saunders.

Kirkpatrick, B., Buchanan, R. W., Ross, D. E., & Carpenter, W. T., Jr. (2001). A separate disease within the syndrome of schizophrenia. *Archives of General Psychiatry, 58*, 165–171.

Kirkpatrick, B., Fenton, W. S., Carpenter, W. T., Jr., & Marder, S. R. (2006). Consensus statement on negative symptoms. *Schizophrenia Bulletin, 32*, 214–219.

Kirsch, I. (1994a). Clinical hypnosis as a nondeceptive placebo: Empirically derived techniques. *American Journal of Clinical Hypnosis, 37*(2), 95–106.

Kirsch, I. (1994b). Defining hypnosis for the public. *Contemporary Hypnosis, 11*(3), 142–143.

Kirsch, I. (2009). Antidepressants and the placebo response. *Epidemiology and Psychiatric Sciences, 18*, 318–322.

Kirsch, I. (2010). *The emperor's new drugs: Exploding the antidepressant myth.* New York: Basic Books.

Kirsch, I., & Braffman, W. (2001). Imaginative suggestibility and hypnotizability. *Psychological Science, 10*, 57–61.

Kirsch, I., Moore, T. J., Scoboria, A., & Nicholls, S. S. (2002). The emperor's new drugs: An analysis of antidepressant medication data submitted to the U.S. Food and Drug Administration [Electronic version]. *Prevention and Treatment, 5*, np.

Kirsch, I., Scoboria, A., & Moore, T. J. (2002). Antidepressants and placebos: Secrets, revelations, and unanswered questions. *Prevention and Treatment, 5*, np.

Kirschneck, C. R., Ömer, P., Proff, P., & Lippold. C. (2013). Psychological profile and self-administered relaxation in patients with craniofacial pain: A prospective in-office study. *Head and Face Medicine, 9*, 31.

Kirsh, S. J. (2011). Children, adolescents, and media violence: A critical look at the research (2nd ed.). Washington, DC: Sage.

Kirshner, H. S. (2012). Primary progressive aphasia and Alzheimer's disease: Brief history, recent evidence. *Current Neurology and Neuroscience Reports*, 12(6), 709–714.

Kishi, T., & Elmquist, J. K. (2005). Body weight is regulated by the brain: A link between feeding and emotion. *Molecular Psychiatry, 10*, 132–146.

Kishi, T., Yoshimura, R., Fukuo, Y., Kitajima, T., Okochi, T., Matsunaga, S., Inada, T., Kunugi, H., Kato, T., Yoshikawa, T., Ujike, H., Umene-Nakano, W., Nakamura, J., Ozaki, N., Serretti, A., Correll, C. U., & Iwata, N. (2011). The CLOCK gene and mood disorders: A case-control study and meta-analysis. *Chronobiology International*, 28(9), 825–833.

Kisilevsky, B. S., Hains, S. M. J., Lee, K., Xie, X., Huang, H., Ye, H. H., et al. (2003). Effects of experience on fetal voice recognition. *Psychological Science, 14*, 220–224.

Kitano, H., Chi, I., Rhee, S., Law, C., & Lubben, J. (1992). Norms and alcohol consumption: Japanese in Japan, Hawaii, and California. *Journal of Studies on Alcohol, 53*, 33–39.

Kitayama, N., Vaccarino, V., Kutner, M., Weiss, P., & Bremner, J. D. (2005). Magnetic resonance imaging (MRI) measurement of hippocampal volume in posttraumatic stress disorder: A meta-analysis. *Journal of Affective Disorders, 88*, 79–86.

Kitayama, S. (2013). The world of cultural neuroscience. *APS Observer, 26*. 10, 1–4.

Kitayama, S., & Markus, H. R. (1992, May). *Construal of self as cultural frame: Implications for internationalizing psychology.* Paper presented to the Symposium on Internationalization and Higher Education, Ann Arbor, Michigan.

Kitayama, S., Park, H., Sevincer, A., T., Karasawa., M., & Uskul, A. K. (2009). A cultural task analysis of implicit independence: Comparing North America, Western Europe, and East Asia. *Journal of Personality and Social Psychology, 97*, 236–255.

Kitayama, S., & Uchida, Y. (2003). Explicit self-criticism and implicit self-regard: Evaluating self and friend in two cultures. *Journal of Experimental Social Psychology, 39*, 476–482.

Kjaer, T. W., Bertelsen, C., Piccini, P., Brooks, D., Alving, J., & Lou, H. C. (2002). Increased dopamine tone during meditation-induced change of consciousness. *Cognitive Brain Research, 13*, 255–259. doi:10.1016/j.appdev.2008.12.031.

Klahr, A. M., & Burt, S. A. (2104). Elucidating the etiology of individual differences in parenting: A meta-analysis of behavioral genetic research. *Psychological Bulletin, 140*, 544–586.

Klahr, A. M., McGue, M., Iacono, W. G., & Burt, S. (2011). The association between parent–child conflict and adolescent conduct problems over time: Results from a longitudinal adoption study. *Journal of Abnormal Psychology, 120*(1), 46–56. doi:10.1037/a0021350.

Klahr, D., & Simon, H. (1999). Studies of scientific discovery: Complementary approaches and convergent findings. *Psychological Bulletin, 125*, 524–543.

Klasios, J. (2013). Cognitive traits as sexually selected fitness indicators. *Review of General Psychology, 17*(4), 428–442.

Klaus, M. H., & Kennell, J. H. (1976). *Maternal infant bonding: The impact of early separation or loss on family development.* St. Louis: Mosby.

Kleber, B., Veit, R., Birbaumer, N., Gruzelier, J., & Lotze, M. (2009). The brain of opera singers: experience-dependent changes in functional activation. *Cerebral Cortex, 20*(5), 1144–1152.

Klein, D. N. (1993). False suff ocation alarms, spontaneous panics, and related conditions: An integrative hypothesis. *Archives of General Psychiatry, 50*, 306–316.

Klein, D. N. (2010). Chronic depression: Diagnosis and classifi cation. *Current Directions in Psychological Science, 19*, 96–100.

Klein, D. C., & Seligman, M. E. P. (1976). Reversal of performance deficits and perceptual deficits in learned helplessness and depression. *Journal of Abnormal Psychology, 85*, 11–26.

Klein, D. N., Santiago, N. J., Vivian, D., Blalock, J. A., Kocsis, J. H., Markowitz, J. C., et al. (2004). Cognitive-behavioral analysis system of psychotherapy as a maintenance treatment for chronic depression. *Journal of Consulting and Clinical Psychology, 72*, 681–688.

Klein, F. (1990). The need to view sexual orientation as a multivariable dynamic process: A theoretical perspective. In McWhirter, D. P., Sanders, S. A., & Reinisch, J. M. (Eds.), *Homosexuality/heterosexuality: Concepts of sexual orientation. The Kinsey Institute series* (Vol. 2, pp. 277–282). New York: Oxford University Press.

Klein, H., & Shiffman, K. S. (2011). Bang bang, you're … NOT dead and you're … NOT even hurt?! Messages provided by animated cartoons about gun violence. *International Journal of Child and Adolescent Health, 4*(3), 265–276.

Klein, H. J., Noe, R. A., & Wang, C. (2006). Motivation to learn and course outcomes: The impact of delivery mode, learning goal orientation, and perceived barriers and enablers. *Personnel Psychology, 59*, 665–702.

Klein, M. (1975). *The writings of Melanie Klein: Vol. 3.* London: Hogarth Press.

Klein, P. D. (1997). Multiplying the problems of intelligence by eight: A critique of Gardner's theory. *Canadian Journal of Education, 22*, 377–394.

Kleinknecht, R. A. (1994). Acquisition of blood, injury, and needle fears and phobias. *Behaviour Research and Therapy, 32*, 817–823.

Kleinman, A. (1991, April). *Culture and DSM-IV: Recommendations for the introduction and for the overall structure.* Paper presented at the National Institute of Mental Health-sponsored Conference on Culture and Diagnosis, Pittsburgh, PA.

Kleinspehn-Ammerlahn, A., Kotter-Gruhn, D., & Smith, J. (2008). Self-perceptions of aging: Do subjective age and satisfaction with aging change during old age? *Journals of Gerontology, Series B: Psychological Sciences and Social Sciences, 63B*, P377–P385.

Kleschevnikov, A. M., Belichenko, P. V., Salehi, A., & Wu, C. (2012). Discoveries in Down syndrome: Moving basic science to clinical care. *Progress in Brain Research, 197*, 199–221.

Kline, S., & Groninger, L. D. (1991). The imagery bizarreness effect as a function of sentence complexity and presentation time. *Bulletin of the Psychonomic Society, 29*, 25–27.

Klinesmith, J., Kasser, T., & McAndrew, F. T. (2006). Guns, testosterone, and aggression: An experimental test of a mediational hypothesis. *Psychological Science, 17*, 568–571.

Kling, K. C., Hyde, J. S., Showers, C. J., & Buswell, B. N. (1999). Gender differences in self-esteem: A meta-analysis. *Psychological Bulletin, 125*, 470–500.

Klingberg, T. (2010). Training and plasticity of working memory. *Trends in Cognitive Science, 14*(7), 317–324.

Klintschar, M., & Heimbold, C. (2012). Association between a functional polymorphism in the MAOA gene and sudden infant death syndrome. *Pediatrics, 129*(3), e756–e761.

Klintsova, A. Y., & Greenough, W. T. (1999). Synaptic plasticity in cortical systems. *Current Opinion in Neurobiology, 9*, 203–208.

Kloep, M., & Hendry, L. B. (2010). Letting go or holding on? Parents' perceptions of their relationships with their children during emerging adulthood. *British Journal of Developmental Psychology, 28*(4), 817–834. doi:10.1348/ 026151009X480581.

Klossek, U. M. H., Russell, J., & Dickinson, A. (2008). The control of instrumental action following outcome devaluation in young children aged between 1 and 4 years. *Journal of Experimental Psychology: General, 137*, 39–51.

Klug, H. J. P., & Maier, G. (2014). Linking goal progress and subjective well-being: A meta-analysis. *Journal of Happiness Studies.* Epub January 9, 2014.

Kluger, A. N., & DeNisi, A. (1998). Feedback interventions: Toward the understanding of a double-edged sword. *Current Directions in Psychological Science, 7*, 67–72.

Knack, W. A. (2009). Psychotherapy and Alcoholics Anonymous: An integrated approach. *Journal of Psychotherapy Integration, 19*, 86–109.

Knafo, A., Israel, S., & Ebstein, R. P. (2011). Heritability of children's prosocial behavior and differential susceptibility to parenting by variation in the dopamine receptor D4 gene. *Development and Psychopathology, 23*(1), 53–67.

Knafo, A., Zahn-Waxler, C., Van Hulle, C., Robinson, J. L., & Rhee, S. H. (2008). The developmental origins of a disposition toward empathy: Genetic and environmental contributions. *Emotion, 8*, 737–752.

Knapp, S. J. (Ed.). (2011a). *APA handbook of ethics in psychology: Volume 1: Moral foundations and common themes.* Washington, DC: American Psychological Association.

Knapp, S. J. (Ed.). (2011b). *APA handbook of ethics in psychology: Volume 2: Practice, teaching, and research.* Washington, DC: American Psychological Association.

Knauper, B., McCollam, A., Rosen-Brown, A., Lacaille, J., Kelso, E., & Roseman, M. (2011). Fruitful plans: Adding targeted mental imagery to implementation intentions increases fruit consumption. *Psychology and Health, 26*, 601–617. doi: 10.1080/08870441003703218

Knöpfel, T., Lin, M. Z., Levskaya, A., Lin, T., Lin, J. Y., & Boyden, E. S. (2010). Toward the second generation of optogenetic tools. *Journal Of Neuroscience, 30*(45), 14998–15004. doi:10.1523/JNEUROSCI.4190-10.2010.

Knopman, D. S. (2006). Dementia and cerebrovascular disease. *Mayo Clinic Proceedings, 81*(2), 223–230.

Kobau, R., Seligman, M. E. P., Peterson, C., Diener, E., Zack, M. M., Chapman, D., & Thompson, W. (2011). Mental health promotion in public health: Perspectives and strategies from positive psychology. *American Journal of Public Health, 101*, 1–9.

Kochanek, K.D., Xu, J., Murphy, S. L., Minino, A. M., Kung, H.-C. (2011). Deaths: Preliminary data for 2009. *National Vital Statistics Reports, Division of Vital Statistics, 4*(59).

Kochanska, G., Aksan, N., & Joy, M. E. (2007). Children's fearfulness as a moderator of parenting in early socialization: Two longitudinal studies. *Developmental Psychology, 43*, 222–237.

Kochanska, G., & Kim, S. (2013). Early attachment organization with both parents and future behavior problems: from infancy to middle childhood. *Child Development, 84*, 283–296.

Koechlin, E., & Hyafil, A. (2007). Anterior prefrontal function and the limits of human decision-making. *Science, 318*, 594–598.

Koenig, L. B., Haber, J., & Jacob, T. (2011). Childhood religious affiliation and alcohol use and abuse across the lifespan in alcohol-dependent men. *Psychology of Addictive Behaviors, 25*(3), 381–389. doi:10.1037/a0024774.

Koerner, N., Vorstenbosch, V., & Antony, M. M. (2012). Panic disorder. In P. Sturmey & M. Hersen (Eds.), *Handbook of evidence-based practice in clinical psychology, Vol 2: Adult disorders* (pp. 285–311). Hoboken, NJ: Wiley.

Kogan, M. D., Blumberg, S. J., Schieve, L. A., Boyle, C. A., et al. (2009). Prevalence of parentreported diagnosis of autism spectrum disorder among children in the U.S., 2007. *Pediatrics, 124*, 1395–1403.

Koger, S. M., Schettler, T., & Weiss, B. (2005). Environmental toxicants and developmental disabilities: A challenge for psychologists. *American Psychologist, 60*, 243–255.

Koh, H. K., Blakey, C. R., & Roper, A. Y. (2014). Healthy People 2020: A report card on the health of the nation. *JAMA, 311*(24), 2475–2476.

Kohlberg, L., & Gilligan, C. (1971). The adolescent as a philosopher: The discovery of the self in a postconventional world. *Daedalus, 100*, 1051–1086.

Kohli, M. A., Salyakina, D., Pfennig, A., Lucae, S., et al. (2010). Association of genetic variants in the neurotrophic receptor–encoding gene NTRK2 and a lifetime history of suicide attempts in depressed patients. *Archives of General Psychiatry, 67*, 348–359. doi:10.1001/archgenpsychiatry.2009.201

Kohn, A. (1993). *Punished by rewards: The trouble with gold stars, incentive plans, A's, praise, and other bribes.* Boston: Houghton Mifflin.

Kohn, H. K., Blakey, C. R., & Roper, A. Y. (2014). Healthy people 2020: A report card on the health of the nation. *JAMA, 311*(24), 2199–2200.

Köhn, M., Persson, L. U., Bryngelsson, I. L., Anderzén-Carlsson, A., & Westerdahl, E. (2013). Medical yoga for patients with stress-related symptoms and diagnoses in primary health care: a randomized controlled trial. *Evidence Based Complementary and Alternative Medicine.* Epub February 26, 2013.

Kohn, N. W., Paulus, P. B., & Choi, Y. (2011). Building on the ideas of others: An examination of the idea combination process. *Journal of Experimental Social Psychology, 47*(3), 554–561. doi:10.1016/j.jesp.2011.01.004.

Kohnert, K. (2004). Cognitive and cognate-based treatments for bilingual aphasia: A case study. *Brain and Language, 91,* 294–302.

Kohut, H. (1984). Selected problems of self-psychological theory. In J. D. Lichtenberg & S. Kaplan (Eds.), *Reflections on self psychology* (pp. 387–416). Hillsdale, NJ: Erlbaum.

Kolata, G., & Markel, H. (2001, April 29). Baby not crawling? Reason seems to be less tummy time. *New York Times.*

Kolb, B., Gorny, G., Li, Y., Samaha, A.-N., & Robinson, T. E. (2003). Amphetamine or cocaine limits the ability of later experience to promote structural plasticity in the neocortex and nucleus accumbens. *Proceedings of the National Academy of Sciences, 100,* 10523–10528.

Komorita, S. S. (1984). Coalition bargaining. In L. Berkowitz (Ed.), *Advances in experimental social psychology* (Vol. 18, pp. 184–246). New York: Academic Press.

Kontoghiorghes, C. (2004). Reconceptualizing the learning transfer conceptual framework: Empirical validation of a new systemic model. *International Journal of Training and Development, 8,* 210–221.

Koob, G., & Kreek, M. J. (2007). Stress, dysregulation of drug reward pathways, and the transition to drug dependence. *American Journal of Psychiatry, 164,* 1149–1159.

Koob, G. F., & Bloom, F. E. (1988). Cellular and molecular mechanisms of drug dependence. *Science, 242,* 715–723.

Koob, G. F., & Volkow, N. D. (2010). Neurocircuitry of addiction. *Neuropsychopharmacology, 35,* 217–238.

Koppel, R. H., & Storm, B. C. (2014). Escaping mental fixation: Incubation and inhibition in creative problem solving. *Memory, 22*(4), 34034–8.

Koppenaal, L., & Glanzer, M. (1990). An examination of the continuous distractor task and the "long-term recency effect." *Memory & Cognition, 18,* 183–195.

Koppes, L. L. (1997). American female pioneers of industrial and organizational psychology during the early years. *Journal Of Applied Psychology, 82*(4), 500–515. doi:10.1037/0021-9010.82.4.500.

Koranyi, N., Gast, A., & Rothermund, K. (2013). "Although quite nice, I was somehow not attracted by that person": Attitudes toward romantically committed opposite-sex others are immune to positive evaluative conditioning. *Social Psychological and Personality Science, 4*(4), 403–410.

Korczyn, A. D., Vakhapova, V., & Grinberg, L. T. (2012). Vascular dementia. *Journal of Vascular Dementia, 322*(1–2), 2–10.

Koretz, D., Lynch, P. S., & Lynch, C. A. (2000, June). The impact of score differences on the admission of minority students: An illustration. *Statements of the National Board on Educational Testing and Public Policy, 1,* 1–15.

Korman, M., Doyon, J., Doljansky, J., Carrier, J., Dagan, Y., & Karni, A. (2007). Daytime sleep condenses the time course of motor memory consolidation. *Nature Neuroscience, 10,* 1206–1213.

Korochkin, L. I. (2000). New approaches in developmental genetics and gene therapy: Xenotransplantation of Drosophila embryonic nerve cells into the brain of vertebrate animals. *Genetika, 36,* 1436–1442.

Koschwanez, H. E., Kerse, N., Darragh, M., Jarrett, P., Booth, R. J., & Broadbent, E. (2013). Expressive writing and wound healing in older adults: A randomized controlled trial. *Psychosomatic Medicine, 75*(6), 581–590.

Kossowsky, J., Wilhelm, F. H., Roth, W. T., & Schneider, S. (2012). Separation anxiety disorder in children: Disorder-specific responses to experimental separation from the mother. *Journal of Child Psychology and Psychiatry, 53*(2), 178–187. doi:10.1111/j.1469-7610.2011.02465.x

Koten, J. W., Jr.; Wood, G.; Hagoort, P.; Goebel, R.; et al. (2009). Genetic contribution to variation in cognitive function: An fMRI study in twins. *Science, 323,* 1737–1740.

Kothari, R., Skuse, D., Wakefield, J., & Micali, N. (2013). Gender differences in the relationship between social communication and emotion recognition. *Journal of the American Academy of Child & Adolescent Psychiatry, 52*(11), 1148–1157.

Kouider, S., & Dupoux, E. (2005). Subliminal speech priming. *Psychological Science, 16,* 617.

Koukopoulos, A., Sani G., & Ghaemi, S. N. (2013). Mixed features of depression: Why DSM-5 is wrong (and so was DSM-IV). *British Journal of Psychiatry, 203*(1), 3–5.

Kounios, J. Frymiare, J. L., Bowden, E. M., Fleck, J. L., Subramaniam, K., Parrish, T. B., & Jung-Beeman, M. (2006). The prepared mind: Neural activity prior to problem presentation predicts subsequent solution by sudden insight. *Psychological Science, 17,* 882–890.

Koustanaï, A., Van Elslande, P., & Bastien, C. (2012). Use of change blindness to measure different abilities to detect relevant changes in natural driving scenes. *Transportation Research: Part F, 15*(3), 233–242. doi:10.1016/j.trf.2011.12.012.

Kouyoumdjian, H. (2004). Influence of unannounced quizzes and cumulative exams on attendance and study behavior. *Teaching of Psychology, 31,* 110–111.

Kozak, M. J., Liebowitz, M. R., & Foa, E. B. (2000). Cognitive behavior therapy and pharmacotherapy for obsessive-compulsive disorder: The NIMH-sponsored collaborative study. In W. K. Goodman, M. V. Rudorfer, & J. D. Maser (Eds.), *Obsessive-compulsive disorder: Contemporary issues in treatment* (pp. 501–530). Mahwah, NJ: Erlbaum.

Kozorovitskiy, Y., Gross, C. G., Kopil, C., Battaglia, L., McBreen, M., Stranahan, A. M., et al. (2005). Experience induces structural and biochemical changes in the adult primate brain. *Proceedings of the National Academy of Sciences, 102,* 17478–17482.

Krain, A. L., & Castellanos, F. X. (2006). Brain development and ADHD. *Clinical Psychology Review, 26,* 433–444.

Krakauer, J. (1997). *Into thin air.* New York: Villard.

Kramár, E., Babayan, A., Gavin, C., Cox, C., Jafari, M., Gall, C., & … Lynch, G. (2012). Synaptic evidence for the efficacy of spaced learning. *Proceedings Of The National Academy Of Sciences Of The United States Of America, 109*(13), 5121–5126.

Kramer, A. F., Larish, J. L., Weber, T. A., & Bardell, L. (1999). Training for executive control: Task coordination strategies and aging. In D. Gopher & A. Koriat (Eds.), *Attention and performance XVII: Cognitive regulation of performance: Interaction of theory and application* (pp. 617–650). Cambridge, MA: MIT Press.

Kramer, G. P., Bernstein, D. A., & Phares, V. (2013). *Introduction to clinical psychology* (8th ed.) Upper Saddle River, NJ: Prentice Hall.

Kramer, G. P., Bernstein, D. A., & Phares, V. (2014). *Introduction to clinical psychology* (8th ed). Upper Saddle River, NJ: Pearson.

Krantz, D., Contrada, R., Hill, D., & Friedler, E. (1988). Environmental stress and biobehavioral antecedents of coronary heart disease. *Journal of Consulting and Clinical Psychology, 56,* 333–341.

Krantz, D., & Durel, L. (1983). Psychobiological substrates of the Type A behavior pattern. *Health Psychology, 2,* 393–411.

Krantz, D. S., & McCeney, M. K. (2002). Effects of psychological and social factors on organic disease: A critical assessment of research on coronary heart disease. *Annual Review of Psychology, 53,* 341–369.

Kraut, R., Olson, J., Banaji, M., Bruckman, A., Cohen, J., & Couper, M. (2004). Psychological research online: Report of board of scientific affairs' advisory group on the conduct of research on the Internet. *American Psychologist, 59,* 105–117.

Krauzlis, R. J. (2002). Reaching for answers. *Neuron, 34,* 673–674.

Krauzlis, R. J., & Lisberger, S. G. (1991). Visual motion commands for pursuit eye movements in the cerebellum. *Science, 253,* 568–571.

Krebs, D. L. (2005). The evolution of morality. In D. Kin & M. Buss (Eds), *The handbook of evolutionary psychology,* Hoboken, NJ: John Wiley & Sons.

Kreek, M. J., Zhou, Y., Butelman, E. R., & Levran, O. (2009). Opiate and cocaine addiction: From bench to clinic and back to the bench. *Current Opinion in Pharmacology, 9*(1), 74–80.

Kremen, W. S., & Lyons, M. J. (2011). Behavior genetics of aging. In K. W. Schaie & S. L. Willis (Eds.), *Handbook of the Psychology of Aging* (7th ed., pp. 93–108). San Diego, CA: Academic Press/Elsevier Science.

Kreppner, J. M., Rutter, M., Beckett, C., Castle, J., Colvert, E., Groothues, C., Hawkins, A., O'Connor, T. G., Stevens, S., & Sonuga-Barke, E. J. S. (2007). Normality and impairment following profound early institutional deprivation: A longitudinal follow-up into early adolescence. *Developmental Psychology, 43,* 931–946.

Kreuger, R. F., & Johnson, W. (2008). Behavioral genetics and personality: A new look at the integration of nature and nurture. In O. John, R. Robins, & L. Pervin (Eds.), *Handbook of personality: Theory and research* (3rd ed., pp. 287–310). New York: Guilford.

Krieger, N., Carney, D., Lancaster, K., Waterman, P. D., Kosheleva, A., & Banaji, M. (2010). Implicit measures reveal evidence of personal discrimination. *American Journal of Public Health, 100,* 1485–1492.

Krieglmeyer, R., Deutsch, R., De Houwer, J., & De Raedt, R. (2010). Being moved: Valence activates approach-avoidance behavior independently of evaluation and approach-avoidance intentions. *Psychological Science, 21*(4), 607–613. doi:10.1177/0956797610365131.

Kring, A. M., & Caponigro, J. M. (2010). Emotion in schizophrenia: Where feeling meets thinking. *Current Directions in Psychological Science, 19*(4), 255–259. doi:10.1177/0963721410377599.

Kring, A. M., Germans Gard, M., & Gard, D. E. (2011). Emotion deficits in schizophrenia: Timing matters. *Journal Of Abnormal Psychology, 120*(1), 79–87. doi:10.1037/a0021402.

Kringelbach, M. L., Stein, A., & van Hartevelt, T. J. (2012). The functional human neuroanatomy of food pleasure cycles. *Physiology & Behavior, 106*(3), 307–316.

Kristof, N. D. (1997, August 17). Where children rule. *New York Times Magazine.*

Krizman, J., Marian, V., Shook, A., Skoe, E., & Kraus, N. (2012). Subcortical encoding of sound is enhanced in bilinguals and relates to executive function advantages. *Proceedings of the National Academy of Sciences of the United States of America, 109*(20), 7877–7881. doi:10.1073/pnas.1201575109.

Kroll, J. F., Bobb, S. C., & Hoshino, N. (2014). Two languages in mind: Bilingualism as a tool to investigate language, cognition, and the brain. *Current Directions in Psychological Science, 23*(3), 159–163.

Kroneisen, M., & Bell, R. (2013). Sex, cheating, and disgust: Enhanced source memory for trait information that violates gender stereotypes, *Memory, 21*(2), 167–181.

Krosch, A. R., Figner, B., & Weber, E. U. (2012). Choice processes and their post-decisional consequences in morally conflicting decisions. *Judgment and Decision Making, 7*(3), 224–234.

Krosnick, J. A., Betz, A. L., Jussim, L. J., & Lynn, A. R. (1992). Subliminal conditioning of attitude. *Personality and Social Psychology Bulletin, 18,* 152–162.

Krotzer, C. (2013). Man carrying umbrella, not rifle, was on his usual route. *The Olympian*, March 20, 2013.

Krstic, D., & Knuesel, I. (2013). Deciphering the mechanism underlying late-onset Alzheimer disease. *Nature Review Neuroscience, 9*(1), 25–34.

Krueger, F., McCabe, K., Moll, J., Kriegeskorte, N., Zahn, R., Strenziok, M., Heinecke, A., & Grafman, J. (2007). Neural correlates of trust. *Proceedings of the National Academies of Science, 104*(50), 20084–20089.

Krueger, R. F., Markon, K. E., & Bouchard, T. J., Jr. (2003). The extended genotype: The heritability of personality accounts for the heritability of recalled family environments in twins reared apart. *Journal of Personality, 71,* 809–833.

Kruger, J., Wirtz, D., & Miller, D. T. (2005). Counterfactual thinking and the first instinct fallacy. *Journal of Personality and Social Psychology, 88,* 725–735.

Krykouli, S. E., Stanley, B. G., Seirafi, R. D., & Leibowitz, S. F. (1990). Stimulation of feeding by galanin: Anatomical localization and behavioral specificity of this peptide's effects in the brain. *Peptides, 11*(5), 995–1001.

Kubilius, J., Wagemans, J., & de Beeck, H. (2011). Emergence of perceptual Gestalts in the human visual cortex: The case of the configural-superiority effect. *Psychological Science, 22*(10), 1296–1303. doi:10.1177/0956797611417000.

Kubzansky, L. D., Davidson, K. W., & Rozanski, A. (2005). The clinical impact of negative psychological states: Expanding the spectrum of risk for coronary artery disease. *Psychosomatic Medicine, 67*(S1), S10–S14.

Kuczkowski, K.M. (2009). Caffeine in pregnancy. *Archives of Gynecology and Obstetrics, 280,* 695–698.

Kuhl, B. A., Bainbridge, W. A., & Chun, M. M. (2012). Neural reactivation reveals mechanisms for updating memory. *The Journal of Neuroscience, 32*(10), 3453–3461. doi:10.1523/JNEUROSCI.5846–11.2012

Kuhn, D., & Franklin, S. (2006). The second decade: What develops (and how)? In W. Damon & R. M. Lerner (Series Eds.) & D. Kuhn & R. Siegler (Vol. Eds.), *Handbook of child psychology: Vol. 2. Cognition, perception, and language* (6th ed.). New York: Wiley.

Kuhnen, C. M., & Knutson, B. (2005). The neural basis of financial risk taking. *Neuron, 47,* 763–770.

Kumar, V. K., & Farley, F. (2009). Structural aspects of three hypnotizability scales: Smallest space analysis. *International Journal of Clinical and Experimental Hypnosis, 57,* 343–365.

Kuncel, N. R., & Hezlett, S. A. (2010). Fact and fiction in cognitive ability testing for admissions and hiring decisions. *Current Directions in Psychological Science, 19*(6), 339–345. doi:10.1177/0963721410389459.

Kuncel, N. R., Hezlett, S. A., & Ones, D. (2004). Academic performance, career potential, creativity, and job performance: Can one construct predict them all? *Journal of Personality and Social Psychology, 86,* 148–161.

Kuncel, N. R., Ones, D. S. & Sackett, P. R. (2010). Individual differences as predictors of work, educational, and broad life outcomes. *Personality and Individual Differences, 49,* 331–336.

Kunen, S., Niederhauser, R., Smith, P. O., Morris, J. A., & Marx, B. D. (2005). Race disparities in psychiatric rates in emergency departments. *Journal of Consulting and Clinical Psychology, 73,* 116–126.

Kuo, L. E., Kitlinska, J. B., Tilan, J. U., Li, L., Baker, S. B., Johnson, M. D., Lee, E. W., Burnett, M. S., Fricke, S. T., Kvetnansky, R., Herzog, H., & Zukowska, Z. (2007). Neuropeptide Y acts directly in the periphery on fat tissue and mediates stress-induced obesity and metabolic syndrome. *Nature Medicine 13,* 803–811.

Kuo, Y.-L., Liao, H.-F., Chen, P.-C., Hsieh, W.-S., & Hwang, A.-W. (2008). The influence of wakeful prone positioning on motor development during the early life. *Journal of Developmental & Behavioral Pediatrics, 29*(5), 367–376.

Kupfer, D. J., & Regier, D. A. (2010). Why all of medicine should care about DSM-5. *Journal of the American Medical Association, 303,* 1974–1975.

Kupfer, D. J., & Regier, D. A. (2011). Neuroscience, clinical evidence, and the future of psychiatric classification in DSM-5. *The American Journal of Psychiatry, 168*(7), 672–674. doi:10.1176/appi.ajp.2011.11020219.

Kurdek, L. A. (2005). What do we know about gay and lesbian couples? *Current Directions in Psychological Science, 14,* 251–254.

Kurita, H. (2012, March). Is recovery from a pervasive developmental disorder possible?. *Psychiatry & Clinical Neurosciences.* pp. 85–86. doi:10.1111/j.1440-1819. 2011.02309.x.

Kurtz, L. F. (2004). Support and self-help groups. In C. D. Garvin, L. M. Gutierrez, & M. J. Galinsky (Eds.), *Handbook of social work with groups* (pp. 139–159). New York: Guilford Press.

Kurz, M. W., Kurz, K. D., & Farbu, E. (2013). Acute ischemic stroke—From symptom recognition to thrombolysis, *Acta Neurologica Scandinavia.* Supplementum, (196), 57–64.

Kush, J. C., Spring, M. B., & Barkand, J. (2012). Advances in the assessment of cognitive skills using computer-based measurement. *Behavior Research Methods, 44*(1), 125–134. doi:10.3758/s13428–011–0136–2.

Kushner, M. G., Thuras, P., Kaminski, J., Anderson, N., et al. (2000). Expectancies for alcohol to affect tension and anxiety as a function of time. *Addictive Behaviors, 25,* 93–98.

Kwan, M., Greenleaf, W. J., Mann, J., Crapo, L., & Davidson, J. M. (1983). The nature of androgen action on male sexuality: A combined laboratory-self-report study on hypogonadal men. *Journal of Clinical Endocrinology and Metabolism, 57,* 557–562.

Kwan, V. Y., Wojcik, S. P., Miron-shatz, T., Votruba, A. M., & Olivola, C. Y. (2012). Effects of symptom presentation order on perceived disease risk. *Psychological Science, 23*(4), 381–385. doi:10.1177/0956797611432177.

Kwate, N. O. A. (2001). Intelligence or misorientation? *Journal of Black Psychology, 27,* 221–238.

Kymalainen, J. A., Weisman, A. G., Resales, G. A., & Armesto, J. C. (2006). Ethnicity, expressed emotion, and communication deviance in family members of patients with schizophrenia. *Journal of Nervous and Mental Disease, 194,* 391–396.

Kyrios, M., Sanavio, E., Bhar, S., & Liguori, L. (2001). Associations between obsessive-compulsive phenomena, affect, and beliefs: Cross-cultural comparisons of Australian and Italian data. *Behavioural and Cognitive Psychotherapy, 29,* 409–422.

Labouvie-Vief, G. (1982). Discontinuities in development from childhood. In T. M. Field, A. Huston, H. C. Quay, L. Troll, & G. E. Finley (Eds.), *Review of human development.* New York: Wiley.

Labouvie-Vief, G. (1992). A new-Piagetian perspective on adult cognitive development. In R. J. Sternberg & C. A. Berg (Eds.), *Intellectual development.* New York: Cambridge University Press.

Lacayo, A. (1995). Neurologic and psychiatric complications of cocaine abuse. *Neuropsychiatry, Neuropsychology, and Behavioral Neurology, 8,* 53–60.

Lacor, P. N. (2007). Advances on the Understanding of the Origins of Synaptic Pathology in AD. *Current Genomics, 8*(8), 486–508.

Ladd, G. (2005). *Peer relationships and social competence of children and youth.* New Haven, CT: Yale University Press.

Ladd, G. W., & Troop-Gordon, W. (2003). The role of chronic peer difficulties in the development of children's psychological adjustment problems. *Child Development, 74,* 1344–1367.

Lader, M. (2011). Benzodiazepines revisited—will we ever learn? *Addiction, 106*(12), 2086–2109.

Laeng, B., Sirois, S., & Gredebäck, G. (2012). Pupillometry: A window to the preconscious? *Perspectives on Psychological Science, 7*(1) 18–27doi:10.1177/ 1745691611427305.

Lagerspetz, K. M. J., & Lagerspetz, K. Y. H. (1983). Genes and aggression. In E. C. Simmel, M. E. Hahn, & J. K. Walters (Eds.), *Aggressive behavior: Genetic and neural approaches.* Hillsdale, NJ: Erlbaum.

Lagopoulos, J., & Malhi, G. S. (2008). Transcranial magnetic stimulation. *Acta Neuropsychiatrica, 20*(6), 316–317.

Lahey, B., Rathouz, P., Lee, S., Chronis-Tuscano, A., Pelham, W., Waldman, I., & Cook, E. (2011). Interactions between early parenting and a polymorphism of the child's dopamine transporter gene in predicting future child conduct disorder symptoms. *Journal of Abnormal Psychology, 120*(1), 33–45.

Lahey, B. B., Loeber, R., Burke, J. D., & Applegate, B. (2005). Predicting future antisocial personality disorder in males from a clinical assessment in childhood. *Journal of Consulting and Clinical Psychology, 73,* 389–399.

Lahey, B. B., Loeber, R., Hart, E. L., Frick, P. J., & Applegate, B. (1995). Four-year longitudinal study of conduct disorder in boys: Patterns and predictors of persistence. *Journal of Abnormal Psychology, 104,* 83–93.

Lahey, B. B., Van Hulle, C. A., Keenan, K., Rathouz, P. J., D'Onofrio, B. M., Rodgers, J. L., & Waldman, I. D. (2008). Temperament and parenting during the first year of life predict future child conduct problems. *Journal of Abnormal Child Psychology, 36,* 1139–1158.

Lai, C. S. L., Fisher, S. E., Hurst, J. A., Vargha-Khadem, F., & Monaco, A. P. (2001). A forkhead-domain gene is mutated in severe speech and language disorder. *Nature, 413*, 519–523.

Lakhi, S., Snow, W., & Fry, M. (2013). Insulin modulates the electrical activity of subfornical organ neurons. *NeuroReport, 24*(6), 329–334.

Lakin, J. L., & Chartrand, T. L. (2003). Using nonconscious behavioral mimicry to create affiliation and rapport. *Psychological Science, 14*, 334–339.

Lally, P., van Jaarsveld,, C. H. M., Potts, H. W. W., & Wardle, J. (2010). How are habits formed: Modeling habit formation in the real world. *European Journal of Social Psychology, 40*, 998–1009. doi:10.1002/ejsp.674.

Lamb, M. E. (Ed.). (1997). *The role of the father in child development* (3rd ed.). New York: Wiley.

Lamb, M. E., & Ahnert, L. (2006). Nonparental child care. In W. Damon & R. M. Lerner (Series Eds.) & K. A. Renninger & I. E. Sigel (Vol. Eds.), *Handbook of child psychology: Vol. 4. Child psychology in practice* (6th ed.). New York: Wiley.

Lamb, M. E. & Lewis, C. (2010). The development and significance of father-child relationships in two-parent families. In M. E. Lamb (Ed.), *The role of the father in child development* (5th ed., pp. 94–153). Hoboken NJ: Wiley.

Lamberg, L. (2004). Impact of long working hours explored. *Journal of the American Medical Association, 292*, 25–26.

Lambert, M. J. (2013). The efficacy and effectiveness of psychotherapy. In M. J. Lambert (Ed.), *Bergin and Garfield's handbook of psychotherapy and behavior change* (6th ed.) (pp. 169–218). Hoboken, NJ: Wiley.

Lamm, E., & Jablonka, E. (2008). The nurture of nature: Hereditary plasticity in evolution. *Philosophical Psychology, 21*(3), 305–319.

Landolt, A. S., & Milling, L. S. (2011). The efficacy of hypnosis as an intervention for labor and delivery pain: A comprehensive methodological review. *Clinical Psychology Review, 31*(6), 1022–1031.

Landgren, M., Svensson, L., Stromland, K., & Gronlund, M. A. (2010). Prenatal alcohol exposure and neurodevelopmental disorders in children adopted from eastern Europe. *Pediatrics, 125*, e1178–e1185.

Landsdale, M., & Laming, D. (1995). Evaluating the fragmentation hypothesis: The analysis of errors in cued recall. *Acta Psychologica, 88*, 33–77.

Landy, F. J. (1992). Hugo Münsterberg: Victim or visionary? *Journal Of Applied Psychology, 77*(6), 787–802. doi:10.1037/0021–9010.77.6.787.

Lang, A. R., Goeckner, D. J., Adesso, V. J., & Marlatt, G. A. (1975). Effects of alcohol on aggression in male social drinkers. *Journal of Abnormal Psychology, 84*, 508–518.

Lang, J. W. B., & Lang, J. (2010). Priming competence diminishes the link between cognitive test anxiety and test performance: Implications for the interpretation of test scores. *Psychological Science, 21*, 811–819. Epub 2010 Apr 30.

Lang, P. J. (1995). The emotion probe: Studies of motivation and attention. *American Psychologist, 50*(5), 372–385.

Lang, P. J., & Melamed, B. G. (1969). Avoidance conditioning therapy of an infant with chronic ruminative vomiting. *Journal of Abnormal Psychology, 74*, 1–8.

Lang, T. J., Blackwell, S. E., Harmer, C. J., Davison, P., & Holmes, E. A. (2012). Cognitive bias modification using mental imagery for depression: Developing a novel computerized intervention to change negative thinking styles. *European Journal of Personality, 26*(2), 145–157. doi:10.1002/per.855.

Langan, M. (2011). Parental voices and controversies in autism. *Disability & Society, 26*, 193–205. doi:10.1080/09687599.2011.544059

Lange, C., & Byrd, M. (2002). Differences between students' estimated and attained grades in a first-year introductory psychology course as a function of identity development. *Adolescence, 37*(145), 93–108.

Langleben, D. D., & Moriarty, J. C. (2013). Using brain imaging for lie detection: Where science, law, and policy collide. *Psychology, Public Policy, and Law, 19*(2), 222–234.

Lansford, J. E., Chang, L., Dodge, K. A., Malone, P. S., Oburu, P., Palmerus, K., Bombi, A. S., Zelli, A., Tapanya, S., Chaudhary, N., Deater-Deckard, K., Make, B., & Inn, N. (2005). Cultural normativeness as a moderator of the link between physical discipline and children's adjustment: A comparison of China, India, Italy, Kenya, Philippines, and Thailand. *Child Development, 76*, 1234–1246.

Lansu, T. A. M., Cillessen, A. H. N., & Karremans, J. C. (2013). Adolescents' selective visual attention for high-status peers: The role of perceiver status and gender. *Child Development*, Epub July 18, 2013.

Lantz, J. (2004). Research and evaluation issues in existential psychotherapy. *Journal of Contemporary Psychotherapy, 34*, 331–340.

Lanzenberger, R. R., Mitterhauser, M., Spindelegger, C., Wadsak, W., Klein, N., Mien, L. K., et al. (2007). Reduced serotonin-1a receptor binding in social anxiety disorder. *Biological Psychiatry, 61*, 1081–1089.

Lapierre, L. M., & Allen, T. D. (2006). Work-supportive family, family-supportive supervision, use of organizational benefits, and problem-focused coping: Implications for work-family conflict and employee well-being. *Journal of Occupational Health Psychology, 11*, 169–181.

Lareau, C. R. (2013). Civil commitment and involuntary hospitalization of the mentally ill. In R. K. Otto & I. B. Weiner (Eds.), *Handbook of psychology, Vol. 11: Forensic psychology* (2nd ed.) (pp. 308–331). Hoboken, NJ: Wiley.

Larrick, R. P., Timmerman, T. A., Carton, A. M., & Abrevaya, J. (2011). Temper, temperature, and temptation: Heat—related retaliation in baseball. *Psychological Science, 22*(4), 423–428. doi:10.1177/0956797611399292.

Larsen, J. T., & Green, J. D. (2013). Evidence for mixed feelings of happiness and sadness from brief moments in time. *Cognition & Emotion, 27*(8), 1469–1477.

Larsen, J. T., McGraw, A. P., Mellers, B. A., & Cacioppo, J. T. (2004). The agony of victory and thrill of defeat: Mixed emotional reactions to disappointing wins and relieving losses. *Psychological Science, 15*, 325–330.

Larsen, R., & Buss, D. M. (2005). *Personality psychology: Domains of knowledge about human nature* (2nd ed.). New York: McGraw-Hill.

Larsen, R. J., & Buss, D. M. (2010). *Personality psychology: Domains of knowledge about human nature* (4th ed). New York: McGraw-Hill.

Larson, E. B., Wang, H., Bowen, J. D., McCormick, W. C., Teri, L., Crane, P., & Kukull, W. (2006). Exercise is associated with reduced risk of incident dementia among persons 65 years of age and older. *Annals of Internal Medicine, 144*, 73–81.

Larson, G. E., & Saccuzzo, D. P. (1989). Cognitive correlates of general intelligence: Toward a process theory of g. *Intelligence, 13*, 5–32.

Larson, J. R., Jr., Christensen, C., Franz, T. M., & Abbott, A. S. (1998). Diagnosing groups: The pooling, management, and impact of shared and unshared case information in team-based medical decision making. *Journal of Personality and Social Psychology, 75*, 93–108.

Larson, R. W., & Verma, S. (1999). How children and adolescents spend time across the world: Work, play, and developmental opportunities. *Psychological Bulletin, 125*, 701–736.

Larsson, H., Andershed, H., & Lichtenstein, P. (2006). A genetic factor explains most of the variation in the psychopathic personality. *Journal of Abnormal Psychology, 115*, 221–230.

Larzelere, R. E. (1996). A review of the outcomes of parental use of nonabusive or customary physical punishment. *Pediatrics, 98*, 824–828.

Larzelere, R. E., Cox, R. B., & Smith, G. L. (2010). Do nonphysical punishments reduce antisocial behavior more than spanking? A comparison using the strongest previous causal evidence against spanking. *BMC Pediatrics, 10*:10.

Laska, K. M., Gurman, A. S., & Wampold, B. E. (2013). Expanding the lens of evidence-based practice in psychotherapy: A common factors perspective. *Psychotherapy*, Epub December 13, 2013.

Latané, B. (1981). The psychology of social impact. *American Psychologist, 36*, 343–356.

Latané, B., & Rodin, J. (1969). A lady in distress: Inhibiting effects of friends and strangers on bystander intervention. *Journal of Experimental Social Psychology, 5*, 189–202.

Latendresse, S. J., Bates, J. E., Goodnight, J. A., Lansford, J. E., Budde, J. P., Goate, A., Dodge, K. A., Pettit, G. S., & Dick, D. M. (2011). Differential susceptibility to adolescent externalizing trajectories: Examining the interplay between CHRM2 and peer group antisocial behavior. *Child Development, 82*, 1797–1814.

Latham, G. P. (2004). Motivate employee performance through goal-setting. In E. A. Locke (Ed.), *Handbook of principles of organizational behavior* (pp. 107–119). Malden, MA: Blackwell.

Latham, G. P., Skarlicki, D., Irvine, D., & Siegel, J. P. (1993). The increasing importance of performance appraisals to employee effectiveness in organizational settings in North America. In C. L. Cooper & I. T. Robertson (Eds.), *International review of industrial and organizational psychology 1993* (pp. 87–132). Chichester, UK: Wiley.

Lau, J., Molyneaux, E., Telman, M., & Belli, S. (2011). The plasticity of adolescent cognitions: Data from a novel cognitive bias modification training task. *Child Psychiatry and Human Development, 42*(6), 679–693.

Lau, M. A., Pihl, R. O., & Peterson, J. B. (1995). Provocation, acute alcohol intoxication, cognitive performance, and aggression. *Journal of Abnormal Psychology, 104*, 150–155.

Laudan, L. (2012). Eyewitness identifications: One more lesson on the costs of excluding relevant evidence. *Perspectives on Psychological Science, 7*(3), 272–274. doi:10.1177/1745691612443065.

Laughery, K. R. (1999). Modeling human performance during system design. In E. Salas (Ed.), *Human/technology interaction in complex systems* (Vol. 9, pp. 147–174). Stamford, CT: JAI Press.

Laughlin, P. L. (1999). Collective induction: Twelve postulates. *Organizational Behavior and Human Decision Processes, 80*, 50–69.

Laumann, E. O., Gagnon, J. H., Michael, R. T., & Michaels, S. (1994). *The social organization of sexuality: Sexual practices in the United States*. Chicago: University of Chicago Press.

Laumann, E. O., & Michael, R. T. (Eds.). (2000). *Sex, love, and health in America: Private choices and public policies.* Chicago: University of Chicago Press.

Laurin, K., Kay, A. C., & Fitzsimons, G. J. (2012). Reactance versus rationalization: Divergent responses to policies that constrain freedom. *Psychological Science, 23*(2), 205–209. doi:10.1177/0956797611429468.

Laursen, B., Bukowski, W. M., Aunola, K., & Nurmi, J.-E. (2007). Friendship moderates prospective associations between social isolation and adjustment problems in young children. *Child Development, 78,* 1395–1404.

Lauvin, M. A., Martineau, J., Destrieux, C., Andersson, F., Bonnet-Brilhault, F., Gomot, M., El-Hage, W., & Cottier, J. P. (2012). Functional morphological imaging of autism spectrum disorders: current position and theories proposed. *Diagnostic and Interventional Imaging, 93*(3), 139–147.

Lavault, S., Dauvilliers, Y., Drouot , X., Leu-Semenescu, S., Golmard, J. L., Lecendreux, M., Franco, P., & Arnulf, I. (2011). Benefit and risk of modafinil in idiopathic hypersomnia vs. narcolepsy with cataplexy. *Sleep Medicine, 12*(6), 550–556.

Lavoie, M.-P., Lam, R. W., Bouchard, G., Sasseville, A., et al. (2009). Evidence of a biological eff ect of light therapy on the retina of patients with seasonal aff ective disorder. *Biological Psychiatry, 66,* 253–258.

Law, D. J., Pellegrino, J. W., & Hunt, E. B. (1993). Comparing the tortoise and the hare: Gender differences and experience in dynamic spatial reasoning tasks. *Psychological Science, 4,* 35–40.

Law, W., Elliot, A. J., & Murayama, K. (2012). Perceived competence moderates the relation between performance-approach and performance-avoidance goals. *Journal of Educational Psychology.* doi:10.1037/a0027179.

Lawder, R. R., Grant, I. I., Storey, C. C., Walsh, D. D., Whyte, B. B., & Hanlon, P. P. (2011). Epidemiology of hospitalization due to alcohol-related harm: Evidence from a Scottish cohort study. *Public Health, 125*(8), 533–539. doi:10.1016/j.puhe.2011.05.007

Lawless, H. T., & Engen, T. (1977). Associations to odors: Interference, memories and verbal learning. *Journal of Experimental Psychology, 3,* 52–59.

Lawrence, N. K. (2013). Cumulative exams in the introductory psychology course. *Teaching of Psychology, 40*(1), 15–19.

Layzer, C., Rosapep, L., & Barr, S. (2013). A peer education program: Delivering highly reliable sexual health promotion messages in schools. *Journal of Adolescent Health, 54*(3 Supplement l), S70–S77.

Lazarus, A. A. (1971). *Behavior therapy and beyond.* New York: McGraw-Hill.

Lazarus, R. S. (1966). *Psychological stress and the coping process.* New York: McGraw-Hill.

Lazarus, R. S. (1991). Progress on a cognitive-motivational-relational theory of emotion. *American Psychologist, 46,* 819–834.

Lazarus, R. S. (1999). *Stress and emotion: A new synthesis.* New York: Springer.

Lazarus, R. S., & Folkman, S. (1984). *Stress, appraisal, and coping.* New York: Springer-Verlag.

Lazarus, R. S., Opton, E. M., Nomikos, M. S., & Rankin, M. O. (1965). The principle of short-circuiting of threat: Further evidence. *Journal of Personality, 33,* 622–635.

Leadbeater, B. J., & Hoglund, W. L. G. (2009). The effects of peer victimization and physical aggression on changes in internalizing from first to third grade. *Child Development, 80,* 843–859.

Leal, S., & Vrij, A. (2010). The occurrence of eye blinks during a guilty knowledge test. *Psychology, Crime & Law, 16*(4), 349–357. doi:10.1080/10683160902776843.

Leal, S. L., & Yassa, M. A. (2013). Perturbations of neural circuitry in aging, mild cognitive impairment, and Alzheimer's disease. *Ageing Research Reviews, 12*(3), 823–831.

Leamon, M. H., Wright, T. M., & Myrick, H. (2008). Substance-related disorders. In R. E. Hales, S. C. Yudofsky, & G. O. Gabbard (Eds.) *Textbook of psychiatry* (pp. 365–406). Washington, DC: American Psychiatric Publishing.

Leary, M. R. (2010). Affiliation, acceptance, and belonging: The pursuit of interpersonal connection. In S. T. Fiske, D. T. Gilbert, & G. Lindzey (Eds.), *Handbook of social psychology* (5th ed., Vol. 2, pp. 864–897). Hoboken, NJ: Wiley.

Leavell, A. S., Tamis-LeMonda, C. S., Ruble, D. N., Zosuls, K. M., & Cabrera, N. J. (2012). African American, White and Latino fathers' activities with their sons and daughters in early childhood. *Sex Roles, 66,* 53–65.

Lebel, C., & Beaulieu, C. (2011). Longitudinal development of human brain wiring continues from childhood into adulthood. *Journal of Neuroscience,* 31(30), 10937–10947. doi:10.1523/JNEUROSCI.5302-10.2011

LeBlanc, M. M., & Barling, J. (2004). Workplace aggression. *Current Directions in Psychological Science, 13,* 9–12.

LeBlanc, M. M., Dupre, K. E., & Barling, J. (2006). Public-initiated violence. In K. E. Kelloway, J. Barling, & J. J. Hurrell (Eds.), *Handbook of workplace violence* (pp. 261–280). Thousand Oaks, CA: Sage.

Lederbogen, F., Kirsch, P., Haddad, L., Streit, F., Tost, H., Schuch, P., & Meyer-Lindenberg, A. (2011). City living and urban upbringing affect neural social stress processing in humans. *Nature, 474*(7352), 498–501. doi:10.1038/nature10190.

Leding, J. K. (2012). Working memory predicts the rejection of false memories. *Memory, 20*(3), 217–223. doi:10.1080/09658211.2011.653373.

LeDoux, J. E. (1995). Emotion: Clues from the brain. *Annual Review of Psychology, 46,* 209–235.

Lee, C. M., Ryan, J. J., & Kreiner, D. S. (2007). Personality in domestic cats. *Psychological Reports, 100*(1), 27–29.

Lee, C. W., Taylor, G., & Drummond, P. D. (2006). The active ingredient in EMDR: Is it traditional exposure or dual focus of attention? *Clinical Psychology & Psychotherapy, 13*(2), 97–107.

Lee, E. O., & Emanuel, E. J. (2013). Shared decision making to improve care and reduce costs. *New England Journal of Medicine, 368,* 6–8.

Lee, K., Ogunfowora, B., & Ashton, M. C. (2005). Personality traits beyond the big five: Are they within the HEXACO space? *Journal of Personality, 73,* 1437–1463.

Lee, M. S., Kim, J. I., Ha, J. Y., Boddy, K., & Ernst, E. (2009). Yoga for menopausal symptoms: A systematic review. *Menopause, 16,* 602–608.

Lee, S., Colditz, G., Berkman, L., & Kawachi, I. (2003). Caregiving to children and grandchildren and risk of coronary heart disease in women. *American Journal of Public Health, 93,* 1939–1944.

Lee, S. W. S., & Schwarz, N. (2010, May 7). Washing away postdecisional dissonance. *Science, 328*(5979), 709. doi:10.1126/science.1186799.

Lee, Y. S., & Silva, A. J. (2009). The molecular and cellular biology of enhanced cognition. *National Review of Neuroscience, 10*(2), 126–140.

Leeds, A. M. (2009). *A guide to the standard EMDR protocols for clinicians, supervisors, and consultants.* New York: Springer.

Leer, A., Engelhard, I. M., Altink, A., & van den Hout, M. A. (2013). Eye movements during recall of aversive recall of aversive memory decreases conditioned fear. *Behaviour Research Therapy, 51*(10), 633–640.

Legare, C. H., & Gelman, S. A. (2008). Bewitchment, biology, or both: The co- existence of natural and supernatural explanatory frameworks across development. *Cognitive science, 32,* 607–642.

Legault, L., Gutsell, J. N., & Inzlicht, M. (2011). Ironic effects of antiprejudice messages: How motivational interventions can reduce (but also increase) prejudice. *Psychological Science, 22*(12), 1472–1477. doi:10.1177/0956797611427918.

Legerstee, M., Anderson, D., & Schaffer, A. (1998). Five- and eight-month-old infants recognize their faces and voices as familiar and social stimuli. *Child Development, 69,* 37–50.

Lehman, H. E. (1967). Schizophrenia: IV. Clinical features. In A. M. Freedman, H. I. Kaplan, & H. S. Kaplan (Eds.), *Comprehensive textbook of psychiatry.* Baltimore: Williams & Wilkins.

Leibel, R. L., Rosenbaum, M., & Hirsch, J. (1995). Changes in energy expenditure resulting from altered body weight. *New England Journal of Medicine, 332*(10), 621–628.

Leibowitz, H. W., Brislin, R., Perlmutter, L., & Hennessy, R. (1969). Ponzo perspective illusion as a manifestation of space perception. *Science, 166,* 1174–1176.

Leibowitz, S. F. (1992). Neurochemical-neuroendocrine systems in the brain controlling macronutrient intake and metabolism. *TINS, 15,* 491–497.

Leifer, B. P. (2009). Alzheimer's disease: Seeing the signs early. Journal of the American Academy of Nurse Practioners, 21(11), 588–595.

Leigh, B. C., & Stacy, A. W. (2004). Alcohol expectancies and drinking in different age groups. *Addiction, 99,* 215–227.

Leiner, H. C., Leiner, A. L., & Dow, R. S. (1993). Cognitive and language functions of the human cerebellum. *Trends in Neuroscience, 16,* 444–447.

Leinhardt, G., & Knutson, K. (2004). *Listening in on museum conversations.* Walnut Creek, CA: AltaMira Press.

Leippe, M. R., Manion, A. P., & Romanczyk, A. (1992). Eyewitness persuasion: How and how well do fact finders judge the accuracy of adults' and children's memory reports? *Journal of Personality and Social Psychology, 63,* 181–197.

Leising, D., & Zimmermann, J. (2011). An integrative conceptual framework for assessing personality and personality pathology. *Review of General Psychology.* Advance online publication. doi10.1037/a0025070.

Lemaire, P. (2010). Cognitive strategy variations during aging. *Current Directions in Psychological Science, 19*(6), 363–369. doi:10.1177/0963721410390354.

Lemmer, B., Kern, R. I., Nold, G., & Lohrer, H. (2002). Jet lag in athletes after eastward and westward time-zone transition. *Chronobiology International, 19,* 743–764.

Lemoine, P., Kermadi, I., Garcia-Acosta, S., Garay, R. P., & Dib, M. (2006). Double-blind, comparative study of cyamemazine vs. bromazepam in the benzodiazepine withdrawal syndrome. *Progress in Neuro-Psychopharmacology & Biological Psychiatry, 30,* 131–137.

Lemos, G. C., Almeida, L. S., & Colom, R. (2011). Intelligence of adolescents is related to their parents' educational level but not to family income. *Personality and Individual Differences, 50*(7), 1062–1067. doi:10.1016/j.paid.2011.01.025.

Lenneberg, E. H. (1967). *Biological foundations of language*. New York: Wiley.

Lenzenweger, M. F., McLachlan, G., & Rubin, D. B. (2007). Resolving the latent structure of schizophrenia endophenotypes using expectation-maximization-based finite mixture modeling. *Journal of Abnormal Psychology, 116*, 16–29.

Lepore, S. J. (1995). Cynicism, social support, and cardiovascular reactivity. *Health Psychology, 14*, 210–216.

Leppänen, J. M., & Nelson, C. A. (2012). Early development of fear processing. *Current Directions in Psychological Science, 21*, 200–204. doi:10.1177/ 0963721411435841.

Lepper, M. R. (1983). Social-control processes and the internalization of social values: An attributional perspective. In E. T. Higgins, D. N. Ruble, & W. W. Hartup (Eds.), *Social cognition and social development* (pp. 294–330). New York: Cambridge University Press.

Lepper, M. R., & Greene, D. (Eds.). (1978). *The hidden costs of reward*. Hillsdale, NJ: Erlbaum

Lerner, J. S., Gonzalez, R. M., Small, D. A., & Fischhoff, B. (2003). Effects of fear and anger on perceived risks of terrorism: A national field experiment. *Psychological Science, 14*, 144–150.

Leslie, K., Chan, M. T., Myles, P. S., Forbes, A., & McCulloch, T. J. (2010). Posttraumatic stress disorder in aware patients from the B-aware trial. *Anesthesia and Analgesia, 110*(30), 823–828.

Leung, A. K.-y., Kim, S., Polman, E., Ong, L. S., Lin, Q., Goncalo, J. A., & Sanchez-Burks, J. (2012). Embodied metaphors and creative "acts." *Psychological Science*. Published online first. doi:10.1177/0956797611429801.

Leung, H. T., & Westbrook, F. R. (2008). Spontaneous recovery of extinguished fear responses deepens their extinction: A role for error-correction mechanisms. *Journal of Experimental Psychology: Animal Behavior Processes, 31*, 277–288.

Leunis, N., Boumans, M. L., Kremer, B., Din, S., Stobberingh, E., Kessels, A. G., Kross, K. W. (2013). Application of an electronic nose in the diagnosis of head and neck cancer. *Laryngoscope*, October 19, 2013.

Levenson, H. (2003). Time-limited dynamic psychotherapy: An integrationist perspective. *Journal of Psychotherapy Integration, 13*, 300–333.

Levenson, R. W., Ekman, P., & Friesen, W. V. (1990). Voluntary facial action generates emotion-specific autonomic nervous system activity. *Psychophysiology, 27*(4), 363–384.

Levenson, R. W., Ekman, P., Heider, K., & Friesen, W. V. (1992). Emotion and autonomic nervous system activity in the Minangkabau of West Sumatra. *Journal of Personality and Social Psychology, 62*(6), 972–988.

Levin, B., & Bhardwaj, A. (2013). Chronic traumatic encephalopathy: A critical appraisal. *Neurocritical Care*, epub November 5, 2013.

Levin, K. H., Copersino, M. L., Heishman, S. J., Liu, F., Kelly. D. L., Boggs, D. L., & Gorelick, D. A. (2010). Cannabis withdrawal symptoms in non-treatment-seeking adult cannabis smokers. *Drug and Alcohol Dependence, 111*(1–2), 120–127.

Levine, M. W., & Shefner, J. M. (1981). *Fundamentals of sensation and perception*. Reading, MA: Addison-Wesley.

Levine, R., Sato, S., Hashimoto, T., & Verna, J. (1995). Love and marriage in eleven cultures. *Journal of Cross-Cultural Psychology, 26*, 554–571.

Levine, R. V., Reysen, S., & Ganz, E. (2008). The kindness of strangers revisited: A comparison of 24 US cities. *Social Indicators Research, 85*, 461–481.

Levine, S. (1999, February 1). In a loud and noisy world, baby boomers pay the consequences. *International Herald Tribune*.

Levine, T. P., Lester, B., Lagasse, L., Shankaran, S., Bada, H. S., Bauer, C. R., Whitaker, T. M., Higgins, R., Hammond, J., & Roberts, M. B. (2012). Psychopathology and special education enrollment in children with prenatal cocaine exposure. *Journal of Developmental and Behavioral Pediatrics, 33*, 377–386.

Levinson, D. F. (2006). The genetics of depression: A review. *Biological Psychiatry, 60*, 84–92.

Levinson, D. F., Evgrafov, O. V., Knowles, J. A., Potash, J. B., Weissman, M. M., Scheftner, W. A., et al. (2007). Genetics of recurrent early-onset major depression (GenRED): Significant linkage on chromosome 15q25-q26 after fine mapping with single nucleotide polymorphism markers. *American Journal of Psychiatry, 164*, 259–264.

Levinson, D. J., Darrow, C. N., Klein, E. B., Levinson, M. H., & McKee, B. (1978). *The seasons of a man's life*. New York: Knopf.

Levinthal, B. R., & Franconeri, S. L. (2011). Common-fate grouping as feature selection. *Psychological Science, 22*(9), 1132–1137. doi:10.1177/0956797611418346.

Levinthal, C. F. (2001). *Drugs, behavior, and modern society* (3rd ed.). Boston: Allyn & Bacon.

Levitsky, D. A., & DeRosimo, L. (2010). One day of food restriction does not result in an increase in subsequent daily food intake in humans. *Physiology & Behavior, 99*(4), 495–499. doi:10.1016/j.physbeh.2009.12.020.

Levitsky, D. A., & Pacanowski, C. (2011). Losing weight without dieting. Use of commercial foods as meal replacements for lunch produces an extended energy deficit. *Appetite, 57*(2), 311–317. doi:10.1016/j.appet.2011.04.015.

Levy, B. R., Slade, M. D., Kunkel, S. R., & Kasl, S. V. (2002). Longevity increased by positive self-perceptions of aging. *Journal of Personality & Social Psychology, 83*(2), 261–270.

Levy, R., & Ablon, J. S. (Eds.) (2009). *Handbook of evidence-based psychodynamic psychotherapy: Bridging the gap between science and practice*. Totowa, NJ: Humana Press.

Levy-Shiff, R. (1994). Individual and contextual correlates of marital change across the transition to parenthood. *Developmental Psychology, 30*, 591–601.

Lewicki, P. (1992). Nonconscious acquisition of information. *American Psychologist, 47*, 796–801.

Lewinsohn, P. M., Joiner, T. E., & Rohde, P. (2001). Evaluation of cognitive diathesis-stress models in precicting Major Depressive Disorder in adolescents. *Journal of Abnormal Psychology, 110*, 203–215.

Lewinsohn, P. M., & Rosenbaum, M. (1987). Recall of parental behavior by acute depressives, remitted depressives, and nondepressives. *Journal of Personality and Social Psychology, 52*, 611–619.

Lewis, G. J., & Bates, T. C. (2010). Genetic evidence for multiple biological mechanisms underlying in-group favoritism. *Psychological Science, 21*(11), 1263–1268. doi:10.1177/0956797610387439.

Lewis, J. E. (2008). Dream reports of animal rights activists. *Dreaming, 18*, 181–200.

Lewis, J. W., Brefczynski, J. A., Phinney, R. E., Janik, J. J., & DeYoe, E. A. (2005). Distinct cortical pathways for processing tool versus animal sounds. *Journal of Neuroscience, 25*(21), 5148–5158.

Lewis, K. L., Hodges, S. D., Laurent, S. M., Srivastava, S., & Biancarosa, G. (2012). Reading between the minds: The use of stereotypes in empathic accuracy. *Psychological Science*, DOI: 10.1177/0956797612439719 (published online first).

Lewis-Fernández, R., Hinton, D. E., Laria, A. J., Patterson, E. H., Hofmann, S. G., Craske, M. G., & Liao, B. (2010). Culture and the anxiety disorders: Recommendations for DSM-V. *Depression & Anxiety 27*(2), 212–229. doi:10.1002 /da.20647.

Lewis-Morrarty, E., Dozier, M., Bernard, K., Terracciano, S. & Moore, S. (2012). Cognitive flexibility and theory of mind outcomes among foster children: Preschool follow-up results of a randomized clinical trial. *Journal of Adolescent Health, 51*, S17–S22.

Lewison, G. G., Roe, P. P., Wentworth, A. A., & Szmukler, G. G. (2012). The reporting of mental disorders research in British media. *Psychological Medicine, 42*(2), 435–441. doi:10.1017/S0033291711001012.

Lewkowicz, D. J., & Hansen-Tift, A. M. (2012). Infants deploy selective attention to the mouth of a talking face when learning speech. *Proceedings of the National Academy of Sciences of the United States of America, 109*(5), 1431–1436. doi:10.1073/pnas.1114783109.

Lewontin, R. (1976). Race and intelligence. In N. J. Block & G. Dworkin (Eds.), *The IQ controversy: Critical readings* (pp. 107–112). New York: Pantheon.

Ley, J. M., Bennett, P. C., & Coleman, G. J. (2009). A refinement and validation of the Monash Canine Personality Questionnaire (MCPQ). *Applied Animal Behaviour Science, 116*(2–4), 220–227.

Leyro, T. M., Zvolensky, M. J., & Bernstein, A. (2010). Distress tolerance and psychopathological symptoms and disorders: A review of the empirical literature among adults. *Psychological Bulletin, 136*, 576–600.

Lezak, M. D., Howieson, D., Bigler, E. D., & Tranel, D. (2012). Neuropsychological Assessment, 5th ed. Oxford University Press.

Lezak, M. D., Loring, D. W., & Howieson, D. B. (2004). *Neuropsychological assessment* (4th ed.). New York: Oxford University Press.

Li, D.-K., Petitti, D. B., Willinger, M., McMahon, R., et al. (2003). Infant sleeping position and the risk of sudden infant death syndrome in California, 1997–2000. *American Journal of Epidemiology, 157*, 446–455.

Li, N., & Bartlett, C. W. (2012). Defining the genetic architecture of human developmental language impairment. *Life Sciences, 90*(13–14), 469–475.

Li, N., Downey, J. E., Bar-Shir, A., Gilad, A. A., Walczak, P., Kim, H., & Pelled, G. (2011). Optogenetic-guided cortical plasticity after nerve injury. *Proceedings of the National Academy of Sciences of The United States Of America, 108*(21), 8838–8843. doi:10.1073/pnas.1100815108.

Li, N. P., Yong, J. C., Tov, W., Sng, O., Fletcher, G. J. O., Valentine, K. A., Jiang, Y. F., & Balliet, D. (2013). Mate preferences do predict attraction and choices in the early stages of mate selection. *Journal of Personality and Social Psychology, 105*(5), 757–776.

Li, S., Cullen, W., Anwyl, R., & Rowan, M. J. (2003). Dopamine-dependent facilitation of LTP induction in hippocampal CA1 by exposure to spatial novelty. *Nature Neuroscience, 6*, 526–531.

Li, S. C., Lindenberger, U., Hommel, B., Aschersleben, G., Prinz, W., & Baltes, P. B. (2004). Transformations in the couplings among intellectual abilities and constituent cognitive processes across the life span. *Psychological Science, 15*, 155–163.

Li, W., Dowd, S. E., Scurlock, B., Acosta-Martinez, V., & Lyte, M. (2009). Memory and learning behavior in mice is temporally associated with diet-induced alterations in gut bacteria. *Physiology & Behavior, 96*(4–5), 557–567.

Li, Y., Johnson, K. A., Cohen, A. B., Williams, M. J., Knowles, E. D., & Chen, Z. (2012). Fundamental(ist) attribution error: Protestants are dispositionally focused. *Journal of Personality and Social Psychology, 102*(2), 281–290.

Li, Y., Zheng, H., Witt, C. M., Roll, S., Yu, S. G., Yan, J., Sun, G. J., Zhao, L., Huang. W. J., Chang, X. R., Zhang, H. X., Wang, D. J., Lan, L., Zou, R., Liang, F. R. (2012). Acupuncture for migraine prophylaxis: a randomized controlled trial. *CMAJ*, Epub January 9, 2012.

Li Cavoli, G., Mulè, G., & Rotolo, U. (2011). Renal involvement in psychological eating disorders. *Nephron Clinical Practice, 119*(4), c338–c341. doi:10.1159/ 000333798.

Liao, H., & Rupp, D. E. (2005). The impact of justice climate and justice orientation on work outcomes: A cross-level multifoci framework. *Journal of Applied Psychology, 90*, 242–256.

Liben, L. (1978). Perspective-taking skills in young children: Seeing the world through rose-colored glasses. *Developmental Psychology, 14*, 87–92.

Lichenstein, R., Smith, D. C., Ambrose, J. L., & Moody, L. A. (2012). Headphone use and pedestrian injury and death in the United States: 2004–2011. *Injury Prevention*. Advance online publication. doi: Inj Prev doi:10.1136/ injuryprev-2011-040161.

Lichtenstein, E., Zhu, S.-H. , & Tedeschi, G. J. (2010). Smoking cessation quitlines: An underrecognized intervention success story. *American Psychologist, 65*(4), 252–261. doi:10.1037/a0018598.

Lichtman, J., & Denk, W. (2011). The big and the small: Challenges of imaging the brain's circuits. *Science, 334*(6056), 618–623.

Lickey, M., & Gordon, B. (1991). *Medicine and mental illness: The use of drugs in psychiatry*. San Francisco: Freeman.

Lickliter, R. (2008). The growth of developmental thought: Implications for a new evolutionary psychology. *New Ideas in Psychology, 26*(3), 353–369.

Liddle, J. R., Shackelford, T. K., & Weekes–Shackelford, V. A. (2012). Why can't we all just get along? Evolutionary perspectives on violence, homicide, and war. *Review of General Psychology, 16*, 24–36. doi:10.1037/a0026610.

Lidwall, U., & Marklund, S. (2011). Trends in long-term sickness absence in Sweden 1992–2008: The role of economic conditions, legislation, demography, work environment and alcohol consumption. *International Journal of Social Welfare, 20*(2), 167–179. doi:10.1111/j.1468-2397.2010.00744.x

Lieberman, M. D. (2012). A geographical history of social cognitive neuroscience. *Neuroimage, 61*(2), 432–436.

Lieberman, P. (1991). *Uniquely human*. Cambridge, MA: Harvard University Press.

Liebert, R. M., & Spiegler, M. D. (1994). *Personality: Strategies and issues*. Pacific Grove, CA: Brooks/Cole.

Liechti, M. E., Gamma, A., & Vollenweider, F. X. (2001). Gender differences in the subjective effects of MDMA. *Psychopharmacology, 154*, 161–168.

Liechti, M. E. & Markou, A. (2008). Role of the glutamatergic system in nicotine dependence: implications for the discovery and development of new pharmacological smoking cessation therapies. *CNS Drugs, 22*(9), 705–724.

Lievens, F., Harris, M. M., Van Keer, E., & Bisqueret, C. (2003). Predicting cross-cultural training performance: The validity of personality, cognitive ability, and dimensions measured by an assessment center and a behavior description interview. *Journal of Applied Psychology, 88*, 476–489.

Lievens, F., Peeters, H., & Schollaert, E. (2008). Situational judgment tests: A review of recent research. *Personnel Review, 37*, 426–441.

Light, K. C., Girdler, S. S., Sherwood, A., Bragdon, E. E., Brownley, K. A., West, S. G., & Hinderliter, A. L. (1999). High stress responsivity predicts later blood pressure only in combination with positive family history and high life stress. *Hypertension, 33*, 1458–1464.

Light, L. K., Grewen, K. M., Amico, J. A., Brownley, K. A., West, S. G., Hinderliter, A. L., et al. (2005). Oxytocinergic activity is linked to lower blood pressure and vascular resistance during stress in postmenopausal women on estrogen replacement. *Hormones and Behavior, 47*, 540–548.

Lilienfeld, S. O. (2007). Psychological treatments that cause harm. *Perspectives on Psychological Science, 2*, 53–70.

Lilienfeld, S. O. (2011a). Distinguishing scientific from pseudoscientific psychotherapies: Evaluating the role of theoretical plausibility, with a little help from Reverend Bayes. *Clinical Psychology: Science and Practice, 18*, 105–112.

Lilienfeld, S. O. (2011b). Public skepticism of psychology: Why many people perceive the study of human behavior as unscientific. *American Psychologist*. Advance online publication. doi:10.1037/a0023963.

Lilienfeld, S. O., Ammirati, R., & Landfield, K. (2009). Giving debiasing away: Can psychological research on correcting cognitive errors promote human welfare? *Perspectives on Psychological Science, 4*, 390–398.

Lilienfeld, S. O., & Arkowitz, H. (2007, December). EMDR: Taking a closer look. *Scientific American, 17*(4), 10–11.

Lilienfeld, S. O., & Lynn, S. J. (2003). Dissociative identity disorder: Multiple personalities, multiple controversies. In S. O. Lilienfeld & S. J. Lynn (Eds.), *Science and pseudoscience in clinical psychology* (pp. 109–142). New York: Guilford.

Lilienfeld, S. O., Lynn, S. J., Namy, L. L., & Wolff, N. J. (2009). *Psychology: From inquiry to understanding*. Boston: Pearson.

Lilienfeld, S. O., Ritschel, L. A., Lynn, S. J., Cautin, R. L., & Latzman, R. D. (2013). Why many clinical psychologists are resistant to evidence-based practice: root causes and constructive remedies. *Clinical Psychology Review, 33*(7), 883–900.

Lim, J., & Dinges, D. F. (2010). A meta-analysis of the impact of short-term sleep deprivation on cognitive variables. *Psychological Bulletin, 136*, 375–389.

Lim, V. K. G., Teo, T. S. H., & Loo, G. L. (2003). Sex, financial hardship and locus of control: An empirical study of attitudes towards money among Singaporean Chinese. *Personality and Individual Differences, 34*, 411–429.

Lin, J. (2013). Do video games exert stronger effects on aggression than film? The role of media interactivity and identification on the association of violent content and aggressive outcomes. *Computers in Human Behavior, 29*(3), 535–543.

Lin, K. M., Smith, M. W., & Ortiz, V. (2001). Culture and psychopharmacology. *Psychiatric Clinics of North America, 24*, 523–538.

Lin, L., Umahara, M., York, D. A., & Bray, G. A. (1998). Beta-casomorphins stimulate and enterostatin inhibits the intake of dietary fat in rats. *Peptides, 19*, 325–331.

Lin, T., Chen, S., Huang, T., Chang, C., Chuang, J., Wu, F., & . . . Jen, C. J. (2012). Different types of exercise induce differential effects on neuronal adaptations and memory performance. *Neurobiology of Learning and Memory, 97*(1), 140–147. doi:10.1016/j.nlm.2011.10.006.

Lin, Y., Wu, M., Yang, C., Chen, T., Hsu, C., Chang, Y., et al. (2008). Evaluation of assertiveness training for psychiatric patients. *Journal of Clinical Nursing, 17*, 2875–2883.

Linde, K., Allais, G., Brinkhaus, B., Manheimer, E., Vickers, A., & White, A. R. (2009). Acupuncture for tension-type headache. *Cochrane Database Systematic Review, 1*, article no. CD007587. Retrieved March 25, 2009, from http://mrw. interscience. wiley.com/cochrane/clsysrev/articles/CD007587/frame.html.

Linden, D. J., Oosterhof, N. N., Klein, C., & Downing, P. E. (2012). Mapping brain activation and information during category-specific visual working memory. *Journal of Neurophysiology, 107*(2), 628–639. doi:10.1152/jn.00105.2011.

Lindner, I., Echterhoff, G., Davidson, P. R., & Brand, M. (2010). Observation inflation: Your actions become mine. *Psychological Science, 21*(9), 1291–1299. doi:10.1177/0956797610379860.

Lindsay, D. S., Hagen, L., Read, J. D., Wade, K., & Gary, M. (2004). True photographs and false memories. *Psychological Science, 15*, 149–154.

Lindvall, O., & Kokaia, Z. (2010). Stem cells in human neurodegenerative disorders: Time for clinical translation? *Journal of Clinical Investigation, 120*, 29–40. doi:10.1172/JCI40543.

Lippa, R. A. (2003). Are 2D:4D finger-length ratios related to sexual orientation? Yes for men, no for women. *Journal of Personality and Social Psychology, 85*, 179–188.

Lipscomb, S. T., Leve, L. D., Harold, G. T., Neiderhiser, J. M., Shaw, D. S., Ge, X., & Reiss, D. (2011). Trajectories of parenting and child negative emotionality during infancy and toddlerhood: A longitudinal analysis. *Child Development, 82*,1661–1675.

Lisman, J., Yasuda, R., & Raghavachari, S. (2012). Mechanisms of CaMKII action in long-term potentiation. *Nature Reviews Neuroscience, 13*(3), 169–182.

Lissek, S., Kaczkurkin, A. N., Rabin, S., Geraci, M., Pine, D. S., & Grillon, C. (2014). Generalized anxiety disorder is associated with overgeneralization of classically conditioned fear. *Biological Psychiatry, 75*(11), 909–915.

Liston, C., McEwen, B. S., & Casey, B. J. (2009). Psychosocial stress reversibly disrupts prefrontal processing and attentional control. *Proceedings of the National Academy of Sciences, 106*, 912–917.

Litwin, H., & Shiovitz-Ezra, S. (2006). The association between activity and well-being in later life: What really matters? *Aging and Society, 26*, 225–242.

Liu, G., & Akira, H. (1994). Basic principle of TCM. In Liu, G., Akira, H. (Eds.), *Fundamentals of acupuncture and moxibustion*. Tianjin, China: Tianjin Science and Technology Translation and Publishing Corporation.

Liu, J., Raine, A., Venables, P. H., & Mednick, S. A. (2004). Malnutrition at age 3 years and externalizing behavior problems at ages 8, 11, and 17 years. *American Journal of Psychiatry, 161*, 2005–2013.

Liu, J., Zhao, L., Xue, Y., Shi, J., Suo, L., Luo, Y., Chai, B., Yang, C., Fang, Q., Zhang, Y., Bao, Y., Pickens, C. L., & Lu, L. (2014). An unconditioned stimulus retrieval extinction procedure to prevent the return of fear memory. (2014). *Biological Psychology*, Epub April 3, 2014.

Liu, R. T., & Miller, I. (2014). Life events and suicidal ideation and behavior: A systematic review. *Clinical Psychology Review, 34*(3), 181–192.

Liu, W. Y., Weber, B., Reuter, M., Markett, S., Chu, W. C., & Montag, C. (2013). The big five of personality and structural imaging revisited: A VBM-DARTEL study. *Neuroreport, 24*, 375–380.

Liu, Y. P., Lang, B. T., Baskaya, M. K., Dempsey, R. J., & Vemuganti, R. (2009). The potential of neural stem cells to repair stroke-induced brain damage. *Acta Neuropathologica, 117*, 469–480. Epub 2009 Mar 13.

Liuzza, M., Cazzato, V., Vecchione, M., Crostella, F., Caprara, G., & Aglioti, S. (2011). Follow my eyes: the gaze of politicians reflexively captures the gaze of ingroup voters. *Plos One, 6*(9), e25117.

Lively, W. M. (2001). Syncope and neurologic deficits in a track athlete: A case report. *Medicine and Science in Sports and Exercise, 33*, 345–347.

Livesley, W. J. (2005). Behavioral and molecular genetic contributions to a dimensional classification of personality disorders. *Journal of Personality Disorders, 19*, 131–155.

Livingston, R. W., Rosette, A., & Washington, E. F. (2012). Can an agentic Black woman get ahead? The impact of race and interpersonal dominance on perceptions of female leaders. *Psychological Science, 23*, 354–358. doi:10.1177/0956797611428079.

Lizardi, D., Oquendo, M. A., & Graver, R. (2009). Clinical pitfalls in the diagnosis of *ataque de nervios*: A case study. *Transcultural Psychiatry, 46*, 463–486.

Lleras, A., & Moore, C. M. (2006). What you see is what you get: Functional equivalence of a perceptually filled-in surface and a physically presented stimulus. *Psychological Science, 17*, 876–881.

Llewellyn, C. H., Trzaskowski, M., van Jaarsveld, C. H. M., Plomin, R., & Wardle, J. (2014). Satiety mechanisms in genetic risk of obesity. *JAMA Pediatrics, 168*(4), 338–344.

Lobue, V., & Deloache, J. (2011). Pretty in pink: The early development of gender-stereotyped colour preferences. *The British Journal of Developmental Psychology, 29*(Pt 3), 656–667. doi:10.1111/j.2044–835X.2011.02027.x.

LoBue, V., & DeLoache, J. S. (2010). Superior detection of threat-relevant stimuli in infancy. *Developmental Science 13*(1), 221–228. doi:10.1111/j.1467–7687.2009.00872.x.

LoBue, V., Nishida, T., Cynthia, C., DeLoache, J. S., & Haidt, J. (2011). When getting something good is bad: even three-year-olds react to inequality. *Social Development, 20*(1), 154–170. doi:10.1111/j.1467–9507.2009.00560.x.

Locke, E. A. (2000). Motivation, cognition, and action: An analysis of studies of task goals and knowledge. *Applied Psychology: An International Review, 49*, 408–429.

Locke, E. A., & Latham G. P. (1990). *A theory of goal setting & task performance.* Englewood Cliffs, NJ: Prentice Hall.

Locke, E. A., & Latham, G. P. (2002). Building a practically useful theory of goal setting and task motivation: A 35-year odyssey. *American Psychologist, 57*, 705–717.

Lockley, S. W., Barger, L. K., Ayas, N. T., Rothschild, J. M., Czeisler, C. A., Landrigan, C. P. & the Harvard Work Hours, Health and Safety Group. (2007). Effects of health care provider work hours and sleep deprivation on safety and performance. *Joint Commission Journal on Quality and Patient Safety, 33*(11 Suppl), 7–18.

Locurto, C. (1991). Beyond IQ in preschool programs? *Intelligence, 15*, 295–312.

Loehlin, J. C. (1989). Partitioning environmental and genetic contributions to behavioral development. *American Psychologist, 44*, 1285–1292.

Loehlin, J. C. (2010). Environment and the behavior genetics of personality: Let me count the ways. *Personality And Individual Differences, 49*(4), 302–305. doi:10.1016/j.paid.2009.10.035.

Loehlin, J. C. (2011). Genetic and environmental structures of personality: A cluster-analysis approach. *Personality and Individual Differences, 51*, 662–666.

Loehlin, J. C., & Martin, N. G. (2011). The general factor of personality: Questions and elaboration. *Journal of Research in Personality, 45*, 44–49.

Loehlin, J. C., & Martin, N. G. (2013). General and supplementary factors of personality in genetic and environmental correlation matrices. *Personality and Individual Differences, 54*, 761–766.

Loewenstein, G. (1994). The psychology of curiosity: A review and reinterpretation. *Psychological Bulletin, 116*(1), 75–98.

Lofquist, D., Lugaila, T., O'Connell, M., & Feliz, S. (2012, April). Households and families: 2010 (2010 Census Briefs, No. C2010BR-14). Retrieved from http:// www.census.gov/prod/cen2010/briefs/c2010br-14.pdf.

Loftus, E. F. (1992). When a lie becomes memory's truth: Memory distortion after exposure to misinformation. *Psychological Science, 3*, 121–123.

Loftus, E. F. (1997a). Memory for a past that never was. *Current Directions in Psychological Science, 6*, 60–65.

Loftus, E. F. (1997b). Repressed memory accusations: Devastated families and devastated patients. *Applied Cognitive Psychology, 11*, 25–30.

Loftus, E. F. (1998). The price of bad memories. *Skeptical Inquirer, 22*, 23–24.

Loftus, E. F. (2003, January). *Illusions of memory.* Presentation at the 25th Annual National Institute on the Teaching of Psychology, St. Petersburg Beach, Florida.

Loftus, E. F. (2004). Memories of things unseen. *Current Directions in Psychological Science, 13*, 145–147.

Loftus, E. F., & Davis, D. (2006). Recovered memories. *Annual Review of Clinical Psychology, 2*, 469–498.

Loftus, E. F., & Hoffman, H. G. (1989). Misinformation and memory: The creation of new memories. *Journal of Experimental Psychology: General, 118*, 100–104.

Loftus, E. F., & Ketcham, K. (1994). *The myth of repressed memory: False memories and allegations of sexual abuse.* New York: St. Martin's Press.

Loftus, E. F., & Palmer, J. C. (1974). Reconstruction of automobile destruction: An example of the interaction between language and memory. *Journal of Verbal Learning and Verbal Behavior, 13*, 585–589.

Loftus, E. F., & Pickrell, J. E. (1995). The formation of false memories. *Psychiatric Annals, 25*, 720–725.

Logie, R. H. (2011). The functional organization and capacity limits of working memory. *Current Directions in Psychological Science, 20*(4), 240–245. doi:10.1177/0963721411415340.

Logue, A. W. (1985). Conditioned food aversion in humans. *Annals of the New York Academy of Sciences, 104*, 331–340.

Loher, B. T., Noe, R. A., Moeller, N. L., & Fitzgerald, M. P. (1985). A meta-analysis of the relation of job characteristics to job satisfaction. *Journal of Applied Psychology, 70*, 280–289.

Lohman, D. F. (2004). Aptitude for college: The importance of reasoning tests for minority admissions. In R. Zwick (Ed.), *Rethinking the SAT: The future of standardized testing in college admissions* (pp. 41–56). New York: RoutledgeFalmer.

Lohman, D. F. (2005). The role of non-verbal ability tests in identifying academically gifted students: An aptitude perspective. *Gifted Child Quarterly, 49*, 111–138.

Lohman, D. F., & Hagen, E. (2001). *Cognitive abilities test (Form 6): Interpretive guide for teachers and counselors.* Itasca, IL: Riverside.

Lohr, J. M., Hooke, W., Gist, R., & Tolin, D. F. (2003). Novel and controversial treatments for trauma-related stress disorders. In S. O. Lilienfeld, S. J. Lynn, & J. M. Lohr (Eds.), *Science and pseudoscience in clinical psychology* (pp. 243–272). New York: Guilford Press.

LoLordo, V.M., & Overmier, J. B. (2011). Trauma, learned helplessness, its neuroscience, and implications for posttramautic stress disorder. In T. R. Schachtman & S. Reilly (Eds.), *Associative learning and conditioning theory.* Oxford: Oxford University Press.

Lombard, C., Deeks, A., Jolley, D., Ball, K., & Teede, H. (2010). A low-intensity, community-based lifestyle programme to prevent weight gain in women with young children: Cluster randomised controlled trial. *British Medical Journal, 341*, c3215.

London Daily Telegraph. (1998, September 19). "'Cat' that turned out to be a clock." *London Daily Telegraph.*

Long, J. K., & Andrews, B. V. (2011). Fostering strength and resiliency in same-sex couples. In J. L. Wetchler (Ed.), *Handbook of clinical issues in couple therapy* (2nd ed.) (pp. 225–246). New York: Routledge/Taylor & Francis Group.

Long, K., Reger, N., & Adams, G. (2013). NeuroRehabilitation, epub November 27, 2013.

Longo, M. R., & Haggard, P. (2010). An implicit body representation underlying human position sense. *Proceedings of the National Academy of Sciences of the United States of America, 107*(26), 11727–11732.

Longo, N., Klempay, S., & Bitterman, M. E. (1964). Classical appetitive conditioning in the pigeon. *Psychonomic Science, 1*, 19–20.

Lopez, S. R. (1989). Patient variable biases in clinical judgment: Conceptual overview and methodological considerations. *Psychological Bulletin, 106*, 184–203.

Lopez-Garcia, E., van Dam, R. M., Li, T. Y., Rodriguez-Artalejo, F., & Hu, F. B. (2008). The relationship of coffee consumption with mortality. *Annals of Internal Medicine, 148*, 904–914.

Lorenzo, G. L., Biesanz, J. C., & Human, L. J. (2010). What is beautiful is good and more accurately understood: Physical attractiveness and accuracy in first impressions of personality. *Psychological Science, 21*(12), 1777–1782. doi:10.1177/0956797610388048.

Losh, S. C., Tavani, C. M., Njoroge, R., Wilke, R., & McAuley, M. (2003). What does education really do? Educational dimensions and pseudoscience support in the American general public, 1979–2001. *Skeptical Inquirer, 27*, 30–35.

Loughnan, S., Kuppens, P., Allik, J., Balazs, K., de Lemus, S., Dumont, K., Gargurevich, R., Hidegkuti, I., Leidner, B., Matos, L., Park, J., Realo, A., Shi1, S., Sojo, V. E., Tong, Y.-Y., Vaes, J., Verduyn, P., Yeung, V., & Haslam, N. (2011). Economic inequality is linked to biased self-perception. *Psychological Science, 22*(10) 1254–1258. doi:10.1177/0956797611417003.

Lourida, I., Soni, M., Thompson-Coon, J., Purandare, N., Lang, I. A., Ukoummune, O. C., & Llewellyn, D. J. (2013). Mediterranean diet, cognitive function, and dementia: A systematic review. *Epidemiology, 24*(4), 479–489.

Lovell, B., Moss, M., & Wetherell, M. (2012). The psychosocial, endocrine and immune consequences of caring for a child with autism or ADHD. *Psychoneuroendocrinology, 37*(4), 534–542. doi:10.1016/j.psyneuen.2011.08.003.

Lovibond, P. F., Mitchell, C. J., Minard, E., Brady, A., & Menzies, R. G. (2009). Safety behaviours preserve threat beliefs: Protection from extinction of human fear conditioning by an avoidance response. *Behaviour Research and Therapy, 47,* 716–720.

Löwe, B., Mundt, C., Herzog, W., Brunner, R., Backenstass, M., Kronmueller, K., & Henningsen, P. (2008). Validity of current somatoform disorder diagnoses: Perspective for classification in DSM-V and ICD-11. *Psychopathology, 41,* 4–9.

Lubinski, D. (2004). Introduction to the special section on cognitive abilities: 100 years after Spearman's (1904) "'General intelligence,' objectively determined and measured."*Journal of Personality and Social Psychology, 86,* 96–111.

Lubinski, D., & Benbow, C. P. (1995). An opportunity for empiricism [Review of the book *Multiple intelligences: The theory in practice*]. *Contemporary Psychology, 40,* 935–938.

Lubinski, D., Benbow, C. P., Webb, R. M., & Bleske-Rechek, A. (2006). Tracking exceptional human capital over two decades. *Psychological Science, 17*(3), 194–199.

Lubinski, D., Webb, R. M., Morelock, M. J., & Benbow, C. P. (2001). Top 1 in 10,000: A 10 year follow-up of the profoundly gifted. *Journal of Applied Psychology, 86,* 718–729.

Luborsky, L. (1972). Another reply to Eysenck. *Psychological Bulletin, 78,* 406–408.

Luborsky, L., Rosenthal, R., & Diguer, L. (2003). Are some psychotherapies much more effective than others? *Journal of Applied Psychoanalytic Studies, 5*(4), 455–460.

Luborsky, L., Singer, B., & Luborsky, L. (1975). Comparative studies of psychotherapies: Is it true that everyone has won and all must have prizes? *Archives of General Psychiatry, 32,* 995–1008.

Luby, J. L. (2010). Preschool depression: The importance of identifi cation of depression early in development. *Current Directions in Psychological Science, 19,* 91–95.

Lucas, J. A. (2005). Disorders of memory. *Psychiatric Clinics of North America, 28*(3), 581–597.

Lucas, R. E. (2007). Adaptation and the set-point model of subjective well-being: Does happiness change after major life events? *Current Directions in Psychological Science, 16,* 75–79.

Lucas-Thompson, R., & Clarke-Stewart, K. A. (2007). Forecasting friendship: How marital quality, maternal mood, and attachment security are linked to children's peer relationships. *Journal of Applied Developmental Psychology, 28,* 499–514.

Luchins, A. S. (1942). Mechanization in problem solving: The effect of *Einstellung*. *Psychological Monographs, 54*(6, Whole No. 248).

Luders, E., Clark, K., Narr, K. L., & Toga, A. W. (2011). Enhanced brain connectivity in long-term meditation practitioners. *NeuroImage, 57*(4), 1308–1316

Luguri, J., Napier, J., & Dovidio, J. (2012). Reconstruing intolerance: Abstract thinking reduces conservatives' prejudice against nonnormative groups. *Psychological Science, 23,* 756–763.

Luhrmann, T. M. (2008). "The street will drive you crazy": Why homeless psychotic women in the institutional circuit in the United States often say no to offers of help. *American Journal of Psychiatry, 165,* 15–20.

Luk, G., Bialystok, E., Craik, F. M., & Grady, C. L. (2011). Lifelong bilingualism maintains white matter integrity in older adults. *The Journal of Neuroscience, 31*(46), 16808–16813. doi:10.1523/JNEUROSCI.4563–11.2011.

Luna, D., Ringberg, T., & Peracchio, L. A. (2008). One individual, two identities: Frame switching among biculturals. *Journal of Consumer Research, 35*(2), 279–293.

Luna, K., & Martín-Luengo, B. (2012). Confidence–accuracy calibration with general knowledge and eyewitness memory cued recall questions. *Applied Cognitive Psychology, 26*(2), 289–295. doi:10.1002/acp.1822.

Lund, T., Labriola, M., Christensen, K. B., Bultmann, U., & Villadsen, E. (2006). Physical work environment risk factors for long-term sickness absence: Prospective findings among a cohort of 5357 employees in Denmark. *British Medical Journal, 332,* 449–452.

Luntz, B. K., & Widom, C. S. (1994). Antisocial personality disorder in abused and neglected children grown up. *American Journal of Psychiatry, 151,* 670–674.

Lupica, M. (2013). Morbid find suggests murder-obsessed gunman Adam Lanza plotted Newtown, Conn.'s Sandy Hook massacre for years. *New York Daily News,* March 17, 2013.

Luria, Z. (1992, February). *Gender differences in children's play patterns.* Paper presented at University of Southern California, Los Angeles.

Lussier, J. P., Heil, S. H., Mongeon, J. A., Badger, G. J., & Higgins, S. T. (2006). A meta-analysis of voucher-based reinforcement therapy for substance use disorders. *Addiction, 101,* 192–203.

Lustig, R. H., Sen, S., Soberman, J. E., & Velasquez-Mieyer, P. A. (2004). Obesity, leptin resistance, and the effects of insulin reduction. *International Journal of Obesity, 28,* 1344–1348.

Luthar, S. S., & Barkin, S. H. (2012). Are affluent youth truly "at risk"? Vulnerability and resilience across three diverse samples. *Development and Psychopathology, 24,* 429–449.

Lutz, D. J., & Sternberg, R. J. (1999). Cognitive development. In M. H. Bornstein & M. E. Lamb (Eds.), *Developmental psychology: An advanced textbook* (4th ed.). Mahwah, NJ: Erlbaum.

Lv, P., Hu, X., Lv, J., Han, J., Guo, L., & Liu, T. (2014). A linear model for characterization of synchronization frequencies of neural networks. *Cognitive Neurodynamics, 8*(1), 55–69.

Lybarger, J. E., & Monteith, M. J. (2011). The effect of Obama saliency on individual-level racial bias: Silver bullet or smokescreen? *Journal of Experimental Social Psychology, 47*(3), 647–652.

Lydon, J, Fitzsimons, G, & Naidoo, L. (2003). Devaluation versus enhancement of attractive alternatives: A critical test. *Personality and Social Psychology Bulletin, 29,* 349–359.

Lykken, D. T. (1998a). The genetics of genius. In A. Steptoe (Ed.) *Genius and mind: Studies of creativity and temperament* (pp. 15–37). New York, NY: Oxford University Press.

Lykken, D. T. (1998b). *A tremor in the blood: Uses and abuses of the lie detector.* Cambridge, MA: Perseus Publishing.

Lykken, D. T. (1999). *Happiness: What studies on twins show us about nature, nurture, and the happiness set point.* New York: Golden Books.

Lyman, D. R., & Gudonis, L. (2005). The development of psychopathy. *Annual Review of Clinical Psychology, 1,* 381–407.

Lyn, H., Greenfield, P. M., Savage-Rumbaugh, S., Gillespie-Lynch, K., & Hopkins, W. D. (2011). Nonhuman primates do declare! A comparison of declarative symbol and gesture use in two children, two bonobos, and a chimpanzee. *Language & Communication, 31*(1), 63–74. doi:10.1016/j.langcom.2010.11.001.

Lynall, M.-E., Bassett, D. S., Kerwin, R., McKenna, P. J., et al. (2010). Functional connectivity and brain networks in schizophrenia. *Journal of Neuroscience, 30,* 9477–9487.

Lynn, R. (2006). *Race differences in intelligence: An evolutionary analysis.* Augusta, GA: Washington Summit Publishers.

Lynn, R., & Mikk, J. (2007). National differences in intelligence and educational attainment. *Intelligence, 35,* 115–121.

Lynn, S. J., Lilienfeld, S. O., & Lohr, J. M. (Eds.). (2003). *Science and pseudoscience in clinical psychology.* New York: Guilford Press.

Lynn, S. J., Lilienfeld, S. O., Merckelbach, H., Giesbrecht, Y., McNally, R. J., Loftus, E. F., Bruck, M., Garry, M., & Malaktaris, A. (2014). The trauma model of dissociation: Inconvenient trutsh and stubborn fictions. Comment on Dalenberg et al. (2012). *Psychological Bulletin, 140*(3), 896–910.

Lynn, S. J., Lilienfeld, S. O., Merckelbach, H., Giesbrecht, T., & Van Der Kloet, D. (2012). Dissociation and dissociative disorders: Challenging conventional wisdom. *Current Directions in Psychological Science, 21,* 48–53. doi:10.1177/ 0963721411429457.

Lynn, S. J., Myers, B., & Malinoski, P. (1997). Hypnosis, pseudomemories, and clinical guidelines: A sociocognitive perspective. In J. D. Read & D. S. Lindsay (Eds.), *Recollections of trauma: Scientific evidence and clinical practice. NATO ASI series: Series A: Life sciences* (Vol. 291, pp. 305–336). New York: Plenum Press.

Lynn, S. J., & Rhue, J. W. (1986). The fantasy-prone person: Hypnosis, imagination, and creativity. *Journal of Personality and Social Psychology, 51,* 404–408.

Lynn, S. J., Vanderhoff, H., Shindler, K., & Stafford, J. (2002). Defining hypnosis as a trance vs. cooperation: Hypnotic inductions, suggestibility, and performance standards. *American Journal of Clinical Hypnosis, 44,* 231–240.

Lyon, L. (2009, May 8). 7 criminal cases that invoked the "sleepwalking defense." *U.S. News & World Report.* Retrieved from http://health.usnews.com.

Lyubomirsky, S., King, L., & Diener, E. (2005). The benefits of frequent positive affect: Does happiness lead to success? *Psychological Bulletin, 131,* 803–855.

Lyubomirsky, S., & Nolen-Hoeksema, S. (1995). Effects of self-focused rumination on negative thinking and interpersonal problem solving. *Journal of Personality and Social Psychology, 69,* 176–190.

Ma, M. (2007). Encoding olfactory signals via multiple chemosensory systems. *Critical Reviews in Biochemistry and Molecular Biology, 42*(6), 463–480.

Ma, S. H., & Teasdale, J. D. (2004). Mindfulness-based cognitive therapy for depression: Replication and exploration of differential relapse prevention effects. *Journal of Consulting and Clinical Psychology, 72,* 1–40.

Ma, Y., Wang, C., & Han, S. (2011). Neural responses to perceived pain in others predict real-life monetary donations in different socioeconomic contexts. *Neuroimage, 57*(3), 1273–1280. doi:10.1016/j.neuroimage.2011.05.003.

Maandag, N. J., Coman, D., Sanganahalli, B. G., Herman, P., Smith, A. J., Blumenfeld, H., et al. (2007). Energetics of neuronal signaling and fMRI activity. *Proceedings of the National Academies of Sciences, 104*(51), 20546–20551.

MacAndrew, C., & Edgerton, R. B. (1969). *Drunken comportment*. Chicago: Aldine.

McCabe, D. P., Castel, A. D., & Rhodes, M. G. (2011). The influence of fMRI lie detection evidence on juror decision-making. *Behavioral Sciences & the Law, 29*(4), 566–577. doi:10.1002/bsl.993.

Maccoby, E. E., & Martin, J. A. (1983). Socialization in the context of the family: Parent-child interaction. In E. M. Hetherington (Ed.) and P. H. Mussen (Series Ed.), *Handbook of child psychology: Vol. 4. Socialization, personality, and social development* (pp. 1–101). New York: Wiley.

MacDonald, K., MacDonald, T. M., Brune, M., Lamb, K. Wilson, M. P., Golshan, S., & Feifel, D. (2013). Oxytocin and psychotherapy: A pilot study of its physiological, behavioral and subjective effects in males with depression. *Psychoneuroendocrinology, 36*, 2831–2843.

MacDonald, M., & Bernstein, D. A. (1974). Treatment of a spider phobia with in vivo and imaginal desensitization. *Journal of Behavior Therapy and Experimental Psychiatry, 5*, 47–52.

MacDonald, S.W. S., Hultsch, D. F., & Dixon, R. A. (2011). Aging and the shape of cognitive change before death: Terminal decline or terminal drop? *The Journals of Gerontology, 66B*, 292–301.

MacEvoy, S. P., & Paradiso, M. A. (2001). Lightness constancy in primary visual cortex. *Proceedings of the National Academy of Sciences, 98*, 8827–8831.

Machaalani, R., Say, M., & Waters, K. A. (2011). Effects of cigarette smoke exposure on nicotinic acetylcholine receptor subunits a7 and b2 in the sudden infant death syndrome (SIDS) brainstem. *Toxicology and Applied Pharmacology, 257*(3), 396–404.

MacInnis, C. C., Busseri, M. A., Choma, B. L., & Hodson, G. (2013). The happy cyclist: Examining the association between generalized authoritarianism and subjective well-being. *Personality and Individual Differences, 55*(7), 789–793.

Mack, A. (2003). Inattentional blindness: Looking without seeing. *Current Directions in Psychological Science, 12*, 180–184.

Mack, A., & Rock, I. (1998). *Inattentional blindness*. Cambridge, MA: MIT Press.

Mackenzie, C. S., Erickson, J., Deane, F. P., & Wright, M. (2013). Changes in attitudes toward seeking mental health services: A 40-year cross-temporal meta-analysis. *Clinical Psychology Reviews, 34*(2), 99–106.

Mackenzie, R., & Watts, J. (2011). Including emotionality in tests of competence: How does neurodiversity affect measures of free will and agency in medical decision making?. *AJOB Neuroscience, 2*(3), 27–36. doi:10.1080/21507740. 2011.580491.

Mackinnon, S. P., Jordan, C. H., & Wilson, A. E. (2011). Birds of a feather sit together: Physical similarity predicts seating choice. *Personality And Social Psychology Bulletin, 37*(7), 879–892. doi:10.1177/0146167211402094.

MacLean, K. A., Ferrer, E., Aichele, S. R., Bridwell, D. A., et al. (2010). Intensive meditation training improves perceptual discrimination and sustained attention. *Psychological Science, 21*, 829–839.

Macleod, C., & Mathews, A. (2012). Cognitive bias modification approaches to anxiety. *Annual Review of Clinical Psychology, 8189–8217*.

MacLeod, C. M., Gopie, N., Hourihan, K. L., Neary, K. R., & Ozubko, J. D. (2010). The production effect: Delineation of a phenomenon. *Journal Of Experimental Psychology: Learning, Memory, And Cognition, 36*(3), 671–685. doi:10.1037/a0018785.

MacMillan, H. L., Fleming, J. E., Steiner, D. L., Lin, E., Boyle, M. H., Jamieson, E., et al. (2001). Childhood abuse and lifetime psychopathology in a community sample. *American Journal of Psychiatry, 158*, 1878–1883.

MacMillan, N. A., & Creelman, C. D. (2004*). Detection theory: A user's guide* (2nd ed.). Hillsdale, NJ: Erlbaum.

MacQuarrie, B., & Belkin, D. (2003, September 29). Franklin Park gorilla escapes, attacks 2. *Boston Globe*. Retrieved from http://www.boston.com.

MacQueen, G. M., Campbell, S., McEwen, B. S., Macdonald, K., et al. (2003). Course of illness, hippocampal function, and hippocampal volume in major depression. *Proceedings of the National Academy of Sciences, 100*, 1387–1392.

Macrae, C. N., & Quadfl ieg, S. (2010). Perceiving people. In S. T. Fiske, D. T. Gilbert, & G. Lindzey (Eds.), *Handbook of social psychology* (5th ed., Vol. 2, pp.428–464). Hoboken, NJ: Wiley.

Maddi, S. R., & Khoshaba, D. M. (2005). *Resilence at work*. New York: American Management Association.

Madon, S., Willard, J., Guyll, M., & Scherr, K. C. (2011) Self-fulfilling prophecies: Mechanisms, power, and links to social problems. *Social and Personality Psychology Compass, 5*, 578–590

Magid, M., Truong, L., Trevino, K., & Husain, M. (2013). Efficacy of right unilateral ultrabrief pulse width ECT: A preliminary report. *The Journal of ECT, 29*, 258–264.

Magni, L. R., Purgato, M., Gastaldon, C., Papola, D., Furukawa, T. A., Cipriani, A., & Barbui, C. (2013). Fluoxetine versus other types of pharmacotherapy for depression. *Cochrane Database of Systemic Reviews, 7*, CD004185.

Maguire, E. A., & Hassabis, D. (2011). Role of the hippocampus in imagination and future thinking. *PNAS Proceedings of the National Academy of Sciences of The United States Of America, 108*(11), doi:10.1073/pnas.1018876108.

Maier, S. F., & Watkins, L. R. (2000). The immune system as a sensory system: Implications for psychology. *Current Directions in Psychological Science, 9*, 98–102.

Majid, A., Evans, N., Gaby, A., & Levinson, S. (2011). The grammar of exchange: a comparative study of reciprocal constructions across languages. *Frontiers in Psychology, 234*.

Malamuth, N., & Addison, T. (2001). Helping and altruism. In G. Fletcher & M. Clark (Eds.), *Blackwell handbook of social psychology: Interpersonal processes* (pp. 162–195). Oxford, UK: Blackwell.

Malamuth, N. M. (1998). The confluence model as an organizing framework for research on sexually aggressive men: Risk moderators, imagined aggression, and pornography consumption. In R. G. Geen & E. Donnerstein (Eds.), *Human aggression* (pp. 230–247). San Diego: Academic Press.

Malamuth, N. M., Addison, T., & Koss, M. (2000). Pornography and sexual aggression: Are there reliable effects and can we understand them? *Annual Review of Sex Research, 11*, 26–91.

Malamuth, N. M., Hald, G., & Koss, M. (2012). Pornography, individual differences in risk and men's acceptance of violence against women in a representative sample. *Sex Roles, 66* (7– 8), 427–439.

Malarkey, W. B., Kiecolt-Glaser, J. K., Pearl, D., & Glaser, R. (1994). Hostile behavior during marital conflict alters pituitary and adrenal hormones. *Psychosomatic Medicine, 56*, 41–51.

Maldonado, R., Valverde, O., & Berrendero, F. (2006). Involvement of the endocannabinoid system in drug addiction. *Trends in Neuroscience, 29*, 225–232.

Malenka, R. C. (1995). LTP and LTD: Dynamic and interactive processes of synaptic plasticity. *The Neuroscientist, 1*, 35–42.

Malenka, R. C., & Nicoll, R. A. (1999). Long-term potentiation—a decade of progress? *Science, 285*, 1870–1874.

Malgrange, B., Rigo, J. M., Van de Water, T. R., Staecker, H., Moonen, G., & Lefebvre, P. P. (1999). Growth factor therapy to the damaged inner ear: Clinical prospects. *International Journal of Pediatric Otorhinolaryngology, 49*(Suppl. 1), S19–S25.

Malhotra, S. (2008). Impact of the sexual revolution: Consequences of risky sexual behaviors. *Journal of American Physicians & Surgeons, 13*(3), 88–90.

Maljaars, P. W. J., Peters, H. P. F., Mela, D. J., & Masclee, A. A. M. (2008). Ileal brake: A sensible food target for appetite control. A review. *Physiology & Behavior, 95*(3), 271–281.

Mallick, B. N. & Singh, A. (2011). REM sleep loss increases brain excitability: Role of noradrenaline and its mechanism of action. *Sleep Medicine Reviews, 15*(3), 165–178.

Malmberg, K. J., Criss, A. H., Gangwani, T. H., & Shiffrin, R. M. (2012). Overcoming the negative consequences of interference from recognition memory testing. *Psychological Science, 23*(2), 115–119. doi:10.1177/0956797611430692

Mamede, S., van Gog, T., van den Berge, K., Rikers, R. P., van Saase, J. M., van Guldener, C., & Schmidt, H. G. (2010). Effect of availability bias and reflective reasoning on diagnostic accuracy among internal medicine residents. *JAMA: Journal of the American Medical Association, 304*(11), 1198–1203. doi:10.1001/jama.2010.1276.

Manahan, V. J. (2004). When our system of involuntary civil commitment fails individuals with mental illness: Russell Weston and the case for effective monitoring and medication delivery mechanisms. *Law and Psychology Review, 28*, 1–33.

Manard, M., Carabin, D., Jaspar, M., & Collette, F. (2014). Age-related decline in cognitive control: The role of fluid intelligence and processing speed. *BMC Neuroscience, 15*, 7.

Mandara, J., Gaylord-Harden, N. K., Richards, M. H., & Ragsdale, B. L. (2009). The effects of changes in ethnic identityand self-esteem on changes in African American adolescents'mental health. *Child Development, 80*, 1660–1675.

Mandelid, L. J. (2003). Dodofugl-dommen og psykoterapeuters credo. [The Dodo-bird verdict and the beliefs of psychotherapists]. *Tidsskrift for Norsk Psykolog forening, 40*(4), 307–312.

Maner J. K., & Kenrick D. T (2010). Evolutionary social psychology In R. Baumeister & E. Finkel (Eds.) *Advanced social psychology: The state of the science* (pp. 613–654). New York, NY: Oxford.

Maner, J. K., Luce, C. L., Neuberg, S. L., Cialdini, R. B., Brown, S., & Sagarin, B. J. (2002). The effects of perspective taking on motivations for helping: Still no evidence for altruism. *Personality and Social Psychology Bulletin, 28*, 1601–1610.

Manfield, P., & Shapiro, F. (2004). Application of eye movement desensitization and reprocessing (EMDR) to personality disorders. In J. J. Magnavita (Ed.), *Handbook of personality disorders: Theory and practice* (pp. 304–328). New York: Wiley.

Mangels, J. A., Good, C., Whiteman, R. C., Maniscalco, B., & Dweck, C. S. (2012). Emotion blocks the path to learning under stereotype threat. *Social Cognitive and Affective Neuroscience, 7*(2), 230–241. doi:10.1093/scan/nsq100.

Mann, J. J., Apter, A., Bertolote, J., Beautrais, A., Currier, D., Haas, A., et al. (2005). Suicide prevention strategies: A systematic review. *Journal of the American Medical Association, 294,* 2064–2074.

Mann, K., Roschke, J., Nink, M., Aldenhoff, J., Beyer, J., Benkert, O., & Lehnert, H. (1992). Effects of corticotropin-releasing hormone administration in patients suffering from sleep apnea syndrome. *Society for Neuroscience Abstracts, 22,* 196.

Mannix, R., Meehan, W. P., Mandeville, J., Grant, P. E., Gray, T., & Berglass, J. et al. (2013). Clinical correlates in an experimental model of repetitive mild brain injury. *Annals of Neurology, 74(1),* 65–75.

Manolis, A. J., Poulimenos, L. E., Kallistratos, M. S., Gavras, I., & Gavras, H. (2013). Sympathetic overactivity in hypertension and cardiovascular disease. *Current Vascular Pharmacology,* Epub July 31, 2013.

Manrique, M., Sanhueza, I., Manrique, R., & de Abajo, J. (2014). A new bone conduction implant: Surgical technique and results. *Otology & Neurotology, 35(2),* 216–220.

Manto, M. (2008). The cerebellum, cerebellar disorders, and cerebellar research—Two centuries of discoveries. *Cerebellum, 7(4),* 505–516.

Manto, M. (2012). Toxic agents causing cerebellar ataxias. *Handbook of Clinical Neurology, 103,* 201–213.

Manuck, S., & McCaffery, J. M. (2014). Gene-environment interaction *Annual Review of Psychology, 65,* 41–70.

Maraj, S., Figueredo, V. M., & Lynn, M. D. (2010). Cocaine and the heart. *Clinical Cardiology, 33(5),* 264–269.

Marceau, K., Horwitz, B. N., Narusyte, J., Ganiban, J. M., Spotts, E. L., Reiss, D., & Neiderhiser, J. M. (2013). Gene-environment correlation underlying the association between parental negativity and adolescent externalizing problems. *Child Development, 84(6),* 2013–2046.

March, E., & Bramwell, A. (2012). Sex differences in mate preferences in Australia: Exploring evolutionary and social-economic theories. *Journal of Relationships Research, 3,* 18–23.

Marchman, T. (2008, October 24). You Call That Bling? *Wall Street Journal—Eastern Edition, 252*(98).

Marcus, G. F. (1996). Why do children say "breaked"? *Current Directions in Psychological Science, 5,* 81–85.

Marcus, S. V. (2008). Phase 1 of integrated EMDR: An abortive treatment for migraine headaches. *Journal of EMDR Practice and Research, 2*(1), 15–25.

Marcus Jenkins, J. V., Woolley, D. P., Hooper, S. R., & De Bellis, M. D. (2013). Direct and indirect effects of brain volume, socioeconomic status and family stress on child IQ. *Journal of Child and Adolescent Behavior, 1,* 107.

Marenco, S., & Weinberger, D. R. (2000). The neurodevelopmental hypothesis of schizophrenia: Following a trail of evidence from cradle to grave. *Developmental Psychopathology, 12,* 501–527.

Marewski, J. N., & Schooler, L. J. (2011). Cognitive niches: An ecological model of strategy selection. *Psychological Review, 118*(3), 393–437. doi:10.1037/a0024143.

Mariën, P., Ackermann, H., Adamaszek, M., Barwood, C. H., Beaton, A., Desmond, J., De Witte, E., Fawcett, A. J., Hertrich, I., Küper, M., Leggio, M., Marvel, C., Molinari, M., Murdoch, B. E., Nicolson, R. I., Schmahmann, J. D., Stoodley, C. J., Thürling, M., Timmann, D., Wouters, E., & Ziegler, W. (2013). Consensus Paper: Language and the Cerebellum: An Ongoing Enigma. *Cerebellum.* Epub December 7, 2013.

Markey, P. M., & Markey, C. N. (2010). Vulnerability to violent video games: A review and integration of personality research. *Review of General Psychology, 142*(2), 82–91. doi:10.1037/a0019000.

Markman, E. M. (1994). Constraints children place on word meanings. In P. Bloom (Ed.), *Language acquisition: Core readings* (pp. 154–173). Cambridge, MA: MIT Press.

Markus, H. R. (2008). Pride, prejudice, and ambivalence: Toward a unified theory of race and ethnicity. *American Psychologist, 63*(8), 651–670.

Markus, H. R., & Kitayama, S. (1997). Culture and the self: Implications for cognition, emotion, and motivation. In L. A. Peplau & S. Taylor (Eds.), *Sociocultural perspectives in social psychology* (pp. 157–216). Upper Saddle River, NJ: Prentice Hall.

Markus, H. R., & Kitayama, S. (2010). Cultures and selves: A cycle of mutual constitution. *Perspectives on Psychological Science, 54,* 420–430.

Markus, H. R., Kitayama, S., & Heiman, R. J. (1996). Culture and "basic" psychological principles. In E. T. Higgins & A. W. Kruglanski (Eds.), *Social psychology: Handbook of basic principles* (pp. 857–913). New York: Guilford.

Marques, S., Batalha, V. L., Lopes, L. V., & Outeiro, T. F. (2011). Modulating Alzheimer's disease through caffeine: A putative link to epigenetics. *Journal of Alzheimer Disease, 24*(Suppl 2), 161–171.

Marsh, A. A., Ambady, N., & Kleck, R. E. (2005). The effects of fear and anger facial expressions on approach- and avoidance-related behaviors. *Emotion, 5,* 119–124.

Marshall, G. N., Miles, J. N. V., & Stewart, S. H. (2010). Anxiety sensitivity and PTSD symptom severity are reciprocally related: Evidence from a longitudinal study of physical trauma survivors. *Journal of Abnormal Psychology, 119,* 143–150.

Marshall, S. J., Biddle, S. J., Gorely, T., Cameron, N., & Murdey, I. (2004). Relationships between media use, body fatness and physical activity in children and youth: A meta-analysis. *International Journal of Obesity, 28,* 1238–1246.

Martens, M. H. (2011). Change detection in traffic: Where do we look and what do we perceive? *Transportation Research Part F: Traffic Psychology and Behaviour, 14*(3), 240–250. doi:10.1016/j.trf.2011.01.004.

Martens, W. H. J. (2004). The terrorist with antisocial personality disorder. *Journal of Forensic Psychology Practice, 4,* 45–56.

Marti, E., & Rodriguez, C. (Eds.) (2012). *After Piaget.* Piscataway, NJ: Transaction Publishers.

Marti, P. R., Singleton, C. K., & Hiller-Sturmhofel, S. (2003). The role of thiamine deficiency in alcoholic brain disease. *Alcohol Research Health, 27*(2), 134–142.

Martin, C. L., Kornienko, O., Schaefer, D. R., Hanish, L. D., Fabes, R. A., & Goble, P. (2013). The role of sex of peers and gender-typed activities in young children's peer affiliative networks: A longitudinal analysis of selection and influence. *Child Development, 84,* 921–937.

Martin, C. L., & Ruble, D. R. (2009). Patterns of gender development. *Annual Review of Psychology, 61,* 353–381. doi:10.1146/annurev.psych.093008.100511

Martin, G., & Pear, J., (2010) *Behavior Modification: What it is and how to do it.* (9th Edition) Pearson: San Francisco.

Martin, J. A., Hamilton, B. E., Ventura, S. J., Osterman, M. J., K., Kirmeyer, S., Mathews, T.J., & Wilson, E. C. (2011). Births: Final data for 2009. *National Vital Statistics Reports, 60*(1). Washington, DC: U. S. Department of Health and Human Services, Centers for Disease Control and Prevention, National Center for Health Statistics, National Vital Statistics System. Retrieved from http://www.cdc.gov/nchs/data/nvsr/nvsr60/nvsr60_01.pdf.

Martin, J. G. A., & Réale, D. (2008). Temperament, risk assessment and habituation to novelty in eastern chipmunks, Tamias striatus. *Animal Behaviour, 75*(1), 309–318.

Martin, R. A. (2001). Humor, laughter, and physical health: Methodological issues and research findings. *Psychological Bulletin, 127,* 504–519.

Martinez, C. R., & Forgatch, M. S. (2001). Preventing problems with boys' noncompliance: Effects of a parent training intervention for divorcing mothers. *Journal of Consulting and Clinical Psychology, 69,* 416–428.

Martinez, D., Gil, R., Slifstein, M., Hwang, D.-R., Huang, Y., Perez, A., et al. (2005). Alcohol dependence is associated with blunted dopamine transmission in the ventral striatum. *Biological Psychiatry, 58,* 779–786.

Martinez, M. (2000). *Education as the cultivation of intelligence.* Mahwah, NJ: Erlbaum.

Martínez-Amorós, E., Cardoner, N., Soria, V., Gálvez, V., Menchón, J. M., & Urretavizcaya, M. (2012). Long-term treatment strategies in major depression: A 2-year prospective naturalistic follow-up after successful electroconvulsive therapy. *Journal of ECT, 28*(2), 92–97.

Martinez-Taboas, A. (2005). The plural world of culturally sensitive psychotherapy: A response to Castro-Blanco's (2005) comments. *Psychotherapy: Theory, Research, Practice, Training, 42,* 17–19.

Martiniuk, A. L., Senserrick, T., Lo, S., Williamson, A., Du, W., Grunstein, R. R., Woodward, M., Glozier, N., Stevenson, M., Norton, R., & Ivers, R. Q. (2013). Sleep-deprived young drivers and the risk for crash: The DRIVE prospective cohort study. *JAMA Pediatrics, 167*(7), 647–655.

Martin-Santos, R., Fagundo, A. B., Crippa, J. A., Atakan, Z., et al. (2010). Neuroimaging in cannabis use: A systematic review of the literature. *Psychological Medicine, 40,* 383–398.

Martiny, K., Lunde, M., & Bech, P. (2010). Transcranial low-voltage pulsed electromagnetic fields in patients with treatment-resistant depression. *Biological Psychiatry, 68,* 163–169.

Martiny, S. E., Roth, J., Jelenec, P., Steffens, M. C., & Croizet, J. (2012). When a new group identity does harm on the spot: Stereotype threat in newly created groups. *European Journal of Social Psychology, 42*(1), 65–71. doi:10.1002/ejsp.840.

Marzoli, D., Custodero, M, Pagliara, A., & Tommasi, L. (2013). Sun-induced frowning fosters aggressive feelings. *Cognition & Emotion, 27*(8), 1513–1521.

Masi, C. M., Chen, H. Y., Hawkley, L. C., & Cacioppo, J. T. (2011). A meta-analysis of interventions to reduce loneliness. *Personality and Social Psychology Review, 15,* 219–266.

Maslach, C. (2003). Job burnout: New directions in research and intervention. *Current Directions in Psychological Science, 12,* 189–192.

Masland, R. H. (2001). Neuronal diversity in the retina. *Current Opinion in Neurobiology, 11,* 431–436.

Maslow, A. H. (1943). A theory of human motivation. *Psychological Review, 50,* 370–396.

Maslow, A. H. (1954). *Motivation and personality*. New York: Harper.

Maslow, A. H. (1970). *Motivation and personality* (2nd ed.). New York: Harper & Row.

Maslow, A. H. (1971). *Toward a psychology of being*. Princeton, NJ: Van Nostrand.

Mass, R., Hölldorfer, M., Moll, B., Bauer, R., & Wolf, K. (2008). Why we haven't died out yet: Changes in women's mimic reactions to visual erotic stimuli during their menstrual cycles. *Hormones and Behavior, 55*(2), 267–271.

Masson, M. E. J., & MacLeod, C. M. (1992). Reenacting the route to interpretation: Enhanced perceptual identification without prior perception. *Journal of Experimental Psychology: General, 121,* 145–176.

Mast, T. G., & Samuelsen, C. L. (2009). Human pheromone detection by the vomeronasal organ: Unnecessary for mate selection? *Chemical Senses, 34,* 529–531.

Masten, A. S. (2013). Risk and resilience in development. In P. D. Zelazo (Ed.), *Oxford handbook of developmental psychology. Vol 2. Self and other* (pp. 579–607). New York: Oxford University Press.

Masten, A. S., & Tellegen, A. (2012). Resilience in developmental psychopathology: Contributions of the Project Competence Longitudinal Study. *Development and Psychopathology, 24,* 345–361.

Masters, J. C., Burish, T. G., Hollon, S. D., & Rimm, D. C. (1987). *Behavior therapy: Techniques and empirical findings* (3rd ed.). San Diego: Harcourt Brace Jovanovich.

Masters, W. H., & Johnson, V. E. (1966). *Human sexual response*. Boston: Little, Brown & Co.

Masuda, T., Gonzalez, R., Kwan, L., & Nisbett, R. E. (2008). Culture and aesthetic preference: Comparing the attention to context of East Asians and Americans. *Personality and Social Psychology Bulletin, 34*(9), 1260–1275.

Mataix-Cols, D., Turner, C., Monzani, B., Isomura, K., Murphy, C., Krebs, G., & Heyman, I. (2014). Cognitive-behavioural therapy with post-session D-cycloserine augmentation for paediatric obsessive-compulsive disorder: pilot randomised controlled trial. *British Journal of Psychiatry, 204*(1), 77–78.

Mather, M., Canli, T., English, T., Whitfield, S., et al. (2004). Emotionally valenced stimuli in older and younger adults. *Psychological Science, 15,* 259–263.

Mather, M., & Carstensen, L. L. (2005). Aging and motivated cognition: The positivity effect in attention and memory. *Trends in Cognitive Sciences, 9,* 496–502.

Mather, M., & Lighthall, N. R. (2012). Risk and reward are processed differently in decisions made under stress. *Current Directions in Psychological Science, 21*(1) 36–41. doi:10.1177/0963721411429452.

Mathern, G. W., & Miller, J. W. (2013). Outcomes for temporal lobe epilepsy operations may not be equal: A call for an RCT of ATL vs. SAH. *Neurology, 80,* 1630–1631.

Mathew, S. J., Amiel, J. M., & Sackeim, H. A. (2005). Electroconvulsive therapy in treatment-resistant depression. *Primary Psychiatry, 12,* 52–56.

Mathieu, M. T., & Gosling, S. D. (2012). The accuracy or inaccuracy of affective forecasts depends on how accuracy is indexed: A meta-analysis of past studies. *Psychological Science, 23,* 161–162.

Mathy, F., & Feldman, J. (2012). What's magic about magic numbers? Chunking and data compression in short-term memory. *Cognition, 122*(3), 346–362. doi:10.1016/ j.cognition.2011.11.003.

Matlin, M. W. (1998). *Cognition* (4th ed.). Fort Worth, TX: Harcourt Brace.

Matson, J., Sevin, J., Fridley, D., & Love, S. (1990). Increasing spontaneous language in autistic children. *Journal of Applied Behavior Analysis, 23,* 227–223.

Matson, J. L., & Boisjoli, J. A. (2009). The token economy for children with intellectual disability and/or autism: A review. *Research in Developmental Disabilities, 30,* 240–248.

Matsuda, I., Nittono, H., & Allen, J. J. (2013). Detection of concealed information by P3 and frontal EEG asymmetry. *Neuroscience Letters, 537,* 55–59.

Matsumoto, D. (2000). *Culture and psychology: People around the world*. Belmont, CA: Wadsworth.

Matsumoto, D., & Ekman, P. (1989). American-Japanese cultural differences in intensity ratings of facial expressions of emotion. *Motivation and Emotion, 13,* 143–157.

Matsumoto, D., & Juang, L. (2013). *Culture & Psychology* (5th ed.). Belmont, CA: Cengage Learning.

Matsumoto, D., & Willingham, B. (2006). The thrill of victory and the agony of defeat: Spontaneous expressions of medal winners of the 2004 Athens Olympic games. *Journal of Personality and Social Psychology, 91,* 568–581.

Matsumoto, D., & Willingham, B. (2009). Spontaneous facial expressions of emotion of congenitally and noncongenitally blind individuals. *Journal of Personality and Social Psychology, 96,* 1–10.

Matsumoto, D., Yoo, S. H., Hirayama, S., & Petrova, G. (2005). Development and validation of a measure of display rule knowledge: The display rule assessment inventory. *Emotion, 5,* 23–40.

Mattanah, J. F., Hancock, G. R., & Brand, B. L. (2004). Parental attachment, separation-individuation, and college student adjustment: A structural equation analysis of mediational effects. *Journal of Counseling Psychology, 51,* 213–225.

Mattar, A. A. G., & Gribble, P. L. (2005). Motor learning by observing. *Neuron, 46,* 153–160.

Matthews, G. (2008). Reinforcement Sensitivity Theory: A critique from cognitive science. In P. J. Corr (Ed.) *The reinforcement sensitivity theory of personality* (pp. 482–507). Cambridge: Cambridge University Press.

Matthews, K. A. (2013). Matters of the heart: Advancing psychological perspectives on cardiovascular diseases. *Perspectives on Psychological Science, 8*(6), 676–678.

Matthews, K. A., Katholi, C. R., McCreath, H., Whooley, M. A., Williams, D. R., Zhu, S., et al. (2004). Blood pressure reactivity to psychological stress predicts hypertension in the CARDIA study. *Circulation, 110,* 74–78.

Matyas, G. S. (2004). Using MMPI special scale configurations to predict police officer performance in New Jersey. *Applied HRM Research, 9,* 63–66.

Maurer, D., & Lewis, T. (2013). Human visual plasticity: Lessons for children treated with congenital cataracts. J. K. E. Stephens & L. R. Harris (eds.), *Plasticity in sensory systems* (pp. 75–93). New York: Cambridge University Press.

May, G. L., & Kahnweiler, W. M. (2000). The effect of a mastery practice design on learning and transfer in behavior modeling training. *Personnel Psychology, 53,* 353–373.

May, R. (1969). *Love and will*. New York: Norton.

Mayberry, R. I., & Lock, E. (2003). Age constraints on first versus second language acquisition. *Brain and Language, 87,* 369–384.

Mayberry, R. I., Lock, E., & Kazmi, H. (2002). Linguistic ability and early language exposure. *Nature, 417,* 38.

Mayer, D. J., & Price, D. D. (1982). A physiological and psychological analysis of pain: A potential model of motivation. In D. W. Pfaff (Ed.), *The physiological mechanisms of motivation*. New York: Springer-Verlag.

Mayer, F. S., & Sutton, K. (1996). *Personality: An integrative approach*. Upper Saddle River, NJ: Prentice Hall.

Mayer, J. D. (2005). A tale of two visions: Can a new view of personality help integrate psychology? *American Psychologist, 60,* 294–307.

Mayer, R. E. (1992). *Thinking, problem solving, and cognition* (2nd ed.). New York: Freeman.

Mayet, A., Legleye, S., Chau, N., & Falissard, B. (2011). Transitions between tobacco and cannabis use among adolescents: A multi-state modeling of progression from onset to daily use. *Addictive Behaviors, 36*(11), 1101–1105.

Mayet, A., Legleye, S., Falissard, B., & Chau N. (2012). Cannabis use stages as predictors of subsequent initiation with other illicit drugs among French adolescents: Use of a multi-state model. *Addictive Behaviors, 37*(2), 160–166.

Mayeux, R. (2003). Epidemiology of neurodegeneration. *Annual Review of Neuroscience, 26,* 81–104.

Maynard, D. C., Joseph, T. A., & Maynard, A. M. (2006). Underemployment, job attitudes, and turnover intentions. *Journal of Organizational Behavior, 27,* 509–536.

Mazerolle, M., Régner, I., Morisset, P., Rigalleau, F., & Huguet, P. (2012). Stereotype threat strengthens automatic recall and undermines controlled processes in older adults. *Psychological Science, 23*(7), 723–727. Epub 2012 May 18. Doi:10. 11770956797612437607.

Mazoyer, B., Tzouri-Mazoyer, N., Mazard, A., Denis, M., & Mellet, E. (2002). Neural basis of image and language interactions. *International Journal of Psychology, 37,* 204–208.

Mazzoccoli, G. (2011). The timing clockwork of life. *Journal of Biologic Regulators and Homeostatic Agents, 25*(1), 137–143.

Mazzoni, G., Rotriquenz, E., Carvalho, C., Vannucci, M., et al. (2009). Suggested visual hallucinations in and out of hypnosis. *Consciousness and Cognition, 18,* 494–499.

Mazzoni, G. A., & Loftus, E. F. (1996). When dreams become reality. *Consciousness and Cognition, 5,* 442–462.

McAdams, D. P., & Pals, J. L. (2006). A new big five: Fundamental principles for an integrative science of personality. *American Psychologist, 61,* 204–217.

McAndrew, F. T. (2014). The "sword of a woman": Gossip and female aggression. *Aggression and Violent Behavior, 19*(1), 196–199.

McAuley, E. (1992). The role of efficacy cognitions in the prediction of exercise behavior in middle-aged adults. *Journal of Behavioral Medicine, 15,* 65–88.

McAuliff, B. D., Kovera, M. B., & Nunez, G. (2008). Can jurors recognize missing control groups, confounds, and experimental bias in psychological science? *Law and Human Behavior, 33,* 247–257.

McCaffery, E. J., & Baron, J. (2006). Thinking about tax. *Psychology, Public Policy, and Law, 12,* 106–135.

McCall, R.B., Groark, C.J., Fish, L., Muhamedrahimov, R.J., Palmov, O.I., & Nikiforova, N.V. (2013). Maintaining a social-emotional intervention and its benefits for institutionalized children. *Child Development, 84,* 1734–1749.

McCarley, J. S., Kramer, A. F., Wickens, C. D., Vidoni, E. D., & Boot, W. R. (2004). Visual skills in airport-security screening. *Psychological Science, 15,* 302–306.

McCaul, K. D., Hockemeyer, J. R., Johnson, R. J., Zetocha, K., Quinlan, K., & Glasgow, R. E. (2006). Motivation to quit using cigarettes: A review. *Addictive Behaviors, 31,* 42–56.

McClelland, D. C. (1985). *Human motivation.* Glenview, IL: Scott, Foresman.

McClelland, D. C. (1958). Risk-taking in children with high and low need for achievement. In J. W. Atkinson (Ed.), *Motives in fantasy, action, and society* (pp. 306–321). Princeton, NJ: Van Nostrand.

McClelland, D. C., Atkinson, J. W., Clark, R. A., & Lowell, E. L. (1953). *The achievement motive.* New York: Appleton-Century-Crofts.

McClintick, J. N., Xuei, X., Tischfield, J. A., Goate, A., Foroud, T., Wetherill, L., Ehringer, M. A., & Edenberg, H. J. (2013). Stress-response pathways are altered in the hippocampus of chronic alcoholics. *Alcohol, 47*(7), 505–515.

McClintock, C. G., & Liebrand, W. B. G. (1988). Role of interdependence structure, individual value orientation, and another's strategy in social decision making: A transformational analysis. *Journal of Personality and Social Psychology, 55,* 396–409.

McCloskey, M. (1983). Naïve theories of motion. In D. Gentner & K. Stevens (Eds.), *Mental models* (pp. 299–324). Northvale, NJ: Erlbaum.

McCloskey, M. S., Ben-Zeev, D., Lee, R., Berman, M. E., & Coccaro, E. F. (2009). Acute tryptophan depletion and self-injurious behavior in aggressive patients and healthy volunteers. *Psychopharmacology (Berlin), 203,* 53–61. Epub 2008 Oct 23.

McClure, E. B. (2000). A meta-analytic review of sex differences in facial expression processing and their development in infants, children, and adolescents. *Psychological Bulletin, 126,* 424–453.

McConaghy, N., Hadzi-Pavlovic, D., Stevens, C., Manicavasagar, V., Buhrich, N., & Vollmer-Conna, U. (2006). Fraternal birth order and ratio of heterosexual/homosexual feelings in women and men. *Journal of Homosexuality, 51*(4), 161–174.

McCormick, D. A., & Thompson, R. F. (1984). Cerebellum essential involvement in the classically conditioned eyelid response. *Science, 223,* 296–299.

McCormick, E. J., Jeanneret, P. R., & Mecham, R. C. (1972). A study of job characteristics and job dimensions as based on the position analysis questionnaire (PAQ). *Journal of Applied Psychology, 56,* 347–368.

McCrae, R. et al. (2010). The validity and structure of culture-level personality scores: Data from ratings of young adolescents. *Journal of Personality, 78,* 815–838.

McCrae, R., Terracciano, A., & Personality Profiles of Cultures Project (2005). Personality profiles of cultures: Aggregate personality traits. *Journal of Personality and Social Psychology, 89,* 407–425.

McCrae, R. R., & Costa, P. T., Jr. (2004). A contemplated revision of the NEO Five-Factor Inventory. *Personality and Individual Differences, 36,* 587–596.

McCrae, R. R., & Costa, P. T., Jr. (2008). The Five-Factor theory of personality. In O. John, R. Robins, & L. Pervin (Eds.), *Handbook of personality: Theory and research* (3rd ed., pp. 159–181). New York: Guilford.

McCrae, R. R., & Costa, P. T., Jr. (2010). *NEO Inventories: Professional manual.* Lutz, FL: Psychological Assessment Resources, Inc.

McCrae, R. R., Harwood, M. T., & Kelley, S. L. (2011). The NEO Inventories. In T. M. Harwood, L. E. Beutler, & G. Groth-Marnat (Eds.) *Integrative Assessment of Adult Personality* (pp. 252–275). New York: Guilford.

McCrae, R. R., & John, O. (1992). An introduction to the five-factor model and its applications. *Journal of Personality, 60,* 175–215.

McCrae, R. R., Scally, M., Terracciano, A., Abecasis, G. R., & Costa, P. T., Jr. (2010). An alternative to the search for single polymorphisms: Toward molecular personality scales for the five-factor model. *Journal of Personality and Social Psychology, 99,* 1014–1024.

McCullough M. E., & Tabak, B. A. (2010). Prosocial behavior In R. Baumeister & E. Finkel (Eds.) *Advanced social psychology: The state of the science.* (pp. 263–302). New York, NY: Oxford.

McCusker, R. R., Goldberger, B. A., & Cone, E. J. (2003). Caffeine content of specialty coffees. *Journal of Analytical Toxicology, 27,* 520–522.

McCusker, R. R., Goldberger, B. A., & Cone, E. J. (2006). Caffeine content of decaffeinated coffee. *Journal of Analytical Toxicology, 30,* 611–613.

McDermott, K. B. (2002). Explicit and implicit memory. In V. S. Ramachandran (Ed.), *Encyclopedia of the human brain* (Vol. 2, pp. 773–781). New York: Academic Press.

McDermott, K. B., & Chan, J. C. K. (2006). Effects of repetition on memory for pragmatic inferences. *Memory and Cognition.*

McDermott, K. B., & Roediger, H. L. (1998). Attempting to avoid illusory memories: Robust false recognition of associates persists under conditions of explicit warnings and immediate testing. *Journal of Memory and Language, 39,* 508–520.

McDermott, K. B., Szpunar, K. K., & Christ, S. E. (2009). Laboratory-based and autobiographical retrieval tasks differ substantially in their neural substrates. *Neuropsychologia, 47,* 2290–2298.

McDiarmid, M. A., & Condon, M. (2005). Organizational safety culture/climate and worker compliance with hazardous drug guidelines: Lessons from the blood-borne pathogen experience. *Journal of Occupational and Environmental Medicine, 47,* 740–749.

McDonald, G. (2010). The Flynn effect and the demography of schooling. *Teachers College Record, 112*(7), 1851–1870.

McDonald, R., & Siegel, S. (2004). The potential role of drug onset cues in drug dependence and withdrawal: Reply to Bardo (2004), Bossert and Shaham (2004), Bouton (2004), and Stewart (2004). *Experimental and Clinical Psychopharmacology, 12,* 23–26.

McDougall, W. (1908). *An introduction to social psychology.* London: Methuen.

McElvaney, C. (2011). Client evaluations and summaries: How person-centered planning is tainted by a diagnosis. Intellectual And Developmental Disabilities, *49*(3), 203–205. doi:10.1352/1934–9556–49.3.203.

McElwain, N. L., Booth-LaForce, C., & Wu, X. (2011). Infant–mother attachment and children's friendship quality: Maternal mental-state talk as an intervening mechanism. *Developmental Psychology, 47*(5), 1295–1311. doi:10.1037/a0024094.

McEvoy, G. M., & Beatty, R. W. (1989). Assessment centers and subordinate appraisals of managers: A seven-year examination of predictive validity. *Personnel Psychology, 42,* 37–52.

McGarvey, C., McDonnell, M., Hamilton, K., O'Regan, M., & Matthews, T. (2006). An 8-year study of risk factors for SIDS: Bed-sharing versus non-bed-sharing. *Archives of Disease in Childhood, 91,* 318–323.

McGaugh, J. L. (2003). *Memory and emotion.* New York: Columbia University Press.

McGeown, W. J., Venneri, A., Kirsch, I., Nocetti, L., Roberts, K., Foan, L., & Mazzoni, G. (2012). Suggested visual hallucination without hypnosis enhances activity in visual areas of the brain. *Consciousness & Cognition, 21*(1), 100–116. doi:10.1016/j.concog. 2011.10.015.

McGilloway, S., Mhaille, G., Bywater, T., Furlong, M., Leckey, Y., Kelly, P., & Donnelly, M. (2012). A parenting intervention for childhood behavioral problems: A randomized controlled trial in disadvantaged community-based settings. *Journal of Consulting and Clinical Psychology, 80*(1), 116–127. doi:10.1037/a0026304.

McGlynn, S. M., & Schacter, D. L. (1989). Unawareness of deficits in neuropsychological syndromes. *Journal of Clinical and Experimental Neuropsychology, 11*(2), 143–205.

McGorry, P. D., Purcell, R., Goldstone, S., & Amminger, G. P. (2011). Age of onset and timing of treatment for mental and substance use disorders: Implications for preventive intervention strategies and models of care. *Current Opinion in Psychiatry, 24,* 301–306.

McGrath, S. A., Nilsen, A., & Kerley, K. R. (2011). Sexual victimization in childhood and the propensity for juvenile delinquency and adult criminal behavior: A systematic review. *Aggression & Violent Behavior, 16*(6), 485–492. doi:10.1016/ j.avb.2011.03.008.

McGue, M., Elkins, I., Walden, B., & Iacono, W. G. (2005). Perceptions of the parent-adolescent relationship: A longitudinal investigation. *Developmental Psychology, 41,* 971–984.

McHugh, M. C., & Kasardo, A. E. (2012). Anti-fat prejudice: The role of psychology in explication, education and eradication. *Sex Roles, 66*(9–10), 617–627.

McHugh, P. R. (2009). *Try to remember: Psychiatry's clash over meaning, memory, and mind.* Chicago: Dana Press.

McKay, D., & Storch, E. A. (2014). Defining the scope and boundaries of the obsessive-compulsive spectrum. In E. A. Storch & D. McKay (Eds.), *Obsessive-compulsive disorder and its spectrum: A life-span approach* (pp. 3–9). Washington, DC: American Psychological Association.

McKay, M. T., Sumnall, H., Goudie, A. J., Field, M., & Cole, J. C. (2011). What differentiates adolescent problematic drinkers from their peers? Results from a cross-sectional study in Northern Irish school children. *Drugs: Education, Prevention & Policy, 18*(3), 187–199. doi:10.3109/09687637.2010.502160

McLaughlin, K. A., Fox, N. A., Zeanah, C. H., & Nelson, C. A. (2011). Adverse rearing environments and neural development in children: The development of frontal electroencephalogram asymmetry. *Biological Psychiatry, 70*(11), 1008–1015. doi:10.1016/j.biopsych.2011.08.006.

McLaughlin, K. A., & Nolen-Hoeksema, S. (2011). Rumination as a transdiagnostic factor in depression and anxiety. *Behaviour Research and Therapy, 49,* 186–193.

McLeod, J. D., Kessler, R. C., & Landis, K. R. (1992). Speed of recovery from major depressive episodes in a community sample of married men and women. *Journal of Abnormal Psychology, 101,* 277–286.

McLoyd, V. C. (1998). Socioeconomic disadvantage and child development. *American Psychologist, 53,* 185–204.

McMahon, P. (2000, January 31). Oregon man leads life without frills, leaves $9 million to charities, children. *USA Today,* p. 4A.

McMullan, J. L., & Miller, D. (2009). Wins, winning and winners: The commercial advertising of lottery gambling. *Journal of Gambling Studies, 25*(3), 273–295. doi:10.1007/s10899–009–9120–5.

McMurran, M. (2012). Personality disorders. In P. Sturmey & M. Hersen (Eds.), *Handbook of Evidence-based practice in clinical psychology, Vol 2: Adult disorders* (pp. 531–547). Hoboken, NJ: Wiley.

McMurrich, S. L., & Johnson, S. L. (2008). Dispositional rumination in individuals with a depression history. *Cognitive Therapy and Research, 32*, 542–553.

McNally, R. J. (2003). Recovering memories of trauma: A view from the laboratory. *Current Directions in Psychological Science, 12*, 32–35.

McNally, R. J., Clancy, S. A., Barrett, H. M., & Parker, H. A. (2005). Reality monitoring in adults reporting repressed, recovered, or continuous memories of childhood sexual abuse. *Journal of Abnormal Psychology, 114*, 147–152.

McNally, R. J., & Geraerts, E. (2009). A new solution to the recovered memory debate. *Perspectives on Psychological Science, 4*, 126–134.

McNay, E. C., McCarty, R. C., & Gold, P. E. (2001). Fluctuations in brain glucose concentration during behavioral testing: Dissociations between brain areas and between brain and blood. *Neurobiology of Learning and Memory, 75*, 325–337.

McNulty, J. K., & Fincham, F. D. (2012). Beyond positive psychology? Toward a contextual view of psychological processes and well-being. *American Psychologist, 67*(2), 101–110. doi:10.1037/a0024572.

McTigue, K. M., Harris, R., Hemphill, B., Lux, L., Sutton, S., Bunton, A. J., & Lohr, K. N. (2003). Screening and interventions for obesity in adults: Summary of the evidence for the U.S. Preventive Services Task Force. *Annals of Internal Medicine, 139*, 933–949.

McWayne, C. M., Cheung, K., Green Wright, L. E., Hahs-Vaughn, D. L. (2012). Patterns of school readiness among head start children: Meaningful within-group variability during the transition to kindergarten. *Journal of Educational Psychology, 104*(3), 862–878. doi:10.1037/a0028884.

Meadows, G. N., Shawyer, F., Enticott, J. C., Graham, A. L., Judd, F., Martin, P. R., Piterman, L., & Segal, Z. (2014). Mindfulness-based cognitive therapy for recurrent depression: A translational research study with 2-year follow-up. *The Australian and New Zealand Journal of Psychiatry*, Epub March 4, 2014.

Mealor, A., & Dienes, Z. (2012). No-loss gambling shows the speed of the unconscious. *Consciousness & Cognition, 21*(1), 228–237. doi:10.1016/j.concog.2011.12.001.

Meaney, D. F. & Smith, D. H. (2011). Biomechanics of concussion. *Clinics in Sports Medicine, 30*(1), 19–31.

Medin, D. L., Ross, B. H., & Markman, A. B. (2001). *Cognitive psychology* (3rd ed.). Fort Worth, TX: Harcourt.

Mednick, S. C. (2013). Napping helps preschoolers learn. *Proceedings of the National Academy of Sciences, 110*(43), 17171–17172.

Mednick, S., Nakayama, K., & Stickgold, R. (2003). Sleep-dependent learning: A nap is as good as a night. *Nature Neuroscience, 6*, 697–698.

Mefoh, P. C., & Nwanosike, C. L. (2012). Effects of group size and expectancy of reward on social loafing. *IFE Psychologia: An International Journal, 20*(1), 229–-239.

Mehl, M. R., & Pennebaker, J. W. (2003a). The social dynamics of a cultural upheaval: Social interactions surrounding September 11, 2001. *Psychological Science, 14*, 579–585.

Mehl, M. R., & Pennebaker, J. W. (2003b). The sounds of social life: A psychometric analysis of students' daily social environments and natural conversations. *Journal of Personality and Social Psychology, 84*, 857–870.

Mehle, T. (1982). Hypothesis generation in an automobile malfunction inference task. *Acta Psychologica, 52*, 87–116.

Mehler, P. S. (2011). Medical complications of bulimia nervosa and their treatments. *International Journal of Eating Disorders, 44*(2), 95–104. doi:10.1002/eat.20825.

Mehr, S. A., Schachner, A., Katz, R. C., & Spelke, E. S. (2013). Two randomized trials provide no consistent evidence for nonmusical cognitive benefits of brief preschool music enrichment. *PLoS One, 8*(12), e82007.

Mehta, P. H., & Beer, J. (2010). Neural mechanisms of the testosterone-aggression relation: The role of orbitofrontal cortex. *Journal of Cognitive Neuroscience, 22*, 2357–2368.

Meichenbaum, D. (1977). *Cognitive behavior modification: An integrative approach.* New York: Plenum.

Meichenbaum, D. (2009). Stress inoculation training. In W. T. O'Donohue & J. E. Fisher (Eds.), *General principles and empirically supported techniques of cognitive behavior therapy* (pp. 627–630). Hoboken, NJ: Wiley and Sons.

Meier, B. P., Moeller, S. K., Riemer-Peltz, M., & Robinson, M. D. (2011). Sweet taste preferences and experiences predict prosocial inferences, personalities, and behaviors. *Journal of Personality and Social Psychology*, doi:10.1037/a0025253.

Meier, M. H., Caspi, A., Ambler, A., Harrington, H., Houts, R., Keefe, R. S., McDonald, K., Ward, A., Poulton, R., & Moffitt, T. E. (2012). Persistent cannabis users show neuropsychological decline from childhood to midlife. *Proceedings of the National Academy of Sciences, 109*(40), E2657-E2664.

Meiser, T., & Hewstone, M. (2010). Contingency learning and stereotype formation: Illusory and spurious correlations revisited. *European Review of Social Psychology, 21*(1), 285–331.

Melamed, S., Fried, Y., & Froom, P. (2001). The interactive effect of chronic exposure to noise and job complexity on changes in blood pressure and job satisfaction: A longitudinal study of industrial employees. *Journal of Occupational Health Psychology, 6*, 182–195.

Melcangi, R. C., Panzica, G., & Garcia-Segura, L. M. (2011) Neuroactive steroids: focus on human brain. *Neuroscience 191*:1–5.

Mellon, R. C. (2009). Superstitious perception: Response-independent reinforcement and punishment as determinants of recurring eccentric interpretations. *Behaviour Research and Therapy, 47*, 868–875.

Melo, V., Garcia, M., Sandoval, H., Jiménez, H., & Calvo, C. (2011). Quality proteins from edible indigenous insect food of Latin America and Asia. *Emirates Journal of Food & Agriculture (EJFA), 23*(3), 283–289.

Meltzer, H. Y. (2013). Update on typical and atypical antipsychotic drugs. *Annual Review of Medicine, 64*, 393–406.

Melzack, R., & Wall, P. D. (1965). Pain mechanisms: A new theory. *Science, 150*, 971–979.

Menaker, M., & Vogelbaum, M. A. (1993). Mutant circadian period as a marker of suprachiasmatic nucleus function. *Journal of Biological Rhythms, 8*, 93–98.

Mendel, R. R., Traut-Mattausch, E. E., Jonas, E. E., Leucht, S. S., Kane, J. M., Maino, K. K., & Hamann, J. J. (2011). Confirmation bias: why psychiatrists stick to wrong preliminary diagnoses. *Psychological Medicine, 41*(12), 2651–2659. doi:10.1017/S0033291711000808.

Mendell, L. M. (2013). Constructing and deconstructing the gate theory of pain. *Pain, 155*(2), 210–216.

Mendez, I., Viñuela, A., Astradsson, A., Mukhida, K., Hallett, P., Robertson, H., Tierney, T., Holness, R., Dagher, A., Trojanowski, J. Q., & Isacson, O. (2008). Dopamine neurons implanted into people with Parkinson's disease survive without pathology for 14 years. *Nature Medicine, 14*, 507–509.

Mendle, J., Turkheimer, E., & Emery, R. E. (2007). Detrimental psychological outcomes associated with early pubertal timing in adolescent girls. *Developmental Review, 27*, 151–171.

Menon, G. J., Rahman, I., Menon, S. J., & Dutton, G. N. (2003). Complex visual hallucinations in the visually impaired: The Charles Bonnet syndrome. *Survey Ophthalmology, 48*, 58–72.

Mente, A., de Koning, L., Shannon, H. S., & Anand, S. S. (2009). A systematic review of the evidence supporting a causal link between dietary factors and coronary heart disease. *Archives of Internal Medicine, 169*, 659–669.

Merchant, J. A., & Lundell, J. A. (2001). *Workplace violence: A report to the nation.* Iowa City: University of Iowa.

Meredith, E., & Baker, M. (2007). Factors associated with choosing a career in clinical psychology–Undergraduate minority ethnic perspectives. *Clinical Psychology and Psychotherapy, 14*, 475–487.

Merikangas, K. R., Akiskal, H. S., Angst, J., Greenberg, P. E., et al. (2007). Lifetime and 12-month prevalence of bipolar spectrum disorder in the national comorbidity survey replication. *Archives of General Psychiatry, 64*, 543–552.

Merikangas, K. R., He, J.-P., Body, D., Fisher, P. W., et al. (2010). Prevalence and treatment of mental disorders among U.S. children in the 2001–2004 NHANES. *Pediatrics, 125*, 75–81.

Merluzzi, A. (2014). Nonverbal accents: Cultural nuances in emotional expression. *APS Observer, 27*, 15–19.

Merry, T., & Brodley, B. T. (2002). The nondirective attitude in client-centered therapy: A response to Kahn. *Journal of Humanistic Psychology, 42*, 66–77.

Mesquita, B., & Frijda, N. H. (1992). Cultural variations in emotions: A review. *Psychological Bulletin, 112*, 179–204.

Messer, S. B. (2004). Evidence-based practice: Beyond empirically supported treatments. *Professional Psychology: Research and Practice, 35*, 580–588.

Messias, E., Kindrick, K., & Castro, J. (2014). School bullying, cyberbullying, or both: Correlates of teen suicidality in the 2011 CDC youth risk behavior survey. *Comprehensive Psychiatry,* Comprehensive Psychiatry, 55(5), 1063–1068.

Messick, S. (1989). Validity. In R. Linn (Ed.), *Educational measurement* (3rd ed., pp. 13–103). New York: American Council on Education/Macmillan.

Messinger, A., Squire, L. R., Zola, S. M., & Albright, T. D. (2001). Neuronal representations of stimulus associations develop in the temporal lobe during learning. *Proceedings of the National Academy of Sciences, 98*, 12239–12244.

Meston, C. M., & Buss, D. M. (2007). Why humans have sex. *Archives of Sexual Behavior, 36*, 477–507.

Metrik, J., Rohsenow, D. J., Monti, P. M., McGeary, J., Cook, T. A. R., de Wit, H., Haney, M., & Kahler, C. W. (2009). Effectiveness of a marijuana expectancy manipulation: Piloting the balanced-placebo design for marijuana. *Experimental and Clinical Psychopharmacology, 17*(4), 217–225.

Metzinger, T. (Ed.). (2000). Neural correlates of consciousness: Empirical and conceptual questions. Cambridge: MIT Press.

Meuret, A. E., Rosenfield, D., Wilhelm, F. H., Zhou, E., Conrad, A., Ritz, T., & Roth, W. T. (2011). Do unexpected panic attacks occur spontaneously? *Biological Psychiatry, 70*(10), 985–991. doi:10.1016/j.biopsych.2011.05.027

Meuret, A. E., Wolitzky-Taylor, K. B., Twohig, M. P., & Craske, M. G. (2011). Coping skills and exposure therapy in panic disorder and agoraphobia: Latest advances and future directions. *Behavior Therapy, 43,* 271–284.

Meyer, G. J., Finn, S. E., Eyde, L. D., Kay, G. G., Moreland, K. L., Dies, R. R., et al. (2001). Psychological testing and psychological assessment: A review of evidence and issues. *American Psychologist, 56,* 128–165.

Meyer, J. D., & Salovey, P. (1997). What is emotional intelligence? In P. Salovey & D. Sluyter (Eds.), *Emotional development and emotional intelligence* (pp. 3–31). New York: Basic Books.

Meyer, J. M. (2007). Antipsychotic safety and efficacy concerns. *Journal of Clinical Psychiatry, 68*(Supplement 14), 20–26.

Meyer, O., Zane, N., & Cho, Y.I. (2014). Understanding the psychological processes of the racial match effect in Asian Americans. *Journal of Counseling Psychology, 58,* 335–345.

Meyer, R. G. (1975). A behavioral treatment of sleepwalking associated with test anxiety. *Behavior Therapy and Experimental Psychiatry, 6,* 167–168.

Meyer-Bahlburg, H. F. L., Dolezal, C., Baker, S., & New, M. (2008). Sexual orientation in women with classical or non-classical congenital adrenal hyperplasia as a function of degree of prenatal androgen excess. *Archives of Sexual Behavior, 37*(1), 85–99.

Meyer-Lindenberg, A. (2010). From maps to mechanisms through neuroimaging of schizophrenia. *Nature, 468,* 194–202. doi:10.1038/nature09569.

Mezulis, A. H., Abramson, L. Y., Hyde, J. S., & Hankin, B. L. (2004). Is there a universal positivity bias in attributions? A meta-analytic review of individual, developmental, and cultural differences in the self-serving attributional bias. *Psychological Bulletin, 130,* 711–747.

Mezzacappa, E. S., Katkin, E. S., & Palmer, S. N. (1999). Epinephrine, arousal and emotion: A new look at two-factor theory. *Cognition and Emotion, 13,* 181–199.

Michael, R. B., Garry, M., & Kirsch, I. (2012). Suggestion, cognition, and behavior. *Current Directions in Psychological Science, 21*(3), 151–156. doi:10.1177/0963721412446369.

Michael, R. T., Wadsworth, J., Feinleib, J., Johnson, A. M., Laumann, E. O., & Wellings, K. (1998). Private sexual behavior, public opinion, and public health policy related to sexually transmitted diseases: A US-British comparison. *American Journal of Public Health, 88,* 749–754.

Michel, C., Rossion, B., Han, J., Chung, C.-S., & Caldara, R. (2006). Holistic processing is finely tuned for faces of one's own race. *Psychological Science, 17,* 608–615.

Michelena, P., Sibbald, A. M., Erhard, H. W., & McLeod, J. E. (2009). Effects of group size and personality on social foraging: The distribution of sheep across patches. *Behavioral Ecology, 20*(1), 145–152.

Middeldorp, C. M., Cath, D. C., Van Dyck, R., & Boomsma, D. I., (2005). The co-morbidity of anxiety and depression in the perspective of genetic epidemiology: A review of twin and family studies. *Psychological Medicine, 35,* 611–624.

Mieda, M., & Sakurai, T. (2013). Orexin (hypocretin) receptor agonists and antagonists for treatment of sleep disorders. Rationale for development and current status. *CNS Drugs, 27*(2), 83–90.

Miehls, D. (2011). Racism and its effects. In N. R. Heller & A. Gitterman (Eds.), *Mental health and social problems: A social work perspective* (pp. 2–85). New York: Routledge/Taylor & Francis.

Mielke, M. M., Vemuri, P., & Rocca, W.A.(2014). Clinical epidemiology of Alzheimer's disease: Assessing sex and gender differences. *Clinical Epidemiology, 6,* 37–48.

Mikolajczak, M., Gross, J. J., Lane, A., Corneille, O., de Timary, P., & Luminet, O. (2010). Oxytocin makes people trusting, not gullible. *Psychological Science, 21,* 1072–1074. doi:10.1177/0956797610377343.

Mikulincer, M., & Shaver, P. R. (2005). Mental representations of attachment security: Theoretical foundation for a positive social psychology. In M. W. Baldwin (Ed.), *Interpersonal cognition* (pp. 233–266). New York: Guilford Press.

Mikulincer, M., Shaver, P. R., & Berant, E. (2013). An attachment perspective on therapeutic processes and outcomes. *Journal of Personality, 81*(6), 606–616.

Mildner, S., & Buchbauer, G. (2013). Human body scents: Do they influence our behavior? *Natural Product Communications, 8*(11), 1651–1662.

Milev, P., Ho, B. C., Arndt, S., & Andreasen, N. C. (2005). Predictive values of neurocognition and negative symptoms on functional outcome in schizophrenia: A longitudinal first-episode study with 7-year follow-up. *American Journal of Psychiatry, 162,* 495–506.

Milgram, S. (1963). Behavioral study of obedience. *Journal of Abnormal and Social Psychology, 67,* 371–378.

Milgram, S. (1965). Some conditions of obedience and disobedience to authority. *Human Relations, 18,* 57–76.

Milgram, S. (1977, October). Subject reaction: The neglected factor in the ethics of experimentation. *Hastings Center Report* (pp. 19–23).

Milisen, K., Braes, T., Fick, D. M., & Foreman, M. D. (2006). Cognitive assessment and differentiating the 3 Ds (dementia, depression, delirium). *Nursing Clinics of North America, 41*(1), 1–22.

Militec, M. P. (2002). The introduction of feminine psychology to psychoanalysis. *Contemporary Psychoanalysis, 38,* 287–299.

Miller, B. L. (2007). Frontotemporal dementia and semantic dementia: Anatomic variations on the same disease or distinctive entities? *Alzheimer Disease & Associated Disorders, 21*(4), s19–s22.

Miller, D. D., McEvoy, J. P., Davis, S. M., Caroff , S. N., et al. (2005). Clinical correlates of tardive dyskinesia in schizophrenia: Baseline data from the CATIE schizophrenia trial. *Schizophrenia Research, 80,* 33–43.

Miller, E., Tancredi, D. J., McCauley, H. L., Decker, M. R., Virata, M. C. D., Anderson, H. A., Stetkevich, N., Brown, E. W., Moideen, F., & Silverman, J. G. (2012). "Coaching boys into men": A cluster-randomized controlled trial of a dating violence prevention program. *Journal of Adolescent Health Care.* doi:10.1016/j.jadohealth.2012.01.018.

Miller, G. (1956). The magical number seven, plus or minus two: Some limits on our capacity to process information. *Psychological Review, 63,* 81–97.

Miller, G. (2005). Neuroscience: The dark side of glia. *Science, 308,* 778–781.

Miller, G., Tyber, J. M., & Jordan, B. D. (2007). Ovulatory cycle effects on tip earnings by lap dancers: Economic evidence for human estrus? *Evolution and Human Behavior, 28,* 375–381.

Miller, G. A. (1991). *The science of words.* New York: Scientific American Library.

Miller, G. A. (2010). Mistreating psychology in the decades of the brain. *Perspectives on Psychological Science, 5*(6), 716–743. doi:10.1177/1745691610388774.

Miller, G. A., Heise, G. A., & Lichten, W. (1951). The intelligibility of speech as a function of the context of the test materials. *Journal of Experimental Psychology, 41,* 329–335.

Miller, J. (2001). The cultural grounding of social psychological theory. In A. Tesser & N. Schwarz (Eds.), *Blackwell handbook of social psychology: Intraindividual processes* (pp. 22–43). Oxford, UK: Blackwell.

Miller, J. D., Lynam, D., Zimmerman, R. S., Logan, T. K., Leukefeld, C., & Clayton, R. (2004). The utility of the Five Factor Model in understanding risky sexual behavior. *Personality and Individual Differences, 36,* 1611–1626.

Miller, J. G., & Bersoff, D. M. (1994). Cultural influences on the moral status of reciprocity and the discounting of endogenous motivation. *Personality and Social Psychology Bulletin, 20,* 592–607.

Miller, K. F., Smith, C. M., Zhu, J., & Zhang, H. (1995). Preschool origins of cross-national differences in mathematical competence: The role of number-naming systems. *Psychological Science, 6,* 56–60.

Miller, L. C., Putcha-Bhagavatula, A., & Pedersen, W. C. (2002). Men's and women's mating preferences: Distinct evolutionary mechanisms? *Current Directions in Psychological Science, 11,* 88–93.

Miller, L. T., & Vernon, P. A. (1992). The general factor in short-term memory, intelligence, and reaction time. *Intelligence, 16,* 5–29.

Miller, L. T., & Vernon, P. A. (1997). Developmental changes in speed of information processing in young children. *Developmental Psychology, 33,* 549–554.

Miller, N. E. (1959). Liberalization of basic S-R concepts: Extensions to conflict behavior, motivation, and social learning. In S. Koch (Ed.), *Psychology: A study of science* (Vol. 2, pp. 196–292). New York: McGraw-Hill.

Miller, R. R., & Laborda, M. A. (2011). Preventing recovery from extinction and relapse: A product of current retrieval cues and memory strengths. *Current Directions in Psychological Science, 20*(5), 325–329. doi:10.1177/0963721411418466.

Miller, S. L., & Maner, J. K. (2010). Ovulation as a male mating prime: Subtle signs of women's fertility influence men's mating cognition and behavior. *Journal of Personality and Social Psychology, 100*(2), 295–308. doi:10.1037/a0020930.

Miller, T. W., Nigg, J. T., & Miller, R. L. (2009). Attention deficit hyperactivity disorder in African American children: What can we conclude from the past ten years? *Clinical Psychology Review, 29,* 77–86.

Mills, P. E., Cole, K. N., Jenkins, J. R., & Dale, P. S. (1998). Effects of differing levels of inclusion on preschoolers with disabilities. *Exceptional Children, 65,* 79–90.

Milner, B. (1970). Memory and the medial temporal regions of the brain. In K. H. Pribram & D. B. Broadbent (Eds.), *Biology of memory.* New York: Academic Press.

Milner, D. (1983). *Children and race.* Beverly Hills, CA: Sage.

Miltenberger, R. G. (2011). *Behavior modification: Principles and procedures* (5th ed.). New York: Cengage.

Mineka, S., & Zinbarg, R. (2006). A contemporary learning theory perspective on the etiology of anxiety disorders: It's not what you thought it was. *American Psychologist, 61,* 10–26.

Miner, J. L., & Clarke-Stewart, K. A. (2008). Trajectories of externalizing behavior from age 2 to age 9: Relations with gender, temperament, ethnicity, parenting, and rater. *Developmental Psychology, 44,* 771–786.

Minshew, N. J., & Williams, D. L. (2007). The new neurobiology of autism: Cortex, connectivity, and neuronal organization. *Archives of Neurology, 64,* 945–950.

Minson, J. A., & Mueller, J. S. (2012). The cost of collaboration: Why joint decision making exacerbates rejection of outside information. *Psychological Science, 23*(3), 219–224. doi:10.1177/0956797611429132.

Minzenberg, M. J., Jong, H. Y., & Cameron, S. C. (2008). Schizophrenia. In R. E. Hales, S. C. Yudofsky, & G. O. Gabbard (Eds.), *Textbook of psychiatry* (pp. 407–456). Washington, DC: American Psychiatric Publishing.

Minzenberg, M. J., Watrous, A. J., Yoon, J. H., Ursu, S., & Carter, C. S. (2008). Modafinil shifts human locus coeruleus to low-tonic, high-phasic activity during functional MRI. *Science, 322*(5908), 1700–1702.

Miotto, K., Darakjian, J., Basch, J., Murray, S., Zogg, J., & Rawson, R. (2001). Gamma-hydroxybutyric acid: Patterns of use, effects and withdrawal. *American Journal on Addictions, 10,* 232–241.

Miró, J., Huguet, A., & Jensen, M. P. (2014). Pain beliefs predict pain intensity and pain status in children: usefulness of the pediatric version of the survey of pain attitudes. *Pain Medicine.* Epub January 2, 2014.

Mischel, W. (2009). From personality and assessment to personality science. *Journal of Research in Personality, 43,* 282–290.

Mischel, W., & Shoda, Y. (2008). Toward a unified theory of personality: Integrating dispositions and processing dynamics within the cognitive-affective processing system. In O. John, R. Robins, & L. Pervin (Eds.), *Handbook of personality: Theory and research* (3rd ed., pp. 208–241). New York: Guilford.

Mischel, W., Shoda, Y., & Smith, R. (2004). *Introduction to personality: Toward an integration* (7th ed.). New York: Wiley.

Mitchell, C., Hobcraft, J., McLanahan, S. S., Siegel, S. R., Berg, A., Brooks-Gunn, J., Garfinkel, I., & Notterman, D. (2014). Social disadvantage, genetic sensitivity, and children's telomere length. *PNAS, 111*(16), 5944–5949.

Mitchell, D. B. (2006). Nonconscious priming after 17 years: Invulnerable implicit memory? *Psychological Science, 17,* 925–929.

Mitte, K. (2005a). A meta-analysis of the efficacy of psycho- and pharmacotherapy *in* panic disorder with and without agoraphobia. *Journal of Affective Disorders, 88,* 27–45.

Mitte, K. (2005b). Meta-analysis of cognitive-behavioral treatments for generalized anxiety disorder: A comparison with pharmacotherapy. *Psychological Bulletin, 131,* 785–795.

Miyagawa, T., Kawashima, M. Nishida, N., Ohashi, J., Kimura, R., Fujimoto, A., Shimada, M., Morishita, S., Shigeta, T., Lin, L., Hong, S.-C., Faraco, J., Shin, Y.-K., Jeong, J.-H., Okazaki, Y. Tsuji, S., Honda, M., Honda, Y., Mignot, E., & Tokunaga, K. (2008). Variant between CPT1B and CHKB associated with susceptibility to narcolepsy. *Nature Genetics, 40,* 1324–1328.

Miyauchi, S., Misaki, M., Kan, S., Fukunaga, T., & Koike, T. (2009). Human brain activity time-locked to rapid eye movements during REM sleep. *Experimental Brain Research, 92*(4), 657–667.

Mizumori, S. J., Yeshenko, O., Gill, K. M., & Davis, D. M. (2004). Parallel processing across neural systems: Implications for a multiple memory system hypothesis. Neurobiology of Learning and Memory. *Neurobiology of Learning & Memory, 82*(3), 278–298.

Mochizuki-Kawai, H., Yamakawa, Y., Mochizuki, S., Anzai, S., & Arai, M. (2010). Structured floral arrangement programme for improving visuospatial working memory in schizophrenia. *Neuropsychological Rehabilitation, 20*(4), 624–636. doi:10.1080/09602011003715141.

Moen, P., Erickson, W. A., Agarwal, M., Fields, V., & Todd, L. (2000). *The Cornell Retirement and Well-Being Study. Final report.* Ithaca, NY: Bronfenbrenner Life Course Center, Cornell University.

Moffitt, T. E. (2002). Teen-aged mothers in contemporary Britain. *Journal of Child Psychology & Psychiatry & Allied Disciplines, 43,* 727–742.

Moffitt, T. E., Arseneault, L., Belsky, D., Dickson, N., Hancox, R. J., Harrington, H., McConnel, A. R., Brown, C. M., Shoda, T. M., Stayton, L. E., & Martin, C. E. (2011). Friends with benefits: On the positive consequences of pet ownership. *Journal of Personality & Social Psychology, 101*(6), 1239–1252. doi:10.1037/a0024506.

Moffitt, T. E., Caspi, A., & Rutter, M. (2005). Strategy for investigating interactions between measured genes and measured environments. *Archives of General Psychiatry, 62,* 473–481.

Mogenson, G. J. (1976). Neural mechanisms of hunger: Current status and future prospects. In D. Novin, W. Wyrwicka, & G. Bray (Eds.), *Hunger: Basic mechanisms and clinical applications.* New York: Raven.

Mohr, C., Binkofski, F., Erdmann, C., Buchel, C., & Helmchen, C. (2005). The anterior cingulate cortex contains distinct areas dissociating external from self-administered painful stimulation: A parametric fMRI study. *Pain, 114,* 347–357.

Mohr, C., Rohrenbach, C. M., Landis, T., & Regard, M. (2001). Associations to smell are more pleasant than to sound. *Journal of Clinical and Experimental Neuropsychology, 23,* 484–489.

Mohr, P., Rodriguez, M., Slavíčková, A., & Hanka, J. (2011). The application of vagus nerve stimulation and deep brain stimulation in depression. *Neuropsychobiology, 64*(3), 170–181.

Mohtasib, R. S., Lumley, G., Goodwin, J. A., Emsley, H. C., Sluming, V., & Parkes, L. M. (2011). Calibrated fMRI during a cognitive Stroop task reveals reduced metabolic response with increasing age. *Neuroimage.*

Mojzisch, A., & Schulz-Hardt, S. (2010). Knowing others' preferences degrades the quality of group decisions. *Journal of Personality and Social Psychology, 98*(5), 794–808. doi:10.1037/a0017627.

Mokdad, A. H., Marks, J. S., Stroup, D. F., & Gerberding, J. L. (2004). Actual causes of death in the United States, 2000. *Journal of the American Medical Association, 291,* 1238–1245.

Molden, D. C., & Dweck, C. S. (2000). Meaning and motivation. In C. Sansone & J. M. Harackiewicz (Eds.), *Intrinsic and extrinsic motivation: The search for optimal motivation and performance.* San Diego: Academic Press.

Molenberghs, P., Cunnington, R., & Mattingley, J. B. (2012) Brain regions with mirror properties: A meta-analysis of 125 human fMRI studies. *Neurosci Biobehav Rev 36* (1):341–349.

Monane, M., Leichter, D., & Lewis, O. (1984). Physical abuse in psychiatrically hospitalized children and adolescents. *Journal of the American Academy of Child and Adolescent Psychiatry, 23,* 653–658.

Moncrief, W. C., Babakus, E., Cravens, D. W., & Johnston, M. W. (2000). Examining gender differences in field sales organizations. *Journal of Business Research, 49,* 245–257.

Mongrain, M., & Anselmo-Matthews, T. (2012). Do positive psychology exercises work? A replication of Seligman et al. (2005). *Journal of Clinical Psychology, 68*(4), 382–389.

Moniz, E (1948). How I came to perform prefrontal leucotomy. *Proceedings of the First International Congress of Psychosurgery* (pp. 7–18). Lisbon, Portugal: Edicões Atica.

Monroe, S., Thase, M., & Simons, A. (1992). Social factors and psychobiology of depression: Relations between life stress and rapid eye movement sleep latency. *Journal of Abnormal Psychology, 101,* 528–537.

Monstad, K., Propper, C., & Salvanes, K. G. (2011). Is teenage motherhood contagious? Evidence from a natural experiment. *Working Paper No. 11/262.* Centre for Market and Public Organisation, Bristol Institute of Public Affairs. Bristol, UK: University of Bristol.

Moon, R. Y., & Fu, L. (2012). Sudden infant death syndrome: An update. *Pediatrics in Review, 33*(7), 314–320.

Moon, R. Y., Horne, R. S., & Hauck, F. R. (2007). Sudden infant death syndrome. *Lancet, 370*(9598), 1578–1587.

Moon, Y. (2003). Don't blame the computer: When self-disclosure moderates the self-serving bias. *Journal of Consumer Psychology, 13,* 125–137.

Moore, E. R., Anderson, G. C., Bergman, N., & Dowswell, T. (2012). Early skin-to-skin contact for mothers and their healthy newborn infants. *Cochrane Database of Systematic Reviews,* Issue 5. Article No.: CD003519.

Moore, K. A. (2005). *Family strengths: Often overlooked, but real.* Washington, DC: Child Trends.

Moore, K. A. (2009). Teen births: Examining the recent increase. *Child Trends Research Brief.* Retrieved from http://www.childtrends.org/Files/Child _Trends_2009_03_13_FS_TeenBirthRate.pdf

Moore, T. H. M., Zammit, S., Lingford-Hughes, A. Barnes, T. R. E., Jones, P. B., Burke, M., & Lewis, G. (2007). Cannabis use and risk of psychotic or affective mental health outcomes: A systematic review. *The Lancet, 370,* 319–328.

Moran, C. C. (2002). Humor as a moderator of compassion fatigue. In C. R. Figley (Ed.), *Treating compassion fatigue* (pp. 139–154). New York: Brunner-Routledge.

Moran, D. R. (2000, June). *Is active learning for me?* Poster presented at APS Preconvention Teaching Institute, Denver.

Moran, R. (2006). Learning in high-tech and multimedia environments. *Current Directions in Psychological Science, 15,* 63–67.

Moreira, D., Almeida, F., Pinto, M., & Fávero, M. (2014). Psychopathy: A comprehensive review of its assessment and intervention. *Aggression and Behavior, 19*(3), 191–195.

Moreno, S., Bialystok, E., Barac, R., Schellenberg, E., Cepeda, N. J., & Chau, T. (2011). Short-term music training enhances verbal intelligence and executive function. *Psychological Science, 22*(11), 1425–1433. doi:10.1177/ 0956797611416999.

Morewedge, C. K., Gilbert, D. T., & Wilson, T. D. (2005). The least likely of times: How remembering the past biases forecasts of the future. *Psychological Science, 16*(8), 626–630.

Morgan, C. D., & Murray, H. A. (1935). A method for investigating fantasy: The Thematic Apperception Test. *Archives of Neurology and Psychiatry, 34,* 289–306.

Morgenstern, M., Isensee, B., & Hanewinkel, R. (2012). Seeing and liking cigarette advertisements: Is there a "mere exposure" effect? *European Addiction Research, 19*(1), 42–46.

Morikawa, H. & Morrisett, R. A. (2010). Ethanol action on dopaminergic neurons in the ventral tegmental area: Interaction with intrinsic ion channels and neurotransmitter inputs. *International Review of Neurobiology, 91,* 235–288.

Morillo, C., Belloch, A., & Garcia-Soriano, G. (2007). Clinical obsessions in obsessive-compulsive patients and obsession-relevant intrusive thoughts in non-clinical, depressed and anxious subjects: Where are the differences? *Behaviour Research and Therapy, 45,* 1319–1333.

Morin, C. (2011, March). Neuromarketing: The new science of consumer behavior. *Society.* pp. 131–135. doi:10.1007/s12115-010-9408-1.

Morin, C. M., Bélanger, L., LeBlanc, M., Ivers, H., Savard, J., Espie, C. A., Mérette, C., Baillargeon, L., & Grégoire, J.-P. (2009). The natural history of insomnia: A population-based 3-year longitudinal study. *Archives of Internal Medicine, 169,* 447–453.

Morina, N., Wicherts, J. M., Lobbrecht, J., & Proebe, S. (2014). Remission from post-traumatic stress disorder in adults: A systemic review and meta-analysis of long-term outcomes. *Clinical Psychology Review, 34*(3), 249–255.

Morris, L. (2000, December 5). Hold the anaesthetic: I'll hypnotise myself instead. *Daily Mail,* p. 25.

Morris, M. C., Ciesla, J. A., & Garber, J. (2008). A prospective study of the cognitive-stress model of depressive symptoms in adolescents. *Journal of Abnormal Psychology, 117,* 719–734.

Morris, M. C., Evans, D. A., Tangney, C. C., Bienias, J. L., & Wilson, R. S. (2006). Associations of vegetable and fruit consumption with age-related cognitive change. *Neurology, 67,* 1370–1376.

Morris, R. G., & Mograbi, D. C. (2013). Anosognosia, autobiographical memory and self knowledge in Alzheimer's disease. *Cortex,* 49(6), 1553–1565.

Morrison, A., & Chein, J. (2011). Does working memory training work? The promise and challenges of enhancing cognition by training working memory. *Psychonomic Bulletin & Review, 18*(1), 46–60.

Morrison, A. P., French, P., Steward, S. L., K., Birchwood, M., Fowler, D., Guley, A. I., Jones, P. B., Bentall, R. P., Lewis, S. W., Murray, G. K., Patterson, P., Brunet, K., Conroy, J., Parker, S., Reilly, R., Byrne, R., Davies, L. M., & Dunn, G. (2012). Early detection and intervention evaluation for people at risk of psychosis: Multisite randomised controlled trial. *BMJ, 344.* doi:10.1136/bmj.e2233.

Morrison, A. S., & Heimberg, R. G. (2013). Social anxiety and social anxiety disorder. *Annual Review of Clinical Psychology, 9,* 249–274.

Morrison, I., Frangulyan, R., & Riha, R. L. (2011). Beta-blockers as a cause of violent rapid eye movement sleep behavior disorder: A poorly recognized but common cause of violent parasomnias. *American Journal of Medicine, 124*(1), e11.

Morrissette, D. A. (2013). Twisting the night away: A review of the neurobiology, genetics, diagnosis, and treatment of shift work disorder. *CNS Spectrums, 18*(1), 45–53.

Morrissey, T. W., Hutchison, L., & Winsler, A. (2014). Family income, school attendance, and academic achievement in elementary school. *Developmental Psychology, 50*(3), 741–753.

Mortimer, R. G., Goldsteen, K., Armstrong, R. W., & Macrina, D. (1988). *Effects of enforcement, incentives, and publicity on seat belt use in Illinois.* University of Illinois, Dept. of Health & Safety Studies, Final Report to Illinois Dept. of Transportation (Safety Research Report 88–11).

Morton, G. J., Cummings, D. E., Baskin, D. G., Barsh, G. S., & Schwartz, M. W. (2006). Central nervous system control of food intake and body weight. *Nature, 443,* 289–295.

Moscovici, S. (1985). Social influence and conformity. In G. Lindzey & E. Aronson (Eds.), *The handbook of social psychology* (Vol. 2, 3rd ed.). New York: Random House.

Moskowitz, G. B. (2005). *Social cognition: Understanding self and others.* New York: Guilford Press.

Moskowitz, G. B., & Gill, M. J. (2013). Person perception. In D. Reisberg (Ed.), *The Oxford handbook of cognitive psychology* (pp. 918–942). New York: Oxford University Press.

Moskowitz, J. T., Hult, J. R., Bussolari, C., & Acree, M. (2009). What works in coping with HIV? A meta-analysis with implications for coping with serious illness. *Psychological Bulletin, 135,* 121–141.

Moss, E., Bureau, J.-F., Cyr, C., Mongeau, C., & St.-Laurent, D. (2004). Correlates of attachment at age 3: Construct validity of the preschool attachment classification system. *Developmental Psychology, 40,* 323–334.

Mostert, M. P. (2001). Facilitated communication since 1995: A review of published studies. *Journal of Autism and Developmental Disorders, 31,* 287–313.

Motowidlo, S. J., Brownlee, A. L., & Schmit, M. J. (2008). Effects of personality characteristics on knowledge, skill, and performance in servicing retail customers. *International Journal of Selection and Assessment, 16,* 272–280.

Mõttus, R., McNeill, G., Jia, X., Craig, L. C., Starr, J. M., & Deary, I. J. (2011). The associations between personality, diet and body mass index in older people. *Health Psychology, 32*(4), 353–360.

Mousavi-Nasab, S.-M.-H., Kormi-Nouri, R., Sundström, A., & Nilsson, L.-G. (2012). The effects of marital status on episodic and semantic memory in healthy middle-aged and old individuals. *Scandinavian Journal of Psychology, 53,* 1–8.

Moyer, C. A., Donnelly, M. W., Anderson, J. C., Valek, K. C., Huckaby, S. J., Wiederholt, D. A., Doty, R. L., Rehlinger, A. S., & Rice, B. L. (2011). Frontal electroencephalographic asymmetry associated with positive emotion is produced by very brief meditation training. *Psychological Science, 22*(10), 1277–1279. doi:10.1177/0956797611418985.

Mozaffarian, D., Hao, T., Rimm, E. B., Willett, W. C., & Hu, F. B. (2011). Changes in diet and lifestyle and long-term weight gain in women and men. *New England Journal Of Medicine, 364*(25), 2392–2404. doi:10.1056/NEJMoa1014296.

Mroczek, D. K., & Spiro, A., III. (2005). Changing life satisfaction during adulthood: Findings from the Veterans Affairs normative aging study. *Journal of Personality and Social Psychology, 88,* 189–202.

Mucchi-Faina, A., & Pagliaro, S. (2008). Minority influence: The role of ambivalence toward the source. *European Journal of Social Psychology, 38,* 612–623.

Muchinsky, P. M. (2003). *Psychology applied to work* (7th ed.). Belmont, CA: Thomson.

Mudrick, L., Breska, A., Lamy, D., & Deouell, L. Y. (2011). Intergration without awareness: Expanding the limits of unconscious processing. *Psychological Science, 22*(6), 764–770.

Mueller, K. L., Hoon, M. A., Erlenbach, I., Chandrashekar, J., et al. (2005). The receptors and coding logic for bitter taste. *Nature, 434,* 225–229.

Mueser, K. T., & Jeste, D. V. (Eds.) (2009). *Clinical handbook of schizophrenia.* New York: Guilford Press.

Muggleton, N. G., Chen, C. Y., Tzeng, O. J., Hung, D. L., & Juan, C. H. (2010). Inhibitory control and the frontal eye fields. *Journal of Cognitive Neuroscience* [Advance online publication]. doi:10.1162/jocn.2010.21416

Mühlberger, A., Wiedemann, G., Herrmann, M. J., & Pauli, P. (2006). Phylo- and ontogenetic fears and the expectation of danger: Differences between spider- and flight-phobic subjects in cognitive and physiological responses to disorder-specific stimuli. *Journal of Abnormal Psychology, 115*(3), 580–589.

Mukamel, R., Ekstrom, A. D., Kaplan, J., Iacoboni, M., & Fried, I. (2010). Single-neuron responses in humans during execution and observation of actions. *Current Biology, 20*(8), 750–756. doi:10.1016/j.cub.2010.02.045.

Mullen, B. (1986). Atrocity as a function of lynch mob composition: A self-attention perspective. *Personality and Social Psychology Bulletin, 12,* 187–197.

Muller, P. A., Pascual-Leone, A., & Rotenberg, A. (2012). Safety and tolerability of repetitive transcranial magnetic stimulation in patients with pathologic positive sensory phenomena: a review of literature. *Brain Stimulation, 5*(3), 320–329.

Müller, T. D., Föcker, M., Holtkamp, K., Herpertz-Dahlmann, B., & Hebebrand, J. (2009). Leptin-mediated neuroendocrine alterations in anorexia nervosa: Somatic and behavioral implications. *Child and Adolescent Psychiatric Clinics of North America, 18*(1), 117–129.

Mulligan, N. W. (2012). Differentiating between conceptual implicit and explicit memory: A crossed double dissociation between category-exemplar production and category-cued recall. *Psychological Science.* Advance online publication. doi:10.1177/0956797611433335

Mulligan, N. W., & Picklesimer, M. (2012). Levels of processing and the cue-dependent nature of recollection. *Journal of Memory and Language, 66*(1), 79–92. doi:10.1016/ j.jml.2011.10.001.

Mullin, R. E. (2000). *The new handbook of cognitive therapy techniques.* New York: Norton.

Mullins-Sweatt, S. N., Glover, N. G., Derefinko, K. J., Miller, J. D., & Widiger, T. A. (2010). The search for the successful psychopath. *Journal Of Research in Personality, 44*(4), 554–558. doi:10.1016/j.jrp.2010.05.010.

Mullis, I. V. S., Martin, M. O., Gonzales, E. J., & Chrostowski, S. J. (2004). *TIMSS 2003 international mathematics report: Findings from IEA's Trends in International Mathematics and Science Study at the fourth and eighth grades.* Chestnut Hill, MA: Boston College.

Mullis, I. V. S., Martin, M. O., Kennedy, A. M., & Foy, P. (2007). *PIRLS 2006 international report: IEA's Progress in International Reading Literacy Study in primary school in 40 countries.* Chestnut Hill, MA: Boston College.

Mumme, D. L., & Fernald, A. (2003). The infant as onlooker: Learning from emotional reactions observed in a television scenario. *Child Development, 74,* 221–237.

Munakata, Y., Snyder, H. R., & Chatham, C. H. (2012). Developing cognitive control: Three key transitions. *Current Directions in Psychological Science, 21*(2), 71–77. doi: 10.1177/0963721412436807.

Münch M., & Kawasaki, A. (2013). Intrinsically photosensitive retinal ganglion cells: Classification, function and clinical implications. *Current Opinion in Neurology, 26*(1), 45–51.

Munte, T. F., Altenmuller, E., & Jancke, L. (2002). The musician's brain as a model of neuroplasticity. *Nature Reviews: Neuroscience, 3,* 473–478.

Murayama, K., Matsumoto, M., Izuma, K., & Matsumoto, K. (2010). Neural basis of the undermining effect of monetary reward on intrinsic motivation. *Proceedings Of The National Academy Of Sciences Of The United States Of America, 107*(49), 20911–20916. doi:10.1073/pnas.1013305107.

Müri, R. M., Cazzoli, D, Nef, T., Mosimann, U. P., Hopfner, S., & Nyffeler, T. (2013). Non-invasive brain stimulation in neglect rehabilitation: an update. *Frontiers in Human Neuroscience,* ePub June 10, 2013.

Murphy, M. C., Steele, C. M., & Gross, J. J. (2007). Signaling threat: How situational cues affect women in math, science, and engineering settings. *Psychological Science, 18,* 879–885.

Murphy, T. M., Ryan, M., Foster, T., Kelly, C., McClelland, R., O'Grady, J. (2011). Risk and protective genetic variants in suicidal behaviour: Association with SLC1A2, SLC1A3, 5-HTR1B & NTRK2 polymorphisms. *Behavioral and Brain Functions, 7*(22), 1–9.

Murray, B. (2000). Learning from real life. *APA Monitor, 31,* 72–73.

Murray, H. A. (1938). *Explorations in personality.* New York: Oxford University Press.

Murray, J. A., & Terry, D. (1999). Parental reactions to infant death: The effects of resources and coping strategies. *Journal of Social and Clinical Psychology, 18,* 341–369.

Murrough, J.W., Huang, Y., Hu, J., Henry, S., Williams, W., Gallezot, J. D., Bailey, C. R., Krystal, J. H., Carson, R. E., & Neumeister, A. (2011). Reduced amygdala serotonin transporter binding in posttraumatic stress disorder. *Biol Psychiatry 70* (11):1033–1038.

Musa, R., Draman, S., Jeffrey, S., Jeffrey, I., Abdullah, N., Halim, N. A., Wahab, N. A., Mukhtar, N. Z., Johari, S. N., Rameli, N., Midin, M., Nik Jaafar, N. R., Das, S., & Sidi, H. (2014). Post tsunami psychological impact among survivors in Aceh and West Sumatra, Indonesia. *Comprehensive Psychiatry, 55* (Supplement 1), S13–S16.

Musser, E. D., Backs, R. W., Schmitt, C. F., Ablow, J. C., Measelle, J. R., & Nigg, J. T. (2011). Emotion regulation via the autonomic nervous system in children with attention-deficit/hyperactivity disorder (ADHD). *Journal of Abnormal Child Psychology, 39*(6), 841–852. doi:10.1007/s10802-011-9499-1.

Mustanski, B. S., Chivers, M. L., & Bailey, J. M. (2002). A critical review of recent biological research on human sexual orientation. *Annual Review of Sex Research, 13,* 89–140.

Myers, B. J. (1987). Mother-infant bonding as a critical period. In M. H. Bornstein (Ed.), *Sensitive periods in development: Interdisciplinary perspectives.* Hillsdale, NJ: Erlbaum.

Myers, D. G. (2004). *Intuition: Its powers and perils.* New Haven, CT: Yale University Press.

Myers, K. M., & Davis, M. (2007). Mechanisms of fear extinction. *Molecular Psychiatry, 12,* 120–150.

Myers, K. P., & Sclafani, A. (2006). Development of learned flavor preferences. *Developmental Psychobiology, 48,* 380–388.

Na, J., Grossmann, I., Varnum, M.E.W., Kitayama, S., Gonzalez, R., & Nisbett, R.E. (2010). Cultural differences are not always reducible to individual differences. *Proceedings of the National Academy of Sciences of the United States of America, 107,* 6192–6197.

Nadeau, S., & Crosson, B. (1995). A guide to the functional imaging of cognitive processes. *Neuropsychiatry, Neuropsychology, and Behavioral Neurology, 8,* 143–162.

Naidoo, L. J., Scherbaum, C. A., Goldstein, H. W., & Graen, G. B. (2011). A longitudinal examination of the effects of LMX, ability, and differentiation on team performance. *Journal Of Business And Psychology, 26*(3), 347–357. doi:10.1007/s10869-010-9193-2.

Nairne, J. S. (2003). Sensory and working memory. In A. F. P. Healy, R. W. Proctor, & I. B. Weiner (Eds.), *Handbook of psychology: Vol. 4. Experimental psychology* (pp. 423–444). New York: Wiley.

Naito, M., & Miura, H. (2001). Japanese children's numerical competencies: Age- and schooling-related influences on the development of number concepts and addition skills. *Developmental Psychology, 37,* 217–230.

Nakamura, J., & Csikszentmihalyi, M. (2001). Catalytic creativity. *American Psychologist, 56,* 337–341.

Nakano, K., & Kitamura, T. (2001). The relation of the anger subcomponent of Type A behavior to psychological symptoms in Japanese and foreign students. *Japanese Psychological Research, 43,* 50–54.

Nakao, M., & Yano, E. (2006). Prediction of major depression in Japanese adults: Somatic manifestations of depression in annual health examinations. *Journal of Affective Disorders, 90,* 29–35.

Naquin, C. E., Kurtzberg, T. R., & Belkin, L. Y. (2010). The finer points of lying online: E-mail versus pen and paper. *Journal Of Applied Psychology, 95*(2), 387–394. doi:10.1037/a0018627.

Narrow, W. E., Clarke, D. E., Kuramoto, S. J., Kraemer, H. C., Kupfer, D. J., Greiner, L., & Regier, D. A. (2013). *DSM-5* field trials in the United States and Canada, Part III: Development and reliability testing of a cross-cutting symptom assessment for *DSM-5. American Journal of Psychiatry, 170,* 71–82.

Nash, I. S., Mosca, L., Blumenthal, R. S., Davidson, M. H., Smith, S. C., Jr., & Pasternak, R. C. (2003). Contemporary awareness and understanding of cholesterol as a risk factor: Results of an American Heart Association national survey. *Archives of Internal Medicine, 163,* 1597–1600.

Nasoz, F., Lisetti, C. L., & Vasilakos, A. V. (2010). Affectively intelligent and adaptive car interfaces. *Information Sciences, 180*(20), 3817–3836. doi:10.1016/ j.ins.2010.06.034.

Nathan, D. (2011). *Sybil exposed: The extraordinary story behind the famous multiple personality case.* New York, NY US: Free Press.

Nathan, P. E., & Gorman, J. M. (2007). *A guide to treatments that work* (3rd ed.). New York: Oxford University Press.

National Association of Anorexia Nervosa and Associated Disorders. (2002). *Facts about eating disorders.* Retrieved August 26, 2003, from http://www.altrue.net/site /anadweb/content.php?type=1&id=6982.

National Center for Chronic Disease Prevention and Health Promotion. (2002). Trends in Sexual Risk Behaviors Among High School Students—United States, 1991–2001. *Morbidity and Mortality Weekly Report, 51,* 856–859.

National Center for Education Statistics. (2000). *National assessment of education progress.* Washington, DC: NCES.

National Center for Education Statistics. (2002). *Digest of education statistics, 2001.* Washington, DC: Office of Educational Research & Improvement, U.S. Dept. of Education.

National Center for Education Statistics (2014). Fast facts. Retrieved from the World Wide Web at https://nces.ed.gov/fastfacts/display.asp?id=37 on March 25, 2014.

National Center for Health Statistics. (2001). *Births, marriages, divorces, and deaths: Provisional data for January–December 2000.* Hyattsville, MD: Public Health Service.

National Center for Health Statistics. (2007). *Sexual behavior and selected health measures: Men and women 15–44 years of age, United States, 2002.* Hyattsville, MD: U.S. Department of Health and Human Services.

National Center for Health Statistics. (2011). *Births, marriages, divorces, and deaths: Provisional data for January–December 2011.* Hyattsville, MD: Public Health Service.

National Center on Addiction and Substance Abuse. (2004). *National Survey of American Attitudes on Substance Abuse: IX. Teen dating practices and sexual activity.* New York: Author.

National Highway Traffic Safety Administration (2010). *Traffic Safety Facts 2009: Alcohol-Impaired Driving.* Washington, DC: NHTSA.

National Institute of Mental Health (2008b). Study probes environment-triggered genetic changes in schizophrenia. Retrieved March 6, 2009 from http://www .nimh.nih.gov/science-news/2008/study-probes-environment -triggered-genetic-changes-in-schizophrenia.shtml.

National Institute of Mental Health. (1995). *Medications.* Washington, DC: U.S. Department of Health and Human Services.

National Institute of Mental Health. (2004, April 23). *Statement on antidepressant medications for children: Information for parents and caregivers.* Retrieved April 24, 2004, from www.nimh.nih.gov/press/StmntAntidepmeds.cfm.

National Institute of Mental Health. (2006). *The numbers count: Mental disorders in America.* Retrieved August 8, 2006, from http://www.nimh.nih.gov.publicat /numbers.cfm.

National Institute of Mental Health. (2006). The numbers count: Mental disorders in America. Retrieved from http://www.nimh.nih.gov.

National Institute of Mental Health. (2009). Suicide in the U.S.: Statistics and prevention. Retrieved from http://www.nimh.nih.gov.

National Institute of Mental Health. (2012a).Any anxiety disorder among adults. Retrieved from http://www.nimh.nih.gov/statistics/1ANYANX_ADULT.shtml

National Institute of Mental Health. (2012b). Any anxiety disorder among children. Retrieved from http://www.nimh.nih.gov/statistics/1ANYANX_child.shtml

National Institute of Mental Health. (2012c). Specific phobia among adults. Retrieved from http://www.nimh.nih.gov/statistics/1SPEC_ADULT.shtml

National Institute of Mental Health. (2014). The numbers count: Mental disorders in America. Retrieved from http://www.nimh.nih.gov/health/publications/the-numbers-count-mental-disorders-in-America/index.shtml

National Institute on Alcohol Abuse and Alcoholism. (2001). *Alcoholism: Getting the facts.* Bethesda, MD: National Institute on Alcohol Abuse and Alcoholism.

National Institute on Drug Abuse. (2000). Facts about MDMA (Ecstacy). *NIDA Notes, 14.* Retrieved December 13, 2004, from http://drugabuse.gov/NIDA_Notes/NNVol14N4/tearoff.html.

National Institutes of Health. (2001). *Eating disorders: Facts about eating disorders and the search for solutions.* NIH Publication No. 01-4901. Washington, DC: U.S. Department of Health and Human Services.

National Safety Council. (2004). *Reports on injuries in America, 2003.* Itasca, IL: Author.

National Science Foundation, Division of Science Resources Statistics. (2009). *Science and engineering degrees, by race/ethnicity of recipients, 1997-2006.* Arlington, VA.: Author. Retrieved from http://www.nsf.gov/statistics/nsf10300

Navarrete, C. D., McDonald, M. M., Asher, B. D., Kerr, N. L., Yokota, K., Olsson, A., & Sidanius, J. (2012). Fear is readily associated with an out-group face in a minimal group context. *Evolution & Human Behavior, 33*(5), 590-593.

Navarrete-Palacios, E., Hudson, R., Reyes-Guerrero, G., & Guevara-Guzman, R. (2003). Lower olfactory threshold during the ovulatory phase of the menstrual cycle. *Biological Psychology, 63,* 269-279.

Neblett, E. W., Rivas-Drake, D., & Umana-Taylor, A. J. (2012). The promise of racial and ethnic protective factors in promoting ethnic minority youth development. *Child Development Perspectives, 6,* 295-303.

Neher, A. (1991). Maslow's theory of motivation: A critique. *Journal of Humanistic Psychology, 31,* 89-112.

Nehm, R., Ha, M., & Mayfield, E. (2012). Transforming biology assessment with machine learning: Automated scoring of written evolutionary explanations. *Journal of Science Education & Technology, 21*(1), 183-196. doi:10.1007/s10956-011-9300-9.

Nehm, R., & Haertig, H. (2012). Human vs. computer diagnosis of students' natural selection knowledge: Testing the efficacy of text analytic software. *Journal of Science Education & Technology, 21*(1), 56-73. doi:10.1007/s10956-011-9282-7.

Neighbors, C., O'Connor, R. M., Lewis, M. A., Chawla, N., et al. (2008). The relative impact of injunctive norms on college student drinking: The role of reference group. *Psychology of Addictive Behaviors, 22,* 576-581.

Neil, A. L., & Christensen, H. (2009). Efficacy and effectiveness of school-based prevention and early intervention programs for anxiety. *Clinical Psychology Review, 29,* 208-215.

Neill, E., Rossell, S. L., McDonald, S., Joshua, N., Jansen, N., & Morgan, C. J. (2011). Using ketamine to model semantic deficits in schizophrenia. *Journal of Clinical Psychopharmacology, 31*(6), 690-697.

Neisser, U. (1998). *The rising curve: Long-term gains in I.Q. and related measures.* Washington, DC: American Psychological Association.

Neisser, U. (2000a). Memorists. In U. Neisser & I. E. Hyman, Jr. (Eds.), *Memory observed* (2nd ed., pp. 475-478). New York: Worth.

Neisser, U. (2000b). Snapshots or benchmarks? In U. Neisser & I. E. Hyman, Jr. (Eds.), *Memory observed* (2nd ed., pp. 68-74). New York: Worth.

Neisser, U., Boodoo, G., Bouchard, T. J., Boykin, A. W., Brody, N., Ceci, S. J., et al. (1996). Intelligence: Knowns and unknowns. *American Psychologist, 51,* 77-101.

Neitz, J. and Neitz, M. (2011). The genetics of normal and defective color vision. *Vision Research, 51*(7), 633-651.

Nelson, C. A. (1999). Neural plasticity and human development. *Current Directions in Psychological Science, 8,* 42-45.

Nelson, C. A. (2007). A neurobiological perspective on early human deprivation. *Child Development Perspectives, 1,* 13-18.

Nelson, C. A., Thomas, K. M., & de Haan, M. (2006). Neural bases of cognitive development. In W. Damon & R. M. Lerner (Series Eds.) & D. Kuhn & R. Siegler (Vol. Eds.), *Handbook of child psychology: Vol. 2. Cognition, perception, and language* (6th ed., pp. 3-57). New York: Wiley.

Nelson, G., & Prilleltensky, I. (2004). *Community psychology: In pursuit of liberation and wellbeing.* New York: Palgrave Macmillan.

Nelson, J. C., Rahman, Z., Laubmeier, K. K., Eudicone, J. M., McQuade, R. D., Berman, R. M., Marcus, R. N., Baker, R. A., & Sheehan, J. J. (2013). Efficacy of adjunctive aripiprazole in patients with major depressive disorder whose symptoms worsened with antidepressant monotherapy. *CNS Spectrums,* Epub March 18, 2014.

Nelson, K. (1986). Event knowledge and cognitive development. In K. Nelson (Ed.), *Event knowledge: Structure and function in development* (pp. 1-19). Hillsdale, NJ: Erlbaum.

Nelson, P. T., Braak, H., & Markesbery, W. R. (2011). Neuropathology and cognitive impairment in Alzheimer disease: a complex but coherent relationship. *Journal of Neuropathology and Experimental Neurology, 68*(1), 1-14.

Nelson-LeGall, S., & Resnick, L. (1998). Help seeking, achievement motivation, and the social practice of intelligence in school. In S. A. Karabenick (Ed.), *Strategic help seeking* (pp. 39-60). Mahwah, NJ: Erlbaum.

Nemati, A. (2013). The effect of pranayama on test anxiety and test performance. *International Journal of Yoga, 6*(1), 55-60.

Nemeroff, C. B., Weinberger, D., Rutter, M., MacMillan, H. L., Bryant, R. A., Wessely, S., Stein, D. J., Pariante, C. M., Seemüller, F., Berk, M., Malhi, G. S., Preisig, M., Brüne, M., & Lysaker, P. (2013). DSM-5: A collection of psychiatrist views on the changes, controversies, and future directions. *BMC Medicine, 11,* 202.

Nemeth, C. J., Personnaz, B., Personnaz, M., & Goncalo, J. A. (2004). The liberating role of conflict in group creativity: A study in two countries. *European Journal of Social Psychology, 34,* 365-374.

Neovius, M., & Narbro, K. (2008). Cost-effectiveness of pharmacological anti-obesity treatments: a systematic review. *International Journal of Obesity, 32,* 1752-1763.

Nestler, E. J. (2001). Molecular basis of long-term plasticity underlying addiction. *National Review of Neuroscience, 2,* 119-128.

Neubauer, A. C., & Fink, A. (2009). Intelligence and neural efficiency: Measures of brain activation versus measures of functional connectivity in the brain. *Intelligence, 37,* 223-229.

Neubauer, D. N. (2013). Chronic insomnia. *Continuum, 19*(1 Sleep Disorders), 50-66.

Neumann, D. L., & Kitlertsirivatana, E. (2010). Exposure to a novel context after extinction causes a renewal of extinguished conditioned responses: Implications for the treatment of fear. *Behaviour Research and Therapy, 48,* 565-570. doi:10.1016/j.brat.2010.03.002.

Nevin, J. A., Grace, R., Holland S, & McLean A. P. (2001). Variable-ratio versus variable-interval schedules: response rate, resistance to change, and preference. *Journal of the Experimental Analysis of Behavior, 76,* 43-74.

Neville, L. (2012). Do economic equality and generalized trust inhibit academic dishonesty? Evidence from state-level search-engine queries. *Psychological Science, 23*(4), 339-345. doi:10.1177/0956797611435980.

New Israeli law bans underweight models in ads. (2012, 20 March). Retrieved from http://www.foxnews.com/health/2012/03/20/new-israeli-law-bans-underweight-models-in-ads/?test=latestnews.

Newberg, A., Alavi, A., Baime, M., Pourdehnad, M., Santanna, J., & d'Aquili, E. (2001). The measurement of regional cerebral blood flow during the complex cognitive task of meditation: A preliminary SPECT study. *Psychiatry Research, 106,* 113-122.

Newcombe, N., & Fox, N. A. (1994). Infantile amnesia: Through a glass darkly. *Child Development, 65,* 31-40.

Newcombe, N. S., Ambady, N., Eccles, J., Gomez, L., et al. (2009). Psychology's role in mathematics and science education. *American Psychologist, 64,* 538-550.

Newell, A., & Simon, H. A. (1972). *Human problem solving.* Englewood Cliffs, NJ: Prentice Hall.

Newhouse, P., Newhouse, C., & Astur, R. S. (2007). Sex differences in visual-spatial learning using a virtual water maze in pre-pubertal children. *Behavioural Brain Research, 183,* 1-7.

Newman, E. J., & Loftus, E. F. (2012). Clarkian logic on trial. *Perspectives on Psychological Science, 7*(3), 260-263. doi:10.1177/1745691612442907.

Newnam, S., Griffin, M. A., & Mason, C. (2008). Safety in work vehicles: A multilevel study linking safety values and individual predictors to work-related driving crashes. *Journal of Applied Psychology, 93,* 632-644.

Newman, S. D., Keller, T. A., & Just, M. A. (2007). Volitional control of attention and brain activation in dual task performance. *Human Brain Mapping, 28*(2), 109-117.

Newpher, T. M., & Ehlers, M. D. (2008). Glutamate receptor dynamics in dendritic microdomains. *Neuron, 58*(4), 472-497.

Newsom, J. T., Mahan, T. L., Rook, K. S., & Krause, N. (2008). Stable negative social exchanges and health. *Health Psychology, 27,* 78-86.

Ng, C. H., Chong, S., Lambert, T., Fan, A., Hackett, L. P., Mahendran, R., et al. (2005). An inter-ethnic comparison study of clozapine dosage, clinical response, and plasma levels. *International Clinical Psychopharmacology, 20,* 163-168.

Ng, J. Y. Y., Ntoumanis, N., Thøgersen-Ntoumani, C., Deci, E. L., Ryan, R. M., Duda, J. L., & Williams, G. C. (2012). Self-determination theory applied to health contexts: A meta-analysis. *Perspectives on Psychological Science, 7.* Published online first. DOI: 10.1177/1745691612447309.

Ng, K.-Y., Ang, S., & Chan, K.-Yin. (2008). Personality and leader effectiveness: A moderated mediation model of leadership self-efficacy, job demands, and job autonomy. *Journal of Applied Psychology, 93,* 733-743.

Nguyen, B. H., Pérusse, D., Paquet, J., Petit, D., Boivin, M., Tremblay, R. E., & Montplaisir, J. (2008). Sleep terrors in children: A prospective study of twins. *Pediatrics, 122,* e1164–e1167.

Nicassio, P. M., Meyerowitz, B. E., & Kerns, R. D. (2004). The future of health psychology interventions. *Health Psychology, 23,* 132–137.

NICHD Early Child Care Research Network. (2001, April). *Further explorations of the detected effects of quantity of early child care on socioemotional adjustment.* Paper presented at the biennial meetings of the Society for Research in Child Development, Minneapolis.

NICHD Early Child Care Research Network. (2006). Infant-mother attachment classification: Risk and protection in relation to changing maternal caregiving quality. *Developmental Psychology, 42,* 38–58.

NICHD Early Child Care Research Network. (2005). *Child care and child development: Results from the NICHD Study of Early Child Care and Youth Development.* New York: Guilford.

NICHD Early Child Care Research Network. (2006a). Infant-mother attachment classification: Risk and protection in relation to changing maternal caregiving quality. *Developmental Psychology, 42,* 38–58.

NICHD Early Child Care Research Network. (2006b). Child-care effect sizes for the NICHD study of early child care and youth development. *American Psychologist, 61,* 99–116.

Nicholson, A., Fuhrer, R., & Marmot, M. (2005). Psychological distress as a predictor of CHD events in men: The effect of persistence and components of risk. *Psychosomatic Medicine, 67,* 522–530.

Nickerson, R. A., & Adams, M. J. (1979). Long-term memory for a common object. *Cognitive Psychology, 11,* 287–307.

Nicoll, J., & Kieffer, K. M. (2005, August). *Violence in video games: A review of the empirical research.* Paper presented at the 113th annual meeting of the American Psychological Association, Washington, DC.

Nicpon, M., & Pfeiffer, S. (2011). High-ability students: New ways to conceptualize giftedness and provide psychological services in the schools. *Journal of Applied School Psychology, 27*(4), 293–305. doi:10.1080/15377903.2011.616579.

Niederhoffer, K. G., & Pennebaker, J. W. (2002). Sharing one's story: On the benefits of writing or talking about emotional experience. In C. R. Snyder & S. J. Lopez (Eds.), *Handbook of positive psychology* (pp. 573–583). London: Oxford University Press.

Nieuwenhuis, I. L., & Takashima, A. (2011). The role of the ventromedial prefrontal cortex in memory consolidation. *Behavioural Brain Research, 218*(2), 325–334.

Nieuwenhuis, S., Elzinga, B. M., Ras, P. H., Berends, F., Duijs, P., Samara, Z., & Slagter, H. A. (2013). Bilateral saccadic eye movements and tactile stimulation, but not auditory stimulation, enhance memory retrieval. *Brain and Cognition, 81*(1), 52–56.

Nievar, M. A., & Becker, B. J. (2008). Sensitivity as a privileged predictor of attachment: A second perspective on De Wolff and Van IJzendoorn's meta-analysis. *Social Development, 17,* 102–114.

Nigg, J., Nikolas, M., & Burt, S. (2010). Measured gene-by-environment interaction in relation to attention-deficit/hyperactivity disorder. *Journal of the American Academy of Child & Adolescent Psychiatry, 49*(9), 863–873. doi:10.1016/j.jaac.2010.01.025.

Nigg, J. T. (2001). Is ADHD a disinhibitory disorder? *Psychological Bulletin, 127,* 571–598.

Nigg, J. T. (2010). Attention-deficit/hyperactivity disorder: Endophenotypes, structure, and etiological pathways. *Current Directions In Psychological Science, 19*(1), 24–29. doi:10.1177/0963721409359282.

Nijstad, B. A., Stroebe, W., & Lodewijkx, H. F. M. (2003). Production blocking and idea generation: Does blocking interfere with cognitive processes? *Journal of Experimental Social Psychology, 39,* 531–548.

Nikolas, M., Klump, K. L., & Burt, S. A. (2011). Youth appraisals of inter-parental conflict and genetic and environmental contributions to attention-deficit hyperactivity disorder: Examination of GxE effects in a twin sample. *Journal of Abnormal Child Psychology,* 1–12. doi:10.1007/s10802-011-9583-6.

Nikolas, M. A., & Burt, S. A. (2010). Genetic and environmental influences on ADHD symptom dimensions of inattention and hyperactivity: A meta-analysis. *Journal of Abnormal Psychology, 119,* 1–17.

Nikulina, V., Widom, C., & Czaja, S. (2011). The role of childhood neglect and childhood poverty in predicting mental health, academic achievement and crime in adulthood. *American Journal of Community Psychology, 48,* 309–321. doi:10.1007/s10464-010-9385-y.

Nilsson, G. (1996, November). Some forms of memory improve as people age. *APA Monitor, 27.*

Nisbett, R. E. (2003). *The geography of thought.* New York: The Free Press.

Nisbett, R. E., Aronson, J., Blair, C., Dickens, W., Flynn, J., Halpern, D. F., & Turkheimer, E. (2012). Intelligence: New findings and theoretical developments. *American Psychologist, 67*(2), 130–159. doi:10.1037/a0026699.

Nisbett, R. E., & Masuda, T. (2007). Culture and point of view. *Intellectica, 46*(2), 153–172.

Nishimura, K., & Takahashi, J. (2013). Therapeutic application of stem cell technology toward the treatment of Parkinson's disease. *Biological & Pharmaceutical Bulletin. 36*(2), 171–175.

Nishimura, T., Mikami, A., Suzuki, J., & Matsuzawa, T. (2003). Descent of the larynx in chimpanzee infants. *Proceedings of the National Academy of Sciences, 100,* 6930–6933.

Nishino, S. (2011). Hypothalamus, hypocretins/orexin, and vigilance control. *Handbook of Clinical Neurology, 99,* 765–82.

Nobata, T., Hakoda, Y., & Ninose, Y. (2010). The functional field of view becomes narrower while viewing negative emotional stimuli. *Cognition & Emotion, 24*(5), 886–891.

Noble, H. B. (2000, January 25). Outgrowth of new field of tissue engineering. *New York Times.*

Noble, J. M., & Hesdorffer, D. C. (2013). Sports-related concussions: A review of epidemiology, challenges in diagnosis, and potential risk factors. *Neuropsychology Review,* epub November 17, 2013.

Nock, M. K., & Kessler, R. C. (2006). Prevalence of and risk factors for suicide attempts versus suicide gestures: Analysis of the National Comorbidity Survey. *Journal of Abnormal Psychology, 115,* 616–623.

Nokes-Malach, T. J., VanLehn, K., Belenky, D. M., Lichtenstein, M., & Cox, G. (2013). Coordinating principles and examples through analogy and self-explanation. *European Journal of Psychology of Education, 28,* 1237–1263.

Noland, V. J., Liller, K. D., McDermott, R. J., Coulter, M. L., & Seraphine, A. E. (2004). Is adolescent sibling violence a precursor to college dating violence? *American Journal of Health Behavior, 28,* 13–22.

Nolen-Hoeksema, S. (2006). The etiology of gender differences in depression. In C. M. Mazure & G. P. Keita (Eds.), *Understanding depression in women: Applying empirical research to practice and policy* (pp. 9–43). Washington, DC: American Psychological Association.

Nolen-Hoeksema, S. (2012). Emotion regulation and psychopathology: The role of gender. *Annual Review of Clinical Psychology, 8,* 61–87.

Nolen-Hoeksema, S., & Watkins, E. R. (2011). A heuristic for developing transdiagnostic models of psychopathology: Explaining multifinality and divergent trajectories. *Perspectives on Psychological Science, 6*(6), 589–609. doi:10.1177/1745691611419672.

Nolin, R. (2011). Heavier passengers force new guidelines on occupancy rates. *Palm Beach Post.* Retrieved from http://blogs.palmbeachpost.com/travelsmart/2011/04/05/heavier-passengers-force-new-guidelines-on-occupancy-rates/.

Noll, R. B. (1994). Hypnotherapy for warts in children and adolescents. *Journal of Developmental and Behavioral Pediatrics, 15*(3), 170–173.

Nomura, H., Inoue, S., Kamimura, N., Shimodera, S., Mino, Y., et al. (2005). A cross-cultural study on expressed emotion in careers of people with dementia and schizophrenia: Japan and England. *Social Psychiatry and Psychiatric Epidemiology, 40,* 564–570.

Norberg, M. M., Krystal, J. H., & Tolin, D. F. (2008). A meta-analysis of D- Cycloserine and the facilitation of fear extinction and exposure therapy. *Biological Psychiatry, 63,* 1118–1126.

Nørby, S., Lange, M., & Larsen, A. (2010). Forgetting to forget: On the duration of voluntary suppression of neutral and emotional memories. *Acta Psychologica, 133*(1), 73–80. doi:10.1016/j.actpsy.2009.10.002.

Norcross, J. C. (2001). Purposes, processes and products of the task force on empirically supported therapy relationships. *Psychotherapy: Theory, Research, Practice, Training, 38*(4), 345–356.

Norcross, J. C. (2002). *Psychotherapy relationships that work.* New York: Oxford University Press.

Norcross, J. C. (2006). Integrating self-help into psychotherapy: 16 practical suggestions. *Professional Psychology: Research and Practice, 37,* 683–693.

Norcross, J. C. (Ed.) (2011). *Psychotherapy relationships that work: Evidence-based responsiveness* (2nd ed.). New York: Oxford University Press.

Norcross, J. C., Beutler, L. E., & Levant, R. F. (2005). Prologue. In J. C. Norcross, L. E. Beutler, & R. F. Levant (Eds.), *Evidence-based practices in mental health: Debate and dialogue on the fundamental questions* (pp. 3–12). Washington, DC: American Psychological Association.

Norcross, J. C., Koocher, G. P., Fala, N. C., & Wexler, H. K. (2010). What does not work? Expert consensus on discredited treatments in the addictions. *Journal of Addiction Medicine, 4,* 174–180.

Norcross, J. C., Santrock, J. W., Campbell, L. F., Smith, T. P., et al. (2000). *Authoritative guide to self-help resources in mental health.* New York: Guilford Press.

Nordgren, L., & Chou, E. (2011). The push and pull of temptation: the bidirectional influence of temptation on self-control. *Psychological Science, 22*(11), 1386–1390.

Nordsletten, A. E., & Mataix-Cols, D. (2012). Hoarding versus collecting: Where does pathology diverge from play? *Clinical Psychology Review, 32*(3), 165–176. doi:10.1016/j.cpr.2011.12.003.

Norr, A. M., Capron, D. W., & Schmidt, N. B. (2014). Medical information seeking: Impact on risk for anxiety psychopathology. *Journal of Behavior Therapy and Experimental Psychiatry, 45*(3), 402–407.

Norrsell, U., Finger, S., & Lajonchere, C. (1999). Cutaneous sensory spots and the "law of specific nerve energies": History and development of ideas. *Brain Research Bulletin, 48*(5), 457–465.

North, A. C. (2011). The effect of background music on the taste of wine. *British Journal of Psychology,* doi:10.1111/j.2044–8295.2011.02072.x.

North, M. M., North, S. M., & Burwick, C. B. (2008). Virtual reality therapy: A vision for a new paradigm. In L. L'Abate (Ed.), *Toward a science of clinical psychology: Laboratory evaluations and interventions* (pp. 307–320). Hauppauge, NY: Nova Science Publishers.

Norton, A., Zipse, L., Marchina, S., & Schlaug, G. (2009). Melodic intonation therapy: shared insights on how it is done and why it might help. *Ann N Y Acad Sci 1169:* 431–436.

Nosarti, C., Reichenberg, A., Murray, R. M., Cnattingius, S., Lambe, M. P., Yin, L., MacCabe, J., Rifkin, L., & Hultman, C. M. (2012). Preterm birth and psychiatric disorders in young adult life. *Archives of General Psychiatry, 69*(6), 610–617. doi:10.1001/archgenpsychiatry.2011.1374.

Nosko, A., Tieu, T.-T., Lawford, H., & Pratt, M. W. (2011). How do I love thee? Let me count the ways: Parenting during adolescence, attachment styles, and romantic narratives in emerging adulthood. *Developmental Psychology, 47,* 645–657.

Nowak, M. A., Komarova, N. L., & Niyogi, P. (2001). Evolution of universal grammar. *Science, 291,* 114–118.

Noyes, R., & Hoehn-Saric, R. (2006). *The anxiety disorders.* London: Cambridge University Press.

Nugent, N. R., Tyrka, A. R., Carpenter, L. L., & Price, L. H. (2011). Gene-environment interactions: Early life stress and risk for depressive and anxiety disorders. *Psychopharmacology, 214,* 175–196. doi:10.1007/s00213–010–2151-x.

Nunes, L. D., & Weinstein, Y. (2012). Testing improves true recall and protects against the build-up of proactive interference without increasing false recall. *Memory, 20*(2), 138–154. doi:10.1080/09658211.2011.648198.

Nurnberger, J. I., Koller, D. L., Jung, J., Edenberg, H. J., Foroud, T., Guella, I, Vawter, M. P., & Kelsoe, J. R. (2014). Identification of pathways for bipolar disorder: A meta-analysis. *JAMA Psychiatry, 71*(6), 657–664.

Nutt, D. J. (2005). Overview of diagnosis and drug treatments of anxiety disorders. *CNS Spectrums, 10,* 49–56.

Nyberg, L., Petersson, K. M., Nilsson, L. G., Sandblom, J., Aberg, C., & Ingvar, M. (2001). Reactivation of motor brain areas during explicit memory for actions. *Neuroimage, 14,* 521–528.

Nye, C. D., Su, R., Rounds, J., & Drasgow, F. (2012). Vocational interests and performance: A quantitative summary of over 60 years of research. *Perspectives on Psychological Science, 7,* 384–403. doi:10.1177/1745691612449021.

Oatley, K. (1993). Those to whom evil is done. In R. S. Wyer & T. K. Srull (Eds.), *Toward a general theory of anger and emotional aggression: Advances in social cognition* (Vol. 6). Hillsdale, NJ: Erlbaum.

Oberauer, K., & Hein, L. (2012). Attention to information in working memory. *Current Directions in Psychological Science, 21*(3), 164–169. doi:10.1177/0963721412444727.

Obokata, H., Sasai, Y., Niwa, H., Kadota, M., Andrabi, M., Takata, N., Tokoro, M., Terashita, Y., Yonemura, S., Vacanti, C. A., & Wakayama, T. (2014b). Bidirectional developmental potential in reprogrammed cells with acquired pluripotency. *Nature, 505*(7485), 676--80.

Obokata, H., Wakayama, T., Sasai, Y., Kojima, K., Vacanti, M. P., Niwa, H., Yamato, M., & Vacanti, C. A. (2014a). Stimulus-triggered fate conversion of somatic cells into pluripotency. *Nature, 505*(7485), 641--647.

O'Brien, R. J. (2011). Vascular dementia: atherosclerosis, cognition and Alzheimer's disease. *Current Alzheimer Research, 8*(4), 341–344.

O'Brien, T. L. (1991, September 2). Computers help thwart "groupthink" that plagues meetings. *Chicago Sun Times.*

Oboudiyat, C., Glazer, H., Seifan, A., Greer, C., & Isaacson, R. S. (2013). Alzheimer's disease. *Seminars in Neurology, 33*(4), 313–329.

O'Connell, K. (2011). From black box to 'open' brain: Law, neuroimaging and disability discrimination. *Griffith Law Review, 20*(4), 883–904.

Oden, M. H. (1968). The fulfillment of promise: 40-year follow-up of the Terman gifted group. *Genetic Psychology Monographs, 17,* 3–93.

Odgers, C. L., Caspi, A., Nagin, D. S., Piquero, A. R., Slutske, W. S., Milne, B. J., Dickson, N., Poulton, R., & Moffitt, T. E. (2008). Is it important to prevent early exposure to drugs and alcohol among adolescents? *Psychological Science, 19,* 1037–1044.

O'Donohue, W., Fisher, J. E., & Hayes, S. C. (Eds.). (2003). *Cognitive behavior therapy: Applying empirically supported techniques in your practice.* New York: Wiley.

O'Driscoll, M., Brough, P., & Kalliath, T. (2006). Work-family conflict and facilitation. In F. Jones, R. J. Burke, & M. Westman (Eds.), *Work-life balance: A psychological perspective* (pp. 117–142). New York: Psychology Press.

Oeberst, A. (2012). If anything else comes to mind…better keep it to yourself? Delayed recall is discrediting unjustifiably. *Law and Human Behavior, 36*(4), 266–274.

Ogawa, N. & Ueki, H. (2007). Clinical importance of caffeine dependence and abuse. *Psychiatry and Clinical Neurosciences, 61*(3), 263–268.

Ogden, C. L., Carroll, M. D., Kit, B. K., & Flegal, K. M. (2014). Prevalence of childhood and adult obesity in the United States, 2011–2012. *JAMA, 311*(8), 806–814.

Ogilvie, C. A., Newman, E., Todd, L., & Peck, D. (2014). Attachment & violent offending: A meta-analysis. *Aggression and Violent Behavior, 19*(1), 322–339.

Oh, I., & Berry, C. M. (2009). The five-factor model of personality and managerial performance: Validity gains through the use of 360-degree performance ratings. *Journal of Applied Psychology, 94,* 1498–1513.

Ohayon, M. M., & Roth, T. (2003). Place of chronic insomnia in the course of depressive and anxiety disorders. *Journal of Psychiatric Research, 37,* 9–15.

Öhman, A., & Mineka, S. (2003). The malicious serpent: Snakes as a prototypical stimulus for an evolved module of fear. *Current Directions in Psychological Science, 12,* 5–9.

Öhman, A., & Soares, J. J. (1993). On the automatic nature of phobic fear: Conditioned electrodermal responses to masked fear-relevant stimuli. *Journal of Abnormal Psychology, 102*(1), 121–132.

Öhman, A., & Soares, J. J. (1994). "Unconscious anxiety": Phobic responses to masked stimuli. *Journal of Abnormal Psychology, 103*(2), 231–240.

Öhman, A., & Soares, J. J. F. (1998). Emotional conditioning to masked stimuli: Expectancies for aversive outcomes following nonrecognized fear-relevant stimuli. *Journal of Experimental Psychology: General, 127*(1), 69–82.

Öhman, A., Soares, S. C., Juth, P., Lindström, B., & Esteves, F. (2012). Evolutionary derived modulations of attention to two common fear stimuli: Serpents and hostile humans. *Journal of Cognitive Psychology, 24*(1), 17–32.

Öhman, A., Dimberg, U., & Öst, L. G. (1985). Animal and social phobias: A laboratory model. In S. Reiss & R. R. Bootzin (Eds.), *Theoretical issues in behavior therapy.* Orlando, FL: Academic Press.

Ohring, R., Graber, J. A., & Brooks-Gunn, J. (2002). Girls' recurrent and concurrent body dissatisfaction: Correlates and consequences over 8 years. *International Journal of Eating Disorders, 31*(4), 404–415.

Ohta, H., Yamazaki, S., & McMahon, D. G. (2005). Constant light desynchronizes mammalian clock neurons. *Nature Neuroscience, 8,* 267–269.

Oishi, S., Diener, E., Lucas, R. E., & Suh, E. M. (1999). Cross-cultural variations in predictors of life-satisfaction: Perspectives from needs and values. *Personality and Social Psychology Bulletin, 25,* 980–990.

Oishi, S., Schimmack, U., & Diener, E. (2012). Progressive taxation and the subjective well-being of nations. *Psychological Science, 23*(1), 86–92.

Olatunji, B. O. (2006). Evaluative learning and emotional responding to fearful and disgusting stimuli in spider phobia. *Journal of Anxiety Disorders, 20,* 858–876.

Oldenberg, P.-A., Zheleznyak, A., Fang, Y.-F., Lagenaur, C. F., Gresham, H. D., & Lindberg, F. P. (2000). Role of CD47 as a marker of self on red blood cells. *Science, 288,* 2051–2054.

Olds, J. (1973). Commentary on positive reinforcement produced by electrical stimulation of septal areas and other regions of rat brain. In E. S. Valenstein (Ed.), *Brain stimulation and motivation: Research and commentary.* Glenview, IL: Scott, Foresman.

Olds, J., & Milner, P. (1954). Positive reinforcement produced by electrical stimulation of septal areas and other regions of the rat brain. *Journal of Comparative and Physiological Psychology, 47,* 419–427.

O'Leary, C., Leonard, H., Bourke, J., D'Antoine, H., Bartu, A., & Bower, C. (2013). Intellectual disability: Population-based estimates of the proportion attributable to maternal alcohol use disorder during pregnancy. *Developmental Medicine & Child Neurology, 55,* 271–277.

O'Leary, D. S., Block, R. I., Koeppel, J. A., Flaum, M., Schulz, S. K., Andreason, N. C., et al. (2002). Effects of smoking marijuana on brain perfusion and cognition. *Neuropsychopharmacology, 26,* 802–816.

Olfson, M., Blanco, C., Liu, L., Moreno, C., & Laje, G. (2006). National trends in the outpatient treatment of children and adolescents with antipsychotic drugs. *Archives of General Psychiatry, 63,* 679–685.

Olfson, M., Marcus, S. C., & Shaffer, D. (2006). Antidepressant drug therapy and suicide in depressed children and adolescents: A case-control study. *Archives of General Psychiatry, 63,* 865–872.

Oliner, S. P., & Oliner, P. M. (1988). *The altruistic personality: Rescuers of Jews in Nazi Europe.* New York: Free Press.

Olino, K., Mackrell, T. M., Jordan, S. V., & Hayden, P. L. (2013). Structure of observed temperament in childhood. *Journal of Personality, 47,* 524–532.

Olio, K. A. (1994). Truth in memory. *American Psychologist, 49,* 442–443.

Olson, J. M., & Stone, J. (2005). The influence of behavior on attitudes. In D. Albarracín, B. T. Johnson, & M. P. Zanna (Eds.), *Handbook of attitudes* (pp. 223–271). Mahwah, NJ: Erlbaum.

Olson, L. (1997). Regeneration in the adult central nervous system. *Nature Medicine, 3,* 1329–1335.

Olson, S. L., Tardif, T. Z. A., Felt, B., Grabell, A. S., Kessler, D., Wang, L., Karasawa, M., & Hirabayashi, H. (2011). Inhibitory control and harsh discipline as predictors of externalizing problems in young children: A comparative study of U.S., Chinese, and Japanese preschoolers. *Journal of Abnormal Child Psychology, 39,* 1163–1175.

Olsson, A., Ebert, J. P., Banaji, M. R., & Phelps, E. A. (2005). The role of social groups in the persistence of learned fear. *Science, 309,* 785–787.

Olsson, C. J., Jonsson, B., Larsson, A., & Nyberg, L. (2008). Motor representations and practice affect brain systems underlying imagery: An FMRI study of internal imagery in novices and active high jumpers. *The Open Neuroimaging Journal, 2,* 5–13.

Oltmanns, T. F., & Turkheimer, E. (2009). Person perception and personality pathology. *Current Directions in Psychological Science, 18,* 32–36.

Oluigbo, C. O., Salma, A., & Rezai, A. R. (2012). Deep brain stimulation for neurological disorders. *IEEE Review of Biomedical Engineering, 5,* 88–99.

Ölveczky, B. P., Baccus, S. A., & Meister, M. (2003). Segregation of object and background motion in the retina. *Nature, 423,* 401–408.

O'Neill, H. (2000, September 24). After rape, jail—a friendship forms. *St. Petersburg Times,* pp. 1A, 14A.

Ones, D., & Viswesvaran, C. (2001). Personality at work: Criterion focused occupational personality scales used in personnel selection. In R. Hogan & B. Roberts (Eds.), *Personality psychology in the workplace* (pp. 63–92). Washington, DC: American Psychological Association.

Ones, D. S., Dilchert, S., & Viswesvaran, C. (2012). Cognitive abilities. In N. Schmitt (Ed.), *The Oxford handbook of personnel assessment and selection* (pp. 179–224). New York: Oxford University Press.

Ong, A. D., Bergeman, C. S., Bisconti, T. L., & Wallace, K. A. (2006). Psychological resilience, positive emotions, and successful adaptation to stress in later life. *Journal of Personality and Social Psychology, 91,* 730–749.

Ong, A. D. (2010). Pathways linking positive emotion and health in later life. *Current Directions in Psychological Science, 19*(6), 358–362. doi:10.1177/0963721410388805.

Onishi, K. H., & Baillargeon, R. (2005). Do 15-month-old infants understand false beliefs? *Science, 308,* 255–258.

Ono, Y., Kawakami, N., Nakane, Y., Nakamura, Y., et al. (2008). Prevalence of and risk factors for suicide-related outcomes in the World Health Organization Mental Health Surveys Japan. *Psychiatry and Clinical Neurosciences, 62,* 442–449.

Onraet, E., & Van Hiel, A. (2014). Are right-wing adherents mentally troubled? Recent insights on the relationship of right-wing attitudes with threat and psychological ill-being. *Current Directions in Psychological Science, 23*(1), 35–40.

Onyper, S. V., Carr, T. L., Farrar, J. S., & Floyd, B. R. (2011). Cognitive advantages of chewing gum. Now you see them, now you don't. *Appetite, 57*(2), 321–328. doi:10.1016/j.appet.2011.05.313.

Oppel, S. (2000, March 5). Managing ABCs like a CEO. *St. Petersburg Times,* 1A, 12–13A.

Oquendo, M. A., & Mann, J. J. (2000). The biology of impulsivity and suicidality. *Psychiatric Clinics of North America, 23,* 11–25.

Orbell, J. M., van de Kragt, A. J. C., & Dawes, R. M. (1988). Explaining discussion-induced cooperation. *Journal of Personality and Social Psychology, 54,* 811–819.

O'Reardon, J. P., Fontecha, J. F., Cristancho, M. A., & Newman, S. (2007). Unexpected reduction in migraine and psychogenic headaches following rTMS treatment for major depression: A report of two cases. *CNS Spectrums, 12,* 921–925.

Organ, D. W., Podsakoff, P. M., & MacKenzie, S. B. (2006). *Organizational citizenship behavior: Its nature, antecedents, and consequences.* Thousand Oaks, CA: Sage.

Orgilés, M., Espada, J., García-Fernández, J., & Méndez, X. (2009). Relación entre miedos escolares y síntomas de ansiedad por separación infantil. *Revista Mexicana de Psicología, 26*(1), 17–25.

Orgilés, M., Espada, J., García-Fernández, J. M., Méndez, X., & Dolores Hidalgo, M. M. (2011). Most feared situations related to separation anxiety and characteristics by age and gender in late childhood. *Anales de Psicología, 27*(1), 80–85.

Oriña, M. M., W Collins, W. A., Simpson, J. A., Salvatore, J. E., Haydon, K. C., & Kim, J. S. (2011). Developmental and dyadic perspectives on commitment in adult romantic relationships. *Psychological Science, 22,* 908–915. doi:10.1177/0956797611410573.

Ormiston, M. E., & Wong, E. M. (2012). The gleam of the double-edged sword: The benefits of subgroups for organizational ethics. *Psychological Science, 23,* 400–403. doi:10.1177/0956797611431575.

Orne, M. T., & Evans, F. J. (1965). Social control in the psychological experiment: Antisocial behavior and hypnosis. *Journal of Personality and Social Psychology, 1,* 189–200.

Orne, M. T., Sheehan, P. W., & Evans, F. J. (1968). Occurrence of posthypnotic behavior outside the experimental setting. *Journal of Personality and Social Psychology, 9,* 189–196.

Orth-Gomer, K., Schneiderman, N., Wang, H.-X., Walldin, C., et al. (2009). Stress reduction prolongs life in women with coronary disease: Th e Stockholm Women's Intervention Trial for Coronary Heart Disease (SWITCHD). *Circulation: Cardiovascular Quality and Outcomes, 2,* 25–32.

Osnos, E. (2011, January 10). Meet Dr. Freud: Does psychoanalysis have a future in an authoritarian state? *The New Yorker,* 54–63.

Öst, L.-G. (1978). Behavioral treatment of thunder and lightning phobia. *Behavior Research and Therapy, 16,* 197–207.

Öst, L.-G., Hellström, K., & Kåver, A. (1992). One- versus five-session exposure in the treatment of needle phobia. *Behavior Therapy, 23,* 263–282.

Öst, L.-G., Svensson, L., Hellström, K., & Lindwall, R. (2001). One-session treatment of specific phobias in youths: A randomized clinical trial. *Journal of Consulting and Clinical Psychology, 69,* 814–824.

Ostfeld, B. M., Perl, H., Esposito, L., Hempstead, K., et al. (2006). Sleep environment, positional, lifestyle, and demographic characteristics associated with bed sharing in sudden infant death syndrome cases: A population-based study. *Pediatrics, 118,* 2051–2059.

Ostrov, J. M. (2006). Deception and subtypes of aggression during early childhood. *Journal of Experimental Child Psychology, 93,* 322–336.

Otgaar, H., Verschuere, B., Meijer, E. H., & van Oorsouw, K. (2012). The origin of children's implanted false memories: Memory traces or compliance? *Acta Psychologica, 139*(3), 397–403. doi:10.1016/j.actpsy.2012.01.002.

Ouimet, A. J., Covin, R., & Dozois, D. J. A. (2012). Generalized anxiety disorder. In P. Sturmey & M. Hersen (Eds.), *Handbook of evidence-based practice in clinical psychology, Vol 2: Adult disorders* (pp. 651–679). Hoboken, NJ: Wiley.

Overmier, J. B. (2002). On learned helplessness. *Integrative Physiological & Behavioral Science, 37,* 4–8.

Overmier, J. B., & Seligman, M. E. P. (1967). Effects of inescapable shock upon subsequent escape and avoidance learning. *Journal of Comparative and Physiological Psychology, 63,* 23–33.

Overton, D. A. (1984). State dependent learning and drug discriminations. In L. L. Iverson, S. D. Iverson, & S. H. Snyder (Eds.), *Handbook of psychopharmacology* (Vol. 18). New York: Plenum.

Ovsiew, F. (2006). An overview of the psychiatric approach to conversion disorder. In M. Hallet et al. (Eds.), *Psychogenic movement disorders: Neurology and neuropsychiatry* (pp. 112–121). New York: Lippincott Williams & Wilkins.

Owen, J. (2013). Early career perspectives on psychotherapy research and practice: Psychotherapist effects, multicultural orientation, and couple interventions. *Psychotherapy, 50,* 496–502.

Özçalışkan, Ş., & Dimitrova, N. (2013). How gesture input provides a helping hand to language development. *Seminars in Speech & Language, 34*(4), 227–236.

Pachankis, J. E., & Goldfried, M. R. (2004). Clinical issues in working with lesbian, gay, and bisexual clients. *Psychotherapy: Theory, Research, Practice, Training, 41,* 227–246.

Pacheco-Unguetti, A., Acosta, A., Callejas, A., & Lupiáñez, J. (2010). Attention and Anxiety: Different Attentional Functioning Under State and Trait Anxiety. *Psychological Science, 21*(2), 298–304. doi:10.1177/0956797609359624.

Pack, A. A., & Herman, L. M. (2007). The dolphin's (*Tursiops truncatus*) understanding of human gazing and pointing: Knowing what and where. *Journal of Comparative Psychology, 121,* 34–45.

Packer, D. J. (2008). Identifying systematic disobedience in Milgram's obedience experiments: A meta-analytic review. *Perspectives on Psychological Science, 3,* 301–304.

Palazzolo, D. L. (2013). Electronic cigarettes and vaping: A new challenge in clinical medicine and public health. A literature review. *Frontiers in Public Health, 1,* 56, eCollection 2013.

Palincsar, A. S. (2003). Ann L. Brown: Advancing a theoretical model of learning and instruction. In B. J. Zimmerman & D. H. Schunk (Eds.), *Educational psychology: A century of contributions* (pp. 459–475). Mahwah, NJ: Erlbaum.

Palitsky, D. Mota, N. Downs, A. C., & Sareen, J. (2013). The association between adult attachment style, mental disorders, and suicidality: Findings from a population-based study. *Journal of Nervous and Mental Disorders, 201,* 579–586.

Palkovitz, R., Copes, M. A., & Woolfolk, T. N. (2001). It's like . . . you discover a new sense of being: Involved fathering as an evoker of adult development. *Men & Masculinities, 4*(1), 49–69.

Palmer, S. E. (1999). Vision science: Photons to phenomenology. Cambridge, MA: MIT Press.

Palmquist, C. M., & Jaswal, V. K. (2012). Preschoolers expect pointers (even ignorant ones) to be knowledgeable. *Psychological Science, 23*(3), 230–231. doi:10.1177/0956797611427043.

Paloski, W. H. (1998). Vestibulospinal adaptation to microgravity. *Otolaryngology and Head and Neck Surgery, 118,* S39–S44.

Pandit, J. J., Cook, T. M., Jonker, W. R., O'Sullivan, E., & 5th National Audit Project (NAP5) of the Royal College of Anaesthetists and the Association of Anaesthetists of Great Britain, Ireland. (2013). A national survey of anaesthetists (NAP5 baseline) to estimate an annual incidence of accidental awareness during general anaesthesia in the UK. *British Journal of Anaesthesiology, 110*(4), 501–509.

Paoletti, M. G. (1995). Biodiversity, traditional landscapes and agroecosystem management. *Landscape and Urban Planning, 31*(1–3), 117–128.

Paolicelli, R. C., Bolasco, G., Pagani, F., Maggi, L., Scianni, M., Panzanelli, P., Giustetto, M., Ferreira, T. A., Guiducci, E., Dumas, L., Ragozzino, D., & Gross, C. T. (2011) Synaptic pruning by microglia is necessary for normal brain development. *Science 333* (6048):1456–1458.

Paradise, A. (2007). State of the Industry: ASTD's annual review of trends in workplace learning and performance. Alexandria, VA: ASTD.

Parasuraman, R. (2011). Neuroergonomics: Brain, cognition, and performance at work. *Current Directions in Psychological Science 20*(3) 181–186. doi:10.1177/0963721411409176.

Pardini, D. A., Frick, P. J., & Moffitt, T. E. (2010). Building an evidence base for DSM-5 conceptualizations of oppositional defiant disorder and conduct disorder: Introduction to the special section. *Journal of Abnormal Psychology, 119:*4, 683–688. doi:10.1037/a0021441.

Parents Television Council. (2006). *TV bloodbath: Violence on primetime broadcast TV: A PTC state of the television industry report, March.* Retrieved May 24, 2006, from http://www.parentstv.org/PTC/publications/reports/stateindustryviolence/main.asp#_ftn.

Pariente, J., White, P., Frackowiak, R. S., & Lewith, G. (2005). Expectancy and belief modulate the neuronal substrates of pain treated by acupuncture. *NeuroImage, 25,* 1161–1167.

Parise, E., & Csibra, G. (2012). Electrophysiological evidence for the understanding of maternal speech by 9-month-old infants. *Psychological Science, 23,* 728–733. doi:10.1177/0956797612438734.

Park, D. C. (2001, August). *The aging mind.* Paper presented at the annual convention of the American Psychological Association, San Francisco.

Park, D. C., & Huang, C. (2010). Culture wires the brain: A cognitive neuroscience perspective. *Perspectives on Psychological Science, 5*(4), 391–400. doi:10.1177/1745691610374591.

Park, D. C., Lautenschlager, G., Hedden, T., Davidson, N. S., Smith, A. D., & Smith, P. (2002). Models of visuospatial and verbal memory across the adult life span. *Psychology & Aging, 17*(2), 299–320.

Park, G., Lubinski, D., & Benbow, C. P. (2008). Ability differences among people who have commensurate degrees matter for scientific creativity. *Psychological Science, 19,* 957–961.

Park, H. J., Li, R. X., Kim, J., Kim, S. W., Moon, D. H., Kwon, M. H., & Kim, W. J. (2009). Neural correlates of winning and losing while watching soccer matches. *International Journal of Neuroscience, 119*(1), 76–87.

Park, J., & Kitayama, S. (2014). Interdependent selves show face-induced facilitation of error processing: Cultural neuroscience of self-threat. *Social Cognitive and Affective Neuroscience, 9*(2) 201–208.

Park, J. H. (2012). Evolutionary perspectives on intergroup prejudice: Implications for promoting tolerance. In S. Roberts (Ed.), *Applied evolutionary psychology* (pp. 186–200). New York: Oxford University Press.

Parke, R. D. (2002). Fathers and families. In M. H. Bornstein (Ed.), *Handbook of parenting* (2nd ed., pp. 27–63). Mahwah, NJ: Erlbaum.

Parke, R. D., Gailey C., Coltrane, S., & DiMatteo, R. (2012). The pursuit of perfection: Transforming our construction of parenthood and family in the age of new reproductive technologies. In P. Essed & D. T. Goldberg (Eds.), *Clones, fakes and posthumans: Cultures of replication.* Amsterdam: Rodopi.

Parke, R. D., & Buriel, R. (2006). Child development and the family. In W. Damon & R. M. Lerner (Series Eds.) & N. Eisenberg (Vol. Ed.), *Handbook of child psychology: Vol. 3. Social, emotional, and personality development* (6th ed.). New York: Wiley.

Parker, E. S., Cahill, L., & McGaugh, J. L. (2006). A case of unusual autobiographical remembering. *Neurocase, 12,* 35–49.

Parker, G., Gladstone, G., & Chee, K. T. (2001). Depression in the planet's largest ethnic group: The Chinese. *American Journal of Psychiatry, 158,* 857–864.

Parker, J. A., & Bloom, S. R. (2012). Hypothalamic neuropeptides and the regulation of appetite. *Neuropharmacology, 63*(1), 18–30.

Parsons, T. J., Power, C., & Manor, O. (2005). Physical activity, television viewing and body mass index: A cross-sectional analysis from childhood to adulthood in the 1958 British cohort. *International Journal of Obesity, 29,* 1212–1221.

Pascual-Leone, A. (2001). The brain that plays music and is changed by it. *Annals of the New York Academy of Science, 930,* 315–329.

Passie, T., Halpern, J. H., Stichtenoth, D. O., Emrich, H. M., & Hintzen, A. (2008). The pharmacology of lysergic acid diethylamide: A review. *CNS Neuroscience and Therapeutics, 14*(4), 295–314.

Patchin, J. W., & Hinduja, S. (2012). Cyberbullying: An update and synthesis of the research. In J. W. Patchin & S. Hinduja (Eds.), *Cyberbullying Prevention and Response: Expert Perspectives* (pp. 13–35). New York: Routledge.

Patel, K. S., Labar, D. R., Gordon, C. M., Hassnain, K. H., & Schwartz, T. H. (2013). Efficacy of vagus nerve stimulation as a treatment for medically intractable epilepsy in brain tumor patients. A case-controlled study using the VNS therapy Patient Outcome Registry. *Seizure, 22*(8), 627–633.

Pathela, P., Hajat, A., Schillinger, J., Blank, S., Sell, R., & Mostashari, F. (2006). Discordance between sexual behavior and self-reported sexual identity: A population-based survey of New York City men. *Annals of Internal Medicine, 145,* 416–425.

Pati, B. (2011). Inclusive education of children with intellectual disability under education for all (Sarva Shiksha Abhiyan) programme in Orissa. *Social Science International, 27*(1), 123–130.

Patihis, L., Frenda, S. J., LePort, A. K., Petersen, N., Nichols, R. M., Stark, C. E., McGaugh, J. L., & Loftus, E. F. (2013). False memories in highly superior autobiographical memory individuals. *Proceedings of the National Academy of Sciences, 110*(52), 20947–20952.

Patihis, L., Tingen, I. W., & Loftus, E. F. (2013). Memory myths. *Catalyst, 23,* 6–8.

Patkowski, M. (1994). The critical age hypothesis and interlanguage phonology. In M. Yavas (Ed.), *First and second language phonology* (pp. 205–221). San Diego: Singular Publishing Group.

Patterson, C. H. (2000). *Understanding psychotherapy: Fifty years of client-centered theory and practice.* Ross-on-Wye, UK: PCCS Books.

Patterson, C. J. (2002). Lesbian and gay parenthood. In M. H. Bornstein (Ed.), *Handbook of parenting* (2nd ed., pp. 255–274). Mahwah, NJ: Erlbaum.

Patterson, C. J. (2004). *Lesbian and gay parents and their children: Summary of research findings.* Washington, DC: American Psychological Association. Retrieved September 26, 2006, from http://www.apa.org/pi/parent.html.

Patterson, C. J. (2009). Children of lesbian and gay parents: Psychology, law, and policy. *American Psychologist, 64*(8), 727–736.

Patterson, D. R. (2010). *Clinical hypnosis for pain control.* Washington, D.C.: American Psychological Association.

Patton, G. C., McMorris, B. J., Toumbourou, J. W., Hemphill, S. A., Donath, S., & Catalano, R. F. (2004). Puberty and the onset of substance use and abuse [Electronic version]. *Pediatrics, 114*(3), e300–e306.

Pauk, W., & Owens, R. J. Q. (2010). *How to study in college* (10th ed.) Belmont, CA: Wadsworth.

Paukner, A., Ferrari, P. F., & Suomi, S. J. (2011). Delayed imitation of lipsmacking gestures by infant rhesus macaques (*Macaca mulatta*). *PloS One, 6*(12), 1.

Paul, G. L. (1969). Behavior modification research: Design and tactics. In C. M. Franks (Ed.), *Behavior therapy: Appraisal and status* (pp. 29–62). New York: McGraw-Hill.

Paulus, P. B., Kohn, N. W., & Arditti, L. E. (2011). Effects of quantity and quality instructions on brainstorming. *The Journal of Creative Behavior, 45*(1), 38–46. doi:10.1002/j.2162–6057.2011.tb01083.x.

Paulussen-Hoogeboom, M. C., Stams, G. J. J. M., Hermanns, J. M. A., Peetsma, T. T. D., & van den Wittenboer, G. L. H. (2008). Parenting style as a mediator between children's negative emotionality and problematic behavior in early childhood. *Journal of Genetic Psychology, 169,* 209–226.

Paus, T., Keshavan, M., & Giedd, J. N. (2008). Why do many psychiatric disorders emerge during adolescence? *Nature Reviews Neuroscience, 9*(12), 947–957.

Pavitt, C. (2011). Communication, performance, and perceptions in experimental simulations of resource dilemmas. *Small Group Research, 42,* 283–308.

Pavitt, C., High, A. C., Tressler, K. E., & Winslow, J. K. (2007). Leadership communication during group resource dilemmas. *Small Group Research, 38,* 509–531.

Payne, J. D., & Kensinger, E. A. (2010). Sleep's role in the consolidation of emotional episodic memories. *Current Directions in Psychological Science, 19*(5), 290–295.

Payne, J. D., & Nadel, L. (2004). Sleep, dreams, and memory consolidation: The role of the stress hormone cortisol. *Learning and Memory, 11*, 671–678.

Payne, J. D., Tucker, M. A., Ellenbogen, J. M., Wamsley, E. J., Walker, M. P., Schacter, D. L., & Stickgold, R. (2012). Memory for semantically related and unrelated declarative information: The benefit of sleep, the cost of wake. *Plos ONE, 7*(3), doi:10.1371/journal.pone.0033079.

Payne, J. W., Bettman, J. R., & Johnson, E. J. (1992). Behavioral decision research: A constructive processing perspective. *Behavioral decision research: A constructive processing perspective, 43*, 87–131.

Payne, N. A., & Prudic, J. (2009). Electroconvulsive therapy: Part I. A perspective on the evolution and current practice of ECT. *Journal of Psychiatric Practice, 15*, 346–368.

Paz, R., & Pare, D. (2013). Physiological basis for emotional modulation of memory circuits by the amygdala. *Current Opinion in Neurobiology, 23*(3), 381–386.

Pearce, J. M. (2009). Hugo Karl Liepmann and apraxia. *Clinical Medicine, 9*, 466–470.

Pearsall, M. J., Christian, M. S., & Ellis, A. P. J. (2010). Motivating interdependent teams: Individual rewards, shared rewards, or something in between? *Journal of Applied Psychology, 95*, 183–191.

Pekrun, R., Elliot, A. J., & Maier, M. A. (2009). Achievement goals and achievement emotions: Testing a model of their joint relations with academic performance. *Journal of Educational Psychology, 101*(1), 115–135.

Peltola, M. S., Tamminen, H., Toivonen, H., Kujala, T., & Näätänen, R. (2012). Different kinds of bilinguals—Different kinds of brains: The neural organisation of two languages in one brain. *Brain & Language, 121*(3), 261–266. doi:10.1016/ j.bandl.2012.03.007.

Peña-Casanova, J., Sánchez,-Benavides, G., de Sola, S., Manero-Borrás, R. M., & Casals-Coll, M. (2013). Neuropsychology of Alzheimer disease, *Archives of Medical Research, 43*(8), 686–693.

Penedo, F. J., & Dahn, J. (2004). Psychoneuroimmunology and aging. In M. Irwin & K. Vedhara (Eds.), *Psychoneuroimmunology*. New York: Kluwer.

Peng, W. (2009). Design and evaluation of a computer game to promote a healthy diet for young adults. *Health Communication, 24*(2), 115–127. doi:10.1080/ 10410230802676490.

Pennebaker, J. W. (1995). *Emotion, disclosure, and health*. Washington, DC: American Psychological Association.

Pennebaker, J. W. (2000). The effects of traumatic disclosure on physical and mental health: The values of writing and talking about upsetting events. In J. M. Violanti, D. Paton, & C. Dunning (Eds.), *Posttraumatic stress intervention: Challenges, issues, and perspectives* (pp. 97–114). Chicago: Charles C. Thomas.

Pennebaker, J. W., & Chew, C. H. (1985). Deception, electrodermal activity, and inhibition of behavior. *Journal of Personality and Social Psychology, 49*, 1427–1433.

Pennebaker, J. W., & O'Heeron, R. C. (1984). Confiding in others and illness rate among spouses of suicide and accidental death victims. *Journal of Abnormal Psychology, 93*, 473–476.

Penner, L., Brannick, M. T., Webb, S., & Connell, P. (2005). Effects on volunteering of the September 11, 2001 attacks: An archival analysis. *Journal of Applied Social Psychology, 35*, 1333–1360.

Penner, L. A. (2002). Dispositional and organizational influences on sustained volunteerism: An interactionist perspective. *Journal of Social Issues, 58*, 447–467.

Penner, L. A., & Craiger, J. P. (1992). The weakest link: The performance of individual group members. In R. W. Swezey & E. Salas (Eds.), *Teams: Their training and performance* (pp. 57–74). Norwood, NJ: Ablex.

Penner, L. A., & Dovidio, J. F. (2014). Colorblindness and health disparities. In H. A. Neville, M. E. Gallardo, & D. W. Sue (Eds.), *What does it mean to be color-blind? Manifestation, dynamics, and impact*. Washington, DC: APA Press.

Penner, L. A., Dovidio, J., & Albrecht, T. L. (2001). Helping victims of loss and trauma: A social psychological perspective. In J. Harvey & E. Miller (Eds.), *Loss and trauma: General and close relationship perspectives* (pp. 62–85). Philadelphia: Brunner Routledge.

Penner, L. A., Dovidio, J. F., Piliavin, J. A., & Schroeder, D. A. (2005). Prosocial behavior: Multilevel perspectives. *Annual Review of Psychology, 56*, 365–392.

Penner, L. A., & Finkelstein, M. A. (1998). Dispositional and structural determinants of volunteerism. *Journal of Personality and Social Psychology, 74*, 525–537.

Penner, L. A., Fritzsche, B. A., Craiger, J. P., & Friefeld, T. R. (1995). Measuring the prosocial personality. In J. Butcher & C. D. Spielberger (Eds.), *Advances in personality assessment* (Vol. 10, pp. 147–163). Hillsdale, NJ: Erlbaum.

Penner, L. A., Hagiwara, N., Eggly, S., Gaertner, S. L., Albrecht, T. L., & Dovidio, J. F. (2013b). Racial healthcare disparities: A social psychological analysis. *European Review of Social Psychology, 24*, 70–122.

Penner, L. A., & Orom, H. (2009). Enduring goodness: A person-by-situation perspective on prosocial behavior. In M. Mikulnicer & P. Shaver (Eds.), *Prosocial motives, emotions, and behavior* (pp. 55–72). Washington, DC: American Psychological Association.

Penney, L. M., & Spector, P. E. (2005). Job stress, incivility, and counterproductive work behavior (CWB): The moderating role of negative affectivity. *Journal of Organizational Behavior, 26*, 777–796.

Pennington, J., & Knight, T. (2011). Through the lens of hetero-normative assumptions: Re-thinking attitudes towards gay parenting. *Culture, Health & Sexuality, 13*(1), 59–72. doi:10.1080/13691058.2010.519049.

Penninx, B. W., Beekman, A. T., Honig, A., Deeg, D. J., Schoevers, R. A., van Eijk, J. T., van Tilburg, W. (2001). Depression and cardiac mortality: Results from a community-based longitudinal study. *Archives of General Psychiatry, 58*, 221–227.

Penton, R. E., & Lester, R. A. (2009). Cellular events in nicotine addiction. *Seminars in Cell and Developmental Biology, 20*, 418–431.

Peretz, H., & Fried, Y. (2012). National cultures, performance appraisal practices, and organizational absenteeism and turnover: A study across 21 countries. *Journal of Applied Psychology, 97*, 448–459. doi:10.1037/a0026011.

Perfect, T. J., Andrade, J., & Syrett, L. (2012). Environmental visual distraction during retrieval affects the quality, not the quantity, of eyewitness recall. *Applied Cognitive Psychology, 26*(2), 296–300. doi:10.1002/acp.1823.

Pergola, G., Güntürkün, O., Koch, B, Schwarz, M., Daum, I., & Suchan, B. (2012). Recall deficits in stroke patients with thalamic lesions covary with damage to the parvocellular mediodorsal nucleus of the thalamus. *Neuropsychologia, 50*(10), 2477–2491.

Perilloux, C., Easton, J., & Buss, D. (2012). The misperception of sexual interest. *Psychological Science, 23*(2), 146–151.

Perkins, T., Stokes, M., McGillivray, J., & Bittar, R. (2010). Mirror neuron dysfunction in autism spectrum disorders. *J Clin Neurosci 17* (10):1239–1243.

Perkonigg, A., Pfister, H., Stein, M. B., Hofler, M., Lieb, R., Maercker, A., et al. (2005). Longitudinal course of posttraumatic stress disorder and posttraumatic stress disorder symptoms in a community sample of adolescents and young adults. *American Journal of Psychiatry, 162*, 1320–1327.

Perlin, M. L. (2003). Therapeutic jurisprudence and outpatient commitment law: Kendra's Law as case study. *Psychology, Public Policy, and Law, 9*, 183–208.

Perlis, M. L., Sharpe, M., Smith, M. T., Greenblatt, D., & Giles, D. (2001). Behavioral treatment of insomnia: Treatment outcomes and the relevance of medical and psychiatric morbidity. *Journal of Behavioral Medicine, 24*, 281–296.

Perlman, D. M., Salomons, T. V., Davidson, R. J., & Lutz, A. (2010). Diff erential effects on pain intensity and unpleasantness of two meditation practices. *Emotion, 10*, 65–71.

Perls, F. S. (1969). *Ego, hunger and aggression: The beginning of Gestalt therapy*. New York: Random House.

Perls, F. S., Hefferline, R. F., & Goodman, P. (1951). *Gestalt therapy*. New York: Julian Press.

Perovic, S., & Radenovic, L. (2011). Fine-tuning nativism: The 'nurtured nature' and innate cognitive structures. *Phenomenology And The Cognitive Sciences, 10*(3), 399–417. doi:10.1007/s11097-010-9180-0.

Perper, K., & Manlove, J. (2009). Estimated percentage of females who will become teen mothers: Differences across states. *Child Trends Research Brief*. Retrieved from http://www.childtrends.org/Files//Child_Trends-2009_03_19_RB _PercentTeenMothers.pdf.

Perper, K., Peterson, K., & Manlove, J. (2010). Diploma attainment among teen mothers. *Child Trends*, Fact Sheet Publication #2010–01. Washington, DC: Child Trends.

Perrin, J., Merz, S., Bennett, D., Currie, J., Steele, D., Reid, I., & Schwarzbauer, C. (2012). Electroconvulsive therapy reduces frontal cortical connectivity in severe depressive disorder. *Proceedings of the National Academy of Sciences of the United States of America, 109*(14), 5464–5468.

Perrin, M. A., DiGrande, L., Wheeler, K., Thorpe, L., Farfel, M., & Brackbill, R. (2007). Differences in PTSD prevalence and associated risk factors among World Trade Center disaster rescue and recovery workers. *American Journal of Psychiatry, 164*, 1385–1394.

Perry, B. L. (2011). The labeling paradox: Stigma, the sick role, and social networks in mental illness. *Journal of Health & Social Behavior, 52*(4), 460–477. doi:10.1177/ 0022146511408913.

Persons, J. B., Davidson, J., & Tompkins, M. A. (2001). *Essential components of cognitive-behavior therapy for depression*. Washington, DC: American Psychological Association.

Perthen, J. E., Lansing, A. E., Liau, J., Liu, T. T., & Buxton, R. B. (2008). Caffeine-induced uncoupling of cerebral blood flow and oxygen metabolism: A calibrated BOLD fMRI study. *NeuroImage, 40*(1), 237–247.

Pervin, L. A., Cervone, D., & John, O. P. (2005). *Personality: Theory and research.* New York: Wiley.

Pesonen, A.-K., Räikkönen, K., Heinonen, K., Komsi, N., Järvenpää, A.-L., & Strandberg, T. (2008). A transactional model of temperamental development: Evidence of a relationship between child temperament and maternal stress over five years. *Social Development, 17,* 326–340.

Pessiglione, M., Seymour, B., Flandin, G., Dolan, R. J., & Frith, C. D. (2006). Dopamine-dependent prediction errors underpin reward-seeking behaviour in humans. *Nature, 442,* 1042–1045.

Peters, E., Baker, D. P., Dieckmann, N. F., Leon, J., & Collins, J. (2010). Explaining the effect of education on health: A field study in Ghana. *Psychological Science, 21,* (10), 1369–1376. doi:10.1177/0956797610381506.

Peters, E., Hess, T. M., Västfjäll, D., & Auman, C. (2007). Adult age differences in dual information processes: Implications for the role of affective and deliberative processes in older adults' decision making. *Perspectives on Psychological Science, 2,* 1–23.

Peterson, C., Maier, S. F., & Seligman, M. E. (1993). *Learned helplessness: A theory for the age of personal control.* New York: Oxford University Press.

Peterson, C., & Seligman, M. E. P. (1984). Causal explanations as a risk factor for depression: Theory and evidence. *Psychological Review, 91,* 347–374.

Peterson, C., Seligman, M. E. P., Yurko, K. H., Martin, L. R., & Friedman, H. S. (1998). Catastrophizing and untimely death. *Psychological Science, 9,* 127–130.

Peterson, L. R., & Peterson, M. J. (1959). Short-term retention of individual verbal items. *Journal of Experimental Psychology, 58,* 193–198.

Peterson, N. G., Mumford, M. D., Borman, W. C., Jeanneret, P. R., Fleishman, E. A., Levin, K. Y., et al. (2001). Understanding work using the Occupational Information Network (O*NET): Implications for practice and research. *Personnel Psychology, 54,* 451–492.

Peterson, R. S., Smith, D. B., Martorana, P. V., & Owens, P. D. (2003). The impact of chief executive officer personality on top management team dynamics: One mechanism by which leadership affects organizational performance. *Journal of Applied Psychology, 88,* 795–808.

Petitclerc, A., & Tremblay, R. E. (2009). Childhood disruptive behaviour disorders: Review of their origin, development and prevention. *Canadian Journal of Psychiatry, 54,* 222–231.

Petrescu, N. (2008). Loud music listening. *McGill Journal of Medicine, 11*(2), 169–176.

Petrie, K., Fontanilla, I., Thomas, M., Booth, R., & Pennebaker, J. W. (2004). Effects of written emotional expression on immune function in patients with human immunodeficiency virus infection: a randomized trial. *Psychosomatic Medicine, 66,* 272–275, 2004.

Petrie, K. J., & Weinman, J. (2012). Patients' perceptions of their illness: The dynamo of volition in health care. *Current Directions in Psychological Science, 21*(1), 60–65. doi:10.1177/0963721411429456.

Petrovic, P., Dietrich, T., Fransson, P., Andersson, J., Carlsson, K., & Ingvar, M. (2005). Placebo in emotional processing: Induced expectations of anxiety relief activate a generalized modulatory network. *Neuron, 46,* 957–969.

Petrovich, G. D. (2011). Learning and the motivation to eat: Forebrain circuitry. *Physiology & Behavior, 104*(4), 582–589.

Pettigrew, T. F. (2001). The ultimate attribution error: Extending Allport's cognitive analysis of prejudice. In M. A. Hogg & D. Abrams (Eds.), *Intergroup relations: Essential readings* (pp. 162–173). New York: Psychology Press.

Pettigrew, T. F., Tropp, L. R., Wagner, U. & Christ, O. (2011) Recent advances in intergroup contact theory. *International Journal of Intercultural Relations, 35,* 271–280.

Petty, R., & Brinol, P. (2010). Attitude change In R. Baumeister & E. Finkel (Eds.), *Advanced social psychology: The state of the science* (pp. 217–262). New York: Oxford.

Petty, R. E., & Briñol, P. (2012). The elaboration likelihood model. In P. M. Van Lange, A. W. Kruglanski, & E. Higgins (Eds.), *Handbook of theories of social psychology (Vol. 1)* (pp. 224–245). Thousand Oaks, CA: Sage Publications Ltd.

Petzold, G. C., & Murthy, V. N. (2011) Role of astrocytes in neurovascular coupling. *Neuron 71* (5):782–797.

Pexman, P., Rostad, K., McMorris, C., Climie, E., Stowkowy, J., & Glenwright, M. (2011). Processing of ironic language in children with high-functioning autism spectrum disorder. *Journal of Autism and Developmental Disorders, 41,* 1097–1112.

Pfefferbaum, B., Tucker, P., North, C. S., Jeon-Slaughter, H., & Nitéma, P. (2014). Children of terrorism survivors: Physiology reactions seven years following a terrorist incident. *Comprehensive Psychiatry, 55*(4), 749–754.

Pfister, J. A., Stegelmeier, B. L., Gardner, D. R., & James, L. F. (2003). Grazing of spotted locoweed (*Astragalus lentiginosus*) by cattle and horses in Arizona. *Journal of Animal Science, 81,* 2285–2293.

Pham, L. B., Taylor, S. E., & Seeman, T. E. (2001). Effects of environmental predictability and personal mastery on self-regulatory and physiological processes. *Personality & Social Psychology Bulletin, 27,* 611–620.

Phares, E. J. (1976). *Locus of control in personality.* Morristown, NJ: General Learning Press.

Phares, V. (2014). *Understanding abnormal child psychology* (3rd ed.). Hoboken, NJ: Wiley.

Phelps, E. A., & LeDoux, J. E. (2005). Contributions of the amygdala to emotion processing: From animal models to human behavior. *Neuron, 48,* 175–187.

Phelps, E. A., O'Connor, K. J., Cunningham, W. A., Funayama, E. S., Gatenby, J. C., Gore, J. C., & Banaji, M. R. (2000). Performance on indirect measures of race evaluation predicts amygdala activation. *Journal of Cognitive Neuroscience, 12,* 729–738.

Phillips, K. M., Freund, B., Fordiani, J., Kuhn, R., & Ironson, G. (2009). EMDR treatment of past domestic violence: A clinical vignette. *Journal of EMDR Practice and Research, 3,* 192–197.

Phillips, P. E., Stuber, G. D., Heien, M. L., Wightman, R. M., & Carelli, R. M. (2003). Subsecond dopamine release promotes cocaine seeking. *Nature, 422,* 614–618.

Phinney, J. S., Jacoby, B., Silva, C. (2007). Positive intergroup attitudes: The role of ethnic identity. *International Journal of Behavioral Development, 31,* 478–490.

Phipps, M. G., Blume, J. D., & DeMonner, S. M. (2002). Young maternal age associated with increased risk of postneonatal death. *Obstetrics and Gynecology, 100,* 481–486.

Piaget, J. (1952). *The origins of intelligence in children.* New York: International Universities Press.

Piasecki, T. M. (2006). Relapse to smoking. *Clinical Psychology Review, 26,* 196–215.

Pickler, N. (2002, November 19). *NTSB cites fatigue, sleep apnea in fatal train wreck.* Associated Press. Retrieved August 25, 2003, from http://newsobserver.com /24hour/nation/v-print/story/626769p-4807167c.html.

Pierce, J. R., & Aguinis, H. (2013). The too-much-of-a-good-thing effect in management research. *Journal of Management, 39*(2), 313–338.

Pietro, P., Guazzeli, M., Basso, G., Jaffe, K., & Grafman, J. (2000). Neural correlates of imaginal aggressive behavior assessed by positron emission tomography in healthy subjects. *American Journal of Psychiatry, 157,* 1772–1781.

Piko, B. F., Bak, J., Gibbons, F. X. (2007). Prototype perception and smoking: Are negative or positive social images more important in adolescents? *Addictive Behaviors, 32,* 1728–1732.

Piliavin, J. A., Dovidio, J. F., Gaertner, S. L., & Clark, R. D., III. (1981). *Emergency intervention.* New York: Academic Press.

Pillemer, K., & Suitor, J. J. (2002). Explaining mothers' ambivalence towards their adult children. *Journal of Marriage and Family, 64,* 602–613.

Pillmann, F. (2009). Complex dream-enacting behavior in sleepwalking. *Psychosomatic Medicine, 71,* 231–234.

Pinker, S. (1994). *The language instinct: How the mind creates language.* New York: Morrow.

Pinto, J. M. (2011). Olfaction. *Proceedings of the American Thoracic Society, 8*(1), 46–52.

Pintrich, P. R. (2003). Motivation and classroom learning. In W. M. Reynolds & G. E. Miller (Eds.), *Handbook of psychology: Educational psychology, Vol. 7* (pp. 103–122). Hoboken, NJ: John Wiley & Sons Inc.

Pipes, R. B., Holstein, J. E., & Aguirre, M. G. (2005). Examining the personal-professional distinction: Ethics codes and the difficulty of drawing a boundary. *American Psychologist, 60,* 325–334.

Pipitone, R. N., & Gallup G. G., Jr. (2008). Women's voice attractiveness varies across the menstrual cycle. *Evolution and Human Behavior, 29,* 268–274.

Pittler, M. H., Verster, J. C., & Ernst, E. (2005). Interventions for preventing or treating alcohol hangover: Systematic review of randomised controlled trials. *British Medical Journal, 331,* 1515–1518.

Pizza, F., Contardi, S., Antognini, A. B., Zagoraiou, M., Borrotti, M., Mostacci, B., Mondini, S., & Cirignotta, F. (2010). Sleep quality and motor vehicle crashes in adolescents. *Journal of Clinical Sleep Medicine, 6*(1), 41–45.

Plant, E. A., & Sachs-Ericsson, N. (2004). Racial and ethnic differences in depression: The roles of social support and meeting basic needs. *Journal of Consulting and Clinical Psychology, 72,* 41–52.

Plant, K. L., & Stanton, N. A. (2012). Why did the pilots shut down the wrong engine? Explaining errors in context using Schema Theory and the Perceptual Cycle Model. *Safety Science, 50*(2), 300–315. doi:10.1016/j.ssci.2011.09.005.

Platek, S. M., & Singh, D. (2010). Optimal Waist-to-Hip Ratios in Women Activate Neural Reward Centers in Men. *Plos ONE, 5*(2), 1–5. doi:10.1371/journal.pone.0009042.

Pleck, E. H. (2004). Two dimensions of fatherhood: A history of the good dad–bad dad complex. In M. E. Lamb (Ed.), *The role of the father in child development* (4th ed., pp. 32–57). Hoboken, NJ: Wiley.

Plomin, R. (1994). *Genetics and experience: The developmental interplay between nature and nurture.* Newbury Park, CA: Sage.

Plomin, R., DeFries, J. C., McClearn, G. E., & McGuffin, P. (2008). *Behavioral genetics* (5th ed.). New York: Worth.

Plomin, R., & McGuffin, P. (2003). Psychopathology in the postgenomic era. *Annual Review of Psychology, 54,* 205–228.

Plomin, R., & Spinath, F. M. (2004). Intelligence: Genetics, genes, and genomics. *Journal of Personality and Social Psychology, 86,* 112–129.

Ploner, M., Gross, J., Timmermann, L., & Schnitzler, A. (2002). Cortical representation of first and second pain sensation in humans. *Proceedings of the National Academy of Sciences, 99,* 12444–12448.

Pluess, M. & Belsky, J. (2010). Differential susceptibility to parenting and quality child care. *Developmental Psychology 46,* 379.

Plutchik, R., & Conte, H. R. (Eds.). (1997). *Circumplex models of personality and emotions.* Washington, DC: American Psychological Association.

Pogue-Geile, M. F., & Yokley, J. L. (2010). Current research on the genetic contributors to schizophrenia. *Current Directions in Psychological Science, 19*(4), 214–219. doi:10.1177/0963721410378490.

Polanczyk, G., Moffitt, T. E., Arseneault, L., Cannon, M., Ambler, A., Keefe, R. S. E. (2010). Etiological and clinical features of childhood psychotic symptoms. *Arch Gen Psychiatry, 67*:4, 328–338.

Poland, J., & Caplan, P. J. (2004). The deep structure of bias in psychiatric diagnosis. In P. J. Caplan & L. Cosgrove (Eds.), *Bias in psychiatric diagnosis: A project of the association for women in psychology* (pp. 9–23). New York: Aronson.

Poldrack, R. A. (2010). Mapping mental function to brain structure: How can cognitive neuroimaging succeed?. *Perspectives on Psychological Science, 5*(6), 753–761. doi:10.1177/1745691610388777.

Poldrack, R. A., Halchenko, Y. O., & Hanson, S. J. (2009). Decoding the large-scale structure of brain function by classifying mental states across individuals. *Psychological Science, 20,* 1364–1372.

Police Executive Research Forum (2013). *A National Survey of Eyewitness Identification Procedures in Law Enforcement Agencies.* (http://policeforum.org/library/eyewitness-identification/NIJEyewitnessReport.pdf).

Polivy, J., & Herman, C. P. (2002). If at first you don't succeed: False hopes of self-change. *American Psychologist, 57,* 677–689.

Poljac, E., Poljac, E., & Wagemans, J. (2013). Reduced accuracy and sensitivity in the perception of emotional facial expressions in individuals with high autism spectrum traits. *Autism, 17*(6), 668–680.

Pollack, I. (1953). The assimilation of sequentially coded information. *American Journal of Psychology, 66,* 421–435.

Pollatsek, A., Romoser, M. E., & Fisher, D. L. (2011). Identifying and remediating failures of selective attention in older drivers. *Current Directions in Psychological Science 21*(1) 3–7. doi:10.1177/0963721411429459

Pollo, A., & Benedetti, F. (2009). The placebo response: Neurobiological and clinical issues of neurological relevance. *Progress in Brain Research, 175,* 283–294.

Polman, H., Orobio de Castro, B., & van Aken, M. A. G. (2008). Experimental study of the differential effects of playing versus watching violent video games on children's aggressive behavior. *Aggressive Behavior, 34,* 256–264.

Polusny, M. A., & Follette, V. M. (1995). Long-term correlates of child sexual abuse: Theory and review of the empirical literature. *Applied and Preventive Psychology, 4,* 143–166.

Pompili, M., Lester, D., De Pisa, E., Del Casale, A., et al. (2008). Surviving the suicides of significant others: A case study. *Crisis, 29,* 45–48.

Ponomarev, I. (2013). Epigenetic control of gene expression in the alcoholic brain. *Alcohol Research, 35*(1), 69–76.

Poole, D., Bruck, M., & Pipe, M. (2011). Forensic interviewing aids: Do props help children answer questions about touching?. *Current Directions In Psychological Science, 20*(1), 11–15. doi:10.1177/0963721410388804.

Poon, L. W. (2008). What can we learn from centenarians? In C. Y. Read, R. C. Green, & M. A. Smyer (Eds.), *Aging, biotechnology, and the future* (pp. 100–110). Baltimore: Johns Hopkins University Press.

Pope, H. G., Jr., Hudson, J. I., Bodkin, J. A., & Oliva, P. (1998). Questionable validity of "dissociative amnesia" in trauma victims: Evidence from prospective studies. *British Journal of Psychiatry, 172,* 210–215.

Popper, M. (2011). Toward a theory of followership. *Review of General Psychology, 15*(1), 29–36. doi:10.1037/a0021989.

Porges, S. W., Doussard, R. J. A., & Maita, A. K. (1995). Vagal tone and the physiological regulation of emotion. *Monographs of the Society for Research on Child Development, 59*(2–3), 167–186, 250–283.

Porter, J., Anand, T., Johnson, B., Khan, R. M., & Sobell, N. (2005). Brain mechanisms for extracting spatial information from smell. *Neuron, 47,* 581–592.

Porter, R. H. (1991). Human reproduction and the mother-infant relationship. In T. V. Getchell et al. (Eds.), *Taste and smell in health and disease.* New York: Raven Press.

Porter, R. H., Cernich, J. M., & McLaughlin, F. J. (1983). Maternal recognition of neonates through olfactory cues. *Physiology and Behavior, 30,* 151–154.

Porter, R. H., Makin, J. W., Davis, L. B., & Christensen, K. M. (1992). Breast-fed infants respond to olfactory cues from their own mother and unfamiliar lactating females. *Infant Behavior and Development, 15,* 85–93.

Porter, S., & Brinke, L. (2010). The truth about lies: What works in detecting high-stakes deception?. *Legal & Criminological Psychology, 15*(1), 57–75. doi:10.1348/135532509X433151.

Porter, S., & Peace, K. A. (2007). The scars of memory: A prospective, longitudinal investigation of the consistency of traumatic and positive emotional memories in adulthood. *Psychological Science 18,* 435–441.

Porter, S., Yuille, J. C., & Lehman, D. R. (1999). The nature of real, implanted, and fabricated memories for emotional childhood events: Implications for the recovered memory debate. *Law & Human Behavior, 23,* 517–537.

Posener, J. A., DeBattista, C., Williams, G. H., Kraemer, H. C., Kalehzan, B. M., & Schatzberg, A. F. (2000). 24-hour monitoring of cortisol and corticotropin secretion in psychotic and nonpsychotic major depression. *Archives of General Psychiatry, 57,* 755–760.

Posner, J. B., Saper, C. B., Schiff, N. D., & Plum, F. (2007). *Plum and Posner's Diagnosis of Stupor and Coma. (Contemporary Neurology Series. 71.) Fourth edition.* New York, NY: Oxford University Press.

Posner, M. I., Nissen, M. J., & Ogden, W. C. (1978). Attended and unattended processing modes: The role of set for spatial location. In H. L. Pick & I. J. Saltzman (Eds.), *Modes of perceiving and processing information* (pp. 137–157). Hillsdale, NJ: Erlbaum.

Posner, M. I., & Rothbart, M. K. (2000). Developing mechanisms of self-regulation. *Development and Psychopathology, 12,* 427–427.

Posthuma, D., & deGeus, E. J. C. (2006). Progress in the molecular-genetic study of intelligence. *Current Directions in Psychological Science, 15,* 151–155.

Potenza, M. N. (2013). Neurobiology of gambling behaviors. *Current Opinion in Neurobiology, 23*(4), 660–667.

Potter, P. T., & Zautra, A. J. (1997). Stressful life events' effects on rheumatoid arthritis disease activity. *Journal of Consulting and Clinical Psychology, 65,* 319–323.

Pottick, K. J., Bilder, S., VanderStoep, A., Warner, L. A., & Alvarez, M. F. (2008). US patterns of mental health service utilization for transition-age youth and young adults. *Journal of Behavioral Health Services and Research, 35,* 373–389.

Pottick, K. J., Kirk, S. A., Hsieh, D. K., & Tian, X. (2007). Judging mental disorder in youths: Effects of client, clinician, and contextual differences. *Journal of Consulting and Clinical Psychology, 75,* 1–8.

Poulin-Dubois, D., Blaye, A., Coutya, J., & Bialystok, E. (2011). The effects of bilingualism on toddlers' executive functioning. *Journal of Experimental Child Psychology, 108*(3), 567–579. doi:10.1016/j.jecp.2010.10.009.

Pourtois, G., de Gelder, B., Bol, A., & Crommelinck, M. (2005). Perception of facial expressions and voices and of their combination in the human brain. *Cortex, 41,* 49–59.

Povinelli, D. J., & Bering, J. M. (2002). The mentality of apes revisited. *Current Directions in Psychological Science, 11,* 115–119.

Powers, M. B., Halpern, J. M., Ferenschak, M. P., Gillihan, S. J., & Foa, E. B. (2010). A metaanalytic review of prolonged exposure for posttraumatic stress disorder. *Clinical Psychology Review, 30,* 635–641.

Powers, S. I., Pietromonaco, P. R., Gunlicks, M., & Sayer, A. (2006). Dating couples' attachment styles and patterns of cortisol reactivity and recovery in response to a relationship conflict. *Journal of Personality and Social Psychology, 90,* 613–628.

Powley, T. L., & Keesey, R. E. (1970). Relationship of body weight to the lateral hypothalamic feeding syndrome. *Journal of Comparative & Physiological Psychology, 70,* 25–36.

Poyares, D., Guilleminault, C., Ohayon, M. M., & Tufik, S. (2004). Chronic benzodiazepine usage and withdrawal in insomnia patients. *Journal of Psychiatric Research, 38,* 327–334.

Practice guidelines regarding psychologists' involvement in pharmacological issues. (2011). *American Psychologist, 66*(9), 835–849. doi:10.1037/a0025890.

Pradhan, G., Samson, S. L., & Sun, Y. (2013). Ghrelin: Much more than a hunger hormone. *Current Opinion in Clinical Nutrition and Metabolic Care, 16*(6), 619–624.

Pratkanis, A., & Aronson, E. (2001). *The age of propaganda: The everyday use and abuse of propaganda.* New York: W. H. Freeman.

Pratkanis, A. R. (1992). The cargo-cult science of subliminal persuasion. *Skeptical Inquirer, 16,* 260–273.

Pratkanis, A. R., Eskenazi, J., & Greenwald, A. G. (1994). What you expect is what you believe (but not necessarily what you get): A test of the effectiveness of self-help audiotapes. *Basic and Applied Social Psychology, 15,* 251–276.

Prepau, M. J., Lipton, P. A., Eichenbaum, H. B., & Eden, U. T. (2014). Characterizing context-dependent differential firing activity in the hippocampus and entorhinal cortex. *Hippocampus.* E-pub January 16, 2014.

Preciado, P., Snijders, T. B., Burk, W. J., Stattin, H., & Kerr, M. (2012). Does proximity matter? Distance dependence of adolescent friendships. *Social Networks, 34,* 18–31.

Premack, D. (1971). Language in chimpanzees? *Science, 172,* 808–822.

Premack, D., & Premack, A. J. (1983). *The mind of an ape.* New York: Norton.

Prescott, J. W. (1996). The origins of human love and violence. *Pre- and Peri-Natal Psychology Journal, 10,* 143–188.

Pressman, S. D., & Cohen, S. (2005). Does positive affect influence health? *Psychological Bulletin, 131,* 925–971.

Pressman, S. D., & Cohen, S. (2005). Does positive affect influence health? *Psychological Bulletin, 131,* 925–971.

Pressman, S. D., Gallagher, M. W., & Lopez, S. J. (2013). Is the emotion-health connection a "first-world problem"? *Psychological Science, 24*(4), 544–549.

Price, C. J. (2012). A review and synthesis of the first 20 years of PET and fMRI studies of heard speech, spoken language and reading. *Neuroimage, 62*(2), 816–847.

Price, K. H., Harrison, D. A., & Gavin, J. H. (2006).Withholding inputs in team contexts: Member composition, interaction processes, evaluation structure, and social loafing. *Journal of Applied Psychology, 91,* 1375–1384.

Price, M., & Anderson, P. L. (2012). Outcome expectancy as a predictor of treatment response in cognitive behavioral therapy for public speaking fears within social anxiety disorder. *Psychotherapy, 49,* 173–179. doi:10.1037/a0024734.

Price, M., & Hyde, J. (2011). Perceived and observed maternal relationship quality predict sexual debut by age 15. *Journal of Youth & Adolescence, 40*(12), 1595–1606. doi:10.1007/s10964-011-9641-y.

Priego, T., Sanchez, J., Palou, A., & Pico, C. (2010). Leptin intake during the suckling period improves the metabolic response of adipose tissue to a high-fat diet. *International Journal of Obesity, 34,* 809–819.

Prigatano, G. P. (2013). Denial, anosodiaphoria, and emotional reactivity in anosognosia. *Cognitive Neuroscience, 4*(3–4), 201–202.

Prigatano, G. P., Matthes, J., Hill, S. W., Wolf, T. R., & Heiserman, J. E. (2011). Anosognosia for hemiplegia with preserved awareness of complete cortical blindness following intracranial hemorrhage. *Cortex, 47*(10), 1219–1227.

Prikryl, R., Ceskova, E., Kasparek, T., & Kucerova, H. (2006). Neurological soft signs, clinical symptoms and treatment reactivity in patients suffering from first episode schizophrenia. *Journal of Psychiatric Research, 40,* 141–146.

Prince, M., Bryce, R., Albanese, E., Wimo, A., Ribeiro, W., & Ferri, C. P. (2013). The global prevalence of dementia: A systematic review and metaanalysis. *Alzheimer's & Dementia, 9*(1), 63–75.

Prochaska, J. O. (1994). Strong and weak principles for progressing from precontemplation to action on the basis of twelve problem behaviors. *Health Psychology, 13,* 47–51.

Prochaska, J. O., DiClemente, C., & Norcross, J. (1992). In search of how people change: Application to addictive behaviors. *American Psychologist, 47,* 1102–1114.

Program for International Student Assessment. (2005). *Learning for tomorrow's world: First results from PISA 2004.* Paris: OECD.

Pronin, E., Wegner, D. M., McCarthy, K., & Rodriguez, S. (2006). Everyday magical powers: The role of apparent causation in the overestimation of personal influence. *Journal of Personality and Social Psychology, 91,* 218–231.

Proske, E. (2006). Kinesthesia: The role of muscle receptors. *Muscle and Nerve, 34*(5), 545–558.

Pruitt, D. G., & Carnevale, P. J. (1993). *Negotiation in social conflict.* Pacific Grove, CA: Brooks/Cole.

Przybylski, A. K., Weinstein, N., Murayama, K., Lynch, M. F., & Ryan, R. M. (2012). The Ideal self at play: The appeal of video games that let you be all you can be. *Psychological Science, 23*(1), 69–76. doi:10.1177/0956797611418676.

Puetz, A., & Ruenzi, S. (2011). Overconfidence among professional investors: Evidence from mutual fund managers. *Journal of Business Finance & Accounting, 38,* 684–712.

Pulfrey, C., Buchs, C., & Butera, F. (2011). Why grades engender performance-avoidance goals: The mediating role of autonomous motivation. *Journal Of Educational Psychology, 103*(3), 683–700. doi:10.1037/a0023911.

Pulkkinen, L., Kokko, K., & Rantanen, J. (2012). Paths from socioemotional behavior in middle childhood to personality in middle adulthood. *Developmental Psychology, 48,* 1283–1291.

Purves, D., Augustine, G. J., Fitzpatrick, D., Hall, W. C., LaMantia, A-S., & White, L. E. (Eds.). (2011). *Neuroscience.* 5th ed. Sunderland, MA: Sinauer Associates, Inc.

Puvathingal, B. J., & Hantula, D. A. (2012). Revisiting the psychology of intelligence analysis: From rational actors to adaptive thinkers. *American Psychologist, 67*(3), 199–210. doi:10.1037/a0026640.

Pyszczynski, T., Greenberg, J., Koole, S., & Solomon, S. (2010). Experimental existential psychology: Coping with the facts of life. In S. T. Fiske, D. T. Gilbert, & G. Lindzey (Eds.), *Handbook of social psychology* (5th ed., Vol. 2., pp. 724–760). Hoboken, NJ: Wiley.

Quinlivan, D. S., Neuschatz, J. S., Cutler, B. L., Wells, G. L., McClung, J., & Harker, D. L. (2012). Do pre-admonition suggestions moderate the effect of unbiased lineup instructions? *Legal and Criminological Psychology, 17*(1), 165–176. doi:10.1348/135532510X533554.

Quinn, P., & Liben, L. S. (2008). A sex difference in mental rotation in young infants. *Psychological Science, 19,* 1067–1070.

Quinn, P. C., & Bhatt, R. S. (2005). Learning perceptual organization in infancy. *Psychological Science, 16,* 511–515.

Quintana, S. M. (2011). Ethnicity, race, and children's social development. In P. K. Smith & C. H. Hart (Eds.), *Wiley-Blackwell handbook of childhood social development* (2nd ed). Hoboken, NJ: Wiley-Blackwell.

Quintero, G. C. (2013). Role of nucleus accumbens glutamatergic plasticity in drug addiction. *Neuropsychiatric Disease and Treatment, 9,* 1499–1512.

Raaijmakers, J. G. W., & Jakab, E. (2013). Is forgetting caused by inhibition? *Current Directions in Psychological Science, 22*(3), 205–209.

Raaijmakers, Q. A. W., Engels, R. C. M. E., & Van Hoof, A. (2005). Delinquency and moral reasoning in adolescence and young adulthood. *International Journal of Behavioral Development, 29,* 247–258.

Rabasca, L. (1999, July/August). Behavioral interventions can cut the use of restraints. *APA Monitor,* p. 27.

Rabinowitz, J., De Smedt, G., Harvey, P. D., & Davidson, M. (2002). Relationship between premorbid functioning and symptom severity as assessed at first episode of psychosis. *American Journal of Psychiatry, 159,* 2021–2026.

Rachlin, H. (2000). *The science of self-control.* Cambridge, MA: Harvard University Press.

Racsmany, M., Conway, M. A., & Demeter, G. (2010). Consolidation of episodic memories during sleep: Long-term eff ects of retrieval practice. *Psychological Science, 21,* 80–85.

Rada, J. B., & Rogers, R. W. (1973). *Obedience to authority: Presence of authority and command strength.* Paper presented at the annual convention of the Southeastern Psychological Association.

Radel, R., & Clément-Guillotin, C. (2012). Evidence of motivational influences in early visual perception: Hunger modulates conscious access. *Psychological Science, 23*(3), 232–234. doi:10.1177/0956797611427920.

Radford, B. (2005). Voice of reason: Exorcisms, fictional and fatal. *Skeptical Inquirer.* Retrieved August 1, 2005, from http://www.csicop.org/specialarticles/exorcist-rituals.html.

Radvansky, G. A. (1999). Aging, memory, and comprehension. *Current Directions in Psychological Science, 8,* 49–53.

Raffaelli, M., & Crockett, L. J. (2003). Sexual risk taking in adolescence: The role of self-regulation and attraction to risk. *Developmental Psychology, 39,* 1036–1046.

Raggatt, P. T. (1991). Work stress among long-distance coach drivers: A survey and correlational study. *Journal of Organizational Behavior, 12,* 565–579.

Ragusea, A. S. (2012). The more things change, the more they stay the same: Ethical issues in the provision of tele-health. In S. J. Knapp, M. C. Gottlieb, M. M. Handelsman, & L. D. VandeCreek (Eds.), *APA Handbook of Ethics in Psychology, Vol 2: Practice, Teaching, and Research* (pp. 183–196). Washington, DC: American Psychological Association.

Rai, T., & Fiske, A. (2011). Moral psychology is relationship regulation: Moral motives for unity, hierarchy, equality, and proportionality. *Psychological Review, 118*(1), 57–75. doi:10.1037/a0021867.

Raikes, H., Pan, B. A., Luze, G., Tamis-LeMonda, C. S., Brooks-Gunn, J., Constantine, J., et al. (2006). Mother-child bookreading in low-income families: Correlates and outcomes during the first three years of life. *Child Development, 77,* 924–953. doi:10.1080/10683169808401752.

Raine, A., Moffitt, T. E., Caspi, A., Loeber, R., Stouthamer-Loeber, M., & Lynam, D. (2005). Neurocognitive impairments in boys on the life-course persistent antisocial path. *Journal of Abnormal Psychology, 114,* 38–49.

Raineteau, O. (2008). Plastic responses to spinal cord injury. *Behavioural Brain Research, 192,* 114–123.

Rains, G. C., Utley, S. L., & Lewis, W. J. (2006). Behavioral monitoring of trained insects for chemical detection. *Biotechnology Progress, 22,* 2–8.

Raisig, S., Welke, T., Hagendorf, H., & van der Meer, E. (2010). I spy with my little eye: Detection of temporal violations in event sequences and the pupillary response. *International Journal of Psychophysiology, 76,* 1–8.

Rajaram, S., & Barber, S. J. (2008). Retrieval processes in memory. In H. L. Roediger, III (Ed.), *Cognitive psychology of memory.* Oxford: Elsevier.

Rajaratnam, S. M. W., Barger, L. K., Lockley, S. W., Shea, S. A., Wang, W., Landrigan, C. P., O'Brien, C. S., Qadri, S., Sullivan, J. P., Cade, B. E., Epstein, L. J., White, D. P., Czeisler, C. A., for the Harvard Work Hours, Health and Safety Group. (2011). Sleep disorders, health, and safety in police officers. *JAMA, 306*(23), 2567–2578.

Ramachandran, V. S. (1988, August). Perceiving shape from shading. *Scientific American,* 76–83.

Ramachandran, V. S. (2008). *The man with the phantom twin: Adventures in the neuroscience of the human brain.* New York: Dutton.

Ramey, C. T. (1992). High-risk children and IQ: Altering intergenerational patterns. *Intelligence, 16,* 239–256.

Ramar, K., & Olson, E. J. (2013). Management of common sleep disorders. *American Family Physician, 88*(4), 231–238.

Ramirez, S., Liu, X., Lin, P.-A., Suh, J., Pignatelli, M., Redondo, R. L., Ryan, T. J., & Tonegawa, S. (2013). Creating a false memory in the hippocampus. *Science, 341*(6144), 387–391.

Ramo, D. E., Liu, H., & Prochaska, J. J. (2014). A mixed-methods study of young adults' receptivity to using Facebook for smoking cessation: If you build it, will they come? *American Journal of Health Promotion.* Epub February 27, 2014.

Randolph-Seng, B., & Mather, R. D. (2009). Does subliminal persuasion work? It depends on your motivation and awareness. *Skeptical Inquirer, 33,* 49–53.

Ranganath, C. (2010). Binding items and contexts: The cognitive neuroscience of episodic memory. *Current Directions in Psychological Science, 19*(3), 131–137. doi:10.1177/0963721410366805.

Rankin, C. H., Abrams, T., Barry, R. J., Bhatnagar, S., Clayton, D. F., Colombo, J., Coppola, G., Geyer, M. A., Glanzman, D. L., Marsland, S., McSweeney, F. K., Wilson, D. A., Wu, C. F., & Thompson, R. F. (2009). Habituation revisited: An updated and revised description of the behavioral characteristics of habituation. *Neurobiology of Learning and Memory, 92*(2),135–138.

Rapee, R., Kennedy, S., Ingram, M., Edwards, S., & Sweeney, L. (2005). Prevention and early intervention of anxiety disorders in inhibited preschool children. *Journal of Consulting and Clinical Psychology, 73,* 488–497.

Rapoport, J. L., Addington, A. M., & Frangou, S. (2005). The neurodevelopmental model of schizophrenia: Update 2005. *Molecular Psychiatry, 10,* 434–449.

Raskin, N. J., & Rogers, C. R. (2001). Person-centered therapy. In R. J. Corsini & D. Wedding (Eds.), *Current psychotherapies* (6th ed.). Itasca, IL: Peacock.

Raskin, N. J., & Rogers, C. R. (2005). Person-centered therapy. In R. J. Corsini & D. Wedding (Eds.), *Current psychotherapies* (7th ed., pp. 130–165). Belmont, CA: Thomson Brooks/Cole.

Rasmussen, H., Erritzoe, D., Andersen, R., Ebdrup, B. H., et al. (2010). Decreased frontal serotonin 2A receptor binding in antipsychotic-naive patients with first-episode schizophrenia. *Archives of General Psychiatry, 67,* 9–16.

Ratcliff, R., & McKoon, G. (1989). Memory models, text processing, and cue-dependent retrieval. In H. L. Roediger & F. I. M. Craik (Eds.), *Varieties of memory and consciousness.* Hillsdale, NJ: Erlbaum.

Rathbone, D. B., & Huckabee, J. C. (1999). *Controlling road rage: A literature review and pilot study.* Washington, DC: American Automobile Association.

Rattan, A., Good, C., & Dweck, C. S. (2012). "It's ok—Not everyone can be good at math": Instructors with an entity theory comfort (and demotivate) students. *Journal of Experimental Social Psychology, 48*(3), 731–737. doi:10.1016/ j.jesp.2011.12.012.

Rattenborg, N., Lima, S. L., & Amlaner, C. J. (1999). Half-awake to the risk of predation. *Nature, 397,* 397–398.

Raudenbush, B., & Meyer, B. (2002). Effect of nasal dilators on pleasantness, intensity and sampling behaviors of foods in the oral cavity. *Rhinology, 39,* 80–83.

Raudino, A., Woodward, L. J., Fergusson, D. M., Horwood, L. J. (2012). Childhood conduct problems are associated with increased partnership and parenting difficulties in adulthood. *Journal of abnormal child psychology, 40 (2),* 251–63 PubMed: 21904828.

Rawson, K. A., & Dunlosky, J. (2011). Optimizing schedules of retrieval practice for durable and efficient learning: How much is enough? *Journal of Experimental Psychology: General, 140*(3), 283–302. doi:10.1037/a0023956.

Rawson, P. (2006). *Handbook of short-term psychodynamic psychotherapy.* London: Karnac Books.

Ray, L. A.; Miranda, R., Jr.; Tidey, J. W.; McGeary, J. E.; et al. (2010). Polymorphisms of the m-opioid receptor and dopamine D4 receptor genes and subjective responses to alcohol in the natural environment. *Journal of Abnormal Psychology, 119,* 115–125.

Read, S. J., Monroe, B. M., Brownstein, A. L., Yang, Y., et al. (2010). A neural network model of the structure and dynamics of human personality. *Psychological Review, 117,* 61–92.

Reas, D. L., & Grilo, C. M. (2014). Current and emerging drug treatments for binge eating disorder. *Expert Opinion on Emerging Drugs.* Epub January 25, 2014.

Reber, A. S. (1992). The cognitive unconscious: An evolutionary perspective. *Consciousness and Cognition: An International Journal, 1*(2), 93–133.

Redd, M., & de Castro, J. M. (1992). Social facilitation of eating: Effects of social instruction on food intake. *Physiology and Behavior, 52,* 749–754.

Reder, L. M., & Ritter, F. E. (1992). What determines initial feeling of knowing? Familiarity with question terms, not the answer. *Journal of Experimental Psychology: Learning, Memory, and Cognition, 18,* 435–451.

Reed, R. R. (2004). After the holy grail: Establishing a molecular basis for mammalian olfaction. *Cell, 116,* 329–336.

Reed, S. K. (2000). *Cognition* (5th ed.). Belmont, CA: Wadsworth.

Reedy, M. N. (1983). Personality and aging. In D. S. Woodruff & J. E. Birren (Eds.), *Aging: Scientific perspectives and social issues* (2nd ed.). Monterey, CA: Brooks/Cole.

Reeve, C. L., & Bonaccio, S. (2008). Does test anxiety induce measurement bias in cognitive ability tests? *Intelligence, 36,* 526–538.

Reeve, J. (2009). Why teachers adopt a controlling motivating style toward students and how they can become more autonomy supportive. *Educational Psychologist, 44,* 159–175.

Reeve, J. M. (1996). *Understanding motivation and emotion.* New York: Harcourt, Brace, Jovanovich.

Reeves, M. J., & Rafferty, A. P. (2005). Healthy lifestyle characteristics among adults in the United States, 2000. *Archives of Internal Medicine, 165,* 854–857.

Regier, D. A., Narrow, W. E., Clarke, D. E., Kraemer, H. C., Kuramoto, S. J., Kuhl, E. A., & Kupfer, D. J. (2013). *DSM-5* field trials in the United States and Canada, Part II: Test-retest reliability of selected categorical diagnoses. *American Journal of Psychiatry, 170,* 59–70.

Rehm, L. P., & DeMers, S. T. (2006). Licensure. *Clinical Psychology: Science and Practice, 13,* 249–253.

Reich, D. A. (2004). What you expect is not always what you get: The roles of extremity, optimism, and pessimism in the behavioral confirmation process. *Journal of Experimental Social Psychology, 40,* 199–215.

Reich, S. M., Subrahmanyam, K., & Espinoza, G. (2012). Friending, IMing, and hanging out face-to-face: Overlap in adolescents' online and offline social networks. *Developmental Psychology, 48*(2), 356–368. doi:10.1037/a0026980.

Reicher, S.D., Haslam, S.A., & Smith, J.R. (2012). Working toward the experimenter: Reconceptualizing obedience within the Milgram paradigm as identification-based followership. *Perspectives in Psychological Science, 7,* 315–324.

Reid, A. G., Lingford-Hughes, A. R., Cancela, L., & Kalivas, P. W. (2012). Substance abuse disorders. In T. E. Schlaepfer & C. B. Nemeroff (Eds.), *Neurobiology of psychiatric disorders* (pp. 419–431). Amsterdam, Netherlands: Elsevier Science Publishers.

Reimann, M., & Zimbardo, P. G. (2011). The dark side of social encounters: Prospects for a neuroscience of human evil. *Journal of Neuroscience, Psychology, and Economics, 4*(3), 174–180.

Reimer, B., Mehler, B. Coughlin, J. F., Roy, N., & Dusek, J. A. (2010). The impact of a naturalistic hands-free cellular phone task on heart rate and simulated driving performance in two age groups. *Transportation Research Part F: Traffic Psychology and Behaviour, 14*(1), 13–25. doi:10.1016/j.trf.2010.09.002.

Reingold, E. M., Charness, N., Pomplun, M., & Stampe, D. M. (2001). Visual span in expert chess players: Evidence from eye movements. *Psychological Science, 12,* 48–55.

Reinisch, J. M., Ziemba-Davis, M., & Sanders, S. A. (1991). Hormonal contributions to sexually dimorphic behavioral development in humans. *Psychoneuroendocrinology, 16,* 213–278.

Reinoso-Suárez, F., de Andrés, I., & Garzón, M. (2011). Functional anatomy of the sleep-wakefulness cycle: wakefulness. *Advances in Anatomy, Embryology, and Cell Biology, 208,* 1–128.

Reis, B. F., & Brown, L. G. (2006). Preventing therapy dropout in the real world: The clinical utility of videotape preparation and client estimate of treatment duration. *Professional Psychology: Research and Practice, 37,* 311–316.

Reis, H. T., Maniaci, M. R., Caprariello, P. A., Eastwick, P. W, & Finkel, E. J (2011). Familiarity does indeed promote attraction in live interaction. *Journal of Personality and Social Psychology, 101,* 557–570.

Reisenzein, R. (1983). The Schachter theory of emotion: Two decades later. *Psychological Bulletin, 94,* 239–264.

Reiss, A. J., & Roth, J. A. (1993). *Understanding and preventing violence.* Washington, DC: National Academy Press.

Reiss, D., & Marino, L. (2001). Mirror self-recognition in the bottlenose dolphin: A case of cognitive convergence. *Proceedings of the National Academy of Sciences, 98,* 5937–5942.

Reiss, D., Neiderhiser, J. M., Hetherington, E. M., & Plomin, R. (2000). *The relationship code: Deciphering genetic and social influences on adolescent development.* Cambridge, MA: Harvard University Press.

Reitz, C., Tang, M., Schupf, N., Manly, J., Mayeux, R., & Luchsinger, J. (2010). A summary risk score for the prediction of Alzheimer disease in elderly persons. *Archives of Neurology, 67*(7), 835–841.

Remick, A. K., Polivy, J., & Pliner, P. (2009). Internal and external moderators of the effect of variety on food intake. *Psychological Bulletin, 135,* 434–451.

Remulla, A. & Guilleminault, C. (2004). Somnabulism (sleepwalking). *Expert Opinion in Pharmacotherapy, 5,* 2069–2074.

Ren, H., Bolino, M. C., Shaffer, M. A., & Kraimer, M. L. (2013). The influence of job demands and resources on repatriate career satisfaction: A relative deprivation perspective. *Journal of World Business, 48*(1), 149–159.

Ren, J., Li, H., Palaniyappan, L., Liu, H., Wang, J., Li, C., & Rossini, P. M. (2014). Repetitive transcranial magnetic stimulation versus electroconvulsive therapy for major depression: A systematic review and meta-analysis. *Progress in Neuro-Pyschopharmacology and Biological Psychiatry, 51C,* 181–189.

Ren, T. (2002). Longitudinal pattern of basilar membrane vibration in the sensitive cochlea. *Proceedings of the National Academy of Sciences, 99,* 17101–17106.

Rennels, J. L., & Cummings, A. J. (2013). Sex differences in facial scanning: Similarities and dissimilarities between infants and adults. *International Journal of Behavioral Development, 37*(2), 111–117.

Renner, K. H., & Beversdorf, D. Q. (2010). Effects of naturalistic stressors on cognitive flexibility and working memory task performance. *Neurocase, 16,* 293–300. doi:10.1080/13554790903463601

Rentfrow, P. J. (2010). Statewide differences in personality: Toward a psychological geography of the United States. *American Psychologist, 65*(6), 548–558. doi:10.1037/a0018194.

Rescorla, L. A. (1981). Category development in early language. *Journal of Child Language, 8,* 225–238.

Rescorla, R. A. (1968). Probability of shock in the presence and absence of CS in fear conditioning. *Journal of Comparative and Physiological Psychology, 66,* 1–5.

Rescorla, R. A. (1988). Pavlovian conditioning: It's not what you think it is. *American Psychologist, 43,* 151–159.

Rescorla, R. A. (2004). Spontaneous recovery varies inversely with the training-extinction interval. *Learning and Behavior, 32,* 401–408.

Rescorla, R. A. (2005). Spontaneous recovery of excitation but not inhibition. *Journal of Experimental Psychology: Animal Behavior Processes, 31,* 277–288.

Rescorla, R. A., & Wagner, A. R. (1972). A theory of Pavlovian conditioning: Variations in the effectiveness of reinforcement and nonreinforcement. In A. H. Black & W. F. Prokasy (Eds.), *Classical conditioning II.* New York: Appleton Century Crofts.

Reuter, J., Raedler, T., Rose, M., Hand, I., Glascher, J., & Buchel, C. (2005). Pathological gambling is linked to reduced activation of the mesolimbic reward system. *Nature Neuroscience, 8,* 147–148.

Reuter, T. (2011). Fifty years of dark adaptation 1961–2011. *Vision Research, 51*(21–22), 2243–2262.

Revelle, W. (2008). The contribution of Reinforcement Sensitivity Theory to personality theory. In P. J. Corr (Ed)., *The reinforcement sensitivity theory of personality* (pp. 508–527). Cambridge, UK: Cambridge Press.

Reyes-Escogido, L, Gonzalez-Mondragon, E. G., and Vazquez-Tzompantzi, E. (2011). Chemical and pharmacological aspects of capsaicin. *Molecules, 16*(2), 1253–1270.

Reyna, V. F., & Farley, F. (2006). Risk and rationality in adolescent decision making: Implications for theory, practice, and public policy. *Psychological Science in the Public Interest, 7,* 1–44.

Reynolds, C. A., Finkel, D., McArdle, J. J., Gatz, M., Berg, S., & Pederson, N. L. (2005). Quantitative genetic analysis of latent growth curve models of cognitive abilities in adulthood. *Developmental Psychology, 41,* 3–16.

Reynolds, J. S., & Perrin, N. A. (2004). Mismatches in social support and psychosocial adjustment to breast cancer. *Health Psychology, 23,* 425–430.

Reynolds, M. R. (2013). Interpreting the g loadings of intelligence test composite scores in light of Spearman's law of diminishing returns. *School Psychology Quarterly, 28*(1), 63–76.

Rhodes, R. E., Warburton, D. R., & Bredin, S. D. (2009). Predicting the effect of interactive video bikes on exercise adherence: An efficacy trial. *Psychology, Health & Medicine, 14*(6), 631–640. doi:10.1080/13548500903281088.

Riccio, D. C., Millin, P. M., & Gisquet-Verrier, P. (2003). Retrograde amnesia: Forgetting back. *Current Directions in Psychological Science, 12,* 41–44.

Rice, G., Anderson, C., Risch, H., & Ebers, G. (1999). Male homosexuality: Absence of linkage to microsatellite markers at Xq28. *Science, 284,* 665–667.

Rice, W. R., Friberg, U., & Gavrilets, S. (2012). Homosexuality as a consequence of epigenetically canalzed sexual development. *The Quarterly Review of Biology, 87*(4), 343–386.

Richards, D. (2013). Improving outcomes-changing behaviours. *Evidence-Based Dentistry, 14,* 98.

Richards, D. A., & Schat, A. H. (2011). Attachment at (not to) work: Applying attachment theory to explain individual behavior in organizations. *Journal Of Applied Psychology, 96*(1), 169–182. doi:10.1037/a0020372.

Richards, H. J., Benson, V., Donnelly, N., & Hadwin, J. A. (2014). Exploring the function of selective attention and hypervigilance for threat in anxiety. *Clinical Psychology Review, 34*(1), 1–13.

Richards, J. M., & Gross, J. J. (2000). Emotion regulation and memory: The cognitive costs of keeping one's cool. *Journal of Personality and Social Psychology, 79,* 410–424.

Richards, M., Shipley, B., Fuhrer, R., & Wadsworth, M. E. J. (2004). Cognitive ability in childhood and cognitive decline in mid-life: Longitudinal birth cohort study. *British Medical Journal, 328,* 552.

Richards, P. S., & Bergin, A. E. (Eds.). (2000). *Handbook of psychotherapy and religious diversity* (pp. 105–129). Washington, DC: American Psychological Association Press.

Richardson, G. A., Goldschmidt, L., & Larkby, C. (2007). Effects of prenatal cocaine exposure on growth: A longitudinal analysis. *Pediatrics, 120,* e1017–e1027.

Richardson, M., Abraham, C., & Bond, R. (2012). Psychological correlates of university students' academic performance: A systematic review and meta- analysis. *Psychological Bulletin, 138,* 253–387. doi:10.1037/a0026838.

Richardson, R., & Hayne, R. (2007). You can't take it with you: The translation of memory across development. *Current Directions in Psychological Science, 16,* 223–227.

Richardson-Klavehn, A., & Bjork, R. A. (1988). Measures of memory. *Annual Review of Psychology, 39,* 475–543.

Rickels, K., & Rynn, M. (2002). Pharmocotherapy of generalized anxiety disorder. *Journal of Clinical Psychiatry, 63*(Suppl. 14), 9–16.

Ridaura, V. K., Faith, J. J., Rey, F. E., Cheng, J., Duncan, A. E., Kau, A. L., et al. (2013). Gut microbiota from twins discordant for obesity modulate metabolism in mice. *Science, 341*(6150), 1241214.

Riddoch, M. J., Humphreys, G. W., Akhtar, N. A., Allen, H., Bracewell, R. M., & Schofield, A. J. (2008). A tale of two agnosias: Distinctions between form and integrative agnosia. *Cognitive Neuropsychology, 25*(1), 56–92.

Ridley, M. (2000). *Genome: The autobiography of a species in 23 chapters.* New York: HarperCollins.

Rieber, R. W. (2006). *The bifurcation of self: The history and theory of dissociation and its disorders.* New York: Springer.

Rieger, D., Frischlich, L., Wulf, T., Bente, G., & Kneer, J. (2014). Eating ghosts: The underlying mechanisms of mood repair via interactive and noninteractive media. *Psychology of Popular Media Culture.* Epub March 17, 2014.

Riem, M. E., Bakermans-Kranenburg, M. J., Huffmeijer, R., & van IJzendoorn, M. H. (2013). Does intranasal oxytocin promote prosocial behavior to an excluded fellow player? A randomized-controlled trial with cyberball. *Psychoneuroendocrinology, 38*(8), 1418–1425.

Rietschel, M., & Treutlein, J. (2013). The genetics of alcohol dependence. *Annals of the New York Academy of Science, 1282,* 39–70.

Riggio, R. E. (1989). *Introduction to industrial/organizational psychology.* Glenview, IL: Scott, Foresman.

Rihmer, Z. (2001). Can better recognition and treatment of depression reduce suicide rates? A brief review. *European Psychiatry, 16,* 406–409.

Rind, B., Tromovitch, P., & Bauserman, R. (1998). A meta-analytic examination of assumed properties of child sexual abuse using college samples. *Psychological Bulletin, 124,* 22–53.

Rindermann, H., & Ceci, S. J. (2009). Educational policy and country outcomes in international cognitive competence studies. *Perspectives on Psychological Science, 4,* 551–577.

Rinn, W. E. (1984). The neuropsychology of facial expressions: A review of the neurological and psychological mechanisms for producing facial expressions. *Psychological Bulletin, 95,* 52–77.

Rios, R., & Zautra, A. J. (2011). Socioeconomic disparities in pain: The role of economic hardship and daily financial worry. *Health Psychology, 30,* 58–66. doi:10.1037/a0022025.

Rissman, J., Greely, H. T., & Wagner, A. D. (2010). Detecting individual memories through the neural decoding of memory states and past experience. *Proceedings of the National Academy of Sciences, 107,* 9849–9854.

Ritter, M. (2007). Experts link teen brains' immaturity, juvenile crime. *USA Today*. Retrieved from: http://www.usatoday.com/tech/science/2007-12-02-teenbrains_N.htm.

Rizzolatti, G., Fadiga, L., Gallese, V., & Fogassi, L. (1996). Premotor cortex and the recognition of motor actions. *Brain Research: Cognitive Brain Research, 3,* 131–141.

Rob, L. (2012, January 6). Retailers beware shoplifters—and employees. *Colorado Springs Business Journal* (CO).

Robakis, T. K., & Hirsch, L. J. (2006). Literature review, case report, and expert discussion of prolonged refractory status epilepticus. *Neurocritical Care, 4*(1), 35–46.

Robbins, R. A., Nishimura, M., Mondloch, C. J., Lewis, T. L., & Maurer, D. (2010). Deficits in sensitivity to spacing after early visual deprivation in humans: A comparison of human faces, monkey faces, and houses. *Developmental Psychobiology, 52*(8), 775–781.

Robbins, S. B., Lauver, K., Le, H., Davis, D., Langley, R., & Carlstrom, A. (2004). Do psychosocial and study skill factors predict college outcomes? A meta-analysis. *Psychological Bulletin, 130,* 261–288.

Roberts, B. W., Helson, R., & Klohnen, E. C. (2002). Personality development and growth in women across 30 years: Three perspectives. *Journal of Personality, 70,* 79–102.

Roberts, B. W., & Mroczek, D. (2008). Personality trait change in adulthood. *Current Directions in Psychological Science, 17,* 31–35.

Roberts, B. W., Smith, J., Jackson, J. J., & Edmonds, G. (2009). Compensatory conscientiousness and health in older couples. *Psychological Science, 20,* 553–559.

Roberts, B. W., Walton, K. E., & Viechtbauer, W. (2006). Patterns of mean-level change in personality traits across the life course: A meta-analysis of longitudinal studies. *Psychological Bulletin, 132,* 1–25.

Roberts, B. W., Wood, D., & Caspi, A. (2008). The development of personality traits in adulthood. In O. P. John, R. W. Robins, & L. A. Pervin (Eds.), *Handbook of personality: Theory and research* (3rd ed., pp. 375–398). New York: Guilford Press.

Roberts, Y. H., Mitchell, M. J., Witman, M., & Taff aro, C. (2010). Mental health symptoms in youth aff ected by Hurricane Katrina. *Professional Psychology: Research and Practice, 41,* 10–18.

Robertson, E. M. (2012). New insights in human memory interference and consolidation. *Current Biology, 22*(2), R66–R71. doi:10.1016/j.cub.2011.11.051.

Robertson, J., & Robertson, J. (1971). Young children in brief separation: A fresh look. *Psychoanalytic Study of the Child, 26,* 264–315.

Robiner, W. N. (2006). The mental health professions: Workforce supply and demand, issues, and challenges. *Clinical Psychology Review, 26,* 600–625.

Robins, L. N., & Regier, D. A. (Eds.). (1991). *Psychiatric disorders in America: The Epidemiologic Catchment Area study.* New York: Free Press.

Robinson-Cimpian, J. P., Lubienski, S. T., Ganley, C. M., & Copur-Gencturk, Y. (2014). Teachers' perceptions of students' mathematics proficiency may exacerbate early gender gaps in achievement. *Developmental Psychology, 50*(4), 1262–1281.

Robinson, N. M., Zigler, E., & Gallagher, J. J. (2000). Two tails of the normal curve: Similarities and differences in the study of mental retardation and giftedness. *American Psychologist, 55,* 1413–1424.

Robinson, T. N., Borzekowski D. L. G., Matheson, D. M., Kraemer, H. C. (2009). Effects of fast food branding on young children's taste preferences. *Archives of Pediatric and Adolescent Medicine, 161*(8), 792–797.

Robles, T. F., Glaser, R., & Kiecolt-Glaser, J. K. (2005). Out of balance: A new look at chronic stress, depression, and immunity. *Current Directions in Psychological Science, 14,* 111–115.

Rock, I. (1978). *An introduction to perception.* New York: Macmillan.

Rock, I. (1983). *The logic of perception.* Cambridge, MA: MIT Press.

Rodenburg, R., Benjamin, A., de Roos, C., Meijer, A. M., & Stams, G. J. (2009). Efficacy of EMDR in children: A meta-analytic review. *Clinical Psychology Review, 29,* 599–606.

Rodriguez, I., Greer, C. A., Mok, M. Y., & Mombaerts, P. (2000). A putative pheromone receptor gene expressed in human olfactory mucosa. *Nature Genetics, 26,* 18–19.

Roe, K. V. (2001). Relationship between male infants' vocal responses to mother and stranger at three months and self-reported academic attainment and adjustment measures in adulthood. *Psychological Reports, 89*(2), 255–258.

Roediger, H. L., Agarwal, P. K., McDaniel, M. A., & McDermott, K. B. (2011). Test-enhanced learning in the classroom: Long-term improvements from quizzing. *Journal of Experimental Psychology: Applied, 17,* 382–395.

Roediger, H. L., & McDermott, K. B. (2000). Tricks of memory. *Current Directions in Psychological Science, 9,* 123–127.

Roediger, H. L., Meade, M. L., & Bergman, E. T. (2001). Social contagion of memory. *Psychonomic Bulletin and Review, 8,* 365–371.

Roediger, H. L., Putnam, A. L., & Smith, M. A. (2011). Ten benefits of testing and their applications to educational practice. In J. Mestre & B. Ross (Eds.), *Psychology of Learning and Motivation: Cognition in Education* (pp. 1–36). Oxford: Elsevier.

Roediger, H. L., Wixted, J. H., & DeSoto, K. A. (2012). The curious complexity between confidence and accuracy in reports from memory. In L. Nadel & W. Sinnott-Armstrong (Eds.), *Memory and Law,* (pp. 84–118). Oxford: Oxford University Press.

Roediger, H. L., III. (1990). Implicit memory: Retention without remembering. *American Psychologist, 45,* 1043–1056.

Roediger, H. L., III, Gallo, D. A., & Geraci, L. (2002). Processing approaches to cognition: The impetus from the levels-of-processing framework. *Memory, 10,* 319–332.

Roediger, H. L., III, Guynn, M. J., & Jones, T. C. (1995). Implicit memory: A tutorial review. In G. d'Ydewalle, P. Eelen, & P. Bertelson (Eds.), *International perspectives on psychological science: Vol. 2. The state of the art* (pp. 67–94). Hove, UK: Erlbaum.

Roediger, H. L., III, Jacoby, D., & McDermott, K. B. (1996). Misinformation effects in recall: Creating false memories through repeated retrieval. *Journal of Memory and Learning, 35,* 300–318.

Roediger, H. L., III, & Karpicke, J. D. (2006). Test-enhanced learning: Taking memory tests improve long-term retention. *Psychological Science, 17,* 249–255.

Roediger, H. L., III, McDaniel, M., & McDermott, K. (2006). Test enhanced learning. *APS Observer, 19,* 28.

Roediger, H. L., III, & McDermott, K. B. (1995). Creating false memories: Remembering words not presented in lists. *Journal of Experimental Psychology: Learning, Memory, and Cognition, 21,* 803–814.

Roenneberg, T., Kuehnle, T., Juda, M., Kantermann, T., Allebrandt, K., Gordijn, M., & Merrow, M. (2007). Epidemiology of the human circadian clock. *Sleep Med Reviews, 11,* 429–438.

Roesch, R., Zapf, P., & Hart. S. (2010). *Forensic psychology and law.* Hoboken, NJ: John Wiley & Sons.

Roets, A., & Hiel, A. V. (2011). Allport's prejudiced personality today: Need for closure as the motivated cognitive basis of prejudice. *Current Directions in Psychological Science, 20*(6), 349–354. doi:10.1177/0963721411424894.

Roffman, J. L., & Gerber, A. J. (2008). Neural models of psychodynamic concepts and treatments: Implications for psychodynamic psychotherapy. In R. A. Levy & J. S. Ablon (Eds.), *Handbook of evidence-based psychodynamic psychotherapy* (pp. 305–339). Totowa, NJ: Humana Press.

Roffwarg, H. P., Muzio, J. N., & Dement, W. C. (1966). Ontogenetic development of the human sleep-dream cycle. *Science, 152,* 604–619.

Rogeberg, O. (2013). Correlations between cannabis use and IQ change in the Dunedin cohort are consistent with confounding from socioeconomic status. *Proceedings of the National Academy of Sciences,* 110(11), 4251–4254.

Rogers, C. E., Anderson, P. J., Thompson, D. K., Kidokoro, H., Wallendorf, M., Treyvaud, K., & Inder, T. E. (2012). Regional cerebral development at term relates to school-age social–emotional development in very preterm children. *Journal of the American Academy of Child & Adolescent Psychiatry, 51*(2), 181–191. doi:10.1016/j.jaac.2011.11.009.

Rogers, C. R. (1951). *Client-centered therapy.* Boston: Houghton Mifflin.

Rogers, C. R. (1961). *On becoming a person.* Boston: Houghton Mifflin.

Rogers, C. R. (1970). *Carl Rogers on encounter groups.* New York: Harper & Row.

Rogers, C. R. (1980). *A way of being.* Boston: Houghton Mifflin.

Rogers, J., Madamba, S. G., Staunton, D. A., & Siggins, G. R. (1986). Ethanol increases single unit activity in the inferior olivary nucleus. *Brain Research, 385,* 253–262.

Rogers, M. R., & Molina, L. E. (2006). Exemplary efforts in psychology to recruit and retain graduate students of color. *American Psychologist, 61,* 143–156.

Rogers, R. (1995). *Diagnostic and structured interviewing: A handbook for psychologists.* Odessa, FL: Psychological Assessment Resources.

Rogoff, B., & Waddell, K. J. (1982). Memory for information organized in a scene by children from two cultures. *Child Development, 53,* 1224–1228.

Rohrer, D., & Pashier, H. (2007). Increasing retention without increasing study time. *Current Directions in Psychological Science, 16,* 183–186.

Roid, G. H. (2003). *Stanford-Binet Intelligence Scale* (5th ed.). Itasca, IL: Riverside.

Roisman, G. I., Newman, D. A., Fraley, R. C., Haltigan, J. D., Groh, A. M., & Haydon, K. C. (2012). Distinguishing differential susceptibility from diathesis-stress: Recommendations for evaluating interaction effects. *Development and Psychopathology, 24,* 389–409.

Rolland, Y., Andrieu, S., Cantet, C., Morley, J. E., et al. (2007). Wandering behavior and Alzheimer disease: The REAL.FR prospective study. *Alzheimer Disease and Associated Disorders, 21,* 31–38.

Rolls, B. J., Rowe, E. A., & Rolls, E. T. (1982). How sensory properties of foods affect human feeding behavior. *Physiology & Behavior, 29*(3), 409–417.

Rolls, E. T. (2006). Brain mechanisms underlying fl avour and appetite. *Philosophical Transactions of the Royal Society of London, B, 361,* 1123–1136.

Rolls, E. T. (1997). Taste and olfactory processing in the brain and its relation to the control of eating. *Critical Review of Neurobiology, 11,* 263–287.

Rolls, E. T. (2009). Functional neuroimaging of umami taste: what makes umami pleasant? *American Journal of Clinical Nutrition, 90*(3), 804S–813S.

Romeo, R. D., Richardson, H. N., & Sisk, C. L. (2002). Puberty and the maturation of the male brain and sexual behavior: Recasting a behavioral potential. *Neuroscience and Biobehavioral Review, 26,* 381–391.

Roney, J. R., & Simmons, Z. L. (2008). Women's estradiol predicts preference for facial cues of men's testosterone. *Hormones & Behavior, 53*(1), 14–19. doi:10.1016/j.yhbeh.2007.09.008.

Ronnestad, M. H., & Ladany, N. (2006). The impact of psychotherapy training: Introduction to the special section. *Psychotherapy Research, 16,* 261–267.

Rooks, C., Veledar, E., Golberg, J., Bremner, J. D., & Vaccarino, V. (2012). Early trauma and inflammation: Role of familial factors in a study of twins. *Psychosomatic Medicine, 74*(2) 146–152. doi:10.1097/PSY.0b013e318240a7d8.

Roorda, A., & Williams, D. R. (1999). The arrangement of the three cone classes in the living human eye. *Nature, 397,* 520–522.

Rooy, D. L. V., Dilchert, S., Viswesvaran, C., & Ones, D. (2006). Multiplying intelligences: Are general, emotional, and practical intelligences equal? In K. R. Murphy (Ed.), *A critique of emotional intelligence: What are the problems and how can they be fixed?* (pp. 235–262). Mahwah, NJ: Erlbaum.

Rosch, E., Mervis, C. B., Gray, W. D., Johnson, D. M., & Boyes-Braem, P. (1976). Basic objects in natural categories. *Cognitive Psychology, 8,* 382–439.

Rose, A. J., & Rudolph, K. D. (2006). A review of sex differences in peer relationship processes: Potential trade-offs for the emotional and behavioral development of girls and boys. *Psychological Bulletin, 132,* 98–131.

Rose, S. A., Feldman, J. F., Jankowski, J. J., & Van Rossem, R. (2012). Information processing from infancy to 11 years: Continuities and prediction of IQ. *Intelligence, 40,* 445–457.

Roseberry, S., Richie, R., Hirsh-Pasek, K., Golinkoff, R., & Shipley, T. F. (2011). Babies catch a break: 7- to 9-month-olds track statistical probabilities in continuous dynamic events. *Psychological Science, 22*(11), 1422–1424. doi:10.1177/0956797611422074.

Rosellini, L. (1998, April 13). When to spank. *U.S. News and World Report,* pp. 52–58.

Rosen, B. C., & D'Andrade, R. (1959). The psychosocial origins of achievement motivation. *Sociometry, 22,* 188–218.

Rosen, M. L., & López, H. H. (2009). Menstrual cycle shifts in attentional bias for courtship language. *Evolution and Human Behavior, 30*(2), 131–140.

Rosen, R. (1991). *The healthy company.* Los Angeles: Tarcher.

Rosen-Reynoso, M., Alegría, M., Chen, C., Laderman, M., & Roberts, R. (2011). The relationship between obesity and psychiatric disorders across ethnic and racial minority groups in the United States. *Eating Behaviors, 12*(1), 1–8. doi:10.1016/j.eatbeh.2010.08.008.

Rosenbaum, M., & Bennett, B. (1986). Homicide and depression. *American Journal of Psychiatry, 143,* 367–370.

Rosenbaum, R. S., Moscovitch, M., Foster, J. K., Schnyer, D. M., Gao, F., Kovacevic, N., Verfaellie, M., Black, S. E., & Levine, B. (2008). Patterns of autobiographical memory loss in medial-temporal lobe amnesic patients. *Journal of Cognitive Neuroscience, 20*(8), 1490–1506.

Rosenfarb, I. S., Bellack, A. S., & Aziz, N. (2006). A sociocultural stress, appraisal, and coping model of subjective burden and family attitudes toward patients with schizophrenia. *Journal of Abnormal Psychology, 115,* 157–165.

Rosenfarb, I. S., Goldstein, M. J., Mintz, J., & Nuechterlein, K. H. (1995). Expressed emotion and subclinical psychopathology observable within the transactions between schizophrenic patients and their family members. *Journal of Abnormal Psychology, 104,* 259–267.

Rosenfeld, J. P. (1995). Alternative views of Bashore and Rapp's (1993) alternatives to traditional polygraphy: A critique. *Psychological Bulletin, 117*(1), 159–166.

Rosenkranz, M. A., Jackson, D. C., Dalton, K. M., Dolski, I., et al. (2003). Affective style and in vivo immune response: Neurobehavioral mechanisms. *Proceedings of the National Academy of Sciences, 100,* 11148–11152.

Rosenstock, I. M. (1974). Historical origins of the health belief model. *Health Education Monographs, 2,* 328–335.

Rosenthal, R. R. (1966). *Experimenter effects in behavioral research.* New York: Appleton-Century-Crofts.

Ross, C. A. (1997). *Dissociative identity disorder: Diagnosis, clinical features, and treatment of multiple personality.* New York: Wiley.

Ross, E. D., & Monnot, M. (2008). Neurology of affective prosody and its functional–anatomic organization in right hemisphere. *Brain & Language, 104*(1), 51–74.

Ross, M., & Wang, Q. (2010). Why we remember and what we remember: Culture and autobiographical memory. *Perspectives On Psychological Science, 5*(4), 401–409. doi:10.1177/1745691610375555.

Ross, S., & Peselow, E. (2009). The neurobiology of addictive disorders. *Clinical Neuropharmacology, 32,* 269–276.

Ross, S. M., & Ross, L. E. (1971). Comparison of trace and delay classical eyelid conditioning as a function of interstimulus interval. *Journal of Experimental Psychology, 91,* 165–167.

Rosso, C., & Samson, Y. (2013). The ischemic penumbra: The location rather than the volume of recovery determines outcome. *Current Opinion in Neurology,* epub November 23, 2013.

Rost, K., Hsieh, Y. P., Xu, S., Menachemi, N., & Young, A. S. (2011). Potential disparities in the management of schizophrenia in the United States. *Psychiatric Services, 62,* 613–618.

Roth, G., Assor, A., Niemiec, C. P., Deci, E. L., & Ryan, R. M. (2009). The emotional and academic consequences of parental conditional regard. *Developmental Psychology, 45,* 1119–1142.

Roth, H. L., Lora, A. N., & Heilman, K. M. (2002). Effects of monocular viewing and eye dominance on spatial attention. *Brain, 125,* 2023–2035.

Roth, P. L., Huffcutt, A. I., & Bobko, P. (2003). Ethnic group differences in measures of job performance: A new meta-analysis. *Journal of Applied Psychology, 88,* 694–706.

Rothbart, M. (2011). *Becoming who we are: Temperament and personality in development.* New York: Guilford Press.

Rothbart, M. K., & Bates, J. E. (2006). Temperament. In W. Damon & R. M. Lerner (Series Eds.) & N. Eisenberg (Vol. Ed.), *Handbook of child psychology: Vol. 3. Social, emotional, and personality development* (6th ed., pp. 99–166). Hoboken, NJ: Wiley.

Rothbaum, B. O. (2006). Virtual reality in the treatment of psychiatric disorders. *CNS Spectrums, 11,* 34.

Rothbaum, B. O., Hodges, L. F., Kooper, R., & Opdyke, D. (1995). Effectiveness of computer-generated virtual reality graded exposure in the treatment of acrophobia. *American Journal of Psychiatry, 152,* 626–628.

Rothbaum, F., Morelli, G., & Rusk, N. (2010). Attachment, learning and coping: The interplay of cultural similarities and differences. In C.Y. Chiu, Y.Y. Hong, & M. Gelfand (Eds.), *Advances in Culture and Psychology,* Vol. 1, pp. 153–215.

Rothbaum, F., Pott, M., Azuma, H., Miyake, K., & Weisz, J. (2000). The development of close relationships in Japan and the United States: Paths of symbiotic harmony and generative tension. *Child Development, 71,* 1121–1142.

Rothman, L. (2013). FYI, parents: Your kids watch a full-time job's worth of TV each week. *Time Magazine.* November 20, 2013.

Rothschild, A. J. (2010). *Evidence-based guide to antipsychotic medications.* Arlington, VA: American Psychiatric Publishing.

Rottenstreich, Y., & Tversky, A. (1997). Unpacking, repacking, and anchoring: Advances in support theory. *Psychological Review, 104,* 406–415.

Rotter, J. B. (1954). *Social learning and clinical psychology.* New York: Prentice Hall.

Rotter, J. B. (1982). The development and application of social learning theory. New York: Praeger.

Rotundo, M., & Sackett, P. R. (2002). The relative importance of task, citizenship, and counterproductive performance to global ratings of job performance: A policy-capturing approach. *Journal of Applied Psychology, 87*(1), 66–80.

Rouach, N., Koulakoff, A., Abudara, V., Willecke, K., & Giaume, C. (2008). Astroglial metabolic networks sustain hippocampal synaptic transmission. *Science, 322*(5907), 1551–1555.

Rouch, I., Wild, P., Ansiau, D., & Marquie, J.-C. (2005). Shiftwork experience, age, and cognitive performance. *Ergonomics, 48,* 1282–1293.

Rouéché, B. (1986, December 8). Cinnabar. *New Yorker.*

Rouse, S. V. (2007). Using reliability generalization methods to explore measurement error: An illustration using the MMPI2 PSY-5 Scales. *Journal of Personality Assessment, 88,* 264–275.

Roussel, P., Elliot, A. J., & Feltman, R. (2011). The influence of achievement goals and social goals on help-seeking from peers in an academic context. *Learning & Instruction, 21*(3), 394–402. doi:10.1016/j.learninstruc.2010.05.003.

Roussotte, F. F., Sulik, K. K., Mattson, S. N., Riley, E. P., Jones, K. L., Adnams, C. M., & . . . Sowell, E. R. (2012). Regional brain volume reductions relate to facial dysmorphology and neurocognitive function in fetal alcohol spectrum disorders. *Human Brain Mapping, 33*(4), 920–937. doi:10.1002/hbm.21260.

Rovee-Collier, C., & Cuevas, K. (2009). The development of infant memory. In M. L. Courage & N. Cowan (Eds.), *The development of memory in infancy and childhood* (pp 11–41). New York: Psychology Press.

Rovee-Collier, C. (1999). The development of infant memory. *Current Directions in Psychological Science, 8,* 80–85.

Rowe, D. C. (2005). Under the skin: On the impartial treatment of genetic and environmental hypotheses of racial differences. *American Psychologist, 60,* 60–70.

Rowe, D. C., Jacobson, K. C., & Van den Oord, E. J. C. G. (1999). Genetic and environmental influences on vocabulary IQ: Parental education level as moderator. *Child Development, 70,* 1151–1162.

Rowe, M. L., & Goldin-Meadow, S. (2009). Differences in early gesture explain SES disparities in child vocabulary size at school entry. *Science, 323,* 951–953.

Roy, B., Diez-Roux, A. V., Seeman, T., Ranjit, N., et al. (2010). Association of optimism and pessimism with inflammation and hemostasis in the multiethnic study of atherosclerosis (MESA). *Psychosomatic Medicine, 72,* 134–140.

Roy, M., Piche, M., Chen, J.-I., Peretz, I., & Rainville, P. (2009). Cerebral and spinal modulation of pain by emotions. *Proceedings of the National Academy of Sciences, 106,* 20900–20905.

Rozin, P. (1982). "Taste-smell confusions" and the duality of the olfactory sense. *Perception and Psychophysics, 31,* 397–401.

Rozin, P. (2007). Food and eating. In S. Kitayama & D. Cohen (Eds.), *Handbook of cultural psychology* (pp. 391–416). New York, NY: Guilford Press.

Ruan, Y., Zheng, X. Y., Zhang, H. L., Zhu, W., & Zhu, J. (2012). Olfactory dysfunctions in neurodegenerative disorders. *Journal of Neuroscience Research, 90*(9), 1693–1700.

Rubens, A. B., & Benson, D. F. (1971). Associative visual agnosia. *Archives of Neurology, 24,* 304–316.

Rubenwolf, B., & Spörrle, M. (2011). Intuitive decisions: the influence of phonetic and letter frequency recognition heuristics on brand selection decisions. *Neuropsychoeconomics Conference Proceedings*, 43.

Rubin, E. (1915). *Synsoplevede figure*. Copenhagen: Gyldendalske.

Rubin, K. H., Bukowski, W., & Parker, J. G. (2006). Peer interactions, relationships, and groups. In W. Damon & R. M. Lerner (Series Eds.) & N. Eisenberg (Vol. Ed.), *Handbook of child psychology: Vol. 3. Social, emotional, and personality development* (6th ed.). New York: Wiley.

Rubin, M. (2011). Social affiliation cues prime help-seeking intentions. *Canadian Journal Of Behavioural Science/Revue Canadienne Des Sciences Du Comportement, 43*(2), 138–141. doi:10.1037/a0022246.

Rubin, M., Paolini, S., & Crisp, R. J. (2010). A processing fluency explanation of bias against migrants. *Journal Of Experimental Social Psychology, 46*(1), 21–28. doi:10.1016/j.jesp.2009.09.006.

Rubinstein, S., & Caballero, B. (2000). Is Miss America an undernourished role model? *Journal of the American Medical Association, 283,* 1569.

Ruble, D. N., Martin, C. L., & Berenbaum, S. A. (2006). Gender development. In W. Damon & R. M. Lerner (Series Eds.) & N. Eisenberg (Vol. Ed.), *Handbook of child psychology: Vol. 3. Social, emotional, and personality development* (6th ed., pp. 858–932). New York: Wiley.

Ruby, M. B., Falk, C. F., Heine, S. J., Villa, C., & Silberstein, O. (2012). Not all collectivisms are equal: Opposing preferences for ideal affect between East Asians and Mexicans. *Emotion, 12,* 1206–1209.

Rucker, D. D., Dubois, D., & Galinsky, A. D. (2011). Generous paupers and stingy princes: Power drives consumer spending on self versus others. *Journal of Consumer Research, 37,* doi:10.1086/657162.

Rudman, L. A., Greenwald, A. G., Mellott, D. S., & Schwartz, J. L. K. (1999). Measuring the automatic components of prejudice: Flexibility and generality of the Implicit Association Test. *Social Cognition, 17,* 437–465.

Rudolph, A. E., Jones, K. C., Latkin, C., Crawford, N. D., & Fuller, C. M. (2011). The association between parental risk behaviors during childhood and having high risk networks in adulthood. *Drug & Alcohol Dependence, 118*(2/3), 437–443. doi:10.1016/j.drugalcdep.2011.05.003

Rudolph, K. D., Lambert, S. F., Clark, A. G., & Kurlakowsky, K. D. (2001). Negotiating the transition to middle school: The role of self-regulatory processes. *Child Development, 72,* 929–946.

Rudoy, J. D., Voss, J. L., Westerberg, C. E., & Paller, K. A. (2009). Strengthening individual memories by reactivating them during sleep. *Science, 326*(5956), 1079.

Rueckert, L., Baboorian, D., Stavropoulos, K., & Yasutake, C. (1999). Individual differences in callosal efficiency: Correlation with attention. *Brain and Cognition, 41,* 390–410.

Ruhé, H. G., Huyser, J., Swinkels, J. A., & Schene, A. H. (2006). Switching antidepressants after a first selective serotonin reuptake inhibitor in major depressive disorder: A systematic review. *Journal of Clinical Psychiatry, 67*(12), 1836–1855.

Ruitenberg, M. J., & Vukovic, J. (2008). Promoting central nervous system regeneration: Lessons from cranial nerve I. *Restorative Neurology and Neuroscience, 26,* 183–196.

Rule, N., Rosen, K., Slepian, M., & Ambady, N. (2011). Mating interest improves women's accuracy in judging male sexual orientation. *Psychological Science, 22*(7), 881–886.

Rule, N. O., Moran, J. M., Freeman, J. B., Whitfield-Gabrieli, S., Gabrieli, J. E., & Ambady, N. (2011). Face value: Amygdala response reflects the validity of first impressions. *Neuroimage, 54*(1), 734–741.

Rumbaugh, D. M. (Ed.). (1977). *Language learning by a chimpanzee: The Lana project.* New York: Academic Press.

Rumelhart, D. E., & McClelland, J. L. (1986). *Parallel distributed processing: Explorations in the microstructure of cognition: Vol. 1. Foundations.* Cambridge, MA: Bradford.

Runtti, H., Mattila, J., vcan Gils, M., Koikkalainen, J., Soininen, H., & Lötjönen, J. (20143). Quantitative evaluation of disease progression in a longitudinal mild cognitive impairment cohort. *Journal of Alzheimers Disease, 39* (1), 49–61.

Runyan, D. K., Shankar, V., Hassan, F., Hunter, W. M., Jain, D., Paula, C. S., Bangdiwala, S. I., Ramiro, L. S., Munoz, S. R., Vizcarra, B., en Psic, L., & Bordin, I. A. (2010). International variations in harsh child discipline. *Pediatrics, 126*(3), e701–e711. doi:10.1542/peds.2008-2374.

Ruscio, J. (2005). Exploring controversies in the art and science of polygraph testing. *Skeptical Inquirer, 29,* 34–39.

Rushton, J. P., & Jensen, A. R. (2005). Thirty years of research on race differences in cognitive ability. *Psychology, Public Policy, and Law, 11*(2), 235–294. doi:10.1037/1076-8971.11.2.235.

Russell, J. A. (1991). Culture and the categorization of emotions. *Psychological Bulletin, 110,* 426–450.

Russell, J. A. (1994). Is there universal recognition of emotion from facial expression? A review of the cross-cultural studies. *Psychological Bulletin, 155*(2), 102–141.

Russell, J. A. (1995). Facial expressions of emotion: What lies beyond minimal universality? *Psychological Bulletin, 118,* 379–391.

Russell, M. C., Silver, S. M., Rogers, S., & Darnell, J. N. (2007). Responding to an identified need: A joint Department of Defense/Department of Veterans Affairs training program in eye movement desensitization and reprocessing (EMDR) for clinicians providing trauma services. *International Journal of Stress Management, 14*(1), 61–71.

Russo, P., Cesario, A., Rutella, S., Veronesi, G., Spaggiari, L., Galetta, D., Margaritora, S., Granone, P., & Greenberg, D. S. (2011). Impact of genetic variability in nicotinic acetylcholine receptors on nicotine addiction and smoking cessation treatment. *Current Medicinal Chemistry, 18*(1), 91–112.

Rusyniak, D. E. (2011). Neurologic manifestations of chronic methamphetamine abuse. *Neurologic Clinics, 29*(3), 641–655.

Rutkowski, G. K., Gruder, C. L., & Romer, D. (1983). Group cohesiveness, social norms, and bystander intervention. *Journal of Personality and Social Psychology, 44,* 545–552.

Rutkowski, L., Vasterling, J. J., Proctor, S. P., & Anderson, C. J. (2010). Posttraumatic stress disorder and standardized test-taking ability. *Journal Of Educational Psychology, 102*(1), 223–233. doi:10.1037/a0017287.

Rutland, A., Killen, M., & Abrams, D. (2010). A new social-cognitive developmental perspective on prejudice. *Perspectives on Psychological Science, 5,* 279–291.

Rutledge, T., Reis, S. E., Olson, M., Owens, J., Kelsey, S. F., Pepine, C. J., et al. (2004). Social networks are associated with lower mortality rates among women with suspected coronary disease: The National Heart, Lung, and Blood Institute-Sponsored Women's Ischemia Syndrome Evaluation study. *Psychosomatic Medicine, 66,* 882–888.

Rutter, M. (2003). Commentary: Causal processes leading to antisocial behavior. *Developmental Psychology, 39,* 372–378.

Rutter, M. (2006). The promotion of resilience in the face of adversity. In A. Clarke-Stewart & J. Dunn (Eds.), *Families count: Effects on child and adolescent development* (pp. 26–52). New York: Cambridge University Press.

Rutter, M. (2007). Proceeding from observed correlation to causal inference: The use of natural experiments. *Perspectives on Psychological Science, 2,* 377–395.

Rutter, M., O'Connor, T. G., & ERA Study Team. (2004). Are there biological programming effects for psychological development? Findings from a study of Romanian adoptees. *Developmental Psychology, 40,* 81–94.

Ryan, C. S., Casas, J. F., Kelly-Vance, L., Ryalls, B. O., & Nero, C. (2010). Parent involvement and views of school success: The role of parents' Latino and White American cultural orientations. *Psychology in the Schools, 47*(4), 391–405.

Ryan, R., & Hout, M. (2011). Gateway transitions in rural Irish youth: Implications for culturally appropriate and targeted drug prevention. *Journal of Alcohol and Drug Education, 55*(1), 7–14.

Ryan, R. H., & Geiselman, R. E. (1991). Effects of biased information on the relationship between eyewitness confidence and accuracy. *Bulletin of the Psychonomic Society, 29,* 7–9.

Ryan, R. M. (1993). Agency and organization: Intrinsic motivation, autonomy, and the self in psychological development. In J. E. Jacobs (Ed.), *Nebraska symposium on motivation: Developmental perspectives on motivation* (Vol. 40, pp. 1–56). Lincoln: University of Nebraska Press.

Ryan, R. M., & Deci, E. L. (2000). Self-determination theory and the facilitation of intrinsic motivation, social development, and well-being. *American Psychologist, 55,* 68–78.

Rybakowski, J. K. (2014). Response to lithium in bipolar disorder: clinical and genetic findings. *ACS Chemical Neuroscience*, Epub March 14, 2014.

Ryckman, R. A. (2013). *Theories of personality* (10th ed.). Belmont, CA: Cengage Learning.

Ryder, A. G., Yang, J., Zhu, X., Yao, S., Yi, J., Heine, S. J., & Bagby, R. M. (2008). The cultural shaping of depression: Somatic symptoms in China, psychological symptoms in North America? *Journal of Abnormal Psychology, 117,* 300–313.

Rymer, R. (1993). *Genie: A scientific tragedy.* New York: HarperCollins.

Rynders, J., & Horrobin, J. (1980). Educational provisions for young children with Down's syndrome. In J. Gottlieb (Ed.), *Educating mentally retarded persons in the mainstream* (pp. 109–147). Baltimore: University Park Press.

Rynes, S. L., Gerhart, B., & Parks, L. (2005). Performance evaluation and pay for performance. *Annual Review of Psychology, 56,* 571–600.

Rypma, B., & Prabhakaran, V. (2009). When less is more and when more is more: The mediating roles of capacity and speed in brain-behavior efficiency. *Intelligence, 37,* 207–222.

Saarni, C. (2006). Emotion regulation and personality development in childhood. In D. K. Mroczek & T. D. Little (Eds.), *Handbook of personality development* (pp. 245–262). Mahwah, NJ: Erlbaum.

Sabbagh, M. A., Xu, F., Carlson, S. M., Moses, L. J., & Lee, K. (2006). The development of executive functioning and theory of mind: A comparison of Chinese and U.S. preschoolers. *Psychological Science, 17,* 74–81.

Sabin, J. A., Nosek, B. A., Greenwald, A. G., & Rivara, F. P. (2009). Physicians' implicit and explicit attitudes about race by MD race, ethnicity, and gender. *Journal of Healthcare for the Poor and Underserved, 20,* 896–913.

Sachs, J. (1967). Recognition memory for syntactic and semantic aspects of connected discourse. *Perception and Psychophysics, 2,* 437–442.

Sackett, P. R., Borneman, M. J., & Connelly, B. S. (2008). High stakes testing in higher education and employment: Appraising the evidence for validity and fairness. *American Psychologist, 63,* 215–227.

Sackett, P. R., Kuncel, N. R., Arneson, J. J., Cooper, S. R., & Waters, S. D. (2009). Does socio-economic status explain the relationship between admissions tests and post-secondary academic performance? *Psychological Bulletin, 135,* 1–22.

Sackett, P. R., & Lievens, F. (2008). Personnel selection. *Annual Review of Psychology, 59,* 419–450.

Sackett, P. R., & Schmitt, N. (2012). On reconciling conflicting meta-analytic findings regarding integrity test validity. *Journal of Applied Psychology, 97,* 550–556.

Sackett, P. R., Schmitt, N., Ellington, J. E., & Kabin, M. B. (2001). High-stakes testing in employment, credentialing, and higher education: Prospects in a post-affirmative action world. *American Psychologist, 56,* 302–318.

Sacks, D. W., Stevenson, B., & Wolfers, J. (2012). The new stylized facts about income and subjective well-being. *Emotion, 12*(6), 1181–1187.

Sacks, O. (1985). *The man who mistook his wife for a hat.* New York: Summit Books.

Sacks, O. (1992, July 27). The landscape of his dreams. *New Yorker.*

Sacks, O. (2002, October 7). The case of Anna H. *New Yorker,* pp. 62–73.

Sacks, O. (2007). *Musicophilia: A tale of music and the brain.* New York: Knopf.

Sadeh, A. (2005). Cognitive-behavioral treatment for childhood sleep disorders. *Clinical Psychology Review, 25*(5), 612–628.

Sadler, L. S., Swartz, M. K., Ryan-Krause, P., Seitz, V., Meadows-Oliver, M., Grey, M., & Clemmens, D. A. (2007). Promising outcomes in teen mothers enrolled in a school-based parent support program and child care center. *Journal of School Health, 77*(3), 121–130.

Safir, M. P., & Wallach, H. S., & Bar-Zvi, M. (2012). Virtual reality cognitive-behavior therapy for public speaking anxiety: One-year follow-up. *Behavior Modification, 36,* 235–246.

Saffran, J. R., Senghas, A., & Trueswell, J. C. (2001). The acquisition of language by children. *Proceedings of the National Academy of Sciences, 98,* 12874–12875.

Safran, J. D. (2012). *Psychoanalysis and psychoanalytic therapies.* Washington, D.C.: American Psychological Association.

Safren, S. A., Gershuny, B. S., Marzol, P., Otto, M. W., Pollack, M. H. (2002). History of childhood abuse in panic disorder, social phobia, and generalized anxiety disorder. *Journal of Nervous and Mental Disease, 190,* 453–456.

Sagaspe, P., Taillard, J., Bayon, V., Lagarde, E., Moore, N., Boussuge, J., Chaumet, G., Bioulac, B., & Philip, P. (2010). Sleepiness, near-misses and driving accidents among a representative population of French drivers. *Journal of Sleep Research, 19*(4):578–584.

Saguy, A. (2013). *What's wrong with fat?* Cambridge, MA: Oxford University Press.

Sahebzamani, F. M., D'Aoust, R. F., Friedrich, D., Aiyer, A. N., Reis, S. E., & Kip, K. E. (2013). Relationship among low cholesterol levels, depressive symptoms, aggression, hostility, and cynicism. *Journal of Clinical Lipidology, 7*(3), 208–216.

Saiz, P. A., Garcia-Portilla, M. P., Arango, C., Morales, B., Bascaran, M., et al. (2008). Association study between obsessive-compulsive disorder and serotonegic candidate genes. *Progress in Neuro-Psychopharmacology and Biological Psychiatry, 32,* 765–770.

Sakuma, M., Endo, T., & Muto, T. (2000). The development of self-understanding in preschoolers and elementary school children: Analysis of self-descriptions and self-evaluations. *Japanese Journal of Developmental Psychology, 11,* 176–187.

Salas, C. R., Minakata, K., & Kelemen, W. L. (2011). Walking before study enhances free recall but not judgement-of-learning magnitude. *Journal Of Cognitive Psychology, 23*(4), 507–513. doi:10.1080/20445911.2011.532207.

Salas, E., Tannenbaum, S. I., Kraiger, K., & Smith-Jentsch, K. A. (2012). The science of training and development in organizations: What matters in practice. *Psychological Science in the Public Interest, 13,* 74–101. doi:10.1177/1529100612436661.

Salgado-Delgado, R., Tapia Osorio, A., Saderi, N., & Escobar, C. (2011). Disruption of circadian rhythms: A crucial factor in the etiology of depression. *Depression Research and Treatment,* Epub August 8, 2011.

Salgado-Pineda, P. P., Fakra, E. E., Delaveau, P. P., McKenna, P. J., Pomarol-Clotet, E. E., & Blin, O. O. (2011). Correlated structural and functional brain abnormalities in the default mode network in schizophrenia patients. *Schizophrenia Research, 125* (2–3), 101–109. doi:10.1016/j.schres.2010.10.027

Salin-Pascual, R., Gerashchenko, D., Greco, M., Blanco-Centurion, C., & Shiromani, P. J. (2001). Hypothalamic regulation of sleep. *Neuropsychopharmacology, 25*(Suppl. 5), S21.

Salisbury, A. L., Ponder, K. L., Padbury, J. F., & Lester, B. M. (2009). Fetal effects of psychoactive drugs. *Clinical Perinatology, 36,* 595–619.

Salo, R., Ravizza, S., & Fassbender, C. (2011). Overlapping cognitive patterns in schizophrenia and methamphetamine dependence. *Cognitive and Behavioral Neurology,* November 25, 2011 [Epub ahead of print]

Salokangas, R. K. R. (2004). Gender and the use of neuroleptics in schizophrenia. *Schizophrenia Research, 66,* 41–49.

Salovey, P., & Grewal, D. (2005). The science of emotional intelligence. *Current Directions in Psychological Science, 14,* 281–285.

Salthouse, T. A. (2000). Aging and measures of processing speed. *Biological Psychology, 54,* 35–54.

Salvatore, J. E., Kuo, S., Steele, R. D., Simpson, J. A., & Collins, W. (2011). Recovering from conflict in romantic relationships: A developmental perspective. *Psychological Science, 22*(3), 376–383. doi:10.1177/0956797610397055.

Sambunaris, A., & Hyde, T. M. (1994). Stroke-related aphasias mistaken for psychotic speech: Two case reports. *Journal of Geriatric Psychiatry and Neurology, 7*(3), 144–147.

Samuelson, C. D., & Messick, D. M. (1995). When do people want to change the rules for allocating shared resources? In D. Schroeder (Ed.), *Social dilemmas: Perspectives on individuals and groups* (pp. 143–162). Westport, CT: Praeger.

Sanderson, C. A. (2010). *Social psychology.* Hoboken, NJ: Wiley

Sanderson, W. C., Rapee, R. M., & Barlow, D. H. (1989). The influence of an illusion of control on panic attacks induced via inhalation of 5.5% carbon dioxide-enriched air. *Archives of General Psychiatry, 46,* 157–162.

Sandin, S., Lichtenstein, P., Kuja-Halkola, R., Larsson,H., Hultman, C. M., & Reichenberg, & A. (2014). The familial risk of autism. *JAMA, 311*(17), 1770–1777.

Sandman, C. A., Davis, E. P., Buss, C., & Glynn, L. M. (2011). Prenatal programming of human neurological function. *International Journal of Peptides,* 1–9. doi:10.1155/2011/837596.

Sandman, C. A., Davis, E. P., Buss, C., & Glynn, L. M. (2012). Exposure to prenatal psychobiological stress exerts programming influences on the mother and her fetus. *Neuroendocrinology, 95*(1), 8–21. doi:10.1159/000327017.

Sandrini, M., & Cohen, L. G. (2013). Noninvasic brain stimulation in neurorehabilitation. *Handbook of Clinical Neurology, 116,* 499–524.

Sanjuán, P., & Magallares, A. (2013). Coping strategies as mediating variables between self-serving attributional bias and subjective well-being. *Journal of Happiness Studies,* Online journal accessed March 15, 2014.

Saper, C. B., Chou, T. C., & Scammell, T. E. (2001). The sleep switch: Hypothalamic control of sleep and wakefulness. *Trends in Neurosciences, 24,* 726–731.

Saper, C. B., & Scammell, T. E. (2013). Emerging therapeutics in sleep. *Annals of Neurology, 74*(3), 435–440.

Sara, M., & Pistoia, F. (2009). Defining consciousness: Lessons from patients and modern techniques. *Journal of Neurotrauma, 27,* 771–773.

Sarason, B. R., Sarason, I. G., & Gurung, R. A. R. (1997). Close personal relationships and health outcomes: A key to the role of social support. In S. Duck (Ed.), *Handbook of personal relationships* (pp. 547–573). New York: Wiley.

Sarason, I. G., Johnson, J., & Siegel, J. (1978). Assessing impact of life changes: Development of the life experiences survey. *Journal of Clinical and Consulting Psychology, 46,* 932–946.

Sarin, S., Abela, J. R. Z., & Auerbach, R. P. (2005). The response styles theory of depression: A test of specificity and causal mediation. *Cognition and Emotion, 19,* 751–761.

Sarkar, S., & Schmued, L. (2010). Neurotoxicity of ecstasy (MDMA): An overview. *Current Pharmaceutical Biotechnology, 11*(5), 460–469.

Sarrett, J. C. (2011). Trapped children: Popular images of children with autism in the 1960s and 2000s. *Journal of Medical Humanities, 32*(2), 141–153. doi:10.1007/s10912-010-9135-z.

Sattler, C., Erickson, K. I., Toro, P., & Schröder, J. (2011). Physical fitness as a protective factor for cognitive impairment in a prospective population-based study in Germany. *Journal of Alzheimer's Disease, 26*(4), 709–718.

Sattler, D. N., Kaiser, C. F., & Hittner, J. B. (2000). Disaster preparedness: Relationships among prior experience, personal characteristics, and distress. *Journal of Applied Social Psychology, 30,* 1396–1420.

Saucier, G., Akers, L. G., Shen-Miller, S., Knežević, G., & Stankov, L. (2009). Patterns of thinking in militant extremism. *Perspectives on Psychological Science, 4,* 256–271.

Saurat, M.-T., Agbakou, M., Attigui, P., Golmard, J.-L., & Arnulf, I. (2011). Walking dreams in congenital and acquired paraplegia. *Consciousness and Cognition, 20,* 1425–1432.

Savage, J. (2014). The association between attachment, parental bonds and physically aggressive and violent behavior: A comprehensive review. *Aggression & Violent Behavior.* Epub February 22, 2014.

Savage, J., & Yancey, C. (2008). The effects of media violence exposure on criminal aggression: A meta-analysis. *Criminal Justice and Behavior, 35,* 772–791.

Savage-Rumbaugh, E. S. (1990). Language acquisition in a nonhuman species: Implications for the innateness debate. *Developmental Psychology, 23,* 599–620.

Savage-Rumbaugh, E. S., & Brakke, K. E. (1996). Animal language: Methodological and interpretive issues. In M. Bekoff & D. Jamieson (Eds.), *Readings in animal cognition* (pp. 269–288). Cambridge, MA: MIT Press.

Savage-Rumbaugh, E. S., Murphy, J., Sevcik, R. A., Brakke, K. E., et al. (1993). Language comprehension in ape and child. *Monographs of the Society for Research in Child Development, 58,* 1–222.

Savage-Rumbaugh, E. S., Shanker, S. G., & Taylor, T. J. (2001). *Apes, language, and the human mind.* New York: Oxford University Press.

Saveliev, S. V., Lebedev, V. V., Evgeniev, M. B., & Korochkin, L. I. (1997). Chimeric brain: Theoretical and clinical aspects. *International Journal of Developmental Biology, 41,* 801–808.

Savic, I., & Arver, S. (2011). Sex dimorphism of the brain in male-to-female transsexuals. *Cerebral Cortex (New York, N.Y.: 1991), 21*(11), 2525–2533.

Saville, B. K., Zinn, T. E., Neef, N. A., Van Norman, R., & Ferreri, S. J. (2006). A comparison of interteaching and lecture in the college classroom. *Journal of Applied Behavior Analysis, 39,* 49–61.

Savin-Williams, R. C. (2006). Who's gay? Does it matter? *Current Directions in Psychological Science, 15,* 40–44.

Savin-Williams, R. C., & Demo, D. H. (1984). Developmental change and stability in adolescent self-concept. *Developmental Psychology, 20,* 1100–1110.

Savitz, J. B., Price, J. L., & Drevets, W. C. (2014). Neuropathological and neuromorphometric abnormalities in bipolar disorder: View from the medial prefrontal cortical network. *Neuroscience and Biobehavioral Reviews, 42C,* 132–147.

Saxe, G. B. (2004). Practices of quantification from a sociocultural perspective. In K. A. Demetriou & A. Raftopoulos (Eds.), *Developmental change: Theories, models, and measurement* (pp. 241–263). New York: Cambridge University Press.

Saxe, R., Tzelnic, R., & Carey, S. (2007). Knowing who dunnit: Infants identify causal agent in an unseen causal interaction. *Developmental Psychology, 43,* 149–158.

Sayal, K., Heron, J., Golding, J., Alati, R., Smith, G. D., Gray, R., & Emond, A. (2009). Binge pattern of alcohol consumption during pregnancy and childhood mental health outcomes: Longitudinal population-based study. *Pediatrics, 123,* e289–e296.

Sbarra, D. A., Law, R. W., & Portley, R. M. (2011). Divorce and death: A meta-analysis and research agenda for clinical, social, and health psychology. *Perspectives on Psychological Science, 6*(5) 454–474. doi:10.1177/1745691611414724.

Sbarra, D. A., Smith, H. L., & Mehl, M. R. (2012). When leaving your ex, love yourself: Observational ratings of self-compassion predict the course of emotional recovery following marital separation. *Psychological Science, 23,* 261–269. doi:10.1177/0956797611429466.

Scandura, T. A., & Lankau, M. J. (1997). Relationships of gender, family responsibility and flexible work hours to organizational commitment and job satisfaction. *Journal of Organizational Behavior, 18,* 377–391.

Scandura, T. A., & Schriesheim, C. A. (1994). Leader-member exchange and supervisor career mentoring as complementary constructs in leadership research. *Academy of Management Journal, 37,* 1588–1602.

Scarr, S. (1997). The development of individual differences in intelligence and personality. In H. W. Reese & M. D. Franzen (Eds.), *Biological and neuropsychological mechanisms: Life-span developmental psychology* (pp. 1–22). Hillsdale, NJ: Erlbaum.

Scarr, S. (1998). How do families affect intelligence? Social environmental and behavior genetic prediction. In J. J. McArdle & R. W. Woodcock (Eds.), *Human cognitive abilities in theory and practice* (pp. 113–136). Mahwah, NJ: Erlbaum.

Scarr, S., & Carter-Saltzman, L. (1982). Genetics and intelligence. In R. Sternberg (Ed.), *Handbook of human intelligence* (pp. 792–896). Cambridge, UK: Cambridge University Press.

Scarr, S., & Weinberg, R. A. (1976). IQ test performance of black children adopted by white families. *American Psychologist, 31,* 726–739.

Schabracq, M. J. (2003). Organizational culture, stress, and change. In M. J. Schabracq, J. A. M. Winnubst, & C. L. Cooper (Eds.), *Handbook of work and health psychology* (pp.37–62). West Sussex, UK: Wiley.

Schacter, D. L. (2012). Constructive memory: Past and future. *Dialogues in Clinical Neuroscience, 14*(1), 7–18.

Schacter, D. L., Cooper, L. A., Delaney, S. M., Peterson, M. A., & Tharan, M. (1991). Implicit memory for possible and impossible objects: Constraints on the construction of structural descriptions. *Journal of Experimental Psychology: Learning, Memory, and Cognition, 17,* 3–19.

Schacter, D. L., Wagner, A. D., & Buckner, R. L. (2000). Memory systems of 1999. In E. Tulving & F. I. M. Craik (Eds.), *The Oxford handbook of memory* (pp. 627–643). New York: Oxford University Press.

Schachter, S., & Singer, J. (1962). Cognitive, social and physiological determinants of emotional state. *Psychological Review, 69,* 379–399.

Schaefer, J., Sykes, R., Rowley, R., & Baek, S. (1988, November). *Slow country music and drinking.* Paper presented at the 87th annual meeting of the American Anthropological Association, Phoenix, AZ.

Schaefer, M., Heinze, H. J., & Rotte, M. (2008). My third arm: Shifts in topography of the somatosensory homunculus predict feeling of an artificial supernumerary arm. *Human Brain Mapping, 6,* 6.

Schaie, K. W., & Willis, S. L. (in press). The Seattle Longitudinal Study of Adult Cognitive Development. *Bulletin of the International Society for the Study of Behavioral Development.*

Schalkwijk, S., Undurraga, J., Tondo, L., & Baldessarini, R. J. (2014). Declining efficacy in controlled trials of antidepressants: Effects of placebo dropout. *International Journal of Neuropsychopharmacology,* Epub March 13, 2014.

Schalock, R. L., Borthwick-Duff y, S. A., Buntinx, W. H. E., Coulter, D. L., & Craig, E. M. (2009). *Intellectual disability: Definition, classification, and systems of supports* (11th ed.). Washington, DC: American Association of Intellectual and Developmental Disability.

Schanche, E., Stiles, T. C., McCullough, L., Svartberg, M., & Nielsen, G. (2011). The relationship between activating affects, inhibitory affects, and self-compassion in patients with Cluster C personality disorders. *Psychotherapy, 48*(3), 293–303. doi:10.1037/a0022012.

Schapiro, A. C., & McClelland, J. L. (2009). A connectionist model of a continuous developmental transition in the balance scale task. *Cognition, 110,* 395–411.

Schatzberg, A. F., Cole, J. O., & DeBattista, C. (2007). *Manual of clinical psychopharmacology* (6th ed.). Arlington, VA: American Psychiatric Publishing.

Schaubroeck, J., Jones, J. R., & Xie, J. J. (2001). Individual differences in utilizing control to cope with job demands: Effects on susceptibility to infectious disease. *Journal of Applied Psychology, 86,* 265–278.

Scheerer, M., Rothmann, R., & Goldstein, K. (1945). A case of "idiot savant": An experimental study of personality organization. *Psychology Monograph, 58*(4), 1–63.

Scheibert, J., Leurent, S., Prevost, A., & Debrégeas, G. (2009). The role of fingerprints in the coding of tactile information probed with a biomimetic sensor. *Science, 323,* 1503–1506.

Scheier, M. F., Matthews, K. A., Owens, J. F., Magovern, G. J., Lefebvre, R. C., Abbott, R. A., et al. (1989). Dispositional optimism and recovery from coronary artery bypass surgery: The beneficial effects on physical and psychological well-being. *Journal of Personality and Social Psychology, 57,* 1024–1040.

Scheier, M. F., Matthews, K. A., Owens, J. F., Schulz, R., Bridges, M. W., Magovern, G. J., et al. (1999). Optimism and rehospitalization after coronary artery bypass graft surgery. *Archives of Internal Medicine, 159,* 829–835.

Schell, T. L., Martino, S. C., Ellickson, P. L., Collins, R. L., & McCaffrey, D. (2005). Measuring developmental changes in alcohol expectancies. *Psychology of Addictive Behaviors, 19,* 217–220.

Schellenberg, E. (2005). Music and cognitive abilities. *Current Directions in Psychological Science, 14*(6), 317–320. doi:10.1111/j.0963-7214.2005.00389.x.

Schellenberg, E. (2006). Long-term positive associations between music lessons and IQ. *Journal of Educational Psychology, 98*(2), 457–468. doi:10.1037/ 0022-0663.98.2.457.

Schellenberg, E. (2011). Music lessons, emotional intelligence, and IQ. *Music Perception, 29*(2), 185–194. doi:10.1525/MP.2011.29.2.185.

Schenck, C. H., & Mahowald, M. W. (1992). Motor dyscontrol in narcolepsy: Rapid eye movement (REM) sleep without atonia and REM sleep behavior disorder. *Annals of Neurology, 32*(1), 3–10.

Schenk, S., Gittings, D., & Colussi-Mas, J. (2011). Dopaminergic mechanisms of reinstatement of MDMA-seeking behaviour in rats. *British Journal of Pharmacology, 162*(8), 1770–1780.

Schiffman, S. S., Graham, B. G., Sattely-Miller, E. A., & Warwick, Z. (1999). Orosensory perception of dietary fat. *Current Directions in Psychological Science, 7*, 137–143.

Schiller, D., Monfils, M.-H., Raio, C. M., Johnson, D. C., et al. (2010). Blocking the return of fear in humans using reconsolidation update mechanisms. *Nature, 463*, 49–53.

Schiltz, K. K., Witzel, J. G., & Bogerts, B. B. (2011). Neurobiological and clinical aspects of violent offenders. *Minerva Psichiatrica, 52*(4), 187–203.

Schindler, S., Reinhard, M., & Stahlberg, D. (2013). Tit for tat in the face of death: The effect of mortality salience on reciprocal behavior. *Journal of Experimental Social Psychology, 49*(1), 87–92.

Schirmer, A., Teh, K., Wang, S., Vijayakumar, R., Ching, A., Nithianantham, D., & .. Cheok, A. (2011). Squeeze me, but don't tease me: Human and mechanical touch enhance visual attention and emotion discrimination. *Social Neuroscience, 6*(3), 219–230. doi:10.1080/17470919.2010.507958.

Schlaepfer, T. E., & Nemeroff, C. B. (2012). *Neurobiology of psychiatric disorders.* Amsterdam, Netherlands: Elsevier Science Publishers.

Schleicher, D. J., Watt, J. D., & Greguras, G. J. (2004). Reexamining the job satisfaction–performance relationship: The complexity of attitudes. *Journal of Applied Psychology, 89*, 165–177.

Schlicht, E., Shimojo, S., Camerer, C., Battaglia, P., & Nakayama, K. (2010). Human wagering behavior depends on opponents' faces. *Plos One, 5*(7), e11663.

Schlueter, N. N., Ganss, C. C., Pötschke, S. S., Klimek, J. J., & Hannig, C. C. (2012). Enzyme activities in the oral fluids of patients suffering from bulimia: A controlled clinical trial. *Caries Research, 46*(2), 130–139. doi:10.1159/000337105.

Schmader, T. (2010). Stereotype threat deconstructed. *Current Directions in Psychological Science, 19*(1), 14–18. doi:10.1177/0963721409359292.

Schmeichel, B. J., Gailliot, M. T., Filardo, E., McGregor, I., et al. (2009). Terror management theory and self-esteem revisited: The roles of implicit and explicit self-esteem in mortality salience effects. *Journal of Personality and Social Psychology, 96*, 1077–1087.

Schmidt, F. L. (2011). A theory of sex differences in technical aptitude and some supporting evidence. *Perspectives on Psychological Science, 6*(6), 560–573. doi:10.1177/1745691611419670.

Schmidt, F. L., & Hunter, J. E. (2004). General mental ability in the world of work: Occupational attainment and job performance. *Journal of Personality and Social Psychology, 86*, 162–173.

Schmidt, M. F. H., & Tomasello, M. (2012). Young children enforce social norms. *Current Directions in Psychological Science, 21*, 232–236. doi: 10.1177/0963721412448659.

Schmidtke, A., & Hafner, H. (1988). The Werther effect after television films: New evidence for an old hypothesis. *Psychological Medicine, 18*, 665–676.

Schmitt, D. P. (2005). Sociosexuality from argentina to zimbabwe: A 48-nation study of sex, culture, and strategies of human mating. *Behavioral and Brain Sciences, 28*(2), 247–311.

Schmitz, R., Dehon, H., & Peigneux, P. (2013). Lateralized processing of false memories and pseudoneglect in aging. *Cortex, 49*, 1314–1324.

Schnall, S., & Laird, J. D. (2003). Keep smiling: Enduring effects of facial expressions and postures on emotional experience and memory. *Cognition & Emotion, 17*, 787–797.

Schnee, M. E., Lawton, D. M., Furness, D. N., Benke, T. A., & Ricci, A. J. (2005). Auditory hair cell-afferent fiber synapses are specialized to operate at their best frequencies. *Neuron, 47*, 243–254.

Schneider, B. (1985). Organizational behavior. *Annual Review of Psychology, 36*, 573–611.

Schneider, E. B., Sur, S., Raymount, V., Duckworth, J., Kowalski, R. G., Efron, D. T., & Hui, X. et al. (2014). Functional recovery after moderate/severe traumatic brain injury: A role for cognitive reserve? *Neurology, 82*(18), 1636–1642.

Schneider, K. J., & Längle, A. (2012). The renewal of humanism in psychotherapy: A roundtable discussion. *Psychotherapy, 49*(4), 427–429.

Schneider, L. S. (2013). Alzheimer disease pharmacologic treatment and treatment research. *Continuum, 19*(2), 339–357.

Schneider, T. R., Ring, C., & Katkin, E. S. (1998). A test of the validity of the method of constant stimuli as an index of heartbeat detection. *Psychophysiology, 35*, 86–89.

Schneiderman, N. (2004). Psychosocial, behavioral, and biological aspects of chronic diseases. *Current Directions in Psychological Science, 13*, 247–251.

Schofield, H.-L., Bierman, K. L., Heinrichs, B., & Nix, R. L. (2008). Predicting early sexual activity with behavior problems exhibited at school entry and in early adolescence. *Journal of Abnormal Child Psychology, 36*(8), 1175–1188.

Schott, B. H., Henson, R. N., Richardson-Klavehn, A., Becker, C., Thoma, V., Heinze, H. J., & Duzel, E. (2005). Redefining implicit and explicit memory: The functional neuroanatomy of priming, remembering, and control of retrieval. *Proceedings of the National Academy of Sciences, 102*, 1257–1262.

Schredl, M. (2010). Characteristics and contents of dreams. *International Review of Neurobiology, 92*, 135–154.

Schredl, M. & Reinhard, I. (2011). Gender differences in nightmare frequency: A meta-analysis. *Sleep Medicine Reviews, 15*(2), 115–121.

Schreiber, G. B., Robins, M., Striegel-Moore, R., Obarzanek, E., Morrison, J. A., & Wright, D. J. (1996). Weight modification efforts reported by black and white preadolescent girls: National Heart, Lung, and Blood Institute Growth and Health Study. *Pediatrics, 98*, 63–70.

Schroeder, D. A., Penner, L. A., Dovidio, J. F., & Piliavin, J. A. (1995). *The psychology of helping and altruism: Problems and puzzles.* New York: McGraw-Hill.

Schueller, S. M., Muñoz, R. F., & Mohr, D. C. (2013). Realizing the potential of behavioral intervention technologies. *Current Directions in Psychological Science, 22*(6), 478–483.

Schulden, J., Chen, J., Kresnow, M., Arias, I., Crosby, A., Mercy, J., et al. (2006). Psychological responses to the sniper attacks: Washington DC area, October, 2002. *American Journal of Preventive Medicine, 31*, 324–327.

Schultheiss, O. C. (2013). The hormonal correlates of implicit motives. *Social and Personality Psychology Compass, 7*, 52–65.

Schultz, D., & Schultz, S. (2013). *Theories of personality* (10th ed.). Belmont, CA: Cengage Learning.

Schultz, D. P., & Schultz, S. E. (2000). *A history of modern psychology* (7th ed.). Fort Worth, TX: Harcourt Brace.

Schultz, D. P., & Schultz, S. E. (2004). *A history of modern psychology* (8th ed.). Fort Worth, TX: Harcourt Brace.

Schultz, D. P., & Schultz, S. E. (2009). *Theories of personality* (9th ed.). Florence, KY: Cengage Learning.

Schultz, P. W., Nolan, J. M., Cialdini, R. B., Goldstein, N. J., & Griskevicius, V. (2007). The constructive, destructive, and reconstructive power of social norms. *Psychological Science, 18*, 429–434.

Schulz, R. (1978). *The psychology of death, dying, and bereavement.* Reading, MA: Addison-Wesley.

Schulz, R., Beach, S. R., Lind, B., Martire, L. M., Zdaniuk, B., Hirsch, C., et al. (2001). Involvement in caregiving and adjustment to death of a spouse: Findings from the caregiver health effects study. *Journal of the American Medical Association, 285*, 3123–3129.

Schulz-Hardt, S., Frey, D., Luthgens, C., & Moscovici, S. (2000). Biased information search in group decision making. *Journal of Personality and Social Psychology, 78*, 665–669.

Schuman-Olivier, Z., Vago, D. R., Ott, U., & Hopfer, C. (2011). Club drug, prescription drug, and over-the-counter medication abuse: Description, diagnosis, and intervention. In Kaminer, Y. & Winters, K. C. (Eds.), *Clinical manual of adolescent substance abuse treatment.* Arlington, VA, US: American Psychiatric Publishing, Inc.

Schumann, A., Meyer, C., Rumpf, H. J., Hannover, W., Hapke, U., & John, U. (2005). Stage of change transitions and processes of change, decisional balance, and self-efficacy in smokers: A transtheoretical model validation using longitudinal data. *Psychology of Addictive Behaviors, 19*, 3–9.

Schutte, N. S., & Malouff, J. M. (2014). A meta-analytic review of the effects of mindfulness meditation on telomerase activity. *Psychoneuroendocrinology.* ePub January 7, 2014.

Schwabe, L., Nader, K., & Pruessner, J. C. (2014). Reconsolidation of human memory: Brain mechanisms and clinical relevance. *Biological Psychiatry,* Epub March 15, 2014.

Schwabe, L., & Wolf, O. T. (2011). Stress increases behavioral resistance to extinction. *Psychoneuroendocrinology, 36*(9), 1287–1293. doi:10.1016/j.psyneuen.2011.02.002.

Schwartz, A., & Bugental, D. B. (2004). *Infant habituation to repeated stress as an interactive function of child temperament and maternal depression.* Unpublished manuscript.

Schwartz, B. L., & Metcalfe, J. (2011). Tip-of-the-tongue (TOT) states: Retrieval, behavior, and experience. *Memory & Cognition, 39*(5), 737–749.

Schwartz, J. (2004, September 5). Always on the job, employees pay with health. *New York Times,* p. 1.

Schwartz, R. C., & Feisthamel, K. P. (2009). Disproportionate diagnosis of mental disorders among African American versus European American clients: Implications for counseling theory, research, and practice. *Journal of Counseling and Development, 87*, 295–301.

Schwarz, N., & Scheuring, B. (1992). Frequency reports of psychosomatic symptoms: What respondents learn from response alternatives. *Zeutschrift fur Klinische Psychologie, 22,* 197–208.

Schwenck, C., Bjorklund, D. F., & Schneider, W. (2009). Developmental and individual diff erences in young children's use and maintenance of a selective memory strategy. *Developmental Psychology, 45,* 1034–1050.

Schwender, D., Klasing, D., Daunderer, M., Maddler, C., Poppel, E., & Peter, K. (1995). Awareness during general anesthetic: Definition, incidence, clinical relevance, causes, avoidance, and medicolegal aspects. *Anaesthetist, 44,* 743–754.

Schyns, B. (2006). Are group consensus in leader-member exchange (LMX) and shared work values related to organizational outcomes? *Small Group Research, 37,* 20–35.

Scott, K. M., Smith, D. R., & Ellis, P. M. (2010). Prospectively ascertained child maltreatment and its association with DSM-IV mental disorders in young adults. *Archives of General Psychiatry, 67,* 712–719.

Scott, T. F. (2006). The neurological examination. In P. J. Snyder & P. D. Nussbaum (Eds.), *Clinical neuropsychology: A pocket handbook for assessment,* 2nd ed. (pp. 17–33). Washington, DC: American Psychological Association.

Scoville, W. B., & Milner, B. (1957). Loss of recent memory after bilateral hippocampal lesions. *Journal of Neurology, Neurosurgery, and Psychiatry, 20,* 11–21.

Scullin, M. K., & McDaniel, M. A. (2010). Remembering to execute a goal: Sleep on it!. *Psychological Science, 21*(7), 1028–1035. doi:10.1177/0956797610373373.

Seamon, J. G., Punjabi, P. V., & Busch, E. A. (2010). Memorising Milton's Paradise Lost: A study of a septuagenarian exceptional memoriser. *Memory, 18*(5), 498–503. doi:10.1080/09658211003781522.

Seaton, E. K., Yip, T., Morgan-Lopez, A., & Sellers, R. M. (2012). Racial discrimination and racial socialization as predictors of African American adolescents' racial identity development using latent transition analysis. *Developmental Psychology, 48,* 448–458.

Seeley, K. (2006). *Cultural psychotherapy: Working with culture in the clinical encounter.* Northvale, NJ: Aronson.

Seery, M. D. (2011). Resilience: A silver lining to experiencing adverse life events? *Current Directions in Psychological Science, 20,* 390–394.

Segall, M. H., Dasen, P. R., Berry, J. W., & Poortinga, Y. H. (1990). *Human behavior in global perspective: An introduction to cross-cultural psychology.* Elmwood, NY: Pergamon Press.

Segerstrom, S. C., & Sephton, S. E. (2010). Optimistic expectancies and cell-mediated immunity. *Psychological Science, 21,* 448–455.

Segerstrom, S. C., Taylor, S. E., Kemeny, M. E., & Fahey, J. L. (1998). Optimism is associated with mood, coping, and immune change in response to stress. *Journal of Personality and Social Psychology, 74,* 1646–1655.

Seguin, J. R., & Zelazo, P. D. (2005). Executive function in early physical aggression. In R. E. Tremblay, W. W. Hartup, & J. Archer (Eds.), *Developmental origins of aggression* (pp. 307–329). New York: Guilford Press.

Seidler, G. H., & Wagner, F. E. (2006). Comparing the efficacy of EMDR and trauma-focused cognitive-behavioral therapy in the treatment of PTSD: A meta-analytic study. *Psychological Medicine, 36,* 1515–1522.

Selbom, M. & Bagby, M. R. (2010). Detection of overreported psychopathology with the MMPI-2 RF form validity scales. *Psychological Assessment: A Journal of Consulting and Clinical Psychology, 22,* 757–767.

Seligman, M. E. P. (1975). *Helplessness: On depression, development, and death.* San Francisco: Freeman.

Seligman, M. E. P. (1991). *Learned optimism.* New York: Knopf.

Seligman, M. E. P. (1996). Good news for psychotherapy: The *Consumer Reports* study. *Independent Practitioner, 16,* 17–20.

Seligman, M. E. P. (2011). *Flourish: A visionary new understanding of happiness and well-being.* New York: Free Press.

Seligman, M. E. P., Berkowitz, M. W., Catalano, R. F., Damon, W., et al. (2005). The positive perspective on youth development. In D. L. Evans, E. Foa, R. Gur, H. Hendrin, et al. (Eds.), *Treating and preventing adolescent mental health disorders: What we know and what we don't know* (pp. 499–529). New York: Oxford University Press.

Seligman, M. E. P., Castellon, C., Cacciola, J., Shulman, P., Luborsky, L., Ollove, M., & Downing, R. (1988). Explanatory style change during cognitive therapy for unipolar depression. *Journal of Abnormal Psychology, 97,* 13–18.

Seligman, M. E. P., Rashid, T., & Parks, A. C. (2006). Positive psychotherapy. *American Psychologist, 61,* 774–788.

Seligman, M. E. P., & Schulman, P. (1986). Explanatory style as a predictor of productivity and quitting among life insurance agents. *Journal of Personality and Social Psychology, 50,* 832–838.

Seligman, M. E. P., Steen, T. A., Park, N., & Peterson, C. (2005). Positive psychology progress: Empirical validation of interventions. *American Psychologist, 60,* 410–421.

Selle, V., Schalkwijk, S., Vázquez, G. H., & Baldessarini, R. J. (2014). Treatments for acute bipolar depression: Meta-analyses of placebo-controlled, monotherapy trials of anticonvulsants, lithium and antipsychotics. *Pharmacopsychiatry,* Epub February 18, 2014.

Selye, H. (1956). *The stress of life.* New York: McGraw-Hill.

Selye, H. (1975). *Stress without distress.* New York: Signet.

Selye, H. (1976). *The stress of life* (2nd ed.). New York: McGraw-Hill.

Semmler, C., Brewer, N., & Wells, G. L. (2004). Effects of postidentification feedback on eyewitness identification and nonidentification confidence. *Journal of Applied Psychology, 89,* 334–346.

Seo, H., & Lee, D. (2009). Behavioral and neural changes after gains and losses of conditioned reinforcers. *Journal of Neuroscience, 29,* 3627–3641.

Serretti, A., Chiesa, A., Calati, R., Perma, G., Bellodi, L., & De Ronchi, D. (2009). Common genetic, clinical, demographic and psychosocial predictors of response to pharmacotherapy in mood and anxiety disorders. *International Clinical Psychopharmacology, 24,* 1–18.

Servan-Schreiber, D., Schooler, J., Dew, M. A., Carter, C., & Bartone, P. (2006). Eye movement desensitization and reprocessing for posttraumatic stress disorder: A pilot blinded, randomized study of stimulation type. *Psychotherapy and Psychosomatics, 75,* 290–297.

Servan-Schreiber, E., & Anderson, J. R. (1990). Learning artificial grammars with competitive chunking. *Journal of Experimental Psychology: Learning, Memory, and Cognition, 16,* 592–608.

Seto, M. C., Maric, A., & Barbaree, H. E. (2001). The role of pornography in the etiology of sexual aggression. *Aggression and Violent Behavior, 6,* 35–53.

Sevcik, R. A., & Savage-Rumbaugh, E. S. (1994). Language comprehension and use by great apes. *Language and Communication, 14,* 37–58.

Sexton, T. L., Datchi, C., Evans, L., LaFolllette, J., & Wright, L. (2013). The effectiveness of couple and family-based clinical interventions. In M. J. Lambert (Ed.), *Bergin and Garfield's Handbook of Psychotherapy and Behavior Change* (6th ed.) (pp. 587–639). Hoboken, NJ: Wiley.

Shackelford, T. K., Schmitt, D. P., & Buss, D. M. (2005). Universal dimensions of human mate preference. *Personality and Individual Differences, 39,* 447–458.

Shadish, W. R., Cook, T. D., & Campbell, D. T. (2002). *Experimental and quasi-experimental designs for generalized causal inference.* Boston: Houghton Mifflin.

Shadish, W. R., Matt, G. E., Navarro, A. M., & Phillips, G. (2000). The effects of psychological therapies under clinically representative conditions: A meta-analysis. *Psychological Bulletin, 126,* 512–529.

Shaffer, D. R. (1999). *Developmental psychology: Childhood and adolescence.* Pacific Grove, CA: Brooks/Cole.

Shafto, P., Goodman, N. D., & Frank, M. C. (2012). Learning from others: The consequences of psychological reasoning for human learning. *Perspectives on Psychological Science, 7,* 341–351. doi:10.1177/1745691612448481.

Shah, R. (2013). The role of nutrition and diet in Alzheimer disease: A systematic review. *Journal of the American Medical Directors Association, 14*(6), 398–402.

Shahly, V., Berglund, P. A., Coulouvrat, C., Fitzgerald, T., Hajak, G., Roth, T., Shillington, A. C., Stephenson, J. J., Walsh, J. K., & Kessler, R. C. (2012). The associations of insomnia with costly workplace accidents and errors: Results from the America Insomnia Survey. *Archives of General Psychiatry, 69*(10), 1054–1063.

Shalev, A., Ankri, Y., Israeli-Shalev, Y., Peleg, T., Adessky, R., & Freedman, S. (2012). Prevention of posttraumatic stress disorder by early treatment: results from the jerusalem trauma outreach and prevention study. *Archives Of General Psychiatry, 69*(2), 166–176. doi:10.1001/archgenpsychiatry.2011.127.

Shalvi, S., Moran, S., & Ritov, I. (2010). Overcoming initial anchors: The effect of negotiators' dispositional control beliefs., *Negotiation and Conflict Management Research, 3,* 232–248.

Shamah Levy, T., Morales Ruán, C., Amaya Castellanos, C., Salazar Coronel, A., Jiménez Aguilar, A., & Méndez Gómez Humarán, I. (2012). Effectiveness of a diet and physical activity promotion strategy on the prevention of obesity in Mexican school children. *BMC Public Health, 12,* 152.

Shamay-Tsoory, S. G., & Tomer, R. (2005). The neuroanatomical basis of understanding sarcasm and its relationship to social cognition. *Neuropsychology, 19,* 288–300.

Shams, L., Kamitani, Y., & Shimojo, S. (2000). Illusions: What you see is what you hear. *Nature, 408,* 788.

Shanahan, M. J., Hill, P. L., Roberts, B. W., Eccles, J., & Friedman, H. S. (2012). Conscientiousness, health, and aging: The life course of personality model. *Developmental Psychology. Developmental Psychology, 50*(5), 1407–1425.

Shand, M. A. (1982). Sign-based short-term memory coding of American Sign Language and printed English words by congenitally deaf signers. *Cognitive Psychology, 14,* 1–12.

Shankar, A., McMunn, A., Banks, J., & Steptoe, A. (2011). Loneliness, social isolation, and behavioral and biological health indicators in older adults. *Health Psychology: Official Journal of the Division of Health Psychology, American Psychological Association, 30*(4), 377–385.

Shankaran, S., Das, A., Bauer, C. R., Bada, H. S., Lester, B. M., Wright, L. L., & . Poole, W. (2011). Prenatal cocaine exposure and small-for-gestational-age status: Effects on growth at 6 years of age. *Neurotoxicology and Teratology, 33*(5), 575–581. doi:10.1016/j.ntt.2011.04.003.

Shanks, D. R. (1995). *The psychology of associative learning.* New York: Cambridge University Press.

Shapiro, F. (1989a). Efficacy of the eye movement desensitization procedure in the treatment of traumatic memories. *Journal of Traumatic Stress, 2,* 199–223.

Shapiro, F. (1989b). Eye movement desensitization: A new treatment for posttraumatic stress disorder. *Journal of Behavior Therapy and Experimental Psychiatry, 20,* 211–217.

Shapiro, F. (1991). Eye movement desensitization and reprocessing procedure: From EMD to EMD/R—A new treatment model for anxiety and related traumata. *Behavior Therapist, 15,* 133–135.

Shapiro, F. (2001). *Eye movement desensitization and reprocessing: Basic principles, protocols, and procedures* (2nd ed.). New York: Guilford Press.

Shapiro, F., & Forrest, M. S. (2004). *EMDR: The breakthrough therapy for overcoming anxiety, stress, and trauma.* New York: Basic Books.

Shapiro, F. (2005). *EMDR solutions: Pathways to healing.* New York: Norton.

Sharot, T., Shiner, T., Brown, A. C., Fan, J., & Dolan, R. J. (2009). Dopamine enhances expectation of pleasure in humans. *Current Biology, 19*(24), 2077–2080.

Shargorodsky, J., Curhan, S. G., Curhan, G. C., & Eavey, R. (2010). Change in Prevalence of Hearing Loss in US Adolescents. *JAMA: Journal Of The American Medical Association, 304*(7), 772–778.

Shariff, A. F., & Tracy, J. L. (2011). What are emotion expressions for? *Current Directions In Psychological Science, 20*(6), 395–399. doi:10.1177/0963721411424739.

Sharp, T., & Cowen, P. (2011). 5-HT and depression: is the glass half-full? *Current Opinion in Pharmacology, 11*(1), 45–51. doi:10.1016/j.coph.2011.02.003.

Shatzmiller, R. A. (2010, June 17). *Sleep stage scoring introduction/ Historical perspective.* Retrieved from http://emedicine.medscape.com/article/1188142-overview.

Shaw, D. S., Dishion, T. J., Supplee, L., Gardner, F., & Arnds, K. (2006). Randomized trial of a family-centered approach to the prevention of early conduct problems: 2-year effects of the family check-up in early childhood. *Journal of Consulting and Clinical Psychology, 74,* 1–9.

Shechtman, Z. (1992). A group assessment procedure as a predictor of on-the-job performance of teachers. *Journal of Applied Psychology, 77,* 383–387.

Shedler, J. (2010). The efficacy of psychodynamic psychotherapy. *American Psychologist, 65,* 98–109.

Sheehy, R., & Horan, J. J. (2004). Effects of stress inoculation training for 1st-year law students. *International Journal of Stress Management, 11*(1), 41–55.

Sheerin, C. M., Seim, R. W., & Spates, C. R. (2012). A new appraisal of combined treatments for PTSD in the era of psychotherapy adjunctive medications. *Journal of Contemporary Psychotherapy, 42,* 69–76.

Sheldon, C. A., Malcolm, G. L., & Barton, J. J. (2008). Alexia with and without agraphia: An assessment of two classical syndromes. *Canadian Journal of Neurological Sciences, 35,* 616–624.

Sheldon, K. M., & King, L. (2001). Why positive psychology is necessary. *American Psychologist, 56,* 216–217.

Shen, J., & Dicker, B. (2008). The impacts of shiftwork on employees. *International Journal of Human Resource Management, 19,* 392–405.

Shenker, J. (2014, submitted). If you only see trees, is there still forest?Shenker, J. (2005). When you only see trees, is there still a forest? Paper presented at the American Academy of Neurology Annual Meeting, Miami Beach, FL, April.

Shenker, J. I. (2010, February 19). The lady who didn't know she couldn't move, the vanishing mystery woman, and other broken brains that teach. Presentation to fifth annual Conference on Applied Learning in Higher Education, Missouri Western State University, Saint Joseph, MO.

Shenker, J. I. (2013). Reversible Capgras syndrome due to temporal lobe dysfunction. Presentation to the American Neurology Association Annual Meeting, New Orleans.

Shenker, J. I., Wylie, S. A., Fuchs, K., Manning, C. A., & Heilman, K. M. (2004). On-line anosognosia: Unawareness for chorea in real time but not on videotape delay. *Neurology, 63*(1), 159–160.

Shepherd, C., Kohut, J. J., & Sweet, R. (1989). *News of the weird.* New York: New American Library.

Shepherd, R. K., Coco, A., Epp, S. B., & Crook, J. M. (2005). Chronic depolarization enhances the trophic effects of brain-derived neurotrophic factor in rescuing auditory neurons following a sensorineural hearing loss. *Journal of Comparative Neurology, 486,* 145–158.

Shepherd, R. K., & McCreery, D. B. (2006). Basis of electrical stimulation of the cochlea and the cochlear nucleus. *Advances in Otorhinolaryngology, 64,* 186–205.

Shepperd, J. A., Klein, W. P., Waters, E. A., & Weinstein, N. D. (2013). Taking stock of unrealistic optimism. *Perspectives on Psychological Science, 8*(4), 395–411.

Sheppes, G., Scheibe, S., Suri, G., & Gross, J. J. (2011). Emotion-regulation choice. *Psychological Science, 22*(11), 1391–1396. doi:10.1177/0956797611418350.

Sher, K. J., Wood, M. D., Wood, P. K., & Raskin, G. (1996). Alcohol outcome expectancies and alcohol use: A latent variable cross-lagged panel study. *Journal of Abnormal Psychology, 105,* 561–574.

Shera, C. A., Guinan, J. J., & Oxenham, A. J. (2002). Revised estimates of human cochlear tuning from otoacoustic and behavioral measurements. *Proceedings of the National Academy of Sciences, 99*(5), 3318–3323.

Sherif, M. (1937). An experimental approach to the study of attitudes. *Sociometry, 1,* 90–98.

Sherman, R. A., Nave, C. S., Funder, D. C. (2012). Properties of persons and situations related to overall and distinctive personality-behavior congruence. *Journal of Research in Personality, 46,* 87–101.

Sherman, S. J. (1980). On the self-erasing nature of errors of prediction. *Journal of Personality and Social Psychology, 39,* 211–221.

Sherman, S. M. (2007). The thalamus is more than just a relay. *Current Opinion in Neurobiology, 17,* 417–422.

Sherry, J. L. (2001). The effects of violent video games on aggression: A meta-analysis. *Human Communication Research, 27,* 409–431.

Sherwin, B. B., & Gelfand, M. M. (1987). The role of androgen in the maintenance of sexual functioning in oophorectomized women. *Psychosomatic Medicine, 49,* 397–409.

Sherwin, B. B., Gelfand, M. M., & Brender, W. (1985). Androgen enhances sexual motivation in females: A prospective crossover study of sex steroid administration in the surgical menopause. *Psychosomatic Medicine, 47,* 339–351.

Shidlovski, D., & Hassin, R. (2011). When pooping babies become more appealing: the effects of nonconscious goal pursuit on experienced emotions. *Psychological Science, 22*(11), 1381–1385.

Shorey, R. C., Stuart, G. L., Moore, T. M., & McNulty, J. K. (e-pub ahead of print 2013). The temporal relationship between alcohol, marijuana, angry affect, and dating violence perpetration: A daily diary study with female college students. *Psychology of Addictive Behaviors.* Epub November 25, 2013.

Shortt, A. J., Allan, B. D., & Evans, J. R. (2013). Laser-assisted in-situ keratomileusis (LASIK) versus photorefractive keratectomy (PRK) for myopia. *The Cochrane Database of Systematic Reviews, 1,* CD005135.

Sieverding, M., Decker, S., & Zimmermann, F. (2010). Information about low participation in cancer screening demotivates other people. *Psychological Science, 21*(7), 941–943. doi:10.1177/0956797610373936.

Shi, F., Hu, L., & Edge, A. S. (2013). Generation of hair cells in neonatal mice by β-catenin overexpression in Lgr5-positive cochlear progenitors. *PNAS, 110*(34), 13851–6. doi: 10.1073/pnas.1219952110. Epub 2013 Aug 5.

Shiller, R. J. (2001). *Irrational exuberance.* Princeton, NJ: Princeton University Press.

Shin, L. M., Rauch, S. L., & Pitman, R. K. (2006). Amygdala, medial prefrontal cortex, and hippocampal function in PTSD. *Annals of the New York Academy of Sciences, 1071,* 67–79.

Shin, M., Besser, L. M., Kucik, J. E., Lu, C., et al. (2009). Prevalence of Down syndrome among children and adolescents in 10 regions of the United States. *Pediatrics, 124,* 1565–1571.

Shinskey, J. L., & Munakata, Y. (2005). Familiarity breeds searching. *Psychological Science, 16,* 596–600.

Shipstead, Z., Redick, T. S., & Engle, R. W. (2012). Is working memory training effective?. *Psychological Bulletin,* doi:10.1037/a0027473

Shiraev, E. B., & Levy, D. A. (2010). *Cross-cultural psychology: Critical thinking and contemporary applications* (4th ed.). Boston: Allyn & Bacon.

Shiwach, R. S., Reid, W. H., & Carmody, T. J. (2001). An analysis of reported deaths following electroconvulsive therapy in Texas, 1993–1998. *Psychiatric Services, 52,* 1095–1097.

Shneider, L. S. (2013). Alzheimer disease pharmacologic treatment and treatment research. *Continuum, 19*(2), 339–357.

Shneidman, E. S. (1987). A psychological approach to suicide. In G. VandenBos & B. K. Bryant (Eds.), *Cataclysms, crises, and catastrophes: Psychology in action. The master lectures* (Vol. 6, pp. 147–183). Washington, DC: American Psychological Association.

Shoda, Y., & LeeTiernan, S. (2002). What remains invariant? Finding order within a person's thoughts, feelings, and behavior across situations. In D. Cervone & W. Mischel (Eds.), *Advances in personality science* (pp. 241–270). New York: Guilford Press.

Shoda, Y., & Mischel, W. (2006). Applying meta-theory to achieve generalisability and precision in personality science: Comment. *Applied Psychology: An International Review, 55,* 439–452.

Shook, N. J., & Fazio, R. H. (2008). Interracial roommate relationships: An experimental field test of the contact hypothesis. *Psychological Science, 19*(7), 717–723. doi:10.1111/j.1467–9280.2008.02147.x

Shorter, E., & Healy, D. (2007). *Shock therapy: A history of electroconvulsive treatment in mental illness.* Piscataway, NJ: Rutgers University Press.

Shreeve, J. (1993, June). Touching the phantom. *Discover,* 35–42.

Shuffler, M. L., DiazGranados, D., & Salas, E. (2011). There's a science for that. *Current Directions in Psychological Science, 20*(6) 365–372. doi:10.1177/0963721411422054.

Shultz, E., & Malone, D. A. Jr. (2013). A practical approach to prescribing antidepressants. *Cleveland Clinic Journal of Medicine, 80*(10), 625–631.

Shultz, K. S., & Wang, M. (2011). Psychological perspectives on the changing nature of retirement. *American Psychologist, 66*(3), 170–179. doi:10.1037/a0022411.

Shweder, R. A., Much, N. C., Mahapatra, M., & Park, L. (1994). The "big three" of morality (autonomy, community, and divinity), and the "big three" explanations of suffering, as well. In A. Brandt & P. Rozin (Eds.), *Morality and health.* Stanford, CA: Stanford University Press.

Sia, G. M., Clem, R. L., & Huganir, R. L. (2013). The human language–associated gene SRPX2 regulates synapse formation and vocalization in mice. *Science, 342*(6161), 987–991.

Sibbald, M., Panisko, D., & Cavalcanti, R. B. (2011). Role of clinical context in residents' physical examination diagnostic accuracy. *Medical Education, 45*(4), 415–421. doi:10.1111/j.1365–2923.2010.03896.x.

Siber, K. (2005, December). Precious metal. *Skiing, 58*(4), 16E.

Sibley, C. G., & Duckitt, J. (2013). The dual process model of ideology and prejudice: A longitudinal test during a global recession. *The Journal of Social Psychology, 153*(4), 448–466.

Siddique, J., Chung, J. Y., Brown, C. H., & Miranda, J. (2012). Comparative effectiveness of medication versus cognitive-behavioral therapy in a randomized controlled trial of low-income young minority women with depression. *Journal of Consulting and Clinical Psychology, 80,* 995–1006.

Sidney, S., Feng, L., & Kertesz, S. (2011). Association between marijuana exposure and pulmonary function over 20 years. *JAMA, 307*(2), 173–181. doi:10.1001/jama.2011.1961.

Siegel, J. M. (2005). Clues to the functions of mammalian sleep. *Nature, 437,* 1264–1271.

Siegel, J. M., & Rogawski, M. A. (1988). A function for REM sleep: Regulation of noradrenergic receptor sensitivity. *Brain Research Review, 13,* 213–233.

Siegal, M. (1997). *Knowing children: Experiments in conversation and cognition* (2nd ed.). Hove, UK: Psychology Press/Erlbaum/Taylor & Francis.

Siegel, S. (2005). Drug tolerance, drug addiction, and drug anticipation. *Current Directions in Psychological Science, 14,* 296–300.

Siegler, R. S. (2003). Thinking and intelligence. In M. H. Bornstein, L. Davidson, C. L. M. Keyes, & K. A. Moore (Eds.), *Well-being: Positive development across the life course. Crosscurrents in Contemporary Psychology* (pp. 311–320). Mahwah, NJ: Lawrence Erlbaum Associates Publishers.

Siegler, R. S. (2006). Microgenetic analysis of learning. In W. Damon & R. M. Lerner (Series Eds.) & D. Kuhn & R. Siegler (Vol. Eds.), *Handbook of child psychology: Vol. 2. Cognition, perception, and language* (6th ed.). New York: Wiley.

Siep, N., Roefs, A., Roebroeck, A., Havermans, R., Bonte, M. L., & Jansen, A. (2009). Hunger is the best spice: An fMRI study of the effects of attention, hunger and calorie content on food reward processing in the amygdala and orbitofrontal cortex. *Behavioural Brain Research, 198*(1), 149–158.

Siever, L. J. (2008). Neurobiology of aggression and violence. *American Journal of Psychiatry, 165,* 429–442.

Silber, M. H. (2001). Sleep disorders. *Neurology Clinics, 19,* 173–186. 857–868.

Silber, M. H., Ancoli-Israel, S., Bonnet, M. H., Chokroverty, S., Grigg-Damberger, M. M., Hirshkowitz, M., Kapen, S., Keenan, S. A., Kryger, M. H., Penzel, T., Pressman, M. R., & Iber, C. (2007). The visual scoring of sleep in adults. *Journal of Clinical Sleep Medicine, 3*(2), 121–131.

Silverman, K., Evans, A. M., Strain, E. C., & Griffiths, R. R. (1992). Withdrawal syndrome after the double-blind cessation of caffeine consumption. *New England Journal of Medicine, 327,* 1109–1114.

Silverman, M. J. (2012). Effects of melodic complexity and rhythm on working memory as measured by digit-recall performance. *Music and Medicine, 4*(1), 22–27.

Silverstein, L. B. (1996). Evolutionary psychology and the search for sex differences. *American Psychologist, 51,* 160–161.

Silverthorne, C. (2001). Leadership effectiveness and personality: A cross cultural evaluation. *Personality & Individual Differences, 30,* 303–309.

Simavli, S., Kaygusuz, I., Gumus, I., Usluogulları, B., Yildirim, M., & Kafali, H. (2013). Effect of music therapy during vaginal delivery on postpartum pain relief and mental health. *Journal of Affective Disorders.* Epub December 28, 2013.

Simcock, G., & Hayne, H. (2002). Breaking the barrier? Children fail to translate their preverbal memories into language. *Psychological Science, 13,* 225–231.

Simion, F., Cassia, V. M., Turati, C., & Valenza, E. (2003). Non-specific perceptual biases at the origins of face processing. In O. Pascalis & A. Slater (Eds.), *The development of face processing in infancy and early childhood* (pp. 13–25). Hauppauge, NY: Nova Science.

Simmons, A. L. (2012). Distributed practice and procedural memory consolidation in musicians' skill learning. *Journal of Research in Music Education, 59*(4), 357–368. doi:10.1177/0022429411424798.

Simon, S. R., Khateb, A., Darque, A., Lazeyras, F., Mayer, E., & Pegna, A. J. (2011). When the brain remembers, but the patient doesn't: converging fMRI and EEG evidence for covert recognition in a case of prosopagnosia. *Cortex, 47*(7), 825–838.

Simon, W., & Gagnon, J. H. (1986). Sexual scripts: Permanence and change. *Archives of Sexual Behavior, 15,* 97–120.

Simon-Thomas, E. R., Keltner, D. J., Sauter, D., Sinicropi-Yao, L., & Abramson, A. (2009). The voice conveys specific emotions: Evidence from vocal burst displays. *Emotion, 6,* 838–846.

Simons, C. J. P., Tracy, D. K., Sanghera, K. K., O'Daly, O., et al. (2010). Functional magnetic resonance imaging of inner speech in schizophrenia. *Biological Psychiatry, 67,* 232–237.

Simons, D. J., & Ambinder, M. S. (2005). Change blindness: Theory and consequences. *Current Directions in Psychological Science, 14,* 44–48.

Simons, D. J., & Chabris, C. F. (1999). Gorillas in our midst: Sustained inattentional blindness for dynamic events. *Perception, 28,* 1059–1074.

Simons, D. J., & Valk, P. J. L. (2009). Melatonin for commercial aircrew? *Biological Rhythm Research, 40*(1), 7–16.

Simons, T., & Roberson, Q. (2003). Why managers should care about fairness: The effects of aggregate justice perceptions on organizational outcomes. *Journal of Applied Psychology, 88,* 432–443.

Simons-Morton, B. G., Bingham, C., Falk, E. B., Li, K., Pradhan, A. K., Ouimet, M., & Shope, J. T. (2014). Experimental effects of injunctive norms on simulated risky driving among teenage males. *Health Psychology.* Epub January 27, 2014.

Simonton, D. K. (1999). Creativity and genius. In L. Pervin & O. John (Eds.), *Handbook of personality research* (2nd ed., pp. 629–652). New York: Guilford.

Simonton, D. K. (2002). In C. R. Snyder & J. Shane (Eds.), *Handbook of positive psychology* (pp. 189–201). London: Oxford University Press.

Simonton, D. K. (2004). *Creativity in science: Chance, logic, genius, and zeitgeist.* Cambridge, UK: Cambridge University Press.

Simonton, D. K. (2012). Teaching creativity: Current findings, trends, and controversies in the psychology of creativity. *Teaching of Psychology, 39,* 217–222.

Simonton, D. K., & Song, A. V. (2009). Eminence, IQ, physical and mental health, and achievement domain: Cox's 282 geniuses revisited. *Psychological Science, 20,* 429–434.

Simpson, J. A., Collins, W. A., Farrell, A., & Raby, K. L. (2014). The significance of childhood relationships for forming and maintaining adult attachments. In V. Zayas, and C. Hazan (Eds.), *Bases of adult attachment: Linking brain, mind, and behavior.* New York: Springer.

Simpson, J. A., Collins, W. A., & Salvatore, J. E. (2011). The impact of early interpersonal experience on adult romantic relationship functioning: Recent findings from the Simpson 10 Minnesota Longitudinal Study of Risk and Adaptation. *Current Directions in Psychological Science. 20*(6), 355–359. doi:10.1177/0963721411418468.

Simpson, J. A., & Kenrick, D. T. (1997). *Evolutionary social psychology.* Mahwah, NJ: Erlbaum.

Simpson, J. A., Rholes, W. S., & Winterheld, H. A. (2010). Attachment working models twist memories of relationship events. *Psychological Science, 21*(2), 252–259. doi:10.1177/0956797609357175.

Simpson, S., Hurtley, S. M., & Marx, J. (2000). Immune cell networks. *Science, 290,* 79.

Simpson, S. G., McMahon, F. J., McInnis, M. G., MacKinnon, D. F., Edwin, D., Folstein, S. E., et al. (2002). Diagnostic reliability of bipolar II disorder. *Archives of General Psychiatry, 59,* 736–740.

Sinclair, R. C., Hoffman, C., Mark, M. M., Martin, L. L., & Pickering, T. L. (1994). Construct accessibility and the misattribution of arousal. *Psychological Science, 5*(1), 15–19.

Singh, H., & O'Boyle, M. W. (2004). Interhemispheric interaction during global-local processing in mathematically gifted adolescents, average-ability youth, and college students. *Neuropsychology, 18,* 371–377.

Singh, M. K., Kesler, S. R., Hadi Hosseini, S. M., Kelley, R. G., Amatya, D., Hamilton, J. P., Chen, M. C., & Gotlib, I. H. (2013). Anomalous gray matter structural networks in major depressive disorder. *Biological Psychiatry, 74*(10), 777–785.

Singh, S. M., & O'Reilly, R. (2009). (Epi)genomics and neurodevelopment in schizophrenia: Monozygotic twins discordant for schizophrenia augment the search for disease-related (epi)genomic alterations. *Genome, 52*(1), 8–19.

Siti, M. (2004). Hypochondriasis: Modern perspectives on an ancient malady. *Journal of Cognitive Psychotherapy, 18*, 369–370.

Sitser, T., van der Linden, D. B., & Marise P. H. (2013). Predicting sales performance criteria with personality measures: The use of the general factor of personality, the Big Five and narrow traits. *Human Performance, 26*, 26–149.

Sitzmann, T., Brown, K. G., Casper, W. D., Ely, K., & Zimmerman, R. D. (2008). A review and meta-analysis of the nomological network of trainee reactions. *Journal of Applied* Psychology, 93, 280–295.

Sivertsen, B., Øverland, S., Pallesen, S., Bjorvatn, B., Nordhus, I. H., Maeland., J. G., & Mykletun, A. (2009). Insomnia and long sleep duration are risk factors for later work disability. The Hordaland Health Study. *Journal of Sleep Research, 18*(1), 122–128.

Skeem, J. L., Polaschek, D. L., Patrick, C. J., & Lilienfeld, S. O. (2011). Psychopathic personality: Bridging the gap between scientific evidence and public policy. *Psychological Science in the Public Interest, 12*(3), 95–162. doi:10.1177/1529100611426706.

Skinner, B. F. (1938). *The behavior of organisms.* New York: Appleton.

Skinner, B. F. (1961). *Cumulative record* (3rd ed.). Englewood Cliffs, NJ: Prentice Hall.

Skinner, N. F. (2009). Academic folk wisdom: Fact, fiction and falderal. *Psychology Learning & Teaching, 8*(1), 46–50.

Skitka, L. (2010). The psychology of moral conviction. *Social and Personality Psychology Compass, 4*, 267–28.

Skre, I., Onstad, S., Toregersen, S., Lyngren, S., & Kringlin, E. (2000). The heritability of common phobic fear: A twin study of a clinical sample. *Journal of Anxiety Disorders, 14*, 549–562.

Skrobik, Y. (2009). Delirium prevention and treatment. *Critical Care Clinics, 25*, 585–591.

Skroubis, G., Karamanakos, S., Sakellaropoulos, G., Panagopoulos, K., & Kalfarentzos, F. (2011). Comparison of early and late complications after various bariatric procedures: Incidence and treatment during 15 years at a single institution. *World Journal Of Surgery, 35*(1), 93–101.

Slade, E. P., & Wissow, L. S. (2004). Spanking in early childhood and later behavior problems: A prospective study of infants and young toddlers. *Pediatrics, 113*, 1321–1330.

Slamecka, N. J., & McElree, B. (1983). Normal forgetting of verbal lists as a function of their degree of learning. *Journal of Experimental Psychology: Learning, Memory, and Cognition, 9*, 384–397.

Slater, A., Mattock, A., Brown, E., & Bremmer, J. G. (1991). Form perception at birth. *Journal of Experimental Child Psychology, 51*, 395–406.

Slavich, G. M., & Cole, S. W. (2013). The emerging field of human social genomics. *Clinical Psychological Science, 1*(3), 331–348.

Slavin, K. V. (2008). Peripheral nerve stimulation for neuropathic pain. *Neurotherapeutics, 5*(1), 100–106.

Sliwinska-Kowalska, M., & Davis, A. (2012). Noise-induced hearing loss. *Noise & Health, 14*(61), 274–280.

Sloan, R. P., Shapiro, P. A., Gorenstein, E. E., Tager, F. A., et al. (2010). Cardiac autonomic control and treatment of hostility: A randomized controlled trial. *Psychosomatic Medicine, 72*, 1–8.

Sloane, S., Baillargeon, R., & Premack, D. (2012). Do infants have a sense of fairness?. *Psychological Science, 23*(2), 196–204. doi:10.1177/0956797611422072.

Slone, N. C., Reese, R. J., & McClellan, M. J. (2012). Telepsychology outcome research with children and adolescents: A review of the literature. *Psychological Services, 9*(3), 272–292.

Slotnick, S. D., & Schacter, D. L. (2004). A sensory signature that distinguishes true from fales memories. *Nature Neuroscience, 7*, 664–672.

Slovic, P., Peters, E., Finucane, M. L., & MacGregor, D. G. (2005). Affect, risk, and decision making. *Health Psychology, 24*, S35–S40.

Slutske, W. S., Moffitt, T. E., Poulton, R., & Caspi, A. (2012). Undercontrolled temperament at age 3 predicts disordered gambling at age 32: A longitudinal study of a complete birth cohort. *Psychological Science, 23*, 510–516. doi:10.1177/0956797611429708.

Smillie, L. D., Pickering, A. D., & Jackson, C. J. (2006). The new Reinforcement Sensitivity Theory: Implications for personality measurement. *Personality and Social Psychology Review, 10*, 320–335.

Smink, F. R., van Hoeken, D., & Hoek. H. W. (2013). Epidemiology, course, and outcome of eating disorders. *Current Opinion in Psychiatry, 26*(6), 543–548.

Smit, Y., Huibers, M. H., Ioannidis, J. A., van Dyck, R., van Tilburg, W., & Arntz, A. (2012). The effectiveness of long-term psychoanalytic psychotherapy—A meta-analysis of randomized controlled trials. *Clinical Psychology Review, 32*(2), 81–92. doi:10.1016/j.cpr.2011.11.003.

Smith, A. R., Chein, J., & Steinberg, L. (2014). Peers increase adolescent risk taking even when the probabilities of negative outcomes are known. *Developmental Psychology, 50*(5), 1564–1568.

Smith, D. M., Loewenstein, G., Jankovic, A., & Ubel, P. A. (2009). Happily hopeless: Adaptation to a permanent, but not to a temporary, disability. *Health Psychology, 28*, 787–791.

Smith, G. C. S., & White, I. R. (2006). Predicting the risk for sudden infant death syndrome from obstetric characteristics: A retrospective cohort study of 505,011 live births. *Pediatrics, 117*, 60–66.

Smith, G. T., Simmons, J. R., Flory, K., Annus, A. M., & Hill, K. K. (2007). Thinness and eating expectancies predict subsequent binge-eating and purging behavior among adolescent girls. *Journal of Abnormal Psychology, 116*, 188–197.

Smith, L. B., & Sera, M. D. (1992). A developmental analysis of the polar structure of dimensions. *Cognitive Psychology, 24*, 99–142.

Smith, M. L., Glass, G. V., & Miller, T. I. (1980). *The benefits of psychotherapy.* Baltimore: Johns Hopkins University Press.

Smith, P., Frank, J., Bondy, S., & Mustard, C. (2008). Do changes in job control predict differences in health status? Results from a longitudinal national survey of Canadians. *Psychosomatic Medicine, 70*, 85–91.

Smith, P. C., & Kendall, L. M. (1963). Retranslation of expectations: An approach to the construction of unambiguous anchors for rating scales. *Journal of Applied Psychology, 47*, 149–155.

Smith, P. K., & Drew, L. M. (2002). Grandparenthood. In M. H. Bornstein (Ed.), *Handbook of parenting* (2nd ed.). Mahwah, NJ: Erlbaum.

Smith, R. M., Tivarus, M., Campbell, H. L., Hillier, A., & Beversdorf, D. Q. (2006). Apparent transient effects of recent "ecstasy" use on cognitive performance and extrapyramidal signs in human subjects. *Cognitive & Behavioral Neurology, 19*(3), 157–164.

Smith, S., & Freedman, D. G. (1983, April). *Mother-toddler interaction and maternal perception of child temperament in two ethnic groups: Chinese-American and European-American.* Paper presented at the meeting of the Society for Research in Child Development, Detroit, MI.

Smith, S., Weissman, N., Anderson, C., Sanchez, M., Chuang, E., Stubbe, S., & . Shanahan, W. (2010). Multicenter, placebo-controlled trial of lorcaserin for weight management. *The New England Journal Of Medicine, 363*(3), 245–256.

Smith, S. L., & Donnerstein, E. (1998). Harmful effects of exposure to media violence: Learning of aggression, emotional desensitization, and fear. In R. G. Geen & E. Donnerstein (Eds.), *Human aggression* (pp. 230–247). San Diego: Academic Press.

Smith, S. M., & Vela, E. (2001). Environmental context-dependent memory: A review and meta-analysis. *Psychonomic Bulletin and Review, 8*, 203–220.

Smith, S. M., Vela, E., & Williamson, J. E. (1988). Shallow input processing does not induce environmental context-dependent recognition. *Bulletin of the Psychonomic Society, 26*, 537–540.

Smith, T. B., Constantine, M. G., Dunn, T. W., Dinehart, J. M., & Montoya, J. A. (2006). Multicultural education in the mental health professions: A meta-analytic review. *Journal of Counseling Psychology, 53*, 132–145.

Smith, T. E., & Sederer, L. I. (2009). A new kind of homelessness for individuals with serious mental illness? The need for a "mental health home." *Hospital and Community Psychiatry, 60*, 528–533.

Smith, T. W., Uchino, B. N., Berg, C. A., Florsheim, P., Pearce, G., Hawkins, M., Hopkins, P. N., & Yoon, H.-C. (2007). Hostile personality traits and coronary artery calcification in middle-aged and older married couples: Different effects for self-reports versus spouse ratings. *Psychosomatic Medicine 69*, 441–448.

Smith-Crowe, K., Burke, M. J., & Landis, R. S. (2003). Organizational climate as a moderator of safety knowledge–safety performance relationships. *Journal of Organizational Behavior, 24*, 861–876.

Smither, J. W., London, M., & Reilly, R. R. (2005). Does performance improve following multisource feedback? A theoretical model, meta-analysis, and review of empirical findings. *Personnel Psychology, 58*, 33–66.

Smyth, C. L., & MacLachian, M. (2005). Confirmatory factor analysis of the Trinity Inventory of Precursors to Suicide (TIPS) and its relationship to hopelessness and depression. *Death Studies, 29*, 333–350.

Smyth, J. M., Zawadzki, M. J., Santuzzi, A. M., & Filipkowski, K. B. (2014). Examining the effects of perceived social support on momentary mood and symptom reports in asthma and arthritis patients. *Psychological Health*, Epub February 25, 2014

Smoller, J. W. (2008). Genetics of mood and anxiety disorder. In J. W. Smoller, B. R. Sheidley, & M. T. Tsaung (Eds.), *Psychiatric genetics: Applications in clinical practice* (pp. 131–176). Arlington: American Psychiatric Publishing.

Snarey, J., & Hooker, C. (2006). Lawrence Kohlberg. In E. M. Dowling & W. G. Scarlett (Eds.), *Encyclopedia of spiritual and religious development* (pp. 251–255). Thousand Oaks, CA: Sage.

Snarey, J. R. (1994). Cross-cultural universality of social-moral development: A critical review of Kohlbergian research. In B. Puka (Ed.), *New research in moral development* (pp. 268–298). New York: Garland.

Snel, J., & Lorist, M. M. (2011). Effects of caffeine on sleep and cognition. *Progress in Brain Research 190*, 105–117.

Snellingen, T., Evans, J. R., Ravilla, T., & Foster, A. (2002). Surgical interventions for age-related cataract. *Cochrane Database System Review, 2*, CD001323.

Snowden, L. R., & Cheung, F. (1990). Use of inpatient mental health services by members of ethnic minority groups. *American Psychologist, 45*, 347–355.

Sniderman, A. D., LaChapelle, K. J., Rachon, N. A., & Furberg, C. D. (2013). The necessity for clinical reasoning in the era of evidence-based medicine. *Mayo Clinic Proceedings, 88*(10), 1108–1114.

Snyder, A. L., Anderson-Hanley, C., & Arciero, P. J. (2012). Virtual and live social facilitation while exergaming: Competitiveness moderates exercise intensity. *Journal of Sport and Exercise Psychology, 34*(2), 252–259.

Snyder, C. R., & Lopez, S. J. (2009). *Oxford handbook of positive psychology* (2nd ed.). New York: Oxford University Press.

Snyder, C. R., Lopez, S. J., & Pedrotti, J. T. (2010). *Positive psychology: The scientific and practical explorations of human strengths.* Thousand Oaks, CA: Sage.

Snyder, D. M, Goodlin-Jones, B. L., Pionk, M. J., & Stein, M. T. (2008). Inconsolable night-time awakening: Beyond night terrors. *Journal of Developmental and Behavioral Pediatrics, 29*(4), 311–314.

Snyder, M., & Dwyer, P. C. (2013). Altruism and prosocial behavior. In H. Tennen, J. Suls, & I. B. Weiner (Eds.), *Handbook of psychology, Vol. 5: Personality and social psychology* (2nd ed.) (pp. 467–485). Hoboken, NJ: John Wiley & Sons Inc.

Snyder, T. D., Dillow, S. A., & Hoffman, C. M. (2008). *Digest of Education Statistics: 2007* (Report No. NCES 2008–022). Washington, D. C.: National Center for Education Statistics, Institute of Education Sciences, U. S. Department of Education. Retrieved June 9, 2009, from http://nces.ed.gov/programs/digest/d07.

Snyderman, M., & Rothman, S. (1987). Survey of expert opinion on intelligence and aptitude testing. *American Psychologist, 42*, 137–144.

Sofuoglu, M., Sugarman, D. E., & Carroll, K. M. (2010). Cognitive function as an emerging treatment target for marijuana addiction. *Experimental and Clinical Psychopharmacology, 18*(2), 109–119.

Sohlberg, S., & Jansson, B. (2002). Unconscious responses to "mommy and I are one": Does gender matter? In R. F. Bornstein & J. M. Masling (Eds.), *The psychodynamics of gender and gender role.Vol. 10: Empirical studies in psychoanalytic theories* (pp. 165–201). Washington, DC: American Psychological Association.

Sohler, N., & Bromet, E. J. (2003). Does racial bias influence psychiatric diagnoses assigned at first hospitalization? *Social Psychiatry and Psychiatric Epidemiology, 38*, 463–472.

Soken, N. H., & Pick, A. D. (1992). Intermodal perception of happy and angry expressive behaviors by seven-month-old infants. *Child Development, 63*, 787–795.

Solomon, B. D., & Muenke, M. (2012). When to suspect a genetic syndrome. *American Family Physician, 86*(9), 826–833.

Solomon, R. L. (1980). The opponent-process theory of acquired motivation: The costs of pleasure and the benefits of pain. *American Psychologist, 35*, 691–712.

Solomon, R. L., Kamin, L. J., & Wynne, L. C. (1953). Traumatic avoidance learning: The outcomes of several extinction procedures with dogs. *Journal of Abnormal and Social Psychology, 48*, 291–302.

Solomon, S., Greenberg, J., & Pyszczynski, T. (2004). The cultural animal: Twenty years of terror management theory and research. In J. Greenberg, S. L. Koole, & T. Pyszczynski (Eds.), *Handbook of experimental existential psychology* (pp. 13–34). New York: Guilford Press.

Solomonson, A. L., & Lance, C. E. (1997). Examination of the relationship between true halo and halo error in performance ratings. *Journal of Applied Psychology, 82*, 665–674.

Song, H., & Baillargeon, R. (2008). Infants' reasoning about others' false perceptions. *Developmental Psychology, 44*, 1789–1795.

Song, H., Chui, T. Y., Zhong, Z., Elsner, A. E., and Burns, S. A. (2011). Variation of cone photoreceptor packing density with retinal eccentricity and age. *Investigative Ophthalmology and Visual Sciences, 52*(10), 7376–7384.

Song, Z., Li, W., & Arvey, R. D. (2011). Associations between dopamine and serotonin genes and job satisfaction: Preliminary evidence from the Add Health Study. *Journal of Applied Psychology, 96*(6), 1223–1233. doi:10.1037/a0024577.

Sonne, J. L. (2012). Sexualized relationships. In S. J. Knapp, M. C. Gottlieb, M M. Handelsman, & L. D. VandeCreek (Eds.), *APA Handbook of Ethics in Psychology, Vol. 1: Moral Foundations and Common Themes* (pp. 295–310). Washington, DC: American Psychological Association.

Sonnentag, S. (2012). Psychological detachment from work during leisure time: The benefits of mentally disengaging from work. *Current Directions in Psychological Science, 21*, 114–118. doi:10.1177/0963721411434979.

Sorce, J., Emde, R., Campos, J., & Klinnert, M. (1981, April). *Maternal emotional signaling: Its effect on the visual cliff behavior of one-year-olds.* Paper presented at the meeting of the Society for Research in Child Development, Boston, MA.

Sorrentino, R. M., & Roney, C. J. R. (2000). *The uncertain mind: Individual differences in facing the unknown.* Philadelphia: Psychology Press.

Soto, D., Funes, M. J., Guzmán-García, A., Warbrick, T., Rotshtein, P., & Humphreys, G. W. (2009). Pleasant music overcomes the loss of awareness in patients with visual neglect. *Proceedings of the National Academy of Sciences, 106*(14), 6011–6016.

Sowell, E. R., Delis, D., Stiles, J., & Jernigan, T. L. (2001). Improved memory functioning and frontal lobe maturation between childhood and adolescence: A structural MRI study. *Journal of the International Neuropsychological Society, 7*, 312–322.

Sowell, E. R., Peterson, B. S., Thompson, P. M., Welcome, S. E., Henkenius, A. L., & Toga, A. W. (2003). Mapping cortical change across the human life span. *Nature Neuroscience, 6*, 309–315.

Sowell, T. (2005). *Black rednecks and white liberals.* San Francisco: Encounter Books.

Soyka, M. (2013). Nalmefene for the treatment of alcohol dependence: A current update. *International Journal of Neuropsychopharmacology, 18*, 1–10.

Spaans, H. P., Verwijk, E., Comijs, H. C., Kok, R. M., Sienaert, P., Bouckaert, F., Fannes, K., Vandepoel, K., Scherder, E. J., Stek, M. L., & Kho, K. H. (2013). Efficacy and cognitive side effects after brief pulse and ultrabrief pulse right unilateral electroconvulsive therapy for major depression: a randomized, double-blind, controlled study. *Journal of Clinical Psychiatry, 74*(11), e1029–1036.

Spanagel, R., & Weiss, F. (1999). The dopamine hypothesis of reward: Past and current status. *Trends in Neuroscience, 22*, 521–527.

Spangler, G., Fremmer-Bombik, E., & Grossman, K. (1996). Social and individual determinants of infant attachment security and disorganization. *Infant Mental Health Journal, 17*, 127–139.

Spanos, N. P., Burnley, M. C. E., & Cross, P. A. (1993). Response expectancies and interpretations as determinants of hypnotic responding. *Journal of Personality and Social Psychology, 65*(6), 1237–1242.

Sparks, K., Cooper, C., Fried, Y., & Shirom, A. (1997). The effects of hours of work on health: A meta-analytic review. *Journal of Occupational and Organizational Psychology, 70*, 391–408.

Sparks, K., Faragher, B., & Cooper, C. L. (2001). Well-being and occupational health in the 21st century workplace. *Journal of Occupational and Organizational Psychology, 74*, 489–509.

Sparrow, B., Liu, J., & Wegner, D. M. (2011). Google effects on memory: Cognitive consequences of having information at our fingertips. *Science, 333*(6043), 776–778. doi:10.1126/science.1207745.

Spates, C. R., & Rubin, S. (2012). Empirically supported psychological treatments: EMDR. In J. G. Beck & D. M. Sloan (eds.), *The Oxford Handbook of Traumatic Stress Disorders.* DOI: 10.1093/oxfordhb/9780195399066.001.0001

Spear, L. P. (2000). Neurobiological changes in adolescence. *Current Directions in Psychological Science, 9*, 111–114.

Spearman, C. E. (1904). General intelligence objectively determined and measured. *American Journal of Psychology, 15*, 201–293.

Spearman, C. E. (1927). *The abilities of man.* New York: Macmillan.

Speckhard, A. (2002). Voices from the inside: Psychological responses to toxic disasters. In J. M. Havenaar & J. G. Cwikel (Eds.), *Toxic turmoil: Psychological and societal consequences of ecological disasters* (pp. 217–236). New York:

Spears, R., Postmes, T., Lea, M., & Watt, S. E. (2001). A SIDE view of social influence. In J. P. Forgas & K. D. Williams (Eds.), *Social influence: Direct and indirect processes. The Sydney symposium of social psychology* (pp. 331–350). Philadelphia, PA: Psychology Press.

Speckhard, A. (2002). Voices from the inside: Psychological responses to toxic disasters. In J. M. Havenaar & J. G. Cwikel (Eds.), *Toxic turmoil: Psychological and societal consequences of ecological disasters* (pp. 217–236). New York: Plenum.

Specter, M. (2005, May 23). Higher risk. *New Yorker*, 38–45.

Spector, P. E. (1985). Measurement of human service staff satisfaction: Development of the Job Satisfaction Survey. *American Journal of Community Psychology, 13*, 693–713.

Spector, P. E. (2002). Employee control and occupational stress. *Current Directions in Psychological Science, 11*, 133–136.

Spector, P. E. (2003). *Industrial & organizational psychology: Research and practice* (3rd ed.). New York: Wiley.

Spector, P. E., Fox, S., & Domalgaski, T. (2006). Emotions, violence, and counterproductive work behavior. In E. K. Kelloway, J. Barling, & J. J. Hurrell (Eds.), *Handbook of workplace violence* (pp. 29–46). Thousand Oaks, CA: Sage.

Spelke, E. S., Breinlinger, K., Macomber, J., & Jacobson, K. (1992). Origins of knowledge. *Psychological Review, 99*, 605–632.

Spencer, S., Steele, C. M., & Quinn, D. (1997). *Under suspicion on inability: Stereotype threats and women's math performance.* Unpublished manuscript.

Spernak, S. M., Schottenbauer, M. A., Ramey, S. L., & Ramey, C. T. (2006). Child health and academic achievement among former Head Start children. *Children and Youth Services Review, 28*, 1251–1261.

Sperry, R. W. (1968). Hemisphere deconnection and unity in conscious awareness. *American Psychologist, 23*, 723–733.

Sperry, R. W. (1974). Lateral specialization in the surgically separated hemispheres. In F. O. Schmitt & F. G. Wordon (Eds.), *The neurosciences: Third study program* (pp. 5–19). Cambridge, MA: MIT Press.

Spiegel, D. (Ed.). (1994). *Dissociation: Culture, mind, and body.* Washington, DC: American Psychiatric Press.

Spiegler, M. E., & Guevremont, D. C. (2009). *Contemporary behavior therapy* (5th ed.). New York: Cengage Learning.

Spillmann, L., Otte, T., Hamburger, K., & Magnussen, S. (2006). Perceptual filling-in from the edge of the blind spot. *Vision Research, 46*, 4252–4257.

Spinath, B., & Steinmayr, R. (2012). The roles of competence beliefs and goal orientations for change in intrinsic motivation. *Journal of Educational Psychology*, doi:10.1037/a0028115.

Spinath, F. M., Harlaar, N., Ronald, A., & Plomin, R. (2004). Substantial genetic influence on mild mental impairment in early childhood. *American Journal of Mental Retardation, 109*, 34–43.

Spinrad, T. L., Eisenberg, N., Cumberland, A., Fabes, R. A., et al. (2006). Relation of emotionrelated regulation to children's social competence: A longitudinal study. *Emotion, 6*, 498–510.

Spitz, H. H. (1997). *Nonconscious movements: From mystical messages to facilitated communication.* Hillsdale, NJ: Erlbaum.

Spitzer, R. L. (2009, July 2). APA and DSM-V: Empty promises. *Psychiatric Times.* Retrieved from http://www.psychiatrictimes.com/display/article/10168/142584.

Spitzer, R. L., Gibbon, M., Skodol, A. E., & Williams, J. B. W., & First, M. B. (Eds.). (1994). *DSM-IV casebook: A learning companion to the Diagnostic and Statistical Manual of Mental Disorders* (4th ed.). Washington, DC: American Psychiatric Association.

Spörer, N., Brunstein, J. C., & Kieschke, U. (2009). Improving students' reading comprehension skills: Effects of strategy instruction and reciprocal teaching. *Learning And Instruction, 19*(3), 272–286. doi:10.1016/j.learninstruc.2008.05.003.

Sporns, O. (2011). The human connectome: A complex network. *Annals of the American Academy of Sciences, 1224*, 109–125.

Springer, K., & Belk, A. (1994). The role of physical contact and association in early contamination sensitivity. *Developmental Psychology, 30*(6), 864–868.

Springer, S. P., & Deutsch, G. (1989). *Left brain, right brain.* New York: Freeman.

Spychalski, A. C., Quinones, M. A., Gaugler, B. B., & Pohley, K. (1997). A survey of assessment center practices in the U.S. *Personnel Psychology, 50*, 71–90.

Squire, L. R. (1986). Mechanisms of memory. *Science, 232*, 1612–1619.

Squire, L. R. (2009). The legacy of patient H. M. for neuroscience. *Neuron, 61*(1), 6–9.

Srimathi, N. L., Kiran K., S. K. (2011). Self efficacy and psychological well-being among employed women. *Journal of Psychosocial Research, 6*, 95–102.

Srivastava, S., Guglielmo, S., & Beer, J. S. (2010). Perceiving others' personalities: Examining the dimensionality, assumed similarity to the self, and stability of perceiver effects. *Journal of Personality and Social Psychology, 98*, 520–534.

Srivastava, S., John, O. P., Gosling, S. D., & Potter, J. (2003). Development of personality in early and middle adulthood: Set like plaster or persistent change? *Journal of Personality and Social Psychology, 84*, 1041–1053.

Stahl, S. M. (2007). Th e genetics of schizophrenia converge upon the NMDA glutamate receptor. *CNS Spectrums, 12*, 583–588.

Stahl, S. M., Lee-Zimmerman, C., Cartwright, S., & Morrissette, D. A. (2013). Serotonergic drugs for depression and beyond. *Current Drug Targets, 14*(5), 578–585.

Stankov, L. (1989). Attentional resources and intelligence: A disappearing link. *Personality and Individual Differences, 10*, 957–968.

Stanley, B. G., Willett, V. L., Donias, H. W., & Ha-Lyen, H. (1993). The lateral hypothalamus: A primary site mediating excitatory aminoacid-elicited eating. *Brain Research, 63*(1–2), 41–49.

Stanton, A. L., & Low, C. A. (2012). Expressing emotions in stressful contexts: Benefits, moderators, and mechanisms. *Current Directions in Psychological Science, 21*, 124–128. doi:10.1177/0963721411434978.

Starkstein, S. E., Fedoroff, J. P., Price, T. R., Leigguarda, R., & Robinson, R. G. (1992). Anosognosia in patients with cerebrovascular lesions: A study of causative factors. *Stroke, 23*, 1446–1453.

Staudt, M., Grodd, W., Niemann, G., Wildgruber, D., Erb, M., & Krageloh-Mann, I. (2001). Early left periventricular brain lesions induce right hemispheric organization of speech. *Neurology 2001, 57*, 122–125.

Stauffer, J. M., & Buckley, M. R. (2005). The existence and nature of racial bias in supervisory ratings. *Journal of Applied Psychology, 90*, 586–591.

Staw, B. M., & Cohen-Charash, Y. (2005). The dispositional approach to job satisfaction: More than a mirage, but not yet an oasis. *Journal of Organizational Behavior, 26*, 59–78.

Stawski, R. S., Sliwinski, M. J., & Hofer, S. M. (2013). Between-person and within-person associations among processing speed, attention switching, and working memory in younger and older adults. *Experimental Aging Research, 39*(2), 194–214.

Stawskia, R. S., Cichyb, K. E., Piazzac, J. R., Almeidad, D. M. (2013). Associations among daily stressors and salivary cortisol: Findings from the National Study of Daily Experiences. *Psychoneuroendocrinology, 38*(11), 2654–2665.

Stead, L. F., Perera, R., Bullen, C., Mant, D., Hartmann-Boyce, J., Cahill, K., & Lancaster, T. (2012). Nicotine replacement therapy for smoking cessation. *The Cochrane Database of Systemic Reviews, 11*, CD000146.

Steblay, N. K., Wells, G. L., & Douglass, A. B. (2014). The eyewitness post identification feedback effect 15 years later: Theoretical and policy implications. *Psychology, Public Policy, and Law, 20*(1), 1–18.

Steele, C. M. (1997). A threat in the air: How stereotypes shape intellectual identity and performance. *American Psychologist, 52*, 613–629.

Steele, C. M., & Aronson, J. (2000). Stereotype threat and the intellectual test performance of African Americans. In C. Stangor (Ed.), *Stereotypes and prejudice: Essential readings* (pp. 369–389). Philadelphia: Psychology Press/Taylor & Francis.

Steele, K., Schweitzer, M., Prokopowicz, G., Shore, A., Eaton, L., Lidor, A., & … Magnuson, T. (2011). The long-term risk of venous thromboembolism following bariatric surgery. *Obesity Surgery, 21*(9), 1371–1376.

Steele, T. D., McCann, U. D., & Ricaurte, G. A. (1994). 3,4-methylenedioxy-methamphetamine (MDMA, ecstacy): Pharmacology and toxicity in animals and humans. *Addiction, 89*, 539–551.

Stein, A., Malmberg, L.-E., Leach, P., Barnes, J., & FCCC Team (2013). The influence of different forms of early childcare on children's emotional and behavioural development at school entry. *Child: Care, Health and Development, 39*, 676–687.

Stein, D. J. (2006). Specific phobia: A disorder of fear conditioning and extinction. *CNS Spectrums, 11*, 248–251.

Stein, E. (1999). *The mismeasure of desire: The science, theory and ethics of sexual orientation.* New York: Oxford University Press.

Steinberg, L. (1990). Autonomy, conflict, and harmony in the family relationship. In S. S. Feldman & G. R. Elliott (Eds.), *At the threshold: The developing adolescent* (pp. 255–276). Cambridge, MA: Harvard University Press.

Steinberg, L. (2008). A social neuroscience perspective on adolescent risk-taking. *Developmental Review, 28*(1), 78–106.

Steinberg, L., Dornbusch, S. M., & Brown, B. B. (1992). Ethnic differences in adolescent achievement: An ecological perspective. *American Psychologist, 47*, 723–729.

Steinberg, L., Lamborn, S. D., Darling, N., Mounts, N. S., & Dornbusch, S. M. (1994). Over-time changes in adjustment and competence among adolescents from authoritative, authoritarian, indulgent, and neglectful families. *Child Development, 65*, 754–770.

Steinberg, L., & Monahan, K. (2011). Adolescents' exposure to sexy media does not hasten the initiation of sexual intercourse. *Developmental Psychology, 47*(2), 562–576.

Steiner, J. E., Glaser, D., Hawilo, M. E., & Berridge, K. C. (2001). Comparative expression of hedonic impact: Affective reactions to taste by human infants and other primates. *Neuroscience and Biobehavioral Reviews, 25*, 53–74.

Steiner, J. M., & Fahrenberg, J. (2000). Authoritarianism and social status of former members of the Waffen-SS and SS and of the Wehrmacht: An extension and reanalysis of the study published in 1970. *Koelner Zeitschrift fuer Soziologie und Sozialpsychologie, 52*, 329–348.

Steinglass, J., Albano, A., Simpson, H., Carpenter, K., Schebendach, J., & Attia, E. (2012). Fear of food as a treatment target: Exposure and response prevention for anorexia nervosa in an open series. *International Journal Of Eating Disorders, 45*(4), 615–621. doi:10.1002/eat.20950.

Steinglass, J. E., Figner, B., Berkowitz, S., Simpson, H., Weber, E. U., & Walsh, B. (2012). Increased capacity to delay reward in anorexia nervosa. *Journal of the International Neuropsychological Society, 18*(4), 773–780. doi:10.1017/S1355617712000446.

Steinhauser, K. E., Alexander, S. C., Byock, I. R., George, L. K., et al. (2008). Do preparation and life completion discussions improve functioning and quality of life in seriously ill patients? Pilot randomized control trial. *Journal of Palliative Medicine, 11*, 1234–1240.

Stellar, J. E., Manzo, V. M., Kraus, M. W., & Keltner, D. (2011). Class and compassion: Socioeconomic factors predict responses to suffering. *Emotion*, doi:10.1037/a0026508.

Stenfelt, S. (2011). Acoustic and physiologic aspects of bone conduction hearing. *Advances in Otorhinolaryngology*, 71, 10–21.

Stepanikova, I., Triplett, J., & Simpson, B (2011). Implicit racial bias and prosocial behavior. *Social Science Research*, 40, 1186–1195.

Stepanyants, A., & Escobar, G. (2011). Statistical traces of long-term memories stored in strengths and patterns of synaptic connections. *Journal Of Neuroscience*, 31(21), 7657–7669. doi:10.1523/JNEUROSCI.0255–11.2011.

Stephan, K. E., Marshall, J. C., Friston, K. J., Rowe, J. B., Ritzl, A., Zilles, K., & Fink, G. R. (2003). Lateralized cognitive processes and lateralized task control in the human brain. *Science, 301*, 384–386.

Stephens, G. J., Silbert, L. J., & Hasson, U. (2010). Speaker–listener neural coupling underlies successful communication. *PNAS Proceedings of the National Academy of Sciences of the United States of America, 107*(32), 14425–14430. doi:10.1073/pnas.1008662107.

Stephens, R. S., Roffman, R. A., & Simpson, E. E. (1994). Treating adult marijuana dependence: A test of the relapse prevention model. *Journal of Consulting and Clinical Psychology*, 62(1), 92–99..

Steriade, M., & McCarley, R. W. (1990). *Brainstem control of wakefulness and sleep*. New York: Plenum.

Stern, K., & McClintock, M. K. (1998). Regulation of ovulation by human pheromones. *Nature, 392*, 177–179.

Stern, R. A., Riley, D. O., Daneshvar, D. H., Nowinski, C. J., Cantu, R. C., & McKee, A. C. (2011). Long-term consequences of repetitive brain trauma: chronic traumatic encephalopathy. *PM&R, 3*(10 Supplement 2), S460–2467.

Stern, W. L. (1914). The psychological methods of testing intelligence (G. M. Whipple, Trans.). *Educational Psychology Monographs, No. 13*. Baltimore: Warwick & York.

Sternberg, D., & McClelland, J. (2012). Two mechanisms of human contingency learning. *Psychological Science*, 23(1), 59–68.

Sternberg, R. (2009). A duplex theory of love. In R. Sternberg & K. Weis (Eds.), *The new psychology of love* (pp. 184–199). New Haven, CT: Yale University Press.

Sternberg, R. J. (1985). *Beyond IQ: A triarchic theory of human intelligence*. Cambridge, England: Cambridge University Press.

Sternberg, R. J. (1988). *The triarchic mind*. New York: Cambridge Press.

Sternberg, R. J. (1989). Domain generality versus domain specifi city: The life and impending death of a false dichotomy. *Merrill-Palmer Quarterly, 35*, 115–130.

Sternberg, R. J. (1996). *Successful intelligence*. New York: Simon & Schuster.

Sternberg, R. J. (1999). Ability and expertise: It's time to replace the current model of intelligence. *American Educator Spring 1999*, pp. 10–51.

Sternberg, R. J. (2001). What is the common thread of creativity? Its dialectical relation to intelligence and wisdom. *American Psychologist, 56*, 360–362.

Sternberg, R. J. (2004). Culture and intelligence. *American Psychologist, 59*, 325–338.

Sternberg, R. J. (2010). WICS: A new model for school psychology. *School Psychology International, 31*(6), 599–616. doi:10.1177/0143034310386534.

Sternberg, R. J., & Dess, N. K. (2001). Creativity for the new millennium. *American Psychologist, 56*, 332.

Sternberg, R. J., & Grigorenko, E. L. (Eds.). (2004a). *Creativity: From potential to realization*. Washington, DC: APA Books.

Sternberg, R. J., & Grigorenko, E. L. (Eds.). (2004b). *Culture and competence: Contexts of life success*. Washington, DC: APA Books.

Sternberg, R. J., & Kaufman, J. C. (1998). Human abilities. *Annual Review of Psychology, 49*, 479–502.

Sternberg, R. J., Lautrey, J., & Lubart, T. I. (2003). Where are we in the field of intelligence, how did we get here, and where are we going? In R. J. Sternberg, J. Lautrey, et al. (Eds.), *Models of intelligence: International perspectives* (pp. 3–25). Washington, DC: American Psychological Association.

Sternberg, R. J., & Lubart, T. I. (1992). Buy low and sell high: An investment approach to creativity. *Current Directions in Psychological Science, 1*(1), 1–5.

Sternberg, R. J., & The Rainbow Project Coordinators. (2006). The Rainbow Project: Enhancing the SAT through assessments of analytical, practical, and creative skills. *Intelligence, 34*, 321–350.

Sternberg, R. J., Wagner, R. K., Williams, W. M., & Horvath, J. A. (1995). Testing common sense. *American Psychologist, 50*, 912–927.

Sternberg, R. J., & Williams, W. M. (1997). Does the graduate record examination predict meaningful success of graduate training of psychologists? A case study. *American Psychologist, 52*, 630–641.

Sternberg, S. (2011). Modular processes in mind and brain. *Cognitive Neuropsychology, 28*(3–4), 156–208.

Stettler, D. D., Yamahachi, H., Li, W., Denk, W., & Gilbert, C. D. (2006). Axons and synaptic boutons are highly dynamic in adult visual cortex. *Neuron, 49*, 877–887.

Stevens, A. A., & Weaver, K. E. (2009). Functional characteristics of auditory cortex in the blind. *Behavioural Brain Research, 196*, 134–138.

Stevens, J. C., & Pollack, M. H. (2005). Benzodiazepines in clinical practice: Consideration of their long-term use and alternative agents. *Journal of Clinical Psychiatry, 66*(Suppl. 2), 21–27.

Stevens, R. D., & Bhardwaj, A. (2006). Approach to the comatose patient. *Critical Care Medicine, 34*(1), 31–41.

Stevenson, H. (1992). *A long way from being number one: What we can learn from East Asia*. Washington, DC: Federation of Behavior, Psychological and Cognitive Sciences.

Stevenson, R. J., & Boakes, R. A. (2003). A mnemonic theory of odor perception. *Psychological Review, 110*, 340–364.

Stewart, G. L. (2006). A meta-analytic review of relationships between team design features and team performance. *Journal of Management, 32*, 29–55.

Stewart, J. G., & Harkness, K. L. (2012). Symptom specificity in the acute treatment of major depressive disorder: A re-analysis of the treatment of depression collaborative research program. *Journal of Affective Disorders, 137*, 87–97.

Stewart, J. H. (2005). Hypnosis in contemporary medicine. *Mayo Clinic Proceedings, 80*, 511–524.

Stewart-Williams, S. (2004). The placebo puzzle: Putting together the pieces. *Health Psychology, 23*, 198–206.

Stice, E., Marti, C., & Durant, S. (2011). Risk factors for onset of eating disorders: Evidence of multiple risk pathways from an 8-year prospective study. *Behaviour Research & Therapy, 49*(10), 622–627. doi:10.1016/j.brat.2011.06.009.

Stice, E., Ragan, J., & Randall, P. (2004). Prospective relations between social support and depression: Differential direction of effects for parent and peer support? *Journal of Abnormal Psychology, 113*, 155–159.

Stickgold, R., James, L., & Hobson, J. A. (2000). Visual discrimination learning requires sleep after training. *Nature Neuroscience, 3*, 1237–1238.

Stickgold, R., Rittenhouse, C. D., & Hobson, J. A. (1994). Dream splicing: A new technique for assessing thematic coherence in subjective reports of mental activity. *Consciousness and Cognition, 3*(1), 114–128.

Stiegler, M. P., Neelankavil, J. P., Canales, C. C., & Dhillon, A. A. (2012). Cognitive errors detected in anaesthesiology: A literature review and pilot study. *BJA: The British Journal of Anaesthesia, 108*(2), 229–235.

Stilling, R. M., Dinan, T. G., & Cryan, J. F. (2014). Microbial genes, brain & behavior: Epigenetic regulation of the gut–brain axis. *Genes, Brain & Behavior, 13*(1), 69–86.

Stillwell, M. E. (2002). Drug-facilitated sexual assault involving gamma-hydroxybutyric acid. *Journal of Forensic Science, 47*, 1133–1134.

Stipek, D. J. (1983). A developmental analysis of pride and shame. *Human Development, 26*, 42–56.

Stirrat, M., & Perrett, D. I. (2010). Valid facial cues to cooperation and trust: Male facial width and trustworthiness. *Psychological Science, 21*(3) 349–354. doi:10.1177/0956797610362647.

Stoerig, P. & Cowey, A. (1997). "Blindsight in man and monkey". *Brain* 120(3): 535–559.

Stoet, G., & Geary, D. C. (2012). Can stereotype threat explain the gender gap in mathematics performance and achievement? *Review of General Psychology, 16*(1), 93–102. doi:10.1037/a0026617.

Stöllberger, C., Huber, J. O., & Finsterer, J. (2005). Antipsychotic drugs and QT prolongation. *International Clinical Psychopharmacology, 20*(5), 243–251.

Stone, A. A., Schwartz, J. E., Broderick, J. E., & Deaton, A. S. (2010). A snapshot of the age distribution of psychological well-being in the United States. *Proceedings of the National Academy of Sciences, 107*, 9985–9990.

Stone, M., Laughren, T., Jones, M. L., Levenson, M., et al. (2009). Risk of suicidality in clinical trials of antidepressants in adults: Analysis of proprietary data submitted to U.S. Food and Drug Administration. *British Medical Journal, 339*, b2880.

Stone, J., & Fernandez, N. C. (2008). To practice what we preach: The use of hypocrisy and cognitive dissonance to motivate behavior change. *Social and Personality Psychology Compass, 2*, 1024–1051.

Stoney, C. M., & Finney, M. L. (2000). Social support and stress: Influences on lipid reactivity. *International Journal of Behavioral Medicine, 7*, 111–126.

Stoney, C. M., Hughes, J. W., Kuntz, K. K., West, S. G., & Thornton, L. M. (2002). Cardiovascular stress responses among Asian Indian and European American women and men. *Annals of Behavioral Medicine, 24*, 113–121.

Stoney, C. M., & Matthews, K. A. (1988). Parental history of hypertension and myocardial infarction predicts cardiovascular responses to behavioral stressors in middle-aged men and women. *Psychophysiology, 25*, 269–277.

Storm, B. C. (2011). The benefit of forgetting in thinking and remembering. *Current Directions in Psychological Science, 20*(5) 291–295. doi:10.1177/0963721411418469.

Stout, H. (2010, April 30). Antisocial networking. *The New York Times*. Retrieved from http://www.nytimes.com.

St. Pourcain, B., Wang, K., Glessner, J. T., Golding, J., Steer, C., Ring, S. M., Skuse, D. H., Grant, S. F. A., Hakonarson, H., & Smith, G. D. (2010). Association between a high-risk autism locus on 5p14 and social communication spectrum phenotypes in the general population. *American Journal of Psychiatry, xx*. Epub 2010 Jul 15. doi: 10.1176/ appi.ajp.2010.09121789.

Strahan, E. J., Spencer, S. J., & Zanna, M. P. (2005). Subliminal priming and persuasion: How motivation affects the activation of goals and the persuasiveness of messages. In F. R. Kardes, P. Herr, & J. Nantel (Eds.), *Applying social cognition to consumer-focused strategy* (pp. 267–280). Mahwah, NJ: Erlbaum.

Strain, E. C., Mumford, G. K., Silverman, K., & Griffiths, R. R. (1994). Caffeine dependence syndrome: Evidence from case histories and experimental evaluations. *Journal of the American Medical Association, 272*(13), 1043–1048.

Straus, M. A. (2005). Children should never, ever, be spanked no matter what the circumstances. In D. R. Loseke, R. J. Gelles, & M. M. Cavanaugh (Eds.), *Current controversies about family violence* (2nd ed., pp. 137–157). Thousand Oaks, CA: Sage.

Strauss, E., & Wada, J. (1983). Lateral preferences and cerebral speech dominance. *Cortex, 19*(2), 165–177.

Strauss, R. S., & Pollack, H. A. (2001). Epidemic increases in childhood overweight: 1986–1998. *Journal of the American Medical Association, 286*, 2845–2848.

Strayer, D. L., & Drews, F. A. (2007). Cell-phone-induced driver distraction. *Current Directions in Psychological Science, 16*(3), 128–131.

Strick, P. L., Dum, R. P., & Fiez, J. A. (2009). Cerebellum and nonmotor function. *Annual Review of Neuroscience, 32*, 413–434.

Stringhini, S., Sabia, S., Shipley, M., Brunner, E., et al. (2010). Association of socioeconomic position with health behaviors and mortality. *Journal of the American Medical Association, 303*, 1159–1166.

Strohmetz, D. B., Rind, B., Fisher, R., & Lynn, M. (2002). Sweetening the till: The use of candy to increase restaurant tipping. *Journal of Applied Social Psychology, 32*, 300–309.

Strohschein, L. (2005). Household income histories and child mental health trajectories. *Journal of Health and Social Behavior, 46*, 359–375.

Stroop, J. R. (1935). Studies of interference in serial verbal reactions. *Journal of Experimental Psychology, 18*, 643–662.

Stumbrys, T., Erlacher, D., Schädlich, M., & Schredl, M. (2012). Induction of lucid dreams: A systematic review of evidence. *Conscious & Cognition, 21*(3), 1456–75.

Stürmer, T., Hasselbach, P., & Amelang, M. (2006). Personality, lifestyle, and risk of cardiovascular disease and cancer: Follow-up of population based cohort. *British Medical Journal, 332*, 1359.

Su, C. Y., Menuz, K., & Carlson, J. R. (2009). Olfactory perception: Receptors, cells, and circuits. *Cell, 139*, 45–59.

Su, J. C., Tran, A. G. T. T., Wirtz, J. G., Langteau, R. A., & Rothman, A. J. (2008). Driving under the influence (of stress): Evidence of a regional increase in impaired driving and traffic fatalities after the September 11 terrorist attacks. *Psychological Science, 20*, 59–65.

Suarez, M. & Mullins, S. (2008). Motivational interviewing and pediatric Health behavior interventions. *Journal of Developmental and Behavioral Pediatrics, 29*, 417–428.

Subotnik, K. L., Nuechterlein, K. H., Green, M. F., Horan, W. P., et al. (2006). Neurocognitive and social cognitive correlates of formal thought disorder in schizophrenia patients. *Schizophrenia Research, 85*, 84–95.

Subotnik, R. F., Olszewski-Kubilius, P., & Worrell, F. C. (2011). Rethinking giftedness and gifted education: A proposed direction forward based on psychological science. *Psychological Science in the Public Interest, 12*(1), 3–54. doi:10.1177/1529100611418056.

Substance Abuse and Mental Health Services Administration. (2007). *Results from the 2006 National Survey on Drug Use and Health: National findings*. Rockville, MD: Author.

Suddath, R. L., Christison, G. W., Torrey, E. F., Casanova, M. F., & Weinberger, D. R. (1990). Anatomical abnormalities in the brains of monopsychotic twins discordant for schizophrenia. *New England Journal of Medicine, 322*, 789–794.

Suddendorf, T. & Corballis, M. C. (2007). The evolution of foresight: What is mental time travel, and is it unique to humans? *Behavioral and Brain Sciences, 30*, 299–313.

Sue, D. W., & Sue, D. (2008). *Counseling the culturally diverse: Theory and practice* (5th ed.). Hoboken, NJ: Wiley.

Sue, D. W., & Sue, D. (2012). *Counseling the culturally diverse: Theory and practice* (6th ed.). Hoboken, NJ: Wiley.

Sue, S., & Okazaki, S. (1990). Asian-American educational achievements: A phenomenon in search of an explanation. *American Psychologist, 45*, 913–920.

Sue, S., Zane, N., Hall, G. C. N., & Berger, L. K. (2009). The case for cultural competency in psychotherapeutic interventions. *Annual Review of Psychology, 60*, 525–548.

Suh, E., Diener, E., & Fujita, F. (1996). Events and subjective well-being: Only recent events matter. *Journal of Personality and Social Psychology, 70*, 1091–1102.

Sukhotinsky, I., Chan, A. M., Ahmed, O. J., Rao, V. R., Gradinaru, V., Ramakrishnan, C., Deisseroth, K., Majewska, A. K., & Cash, S. S. (2013). Optogenetic delay of status epilepticus onset in an in vivo rodent epilepsy model. *PloS One, 8*(4), e62013.

Sullivan, H. S. (1954). *The psychiatric interview*. New York: Norton.

Sullivan, J. W., & Horowitz, F. D. (1983). The effects of intonation on infant attention: The role of the rising intonation contour. *Journal of Child Language, 10*, 521–534.

Sullivan, P. F., Kendler, K. S., & Neale, M. C. (2003). Schizophrenia as a complex trait: Evidence from a meta-analysis of twin studies. *Archives of General Psychiatry, 60*, 1187–1192.

Suls, J., & Bunde, J. (2005). Anger, anxiety, and depression as risk factors for cardiovascular disease: The problems and implications of overlapping affective dispositions. *Psychological Bulletin, 131*, 260–300.

Suls, J., & Howren, M. (2012). Understanding the physical-symptom experience: The distinctive contributions of anxiety and depression. *Current Directions in Psychological Science, 21*(2), 129–134. doi:10.1177/0963721412439298.

Suls, J., & Rothman, A. (2004). Evolution of the biopsychosocial model: Prospects and challenges for health psychology. *Health Psychology, 23*, 119–125.

Suls, J., & Wan, C. K. (1993). The relationship between trait hostility and cardiovascular reactivity: A quantitative review and analysis. *Psychophysiology, 30*, 1–12.

Sun, Q., Townsend, M. K., Okereke, O. I., Franco, O. H., et al. (2010). Physical activity at midlife in relation to successful survival in women at age 70 years or older. *Archives of Internal Medicine, 170*, 194–201.

Sun, Y. G., Zhao, Z. Q., Meng, X. L., Yin, J., et al. (2009). Cellular basis of itch sensation. *Science, 325*, 1531–1534. Epub 2009 Aug 6.

Suokas, J. T., Suvisaari, J. M., Gissler, M., Löfman, R., Linna, M. S., Raevuori, A., & Haukka, J. (2013). Mortality in eating disorders: A follow-up study of adult eating disorder patients treated in tertiary care, 1995–2010. *Psychiatry Research, 210*(3), 1101–1106.

Suomi, S. (1999). Attachment in rhesus monkeys. In J. Cassidy & P. Shaver (Eds.), *Handbook of attachment* (pp. 181–197). New York: Guilford.

Suomi, S. (2004). Aggression, serotonin, and gene-environment interactions in rhesus monkeys. In J. T. Cacioppo & G. G. Berntson (Eds.), *Essays in social neuroscience* (pp. 15–27). Cambridge, MA: MIT Press.

Suschinsky, K. D., & Lalumière, M. L. (2011). Prepared for anything? An investigation of female genital arousal in response to rape cues. *Psychological Science, 22*(2), 159–165. doi:10.1177/0956797610394660.

Susilo, T., Yovel, G., Barton, J. J., & Duchaine, B. (2013). Face perception is category-specific: Evidence from normal body perception in acquired prosopagnosia. *Cognition, 129*(1), 88–94.

Sussman, A. B., & Shafir, E. (2012). On assets and debt in the psychology of perceived wealth. *Psychological Science, 23*(1), 101–108. doi:10.1177/0956797611421484.

Sutcher, H. (2008). Hypnosis, hypnotizability, and treatment. *American Journal of Clinical Hypnosis, 51*, 57–67.

Suzuki, L. A., & Valencia, R. R. (1997). Race-ethnicity and measured intelligence. *American Psychologist, 52*, 1103–1114.

Suzuki, W. A. (2008). Hippocampal place fields: Relevance to learning and memory. In Mizumori, Sheri J. Y. (Ed.), *Hippocampal place fields*, pp. 218–233. New York: Oxford University Press.

Swaab, D. E., & Hofman, M. A. (1995). Sexual differentiation of the human hypothalamus in relation to gender and sexual orientation. *Trends in Neuroscience, 18*(6), 264–270.

Swain, J., Hancock, K., Hainsworth, C., & Bowman, J. (2013). Acceptance and commitment therapy in the treatment of anxiety: A systematic review. *Clinical Psychology Review, 33*, 965–978.

Swan, G. E. (1996, December). Some elders thrive on working into late life. *APA Monitor*, 35.

Swan, G. E., & Carmelli, D. (1996). Curiosity and mortality in aging adults: A 5-year follow-up of the Western Collaborative Group Study. *Psychology and Aging, 11*, 449–453.

Swaney, W. T. & Keverne, E. B. (2009). The evolution of pheromonal communication. *Behavior and Brain Research, 200*, 239–247.

Swann, W. B., Buhrmeister, M. D., Gómez, A., Jetten, J., Bastian, B., Vázquez, A., Ariyanto, A. et al. (2014). What makes a group worth dying for? Identity fusion fosters perception of familial ties, promoting self-sacrifice. *Journal of Personality & Social Psychology, 106*(6), 912–926.

Swanson, S. A., Crow, S. J., Le Grange, D., Swendsen, J., & Merikangas, K. R. (2011). Prevalence and correlates of eating disorders in adolescents: Results from the national comorbidity survey replication adolescent supplement. *Archives of General Psychiatry, 68*(7), 714–723. doi:10.1001/archgenpsychiatry.2011.22.

Swarte, N. B., van der Lee, M. L., van der Bom, J. G., van den Bout, J., & Heintz, A. P. M. (2003). Effects of euthanasia on the bereaved family and friends: A cross sectional study. *British Medical Journal, 327,* 189.

Swartz, H. A., Zuckoff, A., Grote, N. K., Spielvogle, H. N., Bledsoe, S. E., Shear, M. K., & Frank, E. (2007). Engaging depressed patients in psychotherapy: Integrating techniques from motivational interviewing and ethnographic interviewing to improve treatment. participation. *Professional Psychology: Research and Practice, 38,* 430–439.

Swendsen, J., Burstein, M., Case, B., Conway, K., Dierker, L., He, J., & Merikangas, K. (2012). Use and abuse of alcohol and illicit drugs in US adolescents: Results of the National Comorbidity Survey-Adolescent Supplement. *Archives Of General Psychiatry, 69*(4), 390–398.

Swerdlow, R. H. (2011). Brain aging, Alzheimer's disease, and mitochondria. *Biochimica et Biophysica Acta, 1812*(12), 1630–1639.

Swets, J. A. (1996). *Signal detection theory and ROC analysis in psychology and diagnostics.* New Jersey: Erlbaum.

Swets, J. A., Dawes, R. M., & Monahan, J. (2000). Psychological science can improve diagnostic decisions. *Psychological Science in the Public Interest, 1,* 1–26.

Swift, R. (2010). Medications acting on the dopaminergic system in the treatment of alcoholic patients. *Current Pharmaceutical Design, 16*(19), 2136–2140.

Swithers, S. E., & Hall, W. G. (1994). Does oral experience terminate ingestion? *Appetite, 23*(2), 113–138.

Szameitat, D. P., Kreifelts, B., Alter, K., Szameitat, A. J., Sterr, A., Grodd, W., & Wildgruber, D. (2010). It is not always tickling: Distinct cerebral responses during perception of different laughter types. *Neuroimage, 53*(4), 1264–1271. doi:10.1016/j.neuroimage.2010.06.028.

Szasz, T. (2003). The psychiatric protection order for the "battered mental patient." *British Medical Journal, 327,* 1449–1451.

Szasz, T. (2009). *Coercion as cure.* Edison, NJ: Transaction Publishers.

Szegedi, A., Kohnen, R., Dienel, A., & Kieser, M. (2005). Acute treatment of moderate to severe depression with hypericum extract WS 5570 (St John's wort): Randomised controlled double blind non-inferiority trial versus paroxetine. *British Medical Journal, 330,* 503.

Szmigielski, S. (2013). Cancer risks related to low-level RF/MW exposures, including cell phones. *Electromagnetic Biology and Medicine, 32*(3), 273–280.

Szpunar, K. K. (2010). Episodic future thought: An emerging concept. *Perspectives on Psychological Science, 5,* 142–162.

Szpunar, K. K., Chan, J. C., & McDermott, K. B. (2009). Contextual processing in episodic future thought. *Cerebral Cortex, 19,* 1539–1548. doi:10.1093/cercor/bhn191.

Szpunar, K. K., Watson, J. M., & McDermott, K. B. (2007). Neural substrates of envisioning the future. *Proceedings of the National Academy of Sciences, 104,* 642–647.

Taggar, S., Hackett, R., & Saha, S. (1999). Leadership emergence in autonomous work teams: Antecedents and outcomes. *Personnel Psychology, 52,* 899–926.

Takashima, A., Petersson, K. M., Rutters, F., Tendolkar, I., Jensen, O., Zwarts, M. J., et al. (2006). Declarative memory consolidation in humans: A prospective functional magnetic resonance imaging study. *Proceedings of the National Academy of Sciences, 103,* 756–761.

Takkouche, B., Etminan, M., & Montes-Martinez, A. (2005). Personal use of hair dyes and risk of cancer. *Journal of the American Medical Association, 293,* 2516–2525.

Talarico, J. F., & Rubin, D. C. (2003). Confidence, not consistency, characterizes flashbulb memories. *Psychological Science, 14,* 455–461.

Talmi, D., Grady, C. L., Goshen-Gottstein, Y., & Moscovitch, M. (2005). Neuroimaging the serial position curve: A test of single-store versus dual-store models. *Psychological Science, 16,* 716–723.

Tamashiro, K. L. K., & Bello, N. T. (Eds.) (2008). Special issue on leptin. *Physiology & Behavior, 94*(5).

Tamir, M. (2009). What do people want to feel and why? Pleasure and utility in emotion regulation. *Current Directions in Psychological Science, 18,* 101–105.

Tan, G., Hammond, D. C., & Joseph, G. (2005). Hypnosis and irritable bowel syndrome: A review of efficacy and mechanism of action. *American Journal of Clinical Hypnosis, 47,* 161–178.

Tan, H.-Y., Chen, Q., Sust, S., Buckholtz, J. W., et al. (2007). Epistasis between catechol-Omethyltransferase and type II metabotropic glutamate receptor 3 genes on working memory brain function. *Proceedings of the National Academy of Sciences, 104,* 12536–12541.

Tan, L. (2008). Psychotherapy 2.0: MySpace blogging as self-therapy. *American Journal of Psychotherapy, 62,* 143–163.

Tanaka, A., Koizumi, A., Imai, H., Hiramatsu, S., Hiramoto, E., & de Gelder, B. (2010). I feel your voice: Cultural differences in the multisensory perception of emotion. *Psychological Science, 21*(9), 1259–1262. doi:10.1177/0956797610380698.

Tanaka, H., Taira, K., Arakawa, M., Toguti, H., Urasaki, C., Yamamoto, Y., et al. (2001). Effects of short nap and exercise on elderly people having difficulty sleeping. *Psychiatry and Clinical Neurosciences, 55,* 173–174.

Tanaka, K., & Miyake, Y. (2011). Association between prenatal and postnatal tobacco smoke exposure and allergies in young children. *Journal of Asthma, 48*(5), 458–463. doi:10.3109/02770903.2011.578314.

Tandon, P. S., Zhou, C., Lozano, P., & Christakis, D. A. (2011). Preschoolers' total daily screen time at home and by type of child care. *The Journal Of Pediatrics, 158*(2), 297–300. doi:10.1016/j.jpeds.2010.08.005.

Tandon, R., Keshavan, M. S., & Nasrallah, H. A. (2008). Schizophrenia, "Just the facts" What we know in 2008: 2. Epidemiology and etiology. *Schizophrenia Research, 102*(1–3), 1–18.

Tandon, R., Nasrallah, H. A., & Keshavan, M. S. (2009). Schizophrenia, "just the facts": 4. Clinical features and conceptualization, *Schizophrenia Research, 110,* 1–23.

Tang, T. L., Tang, T. L., & Homaifar, B. Y. (2006). Income, the love of money, pay comparison, and pay satisfaction: Race and gender as moderators. *Journal of Managerial Psychology, 21,* 476–491.

Tang, Y. Y., Ma, Y., Wang, J., Fan, Y., Feng, S., Lu, Q., Yu, Q., Sui, D., Rothbart, M. K., Fan, M., & Posner, M. I. (2007). Short-term meditation training improves attention and self-regulation. *Proceedings of the National Academies of Science, 104,* 17152–17156.

Tannen, D. (2001). *You just don't understand: Women and men in conversation.* New York: HarperCollins.

Tannen, D. (2011). *That's not what I meant!: How conversational style makes or breaks relationships.* New York: Harper.

Tanner, J. M. (1978). *Foetus into man: Physical growth from conception to maturity.* London: Open Books.

Targino, R. A., Imamura, M., Kaziyama, H. H., Souza, L. P., Hsing, W. T., Furland, A. D., Imamura, S. T., & Azevedo Neto, R. S. (2008). A randomized controlled trial of acupuncture added to usual treatment for fibromyalgia. *Journal of Rehabilitation Medicine, 40*(7), 582–588.

Task Force on Sudden Infant Death Syndrome. (2011). SIDS and other sleep- related infant deaths: Expansion of recommendations for a safe infant sleeping environment. *Pediatrics, 128*(5), 1030–1039.

Tassi, P., & Muzet, A. (2001). Defining states of consciousness. *Neuroscience and Biobehavioral Reviews, 25,* 175–191.

Taubenfeld, S. M., Milekic, M. H., Monti, B., & Alberini, C. M. (2001). The consolidation of new but not reactivated memory requires hippocampal C/EBPb. *Nature Neuroscience, 4,* 813–818.

Tavris, C. (2002). The high cost of skepticism. *Skeptical Inquirer, 26,* 41–44.

Tavris, C. (2003). Mind games: Psychological warfare between therapists and scientists. *The Chronicle of Higher Education, 49,* B7–B9.

Taylor, C. A., Manganello, J. A., Lee, S. J., & Rice, J. C. (2010). Mothers' spanking of 3-year-old children and subsequent risk of children's aggressive behavior. *Pediatrics, 125*(5), e1057–e1065. doi:10.1542/peds.2009–2678.

Taylor, G., & Herbert, J. S. (2013). Eye tracking infants: Investigating the role of attention during learning on recognition memory. *Scandinavian Journal of Psychology 54,* 14–19.

Taylor, G., McNeill, A., Girling, A., Farley, A., Lindson-Hawley, N., & Aveyard, P. (2014). Change in mental health after smoking cessation: systematic review and meta-analysis. *BMJ, 348,* g1151.

Taylor, H. A., & Tversky, B. (1992). Spatial mental models derived from survey and route descriptions. *Journal of Memory and Language, 31,* 261–292.

Taylor, J. C., & Downing, P. E. (2011). Division of labor between lateral and ventral extrastriate representation of faces, bodies, and objects. *Journal of Cognitive Neuroscience, 23*(12), 4122–4137.

Taylor, J. G. (2002). Paying attention to consciousness. *Trends in Cognitive Science, 6,* 206–210.

Taylor, S. (2004). Efficacy and outcome predictors for three PTSD treatments: Exposure therapy, EMDR, and relaxation training. In S. Taylor (Ed.), *Advances in the treatment of posttraumatic stress disorder: Cognitive-behavioral perspectives* (pp. 13–37). New York: Springer.

Taylor, S. (2014). Twin studies of the genetic and environmental etiology of obsessive-compulsive and related phenomena. In E. A. Storch & D. McKay (Eds.), *Obsessive-compulsive disorder and its spectrum: A life-span approach* (pp. 347–362). Washington, DC: American Psychological Association.

Taylor, S., & Asmundson, G. J. G. (2008). Hypochondriasis. In J. S. Abramowitz, D. McKay, & S. Taylor. *Clinical handbook of obsessive-compulsive disorder and related problems* (pp. 304–315). Baltimore, MD: Johns Hopkins University Press.

Taylor, S. E. (1999). *Health psychology* (4th ed.). New York: McGraw-Hill.

Taylor, S. E. (2002). *Health psychology* (5th ed.). New York: McGraw-Hill.

Taylor, S. E. (2010). Mechanisms linking early life stress to adult health outcomes. *Proceedings of the National Academy of Sciences, 107,* 8507–8512.

Taylor, S. E., Dickerson, S. S., & Klein, L. C. (2002). Toward a biology of social support. In C. R. Snyder & S. L. Lopez (Eds.), *Handbook of positive psychology* (pp. 556–569). London: Oxford University Press.

Taylor, S. E., Gonzaga, G. C., Klein, L. C., Hu, P., Greendale, G. A., & Seeman, T. E. (2006). Relation of oxytocin to psychological stress responses and hypothalamic-pituitary-adrenocortical axis activity in older women. *Psychosomatic Medicine, 68,* 238–245.

Taylor, S. E., Kemeny, M. E., Reed, G. M., Bower, J. E., & Gruenewald, T. L. (2000). Psychological resources, positive illusions, and health. *American Psychologist, 55,* 99–109.

Taylor, S. E., Klein, L. C., Lewis, B. P., Gruenewald, T. L., Gurung, R. A. R., & Updegraff, J. A. (2000). Biobehavioral responses to stress in females: Tend-and-befriend, not fight-or-flight. *Psychological Review, 107,* 411–429.

Taylor, S. (2014). Twin studies of the genetic and environmental etiology of obsessive-compulsive and related phenomena. In E. A. Storch & D. McKay (Eds.), *Obsessive-compulsive disorder and its spectrum: A life-span approach* (pp. 347–362). Washington, DC: American Psychological Association.

Taylor, S. E., Lerner, J. S., Sherman, K. D., Sage, R. M., & McDowell, N. K. (2003). Are self-enhancing cognitions associated with health or unhealthy biological profiles? *Journal of Personality and Social Psychology, 85,* 605–615.

Teachman, J. D. (2008). The living arrangements of children and their educational well-being. *Journal of Family Issues, 29,* 734–761.

Tedeschi, R. G., & McNally, R. J. (2011). Can We Facilitate Posttraumatic Growth in Combat Veterans?. *American Psychologist, 66*(1), 19–24. doi:10.1037/ a0021896.

Téglás, E., Vul, E., Girotto, V., Gonzalez, M., Tenenbaum, J. B., & Bonatti, L. L. (2011). Pure Reasoning in 12-Month-Old Infants as Probabilistic Inference. *Science, 332*(6033), 1054–1059. doi:10.1126/science.1196404.

Teipel, S. J., Grothe, M., Lista, S., Toschi, N., Garaci, F. G., & Hampel, H. (2013). Relevance of magnetic resonance imaging for early detection and diagnosis of Alzheimer's disease. *Medical Clinics of North America, 97*(3), 399–424.

Teitelbaum, P., & Stellar, E. (1954). Recovery from the failure to eat produced by hypothalamic lesions. *Science, 120,* 894–895.

Tejada-Vera, B. (2013). Mortality from Alzheimer's disease in the United States: Data for 2000 and 2010. *NCHS Data Brief,* (116), 1–8.

Telegraph Correspondent. (2005, April 18). Scratching your cars was art, says vandal. *Daily Telegraph,* p. 5.

Tellegen, A., Lykken, D. T., Bouchard, T. J., Wilcox, K. J., Segal, N. L., & Rich, S. (1988). Personality similarity in twins reared apart and together. *Journal of Personality and Social Psychology, 54,* 1031–1039.

ten Brink, L., Stimson, D., & Carney, D. R. (2014). Some evidence for unconscious lie detection. *Psychological Science, 25*(5), 1098–1105.

ten Brummelhuis, L. L., & Bakker, A. B. (2012). A resource perspective on the work–home interface: The work-home resources model. *American Psychologist,* doi:10.1037/a0027974.

Tenenbaum, E. J., Shah, R. J., Sobel, D. M., Malle, B. F., & Morgan, J. L. (2013). Increased focus on the mouth among infants in the first year of life: A longitudinal eye-tracking study. *Infancy, 18,* 534–553.

Tenenbaum, H. R. (2009). "You'd be good at that!" Gender patterns in parent-child talk about courses. *Social Development, 18,* 447–463.

Tenenbaum, H. R., & Leaper, C. (2003). Parent-child conversations about science: The socializations of gender inequities? *Developmental Psychology, 39,* 34–47.

Teper, R., Inzlicht, M., & Page-Gould, E. (2011). Are we more moral than we think?: Exploring the role of affect in moral behavior and moral forecasting. *Psychological Science, 22*(4), 553–558. doi:10.1177/0956797611402513.

Terbeck, S., Kahane, G., McTavish, S., Savulescu, J., Cowen, P. J., & Hewstone, M. (2012). Propranolol reduces implicit negative racial bias. *Psychopharmacology, 222*(3), 419–424.

Terburg, D., Aarts, H., & van Honk, J. (2012). Testosterone affects gaze aversion from angry faces outside of conscious awareness. *Psychological Science, 23*(5), 459–463. doi:10.1177/0956797611433336.

Terman, L. M. (1906). Genius and stupidity: A study of the intellectual process of seven "bright" and seven "stupid" boys. *Pedagogical Seminary, 13,* 307–373.

Terman, L. M. (1916). *The measurement of intelligence.* Boston: Houghton Mifflin.

Terman, L. M., & Oden, M. H. (1947). *The gifted child grows up: Vol. 4. Genetic studies of genius.* Stanford, CA: Stanford University Press.

Terman, M., & Terman, J. S. (2005). Light therapy for seasonal and nonseasonal depression: Efficacy, protocol, safety, and side effects. *CNS Spectrums, 10,* 647–663.

Terracciano, A., Sanna, S., Uda, M., Deiana, B., et al. (2010). Genome-wide association scan for five major dimensions of personality. *Molecular Psychiatry, 15,* 647–656.

Terrace, H. S., Petitto, L. A., Sanders, D. L., & Bever, J. G. (1979). Can an ape create a sentence? *Science, 206,* 891–902.

Tessari, T., Rubaltelli, E., Tomelleri, S., Zorzi, C., Pietroni, D., Levorato, C., & Rumiati, R. (2011). €1 ≠ €1: Coins versus banknotes and people's spending behavior. *European Psychologist, 16*(3), 238–246. doi:10.1027/1016–9040/a000078.

Tetlock, P. E. (2006). *Expert political judgment: How good is it? How can we know?* Princeton, NJ: Princeton University Press.

Thakkar, R. R., Garrison, M. M., & Christakis, D. A. (2006). A systematic review for the effects of television viewing by infants and preschoolers. *Pediatrics, 118,* 2025–2031.

Thaler, E. R., Kennedy, D. W., & Hanson, C. W. (2001). Medical applications of electronic nose technology: Review of current status. *American Journal of Rhinology, 15,* 291–295.

Thase, M. E. (2011). Antidepressant combinations: Widely used, but far from empirically validated. *Canadian Journal of Psychiatry, 56*(6), 317–323.

Thase, M. E. (2013). Antidepressant combinations: Cutting edge psychopharmacology or passing fad? *Current Psychiatry Reports, 15*(10), 403.

Thelen, E. (1995). Motor development: A new synthesis. *American Psychologist, 50,* 79–95.

Theofilopoulos, S., Goggi, J., Riaz, S. S., Jauniaux, E., Stern, G. M., & Bradford, H. F. (2001). Parallel induction of the formation of dopamine and its metabolites with induction of tyrosine hydroxylase expression in foetal rat and human cerebral cortical cells by brain-derived neurotrophic factor and glial-cell derived neurotrophic factor. *Brain Research: Developmental Brain Research, 127,* 111–122.

Thiering, E., Brüske, I., Kratzsch, J., Thiery, J., Sausenthaler, S., Meisinger, C., & .. Heinrich, J. (2011). Prenatal and postnatal tobacco smoke exposure and development of insulin resistance in 10 year old children. *International Journal of Hygiene & Environmental Health, 214*(5), 361–368. doi:10.1016/j.ijheh.2011.04.004.

Thies, W., Bleiler, L., & Alzheimer's Association (2013). 2013 Alzheimer's disease facts and figures. *Alzheimer's & Dementia, 9*(2), 208–245.

Thiessen, E. D., Hill, E. A., & Saffran, J. R. (2005). Infant-directed speech facilitates word segmentation. *Infancy, 7,* 53–71.

Thomas, A., & Chess, S. (1977). *Temperament and development.* New York: Brunner/Mazel.

Thomas, E. L., & Robinson, H. A. (1972). *Improving reading in every class: A sourcebook for teachers.* Boston: Allyn & Bacon.

Thomas, J. A., & Walton, D. (2007). Measuring perceived risk: Self-reported and actual hand positions of SUV and car drivers. *Traffic Psychology and Behavior, 10,* 201–207.

Thomas, R., & Forde, E. (2006). The role of local and global processing in the recognition of living and nonliving things. *Neuropsychologia, 44*(6), 982–986.

Thompson, G. J., Hurd, P. L., & Crespi, B. J. (2013). Genes underlying altruism. *Biological Letters, 9*(6), 20130395.

Thompson, C., Koon, E., Woodwell, W., Jr., & Beauvais, J. (2002). *Training for the next economy: An ASTD state of the industry report on trend in employer-provided training in the United States.* Washington, DC: American Society for Training and Development.

Thompson, D., Baranowski, T., Buday, R., Baranowski, J., Thompson, V., Jago, R., & Griffith, M. (2010). Serious video games for health: How behavioral science guided the development of a serious video game. *Simulation & Gaming, 41*(4), 587–606. doi:10.1177/1046878108328087.

Thompson, E. H., & Hampton, J. A. (2011). The effect of relationship status on communicating emotions through touch. *Cognition & Emotion, 25*(2), 295–306. doi:10.1080/02699931.2010.492957.

Thompson, E. M., & Morgan, E. M. (2008). "Mostly straight" young women: Variations in sexual behavior and identity development. *Developmental Psychology, 44,* 15–21.

Thompson, G. J., Hurd, P. L., & Crespi, B. J. (2013). Genes underlying altruism. *Biological Letters, 9*(6), 20130395.

Thompson, J. K. (1996). Introduction: Assessment and treatment of binge eating disorder. In J. K. Thompson (Ed.), *Body image, eating disorders, and obesity* (pp. 1–22). Washington, DC: American Psychological Association.

Thompson, P. M., Giedd, J. N., Woods, R. P., Macdonald, D., et al. (2000). Growth patterns in the developing brain detected by using continuum mechanical tensor maps. *Nature, 404,* 190–193.

Thompson, R. A. (2006). The development of the person: Social understanding, relationships, self, conscience. In W. Damon & R. M. Lerner (Series Eds.) & N. Eisenberg (Vol. Ed.), *Handbook of child psychology: Vol. 3. Social, emotional, and personality development* (6th ed.). New York: Wiley.

Thompson, R. A., Lewis, M. D., & Calkins, S. D. (2008). Reassessing emotion regulation. *Child Development Perspectives, 2,* 124–131.

Thompson, R. F. (2009). Habituation: A history. *Neurobiology of Learning and Memory, 92*(2),127–134.

Thompson, V. B., Heiman, J., Chambers, J. B., Benoit, S. C., et al. (2009). Long-term behavioral consequences of prenatal MDMA exposure. *Physiology and Behavior, 96,* 593–601.

Thompson-Brenner, H., Glass, S., & Westen, D. (2003). A multidimensional meta-analysis of psychotherapy for bulimia nervosa. *Clinical Psychology: Science and Practice, 10,* 269–287.

Thomsen, L., Green, E. G. T., & Sidanius, J. (2008).We will hunt them down: How social dominance orientation and right-wing authoritarianism fuel ethnic persecution of immigrants in fundamentally different ways. *Journal of Experimental Social Psychology, 44,* 1455–1464.

Thomson, C. P. (1982). Memory for unique personal events: The roommate study. *Memory & Cognition, 10,* 324–332.

Thoresen, C. J., Kaplan, S. A., Barsky, A. P., Warren, C. R., & de Chermont, K. (2003). The affective underpinnings of job perceptions and attitudes: A meta-analytic review and integration. *Psychological Bulletin, 129,* 914–945.

Thorndike, E. L. (1898). Animal intelligence: An experienced study of the associative process in animals. *Psychological Monographs, 2*(Whole No. 8).

Thorndike, E. L. (1905). *The elements of psychology.* New York: Seiler.

Thorndike, R. L., & Hagen, E. P. (1996). *Form 5 CogAT interpretive guide of school administrators: All levels.* Chicago: Riverside.

Thornton, W. E. (2011). A rationale for space motion sickness. Aviation, Space, and Environmental Medicine, 82(4), 467–468.

Thunberg, T. (1896). Förnimmelserne vid till samma ställe lokaliserad, samtidigt pågående köld-och värmeretning. *Uppsala Läkfören Förhandlingar, 1,* 489–495.

Thurston, I. B., & Phares, V. (2008). Mental health service utilization in African American and Caucasian mothers and fathers. *Journal of Consulting and Clinical Psychology, 76,* 1058–1067.

Tieman, D., Bliss, P., McIntyre, L. M., Blandon-Ubeda, A., Bies, D., Odabasi, A. Z., Rodríguez, G. R., van der Knaap, E., Taylor, M. G., Goulet, C., Mageroy, M. H., Snyder, D. J., Colquhoun, T., Moskowitz, H., Clark, D. G., Sims, C., Bartoshuk, L., & Klee, H. J. (2012).The chemical interactions underlying tomato flavor preferences. *Current Biology, 22*(11), 1035–1039.

Tienari, P., Wynne, L. C., Läksy, K., Moring, J., Nieminen, P., et al. (2003). Genetic boundaries of the schizophrenia spectrum: Evidence from the Finnish Adoptive Family Study of Schizophrenia. *American Journal of Psychiatry, 160,* 1587–1594.

Tierney, J. (2009, March 10). What do dreams mean? Whatever your bias says. *New York Times,* D2.

Tiihonen, J., Kuikka, J., Bergstrom, K., Hakola, P., Karhu, J., Ryynänen, O.-P., & Föhr, J. (1995). Altered striatal dopamine re-uptake site densities in habitually violent and non-violent alcoholics. *Nature Medicine, 1*(7), 654–657.

Tillfors, M., Carlbring, P., Furmark, T., Lewenhaupt, S., et al. (2008). Treating university students with social phobia and public speaking fears: Internet delivered self-help with or without live group exposure sessions. *Depression and Anxiety, 25,* 708–717.

Timko, C., Finney, J. W., & Moos, R. H. (2005). The 8-year course of alcohol abuse: Gender differences in social context and coping. *Alcoholism: Clinical and Experimental Research, 29,* 612–621.

Timms, P. (2005). Is there still a problem with homelessness and schizophrenia? *International Journal of Mental Health, 34,* 57–75.

Tinbergen, N. (1989). *The study of instinct.* Oxford, UK: Clarendon.

Tindale, R. S., & Kameda, T. (2000). "Social sharedness" as a unifying theme for information processing in groups. *Group Processes and Intergroup Relations, 3,* 123–140.

Tindle, H., Belnap, B. H., Houck, P. R., Mazumdar, S., Scheier, M. F., Matthews, K. A., He, F., & Rollman, B. L. (2012). Optimism, response to treatment of depression, and rehospitalization after coronary artery bypass graft surgery. *Psychosomatic Medicine, 74*(2), 200–207. doi:10.1097/PSY.0b013e318244903f.

Todd, P. M., & Gigerenzer, G. (2007). Environments that make us smart: Ecological rationality. *Current Directions in Psychological Science, 16,* 167–171.

Todd, S., Barr, S., Roberts, M., & Passmore, A. P. (2013). Survival in dementia and predictors of mortality: A review. *International Journal of Geriatric Psychiatry, 28*(11), 1109–1124.

Todorov, A., & Porter, J. M. (2014). Misleading first impressions: Different for different facial images of the same person. *Psychological Science,* Epub May 27, 2014

Toffolo, M. J., Smeets, M. M., & van den Hout, M. A. (2012). Proust revisited: Odours as triggers of aversive memories. *Cognition & Emotion, 26*(1), 83–92. doi:10.1080/02699931.2011.555475.

Tohen, M., Zarate, C. A., Jr., Hennen, J., Khalsa, H.-M. K., Strakowski, S. M., Gebre-Medhin, P., et al. (2003). The McLean-Harvard first-episode mania study: Prediction of recovery and first recurrence. *American Journal of Psychiatry, 160,* 2099–2107.

Tolin, D. F. (2010). Is cognitive-behavioral therapy better than other therapies? A metaanalytic review. *Clinical Psychology Review, 30,* 710–720.

Tolman, E. C., & Honzik, C. H. (1930). Introduction and removal of reward and maze performance in rats. *University of California Publication in Psychology, 4,* 257–265.

Tomasello, M. (2006). Why don't apes point? In J. Enfield & S. C. Levinson (Eds.), *Roots of human sociality: Culture, cognition, and interaction* (pp. 506–524). New York: Berg.

Tomasetto, C., Alparone, F., & Cadinu, M. (2011). Girls' math performance under stereotype threat: The moderating role of mothers' gender stereotypes. *Developmental Psychology, 47*(4), 943–949. doi:10.1037/a0024047.

Tomberlin, J. K., Rains, G. C., & Sanford, M. R. (2008). Development of Microplitis croceipes as a biological sensor. *Entomologia Experimentalis et Applicata, 128*(2), 249–257.

Tomes, H. (1999, April). The need for cultural competence. *APA Monitor,* p. 31.

Tomlinson, J. M., Carmichael, C. L., Reis, H. T., & Aron, A., (2010). Affective forecasting and individual differences: Accuracy for relational events and anxious attachment. *Emotion, 10,* 447–453.

Tomova, L., von Dawans, B., Heinrichs, M., Silani, G., & Lamm, C. (2014). Is stress affecting our ability to tune into others? Evidence for gender differences in the effects of stress on self-other distinction. *Psychoneuroendocrinology, 43,* 95–104.

Tonnesen, J., Sorensen, A. T., Deisseroth, K., Lundberg, C., & Kokaia, M. (2009). Optogenetic control of epileptiform activity. *Proceedings of the National Academy of Sciences, 106,* 12162–12167. doi:10.1073/pnas.0901915106.

Topakian, R., & Aichner, F. T. (2008). Vascular dementia: A practical update. *Current Medical Literature: Neurology, 24*(1), 1–8.

Topolinski, S. (2011). I 5683 You: Dialing phone numbers on cell phones activates key-concordant concepts. *Psychological Science, 22*(3), 355–360. doi:10.1177/0956797610397668.

Torges, C. M., Stewart, A. J., & Nolen-Hoeksema, S. (2008). Regret resolution, aging, and adapting to loss: Older adults are better than younger ones at resolving their bereavement-related regrets. *Psychology and Aging, 23,* 169–180.

Torry, Z. D., & Billick, S. B. (2010). Overlapping universe: Understanding legal insanity and psychosis. *Psychiatric Quarterly, 81*(3), 253–262. doi:10.1007/ s11126–010–9134–2

Tosun, L. P., & Lajunen, T. (2009). Why do young adults develop a passion for Internet activities? The associations among personality, revealing "true self" on the Internet, and passion for the Internet. *CyberPsychology & Behavior, 12*(4), 401–406. doi:10.1089=cpb.2009.0006.

Tosun, L. P., & Lajunen, T. (2010). Does Internet use reflect your personality? Relationship between Eysenck's personality dimensions and Internet use. *Computers in Human Behavior, 26,* 162–167. doi:10.1016/j.chb.2009.10.010.

Touzani, K., Puthanveettil, S. V., & Kandel, E. R. (2007). Consolidation of learning strategies during spatial working memory taks requires protein synthesis in the prefrontal cortex. *Proceedings of the National Academy of Sciences, 104,* 5632–5637.

Towfighi, A., & Saver, J. L. (2011). Stroke declines from third to fourth leading cause of death in the United States: Historical perspective and challenges ahead. *Stroke, 42*(8), 2351–2355.

Trabasso, T. R., & Bower, G. H. (1968). *Attention in learning.* New York: Wiley.

Trace, S. E., Baker, J. H., Peñas-Lledó, E., & Bulik, C. M. (2013). The genetics of eating disorders. *Annual Review of Clinical Psychology, 9,* 589–620.

Tracey, T. J. G., Wampold, B. E., Lichtenberg, J. W., & Goodyear, R. K. (2014). Expertise in psychotherapy: An elusive goal? *American Psychologist, 69*(3), 218–229.

Trachtenberg, F. L., Haas, E. A., Kinney, H. C., Stanley, C., & Krous, H. F. (2012). Risk factor changes for sudden infant death syndrome after initiation of back-to-sleep campaign. *Pediatrics, 129*(4), 630–638. doi:10.1542/peds.2011–1419.

Treat, T. A., & Viken, R. J. (2010). Cognitive processing of weight and emotional information in disordered eating. *Current Directions in Psychological Science, 19*(2), 81–85. doi:10.1177/0963721410364007.

Tregear, S., Reston, J., Schoelles, K., & Phillips, B. (2009). Obstructive sleep apnea and risk of motor vehicle crash: Systematic review and meta-analysis. *Journal of Clinical Sleep Medicine, 5*(6), 573–581.

Trevor, C. O. (2001). Interactions among actual ease-of-movement determinants and job satisfaction in the prediction of voluntary turnover. *Academy of Management Journal, 44,* 621–638.

Triandis, H. C., & Trafimow, D. (2001). Cross-national prevalence of collectivism. In C. Sedikides & M. B. Brewer (Eds.), *Individual self, relational self, collective self* (pp. 259–276). New York: Psychology Press.

Trickett, S., Trafton, J., & Schunn, C. D. (2009). How do scientists respond to anomalies? Different strategies used in basic and applied science. *Topics in Cognitive Science, 1*(4), 711–729. doi:10.1111/j.1756–8765.2009.01036.x.

Trierweiler, S. J., Muroff, J. R., Jackson, M. S., Neighbors, H. W., & Munday, C. (2005). Clinician race, situational attributions, and diagnoses of mood versus schizophrenia disorders. *Cultural Diversity & Ethnic Minority Psychology, 11,* 351–364.

Trierweiler, S. J., Neighbors, H. W., Munday, C., Thompson, E. E., Binion, V. J., & Gomez, J. P. (2000). Clinician attributions associated with the diagnosis of schizophrenia in African American and non-African American patients. *Journal of Consulting and Clinical Psychology, 68,* 171–175.

Trifiletti, L. B., Shields, W., McDonald, E., Reynaud, F., & Gielen, A. (2006). Tipping the scales: Obese children and child safety seats. *Pediatrics, 117,* 1197–1202.

Trillin, A. S. (2001, January 29). Betting your life. *New Yorker,* pp. 38–41.

Troisi, J. D., & Gabriel, S. (2011). "Chicken soup really is good for the soul: "Comfort food" fulfills the need to belong. *Psychological Science, 22*(6) 747–753. doi:10.1177/0956797611407931.

Tronick, E. Z., Messinger, D. S., Weinberg, M. K., Lester, B. M., LaGasse, L., Seifer, R., et al. (2005). Cocaine exposure is associated with subtle compromises of infants' and mothers' social-emotional behavior and dyadic features of their interaction in the face-to-face still-face paradigm. *Developmental Psychology, 41,* 711–722.

Trope, Y. (1975). Seeking information about one's own ability as a determinant of choice among tasks. *Journal of Personality and Social Psychology, 32,* 1004–1013.

Trope, Y. (1983). Self-assessment in achievement behavior. In J. Suls & A. G. Greenwald (Eds.), *Psychological perspectives on the self* (Vol. 2, pp. 93–121). Hillsdale, NJ: Lawrence Erlbaum.

Trull, T. J., & Sher, K. J. (1994). Relationship between the five-factor model of personality and Axis I disorders in a nonclinical sample. *Journal of Personality and Social Psychology, 103,* 350–360.

Trumbetta, S. L., Seltzer, B. K., Gottsman, I. I., & McIntyre, K. M. (2010). Mortality predictors in a 60-year follow-up of adolescent males: Exploring delinquency, socioeconomic status, IQ, high school dropout status, and personality. *Psychosomatic Medicine, 72,* 46–52.

Trunzo, J. J., & Pinto, B. M. (2003). Social support as a mediator of optimisim and distress in breast cancer survivors. *Journal of Consulting and Clinical Psychology, 71,* 805–811.

Tryon, W. W. (2005). Possible mechanisms for why desensitization and exposure therapy work. *Clinical Psychology Review, 25,* 67–95.

Tsai, J. L., Knutson, B., & Fung, H. H. (2006). Cultural variation in affect evaluation. *Journal of Personality and Social Psychology, 90,* 288–307.

Tsakiris, M., & Haggard, P. (2005). The rubber hand illusion revisited: Visuotactile integration and self-attribution. *Journal of Experimental Psychology: Human Perception and Performance, 31,* 80–91.

Tsang, J. S., Naughton, P. A., Leong, S., Hill, A. D. K., Kelly, C. J., & Leahy, A. L. (2008). Virtual reality simulation in endovascular surgical training. *Surgeon, 6*(4), 214–220.

Tseng, A., Bansal, R., Liu, J., Gerber, A. J., Goh, S., Posner, J., Colibazzi, T., Algermissen, N., Chiang, I. C., Russell, J. A., & Peterson, B. S. (2013). Using the circumplex model of affect to study valence and arousal ratings of emotional faces by children and adults with autism spectrum disorders. *Journal of Autism and Developmental Disorders.* Epub November 14, 2013.

Tsenkova, V., Boylan, J. M., & Ryff, C. (2013). Stress eating and health. Findings from MIDUS, a national study of U.S. adults. *Appetite, 69,* 151–155.

Tuch, S. A., & Martin, J. K. (1991). Race in the workplace: Black/white differences in the sources of job satisfaction. *The Sociological Quarterly, 32,* 103–116.

Tucker, J. S., Green, H. D., Zhou, A. J., Miles, J. V., Shih, R. A., & D'Amico, E. J. (2011). Substance use among middle school students: Associations with self-rated and peer-nominated popularity. *Journal of Adolescence, 34*(3), 513–519. doi:10.1016/j.adolescence.2010.05.016.

Tucker-Drob, E. M. (2011). Global and domain-specific changes in cognition throughout adulthood. *Developmental Psychology, 47*(2), 331–343.

Tucker-Drob, E. M. (2012). Preschools reduce early academic-achievement gaps: A longitudinal twin approach. *Psychological Science, 23*(3), 310–319. doi:10.1177/0956797611426728.

Tucker-Drob, E. M., & Harden, K. (2012b). Intellectual interest mediates gene × socioeconomic status interaction on adolescent academic achievement. *Child Development, 83*(2), 743–757. doi:10.1111/j.1467-8624.2011.01721.x.

Tucker-Drob, E. M., & Harden, K. (2012a). Early childhood cognitive development and parental cognitive stimulation: Evidence for reciprocal gene-environment transactions. *Developmental Science, 15*(2), 250–259. doi:10.1111/j.1467-7687.2011.01121.x.

Tulving, E. (1983). *Elements of episodic memory.* New York: Oxford University Press.

Tulving, E. (2000). Introduction to memory. In M. S. Gazzaniga (Ed.), *The new cognitive neurosciences* (pp. 727–732). Cambridge, MA: MIT Press.

Tulving, E. (2005). Episodic memory and autonoesis: Uniquely human? In H. S. Terrace and J. Metcalfe (Eds.), *The missing link in cognition: Origins of self-reflective consciousness* (pp. 3–56). New York: Oxford University Press.

Tulving, E., & Psotka, J. (1971). Retroactive inhibition in free recall: Inaccessibility of information available in the memory store. *Journal of Experimental Psychology, 87,* 1–8.

Tuomilehto, J., Lindstrom, J., Eriksson, J. G., Valle, T. T., et al. (2001). Prevention of type 2 diabetes mellitus by changes in lifestyle among subjects with impaired glucose tolerance. *New England Journal of Medicine, 344,* 1343–1350.

Turan, T., Uysal, C., Asdemir, A., & Kilic, E. (2013). May oxytocin be a trait marker for bipolar disorder? *Psychoneuroendocrinology, 38,* 2890–2896.

Turati, C. (2004). Why faces are not special to newborns: An alternative account of the face preference. *Current Directions in Psychological Science, 13,* 5–8.

Turiel, E. (2006). The development of morality. In W. Damon & R. M. Lerner (Series Eds.) & N. Eisenberg (Vol. Ed.), *Handbook of child psychology: Vol. 3. Social, emotional, and personality development* (6th ed.). New York: Wiley.

Turkheimer, E., Haley, A., Waldron, M., D'Onofrio, B., & Gottesman, I. I. (2003). Socioeconomic status modifies heritability of IQ in young children. *Psychological Science, 14,* 623–628.

Turkheimer E., & Harden K.P. (2014). Behavior genetic research methods: testing quasi-causal hypotheses using multivariate twin data. In H. T. Reiss & C. M. Judd (Eds.), *Handbook of research methods in personality and social psychology* (2nd ed). Cambridge, UK: Cambridge University Press.

Turkheimer, E., Pettersson, E., & Horn, E. E. (2014). A phenotypic null hypothesis for the genetics of personality. *Annual Review of Psychology, 65,* 515–540.

Turkheimer, E., & Waldron M. (2000). Nonshared environment: A theoretical, methodological, and quantitative review. *Psychological Bulletin, 126,* 78–108.

Turkington, C. (1987). Special talents. *Psychology Today,* pp. 42–46.

Turnbull, C. (1961). Some observations regarding the experiences and behavior of the Bambuti Pygmies. *American Journal of Psychology, 74,* 304–308.

Turner, R. J., & Lloyd, D. A. (2004). Stress burden and the lifetime incidence of psychiatric disorder in young adults: Racial and ethnic contrasts. *Archives of General Psychiatry, 61,* 481–488.

Turner, S. M., DeMers, S. T., Fox, H. R., & Reed, G. M. (2001). APA's guidelines for test user qualifications: An executive summary. *American Psychologist, 56,* 1099–1113.

Tuschl, R. J. (1990). From dietary restraint to binge eating: Some theoretical considerations. *Appetite, 14*(2), 105–109.

Tversky, A., & Kahneman, D. (1974). Judgment under uncertainty: Heuristics and biases. *Science, 185,* 1124–1131.

Tversky, A., & Kahneman, D. (1981). The framing of decisions and the psychology of choice. *Science, 211,* 453–458.

Tversky, A., & Kahneman, D. (1991). Loss aversion in riskless choice: A reference dependent model. *Quarterly Journal of Economics, 106,* 1039–1061.

Tversky, B., & Tuchin, M. (1989). A reconciliation of the evidence on eyewitness testimony: Comments on McCloskey and Zaragoza. *Journal of Experimental Psychology: General, 118,* 86–91.

Twenge, J. M., Gentile, B., DeWall, C. N., Ma, D., et al. (2010). Birth cohort increases in psychopathology among young Americans, 1938–2007: A cross-temporal meta-analysis of the MMPI. *Clinical Psychology Review, 30,* 145–154.

Tybur, J. M., Bryan, A. D., Magnan, R. E., & Caldwell Hooper, A. E. (2011). Smells like safe sex: Olfactory pathogen primes increase intentions to use condoms. *Psychological Science, 22*(4), 478–480. doi:10.1177/0956797611400096.

Tyler, K. L., & Malessa, R. (2000). The Goltz-Ferrier debates and the triumph of cerebral localizationalist theory. *Neurology, 55*(7), 1015–1024.

Tynes, B. M., Umaña-Taylor, A. J., Rose, C. A., Lin, J., & Anderson, C. J. (2012). Online racial discrimination and the protective function of ethnic identity and self-esteem for African American adolescents. *Developmental Psychology, 48,* 343–355.

Uchida, Y., Kitayama, S., Mesquita, B., & Reyes, J. A. (2001, June). *Interpersonal sources of happiness: The relative significance in Japan, the Philippines, and the United States.* Paper presented at Annual Convention of American Psychological Society, Toronto, Canada.

Uchino, B. N., Smith, T. W., & Berg, C. A. (2014). Spousal relationship quality and cardiovascular risk: Dyadic perceptions of relationship ambivalence are associated with coronary-artery calcification. *Psychological Sciences,* Epub February 5, 2014.

Uddin, M., Aiello, A. E., Wildman, D. E., Koenen, K. C., et al. (2010). Epigenetic and immune function profi les associated with posttraumatic stress disorder. *Proceedings of the National Academy of Sciences, 107,* 9470. doi:10.1073/pnas.0910794107.

Udry, J. R., & Chantala, K. (2003). Masculinity-femininity guides sexual union formation in adolescents. *Personality and Social Psychology Bulletin, 30,* 44–55.

Uhl-Bien, M., Marion, R., & McKelvey, B. (2007). Complexity leadership theory: Shifting leadership from the Industrial Age to the Knowledge Era. *Leadership Quarterly, 18,* 298–318.

Uleman, J. S., & Saribay, S. (2012). Initial impressions of others. In K. Deaux & M. Snyder (Eds.), *The Oxford handbook of personality and social psychology* (pp. 337–366). New York: Oxford University Press.

Ulett, G. A. (2003). Acupuncture, magic, and make-believe. *The Skeptical Inquirer, 27*(2), 47–50.

Um, E., Plass, J. L., Hayward, E. O., & Homer, B. D. (2011). Emotional design in multimedia learning. *Journal Of Educational Psychology,* doi:10.1037/a0026609.

Umbreit, J., Ferro, J., Liaupsin, C. J., & Lane, K. L. (2006). *Functional behavioral assessment and function-based intervention: An effective, practical approach.* Upper Saddle River, NJ: Prentice Hall.

Underdown, J. (2011). Power balance bracelets a bust in tests. *Skeptical Inquirer, 36,* 14–16.

Undurraga, J., & Baldessarini, R. J. (2012). Randomized, placebo-controlled trials of antidepressants for acute major depression: Thirty-year meta-analytic review. *Neuropsychopharmacology, 37*(4), 851–864.

Ungemach, C., Chater, N., & Stewart, N. (2009). Are probabilities overweighted or underweighted when rare outcomes are experienced (rarely)? *Psychological Science, 20,* 473–479.

Ungerleider, L. G., & Mishkin, M. (1982). Two cortical visual systems. In D. J. Ingle, M. A. Goodale, & R. J. W. Mansfield (Eds.), *Analysis of visual behavior.* Cambridge, MA: MIT Press.

United Nations Office on Drugs and Crime. (2007). *Intentional homicide rate per 100,000 population.* Retrieved from http://www.unodc.org/documents/data-and-analysis/IHS-rates-05012009.pdf

Unsworth, N., Fuluda, K., Awh, E., & Vogel, E. K. (2014). Working memory and fluid intelligence: Capacity, attention control, and secondary memory retrieval. *Cognitive Psychology, 71,* 1–26.

Urbach, T. P., Windmann, S. S., Payne, D. G., & Kutas, M. (2005). Mismaking memories. *Psychological Science, 16,* 19–24.

Urquhart, B. L., & Kim, R. B. (2009). Blood-brain barrier transporters and response to CNS-active drugs. *European Journal of Clinical Pharmacology, 65,* 1063–1070.

Urry, H. L., & Gross, J. J. (2010). Emotion regulation in older age. *Current Directions in Psychological Science, 19,* 352–357.

Ursu, S., Kring, A. M., Gard, M., Minzenberg, M. J., Yoon, J. H., Ragland, J., & … Carter, C. S. (2011). Prefrontal cortical deficits and impaired cognition-emotion interactions in schizophrenia. *The American Journal Of Psychiatry, 168*(3), 279–285. doi:10.1176/appi.ajp.2010.09081215

U.S. Bureau of Labor Statistics. (2007). *Injuries, illnesses, and fatalities, 2005.* Washington, DC: U.S. Department of Labor. Retrieved May 9, 2007, from http://www.bls.gov/iif/home.htm#tables.

U.S. Bureau of Labor Statistics. (2012). *Injuries, illnesses, and fatalities: 2012.* Washington, DC: U.S. Department of Labor. Retrieved May 17, 2014 from http://www.bls.gov/iif/#tables.

U.S. Bureau of Labor Statistics. (2014). *Occupational outlook handbook.* Washington, DC: Office of Occupational Statistics and Employment Projections.

U.S. Census Bureau. (2012). Statistical Abstract of the United States. Retrieved from http://www.census.gov/compendia/statab/2012/tables/12s0133.pdf.

U.S. Department of Health and Human Services Office of Applied Studies. (2003). *Results from the 2002 National Survey on Drug Use and Health: Summary of national finding* (DHHS Publication No. SMA 03–3836, NHSDA Series H-22). Rockville, MD: Substance Abuse and Mental Health Services Administration.

U.S. Department of Justice. (1999). *Eyewitness evidence: A guide for law enforcement.* Washington, DC: National Institute of Justice.

U.S. Department of Justice. (2002). *Recidivism of prisoners released in 1994.* Washington, DC: U.S. Department of Justice, Bureau of Justice Statistics.

U.S. Department of Justice. (2007). *Crime characteristics.* Retrieved January 31, 2007, from http://www.ojp.usdoj.gov/bjs/cvict_c.htm#relate.

U.S. Department of Justice, Office of Justice Programs, Bureau of Justice Statistics. (2011). *Workplace violence, 1993–2009: National crime victimization survey and the census of fatal occupational injuries.* (DOJ Publication no. ncj 233231). Retrieved from http://bjs.gov/content/pub/pdf/wv09.pdf

U.S. Department of Labor. (2012). *Employment characteristics of families summary.* Retrieved from http://www.bls.gov/news.release/famee.nr0.htm.

U.S. Surgeon General. (1999). *Mental health: A report of the surgeon general.* Rockville, MD: U.S. Department of Health and Human Services.

Usher, A. (2011). *Annual yearly progress results for 2010–2011.* Washington, DC: Center on Education Policy.

Üstün B., & Kennedy, C. (2009). What is "functional impairment"? Disentangling disability from clinical significance. *World Psychiatry, 8,* 82–85.

Uttal, W. R. (2003). *The new phrenology: The limits of localizing cognitive processes in the brain.* Cambridge, MA: MIT Press.

Uziel, L. (2007). Individual diff erences in the social facilitation eff ect: A review and metaanalysis. *Journal of Research in Personality, 41,* 579–601.

Uziel, L. (2010). Rethinking social desirability scales: From impression management to interpersonally oriented self-control. *Perspectives on Psychological Science, 5,* 243–262.

Vahia, I. V., & Cohen, C. I. (2009). Psychosocial factors. In K. T. Mueser & D. V. Jeste (Eds.), *Clinical handbook of schizophrenia.* (pp. 74–81). New York: Guilford Press.

Vail, K., Arndt, J., Motyl, M., & Pyszczynski, T. (2012). The aftermath of destruction: Images of destroyed buildings increase support for war, dogmatism, and death thought accessibility. *Journal of Experimental Social Psychology, 48*(5), 1069–1081.

Vaitl, D., Birbaumer, N., Gruzelier, J., Jamieson, G. A., Kotchoubey, B., Kubler, A., et al. (2005). Psychobiology of altered states of consciousness. *Psychological Bulletin, 131,* 98–127.

Valdés-Sosa, M., Bobes, M. A., Quiñones, I., Garcia, L., Valdes-Hernandez, P. A, Iturria, Y., Melie-Garcia, L., Lopera, F., & Asencio, J. (2011). Covert face recognition without the fusiform-temporal pathways. *Neuroimage, 57*(3), 1162–1176.

Valenstein, E. S. (Ed.). (1980). *The psychosurgery debate.* San Francisco: Freeman.

Valenza, E., Simion, F., Assia, V. M., & Umilta, C. (1996). Face preference at birth. *Journal of Experimental Psychology: Human Perception and Performance, 22,* 892–903.

Valenza, E., & Bulf, H. (2007). The role of kinetic information in newborns' perception of illusory contours. *Developmental Science, 10*(4), 492–501.

Valkenburg, P. M., & Peter, J. (2007). Preadolescents' and adolescents' online communication and their closeness to friends. *Developmental Psychology, 43*(2), 267–277.

Valkenburg, P. M., & Peter, J. (2009). Social consequences of the Internet for adolescents: A decade of research. *Current Directions in Psychological Science, 18,* 1–5.

Vallerand, R., Paquet, Y., Philippe, F., & Charest, J. (2010). On the role of passion for work in burnout: a process model. *Journal Of Personality, 78*(1), 289–312.

Vallotton, C. D. (2008). Signs of emotion: What can preverbal children "say" about internal states? *Infant Mental Health Journal, 29,* 234–258.

Valuck, R. J., Libby, A. M., Benton, T., D., & Evans, D. L. (2007). A descriptive analysis of 10,000 suicide attempters in the Unites States managed care plans, 1998–2005. *Primary Psychiatry, 14,* 52–60.

Van Allen, J., & Roberts, M. C. (2011). Critical incidents in the marriage of psychology and technology: A discussion of potential ethical issues in practice, education, and policy. *Professional Psychology: Research and Practice, 42*(6), 433–439. doi:10.1037/a0025278.

Van Bezooijen, R., Otto, S. A., & Heenan, T. A. (1983). Recognition of vocal expression of emotion: A three-nation study to identify universal characteristics. *Journal of Cross-Cultural Psychology, 14,* 387–406.

van Dam, R. M., Li, T., Spiegelman, D., Franco, O. H., & Hu, F. B. (2008). Combined impact of lifestyle factors on mortality: prospective cohort study in US women. *British Medical Journal, 337,* a1440.

van den Bos, W., van Dijk, E., Westenberg, M., Rombouts, S. B., & Crone, E. A. (2011). Changing brains, changing perspectives: The neurocognitive development of reciprocity. *Psychological Science, 6*(1), 60–70. doi:10.1177/ 0956797610391102.

van der Helm, E., Gujar, N., Nishida, M,. & Walker, M.P. (2011) Sleep-dependent facilitation of episodic memory details. *PLoS ONE, 6*(11): e27421.

van der Kloet, D., Merckelbach, H., Giesbrecht, T., & Lynn, S. (2012). Fragmented sleep, fragmented mind: The role of sleep in dissociative symptoms. *Perspectives on Psychological Science, 7*(2), 159–175. doi:10.1177/1745691612437597.

van de Ven, N., Zeelenberg, M., & Pieters, R. (2010). Warding Off the Evil Eye: When the Fear of Being Envied Increases Prosocial Behavior. *Psychological Science (Sage Publications Inc.), 21*(11), 1671–1677. doi:10.1177/0956797610385352.

van de Ven, N., Zeelenberg, M., & Pieters, R. (2011). Why envy outperforms admiration. *Personality And Social Psychology Bulletin, 37*(6), 784–795. doi:10.1177/0146167211400421.

Van den Bergh, B. R., & Marcoen, A. (2004). High antenatal maternal anxiety is related to ADHD symptoms, externalizing problems, and anxiety in 8- and 9-year-olds. *Child Development, 75,* 1085–1097.

van den Hout, M. A., & Engelhard, I. M. (2012). How does EMDR work? *Journal of Experimental Psychopathology, 3,* 724–738.

van der Hart, O., Bolt, H., & van der Kolk, B. A. (2005). Memory fragmentation in dissociative identity disorder. *Journal of Trauma & Dissociation, 6*(1), 55–70.

van der Kooy-Hofland, V. C., van der Kooy, J., Bus, A. G., van IJzendoorn, M. H., & Bonsel, G. J. (2012). Differential susceptibility to early literacy intervention in children with mild perinatal adversities: Short and long-term effects of a randomized control trial. *Journal of Educational Psychology, 104,* 337–349. doi:10.1037/a0026984

Van der Molen, J. H. W. (2004). Violence and suffering in television news: Toward a broader conception of harmful television content for children. *Pediatrics, 113,* 1771–1775.

van der Schee, M. P., Palmay, R., Cowan, J. O., & Taylor, D. R. (2013). Predicting steroid responsiveness in patients with asthma using exhaled breath profiling. *Clinical and Experimental Allergy Clinical and Experimental Allergy, 43*(11), 1217–1225.

van Dick, R., Stellmacher, J., Wagner, U., Lemmer, G., & Tissington, P. A. (2009). Group membership salience and task performance. *Journal of Managerial Psychology, 24,* 609–626.

Van Dongen, S., & Gangestad, S. W. (2011). Human fluctuating asymmetry in relation to health and quality: A meta-analysis. *Evolution and Human Behavior, 32*(6), 380–398.

Van Durme, K., Goossens, L., & Braet, C. (2012). Adolescent aesthetic athletes: A group at risk for eating pathology? *Eating Behaviors, 13*(2), 119–122. doi:10.1016/j.eatbeh.2011.11.002.

Van Eerde, W., & Thierry, H. (1996). Vrooms's expectancy models and work-related criteria: A meta-analysis. *Journal of Applied Psychology, 81,* 575–586.

van Geel, M., Vedder, P., & Tanilon, J. (2014). Relationship between peer victimization, cyberbullying, and suicide in children and adolescents. *JAMA Pediatrics*, 168(5), 435–442.

van Haren, N. E. M., Rijsdijk, F., Schnack, H. G., Picchioni, M. M., Toulopoulou, T., Weisbrod, M., Sauer, H., van Erp, T. G., Cannon, T. D., Huttunen, M. O., Boomsma, D. I., Hulshoff Pol, H. E., Murray, R. M., & Kahn, R. S. (2012). The genetic and environmental determinants of the association between brain abnormalities and schizophrenia: The schizophrenia twins and relatives consortium. *Biological Psychiatry, 71,* 915–921.

Vanhaudenhuyse, A., Boly, M., Balteau, E., Schnakers, C., Moonen, G., Luxen, A., Lamy, M., Degueldre, C., Brichant, J. F., Maquet, P., Laureys, S., & Faymonville, M. E. (2009). Pain and non-pain processing during hypnosis: A thulium-YAG event-related fMRI study. *NeuroImage, 47*(3), 1047–1054.

van Hooft, E. J., & Born, M. H. (2012). Intentional response distortion on personality tests: Using eye-tracking to understand response processes when faking. *Journal of Applied Psychology, 97,* 301–316. doi:10.1037/a0025711.

Van Iddekinge, C. H. Roth, P. L. Raymark, P. H., & Odle-Dusseau, H. N. (2012). The criterion-related validity of integrity tests: An updated meta-analysis. *Journal of Applied Psychology, 9,* 499–530.

van IJzendoorn, M. H. (1995). Adult attachment representations, parental responsiveness, and infant attachment: A meta-analysis on the predictive validity of the Adult Attachment Interview. *Psychological Bulletin, 117,* 387–403.

van IJzendoom, M. H., & Juffer, F. (2005). Adoption as a successful natural intervention enhancing adopted children's IQ and school performance. *Current Directions in Psychological Science, 14,* 326–330.

Van Kleef, G. A., Homan, A. C., Beersma, B., & van Knippenberg, D. (2010). On angry leaders and agreeable followers: How leaders' emotions and followers' personalities shape motivation and team performance. *Psychological Science, 21*(12) 1827–1834. doi:10.1177/0956797610387438.

Vanman, E. J., Saltz, J. L., Nathan, L. R., & Warren, J. A. (2004). Racial discrimination by low-prejudiced whites. *Psychological Science, 15,* 711–714.

van Noorden, M. S., van Dongen, L. C., Zitman, F. G., & Vergouwen, T. A. (2009). Gammahydroxybutyrate withdrawal syndrome: Dangerous but not well known. *General Hospital Psychiatry, 31,* 394–396.

Van Oort, F. V. A., vanderEnde, J., Wadsworth, M. E., Verhulst, F. C., & Achenbach, T. M. (2011). Cross-national comparison of the link between socioeconomic status and emotional and behavioral problems in youths. *Social Psychiatry and Psychiatric Epidemiology, 46,* 167–172.

Van Orden, K. A., Witte, T. K., Cukrowicz, K. C., Braithwaite, S. R., et al. (2010). The interpersonal theory of suicide. *Psychological Review, 117,* 575–600.

van Os, J., Kenis, G., & Rutten, B. P. F. (2010). The environment and schizophrenia. *Nature, 468,* 203–212. doi:10.1038/nature09563.

Vansteenkiste, M., Sierens, E., Soenens, B., Luyckx, K., & Lens, W. (2009). Motivational profiles from a self-determination theory perspective: Quality of motivation matters. *Journal of Educational Psychology, 101,* 671–688.

Vansteenkiste, M., Simons, J., Lens, W., Soenens, B., & Matos, L. (2005). Examining the Motivational impact of intrinsic versus extrinsic goal framing and autonomy-supportive versus internally-controlling communication style on early adolescents' academic achievement. *Child Development, 76,* 483–501.

Varnum, M. W., Grossmann, I., Kitayama, S., & Nisbett, R. E. (2010). The origin of cultural differences in cognition: The social orientation hypothesis. *Current Directions in Psychological Science, 19*(1), 9–13. doi:10.1177/0963721409359301.

Varnum, M. E. W., Grossmann, I., Katunar, D., Nisbett, R. E., & Kitayama, S. (2008). Holism in a European cultural context: Differences in cognitive style between Central and East Europeans and westerners. *Journal of Cognition & Culture, 8*(3–4), 321–333.

Vartanian, O., Stewart, K., Mandel, D. R., Pavlovic, N., McLellan, L., & Taylor, P. J. (2012). Personality assessment and behavioral prediction at first impression. *Personality and Individual Differences, 52,* 250–254. doi:10.1016/j.paid.2011.05.024.

Vasey, P. L., & VanderLaan, D. P. (2007). Birth order and male androphilia in Samoan fa'afafine. *Proceedings of the Royal Society: Biological Sciences, 274*(1616), 1437–1442.

Vasquez, M. J. T. (2007). Cultural difference and the therapeutic alliance: An evidence-based analysis. *American Psychologist, 62,* 878–885.

Vasquez, M. J. T., & Jones, J. M. (2006). Increasing the number of psychologists of color: Public policy issues for affirmative diversity. *American Psychologist, 61,* 132–142.

Veale, D. (2009). Body dysmorphic disorder. In M. M. Antony & M. B. Stein, (Eds.). *Oxford handbook of anxiety and related disorders* (pp. 541–550). New York: Oxford University Press USA.

Vecchione, M., Schoen, H., Castro, J. L. G., Cieciuch, J., Pavlopoulos, V., & Caprara, G. V. (2011). Personality correlates of party preference: The Big Five in five big European countries, *Personality and Individual Differences, 51,* 737–742.

Vecera, S. P., Vogel, E. K., & Woodman, G. F. (2002). Lower region: A new cue for figure-ground assignment. *Journal of Experimental Psychology: General, 131,* 194–205.

Vedel, E., & Emmelkamp, P. M. G. (2012). Illicit substance-related disorders. In P. Sturmey & M. Hersen (Eds.), *Handbook of evidence-based practice in clinical psychology, Vol. 2: Adult disorders* (pp. 197–220). Hoboken, NJ: Wiley.

Velik, R. (2010). Why machines cannot feel. *Minds and Machines, 20*(1), 1–18. doi:10.1007/s11023-010-9186-y.

Vemuri, M., Kenna, H. A., Wang, P. W., Ketter, T. A., & Rasgon, N. L. (2011). Gender-specific lipid profiles in patients with bipolar disorder. *Journal of Psychiatric Research, 45,* 1036–1041.

Vemuri, P., Lesnick, T. G., Przybelski, S. A., Machulda, M., Knopman, D. S., Mielke, M. M., Roberts, R. O., Geda, Y. E., Rocca, W. A., Peterson, R. C., & Jack, C. R. (2014). Association of lifetime intellectual enrichment with cognitive decline in the older population. *JAMA Neurology*, Epub June 23, 2014.

Venâncio, C., Magalhães, A., Antunes, L., & Summavielle, T. (2011). Impaired spatial memory after ketamine administration in chronic low doses. *Current Neuropharmacology, 9*(1), 251–255.

Vennemann, M. M., Bajanowski, T., Brinkmann, B., Jorch, G., Sauerland, C., & Mitchell, E. A. (2009a). Sleep environment risk factors for sudden infant death syndrome: The German sudden infant death syndrome study. *Pediatrics, 123,* 1162–1170.

Vennemann, M. M., Bajanowski, T., Brinkmann, B., Jorch, G., Yücesan, K., Sauerland, C., & Mitchell, E. A. (2009b). Does breastfeeding reduce the risk of sudden infant death syndrome? *Pediatrics, 123,* e406–e410.

Verhaeghen, P. (2011). Aging and executive control: Reports of a demise greatly exaggerated. *Current Directions in Psychological Science, 20,* 174–180.

Verhaeghen, P. (2013). Cognitive aging. In D. Reisberg (Ed.), *Oxford handbook of cognitive psychology* (pp. 1014–1035). New York: Oxford University Press.

Verhagen, E. A., ter Horst, H. J., Kooi, E. W., Keating, P., van den Berg, P. P., & Bos, A. F. (2011). Prenatal tobacco exposure influences cerebral oxygenation in preterm infants. *Early Human Development, 87*(6), 401–406. doi:10.1016/j.earlhumdev.2011.03.002.

Vernacchio, L., Corwin, M. J., Lesko, S. M., Vezina, R. M., Hunt, C. E., Hoffman, H. J., et al. (2003). Sleep position of low birth weight infants. *Pediatrics, 111,* 633–640.

Vernet, M. E., Robin, O., & Dittmar, A. (1995). The ohmic perturbation duration, an original temporal index to quantify electrodermal responses. *Behavioural Brain Research, 67*(1), 103–107.

Vernon, P. A., Villani, V. C., Vickers, L. C., & Harris, J. A. (2008). A behavioral genetic investigation of the Dark Triad and the Big 5. *Personality and Individual Differences, 44*(2), 445–452.

Vernon-Feagans, L., Cox, M., & the FLP Key Investigators. (2013). The family life project: An epidemiological and developmental study of young children living in poor rural communities. *Monographs of the Society for Research in Child Development, 78*(5), 1–150.

Verster, J. C., & Volkerts, E. R. (2004). Clinical pharmacology, clinical efficacy, and behavioral toxicity of alprazolam: A review of the literature. *CNS Drug Reviews, 10,* 45–76.

Veru, F., Laplante, D. P., Luheshi, G., & King, S. (2014). Prenatal maternal stress exposure and immune function in the offspring. *Stress, 17*(2), 133–148.

Verwijk, E., Comijs, H. C., Kok, R. M., Spaans, H. P., Stek, M. L., & Scherder, E. J. (2012). Neurocognitive effects after brief pulse and ultrabrief pulse unilateral electroconvulsive therapy for major depression: a review. *Journal of Affective Disorders, 140*(3), 233–243.

Vespa, J., Lewis, J. M., & Kreider, R. M. (2013). America's families and living arrangements: 2012. *Current Population Reports, P20–570.* Washington, D.C.: U.S. Census Bureau.

Vetter, M. L., Cardillo, S., Rickels, M. R., & Iqbal, N. (2009). Narrative review: Effect of bariatric surgery on type 2 diabetes mellitus. *Annals of Internal Medicine, 150*(2), 94–103.

Vetter-O'Hagen, C., & Spear, L. (2012). Hormonal and physical markers of puberty and their relationship to adolescent-typical novelty-directed behavior. *Developmental Psychobiology, 54*, 523–535. doi:10.1002/dev.20610.

Vezzali, L., & Giovannini, D. (2011). Cross-group friendships, social dominance orientation and secondary transfer effect. *TPM-Testing, Psychometrics, Methodology in Applied Psychology, 18*, 181–194.

Vialou, V., Bagot, R. C., Cahill, M. E., Ferguson, D., Robison, A. J., Dietz, D. M., Fallon, B., Mazei-Robison, M., Ku, S. M., Harrigan, E., Winstanley, C. A., Joshi, T., Feng, J., Berton, O., & Nestler, E. J. (2014). Prefrontal cortical circuit for depression- and anxiety-related behaviors mediated by cholecystokinin: Role of ΔFosB. *Journal of Neuroscience, 34*(11), 3878–3887.

Vianello, M., Robusto, E., & Anselmi, P. (2010). Implicit conscientiousness predicts academic performance. *Personality & Individual Differences, 48*, 452–457. doi:10.1016/j.paid.2009.11.019

Vianello, R., & Lanfranchi, S. (2011). Positive effects of the placement of students with intellectual developmental disabilities in typical class. *Life Span and Disability, 14*(1), 75–84.

Vierbuchen, T., Ostermeier, A., Pang, Z. P., Kokubu, Y., et al. (2010). Direct conversion of fibroblasts to functional neurons by defined factors. *Nature, 463*, 1035–1041. Epub 2010 Jan 27.

Vierikko, E., Pulkkinen, L., Kaprio, J., & Rose, R. J. (2006). Genetic and environmental sources of continuity and change in teacher–rated aggression during early adolescence. *Aggressive Behavior, 32*, 308–320.

Vierow, V., Fukuoka, M., Ikoma, A., Dorfler, A., et al. (2009). Cerebral representation of the relief of itch by scratching. *Journal of Neurophysiology, 102*, 3216–3224. Epub 2009 Sep 23.

Vieta, E., Gunter, O., Ekman, M., Miltenburger, C., Chatterton, M. & Astrom, M. (2011). Effectiveness of psychotropic medications in the maintenance phase of bipolar disorder: A meta-analysis of randomized controlled trials. *International Journal of Neuropsychopharmacology, 14*, 1029–1049.

Vieta, E., & Valentí, M. (2013). Pharmacological management of bipolar depression: acute treatment, maintenance, and prophylaxis. *CNS Drugs, 27*(7), 515–529.

Vignovic, J. A., & Thompson, L. F., J. A (2010). Computer-mediated cross-cultural collaboration: Attributing communication errors to the person versus the situation. *Journal of Applied Psychology, 95*, 265–276.

Vincent, C. A., & Richardson, P. H. (1986). The evaluation of therapeutic acupuncture: Concepts and methods. *Pain, 24*, 1–13.

Vines, B. W., Norton, A. C., & Schlaug, G. (2011). Non-invasive brain stimulation enhances the effects of melodic intonation therapy. *Front Psychol 2: article 230* pp. 1–10.

Vinod, K. Y., Yalamanchili, R., Xie, S., Cooper, T. B., & Hungund, B. L. (2006). Effect of chronic ethanol exposure and its withdrawal on the endocannabinoid system. *Neurochemistry International, 49*, 619–625.

Virues-Ortega, J. (2010). Applied behavior analytic intervention for autism in early childhood: Meta-analysis, meta-regression and dose-response meta-analysis of multiple outcomes. *Clinical Psychology Review, 30*, 387–399. Epub 2010 Feb 11.

Visser, B. A., Ashton, M. C., & Vernon, P. A. (2006). Beyond *g*: Putting multiple intelligences theory to the test. *Intelligence, 34*, 487–502.

Visser, B. A., Bay, D., Cook, G. L., & Myburg, J. (2010). Psychopathic and antisocial, but not emotionally intelligent. *Personality and Individual Differences, 48*, 644–648.

Visser, P. S., Krosnick, J. A., & Lavrakas, P. J. (2000). Survey research. In H. T. Reis & C. Judd (Eds.), *Handbook of research methods in social and personality psychology* (pp. 223–252). Cambridge, UK: Cambridge University Press.

Vitlic, A., Lord, J. M., & Phillips, A. C. (2014). Stress, aging and their influence on functional, cellular and molecular aspects of the immune system. *Age*, Epub February 25, 2014.

Vlachou, S., & Markou, A. (2010). GABA receptors in reward processes. *Advances in Pharmacology, 58*, 315–371.

Vocat, R., Saj, A., & Vuilleumier. P. (2013). The riddle of anosognosia: Does unawareness of hemiplegia involve a failure to update beliefs? *Cortex, 49*(7), 1771–1781.

Vocat, R., Staub, F., Stroppini, T., & Vuilleumier, P. (2010). Anosognosia for hemiplegia: a clinical-anatomical prospective study. *Brain, 133*(Pt 12), 3578–3597.

Vogel, I., Brug, J., van der Ploeg, C. P. B., & Raat, H. (2009). Strategies for the prevention of mp3-induced hearing loss among adolescents: Expert opinions from a delphi study. *Pediatrics, 123*, 1257–1262.

Vokey, J. R. (2002). Subliminal messages. In J. R. Vokey & S. W. Allen (Eds.), *Psychological sketches* (6th ed., pp. 223–246). Lethbridge, Alberta, Canada: Psyence Ink.

Vokey, J. R., & Read, J. D. (1985). Subliminal messages: Between the devil and the media. *American Psychologist, 40*, 1231–1239.

Volbrecht, M., & Goldsmith, H. (2010). Early temperamental and family predictors of shyness and anxiety. *Developmental Psychology, 46*, 192–1205.

Volkow, N. D., Tomasi, D., Wang, G., Vaska, P., Fowler, J. S., Telang, F., & .. Wong, C. (2011). Effects of cell phone radiofrequency signal exposure on brain glucose metabolism. *JAMA: Journal of the American Medical Association, 305*(8), 808–814.

Volpicelli, J. R., Ulm, R. R., Altenor, A., & Seligman, M. E. P. (1983). Learned mastery in the rat. *Learning and Motivation, 14*, 204–222.

Volz, J. (2000). Successful aging. The second 50. *APA Monitor, 31*, 24–28.

Von Wright, J. M., Anderson, K., & Stenman, U. (1975). Generalization of conditioned GSRs in dichotic listening. In P. M. A. Rabbitt & S. Dornic (Eds.), *Attention and performance V*. New York: Academic Press.

Voracek, M., & Fisher, M. L. (2002). Shapely centrefolds? Temporal change in body measures: trend analysis. *British Medical Journal, 325*, 1447–1448.

Vos, S. J., Xiong, C., Vi sser, P. J., Jasielec, M. S., Hassenstab, J., Grant, E. A., Cairns, N. J., Morris, J. C., Holtzman, D. M., & Fagan, A. M. (2013). Preclinical Alzheimer's disease and its outcome: A longitudinal cohort study. *Lancet Neurology, 12*(10), 957–965.

Voss, U., Tuin, I., Schermelleh-Engel, K., & Hobson, A. (2011). Waking and dreaming: Related but structurally independent. Dream reports of congenitally paraplegic and deaf-mute persons. *Consciousness and Cognition, 20*(3), 673–687.

Vouloumanos, A., Druhen, M. J., Hauser, M. D., & Huizink, A. T. (2009). Five-month-old infants' identification of the sources of vocalizations. *Proceedings of the National Academy of Sciences, 106*, 18867–18872.

Vrij, A., Leal, S., Mann, S., Warmelink, L., Granhag, P., & Fisher, R. P. (2010). Drawings as an innovative and successful lie detection tool. *Applied Cognitive Psychology, 24*(4), 587–594. doi:10.1002/acp.1627.

Vroom, V. (1964). *Work and motivation*. New York: Wiley.

Vuoksimaa, E., Kaprio, J., Kremen, W. S., Hokkanen, L., et al. (2010). Having a male co-twin masculinizes mental rotation performance in females. *Psychological Science, 21*, 1069–1071.

Vurbic, D., & Bouton, M. E. (2014). A contemporary behavioral perspective on extinction. In F. K. McSweeney & E. S. Murphy (Eds.), *The Wiley-Blackwell handbook of operant and classical conditioning*. New York: Wiley & Sons.

Vygotsky, L. S. (1991). Genesis of the higher mental functions. In P. Light, S. Sheldon, & M. Woodhead (Eds.), *Learning to think: Child development in social context* (Vol. 2, pp. 32–41). London: Routledge.

Vyse, S. A. (2000). *Believing in magic: The psychology of superstition* (Rep. ed.). New York: Oxford University Press.

Vyssoki, B., Praschak-Rieder, N., Sonneck, G., Blüml, V., Willeit, M., Kasper, S., & Kapusta, N. (2012). Effects of sunshine on suicide rates. *Comprehensive Psychiatry, 53*, 535–539.

Waagenaar, W. (1986). My memory: A study of autobiographical memory over six years. *Cognitive Psychology, 18*, 225–252..

Wade, C. (1988, April). *Thinking critically about critical thinking in psychology*. Paper presented at the annual meeting of the Western Psychological Association, San Francisco, CA.

Wade, J. B. (2004). Neuropsychologists diagnose traumatic brain injury. *Brain Injury, 18*(7), 629–643.

Wade-Benzoni, K. A., Tost, L., Hernandez, M., & Larrick, R. P. (2012). It's only a matter of time: Death, legacies, and intergenerational decisions. *Psychological Science 23*, 704–709. doi:10.1177/0956797612443967.

Wagemans, J., Elder, J. H., Kubovy, M., Palmer, S. E., Peterson, M. A., Singh, M., & von der Heydt, R. (2012). A century of Gestalt Psychology in visual perception: I. Perceptual grouping and figure-ground organization. *Psychological Bulletin, 136*(6), 1172–1217.

Wager, T. D., Atlas, L. Y., Leotti, L. A., & Rilling, J. K. (2011). Predicting Individual Differences in Placebo Analgesia: Contributions of Brain Activity during Anticipation and Pain Experience. *Journal Of Neuroscience, 31*(2), 439–452. doi:10.1523/JNEUROSCI.3420-10.2011.

Wagg, J. (2008, October 21). Yamaha Yakidding? Retrieved January 15, 2009, from http://www.randi.org/site/index.php/swift-blog/242-yamaha-yakidding.html.

Wagner, A. D. (1999). Working memory contributions to human learning and remembering. *Neuron, 22*, 19–22.

Wagner, U., Hallschmid, M., Rasch, B., & Born, J. (2006). Brief sleep after learning keeps emotional memories alive for years. *Biological Psychiatry, 60*, 788–790.

Wahl, C., Svensson, Å., & Hydén, C. (2010). Effects of minor phrasing variations in traffic-related questionnaires—Comparison of objective equivalences and respondents' subjective statements. *Transportation Research: Part F, 13*(5), 315–328. doi:10.1016/j.trf.2010.06.002.

Wahlheim, C. N., Finn, B., & Jacoby, L. L. (2012). Metacognitive judgments of repetition and variability effects in natural concept learning: Evidence for variability neglect. *Memory & Cognition, 40*(5), 703–716.

Wai, J., Lubinski, D., & Benbow, C. P. (2005). Creativity and occupational accomplishments among intellectually precocious youth: An age 13 to age 33 longitudinal study. *Journal of Educational Psychology, 97*, 484–492.

Waite, P. J., & Richardson, G. E. (2004). Determining the efficacy of resiliency training in the work site. *Journal of Allied Health, 33*, 178–183.

Waldman, I. D., & Gizer, I. R. (2006). The genetics of attention deficit hyperactivity disorder. *Clinical Psychology Review, 26*, 396–432.

Walker, L. J. (2006). Gender and morality. In M. Killen & J. G. Smetana (Eds.), *Handbook of moral development* (pp. 93–118). Mahwah, NJ: Erlbaum.

Walker, E., Shapiro, D., Esterberg, M., & Trotman, H. (2010). Neurodevelopment and schizophrenia: Broadening the focus. *Current Directions In Psychological Science, 19*(4), 204–208. doi:10.1177/0963721410377744.

Walker, L. (1991). The feminization of psychology. *Psychology of Women Newsletter of Division, 35*, 1, 4.

Walker, L. J. (2006). Gender and morality. In M. Killen & J. G. Smetana (Eds.), *Handbook of moral development* (pp. 93–118). Mahwah, NJ: Erlbaum.

Walker, M. P., & Stickgold, R. (2006). Sleep, memory, and plasticity. *Annual Review of Psychology, 57*, 139–166.

Walkup, J. T., Albano, A. M., Piacentini, J., Birmaher, B., Compton, S. N., Sherrill, J. T., Ginsburg, G. S., Rynn, M. A., McCracken, J., Waslick, B., Iyengar, S., March, J. S., & Kendall, P. C. (2008). Cognitive behavioral therapy, sertraline, or a combination in childhood anxiety. *The New England Journal of Medicine, 359*, 2753–2766.

Wall, T. L., Shea, S. H., Luczak, S. E., Cook, T. A., & Carr, L. G. (2005). Genetic associations of alcohol dehydrogenase with alcohol use disorders and endophenotypes in white college students. *Journal of Abnormal Psychology, 114*, 456–465.

Wallace, J. C., Popp, E., & Mondore, S. (2006). Safety climate as a mediator between foundation climates and occupational accidents: A group-level investigation. *Journal of Applied Psychology, 91*, 681–688.

Wallace, J. R., Allan, K. L., & Tribol, C. T. (2001). Spatial perspective-taking errors in children. *Perceptual and Motor Skills, 92*, 633–639.

Wallace, R. K., & Benson, H. (1972). The physiology of meditation. *Scientific American, 226*, 84–90.

Wallen, K., & Lovejoy, J. (1993). Sexual behavior: Endocrine function and therapy. In J. Shulkin (Ed.), *Hormonal pathways to mind and brain*. New York: Academic Press.

Wallerstein, R. S. (2002). The growth and transformation of American ego psychology. *Journal of the American Psychoanalytic Association, 50*, 135–169. doi:10.1037/a0025751.

Wallis, J. D., Anderson, K. C., & Miller, E. K. (2001). Single neurons in prefrontal cortex encode abstract rules. *Nature, 411*, 953–956.

Walsh, R. (2011). Lifestyle and mental health. *American Psychologist, 66*(7), 579–592. doi:10.1037/a0021769.

Walsh, R., & Shapiro, S. L. (2006). The meeting of meditative disciplines and Western psychology: A mutually enriching dialogue. *American Psychologist, 61*, 227–239.

Walther, E., & Langer, T. (2008). Attitude formation and change though association: An evaluative conditioning account. In R. Prislin & W. B. Crano (Eds.), *Attitudes and Persuasion* (pp. 87–110). New York: Psychology Press.

Walton, G. E., Bower, N. J. A., & Bower, T. G. R. (1992). Recognition of familiar faces by newborns. *Infant Behavior and Development, 15*, 265–269.

Wampold, B. E., Hollon, S. D., & Hill, C. E. (2011). Unresolved questions and future directions in psychotherapy research. In J. C. Norcross, G. R. VandenBos, & D. K. Freedheim (Eds.), *History of psychotherapy: Continuity and change* (pp. 333–356). Washington, D.C.: American Psychological Association.

Wanders, F., Serra, M., & de Jongh, A. (2008). EMDR versus CBT for children with self-esteem and behavioral problems: A randomized controlled trial. *Journal of EMDR Practice and Research, 2*(3), 180–189.

Wanek, J. E., Sackett, P. R., & Ones, D. S. (2003). Towards an understanding of integrity test similarities and differences: An item-level analysis of seven tests. *Personnel Psychology, 56*, 873–894.

Wang, C., Collet, J. P., & Lau, J. (2004). The effect of Tai Chi on health outcomes in patients with chronic conditions: A systematic review. *Archives of Internal Medicine, 164*, 493–501.

Wang, P., & Zheng, S. G. (2013). Regulatory T cells and B cells: Implication on autoimmune diseases. *International Journal of Clinical and Experimental Pathology, 6*(12), 2668–2674.

Wang, P. S., Aguilar-Gaxiola, S., Alonso, J., Angermeyer, M. C., Borges, G., Bromet, E. J., et al. (2007). Use of mental health services for anxiety, mood, and substance disorders in 17 countries in the WHO world mental health surveys. *Lancet, 370*, 841–850.

Wang, P. S., Aguilar-Gaziola, S., Alonso, J., Lee, S., Schoenbaum, M., Ustun, T., . . . & Tsang, A. (2011). Assessing mental disorders and service use across countries: The WHO World Mental Health Survey Initiative. In D. A. Regier, W. E. Narrow, E. A. Kuhl, & D. J. Kupfer (Eds.), *The Conceptual Evolution of DSM-5* (pp. 231–266). Arlington, VA: American Psychiatric Publishing.

Wang, Q. (2008). Emotion knowledge and autobiographical memory across the preschool years: A cross-cultural longitudinal investigation. *Cognition, 108*, 117–135.

Wang, Q., & Peterson, C. (2014). Your earliest memory may be earlier than you think: Prospective studies of children's dating of earliest childhood memories. *Developmental Psychology, 50*(6), 1680–1686.

Wang, S., M., Kain, Z. N., & White, P. (2008). Acupuncture analgesia: I. The scientific basis. *Anesthesia and Analgesia, 106*(2), 602–610.

Wang, W., Chan, S. S., Heldman, D. A., & Moran, D. W. (2010). Motor cortical representation of hand translation and rotation during reaching. *Journal of Neuroscience, 30*, 958–962.

Wang, X., Merzenich, M. M., Sameshima, K., & Jenkins, W. M. (1995). Remodelling of hand representation in adult cortex determined by timing of tactile stimulation. *Nature, 378*, 71–75.

Wang, Y. (2007). Cognitive informatics: Exploring the theoretical foundations for natural intelligence, neural informatics, autonomic computing, and agent systems. *International Journal of Cognitive Informatics and Natural Intelligence, 1*(1), i–x.

Wann, J. P., Poulter, D. R., & Purcell, C. (2011). Reduced Sensitivity to Visual Looming Inflates the Risk Posed by Speeding Vehicles When Children Try to Cross the Road. *Psychological Science, 22*(4), 429–434. doi:10.1177/0956797611400917.

Wansink, B. B., & Wansink, C. S. (2010). The largest Last Supper: Depictions of food portions and plate size increased over the millennium. *International Journal Of Obesity, 34*(5), 943–944. doi:10.1038/ijo.2010.37.

Ward, C. (1994). Culture and altered states of consciousness. In W. J. Lonner & R. S. Malpass (Eds.), *Psychology and culture*. Boston: Allyn & Bacon.

Ward, J. (2013). Synesthesia. *Annual Review of Psychology, 64*, 49–75.

Wark, D. M. (2008). What we can do with hypnosis: A brief note. *American Journal of Clinical Hypnosis, 51*, 29–36.

Warmerdam, L., van Straten, A., Jongsma, J., Twisk, J., & Cuijpers, P. (2010). Online cognitive behavioral therapy and problem-solving therapy for depressive symptoms: Exploring mechanisms of change. *Journal of Behavior Therapy and Experimental Psychiatry, 41*, 64–70.

Warneken, F., Lohse, K., Melis, A. P., & Tomasello, M. (2011). Young children share the spoils after collaboration. *Psychological Science, 22*(2), 267–273. doi:10.1177/0956797610395392.

Warner, B. (2010). Reducing suicidal ideation and depression in older primary care patients: The oldest old and pain. *American Journal of Psychiatry, 167*, 102.

Warren, S. (2011). The case of the malodorous infant: Food choices during pregnancy can have astounding effects. Retrieved from http://scienceline.org/2011/03/ the-case-of-the-malodorous-infant/.

Warrington, E. K., & Weiskrantz, L. (1970). The amnesic syndrome: Consolidation of retrieval? *Nature, 228*, 626–630.

Wasserman, E. A. (1993). Comparative cognition: Beginning the second century of the study of animal intelligence. *Psychological Bulletin, 113*, 211–228.

Wasylkiw, L., MacKinnon, A., & MacLellan, A. (2012). Exploring the link between self-compassion and body image in university women. *Body Image, 9*(2), 236–245.

Wasylyshyn, C., Verhaeghen, P., & Sliwinski, M. J. (2011). Aging and task switching: A meta-analysis. *Psychology and Aging, 26*, 15–20.

Waszczuk, M. A., Zavos, H. M. S., Gregiry, A. M., & Eley, T. C. (2014). The phenotypic and genetic structure of depression and anxiety disorder symptoms in childhood, adolescence, and young adulthood. *JAMA Psychiatry*, Epub June 11, 2014.

Watamura, S. E., Phillips, D. A., Morrissey, T. W., McCartney, K., & Bub, K. (2011). Double jeopardy: Poorer social-emotional outcomes for children in the NICHD SECCYD experiencing home and child-care environments that confer risk. *Child Development, 82*, 48–65.

Watanabe, S., Sakamoto, J., & Wakita, M. (1995). Pigeons' discrimination of paintings by Monet and Picasso. *Journal of Experimental Analysis of Behavior, 63*, 165–174.

Waterhouse, L. (2006a). Inadequate evidence for multiple intelligences, Mozart Effect, and emotional intelligence theories. *Educational Psychologist, 41*(4), 247–255.

Waterhouse, L. (2006b). Multiple Intelligences, the Mozart Effect, and emotional intelligence: A critical review. *Educational Psychologist, 41*(4), 207–225.

Waterman, A. S. (2013). The humanistic psychology-positive psychology divide: Contrasts in philosophical foundations. *American Psychologist, 68*(3), 124–133.

Waters, A. M., Henry, J., & Neumann, D. L. (2009). Aversive Pavlovian conditioning in childhood anxiety disorders: Impaired response inhibition and resistance to extinction. *Journal of Abnormal Psychology, 118*, 311–321.

Watkins, K. E., Smith, S. M., Davis, S., & Howell, P. (2008). Structural and functional abnormalities of the motor system in developmental stuttering. *Brain, 131*, 50–59.

Watson, J. B. (1913). Psychology as the behaviorist views it. *Psychological Review, 20*, 158–177.

Watson, J. B. (1919). *Psychology from the standpoint of a behaviorist*. Philadelphia: Lippincott.

Watson, J. B. (1925). *Behaviorism*. London: Kegan Paul, Trench, Trubner.

Watson, J.C. (2011). Treatment failure in humanistic and experiential psychotherapy. *Journal of Clinical Psychology, 67*, 1117–1128.

Watson, R. T., & Heilman, K. M. (1979). Thalamic neglect. *Neurology, 29*(5), 690–694.

Waugh, C. E., Fredrickson, B. L., & Taylor, S. F. (2008). Adapting to life's slings and arrows: Individual diff erences in resilience when recovering from an anticipated threat. *Journal of Research in Personality, 42*, 1031–1046.

Waytz, A., & Young, L. (2012). The group-member mind trade-off: Attributing mind to groups versus group members. *Psychological Science, 23*, 77–85. doi:10.1177/0956797611423546.

Wearden, A. J., Tarrier, N., Barrowclough, C., Zastowny, T. R., & Rahill, A. A. (2000). A review of expressed emotion research in health care. *Clinical Psychology Review, 20*, 633–666.

Weaver, F. M., Follett, K., Stern, M., Hur, K., Harris, C., Marks, W. J., Jr., et al. (2009). Bilateral deep brain stimulation vs best medical therapy for patients with advanced Parkinson disease: A randomized controlled trial. *Journal of the American Medical Association, 301*(1), 63–73.

Weaver, J. R., Vandello, J. A., & Bosson, Jennifer K. (2012). Intrepid, imprudent, or impetuous?: The effects of gender threats on men's financial decisions. *Psychology of Men & Masculinity*. doi:http://dx.doi.org/10.1037/a0027087.

Webb, T. L., & Sheeran, P. (2006). Does changing behavioral intentions engender behavior change? A meta-analysis of the experimental evidence. *Psychological Bulletin, 132*, 249–268.

Weber, E. U., & Morris, M. W. (2010). Culture and judgment and decision making: The constructivist turn. *Perspectives on Psychological Science, 5*(4), 410–419. doi:10.1177/1745691610375556.

Weber, R. J. (1992). *Forks, phonographs, and hot air balloons: A field guide to inventive thinking*. New York: Oxford University Press.

Wechsler, D. (1939). *The measurement of adult intelligence*. Baltimore: Williams & Wilkins.

Wechsler, D. (1949). *The Wechsler Intelligence Scale for Children*. New York: Psychological Corporation.

Wechsler, D. (2003). *Wechsler Intelligence Scale for Children* (4th ed.). San Antonio, TX: Psychological Corporation.

Wechsler, D. (2008). *Wechsler Adult Intelligence Scale—Fourth edition (WAIS-IV)*. San Antonio, TX: Pearson Assessments.

Wegge, J., & Haslam, S. A. (2005). Improving work motivation and performance in brainstorming groups: The effects of three group goal-setting strategies. *European Journal of Work and Organizational Psychology, 14*, 400–430.

Wegner, D. M., Fuller, V. A. & Sparrow, B. (2003). Clever hands: Uncontrolled intelligence in facilitated communication. *Journal of Personality and Social Psychology, 85*, 5–19.

Weick, J. P., Liu, Y. & Zhang, S.-C. (2011). Human embryonic stem cell-derived neurons adopt and regulate the activity of an established neural network. *Proceedings of the National Academy of Sciences*. Retrieved from http://www.pnas.org/content/early/2011/11/14/1108487108.abstract?etoc. doi:10.1073/pnas.1108487108.

Weihs, K. L., Enright, T. M., & Simmens, S. J. (2008). Close relationships and emotional processing predict decreased mortality in women with breast cancer: Preliminary evidence. *Psychosomatic Medicine, 70*, 117–124.

Weiler, B. L., & Widom, C. S. (1996). Psychopathy and violent behavior in abused and neglected young adults. *Criminal Behaviour and Mental Health, 6*, 253–271.

Weimer, A. A., Sallquist, J., & Bolnick, R. R. (2012). Young children's emotion comprehension and theory of mind understanding. *Early Education and Development, 23*, 280–301.

Weinberg, R. A., Scarr, S., & Waldman, I. D. (1992). The Minnesota transracial adoption study: A follow-up of IQ test performance at adolescence. *Intelligence, 16*, 117–135.

Weinfield, N. S., Sroufe, L. A., & Egeland, B. (2000). Attachment from infancy to early adulthood in a high-risk sample: continuity, discontinuity, and their correlates. *Child Development, 71*, 695–702.

Weiner, R. D., & Falcone, G. (2011). Electroconvulsive therapy: How effective is it? *Journal of the American Psychiatric Nurses Association, 17*, 217–218.

Weingarten, J. A., & Collop, N. A. (2013). Air travel: Effects of sleep deprivation and jet lag. *Chest, 144*(4), 1394–1401.

Weinstein, E. A., & Kahn, R. L. (1955). *Denial of illness: Symbolic and physiological aspects*. Springfield, IL: Thomas.

Weinstein, T. R., Capitanio, J. P., & Gosling, S. D. (2008). Personality in animals. In O. P. John, R. W. Robins, L. A. Pervin (Eds.) , *Handbook of personality: Theory and research (3rd ed.)* (pp. 328–348). New York, NY, US: Guilford Press.

Weis, R., & Cerankosky, B. C. (2010). Effects of video-game ownership on young boys' academic and behavioral functioning: A randomized, controlled study. *Psychological Science, 21*(4), 463–470. doi:10.1177/0956797610362670.

Weisbuch, M., Pauker, K., & Ambady, N. (2009). The subtle transmission of race bias via televised nonverbal behavior. *Science, 326*, 1711–1714.

Weiskopf, N. (2012). Real-time fMRI and its application to neurofeedback. *Neuroimage, 62*(2), 682–692.

Weiss, A., Gale, C. R., Batty, G. D., & Deary, I. J. (2009). Emotionally stable, intelligent men live longer: Th e Vietnam Experience Study cohort. *Psychosomatic Medicine, 71*, 385–394.

Weiss, L. A., & Arking, D. E. (2009). A genome-wide linkage and association scan reveals novel loci for autism. *Nature, 461*, 802–808.

Weiss, S., & Moore, M. (1990). Cultural differences in the perception of magazine alcohol advertisements by Israeli Jewish, Moslem, Druze, and Christian high school students. *Drug and Alcohol Dependence, 26*, 209–215.

Weiss, V. (2007). Percentages of children living in poverty determine IQ averages of nations. *European Journal of Personality*. Special Issue: *European personality reviews, 21*, 761–763.

Weissman, M. M., Markowitz, J. C., & Kierman, G. L. (2007). *Clinician's quick guide to interpersonal psychotherapy*. New York: Oxford University Press.

Weisz, J. R., McCarty, C. A., & Valeri, S. M. (2006). Effects of psychotherapy for depression in children and adolescents: A meta-analysis. *Psychological Bulletin, 132*, 132–149.

Weisz, R. R., & Kazdin, A. E. (2010). *Evidence-based psychotherapies for children and adolescents (2nd ed.)*. New York: Guilford.

Weitzman, M., Rosenthal, D. G., & Liu, Y. (2011). Paternal depressive symptoms and child behavioral or emotional problems in the United States. *Pediatrics, 128*(6), 1126–1134. doi:10.1542/peds.2010–3034

Wells, C., Morrison, C. M., & Conway, M. A. (2013). Adult recollections of childhood memories: What details can be recalled? *Journal of Experimental Psychology 67*(7).

Wells, G. L., & Bradfield, A. L. (1999). Distortions in eyewitness' recollections: Can the postidentification-feedback effect be moderated? *Psychological Science, 10*, 138–144.

Wells, G. L., & Olson, E. A. (2003). Eyewitness testimony. *Annual Review of Psychology, 54*, 277–295.

Wells, G. L., Memon, A., & Penrod, S. D. (2006). Eyewitness evidence: Improving its probative value. *Psychological Science in the Public Interest, 7*, 45–75.

Wells, G. L., Olson, E. A., & Charman, S. D. (2002). The confidence of eyewitnesses in their identifications from lineups. *Current Directions in Psychological Science, 11*, 151–154.

Wells, G. L., Olson, E. A., & Charman, S. D. (2003). Distorted retrospective eyewitness reports as functions of feedback and delay. *Journal of Experimental Psychology: Applied, 9*, 42–52.

Wells, G. L., & Quinlivan, D. S. (2009). Suggestive eyewitness identification procedures and the Supreme Court's reliability test in light of eyewitness science: 30 years later. *Law and Human Behavior, 33*(1), 1–24.

Wells, G. L., Steblay, N. K., & Dysart, J. E. (2012). Eyewitness identification reforms: Are suggestiveness-induced hits and guesses true hits? *Perspectives on Psychological Science, 7*(3), 264–271. doi:10.1177/1745691612443368.

Wells, R., Outhred, T., Heathers, J. A., Quintana, D. S., & Kemp, A. H. (2012). Matter over mind: a randomised-controlled trial of single-session biofeedback training on performance anxiety and heart rate variability in musicians. *PLoS One, 7*(10), e46597.

Wells, S., Graham, K., & West, P. (2000). Alcohol-related aggression in the general population. *Journal of Studies on Alcohol, 61*, 626–632.

Welsh, J. A., Nix, R. L., Blair, C., Bierman, K. L., & Nelson, K. E. (2010). The development of cognitive skills and gains in academic school readiness for children from low-income families. *Journal of Educational Psychology, 102*(1), 43–53. doi:10.1037/a0016738.

Welsh, T. N., Ray, M. C., Weeks, D. J., Dewey, D., & Elliot, D. (2009). Does Joe influence Fred's action? Not if Fred has autism spectrum disorder. *Brain Research, 1248*, 141–148.

Weltzin, T. E., Bulik, C. M., McConaha, C. W., & Kaye, W. H. (1995). Laxative withdrawal and anxiety in bulimia nervosa. *International Journal of Eating Disorders, 17*(2), 141–146.

Wen, C. P, Wai, J. P. M., Tsai, M. K., Yang, T. Y. C., Cheng, T. Y. D., Lee, M.-C., Chan, H. T., Tsao, C. K., Tsai, S. P., & Wu, X. (2011). Minimum amount of physical activity for reduced mortality and extended life expectancy: A prospective cohort study. *The Lancet, 378*, 1244–1253.

Werner, E. (2003, January 28). Police: Sons kill mom, dismember her after seeing it done on "The Sopranos." *Naples Daily News*.

Werth, J. L., Jr.; Welfel, E. R.; & Benjamin, G. A. H. (Eds.). (2009). *The duty to protect: Ethical, legal, and professional considerations for mental health professionals*. Washington, DC: American Psychological Association.

Wertheimer, M. (1923). Laws of organization in perceptual forms. First published as Untersuchungen zur Lehre von der Gestalt II in *Psycologische Forschung, 4,* 301–350. Translation published in Ellis, W. (1938). *A source book of Gestalt psychology* (pp. 71–88). London: Routledge & Kegan Paul.

Wesson, D. W., & Wilson, D. A. (2010). Smelling sounds: Olfactory-auditory sensory convergence in the olfactory tubercle. *Journal of Neuroscience, 30,* 3013–3021.

West, G. L., Anderson, A. K., Bedwell, J. S., & Pratt, J. (2010). Red diffuse light suppresses the accelerated perception of fear. *Psychological Science, 21*(7), 992–999. doi:10.1177/0956797610371966.

West, M. A., Borrill, C. S., & Unsworth, K. L. (1998). Team effectiveness in organizations. In C. L. Cooper & I. T. Robertson (Eds.), *International review of industrial and organizational psychology 1998* (pp. 1–48). Chichester, UK: Wiley.

West, S. A., & Gardner, A. (2010). Altruism, spite, and greenbeards. *Science, 327,* 1341–1344.

West, S. G. (2009). Alternatives to randomized experiments. *Current Directions in Psychological Science, 18,* 299–304.

Westen, D., & Bradley, R. (2005). Empirically supported complexity. *Current Directions in Psychological Science, 14,* 266–271.

Westen, D., Glen, O., Gabbard, G. O., & Ortigo, K. M. (2008). Psychoanalytic approaches to personality. In O. John, R. Robins, & L. Pervin (Eds.), *Handbook of personality: Theory and research* (3rd ed., pp. 61–113). New York: Guilford.

Westen, D., & Morrison, K. (2001). A multidimensional meta-analysis of treatments for depression, panic, and generalized anxiety disorder: An empirical examination of the status of empirically supported therapies. *Journal of Consulting and Clinical Psychology, 69,* 875–899.

Wexler, M. (2005). Anticipating the three-dimensional consequences of eye movements. *Proceedings of the National Academy of Sciences, 102,* 1246–1251.

Whaley, A. L. (2001). Cultural mistrust: An important psychological construct for diagnosis and treatment of African-Americans. *Professional Psychology: Research and Practice, 32,* 555–562.

Whaley, A. L. (2011). Clinicians' competence in assessing cultural mistrust among African American psychiatric patients. *Journal of Black Psychology, 37*(4), 387–406. doi:10.1177/0095798410387133.

Whaley, A. L., & Hall, B. N. (2009). Cultural themes in the psychotic symptoms of African American psychiatric patients. *Professional Psychology: Research and Practice, 40,* 75–80.

Whang, W., Kubzansky, L. D., Kawachi, I., Rexrode, K. M., et al. (2009). Depression and risk of sudden cardiac death and coronary heart disease in women. *Journal of the American College of Cardiology, 53,* 950–958.

Wharton, C. M., Grafman, J., Flitman, S. S., Hansen, E. K., Brauner, J., Marks, A., & Honda, M. (2000). Toward neuroanatomical models of analogy: A positron emission tomography study of analogical mapping. *Cognitive Psychology, 40,* 173–197.

Wheaton, L. A., & Hallett, M. (2007). Ideomotor apraxia: A review. *Journal of the Neurological Sciences, 260*(1–2), 1–10.

Wheeler, L., & Suls, J. (2007). Social comparison: Can we agree on what it is? *Revue Internationale de Psychologie Sociale, 20,* 31–51.

Whimbey, A. (1976). *Intelligence can be taught.* New York: Bantam.

Whitaker, D. J., Morrison, S., Lindquist, C., Hawkins, S. R., O'Neil, J. A., Nesius, A. M., et al. (2006). A critical review of interventions for the primary prevention of perpetration of partner violence. *Aggression and Violent Behavior, 11,* 151–166.

Whitam, F. L., Diamond, M., & Martin, J. (1993). Homosexual orientation in twins: A report on 61 pairs and three triplet sets. *Archives of Sexual Behavior, 22*(3), 187–206.

White, A. T., & Spector, P. E. (1987). An investigation of age-related factors in the age-job satisfaction relationship. *Psychology and Aging, 2,* 261–265.

White, D. P., & Younes, M. K. (2012). Obstructive sleep apnea. *Comprehensive Physiology, 2*(4), 2541–2594.

White, F. J. (1998). Nicotine addiction and the lure of reward. *Nature Medicine, 4,* 659–660.

White, N. M., Packard, M. G., & McDonald, R. J. (2013). Dissociation of memory systems: The story unfolds. *Behavioral Neuroscience, 127*(6), 813–834.

White, S. M. (2006). Talking genes. *Advances in Speech Language Pathology, 8,* 2–6.

Whitman, D., Caleo, S., Carpenter, N., Horner, M., & Bernerth, J. (2012). Fairness at the collective level: A meta-analytic examination of the consequences and boundary conditions of organizational justice climate. *The Journal of Applied Psychology, 97,* 776–791.

Whitney, P. (2001). Schemas, frames, and scripts in cognitive psychology. In N. J. Smelser & P. B. Baltes (Eds.), *International encyclopedia of the social and behavioral sciences* (pp. 13522–13526). New York: Elsevier.

Whitson, L. R., Karayanidis, F., & Michie, P. T. (2012). Task practice differentially modulates task-switching performance across the adult lifespan. *Acta Psychologica, 139,* 124–136.

Whyte, E., Skidmore, E., Aizenstein, H., Ricker, J., & Butters, M. (2011). Cognitive impairment in acquired brain injury: a predictor of rehabilitation outcomes and an opportunity for novel interventions. *PM&R, 3*(6 Supplement 1), S45–S51

Wichers, M. C., Myin-Germeys, I., Jacobs, N., Kenis, G., Dermon, C., Vlietinck, R., et al. (2008). Susceptibility to depression expressed as alterations in cortisol day curve: A cross-twin, cross-trait study. *Biological Psychology, 79,* 80–90.

Wicherts, J. M., & Scholten, A. Z. (2010). Test anxiety and the validity of cognitive tests: A confirmatory factor analysis perspective and some empirical findings. *Intelligence, 38,* 169–178.

Wickens, C. D. (1989). Attention and skilled performance. In D. Holding (Ed.), *Human skills* (pp. 71–105). New York: Wiley.

Wickens, C. D. (1992). *Engineering psychology and human performance* (2nd ed.). New York: HarperCollins.

Wickens, C. D. (2002). Situation awareness and workload in aviation. *Current Directions in Psychological Science, 11,* 128–133.

Wickens, C. D., & Carswell, C. M. (2012). Information processing. In G. Salvendy (Ed.), *Handbook of Human Factors and Ergonomics.* 4th ed. pp. 117–161. Hoboken, NJ: John Wiley & Sons.

Wickens, C. D., Gordon-Becker, S. E., Liu, Y., & Lee, J. D. (2004). *Introduction to human factors engineering* (2nd ed.). Upper Saddle River, NJ: Prentice Hall.

Wicker, B., Keysers, C., Plailly, J., Royet, J. P., Gallese, V., & Rizzolatti, G. (2003). Both of us disgusted in My insula: The common neural basis of seeing and feeling disgust. *Neuron, 40,* 655–664.

Wickham, D. (2001, September 3). Castration often fails to halt offenders. *USA Today.*

Widiger, T. A. (2008). Personality disorders. In J. Hunsley, E. J. Mash (Eds.), *A guide to assessments that work* (pp. 413–435). New York: Oxford University Press.

Widiger, T. A., Livesley, W. J., & Clark, L. A. (2009). An integrative dimensional classification of personality disorder. *Psychological Assessment, 21,* 243–255.

Widom, C. S. (1989). The cycle of violence. *Science, 244,* 160–166.

Widom, C. S. (2000). Childhood victimization: Early adversity, later psychopathology. *National Institute of Justice Journal, 19,* 2–9.

Widom, C. S., Czaja, S. J., & Dutton, M. A. (2008). Childhood victimization and lifetime revictimization. *Child Abuse and Neglect, 32,* 785–796.

Wiens, S., Mezzacappa, E. S., & Katkin, E. S. (2000). Heartbeat detection and the experience of emotions. *Cognition & Emotion, 14,* 417–427.

Wiers, R. W., Eberl, C., Rinck, M., Becker, E. S., & Lindenmeyer, J. (2011). Retraining automatic action tendencies changes alcoholic patients' approach bias for alcohol and improves treatment outcome. *Psychological Science, 22*(4), 490–497. doi:10.1177/0956797611400615.

Wiesner, W. H., & Cronshaw, S. F. (1988). A meta-analytic investigation of the impact of interview format and degree of structure on the validity of the employment interview. *Journal of Occupational Psychology, 61,* 275–290.

Wietek, J., Wiegert, J. S., Adeishvili, N., Schneider, F., Watanabe, H., Tsunoda, S. P., Vogt, A., Elstner, M., Oertner, T. G., & Hegemann, P. (2014). Conversion of channelrhodopsin into light-gated chloride channel. *Science, 344*(6182), 409–412.

Wigfield, A., Eccles, J. S., Schiefele, U., Roeser, R. W., & Davis-Kean, P. (2006). Development of achievement motivation. In W. Damon & R. Lerner (Series Eds.), & N. Eisenberg (Vol. Ed.), *Handbook of child psychology: Vol. 3. Social, emotional, and personality development* (6th ed., pp. 933–1062). Hoboken, NJ: Wiley.

Wiik, K.L., Loman, M.M., Van Ryzin, M.J., Armstrong, J.M., Essex, M.J., Pollak, S.D., & Gunnar, M.R. (2011). Behavioral and emotional symptoms of post-institutionalized children in middle childhood. *Journal of Child Psychiatry and Psychology, 52,* 56–63.

Wijkstra, J., Lijmer, J., Burger, H., Geddes, J., & Nolen, W. A. (2013). Pharmacological treatment for psychotic depression. *Cochrane Database of Systemic Reviews, 11,* CD004044.

Wilcoxon, H. C., Dragoin, W. B., & Kral, P. A. (1971). Illness-induced aversions in rat and quail: Relative salience of visual and gustatory cues. *Science, 171,* 826–828.

Wilford, M. M., & Wells, G. L. (2010). Does Facial Processing Prioritize Change Detection? Change Blindness Illustrates Costs and Benefits of Holistic Processing. *Psychological Science, 21*(11), 1611–1615. doi:10.1177/0956797610385952.

Wilhelm, K., Mitchell, P. B., Niven, H., Finch, A., Wedgwood, L., et al. (2006). Life events, first depression onset, and the serotonin transporter gene. *British Journal of Psychiatry, 188,* 210–215.

Willemsen, R., & Vanderlinden, J. (2008). Hypnotic approaches for alopecia areata. *International Journal of Clinical and Experimental Hypnosis, 56,* 318–333.

Williams, C. L., & Pleil, K. E. (2008). Toy story: Why do monkey and human males prefer trucks? *Hormones and Behavior, 54,* 355–358.

Williams, J. (2008). Working toward a neurobiological account of ADHD: Commentary on Gail Tripp and Jeff Wickens' dopamine transfer deficit. *Journal of Child Psychology and Psychiatry, 49,* 705–711.

Williams, J. A., Zimmerman, F. J., Bell, J. F. (2013). Norms and trends of sleep time among U.S. children and adolescents. *JAMA Pediatrics, 167(1),* 55–60.

Williams, J. E., & Best, D. L. (1990). *Measuring stereotypes: A multination study* (Rev. ed.). Newbury Park, CA: Sage.

Williams, J. H. G., Waiter, G. D., Gilchrist, A., Perrett, D. I., Murray, A. D., et al. (2006). Neural mechanisms of imitation and 'mirror neuron' functioning in autistic spectrum disorder. *Neuropsychologia, 44,* 610–621.

Williams, K. D., & Sommer, K. L. (1997). Social ostracism by coworkers: Does rejection lead to loafing or compensation? *Personality and Social Psychology Bulletin, 23,* 693–706.

Williams, L. E., Bargh, J. A., Nocera, C. C., & Gray, J. R. (2009). The unconscious regulation of emotion: Nonconscious reappraisal goals modulate emotional reactivity. *Emotion, 9,* 847–854.

Williams, L. M. (1994). What does it mean to forget child sexual abuse? A reply to Loftus, Garry, and Feldman (1994). *Journal of Consulting and Clinical Psychology, 62,* 1182–1186.

Williams, N. R., & Okun, M. S. (2013). Deep brain stimulation (DBS) at the interface of neurology and psychiatry. *Journal of Clinical Investigation, 123*(11), 4546–4556.

Williams, R. B. (2001). Hostility and heart disease: Williams et al. (1980). *Advances in Mind-Body Medicine, 17,* 52–55.

Williams, R. J., & Connolly, D. (2006). Does learning about the mathematics of gambling change gambling behavior? *Psychology of Addictive Behavior, 20,* 62–68.

Williams, T. & Williams, K. (2010). Self-efficacy and performance in mathematics: Reciprocal determinism in 33 nations. *Journal of Educational Psychology, 102*(2), 453–466. doi:10.1037/a0017271.

Williams-Piehota, P., Pizarro, J., Schneider, T. R., Mowad, L., & Salovey, P. (2005). Matching health messages to monitor-blunter coping styles to motivate screening mammography. *Health Psychology, 24,* 58–67.

Willis, J., & Todorov, A. (2006). First impressions: Making up your mind after a 100-ms exposure to a face. *Psychological Science, 17,* 592–598.

Willmott L., Harris P, Gellaitry G, Cooper V., Horne R. (2011).The effects of expressive writing following first myocardial infarction: A randomized controlled trial. *Health Psychology, 30,* 642–650.

Wills, T. A., Sandy, J. M., Yaeger, A., & Shinar, O. (2001). Family risk factors and adolescent substance use: Moderation effects of temperament dimension. *Developmental Psychology, 37,* 283–297.

Willyard, C. (2011). Men: A growing minority? *gradPSYCH Magazine,* January 2011, American Psychology Association.

Wilson, A. D., & Baietto, M. (2011). Advances in electronic-nose technologies developed for biomedical applications. *Sensors, 11*(1), 1105–1176.

Wilson,
G. T. (2011). Treatment of binge eating disorder. *Psychiatric Clinics of North American, 34*(4), 773–783.

Wilson, G. T., Nathan, P. E., O'Leary, K. D., & Clark, L. A. (1996). *Abnormal psychology.* Boston: Allyn & Bacon.

Wilson, G. T., Wilfley, D. E., Agras, W. S., & Bryson, S. W. (2010). Psychological treatments of binge eating disorder. *Archives of General Psychiatry, 67,* 94–101.

Wilson, J. M., Straus, S. G., & McEvily, B. (2006). All in due time: The development of trust in computer-mediated and face-to-face teams. *Organizational Behavior and Human Decision Processes, 99,* 16–33.

Wilson, K., & French, C. C. (2006). The relationship between susceptibility to false memories, dissociativity, and paranormal belief and experience. *Personality and Individual Differences, 41,* 1493–1502.

Wilson, R. E., Gosling, S. D., & Graham, L. T. (2012). A review of Facebook research in the social sciences. *Perspectives on Psychological Science, 7,* 203–220. doi:10.1177/1745691612442904.

Wilson, R. S., Begeny, C. T., Boyle, P. A., Schneider, J. A., & Bennett, D. A. (2011). Vulnerability to stress, anxiety, and development of dementia in old age. *The American Journal of Geriatric Psychiatry, 19,* 327–334. doi:10.1097/JGP.0b013e31820119da.

Wilson, R. S., Scherr, P. A., Schneider, J. A., Tang, Y., & Bennett, D. A. (2007). Relation of cognitive activity to risk of developing Alzheimer disease. *Neurology, 69,* 1911–1920.

Wilson, W. J. (1997). *When work disappears: The world of the new urban poor.* New York: Vintage Books.

Wilson-Mendenhall, C., Barrett, L. F., & Barsalou, L. W. (2013). Neural evidence that human emotions share core affective properties. *Psychological Science, 24*(6), 947–956.

Wilt, J., Cox, K. S., & McAdams, D. P. (2010). Exploring the relationships between Eriksonian.

Willyard, C. (2011). Men: A growing minority? *gradPSYCH Magazine,* January 2011, American Psychology Association.

Winer, G. A., Cottrell, J. E., Gregg, V., Fournier, J. S., & Bica, L. A. (2002). Fundamentally misunderstanding visual perception: Adults' belief in visual emissions. *American Psychologist, 57,* 417–424.

Winerman, L. (2005, July/August). A virtual cure. *Monitor on Psychology,* 87–89.

Wing, E. A., Marsh, E. J., & Cabeza, R. (2013). Neural correlates of retrieval-based memory enhancement: An fMRI study of the testing effect. *Neuropsychologia, 51*(12), 2360–2370.

Winkelmayer, W. C., Stampfer, M. J., Willett, W. C., & Curhan, G. C. (2005). Habitual caffeine intake and the risk of hypertension in women. *Journal of the American Medical Association, 294,* 2330–2335.

Winkielman, P., & Berridge, K. C. (2004). Unconscious emotion. *Current Directions in Psychological Science, 13,* 120–123.

Winn, P. (1995). The lateral hypothalamus and motivated behavior: An old syndrome reassessed and a new perspective gained. *Current Directions in Psychological Science, 4,* 182–187.

Winson, J. (1990, November). The meaning of dreams. *Scientific American,* pp. 86–96.

Winter, D. G. (1996). *Personality: Analysis and interpretation of lives.* New York: McGraw-Hill.

Winterer, G. (2006). Cortical microcircuits in schizophrenia—The dopamine hypothesis re-visited. *Pharmacopsychiatry, 39,* S68–S71.

Wintersteen, M. B., Mensinger, J. L., & Diamond, G. S. (2005). Do gender and racial differences between patient and therapist affect therapeutic alliance and treatment retention in adolescents? *Professional Psychology: Research and Practice, 36,* 400–408.

Wise, R. A. & Kiyatkin, E. A. (2011). Differentiating the rapid actions of cocaine. Nature Reviews. *Neuroscience, 12*(8), 479–484.

Wismer Fries, A. B., Shirtcliff, E. A., & Pollak, S. D. (2008). Neuroendocrine dysregulation following early social deprivation in children. *Developmental Psychobiology, 50,* 588–599.

Wismer Fries, A. B., Ziegler, T. E., Kurian, J. R., Jacoris, S., & Pollak, S. D. (2005). Early experience in humans is associated with changes in neuropeptides critical for regulating social behavior. *Proceedings of the National Academy of Sciences, 102,* 17237–17240.

Witkamp, R. (2011). Current and future drug targets in weight management. *Pharmaceutical Research, 28*(8), 1792–1818.

Witkiewitz, K., Bowen, S., Harrop, E. N., Douglas, H., Enkema, M., & Edgwick, C. (2014). Mindfulness-based treatment to prevent addictive behavior relapse: Theoretical models and hypothesized mechanisms of change. *Substance Use & Misuse, 49*(5), 513–524.

Witt, J. K., Linkenauger, S. A., & Proffitt, D. R. (2012). Get me out of this slump! Visual illusions improve sports performance. *Psychological Science, 23*(4), 397–399. doi:10.1177/0956797611428810.

Wixted, J. T. (2004). The psychology and neuroscience of forgetting. *Annual Review of Psychology, 55,* 235–269.

Wixted, J. T. (2005). A theory about why we forget what we once knew. *Current Directions in Psychological Science, 14,* 6–9.

Wixted, J. T., & Mickes, L. (2014). A signal-detection-based diagnostic-feature–Diagnostic model of eyewitness identification. *Psychological Review, 121*(2), 262–276.

Wlodzimirow, K. A., Abu-Hanna, A, Schultz, M. J., Maas, M. A., Bos, L. D., Sterk, P. J., Knobel, H. H., Soers, R. J., & Chamuleau, R. A. (2013). Exhaled breath analysis with electronic nose technology for detection of acute liver failure in rats. *Biosensors & Biotechnology, 53,* 129–134.

Wohl, J. (1995). Traditional individual psychotherapy and ethnic minorities. In J. F. Aponte, R. Y. Rivers, & J. Wohl (Eds.), *Psychological interventions and cultural diversity* (pp. 74–91). Boston: Allyn & Bacon.

Wohlfarth, T., Storosum, J. G., Elferink, A. J. A., van Zweiten, B. J., Fouwels, A., & van den Brink, W. (2004). Response to tricyclic antidepressants: Independent of gender? *American Journal of Psychiatry, 161,* 370–372.

Wojcieszak, M., & Price, V. (2010). Bridging the divide or intensifying the conflict? How disagreement affects strong predilections about sexual minorities. *Political Psychology, 31,* 315–339. doi:10.1111/j.1467-9221.2009.00753.x.

Wojda, U., & Kuznicki, J. (2013). Alzheimer's disease modeling: Ups, downs, and perspectives for human induced pluripotent stem cells. *Journal of Alzheimer's Disease, 34*(3), 563–588.

Wolak, J., Mitchell, K. J., & Finkelhor, D. (2006). *Online victimization of youth: 5 years later.* Alexandria, VA: National Center for Missing & Exploited Children.

Woldt, A. L., & Toman, S. M. (Eds.). (2005). *Gestalt therapy: History, theory, and practice.* Newbury Park, CA: Sage.

Wolfe, J. M., Horowitz, T. S., Van Wert, M. J., Kenner, N. M., Place, S. S., & Kibbi, N. (2007). Low target prevalence is a stubborn source of errors in visual search tasks. *Journal of Experimental Psychology, 136*(4), 623–638.

Wolfe, J. M., & Van Wert, M. J. (2010). Varying target prevalence reveals two dissociable decision criteria in visual search. *Current Biology, 20,* 121–124.

Wolitzky, D. L. (2011). Psychoanalytic theories of psychotherapy. In J. C. Norcross, G. R. VandenBos, & D. K. Freedheim (Eds.), *History of psychotherapy: Continuity and change* (pp. 65–100). Washington, D.C.: American Psychological Association.

Wolpaw, J. R., & Chen, X. Y. (2006). The cerebellum in maintenance of a motor skill: A hierarchy of brain and spinal cord plasticity underlies H-reflex conditioning. *Learning & Memory, 13,* 208–215.

Wolpe, J. (1958). *Psychotherapy by reciprocal inhibition.* Stanford, CA: Stanford University Press.

Wolpert, I. (1924). Die Simultanagnosie: Störung der Gesamtauffassung. Archiv für Psychiatrie und Nervenkrankheiten, vereinigt mit Zeitschrift für die gesamte Neurologie und Psychiatrie, 93, 397–413.

Wong, J., Gordon, E. A., & Heimberg, R. G. (2012). Social anxiety disorder. In P. Sturmey & M. Hersen (Eds.), Handbook of evidence-based practice in clinical psychology, Vol. 2: Adult disorders (pp. 621–649). Hoboken, NJ: Wiley..

Wong, C. G., Gibson, K. M., & Snead, O. C. (2004). From the street to the brain: Neurobiology of the recreational drug gamma-hydroxybutyric acid. *Trends in Pharmacological Science, 25,* 29–34.

Wong, J., Gordon, E. A., & Heimberg, R. G. (2012). Social anxiety disorder. In P. Sturmey & M. Hersen (Eds.), *Handbook of evidence-based practice in clinical psychology, Vol. 2: Adult disorders* (pp. 621–649). Hoboken, NJ: Wiley.

Wong, J. M., Na, B., Regan, M. C., & Whooley, M. A. (2013). Hostility, health behaviors, and risk of recurrent events in patients with stable coronary heart disease: Findings from the Heart and Soul Study. *Journal of the American Heart Association, 2*(5), e000052. doi:10.1161/JAHA.113.000052.

Wong, K. F. E., & Kwong, J. Y. Y. (2005). Between-individual comparisons in performance evaluation: A perspective from prospect theory. *Journal of Applied Psychology, 90,* 284–294.

Wong, N., Ray, P., Stephens, G., & Lewis, L. (2012). Artificial immune systems for the detection of credit card fraud: An architecture, prototype and preliminary results. *Information Systems Journal, 22*(1), 53–76. doi:10.1111/j.1365-2575.2011.00369.x.

Wong, Q. J. J., & Moulds, M. L. (2009). Impact of rumination versus distraction on anxiety and maladaptive self-beliefs in socially anxious individuals. *Behaviour Research and Therapy, 47,* 861–867.

Wood, A. M., & Tarrier, N. (2010). Positive clinical psychology: A new vision and strategy for integrated research and practice. Clinical *Psychology Review, 30*(7), 819–829.

Wood, J. M., Lilienfeld, S. O., Nezworski, M. T., Garb, H. N., Allen, K. H., & Wildermuth, J. L. (2010). Validity of Rorschach inkblot scores for discriminating psychopaths from nonpsychopaths in forensic populations: A meta-analysis. *Psychological Assessment, 22,* 336–349.

Wood, W., & Eagly, A. H. (2002). A cross-cultural analysis of the behavior of women and men: Implications for the origins of sex differences. *Psychological Bulletin, 128,* 699–727.

Wood, W., & Eagly, A. H. (2012). Chapter 2: Biosocial construction of sex differences and similarities in behavior. *Advances in Experimental Social Psychology, 46,* 55–123. doi: http://dx.doi.org/10.1016/B978-0-12-394281-4.00002-7.

Woodcock, A., & Monteith, M. J. (2013). Forging links with the self to combat implicit bias. *Group Processes and Intergroup Relations, 16*(4), 445–461.

Woodhead, M. (1988). When psychology informs public policy: The case of early childhood intervention. *American Psychologist, 43,* 443–454.

Woods, S. C., Schwartz, M. W., Baskin, D. G., & Seeley, R. J. (2000). Food intake and the regulation of body weight. *Annual Review of Psychology, 51,* 255–277.

Woodward, A. L. (2009). Infants' grasp of others' intentions. *Current Directions in Psychological Science, 18,* 53–57.

Woodward, T. S., Moritz, S., Cuttler, C., & Whitman, J. C. (2006). The contribution of a cognitive bias against disconfirmatory evidence (BADE) to delusions in schizophrenia. *Journal of Clinical and Experimental Neuropsychology, 28,* 605–617.

Woodworth, R. S., & Schlosberg, H. (1954). *Experimental psychology.* New York: Holt.

Woody, W. D., Daniel, D. B., & Baker, C. A. (2010). E-books or textbooks: Students prefer textbooks. *Computers & Education, 55,* 945–948. doi:10.1016/j.compedu.2010.04.005.

Woolley, J. D. (1997). Thinking about fantasy: Are children fundamentally different thinkers and believers from adults? *Child Development, 68,* 991–1011.

Worden, B., & Tolin, D. F. (2014). Obsessive-compulsive disorder in adults. In E. A. Storch & D. McKay (Eds.), *Obsessive-compulsive disorder and its spectrum: A life-span approach* (pp. 13–35). Washington, DC: American Psychological Association.

World Health Organization. (2002). *Nutrition: Controlling the global obesity epidemic.* Retrieved December 13, 2004, from http://www.who.int/nut/obs.htm

World Health Organization. (2003). *AIDS epidemic update.* Geneva, Switzerland: Author.

World Health Organization Mental Health Survey Consortium. (2004). Prevalence, severity, and unmet need for treatment of mental disorders in the World Health Organization World Mental Health Surveys. *Journal of the American Medical Association, 291,* 2581–2590.

World Health Organization. (2008). *World health report 2008: Primary health care now more than ever.* Geneva, Switzerland: World Health Organization. Retrieved June 11, 2009, from http://www.who.int/whr/2008/whr08_en.pdf.

World Health Organization. (2009). *World health organization mental health surveys.* Cambridge, MA: Cambridge University Press.

World Health Organization (2012). Depression: What is depression? Retrieved from http://www.who.int/mental_health/management/depression/definition /en/index.html.

Worthington, R. L., Navarro, R. L., Savoy, H. B., & Hampton, D. (2008). Development, reliability, and validity of the Measure of Sexual Identity Exploration and Commitment (MOSIEC). *Developmental Psychology, 44,* 22–33.

Worthy, D. A., Gorlick, M. A., Pacheco, J. L., Schnyer, D. M., & Maddox, W. (2011). With age comes wisdom: Decision making in younger and older adults. *Psychological Science, 22*(11), 1375–1380. doi:10.1177/0956797611420301.

Wright, A. A., Katz, J. S., & Ma, W. (2012). How to be proactive about interference: Lessons from animal memory. *Psychological Science, 23*(5), 453–458. doi:10.1177/0956797611430096.

Wright, A. G. C., Krueger, R. F., Hobbs, M. J., Markon, K. E., Eaton, N. R., & Slade, T. (2013). The structure of psychopathology: Toward an expanded quantitative empirical model. *Journal of Abnormal Psychology, 122,* 281–294.

Wu, C., Cui, B., He, L., Chen, L., & Mobley, W. C. (2009). The coming of age of axonal neurotrophin signaling endosomes. *Journal of Proteomics, 72,* 46–55. Epub 2008 Nov 6.

Wyatt, T. D. (2009). Fifty years of pheromones. *Nature, 457,* 262–263.

Wynne, C. L. (2004). *Do animals think?* Princeton, NJ: Princeton University Press.

Xia, L., & Yin, S. (2013). Local gene transfection in the cochlea (Review). *Molecular Medicine Reports, 8*(1), 3–10.

Xu. J., & Roberts, R. E. (2010). The power of positive emotions: It's a matter of life or death—subjective well-being and longevity over 28 years in a general population. *Health Psychology, 29,* 9–19.

Xue, Y., Luo, Y., Wu, P., Shi, H., Xue, L., Chen, C., & ... Lu, L. (2012). A memory retrieval-extinction procedure to prevent drug craving and relapse. *Science (New York, N.Y.), 336*(6078), 241–245.

Yaffe, K., Fiocco, A. J., Lindquist, K., Vittinghoff, E., et al. (2009). Predictors of maintaining cognitive function in older adults: The Health ABC Study. *Neurology, 72,* 2029–2035.

Yakimovich, D., & Saltz, E. (1971). Helping behavior: The cry for help. *Psychonomic Science, 23,* 427–428.

Yalom, I. D. (1980). *Existential psychotherapy.* New York: Basic Books.

Yamaguchi, Y., Suzuki, T., Mizoro, Y., Kori, H., Okada, K., Chen, Y., Fustin, J-M., Yamazaki, F., Mizuguchi, N., Zhang, J., Dong, X., Tsujimoto, G., Okuno, Y., Doi, M., & Okamura, H. (2013). Mice genetically deficient in vasopressin V1a and V1b receptors are resistant to jet lag. *Science, 342*(6154), 85–90.

Yan, Z., Chi, Y., Wang, P., Cheng, J., Wang, Y., Shu, Q., & Huang, G. (1992). Studies on the luminescence of channels in rats and its law of changes with "syndromes" and treatment of acupuncture and moxibustion. *Journal of Traditional Chinese Medicine, 12*(4), 283–287.

Yang, M. Y., Yang, W. C., Lin, P. M., Hsu, J. F., Hsiao, H. H., Liu, Y. C., Tsai, H. J., Chang, C. S., & Lin, S. F. (2011). Altered expression of circadian clock genes in human chronic myeloid leukemia. *Journal of Biological Rhythms, 26*(2), 136–148.

Yang, Q., Zhang, Z., Gregg, E. W., Flanders, W. D., Merritt, R., & Hu, F. B. (2014). Added sugar intake and cardiovascular diseases mortality among U.S. adults. *JAMA Internal Medicine,* February 3, 2014.

Yang, T., & Kubovy, M. (1999). Weakening the robustness of perspective: Evidence for a modified theory of compensation in picture perception. *Perception and Psychophysics, 61,* 456–467.

Yang, Y., & Wang, G. (2011). A novel emotion recognition method based on ensemble learning and rough set theory. *International Journal Of Cognitive Informatics And Natural Intelligence, 5*(3), 61–72. doi:10.4018/IJCINI.2011070104.

Yang-Teng, F., Decety, J., Chia-Yen, Y., Ji-Lin, L., & Yawei, C. (2010). Unbroken mirror neurons in autism spectrum disorders. *Journal Of Child Psychology & Psychiatry, 51*(9), 981–988. doi:10.1111/j.1469-7610.2010.02269.x.

Yanovski, S. Z., & Yanovski, J. A. (2002). Obesity. *New England Journal of Medicine, 346*(8), 591–602. doi:10.1056/NEJMra012586.

Yanovski, S. Z., & Yanovski, J. A. (2014). Long-term drug treatment for obesity: A systematic and clinical review. *JAMA. 311*(1), 74–86.

Yantis, S. (1993). Stimulus-driven attentional capture. *Current Directions in Psychological Science, 2,* 156–161.

Yarkoni, T. (2010). Personality in 100,000 words: A large-scale analysis of personality and word use among bloggers. *Journal of Research in Personality, 44,* 363–373. doi:10.1016/j.jrp.2010.04.001.

Yarlagadda, A., Helvink, B., Chou, C., Gladieux, K., Keller, A., & Clayton, A. (2008). Glutamic acid decarboxylase (GAD) antibodies in tardive dyskinesia (TD) as compared to patients with schizophrenia without TD and normal controls. *Schizophrenia Research, 105,* 287–288.

Yarnell, L. M., & Neff, K. D. (2013). Self-compassion, interpersonal conflict resolutions, and well-being. *Self and Identity, 12*(2), 146–159.

Yates, J. (2010). Culture and probability judgment. *Social and Personality Psychology Compass, 4*(3), 174–188. doi:10.1111/j.1751-9004.2009.00253.x.

Yearta, S. K., Maitlis, S., & Briner, R. B. (1995). An exploratory study of goal setting in theory and practice: A motivational technique that works? *Journal of Occupational and Organizational Psychology, 68,* 237–252.

Yeo, S. S., Chang, P. H., & Jang, S. H. (2013). The ascending reticular activating system from pontine reticular formation to the thalamus in the human brain. *Frontiers in Human Neurosciences, 7,* 416.

Yeomans, M. R., & Mobini, S. (2006). Hunger alters the expression of acquired hedonic but not sensory qualities of food-paired odors in humans. *Journal of Experimental Psychology: Animal Behavior Processes, 32,* 460–466.

Yerkes, R. M. (Ed.). (1921). Psychological examining in the U.S. Army. *Memoirs of the National Academy of Sciences,* No. 15.

Yesavage, J. A., Noda, A., Hernandez, B., Friedman, L., Cheng, J. J., Tinklenberg, J. R., Hallmayer, J., O'hara, R., David, R., Robert, P., Landsverk, E., Zeitzer, J. M. & the Alzheimer's Disease Neuroimaging Initiative. (2011). Circadian clock gene polymorphisms and sleep-wake disturbance in Alzheimer disease. *American Journal of Geriatric Psychiatry, 19*(7), 635–643.

Yeung, L. M., Linver, M. R., & Brooks-Gunn, J. (2002). How money matters for young children's development: Parental investment and family processes. *Child Development, 73,* 1861–1879.

Yip, T., Douglass, S., & Shelton, J. N. (2013). Daily intragroup contact in diverse settings: Implications for Asian adolescents' ethnic identity. *Child Development, 84,* 1425–1441.

Yip, T., Gee, G. C., & Takeuchi, D. T. (2008). Racial discrimination and psychological distress: The impact of ethnic identity and age among immigrant and United States-born Asian adults. *Developmental Psychology, 44,* 787–800.

Yonas, A., Arterberry, M. E., & Granrud, C. D. (1987). Space perception in infancy. In R. Vasta (Ed.), *Annals of child development* (Vol. 4, pp. 1–34). Greenwich, CT: JAI Press.

Yoo, S.-S., Hu, P. T., Gujar, N., Jolesz, F. A., & Walker, M. P. (2007). A deficit in the ability to form new human memories without sleep. *Nature Neuroscience, 10,* 385–392.

Yoo, W., Shah, D. V., Shaw, B. R., Kim, E., Smaglik, P., Roberts, L. J., Hawkins, R. P., Pingree, S., McDowell, H., & Gustafson, D. H. (2014). The role of the family environment and computer-mediated social support on breast cancer patients' coping strategies. *Journal of Health Communication,* Epub February 10, 2014.

York, J. L., & Welte, J. W. (1994). Gender comparisons of alcohol consumption in alcoholic and nonalcoholic populations. *Journal of Studies on Alcohol, 55,* 743–750.

Yoshimasu, K., Washio, M., Tokunaga, S., Tanaka, K., Liu, Y., Kodama, H., et al. (2002). Relation between Type A behavior pattern and the extent of coronary atherosclerosis in Japanese women. *International Journal of Behavioral Medicine, 9,* 77–93.

Youm, Y., & Laumann, E. O. (2002). Social network effects on the transmission of sexually transmitted diseases. *Sexually Transmitted Diseases, 29,* 689–697.

Youn, S., Kraus, D. R., & Castonguay, L. G. (2012). The treatment outcome package: Facilitating practice and clinically relevant research. *Psychotherapy, 49,* 115–22. doi:10.1037/a0027932

Young, C. B., Wu, S. S., & Menon, V. (2012). The neurodevelopmental basis of math anxiety. *Psychological Science, 23,* 492–501. doi:10.1177/0956797611429134

Young, M. (1971). Age and sex differences in problem solving. *Journal of Gerontology, 26,* 331–336.

Young, M. S., Turner, J., Denny, G., & Young, M. (2004). Examining external and internal poverty as antecedents of teen pregnancy. *American Journal of Health Behavior, 28,* 361–373.

Yu, H., & Neimat, J. S. (2008). The treatment of movement disorders by deep brain stimulation. *Neurotherapeutics, 5*(1), 26–36.

Yu, X., Chen, D., Zhang, Y., Wu, X., Huang, Z., Zhou, H., Zhang, Y., and Zhang, Z. (2012). Overexpression of CXCR4 in mesenchymal stem cells promotes migration, neuroprotection and angiogenesis in a rat model of stroke. *Journal of the Neurological Science,* Epub. January 24.

Yücel, M., Solowij, N., Respondek, C., Whittle, S., Fornito, A., Pantelis, C., & Lubman, D. I. (2008). Regional brain abnormalities associated with long-term heavy cannabis use. *Archives of General Psychiatry, 65,* 694–701.

Yuen, E. K., Goetter, E. M., Herbert, J. D., & Forman, E. M. (2012). Challenges and opportunities in internet-mediated telemental health. *Professional Psychology: Research and Practice, 43,* 1–8.

Yukl, G., & Van Fleet, D. D. (1992). Theory and research on leadership in organizations. In M. D. Dunnette & L. M. Hough (Eds.), *Handbook of industrial and organizational psychology* (Vol. 3, 2nd ed., pp. 147–198). Palo Alto, CA: Consulting Psychologists Press.

Yuma, Y. (2010). The effect of prison crowding on prisoners' violence in Japan: Testing with cointegration regressions and error correction models. *Japanese Journal of Psychology, 81,* 218–225.

Yun, S., Faraj, S., & Sims, H. P. (2005). Contingent leadership and effectiveness of trauma resuscitation teams. *Journal of Applied Psychology, 90,* 1288–1296.

Zabel, K. L., Christopher, A. N., Marek, P., Wieth, M. B., & Carlson, J. J. (2009). Mediational effects of sensation seeking on the age and financial risk-taking relationship. *Personality & Individual Differences, 47*(8), 917–921. doi:10.1016/j.paid.2009.07.016.

Zaccarco, S. J. (2007). Trait-based perspectives of leadership. *American Psychologist, 62,* 6–16.

Zachrisson, H. D., Dearing, E., Lekhal, R., & Toppelberg, C. O. (2013). Little evidence that time in child care causes externalizing problems during early childhood in Norway. *Child Development. 84*(4), 1152–1170.

Zadra, A., Desautels, A., Petit, D., & Montplaisir, J. (2013). Somnambulism: Clinical aspects and pathophysiological hypotheses. *Lancet Neurology, 12*(3), 285–294.

Zadra, A., Desjardins, S., & Marcotte, E. (2006). Evolutionary function of dreams: A test of the threat simulation theory in recurrent dreams. *Consciousness and Cognition, 15,* 450–463.

Zadra, A., & Donderi, D. C. (2000). Nightmares and bad dreams: Their prevalence and relationship to well-being. *Journal of Abnormal Psychology, 109,* 273–281.

Zanigni, S., Calandra-Buonaura, G., Grimaldi, D., & Cortelli, P. (2011). REM behaviour disorder and neurodegenerative diseases. *Sleep Medicine, 12*(Suppl 2), S54-S58.

Zahn-Waxler, C., Shirtcliff, E. A., & Marceau, K. (2008). Disorders of childhood and adolescence: Gender and psychopathology. *Annual Review of Clinical Psychology, 4,* 275–303.

Zahrani, S. S., & Kaplowitz, S. A. (1993). Attributional biases in individualistic and collectivist cultures: A comparison of Americans with Saudis. *Social Psychology Quarterly, 56*(3), 223–233.

Zajonc, R. B. (1965). Social facilitation. *Science, 149,* 269–274.

Zajonc, R. B. (1998). Emotions. In D. Gilbert, S. T. Fiske, & G. Lindzey (Eds.), *Handbook of social psychology* (Vol. 1, 4th ed., pp. 591–634). Boston: McGraw-Hill.

Zakhari, S. (2006). Overview: How is alcohol metabolized by the body? *Alcohol Research and Health, 29,* 245–254.

Zald, D. H., & Pardo, J. V. (1997). Emotion, olfaction, and the human amygdala: Amygdala activation during aversive olfactory stimulation. *Proceedings of the National Academy of Sciences, 94*(8), 4119–4124.

Zalta, A. K., & Keel, P. K. (2006). Peer influence on bulimic symptoms in college students. *Journal of Abnormal Psychology, 115,* 185–189.

Zambelis, T., Paparrigopoulos, T., & Soldatos, C. R. (2002). REM sleep behaviour disorder associated with a neurinoma of the left pontocerebral angle. *Journal of Neurology, Neurosurgery, and Psychiatry, 72,* 821–822.

Zammit, S., Allebeck, P., Andreasson, S., Lundberg, I., & Lewis, G. (2002). Self reported cannabis use as a risk factor for schizophrenia in Swedish conscripts of 1969: Historical cohort study. *British Medical Journal, 325,* 1199.

Zapf, P. A., & Roesch, R. (2011). Future directions in the restoration of competency to stand trial. *Current Directions in Psychological Science, 20*(1), 43–47. doi:10.1177/0963721410396798.

Zatorre, R. J. (2003). Music and the brain. *Annals of the New York Academy of Sciences, 999,* 4–14.

Zawilska, J. B., Skene, D. J., & Arendt, J. (2009). Physiology and pharmacology of melatonin in relation to biological rhythms. *Pharmacological Reports, 61*(3), 383–410.

Zeanah, C. H., Egger, H. L., Smyke, A. T., Nelson, C. A., et al. (2009). Institutional rearing and psychiatric disorders in Romanian preschool children. *American Journal of Psychiatry, 166,* 777–785.

Zeanah, C. H., Smyke, A. T., Koga, S. F., & Carlson, E. (2005). Attachment in institutionalized and community children in Romania. *Child Development, 76,* 1015–1028.

Zeigler-Hill, V., Southard, A. C., Archer, L. M., & Donohoe, P. L. (2013). Neuroticism and negative affect influence the reluctance to engage in destructive obedience in the Milgram paradigm. *The Journal of Social Psychology, 153*(2), 161–174.

Zeman, A. (2001). Consciousness. *Brain, 124,* 1263–1289.

Zeman, A., Britton, T., Douglas, N., Hansen, A., Hicks, J., Howard, R., et al. (2004). Narcolepsy and excessive daytime sleepiness. *British Medical Journal, 329,* 724–728.

Zhai, F., Raver, C., & Jones, S. M. (2012). Academic performance of subsequent schools and impacts of early interventions: Evidence from a randomized controlled trial in head start settings. *Children and Youth Services Review,* doi:10.1016/j.childyouth.2012.01.026.

Zhang, J.-P., Lencz, T., & Malhotra, A. K. (2010). D2 receptor genetic variation and clinical response to antipsychotic drug treatment: A meta-analysis. *American Journal of Psychiatry, 167,* 763–772.

Zhang, L., Jones, C. R., Ptacek, L. J., & Fu, Y. H. (2011). The genetics of the human circadian clock. *Advances in Genetics, 74,* 231–47.

Zhang, P., Jiang, Y., & He, S. (2012). Voluntary attention modulates processing of eye-specific visual information. *Psychological Science, 23*(3), 254–260. doi:10.1177/0956797611424289

Zhang, N. R., & von der Heydt, R. (2010). Analysis of the context integration mechanisms underlying figure–ground organization in the visual cortex. *The Journal of Neuroscience, 30*(19):6482–6496; doi:10.1523/JNEUROSCI. 5168-09.2010.

Zhang, Y., Hoon, M. A., Chandrashekar, J., Mueller, K. L., Cook, B., Wu, D., et al. (2003). Coding of sweet, bitter, and umami tastes: Different receptor cells sharing similar signaling pathways. *Cell, 112,* 293–301.

Zhang, W., & Luck, S. J. (2011). The number and quality of representations in working memory. *Psychological Science, 22*(11), 1434–1441. doi:10.1177/0956797611417006.

Zhao, H., & Seibert, S. E. (2006). The big five personality dimensions and entrepreneurial status: A meta-analytical review. *Journal of Applied Psychology, 91,* 259–271.

Zheng, H., Lenard, N. R., Shin, A. C., & Berthoud, H.-R. (2009). Appetite control and energy balance regulation in the modern world: Reward-driven brain overrides repletion signals. *International Journal of Obesity, 33,* S8–S13.

Zhong, C.-B., Bohns, V. K., & Gino, F. (2010). Good lamps are the best police: Darkness increases dishonesty and self-interested behavior. *Psychological Science, 21*(3), 311–314. doi:10.1177/0956797609360754.

Zhong, C.-B., Strejcek, B., & Sivanathan, N. (2010). A clean self can render harsh moral judgment. *Journal of Experimental Social Psychology, 46,* 859–862. doi:10.1016/j.jesp.2010.04.003.

Zhou, J.-N., Hofman, M. A., Gooren, L. J. G., & Swaab, D. F. (1995). A sex difference in the human brain and its relation to transsexuality. *Nature, 378,* 68–70.

Zhou, N., Lam, S. F., & Chan, K. C. (2012). The Chinese classroom paradox: A cross-cultural comparison of teacher controlling behaviors. *Journal of Experimental Psychology, 104,* 1162–1174.

Zhou, Q., Eisenberg, N., Wang, Y., & Reiser, M. (2004). Chinese children's effortful control and dispositional anger/frustration relations to parenting styles and children's social functioning. *Developmental Psychology, 40,* 352–366.

Zhou, W., Hou, P., Zhou, Y., & Chen, D. (2010). Reduced recruitment of orbitofrontal cortex to human social chemosensory cues in social anxiety. *Neuroimage,* doi:10.1016/j.neuroimage.2010.12.064.

Zhuang, S., Wixted, J. T., Hopkins, R. O., & Squire, L. R. (2011). Impaired capacity for familiarity after hippocampal damage. *Proceedings Of The National Academy Of Sciences Of The United States Of America, 108*(23), 9655–9660. doi:10.1073/pnas.1107247108.

Zickar, M. J., Gibby, R. E., & Robie, C. (2004). Uncovering faking samples in applicant, incumbent, and experimental data sets: An application of mixed-model item response theory. *Organizational Research Methods, 7,* 168–190.

Zigler, E., & Seitz, V. (1982). Social policy and intelligence. In R. J. Sternberg (Ed.), *Handbook of human intelligence* (pp. 586–641). Cambridge, UK: Cambridge University Press.

Zigler, E. F., & Muenchow, S. (1992). *Head Start: The inside story of America's most successful educational experiment.* New York: Basic Books.

Zigurs, I. (2003). Leadership in virtual teams: Oxymoron or opportunity? *Organizational Dynamics, 31,* 339–351.

Zillmann, D. (1984). *Connections between sexuality and aggression.* Hillsdale, NJ: Erlbaum.

Zillmann, D. (1988). Cognition-excitation interdependencies in aggressive behavior. *Aggressive Behavior, 14,* 51–64.

Zillmann, D. (2003). Theory of affective dynamics: Emotions and moods. In J. Bryant & D. Roskos-Ewoldsen (Eds.), *Communication and emotion: Essays in honor of Dolf Zillmann* (pp. 533–567). Mahwah, NJ: Erlbaum.

Zillmann, D., Katcher, A. H., & Milavsky, B. (1972). Excitation transfer from physical exercise to subsequent aggressive behavior. *Journal of Experimental Social Psychology, 8,* 247–259.

Zimmerman, F. J., & Christakis, D. A. (2007). Associations between content types of early media exposure and subsequent attentional problems. *Pediatrics, 120*(5), 986–992.

Zimmerman, F. J., Christakis, D. A., & Meltzoff, A. N. (2007). Associations between media viewing and language development in children under age 2 years. *The Journal of Pediatrics, 151*(4), 364–368.

Zimmerman, F. J., Gilkerson, J., Richards, J. A., Christakis, D. A., et al. (2009). Teaching by listening: Th e importance of adult-child conversations to language development. *Pediatrics, 124,* 342–349.

Zimmerman, M. A. (1990). Toward a theory of learned hopefulness: A structural model analysis of participation and empowerment. *Journal of Research in Personality, 24,* 71–86.

Zimmerman, M. E., Pan, J. W., Hetherington, H. P., Katz, M. J., Verghese, J., Buschke, H., et al. (2008). Hippocampal neurochemistry, neuromorphometry, and verbal memory in nondemented older adults. *Neurology, 70*(18), 1594–1600.

Zinbarg, R. E., & Griffith, J. W. (2008). Behavior therapy. In J. L. Lebow (Ed.), *Twenty-first century psychotherapies: Contemporary approaches to theory and practice* (pp. 8–42). Hoboken, NJ: Wiley.

Zinbarg, R. E., & Mineka, S. (1991). Animal models of psychopathology: II. Simple phobia. *The Behavior Therapist, 14,* 61–65.

Zoellner, L. A., Bedard-Gilligan, M. A., Jun, J. J., Marks, L. H., & Garcia, N. M. (2013). The evolving construct of posttraumatic stress disorder (PTSD): *DSM-5* criteria changes and legal implications. *Psychological Injury and Law, 6,* 277–289.

Zoellner, L. A., Foa, E. B., Brigidi, B. D., & Przeworski, A. (2000). Are trauma victims susceptible to "false memories"? *Journal of Abnormal Psychology, 109,* 517–524.

Zoellner, T., & Maercker, A. (2006). Posttraumatic growth in clinical psychology: A critical review and introduction of a two component model. *Clinical Psychology Review, 26,* 626–653.

Zola-Morgan, S. (1995). Localization of brain function: The legacy of Franz Joseph Gall (1758–1828). *Annual Review of Neuroscience, 18,* 359–383.

Zolotor, A. J., Theodore, A. D., Chang, J. J., Berkoff , M. C., & Runyan, D. K. (2008). Speak softly—and forget the stick: Corporal punishment and child physical abuse. *American Journal of Preventive Medicine, 35,* 364–369.

Zonouzi M., Renzi M., Farrant M., & Cull-Candy S. G. (2011) Bidirectional plasticity of calcium-permeable AMPA receptors in oligodendrocyte lineage cells. *Nat Neurosci 14* (11):1430–1438.

Zou, Z., & Buck, L. B. (2006). Combinatorial effects of odorant mixes in olfactory cortex. *Science, 311,* 1477–1481.

Zou, Z., Li, F., & Buck, L. B. (2005). Odor maps in the olfactory cortex. *Proceedings of the National Academy of Sciences, 102,* 7724–7729.

Zuberbühler, K. (2005). The phylogenetic roots of language. *Current Directions in Psychological Science, 14,* 126–130.

Zubieta, J. K. and Stohler, C. S. (2009). Neurobiological mechanisms of placebo responses. *Annals of the New York Academy of Sciences, 1156,* 198–210.

Zubin, J., & Spring, B. (1977). Vulnerability—A new view of schizophrenia. *Journal of Abnormal Psychology, 86,* 103–126.

Zucker, A. N., Ostrove, J. M., & Stewart, A. J. (2002). College-educated women's personality development in adulthood: Perceptions and age differences. *Psychology & Aging, 17*(2), 236–244.

Zuckerman, M. (1984). Sensation seeking: A comparative approach to a human approach. *Behavioral and Brain Sciences, 7,* 413–471.

Zuckerman, M. (1990). Some dubious premises in research and theory on racial differences. *American Psychologist, 45,* 1297–1303.

Zuckerman, M. (1993). Out of sensory deprivation and into sensation seeking: A personal and scientific journey. In G. G. Brannigan & M. R. Merrens (Eds.), *The undaunted psychologist: Adventures in research* (pp. 45–57). Philadelphia: Temple University Press.

Zuroff, D. C., & Blatt, S. J. (2006). The therapeutic relationship in the brief treatment of depression: Contributions to clinical improvement and enhanced adaptive capacities. *Journal of Consulting and Clinical Psychology, 74,* 130–140.

Zwierzynska, K., Wolke, D., & Lereya, T. (2013). Peer victimization in childhood and internalizing problems in adolescence: A prospective longitudinal study. *Journal of Abnormal Child Psychology, 41,* 309–323.

Zyss, T., Zieba, A., Hese, R. T., Dudek, D., Grabski, B., Gorczyca, P., & Modrzejewska, R. (2010). Magnetic seizure therapy (MST)—A safer method for evoking seizure activity than current therapy with a confirmed antidepressant efficacy. *Neuroendocrinology Letters, 31*(4), 425–437.

NAME INDEX

Stathi, S., 586
Stattin, H., 593
Staub, F., 677
Staudt, M., 74
Stauffer, J. M., 635
Staunton, D. A., 316
Stavropoulos, K., 74
Staw, B. M., 645
Stawski, R. S., 283, 433
Stayton, L. E., 449
Stead, L. F., 319
Steblay, N. K., 198, 199
Steele, C. M., 265, 266, 272, 409
Steele, D., 564
Steele, H., 462
Steele, K., 340
Steele, R. D., 417
Steele, T. D., 320
Steen, T. A., 353, 442, 552
Steer, C., 529
Stefanis C. N., 299
Steffens, D. C., 540
Steffens, M. C., 266
Stegelmeier, B. L., 150
Steil, R., 303
Stein, A., 397
Stein, B., 106
Stein, B. S., 231
Stein, D. J., 501, 507, 514
Stein, E., 350
Stein, M. B., 435
Stein, M. T., 303
Steinberg, L., 76, 77, 170, 270, 271, 400, 408, 409, 410, 472
Steineck, G., 113
Steiner, D. L., 526
Steiner, J. E., 330, 380
Steiner, J. M., 604
Steinglass, J. E., 341
Steinhauser, K. E., 419
Steinman, R., 448
Steinmayr, R., 351
Stellar, E., 337
Stellar, J. E., 614
Stellmacher, J., 619
Stenfelt, S., 101
Stenman, U., 295
Stepanikova, I., 588
Stepanyants, A., 206
Stephan, K. E., 73
Stephens, G., 238
Stephens, G. J., 245
Stephens, R. S., 322
Stephenson, J. J., 301, 306
Steptoe, A., 420, 436
Steriade, M., 305
Sterk, P. J., 106
Stern, K., 107
Stern, M., 78
Stern, R. A., 672
Stern, W. L., 259
Stern, Y., 62
Sternberg, D., 146
Sternberg, M. R., 409
Sternberg, R. J., 239, 240, 259, 268, 273, 274, 277, 278, 387, 414, 552, 595, 596, 666, 667, 669
Sterr, A., 359
Stetkevich, N., 571
Stettler, D. D., 74

Stevens, A. A., 102
Stevens, B. L., 110
Stevens, C., 349
Stevens, J. C., 565
Stevens, N., 301, 401
Stevens, R. D., 677
Stevens, S., 390, 507
Stevenson, B., 354
Stevenson, H., 173
Stevenson, L. A., 368
Stevenson, M., 306
Stevenson, R. J., 106
Steward, S. L. K., 560
Stewart-Williams, S., 111
Stewart, A. J., 418, 419
Stewart, G. L., 655
Stewart, J. G., 568
Stewart, J. H., 311
Stewart, K., 581
Stewart, L., 435
Stewart, M. A., 532
Stewart, M. O., 560
Stewart, N., 231
Stewart, P., 431
Stewart, S. H., 435
Steyerberg, E. W., 568
Stice, E., 340, 342, 518
Stichtenoth, D. O., 321
Stickgold, R., 210, 301, 306, 307, 309
Stiefel, I., 528
Stiegler, M. P., 237
Stiles, J., 77
Stiles, T. C., 545
Stiles, W. B., 555
Stilling, R. M., 336
Stillman, R. C., 192
Stillwell, M. E., 317
Stimson, D., 363
Stinson, F. S., 525, 532
Stipek, D. J., 352
Stirman, S., 556
Stirrat, M., 581
Stobberingh, E., 106
Stockton, S., 566
Stockwell, T., 608
Stoerig, P., 295
Stoet, G., 267
Stohler, C. S., 111
Stokes, M., 71
Stolar, N., 551
Stöllberger, C., 565
Stone, A. A., 418
Stone, D. A., 112
Stone, J., 448, 587
Stone, M., 568
Stone, N. J., 631
Stoner, G., 78
Stoney, C. M., 433, 441, 442, 447, 448
Stoodley, C. J., 60
Stopfer, J. M., 480
Stopp, C., 379
Stopsack, M., 527
Storch, E. A., 506
Stores, G., 301
Storey, C. C., 531
Storm, B. C., 187, 231
Storosum, J. G., 568
Storr, C. L., 436
Stouthamer-Loeber, M., 525
Stowe, R. M., 321

Stowell, J. R., 429, 446
Stowkowy, J., 529
Strahan, E. J., 297
Strain, E. C., 319
Strakowski, S. M., 502, 515
Stranahan, A. M., 77
Strandberg, T., 393
Strauch, I., 299
Straus, M. A., 159
Straus, S. G., 244, 437
Strauss, A., 394
Strauss, B., 552
Strauss, E., 678
Strauss, M. E., 416
Strauss, R. S., 340
Strayer, D. L., 133
Strehl, U., 299
Streisguth, A. P., 379
Streit, F., 430
Strejcek, B., 587
Streng, A., 112
Streri, A., 380
Striano, T., 392
Strick, P. L., 60
Stricker, J. L., 307
Strickland, B. B., 529
Striegel-Moore, R., 341
Stringhini, S., 438
Strites, D. P., 446
Strober, M., 341
Stroebe, W., 244, 297, 340, 552
Strohmetz, D. B., 598
Strohschein, L., 410
Stromland, K., 379
Stromwall, L., 363
Stroop, J. R., 133
Stroppini, T., 677
Stroup, D. F., 427
Strunk, D., 560
Strydom, A., 284
Stuart, G. L., 608
Stubbe, S., 416
Stuber, G. D., 532
Stuckler, D., 435
Stucky, B. D., 405
Studniarek, M., 107
Stueve, A., 431
Stumbrys, T., 308
Sturge-Apple, M. L., 396
Stürmer, T., 471
Su, C. Y., 106
Su, J. C., 242
Su, M., 70
Su, R., 642
Suarez, M., 476
Subotnik, K. L., 522
Subotnik, R. F., 285
Subrahmanyam, K., 408
Subramaniam, K., 167
Subramaniam, M., 568
Substance Abuse and Mental Health Services Administration, 318, 531
Suchan, B., 675
Suddath, R. L., 521
Suddendorf, T., 163
Sudhof, T. C., 75
Sue, D., 496, 561
Sue, D. W., 496, 561
Sue, S., 274, 561
Sugarman, D. E., 322

Sugden, K., 62
Suh, E. M., 354, 355
Suh, J., 69
Sui, D., 312
Suitor, J. J., 418
Sukegawa, S., 172
Sukhotinsky, I., 79
Sulik, K. K., 379
Sullivan, H. S., 542
Sullivan, J. P., 301
Sullivan, J. W., 380
Sullivan, P. F., 520
Suls, J., 436, 447, 448, 509, 512, 578
Sulsky, L. M., 635
Sultan, M. T., 319
Summavielle, T., 321
Sumnall, H., 531
Sumner, P., 295
Sun, G. J., 113
Sun, Q., 420
Sun, S., 675
Sun, Y., 336
Sun, Y. G., 111
Sundarajan-Ramamurti, A., 340
Sundström-Poromaa, I., 111
Sundström, A., 415
Sundvall, J., 449
Suo, L., 548
Suokas, J. T., 341
Suomi, S. J., 41
Suppes, A., 581
Supplee, L., 571
Sur, S., 672
Suri, G., 451
Suschinsky, K. D., 347
Susilo, T., 680
Susser, E. S., 379
Sussman, A. B., 354
Sust, S., 521
Sutcher, H., 310
Sutton-Tyrrell, K., 584
Sutton, K., 264, 350, 351
Sutton, R. M., 581, 586
Sutton, S., 340
Suveg, C., 560
Suvisaari, J. M., 341
Suwaki, H., 317
Suzuki, J., 250
Suzuki, L. A., 269
Suzuki, L. K., 400
Suzuki, T., 304
Suzuki, W. A., 166
Suzuki, Y., 304
Svarer, C., 521
Svartberg, M., 545
Svensson, Å., 32
Svensson, L., 379, 549
Svoboda, K., 77
Swaab, D. E., 349
Swaab, D. F., 346
Swain, J., 546
Swan, G. E., 418, 420
Swaney, W. T., 107
Swann, W. B., 580
Swanson, J., 285
Swanson, N. G., 651
Swanson, S. A., 342
Swarte, N. B., 438
Swartz, H. A., 436, 561
Swartz, M. K., 409

Timmerman, T. A., 611
Timmermann, L., 110
Timms, P., 518
Timpson, N. J., 340
Timulak, L., 545
Tinbergen, N., 330
Tindale, R. S., 243
Tindle, H., 442
Tingen, I. W., 463
Tinklenberg, J. R., 304
Tischfield, J. A., 316
Tissington, P. A., 619
Tivarus, M., 320
To-A-Nan, R., 319
To, S., 401
Tobler, P. N., 167
Todd, K. H., 438
Todd, L., 396, 409, 418
Todd, P. M., 231
Todd, S., 416
Todorov, A., 368, 581
Todorova, E. N., 331
Toffolo, M. J., 191
Toga, A. W., 76, 77, 312
Toguti, H., 301
Tohen, M., 515
Toivonen, H., 249
Tokoro, M., 75
Tokunaga, K., 302
Tokunaga, S., 448
Toler, A., 416
Tolin, D. F., 29, 38, 505, 507, 560, 569
Tolman, E. C., 165, 166
Toman, S. M., 544
Tomasello, M., 252, 404, 597, 612
Tomasetto, C., 266
Tomasi, D., 29, 607
Tomberlin, J. K., 149
Tomelleri, S., 241, 590
Tomer, R., 66
Tomes, H., 561
Tomlinson-Keasey, C., 443
Tomlinson, J. M., 462
Tommasi, L., 363
Tomova, L., 442
Tompkins, M. A., 552
Tondo, L., 517, 565
Tonegawa, S., 69
Tonnesen, J., 79
Tonnessen, F. E., 619
Tononi, G., 293
Topakian, R., 687
Topol, E. J., 427
Topolinski, S., 211
Toppelberg, C. O., 397
Toregersen, S., 506
Torges, C. M., 419
Torigoe, T., 529
Toro, M. A., 21
Toro, R., 76, 77
Torres, A., 529
Torres, B., 293
Torrey, E. F., 521
Torrubia-Beltri, R., 170
Torry, Z. D., 532
Toscano, J. P., 319
Toschi, N., 687
Tossani, E., 504
Tost, H., 430
Tost, L., 579

Tosun, L. P., 465
Tougas, F., 578
Touhara, K., 106
Toulopoulou, T., 521
Toumbourou, J. W., 408
Touzani, K., 208
Towfighi, A., 671
Townsend, M. K., 420
Trabasso, T. R., 223
Trace, S. E., 342
Tracey, I., 110
Tracey, J. L., 367
Tracey, T. J. G., 555
Trachtenberg, F. L., 302
Tracy, D. K., 520
Trafimow, D., 21
Trafton, J., 226
Trakht, I., 304
Trampisch, H. J., 113
Tran, A. G. T. T., 242
Tranel, D., 32, 296, 359, 666
Traut-Mattausch, E. E., 236
Trautwein, U., 470
Treat, T. A., 341
Tregear, S., 302
Treiman, R., 248
Trellakis, S., 106
Tremblay, A., 336
Tremblay, P., 517
Tremblay, R. E., 303
Tremblay, S., 132
Tremplay, R. E., 405, 528
Tressler, K. E., 617
Treutlein, J., 317
Trevathan, E., 529
Trevino, K., 564
Trevor, C. O., 650
Treyens, J. C., 194, 195
Treyvaud, K., 379
Triandis, H. C., 21
Tribol, C. T., 387
Trickett, S., 226
Trierweiler, S. J., 503
Trifiletti, L. B., 339
Triller, A., 74
Triplett, J., 588
Tripp, T. M., 650, 651
Trivendi, M., 570
Troianovski, A., 238
Troisi, J. D., 340
Trojanowski, J. Q., 75, 78
Troland, K., 331
Trommershäuser, J., 241
Tromovitch, P., 527
Tronick, E. Z., 379
Troop-Gordon, W., 402
Trope, Y., 353
Tropp, L. R., 590
Troseth, G. L., 391
Trotman, H., 522
Troughton, E., 532
Troutman, A. C., 161
True, W., 531
Trueswell, J. C., 247
Trull, T. J., 482
Trumbetta, S. L., 438
Trumble, A. C., 35
Trunzo, J. J., 440
Truong, L., 564
Tryon, W. W., 547

Trzaskowski, M., 340
Tsai, H. J., 304
Tsai, J. L., 492, 493
Tsai, M. K., 449
Tsai, P., 597
Tsai, S. P., 449
Tsai, W. Y., 75
Tsakiris, M., 87
Tsang, A., 495
Tsang, J. S., 172
Tsang, W., 635
Tsao, C. K., 449
Tschann, J. M., 431
Tseng, A., 369
Tseng, V., 400
Tsuang, M. T., 342
Tsuchimochi, H., 306
Tsuji, S., 302
Tsujimoto, G., 304
Tsukayama, E., 265
Tsunoda, S. P., 69
Tuch, S. A., 647
Tuchin, M., 198
Tucker-Drob, E. M., 268, 377, 392, 408, 415
Tucker, D. C., 442
Tucker, D. M., 364
Tucker, J. S., 443, 532
Tucker, M. A., 210
Tucker, P., 435
Tufik, S., 301
Tuin, I., 308
Tullis, J., 211
Tully, L., 526
Tulsky, J. A., 419
Tulving, E., 180, 181, 191, 201
Tuohimaa, K., 563
Tuomilehto, J., 449
Tuomisto, M. T., 447
Turan, B., 420
Turan, T., 516
Turansky, A. J., 336
Turati, C., 130, 380
Turiano, N. A., 420
Turiel, E., 406, 412
Turk, D. C., 438
Turkheimer, E., 267, 269, 408, 467, 468, 480
Turkington, C., 286
Turnbull, C., 129
Turnbull, O. H., 308
Turner, C., 569
Turner, J., 409
Turner, N., 651
Turner, R., 306
Turner, R. B., 306, 435, 446
Turner, R. J., 502
Turner, R. N., 591
Turner, S., 556
Turner, S. M., 485, 503
Turton, A. J., 532
Tuschl, R. J., 342
Tuulio-Henriksson, A., 406
Tversky, A., 166, 230, 234, 241, 414
Tversky, B., 198, 227
Tweed, D. B., 122
Twenge, J. M., 477, 491
Twisk, J., 46
Tyber, J. M., 17, 107
Tye, K. M., 69

Tyler, K. L., 667
Tyrka, A. R., 506, 508
Tzelnic, R., 386
Tzeng, W. C., 547
Tzouri-Mazoyer, N., 226

U

U.S. Bureau of Labor Statistics, 637, 654
U.S. Census Bureau, 418, 606
U.S. Department of Justice, 11, 160, 199, 606, 651
U.S. Department of Labor, 397
U.S. Surgeon General, 286
Ubaldi, M., 451
Ubel, P. A., 354
Uchida, Y., 478
Uchino, B. N., 441
Uckert, K., 408
Uda, H., 513
Uddin, M., 506
Udry, J. R., 409
Ueki, H., 319
Uezu, E., 301
Uhl-Bien, M., 655
Uhr, M., 514
Ujike, H., 304
Ukoummunne, O. C., 416
Ulbricht, C., 565
Ulbricht, J., 400
Uleman, J. S., 581
Ulett, G. A., 112
Ullrich, S., 525
Ulm, R. R., 165
Ulriksen, R., 350
Um, E., 171
Um, K., 496
Uma~na-Taylor, A. J., 411
Umahara, M., 338
Umbreit, J., 546
Umene-Nakano, W., 304
Umilta, C., 380
Underdown, J., 38
Underwood, G., 133
Underwood, M. D., 78
Undurraga, J., 565
Ungemach, C., 231
Ungerleider, L. G., 306, 679
Unite, J., 645
United Nations Office on Drugs and Crime, 207
Unrath, A., 71
Unsworth, K. L., 654
Unsworth, N., 276
Updegraff, J. A., 432, 442
Urasaki, C., 301
Urbach, T. P., 209
Urbina, S., 268, 272, 274
Urquhart, B. L., 312
Urretavizcaya, M., 563
Urry, H. L., 419
Ursano, R. J., 435, 436
Ursell, L. K., 336
Ursu, S., 521
Usher, A., 471
Uskul, A. K., 477
Usluogullari, B., 110
Üstün B., 493
Ustun, T., 495, 539
Utley, S. L., 149

SUBJECT INDEX/GLOSSARY

These key terms correspond to those in the American Psychological Association thesaurus and dictionary. Key terms, which appear in boldface, are followed by their definitions.

Berkowitz, Leonard, 610

Between group variations, IQ tests, 270–271

Bias

attribution errors, 583

confirmation, 236

experimenter, 38–39

measuring, 242–243

psychological diagnosis and, 501–503

social perception and, 584

Biased sampling *The process of selecting a group of research participants from a population whose members did not have an equal chance of being chosen,* 40

Big Five model *A view based on studies using factor analysis that suggests the existence of five basic components of human personality: openness, conscientiousness, extraversion, agreeableness, and neuroticism,* 465

Biklen, Douglas, 44

Bilingualism, 249–250

Binet, Alfred, 259

Binge eating disorder *A pattern of sudden, recurrent episodes of eating huge amounts of food, but without purging,* 342–343

Bini, Lucio, 563

Binocular depth cues, 121

Binocular disparity, 121

Biochemical effects of alcohol, 316–317

Biochemistry of hunger, 337–338

Biochemistry of memory, 206

Biofeedback training, 294

Biological approach *An approach to psychology in which behavior and behavior disorders are seen as the result of physical processes, especially relating to the brain and to hormones and other chemicals,* 16

social psychology and, 620

Biological basis of language acquisition, 249

Biological clock, 517

Biological factors

aggression, 607–608

anxiety disorders, 506

autism spectrum disorder, 529

depressive and bipolar disorders, 515–517

gender roles, 405

schizophrenia, 520–521

sexual orientation and, 348–349

Biological preparedness, 507–508

Biological psychologists *Psychologists who analyze the biological factors influencing behavior and mental processes; also called physiological psychologists,* 4

Biological psychology *The psychological specialty focused on the physical and chemical changes that cause, and occur in response to, behavior and mental processes,* 4, 51

Biological trait theories, 466–469

Eysenck's theory, 466–467

Gray's reinforcement sensitivity theory, 467–469

Biological treatments, 562–563

electroconvulsive shock therapy, 563–564

psychosurgery, 563

Biopreparedness to stimuli, 147–148

Biopsychosocial approach *Viewing mental disorders as resulting from a combination of biological, psychological, and sociocultural factors,* 494–497

Biopsychosocial factors, prosocial behavior, 615

Biotechnology, use of to study mental processes, 14–15

Bipolar cells, 95

Bipolar disorders *Conditions in which a person alternates between the two emotional extremes of depression and mania,* 514–515

causes of, 515–518

treatment of with psychoactive medications, 566

Bipolar I disorder, 515

Bipolar II disorder, 515

Birth defects, prenatal exposures and, 378–379

Bisexuality *Sexual desire or behavior that is focused on members of both sexes,* 347

Bislach, Edoardo, 682

Blindness, conversion disorder and, 508–509

Blindsight, 295

Blind spot *The point at which the optic nerve exits the eyeball,* 95

Blood, signals for hunger from, 336–337

Blood-brain barrier *A characteristic of blood vessels in the brain that prevents some substances from entering brain tissue,* 313

Body dysmorphic disorder *An obsessive-compulsive disorder characterized by intense distress over imagined abnormalities of the skin, hair, face, or other areas of the body,* 505

Body-kinesthetic intelligence, 280

Body mass index (BMI), 339

Body senses, 114–115

pain, 110–113

sensing body position, 113–114

touch and temperature, 109–110

Bonding, 392–393. *See also* Attachment

Bottom-up processing *Aspects of recognition that depend first on information about stimuli that come up to the brain from the sensory systems,* 126

understanding speech, 246–247

Bowlby, John, 394

Bradshaw, Gary, 232–233

Brain, 58–59

areas involved in sleeping and dreaming, 305

blood supply to, 671

cerebral cortex, 62

changes in during adolescence, 408

changes in during infancy and childhood, 382

developmental changes in, 76–77

effects of sexual hormones on, 346

fMRI studies of, 69–72

forebrain, 60–62

hindbrain, 59–60

hunger and, 337–338

imaging techniques, 67–72

initiation of voluntary movement, 685

injury, 672

lateralization of, 73–74

lesion analysis, 668–669

localization of function in, 666–667

major structures of, 59

mechanisms of dysfunction, 673

mechanisms of in emotions, 359–360

memory storage areas in, 209–210

midbrain, 60

modules of, 667–668

neurotransmitters in, 78–80

organization of, 64–65

repairing damage to, 74–75

sensory and motor cortex, 62–64

techniques for studying function and structure of, 68

Brain damage

disruption of extrapyramidal and pyramidal motor systems, 359

impact of, 207–209

Brainstem, 60

Brainstorming, 244

Brain structures, memory and, 207–210

Brain waves, electrical activity during sleep, 299–300

Bregman, Elsie Oschrin, 628

Brightness constancy, 123

Brightness *The overall intensity of the wavelengths making up light,* 96

Broca, Paul, 65, 667

Broca's aphasia *A language disorder in which there is a loss of fluent speech,* 65, 683

Broca's area, 65, 71

Brown-Peterson distractor technique *A method for determining how long unrehearsed information remains in short-term memory,* 188

Bulimia *An eating disorder that involves eating massive quantities of food, then eliminating it by self-induced vomiting or laxatives,* 341–342

Bullying, 402

Burnout *A pattern of physical and psychological dysfunctions in response to continuous stressors,* 435

cognitive appraisal and, 437

Bystander effect *A phenomenon in which the chances that someone will help in an emergency decrease as the number of people present increases,* 613

C

Caffeine, 319

Calkins, Mary Whiton, 20

Cannon-Bard theory, 363–364

Cannon's central theory of emotion, 363–364

Canon, Walter, 363–364

Capgras syndrome, 680

Capsaicin, 105

Carbon monoxide, 79

Cardiovascular system, stress and, 446–447

Careers, early adulthood, 417–418

Caregivers

attachment formation and, 392–396

social and emotional development in infants and, 398–399

Carpal tunnel syndrome, 652

Case studies *A research method involving the intensive examination of some phenomenon in a particular individual, group, or situation,* 32, 39

Caspi, Avshalom, 479–480

Catastrophic events

coping with, 429–430

psychological reactions to stress of, 434–435

Catastrophizing, 434, 551

Catecholamines, release of in reaction to stress, 432–433

Category labels, 365

Cattell, James McKeen, 628

Cattell, Raymond B., 276, 464

Causation

correlation and, 35

TV violence and violent behavior in children, 169–171

Cause and effect relationships, experimental exploration of, 35–39

Cells of the nervous system, 51–55. *See also* Nervous system

Central nervous system (CNS) *The parts of the nervous system encased in bone; specifically, the brain and the spinal cord,* 56

plasticity in, 74–76

sensory systems and, 88

Central route to attitude change, 586

Central theory of emotion, 363–364

Central traits, 464

Cerebellum *The part of the hindbrain whose main functions include controlling finely coordinated movements and storing memories about movement but which may also be involved in impulse control, emotion, and language,* 60, 305

Cerebral cortex *The outer surface of the brain,* 62–66

association cortex, 64–66

depression of activity in with opiates, 320

Concepts *Categories of objects, events, or ideas that have common properties,* 223

Conceptual act model of emotion, 365

Concrete operations *According to Piaget, the third period of cognitive development, during which children can learn to count, measure, add, and subtract,* 385

Conditioned reinforcers, 154

Conditioned response (CR) *The response triggered by the conditioned stimulus,* 144

extinction and spontaneous recovery of over time, 145

Conditioned stimulus (CS) *An originally neutral stimulus that now triggers a conditioned response,* 144

Conditioning, language acquisition and, 248–249

Conditions of worth *According to Rogers, circumstances in which an individual experiences positive regard from others only when displaying certain behaviors or attitudes,* 475

Conduct disorders, 528

Conduction deafness, 101

Cones *Photoreceptors in the retina that are less light sensitive than rods but that can distinguish colors,* 94–95

individual differences in types of, 96–97

Confabulation *A characteristic of some neuropsychological disorders in which patients report false memories,* 675

Confidentiality, 561–562

Confirmation bias *The tendency to pay more attention to evidence in support of one's hypothesis about a problem than to evidence that refutes that problem,* 236

Conflicting motives and stress, 356–357

Conformity *Changing one's behavior or beliefs to match those of others, generally as a result of real or imagined (though unspoken) group pressure,* 598–601

Confound *In an experiment, any factor that affects the dependent variable, along with or instead of the independent variable,* 36–37

Confounds

participant expectations, 37–38

random variables, 37

Congruence, 474

Congruence *In client-centered therapy, a consistency between the way therapists feel and the way they act toward clients,* 544

Connectedness, 119

Connectionist models, 162

Conscientiousness, 443, 465, 630

Conscious level *The level of consciousness at which mental activities accessible to awareness occur,* 294–295

Consciousness disturbances *Neuropsychological disorders in which there are impairments in the ability to be aware of the world,* 676–679

Consciousness *The awareness of external stimuli and our own mental activity,* 12, 293

functions of, 13–14

levels of, 294–295

states of, 293–294

Conscious state *The characteristics of consciousness at any particular moment,* 293–294

Consequences Test, 239

Conservation *The ability to recognize that the important properties of substances or objects, such as quantity, volume, or weight, remain constant despite changes in shape, length, or position,* 385

Consolidating memory, 166, 209

Constancy of perception, 122

brightness constancy, 123

shape constancy, 123

size constancy, 123

Constructive memory, 194–196

neural network models and, 196–197

Consummate love, 596

Context, 126

Context-specific memory (context-specific learning) *Memories that are helped or hindered by similarities or differences between the contexts in which they are learned and recalled,* 191

Contingencies, 547–548

Continuity, 118

Continuous reinforcement, 155

Control, learned helplessness and expectations of, 164

Control group *In an experiment, the group that receives no treatment or provides some other baseline against which to compare the performance or response of the experimental group,* 36

Control of attention, measuring changes in across the life span, 283

Control question test, 363

Convenience samples, 40

Conventional level *Moral reasoning that reflects a concern about other people as well as the belief that morality consists of following rules and conventions,* 412

Convergence, 121

Convergent thinking *The ability to apply the rules of logic and what one knows about the world to narrow down the possible solutions to a problem,* 240

Conversion disorder *A somatic symptom disorder in which a person appears to be (but actually is not) blind, deaf, paralyzed, or insensitive to pain,* 66, 508–509, 541

Cooperation *Any type of behavior in which people work together to attain a goal,* 616

promoting, 617–618

Coping

methods for, 452

resources and methods, 438–439

steps for dealing with stress, 451

strategies for, 451–452

ways of, 438–439

Core affect, 365

Cornea *The curved, transparent, protective layer through which light rays enter the eye,* 93

Coronary heart disease, hostility as a risk factor for, 447–448

Corpus callosum *A massive bundle of axons that connects the right and left cerebral hemispheres and allows them to communicate with each other,* 62

lateralization, 73

Correlational studies *Research methods that examine relationships between variables in order to analyze trends in data, test predictions, evaluate theories, and suggest new hypotheses,* 33–34, 39

Correlation coefficient, 34

calculation of for intelligence tests, 263–264

Correlation *In research, the degree to which one variable is related to another,* 33–34

causation and, 35

Correlations of intelligence, 267–268. *See also* Intelligence

Corticosteroids, secretion of in response to stress, 433

Cortisol, 82

secretion of in response to stress, 433

Counseling psychologists *Psychologists who seek to assess, understand, and change abnormal behavior,* 6

Counseling psychology, 6

Counterproductive work behaviors (CWBs), 633

aggression and, 650–651

Couples therapy *A form of therapy that focuses on improving communication between partners,* 552–553

Covert orienting, 132

Crack, 318

Cramming, 211

Cravings, substance abuse and, 315

Creative intelligence, 277–279

Creative skills, 240

Creative thinking, 239–240

Creativity *The capacity to produce original solutions or novel compositions,* 239–240

cognitive and personality characteristics for, 239–240

Credentials, job competence and, 631

Critical incidents, 635

Critical period *An interval during which certain kinds of growth must occur if development is to proceed normally,* 379

Critical period for language acquisition, 249

Critical thinking *The process of assessing claims and making judgments on the basis of well-supported evidence,* 27–28

questions to ask, 28–29

scientific research and, 29–30

statistics and research methods as tools in, 44–45

Cross-cultural psychology, 23

Cross-sectional studies, 282

Crystallized intelligence *The specific knowledge gained as a result of applying fluid intelligence,* 276

measuring changes in across the life span, 283

Cultural background

influence of on behavior, 20–23

influence of on IQ scores, 270–271

Cultural competence, 561

Cultural diversity training, 561

Cultural factors

achievement motivation and, 352

cognitive development and, 389–390

eating and, 338–339

ethnic identity, 410–411

expression of emotion and, 367–369

job satisfaction and, 647

mate selection and, 331

parenting styles and, 400–401

sexuality and, 346–347

temperamental qualities and, 393–394

therapy and, 560–561

Cultural-general disorders, 496

Cultural values

advertising and, 22

altered states of consciousness and, 299

Culture-specific forms of psychological disorders, 496

Culture *The accumulation of values, rules of behavior forms of expression, religious beliefs, occupational choices, and the like for a group of people who share a common language and environment*

clothing and, 597

perception and, 129

personality and, 477–478

forms of expression, religious beliefs, occupational choices, and the like for a group of people who share a common language and environment, 21

Cutaneous senses *Senses including touch, temperature, pain, and kinesthetic perception that are spread throughout the body; also called somatosensory systems,* 109

Cyberchondria, 503

Cyclothymic disorder *A bipolar disorder characterized by an alternating pattern of mood swings that is less extreme than that of bipolar I or bipolar II,* 515

D

Daily hassles, 430

Dark adaptation *The increasing ability to see in the dark as time passes,* 94

Darwin, Charles, influence of on William James' functionalism, 13

activity is confined to sensory perception and motor skills, 384, 386

Sensory adaptation *Decreasing responsiveness to an unchanging stimulus,* 88

Sensory cortex *The parts of the cerebral cortex that receive stimulus information from the senses,* 62–64

Sensory memory *A type of memory that is very brief but lasts long enough to connect one impression to the next,* 183, 185

Sensory neurons *Cells in the nervous system that provide information to the brain about the environment,* 57
touch, 109–110

Sensory receptors, 88

Sensory registers *Memory systems that briefly hold incoming information,* 185

Sensory system elements, 89

Separation anxiety disorder, 529

Sequencing of organizational training, 640–641

Serotonin, 78
association of abnormality of and illness anxiety disorder, 509
hunger suppression and, 337

Set point, 337

Sex hormones *Chemicals in the blood that organize and motivate sexual behavior,* 81, 346
activation of in adolescents, 408
influence of on sexual orientation, 348

Sex offenders, castration of, 346

Sex roles *Patterns of work, appearance, and behavior that a society associates with being male or female,* 404–406. *See also* Gender roles

Sexual activity, adolescents, 409

Sexual aggression, pornography and, 611

Sexual arousal *Physiological arousal that arises from sexual contact or erotic thoughts,* 344, 346–347

Sexual behavior
biology of, 343–344, 346
Kinsey's survey of, 344–345

Sexuality, social and cultural factors in, 346–347

Sexual orientation, 347
factors shaping, 348–350

Sexual relationships, ethical considerations, 561

Sexual response cycle *The pattern of arousal before, during, and after sexual activity,* 343–344, 346

Sexual scripts, 343

Shadow and light, 121

Shape constancy, 123

Shaping *The reinforcement of responses that come successively closer to some desired response,* 154

Shapiro, Francine, 27
experimental investigation of EMDR by, 35–36

Shared decision making, 244

Sherif, Muzafer, 598–599

Shift work, 653

Short-term memory (STM) *A stage of memory in which information normally lasts less than twenty seconds; a component of working memory,* 183
comparison with long-term memory, 189–190
decay and, 201
duration of, 187–188
encoding, 186
storage capacity of, 186–187
working memory and, 186

Short-term psychodynamic psychotherapy, 542

Short-wavelength cones, 97

Shuttle box, 153

Signal detection theory *A mathematical model of what determines a person's report of a near-threshold stimulus,* 90–91

Signals, 146

Significant events, signaling of, 146–148

Similarity, 118
attraction and, 593–594

Simplicity, 31, 118

Simultanagnosia, 680

Singer, Jerome, 364

Situational factors, defining abnormality using, 493

Situational tests, 480

Situation judgment tests (SJTs), 630

Size constancy, 123

Size illusions, 123–124

Size of the majority, conformance and, 600

Skill learning, 173

Skills, industrial and organization assessment of, 629

Skinner, B.F., 14, 151, 545–546

Skinner box, 151

Sleep, 307
reasons for, 303–307
stages of, 299–301 (*See also* NREM sleep; REM sleep)

Sleep apnea *A sleep disorder in which a person briefly but repeatedly stops breathing during the night,* 302

Sleep deprivation *A condition in which people do not get enough sleep; it may result in reduced cognitive abilities, inattention, and increased risk of accidents,* 306–307

Sleep disorders, 301–303, 307

Sleeping pills, 317

Sleep terror disorder (night terrors) *The occurrence of horrific dream images during N3 sleep, followed by a rapid awakening and a state of intense fear,* 303

Sleep-wake rhythms, 303–305

Sleepwalking *A phenomenon that starts primarily in NREM sleep, especially in stage N3, and involves walking while asleep,* 302–303

Sleepy driving, 306

Slow-wave sleep, 300

Small molecules, 78

Smell, 105–107
absolute threshold for, 90
aspects of the sensory system, 108
interaction of with taste, 104–105
newborn sense of, 381

Smoking, prenatal exposure to, 379

Social anxiety disorder (social phobia) *Strong, irrational fears related to social situations,* 504

Social categories, 589

Social cognition *Mental processes associated with people's perceptions of and reactions to other people,* 577

Social-cognitive approach *The view that personality reflects learned patterns of thinking and behavior,* 18, 470
Bandura and reciprocal determinism, 471–472
evaluating, 473
Mischel's cognitive/affective theory, 472–473
Rotter's expectancy theory, 471

Social comparison *Using other people as a basis of comparison for evaluating oneself,* 577–578

Social dependability, 443

Social development
attachment and, 392–393
infancy and childhood, 406

Social dilemmas *Situations in which actions that produce rewards for one individual will produce negative consequences for all if they are adopted by everyone,* 616–617

Social discrimination *Differential treatment of people in certain groups; the behavioral component of prejudice,* 588

Social facilitation *A phenomenon in which the presence of others improves a person's performance,* 618

Social factors
depressive and bipolar disorders, 517–518

expression of emotion and, 367–369
gender roles, 405–406
motivation and, 329
sexuality and, 346–347

Social identity *The beliefs we hold about the groups to which we belong,* 580
obedience and, 605

Social impact of research, 45

Social influence, 596–597
conformity and compliance, 598–602
factors affecting, 606
norms, 597–598
types of, 606

Social interference *A reduction in performance due to the presence of other people,* 618

Socialization *The process by which parents, teachers, and others teach children the skills and social norms necessary to be well-functioning members of society,* 169, 399
gender role development and, 404–406

Social learning, 167–171

Social loafing, 244

Social loafing *Exerting less effort when performing a group task than when performing the same task alone,* 619

Social neuroscience *A specialty that focuses on the influence of social processes on biological processes and on the influence of biological processes on social psychological phenomenon,* 620

Social norms *Learned, socially biased rules that prescribe what people should or should not do in various situations,* 597–598

Social perception *The processes through which people interpret information about others, draw inferences about them, and develop mental representations of them,* 580–581
biases in, 584

Social phobia *Strong, irrational fears related to social situations,* 504

Social psychologists *Psychologists who study how people influence one another's behavior and mental processes, individually and in groups,* 7

Social psychology *The subfield of psychology that explores the effects of the social world on the behavior and mental processes of individuals and groups,* 7, 577
biological psychology and, 620

Social Readjustment Rating Scale (SRRS), 430–431

Social reality, conformance and, 599

Social referencing, 369, 392–393

Social skills, 402

Social skills training, 547

Social support *The friends and social contacts on whom one can depend for help and support,* 440–441
alcohol use and, 531
emotional coping strategy and, 452

Sociocultural diversity, impact of on psychology, 20–23

Sociocultural experience, food selection and, 338–339

Sociocultural factors, hyperactivity and, 528–529

Sociocultural factors influencing abnormality *Characteristics or conditions that can influence the appearance and form of maladaptive behavior,* 496–497
alcohol use disorder, 530–531
anxiety disorders and, 504
schizophrenia, 522
somatic symptom disorders, 509
suicide and, 513–514

Sociocultural factors *Social identity and other background factors, such as gender ethnicity, social class, and culture*
aggression and, 608
psychotherapy and, 560–561

Surface structure *The order in which words are arranged in sentences,* 246
Surveys *A research method that involves giving people questionnaires or special interviews designed to obtain descriptions of their attitudes, beliefs opinions, and intentions*
  designing, 33
  flawed, 34
  limitations of, 33
  validity of, 33
  opinions, and intentions, 32–33, 39
Symbolic reasoning, computer logic and, 238
Symbols
  in language, 245
  use of by children, 384–385
Sympathetic nervous system *The subsystem of the autonomic nervous system that readies the body for vigorous activity,* 57, 361
Sympatho-adreno-medullary (SAM) system, 446–447
  stress responses in, 432–433
Synapses *The tiny gaps between neurons across which they communicate,* 54–55
Synaptic gap, 54
Synchrony, 118
Syndromes *A pattern of symptoms associated with a specific disorder,* 673
Synesthesia, 103–104
Syntax *The set of rules that govern the formation of phrases and sentences in a language,* 245
Systematic desensitization therapy *A behavioral method for treating anxiety in which clients visualize a graduated series of anxiety-provoking stimuli while remaining relaxed,* 149–150, 546–547
Szasz, Thomas, 501

T
Tabula rasa, 12, 375
Taijin kyofusho, 504
Talking cure, 541–542
Tardive dyskinesia, 564–565, 570
Target organs, 81
  emotional response and, 360
Task Force on Promotion and Dissemination of Psychological Procedures, 557–560
Task-motivated leaders *Leaders who provide close supervision, lead by giving directions, and generally discourage group discussion,* 619
Task performance, 633
Taste, 107–108
  absolute threshold for, 90
  aspects of the sensory system, 108
  conditioned aversion, 148
  interaction of with smell, 104–105
  newborn sense of, 381
Taste buds, 107
Taste perception *The sense that detects chemicals in solution that come into contact with receptors inside the mouth; also called gustatory perception,* 104
Taylor, Shelley, 442
T-cells, 446
Teenagers. *See* Adolescents
Telegraphic sentences, 248
Telehealth, 562
Temperament *An individual's basic, natural disposition that is evident from infancy,* 393
  categories of, 479
  differences in, 468
Temperature, touch and, 109–110
Temporal lobe, 62
Tend and befriend, 442

Teratogens *Harmful substances, such as alcohol and other drugs, that can cause birth defects,* 379
Terman, Lewis, 259
Terman Life Cycle Study, 443–444
Terminal drop *A sharp decline in mental functioning that tends to occur in late adulthood, a few months or years before death,* 419
Terrace, Herbert, 251
Terror management theory, 578–579
Test anxiety, 266–267
Test *A systematic procedure for observing behavior in a standard situation and describing it with the help of a numerical scale or a category system,* 263
Testing effects, 282
Testosterone, 81, 346
  aggression and, 607–608
Textbooks, PQ4R method for reading, 212
Thalamus *A forebrain structure that relays signals from most sense organs to higher levels in the brain and plays an important role in processing and making sense out of this information,* 60
  role of in schizophrenia, 521
Thematic Apperception Test, 350, 481
Theoretical criterion, 632–633
Theories, 539. *See also* specific theories
  arousal, 332–333
  attachment, 394, 461–462
  biological trait, 466–469
  Cannon-Bard, 363–364
  decay, 200–201
  dissociation, 311
  drive reduction, 331–332
  excitation transfer, 365
  humanistic, 473–476
  incentive, 333
  object relations, 461
  opponent-process, 97–98
  place, 102
  psychoanalytic, 457
  role of, 30–31
  signal detection, 90–91
  social-cognitive, 470–473
  trichromatic, 97
  volley, 103
Theory *An integrated set of propositions that can be used to account for, predict, and even suggest ways of controlling certain phenomena,* 30
Therapeutic punishment, 159–160
Therapeutic relationship, 539
  rules and rights in, 561–562
Therapists, 539. *See also* specific types
Thinking strategies
  formal reasoning, 228–229
  informal reasoning, 229–231
Thinking *The manipulation of mental representations,* 220–221
Thorndike, Edward L., 150–151, 628
Thought
  basic functions of, 219–222
  blocking, 519
  broadcasting, 519
  ingredients of, 227
  insertion, 519
  mental representations, 223–227
  withdrawal, 519
Thought processes, emotional alteration of, 358
Three-dimensional perception of distance, 120–121
Timbre *The quality of a sound that identifies it,* 100
Timing of stimuli, 146–147
Tip-of-the-tongue phenomenon, 194
Titchener, Edward, 12

Token economy program *A system for improving the behavior of clients in institutions by rewarding desirable behaviors with tokens that can be exchanged for various rewards,* 548
Tolerance, 150
Top-down processing *Aspects of recognition guided by higher-level cognitive processes and by psychological factors such as expectations,* 126–127, 474
  understanding speech, 246–247
Total safety culture, 654
Touch
  absolute threshold for, 90
  adapting to stimuli, 109
  encoding, 109
  sensing temperature, 109–110
Toxic substances, prenatal exposure to, 378–379
Trainee-learning criteria, 642
Training employees, 638
  assessing needs, 639
  designing programs for, 639–641
  evaluating programs for, 641–642
Training-level criteria, 642
Training needs assessment, 639
Trait approach *A perspective on personality that views it as the combination of stable characteristics that people display over time and across situations,* 463–464
  criticisms of, 472–473
  evaluation of, 469–470
Tranquilizing medications (anxiolytics) *Medications that reduce tension and symptoms of anxiety,* 566
Transactional leaders, 619–620
Transcranial magnetic stimulation (TMS), 68, 72, 668–669
  use of in pain management, 111
Transduction *The process of converting incoming physical energy into neural activity,* 88
Transfer-appropriate processing model of memory *A model that suggests that memory depends on how the encoding process matches up with what is later retrieved,* 182
Transference, 542
Transfer of training, 639–640
Transformational leaders, 619–620
Trauma-related disorders, 506
Traumatic brain injury (trauma) *An impact on the brain caused by a blow or sudden, violent movement of the head,* 672
Traumatic memories, repression and recovery of, 202–205
Treatment, basic features of, 539–541
Triarchic theory of intelligence, 277–279
Trichromatic theory *A theory of color vision stating that information from three types of visual elements combines to produce the sensation of color,* 97
Tricyclic antidepressants (TCAs), 565, 570
Trump, Donald, 331
Tsarnaev, Tamerlan and Dzhokhar, 577
Turnover, job dissatisfaction and, 650
TV violence
  aggression and, 608
  observational learning and, 169–171
Twin studies, 42–43
  anxiety disorders, 506
  depressive and bipolar disorders, 515–517
  inheritability of schizophrenia, 521
  job satisfaction, 648–649
  personality traits, 467–469
Two-dimensional location, 119–120
Two-group experiment, 36
Tympanic membrane (eardrum) *A tightly stretched membrane in the middle ear that generates vibrations that match the sound waves striking it,* 100–101